HOUGHTON MIFFLIN SOCIAL STUDIES

To See a World

World Cultures and Geography

TEACHER'S EDITION

Beverly J. Armento
J. Jorge Klor de Alva
Gary B. Nash
Christopher L. Salter
Louis E. Wilson
Karen K. Wixson

Houghton Mifflin Company • Boston
Atlanta • Dallas • Geneva, Illinois • Princeton, New Jersey • Palo Alto • Toronto

Contents

Program Components T4

Program Overview T6

Professional Handbook

Social Studies and the Thinking Curriculum T30
Access to Social Studies for Limited English Proficient Students T32
Teaching Multicultural Perspectives T33
Using Collaborative Learning in Social Studies T34
Developing Concepts and Vocabulary T36
The Role of Literature T38
Writing, Thinking, and Learning T39
The Role of Assessment in Houghton Mifflin Social Studies T40

Scope and Sequence T41

Student Text

Table of Contents vi
About Your Book xiv
Map and Globe Handbook with Teaching Notes G1
Student Pages with Teaching Notes 1
Time/Space Databank 659

Acknowledgments

Photograph on page T4 by Ralph J. Burke. All contemporary author and student photographs on pages T6–T28 by Jeff Schewe. Author photographs on pages T12 and T18 by Reneé Fraser. Photograph on page T41 by Peter Bosy.

1999 Impression

Printed in U.S.A.
Student's Edition ISBN: 0-395-80932-0
Teacher's Edition ISBN: 0-395-80938-X
34567-VH-03 02 01 00

Development by Ligature, Inc.

Student Text with Teaching Notes

The Houghton Mifflin Social Studies Teacher's Edition provides reduced Student Text pages with accompanying teacher's notes. Two pages of additional teacher information precede each chapter.

Openers

On unit and chapter openers, the teacher's margins present strategies where they are most useful—at the point of use.

The gray side margins offer suggestions for previewing the chapter to come and for discussing the images on the opener pages.

The bronze bottom margins contain a unit bibliography and chapter background information.

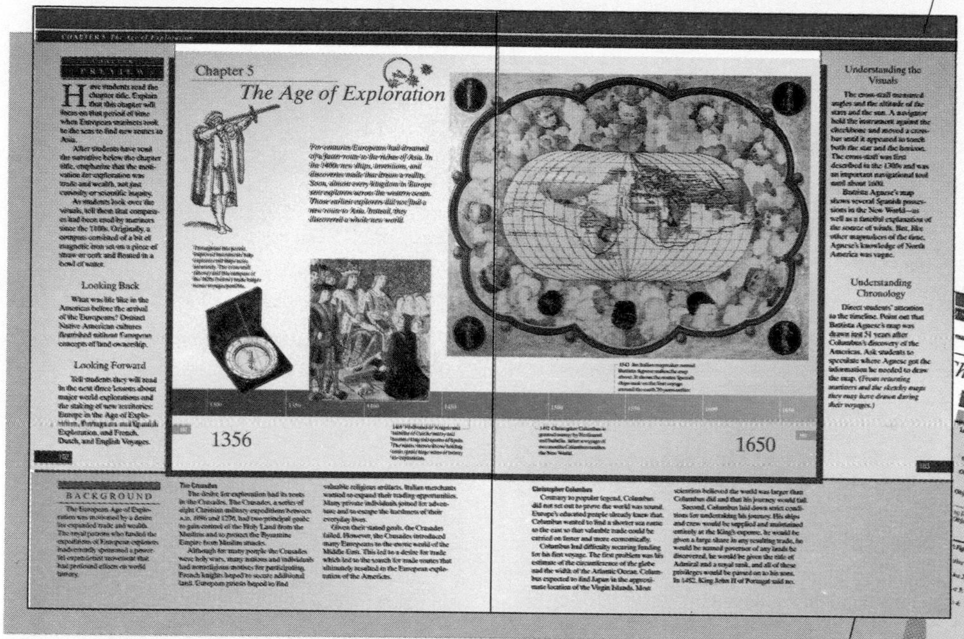

PREVIEW
Chapter 5
The Age of Exploration
Looking Back
Looking Forward
Understanding the Visuals
Understanding Chronology
1356
1650
BACKGROUND

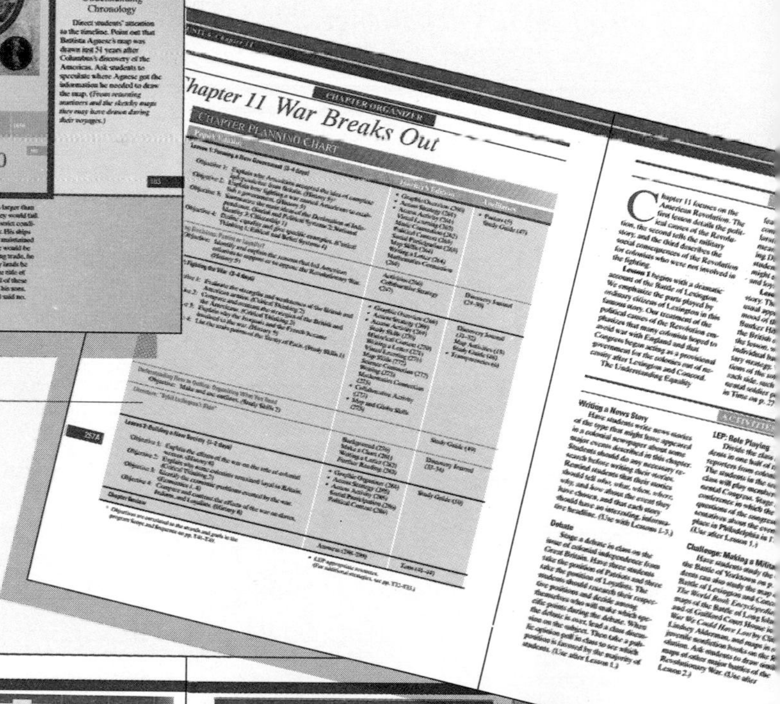

CHAPTER ORGANIZER
Chapter 11 War Breaks Out
CHAPTER PLANNING CHART

Chapter Interleaves

Two pages immediately preceding each chapter provide a Chapter Organizer, a Chapter Rationale, and Chapter Activities and Projects.

Lesson Pages

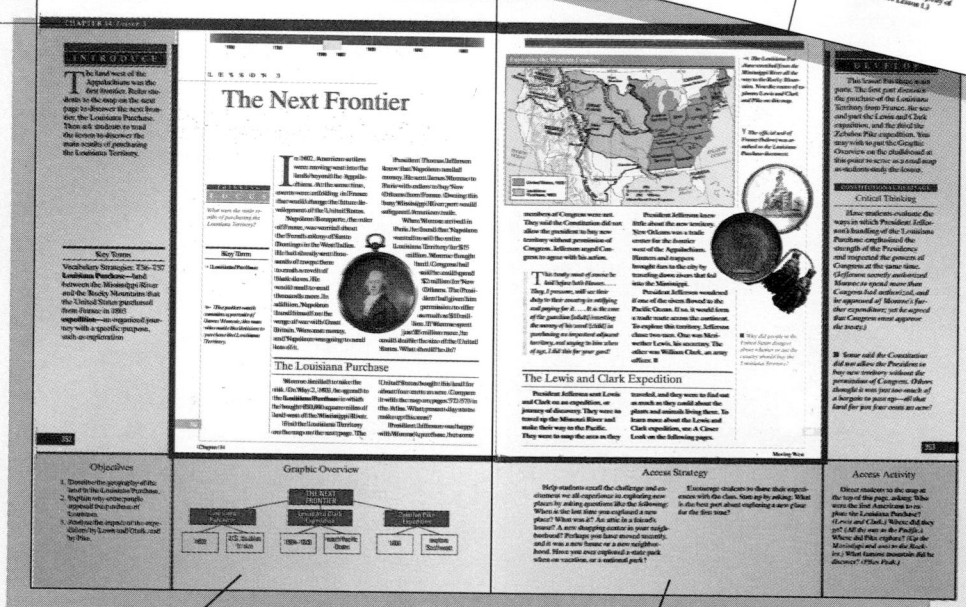

The design of the teacher's margins of all lesson pages continues the two distinct channels of information that were established on the opener pages.

The gray side margins present the three-part lesson plan: Introduce, Develop, Close. Again, critical teaching notes are located at point of use.

The bronze bottom margins offer long-range support, including lesson Objectives and additional Context information, plus a wealth of activities and extensions.

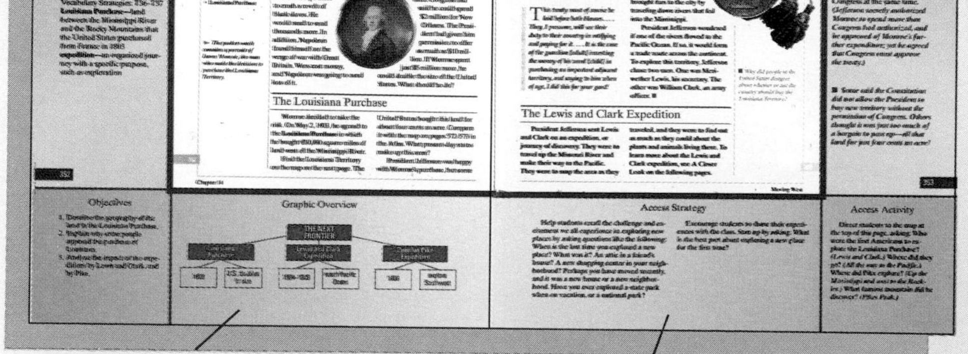

INTRODUCE
The Next Frontier
The Louisiana Purchase
The Lewis and Clark Expedition
DEVELOP
Objectives
Graphic Overview
Access Strategy
Access Activity

The Graphic Overview summarizes the major concepts of the lesson (see pages T36–T37).

The Access Strategy offers special tips for meeting the needs of LEP and other students (see pages T32–T33).

Program Components

Pictured here is a sampling of pages from Houghton Mifflin Social Studies. In addition to lesson pages and special features, the Student Text includes an array of appendices appropriate to each level. The Teacher's Edition provides instructional strategies and activities in the form of interleaf pages and point-of-use notes, as well as other features to support your teaching. Houghton Mifflin Social Studies also includes a wealth of Ancillaries to help you assess students' learning and enrich their social studies experience.

UNIT 1 Lesson 2
We Are a Team

Big Book

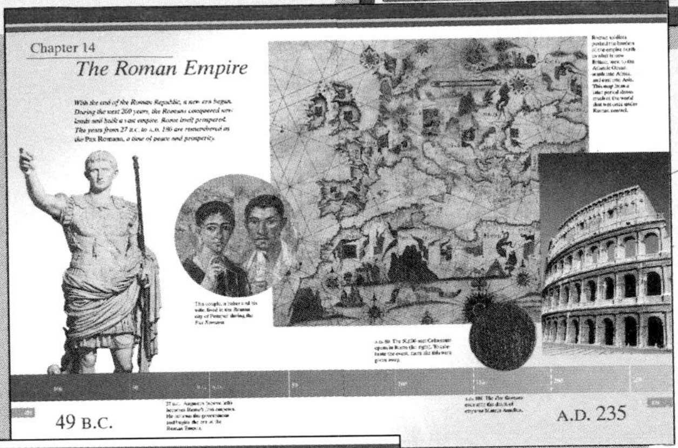
Chapter 14
The Roman Empire
49 B.C.
A.D. 235

Grade 6 Student Text

CHAPTER 7 Lesson 1
INTRODUCE
A New Settlement in Virginia
DEVELOP
Key Terms
Objectives
Access Strategy
Access Activity

Grade 5 Teacher's Edition

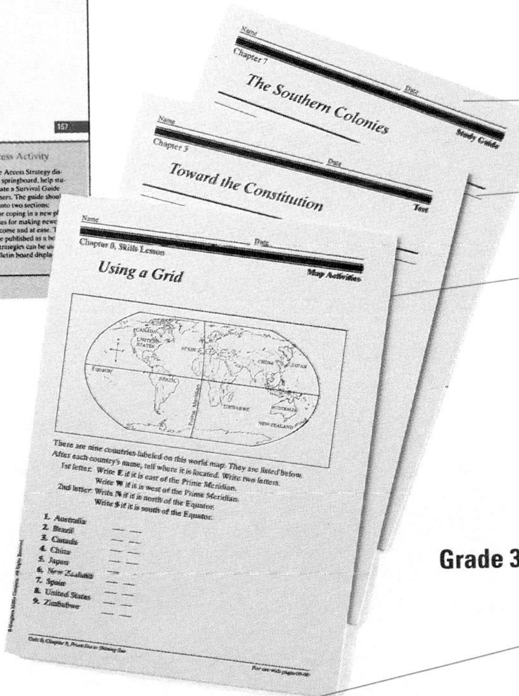
Chapter 7
The Southern Colonies
Study Guide
Chapter 5
Toward the Constitution
Chapter 6, Skills Lesson
Using a Grid
Map Activities

Grade 3 Ancillaries

A MOMENT IN TIME
A Forty-niner
2:30 P.M., August 15, 1850
A mountain stream near Sacramento

Grade 4 Ancillaries

HOUGHTON MIFFLIN SOCIAL STUDIES

Bookshelf

PROGRAM COMPONENTS

Grade	K	1	2	3	4	5	6	7	6/7	8
BIG BOOK	■									
STUDENT TEXT		■	■	■	■	■	■	■	■	■
Our Constitution Today										■
Constitution						■				■
Declaration of Independence						■				■
Additional Primary Sources										■
Minipedia					■	■	■	■	■	■
Atlas		■	■	■	■	■	■	■	■	■
Geographic Glossary		■	■	■	■	■	■	■	■	■
Gazetteer				■	■	■	■	■	■	■
Biographical Dictionary					■	■	■	■	■	■
Glossary		■	■	■	■	■	■	■	■	■
TEACHER'S EDITION	■	■	■	■	■	■	■	■	■	■
Professional Handbook	■	■	■	■	■	■	■	■	■	■
Instructional Strategies	■	■	■	■	■	■	■	■	■	■
Additional Literature Selections	■	■	■	■						
ANCILLARIES	■	■	■	■	■	■	■	■	■	■
Study Guide		■	■	■	■	■	■	■	■	■
Tests		■	■	■	■	■	■	■	■	■
Map Masters		■	■	■	■	■	■	■	■	■
Overhead Transparencies		■	■	■	■	■	■	■	■	■
Home Involvement Booklet		■	■	■	■	■	■	■	■	■
Study Prints		■	■	■	■	■	■	■	■	■
Discovery Journal		■	■	■	■	■	■	■	■	■
Posters	■	■	■	■	■	■	■	■	■	■
Periodic Learning Inventory				■	■	■			■	
Exploring Your Community				■						
BOOKSHELF	■	■	■	■	■	■	■	■	■	■

Houghton Mifflin Social Studies:

Working With You to Develop Literate Citizens

*"All who have meditated
on the art of governing human beings
have been convinced that the fate of empires
depends on the education of youth."*

Aristotle

The goal of Houghton Mifflin Social Studies is the development of literate citizens—individuals with the knowledge, skills, and civic values they need to become active and reflective participants in the world of the twenty-first century. Our program weaves together knowledge, skills, and citizenship to form an integrated program. And because we focus on depth rather than breadth, our program helps you take the time to truly captivate, develop, question, and stretch your students. Take a moment and discover some of the ideas and people that make this program a powerful classroom tool.

A Program Based on In-Depth Learning

Whatever the task, we all know that doing something well takes time. Becoming a literate citizen is no exception. Students need time to explore topics, to practice skills in meaningful contexts, and to relate their learning to the world in which they live.

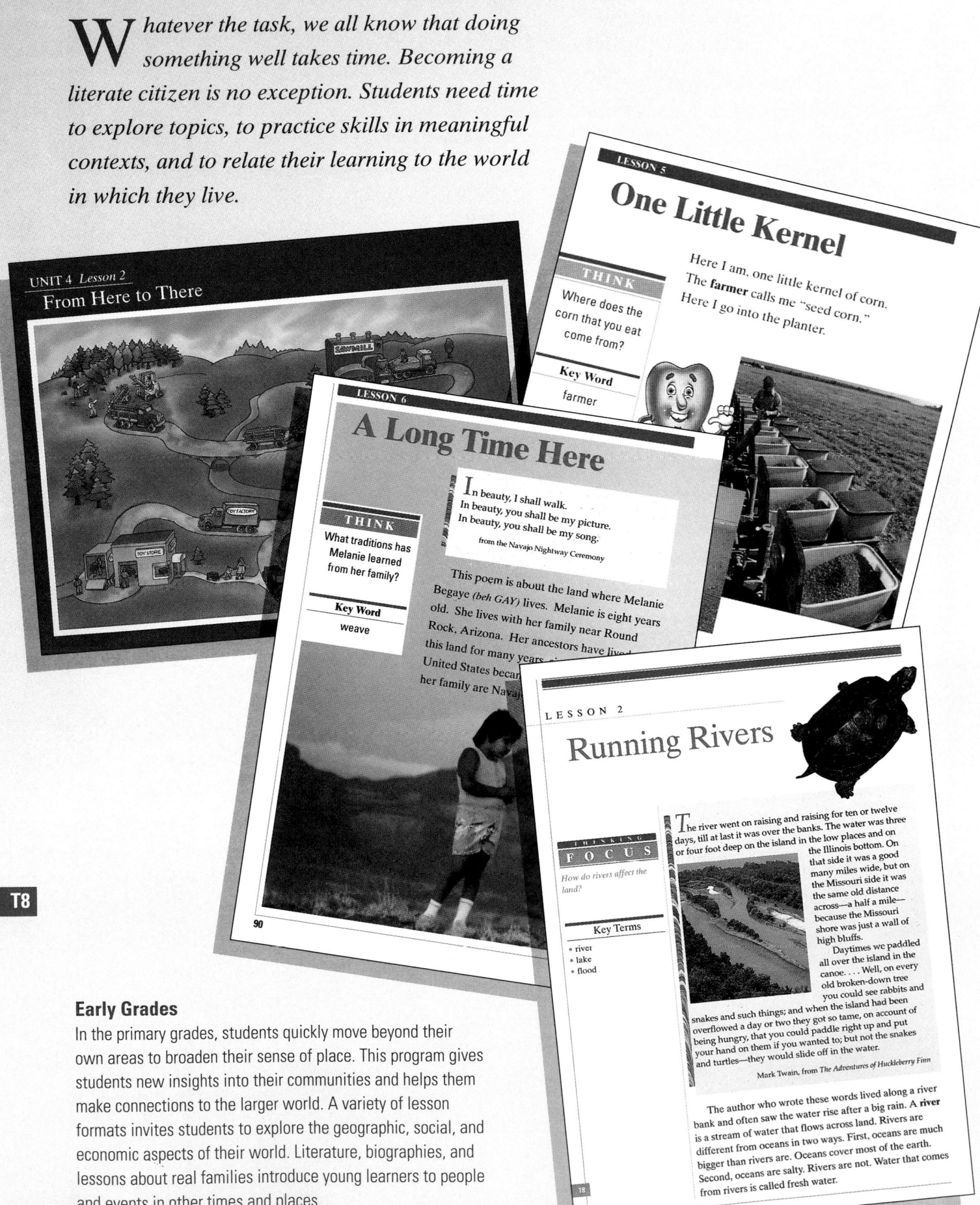

UNIT 4 Lesson 2
From Here to There
SAWMILL
TOY FACTORY
TOY STORE

LESSON 5

One Little Kernel

THINK

Where does the corn that you eat come from?

Key Word

farmer

Here I am, one little kernel of corn.
The **farmer** calls me "seed corn."
Here I go into the planter.

LESSON 6

A Long Time Here

THINK

What traditions has Melanie learned from her family?

Key Word

weave

In beauty, I shall walk.
In beauty, you shall be my picture.
In beauty, you shall be my song.

from the Navajo Nightway Ceremony

This poem is about the land where Melanie Begaye *(beh GAY)* lives. Melanie is eight years old. She lives with her family near Round Rock, Arizona. Her ancestors have lived this land for many years United States becar her family are Nava

90

LESSON 2

Running Rivers

THINKING FOCUS

How do rivers affect the land?

Key Terms

- river
- lake
- flood

The river went on raising and raising for ten or twelve days, till at last it was over the banks. The water was three or four foot deep on the island in the low places and on the Illinois bottom. On that side it was a good many miles wide, but on the Missouri side it was the same old distance across—a half a mile—because the Missouri shore was just a wall of high bluffs.

Daytimes we paddled all over the island in the canoe. . . . Well, on every old broken-down tree you could see rabbits and snakes and such things; and when the island had been overflowed a day or two they got so tame, on account of being hungry, that you could paddle right up and put your hand on them if you wanted to; but not the snakes and turtles—they would slide off in the water.

Mark Twain, from *The Adventures of Huckleberry Finn*

The author who wrote these words lived along a river bank and often saw the water rise after a big rain. A **river** is a stream of water that flows across land. Rivers are different from oceans in two ways. First, oceans are much bigger than rivers are. Oceans cover most of the earth. Second, oceans are salty. Rivers are not. Water that comes from rivers is called fresh water.

18

Early Grades

In the primary grades, students quickly move beyond their own areas to broaden their sense of place. This program gives students new insights into their communities and helps them make connections to the larger world. A variety of lesson formats invites students to explore the geographic, social, and economic aspects of their world. Literature, biographies, and lessons about real families introduce young learners to people and events in other times and places.

Upper Grades

In the upper grades, students continue to study in depth. For example, in the fifth grade students study American history and geography from the first appearance of the American Indians to the modern era. In the eighth grade students focus on the period from the Constitutional Convention to the early 1900s. In the sixth grade they study selected periods of ancient history. In the seventh grade they explore world civilizations and European history from the Fall of Rome to the Enlightenment. In an alternate text for either sixth or seventh grade, students trace the development of selected world cultures from the ancient past to the present. By narrowing the chronological focus, we give students time to take an in-depth, multi-perspective look at the world they live in.

LESSON 2
The Railroad Is Born
Theodore Judah stood on a mountain peak, looking at the scene before him. At his feet, a rocky cliff dropped sharply into a valley 1,000 feet below. It was as if the mountains had put up a great stone stop sign in his path.
THINKING FOCUS
What problems did Theodore Judah and the Big Four have to solve before they could build the transcontinental railroad?
Key Terms
survey
invest
These are the mountains that Judah was hoping to build a railroad over. Does it surprise you that some people thought he was crazy?
LESSON 2
Coming to America
THINKING FOCUS
What were the lives of immigrants like in the United States between 1870 and 1914?
LESSON 1
Exploring, Trading, and Converting
THINKING FOCUS
Why did explorers in the 1400s risk their lives to explore unknown parts of the world?
Key Terms
monopoly
LESSON 3
Daily Life in Ancient Rome
THINKING FOCUS
How was daily life different for rich and poor Romans?
Key Terms
rhetoric
ritual
LESSON 3
The Changing World of American Indians
The only way to check and stop this evil is for all the red men to unite in claiming a common and equal right in the land . . . for it never was divided, but belongs to all, for the use of each.... No part has a right to sell, even to each other, much less to strangers.
So spoke Shawnee chief Tecumseh (ti KUM se) as he condemned and canceled the sale of Indian land to the U.S. government in 1809. Tecumseh had enlisted southern and northern warriors along the Mississippi Valley for a major united effort to recover lands lost to the white people. He was determined to hold the Ohio River as the boundary dividing the United States and Indian country.
As governor of the Indiana Territory, William Henry Harrison was also determined to defend white pioneers who invaded and settled in Indian territories. In 1810, Harrison met the Shawnee leader face to face at Vincennes, Indiana. As their talks began, Harrison's interpreter told Tecumseh, "Your father requests
He argued that the U.S. government had no real right to lands ceded, or transferred, to whites without the consent of all American Indians. Tecumseh shouted, "Sell a country! Why not sell the air, the clouds, and the great sea?"
The Great Spirit gave this great island to his red children. He placed the whites on the other side of the big water. They were not contented with their own, but came to take ours from us. They have driven us from the sea to the lakes—we can go no farther."
THINKING FOCUS
What were the different responses of the various American Indian peoples when their ancestral lands were threatened?
Key Terms
revitalization
cultural accommodation
Tecumseh is shown here saving American prisoners during the War of 1812.

Beverly Armento on

Integrating Social Studies

"In this program we've enriched the content of social studies by drawing on knowledge from history, geography, and economics, as well as from the expressive arts and the humanities. Developing meaningful knowledge of the social world is a major goal of this program."

In my daily life and in my work I use economics and the humanities as a way to step into social studies. But the goal of this program isn't simply to learn economics, or history, or geography. The goal is the development of an informed, active, caring decision maker who draws on meaningful knowledge, who has well-developed skills, who has a sense of what's important and what's not, and who is then able to take all of that and apply it to social issues."

Beverly Jeanne Armento
Professor of Social Studies Education
Director of the Center for Business and Economic Education
Georgia State University, Atlanta

Teacher's Edition Point-of-Use Notes

"To help you integrate knowledge from a wide range of sources, we developed a convenient Teacher's Edition, with teaching notes that support the integration."

[Gr]aphs and Charts

"[Thes]e visuals help us get a picture of how [id]eas relate to one another. The graphic [aid]s are a way we can show these [rel]ationships."

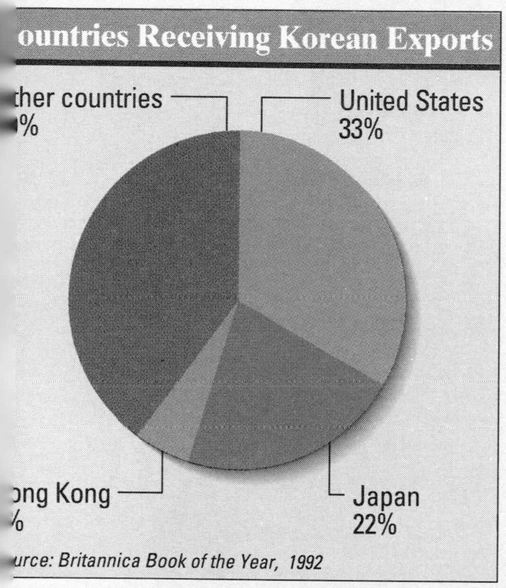

[C]ountries Receiving Korean Exports
[O]ther countries
[..]%
United States
33%
[H]ong Kong
[.]%
Japan
22%
[So]urce: Britannica Book of the Year, 1992

the common elements among these countries, too. *(Close to the ocean; trade important to economy)*

■ *Singapore lies halfway between the major trading centers of India and China and has a deep, wide harbor—perfect for docking ships.*

SOCIAL SYSTEMS

Map and Globe Skills

Ask students to refer to the cartogram on page 689 of the Atlas. Have them compare Indonesia's population density to that of other countries, including Singapore and Vietnam. Then ask them to find Indonesia on the GNP cartogram on page 375 of Chapter 16. Encourage students to make generalizations based on their findings. *(Indonesia's population is extremely dense, and its GNP is relatively large.)*

396

How Do We Know?

HISTORY In 1891, Dutch scientist Eugene Dubois found a human fossil on Java. It was found in stream deposits on the Solo River. He named it Java man. Some scientists have concluded that Java man lived between 500,000 and 1 million years ago.

▼ This famous mosque in Banda Aceh, Indonesia, combines elements of style from Arabia and India.

Indonesia: A Varied Nation

With a population of about 190 million people, Indonesia is the world's fifth largest country. However, its people are divided by geography. The country is made up of more than 13,600 islands, spread out across 3,000 miles of sea. So, from east to west, Indonesia covers about the same number of miles as the distance from northern Maine to southern California. More than half of the people live on the island of Java where Jakarta, the nation's capital city, is located. Many of the other islands are not inhabited.

Beginning thousands of years ago, people from diverse cultures brought many religions to Indonesia. From India came Buddhism and Hinduism. From the Middle East came Islam. From Europe came Christianity. Today about 87 percent of the people practice Islam, making Indonesia the world's largest Muslim nation.

Today the nation is committed to tolerance of its many religions, including those that combine religious practices. Many people, for example, practice a religion that combines Hinduism, Buddhism, and local customs.

The large number of ethnic groups and languages also reflect the nation's cultural diversity. There are more than 300 distinct ethnic groups in Indonesia. About 25 languages and about 250 different dialects are spoken. The national language is Bahasa Indonesia, which has its roots in Malay, the language of early Sumatran traders.

From 1619 to World War II, the Dutch gradually gained control and colonized what is now Indonesia. Then, like the Philippines, it was conquered by Japan. After World War II, Indonesia gained independence from the Dutch. Since 1967 a military dictator has ruled there.

Today Indonesia joins Singapore as a growing economic force in the Pacific Rim area of the world (see the Atlas map of the Pacific Rim region on page 684). Indonesia is a

Chapter 17

Access Activity

Explain that Indonesia is a nation of many religions and ethnic groups. Ask students to compare this fact about Indonesia with what they know about diversity in ...

Access Strategy

Help students understand the role geography plays in a nation's development by staging a game. Divide the class into three groups, and give each group one of the following economic goals: prosperity through shipbuilding, trade, and fishing; good farming and easy distribution of produce; and large cities with successful industries.

Have each group represent one nation and develop a geographical "wish list" that would help it achieve its economic goals. Have groups share their lists with the rest of the class. *(For example, a nation with a harbor and abundant forests would be ideal for shipbuilding, trade, and fishing; one with a fertile river valley would be perfect for farming and transport of produce; and one with flat land and a stable climate would support urban areas and industrialization.)*

Explain that Southeast Asian nations fit the first category, but some, like Singapore, have industry as well.

Literature and the Arts

"In my mind, literature, art, and music belong naturally in social studies. That's the way I've been teaching social studies for 26 years."

LITERATURE

The Captive

Scott O'Dell

As the Spaniards began to explore and settle the Caribbean islands and Central and South America, they brought with them Christian missionaries. These representatives of the Church were intent on bringing Christian beliefs to the peoples living in the Western Hemisphere in the 16th century. Scott O'Dell tells a gripping tale of a young seminary student, Julian Escobar, who stands up to the leaders of an expedition when they enslave the island people and force them to mine gold. As you read the excerpt from The Captive, try to answer this question: Why was Julian angry about the happenings on the island?

By noon Señor Guzmán had collected his band, six in as well as the lone Indian who knew whe... hidden in the past and where t... and Esteban, our translator. A... oughly mistrusted... along

Jorge Klor de Alva on

Teaching Appreciation of Cultural Pluralism

"First, all boys and girls need to see people like themselves in their textbooks. Then students will be ready to respect others who are different from themselves."

Attitudes about gender, race, and ethnicity develop early and crystallize by the upper elementary grades. To counteract the negative stereotypes that influence children, respect for cultural diversity must pervade the social studies curriculum. Lessons with a multicultural cast of characters help students appreciate why people are different and how these differences enrich our society. By also stressing our common interests as people and our individual uniqueness, we provide students with a balanced understanding of human experience."

J. Jorge Klor de Alva
Professor of Anthropology
Princeton University

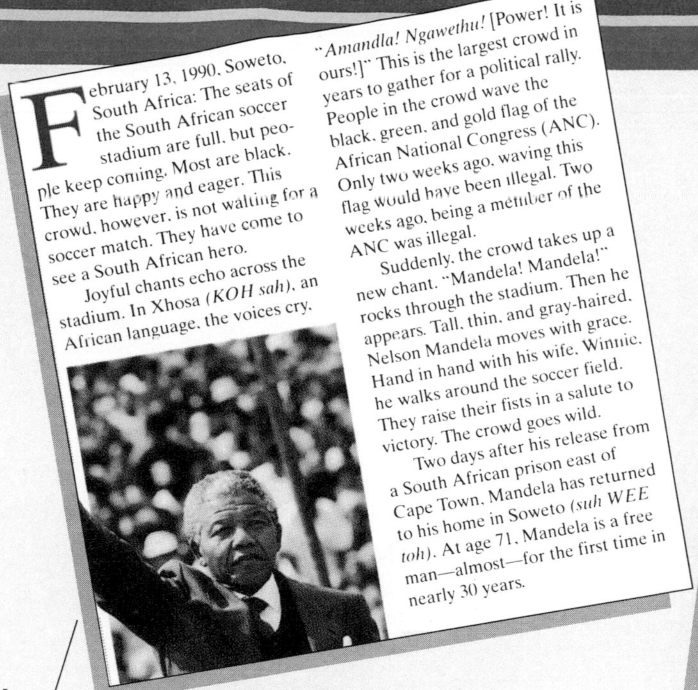
February 13, 1990, Soweto, South Africa: The seats of the South African soccer stadium are full, but people keep coming. Most are black. They are happy and eager. This crowd, however, is not waiting for a soccer match. They have come to see a South African hero.

Joyful chants echo across the stadium. In Xhosa (*KOH sah*), an African language, the voices cry, "*Amandla! Ngawethu!* [Power! It is ours!]" This is the largest crowd in years to gather for a political rally. People in the crowd wave the black, green, and gold flag of the African National Congress (ANC). Only two weeks ago, waving this flag would have been illegal. Two weeks ago, being a member of the ANC was illegal.

Suddenly, the crowd takes up a new chant. "Mandela! Mandela!" rocks through the stadium. Then he appears. Tall, thin, and gray-haired, Nelson Mandela moves with grace. Hand in hand with his wife, Winnie, he walks around the soccer field. They raise their fists in a salute to victory. The crowd goes wild.

Two days after his release from a South African prison east of Cape Town, Mandela has returned to his home in Soweto (*suh WEE toh*). At age 71, Mandela is a free man—almost—for the first time in nearly 30 years.

Human Stories

"No description of an unfamiliar culture captures a student's interest or builds understanding the way a well-told empathetic story does."

Cultural Context

"By exploring constellations of characteristics, such as those surrounding home and religious life, the workplace, and government, students develop a holistic view of a culture."

A CLOSER LOOK

The Emperor's Tomb

Workers digging at Lintong, China, in 1974 discovered a huge buried army. For more than 2,000 years, it stood in an underground chamber, ready for battle. Over 6,000 life-size warriors and horses, made of sculpted clay, guarded the nearby tomb of Qin Shihuangdi, China's first emperor. The entire tomb site has not yet been dug up. It may hide many other treasures of his empire.

Who needs a clay army? The emperor united China through warfare. Guards protected him from attack. They may have been the models for his clay warriors, meant to protect him after he died.

Archaeologists estimate that 700,000 workers built the tomb and clay army in 36 years. Here two archaeologists measure the nearly six-foot height of a warrior.

Special tools are needed to scrape and brush away dirt from the ancient figures so that they are not damaged.

119

Artifacts

"Seeing things used by people from other times and places allows these people to become more real to students."

Life in the City

China's cities bustle with people and bicycles. Many houses and apartments have only two or three rooms. Furniture is simple. Posters and family pictures may decorate the walls. Because indoor space is tight, people like to spend time outside. In city parks, they can play games and listen to singers and storytellers. They can also practice *tai chi chuan (ty chee chwahn)*. It is an ancient form of slow-motion exercise.

A worker's life is controlled by the *danwei*, or **work unit.** Everyone in China belongs to a work unit. A work unit might include, for example, all the workers in a certain factory.

The work unit takes care of all the family's needs. It provides housing and medical care. It may even throw dance parties or show a movie. It also takes care of schooling for young people.

Over time, a typical factory worker can earn enough to buy a refrigerator or a washing machine. An unskilled worker's family may have to make do with a tiny concrete apartment. The family may have to share a kitchen and toilet with other families. But a skilled worker can move into roomier quarters.

For typical factory workers, the day starts at 6:00 A.M. The factory loudspeaker begins broadcasting music and announcements. Then it is time for breakfast—perhaps fried dough and sweet soup. Most workers ride to the factory on bicycles. They return home for lunch, then go back to the factory until 4:00 P.M.

After work, young people may listen to Chinese rock 'n' roll on their tape decks. Or they may play video games set up on the street. Grownups may watch television or go to a teahouse or a restaurant. ■

Like the Kans from Beijing, many Chinese families have parents, grandparents, and one child.

The streets in China's villages are busy with activity. This woman is selling noodles, a popular

Gary Nash on
Teaching History

"Pick any movement you want in history, pick any great event, and as soon as you dig in you begin to see that the person in the street or the worker in the factory or the farmer in the field was involved in that movement."

No one would think of writing a textbook without Abraham Lincoln or Julius Caesar. So it's not that we're completely changing the old vision in which famous people were carved in marble. I think for students we're making history more real, more accessible, more exciting, and more accurate by showing that great people were always interacting with ordinary people. History is the better for it. Women, minorities, and the working person can now find themselves in the historical pageant, the historical process."

Gary B. Nash
Professor of History
UCLA

Across Time and Space

"Part of humanizing history is to show the connection of people in history to people today. Across Time and Space is a feature that makes those connections."

Great People

"Many famous people had grave doubts even in their twenties and thirties about what they were doing; they were still searching. In this program we try to make great people more human, so they're not cardboard heroes."

Across Time & Space

Martin Luther and Martin Luther King, Jr., share more than a name. Both led reform movements that changed the way people live and think. King's policy of civil disobedience promoted racial equality in the United States during the 1950s and 1960s. Under his leadership, the civil rights movement helped reform U.S. society.

All the People

"My research and my writing have focused on people who have been left out of the history books: Native Americans, slaves, women, working people—people whose lives are another thread of the historical tapestry."

Kit Salter on

Teaching Geographic Themes

"Geography is essential to a good education because all of the human drama has been played out in an environmental setting, on an environmental stage. Climate, resources, the presence of some peoples, the absence of others are all elements of geography that give character to the events we're studying."

In geography, we create an initial framework—the patterns of the human use of the earth—then we try to figure out how to study these patterns, and make sense of the landscape. The five fundamental themes of geography are tools we use to make sense of a place.

- Location: What are an area's absolute and relative locations?
- Place: What is its physical environment and what are the patterns of its cultural landscape?
- Human-Environmental Interaction: How have people modified the landscape?
- Movement: What are the effects of the movement of goods, people, and ideas?
- Region: What are the knowable, regional segments of the land?"

Christopher L. Salter
Professor and Chair
Department of Geography
University of Missouri, Columbia

Different Kinds of Maps
"In this global age, geographic literacy is essential. Maps provide a wealth of useful information and insight for students who learn to interpret them."

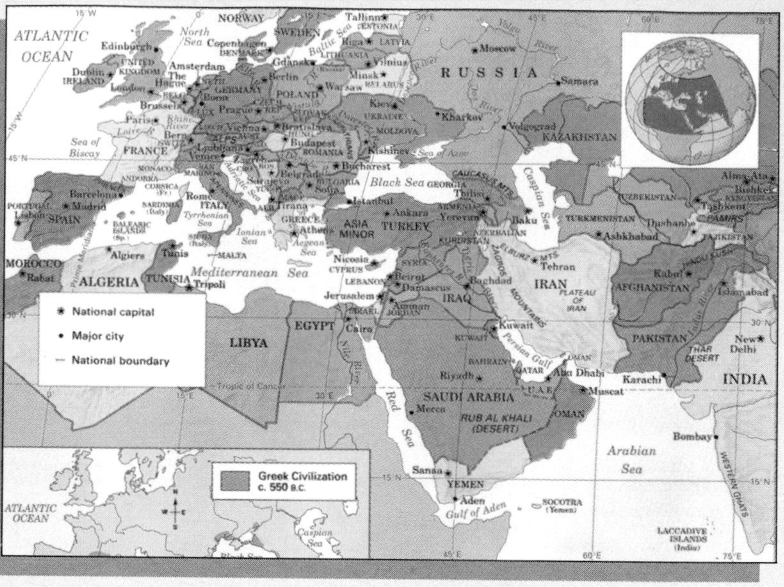
ATLANTIC OCEAN
NORWAY
SWEDEN
RUSSIA
KAZAKHSTAN
FRANCE
SPAIN
ITALY
GREECE
TURKEY
ASIA MINOR
Black Sea
Caspian Sea
Mediterranean Sea
MOROCCO
ALGERIA
TUNISIA
LIBYA
EGYPT
IRAQ
IRAN
AFGHANISTAN
PAKISTAN
INDIA
SAUDI ARABIA
RUB AL KHALI (DESERT)
OMAN
YEMEN
Arabian Sea
Red Sea
National capital
Major city
National boundary
Greek Civilization c. 550 B.C.

Primary Source Maps
"Students have faced the challenge of having to find their way in an unfamiliar place. They will identify with the importance of early mapmakers."

UNDERSTANDING TOPOGRAPHY

Analyzing Elevation Maps

Here's Why

If you plan a bicycle route to avoid hills or to go around a lake, you are showing that you understand topography—the natural surface features of the land.

Studying topography gives you more than information about possible routes. Understanding topography can also help you find out more about the land, its people, and its wildlife. For example, understanding topography can help you study the animals in any given place.

Here's How

Imagine you are a naturalist looking for the Sumatran rhinoceros, an animal that is close to extinction. From your study, you know that the Sumatran rhinoceros feeds on bamboo and fruit. On the island of Sumatra, this rhinoceros lives only in highlands and mountain forests.

How would you plan a trip that would take you across the island of Sumatra in search of this rhinoceros? You might begin by looking at the map and the diagram on this page.

The map uses color to show different ranges in elevation, or height, above sea level. The key shows the elevations represented by each color. The diagram below the map shows the elevation of one route across the island of Sumatra.

Study both the map and the diagram. Based on what you know about the rhino and the information on the map, would you expect to find the Sumatran rhinoceros along this route? Why or why not?

Western Indonesia: Physical and Profile Map

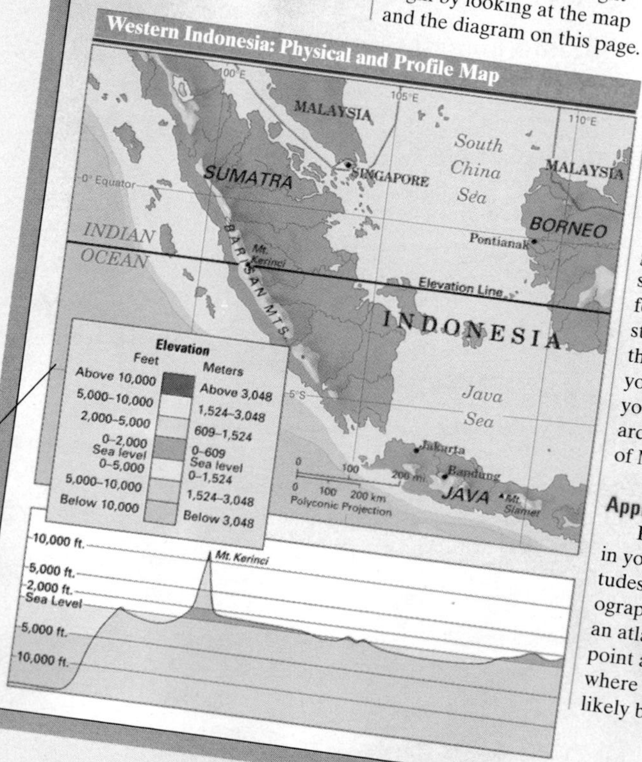
MALAYSIA
SUMATRA
SINGAPORE
South China Sea
MALAYSIA
BORNEO
Pontianak
INDIAN OCEAN
BARISAN MTS.
Mt. Kerinci
Elevation Line
INDONESIA
Java Sea
Jakarta
Bandung
JAVA
Mt. Slamet
0° Equator
100°E
105°E
110°E
5°S
Elevation
Feet
Meters
Above 10,000
5,000–10,000
2,000–5,000
0–2,000
Sea level
0–5,000
5,000–10,000
Below 10,000
Above 3,048
1,524–3,048
609–1,524
0–609
Sea level
0–1,524
1,524–3,048
Below 3,048
Polyconic Projection
10,000 ft.
5,000 ft.
2,000 ft.
Sea Level
5,000 ft.
10,000 ft.
Mt. Kerinci

Try It

Your friend is a naturalist studying the clouded leopard, another endangered animal living in Sumatra. According to her information, the clouded leopard lives in evergreen forests that range from sea level to a height of 6,600 feet. Your friend wants to study the clouded leopard in the wild. Would you invite your friend to join you on your route? Would this leopard be likely to live at the top of Mount Kerinci?

Apply It

Research an animal found in your state. At what altitudes does it live? Find a topographic map of your state in an atlas. Use the map to pinpoint areas in your state where the animal would most likely be found.

399

Southeast Asia

Map Skills
"Students routinely use signposts, direction, and other geographic aids. With help, students can become equally skilled at using such map aids as the scale and grid."

Louis Wilson on

Teaching Multiple Perspectives

"A mature understanding of history and culture is empathetic as well as intellectual. As students learn to identify with the feelings and aspirations of those around them, you can extend this identification to people in other times and places."

To meet the challenges of this global age, children must learn to understand those beyond their own circle of associations. You can encourage this response by asking students, "What would it be like?" and "How would you feel?" as they study other cultures and historical periods. Lessons should focus on the beliefs and values underlying a people's history and culture. What starts as curiosity can blossom into empathy in a learning environment where every person is accorded dignity and a respectful hearing."

Louis E. Wilson
Associate Professor of Afro-American Studies
Smith College

Y*ou could hardly see the sea. The Spanish fleet was stretched out in the form of a half moon. . . . The masts and rigging, the towering sterns and prows which in height and number were so great that they dominated the whole [scene], caused horror mixed with wonder and gave rise to doubt whether that campaign was at sea or on land. . . .*

In Their Own Words

"Primary source quotes allow characters in the lessons to express their beliefs and feelings directly to the students."

Photos and Illustrations

"Visualizing people in an unfamiliar setting helps the child imagine being in their place. Relating in this way is a first step toward empathy."

EXPLORING

Japanese and U.S. Schools

You can learn a great deal about another country by finding out about its schools. Education is one way in which a society passes its values and knowledge to the next generation. What is school like in Japan?

Who cleans your school? In Japan the students themselves sweep the floors of their classrooms daily.

Find Out

Look for answers to each of your questions. If an answer gives you an idea for another question, add it to your list.

Divide your information into two groups: ways in which U.S. and Japanese schools are alike and ways in which they are different. Did you find more similarities or more differences?

Get Ready

You'll need a notebook, a pen, and some books or magazines with information about schools in Japan.

Make a list of questions you want to answer: What time does school begin and end for Japanese students your age? Do they have dress codes? What about after- ... ? Do students move

新編 新しい社会(地理)

This is the cover of a ... textbook

Social Participation

"Class activities should summon affective as well as cognitive responses from students. Personal involvement in another period or culture leads naturally to identification with the people there."

Karen Wixson on

Making Instruction Considerate

"Instructional design really is a model of the thinking process that most of us learn to engage in through experience. Considerate instructional design makes the thinking process explicit. It helps the students become conscious of the thinking process."

Being considerate of the student means working out an instructional design that helps the student learn. The text, for example, must have a logical flow of information, and the lessons, chapters, and units must be woven together by meaningful transitions. There must also be unity in the focus of the text so that the student stays with the big ideas. Instructional supports in the text, such as headings, graphics, and charts, have to relate to important information in a way that guides the learner through the text. Finally, the material has to be appropriate to the audience."

Karen K. Wixson
Associate Professor of Education
University of Michigan, Ann Arbor

Scholar's Margin

"We designed an area outside the text body. We call it the Scholar's Margin. It was developed to guide student reading by focusing students on important ideas."

les, cucumbers, apricots, and dates ere grown in Babylonia. Pears, mons (called Persian apples by the Greeks), honey, and pistachio nuts ame from Persia itself. Coins made y the Persian government had the ame value all through the empire, aking it easier for people to buy nd sell goods. Banks loaned money nd even took checks.

Caravans of merchants moved long the 1,677 miles of the Royal Road built by Darius. It took them bout 90 days to travel from Sardis Susa, the Persian capital (see ap above). Relays of the shah's essengers, riding swift horses, aveled the road in about a week.

onquest and Revival

Even before Darius I died in 86 B.C., some of the satrapies re- olted. Persia fought several wars ith the Greek city-states (see Chapter 7). In 330 B.C. Persia fell to he army of Alexander the Great.

Across Time & Space

On April 3, 1860, the first pony express riders dashed off with the U.S. mail. They were copying the system Darius I had set up about 2,300 years earlier. "Nothing stops these couriers from covering their allotted stage . . . ," a Greek historian wrote of the Persian messengers, "neither snow, rain, heat, nor darkness." His words are still used by the U.S. Postal Service.

209

Iran

MAKING DECISIONS

Should Puerto Rico Be the 51st State?

Puerto Rico is a Latin American nation . . . except for political expression of the fact.

Puerto Rican Senator Fernando Martin

One half of the electorate in Puerto Rico would stand to gain economically and personally from a vote for statehood.

Former Governor Rafael Hernández Colón

Background

Consider these facts:

- Puerto Rico is an island about half the size of New Jersey.
- Puerto Rico's population is about 3.5 million people.
- Spanish is the island's official language.
- About 40 percent of the population speak some English.
- The island's per capita [per person] income is about $6,000.
- Its per capita income is higher than that of most other Caribbean islands.
- Its per capita income is about half that of Mississippi, the poorest state.
- Its unemployment rate is about 14 percent, higher than any state's.

U.S. involvement in Puerto Rico dates back to 1898. Up to that time, Puerto Rico had been a Spanish territory.

In April 1898 the United States went to war with Spain. The war lasted only four months. In that time the United States smashed Spanish fleets near the Philippines and Cuba. In July U.S. troops occupied Puerto Rico with little opposition. After the war Puerto Rico became a U.S. territory.

The following are other important dates in U.S.–Puerto Rican relations:

- **1917** Puerto Ricans were granted U.S. citizenship.
- **1948** Puerto Ricans elected their first governor.
- **1952** The island received U.S. commonwealth status. Thus, Puerto Rico would have its own government and constitution.
- **1967** Puerto Ricans voted to continue commonwealth status.

Luis Muñoz Marín
USA
05
Governor, Puerto Rico

▲ *Luis Muñoz Marín was elected the first governor of Puerto Rico in 1948.*

638

Chapter 27

Making Decisions

"Our Making Decisions features give students a map of the process of decision making. Decisions made in history are connected with current concerns."

Questions

"The Scholar's Margin questions, preceded by a red box, and the Review questions were designed to help students check their understanding of important points in the lesson."

ncreased manufacturing the d over has also damaged the ronment. Toxic, or poisonous, ke from industry and cars fills

come extinct, it is gone forever. The chart on this page lists some endangered species found in the United States and Puerto Rico. ■

■ *In what ways do humans shape the earth?*

REVIEW

1. **FOCUS** How do people interact with the natural world?
2. **GEOGRAPHY** What are some ways people are harming the environment?
3. **GEOGRAPHY** The radioactive waste that people create can't be thrown away because it doesn't decompose, or become part of the soil, like most other trash. So the United States is considering putting it all in one place and creating some sort of symbol that would alert everyone for thousands of years to KEEP OUT. What kind of symbol do you think would be most effective?
4. **CRITICAL THINKING** President Franklin D. Roosevelt once wrote, "The nation that destroys its soil destroys itself." What do you think he meant by this statement?
5. **ACTIVITY** Choose one of the animals listed on the Endangered Species chart on this page. Research your choice. Then write two or three paragraphs explaining what effect the extinction of this animal might have on the rest of the world. Illustrate your paragraph with a picture of the animal.

35

Exploring Geography

A Program That Captivates

Teachers and authors worked together to develop a program that reaches out and captivates a child. Together we developed books that students want to read, that capture student attention.

captivate

A Moment in Time

A Tea Master

Noon, October 3, 1992
A tearoom in Kyoto, Japan

Ladle (Hishaku)
With a graceful gesture, he dips the bamboo ladle. For years he has practiced each movement of the ceremony.

Kettle (Kama) and Brazier (Furo)
Hot coals in a brass *furo* heat water in his cast iron kettle. The sound of water in the *kama* reminds him of wind blowing through trees. Tea masters have heard this sound for centuries.

Tea Scoop (Chashaku)
He gives his bamboo scoop a special name—*akatonbo*. This is the name of a red dragonfly common in autumn. His tea ceremony honors the fall season.

Whisk (Chasen)
He rinses his whisk before stirring thin tea for his guests. Purity is important in sharing tea.

Tea Powder Container (Natsume)
Earlier this morning he poured green tea powder into his *natsume* to resemble a mountain. His guests appreciate the image from nature.

Tea Bowl
His tea bowls are simple and imperfect, as things are in nature. His favorite bowl has a faint crack shaped like an old vine in his garden.

369

A Moment in Time
This feature allows students to get an in-depth look at people, objects, and places. History and geography come alive in the middle of every-day activities.

A Story Well Told
Each lesson begins with a hook—an engaging passage—sometimes taken from a primary source or a piece of literature. What follows is a well-told story, presented in a meaningful way.

Teacher's Edition Notes
Convenient teacher's notes, like the Understanding the Visuals feature, give you additional information to make your instruction relevant and engaging.

6000 | 5000 | 4000 | 3000 | c. 2600 | B.C. | A.D. | c. 350 | 1000

L E S S O N 3

Great Achievements

He was counselor to the king, high priest of the sun, astrologer, and wise man. He was both a scribe and a sculptor. In a sense, Imhotep *(ihm HOH tehp)* represents the genius of Egypt.

About 2650 B.C., Egypt's King Djoser *(DZOH suhr)* asked Imhotep to design the grandest tomb ever. The result was Egypt's first pyramid and the first large monument of cut stone in the world. The Step Pyramid, at Saqqara *(suh KAHR uh)*, rose in six levels to a height of more than 200 feet.

Imhotep was most likely a doctor, too, and a brilliant one. He was one of the first people to study how the body worked. He may have known, for example, that blood runs through the body. This fact had to be discovered again by modern medicine 4,000 years later.

Egyptian medicine was famous in the ancient world. Egyptian doctors treated patients in Assyria and beyond. In the *Odyssey*, the Greek poet Homer summed up the world's admiration of Egyptian medicine. He wrote of Egypt,

> Where the rich plantations grow herbs of all kinds, maleficent [harmful] and healthful; and no one else knows medicine as they do, the Egyptian heirs of Paian, the healing god.

Imhotep was so admired that cultures in Egypt and beyond made him a God of medicine. For thousands of years, people prayed to him in the hope of being healed.

THINKING FOCUS

What lasting effects did the Egyptians and the Nubians have on the world?

Key Term

- papyrus

In Greece, Imhotep was worshiped as a God and was identified with the Greek God of medicine, Asclepius.

Egypt's Place in History

The works of Imhotep, like those of Egypt itself, lived on. Egyptian ideas spread throughout the ancient world. Some still affect our lives today.

Spread of Egyptian Culture

Trade was one way the ideas of Egypt traveled. Egypt exported paper, pottery, grain, and other goods. An Egyptian statue found on the island of Crete may have been brought there about 1700 B.C.

93

Understanding the Visuals

Direct the students' attention to the picture of the Guatemalan schoolboys on this page. About 20 different languages, mostly of Mayan origin, are spoken in Guatemala. Remind students of the Mayan civilization they learned about in Chapter 6.

Invite students to examine the fish-shaped tapestry on these pages. Dating from A.D. 1000, this textile originated in the central coast region of Peru. Ask students what the design might tell them about the early Peruvians. *(Fish, and probably fishing, were important to them.)*

The Earliest Humans, 2,400,000–15,000 B.C.

2,400,000 B.C. Date of oldest human fossil and oldest stone tools

1,600,000 B.C. Date of oldest *Homo erectus* fossils

900,000 B.C. *Homo sapiens* first appears.

2,500,000 | 2,000,000 | 1,500,000 | 1,000,000

2,000,000 B.C. Upright *Homo erectus* first appears.

50,000 B.C. Hunter-gatherer societies emerge.

15,000 B.C. Hunter-gatherer societies begin to farm.

Timelines
Timelines draw students into the chronology of history. Timelines help students relate images, ideas, events, and places in temporal order.

A Program That Develops

Developing and deepening student understanding of conceptual knowledge is a key part of forming literate citizens. Enriching student awareness of important ideas is one of the fundamental goals of this program. We include features that help you develop a deeper understanding of knowledge in your students.

develop

Understanding
The Understanding feature takes an in-depth look at an important lesson concept. This feature allows students to relate concepts to ideas they already know.

UNDERSTANDING NATURAL RESOURCES

Since the beginning of time, natural forces have shaped and changed our earth. During the ice ages, massive glaciers inched across the land, carving out lakes and ponds in their paths. The powerful force of earthquakes has pushed precious metals like gold and silver up from deep inside of the earth, while reshaping the face of the earth. Wet, cold climates of northern regions have produced forests of towering trees spreading far ...s the land.

Nature and Human Needs

Humans have come to depend on these products of nature for their survival. Fresh water from lakes and ponds can meet the water needs of entire communities. Lumber from the trees of the north is used to make strong and sturdy houses. Oil and natural gas found deep within the earth provide energy to run factories and businesses and to heat homes. Metals such as gold, silver, and copper are used to make tools and valuable jewelry.

Resources You Use

These materials that humans find in nature and use for their needs are called natural resources. Without natural resources, life as you know it would not exist. Look around you, and you will see many examples of natural resources. A short list might include the electricity that powers your television set, the plastic (produced from oil) wrapper on your sandwich, the steel used to build your family's car, and the water that runs through your home.

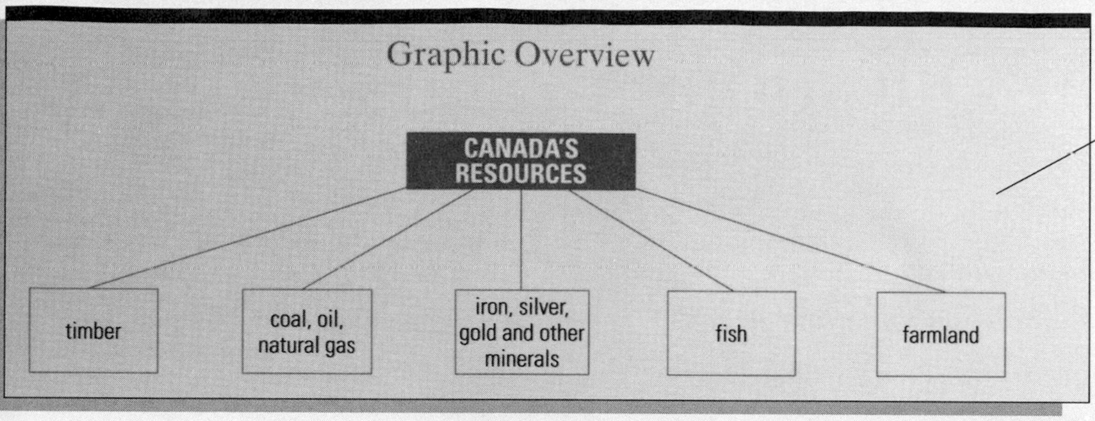

Graphic Overview
CANADA'S RESOURCES
timber
coal, oil, natural gas
iron, silver, gold and other minerals
fish
farmland

Graphic Overviews
Graphic Overviews in the Teacher's Edition give you a new way to organize knowledge. Each is a visual map to learning.

Photographs and Illustrations
Visual learning is a special way to help students develop their knowledge. It also helps to reach students who might otherwise be unreachable.

DEVELOP

Direct students to the map on page 653 and explain that the separate nations of North Korea and South Korea were for many centuries the single country of Korea. Ask what countries are nearby. *(China, Russia, and Japan)* To get a better idea of the size and location of Korea, refer your students to the map of Eurasia on pages 682–683 of the Atlas. Help students identify Korea as a peninsula; tell them that Korea's geographic isolation was yet another reason it was called the Hermit Kingdom. Explain that this lesson will tell about ancient Korea and about what life is like in South Korea today.

Teacher's Edition Notes
The Teacher's Edition point-of-use notes supply you with background knowledge and ideas to help you develop in students a deeper understanding of a subject.

A Program That Questions

Helping students think about ideas and issues involves getting them to question and think in a critical way. We developed a program with solid critical thinking strategies and a thorough assessment component.

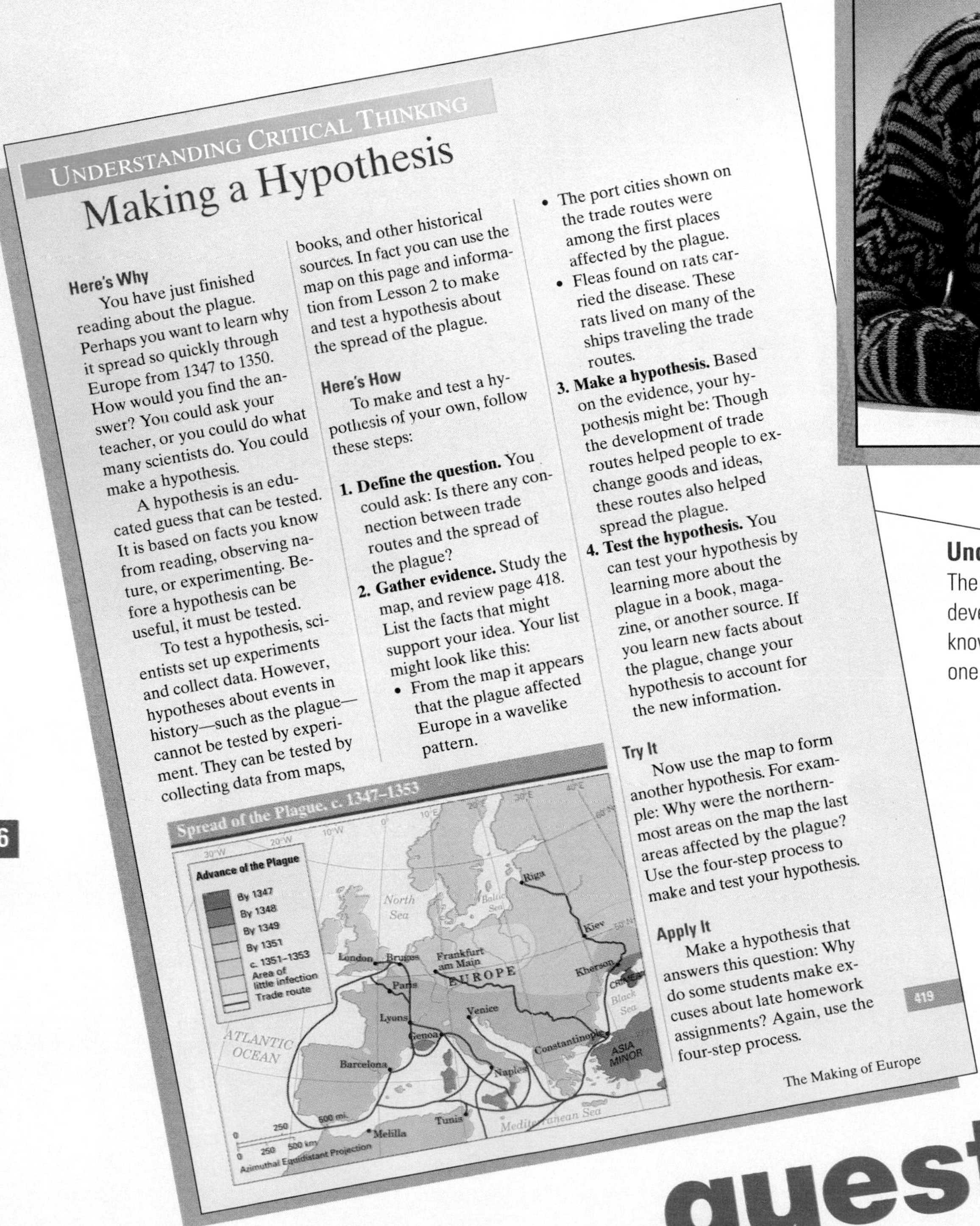

UNDERSTANDING CRITICAL THINKING

Making a Hypothesis

Here's Why

You have just finished reading about the plague. Perhaps you want to learn why it spread so quickly through Europe from 1347 to 1350. How would you find the answer? You could ask your teacher, or you could do what many scientists do. You could make a hypothesis.

A hypothesis is an educated guess that can be tested. It is based on facts you know from reading, observing nature, or experimenting. Before a hypothesis can be useful, it must be tested.

To test a hypothesis, scientists set up experiments and collect data. However, hypotheses about events in history—such as the plague—cannot be tested by experiment. They can be tested by collecting data from maps, books, and other historical sources. In fact you can use the map on this page and information from Lesson 2 to make and test a hypothesis about the spread of the plague.

Here's How

To make and test a hypothesis of your own, follow these steps:

1. **Define the question.** You could ask: Is there any connection between trade routes and the spread of the plague?
2. **Gather evidence.** Study the map, and review page 418. List the facts that might support your idea. Your list might look like this:
   - From the map it appears that the plague affected Europe in a wavelike pattern.
   - The port cities shown on the trade routes were among the first places affected by the plague.
   - Fleas found on rats carried the disease. These rats lived on many of the ships traveling the trade routes.
3. **Make a hypothesis.** Based on the evidence, your hypothesis might be: Though the development of trade routes helped people to exchange goods and ideas, these routes also helped spread the plague.
4. **Test the hypothesis.** You can test your hypothesis by learning more about the plague in a book, magazine, or another source. If you learn new facts about the plague, change your hypothesis to account for the new information.

Try It

Now use the map to form another hypothesis. For example: Why were the northernmost areas on the map the last areas affected by the plague? Use the four-step process to make and test your hypothesis.

Apply It

Make a hypothesis that answers this question: Why do some students make excuses about late homework assignments? Again, use the four-step process.

Spread of the Plague, c. 1347–1353

Advance of the Plague
By 1347
By 1348
By 1349
By 1351
c. 1351–1353
Area of little infection
Trade route
North Sea
Riga
Kiev
London
Bruges
Frankfurt am Main
EUROPE
Paris
Kherson
CRIMEA
Black Sea
Lyons
Venice
Genoa
Constantinople
ASIA MINOR
ATLANTIC OCEAN
Barcelona
Naples
Tunis
Melilla
Mediterranean Sea
Azimuthal Equidistant Projection

419

The Making of Europe

Understanding

The Understanding feature helps integrate the development of skills with the learning of knowledge. In this program, Critical Thinking is one of the central skill strands.

question

Access Strategy

Ideas to help you aid students with limited English proficiency and students with little prior knowledge of a subject are parts of the Access Strategy feature in the Teacher's Edition.

Access Strategy

Have students analyze the photographs on pages 127 (Machu Picchu), 138 (mountain peaks), and 141 (mountain trail). What kind of land surface appears in all of the photos? *(Mountains)* Now have students use the map on this page to confirm their answer. Tell students that the Andes have a number of peaks that are higher than Mount McKinley, the highest peak in North America. Discuss with students what problems people would have living in such an environment. On the map on this page, point out the large rivers that run from south to north between the mountains. The effect of this is that travelers going from west to east must cross three or four parallel mountain ranges and large rivers. One reason why Machu Picchu remained hidden for so long is its location above cliffs and between two deep river valleys.

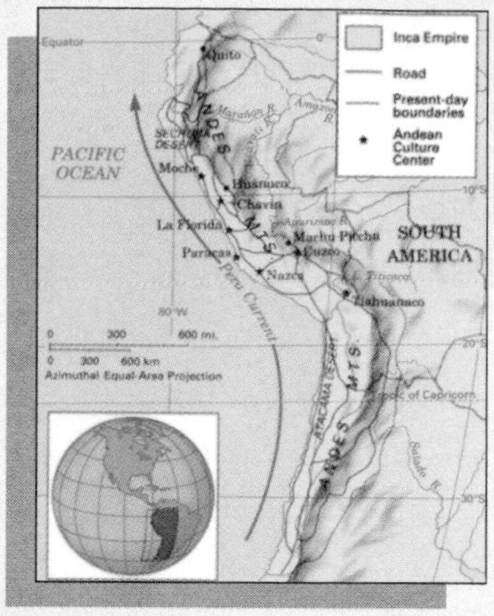

Inca Empire
Road
Present-day boundaries
Andean Culture Center
PACIFIC OCEAN
SOUTH AMERICA
Quito
Moche
Huanuco
Chavín
La Florida
Machu Picchu
Cuzco
Paracas
Nazca
Tiahuanaco
Peru Current
ANDES MTS.
Tropic of Capricorn
Azimuthal Equal-Area Projection

Making Decisions

Students are actively engaged in addressing important issues in this program. This feature helps students develop decision-making skills.

MAKING DECISIONS

Rain Forests: Preserve Them? Use Them?

We simply cannot replace this invaluable resource once it is gone. The rain forests . . . once lost, can never be regained. Every second of every day, we are losing a tropical forest the size of a football field.

Hon. John E. Porter
U.S. Representative, Illinois

How can Brazil be expected to control its economic development, [Brazil's President José Sarney] asks, when it is staggering under a $111 billion foreign-debt load? By what right does the U.S. . . . lecture poor countries like Brazil on their responsibilities to mankind?

Time, September 18, 1989

Background

From the air Brazil's great forests look like a giant, green cushion. Once the earth nourished many such rain forests. Now only a few remain. The loss of these rain forests affects the entire world.

How? Like all plants, the huge trees of the forest take in carbon dioxide from the air. They use this gas to make their food. In the process, they release oxygen into the atmosphere. The enormous forests, therefore, help balance the carbon dioxide and the oxygen in the earth's atmosphere. When the trees are cut down, we reduce the amount of carbon dioxide taken from the air. At the same time, we are burning more gasoline and other fossil fuels, releasing more carbon dioxide into the air. Some scientists predict that this buildup of carbon dioxide in the atmosphere will cause the world's climates to grow warmer and warmer. We cannot foresee all the results of this global warming. One possibility, though, is that fertile farmland could someday become barren desert.

A close look at the rain forests reveals bare patches, some as big as Connecticut. Other effects of deforestation are more difficult to see. When trees go, so do mammals, plants, insects, and birds. Species as unique as the frogs shown here may also become extinct if this trend continues. Such extinctions could have far-reaching effects. For example, many of our medicines come from plants. What if a plant growing in a rain forest today contains a cure for a form of cancer? What if the plant becomes extinct as the forest shrinks?

Roots of the Problem

If you look only at the effects of this loss of the rain forests, the solution may seem clear: Put a stop to it. To see how complicated the problem really is, you have to study the causes—the reasons for clearing the rain forests.

As you have read, Brazil has a large and rapidly growing population. Providing jobs and housing requires space. Some forests are cleared to build homes, factories, roads, and bridges.

Like most other countries, Brazil wants to keep a balance of trade. This means that Brazil tries to sell to other nations as much as it buys from them. Brazil imports steel and other products. It exports beef, rubber, and lumber. Forests are cleared to provide grazing land for cattle. Lumber, of course, comes from the forests.

In addition, Brazilian miners bring 70 tons of gold a year out of the rain forests. Some areas of the forests are cleared to give the miners room to work.

Brazilians want to raise their standard of living. If the rain forests can be useful, why shouldn't they benefit the nation in which they grow?

Decision Point

1. After reading about the problem of the rain forests, what questions do you have?
2. Where would you look for more information about global warming? About Brazil's economy?
3. Are there ways to both preserve and use the rain forests? How can you find out?
4. Choose one topic related to the rain forest problem. What more do you need to know about it? Find the information in newspapers and magazines.
5. Discuss the new information you and your classmates found. Based on this limited information, what ideas and alternatives can you suggest?

566

Chapter 24

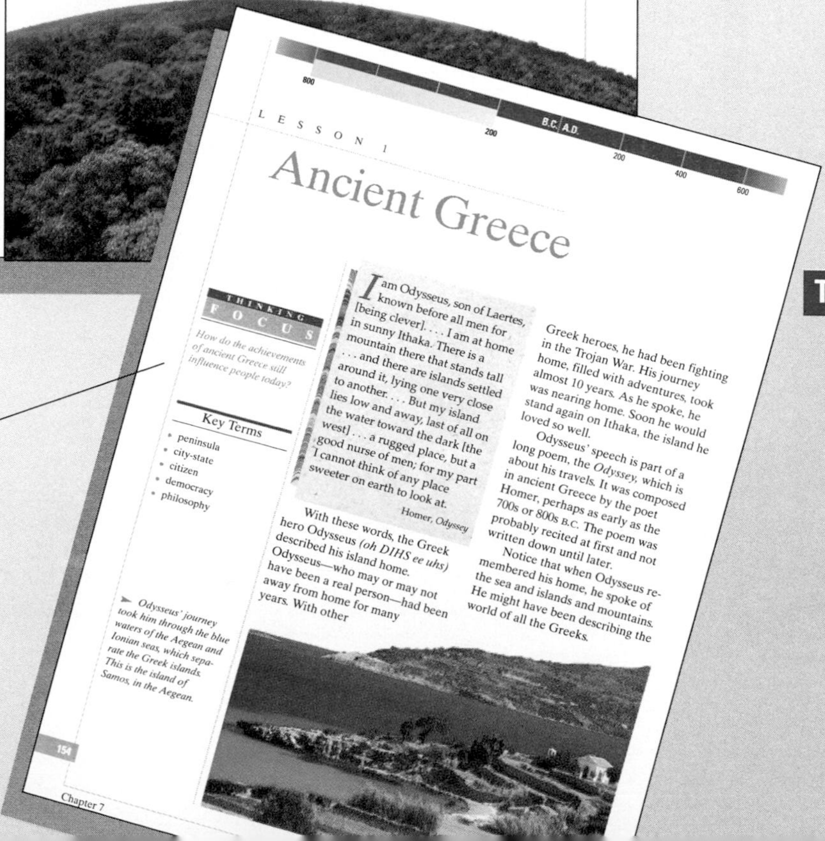

800 200 B.C. A.D. 200 400 600

L E S S O N 1

Ancient Greece

THINKING FOCUS

How do the achievements of ancient Greece still influence people today?

Key Terms
- peninsula
- city-state
- citizen
- democracy
- philosophy

I am Odysseus, son of Laertes, known before all men for [being clever]. . . . I am at home in sunny Ithaka. There is a mountain there that stands tall . . . and there are islands settled around it, lying one very close to another. . . . But my island lies low and away, last of all on the water toward the dark [the west] . . . a rugged place, but a good nurse of men; for my part I cannot think of any place sweeter on earth to look at.

Homer, *Odyssey*

With these words, the Greek hero Odysseus *(oh DIHS ee uhs)* described his island home. Odysseus—who may or may not have been a real person—had been away from home for many years. With other Greek heroes, he had been fighting in the Trojan War. His journey home, filled with adventures, took almost 10 years. As he spoke, he was nearing home. Soon he would stand again on Ithaka, the island he loved so well.

Odysseus' speech is part of a long poem, the *Odyssey*, which is about his travels. It was composed in ancient Greece by the poet Homer, perhaps as early as the 700s or 800s B.C. The poem was probably recited at first and not written down until later.

Notice that when Odysseus remembered his home, he spoke of the sea and islands and mountains. He might have been describing the world of all the Greeks.

Odysseus' journey took him through the blue waters of the Aegean and Ionian seas, which separate the Greek islands. This is the island of Samos, in the Aegean.

154

Chapter 7

Thinking Focus

The Thinking Focus question sets up a purpose for the lesson. It centers students' attention as they read.

A Program That Stretches

Effective instruction encourages students to go beyond the classroom to seek an understanding of the social world. You have asked us to come up with ideas that help you stretch student learning and to provide extra resources that enrich students' educational experience.

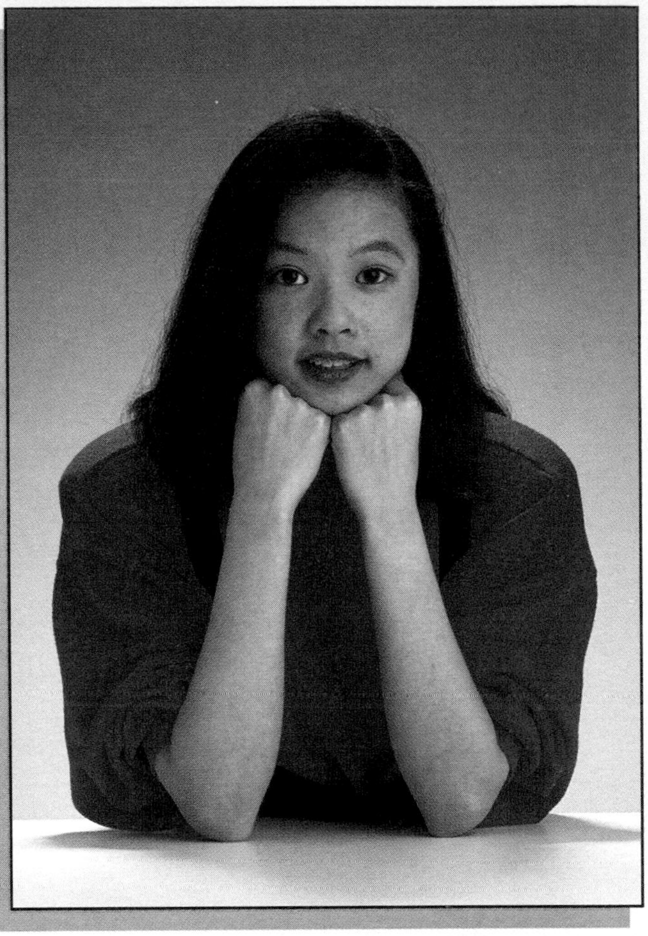

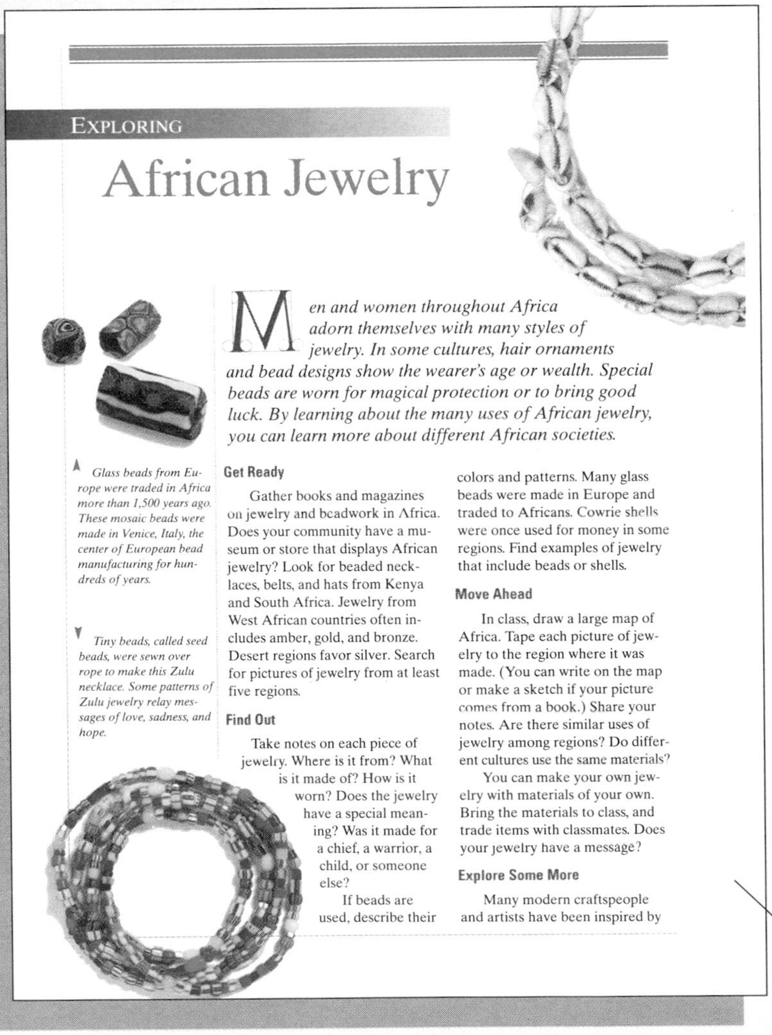

EXPLORING

African Jewelry

Men and women throughout Africa adorn themselves with many styles of jewelry. In some cultures, hair ornaments and bead designs show the wearer's age or wealth. Special beads are worn for magical protection or to bring good luck. By learning about the many uses of African jewelry, you can learn more about different African societies.

▲ *Glass beads from Europe were traded in Africa more than 1,500 years ago. These mosaic beads were made in Venice, Italy, the center of European bead manufacturing for hundreds of years.*

▼ *Tiny beads, called seed beads, were sewn over rope to make this Zulu necklace. Some patterns of Zulu jewelry relay messages of love, sadness, and hope.*

Get Ready

Gather books and magazines on jewelry and beadwork in Africa. Does your community have a museum or store that displays African jewelry? Look for beaded necklaces, belts, and hats from Kenya and South Africa. Jewelry from West African countries often includes amber, gold, and bronze. Desert regions favor silver. Search for pictures of jewelry from at least five regions.

Find Out

Take notes on each piece of jewelry. Where is it from? What is it made of? How is it worn? Does the jewelry have a special meaning? Was it made for a chief, a warrior, a child, or someone else?

If beads are used, describe their colors and patterns. Many glass beads were made in Europe and traded to Africans. Cowrie shells were once used for money in some regions. Find examples of jewelry that include beads or shells.

Move Ahead

In class, draw a large map of Africa. Tape each picture of jewelry to the region where it was made. (You can write on the map or make a sketch if your picture comes from a book.) Share your notes. Are there similar uses of jewelry among regions? Do different cultures use the same materials?

You can make your own jewelry with materials of your own. Bring the materials to class, and trade items with classmates. Does your jewelry have a message?

Explore Some More

Many modern craftspeople and artists have been inspired by

stretch

Explore

Our Explore feature provides opportunities for students to try to find out new things for themselves.

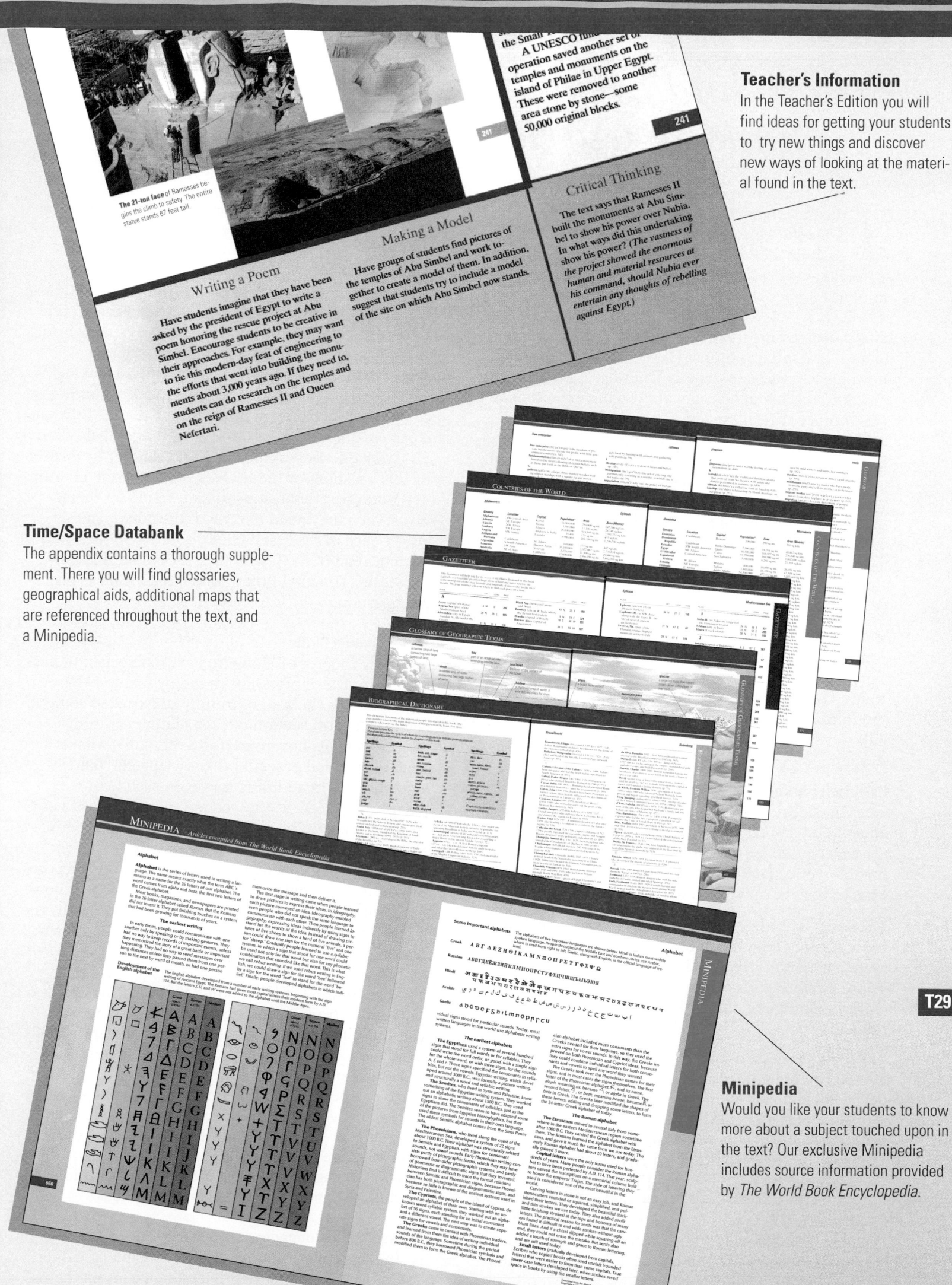

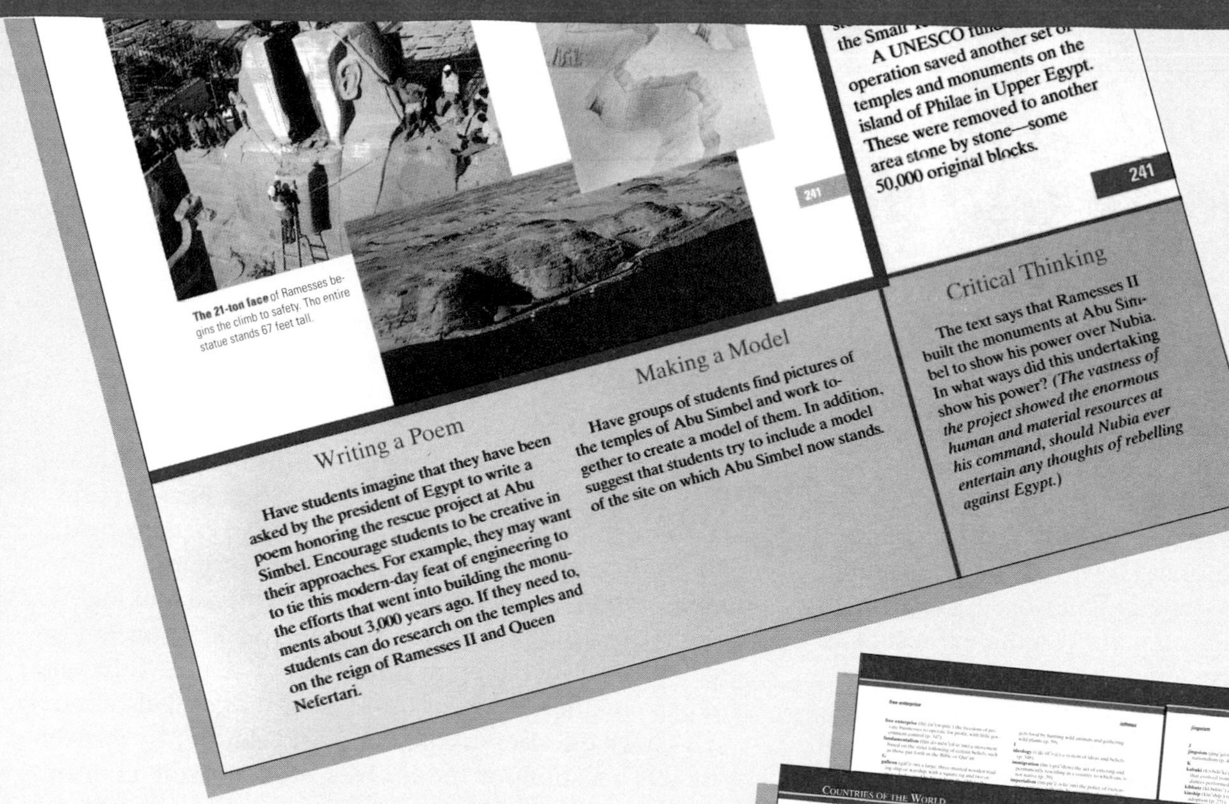
A UNESCO ... operation saved another set of temples and monuments on the island of Philae in Upper Egypt. These were removed to another area stone by stone—some 50,000 original blocks.
241
241
The 21-ton face of Ramesses begins the climb to safety. The entire statue stands 67 feet tall.
Writing a Poem
Have students imagine that they have been asked by the president of Egypt to write a poem honoring the rescue project at Abu Simbel. Encourage students to be creative in their approaches. For example, they may want to tie this modern-day feat of engineering to the efforts that went into building the monuments about 3,000 years ago. If they need to, students can do research on the temples and on the reign of Ramesses II and Queen Nefertari.
Making a Model
Have groups of students find pictures of the temples of Abu Simbel and work together to create a model of them. In addition, suggest that students try to include a model of the site on which Abu Simbel now stands.
Critical Thinking
The text says that Ramesses II built the monuments at Abu Simbel to show his power over Nubia. In what ways did this undertaking show his power? (The vastness of the project showed the enormous human and material resources at his command, should Nubia ever entertain any thoughts of rebelling against Egypt.)

Teacher's Information

In the Teacher's Edition you will find ideas for getting your students to try new things and discover new ways of looking at the material found in the text.

Glossary
Countries of the World
Gazetteer
Glossary of Geographic Terms
Biographical Dictionary

Time/Space Databank

The appendix contains a thorough supplement. There you will find glossaries, geographical aids, additional maps that are referenced throughout the text, and a Minipedia.

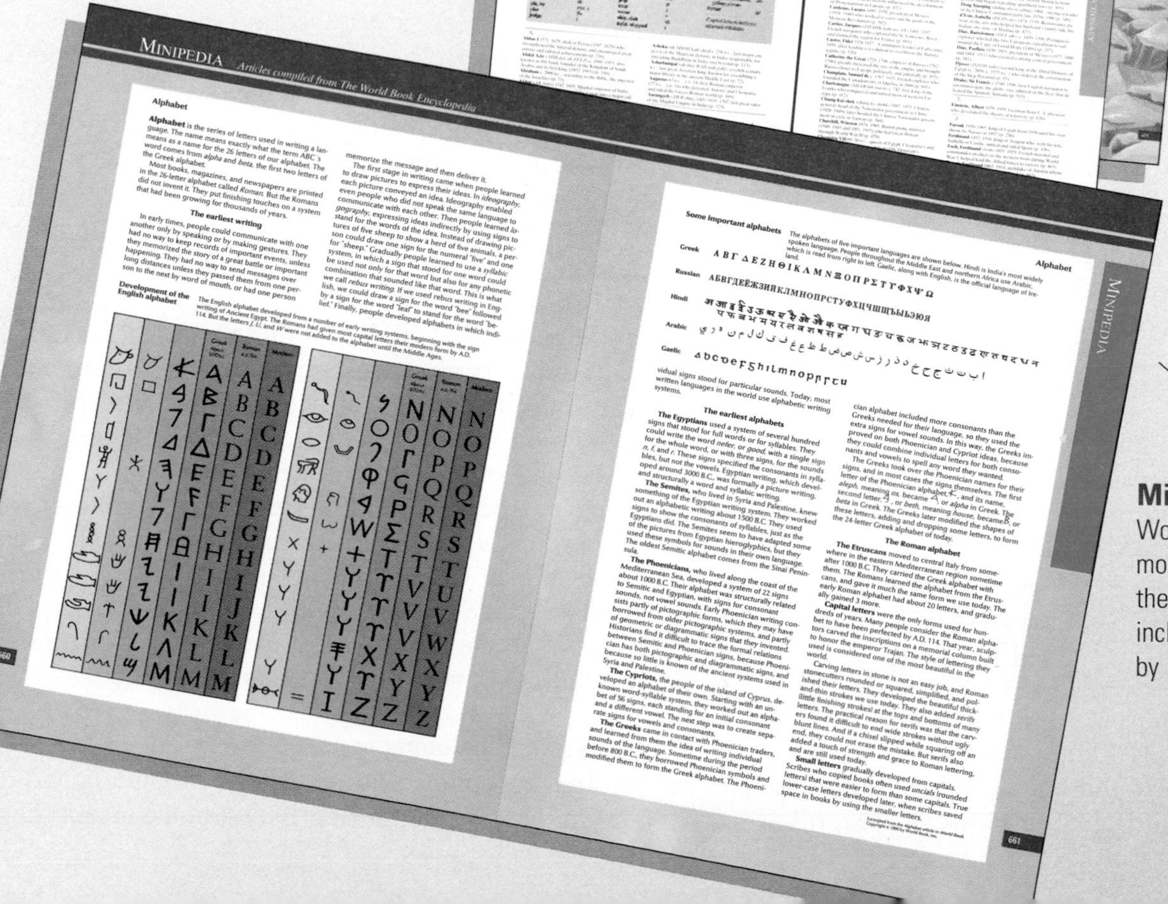
Minipedia Articles compiled from The World Book Encyclopedia
Alphabet
The earliest writing
Some important alphabets
The earliest alphabets
The Roman alphabet
Minipedia
660
661

Minipedia

Would you like your students to know more about a subject touched upon in the text? Our exclusive Minipedia includes source information provided by *The World Book Encyclopedia*.

Social Studies and the Thinking Curriculum

The development of reflective and knowledgeable thinkers and decision makers is an important goal of instruction in social studies as well as in other curriculum areas. Many educators have traditionally approached thinking in terms of a hierarchy of skills in which young students master basic skills before progressing to "higher-order" skills such as analysis and interpretation. However, recent research indicates that these so-called higher-order skills are crucial to successful learning at even the earliest ages.

Another critical aspect of the new research on learning is that knowledge and skills must be developed together, and not as isolated elements. The dual agenda of knowledge and skills is an important part of the Houghton Mifflin program.

Instead of focusing on a rigid hierarchy of thinking skills, effective instruction takes into account many aspects of thinking. The following definitions describe four key aspects of thinking as they are used in Houghton Mifflin Social Studies.

Metacognition: Simply put, *metacognition* means being aware of our thinking as we perform tasks and using that awareness to monitor and direct what we are doing. This ability is exercised by all skilled readers and thinkers, and it is crucial to model metacognitive skills for students so that they can become independent learners.

Critical Thinking: Although *critical thinking* is a major focus in education today, the term is often ambiguously understood. Houghton Mifflin Social Studies adopts the widely used definition of critical thinking as reasonable, reflective thinking that is focused on deciding what to believe or what to do.

Thinking Skills: In Houghton Mifflin Social Studies, the term *thinking skills* refers to basic mental tasks such as observing, comparing, classifying, or predicting. These discrete skills can be learned and then used in metacognition, critical thinking, and other thinking processes.

Thinking Processes: The term *thinking processes* refers to goal-oriented processes such as problem solving and decision making that involve a variable but predictable sequence of thinking skills.

Houghton Mifflin Social Studies Features That Promote Thinking

Because thinking is central to all instruction and learning, Houghton Mifflin Social Studies integrates metacognition, critical thinking, thinking skills and thinking processes throughout. However, several features are particularly effective devices for promoting the development of skilled thinkers.

Scholar's Margin

In every lesson of Houghton Mifflin Social Studies, the outside margin of each page is a Scholar's Margin devoted to helping students take charge of their own learning. In other words, it is there to promote metacognition. Each lesson begins with a Thinking Focus question that alerts students to a key concept or idea they should keep in mind as they read. At the end of each major section of the lesson, they will also find a self-check question in the Scholar's Margin. By answering this question for themselves, students can monitor their own comprehension and determine for themselves when they need to reread. If students can answer each of these self-check questions, when they reach the end of the lesson they should be able to answer the Thinking Focus, which reappears as the first question in the lesson Review.

Understanding Skills

Every chapter of Houghton Mifflin Social Studies contains one or more Understanding features that teach students skills in a carefully constructed context. The Here's How section of each feature carefully teaches students how to perform the skill—what is sometimes called procedural knowledge or "knowledge of how." In addition, however, each feature begins with a Here's Why section that addresses a critical but often overlooked aspect of thinking—conditional knowledge or "knowledge of why and when." This section helps students to understand the purposes for which they would use the skill and to identify conditions under which it would be useful. As a result, students learn not just how to use a skill but also how to determine for themselves when it would be useful to apply the skill.

Many of the Understanding Skills features focus on skills drawn from our Critical Thinking strand. Students have the opportunity to practice and apply skills of defining and clarifying problems and issues, evaluating and judging information, identifying alternative perspectives and solving problems and drawing conclusions. At every grade level, students work with these "higher-order" skills. What progresses from grade to grade is the difficulty of the information about which students are thinking and the sophistication of the context in which these skills are applied.

Understanding Concepts

In most chapters another type of Understanding feature provides an in-depth look at a concept that is key to that chapter. These features provide support for students in the important thinking process of concept formation. They provide extended definitions and present examples and nonexamples of the concept. These features also help students identify the major attributes of the concept and relate it to other concepts they have learned previously.

Making Decisions

Because a key goal of social studies instruction is the development of citizens who can make informed and responsible decisions, the process of decision making is a particularly appropriate thinking process to emphasize in social studies. The Making Decisions features in Houghton Mifflin Social Studies provide the opportunity for students to analyze important decisions in history and utilize the thinking skills that make up the decision-making process.

These features have been developed on the basis of a five-step model of decision making that maps out the sequence of critical thinking skills involved in making decisions:

1. Recognize the need for a decision.
2. Define the goals and values involved.
3. Acquire and evaluate necessary information.
4. Identify and analyze possible alternatives.
5. Choose the best alternative.

As this model demonstrates, the process of decision making involves all of the major strands of social studies instruction: knowledge, skills, and values. Thus these features provide a powerful tool for integrated learning and thinking.

A Classroom Climate That Promotes Thinking

One thing that distinguishes proficient thinkers and decision makers from poorer ones is not so much the skills they possess as their motivation and tendency to use them. Because thinking is hard work, students need not only to know how to do it but also to have their own powerful reasons for wanting to think critically and reflectively. The role of the teacher is crucial in helping students become motivated and active thinkers. In particular, researchers point to the importance of modeling skillful thinking for students and of establishing a classroom environment that encourages and values thinking.

Modeling can take a variety of forms. For example, you as a teacher can model for students ways of becoming aware of your own thinking and using that awareness to control what you are doing. You may start by verbalizing for students your internal thought processes as you process new information. This "thinking out loud" may include

- assessing your current knowledge ("Do I know the meaning of all the words in this text?" or "Do I understand the legend on this map?")
- setting goals ("What do I want to know or be able to do when I'm through?")
- checking your progress as you go along ("Do I understand what I just read?" or "Am I closer to my goal now than when I started?")

Teachers also play a vital role in modeling attitudes and dispositions that are essential to successful thinking and learning. Important first steps include modeling and reinforcing such basic attitudes as "hard work pays off" and "it's important to learn from mistakes." Teachers also provide a major service to students by exemplifying important dispositions of critical thinking, such as:

- seeking a clear statement of a question
- using and mentioning credible sources
- seeking reasons
- looking for alternatives and alternative viewpoints
- being open-minded
- changing one's position when the evidence merits

In addition to the teacher, student interaction can also play an important role in developing skilled thinkers. This is one reason why collaborative learning can be a powerful approach (see page T34). More capable students can model for peers effective ways of approaching problems, analyzing text, and organizing their work. Students in groups may also support each other in carrying out complicated tasks. By working collaboratively, the group can succeed at a task that individual students could not handle alone.

Finally, the social setting of the classroom can communicate to students that all aspects of thinking are valued. Through their behavior and interactions, teachers and students can convey the message that questioning, interpreting, and trying many possibilities are as important as "getting the right answer."

For Further Reading

Laughlin, Margaret A., H. Michael Hartoonian, Norris M. Sanders, eds. *From Information to Decision Making: New Challenges for Effective Citizenship.* Washington, D.C.: National Council for the Social Studies (Bulletin No. 83), 1989.

Marzano, Robert J., et al. *Dimensions of Thinking: A Framework for Curriculum and Instruction.* Alexandria, Va.: Association for Supervision and Curriculum Development, 1988.

Access to Social Studies for Limited English Proficient Students

Because of rapid demographic changes nationwide, many school districts now enroll a significant number of students whose first language is not English. In most cases, Limited English Proficient (LEP) students in a school have widely different educational backgrounds and function at a broad range of achievement levels. Students who are completely non-English speaking may need to access social studies through their first language while acquiring English. As pupils reach intermediate-level fluency in English, they usually can comprehend content taught in the new language when teachers make effective use of context clues, such as facial expressions, gestures, and props.

Features of Houghton Mifflin Social Studies That Promote Access

Houghton Mifflin Social Studies has been designed to facilitate maximum access to social studies concepts for students from a wide variety of cultural and linguistic backgrounds. The unique Visual Learning strand and prominent instructional visuals throughout the program provide a channel of access for LEP students. Additional LEP-appropriate features are clearly identified for you in the Unit Organizer chart that precedes each unit, including:

- LEP Unit Activities
- Access Strategies and Activities
- Graphic Overviews
- Visual Learning Strategies

Strategies for Accessible Instruction

Teachers of LEP students should consider the following suggestions.

1. **Use language-sensitive techniques** to lower the language barrier for intermediate fluency LEP students. These techniques include:
   - using gestures and facial expressions
   - modeling the desired performance
   - using visuals and props
   - simplifying speech
   - showing a sample of the finished product
   - breaking down complicated tasks into subtasks
   - checking frequently for understanding
2. **Build background knowledge** necessary to unlock key concepts in the lesson, using the TE Access Strategy and discussion of the Study Prints, Posters, and Overhead Transparencies.
3. **Tap prior knowledge** by having pupils brainstorm what they already know about the topic, do quick-writes, and use Venn diagrams (T36) to show similarities and differences among ideas or events.
4. **Preteach only essential vocabulary** for understanding the key concepts in a lesson. Where possible, introduce families of words in context with interactive activities (see T36–T37).
5. **Utilize collaborative learning** activities that enable pairs and small groups of students to read selected sections of text together (see T34–T35).
6. **Use oral and visual language** by talking through the Graphic Overview and Thinking Focus for each new lesson to help LEP students focus on key concepts.

Social Studies and the Overall LEP Program

There is no simple way to eliminate completely the language barrier to social studies for LEP students. LEP youngsters are most successful when they have a program that enables them to achieve functional fluency in English quickly. Such a program begins with intensive English as a second language (ESL) lessons designed to teach the basics of English. Then an advanced ESL program might teach social studies vocabulary and build conceptual background to enable students to derive maximum benefit from the Houghton Mifflin Social Studies program.

In addition to a sequential English language development program, students who are in the initial phases of acquiring English may need primary language support to comprehend fully the key concepts in the program. To benefit all students, Houghton Mifflin Social Studies has been designed to facilitate access to grade-level social studies through instructional strategies that are grounded in language and learning theory as well as good teaching.

For Further Reading

Cantoni-Harvey, G. *Content-Area Language Instruction: Approaches and Strategies.* Reading, Mass.: Addison-Wesley, 1987.

Crandall, J. A., D. Christian, and D. J. Short. *How to Integrate Language and Content Instruction: A Training Manual.* Berkeley, Cal.: Center for Language Education and Research, University of California, 1989.

Richard-Amato, P. A. *Making It Happen: Interaction in the Second Language Classroom from Theory to Practice.* New York: Longman, 1988.

Teaching Multicultural Perspectives

Three important changes in the United States during the last 25 years have profoundly affected the content and methods of social studies education. First, Asians and Latin Americans have become the largest immigrant groups. Newcomers from these and other parts of the world have dramatically altered the demographic composition of most classrooms.

Second, more than ever before, scholars have focused on the historical and social reality of gender, ethnic, and racial groups. This research has resulted in the reevaluation of the roles these groups have played in the making of the United States. Today we can accurately document the contributions made and the difficulties faced by all groups.

Third, the momentous social and political changes resulting from the civil rights movement and the more recent affirmation of cultural distinctions have led to widespread concern with ethnic and racial identity. Expressions of this concern have ranged from celebration to censure.

Instructional Goals and Strategies

With today's heightened awareness of cultural diversity comes the responsibility to address cultural differences with respect and common sense. Houghton Mifflin Social Studies assists you in fulfilling that responsibility. The multicultural perspectives employed throughout the series promote three important goals.

1. **Facilitating readiness to learn in the classroom:** Students who encounter people like themselves in the pages of their textbooks will be more at ease in the school setting and will gain the sense of belonging that prepares them to learn. The variety of foreign-born students in today's classrooms makes inclusive representation more difficult than ever before. Teachers and textbooks must be sensitive to a wide range of cultural differences.

   Houghton Mifflin Social Studies achieves inclusiveness through empathetic descriptions of the aspirations and achievements of all groups. Multicultural representation occurs not only for the United States, but also for other past and present societies.

2. **Providing a more accurate representation of historical events and the world today:** To achieve the second goal, the program incorporates the most recent applicable scholarship in history, geography, anthropology, and the other social sciences. The aim is to represent factually the relevant groups and individuals—mainstream or minority—that have contributed to the making of the United States and other nations, while avoiding the suggestion that all cultures have been equally prominent in all times and places. Controversial matters are dealt with in an accurate manner, free of bias. Instructional materials make use of primary sources and quotations to present the positions of the affected actors in their own words. This, in turn, can help teachers bring life to the perspectives significant to the issues, events, and processes that have shaped our nation and the world. Multiple perspectives provide a stage for students to explore, debate, and make informed judgments regarding contrasting interpretations of human events.

3. **Encouraging respect for ethnic, cultural, and social differences:** The third goal requires balanced descriptions of ethnic, racial, and religious groups. Group or individual descriptions are carefully scrutinized to avoid language that might appear patronizing, stereotypical, or demeaning. In addition, HMSS represents ways of living, occupations, and religions of all peoples with accuracy and without value judgments. Ethnic and racial groups appear in leadership, problem-solving, and decision-making roles appropriate to their participation in society. This commitment to accurate representation allows exploration of the barriers that have restricted choices for racial and ethnic groups and for women.

   HMSS includes a discussion of religious and ethical beliefs in contexts where such beliefs strongly influence the culture or historical trajectory of a group. With respect to religion, descriptions are factual and not judgmental. Care is taken that no belief system is ridiculed, trivialized, or portrayed as inferior.

   What students read about people from other historical periods and other cultural backgrounds profoundly affects the students' attitudes. The goal of HMSS is to help students understand and respect all peoples as equals.

For Further Reading

Banks, James. *Teaching Strategies for Ethnic Studies.* Boston: Allyn and Bacon, 1991.

Hernandez, Hilda. *Multicultural Education.* Columbus, Oh.: Merrill Publishing Company, 1989.

Nash, Gary. *A Teacher's Guide to Multicultural Perspectives in Social Studies.* Boston: Houghton Mifflin Company, 1991.

Using Collaborative Learning in Social Studies

Collaborative learning is a strategy or structure for learning that can be adapted to many lessons and activities. There are many models or approaches to collaborative learning (or cooperative learning), but all of these models share certain basic characteristics:

- Students work face to face in heterogeneous groups.
- Each member of the group has a clearly defined role and is individually accountable.
- Each member makes an important contribution to the success of the group's effort ("positive interdependence").

In addition to the advantages that it offers in all curriculum areas, collaborative learning is an especially appropriate strategy for social studies. Working together in collaborative groups is an excellent way to develop students' skills of social participation, always a key goal of the social studies curriculum.

As a teacher, you should feel free to take collaborative learning at your own pace. You may wish to begin with simple strategies in which students work in pairs. As both you and your students become comfortable with this approach to learning, you can tackle more elaborate activities involving groups of four or five.

Your Role as Teacher

It is important to bear in mind that collaborative learning supplements direct instruction—it does not replace it. As always, the teacher provides the solid instruction that is the basis for learning. And simply putting students in groups and giving them an interesting assignment does not lead to successful collaborative learning. Instead, you as teacher play the key role of providing structure, guidance, and feedback. In a very real sense, your role becomes that of coach or facilitator.

An important ingredient in the success of collaborative groups is effective use of interpersonal skills. As facilitator, you can help groups identify ahead of time the kinds of interpersonal skills that will be important to the task they are undertaking. These skills may range from something as simple as speaking quietly to more complex skills such as encouraging participation and giving constructive criticism. Modeling these skills for students and helping students practice them are important parts of your role.

Another area in which student groups need support is in learning to manage the process of group interaction. It is usually easier for students to divide up tasks such as research and writing than it is for them to make sure that someone keeps the group on target and monitors their progress. Supporting and guiding students in these process tasks can help assure the success of the group's efforts.

Practical Tips

1. It takes time for group members to become comfortable with one another and work together effectively. You may want to begin by having groups engage in some simple brainstorming activities just to become acquainted and begin to develop trust. For the same reason, it is usually best to keep groups together for at least several weeks before regrouping.
2. To promote the development of interpersonal skills, you may wish to provide reinforcement to groups for exhibiting particular social skills in their work together.
3. Try to build in time for groups to evaluate their performance after completing an activity. How well did they do not only with the academic task but with their interpersonal and group processes? What lessons can they apply to future collaborative efforts?

Strategies

The following strategies can be adapted to many lessons and activities in Houghton Mifflin Social Studies. For more information about these and other strategies, see For Further Reading on page T35.

Three-Step Interview

Procedures: Students work in pairs to interview each other about an assigned topic.

1. One student interviews the other about the topic.
2. The students switch roles as interviewer and interviewee.
3. Each student then shares with the group what he or she learned during the interview.

Uses: The Three-Step Interview can be used effectively to build background knowledge in conjunction with the Introduce part of the Teacher's Edition lesson. You can use the notes under Introduce to formulate a question for the interview, such as "What do you know about [topic of lesson]?" As an option for the Close part of the lesson, occasionally you might also have students do a Three-Step Interview on a question such as "What's the most important thing you learned about [topic of lesson]?" or "What else would you like to know about [topic]?"

Benefits: Promotes participation, listening skills, divergent thinking

Jigsaw

Procedures: In the Jigsaw strategy each member of the team becomes "expert" about a particular topic related to a larger team project. Team members then share information to prepare a presentation or solve a problem. Following are the main steps:

1. Identify several manageable topics related to a larger topic or concept.
2. Set up an "expert" group for each topic made up of one member from each team.
3. Have expert groups work together to research their topic.
4. Experts return to their original teams and share what they have learned.
5. You as teacher may assign the teams a particular format for presenting their findings, or you may let teams select for themselves the formats they wish to use.

Uses: The Jigsaw approach can be used with many of the Collaborative Learning activities in the Chapter Reviews. It is particularly effective in helping students to prepare for informed debate or to acquire and present new information.

Benefits: Promotes interdependence, helps students discover connections among concepts and bodies of information

Group Investigation

Procedures: Students work in teams to prepare a presentation or project to share with the class. Students form teams based on a shared interest in the topic and divide the work so that each student on a team has a definite task to perform.

Uses: This strategy is helpful to students in synthesizing information from several sources, including interviews and library research. Many Chapter Review activities lend themselves to this approach.

Benefits: Promotes organizational and presentation skills; helps students direct their own learning

Pair Debate

Procedures: Students debate an issue in pairs. First, each student defends one side of the issue; then pairs switch partners, and each student must defend the other side of the same issue.

Uses: Pair Debate can be used as an effective Close for many lessons, especially those that deal with conflict or controversy in history.

Benefits: Promotes role-taking, knowing, and respecting different points of view

For Further Reading

Aronson, E., et al. *The Jigsaw Classroom.* Beverly Hills, Cal.: Sage Publications, 1978.

Johnson, D. W., R. T. Johnson, E. J. Holubec, and P. Roy. *Circles of Learning: Cooperation in the Classroom.* Alexandria, Va.: Association for Supervision and Curriculum Development, 1984.

Kagan, S. *Cooperative Learning: Resources for Teachers.* San Juan Capistrano, Cal.: Resources for Teachers, 1989.

Slavin, R. E., et al., eds. *Learning to Cooperate, Cooperating to Learn.* New York: Plenum Press, 1985.

Developing Concepts and Vocabulary

Vocabulary instruction plays an important role in social studies, as it does in all content area reading. But teaching students a social studies term usually does not mean teaching them a new label for a concept that they already have. In most cases, it means teaching students an unfamiliar concept.

Houghton Mifflin Social Studies integrates vocabulary instruction with the teaching of other concepts and knowledge. Always the emphasis is on starting with what students already know and linking that prior knowledge to new concepts and information. This approach is solidly grounded in research that shows that knowledge is not just unrelated facts but sets of relationships. We learn new information by relating it to what we already know.

Many features of this Teacher's Edition will help you help your students activate their prior knowledge and link new concepts. The Unit Previews, the Chapter Overviews, and the Introduce portion of each lesson provide useful strategies. The Graphic Overviews can also help you show your students connections among the key ideas in each lesson. And in the students' own books, the Connect question in each lesson Review helps students link what they have learned in that lesson to previous learning.

Effective Vocabulary Instruction

Much research has shown that some approaches to teaching vocabulary are far more effective than others. In general, approaches that involve just learning definitions or synonyms for new terms are not highly effective. The knowledge gained from definitions is too limited to provide mastery of new terms. In contrast, the most successful approaches to vocabulary expose students to in-depth knowledge and frequent opportunities to use new terms in meaningful contexts.

Houghton Mifflin Social Studies reflects these characteristics of effective vocabulary and concept instruction in its selection of Key Terms. The Key Terms listed for any lesson are terms that are related to an important idea in that lesson and are terms that students will encounter frequently in their social studies reading.

Vocabulary Strategies

The strategies that follow present useful options for preteaching vocabulary for any lesson. There are, of course, many other effective strategies you may also choose to use, but these strategies will help your students develop the deep knowledge of new terms they will need to make the words part of their own social studies vocabulary.

Semantic Feature Analysis

This strategy is particularly effective in helping students identify connections among related concepts. For this reason, it works best with terms that are closely related in meaning.

1. On the chalkboard or an overhead, write a list of words that share some properties.
2. Have students suggest features that at least one of the words possesses. List these features in a row across the top of the board or transparency.
3. Have students fill in the matrix with pluses (+) and minuses (–) to show whether or not a word has the given feature. (Depending on the set of words, you may need to use question marks or zeros for features that do not apply to some terms.)

Example:

	high	large	flat top	steep sides
hill	+	–	–	+
mountain	+	+	–	+
mesa	+	–	+	+
butte	+	+	+	+

This activity can be made open-ended by having students add other related terms and features and continue filling in the matrix.

Venn Diagram

A Venn diagram can also be used effectively for semantic feature analysis. Borrowed from the field of mathematics, a Venn diagram is a pictorial representation that uses intersecting circles to show features shared by two or more concepts and features peculiar to each concept.

Example:

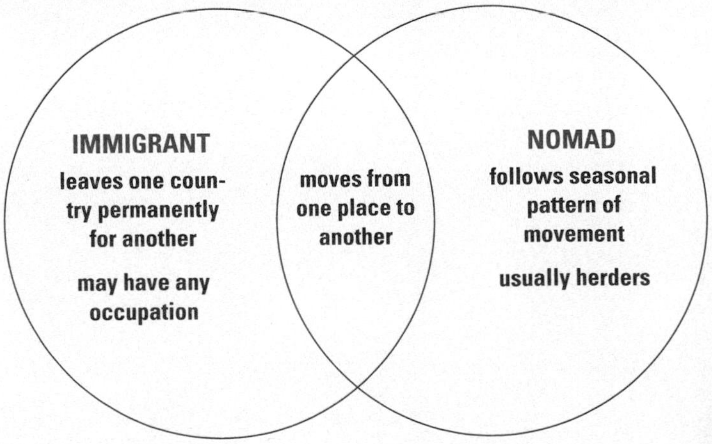
IMMIGRANT
leaves one country permanently for another
may have any occupation
moves from one place to another
NOMAD
follows seasonal pattern of movement
usually herders

Graphic Overview

Graphic overviews like the ones provided in the Teacher's Edition for each lesson are visual representations of relationships among sets of ideas or events. You can use graphic overviews effectively in a wide variety of ways in the classroom:

1. Present the Graphic Overview before the lesson to provide an advance organizer for students.
2. Have students start a graphic overview for the lesson based on their prior knowledge and their preview of the lesson. As they read the lesson, students can add to, change, and refine their graphic overviews.
3. Have students complete a graphic overview to review and summarize a lesson or chapter.

Contextual Redefinition

The strategy called contextual redefinition explicitly teaches students to use context as a clue to meaning. Because all Key Terms in Houghton Mifflin Social Studies are clearly defined in context, this strategy can be easily used with any lesson.

1. Present the words in isolation. Write each Key Term on the board or an overhead, and ask students to supply a meaning for each word. Students should defend their suggestions and come to consensus on the best definition.
2. Have students read the sentence from the lesson in which the term appears in boldface (dark type). Then students again suggest definitions and defend their suggestions. In this way, more skilled readers model for other students the thinking processes involved in formulating a definition from context.
3. Have students consult the Glossary, if appropriate, to confirm the definition.

Prior Knowledge

This strategy, based on the Pre-Reading Plan (PReP) developed by Judith Langer, is useful for activating and assessing students' prior knowledge. It can be used effectively with Key Terms that are important concepts in the lesson, but it may also be used with other concepts that are not being explicitly taught as vocabulary. This strategy works best when carried out with groups of about 10 students.

1. Preview the lesson and list key concepts important to understanding the text.
2. Use the following questions as the basis for a discussion about each concept:
   - What comes to mind when you hear ___? (Write the students' responses on the board.)
   - What made you think of ___? (responses to first question)
   - Given our discussion, what new ideas can you add about ___?
3. Have students work in groups of two or three to arrange words listed on the board into some sensible order.
4. Evaluate student responses as follows:
   - much prior knowledge: precise definitions, analogies, conceptual links among concepts
   - some prior knowledge: examples and characteristics but no connections or relations
   - little prior knowledge: sound alikes or look alikes, associated experiences, little or no meaning relations

After students have read the lesson, you may wish to follow up by

- Discussing how the text ideas relate to the ideas discussed prior to reading.
- Having students redo the organizing activity (number 3 above) and compare their results with what they did prior to reading. (This technique can serve as an informal learning assessment.)

For Further Reading

Moore, David W., John E. Readence, and Robert J. Rickelman. *Prereading Activities for Content Area Reading and Learning.* Newark, Del.: International Reading Association, 1989.

Nagy, William E. *Teaching Vocabulary to Improve Reading Comprehension.* Urbana, Ill.: ERIC Clearinghouse on Reading and Communication Skills, 1988.

The Role of Literature and Primary Sources

In a well-designed social studies curriculum, students come face to face with a full range of human experience in many times and places—including economic and social conditions, values and customs, as well as geographic conditions and historical events. To convey the richness of this experience, a textbook must employ a variety of modes of presentation: exposition, narration, description, and visual presentation. The inclusion of literature and primary sources can enhance the effectiveness of all these modes of presentation.

Houghton Mifflin Social Studies integrates literature and primary sources throughout the program. Students have the opportunity to read both literature written by people of the periods they are studying as well as literature about these periods. Every unit of Houghton Mifflin Social Studies includes at least one full-length literature selection. In addition, many lessons include shorter excerpts from literature. Most chapters also make extensive use of primary sources, such as letters, speeches, diaries, and newspaper accounts as well as official documents. In Grades 5 and 8, the Time/Space Databank also includes a collection of important primary source documents.

The major function of the literature in Houghton Mifflin Social Studies is to help students develop empathy for the experiences of people in other times and places. Through reading stories, legends, and poems, students can gain insight into the thoughts, feelings, and experiences of people who lived the history they are studying. Literature also infuses perspective by letting students read the words of people who viewed events in a particular way because of their own experience and place in society.

Using Literature

The major literature selections in Houghton Mifflin Social Studies are found before or after lessons at their most appropriate point of use. Sometimes literature provides an engaging point of entry for students into a new topic or period. Other times it expands on or exemplifies ideas of events that students have studied in a previous lesson. In either case, the use of the literature should be response centered. The goal is not to have students analyze the literature but rather to have them respond to it in ways that help students in the following ways:

- enrich understanding of other times and places
- promote the development of historical empathy
- broaden perspectives on historical events
- deepen appreciation of the ways in which events and ideas affect people's daily lives

The Teacher's Edition notes with each literature selection provide suggested activities and strategies for student response to literature. In addition, each unit opener spread in the Teacher's Edition lists the titles from the Houghton Mifflin Social Studies Bookshelf that relate to that unit. On those same pages, you will also find a bibliography that includes other literature appropriate for use with the unit.

Using Primary Sources

Diaries, letters, newspaper accounts, and other primary documents also let people of the past speak directly to students. Reading these sources exposes students to opposing opinions, alternative points of view, and immediate accounts of how events affected people in various walks of life. In this way, students also begin to develop familiarity with many of the kinds of evidence that historians use and interpret.

For Further Information

A valuable source of information on recently published literature is the annual bibliography of outstanding children's trade books in the field of social studies that appears in the April/May issue of Social Education, published by the National Council for the Social Studies.

Writing, Thinking, and Learning

Research has long supported the belief that writing fosters learning. In social studies, it is no surprise that a program rich in writing activities will provide a wide range of in-depth learning experiences.

Houghton Mifflin Social Studies gives students a multitude of writing opportunities that involve inquiry, discovery, and problem solving, as well as the integration of information. In this program, students use a variety of thinking skills and processes as they write: they identify, recall, define, explore, classify, order, select; they analyze content, synthesize choices, and evaluate conclusions. This process of learning through writing is both powerful and engaging.

Integration of Writing

Student Text: An abundance of writing activities is included in the reviews in the students' books. Each activity challenges the student to apply the appropriate thinking skills to the content of the lesson in a meaningful way.

Teacher's Edition: Unit and Chapter Projects and Activities provide numerous writing opportunities:

- LEP activities that help bridge the language gap from visual to oral to written communication
- individual writing projects and activities covering a variety of formats, purposes, and points of view
- collaborative writing activities
- challenging longer-term writing projects that encourage more research and investigation

Writing activities in the side columns and bottom panel notes focus on skills, content, or values.

Ancillaries: The Discovery Journal is a thoughtful, balanced blend of structured and free-response writing activities correlated to the special features of the Student Text. The other ancillaries also provide many opportunities for writing.

What Your Role Can Be

As Facilitator: You play a key role in providing structure, guidance, and feedback to any student writer. Younger writers need to be encouraged to use pictures and invented spellings to convey their ideas. All students need first to get their ideas down, massage them, and revise them. Then they can polish and refine the final expression and structure. Offer support and encouragement throughout this process.

As Model: Whenever feasible, participate in group or paired writing activities. Most of the Strategies for Accessible Instruction (T32–T33) are also excellent techniques for building students' confidence.

As Evaluator: Students need to know what is expected of them in any given writing situation. Provide constructive criticism; become the writing coach. Promote a mix of evaluation modes: self-evaluation, peer evaluation, group analysis, conferencing. You may want to have students keep long-term journals or writing "portfolios" that are evaluated in a holistic manner. If students feel that every written assignment is scrutinized and rigorously graded, they may be reluctant to explore and experiment. And without exploration, there is no discovery, no development of the writing craft.

The Computer Connection

More and more elementary schools are providing students increased access to computers for a variety of learning experiences. In particular, word processing is playing a growing role in the composing process across the curriculum. Students of all ages compose on keyboards. Word processing makes the task of rethinking, revising, and recomposing a less tedious, less cumbersome operation. Using word processing for many writing activities in Houghton Mifflin Social Studies is an excellent way for students to explore and experiment as they think, learn, and write.

For Further Reading

Holbrook, H. T. *Writing to Learn in the Social Studies.* Urbana, Ill.: ERIC Clearinghouse on Reading and Communication Skills, 1987.

Lake, D. T. "Teaching Writing in the 1990's." *English Journal* (November 1989): 73–74.

Langer, Judith A., and Arthur N. Applebee. *How Writing Shapes Thinking: A Study of Teaching and Learning.* Urbana, Ill.: National Council of Teachers of English (NCTE research report; no. 22), 1987.

Millett, Nancy Carlyon. *Teaching the Writing Process.* Boston, Mass.: Houghton Mifflin Company, 1990.

The Role of Assessment in Houghton Mifflin Social Studies

Making assessment more authentic is a major theme in education today. Teachers and researchers alike have pointed to the need to broaden the range of assessment techniques. In social studies, measurement should assess not just recalling facts but also understanding concepts, developing a flexible repertoire of skills, and gaining insight into civic values and responsibilities.

Because the instructional goals of Houghton Mifflin Social Studies go beyond the learning of discrete facts and skills, a variety of assessment approaches evaluate students' ability to relate ideas and concepts, to apply skills, and to think critically. Accordingly, Houghton Mifflin Social Studies provides a comprehensive assessment program that

- includes features of the Student Text, Teacher's Edition, and ancillaries as well as separate Chapter Test and Periodic Learning Inventory components
- provides components for each of the three major strands in the curriculum: Knowledge, Skills, and Civic Values and Understanding (Citizenship)
- includes but is not limited to paper-and-pencil tests; other modes of assessment include teacher evaluation of student performance, student cvaluation of personal progress, and peer evaluation
- provides opportunities for student participation

Assessment Components

Tests: A four-page test in blackline master form is provided for each chapter. These tests assess each of the three strands and are structured as follows:

- Part I consists of a variety of short-answer formats.
- Part II consists of free-response questions, including at least one longer "essay" question.

Periodic Learning Inventory: This ancillary includes blackline masters for mid-year and year-end assessments. While chapter tests measure students' mastery of text content, these assessments measure their ability to learn and apply what they read in social studies. Each assessment includes the following:

- A reading selection related to a text unit
- Survey questions on the reading
- A summary task
- Application activities
- Self-evaluation questions

Student Text Features: Houghton Mifflin Social Studies has built into its Student Text many instructional features that can also be used to serve an assessment function. These features are found within lessons, special feature pages, and the Chapter Review. The chart on this page identifies these features.

Teacher's Edition Features: You may also choose to use for assessment purposes many of the activities and strategies provided in the Chapter Organizers and lesson notes in the Teacher's Edition. These features are also identified in the chart.

Discovery Journal: The writing activities in this ancillary component provide ongoing opportunities for informal assessment of student progress.

Profile Sheets: In the Test booklet you will find a profile sheet that you can reproduce for each student to monitor progress and chart performance on the full range of assessment measures.

Assessment Components in Houghton Mifflin Social Studies

This chart identifies the assessment components, the strands they assess (K=Knowledge, S=Skills, C=Citizenship), and the mode of evaluation in which they can be used (T=Teacher, S=Self, P=Peer).

TEXT	STRANDS ASSESSED			EVALUATION MODE		
	K	S	C	T	S	P
Tests						
Part I	•	•		•		
Part II	•	•	•	•		
Periodic Learning Inventory	•	•	•	•	•	
Student Text						
Chapter Review						
Reviewing Key Terms	•			•		
Exploring Concepts	•			•		
Reviewing Skills		•		•		
Using Critical Thinking	•	•		•		
Preparing for Citizenship	•		•	•	•	•
Lesson Items						
Focus Questions	•			•		
Review	•	•	•	•		
Self-check questions	•				•	
Understanding Skills:		•		•	•	
Try It and Apply It						
Making Decisions		•	•	•	•	•
Exploring	•	•		•	•	•
Teacher's Edition						
Chapter Activities	•	•	•	•	•	•
Collaborative Learning	•	•	•			•
Close (lesson part 3)	•			•	•	•
Skill Activities		•		•		
Discovery Journal	•	•	•	•	•	

SCOPE AND SEQUENCE

This Scope and Sequence has been designed to provide students with the comprehensive knowledge, civic values, and intellectual skills they will need to meet the challenge of citizenship in the 21st century. The three strands of the program have been tightly integrated at all levels, so that skills are always taught in the context of the lesson content, and knowledge is enhanced by the application of sound values. The goals of each strand are listed on the following two pages. References in the Teacher's Edition key all learning objectives to these goals. Typically the student is introduced to a subject or skill at an early level, taught to actively use it at an intermediate level, and encouraged to analyze and critique it at an advanced level.

Knowledge and Understanding

History
Geography
Economics
Culture
Ethics and Belief Systems
Social and Political Systems

Civic Understanding and Values

National Identity
Constitutional Heritage
Citizenship

Skills

Study Skills
Visual Learning
Map and Globe Skills
Critical Thinking
Social Participation

● KNOWLEDGE AND UNDERSTANDING

HISTORY

1. Develop an understanding of the reasons for studying history and of the relationships between the past and the present
2. Develop an awareness of the ways in which we learn about the past and the methods and tools of the historian
3. Create a sense of empathy for the past
4. Understand the meaning of time and chronology
5. Analyze the sometimes complex cause-and-effect relationships of ideas and events, recognizing also the effects of the accidental and irrational on history
6. Understand the reasons for both continuity and change
7. Recognize the interrelatedness of geography, economics, culture, belief systems, and political systems within history
8. Comprehend the history of women, minorities, and the full range of social classes, not just the history of the elite or the notable individual

GEOGRAPHY

1. Develop locational skills and understanding
2. Develop an awareness of place
3. Understand human and environmental interaction
4. Understand movement of people, goods, and ideas
5. Understand world regions and their historical, cultural, economic, and political characteristics

ECONOMICS

1. Identify and apply basic concepts of economics (basic wants and needs, scarcity, choices, decision making, opportunity costs, resources, production, distribution, consumption, markets, labor, capital)
2. Develop an awareness of past and present exchange systems
3. Recognize and analyze the economic systems of various societies, including the United States, and their responses to the three basic economic questions: what to produce (value), how and how much to produce (allocation), and how to distribute (distribution)
4. Recognize the economic global interdependence of societies
5. Recognize the impact of technology on economics

▲ CIVIC UNDERSTANDING AND VALUES

NATIONAL IDENTITY

1. Develop an appreciation for the multicultural, pluralistic nature of U.S. society
2. Understand the basic principles of democracy
3. Understand and appreciate American ideals, as expressed in historical documents, speeches, songs, art, and symbolic representations and activities
4. Recognize that the American patriotic ideals are not yet fully realized and that to be protected they must constantly be reaffirmed

CONSTITUTIONAL HERITAGE

1. Develop an appreciation for the balance of power established by the Constitution between majority and minority, the individual and the state, and government by and for the people
2. Understand the historical origins of the Constitution and how it has been amended and changed over time
3. Recognize the Constitution as an expression of democratic ideals that is reinterpreted from time to time

CITIZENSHIP

1. Recognize the reciprocal relationship between the individual and the state in a democracy
2. Understand and appreciate the kind of behavior necessary for the functioning and maintenance of our democratic society
3. Learn the duties and method of selection of our leaders
4. Develop a respect for human rights, including those of individuals and of minorities
5. Develop an understanding and appreciation for the rational settlement of disputes and for compromise
6. Recognize the special strategies required to allow the different elements within our pluralistic society to live together amicably
7. Develop an understanding of the processes that have led to the fall of democracies

■ SKILLS

STUDY SKILLS

1. Locate, select, and collect information by interviewing or by using appropriate reference materials
2. Organize information from reference sources to address issues or problems
3. Present information convincingly in spoken or written forms

VISUAL LEARNING

1. Develop careful and directed observation of images, objects, and the environment
2. Understand, use, and create graphic information (timelines, charts, tables, other graphic organizers, graphs, diagrams)
3. Interpret and respond to photographs, paintings, cartoons, and other illustrative materials
4. Understand and use symbols
5. Express meaning through sensory forms of representation

MAP & GLOBE SKILLS

1. Identify and use map and globe symbols; identify and use different map projections
2. Understand and use locational terms; locate places and positions on a map or globe
3. Interpret and use directional terms and symbols on a map or globe
4. Understand and use terms to describe relative size and distance; identify and use map scales
5. Construct and use maps and geographic models

CULTURE

1. Understand that culture encompasses all aspects of a human society that are learned, not inherited, and know how culture is transmitted
2. Develop an appreciation for the rich complexity of a society's culture and an understanding of how the parts of a culture interrelate
3. Recognize and appreciate the multicultural and multiethnic dimensions of our society and the contributions made by various groups
4. Appreciate the cultural similarities and differences that exist among societies of different times and places
5. Recognize the roles everyday customs and beliefs, along with rituals, literature, and the arts play in reflecting the ideals of a people and in projecting a people's image of themselves to the world
6. Learn about the beliefs, legends, and myths, along with the heroes and heroines, of cultures from different times and places

ETHICS & BELIEF SYSTEMS

1. Recognize that all societies have ideals and standards of behavior
2. Understand that the ideas people profess affect their actions
3. Recognize the importance of religion in human society and its influence on history
4. Become familiar with the basic ideas of major religions and ethical traditions of other times and places
5. Develop an understanding of how different societies have tried to resolve ethical issues when conflicts occur between individuals, groups, and societies

SOCIAL & POLITICAL SYSTEMS

1. Develop an awareness of the reciprocal relationship between the individual and various social and political groups: family, community, and nation
2. Understand the role of law and its relationship to social and political systems
3. Develop an appreciation for the tension between opposing ideals in human affairs
4. Develop an awareness of the structure of social classes and the changes in status of women and racial and ethnic minorities in U.S. society and other societies
5. Understand comparative political systems, past and present
6. Understand the complex relationship and interdependence that exists among the world's nations

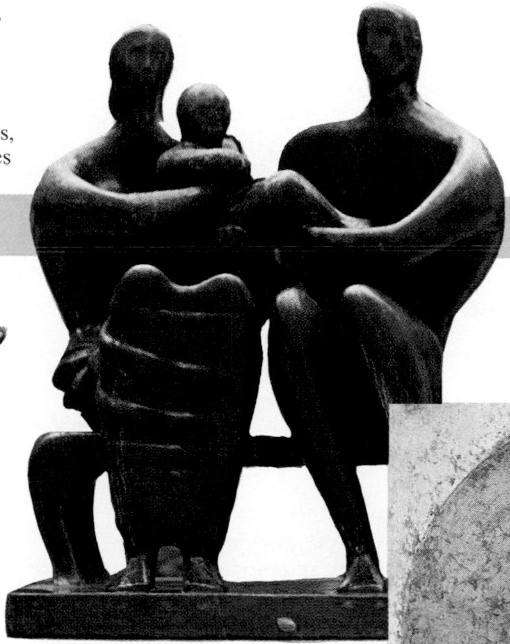

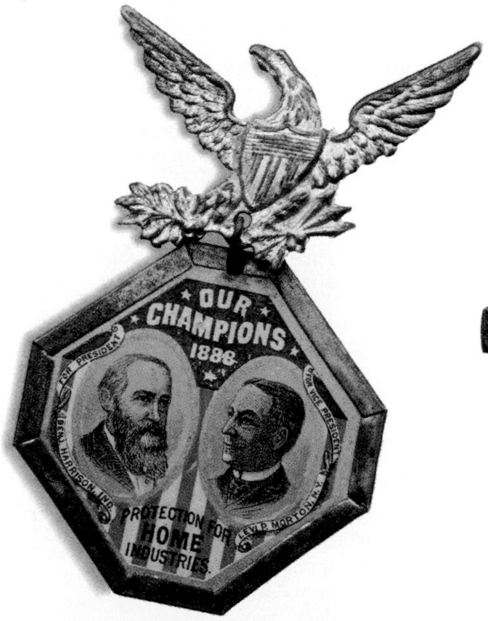
OUR
CHAMPIONS
1888
FOR PRESIDENT
PROTECTION FOR
HOME
INDUSTRIES

CRITICAL THINKING

1. Define and clarify problems, issues, and ideas
2. Evaluate and judge information related to a problem, an issue, or an idea
3. Solve problems and draw conclusions related to an issue or idea*

*Critical thinking is taught both in a problem-solving and in a decision-making context.

SOCIAL PARTICIPATION

1. Develop interpersonal skills
2. Work successfully in groups

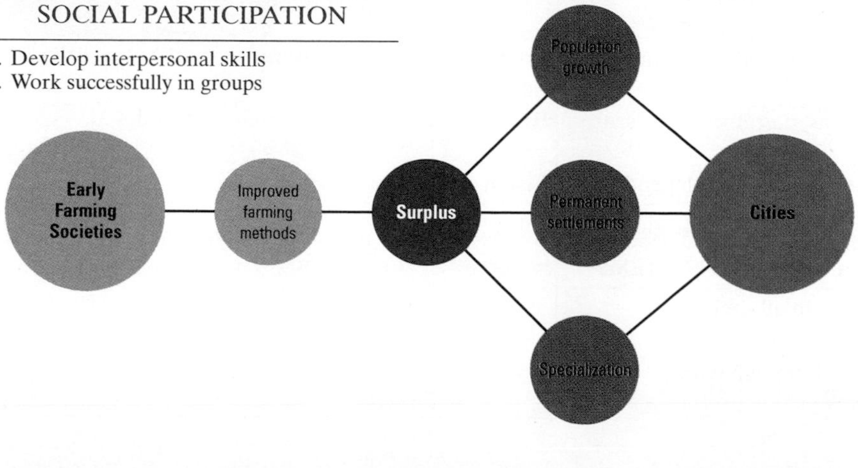
Early Farming Societies
Improved farming methods
Surplus
Population growth
Permanent settlements
Specialization
Cities

• KNOWLEDGE AND UNDERSTANDING

Grade	K	1	2	3	4
HISTORY					
1. Links to the past	Compare travel now and long ago	Parents and grandparents	Discuss traditions and their origins		State, region names Family histories
2. How we know	--	Family histories		Physical evidence Journals of pioneers	Primary sources Artifacts
3. Empathy	Identification through literature		Through biographies	With real people of the past	Past settlers of the state, region
4. Time and chronology	Understand and use time sequence terms Identify seasons of the year			Read and use timelines	
5. Cause and effect	Introduce through group dynamics	Changes in community	Effects of war	Migration and settlement	Settlement and expansion
6. Continuity and change	In individuals, families	In community	Family history How needs were met, long ago and today	Bust of boom town	Of region over time
7. Interrelatedness	Of economics with history	Of geography with history	Origins of Thanksgiving	Of geography, economics with history	Of geography, economics, culture
8. Women, minorities	Through stories, illustrations	Diversity of people presented			Roles in early U.S. societies
GEOGRAPHY					
1. Location	The self in space	Home, school, community	Beyond the neighborhood	Relative location	Factors that influence locations
2. Place	Elementary land and water forms	Map locations Identify and analyze microenvironments	Global climates	Place characteristics	Rural/urban areas
3. Human-environment interaction	Adjustment of dress to climate	Environmental changes in area		Community changes and interactions	Interactions at different times
4. Movement	Movement of goods and people			Historical movements of people	Reasons for migrations
5. Regions	--	--	Identify other regions	Regional characteristics	Nature and characteristics of regions
ECONOMICS					
1. Basic concepts	Wants and needs	Discuss how needs are met Identify and discuss community jobs		How needs are met over time, space	How wants are met over time
2. Exchange systems	Role-playing (stores)	Trade of surpluses	How immigrants learn systems	American Indian exchange systems	Use of barter, money History of businesses
3. Basic economic questions	Distribution of goods from production to market		Production and distribution		Economic cycles
4. Interdependence	--	Interdependence of producers and consumers	Inventions	Between communities	In, between regions In natural disasters
5. Technology	--	--	--	Production and transportation	Post World War II Pollution
CULTURE					
1. Definition and transmission	Appreciation through participation		Role of family	How transmitted	
2. Complexity of culture	Identify through literature		Compare traditions	American Indians	In state's, region's history
3. Multicultural society	--	--	Biographies	American Indians	Contributions to local history
4. Similarities and differences	Compare through literature			American Indians	Other groups in region
5. Customs, literature, rituals, arts	Recognize and respond through examples			Of other times and places	Throughout area's history
6. Beliefs, myths, and legends	Listen and respond to folk tales			American Indians, cowboys, settlers	
ETHICS & BELIEF SYSTEMS					
1. Present in all societies	--	--	--	American Indian societies	Historical past in state, region
2. Ideas affect behavior	--	--	--	American Indian societies	Role of missionaries Beliefs of immgrants

5	6	7	6/7	8
Origins of today's institutions Cultural heritage of self, others		Global interaction today		Personal, national identity Redefinition of the past
Historian's techniques; archaeologist's discoveries Limitations of information about the past				Historical record, newspapers, photos
With pioneers, slaves, American Indians	With ancient people Through literature, art, primary sources, artifacts	With past people	With other cultures	With pioneers, American Indians, slaves, immigrants
Use of B.C./A.D.	Developments in concurrent civilizations			
Analysis of settlement, expansion, wars	Of territorial expansion, cultural diffusion	Of exploration, reformation, technology	Of expansion, cultural diffusion, technology	Of settlement, expansion, Industrial Revolution
Analyze reasons for	Steps to civilizations Analysis of a civilization over time			Regional development, urbanization
Of belief systems	Of trade, religion, and immigration in the spread of ideas Of class structure			Of belief systems Of class structure
Role of ethnic groups and women in early U.S.	Women, and social classes, and minorities in ancient cultures and past societies		In modern societies	Diverse groups in U.S. history
Why different activities are in different locations	Evaluate reasons for a city's location	Historical significance of a city's location		Competition for locations
Comparative historical analysis of places	Influences of physical, cultural geography on history		Influence today	Effect of place on population distribution
Use of natural resources Impact of technology	Origin of the city Environmental changes	Changes in cities Impact of technology		Use of natural resources
Migrations of people Movement of goods	Ancient migrations Ancient trade routes	Global movements	World migrations and trade routes	Migrations to America
Compare/contrast of regions over time	Identify and analyze criteria used to define regions			
Distribution of resources	How wants met long ago Scarcity; specialization	In different societies Rise of merchant class	Scarcity; surplus; specialization	Colonial markets Divisions of labor
Early exchange systems Role of trade routes		Banking systems	Early exchange systems Role of trade routes	Trade partnerships
In early U.S. history Role of government	In ancient times	At different times and places in the past	In present societies	Analyze econ. decisions Roles of governments
Between people, states, nations	Ancient global trade Transportation changes	International trade routes	Global trade Transportation changes	Debtor/lender nations Imports/exports
Industrial Revolution	Effects of new technologies	Key inventions in world history	Effects on past and present societies	Industrial revolution; mass production
Role of education	Define culture Analyze how culture is transmitted	Identify culture		
Identify in U.S. at different time periods	Analyze in prehistoric, ancient cultures	Analyze other cultures	Analyze past and present world cultures	Analyze in U.S. historically
Contributions of Indians, blacks, immigrants	Identify origins of contemporary cultures in the past		Subculture contributions	Contributions of Indians, slaves, immigrants
Interactions and conflicts of cultures in U.S.	Analyze interaction and conflict in other cultures			Among U.S. population interaction and conflict
Understand and appreciate cultural images presented				Analyze cultural images presented
Analyze heroes, heroines	Importance in ancient, past, and present cultures			Analyze American legends, tall tales
In historical past in state, region, country	Comparison of past societies		Comparison of past and present societies	Analyze past ethical standards in U.S. history
Pilgrims, puritans, attitudes about slavery	Buddhist, Jewish, Christian examples	Crusades, from two points of view	Examples from major world religions	The Great Awakening Church and abolitionists

Grade	K	1	2	3	4
ETHICS & BELIEF SYSTEMS					
3. Influence of religion	--	--	--	Among American Indians, Pilgrims	Conflict between belief systems
4. Basic belief systems	--	--	--	Of American Indians	
5. Resolution of ethical issues	Introduce through literature			Discuss examples in literature	
SOCIAL & POLITICAL SYSTEMS					
1. Belonging to groups	Recognize membership in groups Identify public/private sectors			Responsibilities of individual to group	Political sub-units
2. Law	Recognize and observe the need for rules			Community laws	Who enforces laws
3. Opposing ideals	--	--	--	American Indians and settlers	Conflicting goals in state, regional history
4. Social structure	--	--	--	In other societies, times	Differences over time
5. Comparative political systems	--	--	--	Recognize differences	Recognize variety of political systems
6. Global interdependence	Recognize world neighbors	Recognize interdependence	Recognize other nations	International trade	Trade, foreign affairs

▲ CIVIC UNDERSTANDINGS AND VALUES

Grade	K	1	2	3	4
NATIONAL IDENTITY					
1. Pluralism	Recognize national identity Recognize diversity of U.S. citizens			Through examples	
2. Democracy	Practice through classroom examples			Through historic, contemporary examples	
3. American ideals and symbols	Recognize flag, songs	Learn national symbols, Pledge of Allegiance, patriotic songs			Learn state symbols
4. Need for reaffirmation of ideals	--	--	--	Conservation of resources	Focus on state's or region's future
CONSTITUTIONAL HERITAGE					
1. Balance of power	Fair treatment of all in the classroom			In other societies, state, U.S. government	Examples in state, regional history
2. Origin of Constitution	--	--	--	--	State constitutions
3. Reinterpretation of ideals	--	--	--	--	Changes in state laws over time
CITIZENSHIP					
1. Individual and state	Classroom examples			Conservation Community service	Through examples in state history
2. Democratic behavior	Recognize problems that arise in groups			Need for rules and government	Need for rules Violations in past
3. Selection of leaders	--	--	Identify office of U.S. president	Awareness of U.S. election process	Selection of state leaders
4. Human rights	Develop respect for others			Examples in the past	Examples in state history
5. Settlement of disputes	Through classroom examples			In community government	Through examples in state history
6. Strategies for pluralism	--	Through classroom examples			Through examples in state history
7. How democracies fail	--	--	--	--	--

5	6	7	6/7	8
Pilgrims, puritans, attitudes towards slavery	Spread through missionaries, diffusion	Split among Christians; Islam; missionaries	Spread of world religions Conflict among groups	Slavery; Manifest Destiny; 2nd Great Awakening
Of American Indians, slaves, immigrants	Origins, early history of major world religions	Origins, history of Islam; Japanese Buddhism	Origins, history, present beliefs of major religions	Of Indians, slaves, early immigrants
Freedom to dissent; slavery; tolerance	Examples from ancient civilizations	Through religious wars	Past and present examples	Attempts to resolve slavery issue
Early U.S. political units Origins of public/private	Identify social, political units in ancient times	Identify world social and political units in past societies	In modern societies	Conflicting group memberships in U.S. history
Reinterpretations of law over time	Identify origins of law	Recognize non-Roman systems of law	Origins of law International law	How law is enacted, changed; dissent
In early U.S. history	In and among prehistoric, ancient societies	In and among world societies, over time	In modern cultures	At various times in U.S. history
Analyze reasons for changes	Analyze social status and change In ancient times	In past times	In past and present	Analyze reasons for change
Of American Indian, British, French, Spanish	Among ancient civilizations	Note changes over time	Among world's nations	Among nations that have affected U.S. history
Identify relationships of U.S. with others	Identify and analyze interdependence In ancient times	In past times	In past and present	History of U.S. relationship with other nations

5	6	7	6/7	8
Origins of pluralism	Discuss identities of ancient civilizations	Discuss identities of other nations In past times	In past and present	Tensions of assimilation
History of democracy in U.S.	Origins of democracy In ancient times	Within history	Ancient and past origins	History and development of U.S. democracy
As expressed in U.S. history	Symbols of other nations and empires In ancient times	In past times	In past and present	As expressed in U.S.history
Identify past crises in U.S. history	Compare and contrast U.S. with examples From ancient times	From past times	From other places	Identify and discuss past crises in U.S.
Checks and balances Historical examples	Balance of power In ancient times	In past times	In past and present	Checks and balances Historical examples
Writing of Constitution Passage of amendments	– –	Influence of Enlightenment ideas	– –	Writing of Constitution Passage of amendments
Meaning then and now	– –	– –	– –	Discuss reasons for reinterpretations
Identify examples in U.S. history	Identify examples in ancient times	Identify examples in other societies	Examples in past and present societies	Analyze examples in U.S. history
Discuss examples in U.S. history	Analyze behavior in ancient times	Analyze behavior in other societies	Analyze past and present societies	Discuss examples in U.S. history
Analyze, using past U.S. examples	Compare selection process of long ago	Compare selection process of other societies		Analyze, using past U.S. examples
Evaluate cases from U.S. history	Discuss minority rights long ago	Discuss minority rights in past world cultures	Present-day cases	Evaluate cases from U.S. history
Identify examples from U.S. history	Analyze disputes in ancient times	Analyze disputes in other societies	Examples from past and present societies	Analyze examples from U.S. history
Identify examples from U.S. history	Analyze pluralism in ancient times	Analyze pluralism in other societies	Present-day examples	Analyze examples from U.S. history
Identify crises in U.S. history	Analyze why past democracies failed	Analyze why past democracies failed		Analyze crises in U.S. history

■ SKILLS

Grade	K	1	2	3	4
STUDY SKILLS					
1. Collecting information	Interview others Visit a library	Learn book parts Picture dictionary	Use a library; reference materials Interview for information		Use catalog
2. Organizing information	Listen and retell story	Identify and make categories	Identify main ideas and details	Summarize paragraph	Combine facts Give directions
3. Presenting information	Tell events in sequence		Tell events and ideas in sequence Write simple paragraphs		Oral discussion Write reports
VISUAL LEARNING					
1. Observation	Classroom materials	School, neighborhood	Neighborhood, community features		Regional features
2. Timelines	Know the seasons	Read and make simple timelines			Read U.S. time zone maps
Graphic organizers	Use a chart	Read charts, tables			
Graphs	Use simple picture, bar graphs	Read and make picture, bar graphs		Read line, circle graphs	Read bar graphs
Diagrams	– –	Read process and cut-away diagrams, cross-section diagrams			Read and use variety of diagrams
3. Interpretation	State main idea of illustrations	Gather information from and respond to photos, illustrations, fine art			Interpret illustrations, cartoons
4. Symbols	Traffic signs U.S. flag	National symbols; flag			State symbols
5. Visual self-expression	Drawings, constructions	Class activities			
MAP & GLOBE SKILLS					
1. Symbols	Compare maps, photos, and real environments		Color as symbol Continents, oceans	Read a physical map Use a map key, rose	Area characteristics Making symbols
2. Location	Use simple locational terms		Use grids to find locations Relative location	Latitude, longitude	Hemispheres Global reference points
3. Direction	Orient self in space; use directional terms		Cardinal directions Describe routes	Intermediate direction Follow map routes	Use directional terms for routes
4. Scale and distance	Use relative terms	Judge relative sizes, distances		Use map scale Time/distance	Use large and small-scale representations
5. Construction and use	Construct table or floor 3-D maps of community, neighborhood				Make a map
CRITICAL THINKING					
1. Define and clarify	Similarities and differences Organize categories	Formulate questions		Identify problems or central issues	
2. Evaluate and judge	Identify evidence	Sequence of events		Evidence supporting main idea	Facts vs. opinions Evaluate information
3. Solve and conclude	Identify cause and effect Draw conclusions based on evidence			Cause and effect If/then statements	Draw conclusions
SOCIAL PARTICIPATION					
1. Interpersonal	Develop self-respect and confidence; Develop good listening skills			Others' points of view; Express one's own ideas	Listen to others
2. Group work	Show willingness to participate in group activities	Accept decisions	Practice collaborative learning roles	Identify goals	Participate in discussions

5	6	7	6/7	8
Use a library catalog Interview for information	Use atlas; primary sources	Use Readers' Guide Conduct interviews	Use primary and secondary sources	Use special reference resources
Take notes, make outlines	Identify text patterns	Code notes Interpret primary sources	Interpret text patterns	Code notes Make bibliography cards
Develop oral discussion skills Plan and write reports		Use a variety of oral and written genres, debates, and skits to present reports		
Apply to historical artifacts, photographs, fine art				
Understand B.C./A.D.	Read and make telescopic and parallel timelines			
Read charts, tables	Read and make cluster, cause-and-effect graphic organizers			
Make line graphs	Compare graphs	Choose, assess graphs	Compare graphs	Choose, assess graphs
Read and use variety of diagrams	Analyze cross-section, process diagrams			
Interpret illustrations Compare media	Identify limitations of illustrative materials Interpret artifacts			
Learn history of national symbols	Religious, historical symbols			History of U.S. symbols
As class activities	Making a mural			
Parallels/meridians tied to earth/sun	Read cartograms Draw inferences	Use topographical map	Read cartograms, seabed profile	Make inferences Relate routes/topography
Use latitude/longitude to locate, specify places		Earth/sun relationship and time of day	Compare two maps	Analyze locations
Trace explorers' routes	Formulate hypotheses Movement of people over time			Cultural diffusion
Evaluate large and small-scale maps	Compute distances and travel time	Read vertical profiles Trace and analyze routes		
Use landmarks to draw map	Make a map	Make a vertical profile		Design map based on information given
Ask good questions	Interpret values and ideologies of individuals, groups	Identify central issues	Recognize assumptions	Analyze points of view
Identify facts, opinions	Distinguish among facts, opinions, and reasoned judgments	Recognize bias	Evaluate arguments	Judge bias, propaganda Analyze arguments
Interpret cause and effect Draw conclusions from evidence		Make hypotheses Predict consequences		Compare causes/effects Identify alternatives
Recognize the social needs of others Provide positive feedback		Identify and overcome stereotypes Recognize and respect others' points of view		
Participate in setting and planning goals Develop collaborative learning roles		Analyze and support group decisions	Identify and settle conflicts	Appreciate and practice compromises

To see a World *in a Grain of Sand*
And a Heaven in a Wild Flower,
Hold Infinity in the palm of your hand
And Eternity in an hour.

William Blake

Beverly J. Armento
J. Jorge Klor de Alva
Gary B. Nash
Christopher L. Salter
Louis E. Wilson
Karen K. Wixson

To See a World

World Cultures and Geography

Houghton Mifflin Company • Boston
Atlanta • Dallas • Geneva, Illinois • Princeton, New Jersey • Palo Alto • Toronto

Consultants

Khalid Yahya Blankinship
Assistant Professor of Religion
Temple University
Philadelphia, Pennsylvania

Kees W. Bolle
Professor Emeritus of History
University of California
Guest Professor, Religion, Reed College
Portland, Oregon

Mark Cummings
Editor in Chief
Encyclopedia Americana
Grolier, Incorporated
Danbury, Connecticut

Charles C. Haynes, Ph.D.
Executive Director
First Liberty Institute at George Mason University
Fairfax, Virginia

Mary N. MacDonald
Assistant Professor of Religious Studies
LeMoyne College
Syracuse, New York

Shabbir Mansuri
Director, Council on Islamic Education
Tustin, California

The Most Reverend Desmond M. Tutu, D.D. F.K.C.
Bishopscourt, Claremont
Cape Town, Republic of South Africa

Taitetsu Unno
Jill Ker Conway Professor of Religion and East Asian Studies
Smith College
Northampton, Massachusetts

Rabbi Alfred Wolf, Ph.D.
Director, Skirball Institute on American Values
American Jewish Committee
Los Angeles, California

Teacher Reviewers

Linda Crain
Broward County Schools
Ft. Lauderdale, Florida

B. J. Dancer
Ector County Independent School District
Odessa, Texas

Susan M. Denhardt
Glenwood Middle School
Glenwood, Maryland

Glenn Diedrich
Walker Middle School
Milwaukee, Wisconsin

William F. Frew
Whitney Young Intermediate School
Cleveland, Ohio

Joyce Hecht-Hulslander
Largo Middle School
Pinellas County School Board
Clearwater, Florida

Jeanie Heginbotham
Baxter Elementary School
Anchorage, Alaska

Beverly Leonard
Blue Springs R-IV School District
Blue Springs, Missouri

Nancy Meyer, R.S.M.
Archdiocese of Cincinnati
Cincinnati, Ohio

Kathy J. Nye
Baltimore County Public Schools
Baltimore, Maryland

Virginia Tang
Woodland School
Weston, Massachusetts

Bonnie S. C. Wood
Tumwater Middle School
Tumwater, Washington

Printed in the U.S.A.

ISBN: 0-395-80932-0
123456-VH-99 98 97 96

Development by Ligature, Inc.

Acknowledgments

Grateful acknowledgment is made for the use of the material listed below.

The material in the Minipedia is reprinted from *The World Book Encyclopedia* with the expressed permission of the publisher. © 1993 by World Book, Inc.

–Continued on page 723.

From Your Authors

They were probably some of the world's first exchange students. They came from China, Tibet, and as far away as Japan. During the fourth century, students from all over Asia filled the classrooms of the University at Nalanda. It was a long trip to northern India, but worth it.

So begins the story of a real event in the culture of ancient India. Could college students from 1,600 years ago and halfway around the world have anything to do with you? Well, as Chapter 14 explains, you can thank such ancient scholars for your math homework tonight. That's right. Indian mathematicians invented the number system that you use today.

In this book you'll find many surprising connections to cultures from distant times and remote places. Your world has been shaped by the customs and decisions of many people—ordinary people as well as great leaders. Ideas you believe in may have been passed to you through many generations and many countries. Things we take for granted—from marriage to makeup to marathons—have roots in the past.

Many present-day people affect your life as well, even though you've never met them. That's why in this book you'll read about modern as well as ancient cultures. While there isn't time to visit every culture, you'll touch down in many fascinating places.

We hope that as you proceed, you'll ask questions like these: "Why did people settle here?" "What makes this culture unique?" "What would it be like to grow up in this society?"

Most of all, we hope you catch the excitement of thinking about your world—its past, present, and future.

Beverly J. Armento
Professor of Social Studies
Director, Center for Business and Economic Education
Georgia State University

Gary B. Nash
Professor of History
University of California—Los Angeles

Louis E. Wilson
Associate Professor
Department of Afro-American Studies
Smith College

J. Jorge Klor de Alva
Professor of Anthropology
Princeton University

Christopher L. Salter
Professor and Chair
Department of Geography
University of Missouri

Karen K. Wixson
Associate Professor of Education
University of Michigan

Contents

About Your Book xiv

Map and Globe Handbook xx

UNIT 1 Looking at the World 1	Chapter 1 *Exploring Culture* 2	Lesson 1 *A World of People* 4
		Lesson 2 *What Shapes and Changes Cultures?* 12
		Lesson 3 *How Do We Learn about Culture?* 20
	Chapter 2 *Exploring Geography* 26	Lesson 1 *Location and Place* 28
		Lesson 2 *Interaction* 32
		Lesson 3 *Movement* 38
		Lesson 4 *Regions* 42
UNIT 2 Origins of Today's World 50	Chapter 3 *The Fertile Crescent* 56	Lesson 1 *Life in Prehistoric Times* 58
		Lesson 2 *Ancient Mesopotamia* 66
		Lesson 3 *The Origins of Judaism* 73
	Chapter 4 *Ancient Egypt and Nubia* 80	Lesson 1 *Kingdoms on the Nile* 82
		Lesson 2 *Ancient Cultures Linked Together* 87
		Lesson 3 *Great Achievements* 93
	Chapter 5 *Two Early Asian Civilizations* 100	Lesson 1 *Ancient India* 102
		Lesson 2 *Hinduism and Buddhism* 108
		Lesson 3 *Ancient China* 114
		Lesson 4 *China's Cultural Heritage* 117
	Chapter 6 *Early Civilizations in the Americas* 126	Lesson 1 *Early Americans* 128
		Lesson 2 *Aztec Civilization* 132
		Lesson 3 *Andean Civilizations* 138
UNIT 3 The Mediterranean and Southwest Asia 146	Chapter 7 *The Mediterranean World* 152	Lesson 1 *Ancient Greece* 154
		Lesson 2 *Ancient Rome* 168
		Lesson 3 *Early Christianity* 175
	Chapter 8 *The Arabian Peninsula* 182	Lesson 1 *Islam Develops* 184
		Lesson 2 *The Spread of Islam* 189
		Lesson 3 *Saudi Arabia Today* 193
	Chapter 9 *Iran* 202	Lesson 1 *Iran's Land and Traditions* 204
		Lesson 2 *Iran's Proud Legacy* 208
		Lesson 3 *Modern Iran* 213

UNIT 4 Africa 220

Chapter 10 *Egypt* 226
Lesson 1 *Rulers from the North* 228
Lesson 2 *Islamic Egypt* 232
Lesson 3 *A Trip Down the Nile* 239

Chapter 11 *Mali* 246
Lesson 1 *From Empire to Colony* 248
Lesson 2 *Mali and Its People* 255
Lesson 3 *Republic of Mali* 259

Chapter 12 *Ghana* 266
Lesson 1 *The Asante: A People of Tradition* 268
Lesson 2 *Growth and Change* 273
Lesson 3 *A New Nation* 280

Chapter 13 *South Africa* 290
Lesson 1 *A Divided Land* 292
Lesson 2 *The Fight for Land* 296
Lesson 3 *A New South Africa* 304

UNIT 5 Asia 310

Chapter 14 *India* 316
Lesson 1 *A Hindu Empire* 318
Lesson 2 *Foreign Rulers* 322
Lesson 3 *Modern India* 329

Chapter 15 *China* 338
Lesson 1 *Mandate of Heaven* 340
Lesson 2 *China after Mao* 347
Lesson 3 *China Today* 351

Chapter 16 *Japan* 358
Lesson 1 *Island Culture* 360
Lesson 2 *History of Japan* 366
Lesson 3 *Japan Today* 374

Chapter 17 *Southeast Asia* 384
Lesson 1 *The Geography of Southeast Asia* 386
Lesson 2 *The Philippines* 390
Lesson 3 *Singapore, Indonesia, and Vietnam* 395

UNIT 6 Europe 402

Chapter 18 *The Making of Europe* 408
Lesson 1 *The Power of the Church* 410
Lesson 2 *Feudal Europe* 414
Lesson 3 *The Renaissance* 424
Lesson 4 *The Reformation* 430

Chapter 19 *The Rise of Spain, Great Britain, and Russia* 436
Lesson 1 *Spain: The First Modern Empire* 438
Lesson 2 *Great Britain's Sea Empire* 444
Lesson 3 *Russia's Land Empire* 452

Chapter 20 *Europe: 1900 to the End of the Cold War* 458
Lesson 1 *World War I* 460
Lesson 2 *Russia Becomes the Soviet Union* 464
Lesson 3 *World War II and the Cold War* 468

Chapter 21 *Europe and Russia Today* 478
Lesson 1 *Europe Today* 480
Lesson 2 *Western Europe Today* 484
Lesson 3 *Eastern Europe Today* 490
Lesson 4 *Russia and the Former Soviet Republics* 493

UNIT 7 500
The Caribbean, Central and South America

Chapter 22 *The Caribbean* 506
- Lesson 1 *Geography of the Caribbean* 508
- Lesson 2 *The Caribbean: Cradle of the Americas* 512
- Lesson 3 *The Caribbean Today* 518

Chapter 23 *Central and South America* 526
- Lesson 1 *The Land and Its History* 528
- Lesson 2 *South America* 536
- Lesson 3 *Central America* 542

Chapter 24 *Brazil* 548
- Lesson 1 *The History of Brazil* 550
- Lesson 2 *The Geography and Economy of Brazil* 555
- Lesson 3 *Brazil Today* 562

UNIT 8 570
North America

Chapter 25 *Mexico* 576
- Lesson 1 *The Forming of Mexico* 578
- Lesson 2 *Regions and Resources* 584
- Lesson 3 *A Blending of Cultures* 588

Chapter 26 *Canada* 596
- Lesson 1 *Geography and Native Peoples* 598
- Lesson 2 *History of Canada* 601
- Lesson 3 *Canada Today* 607

Chapter 27 *From Many, One Nation* 616
- Lesson 1 *Land of Diversity* 618
- Lesson 2 *People from Many Lands* 622
- Lesson 3 *For the Good of All* 632

Chapter 28 *The United Nations, Israel, and South Korea* 642
- Lesson 1 *The United Nations* 644
- Lesson 2 *Israel and the United Nations* 648
- Lesson 3 *South Korea and the United Nations* 653

Time/Space Databank 659

- Minipedia 660
- Countries of the World 674
- Atlas 678
- Glossary of Geographic Terms 690
- Gazetteer 692
- Biographical Dictionary 696
- Glossary 701

- Index 708
- Acknowledgments 723

Understanding Skills

Each Understanding Skills feature gives you the opportunity to learn and practice a skill related to the topic you are studying.

Fact, Judgment, and Opinion: Evaluating Information 18
Thematic Maps: Comparing Two U.S. Maps 46
Graphic Organizers: Using a Flow Chart 61
Visual Evidence: Interpreting Egyptian Art 96
Organization: Identifying Patterns 107
Evidence: Identifying Main Ideas 143
Conclusions: Comparing Greece and Rome 174
Historical Sequence: Making Parallel Timelines 199
Current Events: Making Predictions 217
Historical Evidence: Evaluating Sources 238
Arguments: Identifying Supporting Evidence 263
Critical Thinking: Interpreting Proverbs 272
Note-Taking: Recording Information 303
Reference Sources: Using the *Readers' Guide* 328
Written Reports: Presenting Information 355
Cartograms: Interpreting Symbols 372
Topography: Analyzing Elevation Maps 399
Critical Thinking: Making a Hypothesis 419
Graphic Information: Comparing Graphs 451
Visual Learning: Interpreting Political Cartoons 475
Conflict: Resolving Conflicts Peacefully 483
Others: Using Constructive Criticism 517
Oral Reports: Presenting Information 541
Critical Thinking: Recognizing Assumptions 554
Historical Evidence: Interpreting Artifacts 583
Diagrams: Reading a Process Diagram 606
Relationships: Identifying Stereotypes 637

Exploring

The story of the past is hidden all around you in the world of the present. Exploring pages tell you the secrets of how to find it.

Greek Architecture in Your Community 162
African Jewelry 278
Japanese and U.S. Schools 380

Making Decisions

Much of history is made of people's decisions. These pages take you step-by-step through fascinating problems from history and today. What will you decide?

Where Should We Put Our Trash? 36
The Great Wall 122
Voting For or Against a United Europe 488
Rain Forests: Preserve Them? Use Them? 566
Should Puerto Rico Be the 51st State? 638

Understanding Concepts

Each Understanding Concepts feature gives you more information about a concept that is important to the lesson you are reading.

Cultural Diffusion 15
Natural Resources 34
Dynasty 84
Empire 136
Democracy 157
Kinship 270
Social Justice 306
Communism 345
Feudalism 367
Colonialism 440
Genocide 471
Inflation 560
Borders 586
Naturalization 626

Literature

Throughout history people have expressed their deepest feelings and beliefs through literature. Reading these stories, legends, poems, and shorter passages that appear in the lesson will help you experience what life was like for people of other places and times.

A World of Poems 10
"The Luring of Enkidu" from *Gilgamesh,* retold by Bernarda Bryson 62
"Demeter and Persephone" from *Book of Greek Myths,* retold by Ingri and Edgar Parin D'Aulaire 164
"The Cow-Tail Switch" retold by Harold Courlander and George Herzog 284
Japanese Poetry, written by Sanpū, Bashō, and Gokason 364
Chapter Six from *Valentine & Orson,* re-created and illlustrated by Nancy Ekholm Burkert 420
From *The Captive,* by Scott O'Dell 534
"Ginger for the Heart" from *Tales from Gold Mountain,* by Paul Yee 628

Primary Sources

Reading the exact words of the people who made and lived history is the best way to get a sense of how they saw themselves and the times in which they lived. You will find more than 50 primary sources throughout this book including the following:

Guglielmo Marconi 12
Elihu Burritt, from *The Irish Potato Famine: Victims of the Great Hunger* 38
The Ten Commandments 76
Homer, from the *Odyssey* 93
Ashoka, Rock Edict I 113
John Lloyd Stephens, *Incidents of Travel in Central America, Chiapas, and Yucatán* 131
"Pericles' Funeral Speech," from Thucydides, *The Peloponnesian War* 158
Ar-Razi's diagnosis of smallpox from *al-Judari wa Hasbah,* A.D. 910 189
Barry Rosen, *444 Days: The Hostages Remember* 216
Arab historian Ibn Khaldun, description of 14th-century Cairo 232
Leo Africanus, diary account of life in ancient Mali 253
Kwame Nkrumah, *I Speak of Freedom* 280
Nelson Mandela 294
Turkish Sultan Mahmud of Ghazna 322
Xiao Wenxin, Chinese teacher 351
Tokugawa Ieyasu, a decree on proper behavior 368
Pope Pius XII 394
Martin Luther, *Ninety-Five Theses* 430
Columbus, from *History of the Indies,* by Bartolomé de las Casas 442
Anne Frank: The Diary of a Young Girl 470
Nickolai Karanko, a Ukrainian teenager, on democracy 495
Unnamed survivor of Haitian revolution 515
Rigoberta Menchú 542
From the letter of Pero Vaz de Caminha to King Manuel, written at Porto Seguro, Brazil, May 1, 1500 551
Miguel Hidalgo y Costilla, *Grito de Delores* 580
Captain James Cook 600
Von, Vietnamese immigrant 632
From the Preamble to the United Nations Charter 644

A Closer Look

Take a closer look at the objects and pictures spread out on these special pages. With the clues you see, you'll become a cultural detective.

The Great Migration 40
Cuneiform Writing 70
The Emperor's Tomb 119
Inca Highways 141
Arabian Hospitality 195
Persian Miniatures 211
The Rescue of Abu Simbel 241
Kente Cloth 275
Mining in South Africa 300
Monsoons 330
The Voyages of Zheng He 343
Volcanoes 388
Britain, Transplanted 449
The Last Czar 466
European Currency 486
Steel Drums 521
The Amazon River 558
Día de los Muertos 592
Canadian Animation 611

A Moment in Time

A person is frozen at an exciting moment. You'll get to know these people by reading about where they are and the objects around them.

An Anthropologist 22
A Nubian Princess 91
A Roman Engineer 172
A Mali Metalsmith 252
A Tea Master 369
A Crusader 417
A Gaucho 538
A Gulf War Soldier 634

Charts, Diagrams, and Timelines

The visual presentations of information help give you a clearer picture of the people, places, and events you are studying.

What Is Culture? 6
Institutions and Culture 9
Technology and Culture 17
Endangered Species 35
What's in Our Garbage? 37
Major Rivers of the Ancient World 54
The Earliest Humans, 2,400,000–15,000 B.C. 60
Steps Toward Civilization 61
The Ten Commandments 76
Ancient Egypt and Nubia, 3000 B.C.–c. A.D. 350 85
Building the Great Pyramid, 2500s B.C. 88
The Meroitic Alphabet 95
The Four Noble Truths 111
The Eightfold Path 112
Ancient and Modern Writing 117
Dynasties and Inventions of China, 1766 B.C.–A.D. 1279 120
Aztec Exchange Rates, c. 1525 134
Regional Rainfall 150
How an Aqueduct Works 171
Performing the Pilgrimage 184
Five Pillars of Islam 187
Largest Muslim Populations 190
Wheat Production, 1975–1990 198
Making Parallel Timelines 199
Society under the Pahlavis 214
Oil Production in Iran 215
African Population 225
Religious Groups in Egypt 242
Populations Compared by Age, 1990 261
Cocoa Prices, 1955–1965 281
Population and Land 294
Creation of Modern South Africa 298
Famous Mountains 314
Pacific Rim Trading Partners 315
City Population Density 315
Major Religions of India 333
Literacy Rate 334
China's Population 348
Camera Production 374
East vs. West: Church and Culture 413
Medieval Life: Serfs and Lords 415
Spain's Empire, 1492–1898 441
Foods in the Columbian Exchange 442
Great Britain's Empire, 1600–1931 445
World Trade, 1780–1820 451
World Trade, 1820 451
Russia's Empire, 1462–1917 453
Modern Europe and Russia 470
Per Capita Income in Europe and the United States 485
Comparing Canals 505
The Largest Caribbean Islands 520
Vertical Zones 528
Central America 530
South America 531
Population, 1818 552
War and Revolution 581
Mexican Exports, 1981–1989 587
How a Lock Works 606
Acid Rain 612
Patterns of U.S. Immigration, 1820–2000 625
Projected U.S. Population, 1990–2090 633
The Founding of Israel 649
Population of Israel 650
Population 652
The History of Korea 654
Countries Receiving Korean Exports 655

Maps

Each culture has been shaped by the places in which it developed. Each map in this book tells its own story about these cultures and regions.

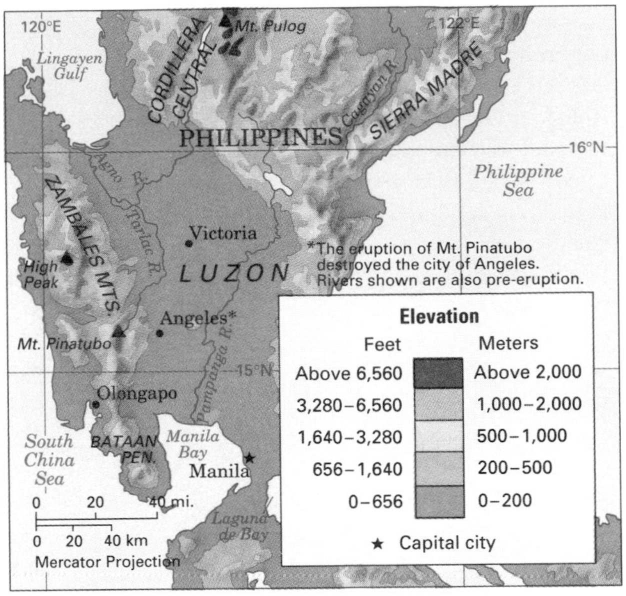
120°E
122°E
16°N
15°N
Lingayen Gulf
CORDILLERA CENTRAL
Mt. Pulog
Cagayan R.
SIERRA MADRE
PHILIPPINES
Philippine Sea
Agno R.
ZAMBALES MTS.
Tarlac R.
Victoria
LUZON
High Peak
*The eruption of Mt. Pinatubo destroyed the city of Angeles. Rivers shown are also pre-eruption.
Angeles*
Mt. Pinatubo
Pampanga R.
Olongapo
South China Sea
BATAAN PEN.
Manila Bay
Manila
Laguna de Bay
0 20 40 mi.
0 20 40 km
Mercator Projection
Elevation
Feet
Meters
Above 6,560
Above 2,000
3,280–6,560
1,000–2,000
1,640–3,280
500–1,000
656–1,640
200–500
0–656
0–200
★ Capital city

Korea and Japan: Political G1
Australia: Political G2
Mexico City: A Downtown Section G3
The World: Hemispheres G4
Southeast Asia: Political G5
Mercator Projection G6
Peters Projection G6
Goode Projection G7
Robinson Projection G7
Africa: Physical and Profile Map G9
Time Zones of the Western Hemisphere G10
Roman Expansion, 338 B.C.–133 B.C. G11
The Conquests of Alexander the Great G12
Argentina: Land Regions G13
Argentina: Population Density G13
African Migration and Language G14
United States: Regions 43
World: Regions 44
United States: Physical Regions 46
United States: Land Use and Resources 47
Africa: Annual Precipitation 49
Early Civilizations 53
Early Farming Areas 59
Fertile Crescent, 6000–2000 B.C. 67
Assyrian and Babylonian Empires 71
Ancient Egypt and Nubia 83
Ancient Cities of the Nile 86
Ancient Trade Routes and Resources, c. 2500 B.C. 104
China: Physical 115
Early Migration to the Americas 129
Mesoamerican Civilizations, 1200 B.C.–A.D. 1521 130
Andean Civilizations, 2500 B.C.–A.D. 1532 139
Western Eurasia: Political 149
Greek Civilization, c. 550 B.C. 149
Persian Empire, c. 500 B.C. 149
Roman Empire, c. A.D. 117 149
Western Eurasia: Climate 150
Greek City-States and Trade Routes, c. 550 B.C. 155
Rise of the Roman Empire, 338 B.C.–A.D. 117 169
Spread of Early Christianity by A.D. 395 178
Performing the Pilgrimage 184
The Expansion of Islam, A.D. 622–750 190
Modern Iran 205
Empires of Persia 209
Persian Gulf Oil Production, 1991 215
Africa: Political 223
The Expanding Deserts of Africa 224
Major Grain–Producing Areas of the Roman Empire 230
Expansion of the Ottoman Empire 234
Egypt: Population, 1990 240
Mali Empire, c. 1337 250
Songhai Empire, c. 1500 250
French Occupation, 1924 251
Modern Mali 251
Western Africa: Vegetation Regions 256
Ashanti Empire, 1820 269
Modern Ghana 282
South Africa, 1990 294
Groups Living in Southern Africa, c. 1400 297
Southern Africa, 1854 298
Asia: Political 313
Asia: Rainfall and Monsoon Winds 314
The Gupta Empire, c. A.D. 400 318
Muslim Rule and Indian Resistance, c. 1700 324
The Indian Subcontinent: Physical 331
Indian States and Languages, 1993 333
The Mongol Empire in China, c. 1294 341
Modern China: Population and Arable/Non-arable Land 348
Dialects in China, 1950 355
Japan: Physical 361

World: Political 372
World: Petroleum Resources 373
World: Gross National Product 375
Southeast Asia: Political 387
Manila Galleon Trade Routes, 1565–1815 391
Western Indonesia: Physical and Profile Map 399
Northern Philippines: Physical 401
Europe: Political 404
Europe: Areas Affected by Acid Rain 406
Division of the Christian World, c. A.D. 950 413
Feudal Europe, c. 1100 416
Spread of the Plague, c. 1347–1353 419
The Spread of Protestantism, c. 1560 433
Spanish Empire, c. 1600 441
British Empire, c. 1860 445
Russian Empire, c. 1600 453
People of Europe, 1914 462
Berlin and Germany, 1989 473
Eastern and Western Europe, 1993 481
The European Economic Community, 1993 485
Russia Today 494
Central and South America: Political 503
Central and South America: Vegetation Regions 504
Caribbean: Natural Resources 509
European Presence in the Caribbean 514
Indentured Servants to the Caribbean 516
Central and South America: Climate Regions 529
Central America: Major Products 543
Brazil: Geographic Regions 551
Brazil: Resources and States 557
North America: Political 573
The Last Ice Age, c. 16,000 B.C. 574
Volcanoes and Earthquakes since 1900 574
Mexico: Changing Borders, 1835–1853 580
Mexico: Physical Regions and Resources 585
Mexico: Population, 1990 590
Canada: Vegetation Regions 599
Mackenzie's Explorations 602
Four Peaks of U.S. Immigration 624
Peace Missions of the United Nations 647
Changing Boundaries of Palestine and Israel 649
Israel and the Occupied Territories, 1993 652
North and South Korea, 1993 653
World: Political 678
World: Physical 680
Eurasia: Political/Physical 682
Pacific Rim: Political/Physical 684
Africa: Political/Physical 685
North America: Political/Physical 686
South America: Political/Physical 687
World: Religions 688
World: Climate 688
World: Land Use, Land and Ocean Resources 689
World: Population 689

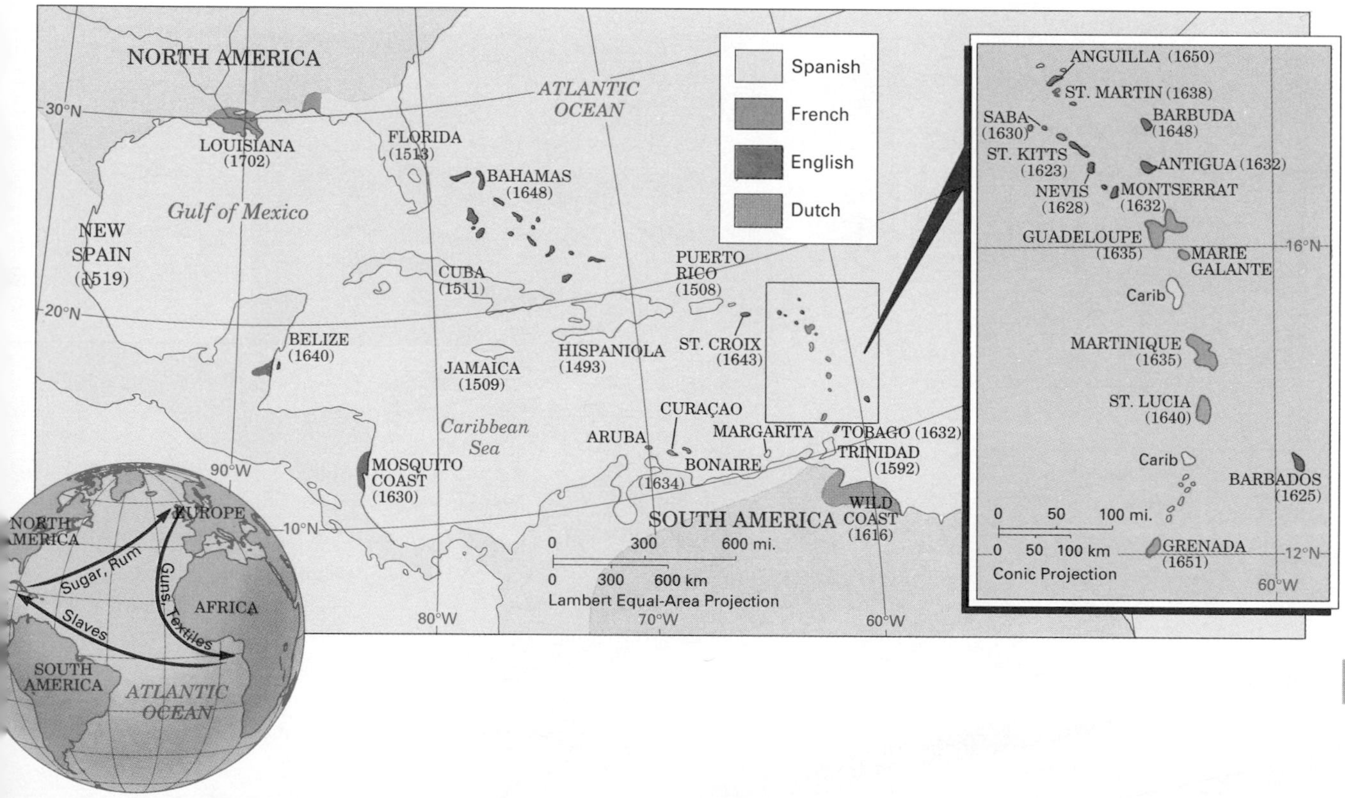

NORTH AMERICA
ATLANTIC OCEAN
Spanish
French
English
Dutch
30°N
LOUISIANA (1702)
FLORIDA (1513)
BAHAMAS (1648)
Gulf of Mexico
NEW SPAIN (1519)
CUBA (1511)
PUERTO RICO (1508)
20°N
BELIZE (1640)
JAMAICA (1509)
HISPANIOLA (1493)
ST. CROIX (1643)
CURAÇAO
Caribbean Sea
ARUBA
MARGARITA
TOBAGO (1632)
TRINIDAD (1592)
BONAIRE (1634)
MOSQUITO COAST (1630)
90°W
10°N
SOUTH AMERICA
WILD COAST (1616)
0 300 600 mi.
0 300 600 km
Lambert Equal-Area Projection
80°W
70°W
60°W
ANGUILLA (1650)
ST. MARTIN (1638)
SABA (1630)
BARBUDA (1648)
ST. KITTS (1623)
ANTIGUA (1632)
NEVIS (1628)
MONTSERRAT (1632)
GUADELOUPE (1635)
16°N
MARIE GALANTE
Carib
MARTINIQUE (1635)
ST. LUCIA (1640)
Carib
BARBADOS (1625)
0 50 100 mi.
0 50 100 km
GRENADA (1651)
12°N
Conic Projection
60°W
NORTH AMERICA
EUROPE
Sugar, Rum
Guns, Textiles
Slaves
AFRICA
SOUTH AMERICA
ATLANTIC OCEAN

Starting Out

What makes this textbook so special? This book is about a whole world of people and landscapes. It is about your world—the one that exists today, and the one you will live in during the 21st century.

Unit Opener Striking images introduce each unit. Your journey to the various countries and cultures of the world begins here.

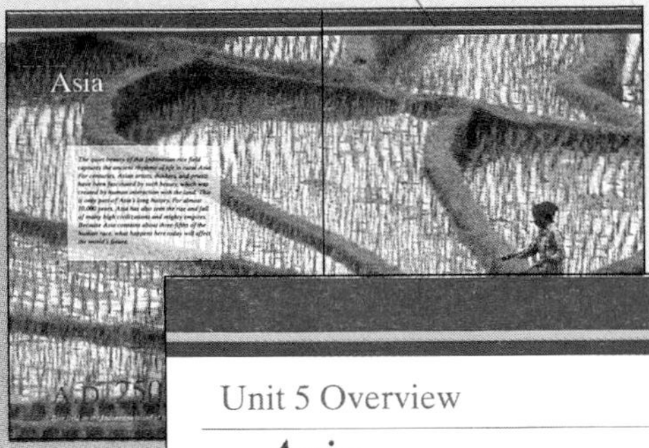
Asia

Unit Overview These four pages of maps and charts help you get the big picture—of a continent or other large region.

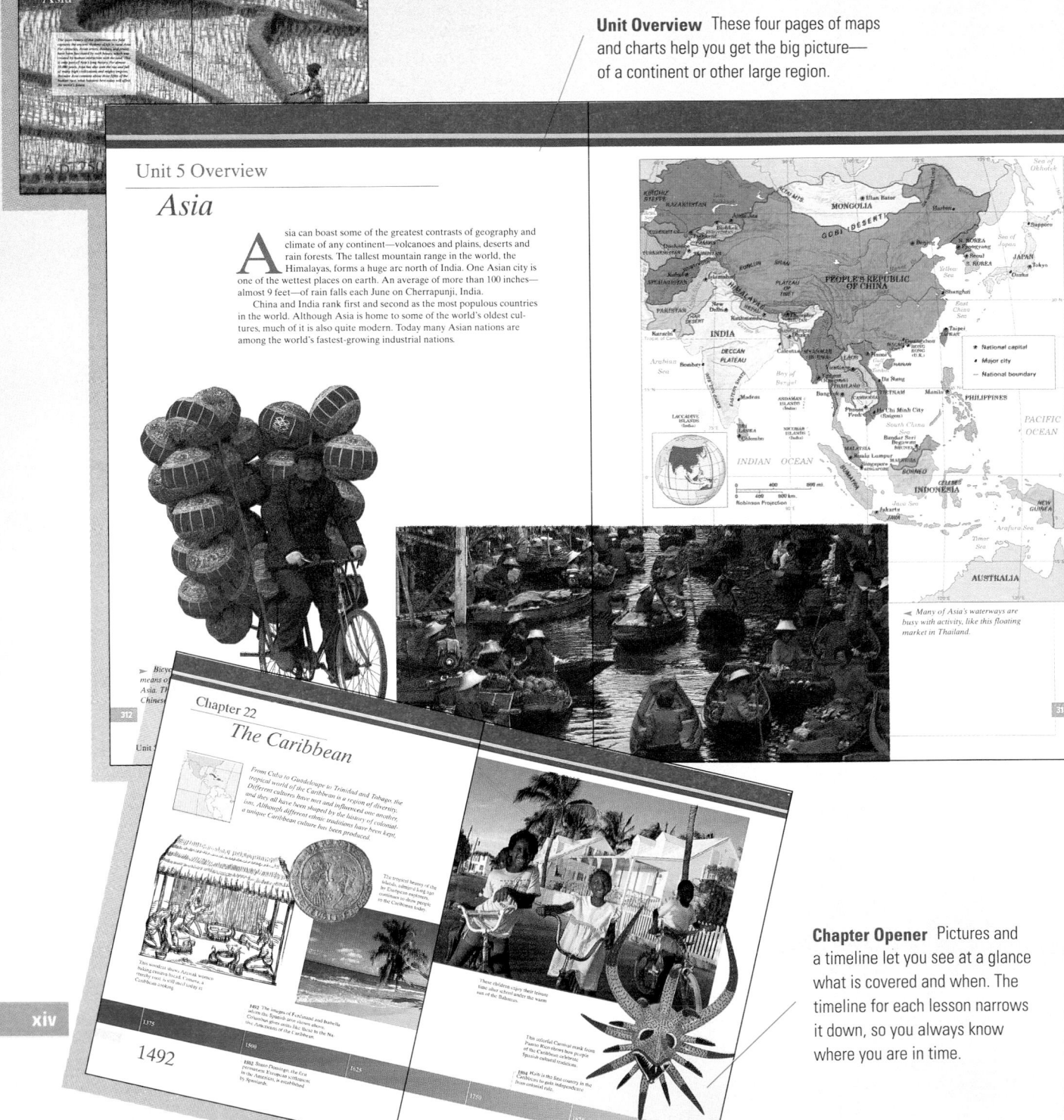

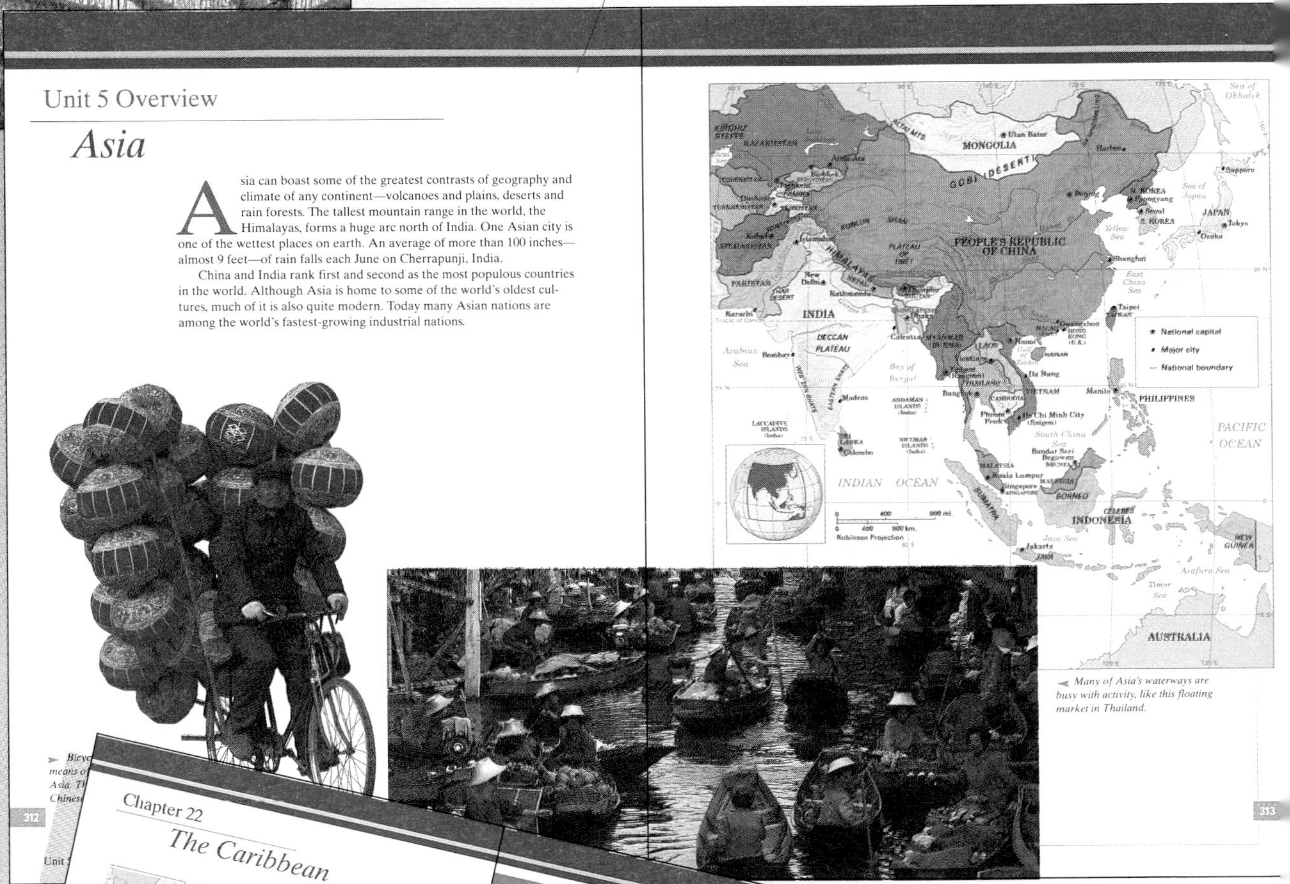
Unit 5 Overview

Asia

Asia can boast some of the greatest contrasts of geography and climate of any continent—volcanoes and plains, deserts and rain forests. The tallest mountain range in the world, the Himalayas, forms a huge arc north of India. One Asian city is one of the wettest places on earth. An average of more than 100 inches—almost 9 feet—of rain falls each June on Cherrapunji, India.

China and India rank first and second as the most populous countries in the world. Although Asia is home to some of the world's oldest cultures, much of it is also quite modern. Today many Asian nations are among the world's fastest-growing industrial nations.

MONGOLIA
GOBI DESERT
PEOPLE'S REPUBLIC OF CHINA
INDIA
JAPAN
PHILIPPINES
INDONESIA
AUSTRALIA
INDIAN OCEAN
PACIFIC OCEAN
National capital
Major city
National boundary

Many of Asia's waterways are busy with activity, like this floating market in Thailand.

312

313

Chapter 22

The Caribbean

From Cuba to Guadeloupe to Trinidad and Tobago, the tropical world of the Caribbean is a region of diversity. Different cultures have met and influenced one another, and they all have been shaped by the history of colonialism. Although different ethnic traditions have been kept, a unique Caribbean culture has been produced.

1375
1492
1500
1625
1750
1875

Chapter Opener Pictures and a timeline let you see at a glance what is covered and when. The timeline for each lesson narrows it down, so you always know where you are in time.

500 B.C. A.D. 500 639 TODAY

LESSON 2

Islamic Egypt

It is the metropolis of the universe, the garden of the world, the nest of the human species. . . . [It is] the glory of Islam and the orchard of the world.

THINKING FOCUS

How did Egypt become an Islamic nation?

Key Terms
- sultan
- isthmus

These words are from the Arab historian Ibn Khaldun *(IHB uhn kal DOON)*. The place he described was a city in the Egyptian desert, al-Qahirah *(ahl KUH hee ruh)*. We know it as Cairo *(KY roh)*.

According to one legend, the birth of Cairo happened this way: In A.D. 969 a group of Shiite Muslims prepared to break ground for a new city. They hired astrologers to tell them when the digging should begin. Workers raised their shovels. The astrologers watched the sky. When the moment arrived, they would give the signal to begin by pulling on a bell rope.

The planet Mars rose in the sky, but before the astrologers could give the signal, a raven landed on the rope and jingled the bells. The new city was named al-Qahirah, Arabic for Mars the victorious.

Whatever the true story of Cairo's founding, the city quickly grew. By the 1300s, Cairo was the greatest city in all of Africa, Europe, and Southwest Asia.

Arab Rule

The Arab Muslims came to Egypt in A.D. 639, when the Byzantines ruled. Like Alexander the Great, the Arabs entered Egypt with little trouble. The Byzantine Empire was too weak to fight. In addition, Egyptian Christians still disliked the Byzantines because of the split with the church at Constantinople.

Arab rule was fairly mild. The Arab ruler, Caliph Umar, did not allow Muslims to take Egyptian land. Instead, Egypt had to pay tribute. "Tribute is better than booty [stolen goods]," Umar said. "It lasts longer."

The Arabs also demanded tribute from Egypt's ancient neighbor, Nubia (see Chapter 4). A treaty made during the mid-600s required Nubia, which was then largely Christian, to do business with Muslim traders, build a mosque, and send 360 slaves to Cairo each year. Yet the treaty also required Cairo to send yearly gifts of food, horses, and cloth to Nubia.

An Islamic Nation

Like Egypt's Greek and Roman rulers, the Arabs allowed the Egyptians to worship as they chose. Although many Egyptians remained Christians, Egypt slowly became an Islamic nation.

The message of Islam, its five basic duties, and the caring community that it provided appealed to the people of the Nile. The practices of Islam were, in some respects, familiar. Like the beliefs of the ancient Egyptian religion and of Christianity, Islam gave Egyptians hope even when the Nile failed. It was the hope of a paradise that worshipers would enter after death.

The Rise of Cairo

Besides a new religion, the Arabs brought Egypt a new culture. Shortly after arriving in Egypt, they built a new capital called al-Fustat *(ahl FUH staht)* on the banks of the Nile. Later a newer capital was built at a site not far from al-Fustat. This new capital was Cairo.

The map on page 685 of the Atlas shows why the Arabs moved the capital from Alexandria. This capital of the Ptolemies bordered the Mediterranean Sea. The Greeks and Romans who had ruled Egypt from Alexandria looked across the sea, toward their homelands in Greece and Italy. The Arabs had little use for a capital that had to be defended from attack by sea. From Cairo the Arabs' ties lay southeast, toward the Muslim holy city of Mecca.

How Do We Know?

CULTURE *The writings of Ibn Khaldun (1332–1406) give a picture of how people lived in old Cairo. An Arabian born in Tunis, Ibn Khaldun used aspects of culture, such as geography and family ties, to understand societies of the past. Before settling in Cairo, he advised rulers in North Africa and Spain.*

Across Time & Space

An earthquake that hit Cairo on October 12, 1992, did a great deal of damage to the city's modern buildings. The pyramids and Sphinx outside the city fared better. The 40-second quake wiped out many older homes and killed hundreds of people.

The Muslim ruler Saladin built this fortress, the Citadel of Cairo, to protect Egypt from Christian invaders.

232 Chapter 10

Important Connections *Across Time & Space* connects what you're reading to events that happened centuries ago or continents away. *How Do We Know?* explains where information about a particular culture comes from.

Thinking Focus This question is a guide suggesting what to keep in mind as you read a lesson.

Key Terms As you read a lesson, watch for these words and phrases listed on the lesson's opening page. Each term is highlighted in heavy black type and is defined, both in the lesson and the Glossary.

A Closer Look From the lavish life of a Russian czar to exploding volcanoes, special subjects get extra attention on these pages.

A MOMENT IN TIME
A Nubian Princess
9:11 A.M., May 10, 1341 B.C.
In the home of a Nubian royal family
Makeup
Earrings
Jewel Box
Gown
Cat
Sandals
LOOK
Chapter 20

A Moment in Time In these features, time stops for a moment in the daily lives of people from many cultures.

Continuing On

As you read about different peoples and their cultures, you'll need a variety of tools to help you understand and remember them. The many features shown here are useful guides for learning and remembering.

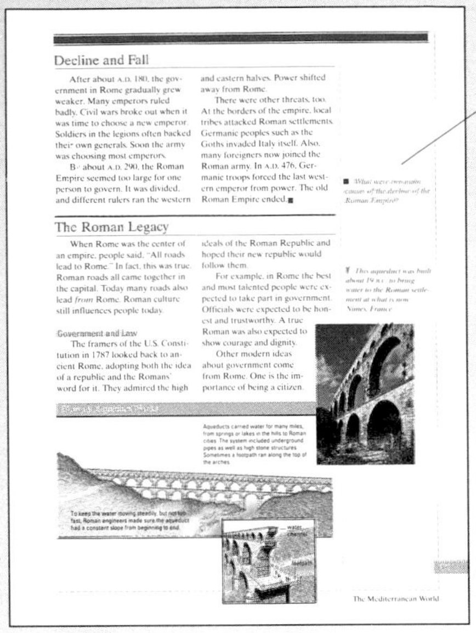

Decline and Fall
The Roman Legacy
Government and Law
The Mediterranean World

Charts and Graphs Information is presented in different ways to make it easier to understand. This is a diagram of an aqueduct.

Lesson Titles and Subtitles Red titles in the text tell you the main topics discussed. Blue titles are subtopics.

Margin Checks Find the red square at the end of the text. Match it to the square in the margin. If you can answer the question there, you probably understood what you have just read.

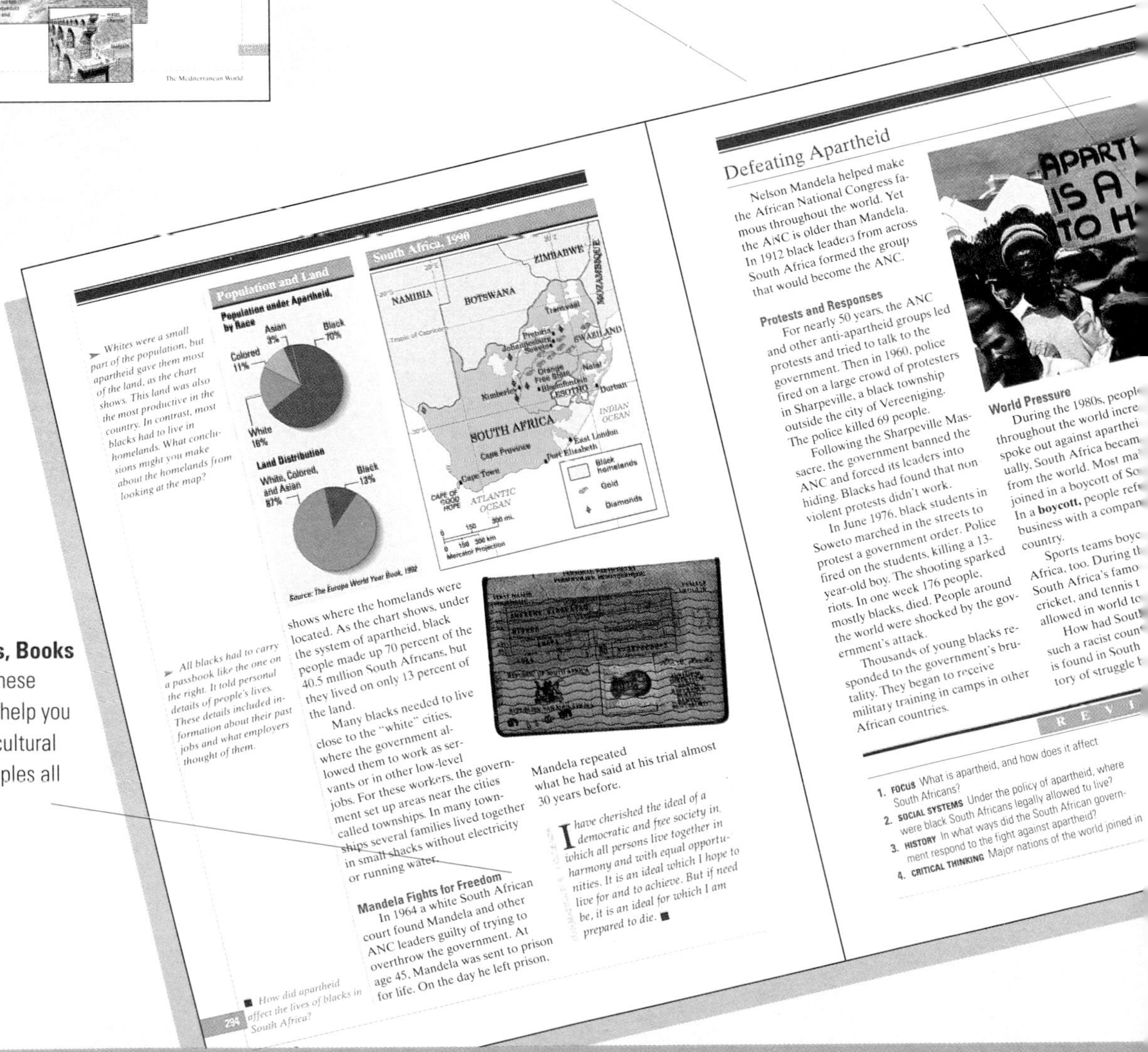

Population and Land
Population under Apartheid, by Race
Asian 3%
Black 70%
Colored 11%
White 16%
Land Distribution
White, Colored, and Asian 87%
Black 13%
Source: The Europa World Year Book, 1992
South Africa, 1990
NAMIBIA
BOTSWANA
ZIMBABWE
MOZAMBIQUE
SWAZILAND
SOUTH AFRICA
LESOTHO
INDIAN OCEAN
ATLANTIC OCEAN
Cape Town
Durban
Kimberley
Port Elizabeth
East London
Black homelands
Gold
Diamonds
Whites were a small part of the population, but apartheid gave them most of the land, as the chart shows. This land was also the most productive in the country. In contrast, most blacks had to live in homelands. What conclusions might you make about the homelands from looking at the map?
shows where the homelands were located. As the chart shows, under the system of apartheid, black people made up 70 percent of the 40.5 million South Africans, but they lived on only 13 percent of the land.
Many blacks needed to live close to the "white" cities, where the government allowed them to work as servants or in other low-level jobs. For these workers, the government set up areas near the cities called townships. In many townships several families lived together in small shacks without electricity or running water.
All blacks had to carry a passbook like the one on the right. It told personal details of people's lives. These details included information about their past jobs and what employers thought of them.
Mandela Fights for Freedom
In 1964 a white South African court found Mandela and other ANC leaders guilty of trying to overthrow the government. At age 45, Mandela was sent to prison for life. On the day he left prison,
Mandela repeated what he had said at his trial almost 30 years before.
I have cherished the ideal of a democratic and free society in which all persons live together in harmony and with equal opportunities. It is an ideal which I hope to live for and to achieve. But if need be, it is an ideal for which I am prepared to die.
How did apartheid affect the lives of blacks in South Africa?
294
Defeating Apartheid
Nelson Mandela helped make the African National Congress famous throughout the world. Yet the ANC is older than Mandela. In 1912 black leaders from across South Africa formed the group that would become the ANC.
Protests and Responses
For nearly 50 years, the ANC and other anti-apartheid groups led protests and tried to talk to the government. Then in 1960, police fired on a large crowd of protesters in Sharpeville, a black township outside the city of Vereeniging. The police killed 69 people.
Following the Sharpeville Massacre, the government banned the ANC and forced its leaders into hiding. Blacks had found that non violent protests didn't work.
In June 1976, black students in Soweto marched in the streets to protest a government order. Police fired on the students, killing a 13-year-old boy. The shooting sparked riots. In one week 176 people, mostly blacks, died. People around the world were shocked by the government's attack.
Thousands of young blacks responded to the government's brutality. They began to receive military training in camps in other African countries.
World Pressure
1. FOCUS What is apartheid, and how does it affect South Africans?
2. SOCIAL SYSTEMS Under the policy of apartheid, where were black South Africans legally allowed to live?
3. HISTORY In what ways did the South African government respond to the fight against apartheid?
4. CRITICAL THINKING

Letters, Diaries, Books Passages from these primary sources help you understand the cultural traditions of peoples all over the world.

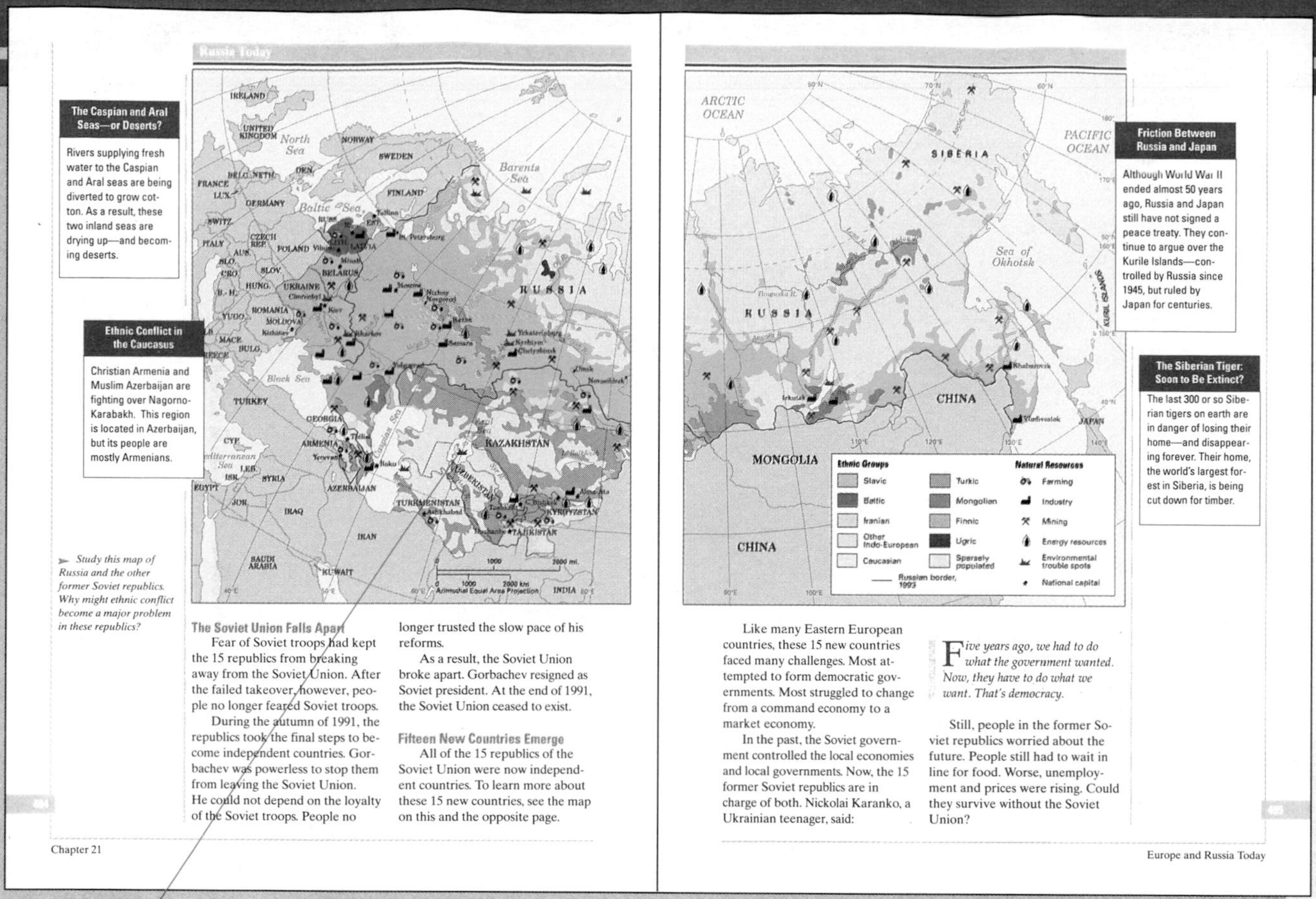

Russia Today

The Caspian and Aral Seas—or Deserts?

Rivers supplying fresh water to the Caspian and Aral seas are being diverted to grow cotton. As a result, these two inland seas are drying up—and becoming deserts.

Ethnic Conflict in the Caucasus

Christian Armenia and Muslim Azerbaijan are fighting over Nagorno-Karabakh. This region is located in Azerbaijan, but its people are mostly Armenians.

Study this map of Russia and the other former Soviet republics. Why might ethnic conflict become a major problem in these republics?

The Soviet Union Falls Apart

Fear of Soviet troops had kept the 15 republics from breaking away from the Soviet Union. After the failed takeover, however, people no longer feared Soviet troops.

During the autumn of 1991, the republics took the final steps to become independent countries. Gorbachev was powerless to stop them from leaving the Soviet Union. He could not depend on the loyalty of the Soviet troops. People no longer trusted the slow pace of his reforms.

As a result, the Soviet Union broke apart. Gorbachev resigned as Soviet president. At the end of 1991, the Soviet Union ceased to exist.

Fifteen New Countries Emerge

All of the 15 republics of the Soviet Union were now independent countries. To learn more about these 15 new countries, see the map on this and the opposite page.

Like many Eastern European countries, these 15 new countries faced many challenges. Most attempted to form democratic governments. Most struggled to change from a command economy to a market economy.

In the past, the Soviet government controlled the local economies and local governments. Now, the 15 former Soviet republics are in charge of both. Nickolai Karanko, a Ukrainian teenager, said:

Five years ago, we had to do what the government wanted. Now, they have to do what we want. That's democracy.

Still, people in the former Soviet republics worried about the future. People still had to wait in line for food. Worse, unemployment and prices were rising. Could they survive without the Soviet Union?

Friction Between Russia and Japan

Although World War II ended almost 50 years ago, Russia and Japan still have not signed a peace treaty. They continue to argue over the Kurile Islands—controlled by Russia since 1945, but ruled by Japan for centuries.

The Siberian Tiger: Soon to Be Extinct?

The last 300 or so Siberian tigers on earth are in danger of losing their home—and disappearing forever. Their home, the world's largest forest in Siberia, is being cut down for timber.

Chapter 21 — Europe and Russia Today

Maps You'll find maps showing landforms, oceans, waterways, ancient empires, trade routes, migrations, and brand new countries only weeks or months old.

More Understanding A second type of Understanding feature looks at concepts—the big ideas that help you put all the pieces together. This feature defines dynasties.

Understanding . . . Two kinds of Understanding features give you tools for learning. One covers skills you'll need throughout your life, such as Understanding Topography, which explains how to read elevation maps.

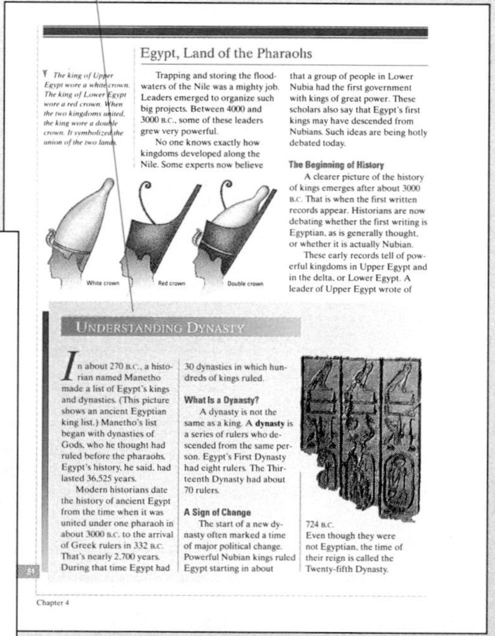

Egypt, Land of the Pharaohs

The king of Upper Egypt wore a white crown. The king of Lower Egypt wore a red crown. When the two kingdoms united, the king wore a double crown. It symbolized the union of the two lands.

Trapping and storing the floodwaters of the Nile was a mighty job. Leaders emerged to organize such big projects. Between 4000 and 3000 B.C., some of these leaders grew very powerful.

No one knows exactly how kingdoms developed along the Nile. Some experts now believe that a group of people in Lower Nubia had the first government with kings of great power. These scholars also say that Egypt's first kings may have descended from Nubians. Such ideas are being hotly debated today.

The Beginning of History

A clearer picture of the history of kings emerges after about 3000 B.C. That is when the first written records appear. Historians are now debating whether the first writing is Egyptian, as is generally thought, or whether it is actually Nubian.

These early records tell of powerful kingdoms in Upper Egypt and in the delta, or Lower Egypt. A leader of Upper Egypt wrote of

UNDERSTANDING DYNASTY

In about 270 B.C., a historian named Manetho made a list of Egypt's kings and dynasties. (This picture shows an ancient Egyptian king list.) Manetho's list began with dynasties of Gods, who he thought had ruled before the pharaohs. Egypt's history, he said, had lasted 36,525 years.

Modern historians date the history of ancient Egypt from the time when it was united under one pharaoh in about 3000 B.C. to the arrival of Greek rulers in 332 B.C. That's nearly 2,700 years. During that time Egypt had 30 dynasties in which hundreds of kings ruled.

What Is a Dynasty?

A dynasty is not the same as a king. A **dynasty** is a series of rulers who descended from the same person. Egypt's First Dynasty had eight rulers. The Thirteenth Dynasty had about 70 rulers.

A Sign of Change

The start of a new dynasty often marked a time of major political change. Powerful Nubian kings ruled Egypt starting in about

724 B.C. Even though they were not Egyptian, the time of their reign is called the Twenty-fifth Dynasty.

Chapter 4

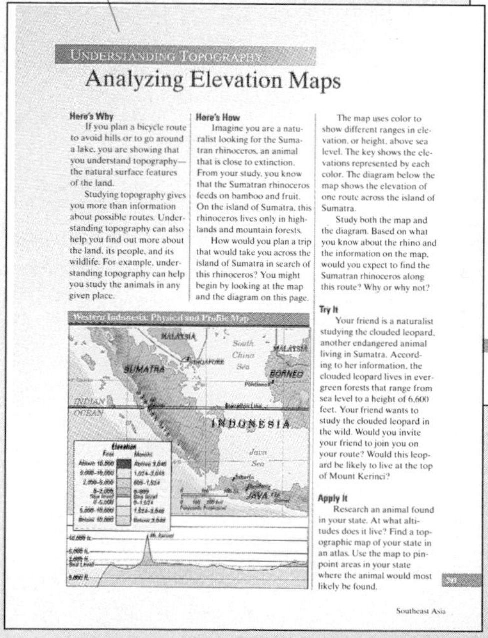

UNDERSTANDING TOPOGRAPHY

Analyzing Elevation Maps

Here's Why

If you plan a bicycle route to avoid hills or to go around a lake, you are showing that you understand topography—the natural surface features of the land.

Studying topography gives you more than information about possible routes. Understanding topography can also help you find out more about the land, its people, and its wildlife. For example, understanding topography can help you study the animals in any given place.

Here's How

Imagine you are a naturalist looking for the Sumatran rhinoceros, an animal that is close to extinction. From your study, you know that the Sumatran rhinoceros feeds on bamboo and fruit. On the island of Sumatra, this rhinoceros lives only in highlands and mountain forests.

How would you plan a trip that would take you across the island of Sumatra in search of this rhinoceros? You might begin by looking at the map and the diagram on this page.

The map uses color to show different ranges in elevation, or height, above sea level. The key shows the elevations represented by each color. The diagram below the map shows the elevation of one route across the island of Sumatra.

Study both the map and the diagram. Based on what you know about the rhino and the information on the map, would you expect to find the Sumatran rhinoceros along this route? Why or why not?

Try It

Your friend is a naturalist studying the clouded leopard, another endangered animal living in Sumatra. According to her information, the clouded leopard lives in evergreen forests that range from sea level to a height of 6,600 feet. Your friend wants to study the clouded leopard in the wild. Would you invite your friend to join you on your route? Would this leopard be likely to live at the top of Mount Kerinci?

Apply It

Research an animal found in your state. At what altitudes does it live? Find a topographic map of your state in an atlas. Use the map to pinpoint areas in your state where the animal would most likely be found.

Western Indonesia: Physical and Profile Map

Southeast Asia

Reviews At the end of the lesson, take time to review what you've read. These questions and activities help you focus on the lesson and connect it to what you've already learned. A Chapter Review then ties all the lessons together.

Also Featuring

Each unit includes special features and learning activities to increase your understanding. At the back of this book, you'll find more information in the Time/Space Databank, including an atlas of world maps.

Map and Globe Handbook
At the very front of the book, you'll find a resource section on maps, globes, and geographic skills. Reviewing this section will help you make sure that you can use all the maps in your textbook.

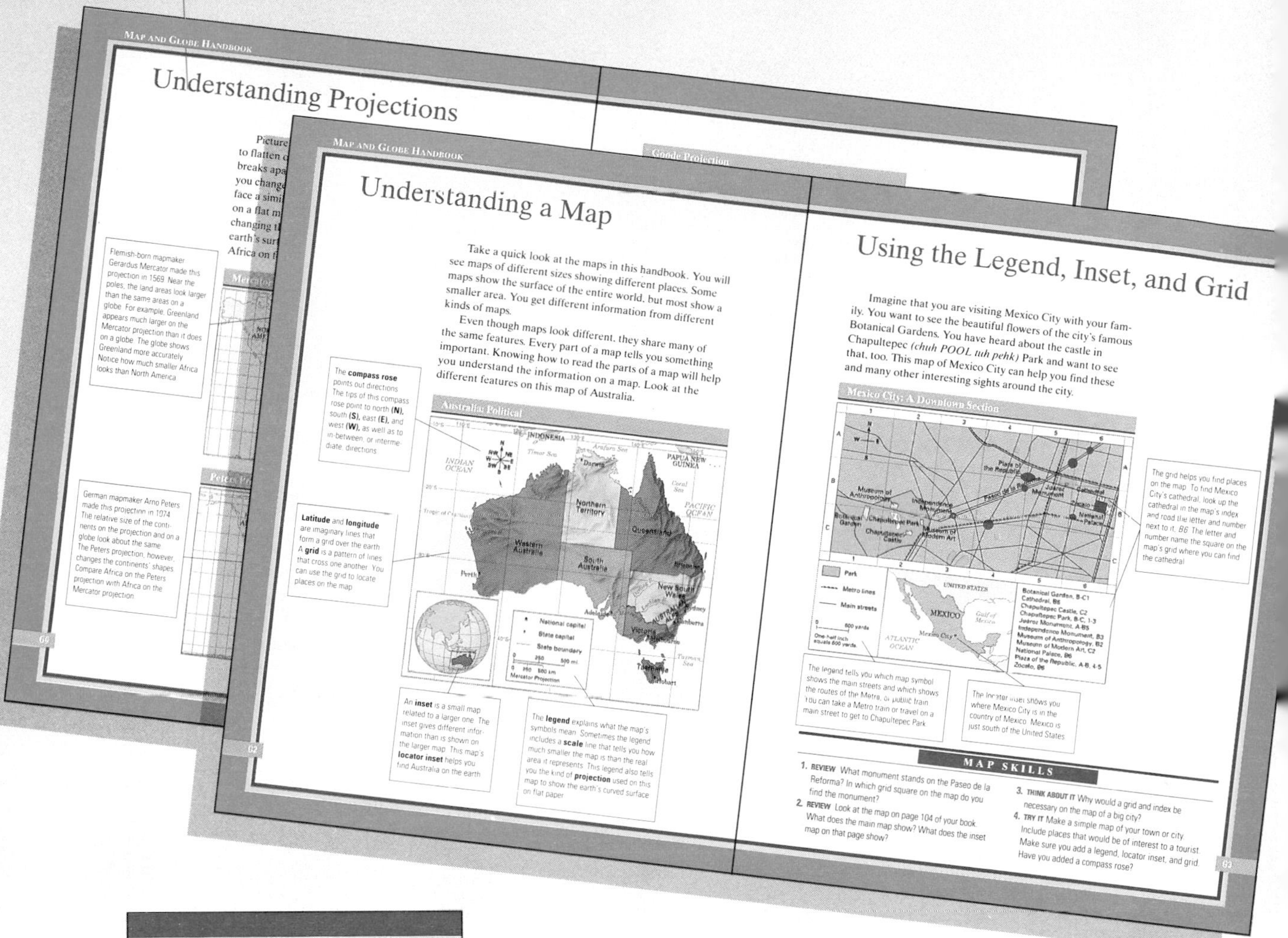

MAP AND GLOBE HANDBOOK
Understanding Projections
MAP AND GLOBE HANDBOOK
Understanding a Map
Take a quick look at the maps in this handbook. You will see maps of different sizes showing different places. Some maps show the surface of the entire world, but most show a smaller area. You get different information from different kinds of maps.
Even though maps look different, they share many of the same features. Every part of a map tells you something important. Knowing how to read the parts of a map will help you understand the information on a map. Look at the different features on this map of Australia.
Australia: Political
Using the Legend, Inset, and Grid
Imagine that you are visiting Mexico City with your family. You want to see the beautiful flowers of the city's famous Botanical Gardens. You have heard about the castle in Chapultepec (chuh POOL tuh pehk) Park and want to see that, too. This map of Mexico City can help you find these and many other interesting sights around the city.
Mexico City: A Downtown Section
MAP SKILLS

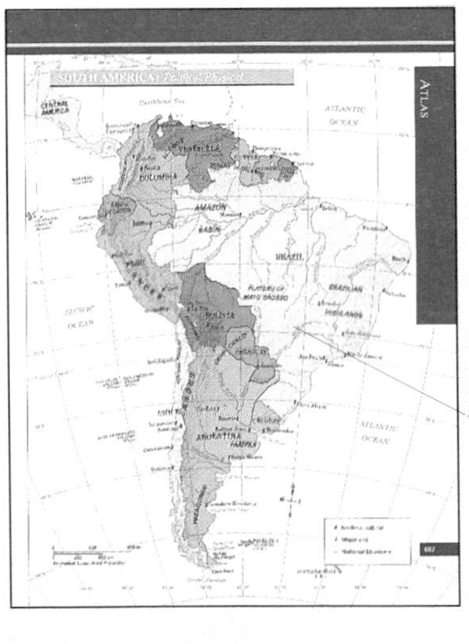

ATLAS

Atlas The Atlas adds to the wealth of maps in this book. Special maps also show languages, religions, climates, and resources.

Literature Stories and writing are an important part of every culture. Each unit includes a work of literature that relates to the topic you are studying. These haiku were written by Japanese poets.

LITERATURE
Japanese Poetry

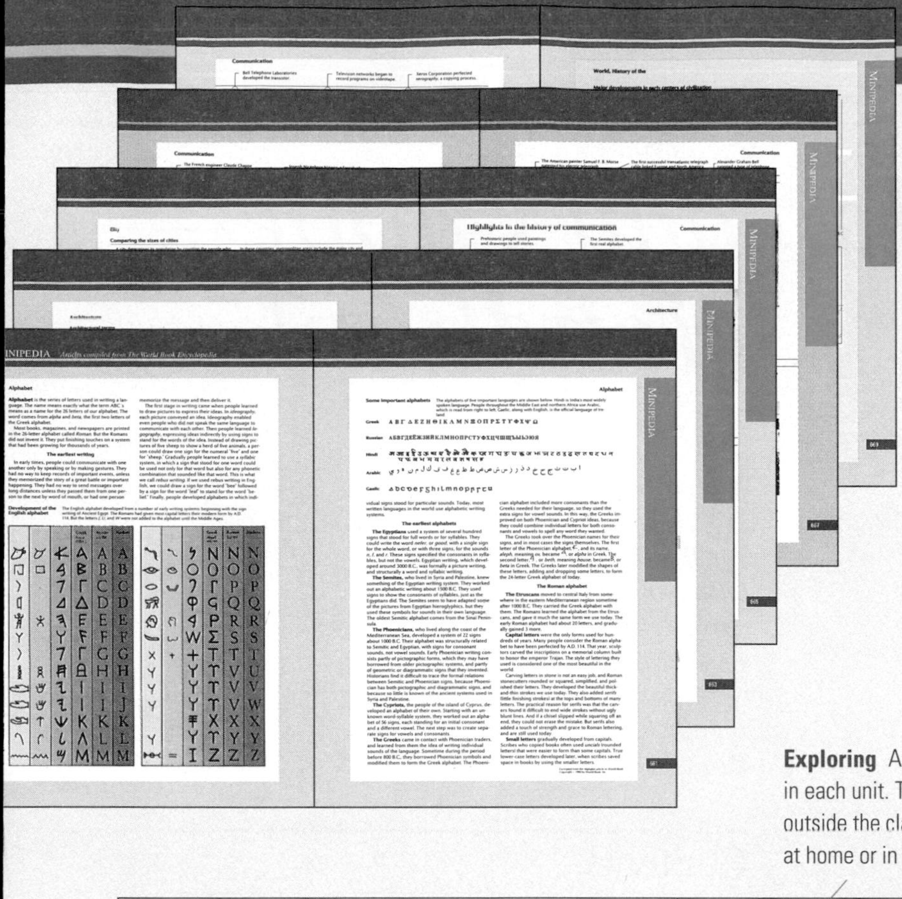
MINIPEDIA
Alphabet
Some important alphabets
Development of the English alphabet
The earliest writing
The earliest alphabets
The Roman alphabet

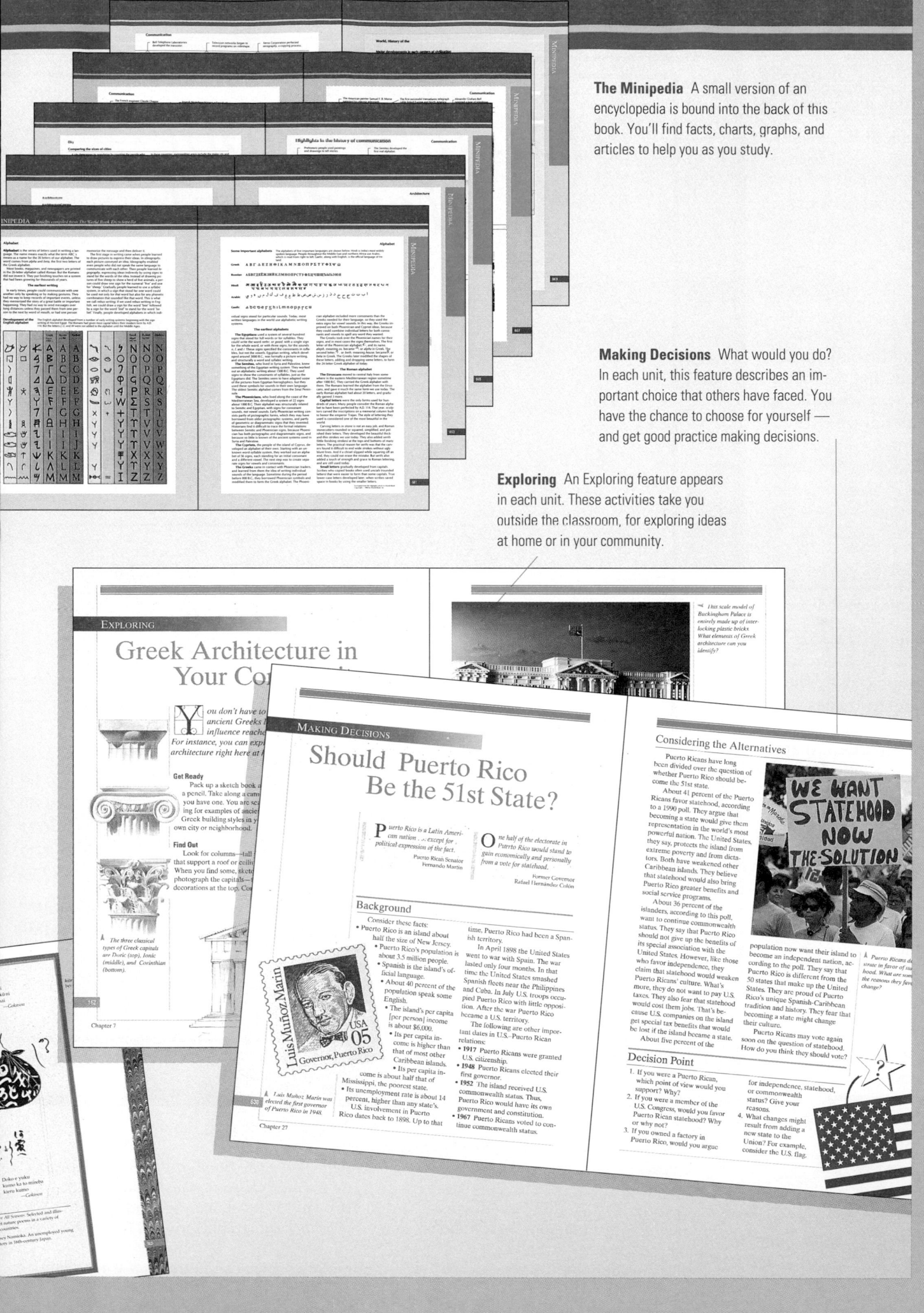

The Minipedia A small version of an encyclopedia is bound into the back of this book. You'll find facts, charts, graphs, and articles to help you as you study.

Making Decisions What would you do? In each unit, this feature describes an important choice that others have faced. You have the chance to choose for yourself — and get good practice making decisions.

Exploring An Exploring feature appears in each unit. These activities take you outside the classroom, for exploring ideas at home or in your community.

EXPLORING
Greek Architecture in Your Co
You don't have to
ancient Greeks
influence reache
For instance, you can exp
architecture right here at
Get Ready
Pack up a sketch book a
a pencil. Take along a cam
you have one. You are se
ing for examples of ancie
Greek building styles in y
own city or neighborhood.
Find Out
Look for columns—tall
that support a roof or ceilin
When you find some, sket
photograph the capitals—
decorations at the top. Co
The three classical types of Greek capitals are Doric (top), Ionic (middle), and Corinthian (bottom).
152
Chapter 7
This scale model of Buckingham Palace is entirely made up of interlocking plastic bricks. What elements of Greek architecture can you identify?
MAKING DECISIONS
Should Puerto Rico Be the 51st State?
Puerto Rico is a Latin American nation . . . except for political expression of the fact.
Puerto Rican Senator Fernando Martín
One half of the electorate in Puerto Rico would stand to gain economically and personally from a vote for statehood.
Former Governor Rafael Hernández Colón
Background
Consider these facts:
• Puerto Rico is an island about half the size of New Jersey.
• Puerto Rico's population is about 3.5 million people.
• Spanish is the island's official language.
• About 40 percent of the population speak some English.
• The island's per capita [per person] income is about $6,000.
• Its per capita income is higher than that of most other Caribbean islands.
• Its per capita income is about half that of Mississippi, the poorest state.
• Its unemployment rate is about 14 percent, higher than any state's.
U.S. involvement in Puerto Rico dates back to 1898. Up to that time, Puerto Rico had been a Spanish territory.
In April 1898 the United States went to war with Spain. The war lasted only four months. In that time the United States smashed Spanish fleets near the Philippines and Cuba. In July U.S. troops occupied Puerto Rico with little opposition. After the war Puerto Rico became a U.S. territory.
The following are other important dates in U.S.–Puerto Rican relations:
• 1917 Puerto Ricans were granted U.S. citizenship.
• 1948 Puerto Ricans elected their first governor.
• 1952 The island received U.S. commonwealth status. Thus, Puerto Rico would have its own government and constitution.
• 1967 Puerto Ricans voted to continue commonwealth status.
Luis Muñoz Marín
USA 05
Governor, Puerto Rico
Luis Muñoz Marín was elected the first governor of Puerto Rico in 1948.
638
Chapter 27
Considering the Alternatives
Puerto Ricans have long been divided over the question of whether Puerto Rico should become the 51st state.
About 41 percent of the Puerto Ricans favor statehood, according to a 1990 poll. They argue that becoming a state would give them representation in the world's most powerful nation. The United States, they say, protects the island from extreme poverty and from dictators. Both have weakened other Caribbean islands. They believe that statehood would also bring Puerto Rico greater benefits and social service programs.
About 36 percent of the islanders, according to this poll, want to continue commonwealth status. They say that Puerto Rico should not give up the benefits of its special association with the United States. However, like those who favor independence, they claim that statehood would weaken Puerto Ricans' culture. What's more, they do not want to pay U.S. taxes. They also fear that statehood would cost them jobs. That's because U.S. companies on the island get special tax benefits that would be lost if the island became a state.
About five percent of the population now want their island to become an independent nation, according to the poll. They say that Puerto Rico is different from the 50 states that make up the United States. They are proud of Puerto Rico's unique Spanish-Caribbean tradition and history. They fear that becoming a state might change their culture.
Puerto Ricans may vote again soon on the question of statehood. How do you think they should vote?
WE WANT STATEHOOD NOW
THE SOLUTION
Puerto Ricans demonstrate in favor of statehood. What are some of the reasons they favor change?
Decision Point
1. If you were a Puerto Rican, which point of view would you support? Why?
2. If you were a member of the U.S. Congress, would you favor Puerto Rican statehood? Why or why not?
3. If you owned a factory in Puerto Rico, would you argue for independence, statehood, or commonwealth status? Give your reasons.
4. What changes might result from adding a new state to the Union? For example, consider the U.S. flag.
Doko e yuku
kumo ka to mireba
kieru kumo
—Gokason

OVERVIEW

Ask students to imagine they are about to lead a tour around the world. Explain that, as tour guides, they will have to know how to find places and how to read maps. They will also need to know how to use maps to find information about countries. Page through the Map and Globe Handbook with students. Tell them that the skills the handbook teaches will guide them not only in their around-the-world tour but also in mentally traveling through history and in reading maps in real-life situations.

Looking Forward

Each section in the Map and Globe Handbook covers a specific geographic skill. The entire handbook provides a self-contained reference tool that students can access at any time. Some map captions within the text refer to a particular handbook section for additional help in understanding the text map. You may prefer to teach the handbook as a separate unit early in the school year or to teach sections of it throughout the year.

Map and Globe Handbook

You are about to begin a journey through space and time. First you'll visit Korea and Japan, and then Australia. You'll go to Africa to scale the heights of Mt. Kilimanjaro. Later, you will follow the ancient route of Alexander the Great's army. By using maps and globes, you can explore lands nearby or on the other side of the world.

Your adventure begins in the pages of this handbook, which will help you unlock the secrets of maps and globes. Turn to page G1, and get ready to start your journey.

Contents

Mapping Our Planet **G1**
Understanding a Map **G2**
Using the Legend, Inset, and Grid **G3**
Understanding Globes and Hemispheres **G4**
Using Latitude and Longitude on Maps **G5**
Understanding Projections **G6**
Observing the Seasons **G8**
Reading Different Kinds of Maps
A Physical Map with a Profile **G9**
A Time Zone Map **G10**
A Historical Map **G11**
A Route Map **G12**
Comparing Maps **G13**
A Cultural Map **G14**
Using Geographic References **G15**

Bibliography

Books for Students

Blandford, Percy W. *The New Explorer's Guide to Using Maps and Compasses.* Blue Ridge Summit, Pa.: TAB Books, 1992. Advanced readers will enjoy this guide to real and vicarious explorations.

Cultural Atlas for Young People Series. New York: Facts on File, 1974–1976. This six-volume set of historical atlases will be useful for reports and projects this year.

Exploring Your World: The Adventures of Geography. Washington, D.C.: National Geographic Society, 1990. Photographs illustrate this useful encyclopedia of geography.

Weiss, Harvey. *Maps: Getting from Here to There.* Boston: Houghton Mifflin, 1991. This book presents important geographic concepts, including contour lines and marine charts.

Books for Teachers

Bell, Neill. *The Book of Where; or, How to Be Naturally Geographic.* Boston: Little Brown, 1982. A humorous and creative approach to geography projects for students.

McVey, Vicki. *The Sierra Club Wayfinding Book.* Boston: Little Brown, 1989. This combination how-to and activity book is an excellent source of geographic projects and games.

Mapping Our Planet

A map is a representation of all or part of the earth's surface. Look at the pictures and map on this page. The picture on the right shows our planet in space. You can hardly see any details of the land. The picture below shows a smaller area of the earth. You can see the islands of Japan. You can also see North and South Korea and other parts of the East Asia coast. Now look at the map of the same area. Notice how carefully the mapmaker has drawn the shapes and sizes of the coastal lands and islands. The map is like a diagram of the area in the picture.

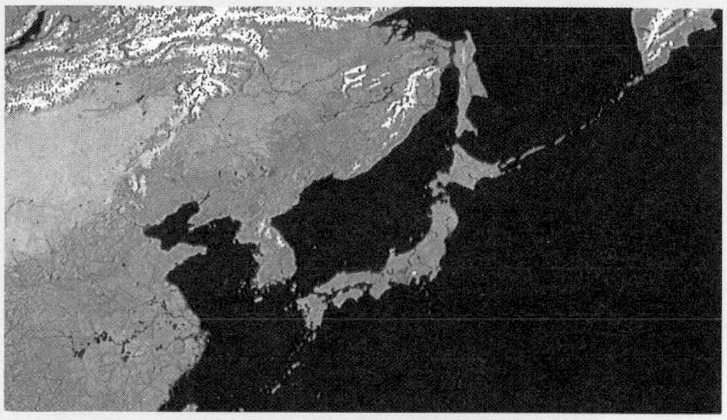

◄ *You can see that Japan is really many islands and that North and South Korea are on a peninsula. In both pictures, computers have added color to make the images clearer.*

Korea and Japan: Political

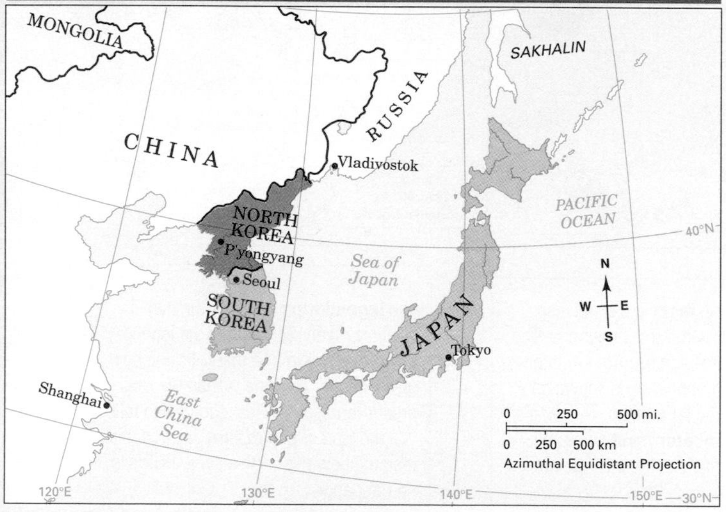
MONGOLIA
CHINA
RUSSIA
SAKHALIN
Vladivostok
NORTH KOREA
P'yongyang
Seoul
SOUTH KOREA
Sea of Japan
PACIFIC OCEAN
JAPAN
Tokyo
Shanghai
East China Sea
N
W
E
S
0 250 500 mi.
0 250 500 km
Azimuthal Equidistant Projection
40°N
30°N
120°E
130°E
140°E
150°E

◄ *Look at the coastline of Japan on the map and in the photo above it. Check to see how accurately the mapmaker drew this coastline.*

CLASS ACTIVITY

Ask students to describe the differences between the images shown here. The photo on the right shows half of the earth from far out in space. The rectangle on that photo marks the smaller area of the earth's surface that appears in the photo on the left and in the map below it. Help students generate a basic map definition based on the comparisons they see here. Explain that a map is a specific kind of drawing to represent all or part of the earth's surface. Tell students that is what this progression shows.

GEOGRAPHY

Visual Learning

Have students study the photo of Asia's east coast and then decide on other cities or features they could add to the map. Have them use the Atlas map on pages 682–683 as a reference. You might want to share with students the technique used to create the images of the earth. Thousands of separate images are recorded by meteorological satellites. These images are then put into a vast database, from which a graphics computer generates the composite photo on this page. The photos here are computer-enhanced to remove clouds for a clearer view. The computer also creates brighter colors to highlight features.

Visual Learning

Have students draw and color their own versions of a satellite-image picture of North America, using the images of Asia and the earth on this page as a style guide, and the map of North America on page 686 as a factual guide.

Project

Have students work together to make a photo-to-map display. Assign some to photograph the area around their school or neighborhood. Students might take photos from the top floor of a building. If this is not possible, have students look for panoramic pictures in books. Students should then make maps based on their photos. Display the photo-map sets for school viewing.

Objectives

1. Compare a map and photograph of the same geographic area to determine the features being shown. (Visual Learning 1, Map and Globe Skills 1)
2. Compare a map and photograph to see how a map is a diagram of a real place. (Visual Learning 1)

CLASS ACTIVITY

Have students list some information they can learn from a quick look at the map of Australia. *(Among many other facts, students can learn that the capital of Australia is Canberra and that other important Australian cities are Sydney, Brisbane, Perth, and Melbourne. Students can learn the Australian states, including the island state of Tasmania.)* Call attention to some of the parts of the map they can use to gain information, such as the locator inset, the lines of latitude and longitude, the legend, and the compass rose. Point out that these features are standard on most maps. If students learn to use the main parts on one map, they can read other maps.

Geography Theme: Location

Using the information shown on this map and in atlas maps, help students make up absolute and relative location statements about Australia. Latitude and longitude can be used to describe the location of Australia relative to other lands in the region, such as Indonesia and Papua New Guinea, as well as to describe Australia's absolute location, or where it is located on the earth. The latitude and longitude lines, the locator globe, and the compass rose will help in supplying the location information.

Understanding a Map

Take a quick look at the maps in this handbook. You will see maps of different sizes showing different places. Some maps show the surface of the entire world, but most show a smaller area. You get different information from different kinds of maps.

Even though maps look different, they share many of the same features. Every part of a map tells you something important. Knowing how to read the parts of a map will help you understand the information on a map. Look at the different features on this map of Australia.

The **compass rose** points out directions. The tips of this compass rose point to north **(N)**, south **(S)**, east **(E)**, and west **(W)**, as well as to in-between, or intermediate, directions.

Latitude and **longitude** are imaginary lines that form a grid over the earth. A **grid** is a pattern of lines that cross one another. You can use the grid to locate places on the map.

Australia: Political

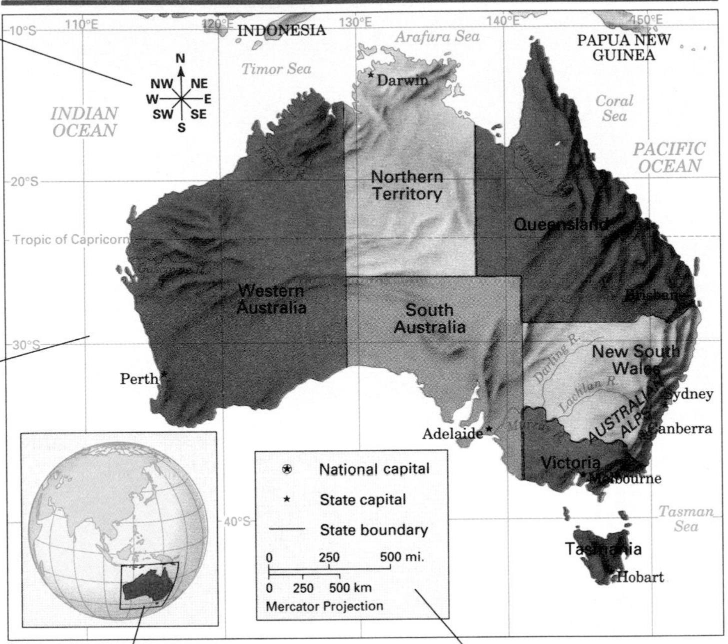
10°S
110°E
120°E
130°E
140°E
150°E
INDONESIA
Arafura Sea
Timor Sea
PAPUA NEW GUINEA
Darwin
N
NW
NE
W
E
SW
SE
S
INDIAN OCEAN
Coral Sea
PACIFIC OCEAN
20°S
Northern Territory
Queensland
Tropic of Capricorn
Western Australia
South Australia
Brisbane
30°S
Perth
New South Wales
Darling R.
Lachlan R.
Sydney
AUSTRALIAN ALPS
Canberra
Adelaide
Victoria
Melbourne
40°S
Tasman Sea
Tasmania
Hobart
National capital
State capital
State boundary
0
250
500 mi.
0
250
500 km
Mercator Projection

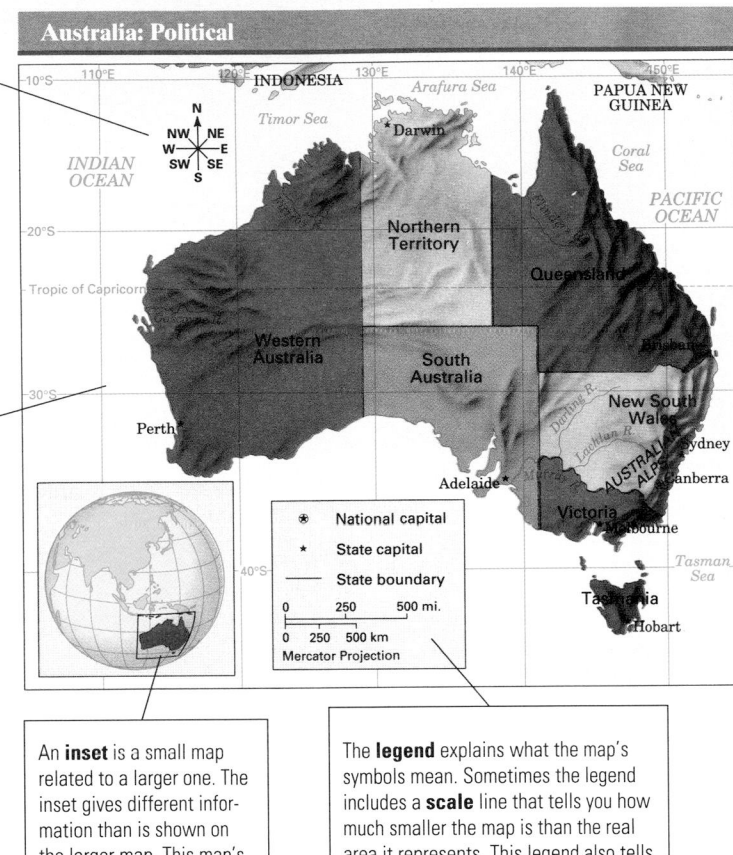

An **inset** is a small map related to a larger one. The inset gives different information than is shown on the larger map. This map's **locator inset** helps you find Australia on the earth.

The **legend** explains what the map's symbols mean. Sometimes the legend includes a **scale** line that tells you how much smaller the map is than the real area it represents. This legend also tells you the kind of **projection** used on this map to show the earth's curved surface on flat paper.

Objectives

1. Interpret the meaning of map symbols. (Map and Globe Skills 1)
2. Locate cities and other features on a map. (Map and Globe Skills 2)

Mathematics Connection

Review the concept of scale by first having students mark the edge of a piece of paper to match the length of the map's scale line. Students can then use the edge of the paper to calculate the number of miles or kilometers between selected cities. Explain that most people in the world express distances using the metric system, which is based on units of 10. One kilometer is 0.62 mile. One mile is 1.609 kilometers.

Research Project

Students should examine atlases and road maps to see how many different symbols they can find. Cities may have circles of various sizes based on population. Capital cities may use a star. Many symbols are stylized representations for the item on the map—a tiny airplane stands for an airport, a cross may be a church, and crossed swords can stand for a battle site. Have students copy as many different symbols as possible and then share their findings with the class.

Using the Legend, Inset, and Grid

Imagine that you are visiting Mexico City with your family. You want to see the beautiful flowers of the city's famous Botanical Gardens. You have heard about the castle in Chapultepec *(chuh POOL tuh pehk)* Park and want to see that, too. This map of Mexico City can help you find these and many other interesting sights around the city.

Mexico City: A Downtown Section

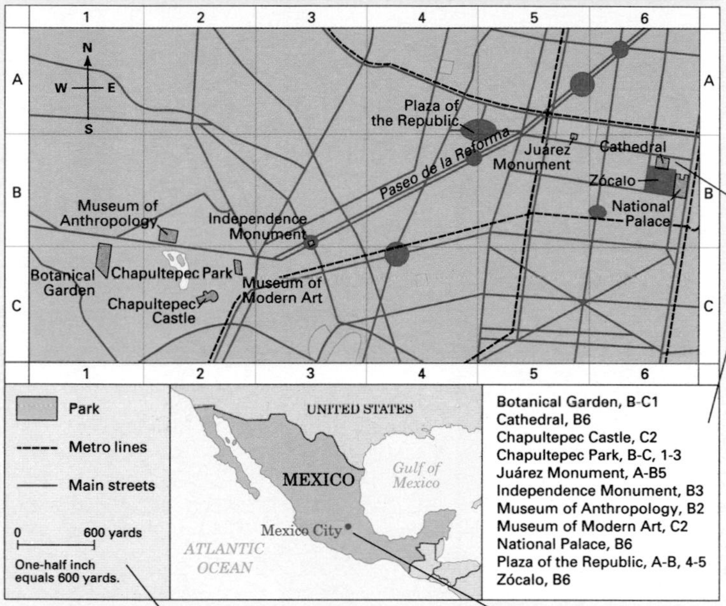

1 2 3 4 5 6
A B C
N S E W
Plaza of the Republic
Paseo de la Reforma
Juárez Monument
Cathedral
Zócalo
National Palace
Museum of Anthropology
Independence Monument
Botanical Garden
Chapultepec Park
Chapultepec Castle
Museum of Modern Art
Park
Metro lines
Main streets
0 600 yards
One-half inch equals 600 yards.
UNITED STATES
MEXICO
Gulf of Mexico
Mexico City
ATLANTIC OCEAN
Botanical Garden, B-C1
Cathedral, B6
Chapultepec Castle, C2
Chapultepec Park, B-C, 1-3
Juárez Monument, A-B5
Independence Monument, B3
Museum of Anthropology, B2
Museum of Modern Art, C2
National Palace, B6
Plaza of the Republic, A-B, 4-5
Zócalo, B6

The grid helps you find places on the map. To find Mexico City's cathedral, look up the cathedral in the map's index and read the letter and number next to it, *B6*. The letter and number name the square on the map's grid where you can find the cathedral.

The legend tells you which map symbol shows the main streets and which shows the routes of the Metro, or public train. You can take a Metro train or travel on a main street to get to Chapultepec Park.

The locator inset shows you where Mexico City is in the country of Mexico. Mexico is just south of the United States.

MAP SKILLS

1. **REVIEW** What monument stands on the Paseo de la Reforma? In which grid square on the map do you find the monument?
2. **REVIEW** Look at the map on page 104 of your book. What does the main map show? What does the inset map on that page show?
3. **THINK ABOUT IT** Why would a grid and index be necessary on the map of a big city?
4. **TRY IT** Make a simple map of your town or city. Include places that would be of interest to a tourist. Make sure you add a legend, locator inset, and grid. Have you added a compass rose?

CLASS ACTIVITY

Ask students to visualize what a map of their school's neighborhood would look like. Ask them what places and streets would be shown. Discuss the fact that city maps and other local maps show much more detail than do maps of larger areas. Students could expect to find a particular street on a city map but never on a map of the United States. Talk about the ways in which a city map is useful to tourists—if they know how to use the grid and legend on the map.

GEOGRAPHY

Map and Globe Skills

Ask students to make up and answer questions about Mexico City based on the locator inset. *(Example: Where is Mexico City in Mexico? or Mexico City lies between what bodies of water?)*

GEOGRAPHY

Map and Globe Skills

Have students pair up to do a map and globe activity. One student in a pair will name sites in Mexico City, and the other student will name the grid square or squares for each site.

Answers to Map Skills

1. The Independence Monument is on the Paseo de la Reforma. It is in square B3.
2. The main map shows ancient trade routes and resources of Southwest Asia; the inset is a locator map.
3. Road maps of a big city must show many streets and places very close together. Without a grid and index, it would be very difficult for someone to locate an unfamiliar place on a large and detailed map.
4. The maps may focus on one area of a larger community. Help students prepare their maps by offering suggestions on coverage, places of interest, and symbols.

Objectives

1. Use a locator inset map to find out where an area is located in a larger area. (Map and Globe Skills 2)
2. Describe locations using a map grid. (Map and Globe Skills 2)
3. Interpret map symbols by using a legend. (Map and Globe Skills 1)

CLASS ACTIVITY

Hold up a globe and ask students if they can name the different hemispheres. Point out that the word *hemisphere* means "half sphere." Help students see the major dividing lines that are superimposed on the globe. Ask students to name the hemispheres in which they live. *(The United States is in the Western and Northern hemispheres.)*

GEOGRAPHY

Map and Globe Skills

Ask students to name cities, countries, or continents that lie on the equator. They should use the Atlas maps on pages 678–687 for reference. Then ask for citics along the prime meridian and 180º longitude line. Explain that the countries of the world did not decide on the location of the prime meridian until 1884, when the city of Greenwich, near London in England, was chosen to be located at 0° longitude. Point out that a small part of Europe and Africa are west of the prime meridian. However, Europe and Africa are usually considered to be in the Eastern Hemisphere.

Understanding Globes and Hemispheres

Northern Hemisphere
Detroit

Southern Hemisphere
Melbourne

Western Hemisphere
Rio de Janeiro

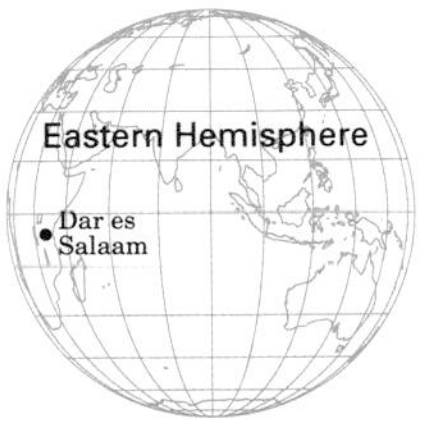
Eastern Hemisphere
Dar es Salaam

Above, you can see the four hemispheres and a major city in each.

Both maps and globes show the location of land and water on the earth. However, a globe does something a flat map can't do. A globe shows that the earth is shaped like a ball, or sphere. Geographers use certain imaginary lines of latitude and longitude on the globe to divide the earth into halves, or hemispheres. When you want to locate a place on a globe, it helps to know in which hemisphere the place can be found.

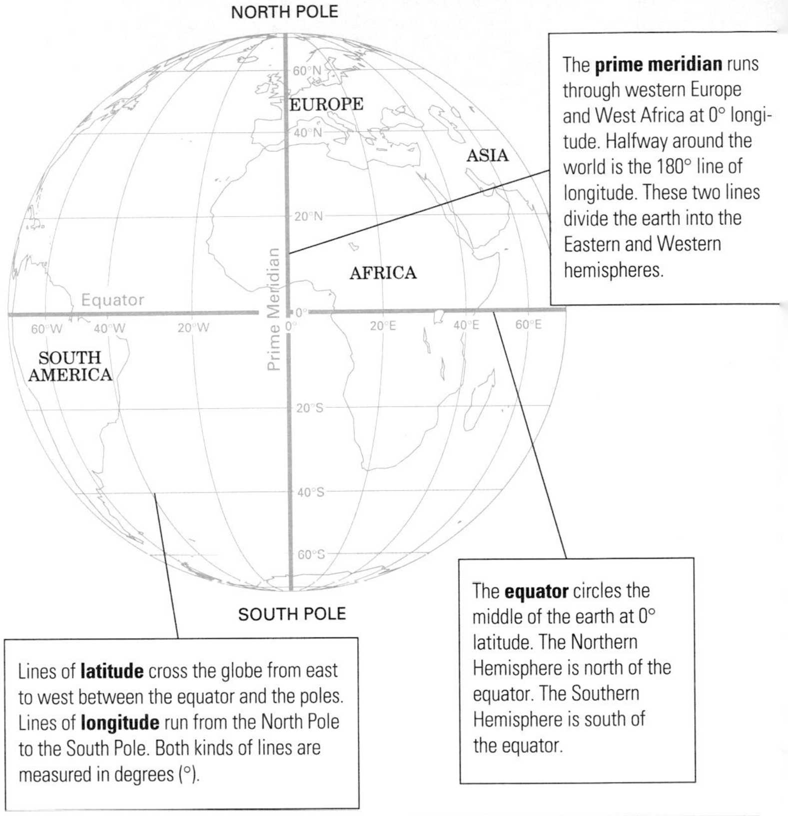
NORTH POLE
60°N
EUROPE
40°N
ASIA
20°N
AFRICA
Equator
Prime Meridian
0°
60°W
40°W
20°W
20°E
40°E
60°E
SOUTH AMERICA
20°S
40°S
60°S
SOUTH POLE
The **prime meridian** runs through western Europe and West Africa at 0° longitude. Halfway around the world is the 180° line of longitude. These two lines divide the earth into the Eastern and Western hemispheres.
Lines of **latitude** cross the globe from east to west between the equator and the poles. Lines of **longitude** run from the North Pole to the South Pole. Both kinds of lines are measured in degrees (°).
The **equator** circles the middle of the earth at 0° latitude. The Northern Hemisphere is north of the equator. The Southern Hemisphere is south of the equator.

GLOBE SKILLS

1. **REVIEW** Why is it helpful to know the four hemispheres of the earth?
2. **THINK ABOUT IT** One continent lies in four hemispheres. What continent is it and how is this possible?
3. **TRY IT** Find three countries on a globe. Give the name of each country to a classmate. Have each classmate find the country on the globe and tell you the two hemispheres in which it lies.

Objectives

1. Identify the four hemispheres of the earth on a globe. (Map and Globe Skills 2)
2. Locate the prime meridian and 180º longitude line on a map or globe. (Map and Globe Skills 2)

Answers to Globe Skills

1. Knowing its hemisphere helps you locate an unfamiliar place on the earth. Atlases sometimes identify places by the degrees of east or west longitude and north or south latitude.
2. Africa is in all four hemispheres. Both the equator and the prime meridian run through Africa.
3. Answers will vary. Students should try to name countries in different hemispheres.

Collaborative Learning

In pairs or small groups, students should take turns closing their eyes and randomly pointing to a place on a globe or world map. When they open their eyes, they should name the location and the hemispheres in which they "landed." Other group members should confirm answers.

Using Latitude and Longitude on Maps

Suppose someone asks you the location of the small country of Singapore. You might say it is in Southeast Asia. If you need to tell exactly where Singapore is, you can give its latitude and longitude. Singapore is located at about 1° north latitude and 103° east longitude. That means Singapore lies one degree north of the equator and 103 degrees east of the prime meridian.

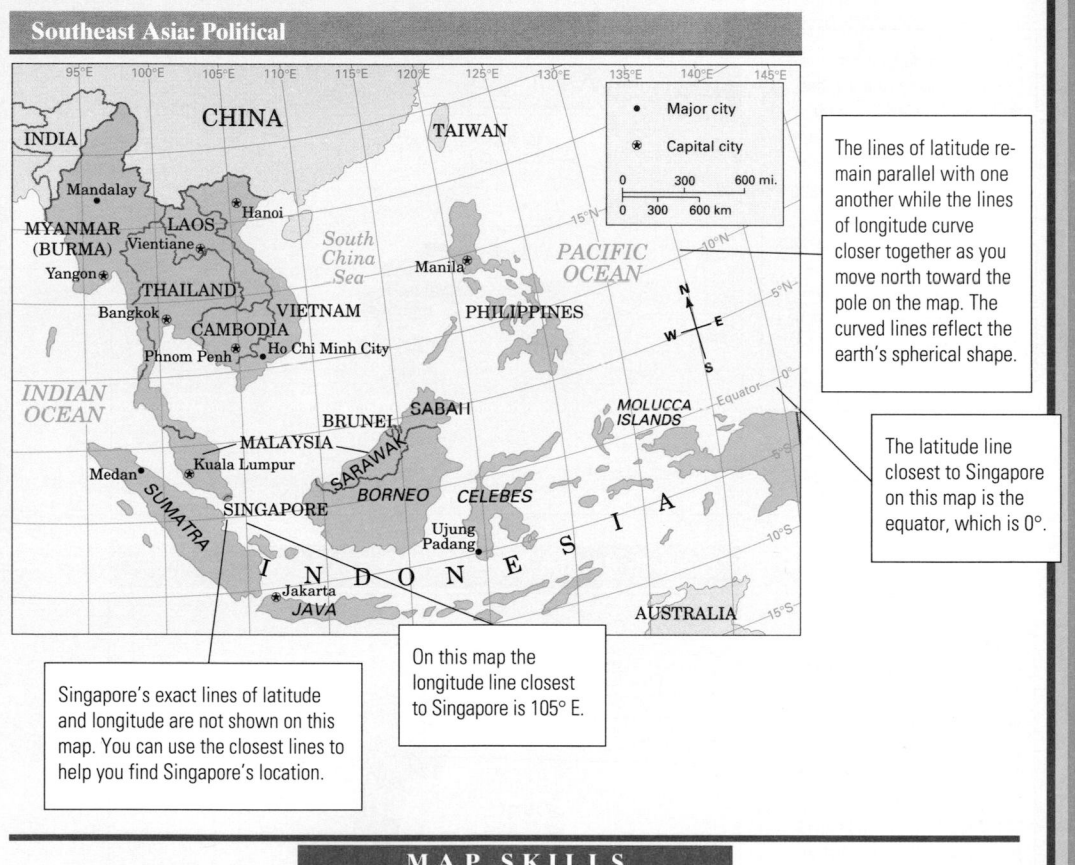

Southeast Asia: Political

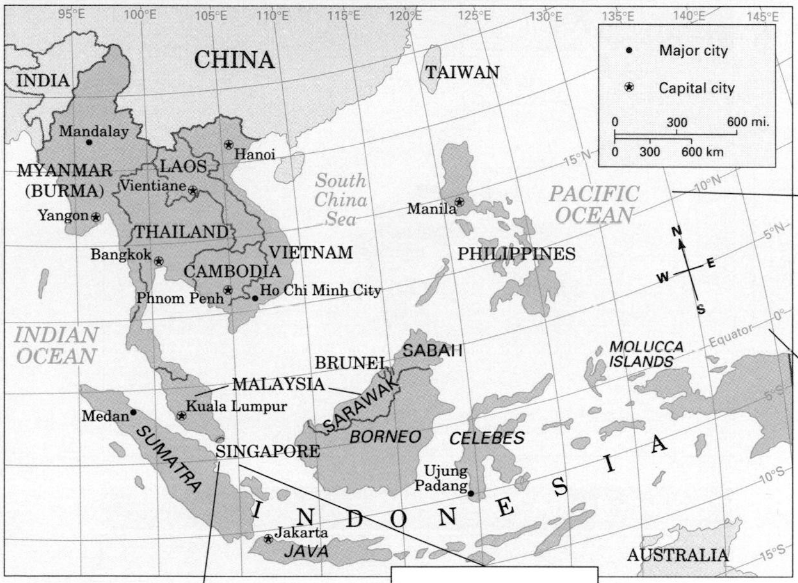

95°E
100°E
105°E
110°E
115°E
120°E
125°E
130°E
135°E
140°E
145°E
Major city
Capital city
0 300 600 mi.
0 300 600 km
CHINA
INDIA
TAIWAN
Mandalay
Hanoi
MYANMAR (BURMA)
LAOS
Vientiane
South China Sea
Yangon
Manila
PACIFIC OCEAN
THAILAND
Bangkok
VIETNAM
PHILIPPINES
CAMBODIA
Phnom Penh
Ho Chi Minh City
INDIAN OCEAN
BRUNEI
SABAH
MOLUCCA ISLANDS
MALAYSIA
SARAWAK
Kuala Lumpur
Medan
SUMATRA
SINGAPORE
BORNEO
CELEBES
Ujung Padang
INDONESIA
Jakarta
JAVA
AUSTRALIA
15°N
10°N
5°N
Equator
5°S
10°S
15°S
N
S
E
W

The lines of latitude remain parallel with one another while the lines of longitude curve closer together as you move north toward the pole on the map. The curved lines reflect the earth's spherical shape.

The latitude line closest to Singapore on this map is the equator, which is 0°.

On this map the longitude line closest to Singapore is 105° E.

Singapore's exact lines of latitude and longitude are not shown on this map. You can use the closest lines to help you find Singapore's location.

MAP SKILLS

1. **REVIEW** Use latitude and longitude to tell the location of Ujung Padang on the island of Celebes in Indonesia.
2. **THINK ABOUT IT** How could you use latitude and longitude to tell the location of an entire nation, such as Vietnam in Southeast Asia?
3. **TRY IT** Use a globe or atlas to find the lines of latitude and longitude closest to your city or town.
4. **TRY IT** Look at the map of Eurasia on pages 682–683. List European and Asian cities located near 45° N latitude and cities near 45° E longitude.

CLASS ACTIVITY

Ask students to imagine that they are on a ship sailing from Taiwan to Manila and are lost in the South China Sea. They have to send an SOS for help in identifying their exact location. They began their trip on the northern tip of Taiwan. Now they have been blown off course by a storm about 400 miles west of Manila in the Philippines. At what degrees of longitude and latitude shown on the map is the ship? *(115° E longitude, 15° N latitude)* Discuss how degrees of latitude and longitude give an exact location for any place on earth.

GEOGRAPHY

Map and Globe Skills

Have students identify the latitude and longitude degrees of cities on the map of Southeast Asia. They may refer to the Atlas map of the Pacific Rim on page 684. Discuss how to show both latitude and longitude in degrees *(for example: 3° N, 105° E)*.

Geography Theme: Location

Ask students what makes location by degrees of latitude and longitude so exact. Discuss the fact that a specific longitude and latitude identify a fairly limited area.

Answers to Map Skills

1. Ujung Padang is 5° S latitude, 119° E longitude.
2. You can tell the lines of latitude and longitude between which a nation lies. Vietnam lies between 102° E and 109° E longitude and between 8° N and 23° N latitude.
3. Locations will vary.
4. Cities near 45° N latitude include Venice, Belgrade, Bucharest, and Harbin. Cities at 45° E longitude are Volgograd, Tbilisi, Baghdad, and Aden.

Project

Use a large wall map of the United States to set up a "Find That Place" display. Have students write a city's name on an index card, and that city's coordinates of latitude and longitude on the reverse side of the card. Students may practice finding locations named on the cards.

Objectives

1. Locate places on a map using degrees of latitude and longitude. (Map and Globe Skills 1)
2. Estimate degrees of latitude and longitude when locations do not lie on labeled lines. (Map and Globe Skills 1)

CLASS ACTIVITY

Display a globe next to a small, flat world map. Ask students if they could fit the map on the globe, smooth it down, and produce a "new" globe. Why or why not? *(Students should see that the flat map's rectangular shape would not fit perfectly to produce a globe that is narrower at the top and bottom than in the middle.)* Explain that a projection is a system for mapping the spherical earth on a flat surface. Discuss why a globe's spherical shape cannot be flattened and remain accurate.

GEOGRAPHY
Visual Learning

Have students compare the different projections. Ask them to describe in their own words how the projections look different. Which one(s) look most familiar to them? Discuss possible reasons. For example, one projection may have continents that resemble the shapes of the continents on the globe, or a projection may be the one most often used in their books.

Understanding Projections

Picture yourself peeling an orange. Once you finish, try to flatten out the peel. What happens? Most likely, the peel breaks apart. Because the peel is shaped like a sphere, or ball, you change its shape when you try to flatten it. Mapmakers face a similar problem when they show the sphere-shaped earth on a flat map. Each map uses a certain projection, or way of changing the size or shape of oceans and continents on the earth's surface. Compare the shape and size of the continent of Africa on four projections.

Flemish-born mapmaker Gerardus Mercator made this projection in 1569. Near the poles, the land areas look larger than the same areas on a globe. For example, Greenland appears much larger on the Mercator projection than it does on a globe. The globe shows Greenland more accurately. Notice how much smaller Africa looks than North America.

Mercator Projection

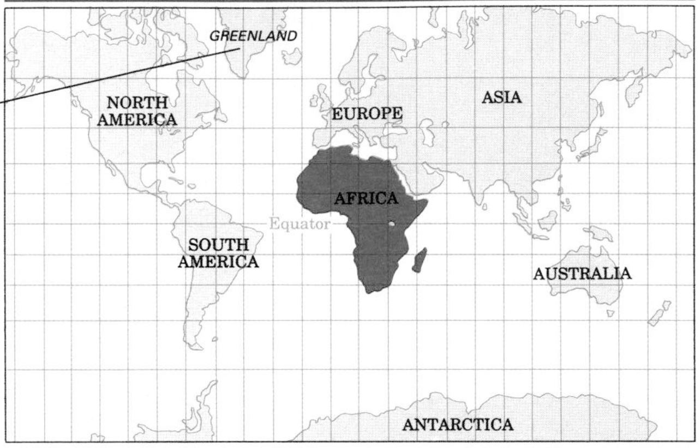
GREENLAND
NORTH AMERICA
EUROPE
ASIA
AFRICA
Equator
SOUTH AMERICA
AUSTRALIA
ANTARCTICA

German mapmaker Arno Peters made this projection in 1974. The relative size of the continents on the projection and on a globe look about the same. The Peters projection, however, changes the continents' shapes. Compare Africa on the Peters projection with Africa on the Mercator projection.

Peters Projection

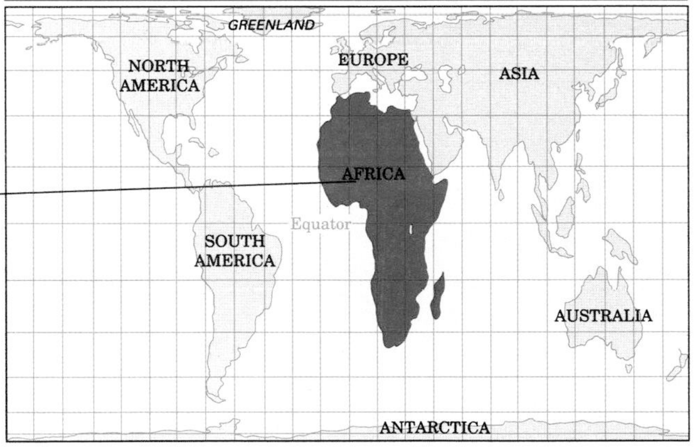
GREENLAND
NORTH AMERICA
EUROPE
ASIA
AFRICA
Equator
SOUTH AMERICA
AUSTRALIA
ANTARCTICA

Objectives

1. Recognize the differences between world map projections. (Visual Learning 1)
2. Explain why flat maps distort the earth's shape and how projections try to minimize the distortion. (Map and Globe Skills 1)

Access Strategy

Peel some oranges in class with students. Try making a careful vertical slice from top to bottom and have class members carefully pull the peel off without tearing it. Flatten and mount a few samples on construction paper as tangible examples of trying to project a sphere onto a flat surface.

Research

Have students bring in examples of world maps and identify which type of projection each uses. Ask students to explain the advantages of each projection and when each is likely to be used. Also have them explain the disadvantages of any particular projection and when it would not be useful.

Goode Projection

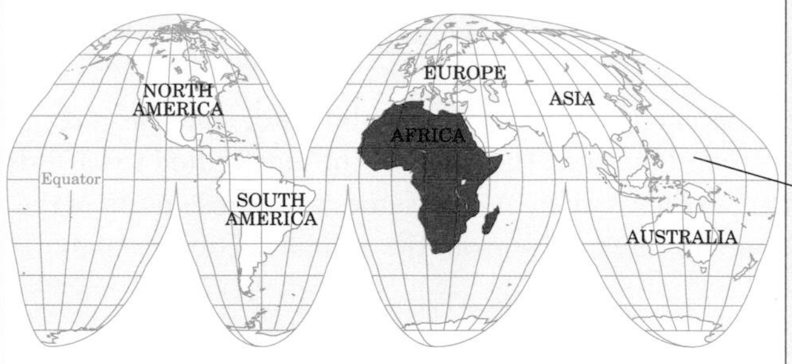
NORTH AMERICA
EUROPE
ASIA
AFRICA
Equator
SOUTH AMERICA
AUSTRALIA

In 1923 American mapmaker Paul Goode created a projection showing the continent sizes and shapes as they appear on a globe. Because this projection divides the earth into segments, or pieces, near the poles, the distances between places cannot be easily measured.

Robinson Projection

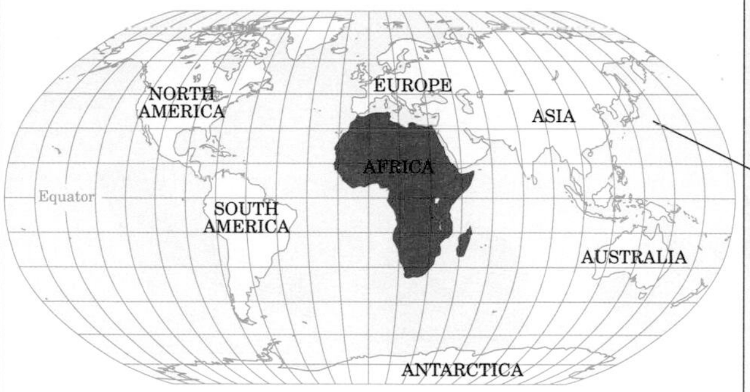
NORTH AMERICA
EUROPE
ASIA
AFRICA
Equator
SOUTH AMERICA
AUSTRALIA
ANTARCTICA

Another American mapmaker, Arthur Robinson, made this projection in 1963. The sizes, shapes, and distances of land and water areas on this projection are closest to the ones on a globe. Most of the world maps in this book use the Robinson projection.

MAP SKILLS

1. **REVIEW** Which projections show Africa closest to the way it looks on a globe?
2. **THINK ABOUT IT** Look at Africa on the Mercator projection and the Goode projection. Why do you think Africa looks alike on the two projections when Greenland and other areas at the top of the projections are so different? Use a globe to help you answer the question.
3. **TRY IT** Find the land areas of Greenland, Antarctica, and Africa on a globe and trace them. Compare each tracing to the same area on a flat world map. They will not be exactly the same because your globe and map are different sizes. Notice differences in the shapes of the land areas. Which shapes show the most change? Why did the changes occur?

CLASS ACTIVITY

Have students look through the maps in their textbook and find the type of projection used with each map. Suggest that students make a chart listing the types of projections in one column. The second column should show the number of times each projection was used. The third column should ask for the student's explanation of why this type of projection seemed best suited to the kind of map produced. Students may need to consult cartography or geography books to help in their explanations.

GEOGRAPHY
Visual Learning

Examine the Goode projection with students. Ask them to imagine the segments fitting together as if they were a pattern for a ball; the segments could be sewn together to meet at one point.

Answers to Map Skills

1. The Mercator, Goode, and Robinson projections show Africa closest to its shape on a globe.
2. The Mercator projection fills in the land and water at the poles, stretching the shape of land and making it appear much larger. Africa, however, is at the equator, where distortion is much less, so the continent changes little in both the Mercator and Goode projections.
3. Greenland and Antarctica should be changed the most and Africa the least. All world maps are drawn according to one projection or another. The changes in shape occur because a projection's distortion is most noticeable on the land areas near the poles.

Project

Have interested class members experiment with making a projection. Using a basketball, a soccer ball, or similar object, they should try to make a cover that fits snugly on it. They can use paper or fabric for their cover. Ask students how their final product is different from standard map projections.

CLASS ACTIVITY

Draw a chart with the following headings on the chalkboard: *Location, Season,* and *Position of the Sun.* Have students take turns coming to the chalkboard, each writing an entry under *Location* and then filling in a season and the appropriate sun position.

GEOGRAPHY

Visual Learning

Find North America and the current season on the diagram. If the current month is not March, June, September, or December, have students decide in what position the globe should be for the current month. Discuss your current temperature pattern and how this is related to the season because of the tilt of North America's hemisphere either toward or away from the sun. Explain that the seasons have greater variety in most parts of the United States than in countries close to the equator. Use the diagram to show how the sun's rays change much less from summer to winter close to the equator than they do farther north or south on the earth, where the angle of the sun changes a great deal. While most of the United States has four seasons, regions along the equator may have only rainy and dry seasons.

Observing the Seasons

Why do the seasons have to change? Why can't you enjoy your favorite weather all year long? The diagram below gives the answer.

Seasons change because the earth tilts or slants as it revolves around the sun. The parts of the earth tilted toward the sun have warm weather. At the same time, those parts of the earth that are tilted away from the sun have cooler weather.

The Northern and Southern hemispheres each tilt toward the sun for about six months and away from the sun for six months. In June when the North Pole tilts toward the sun, the Northern Hemisphere has summer while the Southern Hemisphere has winter.

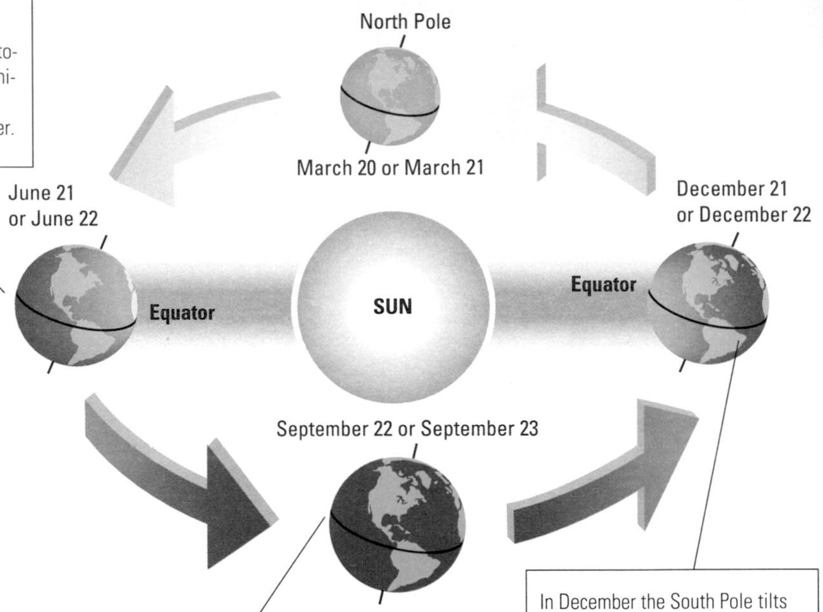
North Pole
March 20 or March 21
June 21
or June 22
December 21
or December 22
Equator
SUN
Equator
September 22 or September 23

This Indonesian mother uses an umbrella to protect herself and her baby from the hot sun. Indonesia lies on the equator where the weather is hot all year round.

On two days each year, both hemispheres are about the same distance from the sun. In the United States those days are the first day of spring (March 20 or 21) and the first day of autumn (September 22 or 23).

In December the South Pole tilts toward the sun bringing summer to the Southern Hemisphere. At the same time, the Northern Hemisphere tilts away from the sun and has winter.

GLOBE SKILLS

1. **REVIEW** When does summer begin in Australia? Why?
2. **THINK ABOUT IT** What season is it right now in the nation of Chile in South America? How do you know?
3. **TRY IT** Place a ball on a table. Hold a smaller ball and move it around the larger ball. Draw two dots on the smaller ball, one for the North Pole and the other for the South Pole. Watch how its position changes in relation to your "sun." Use the balls to explain to a classmate why winter in the Northern Hemisphere begins in December.

Objectives

1. Understand the change of seasons. (Map and Globe Skills 1)
2. Find North America on a diagram and trace its seasonal path through the year. (Map and Globe Skills 2)
3. Explain why seasonal change is opposite in the Northern and Southern hemispheres. (Map and Globe Skills 2)

Answers to Globe Skills

1. Summer begins on December 21 or 22 in Australia because the Southern Hemisphere tilts toward the sun at that time.
2. If it is spring in the Northern Hemisphere (where students are), then it is autumn in the Southern Hemisphere, where Chile is located. Students can tell by looking at the diagram and at a globe.
3. Make sure students keep the smaller ball slanted slightly so they can see it tilting toward and away from the sun.

Identifying the Seasons

Have students make a chart. Assign several arbitrary dates and several specific locations for the class to find on a globe or world map. Their chart should tell which season each date represents for each location. For example, on April 10 it would be spring in Miami, Florida. Make a sample of chart headings on the chalkboard for students to follow: *Date, Location,* and *Season.*

Reading Different Kinds of Maps

Maps do more than show the shape of the land. Study the maps on the following pages and think about what you learn.

A Physical Map with a Profile

A physical map shows the elevation of land, or its height compared to sea level. Sometimes a physical map includes a diagram called a profile. The profile below shows a side view of the mountains, hills, and flat lands you would see in the area marked by the red line on the map.

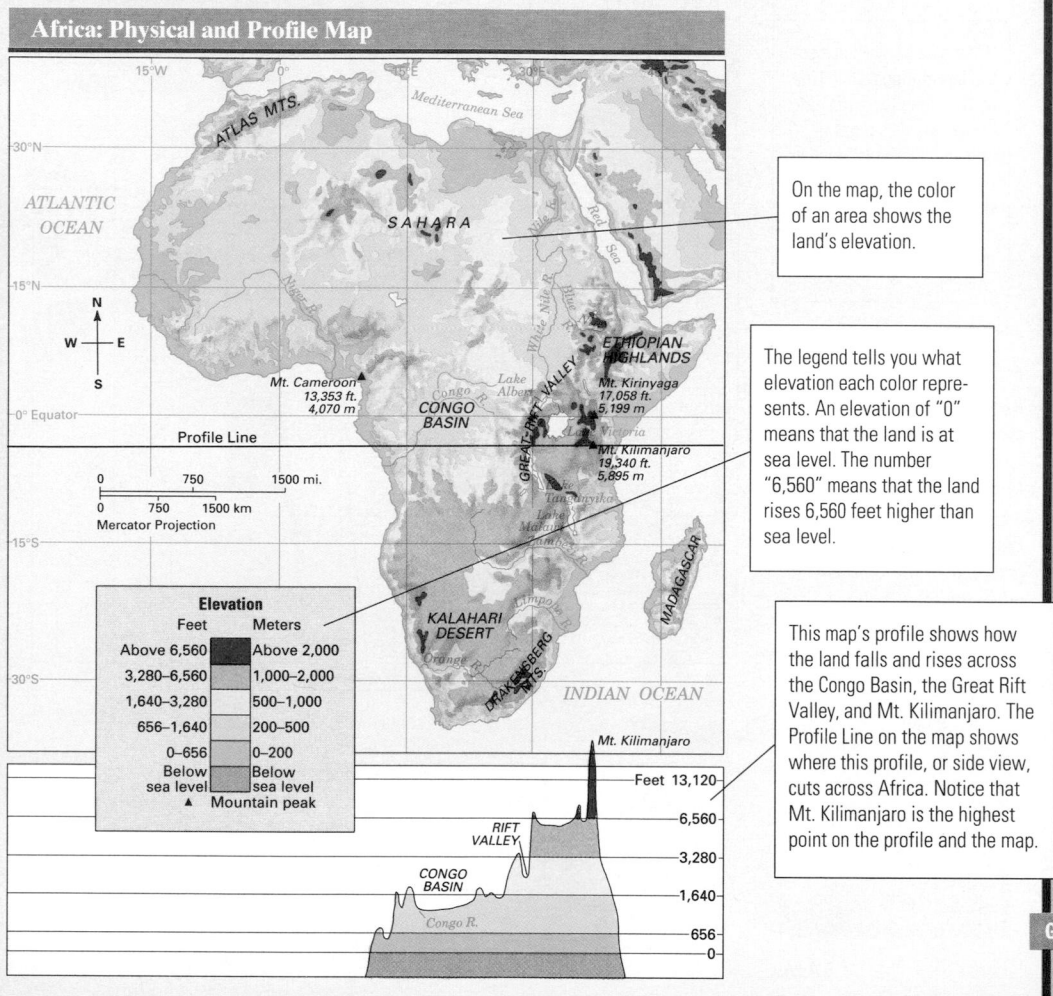

Africa: Physical and Profile Map

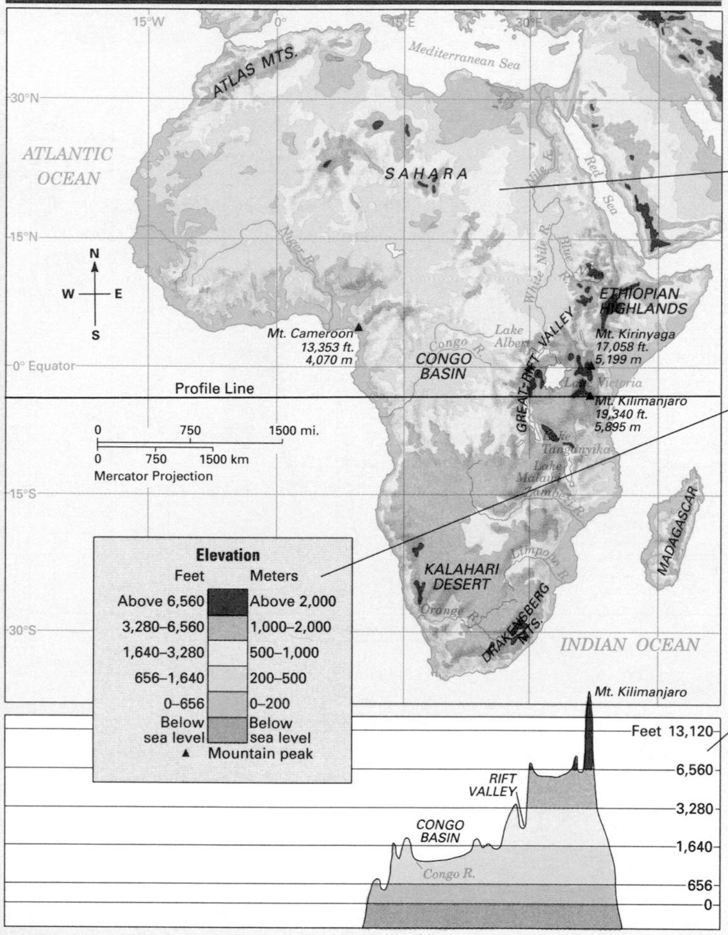

15°W
0°
15°E
30°E
30°N
15°N
0° Equator
15°S
30°S
ATLAS MTS.
Mediterranean Sea
ATLANTIC OCEAN
SAHARA
Niger R.
Nile R.
White Nile R.
Blue Nile R.
Red Sea
ETHIOPIAN HIGHLANDS
Mt. Cameroon 13,353 ft. 4,070 m
Congo R.
CONGO BASIN
Lake Albert
GREAT RIFT VALLEY
Mt. Kirinyaga 17,058 ft. 5,199 m
Lake Victoria
Mt. Kilimanjaro 19,340 ft. 5,895 m
Lake Tanganyika
Lake Malawi
Zambezi R.
Profile Line
N
W
E
S
0
750
1500 mi.
0
750
1500 km
Mercator Projection
KALAHARI DESERT
Limpopo R.
Orange R.
DRAKENSBERG MTS.
MADAGASCAR
INDIAN OCEAN
Elevation
Feet
Meters
Above 6,560
Above 2,000
3,280–6,560
1,000–2,000
1,640–3,280
500–1,000
656–1,640
200–500
0–656
0–200
Below sea level
Below sea level
▲ Mountain peak
Mt. Kilimanjaro
Feet 13,120
6,560
3,280
1,640
656
0
RIFT VALLEY
CONGO BASIN
Congo R.

On the map, the color of an area shows the land's elevation.

The legend tells you what elevation each color represents. An elevation of "0" means that the land is at sea level. The number "6,560" means that the land rises 6,560 feet higher than sea level.

This map's profile shows how the land falls and rises across the Congo Basin, the Great Rift Valley, and Mt. Kilimanjaro. The Profile Line on the map shows where this profile, or side view, cuts across Africa. Notice that Mt. Kilimanjaro is the highest point on the profile and the map.

CLASS ACTIVITY

Review the types of maps students have used. Ask students what other kinds of maps they can think of. Discuss how varied maps are and how many different kinds of information they show. Ask if students have ever seen a landform profile, such as the one on this physical map of Africa.

Geography Theme: Place

Have the class consider what the profile shows in Africa. *(Students may mention Mt. Kilimanjaro, the Rift Valley, or the Congo Basin.)* Ask students if the profile adds to the information shown on the physical map or just shows the map information in a different way. *(Students may answer that the profile gives them a better image of the comparative elevations of different areas.)*

GEOGRAPHY

Map and Globe Skills

Have the class examine the map and find out the elevation of most of the land along the Nile River. Find the area where you live on the physical map on page 680. Find a place in Africa that is in the same elevation range.

Map Activity

Have students use the physical map of North America on page 686 in the Atlas to make a map of their state with a landform profile. They should also check other atlases or an almanac for additional information on the physical features of their state. Remind them to draw a line through the profiled area on the map. Their maps should have labels. The profile should have elevations noted, but students need not color in all the elevations on the map.

Objectives

1. Use a landform profile with a physical map to find details about land. (Map and Globe Skills 2)
2. Use a time zone map to understand time zone changes. (Map and Globe Skills 2)
3. Use a historical map to trace growth of civilizations. (Map and Globe Skills 2)

(continued on p. G10)

CLASS ACTIVITY

Discuss the time in different parts of the country and different parts of the world. Ask students if crossing from one time zone to another has affected them in any way. Encourage then to tell how the speed of modern communication and travel can disrupt lives on the "human time clock." For example, some students may have crossed six to eight time zones on an airplane flight from the United States to Europe. Not only have they "lost" several hours by going east, but they also have spent many hours' flying time. Returning home, they "gained" the time back, but the body must readjust. Other effects of time zones on our lives occur in television programming, long-distance telephone calls, and even ordering and sending things. Point out that some international financial and securities markets operate on a 24-hour basis, which necessitates extraordinary work hours. Discuss if there are ways to "beat the clock."

GEOGRAPHY

Map and Globe Skills

Have students find their time zone on the map. What other cities share the same time zone? Students may need to refer to an atlas.

Map and Globe Handbook

A Time Zone Map

When you want to call a friend in another part of the country, think about the time zone where your friend lives. When it is 12:00 noon in Los Angeles, California, the time is 10:00 A.M. in Honolulu, Hawaii, and 3:00 P.M. in Miami, Florida.

Before official time zones existed, people had difficulty planning travel and doing business far from their homes. Each area set its own time. In order to end the confusion, government leaders agreed in 1884 to divide the earth into 24 time zones.

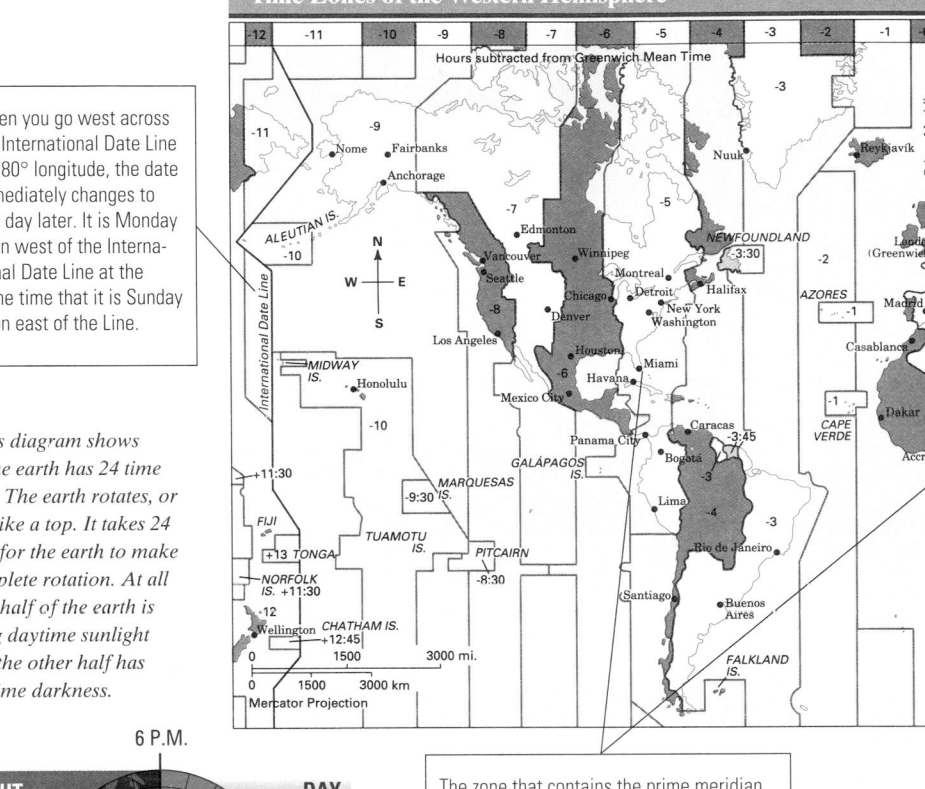

Time Zones of the Western Hemisphere

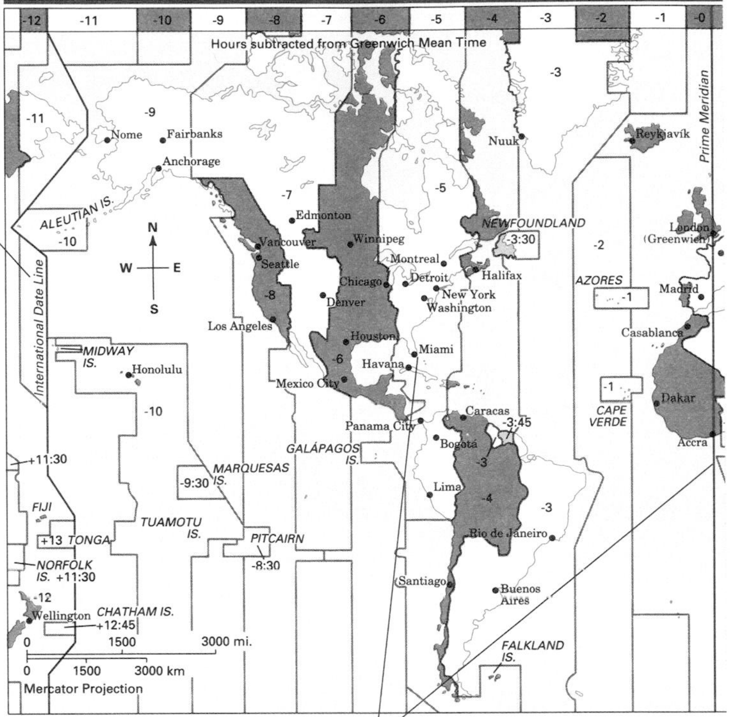

Hours subtracted from Greenwich Mean Time
-12
-11
-10
-9
-8
-7
-6
-5
-4
-3
-2
-1
-0
Prime Meridian
International Date Line
Nome
Fairbanks
Anchorage
ALEUTIAN IS.
Edmonton
Vancouver
Seattle
Winnipeg
Montreal
Detroit
Chicago
Denver
New York
Washington
Halifax
Los Angeles
Houston
Miami
Havana
Mexico City
Nuuk
Reykjavík
NEWFOUNDLAND
-3:30
London (Greenwich)
AZORES
Madrid
Casablanca
Dakar
CAPE VERDE
Accra
MIDWAY IS.
Honolulu
Panama City
Caracas
-3:45
Bogotá
GALÁPAGOS IS.
MARQUESAS IS.
-9:30
Lima
FIJI
+13 TONGA
TUAMOTU IS.
PITCAIRN
-8:30
NORFOLK IS. +11:30
+11:30
Rio de Janeiro
Santiago
Buenos Aires
Wellington
CHATHAM IS.
+12:45
FALKLAND IS.
0 1500 3000 mi.
0 1500 3000 km
Mercator Projection
N
S
E
W

When you go west across the International Date Line at 180° longitude, the date immediately changes to one day later. It is Monday noon west of the International Date Line at the same time that it is Sunday noon east of the Line.

The zone that contains the prime meridian is the starting point of the time zone map. West of the prime meridian, the time gets earlier. Miami is in the "-5" time zone that is five hours earlier than the prime meridian time zone.

This diagram shows why the earth has 24 time zones. The earth rotates, or spins like a top. It takes 24 hours for the earth to make a complete rotation. At all times, half of the earth is getting daytime sunlight while the other half has nighttime darkness.

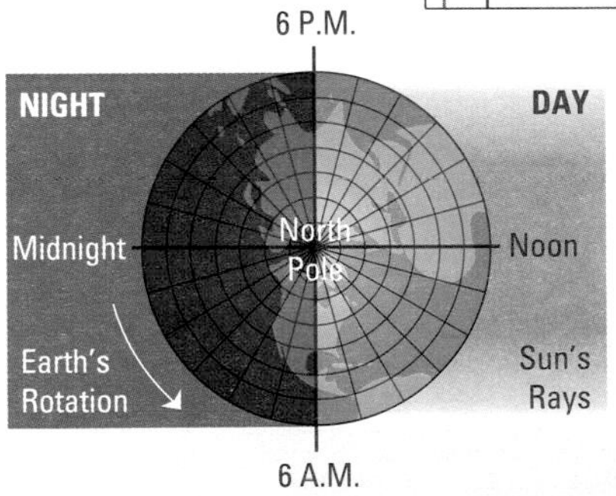

6 P.M.
NIGHT
DAY
Midnight
North Pole
Noon
Earth's Rotation
Sun's Rays
6 A.M.

G10

Objectives

(continued)

4. Follow events on a route map. (Map and Globe Skills 2)
5. Identify land regions by reading a physical map. (Map and Globe Skills 4)
6. Understand a population density map. (Map and Globe Skills 4)
7. Follow the spread of a language on a cultural map. (Map and Globe Skills 3)

Research

Starting with your current hour, have students make a chart telling what time it is in several other locations throughout the world. Students will need to consult a world time zones map in an encyclopedia or other reference book. If you prefer to stay within the Western Hemisphere, students can rely on the map on this page. If students wish to include places not labeled on this map, direct them to an Atlas map in the back of the book.

Background

Explain the meaning of A.M. (*ante meridiem,* or "before noon") and P.M. (*post meridiem,* or "after noon"). The confusion caused in determining whether 12:00 noon is A.M. or P.M. led to the development of the 24-hour clock, which uses four digits. By this reckoning 1200 is 12:00 noon. Midnight is 2400 or 0000. The military services use the 24-hour clock. Modern science has enabled people to tell time in increasingly precise terms, to the millionth of a second.

CLASS ACTIVITY

Ask students if a map could show how the United States has changed over two hundred years. If so, what kinds of changes could be shown? *(Focus attention on territorial growth.)*

Talk about how historical maps, such as this one of the ancient Roman Republic, often show expansion of a nation over time.

Geographic Theme: Movement

Have students examine the directions in which Roman power spread. Ask them to imagine the kinds of change that may have come to lands conquered by Rome. Indicate the importance of the Mediterranean Sea to Roman expansion. Its name means "middle of the earth." Show how other early civilizations also used the Mediterranean for trade and settlement.

A Historical Map

Historical maps tell about the history of a group of people or a part of the world. These maps give information about countries that existed in the past. Some of these maps show how the boundaries of an area have changed over time. The historical map below gives information about the land controlled by Rome from 338 B.C. to 133 B.C. The map shows three stages in the expansion of the lands controlled by Rome.

Roman armies conquered most of this peninsula by 270 B.C. This land, gained during the second stage of Roman expansion, appears in orange on the map.

Roman Expansion, 338 B.C.–133 B.C.

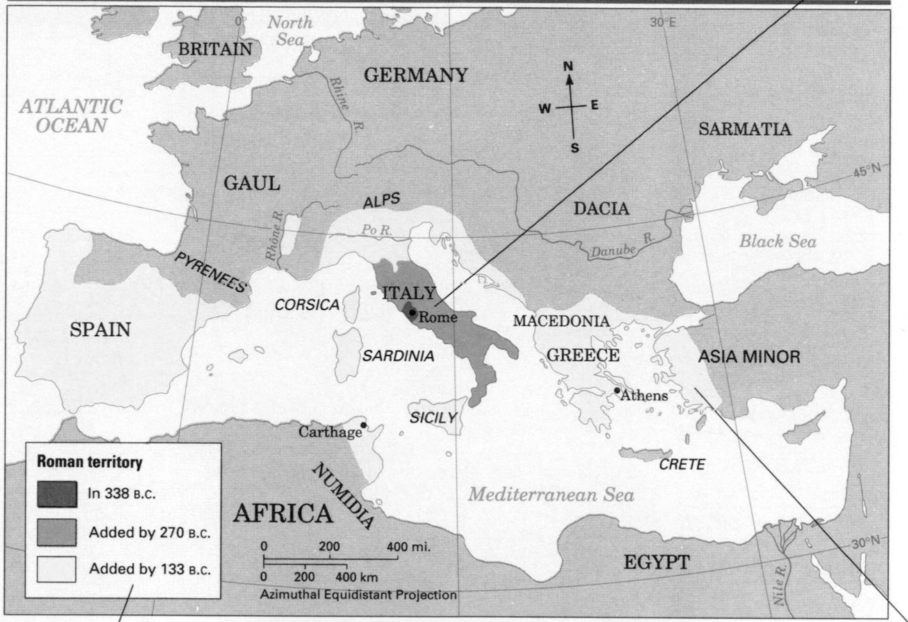

North Sea
BRITAIN
GERMANY
ATLANTIC OCEAN
Rhine R.
N
W
E
S
30°E
SARMATIA
45°N
GAUL
ALPS
Po R.
DACIA
Rhone R.
Danube R.
Black Sea
PYRENEES
CORSICA
ITALY
Rome
MACEDONIA
SPAIN
SARDINIA
GREECE
ASIA MINOR
Athens
SICILY
Carthage
CRETE
Roman territory
In 338 B.C.
Added by 270 B.C.
Added by 133 B.C.
NUMIDIA
AFRICA
Mediterranean Sea
0 200 400 mi.
0 200 400 km
Azimuthal Equidistant Projection
30°N
EGYPT
Nile R.

The legend explains the meaning of each color used on the map. Areas of the same color represent the land gained during one time period. In 338 B.C., the land controlled by Rome included only the city and the area around it.

The land under Roman control more than doubled during the third stage of expansion, between 270 B.C. and 133 B.C. Land added during this stage has the color yellow.

◄ *Roman engineers built aqueducts to carry water between towns. This one near Nîmes, France, was built in the first century A.D.*

Collaborative Learning

Have students work in small groups and choose a present-day country that was once completely or partly ruled by the Roman Empire. Each group must select a country different from that chosen by the others. Each group should then make two maps of their country: one reflecting Roman control and the other a modern political map. The earlier map needs to show general area, cities if possible, and perhaps rivers and other natural features that can be identified. The modern-day map should show current borders, cities, and other appropriate features. Students will need to use atlases and other reference books to find the information. When the maps are completed, have a spokesperson for each group explain how much influence ancient Rome had on their country. The spokesperson should use the maps to discuss such topics as the extent of Rome's control and the names the Romans gave to present-day cities.

Project

Have students make a historical map of an imaginary land. They can make up the name of their country or kingdom, choose a time period, and show different periods of expansion. Be sure to have them include a compass rose and legend that explains the colors used.

CLASS ACTIVITY

Ask students to plan a trip and mark their travel route on a map. Then ask them to think of various travelers or explorers, such as Marco Polo, Columbus, or Magellan, and how such voyages could be shown on a map *(with arrows across the land and water)*. Discuss route maps and how they show where people travel. Inform students that route maps can also show movement because of trade, military maneuvers, and migration. The latter might include the colonization by Phoenicians and Greeks throughout the Mediterranean world, the expansion of the Arab peoples, the movement of African peoples throughout that continent, the diaspora of the Jews, and the emigration of Europeans throughout the earth following their period of exploration.

HISTORY

Map and Globe Skills

Have students trace Alexander's route on the map. Ask a few volunteers to take turns describing the path of the empire, following the arrows and mentioning directions traveled and places reached. Consider how this map differs from the historical map of Rome on page G11 and how the two maps are similar.

A Route Map

A route map shows the movement of people or goods across an area. Some route maps show the paths explorers used. Other route maps show the roads to take on a family trip. This route map shows the path Alexander's army followed.

Alexander the Great set out from Macedonia in southeastern Europe to conquer the mighty Persian Empire. Follow the heavy line on this route map to see where Alexander and his troops traveled.

Alexander's route starts at Pella in Macedonia. Alexander and his troops left Pella in 334 B.C.

The map area colored yellow shows Alexander's empire at its height—around 323 B.C.

The Conquests of Alexander the Great

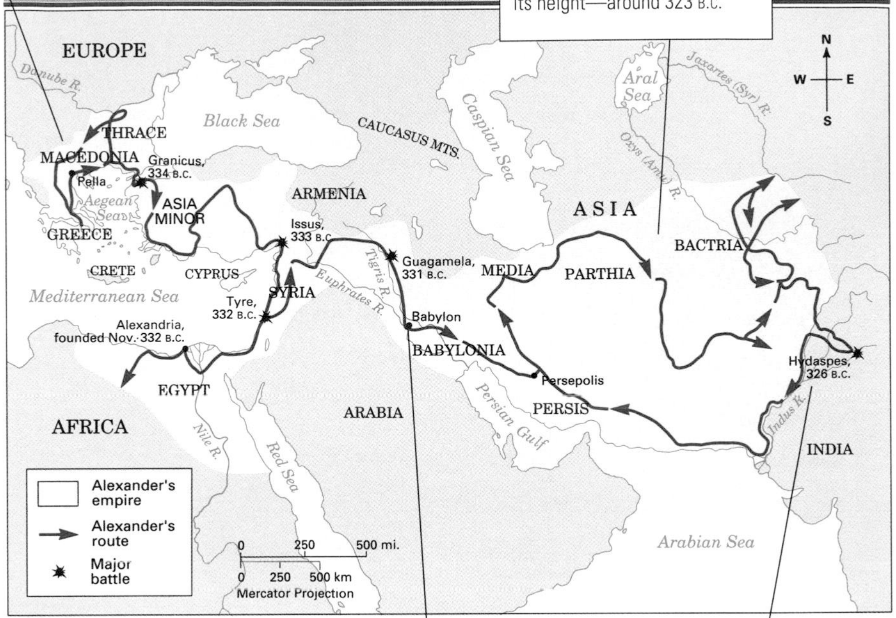

EUROPE
Danube R.
THRACE
Black Sea
CAUCASUS MTS.
Caspian Sea
Aral Sea
Jaxartes (Syr) R.
Oxus (Amu) R.
MACEDONIA
Pella
Granicus, 334 B.C.
Aegean Sea
ASIA MINOR
ARMENIA
ASIA
GREECE
Issus, 333 B.C.
Guagamela, 331 B.C.
MEDIA
PARTHIA
BACTRIA
CRETE
CYPRUS
SYRIA
Tigris R.
Euphrates R.
Mediterranean Sea
Tyre, 332 B.C.
Babylon
Alexandria, founded Nov. 332 B.C.
BABYLONIA
Persepolis
Hydaspes, 326 B.C.
EGYPT
PERSIS
Persian Gulf
AFRICA
ARABIA
Nile R.
Red Sea
Indus R.
INDIA
Arabian Sea
Alexander's empire
Alexander's route
Major battle
0 250 500 mi.
0 250 500 km
Mercator Projection
N
W
E
S

Alexander's route led back to Babylon, the capital of his empire. Alexander died there in 323 B.C. after a sudden illness. He did not leave an heir to his empire. These lands were divided up among Alexander's generals, who established kingdoms of their own.

Alexander reached northwest India in 326 B.C. and defeated the army of the Indian prince Porus. Alexander planned to continue across India, but his troops rebelled. Instead, he sailed down the Indus River, then led his troops west. Notice how the arrows point south, then west.

Alexander the Great lived only 33 years (356–323 B.C.) but changed the world of his time.

Background

Alexander was only 20 years old when his father Philip was assassinated and he became king of Macedonia. Alexander set out to conquer the Persian Empire. With superior battle plans and well-trained troops, he defeated much larger armies to become one of the world's masters of military strategy and a legendary hero. Refer to Chapter 10.

Language Connection

Have interested students pick a favorite story in which travel is a prominent theme. Tell them to see if they can make a route map that follows the travel route in the book. Stories of settlers traveling to the American West are possibilities, as are stories of immigrants traveling to the United States. Students may choose to describe travel to imaginary lands, such as those described by Jonathan Swift in *Gulliver's Travels* or by Francis Parkman in *The Oregon Trail*. They should also check travel sources in their school or public libraries. Have students title their maps and give the name of the book. They should include a brief paragraph summarizing what the map shows.

Comparing Maps

These two maps show different facts about the country of Argentina. The land regions map shows the main physical areas in Argentina. The population density map shows the number of people in different areas of Argentina. You can compare the maps to figure out why people in Argentina live where they do.

Argentina: Land Regions

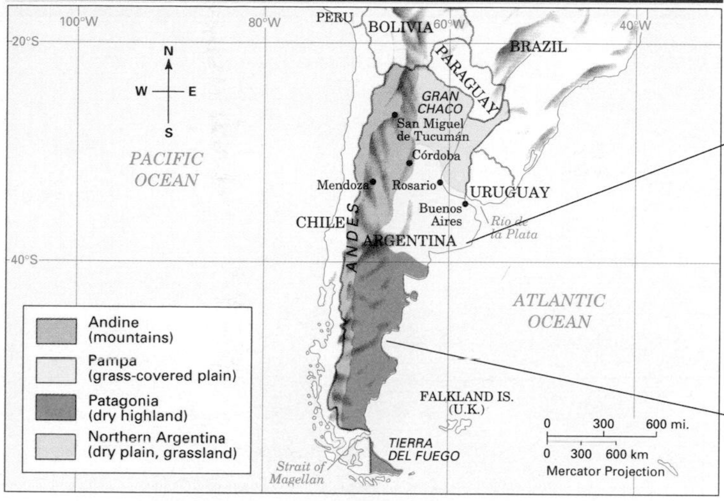

100°W
80°W
60°W
40°W
20°S
40°S
N
W
E
S
PERU
BOLIVIA
BRAZIL
PARAGUAY
GRAN CHACO
San Miguel de Tucumán
Córdoba
PACIFIC OCEAN
Mendoza
Rosario
URUGUAY
Buenos Aires
Río de la Plata
CHILE
ANDES
ARGENTINA
ATLANTIC OCEAN
Andine (mountains)
Pampa (grass-covered plain)
Patagonia (dry highland)
Northern Argentina (dry plain, grassland)
FALKLAND IS. (U.K.)
TIERRA DEL FUEGO
Strait of Magellan
0 300 600 mi.
0 300 600 km
Mercator Projection

The pampas, a large plain, extends from the Atlantic coast inland to central Argentina. The land here is fertile and good for farming. Buenos Aires, Argentina's capital, is in this region on the coast.

Patagonia, Argentina's dry and windy plateau, extends from the coast to the Andes Mountains, south of the pampas. Patagonia has poor soil for farming. Sheep ranchers, who need a lot of land for grazing, can make a living here.

Argentina: Population Density

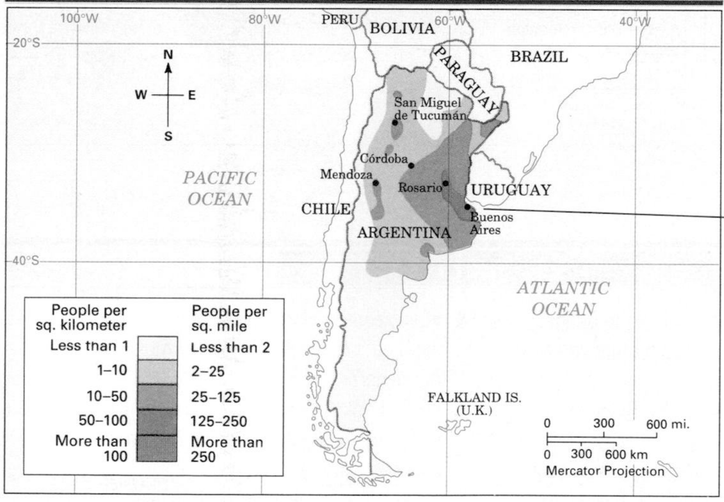

100°W
80°W
60°W
40°W
20°S
40°S
N
W
E
S
PERU
BOLIVIA
BRAZIL
PARAGUAY
San Miguel de Tucumán
Córdoba
Mendoza
PACIFIC OCEAN
Rosario
URUGUAY
CHILE
Buenos Aires
ARGENTINA
ATLANTIC OCEAN
People per sq. kilometer
People per sq. mile
Less than 1
Less than 2
1–10
2–25
10–50
25–125
50–100
125–250
More than 100
More than 250
FALKLAND IS. (U.K.)
0 300 600 mi.
0 300 600 km
Mercator Projection

The population map shows that Buenos Aires has more than 250 people per square mile. In most parts of the world, the greatest number of people live in fertile, low-lying lands, where enough rain falls to grow the crops needed to feed them.

CLASS ACTIVITY

Ask students to think of possible ways two maps could be used together. Suppose the class were using a map of bike trails in their region and another map of picnic areas or camping grounds. Suppose they had a map showing crops grown in their state and a climate map. Ask students whether such maps can be used together to help us draw conclusions and gain more information.

Geography Theme: Region

Have the class name some land regions in Argentina. Ask them if climate and elevation have something to do with the differences in the regions. *(Students may discuss the differences between the Andes mountains, the grass-covered plain of Pampas, the dry highlands of Patagonia, and the dry plain and grassland of northern Argentina.)*

GEOGRAPHY
Map and Globe Skills

Have students look for other areas of low population density in Argentina besides Patagonia. Ask what they think might be reasons for the low density, using the other map to help form their opinion.

Background

Argentina's population is 86 percent urban; 3 million of its 33 million people live in Buenos Aires, the capital. Argentines are ethnically diverse. About 15 percent are of Indian or mixed descent, while 85 percent are white (mainly Spanish or Italian). Argentina belonged to the Spanish Empire until it achieved independence in 1816. Spanish is the official language. Argentina had a long series of military governments, but democracy was restored in the late 1980s. Refer to Chapter 23.

Collaborative Learning

Have students work in small groups and choose a country on which to base a map booklet. Using the maps in this book as well as those in encyclopedias and other resources, students should make a physical map, a population density map, a land use map, and a product map of their chosen country. The booklet should also contain a brief written report of students' conclusions focusing on how land and resources affect population density.

Visual Learning

Have students compare the United States with other countries on the population cartogram on page 689 in the Atlas. Ask why students think there is high or low density in certain places. They should use the physical map, resource map, or other maps in the Atlas for their answers.

CLASS ACTIVITY

Have students look at the map of Bantu migration and decide in what ways it is different from other route maps they have seen. Explain that more than 2,500 years ago the Bantu began a mass migration from their home in central Africa to other parts of the continent. As the map shows, the Bantu still live in Africa, with the Bantu language spread across the areas to which they migrated. Point out that the arrows on this map tell where the Bantu migrated. Students will learn more about Bantu migration in Chapter 13.

GEOGRAPHY

Map and Globe Skills

Have students describe where the Bantu migrated within Africa, based on the directions of the arrows. Where could students expect to find Bantu groups today? Use the Atlas map on page 685 to name the countries. Discuss the ways in which the spread of the Bantu culture may have affected other groups in Africa. Note that culture includes all parts of a people's way of life—their tools, clothing, music, foods, crafts, language, religion, customs, and government. Ask students if they can think of other cultural migrations in history.

A Cultural Map

A people's culture includes everything that is part of their way of life. Cultural maps can show how all or part of one group's culture spread and influenced other people. This map shows what happened as a result of the Bantu migration in Africa.

African Migration and Language

Arrows show the directions of the Bantu migrations from the interior of Africa, starting more than 2,500 years ago. As they traveled, they split off into many smaller groups with similar languages. To which part of Africa did the Bantu bring their language and culture?

The map uses color to show the area where the Bantu language spread and the areas where other major languages not related to Bantu are spoken in Africa.

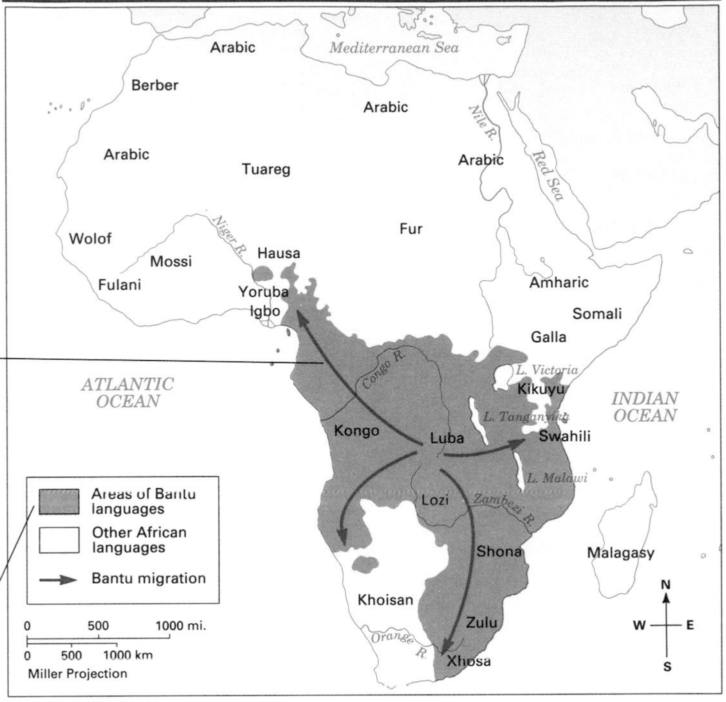
Arabic
Mediterranean Sea
Berber
Arabic
Nile R.
Arabic
Tuareg
Arabic
Red Sea
Wolof
Niger R.
Hausa
Fur
Mossi
Fulani
Yoruba
Igbo
Amharic
Somali
Galla
Congo R.
L. Victoria
Kikuyu
ATLANTIC OCEAN
INDIAN OCEAN
L. Tanganyika
Kongo
Luba
Swahili
L. Malawi
Lozi
Zambezi R.
Areas of Bantu languages
Other African languages
Bantu migration
Shona
Malagasy
Khoisan
Zulu
Orange R.
Xhosa
0 500 1000 mi.
0 500 1000 km
Miller Projection
N
W
E
S

MAP SKILLS

1. **REVIEW** Which has a higher elevation, the Congo Basin or the Rift Valley? What map feature can help you answer this question quickly?
2. **REVIEW** Look at the map on page 234. By what year did the Ottomans gain land in Egypt?
3. **REVIEW** Compare the map of climate regions on page 529 with the Atlas map on page 689 showing land use. What kind of climate do most of the large farming regions of South America have?
4. **THINK ABOUT IT** How would the route map of Alexander the Great's conquests help you write a report about Alexander?
5. **TRY IT** Think of three to five places in the United States you would like to visit. Then imagine your family going on a two-week vacation to see these places. You might travel by car, plane, train, or even boat. Trace a map of the United States. On it, draw a route map of your imaginary vacation.

Background

Early Bantu groups had advanced farming and ironworking methods. The migration, one of the largest in history, took place gradually over centuries. Today, about 300 different Bantu groups make up a large part of the population of nearly all African countries below 5° north latitude.

Answers to Map Skills

1. The Rift Valley has a higher elevation. The landform profile on page G9 shows this.
2. The Ottoman Turks gained land in Egypt by 1520.
3. Most large farming regions of South America have a humid subtropical climate.
4. Sample answer: Alexander the Great's route map shows where he led his troops, when and where major battles took place, and which areas he conquered. The map would be a good visual aid for an oral report.
5. Maps will vary. Students should make sure that their trip can be accomplished within a two-week period.

Using Geographic References

What countries border El Salvador? What does a volcano look like? Where is Haiti? The different parts of the Time/Space Databank on pages 659–708 of this book will help you answer many geography questions.

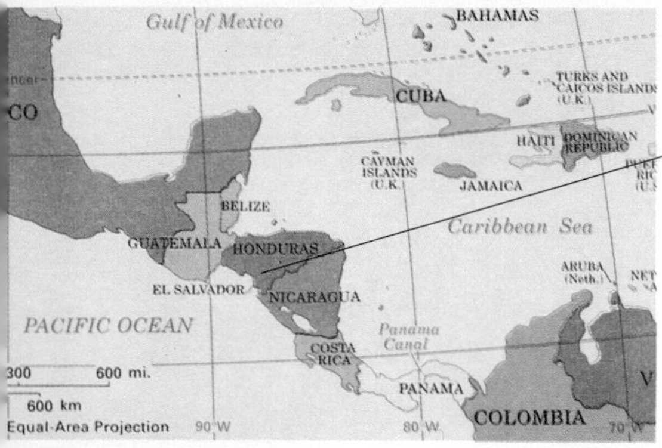
Gulf of Mexico
BAHAMAS
CUBA
TURKS AND CAICOS ISLANDS (U.K.)
HAITI
DOMINICAN REPUBLIC
CAYMAN ISLANDS (U.K.)
JAMAICA
BELIZE
GUATEMALA
HONDURAS
Caribbean Sea
ARUBA (Neth.)
EL SALVADOR
NICARAGUA
PACIFIC OCEAN
Panama Canal
COSTA RICA
PANAMA
COLOMBIA
600 mi.
600 km
Equal-Area Projection
90°W
80°W
70°W

The Atlas on pages 678–689 has maps of the world and continents. This segment from the Atlas shows the northwest corner of South America, Central America, and major islands in the Caribbean Sea. You can see that El Salvador is bordered by two countries, Guatemala and Honduras.

The Glossary of Geographic Terms on pages 690–691 shows some of the earth's natural features. This entry for volcano tells you what a volcano is and shows a picture of what one looks like.

This entry from page 692 of the Gazetteer tells you where the city of Alexandria, Egypt, is. It tells the city's latitude and longitude and on what page you can find Alexandria on a map.

A			
Accra (capital of Ghana)	6°N	0°	**282**
Aegean Sea (part of the Mediterranean Sea)	39°N	25°E	**155**
Alexandria (city in Egypt founded by Alexander the Great)	31°N	30°E	**178**
altiplano (high plateau, as in the Andes region)	19°S	68°W	**687**
Amazon R. (in South America; largest in the world)	1°S	52°W	**557**

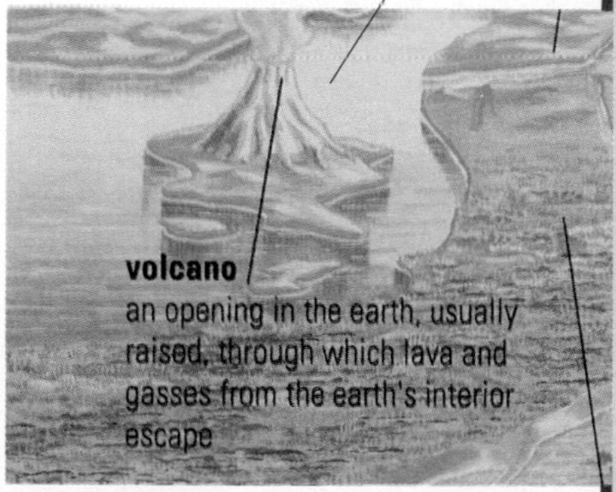
volcano
an opening in the earth, usually raised, through which lava and gasses from the earth's interior escape

MAP SKILLS

1. **REVIEW** Which part of the Time/Space Databank will have a map of the world's vegetation regions? Look at the vegetation map there and find out which continent is mostly desert.
2. **REVIEW** What is the exact location of Cairo, Egypt? On what page of your book will you find a map of Cairo?
3. **THINK ABOUT IT** What is the difference between a canyon and a cliff? Which part of the Time/Space Databank helped you answer this question?
4. **TRY IT** Suppose you are the new editor of the Time/Space Databank. You decide to add more information to the Glossary of Geographic Terms. Pick two geographic features, write their definitions, and draw pictures of them.

CLASS ACTIVITY

Ask geographic fact questions such as the following: What is the capital of Canada? What is the capital of Japan? Where is Austria located in Europe? Where is Russia? Where does the Nile River flow? What is a plateau? Inform students that these answers can be found in this book and in encyclopedias, atlases, and dictionaries. Ask students to leaf through the Time/Space Databank on pages 659–695.

GEOGRAPHY
Study Skills

Ask questions with answers that can be found specifically in the Atlas, Glossary of Geographic Terms, or Gazetteer, and have students decide the ways in which each source is helpful. (Sometimes more than one source may provide the same answers.) Then have students compose several questions and exchange their list with a partner to answer each other's questions.

Answers to Map Skills

1. The Atlas would have this map. Australia is mostly desert.
2. Cairo is 30° N, 31° E. The map is on page 240.
3. A canyon is a valley with steep sides. A cliff is a steep edge of a mountain, hill, or plain. Both terms are defined in the Glossary of Geographic Terms.
4. Answers will vary. Direct students to detailed current atlases and other reference tools for their additions.

Objectives

1. Use Atlas maps to find geography information. (Map and Globe Skills 1)
2. Use the Gazetteer to identify places and to find them on maps using their latitude and longitude coordinates. (Visual Learning 2)
3. Use the Glossary of Geographic Terms to find definitions and illustrations of specific geographic features. (Visual Learning 1)

UNIT
PREVIEW

Have students read the unit title, Looking at the World. Explain that this unit will examine how people in many places interact in various ways with the world around them. Ask a volunteer to read the text paragraph while the other students study the photograph. Then ask them to define *culture* and *geography,* the main topics of this unit. Then ask how the photograph shows these concepts. For example, how does geography affect the climber? *(He enjoys climbing steep mountains.)* How is he a part of his culture? *(He wears special clothing; he will later go home and share his adventure with other people.)*

Looking Forward

These first chapters introduce two major concepts that will guide the textbook's approach to various regions:
Chapter 1 *Exploring Culture*
Chapter 2 *Exploring Geography*

The terms and concepts that students learn in Unit 1 are basic to subsequent units.

Unit 1

Looking at the World

A mountain climber raises his arms in triumph as he reaches the peak of Mont Blanc, France. This moment of celebration is a solitary one, for the man is alone in this barren and cold place. Soon, however, he will come down from the mountain. He will return to the lowlands where people make their homes on farms and in villages. There he will be able to tell others of his experience and to share his achievement.

Mountain climber atop Mont Blanc, France

BIBLIOGRAPHY

Books for Students
Lyttle, Richard B. *Land Beyond the River: Europe in the Age of Migration.* New York: Atheneum, 1986. Discussion of the migrations of European peoples. Nonfiction.

Moss, Carol. *Science in Ancient Mesopotamia.* New York: Watts, 1988. An account of the scientific achievements of this early civilization. Nonfiction.

Olliver, Jane, ed. *The Warwick Atlas of World History.* New York: Warwick, 1988. The history of the world through maps, photographs, and drawings. Nonfiction.

Books to Read Aloud
Hamilton, Virginia. *In the Beginning: Creation Stories from Around the World.* San Diego: Harcourt Brace Jovanovich, 1988. A rich collection of stories from many cultures. Fiction.

Johanson, Donald C., and Kevin O'Farrell. *Journey from the Dawn: Life with the World's First Family.* New York: Villand Books, 1990. The story of the oldest human ancestor, known as "Lucy," who was discovered in Ethiopia. Nonfiction.

Books for Teachers
The History of Science and Technology: A Narrative Chronology. New York: Facts on File, 1988. A two-volume set that covers prehistoric times to the present. Nonfiction.

Understanding the Photograph

The lone figure in this photo stands atop Mont Blanc ("white mountain"), the highest peak in Europe (15,771 ft.; 4,807 m). Part of the Alps, the mountain is on the French-Italian border. A French doctor and his companion were the first to reach the summit; they accomplished this feat in 1786. Today, tramways and resorts dot the area. A tunnel seven-and-a-half miles long, joining Chamonix, France, and Courmayeur, Italy, passes through Mont Blanc.

Understanding Chronology

In this unit, rather than exploring specific chronological events, students will learn about concepts and factors that determine and affect history. (Although chronological events are often used as examples, the concepts explored are essentially nonchronological.) Students will apply these concepts to particular times and places in subsequent chapters.

Miller-Lachmann, Lyn. *Our Family, Our Friends, Our World: An Annotated Guide to Significant Multicultural Books for Children and Teenagers.* New Providence, N.J.: Bowker, 1992. Annotations to books that have significant multicultural themes. Nonfiction.

Other Resources

Recordings

Walk A Mile—Vitamin L. Loveable Creature Music, distributed by Alcazar. Recording of a multiethnic group of adults and teens mixing blues, reggae, and pop.

Software

Our World: Yesterday & Today. Scott Foresman, 1988. A database/material generator program with activities covering world geography and culture.

CHAPTER ORGANIZER

Chapter 1 Exploring Culture

CHAPTER PLANNING CHART

Pupil's Edition	Teacher's Edition	Ancillaries
Lesson 1: A World of People (2–3 days) Objective 1: Understand common human needs and life experiences. (Culture 1, 4) Objective 2: Understand what culture is and why all people live within cultural patterns. (Culture 2)	• Graphic Overview (4) • Access Strategy (5) • Access Activity (5) • Visual Learning (6) Writing a Letter (6) Art Connection (7) Music Connection (7) Study Skills (7) Social Participation (8) Writing a News Account (8) Political Context (8)	Study Guide (1)
Literature: A World of Poems	• Access Strategy (11)	Discovery Journal (1)
Lesson 2: What Shapes and Changes Cultures? (2–3 days) Objective 1: Understand how physical environment affects culture. (Geography 3) Objective 2: Understand how social interaction affects culture. (Culture 1) Objective 3: Understand how ideas and technology affect culture. (Culture 5)	• Graphic Overview (12) • Access Strategy (13) • Access Activity (13) Study Skills (14) Language Arts Connection (14) Cultural Context (15) Critical Thinking (15) Study Skills (16) Science Connection (16)	Study Guide (2) Discovery Journal (2)
Understanding Fact, Judgment, and Opinion Objective: Demonstrate how recognizing facts, reasoned judgments, and opinions can help determine the reliability of information. (Critical Thinking 2)	Science Connection (18) • Visual Learning (19)	Study Guide (3) • Study Prints (1)
Lesson 3: How Do We Learn about Culture? (1–2 days) Objective 1: Understand how people learn about their own culture and other cultures. (History 1, 2; Culture 1) Objective 2: Explain how anthropologists study cultures. (History 2; Culture 1) Objective 3: Appreciate the value of all cultures. (Culture 4)	• Graphic Overview (20) • Access Strategy (21) • Access Activity (21) • Visual Learning (22) Investigating (22) Collaborative Learning (22)	Study Guide (4) Discovery Journal (3)
Chapter Review	Answers (24–25)	Tests (1–4)

* Objectives are correlated to the strands and goals in the program Scope and Sequence on pages T41–T49.

• LEP appropriate resources. (For additional strategies, see pages T32–T33.)

CHAPTER RATIONALE

Chapter 1 sets the stage for the study of world cultures throughout the book. The chapter introduces the concept of culture—what it is, how it develops and changes, and how it is learned. Students see that they themselves are part of a culture that shapes the way they live. By becoming aware of their own and others' surroundings, students develop a framework for their journey through cultures past and present.

In **Lesson 1** students explore in depth the meaning of culture. Concrete examples of customs, institutions, and beliefs make this complex and abstract concept meaningful to students. Examples show what all cultures have in common as well as how groups of people express their identity. Students are encouraged to think about how culture is important to them and, thus, how it is important in the lives of people everywhere. *A World of Poems,* which contains poems written by children from different nations around the world, helps students gain insight into common experiences and feelings.

Lesson 2 describes the forces that shape and change cultures. The goal of the lesson is to explain ways in which cultures change and evolve. Students see how physical environment influences cultures as people attempt to meet their basic needs for food, clothing, and shelter. Next, students examine how the interaction among cultural groups can shape cultures. The lesson places special emphasis on the process of cultural diffusion, through which elements of one culture spread to another. Next, students explore how advances in technology affect cultures. Familiar examples—the car and the television—show how students' own lives have been affected by technological innovation. Finally, a feature on Understanding Fact, Judgment, and Opinion gives students guidance in evaluating information.

Lesson 3 establishes a global purpose for the study of world cultures. This lesson explains that understanding how cultures both differ from and resemble our own can better enable people to share the planet harmoniously. Students read that from birth they have learned about their own culture through their family, school, and community, as well as through the news media and the arts. They learn about other cultures through interaction with people from different ethnic groups and by studying the social sciences. We highlight one of these social sciences, anthropology, in A Moment in Time. Students are encouraged to learn about other cultures, in part to dispel prejudice and racism.

We encourage teachers to develop students' understanding of human rights issues as they study this and succeeding chapters in the book. For resources on these issues, contact Amnesty International USA Educators' Network, 322 Eighth Avenue, New York, NY 10001, (212) 807-8400, or the Southern Poverty Law Center, 400 Washington Avenue, Montgomery, AL 36104, which publishes *Teaching Tolerance,* a biannual magazine for teachers.

ACTIVITIES & PROJECTS

Bulletin Board

Direct students to find newspaper and magazine articles about cultures other than the United States. Divide a class bulletin board into sections corresponding to the unit titles of this book (for example, The Mediterranean and Southwest Asia; Africa). Have students tack their articles to the bulletin board in the appropriate sections. You may wish to repeat this assignment monthly or make it an ongoing activity. Students can use these articles for information as they work through the units of the book. (Use after any lesson.)

Challenge: Collaborative Learning

Have small groups of students leaf through the book. Direct each group to choose a foreign culture that particularly interests all members of the group. Ask each group member to research a particular aspect of the chosen culture. Refer students to the diagram on page 6 for help in choosing the aspect they want to investigate. When students have gathered their information, each group can integrate the information into a report. Have one member of each group read the group's report to the class. (Use after any lesson.)

LEP: Making a Mural

Refer students to the photograph of the mural on page 20. Ask students to think about the people, places, and events that they would highlight in a mural depicting U.S. culture today. Tell students to draw or paint one of these people, places, or events on a piece of colored paper or construction paper. Assemble students' creations into a class mural. (Use after Lesson 3.)

Basic: Writing a Report

Ask students to imagine that they are anthropologists on assignment to study their community. Have them choose a place in the community (for example, a grocery store, bus stop, or busy street corner) where they can observe a sufficient number of people to be able to generalize about human behavior. Instruct students to take notes on what people are wearing, how they walk, what they are doing, and how they relate to one another. Then have students write a one-page report summarizing their observations. Encourage them to use these observations to draw conclusions about U.S. culture. (Use after Lesson 3.)

CHAPTER PREVIEW

Have students read the chapter title and the text that follows. Now have them look over the visuals on pages 2 and 3, and explain that the people pictured represent some of the many different cultures in the world. Have students read the captions. Then ask them what the pictures tell them about the meaning of culture. *(Education is part of culture. Culture has something to do with art. The weavings and the paintings shown here represent very different cultures. Culture involves traditions, as shown by these Korean girls, who are taking part in a celebration. Culture also involves writing and literature, such as the work of Wole Soyinka.)*

Looking Forward

Explain that education, art, traditions, and writing are only parts of culture. Tell students that in the next three lessons—A World of People, What Shapes and Changes Cultures?, and How Do We Learn About Culture?—they will learn more about culture.

In Lesson 1, they will learn about the many parts of life that make up culture. They will also discover how cultures around the world are alike and how they are different.

Chapter 1

Exploring Culture

The people in the pictures on these pages are from different places in the world. Yet they are doing many of the same things that you might do. Some are talking together. Some are celebrating a holiday, as you might celebrate your birthday or the Fourth of July. Some are working with their hands to make something beautiful. No matter where people live, they all work, play, and learn, and they observe important events. The different ways in which they do these things is the subject of this chapter.

RESPONSIBLE LEADERS
ARE COMMITTED TO...
...RESPECTING THEIR ENVIRONMENT AND THE PEOPLE IN IT.
...HONESTY.
...USING MISTAKES AS LEARNING TOOLS.
...GOING THE EXTRA MILE.
MR DEMAREST
MR MC MACKIN
GRADE 5

These sixth-grade students represent many different cultures, yet share the responsibility of being citizens of the world.

BACKGROUND

The term *culture* refers to a people's way of life. It includes their customs, institutions, beliefs, ideas, technology, and more. Anthropologists have helped us understand present cultures as well as ancient ones. By studying the tools of ancient peoples, anthropologists have been able to put together a partial picture of early cultures.

What Constitutes Culture

In its broadest sense, a culture is the specific pattern in which a human group does everything that is not the result of biological inheritance. The culture of a group is the artifacts—tools, weapons, and ornaments—behaviors, and ideas that the group produces. Culture, therefore, is something that must be taught anew to each generation through the family, the community, and the educational system.

Culture differentiates human beings from animals. Animals do display some of the traits that we think of as cultural. Some animals live and hunt in groups. They have different behavior patterns, such as displaying friendly or hostile signals. However, only humans make extensive use of language and symbols, allowing us to accumulate and build on ideas.

History of Human Culture

A timeline of human culture would show humans beginning to make and use tools around 2.4 million years ago. Using tools is the first step in the development of culture, followed by creating artwork and simple

This Mexican woman sells her weavings to tourists.

Wole Soyinka of Nigeria, the first black African to win the Nobel Prize in literature, is interviewed in Stockholm in 1986. Soyinka won the prize that year for his plays, poems, and novels.

Korean girls take part in a harvest festival.

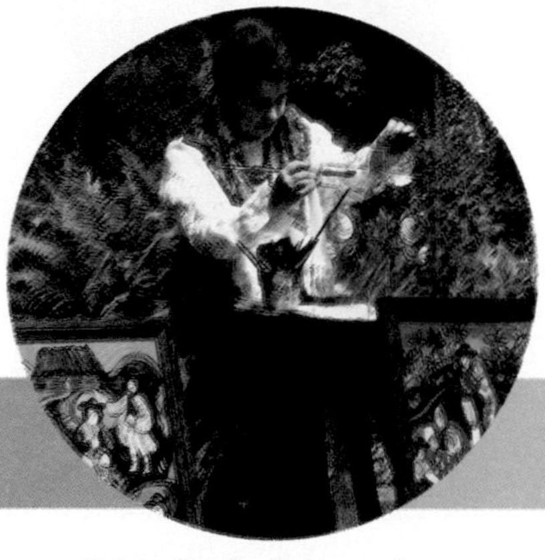

Painter Ewelina Peksowa of Poland displays her paintings done on glass.

Understanding the Visuals

Encourage students to speculate about ways in which they are like the people pictured on these two pages and ways in which they are different. Tell students that the different ways people do things make up their culture. Invite students to examine the photo of the Mexican woman with her weavings. Explain to students that the weavings are an example of Mexican artistic tradition. Then call attention to the Polish woman with her paintings on glass. Tell students that these paintings are one example of the traditional art of the Poles.

ceremonies. Farming, which began around 15,000 B.C., allowed people to create permanent settlements, which in turn led to further cultural growth. As populations grew, people had greater contact with one another. Two more important features of culture, the growth of cities and the development of writing, occurred around 3500 B.C. Writing allowed people to record their ideas and to communicate over long distances.

Changing Cultural Patterns

As the history of human culture shows, cultures are not static sets of unique traits—such as languages, religions, or customs. Instead, they are continually undergoing change. Change occurs as cultures respond to transformations in the physical and social environment and to innovations created by the culture or introduced from the outside. The study of the general idea of culture and of particular cultural patterns is the subject of the social studies, particularly history, geography, and anthropology.

INTRODUCE

Have students read the lesson title, A World of People. Tell them that people everywhere live in groups and that each group has its own culture, or way of life. Have students read the Thinking Focus and speculate about why culture is important to all people. Have students read the lesson to find out more about what culture is and how it helps people make sense of their world in order to be able to live in it.

Key Terms

Vocabulary Strategies: T36–T37

culture—everything a person must learn to live as a member of a group

custom—a way of doing things that has become accepted by a group

institution—an organization created by a people to do what one of its members alone cannot do

belief—an idea a person holds to be true

value—a belief about the right way to live and about how a person ought to behave

L E S S O N 1

A World of People

THINKING FOCUS

Why is culture important to people everywhere?

Key Terms

- culture
- custom
- institution
- belief
- value

Dear Kenji,

My name is Lilla. I live in Chicago, which is a big city here in the United States.

I am in middle school. My favorite subject in school is English. I also like science. After school on Mondays, I go to soccer practice. Most days I have homework to do. My mom says I have to finish my homework before I can watch TV.

I like Saturdays best because I can go to a friend's house to listen to music and talk. Sometimes, my friends and I go shopping. This week I bought a new pair of sneakers for school. My old ones were a mess!

I hope you will write and tell me all about yourself.

Your pen pal,
Lilla

Dear Lilla,

Thank you for your letter. I am happy to have a pen pal from the United States.

I am twelve years old. My favorite subject is Japanese. I study Japanese and other subjects every day in school and at home after school. Some days I also go to classes in kendo, an old martial art.

On Sundays, I like to meet my friends for ice cream and shopping. Last week I bought a new T-shirt. I do not wear it to school, however. I wear a uniform to school.

Please write again soon.

Your pen pal,
Kenji

Lilla and Kenji have just become pen pals. They are discovering that they have a lot in common. They both enjoy shopping and being with their friends. They both go to school, where they study a language. They are learning that there are differences between them, too. The languages they study are different. So are the clothes they wear to school and the sports they play.

Through their letters Lilla and Kenji tell each other about the things friends talk about—school, sports, clothes, hobbies, and so on. As they write to each other, they also learn about how someone in another country lives. In other words, they learn about a different culture.

Objectives

1. Understand common human needs and life experiences.
2. Understand what culture is and why all people live within cultural patterns.

Graphic Overview

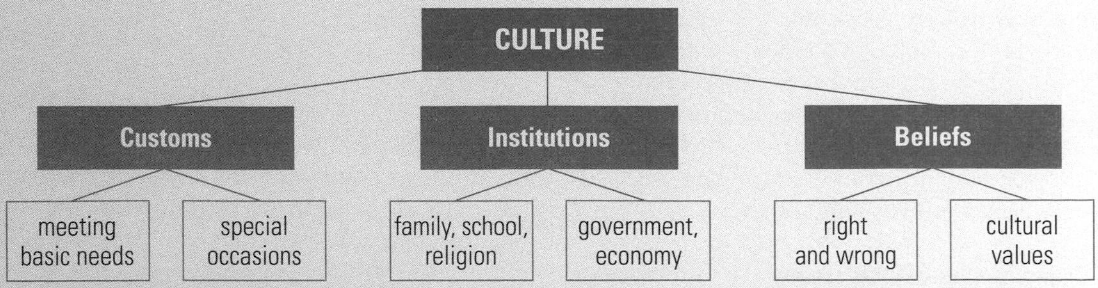
CULTURE
Customs
Institutions
Beliefs
meeting basic needs
special occasions
family, school, religion
government, economy
right and wrong
cultural values

What Is Culture?

What do you notice about the girl in the picture on this page? Perhaps you notice her clothing or the things she is carrying. Almost everything you notice tells you something about her culture. **Culture** is everything a person must learn to live as a member of a group. It includes ways of making things, behaving, and thinking. It includes the types of food, clothing, and shelter that a group uses. It may include a shared religion, language, and forms of art. It even includes ways of having fun and being sad, and of making a living.

The diagram on page 6 can help you understand culture. It shows all the ways of looking at or thinking about culture that are common to most groups the world over.

Cultures Are Alike and Different

As you read this book, you will learn about the cultures of the world. You will see how they are alike and how they are different. You will see that people all over the world have many of the same needs. For example, all people need food, clothing, and shelter. Culture shapes the way people meet their needs. Culture determines what foods people eat and what a group's clothing and shelters look like.

People of all nations also share the same experiences of change, such as birth, childhood, adulthood, old age, and death. They celebrate many of the same events, such as marriage or the birth of a baby. These celebrations differ from culture to culture, however. People everywhere are sad about many of the same losses and failures, too. Culture shapes what people do as they face these losses. For example, people of different cultures act differently when a loved one dies.

▲ *This girl is from the United States. What do you notice about her that tells you about her culture?*

DEVELOP

Use the visuals and text to provide examples of aspects of culture. Whenever possible, ask students to compare and contrast images, for example the girl from the United States and the boys from Japan pictured on page 4. Ask students to draw conclusions about the role of culture in people's lives, based on what they see in the pictures. *(In this case, culture influences clothing styles, hairstyles, and what type of clothing is considered appropriate for school.)*

◄ *Students may mention that the girl's books and backpack show that she goes to school; her hairstyle and clothing are common in her culture.*

Access Strategy

Ask students to imagine a typical school day. Have them name some of the activities that take place. These might include choosing clothes, eating breakfast, taking the bus to school, attending classes, talking with friends, watching television, or playing a sport. Explain to students that their culture is made up of what are considered to be acceptable ways of doing these and other everyday things. Culture includes what students wear, what they eat, how they get to school, what they study, what they do with their friends, and how they spend their free time.

Next, call attention to the picture of the girl on this page. Ask students to imagine themselves pictured in her place. What would people notice about them that tells about their culture? Encourage students to name items or to describe themselves as they imagined themselves to look.

Access Activity

Ask students whether they have ever had a pen pal. Have them imagine that they are writing a letter to a pen pal in another country. What would they want to tell the pen pal about their daily life? What would they want to know about their pen pal's life?

CULTURES

Critical Thinking

Sometimes, differences in customs can present difficulties for people visiting other cultures. Ask students to think of why this is so. *(The visitor might unknowingly do something that is considered rude or inappropriate or might not know what is expected in certain social situations. The visitor might not like the food served or the clothing used.)* Ask students how these difficulties might be overcome. *(Visitors might read about their hosts before visiting them to better understand their values and customs.)*

CULTURE

Study Skills

Have students read the text on this page, and ask them to make a list of customs of their culture. Remind students to be as specific as possible in describing each custom. For example, students may mention that one custom is to say "hello" after picking up the telephone to answer a call. *(Students' lists may include marriage and funeral customs, manners, customs related to feasts and festivals, or any other aspects of culture that are a matter of custom.)*

A baby learns about its culture from the moment it is born.

Cultures Include Customs

Ways of doing things that have become accepted by a group are called **customs.** Customs vary from culture to culture. For example, in all countries people get married. They differ, however, in the way they marry. In the United States, at many weddings the bride and the groom feed wedding cake to each other. Jewish couples smash a glass at their ceremonies. In Ethiopia friends of the groom pretend to kidnap the new bride.

The rules about marriage also differ from place to place. In some parts of the world, people marry at an early age. In other places people marry when they have grown up. In some cultures people can have more than one husband or wife at the same time. In the United States, people usually choose their own husbands and wives. In some countries, parents choose the person their son or daughter will marry.

All over the world, people are sorrowful about the deaths of loved ones. However, ceremonies to honor the dead can be very different. After a Hindu funeral procession, the body is burned. Some groups of Australian aborigines place the dead in trees.

Manners are also a matter of custom. In the United States, it is acceptable for people to rest their hands in their laps while at the table. In Germany children are taught that polite Germans rest their wrists on the edge of the table. In the United States, it is the custom to hold a fork in the right hand. In Germany the fork is usually held in the left hand.

The feasts and the festivals celebrated by a group are also customs.

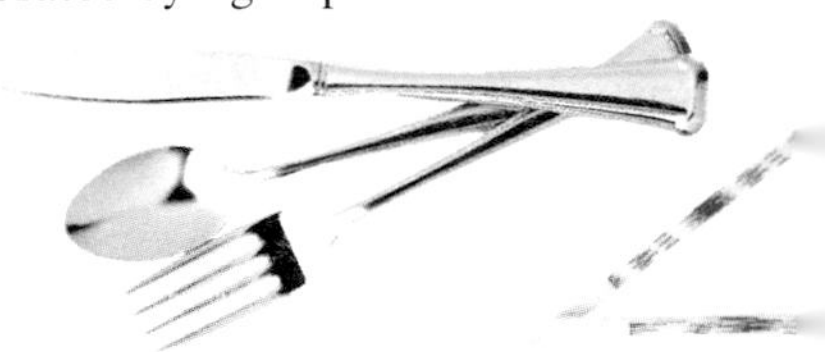

What Is Culture?

This diagram shows that culture is made up of many different parts of the life of a people.

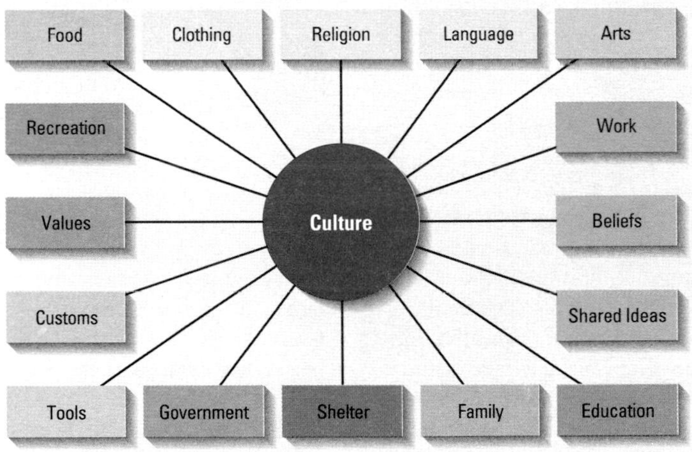
Food
Clothing
Religion
Language
Arts
Recreation
Work
Values
Culture
Beliefs
Customs
Shared Ideas
Tools
Government
Shelter
Family
Education

Visual Learning

Have students examine the diagram on this page and give examples of each of the categories from their own culture and, whenever possible, from other cultures. Tell students that although many of the things they do on a daily basis may seem natural to them, these things may be quite different from the way people in other cultures do things.

Writing a Letter

Have students write to an imaginary pen pal from another culture, describing the celebration of a U.S. holiday of their choosing. Remind students to include specific details because the events they describe will probably be unfamiliar to their pen pal.

HAPPY
NEW YEAR

These objects are used in New Year's Eve celebrations in the United States.

Many cultures celebrate the coming of spring. In Italy residents of Florence celebrate the Festa Del Gallo, or cricket festival, on the 40th day after Easter. They say that the cricket's song heralds the coming of spring. For hundreds of years in Great Britain, the first of May has meant a celebration. A May queen is crowned, and people dance around a ribbon-wrapped maypole.

People in almost every country celebrate the new year with a holiday. On New Year's Eve, many people in the United States celebrate with parties and dancing. They hang banners and blow noisemakers like the ones shown above.

Many people the world over celebrate the new year on dates established by their religion. For example, the Jewish New Year, called Rosh Hashanah, is observed during September or early October. The Chinese New Year is celebrated for a month beginning in late January or early February. The objects you see below are used in celebrations of the Chinese New Year.

Shared ceremonies, manners, celebrations, foods, clothing, and so on are an important part of a culture. They draw the people of a culture together as a group.

Cultures Include Institutions

In order to live together as a group, a people must organize orderly ways of doing certain jobs. An **institution** is an organization created by a people to do what one of its members alone cannot do.

Many items used in celebrations of the Chinese New Year are red or orange. These colors are thought to bring good luck. The banner at the right shows characters of the Chinese language that mean "Happy New Year." The red paper square at the left says "good luck"; the one to the right of it says "spring."

福
春
23
賀新禧

CULTURE

Critical Thinking

Point out to students that "culture" is not the same as "country." Point out that although people sometimes speak of an American culture, there are many different cultures in North America. These cultures vary according to region, ethnic group, and other factors. Based on the definition of culture in the text, do students think there is such a thing as an elementary-school, middle-school, or high-school culture? *(Some students may think that there is a school culture because fashions, slang, and appropriate behavior are different in each school. Others may feel that the differences are not strong enough for each school to be considered a distinct culture.)*

Art Connection

Cultures often develop distinctive art. Have students research the art of a culture of their choice and bring to class one or more books showing examples. Ask each student to examine the examples and to list up to five characteristics of the art of this culture (colors, materials, subjects, and so on). Then have students work in small groups, showing the pictures and sharing what they have read and observed about them.

Music Connection

Ask students if they can name the song that is traditionally sung in the United States at the stroke of midnight on New Year's Eve. Share with them the words to "Auld Lang Syne," and explain that this song comes from Scotland. You may wish to have students research how the song passed into U.S. culture.

Study Skills

Have students work in groups to research a holiday or festival in a different culture. Have them make a drawing or collage of it. Make a large calendar for the coming year, and hang it on a wall. Ask students to paste their artwork in the appropriate space on the calendar, and to tell the other students what the holiday is about and how they have chosen to illustrate it.

CULTURE

Visual Learning

Using examples from magazines such as *National Geographic,* discuss with students the influence of culture on the kinds of structures that are built in a place. Point out, for instance, that some cultures have marketplaces instead of shopping centers. The importance that people place on a building, as well as how it looks, varies from one culture to another. For example, in Chapter 18 students will learn about medieval European culture, in which the cathedral was the central structure in a town. Review the definition of *institution,* and have students identify the institution that is connected to each of the structures discussed.

At the right a farm family is shown loading hay into a horse-drawn cart in the Slovak Republic. The photograph below shows shelters of Inuit families living in the Arctic.

The family is perhaps the oldest institution. It came into being because human infants need protection and education for a long time. Therefore, the family has been one of the most important institutions in the world. The pictures on this page show families in different parts of the world.

Families teach many important things—how to speak, how to dress and eat, and how to behave. People rely on another institution—the school—to teach other things they need or want to know. In schools experienced people teach knowledge and skills that students will need to survive in their culture. Many adults go back to school again and again to gain new knowledge and skills.

Government is another important institution. Through government, people can make decisions, enforce rules, settle disagreements, and live together in an orderly way.

The economic system of a culture is also an institution. An economic system allows people to sell or trade what they have and get what they need.

In most cultures people share another of the oldest institutions—religion. Religion helps people in their search to understand how the world came to be, why people are born, and what happens to them after death.

Institutions usually have special buildings in which to carry out their purposes. The building pictured on page 9 has a special purpose too. What is this building used for? The table on page 9 describes other buildings and their uses.

Cultures Include Beliefs

People of all cultures have certain ideas in which they believe. An idea a person holds to be true is a **belief.** Many beliefs are ideas you accept as true that can't be proven correct or incorrect by scientific experiment or measurement. Beliefs often have to do with things that are difficult to measure, such as good or evil, or whether something is beautiful or ugly.

Beliefs are an important part of culture. This doesn't mean that all

Social Participation

Have students work in groups to create and perform a short skit on one of the following: adults being introduced to one another; family members attending a middle-school graduation ceremony; shoppers making purchases with the help of a salesclerk. In a discussion afterward, ask students to identify the aspects of culture each skit addressed.

Writing a News Account

Ask each student to choose one aspect of U.S. culture—for example, beliefs about the right way to behave. Have students write three questions about their topic, interview several other students, and write news reports about their findings. Before students begin, discuss the difference between opinions and facts. Explain that students will be writing about others' opinions about U.S. culture. Remind them to use expressions such as "according to one student . . ." and "the student said that . . ."

Political Context

Point out to students that some cultures in the United States today struggle to survive because they lack political power. Many Native American cultures, for example, are gradually losing their traditional ways of life, including the ways they meet their basic needs for food, clothing, and shelter, as well as arts, language, songs, rituals, and so on.

Institutions and Culture

RESTAURANT

Building	School	Skyscraper	Houses of Worship	Stores and Restaurants
Social group	Students and teachers	Office workers	Religious groups	Merchants and customers
Purpose of building	Schools are used for education of students. Teachers and groups of students work together in classrooms.	Skyscrapers provide office space for workers and for storing records.	Houses of worship inspire and educate people about their faith. They provide a place for worship services.	Stores display goods for sale. They have signs to identify them and their products.

members of a cultural group have exactly the same beliefs. It does mean, however, that many members of the group share a large number of beliefs. For example, most persons in the United States believe that people should be free to speak their minds. In some cultures, however, it is considered rude or ugly to say publicly that you disagree with someone, even if you do.

In every culture people are expected to behave in ways that are considered "right" or "good." If they act in ways that are considered "wrong" or "bad," they will be shamed or punished. Often beliefs about right and wrong are part of religion.

Beliefs that people hold about the right way to live and about how a person ought to behave are called **values.** Cultural values are the ideas, qualities, and institutions people prize most. They are used to define individuals and members of a group. Shared beliefs and values draw people closer together, just as a group's customs and institutions do. ■

LUNCH

◄ *A restaurant in Tacoma, Washington, is built in the shape of a teapot.*

■ *How does your culture help you live in the world?*

REVIEW

1. **FOCUS** Why is culture important to people everywhere?
2. **CULTURE** Describe some customs or celebrations that are important in your culture.
3. **BELIEF SYSTEMS** Why are some beliefs hard to measure or prove?
4. **CRITICAL THINKING** Which of the institutions described in the lesson do you think is most important to you? Why?
5. **WRITING ACTIVITY** Ask your parents to talk about how the culture in which your grandparents grew up is different from your culture today. Then write a paragraph or two describing these differences.

HISTORY

Visual Learning

Tell students that beliefs and values vary not only from one place to another, but also from one time period to another. Have students explore their new textbook, glancing through the table of contents and the pictures. Tell them that they'll be studying cultures from around the world and from the earliest peoples until today. Explain that each time period, like each area of the world, has its own cultural characteristics.

■ *Students' answers should indicate that culture includes the customs, institutions, and beliefs that members of a culture need to live and work together.*

CLOSE

Read and discuss the Thinking Focus. Then create a bulletin-board display with students. Label it "Culture includes . . . ," and ask students to name all the aspects of people's lives they can think of that are affected by their culture. Write each idea on a circle of construction paper. Group the circles into the categories Customs, Institutions, and Beliefs. Have students find pictures of people or places from a variety of cultures to illustrate the concepts included on the bulletin board.

Answers to Review Questions

1. Without culture people would not know how to meet their basic needs for food, clothing, and shelter. The customs, institutions, and beliefs that are part of culture help people live together in an orderly way.
2. Students may describe Thanksgiving dinner, Fourth-of-July fireworks, or other celebrations common to their culture.
3. Beliefs often have to do with ideas, such as good or evil, or judgments, such as beauty or ugliness, that cannot be proved or measured.
4. Students may choose family, school, religion, the government, or the economic system. They should defend their choices with examples.
5. Students' paragraphs might highlight ways in which technology, family life, and the economy differed in their grandparents' youth.

Homework Options

Ask students to research a food from an unfamiliar culture. Have them write a paragraph about the food, including such information as how it is prepared and when and how it is served. Encourage students to include a picture when possible. Display the completed assignments.

Study Guide: page 1

INTRODUCE

These poems may help students see that in many ways human beings are alike, no matter in what country they live. The writers of these poems come from the United States, the Philippines, Canada, and China; yet they express universal experiences, emotions, hopes, and fears. The poems are from *Miracles: Poems by Children of the English-speaking World.* The poem by Chan Fang-Sheng is from *All the Silver Pennies,* edited by Blanche Jennings Thompson.

READ AND RESPOND

To help students make connections between the poems, ask them to consider the following questions as they read alone or together: What experience did each writer choose to describe? What can you tell about the writer's feelings from the poem? Have you ever felt the way the writer has? If so, when and why?

Before students read, point out the vocabulary words and unfamiliar terms defined in the margins. Be sure they understand what the words mean; help with pronunciation if necessary.

In Lesson 1 you read that the world is home to many different cultures. In the next lesson you will read that cultures are shaped by nature and by the coming together of different peoples. Here young poets share their thoughts about nature and about the world as they see it.

LITERATURE

A World of Poems

People around the world share many of the same feelings. Some of these poems were written by children from different nations. As you read, think about the special feelings the poets have about the world and their place in it.

I Love the World

I love you, Big World.
I wish I could call you
And tell you a secret:
That I love you, World.
—Paul Wollner, age 7, United States

The Pier

pier a structure extending into water for use as a landing place for boats

One very nice day I went to the pier,
There were lots of noises that I could hear,
There I saw so many ships.
They were buzzing; buzzing, buzzing
I couldn't stand it, there was so much noise—
As if the place was full of naughty schoolboys.
However, I didn't want to leave. I had to be brave
Because I was enjoying myself, looking at the waves.
Soon I had to go; night had come, lights went on,
The day had brought me so much fun.
That night I could not sleep; I wanted to sing,
Of ships and waves and bells that ring.
—Enrique Lozada, age 10, Philippines

A Wish

I want to climb the santol tree
That grows beside my bedroom window
And get a santol fruit.
I want to climb the tree at night
And get the moon the branches hide.
Then I shall go to bed, my pockets full,
One with the fruit, the other with the moon.
—Tonas Santos, age 7, Philippines

Thematic Connections

Social Studies: Culture/Reflecting a people's inner life

Houghton Mifflin Literary Readers: Poetry/Moving the World

Background

The first four poems are written by children who live in countries where English is spoken as the primary or secondary language. The editor of the anthology in which they appear, Richard Lewis, taught literature and creative writing in a New York City elementary school in the early 1960s. There, he became fascinated by the quality of children's poetry—its depth of feeling and its clarity—and he decided to put together an international collection. With the support of UNESCO (United Nations Educational, Scientific, and Cultural Organization), he embarked on a world tour that put him in touch with children in such places as New Zealand, Kenya, and India. These four poems are from that collection.

"Sailing Homeward," on the other hand, was written in Chinese and translated by Arthur Waley. If there is anyone in your class who speaks Chinese, it might be interesting to have him or her translate the poem back into its original language and read it for the class.

Winter

Animals are restless
Birds are in flight,
Butterflies are not out.
Leaves; a gray blanket,
Winter lurks near.

Icy fingers grasp the world.
Snow falls; graceful, beautiful,
    undisturbed.
Silence creeps about.

—John Constant, age 10, Canada

lurks lies in wait

Sailing Homeward

Cliffs that rise a thousand feet
Without a break,
Lake that stretches a hundred miles
Without a wave,
Sands that are white through all the year
Without a stain,
Pine-tree woods, winter and summer
Evergreen,
Streams that forever flow and flow
Without a pause,
Trees that for twenty thousand years
Your vows have kept,
You have suddenly healed the pain of a traveler's heart,
And moved his brush to write a new song.

—Chan Fang-Sheng, China
—Arthur Waley, Translator

vows promises

Further Reading

The Cay. Theodore Taylor. Phillip, shipwrecked in the West Indies, learns to respect the dark-skinned people he finds there.

The Desert Is Theirs. Byrd Baylor. The author describes the characteristics of the desert and its plant, animal, and human life.

Talking to the Sun: An Illustrated Anthology of Poems for Young People. Kenneth Koch and Kate Farrell. This collection of poems combines beautiful works of art from the Metropolitan Museum of Art in New York with poems for young people. The poems include African chants, Japanese haiku, American Indian verse, and much more.

◄ John Constant, who lives in Canada, describes the kind of winter he knows best. Ask students what details they would choose to describe winter in the place where they live. *(Answers will depend on the part of the United States where students live.)*

EXTEND

Have students write a short poem of their own about how they would feel returning home after a long time away. Like Chan Fang-Sheng, they might wish to describe familiar or comforting sights in their poems.

Access Strategy

To help students prepare for reading the poems on these pages, tell them that all but one of the poems are related to nature topics. Ask students to scan the poems and look for nature words. List the words on the chalkboard. *(For example: waves, tree, moon, fruit, animals, birds, snow, leaves, cliff, lake, sands, pine-tree woods)* Then ask volunteers to read the poems aloud.

Further Reading

You may want to have your students look in the school or local library for more poems by people from other countries.

INTRODUCE

Have students name some basic human needs. *(Students may name food, water, shelter, clothing, education, love, human rights, or others.)* Then read the Thinking Focus, and have students speculate about factors that might influence the ways in which different cultures meet people's needs. How, for instance, might a culture in a very cold climate differ from a culture in a very hot one? *(Possible answers include differences in the types of clothing and shelter and the kinds of plants and animals that live in the area and that provide food.)* Have students read the lesson to learn more about factors that shape cultures.

Key Terms

Vocabulary Strategies: T36–T37

environment—the things by which people are surrounded, including air, land, living things, and climate
social interaction—contact between people, in which they communicate and do things with one another
cultural diffusion—the spread of elements of one culture to another
technology—tools and machines and the knowledge and skills needed to make and use them

L E S S O N 2

What Shapes and Changes Cultures?

THINKING FOCUS

What factors influence the way cultures develop and change?

Key Terms

- environment
- social interaction
- cultural diffusion
- technology

In 1901 in a hut in Newfoundland, Canada, Guglielmo Marconi *(gool YEHL moh mahr COH nee)* listened on an earphone. Suddenly, he heard a tapping sound. The world's first wireless transatlantic radio message had just been sent through the airwaves from Great Britain. Later, he would say:

I now felt for the first time absolutely certain that the day would come when mankind would be able to send messages without wires not only across the Atlantic but between the farthermost ends of the earth.

Physical Environment and Culture

Marconi's invention soon enabled people to send messages around the world in a matter of minutes. With advances in communication, cultures came into contact with one another more than ever before. This contact has helped to shape the world's cultures.

Before rapid communication, cultures changed more slowly, and natural surroundings did much to shape them. Physical, or natural, environment has always been an important factor in shaping culture. **Environment** includes things by which people are surrounded. Physical environment includes all natural features such as air, land, living things,

▼ *A woman makes good use of a waterway in her area. She lives on a houseboat in Pakistan.*

Objectives

1. Understand how physical environment affects culture.
2. Understand how social interaction affects culture.
3. Understand how ideas and technology affect culture.

Graphic Overview

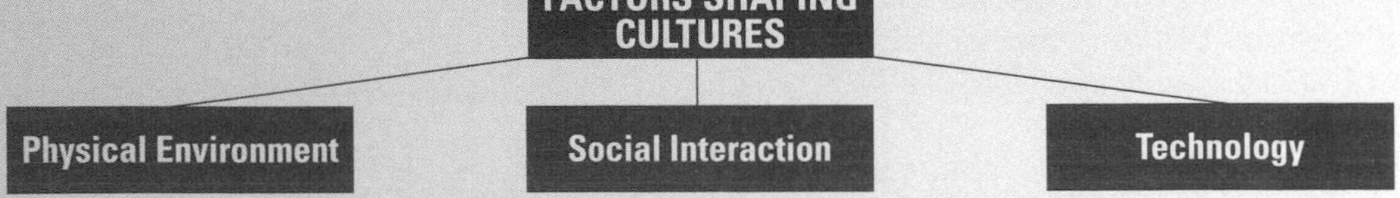
FACTORS SHAPING CULTURES
Physical Environment
Social Interaction
Technology

◄ *As a temporary shelter, this igloo in the Canadian Arctic provides warmth and protection from the wind.*

and climate found in a particular area. An example of physical environment can be seen in the picture on page 12 of a waterway in Pakistan.

Natural features help shape culture in many ways. For example, for thousands of years people have lived near the Arctic Circle. To adapt to this climate of continuous cold, they dressed in animal furs. When hunting, they built temporary shelters, like the one shown above, from snow and ice. Today people still live in the Arctic, and their culture is still shaped by the cold. It has changed, however. For example, many people now use snowmobiles to travel over the snow-covered ground.

A culture adapted to the Arctic probably could not survive in the world's deserts. Some people who live in deserts must travel from place to place looking for water and new pastureland for the animals they herd. They use tents for shelters because they are easy to move and small enough to carry. Like the man in the picture to the right, people take advantage of the desert sun.

Physical Environments Change

A change in physical environment can change culture. The people of Africa's Sahel, an area south of the Sahara, were nomads. When there were rains, they moved through the Sahel in search of pasture for their herds of cattle, camels, goats, and sheep. During periods of little rain, they moved south to more fertile areas.

In 1968, however, the Sahel entered a continuing period of little rain. At the same time, people there came to rely more and more on farming. They settled down to plant crops and graze cows and sheep, no longer herding their animals to new pastures. Because of the lack of rain and because the people used the same lands continuously for farming and grazing, the grass that covered the soil was destroyed. This made it possible for the desert to creep southward, taking over hundreds of thousands of square miles of grassland. Thus, the people of the Sahel lost the land they had once moved to. As a result, those who had survived by following the rains lost their way of life. ■

▼ *A man in the desert of Saudi Arabia talks on a solar-powered telephone.*

■ *In what ways does physical environment help shape cultures?*

DEVELOP

Point out that in this lesson students will read about three major factors that influence cultures—physical environment, social interaction, and technology. Draw the Graphic Overview on the chalkboard, and tell students that in this lesson they will see examples of how each factor, such as the climate in which a culture exists or the introduction of a piece of machinery, can help shape a culture.

■ *Natural surroundings such as air, land, living things, and climate influence the ways people meet their basic needs for food, clothing, and shelter.*

Access Strategy

Have students examine the images and accompanying captions on these two pages. Point out that the people in these pictures are making use of features of the natural environment available to them. Have students name those features. *(Water, snow, sun)* Then ask students what natural features people in their own area use. For example, what are the houses made of? *(Students will mention various materials.)* Point out that although many houses are made of wood, in areas where there are not many trees, houses may be made of other plants, such as bamboo; or they may be made of stone, brick, adobe, or other materials. Are there rivers or other bodies of water nearby? If so, how do people use them? *(Answers may include using water resources to produce electricity or for transportation of goods.)* How do people use the area's climate and plant and animal life to meet their needs? *(Answers may include farming and fishing.)*

Access Activity

Ask students to look around their own homes for examples of ways in which the physical environment of their area affects the way they live. Have students work in small groups to discuss their findings. *(Students may mention clothing appropriate for the climate in their area; the need to heat or cool their homes; or items used for recreation.)*

SOCIAL SYSTEMS

Study Skills

Have students read the description of the Apache coming-of-age ceremony on this page. Explain that for the Apache, becoming an adult means expressing one's willingness to carry on the Apache culture. The young woman in the photograph must be able to recount the story of her people's origins. She also must become responsible for the well-being of her people. Ask students to write two or more paragraphs on what it means, in their opinion, to become an adult. Is there a certain time that they think marks this coming of age? How will they know when they are adult? Will they have new responsibilities? What will these be?

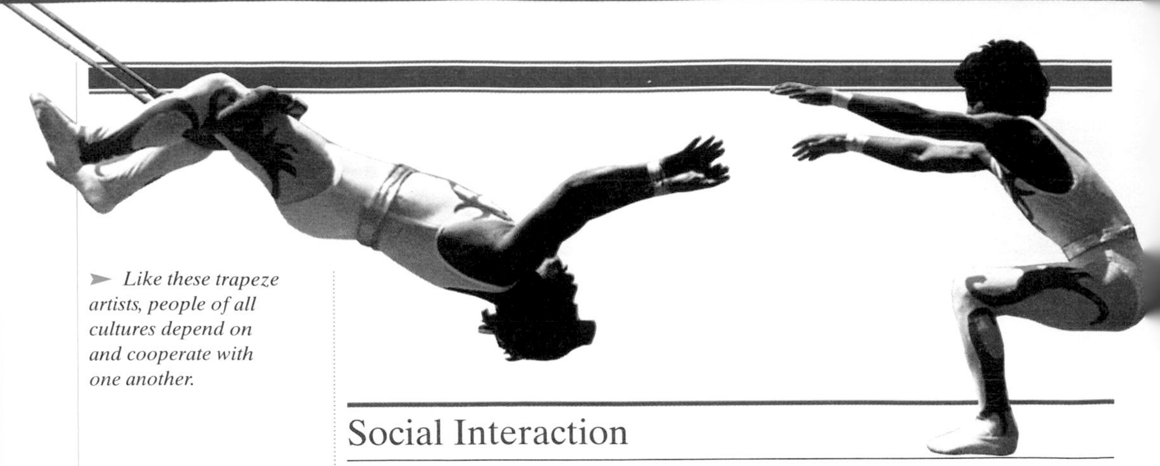

Like these trapeze artists, people of all cultures depend on and cooperate with one another.

Social Interaction

Within a culture, people constantly come in contact with one another. This contact, in which people communicate and do things with one another, is called **social interaction.** Social interaction is essential to the trapeze artists shown on these pages. They must communicate with one another as they plan, practice, and perform amazing acts of skill.

Special ceremonies and celebrations are an important part of social interaction within a culture. For instance, the young Apache woman in the photograph below is taking part in a ceremony that marks her coming of age as an adult. She is dressed in buckskin and jewelry and is guided through the ceremony by her godmother.

During the ceremony, which continues for four days, Apache elders join in singing chants. In turn, the young woman acts out for everyone the story of the origins of her people. Then she is instructed by her godmother in her responsibilities as an adult, that is, in how she is supposed to interact with others. At the close of the ceremony, she dances from sunrise to sunset for the well-being of her people. Like generations of Apache women before her, the young woman completes an essential ritual that communicates to everyone her willingness to be part of her culture.

Social interaction also occurs when whole cultures come into contact with each other. Social interaction between cultures often

In Whiteriver, Arizona, an Apache woman takes part in a ceremony celebrating the beginning of her life as an adult.

Study Skills

Have students research the impact of many cultures in the United States. Have students describe cultural elements, such as food, music, or customs, that have become part of U.S. culture.

Language Arts Connection

Language is an element of culture that changes with social interaction just as other aspects of culture do. The English language, for example, began as a Germanic dialect spoken by the Angles, Saxons, and Jutes, peoples who invaded and settled in Britain in the fifth century A.D. Their language was later influenced by the invasion of Scandinavians in the eighth and ninth centuries. The Scandinavians, who spoke a similar dialect, gave English several sets of synonyms, such as *craft* and *skill* and *wish* and *want,* as well as other words similar to English words but with slightly different meanings; these include *shriek* and *screech, scatter* and *shatter, skirt* and *shirt.* In 1066 invading French-speakers from Normandy brought even greater changes to English. Because the Normans ruled England, many English words relating to government come from French, such as *judge* and *court.* Modern English has about 7,000 words of Norman origin.

brings changes to each of them. Sometimes, elements of one culture spread to the other. This is called **cultural diffusion.**

Examples of cultural diffusion occurred after the Spaniards had come to Mexico in the 1500s. The Spaniards had brought many things with them, including horses, cattle, and sheep. The use of horses spread rapidly, and soon many American Indian groups rode horses. The wild cattle became the longhorns that helped shape culture in the southwestern United States. The Navajo borrowed sheep raising from the Spaniards and turned the making of wool blankets into an art form. Understanding Cultural Diffusion below will tell you more. ■

■ *How does cultural diffusion change cultures?*

Understanding Cultural Diffusion

Can you imagine pizza or spaghetti without the tangy flavor of tomatoes, or a hamburger without French-fried potatoes? Yet 500 years ago, tomatoes and potatoes grew only in the Americas. People in Italy and France had never tasted them. European explorers who came to the Americas in the 1500s took these foods back home. They quickly became part of European culture. This process has gone on all over the world.

Ideas as well as foods have spread from one culture to another. For example, new farming methods, such as irrigation and the use of plows, were developed in Southwest Asia and spread to many cultures in Europe and elsewhere.

What Is Cultural Diffusion?

The process you have been reading about is called cultural diffusion. The term *diffusion* is used in science. For example, a drop of ink in a glass of water will gradually diffuse, or spread out, until it colors all the water in the glass. In the process of cultural diffusion, an idea or method spreads from one culture to another.

The Spread of Culture

Long ago, mountains, deserts, and oceans kept different groups of people apart. Still, whenever groups of people met—by accident, for trade, or even in war—cultural diffusion might occur. Someone might sample a new food or admire the way a spear point or pottery bowl was made. He or she took the new idea home, making it part of another culture.

Many languages and ways of writing them spread by cultural diffusion. So did religions, farming methods, and skills such as working with metals.

Today, modern travel and communication have shrunk distances. People encounter different cultures often, sometimes every day. As a result, cultural diffusion can occur more often than in the past. You may play a Japanese computer game or watch a program on a television set manufactured in Japan. Japanese students enjoy U.S. rock music, fast foods, fashions, and sports.

GEOGRAPHY

Study Skills

Have students read Understanding Cultural Diffusion. Discuss with them the ways in which cultures came into contact with one another before the 20th century. Explain that travelers, traders, explorers, missionaries, and conquerors, traveling by sea and over land, brought with them ideas that were adopted by the cultures with which they came into contact. Sometimes whole civilizations moved, resulting in social interaction between different cultures. Then invite students to name modern means of transportation and communication that make interaction between cultures more common today. *(Airplanes, telegraphs, telephones, television, computers, modems, fax machines, satellites, and so on)*

■ *As cultures come into contact with one another, elements of one culture are adopted by another.*

Cultural Context

To help students understand cultural diffusion, explain that it is a two-way street, even when one culture dominates another. For example, vast numbers of Native Americans were killed when Europeans settled in North America, and Native Americans have lost a good deal of their traditional culture. Yet European immigrants were influenced by Native American cultures as well. Examples of cultural elements adopted by Europeans include forms of transportation such as the toboggan and canoe; foods such as peanuts, corn, pineapples, and tomatoes; and many words. Hundreds of place names in the United States, including half of our state names, are of Native American origin.

Critical Thinking

Place a drop of ink in a clear glass of water. Have students describe what happens to the ink. *(It spreads out and seems to disappear, but the water becomes slightly shaded.)* Then ask how this result is like cultural diffusion. *(When people from different cultures interact, each culture is affected by the contact, even when it may seem the effect is only slight.)*

➤ *Students may say the person who owns the Corvette enjoys driving, can afford an expensive car, is adventurous, wants to present a certain image, and so on.*

CULTURE

Critical Thinking

Tell students that manners and customs shape many of their social interactions. Discuss with students several different kinds of social interaction—for example, talking to a teacher and to friends at school. Ask students if they behave differently with people their age than they do with adults. Do they behave differently with their friends than with strangers? Discuss why students' behavior differs. *(Students may say they are more polite, serious, or formal with adults and strangers than with friends.)*

CULTURE

Visual Learning

Have students examine the diagram on page 17 showing changes brought by the invention of the car. Ask them to identify those changes they think are positive and those they think are negative and to explain their reasoning. Then lead students in a discussion of whether the benefits of having cars outweigh the disadvantages.

➤ *Cars play a very important role in the culture of the United States. What kind of person might own this car?*

Technology and Culture

Through cultural diffusion, ideas and technology move from one culture to another. **Technology** means tools and machines and the knowledge and skills needed to make and use them. New technologies change the cultures that adopt them. Changes in farming, transportation, and communication have all shaped and altered cultures around the world.

Advances in Transportation

An early advance in transportation was the steam engine, developed in Great Britain in the early 1800s and used both for water and land travel. The steam engine quickly changed cultures. In the United States, the steam-run locomotive helped create and then end the cowhand culture. In the 1860s, trains made it possible to ship large numbers of cattle to the eastern cities. Therefore, many cowhands were needed to tend huge herds of cattle on unfenced land called the open range. The cowhands took the cattle on long trail drives to railway stations in the "cow towns."

About 30 years later, changes in technology put most of the

➤ *The scene below shows Los Angeles, California, in 1884. At that time, people rode along dirt streets in horse-drawn carriages and trolleys. The picture at the right shows Los Angeles today. The vast majority of people in the Los Angeles area drive to work in cars, vans, or trucks.*

Study Skills

Have students make a diagram illustrating the impact on U.S. culture of an advance in technology other than the car or the television. The name of the technological innovation should go in the center of the diagram, with arrows radiating from it and pointing to its effects. If those effects led to other effects or to other inventions, students can name those as well.

Science Connection

It has been said that the goal of communication technology is to reduce the barriers of space and time. Have students review Highlights in the History of Communication in the Minipedia (pages 665–668), and ask them to reflect on what this expression means by comparing mail delivery by horse, by rail, and by fax or modem. How have developments in communication technology changed U.S. culture? *(Methods of communication are much faster than they once were. This makes it possible to gather information, make decisions, and create products more quickly. Modern communications also make it possible for people separated by great distances to work together.)*

Technology and Culture

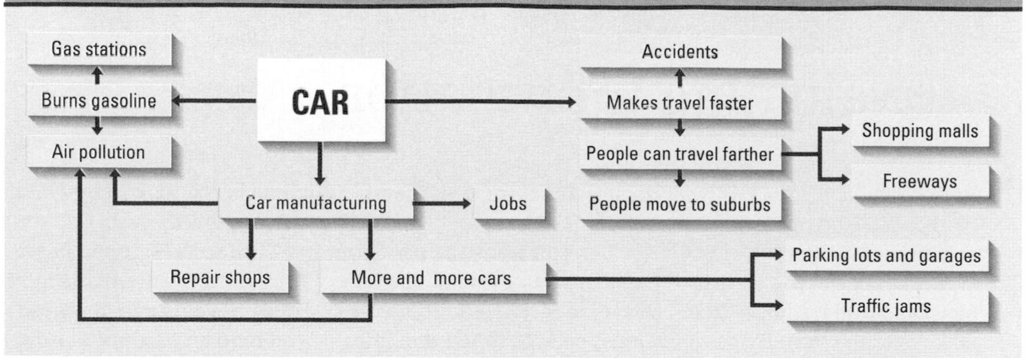

CAR
Gas stations
Burns gasoline
Air pollution
Car manufacturing
Jobs
Repair shops
More and more cars
Accidents
Makes travel faster
People can travel farther
People move to suburbs
Shopping malls
Freeways
Parking lots and garages
Traffic jams

cowhands out of work. The use of barbed wire fences and the spread of farms brought an end to the open range. Railroads expanded to reach the cattle ranches and did away with the need for trail drives. As a result, far fewer cowhands were needed.

Cars brought dramatic changes to culture in the United States. Compare the scenes pictured on page 16. One photo was taken before the invention of the car. The other shows modern downtown Los Angeles.

With the invention of the car, people no longer had to live close to their jobs. Instead, they spread out to live in suburbs. Businesses with drive-in services sprang up near roads across the United States, changing the way people shopped and spent their leisure time. People drove their cars to supermarkets, shopping centers, drive-in banks, and, later, to shopping malls. They traveled to tourist cabins, campgrounds, motels, and resorts. They enjoyed food at drive-in restaurants and films at drive-in theaters. The chart on this page shows not only the benefits but also some problems brought by the car.

▲ *This chart shows the many changes brought about by the invention of the car.*

Advances in Communication

Advances in communication also have changed our culture. For example, television permits almost everyone, wherever they may be, to share in political, cultural, and other experiences. With television, citizens in the United States witness presidential debates and speeches. Television advertising influences what we eat and wear, the cars we drive, what we do for fun, and how we clean our homes. Through television news, people see and hear about what the government is doing every day and what is taking place throughout the world. Television, therefore, has helped build a common culture from one end of the United States to the other. ■

■ *What are some advances in technology that are important in your life?*

REVIEW

1. **FOCUS** What factors influence the way cultures develop and change?
2. **GEOGRAPHY** How does physical environment affect the way people in different cultures meet their basic needs?
3. **CULTURE** Give an example of how each of the following has shaped culture in the United States: physical environment, cultural diffusion, technology.
4. **CRITICAL THINKING** Study the information on pages 665–668 in the Minipedia—Highlights in the History of Communication. What developments in communication are important in your life? Why?
5. **ACTIVITY** Look around your house and list five items that come from other countries. Compare your list with other students' lists.

■ *Students may describe developments in transportation, communication, or other technologies that affect their daily lives.*

CLOSE

Read the Thinking Focus aloud. For each of the three categories—physical environment, social interaction, and technology—have students write newspaper headlines that describe examples of cultural changes discussed in the lesson. An example might be, "Solar Telephone Makes Use of Saudi Sunshine," or "Spaniards Introduce Horse to North America." Have students share their headlines with the class.

Answers to Review Questions

1. Students should indicate that factors of physical environment, including land and water, living things, and climate, influence cultures.
2. Different natural environments create differences in the ways people meet their needs for food, clothing, and shelter.
3. Possible answers: physical environment—many people in the southwestern United States spend much of the year indoors to avoid the desert heat; cultural diffusion—horses and sheep, brought to Mexico by the Spaniards, spread to the cultures of American Indians; technology—the invention of the car resulted in more leisure time spent traveling.
4. Students should provide examples of ways in which advances in communication, for example the telephone and computers, have affected their own lives.
5. Students should recognize that many cultures of the world trade with one another.

Homework Options

Have students approach a parent, grandparent, or other older relative and ask how that relative spent his or her free time as a child. Have students take notes on the information provided.

Study Guide: page 2

UNDERSTANDING FACT, JUDGMENT, AND OPINION

This skills feature teaches students how to identify and distinguish between the facts, reasoned judgments, and opinions that they encounter in reading.

HISTORY

Critical Thinking

Ask students what might happen if a historian were not able to distinguish between fact, reasoned judgment, and opinion. (*The historian might get the wrong impression about historical events and pass on the wrong information to others.*)

UNDERSTANDING FACT, JUDGMENT, AND OPINION

Evaluating Information

Here's Why

People learn about the past in many different ways. Written records, fossils, artifacts, and oral traditions are all keys to the past. By gathering and evaluating these sources, historians form their ideas about past events.

As you study the past, you also need to evaluate historical evidence. To do this, you must be able to tell the difference between facts, reasoned judgments, and opinions.

Look at the picture below of the gigantic stone statues found on Easter Island. This island is located in the Pacific Ocean about 2,300 miles west of Chile.

The Polynesian name for Easter Island is Rapa Nui *(rah puh NOO ee).* Its Chilean name is Isla de Pascua *(EEZ lah day PAHS kwah).*

The statues, called *moai (MOH eye),* were made hundreds of years ago. Suppose you read an account of how these statues were made. How would you know whether or not to believe the account?

Here's How

To decide whether information is accurate, look for facts, reasoned judgments, and opinions. An interpretation that depends on facts and reasoned judgments is likely to be correct. An explanation that offers only opinions has little value.

Read "The Easter Island Story" on page 19. It contains facts, reasoned judgments, and opinions.

Objective

Demonstrate how recognizing facts, reasoned judgments, and opinions can help determine the reliability of information. (Critical Thinking 2)

Science Connection

The social studies are called social sciences because, like other sciences, they attempt to be as accurate as possible in describing facts and events. The scientific method calls for scientists to formulate a hypothesis and then carry out experiments to prove or disprove the hypothesis. Similarly, a historian studying the stone statues on Easter Island can formulate a hypothesis that stones on the island were moved by using logs as levers. However, experimentation will not prove the hypothesis. It will only prove that the hypothesis is possible or not possible. The historian must present the idea as a reasoned judgment, not as fact.

EASTER
ISLAND

A fact is a statement that can be proven. There are many forms of proof. The archaeologists' findings can be proof, or they can come from written sources or direct observation.

Find the statement highlighted in blue in "The Easter Island Story." This statement is a fact because there is proof that it is true. Photographs and other records show the statues and the stone picks that archaeologists found at the volcano.

A reasoned judgment is a statement that is based on fact but has not been proven. Key words such as *probably, perhaps,* and *possibly* can help you identify reasoned judgments.

The statement highlighted in pink is a reasoned judgment. It explains how the statues may have been lifted onto their platforms. Can you find the facts that support this idea? They directly follow the reasoned judgment. People on Easter Island tested this idea in the 1950s. Using three logs as levers and piled stones, they lifted a 25-ton statue. Yet it has not been proven that the statues' makers used logs as levers. It only has been shown that this is possible.

An opinion is a statement of personal preference, feelings, or ideas. Words such as *think* and *feel* often indicate that a statement is an opinion. The statement highlighted in green is an opinion. It tells you how the writer feels about the statues.

Try It

Look again at "The Easter Island Story." Find a fact, a reasoned judgment, and an opinion. Be sure to choose examples that have not been discussed already.

Apply It

Listen to a newscast or read a newspaper or a magazine article. Record one fact, one reasoned judgment, and one opinion. Point out any key words that helped you identify the types of statements.

The Easter Island Story

I think the *moai* of Easter Island are exciting artifacts. They are certain to interest people in the future.

Islanders used stone picks to carve the *moai* from the rock of the extinct volcano Rano Raruku. Both inside and outside of the crater, archaeologists have found many unfinished statues and thousands of stone picks. All of the *moai* are made of a yellow-gray stone called tuff. The tuff comes from the crater walls of Rano Raruku.

The islanders probably dragged the statues from the volcano to the places where they stand now. In the 1950s people from Easter Island tested this idea. They found that it took 180 people to pull a medium-sized statue!

The people who built the statues probably used log levers to lift the statues onto their platforms. Trees grow on the island today. By studying pollen deposits, scientists have learned that there were trees on the island in the past. Also, people in other times and places have used logs for the same purpose.

GEOGRAPHY

Map and Globe Skills

Tell students that Easter Island is one of a scattered group of islands, located in the eastern and southeastern Pacific Ocean and known as Polynesia, which is marked by New Zealand in the south, Hawaii in the north, and Easter Island in the east. Have students look at a map and locate Polynesia and Easter Island. Explain to students that most people on Easter Island speak Polynesian. The rest speak Spanish, because the land of Easter Island is claimed by Chile.

Answers to Try It

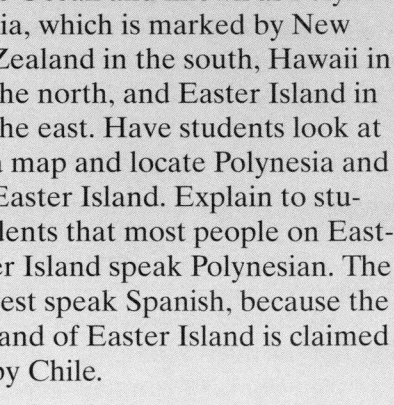

Facts: Islanders used stone picks.
The *moai* are made of tuff.
Tuff comes from the crater walls of Rano Raruku.
In the 1950s it took 180 people to pull a statue.
Trees grow on the island today.
Trees grew on the island in the past.
Reasoned judgment: The islanders probably dragged the statues from the volcano.
Opinion: The *moai* are certain to interest people in the future.

Answers to Apply It

Words that might indicate a reasoned judgment are *believe* and *probably,* when they are linked with factual information. Words like *good, best, think,* or *feel* might be used with opinions. Students' analyses of articles or newscasts should focus on the writers or broadcasters, their purposes, and the amount of factual information connected with their statements.

Visual Learning

Have students look at the picture of the stone statues on page 18. What impression do the statues give students? What kind of facial expressions do the statues have? Point out that the islanders must have valued the statues to make so many and to move them when they are so large and heavy. Allow students to speculate about why the statues were moved.

INTRODUCE

Explain to students that there are many ways of learning about cultures, including firsthand experience, the media and the arts, and various kinds of studies called the social sciences. Read the Thinking Focus, and ask students to imagine different ways they might learn about cultures. Have them read the lesson to find out more about how people learn about culture.

Key Terms

Vocabulary Strategies: T36–T37

media—means of communicating ideas to many people at once, including newspapers, magazines, radio, and television

ethnic group—a group of people who share a common cultural heritage

anthropologist—an expert in the science that studies how people live as cultural groups

prejudice—a dislike or distrust of certain people simply because they are different

racism—acting to deliberately hurt a whole group of people because they look different

L E S S O N 3

How Do We Learn about Culture?

THINKING FOCUS

How do people learn about their own and other cultures?

On your paper, write the answers to the "culture test" below.

1. *Look both ways before you ___ ___ ___.*
2. *___ your hands before you eat.*
3. *The Pilgrims and Native Americans celebrated the first ___.*

Check your answers with the ones below.

The answers are:

1. *cross the street*
2. *Wash*
3. *Thanksgiving*

How did you do?

Key Terms

- media
- ethnic group
- anthropologist
- prejudice
- racism

Our Own Culture

In schools all over the United States, students know the answers to these questions. How did so many people learn the same answers to the same questions?

From the time people are born, they begin to learn about their culture. Knowledge about one's culture usually begins with the family. When a mother puts a spoon into the hand of her two-year-old child, she learns that, in her culture, people eat with spoons. Her family doesn't use chopsticks or eat with the fingers.

Perhaps the child plays with other children in her neighborhood

➤ *A young African American girl studies a mural depicting U. S. history.*

Objectives

1. Understand how people learn about their own culture and other cultures.
2. Explain how anthropologists study cultures.
3. Appreciate the value of all cultures.

Graphic Overview

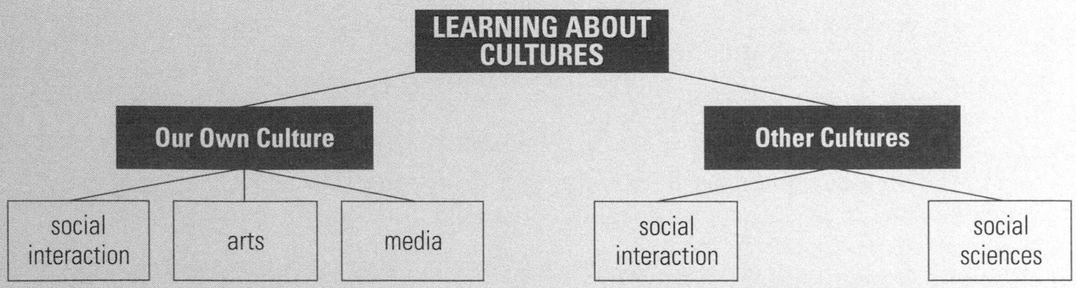
LEARNING ABOUT CULTURES
Our Own Culture
Other Cultures
social interaction
arts
media
social interaction
social sciences

◄ *Children everywhere learn much about their culture from family members. Here a six-year-old girl talks with her great-grandmother.*

or goes to daycare. Through these experiences, she learns what behavior is acceptable. For example, she learns to wait her turn. At about five years of age, she starts school. There she learns to read and write her language.

Meanwhile, the community around her also teaches her about her culture. The crossing guard teaches her to use the crosswalk. The food that is offered in local restaurants reveals the foods of her culture. She sees the ways nearby stores decorate for special days such as Halloween and Thanksgiving. Everywhere she goes, she learns about the customs, institutions, beliefs, and values of her community.

Culture is also learned through the media and the arts. Every time you decide you want your hair cut like the model's in a magazine ad or you want to see a movie advertised on television, you are being influenced by the media. Through the **media,** including newspapers, magazines, radio, and television, ideas are communicated to many people at once. The arts also teach culture. The girl in the picture on page 20 is looking at a mural showing scenes of U.S. history. ■

■ *How do the media teach you about your culture?*

Other Cultures

You have read that people learn about their own culture through social interaction that begins at birth. People can learn about other cultures through social interaction with different ethnic groups. An **ethnic group** is a group of people who share a common cultural heritage. There are many ethnic groups in the United States: for example, Chinese Americans and Swedish Americans. In Chapter 11 you will read about ethnic groups in Mali, including the Bambara and the Fulani. By interacting with members of other ethnic groups, it is possible to learn firsthand about their customs and beliefs.

Culture and the Social Sciences

People in school learn about cultures by studying the social sciences, the basis of social studies. The social sciences, including geography, history, economics, sociology, and political science, all teach about culture. Geography, for example, provides a look at how physical environment helps shape culture. The study of history also provides valuable clues to solving

▼ *African Americans celebrate Kwanza, a holiday based on the African festival of the harvest of the first crops. The celebration combines discussions of African American goals and ideals with African practices. People enjoy African foods, dancing, music, and ceremonies honoring ancestors.*

DEVELOP

Tell students that we learn about our own culture as we go about our daily lives, often without realizing that we are learning. When we are young, we assume that the culture we grow up in is simply the way things are everywhere. As we grow older, we realize that there are many other ways of doing things. Ask students why they think it might be valuable to study other cultures. *(Students may offer any of these answers: we gain new ideas; we are able to understand points of view that are different from our own; we get to know ourselves better and see what is unique about our own culture.)*

■ *Students might answer that the media give them ideas about how to dress and behave, what to eat, what to buy, what government should and should not do, and so on.*

Access Strategy

Ask how many students take music lessons. How many play sports? How many have ever been taught a game or a skill by an adult? Tell students that in addition to their parents and teachers, many people take on a teaching role in their lives and pass on cultural information. Now ask how many students listen to the radio, read magazines, or watch television. How many sometimes eat in restaurants? By now all students should have raised their hands. Explain that cultural information is all around us. It is learned and reinforced every day by what we see and do. Have students make a collage of magazine photos of things in their daily life that teach them about their culture. Display the collages.

Access Activity

Have students examine the picture on page 20 without reading the caption. Ask what information the mural gives about the culture that created it. *(The people are of various origins, play drums, and live in a city or town.)* Tell students they have just learned something about the musical instruments, architecture, and people of a past culture.

Note: Expand on students' understanding of the work of an anthropologist by directing their attention to the picture and text on this page.

CULTURE

Visual Learning

Explain to students that many anthropologists experience firsthand the cultures they are studying. They collect evidence by taking part in the community life of the people. Have students name each piece of research equipment this anthropologist needs to record her experiences in the coal mine and tell what each is used for. *(Tape recorder to record noise in the mine, camera to take pictures, notebook to take notes during interviews)*

More About Coal Miners During the 1800s many coal miners lived in settlements run by mining companies. Often they were not paid in cash for their labor but in coupons that they could spend to rent company-owned houses and to buy food in company-owned stores. The company could set prices higher than the miners could afford, so the miners were always in debt to the company. In 1890, workers organized the United Mine Workers of America (UMW) to improve wages and working conditions.

A MOMENT IN TIME

An Anthropologist

9:25 A.M., November 7, 1993
Coal mine, Boone County, West Virginia

Shoulder Bag
She packs a tape recorder. As part of her study, she checks noise levels in the deep mine. She also wants to know how miners adjust to the dangers of their everyday work.

Notebook
Today she notes the tasks of coal loade
Several are teenagers. Loaders are exposed to coal dust, which causes black lung disease.

Camera
She photographs the miners both at work and after their shifts. Her articles will include pictures of union meetings and miners' ball games.

Lunch Pail
She eats underground with men and women of the day crew and totes a durable pail like theirs. They arrive before daylight and leave after dark.

Lantern
Like the miners, she checks her lantern. A b
flame means deadly ga
fumes are present. Her steel-toed boots protec
her from heavy machin
and falling rocks.

Visual Learning

Have students read the text on this page and name the dangers facing coal miners. *(The noise levels in the mine may be dangerous; miners see no daylight; coal dust may lead to black lung disease; deadly gas fumes may be present; heavy machinery and falling rocks present dangers.)*

Investigating

Have students pretend they are anthropologists studying coal miners. Direct them to write four questions that they would ask the miners in order to learn more about their lives and culture.

Collaborative Learning

Have students work in groups of three or four to research the work of an anthropologist such as Margaret Mead or the Leakeys—Louis, Mary, or Richard. Have students write a short profile of the person that includes where the anthropologist has worked; what he or she has tried to learn; what equipment has been used; and how the anthropologist has done the work. Have groups share their profiles with the class.

How Do Anthropologists Learn About People?

An anthropologist studying this scene might ask:

- What are these people doing? Why?
- How is the woman in the white dress related to the man with her?
- How does the woman feel? How do the people watching her feel?

cultural puzzles. History tells what a culture used to be like. It also tells how a culture has changed over time.

The study of economics—how a group uses its resources—adds details to the picture of its culture. So does learning about political science, the study of how political power is distributed in a group.

Perhaps the social science that adds the most to people's knowledge of other cultures is anthropology. One of the aims of this science is to study how people live as a cultural group. A person who is an expert in this science is called an **anthropologist.** In the box above, you can read some questions an anthropologist might ask when studying a group of people. To learn more about the work of an anthropologist, see A Moment in Time on page 22.

The Value of Each Culture

As people learn more about other cultures, they learn to recognize the value of each one. Without this knowledge and understanding, negative prejudices can develop. This kind of **prejudice** is a dislike or a distrust of certain people simply because they are different.

Sometimes, this prejudice grows beyond dislike or distrust. It turns into something far worse, called racism. **Racism** means disliking or distrusting people because they belong to a different group than you do.

As you will read in this book, the earth is home to different peoples with long and amazing histories. Learning to understand and value other cultures is a way of learning to live on the planet all people share. ■

■ *How do the social sciences help people learn about cultures?*

REVIEW

1. **FOCUS** How do people learn about their own and other cultures?
2. **CULTURE** How do geography, history, economics, and political science teach people about culture?
3. **CULTURE** Explain how an anthropologist can learn about a culture by living among its members.
4. **CRITICAL THINKING** Why is it important to learn about other cultures?
5. **WRITING ACTIVITY** Imagine you are an anthropologist studying the classroom behavior of students in your school. Spend your next class observing other students. Jot down your observations. For example, do students raise their hands to answer questions? Do students sit in chairs? Then write a short paragraph describing the cultural details you observed.

ETHICS

Critical Thinking

Point out that prejudice is prejudging someone, judging what they are like before knowing them. Ask how studying the social sciences and learning about other cultures might help someone avoid prejudiced and racist behavior. *(The social sciences help us to understand and appreciate the value of other cultures and to see what all people have in common. They can help us to avoid judging people who are different when we know little about them.)*

CLOSE

Divide the class into three groups. Have one group compile a list of ways in which cultural information is passed on through social interaction. The second group should list ways in which the media and the arts transmit culture. Ask the third to list ways in which the social sciences help us learn about cultures. When students have finished their work, reread the Thinking Focus, and have each group share its ideas.

■ *Answers should indicate that geography, history, economics, and political science help people understand different aspects of culture. In addition, the social science of anthropology focuses on individual cultural groups.*

Answers to Review Questions

1. People learn about their own culture from their families, schools, and communities and from the media and the arts. People learn about other cultures through social interaction with different ethnic groups and by studying the social sciences.
2. Geography shows how physical environment influences culture. History tells what a culture was like in the past and how it has changed over time. Economics teaches how a people uses its resources. Political science teaches about how power is gained and distributed.
3. Anthropologists can observe and ask questions about the customs, beliefs, institutions, and other aspects of the culture.
4. Students should indicate that learning about other cultures can help prevent prejudice and racism.
5. Students' paragraphs may describe behaviors, language, and ways of interacting observed in the classroom.

Homework Options

Have students list the names of the television shows they watch in a week and identify the kinds of information and messages about their culture they get from each of the shows.

Study Guide: page 4

Chapter Review

Reviewing Key Terms

anthropologist (p. 23)	institution (p. 7)
belief (p. 8)	media (p. 21)
cultural diffusion (p. 15)	prejudice (p. 23)
culture (p. 5)	racism (p. 23)
custom (p. 6)	social interaction (p. 14)
environment (p. 12)	technology (p. 16)
ethnic group (p. 21)	value (p. 9)

A. Write a definition for each of the following key terms. Then give an example of each one, based on your own knowledge and experience.

1. custom
2. ethnic group
3. belief
4. institution
5. value
6. media

B. Write the key term that is suggested by each of the following groups of words. Then explain how each group of words relates to the key term.

1. climate, neighborhood
2. conversations, meetings
3. farm machinery, computers
4. language, religion, recreation, arts

C. Explain the relationship between the key terms in each of the following pairs.

1. prejudice, racism
2. social interaction, cultural diffusion
3. belief, value
4. anthropologist, culture
5. environment, technology

Exploring Concepts

A. On your own paper, copy and complete the outline below. Then use it to write a summary of the chapter. For each main idea, write a short paragraph.

I. Culture is the way of life of a people.
  A. Customs
  B. Institutions
  C.
II. Cultures develop and change.
  A.
  B. Social interaction
    1.
    2.
  C.
III. We learn about culture.
  A. Our own culture
  B. Other cultures
    1.
    2.
  C.

B. Answer each question with information from the chapter or a dictionary.

1. In what ways are people of all cultures alike?
2. List at least eight parts of culture that are common to most cultures.
3. Give two examples of ways in which cultures differ.
4. The English language, as it is spoken in the United States, has become enriched with words from many cultures. Explain how this growth of language is an example of cultural diffusion. Then look up each of the following words in an English dictionary: *gumbo, pinto, skunk, kayak.* Identify the word's origin. Then write a brief definition.
5. Technology and invention have also introduced new words and phrases into the English language. Look up the following examples: *motel, turbo, database, sandwich, braille, dahlia.* Tell how the words were created and what they mean.

Answers to Reviewing Key Terms

A. Sample answers:
1. A **custom** is a way of doing something, such as celebrating a holiday, that is accepted by a cultural group.
2. An **ethnic group** is a group of people who share a common cultural heritage, such as Germans and French Canadians.
3. A **belief** is something a person holds to be true, such as a belief in God.
4. An **institution** is an organization, such as a government, created by a people to do what one member could not do alone.
5. A **value** is a belief about the right way to live and behave, such as honesty.
6. **Media** are all means of mass communication, such as newspapers and television.

B. Sample answers:
1. **Environment.** Things that occur in a person's surroundings.
2. **Social interaction.** Forms of communication among people.
3. **Technology.** Examples of tools that help shape culture.
4. **Culture.** Aspects of culture.

C. Sample answers:
1. **Prejudice** is dislike of certain people simply because they are different. When prejudice grows, it can turn into something far worse called **racism.**
2. **Social interaction** among members of different cultures may lead to **cultural diffusion.**
3. A **value** is a **belief** about the right way to live and to behave.
4. An **anthropologist** is a scientist who studies how the people of a **culture** live.
5. **Technology** is part of the **environment,** or people's surroundings.

Answers to Exploring Concepts

A. Sample outline: I. C. Beliefs II. A. Physical environment B. 1. Within a culture 2. Among cultures, leads to cultural diffusion C. Technology III. B. 1. Interaction with other ethnic groups 2. Social sciences C. Recognizing the value of each culture

B. Sample answers:
1. People of all cultures have the same basic needs for food, clothing, and shelter.
2. These include language, arts, work, beliefs, education, family, shelter, government, and technology.
3. Possible answers include differences in foods, clothing, and ceremonies.
4. *Gumbo* is the Bantu (African) word for okra, an ingredient for a soup. *Pinto* is a Spanish word for "spotted." In English, a pinto is a white horse with dark spots. *Skunk* is an Algonquin (Native American) word for a small black and white mammal. *Kayak* is an Inuit word for a canoe-like boat.
5. *Motel,* an overnight reststop, is a combination of *motor* and *hotel. Turbo,* an engine driven by a turbine, is short for "turbosupercharger." *Database,* a term taken from the computer field, means a large collection of information. John Montagu, the fourth earl of Sandwich, asked his servant to make him a dinner (a *sandwich*) that he could eat without silverware. *Braille,* a reading system for the visually impaired, was named after Louis Braille. A *dahlia,* named after botanist A. Dahl, is a flower with large blooms.

Reviewing Skills

1. Guglielmo Marconi received the world's first transatlantic radio message in 1901. How do you know that this statement is a fact?
2. We believe that the cricket's song heralds the coming of spring. What key words tell you that this statement is an opinion?
3. Social scientists think that the family is perhaps the oldest institution. Is this statement a fact, a reasoned judgment, or an opinion? Explain your answer.
4. Customs vary from culture to culture. How do you know that this statement is a fact? Use examples to support your answer.
5. Imagine that you are observing the scene in the picture on page 23. First, you write an exact description of what you see in the picture. Then, you write a statement about what is probably happening in the picture. Finally, you write your feelings and thoughts about the picture. What three types of information are you writing down?

Using Critical Thinking

1. The word *prejudice* contains two Latin word parts: *pre-*, which means "before" and *iudicium,* which means "judgment." Therefore, the literal meaning of prejudice is "a judgment made before." Before what do you think the judgment is made in cases of prejudice?
2. The United States is a multicultural nation. (The word part *multi-* means "many.") What benefits and problems might a multicultural nation have? How, in your opinion, can social interaction and institutions such as schools and government work to solve some of the problems? Explain your answers.
3. Movies made in the United States are seen by people all over the world. Think of a movie you have seen that takes place in the United States. What view of our culture do you think this movie gives? In your opinion, does this movie present a true picture of our culture? Why or why not?

Preparing for Citizenship

1. **GROUP ACTIVITY** The English language, as it is spoken in the United States, contains many idioms. An idiom is a saying that has a meaning different from the meanings of the words that make it up. Such sayings include *by the way, in the meantime, on the other hand,* and *It's up to you.* Idioms are often difficult for people from other cultures to understand. In a small group, make a list of as many of these expressions as possible. Then work together to write definitions for them.
2. **INTERVIEWING** List inventions that have changed your culture in recent years. Then interview older relatives about changes that have occurred during their lifetimes. Report your findings to the class.
3. **WRITING ACTIVITY** On page 15 you read about a change that took place in some American Indian cultures after the Spaniards came to Mexico in the 1500s. Select an American Indian culture to research. Where did the people live, and how did the physical environment shape their culture? What customs, institutions, beliefs, and values were part of the culture? How did the culture change after the arrival of new settlers? Prepare a report to share with the class.
4. **COLLABORATIVE LEARNING** Like many other institutions, a government has special buildings for its activities. With three of your classmates, give a presentation that describes a government building. Choose a building located in your state capital or in the nation's capital. Two can gather information about the building. The other two can prepare a description of the building's purpose, the groups that use it, and the activities that go on there.

Answers to Reviewing Skills

1. This statement can be proved true through written records of the event.
2. The phrase "we believe" is a signal that this is an opinion.
3. Social scientists made a reasoned judgment that the family is the oldest human institution. The claim is based on facts but has not been proved.
4. This statement can be proved through records and by direct observation. Possible examples from the chapter include marriage customs, ceremonies honoring the dead, and customary foods.
5. The three types of information are fact, reasoned judgment, and opinion, respectively.

Answers to Using Critical Thinking

1. Before knowledge, before gathering facts, before social interaction, and so on. Students should express that prejudice is based on lack of information and experience.
2. Benefits: the diffusion of new ideas and an enrichment based on sharing. Problem: prejudice. Social interaction might help to distribute information about different ethnic groups and show that all people have similar needs and feelings. Institutions might solve some of the problems through educational programs and civil rights legislation and enforcement.
3. Students should identify specific films and describe views of our culture that they think the films present. Students should also give reasons why they think these views are or are not accurate.

Answers to Preparing for Citizenship

1. **GROUP ACTIVITY** You may wish to provide assistance in the listing of other U.S. idioms, including current slang.
2. **INTERVIEWING** Stimulate discussion by suggesting that students consider advances in communication, transportation, computer science, medicine, educational materials, food preparation, and so on. Provide ample time for the sharing of interview reports. Have students speculate on how family life might have been different, for example, before television.
3. **WRITING ACTIVITY** Reports should indicate a thorough attempt to research a Native American culture. Discuss how social interaction, cultural diffusion, and environmental factors caused the culture to change.
4. **COLLABORATIVE LEARNING** Students might select the White House, the Pentagon, or the Capitol building, for example. Or they might choose a local court or town hall.

CHAPTER ORGANIZER

Chapter 2 Exploring Geography

CHAPTER PLANNING CHART

Pupil's Edition	Teacher's Edition	Ancillaries
Lesson 1: Location and Place (1–2 days) Objective 1: Identify two ways to describe location. (Geography 1) Objective 2: Describe at least two characteristics of place. (Geography 2)	• Graphic Overview (28) • Access Strategy (29) • Access Activity (29) Critical Thinking (30) Reader's Theater (30)	Study Guide (5) Map Activities (1) • Study Prints (2)
Lesson 2: Interaction (2–3 days) Objective 1: Show how people interact with the natural world. (Geography 3; History 7) Objective 2: Describe positive and negative effects of human interaction with the natural world. (Geography 3)	• Graphic Overview (32) • Access Strategy (33) • Access Activity (33) Map and Globe Skills (34) Geographic Context (34)	Study Guide (6) Discovery Journal (4) Map Activities (2)
Making Decisions: Where Should We Put Our Trash? Objective 1: Understand the developments of waste disposal throughout time, as well as the pros and cons of various methods of disposal. (History 1; Culture 1; Social and Political Systems 2) Objective 2: Identify and decide on the best means of waste disposal. (Geography 5: Economics 5; Critical Thinking 3)		Discovery Journal (5)
Lesson 3: Movement (1–2 days) Objective 1: Give at least two examples of migration. (Geography 4) Objective 2: Explain why people move. (Geography 4)	• Graphic Overview (38) • Access Strategy (39) • Access Activity (39) • Visual Learning (40) Producing a Newspaper (40)	Study Guide (7) Discovery Journal (6) Map Activities (3)
Lesson 4: Regions (2–3 days) Objective 1: Define *region.* (Geography 3, 4, 5) Objective 2: Compare at least two different types of regions. (Geography 4, 5)	• Graphic Overview (42) • Access Strategy (43) • Access Activity (43) Study Skills (44) Political Context (44)	Study Guide (8) Map Activities (4)
Understanding Thematic Maps Objective: Compare thematic maps to learn about regions. (Map and Globe Skills 1)	Research (46) Map and Globe Skills (47)	Study Guide (9) Map Activities (5, 6) Transparency (1)
Chapter Review	Answers (48–49)	Tests (5–8)

* Objectives are correlated to the strands and goals in the program Scope and Sequence on pages T41–T49.

• LEP appropriate resources. (For additional strategies, see pages T32–T33.)

CHAPTER RATIONALE

At each stop on their journey through world cultures, students will examine the role of geography in culture. Chapter 2 prepares students to understand this role by describing the five basic themes of geography—location, place, interaction, movement, and regions.

Lesson 1 defines geography as the study of the earth and the relationship of people with the earth. The lesson then introduces location and place as the descriptive tools of geography that students can use to locate places and to describe the physical and human features of those places. To help students apply what they learn, they are asked to describe the location and features of places near them.

Lesson 2 focuses on the interaction of people with the earth. The aim of the lesson is to give students a sense of the earth as a resource. Examples such as the use of irrigation and deforestation show students not only how humans use and adapt to the world, but also the consequences of human actions for the physical environment.

Lesson 3 explores another aspect of the relationship of people with the earth, that is, the movement of goods, services, people, and ideas around the world. Examples in the text help students understand the causes and effects of human movement.

To study the earth and to understand the relationship of people to the earth, geographers choose to divide the world into regions. **Lesson 4** gives students a tool—the concept of region—for understanding the physical, political, and cultural world. The lesson introduces students to the regions that will be discussed in this book. The maps in the lesson show students how regional designations overlap.

ACTIVITIES & PROJECTS

LEP: Making a Map

Remind students that a landform is a feature on the earth's surface, such as a hill or valley. Have students make a topographical (landform) map of the land around their school. They can begin by photographing the land. Then, using the pictures as a guide, students can create a topographical map using Plasticine. (Use after Lesson 1.)

Basic: A Special-Purpose Map

Have each student create his or her own family safety map. It should include the route from home to the nearest police station, fire station, doctor's office, pharmacy, public transportation, and public telephone. (Use after Lesson 1.)

Challenge: Making Observations

Remind students that people's activities cause both positive and negative changes in the natural world. Tell students to pretend to be sleuths, or detectives, on the lookout for changes in the natural world that have been caused by people. Ask them to recall any such changes that they see as they walk or ride to school. Have them record their observations on a sheet of paper and then share their observations with the class. (Use after Lesson 2.)

Making a Wall Chart

Have students make a wall chart showing the types of regions to which their school district belongs. Categories should include political, climatic, vegetation, and landform regions. (Use after Lesson 4.)

CHAPTER PREVIEW

Read the chapter title aloud. Then direct students to the photograph of the earth on page 27. Ask them to relate the other photographs on this page and page 27 to the earth. *(Possible responses: the signpost shows places on the earth; the volcano is a physical feature on the earth; the minerals are examples of the earth's resources; the beach scene shows people on the earth.)* Note that geography has to do with the earth and its landscapes.

Looking Back

Ask students to recall the title of Chapter 1. *(Exploring Culture)* Remind students that they learned in the previous chapter that the earth is the home of many different peoples. Tell them that in this chapter they will learn more about the earth and the relationship of people to the earth.

Looking Forward

Tell students that in Chapter 2 they will read about five ideas, or themes, of geography—Location and Place, Interaction, Movement, and Regions. Lesson 1 defines geography and introduces the themes of location and place.

Chapter 2

Exploring Geography

A photograph of the earth, taken from outer space, shows a world wrapped in clouds. Close-up photographs show features of the land and evidence of the human, animal, and plant life found on earth. In this chapter you will read about how people study the earth.

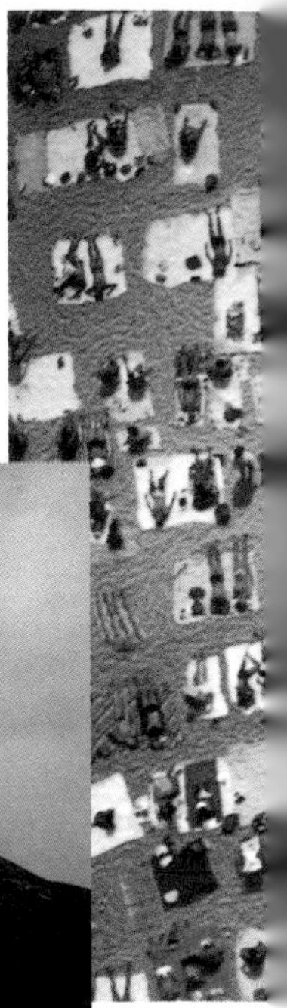

PLYMOUTH 8210
UNION FLAG
HUNGERFORD 8165 MILES
SUZANNE
WHITBY 8247 MILES
UPTON ARMS
MANCHESTER 8317
STRANRAER 8440
NEPAL 10,104
MARSHAM St 8060
TYNECASTLE PARK

Signposts in the Falkland Islands point the long way home for British troops stationed there. Great Britain rules the Falklands, which are located in the South Atlantic Ocean, about 8,000 miles from Britain.

A Hawaiian volcano erupts, sending glowing rivers of lava down its sides.

On the left you see orpiment, or arsenic trisulfide. On the right is malachite, or carbonate of copper. These are just two of the many different kinds of minerals found in the earth.

26

BACKGROUND

People have thought about the earth from the earliest times and have tried to learn more about it. Ancient Greeks, for example, were very interested in the earth and its features. The early Greek philosopher Pythagoras determined that the earth was spherical and that it orbited a ball of fire thought to be the center of the universe.

Pioneers in Geography

Strabo, a Greek geographer who lived about the time of Jesus, wrote a 17-volume work called *Geography.* Two of the volumes discuss geography in general, and the remaining 15 volumes describe various regions. In the second century A.D., the astronomer Ptolemy introduced the idea of latitude and longitude and used these imaginary lines to locate places more precisely. Arab geographers preserved much of Greek knowledge about the earth and passed on this knowledge to Europeans in the Middle Ages. The Europeans modified ancient ideas, especially those of Ptolemy, as they began exploring the world more completely in the 15th and 16th centuries.

Alexander von Humboldt, a German naturalist and writer, helped to set the stage for modern geography. He traveled extensively, even to South and Central America; made observations on a wide range of topics, including altitude, climate, vegetation, population, and use of resources; and used the best instruments available to make measurements and locate places.

People enjoy a day at the beach in Atlantic City, New Jersey.

This photograph of the earth was taken in April 1972 by the spacecraft *Apollo 16.*

Fossils are the remains or imprints of ancient animals and plants. At the right is a fossil trilobite, an ancient marine animal. At the left are fern fossils.

Understanding the Visuals

Apollo 16, which took this photo of the earth from outer space, was part of the lunar mission begun in 1961. The object of the Apollo program was to land astronauts on the moon. The landing was accomplished by *Apollo 11* on July 20, 1969, when Neil A. Armstrong and Edwin E. Aldrin, Jr., became the first people to set foot on the moon. Later Apollo flights also brought astronauts to the moon. *Apollo 16* returned to the earth with lunar rocks and soil.

Fossils, such as those pictured here, are the main source of information about the history of life on the earth. Yet only a very small number of early organisms are preserved in the form of fossils. Generally, to become fossilized, an organism must be buried rapidly, before it begins to decompose, and it must have hard parts that can be preserved. Most fossils are preserved in water environments, such as at the bottom of the sea.

27

Modern Study of the Earth

In North America, President Thomas Jefferson, who had a keen interest in geography, sent Meriwether Lewis and William Clark on an expedition to explore the western territory gained as part of the Louisiana Purchase in 1803. They returned with maps and information about the region. Later surveys of the West excited a great interest in the geography of the United States. In the 20th century many universities throughout the country began to include geography as a program of study.

Geographers around the world have different interests, depending on their country's needs and traditions. In addition to working in more traditional areas such as cartography (map making), geographers today are actively involved in identifying and trying to solve the problems that people have created on the earth, such as pollution, overpopulation, and the destruction of fragile environments.

INTRODUCE

Read the Thinking Focus aloud. Then write the key term *geography* on the chalkboard. Explain that the term comes from the two Greek words *geo,* meaning "of the earth," and *graphein,* meaning "to write." Together they mean "to write about, or study, the earth." Next, write the five themes of geography on the chalkboard—location, place, interaction, movement, and regions. Have students read the lesson to find out more about geography and its themes.

Key Terms

Vocabulary Strategies: T36–T37

geography—the study of the earth and the relationship of people with the earth

landform—a feature on the earth's surface

latitude—a place's distance north or south of the equator

longitude—a place's distance east or west of the prime meridian

L E S S O N 1

Location and Place

THINKING FOCUS

What is geography, and what are its five themes?

Key Terms

- geography
- landform
- latitude
- longitude

Jenny was dreaming. In her dream she was walking along a strange street. Yet much of what she saw was familiar to her. She could tell she was in a city because she saw tall buildings crowded along the sidewalk and dozens of people hurrying past her. She saw a school and a church. She crossed a bridge over a wide river.

Yet some things in this city were not familiar to Jenny. Many of the buildings seemed to be hundreds of years old—much older than the buildings in most U.S. cities. The flags flying from storefronts showed thick stripes of blue, white, and red—not the thin red and white stripes and white stars on blue that make up the U.S. flag.

Do you recognize the city in Jenny's dream? Perhaps the pictures here can help you name it.

All the things Jenny saw in her dream help describe a place: Paris, France. This place has a location. Location and place are two important ways people who study the earth organize information about it. Other important ways are human interaction with the earth; movement of people, goods, and ideas across the earth; and regions of the earth. Location, place, interaction, movement, and regions are known as the five themes of geography.

L'EXPRESS
marie claire
Maison
LOUVRE

➤ *Look closely at these objects. Do you recognize the language that appears on the magazines and the menus? Do you recognize the small souvenir tower at the far right? These objects bring to mind a particular place. Do you know what the place is?*

Objectives

1. Identify two ways to describe location.
2. Describe at least two characteristics of place.

Graphic Overview

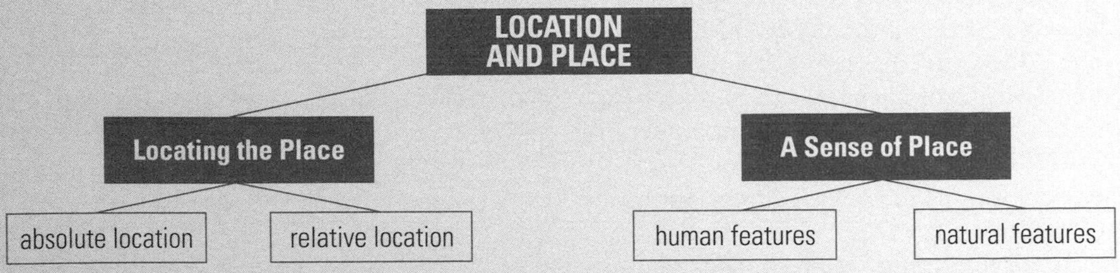
LOCATION AND PLACE
Locating the Place
A Sense of Place
absolute location
relative location
human features
natural features

Locating the Place

Geography is the study of the earth and the relationship of people with the earth. Geography describes physical features of the earth such as the plants, animals, and landforms of an area. A **landform** is a feature on the earth's surface such as a hill, plain, or valley. Geography also looks at how the earth supplies basic human needs for food, clothing, and shelter. In addition, geography explores how people use the earth and how they affect the environment.

Locating places is an important part of geography. Geographers describe location in two ways—absolute location and relative location. Absolute location is identified by a specific address or a point on a map. Relative location is found by looking at where places are in relation to one another.

◄ *The Eiffel Tower is named after Alexandre Eiffel, the engineer who designed it. The tower is an iron framework, 984 feet high. It was completed in 1889.*

A Point on a Map

Using a map is one way to find the location of a place. However, a map usually shows a large area with many places. How can you find one particular place on a map? Mapmakers crisscross maps with two sets of imaginary lines that divide up the map. One set of lines circles the earth east and west, like the equator. These are lines of **latitude.** All lines of latitude are parallel with one another—they never meet. Lines of latitude are measured in degrees (°). The latitude of a place is its distance north or south of the equator.

The other set of lines circles the earth to meet at the North and South poles. These lines, or meridians, of **longitude** are also measured in degrees (°). The longitude of a place is its distance east or west of the prime meridian, a line of longitude that runs through Greenwich, England.

Together, the lines of latitude and longitude create a grid that breaks up a map into smaller parts. The picture of the globe on page 30 shows lines of latitude and longitude. Every place on the earth can be described through the use of latitude and longitude. The absolute location of a place is the point where a specific degree of latitude crosses

CAFE DE FLORE

DEVELOP

Explain that in Lesson 1, students will learn about two of the five themes of geography—location and place. Then draw the framework for the Graphic Overview on the chalkboard. Ask students to fill in details about location and place as they read.

GEOGRAPHY

Map and Globe Skills

Display a large map of the United States or have students turn to the map of North America on page 686 of the Atlas. Then name cities labeled on the map and have students locate each one in two ways: by identifying the place's latitude and longitude, and by describing what the place is near. Sample cities might include Paris, New York, Manila, and Nairobi. For additional help on how to read latitude and longitude, ask students to turn to page G5 in the Map and Globe Handbook. Tell students that they should estimate, or figure out as closely as possible, the latitude and longitude of a place that is not located on the lines shown on the map.

Access Strategy

Have students work in small groups to identify human and natural features of places. Set out a box labeled Human and Natural Features. Give each group old magazines and newspapers, cardboard or poster board, and paste. Tell students to look in the magazines and newspapers for pictures of human and natural features of places. Students should cut out the pictures and paste them on cardboard, label the back of each one Human or Natural, and deposit each picture in the box. Check that the pictures in the box have been correctly identified. Then number the back of each. Finally, hold up each picture and say its number. On a sheet of paper, students should write the number and then *H* or *N* to identify the picture as a human or natural feature. Note that some features, like certain crops and flowers, while natural, have been introduced by people. Discuss whether these should be labeled as human or natural.

Access Activity

Help students understand the terms *absolute location* and *relative location* by asking them where they live. If a student responds with an address, say, "That tells me the exact location, or *absolute location,* of where you live." If a student names places nearby, say, "That tells me what is near where you live, or the *relative location.*"

■ *One way to identify the location of a place is by using latitude and longitude or a street address; the other is to describe the location relative to a known place.*

GEOGRAPHY

Study Skills

Have students write a sense-of-place puzzler about a place of their own choice or one assigned by you. The puzzler should give hints about the place and describe characteristics that make the place unique. Tell students to include at least two natural features and two human features as hints. *(Example: flat plains, fertile soil, large farms, often called "America's breadbasket"; answer: the midwestern United States)* Suggest that students use encyclopedias, travel brochures, or magazines such as *National Geographic* from the school or public library to gather information. Post the puzzlers on a bulletin board so that the whole class may read them and take a guess.

one of longitude. You can read more about using latitude and longitude on page G5 in the Map and Globe Handbook.

■ *Describe two ways to identify the location of a place.*

What Are You Near?

Relative location tells where one place is in relation to another. Giving directions is one way to explain relative location. For example, you might tell a friend how to get to your house from the school that she attends.

A map can also show relative location. The map of a Paris neighborhood on page 31 shows the location of places in relation to one another. ■

A Sense of Place

Location tells you where you are. Paris, for example, is located 49 degrees north of the equator and 2 degrees east of the prime meridian. This doesn't tell you very much about Paris, however. You are probably more interested in its sights—the special buildings, the river, and the stores. All these features give you a sense of place.

When they are describing a certain place—a valley, a desert, a house, a school, a village, a city, or any other place on earth—geographers talk about both the human features and the natural features of this place.

A Human Place

In her dream Jenny recognized a school and a church. She walked along crowded streets and over a bridge. All of these things were built by people. All are human features of Paris. These features illustrate how people affect a place.

➤ *This photograph, taken from the air, shows the city of Paris, France.*

Critical Thinking

Ask students to make two lists: one of the human features in their neighborhood and the other of the natural features. Then ask whether they would prefer to live in a place with more human features, more natural features, or a mix of both. Be sure that they support their point of view.

Reader's Theater

Travel writing is a type of literature that creates a sense of place through words. Students may enjoy giving oral readings from this genre. Bring in books from the school or public library for them to choose from. Possible choices include Sonia Levitan, *Journey to America;* Jean Fritz, *Homesick, My Own Story;* Karen Branson, *Street of Gold;* Madeleine L'Engle, *The Moon by Night;* Roger Lea MacBride, ed., *West from Home: Letters of Laura Ingalls Wilder.* Easy: Pat Brisson, *Kate Heads West.* Challenging: William Least Heat Moon, *Blue Highways.* Recommend that students introduce the passage they have selected by explaining why it appealed to them.

You may find some of the human features of Paris in a city near you, too. Other human features such as the religions practiced, the flags flown, and the languages spoken help make a city—or any area—unique.

A Place in Nature

The place in Jenny's dream also included a river. This river, the Seine, is a natural, or physical, feature of Paris. You can see the Seine flowing through the heart of Paris in the photograph on page 30. Altitude—or the height of a place, usually above sea level—is a physical feature. The land on which Paris is built is about 250 feet above sea level. The climate of an area is also a physical feature. Parisians enjoy a climate with comfortable temperatures and moderate rainfall most of the year.

Both the human features and the physical features found around the world vary dramatically. Housing—a human feature—varies from igloos used as temporary hunting shelters in northern Canada to towering concrete, glass, and steel skyscrapers in Houston, Texas. Climate—a physical feature—ranges from always hot in the tropics to always cold at the poles.

Physical features and human features also change. In 200 years transportation systems in the United States have changed from horses, wagons, and canoes to cars, trains, and planes. The Sahel is a physical feature you read about in Chapter 1. Because of recent periods of little rain, the Sahel is changing as it slowly becomes absorbed by the expanding Sahara. ■

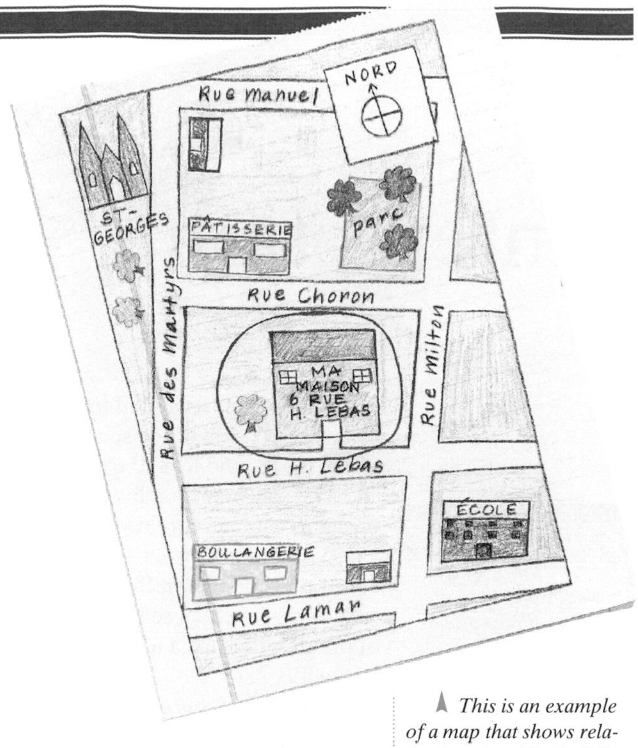

NORD
Rue manuel
ST-GEORGES
PATISSERIE
parc
Rue Chonon
Rue des Martyrs
Rue milton
MA MAISON 6 RUE H. LEBAS
Rue H. Lebas
ECOLE
BOULANGERIE
Rue Laman

▲ *This is an example of a map that shows relative location. The building in the center of the map is labeled* ma maison, *which means "my house." The map shows where this house is located in relation to other places, including a church, and a school* (école).

■ *What two kinds of features are used to describe a place?*

REVIEW

1. **FOCUS** What is geography, and what are its five themes?
2. **GEOGRAPHY** How do lines of latitude and longitude divide the world into a grid?
3. **GEOGRAPHY** Describe two human features and two physical features found where you live.
4. **CULTURE** List three ways climate in your area affects the way you live.
5. **CRITICAL THINKING** Draw a map of your neighborhood. Then compare it with the map of the Paris neighborhood on this page. How are the two places and maps alike? How are they different?
6. **ACTIVITY** Choose four countries from the world map on pages 678 and 679 of your text. Write down the degrees of latitude and longitude that intersect, or cross, in these countries. Then exchange papers with a classmate and take a location quiz. Use the degrees of latitude and longitude on the world map to identify the four countries.

■ *Both human and physical features are used to describe a place.*

CLOSE

Read the Thinking Focus aloud. Ask students to tell what details of location and place they added to their Graphic Overview as they read the lesson. Then on the chalkboard have students draw a street map of the neighborhood around the school to help someone locate the school and understand what makes the neighborhood unique. Have volunteers come to the board to create a street grid and label human and natural features. When the map is finished, ask others to use it to describe the school's absolute and relative locations and to name special characteristics of the school's neighborhood.

Answers to Review Questions

1. Geography is the study of the earth and the relationship of people with the earth. The five themes are location, place, interaction, movement, and regions.
2. Lines of latitude and longitude form a grid by crossing each other and dividing the map into smaller parts.
3. Answers may include buildings, transportation systems, and other human features. Physical features may include bodies of water and landforms such as mountains.
4. Students may describe ways the climate affects what they eat, what they wear, the homes they live in, and so on.
5. Students should indicate that both maps show absolute and relative location. They are different in terms of specific place locations.
6. Students should recognize the importance of latitude and longitude in determining exact location.

Homework Options

Have students use an almanac to identify and describe human and natural features such as the tallest building in the world, the busiest airport, the largest city in the world, the highest mountain, and the longest river. Have them share their findings with the rest of the class.

Study Guide: page 5

INTRODUCE

Ask students to recall the two kinds of features that describe a place. *(Human and natural features)* Explain that some human features of a place may be positive, while others may have a negative effect on the environment. Discuss both the positive and negative ways that people have affected the local community. Read the lesson title and the Thinking Focus. Then tell students that in this lesson they will learn more about the interaction of people with the environment. Interaction, or human-environmental interaction, is one of the five themes of geography.

Key Terms

Vocabulary Strategies: T36–T37
adapt—adjust
deforestation—the process of clearing forests
pollute—make dirty or contaminate
endangered—in danger of dying off
extinct—having died off

L E S S O N 2

Interaction

THINKING FOCUS

How do people interact with the natural world?

Key Terms

- adapt
- deforestation
- pollute
- endangered
- extinct

Matt stumbled to the side of the soccer field and leaned over, his hands on his knees, trying to catch his breath.

"I don't know what's so hard about playing here in Bolivia," he said to his coach. "I seem to be out of breath after just a few minutes of practice."

"Well, La Paz is one of the highest cities in the world," his coach explained. "At 12,000 feet above sea level, the air is thin. Most visitors have more trouble breathing than the people who have lived here a long time. Look out there." The coach motioned toward the mountain peaks in the distance. "Those are the tops of the Andes—and they don't even look very high from here."

Matt stood and gazed at the mountain tops. "You know, Coach, this place is really beautiful. If I had grown up here, I don't think I'd want to leave."

➤ *La Paz, Bolivia's largest city, lies on a broad stretch of high, level land in the Andes of South America. Most people who work in La Paz live on the slopes of the valley that surrounds the city.*

Adapting to Places

Certainly people can enjoy the natural beauty of their surroundings. Yet beauty is not the main factor people consider when they decide where to live. The vast deserts of Africa, for example, may appear beautiful, but few live there.

Where People Live

Most of the world's people live in places that have a comfortable climate, a source of water, fertile soil, and level areas of land. These resources help make it easy to produce food, to build homes, and to

Objectives

1. Show how people interact with the natural world.
2. Describe positive and negative effects of human interaction with the natural world.

Graphic Overview

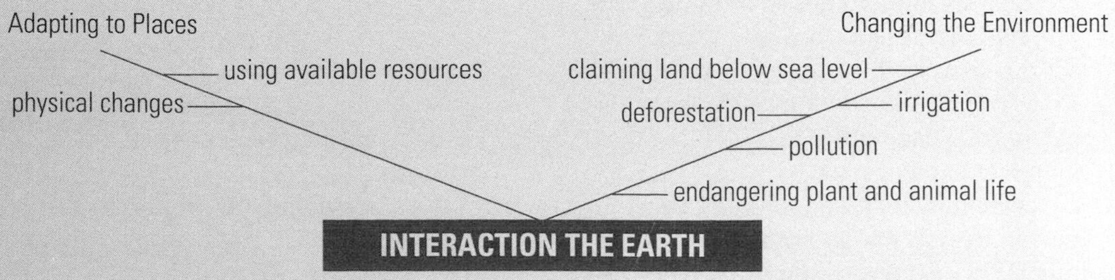
Adapting to Places
using available resources
physical changes
Changing the Environment
claiming land below sea level
irrigation
deforestation
pollution
endangering plant and animal life
INTERACTION THE EARTH

meet the needs of business and industry. In other words, people live where they can find work and meet their basic needs. Understanding Natural Resources on page 34 will tell you more.

We Adapt to Places

Some places in the world meet most human needs. For example, British settlers in the area of Sydney, Australia, found land that could support crops and sheep. The mild climate offered a sufficient growing period and enough rain to provide water for people, farms, and ranches. The nearby harbor provided a way to get goods to market. It's no wonder, then, that Sydney continues to grow and is today Australia's largest city.

Not all areas of the world answer every human need so well. Often people must **adapt**—or adjust—to an area. When pioneers decided to settle the Great Plains of the United States, they found few trees to provide lumber for housing. Yet the climate and soil of the Great Plains did meet many of their needs. So the pioneers adapted. They learned to build houses of sod—chunks of root-tangled earth cut from the land itself.

Sometimes, people's bodies can adapt to their environment. Over the years, the people of the Andes have physically adapted to the lower level of oxygen in the air. They have developed barrel-shaped chests as their hearts and lungs have increased in size. They also breathe more rapidly than people who live at lower altitudes. These physical changes allow them to take in enough oxygen. ■

■ *What factors influence where people live?*

Changing the Environment

Much of what is now the Netherlands was once underwater. The Netherlands grew because the people found a way to claim land that was below sea level. First, they built dikes. Then they drained away the seawater, uncovering soil that could be turned into rich farmland. They added thousands of square miles to their nation. This is

▼ *This photograph of Sydney was taken with a special camera lens that permits a broad view in the shape of an arc, or curve. Sydney is located in the most heavily populated area of Australia.*

DEVELOP

Explain that people interact with their environment in two ways: they either adapt, or adjust, to their environment or they try to change it. Draw the Graphic Overview on the chalkboard. Have students fill in examples of each kind of interaction as they read.

GEOGRAPHY

Social Participation

Have students work together to create a mural that shows as many examples as possible of how people interact with the natural world. Students might work in pairs on different panels of the mural. They should portray how people adapt to the climate and landscape in different locations, as well as how people use the natural world to meet their needs. Encourage students to consult outside resources such as encyclopedias and geography books from the library to make their artwork authentic.

■ *People choose to live in places where they can find work and can meet their basic needs. They may also consider natural beauty when choosing a place to settle.*

Access Strategy

Ask students to scan the photos in the lesson and explain what is going on in each. Then ask them in what ways the photos show humans interacting with the natural world. How do the types of interaction differ? Introduce the key terms of the lesson as they relate to the lesson's photos. *(For example, the photo of La Paz suggests the idea that people* adapt *to their environment; the photo of the rain forest shows the effects of* deforestation.*)*

You may wish to show students pictures in books or magazines from the school or public library that illustrate the concept of human-environmental interaction. When students understand the concept of interaction and the key terms, have them draw a picture that illustrates one of the key terms. Assemble students' drawings in a picture dictionary.

Access Activity

Ask students to describe what they have eaten that day, what they are wearing, and where they live. Ask where their food came from, why they chose to wear what they have on, and what materials were used to build their homes. Students' answers should include observations about their environment—climate, landscape, and available resources.

GEOGRAPHY

Critical Thinking

Ask students to describe how the following features and activities change the environment: dikes, irrigation canals, terracing, slash-and-burn farming, industries. Discuss the positive and negative effects of each. Under what circumstances do the positive effects of a human change in the environment outweigh the negative? When do the negative effects of a change outweigh the positive? *(Students should show an awareness of both the positive and negative effects resulting from human-environmental interaction.)*

GEOGRAPHY

Study Skills

Ask students to define the term *natural resources. (The materials that humans find in nature and use for their needs)* Give them one minute to name all the natural resources they can see from where they are sitting. *(Examples: air, trees, water, sunlight)* Should the following be considered natural resources: coal, oil, natural gas, waterfalls, wind, natural beauty? Are animals a natural resource? *(Students' answers should reflect an understanding of the definition of natural resources.)*

only one of the ways in which humans shape their environment.

Using the Land

People have found ways to use many kinds of places for farmland. Starting thousands of years ago, they have brought water from rivers and wells to dry and desert areas. People have cut into mountains and hills to create flat areas called terraces and planted crops there. From China to Peru, terracing is still practiced.

Human Impact

You have been reading about ways people interact with the environment. In this interaction, or give-and-take, between people and the environment, humans can also do harm. For example, when people first began to plant crops, they developed the slash-and-burn method. They cut down trees and plants, let them dry out, and then set fire to what remained. They farmed the cleared land until its nutrients were used up. Then the people moved on to slash and burn another area.

This farming method has been a way of life for thousands of years in parts of Africa, Central America,

➤ *The photograph at the right shows an area of rain forest that has been destroyed.*

Understanding Natural Resources

Since the beginning of time, natural forces have shaped and changed our earth. During the ice ages, massive glaciers inched across the land, carving out lakes and ponds in their paths. The powerful force of earthquakes has pushed precious metals like gold and silver up from deep inside of the earth, while reshaping the face of the earth. Wet, cold climates of northern regions have produced forests of towering trees spreading far across the land.

Nature and Human Needs

Humans have come to depend on these products of nature for their survival. Fresh water from lakes and ponds can meet the water needs of entire communities. Lumber from the trees of the north is used to make strong and sturdy houses. Oil and natural gas found deep within the earth provide energy to run factories and businesses and to heat homes. Metals such as gold, silver, and copper are used to make tools and valuable jewelry.

Resources You Use

These materials that humans find in nature and use for their needs are called natural resources. Without natural resources, life as you know it would not exist. Look around you, and you will see many examples of natural resources. A short list might include the electricity that powers your television set, the plastic (produced from oil) wrapper on your sandwich, the steel used to build your family's car, and the water that runs through your home.

Map and Globe Skills

Distribute outline maps of the United States to students or have them trace the map on page 43 on a sheet of paper. Then direct them to encyclopedias and almanacs to find information about the location of natural resources in the United States. Tell students to use the information as a guide in illustrating the location of one or two kinds of resources on their maps.

Geographic Context

Natural resources are often classified as renewable or nonrenewable. Renewable resources are living things that can reproduce themselves, such as trees. Nonrenewable resources are nonliving and cannot be replaced once they are used up. Minerals and fossil fuels such as oil and coal are nonrenewable.

This classification is not completely satisfactory, however, since technically speaking, some nonliving resources such as coal could be replaced over an extremely long period of time. Also, renewable resources would quickly become nonrenewable if the rate of use went beyond the resource's ability to reproduce in a certain period of time. Therefore, it is important to be aware of how long it takes to replace whatever amount is used of a particular resource.

Endangered Species

Endangered Species	Species Habitat	Threat	Progress Toward Saving Species
Gray bat	caves, mines, and crevices in rocks in southeastern U.S.	cave exploration, pesticides, deforestation	Population has increased greatly since 1985.
Northern Right whale	shallow ocean waters in Northern Hemisphere	hunted almost to point of extinction	Population has increased little if any since 1935.
Puerto Rican parrot	lowland forest of Puerto Rico	deforestation, logging, hunting, pet industry	A fragile population of 20–25 birds is slowly increasing.
California condor	caves and crevices in the costal moutain range of central California	pesticides and other poisons	Today there are about 60 birds in captivity.

South America, Southeast Asia, and some Pacific islands. Its limited use does not do permanent damage to the land. However, when millions of people do it, aided by giant bulldozers and cutting machines, slash-and-burn becomes a problem. Today **deforestation**—the process of clearing forests—is having a tremendous impact on the environment. For example, widespread logging and cattle ranching are destroying the rain forests of the Amazon. In the picture that appears on page 34, you can see an area of rain forest that has been cleared and burned.

Increased manufacturing the world over has also damaged the environment. Toxic, or poisonous, smoke from industry and cars fills our air. Oil spills and industrial sewage **pollute**—make dirty or unusable—our oceans. Waste dumps contain toxic materials. Even our own homes help pollute the earth, as you will see when you read Where Should We Put Our Trash? on pages 36–37.

Damage to the environment through deforestation and pollution has endangered the earth's plant and animal life. **Endangered** plant and animal species are in danger of becoming **extinct,** or dying off. Once a species has become extinct, it is gone forever. The chart on this page lists some endangered species found in the United States and Puerto Rico. ■

▲ *In 1982 scientists began a program to capture all wild California condors. The last of these wild birds was captured in 1987. Since then, several condors have been born and raised in captivity. Some condors born in captivity have been returned to the wild. Nevertheless, the future of the bird remains in doubt.*

■ *In what ways do humans shape the earth?*

REVIEW

1. **FOCUS** How do people interact with the natural world?
2. **GEOGRAPHY** What are some ways people are harming the environment?
3. **GEOGRAPHY** The radioactive waste that people create can't be thrown away because it doesn't decompose, or become part of the soil, like most other trash. So the United States is considering putting it all in one place and creating some sort of symbol that would alert everyone for thousands of years to KEEP OUT. What kind of symbol do you think would be most effective?
4. **CRITICAL THINKING** President Franklin D. Roosevelt once wrote, "The nation that destroys its soil destroys itself." What do you think he meant by this statement?
5. **ACTIVITY** Choose one of the animals listed on the Endangered Species chart on this page. Research your choice. Then write two or three paragraphs explaining what effect the extinction of this animal might have on the rest of the world. Illustrate your paragraph with a picture of the animal.

CLOSE

Read the Thinking Focus aloud. Then create and play a game called Interaction to answer the question. Divide the class into teams, and give each team three index cards. Tell the teams to think of three situations that require people to interact with the natural world. Using a different card for each situation, teams should write a short description of each situation on a card. A card might read: *You wake up to find that a foot of snow has fallen overnight. You want to make money shoveling snow.* Or: *A river separates a city from the towns where many of its workers live.* Collect the cards from each team. Then read to one of the teams a card that was created by another team. The answering team should say "adapt" or "change," depending on the situation described. This team should also explain how people might adapt to or change the environment to meet their needs in the situation.

■ *Humans shape the earth as they irrigate and clear the land, plant crops, use natural resources, and create waste.*

Answers to Review Questions

1. Students should indicate that the earth—with its varying climates, landforms, and other geographic features—shapes people's lives, and that people, through agriculture and industry, shape the environment.
2. Large-scale deforestation is destroying rain forests such as the Amazon. Wastes from industry, homes, and vehicles pollute land, water, and air.
3. Answers will vary. Students should keep in mind, however, that writing in English might not be ideal since English might not be understood thousands of years from now.
4. President Roosevelt probably meant that without fertile soil, farmers cannot grow the food needed to feed the nation. The nation will then become dependent on other nations for the most basic of needs—food.
5. Student paragraphs should indicate how the extinction would alter nature's balance.

Homework Options

Have students write a letter to the editor of a local newspaper that argues for taking measures to save an endangered animal or plant. Review students' letters and select a sampling to be read to the class by their authors. Then select one to be sent to the newspaper.

Study Guide: page 6

DECISION-MAKING PROCESS

1. Recognize the need for a decision.
2. Define the goals and values involved.
3. Acquire and evaluate necessary information.
4. Identify and analyze possible alternatives.
5. Choose the best alternative.

This Making Decisions feature, Where Should We Put Our Trash? uses Step 1 of the decision-making process.

HISTORY

Critical Thinking

Write *responsible stewardship* on the chalkboard. Note that the phrase is found in the opening quotation on this page. Explain that a steward is someone who takes care of or is in charge of things, and that stewardship is the job of taking charge of something. Have students recall from their reading ways in which people have dealt with their trash over the ages. Then have students debate which methods were examples of responsible stewardship. Stress that students should use sound reasoning to back up their points of view.

MAKING DECISIONS

Where Should We Put Our Trash?

We are running out of landfill space. More important, is the issue really "available space" or is it a question of our right to dig a hole whenever we feel the need to bury our garbage because it seems easier than the role of responsible stewardship [caretaking]?

Peter L. Grogan, president of the National Recycling Coalition

What most people don't know about landfills could fill a landfill. At the current rate, if all the nation's solid waste for the next 500 years were piled or buried in a single landfill to a depth of 100 yards, . . . this "national landfill" would require a square site less than 20 miles on a side.

Clark Wiseman, professor of economics, Gonzaga University

Background

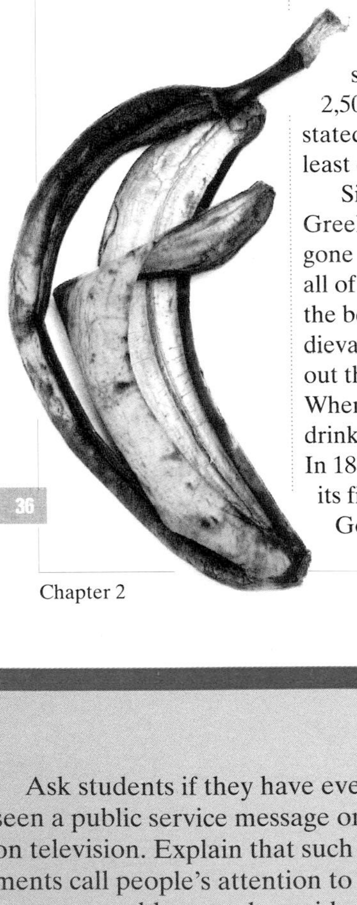

The first record of a city's plan for trash disposal comes from the Greek city-state of Athens, more than 2,500 years ago. The law simply stated that waste was to be taken at least one mile from the city.

Since the time of the ancient Greeks, the disposal of trash has gone through many changes. Not all of these changes have been for the better. City dwellers in medieval Europe simply tossed trash out their windows into the street. When the garbage seeped into the drinking water, people became sick. In 1885 the United States opened its first garbage incinerator on Governor's Island in New York City. Since then, the need for new methods of trash disposal has grown as the amount of trash has grown.

Since World War II the number of products we use once or twice and then throw away has grown considerably. The list includes disposable diapers, razors, fast-food containers, and much, much more.

In 1960 approximately 2.7 pounds of trash were discarded each day for every man, woman, and child in the United States. Today, each person in the United States discards about 4 pounds of trash per day, or one-half ton per year. This is roughly twice the amount as in Japan and Western Europe.

Objectives

1. Understand the developments of waste disposal throughout time, as well as the pros and cons of various methods of disposal.
2. Identify and decide on the best means of waste disposal.

Activity

Ask students if they have ever heard or seen a public service message on the radio or on television. Explain that such announcements call people's attention to important issues or problems and provide them with information. Tell students to write a public service announcement for broadcast entitled "Call to Decision: Where Should We Put Our Trash?" Students should use data and ideas only from this lesson in their message. Emphasize that they should recast the information in their own words, although they may quote the individuals quoted in the lesson. Encourage students to use their creativity to make their messages catchy. Have students "broadcast" their messages to the rest of the class.

Considering Alternatives

The diagram at the right shows what makes up our trash. What should we do with these waste materials? One alternative is to bury solid waste in landfills. Another is to recycle it. Products that can be recycled include glass, aluminum, paper, plastics, and vegetable waste (made into compost). A third alternative is incineration, that is, burning waste to greatly reduce its size. By 1990, U.S. residents were throwing away about 73 percent of their trash in landfills, incinerating about 14 percent, and recycling about 13 percent.

Landfills have given rise to the slogan NIMBY (Not In My Backyard). No one wants a landfill next door. Landfills are unsightly, smelly, and unsafe.

Recycling sounds like a good idea, but most communities can't afford to collect and recycle their citizens' waste. They have barely enough resources to provide police and fire protection, schools, and town dumps. In addition, industries that make new things from recycled materials are still trying to keep up with even the small amount being recycled.

Burning trash has advantages and disadvantages. Some incinerators burn waste to produce steam and electricity. In the process, however, foul odors, toxic gases, and gritty smoke are produced. In 1992 the United States had 140 waste-to-energy plants in operation. The building of more waste-to-energy plants was blocked, however, when citizens became concerned about the plants' impact on their local environments.

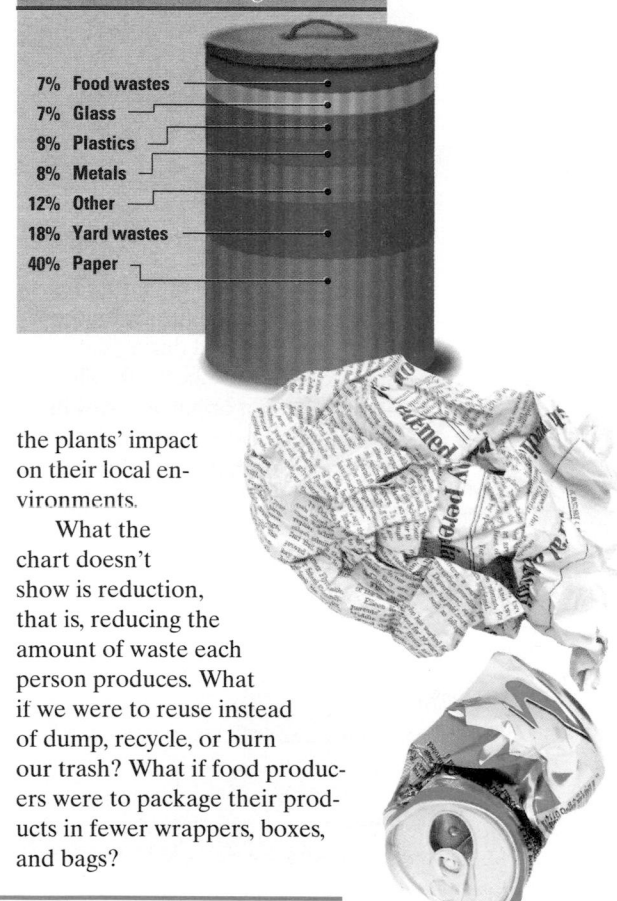

What's in Our Garbage?

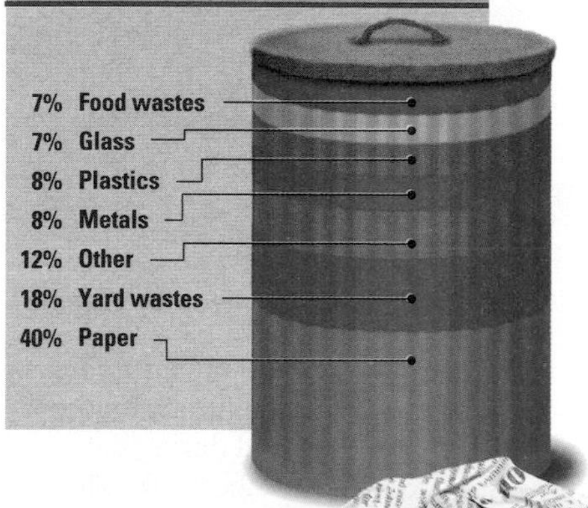

7% Food wastes
7% Glass
8% Plastics
8% Metals
12% Other
18% Yard wastes
40% Paper

What the chart doesn't show is reduction, that is, reducing the amount of waste each person produces. What if we were to reuse instead of dump, recycle, or burn our trash? What if food producers were to package their products in fewer wrappers, boxes, and bags?

Decision Point

1. What are the advantages of each kind of waste management discussed above? What are the disadvantages of each one?
2. How does your community handle its waste? Do you think this is the most effective way?
3. List at least 10 ways that you yourself can reduce the amount of waste you generate.

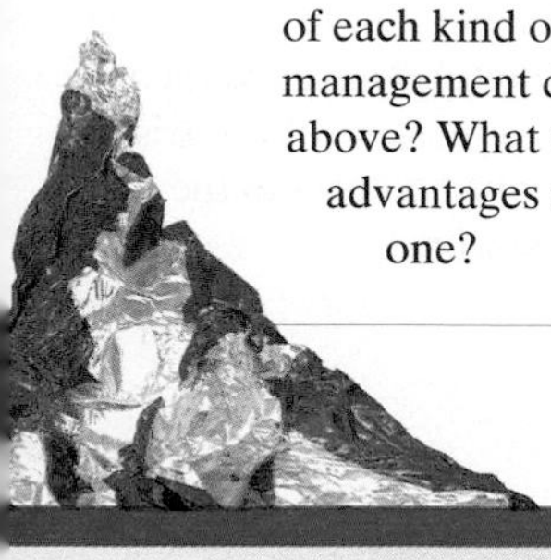

GEOGRAPHY

Visual Learning

Divide the class into small groups and have each group design a poster that illustrates the pros and cons of one of the ways of dealing with trash mentioned in the section Considering Alternatives. Members of each group may consult and choose a method named in the text, or you may assign a method to each group in order to cover all those mentioned. Students should brainstorm pros and cons rather than research them. Display and discuss students' work.

Answers to Decision Point

1. Landfills: advantage—provide a place to store trash; disadvantages—unsightly, smelly, and unsafe. Recycling: advantage—resources are not wasted; disadvantages—most communities can't afford to recycle; the recycling industry can't keep up with demand. Incineration: advantage—some incinerators produce steam and electricity; disadvantage—air pollution.
2. Students' answers should show an awareness of the issues involved in managing waste and the effect of waste-management decisions on the local community.
3. Examples include using cloth rather than paper bags, using both sides of a sheet of paper, and buying products with the least amount of packaging.

Collaborative Strategy

A recommended strategy for this lesson is a jigsaw strategy. For further information, turn to page T35.

INTRODUCE

Remind students that people often adapt to their environment, making changes in how they live with or use natural resources. Write *adapt* on the chalkboard. Then ask students what they could do if they did not want or were not able to adapt to their environment. *(Students may answer that they would move.)* Write *move* on the chalkboard. Read the lesson title and the Thinking Focus. Explain that in this lesson students will read about the movement of goods, ideas, services, and people.

Key Terms

Vocabulary Strategies: T36–T37

immigration—the movement of people to a new homeland

migration—movement from one place to another

emigrant—a person who has left his or her native land to make a home in another country

rural—farming areas

LESSON 3

Movement

THINKING FOCUS

What are the causes and the effects of human movement around the world?

Key Terms

- immigration
- migration
- emigrant
- rural

We entered [a cabin] and found a single child about three years old lying on a kind of shelf, with its little face resting upon the edge of the board and looking steadfastly out at the door as if for its mother. It never moved its eyes as we entered, but kept them fixed toward the entrance. It is doubtful whether the poor thing had a mother or father left to her. . . . Never have I seen such bright, blue, clear eyes looking so steadfastly at nothing.

Elihu Burritt, from *The Irish Potato Famine: Victims of the Great Hunger*

This description of a starving child was written after the author had visited Ireland during the potato famine in the 1840s. The potato did not originally grow in Ireland. Instead, explorers returning from South America brought the potato back with them. It grew so well in Irish soil that it became Ireland's main food. When a disease wiped out the potato crop, a million people died, and more than a million left their homeland. All this movement and change was caused by the little, round root crop called the potato.

Samuel B. Waugh painted this scene, entitled The Bay and Harbor of New York, *in 1855. It shows people arriving by ship to make their home in the United States.*

People, Goods, and Ideas

Movement of goods, services, and ideas around the world is one way in which people interact with the environment. Bringing the potato from South America, for example, eventually offered a new, very healthful food source to many nations, including China, India, and the United States. This movement of the potato—in spite of the Irish tragedy—proved helpful to the people of the world.

Objectives

1. Give at least two examples of migration.
2. Explain why people move.

Graphic Overview

Causes		Migration		Effects
• push factors • pull factors	→	Migration	→	• Goods, services, and ideas travel with people. • Movement of goods, services, and ideas benefits people.

Goods and Services

In fact, the movement of goods and services usually benefits humans. This movement is one of the things that allows humans to adapt to their environment. For example, wheat is the world's most important food crop. Western European countries do not produce enough wheat to meet their own needs. So vast amounts of wheat are sold to these countries by countries that produce a surplus of the crop.

Ideas

Ideas, like goods and services, also move throughout the world. In the early days, people could not write. They passed on information by speaking. The Egyptians were among the first to develop a form of picture writing. When the Semites learned of it, they used it to create an alphabet. The Semites passed this new idea to the Phoenicians, who made changes to it and passed it along to the Greeks. The Greeks introduced it to the Etruscans, who moved the idea along to the Romans. Eventually, the alphabet became our ABCs.

U.S. Immigration

How do goods, services, and ideas get from one place to another? Often they travel with people who are themselves moving. In this way the idea of an alphabet was spread throughout the ancient world.

Today people still bring goods, services, and ideas with them when they move. For example, people from many nations have moved to the United States. In fact, our nation was built on **immigration,** or the movement of people to a new homeland. Immigrants—people who come to a country to live permanently—bring with them the clothing, foods, celebrations, ideas, and skills that are part of their way of life. ■

▲ *This photograph shows a restored Union Pacific passenger train, one of the first trains used to carry travelers across the United States.*

■ *Give an example of how the movement of goods, services, or ideas has benefited people.*

People in Motion

People move for a variety of reasons. The people of the Sahel, about whom you read in Chapter 1, move from the Sahel to the south, then back again, according to the rains. This is called **migration,** or movement from one place to another. Mexico's Tarahumara Indians migrate with the seasons, living high in the Sierra Madre most of the year but moving down the mountainsides during the winter.

In the United States many farm workers migrate as various crops ripen and are ready for harvesting. For example, in California migrant workers harvest lettuce in the Salinas Valley along the southern coast.

DEVELOP

Have students scan the lesson's photos and headings. Point out that the headings express the main ideas of the lesson and that these main ideas are supported by the text that follows each heading. Have students copy the headings and subheadings onto a sheet of paper and then, as they read, have them write down the main idea of the text under each heading. Ask them to list additional examples of each idea under the appropriate headings.

■ *Students may mention bringing food or other products to areas that do not have them. They may also mention ideas such as the alphabet, which we use today thanks to the spread of ideas from ancient and faraway places.*

CULTURE

Social Participation

Ask students to give examples of migration—such as people of the Sahel and the Tarahumara—discussed in the lesson. Have them work in pairs using encyclopedias to learn more about these groups and their migrations. Ask students to share their findings with the class.

Access Strategy

Help students distinguish between temporary and permanent migrations. Point out the reasons why people sometimes move to another place for a short period of time. *(Vacations, visits)* Then, note that when people move to a place and stay there, the move has consequences that are different from those of a temporary move. *(Such as the need for permanent housing and a new job)*

Next, ask students to raise their hands if they have ever traveled somewhere, stayed for a while, and then returned home. Have them tell where they went, why, and what they did. *(Many will answer that they went on vacation and visited special sights or family and friends.)* Explain that such trips are temporary migrations. Then ask if they have ever moved away and stayed there to live. Have them tell where they went, why, and what life was like in their new home. Explain that such moves are permanent migrations.

Access Activity

Have students create a bulletin board display that illustrates reasons that people would move to the students' city or town. The display might include postcards, maps, and if available, brochures published by the local chamber of commerce. Students should supplement these materials with their own maps and drawings.

Note: This Closer Look can be used as an additional example of movement as described on pages 39 and 41.

CULTURE

Visual Learning

Jacob Lawrence, whose painting appears to the right, is one of the nation's leading African American artists. In his paintings Lawrence often uses browns and blacks for shadows outlined against a background of bright colors. This technique, combined with his preference for simple, angular figures, often gives his paintings the look of posters. Ask students how the composition of the painting emphasizes the concept of migration. *(The crowds; people carrying belongings)*

More About the Great Migration Migrants who left their homes in the South often journeyed more than 1,000 miles. From Birmingham to New York by train is 1,204 miles; from New Orleans to Detroit is 1,096 miles. Help students appreciate these distances by finding these cities on the map of North America on page 686 of the Atlas.

A CLOSER LOOK

The Great Migration

Over several decades beginning in the late 1800s, millions of African Americans left the South. Black recruiters and newspapers from northern cities told of a better life there. Families and individuals moved to Chicago, Detroit, New York City, and other factory centers. From 1916 to 1930, the blacks who headed north created the largest single internal migration in United States history.

Why leave? Southerners had passed laws unfair to African Americans. Also, the amount of farm work declined. Jobs at mills, mines, and docks paid too little or went to white workers.

CHICAGO
NEW YORK
ST. LOUIS

Black men and women packed and traveled to the North, where they hoped to find better-paying jobs. Also, fewer laws restricted their freedom.

Noted African American artist Jacob Lawrence painted a series of panels of the Great Migration. Most migrants traveled by train. They arrived amid crowds of strangers, noise, and the faster pace of a northern urban culture.

Visual Learning

Have students look closely at the photo of the migrating family and the painting by Jacob Lawrence and read the captions. Encourage students to speculate about the thoughts and emotions of the migrants as they left behind everything that was old and familiar and arrived in a place that was new and unknown.

Producing a Newspaper

Explain to students that a number of newspapers published by African Americans in the North and the South aggressively encouraged migration. One, however, stood out among the rest—the Chicago *Defender.* Founded by a migrant named Robert Abbott, it was described by the poet Carl Sandburg as "the big cause of the 'Northern fever' and the big exodus from the South." The *Defender* appeared weekly with headlines underlining the troubles of African Americans in the South, other items of news, want ads for jobs in Chicago, cartoons, photos, editorials, and even "migration poems." Have students work in groups to create an issue of a newspaper like the Chicago *Defender.* Tell students to use the information in their book and in sources from the school and public library to compose articles, visuals, editorials, and poems that capture the spirit of the Great Migration.

Then they move on. Such workers travel throughout the state, harvesting whatever crops are in season.

For other people, the move is permanent. For example, many Irish immigrants who fled the potato famine in the 1840s settled permanently in the United States. You can read about another example of migration—the African American movement from the South to the North within the United States—in A Closer Look on page 40.

Problems at Home

In the examples of migration you have read about so far, something was pushing people away from where they were. Sometimes the push comes from the climate. People in the Sahel move with the rainfall; the Tarahumara migrate with the temperature. Sometimes the push comes from changes in job opportunities in an area, for example, when a factory closes.

Many who migrate permanently also are pushed to move. As you read, in the 1840s Irish **emigrants**—people who have left their native land to make their home in another country—did so because of the push of starvation. Many of these emigrants came from **rural,** or farming, areas. When they reached the United States, they settled in cities, where they had to become accustomed to city life.

Opportunity and Community

Yet even as they say their goodbyes, immigrants often look forward with hope to their new home. Usually, new opportunities wait for them there. Perhaps the climate is better, the food is more plentiful, or more jobs are available. Perhaps the new land promises trade opportunities or religious freedom. All of these factors are called pull factors—attractions pulling people away from their homes and toward their new destinations. ■

The movement of human beings and their technology has extended into outer space. This photograph, taken on May 13, 1992, shows U.S. astronauts outside the spacecraft Endeavour, *rescuing a satellite from its orbit around the earth.*

■ *Why do people move from place to place?*

NASA
HUGHES

REVIEW

1. **FOCUS** What are the causes and the effects of human movement around the world?
2. **CULTURE** When do people choose to move away rather than adapt to their environment?
3. **GEOGRAPHY** Give examples of push and pull factors.
4. **CRITICAL THINKING** Why do you think geographers study the movement of people, goods, services, and ideas?
5. **ACTIVITY** Imagine you have been put in charge of creating an advertisement that will entice people to settle on the moon. Choose a pull factor you think will work and use it to draw a poster that will attract moon pioneers.

GEOGRAPHY

Critical Thinking

Ask students to explain in their own words what push and pull factors are. *(A push factor is something that makes people move away from where they were, and a pull factor is something that attracts people to a new place.)* Then have students write a few paragraphs in response to these questions: What might push your family to leave where you live? What might pull them to move to another place? *(Students' responses should show an understanding of the difference between push and pull factors.)*

■ *Students should indicate that movement from place to place is created by both push and pull factors.*

CLOSE

Have students compare the examples of main ideas that they wrote down as they read the lesson. Then draw the first two boxes of the Graphic Overview on the chalkboard. Ask students to fill in the third box, labeled Effects. Read the Thinking Focus aloud. Point out that studying the Graphic Overview will help students answer the question.

Answers to Review Questions

1. People move because of factors that push them away from their homeland and pull them toward a new place. Human movement causes the spread of goods, services, and ideas.
2. People move when they cannot survive in their environment or when another environment offers better opportunities.
3. Push factors include changes in climate, lack of jobs, and famine. Pull factors include new jobs, better climate, more plentiful food, trade opportunities, and religious freedom.
4. By studying movement, geographers can better understand people's relationship with and impact on a particular area.
5. Posters should reflect an appropriate pull factor for their goal of creating a desire to go to the moon. Students might use a pull factor such as adventure, free land, or mining rights.

Homework Options

Have students check the newspaper for a week to find articles on the movement of people around the world. Students may bring in articles they find and give oral summaries of them, or if they are unable to bring in articles, they may hand in written summaries.

Study Guide: page 8

INTRODUCE

Ask for three volunteers to dramatize the opening scenario to this lesson. One student should narrate, and the other two should play the parts of James and Harry. When the skit has been performed, ask students what word the boys used to refer to areas in their school. *(Region)* Read the lesson title and the Thinking Focus, and remind students that regions are one of the five themes of geography. Have them read the lesson to find out more about regions in the United States and the world.

Key Terms

Vocabulary Strategies: T36–T37

region—an area that has shared features that set it apart from surrounding areas

urban—having to do with a city and the area around it

➤ *Possible answers include the gym, auditorium, and principal's office.*

LESSON 4

Regions

THINKING FOCUS

Why do geographers divide the world into regions?

Key Terms

- region
- urban

James jumped off the bus and waved to Harry.

"Hey, Harry!" he shouted over the din of the student crowd. "I'll meet you in the social region."

James ran down the hall to his locker, where Harry was waiting for him.

"Listen, I have something to tell you," James said. "Can you meet me in the food region at 12 sharp?"

"That's gonna be tough," Harry explained. "I have to come all the way from the exercise region and stop at the administration region to pick up a note from my dad. I'll be there as soon as I can."

Regions in the United States

In real life nobody talks the way James and Harry just did. Yet you knew exactly what areas of the school they were talking about. The social region includes the locker area and the halls. The food region is the cafeteria and the kitchen. The exercise region is the gym and the playing fields. The administration region is the office and the nurse's room. Each area can be called a region because the places in this area have certain characteristics, or features, in common. A **region** is an area that has shared features that set it apart from surrounding areas.

Like a school, the world can be divided into regions. Geographers do this so they can study the features of particular regions and how they differ. Even the world's countries, including the United States, can be divided into regions.

➤ *This cafeteria has tables, chairs, trays, and other equipment for serving and eating meals. Other areas of a school also have special purposes. What areas are used for special purposes in your school?*

Objectives

1. Define *region.*
2. Compare at least two different types of regions.

Graphic Overview

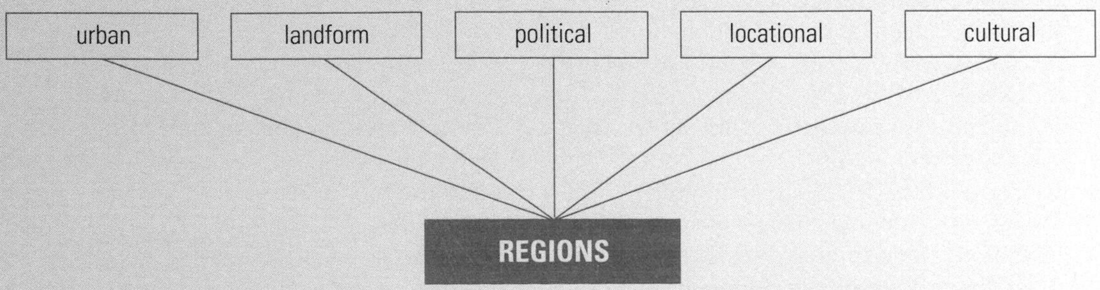
urban
landform
political
locational
cultural
REGIONS

Geographers can define a region by almost any feature. They name the region by the characteristic the area shares. For example, the word **urban** means "city." So an urban region is a city and the area around it. A climatic region is an area that shares a particular climate. Other types of regions include vegetation regions and landform regions. Often, regions are illustrated on thematic maps. You'll read more about this kind of map on pages 46–47.

Your school district is another example of a region—an educational region. The school district also is a political region, with a ruling group voted on by residents.

States as Political Regions

The United States has many levels of political regions. A school district is one; your city is another; your county (in Louisiana, parish) is another. There are also 50 larger regions, each with its own government, each with its own unchanging boundaries. You have probably already guessed that these are the states.

Regions by Location

Look at the map of the United States on this page. Locate the region called the Northeast. You probably knew to look in the upper right-hand corner of the map, because the region's name gives directions to the place. You know it is both in the north and in the east.

The map divides the United States into six regions. The area included in each region shares certain features. For example, much of the Midwest is flat, with fertile land used for farming. On the other hand, the Rocky Mountain region is named after a high mountain range. The mountains have many rich metal deposits. Because of these natural resources there is much mining in this region. Much of the Southeast is characterized by a long coastal plain and a climate that is warm and wet. ■

▼ *The map below shows the United States divided into six regions. Find your state on the map. In what region is it located? How do you think your state is like others in the same region?*

■ *List three examples of political regions found in the United States.*

United States: Regions

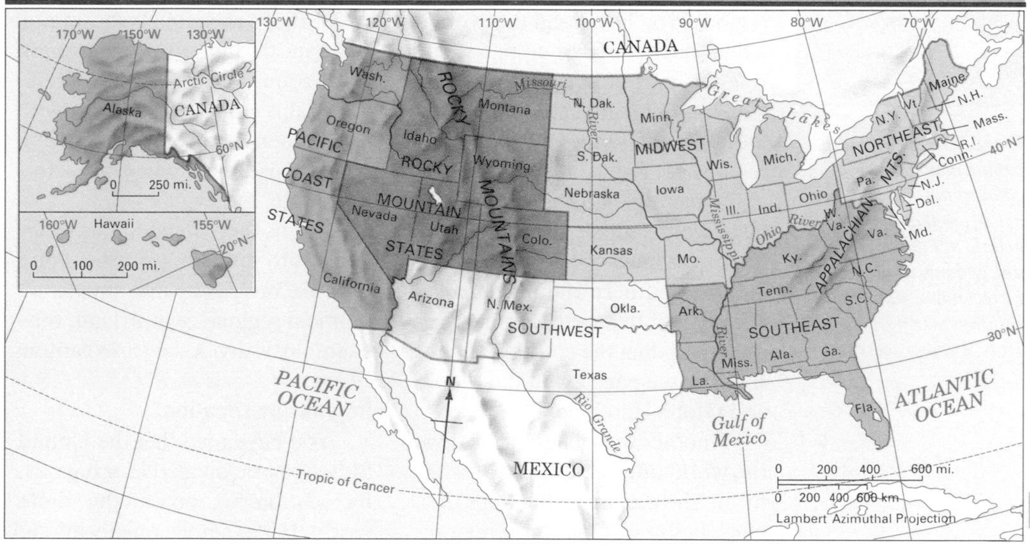

170°W
150°W
130°W
Arctic Circle
Alaska
CANADA
60°N
250 mi.
160°W
Hawaii
155°W
20°N
100
200 mi.
130°W
120°W
110°W
100°W
90°W
80°W
70°W
CANADA
Wash.
Oregon
Idaho
Montana
Wyoming
Nevada
Utah
Colo.
California
Arizona
N. Mex.
PACIFIC COAST STATES
ROCKY MOUNTAIN STATES
ROCKY MOUNTAINS
Missouri
N. Dak.
S. Dak.
Nebraska
Kansas
Okla.
Texas
SOUTHWEST
Minn.
Iowa
Mo.
Wis.
Mich.
Ill.
Ind.
Ohio
MIDWEST
Great Lakes
Mississippi River
Ohio River
Ky.
Tenn.
Ark.
La.
Miss.
Ala.
Ga.
Fla.
S.C.
N.C.
Va.
W. Va.
SOUTHEAST
APPALACHIAN MTS.
Pa.
N.Y.
Vt.
N.H.
Maine
Mass.
R.I.
Conn.
N.J.
Del.
Md.
NORTHEAST
40°N
30°N
PACIFIC OCEAN
ATLANTIC OCEAN
Gulf of Mexico
MEXICO
Rio Grande
Tropic of Cancer
N
0 200 400 600 mi.
0 200 400 600 km
Lambert Azimuthal Projection

DEVELOP

Direct students' attention to the parallel structure of the two parts of the lesson. Note that the main sections of the text and some subsections under them have similar headings. Point out that there is a map for each of the main sections. Encourage students to use the section and subsection headings and the maps to orient themselves as they study the lesson.

GEOGRAPHY

Map and Globe Skills

Direct students to study the map of the regions of the United States on this page. Have them locate the Southeast. The text states that the Southeast is mostly a coastal plain. Have students define *coastal plain.* *(Relatively flat land that borders the edge of the ocean)*

◄ *Students should locate their state's region by color. Answers should reflect an awareness of landforms, climate, and vegetation.*

■ *Political regions found in the United States include the 50 states; counties, townships, or parishes; cities; and school districts.*

Access Strategy

To help students understand the concept of overlapping regions, create three kinds of overlapping regions in the class. First, divide the class into four regions according to location, and designate which desks belong to each region. You might name the regions according to their location: for instance, Door, Window, Chalkboard, and Closet. Then put pencils on one adjacent group of desks and pens on the rest of the desks. Point out that these two regions are called Pen and Pencil. Last, choose three colors that students are wearing, such as red, blue, and green. Have students wearing red sit at desks in one area, those wearing blue sit in another, and those in green in another. Point to the three groups and announce that they are the Red, Blue, and Green regions.

Call on students to name the three regions in which they are sitting. Conclude by observing that the regions overlap.

Access Activity

To help students understand the levels of political regions, draw a set of concentric circles with the students' community, state, and country. Next, have students locate Paris, France, and Europe on page 682 of the Atlas. Explain that starting from Paris, they are moving from a smaller political region to the larger one of France and then to the still larger one of Europe.

GEOGRAPHY

Social Participation

Have students turn to the world map on pages 678–679 of the Atlas. Ask each student to write down the name of a country on a file card. Collect the cards and divide students into two teams. Read the name of each country aloud, and have students use the map shown here to help them name the world region to which the country belongs. Award points for the team that identifies the answer correctly.

GEOGRAPHY

Critical Thinking

Ask students what could make a region change. *(Migration of people, rise of new industries, politics, war)* Point out that students will be reading about these changes in many future lessons.

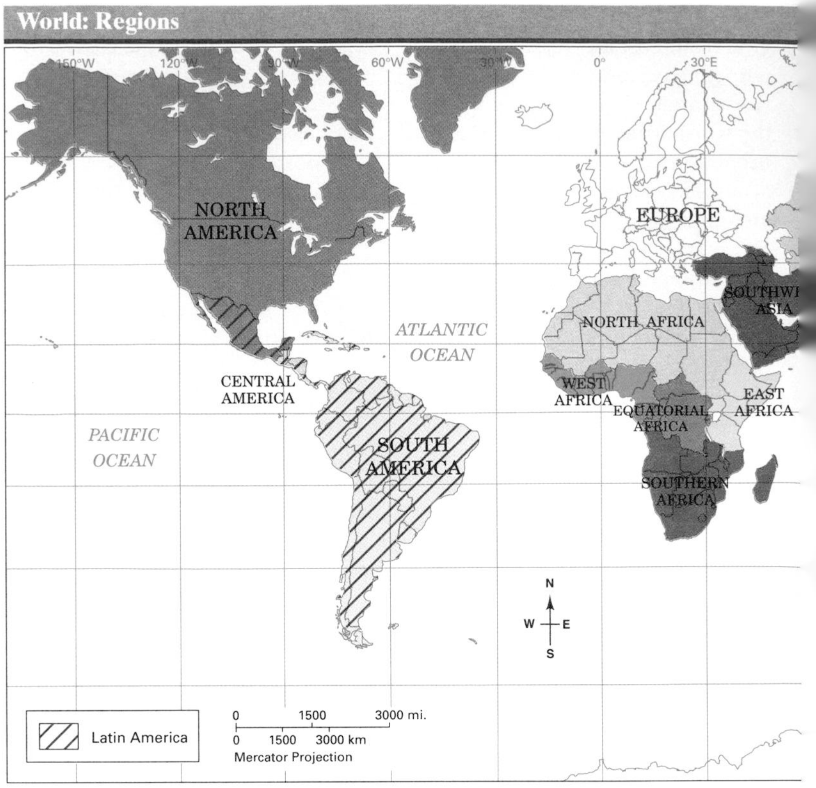
World: Regions
150°W
120°W
60°W
30°W
0°
30°E
NORTH AMERICA
EUROPE
SOUTHWEST ASIA
NORTH AFRICA
ATLANTIC OCEAN
CENTRAL AMERICA
WEST AFRICA
EQUATORIAL AFRICA
EAST AFRICA
PACIFIC OCEAN
SOUTH AMERICA
SOUTHERN AFRICA
N
W
E
S
Latin America
0 1500 3000 mi.
0 1500 3000 km
Mercator Projection

➤ *The map on these pages shows different regions of the world. Some regions are identified by their location, for example, North, Central, and South America. The continent of Africa is also divided into regions by location. Latin America, a cultural region, is marked with diagonal lines.*

▲ *Guatemala has more people than any other country in Central America. More than half the people of Guatemala are descendants of the Maya. Here, Indian women and children take part in a Holy Week procession.*

Regions of the World

One area can be part of several regions. You have read that your school district makes up one region. It is also part of larger political regions—your state and the United States. In the same way, the world's regions overlap.

Some regions of the world are huge. For example, the regions we refer to as the Northern Hemisphere and the Southern Hemisphere each occupy half the earth. For help in understanding the concept of hemispheres, see page G4 in the Map and Globe Handbook.

Another way geographers divide the world into regions is by landform. The picture of the Alps on page 45 shows a landform region.

Countries as Political Regions

Perhaps the regions most familiar to us are the world's countries. Each country can be considered a political region. Each has its own government and court system. Each provides certain services to its people.

Just as the United States is divided into states, many other countries are broken up into smaller political regions. Switzerland, for example, is divided into 23 cantons.

Regions by Location

You have read that the United States can be divided into regions by location. So, too, can the whole world. For example, one locational

Study Skills

Ask students to use encyclopedias in the school or public library to research a world region and write a one-page report. Students' reports should identify the countries included in the region and explain briefly what climatic, landform, historical, or cultural features help unite the region.

Political Context

Political regions smaller than a nation but larger than a city or town can be found in many countries. Some, like the U.S. states and the Swiss cantons, are governing units with their own institutions and specific responsibilities. Others have no political functions but represent an earlier division of territory according to ethnic, cultural, language, or other features. Some are rooted in tradition, having existed before the nation itself came into being, while others were set up by national governments to perform certain administrative functions.

The *régions* of France are an example of both the traditional region and the contemporary administrative unit. Their boundaries in many cases follow the lines of the provinces that existed before the French Revolution. The new regions, however, were created for a new era by the French government under Charles de Gaulle in the second half of the 20th century.

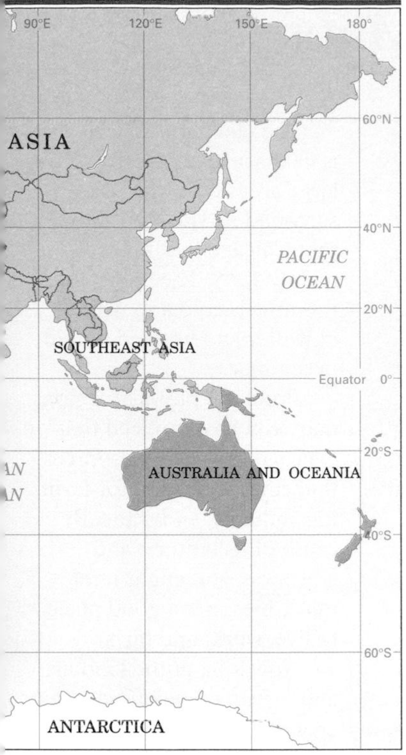
90°E
120°E
150°E
180°
60°N
ASIA
40°N
PACIFIC
OCEAN
20°N
SOUTHEAST ASIA
Equator 0°
20°S
AUSTRALIA AND OCEANIA
40°S
60°S
ANTARCTICA

The Alps are the largest mountain system in Europe. The entire system is about 750 miles long. At their widest point, the Alps are about 125 miles wide. At their narrowest point, they cover about 75 miles.

region is South America. This region includes all the countries on this continent. Locate South America on the world map above. Then look at the continent of Africa on the map. Into what locational regions has Africa been divided?

Cultural Regions

The world can also be divided into cultural regions. In this type of region, the people share cultural features, such as language and clothing. A cultural region can be very small. One example is the region around Lancaster, Pennsylvania, known as Amish country. Here the Amish culture has changed little in 200 years. The Amish share a common religion. Their beliefs require farming as a way of life, but they often refuse to use modern farm machinery. The Amish shun the use of telephones, electricity, and automobiles.

Other cultural regions of the world are vast. Latin America is a cultural region that includes Mexico and most of the countries of the Caribbean, Central America, and South America. Latin Americans share common languages. The majority of the people speak Spanish or Portuguese. ■

■ Give three examples of shared features that might be found in a cultural region.

■ *Examples of shared features found in a cultural region include language, religion, clothing, customs, and beliefs.*

REVIEW

1. **FOCUS** Why do geographers divide the world into regions?
2. **GEOGRAPHY** Name five kinds of regions mentioned in this lesson.
3. **GEOGRAPHY** Locate your community on a map. List three regions of which it is a part.
4. **CRITICAL THINKING** Why is the United States considered one of the world's political regions?
5. **WRITING ACTIVITY** Remember that geographers can create a region by using just about any feature. Choose a crop you know is grown in the United States. Research it in an encyclopedia. Then write a paragraph describing the region in which this crop is found. What states are included in the region?

CLOSE

Read the Thinking Focus aloud. Then draw the Graphic Overview on the chalkboard. Hand out file cards on which you have written the name of a state in the United States. Have students use the map on page 43 to name the region to which each state belongs. They may also name landform and climatic regions as they are able.

Answers to Review Questions

1. Geographers divide the world into regions to study the features of a particular region and how they differ.
2. Answers include political, landform, climatic, cultural, and political.
3. Students' communities may be political regions in and of themselves or part of a nearby urban region. In addition, communities will also be part of a vegetative region, a climatic region, and a landform region.
4. The United States is an independent country with its own government. Like other countries, it is a political region.
5. Students should be able to locate their crop's region on a map of the United States. You may also wish to have them locate other parts of the world where this crop is grown. Can they draw any conclusions about the climates of these other areas and the climate of the U.S. region where their crop is grown?

Homework Options

Have students design a post card that portrays their state's regions. On the picture side, students should represent several regions of the state visually. Then tell them to imagine they are tourists visiting the state. Have them write a message on the reverse that describes features of the state's different regions.

Study Guide: page 9

UNDERSTANDING THEMATIC MAPS

This skills feature compares a topographic map and a land use map and teaches students what they can learn from thematic maps.

ECONOMICS

Social Participation

Divide the class into three teams. Each team should choose one urban area and one rural area on the two maps in the feature. Tell team members to study and compare the maps in order to suggest how geographic factors may have influenced land use in the two areas. Ask the teams to explain the possible relationship between topography and land use for each area. You may extend the activity by giving each team a different location. Then allow the teams a brief consultation period in which to analyze the two maps and suggest a connection between the physical features and the economic activities in their location. Each team in turn can then share ideas with the rest of the class.

UNDERSTANDING THEMATIC MAPS

Comparing Two U.S. Maps

Here's Why

No single map can show you everything about a region. In fact, there are different kinds of maps, each showing a particular kind of information. For example, one kind of map may show rainfall in a region. Another kind may show elevation, and another kind of map may show land use.

You often can learn more by comparing two maps of the same region than you can by looking at one map alone. For example, you can compare physical regions maps with land use maps of the United States. Using the maps together will help you see how the physical features of our country affect our land use.

Here's How

Look at the map of physical regions on this page. It shows physical features such as mountains, lakes, and rivers. A map key explains which colors on the map stand for which elevations.

Now study the land use and resources map of the United States on the facing page. This map shows you what types of economic activities are found in different areas of the United States.

Compare the two maps. How have geographic factors influenced land use in Chicago, Illinois? First, find Chicago on the physical regions map. You can see that it is located at the southwestern tip of Lake Michigan.

The elevation of Chicago is near sea level. Notice that large areas of lowlands also surround it. The map shows that Chicago is at approximately 42°N. The climate in this area is cold and windy in winter and hot and humid in summer.

From the physical regions map, you have noticed that Chicago has water resources that could be useful for farming, industry, and trade. Because of its latitude and elevation, you might infer that Chicago is a good place to live, work, and farm.

Now look at the land use and resources map to see what economic activities are important to Chicago. The map's key tells you that Chicago is

United States: Physical Regions

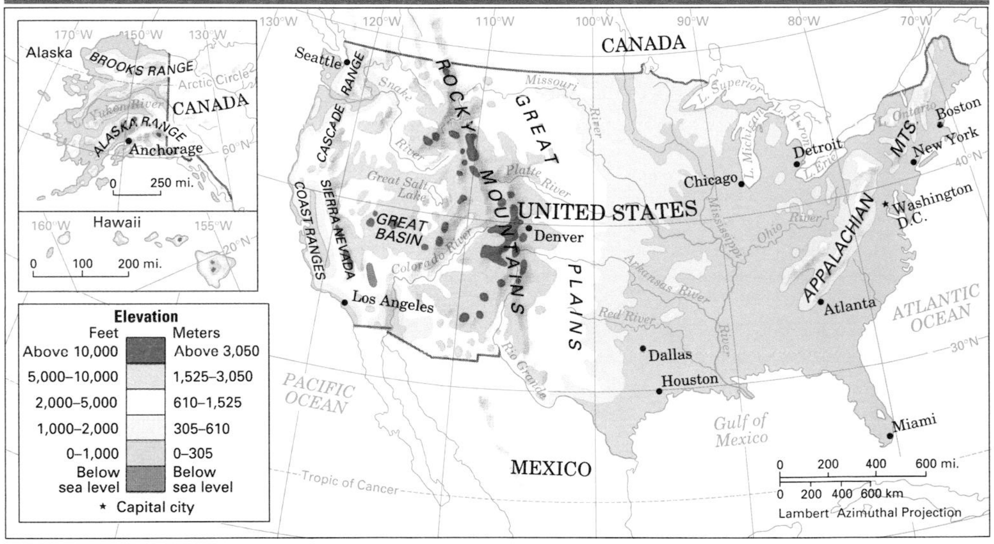

Alaska
BROOKS RANGE
Arctic Circle
Yukon River
ALASKA RANGE
Anchorage
CANADA
250 mi.
Hawaii
0 100 200 mi.
Elevation
Feet / Meters
Above 10,000 / Above 3,050
5,000–10,000 / 1,525–3,050
2,000–5,000 / 610–1,525
1,000–2,000 / 305–610
0–1,000 / 0–305
Below sea level / Below sea level
★ Capital city
CANADA
Seattle
CASCADE RANGE
COAST RANGES
SIERRA NEVADA
Snake River
Great Salt Lake
GREAT BASIN
Colorado River
Los Angeles
ROCKY MOUNTAINS
GREAT PLAINS
Missouri River
Platte River
UNITED STATES
Denver
Rio Grande
Red River
Arkansas River
Dallas
Houston
Mississippi River
Ohio River
Chicago
L. Michigan
L. Superior
L. Erie
L. Ontario
Detroit
Boston
New York
Washington D.C.
APPALACHIAN MTS.
Atlanta
Miami
ATLANTIC OCEAN
PACIFIC OCEAN
Gulf of Mexico
MEXICO
Tropic of Cancer
0 200 400 600 mi.
0 200 400 600 km
Lambert Azimuthal Projection

Objective

Compare thematic maps to learn about regions. (Map and Globe Skills 1)

Research

Tell each student to choose a different country. Ask them to use the school or public library to find encyclopedias, atlases, and other references that have thematic maps of the country of their choice. Then have each student write a profile of the country based on a study and comparison of the thematic maps.

in an urban and industrial area. Most of the surrounding land is used for farming.

Now find Anchorage, Alaska, on the physical regions map. You can see that it is located near the Arctic Circle, at approximately 60°N. This area has long, cold winters. Notice that the elevation of Anchorage is near sea level, with higher elevations nearby.

From the physical regions map, you can tell that because of the latitude and elevation, farming would be difficult if not impossible near Anchorage. You might also infer that few people would live and work in the area.

Now look at the land use and resources map to see what economic activities are found in Anchorage. The map's key tells you that mining and drilling for oil and natural gas are important activities in this area. The key also shows that some of the area around Anchorage is forests. Notice, too, that large areas of this region have little land use.

Try It

Find the Rocky Mountains on the physical regions map. These mountains are the most rugged area of the United States. Now study the land use map. What is the main land use in the Rocky Mountain region? Then look at the eastern coast of the United States. What is the main land use in this region? What geographic features might explain the differences in land use between the two regions?

Finally, locate some urban and industrial areas on the land use map. What information from the physical regions map might explain why these urban and industrial areas are located where they are?

Apply It

Find physical regions and land use maps of your state in an encyclopedia or an atlas. Compare the maps. Then write a short report about how information from the physical regions map helps explain the locations of cities and land use.

United States: Land Use and Resources

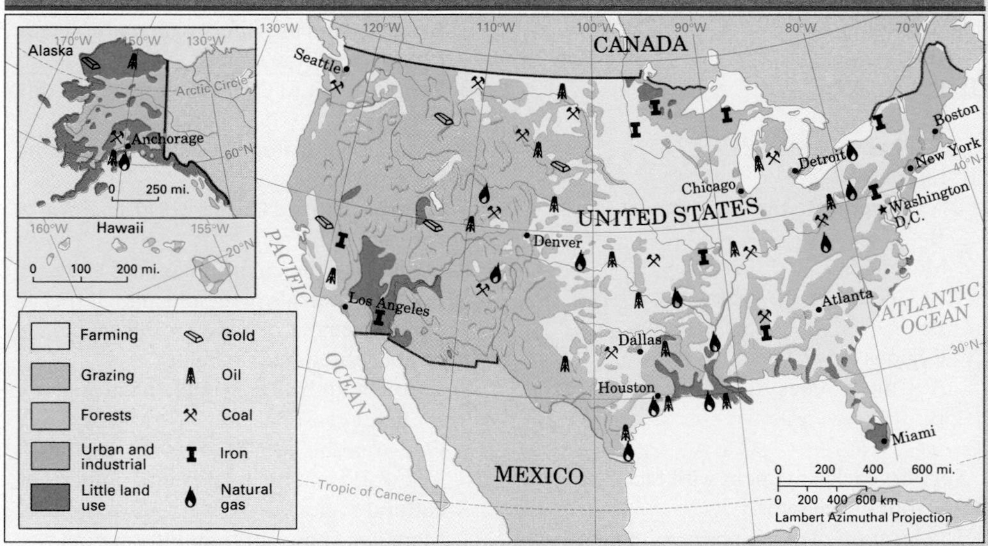

Alaska
Arctic Circle
Anchorage
250 mi.
Hawaii
100
200 mi.
CANADA
UNITED STATES
MEXICO
Seattle
Los Angeles
Denver
Dallas
Houston
Chicago
Detroit
Boston
New York
Washington D.C.
Atlanta
Miami
PACIFIC OCEAN
ATLANTIC OCEAN
Tropic of Cancer
Farming
Grazing
Forests
Urban and industrial
Little land use
Gold
Oil
Coal
Iron
Natural gas
0 200 400 600 mi.
0 200 400 600 km
Lambert Azimuthal Projection

HISTORY

Critical Thinking

When students are familiar with the topographic and land use maps in this feature, ask: Which of the two maps would have looked different 150 years ago? Why? *(Students should respond that the land use map would have been different 150 years ago. People in some areas of the United States used the land in different ways. The topographic map would have looked the same, because the physical features of the United States have not changed radically since then.)* Encourage students to hypothesize about how a land use map from 150 years ago might have looked. *(Students may suggest that more of the land would have been farmed, there would have been fewer and smaller industrial centers, mining might have gone on in places that are now mined out, and some economic activities now common might not have existed then.)*

Answers to Try It

Because of its cold winters and topography, the Rocky Mountain region is primarily used for grazing and mining, while the east coast's low lands and more temperate climate allow for farming and urban and industrial use.

Students should cite the availability of transportation routes, especially waterways, as well as proximity to natural resources and farming areas as reasons for industrial cities to be located where they are.

Answers to Apply It

You may want to encourage students to create a bulletin board display that shows land use and topographical features of your state.

Map and Globe Skills

Tell students to locate a third thematic map of the United States in an atlas or encyclopedia. Have them compare the two maps in this feature to the third map and make inferences about connections among the three maps. Give students three to five minutes each to present their interpretations of the maps.

Chapter Review

Reviewing Key Terms

adapt (p. 33)
deforestation (p. 35)
emigrant (p. 41)
endangered (p. 35)
extinct (p. 35)
geography (p. 29)
immigration (p. 39)
landform (p. 29)
latitude (p. 29)
longitude (p. 29)
migration (p. 39)
pollute (p. 35)
region (p. 42)
rural (p. 41)
urban (p. 43)

A. Read each pair of words. Write a sentence telling how the words in each pair are related.
1. landform, geography
2. rural, urban
3. latitude, longitude
4. endangered, extinct
5. emigrant, immigration
6. adapt, extinct
7. region, landform

B. Write the key term that means about the same as each of the following words or phrases.
1. to make something dirty
2. movement from one place to another
3. adjust
4. the clearing away of trees
5. an area with shared features

C. Give an example of each of the following descriptions.
1. An urban area in the United States
2. An endangered animal
3. A substance that may pollute the environment
4. A place that might be spoiled by deforestation
5. A landform that might contain trees

Exploring Concepts

A. Copy and complete this outline.

I. Location
  A. Absolute
  B.
II. Place
  A.
  B. Physical features
III. Interaction
  A. Adapting to the environment
  B.
IV. Movement
  A. Goods, services, ideas
  B.
V. Regions
  A. United States Regions
  B.

B. Support each statement with facts and details from the chapter.
1. The location of every place on the earth can be described through the use of latitude and longitude.
2. Geographers use human and natural features to describe a place.
3. People adapt to their environment in different ways.
4. Throughout history, people have changed the environment.
5. Humans depend on the world's natural resources.
6. Damage to the environment has endangered the earth's plant and animal species.
7. The movement of goods, services, and ideas has benefited human beings.
8. Throughout history, people have migrated for many reasons.
9. One area can be part of several regions.
10. The world can be divided into political or cultural regions.
11. Maps can show different information.

Answers to Reviewing Key Terms

A. Sample answers:
1. A function of **geography** is to describe **landforms**—physical features on the earth's surface such as hills and valleys.
2. A **rural** area is a farming region, and an **urban** area is a city and the area around it.
3. Lines of **latitude** circle the earth from east to west, while lines of **longitude** meet at the North and South poles.
4. An **endangered** species may die out, or become **extinct.**
5. **Immigration** is the movement of people to a new homeland; an **emigrant** is a person who has left his or her native land to move to another country.
6. To **adapt** is to adjust to the environment. Species that don't adapt may become **extinct.**
7. A **region** is an area with shared features, while a **landform** is a physical characteristic.

B. Answers:
1. pollute; 2. migration; 3. adapt; 4. deforestation; 5. region

C. Sample answers:
1. Chicago (or any city); 2. California condor; 3. nuclear waste; 4. rain forest; 5. mountain

Answers to Exploring Concepts

A. Answers:
I. B. *Relative;* II. A. *Human features;* III. B. *Changing the environment;* IV. B. *People,* 1. *Push factors,* 2. *Pull factors;* V. B. *Regions of the World*

B. Sample answers:
1. Latitude tells how far north or south of the equator a place is. Longitude tells how far east or west of the prime meridian a place is. The lines of latitude and longitude that intersect at a particular place describe the absolute location of that place.
2. Human features of a place include items built by humans; for example, buildings and roads. Physical features include landforms, climate, plants, and other features occurring in nature.
3. People adapt to places by using the natural resources they find, like the sod the Great Plains settlers used to build homes.
4. Human changes to the environment include irrigation canals, deforestation, pollution, and the creation of waste dumps.
5. Humans depend on natural resources for survival. Examples include water, soil, trees, minerals and metals, oil, coal, and natural gas.
6. Rain forests are being destroyed. Many plants and animals have become extinct or endangered because of human activities.
7. The movement allows people to better adapt to their environment and to learn more effective ways of doing things.
8. People have moved to find better climates, farmland, and jobs.
9. An area can be part of political regions—a school district and a state; cultural regions—the Amish community in Pennsylvania; and locational regions.
10. Cultural regions can overlap with political regions. For example, South America is a cultural region in which most people speak Spanish or Portuguese. It is divided into political regions such as Brazil and Peru.
11. Maps may include political, topographical, climate, and land use information.

Reviewing Skills

1. Study this map. Different colors show the average annual, or yearly, amount of rainfall in various regions of Africa. Which regions get the most rain per year? Which regions get the least?
2. Study the map on page 224. It shows how Africa's deserts are spreading. Use both maps of Africa to describe features that are shared by the northern and southwestern regions of Africa. Make a reasoned judgment about how these features are related.
3. Some plant and animal species are in danger of becoming extinct. Is this statement a fact, a reasoned judgment, or an opinion? How do you know?
4. Study the map on page 44. It shows different regions of the world. Make a reasoned judgment about how rainfall helps define regions on the continent of Africa.

Africa: Annual Precipitation

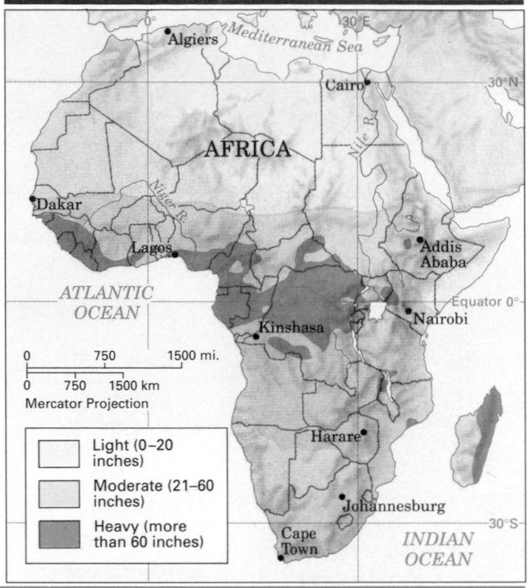

Algiers
Mediterranean Sea
30°E
30°N
Cairo
AFRICA
Nile R.
Niger R.
Dakar
Lagos
Addis Ababa
ATLANTIC OCEAN
Equator 0°
Nairobi
Kinshasa
0 750 1500 mi.
0 750 1500 km
Mercator Projection
Light (0–20 inches)
Moderate (21–60 inches)
Heavy (more than 60 inches)
Harare
Johannesburg
30°S
Cape Town
INDIAN OCEAN

Using Critical Thinking

1. Make a chart to compare the physical and human features of an urban region and a rural region. Then tell which type of region you would prefer to live in, and why.
2. Think about the physical environment, including the climate and other natural features, of the area in which you live. Make a list of ways people have adapted to the environment of your area, for example, building bridges over rivers, heating homes, or bringing water from far away. Then make a list of ways that you personally adapt to your environment.
3. Describe some pull factors that you think might encourage people to move to your area. What might be some push factors causing people to move away from your area?

Preparing for Citizenship

1. **INTERVIEWING** Interview family members about where they have moved during their lifetime and why. Share your findings with the class.
2. **ART ACTIVITY** Make a poster to persuade people to protect the environment from deforestation or a specific form of pollution or to save a specific animal or plant species from extinction. Combine pictures and written facts to make your message clear.
3. **COLLABORATIVE LEARNING** With three classmates, choose a country in Africa or South America. Report on:
   a. the absolute location of its capital city
   b. its relative location (What countries are its neighbors?)
   c. its physical features, major products, and natural resources
   d. its major cultural groups and some of their customs
   e. pull factors that might attract immigrants and push factors that might lead to emigration
   f. adaptations to the local environment

Answers to Reviewing Skills

1. Regions with the most rain include the west coast of Africa, between Dakar and Lagos; the land along the west coast south of Lagos to about the equator; and the central region of Africa around the equator. Regions with the least rain include the entire northern section, from the Mediterranean down to about 15° N latitude; and the southwestern region, from Cape Town northward to about 20°S latitude.
2. The northern and southwestern regions share very light annual rainfall (0–20 inches on average). The regions are largely desert or land that is at high risk of becoming desert. The lack of rain contributes to the desert conditions.
3. A fact; observation has shown that species have become extinct and that species with few surviving members are in danger of extinction.
4. Rainfall helps define regions in Africa because areas with heavy rainfall share certain characteristics such as lush vegetation, while areas with little rain share other characteristics.

Answers to Using Critical Thinking

1. Physical features of urban regions include trees, grass, and rivers. Human features include skyscrapers, subways, and monuments. Physical features in rural regions include mountains, forests, and lakes. Human features include farms, highways, and houses.
2. Students might mention wearing warm clothing if the region is cold in winter or using air conditioning in hot weather.
3. Students might mention climate or other physical features, as well as human features such as jobs and housing.

Answers to Preparing for Citizenship

1. **INTERVIEWING** Students' lists should include factors drawn from personal knowledge, as well as reasoned judgments based on material in the chapter.
2. **ART ACTIVITY** Posters should combine artwork with facts drawn from the chapter.
3. **COLLABORATIVE LEARNING** Reports should show that students can use longitude and latitude lines to determine absolute location; research geographic facts; research the cultural life of the area; make reasoned judgments about pull and push factors; and make observations about how people adapt to their environment.

UNIT PREVIEW

Using a large world map or overhead projection, show students Southwest Asia, China, and India. Ask students to pick out the major river systems in the region. Inform them that the earliest civilizations had their origins near rivers. Ask students to think of reasons that ancient civilizations began near rivers. *(Possible reasons: People needed water to drink; they also used rivers for travel, trade, and irrigation.)*

Looking Back

In Unit 1 students learned about cultural and geographic factors that influence how people live. As they read Unit 2, ask students to identify the cultural and geographic factors that enabled early civilizations to develop.

Looking Forward

In the next four chapters, students will learn about many ancient civilizations, as well as about the beginnings of several major world religions:

Chapter 3 *The Fertile Crescent*
Chapter 4 *Ancient Egypt and Nubia*
Chapter 5 *Two Early Asian Civilizations*
Chapter 6 *Early Civilizations in the Americas*

Unit 2
Origins of Today's World
The exchange of goods and ideas has taken place from the beginning of human experience. Two thousand years ago, the Silk Road passed through these mountains, allowing the great civilizations of China and Rome to trade silk, gold, and silver. The ancient world was crisscrossed with long trading routes, some of which, like the caravan track below, are still in use.
Prehistory
50

A caravan travels through the Pamirs, a mountain range in central Asia with rocky peaks and deep, narrow valleys.

BIBLIOGRAPHY

Books for Students

Chadefaud, Catherine, and Jean-Michel Coblence. *The First Empires.* Trans. Anthea Ridett. Morristown: Silver Burdett, 1988. Description of the early empires of Asia and Africa. Nonfiction.

Coblence, Jean-Michel. Trans. Jane Lamb. *Asian Civilizations.* Englewood Cliffs: Silver Burdett, 1988. An overview of the ancient cultures of China, India, and Japan. Nonfiction.

Mysteries of the Ancient Americas. Pleasantville: Reader's Digest, 1986. Illustrated descriptions of the Americas before the arrival of Columbus. Nonfiction.

Books to Read Aloud

Bierhorst, John, ed. *The Hungry Woman: Myths and Legends of the Aztecs.* New York: Morrow, 1984. A collection that reveals the culture and history of the Aztecs. Fiction.

DeRoin, Nancy, ed. *Jataka Tales.* Boston: Houghton Mifflin, 1975. A collection of 30 Buddhist fables and stories. Fiction.

Fisher, Leonard Everett. *Pyramid of the Sun, Pyramid of the Moon.* New York: Macmillan, 1988. A history of the Aztec, Toltec, and Chichmec empires and of the pyramids of the valley of Mexico. Nonfiction.

A.D. 1532
51

Understanding the Photograph

This photograph shows a river cutting through the Pamirs in Afghanistan. The Pamirs, a mountain range in central Asia, straddles China, Pakistan, Tajikistan, and Afghanistan. (Point out its location on the map you used to preview the unit.) Snow and ice melting high in mountain ranges like this one form rivers that flow down the slopes. Over time, the rivers may create fertile valleys at the base. Major rivers like the Nile, the Tigris and the Euphrates, the Indus, and the Chang Jiang (the Yangtze) provided water for the early civilizations of Egypt, Mesopotamia, India, and China.

Understanding Chronology

The ancient civilizations treated in this unit span about 4,500 years of history. Ancient Egypt and Nubia existed at about the same time as Babylonia and Assyria (3000–1500 B.C.). In Asia, the Qin dynasty in China (221–206 B.C.) paralleled part of the Maurya Empire in India (322–187 B.C.) The best-known American civilizations—the Maya, the Aztec, and the Inca—flourished in later periods, although other cultures in the Americas developed earlier.

Books for Teachers

Schele, Linda, and David Friedel. *A Forest of Kings: The Untold Story of the Ancient Maya.* New York: Morrow, 1990. Magnificent photographs and illustrations, along with archaeologists' findings about Mayan civilization. Nonfiction.

Starr, Chester G. *A History of the Ancient World.* 4th ed. New York: Oxford University Press, 1991. Basic reference on the Middle East, China, India; the rise and fall of Rome; and the spread of Christianity. Nonfiction.

Other Resources

Visual Media

Legacy. Ambrose Video Publications, 1991. A six-part series on ancient civilizations.

Software

The Second Voyage of the Mimi: Maya Math. WINGS for Learning, 1990. A simulation program that explores Mayan math and astronomy.

HOUGHTON MIFFLIN SOCIAL STUDIES

Bookshelf

Perl, Lila. *Mummies, Tombs, and Treasure: Secrets of Ancient Egypt.* New York: Clarion Books, 1987. Egyptian beliefs about death and afterlife are revealed through an investigation of mummies and tombs.

INTRODUCE

Ask students what the word *ancient* means. Explain that historians use the word *ancient* to refer to very early civilizations, such as those shown on the map on page 53. Point out the Mayan carving of the woman weaving. What does it show about Mayan culture? *(Accomplished in the arts, traded goods, had looms and tools for carving in stone)*

Ask students to locate the ancient Mesoamerican civilization on the historical map on page 53. Using the inset map on page 678, explain that Mayan peoples lived in settlements throughout what are now southern Mexico, Guatemala, Belize, El Salvador, and Honduras.

Learning from the Photograph

Refer to the photograph of the Chang Jiang. Locate the Chang Jiang on a modern map of China on pages 682–683. Explain that westerners have used the name Yangtze for this river. Point out where it originates in the highlands of western China and empties into the East China Sea. Ask students to imagine that they are flying over the Chang Jiang. As they fly from west to east, how would the scene below them change? *(From mountains to hills, plains, and lowlands)*

Unit 2 Overview

Origins of Today's World

Imagine that you are an archaeologist looking through the bits and pieces left behind by people who lived thousands of years ago. With slow, careful work, you find a few objects that help tell the story of these ancient people: a piece of pottery, a farming tool, a necklace. Who were these people? How did their culture begin?

From China to the Americas, cultures all shared similar beginnings. People spent much of their time hunting and looking for food. They did not live in any single place but traveled together in small groups. As they learned to plant seeds and tame animals, they began to live together near their fields and herds.

In some places people were able to grow more food than they needed. This allowed some people time for tasks like making pottery or weaving cloth. Communities traded these goods. Villages grew into cities, and cities began to trade ideas as well as goods. In time people developed writing, government, religion, art, and architecture.

Thousands of years ago, Chinese lived on the shores of the Chang Jiang. Today the Chang Jiang and its branches form one of China's most important trade routes.

This ancient Mayan clay figure shows a woman weaving. Weaving—often with brightly colored threads and complicated patterns—is still popular in Latin America today.

Objectives

1. Identify the locations of some ancient civilizations.
2. Understand the importance of rivers for ancient peoples.
3. Identify some of the most important contributions ancient peoples gave to the world.

Collaborative Learning

Divide the class into teams. Ask students to project themselves 2,000 years into the future. A team of archaeologists is digging around their neighborhood or school. What would the archaeologists find? Ask each team to list four or five artifacts that represent something important about life in their town. *(Students might list books, hobbies, music, sports, food, clothing, movies, and so on.)* Ask a spokesperson from each team to share the team's list and explain what these artifacts might show to archaeologists of the future.

If possible, have students choose 10 obtainable items from the teams' lists that represent what their lives are like today and actually prepare a time capsule in some kind of waterproof container that can be labeled with a date. With the help of a custodian, perhaps students can actually bury the time capsule for future students to excavate.

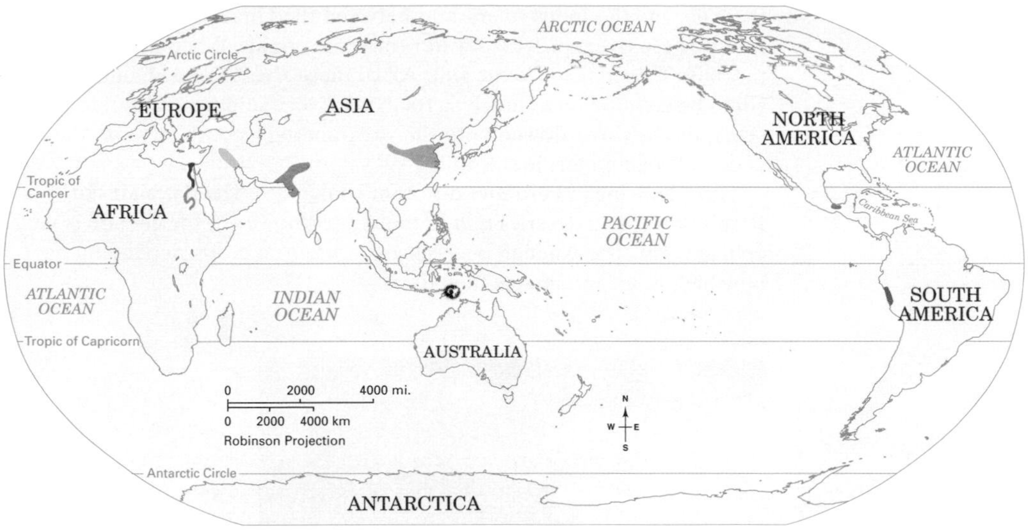
ARCTIC OCEAN
Arctic Circle
EUROPE
ASIA
NORTH AMERICA
ATLANTIC OCEAN
Tropic of Cancer
AFRICA
Caribbean Sea
PACIFIC OCEAN
Equator
ATLANTIC OCEAN
INDIAN OCEAN
SOUTH AMERICA
Tropic of Capricorn
AUSTRALIA
0 2000 4000 mi.
0 2000 4000 km
Robinson Projection
N W E S
Antarctic Circle
ANTARCTICA

▲ *Early civilizations existed between 3500 B.C. and A.D. 900. On the world map above, identify the location of each civilization depicted on the smaller maps below.*

▼ *The maps below show seven early civilizations in detail.*

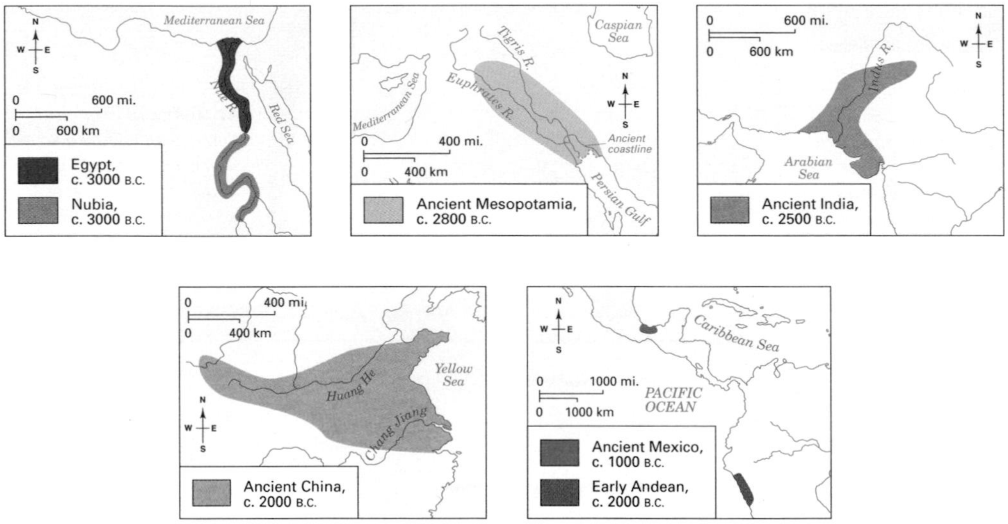
Mediterranean Sea
Nile R.
Red Sea
0 600 mi.
0 600 km
Egypt, c. 3000 B.C.
Nubia, c. 3000 B.C.
Caspian Sea
Tigris R.
Euphrates R.
Mediterranean Sea
Ancient coastline
Persian Gulf
0 400 mi.
0 400 km
Ancient Mesopotamia, c. 2800 B.C.
0 600 mi.
0 600 km
Indus R.
Arabian Sea
Ancient India, c. 2500 B.C.
0 400 mi.
0 400 km
Huang He
Yellow Sea
Chang Jiang
Ancient China, c. 2000 B.C.
Caribbean Sea
0 1000 mi.
0 1000 km
PACIFIC OCEAN
Ancient Mexico, c. 1000 B.C.
Early Andean, c. 2000 B.C.

Learning from Maps

Refer to the locator map at the top of the page to indicate where many ancient peoples settled. Then, directing students to the historical maps below, ask what the settlements of ancient civilizations had in common. *(Most were located in warm climates and near rivers or major bodies of water.)* Explain that the word *Mesopotamia* is Greek for "land between the rivers." Brainstorm why ancient peoples might have chosen to settle near major rivers and other bodies of water. *(Water was necessary for survival—for growing food and drinking.)*

Art Connection

Invite a guest weaver to teach the class the basics of hand weaving and, if possible, to demonstrate weaving on a simple loom. Make sure that students learn the terms *warp* (the set of threads that extends along the length of the fabric) and *woof* or *weft* (the set of threads that runs at right angles to the warp).

Explain that many ancient peoples knew how to weave. Archaeologists sometimes find fragments of woven cloth at sites where ancient cultures once lived. Have students design and make hand weavings of their own using paper strips or strips of cloth brought from home. Display the students' work on a classroom or school bulletin board.

Map and Globe Skills

Have students write the approximate latitude and longitude of each civilization on the maps on this page. *(Egypt: 24°–32°N, 30°–36°E; Mesopotamia: 30°–38°N, 40°–48°E; Indus River valley: 24°–30°N, 66°–72°E; China: 30°–38°N, 105°–120°E; Mesoamerica: 14°–22°N, 86°–102°E)*

LOOK AND RESPOND

Ask students to look at the images on these two pages. Read each caption with the class. Instruct students to generalize from the captions and images about life in ancient civilizations. List their ideas on the chalkboard or on a large sheet of paper. *(Students should recognize that early people needed a source of water to grow plants; adapted to different environments; organized their societies; and developed formal religions.)*

Learning from the Chart

Refer to the chart of rivers on this page. Go over the name of each river and its length. Ask students which river is the longest and which river is the shortest. *(The Nile is the longest; the Tigris is the shortest.)* Ask students to locate the Mississippi, Amazon, Zaire (Congo), and Chang Jiang rivers in a world almanac or on the Atlas maps on pages 678–687 in their texts. Direct students to write down the lengths of these rivers and compare them with the lengths of the rivers listed on the chart.

Explain that ancient peoples built settlements all along the land through which these rivers flowed. The thousands of miles of waterways connected one settlement to another. The waterways were a means for trading both goods and ideas.

The Land and People

The world's first cultures developed along the Tigris and Euphrates, the Nile, and the Indus rivers, and between the Huang He and Chang Jiang. These rivers provided water for thirsty fields. When they flooded, they also helped fertilize the soil. All of these rivers flooded, but none could be counted on as much as the Nile. Every summer for hundreds of years, the Nile overflowed onto the surrounding land. Afterward, the water left behind fertile soil called silt.

People living in Peru met different challenges. The flat plains of Peru's coast are a desert. High in the Andes, however, the climate is very cold at night. The Andean peoples grew different crops, depending on how high in the mountains they lived.

▲ *Ancient peoples depended on rivers and lakes for trade, transportation, and water for their fields. In reed boats like these, people traded along the Tigris and Euphrates.*

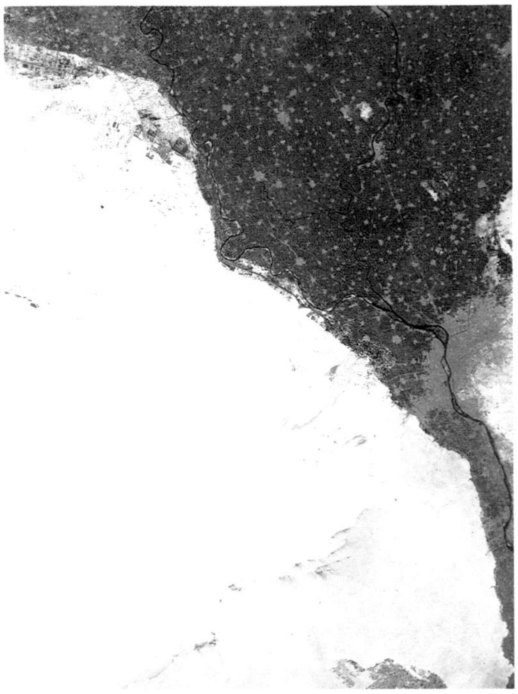

◄ *Today, as in ancient times, people settle near water. This infrared photo of the Nile delta is red where people live. The desert appears as a vast wasteland.*

► *The Nile is the world's longest river. Long or short, all the rivers of the ancient world were necessary to support life.*

Major Rivers of the Ancient World

River	Length
Tigris	1,180 miles 1,899 km
Euphrates	1,739 miles 2,799 km
Indus	1,800 miles 2,897 km
Huang He	2,900 miles 4,667 km
Nile	4,180 miles 6,690 km

Source: Information Please Almanac, 1992

Writing to Learn

After students have read Chapter 3, Lesson 2, have them list on the left side of a chart the five features of civilization. Direct students to list each civilization covered in the unit on the top of the chart and fill in the chart with as much descriptive information as possible. At the end of the unit, have students compare and contrast these civilizations.

Music Connection

Tell students that many of the instruments played thousands of years ago are still being played today. Some examples are the drum, flute, rattle, and panpipe in the mountains of Peru and the drum, lute, cymbals, and harp in India. Play a tape of traditional music from either the Andes or India. If possible, invite musicians to play for the class and to explain the origins of the songs and instruments.

Throughout the ancient world, people worked together to complete large tasks, including feeding the hungry people of a growing city or building a temple. To get the job done, people divided the work. Someone became a carpenter or a stonecutter. Some people worked to keep everything organized.

Ancient peoples invented mathematics and systems of writing to help them with measurements and keeping records. With the invention of writing, people no longer had to depend on memory to keep track of information and ideas. They could easily pass down more complex ideas and longer histories from one generation to the next.

Today people from Peru's coast still trade tropical foods, such as bananas, for foods grown in the mountains.

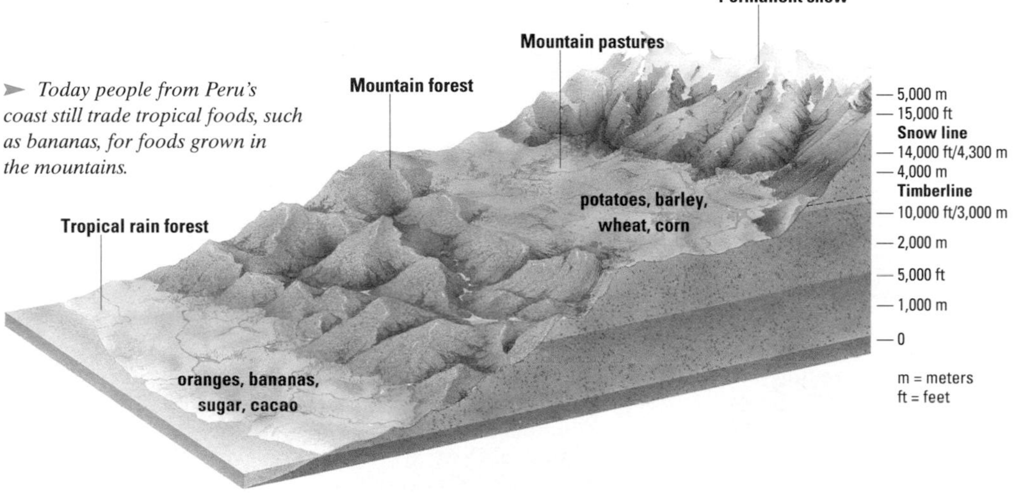
Permanent snow
Mountain pastures
Mountain forest
Tropical rain forest
potatoes, barley, wheat, corn
oranges, bananas, sugar, cacao
5,000 m
15,000 ft
Snow line
14,000 ft/4,300 m
4,000 m
Timberline
10,000 ft/3,000 m
2,000 m
5,000 ft
1,000 m
0
m = meters
ft = feet

Constructing these ancient buildings required a high level of organization as well as enormous skill.

Egypt's kings and queens were buried in huge pyramids. The largest measured more than 481 feet (146 meters) high.

Ancient Mesopotamians built temples on top of pyramid-shaped towers called ziggurats. The largest was about 160 feet (48 meters) high.

A wide stairway leads to what was once a temple at the top of this Mayan pyramid, El Castillo. It is 75 feet (23 meters) high and has 364 stairs.

Learning from the Photographs

Have students study the three photographs at the bottom of this page. Then refer students to the locator map on page 53 to identify the areas where the ancient Egyptians, Mesopotamians, and Maya lived.

Ask students what knowledge and skills the ancients must have had to be able to build these structures. *(Math, especially geometry, physics, and a means for hauling materials)* What do these structures tell us about how these people lived? *(There must have been large numbers of laborers and a strict division of labor.)*

ENRICH

Ancient cultures investigated many principles related to health. For example, the Chinese used acupuncture before about 2500 B.C. Invite an acupuncturist to speak to the class or have the students research acupuncture. What is it? *(A traditional Chinese procedure used as a pain reliever, a cure for diseases, and a treatment to improve general health)* How does it work? *(Needles are inserted into specific points in the body to rectify an "imbalance" in the body.)*

Debate

Arrange a library trip to show students how to use newspaper indexes and microfilm. Ask students to research news accounts of the bombings of Iraq during Operation Desert Storm in 1991. (Students will read more about Operation Desert Storm in Unit 3.) Encourage them to look for information telling how close the bombs came to hitting important archaeological sites from ancient Mesopotamia. Have students report on their findings.

Organize a debate on the question "Should there be international laws protecting archaeological sites from warfare of any kind? Why or why not?" Students should form debate teams. Each team should write down three or four reasons defending its position and support these reasons with facts and examples from the team's research. Invite students from other classes to witness the debate.

Collaborative Learning

Illustrate the origins of written language by listing the words *happiness, evil, love, beauty,* and *hatred* on the chalkboard. Divide the class into teams, and ask each team to invent a symbol for each idea. You may want to show students an illustration of a Chinese character as an example. Have teams decipher the other teams' symbols.

CHAPTER ORGANIZER

Chapter 3 The Fertile Crescent

CHAPTER PLANNING CHART

Pupil's Edition	Teacher's Edition	Ancillaries
Lesson 1: Life in Prehistoric Times (3–4 days) Objective 1: Describe how the earliest peoples lived. (History 2, 5) Objective 2: Explain how agriculture affected human history. (History 5; Geography 3)	• Graphic Overview (58) • Access Strategy (59) • Access Activity (59)	Study Guide (10)
Understanding Graphic Organizers Objective: Read and interpret a flow chart. (Visual Learning 2, 4)		Study Guide (11)
Literature: The Luring of Enkidu	• Access Strategy (63) Writing a News Account (64) • Illustrating (65)	Discovery Journal (7)
Lesson 2: Ancient Mesopotamia (2–3 days) Objective 1: Describe the reasons for the rise of civilization in Mesopotamia. (History 5; Geography 2; Culture 2) Objective 2: Describe the major achievements of the Mesopotamian civilizations. (History 1)	• Graphic Overview (66) • Access Strategy (67) • Access Activity (67) • Visual Learning (68) Cultural Context (68) Historical Context (69) Economic Context (69) Critical Thinking (69) • Visual Learning (70) Collaborative Learning (70) Mathematics Connection (71) • Visual Learning (71)	Study Guide (12) Map Activities (7) Discovery Journal (8)
Lesson 3: The Origins of Judaism (2–3 days) Objective 1: Describe the early history of the Jewish people. (History 1, 6; Geography 4) Objective 2: Explain the major teachings of modern Judaism. (Ethics and Belief Systems 3, 4)	• Graphic Overview (73) • Access Activity (74) • Access Strategy (74) Historical Context (75) • Visual Learning (75) Social Participation (76) Research (76)	Study Guide (13)
Chapter Review	Answers (78–79)	Tests (9–12)

* Objectives are correlated to the strands and goals in the program Scope and Sequence on pages T41–T49.

• LEP appropriate resources. (For additional strategies, see pages T32–T33.)

CHAPTER RATIONALE

Chapter 3 introduces students to the ways of life of early humans and describes some of the first societies in the Fertile Crescent. We have structured the chapter so that the historical developments described in the first two lessons undergird the third lesson, which details the history of the Israelites and Judaism.

Lesson 1 opens with an archaeologist creating stone tools as ancient peoples did. The lesson briefly sketches early human development, stressing important features of ancient hunter-gatherer societies. Next, the lesson describes the changes agriculture brought to these societies. Key developments highlighted in the text are included on the lesson timeline on page 60.

Lesson 2 introduces the time period of the earliest Mesopotamian civilizations by asking students to imagine that they are digging an irrigation canal in ancient Sumer. We have selected three of these early civilizations—Sumer, Babylonia, and Assyria—to describe in depth throughout the lesson. These regions are indicated on the maps on pages 67 and 71. Students are also conducted on an imaginary tour through Ur and urged to identify features that made it one of the earliest civilizations in the world. We highlight one of these features, the existence of written records, in A Closer Look at Cuneiform Writing on page 70. Understanding Graphic Organizers on page 61 shows students how to represent visually some of the factors that gave rise to early civilizations. Finally, in the literature selection from an ancient tale from *Gilgamesh,* students will read one of Mesopotamia's most enduring legends.

Lesson 3 chronicles the development of Judaism. As we trace the history of the Israelite people from the time of their biblical ancestor Abraham, we place special emphasis on the monotheistic nature of the Israelites' faith. We also highlight the Torah—the first five books of the Hebrew Scriptures—and the Talmud, a collection of the laws and customs in Jewish tradition. The chapter closes with a description of Judaism in the world today.

Throughout Lesson 3 we use the New Revised Standard Version of the Hebrew Scriptures, since it is widely accepted by Jews and is recommended by Hebrew scholars as being a faithful translation of the original manuscripts. As students work through the lesson, teachers should be sensitive to the particular concerns of Jewish as well as non-Jewish students. We highly recommend supplementing the material in the lesson with material about the prominent Jewish holy days and how they are observed today.

ACTIVITIES & PROJECTS

Bulletin Board

Direct groups of students to illustrations of what early humans might have looked like and photographs of bones and fossils that have been found. Then have students photocopy and arrange the illustrations and photographs on a wall or a bulletin board in their proper order, according to the evolution of the species they represent. (Use after Lesson 1.)

Basic: Writing a Report

Have students research and write a report about one of the Sumerian, Babylonian, or Assyrian Gods or Goddesses. Among the questions students might address in their reports are the following: What realm (for example, nature, war) was the deity said to control? How was the deity thought to interact with humans? What kind of relationship was the deity believed to have had with other Gods and Goddesses? Select a variety of student reports, and ask their authors to read them aloud to the class. (Use after Lesson 2.)

Challenge: Research

Many Jewish adolescents participate in a religious ritual and celebration called a bar mitzvah (for boys) or a bat mitzvah (for girls) at about 13 years of age. Have students research this ritual and celebration. Ask them to find out what adulthood means for Jews, what the ritual entails, and how the event is celebrated. Encourage students to interview, if possible, a young person—possibly a classmate—who has gone through the bar or bat mitzvah. Then have students make a presentation to the class. (Use after Lesson 3.)

Collaborative Learning

Have students look again at the photograph of a Seder meal on page 77. Tell students that Jews eat the Seder meal at Passover each year to commemorate the Israelites' Exodus from slavery in Egypt. The meal follows a prescribed ritual and involves many symbolic foods. Divide the class into groups, and have each group come up with its own celebration of freedom. Encourage students to think of foods, clothing, and rituals to include. Then ask each group to share its celebration ideas with the class. (Use after Lesson 3.)

LEP: Making a Map

Locate a map of ancient Israel and Egypt in a historical atlas. Have students trace the outlines of these countries onto their own papers. If a climate map is available, have them add symbols or colors to represent the climatic features. Then, using the scale on the source maps, have them determine how far the Israelites might have traveled from Egypt to Canaan following the Exodus. Help students calculate how long the trip might have taken, given that the Israelites were on foot and were traveling with children and animals. How does this calculation differ from the Bible's account, which tells that the Israelites were in the wilderness for 40 years? What explanations can students think of? (Use after Lesson 3.)

CHAPTER PREVIEW

Ask students the meaning of the word *fertile. (Rich, good for growing crops)* Then direct them to look at the map on page 67 and to explain why the chapter is called The Fertile Crescent. *(The rich land area is somewhat crescent-shaped.)* Point out that this chapter covers changes in human societies that occurred over a very long period of time. Ask students to describe clues from the images on these two pages that show the long time period covered in this chapter. *(Stone tool on this page; Torah scroll with written language and elaborate decoration on the next page)*

Looking Forward

Tell students that in the next three lessons—Life in Prehistoric Times, Ancient Mesopotamia, and The Origins of Judaism—they will learn how people in one part of the world made the change from a very simple life to a more complex life. Lesson 1 describes how prehistoric people changed from hunting and gathering to agriculture as a means of getting food.

Chapter 3
The Fertile Crescent

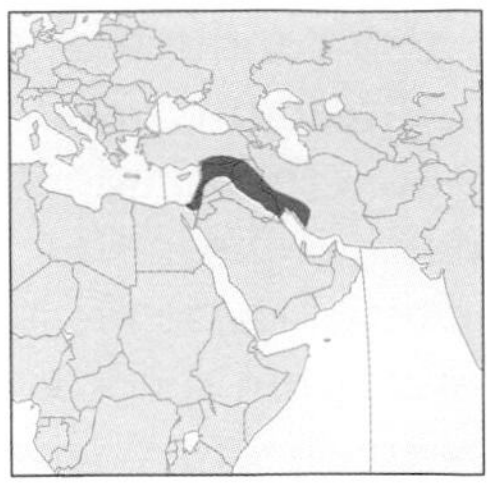

The Fertile Crescent, a band of land that crosses Southwest Asia, was one of the world's first farming areas. Early peoples tended crops and herded animals in the rich soil of its river valleys. In time they settled in cities and built complex civilizations. The Israelites established one of these civilizations in a part of the Fertile Crescent called Canaan.

Early peoples developed the first stone tools. They used bowl-shaped querns like this one to grind wild grains into flour.

Prehistory The earliest human development takes place over millions of years. Much later, in ancient Sumer, people begin to produce written records.

Prehistory	8500	6800	5100

about 9000 B.C. Sheep begin to be raised for their meat and, later, for their wool. Today shepherds like the Syrian man above continue to tend flocks of sheep.

Prehistory

BACKGROUND

It has been estimated that only one percent of our past can be studied through written records; the remaining 99 percent is the province of archaeologists. Thus, it is through archaeologists' study of fossils and artifacts that we learn about prehistoric humans and the first stages of civilization.

The Earliest People

Paleontologists disagree about the direct origin of modern humans; the small amount of evidence available and the difficulty of dating this evidence have made drawing conclusions difficult. For example, to determine the age of what is now thought to be the earliest human fossil, scientists have only a three-inch-long fragment that was found in Kenya. The fragment would have hinged the jaw bone of an early skull.

Not all scientists approach prehistory from a similar framework. Some scientists view human origins in predominantly religious terms. These scientists interpret physical evidence according to one of a variety of accounts of human creation provided in religious writings.

Despite the debates, however, a general consensus among scientists suggests that an early human-like genus called *Australopithecus (aw stray loh PIHTH ih kuhs)* appeared as early as eight million years ago. Fossils of *Australopithecus,* found in southern and eastern Africa, show that it walked upright and had a brain about the size of a chimpanzee.

The Assyrians knew periods of great power. Archaeologists have found stone sculptures like this battle scene in ancient Assyrian temples and palaces.

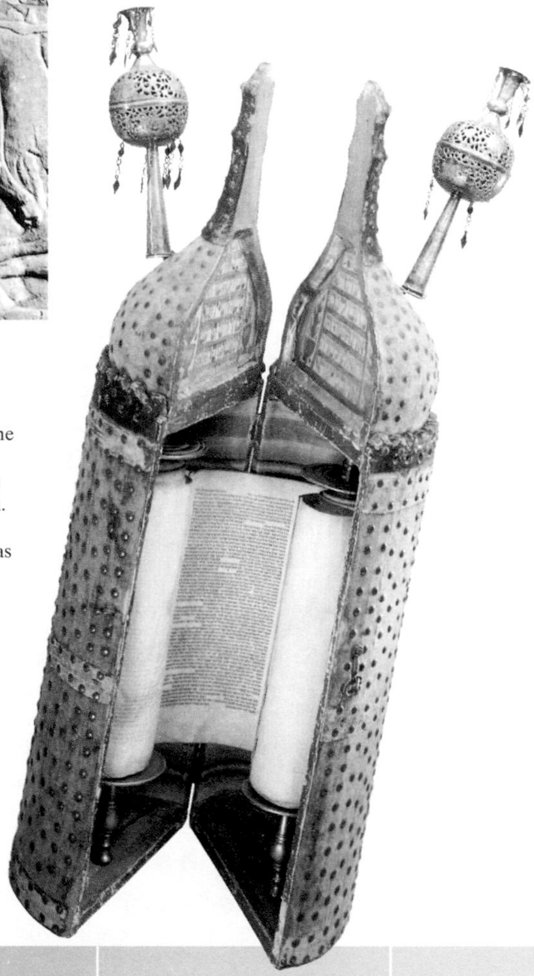

Elaborate cases like this one protect some scrolls of the Torah, a group of religious writings central to Judaism. They are handwritten by trained scribes today, just as they were in ancient days.

about 2000 B.C. Abraham moves with his family from the town of Haran to Canaan, an area of Mesopotamia that later will be called Israel.

3400 | 1700 | B.C. | A.D. | 1700

about 3500 B.C. The civilization of Sumer begins. By 3100 B.C. Sumerians invent writing.

A.D. 70

Understanding the Visuals

Relate the images on these pages to their modern counterparts. People still grind grain for flour and nations still go to war, for example. Have students consider how modern pictures of milling grain, cultivating land, or fighting would differ from the pictures shown here. You may want to have students find appropriate pictures of modern devices or technology for comparison.

Understanding Chronology

Direct students' attention to the timeline. Explain that since the Middle Ages, Western historians have employed a dating system that centers on the date that early Christians believed marked the birth of Jesus. Years are labeled B.C. ("before Christ") or A.D. (*anno Domini,* "in the year of the Lord").

However, some calendars are based on other religions. For example, the Muslim calendar centers on the date of Muhammad's emigration from Mecca to Medina (A.D. 622). Because of variations such as these, many people choose to label years using abbreviations B.C.E., which means "before the Common Era" and C.E., "Common Era." Tell students that they will learn more about dating systems in Lesson 3.

Just how humans descended from *Australopithecus* is greatly debated. A descendant called *Homo habilis* seems to have diverged from the australopithecine line. Some scientists think that *Homo habilis* and *Australopithecus* existed concurrently and that the latter eventually became extinct.

The Fossil Record

The fossil record shows the appearance of *Homo habilis,* of the *Homo* genus, as early as 2.5 million years ago. This species was more slender than *Australopithecus* and had a larger brain. The direct descendant from *Homo habilis* was called *Homo erectus,* fossils of which have been found in Africa, Indonesia, China, and Germany. *Homo erectus* had an even larger brain capacity than *Homo habilis,* used tools, and made fire. *Homo erectus* appeared about 2 million years ago.

There is no consensus of opinion about the relationship of these early species to modern humans. Some scientists speculate that *Homo sapiens* descended directly from *Homo erectus.* Other scientists argue that *Homo erectus* became extinct without evolving further.

Prehistoric Population Growth

The change from hunting and gathering to agriculture meant the regular creation of a food surplus for the first time. One result of this surplus was that populations were able to grow. It has been estimated that about five million people inhabited the world around 8000 B.C.; in A.D. 1000, 340 million; in 1800, 907 million; in 1900, 1.6 billion; in 1970, 3.7 billion; and today, 5.2 billion.

INTRODUCE

Read the lesson title, Life in Prehistoric Times. Ask students what the basic requirements for life are, and list them on the chalkboard. *(Food, shelter, clothing)* Have students read the Thinking Focus, and ask them to think about the sources of food. How do they get food now? *(Primarily from a store)* How might people have obtained food before stores existed? *(Accept a variety of answers.)* Have students read the lesson to learn about changes in the way early peoples obtained food.

Key Terms

Vocabulary Strategies: T36–T37

archaeologist—a scientist who studies objects from the past to learn how people once lived

hunter-gatherer—a person who lived by killing wild animals and collecting wild plants

prehistoric—the time before people developed record-keeping

agriculture—the practice of growing plants and raising animals for food

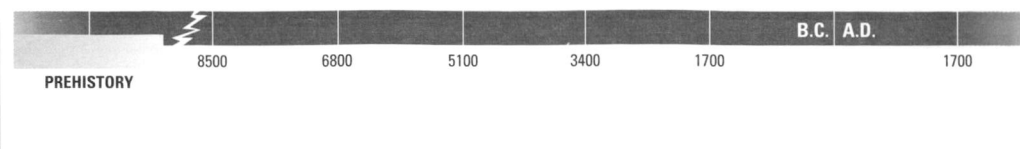

PREHISTORY | 8500 | 6800 | 5100 | 3400 | 1700 | B.C. | A.D. | 1700

L E S S O N 1

Life in Prehistoric Times

THINKING FOCUS

How did prehistoric peoples' ways of getting food change with the passing of time?

Key Terms

- archaeologist
- hunter-gatherer
- prehistoric
- agriculture

You are watching a woman make tools. She puts her foot on a rock to keep it steady. She holds a chisel-like tool called a punch and a hammer, each made from an antler. Working quickly but with care, she splits long, thin pieces from the rock. In a matter of minutes, she has made several blades. They are as sharp as modern knives. The edges are so thin that light shows through them.

Who is this tool maker? She is an **archaeologist** *(AHR kee AHL uh jihst)*. She studies the things people leave behind. Now she is testing how early peoples made stone tools.

If you could ask her why she's interested in archaeology, she might look up with a surprised smile. "Without those first tool makers," she'd say, "we would never have the tools we use today. Our modern ways have deep roots in the world of the earliest peoples."

Lives of the Earliest Peoples

Archaeologists estimate that the earliest human ancestors walked the earth about 2,400,000 years ago. Imagine a one-year calendar with one page for every day. It might be about an inch thick. Then imagine that this calendar showed 2,400,000 years. It would be more than 37 miles thick!

These early ancestors might not actually be called people, but in many ways they looked and acted like humans. They walked on two feet and made tools from rocks and bones.

The kind of humans called *Homo sapiens (HOH moh SAY pih uhnz)* did not develop until about 900,000 years ago. Archaeologists estimate that by around 15,000 B.C., *Homo sapiens* had spread from their first home in Africa to Siberia, the Americas, and Australia. The billions of human beings alive today are *Homo sapiens.*

How did these early peoples live? They were **hunter-gatherers,** which means they

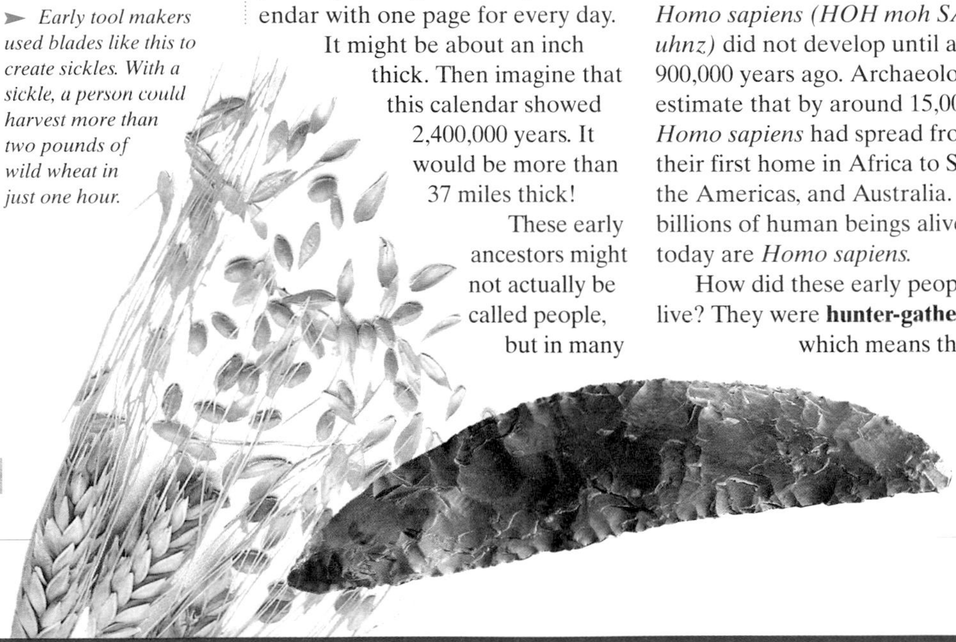

➤ *Early tool makers used blades like this to create sickles. With a sickle, a person could harvest more than two pounds of wild wheat in just one hour.*

Objectives

1. Describe how the earliest peoples lived.
2. Explain how agriculture affected human history.

Graphic Overview

Hunter-Gatherer Societies → Agricultural Societies → Permanent Settlements hunted animals and gathered wild plants to eat. On page 58 you can see a blade from a tool that might have been used to cut wild wheat, as well as a kind of wheat that was gathered. Some archaeologists believe that very early peoples were also scavengers. That is, they ate prey already killed by animals like saber-toothed tigers.

Most hunter-gatherers lived in **prehistoric** times—that is, before people developed record-keeping. As a result, we must get our knowledge about hunter-gatherers from nonwritten evidence. ■

■ How did hunter-gatherers obtain food?

Farming Changes the World

A big change in the way people lived began about 17,000 years ago. No one knows exactly how this change occurred. It took thousands of years to develop and happened in different places and at different times around the world.

People Begin to Farm

The big change was that many people stopped depending only on hunting and gathering for their food supply. They found they could capture some animals and keep them for the milk, wool, and meat they provided. Also, instead of eating all the grains and seeds they gathered, people began to save some to plant later. In this way they could be sure they would have food to eat in the following year. Growing plants for food in this way is called **agriculture.**

Of course, not all the places where people lived were good for farming. You can see where the earliest agriculture developed by studying the map below.

Results of Farming

Agriculture brought tremendous changes to human societies.

▼ About 8000 B.C. people learned to raise animals for the food they provided. This sculpture from about 2600 B.C. shows the pouring of fresh milk.

Early Farming Areas

135°W
90°W
45°W
0°
45°E
90°E
ASIA
EUROPE
NORTH AMERICA
ANATOLIA c. 8000 B.C.
FERTILE CRESCENT 8000–5000 B.C.
HUANG HE VALLEY c. 5000 B.C.
45°N
ATLANTIC OCEAN
NILE RIVER VALLEY c. 6000 B.C.
INDUS RIVER VALLEY c. 2500 B.C.
PACIFIC OCEAN
MESOAMERICA c. 7000 B.C.
AFRICA
Equator 0°
SOUTH AMERICA
INDIAN OCEAN
PACIFIC OCEAN
AUSTRALIA
45°S
0 2000 4000 mi.
0 2000 4000 km
Mercator Projection

◄ By 8000 B.C. people were farming successfully in some regions around the world. For help in using latitude and longitude to locate these regions, see page G5 in the Map and Globe Handbook. What similarities among farming regions can you identify from their location on this map?

DEVELOP

The goal of this lesson is to ground students in the broad period of early human history, giving them a sense of how long humans have lived and how a change from hunting and gathering to agriculture resulted in the development of larger and more organized societies. To give students a sense of the period covered in this lesson, display the Graphic Overview of the lesson, and have students refer to the timeline on page 60 as well as to the timeline in the Chapter Opener.

■ *Hunter-gatherers hunted animals and collected wild plants to eat. They may also have scavenged, or eaten animals that had already died.*

◄ *All of the areas shaded on the map are located in the same latitude range, between the equator and 45° north. Students might answer that these areas have mild climates and long growing seasons, conditions favorable for farming. Some students might guess that some of these areas center on a large river that provides water for the land in the region.*

Access Strategy

Locate in a library and bring to class information about and, if possible, photographs of the modern San of southern Africa or other modern hunter-gatherer societies. After sharing these materials with the students, tell them that hunting and gathering was the way of life of all early humans. While it is often presumed that hunting provided these societies with most of their food supply, as much as two-thirds of the food was obtained through gathering.

In early and modern hunter-gatherer societies, women and children did and still do the gathering, sometimes far from home. Yet it is a mistake to assume that all early cultures divided labor between the sexes similarly. Tell students that throughout history the work that men and women have done in any given culture has varied, in part according to the physical environment in which that culture developed.

Access Activity

Have students imagine that they are lost (as a group) in the wilderness in late August. They have almost no food, one pack of matches, and one blanket each. Explain that, in essence, they have become hunter-gatherers. Have students brainstorm survival plans, and record them on the chalkboard.

HISTORY

Study Skills

Explain to students that anthropologists have discovered fossil remains of *Homo habilis* and *Homo erectus,* two prehistoric species of humans that lived before *Homo sapiens.* Have students use reference materials to learn what these early people looked like, how they lived, and where fossil evidence of each has been found.

■ *Prehistoric people who had learned to farm were likely to build villages and towns. They needed rules about whose land was whose and laws about how to behave toward one another. People were healthier, and populations grew. Also, since they had more than enough food to live, not everyone had to farm.*

CLOSE

Have students answer the Thinking Focus by naming ways that the shift from hunting and gathering to agriculture changed the way people lived. List these changes on the chalkboard. Encourage students to discuss the pros and cons of these transformations, including the development of cities and laws, the growth of populations, and the emergence of specialization.

The Earliest Humans, 2,400,000–15,000 B.C.

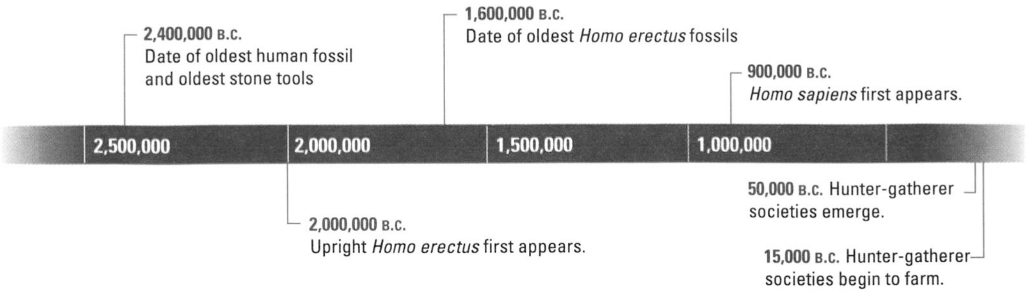
2,400,000 B.C.
Date of oldest human fossil and oldest stone tools
1,600,000 B.C.
Date of oldest *Homo erectus* fossils
900,000 B.C.
Homo sapiens first appears.
2,500,000
2,000,000
1,500,000
1,000,000
50,000 B.C. Hunter-gatherer societies emerge.
2,000,000 B.C.
Upright *Homo erectus* first appears.
15,000 B.C. Hunter-gatherer societies begin to farm.

▲ *Archaeologists have estimated the dates of important developments in early human history. The timeline shows some of these dates.* Homo erectus *is the direct ancestor of* Homo sapiens, *or modern human beings.*

➤ *These sheep are pictured in one of two mosaics that were discovered in 1927 in a royal grave at the ancient city of Ur. You can locate Ur on the map on page 67.*

■ *What changes did agriculture bring to the way early peoples lived?*

As you know, farmers must pull weeds, chase away birds, and care for their plants. As prehistoric peoples took up farming, they tended to stay near their crops. They began to breed and raise the animals they had captured. Since people were now in the same place all the time, they began to build permanent shelters.

Because people had more food, they were healthier. Healthier parents meant that fewer babies died and adults lived longer. Populations grew, and groups of shelters developed into villages and towns.

As farming methods improved, fewer people had to farm. Some people could spend more time making pots or weaving cloth, while others could be full-time religious leaders.

As the population grew, people needed new ways to get along. They needed rules to help divide the land and the crops. They also needed rules to govern how people behaved in the growing communities.

The coming of agriculture began a chain of events that changed the world completely. As you will read in the next lesson, this single change eventually led to very complex human societies. ■

REVIEW

1. **FOCUS** How did prehistoric peoples' ways of getting food change with the passing of time?
2. **HISTORY** How have we learned about the ways early peoples developed and lived?
3. **HISTORY** What kind of evidence must be used to learn about prehistoric peoples? Why?
4. **CULTURE** How did agriculture begin to develop?
5. **CRITICAL THINKING** Early peoples had many uses for blades like the one described at the beginning of this lesson. Name some possible uses for such blades, and think of similar tools we have today that might serve the same uses.
6. **ACTIVITY** Imagine that you are shipwrecked on a large, deserted island. In a small group with your classmates, discuss how you can find ways to grow plants and raise animals.

Homework Options

Have students select a favorite food and then discover where it comes from, who grows it, and how it reaches them. Students can read labels on food products, talk to grocery-store personnel, or do library research. Have students write one-page reports on their discoveries.

Study Guide: page 10

Answers to Review Questions

1. People initially got their food by hunting and gathering. As time passed, people learned to grow plants and breed animals.
2. We have learned what we know about early human life and development through the study of excavated fossils and artifacts.
3. We must use nonwritten evidence, such as stone tools, to learn about prehistoric peoples because they left no written records.
4. Hunter-gatherers began to capture animals and to save grains and seeds for planting.
5. Early peoples may have used blades for killing and skinning animals, gathering plants, and cutting food. For these purposes today, people might use knives, machetes, saws, pruning shears, and scissors.
6. Plants might be cultivated by obtaining the seeds from plants growing wild on the island. If there are animals on the island, they might first be enclosed in a pen built of natural materials. Then they could be used for food and for breeding.

UNDERSTANDING GRAPHIC ORGANIZERS

Using a Flow Chart

Here's Why

Graphic organizers are pictures and words that show one idea or the relationship among many ideas. A flow chart is one type of graphic organizer. A flow chart shows how one event causes another or how several steps make up a process.

Suppose you wanted to get a better understanding of how farming helped the development of early civilizations. By clearly listing the ideas in order, a flow chart can help you study.

Here's How

Look at the flow chart below. First, read the title of the flow chart, Steps Toward Civilization. The title tells you what information the flow chart contains.

Now look at the flow chart itself. You can see that the arrows between the boxes point to the right. These arrows tell you in what direction to read the flow chart. Begin by reading the first box on the left, called Farming.

The arrows in the flow chart mean "leads to." If you read the first box, the arrow, and the second box, you can say, "Farming led to surplus food."

Next, the second box and the three arrows tell you that surplus food in early societies led to the three results listed: settlements expanded, the population increased, and people began working at specialized jobs, such as constructing buildings. Finally, read the flow chart from beginning to end: Farming led to surplus food, which led to settlements expanding, to an increase in population, and to people working at specialized jobs, such as constructing buildings.

Compare this flow chart with the material about early farming in Lesson 1. Does the flow chart make the text you read easier to understand? Why or why not?

Try It

Try creating your own flow chart to summarize the following information. Be sure to give your flow chart a title.

- A growing population in Mesopotamia led to a need for more farmland.
- The need for more farmland led to a need for more irrigation.
- More irrigation led to the rise of administrators to manage these irrigation projects.
- More irrigation led to larger crews of workers to take care of the irrigation canals.

Use your chart to help you understand Lesson 2.

Apply It

Make a flow chart that shows a series of events in your life, such as what happens when you get up late for school, or what happens when school is canceled because of the weather. Model your flow chart after the chart on this page.

Steps Toward Civilization

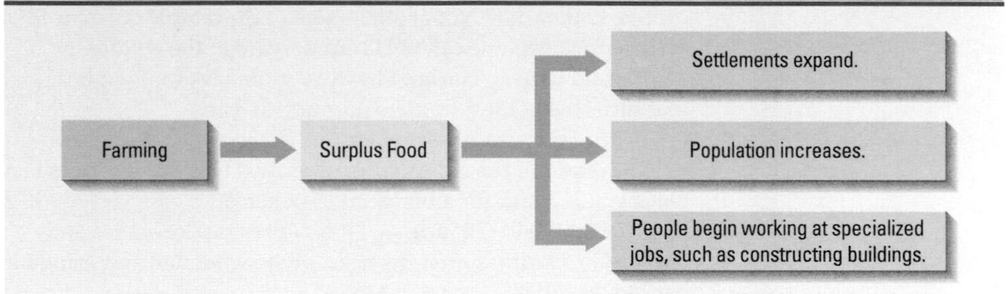
Farming
Surplus Food
Settlements expand.
Population increases.
People begin working at specialized jobs, such as constructing buildings.

61

UNDERSTANDING GRAPHIC ORGANIZERS

This skill page uses the information in Lesson 1 to teach students how to use a simple flow chart.

CITIZENSHIP

Visual Learning

Prepare students for the Try It and Apply It activities by creating a flow chart on the chalkboard. Select a topic of concern in your school or community. For example, concern about waste *leads to* a paper-recycling program, *leads to* a fund-raising opportunity for the students, *leads to* a special field trip.

CULTURE

Study Skills

Flow charts are used in many areas of modern life. Bring in examples of flow charts used in decision-making or manufacturing, for example. Students can ask family or friends for examples as well.

To help students understand these charts, you may have to teach simple decision-points. These are usually shown on a flow chart by a diamond shape representing a yes-or-no question. The answer to the question determines where to go next on the chart.

Answers to Try It

Students' flow charts should contain the following items of information in the following order, in boxes connected by arrows.

Growing population in Mesopotamia
Need for more farmland
Need for more irrigation

The last box should be connected to two boxes containing the following items.

Rise of administrators to manage irrigation
Large crews of workers to take care of the irrigation canals

Answers to Apply It

Make sure that students' flow charts show an accurate chain of events and are appropriately titled. You may want to have students exchange flow charts with partners. Each student should write a sentence that summarizes the progression of ideas in the partner's flow chart.

Objective

Read and interpret a flow chart. (Visual Learning 2, 4)

INTRODUCE

The story of Harim's taming and luring of the wild man, Enkidu, is taken from the book *Gilgamesh* by Bernarda Bryson. While early civilizations on every continent used myths and legends to explain many aspects of their existence, the story of Gilgamesh may be one of the oldest. This story was first written in cuneiform, a system of writing that the Sumerians developed and that students will study in this chapter.

READ AND RESPOND

Students may not be familiar with the writing style the author uses to tell this myth. For this reason, guided reading may be necessary. As the students read the story, remind them that it is a legend. Ask students to consider these questions as they read: What are the best ways to approach a stranger? How do you bring out the best in another person? After they have read the story, students may find it easier to understand if they present it as a play.

Before students read, point out the vocabulary words and unfamiliar terms defined in the margins. Be sure they understand what the words mean; help with pronunciation if necessary.

LITERATURE

The Luring of Enkidu

Retold by Bernarda Bryson

Myths about the Mesopotamian king Gilgamesh are some of the oldest stories in the world. They have been retold many times. This selection from Bernarda Bryson's book Gilgamesh *describes Enkidu, a wild man who lives with animals. In this passage, Enkidu begins to learn the ways of humans.*

The poems and stories about Gilgamesh are based on an actual hero-king of ancient Mesopotamia, the region that you will read about in Lesson 2.

"The hair springs out of his head like a field of grain, and he has the horns of a wild beast!"

"If he stole your catch of game, my son, why didn't you stop him?"

"He is taller and more powerful than Gilgamesh the King. I was numbed with fear!"

"If what you say is true, son, then we must report the matter to the King. But if you have lied, we will be in disgrace forever!"

The shepherd and his son went into the city of Uruk to make their complaint. But there the populace were already spreading rumors about the wild man. Some said, "He is covered with hair from head to foot," and others, "He is taller than a giant and eats grass with the gazelles!"

populace people

It was the eldest of the elders who led the hunter and his father before the King. "O Gilgamesh," said the elder, "there is a wild man that terrorizes the countryside. He robs the hunter of his game and disperses the herds of the shepherd. He turns all who see him numb with fear—indeed I've heard that he is taller and more powerful than Gilgamesh the King!"

disperses scatters, sends away

Gilgamesh, who feared nothing, might have been expected to say, "Then it's I who will go out and subdue him and bring him captive to the city!" Not at all; he sent to the temple of Ishtar for a certain priestess, one called Harim, servant of the goddess.

subdue quiet, conquer

He said to her, "Harim, I have a certain task for you; it is one that turns the boldest hunters numb with fear!"

"Then I am afraid," said Harim.

The eldest of the elders spoke angrily, "This is not a girl's task, O King; it is a task for a brave man—a hero!"

"Tut tut," said Gilgamesh. "It is a girl's task of smiles and charm. Go, Harim; soften the heart of the wild man and bring him back to the city!"

62

Thematic Connections

Social Studies: Culture/Mythology and legends

Houghton Mifflin Literary Readers: Traditional Tales/Timeless Tales

Background

The story of Gilgamesh is thought to be the oldest story ever written. Long before the first version was written down, however, people were telling the legend of Gilgamesh. The legend may be based on a real king who ruled in Mesopotamia sometime between 2500 and 2000 B.C.

According to the legend, King Gilgamesh was one part human and two parts God. He was the strongest, most powerful person in the land. Because Gilgamesh ruled harshly, a God or Goddess created Enkidu, a man in the image of Gilgamesh but wild in spirit and savage in looks. "The Luring of Enkidu" tells how and why Gilgamesh chose the kind and gentle priestess Harim to subdue the savage Enkidu.

This retelling of the legend is not based on any particular translation but rather on the author's cumulative readings of the texts. Her objective is to make the ancient story understandable and interesting to young readers.

Harim was led by the hunter to the edge of the forest, and she noted that he began to tremble with fear. "Go back to the hut of your father," she commanded. "If I can tame the wild man, I will lead him into the city alone."

The hunter was shamed by the girl's bravery. "Do not enter the forest, O Harim; I myself will go." But the priestess laughed at him and sent him home.

She went among the dark cedars; she listened to the sounds of birds and of monkeys chattering. She noted the bits of sunlight that filtered through the branches and lit up the flowers, moss, and bracken on the forest floor. "How peaceful a place this is! How could any evil thing lurk here?" Harim found a fresh spring bubbling with cool water. She sat beside it on a stone, untied her sandals, and dipped her feet in the water.

bracken ferns

Enkidu came to the place with the small wild horse and the gazelle. As they drew near, the two beasts became nervous, sniffed the air, and fled. But Enkidu stood still; he wondered what new danger was near, what unknown beast might have come to the water.

When he saw the girl sitting there his breath failed and he was overcome. He had not yet seen a human being, and this creature seemed to him the most admirable, the most enchanting being that he had ever seen. He stood quietly in order not to frighten her.

Harim gazed at this giant figure, his soaring horns, and his unkempt looks and would have run away, but she could not move. She opened her mouth to scream and could not make a sound. She was numb with terror. And Enkidu noting this remained quiet; he had made friends with many timid creatures and he knew their ways.

unkempt rough, uncombed

When the priestess saw the gentleness of his manner, her courage returned to her somewhat. She called out shyly, "Hello!"

Enkidu knew no words. He could babble somewhat as the monkeys did. He could bark quite like a fox, or trill like many birds. He had various calls of greeting for his wild friends, but this new animal made sounds that he could not understand.

He neither barked nor roared, but stood perplexed looking at the girl. Again she spoke, and now held out her hands to him in greeting.

perplexed puzzled, confused

Enkidu approached slowly and sat on the earth beside the white feet of Harim. She said all sorts of things to him and he understood nothing. She asked him many questions and he could not reply. But he felt ecstasy in his heart, and great contentment in merely sitting beside her.

ecstasy great joy

How easy was her conquest of Enkidu! Harim smiled, but she now began to feel a new sort of fear. How could she lead this great fellow, so gentle and so innocent, back to the city of Uruk? Would

◄ Why was Harim afraid for Enkidu? *(He was gentle and innocent and did not know that people could be unkind and cruel.)*

Access Strategy

Before students read this story, ask them if they ever decide to like or dislike people because of the way they look. Do they ever make a quick judgment about people without giving them a chance to show their true nature? Explain that people or animals sometimes seem frightening because they are frightened themselves. In the story of Enkidu, they will see a character whose inner being and outward appearance are very different.

jeer make fun of

myriad many, countless

eminent outstanding

the people set on him and kill him? Would they jeer at him? Would the King have him put into a cage and carried through the streets on the backs of soldiers? She shuddered.

No, first she must teach him the ways of people, the conformity of life.

"Al-ka ti-ba i-na ga-ag-ga-ri!" said Harim. "Come, rise from the ground!" But the wild man did not understand. Thus, she taught him the word for standing, and then after that, the word for sitting. She taught him the words for walking, running, talking, laughing, eating, and he repeated each one, learning it. She taught him the words for trees and for stones and for water, for earth and for the trailing vines that grew beside the spring, and for the spring itself. She taught him the words for feet and hands and the names of all the fingers and all the myriad words of love.

Thus patiently, Harim taught Enkidu to be like ordinary men. She cut his hair and combed it in the way of people of the city. She made him bathe; she tore her long tunic into two parts, making of one-half a garment for Enkidu, keeping the other half for herself.

Again she spoke to him, and now he understood, "A-na-tal-ka En-ki-du ki-ma ili ta-ba-as-si!"—"I gaze upon you, Enkidu; you are like a god!"

He brought her gifts—all the things that he had come to know and love in the forest and from the open steppes; wild cucumbers and cassia melon, grapes and figs and caper buds from the dry rocks. He brought her blossoms of golden mimosa and fragrant branches of jasmine.

After some time had passed Harim said, "Now I will lead Enkidu out among the people and everyone will admire him!" But still she feared for his life so she took him first to the hut of the shepherd.

At the edge of the forest Enkidu stopped and turned back. He was overcome with regret; how could he leave forever his friends of the woods and wild places? Who would protect them? Who would release them from the traps? How could he leave behind his friend the little wild horse, or the gazelle, the rabbits, the monkeys that had taught him to play games?

But as he approached they leaped away startled. The rabbit hid trembling in the grass and the birds took off with a wild flutter of wings.

Enkidu threw himself to the ground weeping. "O Harim, what have I done? How have I made all my friends into strangers? Why do they run from me?"

"Enkidu is no longer a wild creature. He is no longer a beast of the forest and the open plain. Enkidu is now a man. He will live among men and be eminent among men!"

Enkidu followed regretfully as the priestess led him toward the hut of the shepherd. This man greeted him with awe and

Writing a News Account

Have students write a news account of the day that Enkidu arrived in the city. Remind students to describe Enkidu in detail. Encourage them to use their imaginations to describe Enkidu's appearance. Have them also describe the crowd, the crowd's reaction to seeing Enkidu, and any other aspects of the scene that might be interesting. Students may want to illustrate their accounts and display them on a bulletin board.

admiration, but his son fled from the place and hid in the sheepfold. After some time he returned, running. "Father, a lion has entered the fold! It is devouring the lambs!"

Enkidu went to the sheepfold where again he wrestled with the lion, his friend who no longer knew him. Again he overcame the beast, but he let it go free. He lifted the lambs gently, washing and tending the ones that bled. To his great joy they did not shun him or run away. Neither did the young calves nor the barnyard fowl. A dog followed him wagging its tail. A cat smoothed its fur against his legs, and again he was content.

In the hut of the shepherd Enkidu learned to sit on a chair and to wash his hands before eating. He learned how to care for animals, to make plants grow, and to build with mud and brick and reeds. He learned to play on a flute. He ate bread. There he drank the juice of the wild grape. His face shone, he rejoiced; he sang.

Harim smiled. "Now Enkidu has become like a man, we shall go into the city!"

Further Reading

He Who Saw Everything: The Epic of Gilgamesh. Anita Feagles. This book and *Gilgamesh and Other Babylonian Tales* are other versions of the Gilgamesh epic.

In the Land of Ur: The Discovery of Ancient Mesopotamia. Hans Bauman. The author describes archaeological finds in Mesopotamia and tells what they reveal about the ancient civilizations of that area.

A Song for Gilgamesh. Elizabeth Jamison Hodges. The story of a Sumerian potter is woven in with a myth about the hero-king Gilgamesh and his journey to the Land of the Living.

The Three Brothers of Ur. Jennifer G. Fyson. Here is an adventure story about three boys in the ancient city of Ur. The story also teaches about the boys' religion and customs.

◄ Do you think it was right for Gilgamesh to have Enkidu tamed? *(Accept all responses, and encourage students to give sound reasons to support their viewpoints.)*

EXTEND

Have students find out more about the history of the legend of Gilgamesh. Ask them to look specifically for this information: where the written legend was found, what other parts of the story of Gilgamesh exist, and how the legend began.

Illustrating

Students may better understand the relationship between Gilgamesh and Enkidu if the creation of Enkidu is explained in more detail. If possible, obtain the book *Gilgamesh* by Bernarda Bryson, and read the chapter "Uruk-of-the-Walls" to the class. Have students discuss what it would be like to awake in totally unfamiliar surroundings and not know who they are. Have students make an illustration of Enkidu's life in the forest.

Further Reading

You may want to have your students look in the school or local library for collections of other legends about Gilgamesh or other heroes of ancient Mesopotamia.

INTRODUCE

The Fertile Crescent appears on the map on page 59 as one of the areas where the change from hunting and gathering to agriculture occurred. Now students will learn about three cultures that developed in a part of the Fertile Crescent called Mesopotamia.

Have students look at the map on the next page and name the two rivers that serve as boundaries of Mesopotamia. *(Tigris, Euphrates)* Tell students that the word *Mesopotamia* comes from two Greek words: *meso,* "between," and *pot,* "river." (A related word, *hippopotamus,* means "river horse.")

Key Terms

Vocabulary Strategies: T36–T37

irrigation—a system for supplying land or crops with water

civilization—a society that shows evidence of agricultural surplus, specialization of labor, class structure, government, and other features of culture

surplus—a supply of something, such as food, beyond what is needed

specialization of labor—the division of work in which a person does only one kind of job

class—a social level distinguishing one group of people from another on the basis of social position, wealth, or occupation

PREHISTORY 8500 6800 5100 3500 612 B.C. A.D. 1700

L E S S O N 2

Ancient Mesopotamia

THINKING FOCUS

What were the major achievements of the civilizations of ancient Mesopotamia?

Key Terms

- irrigation
- civilization
- surplus
- specialization of labor
- class

With an enormous heave, you lift one last shovelful of earth onto the growing pile a few feet away. Then, taking a rest, you stand up straight and look around. The time is about 4,000 years ago. You are knee deep in a canal that brings water from the Euphrates *(yoo FRAY teez)* River to your field.

Behind you are the walls and towers of the city of Ur. The king's palace, the temples of the Gods, and the homes of many traders and craftsworkers are located within these walls.

You are a canal digger. Sometimes, you feel important. Without your work, the farms that feed the people of Ur would dry up. At other times, like now, you just feel tired. You wipe away the sweat on your forehead with the back of your hand and again lean over your shovel. Time to get back to work!

➤ *One factor that enabled Mesopotamia to become a powerful culture was the richness of the soil along its rivers. Here a section of the Tigris River flows between the modern cities of Baghdad and Mosul.*

Objectives

1. Describe the reasons for the rise of civilization in Mesopotamia.
2. Describe the major achievements of the Mesopotamian civilizations.

Graphic Overview

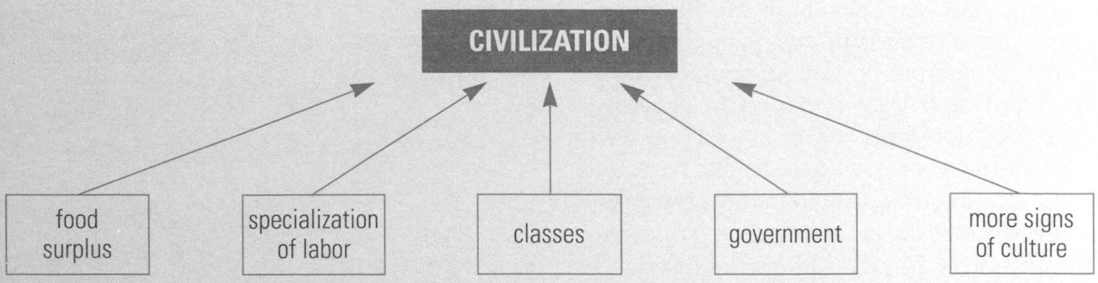
CIVILIZATION
food surplus
specialization of labor
classes
government
more signs of culture

Fertile Crescent, 6000–2000 B.C.

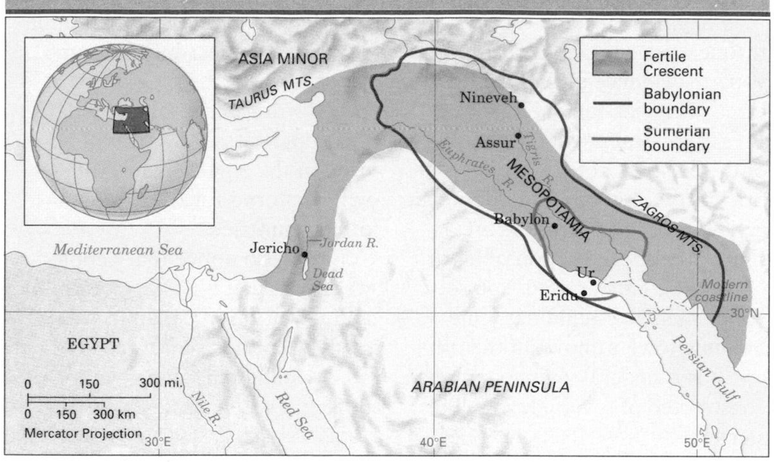
ASIA MINOR
TAURUS MTS.
Nineveh
Assur
Tigris R.
Euphrates R.
MESOPOTAMIA
ZAGROS MTS.
Babylon
Mediterranean Sea
Jericho
Jordan R.
Dead Sea
Ur
Eridu
Modern coastline
30°N
EGYPT
Persian Gulf
ARABIAN PENINSULA
Nile R.
Red Sea
0 150 300 mi.
0 150 300 km
Mercator Projection
30°E
40°E
50°E
Fertile Crescent
Babylonian boundary
Sumerian boundary

The Fertile Crescent extends over parts of what are now Turkey, Iran, Iraq, Syria, Lebanon, Jordan and Israel. Mesopotamia made up much of the Fertile Crescent. Sumer was centered between the Tigris and Euphrates rivers.

Sumer: An Early Civilization

The city of Ur was in Sumer *(SOO muhr),* a land in southern Mesopotamia *(mehs uh puh TAY mee uh).* Sumer was one of the early cultures that arose after people began a farming life. It developed about 5,500 years ago.

The Fertile Crescent

The map on this page shows that Mesopotamia is the area between the Tigris *(TY grihs)* and Euphrates rivers. In fact, in Greek the word Mesopotamia means "land between the rivers." This area covers most of present-day Iraq.

Mesopotamia was part of the Fertile Crescent—an area of land that crosses Southwest Asia. The Fertile Crescent stretches from the Taurus Mountains in the north (now part of Turkey) to modern Israel in the south and the Persian Gulf in the east. Plants grow well in the Fertile Crescent because it has water. Much of this water, however, comes from rivers rather than rain. For this reason **irrigation,** or a system for watering crops, was necessary for the farms around Mesopotamian cities like Ur.

What Is a Civilization?

Civilizations have been defined in different ways. Most scholars agree that when a society develops enough for cities to form, it becomes a **civilization.**

The civilizations of the Fertile Crescent shared at least five specific features. The first was an agricultural **surplus,** or a supply of extra food. A surplus made the other features possible.

Specialization of labor, the second feature, meant that people had specific jobs. These jobs were divided into social levels, or **classes.** This was the third feature. Civilizations also had a form of government, including a system of laws. A government was the fourth feature.

Further evidence of a complex culture was the fifth feature. As you have read, culture includes art, architecture, religion, and music. The first complex cultures also kept written records.

Across Time & Space

Archaeologists try to find out specific dates for important events, such as when Sumer began. However, when early written records cannot be found, archaeologists can only estimate these dates. To show that a date is an estimate, they often use the Latin word circa, *meaning "approximately." Circa is often abbreviated* c. *or* ca.

DEVELOP

This lesson looks at the development of three neighboring civilizations: Sumer, Babylonia, and Assyria. Each of these civilizations developed significant ideas and objects, some of which are still used today. Instruct students to identify these ideas and objects as they read the lesson.

CULTURE

Critical Thinking

Ask students if they think that the United States shows evidence of the five features of civilization described on this page. Draw a chart on the chalkboard that lists these five features. Then have students fill in the chart with examples that show how the United States meets the requirements of a civilization.

CULTURE

Study Skills

Tell students that the Latin word *circa,* which literally means "around," serves as the root of many modern English words. Give students examples of these words, and have students think of others. *(Circumference, circulate, circle)* Discuss how each word incorporates the meaning of "around" or "approximately."

Access Strategy

Bring to class, or have students collect, pictures illustrating irrigation, dams, and other means of managing water resources. These can be found in magazines, encyclopedias, or other books. Lead a discussion about water and its uses. Ask students how they use water, where the water comes from, and how it reaches them.

Stress the special importance of water for farmers, and ask students to tell what they know about irrigation today. Point out that some modern methods of irrigation are similar to those developed more than 5,000 years ago in Mesopotamia. These modern irrigation systems still have the same purposes: to control flooding, to water crops, and to save water for later use.

Access Activity

Cultural achievements in music, literature, and the fine arts are a part of every civilization. Create a cultural profile of the class on the chalkboard. List the names of students who like to draw, write, dance, and so forth. Every student should be represented in at least one category. Tell students that the people of Sumer, Babylonia, and Assyria also cultivated many arts.

HISTORY

Social Participation

Talk about how archaeologists must piece together information about vanished civilizations. Sometimes it's difficult to figure out an item's use or to interpret its meaning.

Divide the class into groups. Ask each group to describe how archaeologists in A.D. 4000 might interpret these "finds" from our civilization: couches and chairs facing a TV; the cages and enclosures of a zoo; a doghouse; a lawn mower; a playground; a transit garage full of buses. Have each group select one person to share the group's interpretations with the class.

NATIONAL IDENTITY

Critical Thinking

Often, archaeologists can tell where objects came from by the way they are made and what they look like. Have students look at the picture of the lyre on this page. Because archaeologists found many objects decorated with bulls' heads when they excavated Ur, they know that similar objects excavated somewhere else may have come from Ur.

Ask students what items in your classroom would tell a stranger that it is a classroom in the United States. *(Pictures of U.S. Presidents or heroes; a U.S. flag; newspapers)*

This lyre decorated with a bull's head was made to look like one used at Ur around 2500 B.C.

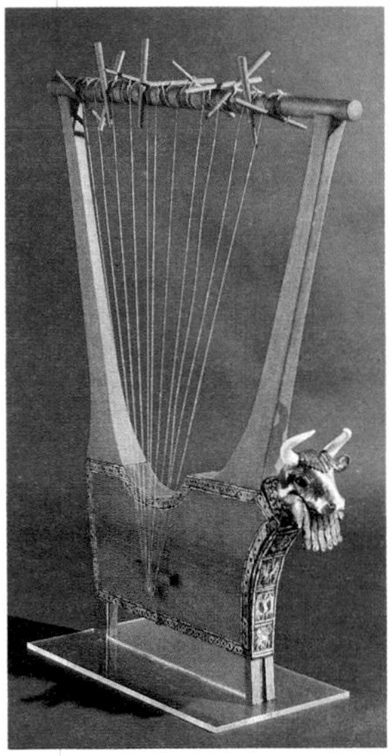

In the center of Ur, the ziggurat, other temples, and nearby buildings were set off as a religious place within the city.

Life in the City of Ur

Imagine you could take a walk through ancient Ur. All around, you see evidence of the five features of civilization.

As you walk toward the center of the city, you notice carpenters, bricklayers, and other builders. The activities of these workers are a sign of the specialization of labor.

As you look around, you see various kinds of buildings. One building towers above all the others. It is a ziggurat, a huge temple constructed of several levels, like steps.

A ziggurat dominated many Mesopotamian cities. Each ziggurat was dedicated to a specific God, who was believed to rule over the city. You can see a diagram of a ziggurat on this page. Near the ziggurat is a large palace where the king lives.

What do the size and richness of the ziggurat and the palace tell you? The ziggurat indicates that the worship of Ur's God is of the greatest importance to the people of Ur. The location of the palace next to the ziggurat signifies the key role played by the king who lives in the palace.

Around the ziggurat you notice a great deal of activity. From all directions people are bringing the produce of their farms to the city. These riches of the region include vegetables, dates, sesame seeds, and wool. Some of these goods will be used by people of the upper classes, some will be used in the ziggurat, and some will be stored for trading with other countries.

You also notice that people wear different kinds of clothing and jewelry. Some people are obviously wealthier, better fed, and better dressed than others—a sign of different social classes.

Social Classes

In Sumer the upper class included priests, soldiers, and government officials. Some of these officials ran the irrigation system. Others collected taxes and fees, while some served priests in the ziggurat.

Merchants, shopkeepers, teachers, farmers, and laborers belonged to the middle class. The lowest class was made up of slaves. Some slaves were people taken prisoner during wars.

On a walk through the king's palace, you notice someone playing a harp decorated with the carved head of a bull. This tells you that Sumerians enjoy music and make beautiful objects, both signs of a people's culture.

When you go to the ziggurat itself, you are at the heart of Ur's culture. There priests are worshiping some of Sumer's hundreds of Gods. There, too, the goods of the entire civilization are gathered. Scribes or priests are keeping track of the wool, grain, and other products brought to the ziggurat. To record these products, the scribes or priests write on clay tablets.

Visual Learning

In Sumer, symbols for commodities, such as grain, were combined with symbols for quantities, such as full sacks, to record harvests and trade transactions. Have students design symbols that show something like the number of books issued to each student or the quantity of items in the school cafeteria. Discuss how these symbols could eventually result in an alphabet.

Cultural Context

The archaeologist Sir Leonard Woolley is famous for excavations he made from 1922 to 1934 at the site of the ancient city of Ur. His most spectacular discoveries were unearthed at Ur's royal cemetery, which dates from about 2650 B.C. to about 2550 B.C.

Woolley excavated 16 royal graves. They show an elaborate burial ritual for members of royalty, including human sacrifices ranging from half a dozen to more than 70 victims in a grave.

After a royal corpse had been entombed, court members, servants, and charioteers with their chariots proceeded down a ramp into the open pit. Each person carried a cup of poison. When all had taken their places, they drank their death potions. Musicians played their harps and lyres until the poison took effect (a few were found with fingers still entwined among the strings). When the bodies were still, the grave was filled in. Woolley found no signs of struggle.

Some Sumerian Achievements

The Sumerians were important thinkers and inventors. They excelled in the fields of science and mathematics. In fact, Sumerian mathematics was so advanced that we still use some of it today.

For example, it was the Sumerians who created a system for subdividing a day and a year. Their year was made up of 12 months. Their system of mathematics divided a circle into 360 equal parts.

The Sumerians also discovered the importance of wheels. They made wheels out of wood. These wheels were used to build vehicles for farming, trade, and war. Even though we don't know who built the very first wheel, we do know that the Sumerians had wheels about 5,500 years ago. If you don't think that the wheel is an important invention, just try to imagine what your life would be like today without it. ■

The invention of the wheel allowed the Sumerians to build vehicles, such as chariots. This copper figurine of an animal-drawn chariot was found in a Sumerian temple.

■ *Give an example of each of the five features of civilization found at Ur.*

The Babylonians

About 1800 B.C. another Mesopotamian civilization arose. We call it Babylonia. Look for it on the map on page 67. The city of Babylon, in southern Mesopotamia, was the center of Babylonia. The king who first brought together various cities of Mesopotamia to form Babylonia was Hammurabi *(hah mu RAH bee)*. He ruled for more than 42 years, from 1792 to 1750 B.C.

Hammurabi is also known for recording a system of laws called the Code of Hammurabi. This code is considered one of the most important law codes in history. It is a description of what to do in specific cases. There are 282 laws contained in the code.

Many of these laws help us understand the treatment of women in Babylonian society. For example, the code says that if a woman was divorced, she could take back the money her parents had given her husband when she was married. If a woman's husband died, she would have the use of his property.

Other laws give us an idea of what life was like in cities such as Babylon. One law tells us what happened if an ox stabbed someone with its horn and caused that person's death. The code says that in such an event, the owner of the ox had to pad its horns, tie it up, or take responsibility for any further harm the ox might cause.

Archaeologists found the Code of Hammurabi engraved on a large stone structure called a stele (STEE lee). *This engraving at the top of the stele shows one of the Babylonian Gods giving the rod and ring to King Hammurabi, which signified his right to rule.*

GEOGRAPHY

Critical Thinking

Have students reread pages 67 through 69, listing other kinds of technology besides irrigation that the Sumerians used because of their physical environment. *(The chariot, the wheel)* In class, discuss how the environment may have stimulated the use of these things. (In talking about the wheel, in use around 3500 B.C., be sure to refer to the Sumerians' extensive trade, the need to transport goods, and the existence of draft animals.)

■ *The following are examples of the five features of civilization found at Ur: surplus—some of the goods brought to the ziggurat were stored for trading with other countries; specialization—builders, priests, merchants; social classes—wealthy and ordinary (or common) people, differentiated by appearance; government—the king and officials; other cultural features—music, religion, record-keeping.*

Historical Context

The world's great civilizations arose where they did largely because people could develop a stable food supply in those regions. In addition to Mesopotamia, by 1500 B.C. there were river-valley civilizations along the Nile in Egypt, the Indus in what is today Pakistan, and the Huang He in China. Turn to the map on page 59 to review the locations of these civilizations. These areas and others that were not located in river valleys will be studied in later chapters.

Economic Context

To give students a fuller understanding of Mesopotamian culture, tell them that clay was ancient Mesopotamia's most important raw material. Buildings were almost exclusively constructed of clay, including the massive walls built around cities. Sun-dried bricks were cheap, easily obtained, and suitable for a climate with little rainfall. A great variety of clay figurines and pottery artifacts still exist. Perhaps most important, clay was the vehicle for cuneiform writing.

Critical Thinking

Encourage students to explain what society would be like today without a system of writing. *(Possible answers: Most scientific and technological advances would not be possible. All communication would be done face-to-face. All teaching and learning would be done orally.)*

Note: You may wish to use this Closer Look as an extension of the discussion of Life in the City of Ur on page 68.

CULTURE

Critical Thinking

Have students study the pictures and read the captions. Discuss the many ways writing is used in our society to communicate ideas and information. Have students work in pairs to "write" to one another using only pictographs or coded symbols. Ask students to explain why this type of writing is more difficult to use than alphabetic writing, such as English.

More About Cuneiform Writing
Translating cuneiform is difficult. Many of the characters can represent either a word or a syllable, depending upon how it was used and when and where it was written. As cuneiform was adapted by different ancient peoples, the same character took on completely different meanings. Sumerian and Babylonian cuneiform was the most complex: it used about 600 characters. Some of the more complicated characters contained 30 or more wedge-shaped elements. For more on ancient writing systems, see the Minipedia, pages 660–661.

A CLOSER LOOK

Cuneiform Writing

The ancient Sumerian people, who lived in what is now southern Iraq, were the first to invent writing. At first, scribes drew simple pictures on wet clay tablets, probably to keep track of cows or sacks of grain. Over many centuries, beginning about 3100 B.C., their marks became more complex. This newer script, called cuneiform, could capture ideas such as "life" or "light" in symbols.

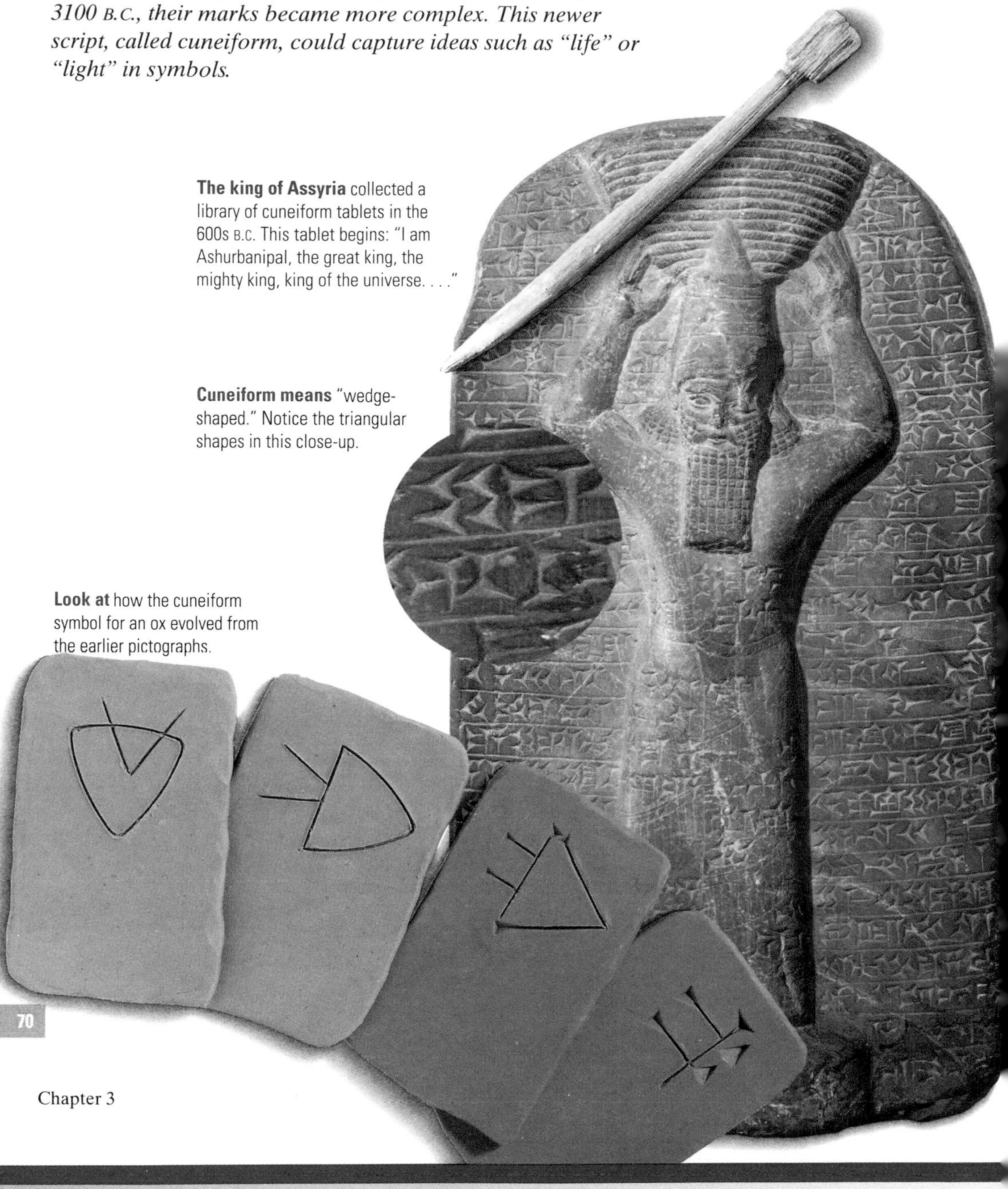

A writing tool, called a stylus, looked like this. Carved from reed or wood, it was pressed into clay to create cuneiform symbols.

The king of Assyria collected a library of cuneiform tablets in the 600s B.C. This tablet begins: "I am Ashurbanipal, the great king, the mighty king, king of the universe. . . ."

Cuneiform means "wedge-shaped." Notice the triangular shapes in this close-up.

Look at how the cuneiform symbol for an ox evolved from the earlier pictographs.

Visual Learning

Have students experiment with cuneiform writing using sticks with wedge-shaped tips, and clay or some other soft medium. Then have students try to fashion the ends of the sticks into other shapes and observe what kinds of indentations they make.

Collaborative Learning

Divide the class into groups. Ask each group to think about changes that occurred in societies once a system of writing was introduced and people learned to read. Tell the class that they will work together in their groups to research and prepare a report on these changes. Each group member should have a task, such as researcher, recorder, editor, illustrator, or presenter. Suggest that students think about the impact of writing and reading on a society's economy, government, religion, arts, and class system. Each group should prepare a brief oral report for the class. Allow time for the class to compare and contrast the conclusions of the different groups. (As you lead this activity, you may find useful *The Domestication of the Savage Mind* by Jack Goody.)

Another law gives the punishment for a builder who "has built a house for a man and has not made his work sound, so that the house he has made falls down and causes the death of the owner of the house." According to the Code of Hammurabi, such a builder should be put to death.

As important and interesting as the Code of Hammurabi is, it was not a law code like those we have today. Instead it was a description of the way Hammurabi felt the laws *should* be. When we examine actual law cases from Babylonian times, we see that the code itself never became the law of the land. ■

■ How do Hammurabi's laws show what life was like in ancient Babylonia?

The Assyrians

North of Babylonia another Mesopotamian civilization arose and became powerful about 1350 B.C. This civilization was Assyria *(uh SIHR ee uh)*. Find Assyria on the map on this page.

The Struggle for Empire

The Assyrians developed powerful armies equipped with iron weapons. With these armies they conquered the lands up to the Mediterranean Sea. At times the Assyrians controlled Babylonia as well. They even overran far-off Egypt. The Assyrians formed a large empire, or a state in which one ruler controls several kingdoms or territories.

The conquered peoples often rebelled. Some of them drove the Assyrians away. At other times rebellions failed, and conquered peoples were killed or exiled. Historians have wondered why the Assyrians had such a hard time holding onto their empire. Some think they have found an explanation in Assyrian art.

Much of Assyrian art portrays battle scenes. In these scenes the Assyrians are often shown killing their enemies. Some historians have suggested that conquered peoples may have rebelled against Assyrian rule because there was no other way to escape Assyrian cruelty.

Other historians point out, however, that the Assyrians were no worse than other rulers of the time. We don't know yet why the Assyrians ruled some areas for such a short time. Maybe we never will.

After many periods of strength and weakness, the Assyrians fell from power. In 612 B.C. the last Assyrian capital, Nineveh, was captured by the Medes, people from what is now Iran.

How Do We Know?

HISTORY *We have learned most of what we know about ancient times and peoples from the science of archaeology. All over the world archaeologists carefully dig up ancient artifacts, or tools and other objects made by early humans. By studying these artifacts, archaeologists can determine their age, what they were used for, and something about the culture of the people who made them.*

Assyrian and Babylonian Empires

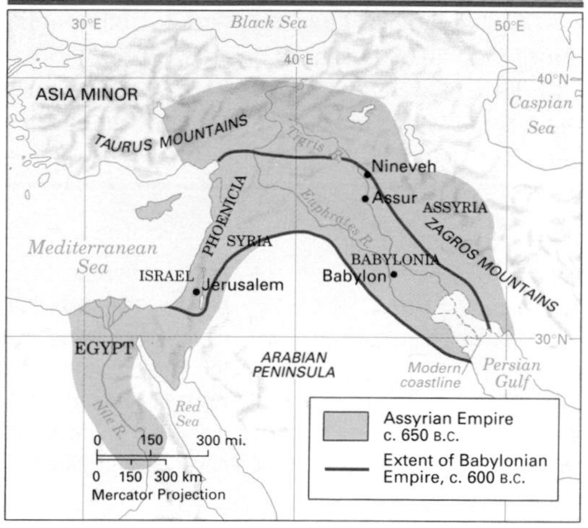
30°E
Black Sea
40°E
50°E
40°N
ASIA MINOR
Caspian Sea
TAURUS MOUNTAINS
Tigris R.
Nineveh
Assur
ASSYRIA
PHOENICIA
Euphrates R.
ZAGROS MOUNTAINS
Mediterranean Sea
SYRIA
BABYLONIA
ISRAEL
Jerusalem
Babylon
30°N
EGYPT
ARABIAN PENINSULA
Modern coastline
Persian Gulf
Nile R.
Red Sea
0 150 300 mi.
0 150 300 km
Mercator Projection
Assyrian Empire c. 650 B.C.
Extent of Babylonian Empire, c. 600 B.C.

◄ This map shows the Assyrian Empire about 650 B.C. Early in their success, the Assyrians defeated Babylon and raided lands as far west as Egypt.

■ Even though the Code of Hammurabi represents the way Hammurabi thought the laws should be, students may infer the following about Babylonia: divorced and widowed women lost access to their husbands' property; oxen wandered about the streets; builders sometimes failed to do a careful job.

GEOGRAPHY

Map and Globe Skills

Direct students to look at the map on this page. To be sure they can interpret the key, ask which was larger, the Assyrian Empire c. 650 B.C. or the Babylonian Empire c. 600 B.C., and why they think this might be so. *(The Assyrian Empire, because their iron weapons enabled them to conquer many surrounding lands)*

CULTURE

Critical Thinking

In southern Mesopotamia rainfall was light, so farmers invented ways to irrigate their crops. In northern Mesopotamia there was more rainfall, so irrigation was not as crucial. Ask students how these facts might have contributed to the Assyrians' drive to build their empire. *(Because not all Assyrians had to spend their time building and maintaining an irrigation system, they had the time and energy available to expand their empire.)*

Mathematics Connection

Lessons 1 and 2 cover a very long period of time. Have students use the lesson timelines to create math problems that demonstrate these long periods. For example, ask them to figure out about how long it took the first humans to develop agriculture. *(2,400,000 – 15,000 = 2,385,000 years)* Then ask them how many years are covered in Lesson 2. *(3500 – 612 = 2888 years)* For contrast, have them use almanacs or books such as *The Timetable of History* by Bernard Grum (Simon and Schuster, 1991) to consider the rate of modern change. For example, they can find out how many years elapsed between the time the first airplane flew and humans first landed on the moon. *(1969 – 1903 = 66 years)* Ask students why they think the rate of change has accelerated in modern history. *(Possible answer: Because of the quicker communication of ideas and the development of technology, such as electronics)*

Visual Learning

Have students create their own objects out of clay in the style of the figurine on page 69. They may wish to create figures, buildings, gates, ziggurats, or relief sculptures. Encourage students to research more Mesopotamian art before they begin their projects.

BELIEF SYSTEMS

Study Skills

Tell students that people in ancient civilizations thought of religion differently from the way most people do today. In ancient times religion was completely integrated into all facets of life. It provided the basic principles upon which all law, ethics, science, art, and other activities were based. A people's religion was a way of seeing and living that, in effect, was the "glue" that held early civilizations together.

Have students look back at the stele on which the Code of Hammurabi is engraved, on page 69. What evidence on the stele might indicate that law and religion were linked for the Babylonians? *(The top of the stele shows the rod and ring, symbols of authority, being given to Hammurabi by a Babylonian God.)*

■ *The Assyrians may have been extremely cruel to the people they conquered.*

CLOSE

Answer the Thinking Focus. Then ask students how life in modern civilizations would be different if Sumer, Babylonia, and Assyria had not contributed those achievements.

➤ In the ruins of Assyrian temples and palaces, archaeologists have found many reliefs. These are stone sculptures that project out from the walls, giving a three-dimensional effect. This relief shows an official giving information to two scribes.

Across Time & Space

Many of the letters of your alphabet were developed 4,000 years ago by the Phoenicians, a trading people who lived along the coast of the eastern Mediterranean Sea. Their names for the first two letters were alef *and* bet. *The Greeks later changed the names of the first two letters to* alpha *and* beta. *From these letters we get our word* alphabet.

■ *What reason do some historians give to explain why the Assyrians often failed to keep control of their conquered peoples?*

Ashurbanipal's Library

Besides its importance as the Assyrian capital, Nineveh is famous for another reason. One of the world's first great libraries was at Nineveh. The last great king of the Assyrians, Ashurbanipal *(ah shur BAH nuh pahl)*, created the library. Ashurbanipal's library included books on fables, proverbs, religion, magic, law, science, folktales, and ancient stories. Some of the books were written in the Sumerian language and some in the Babylonian language.

Archaeologists have uncovered more than 20,000 of these "books." All of them are clay tablets. These tablets may have made up only a small part of the collection Ashurbanipal once had.

When archaeologists found Ashurbanipal's library, they did not know that the Sumerian language existed. By studying Ashurbanipal's Sumerian books and comparing them with others that had been found elsewhere, scholars learned to read Sumerian.

It is fortunate for us that Ashurbanipal collected books. Such a large library can tell us a great deal about the Sumerians and other peoples of the time. If Ashurbanipal had not loved knowledge and books so much, we would know far less about Mesopotamia than we do. ■

REVIEW

1. **FOCUS** What were the major achievements of the civilizations of ancient Mesopotamia?
2. **CULTURE** List and explain three features that make up a civilization.
3. **CULTURE** Give one example of a Sumerian idea that influences our culture today.
4. **CRITICAL THINKING** How might specialization of labor have encouraged social classes to develop in Sumer?
5. **CRITICAL THINKING** Can you think of examples of modern laws that resemble laws from the Code of Hammurabi? List as many as you can think of, and tell how they are similar to those in the Code of Hammurabi.
6. **WRITING ACTIVITY** Write a short story describing how a day in your life would be different if the wheel had never been invented.

Homework Options

Have students choose one social class in a Mesopotamian society and write a paragraph that describes what they imagine life would have been like for a member of that class. Suggest that students mention daily routines, special events, work schedules, contact with others, family life, and so on.

Study Guide: page 12

Answers to Review Questions

1. These civilizations used irrigation; excelled at science and mathematics; used the wheel; developed a legal code; assembled a large library; and used iron weapons.
2. Students' answers should explain three of the following: agricultural surplus, specialization of labor, social classes, government, and other signs of a complex culture.
3. Possible answers include division of a year into 12 months and use of the wheel.
4. People who performed jobs perceived as more valuable than others might have been given higher status; thus, a higher and lower class would have formed.
5. Possible answers include fines for littering or for traffic violations, and community-service sentences for certain offenses. Like laws in the Code of Hammurabi, these laws tell what to do in specific cases.
6. Accept a variety of responses. Encourage students to provide vivid details.

PREHISTORY
8500
6800
5100
3400
2000
B.C. A.D.
70
1700

L E S S O N 3

The Origins of Judaism

About 2000 B.C. a man named Abraham lived with his family in a Mesopotamian town called Haran. People in Haran, as in the rest of Mesopotamia, worshiped many Gods.

Abraham, however, worshiped only one God. Today, **monotheism,** or the belief in only one God, is shared by Christians, Muslims, Jews, and millions of other people all over the world. Most scholars agree that 4,000 years ago, however, monotheism was rarely practiced. Abraham started a tradition that lasted and spread over most of the world.

THINKING FOCUS

What are the main teachings of Judaism?

The Promise of Land

Abraham's story is told in a collection of religious writings called the Bible. The Jewish Bible is made up of 24 books that tell the story and the teachings of early Judaism. The Christian Bible includes the entire Jewish Bible under the name Hebrew Scriptures or Old Testament. It is bound together with the New Testament, a collection of 27 books that tell the story and the teachings of early Christianity. Stories about Abraham are also found in the Muslim Qur'an.

Archaeologists continue to discover artifacts and writings that help us understand Abraham's time. Even so, for his story and for information about early Judaism, the Bible is our best source.

From the book of Genesis, the first book of the Bible, we learn that when Abraham was 75 years old, God spoke to him in Haran. God said to him:

> *Go from your country and your kindred [family] and your father's house to the land that I will show you. I will make of you a great nation, and I will bless you, and make your name great, so that you will be a blessing. . . ."*
>
> Genesis 12:1–2

According to Genesis, Abraham obeyed God's command. He left Haran and journeyed to Canaan, an area just to the east of the Mediterranean Sea. There God promised to give this land to Abraham and his descendants. Abraham, his family, and his descendants

Key Terms

- monotheism
- Torah
- prophet
- rabbi
- Talmud

▼ *The ancient Hebrew alphabet was made up only of consonants. Beginning about A.D. 800, scribes added small symbols to the consonants to represent vowels. Here are the first two words—read from right to left—of chapter 17 in Genesis.*

וַיְהִי אַבְרָם

INTRODUCE

This lesson teaches students about the history and beliefs of the Jewish people. Have students read the Thinking Focus, and ask them to recall what they may already know about Judaism. Remind them that Judaism is one of the world's major religions.

Have students look at the timeline at the top of this page. Help them see that more than 2,000 years will be covered in this lesson. Review the names of the three Mesopotamian civilizations studied in the last lesson. *(Sumer, Babylonia, Assyria)* Tell students that in this lesson they will read about a group of people from Mesopotamia who have kept their religious identity for about 4,000 years.

Key Terms

Vocabulary Strategies: T36–T37

monotheism—the belief that there is only one God

Torah—the first five books of the Bible, containing the laws and early history of the Jews

prophet—a religious leader who reminded the Jews of their responsibilities to God

rabbi—a teacher who interprets Jewish law; the ordained leader of a Jewish synagogue

Talmud—a collection of books containing the laws and customs that developed in the Jewish tradition

Graphic Overview

God promises Canaan to Abraham ➤ **Jacob leaves Canaan for Egypt** ➤ **Moses leads Exodus** 12 tribes settle in Canaan ➤ **Kingdom of Israel / Kingdom of Judah** ➤ **Period of Exile**

Objectives

1. Describe the early history of the Jewish people.
2. Explain the major teachings of modern Judaism.

DEVELOP

Ask students to read the opening paragraphs of the lesson and the section called The Promise of Land to find out what major change in religious belief was represented by the biblical story of Abraham. *(Monotheism, a belief in one God instead of many)* Ask students how they think Abraham was treated by other people during his time. *(They may have thought he was odd, wrong, foolish, or even mad.)*

CULTURE

Critical Thinking

Many African American spirituals were inspired by Bible stories of the ancient Jews. Bring in recordings of "Let My People Go," "Deep River," and other spirituals. Ask students to relate the references in each song to the experiences of the ancient Jews who were enslaved in Egypt and to the experiences of enslaved African Americans in the United States.

▲ *One belief central to Judaism is that God gave a set of laws to Moses after the Israelites had left Egypt in the Exodus. This painting illustrates a manuscript page of the Torah in the Bible of St. Paulo di Muri de Roma in Italy. It shows Moses receiving the laws of the Torah from God and presenting them to the Israelites.*

remained faithful to God even though other people in Canaan worshiped many Gods.

Abraham's grandson Jacob, who was also called Israel, had 12 sons. When a serious food shortage threatened the region, Jacob and his family left Canaan. They moved to the nearby country of Egypt.

In Egypt, Jacob prospered, and his family grew rapidly. Each of his sons became the ancestor of an entire tribe. The members of the 12 tribes came to be known as the Israelites.

The Exodus

For hundreds of years, the Israelites were treated well by the Egyptians. Then one of the Egyptian kings began to treat the Israelites as slaves. He made the Israelites work on various building projects.

In time a leader named Moses arose among the Israelites. The Bible tells us that God instructed Moses to lead the Israelites out of Egypt. Their passage from slavery to freedom, called the Exodus, is still celebrated by Jews in their annual Passover festival.

According to the Bible, Moses led the Israelites through the wilderness for 40 years. Early in their journey, they stopped at Mount Sinai. There God gave them a set of laws called the Ten Commandments.

Through Moses, God gave the Israelites other laws and instructions as well. These laws are included in the first five books of the Bible, which together are called the **Torah.** The word Torah means "instruction." The Torah also includes stories about the beginning of the world and early times up to the death of Moses.

Some of the laws in the Torah are like the laws in the Code of Hammurabi and many modern laws. They tell what should be done in specific legal cases. Other laws in the Torah give instructions for worship. They describe behavior on holy days that Jews still celebrate, such as Rosh Ha-Shanah *(rawsh huh SHAW nuh),* the New Year; Yom Kippur *(yawm KIHP uhr),* the Day of Atonement; and Pesach *(PAY sahkh),* the Passover.

The Torah also gives basic rules for living a good life. The best known rules are the Ten Commandments. Also important is the instruction "Love your neighbor as yourself," found in the book of Leviticus.

Access Activity

Write the first key term, *monotheism,* on the chalkboard. Tell students that the prefix *mono-* comes from the Greek word *monos,* which means "single" or "alone." The root *-the-* comes from *theos,* which means "God." Ask students how understanding word origins can help them determine the meaning of *monotheism.*

Access Strategy

Exodus means "a going out." The Israelites went out of Egypt to escape slavery. Discuss current examples of people leaving their homeland due to famine, political events, or other reasons. Compare these current events with the Exodus described in this lesson.

Ask for volunteers to share personal experiences of moving. Why did they move? *(Possible answers: to find better housing, to live with adoptive parents, because a family member got a new job)* What was pleasant or difficult about moving? *(Pleasant: getting a new start, making friends; difficult: leaving friends, getting used to a new place)*

Then ask how moving as an individual or as a family might be different from moving as a group of individuals or families. What feelings might people in the current-events stories have about their exodus? *(Possible answer: fear, because for many people leaving is not a "choice" and because they may have no new place to go)*

◄ *In ancient Jerusalem the temple was the center of worship. This model shows what the temple that Solomon built might have looked like.*

Jerusalem and the Temple

The people who lived in Canaan when the Israelites arrived were called Canaanites. Scholars disagree about whether the Israelites fought with the Canaanites or settled among them peacefully. Nevertheless, by about 1200 B.C. the Israelites controlled Canaan. They regarded it as the land God had promised to Abraham.

For about 200 years after the Israelites had settled in Canaan, there was little unity among the tribes. People called judges brought the tribes together at times of emergency. Kings ruled a united Israel for the following 100 years. One of these kings, David, made Jerusalem the capital of Israel in about 1000 B.C. Another king, David's son Solomon, built a great temple at Jerusalem. You can see what the temple might have looked like in the picture on this page.

The temple became the center of the Israelites' religious life. People came to the temple to worship, pray, and offer sacrifices to God. They also sang and recited songs called psalms. The book of Psalms in the Bible is a collection of these temple songs and similar poems that were composed later. ■

Independent Kingdoms

Israel's unity did not last long. By about 900 B.C., after the reign of Solomon, the kingdom had split into two parts, each with its own king. The new northern kingdom was home to 10 of the 12 Israelite tribes. It kept the name Israel. The new southern kingdom was called Judah after the tribe of that name. Residents of Judah were known as Judeans. In later years they were called Jews and their religion was called Judaism.

The Prophets

The Bible tells that during the time of the divided kingdoms, many kings did not worship only the one God. They also allowed the people to worship other Gods. In addition, they allowed the rich to take advantage of the poor.

Across Time & Space

In A.D. 525, a Christian monk named Dionysius Exiguus introduced the system used today to number the years. He began with the year when many believed Jesus was born. The initials A.D. mean "anno Domini," or "in the year of the Lord." The initials B.C. mean "before Christ." Some non-Christians and Christians alike prefer to use the initials C.E., meaning "common era," and B.C.E., meaning "before common era."

■ *What were the different types of laws given in the Torah?*

ETHICS

Study Skills

Tell students that the biblical prophets were people who claimed to hear what God had to say to the Jews. The prophets recognized the ways in which the Jews had disregarded God's laws and warned the people of coming destruction if they did not change their behavior.

Today, prophets are not necessarily religious figures. Modern prophets proclaim what they see as the truth about society's ills and warn of possible dire consequences. Rachel Carson, author of *Silent Spring,* was a modern prophet of environmental disaster. Nelson Mandela's views about the elimination of apartheid in South Africa are an example of modern prophecy about civil rights. Assign groups of students to find out more about Carson, Mandela, or another modern prophet and to prepare an illustrated, written report. *(Other possible subjects include Elizabeth Cady Stanton, Sojourner Truth, Alexander Solzhenitsyn, Mohandas Gandhi, and Thurgood Marshall.)*

■ *Laws in the Torah tell what should be done in specific legal cases, give instructions for worship, and like the Ten Commandments, give basic rules for living a good life.*

Historical Context

To give students a greater understanding of Abraham and his descendants, tell them that the Bible says that Abraham's name was originally Abram. When Abram settled in Canaan, God changed his name to Abraham, meaning "father of many nations." Abraham's grandson was named Jacob. The Bible records that God visited Jacob as an angel and wrestled with him. Then God changed Jacob's name to Israel, which means "one who wrestles with God." Canaan came to be known as the land of Israel. Jacob (Israel) had twelve sons, after whom the twelve tribes of Israel were named: Reuben, Simeon, Levi, Judah, Issachar, Zebulun, Joseph, Benjamin, Dan, Naphtali, Gad, and Asher.

Israel divided into two kingdoms following the death of Solomon in 922 B.C. Ten tribes split away to the north to form the kingdom of Israel. The tribes of Benjamin and Judah formed the kingdom of Judah to the south, keeping Jerusalem as the capital.

Visual Learning

Ask students to look at the model on this page to see what Solomon's temple might have looked like. The Bible says that the temple floor was about 60 cubits long by 20 cubits wide. In the Hebrew Scriptures, a cubit is about 17.5 inches. Ask students to estimate how large the temple was in feet. *(About 87.5 feet long by about 29 feet wide)*

BELIEF SYSTEMS

Critical Thinking

Explore with students reasons that the Jews' homeland was so important to them. Write the word *land* on the chalkboard and circle it. Create a word web of ideas Jews associated with the land, and connect the circles around these ideas to the central circle. *(Possible ideas: Exodus; promised by God; Jacob's 12 sons)* Then discuss how each of these ideas held a deep significance for the Jews. Talk about the effect of the exile on the Jews, based on the significance of the land.

HISTORY

Social Participation

Direct students to look at the Hebrew characters on page 73. Tell students that the Hebrew Scriptures (or Old Testament in the Christian Bible) were originally written in ancient Hebrew. These writings, together with archaeological findings, provide all we know about the ancient Israelites and the early Jews. In time these writings were translated into Greek, Latin, and, eventually, hundreds of modern languages, including English. If possible, invite a rabbi or Jewish scholar to read a Hebrew passage aloud to the class.

The Ten Commandments

1. I am the LORD your God. . . . You shall have no other gods before me.
2. You shall not make for yourself an idol [image of a God]. . . . You shall not bow down to them or worship them. . . .
3. You shall not make wrongful use of the name of the LORD your God
4. Remember the sabbath day, and keep it holy. . . .
5. Honor your father and your mother, so that your days may be long in the land that the LORD your God is giving you.
6. You shall not murder.
7. You shall not commit adultery.
8. You shall not steal.
9. You shall not bear false witness against your neighbor.
10. You shall not covet . . . anything that belongs to your neighbor.

Source: The Holy Bible, New Revised Standard Version, 1989

➤ *Although the Ten Commandments were recorded thousands of years ago, many Jews and Christians today still regard them as all-important rules.*

The Bible includes a number of books named for prophets who lived during this time. The **prophets** were religious leaders who were disturbed by the people's actions. The prophets reminded the people of their relationship with God. They preached that the Israelites and the Judeans should worship only the one God of Abraham. They urged the people to treat one another fairly as God had commanded them. If the people failed to obey God, the prophets warned, their land would be destroyed.

The prophets also gave the people hope. They assured the Israelites and the Judeans that God would bring them back even if enemies forced them out of their homeland.

A Period of Exile

In about 722 B.C., the Assyrians destroyed the northern kingdom of Israel. They resettled the Israelites in other parts of the Assyrian Empire. However, the kingdom of Judah remained.

By about 610 B.C., the Babylonians and the Medes had defeated the Assyrians. Under King Nebuchadnezzar, the Babylonians took over Judah in 586 B.C., destroyed the temple, and burned Jerusalem. Nebuchadnezzar forced thousands of Judeans to move to Babylon.

In Babylon the exiled Jews were allowed to live in settlements, farm, and trade. Still, living far from their beloved homeland among people who worshiped many Gods was a test of their faith. One of the psalms records the Jews' struggle: "By the rivers of Babylon —there we sat down and there we wept when we remembered Zion [Jerusalem]. . . . How could we sing the Lord's song in a foreign land?"

The Jews met this test with renewed faith. Now they stressed the importance of their laws and religious traditions even more than they had before the exile.

In 539 B.C. an empire called Persia conquered Babylon. In the following year, the Persian king allowed the Jews to return to their land. They built a new temple in Jerusalem and began to worship in it. Much later, in A.D. 70, the Romans destroyed this second temple in a war against the Jews. They never rebuilt their temple.

From Past to Present

How was it possible for the Jews to maintain their faith without

Across Time & Space

Today during worship services in some synagogues, the Torah is carried in a procession to a reading desk. There passages are read aloud or chanted in an ancient melody. Before and after the reading of the Torah, the congregation recites prayers and blessings. The service varies depending on the day of the week and the time of day.

Social Participation

Ask students to imagine that they are modern prophets. Have each student give a short speech alerting the rest of the class to a particular social problem that presently exists in the local community, in the nation, or elsewhere in the world. Have students outline the specific steps that must be taken to correct this problem.

Research

Point out that the word *God* appears on U.S. coins ("In God We Trust"), in the Pledge of Allegiance (". . .one nation under God"), and in the oath that witnesses take before addressing a court of law (". . . so help me God"). Ask them what they think this indicates about the relationship between religion and government in the United States.

You may wish to assign small groups to do some research and to report to the class about the relationship between religion and government in one of the following: the Massachusetts Bay Colony, the modern United States, modern Israel, the former Soviet Union, Germany just before World War II, or modern Northern Ireland.

a common land or temple? The answer: A group of teachers, a set of books, and a new place to meet for prayer created a portable homeland for the Jews.

The teachers are called **rabbis.** The word *rabbi (RAB eye)* means "master" or "teacher." Beginning in the first century A.D., rabbis taught the Jews how to live by the instructions of the Torah and the prophets, even if they could no longer worship at the temple.

Early rabbis created the **Talmud,** a collection of books containing the laws and customs that developed in the Jewish tradition. The Talmud was completed in Babylonia in the sixth century.

The place for prayer is called the synagogue *(SIHN uh gahg).* The word *synagogue* means "meeting" or "gathering" in Greek. Ever since the exile in Babylon, Jews have been meeting for prayer in synagogues. Synagogues can be built anywhere, but they always face in the direction of Jerusalem.

Today there are more than 17 million Jews in the world. About seven million live in the United States, and about four million in the modern State of Israel. Guided by rabbis who interpret the Talmud, Jews worship in synagogues around the world. Wherever they live, they honor the tradition they believe began almost 4,000 years ago with their ancestor Abraham. ■

The six-pointed Star of David was used in ancient times by several civilizations as a magical sign or decoration. In the 1600s it was used for the first time as a general symbol of Judaism.

Today Jewish families around the world celebrate holy days. Here a family celebrates a Seder meal at Passover.

■ *What helps modern Jews hold onto their traditions?*

■ *The Torah and other Hebrew Scriptures, the rabbis who interpret the Torah, the Talmud, and the synagogue have helped Jews hold onto their religious traditions.*

REVIEW

1. **FOCUS** What are the main teachings of Judaism?
2. **GEOGRAPHY** Why did Jacob leave the land that he believed God had promised to his grandfather?
3. **ETHICS** What was the role of the prophets in ancient Israel and Judah?
4. **BELIEF SYSTEMS** What are the Torah and the Talmud?
5. **CRITICAL THINKING** Give an example of an event in Jewish history that cannot be proven or disproven by archaeologists.
6. **ACTIVITY** Find out about Jewish holy days such as Rosh Ha-Shanah or Yom Kippur. Write one or two paragraphs describing one of these holy days and its ceremonies.

CLOSE

Have students answer the Thinking Focus, recalling the major change in belief that marked the beginning of ancient Judaism. *(The change from belief in many Gods to monotheism, the belief in one God)* Have them recall from the chapter some of the difficulties that Jews have faced over the past 4,000 years or so. *(These include moving to Egypt, the Exodus to Canaan, the destruction of the temple, the exile to Babylon, the Roman invasion. Many students may also be aware of the Holocaust. Some may have family members who were victims or survivors of the Holocaust. Students may also mention the present struggles in Israel.)* Tell students that they will learn more about the recent history of the Jews in Chapters 7, 19, 20, and 28.

Answers to Review Questions

1. Judaism teaches that there is only one God; that God promised the land of Canaan to Abraham and his descendants; and that God gave them laws, recorded in the Torah, that instruct them how to live a good life.
2. Jacob left Canaan because a serious food shortage threatened the region.
3. The prophets reminded the Jews of their relationship with God, urged them to treat one another fairly, and warned the Jews that their land would be destroyed if they failed to obey God.
4. The Torah is the collection of the first five books of the Bible. The Talmud is a collection of books that contain the laws and customs that developed in Jewish tradition.
5. Direct quotations and people's thoughts mentioned in the Bible cannot be proved or disproved by archaeologists.
6. Students should include specific details about the meaning of the holy day and the ceremonies performed on that day.

Homework Options

The Golden Rule is a common rule for living that is reflected in many sacred and secular writings. It can be stated, "Treat others the way you want to be treated." Have students think of five "rules for living" that they try to follow. Then they can prepare a poster illustrating their rules.

Study Guide: page 13

Chapter Review

Reviewing Key Terms

agriculture (p. 59)
archaeologist (p. 58)
civilization (p. 67)
class (p. 67)
hunter-gatherer (p. 58)
irrigation (p. 67)
monotheism (p. 73)
prehistoric (p. 59)
prophet (p. 76)
rabbi (p. 77)
specialization of labor (p. 67)
surplus (p. 67)
Talmud (p. 77)
Torah (p. 74)

A. Read each pair of words. Write a sentence telling how the words in each pair are related.

1. agriculture, irrigation
2. civilization, surplus
3. specialization of labor, class
4. hunter-gatherer, prehistoric
5. archaeologist, civilization

B. Each statement below contains one or more key terms from the chapter. Decide whether each statement is correct or incorrect. Give reasons to support your decision using information in the chapter.

1. A surplus of food led to the specialization of labor.
2. Archaeologists study the written records of people who lived in prehistoric times.
3. Hunter-gatherers in the Fertile Crescent developed an important civilization 50,000 years ago.

C. Use a dictionary to find the origin of the following words. Then explain how the meaning of each word applies to Judaism.

1. Talmud
2. monotheism
3. Torah
4. prophet
5. rabbi

Exploring Concepts

A. The timeline below gives important dates and events in the history of ancient Mesopotamia. Copy the timeline on your own paper and complete it by filling in the missing events.

B. Answer each question with information from the chapter.

1. What big change in the way people lived occurred about 17,000 years ago?
2. What helped the people of Mesopotamia to be successful in farming?
3. Why is the area of land that crosses Southwest Asia called the Fertile Crescent?
4. Name the civilizations that developed in Mesopotamia. What kinds of evidence still exist to tell us about these civilizations?
5. What event do Jews celebrate in their annual Passover festival?
6. Compare the laws in the Code of Hammurabi with the laws in the Torah.

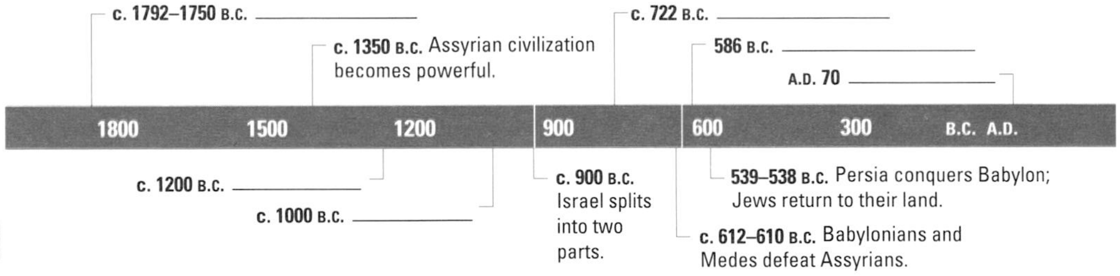
c. 1792–1750 B.C.
c. 1350 B.C. Assyrian civilization becomes powerful.
c. 722 B.C.
586 B.C.
A.D. 70
1800
1500
1200
900
600
300
B.C. A.D.
c. 1200 B.C.
c. 1000 B.C.
c. 900 B.C. Israel splits into two parts.
539–538 B.C. Persia conquers Babylon; Jews return to their land.
c. 612–610 B.C. Babylonians and Medes defeat Assyrians.

Answers to Reviewing Key Terms

A. Sample answers:

1. In some areas, **agriculture** was possible only if farmers developed a system of **irrigation.**
2. An agricultural **surplus** made all the other features of ancient **civilization** possible.
3. The **specialization of labor** led to the development of social levels, or **classes.**
4. Most **hunter-gatherers** lived in **prehistoric** times.
5. **Archaeologists** study the past, including early **civilizations.**

B. Sample answers:

1. The statement is correct. A **surplus** of food made all other features of a civilization possible, including **specialization of labor.**
2. The statement is incorrect. **Prehistoric** time is the time before people invented record-keeping.
3. The statement is incorrect. Ancient **hunter-gatherers** did not build cities and therefore had no **"civilization."**

C. Sample answers:

1. **Talmud** is a Hebrew word. The Talmud is a collection of books containing the laws and customs of Jewish tradition.
2. **Monotheism** is from the Greek words *monos,* "single, alone," and *theos,* "God." Abraham began a religious tradition based on monotheism.
3. **Torah** is a Hebrew word meaning "law" or "instruction." The Torah contains the first five books of the Bible.
4. **Prophet** is from the Greek words *pro,* "before," and *phanai,* "to speak." The prophets were religious leaders who warned the Jews that their behavior could bring about the destruction of their land.
5. **Rabbi** is from the Hebrew word *rab,* "master," plus *-î,* "my." Rabbis teach the Jews how to live by the instructions of the Torah and the prophets.

Answers to Exploring Concepts

A. Sample answers:

c. 1792–1750 B.C. Hammurabi rules Babylonia and issues Code of Hammurabi.
c. 1200 B.C. Israelites control Canaan.
c. 1000 B.C. David makes Jerusalem the capital of Israel.
c. 722 B.C. Assyrians destroy northern kingdom of Israel.
586 B.C. Babylonia takes over Judah, destroys temple, and burns Jerusalem.
A.D. 70 Romans destroy Jews' second temple.

B. Sample answers:

1. Most people stopped being hunter-gatherers. They learned to raise animals, and they began to grow plants.
2. Farming was successful because of the rich soil and the abundance of water.
3. The Fertile Crescent is so called because the land is rich and roughly crescent-shaped.
4. Civilizations: Sumer, Babylonia, Assyria, and Israel. Evidence: a variety of artifacts and a living religion.
5. Jews celebrate Passover to commemorate Moses' leading the Israelites out of Egypt in the Exodus.
6. Some of the laws in the Torah, like the laws in the Code of Hammurabi, tell what should be done in specific cases. Other Torah laws give instructions for worship and for behavior on holy days. Still others give rules for living a good life.

Reviewing Skills

1. Create a flow chart to summarize information in Lesson 3. Make a flow chart from the following facts. Be sure to give your flow chart a title.
   - A food shortage in Canaan caused Abraham's grandson Jacob and his family to move to Egypt.
   - The move to Egypt led to the enslavement of the Jews by an Egyptian king.
2. Look at the map of the Fertile Crescent on page 67. Then find a precipitation map of the region in an encyclopedia or atlas. Study the two maps. What is the annual precipitation in this area? How does this fact help explain why Mesopotamian farmers needed to irrigate the land?
3. Which map in the Atlas of this book tells you the names of the countries that lie within the Fertile Crescent region today? List these countries and their capital cities.

Using Critical Thinking

1. Archaeologists often try to make tools from stone and other materials the way early peoples made them. Why do you think they do this?
2. A surplus of food was probably the most important feature of civilizations in the Fertile Crescent because it made all the other features of civilization possible. Why do you think this is so? Explain your answer.
3. One of the main principles of the Code of Hammurabi is that "the strong shall not injure the weak." Do you think the laws we have today are based on this principle? Explain your answer.
4. The prophets in ancient Israel told the Jews that they had strayed from a proper life and warned them that destruction would result if they did not correct their ways. What do modern environmental prophets tell us about the way our society operates today?
5. During their exile in Babylon from 586 to 539 B.C., the Jews' faith was greatly tested. Why might this exile have been so difficult for the Jews?

Preparing for Citizenship

1. **WRITING ACTIVITY** As you read in this chapter, the Jews have a rich tradition that began long ago with their ancestor Abraham. Interview a Jewish family member or other person who lives in your community. Find out about Jewish customs, beliefs, religious services, holidays, and traditions. Write a short report about one holiday or tradition.
2. **COLLECTING INFORMATION** Ashurbanipal's library included books on fables, proverbs, religion, magic, law, science, folktales, and ancient stories. Visit your school or local library. What system does the library use to classify books? What are the main groups into which the books are classified? Share your information with the class.
3. **GROUP ACTIVITY** In ancient times, irrigation for watering crops was necessary to feed growing populations in cities like Ur. In small groups, discover how farmers today try to increase food production. What methods do they use? How successful have these methods been? Are any of these methods dangerous? Then decide how to present your findings to the class.
4. **COLLABORATIVE LEARNING** Many of the crops that Mesopotamian farmers grew are still grown in the Middle East today. Find out what these foods are and how they are prepared. Then plan a Middle Eastern meal. In small groups, prepare some Middle Eastern dishes to serve to your classmates. You may wish to invite friends and parents to your dinner.

Answers to Reviewing Skills

1. Make sure that students' flow charts show an accurate chain of events and have a title.
2. On average, from 10 to 20 inches of precipitation fall annually between the Tigris and Euphrates rivers. A small area bordering the Tigris River receives 20 to 40 inches. Since so little rain fell, Mesopotamian farmers needed to irrigate their fields.
3. Students should consult the map of Eurasia on pages 682 and 683. They should identify the following countries and capitals: Israel, Jerusalem; Jordan, Amman; Kuwait, Kuwait; Iraq, Baghdad; Iran, Tehran; Syria, Damascus; Lebanon, Beirut; Turkey, Ankara.

Answers to Using Critical Thinking

1. Trying to figure out how early peoples made tools gives archaeologists a better understanding of what those peoples' lives were like and what materials were available to them.
2. Without a surplus of food, everyone in a community has to help with the growing and gathering of food and therefore has little or no time for any other activities. Thus, there could be no specialization of labor, social classes, government, or further signs of culture.
3. Most students will agree that many of our laws are designed to protect the "weak" in society. Encourage students to cite examples of laws that pertain to family relations, such as divorce, adoption, and property laws; and laws that protect civil rights.
4. Modern environmental prophets point out that society dumps huge amounts of pollutants all around us every year. They warn that if we do not learn to change our behavior, we will ruin plant and animal life, including our own.
5. The Jews in exile experienced a test of faith because they no longer had one land and temple to unify them. Also, living amid the Babylonians, who worshiped many Gods, might have tempted the Jews to give up their monotheism.

Answers to Preparing for Citizenship

1. **WRITING ACTIVITY** You may wish to have students hand in their interview questions and notes as well as their reports, so that you can make suggestions about their note-taking or writing processes.
2. **COLLECTING INFORMATION** The library may use the Library of Congress system, Dewey decimal system, or another classification system. You may wish to have students make a chart listing the different classes, or categories, of books.
3. **GROUP ACTIVITY** Encourage students to write to the United Nations Food and Agriculture Organization in New York City for information. Students may wish to present their findings on a poster or mural, or in an oral or written report.
4. **COLLABORATIVE LEARNING** Students may need help locating recipes, obtaining ingredients, and/or preparing the dishes. You may find the following cookbooks useful: Rose Avadanian, *Kitchen Kapers;* Rose Dosti, *Middle Eastern Cooking;* Harry G. Nickles, *Middle Eastern Cooking;* and Claudia Roden, *A Book of Middle Eastern Food.*

CHAPTER ORGANIZER

Chapter 4 Ancient Egypt and Nubia

CHAPTER PLANNING CHART

Pupil's Edition	Teacher's Edition	Ancillaries
Lesson 1: Kingdoms on the Nile (2–3 days) Objective 1: Show how the Nile River supported the growth of civilizations. (Geography 2, 3) Objective 2: Compare and contrast the development of Egypt with that of Nubia. (Geography 4; Economics 2)	• Graphic Overview (82) • Access Strategy (83) Geographic Context (83) • Access Activity (83) Study Skills (84) Historical Context (84) Religious Context (84) Historical Context (85) Cultural Context (85) Critical Thinking (85)	Study Guide (14) Map Activities (8) Discovery Journal (9) • Study Prints (3)
Lesson 2: Ancient Cultures Linked Together (2–3 days) Objective 1: Describe how Egyptian society was organized. (Social and Political Systems 1) Objective 2: Show how religion influenced Egyptian life and culture. (Ethics and Belief Systems 2, 3) Objective 3: Explain how Nubia and Egypt affected each other's cultures. (Culture 1, 4)	• Graphic Overview (87) • Access Activity (88) • Access Strategy (88) Cultural Context (89) • Visual Learning (89) Social Participation (90) Art Connection (90) Geographic Context (90) Map and Globe Skills (91) Role-Playing (91) • Visual Learning (91)	Study Guide (15) Discovery Journal (10) Posters (9)
Lesson 3: Great Achievements (3–4 days) Objective 1: List achievements for which Egypt is remembered. (Culture 3; History 1) Objective 2: Describe the cultural changes that occurred during Nubia's Meroitic period. (Culture 4)	• Graphic Overview (93) • Access Activity (94) • Access Strategy (94)	Study Guide (16)
Understanding Visual Evidence Objective: Show how art can be a source of information about people of the past. (Visual Learning 1, 3)	Writing a Story (96) • Analyzing Art (96)	Study Guide (17)
Chapter Review	Answers (98–99)	Tests (13–16)

* Objectives are correlated to the strands and goals in the program Scope and Sequence on pages T41–T49.

• LEP appropriate resources.
(For additional strategies, see pages T32–T33.)

CHAPTER RATIONALE

Students may have some knowledge of ancient Egypt due to the popularizing of Egyptian motifs in clothing and art and stories of famous rulers such as Tutankhamon, Hatshepsut, and Ramesses II. Like many people, however, they may not have heard of the ancient civilization of Nubia, whose history is so closely tied to that of Egypt.

This chapter condenses some of the political history of dynastic Egypt in order to focus on the cultural relationship between Egypt and Nubia. Archaeological discoveries in this century have yielded plentiful information on Nubian civilization. They show Nubia to be at the center of a vibrant African trading economy, a key element in the flourishing of Egyptian civilization, and a distinct and significant culture in its own right. Any study of Egypt is incomplete without looking at the parallel development of Nubia.

Lesson 1 focuses on the geography of the Nile and on political development along the river valley. It establishes the relationship between Egypt and Nubia and outlines the main historical periods for each. Teachers can reinforce students' understanding of Egypt's three main dynastic periods—the Old, Middle, and New Kingdoms—by referring students to the timeline on page 85 and to the Understanding Dynasty feature on page 84. You might want to copy the timeline on the chalkboard as a reference.

The lesson begins with the desertification of the Sahara, which caused African peoples to concentrate in the Nile Valley. This story will help students understand the relationship of Egypt and Nubia to the rest of Africa. Nubia's role as a supplier of goods from east and central Africa to Egypt also highlights the connection of Nile dwellers to people in tropical Africa. The lesson then shows how the desire for control of the lucrative Nile trade led to rivalries between Nubia and Egypt.

Lesson 2 looks at key aspects of Egyptian and Nubian cultures. It focuses on two periods of time in which each culture greatly affected the other: when Egypt ruled all of Nubia and Nubia ruled all of Egypt. A Moment in Time on page 91 emphasizes the interaction of the two cultures; it depicts a Nubian princess bringing gifts to the Egyptian pharaoh. The story of ancient Egypt concludes with the Assyrian invasion in 671 B.C., which marked the decline of Egypt's Pharaonic age. (Egypt's history from the Ptolemaic period to the present is covered in Chapter 10.) The chronology of Nubia, however, continues in Lesson 3.

Lesson 3 briefly summarizes the effects of Egypt and Nubia on their own time and on world history. We make mention of the lively ongoing debate about the relationship between Egypt and Greece and the assertion that the Greeks may have borrowed cultural concepts from the Egyptians. We hope students will begin to see that the study of ancient cultures is exciting and quickly changing, raising as many questions as it answers. To conclude, we look at the last major kingdom in Nubia, the kingdom of Meroë, which ended in A.D. 350. The chapter ends by showing how Nubian culture survives to this day in the country of Sudan.

ACTIVITIES & PROJECTS

LEP: Interpreting Rock Paintings

After students read the first page of Lesson 1, refer them to the rock painting at the top of the page. Point out the use of varying colors, which were made with natural substances. Have students look in books and encyclopedias for other pictures—preferably in color—of rock paintings. Call on students to display the pictures they find, and ask them questions such as these: Where were the paintings found? What people, animals, plants, or other items are depicted? What activities are taking place? Does the style of painting appear to be realistic, or symbolic? Do the colors seem to have any particular significance? Which painting is your favorite? Why? (Use during Lesson 1.)

Basic: Oral Presentation

Have students pretend they are Egyptian farmers. It is the end of the flood season, and they have just finished working at King Khufu's pyramid complex at Giza. Ask students to role-play their return home. What would they tell their families about their experiences? Direct them to enliven their role-playing with details about their jobs, the site, people they met, and their attitudes toward the pharaoh and toward their contribution to his journey into the afterlife. (Use after Lesson 2.)

Challenge: Critical Thinking

Have students answer these questions in a few paragraphs: Overall, do you think Nubia benefited by having Egypt as a neighbor? Why or why not? Give examples to support your reasoning. (Use after Lesson 3.)

CHAPTER PREVIEW

Have students read the chapter title and the narrative that follows it. Ask students to speculate why Egypt was called "the gift of the Nile." Ask students why Nubia might also be considered a gift of the Nile. Have them read the lesson to compare their ideas with the text.

Looking Back

Review with students what they learned in Chapter 3 about the importance of rivers to the development of Mesopotamia.

Looking Forward

Tell students they will read about two great African civilizations, ancient Egypt and Nubia, in Lessons 1 through 3: Kingdoms on the Nile, Ancient Cultures Linked Together, and Great Achievements.

The first lesson focuses on the geography of the Nile Valley and the interlocked political histories of ancient Egypt and Nubia.

Chapter 4
Ancient Egypt and Nubia

An ancient historian called Egypt "the gift of the Nile." The Nile River created a valley of bountiful land in the harsh African desert, giving everything Egyptians needed to live. Yet Egypt was not the Nile's only gift. Farther south, where the river runs through a rocky land, was another great civilization called Nubia. Located at a crossroads of trade, Nubia was home to mighty kingdoms.

Egyptians prepared for what they believed would be life after death. This couple is shown enjoying a bountiful harvest in paradise.

6000 | **5000** | **4000** | **3000**

6000 B.C.

c. 6000 B.C. The first culture of the Nile Valley begins in Nubia. Cultures in Egypt develop soon after.

c. 3000 B.C. Powerful kingdoms develop in Egypt and Nubia.

80

BACKGROUND

The Nile River, source of water and food, was the giver of life in the deserts of Egypt and Nubia. Because of the reliable flow of the Nile, life was less difficult in Egypt and Nubia than in Mesopotamia. Both the Egyptians and Nubians practiced religious customs that included a belief in an afterlife. Most of what we know today about the two cultures is the result of their preparations for the afterlife.

Nubia's Buried Treasures

The scant written evidence of ancient Nubia that exists today is, for the most part, untranslatable so far. Therefore, objects found buried with the dead reveal much of what is known about early Nubian beliefs and life. Graves in Lower Nubia have contained personal objects, such as jewelry and cosmetics. These items were buried as gifts to the deceased. Sometimes included in the graves were items of clothing, such as belts, leather loincloths, feathers to wear in the hair, and leather caps.

The most revealing objects, however, are the pieces of Nubian pottery. The artistry of the handmade pottery is especially evident in the so-called black-topped ware, shown on the timeline on the next page. These distinctive pots had polished red exteriors and shiny black rims and interiors. The "eggshell" pottery, with its thin walls painted on the outside with red ochre, is the finest type of early Nubian pottery. The existence of pottery indicates a settled aspect to the early Nubian lifestyle.

Egypt and Nubia ruled each other at various times. This led to a mixing of cultural traditions. This piece of gold jewelry, found in the tomb of a Nubian queen, shows the outstretched wings of the Egyptian Goddess Isis.

From about 2600 to 2100 B.C., Egyptian kings built massive tombs and monuments, such as the pyramids and the lionlike Sphinx, shown here.

After Nubian rule of Egypt ended, Nubian kings such as Senkamenisken, shown here, still used the title "King of Upper and Lower Egypt."

2000 | 1000 | B.C. A.D. | 1000

c. 2000 B.C. Nubia's powerful Kerma kingdom produces some of Africa's finest pottery.

81

A.D. 350

Understanding the Visuals

This granite statue of King Senkamanisken, who ruled Nubia from 643 to 623 B.C., stands nearly five feet tall. It was excavated from the Nubian site of Jebel Barkal, a temple built at Napata in about 1450 B.C. The temple—built on a steep, lone mountain where the God Amon was thought to reside—became one of Nubia's most important religious centers. This statue of the king, who ruled from the capital city of Napata, now stands in the Museum of Fine Arts, Boston, Massachusetts.

Temples at Jebel Barkal were built not only for Amon but also for Egyptian Goddesses, including probably Isis. She is depicted in the piece of gold jewelry shown here, which was found in the tomb of a Nubian queen. Egyptian Goddesses were honored as divine mothers.

Understanding Chronology

Point out the parallel development of independent kingdoms in Egypt and Nubia. Both peoples benefited from the rich resources of the Nile River. Each ruled the other at various times, leading to a blending of ideas, religious beliefs, and cultural traditions.

Beautiful pottery also filled the graves of rich Nubian rulers from the period from about 3100 to 2800 B.C. In addition to pottery, the graves contained gold, ivory, and jewelry, much like the tombs of wealthy Egyptian kings.

Egypt's City in the Sand

Egyptian civilization evolved simultaneously with that of Nubia. Like the Nubians, the Egyptians used the resources of the Nile to achieve wealth and power. Yet despite the rapid development of Egyptian society, until recently ancient Egypt was not widely believed to have urban sites on the scale of Mesopotamian cities. That view is now changing.

Very recently archaeologists at Giza uncovered what may be the first evidence of large Egyptian cities. Digs beginning in 1989 uncovered the remains of a granary and bakery, as well as pottery and fishhooks. The thousands of workers building the pyramids may have created a good-sized city, with crops and livestock to feed them. The evidence also debunks the age-old theory that the pyramids were built using mainly slave labor. In fact, evidence shows that many workers took pride in the remarkable tasks they accomplished in the Egyptian desert.

INTRODUCE

Ask students to read the Thinking Focus. Point out that ancient Nubia was the first culture to develop along the Nile River and was located in a land of cataracts, or steep rapids. Have students speculate on differences in development between Egypt and Nubia. Write the list on the chalkboard, and have students read the lesson for confirmation.

Key Terms

Vocabulary Strategies: T36–T37

delta—a triangle-shaped deposit of soil near the mouth of a river

cataract—steep rapids in a river; a large waterfall

dynasty—a succession of rulers from the same family

pharaoh—a king of ancient Egypt; from an Egyptian word meaning "great house"

B.C.
A.D.
6000
350
1000

LESSON 1

Kingdoms on the Nile

THINKING FOCUS

Describe differences in the way kingdoms developed in ancient Egypt and ancient Nubia.

Key Terms

- delta
- cataract
- dynasty
- pharaoh

➤ *This photograph shows how suddenly the green banks of the Nile turn into desert. The rock painting above shows Stone Age people herding cattle in what is now desert. Rock art has been found throughout the Sahara, including a 25-foot-long painting of a rhinoceros.*

If you stood on the green banks of Egypt's Nile River and began walking west, the green under your feet would vanish within a few miles. Facing you would be a landscape of blistering sand that stretches across the entire continent of Africa.

This desert, the Sahara, is the largest on the earth. Its treeless land and soaring temperatures make life there nearly impossible. Yet the Sahara was not always so empty. At one time the desert was a green grassland. People roamed the land. They fished, herded cattle, and hunted animals such as giraffes, elephants, and birds.

Prehistoric rock paintings like the one above show that the Sahara once supported human and animal life. Such colorful paintings have been found throughout the desert.

The last time the Sahara was green was about 8,000 years ago. As it dried out, animals and people spread in all directions, seeking better land. Many were attracted to the fresh water and fertile land of the Nile Valley.

These refugees from the desert joined peoples who had been living along the Nile for thousands of years. In time the blending of these desert and river peoples created two great civilizations.

Objectives

1. Show how the Nile River supported the growth of civilizations.
2. Compare and contrast the development of Egypt with that of Nubia.

Graphic Overview

Expansion of Sahara drives Africans into Nile Valley. → Kingdoms develop in Egypt and Nubia. → Egypt and Nubia coexist peacefully. → Egypt and Nubia conquer and rule each other at various times.

The Gift of the Nile

Each year in late spring, monsoons from the Indian Ocean dump tons of rain on the highlands of east-central Africa. The water rushes downward, swelling a river called the Blue Nile. At the city of Khartoum *(kahr TOOM),* the Blue Nile joins the White Nile to form the Nile River. Locate the Nile and its branches on the map on this page and in the Atlas on page 685.

Geography of the Nile

The powerful Nile River digs a long, deep ditch in the Sahara. A thin strip of fertile land lines the riverbanks. The Nile flows from south to north. That is why the southern, higher part is called the Upper Nile. The northern, lower end is the Lower Nile.

Near the mouth of the river, the Lower Nile fans out into a marshy, triangle-shaped area called a **delta**. There the fresh waters of the Nile empty into the salty Mediterranean Sea. From its source at the start of the White Nile to the delta, the river flows 4,132 miles, making it the world's longest river.

While the Nile flows north, the winds in the valley blow south. This makes boat travel easy, since you can drift downstream and sail upstream. From the delta southward, there is clear sailing for 750 miles. Then suddenly a pile of giant boulders looms ahead. The river bends and crashes around this area of rocky rapids called a **cataract**. Find the Nile's six cataracts on the map.

A Fruitful Valley

The land of the cataracts was home to an ancient civilization called Nubia. It was located in what is today southern Egypt and the northern part of the country of Sudan.

Until this century historians knew little about the people of Nubia. They knew much more about Nubia's northern neighbor, ancient Egypt. Yet Nubia and Egypt were closely tied throughout their ancient history.

The first culture along the Nile began in Nubia, near the modern-day city of Khartoum, south of the Sixth Cataract. This part of Nubia had a climate like that of central Africa—hot and rainy. Pieces of pottery from this fertile region show that the Khartoum culture may date back to 6000 B.C.

Other Nile cultures developed over thousands of years, as the drying of the Sahara pushed more people into the valley. These people brought a knowledge of how to grow grains, such as barley. As in Mesopotamia, people in small communities began working together to capture the floodwaters for farming. They used mud from the river's banks to make bricks for houses. The Nile provided everything they needed to live. ■

Ancient Egypt and Nubia

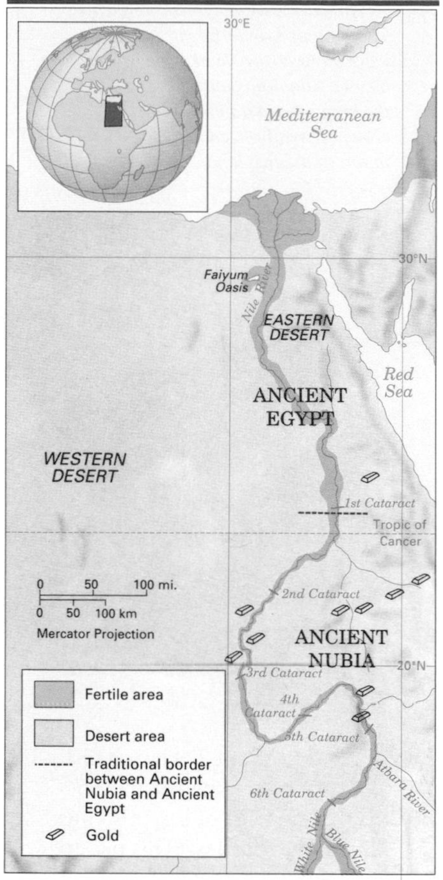

30°E
Mediterranean Sea
30°N
Faiyum Oasis
Nile River
EASTERN DESERT
Red Sea
ANCIENT EGYPT
WESTERN DESERT
1st Cataract
Tropic of Cancer
0 50 100 mi.
0 50 100 km
Mercator Projection
2nd Cataract
ANCIENT NUBIA
20°N
3rd Cataract
4th Cataract
5th Cataract
6th Cataract
Atbara River
White Nile
Blue Nile
Fertile area
Desert area
Traditional border between Ancient Nubia and Ancient Egypt
Gold

▲ *Study the map. Write down two words or phrases that describe the geography of the Nile Valley. Next, look at the inset map. It shows the location of the Nile Valley in the world. For help in using an inset map, see page G3 in the Map and Globe Handbook.*

■ *Why was the Nile Valley a likely place for civilizations to develop?*

DEVELOP

Point out that Lesson 1 describes the importance of the Nile River to the growth of Egypt and Nubia. Trace the Upper Nile and Lower Nile on the map on this page. Tell students to study the map and answer the question in the caption. *(Sample answers: long; surrounded by desert; water; gold; fertile land)* Suggest that as they read, students should compare how ancient Egypt and Nubia used the resources of the Nile to develop their civilizations.

GEOGRAPHY

Critical Thinking

After students read the section entitled Geography of the Nile, ask them in what direction most rivers of the United States flow. *(South)* Then ask them in what direction the Nile River flows. *(North)* Tell them that in ancient Egyptian writing, the symbol meaning "to travel north" is a flat boat, while the symbol for "to travel south" is a sailboat. Ask them to explain why this was so. *(Boats could float north on the Nile's currents and sail south on the southerly winds.)*

■ *The river provided many important things people needed to live.*

Access Strategy

Give each student a small trinket, such as a sticker. Ask them who gave them the gift. *(You)* Who received the gift? *(They did.)* Now remind them that Egypt has been called "the gift of the Nile." Help them to understand this quotation by answering these questions: What was the "gift"? *(The plentiful resources of Egypt)* Who received this gift? *(The people of ancient Egypt)* Where did the gift come from? *(The Nile River)* What kind of resources might the river have given the Egyptians? *(Answers include water for drinking, crops, and transportation; rich soil for farming and plants for food and for grazing; fish and wildlife; mud for bricks.)*

Geographic Context

When the Nile River flooded its banks, it left behind a thin layer of rich soil. The Egyptians called this fertile soil "black land." They never feared stripping the soil of its richness, because every summer the Nile flooded, replenishing the soil with minerals.

Access Activity

Direct students to the modern-day photo of the Nile on page 82. Ask students to list pairs of words that suggest the contrasts shown in the photo. *(Wet/dry, fertile/barren, green/brown)* Point out that these contrasts characterize ancient Egypt and Nubia.

POLITICAL SYSTEMS

Critical Thinking

Have students study the illustrations and captions on this page that explain the union of Upper Egypt and Lower Egypt. Ask if they can think of any other political unions. *(The unification of East and West Germany; the United States)* Ask students to name possible advantages of a unified Egypt. *(Sample answers: better defense, access to resources in both north and south)*

HISTORY

Study Skills

Have students study the timeline on the next page. Point out the period when Egypt was unified under one pharaoh, c. 3000 B.C. Explain that a succession of pharaohs from one family ruled in each dynasty. Thirty dynasties ruled during Egypt's history, which is divided into three eras—the Old Kingdom, the Middle Kingdom, and the New Kingdom. Ask students to locate the three eras on the timeline. Have students read Understanding Dynasty to learn more about Egypt's governing system.

Egypt, Land of the Pharaohs

The king of Upper Egypt wore a white crown. The king of Lower Egypt wore a red crown. When the two kingdoms united, the king wore a double crown. It symbolized the union of the two lands.

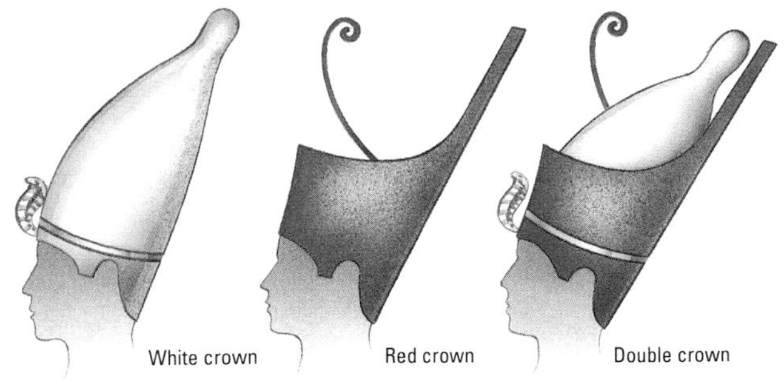
White crown
Red crown
Double crown

Trapping and storing the floodwaters of the Nile was a mighty job. Leaders emerged to organize such big projects. Between 4000 and 3000 B.C., some of these leaders grew very powerful.

No one knows exactly how kingdoms developed along the Nile. Some experts now believe that a group of people in Lower Nubia had the first government with kings of great power. These scholars also say that Egypt's first kings may have descended from Nubians. Such ideas are being hotly debated today.

The Beginning of History

A clearer picture of the history of kings emerges after about 3000 B.C. That is when the first written records appear. Historians are now debating whether the first writing is Egyptian, as is generally thought, or whether it is actually Nubian.

These early records tell of powerful kingdoms in Upper Egypt and in the delta, or Lower Egypt. A leader of Upper Egypt wrote of

Understanding Dynasty

In about 270 B.C., a historian named Manetho made a list of Egypt's kings and dynasties. (This picture shows an ancient Egyptian king list.) Manetho's list began with dynasties of Gods, who he thought had ruled before the pharaohs. Egypt's history, he said, had lasted 36,525 years.

Modern historians date the history of ancient Egypt from the time when it was united under one pharaoh in about 3000 B.C. to the arrival of Greek rulers in 332 B.C. That's nearly 2,700 years. During that time Egypt had 30 dynasties in which hundreds of kings ruled.

What Is a Dynasty?

A dynasty is not the same as a king. A **dynasty** is a series of rulers who descended from the same person. Egypt's First Dynasty had eight rulers. The Thirteenth Dynasty had about 70 rulers.

A Sign of Change

The start of a new dynasty often marked a time of major political change. Powerful Nubian kings ruled Egypt starting in about

724 B.C. Even though they were not Egyptian, the time of their reign is called the Twenty-fifth Dynasty.

Study Skills

Have students identify names of famous Egyptian rulers, either from this book or from an encyclopedia. Have students select one ruler to write about. Direct students to prepare a one- or two-page summary of the ruler's achievements. Ask students what impact the ruler had on Egypt and, if applicable, on Nubia.

Historical Context

Egypt's Old, Middle, and New Kingdoms are distinguished by achievements of each period. The giant pyramids were built during the Old Kingdom, an age that lasted about 400 years. During the Middle Kingdom, Egypt's political and economic strength grew. By the end of this era, pharaohs no longer built great tombs. The New Kingdom is characterized as the era of Egypt's greatest political power.

Religious Context

During the Old Kingdom, pharaohs were buried under or within pyramids. The pyramid formed only a part of a large burial complex made up of pyramids, temples, ramps, and other small buildings. These huge complexes were built largely by Egyptians who were unable to work on their farms during the annual flood seasons.

Ancient Egypt and Nubia, c. 3000 B.C.–c. A.D. 350

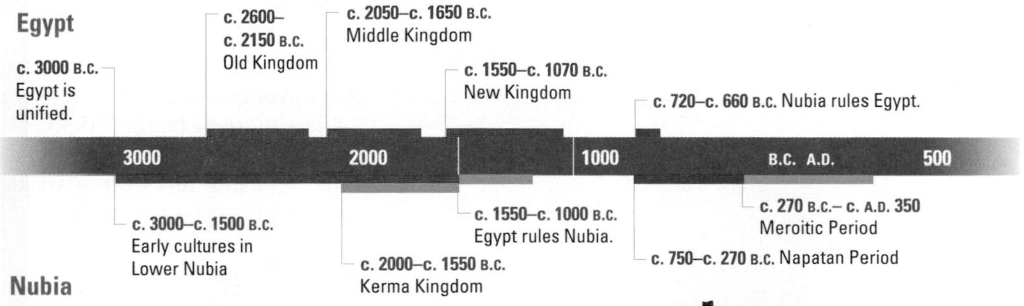
Egypt
c. 3000 B.C. Egypt is unified.
c. 2600–c. 2150 B.C. Old Kingdom
c. 2050–c. 1650 B.C. Middle Kingdom
c. 1550–c. 1070 B.C. New Kingdom
c. 720–c. 660 B.C. Nubia rules Egypt.
3000
2000
1000
B.C. A.D.
500
c. 3000–c. 1500 B.C. Early cultures in Lower Nubia
c. 2000–c. 1550 B.C. Kerma Kingdom
c. 1550–c. 1000 B.C. Egypt rules Nubia.
c. 270 B.C.– c. A.D. 350 Meroitic Period
c. 750–c. 270 B.C. Napatan Period
Nubia

how he had conquered Lower Egypt to form one country. This union marks the start of Egypt's First Dynasty. See Understanding Dynasty on page 84.

Kings and Kingdoms

Thirty dynasties ruled Egypt for nearly 3,000 years. Historians divide Egypt's ancient past into three periods, called kingdoms. On the timeline above, trace Egypt's Old, Middle, and New kingdoms.

At the start of each kingdom, Egypt prospered. Often the king, called the **pharaoh** *(FAIR oh),* was strong and wise. Near the end of each period, Egypt declined because of weak pharaohs, civil wars, or famine.

In normal times the pharaoh, usually a man, had absolute power. Much of Egypt's land and wealth belonged to him. He controlled taxes, trade, irrigation, and mining.

Many colorful leaders ruled Egypt. Although few rulers were women, one queen, Hatshepsut *(haht SHEHP soot),* rose to great power. She led her country into a time of peace and wealth. King Ramesses II *(RAM ih seez)* built great monuments. Another king, Akhenaton *(ah kuh NAHT uhn),* is famous for his failed attempt to make Egypt a monotheistic country.

The pharaohs had a large appetite for wealth, especially gold. Foreigners believed that, in Egypt, gold was as common as dust. What they did not know was that Egypt got much of its wealth from its southern neighbor—Nubia. ■

▲ *The timeline shows the main historical periods of Egypt and Nubia. The large mask (at left) is of one of Egypt's most famous rulers. He was the boy king Tutankhamon* (toot ahng KAH muhn), *who died at age 18.*

■ *Who were the pharaohs, and what powers did they have?*

Nubia, a Crossroads of Trade

Nubia became united more slowly than did Egypt, largely because of its rocky land. To this day, a region south of the Second Cataract is called "belly of rock." The rough terrain made travel, communication, and cooperative farming difficult.

Yet Nubia had other resources. These resources led to the growth of trade, which in turn spurred the development of wealthy kingdoms.

Growth of Trade

Hidden in the rocky sands of eastern and western Nubia was a treasure chest of gold and other minerals. Locate Nubia's gold deposits on the map on page 83. The Nubian Nile was home to valuable

How Do We Know?

CULTURE *No one knows what the early Nubians called their land. The Egyptians called Lower Nubia* Ta-Sety, *or "Land of the Bow"—a reference to the Nubians' famed archery skills.*

CULTURE

Visual Learning

Collect pictures of the excavation of Tutankhamon's tomb from sources such as *National Geographic* magazine. Have students examine closely the pictures of the artifacts, along with the portrait mask of Tutankhamon shown here. Call on volunteers to make hypotheses about Egyptian culture and society based on these artifacts. *(Possible answers: the Egyptians had elaborate burial rites; they believed in an afterlife; they valued gold and other precious gems and minerals; they had a written language based on symbols—hieroglyphics.)*

■ *Pharaohs were Egyptian kings. They had absolute power and controlled Egypt's resources and enterprises.*

Historical Context

Not until 1922, when British Egyptologist Howard Carter discovered the tomb of Tutankhamon, did the boy king become one of Egypt's most well-known rulers. After his sudden death at age 18, Tutankhamon was condemned by his former general, Horemheb. Horemheb later became pharaoh, and Tutankhamon's tomb and monuments were forgotten.

Cultural Context

In the early 1900s, Egypt built a dam at Aswan. Rising waters behind the dam flooded parts of Lower Nubia. Before the flooding, George Andrew Reisner headed an archaeological excavation of the region. Reisner, curator of the Museum of Fine Arts, Boston, rescued many Nubian objects from destruction. His work launched the modern study of long-ignored Nubian cultures.

Critical Thinking

Have students read the section entitled Nubia, a Crossroads of Trade. Then direct students to the map on page 83, which locates Nubia's gold deposits. Help students reach the conclusion that Nubia's gold trade with Egypt was profitable and that it became a strong reason for competition between the two kingdoms.

GEOGRAPHY

Study Skills

Have several students work together to make a chart comparing and contrasting the natural resources of Egypt with those of Nubia. Have them show similarities and differences in availability of resources such as gold and other minerals, ebony, ivory, stone, and farmland. Display their chart in the classroom.

➤ *They were in Upper Nubia.*

■ *Nubia's mineral and animal resources brought it great wealth from trade, but they also made it a tempting target for control by the Egyptian pharaohs.*

CLOSE

Play a game of hangman to review words in the lesson, including the Key Terms on page 82. Have volunteers lead the class, but ask them to whisper the words to you so that you can make sure they provide enough letter spaces on the chalkboard. As each term is guessed, call for an explanation of it. Start the game yourself with *pyramid*.

➤ *Where were most of Nubia's capitals—in Lower Nubia or Upper Nubia?*

Ancient Cities of the Nile

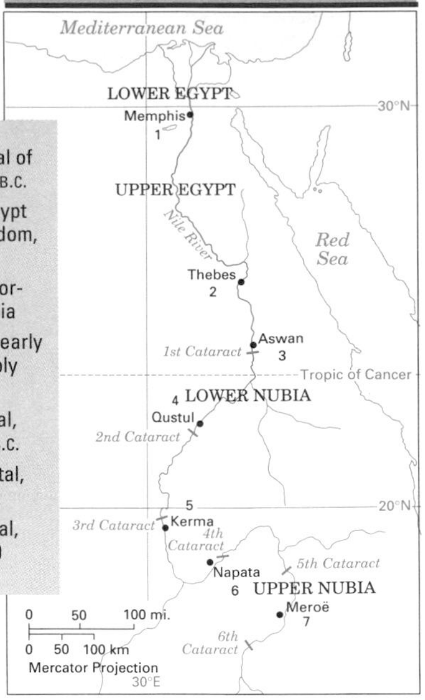
Mediterranean Sea
LOWER EGYPT
Memphis
1
30°N
UPPER EGYPT
Nile River
Red Sea
Thebes
2
1st Cataract
Aswan
3
Tropic of Cancer
4 LOWER NUBIA
Qustul
2nd Cataract
5
20°N
3rd Cataract
Kerma
4th Cataract
Napata
6 UPPER NUBIA
5th Cataract
Meroë
7
6th Cataract
0 50 100 mi.
0 50 100 km
Mercator Projection
30°E

1. **Memphis** First capital of united Egypt, c. 3000 B.C.
2. **Thebes** Capital of Egypt during the New Kingdom, c. 1550 B.C.
3. **Aswan** Traditional border of Egypt and Nubia
4. **Qustul** Burial site of early Nubian rulers, possibly kings
5. **Kerma** Nubian capital, c. 2000 B.C.– c. 1550 B.C.
6. **Napata** Nubian capital, c. 750 B.C.– c. 270 B.C.
7. **Meroë** Nubian capital, c. 270 B.C.– c. A.D. 350

living resources as well. Hippopotamuses, giraffes, ostriches, and other animals roamed the wilderness. A growing human population had driven many of these animals out of Egypt, so the Egyptians eagerly sought them from Nubia.

➤ *Late in its history, Kush was ruled by queens, like the one shown in this silver mask.*

Besides its own goods, Nubia also had access to products from the rain forests of central Africa to the south. Nubian traders got luxury goods from the south and sold them to Egypt and Southwest Asia. One Egyptian trader returned from Nubia with "three hundred donkeys laden with incense, ebony, panther skins, elephants' tusks, throw sticks, and all sorts of good products."

■ *How did resources bring both benefits and problems to Nubia?*

Competition for Power

In time Nubia's trading kingdoms grew to rival the power of Egypt. During its ancient history, Egypt often sought to control Nubia's mines and trade. In times when Egypt's government was strong, powerful pharaohs pushed south, seizing parts of Nubia. In times of weakness, Egyptian forces withdrew.

The Egypt-Nubia border shifted many times. During Egypt's Old Kingdom, the pharaohs often controlled Lower Nubia. After 2000 B.C., however, powerful kingdoms arose in Upper Nubia, a region the Egyptians called Kush.

During the next 1,500 years, Egypt and Nubia often competed for power. In the time of Egypt's New Kingdom, Egypt ruled all of Nubia. Kings from Kush later ruled all of Nubia and Egypt. The map above shows capitals and key cities along the Nile.

When armies crossed the Egypt-Nubia border, parts of their culture crossed over, too. In Lesson 2 you'll read about the cultures of Egypt and Nubia and see how each affected the culture of the other. ■

REVIEW

1. **FOCUS** Describe differences in the way kingdoms developed in ancient Egypt and ancient Nubia.
2. **GEOGRAPHY** How did changes in the climate and land of the Sahara affect the Nile Valley?
3. **HISTORY** What is a dynasty?
4. **CRITICAL THINKING** Why might the Nile's cataracts have affected the history of Egypt and Nubia?
5. **WRITING ACTIVITY** Pretend you are the boy king, Tutankhamon. Write an order for products that you would like to get from Nubia.

Homework Options

Have students write a short paragraph summarizing how the Nile River supported the growth of Egypt and Nubia.

Study Guide: page 14

Answers to Review Questions

1. Egypt united into a single state around 3000 B.C. It was governed by powerful pharaohs. Nubia probably had kings at about the same time as Egypt, but it was slower to unite into a single state because of its geography. It had several different centers of power during the course of its history.
2. As the Sahara expanded, animals and the people who hunted them were attracted to the fertile land of the Nile Valley.
3. A dynasty is a series of rulers who all descended from the same person.
4. Possible answers: The cataracts slowed travel between Egypt and Nubia, making trade—or invasion—more difficult. The cataracts acted as borders between the two kingdoms.
5. Answers include animals, gold and other minerals, and products from central Africa, such as incense, ivory, and throw sticks.

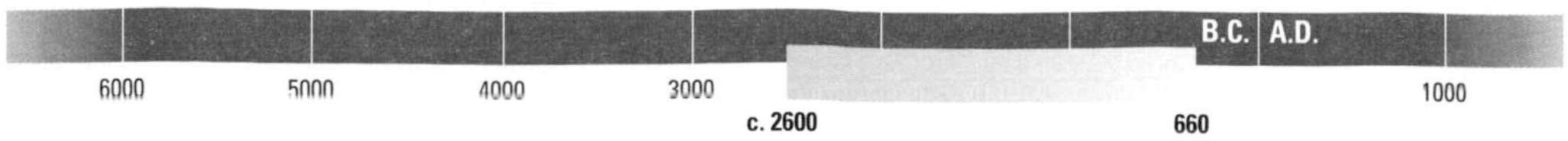
B.C. | A.D.
6000
5000
4000
3000
1000
c. 2600
660

L E S S O N 2

Ancient Cultures Linked Together

For hundreds of years, ancient Egyptian was a lost language. It had begun to fade from use after about A.D. 500, as new languages spread down the Nile. People forgot how to speak the language or read the writing.

Yet all over Egypt, the beautiful symbols of the dead language lived on—in temples, pyramids, and books. The Egyptians wrote in **hieroglyphics** *(hy uhr uh GLIHF ihks),* a script that uses pictures to stand for ideas, words, or letters. The hieroglyphics, and what they told of Egyptian life, remained a mystery until the early 1800s.

In 1799 French soldiers were building a fort near Rosetta, a village in the Nile delta. There they dug up a black stone covered with writing. This object became one of the world's most famous artifacts. It is called the Rosetta stone.

Inscribed on the stone was the same message in three scripts—two forms of ancient Egyptian as well as ancient Greek. The Greek, a known language, gave clues to the meaning of the Egyptian symbols. In time, scholars decoded the more than 700 Egyptian hieroglyphs.

THINKING FOCUS

Summarize key facts about Egyptian and Nubian culture.

Key Terms

- hieroglyphics
- scribe
- afterlife
- mummy

◄ *The Rosetta stone is nearly four feet high and two and one-half feet wide. Its message praising the Greek king Ptolemy V* (TAHL uh mee) *was written in 196 B.C.*

Egyptian Society

The Egyptians left volumes of written material—tax records, poetry, religious books, textbooks, and military reports. Once hieroglyphics could be read, they shed new light on this ancient culture.

Egyptian families lived much like people today. Marriage was important, and husbands were urged to respect their wives. Parents taught their children to work hard and to obey. Although children often did chores at an early age, they also enjoyed dolls, games, and sports.

Egyptians loved to look good, too. People who could afford them used makeup, hairpins, wigs, and perfumes. Although few people were rich, life for many was good.

Nearly every Egyptian was in the service of someone at a higher level of society. The society was

INTRODUCE

Direct students to read the Thinking Focus. Explain that some of what we know about Egypt and Nubia was recorded in Egyptian hieroglyphics.

Now draw attention to the photograph of the Rosetta stone on this page. Tell students that the deciphering of the Rosetta stone unlocked the mystery of ancient Egyptian hieroglyphics. To simulate deciphering the hieroglyphics, have students take turns writing cryptograms on the chalkboard or overhead projector. Have the class decipher them.

Key Terms

Vocabulary Strategies: T36–T37

hieroglyphics—writing system used by the ancient Egyptians, in which pictures stand for ideas, words, or letters

scribe—in ancient Egypt, a skilled writer who kept records and wrote letters

afterlife—a life believed to follow death

mummy—a human or animal body embalmed after death according to the practice of the ancient Egyptians

Graphic Overview

EGYPT'S EFFECT ON NUBIA
- Spread religious culture, including the worship of Egyptian Gods and building of pyramids
- Conquered and ruled Nubia; controlled resources and trade; required tribute; took hostages

NUBIA'S EFFECT ON EGYPT
- Provided resources such as minerals that Egypt needed to grow rich and powerful
- Conquered and ruled Egypt; respected Egyptian traditions; helped restore lost Egyptian culture

Objectives

1. Describe how Egyptian society was organized.
2. Show how religion influenced Egyptian life and culture.
3. Explain how Nubia and Egypt affected each other's cultures.

DEVELOP

Introduce the Graphic Overview to point out the main parts of the lesson. Suggest that as students read Lesson 2, they should think about how and why the cultures of ancient Egypt and Nubia were so strongly linked together.

Remind students that in Lesson 1 they read about artifacts, such as pottery, that were buried with the early Nubians. These artifacts have revealed much about ancient Nubian life. Ask students to connect that idea with what they've just read about Egyptian hieroglyphics.

■ *Slaves were the lowest layer, followed by farmers, skilled workers, scribes, priests, and the pharaoh.*

organized into several levels. From the Middle Kingdom on, slaves made up the lowest level. Next came farmers. Most labored on the farms of wealthy landowners or of the pharaoh. During flood seasons, they built monuments for the pharaoh and served in the army.

On the level above the farmers were the skilled laborers—carpenters, bakers, and jewelers. Above them were the scribes. A **scribe** had the important job of writing. Scribes kept records and wrote letters. Above the scribes were the priests, who worked in the temples.

At the top of society was the all-powerful pharaoh. Thought to be Gods or godlike, the pharaohs were surrounded with wealth and beauty. In fact, the word *pharaoh* means "great house," a reference to the king's grand palace.

Pharaohs were honored in death as well as in life. You can witness this fact at the ancient site of Giza. ■

■ *Describe the layers of Egyptian society.*

The Great Monument Builders

On the plain of Giza near present-day Cairo, stone structures rise out of the sand. The tallest is 40 stories high and covers an area the size of seven city blocks. If it were hollow, four of the world's largest cathedrals could fit inside it. It is the Great Pyramid.

The Pyramids at Giza

The Great Pyramid was the burial tomb of Khufu *(KOO foo)*, a king in the 2500s B.C. The structure consists of 2.3 million blocks of limestone, most weighing more than two tons. During Khufu's reign thousands of men labored to build the pyramid. One group of workers proudly painted its name—"The Craftsmen Gang"—on a wall deep inside the pyramid. Once in place, the outer blocks were so snug that a knife blade could not fit between them.

Two other pyramids at Giza belonged to Khufu's descendants. The fourth structure is the Sphinx, a stone creature nearly as long as a football field. The Sphinx has the body of a lion and the face of a man, thought to be King Khafre *(KHAH frah)*.

Most of the pyramids were built during Egypt's Old Kingdom. More than 80 pyramids survive to this day. Egyptians hoped that the

Across Time & Space

Khufu's pyramid may have been built in about 23 years. Was this really possible? In 1991 U.S. archaeologists did an experiment at Giza to find out. Using ropes, ramps, and ancient-style tools, 12 stonecutters built a small pyramid in only 21 days. At this rate a king's crew of about 400 stonecutters could have completed the task.

Building the Great Pyramid, 2500s B.C.

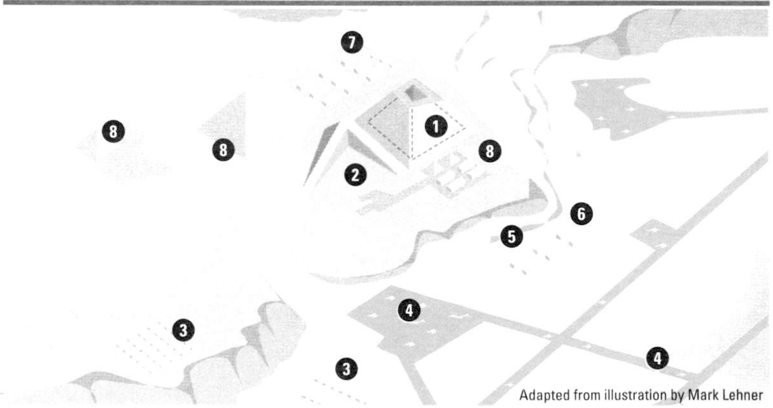
Adapted from illustration by Mark Lehner

➤ *This is an archaeologist's drawing of what the construction site at Giza might have looked like. Shown here are: (1) Great Pyramid of Khufu; (2) ramps; (3) villages for workers; (4) harbor canals; (5) quarries; (6) Khufu's palace complex; (7) tombs of royal relatives and officials; (8) future sites of pyramids of Menkaure, Khafre, and the Sphinx.*

Access Activity

Guide students to use the diagram on this page to develop a list of jobs that workers might have done at Giza. *(Piloting and unloading supply boats; digging and hauling rock from the quarries; building the pyramids; decorating and painting interior rooms; growing and preparing food for workers)* Ask which jobs students would have preferred to do.

Access Strategy

Have students look again at the picture of the Great Pyramid and Sphinx on page 80. Then ask them to locate the two monuments on the diagram on this page. Point out that the pyramids at Giza are among ten built at that site along the Nile River outside of modern-day Cairo between about 2600 and 2500 B.C. Khufu's Great Pyramid was made of more than 2 million stone blocks and is 450 feet high.

Explain that by comparison, the giant stone faces of the presidents on Mount Rushmore are about 60 feet high; the Washington Monument, 555 feet; the Empire State Building, 1250 feet. Sketch an outline of these structures and the Great Pyramid on the chalkboard, drawing them roughly to scale. You may want to add a sketch of any local building or monument that would serve as an appropriate comparison to the pyramid.

monuments would cause the pharaohs' names to be remembered. This would fulfill their belief that "to speak the name of the dead is to make him live again." Indeed, the names of Khufu and his successors are still spoken after more than 4,000 years.

Preparing for the Afterlife

Egyptians were once thought to be a gloomy people because they were so concerned about death. Actually, they hoped that the good things they had in this life would continue in the next.

Egyptian religion taught that achieving a happy **afterlife,** or life after death, was not easy. Egyptians believed that the soul is judged and faces either miserable punishment or a happy afterlife.

This journey is described in the Book of the Dead, a collection of chants, spells, and religious texts found in Egyptian tombs. One spell is from the tomb of a scribe named Ani *(ah NEE)*. (See the painting above.) In the text Ani appears before a jury of 42 Gods to prove that he has lived an honest life.

▲ *The jackal God Anubis* (uh NOO bihs) *weighs Ani's heart against the feather of truth. Egyptians believed that if their hearts were heavy with sin, they would die a permanent death. If their hearts passed the test, they would go on to a happy afterlife.*

> *I have not made [anyone] hungry, I have not made [people] to weep, I have not killed, . . . I have not taken the milk from the mouths of children, I have not deprived the herds of their pastures,. . . . I have not built a dam on flowing water. . . . I am pure, pure, pure, pure!*
>
> Book of the Dead, Spell 125

A Royal Burial

No burial was more important than the pharaoh's. When Khufu's pyramid was completed, workers filled it with treasures he would need in the afterlife—furnishings, gold, jewels, and even games.

Egyptians believed that without a body, a person's spirit could not enjoy the afterlife. They invented a process called embalming to slow the normal decay of the body after death. Embalming changed the body into a **mummy.**

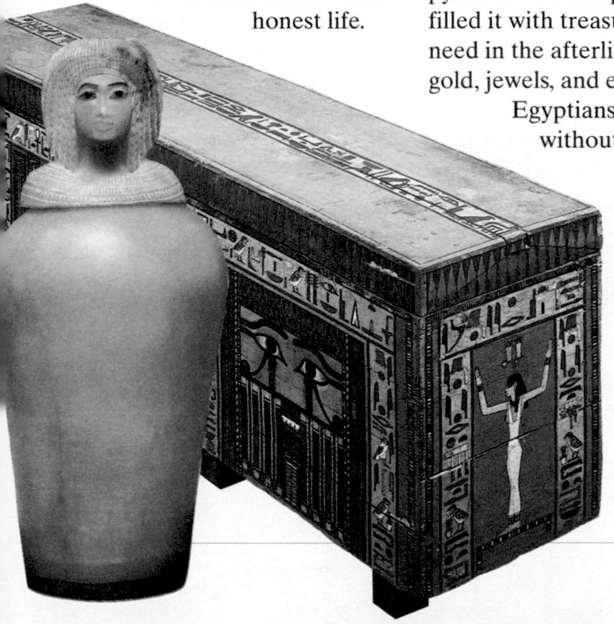

◄ *To make a mummy, embalmers removed some of the organs from the body and put them into canopic* (kuh NOH pic) *jars, like the jar on the left. They filled the body with sawdust or linen and dried it for 40 days in salt. The body was then coated in hot tree sap and wrapped in linen. The mummy was often placed in a beautiful coffin.*

BELIEF SYSTEMS

Study Skills

Have students study the painting and caption at the top of the page. Explain that Egyptians placed a scarab—a small ceramic or stone beetle—over the heart of a mummy to keep the heart from speaking against its owner during judgment. Have students research what other items were buried with the mummies, and why.

BELIEF SYSTEMS

Visual Learning

Draw students' attention to the colorful hieroglyphics painted on the coffin shown here. Note the pair of eyes painted on the side, and explain that the eyes were supposed to (at least symbolically) allow the dead person to look toward the east, into the land of the living. Ask students why this idea would have made sense according to Egyptian religion. *(Because Egyptians believed in an afterlife)*

Cultural Context

To help students understand the origins of pyramid building, explain that the first structure, the Step Pyramid at Saqqara, was built in about 2650 B.C. for King Djoser. The importance of Djoser's pyramid lies not only in its design, but also in its use of permanent stone instead of perishable mud bricks. This change resulted in the preservation of much that gives us our knowledge of Egyptian civilization.

Before Djoser's time, the tombs of Egyptian pharaohs consisted of a burial pit that lay below a low, flat mud-brick structure known as a mastaba. The mastaba was meant to protect the body of the deceased and hold some belongings. The outside was often painted and paneled, perhaps to resemble the homes of the living. The design for Djoser's pyramid may have been an effort to create a mastaba worthy of a pharaoh. Pyramids were built only for royalty. It is thought that ordinary people were buried in simple pit graves, sometimes with a few possessions.

Visual Learning

Read aloud the caption for the painting shown here. Note that in Egypt, Gods were often portrayed with animal heads. Have students research other Egyptian animal Gods, then do a drawing and brief description of one of them. Note the Egyptian style of drawing figures: the torsos usually face forward and are flat and two-dimensional. Heads are often turned sideways.

■ *The magnificence of the pyramids reflects the importance of the pharaoh. The contents of the pyramids reflect the Egyptians' belief that the dead and their belongings went into an afterlife.*

BELIEF SYSTEMS

Study Skills

Have students study the photo and caption of the gold earring. Direct them to use the school library to research the God Amon and write a paragraph on his significance and on ways in which he was depicted in paintings and sculpture.

HISTORY

Critical Thinking

Tell students that the Egyptian name for Lower Nubia was Ta Sety, "land of the bow." Ask if anyone can guess why. *(The Nubians were famed archers.)* Then choose a volunteer to read aloud the definition of *mercenary* from a dictionary. *("A professional soldier who is hired to serve in a foreign army."*—The American Heritage Dictionary of the English Language*)* Ask students how this word might apply to the Nubians. Point out that in fact, Nubian archers were hired as mercenaries by Egypt and by countries as far away as Crete and Persia.

■ *What do the pyramids reveal about the beliefs of the ancient Egyptians?*

When Khufu died, his mummy was placed in the tomb. After a final prayer, workers slid stone blocks into the doorway to seal the tomb—forever, they hoped. Despite these efforts, thieves found their way through secret vaults and false rooms and stole Khufu's mummy and all of his treasures.

Egyptian beliefs had deep roots that developed over thousands of years. These beliefs governed the daily life of every Egyptian from farmers to pharaohs. So powerful were Egypt's customs that they also influenced other cultures—particularly the neighboring peoples of Nubia. ■

Nubia's Unique Culture

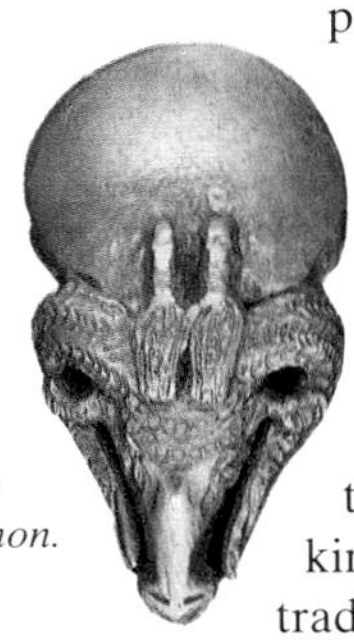

➤ *This earring shows the blending of Nubian and Egyptian cultures. The earring is the head of a ram, a Nubian God. Egyptians used the ram to represent the God Amon.*

Egyptians and Nubians had close contact from very early times, so it's not surprising that each group passed on ideas to the other.

Nevertheless, Nubian culture had a flavor quite different from that of Egypt. While Egyptian pharaohs were building the pyramids, the peoples of Lower Nubia carried on their own traditions. Nubian kings gained great wealth from trade. Nubian soldiers became famous for their archery skills. Because farming took hold slowly in the rocky region, many Nubians raised cattle and hunted and traded for food.

The Rise of Kush

After 2000 B.C. much of Nubia's cultural change took place in the Upper Nubian kingdom of Kush. At Kerma, the Kushite capital from about 2000 to 1550 B.C., workers made knives and tools. Other workers made attractive jewelry. Skilled carpenters carved elegant furniture. Potters in Kerma made some of Africa's finest pottery.

Kerma's kings grew strong enough to capture much of Upper Egypt. In 1550 B.C., however, Egypt struck back. The pharaoh's army marched into Kush, smashed Kerma's walls, and burned the city.

Under Egyptian Rule

For the next 550 years, Egypt ruled all of Nubia. Nubians had to bring payments of gold and other wealth to the pharaoh each year. A Moment in Time on page 91 shows a Nubian princess preparing to take an offering to the pharaoh.

The pharaohs put the Nubians to work. Many were forced to mine gold. To keep the Nubians from rebelling, an official of the pharaoh,

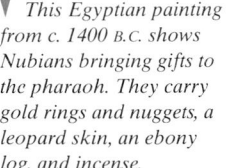

▼ *This Egyptian painting from c. 1400 B.C. shows Nubians bringing gifts to the pharaoh. They carry gold rings and nuggets, a leopard skin, an ebony log, and incense.*

Social Participation

Have students create a large picture map of Egypt and Nubia. Some can copy the map on page 83 onto a large poster board or mural paper. Others can draw a pyramid, temple, or monument, either from this book or an encyclopedia. Students might draw on separate paper and attach their drawings to the appropriate place on the map.

Art Connection

The artifacts and paintings from their tombs tell us much about the daily lives of the ancient Egyptians. (See pages 96–97.) Suggest that students work in pencil, paint, or clay to portray themselves in daily life, showing something that could be of interest to archaeologists 3,000 years in the future.

Geographic Context

Nubian place names can be confusing. Kerma refers to the city in Upper Nubia as well as to the culture and the kingdom that arose there. The Egyptians called the Kerma kingdom Kush. Later, Egypt divided Nubia into a northern province, Wawat, and a southern one, Kush. This southern region, home to the powerful kingdoms of Napata and Meroë, corresponds to Upper Nubia. Hence, this text uses Kush to mean Upper Nubia.

A Moment in Time

A Nubian Princess

9:11 A.M., May 10, 1341 B.C.
In the home of a Nubian royal family

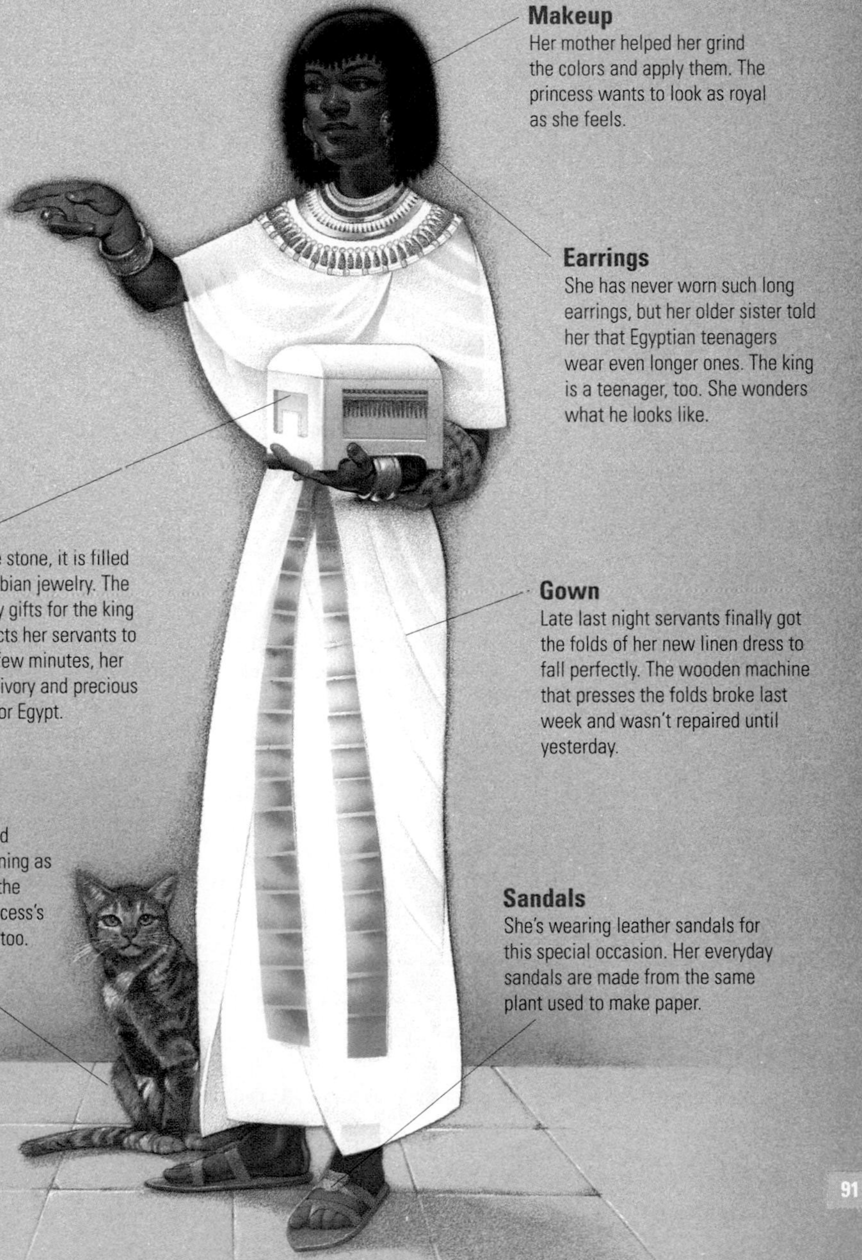

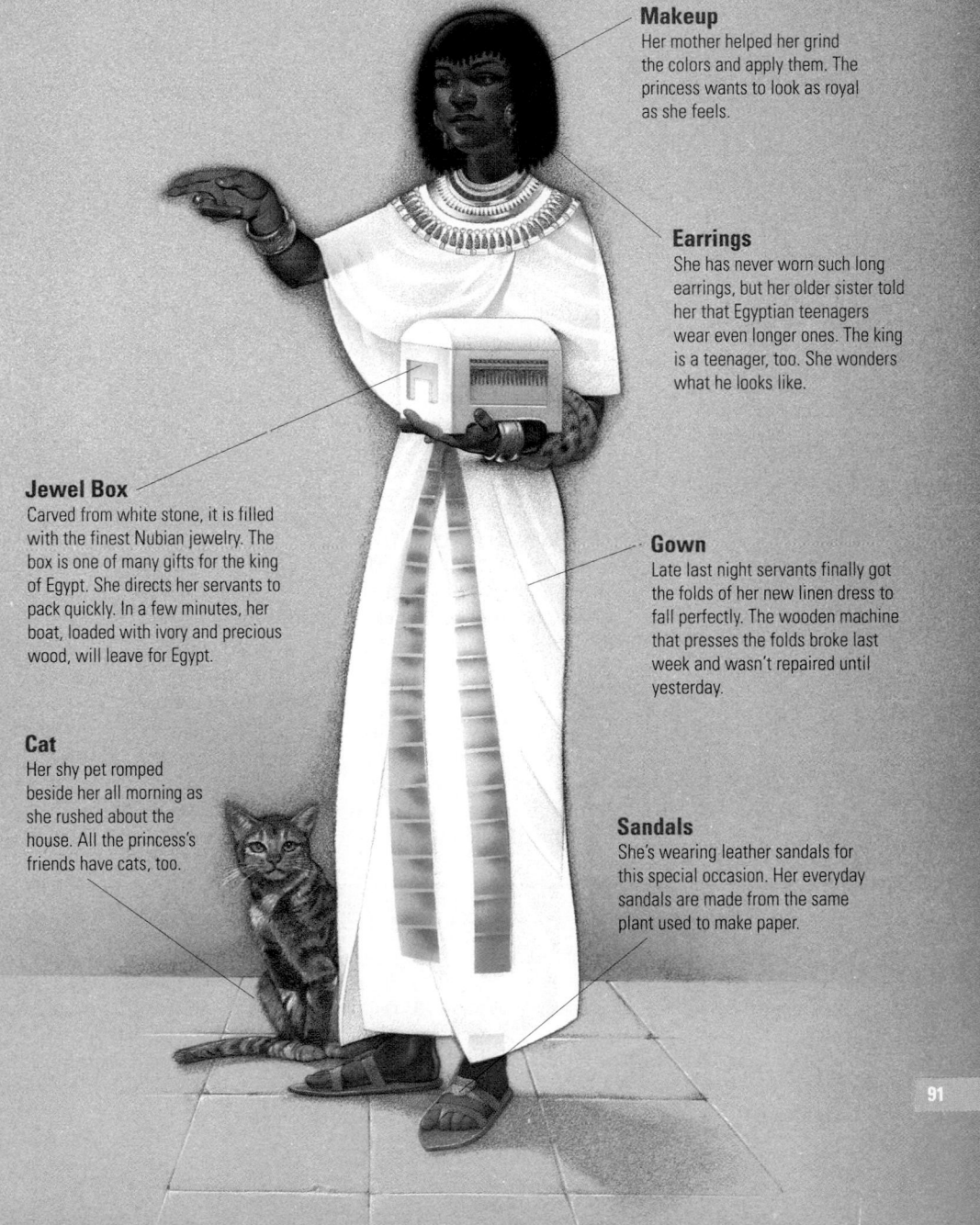

Makeup
Her mother helped her grind the colors and apply them. The princess wants to look as royal as she feels.
Earrings
She has never worn such long earrings, but her older sister told her that Egyptian teenagers wear even longer ones. The king is a teenager, too. She wonders what he looks like.
Jewel Box
Carved from white stone, it is filled with the finest Nubian jewelry. The box is one of many gifts for the king of Egypt. She directs her servants to pack quickly. In a few minutes, her boat, loaded with ivory and precious wood, will leave for Egypt.
Gown
Late last night servants finally got the folds of her new linen dress to fall perfectly. The wooden machine that presses the folds broke last week and wasn't repaired until yesterday.
Cat
Her shy pet romped beside her all morning as she rushed about the house. All the princess's friends have cats, too.
Sandals
She's wearing leather sandals for this special occasion. Her everyday sandals are made from the same plant used to make paper.

Note: Use this feature after page 90 to help create empathy for Nubians under Egyptian rule. The time depicted here corresponds to the rule of the boy king, Tutankhamon. You may want to remind students of the mask of Tutankhamon that they saw on page 85.

More About Nubia Egypt ruled Nubia much like a colonial province for more than 500 years, from about 1550 B.C. to 1000 B.C. Egyptian kings left their mark on Nubia by building many exquisite temples. During the Eighteenth Dynasty, temple building extended southward into Upper Nubia. The dynasty's greatest builder was Amenhotep III. His son, Akhenaton, continued the activity in Nubia. But by the time his son-in-law, Tutankhamon, took the throne, Egypt had grown politically unstable. The Nubian temples of the young king are smaller, minor ones.

Map and Globe Skills

Tell students that the princess comes from Amara, an administrative capital of Upper Nubia during Egyptian rule. Amara lay on the east and west banks of the Nile about halfway between the Second and Third Cataracts. Using the map on page 86, have students find the approximate location of Amara. Then ask them to trace the princess's route down the Nile to the Egyptian capital of Thebes. They can then use the scale of miles to calculate the length of her journey. *(About 225 miles)*

Role-Playing

Direct students to role-play the princess's meeting with King Tutankhamon. You may want to have students research the king's life before beginning. Discuss the fact that the princess is presenting the young king with gifts and that he will probably give her gifts in return. Although Nubia is under Egyptian control, it is very important to Egypt, so he will treat the princess with great respect.

Visual Learning

The Nubian princess is about to have an audience with the pharaoh, Tutankhamon. On the chalkboard, list the special items she is wearing and bringing on this trip. *(New dress, leather sandals, long earrings, a white stone box containing fine jewelry, and ivory and wood)* Have students list special items they would wear or bring on a trip to meet the President.

■ *They tried to impose their culture on Nubia. Sons of Nubian rulers were raised in Egypt so they would bring Egyptian culture home. Nubians also were forced to mine gold for Egypt.*

HISTORY

Critical Thinking

Tell students that Taharka was the last and greatest of Egypt's Nubian kings. An inscription near Dahshur describes a 30-mile marathon performed by Taharka's troops. They ran at night to avoid the desert heat. The king rode on horseback alongside his runners. Ask students what conclusions they can draw from the story. *(Examples: The army was vital to the state; a spirit of camaraderie existed between Taharka and his soldiers; Taharka liked to test his soldiers' endurance.)*

■ *The Nubians did not force their customs on Egyptians. In fact, they helped restore old Egyptian customs. Egypt tried to force Nubians to adopt Egyptian customs.*

CLOSE

Write the Thinking Focus on the chalkboard. Then have students write answers to it on the chalkboard.

■ *How did the Egyptians affect Nubian culture?*

called the King's Son of Kush, kept watch over local rulers. He had their sons sent to Egypt as hostages. In time these sons, raised in Egypt, returned home to rule, bringing Egyptian culture with them. ■

Nubia Influences Egypt

➤ *These Kushite pyramids are smaller and steeper than those of Egypt. Like the Egyptians, Nubians also buried small tablets under the pyramid. They thought the tablets, shown below, had power to protect the tomb.*

Eventually, facing problems at home, Egypt retreated from Nubia. Left alone, the Kushites built a new capital at a city called Napata *(NAP uh tuh)*. From this city, in the 700s B.C., Kush invaded and conquered Egypt. A Nubian king took the throne in Lower Egypt. A Nubian princess ruled Upper Egypt.

Restoring Egyptian Culture

Nubian rulers did not force the Egyptians to follow Nubian customs. Instead, Kushite kings helped to bring back forgotten parts of Egypt's own culture. They added to old temples and built new ones in the Egyptian fashion. Their art mixed styles from Egypt's past.

During this time Nubians adopted many Egyptian ideas. They built their own pyramids and began to mummify their dead.

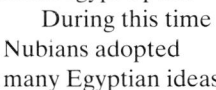

■ *Contrast Egyptian rule of Nubia with Nubian rule of Egypt.*

End of an Era

Nubian rule in Egypt lasted only about 60 years. The Assyrians, spreading their huge empire into Egypt (see Chapter 3), drove the Kushites back to their homeland.

After the Assyrian invasion, Egypt never regained its full strength. However, as you will read in the next lesson, the height of Nubian culture was yet to come. ■

REVIEW

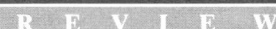

1. **FOCUS** Summarize key facts about Egyptian and Nubian culture.
2. **HISTORY** How did writing help civilization to develop in Egypt?
3. **BELIEF SYSTEMS** Reread the quotation from the Book of the Dead on page 89. How does the Egyptian sense of right and wrong compare with your own?
4. **BELIEF SYSTEMS** Many people today think of tombs as sad places. How was the Egyptian belief different?
5. **CRITICAL THINKING** Why might Egypt have wanted to "Egyptianize" Nubia?
6. **WRITING ACTIVITY** List the things you would want to take with you into the afterlife if you were a pharaoh.

Homework Options

Ask students to list the preparations believed necessary for an Egyptian king to journey into the afterlife.

Study Guide: page 15

Answers to Review Questions

1. Egyptian society was highly structured and based on farming. It was governed by religious beliefs in the afterlife. We know much about Egyptian life from the writings Egyptians left behind. Less is known about Nubia, but we do know that Nubians were skilled archers, craftspeople, and traders. They preserved their own customs while adopting some Egyptian customs.
2. Egyptians could send messages and keep written records, such as tax records, that helped society to function.
3. Answers should reflect an understanding of the quotation.
4. Tombs were places from which Egyptians hoped to travel to a happy afterlife.
5. Sample answers: Egyptians were proud of their culture and wanted others to adopt it. They wanted Nubians to become like them so Nubia would remain loyal to Egypt.
6. Ask students to scan pages 89–90 before answering.

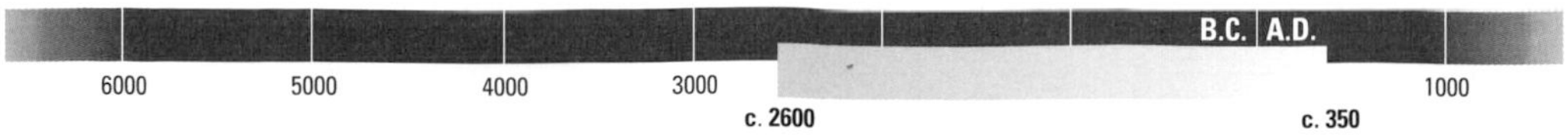
B.C. A.D.
6000
5000
4000
3000
1000
c. 2600
c. 350

L E S S O N 3

Great Achievements

He was counselor to the king, high priest of the sun, astrologer, and wise man. He was both a scribe and a sculptor. In a sense, Imhotep *(ihm HOH tehp)* represents the genius of Egypt.

About 2650 B.C., Egypt's King Djoser *(DZOH suhr)* asked Imhotep to design the grandest tomb ever. The result was Egypt's first pyramid and the first large monument of cut stone in the world. The Step Pyramid, at Saqqara *(suh KAHR uh),* rose in six levels to a height of more than 200 feet.

Imhotep was most likely a doctor, too, and a brilliant one. He was one of the first people to study how the body worked. He may have known, for example, that blood runs through the body. This fact had to be discovered again by modern medicine 4,000 years later.

Egyptian medicine was famous in the ancient world. Egyptian doctors treated patients in Assyria and beyond. In the *Odyssey,* the Greek poet Homer summed up the world's admiration of Egyptian medicine. He wrote of Egypt,

> Where the rich plantations grow herbs of all kinds, maleficent [harmful] and healthful; and no one else knows medicine as they do, Egyptian heirs of Paian, the healing god.

Imhotep was so admired that cultures in Egypt and beyond made him a God of medicine. For thousands of years, people prayed to him in the hope of being healed.

THINKING FOCUS

What lasting effects did the Egyptians and the Nubians have on the world?

Key Term

- papyrus

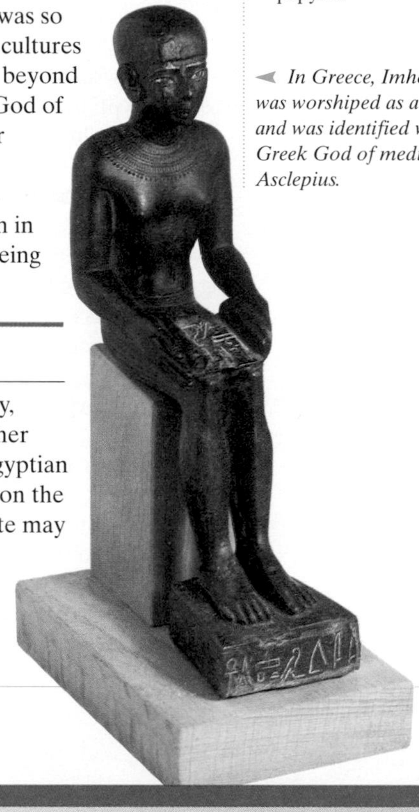

In Greece, Imhotep was worshiped as a God and was identified with the Greek God of medicine, Asclepius.

Egypt's Place in History

The works of Imhotep, like those of Egypt itself, lived on. Egyptian ideas spread throughout the ancient world. Some still affect our lives today.

Spread of Egyptian Culture

Trade was one way the ideas of Egypt traveled. Egypt exported paper, pottery, grain, and other goods. An Egyptian statue found on the island of Crete may have been brought there about 1700 B.C.

INTRODUCE

Read the Thinking Focus aloud. Review the features of the ancient Egyptian and Nubian civilizations studied in Lessons 1 and 2. Have students speculate on the achievements for which each culture is remembered. Write the list on the chalkboard, and have students read the lesson for confirmation.

Key Term

Vocabulary Strategies: T36–T37

papyrus—a plant and a type of paper made from the core of the plant

Graphic Overview

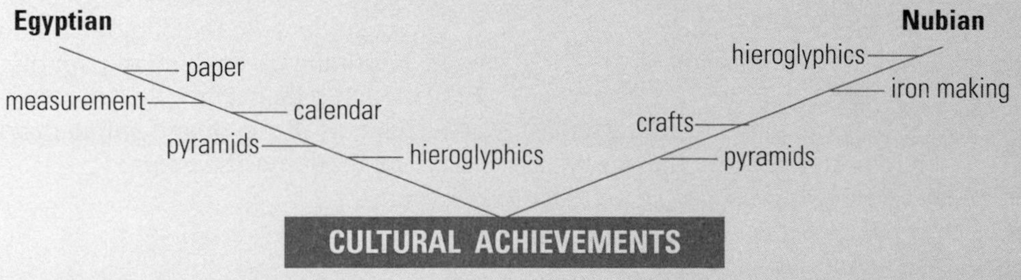
Egyptian
paper
measurement
calendar
pyramids
hieroglyphics
Nubian
hieroglyphics
iron making
crafts
pyramids
CULTURAL ACHIEVEMENTS

Objectives

1. List achievements for which Egypt is remembered.
2. Describe the cultural changes that occurred during Nubia's Meroitic period.

DEVELOP

Tell students about the Greek historian Herodotus, who made a grand tour of ancient Egypt in the 400s B.C. He wrote, "About Egypt I shall have a great deal more to relate [tell] because of the number of remarkable things which the country contains. . . ." Invite students to take their own grand tour of Egypt in this lesson, taking notes as they go. Then have students write a brief description of it.

■ *They spread through trade and through foreign visitors such as Herodotus.*

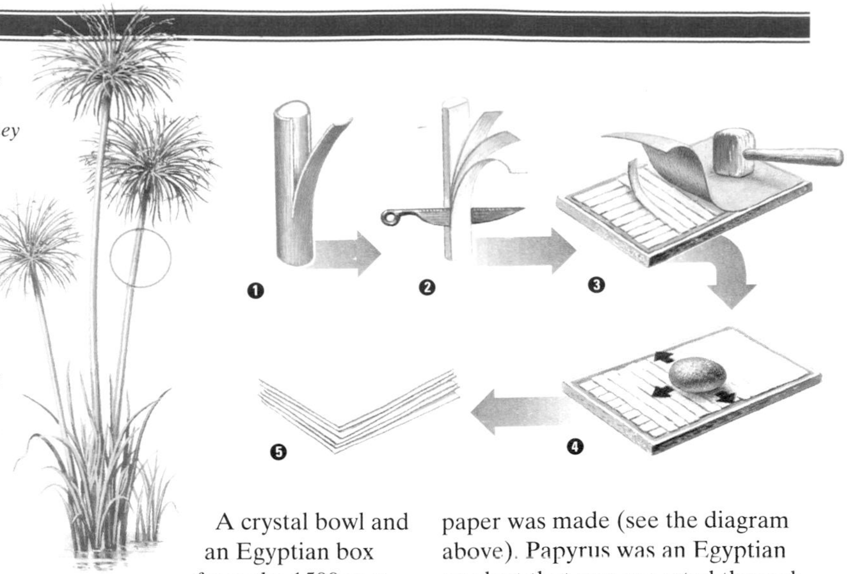
1
2
3
4
5

➤ *(1) Egyptians cut the stem of the papyrus and removed the core. (2) They cut the core into strips, (3) put one layer across another, and beat them into a single sheet. (4) Then they polished the sheet with a stone and (5) trimmed the edges. The papyrus below is from the largest Egyptian math textbook ever found. It asks questions about the geometry of triangles.*

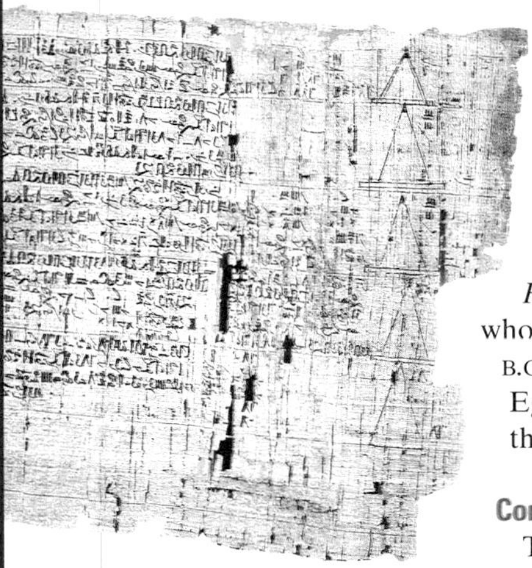

A crystal bowl and an Egyptian box from the 1500s B.C. have been discovered in tombs in Greece. Many scholars now believe that Egypt influenced Greek culture.

One Greek visitor was amazed by Egyptian culture. Herodotus *(hih RAHD uh tuhs),* a historian who sailed the Nile in the 400s B.C., wrote lively accounts of Egyptian customs, such as the building of the pyramids.

Contributions to the World

The page you are reading now is one of the gifts that ancient Egypt passed on to the world. It had its origins in **papyrus** *(puh PY ruhs),* the plant from which the paper was made (see the diagram above). Papyrus was an Egyptian product that was exported throughout the Mediterranean region.

Egyptians also invented a 12-month, 365-day calendar. Their system was later used by the Romans and is the basis for today's calendar.

To build their pyramids, the Egyptians needed to be able to measure exactly. The base of the Great Pyramid is within about 1½ inches of being perfectly square.

The Greeks said that they had learned how to measure areas and angles from the Egyptians. They in turn improved and passed on this knowledge to us as geometry.

The age of Egypt's pharaohs died out in 332 B.C., when the Greeks took control. You will read about Egypt under foreign rule in Chapter 10. ■

■ *How did Egyptian achievements and ideas spread beyond Egypt?*

Nubia's Place in History

Long after Egypt had fallen to the Greeks, Nubian culture lived on. The city of Meroë *(MEHR oh ee),* beyond the Fifth Cataract, became the capital of Kush in 270 B.C. The kingdom of Meroë, which lasted until A.D. 350, was Nubia's last major kingdom—and its finest.

Meroë covered a square mile, a huge size for an ancient city. It was in a fertile region of Kush. This part of the Nile had broad banks and rich soil. Good rainfall during

Access Activity

Have students reflect on their own achievements or those of their community. Ask volunteers to describe aloud what achievements they wish themselves or their community to be remembered for.

Access Strategy

Have students list types of paper used for drawing or writing. *(Newspaper, notebook paper, construction paper, book paper, glossy magazine paper)* Ask them to imagine having to use Mesopotamian-style clay tablets instead of paper. Then they can understand the impact that Egyptian papyrus made on the world. These lightweight sheets, which could be rolled up, were used by writers from Spain to Syria. Egypt, with its ample supplies of the tall papyrus reed, was the world's only supplier of papyrus sheets until about the A.D. 1100s, when rag and wood-pulp paper came along.

Direct students to the diagram on this page describing the making of papyrus. Explain that paper is only one of many achievements of Egypt and Nubia that they will read about in this lesson.

the summer and fall made farming and cattle grazing possible.

The Mystery of Meroë

Find Meroë on the map on page 86, and notice its distance from Egypt. Far from Egypt's influence, Nubian culture took its own course during the Meroitic period.

For example, the Nubians at Meroë created their own language and hieroglyphics. Unfortunately, no one has yet figured out how to read the mysterious language.

Meroitic religion shows a break with Egyptian traditions. Egypt's God Amon was still the most important, but a Nubian Lion-God was next. Kings were still buried in pyramids, but the Kushites returned to older Nubian customs, such as placing the body on a bed instead of in a coffin.

As always, Nubia was a crossroads for African trade. Now, however, the Nubians had a new product of their own: iron. Archaeologists have found huge piles of slag, a product of iron making, at Meroë.

Trade brought Nubians into contact with other cultures. Meroitic art shows Egyptian, Greek, Roman, and central African influences. Nubian graves contained numerous items of bronze, glass, and silver from all over the Mediterranean region.

The Meroitic Alphabet

Hieroglyph				
Cursive	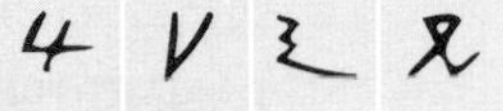			
Sound	i	b	k	d

◄ *These are a few of the 23 Meroitic hieroglyphs, as well as the cursive characters that evolved from them.*

After about A.D. 200, the world began to bypass Nubia, as traders found new routes through the Sahara. Meroë became weak, and in the middle A.D. 300s, it fell to conquerors from the nearby desert.

Survival of Customs

Great kingdoms never rose again in Nubia. However, Nubia makes up part of the modern nation of Sudan. There, Nubian customs survive today. Beautiful pottery, baskets, and furniture are still made in the ancient style. In some parts of Sudan, people use wooden pillows much like ancient Nubian headrests.

Today's Nubians, like the young girl in this picture, are a living part of the ancient culture. After more than 35 centuries, Nubia endures. ■

▼ *This Sudanese girl braids her hair just as the ancient Nubians did.*

■ *Why can it be said that Nubian culture became more independent during the Meroitic period?*

■ *Nubians invented their own language and hieroglyphics; they adopted new burial practices; they began to manufacture iron.*

REVIEW

1. **FOCUS** What lasting effects did the Egyptians and the Nubians have on the world?
2. **GEOGRAPHY** Find Meroë on the map on page 86. How did location and geography help to make Meroitic culture independent?
3. **CULTURE** State in your own words the quotation from the Greek poet about medicine in Egypt.
4. **CULTURE** What was papyrus, and how was it made?
5. **HISTORY** What brought about the fall of the kingdom of Meroë?
6. **CRITICAL THINKING** In your opinion, did the ancient world know less about Nubia than about Egypt?
7. **ACTIVITY** Invent your own writing, using symbols to represent letters, words, or ideas. Write a short paragraph in your hieroglyphics, and have a classmate try to read it.

CLOSE

Have students answer the Thinking Focus by taking turns listing achievements for which Egypt and Nubia are remembered. Direct each student to write one or two words, the goal being to create diagrams of achievements for each civilization.

Answers to Review Questions

1. The Egyptians gave us paper, our yearly calendar, and the beginnings of geometry. The Nubians passed on parts of their culture, such as the making of crafts.
2. Far away from Egypt and its cultural influence, Meroë developed its own traditions.
3. Sample answer: "In Egypt herbs used for medicine grow in fertile fields. Some are harmful; some aid in healing. No one knows medicine like the Egyptians, for they are descended from Paian, the God of healing."
4. Papyrus was a kind of paper made from a plant of the same name. Strips of the core were layered, beaten, and polished.
5. Traders found routes that bypassed Nubia. Meroë became weak and was conquered by the nearby desert peoples.
6. Sample answer: Fewer visitors could reach Nubia and write about it; Nubian writing cannot be read.
7. Encourage students to study samples of Egyptian hieroglyphics.

Homework Options

Have students use school or public library resources to find out more about the history of papermaking. Students should summarize their findings in a couple of paragraphs.

Study Guide: page 16

UNDERSTANDING VISUAL EVIDENCE

This feature uses an Egyptian wall painting to teach students how art can be used as a source of information about people of the past.

CULTURE

Visual Learning

Point out to students that art is a rich source of information about the daily life and beliefs of people of the past. Emphasize that much of what is known about early people has been learned from studying their art. Refer students to the three questions in Here's How before they look at the wall painting. Continue by asking them to relate details from each register of the painting. List on the chalkboard the details that students observe.

UNDERSTANDING VISUAL EVIDENCE

Interpreting Egyptian Art

Here's Why

One way to learn about the daily lives and the beliefs of people of the past is to study their art. Suppose you want to learn more about what life was like in Thebes, the capital of Egypt at the time of the New Kingdom. Art from this time period is rich in information about daily life. Yet first you must know how to interpret art from the past.

Here's How

When you look at art from the past, ask yourself these questions:

1. What was its purpose?
2. What is its main subject?
3. What does it tell you about the past?

The illustration on these pages is from a wall painting found in a tomb in Thebes. The tomb, which dates from about 1380 B.C., belonged to Nebamun (*NEHB uh muhn*) and Ipuky (*ee POO kee*). Both were important artists who worked for the king.

Now ask: What was the artist's purpose? Why was the painting created? A tomb artist's purpose was to help ensure a happy afterlife for the person buried in the tomb.

Next, what is the main subject of the painting? To answer this question, you need to figure out who is shown in the painting and what each person is doing.

Notice that the painting is divided into horizontal sections, called registers. Look at the large, seated figure to the left of the registers. In Egyptian paintings, people of high rank are often shown as being larger than the others. In this case the large figure is a supervisor.

Look at the man on the far left of the upper register. He is weighing gold rings against a counterweight shaped like a bull's head. The four seated men in the upper register are all carving symbols. To the right, two craftsmen are fitting the symbols into a framework. They are building a catafalque (*KAT uh fawlk*), an ornamental structure used in funerals.

Now look at the lower register. Here you see six artisans at work. To their left, two men show finished objects to their supervisor.

Now do you know what the painting is about? If you guessed that it shows a royal workshop of artisans, you are right. Both Nebamun and Ipuky were supervisors in the

Objective

Show how art can be a source of information about people of the past. (Visual Learning 1, 3)

Writing a Story

Have students write a short story about life in a royal workshop, using the details about the painting that the class listed on the chalkboard.

Analyzing Art

Ask students to find another example of an Egyptian wall painting in a book on Egypt, the history of art, or world history. Tell them to interpret the painting, using the methods they learned. Ask students to write a paragraph explaining their interpretation.

royal workshop. The items being made were for the king's tomb.

Next, consider the third question. What does the painting tell you about the past? Most important, it shows how deeply the Egyptians believed in the afterlife. As you can see, much effort went into the crafting of items for the next life.

The painting also tells you about Egyptian customs. For example, think about how the people in the painting are dressed. Notice that the supervisor wears a large ornamental collar and a thin, full-length garment. The workers, however, dress in simple cloths wrapped at the waist.

Try It

Look closely at the lower register. Try interpreting the rest of the painting by answering the following questions. What are the six seated men in the lower register making? What kinds of tools are they using? What does this tell you about ancient Egyptian technology? What are the workers wearing? What does this say about Egypt's climate?

Apply It

Now that you have studied some skills for interpreting wall paintings, try your hand at making a painting of your own. Working alone or in a small group, create a mural that shows a scene from your daily life. For example, you might paint a scene from the lunchroom. Or you could paint a scene of your classroom or a special area such as the library. Be sure to show a number of different activities in detail. Display your murals. Then study and interpret one another's paintings.

CULTURE

Critical Thinking

Point out to students that the value of art to the study of history is based largely on the interpretation of the art. To help students with their interpretation, review the observations they made earlier. Be sure students are clear about the purpose of the painting. *(To help ensure a happy afterlife for the person buried in the tomb)*

Ask students what conclusion they can draw from knowing how much effort Egyptians put into preparing for the next life. *(Students can conclude that the Egyptians felt strongly about the importance of the afterlife.)*

Answers to Try It

Vases, jewelry, figurines; woodcarving and painting tools; the tools shown are very simple ones; the painting emphasizes the cooperation and dedication of the artisans over technological achievement; cloths wrapped around their waists; it was probably hot.

Answers to Apply It

Students should demonstrate that they have studied the details of the painting and drawn their own conclusions about it.

Study Skills

Ask students to make a list of questions they could use to help them interpret a painting from another region or time period.

Answers to Reviewing Key Terms

A. Answers:

1. **Papyrus** is from the Greek word *papuros.* Papyrus is the plant from which the Egyptians made paper and the name for the paper made from that plant.
2. **Cataract** is from the Greek *katarassein,* "to dash down." The Nile has six cataracts, or rocky rapids.
3. **Scribe** is from the Latin word *scribere,* "to write." Egyptian scribes had the job of writing.
4. **Hieroglyphics** is from the Greek *hierogluphikos,* "sacred carving." Egyptians and Nubians wrote in hieroglyphics, which uses pictures to stand for ideas, words, or letters.
5. **Delta** is of Phoenician origin. At its mouth, the Nile fans out into a delta, which is a marshy, triangle-shaped area.
6. **Dynasty** is from the Greek *dunasteia,* "lordship." A dynasty is a line of rulers who are related. Dynasties ruled ancient Egypt.

B. Sample answers:

1. An Egyptian **dynasty** is a line of **pharaohs,** or rulers.
2. **Scribes** wrote in **hieroglyphics.**
3. The Nile River has a **delta** and six **cataracts.**
4. To prepare the body of a dead person for the **afterlife,** Egyptians made it into a **mummy.**

C. Answers:

1. Incorrect. The pharaoh was buried with great care. A **dynasty** was a line of pharaohs.
2. Correct. **Hieroglyphics** is a script that was used to recount the conquests of a **pharaoh.**
3. Correct. In hopes of achieving a happy **afterlife,** they built pyramids and made **mummies.**
4. Incorrect. Egyptian **scribes** were writers who themselves used that writing system.

Chapter Review

Reviewing Key Terms

afterlife (p. 89)
cataract (p. 83)
delta (p. 83)
dynasty (p. 85)
hieroglyphics (p. 87)
mummy (p. 89)
papyrus (p. 94)
pharaoh (p. 85)
scribe (p. 88)

A. Use a dictionary to find the origins of the following words. Then explain how the meaning of each word applies to Egypt and/or Nubia.

1. papyrus
2. cataract
3. scribe
4. hieroglyphics
5. delta
6. dynasty

B. Read each pair of words. Write a sentence telling how the words in each pair are related.

1. pharaoh, dynasty
2. scribe, hieroglyphics
3. delta, cataract
4. afterlife, mummy

C. Each statement below contains one or more key terms from the chapter. Decide whether the statement is correct or incorrect. Give reasons to support your decision using information in the chapter.

1. Because nearly all Egyptians considered the dynasty to be godlike, they buried it with great care.
2. Colorful hieroglyphics written on the temple walls explained how the pharaoh defeated his enemies.
3. The Egyptians' belief in an afterlife resulted in the construction of the pyramids and the practice of making mummies.
4. For more than 1,000 years, scribes tried but failed to decipher the writing system of ancient Egypt.

Exploring Concepts

A. Compare and contrast Egypt and Nubia by copying and completing the following chart.

	Egypt	Nubia
Major resources		
Customs and beliefs		
Contributions		

B. Answer each question with information from the chapter.

1. Why do historians know more about Egyptian civilization after 3000 B.C. than before that time?
2. Why did powerful leaders emerge in the Nile Valley?
3. Why did the Greek historian Herodotus call Egypt "the gift of the Nile"?
4. What effect did trade have on the history of Nubia?
5. Why did the Egypt-Nubia border shift so many times over the years?
6. The Assyrians and, later, the Greeks invaded Egypt. What geographic features protected Egypt from invaders, and what features made it open to invaders?
7. Why were historians able to learn more about ancient Egypt after the early 1800s than they had before?
8. Why did the Egyptians mummify the dead before burial?
9. How did religion influence the Egyptians?
10. Why does Imhotep "represent the genius of Egypt"?

Answers to Exploring Concepts

A. Sample answers:

Resources (Egypt): Nile River, fertile land; (Nubia): Nile River, minerals, animals

Customs (Egypt and Nubia): believed in afterlife and multiple Gods, mummified bodies, built pyramids

Contributions (Egypt): paper, calendar, mathematics; (Nubia): iron, jewelry, furniture, pottery

B. Sample answers:

1. Written records appeared in about 3000 B.C.
2. They were needed to organize projects such as flood control.
3. The river gave Egyptians what they needed to live, such as fertile lands and water.
4. It gave rise to civilizations in Nubia and led to invasions by Egypt.
5. When Egypt's rulers were strong, they invaded Nubia. When Nubian rulers were strong, they invaded Egypt.
6. Deserts protected Egypt, but the Mediterranean Sea left it open to attack.
7. The Rosetta stone, found in 1799, made Egyptian hieroglyphics readable.
8. Mummification slowed the decay of the body; they thought this was needed to enjoy the afterlife.
9. It governed all aspects of life and influenced art, architecture, and burials.
10. Imhotep embodied the achievements of Egyptian culture. He was a scribe, a sculptor, an astrologer, a high priest, a counselor to the king, an architect, and probably a doctor.

Reviewing Skills

Using what you learned about Egyptian art on pages 96 and 97, evaluate the Egyptian painting on page 90. What do you think was the painting's purpose? What are the people in the painting doing? What are they carrying? What does the painting tell you about the history of Egypt and Nubia?

Using Critical Thinking

1. Historians have a wealth of information about the Egyptians who lived in ancient times. Yet they know much less about the culture of the ancient Nubians. How might this lack of information be explained? Explain your reasoning.
2. On the plain of Giza, various Egyptian pharaohs ordered and supervised the building of four enormous stone structures. The largest, the Great Pyramid, is 40 stories high and covers an area the size of seven city blocks. What were some of the factors that enabled the pharaohs to erect such impressive monuments?
3. Egypt's customs were so powerful that they influenced other cultures. What U.S. customs do you think have influenced other cultures around the world? Do you think that U.S. customs have had a good or bad effect on other cultures? Give examples to support your answer.
4. Although Egypt tried to "Egyptianize" Nubia, Nubian rulers did not force the Egyptians to follow Nubian customs. Instead, the Nubians adopted many Egyptian ideas and helped to bring back forgotten parts of Egypt's own culture. What do you think this reveals about the Nubians?

Preparing for Citizenship

1. WRITING ACTIVITY Ancient Egypt and Nubia each influenced the culture of the other. Other cultures have influenced the culture of the United States. Describe a custom of your family or a family you know and explain its origin.
2. COLLECTING INFORMATION The Egyptians believed that "to speak the name of the dead is to make him alive again." Thus, they built great temples and pyramids, hoping that the monuments would cause the pharaohs' names to be remembered. Over the years, the people in your community may have erected monuments, statues, or plaques to honor people and to keep their memory alive. Find such a monument, describe it, and explain why it was erected. Does it reveal anything interesting about the culture of the people who built it or of those whom it honors? If possible, include a photograph or drawing of the monument with your description.
3. GROUP ACTIVITY In ancient times Egypt got many natural resources from Nubia. Today the United States imports from other countries many of the natural resources on which its industries depend. In a small group, make a list of resources the United States imports and the countries from which the resources come. Then draw a map of the world, and label the countries and the resources that they export to the United States.
4. COLLABORATIVE LEARNING Migration is an important part of the history of the United States, just as it was in the early development of the Nile Valley. In small groups prepare a presentation on a migrant culture in the United States. Have one person research and take notes on the reasons that the migration took place. Have another find photographs, artifacts, or articles from that time period. The group can choose a representative, or the entire group can present your findings to the class.

Answers to Reviewing Skills

The painting, which shows Nubians bringing gifts to the pharaoh, was probably meant to show the power and wealth of the pharaoh. The Nubians carry gold rings and nuggets, a leopard skin, an ebony log, and incense. The painting tells you that Egypt controlled Nubia at that time, and it also shows the wealth of resources the Nubians had. It also tells you what the Egyptians thought the Nubians looked like.

Answers to Using Critical Thinking

1. The Egyptians left volumes of written records. Scholars and historians were able to decipher the writings because of the discovery of the Rosetta stone. Also, archaeologists uncovered many artifacts in Egyptian monuments that tell about life in ancient Egypt. Early Nubians had no written language, so they left no written records. As a result, even ancient peoples knew little about the Nubians. Although the Meroitic Nubians left written records, scholars have been unable to decipher them.
2. Building the pyramids required a huge labor force. Fortunately for the pharaohs, farmers were available for work during the flood season. In addition, the Egyptians had the necessary technical skills—they knew how to make exact measurements.
3. Answers might include skyscrapers, baseball, shopping malls, rock music, clothing styles, as well as this country's love for gadgets, fast cars, and fast food. Answers should be supported with good reasoning.
4. Allow for speculation. For example, the Nubians of this time apparently admired and respected Egyptian culture. Perhaps the Nubians were a more tolerant people.

Answers to Preparing for Citizenship

1. WRITING ACTIVITY Students may mention religious celebrations, food, and social customs that have their origins in another culture.
2. COLLECTING INFORMATION Encourage students to examine statues, monuments, and plaques on historic buildings in their community. Information about the people being commemorated is probably available at the local library or could be obtained from a local historical society.
3. GROUP ACTIVITY An almanac and an encyclopedia as well as texts such as *Exploring Your World: The Adventure of Geography* (National Geographic Society, 1989) are good sources of information on world trade.
4. COLLABORATIVE LEARNING Encourage students to list the names of peoples who have migrated to the United States including recent migrants—Haitians, Vietnamese, Laotians, and other people from Central and South America and Asia. Have students check the card catalogue in the library and the *Readers' Guide to Periodical Literature* for information on migrant cultures.

CHAPTER ORGANIZER

Chapter 5 *Two Early Asian Civilizations*

CHAPTER PLANNING CHART

Pupil's Edition	Teacher's Edition	Ancillaries
Lesson 1: Ancient India (2–3 days) Objective 1: Describe the Indus Valley civilization. (History 1) Objective 2: Describe the ancient trade network of which the Indus Valley was a part. (Economics 3, 4) Objective 3: Describe the arrival of the Aryans and their contributions to Indian culture. (Culture 1, 4)	• Graphic Overview (102) • Access Strategy (103) • Access Activity (103) Social Participation (104) Social Context (104) Cultural Context (105)	Study Guide (18) Map Activities (9)
Understanding Organization Objective: Identify and use organizational patterns in written material. (Study Skills 1)	Identifying Patterns (107)	Study Guide (19)
Lesson 2: Hinduism and Buddhism (1–2 days) Objective 1: Understand the main teachings of Hinduism and Buddhism. (Ethics and Belief Systems 4, 5) Objective 2: Explain how the origins of Hinduism and Buddhism are linked to the Vedic tradition. (Ethics and Belief Systems 3)	• Graphic Overview (108) • Access Strategy (109) • Access Activity (109) Study Skills (110) Religious Context (110) Historical Context (111) • Study Skills (111) • Visual Learning (112) Historical Context (112)	Study Guide (20)
Lesson 3: Ancient China (1–2 days) Objective 1: Describe the geography of ancient China. (History 7; Geography 5) Objective 2: Describe patterns in Chinese history. (History 4, 6)	• Graphic Overview (114) • Access Strategy (115) • Access Activity (115)	Study Guide (21)
Lesson 4: China's Cultural Heritage (2–3 days) Objective 1: Describe how the Chinese writing system has helped to unify China. (History 5; Culture 1) Objective 2: Describe the influence of Confucianism on China's cultural heritage and social structure. (Ethics and Belief Systems 4, 5) Objective 3: Describe the great Chinese achievements and inventions. (Economics 5)	• Graphic Overview (117) • Access Activity (118) • Access Strategy (118) Research (119) Journal Writing (119) • Visual Learning (119) Cultural Context (120)	Study Guide (22) Discovery Journal (11)
Making Decisions: The Great Wall Objective 1: Recognize the dangers to the emperor and the empire. (History 3, 5) Objective 2: Define the goals for building the Great Wall. (Critical Thinking 2; History 3, 5) Objective 3: Evaluate the negative and positive effects of building the Great Wall. (Critical Thinking 2; History 5)		Discovery Journal (12)
Chapter Review	Answers (124–125)	Tests (17–20)

* Objectives are correlated to the strands and goals in the program Scope and Sequence on pages T41–T49.

• LEP appropriate resources.
(For additional strategies, see pages T32–T-33.)

CHAPTER RATIONALE

Chapter 5 focuses on the ancient civilizations of India and China. Like the cultures of ancient Egypt and Mesopotamia, those of India and China arose in river valleys. There water and rich soil supported farming and the development of crafts and complex societies.

Lesson 1 opens with the discovery of the remains of ancient cities in the Indus Valley of what is now Pakistan. Mohenjo-Daro, Harappa, and other Indus Valley cities were centers of a highly organized society. In time, this society declined, perhaps because of drought, earthquakes, changes in river paths, or invasion.

Although India's civilization has been marked by continuity from ancient times to the present, it has experienced recurring invasions. The first new group was the Aryans, who began migrating into India about 1500 B.C. They introduced new religious beliefs and a new social system based upon rigid classes, or castes.

Lesson 2 deals with the two major religions that arose in India and became vital parts of that civilization. The mingling of Aryan and indigenous beliefs and practices led to Hinduism, which remains the major religion of India today. Based on a philosophy of life as the search for truth, Hindu practice includes the worship of a personal God or Gods and a belief in reincarnation.

Buddhism arose in part as a result of the religious doubt and experimentation occurring in India in the 6th century B.C. It too represents a philosophy of life based on the search for enlightenment. Emperor Ashoka sought to strengthen Buddhism in India. The religion also spread to East and Southeast Asia.

Lesson 3 presents China as an ancient civilization that remained apart, without the invasions that influenced India's development. Chinese civilization has been continuous to the present day. China's long history has been characterized by the rise and fall of dynasties and the importance of family. Throughout China's history, each dynasty has claimed to have the Mandate of Heaven, divine sanction for the emperor's rule.

Lesson 4 introduces students to the unique achievements of China's civilization. These achievements had the effect of unifying the country and providing continuity. One was a special style of writing. Another was a shared set of values and the belief in a moral order, expressed in the teachings of Confucius.

Students will see that the culture of China was highly creative, excelling in the development and application of new technologies. The Chinese discovered ways to make silk and paper; they invented gunpowder; and they developed a process for printing. China also carried out huge projects, such as the building of the Great Wall. Today archaeologists are gaining new information about China's early history from the discovery of an emperor's tomb.

ACTIVITIES & PROJECTS

LEP: Labeling a Map

Provide students with an outline map of South and Southwest Asia or have them trace the text map on page 104 as far west as the tip of the Arabian Peninsula. Have them label the following: Indus River, Arabian Sea, Mohenjo-Daro, and the Khyber Pass. Refer students to the map on page 104 and ask them what landforms are found to the northwest and north of the Indus Valley. (Use after Lesson 1.)

Writing a Report

After students have read the sections in Lesson 2 entitled Teachings of Buddhism and Siddhartha's Search, ask them to write two paragraphs describing the character traits they associate with Siddhartha. For each trait, they should give an example from the Buddha's life or teachings. (Use after Lesson 2.)

Challenge: Critical Thinking

Write the following five relationships on the chalkboard: *father and son; elder brother and younger brother; husband and wife; friend and friend; ruler and subject.* Point out that Confucius considered these the five basic relationships in society and taught that each requires a strict pattern of duties. For example, a father is to be loving and set a good example; a son is to obey and respect his father. Have students write a short list of duties for the two people in each of the five relationships. (Use after Lesson 4.)

Bulletin Board

Begin the first half of a two-part display comparing the ancient civilizations of India and China. Consider achievements in religion, the arts, science and technology, social life, economics, and politics. Have students sketch or draw illustrations, clip pictures from magazines, or photocopy book illustrations and color them. All bulletin board items should be accompanied by captions written in complete sentences. Each student is responsible for at least one contribution. (Use after Lesson 4.)

Basic: Making a Mural

Direct students to the timeline on pages 120 and 121. Have them identify the achievements of the Shang, Qin, Han, Tang, and Song dynasties. Have students make a mural depicting the main contributions of each dynasty. Where possible, they should show examples of the lifestyle of each era. (Use after Lesson 4.)

CHAPTER PREVIEW

Have students read the chapter title and opening narrative. Tell them that in this chapter they will read about the cultures of ancient India and China. Ask what difference the opening paragraph suggests between these two cultures. *(It suggests that India's culture combined the influences of many peoples, whereas China's tended to grow in isolation.)*

Looking Back

Remind students that in Chapter 4 they read about the importance of the Nile to ancient Egypt and Nubia. Explain that ancient civilizations in India and China also arose in river valleys.

Looking Forward

Tell students that in Lessons 1–4—Ancient India, Hinduism and Buddhism, Ancient China, and China's Cultural Heritage—they will read about the development of two early Asian civilizations.

Lesson 1 explores ancient India, a civilization shaped by the cultures of the early Indus people and the Aryans who later migrated into India.

Chapter 5
Two Early Asian Civilizations

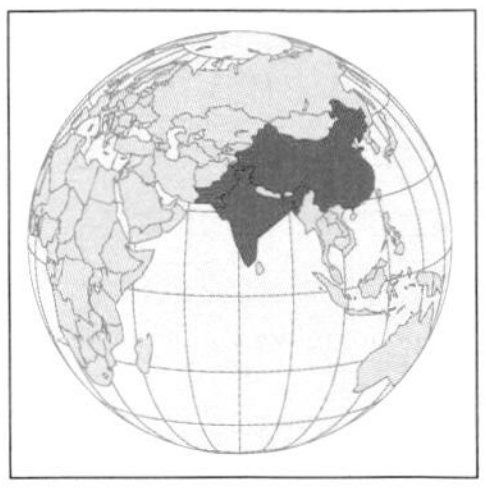

Like the brightly colored cloth woven in India for thousands of years, the culture of India has been fashioned from many strands. India accepted peoples and ideas from many places. China, surrounded by towering mountains and vast deserts, has a culture that grew with little outside influence. Both civilizations developed traditions that live on into the present.

More than 4,000 years ago, people in the Indus Valley were weaving cotton cloth. Hand looms like this are used today in some parts of India.

Great Hindu poems include a tale about a hero named Rama, one form of a Hindu deity. Indian children today still act out this tale.

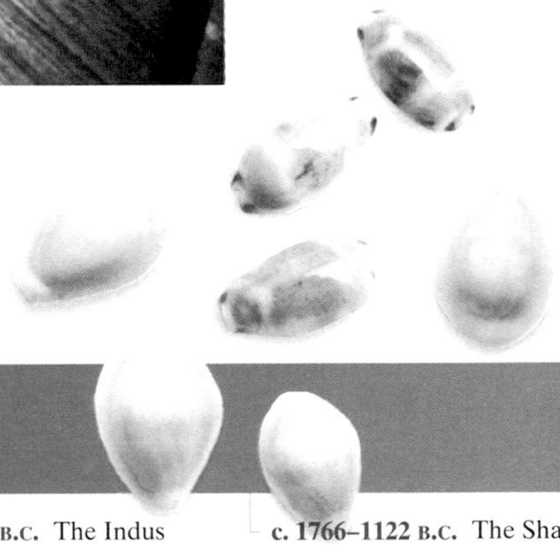

2500 | 2000 | 1000

2500 B.C.

c. 2500–1750 B.C. The Indus Valley civilization flourishes along the Indus River.

c. 1766–1122 B.C. The Shang dynasty, one the earliest known dynasties of China, rul the land. The shells of cowries, a kind of s that lives in warm seas, serve as a form of money during this time.

BACKGROUND

The civilizations of modern India and China are rooted in the past. More than 4,000 years ago, people in Indus Valley cities started a tradition of weaving cotton cloth that has carried through to modern India. When Aryan invaders pushed into the Indian subcontinent about 1500 B.C., they too left their mark. Their legacy includes a caste system that still dominates India's society and the Vedas, sacred hymns and poems still read by Hindus today. Their language, Sanskrit, forms the base of modern Hindi.

China, one of the world's oldest continuous civilizations, takes its name from the Qin dynasty (221–206 B.C.). The Qin legacy also includes a simplified, standardized writing system and the first Chinese civil-service system. Shi huangdi of the Qin dynasty is often called China's first emperor because he conquered a vast region and united it under his rule. To keep out invaders, he ordered the joining of sections of wall on the frontier to form what would become the 1,500-mile Great Wall.

The Arts and Religions of Early India

Each culture in India's long history had special qualities and made unique contributions. A truly remarkable era, however, was the Gupta Period (A.D. 320–550), when the arts reached their peak. This period is often called the Classical Age of India. Chandragupta II (c. A.D. 376–415), the most noted

Buddhism spread from India to China during the Han dynasty. This Chinese bronze sculpture shows the Buddha in a posture of meditation.

B.C. | A.D. | 500 | 1000 | 1500

c. 124 B.C. A university is established to train Chinese government officials. Civil service examinations, stamped with seals like the one above, later come into use.

A.D. 960–1279 Sung dynasty rules in China. The compass is invented.

A.D. 1500

Understanding the Visuals

The children in the photograph are the principal actors in the *Ram Lila,* a play about Rama, hero of the Indian epic *Ramayana.* It tells the story of Prince Rama, whose wife, Sita, is captured by a demon. In rescuing Sita, Rama is helped by monkeys, including the monkey god Hanuman. Each year during a 10-day festival in northern India, young actors wearing elaborate costumes and masks act out scenes from the epic.

Buddhism, founded by Siddhartha Gautama about 2,500 years ago, became one of India's major religions. From India it spread to China and to Southeast Asia. It remains one of Asia's major religions.

Understanding Chronology

Refer the students to the timeline. To demonstrate the parallels in time between events in India and China, point out that as the Shang dynasty arose in China, the Aryans migrated into the Indus Valley in India. The Shang dynasty is the first Chinese dynasty that has been documented through archaeology. However, legends tell of an earlier dynasty, the Xia, arising about 2000 B.C.

of the Gupta rulers, was a devoted patron of the arts. Among the gifted writers of that time was Kalidasa, a great Sanskrit poet. His writings and the myths and epics of ancient India remain important works of world literature.

The origins of Hinduism, the major religion of modern India, can be traced back to 1500 B.C., and its literature to before 1000 B.C. Other religions practiced in India today include Buddhism, Islam, Sikhism, Jainism, and Christianity.

The Arts and Religion of Ancient China

Throughout the dynasties of ancient China, many inventions and ideas flourished. The Han dynasty (202 B.C.–A.D. 220) created a society so remarkable that the Chinese still refer to themselves as Han people. Under the Han dynasty, the arts flourished. A new form of poetry, *fu,* developed. *Fu* combined rhyme and prose in descriptive compositions that were long and entertaining. Lacquer, developed during the Shang dynasty, was perfected by the Han and used to coat art objects and furniture. Another Han achievement included the invention of paper.

Commerce, too, thrived under Han rule. Emperors aided the development of the Silk Road, which linked China with Southwestern Asia and the Mediterranean region.

INTRODUCE

Review with students important characteristics of the Egyptian and Sumerian civilizations studied in earlier chapters. Then ask students to read the Thinking Focus. Have students speculate on which of these characteristics the Indus Valley civilization might have in common with those civilizations. Write the list on the chalkboard, and have students read the lesson for confirmation.

Key Terms

Vocabulary Strategies: T36–T37
tributary—a stream or river that flows into a larger stream or river
caste—a class system based on birth, hereditary rank, profession, or the like
untouchable—one who falls outside the Hindu social system, is excluded from Hindu rituals, and is considered impure

2700 2500 600 B.C. | A.D. 900 1800

LESSON 1

Ancient India

THINKING FOCUS

What are the ancient origins of Indian civilization?

Key Terms

- tributary
- caste
- untouchable

The sun beats down on this dusty place. Temperatures climb to 120°F. Very little grows here, even though the Indus River flows just a few miles away. Yet in this near-desert in 1922, Indian archaeologist R. D. Banerji found small stone seals, or stamps used to make marks in soft clay or wax. He guessed that the seals, carved with writing and images of animals, had been made by people of an ancient civilization. How could the animals on the seals—a tiger, buffalo, and rhinoceros—have lived here? Indeed, how could a civilization have existed here at all?

To find out, scientists began in 1924 to dig at this site, a ruined city called Mohenjo-Daro *(moh hehn joh DAHR oh)*. Using hand scoops and brushes, the scientists removed the dust and dirt that covered the ruins. Ancient tools, pots, and even toys were brought to light. What they found confirmed Banerji's hunch, but on a greater scale than he imagined. The city was thousands of years older than any discovered before in India. Mohenjo-Daro was thriving as long ago as 2500 B.C.

Archaeologists do not know what finally ended life in Mohenjo-Daro. Was it an earthquake? A flood? An invasion? Or was it deforestation? There is some evidence for each of these. Perhaps a combination of them brought the city down.

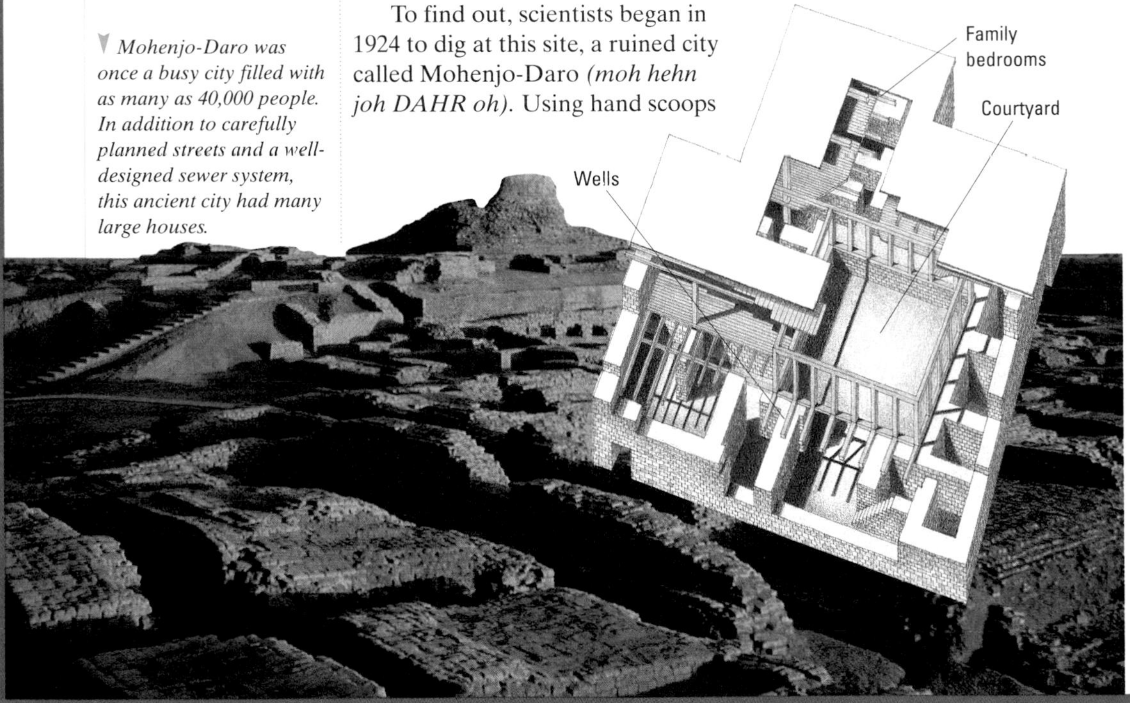
Family bedrooms
Courtyard
Wells

Mohenjo-Daro was once a busy city filled with as many as 40,000 people. In addition to carefully planned streets and a well-designed sewer system, this ancient city had many large houses.

Objectives

1. Describe the Indus Valley civilization.
2. Describe the ancient trade network of which the Indus Valley was a part.
3. Describe the arrival of the Aryans and their contributions to Indian culture.

Graphic Overview

Indus Valley Culture
- River valley farming
- Large cities
- Widespread trade

Aryan Culture
- Migration into India
- Conquest of Indus region
- Settlement across northern India

Migration

Indian Culture
- Hinduism
- Vedas
- Sanskrit language
- Rigid caste system

A Great River Civilization

Historians believe Mohenjo-Daro was the southern center of a widespread civilization. The northern center was Harappa, about 400 miles away on a tributary of the Indus River. A **tributary** is a stream or river that feeds into a larger stream or river. About 70 other sites have been discovered in the Indus Valley. They are scattered across a vast plain about three times the size of California.

These sites are part of the same civilization. The buildings, streets, and sewers were made in the same way. Even the baked bricks used in construction are the same size.

The cities were laid out in a grid pattern, with streets crossing at right angles to one another. The two major cities had a large fortresslike building, which may have been as high as five stories. The building contained a place to store grain, an assembly hall, and a public bath. These public baths were similar to those found in Indian cities today.

In ancient times the Indus River often flooded. The flood waters left behind a rich soil in which crops such as wheat, barley, rice, and cotton grew well.

The Indus Valley also had enough rainfall for farming. The strong monsoon winds of Asia created a regular wet season. See A Closer Look in Chapter 14 to find out more about monsoons. ■

Across Time & Space

The Indus Valley is no longer a well-watered plain. The Indus River passes through a dry, desertlike landscape. This area might have been altered by a change in climate, along with deforestation and overgrazing.

■ *What geographic features made possible the growth of a civilization in the Indus Valley?*

An Ancient Trade Network

At sites both in the Indus Valley and far from it, archaeologists have uncovered evidence of an ancient trade network. Once more, clues have come from the seals.

Evidence of Trade

Historians think that merchants used seals, like the one shown on page 104, to mark their property. The seals were made of a soft stone called steatite *(STEE uh tyt),* on which pictures of animals were carved. Above the animals is writing that has never been decoded and that is unlike any other ancient writing.

Some of these seals turned up in ancient Southwest Asian cities. Archaeologists date a seal found in the Sumerian city of Ur to about 2200 B.C. What goods might have been traded by the people of the Indus Valley with Southwest Asia? Once again, a seal gives a clue. On the back of one of the seals is the imprint of coarse cloth. At this time the Indus Valley people were spinning and weaving cotton. Perhaps they exported cloth to Mesopotamia. The

SHABINA

▲ *These flat-bottomed boats are used today for fishing in the Indus River. Boats similar to these may have been used by the people of the ancient Indus Valley civilization.*

DEVELOP

Have students study a large classroom map of South Asia, or have them look at the map on page 104. Point out the Indus Valley and trace the course of the Indus. Ask students to think of reasons why the river was important to the growth of civilization there. *(It was a communication route between towns, a source of water and rich soil for farming, and a transportation route for trade.)*

■ *The Indus floods brought rich soil for farming. Monsoons provided enough rain to grow crops.*

CULTURE

Critical Thinking

Encourage students to brainstorm other possible uses of the stone seals. Ask them what types of seals are used today and for what purposes. *(Rubber stamps—date, to show bill payment, signature reproduction, ownership; trademarks—product and product-name protection)*

Access Strategy

Ask students to draw a brick on a sheet of paper and color it. Give no other directions. Collect the papers, and then pass out white paper. Ask students to draw a brick four inches long by two inches high and to color it light brown. Show a model. Collect the papers and display a variety of the first bricks. Have students pretend they are archaeologists who have just unearthed these bricks. What clues do they give about the civilization being excavated? *(The civilization had no standard measurements; workers were not skilled; buildings from such bricks would be poorly constructed.)* Hold up the second drawings of the bricks. What do they indicate? *(Standard measurements, more skilled craftspeople, and supervision of the work.)* Bricks found at Harappa and Mohenjo-Daro were like the second set. Discuss what that means in terms of the civilization there. *(It was a highly structured civilization with central planning and supervision of projects.)*

Access Activity

Have students make their own seals. Cut raw potatoes in halves and distribute to the class. Students can carve a design in the cut end with a blunt table knife. Students might also use scissors to cut pieces of inner tube, gluing them in a design on cardboard. To print, use acrylic paint and a hand roller. Using the roller, apply a thin layer of paint to the potato or inner tube pieces.

GEOGRAPHY

Map and Globe Skills

Have students study the map of ancient trade routes on this page. You may wish to have them review how to read a route map in the Map and Globe Handbook, page G12. Point out the various trade routes. To show how far Indus Valley traders traveled, draw the scale for the map on the chalkboard and review the meaning of the scale. Ask students to determine the distance between the Indus Valley and northern Syria *(About 2,000 miles)* and the distance between the Indus Valley and the Nile in Egypt *(About 2,400 miles).*

■ *Civilizations that traded with the Indus Valley included Sumer, Mesopotamia, Persia, Afghanistan, and Egypt.*

Ancient Trade Routes and Resources, c. 2500 B.C.

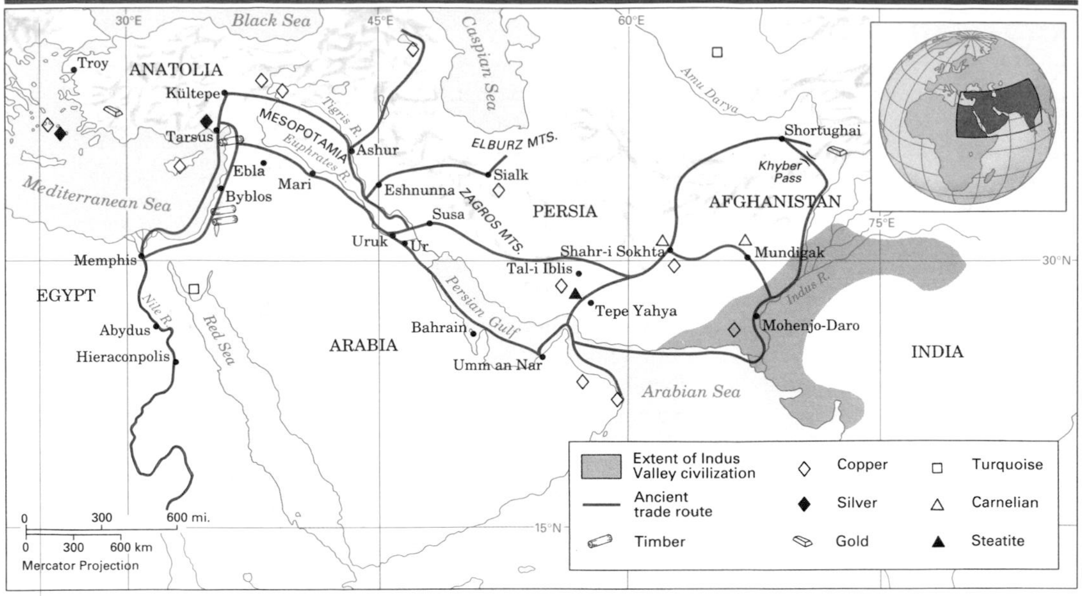

30°E
Black Sea
45°E
Caspian Sea
60°E
Troy
ANATOLIA
Kültepe
Tarsus
MESOPOTAMIA
Tigris R.
Euphrates R.
Ashur
ELBURZ MTS.
Sialk
Ebla
Mari
Byblos
Mediterranean Sea
Eshnunna
ZAGROS MTS.
Susa
PERSIA
Uruk
Ur
Memphis
EGYPT
Nile R.
Red Sea
Abydus
Hieraconpolis
ARABIA
Bahrain
Persian Gulf
Umm an-Nar
Shahr-i Sokhta
Tal-i Iblis
Tepe Yahya
Amu Darya
Shortughai
Khyber Pass
AFGHANISTAN
75°E
Mundigak
Indus R.
30°N
Mohenjo-Daro
INDIA
Arabian Sea
15°N
0 300 600 mi.
0 300 600 km
Mercator Projection
Extent of Indus Valley civilization
Ancient trade route
Timber
Copper
Silver
Gold
Turquoise
Carnelian
Steatite

▲ *As the map shows, many of the trade routes used by people of the Indus Valley civilization followed waterways.*

large granaries discovered at the Indus Valley sites suggest that the people grew more grain than they needed to feed themselves. Perhaps they shipped wheat and barley to Southwest Asia also.

Other Trading Goods

Jewelry and beads are other clues archaeologists use to work out puzzles about the past. Shown below is a necklace made of glazed pottery beads from the Indus Valley. Similar beads have been found in Syria. Other beads from the Indus Valley have been found in Sumerian sites.

Neither the ocean to the south nor the mountains to the north were barriers to Indus Valley traders. At Lothal, an Indus Valley site near the Arabian Sea, archaeologists have found the ruins of a dockyard. From there, ships could have sailed up the Persian Gulf to Mesopotamia. By means of overland caravans, the Indus Valley people obtained gemstones and metals from Iraq, Iran, Afghanistan, and central Asia.

At Harappa archaeologists have found metal pins, ax heads, and vases from Southwest Asia. At Lothal they have dug up a seal that most likely came from the area of the Persian Gulf.

The Indus Valley civilization came to an end around 1750 B.C. One of its contributions is still important to us. The next time you put on a T-shirt, remember that cotton cloth was one of this civilization's gifts to the world. ■

▼ *Beads and seals from the Indus Valley were found as far away as Mesopotamia.*

■ *Which civilizations of the ancient world traded goods with the people of the Indus Valley?*

Social Participation

Have students work in small groups to draw, on a large sheet of paper, their own plan for a city. Have them decide what they want at the center of town. *(A library, school, park, and so on)* Also have them decide how they want to lay out the streets, houses, and shopping centers.

Social Context

Harappa kept its public buildings safe by building them on a citadel mound that rose about 30 to 50 feet high and covered about 16 acres. A notched wall encircled it all. The city fanned out below the citadel. From the citadel, you could see workers' dwellings, much smaller than the homes of the wealthy. A functional plainness typified the architecture throughout Harappa.

Harappa's granaries were located north of the citadel. The fields around the city were planted with wheat, barley, and peas. The people grew sesame, too, pounding the seeds to extract the oil. In the farm areas you could see cattle as well as sheep and pigs. As with farms today, those of Harappa had their share of dogs and cats.

Arrival of the Aryans

No one knows what happened to the people of the Indus Valley civilization. Many factors may have brought an end to the civilization. Soon another group of people, who called themselves Aryans *(AIR ee uhnz),* or "nobles," moved into the Indus Valley region from the north. They brought with them a new language, Sanskrit; new Gods; and a new social structure. Their arrival changed the course of Indian history.

▲ *Aryans made their way through passes like this one in the Hindu Kush.*

Indo-European Migrations

Long before they reached India, the Aryans had lived in the grasslands near the Black and Caspian seas. They were part of a group we call the Indo-Europeans.

The Indo-Europeans were people who herded cattle, goats, and sheep. They had tamed the horse and developed a chariot that had sturdy wheels with spokes. These speedy chariots allowed them to move freely over large areas and to wage war more effectively than warriors on foot.

About 2000 B.C. conditions in their homeland caused the Indo-Europeans to go on the move. Perhaps their pasture lands had dried out. Or perhaps their population had grown so large that they needed more land. Whatever the reason, huge numbers of Indo-Europeans began migrating to new regions. Some groups went west and south. Others, like the Aryans, moved southeast toward India.

By around 1500 B.C., the first Aryans had found their way through the high passes in the Hindu Kush. The Hindu Kush is a mountain range along the northwestern edge of India. The passes there would serve as highways for other migrating and invading peoples over the next 3,000 years.

The Aryan Religion

The early Aryans lived in houses built of bamboo or wood, which decayed and left no evidence for later archaeologists. The Aryans, however, did leave a poetic record. Their beliefs and daily life are recorded in the Vedas *(VAY duhs),* a collection of sacred hymns and poems. The oldest collection, the Rig-Veda, existed by 1500 B.C. The Vedas were not written down, but were passed on through an oral tradition.

The Vedas are the main source of information about the Aryan people and their way of life. For this reason, historians call the time in India from about 1500 to 600 B.C. the Vedic period.

The Aryans brought with them to India a religion based on many Gods. Priests worshiped by sacrificing food and drink to these Gods in

Across Time & Space

As groups of Indo-Europeans moved into new homelands, they took their language with them. Language experts have discovered that many of the languages spoken in Europe and India today have the same root: the language spoken by Indo-Europeans. These include German, Greek, Indo-Iranian, and the Romance languages such as French, Spanish, and Italian.

CULTURE

Visual Learning

Nearly half the people in the world today speak a language that stems from the Indo-European language family. This wide distribution resulted from the far-flung Indo-European migrations. Indo-European languages of today include English, Spanish, German, French, Italian, Russian, Dutch, Swedish, Norwegian, Polish, and Hindi. Draw on the chalkboard a pie graph showing the world's main language families: Indo-European—47 percent; Sino-Tibetan—22 percent; Black African—8 percent; all others—23 percent. Have students copy and color it.

Cultural Context

The Aryans who migrated into the Indus Valley brought with them a totally different culture. The Aryans lived in tribal villages, rather than elaborate cities. Although they did not have a written language, they had an oral tradition. Their spoken language had a rich vocabulary, which was displayed in the poetry they created. They also had highly developed rituals. Their military techniques were outstanding.

Study Skills

Have students working in small groups do research to create a language tree with Indo-European as the "trunk" of the tree.

SOCIAL SYSTEMS

Critical Thinking

Review with students the four classes of the social system developed by the Aryans. Then ask students if they can think of any systems similar to this in contemporary U.S. culture. *(Answers might include the hierarchy within business organizations or status according to wealth, family heritage, or education.)*

■ *The Vedas tell us that the Aryan religion was based on many Gods and that Aryan society was divided into four classes of people.*

CLOSE

Write the Thinking Focus on the chalkboard. Then have volunteers list the origins of Indian civilization. *(The Indus Valley civilization and the Aryan civilization)*

A Vedic fire is still used at upper-caste Hindu weddings. During the ceremony, the Brahmin chants verses from the Vedas.

a sacred fire. To keep the earth's natural forces in balance, Aryan priests fed the ritual fires with melted butter and sang Vedic hymns to the Gods. Because rituals played an important role in their religion, priests became very powerful in Aryan society.

A New Social System

The Aryans introduced into India a new social system made up of four *varnas,* or classes, of people. At the top were the priests, or Brahmins. Next were the ruler and his warriors. The third class were merchants and farmers, while the fourth class consisted of servants.

Only the males of the top three classes were allowed to study the Vedas. They were called the "twice born" because they had a second, ritual birth, after which they began their studies.

Each of the classes contributed something important to the society. Priests performed religious rituals. Kings and warriors ruled and protected the society. The third class of merchants and farmers supplied food, clothing, and other goods. The fourth class served the others.

Within each class were subgroups, called *jatis.* A person was born into a *jati* and stayed there his whole lifetime. He married within his subgroup and did the same kind of work as all the others in that *jati.* The Portuguese later gave the name caste system to this social structure. Today, **caste** means a unit into which a person is born and cannot change.

The Aryans were very concerned with ritual cleanliness and ranked jobs according to their purity. The people who performed the dirtiest tasks, such as dealing with dead bodies, fell completely outside the social system. They were known as **untouchables,** because people believed that their impurity could be transferred through touch.

The caste system has continued in India up to modern times. However, as you will read in Chapter 14, Indian reformers have worked to correct some of the injustices of the caste system. ■

■ *What do the Vedas reveal about Aryan society and religion?*

REVIEW

1. **FOCUS** What are the ancient origins of Indian civilization?
2. **GEOGRAPHY** Why is the Indus Valley civilization considered a great river civilization?
3. **CULTURE** What was the caste system of Aryan society? How did it influence the Aryan way of life?
4. **CRITICAL THINKING** Since the Vedas were composed by Aryans, the information in them is presented from an Aryan point of view. Why is it important to consider point of view?
5. **ACTIVITY** On a map of Europe and Asia, locate the original home of the Aryan people. Trace their route through the Khyber Pass, one of the passes in the Hindu Kush. Show how Aryan settlements spread from the Indus River down to the Ganges River Valley.

Homework Options

Have students write their own myth or Vedic-style poem, setting it in ancient Aryan times.

Study Guide: page 18

Answers to Review Questions

1. Indian civilization originated in the Indus River Valley and was greatly influenced by the arrival of the Aryan people.
2. It developed along the Indus River and its tributaries. It had large, well-planned cities, farming, and extensive trade with other civilizations.
3. The caste system was a social structure made up of four *varnas,* or castes. The highest caste included the priests, or Brahmins; the second included the ruler and warriors; the third consisted of merchants and farmers; and the fourth was made up of servants. It provided for the needs of the society, but it was very rigid and, by contemporary standards, unjust in many ways.
4. The Vedas show how the Aryans viewed themselves and their world. A single viewpoint, however, is only one perspective and thus may reflect bias.
5. Students should refer to the map on page 104.

UNDERSTANDING ORGANIZATION

Identifying Patterns

Here's Why

Writers use different patterns to organize what they write. The chart below explains some of the most common patterns of organization: chronological, spatial, cause and effect, and compare and contrast.

The chart also gives you clue words to help you identify each pattern. Recognizing these patterns when you read can help you improve your understanding of the material.

Here's How

Find the section on Indo-European Migrations on page 105. It is an example of a chronological, or time-related, pattern. This section describes events in the order in which they happened. Notice that dates are used: "about 2000 B.C." and "by around 1500 B.C." Words that describe time relationships such as "the first" are clues, too.

A cause-and-effect pattern shows which events made other events happen. The story on page 102 is an example of a cause-and-effect pattern. We learn that stone seals found in the near-desert of the Indus Valley led archaeologists to discover the ruins of Mohenjo-Daro and the ancient civilization that once thrived there.

Spatial patterns describe people, places, things, and events. A spatial pattern gives you a visual "snapshot" of what is being described. The description of the Indus Valley in the first paragraph of page 103 is an example of spatial organization.

Compare-and-contrast patterns can show similarities or differences between two subjects. They may show both similarities and differences. In A Great River Civilization, on page 103, the writer shows similarities between the ancient cities of Mohenjo-Daro and Harappa.

Writers use many patterns to organize their work. Often, especially in long passages, you will find a combination of several patterns.

Try It

Turn to the first paragraph of the section A New Social System on page 106. Tell what organizational pattern is used in this paragraph. How did you identify the pattern?

Apply It

Find an article in a magazine or a newspaper that uses one of the organizational patterns explained on this page. Name the pattern and explain how you identified it.

How to Identify Patterns of Organization in Your Reading

Pattern	Definition	Some Clue Words
Chronological	Explains the order in which events happened	as soon as, at last, first, second, third, next, then, before, after, finally, while, by, until
Spatial	Describes people, places, things, or events	above, across, beside, behind, below, beyond, east, farther, in front of, inside, lower, near, next to, north, outside, south, under, within, west; names of places
Cause and effect	Tells what events caused others	as a result, because, consequently, if, nevertheless, since, so, therefore, then
Compare and contrast	Describes similarities or differences between two or more events, ideas, people, and places	although, by contrast, by comparison, compared to, relatively, similarly, unlike

UNDERSTANDING ORGANIZATION

This skills feature uses sections of Lesson 1 to teach students to identify patterns of organization in written material.

HISTORY

Critical Thinking

Point out the importance of being able to identify patterns of organization in written material. Then direct students to read Here's How. With the class, list on the chalkboard the clue words found in the section Indo-European Migrations, on page 105. *(Long before, about 2000 B.C., began migrating, around 1500 B.C., over the next 3,000 years)* Then divide the class into small groups. Have them create a timeline based on the chronological pattern found in the section.

Identifying Patterns

Have students use the chart on this page to identify organization patterns in two magazine or newspaper articles. Collect the articles, number them, and tack them up on the bulletin board. Divide the class into groups and have them go to the bulletin board, one group at a time. Have students write down, on a sheet of paper with corresponding numbers, the organization patterns they identify.

Answers to Try It

The paragraph is arranged in a spatial pattern. The clue words are *top* and *next.*

Answers to Apply It

Students should use the chart on this page to identify and explain the organizational pattern they have found.

Objective

Identify and use organizational patterns in written material. (Study Skills 1)

INTRODUCE

Have students read the Thinking Focus. Tell them that Hinduism and Buddhism are major world religions that started in India. While both have millions of followers, Hinduism is the main religion in India today. Ask students what they know about Hinduism and Buddhism. Write their answers on the chalkboard. As they read, they can correct misconceptions. Ask them also to consider the similarities and differences between Hinduism and Buddhism.

Key Terms

Vocabulary Strategies: T36–T37

Hinduism—the major religion and way of life in India

reincarnation—the belief in rebirth of the soul in another body

Buddhism—a religion that was founded in India by Siddhartha Gautama and that emphasizes nonviolence and freedom from worldly desires

B.C. | A.D.

2700 1800 **1500** **650** 900 1800

LESSON 2

Hinduism and Buddhism

THINKING FOCUS

What are the origins and main teachings of Hinduism and Buddhism?

Key Terms

- Hinduism
- reincarnation
- Buddhism

All over India on this night when there is no moon, women light hundreds of small oil lamps. They place them in windows and in rows along the rooftops of their houses.

Members of merchant castes say that the lamps are meant to light the way into their homes for Lakshmi, the Goddess of wealth and good fortune. In Bengal, a state in eastern India, the lamps are lit for the Goddess the people call Kali. Still other Hindus say that the lamps honor Rama, who on this night returned to his palace after 14 years in exile.

In some parts of India, this is the first day of the Hindu New Year. It is also the fourth day of Divali, one of the most important Hindu festivals of the year. It is a time for visiting, exchanging gifts, and wearing new clothes.

➤ *Lamps burn brightly when Hindus mark their new year. The celebration falls in October or November, according to a lunar calendar.*

The Hindu Way of Life

The celebration of Divali begins in late October. Throughout India, Hindus observe this festival of lights in ways that are both similar and different. The deities they worship appear in many different forms and are known by many different names. Yet Hindus all share certain beliefs, values, and traditions. Some of these go back to Vedic times or even earlier. Other beliefs and practices are more recent in origin.

It is this mix of old and new that is **Hinduism,** the major religion in India today. Hinduism is also a distinctive way of life for over 700 million followers.

Objectives

1. Understand the main teachings of Hinduism and Buddhism.
2. Explain how the origins of Hinduism and Buddhism are linked to the Vedic tradition.

Graphic Overview

	Origin	Objective	Means
Hinduism	ancient Aryan beliefs	spiritual freedom	devotion to God(s); wisdom; right actions; reincarnation; sacrifice
Buddhism	teachings of Siddhartha Gautama	achieve nirvana	free self from wants; reincarnation cycle; practice nonviolence

The Search for Truth

As the Vedic period drew to a close in about 600 B.C., some people in India began to ask difficult questions. Why are some people born into a life of ease and others into poverty? What happens after death? How should we live our lives before death? The answers to these questions helped shape Hinduism as it is known today.

Common to all Hindus is the search for truth, for a true understanding of what the world is really like. Hindus believe that the world they live in now is not real but only *maya,* illusion. *Maya* keeps the individual soul, *atman,* from knowing the world soul, Brahman. The goal of life, then, is to become free of *maya,* and to be united with the world soul, Brahman.

Hinduism teaches three ways to achieve this goal. One way is through devotion, such as worship of a personal deity; another way is through wisdom; and a third way is through right actions. However, to reach the goal by any of these three ways requires a very long time—more than any one lifetime provides. From this idea developed the belief in **reincarnation,** the rebirth of the soul in a new body after death.

In Hinduism, how quickly the soul advances toward freedom depends on the karma that a person has built up. Karma is the sum of all the good and bad actions of the soul's previous lives. Hindus believe that everything a person does influences the status of that person's current or future life.

Gods and Goddesses

You could be a Hindu and work toward the goal of spiritual freedom, and not believe in any personal God at all. However, most Hindus are helped toward their goal by worshiping a personal God. Hindu Gods are usually a form of Vishnu, Shiva, or of the mother Goddess, Shakti.

Usually a person worships the same deity as other members of his or her family, caste, or community. All Hindus, however, are free to choose their own personal deity.

The stories and art of India are rich with tales of Gods and Goddesses and of the various forms they have taken to appear on earth. Vishnu is said to have appeared already in nine of his ten different forms. Some of these include a fish; a man-lion; Rama, the ideal human; and Krishna, the divine cowherder.

Temple and Family Worship

Brahmin priests perform temple worship services called *pujas.* Priests also conduct major religious ceremonies, such as weddings.

Most Hindus, however, keep images of their personal deities in their homes and perform the daily *pujas* themselves. In a *puja,* the deity is treated much like an honored guest. The God or Goddess is first woken up from sleep. Then it is offered water, perfume, flowers, and food.

Life's Four Stages

Hindus who choose the path of right action are encouraged to

The Hindu God Shiva dances on the body of a demon to free the world of illusion. The surrounding circle of fire represents the cycle of creation, destruction, and rebirth.

How Do We Know?

RELIGION *We know about Hindu Gods, myths, and religious duties from two long poems called epics. The Mahabharata is the story of a war between two families. The Ramayana is the account of Rama's exile in the forest and of the capture of his wife, Sita, by a demon king.*

DEVELOP

Tell students that the origins of Hinduism and Buddhism are linked to the Vedic tradition. Copy the Graphic Overview incompletely on the chalkboard. Suggest that students complete the chart as they read.

CULTURE

Critical Thinking

Ask students to speculate about how the caste system of the Vedic period helped Hinduism survive through the years. *(The system required people to live and work within their own social groups. The traditions of the Vedic period instilled in the followers of Hinduism a belief in the importance of class and duty.)*

Access Strategy

Storytellers of ancient India could spin wonderful fables and fairy tales. Such stories suggest the cultural richness of ancient India. Some tales made their way westward to the storybooks of Europe. Here's one that students might like to hear:

A wealthy man of India owned a mongoose, a tiny, furry animal with a long tail. It was his beloved pet. One day he left the mongoose to take care of a baby. When he returned home, the mongoose met him with blood smeared on its mouth. The man thought the mongoose had killed the baby. In anger, he slew his beloved pet. Then, sadly, he discovered the baby, fast asleep. Near its cradle lay a dead cobra, the most poisonous of snakes.

European storytellers changed the mongoose to a dog, and the cobra to a wolf to suit Western culture. Yet the lesson is the same. Do you know what it is? *(Students may suggest that one should not jump to conclusions.)*

Access Activity

Tell students that the *Panchatantra* is a collection of tales and sayings that includes advice on personal conduct. What type of conduct does this *Panchatantra* quotation advise: "Since food and drink are not always available for mortals, when one has got a generous supply of it, he should make use of it little by little." *(That one should not be wasteful)*

■ *Hinduism provides a model for how to conduct one's life at each stage. Also, Hinduism teaches that all one's actions contribute to the good and bad karma that affect a person, not only in this life, but in future lives.*

CITIZENSHIP

Critical Thinking

Tell students that Siddhartha was a young man during times of unrest in India. Ask them if we are also living in a time of unrest. If so, what are some causes of the unrest? How are these similar to or different from those in the time of the Buddha? *(Answers may include such causes as racial tensions, poverty, crime, and abuse of drugs. The causes in the time of the Buddha were people's questions about suffering and how to avoid it.)*

■ *In what ways is Hinduism a complete way of life?*

carry out the duties of their caste. They are also guided by an ideal of life that is divided into four stages. In the first stage, a young boy studies the Vedas with a teacher. In the second stage of life, a young man marries and becomes a householder.

In the third stage, the householder puts aside everything that he owns and retires to the forest to meditate, or reflect. During the fourth stage, a man gives up everything, including caste identity, to move about the country. ■

Teachings of Buddhism

The story of another great world religion, Buddhism, begins in a small kingdom in northern India about 2,500 years ago. The king had a son named Siddhartha Gautama *(sihd DAHR tah GAW tah mah)*. At the time of his birth, wise men predicted that the child would grow up to be either a great king or a great spiritual leader.

The king did not want his son to lead the life of a wandering holy man, so he tried to protect the prince from any signs of suffering. No sick, old, or poor people were allowed in the palace or in the streets near the palace.

In the end his father's efforts failed. While away from the palace, the young prince saw an old man. Later, he saw a sick man, and on another day a dead man. Siddhartha realized that he, too, would grow old and die. Was there no way to escape life's sorrows?

➤ *The young Siddhartha (center) is pictured in the royal palace in this modern copy of an Ajanta cave painting. Near Ajanta, India, cave walls are covered with paintings, some dating back to about 200 B.C., around 300 years after Siddhartha lived.*

Then the prince saw a wandering holy man who owned only a single food bowl. In spite of his great age and poverty, the holy man seemed content. Siddhartha decided to give up his riches, to leave the palace, and to search for a way to end suffering in the world.

The story of Siddhartha's birth and childhood may be legend. However, a prince by that name did live in what is now India, from about 563 to 483 B.C. Siddhartha wandered throughout the land, seeking truth by which to live. In time, these ideas became known as **Buddhism,** a major religion of the world today.

Siddhartha's Search

Siddhartha's search for truth took place at a time of great religious activity on the Indian subcontinent. Many others were asking similar questions: Why do people suffer? How can suffering be avoided?

On his journey, Siddhartha met great religious teachers of the day, but he found no answers. He then decided to look within himself for wisdom. Sitting in the shade of a fig

Study Skills

According to Hinduism, a God can appear on the earth in various forms called incarnations. Ask students to explain the difference between incarnation and reincarnation. *(Incarnation refers to a deity embodied in fleshly form. Reincarnation happens to humans. According to Hinduism, at death a person's soul enters another living form.)*

Religious Context

Today the majority of the world's Buddhists live in Asia, especially in Sri Lanka, the countries of Southeast Asia, Tibet, Mongolia, and Japan. The man who established this religion had been born to the warrior caste. He willingly gave up his position and wealth to search for truth. His quest led to the founding of a pragmatic and compassionate way of life nearly five centuries before the Christian era. According to Buddhist teachings, others can also attain such enlightenment. When they do, they will become buddhas, too. However, the title *the Buddha* is reserved for Siddhartha Gautama.

At a time when India's caste system was firmly in place, the Buddha believed in equal status for everyone. He spent about 40 years explaining his views of the causes and cures of human suffering. To many Buddhists, the Buddha represents what Jesus stands for in the eyes of Christians.

tree, he vowed not to leave until he found his answers.

After 49 days of deep thought, Siddhartha discovered the truth he sought. He believed he had found a way to escape suffering. Understanding flooded his mind like a great light. From that time on, he was called the Buddha, meaning "the enlightened one." He had reached the height of understanding that Buddhists call enlightenment.

The Buddha sent his first followers in all directions to spread the Buddhist *dharma,* or law. The Buddha traveled and taught, stopping wherever people would listen. He lived his days in peace, teaching and preaching until his death at the age of 80.

The Way of the Buddha

Following his days of deep thought beneath the fig tree, the Buddha spoke of his Four Noble Truths. These teachings give the Buddhist view on why people suffer and how suffering can be avoided. The chart on this page explains these beliefs.

The Buddha rejected many ideas of his day. He did not believe in *atman,* the individual soul of Hinduism. He had no use for Brahmin or Vedic sacrifices, which required killing animals. He also rejected the caste system, which gave people little choice about how to live their lives.

The Buddha taught that nothing in this world lasts forever. Everyone gets old, most get sick, and all die. He said that people suffer because they want what they cannot have. If they can rid themselves of their wants, he taught, then they would be free. They would be enlightened.

The Chain of Rebirth

Although they have different ideas about the soul, both Buddhists and Hindus believe in reincarnation. Good karma, collected by following Buddhism's Eightfold Path, takes a person closer to enlightenment.

The chain of birth, suffering, death, and rebirth continues until enlightenment is gained. Once enlightened, a person is finally free from further rebirth with all of its earthly suffering. Buddhists call this state nirvana. Nirvana means "blowing out," like blowing out a candle. At that moment a person wants nothing, not even to live or to die or to be reborn.

(top) The Buddha received his enlightenment beneath a sacred tree. This sculpture stands about two feet high. (below) In the Four Noble Truths, the Buddha explained his beliefs about suffering.

The Four Noble Truths
1. Human life is full of suffering and sorrow.
2. Suffering and sorrow are caused by people's greedy desires for power, pleasure, and possessions.
3. Suffering and sorrow will end when people overcome their greed.
4. People can overcome their greed and uncontrolled desires by adopting the Eightfold Path. This path gives eight ways of living a correct, or right, life.

SOCIAL SYSTEMS

Critical Thinking

Have students look at the second Noble Truth in the chart on this page. Ask them to give examples from their own lives of suffering caused by someone's desire for power. *(An example might include a child always bossing his or her brothers and sisters.)* What are examples of suffering caused by pleasure? *(These might include eating too much junk food and not feeling well afterward.)* What are examples of suffering caused by possessions? *(These might include owning precious things but having the burden of caring for them or worrying they will be stolen.)*

CULTURE

Critical Thinking

Have students complete the Study Skills activity below. Using their lists of the reasons the Buddha's teachings were accepted by some, students should speculate on why others did not. Students should consider the caste system and who would lose the most power. *(Priests might have been threatened by Buddha's teaching that people are equal. They might have used their powerful positions to influence people against Buddhism.)*

Historical Context

In India the wheel has become a symbol of *dharma.* Legend relates that the Buddha was born with wheel imprints on the palms of his hands and the soles of his feet. Also, the basics of the Buddha's teachings—the Four Noble Truths and the Eightfold Path—are contained in his Sermon on Setting in Motion the Wheel of Truth.

Many centuries later Mohandas K. Gandhi (1869–1948) used the spinning wheel to symbolize economic independence for India. A spiritual leader as well as a political leader, Gandhi was committed to India's total independence from British rule. Like the Buddha, he advocated nonviolence.

After gaining independence in 1947, India adopted a flag with a wheel. Set against a background of three wide stripes in white, green, and orange is the ancient Wheel of Truth.

Study Skills

Tell students to list the reasons that the Buddha's teachings appealed to some people. *(He offered the hope of peace to everyone; he rejected the caste system that placed people in a certain social group for a lifetime; and he opposed animal sacrifices.)*

BELIEF SYSTEMS

Study Skills

Have students read the section called A Great Buddhist Ruler on page 113. Share with them the information from the Historical Context on this page. Then have students make a chart of Ashoka's actions before and after his conversion to Buddhism. In the Before column, they should list his going to war and the conquering of Kalinga. The After column should include reference to edicts, support of *ahimsa,* his view of his subjects, social reforms, and missionaries.

■ *According to Buddhist beliefs, the ways of the Eightfold Path are right view, right resolve, right speech, right conduct, right livelihood, right effort, right mindfulness, and right concentration. Those who live by these rules will eventually reach enlightenment and will be freed from the cycle of rebirth with all its suffering and sorrow.*

➤ The Four Noble Truths and the Eightfold Path together are the heart of the Buddha's teachings.

The Eightfold Path

Way	Description
Right view	Believing in the Four Noble Truths and the Eightfold Path
Right resolve	Making a firm decision to live according to the Eightfold Path
Right speech	Speaking in a manner that doesn't harm others: not gossiping, lying, or using angry words
Right conduct	Acting in a way that doesn't harm others: not killing, not stealing, and also not acting selfishly
Right livelihood	Earning a living in a way that doesn't harm others
Right effort	Striving to get rid of any evil within oneself
Right mindfulness	Paying attention to every state of the body, mind, and feeling
Right concentration	Thinking deeply for answers to problems

The Three Jewels

Buddhists say that their tradition is made up of three parts, called the Three Jewels. These are the Buddha; his *dharma,* or teachings; and the *sangha (SAHN guh),* or religious community. The *sangha* is made up of monks, nuns, and everyday followers.

Gradually Buddhist missionaries spread their beliefs beyond India. They first traveled to the island of Ceylon, now called Sri Lanka. By about A.D. 650, Buddhism had reached China, Korea, Japan, Tibet, Burma, and other areas of Southeast Asia.

Although Buddhism became less popular in India over the years, it gained followers in other countries. Today more than 300 million people throughout the world are Buddhists. ■

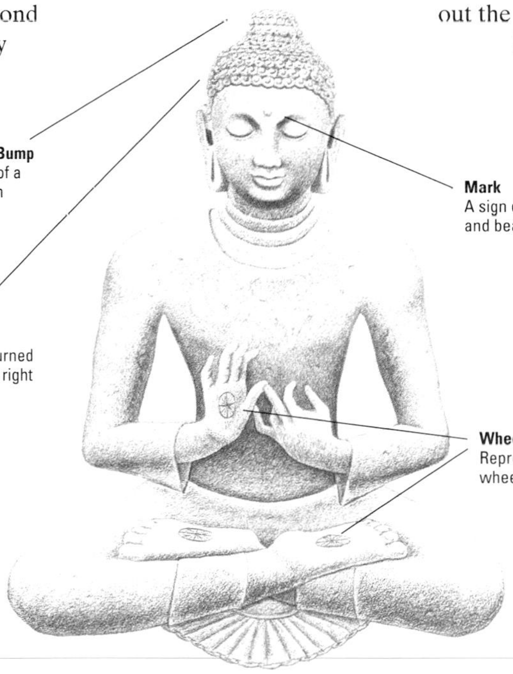
Wisdom Bump
The sign of a great man
Mark
A sign of wisdom and beauty
Curls
Snaillike, turned toward the right
Wheel Imprints
Represents *dharma,* the wheel of the law

➤ The image of the Buddha is identified by several symbolic marks on his body.

■ *What is the Eightfold Path, and what is its importance?*

Visual Learning

Bring in art books, encyclopedias, and books on Asian countries and culture. Have students look in them for photos of the Buddha, which you can photocopy and display around a large class map. Run strings to the countries of origin. Discuss the different ways artists of various cultures have pictured the Buddha.

Historical Context

As evidenced on a rock edict, Ashoka lamented over the Kalinga War (see facing page). Referring to himself as the Beloved of the Gods, he conveyed his feelings about the Kalinga slaughter on a pillar:

"One hundred and fifty thousand persons were thence carried away captive, one hundred thousand were slain, and many times that number died. . . . Thus arose the Beloved of the Gods' remorse for having conquered the Kalingas."

After his conversion to Buddhism, Ashoka relaxed the harsh justice meted out in domestic matters. For weary travelers he established rest houses and planted fruit trees along roadsides, providing both food and shade. Wells also were dug at intervals. He had medicinal herbs cultivated, supplying them to both people and animals. To make sure his reforms were carried out, Ashoka appointed special inspectors to tour his provinces.

A Great Buddhist Ruler

The worldwide spread of Buddhism began with the emperor Ashoka *(ah SHOH kah)*. A faithful follower of Buddhism, he was the first ruler to send missionaries beyond India's borders.

Ashoka's Conversion

Ashoka belonged to a line of conquering kings known as the Mauryas *(MOW ree uhz)*, who ruled India from about 324 to 187 B.C. They built the first great Indian empire. It was probably the largest Indian empire in the country's history.

Soon after Ashoka came to power in 273 B.C., he went to war. He conquered Kalinga, an independent area in eastern India, in a series of bloody battles. The violence may have turned Ashoka toward Buddhism.

Ashoka's Edicts

During the rest of his rule, Ashoka sent out Buddhist missionaries. He also spelled out his beliefs in edicts, or public announcements. Ashoka had these edicts carved into rocks and pillars around the empire. Beautiful carvings like the one shown on this page often decorated the tops, or capitals, of pillars.

Rock Edict I explains Ashoka's support of *ahimsa (uh HIHM sah)*, the Buddhist belief in nonviolence. It forbids harming any humans or animals.

> *No living creature shall be slaughtered here. . . . Many hundreds of thousand living creatures were formerly slaughtered every day for curries in the kitchens of His Majesty. At present, when this edict on Dharma is inscribed, only three living creatures are killed daily, two peacocks and a deer. . . . In the future, not even these three animals shall be slaughtered.*

The Kalinga Edict II in eastern India shows how Ashoka felt toward his people:

> *All men are my children. Just as I seek the welfare and happiness of my own children in this world and the next, I seek the same things for all men.*

Ashoka's nonviolent style of ruling did not last. After his death, the empire broke up into little warring kingdoms. In spite of this bloodshed, the peaceful message of Buddhism continued to spread. ■

This lion capital sits atop an Ashokan pillar. India's national emblem is patterned after it.

■ *How did Ashoka's Buddhist beliefs influence his rule?*

REVIEW

1. **FOCUS** What are the origins and main teachings of Hinduism and Buddhism?
2. **HISTORY** What does Hinduism owe to the Vedic religion?
3. **GEOGRAPHY** Trace a map of Asia. Color areas where Buddhism had spread by A.D. 650.
4. **CRITICAL THINKING** Which groups of people in ancient India were most likely to become Buddhists?
5. **WRITING ACTIVITY** In 50 words or less, write a pillar edict as Ashoka might have done. In your edict, instruct people how to act toward other human beings and toward animals. Draw your pillar. Design a carving for its capital.

■ *Ashoka subscribed to the Buddhist belief in nonviolence. He prohibited the slaughter of animals and felt the same responsibility toward his subjects as he did toward his children. He had his edicts carved on top of pillars and sent missionaries to spread Buddhist* dharma *beyond his realm.*

CLOSE

Review the Thinking Focus with students. Write the headings *Hinduism* and *Buddhism* on the chalkboard. Have students take turns writing features of each religion under the appropriate heading; the goal is to create a diagram of the main features of Hinduism and Buddhism.

Answers to Review Questions

1. Hinduism is a mix of ideas, beliefs, and practices from the Vedic period and from more recent times. Hindus believe that this world is an illusion and that the spiritual goal is to be reunited with the world soul. Buddhism arose from the teachings of the Buddha. It teaches that the only way to escape the suffering that accompanies the chain of rebirth is to rid oneself of wants by following the Eightfold Path.
2. From the Vedic religion came the Vedas, sacred texts of Hinduism and the caste system. Brahmin priests still perform important ceremonies, such as weddings.
3. Shaded areas: Ceylon (now Sri Lanka), China, Korea, Japan, Tibet, and Burma (now Myanmar).
4. Those most unhappy with their caste might have been most attracted to Buddhism.
5. Students' edicts should convey an attitude of nonviolence and responsibility toward other human beings and animals.

Homework Options

Ask students to outline the lesson. The next day have them work in groups to ensure that they have included the key points.

Study Guide: page 20

INTRODUCE

Ask students to recall the ancient civilizations of Mesopotamia, Egypt, and India. Where did these civilizations first develop? *(Along rivers)* Where do the students think Chinese civilization might have developed? *(Also along rivers)* Why would rivers have provided a natural location for development? *(Water for animals, people, and crops; fish for food; rich soil; aid to communication and trade)*

Key Term

Vocabulary Strategies: T36–T37

Mandate of Heaven—support that the power of heaven gave to a Chinese emperor who ruled well

2700
1766
1122
900
B.C. | A.D.
900
1800

LESSON 3

Ancient China

THINKING FOCUS

What are some major patterns that appear throughout early Chinese history?

Key Term

- Mandate of Heaven

The towering heights of the
Southern Mountains
Soar dizzily like a stack
of cooking pots,
Their sides are furrowed with
ravines and valleys. . . .
While from their folds the
mountain streams leap and
tumble,
Spilling out upon the level
plains,
There they flow a thousand
miles along smooth beds,
Their banks lined with dikes
Blanketed with green orchids.

From "The Shang-lin Park"

Imagine traveling through a landscape like this. Your trip would be a long one, and the sights would be incredible. Over this vast distance, you'd see huge mountains, powerful rivers, and sweeping, green plains. These are some of the features of China, as the poet Sima Xiangru *(suh mah shahng roo)* described them more than 2,000 years ago.

Surrounding China are mountains, deserts, and the Pacific Ocean. These natural barriers set the ancient Chinese apart from other cultures. Thinking they were at the center of the world, they called their land the Middle Kingdom. Dating back over 4,000 years, China is the world's oldest continuous civilization.

➤ *High peaks, fertile plains, desert wastes—these are some of the varied landforms of China.*

Objectives

1. Describe the geography of ancient China.
2. Describe patterns in Chinese history.

Graphic Overview

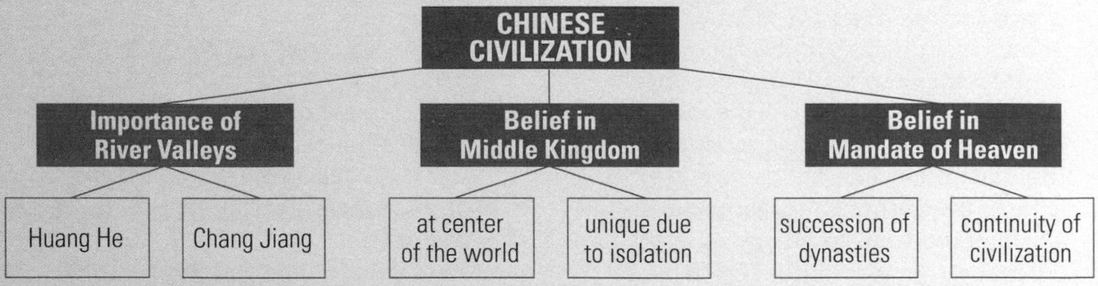

CHINESE CIVILIZATION
Importance of River Valleys
Belief in Middle Kingdom
Belief in Mandate of Heaven
Huang He
Chang Jiang
at center of the world
unique due to isolation
succession of dynasties
continuity of civilization

China's Geography

Look carefully at the physical map of China on this page. You can see that China is a vast and varied land. Different landforms and climates cause ways of life to differ from one region to another.

The Himalayas in southwestern China are the world's highest mountains. Grasslands as well as barren deserts stretch across north and northwest China. In the southwest is Tibet, a land of high-altitude plateaus and mountain ranges where little grows. The climate here is dry and very cold.

The Plateau of Tibet is the source of the Huang He *(hwahng hoh)*, one of China's major rivers. On the map, trace the Huang He, which means "Yellow River," across northeastern China. Notice how low and flat the land becomes as the river nears the ocean. This plain contains rich soil, thanks to the river floods.

Across central and southern China flows the Chang Jiang *(chahng jyahng)*. The basin of this river, called the Yangtze *(YANG see)* in English, is another area of rich farmland. Farmers use the river to send their crops to Pacific ports.

Eastern China is much better suited to farming than western China. In addition to fertile soil, eastern China benefits from rains brought by the monsoons of southern Asia. ■

▼ *As the map shows, nature built a wall around China with mountains, plateaus, seas, and deserts.*

■ *Why is eastern China better suited to farming than western China?*

ina: Physical

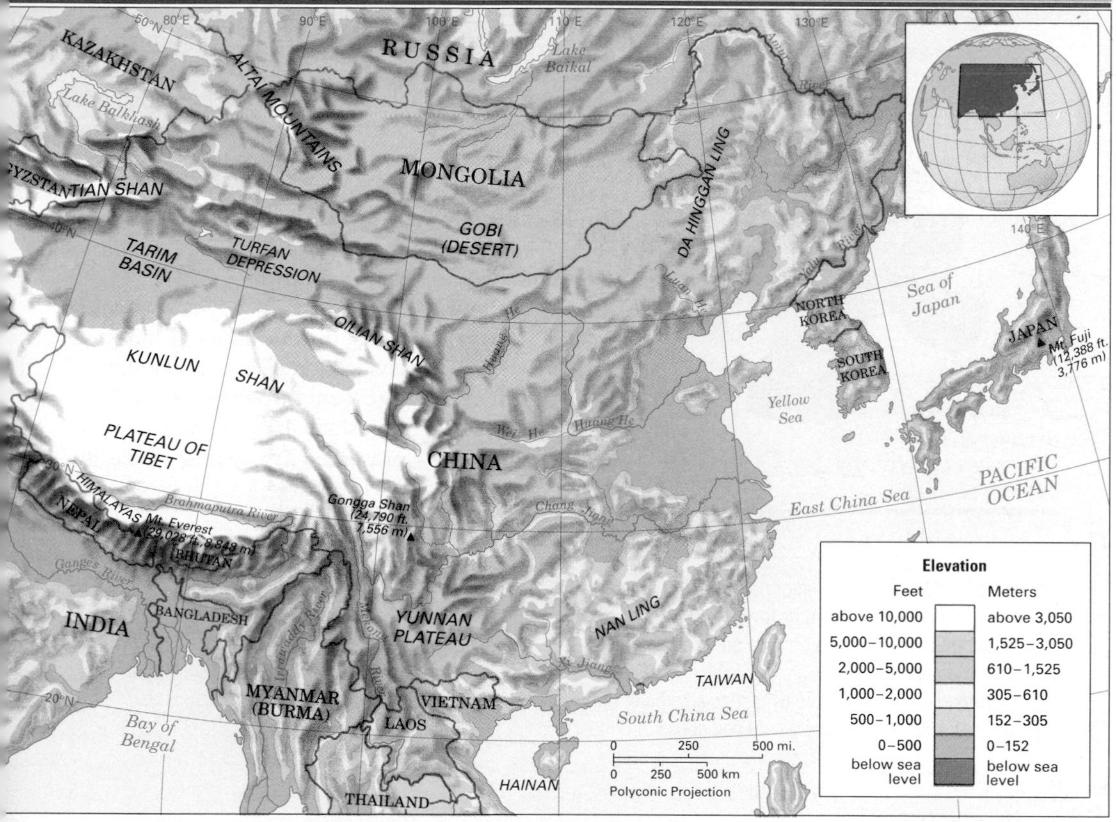

RUSSIA
KAZAKHSTAN
Lake Balkhash
ALTAI MOUNTAINS
Lake Baikal
MONGOLIA
TIANSHAN
TARIM BASIN
TURFAN DEPRESSION
GOBI (DESERT)
DA HINGGAN LING
QILIAN SHAN
KUNLUN
SHAN
PLATEAU OF TIBET
CHINA
HIMALAYAS
Mt. Everest
NEPAL
BHUTAN
Brahmaputra River
Gongga Shan (24,790 ft. 7,556 m)
Ganges River
INDIA
BANGLADESH
YUNNAN PLATEAU
NAN LING
MYANMAR (BURMA)
VIETNAM
LAOS
THAILAND
HAINAN
Bay of Bengal
South China Sea
TAIWAN
East China Sea
Yellow Sea
Sea of Japan
NORTH KOREA
SOUTH KOREA
JAPAN
Mt. Fuji (12,388 ft. 3,776 m)
PACIFIC OCEAN
Wei He
Huang He
Chang Jiang
Xi Jiang
Elevation
Feet | Meters
above 10,000 | above 3,050
5,000–10,000 | 1,525–3,050
2,000–5,000 | 610–1,525
1,000–2,000 | 305–610
500–1,000 | 152–305
0–500 | 0–152
below sea level | below sea level
0 250 500 mi.
0 250 500 km
Polyconic Projection

DEVELOP

Tell students that in this lesson they will learn about China, one of the world's oldest continuous civilizations. On a large map of the world, point out the area that is China. Point out the natural barriers of mountains (Himalayas), desert (Gobi), and water (Pacific Ocean) that surround China. Tell students that these natural barriers influenced the development of China's civilization because they isolated and protected it. Ask students to speculate about why the ancient Chinese called their land the Middle Kingdom. *(They considered China the center of the world.)*

■ *In eastern China the land is relatively flat, the soil is fertile, and there is enough rainfall to support farming. Western China is much colder and drier.*

Access Strategy

Have students locate China on a world map or globe. Tell them that China is about 20,000 square miles larger than the United States. Using the physical map on this page, find the geographic barriers that separate China from other countries. Ask students to name possible advantages and disadvantages of geographic isolation. *(Advantages: protection from enemies, protection of unique culture; disadvantages: no exposure to beneficial ideas and customs of other cultures)* Ask students what geographic barriers divide China into separate regions. *(Mountain ranges and hilly areas, huge distances)* What features unify China? *(Large coastal plain, river valleys)* What factors besides geography could unite people there? *(A common written language, culture, religion, traditions, a stable and powerful government)* Encourage students to look for these factors as they read the lesson.

Access Activity

Have students find China on the map on page 53. Then have them locate the Huang He (Yellow River) there and on the map on this page. Explain that the Huang He has the same importance as the Tigris and Euphrates, the Nile, and the Indus. Ask students what these rivers had in common. *(Their valleys were the homes of ancient civilizations.)*

HISTORY

Critical Thinking

Remind students that a *dynasty* is a series of rulers from the same family. Among Shang rulers, power was often passed from brother to brother. The Shang dynasty fell in the mid-1000s B.C. Have students list problems an emperor of China might have faced. *(Answers include large land area to govern, frequent wars with neighbors.)* Ask students to speculate on why, in spite of rising and falling dynasties, Chinese civilization continued. *(Answers include people's belief in the Mandate of Heaven and their sense of continuity of past, present, and future.)*

■ *The Chinese believed that it gave the support of heaven to a Chinese emperor who ruled well. If he ruled badly, he lost the mandate and could be overthrown. The idea enabled China to rid itself of bad rulers.*

CLOSE

Write the Thinking Focus on the chalkboard. Then have volunteers identify patterns in Chinese history. *(Rise and fall of dynasties and the Mandate of Heaven)*

Patterns in Chinese History

Shang craftworkers created this 14-inch-high bronze vessel in the shape of a man within a tiger's open jaws. No one knows whether the tiger is protecting the man or eating him. What do you think?

■ *What was the importance of the Mandate of Heaven?*

As in Mesopotamia and India, civilization in China started beside a river. The Shang, the first dynasty to leave historical records, ruled a large area of eastern China between the Yellow and Yangzte rivers. At this time, Shang China was farmland, but there were also towns and walled cities. Shang rule lasted from about 1766 to 1122 B.C.

The Rise and Fall of Dynasties

How did Shang power come to an end? The answer to this question shows a pattern that repeated itself many times in Chinese history. Shang rulers feared raids from people outside their territory. For protection the Shang rulers sought the help of the Zhou *(joh)* people, who lived west of Shang territory, in patrolling the borders. The Zhou people soon came to believe that Shang rulers were corrupt and immoral, and conflict erupted between the two forces. Eventually, the Zhou leader overthrew the Shang king and started his own dynasty.

Chinese history has gone through many changes of dynasty. A new dynasty usually rose after a period of civil war and unrest. When a new ruling family came to power, it often built up the economy and strengthened Chinese power along the northern and western frontiers.

As the dynasty aged, the central government weakened. Groups along the frontiers took advantage of this weakness. Sometimes they joined with local lords to overthrow a dynasty.

The Mandate of Heaven

Starting with the Zhou dynasty, the Chinese have believed that their emperor ruled through the **Mandate of Heaven.** Heaven to them was a power that demanded right behavior and good government. Heaven gave its support, or mandate, to a good ruler. If the emperor did not rule well, he lost the Mandate of Heaven. Then he could be overthrown.

The end of a dynasty did not signal the downfall of Chinese civilization. Even though the empire went through periods of unrest, Chinese civilization was preserved as a distinct whole. ■

REVIEW

1. **FOCUS** What are some major patterns that appear throughout early Chinese history?
2. **GEOGRAPHY** Of what importance are the Huang He and Chang Jiang?
3. **HISTORY** How and why did dynasties change in China?
4. **CRITICAL THINKING** Where would you guess that most people in China live? Why?
5. **WRITING ACTIVITY** Imagine that you are an ancient Chinese ruler. Write a journal entry describing what problems you are facing as your country's leader. How would you propose to solve them?

Homework Options

Refer students to the Key Term at the beginning of the lesson. Have them write a paragraph about how the Mandate of Heaven relates to the pattern of rising and falling dynasties in Chinese history.

Study Guide: page 21

Answers to Review Questions

1. China's history is marked by the rise and fall of dynasties, and the ruler's claim to possess the Mandate of Heaven. Chinese civilization has been continuous for almost 4,000 years.
2. These rivers have valleys with rich soil, and they provide water for farming. They also provide trade routes.
3. When loss of faith in a dynasty occurred, opposition leaders often gained control. The new dynasty usually strengthened the country and then became weak or corrupt, resulting in its overthrow.
4. People are concentrated in southern and eastern China—areas with the most level land and the best climates for farming.
5. Problems include floods destroying farmland and causing famines, and raids from bordering peoples. Solutions include dike-building projects to control flooding and the stationing of soldiers along the frontier to stop invaders.

B.C. A.D.
2700
1766
1279
1800

L E S S O N 4

China's Cultural Heritage

What strange bones! In their fields, some Chinese farmers found oddly polished bones with strange markings. One man thought they came from dragons. Many Chinese believed that ground-up dragon bones could cure the sick. Knowing their value as medicine, the farmer sold all the bones he found.

Some of the bones turned up in medicine shops in Beijing. In 1899, Chinese scholars guessed that the markings were a form of ancient writing.

The designs on the bones proved to be the oldest known writing in East Asia. Yet the ancient writing was enough like modern Chinese for scholars to read nearly 1,500 words.

The bones were used as oracles, or predictors of things to come. Though meant for looking into the future, these bones make it possible for us to look back into China's ancient past.

Tracing the source of the bones led scholars all the way back to Anyang, the capital of one of China's first dynasties. The scholars were delighted. By decoding the writing on the oracle bones, they had unlocked China's past.

For about 4,000 years, the written language has helped to hold the people of China together. Though the spoken language differed from region to region, the written language was the same. Educated people throughout China used it to communicate with one another for generations.

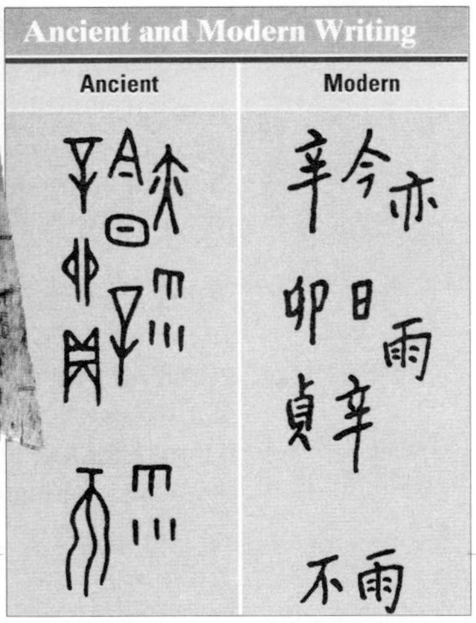
Ancient and Modern Writing
Ancient
Modern
辛今亦
卯日雨
貞辛
不雨

◄ *The chart compares an example of oracle bone writing with its modern Chinese counterpart. Both have the same meaning: "On this day . . . it is divined whether on this . . . day it will rain—or not rain."*

THINKING FOCUS

What factors have helped make China the oldest continuous civilization in the world?

Key Term

- Confucianism

INTRODUCE

Remind students that ancient China was isolated from other civilizations by geographic barriers, although some outside contacts were maintained—for example, by means of the Silk Road reaching to Southwest Asia. Then read the Thinking Focus with the class. Tell them to keep it in mind as they read the lesson. They should also keep in mind the effect of traditional patterns in China's history.

Key Term

Vocabulary Strategies: T36–T37

Confucianism—an ethics system based on the teachings of Confucius, which emphasize devotion to family

Graphic Overview

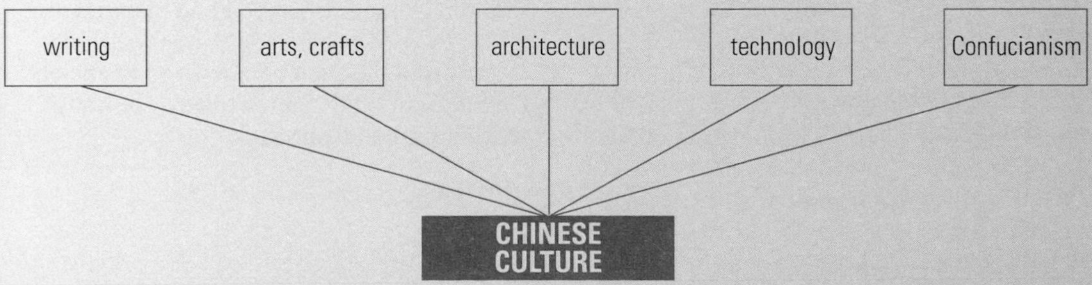
writing
arts, crafts
architecture
technology
Confucianism
CHINESE CULTURE

Objectives

1. Describe how the Chinese writing system has helped to unify China.
2. Describe the influence of Confucianism on China's cultural heritage and social structure.
3. Describe the great Chinese achievements and inventions.

DEVELOP

Tell students that in this lesson they will learn about Chinese values, achievements, and inventions. Explain that Confucianism was one of the strongest influences on China's cultural heritage. Ask students to read the Key Term—Confucianism—and its definition. Have students speculate on the characteristics of Confucianism that might have affected human conduct and government policies in ancient China. *(These characteristics might be sincerity, loyalty, kindness, respect, and ruling by example.)*

BELIEF SYSTEMS

Critical Thinking

Explain to students that Confucius taught that people should be sincere, loyal, and respectful in all relationships. Confucius also taught that children should respect their parents and grandparents at all times. Ask students to decide if Confucianism differs from people's feelings toward relatives today. What attitudes toward the living and the dead would Confucianism encourage? *(It would encourage respect for the past, respect for elders, respect for family relationships, and a sense of continuity among past, present, and future.)*

Confucianism and the Social Heritage

Since ancient times, respect for elders, ancestors, and the past have been key parts of Chinese culture. These values have helped hold Chinese civilization together for many thousands of years. They have been passed on by rituals and by the writings of China's great thinkers. Perhaps the best known is K'ung Ch'iu *(kung chee oo),* or Confucius, as he is known in the West.

➤ *The brush strokes at the top represent the Chinese word for* man. *The two middle strokes represent the number* two. *When written together, these characters change to form* jen*—one person existing in harmony with another. The relationship between two people is central to Confucianism.*

Confucius the Teacher

Confucius was born in 551 B.C. and was one of the best-educated men in China. He taught many new ideas on how to improve government and society. These ideas, known as **Confucianism,** still influence Chinese thought after almost 2,500 years.

Confucianism isn't a religion, but it gives people a code of right and wrong behavior. A central idea of Confucianism is *jen. Jen* means "human-heartedness," or loving others. In order to practice *jen,* Confucius said, "Do not do to others what you do not wish yourself."

Five Basic Relationships

Confucius taught that there are five basic relationships. They are those between ruler and subject, father and son, older and younger brother, husband and wife, and friend and friend. In each relationship, people should be sincere, loyal, and respectful.

Three of Confucius's basic relationships are among family members. The family has always been the most important unit in Chinese society. Confucius believed that children should respect their parents at all times.

Over the centuries, Chinese homes have reflected Confucius's ideas about the importance of the family. Children would live with their parents and grandparents and perhaps even aunts and uncles. At the age of 15 or 16, a son might bring his new wife into the family home. A married daughter would move to her husband's home. Family members were buried near the home, and their descendants made offerings to their spirits.

▼ *The family has been central to Chinese life throughout its history. This painting shows a family giving thanks before its family shrine.*

Rulers and Their Subjects

Confucius used the family as a model for how the rest of society should work. A ruler, he believed, should act like a good father. Ruled by a wise and good leader, people

Access Activity

Read aloud these sayings from Confucius: "The gentleman first practices what he preaches and then preaches what he practices." "Do not do to others what you would not want others to do to you." Discuss these quotations. Do students know any similar quotations? *("Do unto others as you would have them do unto you"* and *"Love thy neighbor as thyself."—the Bible)*

Access Strategy

On August 28, 1963, Martin Luther King, Jr., gave a speech that still echoes in the minds of many Americans. In it, he said, over and over, "I have a dream." King said he dreamed that his four children would live in a country in which people would judge them by their character, not by the color of their skin.

Using this speech, remind students that when people speak, they often reveal their beliefs. King's words showed his belief that changes were needed in U.S. society.

Throughout history men and women have said things that influenced and inspired others, in their own time and sometimes long afterward. One such person lived in ancient China during the Zhou dynasty. He was a teacher named Confucius.

A Closer Look

The Emperor's Tomb

Workers digging at Lintong, China, in 1974 discovered a huge buried army. For more than 2,000 years, it stood in an underground chamber, ready for battle. Over 6,000 life-size warriors and horses, made of sculpted clay, guarded the nearby tomb of Qin Shi huangdi, China's first emperor. The entire tomb site has not yet been dug up. It may hide many other treasures of his empire.

Archaeologists estimate that 700,000 workers built the tomb and clay army in 36 years. Here two archaeologists measure the nearly six-foot height of a warrior.

Who needs a clay army? The emperor united China through warfare. Guards protected him from attack. They may have been the models for his clay warriors, meant to protect him after he died.

Special tools are needed to scrape and brush away dirt from the ancient figures so that they are not damaged.

Note: You may wish to use this Closer Look in relation to the section Protection Against Foreigners on page 121 or to Making Decisions on page 122.

GEOGRAPHY

Visual Learning

Tell students that the imperial tomb is located about 22 miles east of Xi'an, a city in Shaanxi Province. Ask students to find the approximate location on a classroom map. What river is to the north? *(The Wei He)* What mountain is nearby? *(The Li)* Ask students to speculate on the emperor's reasons for placing the underground army in this location. *(Students might guess that the location was isolated, to safeguard against invasion.)*

More About the Emperor's Tomb
Sima Qian, a historian who lived 100 years after the death of Shi huangdi, described the emperor's tomb as an underground palace. In his history Sima Qian wrote that the floor of the tomb was a map of the empire. The ceiling illustrated the heavens.

119

Research

Assign small groups to research the archaeological excavation of the terra-cotta army in Lintong. What does the first emperor's underground army teach about Chinese art prior to the Han dynasty? *(The variety and details found in the sculptures suggest skilled artisans who were familiar with their subject matter. Such variety in form was not known to exist prior to the Han dynasty, until the discovery of the underground army.)*

Journal Writing

Behind the magnificent collection of terra-cotta figures is the labor of thousands of drafted artisans and workers. Have students brainstorm and write entries for a group journal that re-creates the workdays of one of the artisans. To help them imagine a day in the life of one of the artisans, remind students of how the figures were made.

Visual Learning

The heads of the terra-cotta warriors were pressed by molds and finished by hand. Ears, lips, and eyes were added later, making the warriors look different from one another. Ask students what information an archaeologist might learn from the figures. *(The skill level of artisans, the size of the army, and the armor, weaponry, and clothing used)*

CULTURE

Critical Thinking

Point out that because the written language was the same throughout China, it could be read and understood by people in different regions, even though their spoken languages were not the same. Written records and books also linked Chinese people to their past. What effect would these cultural factors have on China politically? *(They would help to unify China into a single state.)*

■ *The teachings of Confucius stressed the value of the family, of merit, and of good government through honesty and by setting a good example. His lessons helped to preserve Chinese civilization through the centuries.*

Dynasties and Inventions of China, 1766 B.C.–A.D. 1279

1600 — 1200 — 400

c.1766–1122 B.C. Shang Dynasty; development of writing

221–206 B.C. Qin Dynasty; connection of Great Wall

206 B.C.–A.D.220 Han Dynasty; invention of paper

would be wise and good, too.

Confucius believed in traditional Chinese values such as obedience and order, but his ideas about government were new. Instead of laws and punishment, Confucius thought that government should be based on goodness. He said, "If the ruler himself is upright, all will go well, even though he does not give orders."

The Civil Service

Laws, however, were an accepted part of Chinese civilization. To carry them out, the emperor had a huge body of government workers called the civil service. Confucius taught that government officials should earn their jobs through education and talent. They should not use family connections to get their jobs, as so many did. He gave this advice: "Don't worry about not being in office; worry about qualifying yourself for office."

■ *What contributions did the teachings of Confucius make to Chinese civilization?*

Many years after Confucius, China set up a system of examinations by which civil servants, or government workers, were chosen. To pass the exams, students had to read and write well. They also had to know the writings of the Confucian classics.

The civil service was an important unifying force in Chinese history. In spite of rebellions, invasions, and changing dynasties, the civil service helped preserve Chinese civilization. This class of well-educated people helped China produce some of the most dazzling achievements of the ancient world. ■

Chinese Achievements

Take a good look at this book. In every way, it seems to belong to modern Western civilization. Yet it is in your hands today because of several key Chinese inventions. The Chinese are responsible for many achievements that have changed the course of world history.

Silk, Paper, and Printing

Did you ever stop to think what people wrote on before there was paper? In ancient China, scribes used soft brushes to copy words, character by character, onto pieces of silk. Silk was made from the cocoons of silkworms. How to make silk was one of China's best-guarded secrets.

According to legend, Emperor Ho-ti was tired of writing on silk. To please him, a courtier figured out how to make paper from the inner bark of the mulberry tree in about A.D. 105.

Paper replaced silk for many written documents, but painting characters still took a lot of time.

Cultural Context

The Chinese valued highly the stone called jade. One Chinese source said of jade that it shines like benevolence; that it is strong and dependable like wisdom; that, like justice, it has edges that are sharp but do not cut; and that, like truth, it does not hide its flaws. The Chinese believed that jade was endowed with magic and curative properties.

Jade, which is found in colors ranging from dark green to white, has been carved by the Chinese throughout their history. In fact, hand tools used for jade carving have been found from the Chinese Neolithic period. The early Chinese worked jade into axes, knives, and blades. As metal replaced stone for tools, jade was carved into ritual objects such as jewelry and figures of people and animals. In addition, the Chinese made sets of musical jade stones that produced clear, mellow notes when struck.

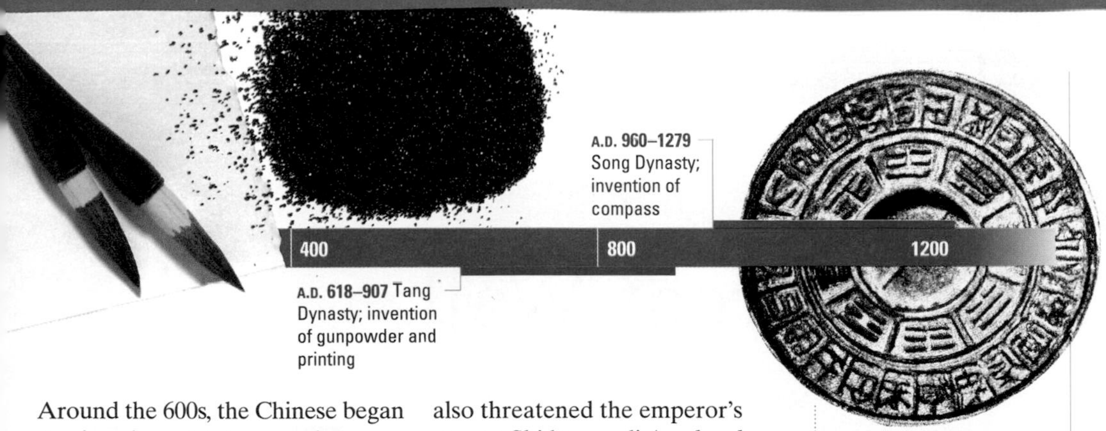
A.D. 960–1279 Song Dynasty; invention of compass
400
800
1200
A.D. 618–907 Tang Dynasty; invention of gunpowder and printing

Trace some of the great achievements and dynasties of ancient China.

Around the 600s, the Chinese began carving characters on wooden blocks. By applying ink to these blocks, and then pressing the blocks onto paper, the Chinese were able to print many copies quickly. Printing with wood blocks would not start in Europe until the 1400s.

Protection Against Foreigners

Some products from China began reaching Europe about 2,000 years ago. Silk was in great demand. Traders carried it over the Silk Road, from China across Asia and the Middle East to the Mediterranean. These traders, however, were not Chinese. The emperors of China did not want certain secrets to leak out. They even threatened death to anyone who told an outsider the secret of silk or gave away a silkworm.

Preserving and protecting the Middle Kingdom and its culture were of the highest importance to the rulers. They feared invasions by warlike peoples to the north and west. Invaders threatened farming, on which China depended. They also threatened the emperor's power. Shi huang-di *(see hwahng dee)* was the first ruler to unite large parts of China. To keep out invaders and strengthen his control, he ordered a huge wall to be built in 221 B.C. (see A Closer Look on page 119).

Gunpowder

In spite of its size, the Great Wall was not very successful in keeping out invaders. Warfare was a common ingredient in Chinese history. In addition to fighting off invaders, the Chinese went through periods of fighting among themselves. The need for new weapons seemed constant.

Perhaps the most famous Chinese invention is gunpowder. By the 900s, the Chinese had figured out how to make gunpowder fuses for flamethrowers. They also invented the fire-lance, an early kind of gun. By the 1000s, the Chinese were developing gunpowder rockets, flares, fireworks, grenades, and bombs. Not for several hundred years would Europe do the same. ■

■ *How have Chinese inventions influenced the world beyond China's borders?*

REVIEW

1. **FOCUS** What factors have helped make China the oldest continuous civilization in the world?
2. **HISTORY** How did the oracle bones provide a window into China's past?
3. **ETHICS** Explain the principle of *jen* in your own words.
4. **CRITICAL THINKING** Which of the achievements of Chinese civilization described here do you think is the most important? Why?
5. **ACTIVITY** For each of Confucius's five relationships, make up a rule that could be applied in today's world. Do you think Confucius would agree with your rules? Why or why not? Share your ideas with your class.

◄ Shang dynasty: development of writing; Qin dynasty: connection of the sections of the Great Wall; Han dynasty: invention of paper; Tang dynasty: invention of gunpowder and printing; Song dynasty: invention of compass

■ *Printing and paper have speeded communications everywhere. The invention of gunpowder made hunting more effective, but it also caused warfare to become more costly in terms of human lives. China's inventions have challenged people in other societies to copy them.*

CLOSE

Read the Thinking Focus aloud. Then have students scan the lesson in preparation for writing questions for a Quiz Bowl game. Encourage them to form questions about the following topics: the Chinese writing system, Confucianism, and Chinese achievements and inventions. Divide the class into two teams. Have them exchange their questions, read them, and then answer them to see which team can answer more.

Answers to Review Questions

1. Factors include China's isolation, its writing system, the teachings of Confucius about respect for elders, the civil service system, and an educated class.
2. The oracle bones contained the oldest known form of Chinese writing. Because this writing was similar to modern Chinese, scholars could read the bones and learn about life during the Shang dynasty.
3. It teaches that people should treat others as they would want to be treated.
4. Students should support their answers with a discussion of one of the achievements listed in the text.
5. Answers should reflect an understanding of the teachings of Confucius.

Homework Options

Refer students to the Key Term at the beginning of the lesson. Have them write a paragraph explaining how Confucianism relates to the development of China.

Study Guide: page 22

DECISION-MAKING PROCESS

1. Recognize the need for a decision
2. Define the goals and values involved
3. Acquire and evaluate necessary information
4. Identify and analyze possible alternatives
5. Choose the best alternative

In this lesson students will use steps 1, 2, and 3 of the decision-making process.

HISTORY

Study Skills

Have students identify several reasons given in the textbook for building the Great Wall. *(Protection along the northern border; a way for the emperor to get rid of enemies, including enemy soldiers—putting them to work in a distant place)* What else might the emperor have done to solve his problems? *(Have men guard the northern border; have enemies build roads or public buildings; imprison enemies or put them to death)*

MAKING DECISIONS

The Great Wall

Had the Great Wall not already existed, Yangdi [the second Sui emperor] would certainly have conceived it. As it was, he had to be content with rebuilding it.

Robert Silverberg,
20th-century historian

➤ *The Great Wall still snakes for thousands of miles across modern China. However, the wall that is still standing is not Shi huangdi's wall, but a later version, built during the Ming dynasty.*

Background

Records show that Yangdi's rebuilding of the Great Wall in A.D. 607 required more than one million workers. More than half of them died of overwork or fled the harsh conditions.

The original building of the Great Wall, begun in 221 B.C., also involved a huge work force. Shi huangdi, the Qin emperor who thought of this project, connected shorter walls that had been built along China's northern border centuries before. He also extended the wall for hundreds of miles. The resulting wall was and still is the longest structure on the earth.

Before beginning any massive work, such as the building of the Great Wall of China, a wise decision maker will try to weigh the benefits and the costs of the project. We can look at historical events to try to compare the benefits and the costs of building the Great Wall of China.

These coins, which were issued by Shi huangdi, were the standard currency throughout the empire at the time when the Great Wall was being built.

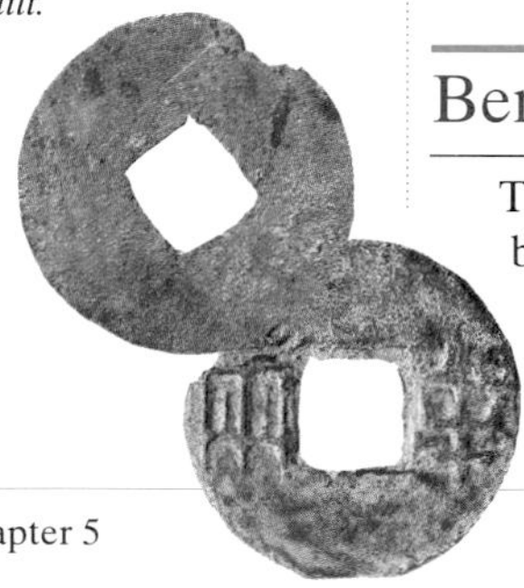

Benefits and Costs of the Great Wall

The most obvious benefit of building the Great Wall was protection. The wall helped prevent wandering horsemen from invading China's farms along the northern border. Also, it kept farmers living along the border from joining the nomads.

Building the Great Wall helped Shi huangdi to get rid of his

Objectives

1. Recognize the dangers to the emperor and the empire. (History 3, 5)
2. Define the goals for building the Great Wall. (Critical Thinking 2; History 3, 5)
3. Evaluate the negative and positive effects of building the Great Wall. (Critical Thinking 2; History 5)

Activity

Tell students to imagine what it might have been like to live in China in 221 B.C., when Shi huangdi decided to begin building the Great Wall. Encourage them to speculate about the following: the northern farmers' opinions of the Great Wall; the disloyal soldiers' thoughts about it; worker-management problems; the emperor's point of view; the nomads' point of view; and the Chinese people's attitude toward the building project.

After some discussion, have students write news stories about the building project. Tell students that they can use graphs, charts, and political cartoons to make their reports more interesting; they might also work in teams and present their news reports in interview form. Finally, have students present their reports as if they were appearing on the evening news.

enemies. He ordered them to work on distant parts of the wall. He also sent soldiers to work on the wall. As a result, the soldiers could not band together and rise up against the emperor.

However, it is estimated that building Shi huangdi's wall required more than 300,000 workers. Most of them were drafted against their will. Thousands of farmers and merchants were required to supply the workers with food, clothing, tools, and shelter. Most of these supplies never made it to the work sites; bandits roaming the countryside robbed the supply caravans.

The work of constructing the wall was so difficult and living conditions were so harsh that thousands of workers died. Often they were buried in the wall itself. Thus, the Great Wall of China gained the gruesome title of "the world's longest cemetery."

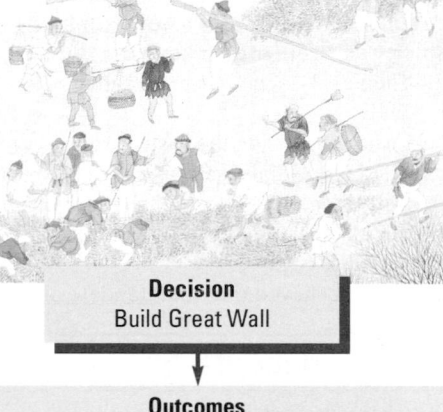

Sturdy horses, like the one at the left, carried nomads who raided China's northern border. In response, the Great Wall was built, using labor-intensive construction methods as shown. Study the chart for a comparison of the Great Wall's long-range benefits and short-term costs.

Decision
Build Great Wall

Outcomes	
• People are safer.	• Many laborers die.
• More farmers stay on farms.	• People become poorer.
• Fewer threats to emperor arise.	• Supply caravans are often attacked.

Decision Point

1. What were the benefits of constructing the Great Wall of China? What were the costs?
2. Do you think these were the only benefits and costs of the Great Wall? Where would you look to find more information about the role of the Great Wall in Chinese history?
3. Based on the information on these pages and any other information you have found, do you think the benefits and costs of building the Great Wall balanced out? Explain.
4. Collect information from newspapers and magazines about upcoming plans for large government projects in the United States. Discuss the projected benefits and costs of each project. Decide which projects you would support and which you would oppose.

HISTORY

Critical Thinking

Draw students' attention to the chart on this page. Have a volunteer read the left side of the chart—the positive outcomes of the building of the Great Wall. Ask if the positive outcomes lasted over time. *(Yes. Emperor Yangdi still relied on the Great Wall for defense 800 years after it was built.)* Then have a volunteer read the right side of the chart. Ask students why they think Emperor Shi huangdi decided to continue building the Great Wall even when its drawbacks became apparent. *(The emperor saw the negative outcomes as short-term costs, while he saw the wall's benefits as lasting into the future.)* Discuss with students the values, both positive and negative, reflected in the building of the Great Wall. *(For example, the emperor cared more for his own survival and the survival of his empire than for the lives of the Chinese people.)*

Answers to Decision Point

1. The benefits were that the people were safer, more farmers stayed on their farms, and there were fewer threats to the emperor. The costs were that many laborers died, the people became poorer, and caravans of supplies traveling to the wall were often attacked.
2. Students will probably say that they could learn about additional benefits and costs by consulting encyclopedias and history textbooks.
3. Students answering yes might say that the benefits of building the Great Wall were much longer lasting than the costs. Those answering no might say that the abuse of human life can never be balanced by any positive outcomes.
4. Possible government projects might be construction of federal office buildings and dams, military base expansion, or road improvements.

Collaborative Strategy

For a collaborative learning strategy you can use with this lesson, refer to pages T34–T35.

Chapter Review

Reviewing Key Terms

Buddhism (p.110)
caste (p.106)
Confucianism (p.118)
Hinduism (p.108)
Mandate of Heaven (p.116)
reincarnation (p.109)
tributary (p.103)
untouchable (p.106)

A. Each statement below uses a key term from this chapter. Tell whether each key term is used correctly. Then explain the reason for your answer.

1. People who fell outside the caste system were called untouchables.
2. Buddhism teaches that in order to reach enlightenment, a person must do the duties of his or her caste.
3. The Chinese believed that the Mandate of Heaven gave the emperor unlimited power to rule; no one could ever question anything he did.
4. According to Confucianism, all people are equal; therefore, no one owes obedience to anyone else.

B. Use a dictionary to find the origins and the definitions of the following words. Then explain how the meaning of each word applies to India.

1. tributary
2. caste
3. reincarnation
4. untouchable
5. Hinduism

Exploring Concepts

A. In this chapter you have read about three important systems of belief in Asia. The chart below will help you compare them. Copy and complete this chart.

Belief system	Goal of life	How to achieve goal
Hinduism		
Buddhism		
Confucianism	right behavior	

B. Answer each question with information from the chapter.

1. Why were archaeologists excited about the discovery of the Mohenjo-Daro and Harappa sites in India?
2. What evidence do we have that the Indus Valley civilization was centrally planned?
3. How did its geographic location affect how people made a living in the ancient Indus Valley?
4. What do we know about the Aryans from the Vedas?
5. According to legend, why did Siddhartha Gautama give up his riches to search for a way to end suffering in the world?
6. How did geography influence the development of a distinctive Chinese culture?
7. How did China's system of writing contribute to stability in the empire?
8. What evidence can you give that the emperors of ancient China shunned the outside world?

Answers to Reviewing Key Terms

A. Sample answers:

1. Correct. They were called **untouchable** because people thought their impurity could be transferred by touch.
2. Incorrect. The caste system is irrelevant to **Buddhism.**
3. Incorrect. The **Mandate of Heaven** could be withdrawn, and the emperor could be overthrown if he did not rule wisely.
4. Incorrect. **Confucianism** teaches that society is based on relationships ordered by obedience, such as ruler and subject.

B. Sample answers:

1. **tributary:** from the Latin word *tributarius,* which means "of tribute," something given to a superior. Tributaries of a river are its feeder rivers. In ancient India, settlements grew up along tributaries of the Indus River.
2. **caste:** from a Portuguese word meaning "breed" or "race," which is from the Latin word for "pure." In India each caste is a separate group of people.
3. **reincarnation:** from Latin words meaning "again," "in," and "flesh." It means rebirth of the soul in a different body and is a central belief of Hinduism.
4. **untouchable:** from English words meaning "not," "touch," and "able." In India this term refers to a group of people considered impure.
5. **Hinduism:** from the Old Persian word *Hindu,* referring to the religion and dominant culture of India.

Answers to Exploring Concepts

A. Sample answers:

Hinduism: purified soul, to be absorbed back into world soul; fulfill caste duties, live by Hinduism's teachings. **Buddhism:** enlightenment; Eightfold Path. **Confucianism:** right behavior; practice *jen,* be sincere, loyal, respectful in each of five relationships.

B. Sample answers:

1. The sites showed the existence of highly developed civilizations in ancient India.
2. All the settlements were laid out and built in the same way.
3. Fertile soil and adequate rainfall made the Indus Valley a good place for farming. In addition, its location on the Arabian Sea made trading with other peoples possible.
4. Aryan society had four classes, each of which consisted of many castes. Because religious rituals were important, the priests held a great deal of power.
5. Siddhartha Gautama saw an old man, a sick man, and a dead man, and realized that he, too, would grow old and die. Then he saw an impoverished wandering holy man who seemed very content. He decided to follow the man's example.
6. China was bounded on the south and west by mountains; on the north by deserts; and on the east by the Pacific Ocean, setting it apart from other cultures.
7. The Chinese written language was the same all over the empire, even though the spoken language differed.
8. They forbade Chinese to trade directly with other countries to protect the secrets of how to make silk and paper. They also built the Great Wall to keep invaders out.

Reviewing Skills

Use the clue words in the chart on page 107 to help you answer each of the following questions in a brief paragraph.

1. What were some of the most important events that helped to establish Chinese civilization? Use chronological organization in your answer.
2. Describe the area of China where civilization developed. Use spatial organization in developing your answer.
3. Explain why the population of China was concentrated in the area you just described. Use cause-and-effect organization in your answer.
4. How was ancient China like ancient India? How was it different? Be sure to include both comparisons and contrasts in the answer that you give.

Using Critical Thinking

1. The caste system still exists in India today, although it is not so rigid as in ancient times. Compare this kind of social organization with U.S. society today.
2. The success of crops and trade depended on the regular monsoons. What might have happened if the monsoon was early or late?
3. In the Buddha's time, priests, rulers, and warriors were in the upper classes. How might they have felt about Buddhism? Why?
4. Confucius said, "Riches and honor are what everyone desires, but if they can be gained only by doing evil, they must not be held." What do you think it would take to get government leaders to follow this advice today?
5. The emperors of ancient China did not want the rest of the world to know the secrets of making silk and paper. Do we have similar laws protecting our technology today? Do you think such laws are a good idea? Why or why not?

Preparing for Citizenship

1. **WRITING ACTIVITY** Just as archaeologists did at Mohenjo-Daro, scientists one thousand years from now may start digging up your community for evidence of a past civilization. Write a brief description of what you think they will find. Then tell how they might think these artifacts were used in the late 20th century.
2. **COLLECTING INFORMATION** Archaeologists learn about ancient life and culture by unearthing old cities and artifacts. Based on what they find, archaeologists try to piece together a picture of what life must have been like in the past. Your community has a past. Discover any traces left from its past inhabitants. You could interview older residents; research photographs, maps, and books; or study the buildings and land. Share your research with the class. Explain what you think life was once like in your community.
3. **COLLABORATIVE LEARNING** In this chapter you have read about three of the world's most important systems of belief: Hinduism, Buddhism, and Confucianism. What would each system have to say about proper conduct and attitudes in the classroom? Working with a small group of classmates, choose a different belief system. Your group should develop a list of classroom rules that reflect the values of one of the three belief systems. Here are some questions to get your group discussion started:
(1) What is the purpose of education?
(2) What are the teacher's duties?
(3) What are the students' duties?
Have a member of your group present the rules to the class. In class discussion, compare the three sets of rules. Which sets are more alike? Which rules do you think would create the best climate for learning?

Answers to Reviewing Skills

Sample answers:

1. The first dynasty to leave historical records was the Shang, which lasted from 1766 to 1122 B.C. Next came the Zhou dynasty. By overthrowing the Shang, they set up a pattern that would be repeated often. The Zhou established the belief in the Mandate of Heaven.
2. Chinese civilization began in eastern China. Unlike western China, which has mountains and deserts, eastern China has extensive river systems, broad flat plains, and a moist climate.
3. In ancient times large numbers of people could live only where farming was possible. Because rivers in eastern China frequently flooded, the soil was enriched by silt. Fertile soil, combined with the monsoons of southern Asia, made the area good farmland.
4. Both civilizations began along rivers and developed highly organized societies. Chinese geography and sense of superiority kept China apart from the rest of the world. India traded with many lands and experienced Aryan migrations and the mingling of cultures.

Answers to Using Critical Thinking

1. In the caste system, people belong to one group for their entire lives. In U.S. society, in theory, anyone can go "from rags to riches." In reality, we have different status groups too, but they are not rigid.
2. If the monsoon was early, farmers might not be ready to plant their crops, and trade by sea might be delayed or caught in storms. If the monsoon was late, the land would dry out.
3. Students may answer that these people might have feared Buddhism, which rejected the caste system, changed certain rituals, and encouraged peace.
4. Students might mention close scrutiny by the press, congressional hearings, or yearly public reviews.
5. Yes. Students may disagree about the need for laws prohibiting the export of defense-related and computer technology.

Answers to Preparing for Citizenship

1. **WRITING ACTIVITY** Answers may include ideas such as these: Future archaeologists might find aluminum soda cans, cassette tapes, and broken television sets. They might think that people in the late 20th century created a lot of trash.
2. **COLLECTING INFORMATION** All the information that students find will provide a framework for telling what life was once like in the community.
3. **COLLABORATIVE LEARNING** Answers may include ideas such as these:

Hindu Rules: The goal of education is to teach members of the student caste all the laws of their caste.

Buddhist Rules: The goal of education is enlightenment. Therefore, students should learn the ways of the Eightfold Path.

Confucian Rules: The teacher must demonstrate "human-heartedness" and responsibility in all actions. Students must show respect for their teachers.

CHAPTER ORGANIZER

Chapter 6 *Early Civilizations in the Americas*

CHAPTER PLANNING CHART

Pupil's Edition	Teacher's Edition	Ancillaries
Lesson 1: Early Americans (2–3 days) Objective 1: Explain how people first came to the Americas and how they lived. (History 2; Geography 1, 4) Objective 2: Identify the Olmec and Mayan civilizations and the environments in which they developed. (Geography 2, 5; Culture 2) Objective 3: Explain the special characteristics and achievements of Mayan civilization. (Culture 2, 5, 6; Ethics and Belief Systems 3)	• Graphic Overview (128) • Access Strategy (129) • Access Activity (129) Critical Thinking (130) Science Connection (130)	Study Guide (23) Map Activities (10) Transparency (2) • Study Prints (4)
Lesson 2: Aztec Civilization (2–3 days) Objective 1: Trace the Aztec rise to power. (History 5, 6, 7) Objective 2: Relate the products of the Aztec market to the environment. (Geography 4; Economics 2, 3) Objective 3: Explain Aztec religious beliefs and their impact on society. (Culture 2; Ethics and Belief Systems 3, 4; Social and Political Systems 4) Objective 4: Relate Aztec religious beliefs to the expansion of their empire. (Ethics and Belief Systems 2; Social and Political Systems 1, 5)	• Graphic Overview (132) • Access Strategy (133) • Access Activity (133) Social Participation (134) Collaborative Learning (134) Cultural Context (134) Geographic Context (135) Social Context (135) • Visual Learning (135) Critical Thinking (136) Language Arts Connection (136) Writing (136)	Study Guide (24) Discovery Journal (13)
Lesson 3: Andean Civilizations (3–4 days) Objective 1: Relate the rise of Andean civilizations to the environment. (History 7; Geography 2, 3) Objective 2: Identify the Inca and the main characteristics of their way of life. (Culture 4; Ethics and Belief Systems 3) Objective 3: Explain the distribution of resources and labor in the Inca Empire. (Economics 1, 3; Social and Political Systems 1)	• Graphic Overview (138) • Access Strategy (139) • Access Activity (139) Critical Thinking (140) Social Context (140) Writing a Journal Entry (141) Research (141) • Visual Learning (141)	Study Guide (25) Discovery Journal (14)
Understanding Evidence Objective: Identify main ideas and supporting details in paragraphs. (Study Skills 2)		Study Guide (26)
Chapter Review	Answers (144–145)	Tests (21–24)

* Objectives are correlated to the strands and goals in the program Scope and Sequence on pages T41–T49.

• LEP appropriate resources. (For additional strategies, see pages T32–T33.)

CHAPTER RATIONALE

Chapter 6, which focuses on early civilizations in the Americas, concludes the unit on early civilizations. From the arrival of the first Americans from Asia, we trace the growth of major civilizations in the Americas. These civilizations gave rise to the Aztecs in Mesoamerica and the Inca in Andean South America.

Lesson 1 introduces students to the many unknowns about early life in the Americas. Archaeologists look for evidence about such questions as who the first Americans were, when they first reached the Americas, what routes they followed, and how they lived. Students will find that many of these questions do not have firm answers and that the search for evidence continues.

A life of hunting and gathering gave way in time to farming. The domestication of corn was a major breakthrough because it provided a staple food. In Mesoamerica centers of population arose where in time civilizations were to develop. The first of these was the Olmec, followed by the brilliant civilization of the Maya. Along with other major accomplishments, the Maya developed a written language, which marks the transition from prehistory, based on archaeological evidence, to history, based on written records.

Lesson 2 considers the Aztecs, the last of the Mesoamerican cultures, in terms of their society, religion, culture, and empire. Their capital, Tenochtitlan, became one of the world's great cities of its time. Because of an all-pervasive religion, Aztec society was highly organized and carefully regulated. Students read that conquest and the building of an empire were the sources of both strength and weakness for the Aztecs. While increased power and wealth strengthened the empire, the large-scale conquests and the taking of captives for sacrifice caused resistance among conquered peoples.

Lesson 3 on Andean civilizations in South America parallels the preceding lesson on the Aztecs. The first part of Lesson 3 introduces new archaeological findings about pre-Inca peoples and cultures. These findings indicate that the earliest of the Andean civilizations arose a thousand years before that of the Olmec in Mesoamerica. Located on the coast, this culture was unique among early civilizations in its dependence on the sea, rather than farming, for food.

The relation between peoples and their environment is a key focus here. From the start Andean peoples had to overcome major problems caused by their environment. Thus, students read about various ways which Andean peoples interacted with their environment.

Each succeeding Andean civilization built upon the skills, arts and crafts, and technology of its predecessors, culminating with the Inca. An in-depth study of the Inca includes their society, religion, culture, and empire. Unlike the Aztecs, the Inca kept a highly centralized control of their empire. Their system began to weaken even before the European conquest.

ACTIVITIES & PROJECTS

Basic: Drawing

Mesoamerica and the Andean region had many very highly skilled artists and craftspeople. Provide library books and magazines showing the arts of both regions. Ask students to copy or originate drawings that represent the work of artists and craftspeople in either region. (Use after any lesson.)

LEP: Decorating a Wall Map

Provide a large wall map of Mesoamerica and another of the Andean region centered on Peru. Have students cut out their works created in the previous activity and place them on the map in the appropriate location. Encourage students to tell how their drawings represent the particular culture. (Use after any lesson.)

Challenge: Research

Have students use library resources to research the story of the domestication of corn and other crops native to Mesoamerica as well as potatoes and other foods native to Andean civilizations. Ask students to prepare a one-minute oral report on their findings. (Use after Lessons 1 or 3.)

LEP: Collaborative Learning

Have students plan a Mesoamerican or an Andean feast. Divide the class into groups and assign them research topics: Foods, Music, Dances, and Games. Students should plan a way to pay for the food, which can be prepared by class volunteers. Have students work with their other classmates to use the library to research the appropriate foods, music, dances, and games. The library may also have tapes of early Mesoamerican and Andean music. (Use after Lesson 3.)

Role Playing

Have students role play villagers that have recently been conquered by the Inca. Remind students that the Inca were very strict and exercised total control over their subjects' lives.

Have several students play the role of Inca officials who have arrived to take a census and divide the villager's land. Two or three students can play the roles of town officials, who must explain to the villagers what has happened and what will be expected of them under the new regime. Another half-dozen students can be villagers who will ask questions about the new regime and will raise questions about its policies.

This situation may be played as one scene among all three parties or as two separate scenes—one involving the Inca and local officials, the second involving the local officials and the villagers. (Use after Lesson 3.)

CHAPTER PREVIEW

Ask students to read the chapter title and the paragraph that follows. Have them look at the photographs on these two pages and read the captions for them. What information do the photographs provide about early civilizations of the Americas? *(People of these early civilizations knew how to carve stone; kept track of time; could build a great city high in the mountains; used pack animals.)*

Looking Back

Review with students the world and regional maps on page 53 of the Unit 2 Overview. Have students identify where the civilizations introduced in Chapters 3, 4, and 5 flourished. *(Mesopotamia in Southwest Asia, Egypt and Nubia in Africa, and India and China in Asia)*

Looking Forward

Have students identify the map on page 53 that shows the early American civilizations. Tell students they will be reading about these in the next three lessons: Early Americans, Aztec Civilization, and Andean Civilizations.

Lesson 1 begins with the migration of the earliest Americans from Asia.

Chapter 6

Early Civilizations in the Americas

The Atlantic and Pacific oceans form a vast barrier that separates the Americas from other continents. In time people settled in the Americas and developed unique ways of life that became great civilizations. Among these people were the Olmec, the Maya, the Aztecs, and the Inca.

The Olmec sculptured enormous, stone heads that weigh up to twenty tons and stand nine feet tall.

The Mayan Temple of the Warriors at Chichén Itzá is a pyramid with a temple at the top. The statue holds a bowl, perhaps for offerings.

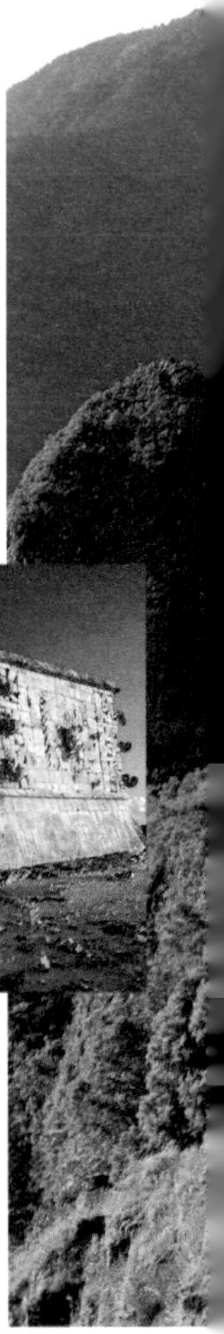

Machu Picchu, the "lost city of the Inca," was unknown to the outside world until 1911. The llama, a relative of the camel, is the main pack animal used in the Andes.

15.000	14,500		1000	500

14,000 B.C.

1000 B.C. Chavín civilization emerges in the Andes.

BACKGROUND

In the last decade, new discoveries have radically changed scholars' views of the archaeology and prehistory of the Americas. Analyses of blood and teeth have established that the first Americans came from Asia. The date of their arrival, however, is highly controversial. According to an article in the November 1992 *Scientific American,* evidence supporting a theory of three waves of migration is growing. Both genetic and linguistic analyses of Native American populations support this view.

The Maya and the Aztecs

Because much of archaeologists' knowledge about the Maya and Aztecs was, until recent years, based on archaeological evidence rather than on written records, many aspects of these civilizations remained unknown. Today, the decoding of Mayan glyphs has provided new understandings of Mayan culture, history, and world view. For example, we now know that the Maya believed in a soul-force that scholar Linda Schele compares to "The Force" in George Lucas's "Star Wars" films. Furthermore, our view of the Maya as an essentially peaceful people has changed. Translation of their glyphs has shown that they fought many wars with their neighbors. The glyphs thus became a written record of historical events.

Recent studies of Aztec codices have also provided new understandings of Aztec culture. Codices were books made of fig-bark

s huge stone carving represented Aztec ideas he creation of the world, the universe, and the :ecs' role in the universe. Called the Calendar ne, the carving was set near the Great Temple Tenochtitlan.

1325 Aztecs build Tenochtitlan.

B.C. | A.D. | 500 | 1000 | 1550

A.D. 250 Mayan civilization thrives in Mesoamerica.

A.D. 500 Teotihuacan is at its height.

A.D. 1532

Understanding the Visuals

Archaeologists believe that the Olmec, to make enormous sculptures like the one on the previous page, dragged huge rocks to rivers and floated them on rafts to their final location.

This carved stone, which is 12 feet wide and weighs more than 26 tons, shows the Aztecs' beliefs about the universe and their place in it They believed time was composed of cycles of 52 years. When each cycle ended, a new one began. The Aztecs focused on cycles of time to assure the continuation of life and the universe.

Understanding Chronology

Point out the break in the timeline and ask what it means. (A break also appeared in the timeline for Chapter 3, pages 56–57.) Review the term *prehistoric,* introduced on page 59, and tell students that Lesson 1 begins in the prehistoric era.

Students should know that Andean cultures existed about ten times longer than the time since the Spanish conquest of Peru.

paper or deerskin, in which genealogies, calendars, religious ideas, myths, and historical events were recorded. The codices show that the Aztecs were very strict with their children. Disobedient children might be forced to sleep on the cold ground.

Andean Cultures

Neither the Chavín nor the Moche culture, which were early Andean civilizations, ever created a written language. The skill of Moche craftspeople in depicting scenes from daily life on pottery and jewelry, however, is so great that scholars hope to learn a great deal more about this ancient culture from recent discoveries.

Machu Picchu

The Inca city of Machu Picchu lies one and a half miles high between two mountain peaks in Peru. The city was discovered by explorer Hiram Bingham. Enough food was grown on the terraces outside Machu Picchu to feed the whole community. Some terraces were located near the top of the central peak.

INTRODUCE

Tell students that the earliest human beings are believed to have lived in Africa. Review with students the maps of civilizations in the Unit 2 Overview on page 53. Then have them locate the specific civilizations they will study in this chapter. *(Mesoamerica and western South America)* Point out that the Americas are the only major continents that did not have inhabitants during most of prehistory. Then direct students to the Thinking Focus, and ask them how they think people traveled from Asia to the Americas.

Key Terms

Vocabulary Strategies: T36–T37

glacier—a great mass of ice

diversity—variety or points of difference

rain forest—a damp jungle located in the humid tropics (composed of leaf trees, not evergreens such as pine)

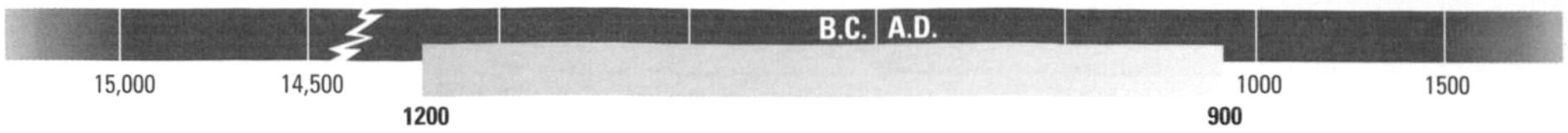

B.C. | A.D.
15,000
14,500
1200
1000
900
1500

LESSON 1

Early Americans

THINKING FOCUS

How did people first come to the Americas?

Key Terms

- glacier
- diversity
- rain forest

Who were the first Americans? Where did they come from? When did they arrive? How did they get here? Archaeologists have spent years trying to answer these questions. They look for signs of human life, such as the remains of humans, fireplaces, and tools. This search is still going on.

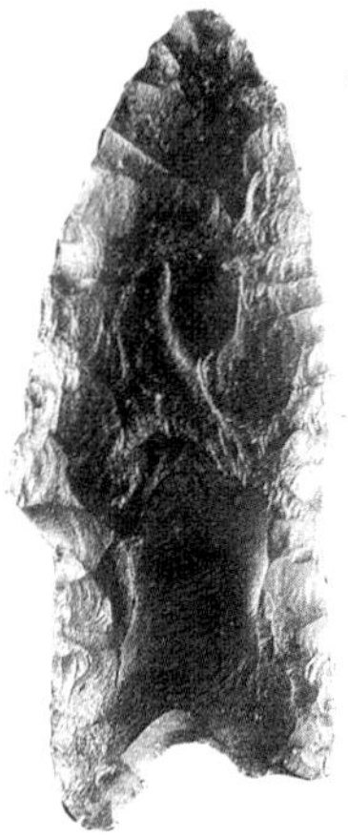

➤ *Clovis points, usually made of flint, a kind of quartz, were fitted onto spear shafts.*

The earliest Americans came from Asia. They arrived by way of a land bridge that once existed between Asia and North America. In the distant past, great masses of ice, or **glaciers,** covered much of northern Europe, Asia, and North America. The glaciers held so much water that ocean depths were as much as 300 feet less than what they are today. This exposed a wide landmass between Asia and North America. Today, scientists call this area Beringia. The map on page 129 shows the location of Beringia.

Across Time & Space

In 1990 U.S. President George Bush and Soviet President Mikhail Gorbachev planned the Beringian Heritage International Park. The park will protect the culture of the people in the region along with wildlife and other resources.

The First Americans

Archaeologists disagree about the time when people first came to the Americas. Was it within the past 10,000 to 15,000 years? Was it twice that long ago? The actual time is a mystery. Scientists know that stone spearheads found near Folsom and Clovis, New Mexico, date to 11,500 years ago.

In the past 10 years, however, scientists have found signs that people may have arrived much earlier. Bones of a mammoth that may have been killed by humans have been found in a Canadian cave. These bones date to 15,500 years ago. Remains of animal bones and objects that may have been tools have been found in Brazil. The bones are 17,000 years old. In 1992 the archaeologist Richard MacNeish, in Orogrande, New Mexico, found what he thinks are signs of human life dating to 55,000 years ago. The debate about the time—and the evidence itself—continues today.

Some scientists now think that Asians came to the Americas in at least three waves. These scientists, who study language, believe that early Americans can be divided into three groups. Scientists still disagree

Objectives

1. Explain how people first came to the Americas and how they lived.
2. Identify the Olmec and Mayan civilizations and the environments in which they developed.
3. Explain the special characteristics and achievements of Mayan civilization.

Graphic Overview

Early American societies developed in a pattern like that of other societies.

Hunter-Gatherers
- Small nomadic bands
- No permanent structures
- Diversity of lifestyles, cultures

→

Learn How to Plant Crops and Domesticate Animals

→

Farmers
- Settlements with many people
- Permanent structures
- Single culture within a region
- Network of trade

about the route people took. Some scientists think that hunters crossed the Beringian plain by an inland route, following herds of caribou and woolly mammoths. This route is shown on the map opposite. Other scientists think that people traveled by foot or in skin boats along the warmer coast of Beringia. There they could live on fish, sea mammals, and birds.

Hunting-Gathering Societies

Bands of people kept moving southward in search of food. They found mammoths, herds of bison, and other large, grazing animals on the plains of North America.

Over time, small bands of hunter-gatherers occupied an area from the Great Plains to the Andean mountains. They lived apart from one another in widely scattered areas.

The **diversity,** or variety, of plant and animal life in the various geographic regions meant that people in the regions needed different skills in order to survive. They developed belief systems and ways of living that also showed diversity.

Origins of Farming

Sometime between 7000 and 6000 B.C., people began to turn from hunting-gathering to farming. This change took place first in Mesoamerica, the region shown on the map on page 130. Most of Mesoamerica lies in the tropics, where the climate is hot and wet.

Along the swampy coasts of the Gulf of Mexico, farmers began to clear the land and plant crops. The first people to grow corn, however, lived in the highlands of central Mesoamerica. Corn soon became the basic food of early Mesoamericans. Just as wheat supported civilizations in the Fertile Crescent, corn supported the rise of civilizations in early Mesoamerica. ■

Early Migration to the Americas

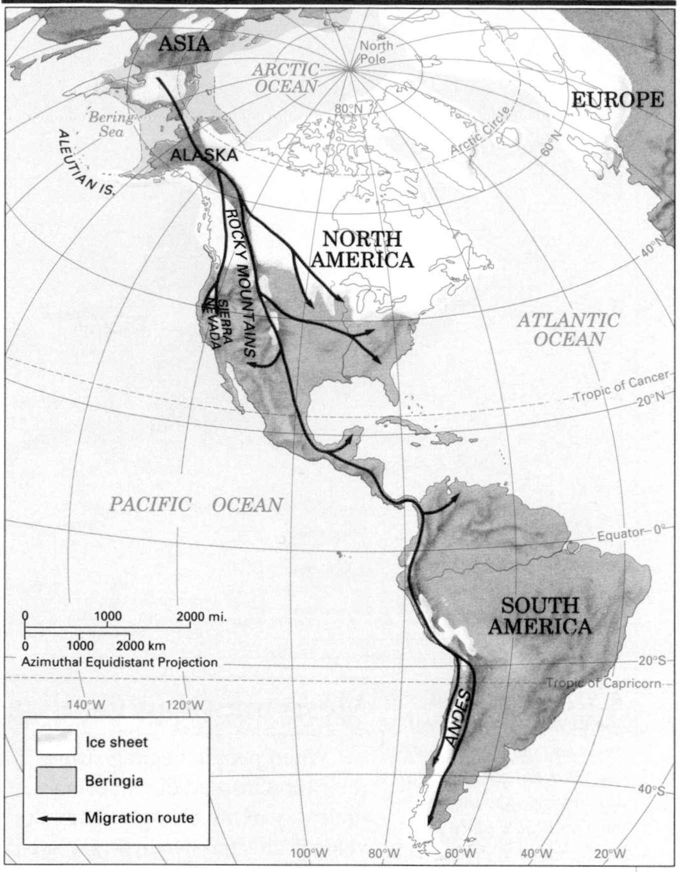

ASIA
North Pole
ARCTIC OCEAN
80°N
EUROPE
Bering Sea
ALEUTIAN IS.
ALASKA
Arctic Circle
60°N
ROCKY MOUNTAINS
NORTH AMERICA
40°N
SIERRA NEVADA
ATLANTIC OCEAN
Tropic of Cancer 20°N
PACIFIC OCEAN
Equator 0°
0 1000 2000 mi.
0 1000 2000 km
Azimuthal Equidistant Projection
SOUTH AMERICA
20°S
Tropic of Capricorn
ANDES
140°W
120°W
Ice sheet
Beringia
Migration route
40°S
100°W
80°W
60°W
40°W
20°W

▲ *Beringia was located in the region of today's Bering Sea, as this route map shows. What became of Beringia? For help in using a route map, see page G12 of the Map and Globe Handbook.*

◄ *Early farmers in Mesoamerica learned to grow such plants as corn, chilies, and peanuts.*

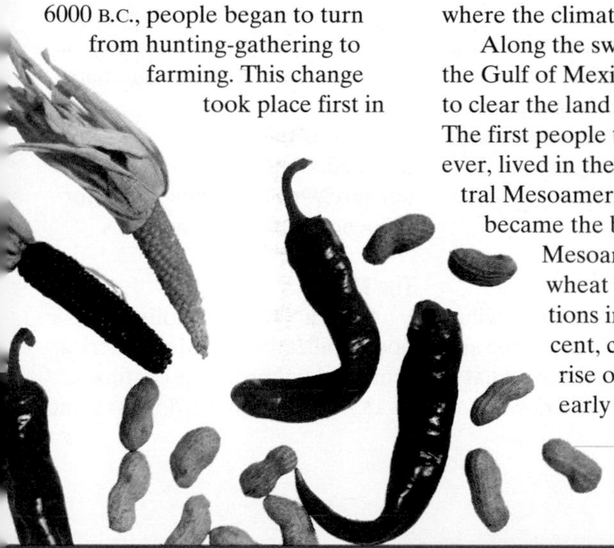

■ *How did people's ways of living change in the Americas?*

DEVELOP

Have students study the map on this page or display Transparency 2, Early Migration to the Americas. Trace with students the different routes people followed. What factors might account for the location of the routes? *(Mountain ranges, location of glaciers)* Page G12 of the Map and Globe Handbook can be used to provide additional practice in using route maps.

Discuss with students why early people migrated. *(To find food, escape enemies)* Point out that the migration from Asia took place over thousands of years and covered enormous distances. As they moved, people had to adapt their culture to new food sources and new environments.

◄ *When the climate had warmed and the glaciers had melted, the sea level rose and covered Beringia. That landmass is now under the Bering Sea.*

■ *The migrants from Asia were hunter-gatherers who lived by hunting, fishing, and gathering foods in the wild. That way of life continued for a long time. Around 7000 B.C. people in Mesoamerica began to farm. Over several centuries the population increased. Later still, cities began to develop.*

Access Strategy

Ask students what they would bury in a time capsule to let people in the future know how people today lived, worked, and entertained themselves. Have each student make a list of five to ten items and then share it with the class. Keep track of these items on the chalkboard to see if common items occur.

Then tell students that because of the moisture and the acidic soil in the area where the Olmec and Maya lived, only a small number of artifacts from their culture have survived. Stone columns and figures could survive these conditions, but articles made of wood, cloth, plant fibers, animal skins, and even bones and shells decayed quickly. Point out that the information gathered by historians from these artifacts is incomplete. For example, religion may have played only a small part in a culture. Yet, if all that remains of the civilization are its religious artifacts, scholars might tend to overemphasize the importance of religion in that culture.

Access Activity

Refer students to the map of Mesoamerican civilizations on the next page. Locate the Olmec and Mayan civilizations. Ask students what they can tell about these geographic regions from the map. *(The regions are within the tropics; several rivers are in the area; they are bordered by the Pacific Ocean, the Gulf of Mexico, and the Caribbean Sea.)*

➤ *Mesoamerica was a favorable location for the development of civilizations because of its climate and environments. The variety of environments and their different products encouraged the growth of trade. The organization and interaction required by trade led to a complex social life and specialization and eventually to the growth of civilization.*

GEOGRAPHY

Critical Thinking

To help students understand the geography of the lands of the Olmec and the Maya, point out that these areas actually contained three main geographic regions: a swampy lowland area south of the Gulf, a mountainous area south of that, and a lowland plain on the Yucatan Peninsula. Tell students that although the entire region is in the tropics, the climate varies. The lowland area south of the Gulf is hot and wet, with rain forests. The climate of the Yucatan is actually dry, with little rain. The mountain climate varies with the elevation.

Ask students to imagine that they live in one of these regions. What special problems does each region offer? *(Swamps: hot and humid, with flooding from rains; dry plain: hot and dry, with water supply limited; mountains: colder, hard to grow crops)*

Mesoamerican Civilizations, 1200 B.C.–A.D. 1521

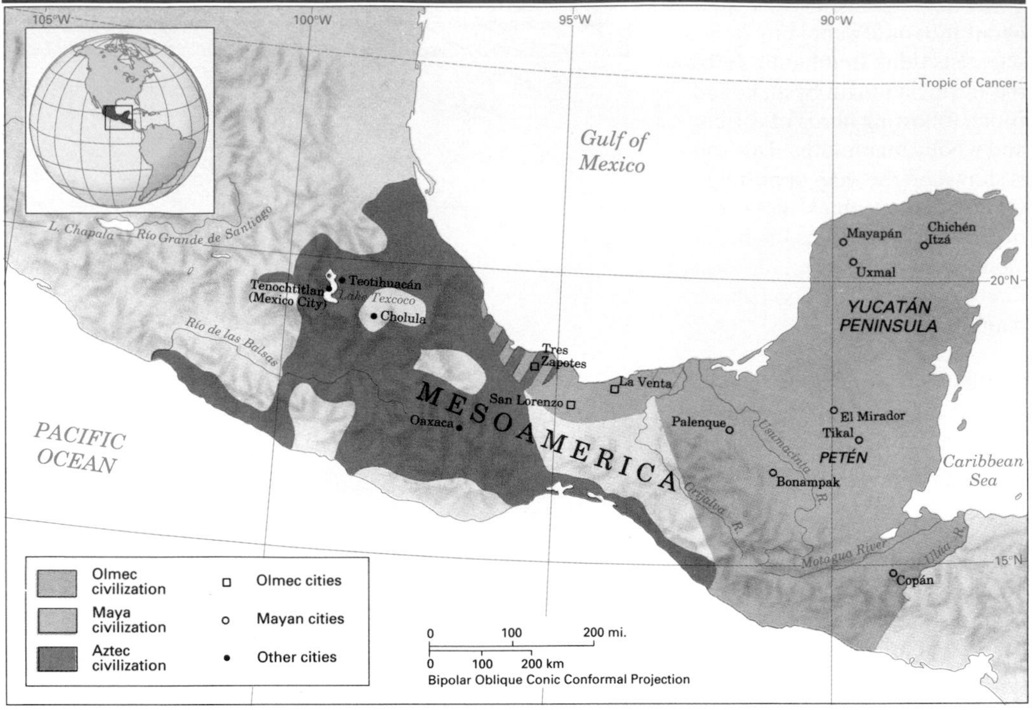
105°W
100°W
95°W
90°W
Tropic of Cancer
Gulf of Mexico
L. Chapala
Rio Grande de Santiago
Tenochtitlan (Mexico City)
Teotihuacán
Lake Texcoco
Cholula
Río de las Balsas
Tres Zapotes
La Venta
San Lorenzo
Oaxaca
MESOAMERICA
PACIFIC OCEAN
Mayapán
Chichén Itzá
Uxmal
20°N
YUCATÁN PENINSULA
Palenque
El Mirador
Tikal
PETÉN
Bonampak
Caribbean Sea
Copán
Motagua River
15°N
Olmec civilization
Maya civilization
Aztec civilization
Olmec cities
Mayan cities
Other cities
0 100 200 mi.
0 100 200 km
Bipolar Oblique Conic Conformal Projection

▲ *This map shows the major Mesoamerican cultures and their cities. Judging from the geography of this region, why might it be a favorable place for civilizations to develop?*

Mesoamerican Civilizations

When people begin growing their food instead of gathering it, their way of life changes. They develop crafts and live in larger settlements. Cities grew slowly in Mesoamerica, but in time they became centers of new civilizations.

The Olmec

The earliest of these civilizations was the Olmec. Its people lived in the **rain forest,** or damp jungle, along the coast of the Gulf of Mexico.

Religion was the driving force of the Olmec and the civilizations that followed. Knowing that their way of life depended on a good harvest, farmers prayed to their Gods. When rain or sunshine failed, people turned to their priests.

The Olmec built large temples where priests held religious ceremonies. Priests also developed the first calendar in the Americas. To record time and events, they used systems of counting and writing in which pictures stood for numbers and ideas.

In time the Olmec civilization declined, though archaeologists are not sure why. It remained a major influence on later civilizations.

The Maya

One of the most highly developed civilizations of Mesoamerica remained unknown for centuries. In 1839, John Lloyd Stephens came

➤ *The Olmec frequently used jade in their carvings. This one, which is part human and part animal, may have been a religious carving.*

Critical Thinking

Archaeological evidence doesn't usually give information about why a civilization has declined. Ask students to suggest possible reasons for the decline of the Olmec civilization. *(Answers will vary, but reasons for decline might include natural disasters, droughts and famine, destruction by another people, or civil war.)*

Science Connection

Scientists date archaeological finds by measuring the amount of carbon 14 they contain; this is called carbon dating. Carbon 14 has a half-life of 5,700 years; in other words, half the carbon 14 in an object will decay over that amount of time. Since carbon is found only in living organisms, such inorganic objects as tools and jewelry cannot be dated using this method. However, shreds of flesh, bone, blood, or plant matter found on or near an arrowhead, for example, can be dated.

Have students create an example of archaeological layering. Using a large glass or clear plastic container, have students freeze a layer of water into ice. Then add materials such as leaves and seeds, add more water, and freeze. Repeat the layering until a number of layers are formed. Then turn the frozen block out of its container and set it in its original position. Ask what the layers would represent to an archaeologist. Which layer would be the oldest and which the most recent?

across an amazing sight as he hacked his way through the rain forests of Central America. Stephens was led by local Maya to the ruins of an ancient city. It would prove to be Copán *(koh PAHN),* a great Mayan city. Stephens later described his feelings about the discovery.

> *The beauty of the sculpture, the solemn stillness of the woods, disturbed only by the scrambling of monkeys and the chattering of parrots, the desolation [loneliness] of the city, and the mystery that hung over it, all created an interest higher, if possible, than I had ever felt among the ruins of the Old World.*
>
> quoted from *Incidents of Travel in Central America, Chiapas, and Yucatán*

The Mayan civilization flourished from about A.D. 250 to 900. The map on page 130 shows its location. For the present-day countries of this region, see the Atlas map on page 686.

▲ *Chichén Itzá, one of the last great Mayan cities, is known for its beautiful temples, such as this Temple of Kukulcán. The detail shows a painting from the Mayan book known as the* Dresden Codex.

Mayan Achievements

Like the Olmec, the Maya built huge religious centers with pyramid temples, palaces, and plazas. Colorful murals adorned the rooms, and sculptures decorated the outside walls. At the height of Mayan civilization, at least 100 cities dotted the region.

By observing the sun and the moon, Mayan priests perfected two calendars. One was a 365-day calendar that kept track of the seasons for planting and harvesting. The other, a 260-day calendar, recorded the times for religious ceremonies.

The Maya also developed a system of numbers that was similar to the Arabic system that we use. In their writing the Maya used hieroglyphics, with symbols standing for ideas. The Maya were great artists, too. Paintings on the walls of their palaces and temples show vivid scenes of their lives.

For many years the meaning of these glyphs remained a mystery. In recent years, however, scholars have translated them. The translations have finally given scholars a written history of the Maya. John Lloyd Stephens had sensed correctly the brilliant and complex civilization that lay within the ruins he saw. ■

■ *What were some of the achievements of the Olmec and the Maya?*

R E V I E W

1. **FOCUS** How did people first come to the Americas?
2. **HISTORY** What different ideas do scientists have about the time when people came to the Americas?
3. **GEOGRAPHY** Why was the Gulf coast a favorable place for a civilization to develop?
4. **CRITICAL THINKING** Raising corn was an important step for Mesoamerica. Why is a surplus of food necessary in order for a civilization to develop?
5. **ACTIVITY** Write a paragraph describing the ruins of Copán as Stephens might have seen them.

HISTORY

Study Skills

Invite an archaeologist from a local museum to speak to the class. Request that artifacts be brought that can be described in terms of their material, place of discovery, age, and significance. Encourage students to ask questions about the work of the museum and the discovery of these particular artifacts.

■ *The Olmec developed ways of farming, a complex religion, a calendar, and a system of counting and writing in pictures. Based in part on Olmec achievements, the Maya went on to develop two calendars based on knowledge of astronomy, a system of numbers similar to ours, a system of writing that used hieroglyphics, and more than 100 cities.*

CLOSE

Draw the Graphic Overview on the chalkboard, and use it to review the main points of the lesson.

Reread the Thinking Focus. Ask students why we know more about the Olmec and Maya than about the earliest Americans. *(There are many more archaeological remains of the Olmec and Maya, and the Maya left written records.)*

Answers to Review Questions

1. The Americas were settled by people who migrated from Asia by way of the Beringia land bridge. Some may have come by an inland route, and others along the coast.
2. Some scientists think that people first came to the Americas about 11,500 years ago, as indicated by the Folsom and Clovis points. Other scientists think that people came to the Americas much earlier.
3. The area was favorable for the development of civilization due to its hot, wet climate. The climate allowed crops to be grown easily.
4. Having a surplus of food allows some individuals to do things other than obtain food every day. While some people produce food, others carry on the activities of religion, government, and trade; develop crafts; and do the heavy work.
5. Answers will vary but may include mention of the ruins of pyramids, temples, palaces, plazas, sculptures, and murals.

Homework Options

Have students create an ad for the proposed Beringian Heritage International Park discussed in Across Time & Space on page 128. Encourage them to consider what season would be best for tourism and what a tourist is likely to see and experience while visiting the park.

Study Guide: page 23

INTRODUCE

Have students turn to the map of Mesoamerican civilizations on page 130. Explain that in this lesson they will be learning about the Aztecs, the last of the Mesoamerican civilizations to exist before Spanish explorers arrived in the early 1500s. Ask students to keep the Thinking Focus in mind as they read. The answer to the question provides insight into the course that Aztec civilization followed.

Key Terms

Vocabulary Strategies: T36–T37

barter—to trade goods or services without the use of money

currency—any form of money used as a basis of exchange

tribute—forced payment in the form of goods, services, or currency made by a conquered people

15,000 | 14,500 | 1000 | 500 | B.C. | A.D. | 500 | 1000 | 1325 1520

LESSON 2

Aztec Civilization

THINKING FOCUS

How did the Aztecs view their place in the world as a whole?

Key Terms

- barter
- currency
- tribute

This jade mask is from Teotihuacan, a great religious center before the rise of Tenochtitlan. The Aztecs borrowed many ideas from Teotihuacan.

Against the waters of Lake Texcoco, the island city gleamed white in the sun. Around it stretched lush green gardens built up on the lake. Wide causeways, or raised earthen roads, linked the city to the mainland. From the hills beyond, a raised channel carried fresh water to the city. A wide dike crossing the lake protected the gardens from the salt waters of the lake. This was Tenochtitlan (*teh nawch TEE tlahn*), capital of the Aztec Empire and center of Aztec life. The Aztecs believed they were the People of the Sun, chosen to carry out the Sun God's work.

The Aztecs loved their city so much that they wrote praises to it in their poetry.

Proud of itself
is the city of Mexico-
Tenochtitlán.
Here no one fears to die in war.
Have this in mind, oh princes,
do not forget it.
Who could conquer Tenochtitlán?
Who could shake the foundations
of heaven?

Cantares Mexicanos

Nearby was the great market center that shared the island with Tenochtitlan. This was Tlatelolco (*tlah teh LOHL koh*). Here, goods from all over the empire were traded. People throughout Mesoamerica came to Tlatelolco. Its huge open-air plaza was the center of everyday life for the people of Tenochtitlan.

The Aztecs

The Aztec people, or Mexica (*mehk SHEE kuh*), were the last to appear in Mesoamerica before the Spanish conquest. When the Aztecs first appeared in the Valley of Mexico in the 1200s, they were a wandering, desperate group. They said of themselves, "... they had no houses, they had no lands, they had no woven capes as clothing ..." What they did have, however, was a belief in their own special destiny. In time, these people were to build their great city and carve out a mighty empire.

Origin of the Aztecs

The Aztecs came to the Valley of Mexico from the northwest. Changes in climate may have forced them to seek better land. When they arrived in the valley, they found the best lands already taken. For a while the Aztecs lived on other people's land, but they were soon forced to move on.

Objectives

1. Trace the Aztec rise to power.
2. Relate the products of the Aztec market to the environment.
3. Explain Aztec religious beliefs and their impact on society.
4. Relate Aztec religious beliefs to the expansion of their empire.

Graphic Overview

Aztecs Seek a Land of Their Own Settle island in Lake Texcoco. → **Island Too Small** Aztecs construct canals and artificial islands. → **Islands Too Marshy to Support Buildings** Aztecs drive huge wooden poles into ground. → **Rebellions by Conquered Peoples** Aztecs use military force to subdue rebels.

In the course of wandering, the Aztecs worked and became soldiers for another group of people. Again, conflicts forced them to flee. They found a home on a small island surrounded by marshes at the western edge of Lake Texcoco.

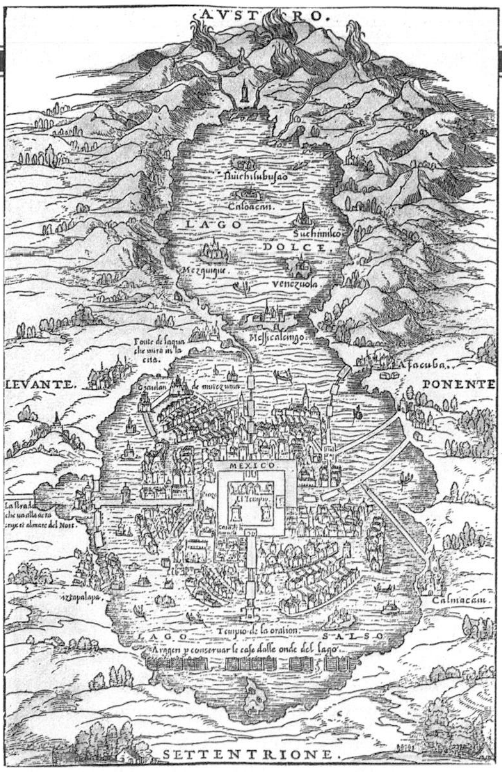

LAGO
DOLCE
LEVANTE.
PONENTE
MEXICO
SETTENTRIONE.

◄ *This map of Tenochtitlan, drawn after the Spanish conquest, shows many details of the city. What features of the city can you identify? What can you tell from the map about the artist's idea of the city?*

Tenochtitlan: The Capital

According to their history, when the Aztecs arrived on their island in 1325, they saw an eagle sitting on a prickly pear cactus and holding a snake in its beak. To the Aztec priests, this was a sign that they should build their capital here. They called the site Tenochtitlan, Place of the Prickly Pear Cactus on a Rock.

First, the Aztecs set out to enlarge their small island. In shallow areas along the shore of the island, they cut canals through the marshes. Between the canals they heaped up a mass of weeds to form solid islands. On top of the weeds, they layered mud brought up from the bottom of the lake. On these islands, called *chinampas (chih NAM pahs),* farmers could grow at least two crops each year. With a stable food supply, the population grew. The time had now come for the Aztecs to enlarge and improve their city.

The Aztecs became highly skilled in engineering. They built causeways for roads; raised channels to carry fresh water; and dikes, or earthen banks, to keep the salt water of the lake out of their gardens. They also enlarged the city itself.

Building a city is difficult at best. For the Aztecs, it posed special problems. To keep buildings from sinking into the soft, marshy land, workers had to drive huge wooden poles into the ground for support. Because no building materials existed on the island, everything had to be brought there. The Aztecs, however, had neither wheeled vehicles nor large animals to pull them. Instead, they depended on human power, along with boats, for transporting goods. They also lacked metal tools.

In the central part of the city, the Aztecs built a great plaza, the main ceremonial center of the city. Facing the plaza was the Great Temple, which was built on top of a pyramid that rose to a height of about 97 feet. A number of other temples also faced the plaza. Beyond the temples were the palace of the ruler, the homes of the nobles, and many of the government buildings. Farther out were the houses of the common people.

DEVELOP

Tell students that the Aztecs solved many problems in building their civilization and expanding their empire. However, they failed to solve one crucial problem. They could not win the loyalty of the people they conquered. Tell students that failing to solve this problem would contribute to the downfall of Aztec civilization.

◄ *Features include roads, waterways, bridges, temples, castles, and other buildings. The map shows the city as well-organized, surrounded by water, and well-defended. A templelike structure can be seen in the middle, with the rest of the city built around it.*

BELIEF SYSTEMS

Critical Thinking

Ask students how the Aztecs' belief that they were chosen to carry out their God's work might have influenced them. *(This belief may have encouraged the Aztecs to build a great city; to make sacrifices for the good of the community; to live a proper life; to accept a highly organized society; and to expand the empire by conquering their neighbors.)*

Access Strategy

Have students look at the photos, illustrations, and charts in this lesson to see what they show about the Aztecs. For example, on the next page they see a stone sculpture of an Aztec porter carrying corn. This figure reveals that the Aztecs knew how to carve stone. The sculpture also provides evidence that the Aztecs were farmers and were able to grow corn. It suggests that goods were transported by human labor. Other photographs and illustrations offer information about Aztec rituals, architecture, jewelry, city life, economics, and natural resources.

Access Activity

Ask students to study the map of Tenochtitlan on this page. How is the role of religion in Aztec life revealed by the plan of the city? *(The temple is in the middle, suggesting that it was the focus of the entire city and its people.)* Would students expect religious leaders or political leaders to be more powerful in Aztec society? *(Religious leaders)*

ECONOMICS

Critical Thinking

Explain to students the differences between an economy based on bartering and one based on the use of currency. Have students hypothesize about the advantages and disadvantages of a barter economy. Why did people begin to use currency instead of barter? *(Currency makes trade easier and more efficient.)* Point out that barter may be appropriate at one stage of economic development, whereas currency may be more suitable at another. However, barter remains a valid method in situations such as the exchange of services within a neighborhood.

■ *Trade was important because it served as a binding force that kept the empire not only wealthy and powerful, but united. The market of Tlatelolco was the economic center of the Aztec Empire. Here people from all classes of society came to barter, visit, and share news. Thus, the market had both an economic and a social function.*

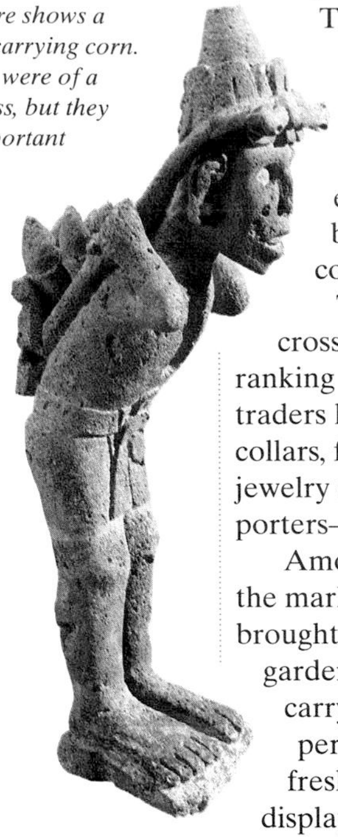

This Aztec stone sculpture shows a porter carrying corn. Porters were of a low class, but they did important work.

Tlatelolco: The Market

In the northern part of the capital lay the great market of Tlatelolco. It was the main crossroads for trade in the Aztec Empire. Here all kinds of goods were at hand—fruits and vegetables, cooking pots, brooms, herbs, jewels, and colored feathers.

The market was also a crossroads for people. High-ranking nobles, priests, merchants, traders leading slaves harnessed in collars, feather workers, farmers, jewelry makers, potters, and porters—all visited the market.

Among those selling goods in the market were women who brought produce from their own gardens. People came by canoe, carrying their tomatoes, peppers, squash, and fruit, all fresh from the *chinampas.* They displayed these wares in baskets in one section of the market.

Many products in the market differed according to the region that produced them. From the steaming coastal plains came cotton, vanilla, and cacao beans, used to make chocolate. Milder lowland areas grew fruits of all kinds, as well as tomatoes, avocados, and peppers. The Gulf coast and inland salt lakes produced salt, a major item of trade. From highland forests came wood for fire and for building.

The goods that traders brought to the market also differed from region to region and even from village to village. Workers in the old city of Teotihuacan *(teh uh tee WAH kahn)* fashioned knives and spearheads from obsidian, a black volcanic glass. In Xochimilco *(soh chee MEEL koh)* highly skilled workers made jewelry and small figures from jade. Feather workers created gleaming and colorful shields, headdresses, and fans.

The Aztecs did much of their buying and selling by **barter,** the exchange of one item for another without the use of money. At times they did use some forms of money. Cacao beans were the most common form of **currency,** or money. The Aztecs also used gold dust and cotton cloaks as currency.

Markets and Trade

The market at Tlatelolco was held every day of the week. The fifth day, the last day of the Aztec week, was by far the busiest. On this day, 40,000 to 50,000 people met to barter, visit, and share news.

Though Tenochtitlan had the largest market in the empire, every community held a market on a regular basis. These smaller markets were held just once every five days. They offered mostly food and household items, though at times they also had luxury goods.

Luxury items came from many different sources. To get these goods, merchants traveled along ancient trade routes. One route led to the Pacific coast. There merchants traded for shells, turquoise, and jade. Another route led south to Guatemala. There merchants traded for precious stones, cacao, and feathers of parrots, macaws, and quetzal *(KEHT zuhl)* birds. ■

Rates of exchange were important to the Aztecs. Because cacao beans were rare and precious, they could be used as money.

■ *Why was trade important to the Aztecs?*

Aztec Exchange Rates, c. 1525

1 Cotton cloak = 100 Cacao beans

Item	Price
Dugout canoe	1 Cotton cloak
Gold lip-plug	25 Cotton cloaks
Feather cloak	100 Cotton cloaks
String of jade beads	600 Cotton cloaks

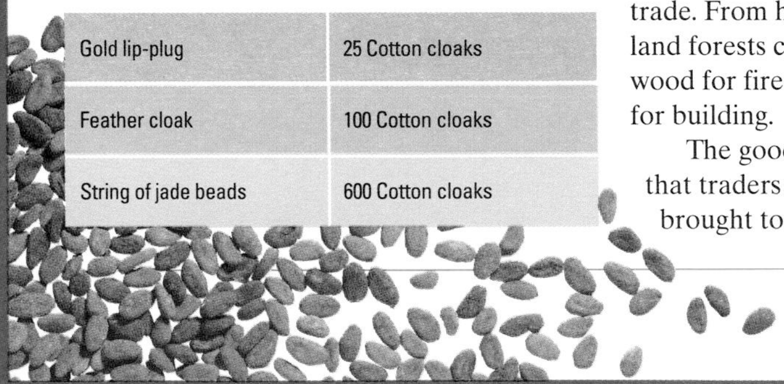

Social Participation

Divide the class into several small groups. Explain that the variety of goods in the market reflects some of the occupations of Aztec workers. Ask the groups to list some of these occupations and the goods they produced. *(Different professions include: farmers, artisans, merchants, traders, feather workers, jewelry makers, potters, porters, and woodcutters.)*

Collaborative Learning

Have small groups of students work together to develop a written rate of exchange for goods and services that students could barter among themselves. Choose one member of the group to write the ideas down. Each member of the group should contribute ideas through brainstorming. The group will need to come to a consensus about the final list. Examples might be three erasers for one pencil or pen, or one carton of milk in exchange for returning a book to the library.

Cultural Context

To provide further information about Aztec culture, explain that the Aztec language was Nahuatl *(NAH waht uhl).* It provides insight into Aztec society and values. For example, children were usually called "beloved children." Nahuatl has given us such words as *avocado, tomato, chocolate, tamale,* and *chili.* Today, about a million Mexicans of Aztec ancestry continue to speak that language with few changes.

The Aztec Way of Life

In Aztec society each person had a particular role. Nobles served as judges, rulers of cities, and generals in the army. Priests carried out religious duties. Merchants brought goods from distant markets. Skilled artisans made luxury items, and the common people farmed, fished, hunted, and made items for everyday use. Together, the different classes formed an orderly, highly organized society united by its beliefs.

Religion

Like the other peoples of Mesoamerica, the Aztecs were very religious. Many of their daily activities included religious rituals, or ceremonies. Their beliefs influenced their economy, their way of governing, and their ways of waging war.

The Aztecs believed that the God of the sun and war, Huitzilopochtli *(hweets y loh PAWCH tlee),* was in a constant fight with the forces of darkness. For the God to remain strong and continue his struggle, the Aztecs believed that he and the other Gods needed regular sacrifices that included human blood. At the dedication of Tenochtitlan's Great Temple in 1487, Aztec priests may have sacrificed thousands of captives.

The Aztecs also believed that fate influenced each person's life. The date of one's birth, for example, influenced the course of one's whole life—and even one's death. It was important to choose the best possible day for naming an infant, planting crops, or crowning a ruler. This focus on time explains in part the importance of calendars for the Aztecs. The Aztecs also believed in omens, or signs that told the future. Such omens might be found in the call of birds or the way that certain animals acted.

Because they believed in fate, the Aztecs did not always fear or

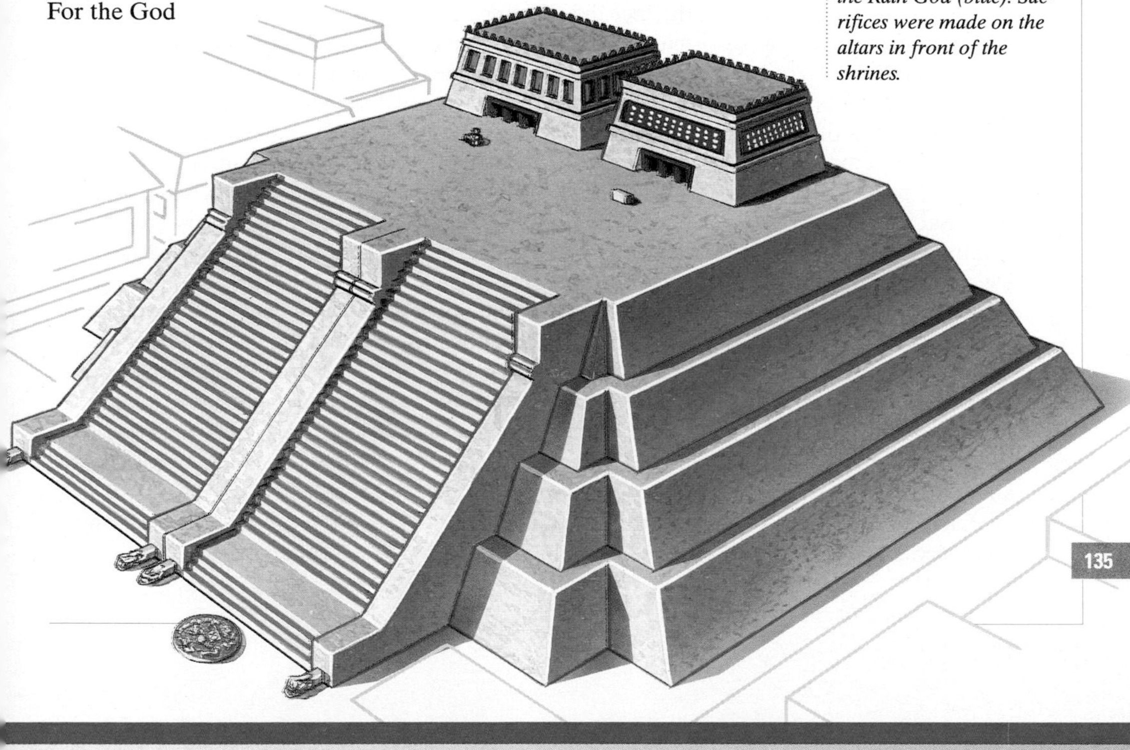

The Great Temple of Tenochtitlan was sacred to Huitzilopochtli, the Aztec God of the sun and war. This is an artist's idea of how the temple may have looked. Priests climbed the double staircase leading to the shrines for Huitzilopochtli (red) and Tlaloc, the Rain God (blue). Sacrifices were made on the altars in front of the shrines.

BELIEF SYSTEMS

Critical Thinking

To help students understand Aztec religious beliefs, explain that the concept of sacrifice was very important to the Aztecs. One kind was human sacrifice, which involved victims captured in war. Another kind was self-sacrifice, done through the letting of blood— for example, by pricking a finger. Have students consider the extent to which the Aztec practice of sacrifice influenced the course of their civilization. *(It kept individuals subordinate to the religion and the state. It also led to the expansion of the empire as more and more captives were needed. The practice created ill will toward the Aztecs among the people they conquered.)*

Geographic Context

To give students a clearer understanding of the importance of Tenochtitlan, tell them that it covered more than five square miles on the island and on built-up land in Lake Texcoco. The population in 1519 was about 200,000 people, perhaps the largest in any Mesoamerican city at that time. Today, Mexico City stands where Tenochtitlan was located. Lake Texcoco no longer exists; the Spaniards drained it to provide more room for settlement.

Social Context

To aid students' understanding of Aztec society, explain that at the top of the social pyramid was the Aztec ruler. By the late 1400s, he was not only regarded as a mere human but also as a living God. No ordinary person could touch him or look at him. The ruler was always chosen from the same family and was usually the brother or son of his predecessor. He usually lived in luxury in a huge palace. A civil and military council advised the ruler on matters of state and war.

Visual Learning

Have students look carefully at the illustration of the Aztec temple on this page. Ask them to suggest some of the skills, technologies, and types of knowledge a society would need in order to build such a structure. *(Answers will include mathematics, engineering, stone cutting, measuring, architecture, transporting materials, and coordinating the activities of large groups of laborers.)*

SOCIAL SYSTEMS

Critical Thinking

Ask students to list the advantages and disadvantages of living in a society in which classes are strictly ordered and defined. *(Students might list advantages as stability and peace; disadvantages include the rigidity of the system and the lack of upward mobility and choice. Eventually a rigid class system might lead to conflict within the society.)*

HISTORY

Critical Thinking

Would the Aztec Empire have fallen even if the Spaniards had not arrived? Ask students to argue this question, pro and con. *(Answers will vary but should mention the hostility felt toward the Aztecs by conquered peoples. Students should also consider the extent to which Aztec culture penetrated into other cultures, so that the cultures became more alike.)*

This scene from the Aztec Codex Mendoza *shows stages in the life of a warrior. The stages begin with taking the first captive and end with becoming a general.*

resist death. To be sacrificed to the Gods was in fact an honor. At times rulers even sacrificed members of their own families. All Aztecs viewed such actions as a sacred part of their religion.

Aztec Society

The Aztec way of life was an orderly one. Each level of society was divided into several groups. The highest-ranking nobles ruled large city-states. Lesser nobles ruled smaller cities and towns or served as judges or generals in the army. Between the nobles and the commoners were the traveling merchants and the most highly skilled artisans.

Each class lived by strict rules of conduct. For example, the rules

Understanding Empire

During the two centuries from about 1300 to 1520, the Aztecs built the last great empire in Mesoamerica. At the same time, the Inca in South America built a huge Andean empire, also the last of its kind. In the space of a few years, both empires fell under the threat of another entirely alien empire—the Spanish Empire.

What is an empire? An empire is a political unit in which one powerful state rules over others. Large in area, empires usually include peoples with both similar and different cultures. Differences may include language, customs, religion, and ways of life.

Once a people such as the Aztecs build an empire, they must decide how to govern it. This control can take different forms. Sometimes the ruling state keeps direct control over the lives of the conquered peoples, as the Inca did. The Inca demanded that conquered peoples adopt their language, customs, religion, and way of life. You will read about the Inca in the next lesson.

The Aztecs, however, did not try to interfere with the language and local customs of the peoples they conquered. They did not set out to control local governments. Instead, they appointed Aztec governors and tax collectors. They also placed soldiers in key locations to ensure control over the area. The Aztecs allowed local rulers to remain in office as long as regular payments of taxes were made to the Aztecs.

The collecting of tribute—a tax paid by conquered peoples, to the conquerors—is another feature of an empire. The new rulers may demand that tribute payments be made on a regular basis, as the Aztecs did, or only as the empire needs it.

The Aztecs and the Inca built empires every bit as real as the empires of the Persians, Romans, and other ancient peoples you will read about in this book. They all conquered other states, extended their control over a large area, and demanded tribute from the peoples they ruled. However, they also risked causing hatred among the conquered peoples.

Critical Thinking

Discuss how the Aztecs treated the people they conquered. What were the advantages and disadvantages of this system? *(Possible advantages for the Aztecs: the system brought wealth through tribute and provided captives for sacrifices. Possible disadvantages: the system caused loss of life and resentment toward the Aztecs among conquered peoples.)*

Language Arts Connection

On the board write this poem about one Aztec God:

He mocks us.
As he wishes, so he wills.
He places us in the palm of his hand,
He rolls us about;
Like pebbles we roll, we spin. . . .
We make him laugh,
He mocks us.

Have students speculate on the meaning of the poem. How did the Aztecs see their relationship to this God? How did they feel about their place in the world as humans?

Writing

Have students choose one class of Aztec society and write a paragraph describing life as a member of that class. Students should review their text and also read more about Aztec life in library books. The paragraphs may be written as a diary entry or as a letter to a friend.

told what kind of clothing people could wear. Only nobles of the highest rank could wear expensive cotton cloaks. Everyone in Aztec society was expected to lead a proper life. Parents taught their children to be honest, to respect authority, and to work hard.

Literature and the Arts

The Aztecs adopted some of their customs and ideas from other peoples in Mesoamerica. They took many of their religious beliefs and art from different groups. Even the calendar was borrowed from other peoples. However, the Aztecs changed these crafts and ideas to make them their own. You have seen the great city they planned and built. They were also skilled sculptors who made fine stone carvings and figures of turquoise and jade. As poets, they wrote beautiful verses that often expressed a sense of sadness. ■

■ *How did religion influence Aztec life?*

■ *Religion influenced the daily activities, the economy, the method of governing, and the way of waging war of the Aztec.*

A Powerful Empire

The Aztecs began their conquests in the name of their Sun and War God Huitzilopochtli. They expanded their rule, first over nearby cities and then over regions beyond the Valley of Mexico. In time, their city-state became an empire. Their goal was in part religious—to gain captives to sacrifice. They also sought wealth.

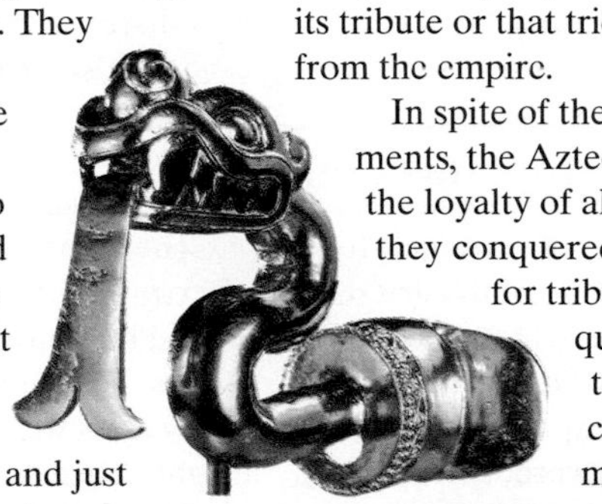

At its height the Aztec Empire included about 400 to 500 small states and perhaps as many as 15 million people. It reached from the Pacific Ocean to the Gulf of Mexico and just into present-day Guatemala.

From conquered peoples, the Aztecs collected **tribute,** payment in the form of goods, services, or currency. Tribute had to be paid regularly and when demanded. The Aztecs sent officials to each conquered province to collect the payments. If a province rebelled, the Aztecs doubled the amount to be paid. Thus, the Aztecs held their empire together by force. They sent troops to any city that failed to send its tribute or that tried to escape from the empire.

In spite of their achievements, the Aztecs failed to win the loyalty of all of the people they conquered. The demand for tribute and the quest for captives to sacrifice caused resentment and anger among many of the conquered groups. When the time came, these conquered peoples would be eager to join the Spaniards in defeating the Aztec Empire. ■

How Do We Know?

HISTORY *One source of information about the Mesoamericans is their record books. Each book is known as a codex. These codices tell about important events and customs. The Aztecs made hundreds of codices, but only a few remain. The* Codex Mendoza *was made by Aztec artists after the Spanish conquest.*

◄ *Aztec rulers and nobles sometimes wore gold lip plugs as jewelry to show their high status.*

■ *Why did the Aztecs seek to create an empire?*

■ *The Aztecs believed they were chosen to rule over other peoples. In the name of the Sun God, they began a series of conquests. The establishment of the empire was due in large part to their religious beliefs. The Aztecs believed their Gods needed human blood to sustain them. Thus, people sacrificed prisoners taken in combat.*

REVIEW

1. **FOCUS** How did the Aztecs view their place in the world as a whole?
2. **SOCIAL SYSTEMS** What problems did the Aztecs face in building the city of Tenochtitlan?
3. **BELIEF SYSTEMS** How did the Aztecs look upon fate?
4. **CRITICAL THINKING** The Aztecs had worked very hard to establish their own nation. Why then did they set out to conquer neighboring cities?
5. **ACTIVITY** Draw a picture showing some of the people in the market at Tlatelolco.

CLOSE

Draw on the chalkboard two of the problem and solution boxes from the Graphic Overview on page 132. Then ask students to work in small groups to find other examples of problems the Aztecs faced and the solutions they applied. Add these suggestions to the chart. Then ask students to reread the Thinking Focus and to answer it.

Answers to Review Questions

1. The Aztecs believed they were the People of the Sun. To keep their Gods strong required regular human sacrifices.
2. Because Tenochtitlan was located on a marshy island, the Aztecs had to drive wooden poles into the soft ground to make a firm base. The island had no building materials, so everything had to be brought in. Because the Aztecs had neither wheeled vehicles nor draft animals, goods were moved by boat or human power.
3. The Aztecs thought fate influenced each person's life. They did not fear death, although they did not welcome it. Sacrifice was considered an honor.
4. The Aztecs believed that the Sun God was in a constant fight with the forces of darkness and that the Sun God needed human blood to keep up his strength. Therefore, they sought captives to use as sacrifices.
5. Pictures should show some of the people in the market as well as some of the goods.

Homework Options

Ask students to imagine that they are among the first Europeans to encounter the Aztecs. Have them write a letter to a friend or relative describing their impressions of either Aztec civilization or the city of Tenochtitlan.

Study Guide: page 24

INTRODUCE

Refer students to the maps of North and South America on pages 686–687. Review the location of Mesoamerica there. Tell students that at the same time that the Olmec, Maya, and Aztec cultures were thriving in Mesoamerica, other civilizations existed in what is now Peru. Have students locate the Andean region on the map on the next page. Read the Thinking Focus and ask students to speculate on reasons why water was so important. Tell them that the Andean cultures, which will be discussed in this lesson, were as wealthy, technically advanced, and politically powerful as Mesoamerican cultures. At the same time, they were unique in many ways.

Key Terms

Vocabulary Strategies: T36–T37

elevation—the height of land above sea level

distribution—the way goods and resources are divided and distributed

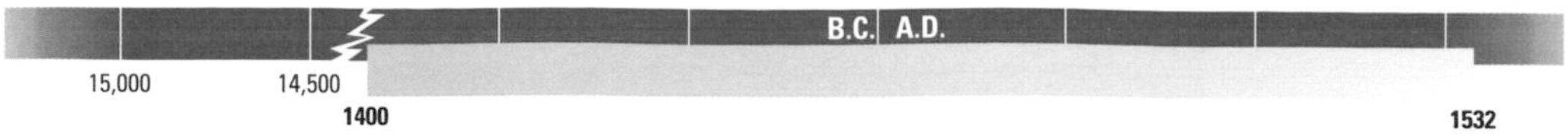
B.C. A.D.
15,000
14,500
1400
1532

L E S S O N 3

Andean Civilizations

THINKING FOCUS

Why was water such an important resource to Andean peoples?

Key Terms

- elevation
- distribution

A second center of early American civilization arose on the west coast of South America. Until recent years, the best-known people of this region were the Inca. They lived in the high Andes of Peru at about the same time as the Aztecs in Mesoamerica. Archaeologists wondered if earlier peoples might have existed in the region. Might earlier peoples—like the Olmec and the Maya in Mesoamerica—have built civilizations in this region before the Inca?

Archaeologists have learned in the past 20 years that such civilizations did indeed exist. In fact the earliest of these cultures arose a thousand years before the Olmec. In their harsh desert and mountain environments, Andean peoples built unique civilizations.

How could people live in such a harsh land? What were special features of their cultures? Archaeologists are still finding answers to these questions. Each year brings new discoveries about these earliest South American civilizations.

Environments and Cultures

Peru is a land of extremes. Its coastal desert—one of the driest on the earth—stretches for 1,500 miles along the Pacific Ocean. Few rivers cross this great expanse. Inland, the Andes reach skyward, their peaks covered with snow.

Six to ten peaks of the Peruvian Andes rise to more than 20,000 feet. Even the passes are high. The pass for crossing the mountains east of Cuzco is above 16,000 feet.

The climate of Peru is also one of extremes. The coastal desert is cooled by winds off the cold ocean waters. The climate in the mountains varies with **elevation,** or height above sea level.

The earliest Andean cultures arose on the coast. Archaeologists have found that the peoples here, unlike the farmers of Egypt and Mesopotamia, lived mainly on fish. In time these Andean peoples learned to grow plants along the rivers.

For the early Andean peoples, the lack of fresh water was a problem. With almost no rain in their desert home, they had to seek other sources. Because of their

Objectives

1. Relate the rise of Andean civilizations to the environment.
2. Identify the Inca and the main characteristics of their way of life.
3. Explain the distribution of resources and labor in the Inca empire.

Graphic Overview

ANDEAN ENVIRONMENT
Shortage of Fresh Water
Desert on Long Coastline
Extremely High Mountains

elevations, the peaks of the Andes are covered with snow and deep-frozen glaciers. As these melt in spring and summer, rivers of runoff fall down the slopes and cross the desert. These rivers dry up for months each year, however. To keep a good supply of water, the early Andean peoples built storage ponds and irrigation canals to hold the runoff.

In the coastal settlements, the first signs of civilization appeared.

Here people built huge buildings and pyramids made of stone. Some of these structures may date back to the time of the pyramids in ancient Egypt. Other peoples settled on the altiplano, the high plateau. There they built canals, terraces, temples, and storehouses.

Andean Civilizations, 2500 B.C.–A.D. 1532

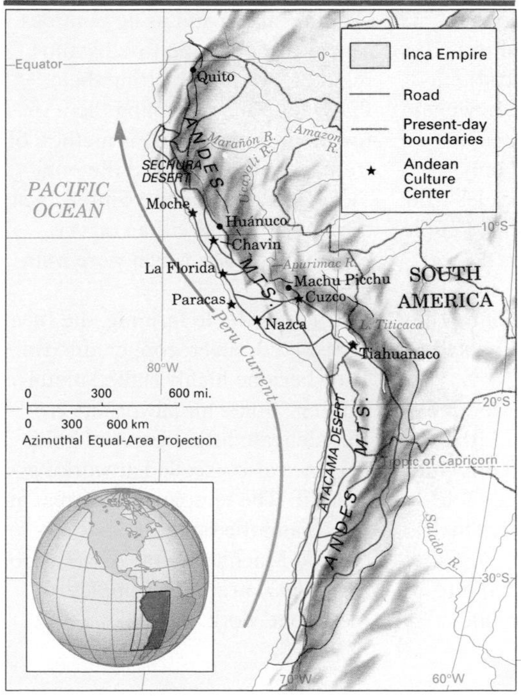
Inca Empire
Road
Present-day boundaries
Andean Culture Center
Equator
0°
Quito
ANDES
Marañón R.
Amazon R.
Ucayali R.
SECHURA DESERT
PACIFIC OCEAN
Moche
Huánuco
Chavín
10°S
La Florida
Apurimac R.
Machu Picchu
Cuzco
SOUTH AMERICA
Paracas
Nazca
L. Titicaca
Tiahuanaco
Peru Current
MTS.
80°W
0 300 600 mi.
0 300 600 km
Azimuthal Equal-Area Projection
20°S
ATACAMA DESERT
Tropic of Capricorn
Salado R.
30°S
70°W
60°W

The Chavín

In time a new culture, the Chavín *(chah VEEN),* appeared and spread across northern Peru. Chavín civilization reached its height between 1000 B.C. and 200 B.C. Chavín de Huantar, with its great temple, was the main center.

The Chavín culture is known for its stone carvings and its pottery and weaving. It borrowed some of its ideas and designs from earlier cultures, and it remained the base for later Andean civilizations.

The Moche

Another civilization that arose in Peru was the Moche *(MOH cheh).* It flourished from A.D. 100 to 800. The Moche culture was known for its pottery, wall paintings, and beautiful cotton and wool cloth.

Moche culture gained new fame in 1987. In that year, archaeologists discovered tombs of Moche rulers. The tombs were filled with gold and copper ornaments set with jewels. The finds showed that the Moche were among the greatest artists of the ancient world.

The Moche traded far and wide. Jewels came from present-day Chile, jaguar skins and feathers from the Amazon rain forests, and shells and gems from present-day Ecuador and Colombia. These riches were used in the temples and in tombs. ■

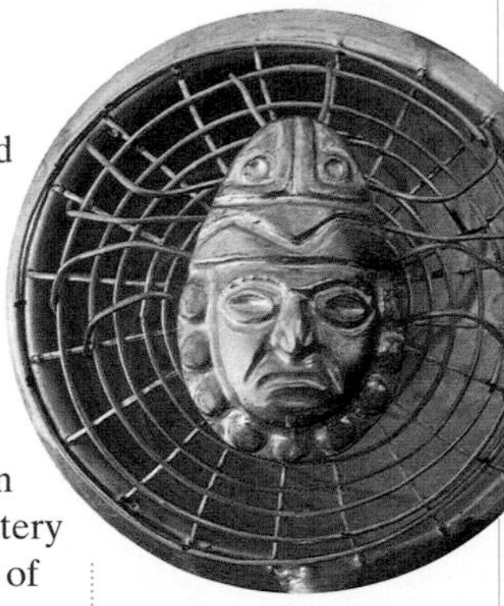

▲ *The Moche were highly skilled at working in gold. Here a gold spider, shown above and opposite, rests in its golden web. Notice that the artist has shown the spider with a human face.*

◄ *Deserts and mountains separated the early Andean peoples into many small settlements. Later, regional cultures appeared. What centers of these cultures appear on the map?*

■ *What knowledge have archaeologists recently gained about Andean cultures?*

DEVELOP

Tell students that this lesson describes the ancient peoples of the Andes and explains how they built great civilizations amid the harsh deserts and steep mountains of western South America. Ask students to list some of the problems people experience living in desert and mountain environments. *(Answers should include limited water supply, difficulty in growing food, and transportation problems.)*

GEOGRAPHY

Study Skills

Have students make a drawing of the different sources of water that the Andean people depended on. Use this activity to start a discussion of the importance of water and water conservation in this region.

◄ *Regional cultural centers include La Florida, Chavín, Paracas, Moche, Nazca, Tiahuanaco, and Cuzco.*

■ *Archaeologists have found that a number of major Andean cultures existed before the Inca. The earliest of these cultures arose a thousand years before the Olmec. It began on the coastal plain. Its people lived mainly from the sea.*

Access Strategy

Have students analyze the photographs on pages 127 (Machu Picchu), 138 (mountain peaks), and 141 (mountain trail). What kind of land surface appears in all of the photos? *(Mountains)* Now have students use the map on this page to confirm their answer. Tell students that the Andes have a number of peaks that are higher than Mount McKinley, the highest peak in North America. Discuss with students what problems people would have living in such an environment. On the map on this page, point out the large rivers that run from south to north between the mountains. The effect of this is that travelers going from west to east must cross three or four parallel mountain ranges and large rivers. One reason why Machu Picchu remained hidden for so long is its location above cliffs and between two deep river valleys.

Access Activity

After students have studied the map on this page, ask them the following question: Why do you think the Inca expanded their empire mainly north and south rather than east and west? *(The Andes blocked eastward expansion; river valleys and mountain ranges run mainly north and south.)*

GEOGRAPHY

Study Skills

Ask students to read on this page how the Inca used their natural resources. Have students take notes as they read. Then have them complete a chart listing natural resources in the first column and the uses for each resource in the second column. *(Resources: potatoes [food], llamas and alpacas [food, wool, means of transport]; gold, silver, copper, and tin [mainly sculpture and decorative uses]; stone [buildings])*

■ *The power to rule belonged to the Inca—the emperor and the nobles who were members of his family. As the Son of the Sun, he was worshiped almost as a god. All activities of the empire, such as farming, mining, weaving, and constructing buildings and roads, were done in his name. Gold was his special property.*

The Inca

A number of outstanding cultures arose after the Moche. The last and greatest of these was the Inca. Like the Aztecs, the Inca began as a small, struggling group and were latecomers to their region. In about A.D. 1200, they moved into the valley near Cuzco. Also like the Aztecs, the Inca saw themselves as a chosen people. They borrowed many ideas from earlier cultures. Often, however, they destroyed the remains of those cultures or took credit for the cultures' achievements.

▲ *Andean artists excelled at weaving cloth. This weaving, part of a sleeve, is from the north coast before the Inca conquest. It is made of wool from a llama or an alpaca and cotton. Andean peoples valued decorative fabrics.*

Inca Rule

Today, the term *Inca,* which means "sun," is applied to all the people of this culture. To the Inca themselves, however, the term referred only to the emperor and to the nobles who were members of his family. People believed that the Inca was descended directly from the sun. They called him the Son of the Sun. They worshiped not only the sun itself but also the Inca.

The Inca had total power. He made all the main decisions that affected his people. He also directed the use of land and wealth. Gold—"the sweat of the sun"—was his special property.

Inca society was divided into separate classes, but everyone worked for the Inca. The men of the villages worked in the fields. They also worked on roads, terraces, canals, and temples. Some served in the army, mined gold and silver, or served as runners who carried messages over the royal roads. Women, too, worked for both family and state. They spun and wove wool for clothing for the Inca, the members of his court, and the soldiers. Women also prepared food for the soldiers and the men working on state projects.

■ *What was the emperor's role in Inca society?*

A Rural Way of Life

The Incan way of life was centered on the land. Farming was the main occupation. Inca farmers built canals, terraces, and storage ponds, and raised a variety of crops. People raised llamas and alpacas at higher elevations. Inca artists used the wool to weave beautiful cloth.

Inca farmers developed special ways of raising and using potatoes. They preserved potatoes by allowing them to freeze, letting them thaw, and then trampling them to force out the water. This method of freeze-drying preserved the potatoes for use during the winter. Inca farmers grew more than 60 varieties of potatoes, which were a staple food.

In addition to farming, the Inca mined gold, silver, copper, and tin. They became highly skilled metalworkers. Some metalworkers created delicate little figures of gold. The Inca also excelled at working in stone. The temple and fortress at Cuzco and the buildings and terraces at Machu Picchu *(MAH choo PEE choo)* are fine examples of Inca stone work. ■

Critical Thinking

Tell students the Inca forced conquered peoples to adopt their language. Ask students to list the ways a common language might have promoted unity within the Inca Empire. *(Government officials could communicate with the leaders of subject peoples; members of the army could understand their superiors and each other.)*

Social Context

To help students understand the structure of Inca society, explain that it was made up of clans called *ayllus.* Members of each *ayllu* believed that they were descended from a common ancestor. The descendants of Inca rulers formed the royal *ayllus* in Cuzco. They held the most important posts in the government and the religious hierarchy, which were handed down to their sons after they died. Those who belonged to lesser nobility included members of the Inca peoples surrounding Cuzco and chieftains of conquered peoples.

The nobility enjoyed numerous rights and privileges. Cuzco nobles wore earplugs as symbols of their position. Only they could wear fine clothing and gold and silver jewelry. Only children of the nobility went to school. They studied Inca religion, law, history, poetry, music, and astrology. Nobles were punished less severely than the ordinary citizen for the same crime.

A CLOSER LOOK

Inca Highways

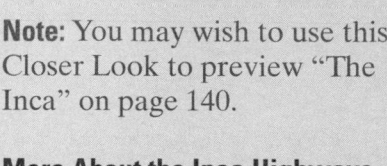

Rivers, mountains, jungles, and deserts once separated the peoples of western South America. When the Inca built a great network of stone roads, they connected many groups and created an empire. The roads covered more than 10,000 miles. Inca runners sprinted along them to relay messages. In five days a message could travel the length of present-day Peru.

Foods of the Inca included potatoes, maize, beans, chili peppers, and sun-dried meats.

A *quipu* was like an adding machine made of strings. The Inca tied knots in the strings to count llamas, gold, or the foods they sent to villages in need.

Roadside shelters were spaced about a day's journey apart. Here, weary travelers could find food or safely rest.

Steep steps climbed into mountainous regions. Suspension bridges crossed deep gorges and streams.

Note: You may wish to use this Closer Look to preview "The Inca" on page 140.

More About the Inca Highways
Roads like the one shown on this page were used only for government business, which included trade as well as administration. Roads were carefully designed to handle the kind of traffic using them, such as pedestrians or llamas. Minor roads were barely three feet wide, while major thoroughfares could be as wide as fifty feet across. The two principal Inca highways ran from north to south. One ran along the coast; the second followed the Andean range, connecting the cities of Quito and Cuzco.

HISTORY

Critical Thinking

Point out to students that the Inca roads amazed the Spaniards who arrived in the 1500s. The Inca highways were adapted to more varied terrains than those in Europe at the time. Ask students how these same roads that united the Inca Empire may have helped bring the empire down. *(The roads made travel easier for the Spaniards, enabling them to conquer the Inca Empire all the more easily.)*

Writing a Journal Entry

Ask students to imagine what it was like to be a messenger along an Inca highway. Ask them to write a journal or diary entry about a typical day. Encourage students to write a detailed entry and to try to capture some of the excitement and challenges of the job.

Research

Students might research other methods of communication within the Inca Empire, such as the Quechua language and the use of *quipus* for keeping records. Have students use the card catalog in their local library to find sources of information.

Visual Learning

Have students study the images on this page. Use the Inca Highways feature to start a discussion on the difficulty of ruling a territory as large as the Inca Empire and of carrying on trade. Discuss how roads may have helped solve these problems.

■ *The Inca state controlled the distribution of goods. Resources were distributed according to need.*

CLOSE

Refer students back to the Graphic Overview on page 138 and note the three environmental factors shown there. Remind students that the Andean environment differed greatly from the river valley environments where the civilizations of Egypt, Mesopotamia, India, and China had developed. Ask how each of the factors in the Graphic Overview influenced the development of Andean civilizations. Have students begin with the Thinking Focus, which relates to the first factor in the Overview, and to continue with the other two factors. *(Shortage of fresh water: people built irrigation canals, dams, and ponds to conserve water. Desert on long coastline: people at first got their food from the sea; later they farmed, using irrigation. Extremely high mountains with steep slopes: people adapted their use of land and resources to the elevation; terraced slopes to gain farmland.)*

A Widespread Empire

In 1438 Pachacuti *(pah chah KOO tee)*, the ninth Inca emperor, set out to unite the peoples of the Andean region into one powerful empire. In less than 90 years, he and the rulers after him spread their control over about 12 million people. The empire stretched for nearly 2,500 miles.

The Inca imposed their government, law, religion, and language on each group they conquered. They allowed local officials to keep their positions as long as they remained loyal to the emperor. If local groups resisted, the Inca sometimes moved whole villages to the Inca homeland. The empty rebel villages were filled with loyal Inca subjects, who would teach Inca ways.

Soon after a conquest, officials took a census, or count of the people, of the region. They divided the fields into three parts: one for the Gods, one for the Inca, and one for the members of the community.

Unlike the Aztec method of exchanging goods through markets, the Inca state set the **distribution,** or handing out, of goods. It divided the resources and distributed them according to need.

The Inca way of life was highly organized with the Inca himself as the center of power. However, if some misfortune happened to the Inca, who would be in command? Later, even before the Spaniards arrived, the empire had been weakened by disease and war. ■

➤ *The people of Peru still celebrate the Inca pageant called Inti Raymi. Held annually on June 24, it honors the sun.*

■ *How were goods distributed in Inca society?*

R E V I E W

1. **FOCUS** Why was water such an important resource to Andean peoples?
2. **HISTORY** How did a recent discovery gain fame for the Moche?
3. **CULTURE** How did the Inca impose their culture on conquered peoples?
4. **CRITICAL THINKING** Empires always risk the danger of revolt. Why do you think Andean peoples were less likely than Mesoamericans to resist their rulers?
5. **ACTIVITY** A number of cultures besides the Chavín, Moche, and Inca developed in Peru. Look back at the centers of these cultures on the map on page 139. Then prepare a report on one of these early Andean cultures.

Homework Options

Ask students to imagine that they live in the Inca Empire. They might imagine that they are a villager who has been conquered by the Inca, an Inca noble, a road builder, a farmer, a weaver, or a homemaker. Have them write an account describing daily life from that person's perspective.

Study Guide: page 25

Answers to Review Questions

1. In the Andean region, the coastal area was mostly desert. Water from melting snows in the mountains was seasonal.
2. Recently archaeologists discovered Moche tombs filled with gold and copper ornaments set with jewels. The finds show that the Moche were great artists.
3. The Inca made conquered peoples accept their government, law, religion, and language.
4. The Inca system of rule gave security to conquered peoples, so long as they conformed to Inca demands. The price was the gradual loss of their culture. The Aztec system of empire provided no such security because conquered peoples had to pay heavy tribute and captives were used for sacrifice. However, groups were able to retain their own cultures.
5. Students should prepare a report on one of the following cultures: La Florida, Paracas, Nazca, or Tiahuanaco.

UNDERSTANDING EVIDENCE

Identifying Main Ideas

Here's Why

When you read, you need to determine what the writer wants you to understand. Identifying the main idea is the key to getting the most out of anything you read. For example, if you were asked to tell someone what you read in Lesson 3 about the Inca Empire, you would need to use this skill.

Here's How

The main idea of a paragraph is often stated in the topic sentence. This sentence, which is usually the first or last sentence, tells what the paragraph is about. The other sentences of the paragraph provide facts and details that support the main idea.

The main idea of a large section of a lesson may be found in a topic paragraph. Like a topic sentence, a topic paragraph tells you the main idea of the section. The other paragraphs in the section build on and support the topic paragraph.

Look at the summary of the Lesson 3 section, The Inca (box). In this example, a topic paragraph begins the passage. As you can tell from the green highlighting, the paragraph asks why the Inca were successful. Supporting details, highlighted in blue, explain what led to the Inca's success in creating a great civilization.

The main idea of a passage is not always stated in a topic paragraph. For example, if the passage did not include the first paragraph, you would need to look at the rest of the passage for a common idea or ideas. You would study the supporting details to determine the unstated main idea.

Look at the passage. Blue highlights the part of each sentence that tells about some major accomplishment of the Inca. When you determine what these sentences have in common, you can come up with the main idea of the section.

Try It

Turn to page 142 and reread the section called A Widespread Empire. Write the main idea of that section on your paper. Now list several supporting facts or details that reinforce the main idea.

Apply It

Find a magazine article about a topic that interests you. Read the article to get an idea of its content. Then identify the topic sentence or the topic paragraph of the article. Describe how the other sentences or paragraphs in the article support the main idea.

The Inca

The last and greatest of the Andean civilizations was that of the Inca. They began as a small, struggling group but built a vast empire. What factors led to their success?

The Inca people believed their ruler, the Inca, was descended from the sun. Thus, he was not only an emperor but also a God to be worshiped. As ruler, he oversaw the distribution of land, resources, and food. The state also carried on public projects such as building irrigation works and highways. Everyone owed service to the state. Though the Inca demanded much from the people, he also took care of them in time of need.

The Inca way of life was based mainly on farming. Men of the villages worked on the land and on public projects. At high elevations they raised llamas and alpacas. The Inca people also mined valuable minerals such as gold, silver, and copper. Besides caring for their families, Inca women wove cloth and prepared food for the state.

The Inca culture supported many craftworkers, such as metal workers and weavers of beautiful fabrics. Their work shows the accomplishments of the Inca culture.

UNDERSTANDING EVIDENCE

This skills feature teaches students how to identify the main idea in paragraphs and in longer written pieces.

POLITICAL SYSTEMS

Critical Thinking

The Inca Empire dictated every facet of daily life for its subjects, even to the cleanliness of peasant huts. Everyone was expected to work; for example, the blind were given jobs picking seeds from cotton bolls or husking corn. However, anyone who could not work was cared for: a mine worker who was sick was sent home immediately. Most people were not allowed to own anything beyond personal possessions and lived at a basic level of survival.

Ask students to discuss the advantages and disadvantages of such a government. Would they choose to live in that kind of system? Why or why not? In what ways, if any, would they prefer it to other systems?

Answers to Try It

The main idea of the section is: The Inca developed a large and powerful empire. Supporting details include: after 1438, Inca rulers spread their control over 12 million people; the empire stretched for nearly 2,500 miles; rulers imposed Inca cultures on conquered peoples; a census was taken after each conquest; resources were distributed according to need; the Inca ruler was the center of power.

Answer to Apply It

Check to see that students have correctly identified the main idea of the article as well as the correct supporting details. You may want to have students share their articles in small groups.

Objective

Identify main ideas and supporting details in paragraphs. (Study Skills 2)

Chapter Review

Reviewing Key Terms

barter (p.134)
currency (p.134)
distribution (p.142)
diversity (p.129)
elevation (p.138)
glacier (p.128)
rain forest (p.130)
tribute (p.137)

A. Read each pair of words. Write a sentence telling how the words in each pair are related.

1. rain forest, diversity
2. barter, currency
3. glacier, elevation

B. Each statement below contains a key term from the chapter. Decide whether each statement is correct or incorrect. Give reasons to support your decision using information in the chapter.

1. When glaciers covered much of Asia and North America, people could not travel from one continent to the other.
2. The tribute that conquered peoples paid to the Aztecs helped to unify the empire.
3. People in the Inca Empire were well cared for in times of need because the ruler controlled the distribution of goods.
4. The diversity of plant and animal life in Mesoamerica led to the growth of markets.

Exploring Concepts

A. Most empires have certain traits in common. These are listed on the chart below. Copy and complete the chart. Write one or more sentences telling how the Aztec Empire illustrated each trait.

Common Traits of Empires	Examples from Aztec Empire
Rule by a powerful state over lesser, conquered states	
A system for ruling the conquered states	
The taking of tribute or payments from conquered peoples	goods, services, or currency often taken by force

B. Answer each question with information from the chapter.

1. Why are recent discoveries in Canada, Brazil, and New Mexico important to archaeologists?
2. Why did priests have a high rank in Mesoamerican societies?
3. In what ways did the earliest Andean civilization differ from Olmec civilization in Mesoamerica?
4. What basic technologies did Mesoamerican and Andean peoples lack when they built their huge projects?
5. On what kinds of resources and materials did the people of Mesoamerica and the Andes rely most? Why might they have valued these things?
6. How were the Aztec and Inca civilizations alike? How were they different?
7. What special methods of farming did the Aztecs and the Inca use?
8. How were Andean peoples able to live and thrive in their difficult environment?

Answers to Reviewing Key Terms

A. Sample answers:

1. A wide **diversity** of plant and animal life can be found in **rain forests** in the tropics.
2. Although the Aztecs did use some forms of **currency,** they did most of their buying and selling by **barter,** the exchange of one item for another.
3. Many rivers in Peru have their sources in **glaciers,** large masses of ice that are found in the higher **elevations** of the Andes.

B. Answers:

1. The statement is not correct. Because **glaciers** trapped so much water, sea levels fell, exposing a land bridge between Asia and North America.
2. The statement is not correct. The **tribute** that Aztecs collected caused much resentment among conquered peoples.
3. The statement is correct. Because the state controlled the **distribution** of goods, it could apportion according to needs.
4. The statement is correct. Because Mesoamerica had a **diversity** of plant and animal life, a variety of goods was available.

Answers to Exploring Concepts

A. Sample answers to Examples from Aztec Empire:

1. The Aztecs conquered neighboring states and then more distant ones.
2. The Aztecs did not interfere with local customs or government. They appointed Aztec governors and tax collectors and placed soldiers in conquered lands.
3. Goods, services, or currency were often taken by force.

B. Sample answers:

1. These discoveries indicate that people may have come to the Americas much earlier than archaeologists once thought.
2. To ensure a good crop, people turned to the priests, who were believed to be the link to the Gods.
3. The earliest Andean civilization differed from the Olmec in its basic food—fish; its time—a thousand years before the Olmec; and its environment—a desert, not a rain forest.
4. Aztec engineers had neither wheeled vehicles nor draft animals. Inca engineers also lacked wheeled vehicles and draft animals except the llama.
5. Both societies valued corn and other agricultural and natural resources. Mesoamericans treasured materials such as jade. Andean peoples valued textiles. They valued gold as a material for religious and decorative uses.
6. Both the Aztecs and the Inca were latecomers to their region. Both believed they were a chosen people, borrowed from earlier cultures, and established an empire. They were different in their methods of ruling their empires and in the way goods were distributed.
7. The Aztecs used *chinampas*. The Inca terraced steep mountainsides, developed large irrigation systems, and adapted crops to elevation.
8. To get water for crops, they built irrigation canals. They raised crops suited to their varied climates. At high elevations, they raised grazing animals such as the llama. To gain farm lands on steep slopes, they built terraces.

Reviewing Skills

1. Turn to pages 130–131 and reread the section called Mesoamerican Civilizations. Write the main idea of that section on your paper. Then list as many supporting facts or details as you can find that reinforce the main idea.
2. Look at the picture from the *Codex Mendoza* on page 136 and read the caption. What does the picture show? What does it tell you about Aztec civilization?
3. Imagine you are an archaeologist who has just discovered an ancient city in the Peruvian desert. What questions will you try to answer about your find? In what ways might it change people's thinking about early Andean cultures?

Using Critical Thinking

1. Sir Isaac Newton once wrote, "If I have seen further [than other men] it is by standing on the shoulders of Giants." What do you think he meant by that statement? Do you think the same could be said of the Aztec and the Inca civilizations? Explain your answer.
2. Although the Aztecs and the Inca borrowed many ideas from earlier cultures, they often destroyed elements of those cultures. What do you think accounts for this action?
3. Although at times they used currency, the Aztecs did much of their buying and selling by barter. In your opinion, why is barter rarely used today?
4. The cultures that flourished in Mesoamerica and in the Andes are known for their art work, literature, buildings, monuments, and feats of engineering. What do you think people a thousand years from now will consider outstanding about U.S. culture today? Explain your answer.

Preparing for Citizenship

1. **WRITING ACTIVITY** The Aztecs and the Inca conquered and ruled other peoples. If you were a member of a conquered group, in which empire would you have preferred to live? Write an essay to answer this question, including the reasons for your choice.
2. **COLLECTING INFORMATION** Archaeologists find, record, and interpret various forms of evidence about life long ago. Your community also has a past. What evidence exists about earlier inhabitants? You could interview older residents; research photographs, maps, and books; or study the buildings and land to obtain information about earlier times in your community. Share your information with the class.
3. **GROUP ACTIVITY** The Inca built highways to aid the movement of people and goods to distant parts of their empire. The same needs for transportation exist today. Working in small groups, study the various forms of transportation in your state or community. What different types are there? What special purposes does each serve? What routes or places does it connect? Share your findings with the class.
4. **COLLABORATIVE LEARNING** The products that Aztec farmers and artisans brought to market differed from region to region. Working in small groups, prepare a display of food products, from different parts of the United States and from other countries, that are available in your area. Have several students collect products from different regions and countries. Have others locate, on a map of the United States or the world, the regions and countries from which each item comes. Other students might write a brief description of each product and the way it is used. Group members should then decide together how to present the findings to the class.

Answers to Reviewing Skills

1. The main idea of the section is that Mesoamerica became the scene of major civilizations. The Olmec developed the first one in the rain forests along the Gulf of Mexico. They developed farming and built places of worship that became centers of population. Their civilization became the base for later ones, such as the Maya and Aztecs. The Maya created a brilliant civilization that included great paintings, sculptures, architecture, and a written language. The Aztecs later built their great center of religion and government at Tenochtitlan. They went on to conquer an empire.
2. It shows the stages of a warrior's career and indicates the Aztecs' concern with military life.
3. You will try to answer such questions as: What people built this city? When did they live? What were some special features of the city, such as temples, storehouses, palaces, and homes of different classes? How did people live and get their food?

Answers to Using Critical Thinking

1. Newton's discoveries depended on the work of scientists who came before him. The achievements of a civilization are built upon the achievements of civilizations that precede it.
2. Some students may suggest that when empires are established by force, the cultures of the conquered peoples are ruined in warfare. Other students may suggest that the destruction of a culture is deliberate.
3. Most students will suggest that barter is rarely used in modern societies because it is a cumbersome method of exchanging goods.
4. Answers will probably range from democratic traditions and laws to skyscrapers, space exploration, achievements in science and industry, rock music, musical comedies, television, and so forth.

Answers to Preparing for Citizenship

1. **WRITING ACTIVITY** Discuss the form of an essay with students. Encourage students to state their choice clearly and to present facts and details to support it.
2. **COLLECTING INFORMATION** Students may need help in identifying older residents to interview, using the local library, and photographing historic buildings, monuments, businesses, and public buildings.
3. **GROUP ACTIVITY** Brainstorm with students to develop a list of the kinds of transportation available in their community. Make highway maps, bus and train schedules, and other types of information available in class. Also make chart paper or graph paper available for preparing displays.
4. **COLLABORATIVE LEARNING** Discuss with students where they can procure products—for example, supermarkets, delicatessens, open-air stands, and their own homes. Supermarkets often have signs or labels identifying the country of origin. Encourage students to bring products that are special to their own cultures.

UNIT PREVIEW

Show students the area around the Mediterranean Sea and the Southwest Asia on a large world map. Ask them to suggest how customs, beliefs, and other aspects of culture might have traveled between Southwest Asia and Italy and Greece in Europe. (*Traveled across the Mediterranean Sea.*)

Read the text paragraph aloud and ask students if they can identify some ideas that began in this part of the world. In this unit they will study the origins of two great religions—Christianity and Islam—as well as the sources of many basic ideas of modern culture.

Looking Back

In Unit 2 students learned about cultures in Asia, Africa, and the Americas.

Looking Forward

Students will be studying three distinct regions in the next three chapters:

Chapter 7 *The Mediterranean World*
Chapter 8 *The Arabian Peninsula*
Chapter 9 *Iran*

Unit 3

The Mediterranean and Southwest Asia

The lands around the Mediterranean Sea have been the birthplace of powerful ideas about government, learning, and the arts that still influence people today. From the eastern Mediterranean and nearby Southwest Asia came three great world religions—Judaism, Christianity, and Islam. Some ideas were spread by force, perhaps by mighty armies like this Roman cavalry. Other ideas spread through trade, or simply through their appeal to the human spirit.

B.C.

... of column honoring ... Antoninus Pius, Roman ... –161

BIBLIOGRAPHY

Books for Students

Caselli, Giovanni. *The Roman Empire and the Dark Ages.* New York: Bedrick, 1985. Re-creation of the history of Rome from objects used by the people. Nonfiction.

Coolidge, Olivia. *The Golden Days of Greece.* New York: Crowell, 1968. Descriptions of everyday life in Athens and Sparta. Nonfiction.

Husain, Akbar. *The Revolution in Iran.* Vero Beach, Fla.: Rourke, 1988. Depiction of events that led to the Shah's downfall and the revolution in Iran. Nonfiction.

Tames, Richard. *The Muslim World.* Morristown: Silver Burdett, 1983. An introduction to Islam and its role in the world. Nonfiction.

Books to Read Aloud

Colum, Padraic. *The Children's Homer: The Adventures of Odysseus and the Tale of Troy.* New York: Collier's, 1982. A retelling of the story of Odysseus by the Irish poet. Fiction.

McVitty, Walter. *Ali Baba and the Forty Thieves.* New York: Abrams, 1989. Illustrated retelling of a famous Arabian Nights tale from the Golden Age of Muslim culture. Fiction.

Today

Understanding the Photograph

The carved relief shows Roman soldiers of a cavalry legion engaged in various soldierly tasks. Ask students to study the men's faces and to describe what kind of people they seem to be. Point out the standards carried by the soldiers in the center, and explain that these were the symbols of the different legions, or fighting units.

Understanding Chronology

This unit covers a long time span, from 1500 B.C. to the present. Be sure to have students note the chapter timelines to see the chronological relationships between the cultures of Greece, Rome, the Arabian Peninsula, and Iran. You may want to keep an ongoing parallel timeline on the chalkboard during your study of the unit.

Other Resources

Books for Teachers

Dekmejian, Hrair. *Islam in Revolution: Fundamentalism in the Arab World.* Syracuse: Syracuse University Press, 1985. History of the fundamentalist movement in Islam. Nonfiction.

Lane Fox, Robin. *Pagans and Christians.* New York: Knopf, 1987. An account of the transition of Rome from pagan to Christian. Nonfiction.

Software

Ancient Rome. Teach Yourself Computer Software, Inc., 1986. A two-disk tutorial with 24 pictures covering topics such as food, games, dress, books, and buildings.

Iraq Stack. Techware Corp., 1991. A hypercard stack that allows students to deal with issues related to the Gulf War.

Houghton Mifflin Social Studies

Bookshelf

McLean, Mollie, and Anne Wiseman. *Adventures of the Greek Heroes.* Boston: Houghton Mifflin, 1989. Stories of Greek heroes such as Hercules and Theseus come alive in this illustrated volume.

INTRODUCE

The name *Mediterranean* comes from two Latin words: *medius,* "middle," and *terra,* "land." Have students read the unit title and the text on this page. Explain that many early cultures, such as China's, believed that their culture was at the center, or middle, of the world.

Point out the photograph of the statue of the Greek charioteer and mention that the Olympics are just one example of the long-lasting influence of the Mediterranean region. Have students suggest any other examples they know of Roman or Greek influences. *(Architecture, myths, law)*

Note the photograph of the Southwest Asian landscape. As it shows, much of Southwest Asia is very dry. The Arabian Desert alone stretches for 900,000 square miles. In this region the ancient Persians built a mighty empire. As students have read, Judaism originated in Southwest Asia; as they will learn in this unit, two other great religions began here later. Have students consider how people developed cultures in such a dry environment. *(Nomadic lifestyles, crops that require little rain, irrigation projects)*

Unit 3 Overview

The Mediterranean and Southwest Asia

The Olympic Games were first held in Olympia, Greece, in 776 B.C. Early events included chariot racing. This statue of a charioteer is from the Greek city of Delphi.

The Mediterranean and Southwest Asia lie at the meeting point of three great continents—Africa, Asia, and Europe. Many ancient traditions began in this region and then spread throughout these continents and beyond.

Greece and Italy reach far into the Mediterranean Sea. The ancient Greeks used the sea for trade and expansion of power. In their turn, the Romans conquered the Greeks. Then they went on to build a mighty empire. Much of Roman culture, however, copied Greek arts, religion, literature, and science.

The effects of these ancient cultures are still in evidence today. Greek-style buildings are found in many modern cities. Some of today's governments are built on Roman ideas of law and citizenship. Three world religions—Judaism, Christianity, and Islam—spread quickly outward from Southwest Asia. These religions remain major forces in the lives of peoples around the world.

Much of Southwest Asia has a desert climate. These olive trees and other plants grow near the few areas that have water.

Objectives

1. Identify three ancient empires that held power in the Mediterranean and Southwest Asia.
2. Describe the components of a Mediterranean climate.
3. Understand that three major world religions began in this region.

Economic Context

Although petroleum in the Arabian Desert had been known about for centuries, it wasn't considered a significantly useful resource until the 20th century. Oil was found in Saudi Arabia and Kuwait in 1938 and in Iran in 1908. In 1992 this area produced about 13 million barrels of oil a day. Saudi Arabia, Iran, Iraq, Kuwait, Oman, Qatar, and the United Arab Emirates hold more than half of the known oil reserves in the world.

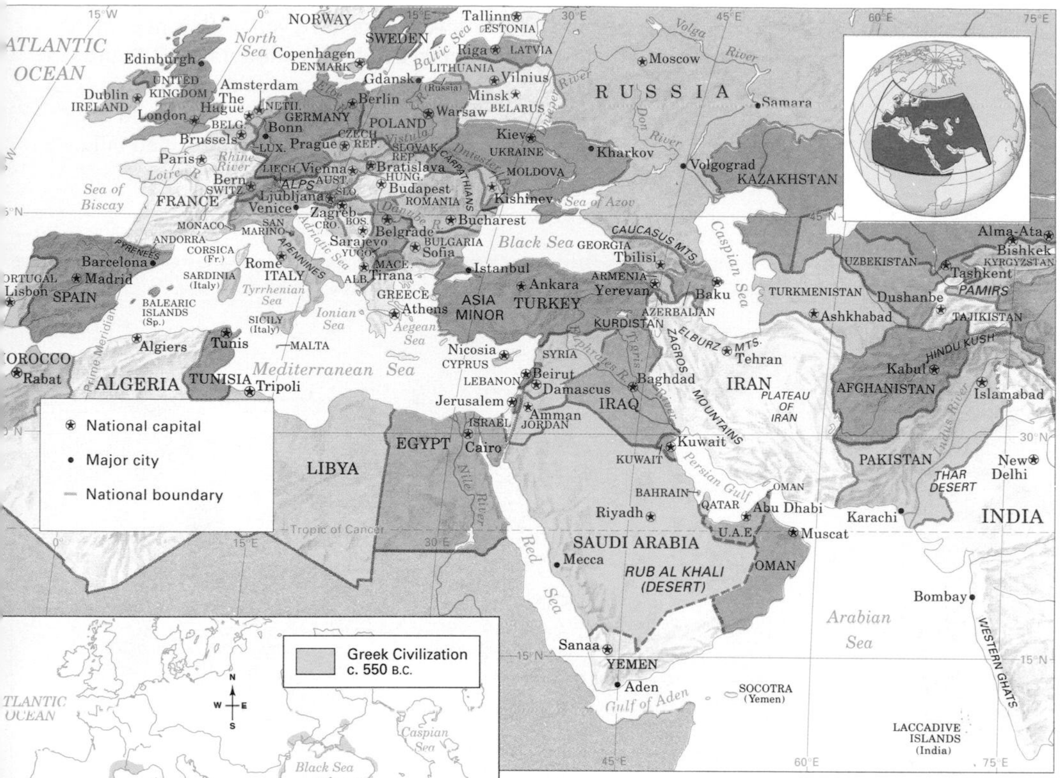
National capital
Major city
National boundary
ATLANTIC OCEAN
NORWAY
SWEDEN
North Sea
Baltic Sea
Edinburgh
UNITED KINGDOM
IRELAND
Dublin
London
Copenhagen
DENMARK
Amsterdam
The Hague
NETH.
Brussels
BELG.
LUX.
Paris
FRANCE
Sea of Biscay
Bonn
GERMANY
Berlin
Prague
CZECH REP.
POLAND
Warsaw
Gdansk
(Russia)
LITHUANIA
Vilnius
Minsk
BELARUS
Riga
LATVIA
Tallinn
ESTONIA
Moscow
RUSSIA
Samara
Volga River
Don River
Kiev
UKRAINE
Kharkov
Volgograd
KAZAKHSTAN
MOLDOVA
Kishinev
Sea of Azov
Vienna
AUST.
Bratislava
SLOVAK REP.
Budapest
HUNG.
ROMANIA
Bucharest
Bern
SWITZ.
LIECH.
ALPS
Ljubljana
SLO.
Zagreb
CRO.
BOS.
Sarajevo
Belgrade
YUGO.
Venice
MONACO
SAN MARINO
ANDORRA
PYRENEES
Barcelona
Madrid
SPAIN
PORTUGAL
Lisbon
CORSICA (Fr.)
SARDINIA (Italy)
BALEARIC ISLANDS (Sp.)
Rome
ITALY
APENNINES
Tyrrhenian Sea
Adriatic Sea
SICILY (Italy)
Ionian Sea
MALTA
MACE.
Tirana
ALB.
GREECE
Athens
Aegean Sea
BULGARIA
Sofia
Istanbul
Black Sea
Ankara
ASIA MINOR
TURKEY
GEORGIA
Tbilisi
CAUCASUS MTS.
ARMENIA
Yerevan
AZERBAIJAN
Baku
Caspian Sea
KURDISTAN
Nicosia
CYPRUS
SYRIA
LEBANON
Beirut
Damascus
Jerusalem
ISRAEL
Amman
JORDAN
IRAQ
Baghdad
Euphrates R.
Tigris R.
ZAGROS MOUNTAINS
ELBURZ MTS.
Tehran
IRAN
PLATEAU OF IRAN
TURKMENISTAN
Ashkhabad
UZBEKISTAN
Tashkent
Dushanbe
TAJIKISTAN
PAMIRS
Alma-Ata
Bishkek
KYRGYZSTAN
HINDU KUSH
Kabul
AFGHANISTAN
Islamabad
Indus River
PAKISTAN
THAR DESERT
New Delhi
INDIA
Karachi
Bombay
WESTERN GHATS
Arabian Sea
LACCADIVE ISLANDS (India)
MOROCCO
Rabat
Algiers
ALGERIA
Tunis
TUNISIA
Tripoli
Mediterranean Sea
LIBYA
EGYPT
Cairo
Nile River
Tropic of Cancer
Red Sea
Kuwait
KUWAIT
Persian Gulf
BAHRAIN
QATAR
Abu Dhabi
U.A.E.
Muscat
OMAN
Riyadh
SAUDI ARABIA
Mecca
RUB AL KHALI (DESERT)
Sanaa
YEMEN
Aden
Gulf of Aden
SOCOTRA (Yemen)
15°W
0°
15°E
30°E
45°E
60°E
75°E
45°N
30°N
15°N

The map above shows modern Europe and Southwest Asia.

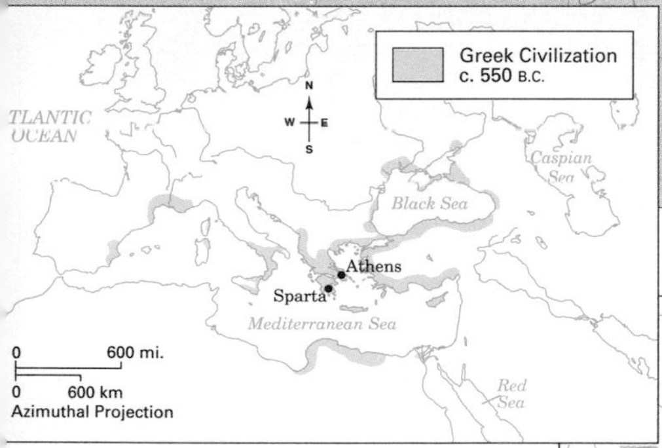
Greek Civilization c. 550 B.C.
N
W
E
S
ATLANTIC OCEAN
Caspian Sea
Black Sea
Athens
Sparta
Mediterranean Sea
Red Sea
0
600 mi.
0
600 km
Azimuthal Projection

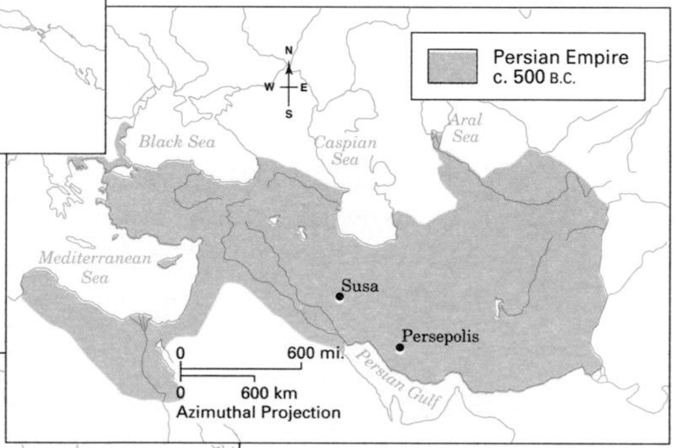
Persian Empire c. 500 B.C.
N
W
E
S
Aral Sea
Black Sea
Caspian Sea
Mediterranean Sea
Susa
Persepolis
Persian Gulf
0
600 mi.
0
600 km
Azimuthal Projection

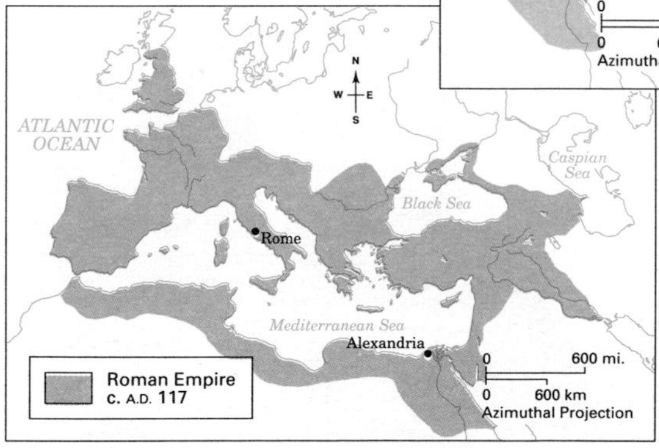
N
W
E
S
ATLANTIC OCEAN
Caspian Sea
Black Sea
Rome
Mediterranean Sea
Alexandria
Roman Empire c. A.D. 117
0
600 mi.
0
600 km
Azimuthal Projection

The ancient empires of Greece (above left), Persia (above), and Rome (left) stretched for thousands of miles across two geographic regions—the Mediterranean and Southwest Asia.

Learning from Maps

Have students compare the maps of the three ancient empires with the modern map of this region. Ask for volunteers to locate the countries that, had they existed hundreds of years ago, would have been part of each empire. Then ask them which empire appears to extend farthest east on the maps *(Persian Empire);* which stretches farthest west *(Roman Empire);* and which civilization was earliest in time *(Greek).*

Have students compare the map of the Persian Empire with the modern map to identify the modern country where Persepolis was located. *(Iran)* Tell students that the countries of Southwest Asia, also called the Middle East, have often been a battleground. In ancient times they were a land bridge connecting Asia, Africa, and Europe. Today they are politically volatile mainly because of their oil reserves.

149

Historical Context

The Olympic Games began in Greece probably at least 3,000 years ago. Although the first recorded festival was held in 776 B.C., historians believe that the games were perhaps 500 years old by that time. Just as they are now, the games were held every four years. The Olympic Games held such an important place in Greek life that time was measured by the interval between them, called an Olympiad.

In A.D. 394, the Olympic Games were abolished by the Roman Emperor Theodosius I. Then in 1887, a French nobleman, Baron Pierre de Coubertin, thought of reviving the games. Nine years later, in 1896, the first modern Olympic Games were held in Athens, Greece.

Map and Globe Skills

Have students use the map scales to estimate how far the Mediterranean Sea stretches from east to the west. *(About 2,500 miles or 4,000 kilometers)* Remind students that a *strait* is a narrow passage of water between two bodies of land. Ask students to find the Strait of Gibraltar and the Bosporus (strait separating Europe from Asia).

LOOK AND RESPOND

Have students scan the images on these two pages. List their observations and impressions on the chalkboard.

Learning from the Graphics

Ask students to look at the bar graph and tell which city has the most rain *(Rome)* and which the least *(Riyadh)*. Have students find Athens, Rome, Tehran, and Riyadh on the political map on page 149. Then ask them to use that map and the climate map on this page to determine in which climate zones these cities are located. *(Rome and Athens—Mediterranean, Tehran—semiarid, Riyadh—desert)* Then ask students to speculate on how different patterns of climate might affect population. *(Students may suggest that population will be larger in areas with moderate temperature and sufficient rainfall.)* Have them verify their speculations by comparing the world population cartogram in the Atlas on page 689 with this climate map.

The Land and People

The Mediterranean and Southwest Asia have very different climates. When clouds from the Mediterranean Sea hit the mountains of Southwest Asia, they drop their rain. As a result, the land east of the mountains gets very little rain. For this reason, much of Southwest Asia is hot and dry. Areas near the Mediterranean Sea have warm, dry summers and mild, rainy winters.

➤ Regions circling the Mediterranean receive plenty of rainfall during winter. To the west, however, the land becomes desert.

Western Eurasia: Climate

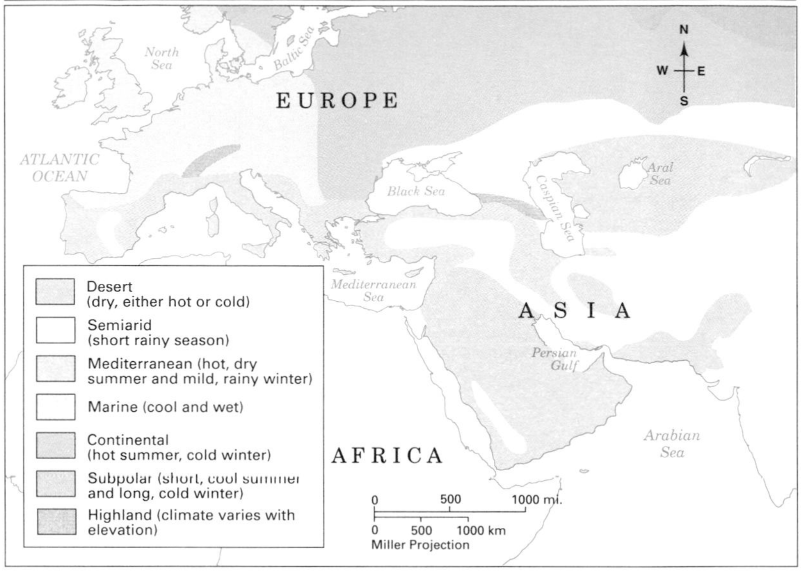
North Sea
Baltic Sea
EUROPE
N
W
E
S
ATLANTIC OCEAN
Black Sea
Caspian Sea
Aral Sea
Mediterranean Sea
ASIA
Persian Gulf
Arabian Sea
AFRICA
Desert (dry, either hot or cold)
Semiarid (short rainy season)
Mediterranean (hot, dry summer and mild, rainy winter)
Marine (cool and wet)
Continental (hot summer, cold winter)
Subpolar (short, cool summer and long, cold winter)
Highland (climate varies with elevation)
0 500 1000 mi.
0 500 1000 km
Miller Projection

▲ Frankincense comes from trees grown in Africa and Southwest Asia. In ancient times it was burned during religious celebrations and was a major trading item. Today it is used in perfumes.

➤ Saudi Arabia receives less rainfall than almost any other place in the world.

Regional Rainfall

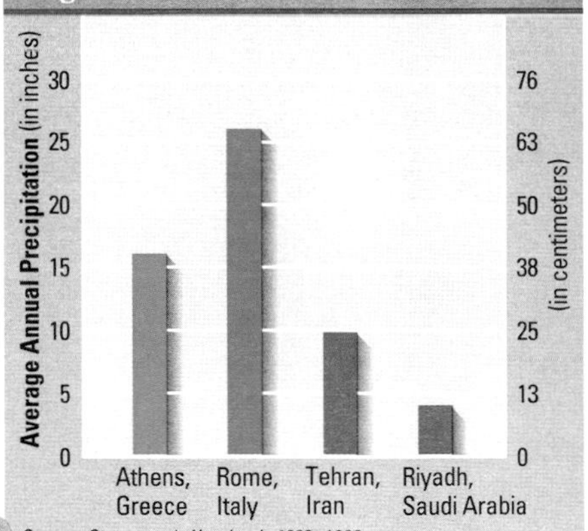
Average Annual Precipitation (in inches)
30
25
20
15
10
5
0
76
63
50
38
25
13
0
(in centimeters)
Athens, Greece
Rome, Italy
Tehran, Iran
Riyadh, Saudi Arabia

Source: Statesman's Yearbook, 1992–1993

▼ Pistachios grow in the dry climate of the eastern Mediterranean and Southwest Asia.

150

Writing to Learn

Ask students to write a paragraph summarizing what they know about one of the following subjects: life in ancient Greece or Rome, the origins of Christianity and Islam, life in Saudi Arabia or Iran today. After they have read the unit, have them revise their paragraph in view of what they have learned.

Making a Map or a Model

Tell students that many ancient Roman roads are still used today. Interested students might like to make a map showing the large network of these roads or construct a model that demonstrates how such a road was constructed (see TE page 172).

Language Arts Connection

Remind students that the word *monotheism* comes from Latin and Greek roots for the words that mean "one" and "God." Tell them that many other words use the Latin roots for numbers: *mono-*, *bi-*, and *tri-*, for example. Have teams of students see which one can generate the longest list of words beginning with one of these prefixes. Encourage students to find out the meanings of all the words they write.

Three world religions began in Southwest Asia. The development of Judaism began when a shepherd named Abraham left Mesopotamia to settle in what is now Israel. His descendants were called Israelites, the ancestors of the Jews. Christianity began almost 2,000 years later and was based on the teachings of Jesus, who had been raised in the traditions of Judaism. In the early seventh century, Muhammad, the founder of Islam, began preaching in Mecca, Saudi Arabia. Today these religions are practiced throughout the world.

*Followers of Islam face toward the **holy** city of Mecca when they pray.*

This boy is celebrating his Bar Mitzvah, a ceremony in which he will become a full member of the Jewish community.

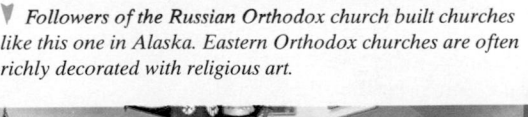

Followers of the Russian Orthodox church built churches like this one in Alaska. Eastern Orthodox churches are often richly decorated with religious art.

Learning from Photographs

Have students study the photographs and the accompanying captions. Ask students what all three pictures have in common. *(In each religious ritual pictured, participants are wearing special clothing, holding special objects, or performing special gestures.)* Ask if students know anything more about the particular religions pictured that they might like to share with the class.

You might want to tell students that the Jewish Torah or Bible in the picture is handwritten on a scroll made of animal skins by a specially trained scribe. If the scribe makes a mistake on any section of the scroll, it cannot simply be thrown away, but must be buried in a special ceremony.

ENRICH

Have students recall the meaning of the word *monotheism*. What religions do they know that are monotheistic? *(Judaism, Christianity, Islam)* Ask students to recall what they read about the religions of the ancient Egyptians and Nubians. Ask if these religions were based on monotheism. *(No. The ancient Egyptians and Nubians worshiped many Gods.)*

Mathematics Connection

Point out to students that they probably are familiar with Roman numerals, the numbering system used in the Roman Empire. For example, the Table of Contents and other introductory pages in this textbook are identified by Roman numerals. Have a pair of volunteers make a poster for the classroom that shows the various letters and their value. Ask all students to look for other examples of Roman numerals (on buildings, for example) and decipher them.

Research

Encourage pairs of students to visit local travel agents to get brochures about Mediterranean resorts and combine the glossy photos on a bulletin board, arranged by country. For fun, they can find out how much a trip to one of these resorts would cost if they were to make a plane reservation today. Who in your classroom can come up with the least expensive flight?

Collaborative Learning

Divide the class into groups, each of which will research the religious beliefs of early Greeks, Romans, Persians, Jews, Christians, or Muslims. Ask groups first to make a list of questions to guide their research and then assign questions to individuals or pairs. As a group, they should present their research to the class.

CHAPTER ORGANIZER

Chapter 7 The Mediterranean World

CHAPTER PLANNING CHART

Pupil's Edition	Teacher's Edition	Ancillaries
Lesson 1: Ancient Greece (3–4 days) Objective 1: Describe how Athens and Sparta differed. (Culture 2, 4; Social and Political Systems 1) Objective 2: Explain how Athenian democracy developed. (History 5; Ethics and Belief Systems 1; Social and Political Systems 2, 5) Objective 3: Describe two achievements of the Greeks and explain their significance. (History 5, 6; Culture 5, 6)	• Graphic Overview (154) • Access Strategy (155) • Access Activity (155) Study Skills (156) Historical Context (156) Language Arts Connection (157) Political Context (157) • Visual Learning (157) Critical Thinking (158) Political Context (158) Art Connection (159) • Visual Learning (159) Study Skills (160) Cultural Context (160)	Study Guide (27) Discovery Journal (15) • Study Prints (5)
Exploring: Greek Architecture in Your Community Objective 1: Describe the three types of Greek capitals and give the correct terms for some general features of ancient Greek architecture. (Culture 1) Objective 2: Name some uses of Greek architectural style in present-day buildings. (History 1, 2, 7; Culture 4)		Discovery Journal (16)
Literature: "Demeter and Persephone"	• Access Strategy (165) Illustrating (166, 167)	Discovery Journal (17)
Lesson 2: Ancient Rome (2-3 days) Objective 1: Describe how Rome grew under the Republic and the empire. (Culture 1, 2) Objective 2: Describe what life was like in ancient Rome and its empire. (Culture 4; Ethics and Belief Systems 1) Objective 3: Explain why the Roman Empire fell. (History 3, 5; Social and Political Systems 2) Objective 4: Describe the importance of the legacies from ancient Rome. (History 5, 6)	• Graphic Overview (168) • Access Strategy (169) • Access Activity (169) Social Participation (170) Cultural Context (170) Economic Context (170) Social Context (171) Science Connection (171) • Visual Learning (171, 172) Collaborative Learning (172)	Study Guide (28) Map Activities (11) Discovery Journal (18)
Understanding Conclusions Objective: List and apply the steps used in drawing conclusions from evidence. (Critical Thinking 3)		Study Guide (29)
Lesson 3: Early Christianity (1-2 days) Objective 1: Explain the origins of Christianity. (Ethics and Belief Systems 4) Objective 2: Describe the ways in which Christianity was spread. (Culture 1)	• Graphic Overview (175) • Access Activity (176) • Access Strategy (176) Historical Context (177) Critical Thinking (177) Critical Thinking (178) Language Arts Connection (178)	Study Guide (30)
Chapter Review	Answers (180–181)	Tests (25–28)

* Objectives are correlated to the strands and goals in the program Scope and Sequence on pages T41–T49.

• LEP appropriate resources. (For additional strategies, see pages T32–T33.)

CHAPTER RATIONALE

Throughout Unit 2, students have become acquainted with early civilizations in Asia, Africa, and the Americas. Now Chapter 7 looks at some of the foundations of Western civilization—the heritage of classical Greece and Rome and the early beginnings of Christianity.

The chapter describes these influences in their geographic setting in the Mediterranean world. Although we in the United States have been shaped by many other cultures, the ancient Mediterranean is still the source of important ideas about the ways we live, create, govern, and think about right and wrong.

To help readers understand the physical setting, the opening of **Lesson 1** emphasizes the influence of geography on the Greek way of life. The lesson begins with a quotation from Homer's *Odyssey,* in which Odysseus tells about his island home. The quotation appears with a photograph of the Greek islands, a map, and a description of the geography of Greece.

While students read about the historical background of ancient Greece, the main focus is on the Greeks' belief in excellence and individual creativity. The chapter acquaints readers with some of the Greeks' achievements in art, architecture, sports, and literature, pointing out ways in which these continue to influence us.

From Greece we move to ancient Rome, its successor as the leading power in the Mediterranean world. **Lesson 2** gives an overview of Rome's history and its growth into a powerful empire. The lesson also provides colorful insights into daily life. Again, the emphasis is on the continuing influence of Rome—in government, engineering, and language. The feature A Moment in Time highlights an engineer surveying a Roman road.

Lesson 3 gives a clear, accurate introduction to the origins of Christianity, set in its historical context within the Roman Empire. This lesson traces the growth of Christianity throughout the Mediterranean world, from its beginnings until its establishment as the religion of the later Roman Empire.

ACTIVITIES & PROJECTS

Basic: Bulletin Board

Have students look in used magazines (on architecture, travel, theater, and the like) and newspapers to collect both pictures and articles that reflect the modern heritage from ancient Greece and Rome. Arrange the pictures and the articles on the bulletin board under headings such as Architecture, Theater, Painting and Sculpture, Mythology and Literature, Government, and Engineering. (Use after Lesson 1.)

LEP: Collaborative Learning

Have students plan a lunch-hour or after-school banquet featuring foods that the ancient Greeks might have enjoyed. Divide the class into groups and have them research these areas: food, music and dance, and clothing. Student volunteers can make a simple meal featuring (for instance) Greek bread, cheese, olives, honey, and fruit. They may also enjoy visiting a Greek bakery or restaurant for contemporary foods. The library may be able to supply a tape of Greek music for one group to teach their classmates Greek folk dances. The clothing group can demonstrate how to drape and belt a sheet into a simple *chiton* or *peplos.* (Use after Lesson 1.)

Challenge: Writing a Play

Ask students to read some Greek or Roman myths to get acquainted with the different (but comparable) Gods and Goddesses of Rome. Have a group of three or four students choose a Greek or Roman myth and write a script for a short play to present in class. (Use after Lesson 2.)

Making a Map

Supply students with a political map of the modern Mediterranean world. Have them fasten a piece of tracing paper over the map and draw the outline of the Roman Empire's boundaries in A.D. 117 (text page 169). Ask them to list the modern countries that were once wholly or partly within the empire. (Use after Lesson 2.)

Challenge: Research

The Christian church has changed and has grown since the fourth century. Have students do research to make a chart that shows the different major branches and denominations of contemporary Christianity. (Use after Lesson 3.)

CHAPTER PREVIEW

Ask a student to read aloud the chapter title and the text that follows it. To follow up on the idea of the Mediterranean's influence, direct students to the world map on pages 680–681 in the Atlas and ask them to find the Mediterranean Sea. Then have them look at the maps on pages 155, 169, and 178 to locate ancient Greece, ancient Rome, and Judea in the eastern Mediterranean, where Christianity began. Ask students to think of examples of how Greek culture, Roman culture, and the Christian religion are closely linked with ideas we have today about each of the following: what is beautiful, what is just, and what is right or wrong.

Looking Forward

Tell students that in the next three lessons—Ancient Greece, Ancient Rome, and Early Christianity—they will learn about three ways of life from the ancient Mediterranean world that still have a great influence on people today.

Lesson 1 portrays ancient Greece from three standpoints: geography, history and daily life, and culture.

Chapter 7
The Mediterranean World

On a globe, the Mediterranean is a small sea. Yet it touches the shores of three continents. Many peoples who lived here developed remarkable new ideas. Rich cultures developed in Greece and Rome. The Christian religion began and grew in the eastern Mediterranean. From the Mediterranean world come many of our ideas about what is beautiful, what is just, and what is right and wrong.

438 B.C. The Parthenon, a temple to the Goddess Athena (shown left), is completed as part of Pericles' ambitious building program for Athens. The temple still stands on the Acropolis in modern Athens.

800 | 600 | 400 | 200

800 B.C.

343 B.C. The Greek philosopher Aristotle becomes the tutor of young Alexander of Macedonia, who will grow up to be known as Alexander the Great.

BACKGROUND

Civilizations in the Mediterranean developed over many centuries. The earliest were the Minoan (on Crete) and the Mycenaean (on the Greek mainland and on other islands). After those cultures fell, about 1100 B.C., Greek villages developed in isolation. By about 800 B.C., small towns and the lands around them joined to form city-states. The peninsula's rugged terrain hindered further growth, however. No city-state could grow large enough to control the others for long.

In Italy, by contrast, Rome had an ideal location in the center of the Italian peninsula, with easy access to the sea. The city was able, therefore, to form a huge and long-lived empire.

Powerful City-States

Among the Greek city-states, two were outstanding. In 430 B.C., Pericles, the leader of Athens, boasted, "Our city is an education to Greece." Arts, science, and democratic government flourished there. Although Athens was once ruled by tyrants and oligarchies, steps toward democracy were taken in the sixth century by the Athenian statesmen Solon, who reformed the law, and Cleisthenes, who proposed changes that led to democracy. Under democracy, Athenian culture thrived.

Sparta emerged as the other dominant city-state. At first, it was a center for music, poetry, dance, fine bronze work, and pottery.

Suedia
Bergen
S. Nicolas
Nougrod
Tartar
Volga
Moſkow
Cracow
Gallia
Buda
Wien
Italia
Corsica
Natolia
Candia
Cyprus
Barba-
ria.
Berdoa
Albaidi
Aegyptus
AFRICA.
Borno
Nubia

Roman soldiers pushed the borders of the empire north to Britain, west to the Atlantic Ocean, south into Africa, and east into Asia. This map from a later period shows much of the world that was once under Roman rule.

When the new Colosseum opened in Rome in A.D. 80, the emperor Titus sponsored 100 days of public shows of gladiator fights and of wild animals.

A.D. 312 The Roman emperor Constantine becomes a Christian. As Christianity spreads, the cross (carried by a dolphin in this carving) becomes one of its most important symbols.

B.C. | A.D. | 200 | 400 | 600

58–46 B.C. Julius Caesar conquers Gaul for Rome and invades Britain. He defeats his opponents, returns to Rome a hero, and soon is a powerful ruler.

A.D. 476

153

Understanding the Visuals

The well-known Mourning Athena (far left, facing page) was found south of the Parthenon. This relief (1.75 feet high) dates from 460 B.C. and is made of marble from the Aegean island of Paros. It shows Athena in helmet and simple peplos (a long, straight wool garment) leaning against her lance, apparently pondering the inscription on the stele before her, which may be a funeral marker.

In the era of its greatest use, the Colosseum (left) was called the Flavian Amphitheater after the emperors of that family—Vespasian, Titus, and Domitian—under whom it was built. It became known as the Colosseum in medieval times. The structure has different types of columns (Doric, Ionic, Corinthian) at each level. There were originally 80 entrances for the crowds who came to the Colosseum.

Understanding Chronology

Direct students' attention to the timeline. Ask how many centuries separated the completion of the Parthenon at Athens and the opening of the Colosseum at Rome. *(More than five centuries passed: 438 B.C. to A.D. 80.)*

Gradually, Sparta changed. Education switched from arts and sports to harsh military training. In time, the disciplined Spartan military machine defeated Athens. Conflicts among the city-states of Greece eventually led to their decline, and they ultimately fell to outside invaders.

A City with an Empire

As the Greek city-states were weakening, Rome was growing. It expanded slowly at first, as its citizens fought nearby tribes. By 338 B.C., Rome dominated Latium and southern Etruria. The Roman custom of giving newly conquered peoples Roman citizenship gave Rome a basis for future strength—increased loyalty and the ability to put more soldiers into the field than any opponent. Within two generations Romans held all of Italy. Under the leadership of Augustus, Rome's first emperor, the Roman Empire was established, and it advanced into Europe as far as the Danube and the Rhine. With the death of the emperor Marcus Aurelius in A.D. 180, the period of peace and prosperity (Pax Romana) ended. Rome began to decline.

As the power of the empire waned, the power of the Christian Church increased. Congregations were established throughout Roman territory. Outside invaders weakened Rome still more. After Rome fell, the eastern capital of Constantinople flourished as the center of the Byzantine Empire.

INTRODUCE

Use the Table of Contents to review some of the earlier cultures the class has studied (for example, Mesopotamia, Nubia, India, China, Mesoamerica). Recall some achievements of each. Then read aloud the last two sentences of this lesson, on page 161. Ask students what these statements tell them about the achievements of the ancient Greeks. *(The Greeks were accomplished in literature, the arts, and architecture.)* Link this idea to the Thinking Focus, pointing out that the achievements of the Greeks in these fields still influence people today. Tell students to watch for these achievements—and others—as they read the lesson.

Key Terms

Vocabulary Strategies: T36–T37

peninsula—a piece of land that extends into a body of water

city-state—an independent town, with the land around it

citizen—a person who has full rights and duties in a state

democracy—a government in which the people make the laws and decisions

philosophy—the love of knowledge or wisdom

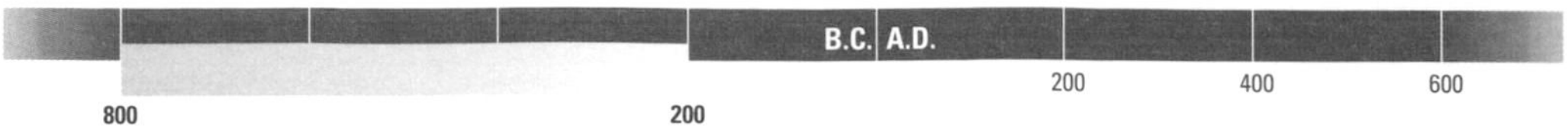

B.C. A.D.
800
200
200
400
600

L E S S O N 1

Ancient Greece

THINKING FOCUS

How do the achievements of ancient Greece still influence people today?

Key Terms

- peninsula
- city-state
- citizen
- democracy
- philosophy

> I am Odysseus, son of Laertes, known before all men for [being clever]. . . . I am at home in sunny Ithaka. There is a mountain there that stands tall . . . and there are islands settled around it, lying one very close to another. . . . But my island lies low and away, last of all on the water toward the dark [the west] . . . a rugged place, but a good nurse of men; for my part I cannot think of any place sweeter on earth to look at.
>
> Homer, *Odyssey*

With these words, the Greek hero Odysseus *(oh DIHS ee uhs)* described his island home. Odysseus—who may or may not have been a real person—had been away from home for many years. With other Greek heroes, he had been fighting in the Trojan War. His journey home, filled with adventures, took almost 10 years. As he spoke, he was nearing home. Soon he would stand again on Ithaka, the island he loved so well.

Odysseus' speech is part of a long poem, the *Odyssey,* which is about his travels. It was composed in ancient Greece by the poet Homer, perhaps as early as the 700s or 800s B.C. The poem was probably recited at first and not written down until later.

Notice that when Odysseus remembered his home, he spoke of the sea and islands and mountains. He might have been describing the world of all the Greeks.

Odysseus' journey took him through the blue waters of the Aegean and Ionian seas, which separate the Greek islands. This is the island of Samos, in the Aegean.

Objectives

1. Describe how Athens and Sparta differed.
2. Explain how Athenian democracy developed.
3. Describe two achievements of the Greeks and explain their significance.

Graphic Overview

GREEK CULTURE
Art and Architecture
Literature
Ideas
sculpture, pottery
temples, theaters
drama, poetry
history
science, philosophy
government

Greek City-States and Trade Routes, c. 550 B.C.

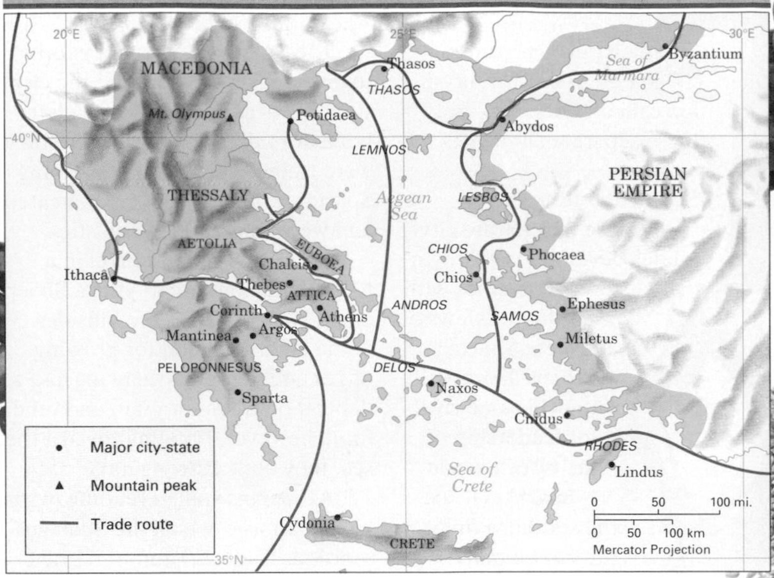

20°E
25°E
30°E
40°N
35°N
MACEDONIA
Mt. Olympus
Potidaea
Thasos
THASOS
Sea of Marmara
Byzantium
Abydos
LEMNOS
THESSALY
Aegean Sea
LESBOS
PERSIAN EMPIRE
AETOLIA
EUBOEA
Chalcis
CHIOS
Chios
Phocaea
Ithaca
Thebes
ATTICA
Corinth
Athens
ANDROS
SAMOS
Ephesus
Miletus
Mantinea
Argos
PELOPONNESUS
DELOS
Naxos
Sparta
Cnidus
RHODES
Lindus
Sea of Crete
Cydonia
CRETE
Major city-state
Mountain peak
Trade route
0 50 100 mi.
0 50 100 km
Mercator Projection

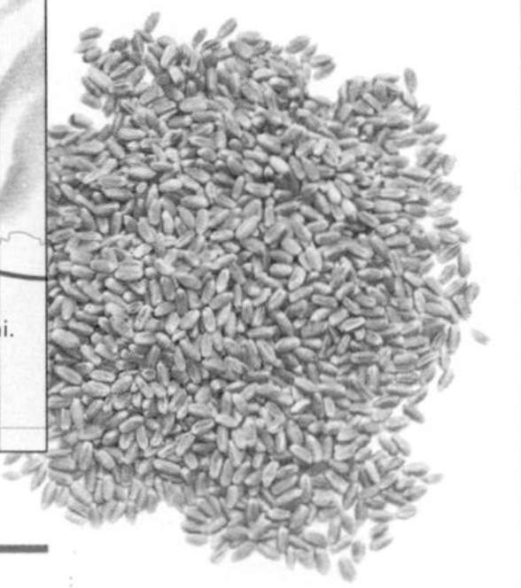

The Setting

To understand Odysseus' feelings about his home, look at the map above. Much of what is now Greece is a triangular piece of land that extends into the sea. That is, the Greek mainland is a **peninsula,** a word that means "almost island." Greece also includes many islands clustered in the sea nearby.

The map also shows clearly that rugged mountains cross the Greek landscape. Land and sea, mountains and valleys—these are the geographic contrasts in which ancient Greek culture developed.

Land and Sea

Like most other peoples in ancient times, the Greeks raised crops and herded animals for food. However, Greece is so hilly that fields with good soil are small and scarce. The Greeks could not grow all the food they needed.

As a result, the Greeks turned to the sea. They were fishers and sea traders as well as farmers. The Greeks sailed from island to island but tried not to lose sight of land.

Traders brought home products that the Greeks needed. Still, the lack of good farmland often meant food shortages at home. One solution was to send settlers to start new cities elsewhere.

As a result, ancient Greece included cities in what are now France, Spain, Italy, Russia, and Turkey. Modern Marseilles *(mahr SAY),* France, for instance, began as a Greek settlement. The new cities traded and sometimes fought with each other. Their people were thoroughly Greek in lifestyle.

Mountains and Valleys

In Greece, settlements were cut off from one another by mountains and the sea. Each city developed its own laws and its own government. An independent town, with the land around it, was called a **city-state**.

▲ *The main crops grown in the rugged land of Greece were olives, grapes, and grain. Notice how mountains and sea separate the city-states. Which ones were in the Peloponnesus?*

DEVELOP

Suggest that students use the map on this page as a point of reference as they read the lesson. Ask students to describe what the map shows. *(Students may mention land, sea, specific landforms such as islands or mountains, and place names.)* Instruct students to look for other elements of the lesson, such as photographs and text heads, that relate to what the map shows. *(Students may note the section title The Setting; the key terms* peninsula *and* city-state; *the photograph of Samos on page 154; and the heads Land and Sea, Mountains and Valleys, Sparta and Athens.)*

◄ *City-states in the Peloponnesus include Sparta, Mantinea, Argos, and Corinth.*

Access Strategy

Ask students if they remember the most recent Olympic Games or if they have seen films or televison clips of the games. Help them recall the lighting of the Olympic torch, which is part of the opening ceremonies. Explain that the torch is lit in Olympia, Greece, and brought to the current site of the games by relays of cross-country runners over a period of several weeks before the games begin. (The torch sometimes travels by plane or ship as well.) The last runner brings the torch into the stadium and lights the flame, which burns until the games are over. Find out whether students know the connection between the Olympic Games and ancient Greece. Explain that the idea of the Olympic Games, along with many of its traditions, developed about 2,700 years ago in ancient Greece. Then point out that this is only one of the many things that we have inherited from the ancient Greeks, who are the subject of this lesson.

Access Activity

Direct students' attention to the map, pointing out how color and shadings show mountains and valleys. Then have them point out the mainland, the islands, and the seas; ask them to find specific islands such as Ithaca, Odysseus' home, and Samos, shown in the photograph.

SOCIAL SYSTEMS

Critical Thinking

Emphasize that ancient Greece was not a nation as Greece is today, but a collection of independent city-states. Cite the distinction between Sparta and Athens as an example of the great differences between city-states. Divide the class into "Spartans" and "Athenians." Call on students at random to make a statement about how "their" city-state differs from the other.

Then ask whether they think that modern cities within the same country are likely to be as different as Sparta and Athens. Why or why not? *(Not as geographically separate, a common national culture)* What features of the modern world tend to make cities more alike? *(Television, fast transportation, and other communication)*

■ *Because the peninsula lacked good soil, many Greeks turned to the sea for fishing and trade. Food shortages were also a reason for trade and for starting new settlements. City-states were separated by mountains or the sea and developed independently.*

Spartans encouraged sports for both women and men. This bronze statue, from about 520 B.C., shows a girl running.

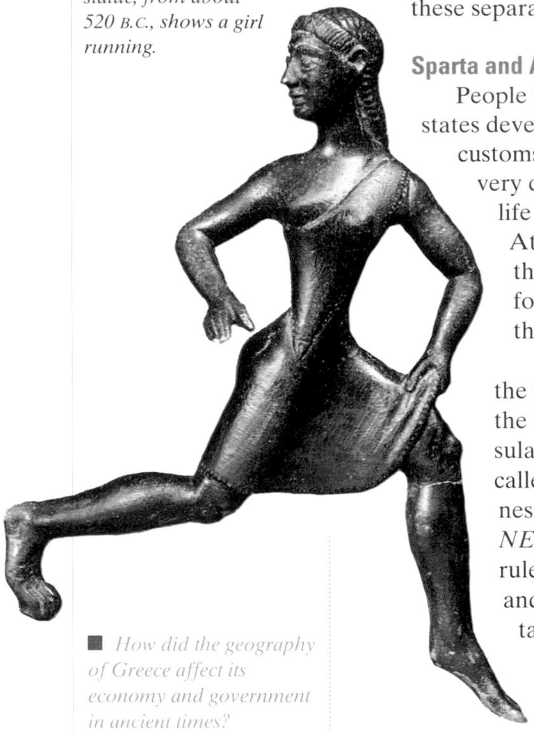

■ *How did the geography of Greece affect its economy and government in ancient times?*

The map on page 155 shows major city-states. There was no single nation called "Greece"—only these separate city-states.

Sparta and Athens

People in separate city-states developed their own customs. Two cities with very different views of life were Sparta and Athens. Eventually they became rivals for leadership of the Greek world.

Sparta is near the southern tip of the Greek peninsula, in a hilly region called the Peloponnesus *(pehl uh puh NEE suhs)*. It was ruled by two kings and a council. Spartans valued physical courage, strength, and bravery in war.

The Spartans expected people to give their first loyalty to the city-state. Boys as young as seven left home for military camps where they were trained to be soldiers. Young Spartan women also were educated and were trained in gymnastics.

Athens is farther north, in a forested region called Attica. Sheep and goats grazed on the hillsides. Some land was good for growing olives and grapes. Athenians had to depend on trade for grain and other food, however. Looking toward the sea, they built a strong navy.

Athenians valued reading, writing, and music, which the Spartans scorned. They also admired bravery in battle. They ran, wrestled, and did other gymnastics to keep both body and mind fit. At its height, Athens did not have a king. It was sometimes ruled by its people, sometimes by one strong ruler.

Both Athenians and Spartans were scornful of the others' way of life. It was partly these differences that made the two cities rivals. ■

The Golden Age

A time of prosperity, creative art, and rich culture is often called a golden age. In Greece, the Golden Age lasted from about 500 B.C. to 338 B.C. Much of the Greek art, literature, and ideas that people admire today come from this period. However, Greece's Golden Age was also an age of war.

From Kings to Democracy

Before about 600 B.C., the city-states of Greece were ruled by kings. By the start of the Golden Age, the government of most Greek city-states included some kind of an assembly, a gathering of the people.

The Assembly in Athens, in fact, governed the city. People met there to vote on questions of defense, trade, and other issues. Only Athenian citizens could vote in the Assembly. A **citizen** is a person who has full rights and duties in a state. For example, a citizen may have both the right to vote and the duty to serve in the army.

Only a small number of Athenians—about 15 to 20 percent—were citizens. All were men. Athenian women had certain privileges, and they could pass citizenship on to their sons. They were not voting citizens, though, and they could not

Study Skills

Have students research how being a citizen in another democratic nation (such as Germany, India, or Mexico) differs from being a U.S. citizen. For instance, must all citizens serve in the army? Are citizens required to vote?

Historical Context

"Suppose . . . that the city of Sparta were to become deserted and that only the temples and foundations of buildings remained," suggested the fifth-century Greek historian Thucydides. "I think that future generations would, as time passed, find it very difficult to believe that the place had really been as powerful as it was represented to be." In fact, little evidence of Sparta's power does remain. According to Thucydides, Sparta had "no temples or monuments of great magnificence," as Athens did. In addition, in his time Sparta did not have walls around it, relying on its soldiers and the hills that surrounded it for its defense. Today, visitors find walls and ruins of a later period but little of Sparta's heroic past, except for traces of sacred areas such as the sanctuary of Artemis. The few other early sites include a shrine to King Menelaus and his wife, Helen of Troy.

own anything except their clothes, jewelry, and slaves. Upper-class women lived restricted lives inside their homes.

Children and most foreigners were not citizens. Neither were slaves. Slavery was common in many ancient cultures. Most slaves in Athens had been captured in war or were so deep in debt that they had to sell themselves into slavery.

The limits on citizenship meant that all Athenians were governed by a small group of men. From 80 to 85 percent of the people had no say in important decisions. Still,

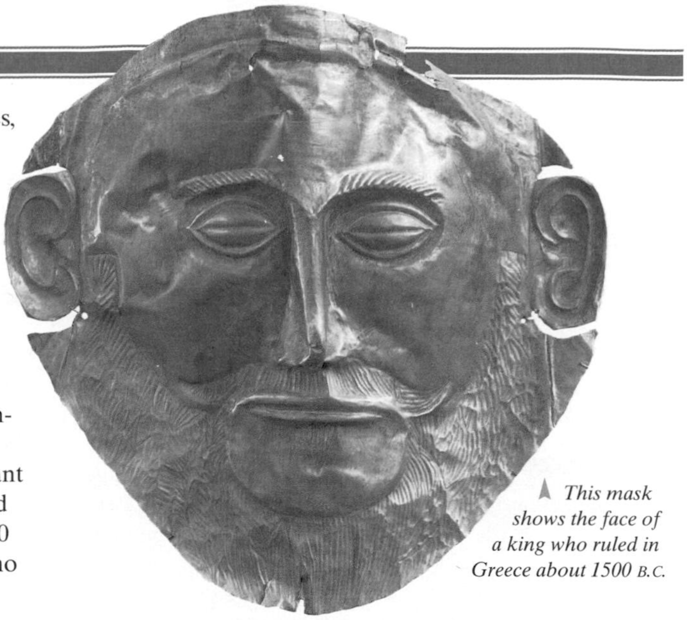

▲ *This mask shows the face of a king who ruled in Greece about 1500 B.C.*

UNDERSTANDING DEMOCRACY

Throughout ancient history, kingdoms and nations were ruled by one powerful ruler or a small group of people. Then, in the sixth century B.C., people of the Greek city-states made a change. Several city-states organized the first lasting democracies—governments in which people ruled themselves. Because historians wrote the most about the city-state of Athens, people still study it today as the birthplace of democracy.

Rule of the People

A democracy is a form of government in which all citizens may take part in governing. The word comes from two Greek words: *demos,* meaning "people," and *kratos,* meaning "power." In any democracy, it is the people who hold the power. Athenian democracy, however, was not like democracy in the United States and other nations today.

Forms of Democracy

There are two types of democracies—direct and representative. In a *direct democracy,* such as Athens, each citizen decides and votes on important issues. Athenian citizens cast their votes with tokens like those at the left. In a *representative democracy,* citizens elect a group of people to make decisions about government.

Direct democracies work best in small communities, such as the early Greek city-states or small towns today. In countries or even big cities, it would be impractical for everyone to meet together to discuss and vote on issues. That is why modern democratic countries have representative democracy. In the United States, citizens vote to elect men and women who will represent them in Congress.

In the future, television and electronics might change how democracy works. With an "electronic town meeting," citizens might be able to sit at home, listen to debates, and vote directly, just as citizens did long ago in the Assembly at Athens.

CITIZENSHIP

Social Participation

Democracies differ all over the world. Have the class work together to create a bulletin board showing democracy in its many forms. Divide the students into teams. Each team can be responsible for investigating the form of democracy practiced in one country. You might choose from the following: Japan, Mauritius, Zimbabwe, the Netherlands, Costa Rica, India, Western Samoa, or Pakistan. The display should include a world map that shows the location of the countries, a chart comparing forms of democracy, and photos or student drawings of expressions of democracy in the different countries.

Language Arts Connection

Many terms relating to government come from Greek. Review the etymology of *democracy* given in the Understanding Democracy feature. Then introduce the word *monarchy,* explaining that it is from two Greek words: *monos,* "one," and *arche,* "rule." Tell students to look up these words in a dictionary: *aristocracy, autocracy, plutocracy, technocracy; hierarchy, matriarchy, oligarchy, patriarchy.* Then have them compile a glossary of these terms and their meanings.

Political Context

In Athens only a small percentage of men could take part in the democracy. In U.S. history there have also been limits on who can vote. African Americans' right to vote was first protected in 1870. Women could not vote nationally until 1920, and many Native Americans could not vote until 1948. Some Americans are excluded from voting. Ask students to find out who is excluded and why. *(Certain criminals, people under age 18)* Then ask whether they think such exclusions are fair.

Visual Learning

The mask on this page was found by the archaeologist Heinrich Schliemann in a royal grave at Mycenae in 1876. Have students suggest what material the sculptor used. *(Beaten gold)* What does the mask show about the culture? About the person it represents? *(It shows wealth and skillful crafting; it shows that the person was important.)*

CULTURE

Critical Thinking

Discuss with students what constitutes a golden age. *(Prosperity, creative art, rich culture)* Then have them discuss whether or not we live in a golden age. To extend this into an activity, ask students who think this is a golden age to collect pictures from used magazines to create a collage showing aspects of life that support their viewpoint. Students who disagree can make a collage to show their ideas. Display students' artwork on the bulletin board.

HISTORY

Critical Thinking

Point out the seeming contradiction of the outcome of the Peloponnesian War: Sparta gave little to the world, except certain memorable examples of physical courage. Athens has come to stand for Greece's greatness in thought, art, and science. Yet Athens lost the war. Tell students that the Spartan victory in the war has puzzled people for more than 2,000 years. Ask them whether they find a lesson in Athens's defeat and Sparta's victory.

■ *Athens became a leader by using its fleet to protect its island neighbors. This defensive alliance developed into an empire that made the city wealthy and powerful.*

Pericles' rule in Athens was the height of the Golden Age. He was not only a political and military leader but also a person who loved the arts. This statue shows him wearing a military helmet.

ΠΕΡΙΚΛΗΣ

a government in which groups of people—not one ruler—make the laws was something new in the ancient world. It is called a **democracy**.

You can learn more about how it works by reading Understanding Democracy on page 157.

Athens Becomes a Leader

The Greek city-states were not the only powers in the eastern Mediterranean region. Greece's neighbor to the east was the huge Persian Empire. (Part of the Persian Empire is shown on the map on page 155.)

In about 499 B.C., the Greek city-states went to war with Persia. Persian forces were much larger, but the city-states banded together. With great courage and clever strategy, the Greeks won. Two of their greatest victories were at Marathon and Salamis.

After the war with Persia, Athens became the leader of a group of city-states. Its navy protected them from attack. These cities formed a small empire, which made Athens rich and powerful. Sparta headed another group of city-states. They were its neighbors in the southern part of the peninsula.

The years from about 460 to 430 B.C. were the height of Athens's Golden Age. Poets, playwrights, and sculptors worked to create beautiful works of art that still inspire people today. The Athenian leader Pericles *(PEHR ih kleez)* made the city beautiful, too.

Pericles hired architects and sculptors to build new buildings in the heart of Athens. On the top of the central hill was the Parthenon. This temple honored Athena, the city's chief Goddess. A great gold and ivory statue of Athena stood inside its columns. Although the Parthenon has been damaged since Pericles' time, the white marble temple still stands in Athens today.

Cultures in Conflict

Athens's growing power made the Spartans nervous. In 431 B.C. the two rivals began a destructive war. Fighting continued off and on for about 25 years. Historians refer to this time period as the Peloponnesian War. In many ways it was a war between two different cultures. Early in the war, Pericles said:

> *It is worth remembering some of the great differences between our way of life and that of our enemies. . . . Our city is open to all the world and everyone is free to look at what he likes in it. This is because we rely not on secret weapons, but on our own real courage and loyalty. There is a difference too in our educational systems. The Spartans, from their earliest boyhood, are submitted to the most strict and laborious training in courage. We pass our lives without all these restrictions, and yet we are just as ready to face danger as they are when the moment comes.*
>
> "Pericles' Funeral Speech," about 430 B.C., from Thucydides, *The Peloponnesian War*

A few months later, many Athenians, including Pericles, died in a dreadful epidemic. As the war went on, people on both sides suffered greatly. Sparta won a final victory in 405 B.C. It captured the Athenian navy and surrounded the city. With their supplies of food cut off, the starving Athenians eventually had to surrender. ■

■ *How did Athens become a leader among the city-states?*

Critical Thinking

Ask a student to volunteer to read aloud the passage from Pericles' speech. Then have students recall what they have read earlier about Sparta and Athens and the things each city considered important. Have them discuss or list what they personally consider important values and attitudes for a city or a nation.

Political Context

Pericles was most influential as a leader in the two decades of the 440s and 430s B.C. His masterful use of rhetoric in the Assembly was necessary. Although Athens had no political parties, strong factions backed different viewpoints on issues. Even Pericles sometimes lost the Assembly's support. He was once dismissed from his position as general, and fined.

The Athenians chose Pericles to deliver the funeral speech quoted above on the basis of his skill and originality as a speaker. The occasion was a public military funeral for Athenian soldiers killed during the first year of fighting in the war with Sparta. Pericles went beyond the occasion to comment on his own feelings about Athenian values and Athens's place in history. It was most likely the transcendent themes of the speech that led Thucydides to quote it when, in the later years of the Peloponnesian War, he wrote his *History*.

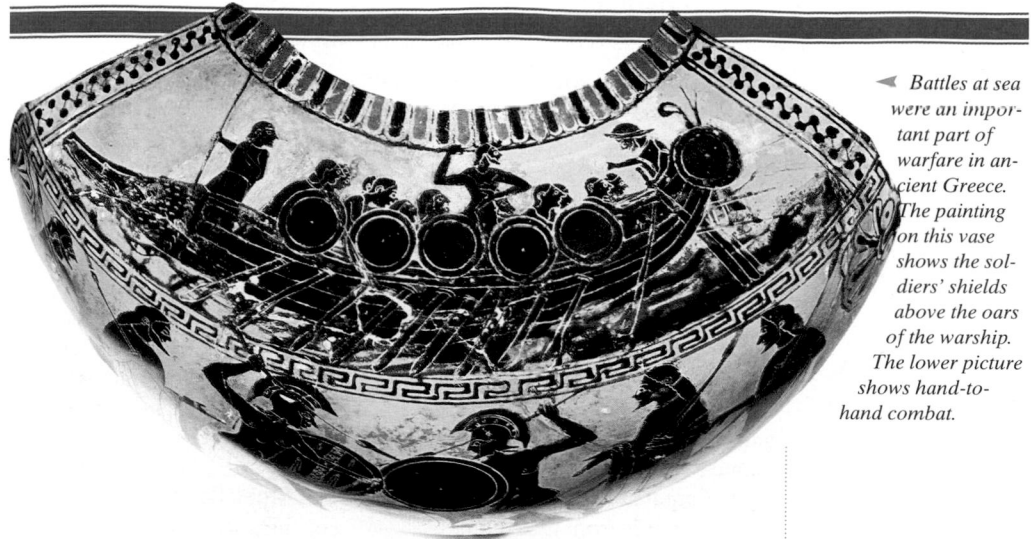

Battles at sea were an important part of warfare in ancient Greece. The painting on this vase shows the soldiers' shields above the oars of the warship. The lower picture shows hand-to-hand combat.

The Greek Heritage

After the Peloponnesian War, Greek city-states continued to fight among themselves. The wars drained their money and energy. In 338 B.C. King Philip of Macedonia, a large region north of Greece, took over the entire peninsula.

Philip's son Alexander was brought up to admire the culture of Greece. As Alexander the Great, he later went on to conquer most of the world the Greeks knew about. You will read about Alexander in Chapter 10. His conquests helped spread Greek culture to a wide area.

Greek Religion

The Greeks worshiped many Gods that they believed looked like—and often acted like—human beings. Myths, or stories, were told about the Gods and their adventures. Myths were not just good stories but looked into human nature and the relationships between Gods and humans. Writers and artists still use stories and symbols from the Greek myths. People still enjoy reading them.

There were 12 main Greek Gods. They were seen as members of a large family who fought, got jealous, and otherwise behaved in very human ways. Their home was Mount Olympus.

Zeus, as head of the family, was called "the father of Gods and men." He ruled the sky, while his brothers Poseidon and Hades ruled the sea and the underworld. His wife Hera protected the home.

Greek cities often chose one God or Goddess as their special protector. People also came under their protection. Each God also looked after certain crafts and ideas. For example, Zeus's daughter Athena was the Goddess of wisdom and war as well as crafts such as spinning thread and weaving cloth. Her special city was Athens.

Before making important decisions, the Greeks wanted to make

This fragment of a Roman mosaic shows the young conqueror Alexander the Great on his favorite war horse, Bucephalus. Because of Alexander's conquests, Greek culture spread to many areas.

BELIEF SYSTEMS

Social Participation

Divide the class into six groups and assign each group two of these major Olympian Gods: Zeus, Hera, Poseidon, Hades, Athena, Apollo, Artemis, Aphrodite, Hermes, Ares, Hephaestus, or Hestia. For a larger class, include other interesting deities, such as Demeter, Dionysus, the Muses, and the Fates. Tell the groups to research the following: an epithet, or descriptive nickname, for each God; an attribute or object associated with him or her; the God's relationship to other deities; and an entertaining myth about each. Have the groups present their findings orally, with each member participating.

Art Connection

Bring in a poster or another large picture of the Parthenon, a temple built to honor the Goddess Athena. (A small picture of it appears in the Chapter Opener.) Ask students why they think it was considered the most beautiful building in ancient Greece. Explain that art historians praise the Parthenon's proportions. Despite its size, the building seems light, not heavy.

Visual Learning

Vase paintings like those on this page and on page 161 tell us much of what we know about how Greeks looked, dressed, fought, lived, worked, and played. Ask students to study both paintings carefully and point out the details they see.

BELIEF SYSTEMS

Critical Thinking

Despite the differences among Greek city-states, Greeks of all cities visited certain sanctuaries, or holy places. One was the temple to Apollo at Delphi, located on the slopes of Mount Parnassus. Government leaders and private individuals consulted the oracle. Apollo's messages were given through a priestess, the Pythia, who spoke while in a trance. The oracle was famous for giving answers that were so ambiguous they could not be proved wrong.

Ask students what they think of this mode of decision-making. Challenge them to think of questions and responses that can be interpreted the way the listener wishes. *(Two examples are "If you take that action, someone will be unhappy" and "The next weeks will bring change.")*

sure the Gods approved. One way to find out was to visit the oracle at one of more than 200 special temples. There, people's questions about the future were answered. Many people asked advice from Apollo, a son of Zeus. He was a popular God, considered the God of truth. His best-known temple was at Delphi.

Greeks honored their Gods at festivals, with dances, songs, and athletic games. The most famous games were the ancient Olympic Games, which honored Zeus. Athletes competed mainly for fame and for honors from their home cities. The prize was a wreath of leaves. There are records of Olympic Games every four years from 776 B.C. to A.D. 217.

Greek Philosophers

The Greek word **philosophy** means the love of knowledge of all kinds. For Greek philosophers, studying philosophy was a way to discover what the universe was like and how to live correctly.

One Athenian philosopher, Socrates *(SOK ruh teez),* used an unusual way of teaching. Instead of telling his students what they should know, he asked careful questions. As students tried to answer, they learned how to think.

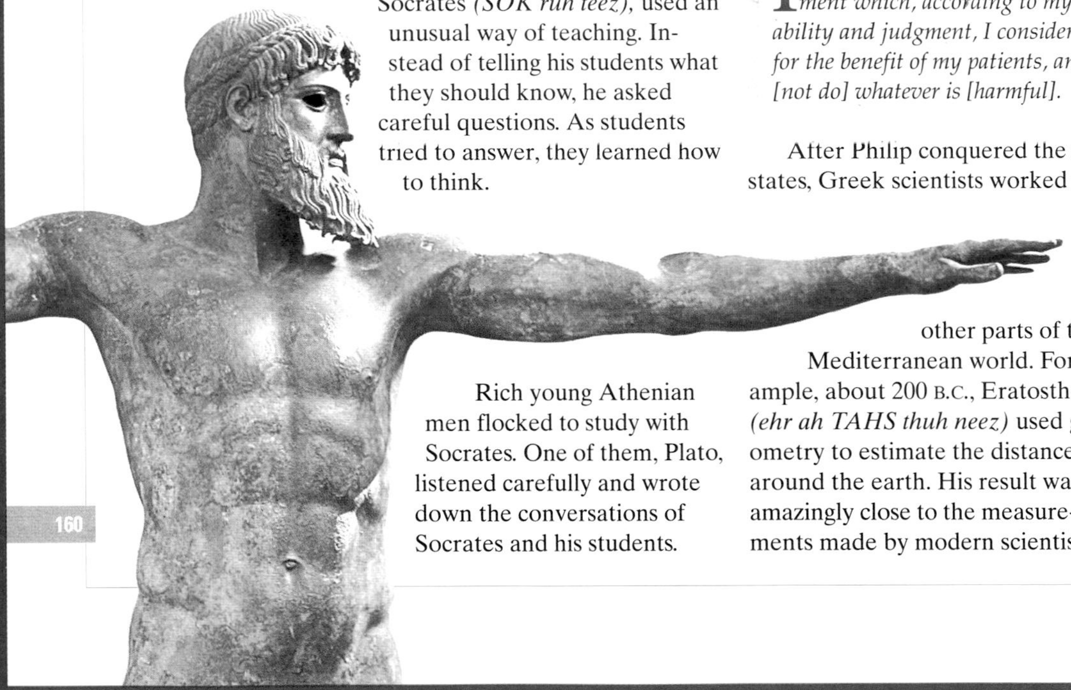

This statue is thought to show Zeus, ruler of the sky, getting ready to throw a thunderbolt. Notice how real—but how perfect—the figure appears.

Rich young Athenian men flocked to study with Socrates. One of them, Plato, listened carefully and wrote down the conversations of Socrates and his students. Plato's works and Socrates' ideas are still studied today.

One of Plato's students, Aristotle *(AIR ihs taht uhl),* became as famous as his teacher. He explored many fields—science, drama, government. His ideas were studied and followed for centuries. Students today still learn Aristotle's theories about drama and poetry. As the teacher of Alexander the Great, Aristotle taught him to love Greek culture.

Ancient Greek Science

For the ancient Greeks, science and philosophy went together in understanding the world. Greek scientists asked "why" about things they saw. For example, in about 400 B.C., Hippocrates *(hih PAHK ruh teez)* taught medicine. He trained doctors to look for physical causes of illness, not to blame it on the anger of the Gods. Doctors today still take an oath named after Hippocrates. This is part of it:

> *I will follow that method of treatment which, according to my ability and judgment, I consider for the benefit of my patients, and [not do] whatever is [harmful].*

After Philip conquered the city-states, Greek scientists worked in other parts of the Mediterranean world. For example, about 200 B.C., Eratosthenes *(ehr ah TAHS thuh neez)* used geometry to estimate the distance around the earth. His result was amazingly close to the measurements made by modern scientists.

Study Skills

Modern theater, movies, and television derive much more from Greek drama than just the ideas of comedy and tragedy. Have students research the Greek theater and some of its elements that are still used today (such as theater-in-the-round).

Cultural Context

Olympia, home of the ancient Olympic (or Olympian) Games, was the main sanctuary of Zeus, whom the games honored. The site, near the river Alpheus, also had other shrines, as well as statues of winning athletes. The early Olympic Games lasted one day and featured just running and wrestling. Most of the early victors were Spartans. After the seventh century B.C., more city-states began to take part. Athletes came from throughout the Greek world to compete.

On the first day, there were sacrifices to Zeus. Competitors and judges took an oath to be fair. The next three days included foot and chariot races, wrestling, boxing, and jumping. There were also combined events such as the pentathlon: running, jumping, javelin throwing, discus throwing, and wrestling. On the final day, more sacrifices were performed. Victors were entertained at a banquet and crowned with wreaths of olive leaves.

A Lasting Artistic Vision

You have read how the ancient Greeks left their mark on government, history, philosophy, and science. They also produced striking works of literature, art, and architecture. You can find out more about the influence of Greek architecture in the feature on the next two pages.

The most famous Greek authors of the Golden Age wrote plays. In comedies, or humorous plays, they poked fun at politicians and current events. In tragedies, writers showed how fate and people's own unwise actions led them into disaster.

Today, if you watch a "situation comedy" or a Shakespearean tragedy, you are seeing a kind of play that was first created by the ancient Greeks. Audiences came to huge outdoor theaters where these plays were given. Playwrights competed to write the best new comedy or tragedy for a festival.

Greek artists of the Golden Age created magnificent sculptures. They tried to show both humans and Gods as perfect. Look at the statue of the God Zeus on page 160. What impression does it give you?

Over the course of 2,500 years, many of the great Greek plays and other writings have been lost. Vases, statues, and buildings have been broken or damaged. Still, the Greek heritage is an amazing one. Anyone today who wants to be a writer, artist, or architect needs to know what was done long ago in Greece. ■

◄ *Greek vases (left) were often decorated with paintings, usually in black or red. They show scenes from the myths and from everyday life—how the Greeks dressed, fought, lived, and worked. Greek theaters were outdoors, like this one (below) at Epidaurus.*

■ *Identify three things in modern U.S. culture that you can trace back to ancient Greece.*

■ *Possible answers include the Olympic Games, comedy and tragedy in drama, the Socratic method in teaching, modern methods of science, and architectural styles.*

REVIEW

1. **FOCUS** How do the achievements of ancient Greece still influence people today?
2. **GEOGRAPHY** In Chapter 2, you read about different kinds of regions. What different regions can you identify for ancient Greece?
3. **CULTURE** Describe how Athens and Sparta differed in the way young people were educated.
4. **SOCIAL AND POLITICAL SYSTEMS** How was Athens governed during the Golden Age?
5. **CRITICAL THINKING** How did Greek scientists like Hippocrates set the stage for the way modern scientists work?
6. **ACTIVITY** Many familiar words refer to the Greek myths. Look up the following words in a dictionary to find the meaning and the name of the Greek God or hero to which it refers: *narcissus* (flower), *arachnid, echo, atlas, Herculean.* Then look in a book of Greek myths to read the story behind one of the words.

CLOSE

Read the Thinking Focus aloud. Then draw the upper boxes of the Graphic Overview on the chalkboard, with lines leading from Art and Architecture, Literature, and Ideas to several boxes that you have drawn but left empty. Have students supply categories or specific names to fill the boxes. *(For example, sculpture, Parthenon; tragedy, history, comedy; Socrates, Aristotle, science, medicine)* Suggestions do not have to match the original Graphic Overview but should show that students recall the achievements of ancient Greece.

Answers to Review Questions

1. Many modern countries are democracies. Greek models and ideas still influence drama, science, philosophy, art, and architecture.
2. Recalling Chapter 2, students may identify political regions (city-state), landform regions (peninsula, islands, mountains, sea), or cultural regions (Athens, Sparta).
3. Spartan education emphasized physical skill and (for boys) military training. Athenian education, mostly for males, included reading, writing, and music along with physical training.
4. An Assembly of citizens, all free men, voted directly on issues. Women, children, slaves, and foreigners were not citizens.
5. Students should note that the Greeks were curious about the natural world. Although their myths explained the world, they began to look for physical, not magical, causes for natural events.
6. Students can read myths aloud to the class.

Homework Options

Tell students to imagine that they are Greeks of the Golden Age who have traveled into the future to our time. Ask each one to write a short diary entry, telling what familiar things and Greek influences he or she sees today. Encourage students to be imaginative.

Study Guide: page 27

DISCOVERY PROCESS

Students will use the following steps in the discovery process to complete the activity:

Get Ready Search the neighborhood for ancient Greek building styles.

Find Out Photograph or sketch buildings and record their locations, names, and uses.

Move Ahead Check sketches with the Minipedia. Compare lists with other students. Create a mural about classical Greek architecture.

Explore Some More Read about classical architecture.

Materials Needed: Sketchbook, pencil, camera (if available).

CULTURE

Visual Learning

Discuss the illustrations on this page. Ask students how the tops of the columns, or capitals, differ. *(The first is plain; the second is a simple scroll; the third is elaborately carved.)* Explain that the three styles developed in different parts of Greece.

Have students imagine the amount of work that stone cutters did on each type of capital and ask them which type they would prefer to work on as a sculptor. *(Students might say Doric, because it is simple, or Corinthian, because it would be a challenge.)*

EXPLORING

Greek Architecture in Your Community

You don't have to travel to Greece to see what the ancient Greeks left to the modern world. Their influence reached far beyond their own borders. For instance, you can explore the Greek contribution to architecture right here at home.

▲ *The three classical types of Greek capitals are Doric (top), Ionic (middle), and Corinthian (bottom).*

Get Ready

Pack up a sketch book and a pencil. Take along a camera if you have one. You are searching for examples of ancient Greek building styles in your own city or neighborhood.

Find Out

Look for columns—tall pillars that support a roof or ceiling. When you find some, sketch or photograph the capitals—the decorations at the top. Compare your sketch with those at the left. Are the capitals simple Doric, graceful Ionic, or elegant Corinthian?

Record the location of the building and its name, if it has one. Write down what it is used for: Is it a house? A store? A government building? A bank?

Move Ahead

Back in your classroom, compare your sketches or photographs with the drawings of the capitals on

PEDIMENT
CORNICE
FRIEZE
ARCHITRAVE
CAPITAL
SHAFT
COLUMN
BASE
STYLOBATE
CREPIDOMA

Objectives

1. Describe the three types of Greek capitals and give the correct terms for some general features of ancient Greek architecture. (Culture 1, 2)
2. Name some uses of Greek architectural styles in present-day buildings. (History 1, 2, 7; Culture 4)

Activities

After students have completed the steps outlined in the lesson, ask them where they could find out more about ancient Greek architecture. *(Encyclopedias; architectural magazines and journals; museums;* National Geographic, Smithsonian *magazines)* Have students write the architectural terms from the drawing at the bottom of this page; then have them add definitions and sketches to illustrate the terms. Ask students to look for examples of Greek architecture (sketches and photographs) to share with the class. Display the examples around the classroom. Discuss the function of each building part and the figures that decorate it.

Divide students into groups and provide each group with scratch paper, a large piece of sketch paper, and colored pencils or markers. Tell them that each group will role-play an architectural firm whose current project is to create a design for a class clubhouse; the design must include areas for study,

◄ *This scale model of Buckingham Palace is entirely made up of interlocking plastic bricks. What elements of Greek architecture can you identify?*

these pages and in the Architecture entry of the Minipedia, on pages 662 and 663. Correct your sketches or labels, if necessary.

Make a list of all the buildings you and your classmates saw. How many are there? What are the buildings used for?

Your class can draw a large mural showing the classical Greek architecture you found in your exploration. You can also combine many of the drawings and the photographs in a collage.

Explore Some More

Use the architectural terms on pages 662 and 663 to identify features of other buildings you find in your city or neighborhood. For example, some of the buildings you see may have a round dome.

The ancient Romans were the first people to borrow the Greek style. Since then, it has been copied often and in many places. In the late 1700s, architects in the United States imitated Greek architecture. Historians call this time the Federalist period of American arts.

Since Greece was the world's first democracy, Greek building styles symbolized the ideals of the new nation. The buildings were statements in stone, reminders of the people's right to govern themselves.

▼ *Early Greek temples were painted in many bright colors. As you explore your neighborhood, do you find colors used together with elements of Greek architecture?*

◄ *Buckingham Palace has Greek columns, cornices, and pediments. (If necessary, help students identify Buckingham Palace as the main residence of the British monarch.)*

◄ *Most Greek-style buildings, including Greek Revival, are plain stone or painted white.*

BELIEF SYSTEMS

Critical Thinking

Point out that the features of Greek architecture originated in temples to the Greek Gods and Goddesses. A temple was a "house" for the deity and usually contained an image of the God or Goddess to whom it was dedicated. Services honoring the Gods were held outside the building, however. Later these architectural features were used in secular buildings such as marketplaces.

Have students name some of the types of buildings in the Greek style that they found. Why do they think this style of architecture was chosen? Do the buildings give students a sense of respect, honor, wonder, or awe?

Another architectural form that originated in ancient Greece is the amphitheater, which often utilized the slope and curve of a natural hillside. (See the photo on page 161.) Greek theater, too, was religious in origin.

recreation, and eating. Each group should list the qualities they wish to reflect in their drawings. Then have them list the types of rooms and facilities they want their clubhouse to have.

Finally, the members of the group should bring their ideas together into one drawing or architectural plan. Display all the different plans where the class can study them closely. Have the whole class judge the final designs.

Collaborative Strategy

A recommended strategy for this lesson is Group Investigation. For further information turn to pages T34–T35.

INTRODUCE

Like other early cultures, the Greeks often explained natural cycles and occurrences through stories about their Gods and Goddesses. This retelling of the myth of Demeter and Persephone is from Ingri and Edgar Parin D'Aulaire's *Book of Greek Myths.* The selection helps to illustrate the discussion of Greek religion in this chapter. You may wish to have students review the cycle of the seasons on page G8 of the Map and Globe Handbook before they read the literature selection.

READ AND RESPOND

Students unfamiliar with the Greek myths will benefit from a guided reading of this longer selection. As students read, ask them to think about these questions: How does the myth explain the cycle of the seasons? How does it show the importance of grain to people's lives?

Before students read, point out the vocabulary words and unfamiliar terms defined in the margins. Be sure they understand what the words mean; help with the pronunciation of Greek names if necessary.

LITERATURE

Demeter and Persephone

Retold by Ingri and Edgar Parin D'Aulaire

As you read in Lesson 1, Greek myths are not just stories about Gods and humans. They also tell us a great deal about how the Greeks saw their world.

Although Demeter was not one of the major Goddesses of Mount Olympus, the Greek people loved her dearly. She was the Goddess who helped them plant and harvest crops, especially the grain used to make bread and flour. (Even Demeter's hair was the golden color of ripe grain.) As you read this myth, think about the events in nature that it explains.

Persephone (per SEF uh nee)

Demeter (dih MEET ur)

Hades God of the underworld, brother of Zeus

nymphs young Goddesses of nature

dismal gloomy

Persephone grew up on Olympus and her gay laughter rang through the brilliant halls. She was the daughter of Demeter, goddess of the harvest, and her mother loved her so dearly she could not bear to have her out of her sight. When Demeter sat on her golden throne, her daughter was always on her lap; when she went down to earth to look after her trees and fields, she took Persephone. Wherever Persephone danced on her light feet, flowers sprang up. She was so lovely and full of grace that even Hades, who saw so little, noticed her and fell in love with her. He wanted her for his queen, but he knew that her mother would never consent to part with her, so he decided to carry her off.

One day as Persephone ran about in the meadow gathering flowers, she strayed away from her mother and the attending nymphs. Suddenly, the ground split open and up from the yawning crevice came a dark chariot drawn by black horses. At the reins stood grim Hades. He seized the terrified girl, turned his horses, and plunged back into the ground. A herd of pigs rooting in the meadow tumbled into the cleft, and Persephone's cries for help died out as the ground closed again as suddenly as it had opened. Up in the field, a little swineherd stood and wept over the pigs he had lost, while Demeter rushed wildly about in the meadow, looking in vain for her daughter, who had vanished without leaving a trace.

With the frightened girl in his arms, Hades raced his snorting horses down away from the sunlit world. Down and down they sped on the dark path to his dismal underground palace. He led weeping Persephone in, seated her beside him on a throne of black marble, and decked her with gold and precious stones.

Thematic Connections

Social Studies: Belief Systems/ Importance of religion in human society

Houghton Mifflin Literary Readers: Traditional Tales/Timeless Tales

Background

The Greek myths were traditional tales about Gods and Goddesses, originally told orally. The tales had many variations because each city-state tended to have its own deities and traditions.

Between 600 and 200 B.C., some of these tales were written down. Known collectively as the Homeric Hymns, they were attributed to the Greek poet Homer (although they actually are probably the work of many authors). Each of the poems celebrated a particular deity's lineage and achievements. At religious festivals, bards, or minstrels, sang the hymns as introductions to their longer songs. Homer's epic poems, the *Iliad* and the *Odyssey,* also include well-known stories about the Greek Gods and Goddesses.

Ingri and Edgar Parin D'Aulaire wrote and illustrated numerous children's books in the United States and abroad. Their book *Abraham Lincoln* won the Caldecott Medal in 1940.

But the jewels brought her no joy. She wanted no cold stones. She longed for warm sunshine and flowers and her golden-tressed mother.

Dead souls crowded out from cracks and crevices to look at their new queen, while ever more souls came across the Styx and Persephone watched them drink from a spring under dark poplars. It was the spring of Lethe, and those who drank from its waters forgot who they were and what they had done on earth. Rhadamanthus *(rad ah MAN thus)*, a judge of the dead, dealt out punishment to the souls of great sinners. They were sentenced to suffer forever under the whips of the avenging Erinyes. Heroes were led to the Elysian fields, where they lived happily forever in never-failing light.

Around the palace of Hades there was a garden where whispering poplars and weeping willows grew. They had no flowers and bore no fruit and no birds sang in their branches. There was only one tree in the whole realm of Hades that bore fruit. That was a little pomegranate tree. The gardener of the underworld offered the tempting pomegranates to the queen, but Persephone refused to touch the food of the dead.

Wordlessly she walked through the garden at silent Hades' side and slowly her heart turned to ice.

Above, on earth, Demeter ran about searching for her lost daughter, and all nature grieved with her. Flowers wilted, trees lost their leaves, and the fields grew barren and cold. In vain did the plow cut through the icy ground; nothing could sprout and nothing could grow while the goddess of the harvest wept. People and animals starved and the gods begged Demeter again to bless

Styx (stihks) river across which souls of dead are carried

Erinyes (ih RIN eez) the furies, mythological creatures who pursued and punished sinners

barren without fruit

◄ How does Demeter show her grief when Persephone vanishes? *(She forbids anything on the earth to grow. Flowers wilt; fields are barren; people and animals go hungry.)*

Access Strategy

Help students understand that throughout history people have developed myths, or stories, to explain natural phenomena and the processes of life. Explain to students that ancient Greek mythology was peopled with a large number of Gods, Goddesses, and human beings. Many of these figures remain symbolically powerful in modern culture.

Before reading the selection, students may need a brief introduction to further major figures and locations that appear in this myth.

Mount Olympus—the home of the major Gods and Goddesses

Elysian Fields—a peaceful place where the souls of good people went after death

Zeus—the chief of the Gods and Goddesses and the father of some of them; lived at the top of Mount Olympus the earth. But she refused to let anything grow until she had found her daughter.

Bent with grief, Demeter turned into a gray old woman. She returned to the meadow where Persephone had vanished and asked the sun if he had seen what had happened, but he said no, dark clouds had hidden his face that day. She wandered around the meadow and after a while she met a youth whose name was Triptolemus *(trihp toh LAY muhz)*. He told her that his brother, a swineherd, had seen his pigs disappear into the ground and had heard the frightened screams of a girl.

Demeter now understood that Hades had kidnapped her daughter, and her grief turned to anger. She called to Zeus and said that she would never again make the earth green if he did not command Hades to return Persephone. Zeus could not let the world perish and he sent Hermes down to Hades, bidding him to let Persephone go. Even Hades had to obey the orders of Zeus, and sadly he said farewell to his queen.

Hermes (HER meez) Son of Zeus and messenger of the Gods.

Joyfully, Persephone leaped to her feet, but as she was leaving with Hermes, a hooting laugh came from the garden. There stood the gardener of Hades, grinning. He pointed to a pomegranate from which a few of the kernels were missing. Persephone, lost in thought, had eaten the seeds, he said.

Then dark Hades smiled. He watched Hermes lead Persephone up to the bright world above. He knew that she must return to him, for she had tasted the food of the dead.

When Persephone again appeared on earth, Demeter sprang to her feet with a cry of joy and rushed to greet her daughter. No longer was she a sad old woman, but a radiant goddess. Again she blessed her fields and the flowers bloomed anew and the grain ripened.

"Dear child," she said, "never again shall we be parted. Together we shall make all nature bloom." But joy soon was changed to sadness, for Persephone had to admit that she had tasted the food of the dead and must return to Hades. However, Zeus decided that mother and daughter should not be parted forever. He ruled that Persephone had to return to Hades and spend one month in the underworld for each seed she had eaten.

Every year, when Persephone had left her, Demeter grieved, nothing grew, and there was winter on earth. But as soon as her daughter's light footsteps were heard, the whole earth burst into bloom. Spring had come. As long as mother and daughter were together, the earth was warm and bore fruit.

Demeter was a kind goddess. She did not want mankind to starve during the cold months of winter when Persephone was away. She lent her chariot, laden with grain, to Triptolemus,

➤ How does the myth illustrate the yearly cycle of nature? *(When Persephone must leave the earth, it becomes fall and then winter, when plants wither or disappear. When Persephone returns to Demeter and the world of light, plants grow again, bloom, and give fruit. This period corresponds to spring and summer.)*

➤ Why was Demeter's gift so important to humankind? *(Demeter showed humans how to sow and reap grain so that they would have something to eat in the winter months, when the earth was not producing food.)*

Illustrating a Scene

The Greeks depicted stories about their Gods and Goddesses in sculptures and on painted walls, mosaic floors, and urns and bowls. Have students illustrate a scene from the myth of Demeter and Persephone that captures an important part of the myth. For example, they might want to show Hades capturing Persephone, Persephone eating from the pomegranate tree, Demeter grieving as living things on the earth wither, or the reunion of Demeter and Persephone.

Encourage students to look at pictures of Greek art forms such as the mask on page 157, the sculpture on pages 158 and 160, and the vases on pages 159 and 161. Instruct them to prepare their illustrations in a style similar to that used by the Greeks. Some students may wish to depict all the key scenes in the myth as a continuous mural or a series of panels.

the youth who had helped her to find her lost daughter. She told him to scatter her golden grain over the world and teach men how to sow it in spring and reap it in fall and store it away for the long months when again the earth was barren and cold.

reap to harvest, gather

Further Reading

The Avenger. Margaret Hodges. This exciting historical novel is set at the time of the Battle of Marathon (490 B.C.) between the Greeks and the Persians.

Book of Greek Myths. Ingri and Edgar Parin d'Aulaire. The book includes the myth above as well as other familiar stories.

Greek Gods and Heroes. Robert Graves. The author colorfully retells some classic myths and tales.

EXTEND

The story of Demeter and Persephone explains the seasons. Have students use the school or public library to find a Greek myth that explains another natural phenomena: for example, a myth about the Greek God Apollo explains the cycle of day and night; one about the God Zeus explains thunderstorms; and so forth.

Illustrating a Glossary

Have students research and create an illustrated glossary of selected Greek Gods and Goddesses. Students can write a brief description of the God and Goddess and the role he or she performed in the Greek pantheon. Then they can draw a picture of each deity. Students' drawings should incorporate clothing and activities that represent each deity's importance and responsibilities. *(For example, students might draw Zeus sitting atop Mount Olympus, hurling thunderbolts to the earth.)*

Further Reading

You may want to have students look in the school or local library for other myths about the Greek Gods and Goddesses.

INTRODUCE

Read the excerpt from the *Georgics* aloud. Discuss with students what kind of land and way of life they can picture from the poem. Ask them if ancient Rome sounds like ancient Greece. Emphasize that the two cultures were alike in some ways but quite different in others. Also, have students compare the two lesson timelines to see that much of Roman history falls later than Greece's Golden Age (400s B.C.). Then have a student read the Thinking Focus aloud. Ask students what they expect to discover about the Roman people as they read the lesson. *(They were proud, had a good army, were good at governing, and were skilled engineers.)*

Key Terms

Vocabulary Strategies: T36–T37

republic—a state without a king, in which the people may have a voice

province—a division of the Roman Empire, with a governor appointed by the emperor

legion—a fighting unit of the Roman army

aqueduct—a system for carrying fresh water using both pipes and high, arched stone structures

B.C. | A.D.
753
476
600

LESSON 2

Ancient Rome

THINKING FOCUS

How did Rome rule a huge empire for so long?

Key Terms

- republic
- province
- legion
- aqueduct

This place [Italy] . . . the olive owns, and the joyful herds. From here the war-horse comes, striding in his pride over the plain . . . Remember, too, all the fine cities . . . and the rivers gliding by beneath ancient walls. . . . This land has raised a fierce kind of men . . . Hail, great parent of harvests, land of the God Saturn, hail, great parent of men!

Virgil, *Georgics*, written about 37 B.C.

More than 2,000 years ago, the Roman poet Virgil praised the fertile farmlands and heroic people of Italy. His long poem *Georgics* was written when Rome was powerful but facing great political changes. The poem talked about lasting values. It reflected the pride that Romans had always felt in their home.

In this feeling of pride for their homeland, ancient Romans and Greeks were very similar. In other ways, the people of these two cultures were very different.

The Beginnings

Like Greece, Italy is a long peninsula that juts into the Mediterranean Sea. A chain of mountains runs down the center. Notice on the map that the city of Rome is near the center of Italy, on the Tiber River. Its location helped Rome grow powerful.

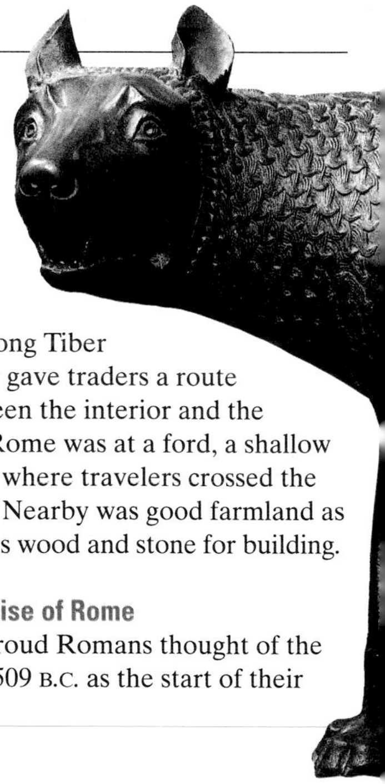

➤ *This statue of a mother wolf is a symbol of the city of Rome. Legend says that a wolf rescued and raised twin babies, Romulus and Remus. They supposedly founded the city in 753 B.C. but later fought. Romulus won, giving the city his name.*

A City on Seven Hills

When Rome began, several tribes of people lived on the Italian peninsula. In the center were the Latins. Etruscans lived to the north and south. Farther south were other tribes as well as Greek city-states.

The early Romans picked a good place for a town. It was built on seven hills that were easy to defend. The long Tiber River gave traders a route between the interior and the sea. Rome was at a ford, a shallow place where travelers crossed the river. Nearby was good farmland as well as wood and stone for building.

The Rise of Rome

Proud Romans thought of the year 509 B.C. as the start of their

Objectives

1. Describe how Rome grew under the Republic and the empire.
2. Describe what life was like in ancient Rome and its empire.
3. Explain why the Roman Empire fell.
4. Describe the importance of the legacies from ancient Rome.

Graphic Overview

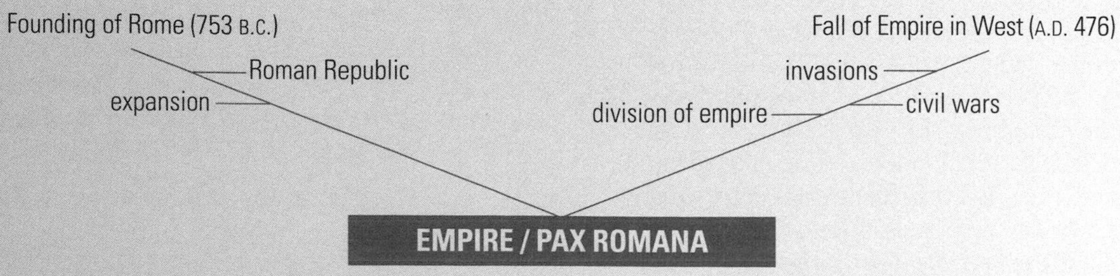
Founding of Rome (753 B.C.)
Roman Republic
expansion
Fall of Empire in West (A.D. 476)
invasions
civil wars
division of empire
EMPIRE / PAX ROMANA

Rise of the Roman Empire, 338 B.C.–A.D. 117

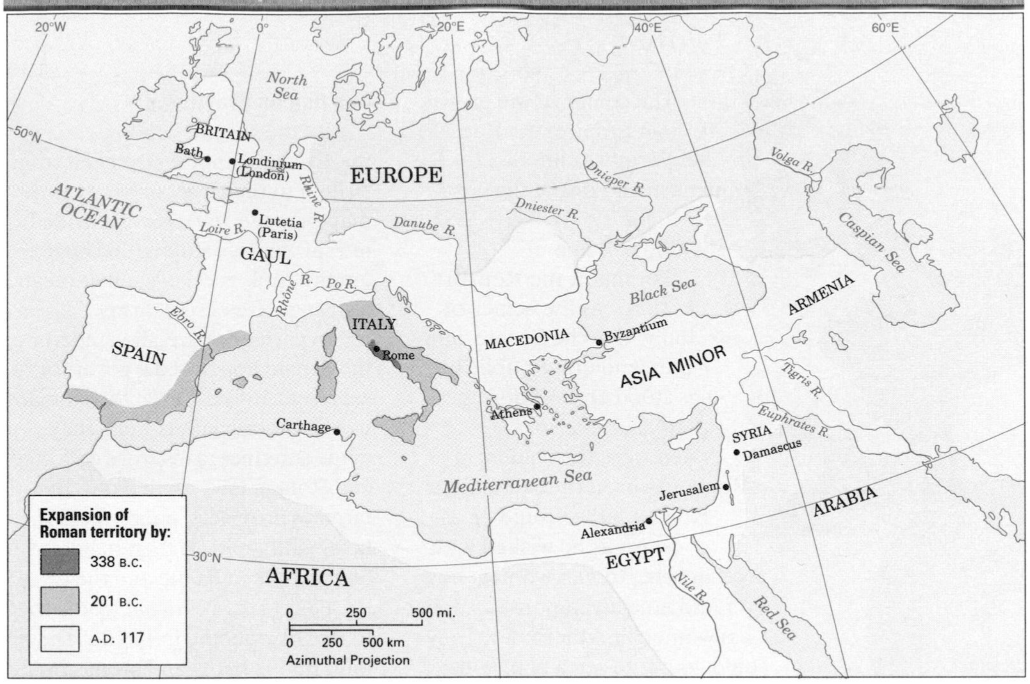
20°W
0°
20°E
40°E
60°E
50°N
30°N
North Sea
BRITAIN
Bath
Londinium (London)
EUROPE
ATLANTIC OCEAN
Lutetia (Paris)
Loire R.
GAUL
Rhine R.
Danube R.
Dnieper R.
Dniester R.
Volga R.
Caspian Sea
Rhône R.
Po R.
Black Sea
ARMENIA
Ebro R.
SPAIN
ITALY
Rome
MACEDONIA
Byzantium
ASIA MINOR
Tigris R.
Euphrates R.
Athens
Carthage
SYRIA
Damascus
Mediterranean Sea
Jerusalem
ARABIA
Alexandria
EGYPT
Nile R.
Red Sea
AFRICA
Expansion of Roman territory by:
338 B.C.
201 B.C.
A.D. 117
0 250 500 mi.
0 250 500 km
Azimuthal Projection

greatness. In that year they overthrew their king, an Etruscan, and set up a new government. It was a **republic**, a state without a king, in which the people have a voice.

Rome was not a democracy like Athens, however. Roman noblemen made up a Senate that advised Rome's leaders. Gradually, the city took over the rest of the Italian peninsula, then began to conquer nearby lands (see page G11 in the Map and Globe Handbook).

Rome's chief rival to the west was the city of Carthage in North Africa, the center of a huge trading empire. For over 100 years, Rome and Carthage fought three wars, called the Punic Wars. Rome won each war. In 146 B.C., Roman soldiers burned Carthage to the ground.

Rome continued to grow by conquering new territory. At home, however, Romans faced problems such as poverty, lack of jobs, and riots in the cities. Civil wars broke out. After more than 400 years, the Republic was in trouble.

By 44 B.C., Julius Caesar, a military hero, was the most powerful and popular man in Rome. Afraid that Caesar would become king, a group of nobles killed him. This did not save the Republic, however.

Rome now became an empire. In 31 B.C., Caesar's adopted son Octavian became sole ruler. As Augustus Caesar, he ruled until A.D. 14. His rule began a 200-year period known as the Pax Romana—the "Roman Peace." Although wars still went on at the empire's borders, Rome itself was at peace.

Roman emperors after Augustus had supreme power. They were sometimes worshiped as Gods. Yet many tried to rule wisely. The early empire was more peaceful and prosperous than the stormy last years of the Republic. ■

▲ *Through wars and military expeditions, the Roman Republic steadily increased its territory over several centuries. How did Rome acquire the territory around Carthage in North Africa?*

■ *How did Rome become an empire?*

DEVELOP

Draw the left-hand side of the Graphic Overview on the chalkboard (up to Empire). Then have a student read aloud the four boldface text heads—A City on Seven Hills, The Rise of Rome, The City of Rome, and The Roman Provinces. Explain that these sections of the lesson tell the story of the events in the diagram: how Rome began as a small town, grew into a city, and then acquired a huge empire, which it divided into provinces.

◄ *Rome acquired its territory in North Africa as a result of the Punic Wars.*

HISTORY

Map and Globe Skills

Point out that the map on this page is yet another way to show the stages in Rome's expansion. Ask students to notice the title of the map and the dates given on it. Then have them explain where it would go on the Graphic Overview. *(It covers the period from Expansion to Empire.)*

■ *First the Romans took control of the Italian peninsula. Then Roman armies conquered most of the lands around the Mediterranean Sea, defeating competitors like Carthage in North Africa.*

Access Strategy

Explain that the Romans borrowed much from Greek culture, that they changed or adapted Greek ideas and models to meet their particular needs, and that they also developed ideas and inventions of their own. Ask students to name cultures that have had a strong influence on life in the United States. *(Students may mention the cultures of Great Britain, Mexico, Africa, and ancient Greece, among others.)*

Draw a web on the board of things that people in the United States have borrowed from other cultures. *(For example, foods from Mexico, Italy, and France; government from Britain; words from Spanish, French, and Native American languages; architectural styles from Mexico and from ancient Greece and Rome; music from Africa)* Then consider with students how the United States has adapted things borrowed from other cultures.

Access Activity

Ask students to identify the geographic features of their neighborhood or city. Discuss with them how the features of the place helped it to grow. Then ask students to name features they would look for if they wanted to settle in a new area. If they had lived in ancient times, would they have looked for other things? *(For example, water, good land)*

GEOGRAPHY

Map and Globe Skills

Have students compare the map on page 169 with the map of earlier Roman expansion in the Map and Globe Handbook, page G11. Have them look first at the earliest stages of Roman expansion, when Rome rather quickly took over most of Italy. Then tell them to compare the areas that Rome held by 133 B.C. with the empire in A.D. 117, 250 years later. Where were the largest areas of new territory? *(Northern and eastern Europe—Gaul [modern France], Britain, Dacia, Illyricum [parts of Romania, Austria, the former Yugoslavia]; also Africa [Egypt] and Asia Minor)* The empire reached its greatest extent as a result of the campaigns of the emperor Trajan, who ruled from A.D. 98 to A.D. 117.

You may also want to have students compare the extent of the Roman Empire with a modern map showing the countries it encompassed.

■ *When they had completed their service, soldiers were given land or paid a bonus. They also became Roman citizens, if they were not already. Some became generals and a few, emperors.*

Daily Life

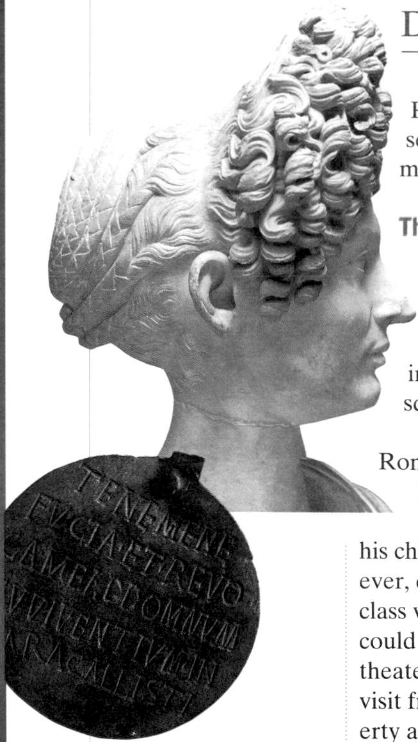

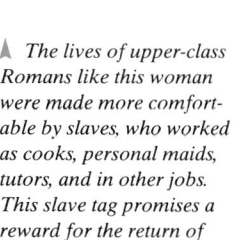

▲ *The lives of upper-class Romans like this woman were made more comfortable by slaves, who worked as cooks, personal maids, tutors, and in other jobs. This slave tag promises a reward for the return of a valuable runaway slave.*

The center of the growing Roman Empire was Rome itself. What was life like for Romans in and out of the city?

The City of Rome

For many, the Roman Forum was the center of daily life. The Senate, temples, and other public buildings stood around this open square.

Men were the leaders in Rome. As head of the family, a Roman father could be as stern as he wished with his children. Roman women, however, did not stay at home as upper-class women in Athens did. They could go out to see a play at the theater, to watch gladiators, or to visit friends. Women owned property and had other legal rights.

Rich and poor lived very differently in Rome. Most people lived in crowded apartment houses, three or four stories high. These rickety buildings often collapsed or caught fire. Wealthy Roman families had their own private houses, built around pleasant courtyards. They owned slaves who did all their everyday work.

Romans enjoyed many kinds of entertainment. Both rich and poor people exercised, bathed, and relaxed at the public baths. Romans also liked to go to the city's huge sports arenas. At the Circus Maximus, as many as 250,000 people could see fast horses and skillful drivers in exciting chariot races. The main sport at the Colosseum was watching gladiators fight hand-to-hand—often to the death—with each other or with wild animals.

The Roman Provinces

By the second century A.D., the Roman Empire stretched from Britain to the Caspian Sea (see the map on page 169). It was divided into **provinces**. Ruling this huge empire took good organization and a strong, often cruel, army.

In each province, the emperor or the Senate appointed a governor to represent Rome. Often the Romans used local officials as well. They made sure that taxes were collected and Roman laws carried out. In farming provinces, people paid their taxes with grain. The grain helped feed people in Rome and the army.

People in provincial towns tried to live like people in Rome. They built public baths and arenas in the Roman style. Being able to say, "I am a Roman citizen" was important in the provinces. Roman laws protected citizens anywhere in the empire. If accused of a serious crime, they could demand a trial in Rome. Only citizens could become officials or army officers.

The Roman army had been important in building the empire. Now it had to guard the empire's frontiers. When people in the provinces resisted Roman rule, soldiers brutally crushed the rebels. Sometimes, thousands died.

The Roman army was divided into about 30 **legions**, or fighting units. A legion typically had about 5,400 soldiers. Army life was hard, but it had rewards. After serving for 20 years, a soldier was given land or a sum of money as well as full citizenship, if he was not already a citizen. Late in the empire, a soldier could rise to become a general or even emperor. ■

■ Why did men want to become soldiers in the Roman army?

Social Participation

Ask students to form small groups to prepare a five-minute skit about daily life in ancient Rome. The skit may take place in the Forum, at home, at a sports arena, and so forth. Students should do outside research to make the scenes authentic. Have the groups perform their skits for each other or for other classes.

Cultural Context

The phrase "bread and circuses" now means short-term government actions to distract people from issues. In Rome, politicians gave out free grain and sponsored "circus" races and events such as gladiatorial contests.

The "thumbs down" sign comes from gladiatorial events. Spectators used it to refuse mercy to a wounded fighter. Most gladiators were criminals or prisoners of war, but some took up the profession for money or love of danger.

Economic Context

The Roman Empire had many natural resources outside the Italian peninsula. They included fertile lands for growing grain in Sicily and Egypt, rich mineral deposits (tin, silver, copper, gold, salt) in Spain and Britain, and marble quarries in Greece. In addition, Asia Minor had thick forests, while vineyards and olive trees grew in Gaul, Spain, North Africa, and Greece. Foods and farm products from the empire included cheese, fruit, honey, wool, wine, and leather.

Decline and Fall

After about A.D. 180, the government in Rome gradually grew weaker. Many emperors ruled badly. Civil wars broke out when it was time to choose a new emperor. Soldiers in the legions often backed their own generals. Soon the army was choosing most emperors.

By about A.D. 290, the Roman Empire seemed too large for one person to govern. It was divided, and different rulers ran the western and eastern halves. Power shifted away from Rome.

There were other threats, too. At the borders of the empire, local tribes attacked Roman settlements. Germanic peoples such as the Goths invaded Italy itself. Also, many foreigners now joined the Roman army. In A.D. 476, Germanic troops forced the last western emperor from power. The old Roman Empire ended. ■

■ *What were two main causes of the decline of the Roman Empire?*

The Roman Legacy

When Rome was the center of an empire, people said, "All roads lead to Rome." In fact, this was true. Roman roads all came together in the capital. Today many roads also lead *from* Rome. Roman culture still influences people today.

Government and Law

The framers of the U.S. Constitution in 1787 looked back to ancient Rome, adopting both the idea of a republic and the Romans' word for it. They admired the high ideals of the Roman Republic and hoped their new republic would follow them.

For example, in Rome the best and most talented people were expected to take part in government. Officials were expected to be honest and trustworthy. A true Roman was also expected to show courage and dignity.

Other modern ideas about government come from Rome. One is the importance of being a citizen.

This aqueduct was built about 19 B.C. to bring water to the Roman settlement at what is now Nîmes, France.

How an Aqueduct Works

Aqueducts carried water for many miles, from springs or lakes in the hills to Roman cities. The system included underground pipes as well as high stone structures. Sometimes a footpath ran along the top of the arches.

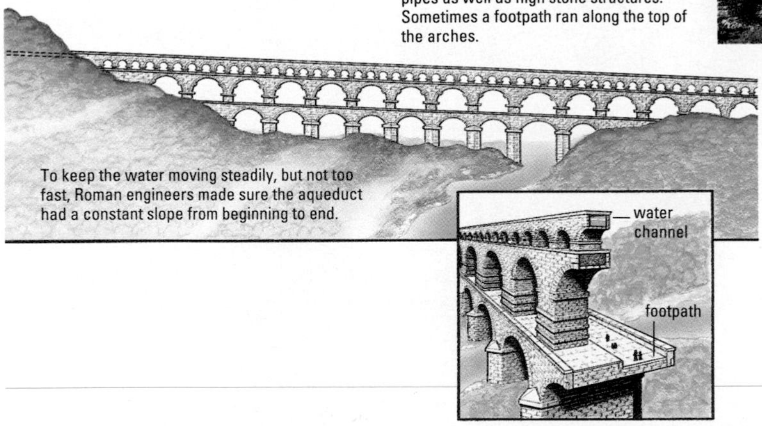
To keep the water moving steadily, but not too fast, Roman engineers made sure the aqueduct had a constant slope from beginning to end.
water channel
footpath

■ *Causes of the decline of the Roman Empire included frequent civil wars over who should become the next emperor and a shift of power from Rome to the eastern part of the empire. Another cause was attacks by tribes along the empire's borders and, later, Germanic invasions of Italy.*

CULTURE

Social Participation

Have students work together in small groups to create posters on the theme Many Roads Lead from Rome. Tell the groups that their posters should illustrate how Roman culture influences people today. Suggest that students use the "road" theme in designing their posters. For example, the poster might show a chariot wheel with Rome as the hub and the Roman legacies (such as language) as the spokes. Or Rome might stand in the center as a city on seven hills, with roads leading away from it bearing labels for its legacies. Display the posters in the classroom.

Social Context

At its greatest extent, the Roman Empire may have had as many as 50 to 70 million people, but it is hard to be exact. Regular censuses were taken but included only citizens—that is, adult males. Population densities were greatest in Italy. Rome itself had about one million people in the early second century A.D. At about A.D. 200, almost 80 percent of all the people in Europe lived within the empire. Thereafter, the population declined steadily for four centuries.

Science Connection

Many examples of Roman skill in architecture still exist today. Have students collect pictures or make their own drawings of existing Roman structures, such as aqueducts, walls, baths, and arenas. Good sources are travel magazines and books on art and architecture. Tell them to label their examples for display as follows: the name of the structure, where it is located, when it was built, what its original purpose was, what it is used for today, and where they found out about it.

Visual Learning

Have students examine the illustrations of an aqueduct on this page, locating the following elements in both the diagrams and the photograph: footpath, stone arches, concrete bases, and water channel. Ask what important feature the larger drawing illustrates. *(The constant slope, which keeps the flow steady)*

Note: Use this Moment in Time, which presents a Roman engineer at work, to build on the students' appreciation of the Romans' engineering skill.

GEOGRAPHY

Visual Learning

Use a map to show students that the section of road this engineer is working on will extend the old Rome-Pisa road all the way to Genoa. Roman builders will eventually continue the road through southern France and down the east coast of Spain to Cadiz.

The section of road will be named for the government official who paid for it. *Via Aemilia Scauri* means "the way (or road) of Aemilius Scaurus."

More About Roman Roads
Roman roads were built to last with little or no repair for up to a century. Some major roads were wide enough for two or more chariots to drive side by side. (There were also smaller side roads and country roads of dirt or gravel.) Although built primarily to move troops, the roads also promoted trade and communication. Roman roads eventually covered about 50,000 miles throughout the empire, making it easier to administer the huge territory.

A MOMENT IN TIME

A Roman Engineer

10:42 A.M., July 26, 109 B.C.
On what will be the Via Aemilia Scauri, outside Pisa

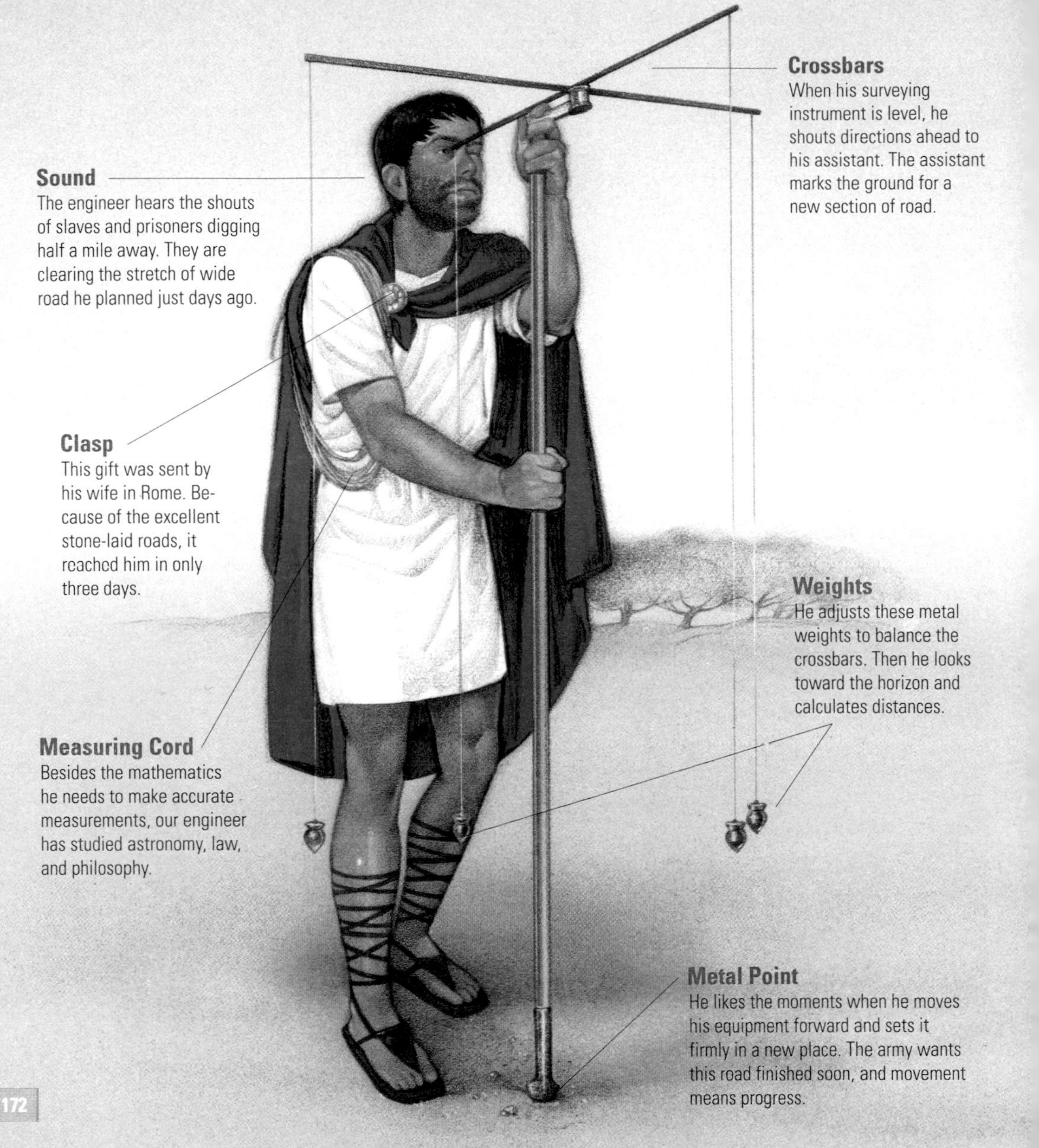
Crossbars
When his surveying instrument is level, he shouts directions ahead to his assistant. The assistant marks the ground for a new section of road.
Sound
The engineer hears the shouts of slaves and prisoners digging half a mile away. They are clearing the stretch of wide road he planned just days ago.
Clasp
This gift was sent by his wife in Rome. Because of the excellent stone-laid roads, it reached him in only three days.
Weights
He adjusts these metal weights to balance the crossbars. Then he looks toward the horizon and calculates distances.
Measuring Cord
Besides the mathematics he needs to make accurate measurements, our engineer has studied astronomy, law, and philosophy.
Metal Point
He likes the moments when he moves his equipment forward and sets it firmly in a new place. The army wants this road finished soon, and movement means progress.
172

Visual Learning

Ask students how they think the engineer used his tools. Like a modern surveyor, his job was to measure distances and angles to lay out the route for the new road. His essential tool—besides his instruments—was a good grasp of geometry. *(A crosspiece with four plumb lines was used to find a level and measure right angles.)*

Collaborative Learning

Have interested students draw a cross section or make a three-dimensional model of a Roman road. These roads had several layers, depending partly on the terrain. After the surveyors measured, builders (often soldiers) dug a ditch, sometimes down to bedrock. A layer of broken bricks, pebbles, and sand or gravel was rammed down solidly, followed by a watertight layer of small stones and another layer of gravel. The road surface was of large flat-topped stones, whose diamond-shaped undersides were stuck into the gravel. The finished roads were slightly slanted so that water would drain off the sides.

Students' models or drawings may include milestones, huge stone pillars that stood at every mile along a Roman road (after 123 B.C.), telling distances and some of the road's history. The Roman mile, from *mille passus,* "a thousand feet," was shorter than the present-day English (and American) mile because the Roman "foot" measure was shorter.

As in Rome, citizens of the United States have both rights and responsibilities. Another is the importance of having written laws so that people can read them for themselves.

Architecture

The Romans were practical people who were good engineers and builders. Roman architects used many rounded arches in their buildings. The Colosseum pictured on page 153 is a good example.

Roman aqueducts were also constructed of stone arches. As you can see in the pictures on page 171, an **aqueduct** carried fresh water into a city. Roman aqueducts still stand in Spain, France, and other places where Rome ruled.

The Romans were also famous for their road system. These roads were well built, with layers of stone and gravel. By A.D. 300 there were 50,000 miles of roads throughout the empire. Roads were built mainly for the army but also helped unite the empire. You can see a Roman road engineer at work in A Moment in Time on the facing page.

Language

Anywhere you traveled in the Roman Empire, you were likely to hear someone speaking Latin. Outside Italy, of course, local people spoke their own languages. Latin was the language of Rome, however. Anyone who wanted to succeed had to learn it.

In many places in the empire, people began to speak an everyday Latin that was different from written Latin. In time, most people stopped speaking their old languages. The local forms of Latin developed into new languages. Because these languages came from the language of Rome, they are called Romance languages. More than 400 million people speak these languages today. The largest number speak Spanish, French, Portuguese, Italian, and Romanian. ■

Across Time & Space

What if you did not know what your country's laws were until you broke one? What if an official could change a law without telling you? That is how things were in most early cultures.

In about 451 B.C., the Roman people insisted that their laws be written down. The laws, called the Twelve Tables, were posted in the Forum. Today people still believe that having written laws helps ensure justice.

◄ A Roman pupil unrolls his scroll to read, while another stands to face the stern-looking teacher.

■ *Name at least three things modern culture has adopted from Roman culture.*

REVIEW

1. **FOCUS** How did Rome rule a huge empire for so long?
2. **GOVERNMENT** How was the government of the Roman Empire different from the government of Athens?
3. **CULTURE** Compare the entertainments that Romans enjoyed with those that people enjoy today. Can you see any similarities?
4. **CRITICAL THINKING** Roman generals often fought among themselves for control of the empire. What kind of rules or laws could have helped prevent this type of fighting?
5. **ACTIVITY** Look at the arches in Roman structures such as the Colosseum or an aqueduct (pages 153 and 171). Then look for similar examples of arches in buildings in your community. Are Roman arches common in any particular type of building? Report your findings to the class.

CITIZENSHIP

Critical Thinking

Across Time & Space points out the importance of written law. Have students recall earlier examples of written law, such as the Code of Hammurabi and the laws of the Torah (see Chapter 3). Have them consider why the Twelve Tables were an important development in ensuring justice. *(They were written at the request of the Roman people, not at the will of a ruler.)*

■ *Modern culture has adopted Roman ideas about government, such as the principle of written laws and the republican ideal. Roman architecture and engineering influenced later builders. The Romance languages grew out of Latin.*

CLOSE

Ask students to reread the Thinking Focus. Then draw the outline of the Graphic Overview on the board, filling in the label only for the Empire/Pax Romana box. Then have students supply all the steps in both the establishment of the empire and its decline. Add additional lines or boxes to accommodate students' suggestions.

Answers to Review Questions

1. The Roman Empire was successful in part because it was well organized. Rome often used local leaders and institutions as part of its rule in the provinces. Roman law made citizenship desirable; good roads and a common official language helped unite the empire. The well-rewarded army supplied force when needed.
2. Athens was a city-state; citizens governed it in a form of direct democracy. In the Roman Empire, the emperor had supreme power; the Senate had limited power.
3. Students may mention theater, chariot races, and gladiators and note that all of these have modern counterparts.
4. Students may answer that if the Romans had had an established legal system for choosing new emperors, they would not have had to fight one another.
5. Suggest that students link this activity with the Exploring feature on Greek architecture in Lesson 1.

Homework Options

Ask students to look around them to find three things that show the Roman legacy. Suggest such common examples as a speed-limit sign (written law), a round arch (architecture), or people speaking Spanish or another Romance language. In class, have students compare their lists.

Study Guide: page 28

UNDERSTANDING CONCLUSIONS

This skills feature uses a three-step process to teach students how to examine evidence and draw conclusions from it.

HISTORY

Critical Thinking

List the three-step process on the chalkboard:

1. Study the evidence.
2. Draw a conclusion.
3. Think about the evidence again.

Emphasize that valid conclusions must be based on factual evidence. To demonstrate, ask students to predict which team is more likely to win a game—one whose record is 1 win and 10 losses or one whose record is 10 wins and 1 loss. Point out that to answer this, they will compare the two teams and draw a conclusion from the evidence. Explain that this skill can help them use information more effectively.

UNDERSTANDING CONCLUSIONS

Comparing Greece and Rome

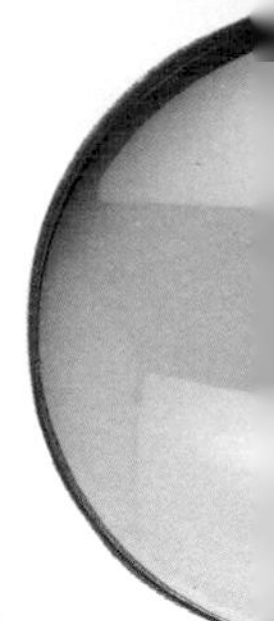

Here's Why

A conclusion is a reasoned judgment based on evidence. To draw your own conclusions, you must first study the facts available and see where they lead.

For example, as you read Lessons 1 and 2, you may have seen both similarities and differences between the cultures of ancient Greece and Rome. What conclusions can you draw about those two cultures?

Here's How

The paragraph on the left below is a summary of facts about Greek and Roman military organization. Use it to draw a conclusion about the strength of Roman legions compared with the armies of the Greek city-states. Follow these steps:

1. **Study the evidence.** As you read, look for facts. The paragraph on military organization includes these important points:
   a. Roman legions had thousands of trained soldiers.
   b. Small Greek armies were made up of citizen-soldiers.
2. **Draw a conclusion.** Use the facts from step 1 along with anything else you know about the subject. Here it is reasonable to conclude that the Roman legions were stronger than the Greek armies. Trained, experienced soldiers are likely to be a stronger force than citizen-soldiers.
3. **Think about the evidence again.** Does it support the conclusion? Be ready to change your conclusion if necessary. During the empire, Roman troops in the legions spent 20 years as soldiers. The legions were well supplied and organized. Certain troops were specially trained. These facts support the conclusion.

Try It

The paragraph on the right below compares Greek and Roman engineering skills. What facts are given? What conclusion can you draw about their relative abilities?

Apply It

Find an article in a local newspaper or magazine. Use the three-step strategy in Here's How to draw a conclusion from it.

Military Organization

The Roman army was a powerful military force. It did not depend only on huge numbers of soldiers but used planning and discipline to defeat its enemies. The small armies of most Greek city-states were made up of citizen-soldiers. In contrast, the Roman army had thousands of trained soldiers who served for 20 years. Roman legions traveled with workers who could make weapons or give medical help, so they seldom needed to return to Rome. In addition, they could adapt to changing battle conditions with troops specially trained as archers, spear throwers, and so forth.

Engineering Skill

The Romans owed much to Greek culture but made many important practical achievements of their own. Engineering skill enabled the Romans to build long-lasting roads throughout the empire. The mountains of Greece, however, made road building difficult, so the Greeks more often traveled by sea. Greek builders skillfully cut and carved stone for their buildings. The Romans, on the other hand, invented a form of concrete, which was strong but lighter than stone. Concrete was used not only for roads but also in huge public works such as bridges, aqueducts, and stadiums.

Objective

List and apply the steps used in drawing conclusions from evidence. (Critical Thinking 3)

Working in Groups

Divide the class into groups of four or five. Assign each group a section of Chapter 7. Have them follow the three-step process to study the evidence (list the facts) in the section, then make a list of conclusions they can draw from those facts. Have the class evaluate the suggested conclusions.

Answers to Try It

Facts: The Romans learned some architectural skills from Greek culture. They made technological advances, such as the invention of a form of concrete, which let them build large, sturdy structures. Possible conclusion: the Greeks were skillful, creative architects, but the Romans were probably better at engineering and technology.

Answers to Apply It

Students should state the evidence presented in the articles and show how it led them to their conclusions.

B.C. A.D.
800
600
400
200
6
400
600

LESSON 3

Early Christianity

It was the middle of the night, but Paul and Silas, two prisoners in the jail at Philippi, were praying and singing. Paul was an **apostle**—a person who spreads the message of a new religion. Suddenly, an earthquake shook the prison. Doors flew open, but the two prisoners did not run away. The jailer was amazed and relieved, for he would have been punished for their escape. He fell to his knees before the prisoners.

Then he brought them outside and said, "Sirs, what must I do to be saved?" They answered, "Believe on the Lord Jesus, and you will be saved, you and your household."

Bible, Acts 16:30–31

The New Testament of the Bible tells how apostles like Paul spread this message to many people during the first century A.D. They spoke about the new beliefs taught by Jesus.

THINKING FOCUS

How did the Christian religion begin and grow?

Key Terms

- apostle
- Gospel

The Life and Message of Jesus

Scholars are not sure of the historical facts of Jesus' life. Many now agree that he was born a Jew about 6 B.C. in the Roman province of Judea. In Rome, Augustus Caesar was still ruling as emperor. Jesus was put to death in Jerusalem in about A.D. 30. His followers later called Jesus "the Christ." This name refers to the holy oil used when kings were chosen. Jesus' followers are called Christians.

The people who first followed Jesus were Jews. Most of his teachings agreed with Jewish beliefs. As a result, the Christian and Jewish faiths share many common ideas. Most of what they teach about right and wrong is the same.

The part of the Christian Bible called the Old Testament includes the same books as the Jewish scriptures. They are a part of belief and worship services for both Christians and Jews. The rest of the Christian Bible is called the New Testament. It is the source of many basic Christian beliefs.

The Gospels

Four books of the New Testament tell how Christians understand the life of Jesus. Matthew, Mark, Luke, and John describe the

The infant Jesus with his mother, Mary, has been a favorite subject for Christian art. This mosaic was made in the sixth century A.D. for a Byzantine church.

INTRODUCE

Tell students that one of the world's major religions had its beginnings in the Roman Empire during the Pax Romana. Ask students whether they can identify the religion. Then have them turn to the map of world religions on page 688 of the Atlas and locate the parts of the world where Christianity is the main religion today. Have a student read the Thinking Focus aloud. Then tell the class that this lesson will look at how Christianity began in the Mediterranean region and then spread to other parts of the world.

Key Terms

Vocabulary Strategies: T36–T37

apostle—a person who spreads the message of a new religion

Gospel—one of four books of the New Testament, telling the story of Jesus' life and teachings

Graphic Overview

Spread of Christianity

Judea (A.D. 30) Jesus' followers spread Gospel message.	→	**Roman Empire (by A.D. 395)** Paul and later missionaries establish new congregations.	→	**Asia, Africa, Americas (today)** Colonizers and missionaries spread religion worldwide.

Objectives

1. Explain the origins of Christianity.
2. Describe the ways in which Christianity was spread.

DEVELOP

Explain that this lesson traces the beginnings and growth of the Christian religion, which took place during the Pax Romana and the later years of the Roman Empire. Have students compare the lesson timeline with the one for Rome on page 168. Point out that some of the events in this lesson tie directly to historical dates, while the exact dates of other events are not known.

HISTORY

Critical Thinking

Some students will be confused by seeing the date of Jesus' birth given as 6 B.C. Ask students to recall how the dates for B.C. and A.D. were set. (See Chapter 3, Across Time & Space, page 75.) Have them discuss the kinds of evidence scholars might look for to establish the date of an event like Jesus' birth.

Both Christian and Jewish scriptures were originally written down in several different languages and versions. This ancient manuscript in Greek is part of Psalms, a book of the Old Testament.

How Do We Know?

HISTORY *No one person sat down and wrote a book called the New Testament. The books in it were written during the first and second centuries A.D. Church scholars argued for centuries about which books to include.*

The New Testament begins with the four Gospels. Next, the Acts of the Apostles gives some history of the early Church. Letters from Paul and other apostles make up most of the rest.

message of God's forgiveness that Jesus taught. These books are called the **Gospels**, meaning "good news."

According to Luke, at about age 30, Jesus began to travel and teach. He preached to large crowds about the kingdom of God. He told them he had come as a sign of God's offer of salvation. For Jesus, salvation meant being forgiven by God for your sins so that you could have eternal life. Jesus said that those who truly repented for their sins could enter God's kingdom. He chose 12 apostles to help him spread his message.

The Gospels say that Jesus performed miracles, which were seen as signs of the coming kingdom of God. They tell how he healed the sick, walked on water, and brought the dead back to life.

The Teachings of Jesus

Jesus followed Jewish tradition in teaching that it was important to forgive people. He said, "For if you forgive others their [wrongdoings], your heavenly Father will also forgive you" (Matthew 6:14). Even though humans did not deserve to be forgiven, Jesus said, God offered forgiveness to those who believed in God and were sorry for their sins.

Jesus knew the Jewish scriptures well. One Gospel tells about a lawyer who asked Jesus what part of the Law was the greatest. Jesus answered with verses from the Jewish scriptures:

> *You shall love the Lord your God with all your heart, and with all your soul, and with all your mind." This is the greatest and first commandment. And a second is like it: "You shall love your neighbor as yourself." On these two commandments hang [depend] all the Law and the prophets.*
>
> Bible, Matthew 22:37–40

Jesus' Death and Afterward

According to the Gospels, many people listened to Jesus. They came to believe he was the son of God.

Both Roman officials and local Jewish leaders believed Jesus was dangerous. In about A.D. 30, Jesus was arrested. Under Roman law, he was put to death by crucifixion—fastened to a wooden cross until he died. This was a Roman method for carrying out death sentences.

Jesus' friends were stunned by his death. Christians believe, however, that he was resurrected, or raised from the dead, a few days later. According to the Gospels, Jesus talked to his followers several times after the crucifixion.

For Jesus' followers, the resurrection was a sign of hope. To them, it meant that all who believed in Jesus would gain God's forgiveness and have a life after death. The Christian festival of Easter celebrates the resurrection.

Christians believe that Jesus suffered to save all humanity. In a ritual called Holy Communion or

Access Activity

Draw the Graphic Overview on the chalkboard. Then have students look at the map on page 178. Tell them that both show, in different ways, the spread of the Christian religion. Have students compare the differences and similarities in the information presented by the two graphics.

Access Strategy

Ask students to think of examples in history when one individual had a very strong influence on the basic beliefs of thousands of people. Discuss what effects each person had and how the governments or officials in power during their lives reacted. Ask this question: How is it possible for one individual to be so influential? This lesson explores the effect of one individual, Jesus, upon the beliefs of many Jews and non-Jews, and the reaction of the government of the Roman Empire.

the Lord's Supper, they remember Jesus' last meal with his apostles. He gave them bread and wine as symbols of his suffering. The cross on which Jesus died also became an important Christian symbol. ■

■ *What did Jesus teach about the Jewish Law?*

■ *He taught that it meant that people should love God and one another.*

The Christian Religion

According to the Gospels, Jesus himself told his close friends to spread his message of God's forgiveness for humanity. In one of his last meetings with the apostles, he had said, "Go into all the world and proclaim the good news to the whole creation" (Mark 16:15).

At Jesus' death, some of his followers returned to Jerusalem. The small group was made up of the apostles and several women, including Jesus' mother, Mary.

The Religion Grows

At first, the new religion was guided by such apostles as Peter, James, and John. Later, other people joined in their efforts. They traveled to nearby cities and countries as missionaries, telling people about Jesus' death and resurrection. The map on the next page shows how groups, or congregations, of Christians formed throughout the Roman Empire.

Some features of the Roman Empire helped Christianity spread. Missionaries used the fine Roman roads. They sailed on Roman trading ships. Some could teach in Greek or Latin, which people throughout the empire understood.

On the other hand, the missionaries spreading the new religion often were in danger. Their preaching angered people who still followed the old Gods of Greece and Rome. It also bothered local officials. Some rulers had missionaries arrested and sometimes put to death. In Jerusalem, an angry crowd chased and killed a young preacher named Stephen.

Probably the most famous apostle is Paul, a Jew born in a Greek city in Asia Minor. For years, Paul was one of the officials who arrested and threatened Christians. According to the Bible, as he traveled to Damascus one day, he saw a blinding light and heard Jesus speaking to him. Paul suddenly became a believer.

For the rest of his life, Paul journeyed from one end of the Mediterranean to another. He began new churches and wrote letters to groups in other cities. A Roman citizen, Paul used his citizenship for protection when he was arrested for preaching. The books of the New Testament include Paul's letters to early churches in Rome, Greece, and Asia Minor.

Early Christians in Rome were buried in the catacombs—long underground tunnels on the edge of the city. By the dim light of small oil lamps, Christians made their way through the catacombs to hold services at tombs that had become shrines.

BELIEF SYSTEMS

Study Skills

Remind students that the Old Testament and the Jewish scriptures include the same books, but in different order. In the primary source on the facing page, Jesus quotes from two books of the Torah: Deuteronomy 6:5 and Leviticus 19:18 (see Chapter 3). Have students find out the names of the books of the Torah, the first five books of both the Christian and the Jewish Bible. *(Genesis, Exodus, Leviticus, Numbers, Deuteronomy)*

HISTORY

Map and Globe Skills

Ask students to trace the journeys of the apostle Paul in the Mediterranean region. Tell them they will find primary-source material in the New Testament (Book of Acts, Paul's letters) and secondary-source information in an encyclopedia. Once they have gathered their information, students should draw Paul's route, either drawing their own maps or tracing the map on page 178. Tell them to identify major cities and congregations that Paul visited.

Historical Context

Jesus' teachings might never have spread had it not been for the small group of Jewish men and women in Judea who led the early Christians. At first just a sect within Judaism, they believed that Jesus would soon return to bring the kingdom of God. Differences in belief between Christians and traditional Jews increased. Apostles then made the serious decision to preach to Gentiles, or non-Jews. Soon most Christian converts were non-Jewish peoples.

Critical Thinking

Ask students to consider what motivations led the apostles and other early Christian missionaries to face hardship, danger, and death in spreading their religion. Discuss what ideas today might inspire people to this kind of behavior and dedication. *(Students may suggest work for civil rights or human rights, against apartheid in South Africa, for democracy in China.)*

GEOGRAPHY

Map and Globe Skills

Have students compare the map on this page with the map of the Roman Empire on page 169. Ask them to describe the overlap of the two maps and to comment on the reasons for it. *(For its inhabitants, the Roman Empire was the extent of the "civilized world" at the time. Missionaries could travel on Roman roads or ships. The government of Rome assured some kind of order wherever they went, especially if they were citizens.)*

➤ *The westernmost congregation shown is Cordoba, Spain; the easternmost (named on the map) are those at Antioch and Jerusalem.*

Christianity Gains a Protector

Being a Christian in the Roman Empire was often risky. Some Romans thought the new group was dangerous. Christians did not honor the Roman Gods or accept the Roman emperor as a God. They did not come to public ceremonies or festivals, which honored the Gods. Romans thought this behavior was disloyal to the empire itself. They blamed Christians for fires and other disasters. Christians in both Rome and the provinces were killed, put in prison, or sent to face wild animals in the arena.

Yet, Christians tried to obey Roman law. They also took care of the sick and the needy. Still, their beliefs and actions set them apart from the Roman community.

Gradually, however, the Roman Empire began to accept Christianity along with other religions. Then in A.D. 312, Constantine, who would become Roman emperor, had a vision. It led him to become a strong protector of the Church.

What changed Constantine's mind? According to one source, he was at war with a rival who also wanted to be Roman emperor. The night before the battle, Constantine dreamed that he should paint a Christian symbol on his soldiers' shields. After winning the battle, he became a supporter of Christianity.

Constantine later believed that his support of Christianity made him a successful ruler. He worked hard to make the Roman Empire a Christian empire. His support helped the Church become rich and powerful. Gradually, statues of the old Gods were taken down. In time, Christianity became the official religion of the Roman Empire.

Constantine built himself a city called "New Rome" at the town of Byzantium, near the eastern end of the Mediterranean Sea. In A.D. 330, Constantine made his new city the capital of the Roman Empire. He renamed it Constantinople *(kon stan tih NOH puhl)*. Today it is the city of Istanbul in modern Turkey.

Spread of Early Christianity by A.D. 395

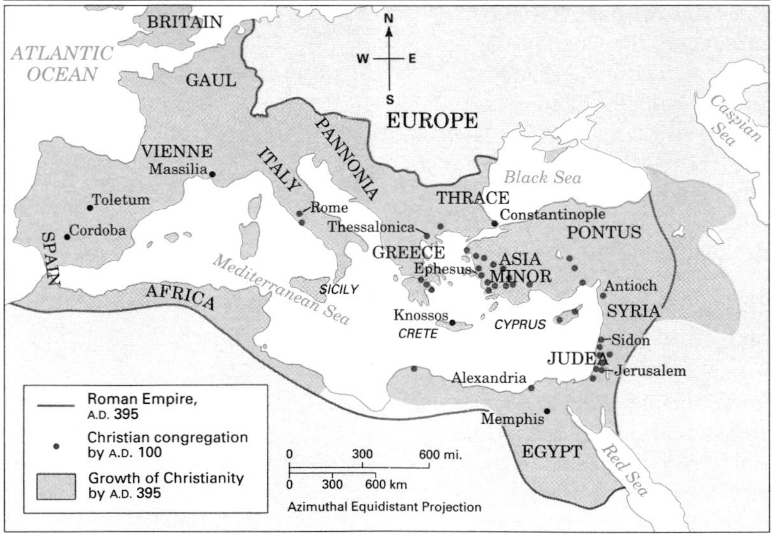
BRITAIN
ATLANTIC OCEAN
GAUL
N
W
E
S
EUROPE
Caspian Sea
VIENNE
Massilia
ITALY
PANNONIA
Black Sea
Toletum
THRACE
Rome
Constantinople
Cordoba
Thessalonica
PONTUS
SPAIN
GREECE
ASIA MINOR
Ephesus
Mediterranean Sea
SICILY
Antioch
AFRICA
SYRIA
Knossos
CRETE
CYPRUS
Sidon
JUDEA
Jerusalem
Alexandria
Memphis
EGYPT
Red Sea
Roman Empire, A.D. 395
Christian congregation by A.D. 100
Growth of Christianity by A.D. 395
0 300 600 mi.
0 300 600 km
Azimuthal Equidistant Projection

➤ *By A.D. 200, missionaries had started Christian congregations from one end of the Mediterranean to the other. What were the easternmost and westernmost Christian settlements?*

Critical Thinking

What if Constantine or another Roman emperor had not converted to Christianity? What would have happened to the new religion? Ask students to speculate about whether the religion would have grown as fast or spread as widely.

Language Arts Connection

The first Christians preserved the story of Jesus' life and teachings largely by word of mouth. Written material included the letters of Paul and other apostles. As the How Do We Know? on page 176 points out, scholars decided later which materials to include. The Bible of the earliest Christians was the New Testament in Greek. Throughout the medieval period, Latin was the language of the Church. The first complete English translation was planned by an English priest named John Wycliffe in about 1380–1381. Since then, many different English translations have been made. Each includes slightly different interpretations. Some are more literary, and some are intended to make the Scriptures understandable to a wider audience. The Bible excerpts in this chapter are from the *New Revised Standard Version.* You may wish to compare and contrast them with those in other Bibles, both Protestant and Catholic.

Christians Discuss Beliefs

By the time of Constantine, the Christian Church was well organized. The first apostles had been mainly teachers. They inspired people by preaching, as Jesus had done. Now local churches needed people to lead them and look after day-to-day business. Those chosen as leaders were called bishops.

Bishops became very important in the Church. They decided what would be taught and made rules for people in their congregations. They looked after the Church's money and property. Power was passed on from bishop to bishop.

A declaration of beliefs became a central part of early Christian services. Because this statement was so important to them, Christians argued about several questions of belief. It was the bishops who decided such questions for the Church as a whole. They wrote letters back and forth about their different points of view. They also held meetings, or councils, to discuss them.

One question was this: Was Jesus a human being, or was he divine, like God? Jesus had suffered and died as a human being. How then, some asked, could he be the son of God, as he had said he was? Perhaps he had been only a great prophet or teacher. Finally, a council of bishops agreed that Jesus was both human and divine.

Still another question was about the Trinity, the idea of "threeness." Christians, like Jews, believe in only one God. Those who believed in the Trinity said that this one God included three "persons:" God the Father, God the Son (Jesus), and the Holy Spirit. Others disagreed. Church scholars argued about the idea for centuries. By the end of the fourth century A.D., however, the Trinity became an official teaching of the Church.

Over later centuries, Christianity spread to many parts of the world. The Atlas map on page 688 shows where followers of Christianity and other religions live today. ■

▲ *This painting depicts Jesus' Last Supper with his small group of 12 apostles. This event is still remembered in Christian religious services. The painting is on a wall of the Roman catacombs.*

■ *Why were bishops important in the early Christian Church?*

R E V I E W

1. **FOCUS** How did the Christian religion begin and grow?
2. **HISTORY** How did the organization of the Roman Empire help the apostles in their work of spreading Jesus' message?
3. **BELIEF SYSTEMS** Why did Christianity seem threatening to some Romans?
4. **CRITICAL THINKING** You have read about the troubled times during the decline of the Roman Empire. How might this have helped the spread of Christianity?
5. **ACTIVITY** In your library, do research to find out more about catacombs like the one shown in the illustration on page 177. Write a three-paragraph report describing what you discovered.

BELIEF SYSTEMS

Study Skills

The outcome of some councils of bishops was an official creed, or declaration of beliefs. The most widely accepted are the Nicene Creed (from the Council of Nicaea in A.D. 325) and the Apostles' Creed (which may go back to second-century models). If it seems appropriate, have students find copies of each of these creeds and bring them to class.

■ *Bishops became necessary as the Church grew. They organized and managed Church property and business; they set up rules for their congregations; they also conferred to settle questions of doctrine.*

C L O S E

Read the Thinking Focus aloud. Then ask students what kind of a diagram or graphic organizer they would draw to illustrate what they have learned about the growth of Christianity. Invite students to put their diagrams on the board and to explain how they show Christianity's growth. If necessary, refer to the original Graphic Overview.

Answers to Review Questions

1. Christianity began in Judea about A.D. 30 with the teachings of Jesus. His followers believed he brought a message of salvation, and they spread their beliefs to many people throughout the Mediterranean in the centuries after Jesus' death.
2. The Pax Romana made travel easier because the Roman Empire was generally at peace during this time. Roman roads and laws, as well as the common use of Greek or Latin, also helped the apostles.
3. Because the Roman religion was so closely linked with the emperor, refusing to honor the Roman Gods seemed like treason.
4. Students may see a connection: People looked to the new faith for security in troubled times. Also, Christianity may have weakened Roman unity.
5. Students' paragraphs should show that they know how to do research to find this type of information.

Homework Options

Tell students to look in art books and other references to find representations of Jesus, the apostles, or scenes from the Bible. Students may share the pictures they have located with the rest of the class and briefly explain what they show.

Study Guide: page 30

Answers to Reviewing Key Terms

A. Sample answers:

1. Yes. Because settlements were cut off from each other by steep mountains, each **city-state** developed its own government.
2. No. A **province** was a division of the empire; it was ruled by Roman laws.
3. No. A **legion** was a division of soldiers in the Roman army.
4. No. As an **apostle,** Paul spread the teachings of Jesus.
5. Yes. The four **Gospels** relate the life of Jesus as seen by his followers.

B. Sample answers:

1. **aqueduct:** from Latin words meaning "water" and "to lead." Roman aqueducts brought water to growing cities.
2. **citizen:** from French and Latin for "city" *(civitas)* and "citizen" *(civis).* A citizen was originally a resident of a city (such as Rome), who had certain rights.
3. **democracy:** from Greek words meaning "the people" and "to rule." Democracy began in the city-states of ancient Greece.
4. **peninsula:** from Latin, meaning "almost an island." Both Greece and Italy are peninsulas.
5. **philosophy:** from Greek words meaning "love" and "wisdom." Philosophy is part of our heritage from ancient Greek culture.
6. **republic:** from Latin words meaning "interest" and "public." The Romans overthrew their king to set up a republic.

Answers to Exploring Concepts

A. Contributions listed in the chart may include:

Greeks: democracy, architecture, mythology, philosophy, arts

Romans: civil engineering (roads, bridges, aqueducts), code of law, military organization, citizenship, Romance languages

B. Sample answers:

1. Hilly terrain meant little good farmland. People herded animals and raised crops, but they also turned to fishing and trade.
2. Greek culture spread as a result of trade, the founding of Greek colonies, and the conquests of Alexander the Great.
3. Pericles was a military, political, and artistic leader who led Athens during the Golden Age and the Peloponnesian War.
4. The Roman Republic was led mainly by the Senate, a group of wealthy nobles. The Roman Empire was governed by one ruler, the emperor; the Senate and the army had some power.
5. People in the provinces lived under Roman law and Roman officials, built houses and public buildings in Roman style, spoke Latin. Roads connected the empire.
6. The army fought wars and conquered territory; later it guarded the frontiers, suppressed rebellions, and sometimes chose emperors.
7. The Old Testament includes the same books as the Jewish scriptures; the New Testament tells about the life and teachings of Jesus and Christianity.
8. At about the age of 30, Jesus began to travel and preach in Judea.
9. Apostles and missionaries spread the Christian religion throughout the Mediterranean world. Roman officials persecuted Christians.
10. Bishops guided local congregations, looked after Church property, and conferred on questions of belief.

Chapter Review

Reviewing Key Terms

apostle (p. 175)
aqueduct (p. 173)
citizen (p. 156)
city-state (p. 155)
democracy (p. 158)
Gospel (p. 176)
legion (p. 170)
peninsula (p. 155)
philosophy (p. 160)
province (p. 170)
republic (p. 169)

A. Each statement below uses a key term from this chapter. Tell whether each key term is used correctly. Then explain the reason for your answer.

1. The rugged geography of Greece contributed to the development of self-governing city-states.
2. Each province of the Roman Empire was like a separate country, with its own laws and rulers.
3. In the Roman army, a legion was a group of generals from which the next emperor would be chosen.
4. As an apostle, Paul arrested and threatened Christians.
5. The four Gospels describe what Christians understand about the life of Jesus.

B. Use a dictionary to find the origin of the following words. Then explain their importance in the ancient Mediterranean world.

1. aqueduct
2. citizen
3. democracy
4. peninsula
5. philosophy
6. republic

Exploring Concepts

A. The cultures of ancient Greece and Rome made many contributions to present-day culture. Copy and complete this chart with information from the chapter. Include at least four items for each culture.

Culture	Contributions
Greeks	tragedy, comedy
Romans	

B. Answer each question with information from the chapter.

1. How did geography affect the way people lived and worked in ancient Greece?
2. How did Greek culture spread to other parts of the ancient Mediterranean world?
3. In what ways was Pericles important in Greek history?
4. How was Roman government different under the Republic and the empire?
5. What were some of the ways in which Roman culture influenced people throughout the Roman Empire?
6. Why was the army so important in Roman history?
7. What different materials do the Old Testament and the New Testament of the Christian Bible include?
8. According to the Gospel of Luke, how and where did Jesus begin to spread his message?
9. How did the Christian religion spread? What obstacles did early Christians face?
10. What was the role of bishops in the early Christian Church?

Reviewing Skills

1. Comparing two maps of the same area can tell you how geography, history, and people's ways of life are related. For example, the maps on pages 169 and 178 show the Mediterranean world in Roman times. Compare the maps to see what they show about the relationship of the Roman world and the spread of Christianity. For instance, what major cities of the empire became the sites of new Christian congregations?
2. From your comparison of the two maps, what conclusions can you draw about the relationship between Rome and the spread of Christianity? Write a statement of your conclusions.
3. Suppose you were a historian doing research on what it was like to be a young student in ancient Rome. What kinds of written sources would you look in to find this kind of information?

Using Critical Thinking

1. In Athens, only free-born males could be citizens or members of the Assembly. Although the Athenian government would not be considered a true democracy today, it is still admired as a model. Write a paragraph telling whether or not you think this is justified.
2. "In Rome, the best and most talented people were expected to take part in government." To what extent is this true in the United States? How would you go about convincing the "best and most talented" people to work in politics and government?
3. Look at the map of Roman expansion on page G11 in the Map and Globe Handbook. Imagine that you are a member of the Roman Senate in 133 B.C., listening to a plan to extend Roman territory. What would be some advantages of doing so? What would be some problems?
4. After Constantine, Christianity became the official religion of the Roman Empire. Do you think it is a good idea for a government to give its support to one religion over all other religions? Why?

Preparing for Citizenship

1. **WRITING ACTIVITY** Although the ancient Greek myths describe the actions of Greek Gods and Goddesses, they actually show much about human nature. Read several Greek myths. Then invent a God or Goddess your own age and write your own myth. How does your main character face one of the problems of growing up?
2. **GROUP ACTIVITY** Citizens in ancient Greece or Rome had both rights and responsibilities. As a class, list rights that United States citizens have. Then develop a list of responsibilities of citizenship. Some are written laws. What are some that are unwritten but still important?
3. **ARTS ACTIVITY** Both Greeks and Romans made mosaics with small stones, tiles, or glass. (The pictures on pages 159 and 175 are mosaics.) Design and make a small mosaic. Your design might show a Greek or Roman God or Goddess, a plant or animal, or a portrait. You can use materials such as colored paper, cellophane, stones, or clay.
4. **COLLABORATIVE LEARNING** The Romans were good engineers and city planners. You have read about their roads, aqueducts, and buildings. Now work as a class to plan a new community of your own. Discuss these questions: What buildings will the community need? What kinds of services? You may want to divide into groups to work on different areas. When your plan has been finished, draw a diagram or an aerial view of your model community, and label all the important parts.

Answers to Reviewing Skills

1. From the maps and their reading of the text, students should understand that Christianity at first spread within the Roman Empire. Major cities with Christian congregations included Alexandria, Jerusalem, Rome, and Byzantium.
2. One possible conclusion is that, despite some persecutions, the Roman Empire helped the spread of Christianity more than it hindered it.
3. Students should suggest primary sources such as letters or journals kept by Roman students, or memoirs or contemporary biographies written by prominent Romans.

Answers to Using Critical Thinking

1. Students might say that Athens represents an important beginning, that giving some members of a community the right to vote is better than no public voice at all. Others might insist that there can be no government by the people when women do not have equal rights and when slavery is allowed.
2. Students may suggest paying public officials high salaries, having leaders who inspire others to go into government service, teaching young people the importance of serving in public office.
3. Advantages include: more wealth and trade from new territory; larger base for recruiting soldiers; new source of slaves. Difficulties include: more distant frontiers to defend; slow communication with frontier.
4. Students may or may not be aware of the principle of separation of church and state established in the U.S. Constitution.

Answers to Preparing for Citizenship

1. **WRITING ACTIVITY** Students might enjoy reading the myth of Pandora. Their own myths might deal with Gods and Goddesses who were too concerned with their appearance, fought with their siblings, or wanted more independence from their parents.
2. **GROUP ACTIVITY** Students' list of rights should include trial by jury, voting, equal justice, freedoms of speech, press, religion, and assembly. Responsibilities list should mention paying taxes, obeying laws, serving in the military and on juries. Unwritten responsibilities might include tolerance, community work.
3. **ARTS ACTIVITY** Help students find appropriate materials. Other examples of mosaics can be found in the chapters on Islam; e.g.,on page 192.
4. **COLLABORATIVE LEARNING** Students should recognize the need for sources of food, water, energy; transportation and communication links; places for working, learning, playing, and meeting; ways to deal with waste and pollution. (A useful resource is David Macaulay's book *City*.)

CHAPTER ORGANIZER

Chapter 8 The Arabian Peninsula

CHAPTER PLANNING CHART

Pupil's Edition	Teacher's Edition	Ancillaries
Lesson 1: Islam Develops (1–2 days) Objective 1: Describe how the religion of Islam developed. (Ethics and Beliefs Systems 1, 4) Objective 2: Identify the five duties of all Muslims. (Ethics and Belief Systems 3) Objective 3: Explain the ties between Islam, Judaism, and Christianity. (Culture 4; Ethics and Belief Systems 4)	• Graphic Overview (184) • Access Strategy (185) • Access Activity (185) Study Skills (186) Religious Context (186) • Art Connection (186) Science Connection (187) Study Skills (187)	Study Guide (31)
Lesson 2: The Spread of Islam (1–2 days) Objective 1: Describe how and where Islam spread. (Culture 1; Ethics and Belief Systems 2, 3) Objective 2: Explain what is meant by the community of Islam. (Ethics and Belief Systems 3; Social and Political Systems 1, 2) Objective 3: Name at least two Muslim achievements in art and science. (Culture 5, 6)	• Graphic Overview (189) • Access Activity (190) • Access Strategy (190) Cultural Context (191) Social Participation (191)	Study Guide (32) Map Activities (12) • Study Prints (6)
Lesson 3: Saudi Arabia Today (2–3 days) Objective 1: Describe how the kingdom of Saudi Arabia was created. (History 4, 5; Geography 5) Objective 2: Name at least four things the rulers of Saudi Arabia do to promote Islam. (Ethics and Belief Systems 1, 2, 3) Objective 3: Explain how Saudi oil resources have led to interdependence. (History 5, 6, 7; Geography 3, 5; Economics 1, 5)	• Graphic Overview (193) • Access Activity (194) • Access Strategy (194) Bulletin Board (195) Research/Investigating (195) • Visual Learning (195) Presenting a Report (196) Social Context (196) Mathematics Connection (197) • Visual Learning (197)	Study Guide (33) Discovery Journal (19)
Understanding Historical Sequence Objective: Demonstrate how to read and plot information on a timeline. (Visual Learning 2)		Study Guide (34)
Chapter Review	Answers (200–201)	Tests (29–32)

* Objectives are correlated to the strands and goals in the program Scope and Sequence on pages T41–T49.

• LEP appropriate resources. (For additional strategies, see pages T32–T33.)

CHAPTER RATIONALE

Chapter 8 focuses on the Arabian Peninsula, which is both the land where Islam developed and a strategic area in the modern world. Interest in the background and beliefs of Islam has steadily grown in recent years. Only by understanding its basic tenets can students begin to comprehend the outlooks and behaviors of a large percentage of the world's population. The lessons in this chapter provide the necessary background for the study of Islamic cultures.

Lesson 1 orients the students to the geographic setting in which Islam developed. By concentrating on the caravan trade and the city of Mecca, we counter the stereotype of Islam as a desert religion. Introducing the world of Islam through the account of a modern pilgrimage helps students recognize the current force of the Islamic faith. This lesson presents the events in Muhammad's life and the basic teachings of Islam to provide the background students need to place Islam along with Judaism and Christianity as a major monotheistic world religion.

In **Lesson 2** the focus shifts from the Arabian Peninsula to the expanding Muslim world. A historical map helps students visualize the phenomenal spread of Islam between A.D. 632 and 750. By focusing on the appeal of Islam rather than the Muslim armies, the lesson works to dispel the myth that Islam was spread largely by the sword. The emphasis on Muslim achievements helps students recognize how much other cultures owe to Islamic scholars, scientists, artists, and mathematicians.

Lesson 3 revisits the Arabian Peninsula—but this time we examine modern life in the kingdom of Saudi Arabia. By reading about Arabian customs and Saudi programs of modernization, students learn how Saudi Arabia is poised between tradition and change. We highlight the tradition of Arabian hospitality in A Closer Look, which features a special building for welcoming diplomats, and explore the Saudis' obligations to protect the holy places of Islam. The lesson focuses on Saudi Arabia less as a Muslim nation than as a nation rich in oil. Saudi oil has led to an interdependence among the industrialized nations—culminating in the Persian Gulf War. The discussion emphasizes the need for Saudis to develop alternative industries in order to secure their economic future.

ACTIVITIES & PROJECTS

Researching

Have students use a current almanac to find the numbers of believers in these major religions: Buddhism, Christianity, Hinduism, Islam, and Judaism. Tell them to present the figures in a simple table. (Use after Lesson 1.)

LEP: Making a Display

Divide the class into small groups of three or four students each. Ask each group to prepare a classroom display on one form of Muslim art. Topics might include Arabesque Patterns, Calligraphy, Ornate Tiles, and Damask. Suggest that students bring in samples of these art objects, if possible, or find pictures of them in library books. (Use after Lesson 2.)

Challenge: Giving an Oral Report

Invite students to research OPEC in the library. Ask them to read and take notes on a recent article about OPEC. Have them list the member nations of OPEC and consult other sources as needed. Then ask each student to present a brief oral report based on the article read, relating their findings to what they learned about modern Saudi Arabia. (Use after Lesson 3.)

Basic: Investigating

To follow up on Across Time and Space in Lesson 2, suggest to students that they look at the night sky—as Muslim astronomers did. Encourage them to chart a few clear constellations over the course of a few days and share their charts and the names of the constellations with the class.

CHAPTER PREVIEW

Have students read the chapter title and the text following it. Direct their attention to the photographs on page 183. Explain that the photo of Mecca shows one of the holy places of Islam, one of the world's great monotheistic religions (religions that center their belief on one God). Point out that the two photographs illustrate both continuity and change. Ask students to read the captions and identify elements of each photograph that give evidence of either continuity or change. *(Continuity—Mecca, a city since before Muhammad's time; Great Mosque and Ka'bah, toward which Muslims turn in worship; change—modern buildings)*

Looking Back

Ask students what other religions based on the belief in one God they have read about. *(Judaism in Chapter 3 and Christianity in Chapter 7)*

Looking Forward

Tell students that this chapter tells about the religion of Islam in three lessons: Islam Develops, The Spread of Islam, and Saudi Arabia Today.

In Lesson 1, students will learn about the origins of Islam.

Chapter 8

The Arabian Peninsula

In the dry climate of the Arabian Peninsula, towns have clustered near water since ancient times. About 1,400 years ago in the town of Mecca, a religious leader named Muhammad began to spread the message of Islam. Since that time Islam has gained followers around the world. Each year hundreds of thousands of worshipers visit Saudi Arabia to affirm their faith at the holy places of Islam.

Verses from the Qur'an, the holy book of Islam, are embroidered with gold thread in intricate Arabic script on this covering for the Ka'bah.

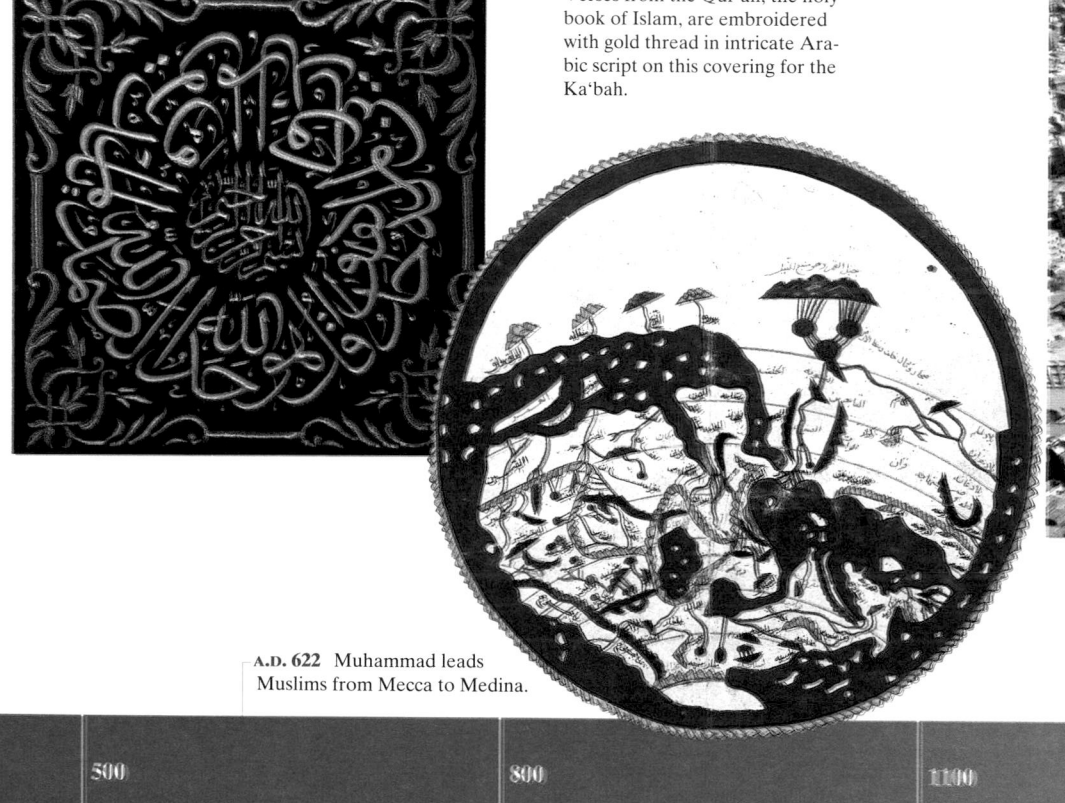

A.D. 622 Muhammad leads Muslims from Mecca to Medina.

500 | 800 | 1100

c. 1154 Al-Idrisi, the greatest Muslim geographer, draws this map. He puts northern Europe at the bottom of the map, so that the reader looks upward toward Arabia.

A.D. 500

BACKGROUND

In the decades and centuries that followed Muhammad's death in A.D. 632, Islam became a major force in the lives of people who inhabit a broad area that spreads over three continents: Asia, Africa, and Europe (see map on page 190). Islam continues to be practiced by a wide range of peoples all over the world.

The Practice of Islam

Islam as practiced is characterized by strict adherence to the rules of prayer, the giving of alms to the poor, fasting, and a pilgrimage to Mecca. For Muslims, Friday is always the holiest day of the week. Like the Christian Sunday and the Jewish Saturday, Fridays for Muslims are the holy day.

Criers typically announce prayer times from mosque towers called minarets. Muslims wash their face, hands, and feet immediately before praying. The prayer leader faces Mecca, and all others kneel behind him. Special movements—such as bowing from the hips and lowering one's face to the ground—often accompany the praying ritual.

The hajj, or pilgrimage to Mecca, is considered by Muslims to be the "Great Festival." The "Lesser Festival" is the celebration after the holy month of fasting. This period is called Ramadan and is the ninth month of the Muslim calendar. Another important celebration happens when a child memorizes the Qur'an. At this time parents throw a party for both their child and the child's teacher.

Riyadh, the capital of Saudi Arabia, has some strikingly modern buildings. This shopping mall is protected from the glaring desert sun by a modern air conditioning system.

Hills surround Mecca, where Muhammad delivered the message of Islam. In the center of the picture is the Great Mosque, within which is the Ka'bah.

1932 Abdul Aziz proclaims the formation of Saudi Arabia.

1400 | 1700 | 2000

Today

Understanding the Visuals

The decorative script in which the verses from the Qur'an are embroidered (page 182) is an example of calligraphy, the art of beautiful writing. Calligraphy (and the arabesque, mentioned later in this chapter) is an art form that gained prominence in part because Islamic tradition discourages the portrayal of human images.

Encourage students to look for other examples of calligraphy pictured in this chapter and in Chapter 9. Calligraphy is also a common form of art in Chinese and Japanese culture.

Call students' attention to the photo of the Great Mosque on this page. In the center of the mosque's large open court is the Ka'bah, a 50-foot-high, boxlike building that Muslims regard as the House of God.

Understanding Chronology

Point out to students that the dates shown on the timeline all use B.C. and A.D. because of their familiarity to U.S. students. In the Muslim world, the timeline would begin 1 A.H., the date of the Hijra (A.H. stands for *anno hegirae,* "year of the Hijra"; see page 186). The Muslim calendar is lunar, and 33 lunar years approximately equal 32 solar years of Western calendars.

A Worldwide Faith

The religion of Islam unites millions of peoples over varied continents and with different cultural heritages. For this reason no one culture can be called the definitive Muslim culture. For example, the Islam followed in Saudi Arabia is from the Wahhabi sect, a strict form of Sunni Islam. Iran, as Chapter 9 will show, combines Shi'a Islam and the Persian language and culture. Neighboring Iraq's people are mainly Shi'as and Arabic speakers. These divisions arose from early disagreements about the status of the caliphs, or Muslim leaders, and still create tensions in the Islamic world. The tropical island nation of Indonesia has the largest Muslim population in the world—over 160 million in 1992—and an official language that is Maylay in origin. The point to be made is not the uniformity of Islam but the great diversity of cultures that share Islam as the dominant faith.

INTRODUCE

Ask students about times they have seen or have been part of a huge crowd (for example, a sports event or a parade). Call their attention to the picture of the Ka'bah on page 186 and the crowd circling it. Discuss what this crowd tells students about Islam. Then have them read the account of a modern pilgrim to Mecca in the lesson opener.

Read the lesson title and the Thinking Focus question aloud. Ask students what elements might have played a part in the development of Islam. *(An inspiring leader; a holy book)*

Key Terms

Vocabulary Strategies: T36–T37

pilgrimage—a religious journey

oasis—a fertile area around a spring or a waterhole

caravan—a long line of people traveling on horses or camels from one oasis to another

mosque—a place for Muslims to worship

➤ *Pilgrims visit Mecca, Mina, and the Plain of Arafat during the hajj.*

800
1100
1400
1700
2000
500
632

L E S S O N 1

Islam Develops

THINKING FOCUS

How did Islam develop?

Key Terms

- pilgrimage
- oasis
- caravan
- mosque

Here I am, O God, at thy Command. Here I am!" The prayer echoes in the dry air of Saudi *(sah OO dee)* Arabia. Hundreds of thousands of people join in. All are Muslims, followers of the religion of Islam. They are making a religious journey, a **pilgrimage,** to the city of Mecca (see map below).

Among them is Mrs. Sara Sahali from the United States. Two days ago, when she left her family in Michigan, it was snowing. Now she is far from home. Yet, in a way, this hot, sunny place also feels like home. Here are the holy places of her religion.

▼ *What places do pilgrims visit during the hajj?*

Mrs. Sahali thinks of the millions of pilgrims who have gone before her. A long time ago, many pilgrims traveled great distances by foot to get to Mecca.

When she reaches Mecca, Mrs. Sahali will join the pilgrims massed around a large, stone building. This place, the Ka'bah *(KAH buh),* is the focus of Muslim worship (see picture on page 186). All Muslims, wherever they are, turn toward Mecca and the Ka'bah when they pray. It symbolizes the unity of their belief in one God.

The most important part of the hajj, or pilgrimage, is a visit to the Plain of Arafat (see map). There the pilgrims spend the day in prayer and worship. Many climb the small hill called the Mount of Mercy. At its foot the prophet Muhammad gave his last sermon while he was on a pilgrimage to Mecca.

Performing the Pilgrimage

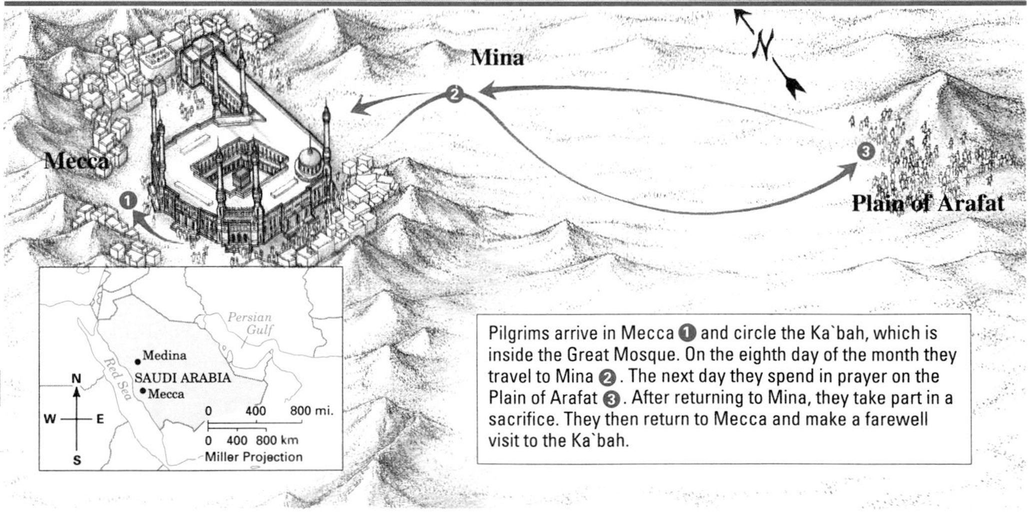

Mina
Mecca
Plain of Arafat
N
Persian Gulf
Medina
SAUDI ARABIA
Mecca
Red Sea
N
W
E
S
0 400 800 mi.
0 400 800 km
Miller Projection

Pilgrims arrive in Mecca ❶ and circle the Ka'bah, which is inside the Great Mosque. On the eighth day of the month they travel to Mina ❷. The next day they spend in prayer on the Plain of Arafat ❸. After returning to Mina, they take part in a sacrifice. They then return to Mecca and make a farewell visit to the Ka'bah.

Objectives

1. Describe how the religion of Islam developed.
2. Identify the five duties of all Muslims.
3. Explain the ties between Islam, Judaism, and Christianity.

Graphic Overview

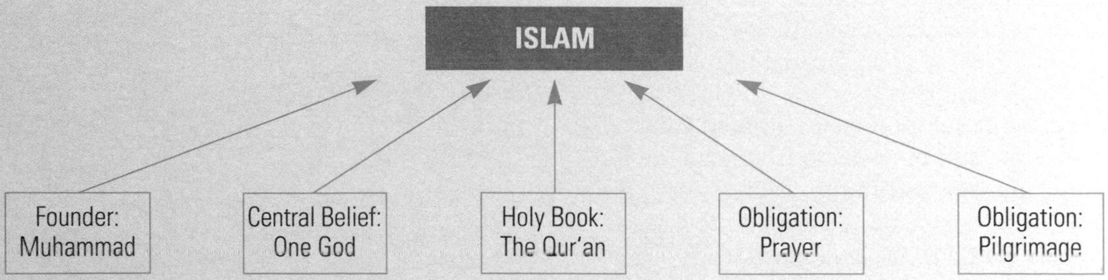

ISLAM
Founder: Muhammad
Central Belief: One God
Holy Book: The Qur'an
Obligation: Prayer
Obligation: Pilgrimage

The Setting

Mecca is in the western part of the Arabian Peninsula. This peninsula is the largest in the world, and lies between the Red Sea and the Persian Gulf. To the south of the peninsula is the Arabian Sea, which is part of the Indian Ocean.

Deserts and Towns

Much of the Arabian Peninsula is a high plain of rocks and sand. There are no rivers. Here and there is an **oasis** *(oh AY sihs)*, a fertile area around a spring or a waterhole. Because water is so precious in this hot, dry land, the oases attracted wandering herders and settlers. Towns grew up around many oases.

The southeastern part of Arabia is called the Empty Quarter. An area the size of Texas, it is covered with dunes of fine, soft sand. People rarely visit this barren region. No rain falls for years at a time, and fierce sandstorms are common.

The mountains along the coasts of the Red Sea and the Arabian Sea are much more inviting. There, enough rain falls for farming. The Yemeni civilization had developed in the southwestern mountains by about 1000 B.C.

Destination Mecca

Traders from southwestern Arabia sailed the seas to India and to eastern Africa, bringing back gems, silk, ivory, and precious spices. On the homeward route, many merchants sailed north on the Red Sea. Some went overland in a caravan. Each **caravan** was a long line of people and camels traveling from one oasis to another. Caravans were like cities on the move. As many as 300 traders, camel drivers, and guards made up each caravan. Up to 2,500 camels were loaded with goods bound for Mecca. From there, other caravans carried the goods farther north.

Mecca was also the goal of Bedouin *(BEHD oo ihn)* families. For hundreds of years, the Bedouin Arabs had been herders. Each group of Bedouins had its own land. When one area was grazed over, the Bedouins moved on, looking for food and water for their herds of camels and sheep. Each group moved in a regular pattern over the lands it had claimed.

The Bedouins went to Mecca to sell the meat and milk from their camels and the wool from their sheep. From the merchants there, they bought grain, swords, and carpets. Then they visited the Ka'bah.

Like most other people in Arabia in the 500s, the Bedouins worshiped many spirits. They thought that spirits lived in the wind and rain and in bushes and stones. At the Ka'bah they prayed to stone and wooden statues that stood for these spirits. ■

▲ *Mecca may have had houses like the ones in this modern Arabian town. Thick walls keep the buildings cool inside.*

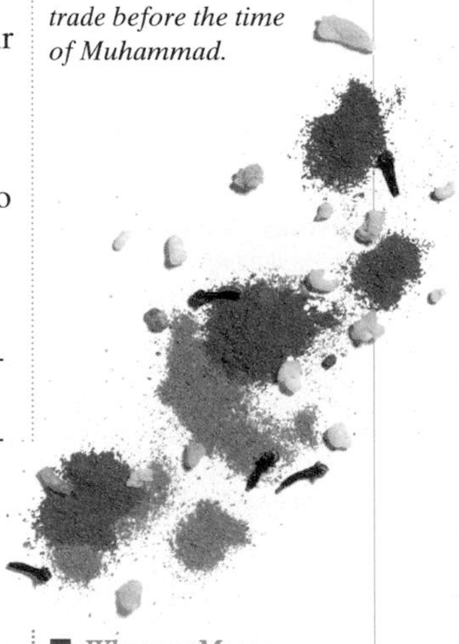

▼ *Frankincense comes from trees in southern Arabia. Incense and spices were valuable items of trade before the time of Muhammad.*

■ *Why was Mecca important to both merchants and Bedouins?*

DEVELOP

Direct students' attention to the two maps on page 184. Help students get their bearings before beginning the lesson. Ask them to connect each place name in the text with a location on one of the two maps. Urge students to refer to the maps frequently as they read. Point out that the map of Mecca and its surroundings will help them visualize better the pilgrimage Muslims make to Mecca.

ECONOMICS

Visual Learning

Frankincense, along with other perfumes and spices, contributed to the very profitable Arabian spice trade. The Sumerians, Egyptians, Minoans, Greeks, and Romans used these substances in medical prescriptions, religious rituals, cremation, embalming, and the anointing of rulers. Ask students to name some spices they use in their homes. Where do they come from? *(Some possible answers are vanilla from Madagascar, saffron from Spain, paprika from Hungary.)*

■ *Mecca was on the trade route between southwestern Arabia, India, and eastern Africa; Bedouins went to Mecca to buy and sell goods and to worship at the Ka'bah.*

Access Strategy

Explore the concept of pilgrimage with students. Ask them whether they have ever made a special trip to visit someone they care about or to see an important sight. Allow students time to recall any such journeys they may have had. Encourage them to think about preparations they made for their trip and what they carried with them. What thoughts did they have before leaving, en route, and upon arriving at their destination? Students may share their experiences with the rest of the class orally or draw a picture that represents their trip.

Explain that people sometimes make pilgrimages, often over great distances, to places that are important to their religion. Draw parallels, if possible, between details offered in student descriptions and aspects of a religious journey (preparations, feelings of anticipation and awe). Point out to students that the pilgrimage is one important part of the religion of Islam (see the table on page 187).

Access Activity

Divide the class into groups of four, and ask each group to discuss what they already know and what they would like to know about Islam. Ask each group to share three points with the class. Help students frame questions they hope to have answered through their study of this lesson.

BELIEF SYSTEMS

Critical Thinking

Tell students that the contemporary use of the word *mecca* designates a place that is the center of an activity or the goal of a specific group, as in these sentences: Broadway is the mecca of theater; she finally sang in Nashville, a mecca for country singers. Students may suggest others. Use the activity as a springboard for a discussion of Mecca's importance both to pre-Islamic Arabs and to Muslims.

Muhammad and Islam

Each year the Ka'bah is covered with a new cloth woven by hand. Verses from the Qur'an are embroidered on it in gold.

Only a small number of people in the Arabian Peninsula were Bedouins. Most Arabs lived in towns like Mecca.

Trade made Mecca a busy, noisy town. Here the prophet Muhammad was born about the year A.D. 570. Orphaned at an early age, Muhammad was brought up by relatives. He became a successful merchant and married Khadijah *(kah DEE juh),* the woman for whom he worked.

Muhammad's Vision

Muhammad often felt he needed to get away from Mecca's noise and bustle. He went out to the quiet, empty mountains near the town. According to Islamic tradition, around the year 610, when Muhammad was about 40 years old, he had a vision. This experience changed his life—and the lives of millions of other people around the world.

In the silence of the mountains, Muhammad was amazed to hear a voice. The voice seemed to come from everywhere at once. "Recite!" the voice thundered. "Recite in the name of thy Lord!" Twice more the message was repeated. Then Muhammad saw a figure looming against the sky. The figure told Muhammad that he had been chosen to be the prophet of God.

Muhammad rushed back to Mecca to tell Khadijah. She was filled with joy that her husband had been chosen as a prophet of God.

Spreading the Word

Urged on by Khadijah, Muhammad began to preach to other people in Mecca. "There is only one God," he said, using the Arabic word *Allah* for God. He urged the people of Mecca to follow God's word and lead good lives. Several of his friends and members of his family became Muslims, followers of Islam. The word *Islam* means "submission to God." A person who accepts Islam is willing to follow God's teachings in all parts of life.

At first most Meccans did not accept Muhammad's message. They did not want to give up their old religion. They also may have feared that Islam would end the profitable trade with the Bedouins. Some of the people of Mecca threatened the Muslims.

In 622 Muhammad and his followers moved to Yathrib *(YATH ruhb),* about 200 miles north of Mecca. Islam already had supporters there. Soon, Yathrib (now called Medina) became known as Medinat an-Nabi, City of the Prophet. There Muhammad and his followers put up a simple house. It became Islam's first **mosque,** a place to worship.

The migration to Medina is known as the Hijra *(HEEJ ruh).* Muslims begin their calendar on the date the Hijra occurred. The year A.D. 622 is the year 1 A.H.—the first year of the Hijra. (A.H. is Latin for *anno hegirae,* "year of the Hijra," just as the Christian date A.D., *anno domini,* is Latin for "year of the Lord.")

How Do We Know?

HISTORY *Many pilgrims made the hajj in caravans. In the 1600s poet George Sandys wrote from Cairo, Egypt, "Forty easie days journey it is distant from hence: divided by a wildernesse of sand . . . thorow which they are guided . . . by stars, as ships in the Ocean."*

Study Skills

Tell students to prepare a written report on the city of Mecca. Have them include the following: the city's origins as a trading center, its development as a religious destination, and its continued role in the life of modern-day pilgrims. Direct students to reference materials (encyclopedias and books on Islam). Ask volunteers to read their reports to the class.

Religious Context

To help the students understand the modern-day continuity of the Five Pillars of Islam, tell them that Malcolm X—the U.S. black militant leader—made the hajj in the 1960s. He wanted to affirm his commitment to orthodox Islam by traveling to Mecca and praying at the Great Mosque. Like most other 20th-century Muslims who live outside Southwest Asia, Malcolm X arrived in Saudi Arabia by airplane.

Art Connection

Have students look at the calligraphic Arabic writing on page 188, and invite them to make nameplates for themselves using a calligraphic style. Guide them in creating an intricate script, providing in-class samples of calligraphy if possible. Remind the class that calligraphy is an art common to Japanese and Chinese cultures, as well as the Muslim world.

Return to Mecca

Within eight years of the Hijra, thousands of Arabs had become Muslims. With his followers Muhammad returned to Mecca. He destroyed the idols in the Ka'bah and restored it as the center of worship of one God. Later, the Great Mosque was built around it (see page 183).

Muhammad told the Muslims that they should honor the Ka'bah as the house of God. Muslims believe that Abraham rebuilt the original Ka'bah. They honor him as the founding father of the religions based on the belief in one God.

Until his death in 632, Muhammad continued to preach. His followers wrote down what he said on "bits of parchment, thin white stones, and leafless palm branches." These messages were gathered into the Qur'an, Islam's holy book. ■

■ *Why is the Hijra important to Muslims?*

The Teachings of Islam

Because Islam developed in Arabia, some people think of it as a desert religion. Yet Islam developed in the towns of the Arabian Peninsula. As Islam spread, it flourished in the cities.

The Qur'an

The rules guiding the lives of all Muslims are set forth in the Qur'an (sometimes spelled Koran). The table on this page shows the duties of all Muslims. The same duties apply to both men and women.

Under the laws of the Qur'an, the rights of women were broadened. Women can own and inherit property. Although a man may have as many as four wives, he must support all of them equally. A man can divorce his wife easily, but she may keep any money or property she had when she married.

The Qur'an is organized in chapters called suras. It is written in Arabic, the language spoken by the first Muslims (see the Minipedia, pages 660–673, for the Arabic alphabet). Passages such as the one on the next page have inspired faithful Muslims for centuries.

◄ *During the hajj, rich and poor pilgrims dress alike. Men wear two pieces of seamless white clothing called an* ihram. *Women cover their heads and wear simple dresses.*

Five Pillars of Islam

Duty	What Muslims Do
Shahada	They express their faith by saying, "There is no god but God, and Muhammad is the messenger of God."
Salat	They pray five times a day–dawn, midday, late afternoon, sunset, and night–while facing toward Mecca.
Zakat	They give a portion of their income to the poor and to public charities.
Sawm	They fast during Ramadan, the ninth month of the Muslim year. They do not eat or drink between sunrise and sunset.
Hajj	If they are in good health and can afford it, all Muslims must make the pilgrimage to Mecca once in their lifetime.

BELIEF SYSTEMS

Study Skills

Pair students and supply each pair with five index cards. Tell students to make index cards that reflect the information about the Five Pillars of Islam in the table on this page. Students should write the Arabic word for each duty and its translation on one side of each card. On the other side, they should write an explanation of the duty in their own words. After students study the table, have them use the cards to test each other's comprehension of the Five Pillars of Islam.

■ *The Hijra (A.D. 622) marks the date of Muhammad's migration from Mecca to Medina; it is the date at which the Muslim calendar begins.*

Science Connection

The hajj, or pilgrimage, takes place during the 12th month of the Muslim year. It occurs at a slightly different time each year because Muslims use a lunar calendar that measures months from one new moon to the next. The lunar year is 354 days long, 11 days shorter than the 365-day solar year of the Gregorian calendar used in Europe, the United States, and many other parts of the world. Thus, every year the hajj occurs 11 days earlier on the Gregorian calendar.

Remind students that the Muslim calendar begins on the date that the Hijra occurred (July 16, 622). Thus, this date became the first day of the first month of the first year A.H. The months of the Muslim calendar are true lunar months, so neither the years nor the months of the Muslim calendar coincide with the Gregorian calendar. For example, January 1, 1991, fell on 14 Jumada II, the sixth month of the year 1411 A.H.

Study Skills

Have students research these facts about the Muslim calendar: the names of the months and the religious significance of the months. Suggest that the class make a calendar of the Gregorian year with a synchronous calendar of the Islamic year alongside it for comparison.

BELIEF SYSTEMS

Critical Thinking

Point out that after Muhammad died, his companions collected all the revelations he had received into one complete book. Ask students why Muslims thought it important to write down Muhammad's messages from God, or Allah. *(If the message of Allah had not been written down, parts might have been forgotten, remembered incorrectly, or lost. Also, the written text helped settle disputes and teach converts.)*

■ *All Muslims believe that there is only one God, that Muhammad was the messenger of God, and that the Qur'an is God's message that Muhammad delivered to the Muslims.*

CLOSE

Divide the class into groups of four. Tell them that you will ask each group the question, "How did Islam develop?" The members of each group will answer briefly in turn *who, what, where,* and *when* in response to the general question *how.* Tell the groups to decide in advance which member will answer each question. (Notice that the answer to *what* should focus on beliefs and practices.)

It is He who fashioned for you hearing, eyes and hearts
(but little do you give thanks),
and it is He who scattered you through the earth
(and to Him shall you be mustered [returned]),
and it is He who causes you to die, and to live,
and to Him belongs the alternation of night and day:
will you not understand?

From Sura 23, the Qur'an

Flowing Arabic script makes this handwritten page of the Qur'an a work of art. This passage is in the oldest style of written Arabic.

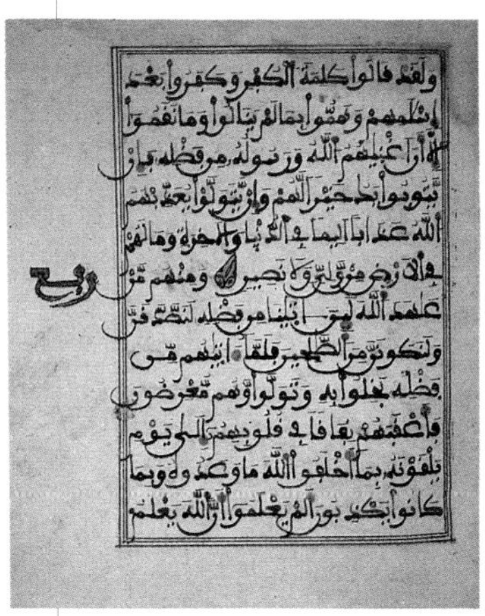

■ *What basic beliefs do all Muslims share?*

Ties with Other Religions

Muslims called the Jews and Christians People of the Book, meaning the Bible. The Qur'an has many ideas that parallel ideas from the Jewish Scriptures and the Christian Bible. All three religions look on Abraham as a founder and regard the Jewish prophets as messengers of God. Muhammad believed that he belonged to the same line of prophets as the prophets of the Jews and the Christians.

As a trader, Muhammad doubtless had contact with Jews and Christians. Many Jews lived in Medina, and there were Christian Arabs living in southern Arabia and East Africa.

There are important differences among the three religions. While all three believe in one God, most Christians speak of God as a Trinity and believe that Jesus was the son of God. Neither Muslims nor Jews believe that Jesus was divine. Muslims look on Jesus as a prophet, although Jews do not. Although Muslims regard Muhammad as the last and greatest of the prophets, they do not think he was divine.

Muhammad taught his followers that God's message in the Bible had been misunderstood. Muhammad said that the message of God in its pure form appears in the Qur'an.

Both the Qur'an and the Hebrew Scriptures are very much concerned with daily living. Both deal with the regulation of some parts of daily life—food, dress, customs of the home, and so forth—more than do the Christian Scriptures.

After Muhammad's death, Islam spread to lands outside Arabia. Many people there became Muslims, but many Christians and Jews kept their faith. The Muslim rulers generally allowed these People of the Book to practice their own beliefs. ■

REVIEW

1. **FOCUS** How did Islam develop?
2. **ECONOMICS** Why did Mecca attract both merchants and Bedouins?
3. **BELIEFS** What are the five duties of all Muslims?
4. **CULTURE** Compare the teachings of Islam with the teachings of Judaism and Christianity. In what ways are the three religions alike? In what ways are these religions different?
5. **CRITICAL THINKING** Most religions have holy places that worshipers visit on pilgrimages. Christians may make a pilgrimage to Rome, and Jews go to the State of Israel. What makes the hajj of Islam different from the pilgrimages made by people of other faiths?
6. **MAP ACTIVITY** Use the modern political map in the Atlas (pages 682–683) to list the countries that are now located within the Arabian Peninsula.

Homework Options

Have students write sentences using each of the key terms in this lesson. Ask for volunteers to read their sentences aloud to the class.

Study Guide: page 31

Answers to Review Questions

1. According to Muslim tradition, Muhammad became the prophet of Islam. His message of one God quickly spread.
2. Mecca was on a trade route and was also the place where Bedouins worshiped spirits whose idols were kept at the Ka'bah.
3. A Muslim's duties are to state belief in one God, to pray five times daily, to give charity to the poor, to fast during Ramadan, and to make the hajj to Mecca if possible.
4. All three religions share the belief in one God and view the Jewish prophets as messengers of God. Although Christians believe that Jesus was divine, Jews and Muslims do not. Muslims believe that only the Qur'an has the message of God in its pure form.
5. Unlike pilgrimages of other faiths, the hajj should be taken by all devout Muslims.
6. Saudi Arabia, Kuwait, Yemen, Qatar, Bahrain, Oman, and the United Arab Emirates are there now.

500 632 1100 1400 1700 2000

L E S S O N 2

The Spread of Islam

After 632 Islam spread to many new lands. A golden age of learning developed. One feature of this age was an interest in science, especially medicine. Many medical advances came from Persia to the northeast of the Arabian Peninsula (see Chapter 9). A doctor there named ar-Razi was the first to make a careful study of smallpox.

Ar-Razi's work made it possible to make an accurate **diagnosis,** or identification, of disease. For centuries doctors in Europe used his diagnosis of smallpox, quoted at the right, as a model. Ar-Razi's diagnosis describes how a patient with smallpox looked and felt.

The eruption of the Small-Pox is preceded by a continued fever, pain in the back, itching in the nose, and terrors in sleep. . . . then also a pricking which the patient feels all over his body; a fullness of the face, which at times goes and comes; an inflamed color, and vehement redness in both the cheeks; . . . a heaviness of the whole body; . . . a pain in the throat and chest, with a slight difficulty in breathing, and cough; a dryness of the mouth, thick spittle, and hoarseness of the voice; pain and heaviness of the head. . . .

From *al-Judari wa Hasbah,* A.D. 910

THINKING FOCUS

Why is the period from 700 to 1100 called a golden age of Muslim culture?

Key Terms

- diagnosis
- caliph

The Caliphs Spread Islam

When Muhammad died, his followers worried because he had not named a successor. Who would lead the Muslims? One of Muhammad's closest followers, Abu-Bakr *(AH boo BAH kuhr),* tried to ease their fears. "O men, if you worship Muhammad, Muhammad is dead; if you worship God, God is alive."

The Early Caliphs

A group of leading Muslims met to choose a **caliph** *(KAY lihf),* a successor to Muhammad. The caliph was not expected to act as a prophet. His job was to serve as head of the Muslim state and be the defender of the faith. Abu-Bakr was chosen as the first caliph.

This painting from a Persian book shows a pharmacist mixing cough syrup. The written text gives the formula for the medicine.

189

INTRODUCE

Ask a student to read the Lesson 2 title and the Thinking Focus aloud. Have students scan the headings in the lesson and consider how they relate to the lesson title and focus question. Write on the chalkboard the inferences students draw from the lesson headings about the spread and flowering of Islam. Tell students to read the lesson to determine the validity of the inferences they have drawn.

Key Terms

Vocabulary Strategies: T36–T37

diagnosis—the identification of disease

caliph—a successor to Muhammad

Graphic Overview

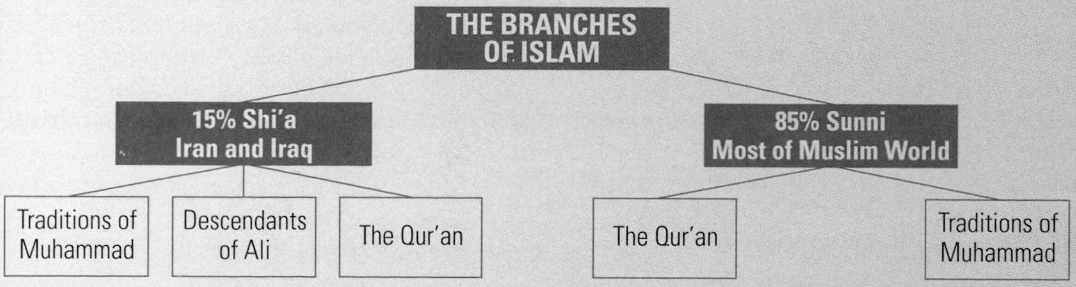
THE BRANCHES OF ISLAM
15% Shi'a Iran and Iraq
85% Sunni Most of Muslim World
Traditions of Muhammad
Descendants of Ali
The Qur'an
The Qur'an
Traditions of Muhammad

Objectives

1. Describe how and where Islam spread.
2. Explain what is meant by the community of Islam.
3. Name at least two Muslim achievements in art and science.

DEVELOP

Suggest to students that they view the spread of Islam as a series of causes and effects. For example: Muhammad died (cause); Muslim leaders met to choose a successor (effect). Instruct students, as they read the text, to look for cause-and-effect links. Students might set up a two-column chart, with column heads *Cause* and *Effect,* on which to register connections between events or achievements in the history of Islam.

GEOGRAPHY
Map Skills

Read aloud sentences from the text that contain place names. Have students refer to the labels and color key on the map on this page to determine when Islam spread to each place named. Then tell students to use the map on pages 682–683 in the Atlas to locate the modern countries that were part of the Muslim lands in 632. *(Saudi Arabia, Yemen, Oman, and the United Arab Emirates)*

➤ *The first four caliphs added the areas colored light orange; the Umayyads added areas in yellow.*

The Expansion of Islam, A.D. 622–750

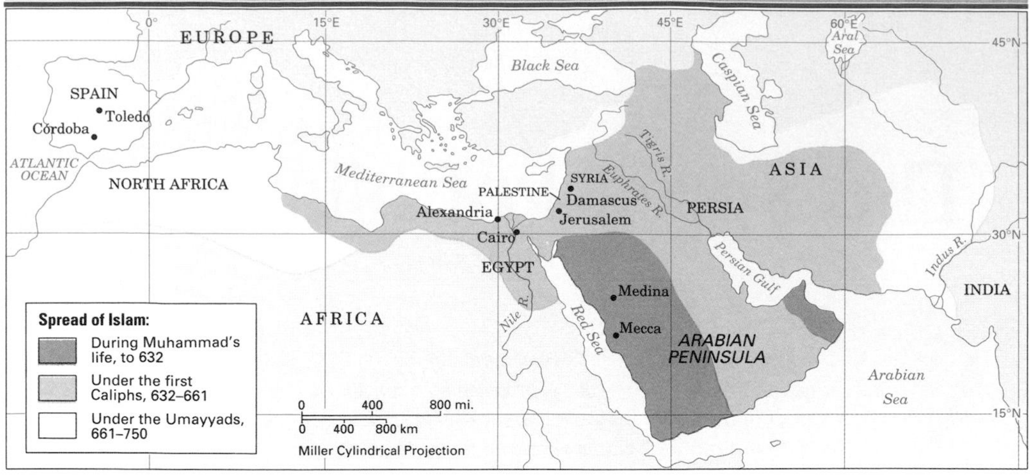
EUROPE
Black Sea
SPAIN
Toledo
Córdoba
ATLANTIC OCEAN
NORTH AFRICA
Mediterranean Sea
PALESTINE
SYRIA
Damascus
Jerusalem
Alexandria
Cairo
EGYPT
Caspian Sea
Tigris R.
Euphrates R.
ASIA
PERSIA
Persian Gulf
Indus R.
INDIA
Aral Sea
Medina
Mecca
Red Sea
Nile R.
AFRICA
ARABIAN PENINSULA
Arabian Sea
Spread of Islam:
During Muhammad's life, to 632
Under the first Caliphs, 632–661
Under the Umayyads, 661–750
0 400 800 mi.
0 400 800 km
Miller Cylindrical Projection
0°
15°E
30°E
45°E
60°E
45°N
30°N
15°N

▲ *This map shows the spread of Islam. What areas did the first four caliphs add? What areas did the Umayyads add? For help in reading a historical map, see page G11 in the Map and Globe Handbook.*

He and the next three caliphs helped spread Islam beyond the Arabian Peninsula.

A Split among Muslims

The next group of caliphs came from the Umayyad *(oo MY ad)* family. The Umayyads gained power after the murder of the fourth caliph, Ali *(ah LEE),* in A.D. 661. Ali was married to Muhammad's daughter Fatima *(FAHT uh muh).* Muslims who supported Ali refused to recognize the Umayyad caliphs. Fighting between the two groups of Muslims led to the murder of Ali's son Husayn in 680.

Today there are still two main groups of Muslims. The larger group is known as Sunni *(SUN ee).* Sunni Muslims believe that the only sources of Islam are the Qur'an—that is, the word of God—and the traditions of Muhammad. Their name comes from the *sunna,* the deeds and sayings of Muhammad and the actions he permitted. More than 85 percent of the world's Muslims are Sunnis.

▼ *The chart does not include large countries with a small percentage of Muslims. For example, in 1990 about 2 percent of the U.S. population of about 250 million were Muslims.*

Largest Muslim Populations

Country	Muslim Populations	Percent
Indonesia	160,330,500	87
Pakistan	118,170,700	97
Bangladesh	96,472,400	87
India	95,298,691	11
Iran	59,103,000	99
Turkey	58,608,000	99
Egypt	50,130,000	90
Nigeria	43,248,000	48
Morocco	25,938,000	99
Ethiopia	24,435,000	45

Sources: 1992 World Population Data Sheet, Population Reference Bureau, 1992; The Europa World Year Book, 1991

The smaller group of Muslims is known as Shi'a *(SHEE uh)* or Shiites. Most Shi'as live in Iran and Iraq. Their name means "party" and refers to Ali's supporters. The Shi'as believe there are three sources of Islam: the Qur'an, Muhammad, and Ali's descendants.

The Appeal of Islam

The Umayyads ruled the Muslim state between 661 and 750, adding vast areas to its territory. By 750 all of North Africa was Muslim. Muslim armies also reached central France before Christian forces pushed them back into Spain. To the east, Islam reached India. The map above shows how far Islam spread in about 125 years.

By 750 the Muslim world included people from many countries and walks of life. Islam had followers among city dwellers, people in villages, and farmers in tropical lowlands. Today many countries have large Muslim populations (see chart).

Why did so many people accept Islam? Some welcomed the idea that all Muslims are equal. "Know that every Muslim is a Muslim's

190

Access Activity

Ask students to list the countries named in the chart on this page. Have them locate each country on the Atlas maps of Eurasia and of Africa on pages 682 and 685. Ask students what conclusions they can draw from this information. *(Islam spread to Asia and Africa.)*

Access Strategy

Discuss with students how ideas spread. First, ask students where they get new ideas. *(Family, friends, teachers, books, magazines, radio, television, films)* Then ask them which sources that they named would have been available in the period following Muhammad's death. Give students the opportunity to make observations about how the communication of ideas has changed or has remained the same over the centuries.

Explain that Islam spread by word of mouth and through the written word (the Qur'an). Discuss with students other ways in which new ideas are spread. Have students consider what the following meant in terms of the spread of ideas during Umayyad times: handwritten manuscripts, translations, high rate of literacy.

brother," Muhammad had said. Some were attracted by the idea that all Muslims are joined in a community, or *umma,* that requires the same five duties of all followers (see Lesson 1). Islam provides a guide to daily life that all believers can follow. ■

■ *What caused a split among the followers of Islam?*

Muslim Achievements

As the religion of Islam spread, Muslim culture flowered. From 700 to 1100, Muslim culture experienced a golden age. Many cities in the Muslim world had lighted streets. In some homes fountains cooled the air and pleased the ear with the sound of falling water.

Science and Medicine

The caliphs of the golden age built schools and libraries. Cairo, Egypt, was said to have a library with 100,000 books on history, astronomy, Islamic law, and other subjects. At this time learning in Europe was in decline. Yet the ideas of ancient Greek and Roman writers survived. They were preserved in part because Muslim scholars translated the works into Arabic. As learning revived in Europe, these volumes were translated back into Western languages.

The caliphs also promoted science. Physicists studied light and how the eye sees it. Astronomers kept records of the ways the planets move, and biologists described plants and animals. These scientists learned to look with care at the world around them. They made careful notes of what they saw and did experiments to test their ideas. Today's scientists still use methods like those of Muslim scientists.

Muslims also made advances in mathematics. They brought the use of zero and the Indian numeral system to Southwest Asia. From there these numerals spread to Europe. You know them as our Arabic numerals and use them every day. Muslims also improved on the geometry used by the Greeks and did original work in algebra. In fact, the words *algebra* and *algorithm*—a method for solving problems—both come from the Arabic language.

In Muslim hospitals chemists made oils and ointments to use in medicine. Doctors vowed to care for the sick by repeating the Hippocratic Oath (page 160). They diagnosed diseases and performed surgery. Some devoted their lives to caring for children.

Trade and Geography

Muslim traders regularly moved back and forth from Spain to India and China, using Arabic as a common language. They had maps drawn of trade routes and encouraged travelers to write about their journeys. These accounts added greatly to knowledge of the world.

One of the greatest travelers of all time was Ibn Battuta. In 1325 he set out from Tangier, Morocco, to make the hajj. He returned home 29 years later. During these years Ibn Battuta crossed two continents and traveled 75,000 miles by land and sea.

Across Time & Space

Paintings showing scientists studying the skies reflect Muslim interest in astronomy. The star maps they made show star names that are still used—Altair, Deneb, Rigel, and Aldebaran. All of these names are from the Arabic language.

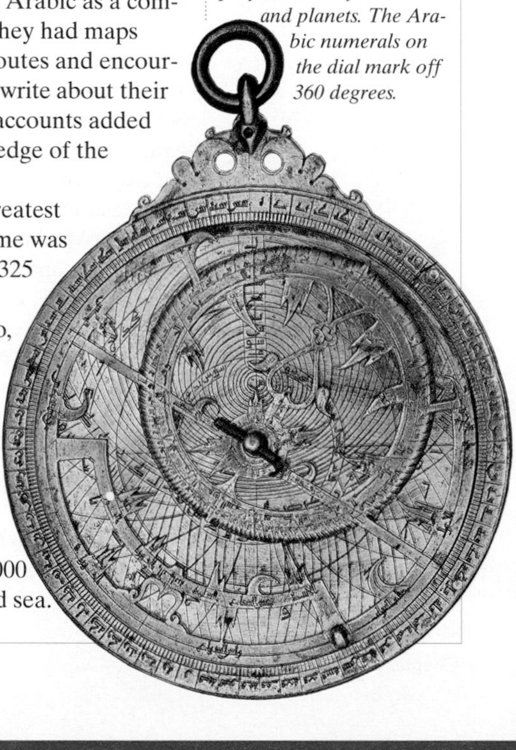

▼ *Muslim scientists used an astrolabe like this one to figure the time for prayers and to find stars and planets. The Arabic numerals on the dial mark off 360 degrees.*

■ *Shi'a Muslims supported Ali and refused to recognize the Umayyad caliphs after the murder of Ali and that of his son Husayn.*

CULTURE

Critical Thinking

Allow students several minutes to study the text under the heading Muslim Achievements. Then have them close their books and write as many advances of the Muslim golden age as they can remember on a sheet of paper. When students have finished, ask them to write one or two paragraphs telling which achievement of the golden age they believe has benefited later ages the most. Tell students to support their ideas with information from the text and provide examples.

Cultural Context

To help students understand intercultural contact, discuss the sharing of foods among cultures. During the golden age of Muslim culture, Muslims developed a cuisine that combined elements from the many cultures with which they came into contact. In fact, the Muslim world was an important source of written recipes between 700 and 1100. Interest in cuisine and the development of cooking techniques can be traced back to the ancient civilizations in the region, particularly to Mesopotamia. The earliest surviving Arabic manuscript treating cookery dates from the late 10th century and comes from Abbasid Iraq.

More interesting, however, is information the manuscript provides about a group of gourmets in Baghdad in the ninth century. This group pooled their cooking traditions and created a cuisine that made the Abbasid capital an unrivaled culinary center with a wide influence. Today yogurt and shish kebab continue this cuisine.

Social Participation

Point out that Arabic has served as a *lingua franca,* or common "international" language, throughout the Muslim world. Note the use of English as an international language today. Then divide the class into groups and hold a debate on these questions: Is an international language necessary today? Should English continue to be the international language?

CULTURE

Critical Thinking

Scholars often point to the way in which Muslim culture took elements from many different sources and made something entirely new from them. Discuss with students how the golden age exemplifies this idea. Encourage them to cite specific details in the text to support their opinions.

■ *Muslims made achievements in astronomy, mathematics, medicine, geography, trade, crafts, and art.*

CLOSE

Read the Thinking Focus aloud. Have each student check the list of inferences they made at the beginning of the lesson, as well as the list of causes and effects. Ask students to complete the following sentence aloud as a group without referring to the text: *The period from 700 to 1100 is called the golden age of Muslim culture because . . .* Their lists will help them fill in the blank.

▲ The Pearl Mosque in India (above) has domes that borrow from Indian styles of architecture. Muslim designs of brightly colored tiles decorate a wall in Fez, Morocco (right).

He described the markets and mosques of Southwest Asia, the frozen plains of Russia, bustling cities in India and China, and the many peoples he met.

Muslim merchants traded in an enormous variety of products. They introduced dozens of plant products to Western Europe, including oranges, lemons, apricots, dates, rice, and sugar. The master swordmakers of Damascus, Syria, invented damascene, a way to inlay gold and silver in steel. Damask, a cloth with a finely woven pattern, was another product from Damascus. From Mosul, Iraq, came the sheer cotton cloth called muslin. Books were bound in cordovan leather from Córdoba, Spain.

Muslim Art

Muslim artists created more than swords, cloth, and books. The Qur'an did not forbid pictures of people and animals. Muhammad and many Muslims, however, felt it was disrespectful. They believed that only God has the power to create life. Muslim artists made writing a form of art. They copied verses from the Qur'an in flowing Arabic script. Beautifully handwritten copies of the Qur'an are among the treasures of Muslim art.

Some Muslim artists, particularly in Iran and India, showed figures of people and animals. Many others made designs out of stone and tiles. They formed patterns of stars, circles, and triangles and copied the shapes of flowers and trees. Complex patterns of intertwined lines are called arabesques. Muslim artists today still use designs like these. ■

■ *What achievements did Muslims make during their golden age?*

REVIEW

1. **FOCUS** Why is the period from 700 to 1100 called a golden age of Muslim culture?
2. **BELIEFS** What are the two main groups of Muslims? Explain what still unites these groups.
3. **CULTURE** What contributions did Muslims make to science and mathematics during the golden age of Muslim culture?
4. **CRITICAL THINKING** Explain what Abu-Bakr meant when he said, "If you worship Muhammad, Muhammad is dead; if you worship God, God is alive."
5. **WRITING ACTIVITY** Using ar-Razi's diagnosis as an example, write a description of the symptoms you noticed when you were feeling ill with a cold, the flu, or some other disease.

Homework Options

Have students make a work of art using patterns of stars, circles, triangles, intertwined lines, or shapes of flowers and trees. Remind them that this is an example of the arabesque style.

Study Guide: page 32

Answers to Review Questions

1. Between 700 and 1100, Muslims sought to expand knowledge; caliphs built schools and libraries and had ancient books translated; Muslims made advances in science, mathematics, art, and medicine.
2. The two groups are Sunnis and Shi'as. Both believe in one God, regard Muhammad as God's prophet and the Qur'an as a holy book, and perform the same five duties.
3. Muslims studied light, recorded the movement of the planets, and described plants and animals. They spread the use of the Indian numeral system, improved geometry, and developed algebra.
4. Abu-Bakr was probably reminding Muslims that Muhammad was a messenger of Allah and not to be worshiped. He died like any other man, whereas God is eternal.
5. Encourage students to be specific in making their diagnoses.

500
800
1100
1400
1700
2000
1932 TODAY

L E S S O N 3

Saudi Arabia Today

For centuries, whenever travelers arrived at a Bedouin's tent, they knew they would be given water, food, and shelter. Today, at the start of a business meeting, the Saudis continue this ancient custom of welcoming guests by offering visitors tea to drink.

Every place in the world has its own customs. In Saudi Arabia many customs are tied to the rules of Islam. For example, Muslims may not drink alcohol or eat pork, which is viewed as unclean.

Cleanliness is an important part of worship for Muslims. Before they pray, they wash their hands, faces, and feet. When they enter a mosque, they take off their shoes to avoid tracking dirt inside.

Islam also influences working hours in Saudi Arabia. At noontime, midafternoon, and sunset, stores and businesses close to allow workers to meet their duty to pray (see table, page 187). On Friday businesses are closed for most of the day. Friday is Islam's holy day, when many people go to a mosque for midday prayers.

Some Saudi social customs combine Bedouin and Muslim practices. Since ancient times, for example, the Arabs have believed that women should dress very modestly. In the Qur'an the wives of Muhammad are advised to wear veils. Muslim women are expected to keep their hair covered, and in Saudi Arabia they usually wear face veils in public. These customs show the mixture of Muslim and Bedouin beliefs and ways of life in modern Saudi Arabia.

THINKING FOCUS

How has oil changed life in Saudi Arabia?

Key Terms

- censor
- desalination

▲ *Muslims remove their shoes when entering a mosque. While praying, they touch the floor with their head and hands.*

◄ *The tiny cups in which tea is served are often decorated with floral designs.*

INTRODUCE

Have students turn back to the map on page 184 and ask a volunteer to tell in what country Mecca is located. *(Saudi Arabia)* Then read the title and the Thinking Focus of Lesson 3. Use the exercise to establish a link between the preceding two lessons on Islam and this lesson. In a brainstorming session, ask students to volunteer what they know about modern Saudi Arabia. Jot their statements on the chalkboard. Students may mention the Persian Gulf War and oil. Tell them that as they read the lesson, they will flesh out their impressions.

Key Terms

Vocabulary Strategies: T36–T37

censor—to examine something and cut out what seems objectionable or stop it from being sold

desalination—the process that removes salt from sea water

Graphic Overview

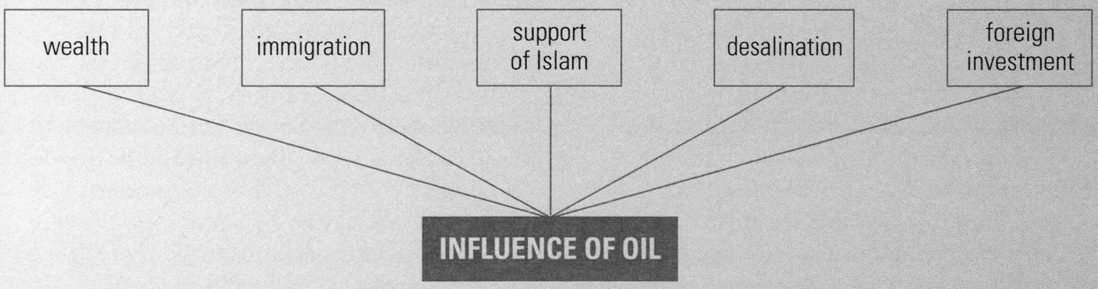
wealth
immigration
support of Islam
desalination
foreign investment
INFLUENCE OF OIL

Objectives

1. Describe how the kingdom of Saudi Arabia was created.
2. Name at least four things the rulers of Saudi Arabia do to promote Islam.
3. Explain how Saudi oil resources have led to interdependence.

DEVELOP

Draw the Graphic Overview on page 193 on the chalkboard. Discuss the graphic's parts and their relationships. Then direct students to look carefully at the lesson to identify headings, text, or visuals that correspond to or reflect the parts of the Graphic Overview. Suggest to students that they may find it helpful to create their own graphic organizer as a study aid after they have read the lesson.

GEOGRAPHY

Map and Globe Skills

Ask students to turn to page 664 in the Minipedia and look for the populations of each of the following cities that is in a Muslim country: Jakarta, Cairo, Teheran (Tehran), Karachi, Baghdad. Have students use the map of Eurasia on pages 682–683 of the Atlas to locate the country in which each of these cities is located.

The Saudi Kingdom

Saudi Arabia is the only country in all the world that is named for its ruling family—the Sauds. If history had been different, it might have been called Rashidi Arabia.

Forming a Kingdom

For many years, the Saud and Rashid families had been enemies. In 1891 the Rashids attacked the Saudi town of Riyadh *(ree YAHD)*. They poured poison into the wells and cut down the date palms. The Sauds fled to the desert on the edge of the Empty Quarter (see page 185). Their leader's 15-year-old son was hidden in a basket strapped to the back of a camel.

The young prince, Abdul Aziz *(AHB dul ah ZEEZ)*, vowed to regain Riyadh. One cold winter's night 11 years later, he and a small raiding party climbed the town wall. At dawn, with a loud war cry, Abdul Aziz attacked. When the battle ended, the Saudi forces had won back Riyadh.

By the early 1920s, Abdul Aziz controlled most of the Arabian Peninsula except Yemen. In 1932 he declared himself king of Saudi Arabia. Today Saudi Arabia welcomes representatives from many nations, as shown in A Closer Look on page 195.

Introducing Modern Ways

King Abdul Aziz often said, "The chief of a tribe is its servant." He liked to talk about his plans with the leading men of different families. He encouraged his subjects to come to him with their problems.

Although Abdul Aziz listened to the advice of others, he was the one who made all the decisions. Saudi Arabia is one of the few nations in the world today that is ruled by one person with nearly absolute power. The Saudi ruler has almost complete control, and his word is law. Yet because Saudi Arabia is a Muslim country, its laws must agree with the rules of Islam.

➤ *During the hajj the tent city on the Plain of Arafat stretches to the horizon. Here the Saudi government provides sanitary areas and tents where pilgrims can rest and eat, get first aid, and find friends and relatives who are lost.*

Access Activity

Ask students whether they have heard the saying "A picture is worth a thousand words." Encourage them to share their thoughts about what the saying means. Then have each student select a photograph in the lesson and explain what it tells about modern Saudi Arabia.

Access Strategy

Probe students' perceptions of change. Suggest that change is part of life. Ask students to think of changes that have been part of their lives. Give students a chance to consider why people sometimes do not want to accept change. *(Fear of the unknown, feel comfortable with familiar ways of doing things, think that change conflicts with beliefs)*

Ask students to think about whether attitudes toward change may alter over time. For example, students may view moving to a new city as a bad change; after they make new friends, however, they often think that the change is good. Tell students to note the changes that the people of Saudi Arabia have experienced in this century. Have them consider whether most Saudis tend to accept these changes. How might the Saudis' modern problems be similar to those of modern U.S. citizens? *(Status of women and immigrants, role of religion, and disputes about the family are problems faced by both nations.)*

A CLOSER LOOK

Arabian Hospitality

In their proud tradition of hospitality, the Saudi Arabians built the Tuwaiq Palace to welcome foreign diplomats to the capital city of Riyadh. Like an ancient oasis, the palace offers protection against the desert sun and winds.

If you walked along the top of the walls, you'd cover the length of more than four football fields.
Inside the limestone walls are guest rooms and offices. The walls reach nearly four stories high.
Bowling alleys, squash courts, a pool, and a gymnasium are all under one white tent.
The white tents are made of fiberglass. All three cover large halls.

When Abdul Aziz first allowed automobiles and cameras into Saudi Arabia, many people opposed him. They said the changes were against the teachings of Islam. One sheik, a religious leader, thought the radio was a tool of the devil. After all, he said, it made words come out of the air!

Abdul Aziz asked, "Would Satan carry God's word?"

The sheik replied, "You know and I know that Satan would never carry the word of God one inch."

The king then led the sheik to the radio. Through the crackle of static, they could hear a voice reading verses from the Qur'an. This convinced the sheik that the radio was not some evil invention.

Changes by Later Kings

Abdul Aziz used similar methods to get roads and railroads built. By the time he died in 1953, Saudi Arabia had modern cities as well as desert villages. Abdul Aziz's son Faisal *(FY suhl),* who came to the throne in 1964, continued his father's policies. He also supported the schools his wife, Iffat *(IHF iht),* set up to teach boys mathematics and science. She also planned schools for girls, courses in typing, and women's health clinics.

When Faisal's half-brother, Fahd, became king in 1982, he used the title Custodian of the Two Holy Mosques. It emphasized the Saud family's duties toward pilgrims. Each year the government provides transportation and shelter for pilgrims. Caravans of tanker trucks carry water to the pilgrims each day, and kitchens supply them with food.

A printing plant supplies Muslims around the world with about 10 million free copies of the Qur'an

Note: You may want to refer to this Closer Look to reinforce the idea of Saudi social customs, discussed on page 193.

CULTURE

Visual Learning

Use this picture to discuss the idea of hospitality in different cultures. In many desert countries, for example, giving water to a guest signifies welcome because water is scarce. Have students supply examples of hospitality from their own homes and school. Encourage them to add to their examples as they read further in this book.

More About Tuwaiq Palace

Point to the different covered areas and the huge tents, which are made of fiberglass. Explain that leading architects from different countries worked on the plans for the diplomatic quarters. The Swedish embassy, for example, used birch wood, which is common in Sweden. Point out that the Saudis wanted to combine old and new—nearby are the ruins of an old fort as well as the modern King Saud University. Remind students of the photographs showing continuity and change on page 183.

Bulletin Board

Set up an international hospitality bulletin board. Have students make drawings or collect pictures from magazines to illustrate examples of hospitality or considerate behavior practiced throughout the world. They might include cartoons criticizing inappropriate behavior.

Research/Investigating

Point out that the word *hospitality* comes from the Latin root *hospes,* which means "host." Have students look up the following words in a dictionary and tell how they are related in meaning to hospitality: *hospice, hospital, host, hostage, hostel.*

Visual Learning

One of the aims of the Saudi government was to have the diplomatic quarters be in harmony with their surroundings. Ask students to identify ways in which the palace blends with the desert. *(Natural-appearing walls of material compatible with desert and curving like dunes, structures like tents in desert)*

■ *The Saudi government supplies Muslim pilgrims with shelter, water, food, and transportation; and free copies of the Qur'an worldwide.*

POLITICAL SYSTEMS

Social Participation

Remind students that the Saudi king, who is descended from Abdul Aziz, rules in accordance with the religion of Islam. Have the class reread pages 194–196 and divide into two groups. Ask one group to write a paragraph on the creation of the Saudi kingdom. Ask the other group to write a paragraph on the government's promotion of Islam. Then ask the groups to read the paragraphs to each other.

ECONOMICS

Critical Thinking

Help students make generalizations about what happens when one country depends on another for basic needs. *(Disagreements may interfere with the delivery of needed goods; countries learn to cooperate.)* Ask what makes the Saudis' oil an especially problematic resource. *(It's depletable, and it will force the Saudis to redevelop eventually.)*

■ *How does the Saud family meet its responsibilities toward Muslims?*

yearly. King Fahd also decided that the Saudi government should pay for the cost of educating the people of the kingdom and providing them with health care.

Programs such as these cost a great deal of money. How do the Saudis pay for them? The answer lies in the oil that is buried under the desert sands. ■

The Impact of Oil

The kingdom Abdul Aziz had created in 1932 was very poor. It is said that the head of the treasury kept all the nation's money in a box in his home! Abdul Aziz knew that oil had been found in desert areas in other countries. In 1933 he agreed to let a U.S. oil company drill in Saudi Arabia. In March 1938 the drills finally made a major strike. The discovery changed Saudi Arabia forever.

Oil Becomes a Weapon

At the end of World War II in 1945, the demand for oil soared. The largest demand came from industrial countries like the United States. When U.S. oil companies could not meet the demand, companies in Saudi Arabia and other countries filled the gap. Saudi oil was cheap, and the supply seemed endless. Saudi Arabia had over one-fourth of the world's known oil reserves. Soon the Saudi princes were collecting millions of dollars in oil profits each year.

By 1960 the Saudis wanted more control of their oil. They met with four other oil-producing nations—Iran, Iraq, Kuwait *(koo WAYT),* and Venezuela—to form the Organization of Petroleum Exporting Countries (OPEC). Eight other nations later joined them. OPEC raised the price of oil and controlled the amount produced.

Then, in 1973, war broke out between the Arab nations and Israel. Like other Arab leaders, Faisal was opposed to Israel. He stopped shipping oil to nations supporting Israel. Oil and gasoline became scarce in the industrial nations, and prices soared. Worried about how much they depended on foreign oil, people in the United States began to look for ways to use less oil.

Five months later the United States agreed to provide support and help for the development of Saudi Arabia. Faisal reluctantly began to ship oil again.

This oil refinery at Ras Tanura is one of the four largest in the world. Oil produces nearly all the kingdom's income. Less than 2 percent of the workers in Saudi Arabia, however, are employed in the oil industry.

Worries about Change

Although the Saudis have set up modern industries, they have held onto many traditional values. Many Saudi women teach, run computers, act as doctors, and work in banks. Yet women are usually separated from male co-workers. Male teachers instruct female students over closed-circuit TV. No woman can stay in a hotel, ride in an airplane, or study abroad without

Presenting a Report

Invite students to research the process of oil production and present a report to the class. Ask them to tell how oil is pumped out of the ground and how it is treated. Students can use the encyclopedia in the school library.

Social Context

To help students understand the idea of censorship, tell them that the Saudi government operates in accordance with the religion of Islam. Islam promotes a sharing of goods, resources, and information for the benefit of the entire Muslim community. For this reason, many things that remain private in the United States would be considered public in Saudi Arabia.

For example, a Westerner visiting Saudi Arabia may have his or her mail opened if there were any suspicion that its contents were critical of Saudi Arabia. The cities of Mecca and Medina exist for Muslims only. Generally, any non-Muslim will be barred from going beyond the city gates.

Despite the legal connection between Islam and the Saudi government, there is still some tension in the Islamic world about Saudi control of Mecca. Students should understand that the Saudi regime is a source of controversy within Islam.

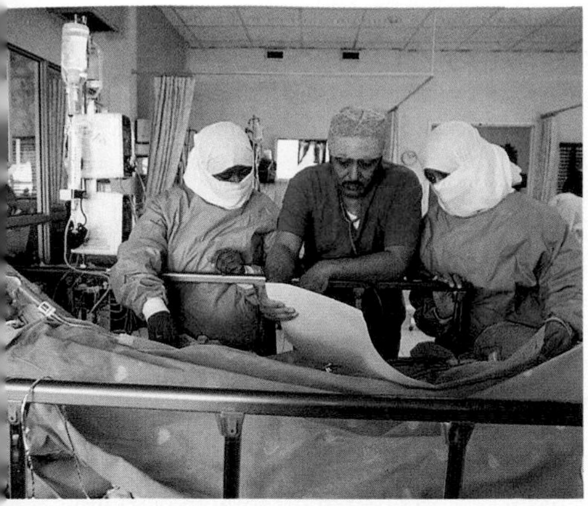

◄ *Fifty years ago Saudi women did not even consider a career in medicine. Today there are women working as both doctors and nurses in the nation's modern hospitals.*

written permission from a male relative or an official sponsor.

The Saudi government censors printed materials, music, and films. To **censor** something is to cut out anything that seems objectionable, or stop it from being sold. Censored books may be removed from libraries and bookstores. In the United States, freedom of speech and the press are basic rights. These rights do not exist in Saudi Arabia, but many Saudis are beginning to demand them.

The Saudis also worry about unrest in Southwest Asia. In the past, civil war in Lebanon, war between Iran and Iraq, and clashes between Israel and the Muslim nations have threatened to tear the region apart. (Find these nations on the Atlas map on pages 682–683.) Also, many Muslim nations have large populations but low incomes. They feel Saudi Arabia should share its wealth with less fortunate Muslims.

War in the Gulf

One of these nations, Iraq, had a special interest in Kuwait, Saudi Arabia's oil-rich neighbor on the Persian Gulf. When Iraq became independent in 1932, it claimed Kuwait. In 1990 Iraq renewed its claims. During a costly war with Iran (page 216), Iraq had borrowed large sums of money from Kuwait and Saudi Arabia, which also had opposed Iran. The Iraqis thought Kuwait should cancel the debt, but Kuwait refused. On August 2, 1990, Iraqi troops invaded Kuwait.

When the Iraqis moved south, King Fahd felt Saudi Arabia was threatened. Industrial nations such as the United States, Germany, and Japan did not want Iraq controlling another major source of oil. The United Nations voted to drive the Iraqis out of Kuwait. Almost all the Arab nations agreed, although Libya, Jordan, and Yemen did not. This was the first time Arab nations had joined forces with the United States for the purpose of attacking another Arab country.

▲ *In modern wars soldiers wear clothing that blends in with the land around them. The "pyramids" in this picture from the Persian Gulf War are really tents designed to blend in with the desert. Saudi troops played an important role in the war.*

In January 1991 multinational troops sponsored by the United Nations launched an attack called Operation Desert Storm. The troops soon drove the Iraqis out of Kuwait.

New Sources of Income

Oil income has helped the Saud family do many things for the nation. Yet scientists know that the world's supply of oil is limited. Once the present supply of oil has been pumped out of the ground, there will be no more.

SOCIAL SYSTEMS

Visual Learning

Have students work in small groups to compose a five-minute television news report on the problems faced by Saudi Arabia. Tell students to work the photographs and graph on pages 197–198 into their reports. For example, the photos on this page might be used with the topics of change (upper left) and regional unrest (right). Have the groups of students deliver the reports to the class.

GEOGRAPHY

Map and Globe Skills

Introduce the idea of strategic locations—places that are important because they control access to important areas. Have students turn to the map of Eurasia in the Atlas (pages 682–683) and locate the Persian Gulf, the waterway between Spain and Morocco, and the straits between the Mediterranean and the Black Sea. Ask students why they think that each is strategic. *(Persian Gulf: source of oil, access to Iran and Asia; Spain-Morocco: access to Mediterranean countries; Mediterranean-Black Sea: access to eastern Europe, western Asia, and Mediterranean countries.)*

Mathematics Connection

The Gulf War was extremely costly. Though many other countries participated and helped defray costs, the financial contribution the United States made to the effort was enormous. Even before Operation Desert Shield became Operation Desert Storm, the shopping list for the troops was huge, totaling $10 billion in the first five months. To give students some idea of the cost of the special personal equipment needed for Desert Shield, write these quantities and prices for certain supplies on the board: 150,000 bottles of sunscreen totaling $219,000; 600,000 tubes of lip balm totaling $99,000; 230,000 tubes of foot powder totaling $80,000; and 40,000 cans of insect repellent for $76,400. Tell students to compute the grand total for these supplies. *($474,400)* Then challenge students to determine the totals for these clothing items: 168,000 chemical protection suits at $68.15 each and 100,000 pairs of goggles at $3.85 each. *(The totals are $11,449,200 and $385,000.)*

Visual Learning

Have students study the picture of the soldiers on this page. Explain that armies in the past often did not try to blend in with their surroundings. The British in the American Revolution, for example, wore bright scarlet coats. Have students discuss the advantages of camouflage, and refer to the soldier depicted in the Moment in Time feature on page 634.

ECONOMICS

Visual Learning

Have students use the graph to figure out approximately how many tons of wheat were produced in each of the years given. Ask them to use this information to infer when the program of desalination came into wide use. *(Probably between 1980 and 1985, since there is a great jump in production in that period)*

CLOSE

Read the Thinking Focus aloud. Write the words *Past, Present,* and *Future* across the board, leaving ample space between the words. Then ask for three volunteers to stand before each of the words. Tell them to write two or three sentences that describe life in Saudi Arabia in their time period. Have other class members write similar sentences at their desks. Then have all the students revisit the ideas they jotted down at the beginning of the lesson.

■ *Saudi Arabia faces the problems of unrest in the Persian Gulf region, possible exhaustion of its oil reserves, and a shortage of local labor.*

Desalination provides water for irrigation so Saudi farmers can grow larger crops. The graph shows how greatly wheat production increased after irrigation became widely used. Today Saudi Arabia produces all the wheat it needs.

The Saud family is trying to develop new sources of income for the country. The Saudis have reopened gold mines. They have started a cement factory, steel mills, and fertilizer plants. Along the coasts they have built plants for the desalination of sea water. The process of **desalination** removes the salt. People can then use the desalinated water for drinking and cooking or for irrigating crops (see the graph).

Wheat Production, 1975–1990

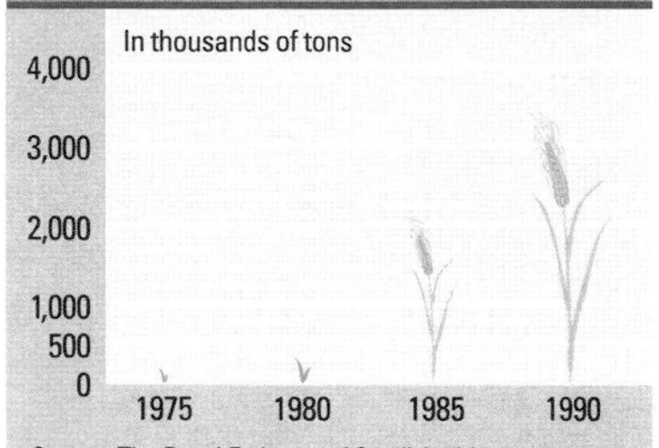

In thousands of tons
4,000
3,000
2,000
1,000
500
0
1975
1980
1985
1990

Source: The Royal Embassy of Saudi Arabia Information Office

Need for Workers

Saudi Arabia has only about 16 million people. There simply are not enough people to do the hard work needed to develop the country as quickly as King Fahd wishes.

Workers are needed to build factories and roads, string electric lines, drive trucks, and work in Saudi stores and banks. Nearly 60 percent of these workers now come from other countries.

Foreign workers are not allowed to bring their wives or families with them. They may not become citizens of Saudi Arabia. Although many foreigners may go home on leave, most return. They know they can earn more money in Saudi Arabia than they can at home.

At first, most foreign workers were Muslims from other Arabic-speaking countries. They found it fairly easy to fit into Saudi society. Now, more and more of these workers come from such countries as Sri Lanka, India, Pakistan, and the Philippines. Many of these workers do not speak Arabic. Some are not even Muslims. In time these foreign workers may come to outnumber the native-born Saudi population.

Saudi Arabia has faced many changes in the 60 years it has taken to become a modern nation. In the years to come, the nation may face even greater changes. ■

■ *What major problems does Saudi Arabia face today?*

REVIEW

1. **FOCUS** How has oil changed life in Saudi Arabia?
2. **BELIEFS** Why did Abdul Aziz have difficulty introducing modern inventions to Saudi Arabia?
3. **ECONOMICS** How do Saudi Arabia and industrial nations such as the United States depend on one another?
4. **CRITICAL THINKING** How would your life change if the world ran out of oil? Where would people get energy?
5. **WRITING ACTIVITY** Coins used in Saudi Arabia bear the words of the Islamic statement of faith: "There is no god but God, and Muhammad is the messenger of God." Examine the sayings found on all U.S. coins. Write a short statement telling what each saying reveals about the United States.

Homework Options

Tell students to pretend that they are foreign workers in Saudi Arabia. Have them write an imaginary letter to their family at home telling about life in Saudi Arabia. Urge students to be creative and use what they have learned about modern Saudi Arabia from this lesson.

Study Guide: page 33

Answers to Review Questions

1. Oil has given the rulers of Saudi Arabia the wealth to provide care for pilgrims, pay for education and health care, and modernize the kingdom.
2. Some Saudi Arabians, including some Islamic leaders, thought that such inventions went against the teachings of Islam.
3. The industrial nations depend on Saudi Arabia for oil. Saudi Arabia depends on these nations for the selling of its oil.
4. Students may answer that loss of oil would affect how they traveled and what they bought (gasoline, plastics, and other products made from petrochemicals). Alternatives might be nuclear or solar energy.
5. U.S. coins bear three mottoes: "Liberty," which expresses the belief in freedom; "In God We Trust," which recognizes the place of religion in U.S. life; and *"E Pluribus Unum,"* which is Latin for "From Many, One," indicating that many people come together to form one nation.

UNDERSTANDING HISTORICAL SEQUENCE

Making Parallel Timelines

Here's Why

Many timelines show you dates from a single culture or nation. Some timelines show links among different groups. They are called parallel timelines because they show parallels among events. For example, some of the events you will read about later in Chapter 21 happened at the same time as some events in this chapter. By using a parallel timeline such as the one below, you can fit together different pieces of history. This will let you compare and contrast the events that happened at the same time.

Here's How

You can follow these steps to make a parallel timeline.

1. **Decide what you want your timeline to do.** You might want to use it to compare the histories of two groups. You might want to show what people were doing when certain events took place. The timeline below shows important dates in technology and Saudi Arabian history.
2. **Decide what span of dates your timeline will show.** The timeline below begins with the year 1930 and ends with 1990. It is divided into 10-year segments.
3. **Gather dates and information about events for your timeline.**
4. **Plot the events near the appropriate dates on the timeline.**

Try It

The list below gives some important inventions that were made after 1930. Copy the timeline below. Add the dates and inventions on the list. Plot the following inventions on the appropriate segment of the timeline.

- 1932, Polaroid glass developed, later used in sunglasses.
- 1938, Ballpoint pen invented.
- 1939, Television shown at the New York World's Fair.
- 1943, First successful electronic computer started operating.
- 1972, Advances made in compact disc technology.

Now, use the timeline you enlarged to answer the following questions.

1. Which invention was made the year Abdul Aziz became king?
2. Which invention helped Saudis keep track of how much oil they produced and sold?
3. Which invention let people in the United States see events as they happened in the Persian Gulf War?

Apply It

Create a parallel timeline. On one part, show events in your life or in your family's history. Use an almanac to find events in U.S. history that happened about the same time.

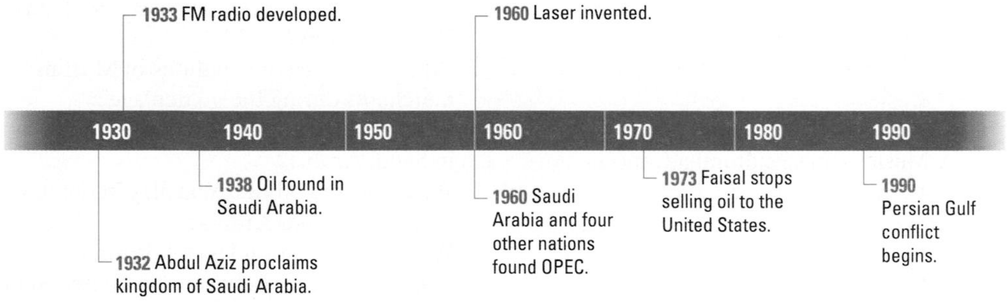

1933 FM radio developed.
1960 Laser invented.
1930
1940
1950
1960
1970
1980
1990
1938 Oil found in Saudi Arabia.
1932 Abdul Aziz proclaims kingdom of Saudi Arabia.
1960 Saudi Arabia and four other nations found OPEC.
1973 Faisal stops selling oil to the United States.
1990 Persian Gulf conflict begins.

UNDERSTANDING HISTORICAL SEQUENCE

In this skills feature, students gain a sense of chronology by adding information to a timeline of events from Chapter 8. This parallel timeline relates Saudi Arabian history to notable modern inventions.

HISTORY

Visual Learning

Divide students into small groups. Provide each group with a regular calendar showing major holidays and a school calendar showing school holidays and vacations. Have each group begin by setting up a timeline divided into 12 one-month segments. Each group should then plot the events on the school calendar on the timeline. Next—using a different color pen or marker—students should add major national and religious holidays in the appropriate places on the timeline. Ask one person from each group to point out the connection between school vacations and national holidays.

Answers to Try It

Check student timelines to be sure that they have understood the principle and placed events in the appropriate places.

1. Polaroid glass for sunglasses (1932)
2. Computer (1943)
3. Television (1939)

Answers to Apply It

Ask students to share their own timelines with the class or with small groups if appropriate. Discuss making the timelines. Was it difficult or relatively easy for the students to find the information they wanted? From whom or where did they get most of their family information?

Objective

Demonstrate how to read and plot information on a timeline. (Visual Learning 2)

Answers to Reviewing Key Terms

A. Sample answers:
1. a religious journey
2. the process of removing salt from seawater
3. a successor to Muhammad
4. identification of disease
5. examine printed materials, music, and movies; cut out or suppress anything that seems objectionable
6. a fertile area around a spring or water hole
7. a place to gather and pray
8. a long line of people and camels traveling from one place to another

B. Sample answers:
1. Merchants traveled overland in **caravans,** moving from one **oasis** to another.
2. At least once in his or her lifetime, a Muslim makes a **pilgrimage** to the holy city of Mecca and worships at the Great **Mosque.**
3. Sometimes a **caliph,** the head of a Muslim state, might ask government officials to **censor** printed materials, music, and movies.
4. On the **pilgrimage** to the holy city, our **caravan** only stopped twice for water and food.

Answers to Exploring Concepts

A. Sample answers:
B. 1. Sunnis believe that only the Qur'an and Muhammad can be the sources of Islam. B. 2. Shi'as believe that the Qur'an, Muhammad, and the descendants of the caliph Ali are all sources of Islam. C. 1. Islam requires the same five duties of all Muslims. C. 2. It provides a guide to life that anyone can follow. C. 3. Under Islamic law, the rights of women have been broadened. D. 1. Physicists study light. D. 2. Biologists describe plants and animals. D. 3. Mathematicians introduce Arabic numerals and the use of zero. D. 4. Sword makers invent damascene. D. 5. Artists use the arabesque design in their work.

B. Sample answers:
1. Mecca is the holy city of Islam toward which Muslims turn when they worship. Each Muslim must make a pilgrimage to Mecca at least once in his or her lifetime.
2. Enough rain falls in the mountains along the Red Sea to support farming.
3. The Meccans did not want to give up their old religion and may have feared that Islam would end trade with the Bedouins.
4. Islamic women can own and inherit property. A divorced wife may keep any money or property she had when she married.
5. People welcomed the idea that all Muslims are equal and are joined in a community that requires the same five duties of all Muslims.
6. Muslim scholars translated the works of ancient Greek and Roman writers into Arabic.
7. The maps and journals of the travels added greatly to knowledge of the world and also introduced a variety of plant products to Western Europe.
8. Muslims may not drink wine or eat pork. Three times a day, businesses close to allow workers to meet their duty to pray. Muslim women are expected to dress modestly.
9. Abdul Aziz gained control of most of the Arabian Peninsula and declared himself

Chapter Review

Reviewing Key Terms

caliph (p. 189)
caravan (p. 185)
censor (p. 197)
desalination (p. 198)
diagnosis (p. 189)
mosque (p. 186)
oasis (p. 185)
pilgrimage (p. 184)

A. Imagine you are playing a game with a partner. Your partner tries to guess which key term you are thinking of. For each key term below, think of a phrase you could give to your partner as a clue. Write each phrase on your own paper. An example has been filled in for you.
1. pilgrimage: a religious journey
2. desalination
3. caliph
4. diagnosis
5. censor
6. oasis
7. mosque
8. caravan

B. Read each pair of words. Write a sentence telling how the words in each pair are related.
1. caravan, oasis
2. pilgrimage, mosque
3. caliph, censor
4. caravan, pilgrimage

Exploring Concepts

A. In about 125 years, Islam spread from Arabia into Africa, Europe, and Asia. Today this religion has one of the largest followings in the world. Copy and complete the following outline.

I. The Spread of Islam
   A. After Muhammad's death, the caliphs begin spreading Islam beyond Arabia.
   B. Muslims split into two groups of believers.
      1.
      2.
   C. The teachings of Islam appeal to many people.
      1.
      2.
      3.
   D. Muslims make cultural advances.
      1.
      2.
      3.
      4.
      5.

B. Answer each question with information from the chapter.
1. What part does Mecca play in the Islamic religion?
2. Why did an early civilization develop in the the southwestern mountains of Arabia?
3. Why were most Meccans slow to accept Muhammad's message?
4. How did the Islamic religion affect the status of women?
5. Why did so many people come to accept Islam?
6. What role did Muslim scholars play in preserving the ideas of ancient Greek and Roman writers?
7. What were the contributions of Muslim merchants during the golden age?
8. What influence does Islam have on customs in Saudi Arabia?
9. What role did Abdul Aziz play in the development of Saudi Arabia?
10. Why was Operation Desert Storm a turning point in relations between the United States and the Arab nations?

Reviewing Skills

1. Look at the timeline on this page. It shows important dates during the golden age of Muslim culture. Using the timeline, figure out the number of years between the time when the Muslim armies began their conquest of Spain and the date when they were expelled by Christian Spain. Did the Crusaders capture Jerusalem before or after the Muslims began their conquest of Spain?
2. Look at the map on page 190 showing the spread of Islam. Imagine that you are a Muslim traveling in a caravan. Using the map scale, figure out how far it is from Mecca to Damascus. If your caravan traveled at 10 miles per hour, how long would the trip take?
3. Imagine that you are keeping a journal of your travels. What kinds of information would you include in your journal?

600 | 800 | 1000 | 1200 | 1400 | 1600 | 1800

- A.D. **711** Muslim conquest of Spain begins.
- A.D. **998** Muslim armies conquer northern India.
- A.D. **1010** Destruction of Christian holy places in Jerusalem ordered.
- A.D. **1099** Crusaders capture Jerusalem.
- A.D. **1492** Muslims expelled from Spain.

Using Critical Thinking

1. Islam, Christianity, and Judaism all expanded from the same part of the world. In fact, Jerusalem is a holy city to all three faiths. What might there have been about this region that encouraged the spread of religious beliefs?
2. After 632, as Islam spread to many lands, a golden age of learning developed. Do you think there is a connection? Explain.
3. After Ali and his son Husayn were murdered, the Muslims split into two groups, the Sunnis and the Shi'as. Do you think they could ever be reunited? Explain.
4. In 1973 Faisal stopped shipping oil to nations supporting Israel. When people in the United States looked for ways to use less oil, however, Faisal began to ship oil again. If he had not resumed oil shipments, how might the events of 1990–1991 in the Persian Gulf have been different?

Preparing for Citizenship

1. COLLECTING INFORMATION Most of the people living in Saudi Arabia are Muslims. Use an almanac to find and list the names of the major religious groups in the United States. Include the number of members each has.
2. ARTS ACTIVITY Muslim artists made writing a form of art. Sometimes, artists in the United States have treated writing as an art form. Collect photographs, pictures, or books that show writing as an art form, or create a work of your own using writing as an art form. Share your collection or your own artwork with the class.
3. GROUP ACTIVITY The Qur'an contains rules guiding the lives of all Muslims. In small groups, make a set of rules for your school. What do you think is good school behavior? Display your rules on a poster.
4. COLLABORATIVE LEARNING People from other countries come to both the United States and Saudi Arabia to live and work. In small groups, give a presentation on the experience of newcomers to the United States. Brainstorm to create a list of questions you would ask a recent immigrant. As a group, decide how to present your findings to the class.

king. He modernized the country and encouraged the building of highways and railroads.

10. For the first time, Arab nations joined forces with the United States for the purpose of attacking another Arab country.

Answers to Reviewing Skills

1. 781 years after
2. about 900 miles (1,400 km); 90 hours
3. Answers may include a description of the geography of the regions visited; a description of the cities and towns; a description of the peoples encountered on the journey—their dress, customs, language, and so forth.

Answers to Using Critical Thinking

1. Possible answers: This area had civilizations that were thousands of years old; contact between different places was frequent, encouraging the spread of ideas.
2. Students will probably recognize a connection between the spread of Islam and the development of a golden age of learning. As Muslims traveled to other lands, they were exposed to different cultures and new ideas that promoted the flowering of Muslim culture.
3. Students may answer that the major difference between Sunni Muslims and Shi'a Muslims is that the latter include Ali as a source of Islam, which Sunnis find unthinkable. Because this difference goes to the heart of Islamic belief, students may suggest that a reunion of Sunnis and Shi'as is unlikely, even though both share the belief in one God and in Muhammad as the prophet.
4. Students may suggest that if Faisal had not lifted the oil embargo, the United States would have continued its efforts to lessen its dependence on oil from the OPEC nations. If alternative fuels had been available when the Iraqis invaded Kuwait, the United States may not have come to the aid of Kuwait and Saudi Arabia in Operation Desert Storm.

Answers to Preparing for Citizenship

1. COLLECTING INFORMATION Students can use an encyclopedia or almanac for their research. Encourage them to prepare a chart of the information they find.
2. ARTS ACTIVITY Students can look through magazines or art books for examples. If they wish to create their own artwork, provide them with drawing paper, felt-tipped markers, newspapers and magazines to cut up, and/or poster paints.
3. GROUP ACTIVITY You may wish to have students discuss the various rules that each group produces and decide which are most conducive to promoting a favorable classroom climate. Supply materials for student posters.
4. COLLABORATIVE LEARNING Before students make their list of questions, discuss the major categories of information they wish to discover. Then have them develop questions that will elicit that information. Students may also need help in locating recent immigrants.

CHAPTER ORGANIZER

Chapter 9 Iran

CHAPTER PLANNING CHART

Pupil's Edition	Teacher's Edition	Ancillaries
Lesson 1: Iran's Land and Traditions (1–2 days) Objective 1: Describe the major landforms and climate in Iran. (Geography 2, 3) Objective 2: Explain why Iran has experienced many movements of people. (Geography 4)	• Graphic Overview (204) • Access Strategy (205) • Access Activity (205) • Visual Learning (206) Historical Context (206)	Study Guide (35)
Lesson 2: Iran's Proud Legacy (1–2 days) Objective 1: Describe the tribute system used by the Achaemenids. (Economics 1, 2, 3) Objective 2: Identify the changes that Islam brought to Iran. (Ethics and Belief Systems 1, 2, 3, 4,) Objective 3: Explain how the Safavids laid the basis for modern Iran. (History 5, 6, 7; Culture 1, 4)	• Graphic Overview (208) • Access Strategy (209) • Access Activity (209) Study Skills (210) Cultural Context (210) Oral Report (211) Research (211) • Visual Learning (211)	Study Guide (36) Discovery Journal (20)
Lesson 3: Modern Iran (2–3 days) Objective 1: Describe the changes the Pahlavis introduced to modernize Iran. (History 5, 6, 7; Culture 1, 4) Objective 2: Explain why the people of Iran overthrew the Pahlavis. (History 1, 5, 6, 7; Social and Political Systems 3) Objective 3: Identify the policies Iran's religious leaders have followed. (Ethics and Belief Systems 1, 2, 3)	• Graphic Overview (213) • Access Activity (214) • Access Strategy (214) Political Context (215) Critical Thinking (215)	Study Guide (37) Map Activities (13) Transparency (3)
Understanding Current Events Objective: Predict consequences based on evidence and experience. (Critical Thinking 3)		Study Guide (38)
Chapter Review	Answers (218–219)	Tests (33–36)

* Objectives are correlated to the strands and goals in the program Scope and Sequence on pages T41–T49.

• LEP appropriate resources. (For additional strategies, see pages T32–T33.)

CHAPTER RATIONALE

Chapter 9 introduces students to Persian culture, one of the world's most richly layered cultures. The chapter also allows students to see how the Muslim culture of Iran differs from that of the Arabian Peninsula. It is critical for students to recognize that although the basic beliefs of Islam do not change, the societies that have adopted this religion reflect a great diversity. They encompass languages other than Arabic, numerous cultures, and many different ways of interpreting Islamic law.

The account of the devastating earthquake that opens **Lesson 1** is a dramatic way of showing students that the people of Iran have overcome numerous natural obstacles in building their nation. The lesson discusses the ingenious ways Iranians have obtained water since ancient times. It identifies some of the language groups in modern Iran. Supplementing the text with study of the map on page 205 will help students recognize that the people of Iran are related to people in several neighboring countries. We then discuss how Zoroastrianism, Islam, and Now Rouz—the New Year's celebration—link the Iranian people of today to their rich past.

Lesson 2 explores some of the facets of that multilayered past, from the amazing Achaemenid ruins at Persepolis to the wonderful city Shah Abbas built in Isfahan. Information on changing beliefs helps students recognize that religion has played a significant role in Persian life since ancient times. Through all the changes, however, Persian language and culture persist as a thread binding past and present.

Lesson 3 concentrates on the 20th century and its sweeping changes. It identifies two main strands that run through the modern period—modernization and Iran's long Islamic heritage—to help students understand why the Islamic revolution of 1979 was a genuine people's revolt. The lesson looks at the hostage crisis and the bitter war with Iraq, which further helped to shape Iranian attitudes. The chapter ends by describing the forces that continue to shape modern Iranian society.

ACTIVITIES & PROJECTS

Collaborative Learning

The Persians built *qanats* to carry water to arid areas as far as 50 miles away from the source. Ask students to find out where their town's water comes from and how it is brought into their schools and homes. One way to do this is to have the class write a letter to the local water department and request that someone come and tell them about the water supply. If possible, arrange a trip to a reservoir, dam, or water treatment plant. (Use after Lesson 1.)

Basic: Making a Wall Map

Point out that about 70 percent of Iran's land is virtually uninhabited. Have students create a wall-sized population map of modern Iran. Suggest that they consult a reference book such as the *Information Please Almanac* to research Iran's population figures and the geographic distribution of its people. (Use after Lesson 1.)

LEP: Making a Mural

Have students reread the passage on page 212 that describes Isfahan at its peak during the reign of Shah Abbas. Put up a continuous piece of butcher paper along a wall. Have students use markers or paint to create a mural of the wonders of 16th-century Isfahan. (Use after Lesson 2.)

Writing a Report

Have students prepare reports on the history of Iran's relations with Iraq. Most of the people in these countries, which share a border, belong to the Shi'a branch of Islam. Suggest that students research the similarities and differences between Iran and Iraq and the events leading to their bitter war of 1980–1988. (Use after Lesson 3.)

Challenge: Research

Religious leaders are very important figures in Iran. Popular support for the Ayatollah Khomeini sent Shah Mohammed Reza into exile. Have volunteers research the special relationship between Shi'a Islamic clerics and their followers. Students can report their findings to the rest of the class. (Use after Lesson 3.)

CHAPTER PREVIEW

Tell students that the modern country of Iran was called Persia for thousands of years prior to 1925. Have students read the chapter title and the paragraph that follows. Point out that this chapter covers a great time span —nearly 2,500 years. Explain that during this long time period, many different peoples came to Persia and that each group made unique contributions to modern Iran.

Looking Back

Explain that like early India ancient Persia has Aryan roots. Ask students to find India and Iran on the map of Eurasia on page 682 of the Atlas. Ask them to name the countries between India and Iran. *(Afghanistan and Pakistan)* Point out that the peoples of these countries all speak Indo-European languages, which are Aryan in origin.

Looking Forward

Tell students that in this chapter they will learn about ancient Persia and modern Iran in three lessons—Iran's Land and Traditions, Iran's Proud Legacy, and Modern Iran. Lesson 1 describes Iran's geography and the traditions of its predominantly Shi'a Muslim population.

Chapter 9

Iran

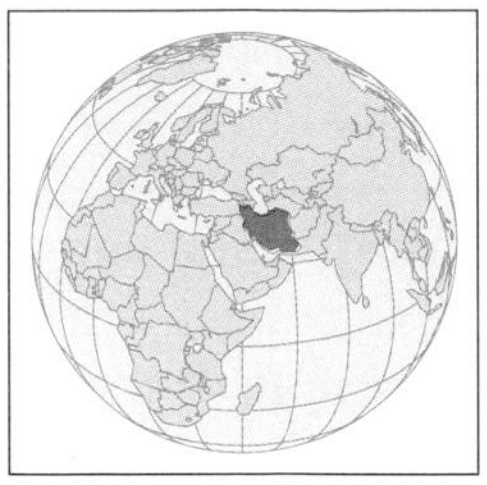

For more than 2,500 years, the Plateau of Iran has been a crossroads for people moving between Asia and the Mediterranean. Here the Persian Empire arose about 550 B.C., and the Zoroastrian religion became important. About A.D. 640 Islam spread to Persia, and 900 years later the Persian ruler turned to the Shi'a branch of Islam. The stage was set for the modern revolution that turned Iran into a republic guided by the teachings of Islam.

Persian artisans were noted for their metalwork. This plate of silver, made about A.D. 350, shows a Sasanian ruler hunting wild boars, a favorite pastime of Persian shahs.

1500	1000	500	B.C.	A.D.

550 B.C. Cyrus the Great forms the Persian Empire.

1500 B.C.

BACKGROUND

The people of Iran *(formerly Persia)* like to quote an ancient Persian proverb: "Defeat makes us invincible," because, although invaded many times over the centuries, Persians always turned their conquerors into Persians. By 550 B.C. Achaemenid rule, under Cyrus the Great, stretched east to Russia and west as far as the Greek city-states along the Ionian coast. By 539 B.C. Cyrus had conquered Babylonia and freed the captive Jews.

A Mighty Persian Empire

Darius, who became ruler in 522 B.C., was known as "The Lawgiver." He chose as his epitaph "My Law—of that they feel fear, so that the stronger does not smite nor destroy the weak." Darius's stone-paved Royal Road and mail system were imitated by both the Greeks and the builders of the famous highways that spanned the Roman Empire.

The Persians, notably under Xerxes and Darius III, tried mightily but failed to conquer Greece. They were beaten by Alexander the Great, who plundered the Persian Empire. According to the Greek historian Plutarch, Alexander needed 20,000 mules and 5,000 camels to carry away Persian treasures.

After the Greeks, Persia was overrun by successive invaders—although some of the most ruthless conquerers were won over by what Persia had to offer them. For example, Tamerlane imposed Turkish rule on Persia in the late 1370s, but Persian arts and letters

Items like this pear, made of gold set in steel, appeared in Persian markets around 1600, during the rule of Shah Abbas I. Artists often made models of fruit because faithful Muslims are promised they will find abundant fruits in paradise.

Today each Iranian bazaar, or market, is a city within a city. Shopkeepers and clerks meet and talk here. During the revolution of 1979, they helped organize protests against the government.

1502 The first Safavid ruler makes Shi'a Islam the official religion in Persia.

500	1000	1500	2000

c. 642 Islam begins to spread in Persia.

c. 1925 Reza Shah begins attempts to modernize Iran.

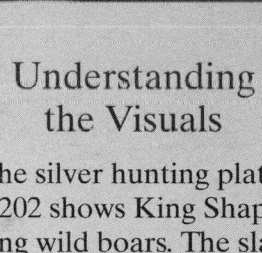

Today

Understanding the Visuals

The silver hunting plate on page 202 shows King Shapur II hunting wild boars. The slaying of beasts by a hero-king was a common motif under the Sasanians, A.D. 227–634. This hunting theme inspired not only silver vessels and ornaments, but wall paintings and stucco designs as well.

Traditional bazaars, like the Isfahan bazaar in the photograph, are the inspiration for the shopping malls found in the United States and other Western countries today. Iran's bazaars are mazes of covered streets lined with shops arranged by specialty. Some streets, for example, have shops that sell only household goods; others sell gold jewelry, groceries, carpets, and antiques. There are no fixed prices. Every purchase, no matter how small, is an occasion for lively discussion and bargaining.

Understanding Chronology

Have students study the timeline. Ask what the timeline indicates as the predominant religion in Iran. *(Islam)* Have students calculate how many years elapsed between the introduction of Islam to Iran and the naming of Shi'a Islam as the official religion of Iran. *(about 860 years)*

remained dominant. By the 18th century, however, a series of invasions crumbled the artistic brilliance of Safavid Persia. The Pahlavis were the last family to rule Persia, which they renamed Iran.

Knowledge is Power

Reza Khan Pahlavi became shah of Iran in 1925. In the spirit of Darius more than 2,000 years before, Reza Shah built the Trans-Iranian railroad, which linked the Persian Gulf to the Caspian Sea. Using the motto "He who has knowledge has power," Reza Shah promoted an ambitious program to teach every Iranian child to read and write. At the same time, Reza Shah's plan to modernize Iran laid the seeds of the downfall of the Pahlavi monarchy. Secularization of the schools, for example, undermined the authority of the Muslim leaders.

Neither East nor West

In a country where the people had very close ties to their Shi'a clerics, the Shah's programs were branded as anti-Islam . In 1979 angry revolutionaries, under the leadership of the Ayatollah Khomeini, ousted Reza Shah's son, Shah Mohammed Reza, and took control of the government. Iran became an Islamic republic. Significantly, the last thing seen by a Western journalist as he left Iran in the mid-1980s was a billboard with the slogan "We are neither East nor West, but Islam."

INTRODUCE

Ask students to recall, from previous chapters, some civilizations that became dominant because of their particular geographic conditions. *(Egyptian, Indian, Inca)* Tell them that Persia's people respond to similar geographic conditions.

Then ask the students to read the Thinking Focus aloud. Suggest that they compare the photograph of the capital city of Tehran on page 205 with the photograph of an Iranian village on page 206. Ask volunteers to explain the similarities of the geographic conditions. *(Students may point out that Iran is a mountainous country: large and small communities, such as Tehran and the village, were settled in valleys.)* Tell students to keep the Thinking Focus in mind as they read the lesson.

Key Terms

Vocabulary Strategies: T36–T37
plateau—level land that is higher than the land around it
arid—very dry

B.C.
A.D.
1500
TODAY

LESSON 1

Iran's Land and Traditions

THINKING FOCUS

What is the land of Iran like?

Key Terms

- plateau
- arid

The clock had just struck midnight in the lonely village of Rudbar. Usually, its farmers and their families were fast asleep. Tonight, however, many of them were awake. They were watching the World Cup soccer match on television. Suddenly, there was a grinding roar. Houses shook. Walls cracked and crumbled. All over the village, roofs crashed down, burying screaming men, women, and children. In less than a minute, almost every building in Rudbar was flattened. With bleeding hands the weeping survivors dug among the rubble, looking for members of their families.

➤ *The Rudbar quake brought down buildings made of concrete as well as houses of dried-mud bricks.*

On that June night in 1990, a single earthquake leveled more than 100 towns in northwestern Iran *(ih RAHN)*. As many as 50,000 Iranians were killed, and more than 100,000 were hurt. About 500,000 people were left without homes, food, water to drink, or blankets to protect them from the chilly nights.

The 1990 earthquake was not the first to hit Iran. Find the Caspian Sea on the map on page 205. People living around the Caspian Sea experience dozens of quakes each year. Iran lies right in the middle of an earthquake zone stretching from Europe's Mediterranean shore to the Pacific Ocean. Most quakes in Iran are minor, but some cause as much damage as the one at Rudbar.

Earthquakes are very destructive forces. Yet they are only one of Iran's challenges. Its landforms and climate cause other problems.

Objectives

1. Describe the major landforms and climate in Iran.
2. Explain why Iran has experienced many movements of people.

Graphic Overview

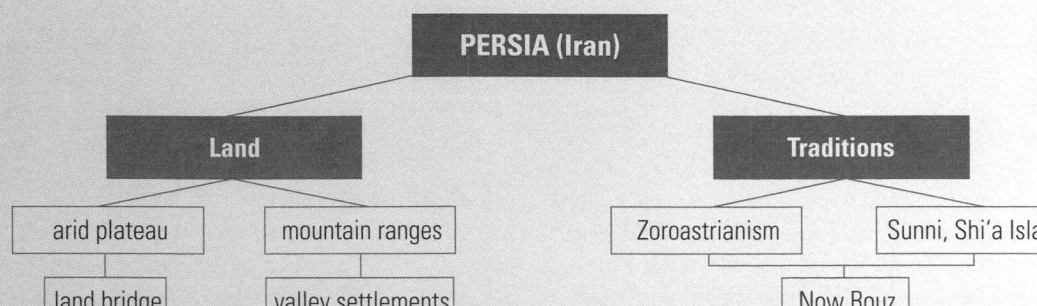

- **PERSIA (Iran)**
  - **Land**
    - arid plateau
      - land bridge
    - mountain ranges
      - valley settlements
  - **Traditions**
    - Zoroastrianism
    - Sunni, Shi'a Islam
      - Now Rouz

The Land of Iran

Iran is a combination of mountains and a huge plateau. A **plateau** is an area of fairly level land that is higher than the land around it. Rising 3,000 to 5,000 feet above sea level, the Plateau of Iran covers more than three-fourths of the country. In its center are two salt deserts, the remains of dried-up lakes.

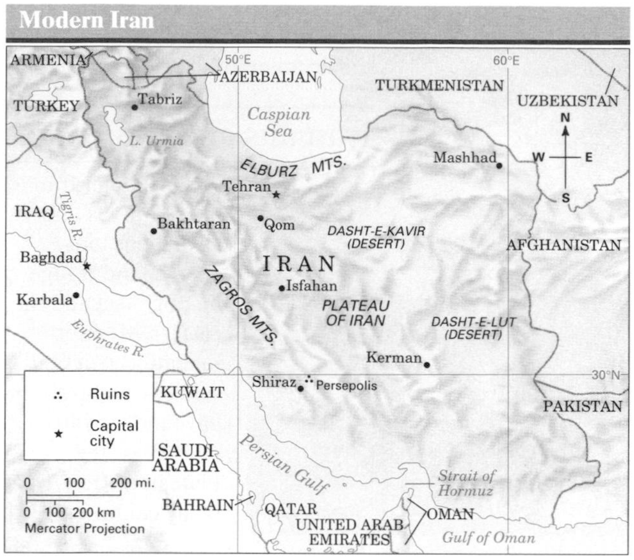
Modern Iran
ARMENIA
AZERBAIJAN
TURKMENISTAN
UZBEKISTAN
TURKEY
Tabriz
Caspian Sea
L. Urmia
50°E
60°E
N
W
E
S
ELBURZ MTS.
Mashhad
Tehran
IRAQ
Tigris R.
Bakhtaran
Qom
DASHT-E-KAVIR (DESERT)
AFGHANISTAN
Baghdad
IRAN
Isfahan
ZAGROS MTS.
Karbala
PLATEAU OF IRAN
DASHT-E-LUT (DESERT)
Euphrates R.
Kerman
30°N
Ruins
Capital city
KUWAIT
Shiraz
Persepolis
PAKISTAN
SAUDI ARABIA
Persian Gulf
0 100 200 mi.
0 100 200 km
Mercator Projection
BAHRAIN
QATAR
Strait of Hormuz
UNITED ARAB EMIRATES
OMAN
Gulf of Oman

▲ *Find the dried-up lakes in the Plateau of Iran. How could they make travel across Iran difficult?*

Iran's Hills and Plains

Most Iranians live on the edge of the plateau, in the foothills and valleys of the mountains. Stretching from northwestern Iran to the Persian Gulf are the mighty Zagros *(ZAG ruhs)* Mountains. In places, rows of these mountains form a wall 150 miles wide. The Elburz Mountains curve along the south shore of the Caspian Sea. They include the highest mountain in Iran, Mount Damavand. More than 18,000 feet high, this mountain's snowcapped peak seems to float above the dusty plateau.

Dust, in fact, is common in this **arid,** or dry, land. Much of the Plateau of Iran gets only a few inches of rain each year. Dry summer winds make the land even more arid. Although forests grow along the Caspian Sea, most of Iran is so arid that crops can be grown only with irrigation.

◄ *Tehran, Iran's modern capital, lies at the foot of Mount Damavand.*

Finding Water

Farmers get water from the rivers after rains and from the snow melting from the mountains. In some places dams store water for irrigation and electric power.

The Iranians also have a special way of getting water. If you flew over the plateau, you would see a line of large holes. They look like huge, round footprints marching for miles across the plateau. These holes lead to an underground water system. This system was created as many as 2,500 years ago.

The ancient Iranians dug deep shafts that reached 30 to 100 feet below the surface. There they tapped into the water table, the

DEVELOP

Read aloud the subheads under The Land of Iran, and have students study the map on this page. Then ask them to note that the Iranian Plateau stretches east of Iran. Ask which two countries this Plateau reaches. *(Afghanistan and Pakistan)* Point out that Iran straddles both Asia and the eastern Mediterranean and has long been regarded as a land bridge over which conquerors and traders alike have traveled.

◄ *The dried-up lakes are salt deserts. They contain no water to help travelers cross Iran.*

GEOGRAPHY

Map and Globe Skills

Refer students to the map on this page. Ask them to name the two major mountain ranges in Iran. *(Zagros and Elburz ranges)* Then refer students to the world climate map in the Atlas on page 688. Ask these questions: Besides the mountain ranges, what major climate features are found in Iran? *(Desert and semiarid climate)* What are the general characteristics of such conditions? *(Students may answer shortages of water, insufficient arable land, and extreme temperatures.)*

Access Strategy

Explain to students that the ability to irrigate land means the difference between life and death for countries with dry, or arid, climates. Invite them to look back at previous chapters to find photographs or drawings of water-conservation projects. *(Two examples are Roman aqueducts, on page 171, and desalination in Saudi Arabia, on page 198.)*

Point out that in very dry lands like Persia, irrigation makes it possible to grow crops. Without enough water, almost no agriculture is possible. Explain that the Persians invented their own unique way to irrigate their land. The system of irrigation that began in ancient Persia is still used in Iran today.

Access Activity

Have students turn to the Glossary of Geographic Terms, on pages 690–691 in the Time/Space Databank. Review the characteristics of a plateau. *(High, level land)* Have students draw pictures of plateaus, using crayons, colored pencils, or markers.

■ *They use irrigation, modern dams, and a system of underground canals called* qanats.

BELIEF SYSTEMS

Critical Thinking

Review the tenets of Zoroastrianism with the class. Point out that many Zoroastrian teachings include some ideas that are present in various other religions. Ask students what earlier religion might have influenced Zoroastrianism. *(Judaism—the idea of free will)* Then ask what later religion may have been influenced by Zoroastrian beliefs. *(Christianity—the tension between good and evil)*

■ How do the Iranians get the water they need?

moisture that is far below the ground. They built underground canals called *qanats (KAH nahts)* to carry water to the fields. These canals followed the slope of the land. The system worked so well that it is still in use. In the darkness 30 to 100 feet below the surface, water flows silently to villages as far as 50 miles away. ■

Iranians and Their Traditions

▲ *Many Iranian villages nestle in mountain valleys.*

Although Iran is mountainous and arid, it has long been a land bridge linking Asia and the eastern Mediterranean. Herders, soldiers, and traders have moved into and across the Plateau of Iran for many centuries.

Peoples and Languages

About 1500 B.C. small groups of people may have begun to drift south from the region around the Aral Sea. (See the Atlas map on page 682.) This casual southward movement probably went on for hundreds of years. Some of the migrating groups traveled south and east in the direction of India. Other groups moved south and then turned westward into Iran.

The southward-moving peoples spoke several related languages. These languages belonged to the Indo-Iranian group, which is part of the far-flung Indo-European family of languages.

Iran's name comes from the Aryan subgroup of Indo-Iranian languages. For many years, however, people in other nations used the name Persia for Iran. The ancient Greeks took this name from Parsa, the name of an Iranian province. We still speak of the ancient Persian Empire, the Persian language, and Persian art and literature. The name of the modern nation, however, is Iran.

Most Iranians now speak modern Persian, called Farsi, or related languages. Azerbaijanis *(ah zuhr by JAH neez)* are the largest minority group in Iran. They speak Azeri, a language related to Turkish. Like the Farsi-speaking majority of Iranians, the Azerbaijanis are Shi'a Muslims.

Across Time & Space

Muslims carried the idea of qanats *from Persia to North Africa. From there the idea spread to arid areas in Spain. The Spaniards carried the use of* qanats *to Mexico. Today the remains of* qanats *can still be seen in south central Mexico. There they are known as* apantles con tragaluces, *"channels with skylights."*

Zoroastrianism

Although Shi'a Islam is the major faith in Iran today, traces remain of some very old beliefs. One of the oldest goes back to Zoroaster *(ZAWR oh ahs tuhr),*

➤ *Iranian women have worn head coverings since ancient times. These Baluchi women are baking bread.*

Visual Learning

Have students study the photograph of the Baluchi women on this page. Bread is one of the world's most widely eaten foods, and at least 40 kinds of flat, or unleavened, bread are baked in Iran. Ask students to use magazine pictures, or their own drawings, to create posters depicting breads common to other parts of the world.

Historical Context

Aryan is a term that has become infamous in this century. Tell students that Aryan is the historic name for the ancient ancestors of the peoples of Iran and India. From their language are descended the Indo-European languages that are widely spoken today.

Explain that the phrase "Aryan race" was borrowed by a group of 19th-century social scientists to describe people who spoke Indo-European languages and, it was claimed, were superior to those they called "non-Aryans."

Tell students that Chapter 21 explains how Adolf Hitler came to power in Nazi Germany in part through appeals to racial superiority based on the idea of an Aryan "race."

Remind students that in Chapter 1, Lesson 3, they learned that a dislike or distrust of certain people simply because they are different is called prejudice. Refer to that same chapter, or to the Glossary on page 706, to have students review the meaning of the word *racism.*

who was born about 628 B.C. His teachings introduced ideas that became important to the religions based on belief in one God.

Zoroaster spoke of a struggle between good and evil. The good, represented by Ahura Mazda, includes light, life, and truth. Opposing good is Ahriman, the lie, a force of evil, darkness, and death. Zoroaster said only Ahura Mazda should be worshiped. He taught that good would finally defeat evil. He made it clear, however, that each person was free to choose between the forces of good and evil. People who lived good lives could expect to go to paradise, or heaven, after they died.

Shi'a Islam

In the 600s Islam reached Iran. Nearly all Iranians today are Muslims, and most of them belong to the Shi'a branch of Islam (see Chapter 8). One of their most important anniversaries each year is Ashura, a time of mourning for the death of Husayn, grandson of Muhammad. During Ashura many Iranians take part in religious plays. These dramas tell the sad story of Husayn's death.

Now Rouz

Muslim and ancient Zoroastrian beliefs can both be found in Now Rouz, the New Year's celebration in Iran. Now Rouz starts on March 21 as the snow is melting and flowers are beginning to bloom.

Weeks before the new year, women begin to clean house, mend clothes, and fix broken household goods. Each family plants seeds of grain in pots inside the house. By March 21 the grain has tender green shoots. Iranians believe that the plants pick up any unhappiness in the home.

Candles or lamps found in each home are a reminder of ancient Zoroastrian beliefs that light stands for good. Each Muslim home proudly shows a copy of the Qur'an, a sign that God comes first in people's lives. When the cannon booms to call in the new year, many Iranians go to the mosque to pray. Others worship at home.

Dressed in new clothes, the Iranians share meals with friends and family. For each person there is a small gift—a toy for a child, a piece of jewelry, scented soap, an article of clothing, or a small plant.

Now Rouz is at least 2,500 years old. One of Iran's greatest rulers even built a city where the New Year's festival could be celebrated. You will read about this city, Persepolis *(puhr SEHP uh lihs),* in the next lesson. ■

▲ *Among the things that might be seen in an Iranian home during Now Rouz are fish in a bowl, grain, an apple, and garlic to keep away evil spirits.*

■ What is Now Rouz?

REVIEW

1. **FOCUS** What is the land of Iran like?
2. **GEOGRAPHY** What problems do Iranians face because of the natural environment?
3. **CULTURE** How are the people of Iran and India connected?
4. **BELIEFS** What two forces did Zoroaster describe?
5. **CRITICAL THINKING** What evidence is there that some cultural traditions followed in Iran are very old?
6. **ACTIVITY** Now Rouz is a family event. What special events does your family celebrate? Write a paragraph telling about one event and what family members might do.

SOCIAL SYSTEMS

Social Participation

Two other traditions of Now Rouz are the following:

As the New Year nears, the family gathers at the table to await the exact moment that it arrives. A leaf suddenly moving on the surface of a bowl of water is said to indicate this.

Families make five days of social calls, and great sums of money are spent on entertaining guests.

Have students describe New Year traditions they enjoy with their families and friends.

■ *Now Rouz is the ancient New Year's celebration that starts on March 21 and is celebrated by Iranian families.*

CLOSE

Have students reread the Thinking Focus. Ask them to include the following categories in their answers: landforms, climate, history, past and present belief systems, and traditions. Suggest they draw a chart by using the Thinking Focus as the heading and placing the four categories down the left-hand side. *(Students may suggest mountains, plateaus, deserts; extremes in climate; Zoroastrianism, Sunni and Shi'a Islam; Now Rouz)*

Answers to Review Questions

1. Three-fourths of Iran is an arid plateau, with mountains (Zagros, Elburz) stretching from the Caspian Sea to the Persian Gulf.
2. Geographic problems that people in Iran face include earthquakes, an arid climate, rugged mountains, and lakes that have become deserts.
3. The people of both Iran and India are descended from migrating groups that spoke Indo-Iranian languages.
4. Zoroaster described the forces of good and evil (light and darkness).
5. The use of candles and lamps during Now Rouz reflects the belief that light represents good, and dates back to the time of Zoroaster, born c. 628 B.C.
6. Students might include such events as birthdays, graduations, and anniversaries. As participants, they might include family and friends; as festivities, they might describe music and dance, typical menus, and games.

Homework Options

Have students write a paragraph that compares and contrasts the geography of your part of the United States with that of Iran. Some students may prefer to write a paragraph that compares and contrasts a facet of Iranian life with their own.

Study Guide: page 35

INTRODUCE

Tell students they will be reading about the families who ruled the Persian empire. Have a student read the Thinking Focus aloud, and ask students to predict the answer. *(New ideas, beliefs, customs, art)* Tell them that Lesson 2 will explain how each group that ruled Persia shaped it in its own way.

Key Terms

Vocabulary Strategies: T36–T37
shah—a ruler of Persia or Iran
satrap—the governor of a province in ancient Persia

B.C.
A.D.
1500
1000
550
1722
2000

LESSON 2

Iran's Proud Legacy

THINKING FOCUS

What did different ruling families contribute to Persia?

Key Terms

- shah
- satrap

A soft breeze kicks up a cloud of dust and swirls it across a huge stone platform. Broad, stone stairs rise from the dusty plain to the platform, which is nearly as long as five football fields. Beside the stairway, long rows of marching men are carved in stone. One is tugging at a snorting horse. Two others hold squirming lion cubs. Others march by leading a prize bull, a pair of woolly rams, and a stately two-humped camel from central Asia. There are men carrying elephant tusks from Africa and jars of gold dust from India. Others hold bolts of fine cloth, gold vases with handles shaped like winged bulls, dishes of food, and a bunch of flowers.

The carvings are at the ruins of Persepolis. Here, 2,500 years ago, Persia's king, the **shah,** received tribute during Now Rouz from the peoples he ruled. Horses for the army came from Media, Persia, and Armenia. Arabia supplied more than 6,600 pounds of frankincense each year as tribute, and the Egyptians provided 120,000 bushels of grain.

The photograph shows the 33 acres of Persepolis as seen from the air. The clothing worn by the tribute bearers, shown in the detailed carving at right, has made it possible to identify the country from which each person came.

Objectives

1. Describe the tribute system used by the Achaemenids.
2. Identify the changes that Islam brought to Iran.
3. Describe how the Safavids laid the basis for modern Iran.

Graphic Overview

Past Rulers of Persia

Rulers	Cultures	Languages
Achaemenids	Tolerance	Persian
Sasanians	Zoroastrianism	Pahlavi (Persian)
Arabs	Sunni Islam	Arabic
Safavids	Shi'a Islam	Persian

Empires of Persia

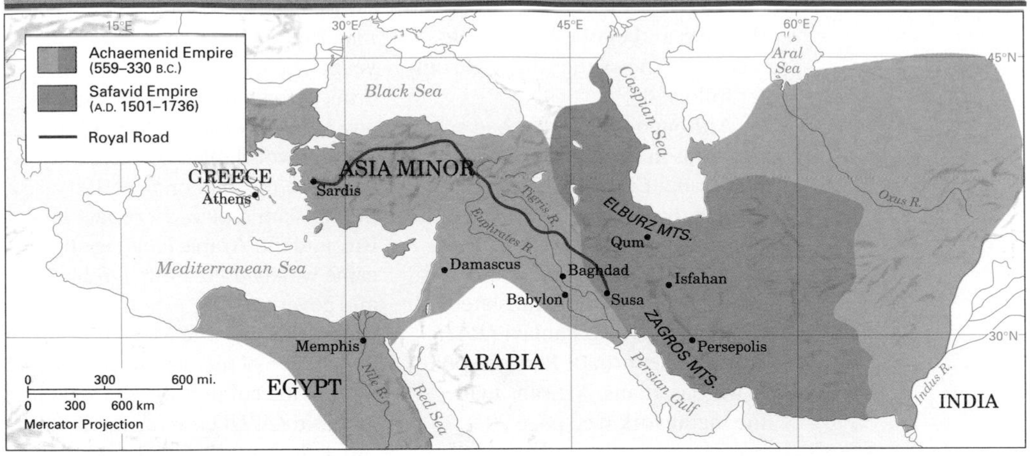
Achaemenid Empire (559–330 B.C.)
Safavid Empire (A.D. 1501–1736)
Royal Road
15°E
30°E
45°E
60°E
45°N
30°N
Black Sea
Caspian Sea
Aral Sea
GREECE
Athens
ASIA MINOR
Sardis
Tigris R.
Euphrates R.
ELBURZ MTS.
Qum
Oxus R.
Mediterranean Sea
Damascus
Baghdad
Isfahan
Babylon
Susa
ZAGROS MTS.
Memphis
Persepolis
ARABIA
Persian Gulf
Indus R.
INDIA
EGYPT
Nile R.
Red Sea
0 300 600 mi.
0 300 600 km
Mercator Projection

▲ *Which lands were part of the Persian Empire but were not part of Safavid Persia?*

A Glorious Past

Persepolis was built by the Achaemenid *(uh KEE muh nuhd)* family. This family ruled the Persian Empire from 550 to 330 B.C.

The Persian Empire

The Persian shahs were noted for their wise rule. An early shah, Cyrus the Great, built the Persian Empire by conquering other lands. Cyrus let conquered peoples keep their own beliefs and customs, however. Cyrus knew he could turn to his army if any people in the empire challenged his rule.

In 522 B.C., Darius I *(duh RY uhs)* came to the throne. Under Darius, the Persian Empire expanded to two million square miles and may have included 10 million people. Darius adopted some ideas from other peoples, such as laws from the Code of Hammurabi, and used them in the Persian government. To make the empire easier to rule, Darius divided it into 20 provinces. He put a Persian official called a **satrap** *(SAH trahp)* in charge of each province, or satrapy. The satrap collected taxes and tribute for the shah. From time to time, inspectors who were called "the eyes of the king" visited the satraps to make sure they were being honest.

Each satrapy supplied what grew best there. Peas, onions, apples, cucumbers, apricots, and dates were grown in Babylonia. Pears, lemons (called Persian apples by the Greeks), honey, and pistachio nuts came from Persia itself. Coins made by the Persian government had the same value all through the empire, making it easier for people to buy and sell goods. Banks loaned money and even took checks.

Caravans of merchants moved along the 1,677 miles of the Royal Road built by Darius. It took them about 90 days to travel from Sardis to Susa, the Persian capital (see map above). Relays of the shah's messengers, riding swift horses, traveled the road in about a week.

Conquest and Revival

Even before Darius I died in 486 B.C., some of the satrapies revolted. Persia fought several wars with the Greek city-states (see Chapter 7). In 330 B.C. Persia fell to the army of Alexander the Great.

Across Time & Space

On April 3, 1860, the first pony express riders dashed off with the U.S. mail. They were copying the system Darius I had set up about 2,300 years earlier. "Nothing stops these couriers from covering their allotted stage . . . ," a Greek historian wrote of the Persian messengers, "neither snow, rain, heat, nor darkness." His words are still used by the U.S. Postal Service.

DEVELOP

Display the Graphic Overview on the chalkboard or overhead projector. Tell students that this lesson will discuss the impact of a succession of ruling families on Persian history and culture. Ask them what challenges the Persian people faced with each new dynasty. *(Students may suggest adapting to a new government, new taxes, a new language, and a new religion.)*

◄ *Achaemenid Persia included the lands west of the Tigris River to the Mediterranean (including parts of Egypt), land north of Greece, a large area east of the Caspian Sea; most of these lands were not part of the Safavid Empire.*

HISTORY

Map and Globe Skills

Refer students to the map titled Empires of Persia on this page. Suggest that students imagine themselves as mounted messengers in the Persian Empire. Have them use the map scale to measure the distance they would have to travel between Persepolis and Memphis. *(About 1,800 miles, or 2,896 kilometers)* Ask what physical barriers might be in the way. *(Students may suggest the Zagros Mountains and the Euphrates River.)*

Access Strategy

Read the poem on page 212 aloud. Tell students that this poem was written by a Sufi poet. Explain that Sufism is an important branch of Islam and that Sufi literature is found in the Arabic, Persian, Turkish, and Urdu languages. Sufi poetry is particularly admired in Islamic countries. Invite students to use the poem to learn more about Persia (now Iran) by answering these questions: What is the inspiration for the poem? *(A Persian carpet)* What does the poet say about the Persian seasons? *(Spring: loveliest; Summer: very hot; Autumn: windy; Winter: icy and snowy)* How do Persians use their gardens? *(To get away from daily problems)*

Access Activity

Refer students to the photograph of the tribute bearers to the Persian Empire on the previous page. Ask a volunteer to read the caption aloud. Then review the definition of *tribute,* on page 707 of the Glossary. Ask what the photograph suggests about the Persian Empire at that time. *(It was a conquering nation, and it was very wealthy.)*

POLITICAL SYSTEMS

Critical Thinking

Tell students that as well as providing resources, such as horses, spices, and grain, the conquered peoples of the Persian Empire paid tribute in talents—oval silver bars weighing about 66 pounds and worth about $2,400 each today. Explain that *talent* meant "burden." Then write on the chalkboard this partial list of tributes from conquered peoples to the Persian Empire:

Ionia: 400 talents
Egypt: 700 talents
Cilicia: 360 talents
Babylonia: 1,000 talents
Armenia: 400 talents

Ask students to brainstorm reasons why the Persians collected tribute in varied amounts. *(Students may suggest that, since all talents weighed the same, each nation paid in proportion to its wealth.)* Based on what they recall from previous chapters, ask students why Babylonia and Egypt were so heavily taxed by Persia. *(They were wealthier than the other conquered nations listed.)*

■ *Alexander's triumph over Persia in 330 B.C. threatened its power as an empire; the Muslim armies' invasions in A.D. 637 threatened its religion and its entire way of life.*

The Map and Globe Handbook, page G12, shows the route Alexander followed.

Although the Greeks had set up kingdoms in Persia, the power of the Persian Empire was gone. In A.D. 224, however, a new family, the Sasanians, tried to revive it. They made Zoroastrianism the only religion in Iran. Scholars translated foreign books into Pahlavi *(PAH luh vee)*, the form of Persian spoken by the Sasanians. Artisans made fine metalwork (see page 202).

■ *What threats did the Persians face between 330 B.C. and A.D. 650?*

Arrival of Islam

Despite attacks from the Roman Empire and from India, the Sasanian Empire lasted more than 400 years. Then, in A.D. 637, Muslim armies began to defeat the Sasanians. By 661 Persia was part of the Muslim world ruled by the Umayyads (see the map on page 190). Sunni Islam replaced Zoroastrianism, and the Arabic language became widely used, both in religion and government.

By this time the Muslim world had people of many different languages and cultures. In A.D. 750 the Abbasid *(AHB uh seed)* family overthrew the Umayyads. The Abbasids encouraged trade and learning. They helped bring about the golden age of Islam (see Chapter 8). ■

Safavid Persia

By the mid-900s, local rulers controlled many of the Muslim lands. Various foreign peoples also invaded Southwest Asia. Finally, in 1502 a powerful new family, the Safavids *(sah FAH weedz)*, came to the Persian throne.

Safavid Rule

The Safavids ruled Persia from 1502 to 1736. They sought to strengthen Persia and its culture. Their work was important at a time when major changes were occurring elsewhere (see the Minipedia, page 672).

The first Safavid shah proclaimed that Shi'a Islam would be the only religion in Persia. Sunni Muslims who refused to become Shi'as were persecuted. Even today, most people in Iran are Shi'a Muslims. The shah also insisted that the Persian language be used in religion. Many Iranians today speak Farsi (modern Persian).

Persian Culture

The greatest Safavid shah was Abbas I, who became Persia's ruler in 1587. Shah Abbas is best remembered for his capital at Isfahan *(ihs fuh HAHN)*. Artists created miniatures like the one in A Closer Look on page 211.

The Shah Mosque in Isfahan is noted for its beautiful tiles that form arabesques of blossoms. From its slender columns, called minarets, Muslims are called to worship.

Study Skills

Review the major differences between Sunni and Shi'a Islam. (See Chapter 8, page 190.) Then ask students to study the text under Safavid Rule, on this page. Ask them to list the ways that Shi'a Islam was adapted by the Safavids to be uniquely Persian. *(Use of the Persian language, rather than Arabic; exclusion of other religions)*

Cultural Context

Isfahan, the capital of Persia under Shah Abbas, reached its height during the 16th century. It was actually larger than Paris at that time, with 600,000 people, 162 mosques, 48 religious colleges, 1,802 merchant depots, and 273 public baths. The city was so beautiful that the people coined the saying, "Isfahan is half the world." It was in Isfahan that the shah commissioned the most beautiful of mosques.

The dome over the Shah Mosque is covered in brilliant blue tiles, intertwined with bands of scarlet and cream-colored flowers.

Isfahan today still has over 200 mosques, palaces, monuments, and bazaars. What was once the Shah's polo ground is now the Royal Square, lined with magnificent trees. A beautiful double-arched bridge crosses the city's Zayandel River.

A Closer Look

Persian Miniatures

Centuries ago, Persian princes left their palaces to spend months traveling the desert. They took their most treasured paintings with them—bound inside books! Persian miniatures illustrated tales and poems. Some paintings were smaller than this page. Artists began studying in their teens to become master painters. After years of practice, they might be asked to paint the leopards or angels in a landscape, or to fill an entire sky with real gold.

Colors! Artists ground precious stones into a fine powder and mixed it with glue for special colors. A deep, vibrant blue came from lapis lazuli. Malachite created a rich green.

The sad but popular story of young Layla and Majnun is told in this miniature from 1490. They fell in love at school but were kept apart by their feuding families.

Painted cases, like this one, once held the pens of calligraphers. Notice the calligraphy—the ornate script—on the painting.

Iran

Note: You may wish to use this feature as an extension of the activity on Persian art at the bottom of this page.

CULTURE

Visual Learning

Calligraphy, the art of beautiful writing, is an important artistic expression in many different cultures and is part of the painting on the left. In the Islamic tradition, the Arabic script is widely used because Arabic is the language of the Qur'an. Ask students to look through the text and to identify other examples of beautiful writing, or calligraphy. *(Students may select the illustrations of Islamic calligraphy on pages 182, 188, and 189, or they may cite examples of Chinese calligraphy in Chapter 5.)* Inform them that Persian paintings were imitated by Mughal artists in India. Suggest that students compare this painting to the Mughal miniature on page 323 in Chapter 14.

More About Persian Miniatures
Persian miniature art is more decorative than realistic, although details of architecture and costumes are amazingly exact. The figures of people, though brilliantly colored, are stiff and flat. Unlike the countries of the Arabian Peninsula, Persia used living forms in its secular, or nonreligious, art.

Oral Report

Have students choose one of the following activities to extend their acquaintance with Persian art. If possible, arrange for them to visit a museum that has a collection of Persian artifacts of the 15th and 16th centuries. You might also have students form groups of four or five to visit a carpet store that specializes in Persian carpets. Students' observations from these field trips should be presented to the class in the form of oral reports.

Research

Ask students to read the caption for the Persian miniature illustrated above. Point out that the story of young lovers kept apart has been a popular theme in literature throughout history. This Persian story is part of a series of romantic poems and was illustrated by the master painter Bihzad. Suggest that students write one-page reports on other works that use parallel themes of tragic young lovers. One example is Shakespeare's *Romeo and Juliet* (published in 1597).

Visual Learning

Suggest students make simple flower designs in the Persian artists' colors. Have them make frames of black construction paper, making sure to have their flower designs touch the edges of the frames. Let them experiment with layers of colored tissue paper, combining the patterns to create brilliant colors that glow when held up to light.

HISTORY

Critical Thinking

Have students read the last paragraph of the lesson, on this page. Explain that this paragraph not only closes this lesson but is a good introduction to the next lesson, on modern Iran. Ask what might be the effect of oil on the Persian economy. *(Will bring new wealth to the area)* How will foreign influences affect Persia? *(Students may suggest industrialization, new social and political systems, displacement of traditional leaders, and resentment against outsiders.)*

■ *The Safavids made Isfahan a center of culture by encouraging fine architecture, skilled weaving and pottery, and the talents of poets and artists.*

CLOSE

Read the Thinking Focus aloud for students. Then write on the chalkboard (or display the Graphic Overview) the names of the chief dynasties, or ruling families, of Persia: the Achaemenids (Cyrus, Darius, and others of their time), the Sasanians, the Arabs, and the Safavids. Have students list, underneath each name, the most important contribution each made. Discuss students' responses.

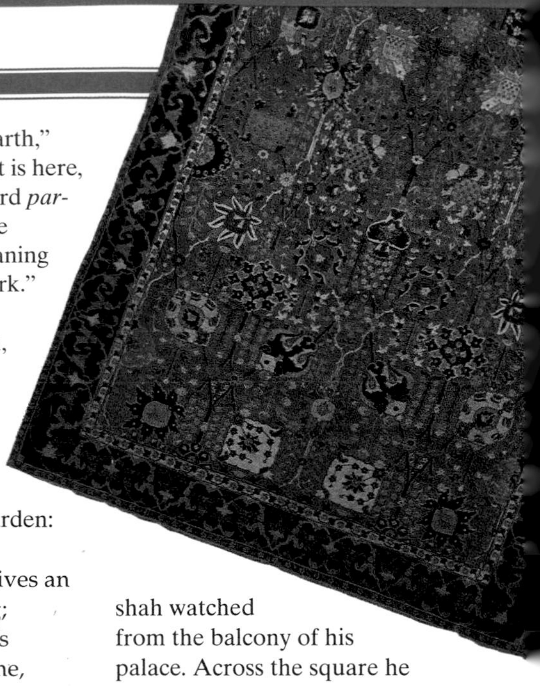

➤ This carpet was woven during the Safavid period, the golden age of carpet making. A wool carpet measuring 9 x 12 feet is made of more than seven million knots, as many as 500 to the square inch. A skilled worker can make 10,000–14,000 of these knots per day.

"If there be a Paradise on earth," exclaimed a Persian poet, "it is here, it is here, it is here!" The word *paradise,* in fact, comes from the Greek word *paradeisos,* meaning "a garden" or "a hunting park." To Persian people familiar with the arid Plateau of Iran, Isfahan did indeed seem a paradise.

Safavid weavers were famous for their fine carpets. One Persian poet compared a carpet with a garden:

> Here in this carpet lives an
> ever-lovely spring;
> Unscorched by summer's
> ardent [burning] flame,
> Safe too from autumn's boisterous gales,
> Midwinter's cruel ice and snow,
> 'Tis gaily blooming still.
> The handsome border is the
> garden wall
> Protecting, preserving the Park
> within
> For refuge and renewal:
> a magic space.
>
> Unknown Sufi poet

A three-mile avenue, shaded by trees, led to the main square in Isfahan. Down a canal in the center of the street flowed water from the river. In a large square at the center of the city, Persians played polo. Troops marched in review as the shah watched from the balcony of his palace. Across the square he could see the heavenly blue tiles of the Shah Mosque.

Shah Abbas brought many artisans to Isfahan. Among them were 300 Chinese skilled in making porcelain and weavers who worked in shops run by the government.

Although Safavid rule ended in 1736, Persia stayed wealthy and powerful until the late 1700s. By 1850, however, it had come under the influence of foreign nations. Great Britain held most of southern Persia, and Russia controlled most of the north. In 1901 Iran agreed to let a British company develop its oil fields located along the Persian Gulf. Persia was on the eve of vast changes. ■

■ *How did the Safavids make Isfahan a center of culture?*

REVIEW

1. **FOCUS** What did different ruling families contribute to Persia?
2. **GOVERNMENT** What did the rulers of the Persian Empire do to make their government strong?
3. **ECONOMICS** How did the Persian rulers meet the costs of governing their empire?
4. **BELIEFS** What part has Islam played in Persian history?
5. **CRITICAL THINKING** Reread the poem above. What does it tell you about the Persian climate? Why do the people cherish gardens?
6. **WRITING ACTIVITY** Imagine you've traveled from a village in Persia to the Isfahan of Shah Abbas. Write a letter home, telling what you've seen. Use the pictures as well as the text to help you write your letter.

Homework Options

Ask students to imagine that they are Persian traders during the time of Darius I. Have them make a list of the things they would pack—to wear, to eat and drink, and to sell—to travel the Royal Road by caravan.

Study Guide: page 36

Answers to Review Questions

1. The Achaemenids ruled through satraps and tolerated different customs. The Sasanians made Zoroastrianism the Persian religion. The Arabs introduced Sunni Islam and the Arabic language. The Safavids made Shi'a Islam the official religion and Persian the language for religion.
2. The shahs divided the Persian Empire into provinces (satrapies) governed by satraps and overseen by "the eyes of the king."
3. The shahs taxed the satrapies and took tribute from them.
4. Muslims brought Sunni Islam to Iran in the 630s, and the Safavid rulers made Shi'a Islam the religion of the country in 1502.
5. The poem mentions the four seasons. The plants growing in gardens contrast with the arid landscape found in much of Iran.
6. Students should note important features such as carpets, the Shah Mosque, the bazaar, and the Persian gardens.

B.C.
A.D.
1500
1000
500
500
1000
1500
1900
TODAY

L E S S O N 3

Modern Iran

It's afternoon in Tehran, the capital of Iran. Ali and his friends have been playing soccer. Now Ali glances at his watch and sees that it's time for supper.

As Ali turns to leave, his friend Ahmad grabs his sleeve. "Don't forget," Ahmad whispers. "Call and tell me if you're coming to hear rock tapes tonight."

Ali glances down at his dusty sneakers. Then he looks at Ahmad. "*Basheh,*" he says. "All right. I will."

While eating supper, Ali and his family talk about Ashura. This event, held in memory of the death of Husayn, unites all Shi'a Muslims (see page 190). Ali's village is famous for its religious plays during Ashura.

For a few minutes Ali's memories of Ashura blot out his worries. Then they begin again. He knows his parents don't want him to hear Ahmad's tapes. Iran's government has censored Western rock music. Even so, sometimes tapes are sold secretly. Some of Ali's friends buy these tapes to listen to at home.

Ali doesn't feel comfortable doing something his parents say is wrong. The values he has learned from his family and the teachings of Islam conflict with his friends' values. The choices Ali has to make reflect the clash of values that are faced by many people in Iran today.

◄ *This is one of the giant floats used during Ashura.*

THINKING FOCUS

Why did the people of Iran take part in a revolution?

Key Terms

- modernize
- exile
- hostage

Changes Made by the Pahlavis

Iran has gone through many changes since 1900. In 1906 protests against the shah led to the creation of an elected assembly and a constitution. In 1925 a cavalry officer named Reza Khan gained power, was named shah, and took the name Pahlavi. The new shah insisted that his country be called Iran, instead of Persia.

Modernizing Iran

Reza Shah Pahlavi wanted Iran to be a powerful industrial nation like the United States and Britain. He began to modernize Iran.

INTRODUCE

Have a student read the Thinking Focus aloud. Ask students what the word *revolution* means to them. *(Students may suggest uprising, revolt; also, whirling around)* Direct students to look up *revolution* on page 706 of the Glossary. Tell them that a revolution often results in the overthrow of one government and its replacement with another. In this lesson they will learn how this happened in modern Iran.

Key Terms

Vocabulary Strategies: T36–T37

modernize—to adopt up-to-date, or modern, ways

exile—removal from one's home or country

hostage—a person held captive until certain terms are met

Graphic Overview

Causes
- Shah seeks to modernize Iran.
- Shah sends Khomeini into exile.
- Shah uses force against opponents.

→ **Shah's Exile Ends Pahlavi Monarchy** →

Effects
- Khomeini returns to Iran.
- Iran becomes an Islamic republic.
- Iran's leaders persecute critics.

Objectives

1. Describe the changes the Pahlavis introduced to modernize Iran.
2. Explain why the people of Iran overthrew the Pahlavis.
3. Identify the policies Iran's religious leaders have followed.

DEVELOP

Display the Graphic Overview on the chalkboard or overhead projector. Tell students that this lesson will discuss the events leading up to, as well as those occurring after, revolution in modern Iran. Explain that the history of modern Iran might be viewed as a series of causes and effects. Instruct the students, as they read the text, to look for cause-and-effect links between events in modern Iran.

CITIZENSHIP
Study Skills

Have students review the section called Changes Made by the Pahlavis, on pages 213–214. Then ask them to list the types of people who probably benefited from the shah's programs and the types of people who did not benefit from those programs. *(Those who benefited may include business people, such as factory managers and merchants, military personnel, and police officers. Those who did not benefit would include religious leaders, small farmers, and poor urban workers.)*

■ *The Pahlavis' policies raised the literacy rate and modernized the country. On the other hand, these policies undermined Islamic beliefs and failed to do much to improve the lives of most of the people.*

➤ *Notice that there are two groups of people ranked as lower-class Iranians.*

Society under the Pahlavis

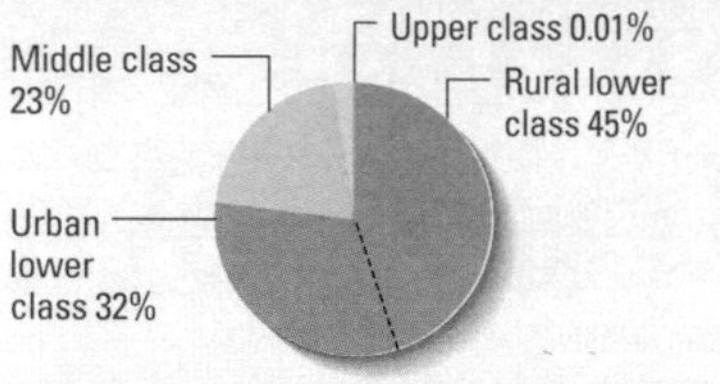
Middle class 23%
Upper class 0.01%
Rural lower class 45%
Urban lower class 32%

Upper class–Pahlavis, army, government office holders

Middle class–shop owners, doctors, office workers, students

Lower classes–farmers, factory workers, unemployed

Source: The Iranian Mojahedin, 1989

▼ *At his coronation the shah and the Empress Farah displayed a fortune in jewels, including a copy of the fabulous Peacock Throne that originally had come from India.*

■ *How did the Pahlavis' policies both help and hurt Iran?*

When a country **modernizes,** it may borrow ideas and ways of doing things from cultures that seem more up-to-date. The shah had factories built to weave cotton and silk, refine sugar, and process food. Roads and power plants were built.

Reza Shah also made social changes. He demanded that Iranians wear Western clothes. The shah built a strong army. He strengthened the school system and tried to weaken the power of Muslim religious leaders.

Not all Iranians liked these changes. Many women felt exposed in Western clothing. Deeply religious Iranians were upset by programs that challenged their Islamic faith. Few benefited from improved farming methods. During the rule of Reza Shah's son, Mohammed Reza, the complaints increased.

Limiting Rights

In 1963 Mohammed Reza set up a plan he called the White Revolution. He used the huge sums Iran was getting for its oil to pay for the changes. Women gained the right to vote, and more Iranians received an education. Between 1956 and 1976, the percentage of people who could read and write tripled, reaching 47 percent.

Although small farmers had gained some land, they did not have the money needed to keep it up. Millions moved to the cities. With fewer people growing crops, Iran had to import the food it needed. The shah had to borrow large sums from the United States. By the 1970s only a small percentage of Iranians were among the rich (see chart above).

When people complained about ties to the United States, among other things, Mohammed Reza censored the newspapers. He outlawed all political parties but his own. With help from the United States, he created SAVAK. This police force used fear to control the people.

In 1971 the shah held a party at Persepolis to celebrate 2,500 years of Iranian history. Heads of state from all over the world were invited. Foreign companies supplied the food and entertainment for the party. However, the event cost the people of Iran about $100 million. Anger at the shah's ties with foreign nations increased. ■

Revolution in Iran

As discontent grew, thousands of Iranians turned to the Ayatollah Khomeini *(koh MAY nee)*, the foremost Iranian Shi'a leader. *(Ayatollah* is the title for a Shi'a religious leader.) Khomeini demanded that the shah leave Iran. The ayatollah claimed that modernization was a U.S. plot against Islam. For these views, Khomeini

Access Activity

Have students examine the photograph of the coronation of the shah and empress of Iran on this page. What does the photograph portray about life under the shah? *(Students may suggest a wealthy ruling family, a love of pomp and ceremony, and a wide gap between Iran's government and common people.)*

Access Strategy

Invite students to recall some causes of the American Revolution. *(No representation in Parliament; unfair trading practices; corrupt British government; dislike of British king)* Ask them how revolutionary ideas are spread. *(Newspapers and other media, gossip, political speeches)* Then ask these questions: What are some of the effects of a revolution? *(A new government, new ideas)* Do you think revolutions always bring about a good change for everyone involved? *(Not necessarily—the Russian Revolution proved to be a failure.)* Tell students that, in this lesson, they will follow the causes and effects of revolution in modern Iran.

◄ *Followers of Ayatollah Khomeini used huge banners to win popular support.*

had been forced to leave Iran in 1964. He spent the next 14 years in **exile,** which means he was not allowed to enter Iran. During his exile in Iraq and France, Khomeini used telephones and tape recordings to keep in touch with his supporters.

A Religious Republic

When a newspaper article attacked the ayatollah in 1978, thousands of Iranians poured into the streets, shouting slogans against the shah. Even police bullets did not stop them. By the end of the year, millions of Iranians were taking part in rallies against the shah.

Mohammed Reza had left Iran in January 1979. Two weeks later, millions of wildly cheering Iranians mobbed the streets of Tehran. They joyfully welcomed Khomeini on his return from exile.

A year later voters approved the forming of an Islamic republic. Some officials in the new government were elected. The Shi'a religious leaders, however, were in control. They wanted Islamic laws to be followed strictly. To enforce these laws, they named a Council of Guardians. Women who did not wear proper clothing could be fined or whipped. Western films and music and foreign businesses were outlawed. The amount of oil to be exported was cut back (see graph). People suspected of being enemies of the Islamic government could be jailed or killed.

How Do We Know?

HISTORY *Khomeini's followers used posters to stir up feeling against the shah. One poster showed Khomeini confronting the shah, who was being attacked by a dragon beside Persepolis. The caption reads: "Anyone who tries to blow out a lamp lighted by God will burn his beard."*

Oil Production in Iran

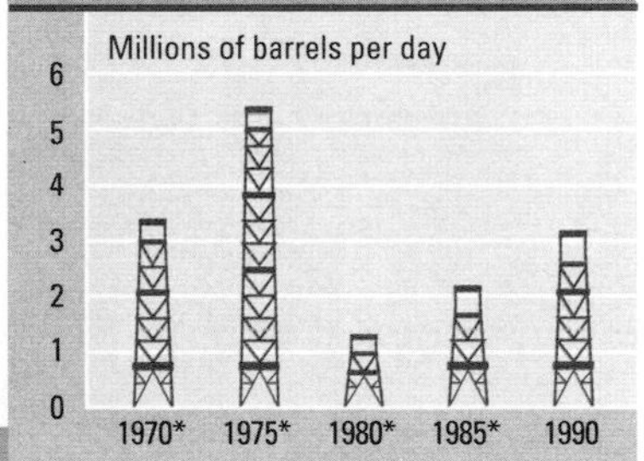

Millions of barrels per day
6
5
4
3
2
1
0
1970*
1975*
1980*
1985*
1990

* Estimates based on daily average for first 6 months
Source: Oil and Gas Journal, 1970-1990

▲ *Under the shah, more than 30,000 tons of crude oil poured into tankers each hour. The Islamic government limited oil production.*

Persian Gulf Oil Production, 1991

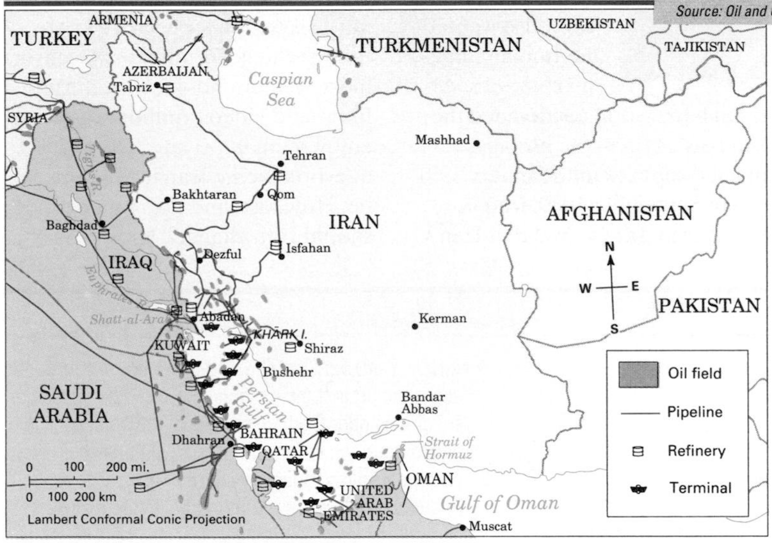

ARMENIA
TURKEY
AZERBAIJAN
Tabriz
Caspian Sea
TURKMENISTAN
UZBEKISTAN
TAJIKISTAN
SYRIA
Mashhad
Tehran
Bakhtaran
Qom
Baghdad
IRAN
AFGHANISTAN
Isfahan
IRAQ
Dezful
Euphrates
Tigris
Shatt-al-Arab
Abadan
Kerman
PAKISTAN
N
W
E
S
KUWAIT
KHARK I.
Shiraz
Bushehr
SAUDI ARABIA
Persian Gulf
Bandar Abbas
Dhahran
BAHRAIN
QATAR
Strait of Hormuz
OMAN
UNITED ARAB EMIRATES
Gulf of Oman
Muscat
Oil field
Pipeline
Refinery
Terminal
0 100 200 mi.
0 100 200 km
Lambert Conformal Conic Projection

◄ *Where does the map show that Iranian oil is produced and refined?*

ECONOMICS

Visual Learning

Have students create a timeline to indicate the major events leading to revolution in modern Iran. Allow them several minutes to skim the text under the heads Changes Made by the Pahlavis, and Revolution in Iran. *(Students may include the following dates: White Revolution begins [1963]; The Persepolis party [1971]; the exile of Ayatollah Khomeini [1964].*

◄ *For the most part, Iranian oil is produced and refined in western Iran, near the Persian Gulf. Refineries are also found in cities.*

Political Context

To help students understand the term *exile,* explain political exile as an expulsion, or voluntary absence, from one's home or country. It was common in ancient Palestine, in Greece, and in Rome. In more recent times, many American colonists who opposed the break with Britain went into exile during the American Revolution; and Russian dissidents—people who spoke out against the government—were sentenced to internal exile in Siberia by both the czars and the Communists who followed.

The Ayatollah Khomeini was exiled from Iran by the shah. Later, the shah, in turn, was forced into exile on the orders of the Ayatollah. Many people, and groups, have used their status as exiles to draw wide attention to their causes. From France, Khomeini conducted a strong opposition movement against the shah. Then, as leader of Iran, the Ayatollah forced into exile many people who were perceived as threats to his Islamic republic.

Critical Thinking

Suggest that students review this page and the following page of the text on Iran after the revolution. Ask them to compare Khomeini's revolutionary programs with the policies of the Iranian leaders that came after his death. *(Khomeini strictly enforced the code of Islam. Opposition forces were jailed or killed. Khomeini's death led to the beginning of a more open society.)*

■ *After a period of terror, in which the religious leadership got rid of opposition, the government has become more democratic. People now enjoy greater freedom, at least at home; some women have been elected to the legislature.*

CLOSE

Have students reread the Thinking Focus on page 213. Then challenge students to summarize the causes of the revolution in Iran in each of the following categories: economic, religious, social, cultural, and political. *(Students may suggest the poverty of most Iranians; popular support for traditional Islam; and anger toward the shah's pro-Western policies, use of a brutal police force, censorship, and prohibition of opposition parties.)*

New Problems

The extent of anti-U.S. feeling became clear in February 1979, when armed bands attacked the U.S. embassy in Tehran.

> *Automatic weapons fire started to rip through the upper floors of the building. The windows were shattered, and the walls were riveted with bullets. We all hit the floor.*
>
> Barry Rosen in *444 Days: The Hostages Remember*

▼ *Iranian women are experiencing greater opportunities in many careers. This woman is a television director.*

A more serious problem arose in November 1979, when Iranian students attacked the embassy. They took more than 60 Americans hostage. A **hostage** is someone held captive until certain demands are met. Iranian students demanded the return of the shah, who was in the United States being treated for cancer. They also wanted the Iranian funds in U.S. banks. Although the world condemned the Iranians' actions, the hostages remained captives until January 1981.

In September 1980, Iraq invaded Iran. Iraq feared that Iran's revolution would spread. Iraq also wanted the Iranian oil fields on the Persian Gulf. Iraq's leaders expected a quick victory, for their army was five times the size of Iran's. Later, the United States and some Arab nations backed Iraq.

The Iranians' devotion to their country, however, stopped the Iraqi advance. Iranian boys as young as 13 joined the army. The war lasted until August 1988. More than one million people had been killed or injured on both sides.

■ *What changes have taken place in Iran since the revolution?*

Changing Policies

After Khomeini died in 1989, different groups tried to get control of the government. The 1992 elections seemed to be a sign of change. Many of the strictest Islamic leaders were defeated. Nine women won seats in the legislature. Foreign companies were again allowed to do business in Iran.

Today Iranian families enjoy new shopping malls. Iranian factories produce stylish *roupooshes,* housecoats women can wear in place of the *chador.* Iranian folk music is no longer censored. Although the government still censors most Western books, rock music, films, and videos, millions of people enjoy them in private. The big question facing Iran now seems to be: How fast, and how much, should Iran change? ■

REVIEW

1. **FOCUS** Why did the people of Iran take part in a revolution?
2. **ECONOMICS** What changes did the Pahlavis make to modernize Iran?
3. **HISTORY** Why did Shah Mohammed Reza choose Persepolis for a major celebration?
4. **HISTORY** Why did Iranian students take hostages?
5. **CRITICAL THINKING** One U.S. foreign policy expert wrote about the protest movements of 1978, "the opposition solidified under the hammer blows of Pahlavi police and military forces." Explain what you think he meant.
6. **WRITING ACTIVITY** Imagine you're a reporter covering Ayatollah Khomeini's return to Iran. Write a story about this moment in history.

Homework Options

Tell students to imagine that they are Iranian students during the time that Ayatollah Khomeini led Iran. They have been sent into exile because they supported the shah. Have them write letters to Khomeini listing their grievances and suggesting ways to make Iran a more democratic country.

Study Guide: page 37

Answers to Review Questions

1. The people resented the cost of modernization and close ties to the United States; devout Muslims felt the shah's policies were undermining Islam.
2. The Pahlavis promoted education, built a strong army, limited the power of the religious leaders, improved transportation, banned traditional dress, and built factories and power plants.
3. Persepolis is a symbol of the glorious days of the Persian Empire and of a powerful shah.
4. The Iranian students wanted the shah returned to Iran. They also wanted Iranian assets that were held in U.S. banks.
5. The more the shah and his army tried to stop the protests, the more determined the protestors became.
6. Students' stories should include a description of the ayatollah, and a statement about why this event was so important.

UNDERSTANDING CURRENT EVENTS

Making Predictions

Here's Why

When you read a mystery novel, you constantly think about what will happen next. The same thing can happen when you read history. In the beginning of Lesson 3, you read about how Reza Shah tried to modernize Iran. You learned how his son's policies divided the Iranian people. You wondered what would happen next. What might the people do to change the shah's policies? Would they allow Mohammed Reza to continue his rule?

Later in Lesson 3, you found the answer: The shah lost his throne during a revolution. The religious leader, Ayatollah Khomeini, and his followers triumphed and set up an Islamic republic.

Knowing the result of one event can help you predict what might happen later in a similar event. Can you predict how the Iranians might react in the future if the religious leaders of their republic fail to improve conditions?

Here's How

To make predictions as accurately as possible, follow these steps:

1. **Review the stated facts.** In Lesson 3 you read about the changes the Pahlavis made. You read about ways they improved transportation and education. You also read how they failed to make life better for most Iranians. The Iranians' protests turned into a revolution that overthrew Mohammed Reza.
2. **Add other knowledge and experience.** This information may come from your own experience or from something you have read. As you read, Iraq invaded Iran partly because the Iraqis believed that Iran's revolution might spread. On the map on page 205, locate other countries that are neighbors of Iran. How might they feel about the unrest in Iran?
3. **Make a prediction.** Use facts from the text and your additional knowledge to guess what will happen. Will the people of Iran ever again revolt against their government? Give reasons for your prediction.

You might predict that the Iranians will revolt again if the government does not improve conditions for the poor. On the other hand, you may point out that, now that Iran is a republic, the people have the choice of voting against leaders they think are failing to make life better. Either prediction may be true. Only time will tell.

Try It

Reread Lesson 3. Follow the three steps in Here's How to predict whether Ali's values might change as he grows older. Will he choose to live by the strict rules of Shi'a Islam? Will he decide that he can accept some Western ideas? Be sure to support your prediction with information from the chapter.

Apply It

Write a sentence predicting how your classmates might respond to each of the following situations. Use the three steps to make each prediction.

1. You and a friend enter the same essay contest, and you win first place.
2. The school principal decides to cancel the end-of-the-year field trip because too many students have not turned in their assignments.

UNDERSTANDING CURRENT EVENTS

This skills feature shows students how to use their knowledge of facts and their personal experience to make predictions about future events.

HISTORY

Critical Thinking

Have students reread the three steps under Here's How. Then offer them some school situations to give them some practice in predicting. For example, you might ask what would happen if a water pipe burst in the school building and half the classrooms flooded.

After they have practiced school-related situations, ask students to make predictions about the future of Iran. Remind them to use the steps under Here's How to ensure that they make logical conclusions.

Answers to Try It

Be sure students support their predictions with evidence from the text. Students may say that while Ali will decide to remain a loyal Muslim, he may choose to adopt values that do not conflict with his beliefs.

Answers to Apply It

Students' predictions should be supported with experiences they have had with their friends and classmates. You may want to ask students to share their experiences and predictions with the class.

Objective

Predict consequences based on evidence and experience. (Critical Thinking 3)

Answers to Reviewing Key Terms

A. Answers:
1. arid
2. satrap
3. satrap
4. modernize
5. hostages

B. Sample answers:
1. The **shah** ruled the Persian Empire and appointed **satraps** to govern the provinces or satrapies.
2. Most of Iran consists of the **Plateau** of Iran, which is **arid** because it receives little rainfall.
3. As part of his program to **modernize** Iran, Reza Shah Pahlavi tried to limit the power of the religious leaders; when Khomeini protested, he was forced into **exile.**
4. Iranian students took Americans **hostage,** demanding that the shah be returned from **exile** in the United States.

Answers to Exploring Concepts

A. Answers:

1. d	2. c	3. g	4. b
5. e	6. h	7. f	8. a

B. Sample answers:
1. The mountains and arid land make travel difficult in Iran.
2. Iranians built underground canals, called *qanats,* to bring water to their arid lands.
3. Iran links Asia and the eastern Mediterranean area.
4. Zoroaster taught that each person was free to choose between the forces of good and evil. People who lived good lives could expect to go to heaven, or paradise.
5. The government minted coins that had the same value throughout the empire, and the Royal Road made travel easier.
6. About A.D. 224 the Sasanians made Zoroastrianism the only religion in Iran. The Muslims introduced Sunni Islam in the 600s, and the Safavids made Shi'a Islam the only religion in 1502.
7. In the early 1500s, the Reformation was taking place in Europe; in 1519–1521, Magellan commanded the first globe-circling voyage; in 1521 Spain defeated the Aztecs; in 1526 Babar invaded India; in 1588, England defeated the Spanish Armada; and the Manchus began to rule China in 1644.
8. Iranian artists excelled in miniature paintings, decorative tiles, and fine carpets and weavings.
9. Unlike the arid lands around it, Isfahan was like a garden, which is what the word *paradise* means. Its streets were lined with trees and flowers, and a channel of water ran through it.
10. The Pahlavis were Reza Khan, who took the name Pahlavi when he took control of the government of Iran, and his son Mohammed Reza.
11. SAVAK was the police force used by Mohammed Reza to control the Iranian people.
12. Khomeini claimed that the shah's modernization program was a U.S. plot against Islam.
13. Many people in Iran are devout Shi'a Muslims and support the religious nature of the republic. At the same time, many want greater freedom to choose their own dress, music, literature, films, and plays.

Chapter Review

Reviewing Key Terms

arid (p. 205)
exile (p. 215)
hostage (p. 216)
modernize (p. 213)
plateau (p. 205)
satrap (p. 209)
shah (p. 208)

A. Each sentence below has two key terms in parentheses. Choose the key term that is correct, and write it on your own paper.
1. The Iranians built *qanats* to bring water to their (arid, plateau) land.
2. The ruler elected a (shah, satrap) to govern the province.
3. People in the provinces paid tribute to the (hostage, satrap).
4. In his efforts to (modernize, exile) Iran, Reza Shah demanded that the people wear Western clothes.
5. In 1979 Iranian students attacked the U.S. embassy and took (hostages, exiles).

B. Read each pair of words. Write a sentence telling how the words in each pair are related.
1. shah, satrap
2. arid, plateau
3. exile, modernize
4. hostage, exile

Exploring Concepts

A. Important dates in the history of Iran are listed below. Following them is a list of events. Copy the list of dates. Beside each date write the letter of the event that took place on that date.
1. 628 B.C.
2. 522 B.C.
3. 330 B.C.
4. A.D. 224
5. A.D. 637
6. 1502
7. 1925
8. 1979

a. An Islamic republic is set up in Iran.
b. Zoroastrianism becomes the official Persian religion.
c. Darius I becomes shah of the Persian Empire.
d. Zoroaster is born.
e. Muslim armies invade Persia.
f. Reza Shah begins to modernize Iran.
g. Alexander the Great conquers the Persian Empire.
h. Shi'a Islam becomes the official Persian religion.

B. Answer each question with information from the chapter.
1. What makes travel difficult in Iran?
2. How did Iranians solve the problem of bringing water to arid lands?
3. How has Iran been a land bridge?
4. Describe the ideas introduced by the teachings of Zoroaster.
5. What two things made it easy for people in the Persian Empire to trade goods?
6. What changes have taken place in Iran's official religion over the centuries?
7. What major changes were occurring in the world during the period of Safavid rule of Persia?
8. Name at least three crafts at which Iranian artisans have excelled.
9. Why did one poet call Isfahan a paradise?
10. Who were the Pahlavis?
11. What was SAVAK?
12. What accusations did Khomeini make against the shah?
13. Name two values that are in conflict in modern Iran.

Reviewing Skills

1. In the 1980s the United States opposed Iran. Will relations between Iran and the United States get better in the 1990s? Use the three steps in Here's How on page 217 to make your prediction. Be sure to support your prediction with information from the chapter.
2. Iraq invaded Iran in 1980. In Chapter 8 you read about Iraq's invasion of Kuwait in 1990 (page 197). Is it likely that Iraq might attack one of its neighbors in the future? Use the information from Chapters 8 and 9 to make a prediction. Be sure to include information shown on the maps.

Using Critical Thinking

1. Why might the first Safavid shah have changed the official religion of Persia from Sunni to Shi'a Islam?
2. One of the important tasks undertaken both by Darius I and by Reza Shah was building roads. Why was this task important?
3. After the shah left Iran in 1979, Shi'a religious leaders took control. Do you think the average Iranian faced more difficult conditions under the shah or under the religious leaders during the 1980s? Explain your answer.
4. Why might strict Islamic law require women to wear the *chador?*

Preparing for Citizenship

1. **COLLECTING INFORMATION** Look through newspapers and magazines for stories that answer the following questions about Iran: Is the area still a center of trade? Do the people who live there still borrow ideas from other cultures? What is life like in Iran today? Collect everyone's stories, and display them on a bulletin board under headings such as Trade in Iran Today or Iranian Culture.
2. **ART ACTIVITY** Persian artisans were skilled metalworkers. One method they used was to cut patterns out of one metal and attach them to another. They also set one metal into another. Use a variation of one of these methods to create a scene from one of the lessons. You might use different colors of foil. As you design and create your scene, think about the talent, materials, effort, and imagination that ancient peoples put into their metalworking.
3. **GROUP ACTIVITY** Both the Pahlavis and the Shi'a religious leaders of the republic told Iranians what type of clothing they should wear. Imagine that officials at your school want to set up a dress code for all students. Divide the class into two groups. One group can develop arguments supporting a uniform dress code. The second group can develop arguments opposing the dress code. Prepare a debate on the topic, "Resolved, that the school should have a dress code for all students." Two to three students should present arguments supporting each side. Choose one student to act as moderator. Stage the debate for the class and judge the results by a vote on the issue.
4. **WRITING ACTIVITY** Iran today, unlike the United States, has a state religion. Write three or four paragraphs describing how your life might change if the United States had a state religion.
5. **COLLABORATIVE LEARNING** The values Iranian youths learn from their families sometimes conflict with the values of their peers. Do the values you learn from your family ever conflict with the values of your classmates? With a few classmates, discuss times when you have faced a conflict of values. Together prepare a short dialogue about one particular conflict of value. Present the dialogue to the class.

Answers to Reviewing Skills

1. Answers will vary. Students may point out that the easing of restrictions on some Western music and books may indicate a gradual improvement of relations between Iran and the United States. Other students may note that the long hostility toward the United States that culminated in the hostage crisis may prevent better relations.
2. As Chapter 8 points out, Iraq went deeply into debt during the Iran-Iraq War, and the Persian Gulf War increased that debt. Students might point out that Iraq may again try to seize neighboring oil fields and/or refineries to diminish its debt. On the other hand, Iraq's debt may prevent it from building a large enough army to attack one of its neighbors.

Answers to Using Critical Thinking

1. Students may speculate that the first Safavid shah followed Shi'a Islam, and wanted to make his own mark on Persian culture.
2. Improved transportation made it easier to move goods and people throughout the kingdom, thus promoting trade. Better roads also made it easier to move an army to keep order or protect the country against invasion.
3. Students will probably conclude that the average Iranian faced restrictions under both the shah and the republic. The shah used SAVAK and the army to prevent resistance. The republic's leaders applied Islamic laws strictly, outlawed Western influences, and banned foreign businesses. Under the shah only a very small percentage of the people prospered. Because of the war with Iraq and the decision to limit oil production, the Islamic republic faced economic problems that made life difficult for the average Iranian.
4. Answers will vary. Some students may infer that according to Islam it is proper that women's bodies be entirely covered so that they can't be seen. Others may infer that wearing the *chador* is a way of expressing devotion to God.

Answers to Preparing for Citizenship

1. **COLLECTING INFORMATION** Students should search past and present newspapers and other sources to gain an understanding of Iranian lifestyles, trade policies, and other pertinent information concerning Iran.
2. **ART ACTIVITY** Provide students with different colors of foil and cardboard they might use as backing. Encourage them to study the examples of Persian metalwork on pages 202 and 203 before creating their scenes.
3. **GROUP ACTIVITY** After the debate, have students discuss how effective each side was in presenting its points. Suggest ways in which debaters might improve their arguments.
4. **WRITING ACTIVITY** Students may suggest that their schools would be run by religious teachers; and that only persons of the state religion could run for political office.
5. **COLLABORATIVE LEARNING** Before students begin their discussion, brainstorm with them to develop a list of possible sources of conflict between the values of their family and those of their peers.

UNIT PREVIEW

Refer students to the large map of Africa on page 223 of the Unit Overview, and have them locate Somalia, where this photograph was taken. Then ask them to place themselves, in their imaginations, in the picture. Have them list what they could observe in this market, using all five senses.

Help students understand that Africa is a huge continent on which there are more than 40 nations. This unit will look in detail at four of them.

Looking Back

In Chapter 8, students read about the rise and spread of Islam from Arabia to North Africa and Europe. Ask students to review events that might have taken the Islamic movement into sub-Saharan Africa. *(Caravan trade across the desert)*

Looking Forward

To help students understand how different African cultures have changed and developed, this unit will treat four nations:
Chapter 10 *Egypt*
Chapter 11 *Mali*
Chapter 12 *Ghana*
Chapter 13 *South Africa*

Unit 4
Africa

Africa is the birthplace of the human species and of the first spoken language, called proto-World. This East African spice market is a reflection of one of the most vital and most ancient of human activities—the exchange of goods. In a great many African cultures, this activity has traditionally been carried out by women.

332 B.C.

Spice market, Somalia, East Africa

BIBLIOGRAPHY

Books for Students
Canesso, Claudia. *South Africa.* New York: Chelsea House, 1989. An overview of the country's society, culture, and history. Nonfiction.

Chiasson, John. *African Journey.* New York: Bradbury Press, 1987. A photojournalist's experiences in West Africa, including Mali, Senegal, and Ethiopia. Nonfiction.

Naylor, Kim. *Mali.* New York: Chelsea House, 1987. An overview of the country's geography, culture, and history.

Books to Read Aloud.
Gordon, Sheila. *The Middle of Somewhere: A Story of South Africa.* New York: Orchard, 1990. The story of a courageous black South African family relocated to a desolate area by the government. Fiction.

Kaye, Geraldine. *Comfort Herself.* London: Deutsch, 1984. Story of the child of an interracial marriage who goes to Ghana to live with her father. Fiction.

Books for Teachers
Davidson, Basil. *Modern Africa.* New York: Longman, 1989. Good overview of the continent today. Nonfiction.

Gunner, Elizabeth. *A Handbook for Teaching African Literature.* London: Heinemann, 1987. A teaching resource including plays,

Today

Understanding the Photograph

Somalia is located on the Horn of Africa, on the east coast of the continent. Its name may be familiar to students from news reports. This photograph shows a typical local African spice market. Long important in African commerce, spices not only enhance the taste of food but also preserve food in an area where refrigeration may be costly or unavailable. Have students note that trading is being conducted by women, which is traditional in much of Africa.

Understanding Chronology

To better understand the chronology of Unit 4, students may want to organize their notes under three headings: Ancient Kingdoms, Colonial Era, and Modern Nations. Students should note that colonialism came to different parts of Africa at different periods but that most African nations had to wait until the mid-20th century to achieve independence.

poetry, prose, and other materials on Africa. Nonfiction.

Hourani, Albert. *A History of the Arab Peoples.* Cambridge: Harvard University Press, 1991. A cultural, historical, and religious history from the seventh century to the 1980s. Nonfiction.

Other Resources

Activity Book

Bartok, M., and C. Ronan, eds. *Stencils: West Africa—Ghana.* Santa Monica: Goodyear, 1993. Fables, activities, crafts, festivals, and other projects related to Ghana.

Visual Media

Africa. Home Vision, 1984. Four video cassettes written and presented by Basil Davidson, a well-known scholar of Africa.

HOUGHTON MIFFLIN SOCIAL STUDIES

Bookshelf

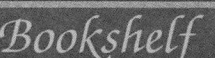

Maartens, Maretha. *Paper Bird.* New York: Clarion Books, 1989. A South African boy uses courage and the kindness of others to face a crisis.

INTRODUCE

Tell students that the African continent covers one-fifth of the earth's land area. Then have them read the unit title and the first paragraph on this page to learn other remarkable facts about Africa. List on the chalkboard some of the continent's other geographic wonders. *(Africa is the second largest continent; the Nile is the world's longest river; Africa is the hottest continent and has huge deserts, rain forests, and mountains.)*

Draw attention to the photographs of the woman carrying the baby and of the city of Nairobi. Point out that because Africa has such varied geography, history, and cultures, its peoples live in different types of places—old cities, new cities, nomadic encampments; they live in deserts, rain forests, and mountains. People also make their living in different ways. Those living in cities could be business executives, teachers, doctors, or factory workers. People living in villages often farm or herd animals.

Ask students to recall from Chapter 1 the factors that shape and change cultures. *(Physical environment, social interaction, and technology)* Tell students that they will see evidence of these influences in each chapter of this unit.

Unit 4 Overview

Africa

Africa is the world's second largest continent. In this vast land are lakes so large that early explorers called them inland seas. Africa is home to the world's longest river—the Nile—and the largest desert—the Sahara. It is the hottest of all the continents. Huge deserts cover much of the land. Grasslands, home to zebras and lions, also spread across wide areas. Africa has many other geographic features too—waterfalls, rain forests, and mountains whose tops are covered with snow all year.

The history of Africa's peoples reaches far into the past. In 1960 scientists Mary and Louis Leakey found pieces of bone in Olduvai Gorge in northern Tanzania. The Leakeys estimated these fragments to be 1.7 million years old—some of the oldest signs of human life found anywhere in the world.

During thousands of years, African peoples settled in every part of the continent. They developed their own customs, languages, and religions. Eventually peoples from other cultures brought new ideas. Sometimes, the meeting of different cultures was peaceful. At other times cultures clashed. Today Africa's peoples blend ancient customs with new ways of life.

Bright colors and bold patterns decorate traditional African clothing.

Nairobi, the capital of Kenya, shows the influence of modern architecture in its tall office and apartment buildings. This photo shows the Nyayo Monument in Nairobi's Central Park.

Objectives

1. Identify the African continent's landforms.
2. Preview some important events in Africa's history.
3. Describe some of Africa's geographic and human resources.

Cultural Context

Africans belong to many ethnic groups and speak more than 800 languages. Most people living in countries of North Africa speak Arabic. Those in central and southern Africa speak the Bantu languages. Swahili, which is a Bantu language, is spoken mostly along the eastern coast.

When European countries explored and colonized Africa, they brought their languages—Portuguese, Dutch, French, English, and German. As a result, European languages are spoken throughout Africa.

In many African countries, people practice Islam. From the mid-600s, Muslim traders from Southwest Asia brought their religion with them as they traveled throughout West African empires such as Ghana, Mali, and Songhai. Today more than 260 million Africans are Muslims, while over 310 million are Christians.

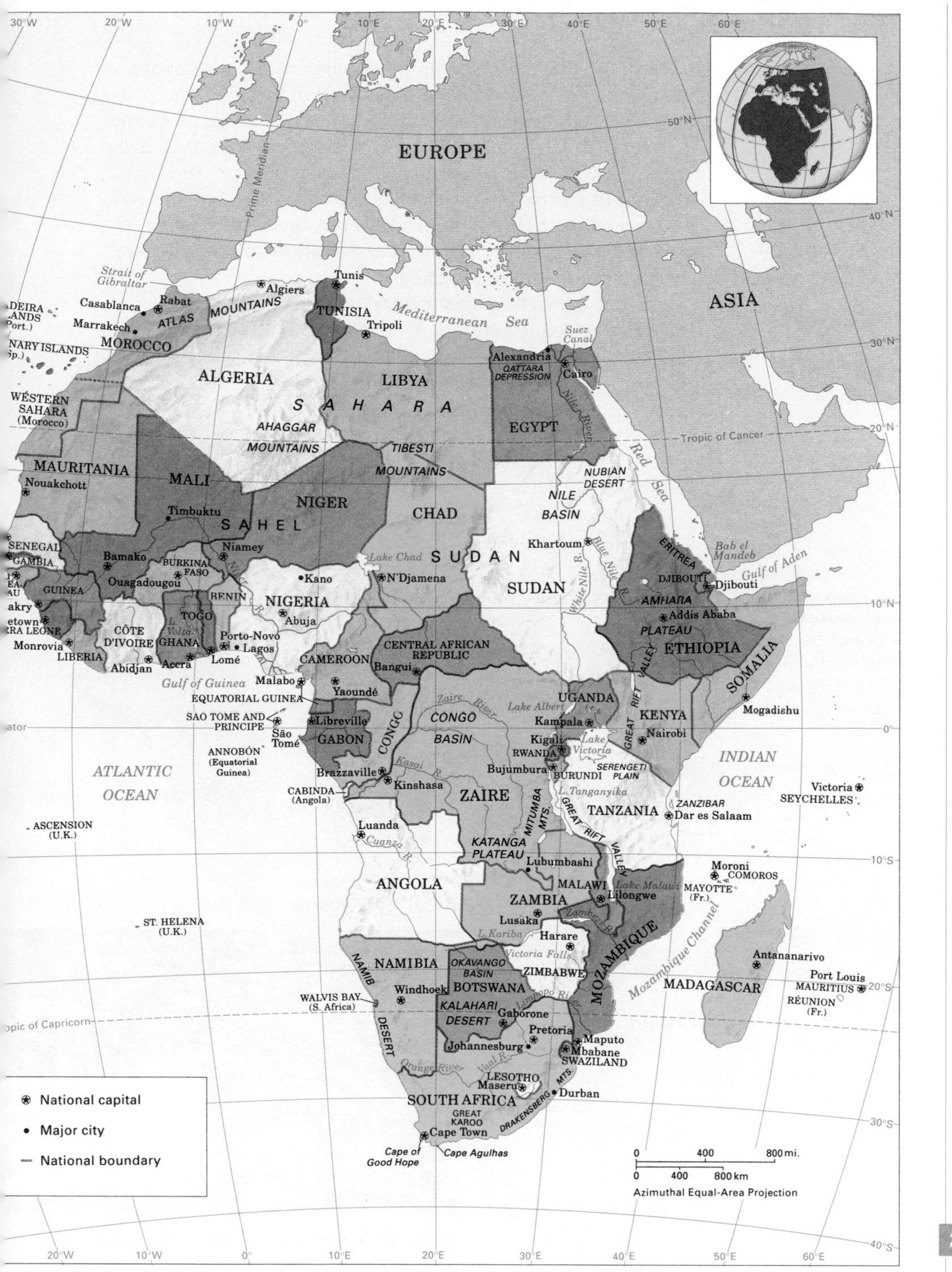
EUROPE
ASIA
Prime Meridian
Strait of Gibraltar
Mediterranean Sea
Suez Canal
Tropic of Cancer
Tropic of Capricorn
Rabat
Casablanca
Marrakech
ATLAS MOUNTAINS
Algiers
Tunis
TUNISIA
Tripoli
MOROCCO
CANARY ISLANDS
ALGERIA
LIBYA
Alexandria
QATTARA DEPRESSION
Cairo
EGYPT
WESTERN SAHARA (Morocco)
S A H A R A
AHAGGAR MOUNTAINS
TIBESTI MOUNTAINS
NUBIAN DESERT
NILE BASIN
Red Sea
MAURITANIA
Nouakchott
MALI
Timbuktu
S A H E L
NIGER
CHAD
SUDAN
Khartoum
Blue Nile R.
White Nile R.
ERITREA
Bab el Mandeb
Gulf of Aden
DJIBOUTI
Djibouti
SENEGAL
GAMBIA
Bamako
BURKINA FASO
Ouagadougou
Niamey
Kano
Lake Chad
N'Djamena
GUINEA
BENIN
NIGERIA
Abuja
AMHARA PLATEAU
Addis Ababa
ETHIOPIA
TOGO
CÔTE D'IVOIRE
GHANA
Porto-Novo
Lagos
Lomé
Accra
Abidjan
Monrovia
LIBERIA
CENTRAL AFRICAN REPUBLIC
Bangui
CAMEROON
Yaoundé
Malabo
EQUATORIAL GUINEA
Gulf of Guinea
SOMALIA
Mogadishu
SAO TOME AND PRINCIPE
São Tomé
Libreville
GABON
CONGO
CONGO BASIN
Zaire River
Lake Albert
UGANDA
Kampala
KENYA
Nairobi
GREAT RIFT VALLEY
Lake Victoria
Kigali
RWANDA
BURUNDI
Bujumbura
SERENGETI PLAIN
ANNOBÓN (Equatorial Guinea)
ATLANTIC OCEAN
INDIAN OCEAN
Brazzaville
Kinshasa
Kasai R.
CABINDA (Angola)
ZAIRE
MITUMBA MTS.
L. Tanganyika
TANZANIA
ZANZIBAR
Dar es Salaam
Victoria
SEYCHELLES
ASCENSION (U.K.)
Luanda
Cuanza R.
KATANGA PLATEAU
Lubumbashi
Moroni
COMOROS
MAYOTTE (Fr.)
ANGOLA
MALAWI
Lake Malawi
Lilongwe
ZAMBIA
Lusaka
Zambezi R.
L. Kariba
Harare
ST. HELENA (U.K.)
NAMIBIA
OKAVANGO BASIN
Victoria Falls
ZIMBABWE
MOZAMBIQUE
Mozambique Channel
Antananarivo
Port Louis
MAURITIUS
MADAGASCAR
RÉUNION (Fr.)
WALVIS BAY (S. Africa)
Windhoek
BOTSWANA
KALAHARI DESERT
Gaborone
Limpopo R.
NAMIB DESERT
Pretoria
Johannesburg
Maputo
Mbabane
SWAZILAND
Orange River
Vaal R.
LESOTHO
Maseru
Durban
DRAKENSBERG MTS.
SOUTH AFRICA
GREAT KAROO
Cape Town
Cape of Good Hope
Cape Agulhas
National capital
Major city
National boundary
0 400 800 mi.
0 400 800 km
Azimuthal Equal-Area Projection
223

Africa

Learning from Maps

Direct students to the locator map at the top of the large map. Have them locate the continent of Africa. Then give students time to study the large map. Ask them to find these countries and their capitals: Egypt *(Cairo),* Mali *(Bamako),* Ghana *(Accra),* and South Africa *(Cape Town* and *Pretoria).* Tell students that the boundaries for many African countries today were created by European colonial powers in the late 1800s. Those boundaries remained largely unchanged after much of Africa regained its independence in the 1960s. Explain to students that they will read about these sweeping changes in Africa in this unit.

Mathematics Connection

Have groups of students use the map scale to find the size of the African continent. They should measure in these directions: north to south; east to west at its widest point; and east to west at its narrowest point. Each group will need a ruler, a copy of the map, and a sheet of paper to calculate their measurements. Agree upon the points from which the measurements will be made. For help using a scale of miles, have students refer to page G2 in the Map and Globe Handbook.

Map and Globe Skills

Have students turn to the world climate map in the Atlas on page 688. Ask them what climate generally exists at the equator in Africa. *(Tropical, wet; hot and rainy all year)* Ask how the climate changes as you move away from the equator. *(The climate becomes drier, turns into desert, then changes to a Mediterranean climate along the northern coast.)*

LOOK AND RESPOND

Have students scan the captions and the images on pages 224 and 225. On the chalkboard make a list of observations and impressions about the people and geography of Africa.

Learning from the Map

Have students study the map of Africa's expanding deserts. How might the landscape of Africa be different in the future? *(More desert)* What effect will this have on Africa's peoples? *(Answers will vary. Some students may say that desertification will force some people to migrate away from the desert, where it is difficult to grow crops or raise animals.)*

The Land and People

Most of Africa is a plateau. Tall mountains rise high above the surrounding land in the north and east of the continent. Along the Great Rift Valley in eastern Africa, the land drops far below sea level. This huge gash in the earth's crust is so deep that many Grand Canyons could fit inside it.

Some of Africa's land is changing. Long periods without water have turned some land to desert. Deserts are also expanding where animals have been allowed to overgraze and people have cut down trees to make farmland.

Parts of Africa have rich mineral deposits. These include diamonds, gold, and uranium. Wild animals are also treated as a valuable resource. Some nations, like Kenya, have created parks where animals such as elephants, lions, and giraffes are protected from poachers—people who hunt illegally.

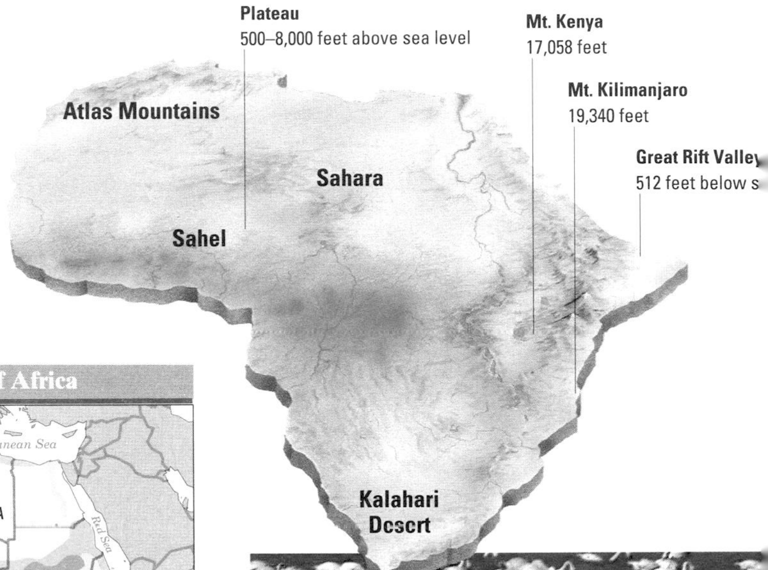
Plateau
500–8,000 feet above sea level
Mt. Kenya
17,058 feet
Mt. Kilimanjaro
19,340 feet
Great Rift Valley
512 feet below s
Atlas Mountains
Sahara
Sahel
Kalahari
Desert

Long periods without rain cause plants to wither and die. Without plant roots to hold the soil, it blows away. Dry sands take its place. This map shows how this process affects some regions in Africa.

The Expanding Deserts of Africa

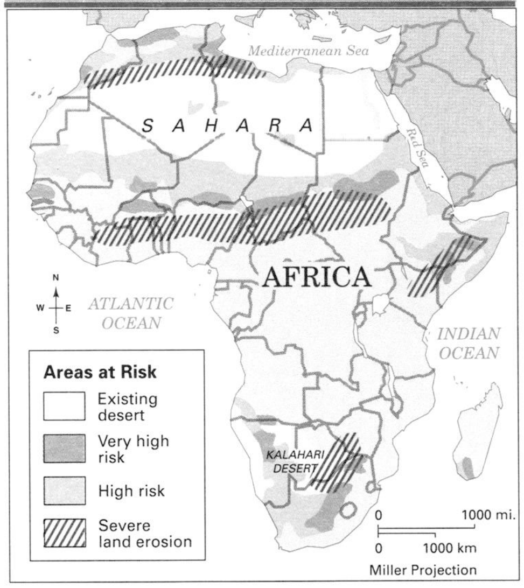
Mediterranean Sea
S A H A R A
Red Sea
AFRICA
ATLANTIC OCEAN
INDIAN OCEAN
KALAHARI DESERT
N
W
E
S
Areas at Risk
Existing desert
Very high risk
High risk
Severe land erosion
0
1000 mi.
0
1000 km
Miller Projection

The Great Rift Valley is home to many of Africa's animals, including these flamingos in Tanzania.

Writing to Learn

Encourage students to write a paragraph describing whatever they know about life in some part of Africa today. After they have read and studied the unit, ask them to revise their paragraphs in view of what they have learned.

Geographic Context

One of Africa's spectacular geographic features is a huge waterfall called Victoria Falls. David Livingstone, a British explorer, named the falls after Queen Victoria in 1855. At one point the falls have a maximum drop of 355 feet. The falls are part of the Zambezi River system, which runs through the countries of Zambia, Mozambique, and Zimbabwe.

Language Arts Connection

Write the word *Sahel* on the board. Have students find Sahel on the illustration above the photograph. Then point out that *Sahel* is the Arab word for "shore" or "border." Have students write an explanation of the way in which the Sahel is a shore. Students may wish to read about the Sahel in an encyclopedia before writing their explanation. Encourage them to use descriptive and precise language.

Important Dates in African History

1200 | 1300 | 1400 | 1500 | 1600 | 1700 | 1800 | 1900

A.D. 1250 Mali becomes the most powerful empire in West Africa.

1497 Navigator Vasco da Gama rounds South Africa's coast.

1670s Osei Tutu forms the Ashanti Empire.

1914 Europeans colonize all of Africa except Ethiopia and Liberia.

1957 Ghana gains its independence from Great Britain.

TODAY South Africa works to end racism.

No other continent has more new nations than Africa. For hundreds of years, Africa was home to busy trading empires. Then, during the 1800s, Europeans colonized most of the continent. Africa finally won its freedom from European control after World War II. Today the continent is made up of more than 50 independent nations.

Africa's peoples belong to hundreds of different cultures and speak as many as 1,000 languages. Most Africans live in villages where they work close to the land as farmers or herders. However, millions of people are moving to the cities. Africa's nations are working to create new manufacturing and other industries to provide jobs for their growing populations.

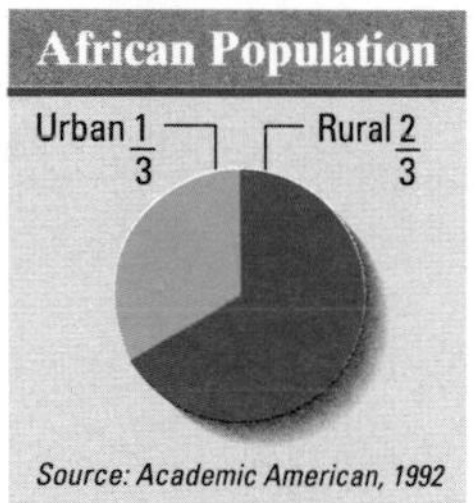
African Population
Urban 1/3
Rural 2/3
Source: Academic American, 1992

More than 200 million of Africa's approximately 700 million people live in cities.

Factory workers prepare sisal fibers to make into mats, rope, and baskets. Baskets like those below are often made by hand.

Learning from the Timeline

Have students study the timeline and the captions. Have them brainstorm a list of reasons Europeans would have wanted to control Africa. *(Raw materials, trade, markets, mineral wealth, competition for territory)*

Learning from the Photograph

The caption explains the work of these factory workers. Sisal is a plant whose fibers are used to make twine. Tell students that the sisal fibers grow in Eastern Africa.

Learning from the Graph

Have students locate Lagos, Nigeria, on the map on page 223. Tell them that Lagos is one of Africa's fastest growing cities. Ask students what percentage of Africans live in urban areas. *(About 33 percent)*

ENRICH

Students can use library resources to research which animals in Africa are endangered. Students' research should answer this question: What is being done to protect endangered animals?

Health Connection

Tell students that the tsetse fly has helped shape the history of Africa. Both Africans and non-Africans went out of their way to avoid areas infested with tsetse flies. The flies are bloodsucking insects that can bite through canvas clothing and even through the hide of a rhinoceros. One bite of the fly can be deadly to both humans and animals. In humans, parasites carried by the fly enter the bloodstream, causing "sleeping sickness." The disease begins with headaches, fever, and joint pain. If the bite goes untreated, the victim succumbs to extreme sleepiness, lapses into a coma, and dies. Until preventive measures were taken early in this century, sleeping sickness killed millions of Africans each year. In the past 10 years, the number of deaths each year has been in the thousands. Have students research malaria, AIDS, and other diseases that affect Africans today.

Collaborative Learning

Divide the class into groups. Each group will prepare a one-page report on a region of Africa, using school library resources. Assign a region (north, east, south, west, central) to each group and explain what countries it includes. Groups should research the geographic features, crops and products, languages, and capitals of the countries in their regions.

CHAPTER ORGANIZER

Chapter 10 Egypt

CHAPTER PLANNING CHART

Pupil's Edition	Teacher's Edition	Ancillaries
Lesson 1: Rulers from the North (2–3 days) Objective 1: List the features of Alexandria that made it an important Mediterranean city. (Geography 2, 4, 5) Objective 2: Describe how conquering groups influenced and were influenced by Egyptian culture. (History 5, 6; Culture 1, 2) Objective 3: Explain the significance of Coptic Christianity. (Ethics and Belief Systems 3, 4)	• Graphic Overview (228) • Access Strategy (229) • Access Activity (229) Map and Globe Skills (230) Historical Context (230)	Study Guide (39) • Posters (1)
Lesson 2: Islamic Egypt (3–4 days) Objective 1: Describe how Arab rule shaped Egypt's culture. (Geography 4; Culture 1) Objective 2: Analyze the effects of Ottoman rule on Egypt. (History 6) Objective 3: Describe the challenges that have faced Egypt in the period of self-rule. (Ethics and Belief Systems 5; Social and Political Systems 3, 6)	• Graphic Overview (232) • Access Strategy (233) • Access Activity (233) Study Skills (234) Historical Context (234, 235) Map and Globe Skills (235) Critical Thinking (236) Making a Bulletin Board (236) Research (236)	Study Guide (40) Map Activities (14)
Understanding Historical Evidence Objective 1: Distinguish between primary and secondary sources. (Study Skills 1) Objective 2: Evaluate the use of primary and secondary sources as authorities on people and events. (Critical Thinking 2)		Study Guide (41)
Lesson 3: A Trip Down the Nile (2–3 days) Objective 1: Explain how the Aswan High Dam is changing life along the Nile. (Economics 1; Geography 3) Objective 2: Contrast old traditions and new trends in Egyptian life. (History 5, 6)	• Graphic Overview (239) • Access Activity (240) • Access Strategy (240) Writing a Poem (241) Making a Model (241) Critical Thinking (241) Study Skills (242) Art Activity (242)	Study Guide (42) Discovery Journal (21)
Chapter Review	Answers (244–245)	Tests (37–40)

* Objectives are correlated to the strands and goals in the program Scope and Sequence on pages T41–T49.

• LEP appropriate resources. (For additional strategies, see pages T32–T33.)

CHAPTER RATIONALE

Chapter 4 explored Egypt's ancient history. This chapter on modern Egypt covers selected themes from the time of Alexander's conquest in 332 B.C. to the present. As in Egypt's earlier history, cultural influences combine with existing lifestyles to form a uniquely Egyptian identity.

This chapter emphasizes dual themes of continuity and change in Egypt. **Lesson 1** discusses the influences of the Greeks, Romans, and Byzantines, highlighting the point that many people who came to rule Egypt were in fact changed by Egypt's rich traditions. The lesson also points out that while repeated conquests brought political change, peasant life along the rural Nile was relatively untouched by these trends.

Lesson 2 traces the history of Egypt under the Arab and Ottoman empires and explains how Egyptians achieved self-rule in this century. The lesson focuses on helping students understand how foreign rule affected Egypt, why Egyptians sought self-rule, and what challenges they faced after achieving it. Chief among those challenges were the protracted and draining war with Israel and the growing Islamic fundamentalist movement that aimed to destabilize Egyptian democracy.

Lesson 3 follows in the footsteps of many visitors to Egypt by taking students on a trip down the Nile. The lesson begins with the building of the Aswan Dam. This provides a vehicle for looking at change throughout the Nile Valley, since the dam has had such tremendous effects on the area. Those effects begin right at Egypt's southern border in what was once ancient Nubia. Students read about how the mammoth Lake Nasser, created behind the dam, inundated this region and displaced thousands of modern-day Nubians. A Closer Look at the Rescue of Abu Simbel tells the fascinating tale of how archaeologists worked round-the-clock to save a famous monument from the rising waters of the Nile. This story and other aspects of the dam project are fertile topics for further exploration by students of any learning level.

ACTIVITIES & PROJECTS

Basic: Collaborative Learning

Have students work in small groups to compile a *Who's Who in Ancient Alexandria.* They should begin by dividing up the task of researching the rulers, astronomers, mathematicians, geographers, and religious scholars who once worked there. (Names include the ruling Ptolemies—as well as the astronomer Ptolemy—Demetrius, Euclid, Eratosthenes, Strato, Archimedes, Strabon, Ctesibius, Philon, Hero, and Philo Judaeus.) Encourage students to find or draw pictures or diagrams relating to the people and their work. Have group members combine their findings and decide in what form to present them—a book, a poster, or a bulletin board. (Use after Lesson 1.)

LEP: Making a Poster

Instruct students to collect images to present as a visual journey down the Nile. Encourage them to look in books and magazines in the public library or school library. Images may include maps as well as pictures. Remind students that the Nile runs north, so a journey *down* the Nile must proceed from south to north. Students may choose to display their findings on a poster, or they may present them orally to the class. (Use after Lesson 3.)

Challenge: Research

Explain to students that the Arab-Israeli peace agreement worked out at Camp David in 1978 followed years of bitter strife between Egypt and its Arab allies and Israel. Invite students to explore the Arab-Israeli conflict further by researching one or more of these topics: the Suez crisis; the Six-Day War; the Yom Kippur War; the Sinai Peninsula and the Gaza Strip; the Camp David Accords; the lives of Menachem Begin and Anwar Sadat. Have them write one or two pages about the topic and explain how it has affected the course of events in the region. (Use after Lesson 3.)

CHAPTER
PREVIEW

Ask a student volunteer to read the chapter title and opening paragraph. Using the map in the Atlas on page 685, have students identify Egypt's location and tell why they think foreign powers sought control of the area. *(Its location in northeastern Africa provided ready access to Europe, Asia, and the rest of Africa as well as to the trade routes fanning out to these three continents from Egypt. The fertile Nile Valley also attracted foreign powers.)*

Looking Forward

Tell students that they will be journeying through time in modern Egypt, from the start of Greek rule in 332 B.C. to the present. Their journey will include these lessons: Rulers from the North, Islamic Egypt, and A Trip Down the Nile.

Lesson 1 describes how the Greeks, Romans, and Byzantines affected Egypt.

Chapter 10

Egypt

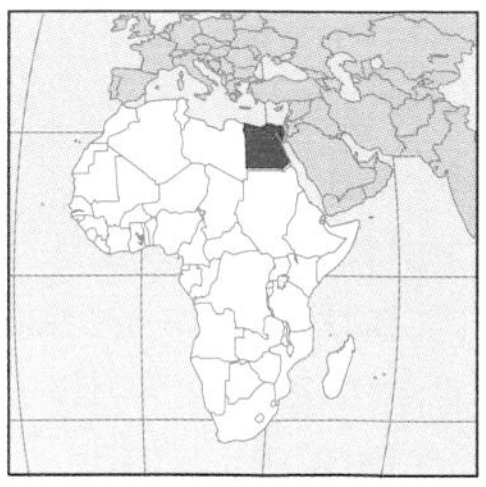

After the days of the ancient pharaohs, Egypt was ruled by foreigners, such as the clever Greek queen Cleopatra and the Muslim hero Muhammad Ali. All of them changed Egypt, and all were changed by it. After nearly 2,300 years of foreign rule, the people of the Nile took back their country. Today Egyptians seek their own solutions for governing their growing nation.

The Romans, who conquered Egypt in 30 B.C., mixed Egyptian customs with their own. Wealthy Romans in Egypt, like this man, were often mummified in the Egyptian style.

A.D. 395 Egypt becomes part of the Christian Byzantine Empire.

500 B.C. A.D. 500

332 B.C.

332 B.C. Alexander the Great conquers Egypt and founds the great city of Alexandria.

A.D. 639 Arabs come to Egypt, bringing Muslim culture.

BACKGROUND

The evolution of modern Egypt was marked by waves of foreign conquest, each triggering changes. Throughout those changing times, the Nile—the world's longest river—has remained a constant resource for Egypt, serving as a major means of transportation and as the single most vital source of water for crops.

Arab Culture in Egypt

Egypt's location and its agricultural riches made it an attractive target for conquest by foreign powers. Greeks, Romans, Byzantines, Ottomans, and Europeans all came to dominate Egypt politically and economically, but it was the Arab Muslims who had the most profound and enduring impact on Egyptian culture.

The Arab rulers who entered Alexandria in A.D. 639 showed respect for Egyptian traditions, but the Egyptians looked down on them. This gave Amr, the Arab governor of Egypt, the chance to make a point. He invited Egyptians and Arabs alike to a three-day banquet. On the first day, he served camel meat as the main course—much to the Egyptians' disgust—and on the second day, Egyptian delicacies. On the third day, Amr paraded his soldiers in battle formation and informed his Egyptian guests: "The first day's entertainment was to show you the plain food of the desert Arabs; the second was to show you that we can also appreciate the finer things in the conquered lands; the third day is to show you that we still retain our [military might]."

Gamal Abdel Nasser led a revolution in 1952 that established Egyptian self-rule. One of his dreams was to build a dam to tame the floods of the Nile. The Aswan High Dam was completed in 1970.

Feeding the huge population along the Nile is one of the many challenges that Egypt faces today.

1000 | 1500 | 2000

A.D. 969 Arab rulers found a new capital, Cairo. In the shadow of the ancient Giza pyramids, Cairo, shown above, reflects the old and new in Egypt today.

Today

Understanding the Visuals

The pyramids at Giza, shown here, were built roughly 4,500 years ago out of limestone blocks. The largest pyramid, the Great Pyramid of Khufu, was originally 481 feet high. This massive monument covers nearly 13 acres—which means that at its base, each side is about the same length as two-and-a-half football fields. It contains more than 2 million blocks, and each block weighs about 2½ tons (5,000 pounds)—the equivalent of fifty 100-pound sixth graders.

Understanding Chronology

Have students study the timeline and the images. Ask them to use the information in the captions to find the approximate points on the timeline for the images of the Roman mummy, the founding of Cairo, and the building of the Aswan High Dam.

His point was that if mutual tolerance did not prevail, Arab force would.

Cultural Tradeoffs

Despite the country's tumultuous history of foreign invasions, the peasant farmers of Upper Egypt, the *fellahin,* still live and work in ways that have remained virtually unchanged for centuries. Like the Nile itself, the *fellahin* represent continuity. They use farming tools such as the *fass,* a short-handled hoe, just as they did in the times of the early pharaohs. Some local funeral rites are still performed according to ancient Egyptian, not Islamic, tradition.

Unlike the *fellahin* of the delta region, those of Upper Egypt have yet to adapt culturally to changes brought about by the Aswan High Dam. The *fellahin* of both regions earn about the same amount of money from farming, but their spending patterns are very different. Upper Egyptian families spend almost twice as much as delta families on cigarettes, meat, sugar, and tea, because tradition demands that they offer hospitality to friends and neighbors. A delta family spends up to 20 percent of its income on education, but in Upper Egypt little is spent on education. The illiteracy rate there is very high. Will the *fellahin* of Upper Egypt remain unaffected by the latest wave of change, or will they, like the ancient Nile, at last yield to irresistible new forces?

INTRODUCE

Have students locate Egypt on the Unit Overview map on page 149. Encourage them to speculate on reasons that Europeans such as the Greeks and Romans would have been interested in taking over Egypt. *(Key location along trade routes)* Ask a volunteer to read the Thinking Focus. Then have students read the lesson to find out about the effects of European rule on Egypt.

Key Terms

Vocabulary Strategies: T36–T37

fellahin—in Egypt, peasant farmers living along the Nile

infrastructure—a system of basic public facilities and services, such as roads and irrigation canals

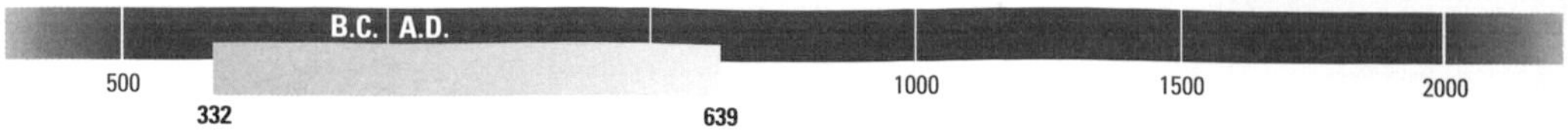

B.C. | A.D.
500
332
639
1000
1500
2000

LESSON 1

Rulers from the North

THINKING FOCUS

How did the Greeks, the Romans, and the Byzantines affect Egyptian culture?

Key Terms

- fellahin
- infrastructure

This stele, or stone marker, was carved on the tomb of a little boy who died in Egypt in about A.D. 225. The boy had a Roman name: Julius Valerius. His father served in the Roman army, which occupied Egypt from 30 B.C. to A.D. 639.

If you look closely at the stele, you can see the influence of three cultures in Egyptian history. The writing that describes the boy is both Greek and Latin. "C. Julius Valerius," it says, "son of C. Julius Severus, a soldier of the second legion Traiana. He lived 3 years." Notice the animals around the boy: At the top are a large bird called a falcon and a type of wild dog called a jackal. They represent Egyptian Gods. At the boy's feet is a creature from Greek mythology called a griffin. After the age of Egypt's pharaohs, three cultures—Egyptian, Greek, and Roman—came together in Egypt, just as they did on the stele of young Julius.

➤ *This stele shows a mixing of traditions that was common among Romans in Egypt. Wealthy Roman families often mummified their dead. They buried the mummies, Roman-style, in underground tombs called catacombs.*

Foreign Pharaohs

Foreigners ruled Egypt most of the time between the fall of the Egyptian pharaohs and modern times. In Chapter 4 you read about the Assyrian invasion of Egypt in 671 B.C. Besides the Assyrians, Egypt was ruled at various times by the Persians and by the Greeks, the Romans, and the Byzantines *(BIHZ uhn teens)*. These groups were followed by many others, including Arabs, Turks, and British. For most of 2,600 years, foreign rulers controlled Egypt.

Egyptians in towns and cities often accepted the foreigners' Gods, and adopted their languages, weapons, and art. However, foreign rule had less effect on the **fellahin** *(feh lah HEEN)*. They were peasant farmers who lived in villages in the Nile delta and along the Upper Nile. As in ancient times, the *fellahin* planted and harvested according to

Objectives

1. List the features of Alexandria that made it an important Mediterranean city.
2. Describe how conquering groups influenced and were influenced by Egyptian culture.
3. Explain the significance of Coptic Christianity.

Graphic Overview

Greek Rule
- new capital, Alexandria
- Egyptian traditions honored
- large Jewish community

→

Roman Rule
- better infrastructure
- Jews, Christians persecuted
- no self-government
- Christianity eventually adopted

→

Byzantine Rule
- Egypt's Christians form Coptic church
- Copts create new written language

the yearly Nile floods. Empires came and went, but their lives changed little.

Alexander's Empire

Legend says that Alexander the Great was called to Egypt by a gray-haired man in a dream. "An island lies where loud the billows roar," the old man declared. "Pharos they call it, on the Egyptian shore." Alexander made the dream come true.

In 332 B.C. Alexander entered Egypt without a battle. Egyptians welcomed him as a hero because he freed them from harsh Persian rule.

Alexander made a pilgrimage to the Siwa *(SEE wuh)* Oasis to worship Egypt's sun God, Amon-Re. Pleased that he honored Egyptian Gods, the priests of Amon-Re gave Alexander their blessing. He left Siwa, tradition says, with the godlike powers of a pharaoh.

Ancient Alexandria

After the death of Alexander in 323 B.C., one of his generals, Ptolemy I *(TAHL uh mee),* ruled Egypt. Ptolemy's dynasty held power for nearly 300 years. Like Alexander, the Ptolemies respected Egyptian traditions. They called themselves pharaohs; they worshiped both Greek and Egyptian Gods.

Ptolemy I completed Egypt's new capital, Alexandria, which Alexander had founded. As the map on page 230 shows, Alexandria lies on the Mediterranean Sea. A lighthouse on the island of Pharos guided ships into the city's harbor. Greeks, Persians, Phoenicians, and Ionians came to settle in Alexandria. During the time of the Ptolemies, the city also was home to the world's largest Jewish community.

One of the greatest wonders of Alexandria was its library and the "living books," or scholars, who came from all over to study there. Alexandrian astronomers were among the first to suggest that Earth is a sphere that travels around the sun. Mathematicians discovered new laws of geometry based on ideas of the ancient pyramid builders. Sky watchers made the first long-range weather predictions. At all hours, Alexandria's scholars might be called upon to advise Egypt's Ptolemaic rulers.

The first three Ptolemies were strong rulers. The Ptolemies grew weak, however, as the Roman Empire grew strong.

Queen Cleopatra

The last of the Ptolemies may be familiar to you. Her name was Cleopatra VII.

By the time Cleopatra became queen in 51 B.C., Rome had a large role in Egypt's affairs. It was only a matter of time before Egypt became part of the Roman Empire. Yet, by making deals with Roman leaders, the clever Cleopatra kept her throne and Egypt's independence for over 20 years. Finally, in 30 B.C., the Romans defeated Cleopatra's forces. The queen refused to surrender; she later took her own life. Control of Egypt passed to Rome. ■

◄ Cleopatra, the first of the Ptolemies to learn her subjects' language, paid tribute to Egyptian Gods. Here she appears on an Egyptian wall carving and, below, on a Roman coin.

Across Time & Space

In time, the library at Alexandria disappeared. Some scholars believe conquering armies destroyed the library. Others think it died out over time as books began replacing papyrus scrolls.

Today, Egypt is building a new library near Alexandria that will contain thousands of historic books. Computers will let people from all over the world use the library's resources.

■ *Give examples to show how Egypt affected its Greek rulers.*

DEVELOP

Have students review what they learned about the ancient Greek and Roman cultures in Chapter 7. Ask a volunteer to describe the location and geography of Egypt, based on the physical map of Southwest Asia on page 149. *(South of Europe; bordered to the north by the Mediterranean Sea and to the east by the Red Sea; mostly desert, with some mountains and a long river)* Ask students to keep these features in mind as they read the lesson.

HISTORY

Visual Learning

Help students make a flow chart showing how one set of foreign rulers gave way to another in Egypt, from the Assyrian invasion in 671 B.C. to the arrival of the Arabs in A.D. 639. The flow charts should show the following progression: Assyrians, Persians, Greeks, Romans, Byzantines, Arabs. Students can also use the chart to keep track of religions that influenced Egyptian culture.

■ *Alexander honored the Egyptian sun God; the Ptolemies ruled as pharaohs; the last Ptolemaic ruler, Cleopatra, learned the Egyptian language and defended Egypt against the Romans.*

Access Strategy

Invite students to look closely at the stele pictured on page 228. What are the three creatures depicted on the marker? *(A falcon, a jackal, and a griffin)* Ask students to think about their earlier study of ancient Egyptian civilization and burial customs. Explain that the falcon on the stele stands for the Egyptian God Horus, the God of the heavens. The jackal stands for the God of the underworld, Anubis, who weighed on a scale of justice the heart of every person who died. He also judged a person's deeds on earth. The griffin was a strange creature from Greek mythology. It had an eagle's wings and head and a lion's body. Griffins were often shown guarding gold or some other treasure. This stele, then, is strong evidence of the mix of cultures in Egypt. As students read the lesson, have them look for other examples of how the Egyptians and their conquerors—the Greeks, Romans, and Byzantines—influenced each other's cultures.

Access Activity

Ask students to think of objects that are common to many civilizations but whose designs or symbols often vary from culture to culture. *(Coins, gravestones, and monuments are examples.)* Have students work in small groups to design a coin that represents their classroom "civilization."

➤ *Rome needed to ensure that grain could be grown and transported from the empire's major grain-producing areas to the city of Rome, which was not sited in a major grain-producing area.*

BELIEF SYSTEMS

Critical Thinking

Explain to students that both Christians and Jews were monotheistic; they believed in one God and refused to worship the Roman emperor as a God. Ask students what relationship this belief might have had to the Romans' persecution of Egypt's Jews and of the early Christians as well. *(The Romans may have persecuted Jews and Christians out of fear that their monotheistic beliefs would spread and undermine Roman authority and rule.)*

■ *Egypt benefited from the Romans' valuable improvements in infrastructure; however, the Romans did not let Egyptians govern themselves, and they discriminated against Egypt's Jews.*

➤ *Looking at this map, why do you think Rome needed to build up the infrastructure of Egypt and other lands it conquered?*

Major Grain-Producing Areas of the Roman Empire

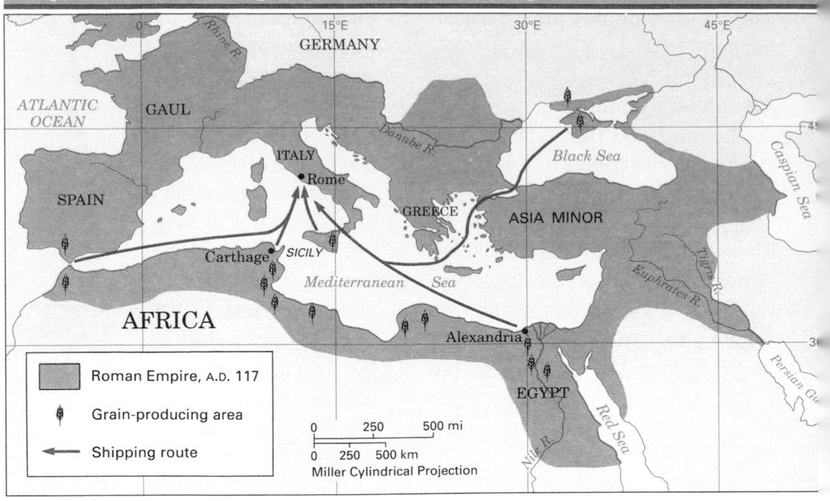
15°E
30°E
45°E
GERMANY
Rhine R.
ATLANTIC OCEAN
GAUL
Danube R.
ITALY
Rome
Black Sea
Caspian Sea
SPAIN
GREECE
ASIA MINOR
Carthage
SICILY
Mediterranean Sea
Euphrates R.
Tigris R.
AFRICA
Alexandria
EGYPT
Nile R.
Red Sea
Persian Gulf
Roman Empire, A.D. 117
Grain-producing area
Shipping route
0 250 500 mi
0 250 500 km
Miller Cylindrical Projection

Roman Times

One ancient historian noted that in the A.D. 200s, Rome gave out free grain to its citizens. The amount of grain needed to feed the city was staggering. It imported 14 million bushels of grain a year. The map on this page shows the role of Egypt in the Roman Empire: to grow grain. For 300 years, until A.D. 300, Egypt sent 150,000 tons of grain a year to Rome.

In some ways, Rome's need for grain helped Egypt. The Romans improved Egypt's **infrastructure,** its system of public services such as roads, harbors, and irrigation canals. New canals helped improve the harvests. Harbors and roads transported grain to Rome. When Roman rule ended, Egypt kept its valuable infrastructure.

Yet some Egyptians suffered under Roman rule. Many wanted to govern themselves, as people in other Roman provinces did, but Rome would not allow it.

Jews, moreover, had fewer rights than other Egyptians under Roman rule. Alexandria's Jews tried to regain rights they had enjoyed under the Greeks. Rome crushed Jewish uprisings so brutally that the Jewish community was almost destroyed. ■

■ *How did Roman rule both help and harm Egypt?*

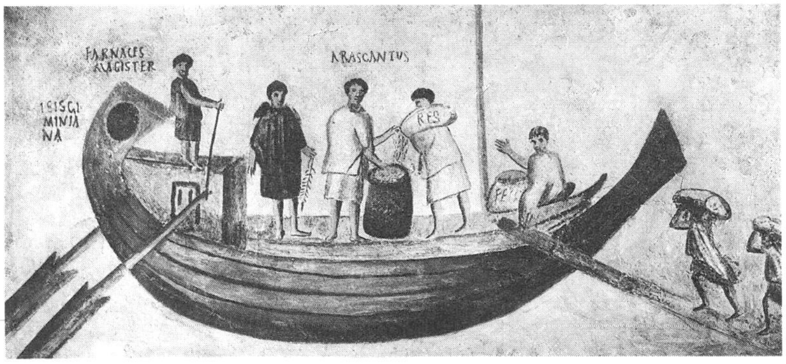
FARNACES MAGISTER
ARASCANTVS

➤ *This painting shows sacks of Egyptian grain being loaded on a barge for shipment to Rome.*

Map and Globe Skills

Invite students to look carefully at the map on this page. Ask them to locate the city of Alexandria, the Nile River, and the Nile delta. Then have students suggest why Alexander wanted to establish Alexandria where he did. *(Good port location for shipping and trading)*

Historical Context

Help students understand the different beliefs held by Coptic and Byzantine Christians. Explain that although Copts make up only about 7 percent of Egypt's present-day population, they played a key role in the early development of Christianity. One Copt, Anthony of Thebes, established a Christian community of hermits in the early A.D. 300s that served as a model for later monasteries. In A.D. 451 the Coptic belief that Jesus was divine in nature was condemned as heresy by the Byzantine Christian church, which held that Jesus was both divine and human. Because of this rift, the Byzantines subjected Egyptians to centuries of persecution. This persecution, combined with a heavy tax burden, fueled Egyptians' resentment of their Byzantine rulers. After the Arab Muslims arrived in A.D. 639, most Egyptian Christians eventually converted to Islam, but several million Copts still live in Egypt today.

Christianity Spreads

During Roman rule in Egypt, a wave of cultural change swept through the country, affecting both the rich and the *fellahin*. For the first time in 3,000 years, Egyptians adopted a new religion. It was Christianity.

In the A.D. 100s, the followers of Jesus brought Christianity to Egypt. In spite of punishment by some Roman rulers, many Egyptians eagerly accepted the new religion. Gradually, monotheism spread through Egypt and south into Nubia (see Chapter 4).

Except for their use of short Coptic phrases, Coptic priests such as these speak mostly in Arabic in services today.

The Byzantines

Although Roman emperors at first opposed Christianity, they later adopted it. In the A.D. 300s, Christianity became the religion of the Roman Empire. At the same time, the empire split into two parts. Egypt was in the eastern part, the Byzantine Empire. The empire's capital, Constantinople, was the center of the Byzantine Christian church.

Coptic Christianity

In the A.D. 400s, arguments arose among Byzantine Christians. Church leaders in Constantinople and Alexandria did not agree on how to explain Christianity. The Egyptian church broke with the Byzantine church, and a new, Egyptian form of Christianity was born. Its followers were called Copts, from the Greek name for Egyptians. The Copts formed a new written language, Coptic, made up of Egyptian words spelled in Greek letters.

Most Egyptians might be Coptic Christians today, if Egypt had not been invaded yet again. In A.D. 639, however, the Muslim Arabs arrived. ■

■ *How did Christianity affect Egypt?*

REVIEW

1. **FOCUS** How did the Greeks, the Romans, and the Byzantines affect Egyptian culture?
2. **CULTURE** Who were the *fellahin*?
3. **CULTURE** Explain how Roman rule affected the Alexandrian Jews.
4. **RELIGION** What is the Coptic language?
5. **CRITICAL THINKING** In your opinion, why did Greek rulers of Egypt have themselves crowned as pharaohs?
6. **WRITING ACTIVITY** Pretend you are Cleopatra VII. You have just received a message from Rome demanding the surrender of Egypt. Draft a reply to the emperor.

POLITICAL SYSTEMS

Map and Globe Skills

To help students grasp the immensity of the Roman Empire, have them refer to the map on page 230. Using the scale provided, ask students to estimate in square miles the area of the Roman Empire, including the Mediterranean Sea. *(About 5,300,000 square miles)* Point out that the United States and China are both about 3,700,000 square miles in area. Discuss the difficulties the Romans might have had in controlling such a vast empire or in promoting loyalty in and among the various regions.

■ *For the first time in about 3,000 years, Egyptians changed their religion, adopting Christianity. Differing beliefs caused a split between Byzantine and Egyptian Christians. Egyptian Christians also developed the new Coptic language.*

CLOSE

Read the Thinking Focus aloud, and then copy the structure of the Graphic Overview on the chalkboard. Ask students to volunteer ideas and information from the lesson to fill in the headings and details for the structure.

Answers to Review Questions

1. The Greeks built Alexandria and made it a great center of learning. The Romans improved Egypt's infrastructure, helping Egypt to grow and transport more food. A religious split under Byzantine rule led to the founding of the Coptic church.
2. The *fellahin* were Egypt's peasant farmers, who lived along the Nile.
3. The Romans discriminated against Jews. When the Jews of Alexandria rose up in protest, Rome's brutal response nearly destroyed their community.
4. It is a language developed by early Christian Egyptians that was made up of Egyptian words spelled in Greek letters.
5. Possible answers: The Greeks respected Egypt's traditions and wanted to continue them; the Greeks wanted to gain favor among the Egyptians.
6. Students' replies might indicate defiance toward Rome and might mention the long, proud history of Ptolemaic rule in Egypt.

Homework Options

Have students draw a scene that shows some aspect of Alexandria under Greek rule. Scenes might include Alexander or Cleopatra honoring Egyptian Gods, scholars studying in the great library or advising Ptolemaic rulers, or ships being guided into harbor by the Pharos lighthouse.

Study Guide: page 39

INTRODUCE

Refer students to the timeline on page 226. Ask them to locate the date when Arab Muslim forces entered Egypt. *(A.D. 639)* Remind students that Egypt was then a province of the Byzantine Empire and that most of its inhabitants were Christian. Invite students to speculate as to why the Arab Muslims wanted to conquer Egypt. *(Students may recall from Chapter 8 that followers of Muhammad wanted to spread Islam. Like the Romans and Byzantines, the Arabs may also have wanted to control Egypt's trade routes and grain supplies.)* Ask students to read the Thinking Focus and then read the lesson to find out how Egypt became an Islamic nation.

Key Terms

Vocabulary Strategies: T36–T37

sultan—a Turkish ruler

isthmus—a narrow strip of land that connects two larger land masses

B.C. A.D.
500 500 639 TODAY

LESSON 2

Islamic Egypt

THINKING FOCUS

How did Egypt become an Islamic nation?

Key Terms

- sultan
- isthmus

It is the metropolis of the universe, the garden of the world, the nest of the human species. . . . [It is] the glory of Islam and the orchard of the world.

These words are from the Arab historian Ibn Khaldun *(IHB uhn kal DOON)*. The place he described was a city in the Egyptian desert, al-Qahirah *(ahl KUH hee ruh)*. We know it as Cairo *(KY roh)*.

According to one legend, the birth of Cairo happened this way: In A.D. 969 a group of Shiite Muslims prepared to break ground for a new city. They hired astrologers to tell them when the digging should begin. Workers raised their shovels. The astrologers watched the sky. When the moment arrived, they would give the signal to begin by pulling on a bell rope.

The planet Mars rose in the sky, but before the astrologers could give the signal, a raven landed on the rope and jingled the bells. The new city was named al-Qahirah, Arabic for Mars the victorious.

Whatever the true story of Cairo's founding, the city quickly grew. By the 1300s, Cairo was the greatest city in all of Africa, Europe, and Southwest Asia.

How Do We Know?

CULTURE *The writings of Ibn Khaldun (1332–1406) give a picture of how people lived in old Cairo. An Arabian born in Tunis, Ibn Khaldun used aspects of culture, such as geography and family ties, to understand societies of the past. Before settling in Cairo, he advised rulers in North Africa and Spain.*

Arab Rule

The Arab Muslims came to Egypt in A.D. 639, when the Byzantines ruled. Like Alexander the Great, the Arabs entered Egypt with little trouble. The Byzantine Empire was too weak to fight. In addition, Egyptian Christians still disliked the Byzantines because of the split with the church at Constantinople.

Arab rule was fairly mild. The Arab ruler, Caliph Umar, did not allow Muslims to take Egyptian land. Instead, Egypt had to pay tribute. "Tribute is better than booty [stolen goods]," Umar said. "It lasts longer."

The Arabs also demanded tribute from Egypt's ancient neighbor, Nubia (see Chapter 4). A treaty made during the mid-600s required Nubia, which

Objectives

1. Describe how Arab rule shaped Egypt's culture.
2. Analyze the effects of Ottoman rule on Egypt.
3. Describe the challenges that have faced Egypt in the period of self-rule.

Graphic Overview

Arab Rule	→	Ottoman Rule	→	Self-Rule
• new culture • new foods • Islam • mild rule • tribute		• Turks, not Arabs • Muslim • sultans ruled • small influences • architecture		• conflict with Israel • Nasser a hero • focus on Arab, African roots • Islamic rule

was then largely Christian, to do business with Muslim traders, build a mosque, and send 360 slaves to Cairo each year. Yet the treaty also required Cairo to send yearly gifts of food, horses, and cloth to Nubia.

An Islamic Nation

Like Egypt's Greek and Roman rulers, the Arabs allowed the Egyptians to worship as they chose. Although many Egyptians remained Christians, Egypt slowly became an Islamic nation.

The message of Islam, its five basic duties, and the caring community that it provided appealed to the people of the Nile. The practices of Islam were, in some respects, familiar. Like the beliefs of the ancient Egyptian religion and of Christianity, Islam gave Egyptians hope even when the Nile failed. It was the hope of a paradise that worshipers would enter after death.

The Rise of Cairo

Besides a new religion, the Arabs brought Egypt a new culture. Shortly after arriving in Egypt, they built a new capital called al-Fustat *(ahl FUH staht)* on the banks of the Nile. Later a newer capital was built at a site not far from al-Fustat. This new capital was Cairo.

The map on page 685 of the Atlas shows why the Arabs moved the capital from Alexandria. This capital of the Ptolemies bordered the Mediterranean Sea. The Greeks and Romans who had ruled Egypt from Alexandria looked across the sea, toward their homelands in Greece and Italy. The Arabs had little use for a capital that had to be defended from attack by sea. From Cairo the Arabs' ties lay southeast, toward the Muslim holy city of Mecca.

Across Time & Space

An earthquake that hit Cairo on October 12, 1992, did a great deal of damage to the city's modern buildings. The pyramids and Sphinx outside the city fared better. The 40-second quake wiped out many older homes and killed hundreds of people.

The Muslim ruler Saladin built this fortress, the Citadel of Cairo, to protect Egypt from Christian invaders.

DEVELOP

Tell students that this lesson explores how Egypt changed over a span of nearly 1,350 years—from A.D. 639 until the 1980s—under the rule of two foreign Muslim powers and finally under self-rule. Remind students of Egypt's long history of foreign rule, and ask them to predict what aspects of Egyptian life would undergo the greatest changes. Have students keep track of the events that affected Egypt during each period of rule by filling in the Graphic Overview as they read the lesson.

BELIEF SYSTEMS

Critical Thinking

Explain that the Muslim Arabs gave the Coptic Christians of Egypt a choice between adopting Islam as their religion or keeping their own religion and paying a tax. Many Egyptians chose to remain Christian; others converted willingly. Over centuries of Arab rule, however, taxation and discrimination became oppressive, and most Copts converted to Islam. Ask students why the Muslim Arabs might have been so tolerant at first. *(Tolerance might encourage cooperation rather than resistance.)*

Access Strategy

Tell students that the building in which they are sitting has a story to tell, a history. Have students begin to reveal that story by discussing the building's age and design and the methods and materials that were used to build it. Then invite students to look at the photograph of the Citadel of Cairo on this page. Point out that this fortress tells a story in stone of some of Egypt's long history.

Arab Muslims built the Citadel's walls in the 1100s—about 500 years after conquering Egypt—from some of the same stone blocks the Egyptians had used in their pyramids over 3,000 years before. The domed mosque within the walls is also a Muslim structure; it was built by Ottoman Muslims in the 1800s, about 300 years after they conquered Egypt. As students read the lesson, they should look for other examples of how these two groups of Muslim conquerors affected Egypt and its people.

Access Activity

Bring in a collection of books that illustrate Roman and Muslim architecture. Ask students to describe similarities and differences in the two styles and in the materials used for construction. Have them pay particular attention to the use of arches and to their various shapes.

■ *In A.D. 969 the Arabs built a new capital, Cairo. It became a center of trade with Europe and Asia, and its university became the center of Islamic learning.*

GEOGRAPHY

Critical Thinking

Remind students that Egypt's capital had been moved in the past to suit the needs of foreign rulers. Refer students to the map on this page. Ask them to speculate why the Ottomans kept Egypt's capital at Cairo, rather than moving it to some other site. *(The Muslim Ottomans' economic and religious interests were likely well served by Cairo's status as a center of trade and Islamic culture.)*

BELIEF SYSTEMS

Critical Thinking

Tell students that when Suleiman I, son of the sultan who conquered Egypt, became sultan in 1520, he was greeted by his subjects, over whom he held absolute power, with the ritual chant: "Be not proud, my sultan. God is greater than you." Ask students what this reveals about Ottoman tradition. *(Belief in the supremacy of God; tradition of humbling the ruler by reminding him of the limits of his power)*

■ *Find facts to support this statement: Under Arab rule, the center of Egyptian culture shifted from Alexandria to Cairo.*

Cairo grew busy and famous. Its bazaars were filled with peddlers selling copper pots and silk. Sugar cane from Egypt and coffee, a new beverage in great demand from neighboring Yemen, were shipped from Cairo to markets in Europe and Asia.

Cairo's al-Azhar University became the center of Islamic learning. Muslims, Jews, and Christians lived side by side in the growing city. ■

Ottoman Rule

Arab dynasties brought a Muslim culture that shapes Egyptian life to this day. While Christianity had little effect on Egypt's language or family life, Muslim rule brought dramatic change. Most Egyptians became Muslims. Arabic replaced Coptic as Egypt's written and spoken language. The Arabs also brought new foods and clothing.

New Muslim Leaders

Arab rule lasted nearly 900 years. Then Egypt's foreign rulers changed again. An Asian people, the Turks, under the command of Selim I, invaded Egypt in 1517. Selim, like many other Turkish rulers, was called a **sultan.** The sultan ruled the vast Ottoman Empire (see the map below).

Although the Ottoman Turks were Muslims, they were not Arab. They had their own culture, clothing, and language. Turkish culture did not replace Arab culture in Egypt. Instead, during the roughly 350-year rule, the Turks changed Egypt in small ways. One example is Cairo's Ottoman-style mosques and houses with beautifully carved balconies.

Ottoman control of Egypt weakened in 1805, when the sultan named a new governor of Egypt. His name was Muhammad Ali.

Expansion of the Ottoman Empire

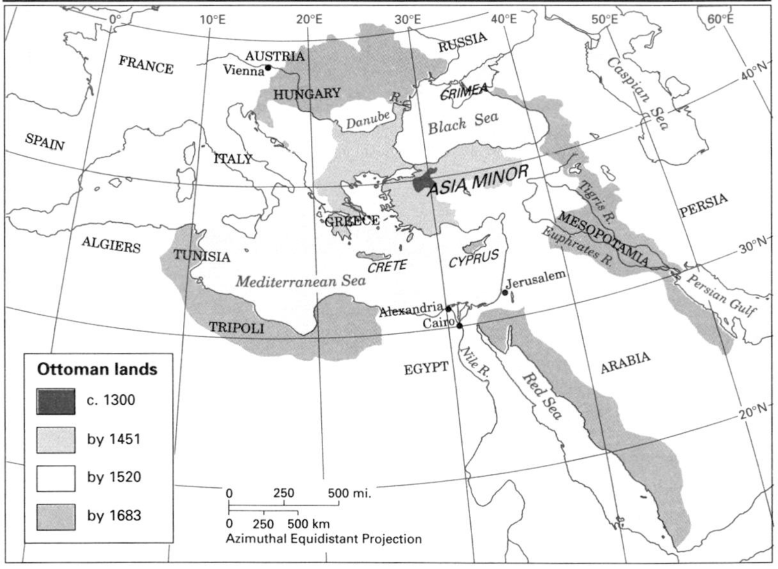
0°
10°E
20°E
30°E
40°E
50°E
60°E
40°N
30°N
20°N
FRANCE
AUSTRIA
Vienna
HUNGARY
RUSSIA
CRIMEA
Danube R.
Black Sea
Caspian Sea
SPAIN
ITALY
ASIA MINOR
GREECE
PERSIA
Tigris R.
MESOPOTAMIA
Euphrates R.
ALGIERS
TUNISIA
CRETE
CYPRUS
Mediterranean Sea
Jerusalem
Persian Gulf
TRIPOLI
Alexandria
Cairo
EGYPT
Nile R.
Red Sea
ARABIA
Ottoman lands
c. 1300
by 1451
by 1520
by 1683
0 250 500 mi.
0 250 500 km
Azimuthal Equidistant Projection

➤ *The Ottoman Empire was named after the empire's founder. On the map, locate the region the Ottomans came from. Find the size of the empire by the year 1520, when it included Egypt.*

Study Skills

One small change the Ottomans brought to Egypt was the *tarboosh,* Egyptian Arabic for "sweating cap." Have students research the *tarboosh* and find out what it looked like, who wore it, and why "sweating cap" was such an apt name for it. *(Worn mainly by Muslim men in the Mediterranean, it was made of felt or cloth and was tightly fitting.)*

Historical Context

The Arab rulers who controlled Egypt from 1171 to 1260 used slaves called Mamelukes—Arabic for "possessed ones"—as bodyguards and soldiers. The Mamelukes were mainly Turks and Circassians from the eastern shores of the Baltic Sea whom the Arabs had bought or kidnapped as children, then raised as Muslims in comfortable—even luxurious—surroundings. After rigorous training in fighting techniques, many rose to high positions in the army. In 1260 the Mamelukes seized power from their Arab masters and took control of Egypt, which they ruled for the next 250 years. Although ruthless, they promoted the development of art and architecture.

The Mameluke dynasty declined in the late 1400s. European explorers had found a sea route to India and Asia, which enabled them to bypass the overland trade routes controlled by Egypt's rulers. This economic loss weakened Mameluke rule, and in 1517 Ottoman Turks seized control of Egypt.

Ali's Vision

Muhammad Ali is often called the founder of modern Egypt. A great admirer of European countries, he wanted Egypt to become rich and modern.

To reach his goal, Muhammad Ali built ships, canals, and harbors. He founded schools for general and medical education. He hired French experts to teach Egyptians new military techniques. His grandson, Ismail, went even further. "My country is no longer in Africa," Ismail declared, "we now form part of Europe."

Muhammad Ali and his grandson helped Egypt's economy grow. Yet the *fellahin* grew poorer than ever. Muhammad Ali and his family owned much of Egypt's land and industries. The *fellahin* had to grow mostly tobacco, cotton, and other crops to sell on the world market, rather than growing food. ■

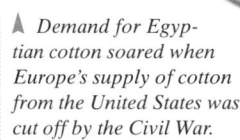

▲ *Demand for Egyptian cotton soared when Europe's supply of cotton from the United States was cut off by the Civil War.*

■ *What was Muhammad Ali's goal, and how did he try to reach that goal?*

The Suez Canal

Muhammad Ali's descendants dreamed of a canal that would join the Red Sea and the Mediterranean Sea. The pharaohs of ancient Egypt had made several attempts to link these bodies of water. Yet their efforts did not last. Desert sands blew into the canal and clogged it. In the mid-1800s, however, there were new reasons to solve these problems.

Building the Canal

By this time, Great Britain had a thriving trade with India. Without a canal, British ships had to make a long journey around the continent of Africa. A canal through the Isthmus of Suez would cut 6,000 miles from the trip. An **isthmus** *(IHS muhs)* is a thin strip of land connecting two larger pieces of land.

Egypt's rulers saw that there was money to be made in a new shipping route through the isthmus. France, hoping to compete with England for world trade, wanted the canal dug as well. A French company made a deal with Egypt to build the Suez Canal.

Britain Seeks Control

The canal opened in 1869. Royalty from all over Europe came to celebrate. To house his guests, the Egyptian ruler, Ismail, built the grand Abdin *(ahb deen)* Palace in Cairo. He adorned Egypt's capital in European style, with wide streets and flowering gardens.

▼ *After taking power in 1952, President Gamal Abdel Nasser told a crowd, "The canal will be run by Egyptians, Egyptians, Egyptians!" Nasser kept his promise. He seized control of the Suez Canal from the British in 1956.*

■ *Muhammad Ali's goal was to make Egypt wealthy and modern, like the nations of Europe. He built new shipping facilities, founded schools, and modern-*

CULTURE

Critical Thinking

Tell students that in 1798 the French invaded Egypt in order to gain control of its land route to India. The next year a French soldier found a tablet, inscribed in three languages, near the Rosetta branch of the Nile. The Rosetta stone revealed the mysteries of ancient Egypt's hieroglyphic writings, as described in Chapter 4. Why was this find significant? *(People could learn what ancient Egyptians had to say about their own culture.)* The British and Turks drove the French from Egypt in 1801, but Western interest in Egypt had been awakened.

Historical Context

In 1869, while the Suez Canal was being completed in Egypt, another major feat of engineering and construction was also reaching completion thousands of miles away in the United States. There, on May 10, 1869, the world's first transcontinental railroad was completed. Tracks laid by workers for the Central Pacific and Union Pacific railroads met in Promontory, Utah, where a golden spike was driven to mark the historic juncture. Both projects—the transcontinental railroad and the Suez Canal—were beneficiaries of a revolution in transportation and technology that was then sweeping Europe and the United States, making long-distance trade more efficient and economical.

Map and Globe Skills

Ask students to look at the map of Africa on page 685. Why was the Suez Canal so important to Egypt's economy? *(Egypt could profit from foreign shipping through the canal; the canal enabled Egyptian goods to reach world markets prior to the age of air transportation.)*

■ *The location of the Suez Canal made it valuable. By joining the Red Sea and the Mediterranean Sea, the canal cut 6,000 miles off the voyage from Europe to India.*

HISTORY

Social Participation

Throughout World War II, Egypt remained under British occupation and control, despite the fact that Britain technically granted Egypt its independence in 1922. Meanwhile, descendants of the Ottoman line still held the throne. Ask students to divide into two groups: the British, who wanted to protect their investment and interests in the Suez Canal; and the Egyptians, who wanted to control their own land. Have the two groups hold a summit conference to reach an agreement on how the canal should be run.

■ *What made the Suez Canal so valuable?*

Ismail's heavy spending came just at the time when the price of Egyptian cotton plunged. In addition, Egypt had gone deeply into debt to pay for the Suez Canal. Ismail got large loans from European banks, but he ran out of money to repay them. Egypt had to sell its share of the canal to Great Britain.

The British government sent soldiers into Egypt, saying it was concerned for its property. Yet the move began a new period of foreign control in Egypt. ■

Egyptians Rule Egypt

In the 1930s Great Britain still controlled Egypt. A descendant of Muhammad Ali, King Farouk, held the throne. Discontent with foreign leaders was growing. In 1935 a 17-year-old Egyptian, Gamal Abdel Nasser *(NAS uhr)* wrote to a friend that Egypt was in a state of "hopeless despair."

> Who can remove this feeling? The Egyptian Government is based on corruption and favours. . . . [W]here is . . . the man to rebuild the country so that the weak and humiliated Egyptian people can rise again and live as free and independent men?

As a student at Egypt's Royal Military Academy, Nasser found people who shared his concern. Many Egyptians wanted to be rid of foreign control.

▼ *Shepheard's Hotel in Cairo was a symbol of the European life of luxury that most Egyptians could never hope to have. On January 26, 1952, Egyptians entered the old hotel and set it afire.*

Egyptians Rebel

King Farouk was part of the problem. Egypt's ruler spent most of his time entertaining Europeans in his two palaces or on one of his many yachts. Egyptians resented the king's free-spending ways.

British soldiers protected Farouk. In 1951 the British suppressed four uprisings of *fellahin*—one at the king's country home. In January 1952 an angry crowd set fire to the European section of Cairo. King Farouk watched from Abdin Palace as Cairo burned. Six months later a group of young army officers, led by Nasser, forced Farouk to flee Egypt on his yacht.

Nasser became the nation's new leader. After more than 2,000 years of foreign control, an Egyptian ruled Egypt once again.

War Burdens Egypt

Farouk left Egypt with a warning for Nasser. "Your task will be difficult," he said. "It is not easy to govern Egypt." Farouk was right. President Nasser and his successor, Anwar Sadat *(suh DAHT)*, faced great challenges.

Among them was a costly conflict with Israel. Israel had become a nation in 1948. It had been created by the United Nations as a

Critical Thinking

Ask students to compare the lifestyle of the *fellahin* with the lifestyle of King Farouk and to list the differences on a chart. *(Answers should show an understanding of the disparity between the poverty of the* fellahin *and the extravagance of the royalty whom they worked to support.)*

Making a Bulletin Board

Suggest that students go through recent newspapers and magazines to find news articles about Egypt. They can share their articles with the class. Then they can create an "Egypt in the News" bulletin board.

Research

Ask students to investigate the role of women in Egypt's present-day culture. Have students describe their findings in a one- or two-page report.

PEACE
PAIX

Jewish state. Egypt and other Arab nations regarded the land that Israel occupied as Arab land. From 1948 to 1973, Israel and Arab nations fought a series of wars in which Egypt lost heavily. By the mid-1970s, President Sadat believed that Egypt would run out of money if it did not make peace.

Israel wanted peace, too. The cost of war, in money and lives, was high. As Sadat's wife, Jihan, wrote to a grieving Israeli woman: "In every soldier who fell in the War . . . there is our son and a part of our soul."

With the help of U.S. President Jimmy Carter, Sadat and Israel's prime minister, Menachem Begin, held peace talks. They signed a peace agreement at Camp David, Maryland, on March 26, 1979. For their efforts, Sadat and Begin won the Nobel Peace Prize.

Questions of Religion and Law

Nasser and the leaders who followed him have tried to help Egypt to support itself. Unlike Ismail, who wanted to make Egypt a part of Europe, they emphasize Egypt's African and Arab heritage.

Today, cultural changes in Egypt are coming not from outside the country, but from inside. Some Egyptians want to do away with their country's European-style democracy. They seek to form a government based on Islamic law, like the government of Iran (Chapter 9).

In the 1970s President Sadat, a Muslim, tried to quiet the growing demand for a new government—a move that angered some Islamic groups. They were further upset when he made peace with Israel. On October 6, 1981, the world was shocked when a member of a Muslim group shot and killed Sadat.

Questions about Egypt's future continue under Sadat's successor, Hosni Mubarak. Many younger people are pushing for a return to Islamic government. College students in Alexandria, for instance, forced their school to make separate classes for men and women.

Changes in government and religion have swept through Egypt many times in the last 2,000 years. Many people wonder if another wave of change is on the way. ■

▲ *Egypt gave the plaque on the left to Israel to celebrate the peace agreement. Shown above, left to right, are Sadat, Carter, and Begin, clasping hands.*

■ *How did Egyptian rulers change Egypt?*

REVIEW

1. **FOCUS** How did Egypt become an Islamic nation?
2. **POLITICAL SYSTEMS** Characterize Arab rule of Egypt and of Nubia.
3. **ECONOMICS** What effect did Ismail have on Egypt?
4. **HISTORY** Why did Egyptians want control of Egypt, and how did they gain control?
5. **CRITICAL THINKING** Contrast the goals of Egyptian leaders Muhammad Ali and Gamal Abdel Nasser.
6. **ACTIVITY** Using the map in the Atlas on page 679, draw a map to show how European ships traveled to India before and after the Suez Canal was built.

CULTURE

Visual Learning

Refer students to the photograph on this page showing the plaque given to Israel by Egypt. Ask them to evaluate its purpose and message and suggest why birds and a woman are shown. *(The plaque commemorates the agreement between Egypt and Israel, and its message is peace. The woman and the doves symbolize peace.)* Have students compare this plaque with the stele on page 228. What elements do the two have in common? *(Both are memorials, have messages written in more than one language, and show a human figure with animal symbols.)*

■ *Egyptian leaders led Egypt into wars—then peace—with Israel, emphasized Egypt's Arab and African heritage, and resisted moves to change Egypt from a democracy to a government based on Islamic law.*

CLOSE

Have students summarize what they have learned by answering the Thinking Focus. As a reteaching activity, let students point out on a wall map the location of Egypt, the place of origin of the Arab Muslims, and the areas that made up the Ottoman Empire.

Answers to Review Questions

1. Arabs brought Islam to Egypt in A.D. 639. Islam appealed to many Egyptians.
2. The Arabs required tribute from both Nubia and Egypt, but in Nubia they provided gifts in return.
3. He helped build up Cairo in a European style but put Egypt into debt. Egypt had to sell its share of the Suez Canal.
4. The extravagance of foreign rulers did not benefit most Egyptians. Egyptians burned Cairo's European section, and Egyptian army officers later ousted King Farouk.
5. Muhammad Ali wanted Egypt to be a European-style nation, run by his family. Nasser embraced Egypt's African-Arab roots and the goal of self-rule.
6. The "before" route: European ships had to sail south around Africa. The "after" route: Ships passed from the Mediterranean Sea through the Suez Canal to the Red Sea, then through the Gulf of Aden to the Indian Ocean.

Homework Options

Have students design a traffic corridor (street, bridge, tunnel, and so on) that would serve as a shortcut from their neighborhood to their school. They should draw a diagram of the area and estimate the travel time or distance their shortcut would save.

Study Guide: page 40

UNDERSTANDING HISTORICAL EVIDENCE

This skills feature uses a quotation from the autobiography of Jihan Sadat, wife of Egypt's late president Anwar Sadat, to help students distinguish between primary and secondary sources and evaluate their use in understanding history.

HISTORY

Critical Thinking

Explain to students that a source can sometimes serve as both a primary and a secondary source of facts—but usually not about the same person or event. For example, the quotation on this page could be used as a secondary source of facts about the Camp David meeting. Why couldn't it serve as a primary source for that event? *(The writer was not present at the meeting.)* Why could the quotation serve as a primary source of facts about Anwar Sadat? *(He spoke directly to the writer about his thoughts and feelings.)* Have students discuss how a writer's bias with regard to a subject could affect the accuracy of primary and secondary sources.

UNDERSTANDING HISTORICAL EVIDENCE

Evaluating Sources

Here's Why

To learn about the past, we use records and accounts of events left behind. You read in Lesson 2 that in 1978, U.S. President Jimmy Carter invited Egyptian president Anwar Sadat and Israeli prime minister Menachem Begin to Camp David for peace talks. Suppose you want to explore Sadat's feelings and thoughts during those difficult talks. Where would you begin?

Hundreds of books, encyclopedia articles, and newspaper reports have been written about Sadat. Therefore, you must be able to evaluate the sources available to you.

Here's How

First, decide whether you want to get your information from a primary source or a secondary source. To tell if a source is primary or secondary, see if it meets the requirements described below.

To figure out if the source meets the description of a primary or a secondary source, you will need to know the answers to these questions: Who wrote it? When was it produced?

With what you now know about primary and secondary sources, which might you choose to find out about Sadat? Remember, you're trying to find information on his thoughts and feelings during the Camp David talks.

You might try an encyclopedia, but such information is secondary—a secondhand source. Instead, you might try a source such as this:

Every night I called Anwar from Paris. And every night his news was more discouraging. President Carter was meeting . . . with my husband and Begin, trying to [solve] their broad differences. . . .

"You sound so tired, Anwar," I said to my husband two days later. I could hear his sigh all the way across the ocean. "It is exhausting to have to fight so hard for peace," he replied.

The writer is Sadat's wife, Jihan. Her book *A Woman of Egypt* was written nine years after the Camp David meetings. Does her writing qualify as a primary source?

Jihan Sadat's account is indeed a primary source of facts about her husband's experiences. It relates her direct discussion with him—even if only by telephone. Her story seems to be based on her own notes or memories.

A few final questions will help you judge the quality of both primary and secondary sources: What is the purpose of the account—to inform, to describe, or to persuade? Does the writer's background or viewpoint affect the accuracy of the account?

Primary Source

- recorded by someone who participated in the event or who was an eyewitness to it
- recorded at the time of the event, or based on memories or notes from the time of the event

Secondary Source

- uses primary sources for information

Try It

Would you use Jihan Sadat's book as your only source for a report on the Camp David meetings? Why or why not?

Apply It

The newspapers and books of today are sources that people of the future will use to learn about our times. Find three sources of information about a recent U.S. President. At least one source should be a primary source. Then list what type of information you might look for in each source. Explain your reasoning.

Objectives

1. Distinguish between primary and secondary sources. (Study Skills 1)
2. Evaluate the use of primary and secondary sources as authorities on people and events. (Critical Thinking 2)

Answers to Try It

No, you should not use Jihan Sadat's book as the only source for the report. Although it is a primary source of information about Anwar Sadat's experiences, it would not be a primary source of information about what went on in the talks. The best sources might include primary sources such as the writings of the leaders who participated or of other officials who were present. Other good sources would be secondary sources such as encyclopedia articles.

Answers to Apply It

Students' responses should demonstrate a knowledge of the difference between primary and secondary sources. Students should understand that primary sources, which are firsthand, often provide personal reactions and other details that secondary sources might not provide.

B.C. A.D.
500
500
1000
1500
1961 TODAY

L E S S O N 3

A Trip Down the Nile

Every summer, from prehistoric times to modern times, Egyptians watched for the yearly appearance of the star Sirius in the sky. Soon after, they knew, the Nile would flood its banks, providing water for the next year's crop—but how much water?

Low floods meant famine. High floods swept away crops, soil, and the mud-brick homes of the *fellahin.* Egypt, "the gift of the Nile," was at the mercy of the river.

Faced with a growing population that needed more farmland to feed itself, Egypt's President Nasser saw only one answer. He ordered a dam to be built on the Nile at the town of Aswan, near the Nile's First Cataract.

A dam had been built there before, but the new one—started in 1961 and completed in 1970—was much larger. The Aswan High Dam stretched more than two miles across and rose to 364 feet. The huge wall, placed in the river's path, would have amazed even the ancient King Khufu. The dam is 17 times the size of his Great Pyramid.

The dam worked like a giant faucet, allowing a controlled amount of water to flow north to the delta. Without the threat of floods, more land could be irrigated and farmed. Hydroelectricity made by the dam provided power for much of Egypt.

In a land slow to change, the Aswan High Dam brought as much change to Egypt as had all the foreigners who governed it. Like a pebble dropped into a pond, the effects of the dam rippled down the Nile Valley.

THINKING FOCUS

Describe how modern changes are affecting life along the Nile.

Key Terms

- felucca
- silt

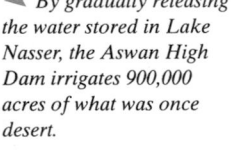

◄ *By gradually releasing the water stored in Lake Nasser, the Aswan High Dam irrigates 900,000 acres of what was once desert.*

INTRODUCE

Ask students to recall what they have already learned about the Nile. *(Students may recall from Chapter 4 and from previous lessons that the Nile is the longest river in the world and that its yearly floods produced fertile farmland for the people of Egypt.)* Have students read the lesson title and the Thinking Focus. Ask them to predict what changes might be affecting life along the Nile today. Then students can read the lesson to discover what these changes are and how they affect life along this great river.

Key Terms

Vocabulary Strategies: T36–T37

felucca—a traditional Egyptian sailboat

silt—particles of soil that are carried and deposited by rivers

Graphic Overview

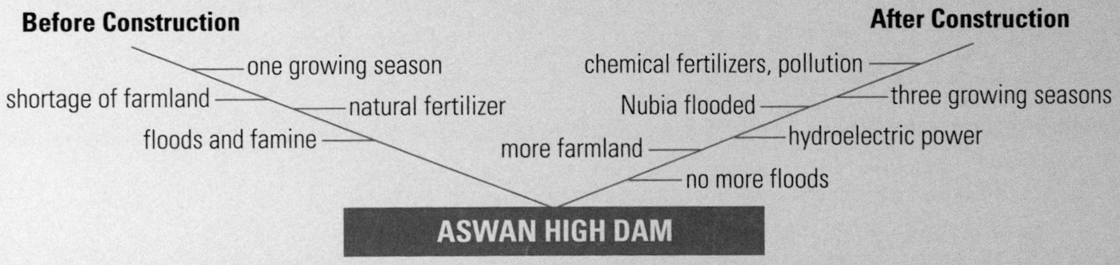
Before Construction
one growing season
shortage of farmland
natural fertilizer
floods and famine
After Construction
chemical fertilizers, pollution
Nubia flooded
three growing seasons
hydroelectric power
more farmland
no more floods
ASWAN HIGH DAM

Objectives

1. Explain how the Aswan High Dam is changing life along the Nile.
2. Contrast old traditions and new trends in Egyptian life.

DEVELOP

Tell students that this lesson compares life along the Nile River before and after the building of the Aswan High Dam. Draw the basic structure of the Graphic Overview on the chalkboard and add the major headings. Ask students to copy it on their own paper and fill in details about the lesson as they read.

GEOGRAPHY

Visual Learning

Refer students to the map on this page. Explain that there is an average of only one person per square mile living in Egypt's desert areas, whereas over 2,500 people are packed into each square mile along the Nile and its delta. Some sources say that up to 99 percent of all Egyptians live along the Nile. Ask students why so many people would live in such a small area. *(They need a reliable supply of water for daily living and for growing crops. In Egypt, only the Nile can meet these needs on the scale required for large numbers of people, so most Egyptians must live crowded along its banks.)*

The Upper Nile

If you traveled the length of Egypt's Nile, you'd find that the dam's effects, both helpful and harmful, have reached into every city, every village, every family. The dam is one of many new changes that have altered Egyptian life forever.

Nubia

To see the effects of the dam, you might start by flying over the region just south of it. The region is now part of Egypt, but it was once the land of Nubia (see Chapter 4). Today, the land has vanished under Lake Nasser. This artificial lake is a reservoir, or body of stored water, which is held back by the dam. The 2,000-square-mile Lake Nasser is one of the world's largest reservoirs.

As water rose behind the dam, it threatened Nubia's ancient monuments. A Closer Look at the rescue of Abu Simbel, on page 241, shows how one historic treasure was saved in the nick of time.

Modern descendants of the ancient Nubians were greatly affected by the dam. Thousands had to leave their homes and move north. Some carried sacks of Nubian soil with them to their new homes.

Aswan

If you head north, as the Nubians did, you come to the town of Aswan. Here, in the shadow of the dam, you can't help but think of how fast Egypt is changing. New hotels look out over palm trees, sand dunes, shimmering water, and the rocks of the First Cataract.

Yet much of Aswan is unchanged. As in ancient days, goods such as animal skins, baskets, and pottery from central Africa make their way to the shops of Aswan.

From Aswan you decide to journey north on an Egyptian sailboat called a **felucca**. Its white sail blows in the wind as you float down the Nile, which now flows quietly year round. In the distance you see the villages where about 60,000 Nubians were relocated after Lake Nasser swallowed their homes.

Along the riverbank, reeds and lilies grow, but the papyrus plant, from which Egyptians once made

About 99 percent of Egypt's population lives along the Nile. As you can see from the map, the population is very concentrated. In fact, the population density is one of the highest in the world. Many Egyptians are farmers, like the man shown to the right, who still use ancient methods of planting and harvesting.

Egypt: Population, 1990

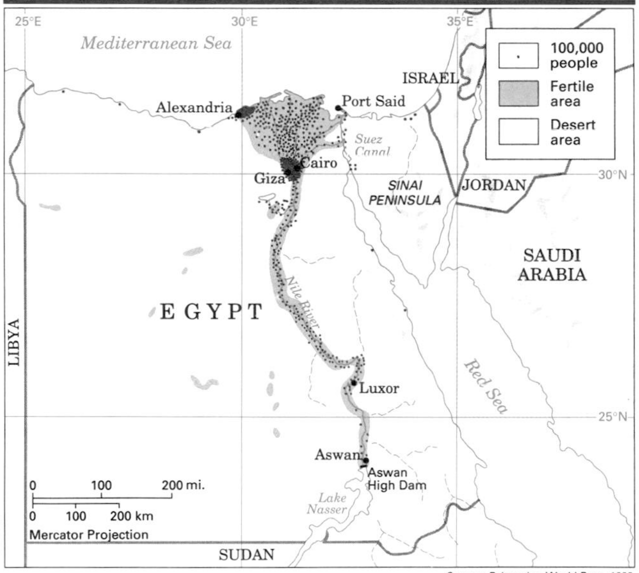

25°E
30°E
35°E
Mediterranean Sea
100,000 people
Fertile area
Desert area
ISRAEL
Port Said
Alexandria
Suez Canal
Cairo
Giza
SINAI PENINSULA
JORDAN
30°N
SAUDI ARABIA
EGYPT
Nile River
LIBYA
Luxor
Red Sea
25°N
Aswan
Aswan High Dam
Lake Nasser
0 100 200 mi.
0 100 200 km
Mercator Projection
SUDAN

Source: Britannica World Data, 1992

Access Activity

To help students visualize the width of the Aswan High Dam, have them identify on a map of their town or city an area that spans a distance of about two miles. Explain that this is roughly the width of the Aswan High Dam.

Access Strategy

Ask students if they have ever experienced a flood firsthand or seen news reports of a flood on television. Ask them to discuss the circumstances surrounding the flood. Was it a regular occurrence that people expected, or were they unprepared for it? What effects did it have on people, land, and property? Explain that the people of Egypt who lived near the Nile depended on yearly floods to provide them with water for living and for growing food. Tell students that in this lesson they will learn about how Egypt tamed the Nile's floods and how that has changed their lives in unexpected ways.

A CLOSER LOOK

The Rescue of Abu Simbel

Ramesses II built monuments along the Nile to show his power over Nubia. For 3,000 years, huge statues of the pharaoh and his family marked the entrances to two temples at Abu Simbel. In the 1960s, however, Abu Simbel was in danger. Nile waters backed up by the Aswan High Dam would soon submerge the site. Engineers from around the world joined Egyptians to move the ancient monuments to a safe place.

Like a giant puzzle, the fragile sandstone temples were cut into more than 1,000 blocks. Some blocks were as heavy as 18 automobiles.

The 21-ton face of Ramesses begins the climb to safety. The entire statue stands 67 feet tall.

Sandstone fragments

The new site is shown in this drawing. The temples are higher and set back from the water's edge. The photograph below was taken before Abu Simbel was moved.

Note: You may want to use this Closer Look as an extension to the discussion of the Aswan High Dam on page 240.

CULTURE

Visual Learning

Have students look closely at the blocks that made up the faces of the statues. Ask them to imagine reassembling all the pieces accurately and to suggest how this could be done. *(By numbering each piece, drawing diagrams of the statues with their numbered pieces, then reassembling the statues according to the numbered diagrams)*

More About the Rescue of Abu Simbel The two temples of Abu Simbel, built in the 1200s B.C., were relocated at a cost of about $40 million, with some 50 countries contributing money and resources to the project. Originally the temples had been carved into a mountainside. Four 67-foot statues of a seated Ramesses II guarded the Great Temple. Four more statues of Ramesses II and two of his wife, Queen Nefertari, stood guard at the entrance of the Small Temple.

A UNESCO fund-raising operation saved another set of temples and monuments on the island of Philae in Upper Egypt. These were removed to another area stone by stone—some 50,000 original blocks.

Writing a Poem

Have students imagine that they have been asked by the president of Egypt to write a poem honoring the rescue project at Abu Simbel. Encourage students to be creative in their approaches. For example, they may want to tie this modern-day feat of engineering to the efforts that went into building the monuments about 3,000 years ago. If they need to, students can do research on the temples and on the reign of Ramesses II and Queen Nefertari.

Making a Model

Have groups of students find pictures of the temples of Abu Simbel and work together to create a model of them. In addition, suggest that students try to include a model of the site on which Abu Simbel now stands.

Critical Thinking

The text says that Ramesses II built the monuments at Abu Simbel to show his power over Nubia. In what ways did this undertaking show his power? *(The vastness of the project showed the enormous human and material resources at his command, should Nubia ever entertain any thoughts of rebelling against Egypt.)*

■ *You might see modern hotels and ancient marketplaces; modern irrigation canals and ancient water wheels; traditional wind-powered feluccas and modern, motorized boats.*

SOCIAL SYSTEMS

Critical Thinking

Explain to students that while most Egyptians live in the Nile Valley, one group is more widely scattered. It is the Bedouins, a nomadic people whose ancestors came from Arabia hundreds of years ago. Many Bedouins herd camels and sheep, moving from place to place just as they have for centuries. The Egyptian government now wants the Bedouins to settle down as farmers. Have students speculate about why the government might want the Bedouins to give up their traditional way of life. *(If the Bedouins gave up herding for farming, they could help Egypt produce more food crops for its growing population, which the country is now struggling to feed.)*

paper, is now hard to find. Here and there, men bathe and women wash clothes in the river. Motorized tourist boats pass by swiftly as you near the next stop.

Luxor

To the ancient Egyptians, the east bank of the Nile was the land of the living, and the west bank was the land of the dead. Today, the city of Luxor celebrates both.

Luxor, on the Nile's east bank, is the place where ancient Thebes once stood. Thebes was Egypt's wealthy capital during the New Kingdom. Today, Luxor attracts wealth from tourism, a key part of Egypt's economy. Here, in the "land of the living," boats and carriages bring visitors. Vendors peddle souvenirs. Tourists cross the river to see the Valley of the Kings. In this rocky valley, 60 ancient rulers were buried, including the boy king, Tutankhamen.

Even in Luxor, about 135 miles north of Aswan, the dam's effects are felt. Irrigation is swelling underground water supplies. The columns of the Temple at Luxor are damaged by salt from the groundwater.

Near Luxor, *fellahin* live much as their ancestors did when mummies were buried in the Valley of the Kings. Water wheels carry irrigation water from river to canal and from canal to ditch. *Fellahin* life has changed, though, since the dam was built. "We can get three crops a year instead of one," a village elder explains. To do so, he must work three times as hard. Yet Egypt grows only half the food it needs. ■

■ *Describe the contrasts you would see along the Upper Nile.*

The Lower Nile

By steamship, you head north from Luxor, passing endless villages and a few industrial cities. In three days' time an unforgettable view appears in the distance. To the west are Giza's ancient pyramids and the Sphinx of Giza. On the east side, deep-green fields suddenly give way to a packed, spreading city—Cairo.

Cairo

Cairo is a city of contrasts. Sleek cars and donkey carts wait side by side in snarled traffic. Women in dresses pass those in Muslim robes. Along the river's edge, European tourists and wealthy Egyptians relax in sailboats and cafés. At night they return to large rooms with lovely river views.

Many people in Cairo, however, live four or five to a room. People without homes have built shacks in the city dump.

Cairo is a magnet city. It attracts Muslims to al-Azhar University. It draws young men from the villages who can't find land to farm. *Fellahin* come with crops to sell.

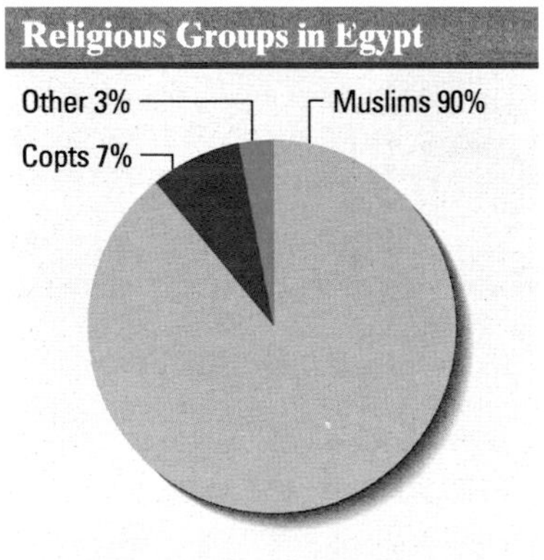

Religious Groups in Egypt
Other 3%
Muslims 90%
Copts 7%

Source: Statesman's Year-Book, 1992

➤ *Of the many cultural influences that are part of Egypt's history, Islam exercises the most powerful force. Most Egyptians are Muslim, as this chart shows. The city of Cairo continues to be a center of Muslim culture.*

Study Skills

Ask students to find out what kinds of foods modern Egyptian families eat. Students should prepare a poster or collage illustrating several typical dishes, complete with recipes if possible.

Art Activity

Have students draw a picture of a busy Cairo market. They can use the description of city life on this page and the next to help them visualize the people, activities, and contrasting lifestyles that can be seen in this city.

▲ *People in Western and Arab dress appear side by side in Cairo.*

In a large open-air market, a delta farmer sells the last of his goods. "Farewell, O oranges!" he cries, taking his baskets home.

The End of the Nile

The map on page 240 shows the delta, where the orange grower lives. This 8,500-square-mile triangle has been called "the greatest vegetable garden on earth." Green fields are planted with wheat, carrots, beans, lettuce, and tomatoes.

A farmer shakes his head when you marvel at the great size of his cauliflower. "Smaller this year than last," he says sadly. Why? "Because of the dam," he replies.

Many people believe that the Aswan High Dam has hurt Egypt's ability to grow food. Before the dam was built, the Nile's floods left a rich substance called **silt** on the land. The silt acted as a natural fertilizer. Now the silt gets caught behind the dam, so farmers must use chemical fertilizers, which pollute irrigation water.

While the dam has caused new problems, Egyptians note that it has saved them from starvation. In the 1980s, when drought brought famine to neighboring Sudan and Ethiopia, Egypt drew on its reservoir of water.

The challenge that faced Egypt in the 1960s, when the dam was built, remains today. Egypt must find a way to feed itself and to protect the river on which it depends. ■

■ *How is life in Cairo different from life in the delta?*

REVIEW

1. **FOCUS** Describe how modern changes are affecting life along the Nile.
2. **HISTORY** Why do tourists come to Luxor?
3. **ECONOMICS** What is Egypt's delta region known for?
4. **CRITICAL THINKING** A dam on the Nile could have been built farther south, in Sudan. Then the Nubians would not have lost their homes. Why would Egypt have wanted the dam to be on Egyptian soil?
5. **WRITING ACTIVITY** Imagine you are an archaeologist in the 1960s who wants to help save Nubian monuments from being flooded by the new reservoir. Write a letter to the editor of an Egyptian newspaper explaining the importance of the rescue and asking people to donate money to the project.

CULTURE

Critical Thinking

Although all children in Egypt are required to attend school, the illiteracy rate remains high—about 45 percent of all adults. Egypt's educational system lacks teachers, school buildings, and funds, and it is severely overcrowded. Have students brainstorm to find ways in which the government could improve the system. *(Suggestions might include volunteer teachers, book donations from wealthier Arab countries, and help from corporations in Cairo.)*

■ *Cairo is a busy, crowded city. The delta is largely a farming area.*

CLOSE

Have students contribute ideas from their own charts to complete the Graphic Overview as a group. Then ask them to answer the Thinking Focus.

Answers to Review Questions

1. The Aswan High Dam is causing pollution but has increased farmland and farm production; the *fellahin* have to work harder. Tourism is bringing money into Egypt's economy. Population growth threatens Egypt's quality of life.
2. They come to visit the Valley of the Kings, where many ancient rulers are buried.
3. It is known for its fertile land and for the abundant fruits, vegetables, and grains that grow there. It has been called "the greatest vegetable garden on earth."
4. Egypt probably wanted to safeguard its control over the flow of the Nile through its territory, because the lives of most Egyptians were at stake. If the dam had been built in another country, Egyptian control could not have been ensured.
5. To get ideas, students might want to review A Closer Look on page 241 as well as the discussion of the role of ancient Egypt in Nubia in Chapter 4.

Homework Options

Have students pick a time period in Egypt between A.D. 639 and the present. Ask them to explain why they would like to have lived during that time and what life would have been like then.

Study Guide: page 42

Answers to Reviewing Key Terms

A. Sample answers:

1. Incorrect. The **fellahin** were Egyptian peasants who farmed the land along the Nile.
2. Correct. Rome improved Egypt's **infrastructure,** or system of roads, bridges, and canals.
3. Correct. The **sultan** was the ruler of the Ottoman Empire.
4. Incorrect. The **Isthmus** of Suez is a narrow strip of land connecting Egypt and the Sinai Peninsula.
5. Incorrect. The **felucca** is an Egyptian sailboat, not a barge.
6. Correct. Since the river no longer floods, the soil along its banks is not renewed with **silt.**

B. Answers:
Arabic: *fellahin,* sultan, felucca
Latin: infrastructure
Greek: isthmus
Other: silt (possibly Danish)

Answers to Exploring Concepts

A. Sample answers:

Greeks: freed Egypt from harsh Persian rule; respected Egyptian traditions; built new capital at Alexandria

Romans: improved Egypt's infrastructure; almost destroyed Jewish community; eventually adopted Christianity

Byzantines: quarreled with church leaders in Alexandria, who then formed the Coptic church

B. Sample answers:

1. Generally, it had little effect. However, the coming of Christianity during Roman rule brought a change of religion for most Egyptians. Arab rule had the biggest impact, since it brought new religion, food, dress, and other cultural changes.
2. The Byzantine rulers were too weak to fight and did not have the support of Egyptians.
3. Both were centers of learning and trade. Each city's location was accessible to the foreign rulers who built it.
4. He modernized Egypt by building ships, canals, harbors, and schools and by improving the economy.
5. It was built as a link between the Mediterranean and the Red seas. It was valuable to the British because it provided a shortcut to India; to the French, who wanted to compete with Great Britain for world trade; and to Egypt, which would receive toll money.
6. Examples include wars with Israel and the movement to create an Islamic government.
7. Today, pressure for change is coming not from powers outside Egypt but from within. Many Egyptians want a return to an Islamic government.
8. The dam provides hydroelectric power. It has enabled more farmland to be brought into production. It also prevents floods and provides a reliable water supply, which helps avoid famine and other disasters.
9. The land of ancient Nubia was flooded by the dam. At Luxor, rising underground water is harming ancient buildings. Along the Upper Nile and in the delta, farmers have to work harder because there are now three growing seasons instead of one. Because floods no longer fertilize the soil, farmers must use chemicals that pour pollution into Mediterranean fishing areas.

Chapter Review

Reviewing Key Terms

fellahin (p. 228)
felucca (p. 240)
infrastructure (p. 230)
isthmus (p. 235)
sultan (p. 234)
silt (p. 243)

A. Each statement below uses a key term from this chapter. Tell whether each key term is used correctly. Then explain the reason for your answer.

1. The fellahin were scholars who came to study at the library in Alexandria.
2. Under Roman rule, Egypt's infrastructure of roads, harbors, and canals was improved.
3. As sultan of the Ottoman Empire, Selim I appointed Muhammad Ali governor of Egypt.
4. The Isthmus of Suez is a narrow body of water that connects the Red Sea and the Mediterranean Sea.
5. Ancient Egyptians used a type of flat barge called a felucca to float large building stones down the Nile.
6. The Aswan High Dam has prevented silt from being deposited along the banks of the Nile.

B. Use a dictionary to look up the origin of each key term. Make a table listing which words come from Arabic, from Latin, and from Greek. Which word does not come from any of these languages?

Exploring Concepts

A. After the fall of the pharaohs, a long series of foreigners left their mark on Egypt. Copy the chart below, then complete all sections. List the ways in which each set of foreign rulers affected Egyptian culture.

Foreign Rulers	Effects on Egypt
Greeks	
Romans	Improved infrastructure
Byzantines	

B. Answer each question with information from the chapter.

1. What effect did foreign rule have on the *fellahin*?
2. Why were the Arabs able to conquer Egypt with little trouble?
3. Compare and contrast ancient Alexandria and Cairo. Why was location important to each?
4. How did Muhammad Ali attempt to make Egypt into a "European-style" nation?
5. Why was the Suez Canal built? To whom was it valuable?
6. "It is not easy to govern Egypt," King Farouk warned Gamal Abdel Nasser. Give examples to support this statement.
7. How are cultural changes occurring in Egypt today different from those that occurred during ancient times?
8. Why is the Aswan High Dam important to Egypt?
9. Which areas along the Nile have felt the harmful effects of the Aswan High Dam?

Reviewing Skills

1. Read the following passage. Tell whether it is a primary or secondary source, and give reasons to support your answer.

> *These were my thoughts about a new war [with Israel]. . . . Such a course would have set us back by more than a century. That is why I chose peace and did not drag my country into war. I found I could achieve the same goals through peace.*
>
> Anwar Sadat

2. Many authors—from the Greek historian Herodotus in the 400s B.C. to modern-day magazine writers—have traveled along the Nile and have written accounts of their journeys. Would such accounts be considered primary sources or secondary sources of information about life along the Nile? If you were doing a report on the geographic features of the Nile, would such an account be your first choice for information? Why or why not?
3. Select five important events in this chapter, and show them on a timeline. For each date, write a sentence to describe why you chose this date.
4. Can you explain how a dam works? What kind of drawing would best support your explanation?

Using Critical Thinking

1. Look at the map of Alexander's conquest on page G12 of the Map and Globe Handbook. Trace Alexander's route. How many years did he travel? Now look at the map of Eurasia on pages 682–683, and retrace the route. About how many miles do you estimate he traveled? Make a list of all the things you think Alexander needed to move his armies such great distances.
2. Democracy means government by the people. If a majority of Egyptians vote to replace their democracy with a government based on Islamic law, do you think that change should be made? Support your answer with reasons.
3. Imagine that you are the Great Sphinx of Giza. Most people think that your eyes are sightless, but of course you can see. Describe changes you have witnessed in Egypt over the past 2,000 years.

Preparing for Citizenship

1. **WRITING ACTIVITY** Think of yourself as a citizen of Egypt today. You are extremely concerned about the environmental problems caused by the damming of the Nile River. What do you think the government should do to help solve these problems? Write a paragraph outlining and explaining your ideas. Compare your ideas with those of your classmates. Which ideas do you think are the most practical?
2. **ART ACTIVITY** Work in small groups to create a travel poster that would invite tourists to visit Egypt today. Begin by discussing what elements of Egyptian culture you want to include. You may want to show the impact of the many foreign influences on Egypt, or you might decide to focus on purely Egyptian achievements. Display your poster in the classroom. Have a spokesperson from your group explain the reasons for your choice of images.
3. **COLLABORATIVE LEARNING** Growing enough food has always been a major concern for the Egyptian people. As a class, do research to find out what are the most common foods eaten in Egypt today. Also find out how and where these foods are grown. Does Egypt need to import any of its key foods? Work together to plan a menu consisting only of Egyptian food.

Answers to Reviewing Skills

1. This is a primary source because it is a first-person account.
2. These would be primary sources, because the writers witnessed life along the Nile. For a report on geography such sources would not be a good first choice. Encyclopedias, atlases, and other sources with basic factual information about the geography would be better starting points.
3. Answers may include 332 B.C., the Greek conquest of Egypt, Alexandria becomes center of learning; 30 B.C., the Romans defeat Cleopatra's forces; A.D. 639, arrival of Arabs in Egypt, beginning of conversion of Egyptians to Islam; 1517, the Ottoman Turks invade Egypt; 1869, opening of Suez Canal; 1952, Nasser leads rebellion and becomes president, Egyptian self-rule begins; 1970, Aswan High Dam, Nile no longer floods, food production grows but so does pollution.
4. A diagram would help explain how a dam controls the flow of a river's water.

Answers to Using Critical Thinking

1. Alexander was on the road for 12 years. In that time, he and his armies covered at least 12,000 miles. To do so, he needed huge supplies of food, pack animals, materials, and workmen to repair and resupply his weapons; sources of fresh troops; and the support of peoples he conquered along the way.
2. Some students may answer that the will of the majority should be followed. Others may say that using a democratic method to destroy democracy makes no sense, and that respect for human rights makes it necessary to preserve democracy at all costs.
3. Student answers might mention the changes in foreign rulers (Greeks, Romans, Byzantines, Arabs, Turks, Europeans) and the different styles of building they brought with them; the building of Cairo beside the Nile; changes in religion; the impact of the Suez Canal; the damming of the Nile and resulting increase in farmland.

Answers to Preparing for Citizenship

1. **WRITING ACTIVITY** Student answers might include requiring farmers to use only organic fertilizers, fining those who use chemical fertilizers, and building water purification plants.
2. **ART ACTIVITY** Posters might show various styles of architecture found in Egypt, such as Greek, Roman, and Ottoman. Or they might contrast ancient and modern Egyptian building projects, like the pyramids and the Aswan Dam.
3. **COLLABORATIVE LEARNING** Foods include bread, vegetables such as corn and beans, fruits such as dates and figs, some milk and cheese, but only a little meat and poultry. Egypt has to import food, especially wheat.

CHAPTER ORGANIZER

Chapter 11 Mali

CHAPTER PLANNING CHART

Pupil's Edition	Teacher's Edition	Ancillaries
Lesson 1: From Empire to Colony (2–3 days) Objective 1: Describe the richness and extent of the empire of Mali. (History 3, 7, 8; Geography 3, 4, 5) Objective 2: Evaluate the importance of trade in the Mali and Songhai empires. (Economics 1, 2, 4; Geography 4) Objective 3: List the several effects of French occupation on the people of Mali. (Culture 4; Ethics and Belief Systems 5)	• Graphic Overview (248) • Access Strategy (249) • Access Activity (249) Study Skills (250) Health Connection (250) Science Connection (251) Political Context (251) Social Participation (251) • Visual Learning (252) Debate (252) Cultural Context (253) • Visual Learning (253)	Study Guide (43) Discovery Journal (22) • Study Prints (7) Transparency (4)
Lesson 2: Mali and Its People (2–3 days) Objective 1: Locate modern Mali and describe its geographic features. (Geography 2) Objective 2: Explain how Mali's people now use their country's land and resources. (History 4, 6; Geography 3, 4, 5; Economics 1)	• Graphic Overview (255) • Access Activity (256) • Access Strategy (256) Writing an Outline (257) Study Skills (257)	Study Guide (44) Map Activities (15)
Lesson 3: Republic of Mali (3–4 days) Objective 1: Explain how drought affects Mali's economy. (Geography 3; Economics 1) Objective 2: Identify the resources Mali has that help the country meet the challenges it faces. (Geography 5; Economics 1)	• Graphic Overview (259) • Access Activity (260) • Access Strategy (260) Science Context (261) • Study Skills (261)	Study Guide (45)
Understanding Arguments Objective: Evaluate an argument for consistency and relevance. (Critical Thinking 1, 2)	Writing an Argument (263)	Study Guide (46)
Chapter Review	Answers (264–265)	Tests (41–44)

* Objectives are correlated to the strands and goals in the program Scope and Sequence on pages T41–T49.

• LEP appropriate resources. (For additional strategies, see pages T32–T33.)

CHAPTER RATIONALE

Traveling southwest from Egypt, our African journey takes us to West Africa. Here students step back in time to examine the great empires of Mali that existed between 1200 B.C. and A.D. 1600. Students also read about the effects of Europeans on the peoples of West Africa in the 18th and 19th centuries as well as the challenges facing today's government in modern Mali.

Lesson 1 illustrates the rich and varied history of West Africa by focusing on two ancient empires—Mali and Songhai located on the southern edge of the Sahara. The lesson describes how the rulers of these empires took advantage of a geographic location that helped them monopolize the lucrative gold and salt trade. Students read about the Muslim traders and travelers who brought their religious beliefs to the region. A main objective of this lesson is to demonstrate how many people of West Africa adopted the faith of Islam. Students will notice Islamic influences in the photograph of the mosque located near the market at Djenné shown on page 251. In market towns along trade routes, Muslim merchants—such as the metalsmith shown in the Closer Look on page 252—opened temporary crafts shops.

In this chapter students will study another example of how colonial powers impose their social and political systems on the peoples they conquer. Four historic maps illustrate the borders of Mali before, during, and after colonial rule. Photos and text work together to point out the impact of French colonialism on the peoples of Mali.

To give students an accurate image of the geography and peoples of modern Mali, **Lesson 2** presents a detailed description of both. Students read about vegetation regions such as the desert, the Sahel, and the savanna, and explore how people have adapted to each environment. The lesson opener gives students a picture of rural life along the Niger River. The lesson makes the point that Mali's rivers are a lifeline to the landlocked country. Students have another opportunity to study the importance of rivers to the way people live. Rivers provide water, food, transportation, and a means of communication among peoples.

Lesson 3 emphasizes the effects of frequent droughts on the peoples of Mali. The lesson compares urban life in the capital city of Bamako with life in Mali's rural villages. The contrasts are striking. You may want students to think about the differences between city and rural life in their area. Although the disparities among education, medical care, and occupations are not as great as in Mali, the comparison helps students understand the reasons for the differences.

ACTIVITIES & PROJECTS

Basic: Writing a Journal Entry

Have students imagine being one of the members of Mansa Musa's court who took the pilgrimage to Mecca in 1324. Then ask them to write a journal entry about any part of the journey they found most interesting. Encourage students to reread the description of the 1324 pilgrimage in their texts on page 248. (Use after Lesson 1.)

LEP: Making a Climate Map

Ask students to use the Atlas map in their text on page 688 and the lesson maps to create a climate map for Africa. If they need help reading the legends, draw their attention to page G3 in the Map and Globe Handbook, Using the Legend Inset. Provide students with graph paper, tracing paper, colored pencils, and crayons to complete their maps. (Use after Lesson 2.)

Challenge: Research

After students have read about the national museum in Bamako, have them use library resources to research the purpose and the use of masks in West African religious ceremonies long ago and today. Students may want to examine art books that show examples of such masks. Ask students to take notes and then write a report about their findings. They can add drawings of masks to illustrate their reports. (Use after Lesson 3.)

Debate

Encourage all students to take part in an open debate of the following statement: The Muslims were a positive influence on the West Africans.

Reader's Theater

A small group of students may obtain an anthology of West African tales from the school library. Have students select a legend or a story to use in a reader's theater production. Encourage students to take roles in the reading and use expressive voices as they present the tale to the class. (Use after any lesson.)

Writing a Story

Have students write an imaginative story from the point of view of a salt trader who visits a market in Timbuktu at the height of its economic importance—some time in the late 1300s. You may want students to refer to their texts and library resources while they work on their stories. (Use after Lesson 1.)

CHAPTER PREVIEW

After they have read the chapter title, ask students to read the paragraph that follows to establish for them that the empire of Mali was at its height between 1200 and 1600. Then explain that colonization, especially in the late 1800s, changed the way of life of the West African people. Help students understand that independence also brought changes and challenges.

Looking Back

Remind students that they have learned about Egypt from ancient to modern times and that their study concentrated on that country's role in North Africa. Explain that now they will read about Mali, a West African country.

Looking Forward

Tell students that they will read about Mali in three lessons—From Empire to Colony, Mali and Its People, and Republic of Mali. In Lesson 1, they will learn about the roots of Mali's Islamic leadership in West Africa as well as about its trade in salt and gold. Their reading will take them from the old empires to present-day Mali and will touch on the French colonization of West Africa.

Chapter 11
Mali

Between 1200 and 1600, West African rulers created kingdoms of great size and richness by controlling Africa's trade in gold and salt. Europeans invaded the region in the 1800s and established colonies. The Europeans changed the way the people of West Africa lived. In 1960 the Republic of Mali became independent of French rule. Today people living in Mali value traditions that date back to the early kings.

For centuries people crossing the desert have carried dried fruits for food.

Gold dinars from North Africa were made of gold brought from the rich empires of West Africa.

The Sankoré Mosque in Timbuktu is one of the oldest in Mali. The mosque was a center of learning in the 1300s.

1300 | 1400 | 1500 | 1600

1324

1324 Mansa Musa, king of Mali, makes a hajj. During his rule from 1307 to 1337, the Mali Empire reaches its greatest extent.

c. 1468 Sonni 'Ali leads the Songhai to victory over the city of Timbuktu, a major center of trade and Islamic learning under Songhai rule.

BACKGROUND

Much of what historians know about ancient Mali comes from the accounts of two travelers: Ibn Battuta, a Muslim explorer in the 1300s, and Leo Africanus, who described Mali during the 1500s.

Ibn Battuta's Caravan

In 29 years of traveling, Ibn Battuta journeyed 75,000 miles—from his home in North Africa to lands south and west. During a two-year trip that began in 1352, he visited Niani, the capital of Mali. As a devout Muslim, Battuta praised the Malians for their devotion to prayer and for their memorizing of the Qur'an. However, he disliked the dress of the women, who went about "without a veil." He gives insights into what traveling with an ancient desert caravan was like in a description of Tjaghaza, the salt-mining center: "We passed ten days of discomfort because the water there is bitter and the place is plagued with flies . . . . Water supplies are laid on [there] . . . for the crossing of the desert . . . which is a ten nights' journey with no water."

Leo Africanus Reports on Mali

The writings of Leo Africanus, who traveled in Mali and Egypt in the early 1500s, were one of Europe's main sources of information about Africa for several centuries. In his Geographical History of Africa, published

People in Mali have worn gold necklaces like this since the time of Mansa Musa.

The people of Mali take pride in modern achievements such as the world's first commercial solar energy project in Diré.

1992 Alpha Oumar Konaré is elected president in Mali's first democratic elections.

1700 | 1800 | 1900 | 2000

1894 Seeking to enrich its colonial holdings, France invades Timbuktu. France rules Mali until 1960.

Today

247

Understanding the Visuals

Have students look at the photos of gold on these pages. The gold dinars and gold jewelry represent the importance of precious metal to Mali's development as a powerful, ancient empire. Gold was the standard currency of West Africa. In some areas during the 1000s, gold dust *(tibr)* was the medium of exchange, while in other areas people traded with unstamped dinars made from pure gold. In the early 1500s, both Djenné and Timbuktu used gold for large transactions. For smaller transactions, however, people used iron or cowries (special shells from the Indian Ocean). It was also common to barter for goods.

Understanding Chronology

Refer students to the timeline. Review the dates, pointing out how relatively recent the French colonization period was.

in 1550, Leo Africanus chronicled the riches of Mali, telling about the abundance of barley, rice, livestock, fish, and cotton. He described Mali in a 1512 visit: "[Mali] . . . borders upon the kingdom of Jenne to the north, and is confined by a desert and arid mountains to the south. To the west there are wild forests which reach the ocean, and to the east it borders upon the territory of Gago [or Songhai]."

Of Gao, he said, "Melons, cucumbers, and excellent pumpkins are abundant and they have enormous quantities of rice. Fresh-water wells are numerous. . . . Its inhabitants are rich merchants who travel constantly about the regions with their wares."

INTRODUCE

As your students read Lesson 1, have them consider the factors that contributed to changes in Mali's economic and political base. To begin the discussion, have students read the title of the lesson and the Thinking Focus. Explain the difference between an empire and a colony. *(An empire is autonomous. It has control of its own government, military, and natural resources—and absorbs the peoples of outlying regions as well. A colony is controlled politically and economically by another government.)* Students will learn more about empires in Chapter 14.

Key Term

Vocabulary Strategies: T36–T37

middleman—a person who buys or sells something on behalf of others

➤ *The Atlas Mountains appear at the top of the map. On the map they look like a stone wall stretching across northern Africa.*

1200
1300
1324
2000
1960

LESSON 1

From Empire to Colony

THINKING FOCUS

How did the empires of Mali and Songhai come to power in West Africa?

Key Term

- middleman

In 1324 the king of the West African kingdom of Mali, Mansa Musa, wanted to fulfill his duty as a follower of Islam. He gave orders to his court to get ready for his pilgrimage to the holy city of Mecca. It was one of the grandest pilgrimages the Islamic world had ever seen.

The king did not travel alone. Thousands of his subjects—officials, his wife, servants, soldiers, and slaves—also made the journey. About 100 camels loaded with gold followed the caravan. They traveled about 3,500 miles across grasslands and desert to reach the holy city of Mecca in what is now Saudi Arabia.

All around the empire, people had helped prepare for the long journey. Leather workers had sewn skin containers to hold water. Servants had loaded camels with gold. Slaves carried huge amounts of food—enough to feed thousands of people for several months.

After months of traveling, Mansa Musa's caravan reached Egypt. They camped near the pyramids for several days before

➤ *This map comes from the Catalan atlas. It was made in the late 1300s. The cartographer drew Mansa Musa holding a golden ball and wearing a golden crown. Can you identify the Atlas Mountains?*

Objectives

1. Describe the richness and extent of the empire of Mali.
2. Evaluate the importance of trade in the Mali and Songhai empires.
3. List the several effects of French occupation on the people of Mali.

Graphic Overview

Mali Empire Trade and Islam grow. → **Songhai Empire** New lands added. → **French Occupation** Mali's people are oppressed. → **Modern Mali** Education and health care suffer.

entering Cairo. The Egyptian ruler let the king from Mali use a palace during his three-month visit. Thankful, Mansa Musa gave away many presents made of gold.

The Egyptians long remembered Mansa Musa's stay. "This man Mansa Musa," one Egyptian recalled, "spread upon Cairo the flood of his generosity: there was no person, officer of the court, or holder of any office . . . who did not receive a sum of gold from him. The people of Cairo earned incalculable sums from him."

Mansa Musa's grand pilgrimage drew the attention of other people living along the caravan routes in North Africa, Southwest Asia, and even Europe. The king's pilgrimage sparked interest from others in the great wealth of West Africa. Mapmakers working at this time started to draw Mansa Musa and the Mali empire on their maps. Once this happened, outsiders began to travel to this great kingdom.

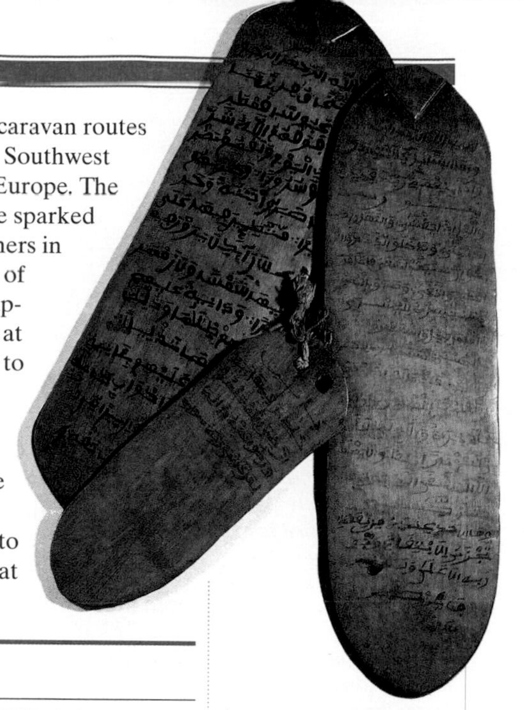

▲ *Students in ancient Mali studied the Qur'an by using boards such as these. They memorized sayings from the Qur'an written on the boards.*

Mali's Golden Age

Under Mansa Musa's rule the West African kingdom of Mali grew to its largest extent. For about 160 years, from 1240 to 1400, much of what is Mali today was ruled by powerful kings. They brought great wealth to their empires by controlling a lively trade in gold. They held political power in the region through strong armies and a network of ambassadors. These representatives from the king were sent to Egypt, Morocco, and to rival kingdoms.

Mali's first king, Sundiata *(sun dee AHT ah),* was Mansa Musa's great uncle. An epic poem tells how Sundiata united many young Malinke *(muh LIHNG kay)* men under his rule.

◄ *Women in Mali today still wear golden beads such as these. The jewelry shows designs from the Muslim world. Arabic letters cover the metal pendant.*

The Roots of Mighty Empires

Sundiata conquered many new lands. Mali gained control over the trading centers of Gao *(gow)* and Djenné *(jen AY).* In these cities traders from north and south of Mali met to exchange salt, gold, and other products.

Traders from North Africa brought salt from mines that lay in the Sahara to the north of Mali. Gold traders brought gold mined in locations south of the empire. The kings of Mali became wealthy by taxing the goods traded there.

A Trading Empire

Market towns along the trade routes grew into small cities. Traders passing through the towns needed housing and supplies. People provided what traders needed. Some people offered rooms where travelers

DEVELOP

Point out that the text structure is chronological. The text begins in 1324, a time when Mali was ruled by a king—Mansa Musa. Students will read about what caused the early empires to rise and fall. Direct students to the map on page 248. This Catalan map was made in 1375 in Majorca, Spain, by the Jewish cartographer Abraham Cresques. Explain that its effect was monumental in that it expanded European thinking about the known land areas of the world. As a result, Europeans became increasingly interested in the gold and other riches of Mali.

ECONOMICS

Critical Thinking

Explain to students that Mansa Musa brought so much gold to Cairo on his visit in 1324 that its value fell drastically. Why? *(Gold values became* deflated, *or went down, because there was a sudden oversupply of gold. In part, the value of gold is determined by its scarcity. In this case there was so much gold that people no longer thought of it as scarce and valuable. So, the price of gold went down.)*

Access Strategy

Read aloud the second and third paragraphs on page 248. Remind students what *caravan* means *(a long line of merchants and camels traveling from one oasis to another).* Then have students make suggestions about what they would want to pack if they were to travel across a region of desert and grasslands. *(Sample answers: water, food, tools, and books)* Why would the camel be a good animal to use for such a trip? *(Camels store water in their hump and can go for long stretches without drinking.)* Tell students that they will learn about two travelers to Mali who explored unknown lands and wrote informative descriptions of what they saw and did.

Access Activity

Have students make a list of all the unfamiliar words in the chapter introduction and in the opening pages of Lesson 1. In addition to proper names, a few words and phrases—such as *solar energy, hajj,* and *mosque*—may require review. Students can work in pairs to practice the pronunciation of these words; then they can work together to research the definitions.

POLITICAL SYSTEMS
Critical Thinking

Have the students use the maps on this page to locate the city of Timbuktu. Explain that Sonni 'Ali captured the city of Timbuktu in 1468. Although he was not an especially fervent Muslim, he welcomed the many devout Muslims who gave the city its reputation as a center for Islamic worship and study. Help students understand that rulers can use power more effectively when people cooperate than they can when people resist their authority. Sonni 'Ali didn't need to antagonize the people of Timbuktu in order to rule.

Songhai leader Sonni 'Ali conquered much of Mansa Musa's empire in the 1400s.

Mali Empire, c. 1337

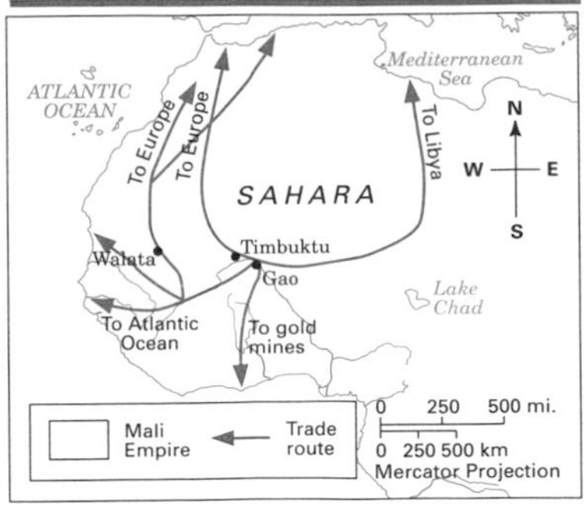

ATLANTIC OCEAN
Mediterranean Sea
To Europe
To Europe
To Libya
SAHARA
N
W
E
S
Walata
Timbuktu
Gao
Lake Chad
To Atlantic Ocean
To gold mines
Mali Empire
Trade route
0 250 500 mi.
0 250 500 km
Mercator Projection

Songhai Empire, c. 1500

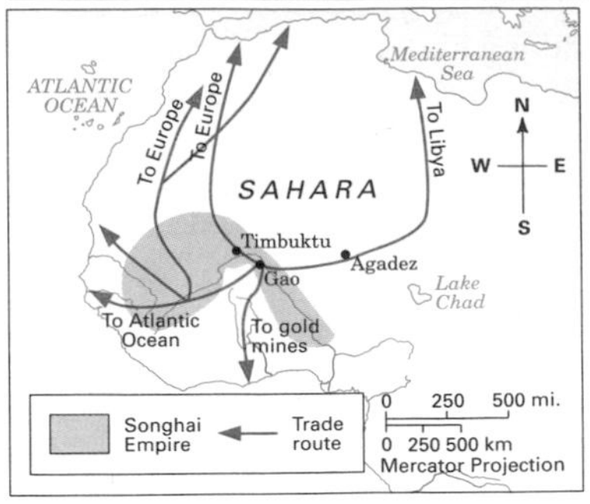

ATLANTIC OCEAN
Mediterranean Sea
To Europe
To Europe
To Libya
SAHARA
N
W
E
S
Timbuktu
Gao
Agadez
Lake Chad
To Atlantic Ocean
To gold mines
Songhai Empire
Trade route
0 250 500 mi.
0 250 500 km
Mercator Projection

Across Time & Space

Salt was also valued in ancient Rome. In A.D. 500, soldiers transported salt on a highway called the Via Salaria *(VEE uh suh LAR ee uh), or Salt Road. The term* salary *comes from the Latin word* salarium, *which means "money paid to soldiers to buy salt."*

could stay. Farmers brought crops to market.

Salt traders from the Sahara entered the city of Timbuktu *(tihm buhk TOO),* their camels bearing huge slabs of salt. Those in charge of the gold mines, south of Timbuktu, did not want the salt traders to see the places where gold was mined. As a result, **middlemen,** people who buy or sell something on behalf of others, ran the trade. The middlemen haggled with the salt and gold traders until they reached a bargain.

Today, people trade salt in an open market in the city of Mopti rather than using middlemen to bargain for goods.

Gold and salt were not the only goods traded in ancient Mali. People living there also traded tusks of ivory from elephants hunted in southern grasslands. They traded the ivory for European cloth brought by Arab traders from cities located in North Africa. The Arab traders exchanged the cloth for other items such as kola nuts and bars of copper and iron offered in Mali's busy trading centers of Gao and Timbuktu.

A Center of Islamic Learning

Sundiata, Mali's first ruler, was not a devout Muslim. Many of the traders who passed through his empire practiced Islam. They brought their religion with them.

Mansa Musa, Sundiata's grandnephew, was a devout Muslim. He encouraged his subjects to practice Islam too. When he returned from Mecca, the king brought with him Islamic scholars and a well-known Spanish architect. He built large mosques in Gao and Timbuktu.

The Muslim explorer Ibn Battuta visited Mali during the reign of Mansa Musa's grandson. You can find a description of Ibn Battuta in the Biographical Dictionary on page 698. Ibn Battuta praised the people of Mali for, he said, "they are devoted to the prayers and keep praying in congregation, which they impose also on their children. If a man does not come early in the morning to the mosque he will not find a place to pray because of the large crowd."

The Songhai Empire

After Mansa Musa died, his brother ruled Mali. He was

Study Skills

Divide students into small groups and assign each group a major trade city—such as Gao, Djenné, or Timbuktu—that existed during either the Mali or the Songhai empires. Instruct the students to work together to prepare a report entitled "[City Name]: Yesterday and Today." Students should divide tasks among the group members.

Health Connection

Explain that today we think of salt as a flavoring rather than as a preservative. However, before refrigeration, salt was used to preserve foods. Explain that spoiled foods spread disease. The need to preserve food with salt was a major reason for the salt trade that existed at the time of the Mali Empire. Some salt deposits were so pure they could be quarried and traded in large slabs. Have students experiment by preserving a slice of bread using salt. Tell them to do the following: Let one slice of bread air-dry, put a second slice in a plastic bag, and place a third slice between two thick layers of table salt. After a week have students compare the results to see which slice of bread is the freshest.

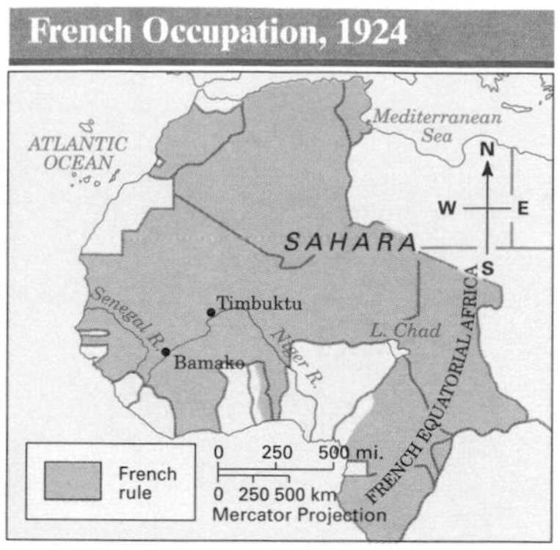
French Occupation, 1924
Mediterranean Sea
ATLANTIC OCEAN
N
W
E
S
SAHARA
Timbuktu
Senegal R.
Niger R.
Bamako
L. Chad
FRENCH EQUATORIAL AFRICA
French rule
0 250 500 mi.
0 250 500 km
Mercator Projection

Modern Mali
Mediterranean Sea
ATLANTIC OCEAN
N
W
E
S
SAHARA
MALI
Timbuktu
Bamako
Lake Chad
Mali
0 250 500 mi.
0 250 500 km
Mercator Projection

In the late 1800s, France invaded Mali. How would you compare the area of French occupation to the area of modern Mali?

followed by weak kings who could not protect Mali's vast territory. By the late 1300s, the empire faced attack from the east.

The river people of Songhai lived along the Niger River. For years the Songhai resisted Mali's control. In the mid-1400s, under the leadership of Sonni 'Ali *(SOH nee AHL ee),* the Songhai built their own empire. It included parts of the old empire of Mali, as you can see on the Songhai map on page 250.

Timbuktu's fame as a center of trade grew under Songhai rule. People also came to the city because it had become a great center of Islamic learning. By the 1500s Timbuktu had 50,000 people living there. The large trading town had three Islamic universities. These were religious schools connected to the mosques.

Leo Africanus, a traveler like Ibn Battuta, visited the Songhai Empire in the early 1500s. His writings were the main source of information Europeans had about Islam for 400 years. He praised the Songhai for the high value they placed on learning.

How Do We Know?

HISTORY *In 1363, toward the end of his life, Ibn Battuta dictated his memoirs to Ibn Juzayy* (IHB uhn joo ZAH ee). *Ibn Juzayy recorded the stories in the form of a book. Ibn Battuta's stories are valuable sources of information for historians.*

After each rainy season, the mosque at Djenné requires repairs. It is partly made of earth, which washes away.

The area of French occupation included most of West Africa and reached to the Atlantic Ocean. Modern Mali is small by comparison and is landlocked, having no access to the ocean except through other countries.

ECONOMICS

Critical Thinking

The Songhai people had lived quietly along the Niger River for years until their leader Sonni 'Ali conquered Timbuktu. What motives might he have had? *(Timbuktu was an important trade route; residents of Timbuktu could act as middlemen and could also levy taxes, which would bring wealth and power to the area.)*

Science Connection

Askia Muhammad, who ruled Songhai from 1493 to 1528, encouraged his people to develop the empire's natural resources. He had them dig many new wells for water, and his engineers designed waterways to bring water to desert regions. The waterways made farming possible far to the north of the Niger. Ask students to locate the area on the World Climate Map in the Atlas on page 688. Use the map to discuss the climate north of the Niger.

Political Context

To show allegiance to the king of Songhai, each group of peoples under his rule was obligated to give him gifts. They usually did that once or twice a year, when a group's chief visited the capital city or when a government representative or tax collector traveled to the provinces. Groups skilled in ironworking might offer iron-tipped spears or arrows for the king's army. Farmers would give food for the king's horses, and Songhai fishers would ship fish by canoes.

Social Participation

Have students imagine conversations between an official from the court of Sonni 'Ali and various members of society—a salt trader, a gold dealer, and a Muslim scholar. Students can discuss the differences in the focus of the conversations. *(Traders and dealers might discuss taxes on their goods. The scholar might remark on the growing interest in Islamic study.)*

Note: You may wish to use this Moment in Time after students have looked at the Mali jewelry on page 249 and have read about metalsmiths on page 253.

CULTURE

Visual Learning

Explain that a metalsmith, called a *numuke,* was always male and was born to his position in West African society. The *numuke* crafted practical items, such as tools and metal parts, and also made jewelry. Have students look at the picture of the metalsmith. Ask them to read the headings that describe the different tools. Explain that an anvil is a metal block on which the metalsmith places the metal. He hammers the heated metal into shape while holding it with pincers. The bellows pumps air into the fire, making the coals burn hotter.

More About Gold Gold has been mined and made into jewelry since ancient times. It is valuable because it is scarce and also because it is soft and can easily be shaped into different forms. To make gold harder, it is often mixed with another metal. The additions are called alloys, and the gold content is measured in karats. Pure gold has 24 karats. Gold that is 12 karats is 12 parts pure gold and 12 parts alloy, for example.

A MOMENT IN TIME

A Mali Metalsmith

8:12 A.M., August 4, 1993
Under a shade tree in Gao, Mali

Jewelry
He finishes a gold earring he will trade today. For generations, traders have sought the finest jewelry from his region. This earring differs little from those made here 200 years ago.
Hammer
He strikes the gold with his hammer. The head of his hammer is made of iron. He crafts iron and other metals besides gold.
Anvil
He treasures his anvil more than any other tool. This one is stable and much harder than the metals he hammers against it.
Files and Pincers
He shares his tools with other smiths who work by the fire. Files smooth jewelry and sharpen blades. Pincers grasp hot metal.
Bellows
In a few minutes, he will take his turn blowing air on the fire's coals with the goatskin bellows. The gusts keep the fire hot so he and the other smiths can soften and shape their metals.
252

Visual Learning

Have students look at the pictures on pages 250–251. Then ask them to draw a mural of a Malian marketplace in the 1300s. Suggest that they use pictures from the previous pages for ideas about clothing. Students can work in groups so that each group shows something different being sold. These items might include salt, gold, cloth, ivory, and foods.

Debate

Divide students into two groups and have them debate whether a non-wealthy country such as Mali should set aside any funds for the development of arts and culture. Have one group support the premise that a sense of self-worth—and ultimately national pride—comes from an enriched cultural life. Have the other group support the premise that a country can improve only by concentrating on developing its economy. (Suggestions for presenting an argument appear on page 263.)

Here in Timbuktu, there are great store of doctors, judges, priests and other learned men, bountifully maintained at the king's cost and charges. And hither are brought divers [different] manuscripts or written books out of Barbary [now Libya], which are sold for more money than any other merchandize.

Leo Africanus

Books were not the only items traded in the markets of Timbuktu. On market days craftspeople set up workshops near the markets. Metalsmiths made hinges and tools of iron and shaped gold into beautiful jewelry. You can find out more about the metalsmiths of Mali in A Moment in Time on page 252.

Like the Mali Empire before it, the Songhai Empire came under attack by outsiders. Moroccan troops rode out of North Africa and attacked the trading cities of Timbuktu and Gao in 1591. The Moroccans were armed with guns. The warriors of Songhai could not succeed against the new weapons.

The vast area that had been the Mali and Songhai empires broke up into smaller states. Various peoples controlled different parts of the old empire from the mid-1700s through the 1800s. Then the French invaded West Africa. ■

■ *What made the rulers of the ancient empires of Mali and Songhai wealthy?*

The French Occupation

In the late 1800s, European nations began to seize huge portions of Africa, including Mali. European nations wanted colonies that could supply raw materials to industries at home. They also wanted colonies to prove they were world powers.

The French wanted to stop the British from grabbing land in West Africa. Look at the first map at the top of page 251. It shows Mali under French rule in 1924. From the mid-1800s to the mid-1900s, France occupied many West African countries that are independent today.

French traders wanted to control a valuable trade in gum arabic. Gum arabic comes from the acacia *(uh KAY shuh)* tree, which grows in the grasslands in southern Mali. In the 1800s, people used gum arabic to dye cloth and starch clothes. The traders asked the French government to set up forts along the Senegal River. The army protected the traders from attack by local people, who were angered by the French invasion of their lands.

CHEMIN DE FER DE DAKAR

▲ *The French left examples of their architecture as well as their language in Mali, as can be seen in this train station.*

Colonial Rule

The French government did build forts along the Senegal River in the 1850s and slowly gained control over western Mali. The forts

NATIONAL IDENTITY

Critical Thinking

Ahmadu, the leader of the Tukulor Empire, was an important person in Mali's history. He resisted French control through diplomatic means and was instrumental in drawing up the Treaty of Nango (1881) in which France recognized his empire's sovereignty and promised not to invade his territory. However, the treaty was never ratified by the French because it promised arms to Ahmadu. Ask students why they think the French would have refused to give him arms. *(Fear of rebellion.)*

■ *Control of the gold and salt trade made the rulers of ancient Mali and Songhai wealthy. The rulers collected taxes on items traded along routes that the empires controlled.*

Cultural Context

The backbone of French occupation rested on a policy known as *assimilation,* whose goal was to educate Malian people to adopt the French culture. Assimilation proved too difficult and costly to impose, and it was replaced by a policy of *association.*

Under this compromise, a limited number of Africans were educated and given positions of control. This policy led to great disparities between the few Africans who were rich and the many who were poor. For the privileged few, it also created a way of life that depended on French subsidies and government jobs.

Visual Learning

Have students examine the photo of the railroad station to see the French influence on Mali's architecture. Point out that while the building is European, the marketplace and the people are Malian. How do native peoples sustain their own cultures in the face of colonialism? *(Keeping up traditional values through rituals, ways of dress, and holidays)*

HISTORY

Critical Thinking

Tell students that in 1880 European countries controlled 10 percent of Africa; but by 1900 only Ethiopia remained fully independent. European countries were vying for control of African countries because the Europeans wanted to expand their power. What other benefits would a colony offer an imperial country? *(Natural resources, cheap labor)*

■ *West Africans did not gain much under French rule. Only a few people were given opportunities such as going to school or working for the government. Many were forced into public-works projects or served as soldiers in the French army.*

CLOSE

Read the Thinking Focus on page 248 aloud. Ask students to write short phrases about why Mali and Songhai rose to power. What economic and political factors contributed? What resources helped? *(Leadership of Mansa Musa, salt and gold trade)*

BANQUE CENTRALE DES ÉTATS DE L'AFRIQUE DE L'OUEST
1000
R.13 D
MILLE FRANCS
07017

After the French colonies became independent, they created a common currency like this 1,000 franc note used in Mali.

were linked by telegraph. The French also began to build a railroad to connect trading centers. The railroad stretched from Kayes on the Senegal River to Bamako. To protect the lands they had invaded, the French put gunboats on the Niger River.

French officials tried to get local leaders to sign treaties that gave the French control over their land. When the leaders refused to sign treaties, the French used the army to force them to give in. By the late 1800s, France had control over what is Mali today.

A small number of Mali's people benefited from French occupation. The French chose Africans to be leaders of each canton, or government unit. These people had power and responsibility. They collected taxes and rounded up laborers for public works projects. In addition, they represented the government to the local people.

Under French rule very few Africans received a good education. Most people did not attend high school or college. Only a few children were able to attend European-run schools.

■ *What did West Africans gain from French rule?*

The French did not allow people to make their own decisions about their lives. The people of West Africa had not chosen French rule, and they were not given the chance to vote. The French forced many Africans to work on building projects such as the construction of the railroad. Some people were forced to fight for France in time of war.

French officials tried to educate canton leaders, hoping that these leaders would agree that French culture was superior. The plan backfired. Instead of trying to become more like the French, the local leaders held more firmly to their own traditions. African leaders started to resist French laws and policies.

Challenges to France

It was dangerous for Africans to challenge French rule. Yet some people did. Herders in the eastern part of West Africa took up arms against the French in 1914. Koumi Diossé, a Bambara leader, refused to make his people work for the French as porters, people who carry baggage from one place to another. He also led a revolt to protest the French army's taking his people to fight for France in World War I.

However, it took many years for the people of Mali to be free of French rule. Not until September 1960 did Mali become an independent country. Modibo Keita became Mali's first president. Under his rule, Mali broke its political and economic ties with France. ■

REVIEW

1. **FOCUS** How did the empires of Mali and Songhai come to power in West Africa?
2. **BELIEF SYSTEMS** What did Ibn Battuta like about the way of life he had observed in Mali?
3. **HISTORY** What did the French do after they invaded West Africa?
4. **CRITICAL THINKING** How did Mansa Musa change the way the people of his empire lived?
5. **ACTIVITY** Suppose you are a cartographer on Mansa Musa's pilgrimage. Make a map of the trip from Timbuktu to Mecca. Use the text and your best ideas to draw your map.

Homework Options

Explain that salt is still used as a preservative but in much smaller quantities. Ask students to check the labels on food products such as cereals and soups; have them record the amount of salt listed. Explain that sodium, or sodium chloride, is another name for salt. Students can report their findings to the class.

Study Guide: page 43

Answers to Review Questions

1. Mali became an empire when the ruler Sundiata conquered many new lands. The Songhai prince Sonni 'Ali conquered lands in the 1400s.
2. Ibn Battuta praised the people of ancient Mali for being devout and faithful Muslims.
3. The French built forts, took control of the gum arabic trade, and built a railroad. They gave a few Africans power by making them canton leaders. They did not allow Africans to vote. Many were forced to pay taxes, work on public building projects, and serve in the army during wartime.
4. Mansa Musa attracted trade to Malian cities and encouraged Islamic scholars and artists to come to the region. Many people throughout the empire adopted Islam.
5. Maps should include: the Sahara, Cairo and Mecca, and the Niger and Nile rivers and should show the route from Mali east across the Sahara, north to Cairo, and south to Mecca.

1200 1300 1400 1500 1600 1700 1800 1900 TODAY

LESSON 2

Mali and Its People

Yassoungo's father is a boatman on the Niger River. He uses a long, flat canoe to bring farm products to open markets. Sometimes, Yassoungo helps his father. They work together, pushing long poles into the muddy river bottom to move the boat.

On this day many people have brought bags of millet and maize to sell at the markets down the river. When his father pulls the canoe close to the river bank, Yassoungo loads the bags onto the boat. The boy listens to the lap of the water against the side of the boat. He looks out across the river and sees many other boats piled high with bags of grain and fresh vegetables.

Yassoungo's father has to turn some people away. There is too much cargo. The boat will get stuck in shallow water if its load is too heavy. In the dry season, the water level in the Niger River falls even farther. Between February and July the water level is so low that large boats cannot travel on the river. At some time during these months, the boy helps his father haul the boat to patch leaks and make new poles.

Most families living along the river catch fish for food. Yassoungo's family also eats vegetables and grains such as rice, millet, sorghum, and maize. They seldom eat meat. Like many other people living in Mali's rural areas, they can't afford it.

THINKING FOCUS

How do the people of Mali use the country's rivers and grasslands?

Key Terms

- landlocked
- Sahel
- drought
- savanna

Farmers raise crops of maize and rice. This large boat is both house and means of transportation for its owners.

INTRODUCE

Have students read the Thinking Focus and look at the Key Terms. These will establish the focus of Lesson 2, which is about how Mali's land and water resources affect the way Malians live. Lesson 1 explained how Mali's history was influenced by the wealth gained from trade in gold and salt. Tell students that in Lesson 2 they will find out more about Mali's geography and its people.

Key Terms

Vocabulary Strategies: T36–T37

landlocked—enclosed by land with no outlets to the sea or ocean

Sahel—the hot, partly dry region in West Africa

drought—a long period without rain

savanna—a region of grasslands and scattered trees

Graphic Overview

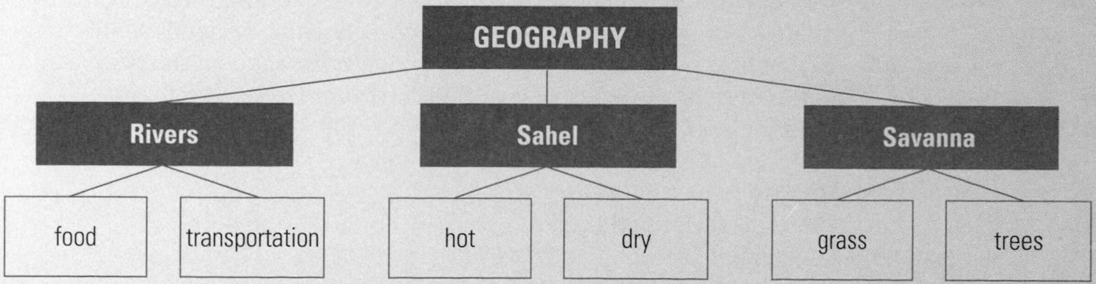
GEOGRAPHY
Rivers
Sahel
Savanna
food
transportation
hot
dry
grass
trees

Objectives

1. Locate modern Mali and describe its geographic features.
2. Explain how Mali's people now use their country's land and resources.

DEVELOP

Draw the Graphic Overview on the chalkboard or project it on an overhead transparency. Point out that the land areas in Mali are diverse, as are its people. Ask a volunteer to define diverse (*varied* or *different*). Have students scan the maps and photos in this lesson to find evidence of diversity in the geography of Mali.

GEOGRAPHY

Map and Globe Skills

Refer students to the following places on the map: the Senegal River, the Niger River, the Sahel, the savanna, and the Sahara. Mention Mali in the context of West Africa, explaining that the tributaries of the Niger and Senegal help link Mali to the Atlantic. Remind students of the discussion of geographic features in Chapter 2, and have them compare Mali's geographic features with those in your region.

➤ *The Sahel is like a shore because it meets the edge of the Sahara, the "sea of sand."*

Land of Mali

Mali is about twice the size of Texas. It is a diverse land. The physical map on this page shows Mali's main vegetation regions. Desert covers the north; grasslands stretch across the south; and a partly arid region lies in between the desert and the grasslands. Most of the people live near Mali's two major rivers.

Mali's Rivers

The Senegal *(sehn ih GAWL)* and the Niger rivers flow through Mali's mostly flat lands. Because Mali is **landlocked,** or enclosed by land, it has no seaports. The Niger is Mali's lifeline to the ocean.

The water from the Niger and Senegal rivers is vital to Mali's population. Without these rivers, people could not raise enough crops and animals to feed themselves.

The Niger flows in a huge arc of about 1,000 miles through southern and central Mali. The Bani River is a tributary of the Niger River. Together, the Niger and the Bani rivers form part of a large flood plain called an inland delta that covers 40,000 square miles in central Mali.

Mali has a rainy season and a dry season. In the rainy season, the Niger and the Bani swell and overflow their banks onto the surrounding plains. The flooding creates a large lake that stretches almost 200 miles in southwestern Mali.

When the flooding passes and the land starts to dry out, grasses begin to grow along the riverbanks. Then herders bring their goats and cattle to feed on the new grass.

▼ *Locate the Sahel region on the map. Why does this Arabic word for* shore *fit this region?*

Western Africa: Vegetation Regions

EUROPE
Mediterranean Sea
MOROCCO
ATLAS MOUNTAINS
TUNISIA
ALGERIA
LIBYA
WESTERN SAHARA (Morocco)
SAHARA
ATLANTIC OCEAN
MAURITANIA
MALI
NIGER
CHAD
Timbuktu
Gao
Lake Chad
Senegal R.
SENEGAL
GAMBIA
Djenné
Mopti
Bamako
Ségou
Niger R.
BURKINA FASO
GUINEA-BISSAU
GUINEA
SIERRA LEONE
CÔTE D'IVOIRE
GHANA
NIGERIA
LIBERIA
TOGO
BENIN
0°
20°E
40°N
20°W
20°N
Equator 0°
Mediterranean vegetation
Desert
Savanna
Sahel
Forest
0 250 500 mi.
0 250 500 km
Mercator Projection

The Sahel

Look at the map of Mali on this page. Find the region called the Sahel *(suh HAYL)*. The **Sahel** is a hot, partly dry region. The word *sahel* comes from the Arabic word meaning *shore* or *coast.* The Sahel is a borderland that lies between the bone-dry Sahara to the north and the wetter grasslands to the south. As the map on this page shows, the Sahel stretches across West Africa, through Mali, and eastward across the continent.

Few plants can grow in this region because at times little or no rain falls there. At other times, too much rain can wash away seedlings. Nevertheless, the Sahel is dotted with scrubby trees and grasses.

Sometimes, there are long periods without rain, or **drought.** During a drought, plants and grasses die.

Access Activity

Have students use the map on this page to locate Mali in West Africa. Ask them to work in pairs to identify Mali's borders and its neighboring countries. Then have them find its population and size in Countries of the World on page 676. Ask them to compare these facts about Mali with the statistics for other countries.

Access Strategy

Bring to class pictures from magazines and books that show the effects of drought and flooding. Suggest that students bring in some pictures, too. Lead a discussion about water and its uses. Talk about the ways the students use water, where the water comes from, and how it reaches them. Stress the importance of water for farmers, and ask students what they know about water problems in your region. Ask students to help you create a list of the effects of drought and flooding. Collect their suggestions, and write them on the chalkboard under two headings. Encourage students to appreciate the demands Mali's geographic features make on the people and how they have learned to adapt.

▲ *In Mali's northern desert, temperatures can reach 140°F, and there is barely any rain. (left) The savanna can receive between 20 and 60 inches of rain each year, enough to grow crops.*

Beginning in the late 1960s, Mali has had several droughts. The droughts have caused so much damage to the Sahel that some parts of the land are more like desert.

The Savanna

South of the Sahel lies a region of grasslands and forests called the **savanna**. This region covers southern Mali. Like the Sahel, it extends across West Africa. In the savanna region, a very wet season follows a very dry season. These conditions are ideal for the growth of grasses and certain trees.

Once many elephants, giraffes, and lions roamed the West African savanna. Hunters have killed many of these animals, however. Animals have also been affected by drought. At these times, the animals could not find enough food or water, so they migrated elsewhere or died.

Most of Mali's people live in the savanna in the southern part of the country. These people are farmers. Generally, enough rain falls each year to support crops as well as animals.

Wooded areas also cover the savanna region. Mango trees, first planted by the French, and shea butter trees are common there. However, the people of Mali use their forests to meet most of their energy needs. Cutting trees for firewood for cooking and heating has caused deforestation in some areas. This problem is so serious that Mali has stove police who make sure that people do not waste wood.

Some farmers in southwestern Mali plant mango and papaya trees alongside grains such as millet. The trees enrich the soil and block the dry wind. The tree roots hold soil. In one village a woman grows seedlings that she gives away to other women. Slowly, Mali's people are bringing back their forests. ■

◄ *The people of the Sahel get water from wells.*

■ How are the Sahel and the savanna regions of Mali different and how are they the same?

ECONOMICS

Critical Thinking

Explain to students that Malian agriculture is a combination of subsistence farming and cash crops.

Subsistence farming means that the crops are raised to feed only the farmer's family; cash crops are raised to be sold to others. Have students suggest some reasons Malians practice subsistence farming. *(Subsistence farming assures them that their food needs will be met, except in cases of severe drought.)*

■ *The Sahel is much drier than the savanna, and the savanna therefore has more grass and trees. Fewer people live in the Sahel. Like the Sahel, the savanna sometimes has very dry spells.*

Writing an Outline

The section of Lesson 2 entitled Land of Mali is useful for teaching or reviewing outlines. Have students prepare an outline, using Land of Mali as the title. Mali's rivers, the Sahel, and the savanna can be their three subheads, labeled A, B, and C. Have students write at least two details, listed as 1 and 2, under each of these subheads. Students can exchange papers to check for accuracy.

Study Skills

Trees found in the savanna include the mango and the papaya. Have students do research to find out more about these trees, presenting their findings in a short oral report. If possible, provide some mango and papaya for the class to taste.

■ *There are eight large ethnic groups and several smaller ones. Each group speaks its own language and usually that of a neighboring people. Many Malians also speak French. Most Malians practice Islam. Different groups grow different kinds of food and trade with each other.*

CLOSE

Read the Thinking Focus on page 255 aloud. Ask students to create a one-sentence opener for a television documentary about Mali's rivers and grasslands. Remind them that the opening sentence should grab the viewer's attention. Have students write their sentences on the chalkboard. These sentences will serve as a review of Mali's important geographic features..

A Multicultural People

For centuries Mali has been a crossroads of many cultures. Today Mali has a population of about nine million people. The population is made up of eight large ethnic groups and several smaller ones.

The Bambara, who live in the geographic center of the country, are Mali's largest ethnic group. They make up one-third of Mali's total population. They are related to the Malinke, whose ancestors lived at the time of Mansa Musa. The Bambara and the Malinke have benefited from education to help them get top positions in the government and the army. However, 81 percent of all Malians are agricultural workers.

The Songhai are a farming people. They live where the Niger River bends. They grow grain crops such as millet and rice. The Fulani are primarily herders. They live around the flood plain of the river.

Each group of people in Mali speaks its own language. Many people also speak the language of a neighboring group of people. When France occupied Mali, French became the official language of the country. It still is today. Malians write in French and speak it in schools and in the cities.

Mali's many peoples generally cooperate with one another. In spite of their diversity, almost all the population is Muslim. Their shared religious beliefs help them understand one another.

Malians also share their trading heritage from ancient times. Today most people depend on trade among themselves. Different groups of people raise different kinds of food. Bozo fishers can trade their catches for grain grown by Bambara farmers. Fulani herders can trade goats' milk for vegetables raised by the Bambara. The peoples of Mali face the challenges of the future with a spirit of cooperation and pride in their cultural traditions. ■

➤ *This Fulani woman comes from one of Mali's many ethnic groups. She wears gold earrings and a necklace. More than 100 years ago men also wore jewelry such as this.*

■ *Name some differences and some similarities among Mali's many peoples.*

REVIEW

1. **FOCUS** How do the people of Mali use the country's rivers and grasslands?
2. **SOCIAL AND POLITICAL SYSTEMS** Compare the role of the Malinke in the empires of Mali and Songhai with their role in the nation of Mali today.
3. **GEOGRAPHY** In what vegetation region of Mali has the number of wild animals decreased?
4. **CRITICAL THINKING** How do the peoples of Mali cooperate with one another?
5. **ACTIVITY** Make a drawing of the regions in Mali. Show details of each region.

Homework Options

Ask students to write a paragraph explaining how the land of Mali is diverse—culturally or geographically. Have them write their description as a "travel guide" that tells visitors what to expect in Mali.

Study Guide: page 44.

Answers to Review Questions

1. Mali's people use the rivers for fishing, irrigation, and transportation. They use the grasslands to graze animals and to grow crops.
2. The Malinke were rulers of the ancient Mali and Songhai empires. Along with the Bambara, they hold top government and army positions in Mali today.
3. Wild animals have decreased on the savanna, where hunting and drought have destroyed many habitats.
4. Most people of Mali share the same religious beliefs and speak the language of a neighboring group. Different groups trade crops, fish, and milk with each other.
5. Students' drawings should show three regions: desert, the Sahel, and the savanna. The desert area should show sand; the Sahel should have scrubby trees and grasses; and the savanna should show grasslands, scattered trees, and farms.

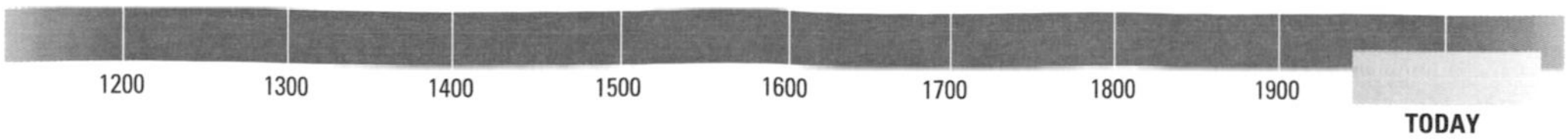
1200
1300
1400
1500
1600
1700
1800
1900
TODAY

LESSON 3

Republic of Mali

Imagine a visit to Bamako, Mali's capital. In Mali's cities, you would see a different side of the country than you have read about in Lessons 1 and 2. In the capital, you see streets lined with business buildings and jammed with cars, buses, and motorbikes. Music blasts from open car windows, and engines roar at stoplights. People crowd the streets selling a little bit of everything. Signs in French advertise supermarkets, hotels, movie theaters, a hospital, and a zoo.

Restaurants serve many delicious African foods. One specialty from Mali is a freshwater fish called *capitaine*. Bamako restaurants, like those in other large cities, offer dishes from around the world—pizza, frog legs, or French-fried potatoes.

A visit to the National Museum takes you away from the hustle and bustle of downtown Bamako to earlier times in Mali's history. Here you see displays of about 4,000 pieces of art made by the Bambara and other peoples. Wood carvings of human figures date back to the time of Mansa Musa's empire. Pieces of colorful woven cloth hang near handsome masks.

You listen as a museum guide talks to a group of schoolchildren. She explains how museum specialists restore artifacts in the collection. As you leave the museum and step into the busy streets of Bamako, you leave behind the interesting stories of Mali's past.

◄ *Carvings, such as this antelope mask made by the Bambara, form part of the living heritage of Mali.*

THINKING FOCUS

What challenges does Mali face today?

Key Term

- life expectancy

◄ *The National Museum is located in busy downtown Bamako.*

INTRODUCE

Prepare students for Lesson 3 by having them recall the information in Lesson 1, about Mali's Golden Age, and in Lesson 2, about the diversity of land and people in Mali. Have students read the Thinking Focus, and then encourage them to predict, briefly, what the challenges might be in modern Mali, based on what they have read so far. *(Improving health care, education, and the weak economy)* After they have read Lesson 3, have students compare their predictions with what they read.

Key Term

Vocabulary Strategies: T36–T37

life expectancy—the number of years that a person can expect to live

Graphic Overview

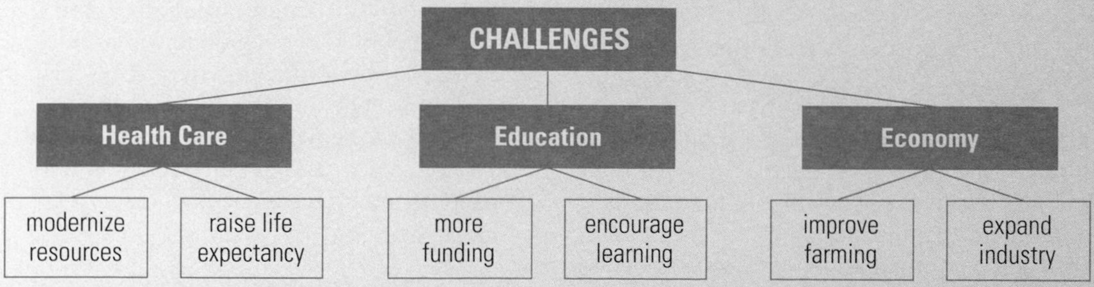
CHALLENGES
Health Care
Education
Economy
modernize resources
raise life expectancy
more funding
encourage learning
improve farming
expand industry

Objectives

1. Explain how drought affects Mali's economy.
2. Identify the resources Mali has that help the country meet the challenges it faces.

DEVELOP

Point out the lesson's problem-solution structure. To help students further understand and relate to the challenges facing Mali, draw a Venn diagram on the chalkboard or on an overhead transparency. In the left circle, write *U.S.* In the right circle, write *Mali.* Label the overlapping area *Shared Challenges.* Then have students consider health care, economy, and education. In the left circle of each diagram, write students' ideas about the ways these same issues challenge the United States. Have students read the lesson to find out about Mali. Then, in the right circle of each diagram, fill in students' predictions about the challenges facing Mali. The center area will show similarities between the United States and Mali.

Drought and Poverty

The modern nation of Mali faces challenges that its earliest empires could not have imagined. Although the early empire of Mali was one of the richest empires in Africa, today the Republic of Mali is one of the poorest countries in the world. Some of Mali's economic problems date back to the time of French occupation. You read about this period of history in Lesson 1. At that time, the region's farming and trade were controlled by the French for their benefit only.

During the late 1800s, farmers in West Africa grew crops such as peanuts, cotton, and rice. They sold the crops to French merchants, who sent the products to France. Other merchants sold French manufactured goods to the West Africans. In this way money paid to farmers for growing crops came back to France when the farmers bought goods they did not make for themselves. The French took both goods and money from the people of West Africa, leaving very little money in the region for the development of other businesses.

Undeveloped Resources

Mali has deposits of bauxite, copper, iron, nickel, and manganese. Using these mineral resources could bring Mali's people needed money. Mining minerals is expensive. Mali does not have the large sums of money needed to dig mines or to build mills or factories to turn these raw materials into finished goods. The government has had to rely on foreign contributions for this money.

Drought Hinders Farming

As you read in Lesson 2, more than half the population of Mali farm, herd animals, or fish. Farming is hard work everywhere, but especially in Mali. Periods of drought make it hard to grow food or raise animals in the Sahel. Drought affects people, animals, and plants.

When plants don't get enough water, they die. As plants wither, their roots no longer hold the soil. In the Sahel the wind blows the bare soil away. As a result the desert expands into what was once grazing land for animals. Herders

In rural areas families build mud brick homes made of two or more round buildings. Each building serves a purpose. One is used as a kitchen, another is a bedroom, and still another is a storeroom or a shelter for animals. People use local materials for building—mud bricks and grass roofs.

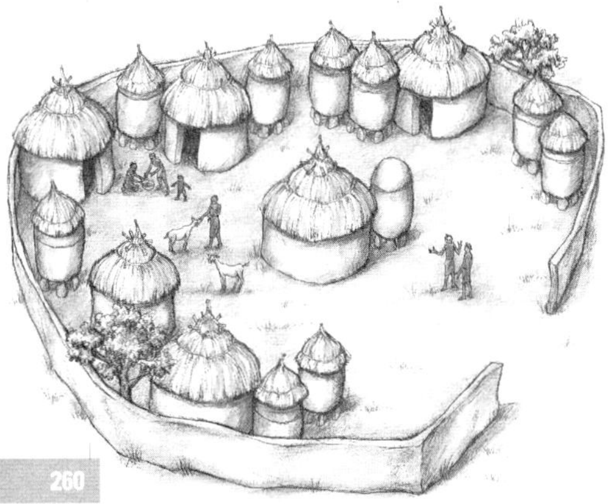

260

Chapter 11

Access Activity

Divide the class into three groups. Then have students brainstorm to come up with possible solutions to the drought problem in Mali. Have them write their ideas on a piece of paper and share their solutions with the whole class. After they have read the lesson, have them compare their ideas with those given in the lesson.

Access Strategy

Have students look at the visuals on pages 259–262 and read the captions. Then have them jot down what they think it would be like living in Mali today, based on what they have seen and read and on what they already know. Have students look at the photo of downtown Bamako on page 259 and compare the environment of the city with that of the countryside. In the city there are transportation and communications systems as well as people working in offices, factories, schools, and small businesses. In the countryside there is farmland but little farm machinery, and there are few cars or telephone wires. Tell students that the rapid growth of cities has brought problems to Mali, just as it has to other parts of the world. The cities face inadequate social services, poor housing, unemployment, and increasing crime.

move to other areas to find food for their goats and cattle. More and more herders rely on the same area to feed their animals. This overgrazing also kills plants and adds to the loss of soil.

During the 1970s and 1980s, two severe droughts occurred in the Sahel. Crops died. People and animals starved. Herders lost cattle and sheep. A group of herders called the Tuareg suffered especially great losses. Between 1970 and 1974, about 20,000 Tuareg left Mali. In search of food, they went to the neighboring countries of Niger and Algeria. Many other herders and farmers moved from rural areas to cities such as Bamako to look for jobs.

However, most people who moved to the cities could not find work. Neither the government nor private industry has the money to develop businesses that could employ the many people who have come to the cities.

Effects of Drought

People eat whatever is available during times of drought. Often the available foods do not give them enough nutrition to stay healthy.

Populations Compared by Age, 1990

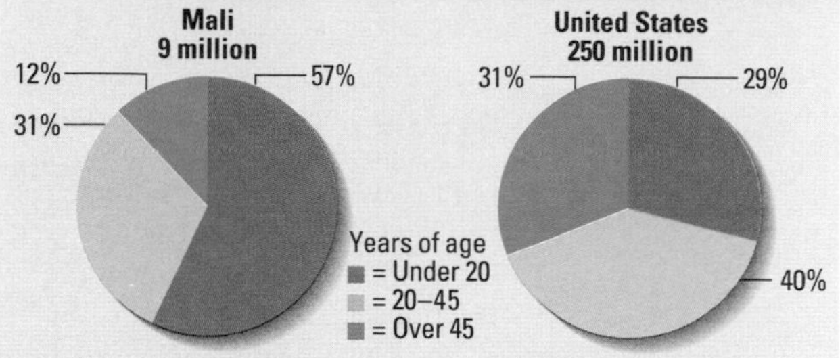

Mali
9 million
12%
57%
31%
United States
250 million
31%
29%
40%
Years of age
= Under 20
= 20–45
= Over 45

Source: United Nations, Department of International Economic and Social Affairs, 1991

The average **life expectancy,** or the number of years that people can expect to live in Mali, is about 48 years. Of each 1,000 babies born in Mali, about 175 babies die during their first year. This is one of the highest infant death rates in the world.

Children living in rural areas do not get the medicines they need to prevent or treat diseases such as measles or malaria. Many children do not live to the age of five.

Most doctors and nurses work in the cities where some people have the money to pay for services. Bamako contains more than 50 percent of Mali's doctors, nurses, and medical supplies. Only 8 percent of Mali's people live in Bamako. Most of the rest of the population lives in rural villages in the savanna or in the Sahel, where there are few health care centers. Rural clinics are often staffed by only one nurse who has no stronger medicine than aspirin to help patients who are sick. ■

▲ The population is growing rapidly in Mali. Most of Mali's people are under 20 years old. The government faces the challenge to provide basic health care for the population.

◄ In rural areas women harvest rice in fields near the Niger River.

■ List two effects of drought in Mali.

GEOGRAPHY

Critical Thinking

Tell students that, as they learned in Chapter 2, droughts affect not only land and plants but also people and animals. During the period from 1970 to 1974, an estimated 50 percent of the livestock in the Sahel and more than 100,000 people died from starvation and disease. Ask students why this occurred. *(As arable lands become desert, people become herders or migrate to new areas where they strip other sections of land. Because there is less food, people have less to eat and become malnourished. This leaves people weakened and susceptible to disease.)*

■ *Drought causes many people to move to urban areas to find work and creates health problems because of lack of proper nutrition due to unavailability of proper foods.*

Science Context

Many areas in Mali produce crops such as millet and maize. These crops are often eaten by a type of grasshopper known as a locust. Locusts fly in swarms, descend on fields, and devour whole crops within minutes. Locust plagues create havoc in the local economy. A locust plague, along with severe droughts, devastated the Malian economy in the 1970s and early 1980s.

Study Skills

Disease causes a high mortality rate in much of Africa, including Mali. Have students research different health problems, including malaria, sleeping sickness, tuberculosis, dehydration, malnutrition, and AIDS. Have students prepare informational sheets on these health problems. Students should include charts or diagrams and statistics on their sheets.

CULTURE

Visual Learning

Have the class study the photo of college students in Bamako. Since many colleges in Mali do not have university-level courses, most Malian students who want higher education go outside their country. The educational system now consists of nine years of basic education, but many students fail exams and do not progress to the ninth grade. Although the situation is improving, women still have considerably less access to education than men do; literacy rates for men are ten times higher than the rates for women.

■ *Mali now has its first democratic government, and its people rely on a rich tradition of respect for leadership.*

CLOSE

Have students answer the Thinking Focus by reviewing the Venn diagram from the beginning of the lesson. Students can use the lesson subheads as major categories to guide the discussion. Write students' ideas on the chalkboard. Compare this list with the students' predictions, made at the beginning of the lesson.

Meeting the Challenges

Mali's government must work to meet the challenges of a weak economy and the effects of drought. Like many other nations throughout the world, Mali's government is turning toward democracy. The government held its first democratic elections in 1992. Voters chose Alpha Oumar Konaré *(AL fuh oo MAHR koh NAHR ay)* as president.

President Konaré is looking to other countries to give more money for education. Drought and expanding desert send farmers and herders to the cities to seek work. These people will need to learn to read in order to work in factories and businesses. Today many children go to school only through the sixth grade.

The riches of ancient Mali are gone. However, some of its glorious past still exists in Mali today. Singing storytellers called *djeli (zehl EE)* pass on Mali's history in songs. The *djeli* songs honor the great deeds of Mali's kings and other leaders since the days of great empires.

▼ *Mali's future depends on the education of its people. These students attend college in Bamako.*

■ *Name two of Mali's resources that can help meet the challenges it faces.*

A hero is born to be a hero.
A numuke [blacksmith] is
born to be a numuke.
A djeli is born to be a djeli.
If I am poor, still I am a djeli.
If I am rich, still I am a djeli.
If my eyes see, still I am a djeli.
If I am blind, still I am a djeli.
In my heart is the spirit of a djeli.
It puts poetry in my mouth
And my mouth sings poetry.
It puts music in my fingers
And my fingers play my ngoni
[musical instrument].
When I was poor I said,
"This is not the meaning of
my life."
When I ruled Jala Bugu I said,
"This is not the meaning of
my life."
The meaning of my life
Is that I will sing for the
Traore family of kings.

Harold Courlander and Ousmane Sako, from *The Heart of the Ngoni*

In future years *djeli* may sing of Mali's present leaders. Their songs may tell of great changes in Mali. ■

REVIEW

1. **FOCUS** What challenges does Mali face today?
2. **GEOGRAPHY** How are the geography and people of Saudi Arabia and Mali alike? How are they different?
3. **CULTURE** What do you think the following saying means: "When a *djeli* dies, it is as though a whole library dies"?
4. **CRITICAL THINKING** Why is it important to preserve the stories and art of Mali's people in places such as the National Museum?
5. **ACTIVITY** Write a newspaper editorial describing the problems that President Konaré faces, and give suggestions for solving them.

Homework Options

Have students read the section called Effects of Drought, on page 261. After they have finished reading, have students write this heading: Ways to Improve Life Expectancy in Mali. Have students list some suggestions: finding new sources of food, improving medical facilities.

Study Guide: page 45

Answers to Review Questions

1. Mali faces the challenges of attracting investors for industries and providing better health care, education, and jobs.
2. Saudi Arabia and Mali both have large regions that are desert. The people in both countries are Muslim. Saudi Arabia is one of the richest countries in the world, whereas Mali is one of the poorest.
3. The songs a *djeli* sings, and the information they convey, are like books in a library.
4. Students might answer that the children need to know their rich heritage. This heritage promotes a sense that the Malians are capable of great achievements.
5. Editorials might mention that the problems President Konaré inherited include poor health care and schools. Students may suggest that Konaré set up more teacher-training programs and seek more help from richer countries.

UNDERSTANDING ARGUMENTS

Identifying Supporting Evidence

Here's Why

People often have different points of view about a situation or an event. A writer presents a point of view in the form of an argument. To evaluate a written argument, you need to be able to find supporting facts, or evidence.

There is a growing debate today in Mali about the environmental effects on a part of the Sahel, a flood plain of the Niger River. Locate the Sahel on the map on page 256. Each year the river, overflowing with summer rains, floods the dry, dusty land. This water lets people here farm and fish. It also supports millions of birds that migrate from Europe to this part of the Sahel each year.

Today drought threatens life in the Sahel. What should be done? One argument is that the natural cycle should be allowed to continue. In this way people can continue to work as herders, farmers, and fishers. Others argue for damming the Niger River and creating large-scale irrigation projects. This would allow people to grow rice.

To evaluate the argument, you must be able to understand the ideas and arguments as they are presented. You must ask which ideas are supported by the most evidence.

People should not interfere with the natural cycle of dryness and flooding in the Sahel. If the area is turned into rice fields, the people have only one way of earning a living—growing rice. In addition, flooding will kill many species of plants and animals. If the cycle is maintained, people can continue to make a living in three ways: fishing, farming, and raising livestock.

Today, because of the decreasing rainfall, people must use the land more wisely. Sometimes animals are lost during windstorms. The number of people who are allowed to farm, raise animals, and fish in the Sahel should be controlled, and only small-scale irrigation projects should be introduced into the area. People and wildlife have lived in the Sahel for thousands of years. Only by taking these measures can they continue to do so.

Main point

Relevant. This emphasizes the main point of the argument.

Irrelevant. This has nothing to do with the main point.

Consistent. This summarizes the argument.

Here's How

As in most other arguments, there are many opinions about the future of the Sahel. The boxed paragraph offers one opinion. To evaluate the argument, first identify its main point: People should not interfere with the natural cycle of the Sahel.

Now, identify the supporting evidence. Are the facts presented relevant—do they fit the point the writer is making? Statements that do not keep to the point are irrelevant. They weaken the writer's position. Then decide whether the facts are consistent—do they agree with other facts presented?

Try It

Is the statement, "The people of Mali have a rich history of ancient kingdoms," relevant or irrelevant to the writer's point? Explain.

Apply It

You can find an argument presented in the editorial pages of your local newspaper. Choose an editorial argument and identify the writer's main point. Then write a paragraph that evaluates the argument using the steps in Here's How.

UNDERSTANDING ARGUMENTS

This skills feature uses information from Lessons 2 and 3 to teach students to evaluate evidence supporting an argument. Students will learn to distinguish between relevant and irrelevant supporting details.

GEOGRAPHY

Critical Thinking

Have students read the overview, Here's Why, which presents two arguments about the future of the Sahel. Ask them to state the two arguments in their own words. *(The first argument favors continuing with the natural cycle; the second argument favors damming the Niger River.)* Next, have students read Here's How and the boxed paragraph in order to understand main points and relevant and irrelevant details. As an extension, write the following two sentences on the chalkboard, asking students to identify them as relevant or irrelevant to the argument:

Rice is not as popular a food in Mali as maize.

In the past interfering with the natural cycle has caused soil problems. *(The first sentence is irrelevant, and the second sentence is relevant.)*

Writing an Argument

Have half the class write arguments that give reasons for forcing Malian medical personnel to work in rural areas before being allowed to work in the cities. Have the other half of the class write a paragraph giving reasons against such a policy. The students should consider the ethical issues involved, as well as the health problems faced by rural Malians. After students have finished writing their arguments, have them exchange papers and evaluate each other's arguments.

Answer to Try It

The statement is irrelevant because it has nothing to do with the future of the Sahel, the topic being discussed.

Answer to Apply It

Check to see that students have identified the writer's main point. If students cannot spot irrelevant facts, suggest that they write the facts down and then determine whether these facts support the writer's main point.

Objective

Evaluate an argument for consistency and relevance. (Critical Thinking 1, 2)

Answers to Reviewing Key Terms

A. Sample answers:

1. Mali is **landlocked.** The country is enclosed by land. The words *land* and *locked* suggest that a region is locked in place by other land.
2. A **middleman** is a person (or *man*) who buys or sells something on behalf of others; is in the *middle* between buyer and seller. In the ancient empire of Mali, middlemen ran the gold trade.
3. **Life expectancy** is the number of years that people can *expect* to *live.* People in Mali have a short life expectancy.

B. Sample answers:

1. A **drought** is a long period without rain. Mali has had so many periods of drought in recent years that farming regions have become deserts.
2. The **Sahel** is a hot, partly dry region that separates deserts from grasslands. The Arabic word *sahel* means "shore" or "coast."
3. A **savanna** is a region of grasslands and forests where grasses, trees, and farm crops grow.
4. **Life expectancy** is the number of years a person can be expected to live. It is affected by health care and food.
5. A **landlocked** country, with no seaport, may not easily trade.

Answers to Exploring Concepts

A. Sample answers:

1235: Sundiata; empire, with king; 1. Mali gained control of the trading centers of Gao and Djenné; 2. The empire controls the gold-salt trade routes.

1307: Mansa Musa; empire, with king; 1. Mansa Musa's pilgrimage displays the great wealth of West Africa; 2. The kingdom of Mali grows to its largest extent.

1468: Sonni 'Ali; empire, with king; 1. Timbuktu becomes a major trading center; 2. Culture flourishes.

1894: France; colonial government; 1. French becomes official language of Mali; 2. Malians' civil rights and education suffer.

1992: Alpha Oumar Konaré; democratic republic, with president; 1. Mali is still a poor nation; 2. President Konaré is trying to improve conditions in Mali.

B. Sample answers:

1. Mansa Musa's pilgrimage to Mecca attracted the attention of many outsiders who, learning of the kingdom's great wealth, began to travel to Mali to trade.
2. Salt traders from North Africa and gold traders from locations to the south of the empire came to Mali, which was located between the two regions.
3. Ibn Battuta, an early Muslim explorer, described the reign of Mansa Musa's grandson. The writings of Leo Africanus praised the Songhai for their learning.
4. The telegraph linked French forts along the Senegal River. The railroad connected trading centers.
5. The French left their language and some examples of architecture.
6. They plant trees to enrich the soil and block the wind.
7. Drought, which leads to soil erosion, makes life difficult for Malian farmers and herders who live in the savanna and the Sahel.
8. The Bambara, Mali's largest ethnic group, live in the center of the country; the Songhai, farming peoples, live near the Niger River; and the Fulani are herders and live around the river's flood plain.

Chapter Review

Reviewing Key Terms

drought (p. 256)
landlocked (p. 256)
life expectancy (p. 261)
middleman (p. 250)
Sahel (p. 256)
savanna (p. 257)

A. A compound word or term is made when two smaller words are combined. Three of the key terms are compound words or terms. On your own paper, write a definition for each of the following key terms that relates to ideas in this chapter. Also write what hints about the definition you get from the two smaller words.

1. landlocked
2. middleman
3. life expectancy

B. Answer the following questions regarding selected key terms.

1. What is a drought, and how have droughts affected farming in modern Mali?
2. What is the Sahel? What two types of land does it separate? What is the meaning of the Arabic word sahel, from which it gets its name?
3. What is a savanna? What types of plants might grow in a savanna?
4. What is a life expectancy? How is it affected by the place in which you live?
5. What does landlocked mean? What effect might being landlocked have on a country?

Exploring Concepts

A. Copy and complete this chart to outline key periods in Mali's history. Use the timeline on pages 246–247 and facts from your reading to help you. In the final column, list at least two facts about that period in Mali's history. Some entries have been filled in for you.

Year	Ruler	Government	Events
1250	Sundiata		
1307			
	Sonni Ali	empire, with king	
1894			French becomes official language of Mali
1992			

B. Answer each question with information from the chapter.

1. How did Mansa Musa's grand pilgrimage to Mecca affect Mali's economic growth during his reign?
2. What role did gold and salt have in making Mali a center of trade?
3. Who are Ibn Battuta and Leo Africanus? What information have they provided for people today about Mali's old empires?
4. How did the French use the telegraph and the railroad to gain control of trade in West Africa?
5. Give two examples of French culture that remain in Mali today.
6. What are the people of Mali doing today to bring the forests back to their country?
7. How have Mali's climate and geography created harsh challenges for its citizens today?
8. Describe the major ethnic groups of Mali. In what areas of Mali is each group located?

Reviewing Skills

1. Reread the section entitled The French Occupation on pages 253–254. Imagine that you are a Malian journalist living in 1898. You are writing an editorial. The title of the editorial is The French Have Made Us Suffer! Write a plan for the editorial. Include the following:
   - a sentence stating the main point of your argument
   - a numbered list of sentences containing information that supports your argument

   Use examples from the chapter as your supporting evidence.
2. Look again at the skill feature in Chapter 10, on page 238. Using the techniques given for identifying sources, write an evaluation of the following source: the song of a modern *djeli* about the empire of Mansa Musa.
3. Imagine that you are a *djeli,* planning to write a song about recent accomplishments by the president of Mali, Alpha Oumar Konaré. What would you need to know in order to write your song? What sources might you use to find that information?

Using Critical Thinking

1. You have read that Mali's food supply is threatened by drought and that its people suffer because medical care and educational opportunities are limited. Imagine that you are advising other nations on ways to help Mali. What specific suggestions would you offer?
2. If you were to move to Mali, where would you choose to live—in the capital city, Bamako, or in the countyside? Explain your answer.
3. In many parts of the world, people of different ethnic groups have great difficulty living together in peace. What factors help Malians to work and live together, despite their differences?

Preparing for Citizenship

1. COLLECTING INFORMATION Life expectancy in Mali is only 48 years, and the nation also has one of the highest death rates for babies. Use an almanac to locate the statistics on life expectancy and infant mortality in the United States. Share your research with the class. Then discuss what factors might make the statistics from Mali and the United States vary.
2. WRITING ACTIVITY Imagine that you are a *djeli* in the United States who has been selected to write a song or a poem about the accomplishments of a famous person. It might be, for example, a political leader, a scientist, a historical figure, an athlete, or a musician. Use your imagination. Share your work with the class.
3. COLLABORATIVE LEARNING The National Museum of Mali exhibits beautiful artifacts that provide a glimpse of Mali's rich history. In a small group, plan and create an exhibit that will provide information about Mali's climate and geography. In your group, create three committees, one for each of Mali's regions—the desert, the savanna, and the Sahel. Refer to pages 256–257. Each committee should discuss and summarize the geographic features of their region. Plan an exhibit that combines written material with diagrams, models, or pictures. Then create the exhibit. When you have finished, all the committees in your group should work together to combine and present the three exhibits to the class. Every member of the group should take on a task. After the groups have presented their exhibits, ask them to get together to discuss what aspects of their group work were successful and what group members could have done to improve the final exhibit.

Answers to Reviewing Skills

1. The students' editorial should include facts and details from pages 253–254 and reflect mastery of the skill feature—evaluating arguments.

   Sample answers:

   Main point: The French colonial government controls all important aspects of our lives, and we are suffering because of it.

   Supporting evidence: They have built forts along the Senegal River, controlling our trade routes; they have forced local leaders to sign treaties giving up their lands; they denied our children a good education; they have forced us to work on building projects.
2. The song of a modern *djeli* about the empire of Mansa Musa would be written after the event took place; the writer is not an eyewitness. It is, therefore, a secondary source.
3. The *djeli* would need specific facts and details about the president's accomplishments. Possible sources include newspapers, magazines, and interviews.

Answers to Using Critical Thinking

1. Sample answers: economic relief to fund health care and educational programs; food and supplies to alleviate the hardships resulting from droughts; scientific planting programs and irrigation systems to replace trees and grasslands; training programs for farmers, teachers, and health-care workers.
2. Students' responses should mention that residents in Bamako have medical centers, schools, museums, and other cultural attractions. However, there are few factories there, so many people cannot find jobs. In rural areas such as the savanna and the Sahel, people live in small villages. Life is difficult, however, because of droughts and inadequate medical facilities.
3. Although each ethnic group speaks a different language, many people also speak French and the language of a neighboring group. Islam also unites the groups, as does the Malians' pride in their past.

Answers to Preparing for Citizenship

1. COLLECTING INFORMATION Students' research should be careful and accurate. In comparing the statistics for the United States and Mali, students should discuss such factors as availability of nutritional foods, access to health care, and the effects of geographic features and climatic crises.
2. WRITING ACTIVITY Students' writing should describe the accomplishments of the subjects they selected.
3. COLLABORATIVE LEARNING The exhibits should include written and graphic materials that effectively illustrate the major geographic features of Mali's three regions.

CHAPTER ORGANIZER

Chapter 12 Ghana

CHAPTER PLANNING CHART

Pupil's Edition	Teacher's Edition	Ancillaries
Lesson 1: The Asante: A People of Tradition (3–4 days) Objective 1: Describe the Asante land and people. (Geography 1, 2; Culture 2) Objective 2: Identify elements of Asante life that are both unique and typical of West African peoples. (Culture 2, 4; Ethics and Belief Systems 1, 4; Social and Political Systems 1)	• Graphic Overview (268) • Access Strategy (269) • Access Activity (269) Critical Thinking (270) Social Context (270)	Study Guide (47) Discovery Journal (23)
Understanding Critical Thinking Objective: Evaluate and interpret proverbs. (Critical Thinking 2)		Study Guide (48)
Lesson 2: Growth and Change (3–4 days) Objective 1: Explain the rise of the Ashanti Empire and its growth in power and wealth. (History 3, 7; Geography 4; Economics 1; Culture 5, 6) Objective 2: Analyze the impact of colonial rule on the Asante way of life. (History 7; Geography 4; Economics 4; Social and Political Systems 3, 6)	• Graphic Overview (273) • Access Activity (274) • Access Strategy (274) Science Connection (275) • Visual Learning (275) Study Skill (276) Historical Context (276)	Study Guide (49) Discovery Journal (24) • Posters (1)
Exploring: African Jewelry Objective 1: Explore the vastness of African culture by taking a look at one facet of it: jewelry and beads. (Culture 5) Objective 2: Explore the origins of various jewelry and bead types. (Culture 1, 2, 4) Objective 3: Explore the global influence of African culture. (Culture 1, 2, 3, 4)		Discovery Journal (25)
Lesson 3: A New Nation (2–3 days) Objective 1: Identify the problems faced by Ghana as a new nation. (History 6; Geography 4; Economics 4) Objective 2: Evaluate the role of old and new traditions in Ghana today. (History 6; Social and Political Systems 1, 3; Citizenship 1, 5, 6)	• Graphic Overview (280) • Access Strategy (281) • Access Activity (281) Critical Thinking (282) Economic Context (282)	Study Guide (50) Map Activities (16)
Literature: The Cow-Tail Switch	• Access Strategy (285) Collaborative Learning (286) Writing a News Account (287)	Discovery Journal (26)
Chapter Review	Answers (288–289)	Tests (45–48)

* Objectives are correlated to the strands and goals in the program Scope and Sequence on pages T41–T49.

• LEP appropriate resources. (For additional strategies, see pages T32–T33.)

CHAPTER RATIONALE

This chapter continues the story of the various cultures and nations of modern Africa. Here we see a traditional African society, the Asante, who are part of the Akan ethnic group of West Africa. The Asante live in Ghana, which became the first independent nation among the African colonies south of the Sahara.

Lesson 1 introduces the Asante through their traditional annual festival, the Odwira. The West African location and rain forest environment of the Asante are described. The Asante are identified as one of the Akan peoples who migrated into the region of modern Ghana between the 1100s and the 1800s. Students will see that the Asante have special customs, such as tracing descent through the matrilineal line. In other ways, the Asante are representative of many West African peoples. Their society is based on kinship, which emphasizes lineage, the descent from a common ancestor. Religion includes worship of a single God as creator, with honor also given to lesser Gods and the spirits of ancestors.

Lesson 2 traces the history of the Asante people and their empire from the late 1600s through the colonial era, which ended in 1957. The lesson opens with the story of Osei Tutu, an Asante leader who formed a union of small Akan states that grew to become the Ashanti Empire. He also devised the symbols, rituals, and kingship that were basic to the nation's identity. Despite contacts with Muslim traders and Europeans, the Asante kept their culture and way of life intact. They traded actively with both groups, even entering the slave trade to obtain firearms and goods for daily life.

In the 1800s Great Britain gained control of the European trade in West Africa. Britain's wish to control the sources of goods brought it into conflict with the Ashanti Empire. In the 1870s Britain set up the Gold Coast colony south of the Asante. After strong resistance, the Asante were made a part of the Gold Coast colony. Yet they kept their cultural traditions and identity.

A new era began after World War II, when a wave of nationalism swept through European colonies in Africa. **Lesson 3** traces the movement for independence in Britain's Gold Coast colony under the leadership of Kwame Nkrumah. In 1957 that colony gained its independence and became the nation of Ghana.

Despite people's high hopes for Ghana's success, problems arose. These were caused by a fall in the price of cocoa, Ghana's main export, and Nkrumah's strong rule. Eventually, rising prices for cocoa brought better times, and new leadership brought reforms in the government.

A more subtle problem for Ghana was to reconcile the new national structure with traditional cultural patterns and institutions. The solution has been to keep traditional ways at the village level, while modernizing and carrying on development at the national level. For the Asante, keeping their traditions is a source of stability in a time of change.

ACTIVITIES & PROJECTS

LEP: Making a Mural

Divide students into four groups. Ask them to paint a mural with scenes representing Lesson 1. Each group will paint one scene. You might suggest possible topics, such as the Odwira as described in the text, an Asante village, a family gathering, or crafts such as weaving or woodcarving. (Use after Lesson 1.)

Basic: Writing

Two people from different cultures might have very different views concerning the same event. Have students write two descriptions of the incident in which the British governor demanded to sit on the Golden Stool: one version that Governor Hodgson might write, the other version that Queen Mother Yaa Asantewa might write. (Use after Lesson 2.)

Investigating

Remind students that part of the United States was once a British colony. Ask them to recall how American colonists felt about British rule. List students' comments on the chalkboard. Then ask how the people of Ghana felt about British rule, and list the comments on the chalkboard. Have students compare the two lists. What conclusions do they draw? (Use after Lesson 2.)

Challenge: Collaborative Learning

Have students read the Declaration of Independence of the United States. Then ask them to write an Asante Declaration of Independence. Several students might develop a list of reasons why the Asante are seeking independence; another group could draw up a list of reasons why they deserve it; and a third group could develop a plan for achieving it. Have students present their Declaration to the class. (Use after Lesson 2.)

Collaborative Learning

Ask students to assume that they have just been appointed to the cabinet of the Ghanaian president. They are preparing for their first working meeting. They must identify areas in which the new nation can improve and grow. Divide the class into three groups, representing political, economic, and social needs. Instruct each group to prepare a list of problems in each area. For each problem they list, students should include ideas for solutions. After they have completed their lists, groups can present their findings to the class. (Use after Lesson 3.)

CHAPTER PREVIEW

Ask students to read the chapter title and the paragraph that follows. Have them look at the photographs and read the captions. What can they tell about Ghana from the photographs? *(Some of Ghana is located in the rain forest; the forest provides wood and gold as resources; Ghanaians value freedom.)*

Looking Back

Have students turn to the map of Africa on page 223 and locate Ghana. Also locate Mali, the nation they have just studied in Chapter 11. Point out that unlike Mali, which is partly desert and is landlocked, Ghana contains savanna and rain forest areas and is located on the coast.

Looking Forward

Tell students that they will read about one West African people, the Asante, in the next three lessons: The Asante: A People of Tradition; Growth and Change; and A New Nation. Tell students that they will learn how the Asante built an empire and how the colony and the empire became a part of the nation of Ghana.

Lesson 1 describes Asante history and traditions.

Chapter 12
Ghana

The rain-forest region of West Africa was the home of many different groups. One of them came to be known as the Asante (uh SAHN tee). From their forest homeland, they built the Ashanti (uh SHAHN tee) Empire and gained wealth through trade. After a time as a colony of Britain, Ashanti and neighboring states founded the modern nation of Ghana. Ghana became the first of the former European colonies in Africa south of the Sahara to become an independent nation.

The rain forest of Ghana provides fine wood for carving. Woodcarvers are highly skilled at their traditional craft.

950	1100	1250	1400

1300s Ancestors of Asante migrate into region of today's Ghana.

1482 Portuguese build fort at Elmin

266

1340

BACKGROUND

Ghana is a country about the size of Oregon and home to about 16 million people. It is considered among the leading countries of Africa because of its long-established culture, wealth of natural resources, and history-making role as the first African colony south of the Sahara to win independence.

West African Trade

From the 700s to the late 1400s, the land of the Asante was on the southern edge of great West African trading empires. In the late 1400s, Europeans entered the West African trade by sea. In 1482 the Portuguese, seeking gold, built a trading post at Elmina. Other Europeans soon followed. By the early 1800s, Britain dominated the West African trade. It then began a quest for territory. From 1901 until 1957, the Ashanti Empire was part of a British colony. In 1957 it gained independence as the nation of Ghana.

Cultural Diversity

The nation of Ghana has at least 75 different cultural groups, each with its own language and customs. Among these are the Akan. The Akan-speaking people migrated into West Africa before the coming of Europeans. During the 1600s several Akan groups united to form the Ashanti state. Their strong sense of cultural identity aided them in becoming a political power.

Throughout their history, Ghana's ethnic groups have preserved their traditions. They still celebrate many of the ancient festivals

The Akosombo Dam on the Volta River provides power for industry. It forms the over-250-mile-long Lake Volta, the world's largest artificial lake.

Nana Konadu Agyeman-Rawlings, wife of Ghana's president, Jerry Rawlings, leads the movement to assure rights and opportunities for women in Ghana.

AD 1957

The Black Star monument in Accra, Ghana's capital, is called Independence Arch. The black star symbolizes all those who fought for freedom.

The rain-forest region of Ghana has for centuries been a major producer of gold. Brass weights like these were used to weigh gold dust when it was traded.

1550 | 1700 | 1850 | 2000

late 1600s Osei Tutu forms Ashanti nation.

1820 Height of Ashanti Empire

1957 Ghana becomes independent.

Today

Understanding the Visuals

Woodcarving, shown on page 266, has a long tradition in West Africa. Many of the carvings have religious meanings. Carved stools are important in Ghana. Ceremonial stools serve as the thrones of chiefs and are symbols of authority.

The Akosombo Dam, built after Ghana became independent, provides hydroelectricity for industries such as the new aluminum industry. Producing aluminum requires a great deal of energy. The new industries are an important addition to the nation's economy.

Nana is an Asante title of respect. Nana Konadu Agyeman-Rawlings takes an active role in improving the position of women in Ghana. She has created a national organization in which women carry out cooperative money-making projects. She has also supported the building of schools and daycare centers throughout the country.

Understanding Chronology

Point out that the timeline encompasses four main eras in Ghanaian history: the Asante migration, the Ashanti nation, the Ashanti Empire, and Ghanaian independence.

and elect local chieftains to lead them and settle disputes. Among the ethnic groups, folktales and proverbs are popular forms of literature. Some of the Akan tales feature Ananse, a spider who overcomes stronger foes by using her wits. Students may enjoy reading these tales for the flavor of Ghanaian life and history they provide.

One of the challenges for modern-day Ghana is how to encourage more cooperation and communication among ethnic groups as a means of building national unity. At the same time, it remains important to preserve the values of these traditional societies.

INTRODUCE

Ask the class to read the lesson title aloud and predict what a "people of tradition" might be like. *(They probably have a rich heritage and many special customs.)* Have students read the Thinking Focus. Ask how a festival relates to the idea of traditions. *(Festivals mark special holidays that are celebrated year after year.)* Point out that the term *Ashanti* refers to a particular kingdom or empire. The term *Asante* is used here to refer to the people of that state. Direct students to read the lesson to learn more about the Asante, their homeland, and their traditions.

Key Terms

Vocabulary Strategies: T36–T37

matrilineal—tracing ancestry through the mother's side of the family

patrilineal—tracing ancestry through the father's side of the family

kinship—being related by common ancestry, adoption, or marriage

lineage—ancestry; the descendants of a common ancestor

B.C. A.D.
1000
1200
1340
TODAY

LESSON 1

The Asante: A People of Tradition

A particular Monday . . . was chosen for the [start] of this ceremony. On that day the reigning King of Ashanti paid a semi-state visit to the [tombs] at Bantama. . . . The king . . . [addressed the ancestral spirits] as follows: "The edges of the years have come round, we are about to celebrate the rites of the odwira; do not permit any evil at all to come upon us and let the new year meet us peacefully."

Captain R. S. Rattray, *Religion and Art in Ashanti*

THINKING FOCUS

What does the Odwira festival mean to the Asante?

Key Terms

- matrilineal
- patrilineal
- kinship
- lineage

Every September the Asante celebrate the great Odwira *(oh DOO ruh)* festival. They give thanks for the yam harvest, honor the spirits of their ancestors, and renew their loyalty to their leader.

Captain Rattray was a British official who witnessed the festival almost a hundred years ago. He also described another part of the ceremony, which takes place 11 days later. This is the royal parade by the Asantehene *(uh sahnt uh HEH nay)*, the Asante king. In this parade the Asantehene follows the Golden Stool, the "shrine and symbol of the national soul" of the Asante. Sheltering the stool is a large umbrella known as "the covering of the nation." Attendants walk alongside the stool, supporting the solid gold bells tied to it. This stool is never used as a seat, and it is treated with great respect.

On the last day of Odwira, Asante chiefs and their attendants once again march to the palace. The Asantehene is carried to the palace in a decorated seat atop his attendants' shoulders. There he awaits the lesser chiefs, who step forward and renew their vow of loyalty. Year after year the Odwira tradition remains unbroken.

The Asantehene is a powerful and respected leader. He maintains order and justice. His heavy gold jewelry shows his wealth and rank as king.

Objectives

1. Describe the Asante land and people.
2. Identify elements of Asante life that are both unique and typical of West African peoples.

Graphic Overview

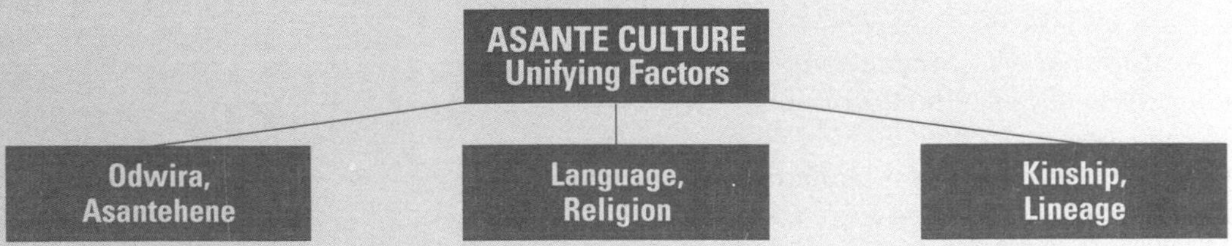
ASANTE CULTURE
Unifying Factors
Odwira, Asantehene
Language, Religion
Kinship, Lineage

Land and People

The roughly two million Asante today make up the largest ethnic group in the modern nation of Ghana. They are citizens of Ghana and live in the Ashanti region. The map Modern Ghana on page 282 shows the location of the present Asante homeland in Ghana.

Geography of Ghana

Ghana, a nation in West Africa, borders the Gulf of Guinea. Ghana is about the size of Oregon. Its location, near the equator and at a low elevation, gives much of it a tropical climate. The Atlas map of Africa on page 685 shows where Ghana is located.

Ghana includes a number of different geographic regions. Along its more than 300-mile coast, no natural harbors exist. Tropical swamps and brush-covered plains stretch 50 miles inland in some places. Farther inland lie humid rain forests. The northern two-thirds of Ghana level out and become savanna. Two large rivers, the Black Volta and White Volta, join to form the huge Volta River, which flows into the Gulf of Guinea.

Origin of the Asante

The ancestors of the Asante came from the savanna north of Ghana. They were members of a large Akan-speaking group that migrated south between the 1100s and 1800s. In time they divided into a number of different states. One of these was Ashanti. Its people, the Asante, settled in the rain forest region.

The warm climate, abundant plant life, and mineral resources of the area helped the Asante prosper. Besides hunting and gathering, they raised crops in clearings in the rain forest. From the forest they harvested kola nuts and mined gold to sell to traders. They also carried on trade with people of the savanna to the north. ■

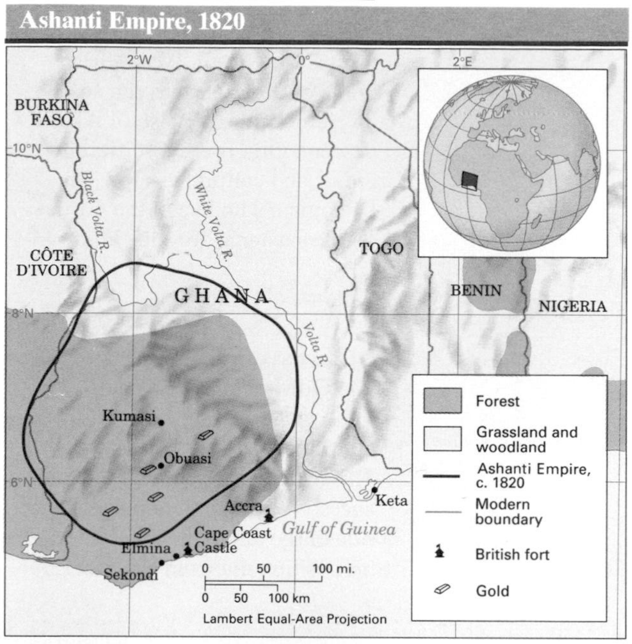

Ashanti Empire, 1820
2°W
0°
2°E
10°N
8°N
6°N
BURKINA FASO
CÔTE D'IVOIRE
GHANA
TOGO
BENIN
NIGERIA
Black Volta R.
White Volta R.
Volta R.
Kumasi
Obuasi
Accra
Keta
Cape Coast Castle
Elmina
Sekondi
Gulf of Guinea
Forest
Grassland and woodland
Ashanti Empire, c. 1820
Modern boundary
British fort
Gold
0 50 100 mi.
0 50 100 km
Lambert Equal-Area Projection

▲ *This map shows the Ashanti Empire at about the time of its first contact with Britain. How large was the Ashanti Empire compared with Ghana today?*

◄ *The dense, tropical rain forest was the homeland of the Asante.*

■ *How did their environment and resources help the Asante prosper?*

DEVELOP

Direct students to look at the map on this page to familiarize themselves with the geography of Ghana. Help students use the map key to identify the vegetation regions that make up modern Ghana. *(Rain forest in the south and west; grassland and woodland in the north and east)* In which region was the Ashanti Empire? *(Mostly rain forest)*

◄ *The Ashanti Empire in 1820 was about one-half as large as Ghana today.*

CULTURE

Critical Thinking

Ghana has more than 75 distinct cultural groups, divided into eight major language groups. The largest language group is the Akan, to which most of the Asante belong. Ask how their language and cultural ties might have helped the Asante to gain influence. *(Having the same language as neighboring groups would enable the Asante to trade readily with them and to form alliances. Having similar traditions would help to bridge any other differences.)*

■ *The tropical environment provided crops for the Asante to harvest; the rain forest provided gold for them to sell.*

Access Strategy

Bring to class items related to a Fourth of July celebration. Ask students what holiday these items bring to mind. *(They are symbols of Independence Day, or the Fourth of July.)* Ask students to suggest similar holidays that are celebrated in other cultures. *(Examples include France's Bastille Day, celebrated on July 14, Mexico's Cinco de Mayo, May 5, and Canada's Canada Day, July 1)* Explain that a holiday celebration is one example of a tradition. Point out that the Fourth of July is a traditional holiday that people in the United States have been celebrating for more than 200 years. Ask volunteers to name other holidays our nation celebrates. *(Sample answers: Labor Day and Thanksgiving)* Remind the class that people in different countries and different ethnic groups follow their own customs and celebrate their own holidays. Tell students that they are going to read about the Asante people, their homeland, and their traditions.

Access Activity

Ask students to reread the literary selection at the top of page 268. Then ask them to suggest special ceremonies or celebrations from their own culture that are similar to those described in the reading. *(Sample answers: A visit to cemeteries suggests Memorial Day; the reference to "new year" suggests the New Year's celebrations.)*

CULTURE

Study Skills

Have students create graphic organizers to show the similarities and differences between the Ashanti kingdom and other West African states. *(Two examples are a Venn diagram of overlapping circles or a chart with check-offs for different characteristics.)*

CITIZENSHIP

Critical Thinking

Direct students to work in small discussion groups to identify advantages and disadvantages of communities and nations based on kinship or ethnic bonds. *(Answers will vary. An advantage might be a shared sense of purpose among kin or the members of an ethnic group. Disadvantages may be a feeling of competition among lineages or groups and the lack of a feeling of national identity.)*

West African Connections

The Asante are one of many groups who live in West Africa. Some of them, such as the coast-dwelling Fante, are also of Akan descent. Others are of different ethnic and cultural groups. The Dagomba, who live in the north on the savanna, are Muslims.

Patterns of Living

Each ethnic group in West Africa has certain unique traditions. The Odwira is a special festival of the Asante. Asante culture is also **matrilineal** *(mat ruh LIHN ee uhl).* This means that people trace their ancestry through their mother's side of the family. A chief inherits his position not from his father but from his mother's brother. Most West African cultures, however, are **patrilineal** *(pat ruh LIHN ee uhl)* and trace their ancestry through the father's side.

Women receive much respect in Asante society. Women can own property and carry on trade. Women also influence decisions about government.

➤ *This young woman is carrying yams to sell at the market in Accra. Market women play an important role in the economy of Ghana.*

Understanding Kinship

When you have a family gathering, who shows up? Grandparents and grandchildren? Aunts and uncles? First and second cousins, nieces and nephews? All of these people are related to you. All of you share kinship.

Africans value kinship and family as the basis of society. Communities are based on family ties. These ties give people in the community a sense of belonging and of caring for each other.

Within an ethnic group, the main unit of kinship is the clan. This is a very large group of families who long ago shared a special ancestor. This ancestor may have lived hundreds of years ago. Yet the people in the clan still feel linked to that person and to everyone else who is related. Within each clan are smaller groups called lineages, made up of a number of families.

The smallest group within a clan is the family. An Asante family is often very large. Wealthy Asante men may have several wives. The family includes these wives, their children, and their relatives. It also includes aunts, uncles, cousins, and grandparents.

Kinship ties are so strong that people who have died are still seen as belonging to the family. In the same way, future children are already seen as members of the family. The naming of a new baby is a special time. The week-old infant is introduced to the kinship group that will play an important role in its life.

Kinship affects each person's life in many ways. It determines not only a person's role within the lineage but also whom a person may marry. It influences one's position in society and what kind of work one may do.

Critical Thinking

Ask students to list characteristics of the traditional roles for Asante men and women. Ask how those roles are similar to and different from the roles of men and women in the United States today. *(Women in both Ghana and the United States fill the role of homemakers, although in the United States men often share this role. Asante tasks and occupations tend to be more gender specific.)*

Social Context

In the matrilineal society of the Asante, the Queen Mother, or Asantehemaa, was very powerful. She was usually the chief's mother or sister. Her role was to advise and guide the Asantehene, and she could assume full powers of leadership if the Asantehene was incapacitated or unavailable. The Queen Mother was a full member of the governing council and judged all cases involving sacred oaths of state. She had jurisdiction over all domestic matters affecting women and members of the royal family. She also had final say over who would succeed a chief. This was a powerful role, since there were no set rules of succession for chiefs.

The Queen Mother (the mother of the Asantehene or another close female relative) is the Asantehene's official adviser.

All West African peoples place great value on **kinship,** or relationship through common ancestors. One important aspect of kinship is **lineage** *(LIHN ee ihj),* a group of several families with the same ancestor.

Most people in West Africa believe in one God, who created all things, and in lesser Gods and spirits. People also believe that their ancestors remain a part of the family. People honor their ancestors with prayer and sacrifice. These practices and beliefs reflect people's view of the world. The music, dance, and art of West Africa often express aspects of people's religion.

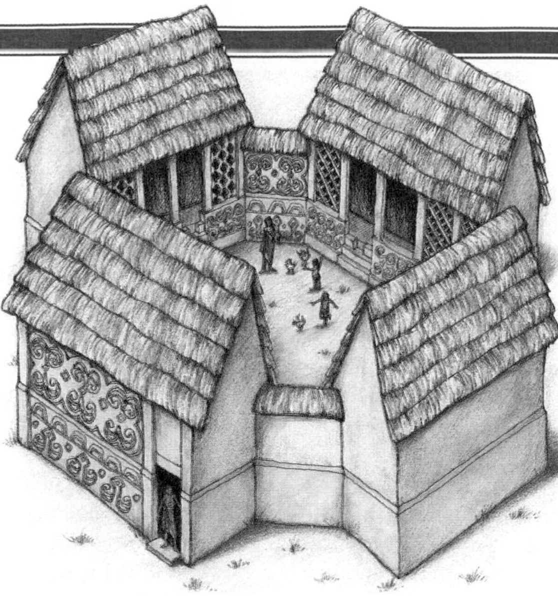

▲ *The houses of an Asante family were built in a circle with low walls between them. The courtyard was a center for family life.*

Traditions of Working

When the Asante had first settled in the rain forest, they lived by hunting and gathering. In time they cleared small areas around their villages and began to farm. They raised yams, millet, rice, beans, and cotton. Land belonged to the clan but was divided among the families of each village.

Over time certain kinds of work became the tasks of men or women. Men cleared the land, hunted, mined for gold, or became skilled craftsmen. Men also wove the richly patterned Kente *(KEHN tay)* cloth. Both men and women worked in the fields. Women sold the produce from crops in the market. Women also managed their households and cared for their families. ■

◄ *Nearly every Asante person owned a wooden stool which was a symbol of the person. This is the stool of an Asante king.*

■ *What has been the role of the family in West African society?*

REVIEW

1. **FOCUS** What does the Odwira festival mean to the Asante?
2. **GEOGRAPHY** Describe the different geographic regions found in Ghana.
3. **CULTURE** What is the role of women in the society and economy of Ghana?
4. **CRITICAL THINKING** The mother of the Asantehene is honored at Odwira. Why do you think this is so?
5. **WRITING ACTIVITY** To the Asante, traditions such as the Odwira festival and symbols such as the Golden Stool and great umbrella gave a feeling of unity. What traditions and symbols does our country have? Write a paragraph explaining why such symbols are important to a people or a country.

CULTURE

Visual Learning

Call students' attention to the illustration of Asante houses. Ask how they think that such a housing style might have reflected or have influenced a community based on kinship. *(The courtyard space may have encouraged interaction among family members. The closeness and shared space probably reflected and strengthened the ties and interdependence within the extended family.)*

■ *The family is the basis of West African society—of lineage and the extended family. Respect for ancestors is a part of the heritage.*

CLOSE

Read the Thinking Focus aloud. To answer the question, have students create invitations to an Odwira festival or posters announcing the festival. They can use large sheets of paper. Suggest that the invitations tell about both the events and the purpose of the festival. Display the invitations and posters. Discuss which ones best capture the spirit of the celebration.

Answers to Review Questions

1. The Odwira festival, the central tradition of the Asante, includes celebration of the yam harvest, honoring the spirits of ancestors, and renewing loyalty to their leader.
2. Ghana's geographic regions include swamps, plains, coastlands, rain forests, and savanna.
3. Women have an established and respected position in Asante society as homemakers, as farmers, as traders in the markets, and as political leaders.
4. The Queen Mother plays an important and established role in the Asante government. People honor the Queen Mother just as they do the Asantehene.
5. Answers will vary, but students may refer to traditions such as the Fourth of July and Thanksgiving. Symbols might include the flag, the eagle, and so on. Such symbols are important for creating a sense of unity.

Homework Options

Ask students to think of ways in which their lives or the lives of their parents might be different if they lived in a kinship-based society. Have them write a paragraph to explain their ideas.

Study Guide: page 47

UNDERSTANDING CRITICAL THINKING

This skills feature examines Ghanaian proverbs to teach students how proverbs reflect the wisdom and morality of the culture from which they came.

CULTURE

Visual Learning

Point out that in Asante culture, many visual effects—such as the patterns in adinkra and Kente cloth—have specific meanings that people recognize and understand. In that sense, they are similar to traffic signs and some advertisments in our culture, which contain symbols that people recognize and interpret. Provide a number of signs or advertisments for the class, or ask students to bring in examples. Display these, and encourage students to identify the symbols and explain their meanings. Have students create their own signs. Display these, and have the class interpret them.

UNDERSTANDING CRITICAL THINKING

Interpreting Proverbs

Here's Why

People sometimes repeat stories or fables in order to teach wisdom or moral lessons. A proverb is similar to the moral of a story; it is a short saying that expresses a well-known truth. Many proverbs can apply to any place in the world and at any time. Others are more specific and reveal something about a particular culture or historical period.

If you read an African proverb, for example, you may learn something about African culture. You may also learn that Africans share many values with your own culture.

Here's How

The proverbs in the box below originated among the Ewe people of Ghana. The proverb about the blacksmith means that when you go to another place, you must learn to behave according to the customs of that place. What clues does the proverb provide about African culture? The reference to blacksmiths suggests their importance. Think of a similar saying from your own culture, such as this: You can be a big fish in a small pond or a small fish in big pond.

Now look at the mask on the right of a European from the west coast of Africa. Read the second proverb about the hat. One interpretation of this proverb might be that if a person wants to give you something, you should beware of why the person is giving it to you. The proverb gives you a clue that Africans do not always find people from outside their culture trustworthy. "Beware of Greeks bearing gifts" is a similar saying.

Try It

Examine the last two proverbs. Analyze both of them, asking the same kinds of questions and using the same kind of thinking you applied to proverbs in Here's How.

Apply It

Your culture has proverbs of its own. Analyze the following proverbs. Discuss how the proverbs provide clues to this culture.

- Haste makes waste.
- A watched pot never boils.
- Anything that can go wrong will go wrong.
- Wisdom is not like money, to be tied up and hidden.

Adinkra cloth, like Kente cloth, is a traditional fabric of the Asante. The designs represent proverbs.

The blacksmith in one village becomes a blacksmith's apprentice in another.

If a [stranger] wants to give you a hat, look at the one he is wearing before you accept it.

You do not become a chief simply by sitting on a big stool.

A stump that stays in a river for a hundred years does not become a crocodile.

Ewe Proverbs, Ghana

Objective

Evaluate and interpret proverbs. (Critical Thinking 2)

Answers to Try It

Possible interpretation of the second to last proverb: You cannot designate yourself as great. Cultural clue: Having a stool to sit on must be a sign of rank.

Possible interpretation of the last proverb: There is a limit to the extent to which a thing can change. Cultural clue: The nature of a thing is permanent.

Answers to Apply It

Possible interpretation and cultural clues:

- Hurrying may cause mistakes that take time to correct: Waste should be avoided.
- Impatience does not make something happen any faster: It is important to be patient.
- The opportunity for error always exists: This culture values accuracy but anticipates mistakes.
- Wisdom should be put to use: This culture values wisdom and seeks the benefits of it.

B.C. A.D.
1000
1200
1400
1600
1700
1900
2000

L E S S O N 2

Growth and Change

In the late 1600s, a young Asante chief, Osei Tutu, asked the chiefs of many clans to join him in forming a military union. He and the other chiefs had many interests in common. They all lived in the rain forest, and they spoke languages that were much alike. Osei Tutu led the other chiefs in defeating the Denkyira, the strongest enemy group in the region. After this victory, the other chiefs accepted Tutu as their leader and as the head of the new Ashanti nation. He became the first Asantehene.

The major symbol of the new nation was the Golden Stool. The idea of a stool was not new; by tradition every chief had his own stool. This Golden Stool, however, was different. Tutu said that it held the spirit of the Ashanti nation. It also stood for the power of the Asantehene. So important was the Golden Stool that no one was supposed to sit on it. It became the most important symbol of the Asante people and nation.

Osei Tutu also proclaimed the Odwira a national celebration to honor the Ashanti nation. Finally, he made the city of Kumasi, a trading center, the nation's political and cultural capital. Kumasi is shown on the map on page 269.

THINKING FOCUS

How did the Ashanti Empire develop?

Key Terms

- export
- import
- cash crop

◄ *This gilded wood carving, the top for a royal umbrella, shows a king holding an egg. If he holds it too tightly, he will crush it. If he holds it too loosely, it will fall and break. What does this carving show about people's feelings toward royal power?*

The Ashanti Empire

Ashanti rulers who came after Osei Tutu added other states to their kingdom. In time they organized these peoples into an empire. The Ashanti Empire was well run, with strong leadership, military power, and wealth from trade. Ashanti kings respected the traditions of conquered peoples. Local chiefs could still rule their own lands as long as they stayed a part of the Ashanti Empire and accepted the Asantehene as their head of state. All had to pay tribute or taxes to the empire.

Ashanti Rule

The Ashanti Empire lasted for over 200 years. At its peak the empire included more than three million people. It was one of the larger empires in West Africa. The map

INTRODUCE

Explain that the Asante were not always a united people. They once lived in small villages based on kinship groups. Over the years they united to form a military and political state and developed a feeling of shared identity. Ask students to predict, based on what they learned in Lesson 1, some of the factors that encouraged the Asante to unite. *(Sample answers include a shared language and culture, similar needs, a similar environment, common enemies, and common trade interests.)*

Key Terms

Vocabulary Strategies: T36–T37

export—to send goods out of the country for sale or trade

import—to bring goods into the country for sale or trade

cash crop—crop raised for export, rather than for food, to gain money for the economy

◄ *The carving shows that people expected the king to have power but to use it wisely and with discretion.*

Graphic Overview

Asante Develop Kingdom and Empire → **Great Britain and Ashanti Empire Compete for Land and Trade** → **Great Britain Adds Ashanti Empire to Gold Coast Colony**

Objectives

1. Explain the rise of the Ashanti Empire and its growth in power and wealth.
2. Analyze the impact of colonial rule on the Asante way of life.

DEVELOP

Before students read the lesson, direct their attention to the timeline on page 273, which shows when the Ashanti Empire developed. Ask students how referring to a timeline might help them understand a region's history. *(It can show the era within a longer time span when certain events took place.)* Suggest that students may want to look at the timeline again after they have read the lesson, to review the era described.

HISTORY
Critical Thinking

Ask students to list some benefits that West Africans gained from the start of trade with European nations. *(They obtained goods such as iron, copper, and cloth; they gained a market for their own products.)* There were also costs or disadvantages to West Africans from that trade. Ask students to predict what those costs might be. *(Sample answers may include domination by foreign traders; lack of a strong, well-rounded economy; loss of population and disruption of culture due to slave trade; and war. Allow for individual opinions.)*

➤ *The Asante were rich in gold and ornaments made of gold. This gold pendant, representing a mudfish, shows the skill of Asante goldsmiths.*

How Do We Know?

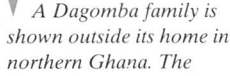

HISTORY *A number of Europeans wrote about their travels among the Asante in the 1800s. The stories told in African oral history also provide a record of events. Today these sources enable historians to study life and events in West Africa at that time.*

▼ *A Dagomba family is shown outside its home in northern Ghana. The Dagomba were a major ethnic group within the Ashanti Empire.*

on page 269 shows the empire in 1820.

As it grew, the Ashanti Empire gained the notice of European nations trading in Africa. In 1817 a British trading group visited Kumasi. One of its members, Thomas Edward Bowdich, later described the scene. As the travelers entered the city, Ashanti soldiers saluted them with gunshots. Flag bearers waved British, Dutch, and Danish flags. Soon Bowdich and his friends were led to the royal palace. There they met the Asantehene, whose kindness and dignity impressed Bowdich. "His manners were majestic, yet courteous," Bowdich wrote in his account.

Growth of Trade

Bowdich's visit to Kumasi was one of the first direct contacts between the Asante and British traders. European traders had, however, been active in West Africa for more than 300 years. The first Europeans to reach West Africa had been the Portuguese, who were seeking gold.

Earlier, gold had been carried overland by Muslim traders. Their caravans had traveled from inland cities of West Africa, such as Timbuktu, north across the Sahara. Now the gold could go by sea and in European ships. In 1482 the Portuguese built a trading post and fort, Elmina, to protect their trade. Soon ships from other European nations joined in the rich West African trade.

One West African group that traded with the Europeans was the Fante. Like the Asante, they were of the Akan ethnic group. They lived in the coastal region—the Gold Coast—between the Asante and the Gulf of Guinea. The Fante controlled trade between inland areas and the European trading posts on the coast. The Asante sold their goods to the Fante, who then sold these to the Europeans.

The Asante produced many goods sought by the Europeans. At first these included gold, hardwood, ivory, animal skins, and salt. In return the Asante obtained new food crops such as plantains, peppers, maize, ground nuts, and cassava from the Americas. They traded for iron and copper bars, textiles, and beads. They also bought luxury goods, such as silk, used in making Kente cloth, which is discussed in A Closer Look on page 275.

In time the trade changed as Europeans began to offer guns. In exchange they wanted slaves. This trade in humans was small at first. It grew, however, to meet the demand for workers in the Caribbean and in Latin America. European trading posts in Africa became scenes of terrible suffering and misery. From 1600 until the 1840s, the demand for slaves disrupted life in West and Central Africa.

In time the Asante too became involved in the slave trade. They

Access Activity

The Golden Stool was a symbol of the Asante people, their empire, and the authority of their leader. Have students draw and label symbols that stand for leadership or authority in other nations—crowns for kings, special seals or insignias, flags, and so on.

Access Strategy

Define the term *empire* ("a number of territories or nations ruled by a single supreme authority"), and have students review the characteristics of empires on page 136. Explain that the Asante people were not always joined in an empire. At first, there were many Akan clans. Later, several clans banded together because they had common interests and needs. Over time, these unified clans conquered other clans. Ask students to imagine that their family lives alone in a wilderness area. Challenge them to list reasons why they might band together with other families. *(Sample answers may include protection, helping one another, and gaining a feeling of community.)* Write these reasons on the chalkboard. Tell students, as they read Lesson 2, to watch for reasons why the Asante united as a kingdom. At the end of the first section, return to the list and discuss specific reasons why Asante groups banded together.

A CLOSER LOOK

Kente Cloth

A proud tradition of weaving continues in West Africa. For centuries Kente (KEHN tay) cloth has been the royal fabric of Ghana, worn by chiefs. Today it is worn by many people in Africa and around the world. Americans of African descent wear it as a sign of pride in their heritage.

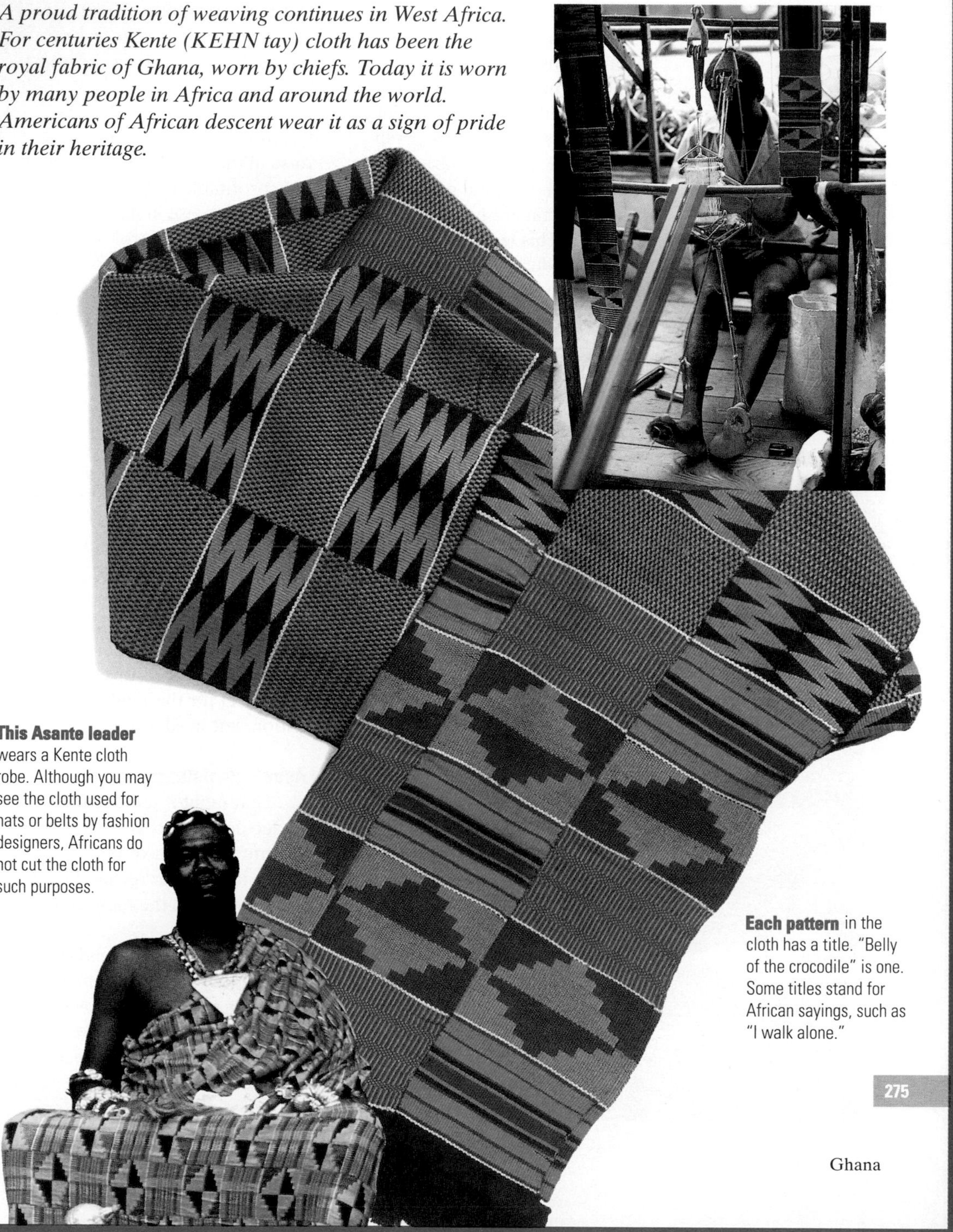

Men weave narrow strips and sew them into a large cloth.

Each pattern in the cloth has a title. "Belly of the crocodile" is one. Some titles stand for African sayings, such as "I walk alone."

This Asante leader wears a Kente cloth robe. Although you may see the cloth used for hats or belts by fashion designers, Africans do not cut the cloth for such purposes.

Ghana

Note: You may wish to tie the discussion of Kente cloth patterns to the skills feature Interpreting Proverbs on page 272. Then ask students to use colored markers to create patterns that illustrate common U.S. or African proverbs.

More About Kente Cloth The Asante may have been weaving Kente cloth as early as the 15th century. As cloth trade between Europe and West Africa increased, West Africans painstakingly unraveled European cloth and rewove it into traditional designs. Kente cloth is not cut and sewed into tailored garments. Men wrap Kente toga-style, while women wrap the fabric around them to form long skirts. Among the Asante only the men weave this traditional cloth, passing the skill down from generation to generation, father to sons, and uncle to nephews.

CULTURE

Visual Learning

Direct students' attention to the photograph of Kwame Nkrumah on page 280. Then have them read the captions and study the images on this page. Ask why Nkrumah might wear the traditional robe of Kente cloth for state occasions. *(He shows that he is proud of his African heritage and honors tradition.)*

Science Connection

West African weavers had to apply an extensive knowledge of the plants and other natural materials in their environment to make the dyes for their fabrics. They used cassava roots for red, cola nuts for brown, and the leaves of a local shrub for blue. Challenge students to find materials for dyes in their own environment. These might include onion skins, berries, beets, and so on. Provide big bowls and heavy spoons (or mortars and pestles, if you can obtain them), water, and strips of unbleached cotton. Instruct students to write their predictions about how the cloth will be affected, then to prepare their "dye" mixtures and allow the cloth to soak overnight. Once the fabric has been dyed, mark an identifier on each strip and wash them all, to see how colorfast the natural dyes are. Wrap up the activity with a discussion of the kinds of knowledge the Asante needed to produce colorful cloth.

Visual Learning

Have students look carefully at the patterns in the illustrations. Ask them to brainstorm what they think the names of two of the patterns might be. *(Accept all reasonable answers.)*

GEOGRAPHY

Map and Globe Skills

To put the colonial history of West Africa in context, have students look at the map of the British Empire on page 445. Ask students to speculate why the British and other Europeans were so interested in establishing colonies all over the world. *(They were competing for overseas territories and markets and could gain wealth from colonial resources and trade.)*

■ *European traders sought slaves to sell in the Americas to work on plantations, in mines, and at many other tasks. The slave trade was very profitable for the Europeans but not for the Africans. The Asante traded in slaves in order to buy firearms and other goods from the Europeans.*

ECONOMICS

Critical Thinking

To show students how trade and politics were linked, review with them the term *middleman*, introduced on page 250. Then ask how this term applies to the Fante, who lived south of the Asante along the coast. *(The Fante were middlemen between the British and the Asante.)*

wanted guns to control their weaker neighbors. To obtain guns, they raided other kingdoms and took captives to sell as slaves.

The slave trade declined by the mid-1800s after a number of European nations stopped buying slaves. At about the same time, church groups in Europe began sending missionaries to spread their religion in Africa. Missionaries built not only churches but also schools where they taught people to read and write. This led in time to new groups of educated people within West African society. However, the teachings of the missionaries questioned traditional African ideas of family and religion.

In those years, British trade with West Africa was increasing. Once again, the kinds of traded goods changed. Along with gold and forest products, the British now sought food crops and raw materials for their factories. Among these products were peanuts, palm oil, cocoa, and cotton. Cocoa, which Asante farmers began to raise in the 1880s, soon became a very profitable crop.

The increase in its trade led Britain to seek control of inland areas in addition to its coastal forts and trading posts. This caused several wars between the British and the Asante, who sought to defend their empire. ■

■ *Why did Europeans trade for slaves, and why did groups like the Asante provide slaves?*

British Colonial Rule

As British power increased in West Africa, Ashanti rule began to weaken. Some groups under Ashanti rule now turned to Britain for support. In 1874, when an Ashanti army invaded lands protected by Britain, an army led by British troops marched on Kumasi. The soldiers burned the city and blew up the royal palace. The Asante remained free, but they lost lands to the British. These lands became part of a new colony, the Gold Coast, set up by Britain. Britain also tried to take over Ashanti trade.

In 1896 the British demanded that the Asante come under British protection. Britain banished the Asantehene and appointed a British governor in his place.

In 1900 Asante chiefs gathered in Kumasi to meet the British governor, Frederick Hodgson. Hodgson greeted the leaders, including Queen Mother Yaa Asantewa. Then he decided to test his power by breaking Asante tradition. He demanded that the Golden Stool be brought to him so that he could sit on it. The Asante leaders, shocked at this show of disrespect for the symbol of their nation, left in silence.

Asante Resistance

That night Asante leaders met to decide what to do. It was Yaa Asantewa who gave the answer. One witness later recalled how she had challenged the men to fight:

> *How can a proud and brave people like the Asante sit back and look while whitemen took away their kings and chiefs, and [shamed] them with a demand for the Golden Stool?*

▼ *Talking drums like this one are carved out of wood and covered with elephant hide. The Asante used drums to send secret messages.*

Study Skill

Talking drums are an example of unwritten communication. Have students research similar forms of communication. They should begin by referring to the Minipedia on pages 665–668. Encourage students to give oral reports or to make sketches or diagrams of their findings. *(Answers may include Morse code, flags used on ships or in weather reporting, and so on.)*

Historical Context

Students may question why the Asante and other West Africans participated in the slave trade. Historians usually point to two main reasons. First, slaves became the "goods" that European traders wanted most—eventually, even more than they wanted gold. Second, the great majority sold as slaves to Europeans were people captured in warfare. Although some criminals or military prisoners had been made slaves by the Asante before the slave trade with Europeans began, these individuals had many more rights than slaves in the Americas. The Asante seldom sold their own citizens, unless they were criminals or political misfits.

◄ *Forts like this one, built by the Dutch at Cape Coast (see map, page 269) in 1662, were places where goods were traded and slaves were held before being shipped overseas. The guns protected the ships from raids by ships from other European countries.*

Stirred by the Queen Mother's words, the Asante agreed to attack. For four months they trapped the British in the fort at Kumasi. Finally, troops rescued the British and defeated the Asante. In 1901 Britain made the Ashanti kingdom part of Britain's Gold Coast colony.

Colonial Rule

Although they had defeated the Asante, the British did not take away all their rights. Chiefs could still rule, but under British control.

Britain expected to profit from its colonies. One way to do this was to **export,** or send overseas, goods from a colony, and sell them elsewhere for a higher price. Another way was to have a colony **import,** or bring into a colony, goods such as cloth and tools from Britain.

The Asante had many products to export—gold, diamonds, hardwoods, kola nuts, palm oil, and cocoa. Cocoa was an example of a **cash crop,** a crop raised to make money rather than to feed people directly.

Colonial trade brought large profits to the British companies but few benefits to colonial peoples. British traders paid low prices to Asante farmers for the cocoa. Asante farmers, however, paid high prices for products such as food, clothing, cars, and trucks imported from Britain. It was the British traders who profited. Most of the profits went back to Britain.

The Asante hated the British system. They pointed out that it was unfair to local producers and that some of the profits should go to the colony and its people. More and more, they spoke out against British rule. ■

▲ *The Queen Mother Yaa Asantewa, shown here dressed for battle, was exiled by the British along with the Asantehene.*

■ *Why did Britain want to make the Asante part of its Gold Coast colony?*

REVIEW

1. **FOCUS** How did the Ashanti Empire develop?
2. **ECONOMICS** How did the Europeans and Asante become trading partners?
3. **GEOGRAPHY** How did the Asante adjust to the changes in trade in the late 1800s?
4. **CRITICAL THINKING** The British imposed their method of trade on colonial peoples. What does this method reveal about Britain's attitudes toward colonial peoples?
5. **ACTIVITY** Imagine you are an Asante leader at the meeting held after the British governor demanded the Golden Stool. Write a one-minute speech telling what you think your fellow Asante should do.

HISTORY

Critical Thinking

Explain that once the Asantehene had been exiled by the British, Yaa Asantewa became ruler. Ask students why they think that the British banished the Asantehene. Do they think that the British accomplished their purpose? *(The British probably wanted to weaken the Asante by depriving them of a strong leader. However, because it was a matrilineal society, the Queen Mother became leader and the British did not accomplish their purpose. When the British finally had realized her strength, they sent her into exile too.)*

■ *The British wanted more control over West African trade and the Asantes' profitable trade.*

CLOSE

Read the Thinking Focus aloud. Have students refer to the timeline on page 273. Ask them to make detailed timelines, showing main events of the period 1700 to 1900.

Answers to Review Questions

1. The Asante chief, Osei Tutu, asked the chiefs of many clans to form a military union. Later rulers added other states to the kingdom. The Asante had military power and wealth from trade.
2. Each had something the other wanted. The Europeans wanted raw materials such as gold and hardwood, and the Asante wanted manufactured goods such as textiles, tools, and firearms.
3. The Asante began to produce more of the crops, minerals, and raw materials that Britain wanted. Cocoa became a major Asante export.
4. The British method of trading took advantage of colonial peoples. It shows that Britain was willing to exploit colonial peoples and probably considered them inferior in terms of technology and civilization.
5. Answers will vary. Students may express Asante anger at Hodgson's action or determination to resist British control.

Homework Options

The decline of the Ashanti Empire was caused in large part by conflict over trade. Have students find an article in a local newspaper or in a magazine showing how trade continues to affect world politics today. They should explain the significance of the articles in terms of trade. Display the articles.

Study Guide: page 49

DISCOVERY PROCESS

Students will use the following steps in the discovery process to complete the activity:
Get Ready Gather books and magazines on African jewelry and beadwork. Collect pictures or sketches of jewelry from at least five African regions.
Find Out Take notes on the appearance and cultural significance of each piece of jewelry. Include examples of jewelry with beadwork or shells.
Move Ahead Draw a large map of Africa and tape pictures of jewelry to the regions from which they come.
Explore Some More Look through magazines and museum catalogs for examples of U.S.-made jewelry that shows African influences. Bring to class pictures of both African and U.S. examples.

Materials needed: Books, magazines, and museum catalogs; paper and pencils; a large sheet of paper; masking tape; markers; possibly materials for handmade jewelry, such as beads, seeds, ribbons, fabric, string, and tapestry needles.

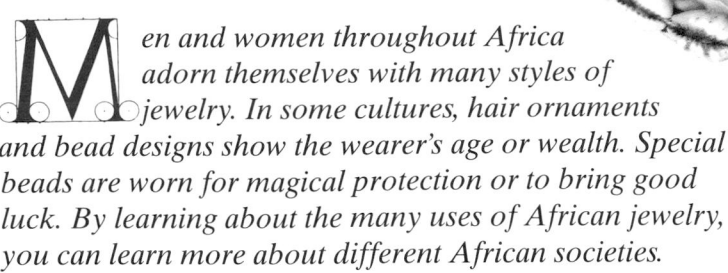

EXPLORING

African Jewelry

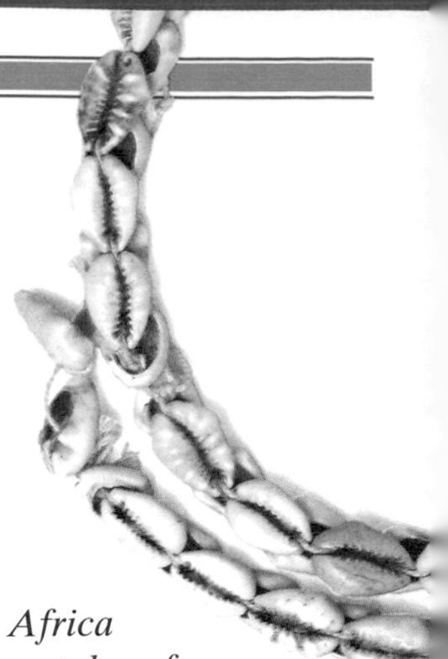

Men and women throughout Africa adorn themselves with many styles of jewelry. In some cultures, hair ornaments and bead designs show the wearer's age or wealth. Special beads are worn for magical protection or to bring good luck. By learning about the many uses of African jewelry, you can learn more about different African societies.

Glass beads from Europe were traded in Africa more than 1,500 years ago. These mosaic beads were made in Venice, Italy, the center of European bead manufacturing for hundreds of years.

Get Ready

Gather books and magazines on jewelry and beadwork in Africa. Does your community have a museum or store that displays African jewelry? Look for beaded necklaces, belts, and hats from Kenya and South Africa. Jewelry from West African countries often includes amber, gold, and bronze. Desert regions favor silver. Search for pictures of jewelry from at least five regions.

Find Out

Take notes on each piece of jewelry. Where is it from? What is it made of? How is it worn? Does the jewelry have a special meaning? Was it made for a chief, a warrior, a child, or someone else?

If beads are used, describe their colors and patterns. Many glass beads were made in Europe and traded to Africans. Cowrie shells were once used for money in some regions. Find examples of jewelry that include beads or shells.

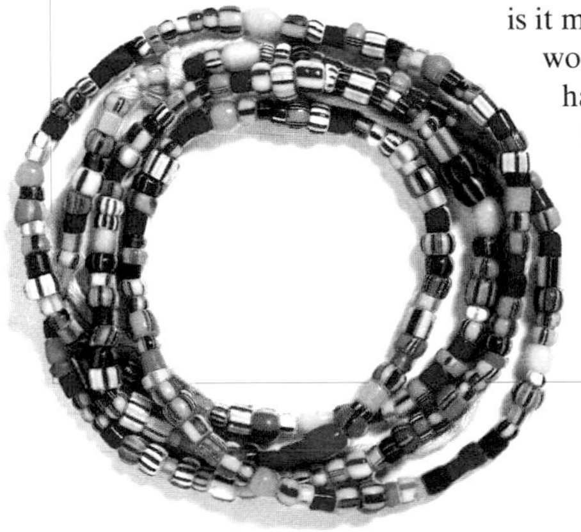

Move Ahead

In class, draw a large map of Africa. Tape each picture of jewelry to the region where it was made. (You can write on the map or make a sketch if your picture comes from a book.) Share your notes. Are there similar uses of jewelry among regions? Do different cultures use the same materials?

You can make your own jewelry with materials of your own. Bring the materials to class, and trade items with classmates. Does your jewelry have a message?

Explore Some More

Many modern craftspeople and artists have been inspired by

Objectives

1. Explore the vastness of African culture by taking a look at one facet of it: jewelry and beads. (Culture 5)
2. Explore the origins of various jewelry and bead types. (Culture 1, 2, 4)
3. Explore the global influence of African culture. (Culture 1, 2, 3, 4)

Activity

Help students organize two surveys: one of traditional uses of jewelry among African men and women; the other of uses of jewelry among men and women in the United States today. Students can work in small teams. For the first survey, they can look at photographs in books on African art, history books, encyclopedias, and so on. For the second, they can use current magazines or actual interviews of people wearing jewelry. Both surveys should identify type of jewelry (necklace, bracelet, earrings, cuff links, and so on) and the gender of the person wearing that jewelry. Lead a discussion of similarities and differences in types of jewelry worn by men and women in the two different cultures. Encourage students to draw conclusions from their findings.

African designs. Now that you are familiar with different styles of African jewelry, look for one-of-a-kind jewelry pieces that are made by U.S. artists. Find examples that show African influences. Your public library may have magazines and catalogs from museums with photographs of examples.

Do you notice African influences in the patterns and choice of materials in the U.S. jewelry? If possible, bring to class pictures of both African and U.S. examples.

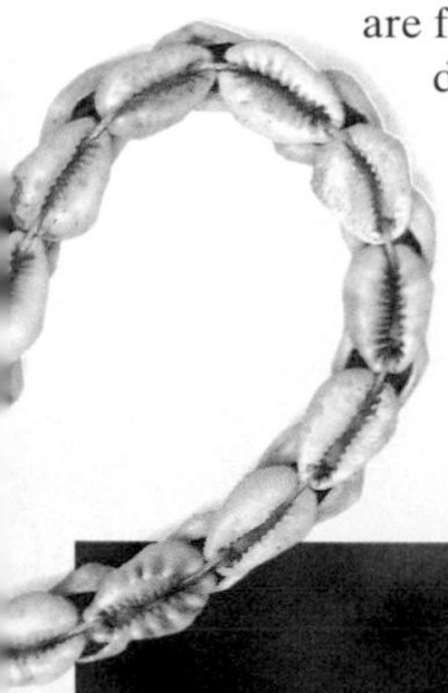

Because the cowrie shell looks like a human eye, it was thought to have magical powers to ward off evil. These shells have been strung for sale. They will be used in making jewelry or masks.

The women in Mauritania braid beads into their hair. The beads are made of glass, silver, amber, and carved stones and shells. Colors have special meaning. Blue stands for the purity of the sky. Violet stands for the dove, which symbolizes love and gentleness.

Amber is sap from trees that lived 40 to 60 million years ago. The sap is fossilized, and its hardness and bright color have made it popular for African jewelry for hundreds of years. Many cultures in Africa value carved amber beads for jewelry.

Ghana

279

CULTURE

Critical Thinking

Ask students to reread the captions accompanying the photos of seed beads and hair braiding. Then have students working in small groups list examples from our own culture of jewelry, clothing, and other apparel used to convey messages. *(Allow for a variety of answers. Examples might include a wedding band revealing that a person is married; a ring showing where someone went to school; a suit symbolizing that a person is attending an important function; or a uniform with a business's name or logo.)*

CULTURE

Visual Learning

Ideas of what is beautiful can differ from culture to culture. Ask students to write a short paragraph telling what they consider to be a beautiful hairstyle. Then ask them to look at the photo of the Mauritanian woman. What does she consider to be a beautiful hairstyle? Ask students to write another paragraph from her point of view.

Collaborative Strategy

One recommended strategy that may be useful in this lesson is positive interdependence, with each member of the group making an important contribution. For further information, turn to pages T34–T35.

INTRODUCE

Ask students to recall from Lesson 2 how the Asante felt about colonial rule. *(They were unhappy with it; they wanted control of their own country.)* Explain that this lesson will show how the people of Ghana obtained independence and what challenges the new nation faced. Ask students to read the Thinking Focus and to consider how Ghana might reconcile old and new ways.

Key Terms

Vocabulary Strategies: T36–T37
nationalism—the desire to control one's own nation
literacy rate—the percentage of the population who can read and write

B.C. A.D. 1000 1200 1400 1600 1800 1951 1993

LESSON 3

A New Nation

THINKING FOCUS

How does Ghana today blend old ways and new?

Key Terms

- nationalism
- literacy rate

➤ *Kwame Nkrumah was Ghana's first prime minister and, later, president. For state ceremonies he often wore the traditional robe of Kente cloth.*

March 6, 1957, was a day of celebration in Accra, the capital of Ghana. On this day Britain's Gold Coast colony became the nation of Ghana. At midnight, the British flag was lowered. Then the red, green, and gold flag of Ghana was raised in its place.

The nation's leader, Kwame Nkrumah *(KWAH may uhng KROO muh)* spoke to the crowds:

> *At long last the battle has ended! And thus Ghana, your beloved country, is free forever. . . . We are prepared to make it a nation that will be respected by any nation in the world.*

Kwame Nkrumah spent much of his life preparing for this moment. He came from a family of the Nzima in the southwestern Gold Coast. As a youth, he left home to attend Catholic mission schools. In time he became a teacher and considered becoming a priest. Then new ideas changed his thinking.

In 1935 Nkrumah went to the United States to study. He wanted to learn how to help Africans win independence. Ten years later Nkrumah left the United States. He felt he had learned much:

> *I saw the Statue of Liberty with her arm raised as if in a personal farewell to me. "You have opened my eyes to the true meaning of liberty," I thought. "I shall never rest until I have carried your message to Africa."*

Ghana: A Nation

Nkrumah returned to Africa in 1947. During his absence the spirit of **nationalism,** the desire to control one's own nation, had spread in Africa. In the Gold Coast, Nkrumah set up a new political party to work for self-government. He also led strikes and other forms of protest. The British put Nkrumah into jail, but this made him more popular.

Objectives

1. Identify the problems faced by Ghana as a new nation.
2. Evaluate the role of old and new traditions in Ghana today.

Graphic Overview

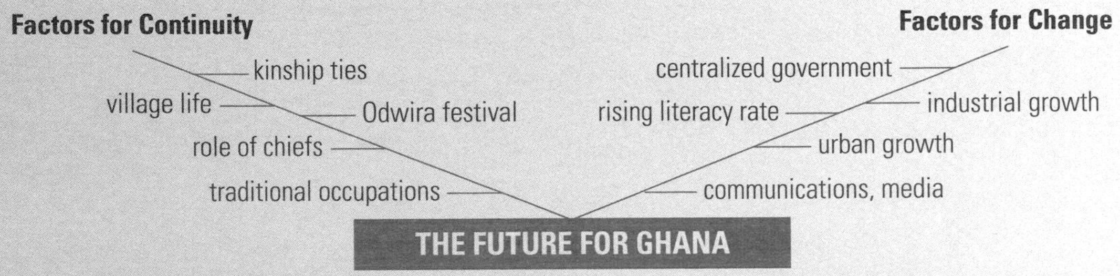
Factors for Continuity
kinship ties
village life
Odwira festival
role of chiefs
traditional occupations
Factors for Change
centralized government
industrial growth
rising literacy rate
urban growth
communications, media
THE FUTURE FOR GHANA

In 1951 the people of the Gold Coast elected Nkrumah's political party to power. This forced the British to release Nkrumah from jail to take his place in the Gold Coast Parliament. There, Africans shared in making laws for the colony. Soon Nkrumah became prime minister, or leader of the colony's Parliament.

As prime minister, Nkrumah worked with the British to prepare the Gold Coast for independence. The British expected this change to take many years, but Nkrumah had other ideas. Soon Britain agreed to grant the colony its independence.

A Difficult Beginning

The Gold Coast became the first African colony south of the Sahara to become an independent nation. It was named Ghana after a great ancient kingdom of West Africa.

Ghana hoped to be a model of success that other African colonies could follow. Indeed, Ghana's future seemed bright. It had many resources and a good system of producing and trading goods. However, independence might also bring problems to Ghana. Would new leaders govern wisely? Could the nation's economy prosper in a worldwide market?

Years of Challenge

The new nation soon faced problems. Ghana counted on cocoa as a cash crop to bring money for developing industries, public projects, and social programs such as schools. If prices for cocoa fell, however, Ghana would have few other crops or products to earn money as exports.

During the 1950s prices for cocoa rose, and money flowed into Ghana. The graph above shows, however, that those good times did not last. In the 1960s world prices for cocoa began to fall. Suddenly, the country was earning less money. This made the government cut its spending for schools, health care, and projects important for the future.

The people of Ghana began to lose confidence in Nkrumah. They felt he had spent money too freely and had gained too much power. In fact, he had ruled as a dictator. In 1966 a group of army officers overthrew Nkrumah. They and the military leaders who followed tried—but often failed—to make reforms to help the country. ■

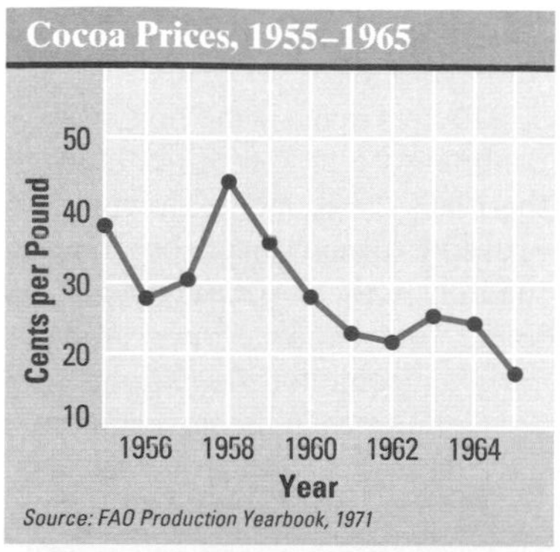

Cocoa Prices, 1955–1965
Cents per Pound
50
40
30
20
10
1956
1958
1960
1962
1964
Year
Source: FAO Production Yearbook, 1971

◄ *This graph shows the decline in the price of cocoa from 1955 to 1965. The fall in prices brought hardship to farmers like these (below). They produce two crops of cocoa a year. Cocoa provides over 40 percent of the money Ghana earns from exports.*

■ *Why did Ghana's economy decline?*

DEVELOP

To help students realize how independence would affect Ghana, ask what kinds of things Ghana might want or need as a nation that it lacked as a colony. *(Answers may include a larger government, more schools, new kinds of economic activity, an army and navy, and more trade and contact with other countries.)* Then ask how Ghana would be able to pay for these things. Encourage students to speculate on a variety of ways. *(Students may point out that taxes would now go to Ghana rather than to Britain. Also, more of the profits from trade might now belong to Ghana.)* Have students note as they read how accurate their answers were.

CULTURE

Visual Learning

Suggest that students preview the photos in this lesson, keeping the Thinking Focus in mind. Ask students what the photographs show about the blending of old and new in Ghana.

■ *Unstable cocoa prices and reliance on a single cash crop were major causes of Ghana's economic decline.*

Access Strategy

It is important for students to understand the economic dangers posed by a country's overdependence on one export. Point out that Ghana's dependence on cocoa was like a store that sells only one item. If the demand for that item goes down, the store could go bankrupt. (A store selling only records, instead of records, cassettes, and CDs, is one example.) Ask students to create another analogy, using a job a teenager might hold. *(Sample answers might include a job shoveling snow that disappears in the summer or babysitting for only one family, whose children will soon grow up.)*

Access Activity

Tell students to imagine that they are Asante children in about 1960. They are facing the decision of whether to stay in the village or move to the city when they grow up. Use questions to build a dialogue with the class about economic changes and what these mean to young people. Bring out the importance of traditions and concerns about the future.

CONSTITUTIONAL HERITAGE

Critical Thinking

Discuss the concept of political party. Ask the students what difference it makes if there is just one political party or more than one. *(Having two parties gives voters a choice; it allows for more discussion and dissent, and thus is more democratic.)* Point out that Nkrumah outlawed all political parties but his own. This was one reason for his overthrow.

➤ *The government had to build a harbor at Tema because the coast of Ghana lacks natural harbors.*

Ghana Today

Across Time & Space

Many Asante now live in New York City. Since they cannot go home to celebrate the Odwira festival, they have brought the festival to New York. Every three years they elect a leader. They pledge their loyalty to him in the same traditional way as in Ghana. The leader helps Ghanaian immigrants in the United States and settles quarrels among local Asante.

Today Ghana is moving more confidently into the future. During the 1980s the economy slowly improved as cocoa prices rose. Unfortunately in the 1990s they began to fall. New exports, however, have earned income for the nation.

Conditions in the government have improved, though slowly. In 1981 Lieutenant Jerry Rawlings, an air force officer, seized power and took control of the government. He promised in May 1992 to allow more than one political party. In November 1992 the people of Ghana elected Rawlings president.

Modern Ghana

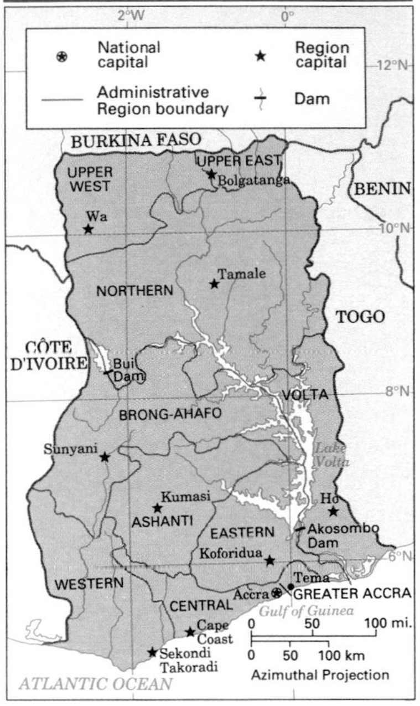

2°W
0°
National capital
Region capital
Administrative Region boundary
Dam
12°N
BURKINA FASO
UPPER EAST
Bolgatanga
UPPER WEST
Wa
BENIN
10°N
Tamale
NORTHERN
TOGO
CÔTE D'IVOIRE
Bui Dam
VOLTA
8°N
BRONG-AHAFO
Sunyani
Lake Volta
Kumasi
ASHANTI
Ho
EASTERN
Akosombo Dam
Koforidua
6°N
WESTERN
Tema
Accra
GREATER ACCRA
CENTRAL
Gulf of Guinea
Cape Coast
Sekondi Takoradi
0 50 100 mi.
0 50 100 km
Azimuthal Projection
ATLANTIC OCEAN

The Asante Today

The nation of Ghana remains rich in its traditions and its different cultures. People still honor the customs and values of their ethnic groups. This is a source of strength in the society.

The government of Ghana is centered at the national level in Accra. Ethnic groups play a part mainly at a regional level, in the 10 units that make up Ghana. These units are shown on the map opposite. Of the 10 units, only one—Ashanti—contains just one distinct group.

All of Ghana's ethnic groups now live in two worlds—traditional and modern. For example, most Asante speak both their traditional language and English, the official language of Ghana. Today's Asantehene is still the traditional leader of the Asante. However, he earns his living as a lawyer.

In the villages, lesser chiefs still play an important part. They help provide for their people's well-being. They also oversee the festivals and other customs of their culture. Thus, they keep traditional ways alive as new changes occur.

➤ *Ghana today is made up of 10 administrative regions. Its main port, Tema, is the outlet for Accra and for exports like aluminum. Why did the government need to build a port at Tema?*

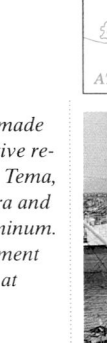

Critical Thinking

Have students locate the Akosombo Dam on the map of Ghana. Then ask how the dam could help to solve these problems: Need for power for industry *(Dam provides electricity.)*; Need for new sources of food *(Lake formed by dam provides fish.)*; Need for water for human use *(Dam increases water supply.)*

Economic Context

Cacao trees are not native to Africa but were brought there from South America in the late 1800s. Today Ghana is the world's largest exporter of cacao beans, producing almost a third of the world's total supply. Many children begin working in the cacao groves at an early age. They care for trees, clear brush, and help with the harvest. Ripe cacao pods, shaped like cucumbers, are chopped from the trees with long knives mounted on poles. Harvesters remove cacao beans from the pods by hand. After the beans have been wrapped in leaves for seven to ten days, workers spread them on platforms to dry for several weeks before they are packed in bags for shipping. The main importers of the cacao beans are the United States, the Netherlands, the United Kingdom, Germany, and Russia.

As the Asante and other groups protect their old ways, they must also adjust to changes. Akuraa, a village of Asante woodcarvers, provides an example of change. Within 20 years its population increased 10 times, as outsiders came to work at a new sawmill. Other strangers made their homes in the village but traveled to Kumasi to work. Suddenly, most villagers were no longer woodcarvers following their traditional craft.

In time the people of the village kept the best of old and new ways. They named a college-educated villager to be the new chief of the community. They also created a new job, chief of the carvers, to see that old traditions were kept.

New Allegiances

Today about one-third of all Ghanaians live in cities like Kumasi and Accra. They have had to learn new ways of living and to deal with new kinds of problems. Many have joined political parties and workers' groups without kinship ties.

Other influences, too, have led to new groups. Public education has raised Ghana's **literacy rate**—the percentage of the population that can read and write. This rising literacy rate benefits everyone. Large numbers of students now attend Ghana's three universities and two medical schools. Some of these students will in time return to the villages of their families. Others will live in cities far removed from family and the support provided by lineage.

Today there is a large group of people working in communications. Ghana has tried to keep a free press, without interference from the government. Hundreds of people work for newspapers, publishing houses, radio, television, and the arts. They bring new issues and ideas to Ghana's 16 million people.

Besides looking to the future, Ghana seeks to preserve its records of the past. Many of its cultural works and treasures did not survive in the villages. Others were lost during the disorder of the slave trade and of colonial rule. The National Cultural Centre at Kumasi works to preserve examples of Asante culture. It also teaches the traditional Asante crafts. Museums in Accra serve the same purposes for the nation as a whole. Traditions of the past are helping the people of Ghana to deal with changes both today and in the future. ■

▲ *Accra, Ghana's capital, is a center for government, education, and business. Crowds of people in modern and traditional dress mingle in the markets and city squares.*

■ *How has Ghanaian society changed since independence?*

REVIEW

1. **FOCUS** How does Ghana today blend old ways and new?
2. **HISTORY** What problems did Ghana face when it became an independent nation?
3. **ECONOMICS** How do changes in the price of cocoa affect Ghana's economy?
4. **CRITICAL THINKING** Kwame Nkrumah had a major influence on the development of Ghana as a nation. Which do you think was greater, the good effects or the bad effects of his influence? Why?
5. **ACTIVITY** Using the Atlas maps on pages 688-689, find and write out the following information about Ghana: religions, climate, population, and land use.

CULTURE

Critical Thinking

Point out that there are still many different languages spoken in Ghana's 10 regions. Ask students why they think that the new nation retained English. *(Having one language aids communication at the national level. If one group's language became the official language, other groups might feel resentful.)*

■ *The society has changed as new groups—such as city dwellers, industrial workers, students, and workers in communications—have emerged. The emergence of more educated people and people of wealth has led to differences in social classes.*

CLOSE

Have students read the Thinking Focus aloud. Have them print the word *Ghana* at the top of a sheet of paper and draw a line down the middle. Then have them write the headings Old and New at the top; of the columns. Ask them to list ways in which Ghana is both old and new. Beginning each statement with "I am . . ." *(For example, I am old when my people celebrate Odwira. / I am new because my government is less than 50 years old.)*

Answers to Review Questions

1. Ghana today is trying to preserve the traditional ways of its various ethnic groups. At the same time, it is encouraging higher education, modernization, the building of industry, and a strong, central government.
2. Ghana had to organize its new government and find money for developing industries, public projects, and social programs.
3. Ghana is dependent on cocoa as its major crop. If the price of cocoa falls, Ghana gets far less income. If prices rise, Ghana has more income.
4. Answers will vary, but students should weigh the value of independence against his later dictatorship.
5. Religions: some Christianity but mainly Other—traditional African religion; climate: most of Ghana has a tropical wet and dry climate; population: the population of Ghana is between 10 and 20 million; land use: farming in the southern half and grazing in the northern half.

Homework Options

Have students use what they have learned about Ghana to write two paragraphs for a travel brochure, telling what places visitors might like to see, and why.

Study Guide: page 50

INTRODUCE

Traditional West African cultures explained many ethical and moral principles through stories. "The Cow-Tail Switch" not only taught a lesson but also entertained. This retelling by Harold Courlander and George Herzog puts into writing a tale that was part of the oral tradition of West Africa. This selection adds narrative detail to what students learn about life in West Africa in Chapters 11 and 12.

READ AND RESPOND

Many students will enjoy reading this story independently, but the dialogue also lends itself to reading aloud. In fact, you may want to replicate the storytelling situation discussed in the head note. If so, read the story aloud, but stop at the point when Ogaloussa is making a decision. Engage the students in a discussion of who should receive the cow-tail switch. Then complete the story and compare decisions.

Before students read, point out the vocabulary words and unfamiliar terms defined in the margins. Be sure they understand what the words mean; help with pronunciation if necessary.

LITERATURE

The Cow-Tail Switch

Retold by Harold Courlander and George Herzog

In traditional West African villages, storytelling was an important part of village life. Stories taught lessons and brought people together. When telling this story, the storyteller often stopped before reaching the end and would ask the listeners to suggest endings for the story. As you read the story, think about how you would end it. Is your ending the same as the one here? If not, why do you think your ending is better?

Lesson 1 describes how leaders in traditional West Africa were entitled to carry certain symbols of authority. In this story the decorated switch—a short braided whip—is one of those symbols.

Near the edge of the Liberian rain forest, on a hill overlooking the Cavally River, was the village of Kundi. Its rice and cassava fields spread in all directions. Cattle grazed in the grassland near the river. Smoke from the fires in the round clay houses seeped through the palmleaf roofs, and from a distance these faint columns of smoke seemed to hover over the village. Men and boys fished in the river with nets, and women pounded grain in wooden mortars before the houses.

cassava (kuh SAH vah) an edible root, source of tapioca

mortar strong container in which things can be ground

Ogaloussa (oh gah LOO suh)

manioc cassava

In this village, with his wife and many children, lived a hunter by the name of Ogaloussa.

One morning Ogaloussa took his weapons down from the wall of his house and went into the forest to hunt. His wife and his children went to tend their fields, and drove their cattle out to graze. The day passed, and they ate their evening meal of manioc and fish. Darkness came, but Ogaloussa didn't return.

Another day went by, and still Ogaloussa didn't come back. They talked about it and wondered what could have detained him. A week passed, then a month. Sometimes Ogaloussa's sons mentioned that he hadn't come home. The family cared for the crops, and the sons hunted for game, but after a while they no longer talked about Ogaloussa's disappearance.

Then, one day, another son was born to Ogaloussa's wife. His name was Puli. Puli grew older. He began to sit up and crawl. The time came when Puli began to talk, and the first thing he said was, "Where is my father?"

The other sons looked across the ricefields.

"Yes," one of them said. "Where is Father?"

"He should have returned long ago," another one said.

Thematic Connections

Social Studies: Social Systems/ Individuals, family, and community

Houghton Mifflin Literary Readers: Traditional Tales/Timeless Tales

Background

In the cultures of West Africa, stories have long been used to entertain, explain, and teach community values. In some African village societies, a person's status was determined by his or her lineage, or family line. Who your ancestors were—mother, father, grandmother, grandfather—meant a great deal, so remembering and honoring them was extremely important. "The Cow-Tail Switch" teaches a lesson about the importance of remembering.

"Something must have happened. We ought to look for him," a third son said.

"He went into the forest, but where will we find him?" another one asked.

"I saw him go," one of them said. "He went that way, across the river. Let us follow the trail and search for him."

So the sons took their weapons and started out to look for Ogaloussa. When they were deep among the great trees and vines of the forest they lost the trail. They searched in the forest until one of them found the trail again. They followed it until they lost the way once more, and then another son found the trail. It was dark in the forest, and many times they became lost. Each time another son found the way. At last they came to a clearing among the trees, and there on the ground scattered about lay Ogaloussa's bones and his rusted weapons. They knew then that Ogaloussa had been killed in the hunt.

One of the sons stepped forward and said, "I know how to put a dead person's bones together." He gathered all of Ogaloussa's bones and put them together, each in its right place.

Another son said, "I have knowledge too. I know how to cover the skeleton with sinews and flesh." He went to work, and he covered Ogaloussa's bones with sinews and flesh.

sinews tendons, muscles

◄ Why didn't Ogaloussa's family look for him before Puli asked his question? *(Family members were too busy with the routine of their lives to do anything about it; they were accustomed to Ogaloussa's going on long hunting trips; sometimes it takes a new person to recognize a problem.)*

Access Strategy

Before students read "The Cow-Tail Switch," ask volunteers to describe traditions from their cultures, religions, or families for remembering ancestors or deceased relatives. *(Visiting cemeteries, displaying photographs, telling stories, lighting candles, holding religious services, keeping shrines)* List these samples on the board. Ask students to point out any similarities they observe.

Help students understand that all cultures have traditions and rituals for remembering ancestors, even though specific practices vary. These traditions are important because they keep us in touch with our family histories. Tell students that in "The Cow-Tail Switch" they will see just how much importance the African villagers placed on remembering their ancestors.

A third son said, "I have the power to put blood into a body." He went forward and put blood into Ogaloussa's veins, and then he stepped aside.

Another of the sons said, "I can put breath into a body." He did his work, and when he was through they saw Ogaloussa's chest rise and fall.

"I can give the power of movement to a body," another of them said. He put the power of movement into his father's body, and Ogaloussa sat up and opened his eyes.

"I can give him the power of speech," another son said. He gave the body the power of speech, and then he stepped back.

Ogaloussa looked around him. He stood up.

"Where are my weapons?" he asked.

They picked up his rusted weapons from the grass where they lay and gave them to him. Then they returned the way they had come, through the forest and the ricefields, until they had arrived once more in the village.

Ogaloussa went into his house. His wife prepared a bath for him and he bathed. She prepared food for him and he ate. Four days he remained in the house, and on the fifth day he came out and shaved his head, because this was what people did when they came back from the land of the dead.

Afterwards he killed a cow for a great feast. He took the cow's tail and braided it. He decorated it with beads and cowry shells and bits of shiny metal. It was a beautiful thing. Ogaloussa carried it with him to important affairs. When there was a dance or an important ceremony he always had it with him. The people of the village thought it was the most beautiful cow-tail switch they had ever seen.

Soon there was a celebration in the village because Ogaloussa had returned from the dead. The people dressed in their best clothes, the musicians brought out their instruments, and a big dance began. The drummers beat their drums and the women sang. The people drank much palm wine. Everyone was happy.

Ogaloussa carried his cow-tail switch, and everyone admired it. Some of the men grew bold and came forward to Ogaloussa and asked for the cow-tail switch, but Ogaloussa kept it in his hand. Now and then there was a clamor and much confusion as many people asked for it at once. The women and children begged for it too, but Ogaloussa refused them all.

Finally he stood up to talk. The dancing stopped and people came close to hear what Ogaloussa had to say.

"A long time ago I went into the forest," Ogaloussa said. "While I was hunting I was killed by a leopard. Then my sons came for me. They brought me back from the land of the dead to my village. I will give this cow-tail switch to one of my sons. All

286

Collaborative Learning

List on the board what each of the sons of Ogaloussa did to bring him back to life. Divide the class into as many groups as there are sons in the story. Have each group prepare an argument stating why that son should receive the cow-tail switch. After students have finished reading the story, have them consider what the moral of the story would have been if "their" son had been given the cow-tail switch. Have one student in each group take notes from the group's discussion and present the group's argument to the class. After all groups have presented their arguments, discuss them as a class, noting the use of logic but avoiding judging the arguments as right or wrong.

of them have done something to bring me back from the dead, but I have only one cow-tail to give. I shall give it to the one who did the most to bring me home."

So an argument started.

"He will give it to me!" one of the sons said. "It was I who did the most, for I found the trail in the forest when it was lost!"

"No, he will give it to me!" another son said. "It was I who put his bones together!"

"It was I who covered his bones with sinews and flesh!" another said. "He will give it to me!"

"It was I who gave him the power of movement!" another son said. "I deserve it most!"

Another son said it was he who should have the switch, because he had put blood in Ogaloussa's veins. Another claimed it because he had put breath in the body. Each of the sons argued his right to possess the wonderful cow-tail switch.

Before long not only the sons but the other people of the village were talking. Some of them argued that the son who had put blood in Ogaloussa's veins should get the switch, others that the one who had given Ogaloussa breath should get it. Some of them believed that all of the sons had done equal things, and that they should share it. They argued back and forth this way until Ogaloussa asked them to be quiet.

"To this son I will give the switch, for I owe most to him," Ogaloussa said.

He came forward and bent low and handed it to Puli, the little boy who had been born while Ogaloussa was in the forest.

The people of the forest remembered then that the child's first words had been, "Where is my father?" They knew that Ogaloussa was right.

For it was a saying among them that a man is not really dead until he is forgotten.

Further Reading

African Myths and Legends. Kathleen Arnott. These tales are about animals, humans, and superhumans.

Behind the Back of the Mountain. Verna Aardema. These are black folktales from southern Africa.

The Cow-Tail Switch and Other West African Tales. Retold by Harold Courlander and George Herzog. This book contains additional West African tales and legends that have been passed down through oral tradition.

The King's Drum and Other Stories. Harold Courlander. Here are tales from many different peoples of Africa.

The Magic Drum: Tales from Central Africa. W. F. P. Burton. The very short stories in this book are similar to fables. They are favorites in the Congo.

◄ What does the last sentence of the story mean? *(It means that someone can stay alive in our memories even after the person has died but that when someone is no longer remembered, then he or she is truly dead.)*

EXTEND

The story of the cow-tail switch touches the importance of remembering and caring for ancestors in West African village society. Have students find more information about rural African customs and prepare short oral reports to be shared with the class.

Writing a News Account

Have students imagine that they are reporters for the *West African Gazette;* they have been sent to cover the miraculous reappearance of Ogaloussa. Have them write their accounts as news stories, including quotations from any of the characters in the story. Students should write catchy headlines for their stories. After they have written rough drafts of their articles, have students proofread and revise, making sure they have corrected all errors and that the story is done in newspaper style, with short, succinct, factual statements. Students should make final copies of their news articles to be displayed or shared.

Further Reading

You may want to have your students look in the school or local library for more collections of African fables and folktales.

Answers to Reviewing Key Terms

A. Sample answers:

1. **Matrilineal** means tracing one's ancestry through the mother's side of the family; **patrilineal** means tracing ancestry through the father's side.
2. **Kinship** means relationship through common ancestors, and **lineage** refers to a group of several families with the same ancestor.
3. **Exports** are goods that one country sells to another; **imports** are goods that one country buys from another.

B. Sample answers:

1. False. By growing **cash crops,** Gold Coast farmers did not produce food to feed their families directly.
2. False. Aroused by a spirit of **nationalism** in the years after World War II, the people of the Gold Coast struggled to gain independence from Great Britain.
3. False. When most of its people can read, a country has a high **literacy rate**.

Answers to Exploring Concepts

A. Sample outline:

I.–The Asante: A People of Tradition
A.–Land and People
1.–*Geography of Ghana*
2.–Origin of the Asante
B.–West African Connections
1.–*Patterns of Living*
2.–*Traditions of Working*
II.–Growth and Change
A.–*The Ashanti Empire*
1.–Ashanti Rule
2.–*Growth of Trade*
B.–British Colonial Rule
1.–*Asante Resistance*
2.–*Colonial Rule*
III.–A New Nation
A.–*Ghana: A Nation*
1.–A Difficult Beginning
2.–*Years of Challenge*
B.–*Ghana Today*
1.–*The Asante Today*
2.–New Allegiances

B. Sample answers:

1. The Odwira festival connected the Asante to their ancestors and renewed support for their leader. The naming of a baby connected it to the kinship system.
2. A warm climate and fertile soil made farming possible; the rain forest provided hunting grounds and wood for carving. Gold was a resource for trade.
3. The Ashanti Empire lasted for more than 200 years and included more than three million people.
4. In return for gold, hardwood, ivory, animal skins, and salt, the Asante obtained food crops, metals, textiles, beads, and luxury goods, such as silk.
5. Increased trade led Britain to seek inland areas, causing wars between the British and the Asante.
6. The Asante invaded lands protected by the British and beseiged the British after the incident of the Golden Stool.
7. In the United States, Nkrumah studied how to help Africans win independence.
8. When cocoa prices fell, Ghana had less income for public needs and projects.
9. The Asante make up the largest ethnic group in Ghana today.
10. People in Ghana today take pride in keeping their traditions. At the same time, many are learning new jobs, speaking English, and gaining an education.

Chapter Review

Reviewing Key Terms

cash crop (p. 277)
export (p. 277)
import (p. 277)
kinship (p. 271)
lineage (p. 271)
literacy rate (p. 283)
matrilineal (p. 270)
nationalism (p. 280)
patrilineal (p. 270)

A. Read each pair of words. Write a sentence telling how the words in each pair are related.

1. matrilineal, patrilineal
2. kinship, lineage
3. export, import

B. Write whether each of the following statements is *true* or *false*. Then rewrite the false statements to make them true. Each new statement should show that you understand the meaning of the key term.

1. By growing <u>cash crops</u>, Gold Coast farmers produced more than enough food to feed their families.
2. Aroused by a spirit of <u>nationalism</u> in the years after World War II, the people of the Gold Coast struggled to remain a colony of Great Britain.
3. When most of its people can read, a country has a low <u>literacy rate</u>.

Exploring Concepts

A. Copy this outline of Chapter 12. Complete the outline with information from the chapter.

I. The Asante: A People of Tradition
  A. Land and People
    1.
    2. Origin of the Asante
  B. West African Connections
    1.
    2.
II. Growth and Change
  A.
    1. Ashanti Rule
    2.
  B. British Colonial Rule
    1.
    2.
III. A New Nation
  A.
    1. A Difficult Beginning
    2.
  B.
    1.
    2. New Allegiances

B. Support each of the following statements with information from the chapter.

1. Traditions helped to unite the Asante people and to give them a sense of belonging to their society.
2. The natural environment helped the Asante to prosper.
3. The Ashanti Empire was one of the larger empires in West Africa.
4. In the beginning, trade with Europeans benefited the Asante.
5. Eventually, trade with the British led to harmful practices.
6. The Asante resisted British expansion in a variety of ways.
7. Kwame Nkrumah gained many new ideas in the United States.
8. Ghana's dependence on one major export crop, cocoa, caused problems for the new nation.
9. The Asante are still an important group in the nation of Ghana.
10. No matter what their ethnic group, today the people of Ghana live in two worlds.

Reviewing Skills

1. Explain each of the following proverbs in your own words. What do these proverbs reveal about U.S. culture?
   a. "Time is money."
   b. "Little strokes fell big oaks."
   c. "Heaven helps those who help themselves."
   d. "Haste makes waste."

   Now write a proverb of your own and explain what it means in terms of your own culture.
2. By looking at a flow chart, you can easily see the order of events. Make a flow chart showing the stages by which Britain took control of the Ashanti Empire. The chart should begin in the 1600s and go to 1900.
3. Storytelling is an important part of West African culture. Why is this tradition valuable to historians?

Using Critical Thinking

1. You read in Chapter 12 that "Traditions of the past are helping the people of Ghana to deal with changes both today and in the future." How do you think that keeping traditions helps people deal with changes in their lives?
2. Compare and contrast the role of kinship in a traditional West African culture and in U.S. culture today.
3. Write a "want ad" or a job description for a future leader of Ghana. List all the skills and qualifications you think a new Ghanaian leader should have in order to deal with the people's needs and problems.
4. In this chapter you read that the people spoke out against British rule. In what ways, if any, did British rule help to prepare the people of the Gold Coast for independence?

Preparing for Citizenship

1. **INTERVIEWING** In traditional West African society, a family's history is handed down by word of mouth from one generation to the next in an oral tradition. Interview members of your family to learn as much as you can of your family's history, focusing on events that have occurred in your own lifetime. If you like, share an event or two from this story with your class.
2. **ARTS ACTIVITY** Go to the library to find pictures of the traditional arts of Ghana. Using clay or papier mâché, make a model of a mask or sculpture that you find interesting. Share your work with the class. What can you learn about the people of Ghana from their art?
3. **WRITING ACTIVITY** Imagine that you are Kwame Nkrumah in his role as prime minister of the Gold Coast in about 1955. Write a rousing political speech that you will use to persuade the British to grant independence to your country. In your role, you may draw on your experience in the United States; on colonial resistance to British rule; on feelings of nationalism among your people; and on the advantages of independence. When you have written your speech, give it in front of the class.
4. **GROUP ACTIVITY** After Ghana became independent, national elections chose Kwame Nkrumah to be prime minister. With a partner, debate whether the Asantehene, the leader of the Asante, should have become prime minister. One of you can take the part of Nkrumah and the other the part of the Asantehene.
5. **COLLABORATIVE LEARNING** As a class, decide which are the major events in the history of the Ashanti Empire and Ghana as told in this chapter. Then divide into small groups, and choose one of these events to dramatize. Your group should choose a narrator, rehearse a brief skit about its event, and present the skit to the whole class.

Answers to Reviewing Skills

1. Sample answers include: (a.) Time is valuable; shows the importance of time. (b.) You can get a big job done in small steps; shows the importance of persistence. (c.) Luck befalls people who help themselves; shows the importance of self-reliance. (d.) Hurrying causes errors that require additional time to correct; stresses thoroughness. Students' proverbs might give advice for modern living.
2. The Asante formed an empire. The Portuguese and British traded goods with the Asante via the Fante and traded guns for slaves. After the slave trade had ended, the British sought gold, food crops, and raw materials. The British seized Asante lands and set up the Gold Coast colony. The British then made the Ashanti kingdom part of the Gold Coast colony.
3. A culture's stories tell of its beliefs, traditions, important events, and leaders or heroes. Historians use the stories to reconstruct the history of various groups and to relate that history to events elsewhere in the world.

Answers to Using Critical Thinking

1. Keeping traditions gives people a sense of belonging to a group when aspects of their lives are changing.
2. Kinship plays a larger role in traditional West African culture than in modern U.S. culture. In the United States, very few families band together as clans. U.S. family members may help one another in hard times, but kinship groups do not influence their position in society as they do in West Africa.
3. Students' ads might specify a person who knows the traditions of Ghana, has experience in dealing with different ethnic groups, knows economics and international trade, and seeks the good of the country.
4. The British established mission schools, encouraged farming, and recognized the achievements of the Asante.

Answers to Preparing for Citizenship

1. **INTERVIEWING** Allow students to tape-record their interviews. Ask students how much new information they have gained about their families and themselves.
2. **ARTS ACTIVITY** If possible, make additional art books available to students. Ghanaians' art can tell us about their interests and beliefs as well as their materials.
3. **WRITING ACTIVITY** Students' speeches may include such topics as Nkrumah's observations about freedom in the United States; the ability of the Asante and other groups to govern themselves; and the need for Gold Coast peoples to benefit fully from their resources, productivity, and trade.
4. **GROUP ACTIVITY** Students should recognize pros and cons for both sides. Nkrumah, a popular leader before independence, was committed to change and modernization. The Asantehene would probably have favored a slower rate of change and maintenance of traditional ways.
5. **COLLABORATIVE LEARNING** Encourage students to identify with the human problems caused by each event.

CHAPTER ORGANIZER

Chapter 13 South Africa

CHAPTER PLANNING CHART

Pupil's Edition	Teacher's Edition	Ancillaries
Lesson 1: A Divided Land (2–3 days) Objective 1: Explain how Nelson Mandela became a symbol of South African injustice. (History 5; Culture 6) Objective 2: Explain how the apartheid system has worked and why it was imposed. (History 1, 7, 8) Objective 3: Describe the growth of the anti-apartheid movement. (Economics 4; Social and Political Systems 3, 6)	• Graphic Overview (292) • Access Strategy (293) • Access Activity (293) Critical Thinking (294) Social Context (294)	Study Guide (51) Map Activities (17) • Posters (1)
Lesson 2: The Fight for Land (3–4 days) Objective 1: Describe the origins of South Africa's main ethnic groups. (History 4, 6) Objective 2: Identify the main events and developments in South African history. (History 7, 8; Geography 4)	• Graphic Overview (296) • Access Strategy (297) • Access Activity (297) Critical Thinking (298) Cultural Context (298) • Music Connection (299) Political Context (299) Critical Thinking (299) • Visual Learning (300) Writing a Letter (300) Political Context (301) Map and Globe Skills (301)	Study Guide (52) Discovery Journal (27)
Understanding Note-Taking Objective: Explain how to extract information from resources and record it efficiently. (Study Skills 1, 2)	Writing a Note Card (303)	Study Guide (53)
Lesson 3: A New South Africa (2–3 days) Objective 1: Identify two problems and two signs of progress in South Africa since the partial lifting of apartheid. (Social and Political Systems 2, 3, 4) Objective 2: List some of the questions that remain unanswered as South Africa looks to the future. (History 7; Social and Political Systems 3, 5)	• Graphic Overview (304) • Access Strategy (305) • Access Activity (305) • Visual Learning (306) Historical Context (306)	Study Guide (54) Discovery Journal (28) • Study Prints (8)
Chapter Review	Answers (308–309)	Tests (49–52)

* Objectives are correlated to the strands and goals in the program Scope and Sequence on pages T41–T49.

• LEP appropriate resources.
(For additional strategies, see pages T32–T33.)

CHAPTER RATIONALE

Chapter 13 examines the history of South Africa through the lens of its crumbling policy of apartheid. South Africa is selected for inclusion in this unit in part because of what students can learn about cultural conflict by studying apartheid and its origins. Apartheid was unique because of the degree to which it legislated segregation; therefore, it merits special consideration as a historical and cultural phenomenon. Understanding Note-Taking on page 303 provides students the opportunity to further research apartheid and its effects.

Although apartheid provides a thematic framework for the chapter, our ultimate goal is to interest students in the remarkable diversity of peoples in South Africa. We place special emphasis on the experiences of two groups, indigenous blacks and white Afrikaners, because of the enormous influence these groups have had on the entire population.

Lesson 1 opens with the 1990 release of Nelson Mandela from prison, inviting students to share the perspective of observers at a Soweto rally where Mandela appears. The lesson then introduces students to apartheid and what it has meant to live under this oppressive system. The graphs and map on page 294 show students the proportion of land occupied by whites and nonwhites and the homelands where most blacks were forced to live under apartheid. The lesson also features important developments in the history of resistance to apartheid.

Lesson 2 traces the history of the early Khoisan and Bantu-speaking peoples and their interactions with European settlers, who began arriving in the 1400s. The lesson emphasizes how the Dutch, German, and French (who collectively called themselves Afrikaners) gained control of the region despite their loss to the British in the South African War of 1899–1902. The Afrikaners used this power to exert control over indigenous blacks and later establish the policy of apartheid. The timeline on pages 298–299 visually summarizes a large portion of the time period covered in the lesson. Students may examine white and nonwhite relations more closely by reading A Closer Look, Mining in South Africa, on page 300.

Lesson 3 takes students to the 1992 Summer Olympic Games in Barcelona, Spain, where two Africans, one black and one white, won first and second places in the women's 10,000-meter race. This event is used to stress the lesson theme, that present-day South Africa is undergoing promising though unsteady change. The lesson reviews recent developments in the dismantling of many apartheid laws and the beginning negotiations between the white government and anti-apartheid leaders. The chapter concludes by registering the volatile uncertainty of South Africa's future. Students are invited to think about apartheid more critically in Understanding Social Justice on page 306.

ACTIVITIES & PROJECTS

Basic: Conducting a Survey

Have students conduct a survey of family members and neighbors on apartheid and South Africa. Among the questions they might ask are: Do you think that apartheid in South Africa has ended? How long do you think that it will take for nonwhites to gain a voice in the South African government? Will opposing groups resort to war, or can an agreement be worked out peacefully? Encourage students also to ask their own questions based on their reading. Students can then present their findings to the class. You may wish to record their findings on the chalkboard and help develop overall conclusions of the survey. (Use after any lesson.)

LEP: Making a Mural

Direct students to find a variety of images of South Africa and its peoples—past and present—in books, newsmagazines, and newspapers. Then have students draw copies of or photocopy the images and assemble them creatively on a wall or a bulletin board in the classroom. You might also wish to assign groups of students to write captions that explain aspects of the mural. Students could then place these captions within the mural. (Use after any lesson.)

Writing a Letter

Tell students that they are to write a letter to the South African president presenting their views on the formation of a new government. Each student's letter might include the following features: a clear statement of the viewpoint; specific suggestions about ways to open the government to nonwhite participation; suggested laws that should be passed; and ways to further desegregate living areas and public places. Encourage students to read their letters aloud in small groups and talk about how the government might implement each student's ideas. (Use after Lesson 3.)

Challenge: Research

Have students locate and look through recent books, magazines, and newspapers to learn about significant events that have taken place in South Africa since 1992. Then ask students to imagine that they are textbook writers. Have them write three or four paragraphs headed South Africa Update that could be added onto Lesson 3 of this chapter. (Use after Lesson 3.)

CHAPTER PREVIEW

Have the students read the chapter title and the timeline text. Ask them to name ways in which people of different ethnic backgrounds and cultures might clash. *(Possible answers include: different languages; different beliefs; competition for land or other scarce resources; unfair treatment of one group by another.)*

Looking Back

Ask students to describe how the people living in Mali and Ghana were treated by the French and the British who colonized there. Explain that European settlers' treatment of the people in South Africa was both similar to and different from their treatment of the people living in Ghana and Mali. Direct students to look for similarities and differences as they read the chapter.

Looking Forward

Explain that in the next three lessons—A Divided Land, The Fight for Land, and A New South Africa—students will read about how South Africa has long been torn by racial conflicts.

Lesson 1 gives students a snapshot of what life was like in South Africa's divided society under the system of apartheid.

Chapter 13

South Africa

"Blacks and whites must come together," says 12-year-old Edward Diholo. "Violence, when will you stop!!!" writes Nthabiseng Nkole, age 14. These young students live in South Africa, a nation that is home to peoples of many colors who take pride in their roots. Color has deeply divided these peoples, and for generations they have fought bitterly to protect their lands and ways of life. Now blacks and whites are trying to come to agreement.

The Khoisan lived throughout the western part of southern Africa for thousands of years. Bantu speakers in the east lived in farm communities such as the one above.

This wealthy Afrikaner, Gert Maritz, was one of the farmers who made the Great Trek to central southern Africa from 1836 to 1840.

1375	1500	1625

1488

1652 The Dutch settle the African cape and import slaves for farming.

BACKGROUND

Until the late 1600s, the Dutch intended their occupation of the Cape of Good Hope to remain a small venture. The sole mission of the Dutch East India Company was to supply the annual fleets of ships with fresh food, water, and supplies; the company did not even expect to make a profit. In time, though, the Dutch and other European settlers fanned out and seized land inhabited by the original peoples, driving them out or enslaving them. By the 1800s the European settlers had forced many indigenous groups from their land and had begun to break their social and cultural traditions. At this time, however, South Africa's development took a unique and even more tragic turn.

The Roots of Divisions

What set South Africa apart from the rest of colonial Africa was the fact that the European settlers began to develop strong cultural ties to the land. With roots in South Africa going back several generations, the descendants of Dutch, German, and French settlers thought of themselves as Africans, not colonizing peoples. Hence, they began calling themselves Afrikaners.

Another key element in South Africa's development was its rich mineral wealth. The discovery of diamonds and gold, in 1867 and 1886, respectively, spurred even more competition for land. After 1870, incoming prospectors forced black South Africans from their land on a large scale. They were used as

This market is located in Cape Town, one of the first settlements established by Europeans in the 1600s.

Children in this Soweto schoolyard and across South Africa look forward to the day when people of all colors are treated as equals.

1750 | 1875 | 2000

1860s Discovery of diamonds brings cities, industry, and waves of English speakers to southern Africa.

1990 Black leader Nelson Mandela is freed from prison. Some unfair laws are repealed.

Today

Understanding the Visuals

Early Bantu-speaking peoples lived in villages similar to the one shown on page 290, which is preserved in Northern Kruger National Park in South Africa. The Late Iron Age culture of Bantu-speaking peoples—which Europeans encountered when they came to the region—was based on farming and herding. Settlements were probably composed of extended families.

Gert Maritz was one of only a handful of wealthy Afrikaner trekkers who sought to flee British colonial rule as well as locate new farmland. This statue of Maritz is at the Voortrekker Museum in Pietermaritzburg. *Voortrekker* means "front trekker," referring to the groups at the vanguard of the migration.

Understanding Chronology

Refer students to the timeline. Ask them to speculate how the population of southern Africa changed between 1652 and the 1860s. *(More European settlers came, pushing Africans off their lands.)* Then ask students how the events of the 1860s might have affected the population. *(The discovery of diamonds and gold intensified the trend of European occupation and control. Africans lost still more land.)*

cheap labor and were segregated by unjust laws. From the 1870s black mine workers resided in all-male compounds far from their families and had to carry passes, while whites could move around freely and live with their families in town. By 1910 blacks had lost all control of South Africa to whites.

Segregation Takes Hold

Widespread racial segregation intensified following the South African War. Racism became institutionalized in South Africa by the 1920s under a policy that later would become apartheid. This effort to completely segregate society came at the very time that segregation in the United States had begun to face significant opposition. Like African Americans in the 1950s, black South Africans crossed racial lines as they moved into the cities in the post–World War II period. They demanded more equitable conditions and political rights. Unlike African Americans, South African blacks constituted a majority of the population. Even so, they had to wait far longer than their U.S. counterparts to achieve even the most basic rights.

The U.S. civil rights movement reached a peak in the 1960s with many notable gains. In South Africa, however, white lawmakers, supported by the courts, the police force, and the armed forces, smothered reform efforts until the 1980s. After decades of division, polarization, and violence in South Africa, many South Africans hope that a permanent reform is finally under way.

INTRODUCE

Have students read the lesson title. Ask them to name factors that might divide different groups of people who live in the same society. *(Answers might include geographic separation, different customs and beliefs, and different rights and freedoms under the law, such as owning land and voting.)* Invite students to speculate how such divisions and separations might affect a society. *(One group of people might live better than the others. Civil war and hostility might arise.)*

Key Terms

Vocabulary Strategies: T36–T37

apartheid—a South African government policy begun in 1948, designed to keep racial groups separate in order to protect the power and privileges of whites

segregation—the separation of people according to their race, ethnic background, religion, or other difference

boycott—a form of protest in which people refuse to do business with a company, a group, or a country

1375 | 1500 | 1625 | 1750 | 1875 | 1912 | TODAY

LESSON 1

A Divided Land

THINKING FOCUS

What is apartheid, and how does it affect South Africans?

Key Terms

- apartheid
- segregation
- boycott

February 13, 1990, Soweto, South Africa: The seats of the South African soccer stadium are full, but people keep coming. Most are black. They are happy and eager. This crowd, however, is not waiting for a soccer match. They have come to see a South African hero.

Joyful chants echo across the stadium. In Xhosa *(KOH sah),* an African language, the voices cry, "*Amandla! Ngawethu!* [Power! It is ours!]" This is the largest crowd in years to gather for a political rally. People in the crowd wave the black, green, and gold flag of the African National Congress (ANC). Only two weeks ago, waving this flag would have been illegal. Two weeks ago, being a member of the ANC was illegal.

Suddenly, the crowd takes up a new chant. "Mandela! Mandela!" rocks through the stadium. Then he appears. Tall, thin, and gray-haired, Nelson Mandela moves with grace. Hand in hand with his wife, Winnie, he walks around the soccer field. They raise their fists in a salute to victory. The crowd goes wild.

Two days after his release from a South African prison east of Cape Town, Mandela has returned to his home in Soweto *(suh WEE toh)*. At age 71, Mandela is a free man—almost—for the first time in nearly 30 years.

Boston Sunday Globe
Mandela to be freed today
De Klerk decree ends 27-year detention
Silber's odyssey in pursuit of truth
New dreams begin for blacks in Soweto

➤ *Mandela was sentenced to life in prison after a seven-month trial without a jury. In one prison he broke bricks and worked in a mine. His release was celebrated around the world.*

Objectives

1. Explain how Nelson Mandela became a symbol of South African injustice.
2. Explain how the apartheid system has worked and why it was imposed.
3. Describe the growth of the anti-apartheid movement.

Graphic Overview

The Rights of Various Groups under Apartheid in the Early 1990s

	Political Rights	Voting Privileges
Whites	all	all
Asians	some	some
Coloreds	some	some
Blacks	very few	none

A Whites-Only Government

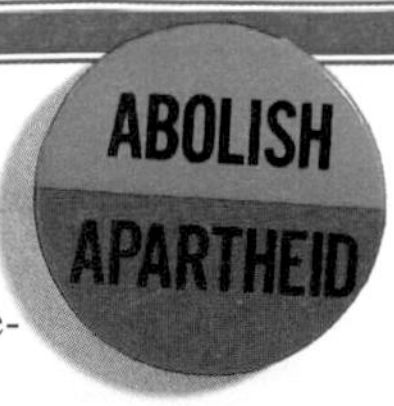

ABOLISH
APARTHEID

Across the world, supporters of Mandela and the anti-apartheid movement wore buttons such as these.

Nelson Mandela had been put in prison because he had protested policies of his country's government. Why did that government let him out of jail? In a sense, South Africa let Mandela go because it hoped to free itself, too. World opinion had recognized that South Africa was an openly racist country.

ABOLISH
APARTHEID
DIVEST NOW

The Republic of South Africa, a country roughly three times the size of California, is located on the southern tip of the African continent. The land is rich in natural resources such as gold, diamonds, platinum, uranium, and coal. About 40.5 million people live here, roughly one-half in rural areas.

South Africa's population, like that of most African countries, including its neighbors Namibia, Zimbabwe, Botswana, Mozambique, and Swaziland, is mostly black. Unlike its neighbors, however, South Africa has a minority white population that runs the government. For decades this government has resisted sharing power with the black majority. It has refused to grant basic rights, including voting rights, to blacks. How has the government been able to do this? ■

■ What makes South Africa different from its neighbors?

Apartheid

Through the early 1990s, the South African government kept its hold on power by creating and enforcing a policy called apartheid *(uh PART hayt).* **Apartheid** was a policy of separation set up in 1948. It defined people in South Africa by color and protected the power of the white government. Apartheid laws labeled every South African white, colored, Asian, or African.

White was supposed to describe people from "pure" European families. *Colored* was a broad term for people of "mixed race" or those who didn't fit any other group. *Asian* was used for people from India as well as for many other Asians. *African* was the term used to describe black Africans.

These terms used by the South African government can be confusing. In this chapter the term *nonwhite* will include the colored, Asian, and African peoples in South Africa. The term *black* will include the African peoples only.

Separate Worlds

Apartheid forced the **segregation,** or separation, of racial groups into two worlds, white and nonwhite. The best schools, hospitals, and public transportation were provided just for whites. There were also separate restaurants, beaches, drinking fountains, train cars, and even park benches. WHITES ONLY signs hung in many public places. Marriage between races was banned.

Apartheid also separated the areas where whites and blacks lived. Large numbers of blacks were crowded into areas called homelands, which were chosen by the government. The map on page 294

BLACKS, COLOUREDS
& ASIANS
ABANTSUNDU, KLEURLINGE
EN ASIËRS

Under apartheid, public facilities were separate and very unequal. For example, nonwhites could use only bathrooms marked for them.

DEVELOP

Have students read the three major headings within the lesson: A Whites-Only Government, Apartheid, and Defeating Apartheid. Explain to students that the idea identified within one heading can lead to the main idea in the next heading. For instance, a whites-only government produced apartheid. Have the students speculate how a whites-only government might affect the man in the picture on page 292, Nelson Mandela. *(He would not be able to participate in such a government.)* Point out that one pronunciation of apartheid sounds like "apart-hate." Invite students to look for reasons why opponents have given apartheid this description.

■ *South Africa is ruled by an all-white minority government that will not let the black majority vote.*

Access Strategy

Have students describe the action in the photograph on this page. *(A black South African child walks in front of a bathroom marked for blacks, coloreds, and Asians.)* Ask students if this scene reminds them of an experience in the history of another country. *(Segregation in parts of the United States before the 1960s)* Explore with students how segregation might have affected this little girl as she grew up.

Next, explain that at one time African Americans in the United States had to ride in the back of public buses and had to give up their seats to white persons. After Rosa Parks, an African American woman in Montgomery, Alabama, was fined for not giving up her seat to a white man, 50,000 African Americans refused to ride on city buses in Montgomery. Start a discussion about how a bus boycott might be effective. *(Loss of revenue would threaten to shut down the city's bus system; city officials might be pressured to change discriminatory bus policies.)*

Access Activity

In 1963 about 200,000 people marched on Washington, D.C., with signs and songs proclaiming "We shall overcome." The marchers protested segregation laws that forced African Americans to use facilities separate from whites and did not let blacks vote. Have students design songs and signs that might be used today to protest a country's policies of segregation.

➤ *Possible answer: The homelands were small, scattered areas far from cities, where most jobs were. Their separation would make cultural and political unity among black groups difficult to achieve.*

SOCIAL SYSTEMS

Visual Learning

Refer students to the map of South Africa on this page. Point out that government policy in 1967 stated that black South Africans "are only temporary residents in the European areas of the republic as long as they offer their labor here." Have students use the map to identify what the government meant by "European areas." *(Areas not designated as black homelands)*

■ *People in nonwhite racial groups had to live in segregated areas and use inferior, segregated facilities.*

➤ *Whites were a small part of the population, but apartheid gave them most of the land, as the chart shows. This land was also the most productive in the country. In contrast, most blacks had to live in homelands. What conclusions might you make about the homelands from looking at the map?*

Population and Land

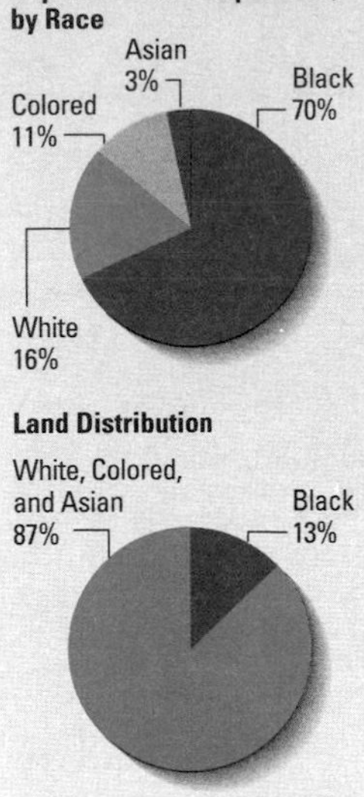
Population under Apartheid, by Race
Asian 3%
Black 70%
Colored 11%
White 16%
Land Distribution
White, Colored, and Asian 87%
Black 13%

Source: The Europa World Year Book, 1992

South Africa, 1990

20°E
30°E
20°S
NAMIBIA
ZIMBABWE
MOZAMBIQUE
BOTSWANA
Tropic of Capricorn
Transvaal
Pretoria
Johannesburg
Soweto
SWAZILAND
Orange Free State
Natal
Kimberley
Bloemfontein
LESOTHO
Durban
30°S
SOUTH AFRICA
INDIAN OCEAN
Cape Province
East London
Port Elizabeth
Cape Town
CAPE OF GOOD HOPE
ATLANTIC OCEAN
0 150 300 mi.
0 150 300 km
Mercator Projection
Black homelands
Gold
Diamonds

➤ *All blacks had to carry a passbook like the one on the right. It told personal details of people's lives. These details included information about their past jobs and what employers thought of them.*

shows where the homelands were located. As the chart shows, under the system of apartheid, black people made up 70 percent of the 40.5 million South Africans, but they lived on only 13 percent of the land.

Many blacks needed to live close to the "white" cities, where the government allowed them to work as servants or in other low-level jobs. For these workers, the government set up areas near the cities called townships. In many townships several families lived together in small shacks without electricity or running water.

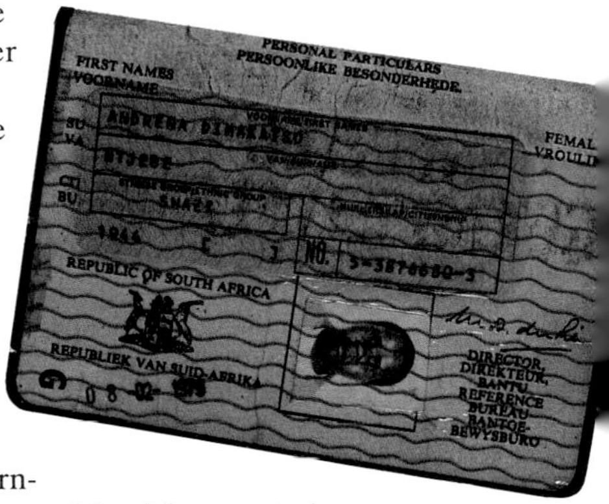
PERSONAL PARTICULARS
PERSOONLIKE BESONDERHEDE
FIRST NAMES
REPUBLIC OF SOUTH AFRICA
REPUBLIEK VAN SUID-AFRIKA
DIRECTOR
DIREKTEUR
BANTU
REFERENCE
BUREAU

Mandela Fights for Freedom

In 1964 a white South African court found Mandela and other ANC leaders guilty of trying to overthrow the government. At age 45, Mandela was sent to prison for life. On the day he left prison, Mandela repeated what he had said at his trial almost 30 years before.

> *I have cherished the ideal of a democratic and free society in which all persons live together in harmony and with equal opportunities. It is an ideal which I hope to live for and to achieve. But if need be, it is an ideal for which I am prepared to die.* ■

■ *How did apartheid affect the lives of blacks in South Africa?*

Critical Thinking

Under apartheid all blacks had to carry a pass at all times. If a black person did not have a pass or had stayed more than six days in a city, he or she could be arrested and imprisoned. Ask students how they would feel if they were subject to such regulations. *(Students might say that they would feel insulted, angry, frustrated, or frightened.)*

Social Context

Help students understand the living conditions of South African townships. During World War II, tremendous numbers of black South Africans migrated to squatter camps on the edges of urban centers. On the southwestern border of Johannesburg, 60,000 to 90,000 squatters formed what became known as the township of Soweto. Lack of sanitation and slum-like conditions plagued the township; in the 1940s one section of Soweto had only 63 water taps for more than 15,000 people.

Townships grew beyond government control until the institution of the Group Areas Act in 1950, which reorganized and segregated the townships. Many areas inhabited by blacks were bulldozed away and zoned as "whites only" land. This social and economic dislocation destroyed whole black communities. Families were split up, as people without jobs were sent to homelands far away. Conditions in the homelands, already overcrowded, became acute.

Defeating Apartheid

Nelson Mandela helped make the African National Congress famous throughout the world. Yet the ANC is older than Mandela. In 1912 black leaders from across South Africa formed the group that would become the ANC.

APARTHEID
IS A CRIME
TO HUMANIT

▲ *Protesters demonstrate in Cape Town, South Africa, just before Mandela's release in 1990. Under apartheid, protest leaders could be jailed for long periods without receiving a trial.*

Protests and Responses

For nearly 50 years, the ANC and other anti-apartheid groups led protests and tried to talk to the government. Then in 1960, police fired on a large crowd of protesters in Sharpeville, a black township outside the city of Vereeniging. The police killed 69 people.

Following the Sharpeville Massacre, the government banned the ANC and forced its leaders into hiding. Blacks had found that nonviolent protests didn't work.

In June 1976, black students in Soweto marched in the streets to protest a government order. Police fired on the students, killing a 13-year-old boy. The shooting sparked riots. In one week 176 people, mostly blacks, died. People around the world were shocked by the government's attack.

Thousands of young blacks responded to the government's brutality. They began to receive military training in camps in other African countries.

World Pressure

During the 1980s, people throughout the world increasingly spoke out against apartheid. Gradually, South Africa became isolated from the world. Most major nations joined in a boycott of South Africa. In a **boycott,** people refuse to do business with a company, group, or country.

Sports teams boycotted South Africa, too. During the boycott South Africa's famous white rugby, cricket, and tennis teams were not allowed in world tournaments.

How had South Africa become such a racist country? The answer is found in South Africa's long history of struggle between peoples. ■

■ *What methods did people use to fight apartheid?*

REVIEW

1. **FOCUS** What is apartheid, and how does it affect South Africans?
2. **SOCIAL SYSTEMS** Under the policy of apartheid, where were black South Africans legally allowed to live?
3. **HISTORY** In what ways did the South African government respond to the fight against apartheid?
4. **CRITICAL THINKING** Major nations of the world joined in a boycott of South Africa. How would refusing to do business with a country affect the economy of that country?
5. **WRITING ACTIVITY** Can you think of any unfair laws today? Would you be willing to protest these laws in public? Why or why not?

HISTORY

Critical Thinking

Explain that Stephen Biko, a black South African journalist, led protests as a student and formed the South African Students' Organization to protest apartheid. The government then "banned" Biko; he could not attend public rallies or be with more than one person, aside from his family, at one time. Police officers arrested and killed Biko in 1977, provoking a worldwide outcry against police brutality in South Africa. Ask students why the government would "ban" and imprison leaders like Biko. *(So they would not spread ideas or organize protests)*

■ *Black South Africans at first protested nonviolently, but some later turned to armed conflict. Other nations instituted economic and sports boycotts.*

CLOSE

Read the Thinking Focus aloud. Ask students to imagine that on this day all apartheid laws and their effects have ended. Have students write a short news report that answers the Thinking Focus. Then ask them to read one anothers' news reports aloud.

Answers to Review Questions

1. Apartheid was a South African policy begun in 1948 that sought to keep racial groups separate to protect the power and privileges of whites. Apartheid segregated all aspects of life and limited the rights of nonwhites.
2. Under apartheid large numbers of black South Africans were allowed to live only in the homelands.
3. Police officers responded with violence against protesters until, under worldwide pressure, the government freed Nelson Mandela and legalized the ANC.
4. A boycott could limit the products a country could sell and consumers could buy. At first, this could harm workers, because companies might reduce wages or cut workers. In time, however, damage to the economy might pressure the government to improve the treatment of its citizens.
5. Students might mention family or school rules or other societal laws that they think are unfair.

Homework Options

Have the students research an anti-apartheid leader in South Africa or a civil rights leader in the movement to end segregation in the United States. Have the students present a short account of the leader's life.

Study Guide: page 51

INTRODUCE

Refer to the world map on pages 678 and 679 in the Atlas. Have students identify South Africa, the Netherlands, the United Kingdom, and India. Point out to students that groups of people from each of these places have affected the history of South Africa. Trace the sea route from the Netherlands to South Africa, and explain that the Dutch settled in South Africa because it was located along trade routes to Asia. Then read aloud, or have a student read, the opening three paragraphs of the lesson. Ask students how they think the European settlers' beliefs about land may have differed from those of the original peoples living in South Africa. *(Sample answer: Original Africans saw land as yielding food and sustenance, while Europeans saw it also as property to own, farm, and sell.)*

Key Terms

Vocabulary Strategies: T36–T37

Afrikaner—the name that descendants of Dutch, German, and French settlers of South Africa called themselves

trek—a journey

1375
1488
1948
2000

LESSON 2

The Fight for Land

THINKING FOCUS

How was the land of southern Africa important to each group of people who lived there?

Key Terms

- Afrikaner
- trek

If you wanted to be a farmer or a rancher today, you would begin by buying a piece of land. Maybe you would put a fence around it or hang a PRIVATE PROPERTY sign.

Not all cultures share the idea that land can be owned as private property. In some places, people have freely used what land they needed. Still, they haven't thought of it as theirs to fence in, buy, or sell.

Some rock paintings like the one on this page show the San hunting eland, a type of antelope.

For thousands of years, southern Africa was such a place. The spacious veld *(vehlt)*—vast grasslands in the interior of the region—was unmarked by fences or permanent buildings.

Early Southern Africans

The veld was far from empty, however. From very early times, three distinct groups of people occupied southern African land.

Peoples of the Western Region

Thousands of years before Europeans arrived, a people called the San *(sahn)* lived in the dry, rocky western part of southern Africa. The San were hunter-gatherers. They hunted antelope, zebras, and elephants. They also gathered wild fruits, berries, and roots.

The San moved constantly, so they didn't build permanent homes. Instead, they stayed in caves or made shelters out of branches or animal skins.

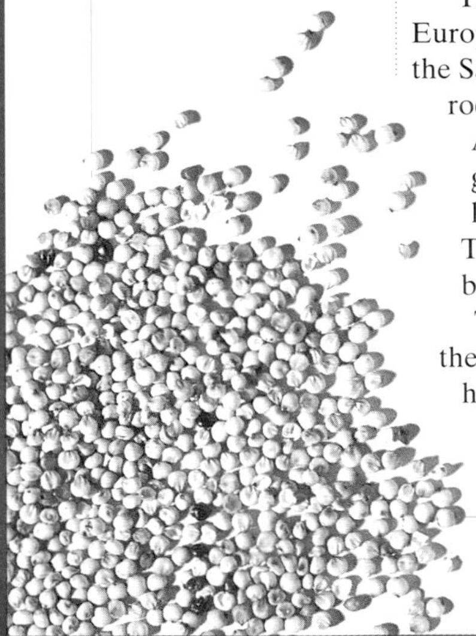

Living alongside the San were a related people called the Khoikhoi *(KOY koy)*. Besides hunting and gathering as the San did, the Khoikhoi also herded cattle and sheep. They lived in shelters made of branches, twigs, and grass.

Historians sometimes refer to both groups together as the Khoisan *(KOY sahn)*. The map on page 297 shows where the Khoisan eventually settled. The Khoisan were not alone in southern Africa, however.

Peoples of the Eastern Region

To the east of the Khoisan lived groups of taller, darker peoples who spoke Bantu languages. These peoples are known as Bantu-speaking peoples. Many of them lived in

Objectives

1. Describe the origins of South Africa's main ethnic groups.
2. Identify the main events and developments in South African history.

Graphic Overview

The Roots of Apartheid

Original peoples live throughout southern Africa. → Europeans threaten cultures of original peoples. → Whites limit rights of nonwhites. → Whites create system of apartheid.

southern Africa as early as A.D. 300. They are the ancestors of most people living in southern Africa today.

Bantu-speaking peoples farmed and herded livestock. They made pottery and mined ore to make iron tools and weapons. The Bantu speakers often stayed in one place. They built lasting homes of stone or clay. Individuals owned livestock, but the land the animals grazed on belonged to the whole group.

The lives of the Bantu-speaking peoples and the Khoisan were to change after the 1400s. That is when Europeans found out about their beautiful land. ■

Groups Living in Southern Africa, c. 1400

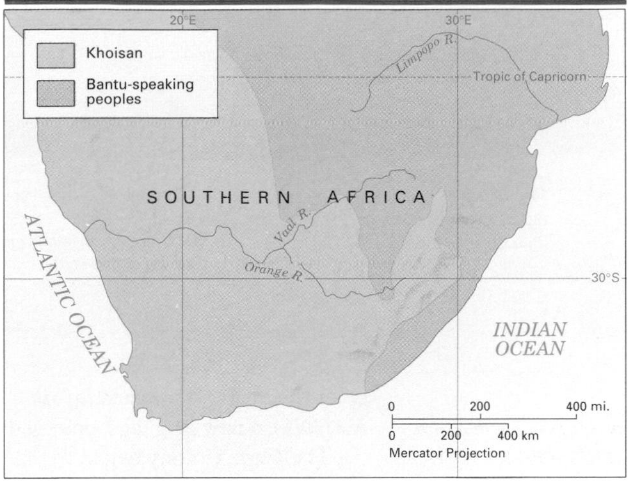

Khoisan
Bantu-speaking peoples
20°E
30°E
Limpopo R.
Tropic of Capricorn
SOUTHERN AFRICA
Vaal R.
Orange R.
30°S
ATLANTIC OCEAN
INDIAN OCEAN
0 200 400 mi.
0 200 400 km
Mercator Projection

The Arrival of the Europeans

In 1488 Bartolomeu Dias *(DEE uhs)*, a Portuguese captain, rounded the southern tip of the African continent. He was searching for a sea route to Asia, the source of much-wanted spices. That southern point came to be called the Cape of Good Hope. It became a regular stop for ships sailing between Europe and Asia. Dias and other early visitors regarded southern Africa as unoccupied and free for the taking.

The Dutch Settle the West

By the 1650s the Dutch had become the leading traders with Asia. In 1652 the Dutch East India Company established an outpost at the cape to supply its many ships with fresh food and water.

The company grew food and traded it with the Khoisan for sheep and cattle. In 1657 the company began giving land on the cape to Dutch settlers to grow food for the fleet. The settlement was known as the Cape Colony.

The land given away had been occupied by the Khoisan for centuries. Not surprisingly, the Khoisan fought to keep their use of the land. European guns and diseases killed many of them. The loss of their lands forced many Khoisan people to work for the Dutch.

The large Dutch farms needed plenty of labor. In addition to hiring Khoisan workers, the colonists brought in slaves from elsewhere in Africa and from Asia. In time the mixing of the Dutch with these African and Asian peoples created a group of Cape Colony residents whom the settlers much later began to call "Cape coloreds."

As more Europeans—especially the Germans and French—joined the Dutch at the Cape Colony, they all began to call themselves **Afrikaners.** The British, who came later, called them Boers. *Boer (bohr)* is the Dutch word for "farmer." The mix of many languages spoken in the colony slowly influenced the Dutch that the Afrikaners spoke.

▲ *Referring to the map, explain how geography affected the early peoples who lived in southern Africa.*

■ *Find two facts in the text that support this statement: The Khoisan and Bantu-speaking peoples were well established in southern Africa centuries before the Europeans arrived.*

➤ *The Bantu speakers planted grains such as sorghum (shown here and on the opposite page) as well as melons, squashes, beans, and yams.*

DEVELOP

Have a volunteer read aloud all the headings of the lesson. Note that many of the headings identify different ethnic groups in South Africa. Encourage students to pay attention to the changing conditions of these ethnic groups as they read the lesson.

◄ *The Khoisan used the drier western lands for hunting, gathering, and grazing. The Bantu-speaking peoples raised crops and grazed cattle in the east, where the climate was moist.*

■ *The statement can be supported by information about ancient San rock paintings and archaeological evidence of Bantu migration as early as A.D. 300.*

HISTORY

Map and Globe Skills

Nelson Mandela was born into a royal family of the Tembu clan, who speak the Xhosa language, one of four major language groups that developed among Bantu-speaking peoples. Refer students to the map on this page, and ask them whether Nelson Mandela's ancestors would have lived in the eastern or western part of southern Africa. *(As Bantu speakers, they probably would have lived in the eastern part.)*

Access Strategy

Tell students that the first people jailed on Robben Island, where Nelson Mandela would once be imprisoned, were two Khoisan herders in 1660 named Herry and Doman. Point out that the Dutch settlers imprisoned Herry and Doman because of a conflict that arose when the two men gave refuge to escaped West Indian slaves.

Explore with students why Khoisan herders might have felt kinship with the escaped slaves. *(Sample answer: The Europeans were causing great hardship to both peoples; both groups were being deprived of their rights and were being badly treated.)* Then discuss what this incident implies about the beliefs of the settlers and their attitudes toward these two groups. *(Guide students to understand that the settlers believed that they had the right to enslave others and had authority over the Khoisan.)*

Access Activity

Ask two volunteers from the class to imagine that each speaks a different language and understands different meanings for common gestures. How would they communicate? What would they try to say? When students have attempted to communicate for a few minutes, discuss how peoples from different cultures learn to communicate.

HISTORY

Visual Learning

For many Afrikaners the Great Trek symbolizes the triumphal escape of Afrikaner trekkers from British rule and the settling of a "promised land" where they were free and independent. Refer students to the painting on the timeline that shows an Afrikaner wagon crossing a river. Have students compare this image of the Great Trek with images they may have seen of westward-bound pioneers on the U.S. frontier. Ask students to describe ways in which the pioneers resembled the trekkers. *(The pioneers thought of western lands as free for the taking; they fought and defeated the original settlers, Native Americans; many pioneers felt guided by their religious beliefs as the trekkers did.)*

➤ *The trekkers did not move north and west because that region was the Kalahari Desert and was not fertile.*

Creation of Modern South Africa

1835–1840s Afrikaners expand north and east, battling Bantu-speaking peoples. This painting depicts Afrikaners on the Great Trek.

1840 | **1850** | **1860**

1840 Mpande becomes head of the Zulu Kingdom, founded by Shaka in the early 1800s.

1860s Diamonds are discovered west of the Orange Free State. The Kimberley diamond mine is pictured on the right.

▲ *Modern South Africa emerged from centuries of conflict and wars over the land and its resources. The timeline above records some of the events that shaped South Africa from 1835 to 1912.*

Over the years, Afrikaans *(af rih KAHNS)*, a new language, emerged.

The Cape Colony began to grow. In search of new farmland, large numbers of Afrikaners headed east and invaded the lands of the Bantu-speaking Xhosa people. In the late 1700s, the Xhosa fought the Afrikaners to defend their homelands.

The Great Trek

By the early 1800s, Great Britain, a rising world power, had taken over the Cape Colony from the Dutch. As British settlers, merchants, and government officials arrived, the new rulers began to make changes. English, not Dutch, became the official language. In the 1830s, slaves in all the British colonies, including the Cape Colony, were freed.

These changes angered many Afrikaner settlers. From 1835 to about 1840, some 6,000 Afrikaner men, women, and children fled British rule. They loaded their belongings, including slaves and servants, into ox-drawn wagons and set off with their slaves and livestock in search of new lands.

The migration became known as the Great Trek. The **trek,** or journey, was long and dangerous. The Afrikaners crossed steep mountains and the huge veld. Most Afrikaners were members of the Dutch Reformed Church and felt guided by their religious beliefs as they made the trek. They believed that God had chosen them to occupy new lands and to rule non-Christian peoples. The Afrikaners saw southern Africa as their rightful home.

The powerful Xhosa blocked the Afrikaners' trek to the east, so the Afrikaners pushed northward.

Southern Africa, 1854

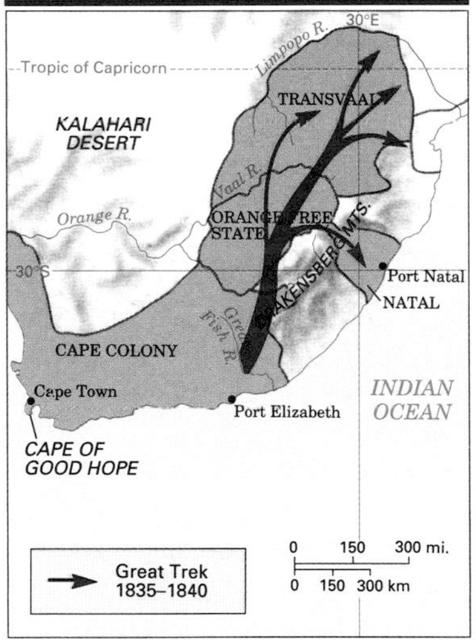
30°E
Tropic of Capricorn
Limpopo R.
TRANSVAAL
KALAHARI DESERT
Vaal R.
Orange R.
ORANGE FREE STATE
30°S
Port Natal
NATAL
CAPE COLONY
Cape Town
Port Elizabeth
INDIAN OCEAN
CAPE OF GOOD HOPE
Great Trek 1835–1840
0 150 300 mi.
0 150 300 km

➤ *The map shows routes that many Afrikaners took on the Great Trek and the Afrikaner and British territories that were created soon afterward. Why did the trekkers move north and east rather than north and west?*

Critical Thinking

Choose a volunteer to reread aloud the first three paragraphs of the lesson, on page 296. Engage students in a discussion of how the Afrikaners' beliefs about land, religion, and ways of life brought them into conflict with others as the Afrikaners made the trek east.

Cultural Context

The British differed from the Afrikaners in the treatment of nonwhite South Africans. Some British ministers on the Cape took blacks into their churches. The Dutch Reformed (Afrikaner) church, on the other hand, created a segregated church in 1857 for "colored" peoples. Some British colonists, called Cape Liberals, believed in the religious and trade education of blacks. Still, even in 1861 "colored" children were not allowed to attend public schools.

Great Britain abolished slavery in 1833, partly due to the belief that free labor was necessary for capitalism to grow. Afrikaners opposed abolition because they wanted to maintain their own economic system of farming and land use. After slavery ended, many blacks chose to work for the higher-paying British settlers rather than the poorer, lower-paying Afrikaner farmers. These cultural conflicts eventually led to the South African War.

1880s Waves of whites and nonwhites come to the Transvaal during the gold rush.

1893 Mohandas Gandhi arrives in South Africa, where he will lead nonwhites in a movement of nonviolent protest.

1899–1902 British defeat Afrikaners in South African War.

UNION OF SOUTH AFRICA
UNIE VAN ZUID AFRICA
2½d
1910

1910 Former British and Afrikaner republics join to become the Union of South Africa. The stamp above is issued, with King George V of England on its face.

1912 African National Congress founded.

1880 | 1890 | 1900 | 1910

The map on page 298 shows the routes they took. Yet the northern regions were the farmlands and pastures of other Bantu speakers.

Even before the Great Trek, many Bantu-speaking peoples had faced tremendous hardship. In the early 1800s, a Bantu-speaking warrior named Shaka had conquered much of the region and formed the Zulu kingdom. Shaka's Zulu army had fought fierce wars of conquest. These wars had killed or uprooted other Bantu-speaking peoples throughout southern Africa. The widespread destruction and scattering of the Bantu-speaking peoples is known as the Mfecane *(uhm fuh KA nay)*.

Because of Shaka's wars, the Bantu-speaking peoples were so scattered that they could not unite to defeat Afrikaner and, later, British invaders. By the late 1800s, the Bantu speakers had lost most of their land. ■

■ *Why did many Afrikaners make the Great Trek?*

A Century of Change

In the 1830s and 1840s, the Afrikaners and Bantu-speaking peoples fought many battles over the land. By 1854 the Afrikaners had won control and had created two new Afrikaner republics, the Transvaal *(trans VAHL)* and the Orange Free State. In these republics, only white men could vote, and slavery was practiced.

Diamonds and Gold

In 1867 diamonds were discovered along the Orange and the Vaal rivers west of the Orange Free State. Settlers found gold in the Transvaal.

Thousands of prospectors from Great Britain, other European countries, the United States, Australia, and elsewhere in Africa poured into the Orange Free State and the Transvaal. Blacks also joined the rush to the mines. Many of them had lost their farmlands to white settlers. Now they were forced to work as laborers in the mines to feed their families. A Closer Look on page 300 tells about life in South Africa's diamond and gold mines today.

By 1896 about 44,000 white miners lived in the Transvaal. With their arrival a new city, Johannesburg, was born. Today Johannesburg is South Africa's largest city.

Across Time & Space

One of the first leaders of the movement for fair treatment in South Africa was Mohandas Gandhi (GAHN dee). *Gandhi, an Indian lawyer who lived in South Africa from 1893 to 1914, led Asians in nonviolent protests against unjust laws. Protesters would break laws intentionally to call attention to the injustice. Later, protesters around the world would use Gandhi's methods.*

BELIEF SYSTEMS

Critical Thinking

Write the word *satyagraha* on the chalkboard. Explain to students that *satyagraha* is the Indian concept of nonviolent protest spread by Mohandas K. Gandhi. Explain that Asians such as Gandhi who were discriminated against in South Africa joined together to resist a law passed in 1906 that required nonwhites to carry passes. Thousands of Asians protested by not registering for passes or by publicly burning them. Explain that such protest is called passive resistance. Ask students to write one or two sentences describing why they think Gandhi chose the word *satyagraha,* meaning "the force that is truth and love," to describe the movement. *(Sample answer: Gandhi believed in the truth of his cause; nonviolent protest demonstrated the force of love.)*

■ *The Afrikaners did not like living under British rule, because English had become the official language, slavery had been outlawed, and Afrikaners wanted more land.*

Music Connection

A distinctive clicking sound, sometimes called a suction stop, is used as a part of the language of some descendants of Nguni clans, such as the Xhosa. The click is made by lifting the back of the tongue against the back roof, or soft palate, of the mouth while holding the teeth or lips together. If possible, locate and play for the class recordings of music by African vocalists such as Miriam Makeba, who incorporates these clicks into her songs.

Political Context

Zulu chief Shaka equipped his warriors with both long spears and short stabbing spears for fighting in close combat. By the mid-1820s Shaka's army controlled an area more than 100 miles in diameter. Shaka ruled through fear. He alone would conduct trials for murder, robbery, rape, adultery, treason, and other crimes. Those found guilty would usually be clubbed to death in a special killing field. Shaka would also kill any clan leader who did not publicly agree with him.

Critical Thinking

Explain to students that Shaka ruled his strong confederation of clans with an iron hand. Ask students how this characteristic might have contributed to Shaka's downfall. *(Families and friends of those killed could become enemies and unite against Shaka.)* Tell students that Shaka was ultimately killed by his personal servant and two of his half-brothers.

Note: You may want to have students read this page after they have read the section Diamonds and Gold on page 299.

More About Mining One of the biggest diamond sites was located on the farm of two Afrikaner brothers named De Beers. Later this site would be called Kimberley, after a British colonial minister.

There were two types of diamond diggings: wet and dry. In wet diggings black workers often waded through deep gravel beds, while white workers sifted through finer rocks. At dry diggings such as Kimberley, thousands of workers stood at the edge of a giant pit where they had staked hundreds of claims.

For decades black laborers confronted disease and inhumane conditions in the mines and the segregated labor camps. Eight percent of black mine workers in the Kimberley mine in the 1870s died, most from pneumonia and smallpox. A smallpox epidemic in 1883 killed more than 500 workers. In 1946, 60,000 mine workers went on strike, demonstrating for better conditions and a minimum wage of 10 shillings (about $2) per day. (Since 1920 black mine workers had earned at least 10 times less than white mine workers.) Police officers put down the strike with force. By the end of the strike, 12 people were dead and more than 1,000 injured.

A CLOSER LOOK

Mining in South Africa

Over the past century, almost half of the world's gold has come from South African mines. Diamonds, silver, platinum, coal, and other metals and ores are also mined there. More than 340,000 workers go underground each workday. The dangers they face include extreme heat, poisonous gases, falling rocks, and explosions.

SOUTH AFRICA

A solid-gold Krugerrand, minted from South African gold, weighs one ounce. Other countries buy South African gold to mint their own coins.

Of the miners who bring the riches out of the ground, black miners have traditionally earned the lowest wages.

Some mines tunnel two miles below the earth's surface. As many as 10,000 miners work in narrow shafts with heavy machines.

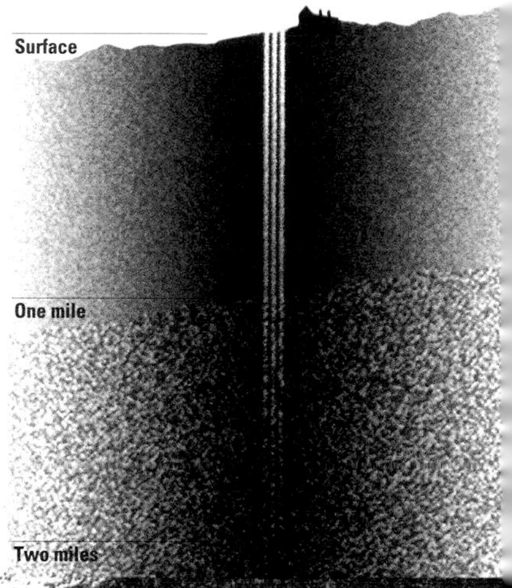
Surface
One mile
Two miles

300

Visual Learning

The Krugerrand was named after Paul Kruger, an Afrikaner who founded the Transvaal and led armies against the British in the South African War. *Rand* is short for Witwatersrand, a region of South Africa known for its rich gold mines. The Krugerrand has become a symbol of South Africa. Have students draw coins that might symbolize their community or state.

Writing a Letter

Explain to students that beginning in the late 1800s, black mine workers were often forced to leave their families for up to a year at a time. The workers lived in segregated, all-male, company-owned compounds where rations were poor and bunks were sometimes made of concrete or cardboard. White laborers, who earned up to 21 times as much as black laborers during apartheid, could live anywhere they pleased. Nevertheless, most black men who were able lived at and worked in the mines, since mining was one of the few types of jobs available to them.

Instruct students to write letters to and from mine workers and their families. As workers, have them describe life in the mines and the compounds. As family members, have them consider the effects on the lives of the women and children who lived in faraway homelands.

Afrikaners Battle the British

As the Cape Colony expanded, the Afrikaner and British settlers disagreed more and more about which group should control the government. In 1899 the Afrikaners and the British began to fight. Both sides recruited blacks to help them. By the end of the South African War (also called the Boer War), thousands of blacks and whites had been killed, and much farmland had been ruined.

The war ended with a British victory in 1902. Bitterness remained for generations, however, between the blacks, the Afrikaners, and the British.

A New Nation

In 1910 the two British colonies, the Cape Colony and Natal *(nuh TAL)*, joined with the Afrikaner republics, the Orange Free State and the Transvaal. Together they formed the Union of South Africa. The timeline on pages 298 and 299 shows some of the events that led to the founding of the union. This new nation, with a strong central government, became part of the British Empire. Refer to the map on page 672 of the Minipedia to locate other nations that were part of the British Empire during this time period.

Blacks, Asians, and coloreds made up most of the population of the new nation. However, under a new constitution, few nonwhites could vote. A former Afrikaner general, Louis Botha *(BOH tuh)*, became prime minister of an all-white government. ■

How Do We Know?

HISTORY *One account of the South African War is found in the diary of Solomon Plaatje* (PLAHT juh), *a black South African interpreter who later became a newspaper editor. He reported that the British had forced Afrikaner families and their black servants into separate concentration camps, where thousands had died of disease.*

■ *What effects did the movement of white settlers have on black African peoples?*

Afrikaner Power

As mining grew, whites and blacks continued to rush to the mines from the countryside. Many whites became diggers in the mines. Blacks, however, often found jobs only as whites' assistants.

More cities sprang up as workers settled near the mines. Gradually, South Africa's economy shifted from farming to industry and from the country to the city. As more and more people moved to the cities, however, jobs became harder and harder to find. Whites began to pass laws that further limited the freedom of nonwhites.

Growing Discrimination

In 1911 South Africa set aside the best jobs at the mines—and the best pay—for whites only. Soon white miners were earning about

▼ *Some Asians were originally brought to South Africa as slaves. The photo below shows a Malayan family long after slavery had ended. Other Asians came as laborers. On the left, Indians arrive in Durban on their way to Natal in the late 1800s.*

CULTURE

Critical Thinking

During the South African War, the British burned Afrikaners' farms and established segregated "refugee camps"—later called concentration camps—where they placed Afrikaners, their families, and the black tenant farmers who worked for them. About 28,000 whites died in the camps, and an incomplete listing of black deaths indicates that more than 14,000 blacks also died. The memory of this brutality against Afrikaners remained in Afrikaner history and culture. Guide students to understand how this episode contributed to Afrikaners' desire for political power. *(Afrikaners grew more unified not only against nonwhites, but also against the British, who had imprisoned them and disagreed with them for decades.)*

■ *The movement of white settlers pushed black South African peoples off their land, forcing most black men into low-paying mine jobs, and ultimately denying black South Africans basic voting rights.*

Political Context

To help students understand the political organization of modern South Africa, explain that following the South African War, the new constitution of the Union of South Africa kept many white privileges intact, although some nonwhite males in the Cape Province could vote and the rights of blacks in certain territories were protected. However, the Union's first government, led by the South African Party, moved quickly to restrict black workers from any skilled labor.

South Africa did not become an independent nation until 1960, when the white electorate of the Union of South Africa voted to become the Republic of South Africa. Many white liberals and English speakers opposed this move because it created an Afrikaner nation independent from Britain. Among them was Helen Suzman, a prominent liberal member of Parliament who became known worldwide for her opposition to apartheid and support for the nonwhite majority.

Map and Globe Skills

One of the photographs on this page shows a Malayan family in South Africa. Help students locate the Malay Peninsula on the Pacific Rim map on page 684 in the Atlas. Discuss with them the change in climate experienced by Asian immigrants to South Africa.

CULTURE

Critical Thinking

For 30 years beginning in the 1920s, South African jazz flourished in the Johannesburg suburb of Sophiatown. Ask students to explore why jazz, which was so dominated by African Americans, would appeal to blacks in South Africa. *(The music often expressed the similar struggles of blacks in both countries.)* In the late 1950s, the government bulldozed Sophiatown off the map.

■ *Evidence includes the 1913 Natives Land Act, pass laws, limitations placed on Asians, and huge wage differences for whites and nonwhites.*

CLOSE

Read the Thinking Focus aloud. Ask students to name each of the ethnic groups mentioned in the chapter that had ties to the land in South Africa. *(Khoisan, Bantu speakers, Afrikaners, British, Asians, and peoples of mixed heritage)* Arrange students into groups, and assign each a different ethnic group. Have students write a paragraph that answers the Thinking Focus for their assigned ethnic group. List all responses on the chalkboard.

➤ Like the Bantu-speaking peoples, many Afrikaners today have strong ties to farming the land and raising livestock. The struggle to get and keep land has long been a part of South Africa's history.

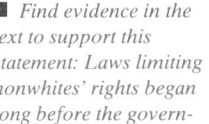

10 times more than black miners. Blacks formed unions to protest their low wages. Yet the mine owners, supported by the government, refused to recognize the unions.

Whites limited blacks' power in still other ways. The Natives Land Act of 1913 made it hard for black South Africans to buy or rent land outside areas set aside for them. These areas, called reserves, quickly became crowded. Thousands of men had to leave their families on the reserves while they worked at white-owned mines and farms. Blacks also needed a pass, or permit, just to go from the reserves to the cities to look for work. These reserves later became homelands under the apartheid policy.

Asians, too, faced new hardships. The British had begun bringing Asians to South Africa in the 1860s to work in the sugar cane fields of Natal. South Africa now passed laws to stop Asians from entering the country and limited the places where they could live.

■ *Find evidence in the text to support this statement: Laws limiting nonwhites' rights began long before the government set up apartheid.*

"A White Man's Land"

Beginning in the early 1900s, some Afrikaners wanted to separate themselves even more from blacks and English-speaking whites. On the one hand, the Afrikaners feared the growing influence of English-speaking whites in both government and business. By the 1930s they were twice as wealthy as Afrikaners. On the other hand, Afrikaners worried about job competition from blacks.

During the 1920s Afrikaners worked to protect white privileges. Afrikaans, along with English, became an official language of South Africa. In 1934, Afrikaners formed the Purified National Party. The party leader said it was the Afrikaners' duty to "make South Africa a white man's land."

The National Party won control of South Africa in 1948. To maintain its power and prevent blacks from gaining equality, the National Party began the policy of apartheid, which means "apartness" in Afrikaans. More than 40 years of apartheid government would follow. ■

REVIEW

1. **FOCUS** How was the land of southern Africa important to each group of people who lived there?
2. **CULTURE** Compare the ways of life of the Khoisan and the Bantu-speaking peoples before Europeans arrived in South Africa.
3. **HISTORY** Why did the government of South Africa pass laws that limited the freedom of nonwhites?
4. **CRITICAL THINKING** Why did the Dutch, Germans, and French in South Africa call themselves Afrikaners?
5. **ACTIVITY** Draw your own Moment in Time that illustrates the culture of one of these groups: the San, the Khoikhoi, or the Bantu speakers.

Homework Options

Give students a list of five historical events in South Africa, such as the Dutch settlement of the Cape and the freeing of Nelson Mandela. Ask students to name the date for each event and create a timeline matching dates to events. In class have students check the dates.

Study Guide: page 52

Answers to Review Questions

1. The San and Khoikhoi hunted and gathered food; the Khoikhoi also grazed cattle. Bantu speakers grew food in the east. Afrikaners established large farms, and Europeans and Africans mined.
2. The Khoisan were hunter-gatherers and herders. They lived in caves or shelters. The Bantu speakers farmed, herded livestock, and mined ore. They built lasting homes of stone or clay.
3. To discourage black migration to urban areas and keep blacks from competing with whites for jobs, the government stopped blacks from owning land and reserved the best jobs for whites.
4. The Dutch, Germans, and French adopted the name Afrikaner because they saw themselves as a distinct African people.
5. Encourage students to think about one of their subjects' activities: hunting and gathering (San), raising cattle (Khoikhoi), or farming (Bantu speakers).

UNDERSTANDING NOTE-TAKING

Recording Information

Here's Why

To make the most effective use of sources such as books, magazines, and newspapers, develop the skill of taking and organizing notes. Suppose you have to prepare a report about life under apartheid. How would you take notes and organize them for your report?

Here's How

As you begin to gather information for your report, write down questions you want your report to answer. For example, you might ask: What were the laws of apartheid? What effect did apartheid have on people's lives?

Once you've written your questions, begin the note-taking process. Write your notes on index cards. On each card, write notes about just one major point. This way you can keep track of information and organize it to prepare for writing your report.

As you take notes, paraphrase what you have read. That is, write the notes in your own words. You may want to shorten this information into brief phrases as shown on the cards below.

Copy the exact words from a source only if you want to use them as a quotation. Make sure to copy the spelling, punctuation, and grammar exactly as it appears in your source. Also, put quotation marks at the beginning and the end of the quotation. This way you can tell it from your paraphrased notes.

Write the source information on each card. Source information includes the author or editor, title, publisher, and date of the source and the page number on which you found the information. You'll need to know this information if you have to go back to the source to check your notes or take more notes. You will also need to name the source if you use any of the information from it in your report.

Using information in a report without naming its source can get you into trouble with your teacher and even with the law. It is against the law to steal other people's ideas and words.

> To protect their power, Afrikaners developed a policy called apartheid. In Afrikaans, the word *apartheid* means "apartness." Apartheid was a complex set of laws designed to bring about total segregation and white domination. For example, people of different races could not eat together, go to the same schools, or ride in the same train cars.

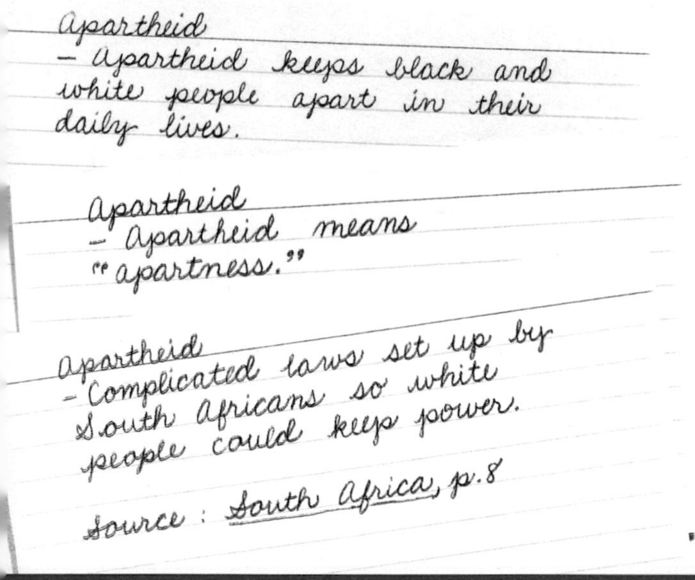
Apartheid
- Apartheid keeps black and white people apart in their daily lives.
Apartheid
- Apartheid means "apartness."
Apartheid
- Complicated laws set up by South Africans so white people could keep power.
Source: South Africa, p.8

Try It

Now turn to Lesson 2, page 298. Write a note card paraphrasing the information about the Great Trek. Record this book as your source.

Apply It

Suppose you are writing a report about Nelson Mandela. Write three or four questions you want to answer, and write two note cards on the material you find for one of the questions.

UNDERSTANDING NOTE-TAKING

This skills feature uses information from the chapter to teach students how to identify important material in their reading and take effective notes.

HISTORY

Critical Thinking

Have students read the section titled A Century of Change beginning on page 299. Ask them what main question the section answers. *(In what ways was the period from the early 1800s to the early 1900s a century of change?)* Write this question on the chalkboard. Then give four index cards to each student. Ask students to identify four major points that the section provides in answer to the question. Instruct students to write on each card a few sentences in their own words about each major point. *(Sample answers: Afrikaners and Bantu-speaking peoples fought many battles for land. Diamonds and gold drew people from all directions to the region. The British and the Afrikaners fought a war for control of southern Africa. Under the constitution of the new Union of South Africa, few nonwhites could vote.)*

Writing a Note Card

Direct students to reread the paragraph describing the proper source information to include on each note card. Then tell them to look again at the sample note card at the bottom of the page. What do they notice about the source information given on the sample card? *(The source information is incomplete on the sample card. It should also name the author, publisher, and date of the source.)* Have students rewrite the source information correctly on their own paper.

Answers to Try It

Check to see that students have acknowledged the source as follows: Beverly Armento, et al., *To See a World,* Houghton Mifflin Company, 1993, page 298.

Answers to Apply It

Sample questions include: Where was Mandela born? What did he like to do as a child? When did he become involved in fighting injustice? How did Mandela become a leader?

Objective

Explain how to extract information from resources and record it efficiently. (Study Skills 1, 2)

INTRODUCE

Read the lesson title aloud. Tell students that photographs like the one on the right could be found in major South African newspapers in 1992. Explain that the picture shows a white South African runner taking a victory lap in the Olympics with a black Ethiopian runner. Solicit students' opinions of why, for many people watching the Games, the incident symbolized change in South Africa. Have students brainstorm headlines that might have accompanied the photograph.

Direct students to read the Thinking Focus. Tell them that they will find out about recent changes in South Africa as they read the lesson.

Key Term

Vocabulary Strategies: T36–T37
social justice—fairness for all, regardless of race, level of income, and way of life

1375
1500
1625
1750
1875
1978 TODAY

L E S S O N 3

A New South Africa

THINKING FOCUS

What are some of the changes that took place in South Africa beginning in 1978?

Key Term

- social justice

Two African women rounded the last lap of the 10,000-meter race. With a final burst of speed, Ethiopia's Derartu Tulu pulled ahead to win the Olympic gold medal. Elana Meyer came close behind to take the silver medal for South Africa.

This moment at the 1992 Olympic Games was thrilling for South Africans. Since 1964 South Africa had been banned from the Olympics. Since 1968 almost no country in the world had played against South African sports teams.

The international sports boycott began to ease when South Africa started changing its policies. In 1991 the International Cricket Council readmitted South Africa as a full member. With the repeal of some of the cruelest apartheid laws, South Africa was allowed to participate in the 1992 Olympics.

After the race Tulu and Meyer hugged each other. Then the two Africans—one black, one white—held hands and ran around the track. Did this scene symbolize a more peaceful future for blacks and whites in Africa? Meyer was hopeful. Later she said of her silver medal, "This is for the new South Africa."

472

Because of apartheid, South Africa was banned from the Olympics for 28 years. When Ethiopia's Derartu Tulu and South Africa's Elana Meyer crossed the finish line in the 1992 women's 10,000-meter race, all of Africa rejoiced.

New Problems, New Progress

By the late 1970s, some white South Africans saw that their country had to change. Yet supporters of apartheid wanted more than ever to prevent the black majority from gaining power. Many South Africans—white and black—began to think that apartheid would end only with a violent war. Others still hoped that the government and the anti-apartheid movement could agree on a peaceful change. What kind of change would solve the country's problems?

Objectives

1. Identify two problems and two signs of progress in South Africa since the partial lifting of apartheid.
2. List some of the questions that remain unanswered as South Africa looks to the future.

Graphic Overview

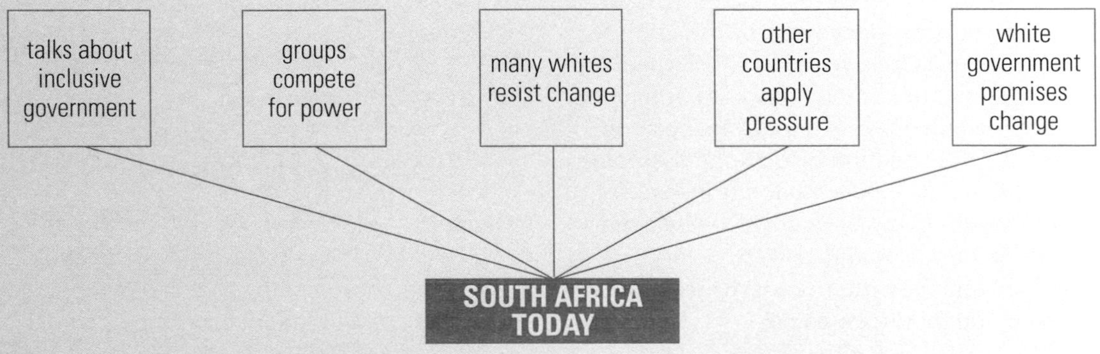
talks about inclusive government
groups compete for power
many whites resist change
other countries apply pressure
white government promises change
SOUTH AFRICA TODAY

Government Reforms

In 1978 the National Party elected P. W. Botha as prime minister. Under Botha's leadership, the government abolished some apartheid laws. Yet it refused to consider demands for equal participation of blacks in government.

Anti-apartheid groups renewed their protests. Police and other officials often met these protests with violence. Nearly 900 people were killed as a result of political violence in 1985 alone. In 1986 Botha declared a national state of emergency. This decree strengthened the power of the police.

More and more whites began to think that, violently or nonviolently, blacks would one day take control of the government. Many thought the best way to prevent a violent takeover was to listen and talk to black leaders. Important white business leaders met with ANC leaders in 1985 to begin talking about how to end apartheid peacefully.

In 1990 a new president, F. W. de Klerk, promised to end apartheid. He abolished many apartheid laws, made the ANC legal, and freed Nelson Mandela. De Klerk also agreed to meet with anti-apartheid leaders to work on forming a new government in which all races would share power fairly.

In 1991 people from all racial groups began holding talks about making a new government and writing a new South African constitution. Many wanted a whole new set of laws to bring about **social justice,** or fairness for people of all races, levels of income, and ways of life. You can read more about social justice on page 306.

Most whites supported the talks with black leaders. Some Afrikaners opposed the talks, though, and said that they would use violence, if needed, to keep whites in power.

Most nonwhite South Africans also supported the talks. They wanted to make sure that they would be fairly represented in any new government that resulted from the talks. This was especially true of the Inkatha Freedom Party (IFP). The IFP was led by Mangosuthu Buthelezi *(boo tuh LEH zee),* chief of the Zulu. Some blacks, however, felt that talking had gone on too long already, with little change in the government's apartheid policies.

▲ *This school in Johannesburg is one of the many schools that became integrated in the early 1990s.*

CITY/STAD DURBAN
CITY OF DURBAN
UNDER SECTION BIS 37 OF THE DURBAN BEACH BY-LAWS. THIS BATHING AREA IS RESERVED FOR THE SOLE USE OF MEMBERS OF THE WHITE RACE GROUP.
STAD DURBAN

▼ *As apartheid laws were abolished, the hated* WHITES ONLY *signs in Durban, South Africa, began to come down.*

DEVELOP

Refer students to the heading New Problems, New Progress on page 304. Ask students to speculate about new progress that might be taking place in South Africa. *(Greater freedoms for nonwhites; talks toward reforming the government)* Then ask the students to speculate about the problems that might come with the ending of apartheid. *(Resistance from some whites; conflict among various groups competing for power in a new government)*

ETHICS

Critical Thinking

Some white people joined the fight against apartheid. In the late 1950s, a group of white women formed an organization called the Black Sash to protest changes in the constitution that deprived nonwhites of their rights. Black Sash members stood in public places wearing white dresses with black sashes and hanging their heads in shame as Parliament members walked by. Ask students why the participation of whites was important in fighting apartheid. *(It showed the government that some whites also opposed apartheid. White participants received media attention. They rallied support among other whites in ways that blacks could not.)*

305

Access Strategy

Refer students to the photograph of the integrated classroom on this page. Then direct them to the photograph of the segregated facility on page 293. Tell students that the latter picture was taken when apartheid laws were in effect, while the picture on this page was taken in the early 1990s. Invite students to discuss what the end of apartheid might mean for schoolchildren. *(The eventual integration of schools; better education for nonwhites; better job opportunities due to better education)*

Then read aloud, or have a student read, the words of Jane Mogase on page 307. Ask students what her words make them think about. Explore with students ways in which Jane Mogase's wishes could be realized. *(Sample answers: Laws could be passed completely desegregating residential areas and schools; successful talks between blacks and whites could bring about peace and equality.)*

Access Activity

Read aloud to students, or have one student read, the primary source material on page 307. Ask students what peace would mean for young people in South Africa. Then have students draw pictures entitled Peace that they might send to a class of schoolchildren in South Africa. Some students may want to brainstorm topic ideas before they begin to draw.

HISTORY

Critical Thinking

Explain to students that Frederick Douglass was a 19th-century African American who escaped slavery and fought to abolish it in the United States. Write on the chalkboard his words: "Power concedes [gives up] nothing without a demand. It never did and it never will." Ask students how Douglass's words could apply to the struggle to end apartheid. *(Apartheid laws would not end without enough political pressure from South Africans and people around the world.)* What forms of "demands" might black South Africans make? *(Strikes, mass protests, and violence to force the government to share power)*

■ *Two problems include opposition toward reform from some whites and the unequal conditions (for example, in housing, jobs, and health care) that remained even after many apartheid laws had been lifted. Two improvements are the ending of key segregation laws and continuing talks between the government and reform leaders.*

Tension among members of all these groups rose. It flared into ongoing violent attacks against both whites and blacks. These attacks continued through the early 1990s.

Signs of Progress

Some observers said that South Africa had come a long way in the early 1990s. The laws that had given high-paying jobs only to whites were cancelled. The hated pass laws were gone. Some white schools were taking nonwhite students. People of all races could legally marry each other and live in the same areas. Restaurants, beaches, and other public places were open to all races. A new constitution was being discussed.

Other observers, however, pointed out that apartheid had not disappeared. Many apartheid laws remained in force. Some people expressed fear that strong apartheid laws could be put back into effect unless nonwhites shared power in the government soon.

The effects of apartheid also had not disappeared. The fear of violence prevented many nonwhites from moving to white areas or from marrying a person from another race. Most blacks still lived in the homelands. There were not enough houses or jobs for blacks. Schools and health care in black areas were still poor.

The most important change of all was also yet to come. The white government still did not share power with the black majority. Blacks like Nelson Mandela still could not vote. ■

■ *Name two major problems and two major improvements in conditions in South Africa today.*

Understanding Social Justice

Do you think it is fair when most of the people in a country cannot vote? Is it fair to allow only white players on a rugby team? Most people would answer no. Under apartheid, though, that is how things were in South Africa. People around the world criticized the country for its lack of social justice.

What Is Social Justice?

Social justice is the idea that a society ought to treat all its members fairly—not just a lucky few. It stems from the idea that all members of a society are equal. Thus, social justice is related to political issues such as fair representation in government and the right to vote. Legal issues, such as the right to proper treatment by police and to a fair trial, are also involved.

Yet social justice cannot be achieved through political and legal action only. Economic and social equality are also needed. No member of society should be excluded from education, jobs, or health care. It is hard, however, to make sure that people who hire workers or give health care are treating all people fairly.

Achieving Social Justice

The changes South Africa made in the early 1990s were a step toward bringing about social justice. However, people's minds and attitudes must also change. That can take a long time.

It is important to remember that South Africa is only one country where achieving social justice is difficult. People all over the world must work to assure everyone of an equal place in human society.

Visual Learning

After students have read Understanding Social Justice on this page, ask them to think of laws and programs through which the United States strives to implement social justice for its citizens. Then have students use these and their own ideas to make a collage that expresses the theme of social justice.

Historical Context

For many opponents of apartheid, the Sharpeville Massacre in March 1960 was the turning point from the use of nonviolent to violent resistance tactics. The ANC and the Pan African Congress (PAC) planned a nonviolent campaign of burning pass books outside police stations on the day of the massacre. Police officers opened fire on the protesters in Sharpeville, killing at least 67 blacks and wounding 186 others, shooting many of them in the back.

As violent government reaction intensified, the ANC and the PAC reasoned that nonviolent resistance would not work in South Africa. Reflecting on this philosophical shift in 1964, Mandela said, ". . . the hard facts were that fifty years of nonviolence had brought the African people nothing but more and more repressive legislation, and fewer and fewer rights." After the Sharpeville Massacre, the ANC founded a military force, *Umkhonto we Sizwe* ("the spear of the nation").

South Africa and the World

The boycotts of many countries in the 1980s began to do great damage to South Africa's economy. Following de Klerk's reforms in the early 1990s, many nations ended their boycotts of South Africa. Still, the country's economy was slow to recover. In addition, continued violence in the townships hurt many South African businesses.

As South Africa looked to the future, many important questions remained unanswered. Would the government continue to talk with black leaders about extending democracy to the nonwhite majority? Would the ANC and other nonwhite groups be able to agree among themselves about how the new government should be formed?

Instead, would talks between the white government and nonwhite groups break down? Would the country be engulfed in a bloody civil war? Would other countries become involved? Would the land and the economy of South Africa be completely destroyed before the white minority shared power equally with all its citizens? South Africans considered these questions as they prepared for change.

In the early 1990s, South Africans faced an uncertain future. Despite the uncertainty, however, young people expressed great hope for their country. In 1992 Jane Mogase *(moh GAH seh)*, a 13-year-old student in Johannesburg, wrote about her dreams.

In a new South Africa we want to help each other and love each other and we want violence to be stopped. . . . We want to do things together and we want to have equal rights and no more war in the world. We want white people to live in our areas and white kids to come to our schools, and we want peace between blacks and whites. ■

Open Hearts
Open Minds
Open City
Be proud.

▲ *To build harmony and cooperation among racial groups, South African opponents of apartheid planned events like the Open City Walk in Cape Town in June 1989.*

■ *What possible outcomes can you think of for South Africa's future?*

REVIEW

1. **FOCUS** What are some of the changes that took place in South Africa beginning in 1978?
2. **CULTURE** Why was South Africa able to participate in the 1992 Olympics?
3. **HISTORY** How did whites and blacks feel about talks between the South African government and black leaders about forming a new government?
4. **CRITICAL THINKING** What items in a new South African constitution would help guarantee the rights of people in all racial groups?
5. **ACTIVITY** Make a chart comparing the viewpoints of some of the political groups who want a say in forming a new South Africa.

■ *Outcomes can range from establishing a new government through peaceful negotiation to violent civil war. Encourage students to think of possible outcomes not mentioned in the text.*

CLOSE

Have students read the Thinking Focus. Draw two yardsticks side by side on the board. Write *1978* in the middle, where the yardsticks join, and write *Today* at both ends. Write *Problems* over the first yardstick and *Progress* over the second. Tell students that the yardsticks represent two timelines. Ask students to name events that fall on both yardsticks. Write student responses in the appropriate places on the chalkboard. *(Possible problems: No vote for nonwhites; violence continues between opposing groups. Possible progress: Many apartheid laws lifted; end of sports boycott; Nelson Mandela freed)*

Answers to Review Questions

1. Changes include P. W. Botha's abolition of some apartheid laws in the late 1970s, white business leaders' meeting with the ANC, and F. W. de Klerk's freeing of Nelson Mandela.
2. South Africa had repealed some of the cruelest apartheid laws.
3. Many whites and blacks alike supported the talks between the government and black leaders. Some whites, however, promised to use violence if necessary to remain in power. Some blacks said that talking had gone on long enough, with little result.
4. A new South African constitution might include measures allowing all racial groups to vote, have a fair trial, and protest.
5. Charts might include whites and nonwhites who want democracy, whites who want to keep power at all costs, blacks who want change immediately, and groups that are competing for power.

Homework Options

Have students write a narrative account of what they think South Africa will be like in the year 2000.

Study Guide: page 54

Answers to Reviewing Key Terms

A. Sample answers:

1. **Apartheid** was a policy of separation set up in 1948 in South Africa to protect the power of the white government.
2. Unfair laws enforced the **segregation** of races into separate and unequal groups.
3. **Afrikaner** is a name that Dutch, German, and French settlers took to distinguish themselves from Europeans who arrived later in South Africa.
4. To protest its unfair policies toward nonwhite residents, many nations joined in a **boycott** of South Africa.

B. Sample answers:

1. **Social justice** is the idea that a society ought to treat all its members fairly. By contrast, the policy of **apartheid** enforced unfair laws against nonwhites in order to protect the power of the white government.
2. **trek**
3. **segregation**
4. The agreement would mean that the group had decided to refuse to do business with the store or company.

Answers to Exploring Concepts

A. Answers:

1912: Black leaders form a group that comes to be called the African National Congress.
1948: The Afrikaners' Purified National Party wins control of South Africa and sets up the policy of apartheid.
1960: The South African government bans the ANC.
1964: ANC leader Nelson Mandela is sentenced to life in prison for trying to overthrow the government.
1990: President F. W. de Klerk frees Nelson Mandela and lifts the ban on ANC membership.

B. Sample answers:

1. The San and Khoikhoi peoples were both hunter-gatherers in the western part of southern Africa. The Khoikhoi also herded cattle and sheep. The San lived in caves or, like the Khoikhoi, made shelters.
2. South Africa's geographic location led it to become a regular stopping place for European traders. The Dutch began growing food to supply Dutch ships with fruit, vegetables, and grain.
3. Europeans felt that the land and resources of South Africa were free for the taking. Over several centuries, they forced Khoisan and Bantu-speaking peoples from the land and established a government that denied rights to nonwhites.
4. The discovery of diamonds and gold brought white prospectors from all over the world. Many became rich. Black Africans were forced to work in the mines for low wages.
5. Beginning in the 1650s, Dutch settlers fought numerous battles against the Khoisan and Bantu-speaking peoples in a successful attempt to take their lands. Shaka waged fierce wars against other Bantu-speaking peoples to establish the Zulu kingdom. From 1899 to 1902, British and Afrikaner settlers fought the South African (or Boer) War. When the National Party established apartheid in 1948, a long period of violence began, as the police suppressed anti-apartheid demonstrations with brutal tactics.

Chapter Review

Reviewing Key Terms

Afrikaner (p. 297)
apartheid (p. 293)
boycott (p. 295)
segregation (p. 293)
social justice (p. 305)
trek (p. 298)

A. In each statement below, a key term has been used incorrectly. Rewrite each sentence using the correct key term.

1. Afrikaner was a policy of separation set up in 1948 in South Africa to protect the power of the white government.
2. Unfair laws enforced the boycott of races into separate and unequal groups.
3. Trek is a name that Dutch, German, and French settlers took to distinguish themselves from Europeans who arrived later in South Africa.
4. To protest its unfair policies toward nonwhite residents, many nations joined in a segregation of South Africa.

B. Answer the following questions regarding selected key terms.

1. What is social justice, and how does it differ from apartheid?
2. Which key term is a synonym for *journey*?
3. Which key term is a synonym for *separation*?
4. If you and your classmates agreed to boycott a store or a company, what would your agreement mean?

Exploring Concepts

A. Copy and complete the timeline below to summarize key events in the history of apartheid and the African National Congress (ANC). On your timeline, place these events at their correct dates:

1. ANC leader Nelson Mandela is sentenced to life in prison for trying to overthrow the government.
2. The Afrikaners' Purified National Party wins control of South Africa and sets up the policy of apartheid.
3. Black leaders form a group that comes to be called the African National Congress.
4. The South African government bans the ANC.
5. President F. W. de Klerk frees Nelson Mandela and lifts the ban on ANC membership.

B. Support each of the following statements with information from the chapter.

1. The San and Khoikhoi peoples, sometimes together referred to as the Khoisan, were both alike and different in their ways of life.
2. South Africa's geographic location and farmland were major features that attracted European traders and settlers.
3. European settlers showed a shocking lack of respect for black South Africans.
4. In South African history, diamonds and gold made a few people rich, but many people in the country remained poor.
5. Violence has played a terrible and continual role in the history of South Africa since the 1650s.

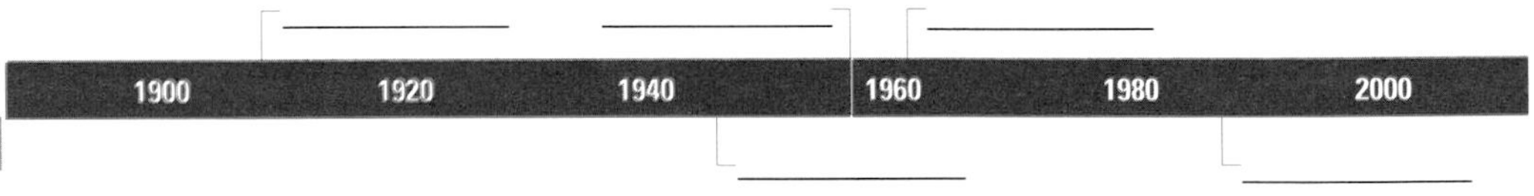
1900
1920
1940
1960
1980
2000

Reviewing Skills

1. In the Atlas, look at the climate map on page 688 and the land use, land, and ocean resources map on page 689. Use the maps to make a chart comparing the climates, land uses, and natural resources of the western and eastern regions of South Africa. Then use your chart to answer these questions:
   • How did the ways of life of the early Khoisan and Bantu-speaking peoples reflect the features of their separate regions?
   • What features led the Afrikaners to migrate to the eastern and northern regions of South Africa during the Great Trek? Why were they seeking these features?
2. Refer to Recognizing Patterns on page 107. Next, reread the first section on page 304. Then, follow these directions:
   • Write a paragraph to summarize the end of the Olympic race and what happened just after the race. Use a chronological pattern. Use clue words to make the pattern clear.
   • Then write a brief paragraph to explain why international sports teams have lifted their boycott of South African teams. Use a cause-and-effect pattern. Use clue words to make the pattern clear.
3. Look again at Understanding Note Taking on page 303. Imagine that you are going to write an article about President F. W. de Klerk's plans to end all of South Africa's apartheid laws. Tomorrow you will interview him. What questions should you ask him to get all the information you need for your article?

Using Critical Thinking

1. In a brief paragraph, explain how each slogan and sentence on the poster on page 307 expresses the goals and dreams of anti-apartheid groups. What other slogans and sentences might you put on an anti-apartheid poster? Explain your answers.
2. Imagine that you are at a conference of international leaders. Your collective goal is to help South Africa grow economically and to enable its citizens to attain full social justice. What suggestions might you offer to the conference? Explain how each suggestion might help the people of South Africa.
3. As the Germans and the French joined the Dutch in South Africa, they all began to call themselves Afrikaners. Why do you think they chose that specific name?

Preparing for Citizenship

1. **COLLECTING INFORMATION** Nelson Mandela's release from prison was celebrated all over the world. Page 292 shows a front-page headline in one U.S. newspaper. How did your local paper report his release? How did local residents react to the news? Do some research at a library. Then interview family members and neighbors. Find out their reactions to Mandela's release. Report your findings to the class.
2. **WRITING ACTIVITY** On page 307 you read about the dreams that one student in South Africa has for her country. What dreams do you have for your country? Write a paragraph that describes those dreams.
3. **COLLABORATIVE LEARNING** In a small group, reread the description on page 292 of the stadium scene. Discuss the feelings people might have had that day, the sounds and sights, and so on. Then work together to create a television news broadcast of the event. Two members of the group should act as reporters on the scene, who explain the events for viewers around the world. Two members should portray Nelson and Winnie Mandela. Other members should portray people in the stadium. Present your broadcast to the class.

Answers to Reviewing Skills

1. Charts should contain the following information: Climate, Western Region: semiarid, desert; Climate, Eastern Region: tropical wet and dry, humid subtropical; Land Use, Western Region: little use, grazing; Land Use, Eastern Region: farming; Natural Resources, Western Region: none; Natural Resources, Eastern Region: coal, gold.

Possible answers to the questions:

- The early Khoisan peoples of the western region were hunter-gatherers and herders. Their land was unsuitable for farming. The Bantu-speaking peoples of the eastern region were farmers and herders. Their lands were more fertile and their climate wetter than in the western region.
- The Afrikaners migrated to the eastern and northern regions because of the favorable climate and farming conditions there.

2. Answers should contain:

- a chronological summary of events at the end of the race. Such clue words as *then, next,* and *finally* should be used.
- a brief explanation stressing that South Africa had repealed some of its cruelest apartheid laws. Such cause-and-effect clue words as *because, since,* or *as a result* should be used.

3. Sample answers: Which laws do you plan to target next? How will you get those laws repealed? How many more laws need to be changed before apartheid is over for good?

Answers to Using Critical Thinking

1. *Open* suggests compassion, open-mindedness, and social justice. *Take part* and *Be proud* encourage all people to work for social justice and to be proud of their efforts. Suggestions for other slogans and sentences should be supported by explanations based on chapter material.
2. Possible answers: Provide economic aid, and guidance toward civil rights legislation. Explanations should contain clear cause-and-effect reasoning.
3. Possible answer: The Afrikaners believed that they were "more" African than later European arrivals and had a greater claim to the land.

Answers to Preparing for Citizenship

1. **COLLECTING INFORMATION** Findings should combine library research with the first-hand observations and memories of primary sources. Allow ample discussion time for the sharing of findings. Emphasize that the memories and observations of different people naturally vary and that there are therefore no "right" and "wrong" answers.
2. **WRITING ACTIVITY** Paragraphs may be extremely personal in nature and should be evaluated not on content but on the student's attempt to express original ideas in a clear way.
3. **COLLABORATIVE LEARNING** Content of the broadcasts should be based on facts presented in the text. Students should effectively portray the triumph of Mandela and the resultant excitement and joy of the assembled crowd. Group members acting as reporters should clearly explain the events, based on the chapter text. Commend groups that work together well by equally contributing ideas and participating in the presentation and by considering the input of all members.

UNIT

PREVIEW

Have students study a large map of Asia. Then direct their attention to the photograph on these pages, and ask volunteers to describe what it shows. Tell them that the photo was taken in Bali, an island in Indonesia. Have them locate Indonesia on the map.

Tell students that this unit will cover three major Asian countries and one region containing several countries. Have them locate India, China, Japan, and the peninsula of Southeast Asia on the map.

Looking Back

Remind students that in Chapter 5 they studied the ancient civilizations of India and China, whose later cultures are covered in this unit. Encourage them to review key concepts of culture and geography in those chapters before they begin reading.

Looking Forward

Students will study three major Asian countries and one important region, each of which has unique cultural traditions.

Chapter 14 *India*
Chapter 15 *China*
Chapter 16 *Japan*
Chapter 17 *Southeast Asia*

Unit 5

Asia

The quiet beauty of this Indonesian rice field captures the ancient rhythms of life in rural Asia. For centuries, Asian artists, thinkers, and priests have been fascinated by such beauty, which was created by human interaction with the land. This is only part of Asia's long history. For almost 10,000 years, Asia has also seen the rise and fall of many high civilizations and mighty empires. Because Asia contains about three-fifths of the human race, what happens here today will affect the world's future.

A.D. 250

310

Rice field on the Indonesian island of Bali

BIBLIOGRAPHY

Books for Students

Bradley, John. *China.* New York: Watts, 1990. A recent history of China, including information on the Tiananmen Square massacre. Nonfiction.

Karan, P. P., ed. *India in the Global Community.* Grand Rapids: Gateway, 1988. A history of India and a description of how its people live. Nonfiction.

Pitts, Forrest R. *Japan in the Global Community.* Grand Rapids: Gateway Press, 1988. A history of Japan, including geography, economics, and social life and customs. Nonfiction.

Withington, William A. *Southeast Asia in the Global Community.* Grand Rapids: Gateway Press, 1988. Tells the history of 10 countries, including Vietnam and Laos. Nonfiction.

Books to Read Aloud

Jaffrey, Madhur. *Seasons of Splendor: Tales, Myths, & Legends of India.* New York: Atheneum, 1985. Folktales and family stories of India. Fiction.

Jagendorf, M. A., and Virginia Weng. *The Magic Boat and Other Chinese Folk Stories.* New York: Vanguard, 1980. A collection of folktales from China. Fiction.

Today
311

Understanding the Photograph

The photograph shows a rice paddy in Bali, one of the main islands in Indonesia. One-half the arable land of Indonesia is devoted to wet-rice cultivation. This region is in the lower latitudes where high temperatures and heavy rainfall provide a good climate for rice-growing. Because rice that is growing needs a constant supply of water, farmers plant it in flooded fields or in low places that get plenty of rain. When the plants are young, the fields look like bright green lakes.

About half the world's people depend on rice as their chief food. Many Asians eat rice three times a day and sometimes have little else to eat. People in India and Japan on average eat more than half a pound of rice everyday. Have students discuss how important rice is in their own diets.

Understanding Chronology

Help students to understand how old these Asian cultures are, compared to the age of the United States. (Have them look back at the timelines in Chapter 5, for instance.) Point out that although these countries have seen many changes, as nations they have remained virtually intact to the present day.

Books for Teachers

Hall, Daniel G. E. *A History of Southeast Asia.* 4th ed. New York: St. Martin's Press, 1981. A classic source on Southeast Asian history. Nonfiction.

Reischauer, Edwin. *The Japanese Today: Change and Continuity.* Cambridge: Harvard University Press, 1988. An overview of Japanese history. Nonfiction.

Wolpert, Stanley. *A New History of India.* 4th ed. New York: Oxford University Press, 1993. A detailed presentation of India's history, politics, and current problems. Nonfiction.

Other Resources

Visual Media

Japan Today. Visual Resources, 1991. A presentation of Japan today.

Software

Where in Time Is Carmen Sandiego? Broderbund, 1990. A simulation game that covers 1,500 years of history.

Houghton Mifflin Social Studies

Bookshelf

Haugaard, Erik Christian. *The Samurai's Tale.* Boston: Houghton Mifflin, 1984. In sixteenth-century Japan, an orphan is adopted by a general and learns to fight as a samurai.

INTRODUCE

Asia, the largest continent, contains 30 percent of the world's land area. The Greeks used the name *Asia* for lands that lay "over there," east of their homeland. The name may also derive from an Assyrian word, *asu,* that means "east." Other terms for the continent also reflect a European perspective: the Far East, the Orient.

Have students read the unit title and the text on this page. Explain that *population density* refers to the number of people on a certain amount of land. For example, the metropolitan area of Jakarta, Indonesia, has a smaller population than the metropolitan area of New York City (about 9.8 million compared with New York's approximately 14.6 million), but those people live in a smaller area. Therefore, Jakarta has a greater population density. Tell students that parts of Asia are sparsely populated, however. Mongolia has only four persons per square mile—while Bangladesh has over 2,000.

Learning from the Photograph

Draw students' attention to the photograph of the floating market in Thailand. Ask students to recall why rivers are valuable. *(Drinking water, transportation, irrigation, energy)*

Unit 5 Overview

Asia

Asia can boast some of the greatest contrasts of geography and climate of any continent—volcanoes and plains, deserts and rain forests. The tallest mountain range in the world, the Himalayas, forms a huge arc north of India. One Asian city is one of the wettest places on earth. An average of more than 100 inches—almost 9 feet—of rain falls each June on Cherrapunji, India.

China and India rank first and second as the most populous countries in the world. Although Asia is home to some of the world's oldest cultures, much of it is also quite modern. Today many Asian nations are among the world's fastest-growing industrial nations.

➤ *Bicycles are an important means of transportation in Asia. This bicyclist carries Chinese lanterns.*

Objectives

1. Identify the Asian continent's geographic features.
2. Describe how climate and geography affect cultures in Asia.
3. Understand the importance of international trade to the economies of Asian countries.

Geographic Context

The Himalayas of Asia include the highest mountains in the world. More than 30 Himalayan peaks rise to heights of more than 24,000 feet above sea level. The world's highest peak, Mount Everest, towers to 29,028 feet.

The name Himalayas was coined by early Indian mountaineers who combined two Sanskrit words, *hima,* meaning "snow," and *alaya,* which means "abode" or "home." Indeed, the Himalayas' tallest peaks rise high above a line of perpetual snow. Drained by 19 major rivers, the Himalayas have a tremendous hydroelectric potential.

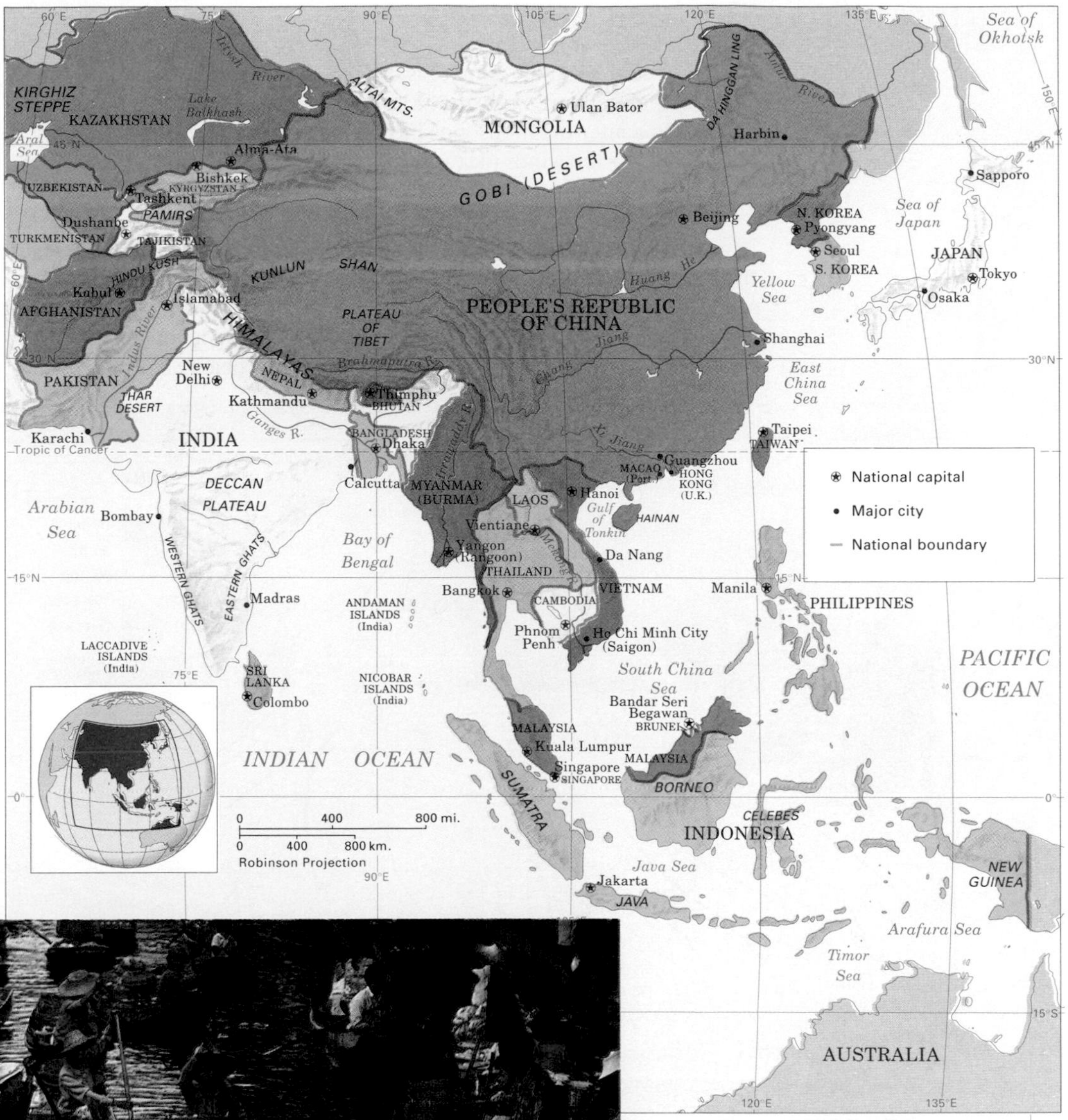
KIRGHIZ STEPPE
KAZAKHSTAN
Lake Balkhash
Aral Sea
Alma-Ata
Bishkek
KYRGYZSTAN
UZBEKISTAN
Tashkent
PAMIRS
Dushanbe
TAJIKISTAN
TURKMENISTAN
HINDU KUSH
Kabul
AFGHANISTAN
Islamabad
PAKISTAN
Indus River
THAR DESERT
New Delhi
Karachi
Tropic of Cancer
INDIA
Kathmandu
NEPAL
Thimphu
BHUTAN
Ganges R.
BANGLADESH
Dhaka
Calcutta
DECCAN PLATEAU
Arabian Sea
Bombay
WESTERN GHATS
EASTERN GHATS
Madras
Bay of Bengal
ANDAMAN ISLANDS (India)
NICOBAR ISLANDS (India)
LACCADIVE ISLANDS (India)
SRI LANKA
Colombo
INDIAN OCEAN
Irtysh River
ALTAI MTS.
Ulan Bator
MONGOLIA
GOBI (DESERT)
KUNLUN SHAN
HIMALAYAS
PLATEAU OF TIBET
Brahmaputra R.
PEOPLE'S REPUBLIC OF CHINA
Huang He
Chang Jiang
Xi Jiang
Beijing
Shanghai
Harbin
DA HINGGAN LING
Amur River
N. KOREA
Pyongyang
Seoul
S. KOREA
Yellow Sea
Sea of Japan
JAPAN
Sapporo
Tokyo
Osaka
Sea of Okhotsk
East China Sea
Taipei
TAIWAN
Guangzhou
MACAO (Port.)
HONG KONG (U.K.)
MYANMAR (BURMA)
Irrawaddy R.
Yangon (Rangoon)
THAILAND
Bangkok
LAOS
Vientiane
Hanoi
Gulf of Tonkin
HAINAN
Mekong R.
Da Nang
VIETNAM
CAMBODIA
Phnom Penh
Ho Chi Minh City (Saigon)
South China Sea
Manila
PHILIPPINES
Bandar Seri Begawan
BRUNEI
MALAYSIA
Kuala Lumpur
Singapore
SINGAPORE
SUMATRA
BORNEO
CELEBES
INDONESIA
Java Sea
Jakarta
JAVA
NEW GUINEA
Arafura Sea
Timor Sea
AUSTRALIA
PACIFIC OCEAN
National capital
Major city
National boundary
0 400 800 mi.
0 400 800 km.
Robinson Projection
60°E
75°E
90°E
105°E
120°E
135°E
150°E
45°N
30°N
15°N
0°
15°S

◄ *Many of Asia's waterways are busy with activity, like this floating market in Thailand.*

313

Asia

Learning from Maps

Give students time to study the map of Asia. Tell them that this unit will focus on the countries of India, China, Japan, the Philippines, Singapore, Indonesia, and Vietnam. Have students locate these countries and their capitals on the map. Then ask them to locate the Chang Jiang in China and the Ganges River in India.

Point out that high mountain systems have formed forbidding natural barriers in Asia, influencing the ease of movements of peoples from one area to another. Ask students what other physical features might protect a civilization from invasion. *(Oceans, seas, rivers, deserts; constructed obstacles such as walls)*

Making a Chart

Tell students that many Asian countries have thriving economies and that they export a variety of products to the United States and other countries throughout the world. Ask students to survey their own homes and make lists of products (shoes and clothing, electronics, toys, foodstuffs, automotives, and so forth) that have been imported from various Asian countries. What do their labels say?

Encourage students to get an adult's help as they survey their homes. Next, ask them to create a chart that lists each product and its country of origin. Then compile a class chart of individual items organized in the categories mentioned above; add other categories if necessary.

Map and Globe Skills

Point out that the continent of Asia stretches across thousands of miles of the earth's surface. Divide the class into pairs. Have them turn to the Atlas map of Asia (pages 682–683) and work together using the map scale to figure out various dimensions: for example, the east-west distance across China; the north-south distance from northern Russia to the southern tip of India.

LOOK AND RESPOND

Ask students to scan the captions and images on the following two pages. Make a list on the chalkboard of their observations and impressions.

Learning from Specialized Maps

Direct students to examine the rainfall map. Ask them from what direction the summer monsoon winds come *(South)* and from what direction the winter monsoon winds come *(North)*. Tell students that these winds are generated by the different rates of heating and cooling of the air over land and over ocean.

Then, ask students to study the areas of heavy rainfall and the areas of light rainfall. What parts of Asia receive the most rainfall annually? Have students compare Asia's rainfall with that of their region of the United States. Direct them to an almanac or a regional weather station for this information. What region of Asia, if any, is similar to their own in rainfall?

The Land and People

In much of Asia, the climate is dry in winter. During the rest of the year, rain falls almost every day. Monsoon winds bring these changes in climate. In winter the monsoons blow from the northeast, bringing dry air. In summer the winds pick up moisture from the warm Indian Ocean. When these winds move over land, they drop heavy rains.

Among Asia's most dramatic geographic features are its mountains. Few people have made the difficult climb to the top of Mount Everest in the Himalayas, the highest point on the earth. Each year, though, thousands of people climb Japan's Mount Fuji. This cone-shaped mountain—once an active volcano—stands high above the surrounding land. To many Japanese, Mount Fuji is a symbol of their nation's beauty.

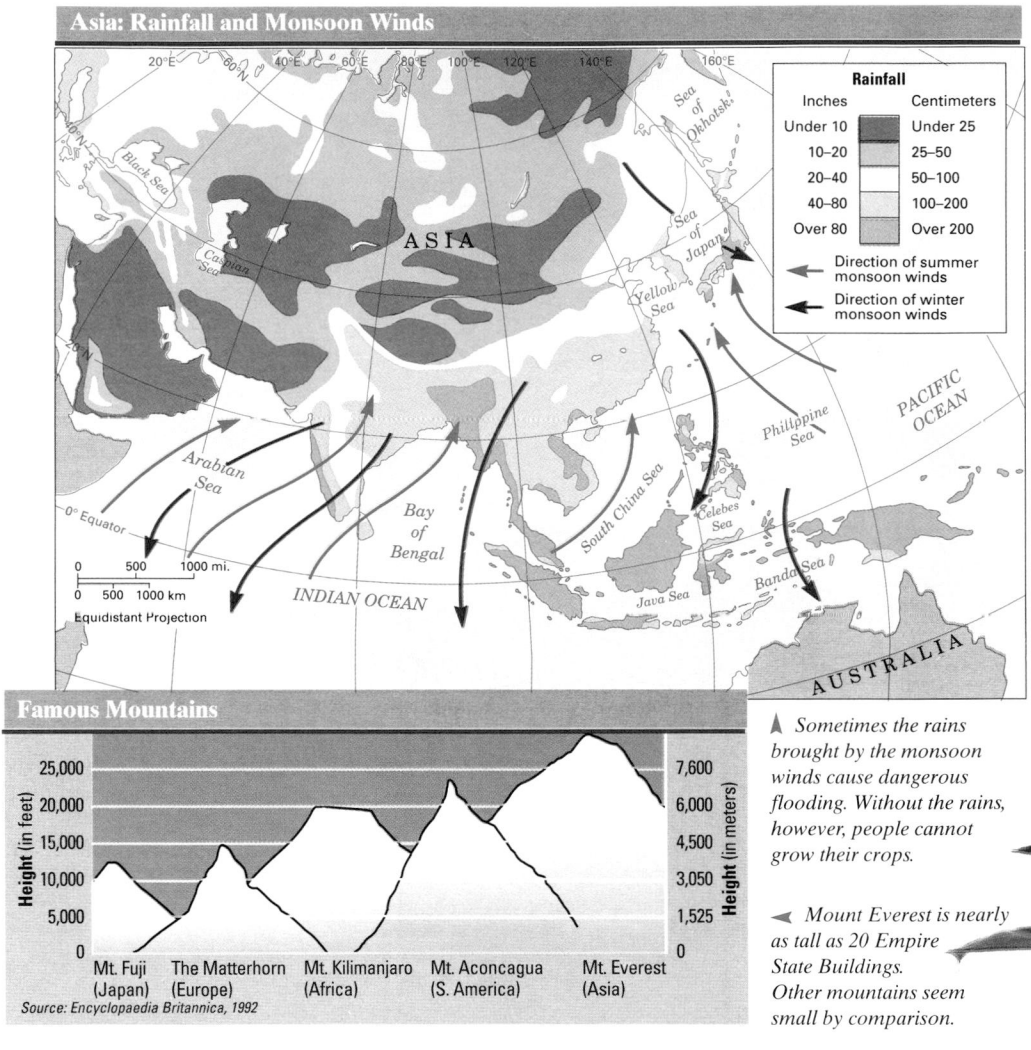

Asia: Rainfall and Monsoon Winds

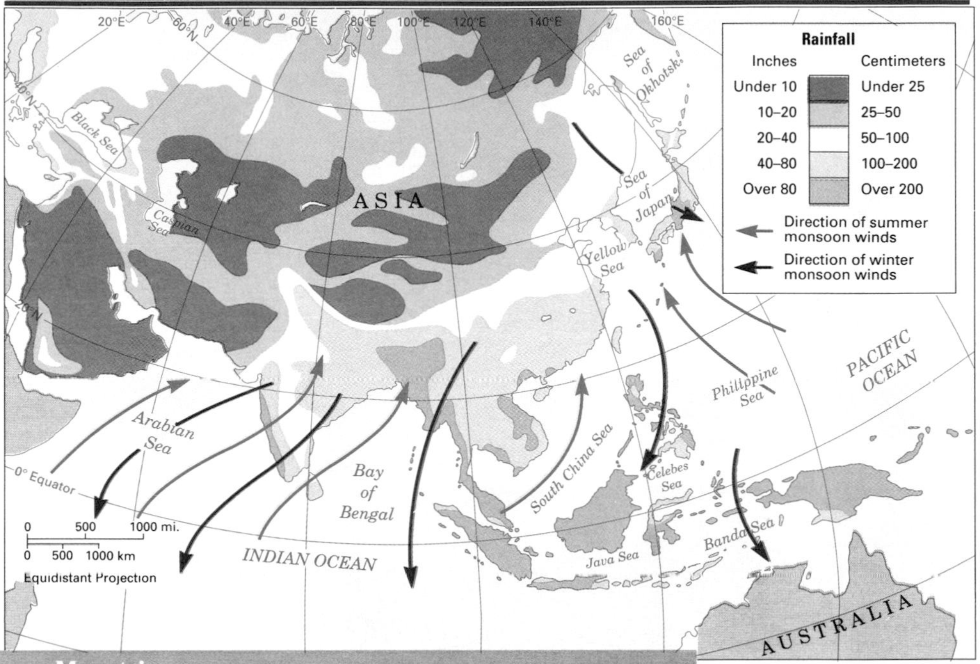
20°E
40°E
60°E
80°E
100°E
120°E
140°E
160°E
Black Sea
Caspian Sea
ASIA
Sea of Okhotsk
Sea of Japan
Yellow Sea
Arabian Sea
Bay of Bengal
South China Sea
Philippine Sea
Celebes Sea
Java Sea
Banda Sea
PACIFIC OCEAN
INDIAN OCEAN
AUSTRALIA
0° Equator
Rainfall
Inches
Centimeters
Under 10
Under 25
10–20
25–50
20–40
50–100
40–80
100–200
Over 80
Over 200
Direction of summer monsoon winds
Direction of winter monsoon winds
0 500 1000 mi.
0 500 1000 km
Equidistant Projection

Famous Mountains

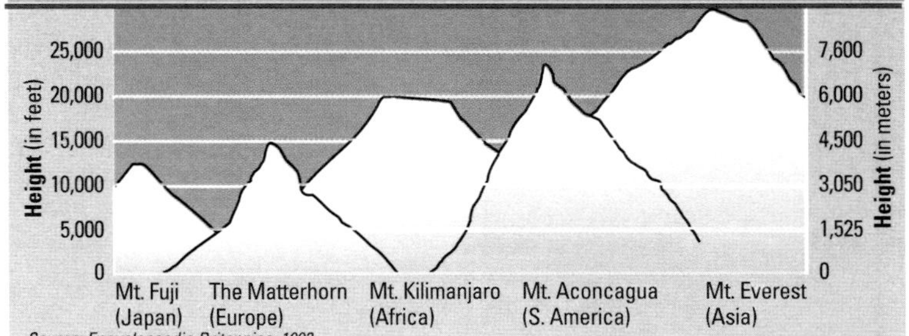
Height (in feet)
25,000
20,000
15,000
10,000
5,000
0
Height (in meters)
7,600
6,000
4,500
3,050
1,525
0
Mt. Fuji (Japan)
The Matterhorn (Europe)
Mt. Kilimanjaro (Africa)
Mt. Aconcagua (S. America)
Mt. Everest (Asia)
Source: Encyclopaedia Britannica, 1992

▲ *Sometimes the rains brought by the monsoon winds cause dangerous flooding. Without the rains, however, people cannot grow their crops.*

◄ *Mount Everest is nearly as tall as 20 Empire State Buildings. Other mountains seem small by comparison.*

Writing to Learn

Encourage students to choose an Asian country they would like to visit and write a paragraph about why they would like to go there. At the end of the unit, ask them to change or add to their reasons or write a new paragraph about a different country.

Economic Context

In addition to the machinery, clothing, oil, office machinery, electronics, clocks, watches, and textiles the Pacific Rim countries export, the developing countries of Asia export rubber, tea, coconut and palm oil, tin, tobacco, iron ore, wool, and hides and skins. Spices, which previously played such an important role in trade with western countries, now form but a tiny part of the total exports of Asia.

Asia's people belong to many ethnic groups and speak many different languages. Although other peoples have brought new customs, Asia has kept its own rich traditions—including music, dance, and theater. A popular form of Indian music, for example, is played on a stringed instrument called a sitar. The traditional Japanese forms of drama—Noh and Kabuki—are still performed today.

The economies of many Asian nations bordering the Pacific Ocean are growing rapidly. This region, called the Pacific Rim, includes Japan, South Korea, Singapore, and other East Asian nations as well as Australia and nations on the west coast of North and South America. These nations trade actively among themselves as well as with other nations.

Pacific Rim Trading Partners

Key: Machinery, Clothing, Oil, Office machines, Electronics, Clocks, Watches, Textiles

Country	Import Partner	Export Partner	Main Exports
Japan	United States	United States	Machinery, Office machines
Philippines	Japan	United States	Machinery, Clothing
Singapore	Japan	United States	Office machines, Oil
Indonesia	Japan	Japan	Oil
South Korea	Japan	United States	Machinery, Textiles
Hong Kong	China	United States	Clothing, Clocks, Watches, Textiles

Source: Europa World Yearbook, 1991

Great changes are taking place in world trade patterns.

Kabuki actors use colorful costumes and heavy makeup to bring characters to life. Scenery, music, and pantomime enliven their performances.

Much of the world's natural rubber comes from rubber trees grown in Malaysia and Indonesia.

Asian cities are some of the most densely populated in the world.

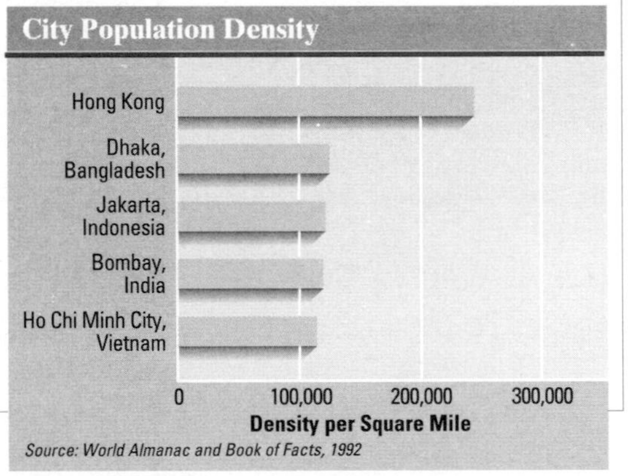
City Population Density
Hong Kong
Dhaka, Bangladesh
Jakarta, Indonesia
Bombay, India
Ho Chi Minh City, Vietnam
0
100,000
200,000
300,000
Density per Square Mile
Source: World Almanac and Book of Facts, 1992

Learning from the Trade Chart

To help students better understand international trade, have them examine the Pacific Rim Trading Partners chart. Walk them through one line of the chart so that they will understand the headings and symbols.

Based on this chart, students should tell which country is the largest importer (Export Partner) of Asian products. *(United States)* From which two countries does the United States import office machines? *(Japan and Singapore)*

Learning from Bar Graphs

Have students study the graph of city population density and locate each of these cities on the map on page 313. Ask why some Asian cities have high population densities *(Near rivers, sufficient rain, arable land)* and why others have low population densities. *(High mountains, cold climate)*

ENRICH

Have students make a chart showing examples of wildlife associated with each Asian country—for example, the panda of China and the Indian elephant. If possible, have them find pictures of the animals.

Health Connection

At 29,028 feet, Mount Everest poses a huge challenge to mountain climbers. The thin air, extreme cold, and roaring wind necessitates detailed preparation and planning before attempting a climb. Students who are interested might like to research the health risks of such challenging mountain climbing *(Frostbite, falls, oxygen deprivation, and so forth)* and present a report about how mountaineers prepare for such climbs and what precautions they take. They may also want to include information on how and why the Sherpa guides can make the climb with less preparation and equipment.

Collaborative Learning

Divide the class into groups, each of which will explore the popular culture of one Asian country: music, art, drama, literature, and food. If possible, have students interview someone who has recently lived in or has visited the country. Have each group present their discoveries as part of a class Cultural Appreciation Day, accompanied by an international lunch.

CHAPTER ORGANIZER

Chapter 14 India

CHAPTER PLANNING CHART

Pupil's Edition	Teacher's Edition	Ancillaries
Lesson 1: A Hindu Empire (2–3 days) Objective 1: Describe the achievements of India's Golden Age. (Culture 2, 3, 4, 5, 6) Objective 2: Describe Hindu village life. (Social and Political Systems 1, 4) Objective 3: Analyze the central role that Hinduism has played in the history of India. (History 7; Ethics and Belief Systems 1, 2, 3)	• Graphic Overview (318) • Access Strategy (319) • Access Activity (319) • Visual Learning (320) Cultural Context (320)	Study Guide (55)
Lesson 2: Foreign Rulers (2–3 days) Objective 1: Describe the Islamic challenge to Hinduism. (History 5, Ethics and Belief Systems 3, 4, 5; Social and Political Systems 3) Objective 2: Explain India's place in Britain's colonial empire. (Social and Political Systems 1, 2, 3) Objective 3: Describe the campaign that led to India's independence. (History 5, 6; Culture 3) Objective 4: Explain the formation of the modern nation of India. (Social and Political Systems 5)	• Graphic Overview (322) • Access Strategy (323) • Access Activity (323) Map and Globe Skills (324) Art Connection (324) Political Context (325) • Visual Learning (325) Social Participation (326) Historical Context (326)	Study Guide (56)
Understanding Reference Sources Objective: Identify elements of an entry to the *Readers' Guide to Periodical Literature* and use the *Readers' Guide* to make a list of entries for a given topic. (Study Skills 1; Critical Thinking 1, 2)		Study Guide (57)
Lesson 3: Modern India (2–3 days) Objective 1: Describe the geographic features that have an impact on Indian life today. (Geography 2, 3, 5; Economics 1, 4, 5) Objective 2: Identify some of the ways that multiculturalism plays itself out in modern India. (Culture 1, 2; Ethics and Belief Systems 3, 4, 5; Social and Political Systems 3, 4) Objective 3: Explain the progress India has made since independence. (Social and Political Systems 6)	• Graphic Overview (329) • Visual Learning (330) Writing a Journal Entry (330) • Access Strategy (331) • Access Activity (331) Critical Thinking (332) Collaborative Activity (332) Religious Context (333) Critical Thinking (333) Map and Globe Skills (334) Science Connection (334)	Study Guide (58) Map Activities (18) Discovery Journal (29) Transparency (5)
Chapter Review	Answers (336–337)	Tests (53–56)

* Objectives are correlated to the strands and goals in the program Scope and Sequence on pages T41–T49.

• LEP appropriate resources. (For additional strategies, see pages T32–T33.)

CHAPTER RATIONALE

In Chapter 14 students will build on what they learned about ancient Indian civilization in Chapter 5 as they explore the development of Indian culture from A.D. 320 to the present. The chapter describes India as one of the world's oldest and most notable civilizations.

Lesson 1 identifies some of the major scientific, cultural, and economic achievements that took place during the years of the Gupta Empire—India's Golden Age. It is important for students to understand that during this time period the main tenets of Hinduism reached final form. Since the time of the Gupta Empire, Hinduism has been the major religion and unifying force of the Indian people.

Lesson 2 examines India under foreign rule—first by Muslim invaders who established the Mughal Empire, and then as a colony of Britain. Throughout the lesson the issues of tolerance and the governing of a conquered people are explored. After explaining how the Indian people were treated under foreign rule, the lesson describes the growth of India's independence movement. Students are introduced to Mohandas K. Gandhi and his use of peaceful civil disobedience as a tool for change. The lesson ends with the achievement of Indian independence.

Lesson 3 presents an overview of the social, economic, and political status of modern India. It gives students the opportunity to understand the multitude of factors that a developing nation must overcome in the course of modernizing. India's challenges range from geographic phenomena such as monsoons to its large and burgeoning population. Students should come away from the lesson appreciating two important ideas about contemporary India: (1) Although it continues to face many difficulties, the nation has made progress in solving many problems; (2) despite being severely tested, India has maintained a democratic form of government.

ACTIVITIES & PROJECTS

Bulletin Board

Divide a bulletin board into four sections, and label the sections *Gupta Empire, Mughal Empire, British Rule,* and *Modern India.* Have students work together to prepare a display representing each period in India's history. Students may choose to design a mural, a collage, a graphic organizer, or any other visual representation of the time period. (Use after each lesson.)

Role-Playing

Choose students to role-play each of the important leaders discussed in this chapter. Have students write a one-page description of what their character looked like or might have looked like, how that character dressed, and what his or her achievements were. Students can then read their descriptions to the class, ending with the question, "Who am I?" The class can guess the role played by each student. (Use after Lesson 3.)

Challenge: Writing an Essay

Ask students to choose a time period in India's history during which they would choose to live as an Indian. Have them compose an essay explaining their choice. (Use after any lesson.)

LEP: Oral Report

Have students examine the illustrations in the chapter. Let them choose one image that they feel represents Indian culture and prepare a brief oral presentation explaining their choice to the class. (Use after Lesson 3.)

Basic: Making a Chart

Have students create a chart on the chalkboard to compare and contrast Indian culture during the periods of Gupta, Mughal, and British rule. Put the names of the three ruling groups across the top of the chart. Down the side of the chart, list attributes for comparison, such as major leaders, life of the Indian people, and achievements. Call on students to come to the board and complete the chart. (Use after Lesson 2.)

CHAPTER PREVIEW

Have students read the chapter title and the paragraph that follows. Point out that this chapter covers a great time span—nearly 1,700 years. Explain that during this long time period, many different people came to India. Tell students that they will read about how the Indian population has maintained ancient traditions in spite of invasions and periods of colonialism.

Looking Forward

Tell students that in Chapter 14 they will continue reading India's story. They will read about the impact of foreign invasions on India's political and social history in Lessons 1–3: A Hindu Empire, Foreign Rulers, and Modern India.

Lesson 1 describes India's Golden Age during the reign of the Guptas, and the early Hindu way of life.

Chapter 14

India

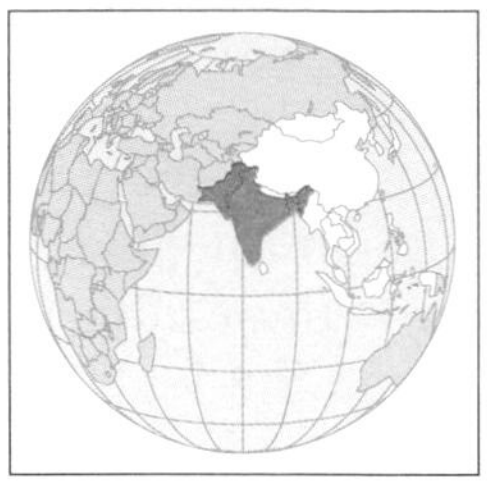

The earliest Indian civilization arose about 4,500 years ago. Gradually, other ancient peoples moved to India. Over the centuries the people blended old and new customs and beliefs into uniquely Indian forms. This wondrous mixture of religious and social traditions continues in India today.

This storekeeper sells powdered dyes and incense to be used during Hindu religious ceremonies.

A.D. 320–550 During India's Gupta dynasty the Hindu religion prospers. These coins were made from gold imported from Rome.

250 | 600 | 950

A.D. 320

1001–1027 Mahmud of Ghazna arrives and establishes a Muslim presence in northern India.

316

BACKGROUND

Each era in India's ancient past had its own richness, but a highlight of its history is the time of the Guptas (A.D. 320–467). During this Golden Age of India, great advances were made in the arts and sciences. In Gupta times, trade also flourished both within and outside India, and the Hindu religion spread throughout the empire.

Religion still plays an important role in the lives of Indian people. Although most Indians follow the Hindu religion, there are also large minority populations of Muslims, Sikhs, and other groups in India. Conflict between the Hindus and Muslims, in particular, has been a recurrent theme throughout Indian history.

Invasion by Outsiders

Muslim rulers called the Mughals ruled India from A.D. 711 to the 1500s. Babur, a descendant of Timur and Genghis Khan, conquered the Delhi Sultanate in 1526 and went on to found the Mughal Empire. Babur passed on the traits of wisdom and kindness to his grandson, Akbar, who would be remembered as the greatest Mughal ruler. Akbar practiced religious tolerance, allowing the primarily Hindu people to live in peace with their Muslim rulers, but many Mughal rulers did not. As a result, the Hindu people rebelled, beginning a pattern of violence between the two groups.

As India's political and social systems were threatened by warring religious groups,

urban ornament like this
, decorated with many
els, was a Muslim symbol
igh rank.

In India today the old and the new exist side by side. This young woman is dressed in traditional clothing. In the cities she walks with people in western clothing.

Under British rule thousands of miles of railroad tracks were built. Today the railroad continues to link the people of India.

1300 | 1650 | 2000

1600–1858 The English East India Company lays the foundation for the British Empire in India.

1947 India becomes an independent nation. Its first prime minister is Jawaharlal Nehru.

Today

Understanding the Visuals

Colorful dyes such as those shown in the Indian shop are used during the spring festival of Holi, a fun-filled day of mischief—not unlike April Fool's Day. People carry buckets of colored water and packages of brightly colored powders. Playfully, they smear the colors and shoot the water at one another.

The young woman in the photograph on the right is wearing a traditional Indian dress called a *sari.* A *sari* is, for an adult woman, about six yards of fabric draped around the waist and over the shoulder.

Understanding Chronology

Refer students to the timeline. Ask them to identify the date of Indian independence. Have students calculate the number of years India spent under some form of British control or direct rule. *(Almost 350 years)* Then remind them that prior to becoming a colony of Great Britain, India had a long history marked by a Golden Age, Muslim invasions, and internal strife.

Europeans took advantage of India as a rich source of raw materials and exotic goods. Great Britain established a stronghold in the late 1800s and maintained control of India for nearly 70 years. The common English words *calico, khaki, madras, bungalow, loot, punch,* and *thug* all come from Indian languages. Through protest, mostly nonviolent protest led by Mohandas Gandhi, the Indian people finally gained independence from Great Britain in 1947.

A Modern Nation Faces Challenges

In 1966 Indira Gandhi was elected prime minister. She was the daughter of the first prime minister of independent India, Jawaharlal Nehru. Gandhi is often described as a symbol of modern India—she was British educated; she was the first woman prime minister of India; and she died at the hands of religious extremists who wanted more independence from the Indian government.

As India faces the 21st century, the world's largest democracy hopes to bring its people a better way of life. The challenges of population control, food supply, ethnic conflict, and equal educational opportunities continue today.

INTRODUCE

Ask students what they can recall about the ancient people of India whom they studied in Chapter 5. *(Students may recall the civilizations of Mohenjo-Daro as well as the migration of the Aryan people.)* Ask students what they recall about the Hindu religion. *(Students may recall ideas about reincarnation, social ranks.)* Have students read the Thinking Focus. Ask them to define the term *Golden Age*. *(A time when a culture is responsible for high achievements)*

Key Term

Vocabulary Strategies: T36–T37
epic—an important or sacred story told or written in the form of a long poem

➤ *Yes, the Ganges River was in the Gupta territory.*

250 320 550 950 1300 1650 2000

LESSON 1

A Hindu Empire

THINKING FOCUS

Why is the period of the Gupta Empire called India's Golden Age?

Key Term

- epic

They were probably some of the world's first exchange students. They came from China, Tibet, and as far away as Japan. During the fourth century, students from all over Asia filled the classrooms of the University at Nalanda. It was a long trip to northern India, but worth it.

The students came to study subjects such as religion, agriculture, art, architecture and medicine. Their teachers at Nalanda and other Indian schools were making amazing discoveries.

Even today these ancient Indian thinkers affect students everywhere. In fact you can thank them for your math homework tonight. Indian mathematicians invented the number system you use today. It is based on nine digits, the zero, and the decimal.

India's Golden Age

The University at Nalanda had eight colleges and three libraries. It blossomed in India during the reign of the Guptas *(GOOP tuhz)*. The Guptas ruled northern India from A.D. 320 to about 550.

The Gupta Empire, c. A.D. 400

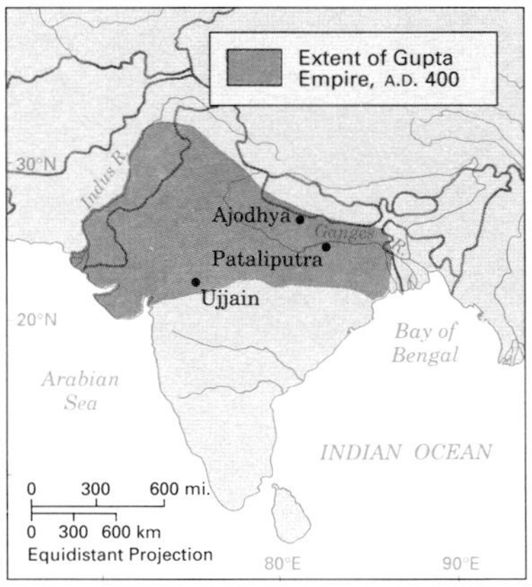
Extent of Gupta Empire, A.D. 400
30°N
Indus R.
Ajodhya
Ganges R.
Pataliputra
Ujjain
20°N
Bay of Bengal
Arabian Sea
INDIAN OCEAN
0 300 600 mi.
0 300 600 km
Equidistant Projection
80°E
90°E

➤ *The Guptas began as rulers of a small kingdom in northeast India. By A.D. 400, Gupta lands covered most of northern India. Find the Ganges River. Was the Ganges River in Gupta territory?*

The founder of the Gupta Empire started as the ruler of a small Indian kingdom. At that time, India had suffered through hundreds of years of invasions. After the Guptas took control, they protected India's borders. For the next 200 years, India was safe from invaders. This was India's Golden Age, a time of learning and great advancement.

Discoveries in Science

Aryabhata *(ah ree ah BAHT uh)* was just one of the many scientists who made important discoveries during Gupta times. He knew that the earth was round and rotated on its axis. In Europe some people

Objectives

1. Describe the achievements of India's Golden Age.
2. Describe Hindu village life.
3. Analyze the central role that Hinduism has played in the history of India.

Graphic Overview

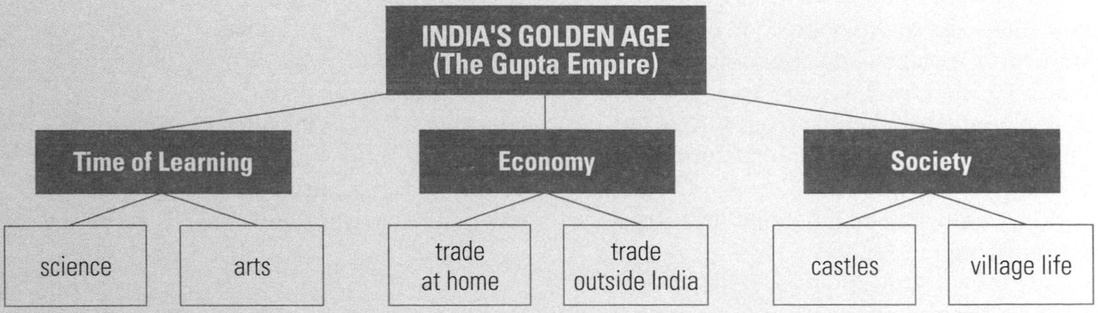
INDIA'S GOLDEN AGE (The Gupta Empire)
Time of Learning
Economy
Society
science
arts
trade at home
trade outside India
castles
village life

still hadn't accepted that fact more than 1,000 years later, when Columbus set out to sea.

Great medical advances were also made. Doctors learned to set broken bones and used plastic surgery to fix scars. They also developed many medicines and knew the importance of cleanliness in stopping the spread of disease.

In the crafts the Guptas made beautiful metalwork. They also improved cloth making. Later, Indian cloth-making methods would be borrowed by the Arabs and by the Europeans. Calico, chintz, and cashmere are all fabrics that were first woven in India.

Achievements in the Arts

Gupta rulers lived in beautiful palaces bustling with activity. The arts flowered under their rule. People throughout Asia, and later in Europe, enjoyed Indian fables and fairy tales. Especially popular was the *Panchatantra (puhn cha TUHN trah),* a collection of fables in which animals speak and act like people.

Before the days of the Guptas, Indians learned about Hindu Gods, myths, and religious duties through two epics. **Epics** are stories told in the form of long poems. These epics were called the *Mahabharata* and *Ramayana.* People learned them by heart from their elders. Then they taught them to the next generation. In Gupta times, these epics were at last written down in the old Sanskrit language of India. (See the Minipedia for more on early alphabets.)

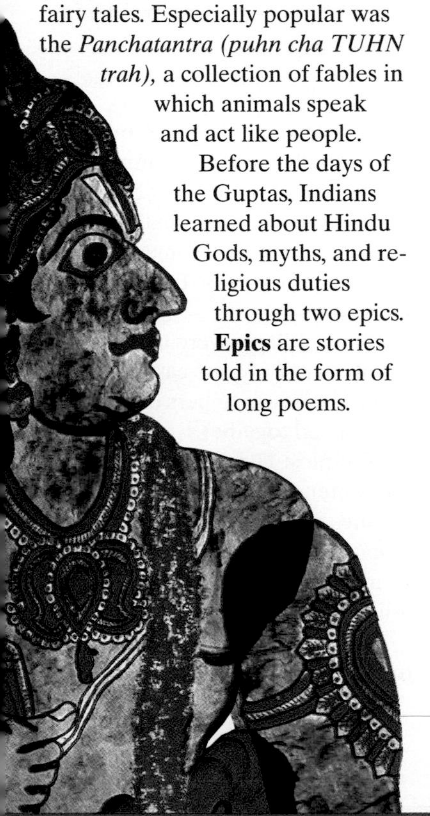

Booming Trade at Home

Wealthy Gupta merchants supported the advances made in science and the arts. Gupta trade routes hummed with activity. Ox-drawn carts loaded with goods for market bumped along the overland trails. The trade routes crossed through desert, forest, and rain forest.

Trade in Indian towns was busy. Food filled the markets and people crowded the cobblestone streets. Most shoppers walked through the markets buying rice, wheat, and sugar. Wealthy people were carried in chairs called litters. They might buy some of the more expensive fruits such as mangoes, melons, pears, and peaches.

Trading Outside India

Trade outside India thrived, too. Westward, Gupta trade routes led to Rome as well as to Africa. Eastward, trade was carried on with China, Southeast Asia, and what is now Indonesia.

Goods coming into the Gupta Empire included gold from Rome, silk from China, and horses from Arabia and Central Asia. In other countries, merchants eagerly bought the Guptas' expensive exports. These exports included gems, pearls, pepper, red dye, ginger, cinnamon, fine cotton cloth, wood such as teak, and perfumes. ■

How Do We Know?

ART *The art from the Gupta Empire gives us a picture of what court life was like during this period. It shows palaces filled with servants, music, and artists.*

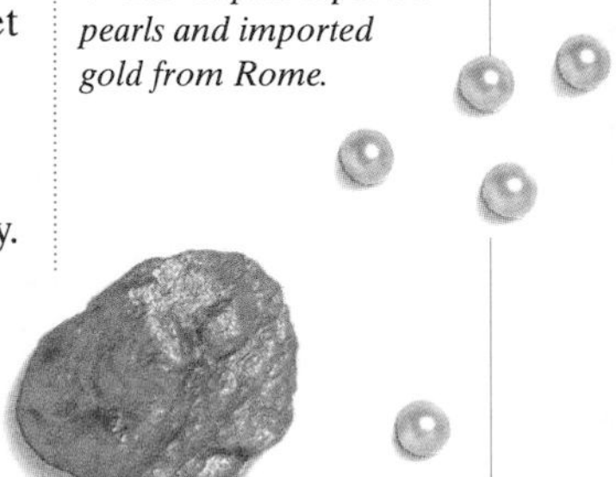

▼ The Guptas exported pearls and imported gold from Rome.

◄ In the Ramayana, *the God Vishnu comes to earth as Rama. In this picture Rama is shown carrying the bow and arrow he uses to save his wife.*

■ *How did trade contribute to advances in arts and science during the Gupta Empire?*

DEVELOP

Have students read through the **boldface** headings on the pages of this lesson to identify the many achievements of India's Golden Age. *(Advances were made in science, the arts, and in trade, both at home and outside India.)* Ask students to list on a sheet of paper the achievements they read about in this lesson. Tell them that the Hindu religion prescribes much of how people live in India. After the students have read pages 320–321, ask them to draw a diagram that explains the influence of Hinduism as a way of life.

CULTURE

Visual Learning

Have students study the image of Rama on this page. What does the image portray about his character? *(He looks regal, noble, powerful.)* Explain that in the epic poem *Ramayana,* Rama is the human form of the Hindu God Vishnu. Rama must save his wife from the demon-king who kidnapped her. Point out that Rama serves as a model for Hindu men. He is handsome, brave, and a loyal husband.

■ *Wealthy merchants paid artists and scientists for their work.*

Access Strategy

You can use the visuals in this lesson to help students develop an appreciation of India's Gupta Empire. Ask students to review the visuals and the map on the first two pages of the lesson and describe what they see. Write their responses on the chalkboard. Do they think that this is a thriving culture or a culture in troubled times? How can they tell? *(A thriving culture is suggested by the extent of the Gupta Empire shown on the map; the imported gold and exported pearls, which represent great wealth; and the regal-looking painting.)* Tell students that the period they will read about is called India's Golden Age.

Access Activity

Have students find India on the world map on page 679 in the Atlas. Ask them how India's location gave its early merchants an advantage in trade. *(Access to a seacoast that faces east and one that faces west allowed them to trade in both directions.)* Ask them to speculate on the problems the Gupta traders had in reaching China. *(Great distances; deserts; mountains)*

SOCIAL SYSTEMS

Critical Thinking

Ask students to summarize their understanding of the caste system. *(The Hindu social structure was determined by a caste system, according to which everyone was born into a specific sector or caste. In the caste system, a person's occupation was thereby determined by birth.)* Ask students to give examples of how they think the caste system differs from how people determine their occupation in the United States. *(People in the United States can choose an occupation that is usually determined by their education and personal interests.)*

Hindu Way of Life

As learning and trade grew in India during the Gupta Empire, the Hindu religion grew, too. Most of Hinduism's main teachings reached final form in the Gupta period. In towns and villages workers built Hindu temples. Hinduism spread throughout both the north and the south of India. Hinduism became India's largest religion, and the number of Buddhists in India grew very small.

➤ *These Hindu people are bathing in the holy Ganges River. Hindu people may travel hundreds of miles to bathe in the river.*

Indian Society

As you read in Chapter 5, the Aryans divided people into four social groups: priests, warriors, merchants and peasants, and servants. These social classes slowly divided into more than 3,000 castes. Children inherit their father's caste.

Caste rules stated whom you could marry and how you could earn a living. In ancient days these castes gave Hindus a sense of security. It was the duty of each caste to care for its members.

At the bottom of the caste system were the untouchables. They were called untouchables because it was said that even their touch could pollute or dirty you. As a result, untouchables were excluded from village life. They were not allowed to drink from the village well. Hindu doctors would not treat their illnesses.

Even today castes remain an important part of life in India. Arranged marriages remain common. Your caste still determines what you can eat. For example, some castes will not eat meat or fish but will eat eggs.

▼ *Villages in the Gupta period looked much as this village in northern India looks today. Notice, however, the modern clothing of the young boys.*

Village Life

The ancient villages of India were usually made up of mud and straw huts. Most people were poor farmers who worked small fields outside the village. Women cooked the family's meals on fires outside the home.

Some villages were made up of members of only one caste. In other villages, members of many castes lived together.

For most Hindus the home was the center of worship. Upper caste families called in priests for ceremonies. In lower caste homes, women performed many of these religious rituals.

Caste councils in each village took care of religious matters. If a

Visual Learning

Have students examine the photograph of the people bathing in the Ganges. Tell them that Hindu people consider the Ganges the most sacred river in India. Ask students to brainstorm other reasons why the Ganges River is important. *(Many cities were built on the Ganges; it is vital to trade; its waters serve the populations settled along its banks.)*

Cultural Context

Students should understand that the group called untouchables was made up of those people who engaged in jobs that, according to the Hindu religion, were thought to be polluting. Polluting activities included killing animals, a category that included fishers; killing or disposing of dead cattle or working with their hides; coming into contact with human bodily fluids such as sweat; and eating the flesh of cattle, pigs, or chickens.

caste member broke a religious law, council members decided the punishment. The worst punishment a person could suffer was to be made an untouchable.

Villages were governed by the *panchayat (puhn CHAH yuht),* a council of five elected people. The members of the council were usually rich farmers or from the higher castes. They collected taxes, ordered the building of roads and wells, and settled fights between feuding villagers.

Today there are some places where village life still looks much as it did in ancient India. Women conduct many of the old rituals, and caste councils are still important. However, changes have slowly taken place.

Villages are still governed by *panchayats,* but they are very different from those of the Guptas. Today there are hundreds of thousands of *panchayats* in India. They work together with the national and state governments to improve village life.

An Indian woman is shown here spinning silk. For hundreds of years, traders from all over the world have eagerly bought fine Indian silk.

Decline of the Gupta Empire

An eyewitness account of India's golden days comes to us from Faxian *(fah shee AHN),* a Buddhist monk from China. He kept a diary while traveling through India in the early A.D. 400s. He wrote that "the people are numerous and happy." His diary tells, too, that there was little crime, and in certain areas hospitals gave free care to the poor and helpless.

About 50 years after Faxian's travels, the Gupta Empire began to decline. Invaders called White Huns swept down from Central Asia. Their attacks weakened the empire, causing it to break up into small kingdoms. By A.D. 467, India's Golden Age was almost over. ■

■ *What is the caste system in India?*

REVIEW

1. **FOCUS** Why is the period of the Gupta Empire called India's Golden Age?
2. **CULTURE** Identify an achievement in science and another in the arts during the Gupta period.
3. **SOCIAL SYSTEMS** Who were the untouchables? Why were they given that name?
4. **CRITICAL THINKING** Meeting someone, falling in love, and choosing your own marriage partner is common in Western countries. How would you feel if your parents told you they had picked a spouse for you? What would you tell them?
5. **ACTIVITY** Imagine you are in charge of bringing foreign students to the University at Nalanda during Gupta times. Using the information in the lesson, create a poster encouraging students to come to study at Nalanda.

■ *The caste system is a Hindu social order based on the existence of specific sectors, or castes, into which a person is born.*

CLOSE

Read the Thinking Focus aloud. Ask students to create one-sentence headlines that answer the question. A sample might be *Nalanda University Is Home to Some of the World's Leading Scholars.* Record all student suggestions on the chalkboard. Then have students evaluate, combine, and revise those headings until they can agree on the headlines that best explain India's Golden Age.

Answers to Review Questions

1. There were advances made in science and art during the period of the Gupta Empire. Trade boomed both within and outside India. Hinduism was strengthened and spread throughout the continent.
2. Gupta scholars wrote down India's ancient epics in the old Sanskrit language; Gupta mathematicians developed the number system used today.
3. Untouchables were Indians living at the bottom of the caste system. They were called untouchables because Hindus believed that just their touch could pollute.
4. Students may point out that, in our society, it would be unusual for parents to select spouses for their children. Students will probably prefer to choose their own marriage partners.
5. Students may design posters that focus on advancements in science and the arts or the university's eight colleges and libraries.

Homework Options

Have students make a "Wall of Fame" chart that illustrates some of the artistic and scientific achievements of the Gupta Empire in India.

Study Guide: page 55

INTRODUCE

Ask a volunteer to read aloud the Thinking Focus. Then ask students if they can name any other cultures they have studied that have been invaded by outsiders. *(Aztec, Roman)* What was the result of these invasions? *(With the help of native allies and through the spread of disease, the Spaniards destroyed the Aztec Empire. The equally bold Germanic invaders helped to bring the Roman Empire to an end.)* Tell students that in this lesson they will learn how outsiders—the Muslims and the British—brought changes to India nearly 500 years after the Gupta Empire.

Key Terms

Vocabulary Strategies: T36–T37

Mughal—people from Central Asia who founded an empire in India

imperialism—one nation under the control of another, as a colony

civil disobedience—the refusal to cooperate or to obey laws believed to be unfair

250 600 950 1000 1947 2000

LESSON 2

Foreign Rulers

The whole country of India is full of gold and jewels, and of the plants which grow there are those fit for making apparel, and aromatic plants and the sugarcane, and the whole aspect of the country is pleasant and delightful. Now, since the inhabitants are chiefly infidels and idolaters, by the order of God [Allah] and his Prophet it is right for us to conquer them.

Turkish Sultan Mahmud of Ghazna

THINKING FOCUS

How did the Mughals and the British affect Indian culture?

Key Terms

- Mughal
- imperialism
- civil disobedience

Seventeen times Mahmud *(mah MOOD)* and his soldiers invaded India between 1001 and 1027. They terrorized Hindu and Buddhist priests, tore down religious shrines, and plundered palaces. Riding on horses, Mahmud's troops defeated the Indians. Hinduism had been the center of Indian life for hundreds of years. Now it was under attack.

Muslim Rule

Mahmud of Ghazna was one of many Muslim invaders who entered India between A.D. 711 and the 1500s. As Muslims spreading the holy word of Islam to unbelievers, they thought their invasions were just. Arab, Turkish, and Mongol armies entered India through the Khyber Pass in the Himalayas.

As you read in Chapter 8, Muslims worship one God. In this way they differ from Hindus who may worship many Gods. Also, the Islamic religion has no caste system. Muslims believe that all people are equal before God. Individuals can change their social status with hard work and luck.

These basic differences in religion and society led to conflict between neighboring Hindu and Muslim states. Some Muslim rulers tried to force Hindus to convert to Islam. In spite of the pressure, many Hindus refused to change their religion or their way of life. The bitterness between Muslims and Hindus that started during this time still divides the Indian people today.

➤ *This finely crafted household object is made of gold. It was probably made in a palace workshop.*

Objectives

1. Describe the Islamic challenge to Hinduism.
2. Explain India's place in Britain's colonial empire.
3. Describe the campaign that led to India's independence.
4. Explain the formation of the modern nation of India.

Graphic Overview

Muslim Invasions
Muslim invasions brought Mughal rule, cultural changes, and ethnic conflict.

→

British Imperialism
British imperialism brought improvements in transportation, communications, and agriculture, but also new ethnic conflict.

→

Opposition to British Rule
Indians protested British rule. Britain granted independence and divided India.

Akbar the Ruler

In 1519, Muslim Turks from Central Asia invaded northern India. They founded the Mughal *(MOO gahl)* Empire. The word **Mughal** comes from the Persian-Indian word for Mongol.

The Mughals built a large and rich empire. Look at the map of India on page 324. Compare it to the map on page 333. What parts of present-day India did the Mughal Empire control?

The greatest Mughal leader was Akbar *(AK bahr)*. He came to power when he was only 13 years old and reigned for 49 years (1556–1605). Akbar showed great tolerance and respect for other religions. He did not try to make Hindus become Muslims. Akbar saw himself as the ruler of all India's people.

During Akbar's reign, the Mughal court became one of the world's leading centers of culture. Akbar invited artists, poets, and musicians to his court. They produced great paintings and other works of art. The Mughals would have a lasting effect on Indian arts and architecture.

Miniature painting reached great heights under the Mughals. The subject of this painting is Akbar. He is in the center of the picture, holding court.

Mughal Rule Ends

The last important Mughal ruler was Aurangzeb *(AWR ehng zehb)*. He ruled from 1658 to 1707. Unlike Akbar, he tried to force Hindus to become Muslims. He forbade the building of new Hindu temples and put a tax on non-Muslims. This caused many rebellions. Many Indians refused to accept Mughal rule.

Look at the map of rebellions on page 324. Locate the Hindu

The Taj Mahal glimmers through the mist behind the boaters. This outstanding example of Mughal architecture took more than 20,000 laborers and 22 years to build. Caravans brought rare, colorful gems from around the world so that the flower designs inside would be the right colors.

DEVELOP

Explain that when outsiders invade a country there is often a period of social and political unrest. The invaders bring their own customs, language, and beliefs and take control of the local population. Ask students to speculate on how India faced invasions by outsiders. Students should give reasons to support their speculations. *(Answers will vary. Some students may say that the Indian culture was strong enough to withstand the invading forces. Others will say that the invaders hurt India, just as the Aztec and Roman empires were harmed by outsiders.)*

HISTORY

Visual Learning

Ask students to look carefully at the painting of the Muslim ruler Akbar on this page. What does it portray about his rule? What does the painting depict about Akbar as a person? *(The painting suggests that Akbar was an approachable ruler, willing to discuss issues with other people. Akbar is directly facing the man with whom he is speaking.)*

Access Strategy

Write the word *imperial* on the chalkboard. Ask students to brainstorm words, ideas, or images that come to mind when they hear this word. *(Kings, queens, castles)* Explain that the word *imperial* comes from the Latin word *imperium,* meaning "command."

Write the word *imperialism* on the chalkboard. Ask students if they can guess what the word might mean. *(Having control over others)* Explain that imperialism is a policy of one nation's having control over others as colonies. Ask students to speculate about how they think people who are taken over might react to outside rulers. *(Angry, afraid)* Explain to students that this lesson describes how the people in India reacted when outsiders invaded their lands.

Access Activity

Read aloud the quotation from the Mahmud of Ghazna on page 322. Ask students to predict what will happen when India is invaded by the sultan's Muslim forces. *(Invaders will steal India's gold and jewels; export its plants and spices; show disrespect to Hindu and Buddhist traditions.)* Explain that students will read more about the Muslim invaders.

➤ *The Marathas and the Rajputs were the two centers of Hindu resistance.*

POLITICAL SYSTEMS

Critical Thinking

Ask students to compare the Mughal rulers Akbar and Aurangzeb. How did the rule of Akbar help to keep the Muslim influence in India? How did the rule of Aurangzeb help to bring Muslim rule to an end? *(Akbar showed respect for the Hindus. He even ate and dressed as a Hindu. Aurangzeb tried to force the Hindus to become Muslims, forbade the building of new Hindu temples, and taxed non-Muslims. Akbar's actions ensured peace; Aurangzeb's rule led to rebellion.)*

■ *Muslims tried to convert Hindus to Islam, which caused tensions that remain today. The Muslims brought new languages and new ideas about art to India.*

Muslim Rule and Indian Resistance, c. 1700

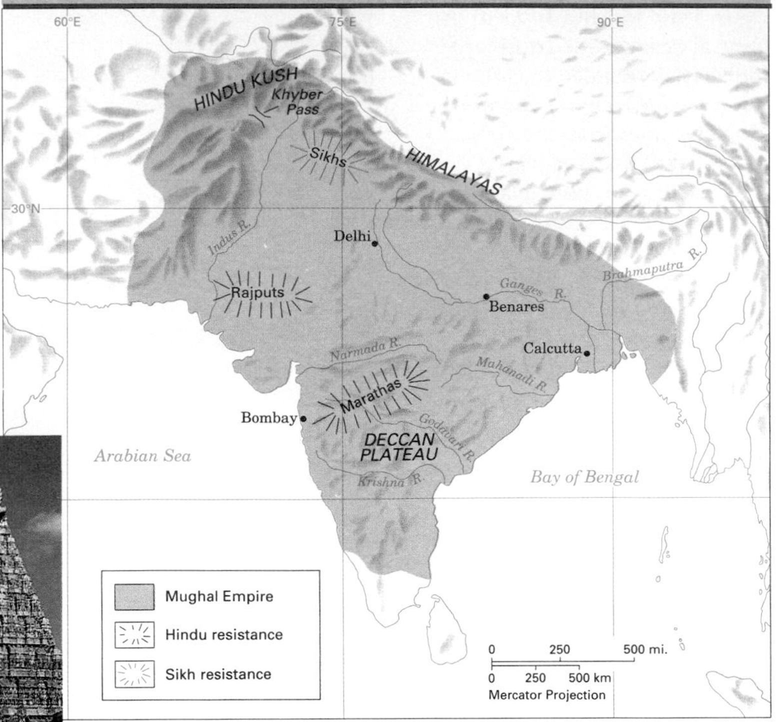
60°E
75°E
90°E
30°N
HINDU KUSH
Khyber Pass
Sikhs
HIMALAYAS
Indus R.
Delhi
Rajputs
Ganges R.
Benares
Brahmaputra R.
Narmada R.
Calcutta
Mahanadi R.
Marathas
Bombay
Godavari R.
DECCAN PLATEAU
Krishna R.
Arabian Sea
Bay of Bengal
Mughal Empire
Hindu resistance
Sikh resistance
0 250 500 mi.
0 250 500 km
Mercator Projection

➤ *The map shows areas of resistance to Mughal rule. The Sikhs were followers of a new faith that blended Islam and Hinduism. Name the two centers of Hindu resistance.*

▼ *This Hindu temple is found in southern India. Its style is very different from the Mughal architecture of the Taj Mahal.*

■ *In what ways did Muslim rule affect India?*

Rajputs. The Rajputs successfully fought Mughal rule and are said to have saved Hinduism in northern India.

The Mughal Empire began to break apart. Once again, India was a collection of kingdoms and small states. Stories of India's splendor and the Mughals' growing weakness spread. Without the Mughals to fear, European nations began to invade by sea. ■

British Rule

For many centuries, Great Britain and other European nations had been attracted by the tea, spices, sugar, indigo, silk cloth, and other products of India and Asia.

It was the Portuguese explorer Vasco da Gama *(VAHS koh dah GAH muh)* who opened the sea route from Europe to India in 1498. Soon trading ships from England, Denmark, and France began arriving in India's harbors.

British East India Company

In the 1600s the ships of the British East India Company anchored in Indian waters. The company built trading posts and forts in Calcutta, Bombay, and Madras. When the Mughal Empire began to fall apart, the East India Company saw the chance to spread its reach.

Step by step the company—a privately owned business—grasped control of more territory. By the

Map and Globe Skills

Have students study the map on this page. Ask them to locate the center of Sikh resistance. *(In the northwest area of the Mughal Empire)* Have students hypothesize which resistance group was best protected by features of physical geography. *(The Sikhs, because they were flanked by the Himalayas and Hindu Kush.)*

Art Connection

The Mughal rulers imported the best Persian artists to create luxurious palaces filled with mosques and thrones decorated with jewels and marble. Walls were engraved with Persian poetry such as "If there is a Paradise on the face of earth, it is this, Oh! It is this, Oh! It is this, Oh!"

Have students look at the photograph at the bottom of page 323. Tell them that the building in the distance is the most famous tomb in the world—the Taj Mahal. What type of structure does it resemble? *(A castle or mosque)* Tell students that the word *mahal* means palace. Explain that the Taj Mahal was built by the Mughal emperor Shāh Jahān in memory of his wife, Mumtāz Mahal, who died in childbirth. Ask students to compare the Taj Mahal with other examples of Islamic art and architecture in previous chapters of their text. (Examples can be found in Chapter 8, page 192, and in Chapter 9, page 210.)

mid-1700s, the British East India Company had become India's most powerful ruler.

When the company's Indian soldiers rebelled, the British government became alarmed. They took over the job of governing India. In 1877 Queen Victoria was crowned empress of India.

The Jewel in the Crown

By the 1800s Britain had become the world's greatest imperial power. It had an empire with colonies all around the world. The colonies supplied Britain, the imperial nation, with raw materials and cheap labor. Usually, the colonies also had to buy goods from Britain. This system in which one nation takes control of another one and makes it a colony is called **imperialism.**

For example, India supplied British textile factories with cotton to be woven into cloth. The cloth was then shipped back to India and sold. British manufacturers made huge profits. The British called India the "Jewel in the Crown" because it was the most valuable colony in the empire. Meanwhile British imperialism was destroying India's own industries.

To keep India running, the British did make improvements. They built railroads, highways, and a telegraph system. They improved irrigation and introduced a postal service. They also allowed some Indians to be educated in Britain. However, the improvements were made on Britain's terms. ■

◄ *The British in India lived well above the means of the average Indian. In British neighborhoods signs were often posted that said* FOR EUROPEANS ONLY.

■ *In what ways did India change under British rule?*

The Move Toward Independence

Many Indians began to say that the British were stealing India's wealth and discriminating against India's people. Indian opposition to British rule grew.

Those Indians who had traveled to England for schooling led the movement to end British rule. While in England, they saw that they did not have the same rights or opportunities as British citizens. When they went home, it did not matter that they had college degrees. The British would not allow them to hold high-ranking jobs in the Indian Civil Service.

Angry at how they were being treated, Indians began organizing. Peasant protests helped to increase the pressure on the British. The cry for independence was picked up across India.

ECONOMICS

Critical Thinking

The British used their Indian colony as a source of raw materials and as a new market for British goods. The British allowed some Indian people to improve their education for the sole purpose of becoming British civil servants. Railways were built from ports to factories, but they were not necessarily of much use to the Indian people. Ask students how they think this economic situation affected the relationship between the British and the Indian people. *(It caused bitterness and resentment.)* You may wish to refer students to Communication in the Minipedia on pages 665–668.

■ *The British brought European ideas to India, helped India develop a widespread communications system, and allowed some Indians to be educated in Britain. They also set in place the institutions that would result in an Indian independence movement. However, Britain destroyed some home industries and encouraged India's ethnic and religious divisions.*

Political Context

To help students understand events leading to British rule in India, explain that the British East India Company hired Indian soldiers to protect their company fortifications and to help them stay in power. To ensure their loyalty, these soldiers, who were called sepoys, were well-trained, paid regularly, and given uniforms by the British. However, a new sense of nationalism was developing in the country, and the sepoys began the first rebellion against the East India Company in 1857. The Sepoy Mutiny was rumored to be triggered when British officers ordered the sepoy soldiers to bite open gun cartridges greased with cow or pig fat. The soldiers' religions wouldn't allow them to obey the order. Hindus could not eat beef; Muslims could not eat pork. The East India Company was able to put down the rebellion in 1858. After the rebellion, the British government decided to take the control of India from the East India Company and put it into government hands.

Visual Learning

Ask students to study the painting on this page. Ask them to compare and contrast the British and the Indian people shown in the painting. *(The British people are relaxing. Western furnishings in the foreground are contrasted with Indian architecture in the background. The Indian people in traditional clothing serve the British people.)*

BELIEF SYSTEMS

Social Participation

Gandhi linked oppression of Hindu's untouchables to British oppression of the Indian people. (Remind students that they can look up *untouchable* in the Glossary on page 707.) Gandhi called the untouchables *Harijans,* a name that means "children of God." Ask students to think about—and discuss—what it might have felt like to be an untouchable and how Gandhi's teachings might have changed their lives.

Mohandas Gandhi

In 1915 an Indian leader by the name of Mohandas *(moh HAHN dahs)* K. Gandhi was gathering a following. Gandhi was a Hindu who had attended law school in Britain. After becoming a lawyer, he spent 21 years in South Africa fighting discrimination against Indians living there. In 1915 he returned to India.

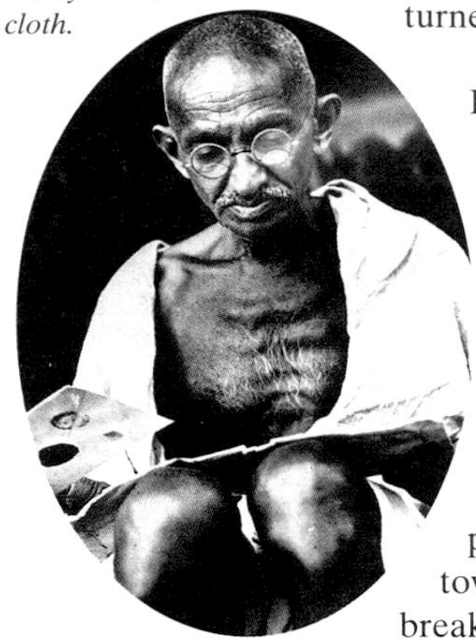

Gandhi wore simple homespun cloth as a symbol of resistance to British rule. Following his lead, millions of Indians refused to buy British-made cloth.

Four years later, the British passed a new series of laws designed to put a stop to Indian demands for more independence. Gandhi told Indians not to obey these laws.

Shortly thereafter, more than 10,000 unarmed Indians held a protest meeting in a town called Amritsar. To break up the meeting, British soldiers were ordered to fire into the crowd. When the rifle shots stopped, about 400 Indians lay dead, and another 1,200 were wounded. After Amritsar, Gandhi became the most well known leader in the fight for Indian independence.

Gandhi didn't believe in war or the use of violence. Yet he did believe in fighting for what was right. The method he used to push the British out of India is called civil disobedience. **Civil disobedience** is the refusal to cooperate or to obey laws that you believe are unfair. You realize that by breaking the law, you may have to go to jail.

Gandhi urged Indians not to buy British goods or pay certain taxes. Across India, Indians refused to work for the British or go to British schools. Millions joined the campaign for independence.

Gandhi was arrested and put in prison many times for his actions. He grew thin from hunger strikes. With each hunger strike, more and more Indians joined the protests.

In 1947 the long independence campaign finally paid off. After World War II, the British decided that the cost of maintaining colonial rule was too high. Britain agreed to give India its independence. With victory in sight, problems between

This 1930 photograph is of a demonstration encouraging Indians not to buy British-made goods. Notice the line of women demonstrators on the right side of the street.

Social Participation

Ask students to find articles related to civil disobedience in newspapers or newsmagazines. Have them share their articles in small groups and discuss the issues at stake and the consequences suffered by the protesters.

Historical Context

To help students understand the role of tradition in India, explain that the wheel is a historic symbol there. Buddhists believe that the Buddha was born with wheel imprints on the palms of his hands and the soles of his feet. Also, the basics of the Buddha's teaching—the Four Noble Truths and the Eightfold Path—are contained in his "Sermon of the Turning of the Wheel of the Law."

The wheel was also an important symbol in the Indian independence movement. To loosen the grip of British-made goods in India, Gandhi proposed that people begin making their own cloth with spinning wheels. The movement spread throughout India, and thousands of peasants produced the simple cotton cloth called *khadi.* India's flag, adopted in 1947, has the ancient symbol called the *Dharma Chakra* (Wheel of Law) set against a background of three wide stripes of white, green, and orange.

Hindus and Muslims surfaced. Many Muslims were worried that the Hindu majority would treat them unfairly. Riots broke out when Muslims asked for their own independent country.

To end the violence, Britain divided India. In the northeast and northwest, where Muslims made up a majority of the population, the British created the Muslim nation of Pakistan. Five months after independence, Gandhi was shot and killed. His assassin was a Hindu who thought Gandhi was too tolerant of Muslims.

A New Nation

One of Gandhi's followers was a young man named Jawaharlal Nehru *(juh wah hur LAHL NAY roo)*. On the eve of independence, Nehru stood ready to become India's first prime minister. As the hands on the clock approached 12, Nehru spoke to the crowd.

> *At the stroke of the midnight hour, when the world sleeps, India will awake to life and freedom. A moment comes, which comes but rarely in history, when we step out from the old to the new, when an age ends, and when the soul of a nation, long suppressed, finds utterance. . .*

On August 15, 1947, India became an independent nation. Huge gatherings cheered with parades and spectacular fireworks. At the same time, millions of Hindus and Muslims fled their homes for religious reasons.

As the Independence Day celebrations faded, India's leaders set about forming a government. India was organized as a democratic republic. In India, every man and woman who had reached the age of 21 was given the right to vote. India was now the world's largest democracy. ■

Across Time & Space

Pakistan was formed as a nation made up of two parts separated by more than 1,000 miles. The government was located in West Pakistan. The people of East Pakistan felt the government discriminated against them. In 1971 civil war broke out. In the same year East Pakistan declared its independence. The new nation was called Bangladesh.

◄ Indira Gandhi was prime minister of India from 1966 to 1977 and from 1980 to 1984. Her father, Jawaharlal Nehru, is on the poster behind her.

■ *How did Mohandas K. Gandhi help India gain independence?*

REVIEW

1. **FOCUS** How did the Mughals and the British affect Indian culture?
2. **POLITICAL SYSTEMS** Compare Akbar's rule of India with the rule of Aurangzeb.
3. **ECONOMICS** Why did the British call India the "Jewel in the Crown"?
4. **HISTORY** How did Indians peacefully protest British rule?
5. **CRITICAL THINKING** Do you think Gandhi's method of civil disobedience could be used to change laws in the United States? Why or why not?
6. **ACTIVITY** Imagine you could meet Mohandas Gandhi. What would you like to know about his life and his beliefs? Make a list of five questions.

■ *Gandhi's civil disobedience campaign mobilized Indians against British rule and eventually pressured Britain into accepting Indian independence.*

CLOSE

Read the Thinking Focus aloud. Create two word webs on the chalkboard. Write *Mughal* in the center of the first web; write *British* in the center of the second. Ask students to brainstorm ways in which these outsiders threatened Indian culture. Have students complete the webs with their ideas.

Answers to Review Questions

1. The Mughals influenced Indian art and religion, and the British influenced education and industrialization in India.
2. Akbar showed great tolerance and respect for other religions. Aurangzeb tried to force Hindus to convert.
3. The British called India the "Jewel in the Crown" because India was the most valuable of all of its colonial possessions.
4. Most Indians followed Gandhi's call for civil disobedience, including boycotts and peaceful public protests. Gandhi also went on several hunger strikes.
5. Answers may include the fact that Rosa Parks and Martin Luther King, Jr., followed a similar course of civil disobedience.
6. Possible answers: (1) How was he raised as a child? (2) Who were his role models? (3) How did his faith shape his protest? (4) What was the most important event in his life? (5) Which thinkers influenced his philosophy of nonviolent protest?

Homework Options

Tell students to imagine that they are Indian activists at the time of Mughal or British rule. Then have them design a petition listing grievances against the foreign rulers that will convince other Indians to join their cause.

Study Guide: page 56

UNDERSTANDING REFERENCE SOURCES

This skills feature uses a sample page from the *Readers' Guide to Periodical Literature* to teach students how to find periodical literature in the library.

CULTURE

Study Skills

Have students review the list of topics shown on the page. Which topics would give them a better understanding of Indian culture? *(Answers may vary but might include Grand Trunk Road, Motion pictures, and Women.)* Which topics would give them a better understanding of the political situation in India today? *(Environmental policy, Public welfare)*

Note: If the *Readers' Guide* is available on computer in the school or local library, you may wish to ask students to use it for the Apply It activity on this page.

UNDERSTANDING REFERENCE SOURCES

Using the *Readers' Guide*

Here's Why

To find current information about a topic, you need to use references other than encyclopedias and books. Magazines and other periodicals can provide recent information about events.

Suppose that you want to find more information about life in India today. How would you find the periodicals?

Here's How

The *Readers' Guide to Periodical Literature* is a set of reference books. It lists articles by topic and year. The boxes below contain entries from the 1991 *Readers' Guide*.

To find an article about life in India today, look under the topic "India." There you will find cross-references, such as "Americans—India." These references tell you that more articles about India today can be found under these headings. What kind of information might you expect to find under the "Americans—India" heading?

Notice that there are also several subheadings under the topic India. One or more articles are listed under each subheading.

Look at the box to your right. It is a key that tells you what kind of information you can find in each entry. Each entry always includes the name of the article, the periodical that published it, and the date. What other information is sometimes given?

Once you find entries that interest you, write the information on a sheet of paper. Look for those magazines and newspapers in the periodicals section of the library.

Try It

Look again at the *Readers' Guide* entries. In what magazine can you find an article about the Hindu-Muslim conflict in India? What is the title of the article? Who wrote it?

Apply It

Think about a holiday or tradition that is part of your ethnic background. Use the *Readers' Guide* to make a list of articles about this topic.

1. Title
2. Cross-References
3. Subject heading
4. Author
5. Illustrations, portraits, maps
6. Periodicals, volume, page numbers, date

INDIA ❶

See also ❷

Americans—India
Bhopal poisonous gas disaster, India, 1984
Calcutta (India)
Environmental policy—India
Grand Trunk Road (India and Pakistan)
Ladakh (India)
Motion pictures—India
Public welfare—India
Securities—India
Wildlife conservation—India
Women—India

Commerce

Russia (Republic)

❸ Russian sale of rocket engine to India [statement, May 11, 1992] R. Boucher. *US Department of State Dispatch* 3:386 My 18 '92

Economic policy

India after the Gandhis. *The Wilson Quarterly* 16:7–8 Spr '92

Foreign relations

India after nonalignment. R. C. Thakur. ❹ bibl f *Foreign Affairs* 71:165–82 Spr '92

United States

See United States—Foreign relations—India

History

British occupation, 1765–1947—Historiography

Marxism and modern India. D. Chakrabarty. ❺ il *History Today* 42:48–51 Mr '92

Nationalism

Marxism and modern India. D. Chakrabarty. il *History Today* 42:48–51 Mr '92

Storm over India [Hindu-Muslim conflict] E. W. Desmond. il (*The New York Review of Books* 39:37–40 My 14 '92) ❻

328

Objective

Identify elements of an entry to the *Readers' Guide to Periodical Literature* and use the *Readers' Guide* to make a list of entries for a given topic. (Study Skills 1; Critical Thinking 1, 2)

Answers to Try It

The New York Review of Books; "Storm over India" by E. W. Desmond.

Answers to Apply It

Holidays and traditions will vary. Check to be sure that students are using the *Readers' Guide* correctly. You may consider taking students to the library to ensure they know how to find the materials once they have identified them in the *Readers' Guide.*

250
600
950
1300
1650
1947
TODAY

L E S S O N 3

Modern India

The monsoon rains were late. In the cities, air conditioners hissed to a halt. Movie houses were limited to one showing a day. Neon signs were turned off, and factories were silenced. In the countryside temperatures rose to more than 110°F, and several people collapsed and died from the heat. Only the arrival of a healthy monsoon could bring relief.

In India the monsoon rains are of great concern, and not only to India's millions of farmers. India's engineers and politicians also worry about them. A good deal of India's electricity is made by water power. If the rains do not come, the cities may lose lights and power. When this happens, India's politicians know they will be blamed for the country's problems. It will be a bad year for those holding elected office.

THINKING FOCUS

How has India progressed since independence ?

Key Term

- subcontinent

India's Geography

Monsoons are only one part of India's fascinating geography. (For more on monsoons, see A Closer Look on page 330.) India has everything from snow-capped mountains to burning desert sands. It also has tropical rain forests and wide river plains that make an ideal place for people to settle. India is truly a country of many different environments.

A World Apart

In the north, two jagged mountain ranges separate India from the rest of the Asian continent. In the south the Indian Ocean and the Arabian Sea separate it. Because the mountain ranges and oceans form natural barriers around India, geographers call India a subcontinent. A **subcontinent** is a large landmass

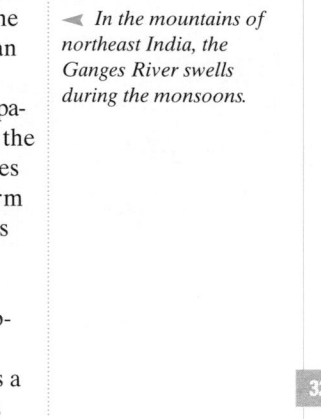

◄ *In the mountains of northeast India, the Ganges River swells during the monsoons.*

INTRODUCE

Have students read the title of the lesson and the Thinking Focus. Then ask them to predict what challenges India faced as it built a new nation. *(Establishing a new government; rebuilding a weak economy; settling the tension between Hindus and Muslims)* Tell students to compare their predictions with the text as they read the lesson.

Key Term

Vocabulary Strategies: T36–T37

subcontinent—a large landmass that is somewhat separate yet still part of a continent

Graphic Overview

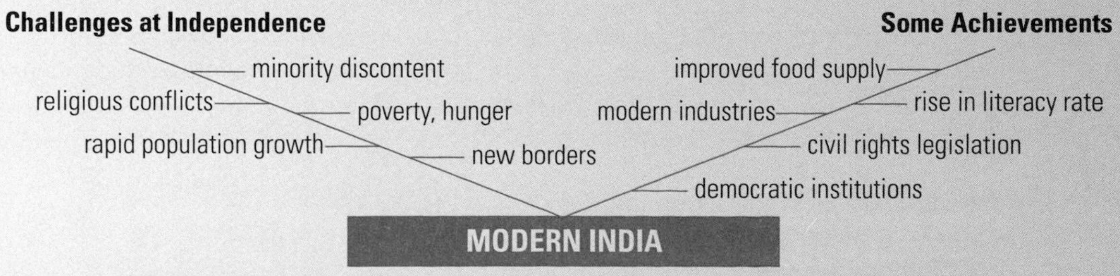
Challenges at Independence
minority discontent
religious conflicts
poverty, hunger
rapid population growth
new borders
Some Achievements
improved food supply
rise in literacy rate
modern industries
civil rights legislation
democratic institutions
MODERN INDIA

Objectives

1. Describe the geographic features that have an impact on Indian life today.
2. Identify some of the ways that multiculturalism plays itself out in modern India.
3. Explain the progress India has made since independence.

Note: You may wish to use this A Closer Look as an extension to the discussion of India's geography beginning on page 329.

More About Monsoons The word *monsoon* comes from the Arabic word meaning "season." Monsoons are often confused with storms such as typhoons. While they bring seriously dangerous rains that strike with near-hurricane force, monsoons are not a single storm, but a rainy season.

Monsoon winds are part of a global system of heat transfer that keeps the earth habitable. Without the monsoons to cause the movement of air and moisture, climate patterns and weather conditions in Asia would be more harsh.

A CLOSER LOOK

Monsoons

May to September is summer monsoon season in India. Strong monsoon winds carry rain to a parched, hot land. When the first rains fall, people celebrate! They will have water to drink, and their crops will survive. Yet the sudden changes in weather can be dangerous. People must look out for mudslides, broken dams, and fierce swirling windstorms called cyclones.

Before the monsoon, dry winds blow dust and grit across the plains. If the monsoon comes late, crops and animals may die in the sweltering heat.

Once it rains, farmers hurry to plant in the wet soil. Fields that were brown and barren become lush with plentiful crops.

Wading through flooded streets or even flooded houses and offices, city people are also joyful for the life-giving rains.

Visual Learning

The bottom photograph shows how India's cities look during monsoon season. Have students research the rainfall in India and in your area in a year by looking in an almanac. How is your area affected by too much or too little rainfall in one year? Ask students to make a bar graph to compare the average rainfall in India with that in your area in a year.

Writing a Journal Entry

Tell students to imagine that they live in India. Using information from A Closer Look and their outside research (if possible), direct students to write two journal entries describing life before and during the monsoon season. Tell students to make their journals as descriptive as possible. For example, you might ask students: How does your home look before the rain? What does the rain sound like? What does the scorching heat feel like on your skin? Students should also write about how the heat and the rain affect their imagined lives, the lives of their families, and the members of their community. You may also want to encourage students to illustrate their journal entries.

The Indian Subcontinent: Physical

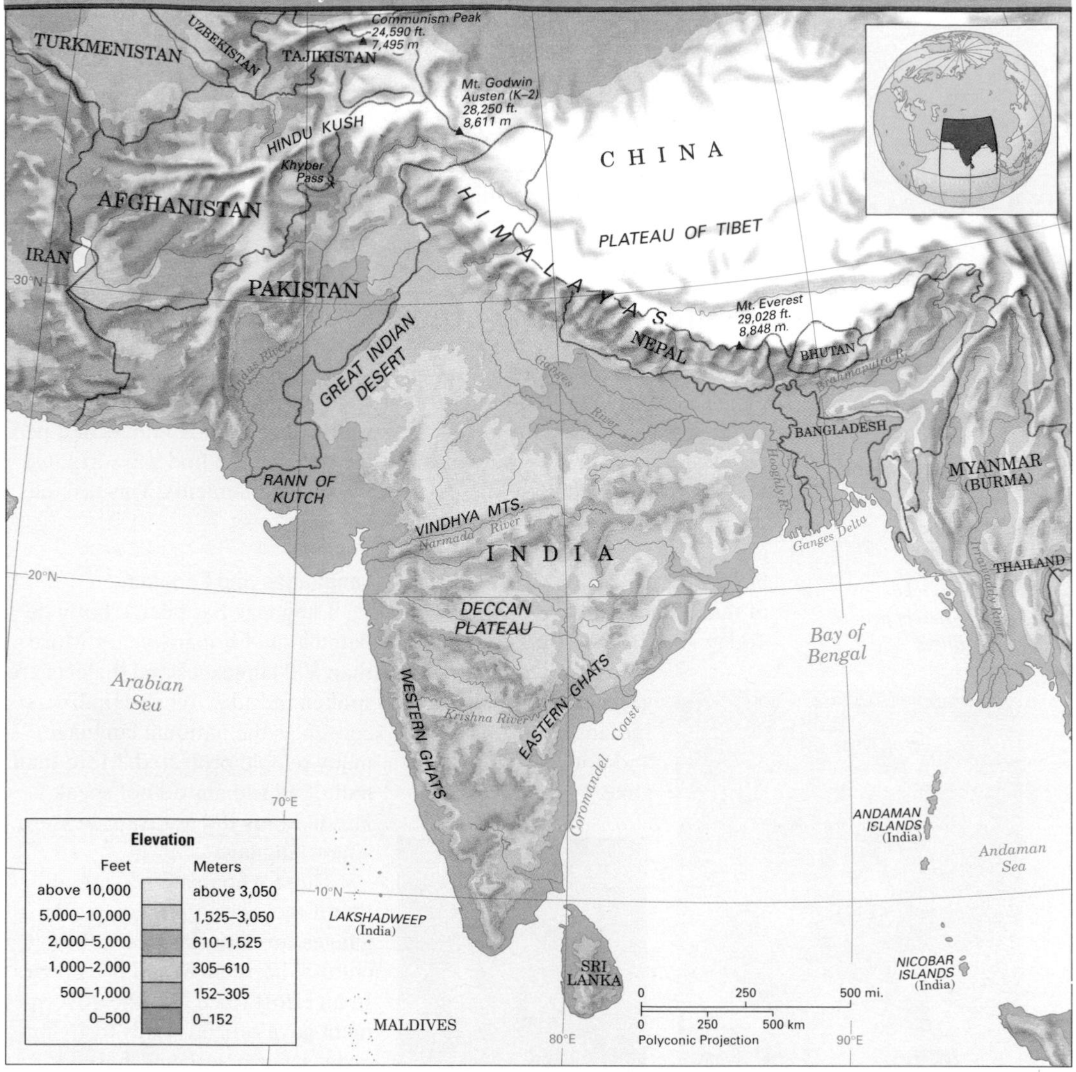

TURKMENISTAN
UZBEKISTAN
TAJIKISTAN
Communism Peak 24,590 ft. 7,495 m
Mt. Godwin Austen (K-2) 28,250 ft. 8,611 m
HINDU KUSH
Khyber Pass
CHINA
AFGHANISTAN
IRAN
30°N
PLATEAU OF TIBET
HIMALAYAS
PAKISTAN
Mt. Everest 29,028 ft. 8,848 m
NEPAL
BHUTAN
GREAT INDIAN DESERT
Indus River
Ganges River
Brahmaputra R.
BANGLADESH
Hooghly R.
RANN OF KUTCH
MYANMAR (BURMA)
VINDHYA MTS.
Narmada River
Ganges Delta
INDIA
THAILAND
20°N
DECCAN PLATEAU
Irrawaddy River
Bay of Bengal
Arabian Sea
WESTERN GHATS
EASTERN GHATS
Krishna River
Coromandel Coast
70°E
ANDAMAN ISLANDS (India)
Andaman Sea
Elevation
Feet
Meters
above 10,000
above 3,050
5,000–10,000
1,525–3,050
2,000–5,000
610–1,525
1,000–2,000
305–610
500–1,000
152–305
0–500
0–152
10°N
LAKSHADWEEP (India)
SRI LANKA
NICOBAR ISLANDS (India)
0
250
500 mi.
0
250
500 km
Polyconic Projection
MALDIVES
80°E
90°E

that is somewhat separate yet still part of a continent.

Find the Himalayas and the Hindu Kush mountains on the map above. What is their elevation? (See the Map and Globe Handbook on page G9 if you need help on how to read physical maps.)

During India's long history, people from all over Asia and Europe have settled in India. Because of its geography, these people are said to have formed a world unto themselves.

New Borders

After independence new maps of India had to be drawn. Important parts of what was once considered India were now gone. These parts became the nations of Pakistan and later Bangladesh.

These changes made many Indians unhappy. Much of the Indus

▲ *Look at the physical map of India. Using the elevation legend, describe northern and southern India. If you were a farmer, where in India would you settle?*

331

DEVELOP

Draw the Graphic Overview on the chalkboard or project it on a screen using an overhead projector. Point out that this lesson will discuss the challenges facing India at independence and India's progress since independence. Ask students to speculate which of India's continuing challenges they think will be most difficult to overcome. *(Population pressure; religious conflicts; food supply)*

◄ *Students might answer that the Indus and Ganges river valleys would support farming.*

NATIONAL IDENTITY

Map and Globe Skills

Following the breakup of colonial India, these countries became independent nations: India and West and East Pakistan (later to divide into Pakistan and Bangladesh). Have students locate each of these countries on the map on this page. Ask why they think many Indians were upset that much of the Indus River Valley—the birthplace of Hinduism and Indian civilization—was in Pakistan instead of India. *(Indians felt that they were losing part of their national history.)*

Access Strategy

Bring to class objects related to national, geographic, religious, and ethnic or family identity. *(You might include a passport, a driver's license, a local newspaper, skis, a copy of the Bible, old family photos, and ethnic foods.)* Ask students to help you classify the objects. *(Classifications may include English as a national language, farming as a local industry, Judaism, Christianity, or other religious beliefs, tacos and pizzas as ethnic foods, and so on.)*

Ask volunteers to share things they do that show their national, religious, or ethnic identity. Point out that in this lesson students will learn how the Indian government is tackling the challenges of group identity along with many other challenges.

Access Activity

To connect the points made in the Access Strategy, have students study the map and chart on page 333. Suggest that students form groups representing the religions of India in the same percentages as shown in the pie chart. Indicate that problems could arise between people of different religions. Have them suggest ways in which cooperation might be achieved.

■ *Pakistan and Bangladesh were carved out of areas once considered part of India, and the remainder of India was divided into states.*

BELIEF SYSTEMS

Visual Learning

Have students look at the photograph of the Sikh priest on this page (top left). Point out that the Sikhs, who follow a blend of Hindu and Muslim beliefs, worship no idols or divine images. Their most sacred object is the book containing the divine scriptures of the Sikh gurus. *Guru* means "divine teacher," and the sacred book was compiled and preserved by the fifth guru of the Sikh believers in the 16th century. According to the Sikh religion, "There is no Hindu, there is no Muslim. There is only One Being who is the Creator. God is One." Ask students to hypothesize why Sikhs are often at odds with other groups in India. *(Possible response: Sikhs owe loyalty to neither Hindus nor Muslims; they want their own country.)*

■ *How did the map of India change after independence?*

River Valley region was now a part of Pakistan.

The leaders of India, however, agreed to the new borders. They felt that it was time to begin building a new nation. Still, conflict between India and Pakistan continued. In some territories they could not agree on who should have control. Sometimes, this led to war.

Indian leaders decided to divide India into states. When the new map was drawn, it showed 25 states and 7 territories. For the first time in its history, India was governed by a central Indian government. ■

A Multicultural Nation

India is a blend of the different people who have settled there over the centuries. Some came as invaders. Others came to trade or to search for a new home.

Each group brought the language, religion, and customs of its homeland. Over time, the majority of these people became Hindus. Today, sharing the Hindu religion helps Indians live together in peace. Yet all Indians are not Hindus, and not all Hindus are alike.

People of different cultural backgrounds don't always get along well. All of India's leaders and people have had to find ways to solve these disagreements. This task has not been easy.

Languages and Peoples

Language has been a hotly debated issue for many years. More than 800 languages and dialects are spoken in India. When Hindi was chosen as the national language, many people protested. More than half of all Indians do not speak Hindi. Many did not want to learn a new language.

Those who protested argued that if they gave up their own languages, an important part of their cultural heritage would disappear. In an effort to be fair, the government gave official status to 15 languages. For now, English is considered an additional official language. It is used a great deal in government and business.

▼ *India is a land of many different peoples and cultures.*

Critical Thinking

Remind students that, besides the 15 official languages, there are more than 800 other languages and dialects spoken in India. Add that English is used in India's Supreme Court and High courts. Ask students why that might cause problems for some people in India. *(Many groups speak their own languages and may not have equal access to government resources.)*

Collaborative Activity

Divide the class into groups. Tell the groups that they will be responsible for making additions to a class bulletin board display entitled India Today. Group members should first collect articles from newsmagazines, newspapers, and summaries of television news reports about events in India. Then the group members together should evaluate all their information and decide which news items should be added to the display. Each news item should be accompanied by a short summary written by team members. Strong visual learners could be responsible for adding photographs and other illustrations to the display.

Once the display is completed, the groups might come together to stage an India Today news broadcast that features the stories on the bulletin board. One group can choose stories, another can decide on anchor people and other issues related to presentation, and so on. You may want to videotape the broadcast.

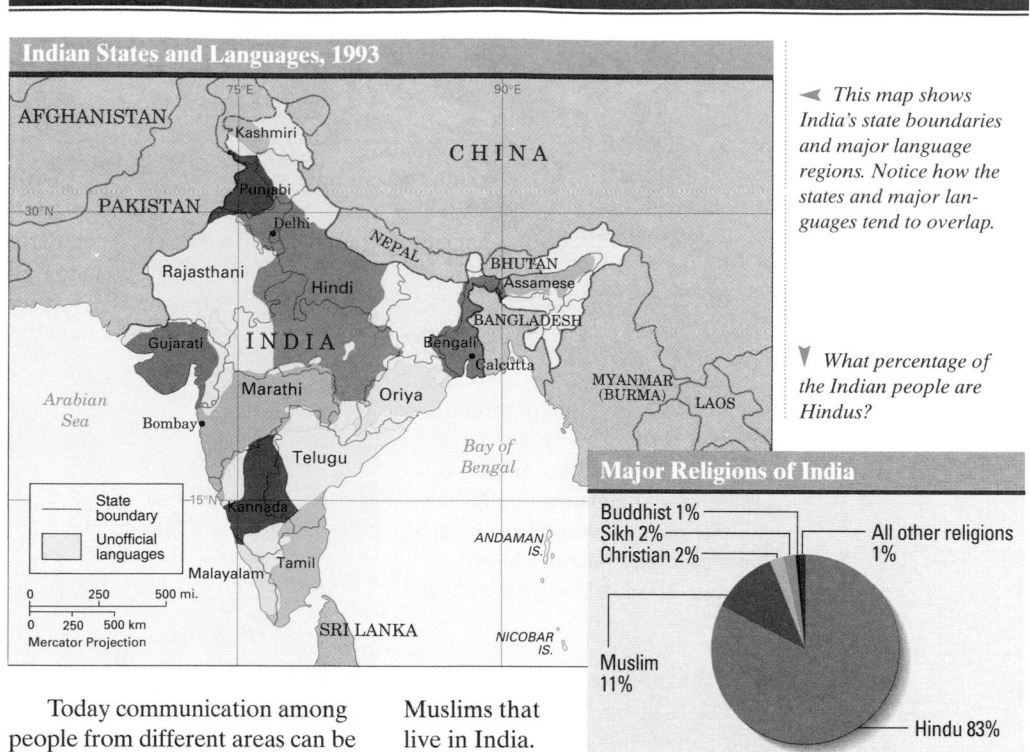

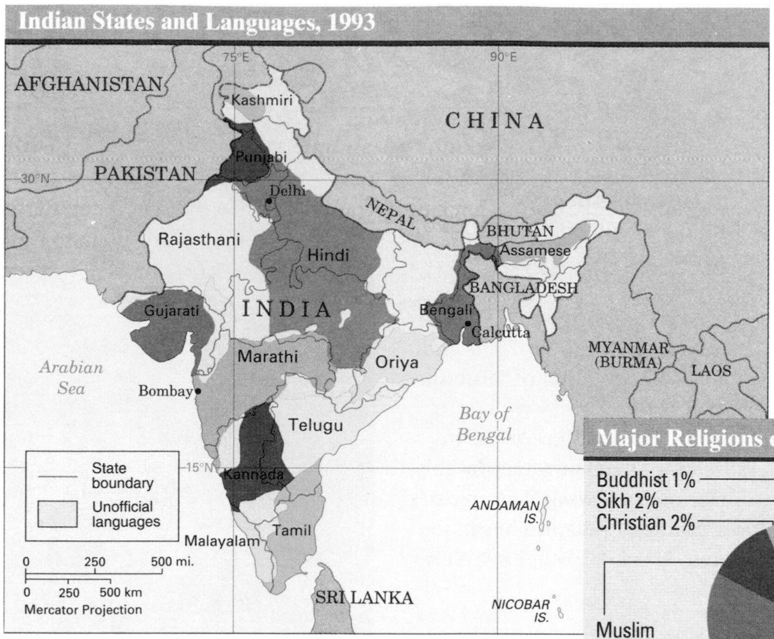
Indian States and Languages, 1993
AFGHANISTAN
PAKISTAN
CHINA
NEPAL
BHUTAN
BANGLADESH
MYANMAR (BURMA)
LAOS
INDIA
SRI LANKA
Kashmiri
Punjabi
Delhi
Rajasthani
Hindi
Assamese
Gujarati
Bengali
Calcutta
Marathi
Oriya
Bombay
Telugu
Kannada
Tamil
Malayalam
Arabian Sea
Bay of Bengal
ANDAMAN IS.
NICOBAR IS.
75°E
90°E
30°N
15°N
State boundary
Unofficial languages
0 250 500 mi.
0 250 500 km
Mercator Projection

◄ *This map shows India's state boundaries and major language regions. Notice how the states and major languages tend to overlap.*

◄ *According to the pie chart, 83 percent of the Indian people are Hindus.*

▼ *What percentage of the Indian people are Hindus?*

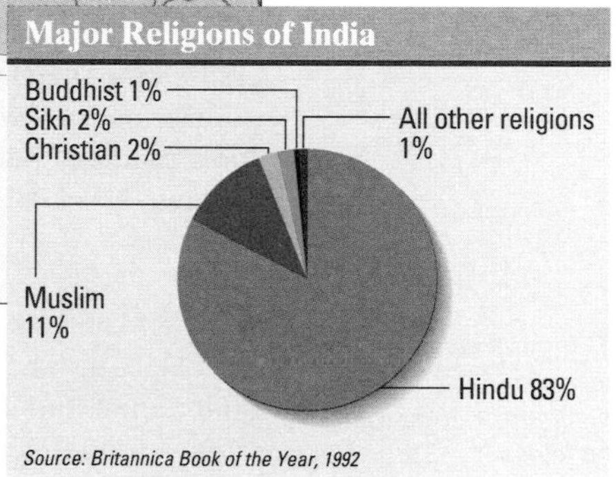
Major Religions of India
Buddhist 1%
Sikh 2%
Christian 2%
All other religions 1%
Muslim 11%
Hindu 83%
Source: Britannica Book of the Year, 1992

Today communication among people from different areas can be difficult. It can also be difficult for the government. India has so many peoples and so many languages that governing it is more like governing the United Nations than a country.

Look at the map at the top of the page. Find where the majority of Hindi-speaking people live.

Religious Differences

After independence many Muslims stayed in India rather than moving to Pakistan. Look at the graph of India's major religions at the right. Notice the percentage of Muslims that live in India. This percentage totals more than 95 million people. Many live in the area where the Mughal Empire first began.

The bitter feelings between Hindus and Muslims can still be felt in India. In the north, fighting sometimes breaks out between the two groups. Muslims say that the Hindu majority discriminates against them in business and government. Like other minority groups in India, they also fear they will lose their culture. ■

■ *What are some of India's cultural challenges?*

■ *Some of India's most noticeable cultural challenges are language diversity and friction between Hindus and Muslims.*

Social Progress

As a new nation, India faced many serious problems. Hunger and disease were common, its people were poorly educated, and the future looked difficult. Since 1947 India has worked hard to make a better life for all of its people. Its leaders have struggled to end the grim poverty under which millions live. Programs have been started to improve the economy, health care, and education.

NATIONAL IDENTITY

Critical Thinking

Although Hindi is one of the official languages of India, only a minority of the people understand it. Point out to students that there are 15 languages printed on India's currency called the rupee.

Ask students how the rupee does or does not reflect the national identity of India. You may want to lead a discussion about having more than one official language in a multicultural nation. What are the advantages? What are the disadvantages? *(Possible responses: advantages—respect is shown for ethnic differences; disadvantages—many people may feel out of the mainstream if theirs is not one of the national languages; communication may be difficult.)*

Religious Context

Tensions between the Hindus and the Muslims in India are centuries old. According to Islamic doctine, "There is no god but God, and Muhammad is the messenger of God." The Hindus, however, believe in many Gods. Hindu temples with their towering gates and walls covered with naked Gods and Goddesses anger many Muslims. Likewise, many Hindus are outraged when Muslims slaughter cows—an animal they consider sacred.

In 1992, a fresh wave of Hindu-Muslim violence broke out in India when devout Hindus began to destroy a 430-year-old Muslim mosque that they believe is located on a Hindu shrine marking the birthplace of Rama, an important Hindu God. The destruction of the mosque prompted widespread violence in India and in neighboring Pakistan and Bangladesh. As many as 700 people died in the rioting.

Critical Thinking

Have students compare the challenges faced by modern India to those experienced by the nation of Mali, another former colony. (Chapter 12). How are they alike? How are they different? *(Alike—seasonal rains and droughts, many ethnic groups, many languages, democratic institutions; different—Mali is predominantly Muslim, India has a higher literacy rate.)*

CULTURE

Visual Learning

Refer students to the chart on this page showing literacy rates in India from 1951 to 1991. Remind them that, according to the chart, more males can read and write than females. Inform students that the literacy rates in 1951, 1961, and 1971 are for the population aged five years and above. The rates in 1981 and 1991 are for the population aged seven years and above. Ask students to suggest how the percentages given for 1981 and 1991 would differ if they were for the population five years and above. *(Possible answer: the percentages would be lower in these years, because usually fewer five- and six-year-olds can read and write than can seven-year-olds.)*

➤ *Students might guess that boys are given more opportunities for education in India.*

➤ *The modern city of Delhi is divided into Old Delhi and New Delhi. This is a photograph of Old Delhi. It is where most of the people live and work. New Delhi is the capital of India.*

A Growing Population

Life has gotten better in India, but its growing population makes progress difficult. Today nearly one-sixth of all the people in the world live in India. Between 1950 and 1990, India's population grew by about 490 million people. This is almost twice as many people as now live in the United States. In 1990 India's population was about 850 million. By the year 2000, India will have a population of more than 1 billion people.

Improved health care has increased the speed at which India's population is growing. The size of India's large population has made progress in solving other problems very slow.

In rural areas such as this, school may be held outdoors or in very simple buildings.

A Higher Living Standard

The British left India a very poor nation. It did not produce enough food to feed all its people, and it had few industries. Also, in general, the Indian people were poorly educated.

Education in India has improved. Look at the line graph below. Literacy is the ability to read and write. The improving literacy rate gives you a good idea of how much education has improved in India. What percentage of boys could read in 1991?

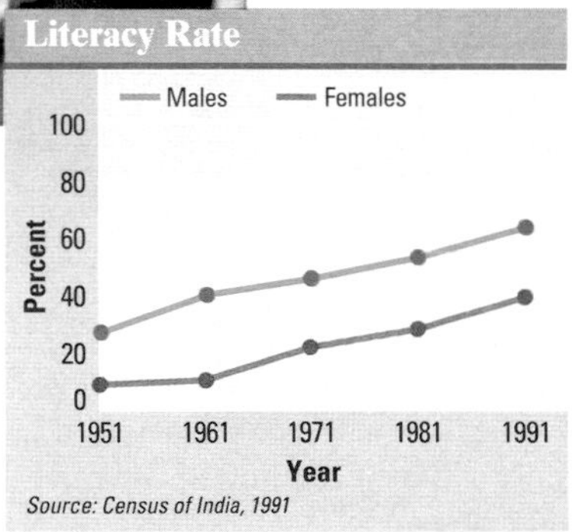
Literacy Rate
Males
Females
100
80
60
40
20
0
Percent
1951
1961
1971
1981
1991
Year
Source: Census of India, 1991

➤ *This graph shows two literacy rates, one for boys and one for girls. Why do you think more boys can read and write than girls?*

To help grow more food, farmers began to use better methods of irrigation and more fertilizers. Indian farmers now grow enough food to hold off famine even when the monsoons fail.

India's industries also have grown. In the villages carpets are made by hand for sale all over the world. Around the cities, factories now produce goods such as appliances and cars.

India has slowly moved forward in the areas of agriculture, industry, and education. Yet there still is much to be done to end poverty.

Map and Globe Skills

Have students locate India's major cities—Bombay, Calcutta, and Delhi, for example—on the map of India on page 333 or in the Atlas on page 682. Tell students to find the population figures for each of these cities and have them discuss why these cities are where they are. Suggest they use a world almanac or similar reference materials.

Science Connection

India's first prime minister, Jawaharlal Nehru, began a series of five-year plans to increase India's agricultural output. After a promising start, disappointing harvests that were the result of monsoons damaged Nehru's plans to free India from its burden of importing food to feed its people.

New ways to boost crop yields were introduced into India and many other developing countries in the 1960s. A worldwide effort, known as the Green Revolution, was launched to increase food production, using new varieties of corn, rice, and wheat. Have students prepare oral reports on the Green Revolution in India in the 1960s. In their reports students should answer questions such as: Why was it called a "revolution?" What nations were involved in the Green Revolution? What was the result of the Green Revolution in India?

Equality for All

One notable feature of the Indian constitution is its goal of full equality for all people. Following in the footsteps of Gandhi, the Indian constitution rejects the caste system and bans laws against untouchables, now called Scheduled Castes.

The constitution requires universities to admit them as students. It also tries to change basic Hindu and Muslim traditions by giving women equal rights with men. It gives women the right to own property. Today Indian women and Scheduled Castes are legally free to pursue careers in government, education, and medicine. In their daily lives, however, equality is still a long way off.

India Today

In India today the old and the new exist side by side. In many villages, there are few modern conveniences. Some houses have electricity, but women still carry water to their homes from wells.

In other villages change is slow, but it is noticeable. It is not unusual to hear the news blaring from a radio or to see a tractor plowing a field. Even the caste system faces challenges from the government and women's groups.

As people move to the cities, modern ways often replace old traditions. In India's crowded cities, office buildings share the sky with ancient temples. Flashy billboards advertise new movies. Men and women in suits and jeans walk side by side with people in traditional clothing. People of different castes and religions mix together.

Modern India is a nation of many people and cultures. With all of its struggles, it moves ahead as the world's largest democracy. ■

MRF-MANSFIELD
BELMONDO
HOUSE FULL!
GOOD NEWS
INDU's achieved 100% capacity utilisation
INDU IS FILM
ABIRAMI
FEAR CITY
NO ENTRY

▼ *Along with the United States and Japan, India is one of the world's largest film producers.*

■ *How has life in India improved?*

CONSTITUTIONAL HERITAGE

Critical Thinking

India is a democratic country. Its constitution is based in large part on the British government system and the U.S. constitution. Ask students to define the word *democracy. (Government by the people)* Ask students to think about India's democratic government in relation to its caste system. Can India have a true democracy while people continue to adhere to the caste system? Why or why not? *(Possible answer: India cannot have a true democracy while people continue to believe that certain groups are born unequal.)*

■ *India has increased its food and industrial production, improved health and education, and attempted to extend equality to all of its citizens, including women and untouchables.*

REVIEW

1. **FOCUS** How has India progressed since independence?
2. **GEOGRAPHY** Describe some of India's different landforms and climates.
3. **SOCIAL SYSTEMS** Why did Indians disagree over their national language?
4. **CRITICAL THINKING** Like India, the United States is also a multicultural nation. How are the United States and India similar, and how are they different?
5. **ACTIVITY** If you could visit India, where would you like to go? Draw a map of India, and mark the places you would like to visit. Tell why you would like to visit these places.

CLOSE

Read the Thinking Focus aloud. To answer the question, ask students to brainstorm ideas for articles that might be put into a magazine called *Indian Progress Report.* Write the ideas on the chalkboard. Have students evaluate ideas and create a final list of articles for the magazine.

Answers to Review Questions

1. Since independence India has improved the quality of life of its people. However, its large and rapidly growing population has made progress slow and expensive. Also, India faces many challenges in uniting its vast and diverse peoples.
2. India's environments range from snow-capped mountains to desert sands. It also has tropical rain forests and wide rivers.
3. More than half of all Indians do not speak Hindi, and many people protested when it was chosen as the national language. Also, language is an integral part of cultural heritage, and people are often reluctant to give up their own language.
4. Indians have not assimilated into a common culture as much as people have in the United States. However, in both countries, people take pride in their cultural heritages.
5. Answers will vary. Students may mention the Khyber Pass, New Delhi, Kashmir, or any number of places.

Homework Options

Imagine you are a representative at an Indian government meeting on agriculture. Name one challenge regarding agriculture facing India today and propose ways the government can meet that challenge.

Study Guide: page 58

Chapter Review

Reviewing Key Terms

civil disobedience (p. 326)
epic (p. 319)
imperialism (p. 325)
Mughal (p. 323)
subcontinent (p. 329)

A. Write whether each of the following statements is *true* or *false.* Then rewrite the false statements to make them true.

1. Information about the Hindu religion can be found in long poems called epics.
2. The Mughals spread the Buddhist religion in India.
3. Under imperialism, Britain allowed India to govern itself.
4. Civil disobedience means refusing to obey laws that you believe are unfair.
5. India is called a subcontinent because it has a hot climate.

B. Write two sentences for each of the words below. Your sentences should show how each word applies to the Hindu religion or to India.

1. epic
2. Mughal
3. imperialism
4. civil disobedience
5. subcontinent

Exploring Concepts

A. Use the chart below to help you summarize the influence of the Gupta, Mughal, and British empires on the history of India. Copy the chart and fill it in with two facts from the chapter about each empire's influence.

Empires	Influences on India
Gupta	There were advances in astronomy, mathematics, and medicine. They include the following: knowledge that the earth rotates on its axis, plastic surgery,and the development of a number system.
Mughal	
British	

B. Support each of the following statements with information from the chapter.

1. Many scientific advancements were made in India during the Gupta period.
2. Most Hindu people still follow a rigid social order.
3. Hindus and Muslims have different religious beliefs.
4. For Great Britain, India was "the Jewel in the Crown."
5. In leading the fight for India's independence from Britain, Mohandas Gandhi used nonviolent methods.
6. India faced many challenges after it had gained independence in 1947.
7. India is a land of many different environments.
8. Language is a hotly debated issue in India.
9. The size of India's population is a matter of concern.
10. One goal of the Indian government is to bring equality to all of India's people.
11. In India today the old and the new exist side by side.

Answers to Reviewing Key Terms

A. Sample answers:

1. True.
2. False. The **Mughals** spread the Muslim religion in India.
3. False. Under **imperialism,** one nation has control of another, which is a colony.
4. True.
5. False. Because it is a large landmass that is somewhat separate from the continent of Asia, India is called a **subcontinent**.

B. Sample answers:

1. You can learn about Hinduism by studying **epic** poems. During the Gupta period the **epics** were written in Sanskrit.
2. During the **Mughal** period, India became one of the world's leading cultural centers. When the **Mughal** Empire had weakened, European nations began to invade India by sea.
3. Through **imperialism,** India became a colony of Great Britain. British **imperialism** hurt the Indian economy.
4. The Indian people used many tactics, including **civil disobedience,** to drive the British out. Gandhi was the recognized leader of the **civil disobedience** movement in India.
5. Two large mountain ranges and two large bodies of water separate India from Asia, making India a **subcontinent.** Because of its **subcontinent** geography, India is said to be a world unto itself.

Answers to Exploring Concepts

A. Sample answers:

Mughal: Islam spread; advances in arts, music, and architecture.

British: improvements in transportation and communication; groundwork for independence.

B. Sample answers:

1. Advances included the knowledge that the earth rotated on its axis, an understanding of cleanliness in stopping the spread of disease, and the development of a number system.
2. The Hindu people still follow the caste system. Most are born into their caste and marry within it.
3. Muslims believe in one God, while the Hindus believe in many Gods.
4. India was Great Britain's most valuable colony, enabling Britain to earn huge profits.
5. Instead of using violence, Gandhi urged Indians not to buy British goods or to pay taxes. He also staged hunger strikes to pressure the British.
6. India had to deal with border disputes, tension between Hindus and Muslims, a struggling economy, and a large number of uneducated citizens.
7. The Indian land includes mountain ranges, deserts, and rain forests.
8. More than 800 languages and dialects are spoken in India. Less than 50 percent of the Indian people speak Hindi, India's first official language.
9. India will probably have a population of more than one billion people by the year 2000 and continue to slow economic progress.
10. The Indian constitution has given full rights to women and untouchables.
11. Examples include ancient villages with radios or tractors, and cities of modern office buildings and ancient temples.

Reviewing Skills

1. Imagine you are writing a report about the challenges facing modern India. Would you try to find books about India in the *Readers' Guide to Periodical Literature*? Explain your answer.
2. Review the *Readers' Guide* material on page 328. Write the name of the cross reference that would give you more information on India's movie industry.
3. Use the information in Lesson 2 to complete this flow chart, entitled "The Road to India's Independence." The flow chart starts with Queen Victoria's being crowned empress of India in 1877 and ends with India's independence in 1947. Copy the flow chart onto a separate sheet of paper. List the important events that occurred between these two dates. Make sure that you list the events in the order in which they happened.

Queen Victoria crowned empress ➡ [ ] ➡ [ ] ➡ [ ] ➡ [ ] ➡ [ ] ➡ India gains Independence

Using Critical Thinking

1. The Gupta Empire, India's Golden Age, was a time of great advancement. Think about the term *golden age*. What characterizes a society during a golden age? Do you think that future historians will use that term to describe the United States today? Why or why not? Give reasons for your answer.
2. Some Mughal leaders encouraged religious tolerance during their rule in India. Other Mughal rulers did not. How did religious freedom benefit Mughal rule? What happened when religious freedom was denied?
3. Mohandas Gandhi once wrote, "No people exists that would not think itself happier under its own bad government than it might really be under the good government of an alien [foreign] power." In this statement does Gandhi support or reject imperialism? Explain your answer.
4. Why would teaching people to read and write be a basic goal of a government trying to improve the standard of living of its citizens?

Preparing for Citizenship

1. **COLLABORATIVE LEARNING** Both India and the United States fought British rule and became independent nations. As a class, compare and contrast India's and the United States' fight for freedom. Divide into small groups. Each group should research a different topic, gathering information on both India and the United States. Some possible topics include (a) the feelings of the colonists toward independence, (b) tactics used by the colonists to gain support for their cause, (c) important Indian and U.S. leaders, (d) important British leaders, and (e) events that led to independence. Be sure to look at the maps in the Atlas to locate where the United States and India are in relation to Great Britain. You may also want to collect quotes and writings from the time. As a class, put the information together in a bulletin-board display entitled "Fighting for Freedom."
2. **WRITING ACTIVITY** Mohandas Gandhi believed in *satyagraha*. *Satya* is a Sanskrit word meaning "truth," and *agraha* means "force." *Satyagraha* can therefore be roughly translated as "truth weapon." In what ways can ordinary citizens use truth as a "weapon" to change government policy?

Answers to Reviewing Skills
Sample answers:
1. No. Only magazine articles are listed in the *Readers' Guide.*
2. Motion pictures—India.
3. Queen Victoria crowned empress; Indians begin to resent British imperial policies that weaken India's economy and discriminate against Indians; Angry Indians begin to organize and pressure is put on the British; Gandhi begins to lead the people in nonviolent rebellion; Indians are killed in the uprising at Amritsar; Millions of Indians join the independence movement; India gains independence.

Answers to Using Critical Thinking
Sample answers:
1. Be sure that students create their own definitions of a golden age—a historical period noted for its achievements. Check that students have supported their opinions with specific facts and examples.
2. For the most part, India lived in peace with its Mughal rulers when they followed policies that fostered religious tolerance. When Hindus were forced to convert to Islam under Aurangzeb, it led to rebellions against Mughal rule.
3. Gandhi rejects imperialism. He thinks that people would rather be free, no matter what the consequences, than be ruled by outsiders.
4. For a nation to improve its standard of living, it must create jobs and modernize its economy. In order to do this, it needs an educated work force. Also, if people can read and write, they can learn more about the world around them and become more aware of social problems.

Answers to Preparing for Citizenship
Sample answers:
1. **COLLABORATIVE LEARNING** Students should report that both countries used nonviolent tactics such as boycotts and civil disobedience. They should also describe how the desire for independence led to violence, in varying degrees, in both countries. Encourage students to find and share writings of these times, including those of Thomas Paine, Mohandas Gandhi, and Jawaharal Nehru.
2. **WRITING ACTIVITY** Students' answers should reflect the idea that people can use their ideas and nonviolent actions as "truth weapons" to expose injustice or ignorance in the hope of changing policy. Actions include writing letters, lobbying government officials, and getting publicity for the cause.

CHAPTER ORGANIZER

Chapter 15 China

CHAPTER PLANNING CHART

Pupil's Edition	Teacher's Edition	Ancillaries
Lesson 1: Mandate of Heaven (1–2 days) Objective 1: Explain the traditional relationship between China's rulers and its people. (Social and Political Systems 2, 4) Objective 2: Explain some factors that contributed to Mao Zedong's rise to power. (History 5, 6; Economics 1; Social and Political Systems 3, 5) Objective 3: Describe the changes that occurred in China after Mao came to power. (Culture 1, 4, 5, 6; Social and Political Systems 3, 5, 6)	• Graphic Overview (340) • Access Strategy (341) • Access Activity (341) Study Skills (342) Political Context (342) Research (343) • Visual Learning (343) Study Skills (344) Historical Context (344) Critical Thinking (345) Social Participation (345)	Study Guide (59) Map Activities (19) Discovery Journal (30, 31)
Lesson 2: China after Mao (2–3 days) Objective 1: Explain the policies of the Communist government in China today. (Social and Political Systems 1, 3, 5) Objective 2: Explain the problems that face China's Communist government in today's world. (Social and Political Systems 6) Objective 3: Explain political protest in China and the government's response. (Social and Political Systems 3, 6)	• Graphic Overview (347) • Access Activity (348) • Access Strategy (348) Cultural Context (349) • Visual Learning (349)	Study Guide (60)
Lesson 3: China Today (2–3 days) Objective 1: Compare urban and rural life in China. (Culture 4; Social and Political Systems 2) Objective 2: Discuss China's potential as a modern nation. (Economics 4, 5)	• Graphic Overview (351) • Access Activity (352) • Access Strategy (352) Economic Context (353) Geography Connection (353) Social Participation (353)	Study Guide (61) • Posters (3)
Understanding Written Reports Objective: Understand and apply the six basic steps for writing a social studies report. (Study Skills 1, 2, 3)		Study Guide (62)
Chapter Review	Answers (356–357)	Tests (57–60)

* Objectives are correlated to the strands and goals in the program Scope and Sequence on pages T41–T49.

• LEP appropriate resources. (For additional strategies, see pages T32–T33.)

CHAPTER RATIONALE

When the topic is China—one of the oldest continuous civilizations in the world—the challenge is to cover great sweeps of time using carefully selected episodes. Chapter 15 picks up where Chapter 5 left off and traces Chinese culture from A.D. 1200 to the present. To make the material manageable for teachers, we focus on themes of contrast and continuity in Chinese history. Since the country's dynastic history can't be covered in depth, this chapter focuses on the contrast between Chinese dynasties and foreign ones. The theme of continuity is explored in the relationship between the Chinese people and their rulers, from past to present.

Finally, the chapter takes a look at China's current economic and political problems. Within the context of contemporary China, students have a chance to view the nation firsthand—from the point of view of people living in the city and in the country today.

Lesson 1 explains the origin and influence of the Mandate of Heaven—the idea that an emperor's right to rule came from heaven. Within this context the lesson scans 800 years of China's history: from the Mongol invaders to the Ming renaissance to the Communist takeover. The lesson also provides a historical look at China's relationship with the West and an overview of its transformation under Mao Zedong.

Lesson 2 reviews some of the reforms and changes China has undergone since the time of Mao, including the gradual introduction of free enterprise, population control measures, and recent contacts with the West. The lesson also illustrates how reforms under Deng Xiaoping increased hopes for more freedom and led to the fledgling "democracy movement" that was crushed at Tiananmen Square.

Lesson 3 takes students inside the lives of two city workers and one farm family and explores life in the *danwei,* or work unit. In the process, students better understand change and continuity in China. Finally, the lesson considers the question: What direction will China's future take?

ACTIVITIES & PROJECTS

Basic: Research

Direct students' attention to the picture of the dragon on page 340. Ask what kinds of ideas and images the dragon symbolizes to them. Explain that the dragon is a legendary creature in many societies. It usually is depicted as a bat-winged, fire-breathing, scaly lizard or snake. Yet not all cultures thought of the dragon as a symbol of evil. Have students research the mythology of the dragon by using history and art books as well as encyclopedias. Ask students to share their findings, including any pictures, with the class. (Use after any lesson.)

LEP: Oral Presentation

Have each student talk to an adult about the past or present head of state that the person most respects. Encourage students to find out what specific qualities of that leader seem to command respect. Have students report their findings to the class. (Use after Lesson 2.)

Challenge: Critical Thinking

Provide students with the following key factors of a free enterprise system:

(1) Private ownership: Instead of being government-owned, most property and businesses are owned by individuals.

(2) Property rights: The government can't take away someone's property without paying for it.

(3) Nongovernmental decision making: Individuals rather than the state decide what goods to produce and how to produce them.

(4) Competition: Most products and services are offered by more than one company, so companies must compete for customers. Competition usually lowers prices, boosts quality, and allows only the best companies to survive.

Have students write a statement explaining whether or not the U.S. economy includes each of these factors. Encourage them to use examples. Then ask them to select one item and speculate how the economy might change if the factor were no longer in effect. (Use after Lesson 2.)

Writing Historical Fiction

Explain that the Chinese government is fighting a traditional bias in favor of male children. Then have students read about the lives of girls in early and contemporary China in the school or public library. Why did families of the past consider it a disadvantage to have daughters? How did this feeling affect girls' lives? Then have students write a one-page report in the form of a short biography of a fictitious Chinese girl in past or recent history. (Use after Lesson 3.)

CHAPTER PREVIEW

Ask students to read the chapter title and the first paragraph. Then ask them to describe how people might feel about an emperor they believe rules with the blessing of heaven. *(They might feel awe and reverence as well as fear of disobeying or questioning him.)* How might this ancient belief influence how modern Chinese feel about their rulers? *(It might encourage respect for strong rulers.)*

Looking Back

Prompt students to recall what they learned in Chapter 5 about the Mandate of Heaven. Point out that China was not the only culture in which rulers were thought to receive deific power. The pharaohs of ancient Egypt were also thought to have godlike powers.

Looking Forward

Tell students that they are going to read about how China has fared under a series of rulers and governments. The next three lessons include: Mandate of Heaven, China after Mao, and China Today.

Lesson 1 describes the history of China from the rise of the Mongol empire to the death of Mao Zedong.

Chapter 15
China

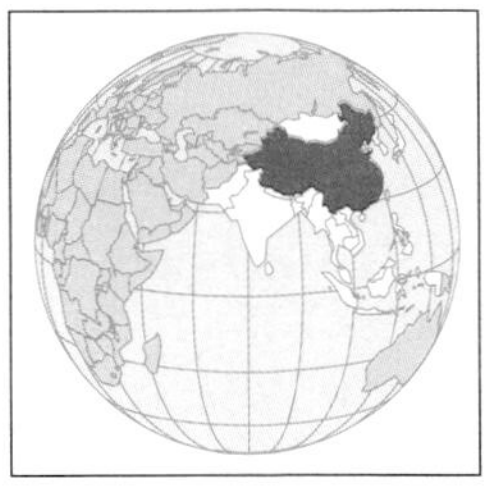

For thousands of years, powerful emperors ruled China. They thought their right to rule came from heaven. During the 20th century, however, China has undergone extraordinary changes. The Communist party came to power in 1949. It took over farms and industries, creating a new society. It changed many ancient traditions. Today China struggles to adapt to the modern world.

The Forbidden City, located in Beijing, includes the palaces where China's emperors once lived. Only members of the emperor's household and certain high officials were allowed to enter the Forbidden City without permission.

1000 | 1200 | 1400

1200

1280 Kublai Khan becomes the first Mongol ruler of China. Mongol rulers, like the emperor pictured above, are the first outsiders to control China.

1368 The Mongols are thrown from power. Under the Ming emperors, China makes advances in education and the arts.

BACKGROUND

Trade goods and trade routes shaped interaction among civilizations all over the world. One of China's most important trade products was silk, and the most important trade route from China to the West was the Silk Road, so named by a 19th-century historian.

The Silk Road

The Silk Road stretched over 4,000 miles from central China to the eastern shore of the Mediterranean Sea. From as early as 200 B.C., traders headed westward with silk, porcelain, and spices and eastward with wool, silver, and gold. People along the route profited by exporting local goods to foreign markets and by taxing goods that passed through their regions. During times of political instability in Asia or Southwest Asia, trade traffic shifted to alternative routes until security was restored.

Transmission of Ideas

The Silk Road was a conduit not only for trade goods but also for ideas. Chinese knowledge of sericulture, papermaking, printing, and gunpowder was probably carried to the West via the Silk Road. Buddhism, a belief system that attracted many Chinese after the fall of the Han Empire and during the Tang Dynasty, was introduced to China from India by missionaries who traveled the Silk Road.

Bicycles are an important form of transportation in China.

For centuries the Grand Canal has been a major Chinese transportation route.

These Chinese coins were made until 1912. A string could be threaded through the hole in the center to make carrying easier.

1949 Mao Zedong announces the victory of communism in China. The nation begins a period of sweeping change.

1600 | 1800 | 2000

1912 A new political party, the Nationalist Party, is established. The last Manchu emperor of China gives up his throne.

Today

Understanding the Visuals

Surrounded by a wall that is 2½ miles long and 35 feet high, the Forbidden City (page 338) is a mammoth complex of hundreds of buildings containing 9,000 rooms—enough to house the entire imperial household. The buildings were converted into museums in 1949, and some are open to the public.

The Grand Canal (shown on this page) is the oldest and longest artificial waterway in the world. It extends for about 1,000 miles, connecting the Chang and Huang rivers. Construction of the canal began in the 500s B.C. Today, many goods from northern China still travel south to Beijing via the canal.

Understanding Chronology

Have students look at the timeline. Ask them how many years the timeline covers. *(About 1,000 years)* Then ask them to figure out how long China has been ruled by the Communist party. *(More than 44 years)* Point out that before the coming of political parties, China was ruled by dynasties of emperors. Remind students that rule by dynasties had its roots in ancient China (Chapter 5).

Contact and Isolation

Mountains, deserts, and the Pacific Ocean isolated China from other cultures along most of its borders. In the north and west, the Chinese built the Great Wall to keep out invaders. Thus the Silk Road in the west and port cities on the southeastern coast were, for the most part, the only avenues of contact between the Chinese and foreign peoples. Rulers limited foreign influence on China by controlling trade traffic at these points. As a result, China experienced long periods of political and cultural isolation.

INTRODUCE

Point out the lesson title and explain that the word *mandate* means "an authoritative command or instruction." Then have students read the Thinking Focus. Ask how a belief in a ruler's mandate from heaven might both help and hinder a country's quest for peace and order. *(It might help because it would give the people great respect for the ruler's decisions and keep them from disagreeing; it would hinder if it caused a ruler to feel arrogant and therefore led him to abuse power.)* Then ask students to continue reading the lesson to find out how this belief has affected China.

Key Terms

Vocabulary Strategies: T36–T37

famine—a scarcity of food

communism—a political, economic, and social system in which the government owns and controls all property and business

A.D.
1000
1200
1976
2000

LESSON 1

Mandate of Heaven

THINKING FOCUS

How has the hope for peace and order guided the Chinese people and their rulers?

Key Terms

- famine
- communism

"The iniquity [evil] of the Shang is full. Heaven commands me to destroy it," declared King Wu, the first ruler of the Zhou *(joh)* dynasty (1122–256 B.C.).

According to that story, Wu described the evil ways of the Shang emperor, Di-xin *(dih shihn)*. Di-xin, he said, had wasted the empire's wealth on palaces, towers, ponds, and pavilions. He had not cared for the temples of his ancestors, nor had he protected the harvest. Di-xin had even "burned and roasted the loyal and good." Therefore, Wu and his followers threw out the Shangs and beheaded Di-xin.

To justify their rule, the Zhous began preaching a new idea. It was called the Mandate of Heaven. The king claimed that his power came from heaven. According to this idea, the king himself was the Son of Heaven.

According to the Mandate of Heaven, a ruler must be just and virtuous and live a moral life. He must also take care of the well-being of the people. If the ruler was not just, did not show proper concern for the people, or lived immorally, heaven would take away his right to rule.

The Mandate of Heaven continued to influence China long after the Zhous lost their power. Years of hunger or unrest might end an emperor's rule. To the people, such troubles showed that their ruler had lost the support of heaven. Without the support of heaven, a ruler had no right to rule. Thus, the people could stop obeying their emperor. They could revolt and take a new ruler, who would bring back peace and order.

The Chinese thinker Mengzi (or Mencius) taught this idea of the right to revolt. A well-known follower of Confucius, Mencius lived in the fourth century B.C.

➤ *The dragon was the symbol of the emperor's great power.*

Objectives

1. Explain the traditional relationship between China's rulers and its people.
2. Explain some factors that contributed to Mao Zedong's rise to power.
3. Describe the changes that occurred in China after Mao came to power.

Graphic Overview

Mongols transportation, trade expanded; Chinese ways rejected; famine, unrest → **Mings** peace, order; art, learning; canals expanded; more famine → **Manchus** Chinese ways adopted; empire expanded; Opium wars; revolution → **Communists** World War II; Great Leap Forward; Cultural Revolution

Mongol Invaders

As you learned in Chapter 5, the Chinese feared invaders entering from the north. For hundreds of years, the Great Wall had protected China from these outsiders. In the early 1200s, however, Mongols from central Asia came around the wall. They burned and looted villages. In 1206, their leader was declared the Genghis Khan *(JEHNG gihs kahn)*, or "Universal Ruler." For the first time, an outsider would control parts of China.

Kublai Khan's Rule

Kublai Khan *(KOO bly kahn)*, a grandson of Genghis Khan, started the Yuan dynasty in 1271. A capable ruler, he rebuilt parts of northern China and repaired the Grand Canal. This transportation route, built in the early 600s, unified China. It connected rivers in the north and south. Each year the canal carried millions of tons of grain.

Trade grew under Kublai's rule. Yak and camel caravans carried goods over the Silk Road. Early Europeans valued silk so much, it was said to be worth its weight in gold.

Most Mongols did not adopt Chinese ways. They had special rights. They did not pay taxes. Mongols were favored over Chinese for government posts. The Chinese resented the Mongols. In fact, China's dislike of foreigners lasted for hundreds of years.

Mongol Rule Challenged

In time, the Chinese challenged Mongol rule. Terrible drought and famine added to the unrest. During a **famine** food is very scarce. More than seven million people starved in the famine. ■

▲ *The Mongol invaders were expert riders. They rode small, sturdy horses like the one above.*

The Mongol Empire in China, c. 1294

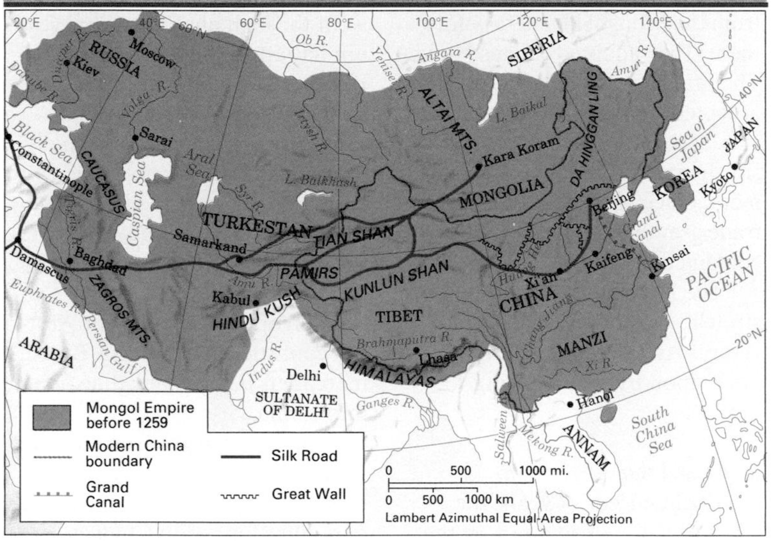

RUSSIA
Moscow
Kiev
Sarai
Black Sea
Constantinople
CAUCASUS
Caspian Sea
Aral Sea
L. Balkhash
TURKESTAN
Samarkand
Baghdad
Damascus
ZAGROS MTS.
Persian Gulf
ARABIA
Kabul
HINDU KUSH
PAMIRS
TIAN SHAN
KUNLUN SHAN
TIBET
Lhasa
HIMALAYAS
Delhi
SULTANATE OF DELHI
SIBERIA
ALTAI MTS.
L. Baikal
Kara Koram
MONGOLIA
DA HINGGAN LING
Beijing
KOREA
JAPAN
Kyoto
Sea of Japan
Kaifeng
Xi'an
Kinsai
CHINA
MANZI
Hanoi
ANNAM
South China Sea
PACIFIC OCEAN
Mongol Empire before 1259
Modern China boundary
Grand Canal
Silk Road
Great Wall
0 500 1000 mi.
0 500 1000 km
Lambert Azimuthal Equal-Area Projection

◄ *In the 1200s the Mongol Empire extended far west into Russia and parts of eastern Europe.*

■ How were the Chinese people treated under Mongol rule?

DEVELOP

Point out that this lesson covers three dynasties. It also covers the enormous changes that China's government has undergone in the 1900s. Suggest that students look for similarities and differences among China's governments during the period covered in the lesson.

Outline the Graphic Overview on the chalkboard, and write the top and side headings. Ask students to copy this framework on a sheet of paper. Encourage students to fill in the details as they read.

GEOGRAPHY

Map and Globe Skills

Ask students to use the map on this page to trace the Grand Canal, the Silk Road, and the Great Wall. Have them compare this map with the map of Asia on page 683. Which modern countries in addition to China did the Mongol Empire include? *(North Korea and South Korea, Pakistan, Afghanistan, Iran, Mongolia, and parts of Russia)*

■ *They were treated poorly. Laws favored the Mongols, who had special rights and did not pay taxes. Mongols were also favored over Chinese for government posts.*

Access Strategy

Remind students that as part of the traditional "bargain" between the rulers and their subjects, Chinese emperors were supposed to be fair and to take care of the well-being of their people. Ask students whether citizens of the United States believe that their Presidents receive a "Mandate from Heaven." Who gives Presidents their mandate? *(The voters)*

Then ask what U.S. voters can do to show how they feel about their government. *(Write letters, hold protest marches, call government officials to express their views, vote for or against officials)* Next, write the words *President* and *Emperor* at the head of two columns on the chalkboard. Ask students to suggest words that describe a good President. In the second column ask them to put a check mark if the same words could apply to an emperor.

Access Activity

Ask students to describe the qualities that make a good leader. Encourage them to name community leaders, school leaders, and heads of state whom they think possess these qualities. What are the most admirable qualities of these leaders? Summarize by writing on the chalkboard one or two adjectives that best describe each leader.

VISUAL LEARNING

Art Connection

Have students find pictures of Ming porcelain in library books and then design their own bowls or vases in a style that was popular during the Ming Dynasty. Each bowl or vase should feature a single design that wraps around the entire piece and tells a story pictorially. Students could draw their designs on paper and, if possible, wrap their drawings around jars or bowls.

■ *The Mings brought peace and order. They rebuilt the Great Wall and reformed government. Learning, trade, and art flourished.*

The Ming Period

In 1368 Chu Yüan-chang led a successful revolt against the Mongols. Chu was a poor farmer, who once begged for food. As founder of the Ming dynasty, he took the reign title Hung-wu.

Early Ming rulers brought peace and order to China. They made new laws. They reformed local government. They built new schools and printed many books.

To increase trade, the Ming expanded the canal system. Cotton, tea, silk, timber, and iron pans called woks could now be shipped to all parts of China.

To protect China, the Ming repaired the Great Wall. They also added on to the old walls. Most of the Great Wall that is seen today was built under the Ming.

To encourage art, the first Ming ruler built a painting academy. Tapestry, calligraphy, and Ming porcelain—known to the outside world as china—also thrived.

Sometimes artists lived in the Ming court. However, one artist, Dai Jin (1388–1462), was sent away from court. He angered the emperor with his painting of a fisher wearing a red jacket. Red was not supposed to be worn by people of the common class.

Famines in the 1620s led to revolts. Once again, the rulers seemed to have lost the Mandate of Heaven. ■

■ *How did China fare under the Mings?*

The Last Dynasty

The Manchus took over the weakened Ming Empire. They came from Manchuria in the northeast. In 1644 these new rulers founded the Qing *(chihng)* dynasty.

The Manchus were different from the Mongol invaders before them. They adopted Chinese ways. The Manchus spoke Chinese. They accepted Confucian ideas of how to rule. Manchus and Chinese worked side by side in the Qing government. Once again, learning, art, and trade grew. Some great libraries contained over 36,000 volumes.

The Manchu Empire now stretched from the east coast to central Asia in the west. China's population tripled, reaching 430 million.

How Do We Know?

HISTORY *Historians have used local census records for taxes to estimate China's population under the emperors. However, people who did not want to pay taxes often avoided being counted. This led census recorders to report too few people in a village. Historians take these factors into account when they estimate population.*

China and the West

For hundreds of years, the Chinese had looked down on the outside world. From the Mongols, they had learned not to trust foreigners. What's more, other countries seemed to have little to offer China.

During the 1800s, the West went through huge changes. Western nations developed great factories that produced many new goods. They also built fleets of ships and powerful new weapons. Merchants from France, Great Britain, and the United States hoped to trade their goods for China's tea, porcelain, and silk.

The Chinese were not as interested in opening trade with Western countries. In response, British merchants began smuggling opium into China.

The Chinese government tried to stop the sale of this habit-forming drug. However, the amount of opium shipped to China grew

Study Skills

Have students use the school or public library to research China under the Mongols, the Mings, or the Manchus. Then ask them to imagine that they live in China during the dynasty they have researched. Have them write a journal entry describing their lives, activities, and outlook.

Political Context

The Manchus' skill for organization resulted in the successful Banner system. In 1601 Manchu leader Nurhachi organized his warriors into four companies of 300 men each. The companies carried banners of different colors—yellow, red, white, and blue. In 1615 four more banners were added. As Manchu conquests increased, the companies each grew to 7,500 men.

Besides its military function, the Banner system played an important administrative role. Taxation, conscription, and census taking were carried out through the banner organization. The banner men lived with their families in times of peace and contributed military troops in times of war.

As the Manchus began to conquer China and Mongolia, they organized their captives under new banners, which then fought beside the old. With these troops, the Manchus were able to conquer China and establish the Qing dynasty.

A Closer Look

The Voyages of Zheng He

While Europeans searched for a sea route to the East, Chinese ambassador Zheng He was exploring the West. His emperor sent Zheng He to display the splendor and power of China and to collect presents along the way, such as beautiful pearls. Under these orders, Zheng He sailed on seven expeditions to southeastern Asia, India, Arabia, and Africa in the early 1400s.

Zheng He, detail from a woodcut by Lo Mou-teng, 1597

Pearls

Fine porcelain and silk were brought along on Zheng He's trips to show off China's wealth.

Zheng He's fleets included more than 300 vessels and carried more than 27,000 men.

Ming vase

Zheng He brought back animals the Chinese had never seen before, including zebras and ostriches. The African kingdom of Malindi sent a giraffe to the Chinese emperor.

The Tribute Giraffe with Attendant *by artist Shen Tu, c.1414*

China

Note: You may wish to use this Closer Look when discussing Ming rulers (page 342).

More About Chinese Junks These vessels, of which there were more than 60 in Zheng He's fleet, were much larger than European ships and capable of weathering even the harshest ocean storms. They had as many as five masts, with sails that were stiffened with bamboo slats so they could be raised and lowered like venetian blinds. Their holds were partitioned with bulkheads, which made it possible to seal off leaking sections until the vessels reached port and repairs could be made. Europeans did not develop similar technology until centuries later.

Research

Have students read more at the library about the voyages of Zheng He. Ask them to trace on a globe or map the course Zheng He followed on these voyages and to compare the voyages with those of European explorers. Ask students how they think the world would be different today if, like the Europeans, the Chinese had established colonies in countries they visited. How might the world be different if Zheng He had reached Europe before Europeans reached China?

Visual Learning

Have students describe the pattern on the Ming vase on this page. *(Scenes of deer)* Explain that Ming porcelain first used floral and abstract designs but later portrayed scenes. The brilliant cobalt blue color was imported from Iran. If sources are available, show students pictures of Blue Willow china. Ask students to describe the scenes.

POLITICAL SYSTEMS

Critical Thinking

Encourage students to role-play a discussion between two Chinese people of the late 1800s, one of whom wants to keep the Manchus in power and the other of whom wants to get rid of the Manchus. What arguments can each present for her or his position? *(In favor of Manchus: getting rid of the Manchus will open the door to Western influence and weaken Chinese traditions; against Manchus: China's troubles prove that the Manchus have lost the Mandate of Heaven, and only a new ruler or government will bring back peace and prosperity.)*

■ *Their acceptance of Chinese ways and their success at maintaining order ensured the support of the people.*

European flags fly over the docks of Guangzhou, a port city in southern China. Before the Opium War, the Chinese allowed Westerners only a limited space in which to carry on trade.

■ *Why do you think the Manchus enjoyed such a long rule in China?*

from 200 chests in 1729 to 30,000 chests in 1839.

The Opium War

In 1839 China and Britain went to war. This Opium War ended in humiliating defeat for China. British ships and weapons easily overwhelmed China's military forces. An 1842 peace treaty gave the island of Hong Kong, located off the southern coast of China, to Great Britain. It also opened five ports to British trade. Soon other Western nations also forced China to give them new trading rights and land.

Angered by this treatment, many Chinese called for change. Some wanted to adopt Western ways. They hoped to use Western technology to protect China. However, others feared the loss of Chinese traditions.

The ruling Manchus were blamed for China's troubles. The Manchus made some efforts to reform. Many Chinese, however, held little hope for real change under the elderly Empress Dowager. At that time she held power for her young nephew.

In 1911 there was a revolution. China was declared a republic. One year later, China's last emperor, Pu Yi, gave up his throne. He was six years old. Thus ended 267 years of Manchu rule. ■

Struggle Toward a New China

The head of the new republic was Sun Yat-sen. Sun wanted to build a Chinese government based on Western democracy.

There was never much chance to try out Sun's ideas. Uniting China proved difficult. Local leaders took control of many areas. Fighting broke out. After Sun's death in 1925, Chiang Kai-shek *(chang ky shehk)* became leader. For a time, he controlled much of China.

One group in Chiang's party pushed for even greater change. Its members believed in communism. Under **communism** the government owns and controls all property and businesses. Chiang feared and fought these Communists. Many were killed. Others fled to the mountains of southeastern China.

Japanese bombing caused death and destruction in many areas of China before and during World War II.

Study Skills

Have students use library resources to research China's climates and terrain in order to evaluate whether these might have hindered Sun Yat-sen in uniting China. Remind them that on the Long March, Mao's troops traveled more than 6,000 miles to evade Sun. Students should consider communication and transportation of that time.

Historical Context

Tea is an ancient beverage. According to Chinese legend, it was first drunk about 2700 B.C., during the reign of the mythical ruler Shen Nung. Tea was first grown in the Chinese province of Szechwan, and by the A.D. 500s, it was also cultivated in Japan.

Desire for tea gradually spread throughout the world, and in the mid-1600s, tea began to replace coffee in England as the beverage of choice. This demand helped force China to open its ports to the West.

The Rise of Mao

In 1931 Japan invaded Manchuria. Then the Japanese moved deeper into China. They dreamed of conquering China and becoming the most powerful nation in the Pacific area. This dream came to nothing.

In 1934, meanwhile, Chiang finally forced the Communists out of the mountains. Mao Zedong *(mow dzuh dahng)* helped lead the Communists in what is called the Long March. For a year, Mao's Red Army fought and marched for 6,000 miles.

In 1945 Japan signed a peace treaty that ended World War II. Japanese troops then left China. The war had exhausted China's resources. Prices were high. Many Chinese had lost faith in Chiang. Fighting

在毛澤東的勝利旗幟下前進

◄ At the height of his power, Mao held huge rallies where he addressed his followers.

Understanding Communism

The idea of communism is an old one. Many people have dreamed of a society that fostered equality. In such a society, everyone would share the land, the factories, the businesses, the wealth.

No country based on the idea of communism existed before 1917. In that year, Communist revolutionaries came into power in Russia. They turned the country into a Communist state.

After a long civil war, the Chinese Communists, under Mao Zedong, took power in 1949. For thousands of years, a small number of people had held most of China's power and wealth. Communism offered the promise of prosperity and equality for all.

In practice, Chinese communism turned out to be different from the idea of communism. The Communists did take over land and factories. They built collective farms where farmers worked together. Production increased.

However, a small number of people still controlled the government in Communist China. Only one party, the Chinese Communist party, was allowed. Many who did not conform to the ideas of the Chinese Communist party were sent to work camps.

Today the Chinese Communist party is still China's only party. The Chinese people have no right to vote, to speak their minds freely, or to practice their religions. What's more, there are still serious economic problems in China that communism has not solved.

ECONOMICS

Critical Thinking

Remind students that Mao gained the support of many peasants during the Long March. Encourage students to speculate about what Mao might have promised the peasants that convinced them to support him. *(Answers include land; an end to hunger; greater security; a higher income for each family; more attention from the government.)*

Critical Thinking

Ask students how the cultural belief in a ruler's Mandate from Heaven may help the Chinese Communists stay in power. *(It may make the Chinese people more accepting of a strong authority figure in government.)* When might the rule of the Communists be in danger? *(If the economy declines too severely, citizens might feel justified in overthrowing their Communist rulers; the gradual spread of Western values and ideas could encourage people to reject communism.)*

Social Participation

Have students use encyclopedias to research some of China's present-day problems, such as political upheaval, overpopulation, health care, and human rights. Then have them work in pairs to brainstorm and present solutions to these problems.

CULTURE

Critical Thinking

Draw two columns on the chalkboard, with a plus sign at the head of one and a minus sign at the head of the other. Ask students to list in the first column ways in which Mao was a successful ruler and in the second column ways in which he was not successful. *(Successes: united China; new building projects; greater equality for women; failures: Great Leap Forward; Cultural Revolution)*

■ *The Communists offered equality and economic security. Their plan to redistribute land appealed to peasants, who were poor and hungry.*

CLOSE

Read the Thinking Focus aloud. Have students explain how the idea of a Mandate from Heaven benefited China in its quest for a peaceful and orderly society. Then divide the class into groups of three or four students each and have them compare the Graphic Overviews that they completed as they read the lesson.

砸碎千年铁锁链，妇女能顶半面天·

▲ *Following the Cultural Revolution, artists were encouraged to create works illustrating the successes of Communist society. This 1978 painting shows that many women entered the work force after the Communists came to power.*

between Chiang's army and the Communists continued.

By 1949 the Communists had captured Beijing, the capital city. To a cheering crowd in Tiananmen *(tyahn ahn mehn)* Square, Mao declared, "Never again will the Chinese be an enslaved people."

Mao Changes China

In the past, strong emperors had held China together. Now Mao united the country. Posters of Mao hung on public buildings everywhere.

Life for many Chinese improved under Mao. The government built new schools. They repaired railroads, riverways, and roads. Doctors were sent to small villages. Women achieved greater equality.

Over time, public ownership of farms, factories, businesses, and stores replaced private ownership. The people worked together in groups known as collectives. Small farms were turned into larger farms of 20 to 30 families. On a farm collective, people shared their work as well as their harvests. These new groups produced more food and goods.

■ *Why were many peasants attracted to communism?*

Mao wasn't satisfied. He wanted more rapid change. In 1958 he designed a new economic plan. It was called the Great Leap Forward. As part of this plan, collectives were united into giant communes. Each one included about 5,000 households. The Communists also organized worker groups. They built bridges, canals, and roads using little more than muscle power.

The Great Leap Forward was mostly a failure. The people became overworked and exhausted. No matter how much they produced, they still received the same pay. To make matters worse, poor harvests and drought led to massive food shortages throughout China.

Many people criticized Mao. His answer to these critics was the Cultural Revolution of 1966. He aimed to destroy old Chinese customs and ideas. He hoped to create a whole new society. The result was 10 years of bloodshed and disorder, much of it caused by students in Mao's "Red Guard." Schools closed. Art treasures and books were destroyed. People were killed if they criticized what was going on. Others were sent to work camps in the countryside where many more died. ■

REVIEW

1. **FOCUS** How has the hope for peace and order guided the Chinese people and their rulers?
2. **HISTORY** Beginning with the Zhous, how did new rulers justify overthrowing a poor or corrupt emperor?
3. **POLITICAL SYSTEMS** How was Manchu rule of China different from Mongol rule?
4. **CRITICAL THINKING** What positive and negative effects did Mao's rule have on the people of China?
5. **WRITING ACTIVITY** Imagine you are a peasant whose farm became part of a collective after the Communist victory in 1949. Now you must work with a group and share the harvest. Write a letter to your sister who lives at another collective. Describe this new situation and how you feel about it.

Homework Options

Locate a reference book such as Bartlett's *Familiar Quotations* in the school or public library. Have students collect some of the sayings of Confucius that Chinese rulers may have taken to heart in their efforts to govern China with virtue and justice.

Study Guide: page 59

Answers to Review Questions

1. Most imperial rulers maintained China's defenses and accepted Confucian ideals, as well as the idea of the Mandate of Heaven. Modern leaders have tried, without success, to establish peace and order by creating equality through Communist principles.
2. Those who sought power pointed to problems such as famine as signs that the old rulers had lost their mandate to govern.
3. Unlike the Mongols, the Manchu adopted Chinese ways; they spoke Chinese and adopted Confucian ideas; they let Chinese hold government jobs.
4. Mao created successful social programs. His early plans increased production. However, the Great Leap Forward and the Cultural Revolution were failures.
5. Some students may say that they feel robbed of their freedom and land and do not like communal living. Others might mention the promise of better living conditions and increased production.

A.D.
1000
1200
1400
1600
1800
1976
TODAY

L E S S O N 2

China after Mao

Changes have come to China since Mao's death in 1976. Moderates took over the government. They favored gradual change instead of the excesses of the Cultural Revolution. Over time, private enterprises came to operate side by side with state-owned businesses. In 1979, two sisters in China planned their future.

So when we heard about the government policy relaxing a bit on private enterprise, the two of us sat up half the night working out how we could open up a restaurant. We did a rough financial estimate and figured it could make money.

They showed their plan to local officials. Before long, the sisters got a license. Now they had a chance to run the first privately owned restaurant in all of China.

These two women were pioneers of the marketplace. Like other pioneers, they faced hardships. They had to deal with competition from other restaurants. They had to face the rising costs of seafood. In the end, the two sisters merged with a state-run restaurant.

Their story shows the benefits and difficulties of **free enterprise** in China. Under free enterprise the government does not control prices or decide how people earn or spend their money. Businesses compete with each other. The best-run businesses survive. Others fail.

THINKING FOCUS

How has Deng's government responded to China's problems?

Key Terms

- free enterprise
- ideology
- dissident

After Mao, Western styles became popular with many young people. Many older people, however, continued wearing the style of the Mao years.

INTRODUCE

Remind students that under Mao, workers earned about the same amount, no matter how much they produced. Ask students what problems this might have caused China's economy. *(China might not have produced as much as it could have; people might have been unwilling to try a new method of production because it wouldn't necessarily benefit them.)* Then ask students to read the Thinking Focus and to predict ways in which the present government might be dealing with these problems. Have them read the lesson to see if their predictions are correct.

Key Terms

Vocabulary Strategies: T36–T37
free enterprise—a system in which the government does not control prices and lets individuals decide how they will earn and spend their money
ideology—a set of ideas and beliefs about human life; for instance, how a society, government, or economy should be organized
dissident—a protester

Graphic Overview

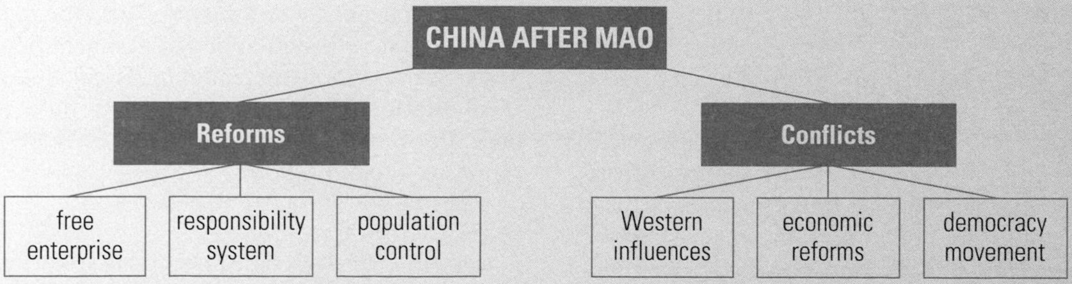
CHINA AFTER MAO
Reforms
Conflicts
free enterprise
responsibility system
population control
Western influences
economic reforms
democracy movement

Objectives

1. Explain the policies of the Communist government in China today.
2. Explain the problems that face China's Communist government in today's world.
3. Explain political protest in China and the government's response.

DEVELOP

Have students read the headings for the lesson. Ask them how China has changed since Mao's death. *(Economic reforms, population controls, contacts with West)*

ECONOMICS

Critical Thinking

Ask students to look at the map on this page. Point out that China has about one-fifth of the world's population. Explain that arable land is land that can be farmed, while nonarable land is land where food cannot be grown because of poor terrain or soil. Then ask students to compare the amounts of arable and nonarable land in China. What problem might be caused by the relationship between China's land and population? *(China has trouble producing enough food to feed its people.)*

■ *Deng introduced limited free enterprise into Communist China. He allowed some people to start small businesses, let farmers earn money from surplus products, and compensated factory workers for excellent performance. He also started a system of bonuses and fines to control population by limiting family size to one child.*

Steering a New Course

"It does not matter whether a cat is black or white, as long as it catches mice," said Deng Xiaoping *(duhng shyow pihng)*.

Deng succeeded Mao in the late 1970s. Mao had never turned from his strict Communist ideals. To Mao, **ideology,** a set of ideas and beliefs, was most important. However, his ideology did not lead to higher production. Deng was more concerned with finding workable solutions to China's problems.

Economic Reforms

Deng understood that people would produce more if they could make a profit from their work. So Deng introduced some free enterprise in China. A few people were permitted to start their own businesses. At the same time, government loosened its control over prices.

Deng also offered opportunities to farmers and factory workers. He got rid of the communes created under Mao. He set up the "responsibility system." Under this system, farmers had to produce a specified amount. If they produced more, they could sell their extra crops for profit. Deng introduced new technology to help make industry more productive. Factory workers who performed with excellence could also earn extra pay.

Social Changes

Deng also tackled the problem of population control. China has the largest population of any country in the world. Over 1.1 billion people live in China. Such a huge population requires vast amounts of food, water, and other supplies. Famines were once a problem in China. Deng wanted everyone to have enough. In 1979 the government began to give bonuses to one-child families. It fined families with more than one child. ■

China is home to over one-fifth of the world's population.

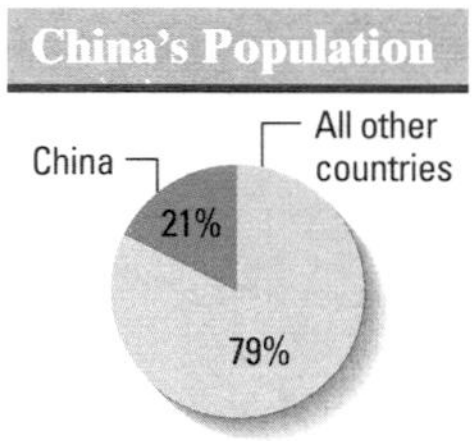
China's Population
China
All other countries
21%
79%

Source: Information Please Almanac, 1992

Much of China's land is mountainous or desert. Most of its people are crowded into the eastern third of the country. This area enjoys a mild climate, plenty of rainfall, and good soil.

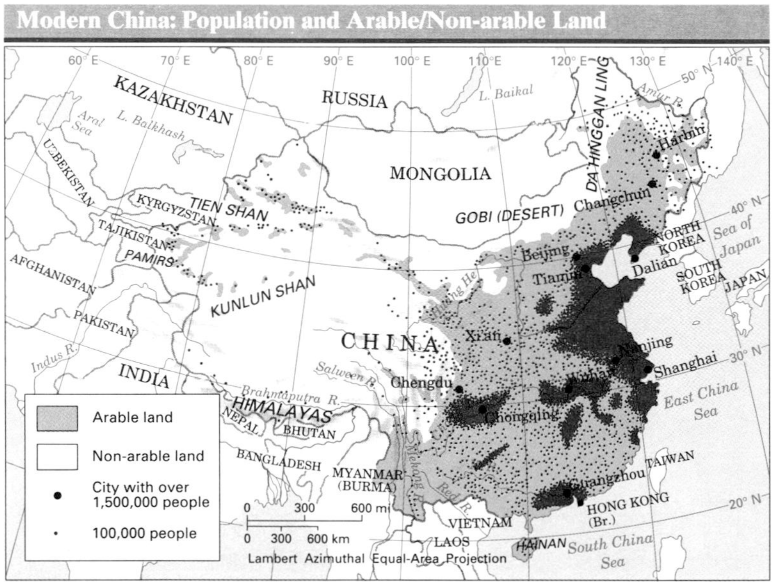
Modern China: Population and Arable/Non-arable Land
60° E
70° E
80° E
90° E
100° E
110° E
120° E
130° E
140° E
50° N
40° N
30° N
20° N
KAZAKHSTAN
RUSSIA
L. Baikal
Aral Sea
L. Balkhash
UZBEKISTAN
KYRGYZSTAN
TAJIKISTAN
PAMIRS
TIEN SHAN
MONGOLIA
GOBI (DESERT)
DA HINGGAN LING
Harbin
Changchun
NORTH KOREA
SOUTH KOREA
JAPAN
Sea of Japan
Beijing
Tianjin
Dalian
AFGHANISTAN
PAKISTAN
KUNLUN SHAN
CHINA
Xi'an
Nanjing
Shanghai
Indus R.
INDIA
Salween R.
Chengdu
Chongqing
East China Sea
Brahmaputra R.
HIMALAYAS
NEPAL
BHUTAN
BANGLADESH
MYANMAR (BURMA)
TAIWAN
Guangzhou
HONG KONG (Br.)
VIETNAM
LAOS
HAINAN
South China Sea
Arable land
Non-arable land
City with over 1,500,000 people
100,000 people
0 300 600 mi
0 300 600 km
Lambert Azimuthal Equal-Area Projection

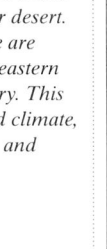

■ *What reforms did Deng Xiaoping introduce to China?*

Access Activity

Find volunteers to put their lunches up for a mock "sale." Have them set prices for their meals. They can lower their prices if their goods aren't selling. Afterward, compare the prices that sellers got for their goods. Why did some sell for more? Explain that in China, the government decided what goods to sell and for how much. This system led to problems.

Access Strategy

Ask students to imagine that there is a 6th-grade basketball player at their school who plays as well as anyone on the 8th-grade team. Should the team's rules be changed to allow this player on the team? Divide students into two groups to debate this question.

Point out that those who want to stick to the established rules and principles of the school value the importance of ideology, or ideas and beliefs. Mao Zedong's government placed great value on ideology. Those students who want to change the rules represent a practical way of thinking. This type of thinking was reflected in the government of Mao's successor, Deng Xiaoping. Read aloud the quotation from Deng at the top of this page. Prompt student reactions and interpretations of the quotation.

New Conflicts

Deng's reforms improved China's economy. At the same time they caused some problems. After the government loosened economic controls, rising prices became a problem. Goods and supplies cost more. Another problem was unemployment. Many people moved to the city after the breakup of the huge farming communes. Some could not find jobs.

Under Mao's strict Communist system, everyone was supposed to "eat out of the same pot." All people would be equal. To reach this goal, the government had controlled the economy. Under Deng, China moved toward limited free enterprise. Some Chinese thought that Deng's reforms undermined the ideals of communism. Some people had bad feelings toward those who were earning more under the "responsibility system." There was also anger at those officials who had grown rich from bribes. For these reasons some people opposed Deng's reforms.

Other Changes

To bring China into the modern world, Deng looked to the West for help. He encouraged Western companies to build factories in China. He let Chinese students study overseas. He invited scientists from other countries to teach in China.

This contact with the West has helped to bring change to China. Many people can now afford consumer goods, such as televisions and watches. What's more, they want to earn more money, like workers in the West. Some Chinese have also started asking for the same rights that people enjoy in Western democracies.

New Questions

For China, change has led to many questions.

- Can Chinese ways survive the influences of the West?
- Can the Communist system survive if China keeps moving toward free enterprise?
- Can China have economic freedom without political freedom? ■

National
SR-18FGH
National
Microwave Oven
NE-6670
HANDLE WITH CARE
DO NOT STEP

▲ *Deng's economic reforms brought more consumer goods to China, including radios, watches, and appliances. This Chinese girl is waiting outside with a new rice cooker and microwave oven.*

■ *What problems came with Deng's reforms?*

The Democracy Movement

Deng's reforms raised people's hopes for more political freedom. Many Chinese, especially students, called on Deng to bring democracy to China.

Student Protest

The democracy movement came to a head in 1989. Thousands of students gathered in Beijing's Tiananmen Square. They came to

SOCIAL SYSTEMS

Critical Thinking

Point out that China remained isolated from the West during much of its history. Have students recall the limited contact China allowed the West during the era of treaty ports and how the debate over isolationism was one of the factors that led to the overthrow of the Manchu dynasty. Ask students how contact with the West has changed China today. *(People have access to consumer goods and are asking for more political freedom.)* Are there ways in which contact with the West might have negative effects on China? *(Negative effects might include the loss of Chinese traditions and values and the possible rise of unemployment.)*

■ *Deng's policies have led to inflation, unemployment, resentment toward those who have benefited from these reforms, discontent with corrupt officials, and uncertainty about the future.*

Cultural Context

China was the first nation to try to reduce its population growth rate. Critics of Deng's efforts to slow population growth point to China's traditional preference for sons, which has led to an unwillingness to stop at one child if that child is a girl.

There is also concern that a generation of single children will be faced with the burden of supporting a much larger generation of elderly parents. Critics point out that incentives to grow more crops have amounted to incentives to have more children to help raise the crops.

Visual Learning

Ask students to look at the photo of consumer goods on this page. Have them use encyclopedias to research China's natural resources and products and make a list of exports that China might sell to the rest of the world. They might also list items labeled "Made in China" that they possess or have seen in stores. Then have students compare their lists in class.

POLITICAL SYSTEMS

Social Participation

Ask students to describe how the Chinese government responded to the student protests in Tiananmen Square. *(The government ordered the troops to fire on the students, killing hundreds.)* Then divide the class into groups of three or four students to brainstorm a list of other ways in which the government could have responded. *(The government could have given the students all or part of what they wanted or agreed to phase in some changes; they could have jailed or fined the dissidents instead of killing them.)*

■ *Protesters wanted reforms such as freedom of speech, freedom of the press, and freedom to demonstrate.*

CLOSE

Read the Thinking Focus aloud. Ask students to respond by creating a problem and solution chart. Have them list each problem with its solution, drawing an arrow between them. Then have students predict whether they think the solution will be successful.

Across Time & Space

In 1986 and 1987 Chinese students protested for democracy at more than 100 universities. One student poster echoed Dr. Martin Luther King, Jr., the African American civil rights leader of the 1960s. It said: I HAVE A DREAM OF DEMOCRACY. I HAVE A DREAM OF LIFE ENDOWED WITH HUMAN RIGHTS.

demand free speech, free press, and the right to hold demonstrations. A protester's poem in a shop window urged people to

Overthrow the old system
Return power to the people
Elect good people to office
And impeach the rotten ones.

The **dissidents,** or protesters, were led by students. Thousands of Chinese citizens joined the protest.

The government appeared uncertain about what to do. Newspeople from around the world were reporting on the events. The government seemed to be worried about world opinion. The protests lasted more than six weeks. Finally, the government ordered the army to surround the square. Some dissidents left. Many others built a statue of the "goddess of democracy." It stood for their dream of greater freedom.

A Brutal Response

On June 4 Chinese troops opened fire in the square. Hundreds of unarmed students were killed. Others fled as tanks took over the square. The democracy movement was forced into hiding. Some protesters were sent to prison. Others left the country. Because of its actions against the students, Deng's government lost the respect of many nations.

These events suggest China is moving toward a free enterprise economy without democracy. Although people are freer to earn money, they do not have the right to speak their minds. Nor can they elect their leaders. ■

➤ *Student protesters in Tiananmen Square built a "goddess of democracy" as part of their protest for greater freedom. Chinese soldiers later attacked the protesters and crushed the democracy movement.*

■ *What did the protesters in Tiananmen Square want?*

REVIEW

1. **FOCUS** How has Deng's government responded to China's problems?
2. **ECONOMICS** Reread the story about the two women who opened China's first privately owned restaurant. What difficulties did they face?
3. **POLITICS** What policy has China's government adopted to control the size of its population?
4. **CRITICAL THINKING** How has Deng's approach to economic problems differed from Mao's?
5. **ACTIVITY** Imagine that you were a student during the time of the Tiananmen Square protests. A protest leader asked you to join the demonstration. Tell how you responded. Explain why.

Homework Options

Have students use newspapers in the public library to research the events that led to the confrontation in Tiananmen Square. Ask them to write several daily journal entries from the point of view of a student. Encourage them to portray the student's feelings of hope, shock, and so on.

Study Guide: page 60

Answers to Review Questions

1. Faced with low productivity, China's government has worked to provide incentives and to modernize its industries. Following the protests in Tiananmen Square, however, it has been unwilling to grant free speech or free elections.
2. They faced rising costs and competition from other restaurants.
3. The government offered incentives to families having only one child, and it fined families that had more than one.
4. Mao believed that Communist ideals would make people work harder. Deng, on the other hand, used economic incentives such as allowing factory workers to earn bonuses for hard work.
5. Students may mention the widespread desire for more freedom. They might also mention concerns for their personal safety. Some might choose not to join the demonstration, saying that it could threaten the stability of their government.

A.D.
1000
1200
1400
1600
1800
TODAY

L E S S O N 3

China Today

China is a vast and varied land. Daily life is different from place to place. In the city or in the country, life in China means hard work. Here's a look at the lives of two Chinese women.

The first, Meng Maying, describes her job as a weaver. She lives in the busy port city of Shanghai, in eastern China. She works in a textile factory. For 22 years she has held this job.

> *For the eight-hour shift, we're on our feet all the time walking up and down the rows of machines. . . . We cannot sit for a moment for fear that there'll be broken ends somewhere. I've never tried to count how far I've walked in the workshop all these years. But I think I've walked a much longer distance than the Red Army's. . . Long March.*
>
> *As a result, my feet are always swollen after a work shift. We all wear flat soled cloth shoes in the workshop.*

The second woman, Xiao Wenxin, lives in rural Hebei *(hoh bay)* Province in northern China. She has taught third and fifth grades for over 20 years. The classrooms in her school are nothing more than clay huts.

By the time Xiao starts her job each day, she has already cooked her meals, taken care of her pigs and chickens, and fed her two children.

> *I arrive at school before 8 o'clock. Four classes in the morning. Go home after 12 o'clock. Three classes in the afternoon. Go home again at 5 o'clock. Then back to the school at 6:30 and coach the students to review or correct homework, or prepare lessons for tomorrow.*

THINKING FOCUS

How is life in China today a mix of old and new ways?

Key Term

- work unit

Children at school wear red scarves, part of the standard uniform from the time of Mao.

INTRODUCE

Remind students that in the last lesson they read about the conflict between old and new ideas of how to govern China. Point out that sometimes old and new ideas can work together to make a peaceful and prosperous society. Then have students read the Thinking Focus. Ask them to read the lesson to see how both new and traditional ways of life are helping the people of China today.

Key Term

Vocabulary Strategies: T36–T37

work unit—in Communist China, a group of people who work together on the same task

Graphic Overview

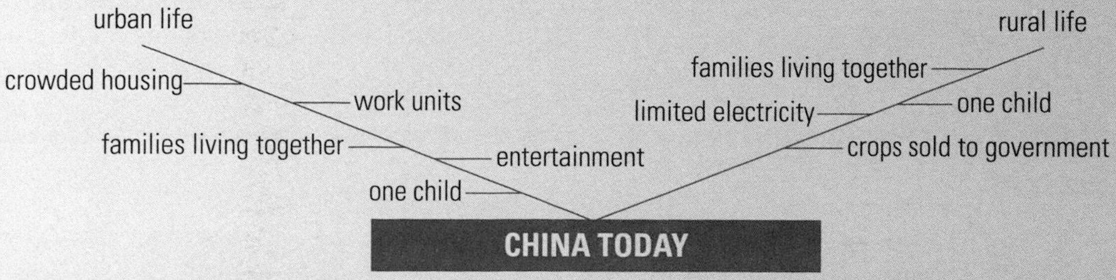
urban life
crowded housing
work units
families living together
entertainment
one child
rural life
families living together
limited electricity
one child
crops sold to government
CHINA TODAY

Objectives

1. Compare urban and rural life in China.
2. Discuss China's potential as a modern nation.

DEVELOP

Ask students to look at the photographs in this lesson. Ask them what they see in the photographs of China today that might cause them to feel optimistic about China's future. *(Possible answers include: Chinese people value education, the family, and work; parts of China are modern, prosperous, and fertile.)*

Rural Life, Urban Life

Feeding China's huge population requires thousands of tons of food and millions of farmers. Cities have grown rapidly since the Communists came to power in 1949. The countryside, however, is still home to most Chinese. Farming is the most common way of life.

A Farm Family

Meet the Kuos. They farm 10 acres of land on China's southeastern coast. Their life is a blend of old ways and modern changes.

Three generations live together in the Kuo household, as Chinese families have done for thousands of years. Following tradition, the Kuos' son brought his bride to live with his family when he married. But unlike Chinese families of old, the son has only one child, a boy. After all, China has a policy of fining families that have more than one child. The boy's name is Vu. Vu is one of China's "little emperors" who get lots of attention.

While Vu is in school, his parents and grandparents do the farm work. They plant their fields with cotton, corn, rice, and wheat. After the harvest, they sell their crops to the government. Under Deng's new policy, they raise another small crop for cash.

The Kuos are far from rich, but their life is comfortable. Many of the Kuos' relatives live nearby. The Kuos' courtyard is often filled with people. Family is important in modern China, as it was in earlier times. People share chores, such as cooking and laundry. There is a washing machine to help, but it can only be run at night. Rural factories use all daytime electricity.

Meals are an important time for families to get together. Family meals usually include soup, rice, vegetables, and fish. Much of the family's food comes from the market in the Kuos' village. Markets in China are often outdoors. They always include large displays of vegetables.

➤ *Hundreds of people crowd the streets of Shanghai. Some of the largest and most densely populated cities in the world are located in China.*

▼ *This train is passing through the Li Valley in southeastern China. The area is so hilly that the farmers build terraces in order to grow their crops.*

Access Activity

Encourage students to discuss the effects of so much hard work on the families they have read about so far in the lesson. Do they think it brings the family members closer together or deprives them of time they would otherwise spend together? Have them give reasons for their opinions.

Access Strategy

Prompt students to discuss how their lives would be different if they lacked labor-saving conveniences such as washing machines, vacuum cleaners and dishwashers. Under such circumstances what chores could they do to help their families? How would the time spent on these chores affect their lives?

Explain that in many parts of China, particularly in rural areas, many families do not have modern conveniences. In the cities, however, many people live like many other urban dwellers, with modern appliances and electronics such as tape players and VCRs.

Life in the City

China's cities bustle with people and bicycles. Many houses and apartments have only two or three rooms. Furniture is simple. Posters and family pictures may decorate the walls. Because indoor space is tight, people like to spend time outside. In city parks, they can play games and listen to singers and storytellers. They can also practice *tai chi chuan (ty chee chwahn)*. It is an ancient form of slow-motion exercise.

▲ *Like the Kans from Beijing, many Chinese families have parents, grandparents, and one child.*

A worker's life is controlled by the *danwei,* or **work unit.** Everyone in China belongs to a work unit. A work unit might include, for example, all the workers in a certain factory.

The work unit takes care of all the family's needs. It provides housing and medical care. It may even throw dance parties or show a movie. It also takes care of schooling for young people.

Over time, a typical factory worker can earn enough to buy a refrigerator or a washing machine. An unskilled worker's family may have to make do with a tiny concrete apartment. The family may have to share a kitchen and toilet with other families. But a skilled worker can move into roomier quarters.

For typical factory workers, the day starts at 6:00 A.M. The factory loudspeaker begins broadcasting music and announcements. Then it is time for breakfast—perhaps fried dough and sweet soup. Most workers ride to the factory on bicycles. They return home for lunch, then go back to the factory until 4:00 P.M.

After work, young people may listen to Chinese rock 'n' roll on their tape decks. Or they may play video games set up on the street. Grownups may watch television or go to a teahouse or a restaurant. ■

◄ *The streets in China's villages are busy with activity. This woman is selling noodles, a popular meal in the wheat-growing regions of northern China.*

■ *How does life in rural China compare with life in the city?*

CULTURE

Critical Thinking

Ask students to describe the purpose of the work unit. *(It takes care of workers' needs, such as housing and medical care.)* What can the work unit be compared to in rural life? *(The collective farm)* What might be some of the advantages and disadvantages of belonging to a work unit? *(The work unit ensures that the basic needs of workers and their families will be met; however, it takes away workers' freedom to make personal choices.)*

■ *Many Chinese families in both urban and rural areas work hard but live in reasonable comfort. Through the work unit, the government plays a large role in people's lives. Modern appliances such as washing machines are making their way into both urban and rural homes.*

Economic Context

Since the 1970s China has decollectivized its agricultural system, allowed growth in the private sector, and shifted its focus from heavy industry such as machines and military equipment to light industry such as consumer goods. Economic growth, however, is limited by a lack of the energy supplies needed to power China's industries and an inadequate system for transporting vital items such as coal. Because of these factors, regional economies vary.

Geography Connection

Have students collect recipes from various regions of China. They can look in Chinese cookbooks in the library or ask friends and neighbors for recipes. How do cooking styles and ingredients vary from region to region? Have students look up any unfamiliar ingredients in encyclopedias. Then on a map of China, locate the regions that are home to the various styles of cooking and ingredients. Examples include noodles in the north and rice and hot peppers in the south.

Social Participation

Have students work in pairs to do research on Hong Kong. Each pair should research one topic, such as geographic location and its effects, early settlers, British involvement, trade and commerce, and the future of Hong Kong. Have students report their findings to the class.

POLITICAL SYSTEMS

Critical Thinking

Point out that most Communist governments in Eastern Europe fell in the late 1980s and early 1990s. Encourage students to discuss what effect this and China's awakening free-market system might have on the future of communism in China. *(Communism in China might be weakened because of the lack of other Communist nations to support it; Western ideas might further undermine communism.)*

■ *China faces the question of how to adapt a Communist society to an economy that allows some free enterprise. Will the government allow China to follow a course like Hong Kong's, or will Hong Kong come under tighter controls?*

CLOSE

Read the Thinking Focus aloud. Have students answer the question by reviewing the lesson and filling in two columns labeled *Old* and *New* with appropriate information. Encourage them to discuss how old ways might help the Chinese people cope with changing times.

China Looks to the Future

China's population is the largest in the world. It is also one of the youngest. About 750 million Chinese are younger than 35 years of age. The future belongs to them.

Hong Kong is busy, crowded, and prosperous. Double-decker buses are just one sign of British influence.

China's Youth

What direction will this future take? This question is hotly debated between young and old in China. Older people remember Mao's revolution. They recall the struggle to build a fairer society. They grew up believing that everyone should work for the common good. For many older people, obeying a ruler is a part of their tradition. They have trouble understanding some of the young people who want "too much" freedom. They don't accept the "get rich quick" attitude of some of China's youth.

Many young people, on the other hand, think the older generation is out of touch with the world. These young people have learned about the West from films and television. They've picked up Western styles of clothing. They've absorbed Western attitudes about money and freedom.

■ *What questions face China as it approaches the 21st century?*

But will these young Chinese be able to put their new ideas into practice? That question is yet to be answered.

Hong Kong

Another big question for China today concerns what will happen to Hong Kong in 1997.

China had to give up the island of Hong Kong to the British in 1842. Since then Hong Kong has become one of the richest markets in Asia. Each year thousands of ships load and unload goods at Hong Kong's busy docks. Hong Kong is also an important manufacturing center. Its factories make textiles, clothing, and appliances.

Hong Kong returns to Chinese control in 1997. China has promised to let Hong Kong keep its free enterprise market. However, after what happened at Tiananmen Square, many people in Hong Kong wonder whether Deng's government will keep its word.

People in China and Hong Kong have questions about their future.

- Will the Communist party extend its tight control over Hong Kong?
- Will mainland Chinese get more freedom, like people in Hong Kong? ■

REVIEW

1. **FOCUS** How is life in China today a mix of old and new ways?
2. **CULTURE** What role does the work unit play in the lives of China's workers?
3. **POLITICS** What are some important questions facing China today?
4. **CRITICAL THINKING** Would you rather be a farmer or a factory worker in China? Give reasons.
5. **WRITING ACTIVITY** Imagine that you could have a pen pal who is your age in China. What would you tell your pen pal about your life? What questions would you like to ask your pen pal? Try writing such a letter.

Homework Options

Have students write a one-page imaginary dialogue in which a young person and an old person discuss the future of China. Students should show the different perspectives of the speakers as well as their different ideas about the future course China should take.

Study Guide: page 61

Answers to Review Questions

1. Farming is still the most common way of life. Several generations of a family still live together. On the other hand, China's one-child policy means families are small. Modern appliances are finding their way into urban and rural households.
2. It provides for most of workers' needs, including jobs, housing, medical care, schooling, and entertainment.
3. Questions include: How much freedom is good? How will Western customs affect China's future? What is the future of China's Communist party?
4. Students might prefer rural life because it is less crowded; they may prefer farm work to factory work. On the other hand, they might prefer the bustle of the city, with its dances and restaurants.
5. Students might tell their pen pals about their families, hobbies, and schools. They might ask their pen pals about their school, family, and work unit.

UNDERSTANDING WRITTEN REPORTS

Presenting Information

Here's Why

Writing a report is a good way to add to your knowledge and to share information with others. Look at the map. It shows some of the different dialects of the Chinese language spoken in China today.

Suppose you were asked to write a report about the many Chinese dialects. Would you know what to do? Where would you begin?

Dialects in China, 1950

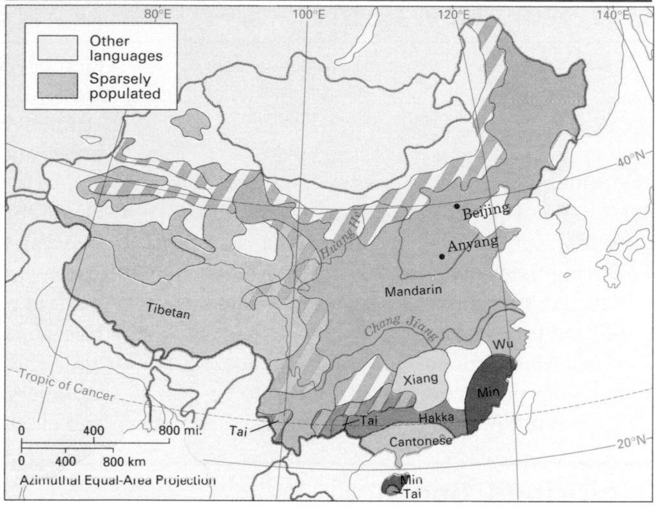
Other languages
Sparsely populated
80°E
100°E
120°E
140°E
40°N
20°N
Beijing
Anyang
Huang He
Chang Jiang
Tibetan
Mandarin
Wu
Xiang
Min
Hakka
Tai
Cantonese
Tropic of Cancer
0 400 800 mi.
0 400 800 km
Azimuthal Equal-Area Projection

Here's How

Here are six basic steps for writing a good report.

1. **Explore your topic.** Make a list of five things you want to know about your topic. Consider narrowing your topic to one of the five questions.
2. **Do research.** You can find general information about China in Chapters 5 and 15, but you should use other sources such as encyclopedias, books, and magazines to help you find information about the Chinese language.
3. **Take notes.** As you read, record information on note cards. Write a different idea on each note card. When you finish taking notes, group the cards according to the main ideas.
4. **Write an outline.** Look at the beginnings of an outline below. The biggest ideas from the note cards become the main points, shown by Roman numerals. Somewhat smaller ideas become subtopics, shown by capital letters. Details are then added, shown by Arabic numerals, and then small letters.
5. **Write a first draft.** Use the items with Roman numerals in your outline as paragraph topic sentences in your report. Use the subtopics as supporting details. Write in complete sentences and paragraphs.
6. **Revise, proofread, and publish.** After completing the first draft, read it over to see how you can improve it and to correct any mistakes you may find. Then prepare the final copy.

I. Dialects are like distinct languages.
  A. Many different dialects are spoken in China today.
    1. Mandarin, the northern dialect, is the official language.
    2. Southern China contains many more dialects than the north.
      a. Most Chinese in the United States speak the Cantonese dialect.

Try It

Follow the first four steps of writing a report. Use this topic: What changes occurred in China under Mao before the Great Leap Forward?

Apply It

Use the first three steps of writing a report to learn more about a hobby of interest to you. Then make an outline.

SOCIAL SYSTEMS

Study Skills

Have students review the text on page 346. Ask volunteers to identify the main ideas of the first three paragraphs under the heading Mao Changes China. *(Mao united the country; life improved for many; public ownership replaced private ownership.)* Have students label these as headings I, II, and III and then complete their outlines by filling in the details.

Answers to Try It

Be sure students' note cards and outlines reflect that for many people life in China under Mao Zedong changed dramatically and that public ownership replaced private ownership. Students' outlines should provide at least two subtopics for each main topic.

Answers to Apply It

Check to be sure that students have sufficiently narrowed their topics. Review outlines and notecards to be sure that they follow the appropriate formats.

Objective

Understand and apply the six basic steps for writing a social studies report. (Study Skills 1, 2, 3)

Answers to Reviewing Key Terms

1. Incorrect. During times of **famine,** the Chinese suffered food shortages, often because of drought and poor harvests.
2. Correct. Mao believed that strict Communist **ideology** was more important than know-how or skills.
3. Incorrect. Under **free enterprise,** there is not much government control. Instead, the marketplace determines prices and production.
4. Incorrect. **Dissidents** are people who speak out against the government in power. The Chinese people do not have freedom of speech.
5. Correct. The **work unit** is responsible for meeting people's basic needs.

Answers to Exploring Concepts

A. Answers:

Mongols: Grand Canal repaired

Mings: the Great Wall repaired; the arts encouraged

Qings: Manchus defeat Mings; Chinese ways adopted

Opium War: five ports opened to western trade; Pu Yi gives up throne

Great Leap Forward: collectives united into communes

B. Sample answers:

1. People did not earn more money. Attempts to reshape China's culture damaged Chinese society.
2. It allows farmers who grow more than their quota to sell the extra crops for profit.
3. It wants to ensure that there are enough resources to meet everyone's needs.
4. In order to modernize China, Deng invited Western companies to build factories in China; he allowed Chinese students to study abroad; and he invited scientists from other nations to teach in China.
5. Dissidents wanted to bring democracy to China, but the government put down the demonstration, and killed many dissidents.
6. When Hong Kong returns to Chinese control in 1997, it may face new controls from the Chinese government. Hong Kong's freedoms may be reduced.

Chapter Review

Reviewing Key Terms

communism (p. 344)
dissident (p. 350)
famine (p. 341)
free enterprise (p. 347)
ideology (p. 348)
work unit (p. 353)

Each statement below uses a key term from this chapter. Tell whether each key term is used correctly. Then explain the reason for your answer.

1. During times of famine, Chinese farmers enjoyed huge harvests, and there was plenty of food for everyone.
2. When Mao Zedong's programs did not lead to higher production, he continued to believe in following a strict Communist ideology, or set of beliefs.
3. Under the free enterprise system, the government controls the economy by setting prices and deciding what farmers will grow and what factories will manufacture.
4. Dissidents in China have always had the freedom to speak their minds because they are the traditional supporters of the government in power.
5. Everyone in China today belongs to a work unit. The work unit is responsible for its members' housing, medical care, education, and even for some leisure activities.

Exploring Concepts

A. Important dynasties and events in Chinese history, from the Mongols to modern times, appear on the timeline below. Copy the timeline on a separate sheet of paper. From the following list, fill in on the timeline the items connected with each dynasty or event:

- Great Wall repaired
- Chinese ways adopted
- Grand Canal repaired
- The arts encouraged
- Five ports opened to western trade
- Pu Yi gives up throne
- Manchus defeat Mings
- Collectives united into communes

B. Answer each question with information from the chapter.

1. Why were the attempts by Mao to create a new society in China costly failures?
2. What is Deng Xiaoping's "responsibility system"?
3. Why does the Chinese government want to limit population growth?
4. Why and how did Deng seek contact with the West?
5. What was the purpose of the demonstrations at Tiananmen Square in 1989? What was the result?
6. What problems will Hong Kong face in 1997?

Mongols ______ Qings ______ Great Leap Forward ______

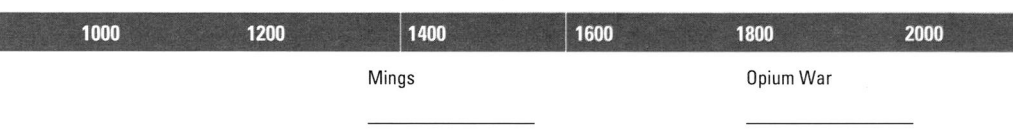

1000 | 1200 | 1400 | 1600 | 1800 | 2000

Mings ______ Opium War ______

Reviewing Skills

1. Reread the sections Steering a New Course, New Conflicts, and The Democracy Movement on pages 348–350. Make a list of five questions you might want to explore if you were writing a report about communism in China today.
2. Choose one question from your list for your report. Explain why you chose it. Which step in the process of presenting information have you completed?
3. Copy the flow chart below and fill in the missing steps.
4. List three sources of information you might look at in the second step of this process.

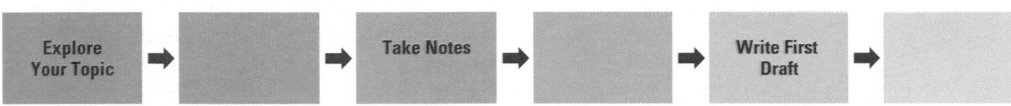

Explore Your Topic ➡ [ ] ➡ Take Notes ➡ [ ] ➡ Write First Draft ➡ [ ]

Using Critical Thinking

1. For centuries the Chinese looked down on other cultures and shut themselves off from the world. In what ways might China have developed differently if it had been open to exchanges of ideas and trade with other countries?
2. Compare life in a Chinese city with life in a U.S. city. What are some important differences? What similarities can you find?
3. "Throughout the history of China, a single strong leader has been a key to stable government." What evidence from the chapter can you find to support this statement?
4. Why do you think that Deng's reforms raised students' hopes for greater freedom in China?

Preparing for Citizenship

1. **WRITING ACTIVITY** Imagine that a Chinese student is coming to study at your school. Write a short essay describing aspects of life in the United States that will be new to him or her. If you like, illustrate your essay with drawings or magazine pictures. Also describe ways you might help the student adapt to your school and your community.
2. **GEOGRAPHY ACTIVITY** Find "50 largest cities of the world" on page 664 of the Minipedia. How many of these cities are in China? Construct a bar graph showing the four countries with the largest cities. What does this graph tell you about China's population?
3. **COLLABORATIVE LEARNING** Who should lead China after Deng Xiaoping? Imagine that Genghis Khan, Hung-wu, Mao Zedong, and Deng Xiaoping came together to discuss what kind of person the new leader should be. Divide the class into four groups. Each group should decide on recommendations that one of these people might make, based on what the group knows of that person's policies and impact on Chinese life. Use reference works or other library books for more information about each leader. Discuss these questions: (1) What values and qualities should the new leader have? (2) What should be the new leader's highest priorities? (3) What kind of leadership style should this person have?

   A speaker from each group should report the leader's recommendations to the class. Is there a class consensus among the leaders about what qualifications China's next leader should have? Then, as a class, imagine that you are Chinese supporters of democracy. How would your recommendations differ from the suggestions of the four leaders listed in the collaborative activity?

Answers to Reviewing Skills

1. Questions include: How does the Communist government control people's lives in China? What has happened to the students who led the democracy movement?
2. Students' chosen questions should resemble the questions suggested above. Choosing a question to answer is part of Step 1, Explore Your Topic.
3. (2) Do Research; (4) Write an Outline; (6) Revise, Proofread, Publish.
4. Books, magazines, and encyclopedias.

Answers to Using Critical Thinking

1. China might have kept pace with other countries in industrial development and might have been better able to defend itself against Western European nations. However, Chinese culture might have been less unique.
2. While the work unit controls life in China, in the United States people have more choice of housing, medical care, and entertainment. In both places young people like to listen to tapes and play video games, and people enjoy watching television and going to restaurants.
3. Strong emperors were able to unite China, bringing peace and prosperity. After the dynasties ended, people continued to obey strong leaders. When leaders lacked strength or when difficulties arose, unrest and revolt ensued.
4. Because of contacts with the West, students were more aware of the freedoms enjoyed by other people and wanted these freedoms for China.

Answers to Preparing for Citizenship

1. **WRITING ACTIVITY** Answers may include what schools are like, what foods Americans eat, what teenagers do for entertainment, and how teenagers feel about their country; ways to help the student may include being friendly and inviting the student to spend time with classmates.
2. **GEOGRAPHY ACTIVITY** Chinese cities are Shanghai, Beijing, Tianjin, Shenyang, Wuhan, Guangzhou, Chongqing, Harbin, and Chengdu (also as of 1997, Hong Kong). China has by far the largest urban population in the world.
3. **COLLABORATIVE LEARNING** Sample answers: Genghis Khan would want a leader with strong military values and skills. Hung-wu might want a leader who would promote trade and the arts. Mao might push for a return to Communist ideology. Deng would want someone who could figure out how to balance a free enterprise economy with Communist control of government.

CHAPTER ORGANIZER

Chapter 16 Japan

CHAPTER PLANNING CHART

Pupil's Edition	Teacher's Edition	Ancillaries
Lesson 1: Island Culture (2–3 days) Objective 1: Analyze the interaction between environment and culture in Japan. (History 7; Geography 3; Economics 1) Objective 2: Describe some of the early influences on the development of Japanese culture. (Culture 1)	• Graphic Overview (360) • Access Strategy (361) • Access Activity (361) Study Skills (362) Political Context (362)	Study Guide (63)
Literature: Japanese Poetry	Collaborative Learning (365)	Discovery Journal (32)
Lesson 2: History of Japan (2–3 days) Objective 1: Describe the importance of the feudal period in Japanese history. (History 8; Social and Political Systems 4) Objective 2: Explain the historical foundation for modern Japan's economic success. (Economics 1, 3, 4, 5) Objective 3: Describe the westernization of Japan following the feudal period. (History 5, 8; Culture 1, 4, 5; Social and Political Systems 5, 6)	• Graphic Overview (366) • Access Strategy (367) • Access Activity (367) Critical Thinking (368) Religious Context (368) Oral Report (369) • Art Connection (369) • Visual Learning (369) Critical Thinking (370) Language Arts Connection (370)	Study Guide (64) Discovery Journal (33, 34) • Study Prints (9)
Understanding Cartograms Objective: Read and interpret a cartogram. (Map and Globe Skills 1, 3, 4, 5)	Math Connection (372) Making a Chart (372)	Study Guide (65) Map Activities (20) Transparency (6)
Lesson 3: Japan Today (3–4 days) Objective 1: Explain the reasons for Japan's economic success in today's world. (History 5; Economics 3, 4, 5) Objective 2: Describe life in contemporary Japan. (History 8; Culture 1, 5; Ethics and Belief Systems 1, 2; Social and Political Systems 1, 2, 4) Objective 3: Identify some of the challenges that Japan faces at home and in the international community. (Social and Political Systems 5, 6)	• Graphic Overview (374) • Access Strategy (375) • Access Activity (375) Social Participation (376) Social Context (376) Music Connection (377) Study Skills (377) Critical Thinking (378) Writing an Editorial (378)	Study Guide (66)
Exploring: Japanese and U.S. Schools Objective 1: Identify similarities and differences between Japanese and American schools. (Study Skills 1, 2) Objective 2: Identify the values reflected by each system. (Ethics and Belief Systems 1, 2, 4)		Discovery Journal (35)
Chapter Review	Answers (382–383)	Tests (61–64)

* Objectives are correlated to the strands and goals in the program Scope and Sequence on pages T41–T49.

• LEP appropriate resources. (For additional strategies, see pages T32–T33.)

CHAPTER RATIONALE

Chapter 16 traces the history of Japan from the arrival of its earliest peoples to the present day. The primary objective of the first two lessons is to describe the geographic and historical factors that explain contemporary Japan's culture and its phenomenal economic success. The chapter then goes on to give students a close-up look at what it is like to live and work in urban Japan.

Lesson 1 focuses on the geographic factors that influenced Japan's development. The chapter demonstrates how nature has influenced or has been incorporated into Japanese life and thought. Lesson 1 also describes the early development of Japanese society and the profound impact that Chinese culture had on Japan. Two concepts are critical to this lesson—the impact of isolation on Japan and the deliberate cultural borrowing that characterizes its history.

Lesson 2 reviews Japan's feudal period, the Tokugawa era of forced isolation, the Meiji Restoration, World War II, and the U.S. military occupation that followed World War II. The lesson makes the point that Japan had a very advanced culture and sophisticated economy centuries before its amazing economic emergence following the war. The text describes the importance of the U.S. occupation period in the rebuilding of Japan's industries following the war. However, it is important for students to understand that while the occupation helped lay the foundation for Japan's industrial emergence, the Japanese people themselves were primarily responsible for the economic success that followed.

Lesson 3 explains how the homogeneous nature of the Japanese and their value system have helped to make the Japanese some of the most productive workers in the world. The lesson gives students a picture of what it is like to live in Tokyo. It also addresses the domestic and international challenges that currently face the Japanese.

ACTIVITIES & PROJECTS

LEP: Making a Map

Refer students to the topographic map on page 361. Have them use clay, a salt-and-flour mixture, or papier-mâché to make a three-dimensional model of Japan based on the map. (Use after Lesson 1.)

Making a Chart

Remind students that Japan experiences more than 1,500 earthquakes a year, although most are mild. Have students work in groups to design a chart of information about earthquakes. Explain that charts can include information on the location of the earth's major earthquakes, their strength, the dates on which they have occurred, damage statistics, and any other data students find. Groups should share their charts. (Use after Lesson 1.)

Collaborative Learning: Research

Tell students that today most Japanese people live in urban areas. Divide the class into four or five groups. Have each group research a different city in Japan today and present a report to the class. (Use after Lesson 3.)

Basic: Reader's Theater

Have students work in groups of five or six to prepare a reader's theater presentation for the class. Have each group choose a time period or event described in the chapter, compose a script, assign roles, gather props, rehearse, and finally present their skit to the class. (Use after any lesson.)

Challenge: Writing a Journal

Ask students to imagine that they could assume the role of any of the members of Japanese society mentioned in the chapter, for example, a courtier during the Heian period, a shogun, a samurai, or a worker in one of Japan's giant companies today. Have students write three or four journal entries about the life of this person. (Use after any lesson.)

CHAPTER PREVIEW

Have students read the chapter title and the introduction. On the chalkboard write the question that appears in the first line of the introduction. Then tell the class to study the pictures and read the captions. Ask students what factors, as indicated by the pictures, seem important to consider in answering this question. *(Geography, group action, art and culture, military power)*

Looking Back

Remind students that in Chapter 15 they learned about Kublai Khan and the Yuan dynasty. Tell students that the Mongols tried to conquer Japan twice. Each time they were unsuccessful because most of their ships were destroyed by a typhoon.

Looking Forward

Tell students that in the next three lessons—Island Culture, History of Japan, and Japan Today—they will learn about Japan's history and culture.

Lesson 1 describes the geographic features of Japan and their effect on the nation's early culture, including its borrowing of Chinese ideas.

Chapter 16
Japan

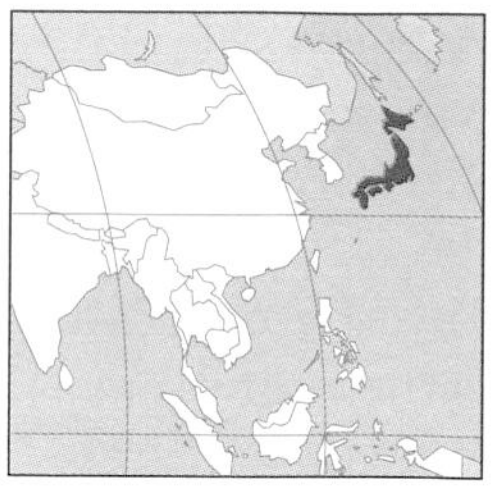

How can one explain the success of the Japanese people in today's world? A small chain of rocky islands that dot the coast of Asia with miles of ocean separating it from its nearest neighbor, Japan was once considered the "end of the earth." Yet it has developed into an economic giant with one of the world's unique and exquisite cultures.

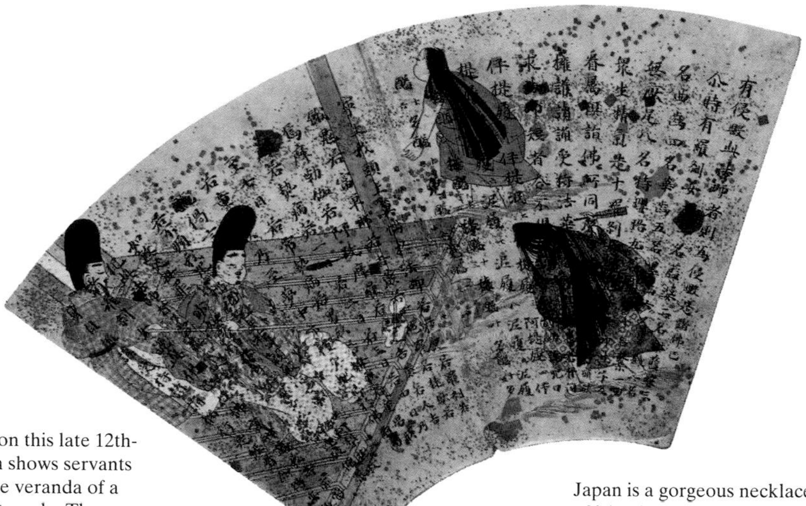

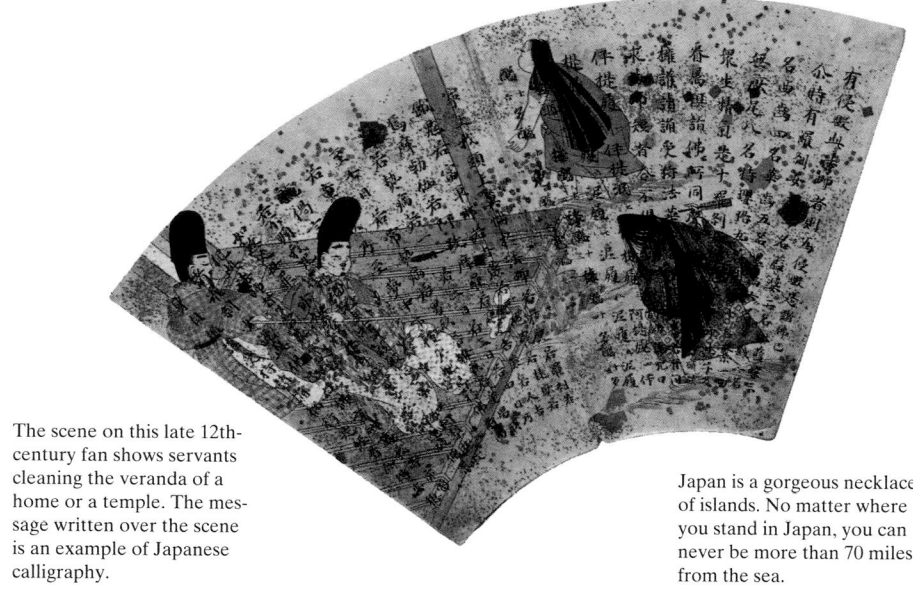

The scene on this late 12th-century fan shows servants cleaning the veranda of a home or a temple. The message written over the scene is an example of Japanese calligraphy.

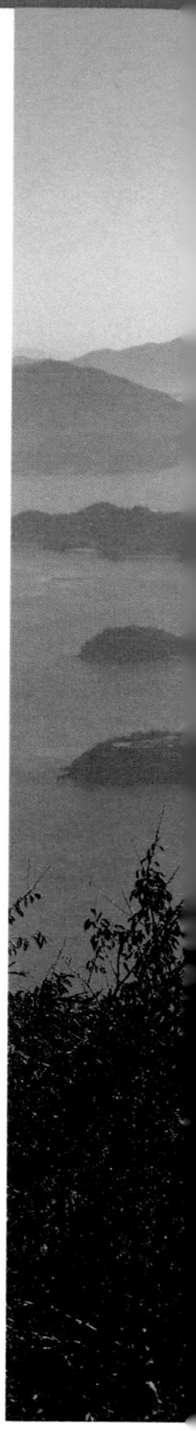

Japan is a gorgeous necklace of islands. No matter where you stand in Japan, you can never be more than 70 miles from the sea.

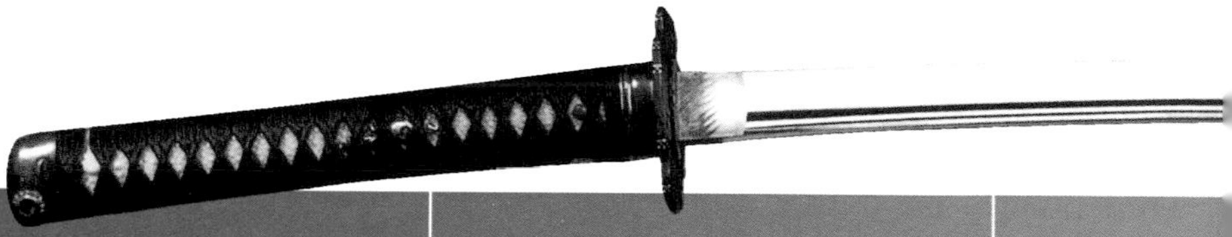

125 | 500 | 875

A.D. 250

A.D. 250–710 Under the rule of the Yamato, Japan is unified, and China becomes its cultural model.

BACKGROUND

Throughout Japan's history, its geography, characterized by a beautiful mountainous landscape, violent natural forces, and a wet climate, has played a major role in shaping Japanese culture. Religion, agriculture, government, and the arts have been influenced by the physical features of the island nation.

The Early Japanese

The first people to settle Japan probably came from Korea, arriving at least as early as 6000 B.C. Later groups also came from the mainland of Asia, bringing with them the knowledge of how to grow rice.

Rice—Backbone of Japan's Economy

Japan's wet climate is ideally suited to the cultivation of rice. Soon after rice was introduced, it became Japan's primary staple crop. It was also the chief medium of exchange in Japan until the 1200s.

Rice growing drastically changed the way of life in early Japan, for unlike hunting and gathering, it required the concerted effort of the entire community. Because rice was so precious, feuding clans often destroyed each other's rice fields or irrigation systems. In the 600s, those caught destroying valuable rice fields received severe punishment.

Chinese Culture in Japan

Chinese Buddhism was introduced into Japan from Korea and China about A.D. 552. Shintoists, fearing Buddhism might eclipse

At this company in Asahikawa, workers start the day by exercising.

These beautiful sword guards, made in the 1700s, separated the sword handle from the blade. The smaller of the two sword guards pictures Buddha and Confucius standing under a pine tree.

1952 The U.S. occupation of Japan ends. Japan continues the rebuilding of its war-torn cities and eventually becomes one of the world's leading economic powers.

1250 | 1625 | 2000

1192 Shogunate begins. Samurai of this period often wore steel swords like the one above made in the 1100s.

1603–1867 The Tokugawa shogunate closes Japan to Western nations. Laws forbid Japanese subjects from leaving the country without permission.

Today

Understanding the Visuals

Like many other aspects of the samurai warrior's life, the creation of his sword included rituals and ceremony. These rituals came mostly from the Shinto religion. For example, some swordsmiths followed Shinto dietary rules while forging a samurai blade. They also wore court robes. The forge would then be decorated with Shinto symbols, such as rope made from straw and cut paper.

The samurai values of hard work, discipline, honor, and loyalty to authority can be seen in the workers of today's Japan. Many workers remain at the same company for their entire professional lives. They are fiercely competitive, while at the same time loyal to their company and coworkers. In turn, the companies extend a wide umbrella of support, including exercise programs such as the one shown here.

Understanding Chronology

Refer students to the timeline. Point out the steady development of a strong national identity and culture continuing into the post–World War II period.

Shinto, reconciled their beliefs with Buddhist doctrine. Today, the majority of Japanese practice both Buddhist and Shinto rituals.

Buddhism sparked an interest in all things Chinese. The Japanese borrowed and adapted a variety of Chinese ideas, including their centralized system of government and parts of the Chinese writing system.

Evolving Cultural Traditions

Every twenty years Japan's most sacred shrine at Ise (EE say) is demolished. It is then rebuilt according to the same design but with new materials. Like that shrine, Japan's society continually rebuilds itself, following the past as a blueprint. Each period of outside influence is blended into a new but uniquely Japanese society.

The Western forces that occupied Japan after its defeat in World War II introduced their popular culture to Japan's youth. In time, blue jeans and rock music arrived.

Western influence has been limited, however, by a historically rigid social structure. Once a young Japanese becomes a *shakaijin* or "member of society," he or she sheds popular culture for traditional roles. For men, this occurs when they go to work; for women, when they marry and, in most cases, become homemakers. Men and women feel pressure to stay within their traditional roles in society in order to keep the social structure intact. In today's world, Japanese culture is still influenced by time-honored conventions.

INTRODUCE

Point out the lesson title. Tell students that the country of Japan is made up of thousands of islands. Ask students to use the map on page 361 to describe the geographic features of the islands of Japan and to name the nearby countries or continents. Have them read the Thinking Focus, and ask them to predict how the fact that Japan is made up of islands might affect its development. Have students read the lesson to confirm or reject their predictions.

Key Terms

Vocabulary Strategies: T36–T37

Shinto—a Japanese religion whose followers believe that all things in the natural world are filled with divine spirits

isolation—the condition of being separated from other people, ideas, or objects

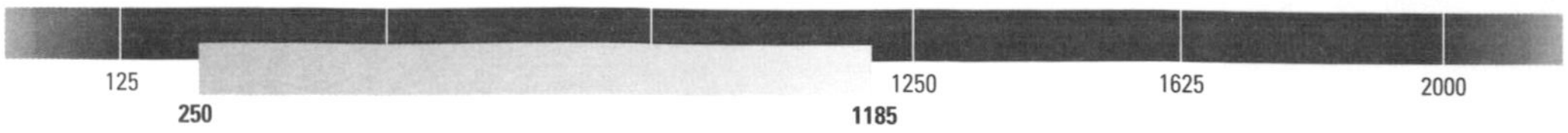
125
250
1250
1185
1625
2000

LESSON 1

Island Culture

THINKING FOCUS

How did Japan's geography affect the development of its culture?

Key Terms

- Shinto
- isolation

In the beginning there was chaos. Then heaven and earth divided, and the Lord of Heaven sent two young Gods, Izanagi and Izanami, to create beauty. Izanagi threw a spear into the ocean. As he pulled the spear out, drops fell and formed the islands of Japan.

This is how the world began, according to Japanese mythology. Today scientists say that volcanoes erupted millions of years ago forming mountains on the floor of the Pacific Ocean. These mountains pushed up out of the ocean and created the islands of Japan.

With its rocky coastlines and forest-covered mountains, Japan is a land of great beauty. Perhaps this is why the Japanese have always shown such an appreciation for the wonders of the natural world.

➤ *The Gods Izanagi and Izanami are shown in this painting. According to a Japanese myth, they created the islands of Japan.*

Land of the Rising Sun

In total area Japan covers a little less land than the state of Montana. As you can see from the map on page 361, Japan has four large islands: Hokkaido *(hah KY doh),* Honshu, Shikoku, Kyushu *(kee OO shoo),* and thousands of smaller islands. These islands stretch about 1,500 miles from north to south. If the islands were placed next to the east coast of the United States, they would reach from Maine to Florida.

The Japanese people do not call their country Japan. They call it either Nihon or Nippon. We get the name Japan from the Chinese pronunciation of Nippon. The word *Nippon* means "where the sun has its origin." This is why Japan is often called the Land of the Rising Sun.

Objectives

1. Analyze the interaction between environment and culture in Japan.
2. Describe some of the early influences on the development of Japanese culture.

Graphic Overview

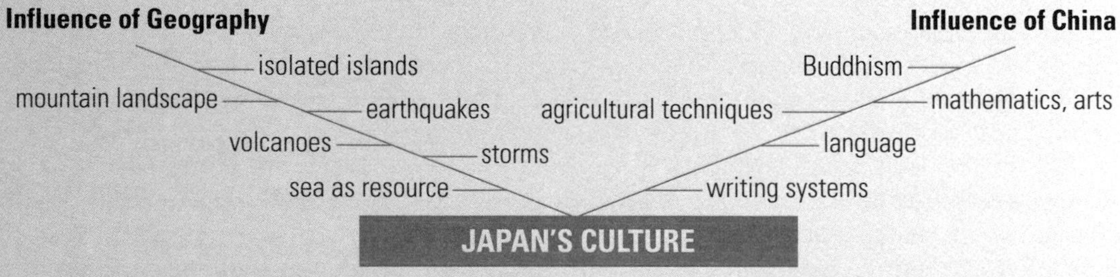
Influence of Geography
isolated islands
mountain landscape
earthquakes
volcanoes
storms
sea as resource
Influence of China
Buddhism
mathematics, arts
agricultural techniques
language
writing systems
JAPAN'S CULTURE

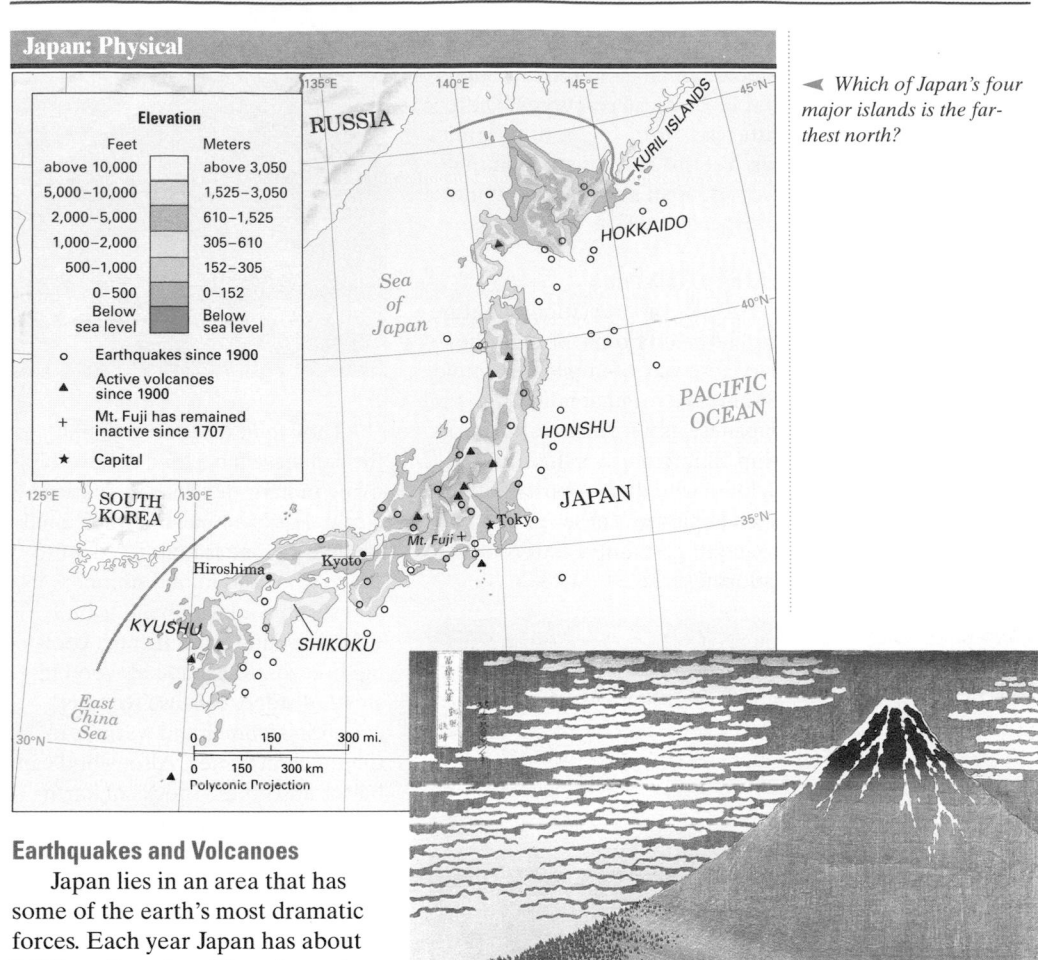

Japan: Physical

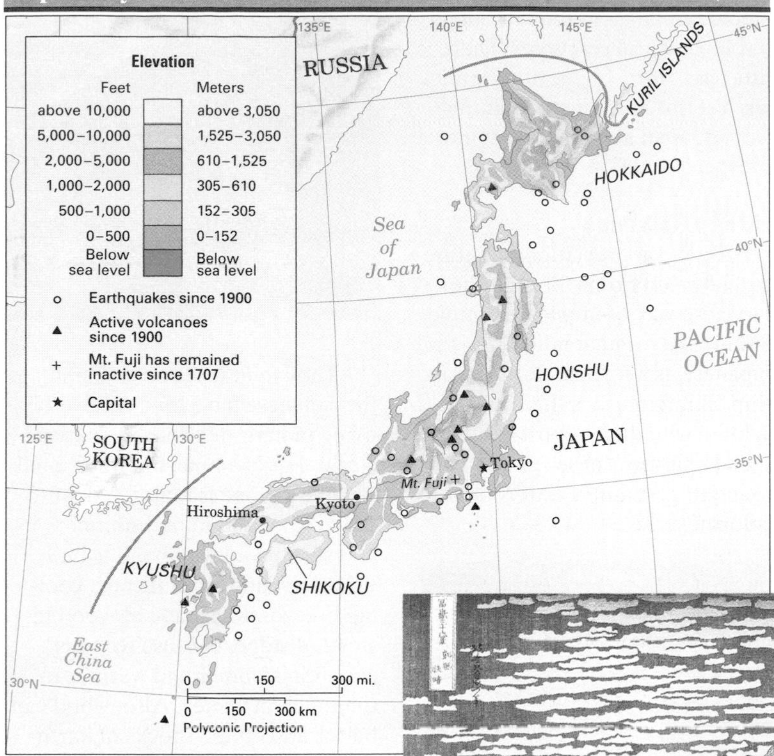

Elevation
Feet
Meters
above 10,000
above 3,050
5,000–10,000
1,525–3,050
2,000–5,000
610–1,525
1,000–2,000
305–610
500–1,000
152–305
0–500
0–152
Below sea level
Below sea level
Earthquakes since 1900
Active volcanoes since 1900
Mt. Fuji has remained inactive since 1707
Capital
RUSSIA
KURIL ISLANDS
HOKKAIDO
Sea of Japan
PACIFIC OCEAN
HONSHU
JAPAN
Tokyo
Mt. Fuji
Kyoto
Hiroshima
SOUTH KOREA
KYUSHU
SHIKOKU
East China Sea
135°E
140°E
145°E
125°E
130°E
45°N
40°N
35°N
30°N
0 150 300 mi.
0 150 300 km
Polyconic Projection

Which of Japan's four major islands is the farthest north?

Mount Fuji is the tallest of Japan's volcanoes. It stands almost 12,390 feet high. Each year thousands of people climb to the Shinto shrine on its peak.

Earthquakes and Volcanoes

Japan lies in an area that has some of the earth's most dramatic forces. Each year Japan has about 1,500 earthquakes. Though most are mild, some cause serious damage. At times earthquakes shake the ocean floor near Japan. These cause tidal waves that smash into the coast, destroying homes and killing people.

Japan also has more than 150 major volcanoes—60 of which are still active. Violent ocean storms sometimes visit Japan. Their heavy winds and rains batter Japan's coasts and flood its valleys.

Natural Resources

Mountains and hills cover most of Japan. Less than 20 percent of the land is suitable for farming. Because of Japan's mild climate and plentiful rainfall, most of this land is used for growing rice. In addition to rice, Japanese farmers grow crops such as soybeans, vegetables, and barley.

The sea has provided another source of food. For centuries fish has been an important part of the Japanese diet. A traditional dinner often includes seafood, such as fish, squid, and octopus, with rice.

DEVELOP

Draw the Graphic Overview on the chalkboard, including only the titles of the two branches. Ask students to copy this chart on a sheet of paper. Explain that the two main branches represent the main influences on early Japanese culture and reflect the structure of the lesson. Have students think about and discuss the geographic isolation of living on an island. Tell students that in this lesson they will learn how Japan's geography affected the cultural development of its early peoples. As students read the lesson, ask them to fill in details in their graphic overviews.

Hokkaido Island is the farthest north of Japan's four major islands.

GEOGRAPHY

Critical Thinking

Have students use the map and the text on this page to describe the significant aspects of Japan's physical geography. *(Volcanoes, earthquakes, mountains)* Then have them list the advantages and disadvantages of living on the islands of Japan. *(Advantages include the sea as a barrier to foreign invaders and a source of abundant seafood; disadvantages include little farmland and few resources.)*

Access Strategy

Ask students if they have ever lived on an island or visited one. Have them imagine what it would be like if the state they live in were in the middle of the Atlantic Ocean or Pacific Ocean. Ask students how the geography of their island would affect the way they live. For example, if their state has little arable farmland—like Nevada, perhaps—they would be forced to look to the ocean and the nearest continent for the resources needed to survive. Ask students what their major industries would probably be, regardless of the geography of their island state. *(Fishing, possibly tourism)* Other points of discussion might include transportation, development of culture in isolation, interaction with people from other states, and military concerns. Point out that the geography of Japan, a mountainous island nation with little fertile land and few natural resources, has greatly affected the development of its people and culture.

Access Activity

Have students locate Japan and the Asian mainland on the map of Eurasia on page 683 in the Atlas. Point out that the mainland is 100 miles from Honshu. Ask students what significance this distance might have on the economic and cultural development of Japan a thousand years ago. *(People would be isolated from mainland cultures; trade would require seaworthy boats.)*

■ *Japanese houses are small, reflecting the land shortage in Japan. Houses are constructed of wood and are elevated from the ground to adapt to the hot summers and earthquakes that frequently shake the islands.*

CULTURE

Critical Thinking

The Japanese adopted only portions of Chinese writing and went on to develop their own distinctive blend of Chinese and Japanese characters. They also replaced Chinese building materials of mud and brick with wood, which is better suited to Japan's more humid climate. Tell students that this is called selective borrowing. Ask them how selective borrowing benefited Japan's culture. *(By borrowing and adapting only selected elements, the Japanese limited outside influences and maintained their own cultural traditions.)*

➤ The "wedded rocks" of this Shinto shrine are linked by a straw rope. In the Shinto religion, the rocks are associated with the Gods who created the islands of Japan.

Other than its mild climate, ample rainfall, and the sea, Japan has few natural resources. There is little coal, iron, oil, or other minerals. Yet this has not stood in the way of Japan's development into a prosperous nation.

Living with Nature

A deep appreciation of nature and its beauty runs through the Japanese way of life. For example, **Shinto,** the original religion of the Japanese, is a form of nature worship. Shinto teaches that the world is filled with divine spirits that are seen in nature. These spirits may be found in a beautiful waterfall or a colorful sunset.

Though nature can be harsh, the Japanese have long believed in living in harmony with the natural world. For example, the traditional Japanese home is built to adapt to Japan's hot and humid summers and short, cold winters. It is built off the ground to let it catch cooling breezes. It is made of wood instead of stone, because wood is cooler in summer and warmer to the touch in winter. Also, wood can better absorb the shocks of earthquakes. The tile roof has overhangs to provide protection from the sun and the rain.

The traditional Japanese home welcomes the outside world. Inner walls are often lightweight paper screens that can be slid back to open up onto a courtyard garden or closed for privacy. ■

■ *How does traditional Japanese housing reflect Japan's geography?*

▲ Most rooms in a traditional Japanese home have little furniture. Straw mats called tatami *cover the floor. At night cotton mattresses called* futons *are rolled out for sleeping.*

Island People

Archaeologists tell us that the first people to live in Japan came from Korea and northeast Asia more than 100,000 years ago. Find South Korea on the map on page 361. Notice how close it is to Japan.

The flow of people into Japan continued into the eighth century A.D. Then it stopped. After this, Japan's seas acted as a natural barrier keeping Japan in **isolation,** or setting it apart. For about the next thousand years, Japanese society grew with little influence from other countries except China.

Early Cultures

In about 4000 B.C., the Jomon *(JOH mahn)* society developed in Japan. The Jomon were fishers and

Study Skills

Have students form research groups to prepare a three-page report on the Shinto religion. Suggest that they use library sources including encyclopedias to find answers to some or all of the following questions: How is Shinto a form of nature worship? How did Shinto react to the introduction of Buddhism in the A.D. 500s? How is Shinto linked to Japanese culture?

Political Context

Partly in response to Chinese influence, the Japanese government underwent a major change during the 7th and 8th centuries. The *ritsu-ryō* system was put into place. The system included *ritsu* laws, which governed criminal actions, and *ryō* laws, which governed civil and administrative actions. The system was modeled on a Chinese system in which the emperor controlled the nation absolutely. However, the Japanese modified the Chinese system where their needs varied. For example, in addition to governing the nation through the *ritsu-ryō* system, the Japanese emperor was also the nation's spiritual leader. In that role, he represented the people before their Gods, interpreting the will of the Gods and offering tribute to them on the people's behalf. Each of the emperor's two roles was carried out by its own branch in the government: the Council of State *(Dajōkan)* dealt with bureaucratic matters, while the Office of Deities *(Jingikan)* dealt with spiritual matters.

hunter-gatherers. In about 200 B.C., the Jomon were replaced by a new group called the Yayoi *(yah YOY).* The Yayoi taught the Japanese how to cultivate rice in water. They also brought metal tools to irrigate and level the land. The Yayoi changed the Japanese to farmers.

Later the Yayoi were replaced by another culture called the Yamato. Under the Yamato rule (A.D. 250–710), Japan became a unified nation. For a short time during the fourth and fifth centuries, the Yamato were powerful enough to gain control of Korea.

From China to Japan

In Korea the Japanese came in contact with Chinese civilization and a new religion, Buddhism. As you read in Chapter 15, China was considered the most advanced civilization in the world at this time. The more the Japanese learned about China, the more they admired what they saw.

When Prince Shōtoku became the ruler in A.D. 593, he sent students to China to learn more about its culture and government. He also welcomed Chinese scholars and artists to Japan. They brought Chinese language, arts, mathematics, and agricultural techniques to Japan.

This cultural borrowing continued for many centuries and deeply affected the way the Japanese thought and lived. Japanese music, architecture, sculpture, and painting went through enormous changes.

Between 794 and 1185, the emperor's court was in the city of Heian *(HAY ahn),* later called Kyoto *(KYOH toh).* During this time, called the Heian period in Japanese history, a culture of refinement and luxury came into being. The Chinese influence could still be seen in this culture. Yet it had been changed into something new and uniquely Japanese.

A good example of how the Japanese adapted Chinese culture is the writing system. Since the Japanese had no writing system of their own, they used the Chinese system. Yet because the languages are very different, some of the Chinese symbols could not express Japanese words or feelings. Over time the Japanese created their own symbols to better express their own language.

Poetry was the favorite form of writing among Japanese courtiers. Courtiers were finely dressed men and women who took part in the social life of the court. After poetry, diaries were the favorite form of writing. Women wrote some of the greatest literature of the age. ■

Across Time & Space

The Japanese imperial line of rulers was started in the fifth century by the Yamato clan. Akihito, who occupies the emperor's throne today, is one of the clan's descendants. Since 770, only males have been allowed to succeed to the throne. Before that time several women ruled Japan as empresses.

■ *How did the early culture of Japan develop?*

REVIEW

1. **FOCUS** How did Japan's geography affect the development of its culture?
2. **CULTURE** What contributions did the Jomon and the Yayoi peoples make to Japanese civilization?
3. **BELIEF SYSTEM** What is the Shinto religion?
4. **CRITICAL THINKING** What are some advantages of a country's developing in isolation from the outside world? Can you think of any disadvantages?
5. **ACTIVITY** Find Japan on the map on page 689 of the Atlas. What does the map tell you about land use in Japan? What else does the map tell you?

POLITICAL SYSTEMS

Critical Thinking

Although Japan borrowed many ideas from Chinese culture, the Japanese shaped these ideas into something unique. During the Heian period, the arts flourished—poetry, painting, sculpture. Ask students what political conditions probably existed in order for the arts to thrive at this time. *(A period of political stability and no attacks from outsiders)*

■ *People migrated to Japan from Korea and northeast Asia. The Japanese changed from fishers and hunter-gatherers to farmers. For most of its early history, Japan developed in isolation with little influence from countries other than China.*

CLOSE

Reread the Thinking Focus aloud. Then have students review the Graphic Overviews they have completed. Ask volunteers what they have added to the Influence of Geography portion of the diagram. *(Possible answers: isolated islands, mountain landscapes, sea as a resource, earthquake zone)*

Answers to Review Questions

1. As an island nation, Japan developed in isolation. Its mountainous terrain meant that there was a shortage of good farmland. This led to the development of a fishing industry. Its climate led to the development of intensive rice planting and special architecture for Japanese houses.
2. The Jomon established one of Japan's earliest cultures. The Yayoi introduced the cultivation of rice in water, metal tools, and irrigation techniques.
3. Shinto is a religion that developed early in Japan's history. It is based on a form of nature worship and is still practiced today.
4. Advantages: people interact more easily because they have similar beliefs and customs; disadvantages: there may be a lack of new ideas.
5. The map shows Japan to be a long chain of islands where fishing is important. It is highly urbanized and industrialized, with forests and some farmland.

Homework Options

Have students read the legend on page 360 and write a paragraph describing what it tells about how the early Japanese felt about themselves. *(They thought their land was created by the Gods and that their rulers descended from the Gods. Therefore, they probably believed that the Gods favored them.)*

Study Guide: page 63

INTRODUCE

Appreciation of the natural world is an enduring element of Japanese culture, as shown by the poems on these pages. In just a few words each poem captures a moment of joy, surprise, beauty, or contemplation. Students have read about the Japanese principle of living in harmony with nature in Lesson 1 of Chapter 16.

READ AND RESPOND

Reading the poems aloud to students in a quiet setting may help them enter the moment presented in each poem. After students listen or read, ask them to think about what the writers saw or sensed that made them want to stop and record the moment.

Before students read, point out the vocabulary words and unfamiliar terms defined in the margins. Be sure students understand what the words mean; help with pronunciation if necessary.

➤ In *haiku* a few words can conjure up a complete scene. Ask students to envision the scene Sanpū experienced in "May rains!" and describe its details. *(Details might include heavy rain and frogs leaping in deep puddles.)*

LITERATURE

Japanese Poetry

Written by Sanpū, Bashō, and Gokason

As you read in Lesson 1, writing poetry has been a popular and well-respected art form in Japan for many centuries.

Japanese poets sometimes use special forms of verse that must have a certain number of lines and syllables. The first three poems on these pages are haiku, *which you may have read (and written) in language arts. They are translated by Kenneth Koch. The others, given in both Japanese and English, are* senryu, *short poems that are usually about everyday events and thoughts.*

May rains!
Now frogs are swimming
At my door.
—Sanpū, 1647–1732

mallow a flowering plant

Beside the road
Mallow flowers bloom—
Now eaten by my horse!
—Bashō, 1644–1694

How cool it feels
To take a noonday nap
With my feet against a wall!
—Bashō, 1644–1694

Thematic Connections

Social Studies: Culture/Projecting an image to the world

Houghton Mifflin Literary Readers: Poetry/Moving the World

Background

Traditionally, *haiku* contain a "season word" and are divided into two rhythmic parts, as in the frog poem by Sanpū. Traditional Japanese *haiku* also contain a limited number of sound symbols. English translations of 10 to 12 syllables are similar in duration to classical *haiku.*

Matsuo Bashō (1644–1694) was a great master of Japanese *haiku.* He emphasized that a *haiku* is a deep kind of seeing in which the writer and the object observed become one.

Senryu (sounds like "send you") are not always easy to distinguish from *haiku.* This form is named after Katai Senryu (1718–1790), a writer who collected humorous longer poems about human nature. *Senryu* tend to emphasize human concerns rather than nature, as in the one on page 365 that starts "When I think." Also, *senryu* do not always speak about the here and now, whereas *haiku* usually do.

The kite with a
full stomach
flies high in the sky.

Hara no ii
tombi kōkū ni
takaka mai

—*Gokason*

kite a large bird, member of the hawk family

When I think it's mine,
how light this big bundle is.

Waga mono to
omoeba karushi
ōzutsumi

—*Gokason*

Wondering
where they're going,
the clouds disappear.

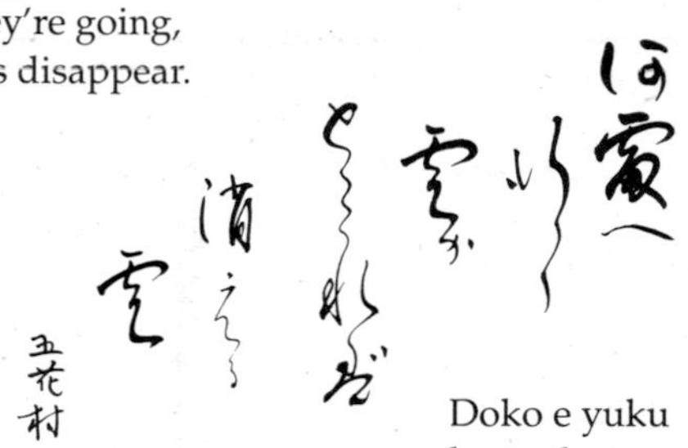

Doko e yuku
kumo ka to mireba
kieru kumo

—*Gokason*

Further Reading

In the Eyes of the Cat: Japanese Poetry for All Seasons. Selected and illustrated by Demi, these delightful short nature poems in a variety of Japanese styles come from different countries.

Valley of the Broken Cherry Trees. Lensey Namioka. An unemployed young samurai and his friend solve a mystery in 16th-century Japan.

➤ What is unsaid in this *senryu* but is suggested by the words "full stomach"? *(The kite has recently swooped down on a prey and eaten it, or the paper kite has filled with air.)*

➤ Which poems present a dramatic moment perceived in an everyday occurrence? *("May rains!" "Beside the road," "The kite," "Wondering")* Which *haiku* presents a single, keenly felt sensation? *("How cool it feels")*

EXTEND

Have students use anthologies to prepare a collection of favorite *haiku.* Students may wish to focus on a particular theme, such as humor, flowers, or animals. (Note: Writing *haiku* is an activity in Lesson 1 of Chapter 16.)

365

Collaborative Learning

Divide the class into groups of six. Each group should assign one poem to every student. After students have read their poems silently, ask them to imagine the moment that led the writer to record it, or to recall a similar moment from their own experience. Then have each student read his or her poem and describe to the group the moment it suggests. For example, the *senryu* "Wondering" may make students think of a windy March day when they saw high puffs of clouds scoot across the sky and disappear beyond the horizon.

Further Reading

You may want to have students look for more examples of traditional and modern *haiku* and *senryu* in the school or local library.

INTRODUCTE

Have students read the Thinking Focus. Explain that in the 1100s, Japan went through several long periods of civil disturbance. Explain that this lesson will describe Japan's unification through war, its period of isolation from the rest of the world, and finally, its renewed interaction with the world through commerce and more war. Ask students to think about the advantages and disadvantages of a policy of isolationism as they read the lesson.

Key Terms

Vocabulary Strategies: T36–T37

shogun—the title of a line of military leaders who ruled Japan for 700 years

samurai—warriors who became a new class in society under the shogun

feudalism—a political system in which lords exchange land for service or military protection

westernize—to adopt the ways of Western nations such as the United States and Great Britain

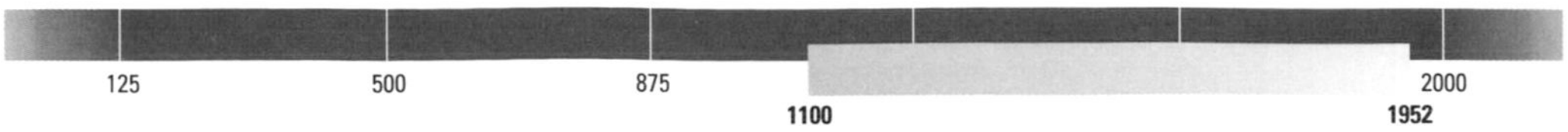
125
500
875
1100
2000
1952

LESSON 2

History of Japan

THINKING FOCUS

Why did the Japanese view the outside world with suspicion?

Key Terms

- shogun
- samurai
- feudalism
- westernize

> Tomoe galloped into their midst, rode up alongside Moroshige, seized him in a powerful grip, pulled him down against the pommel of her saddle. . . . She discarded armor and helmet and fled toward the eastern provinces.
>
> Anonymous, from *The Tale of the Heike*

The passage you just read is from a collection of Japanese tales about war in the 1100s. It was a dangerous age, one in which men—and even a few women, as this description shows—won fame as warriors. It was a time when many swords clashed.

As Japan's nobles closed themselves away in the Kyoto court, warriors rode across the countryside. Inside the luxurious court, well-mannered nobles talked of music and poetry. Outside the court in Kyoto, there was a dangerous situation growing. Slowly the emperor was losing control of Japan.

Shoguns Gain Control

In the 1100s lawlessness was spreading throughout the provinces. People fought for land and power. Looking for help, the court at Kyoto asked nobles in the provinces to help them stop the fighting.

A fierce war broke out between the Taira and Minamoto warrior families. After a long battle, the Minamoto won control. Led by a man called Yoritomo, they set up a new government.

In 1192 the emperor gave Yoritomo the title **shogun,** meaning "the emperor's general." Yoritomo let the emperor and his court remain at Kyoto. The emperor was still called the ruler of Japan. In reality, however, the shogun now ruled Japan.

For about the following 700 years, Japan was ruled by military governments called shogunates. To keep order the shoguns tried to control almost every part of Japanese society and life. Shogunate rule was often cruel.

White Heron Castle near Kyoto was completed in 1609 by a Tokugawa. To reach it, an enemy would have had to pass through 11 barricades. However, the castle was never attacked.

Objectives

1. Describe the importance of the feudal period in Japanese history.
2. Explain the historical foundation for modern Japan's economic success.
3. Describe the westernization of Japan following the feudal period.

Graphic Overview

Isolated Japan

Decline of power of Kyoto court → Rebellion in provinces → Rule by shogun and samurai classes

Japan and the World

Tokugawa shogunate signs treaty with West → Meiji restoration → Japan westernizes

The Samurai

The shogun was supported by nobles who had large estates in the provinces. These nobles were known as *daimyo (DY mee oh).* Each daimyo relied on warriors called **samurai** *(SAM uh ry)* to wage battle against rival clans.

As a reward for their help, the samurai were given small pieces of land or official positions. This system in which people exchange land or services for protection is called **feudalism.** See Understanding Feudalism below.

The samurai became a new class in society. They lived by a code of behavior called *bushido,* or "the way of the warrior." The code called for strict obedience to one's superiors. A samurai was expected to give up his life if his lord wished it. If a samurai failed, he sometimes felt so humiliated that he would kill himself.

Samurai values, such as loyalty, honor, and hard work, spread to people of every class. They became a part of Japanese society. Today these are still values that the Japanese people respect.

From Wars to Unity

In spite of military rule, fighting continued for many centuries. By the mid-1400s, Japan was divided into hundreds of warring states.

Out of the chaos appeared a strong leader in the late 1500s. Oda Nobunaga was a powerful and smart

Samurai armor is made of steel, silk, and bronze. This armor was made between 1338 and 1573.

Understanding Feudalism

You can think of a Japanese samurai in much the same way as you think of a European knight in armor. Both kinds of warriors were part of a political system known as feudalism. In Europe, feudalism began in the 700s and lasted until the 1400s. In Japan, the system began in the 800s and lasted into the 1800s.

What Is Feudalism?

Under feudalism, people exchange land in return for service or military protection. The word *feudalism* comes from the Latin word *feodum,* which means "fief," or "estate." A lord gave a fief to a warrior in return for a pledge of loyalty and military service.

Feudalism Develops

In both Europe and Japan, feudalism developed at a time of political chaos. As governments became weak, people needed a way to protect themselves. In Chapter 18 you will read more about the growth of feudalism in Europe. In Japan, landowners in the provinces depended on samurai warriors to protect their estates and to wage war against rival clans.

Life under Feudalism

In both Europe and Japan, feudal society was divided into separate social classes. Landowners, priests, and warriors were at the top. At the bottom were the peasants who farmed the land.

Most people stayed in the class into which they were born. Each class obeyed rules of behavior, and change was frowned upon.

DEVELOP

Draw the Graphic Overview on the chalkboard. Explain that during the 1100s, Japan's center of government was located in Kyoto. Have students find Kyoto on the map on page 361. Point out that as military leaders in the provinces gradually gained power and fought for control of the government, the central government at Kyoto lost power. Ask students to predict how the rise of the military class (shogun and samurai) might have affected the culture of Japan. *(Japan would be tightly controlled; personal freedoms and opportunities would decline.)*

POLITICAL SYSTEMS

Critical Thinking

The feudal system was structured around an exchange of privileges and obligations among samurai, shogun, daimyo, and peasants. What does each group gain from feudalism? *(Samurai: land, status, power over peasants; shoguns and daimyo: military protection, loyalty; peasants: order, peace)* What obligations did each group have under feudalism? *(Samurai: loyalty to the death to their daimyo or shogun, military service, protection of peasants; daimyo: granting of land to samurai, loyalty to shogun; peasants: obedience to all other groups)*

Access Strategy

Ask students what the United States would be like politically, economically, and culturally if the police force were eliminated in each city and town. Students might suggest that crime would skyrocket. Eventually, people would probably band together for protection. Encourage students to consider that those who were strongest—in numbers, weapons, and physique—would control the land, its economic resources, and the weaker people. In time a new government would emerge, with the strongest military leaders at its head. In order to preserve the new unity, the government might announce a policy of isolation from the rest of the world. No one would be able to leave the United States, and trade and communication with other nations would stop. Ask students to discuss what their own lives might be like in this situation. Tell students that they will read about a similar set of circumstances in Japan's early history.

Access Activity

Direct students to the picture of the samurai suit of armor on this page. Then read aloud the Tokugawa law regarding samurai on page 368. Ask students how they might have felt if they were peasants and they saw a samurai approach them. Ask if they are surprised that the shogunate rule lasted some 700 years with the samurai there to keep order.

POLITICAL SYSTEMS

Study Skills

Point out that strong leaders like Nobunaga and Tokugawa guided Japan away from civil war and away from contact with the rest of the world. Have students make a two-column chart that lists the measures taken by Japanese leaders to unify Japan. Tell them to list in column one each measure taken, and to comment in column two on the effectiveness of each. *(Measures taken: modernize the army, create a strict social order, expel foreigners. Effectiveness: modernizing the army allowed Nobunaga and his successors to unify Japan under one government, a strict social order kept people under control, foreigners were successfully expelled; efforts at isolation were successful for 268 years.)*

CULTURE

Visual Learning

Have students examine the clothing of a samurai family on this page. Point out that the Tokugawa shoguns passed strict laws governing how each class could dress. Emphasize that the samurai, along with the daimyo, belonged to the upper class and had many more freedoms than the rest of Japanese society.

How Do We Know?

HISTORY *For warriors in medieval Japan, the ritual and ceremony of the battle were as important as the battle itself. Stories describing heroism in battle were popular.* The Tale of the Heike, *for example, tells about battles between the Taira and Minamoto clans in the 1100s.*

leader. Instead of swords and arrows, he armed his troops with muskets from Portuguese traders. With his modern army, Nobunaga soon controlled almost half of the country of Japan.

Still more power struggles followed Nobunaga's death. Finally, Nobunaga's assistant general succeeded in unifying Japan under one government. He was succeeded by Tokugawa Ieyasu *(ih yeh YAH soo),* who was named shogun in 1603. The Tokugawa shogunate would last until the 1860s.

The Tokugawa shoguns created thousands of laws limiting what peasants could and could not do. Some laws forbade peasants to leave the land or ride a horse. Other laws described the clothes and hairdos that peasants could wear. These laws were meant to uphold a strict class system. Outside of work, the classes rarely mixed except, perhaps, at a tea ceremony. For more on tea ceremonies, see A Moment in Time on page 369.

At the top of the social classes were the *daimyo* and samurai. Samurai had the freedom to enforce the laws as they saw fit. The following order by Tokugawa Ieyasu makes clear that it was dangerous not to obey a samurai.

> *Farmers, craftsmen and merchants may not behave in a rude manner towards samurai. The word for a rude man is "other-than-expected-fellow" and a samurai is not to be interfered with in cutting down a fellow who has behaved to him in a manner other than is expected.*

Closing the Doors

The Tokugawa shogunate was determined to keep Japan unified. For this reason, the Tokugawas decided to rid Japan of all outsiders. They did not want foreigners introducing new ideas that might lead to rebellion.

Soon after Portuguese traders reached Japan in 1542, Catholic missionaries began to visit Japan. As the number of Japanese who became Christians grew, the shogunate began to see the missionaries as a threat. The Tokugawas feared the missionaries might weaken the loyalty of the Christians. They also feared that *daimyo,* who became rich from foreign trade, might rebel.

Proper clothing for a samurai family often consisted of beautiful, long flowing robes for both the men and the women.

Critical Thinking

Ask students how they think Japanese Christians responded when their religion was outlawed. *(With anger and by worshiping in secret)* Ask how religion in Japan might have developed differently if Christian missionaries had not been outlawed there. *(Shinto might have declined, and Japanese Christians would not have believed that the emperor had divine rights.)*

Religious Context

The Japanese at first welcomed Christianity. Trade with the Portuguese, who brought the Christian missionaries, flourished as a result. Some daimyo even ordered their subjects to convert to Christianity. One such daimyo founded the port of Nagasaki to attract Portuguese trade. Even the great shogun Nobunaga welcomed the missionaries, hoping Christianity would help him undermine well-established rival Buddhist sects. During this period of toleration, some 150,000 to 300,000 Japanese converted to Christianity.

The Tokugawa shoguns later took extreme measures in an effort to uproot Christianity. They forced Christians to publicly forsake their faith. This ritual involved stomping on a Christian icon, which became known as a "treading picture" or *fumi-e.* Nonetheless, some communities, especially on Kyushu, remained secretly Christian until the laws were changed in the 19th century.

MOMENT IN TIME

. Tea Master

n, October 3, 1992
aroom in Kyoto, Japan

Ladle (Hishaku)
With a graceful gesture, he dips the bamboo ladle. For years he has practiced each movement of the ceremony.
Kettle (Kama) and Brazier (Furo)
Hot coals in a brass furo heat water in his cast iron kettle. The sound of water in the kama reminds him of wind blowing through trees. Tea masters have heard this sound for centuries.
Scoop (Chashaku)
ves his bamboo scoop a
al name—akatonbo. This
name of a red dragonfly
non in autumn. His tea
nony honors the fall season.
isk (Chasen)
ses his whisk
e stirring thin
or his guests.
is important
aring tea.
Tea Powder Container (Natsume)
Earlier this morning he poured green tea powder into his natsume to resemble a mountain. His guests appreciate the image from nature.
Tea Bowl
His tea bowls are simple and imperfect, as things are in nature. His favorite bowl has a faint crack shaped like an old vine in his garden.
369

Note: Use this Moment in Time to extend understanding of the Chinese influence on Japanese culture discussed on page 363.

CULTURE

Visual Learning

"A man with no tea in him is not in tune with the universe," says a Japanese proverb. Medieval Zen Buddhists believed that a person could reach this harmony, called satori, through mental exercise and meditation. The tea ceremony developed as part of this meditation. Have students study the picture and captions on this page. Ask students what visual clues show this to be a meditative activity. *(The man is kneeling, and his face seems to express deep concentration.)*

More About the Tea Ceremony
Introduced by Zen monks from China's Sung dynasty, the tea ceremony grew to be an important artistic ritual called *wabi-cha.* This tea ceremony demonstrates the simple quietude (or *wabi*) of Japanese life. The *wabi-cha* has become an artistic expression similar to the art of calligraphy.

In the *wabi-cha, cha-no-yo* (or hot water tea) is served in rustic tea pottery. The shape of the tea bowls varies according to the time of the year. "Winter" bowls are generally deeper than "summer" bowls.

Oral Report

Have students find out more about the traditional arts of Japan. Assign groups to use library resources to research different kinds of Japanese art, such as landscape painting, literature, flower arranging (called *ikebana*), gardening, and drama. Have students take notes and prepare an oral report. They can bring in pictures or other examples of the art they research. Encourage students to find out more about Chinese and other influences on Japanese art.

Art Connection

As a follow-up activity to the oral report, have students work in groups to assemble materials to create a facsimile of a piece of Japanese art. Materials might include rocks, water, sand, and plants for a rock garden; or brush and ink for a landscape painting; or pencils, markers, and paper to write stories or haiku. Have members of each group work separately or together to make Japanese-style works of art. Encourage them to share their creations with the class.

Visual Learning

Ask students to study the picture and explain how the tea ceremony reflects Zen ideals of natural simplicity and small beauties. *(Simple equipment; each element carefully assembled and in its place; serene expression; gentle movements)*

ECONOMICS

Critical Thinking

Emphasize the fact that the Tokugawa shogunate took measures to control the social classes and to isolate Japan in order to preserve its traditional economy and social structure. Ask students what effects these measures had on Japan in the 1600s. *(The merchant class prospered and gained political power. The economy boomed, and education spread to all the classes.)*

■ *The leaders wanted to keep Japan unified. They did not want foreigners introducing new ideas that might disrupt the peace.*

In the early 1600s, the shogunate outlawed Christianity, cut down on European trade, and expelled foreigners. No Japanese person was allowed to leave the country. The Tokugawas began a period of forced isolation. For more than 200 years, Japan had almost no contact with the outside world.

Business Booms

Japan did not stand still during this long period of isolation. Life in the cities was busy. More merchants were hired to bring food, cloth, and other goods to the capital city of Edo—which is now called Tokyo. Merchants became rich from their trade and their political power grew.

During the 1600s, education spread to all classes, and the economy boomed. The samurai learned to read, and many became government officials. By the 1800s Japan was a prospering nation.

Lured by the hope of new trade, Dutch, French, British, and U.S. ships tried to dock in Japanese harbors. Time and time again, the Tokugawas' answer was the same—"Go away!" The Japanese feared that they might fall under the rule of these powerful foreigners. ■

■ *Why did the Tokugawa shogunate close off Japan to outsiders?*

Japan Faces the West

In 1854, eight U.S. warships commanded by Captain Matthew C. Perry steamed into Edo Bay. Perry was determined not to leave empty-handed. He wanted a trade agreement with Japan. Japan could not keep the foreigners out any longer. Faced with the warships' threatening cannons, Japan gave Perry the treaty he wanted.

Soon the Japanese signed similar trade treaties with other Western nations. These treaties all seemed to put the interests of the foreigners ahead of the interests of the Japanese. One treaty went so far as to make foreigners exempt from Japanese law.

Many Japanese people grew very angry. Soon rebels who wanted to overthrow the Tokugawa shogunate made their voices heard all over Japan.

Meiji Restoration

The rebellion was led by a group of young samurai. In 1867 the rebels overthrew the Tokugawa shogunate. Then in 1868 they declared the restoration, or return, of the emperor's rule. This rule was called the Meiji *(MAY jee)*, which means "enlightened rule."

The Meiji leaders felt that the best way to protect Japan from foreigners was to **westernize.** The

During the Meiji Restoration, Japan went through a rapid modernization. This print of Yokohama in 1883 shows a trolley car and the city's first electric streetlight.

Critical Thinking

After the Meiji Restoration, Japan not only ended its isolation from the world, but actively reached out to the West for new ideas. Ask students to speculate about how this dramatic shift in approach might have affected the average Japanese person. *(Changes probably were looked on with fear and distrust by people used to such a closed society.)*

Language Arts Connection

After the Meiji Restoration, Japanese literature was strongly influenced by Western ideas. Just as the nation modernized its technology and transportation, some writers wanted to modernize Japanese literature too. They began to write European-style novels such as Futabatei Shimei's *The Floating Clouds* (1889). Since that time, Japan has produced many exceptional novelists, including Kawabata Yasunari (*Snow Country,* 1948), who in 1968 won the Nobel Prize for his work. You may wish to select a modern Japanese novel to read aloud to the class and then discuss it with students. Interesting Japanese children's literature includes *The Dragon Kite* by Nancy Luenn, *Winds and Wildcat Places* by Kenji Miyazawa, *The Golden Footprints* by Hatoju Muku, *Village of the Vampire Cat* by Lensey Namioka, and *Twenty-Four Eyes* by Sakae Tsuboi.

word *westernizing* means adopting the ways of developed countries in Europe and North America.

Thousands of Japanese students were sent to Germany, France, the United States, and Britain—just as Japan had sent students to China more than 1,300 years earlier. They studied Western business, military science, government, and education. Also, more than 3,000 Western teachers were hired to teach in Japan.

The government began building railroads and telegraph lines. By the end of the Meiji period in 1912, Japan was a modern nation with growing industries. It had a new constitution, compulsory education, and several universities.

Japan in World War II

Japan also wanted to build up an empire of its own. This led to war with China (1894–1895) and Russia (1904–1905). In 1910 Japan took control of Korea and in 1931 seized Manchuria from China.

By 1939 war was raging in both Europe and China. Japan had sided with the United States during World War I, but it joined Germany and the other Axis powers in World War II. Then, on December 7, 1941, without declaring war, Japanese planes attacked U.S. warships in Pearl Harbor, Hawaii. The United States declared war and joined the Allied fight against Germany, Italy, and Japan.

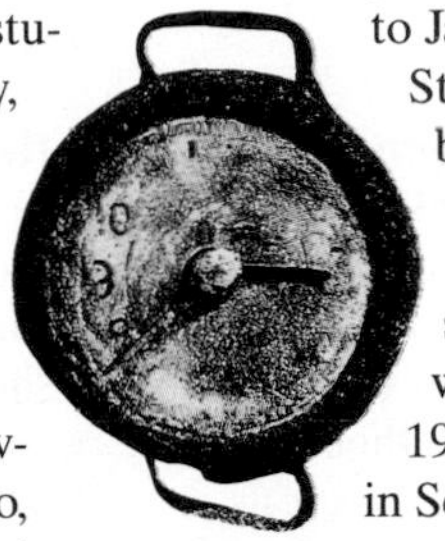

The Allies first defeated Germany and Italy and then turned to Japan. In 1945 the United States dropped atomic bombs on the Japanese cities of Hiroshima and Nagasaki. The Japanese surrendered within a week—on August 14, 1945. A treaty was signed in September.

Recovery

Japan's cities were in ruins, and more than one million Japanese had died. The United States decided that the best way to build a peaceful future was to help the Japanese rebuild their country.

The U.S. Army occupied—controlled—Japan for seven years after the war. Under the leadership of General Douglas MacArthur, the U.S. Army helped rebuild Japan.

During the occupation, Japan adopted a democratic constitution. It gave women the right to vote and outlawed the military forces. Then the United States poured technical know-how and money into rebuilding Japan's industries. By the end of the occupation in 1952, the groundwork had been laid for Japan's booming future. ■

◄ This watch was found in the ruins of Hiroshima. It reads 8:15 A.M.—the exact time the atomic bomb exploded. After Japan surrendered, the U.S. Army helped the Japanese rebuild Japan. In the photograph below, plans are being made to rebuild the Industrial Arts Building in Hiroshima.

■ *How did Japan's attitude toward the West change after the Meiji Restoration?*

REVIEW

1. **FOCUS** Why did the Japanese view the outside world with suspicion?
2. **GOVERNMENT** Describe shogun rule in Japan.
3. **CULTURE** What was *bushido*?
4. **CRITICAL THINKING** What advantages did Japan gain by being occupied by the United States after World War II?
5. **ACTIVITY** Use the information in the lesson to make a timeline that traces Japanese relations with other countries. Include dates from the Tokugawa shogun era to the end of the U.S. occupation in 1952.

ECONOMICS

Critical Thinking

Tell students to list ways in which Japan became westernized. *(Education abroad; bringing Western teachers to Japan; compulsory education; railroad and telegraph construction; industrialization; adoption of a new constitution)* Then ask how these changes helped the Meiji leaders achieve their goal. *(Japan became similar to the West in areas such as business methods, military science, government, and education.)*

■ *Japan's leaders decided to westernize so that they could meet the military and economic challenges of the West.*

CLOSE

Reread the lesson title and Thinking Focus. Then draw a timeline on the chalkboard using the following dates: 1100, 1200, 1300, 1400, 1500, 1600, 1700, 1800, and 1900. Have students work in groups to select events from the lesson that illustrate Japanese history. Then have one volunteer from each group add one or two events on the timeline. *(The timeline should show the rise of feudalism, the creation of the Tokugawa shogunate, the coming of Christianity, and the Meiji Restoration.)*

Answers to Review Questions

1. Isolationism was their tradition, and they were historically apprehensive of unknown cultures. They feared that foreign countries would try to conquer Japan.
2. Shogun rule maintained a very strict social order through laws regulating how each class was to live and work. The samurai were given virtually unlimited power.
3. *Bushido* was the strict code of conduct that the samurai warriors lived by.
4. Advantages gained include the adoption of a democratic constitution, the right to vote given to women, the rebuilding of industries.
5. The timeline should reflect these dates: 1612–1635—Tokugawa shogunate bans outsiders; 1854–1858—Perry arrives, Japan signs trade treaties with U.S.; 1868—Meiji Restoration, westernization; 1904–1938—Japan builds empire; 1941—Japan attacks Pearl Harbor; 1945—U.S. defeats Japan; 1952—U.S. occupation of Japan ends.

Homework Options

Have students interview friends, family, or neighbors about the U.S. and Japanese conflicts in the Pacific during World War II. Have them write a brief report on their findings and present it to the class. Students should verify their findings by reading historical accounts of this period.

Study Guide: page 64

UNDERSTANDING CARTOGRAMS

This skills feature uses a cartogram titled World: Petroleum Resources to teach students how to make comparisons using graphic information.

GEOGRAPHY

Map and Globe Skills

Have students compare the world petroleum resources cartogram and the world political map on these pages. Ask them to describe in one sentence what conclusions they draw about Japan's petroleum resources from their comparison. *(A possible answer is that Japan's petroleum resources are smaller in relative size to other nations than is its geographic size.)* Ask students to point to specific details on each map that support their answer. *(Japan's size on the cartogram is much smaller relative to other countries than its geographic size.)* Explain that such a comparison can help students draw conclusions about a country's strengths and weaknesses.

UNDERSTANDING CARTOGRAMS

Interpreting Symbols

Here's Why

Maps can show statistical information, such as population, rainfall, or resources, in many ways. For example, mapmakers may choose to use a standard map base and then add thematic information, which is explained in a map key. Mapmakers can also use cartograms.

Cartograms are chartlike maps that present statistical information through size. They rarely try to show the actual shape of a country or region. On a cartogram the sizes of real geographic areas are made smaller or larger according to the statistical information. Cartograms allow you to see information at a glance and make comparisons between countries quickly.

Suppose you want to compare Japan's petroleum resources with those of other major industrial nations of the world. Most industrialized nations depend heavily on petroleum for many purposes. Petroleum, often called crude oil, is the source of gasoline and kerosene. It can also be refined and made into products such as paints, plastics, synthetic rubber, soaps, medicines, and explosives. A cartogram can help you learn which countries have the most petroleum and which countries have the least.

Here's How

Look at the maps on these pages. Read the titles. Then find out how each map shows information.

The map below is a political map. It shows the countries of the world. Look carefully at the map. You can use this map as a basis for understanding the cartogram on the next page.

Now look at the cartogram on page 373. Notice that it has no scale of miles. The sentence at the bottom of map tells you that the size of each country is related to the amount of petroleum resources found in each country. The cartogram distorts

World: Political

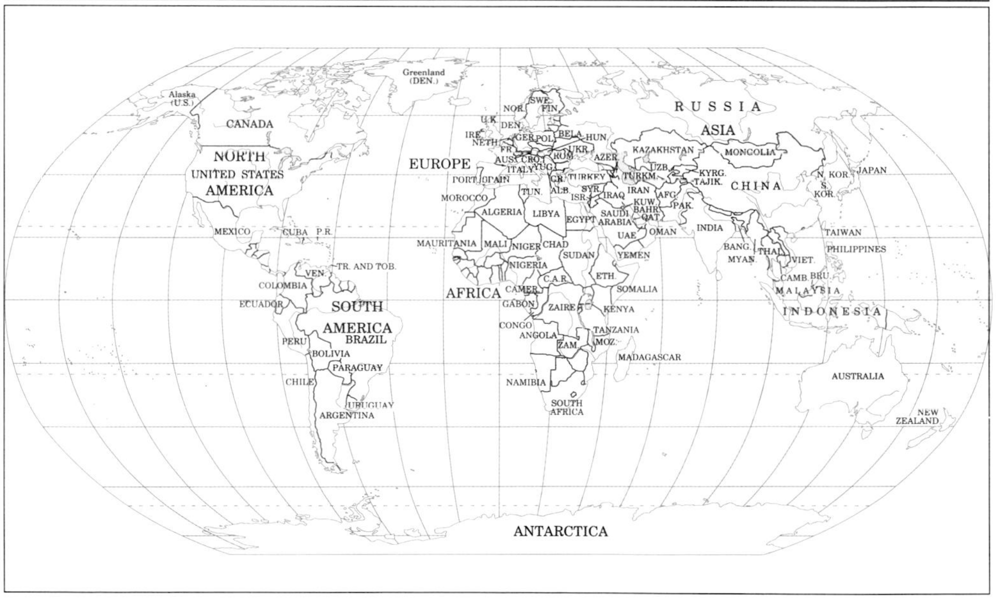
NORTH AMERICA
CANADA
UNITED STATES
SOUTH AMERICA
BRAZIL
EUROPE
AFRICA
ASIA
RUSSIA
CHINA
INDIA
INDONESIA
AUSTRALIA
ANTARCTICA

Objective

Read and interpret a cartogram. (Map and Globe Skills 1, 3, 4, 5)

Math Connection

The former members of the USSR produced more than 250 million metric tons of petroleum per year. Japan produced less than 5 million metric tons. Ask students to compute what percentage of the former USSR's production is represented by Japan's production. *(2 percent)*

Making a Chart

Have groups of students use the map and the cartogram to calculate how many nations produced more than 250 million metric tons of petroleum per year. Then have each group create a chart with two columns—one listing countries that produced more than 250 million metric tons, and one listing countries that produced less than 250 million metric tons. Have students determine how many nations fell into each category. Then have groups compare their findings.

the actual size and shape of countries to show how their natural resources compare.

Find Japan on the map on page 372. This map shows Japan's actual size. On the cartogram, however, Japan looks tiny because of its lack of petroleum resources. Now look at other major industrial countries such as the United States, Germany, and the United Kingdom. How do they compare with Japan in terms of actual size and in terms of petroleum resources?

Try It

Compare the cartogram on this page with the cartogram on page 375. What information does this cartogram show? Now find Japan on each cartogram. On which cartogram is Japan larger? What do these cartograms tell you about the relationship between Japan's economy and its petroleum resources? How does the Japanese economy compare with the economies of the United States, Germany, and the United Kingdom?

Apply It

Find Japan on the World Population Cartogram on page 689. How does the population of Japan compare with the population of the United States?

631
LUFKIN

World: Petroleum Resources

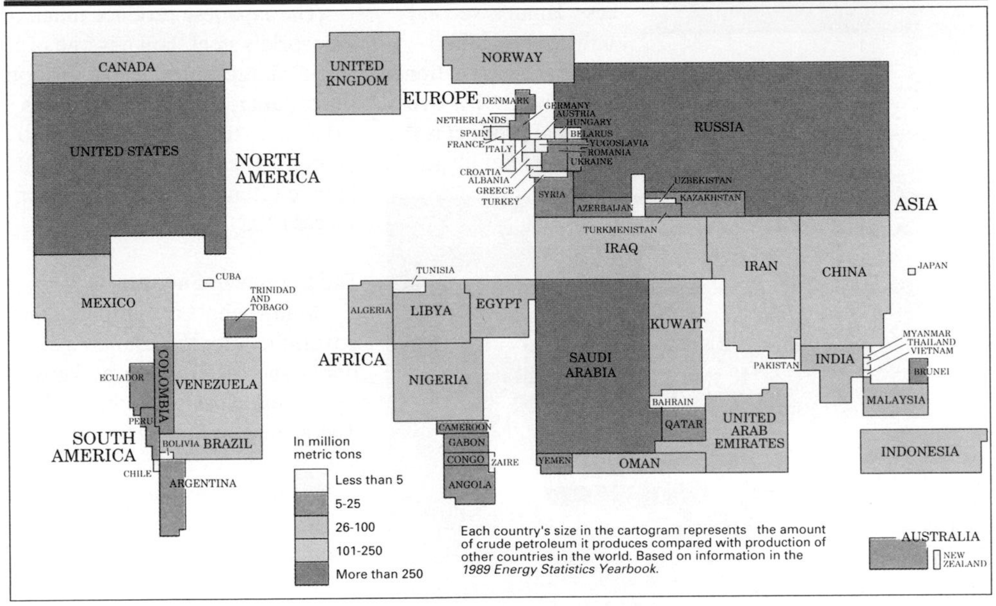
CANADA
UNITED STATES
NORTH AMERICA
MEXICO
CUBA
TRINIDAD AND TOBAGO
ECUADOR
COLOMBIA
VENEZUELA
PERU
SOUTH AMERICA
BOLIVIA
BRAZIL
CHILE
ARGENTINA
UNITED KINGDOM
NORWAY
EUROPE
DENMARK
NETHERLANDS
SPAIN
FRANCE
ITALY
GERMANY
AUSTRIA
HUNGARY
BELARUS
YUGOSLAVIA
ROMANIA
UKRAINE
CROATIA
ALBANIA
GREECE
TURKEY
SYRIA
RUSSIA
UZBEKISTAN
KAZAKHSTAN
AZERBAIJAN
TURKMENISTAN
IRAQ
IRAN
CHINA
ASIA
JAPAN
TUNISIA
ALGERIA
LIBYA
EGYPT
AFRICA
NIGERIA
CAMEROON
GABON
CONGO
ZAIRE
ANGOLA
SAUDI ARABIA
KUWAIT
BAHRAIN
QATAR
UNITED ARAB EMIRATES
YEMEN
OMAN
PAKISTAN
INDIA
MYANMAR
THAILAND
VIETNAM
BRUNEI
MALAYSIA
INDONESIA
AUSTRALIA
NEW ZEALAND
In million metric tons
Less than 5
5-25
26-100
101-250
More than 250
Each country's size in the cartogram represents the amount of crude petroleum it produces compared with production of other countries in the world. Based on information in the *1989 Energy Statistics Yearbook*.

ECONOMICS

Critical Thinking

Petroleum products are extremely important in today's modern societies. Ask students to list some of the ways petroleum products affect their lives. *(Gasoline for transportation of people and goods, oil to heat homes, gasoline to run small machines such as lawn mowers, consumer products made from plastics, chemicals used in fertilizers)* Then ask them to speculate on how limited petroleum resources or their absence might affect a nation's economy and its dependence on other nations.

Answers to Try It

This cartogram shows the world's petroleum resources. Japan is much larger on the cartogram on page 375, which shows Gross National Product, or GNP, of countries of the world. We can say that despite its lack of petroleum resources, Japan has developed a strong economy. According to the latter cartogram, the United States has the strongest economy, and Great Britain's (the United Kingdom's) is weaker than both Japan's and West Germany's, which are about the same.

Answers to Apply It

The population of Japan is smaller than the population of the United States. It appears from the cartogram that Japan has approximately less than half the number of people as the United States.

Study Skills

Explain that in addition to cartograms, students can use maps, graphs, charts, and diagrams to represent and compare information. Ask them to turn to Countries of the World on pages 674–677 in the Time/Space Databank and use one of these graphic tools to compare information about three countries of their choice. Have students share their work.

INTRODUCE

Point out the cartogram on page 375, and explain that Japan has a very successful economy that creates many goods and services (as measured by the total value of its Gross National Product, or GNP). Japan has a high GNP in spite of having very limited natural resources. Have students describe, from their reading of Lessons 1 and 2, some important values in Japanese society. *(Hard work, discipline, duty, loyalty)* Have them read the Thinking Focus aloud and then predict how these values might affect its economic progress.

Key Terms

Vocabulary Strategies: T36–T37

gross national product—the total value of all goods and services a nation produces yearly

standard of living—a measurement of how comfortable people's lives are

homogeneous—of the same kind

trade imbalance—a situation in which a country sells more goods to other countries than it buys or vice versa

125
500
875
1250
1625
1952
TODAY

LESSON 3

Japan Today

THINKING FOCUS

What factors have led to Japan's economic success?

Key Terms

- gross national product
- standard of living
- homogeneous
- trade imbalance

In 1946 about 20 people started a small electronics company. They used a burned-out building in the rubble of downtown Tokyo. There they made the first tape recorders and transistor radios in Japan.

Today this Japanese company—Sony—is one of the biggest companies in the world, with yearly sales of billions of dollars.

Like Sony, the Japanese people and their government also went to work after the war. As part of a national effort, they cleared bombed-out cities and turned them into thriving industrial centers. They bought the newest and most advanced machinery to equip their newly rebuilt factories. Today Japan stands as a leading economic power in the world.

The Japanese Miracle

Take a quick look at worldwide business facts, and you will see Japan's amazing success. Japan is second only to the United States in gross national product (GNP). **Gross national product** is the total value of all goods and services produced yearly by a nation. You can see this on the cartogram on page 375.

The Japanese produce much of the world's steel. Japan is one of the world's largest producers of robots, ships, paper, computers, cameras, videocassette recorders, and automobiles. The list goes on and on. People often call Japan's postwar success "the Japanese miracle."

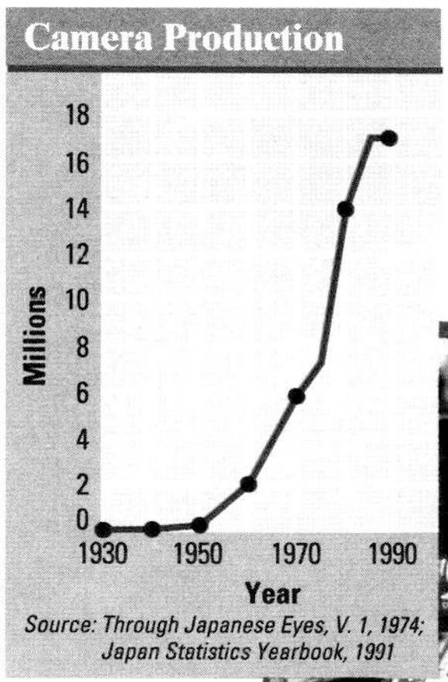
Camera Production
Millions
18
16
14
12
10
8
6
4
2
0
1930
1950
1970
1990
Year
Source: Through Japanese Eyes, V. 1, 1974; Japan Statistics Yearbook, 1991

➤ *By 1960, Japan's economy was taking off. Look at how camera production grew. This photograph shows an assembly line worker in a camera plant.*

The Secrets of Success

Many people credit the Japanese government for the country's economic success. Business and government work closely together in Japan. The government helps companies with money for research. It also helps businesses plan for the future.

Most Japanese, though, will tell you that the secret to their success lies in their people. Since Japan has

Objectives

1. Explain the reasons for Japan's economic success in today's world.
2. Describe life in contemporary Japan.
3. Identify some of the challenges that Japan faces at home and in the international community.

Graphic Overview

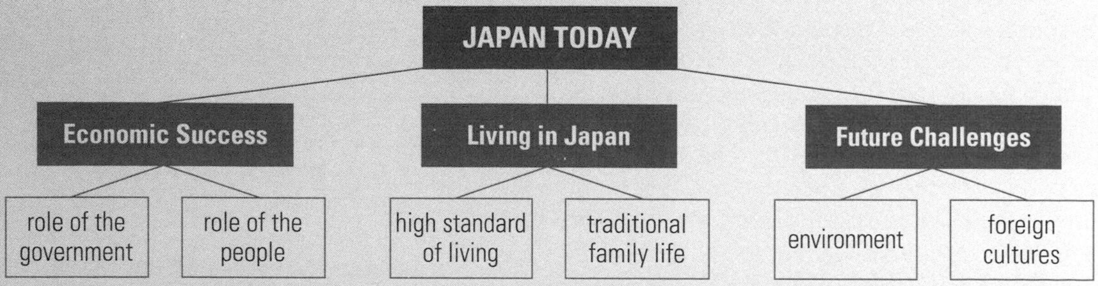
JAPAN TODAY
Economic Success
Living in Japan
Future Challenges
role of the government
role of the people
high standard of living
traditional family life
environment
foreign cultures

World: Gross National Product

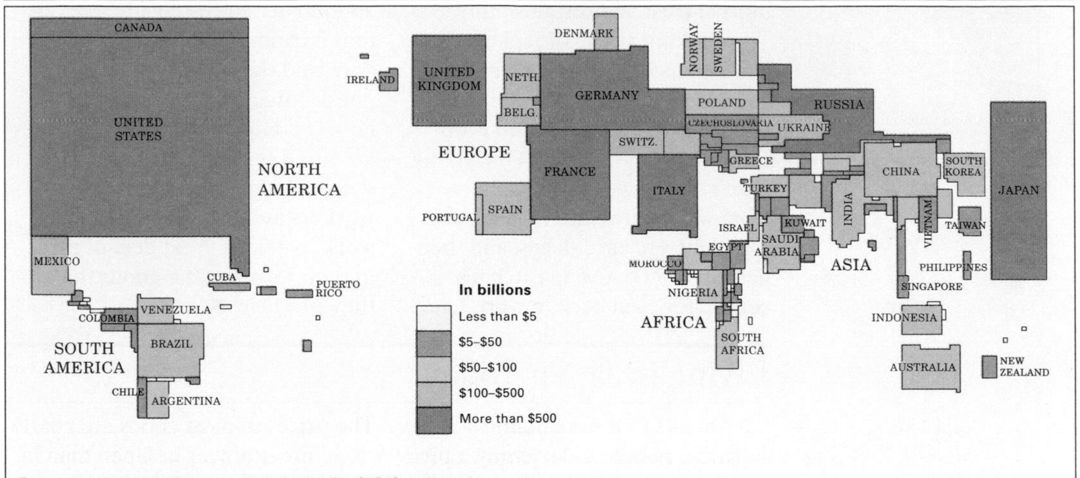
CANADA
UNITED STATES
NORTH AMERICA
MEXICO
CUBA
PUERTO RICO
COLOMBIA
VENEZUELA
BRAZIL
SOUTH AMERICA
CHILE
ARGENTINA
IRELAND
UNITED KINGDOM
DENMARK
NORWAY
SWEDEN
NETH.
BELG.
GERMANY
POLAND
RUSSIA
CZECHOSLOVAKIA
UKRAINE
EUROPE
SWITZ.
FRANCE
ITALY
GREECE
PORTUGAL
SPAIN
TURKEY
ISRAEL
KUWAIT
EGYPT
SAUDI ARABIA
MOROCCO
NIGERIA
AFRICA
SOUTH AFRICA
CHINA
SOUTH KOREA
JAPAN
INDIA
VIETNAM
TAIWAN
ASIA
PHILIPPINES
SINGAPORE
INDONESIA
AUSTRALIA
NEW ZEALAND
In billions
Less than $5
$5–$50
$50–$100
$100–$500
More than $500

Each country's size in the cartogram represents the size of its GNP (Gross National Product) compared with those of other countries in the world. Based on information in *The World Bank Atlas 1991* and *The World Factbook 1991*.

very few natural resources to fuel its industry, it relies on its human resources. In Japan the key to the future has been education.

The Role of Education

One very important reason for Japan's economic success is its highly educated work force. The nation has one of the world's highest literacy rates—99 percent of the Japanese people can read and write. In the United States, this number is about 85 percent.

In addition to being highly educated, the Japanese people share a set of values that make them extremely good workers. Cooperation, hard work, and loyalty are all very important to the Japanese. Children first learn these values at home and then at school.

They are also taught a sense of shared responsibility. Shared responsibility means that everyone pulls together to get a job done. In school or at work, you succeed as your classmates or work mates succeed (see Exploring Japanese and U.S. Schools on pages 380–381).

Today these cultural values have made the Japanese people some of the most productive workers in the world. Like Japanese schools, Japanese companies put great stress on working hard and being part of the group.

From School to Work

As a new workday begins at Matsushita, a Japanese electronics company, the workers gather to recite the company motto. The motto includes the lines, "Alone we are weak, together we are strong. We

▲ *This cartogram shows that Japan has the second highest GNP of any nation in the world—an amazing achievement for a small country with few natural resources.*

▼ *Japanese mothers are often called "education mamas," because they spend a great deal of time helping their children with their schoolwork.*

DEVELOP

Point out that four areas have influenced Japan's economic success—its education, its industry, its values, and its relations with others. These topics reflect the structure of the lesson. Have students think about and discuss the Japanese value of shared responsibility. Ask how a nation might encourage shared responsibility in its people.

Access Strategy

Ask students to imagine that their schoolwork will be graded on the basis of how each of their classmates performs, or that individual sports awards will be given according to the team's record. Then ask them how they might feel about this system and how it might affect their behavior toward their school and teammates. *(Those opposed might feel that the system is unfair and that their achievements might not be recognized. Those in favor of the system might say they would be inspired to help their schoolmates and teammates improve.)* Explain that much of Japan's society is governed by this idea of shared responsibility. Tell them that this lesson explores how the idea has affected Japan's economic success and its social structure.

Access Activity

Encourage students to look at the pictures in the lesson. Tell them to list everything the pictures depict about life in Japan today. Have a volunteer read the captions, and have students react to the Japanese values represented in the words and the images.

BELIEF SYSTEMS

Critical Thinking

Have students read aloud the Matsushita Company's motto that begins on page 375. Ask them to describe the value represented by this policy. *(Each worker is responsible for the success or failure of the whole team.)* Have students list some of the ways this value affects aspects of Japan's society—education, family life, and popular culture, for example. Then ask why they think this value has had such an impact on Japan's economic success.

■ *The Japanese emphasize education because they value a highly skilled work force.*

shall work together as a family in mutual trust and responsibility."

Working at one of Japan's giant companies is often very demanding. In order to get ahead, some male white-collar workers spend little time with their families. One young man's schedule is to arrive home from work between 11:00 P.M. and midnight. He eats, sleeps, and then gets up at 7:00 A.M. to catch his commuter train back to work.

"For the Japanese worker, life and job are so closely interwoven that it cannot be said where one ends and the other begins," says one Japanese writer. In Japan's largest companies, most employees are hired for life. This has created a sense of company loyalty among workers at all levels. As a result, workers take a great deal of pride in their jobs and the goods that they produce. ■

■ *Why is education very important in Japan?*

Living in Japan Today

Thanks to the economic boom, Japanese people today enjoy a high **standard of living.** People's standard of living is usually measured by how comfortable their lives are. In Japan's cities the standard of living is high but costly.

Tokyo, which has a population of more than 12 million people, is Japan's largest city. About 25 percent of the Japanese population lives in the area surrounding Tokyo. It is a modern city filled with high-rise buildings and crowded subways. Most of Japan's best universities are located in Tokyo. Its main shopping district, the Ginza, is famous throughout the world.

Living in Tokyo is expensive. The prices of most goods are nearly three times higher in Japan than in the United States. Food is also very expensive because the government helps Japan's farm families by keeping the price of farm goods high.

In large cities like Tokyo, the cost of owning a home is expensive. Along with the rising standard of living came a demand for better houses. So many people live in the cities, however, and land prices are so high, that few middle-class families can hope to own their own homes. A rather ordinary home, about one hour from downtown Tokyo, costs $500,000.

Family Life

Before World War II, two or three generations of a family often lived together. The oldest son stayed at home and brought his wife to live with him. Today most couples and their children live in small apartments of their own.

Japanese women are still expected to care for the home and the children. Yet it is becoming more common to find women working outside the home. As in the United States, a woman's salary is far below a man's salary. Also,

Tokyo is Japan's political, economic, and cultural center. Once a small fishing village called Edo, it is now one of the world's largest and most sophisticated cities.

Social Participation

Emphasize that Japanese workers often spend as much as 16 hours a day at work, including travel time. While most mothers do not work outside the home, many have begun to do so. Have students work in teams to role-play a scene from a typical day in the life of a Japanese family, including a mother, father, and children.

Social Context

Nemawashi, meaning "rootbinding," is a Japanese version of socializing after work that helps foster the sense of shared responsibility among workers. Coworkers gather in restaurants throughout the Ginza commercial district to share ideas in a friendly setting. Companies feel this practice helps workers identify common goals and avoid jealousies.

Shared responsibility doesn't end when the worker leaves for home. Industry also invites worker loyalty by helping employees cope with the high cost of living in Japan. An employee might pay as little as $80 a month to live in an apartment that is owned or subsidized by the company. The cost of a car or of commuting to work by train, as well as medical care, may also be paid by an employer.

men are far more likely to get the best jobs. Most Japanese women are hired as office workers or at various low-level jobs.

Slowly the traditional attitudes toward Japanese women are changing. One reason for this change has been the impact of the women's rights movement in Western countries. The Japanese government is aware of world opinion and does not want to appear out of step with other modern countries. This has helped strengthen Japan's own feminist movement.

Also, many Japanese companies realize that women are a highly educated resource. In new areas like biotechnology, Japanese women are making progress.

Baseball to Kabuki

In Japan life is more than just going to work and school. The Japanese entertain themselves in many ways. Their choices range from the traditional to the modern.

Sumo, a sport that dates back over 2,000 years, attracts thousands of spectators. Sumo is like wrestling. Huge men, sometimes weighing more than 500 pounds, face off in a ring. They throw, trip, and shove each other. The loser is the first to be forced out of the ring or to touch the ground with any part of his body besides his feet.

In August baseball fever grips Japan as the high school baseball tournaments are played. Today baseball is Japan's most popular spectator sport. The Japanese have professional baseball teams, with names like the Buffalos, the Braves, and the Tigers.

Much like people in the West, the Japanese enjoy many kinds of outdoor recreation. Hiking, skiing, golf, tennis, gardening, and fishing are popular. The Japanese also enjoy indoor sports such as basketball, volleyball, bowling, judo, chess, table tennis, and karate.

In addition to sports, a Japanese family might entertain themselves by going to the Kabuki theater. Kabuki theater goes back hundreds of years to feudal Japan. Kabuki plays range from tales of samurai adventures to stories based on

▲ *This little girl and her grandmother are on a shopping trip. Until the 1950s, it was customary for several generations of a Japanese family to live together.*

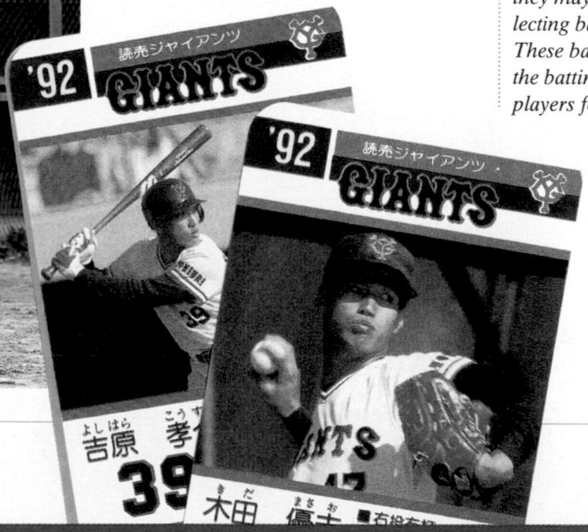
'92
読売ジャイアンツ
GIANTS
'92
読売ジャイアンツ
GIANTS

◄ *These two little girls await the first pitch. Like their U.S. counterparts, they may also enjoy collecting baseball cards. These baseball cards give the batting statistics of two players for the Yomiuri Giants—a very popular team in Japan.*

CULTURE

Study Skills

Tell students that a society's popular culture can reflect elements that are important to that society. Have students make a chart and in one column write down some favorite activities in Japan's popular culture—such as sumo, baseball, kabuki theater, Western music. In a second column, have students write down some of their own favorite activities. Encourage the class to compare the two lists.

Music Connection

Traditional Japanese music is an important part of the popular Bunraku puppet theater. Begun in the 17th century, Bunraku plays use singing or chanting to narrate the puppets' actions. A guitarlike instrument called a *samisen* provides accompanying music. Bunraku music, like other traditional Japanese music, has less melody or tune than Western music. You may wish to bring in some examples of traditional Japanese music for students to hear.

Japanese audiences are used to seeing, and ignoring, three masked puppeteers on the stage for each puppet. Bunraku puppeteering takes many years of practice and often a whole family becomes involved. The puppets, which are about half life size, are considered members of the family. You may wish to bring in some pictures of Bunraku puppets for students to see.

Study Skills

Suggest that students use the text and other library sources to research a popular Japanese sport or recreational activity. Have them bring in pictures or other visual materials to describe their topic to the class. Encourage students to highlight information about the history and current popularity of the sport or other activity.

■ *Many Japanese live in modern cities, can afford a very expensive lifestyle, and entertain themselves with a wide variety of activities.*

ECONOMICS

Critical Thinking

Have students work in groups to create a concept web of the challenges Japan faces in the future. Some branches of the web might be Environment, Social Unrest, and World Economics. Individual students can then contribute details about each branch. Then ask the whole class to participate in creating a final version of the web. Have students comment on how the factors in each branch may hurt or help Japan's future economic progress.

■ *How can you tell that the Japanese enjoy a high standard of living?*

current gossip. Singers and dancers wear fancy costumes and have colorfully painted faces. The "good guys" have white faces, and the "bad guys" have red faces.

Traditional forms of entertainment such as painting and dance continue to be enjoyed by the Japanese. However, Japan has become very westernized. In Tokyo you will see people enjoying many of the same things as you do. Rock music concerts, Western movies, operas, and plays are all popular. ■

Future Challenges

2
4
10
6

These people seem to be enjoying their retirement years, but many of Japan's elderly face a difficult future.

In spite of its economic success, Japan does face challenges in the coming years. The high standard of living that the Japanese people enjoy has come at a price. At home and in foreign countries, there are environmental and political issues that must be faced.

Environment

In their rush to develop industries, the Japanese created serious overcrowding in their cities. Pollution also became a problem. During the 1970s, children went to school wearing face masks to protect themselves from the smog. Industrial waste also flowed into Japan's rivers, poisoning many people.

The Japanese government has attempted to clean up the air and the waterways. By 1990, Japan had some of the toughest environmental protection laws in the world.

Dealing with Others

Japan has also had problems dealing with others, both at home and in foreign countries. At home Japan must face its treatment of minority peoples.

Japan has a very homogeneous population. **Homogeneous** *(hoh muh JEE nee us)* means "the same." The homogeneous nature of the Japanese people has both advantages and disadvantages. On the plus side, it has given the Japanese a strong feeling of unity. On the minus side, many Japanese people do not relate well to people who are not Japanese.

For example, in Japan the Korean population is not treated very well. More than 600,000 Koreans live in Japan. Although most were born in Japan and speak Japanese, they are not treated equally. The same can be said of the growing number of foreign workers living in Japan. Like the Koreans, they face a great deal of discrimination.

Japan's bullet trains travel at speeds of more than 100 miles per hour.

Critical Thinking

Remind students of the isolationist policies Japan has undertaken at various points in its history. Using what they recall from Lessons 1 and 2, ask them how they think this isolationism has contributed to the challenges the nation now faces. *(Japan lacks long-standing ties and friendships with other countries.)*

Writing an Editorial

Tell students that to combat a lack of sunlight caused by the crowding of tall buildings, the city of Tokyo created a policy called *nisshōken,* or sunshine right. Because many Tokyo residents have no central heat, sunshine is very important for warmth. *Nisshōken* requires builders to pay a fine to those who are overshadowed by their buildings. High-rise builders pay households a certain amount for each hour of sunlight lost on a winter day. Cases involving children often result in higher fines. Ask students to imagine they are the editor of a student newspaper in Japan. Have them write an editorial explaining their position for or against the government's policy of *nisshōken.*

Another group, the *burakumin,* are also social outcasts. They are descendants of butchers and leather workers, jobs that were once thought to be unclean. Although Japanese laws ban discrimination against minorities, it is still quite common.

Perhaps Japan's greatest challenge lies in its relationships with people from other countries. Japan's relationship with its trading partners has become a problem in recent years.

Japan sells enormous numbers of cars and high technology products in other countries. However, it limits the amount of goods other countries can export for sale in Japan. This creates a **trade imbalance.** In other words, Japan sells more goods to other nations than it buys from other nations. This is good news from the Japanese point of view. It is bad news for those countries that buy more goods from Japan than they sell to Japan.

Many nations, including the United States, want Japan to fix this trade imbalance. They have asked Japan to allow more foreign goods into the country for sale—which Japan has done. Yet many think that Japan should do more.

The Japanese feel that they are simply being blamed for the economic problems of other countries. They point out that some countries, like the United States, also have favorable trade imbalances—just not with Japan.

Role in the World

In 1945 a U.S. newspaper reporter looked at the bombed-out nation of Japan and predicted that Japan would return to being a small, self-contained nation. Take one look at modern Japan, and you will realize that this reporter was very wrong.

Today other nations expect that Japan will become a leader in world affairs. They want it to play a bigger role in areas such as keeping world peace. So far the Japanese have not decided what their role should be. Still, Japan's future seems bright. Relying on its people and proud heritage, Japan's economic success is likely to continue. ■

Japan has a number of foreign aid programs. In this photograph, South African students are participating in a program designed to teach new ways of increasing agricultural production.

■ *What problems do the Japanese face in their relations with trade partners?*

■ *Japan's trading partners want Japan to allow more foreign goods for sale in Japan. They also want them to play a larger role in solving some of the world's problems.*

CLOSE

Draw the Graphic Overview on the chalkboard. Have students fill in the boxes under the headings *Economic Success, Living in Japan,* and *Future Challenges* with ideas from the lesson to answer the Thinking Focus.

REVIEW

1. **FOCUS** What factors have led to Japan's economic success?
2. **CULTURE** What is it like to work for one of Japan's large companies?
3. **ECONOMICS** Why does a strong economy rely on a good school system?
4. **CRITICAL THINKING** What might other nations do if Japan does not try to correct its trade imbalance?
5. **ACTIVITY** Many Japanese companies think of their employees as family members. In what ways does your classroom work as a family? Make a chart that compares your family with your classroom. Compare such things as goals, decision making, relationships, and so forth.

Answers to Review Questions

1. Government involvement in long-range business plans and a highly educated work force trained to believe in shared responsibility are some of the factors that have led to Japan's economic success.
2. Working for a large company can be very demanding in terms of the hours required on the job. Lifetime employment, however, instills in most workers a great sense of loyalty and pride in their companies.
3. Good school systems produce well-educated workers who are then able to generate good ideas and make quality products that many people will want to buy.
4. Other nations may follow the practice of placing restrictions on Japanese imports.
5. Like parents, teachers are authority figures; students work together like family members with common goals. Unlike parents, teachers have no financial responsibility to students. Family members include a wider range of ages and responsibilities.

Homework Options

Have students write a paragraph explaining Japan's economic success. Tell them to assume their readers are familiar with Japanese history.

Study Guide: page 66

DISCOVERY PROCESS

Students will use the following steps in the discovery process to complete the activity:
Get Ready Gather books or magazines that discuss Japanese schools; list interesting questions.
Find Out Look for answers to the questions.
Move Ahead Create categories of questions on a chart and compare the answers found.
Explore Some More Choose another topic and again investigate similarities and differences between Japan and the United States.

Materials needed: Books, magazines, large sheet of paper, tape, and markers.

CULTURE
Study Skills

Draw attention to the photograph on the left of this page and ask a student to read its caption aloud. Ask students who cleans their school. *(Maintenance staff)* How would they feel if they had to clean the school? Then discuss the caption to the lower illustration on this page. Ask students about the subjects they spend the most time studying. Is social studies second only to English?

EXPLORING

Japanese and U.S. Schools

You can learn a great deal about another country by finding out about its schools. Education is one way in which a society passes its values and knowledge to the next generation. What is school like in Japan?

Who cleans your school? In Japan the students themselves sweep the floors of their classrooms daily.

Get Ready

You'll need a notebook, a pen, and some books or magazines with information about schools in Japan.

Make a list of questions you want to answer: What time does school begin and end for Japanese students your age? Do they have dress codes? What about after-school sports? Do students move from class to class? Does one teacher handle all subjects? What subjects do Japanese schools teach? How much homework do teachers give?

Find Out

Look for answers to each of your questions. If an answer gives you an idea for another question, add it to your list.

Divide your information into two groups: ways in which U.S. and Japanese schools are alike and ways in which they are different. Did you find more similarities or more differences?

新編 新しい社会(地理)

This is the cover of a seventh-grade textbook popular in Japan. Japanese seventh graders spend more time on social studies than on any other subject except Japanese.

Objectives

1. Identify similarities and differences between Japanese and U.S. schools. (Study Skills 1, 2)
2. Identify the values reflected by each system. (Ethics and Belief Systems 1, 2, 4)

Activity

Assign half the students to research the history of Japanese schools and half to research that of American schools. Give each student a question from the categories on the class chart. For example, a student might look for information on the hours in a Japanese school day or week in the 1800s. When the students have finished their research, have them add the facts they found to the class chart in the appropriate areas. Use the information on the chart for a class discussion of the similarities and differences between the two educational systems, and have students speculate on the values represented by some of the facts. Discuss which values are similar and which are different.

Move Ahead

Tape a large sheet of paper to the wall of your classroom. Each student should mention a question that he or she asked. Use the questions to create categories on the chart. For instance, some people may have asked about school hours. If so, a student might write on the chart: Hours in School per Day (or Week).

Do everyone's answers agree? If not, find out where the information came from. Is one magazine or book more recent than another? Does one author have more experience than another?

When the chart has been completed, discuss the information. What Japanese ideas would you like U.S. schools to adopt? Why?

Explore Some More

Choose another area of life in the United States, one you're very familiar with. It might be sports, games, crafts, music, art, or some current concern—animal welfare, the environment, or political campaigns, for instance.

Find out if any Japanese share your interest. If so, do they pursue it in the same way? If not, can you find out why not?

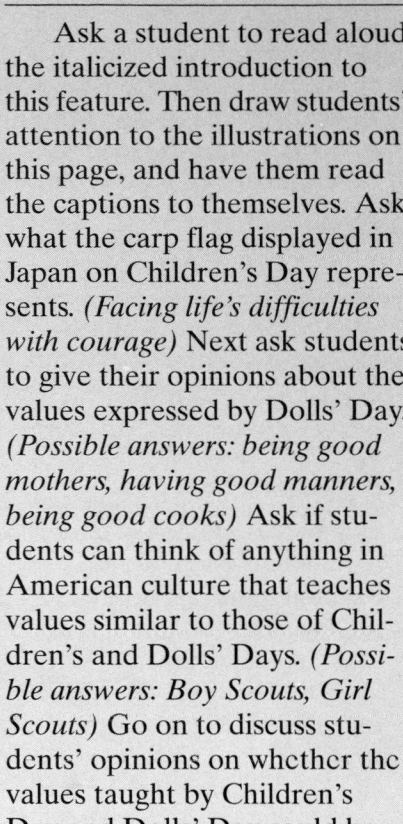

▲ The symbol of the carp—a fish that swims against river currents—is often flown on Children's Day. It inspires boys and girls to face life's difficulties with courage.

◄ Dolls' Day is a school holiday in Japan celebrated on March 3rd. On Dolls' Day young girls display their dolls and hold tea parties where they serve little cakes iced with peach-blossom frosting.

ETHICS

Critical Thinking

Ask a student to read aloud the italicized introduction to this feature. Then draw students' attention to the illustrations on this page, and have them read the captions to themselves. Ask what the carp flag displayed in Japan on Children's Day represents. *(Facing life's difficulties with courage)* Next ask students to give their opinions about the values expressed by Dolls' Day. *(Possible answers: being good mothers, having good manners, being good cooks)* Ask if students can think of anything in American culture that teaches values similar to those of Children's and Dolls' Days. *(Possible answers: Boy Scouts, Girl Scouts)* Go on to discuss students' opinions on whether the values taught by Children's Day and Dolls' Day could be shared by both boys and girls. *(Encourage students to see that indeed they could and should.)*

Activity

Divide students into two groups and tell them they are going to debate whether students should clean their own classrooms at the end of each school day. Assign one group to debate in favor of students cleaning their own classrooms, and the other group to debate in opposition. Allow students time to meet in their groups and list the points they want to make. Tell them to support their points with the values they represent and historical facts from their earlier research.

During the debate, have the groups take turns introducing their points. Let the opposing team respond to each point. When both groups have stated and rebutted each point, have the entire class vote by secret ballot for or against the issue. Count their votes and declare the winning group.

Collaborative Strategy

One recommended strategy that may be useful in this lesson is heterogeneous grouping. For further information, turn to pages T34–T35.

Chapter Review

Reviewing Key Terms

feudalism (p. 367)
gross national product (p. 374)
homogeneous (p. 378)
isolation (p. 362)
samurai (p. 367)
Shinto (p. 362)
shogun (p. 366)
standard of living (p. 376)
trade imbalance (p. 379)
westernize (p. 371)

A. Use a dictionary to find the origins or the definitions of the following words. Then explain how the meaning of each word applies to the history or culture of Japan.

1. homogeneous
2. isolation
3. Shinto
4. samurai
5. shogun

B. Each statement below contains one or more key terms from the chapter. Decide whether the statement is correct or incorrect. Give reasons to support your decision using information in the chapter.

1. In westernizing Japan, the Meiji leaders adopted many ideas from China.
2. During its period of isolation, Japan carried out a brisk trade with foreign nations.
3. Food in Japan is expensive because the Japanese people have such a high gross national product.
4. Like Japan, the United States has a homogeneous population.
5. The current trade imbalance with Japan has caused problems for the United States.

Exploring Concepts

A. Feudalism began in Japan in the 800s and lasted into the 1800s. Copy the following outline and fill in all the blank spaces.

Feudalism in Japan
I. What feudalism is
  A.
  B. Laws uphold a strict social order
    1. Shogun
      a. controls almost every part of Japanese life
      b.
    2. *Daimyo*
      a.
      b.
    3. Samurai
      a.
      b.
    4. Peasants
II. Why feudalism developed
  A.
  B.

B. Answer each question with information from the chapter.

1. What influence did Prince Shotōku and the Heian period have on Japanese culture?
2. What influence did the samurai have on Japanese values? How have these values contributed to Japan's economic success in recent years?
3. How did Japanese society change during the period of isolation in the 1600s and 1700s?
4. What changes occurred in Japan during the Meiji Restoration?
5. How were the Heian and Meiji periods similar?
6. What is it like to live in Japan today?
7. How has the role of women changed in modern Japanese society?
8. What evidence exists today of Western influence in Japan?
9. What challenges does Japan face in the coming years?

Answers to Reviewing Key Terms

A. Sample answers:

1. **Homogeneous** comes from the Greek word *homogenēs. Homo* means "same," and *genos* means "kind." Japan is very homogeneous; that is, most of its people have the same background.
2. **Isolate** comes from the Latin word *insula,* which means "island." Japan is a long chain of islands situated off the coast of Asia. Because of its location, Japanese culture developed in relative **isolation.**
3. **Shinto** comes from the Chinese words *shén,* which means "Gods," and *dào,* which means "way." Shinto, the original religion of the Japanese, is a form of nature worship.
4. **Samurai** is the Japanese word for "warrior." Nobles in feudal Japan relied on the samurai to wage battles against rival clans.
5. **Shogun,** the Japanese word for "general," is of Chinese origin. In 1192, the emperor of Japan gave Yoritomo the title shogun.

B. Answers:

1. Incorrect. China is an Eastern culture, not a Western culture. To westernize is to adopt the ways of developed countries in Europe and North America.
2. Incorrect. During the period of isolation, Japan cut itself off from the outside world.
3. Incorrect. The gross national product does not determine the price of food.
4. Incorrect. The U. S. does not have a homogeneous population; its people are of different origins.
5. Correct. The United States is upset because Japan exports more to the U.S. than it imports.

Answers to Exploring Concepts

Sample answers:

I. A. A system in which people exchange land or services for protection B. 1. b. Rule was often cruel 2. a. Supported the shogun b. Owned large estates 3. a. Fought against rival clans b. Received small pieces of land or official positions from the *daimyo* II. A. Power of the emperor declined B. Lawlessness spread

B. Sample answers:

1. Prince Shotōku sent students to China to learn more about its culture and government. He welcomed Chinese scholars and artists to Japan. During the Heian period, a Japanese culture of refinement and luxury existed.
2. Samurai values such as loyalty, honor, and hard work make the Japanese extremely good workers.
3. Education spread to all classes, and the economy boomed.
4. The Meiji wrote a new constitution, instituted compulsory education, and built several universities.
5. Both were times of cultural borrowing.
6. The Japanese enjoy a high standard of living. Prices of food and housing are high.
7. Women still care for the family, but more are finding outside work. Their pay is far below men's, who get the best jobs.
8. Japan's educational system, its democratic constitution, its cities and industries, its feminist movement, and its popular culture show western influence.
9. Some future challenges are pollution, the cost of living, dealing with such minority groups as Koreans, and the trade imbalance.

Reviewing Skills

1. Look at the World Population cartogram on page 689. Compare the population of Japan with the populations of India and China. Compare this cartogram with the cartogram on page 375. What do these cartograms tell you about the relationship between Japan's economy and its population?
2. Look at the painting on page 360. What was the artist's purpose in painting this picture? Who are the figures in the painting? What are they doing? What does this painting tell you about the Japanese people?
3. What information would you need in order to compare the location of Tokyo with that of Washington, D.C.? Where would you find that information?

Using Critical Thinking

1. Other than its mild climate, ample rainfall, and the sea, Japan has few natural resources. How has this fact influenced the course of Japanese history?
2. Both the Tokugawas and the Meiji leaders feared that Japan might fall under the rule of powerful foreigners. Yet, each government reacted very differently to the threat. How did each government try to protect Japan? Why do you think the policies were so different?
3. Japanese schools and companies put great stress on working hard and on being part of the group. Do you think this is true of schools and companies in the United States today? Give some examples to support your answer.
4. Today, other nations in the world look to Japan to become a leader in world affairs. So far, the Japanese have not decided what their role should be. Why do you think Japan may be reluctant to become a leader in world affairs?

Preparing for Citizenship

1. **WRITING ACTIVITY** The Japanese have shown an appreciation for the beauties of the natural world throughout their history. They often express their appreciation through poetry, such as haiku. A haiku is a Japanese lyric poem of a fixed, 17-syllable form. The first line contains words that equal five syllables. The second line contains words that equal seven syllables. The third line contains words that equal five syllables. Haiku poetry is usually simple, and it usually captures a mood about a scene in nature or a season. Write a haiku poem. Choose your words carefully to stir the reader's imagination.
2. **ARTS ACTIVITY** The traditional Japanese home was built to adapt to Japan's hot, humid summers and short, cold winters. Design a home that is well suited to the region where you live. Share the drawing with your classmates.
3. **GROUP ACTIVITY** Japanese people value cooperation, hard work, and loyalty. Working in small groups, make a list of the values that are important to you and your group. Then try to think of ways to foster these attitudes in your classmates. Share your ideas with the class.
4. **COLLABORATIVE LEARNING** After World War II, many people in the United States believed that the best way to build a peaceful future was to help Japan rebuild. In small groups, debate the following proposition: "Resolved, that the United States' decision to help rebuild Japan has helped build world peace." Two or three students should present arguments in support of the proposition that a healthy Japan was more likely to be a friend than an enemy. Two or three others should present arguments against the proposition that the Japanese should assume full responsibility for rebuilding the nation. Another student should act as moderator. Hold the debate for the class.

Answers to Reviewing Skills

1. The population of Japan is less than that of China and India. Although Japan has a much smaller population than either China or India, it has a higher gross national product, that is, a much stronger economy.
2. The figures in the painting are the Gods Izanagi and Izanami. Izanagi is throwing a spear into the ocean. As he pulls the spear out, drops fall and form the islands of Japan. The painting shows that the Japanese believe their islands are a special place.
3. Students would need to find the longitude and the latitude of the two cities on a political map of the world.

Answers to Using Critical Thinking

1. In the 20th century, Japan set out to establish an empire in order to ensure that it would have a steady supply of raw materials. Its aggressive policies led to war in the Pacific.
2. The Tokugawas began a period of forced isolation in the early 1600s. The Meiji leaders thought that the best way to protect Japan was to modernize through selective borrowing from Western countries. When the Tokugawas came to power, Japan was not technologically at a disadvantage with Western nations. Therefore, isolation was a feasible solution. The Meiji leaders had to deal with a world that was very different. Japan was vulnerable, and isolation was no longer possible.
3. Students will probably suggest that schools and companies in the United States emphasize the goals of the individual rather than those of the group. However, companies in both nations try to teach or encourage the value of hard work.
4. Some students will suggest that Japan has been more interested in developing its economy and industries. Others may suggest that since Japan's constitution outlaws the military, Japan does not have the military forces necessary to play a role in international peacekeeping efforts.

Answers to Preparing for Citizenship

1. **WRITING ACTIVITY** You may wish to read one or two haiku poems to the students or to write a haiku with the students' help.
2. **ARTS ACTIVITY** Discuss with students the climate of the region in which you live and the ways in which people can build houses in order to complement the environment. For example, in warm regions, people may use building materials that do not hold heat; or they may build in a shady place or use light-colored roofs.
3. **GROUP ACTIVITY** Answers will vary. Students could suggest values such as loyalty, individuality, and honesty. These values might be fostered by giving examples of successful role models.
4. **COLLABORATIVE LEARNING** Students should support their opposing positions with details from the chapter.

CHAPTER ORGANIZER

Chapter 17 Southeast Asia

CHAPTER PLANNING CHART

Pupil's Edition	Teacher's Edition	Ancillaries
Lesson 1: The Geography of Southeast Asia (1–2 days) Objective 1: Describe the geography of Southeast Asia. (Geography 1, 2, 5) Objective 2: Explain how the geography of Southeast Asia affects its cultural history. (History 1; Geography 3, 4; Culture 2) Objective 3: Explain the cultural influences of India, China, the Middle East, and Europe. (Culture 4, 5)	• Graphic Overview (386) • Access Strategy (387) • Access Activity (387) • Visual Learning (388) Collaborative Learning (388)	Study Guide (67) Map Activities (21) Discovery Journal (36)
Lesson 2: The Philippines (2–3 days) Objective 1: Explain the history of the Philippines. (History 1, 4, 5) Objective 2: Explain the cultural and historic reasons for the uprising against the Marcos government. (History 1, 6; Culture 2; Ethics and Belief Systems 2, 3) Objective 3: Describe the culture of the Philippines today. (Culture 2)	• Graphic Overview (390) • Access Strategy (391) • Access Activity (391) Study Skills (392) Political Context (392) Art Connection (393) Map and Globe Skills (393)	Study Guide (68) • Posters (3)
Lesson 3: Singapore, Indonesia, and Vietnam (2–3 days) Objective 1: Explain the wide variety of cultures and ways of life in Southeast Asia today. (Culture 4) Objective 2: Compare and contrast Singapore and Indonesia. (Culture 4) Objective 3: Describe some of the challenges facing Vietnam today. (Economics 3, 4; Social and Political Systems 5, 6)	• Graphic Overview (395) • Access Activity (396) • Access Strategy (396) Language Arts Connection (397) • Visual Learning (397)	Study Guide (69) • Study Prints (10)
Understanding Topography Objective: Read and use a topographic map and a vertical profile. (Map and Globe Skills 2, 3)		Study Guide (70) Transparency (7)
Chapter Review	Answers (400–401)	Tests (65–68)

* Objectives are correlated to the strands and goals in the program Scope and Sequence on pages T41–T49.

• LEP appropriate resources. (For additional strategies, see pages T32–T33.)

CHAPTER RATIONALE

Chapter 17 introduces students to the region of Southeast Asia, with emphasis on its ocean-bounded location as a determining factor in its cultural history. Students learn that early traders and explorers from the Middle East and Europe first sailed through the region as they sought the goods and riches of China and India. Students examine the history of the Philippines, from the arrival of Magellan to the present. Finally, a closer study of Singapore, Indonesia, and Vietnam provides contrasting views of life in Southeast Asia today. At the beginning of the chapter, by focusing on the geography of the region, students are encouraged to make connections through all three lessons about how people adapt to their environment over time.

To communicate an immediate impression of Southeast Asia's natural environment, **Lesson 1** begins with a poem written by an Indonesian about the beauty of his homeland. Mainland and island regions are described, as are the climate and resources of Southeast Asia as a whole. A combination political map and population chart orients the students to this region's unique features. Finally, in A Closer Look, the phenomenon of active volcanoes is described.

Lesson 2 traces the history of the Philippines. In order to give students an adequate sense of the Philippines' varied cultural influences, we highlight the colonial domination of this nation by Spain, the United States, and Japan. A focus on World War II and the postwar years reveals the unified spirit of the Filipinos as they rebelled against the Marcos regime, especially during the People Power uprising. By reading about the critical role played by the Catholic church in this movement, students are reminded of the power that religious institutions wield.

In **Lesson 3,** three nations of Southeast Asia—Singapore, Indonesia, and Vietnam—illustrate important geographic, historic, and economic contrasts. Students read about the cultural background of these nations and about what life is like in each of them today. The material on the Vietnam War focuses on the Vietnamese perspective, rather than articulating the tensions within the United States. An emphasis on people and their work gives students concrete details about Southeast Asian social contexts.

ACTIVITIES & PROJECTS

LEP: Performing in a Play

To extend students' appreciation of Indonesian culture, have them work in small groups to create their own shadow puppets and present a shadow puppet show. Students can use their hands as puppets or make simple silhouette cutouts with construction paper and popsicle sticks. Assign characters and a simple plot line, or have students create their own. (Use after Lesson 3.)

Basic: Making a Mural

The geography of Southeast Asia could be the focus of a classroom mural. After Lesson 1 has introduced the students to the island and mainland landforms and vegetation, ask students to choose photos from magazines or draw pictures that illustrate the area. Then invite students to display their illustrations on a mural-sized poster for the class. The mural might take the form of a collage as the students progress through the chapter. Students can add images of people at work, with captions identifying the specific nation. (Use after Lesson 1.)

Writing a Diary Entry

As a follow-up to Lessons 2 and 3, encourage students to write one-paragraph diary entries from the perspective of a Filipino at the time of Magellan and of a Vietnamese today. Ask students to reveal details from the chapter. Choose two or three students to present their entries to the class. (Use after Lessons 2 and 3.)

Challenge: Researching

Encourage groups of students to discuss and make a list of factors that have contributed to Singapore's startling economic success, such as tight government controls, social orderliness, and ethnic tolerance. Interested students may wish to extend this activity by developing a longer list of factors conducive to economic growth and by using their lists to reinterpret what they have learned about the economies of other countries in this chapter, such as the Philippines. (Use after Lesson 3.)

Challenge: Collaboration

The issue of human rights violations is an ongoing controversy in Southeast Asia. Watchdog groups such as Amnesty International and Asia Watch cite serious violations by various governments in the region. Have students work together to research and report on the issue. The report should define the problems and the causes and identify the countries where the problems have occurred. Next, students should report on what is being done to battle the problem. Finally, the group should meet to brainstorm further solutions. Their ideas should form the conclusion of the report. (Use after Lesson 3.)

CHAPTER PREVIEW

Have students read the chapter title. Then ask them to use the map in the Atlas on page 682 to identify some of the countries and islands south of China and east of India, in the area called Southeast Asia. Invite students to discuss the following question: "Why might this area have been called an international crossroads?" *(Explorers and traders passed through the area en route to Europe and Asia.)* Then ask them to read the opening text to test their hypotheses.

Looking Back

Ask students to recall what they learned about trade in China and Japan in Chapters 15 and 16. Tell them to keep in mind the cultures and geography of China and Japan as they study this chapter about the "southern doorway to Asia."

Looking Forward

Tell students that they will learn about Southeast Asia in the three lessons of this chapter: The Geography of Southeast Asia; The Philippines; and Singapore, Indonesia, and Vietnam.

Lesson 1 explores the influence of geography, climate, and resources on Southeast Asian culture and history.

Chapter 17

Southeast Asia

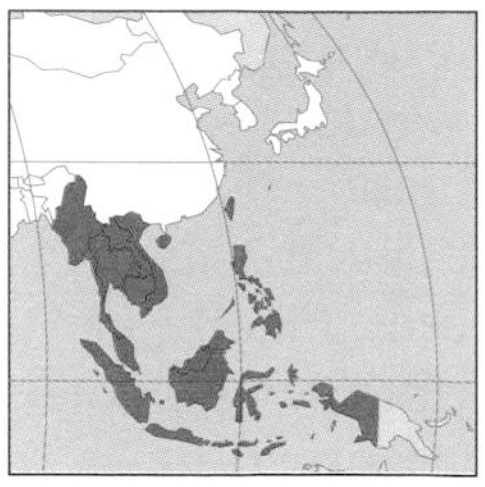

Gold, silks, spices, and precious gems lured the traders and explorers who made their way to Asia. The mainland and islands of Southeast Asia—including Vietnam, the Philippines, and Indonesia—lie at the southern doorway of Asia, surrounded by oceans. As people from Southwest Asia and Europe braved the unknown seas ever more boldly, they discovered that the region between China and India had treasures of its own.

Shadow puppets like these have entertained the people of Indonesia for centuries. They may be used today to tell an ancient Hindu legend or to instruct the people about a government policy.

This Buddha is part of Borobudur, the largest Buddhist temple in the world. Located on the island of Java, it was built in the 700s and 800s.

500	800	1100

384

700

c. 700–1250 Arab traders set up trading routes to India, China, and Southeast Asia. They bring Islam to the area.

BACKGROUND

To understand this lesson, students need to recognize why the region of Southeast Asia was an international "crossroads." Its strategic location between India and China made it attractive to traders as did its riches of spices, precious gems and metals, silk and porcelain, wood, and other raw materials.

Spices: The Main Attraction

Today we use spices such as cinnamon and cloves to enhance the flavor of foods. But in Ferdinand Magellan's day, spices helped to preserve food and to make it edible—not simply more delicious. In the 1600s, spices from Southeast Asia were sometimes as valuable as silver.

Early Maritime Trade Routes

Because of its location, Southeast Asia became a "doorway" between East and West. Before A.D. 500, Arab, Indian, and Chinese merchants followed maritime routes through the Strait of Malacca. Their trade depended on the monsoons. From May to September, these winds blow from the southwest. From December through February, they blow from the northeast. Indian or Arab merchants arriving in the summer had to wait months before the winds changed directions and they could return. Chinese traders arriving in winter waited until summer to leave. As a result, many sailors and traders took up residence in the region for up to six months.

PILIPINAS

Supporters of former Philippine president Corazón Aquino celebrate her victory over Ferdinand Marcos at Camp Crane in the Philippines.

The many religious festivals in the Philippines reflect the people's Christian heritage. Carved wooden masks are worn each year to act out the Easter story.

1898 The United States defeats Spain in the Spanish-American War.

1400 | 1700 | 2000

1521 Ferdinand Magellan claims what is now the Philippines for Spain and brings Christianity to the area.

1957–1975 The Vietnam War is fought between Communist North Vietnam and U.S.-backed South Vietnam.

Today

Understanding the Visuals

Explain that shadow puppets (like those shown on page 384) produce a silhouette, or shadow, when held between a light and a screen. Puppeteers use the shadow puppets to perform favorite folktales as well as Hindu epics. You may want to refer students to the word *epic* on page 703 in the Glossary.

The temple of Borobudur (page 384), situated on the island of Java in Indonesia, was buried under volcanic ash for centuries before its discovery in 1814 by a British army colonel. A group known as the Srivijaya had erected the shrine in the 700s. A strong Buddhist power, the Srivijaya controlled trade through the Strait of Malacca for several centuries.

Understanding Chronology

Refer students to the timeline. Have them identify the nationality and the date of arrival of the first traders to set up routes in Southeast Asia. *(Arabs; c. 700)* Then ask when the first Europeans arrived and where they were from. *(1521; Spain)*

The Lure to Colonize

In this way, colonies sprang up throughout the region. First the Chinese and Indian, next the Arab, and finally the European explorers and traders arrived. With each arrival came new religious and cultural influences—primarily Hinduism, Buddhism, Christianity, and Islam.

The region has experienced considerable social upheaval and suffered the hardships that accompany a diverse cultural environment. Still, one common historical element in the development of the region was the lure of exotic spices, rare gems, and new materials that originally attracted such intense global interest.

INTRODUCE

Have students look at the photograph of Komodo on this page and speculate about the geography of Southeast Asia. Then ask them what they learned in Chapter 1 about how environment shapes culture. *(People adapt their dress, shelter, food, and way of life to the geography, climate, and resources of the place where they live.)* Ask students to read the Thinking Focus and think about possible answers as they learn about the geography and cultural history of the region.

Key Terms

Vocabulary Strategies: T36–T37

archipelago—a group of islands, often formed by volcanoes

typhoon—a violent storm caused by shifting winds

500
800
1100
1400
1700
2000

LESSON 1

The Geography of Southeast Asia

THINKING FOCUS

How has Southeast Asia's geography affected its cultural history?

Key Terms

- archipelago
- typhoon

Near the shores of a lovely
 land
Where waves splatter on sand
And foam spreads in white
 bands
The green sea sprouts islands
Covered with noble mountains,
Islands set in the ocean like
 fountains
Of beauty: my home, my
 Indonesia.

Mohammad Yamin

With these words an Indonesian poet describes the beauty of his homeland in Southeast Asia. In this lesson you will learn how the ocean and geography of this region have played a key role in its history.

A Region Bounded by Ocean

Southeast Asia lies to the south of China and to the east of India. It includes two different land areas: mainland and island Southeast Asia.

The Mainland and the Islands

Mainland Southeast Asia is on an Asian peninsula. Rugged, tall mountain ranges and a series of rivers run from north to south. River valleys along these rivers have rich, moist soil ideal for growing crops. Similar to the river valleys of Egypt, India, and China, the rivers and their floodplains here support life and civilization. The rivers also provide water highways for travel, trade, and the shipment of goods. Vietnam, Thailand, Myanmar (once called Burma), Cambodia, Laos, and Malaysia make up mainland Southeast Asia today.

Indonesia, the Philippines, Singapore, and Brunei are islands or parts of island groups. These island groups are called

Beautiful Komodo, an island in southern Indonesia, is home to the Komodo dragons—the largest known lizards.

Objectives

1. Describe the geography of Southeast Asia.
2. Explain how the geography of Southeast Asia affects its cultural history.
3. Explain the cultural influences of India, China, the Middle East, and Europe.

Graphic Overview

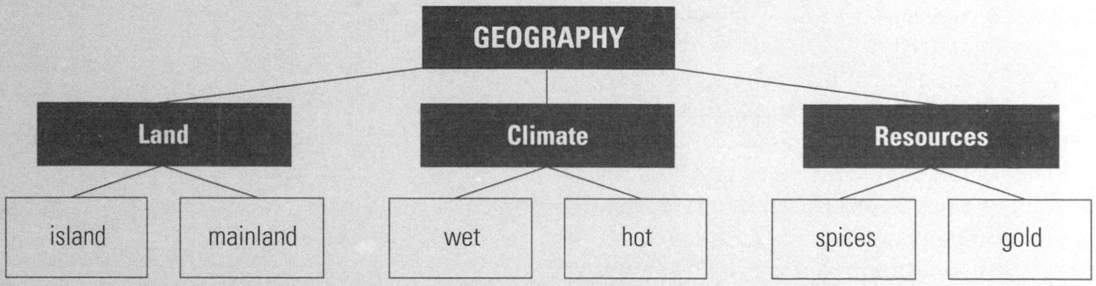
GEOGRAPHY
Land
Climate
Resources
island
mainland
wet
hot
spices
gold

Southeast Asia: Political

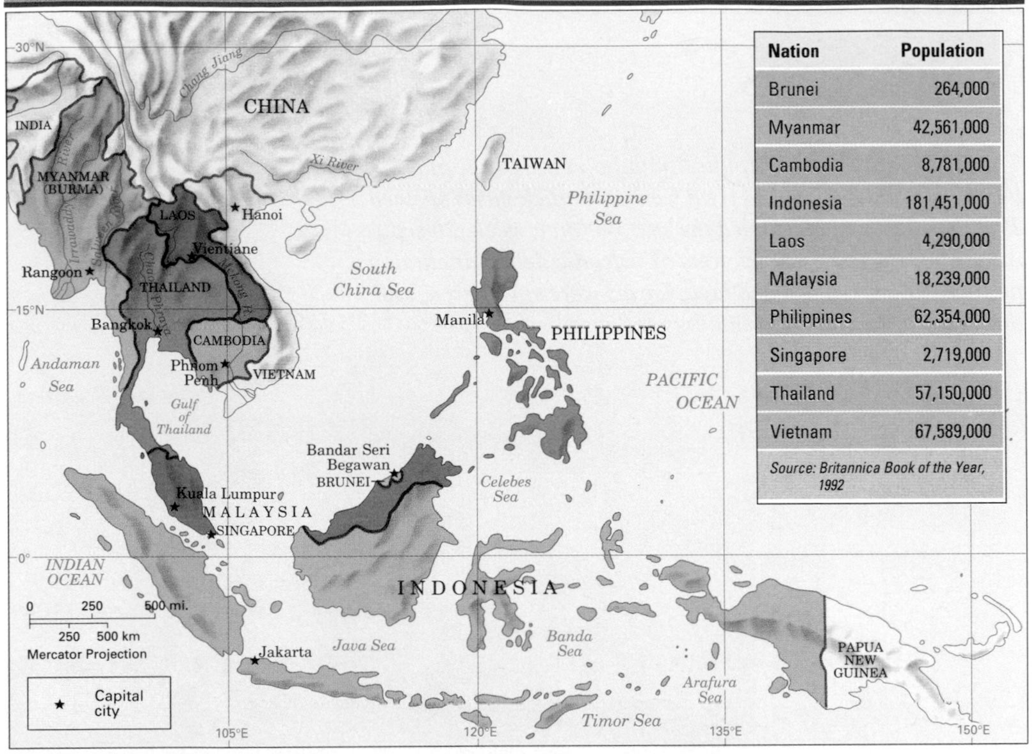
CHINA
INDIA
MYANMAR (BURMA)
LAOS
Hanoi
Vientiane
Rangoon
THAILAND
Bangkok
CAMBODIA
Phnom Penh
VIETNAM
TAIWAN
Philippine Sea
South China Sea
Manila
PHILIPPINES
PACIFIC OCEAN
Andaman Sea
Gulf of Thailand
Bandar Seri Begawan
BRUNEI
Celebes Sea
Kuala Lumpur
MALAYSIA
SINGAPORE
INDIAN OCEAN
INDONESIA
Banda Sea
Java Sea
Jakarta
Arafura Sea
Timor Sea
PAPUA NEW GUINEA
Chang Jiang
Xi River
0 250 500 mi.
250 500 km
Mercator Projection
Capital city
30°N
15°N
0°
105°E
120°E
135°E
150°E

Nation	Population
Brunei	264,000
Myanmar	42,561,000
Cambodia	8,781,000
Indonesia	181,451,000
Laos	4,290,000
Malaysia	18,239,000
Philippines	62,354,000
Singapore	2,719,000
Thailand	57,150,000
Vietnam	67,589,000

Source: Britannica Book of the Year, 1992

archipelagoes *(ahr kuh PEHL uh gohz)*. Most of the islands were formed by volcanoes, some of which are still active. You can read about a recent eruption of a volcano in the Philippines in A Closer Look on page 388.

Climate and Resources

Most of Southeast Asia has a wet, hot climate. The average daily temperature is 80°F, and the average annual rainfall is 60 inches. This climate supports the growth of rain forests. In May, strong, moist monsoon winds blow in from the sea. Although the monsoons can cause drastic floods, their rains are needed for the growing of rice, the major food crop.

The dry season begins when the monsoons switch direction in October. When these winds shift, violent storms called **typhoons** *(ty FOONZ)* often occur. They are similar to the hurricanes that strike the United States in autumn. Typhoons can result in huge damage and loss of life.

The climate of Southeast Asia is ideal for growing spices such as the cloves found in the Moluccas *(muh LUHK uhz)*, or Spice Islands, of eastern Indonesia. Long ago, spices such as pepper, cinnamon, nutmeg, and cloves were extremely valuable. They were used to flavor and preserve foods, and even as medicines. So nations competed to get these spices.

Early traders came to the region for other resources, too. These included gold and gems such as sapphires and diamonds. Today, tin, crude petroleum, teak, and rubber are major resources of the region. ■

▲ *The chart above lists each nation of Southeast Asia with recent population figures. Find each nation on the map. Which nation has the lowest population?*

■ *How are mainland and island Southeast Asia alike and different, in terms of physical geography and climate?*

DEVELOP

Direct students to the map on this page. Explain that many of these islands are isolated from each other as well as from the mainland. As a result, hundreds of distinct cultures developed in this region. Ask them to discuss what it would be like if every state in the United States had a distinct culture, language, and history. *(Communication and a united government would be much more difficult.)*

GEOGRAPHY

Map and Globe Skills

Encourage students to contrast the kind of information they get from the aerial photograph on page 386 to what they get from the map on this page. *(Photo: jagged coastline and sparse vegetation; map: relationships among land masses, sense of scale)* Then have students use the map scale to estimate the total east-west expanse of Southeast Asia. *(Approximately 3,200 miles)*

◄ *Brunei has the lowest population.*

■ *The mainland has tall, rugged mountains and fertile river valleys. Some islands have rain forests, while others have sandy beaches. Both the mainland and the islands have a wet, hot climate.*

Access Strategy

To relate the history of this region to that of other regions the class has studied, review with students what they learned about the beginnings of civilization along river valleys, such as those in Egypt, India, and China. Ask students how rivers help support civilizations in river valleys. *(Rivers provide water for drinking and for growing crops; they offer a means of transporting people and goods; river valleys often have rich soil for growing a variety of crops.)*

Have students break into two groups to debate the pros and cons of life on an island. What would be the advantages of living by the sea? What would be the disadvantages? *(Advantages: plentiful fishing, easy access to ocean trade routes; disadvantages: cultural isolation, exposure to severe weather)*

Access Activity

To help students understand how Southeast Asia came to be a crossroads for culture and trade, have them study the physical map of Eurasia on page 682 of the Atlas. Ask students to locate India and China and verify that Southeast Asia lies roughly halfway between their borders.

Note: You may want to use this Closer Look to extend the discussion about island formation on page 387.

GEOGRAPHY

Visual Learning

Ask students to look at the pumice pictured on this page and imagine this hardened substance as the hot liquid it once was. Some 20 to 30 volcanoes erupt each year, spewing lava over miles of valuable land. Indonesia has 70 active volcanoes, more than any other country. Ask students to check the entry for Mount Pinatubo in the Gazetteer on page 694, and invite them to find out about volcanoes in other places.

More About Volcanoes The earth can be divided into three layers: the crust, the mantle, and the core. The upper mantle consists of magma—hot, molten rock. The crust is made up of giant plates that float on the upper mantle. Volcanoes occur where the magma finds a crack in the giant plates of the earth's crust. Pressure builds up until the crust erupts, spilling forth hot, molten rock. Magma that has reached the earth's surface is called lava.

A CLOSER LOOK

Volcanoes

The 5,770-foot cone of Mount Pinatubo in the Philippines blew up on June 15, 1991. Heavy ash and thick gases spewed 25 miles high and blackened the sky. Within a week, 26 separate eruptions rained down tons of volcanic debris, including pumice, which is hardened lava. Farms were smothered, and thousand of homes and buildings collapsed.

Quiet for 600 years, Mount Pinatubo showed signs of an eruption in time for scientists to alert nearby people. Many safely left the area.

Like these fields in Bali, farmlands near Mount Pinatubo will become fertile again. Ash enriches the soil, but it may take hundreds of years.

Volcanic pumice

Visual Learning

Ask students to study the pictures of farming on this page. Have them speculate about what might be required for Filipino farmers to recover from a volcanic eruption. *(Clearing of debris, increased irrigation)*

Collaborative Learning

To help students understand the consequences of volcanic eruption, have them work in small groups to discuss and then research the following question: "How have volcanoes affected life on the islands of Southeast Asia?" Ask them to work together to develop a chart that compares the effects of volcanoes on three Southeast Asian islands. Suggest that students use the pictures and text on this page as well as other information from the chapter to begin their discussion. Encourage them to use reference works, such as encyclopedias, to extend their knowledge and complete their charts.

A Crossroads of Many Cultures

Since ancient times the sea has linked Southeast Asia with the rest of the world. This region is located halfway between the major trading centers of India and China. Thus, Southeast Asia became a busy intersection of ocean trade and exploration. For centuries traders and seafarers from many parts of the world have sailed in and out of its ports. Many have left cultural influences on the region.

India and China

Four thousand years ago, very advanced civilizations existed along the Indus River in India and the Chang Jiang (or Yangtze River) in China. You read about these civilizations in Chapter 5.

Indian and Chinese traders traveled to Southeast Asia in search of riches. After finding out how valuable the resources of the region were, some of these traders settled in Southeast Asia. Wealthy from trade profits and well educated, they gained power. They married native Southeast Asians and started families. They brought their own cultures to the region, including the religions of Hinduism and Buddhism. Indian and Chinese languages, literature, art, and architecture also became part of the culture of Southeast Asia.

▲ *The vinta boat above is one of a large variety of small, wooden boats used for fishing and inter-island transportation. They continue to sail the oceans of Southeast Asia much as they have for hundreds of years.*

Soon other traders from distant lands discovered that Southeast Asia was a region of riches and a convenient stop between China and India. Beginning in the eighth century, Arab traders from the Middle East established trading colonies in India, China, and Africa. They also set up profitable trading centers in Southeast Asia itself. Today most people of Malaysia and Indonesia practice Islam, the religion that the early Arabian traders brought with them many centuries ago.

East Meets West

In the 1400s, European traders arrived from the West. The Portuguese set up trading bases in the Spice Islands. The Dutch, English, and French came, too. Wanting to share in the riches, Spain sent the explorer Ferdinand Magellan to stake claims. As you will read, Magellan's arrival in 1521 changed forever the history and culture of the Philippines. ■

■ *How did Southeast Asia's geography and natural resources lead other cultures to the region's door?*

REVIEW

1. **FOCUS** How has Southeast Asia's geography affected its cultural history?
2. **GEOGRAPHY** What role have rivers played in the development of Southeast Asian civilization?
3. **ECONOMICS** What attracted traders from Europe, the Middle East, and other parts of Asia to Southeast Asia?
4. **CRITICAL THINKING** Compare the benefits of living along river valleys in Southeast Asia today with the benefits of living in ancient river valley civilizations.
5. **MAPPING ACTIVITY** Draw a map to show the routes that early Chinese and Indian traders may have taken to and from Southeast Asia.

ECONOMICS

Visual Learning

Refer students to the photograph of a vinta boat on this page. Ask how such a vessel might contribute to the economic security of a Southeast Asian society. *(Fishing, trading, and social interactions would be easier with this vessel.)* Encourage students to consider the limitations of the vinta boat. *(Not built for long voyages or for large numbers of passengers)* Remind them that the traders who came through the area from Europe and the Middle East traveled in much larger ships.

■ *The region attracted many explorers because it lies midway between India and China. Its rich natural resources (such as gold, spices, and gems) drew traders from Southwest Asia and, eventually, Europe.*

CLOSE

Have the students answer the Thinking Focus. To review the main points of the lesson, draw the Graphic Overview for this lesson on the chalkboard, leaving out the topics and subtopics. Have students fill in the missing information together.

Answers to Review Questions

1. Because of its position on maritime trade routes, the region attracted explorers, traders, and settlers. The natural resources of the area also drew outsiders there. These people brought their religions, languages, literature, and art to the region.
2. By providing water, food, and trade routes, rivers support civilizations.
3. Traders from Europe and the Middle East were attracted to the region's resources—especially spices, gold, and gems.
4. The benefits today are similar to those of ancient days, including rich soil and easy transport of goods and people. Students may add that although flooding and monsoons still occur, improved weather predictions probably reduce the risks of living in river valleys today.
5. Maps should trace an Indian route through the Strait of Malacca to Malaysia and Indonesia and a Chinese overland route into Vietnam.

Homework Options

Ask students to write a paragraph about an area of the world they would like to explore. Why would they choose that area? How would they travel there? What would they do once they arrived?

Study Guide: page 67

INTRODUCE

Encourage students to recall what they read in Lesson 1 about trade and colonization in Southeast Asia. Ask them to scan the headings and subheadings in this lesson and predict which nations might have influenced Philippine history. *(Spain, United States, Japan)* Have students read the Thinking Focus and then the lesson to find out how other world cultures affected the history of the Philippines.

Key Terms

Vocabulary Strategies: T36–T37

circumnavigate—to sail completely around an area

galleon—a large three-masted sailing ship used for trade

mestizo—a person of mixed ancestry

martial law—the rule of military forces

500 800 1100 1400 1519 TODAY

LESSON 2

The Philippines

THINKING FOCUS

What factors shaped Philippine history?

Key Terms

- circumnavigate
- galleon
- mestizo
- martial law

It is 1519. You are sailing on one of five wooden ships—all smaller than modern-day tugboats. The fleet captain is Ferdinand Magellan, a Portuguese explorer. King Charles I of Spain has sent Magellan to find a western route to the Spice Islands.

The voyage drags on for almost two years. Often the ships are damaged by rough seas. The food runs out, so you eat rats, sawdust, and boiled leather straps. The drinking water is dirty and full of bugs. You watch many of your shipmates die. You are thin, tired, sick, and almost without hope.

Then one morning, you spy mountain peaks on the misty horizon. Soon your small fleet reaches the rocky, palm-fringed coast of an island. You see many other islands dotting the calm waters. You are able to get rice, fruit, and fresh water at one of these islands. At last, you are saved!

Exploration and Colonial History

Magellan and his crew planted the Spanish flag on the shore of what is now the Philippines. One month later, Magellan was killed when he took sides in a war between local peoples. However, his 18 surviving crew members completed the westward voyage back to Spain. They were the first Europeans to **circumnavigate** *(sur kuhm NAV ih gayt),* or sail around, the world.

Magellan's arrival led to three centuries of Spanish control of the Philippine archipelago. It soon became a Spanish colony named Islas Filipinas *(EEZ lahs fee lee PEE nahs),* or the Philippine Islands, in honor of the king of Spain, Philip II.

➤ *The portrait at right is of Ferdinand Magellan. The first circumnavigation of the world, completed by Magellan's crew after his death, added greatly to the world's geographic knowledge.*

Spanish Colonial Rule

The first Spanish settlement in the Philippines was founded in 1565 on the island of Cebu *(seh BOO).* Then, in 1571, the colonial capital was established in Manila on the western coast of the island of Luzon. A governor-general, appointed by the king of Spain, ruled the colony.

Spanish priests traveled throughout the islands converting the Filipinos to Catholicism, the religion of Spain. Church leaders and

Objectives

1. Explain the history of the Philippines.
2. Explain the cultural and historic reasons for the uprising against the Marcos government.
3. Describe the culture of the Philippines today.

Graphic Overview

Spain colonizes islands. ➤ Middle class revolts. ➤ United States defeats Spain. ➤ Japan occupies islands during World War II. ➤ Islands hold free elections.

Manila Galleon Trade Routes, 1565–1815

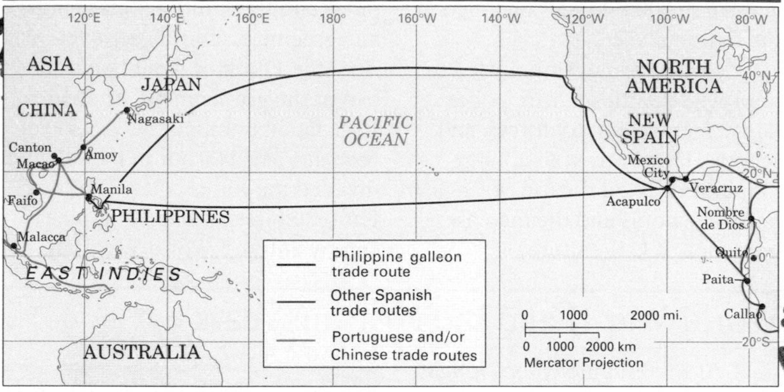
120°E
140°E
160°E
180°
160°W
140°W
120°W
100°W
80°W
40°N
20°N
0°
20°S
ASIA
JAPAN
CHINA
Nagasaki
Canton
Macao
Amoy
Faifo
Manila
PHILIPPINES
Malacca
EAST INDIES
AUSTRALIA
PACIFIC OCEAN
NORTH AMERICA
NEW SPAIN
Mexico City
Veracruz
Acapulco
Nombre de Dios
Quito
Paita
Callao
Philippine galleon trade route
Other Spanish trade routes
Portuguese and/or Chinese trade routes
0 1000 2000 mi.
0 1000 2000 km
Mercator Projection

A round trip for the Manila galleons usually took about a year. About how many miles was the voyage from Mexico back to the Philippines?

Spices like the cinnamon sticks, nutmeg, and peppercorns shown above were part of the galleon shipments.

other Spaniards took control of the land. Soon the Spanish colonizers forced the native people to work for them and to pay taxes to Spain.

Filipino laborers were used, for example, to build galleons for the Spanish. **Galleons** were large three-masted sailing ships used mostly for trade. The galleons built in the Philippines became known as the Manila galleons because Manila was the major port through which goods flowed from east and west. For 250 years, these Spanish galleons sailed the trade route shown on the map above.

Chinese traders brought silks, spices, gems, and items created by Chinese artists to Manila. In Manila, these and other goods from Southeast Asia were loaded onto galleons bound for Mexico and the coast of what is now California. There the goods were traded for silver, which the Chinese desired as payment. Then the galleons returned to Manila to load up with goods again. From Mexico, many of the goods were shipped across the country to the Gulf of Mexico, then across the Atlantic Ocean to Europe.

As a rich trading center, Manila attracted a large group of wealthy Chinese merchants. Many of these merchants married Filipino women, and their children became known as **mestizos** *(mehs TEE zohs)*. The *mestizos* became a new, well-educated, wealthy middle class.

This powerful new middle class rebelled and started a revolution against the Spanish colonial government in 1896. When a truce seemed near, however, the United States came on the scene.

The United States was trying to help Cuba, a Caribbean colony of Spain. Cuba is a large island about 90 miles off the southern coast of Florida. In 1898 the United States declared war against Spain and won the war in four months. As part of the treaty at the end of the Spanish-American War, Spain gave Cuba its independence. Spain gave control of Puerto Rico, Guam, and the Philippines to the U.S. for $20 million. Thus, the Filipinos' fight for independence was ignored. Instead, the Philippines became a colony ruled by the United States.

U.S. Colonial Rule

The Filipinos rebelled against their new colonial masters—the United States. By the time the

The voyage from Mexico back to the Philippines was about 10,000 miles.

DEVELOP

Point out that Lesson 2 unfolds in chronological order, beginning with the exploration and early colonial history of the Philippines. Encourage students to preview the pictures and lesson subheadings for a sense of this chronology. Copy the Graphic Overview onto the chalkboard, as students copy it at their desks. Ask them to add details below each event listed in the chart as they read the lesson.

MAP SKILLS

Critical Thinking

Refer students to the map of European colonial empires in the late 1800s in the Minipedia on page 672. Direct their attention to Southeast Asia, and help them find the Philippines. Ask them to compare the size of the colonial empires of different European nations. Ask them to answer these questions: How many different countries had colonies in Southeast Asia? *(Five: the Netherlands, Great Britain, France, Germany, and Spain)* Why did they value these colonies? *(They valued their resources as well as their strategic locations for trade.)*

Access Strategy

Help students understand the challenges of the early explorers by setting up a scenario of an explorer attempting an important voyage. Ask a group of students to take roles—one as the explorer, a few as crew members, and others as islanders.

Have students tell about the problems of life at sea. *(Damage to ships from bad weather, food supplies running out, little drinking water, loss of direction)* Then have them describe the problems that would arise once they land their ship. *(Learning other languages and customs, being misunderstood, encountering hostility from native peoples)* Explain to the students that they will be reading about a voyage like the one they acted out—Magellan's voyage.

Access Activity

Bring in some cloves, cinnamon, nutmeg, and peppercorns for the students to see and smell. Tell students that spices like these were so rare that they were used as money. Europeans even used them to pay their taxes. Cloves, for example, only grew in a few places, and native peoples of the Spice Islands kept the location secret for as long as possible.

■ *Spanish priests introduced Catholicism; other Spanish colonists took control of the land and forced the original peoples to work for them. Many Chinese merchants married Filipino women, and their offspring rebelled against Spanish control. U.S. colonization brought English to the classrooms and improved health care but resulted in the deaths of thousands of Filipino rebels.*

NATIONAL IDENTITY

Critical Thinking

Ask students whether they think foreign control strengthened or weakened the national identity of the Philippines. Encourage them to discuss the following question in small groups: "Why do you think the Filipino people worked for independence for 50 years?"

CULTURE

Visual Learning

Ask students to study the photograph of the jeepney on this page. The jeepney is the most visible vehicle in the crowded Manila streets. Ask students what the creation of the jeepney shows about the creativity and resourcefulness of the Filipino people. *(They found a creative way to take the "leftovers" of war and turn them into useful products.)*

■ *In what specific ways did the cultures of Spain, China, and the United States affect the history of the Philippines?*

United States crushed the rebellion, about 200,000 Filipinos had died in the fighting.

Colonization eventually led to improved health services, police departments, military forces, and schools. However, at first many Filipinos disliked the use of English in their schools and the increasing influence of U.S. culture.

In 1934 leaders of the Philippines and the United States made an agreement. During a 10-year period, the Filipinos would take control of the government. Then in 1941 Japan bombed the U.S. naval base at Pearl Harbor in Hawaii and invaded the Philippines. Thus, the United States and its Philippine colony entered World War II. ■

World War II and the Postwar Years

U.S. and Filipino troops fought together in the Philippines against Japan. The U.S. general Douglas MacArthur led these combined forces. In April 1942, Japanese troops defeated the U.S. and Filipino forces on the Bataan *(buh TAN)* Peninsula. Victorious, Japan declared the Philippines free of U.S. colonial rule.

MUSIC
225 D

➤ *Colorful new "jeepneys" used as taxis are now made in the Philippines. Filipinos made the first jeepneys by adapting jeeps left behind by the United States after World War II.*

Japanese Occupation

Japan set up an "independent" Philippine republic. However, the Japanese military leaders retained strict control.

In 1944 General MacArthur and U.S. troops returned to the Philippines to fight again. In August 1945, the United States dropped two atom bombs on Japan. Japan surrendered and World War II was over.

On July 4, 1946, the Philippines gained total independence at last. The United States provided aid to rebuild after the war. Much of the old colonial relationship continued.

Many wealthy Filipinos, who had cooperated with the Japanese, became the leaders of the new nation. The poor had openly resisted Japanese control during the war. This created a split between the rich and the poor that continued long after the war. When the people rebelled, Filipino leaders used military force to control unrest.

In 1965, when Philippine army officer Ferdinand Marcos was elected their president, the people believed that the pattern would change. Marcos promised economic reforms to help the poor. He also promised to change treaties to limit the influence of the United States in the Philippines.

From Marcos to Aquino

Ferdinand Marcos kept few of his promises. Seven years after he became president, he declared a state of **martial law.** That is, he placed the country under the rule of

Study Skills

Have students work in pairs to map out countries that Japan invaded and occupied during World War II. Invite them to use reference materials from the school library. Then match each pair of students with another pair to share their maps with one another.

Political Context

To help students understand the class structure that exists in the Philippines today, explain that the Catholic church held significant power under Spanish rule. The church acquired much land, mostly through royal grants. The powerful *mestizo* middle class leased rich farmland from church officials. Those who controlled the land also controlled the resources—and, therefore, the money and power. Over the past hundred years, some *mestizos* have favored reforms. However, wealthy landowners continue to make up a close-knit, privileged class that controls most of the country's wealth.

the military forces. Marcos claimed that only under martial law could he maintain democracy and strict law and order.

Under martial law, Marcos had tremendous power. He and his wife Imelda became very rich, while most Filipinos remained poor. Thousands who opposed Marcos went to jail or "disappeared." In 1983 Senator Benigno Aquino *(beh NEEG noh ah KEE noh),* an important opposition leader, was killed.

His murder horrified and united many Filipinos. In February 1986 they tried to get rid of Marcos through a presidential election. Their candidate was Aquino's widow, Corazón "Cory" Aquino. Even though the election was proved to be a fraud, the government still declared Marcos the winner.

Filipinos were angry, and some of Marcos's own officials were, too. Army Deputy Chief of Staff Fidel Ramos and Defense Minister Juan Ponce Enrile *(ahn REEL ay)* quit. They formed a resistance movement to try to get rid of Marcos.

On February 22, 1986, Marcos sent army tanks to defeat Ramos and Enrile. In response, the Roman Catholic cardinal of Manila spoke on the radio. He urged all citizens to support and protect the resistance leaders.

What happened next became known as the People Power uprising. Nuns and priests, teachers and students, farmers, police officers, business leaders, and mothers with little children formed a barrier across the road leading to the resistance camp. Most wore a yellow ribbon, the symbol of Aquino. The nuns knelt down at the front of the crowd. The tanks hurtled toward them but then stopped. For four days the courageous, nonviolent crowd held off the military forces of Marcos. His soldiers never got through the barrier to the resistance camp.

The People Power uprising succeeded in toppling the corrupt government of Ferdinand Marcos. He and his wife fled the Philippines, and Corazón Aquino became president.

▲ *A Filipino taking part in the uprising holds up a barbed wire ring representing the corrupt Marcos regime. Others prayed using rosary beads like the ones pictured above.*

Across Time & Space

The Roman Catholic church has been a powerful force in the Philippines since the arrival of Magellan. Its continuing influence on the lives of Filipinos was proved by the leadership of the brave nuns and priests who inspired the people during the People Power uprising.

◄ *Under the watch of armed soldiers sent by Marcos, a crowd of Aquino supporters, including several nuns in the foreground, listens to a priest during the uprising.*

BELIEF SYSTEMS

Critical Thinking

Point out to students that most Filipinos—about 80 percent—are Roman Catholic. During the People Power uprising, the Roman Catholic archbishop of Manila, a church leader, supported the resistance; so did many priests and nuns. Ask students how this support affected the outcome of the uprising. *(It contributed to the movement's nonviolent nature and gave moral strength to people.)* Encourage students to speculate on how the outcome might have been different without the support of the Catholic church. *(Resistance leaders may have been in greater danger, and the people might not have felt empowered to express their opposition to Marcos.)*

HISTORY

Visual Learning

Ask students what the photographs on this page show about the People Power uprising. *(The photographs point to its nonviolent character and to the church's involvement.)* Ask them what other Asian nation used nonviolent resistence to force changes in its government. *(India in Chapter 14)*

Art Connection

Have students read the account of the People Power uprising, and ask them to reflect on the events that took place. Then have them draw a picture or make a collage of magazine images that captures the activities in February 1986. Encourage students to write captions for their pictures. Display the artwork on a bulletin board labeled "People Power in the Philippines."

Map and Globe Skills

Challenge students to investigate the rich natural resources of the Philippines and the other islands of Southeast Asia. Using the world land use map in the Atlas on page 689 as a model, they can prepare a large land use and resources chart that lists the name of the country and the natural resources found there.

The Philippines Today

It is up to you to bring to the life you are entering, to the state you must help to form, an energy of true religious faith.

Pope Pius XII

Corazón Aquino had selected these words to appear in her high school yearbook. As president, she put them into action to try to restore civil rights, reform the government, and encourage economic growth. However, she faced many problems, including continued resistance from rebel groups.

In 1992 the first peaceful election in over 25 years took place in the Philippines. The Filipinos chose a new president, Fidel Ramos—the man who had helped to defeat Marcos. He is trying to improve the economy. In recent years, lack of jobs has led to the migration of thousands of Filipinos to the United States and other nations. Land reform is also needed to allow more Filipinos to own their own land.

Approximately 62 million people live in the Philippines today. One of every eight people lives in or around Manila, the center of the government and the economy. About two-thirds of all the country's industries are located there.

The educational system is strong in the Philippines, and the literacy rate is high. According to 1990 figures, about 90 percent of the population aged 15 and over can read and write.

Almost 70 native languages and dialects are spoken in the Philippines. The most widely spoken language is Pilipino *(pihl uh PEE noh)*. It is based on Tagalog, one of the earliest languages. English is also widely spoken.

Today's Filipinos are a people of many different heritages. Malay, Spanish, Chinese, Arab, Japanese, and U.S. influences reflect the nation's history. The Philippines is the only Asian nation that is mostly Christian. ■

➤ *Filipinos today are proud of their heritage. These girls from the Philippine island of Mindanao are wearing traditional, brightly colored, beaded outfits.*

■ *Beginning with World War II, what are the events in Philippine history that led to independence?*

■ *The Japanese occupation forces strictly controlled the Philippines. After the war, those Filipinos who had supported the Japanese used the military to control unrest. During the postwar years, the Philippines relied on U.S. aid to rebuild cities, thus continuing old colonial dependence. Bolstered by the Catholic church, the Filipinos eventually united in a nonviolent uprising to overthrow the government.*

REVIEW

1. **FOCUS** What factors shaped Philippine history?
2. **CULTURE** Describe the trade route between China, the Philippines, and North America under Spanish colonial rule.
3. **SOCIAL SYSTEMS** What did the Filipinos do to bring down the government of Ferdinand Marcos?
4. **CRITICAL THINKING** Imagine that you are a Filipino student. You have studied your nation's history and ways in which the United States both aided and controlled the Philippines. How do you feel about the United States? Explain why some Filipinos may be pro-United States and others may not be.
5. **WRITING ACTIVITY** Imagine that you are one of the participants in the People Power uprising. Write two or three journal entries describing everything that you saw and heard and the people whom you met. Tell what feelings and beliefs led you to oppose Ferdinand Marcos and to join Cory Aquino's followers.

CLOSE

Invite a volunteer to read the Thinking Focus to the class. Have students recall the major chronological events in the lesson and refer to the Graphic Overview they used at the beginning of the lesson. Ask for volunteers to share the details they added below each box of their Graphic Overviews.

Homework Options

Have students write a sentence using each of the key terms in this lesson. The sentences should demonstrate an understanding of each key term.

Study Guide: page 68

Answers to Review Questions

1. Under Spanish rule, Filipinos were encouraged to convert to Catholicism. Under U.S. control, English became the language used in schools. World War II brought Japanese military rule. In 1946 the Philippines gained independence.
2. Goods from China and Southeast Asia arrived in the Philippines; from there they went in galleons to Mexico. There, goods from China and Southeast Asia were traded for silver or sent on to Europe.
3. After Marcos dismissed the election of Corazón Aquino, the Filipinos resisted. When government forces were sent to crush the uprising, the Catholic church urged the people to support the resistance, and Marcos fled the country.
4. The United States made improvements and brought aid, but it also had an increasing influence on the culture.
5. Students should write creatively, basing their entries on facts presented in the text.

500
800
1100
1400
1700
1819
TODAY

L E S S O N 3

Singapore, Indonesia, and Vietnam

An Asian legend tells of a seventh-century Sumatran prince exploring an island off the Malay Peninsula. From offshore, he sees a black-faced tiger. Thinking it is a lion, he names the island Singa Pur, meaning "lion city" in the ancient language of Sanskrit.

In 1857 alone, wild tigers roaming Singapore's tropical forests carried off 300 human victims! Today, tiny Singapore is known as one of the Four Tigers of Asia because of its startling, recent economic success. How did a tiny, tiger-filled rain forest become a major center of business and trade?

THINKING FOCUS

How do Singapore, Indonesia, and Vietnam reflect the wide variety of cultures in Southeast Asia today?

Key Term

- embargo

Singapore: A Thriving City-State

In 1819 the East India Company, a large British trading firm, sent Sir Stamford Raffles to Southeast Asia. He selected Singapore as an ideal location for storing and shipping Asian goods. Singapore, lying halfway between India and China, had just the wide, deep harbor that Raffles sought.

In 1824 when Singapore became part of the British colonial empire, about 11,000 people lived there. By 1911 its population had grown to more than 250,000.

In 1965 Singapore became an independent republic. Today its population of about 2.8 million people are packed into an area of about 242 square miles—less than one-fifth the size of Rhode Island.

Today Singapore is a bustling city and one of the world's busiest ports.

Below, at the left, modern high-rises in Singapore look out over the harbor waters. At the right, a woman sells fish at an open-air market.

INTRODUCE

Ask students to locate the countries of Singapore, Indonesia, and Vietnam on the map of Eurasia in the Atlas on pages 682–683. Ask them to identify a few of the geographic differences among these three countries. *(Students might observe that Vietnam is on the coastal mainland, Singapore is relatively small, and Indonesia is made up of many islands.)* Have students read the Thinking Focus. Tell them that this lesson will illustrate the wide variety of cultures in Southeast Asia.

Key Term

Vocabulary Strategies: T36–T37

embargo—a ban on trade

Graphic Overview

	Singapore	Indonesia	Vietnam
Geography	wide, deep harbor	archipelago	peninsula
Economy	oil, manufacturing	spices, tin, natural gas	farming, U.S. embargo
Colonial Influences	British	Dutch, Japanese	Chinese, French

Objectives

1. Explain the wide variety of cultures and ways of life in Southeast Asia today.
2. Compare and contrast Singapore and Indonesia.
3. Describe some of the challenges facing Vietnam today.

DEVELOP

To help students organize the variety of cultures in Southeast Asia today, copy on the chalkboard the basic structure of the Graphic Overview. Invite students to fill in the chart as they read the lesson. Point out that the lesson focuses on the variety of cultures in the region, but have students think about the common elements among these countries, too. *(Close to the ocean; trade important to economy)*

■ *Singapore lies halfway between the major trading centers of India and China and has a deep, wide harbor—perfect for docking ships.*

SOCIAL SYSTEMS

Map and Globe Skills

Ask students to refer to the cartogram on page 689 of the Atlas. Have them compare Indonesia's population density to that of other countries, including Singapore and Vietnam. Then ask them to find Indonesia on the GNP cartogram on page 375 of Chapter 16. Encourage students to make generalizations based on their findings. *(Indonesia's population is extremely dense, and its GNP is relatively large.)*

It is also a leading center for oil refining, shipbuilding, and manufacturing—including computer parts.

The population is a varied mix of cultures and religions. About 76 percent of the people are Chinese. They are mostly Confucianists, Buddhists, or Taoists. About 15 percent of the people are Malay Muslims. About seven percent of the people are Indian, and they are mostly Hindu.

The government of Singapore has a great deal of control over the lives of its citizens. Singapore, however, is a peaceful, well-ordered society. Most of the people of Singapore enjoy a high standard of living. The government is committed to religious and ethnic tolerance. Singapore, like its larger neighbor Indonesia, has been working to create unity out of a great diversity of peoples and cultures. ■

■ *How did Singapore's location and natural features help it to attract workers and to become a thriving nation?*

How Do We Know?

HISTORY *In 1891, Dutch scientist Eugene Dubois found a human fossil on Java. It was found in stream deposits on the Solo River. He named it Java man. Some scientists have concluded that Java man lived between 500,000 and 1 million years ago.*

Indonesia: A Varied Nation

With a population of about 190 million people, Indonesia is the world's fifth largest country. However, its people are divided by geography. The country is made up of more than 13,600 islands, spread out across 3,000 miles of sea. So, from east to west, Indonesia covers about the same number of miles as the distance from northern Maine to southern California. More than half of the people live on the island of Java where Jakarta, the nation's capital city, is located. Many of the other islands are not inhabited.

Beginning thousands of years ago, people from diverse cultures brought many religions to Indonesia. From India came Buddhism and Hinduism. From the Middle East came Islam. From Europe came Christianity. Today about 87 percent of the people practice Islam, making Indonesia the world's largest Muslim nation.

Today the nation is committed to tolerance of its many religions, including those that combine religious practices. Many people, for example, practice a religion that combines Hinduism, Buddhism, and local customs.

The large number of ethnic groups and languages also reflect the nation's cultural diversity. There are more than 300 distinct ethnic groups in Indonesia. About 25 languages and about 250 different dialects are spoken. The national language is Bahasa Indonesia, which has its roots in Malay, the language of early Sumatran traders.

From 1619 to World War II, the Dutch gradually gained control and colonized what is now Indonesia. Then, like the Philippines, it was conquered by Japan. After World War II, Indonesia gained independence from the Dutch. Since 1967 a military dictator has ruled there.

Today Indonesia joins Singapore as a growing economic force in the Pacific Rim area of the world (see the Atlas map of the Pacific Rim region on page 684). Indonesia is a

▼ *This famous mosque in Banda Aceh, Indonesia, combines elements of style from Arabia and India.*

Access Activity

Explain that Indonesia is a nation of many religions and ethnic groups. Ask students to compare this fact about Indonesia with what they know about diversity in the United States. Have students list a few examples of the variety within their own nation. *(Many kinds of places of worship, ethnic groups, restaurants and stores selling ethnic foods, and so on)*

Access Strategy

Help students understand the role geography plays in a nation's development by staging a game. Divide the class into three groups, and give each group one of the following economic goals: prosperity through shipbuilding, trade, and fishing; good farming and easy distribution of produce; and large cities with successful industries.

Have each group represent one nation and develop a geographical "wish list" that would help it achieve its economic goals. Have groups share their lists with the rest of the class. *(For example, a nation with a harbor and abundant forests would be ideal for shipbuilding, trade, and fishing; one with a fertile river valley would be perfect for farming and transport of produce; and one with flat land and a stable climate would support urban areas and industrialization.)*

Explain that Southeast Asian nations fit the first category, but some, like Singapore, have industry as well.

world leader in the production and export of natural gas, petroleum, and tin. The nation is a major supplier of rubber, coffee, tea, and spices including cloves and nutmeg. Major industries process agricultural and mineral products. The nation is also a leading manufacturer of shoes. Working with Singapore, Indonesia has developed the island of Batam into a thriving industrial park. Several international companies have built manufacturing plants there. ■

▲ *The Indonesian* hudoq *dancer in the foreground is a Christian performing a traditional ceremony to protect the rice crop. A terraced rice field is shown in the background.*

■ *In what specific ways is Indonesia a nation of diversity?*

Vietnam: A War-Torn Nation

Vietnam is a narrow, S-shaped country on the eastern side of the peninsula of Indochina. It is smaller than California but has a population of about 70 million, about twice the population of California.

Throughout much of its history, Vietnam has fought fiercely to maintain its independence. About 2,000 years ago, China conquered Vietnam. Chinese settlers flooded into the region, bringing their religions and cultural influences including Buddhism and Confucianism. In A.D. 939, the Vietnamese drove out the Chinese, but conflicts with China continued for hundreds of years.

Vietnam became a French colony in 1883. Then, like many of its neighbors, it was taken over by Japan during World War II. France tried to regain its colony after the war. A Communist group called the Viet Minh, led by Ho Chi Minh *(hoh chee mihn),* defeated the French colonial power in 1954. Vietnam was divided in half by the terms of the peace treaty. A Communist government ruled North Vietnam. An anti-Communist government supported by the United States ruled South Vietnam. Afraid that the Communists would win, the United States opposed elections that might have unified the country.

In 1957 Ho Chi Minh went to war to unite North and South Vietnam. Communist nations such as China and the former Soviet Union aided North Vietnam. The United States, France, and South Korea later sent troops to aid South Vietnam. Warfare killed hundreds of thousands of people, and much of Vietnam was in ruins. North Vietnam won the Vietnam War in 1975. Communists then reunited North and South Vietnam into one

▼ *Rice is transported along the Mekong River in Vietnam.*

■ *Indonesia's population represents more than 300 ethnic groups, many different religions, and about 25 languages (with about 250 different dialects). Indonesians have established a sense of unity through religious tolerance, national language, and a spirit of national identity.*

ETHICS

Critical Thinking

In 1975 the Indonesian government claimed control of a formerly Portuguese area called East Timor. Human rights organizations maintain that 200,000 people have been killed by the Indonesian military since that year. Ask students to suggest what actions, if any, other countries should take. *(Students might suggest negotiations sponsored by the UN or sanctions against Indonesia by other nations.)*

HISTORY

Study Skills

Help students research the Vietnam War. The text on this page tells of the effects of the war on Vietnam. Ask students to use encyclopedias and to talk with adults at home to learn more about the U.S. role in the war. Have them each share three facts with the class.

Language Arts Connection

Have students listen to the following paragraph about Indonesia's recent political history as you read it aloud:

"The first president of independent Indonesia was Sukarno, who ruled from 1949–1965. Sukarno was a popular, gifted speaker, credited with giving Indonesia its national identity. During his term, there was much political, social, and economic upheaval. In 1965 Suharto overthrew Sukarno's government. In the struggle for power, some 300,000 Communists were slaughtered. Suharto's leadership has been authoritarian, backed by military power."

Ask students to identify the main idea of the paragraph and write a one-sentence summary. *(Since independence, Indonesia's political history has been marked by upheaval.)*

Visual Learning

Encourage students to look at the pictures on this page. Tell them that rice is a basic food throughout Southeast Asia. Have students suggest basic grains in other parts of the world. Ask them how that affects what people eat. *(For example, corn, or maize grain, grows in the Americas, and people eat tortillas and cereal.)*

ECONOMICS

Visual Learning

Invite students to reflect on the fact that bicycles are a major mode of transportation in Vietnam and much of Asia. Have them study the photo on this page and ask them what it reveals about the economy of Vietnam. *(Limited industrialization, low wages for workers, not much fuel for cars)*

■ *Vietnam remains primarily an agricultural, rice-producing nation. About 75 percent of its people live in small villages. Unlike many Southeast Asian countries, Vietnam is not widely involved in world trade because of a U.S. embargo.*

CLOSE

Read the Thinking Focus aloud. Then have students divide into three groups—representing Indonesia, Singapore, and Vietnam—and work together to complete the Graphic Overview started at the beginning of the lesson. A representative from each group should present the examples of geographic and cultural variety to the class.

In Ho Chi Minh City, where bicycles remain a major means of transportation, hopes are high for better days. The price of property has gone up in expectation of renewed relations with the West.

■ *What is life like for the people of Vietnam today?*

country. Other Communist governments took control of the neighboring nations of Laos and Cambodia.

Almost 50 years of waging war have made Vietnam one of the poorest nations in the world. Thousands of craters made by bombs dropped during the Vietnam War remain. Many buildings built by the French still stand in its two major cities, Hanoi and Ho Chi Minh City (formerly Saigon). Yet the buildings are now shabby, and few new ones have been built since the Vietnam War. There are few factories, and many city residents do not have jobs. The nation brims with natural resources, including coal, oil, and timber. However, the government does not have the funds to build processing plants to make use of these resources.

About 75 percent of the Vietnamese live in small villages. They raise rice in the wet, fertile river valleys of the Red River and the Mekong River. Under communism, some Vietnamese work together on large farms called "collectives." They give most of their crops to the government, which distributes them to the people. Recently, the government has allowed the people to keep their crops and sell them privately. Thus, Vietnam has begun to shift to a limited market economy.

The government of Vietnam is trying to improve the economy by renewing trade with the West. However, the United States has had an **embargo,** or a ban on trade, with Vietnam. The United States wants Vietnam to end military involvement in Cambodia. Vietnam must also provide all the facts it has about U.S. military personnel missing in Vietnam since the Vietnam War. In October 1992, Vietnam began to release photos and new information about these U.S. soldiers. This action will help lead to an end to the U.S. trade embargo and to improved relations between the two nations. ■

REVIEW

1. **FOCUS** How do Singapore, Indonesia, and Vietnam reflect the wide variety of cultures in Southeast Asia today?
2. **GEOGRAPHY** Refer to the map of Southeast Asia on page 387. Compare the geography of Indonesia with the geography of Vietnam. How has their geography affected the history of these two countries?
3. **ECONOMICS** Compare and contrast the economic conditions in Singapore with those in Vietnam. Explain the reasons for the differences.
4. **CRITICAL THINKING** You read that Singapore is extremely crowded. What problems do you think overcrowding in a city can cause? Suggest reasonable solutions for solving these problems.
5. **WRITING ACTIVITY** Imagine that you are Sir Stamford Raffles. Write a letter to the East India Company explaining why you chose this location and describing what you saw there.

Homework Options

To relate the concept of trade to the present day, have students look in a newspaper for reports on international trade. Ask them to bring in a sample sentence from one of the articles to share with the class.

Study Guide: page 69

Answers to Review Questions

1. Singapore's population is made up mostly of Chinese, Malay, and Indian ethnic groups. Indonesia has over 300 different ethnic groups, but most of its people practice Islam. Chinese settlers influenced Vietnam with their religious practices of Buddhism and Confucianism.
2. Indonesia's island geography protected it against invasion from China. Vietnam, on the mainland of Asia, was more vulnerable, especially because of its proximity to China.
3. Trade and manufacturing are booming in Singapore. Centuries of war and the U.S. trade embargo have left Vietnam poor.
4. Problems include lack of housing, crowded schools, transmittal of disease, insufficient food and water. Solutions include more high-rise apartments, improved public transportation, and strong health care.
5. Students should write creatively about the ideal natural harbor of Singapore.

UNDERSTANDING TOPOGRAPHY

Analyzing Elevation Maps

Here's Why

If you plan a bicycle route to avoid hills or to go around a lake, you are showing that you understand topography—the natural surface features of the land.

Studying topography gives you more than information about possible routes. Understanding topography can also help you find out more about the land, its people, and its wildlife. For example, understanding topography can help you study the animals in any given place.

Here's How

Imagine you are a naturalist looking for the Sumatran rhinoceros, an animal that is close to extinction. From your study, you know that the Sumatran rhinoceros feeds on bamboo and fruit. On the island of Sumatra, this rhinoceros lives only in highlands and mountain forests.

How would you plan a trip that would take you across the island of Sumatra in search of this rhinoceros? You might begin by looking at the map and the diagram on this page.

The map uses color to show different ranges in elevation, or height, above sea level. The key shows the elevations represented by each color. The diagram below the map shows the elevation of one route across the island of Sumatra.

Study both the map and the diagram. Based on what you know about the rhino and the information on the map, would you expect to find the Sumatran rhinoceros along this route? Why or why not?

Western Indonesia: Physical and Profile Map

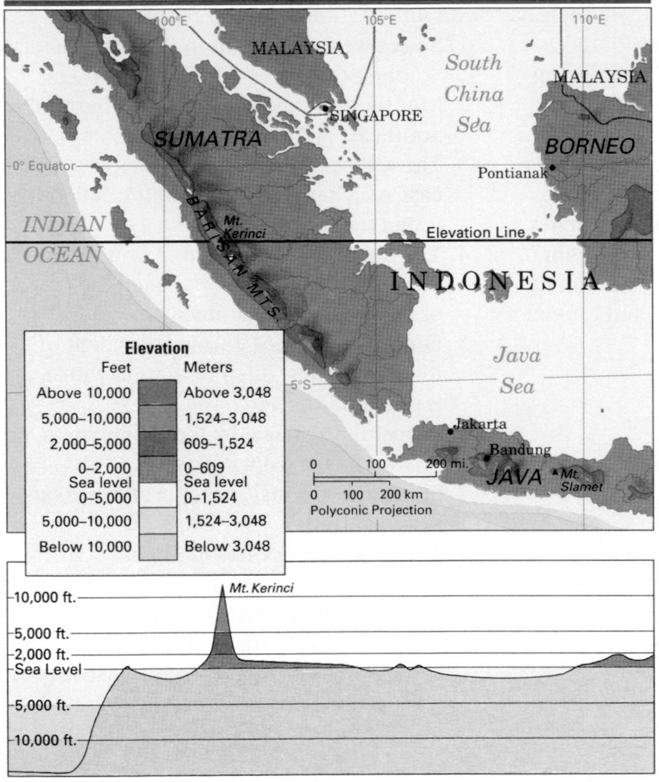

100°E
105°E
110°E
MALAYSIA
SINGAPORE
South China Sea
MALAYSIA
SUMATRA
BORNEO
0° Equator
Pontianak
INDIAN OCEAN
Mt. Kerinci
BARISAN MTS.
Elevation Line
INDONESIA
Java Sea
5°S
Jakarta
Bandung
JAVA
Mt. Slamet
0 100 200 mi.
0 100 200 km
Polyconic Projection
Elevation
Feet / Meters
Above 10,000 / Above 3,048
5,000–10,000 / 1,524–3,048
2,000–5,000 / 609–1,524
0–2,000 / 0–609
Sea level / Sea level
0–5,000 / 0–1,524
5,000–10,000 / 1,524–3,048
Below 10,000 / Below 3,048
Mt. Kerinci
10,000 ft.
5,000 ft.
2,000 ft.
Sea Level
5,000 ft.
10,000 ft.

Try It

Your friend is a naturalist studying the clouded leopard, another endangered animal living in Sumatra. According to her information, the clouded leopard lives in evergreen forests that range from sea level to a height of 6,600 feet. Your friend wants to study the clouded leopard in the wild. Would you invite your friend to join you on your route? Would this leopard be likely to live at the top of Mount Kerinci?

Apply It

Research an animal found in your state. At what altitudes does it live? Find a topographic map of your state in an atlas. Use the map to pinpoint areas in your state where the animal would most likely be found.

UNDERSTANDING TOPOGRAPHY

This skills feature uses an elevation map of western Indonesia and a discussion of the natural habitats of animals to teach students the concept of topography.

GEOGRAPHY

Visual Learning

Encourage students to become more aware of the effects of topography on daily life. Ask students to list ways that streets, buildings, and local vegetation are affected by local topography. How does it affect their lives? *(Students might mention San Francisco cable cars for steep, hilly streets or the growth of conifers, or fir trees, in high-altitude areas. They might conclude that modern technology serves to lessen the effect of topography.)*

Answers to Try It

Yes. The route goes from sea level to 6,600 feet above sea level, which is the region where these leopards live. No. The top of Mount Kerinci is more than 10,000 feet above sea level—higher than where the clouded leopard is usually found.

Answers to Apply It

You may want to refer students to local nature guides and groups for information about the animals. You may want to create a bulletin-board display of a topographical map of your state, with yarn pointing to sites where various animals may be found. Include a fact sheet about each animal on the bulletin board.

Objective

Read and use a topographic map and a vertical profile. (Map and Globe Skills 2, 3)

Answers to Reviewing Key Terms

A. Sample answers:

1. A **galleon** was an early wooden, three-masted sailing ship used primarily for trade. A **typhoon** is a violent storm, similar to a hurricane. A galleon caught in a severe typhoon would be badly damaged and might even sink.
2. The term **martial law** means a system in which a nation is placed under the rule of the military forces. Under such a system, a nation's ruler might rely on soldiers to act as police officers.
3. The **embargo** would ban all U.S. trade with Indonesia.
4. The first **mestizos** were the children of Chinese merchants and Filipino women. The *mestizos* grew up to become a wealthy, well-educated, middle class in the Philippines.

B. Sample answers:

1. To **circumnavigate** is to travel all the way around something. The picture might show an arrow going around the circumference of a circle.
2. An **archipelago** is a group of islands. The picture should feature a group of dots labeled as islands.

Answers to Exploring Concepts

A. Sample answers:

China: Vietnam; Buddhism, Taoism, Confucianism
England: Singapore; an established port
Arabia: Indonesia; Islam
United States: Philippines; economic aid, U.S. culture, English language

B. Sample answers:

1. Spices lured traders and explorers to Southeast Asia.
2. Monsoons bring heavy rains and damaging floods. However, monsoons also create moist conditions for growing rice.
3. European explorers seeking a western route to Asia found that the islands of Southeast Asia were a convenient stopping place. Later, the British established a major trading depot at Singapore.
4. Japan declared the Philippines "independent" of U.S. colonial rule, although the Japanese military retained strict control. Japan helped Indonesia break its colonial ties with the Dutch and forced France to relinquish power in Vietnam.
5. Marcos declared a state of martial law. His opponents were imprisoned or mysteriously disappeared. When citizens held an election, the government declared Marcos the winner, even though there was proof that most citizens had voted against him.
6. Inspired by Catholic leaders, citizens held off the military forces of Marcos and toppled his government.
7. The British established a trading depot in Singapore. Businesses include oil refining, shipbuilding, and manufacturing.
8. Indonesia is made up of more than 13,600 islands, spread across 3,000 miles of sea. There are more than 300 distinct ethnic groups, and about 25 languages and 250 dialects are spoken.
9. In its early history, Vietnam suffered through continuous wars with China. Following World War II, Vietnam went to war against France to drive out the French colonial government. From 1957 to 1975, Vietnam was embroiled in civil war. The damage from that war remains today.

Chapter Review

Reviewing Key Terms

archipelago (p. 387)
circumnavigate (p. 390)
embargo (p. 398)
galleon (p. 391)
martial law (p. 392)
mestizo (p. 391)
typhoon (p. 387)

A. Answer the following questions regarding selected key terms.

1. What is a galleon? What is a typhoon? What might happen to a galleon caught in a severe typhoon?
2. What is meant by the term martial law? Under a system of martial law, what jobs could a nation's ruler give to soldiers?
3. What might occur if the United States declared an embargo on Indonesia?
4. What two cultural groups intermarried to create the first mestizos in Southeast Asia? What success did the mestizos gain?

B. Write a brief definition of the following key terms. Then draw a labeled diagram or picture to illustrate the term's meaning.

1. circumnavigate
2. archipelago

Exploring Concepts

A. Throughout history, the cultures of Southeast Asian nations have been greatly influenced by outside factors. Summarize a few of those outside influences by copying and completing the chart below. The first column lists specific cultures that came to Southeast Asia. Fill in the second column by listing a Southeast Asian nation that shows a lasting influence from that culture. Fill in the final column with a specific example of what the outside culture brought, built, or established in the Southeast Asian nation. The first line has been completed for you as an example.

Outside Culture	Nation	Influence
Spain	Philippines	Roman Catholicism
China		
England		
Arabia		
United States		

B. Support each of the following statements with information from the chapter.

1. Spices were important in the early history of Southeast Asia.
2. Monsoons are both helpful and harmful to Southeast Asia.
3. Throughout its history, the region of Southeast Asia has been a busy intersection for ocean trade.
4. The Japanese occupation of Southeast Asia during World War II weakened the power of the colonial governments.
5. Ferdinand Marcos, former president of the Philippines, ruled his nation with tremendous power.
6. Peaceful resistance by the Philippine people drove Marcos from office.
7. Singapore is a major center of world business and trade.
8. The geography of Indonesia has contributed to the existence of many different languages, religions, ethnic groups, and cultures.
9. The nation of Vietnam has suffered throughout much of its history because of wars and the destruction they caused.

Reviewing Skills

1. Look at the map at the right. Construct a vertical profile of the land at 16°N. What is the highest elevation shown on your vertical profile? What is the lowest elevation shown on your vertical profile?
2. Look at the top photo on page 393. Explain what the barbed wire and yellow ribbon symbolized to the People Power uprising. In your opinion, why did they choose barbed wire as a symbol? Why did they choose a yellow ribbon?
3. Imagine that you are building a museum exhibit that will represent the diversity of Southeast Asia—its land features, its resources, and its ethnic and cultural groups. How would you gather, plan, and organize your ideas and materials?

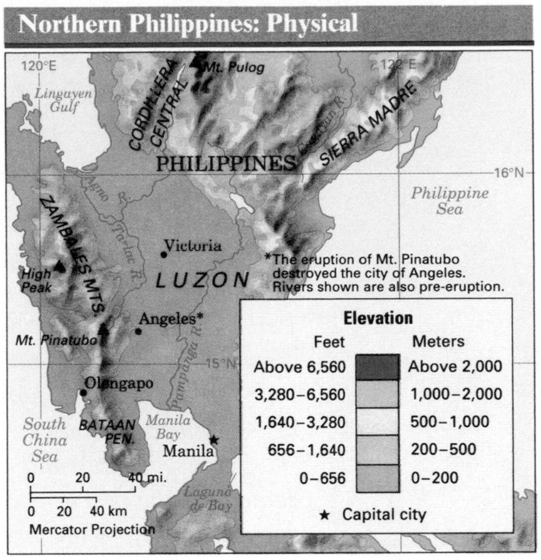
Northern Philippines: Physical
120°E
122°E
16°N
15°N
Lingayen Gulf
Mt. Pulog
CORDILLERA CENTRAL
SIERRA MADRE
PHILIPPINES
Philippine Sea
ZAMBALES MTS.
Victoria
LUZON
High Peak
Angeles*
Mt. Pinatubo
Olongapo
South China Sea
BATAAN PEN.
Manila Bay
Manila
Laguna de Bay
0 20 40 mi.
0 20 40 km
Mercator Projection
*The eruption of Mt. Pinatubo destroyed the city of Angeles. Rivers shown are also pre-eruption.
Elevation
Feet
Meters
Above 6,560
Above 2,000
3,280–6,560
1,000–2,000
1,640–3,280
500–1,000
656–1,640
200–500
0–656
0–200
★ Capital city

Using Critical Thinking

1. Describe the "collective" system of farming that has been practiced by many Vietnamese rice growers. How does this system differ from farming in a free market economy? In your opinion, what are the benefits of collective farming? What are the drawbacks?
2. Magellan's ships were severely damaged during the long voyage that led to the Spaniards arriving at the Philippines. How might the history and modern-day culture of the Philippines have been different if Magellan's ships had never reached their destination?
3. To keep the streets clean, the government of Singapore does not allow people to chew gum. Do you think this is a fair law, or is it too strict? Suggest other ways that the government might solve the problem. Explain why your ideas might be better.

Preparing for Citizenship

1. **COLLECTING INFORMATION** Gather articles and photographs from current newspapers and magazines about recent events and daily life in the nations of Southeast Asia. Include any information you can find about politics, economics, or any other interesting topics. Share your information with the rest of the class.
2. **WRITING ACTIVITY** Imagine that you are the new leader of Indonesia. Write a plan of at least three steps you would take to try to unify the peoples of your diverse nation.
3. **COLLABORATIVE LEARNING** In your community there may be people who have first-hand information regarding past or present events in Southeast Asia. With a partner, brainstorm for ideas concerning individuals you might interview together. You might talk with an Asian who emigrated to the United States, or with a soldier who served in World War II or the Vietnam War. With your partner, prepare your questions. During the interview, listen carefully. Then work together to present your findings to the class. If you cannot conduct an interview, do research with your partner to answer the questions, and then present your findings to the class.

Answers to Reviewing Skills

1. The highest elevation at 16°N are the Sierra Madres. The lowest elevation is sea level or where the Ango River empties into the Lingayen Gulf.
2. The barbed wire represented the corrupt Marcos regime, and the yellow ribbon represented support for Cory Aquino.
3. Answers should indicate logical plans for collecting and presenting information. The list of notes and sketches should indicate thorough and creative use of the skill of identifying main ideas.

Answers to Using Critical Thinking

1. Under the "collective" system of farming, farmers work together on large farms. They give most of the crop to the government, which distributes it evenly to all people. By contrast, in a free-market economy, farmers would own their own farms and sell their crops privately. Possible opinions include: (1) Benefits: all people receive an equal share of the crop; the government makes sure that no one goes without food; the farmers work together without competition. (2) Drawbacks: the farmers are not free to make their own profits; people are not necessarily rewarded for working harder than their peers; the government has too much control over the people's lives.
2. The Spaniards might not have established their cultural influences and dominance. For example, Roman Catholicism might not have become the significant force that it is even today. Another outside culture might have planted its roots in the Philippines and influenced the culture, or the Filipinos might have been left free to develop their own culture without so much outside influence.
3. Opinions regarding the law will vary. Other solutions might include strong antilitter laws, widespread education regarding recycling, and abundant trash receptacles.

Answers to Preparing for Citizenship

1. **COLLECTING INFORMATION** Results should indicate a thorough attempt to gather information about current events and daily life in the nations of Southeast Asia.
2. **WRITING ACTIVITY** Student plans will vary but may suggest such items as improved methods of transportation and communication and the formation of councils of various cultural groups to improve understanding among peoples.
3. **COLLABORATIVE LEARNING** You may wish to provide guidance as students select their interview candidates and prepare their questions, making sure that they approach the assignment with sensitivity and respect regarding the interviewee's experiences. Urge them to send thank-you letters following the interviews. Allow ample classroom time for the presentation of findings. Discuss how firsthand experiences can provide vivid details that make history more interesting.

UNIT PREVIEW

Have students look at the details of the painting on these two pages while a volunteer reads the text paragraph aloud. Ask students how the painting reinforces the ideas in the text about European culture. *(Shows the importance of the past; admiration for ancient Greece and Rome; the influence of classical architecture)* Tell them that events from the past still influence Europeans today.

Looking Back

Remind students that they have read in Chapters 7 and 8 about the influences of ancient Greece and Rome and the origins of Christianity and of Islam.

Looking Forward

In this unit, the chapters examine European history from the fall of Rome to the collapse of the Soviet Union.

Chapter 18 *The Making of Europe*
Chapter 19 *The Rise of Spain, Great Britain, and Russia*
Chapter 20 *Europe: 1900 to the End of the Cold War*
Chapter 21 *Europe and Russia Today*

Unit 6 Europe and Russia

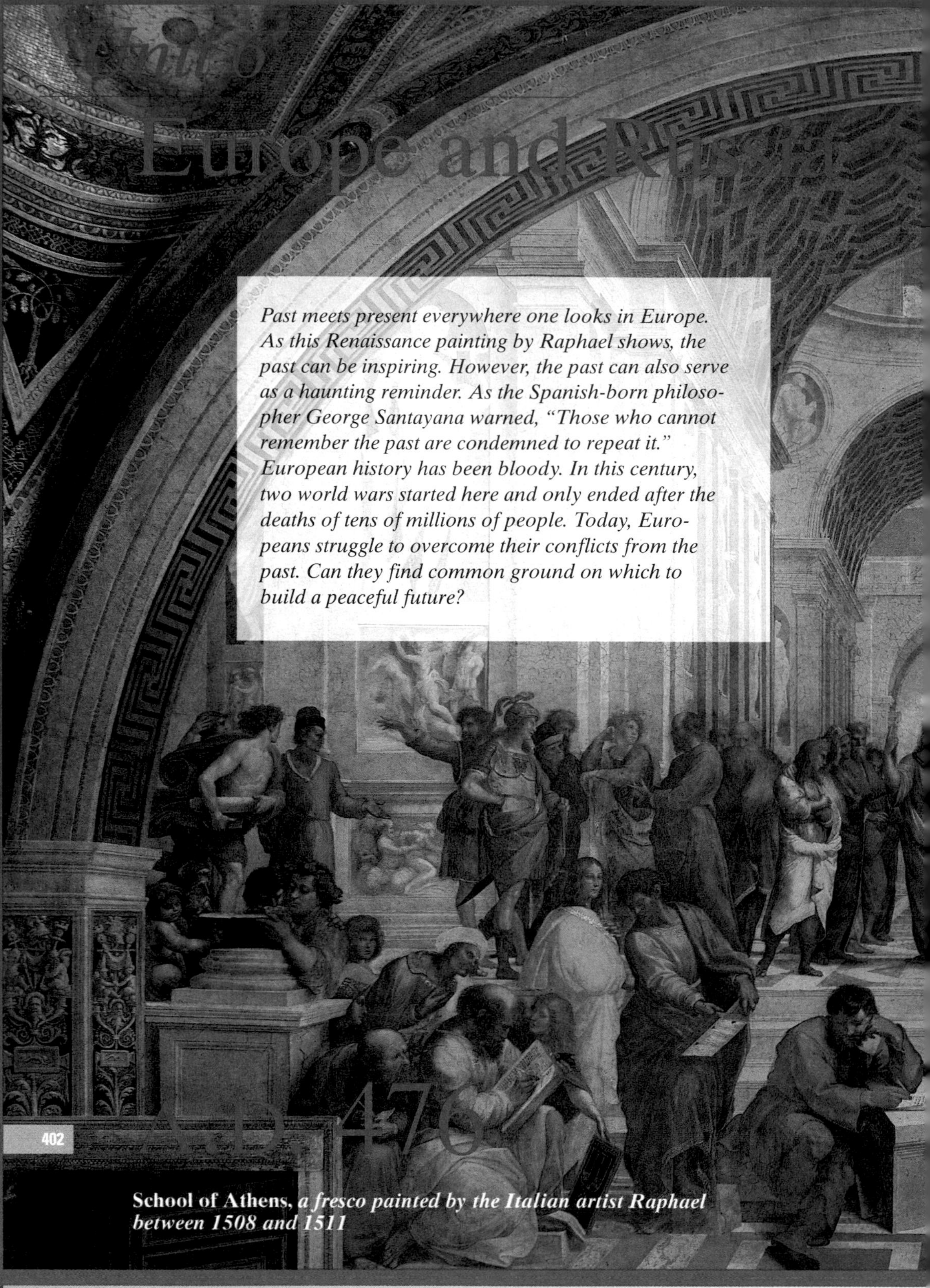

Past meets present everywhere one looks in Europe. As this Renaissance painting by Raphael shows, the past can be inspiring. However, the past can also serve as a haunting reminder. As the Spanish-born philosopher George Santayana warned, "Those who cannot remember the past are condemned to repeat it." European history has been bloody. In this century, two world wars started here and only ended after the deaths of tens of millions of people. Today, Europeans struggle to overcome their conflicts from the past. Can they find common ground on which to build a peaceful future?

A.D. 476

School of Athens, *a fresco painted by the Italian artist Raphael between 1508 and 1511*

402

BIBLIOGRAPHY

Books for Students

Fritz, Jean, and others. *The World in 1492.* New York: Henry Holt, 1992. A multicultural perspective, with sections on each continent and region. Nonfiction.

Resnick, Abraham. *Russia: A History to 1917.* Chicago: Childrens Press, 1983. An account of Russian history from the ninth century to the revolution. Nonfiction.

Roberts, Elizabeth. *Europe 1992: The United States of Europe?* New York: Gloucester, 1990. A description of the European Community. Nonfiction.

Sabbagh, Antoine. *Europe in the Middle Ages.* Trans. Anthea Ridett. Englewood Cliffs: Silver Burdett, 1988. An introduction to medieval society and culture. Nonfiction.

Books to Read Aloud

Finkelstein, Norman H. *The Other 1492: Jewish Settlement in the New World.* New York: Scribner, 1989. A description of the Jews' expulsion from Spain and Jewish influence on Spanish culture. Nonfiction.

Philip, Neil, ed. *Fairy Tales of Eastern Europe.* New York: Clarion Books, 1991. A collection of 22 stories from Eastern Europe and the former Soviet republics. Fiction.

Toda
403

Understanding the Painting

Raphael Sanzio (1483–1520) was the youngest of the great Italian Renaissance trio that also included Michelangelo and Leonardo da Vinci. Many critics think that Raphael's greatest work is *School of Athens,* shown on these facing pages. He painted the fresco on the walls of the papal apartments in the Vatican in Rome. The painting reflects the great interest that Renaissance society had in classical learning. It shows a number of famous Greek philosophers (and some historical and contemporary figures) intently discussing ideas inside a Roman-style building. The central figures are Plato (left) and Aristotle (right); Euclid, Pythagoras, and Socrates also appear.

Understanding Chronology

The chronology of this unit extends from the fall of Rome and the feudal era (A.D. 500–1100) up to the present day. Students should refer to the chapter timelines as they read, to visualize how many—or how few—years pass between major events. For example, the Middle Ages encompassed nearly 700 years, but about two decades elapsed between World War I and World War II.

Books for Teachers

Kennedy, Paul. *The Rise and Fall of the Great Powers: Economic Change and Military Conflict from 1500 to 2000.* New York: Random House, 1987. An examination of the decline of European powers, with a warning about the United States. Nonfiction.

Krause, Axel. *Inside the New Europe.* New York: HarperCollins, 1991. An account of problems facing Europe today. Nonfiction.

Roxburgh, Angus. *The Second Russian Revolution: The Struggle for Power in the Kremlin.* New York: Pharos Books, 1992. A short history of recent power struggles and cultural events. Nonfiction.

Other Resources

Software

Where in Europe Is Carmen Sandiego? Broderbund, 1988. A simulation game in which students learn about Europe's geography, economy, culture, and history.

HOUGHTON MIFFLIN SOCIAL STUDIES

Bookshelf

Macaulay, David. *Castle.* Boston: Houghton Mifflin, 1977. With detailed illustrations, this book shows the step-by-step construction of a medieval castle.

INTRODUCE

Ask a volunteer to read aloud the unit title and the text on this page. Then explain that, to ancient Greek sailors, Europa was the heavily wooded, but sparsely populated, land that lay beyond known civilizations. The Roman Empire and the Christian church eventually extended their influence through much of Europe and left an indelible imprint on many of Europe's languages and cultures. As trade increased during the later Middle Ages, resulting in exchanges of ideas and technologies, the population of European cities swelled. Today Europe boasts a wide variety of cultures spread throughout the continent.

Ask students to look at the photograph. Explain that while Europe today is not as densely populated as many parts of Asia, most Europeans live in cities. Tell students that the percentage of urban dwellers is 95 percent in Belgium, almost 90 percent in the Netherlands, more than 80 percent in Denmark and Sweden, and more than 70 percent in France. Europe has more than one fourth of the world's cities that have populations of more than one million.

Unit 6 Overview

Europe and Russia

Europe is the smallest continent of the world except for Australia. Hundreds of islands and peninsulas make Europe's coast rough and jagged. Away from the coast, however, much of Europe is a wide, fertile plain reaching far into Russia. Yet Europe also has high and beautiful mountains—including the Alps. Great rivers serve as major transportation routes.

Beginning in England in the 1760s, people turned from farms to factories to make their living. New machines helped people make goods much more quickly than in the past. People flocked to where the factories were—in the cities. Today in some nations more than 90 percent of the people live in cities. Europe is a world leader in industry. European goods include machinery, automobiles, and steel.

Most Europeans live in city neighborhoods where shops and markets are within walking distance.

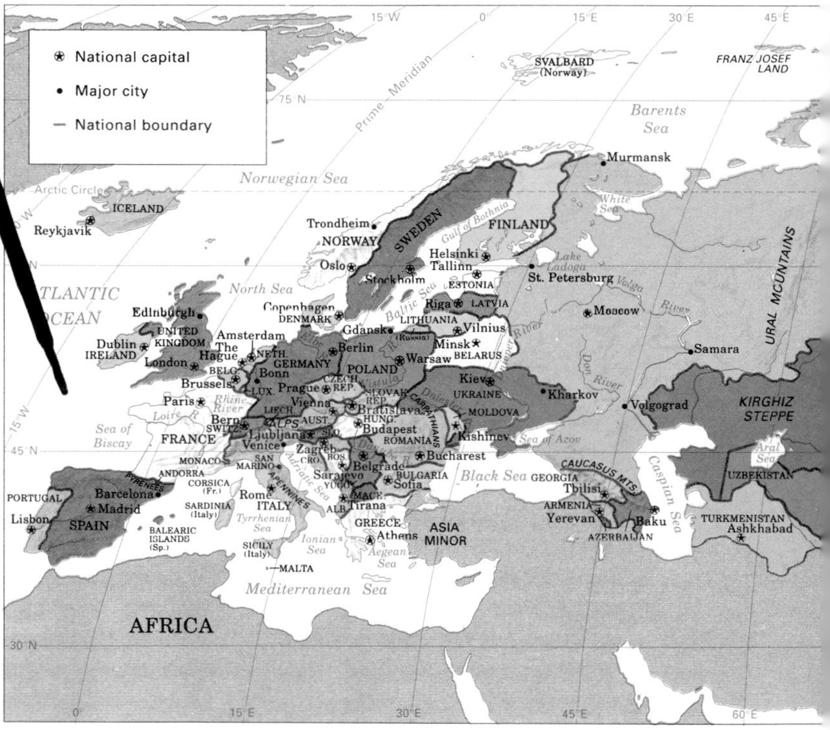
National capital
Major city
National boundary
15°W
0°
15°E
30°E
45°E
60°E
75°N
45°N
30°N
Prime Meridian
Arctic Circle
SVALBARD (Norway)
FRANZ JOSEF LAND
Barents Sea
Norwegian Sea
Murmansk
White Sea
ICELAND
Reykjavik
Trondheim
NORWAY
SWEDEN
Gulf of Bothnia
FINLAND
Helsinki
Tallinn
Oslo
Stockholm
ESTONIA
Lake Ladoga
St. Petersburg
Volga River
ATLANTIC OCEAN
North Sea
Copenhagen
DENMARK
Baltic Sea
Riga
LATVIA
LITHUANIA
Moscow
Edinburgh
UNITED KINGDOM
Dublin
IRELAND
London
Amsterdam
The Hague
NETH.
GERMANY
Bonn
BELG.
Brussels
LUX.
Gdansk
(Russia)
Vilnius
Minsk
BELARUS
Berlin
Warsaw
POLAND
Samara
URAL MOUNTAINS
Prague
CZECH REP.
Vistula
SLOVAK REP.
Kiev
UKRAINE
Dnieper River
Don River
Kharkov
Volgograd
KIRGHIZ STEPPE
Paris
Rhine River
Loire R.
Bern
SWITZ.
LIECH.
ALPS
Vienna
AUST.
Bratislava
HUNG.
Budapest
Dniester
CARPATHIANS
MOLDOVA
Kishinev
Sea of Azov
Aral Sea
Sea of Biscay
FRANCE
Ljubljana
SLO.
Venice
Zagreb
CRO.
BOS.
ROMANIA
Bucharest
Danube R.
MONACO
SAN MARINO
ANDORRA
PYRENEES
Belgrade
Sarajevo
YUGO.
BULGARIA
Sofia
Black Sea
GEORGIA
CAUCASUS MTS.
Tbilisi
Caspian Sea
UZBEKISTAN
PORTUGAL
Barcelona
Madrid
Lisbon
SPAIN
CORSICA (Fr.)
SARDINIA (Italy)
Rome
ITALY
APENNINES
Adriatic Sea
MACE.
ALB.
Tirana
ARMENIA
Yerevan
Baku
AZERBAIJAN
TURKMENISTAN
Ashkhabad
BALEARIC ISLANDS (Sp.)
Tyrrhenian Sea
SICILY (Italy)
Ionian Sea
GREECE
Athens
ASIA MINOR
Aegean Sea
MALTA
Mediterranean Sea
AFRICA

Objectives

1. Preview some important events in Europe's history.
2. Identify some of Europe's diverse cultures.
3. Describe some of the sources of cooperation and friction among Europe's ethnic groups.

Historical Context

To help students realize the impact of European influence around the world, explain that since about the 1500s, Europe has been a generous source of immigrants to less populous parts of the world. Among the factors that induced Europeans to move were: poverty, desire to escape from persecution, and loss of jobs due to economic change.

European immigrants were attracted to other areas primarily because these locations offered new opportunities to make a better living. Huge transfers of Europe's population in the 18th and 19th centuries affected the settlement and economic development of the Americas, Australia, New Zealand, and South Africa—all areas with untapped resources but small populations. Through their involvement in the slave trade, Europeans also caused the forced migrations of Africans to the Americas.

◄ *Moscow, the capital of the former Soviet Union, lies in a part of Russia that has short summers and long, cold winters. Those who go to Red Square today can still see the Kremlin, once the center of government.*

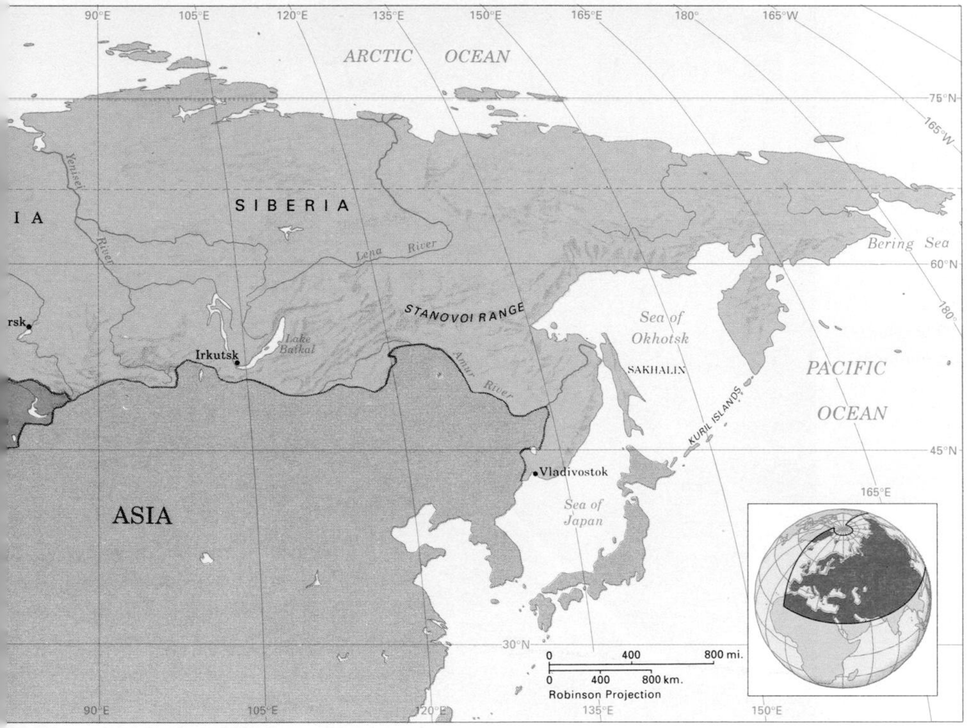

ARCTIC OCEAN
SIBERIA
Lena River
STANOVOI RANGE
Lake Baikal
Irkutsk
Amur River
Sea of Okhotsk
SAKHALIN
KURIL ISLANDS
Bering Sea
PACIFIC OCEAN
Vladivostok
Sea of Japan
ASIA
Yenisei River
90°E
105°E
120°E
135°E
150°E
165°E
180°
165°W
75°N
60°N
45°N
30°N
0 400 800 mi.
0 400 800 km.
Robinson Projection

Learning from Maps

Direct students to the locator map in the lower right corner of the large map on this page. Make sure that they understand the relationship between the two maps. Then give students some time to study the map of Europe on the previous page. Ask them to find these countries and their capitals: Portugal *(Lisbon),* Hungary *(Budapest),* Norway *(Oslo),* Ireland *(Dublin),* Denmark *(Copenhagen),* and Russia *(Moscow).* Tell students that the boundaries for many European countries have changed frequently over the centuries and that many boundaries have been redrawn with the recent fall of communism and the breakup of the Soviet Union into independent republics.

Political Context

To help students understand the new era of European politics, point out that for the first time in history, most European countries today have some form of representative democracy. However, Eastern Europe and the former Soviet republics continue to struggle to build their democracies. The challenge is for Europe and the former Soviet republics to achieve stable governments and avoid returning to dictatorships or one-party rule.

Current Events Bulletin Board

With the breakup of the Soviet Union, the civil war in the former Yugoslavia, and the various treaties of European cooperation, Europe has been prominently featured in the news. Ask students to collect and display newspaper and magazine articles and photographs about Europe today, organized by country or by topic. Then ask students to summarize the articles orally for the class before adding them to the bulletin board.

Map and Globe Skills

Have students turn to the world climate map in the Atlas on page 688. Ask them what climate exists through most of Europe. *(Temperate)* Then have students compare and contrast the latitudes, longitudes, and climates in Europe with those of the United States.

LOOK AND RESPOND

Have students scan the images and the captions on these pages. Ask them to write down their observations about daily life and culture in Europe on a sheet of paper. Collect the papers and write some of their observations on the chalkboard.

Then have students read the first paragraph on this page. List on the chalkboard some of the other languages and cultural or ethnic groups of Europe. *(Examples include Portuguese, English, German, Italian, Czech, and Finnish.)*

Learning from the Map

Direct students to the map on this page. It shows the areas of Europe affected by acid rain. Explain that these acids are formed when fossil fuels (coal, natural gas, and oil) are burned by automobiles, factories, and power plants. Ask students why acid rain might be so widespread in Europe. *(The continent is small, highly industrial, and densely populated. There may be a lack of government regulation.)*

The Land and People

French, Spanish, Romanian, Dutch, Greek, Russian—these are some of the many languages spoken in Europe. From the Mediterranean to the Bering Sea, the people of Europe and Russia speak many languages. They also follow many different traditions.

Europe and Russia's many cultural groups have often found it difficult to feel united. Europeans have fought many wars among themselves. Today, most Europeans hope that people from across the continent can work together to solve problems involving the environment, trade, and ethnic conflict.

Europe: Areas Affected by Acid Rain

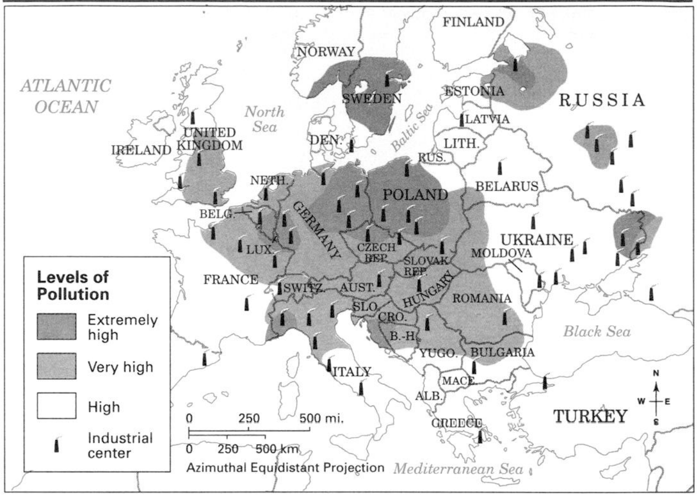

ATLANTIC OCEAN
North Sea
Baltic Sea
Black Sea
Mediterranean Sea
FINLAND
NORWAY
SWEDEN
ESTONIA
LATVIA
LITH.
RUS.
RUSSIA
DEN.
UNITED KINGDOM
IRELAND
NETH.
BELG.
LUX.
GERMANY
POLAND
BELARUS
UKRAINE
MOLDOVA
CZECH REP.
SLOVAK REP.
FRANCE
SWITZ.
AUST.
HUNGARY
SLO.
CRO.
B.-H.
ROMANIA
YUGO.
BULGARIA
ITALY
MACE.
ALB.
GREECE
TURKEY
Levels of Pollution
Extremely high
Very high
High
Industrial center
0 250 500 mi.
0 250 500 km
Azimuthal Equidistant Projection
N
W E
S

Acid rain is formed when gases released by burning oil, coal, and gas mix with water vapor in the air. These acids can be carried hundreds of miles. Acid rain can damage trees and buildings.

The alpenhorn dates back to the time of the Roman Empire. Herders and villagers used the instrument for communication and entertainment.

Edelweiss grows throughout Europe's alpine region.

406

Unit 6 Overview

Writing to Learn

Ask each student to write a letter to a student in a European country. You may want to review their choices of countries to avoid duplications. After reading and studying the unit, students may want to revise and send their letters. Check the public library for information about organizations that will provide the names and addresses of potential penpals.

Science Connection

Have interested students research the problem of acid rain and what is being done to curb its spread. Tell them, for example, that most European countries charge a very high tax on gasoline in order to discourage automobile driving and the subsequent air and water pollution this activity causes.

Encourage students to contact a local office of the Environmental Protection Agency (EPA) or an environmental group to learn what they can do to help prevent acid rain and other forms of pollution. You may also want to encourage students to test the acidity of local lakes, ponds, and rivers to see if acid rain might be affecting their region.

European artists have contributed great literature, music, and painting to the world. Some of the world's most valuable art is housed in the Louvre in Paris. The Louvre was once a palace, home to the kings and queens of France. Today, it is one of the world's largest museums.

Another important European contribution to the world is the British system of government. Great Britain's representative form of government provided an ideal for its colonies throughout the world. When they became independent, many of these colonies adopted Britain's system of government. The most important branch of the British Parliament is the House of Commons, which holds most of the government's power.

Both old and new architecture greet visitors to the Louvre.

The queen of England, Elizabeth II, opens Parliament in the spring of 1992.

England and France have cooperated to build a huge tunnel under the English Channel. Sometimes called the Chunnel, the new tunnel will help unify Europe.

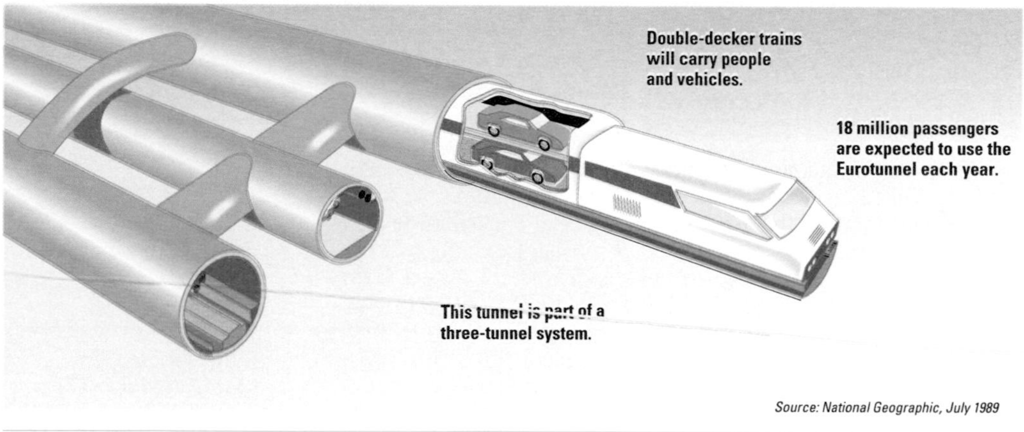
Double-decker trains will carry people and vehicles.
18 million passengers are expected to use the Eurotunnel each year.
This tunnel is part of a three-tunnel system.
Source: National Geographic, July 1989

Learning from the Photographs

Have students study the photographs of the alpine horn player, the opening of the British Parliament, and the I.M. Pei pyramid at the Louvre Museum in Paris. Ask them to observe how the photographs show a blend of the old and the new.

Learning from the Illustration

Ask students what forms of transportation were available for crossing the English Channel prior to the completion of the Eurotunnel or Chunnel *(Boat, plane)* and what additional means will be available once the Chunnel opens *(automobile, train)*. Encourage students to predict what might happen after the Chunnel opens. *(More commuters between the countries; increased cultural exchange and trade)*

ENRICH

Have students make a timeline showing the history of a European country of their choice. They should include early settlements, migrations, and cultural achievements, as well as historical events.

Art Connection

To help students appreciate European art, have them create an arts notebook. Provide a collection of art books for the classroom. For example, you may want to include books about different styles of painting, such as romanticism, impressionism, and cubism. Students may also be interested in books about the lives of European painters, such as Francisco de Goya, Pierre-Auguste Renoir, and Sonia Delaunay. In addition, you may want to include books and magazines on European sculpture, pottery, and fashion.

Encourage students to bring in their own resources as well. During free time, have them examine these materials. Ask students to create an art notebook of their own writings and illustrations based on what they have learned about European art.

Collaborative Learning

Divide the class into groups, each responsible for designing a trip to a different European country. Have groups research national foods, and major cultural and geographical sites. The members of the group should then prepare a presentation for the class.

CHAPTER ORGANIZER

Chapter 18 The Making of Europe

CHAPTER PLANNING CHART

Pupil's Edition	Teacher's Edition	Ancillaries
Lesson 1: The Power of the Church (2–3 days) Objective 1: Describe the influence of the Church during the Middle Ages. (History 5; Culture 6; Ethics and Belief Systems 3) Objective 2: Explain why the Church split into eastern and western branches. (Ethics and Belief Systems 5; Social and Political Systems 3)	• Graphic Overview (410) • Access Strategy (411) • Access Activity (411) Study Skills (412) Historical Context (412) • Art Connection (412)	Study Guide (71)
Lesson 2: Feudal Europe (3–4 days) Objective 1: Describe daily life in feudal Europe. (History 8; Geography 2; Social and Political Systems 1) Objective 2: Explain why the crusades took place. (Ethics and Belief Systems 5; Social and Political Systems 3) Objective 3: Describe the positive and negative effects of increased trade after the crusades. (Economics 4)	• Graphic Overview (414) • Access Strategy (415) • Access Activity (415) Map and Globe Skills (416) Historical Context (416) Making a Mural (416) Writing a Letter (417) Research (417) • Visual Learning (417)	Study Guide (72) Discovery Journal (37)
Understanding Critical Thinking Objective: Explain how historical thematic maps can be used to formulate hypotheses. (Critical Thinking 3; Map and Globe Skills 2, 3)		Study Guide (73) Transparency (8)
Literature: Valentine & Orson	• Access Strategy (421) Collaborative Learning (422)	Discovery Journal (38)
Lesson 3: The Renaissance Objective 1: Describe city life during the Italian Renaissance. (History 3, 8) Objective 2: Explain how the Renaissance spread throughout Europe. (Geography 4; Economics 4; Culture 1) Objective 3: Describe some of the achievements made in the arts and sciences during the Renaissance. (Culture 5)	• Graphic Overview (424) • Access Strategy (425) • Access Activity (425) Study Skills (426) Historical Context (426) Social Context (427) Social Participation (427) • Visual Learning (428) Historical Context (428) Political Context (428)	Study Guide (74) • Study Prints (11)
Lesson 4: The Reformation (2–3 days) Objective 1: Explain the causes of the Reformation. (History 5) Objective 2: Explain how the Reformation spread through Europe. (Geography 4; Culture 1) Objective 3: Discuss the effects of the Reformation. (Social and Political Systems 4)	• Graphic Overview (430) • Access Strategy (431) • Access Activity (431) Social Participation (432) Historical Context (432) Religious Context (432)	Study Guide (75) Map Activities (22)
Chapter Review	Answers (434–435)	Tests (69–72)

* Objectives are correlated to the strands and goals in the program Scope and Sequence on pages T41–T49.

• LEP appropriate resources. (For additional strategies, see pages T32–T33.)

CHAPTER RATIONALE

In Chapter 18 we return to western Europe, beginning with the fall of Rome and ending with the Reformation. Students study changes in European society during this time period that form a link from the ancient world to the modern world. This material serves as the foundation for a better understanding of Europe and its impact on the world.

Lesson 1 focuses on the influence of Christianity on the people of Europe during the early Middle Ages. Christianity was a unifying force in Europe. Students discover how religion dominated daily life. We also illustrate the differences between the western church in Europe and the eastern church in the Byzantine Empire. These differences, such as the dispute over the crowning of Charlemagne as Holy Roman Emperor, help students understand the split of Christianity into the Roman Catholic church and the Eastern Orthodox church.

Lesson 2 explains the causes and effects of both feudalism and the crusades in Europe. Starting with a description of the Viking invasions during the late 700s, the lesson explains how feudalism served Europeans' need for protection and describes feudal life for men and women. A Moment in Time provides students with a realistic portrait of a crusading knight. This feature amplifies the explanation about the crusades—the religious wars fought by Christians and Muslims for control of the Holy Land. We point out the impact of increased trade on Europe at the end of the Middle Ages, especially the devastation wrought by the Great Plague. This lesson is followed by a literature feature, an episode from *Valentine &Orson,* a narrative poem that presents a fanciful tale about medieval life.

Lesson 3 illustrates the Renaissance—a period of renewed emphasis on creativity, learning, and individualism in western Europe. Sparked by the humanists, Renaissance Europeans such as Brunelleschi, Michelangelo, and Leonardo da Vinci, made significant contributions to the arts and sciences. Students read how Renaissance ideas spread from Italy to northern Europe. Finally, they study the life and ideas of pioneers such as Copernicus and Vesalius who were inspired by the Renaissance and helped usher in the Scientific Revolution.

In **Lesson 4** we explain the causes and effects of the Reformation in Europe. On the heels of the Renaissance, the Reformation spread across Europe. Students read about Martin Luther's writings and teachings. These were the foundations of a new denomination, Lutheranism, that greatly influenced other Protestant movements, such as Calvinism. The lesson concludes with a description of the response of the Catholic church to the Reformation.

ACTIVITIES & PROJECTS

Bulletin Board

Have students look through old geographic or art magazines and select images to create a bulletin board display. Photos, pictures, and drawings should capture the various people, places, and events from the Middle Ages, the Renaissance, and the Reformation. Students can then write captions for the images. Ask volunteers to describe to the class the relevance of each picture to the period they are studying.

Basic: Making a Model

Ask students to build a model of a castle, a feudal manor, or a cathedral by using the pictures in this chapter or from another source. Students can use cardboard, clay, construction paper, and natural materials such as pebbles, dirt, and bits of evergreen. Have them identify the functions of the various structures of their model and describe what activities took place there. (Use after Lessons 1 or 2.)

LEP: Role Playing

Divide students into groups of four or five. Have members of each group assume the role of a participant in the crusades—for example, Pope, knight, pilgrim, serf, or Muslim defender. Then have each group work together to act out a scene such as a journey to the Holy Land. (Use after Lesson 2.)

Reader's Theater

Have students develop a skit in which they dramatize a Renaissance encounter between a poor, unknown artist and a wealthy patron. For example, students might choose to show the two negotiating a fair price for a work of art or becoming friends in spite of their differences. Ask students to work together to create props, scenery, and costumes for a performance. (Use after Lesson 3.)

Challenge: Writing a News Account

Have students write a one-page news account about any event discussed in the previous lessons. Students might report on the coronation of Charlemagne, a day in the life of a queen, Michelangelo painting the ceiling of the Sistine Chapel, or Martin Luther writing his *Ninety-Five Theses.* Students should explain who, what, when, and where and should predict the effect the event is likely to have on the lives of people in Europe and the rest of the world.

CHAPTER PREVIEW

Have students read the chapter title and the paragraph that follows it. Ask them to examine the two paintings on these facing pages, and help them see the main difference between the painting styles. *(The medieval painting looks flat, while the Renaissance one gives a sense of depth, drawing the eye to the center of the painting.)* Explain that this change in painting styles represents a shift in ideas about art, science, society, and religion during the period they will be studying.

Looking Forward

Tell students that in the next four lessons—The Power of the Church, Feudal Europe, The Renaissance, and The Reformation—they will study changes in European society over a 1,200-year period.

Lesson 1 focuses on the Church as Europe's most influential power and on its split into the Roman Catholic church and the Eastern Orthodox church.

Chapter 18
The Making of Europe

After the fall of the Roman Empire in A.D. 476, another great power rose from its ruins—the Christian church. People of Europe turned to the Church for protection and guidance. For more than 1,000 years, the Church towered over Europe. It was Europe's most powerful institution. Then, the rise of new ideas changed the way Europeans viewed themselves and the world.

This gold and silver container shows domes that are typical of Byzantine architecture.

In this painting from the Middle Ages, peasant life looks peaceful and happy. In reality, it wasn't. Most European peasants had a hard life and usually died by their thirties.

450	625	800	975

476

800 Charlemagne is crowned "Holy Roman Emperor" by Pope Leo III. Much of western Europe is briefly united under Charlemagne.

800–1054 After years of conflict, the Christian church splits into an eastern and a western branch—the Roman Catholic church and the Eastern Orthodox church.

408

BACKGROUND

During the Middle Ages, the Church grew increasingly powerful in western Europe, helping to unite society. However, resentment also grew over the Church's wealth and power. Leaders of the Reformation rejected the Pope's authority and set up their own churches.

The Power of the Pope

The Pope was both a religious leader and a leader in worldly affairs. He had the power, for example, to crown and depose emperors. He believed that his authority was divinely sanctioned; a statement issued by the papacy in 1075 declared that the Pope could be judged by no one. Although the Pope remained very powerful, between 1100 and 1300, monarchs began to challenge his authority, weakening the papacy. The Church's worldliness led other believers to question its spiritual authority as well.

The Protestant Movement

Martin Luther and other reformers questioned some of the Roman Catholic church's most basic beliefs. The Church had taught that faith and good works led to salvation, the promise of life after death. Luther, however, believed that faith in God alone, apart from good works, led to salvation.

Lutherans also rejected as unnecessary to salvation most of the sacraments, or holy rites of the Roman Catholic church said to be ordained by Jesus. Of the seven Catholic sacraments, Luther recognized only

This Renaissance painting uses perspective to create a sense of depth. It fools the human eye by making objects in the background smaller, which makes them seem farther away.

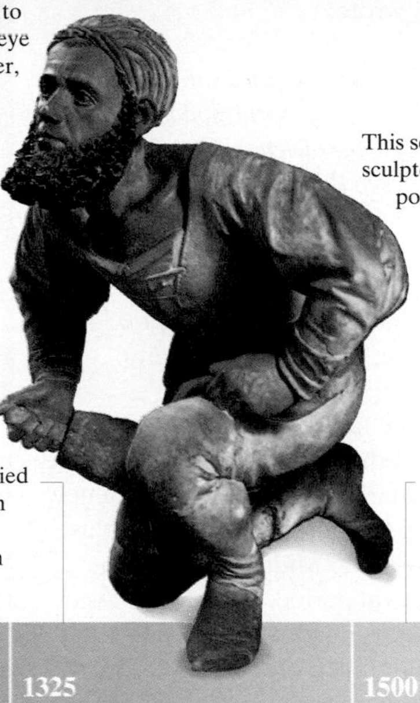

This sculpture by the German sculptor Adam Kraft is a self-portrait that dates back to the late 1400s.

1347 The plague, a disease carried by fleas on rats, spreads through Europe. Although millions die, Europe begins a cultural rebirth soon after—the Renaissance.

1517 Martin Luther calls for the Catholic church to reform. His ideas lead to a religious revolution in Europe—the Reformation.

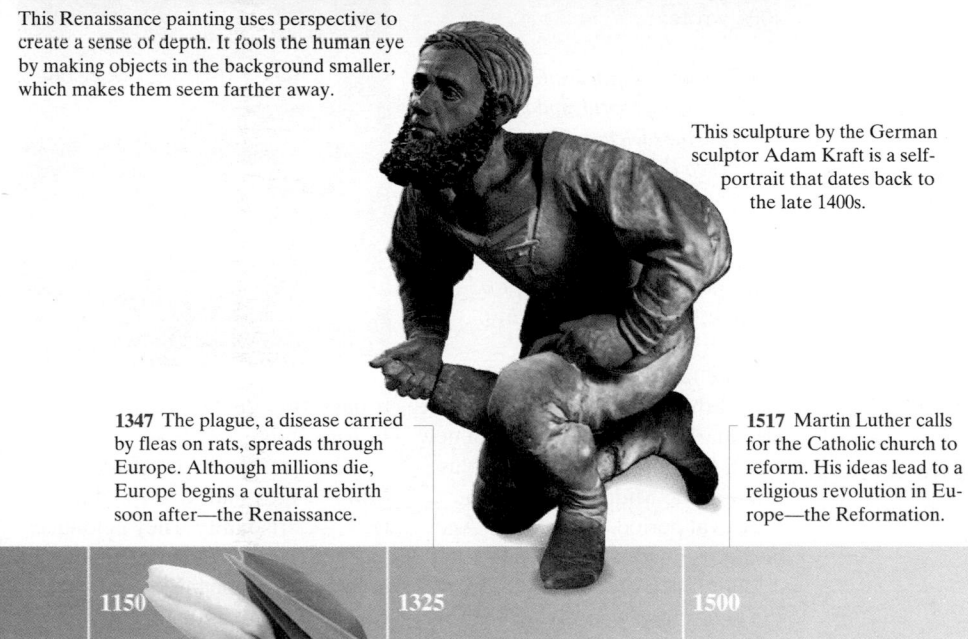

1150 | 1325 | 1500 | 1675

Traders brought tulips to Europe from Constantinople in the 1500s.

1650

Understanding the Visuals

Ask students what goods the peasants shown in the painting on page 408 are working to produce. *(Wool and grain)* This painting is from *Les Tres Riches Heures du Duc de Berry,* a French prayer book made for the brother of the king of France in 1416. It provides prayers for each hour of the day. A calendar included with the book shows seasonal tasks, alternating the activities of the nobility and the peasantry.

Understanding Chronology

Have students examine the images and the timeline. Ask them to name the period of time in which the Christian church dominated European life. *(The Middle Ages)* What do we call the period of cultural rebirth that followed the Middle Ages? *(The Renaissance)* Point out that these two time periods overlap. The Middle Ages lasted from about 475 to about 1450, while the Renaissance is usually dated from about 1350 to about 1650. Have students note that as the Middle Ages were ending, the Renaissance was just beginning. Ask students what other time period overlaps the Renaissance. *(The Reformation)*

two—baptism and holy communion, the commemoration of Jesus' Last Supper.

The Church Reforms

As more and more people left the Church, Roman Catholic leaders realized that reform was necessary. New religious orders such as the Jesuits, founded to help rid the Church of abuses and to carry out missionary work, focused on counteracting the Reformation. These Church reforms were known as the Counter Reformation. The Church also reestablished the Inquisition, or church court, to try to halt the spread of Protestantism.

The Inquisition tried heretics—those whose religious beliefs or practices differed from those authorized by the Church—because they were considered dangerous. Heretics included non-Christians, as well as those who practiced alchemy and witchcraft. First created in the late 12th and early 13th centuries to suppress heretical religious movements, the Inquisition was directed against Protestantism by the Roman Catholic church in the 1500s.

INTRODUCE

Point out the lesson title and have students read the Thinking Focus. Ask them to suggest what the role of Christian churches is in today's society. *(Moral and religious teaching, projects to help the disadvantaged and promote social justice)*

Tell students that during the Middle Ages, the Christian church was the unifying force for many different cultures of Europe, and that the Church was politically powerful and possessed large amounts of land and wealth. Have students read to learn more about the influences of the Church in medieval Europe.

Key Terms

Vocabulary Strategies: T36–T37

clergy—bishops and priests who serve the Church

monastery—a religious community

tithe—a tenth of one's income paid to support a religious institution

450 476 1054 1325 1500 1675

L E S S O N 1

The Power of the Church

THINKING FOCUS

Name two or more ways the Church influenced daily life in Europe during the Middle Ages.

Key Terms

- clergy
- monastery
- tithe

After the fall of Rome in A.D. 476, Germanic tribes, or *volks,* roamed western Europe. They burned cities. They destroyed bridges. To the Romans, it seemed like the end of the world. Where the Roman Empire once had kept peace, now there was war. Orientus, a Roman poet who lived in the 400s, wrote:

> *See how swiftly death comes upon the world, and how many people the violence of war has stricken [hit]. Some lay as food for dogs; others were killed by the flames that licked their homes. In the villages and country houses, in the fields and . . . on every road—death, sorrow, slaughter, fires.*

➤ *After the fall of the Roman Empire, many European cities fell into ruins. Even Rome itself, shown here, was nearly deserted. Some historians have called the Middle Ages the Dark Ages.*

The fall of Rome marked the end of the ancient Roman world. It also marked the beginning of a new era in Europe. Historians call this new era the Middle Ages, or the medieval period. The Middle Ages lasted from about A.D. 476 to 1450.

For much of the Middle Ages, the Germanic *volks* divided Europe into many pieces. Each tribe obeyed its own laws and followed its own customs. Many of these tribal differences still exist in Europe today.

Even so, most Europeans of the Middle Ages shared a common faith—Christianity. They belonged to the Church, headed by the Pope in Rome. Europeans looked to the Church for salvation, or the promise of life after death. They did not question the Pope, nor did they expect life to improve.

Objectives

1. Describe the influence of the Church during the Middle Ages.
2. Explain why the Church split into eastern and western branches.

Graphic Overview

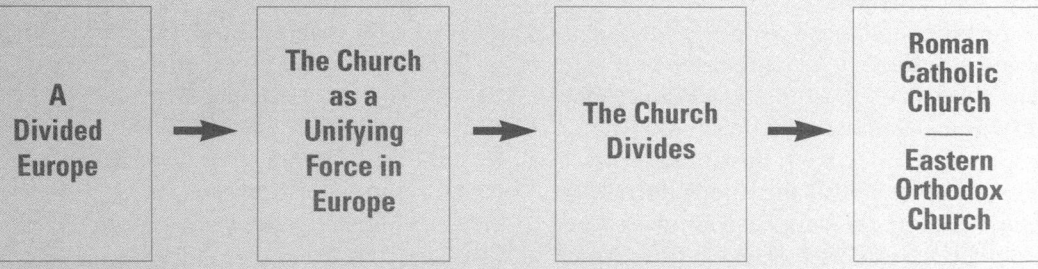

A Divided Europe → The Church as a Unifying Force in Europe → The Church Divides → Roman Catholic Church / Eastern Orthodox Church

One Church, One Faith

During the Middle Ages, the Church was the center of the community. It was the heart of religious life, the center of learning, and a major political force.

The **clergy** were the priests, archbishops, bishops, and cardinals who served the Church. The main duty of priests and bishops was to conduct the worship service, the Mass. Other men who served the Church were called monks. These men lived in a religious community, or **monastery.** Monks led ordered lives. At set times each day, they had to work, pray, study, and teach. Monks also copied the Bible by hand for people to read.

The Church set up religious communities, or convents, for women, too. Women who agreed to follow the convent rules were called nuns. Like monks, nuns spent most of their day working and praying. Nuns also treated people who were ill or dying. However, only a few nuns studied or copied the Bible. In general, most women of the Middle Ages were not taught how to read and write.

Daily Life and the Church

In every village and town, the Church shaped the lives of the common people. Church bells rang when it was time to work, eat, sleep, and go to Mass. People turned to their local priest to bless marriages, baptize babies, comfort the sick, and pray for the dead.

To support the Church, people paid a tithe *(tyth)* each year. A **tithe** equaled one-tenth of a person's income. People could pay their tithes in money, crops, or labor. Church leaders used this income to care for the ill and help the poor. They also used tithes to build huge churches, or cathedrals *(kuh THEE druhls)*.

Cathedrals and Religious Art

Cathedral spires, or tall steeples, towered over many towns during the Middle Ages. Cathedrals were designed to fill people with wonder at the power of God.

Stained glass windows filled the cathedral interiors with beautiful light. Since most people couldn't read, these windows took the place of books. They told stories from the Bible, using colorful pictures that all could understand.

Building a cathedral took a great deal of time and money. Hundreds of workers were needed to cut stone, build walls, and perform other tasks by hand. It could take more than 100 years of hard work to finish a cathedral. Many workers never lived to see one completed. ■

The cathedral at Chartres, France, was built in less than 30 years. Towering over the city, it shows the power of the Church and the faith of its believers during the Middle Ages.

■ *What were some of the duties of the clergy, monks, and nuns during the Middle Ages?*

DEVELOP

Ask students to look at the picture of the cathedral at Chartres on this page. Point out some of the details of the cathedral—carvings, spires, stained glass. What does the size and design of the cathedral suggest about the Church during the Middle Ages? *(The Church was probably extremely wealthy and powerful.)*

■ *The clergy conducted the mass, or worship service. They also blessed marriages and comforted the sick and dying. Monks worked, studied, and taught. They copied the Bible by hand since there were no printing presses. Nuns also worked, prayed, and cared for the sick and dying.*

ETHICS

Critical Thinking

Draw students' attention to the last paragraph on page 410. What was the attitude about life of most Europeans at this time? *(They looked to the Church for salvation and did not expect life to improve.)* How might this attitude have affected the lives of poor peasants? *(They would not try to change their lives or improve the social system in which they lived.)* Who might have benefited from this attitude? *(The Church and monarchs)*

Access Strategy

Ask students to name and draw the most important buildings in their town or city or in a nearby city. *(Students might cite City Hall, banks, schools, or places of worship.)* How can they tell a building's importance? *(They may note central location, large size, large number of people using the building, dignified style of architecture.)* Explain that the church or cathedral was usually the most important building in medieval towns. Point out that students will be reading about how the Church influenced every part of a person's life, from birth to death.

Access Activity

Have students examine the map on page 413. Ask them to identify the two Christian empires and the geographical features of these empires—such as seas, oceans, rivers, and bordering continents. Have them use the Atlas map on page 682 to identify some of the modern nations that now exist in this region. *(Germany, France, Greece, and Turkey)*

CITIZENSHIP

Critical Thinking

Point out that one of the main issues dividing the western and eastern empires of Europe before the Christian church split into its eastern and western branches was this question: Who ruled the Church and who ruled the land? Ask students who ruled the Church and state in the West? *(The Pope ruled the Church, and kings and queens ruled the state.)* In the East? *(The Byzantine emperor ruled both.)*

Ask students to discuss the differences between these social systems and the U.S. government today. Are church and state separate in this country? *(Yes, church and state are legally separate, although the two sometimes work together. Students might note religious references on coins, in prayers given at the opening of Congress, and in the presidential oath of office.)*

A Divided Empire, a Divided Church

Across Time & Space

What is the only city located on two continents? It's Istanbul, Turkey, which spans Europe and Asia. Before 1930 Istanbul was called Constantinople after the Roman emperor Constantine.

In Chapter 7 you read that the Roman Empire split into two parts: a western empire and an eastern empire. This division would also split the Church.

The Eastern Empire

Germanic tribes invaded the western part of the Roman Empire. The eastern part, called the Byzantine *(BIHZ uhn teen)* Empire, stayed rich and powerful. Constantinople *(kahn stan tuh NOH puhl)*, the Byzantine capital, filled western visitors with wonder. It was a city of riches, unlike any city in western Europe. While Rome stood dark at night, Constantinople glowed with streetlights.

The Byzantine Empire differed in other ways from the western empire. The Byzantines took pride in their Greek heritage. Greek was their common language. Priests in the Byzantine Empire spoke Greek during the worship services. Byzantine Christians could understand what their priests said and what they read from the Bible.

In western Europe, priests often did not use the people's everyday language. They spoke mainly Latin, which was the language of the ancient Romans. After A.D. 1000, few people in the West could understand Latin.

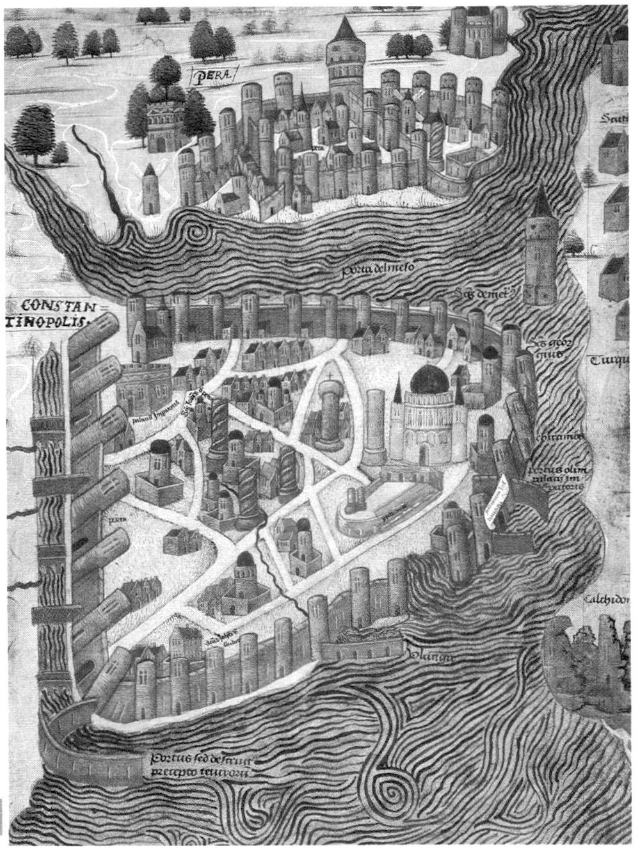
PERA
CONSTAN TINOPOLIS

This map of Constantinople was drawn about 1420. Can you find a dome-roofed cathedral? Compare it with the one on page 411.

The Church Divides

At the core of the differences between East and West was this question: Who ruled the Church, and who ruled the empire? In the East the Byzantine emperor ruled both church and state. In the West the Pope ruled the Church while kings and queens ruled the land.

When Pope Leo III crowned King Charlemagne *(SHAHR luh mayn)* "Holy Roman Emperor" in 800, Byzantine Christians were angry. What right had Pope Leo III to name him emperor? Charlemagne had united western Europe, as the Roman emperors had done centuries before. However, to the Byzantines, the Pope was not head of the Church. To them, the only true leader of the Church was the Byzantine emperor.

For years, these differences caused many disputes in the Church. Finally, in 1054, the Church split in two. The western church became

412

Study Skills

Ask students to research the reign of Charlemagne, using encyclopedias and other reference books. Then have them write a short report describing his accomplishments.

Historical Context

Charlemagne was the first European king after the fall of the western part of the Roman Empire. He was a very able and respected ruler. His coronation as emperor of what would eventually become the Holy Roman Empire illustrated an important point about medieval history—the relationship between church and state. When a Pope crowned a king, the Pope was also demonstrating his own stature and power.

Art Connection

Ask students to study the Byzantine cathedral shown on the map on this page and the cathedral at Chartres, France, on the previous page. You may also want to bring to class library books that show the art and architecture of the Byzantine Empire and western Europe during the Middle Ages. Then have students draw two buildings—such as two cathedrals—one representing Byzantine or eastern styles, the other western.

Division of the Christian World, c. A.D. 950

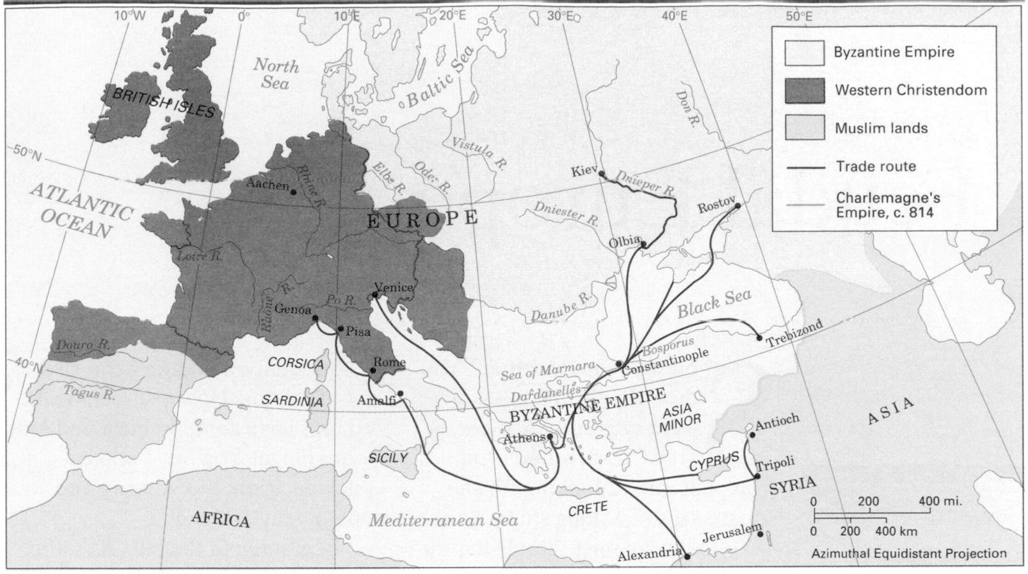
Byzantine Empire
Western Christendom
Muslim lands
Trade route
Charlemagne's Empire, c. 814
BRITISH ISLES
North Sea
Baltic Sea
ATLANTIC OCEAN
EUROPE
Aachen
Rhine R.
Elbe R.
Oder R.
Vistula R.
Don R.
Dnieper R.
Dniester R.
Kiev
Rostov
Olbia
Loire R.
Rhone R.
Po R.
Venice
Genoa
Pisa
Danube R.
Black Sea
Trebizond
Douro R.
Tagus R.
CORSICA
SARDINIA
Rome
Amalfi
Sea of Marmara
Bosporus
Constantinople
Dardanelles
BYZANTINE EMPIRE
ASIA MINOR
ASIA
Athens
Antioch
SICILY
CYPRUS
Tripoli
SYRIA
CRETE
AFRICA
Mediterranean Sea
Jerusalem
Alexandria
10°W
0°
10°E
20°E
30°E
40°E
50°E
50°N
40°N
0 200 400 mi.
0 200 400 km
Azimuthal Equidistant Projection

East vs. West: Church and Culture

	Religious Center	Religious Leader	Church Language	Ruler	Economy	Settlement Patterns	Cultural Influences
East	Constantinople	Emperor, Patriarch	Greek	Emperor	Farming, trade	Rural and urban	Greek, Roman
West	Rome	Pope	Latin	Kings, queens, nobles	Farming	Mostly rural	Roman, Germanic

the Roman Catholic church. The eastern church became the Eastern Orthodox church. As the map and chart above show, two separate Christian cultures developed during the Middle Ages.

After Charlemagne's death in 814, his western empire crumbled. Western Europe was again divided into pieces. The Byzantine Empire, however lasted until 1453. It survived many attacks before it fell to the Ottoman Turks.

During the Middle Ages, western Europe was often in turmoil. War, violence, famine, and disease were common. In the next lesson, you'll read about how the people of Europe tried to protect themselves during these dangerous times. ■

▲ *Study the map and the chart above. How did the location of Constantinople help to support a trading economy?*

■ *How did the language used in the eastern church differ from the one used in the western church?*

REVIEW

1. **FOCUS** Name two or more ways the Church influenced daily life in Europe during the Middle Ages.
2. **HISTORY** Most Europeans of the Middle Ages could not read or write. However, most monks and clergy could. Did the ability to read and write give monks and clergy power over people? Why or why not? If you could not read or write, how would your life be different?
3. **CULTURE** What differences led to the split between the eastern church and the western church?
4. **CRITICAL THINKING** Why did Europeans pay tithes?
5. **ACTIVITY** Learn more about church architecture during the Middle Ages. Research a cathedral or a monastery such as one found on the map above. Draw a diagram or sketch of the building. Use the Minipedia on pages 662 to 663 to label some of the building's most interesting features.

◄ *Constantinople was located at the crossroads between Asia, Africa, and Europe. It had access to the sea trade of the Black Sea, the Aegean Sea, and the Mediterranean Sea.*

You may want to ask students to compare Constantinople with another city located at a cultural crossroads—Manila—which they read about in Chapter 17. *(Both cities were centers of international trade.)*

■ *In the East, the clergy often used Greek, which was a common or everyday language. In the West, however, the clergy often used Latin, the language of the ancient Romans, which few Europeans after A.D. 1000 could understand.*

You may want to have students use pages 660–661 of the Minipedia to help them understand differences in languages.

CLOSE

Have students answer the Thinking Focus. Then draw the diagram from the Graphic Overview on page 410 on the chalkboard. Have students copy the diagram and add details based on the lesson text. Have them exchange diagrams with a partner and compare them.

Answers to Review Questions

1. The Church was at the center of the community. Church bells regulated daily activities; the clergy provided many services. People paid one-tenth of their income to the Church and worked to build cathedrals.
2. In part, yes—people who could not read the Bible had to trust whatever the clergy said it meant. In part, no—the clergy could not control what people knew from experience. Students may note instances when they use reading and writing in their daily lives.
3. The two churches used different languages and disagreed over who was the head of the Church—the Pope or the emperor.
4. Europeans paid tithes because they believed in the Church's teachings and benefited from its services.
5. Refer students to encyclopedias and other library references. They may use pages 662–663 of the Minipedia to label flying buttresses, arches, and columns.

Homework Options

Ask students to draw an outline for a stained glass window that tells a story. Then have them share their pictures and stories with other students in small groups.

Study Guide: page 71

INTRODUCE

Have students read the Thinking Focus. Tell students that many people in medieval Europe were poor and lived in the countryside farming or herding. Remind them that most Europeans lacked basic technology during the early Middle Ages—such as metal-tipped plows—which made life, especially farming, difficult.

Encourage students to imagine what housing, work, and recreation were like in feudal Europe. Then have them read the lesson to learn more about typical feudal life.

Key Terms

Vocabulary Strategies: T36–T37

manor—the castle and estate of a warrior

vassal—a warrior who agreed to become the subject of a ruler in exchange for a manor

serf—a peasant who belonged to the land and was controlled by a manor lord

crusade—a religious war between Christians and Muslims over possession of the Holy Land

knight—an armed soldier on horseback

plague—a deadly disease carried to Europe by rats on trading ships after the crusades

B.C. A.D. 450 | 700 | 1400 | 1500 | 1675

LESSON 2

Feudal Europe

THINKING FOCUS

Describe daily life in feudal Europe.

Key Terms

- manor
- vassal
- serf
- crusade
- knight
- plague

Splash! What was that? You drop the fishing net you were mending. A silent, gray fog surrounds you. You peer into it, looking for the square sails of Viking ships. You see only ocean mist. You listen for the roar of the Viking battle cry. You hear only the waves.

This fog hides all other sights and sounds. You try to convince yourself that what you heard was just a seagull diving for a fish. Sitting down, you pick up the net and start sewing.

The cold air stings your face and numbs your fingers as you work. You laugh at your fright. The rest of your village still sleeps. All is quiet again. Then you hear that splashing sound again.

Suddenly, a dragon head rises out of the fog. Now a ship appears. Vikings have come to burn and loot your village! You must make a quick decision: Do you run and hide or stay and fight?

Beginning in the late 700s, the Vikings sailed from their homes in Scandinavia, which is now Sweden, Norway, and Denmark. Because of a growing population, they sought new lands to conquer and settle.

Vikings were skilled sailors and shipbuilders and ruthless pirates and warriors. They were also farmers, fishers, and traders. Over time, Vikings—who were also called Norsemen or Northmen—settled in what is now Great Britain, Ireland, France, and Russia.

For about 250 years, Vikings plundered, or raided, European towns, monasteries, and cathedrals, especially those along seacoasts and rivers. No one, not even rulers with armies, felt safe from Viking attacks. In England people prayed, "From the fury of the Northmen, deliver us, O Lord."

➤ *Made of walrus ivory, these Viking chess pieces date back to the 1100s. The modern game of chess still reflects the ranks of people in feudal society.*

Objectives

1. Describe daily life in feudal Europe.
2. Explain why the crusades took place.
3. Describe the positive and negative effects of increased trade after the crusades.

Graphic Overview

Feudalism Develops as an Economic, Political, and Social System → **Daily Life in Feudal Europe** → **The Crusades** → **Increased Trade and Contact with Africa and Asia**

Daily Life in Feudal Europe

During the Middle Ages, feudalism developed out of people's need for protection. Feudalism is a social, political, and economic system. European feudalism was like the Japanese feudalism you read about on page 367.

Life on the Feudal Manor

The people of Europe looked to strong rulers—usually kings and queens—for protection. In return the people promised to be loyal to their monarch.

As a reward for loyalty, kings and queens granted land to trusted warriors. Castles, farms, villages, and people usually were included in this grant, or gift. The land and everything on it was a **manor.** In exchange for a manor, a warrior agreed to become the subject, or **vassal** *(VAS uhl)*, of the ruler. Vassals promised to protect and obey their monarch.

Under the feudal system, women had to obey their husbands or fathers. Although women ran the day-to-day affairs of the home, they had few rights. However, noblewomen often were in charge of the entire manor. Some were political and military leaders, such as Queen Margaret I of Denmark. In the late 1300s, she united Denmark, Norway, and Sweden into one Scandinavian state. Others were writers or artists. Marie de France, for example, won fame for her poems, which use some of the legends of King Arthur of England.

Serfs: Backbone of Feudalism

Few people of the Middle Ages were kings or queens. Most were poor peasant farmers.

Some peasants were free, but most were **serfs.** Although serfs were not free, they were not slaves either. Serfs belonged to the land. They could not be bought or sold, unless the land was also. Serfs could leave the land only with their lord's permission or by buying freedom.

Most serfs and free peasants had to pay rent to their manor lord. Most paid rent by working three or more days a week for their lord. Often, serfs and free peasants also had to pay money or crops. ■

▲ *During the Middle Ages, families depended on clay pottery to keep food and drink cool as well as safe from pests such as rats.*

▼ *The pictures on this page were taken from a French book of prayers. The scenes show some of the activities of the farm year.*

Medieval Life: Serfs and Lords

	Land Owned	Food	Clothing	Housing	Income
Serf	Zero to 20 acres	Bread, eggs, poultry, some meat and vegetables	Wool, animal skins, linen	Mud and straw huts; wood and stone houses	A few animals, crops from a few strips of land
Lord	Hundreds to thousands of acres	Meat, game, fish, pastries, spices, vegetables	Wool, silk, linen	Stone and wood castles	Rents, taxes, and services from serfs and peasants

◄ *Use this chart to compare the life of a serf with that of a lord.*

■ *How did the feudal system protect the people of Europe during the Middle Ages?*

DEVELOP

Tell students that feudalism brought some order to a society without a strong central government. Threats came from the Vikings and from other invaders such as the Seljuk Turks, who invaded Southwest Asia in the 11th century. Explain that feudalism offered people security in exchange for loyalty, land, or labor.

Have students examine the Viking chess pieces on page 414 and read the caption. Ask them to name the playing pieces in chess. *(King, queen, bishop, castle—also called rook—knight, and pawns)* You may want to ask students to bring in chess pieces and explain each piece's role in medieval society. *(For example, the king and queen ruled over the pawns, or free peasants and serfs, who worked in the fields.)* Explain that in the game of chess, the value of each piece reflects the power of the person it represents during the Middle Ages.

■ *Vassals were expected to protect and obey the king and queen in exchange for a manor. Likewise, peasants, including serfs, gave labor, cash, or crops to the manor lord in return for protection from invaders.*

Access Strategy

Ask students if serfdom reminds them of another institution in this country. Have them compare serfdom with slavery in the United States. They might note that both serfs and slaves were considered property and had to work very hard, and that both serfdom and slavery were usually for life.

Ask how serfdom and slavery differ. Students might note that slaves were Native Americans or Africans taken from their respective homelands, while serfs came from the areas where they served. Point out that serfs belonged to the land, while slaves belonged to people.

Access Activity

Bonds of loyalty helped hold feudal society together. Discuss the concept of loyalty with students. Ask them to name people that command their loyalty, such as friends and family. Have students assess the strengths and weaknesses of a social structure based primarily on loyalty to one person.

HISTORY

Social Participation

Divide the class into three groups. Have one group represent western Europeans, a second the Byzantines, and a third the Muslims, including the invading Seljuk Turks. Based on what they have read so far, have each group work together to prepare a statement on the role they played in conflicts such as the crusades. Each member of the group should take on a task such as recorder, reporter, or researcher. Groups should get together and discuss their statements.

➤ *The city of Jerusalem was the crusaders' final destination. The power of the Church is illustrated on this map by cathedrals, major monasteries, and universities, all of which were spread throughout Europe.*

■ *The main goal for Christians was to gain control of the Holy Land from the Muslims. In addition, Christians were promised salvation if they died on a crusade. There was also hope of economic gain since the Holy Land was thought to be full of riches.*

The Crusades

God has ordained [ordered] a tournament between Heaven and Hell, and sends to all his friends who wish to defend him, that they fail him not.

From a song of the Second Crusade, 1147

➤ *Often crusaders plundered cities and stole whatever valuables they could carry. Crusaders took this life-sized reliquary, or container of holy items, back to Italy in the early 1200s. They believed it held part of the finger of Nicholas, Bishop of Myra.*

Church leaders used such words to inspire kings and peasants to fight the crusades.

Conflict over the Holy Land

The **crusades** were a series of religious wars that took place from 1095 to 1291. Christians and Muslims fought over the Holy Land, which includes modern Israel. Both wanted to control the holy city of Jerusalem, a sacred place to Jewish, Christian, and Muslim believers.

For most of the Middle Ages, Muslims ruled the Holy Land. Early Muslim rulers allowed all believers to worship in Jerusalem. However, in 1085 the Seljuk Turks captured Jerusalem. Christian pilgrims no longer felt safe.

When the Seljuks also threatened to take Constantinople, the Byzantines asked for help. Christians in Europe resolved to protect the pilgrims and Byzantines—and to capture the Holy Land.

Those who vowed to "take up the cross" in battle became known as crusaders.

▼ *On the map, trace the route of the First Crusade. What city was its destination? How is the power of the Church shown on this map?*

■ *Why did Christians go on the crusades?*

Feudal Europe, c. 1100

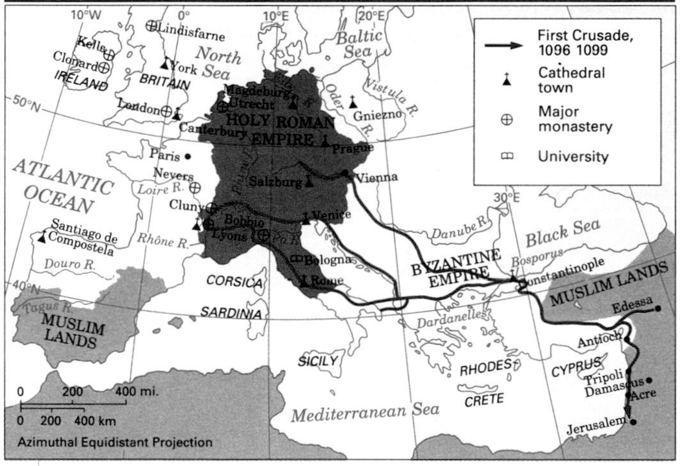
10°W
0°
10°E
20°E
30°E
50°N
40°N
Lindisfarne
Kells
Clonard
IRELAND
BRITAIN
York
North Sea
Baltic Sea
London
Canterbury
Magdeburg
Utrecht
HOLY ROMAN EMPIRE
Oder R.
Vistula R.
Gniezno
Prague
Vienna
Salzburg
Paris
Nevers
Loire R.
Cluny
ATLANTIC OCEAN
Santiago de Compostela
Rhône R.
Lyons
Bobbio
Po R.
Venice
Bologna
Rome
Douro R.
Tagus R.
MUSLIM LANDS
CORSICA
SARDINIA
SICILY
Danube R.
Black Sea
Bosporus
BYZANTINE EMPIRE
Constantinople
MUSLIM LANDS
Edessa
Dardanelles
Antioch
RHODES
CYPRUS
Tripoli
Damascus
Acre
CRETE
Jerusalem
Mediterranean Sea
First Crusade, 1096 1099
Cathedral town
Major monastery
University
0 200 400 mi.
0 200 400 km
Azimuthal Equidistant Projection

Going on a Crusade

Nearly 30,000 crusaders left western Europe in 1096 to fight in the First Crusade. About 4,000 were knights. A **knight** was an armed soldier on horseback. To learn more about the knights of the crusades, read A Moment in Time on the next page. Most crusaders were not knights, but peasant foot soldiers. Women and priests also traveled with the crusaders.

People had several reasons for going on the crusades. First, Church leaders promised salvation for anyone killed on a crusade. Second, crusaders hoped for economic gain. The Holy Land was thought to be full of riches.

The crusades did not turn out to be exciting adventures. Instead, they were bloody wars. Thousands of Muslims and Christians were killed. Jews were often attacked and killed as well. When the crusades ended in the late 1200s, Muslims still ruled the Holy Land. ■

Map and Globe Skills

Point out that the crusades involved a series of wars between three different cultures. Ask students to locate the homelands of the European Christians, the Byzantines, and the Muslims on the map on this page. Discuss what Europeans might have gained from contact with other cultures.

Historical Context

As commerce expanded and the Church became ever more powerful, pilgrimages to Jerusalem became increasingly popular. At the same time, the Byzantine Empire was being threatened by the Seljuk Turks, a nomadic people who ruled much of Southwest Asia. The Byzantine emperor turned to the Pope for aid. In all, at least eight military expeditions—or crusades—were sent to Jerusalem between 1095 and 1270.

Making a Mural

Have the entire class work together to make a large mural showing various elements that went into launching the First Crusade. Students could include pictures of the different types of crusaders, the Pope, horses, weapons, armor, and other supplies the crusaders might have brought along. Encourage them to include a map as well. When the mural is finished, have students use it to tell the story of the First Crusade.

A Moment in Time

A Crusader

3:32 P.M., October 20, 1192
In a field outside Vienna, Austria

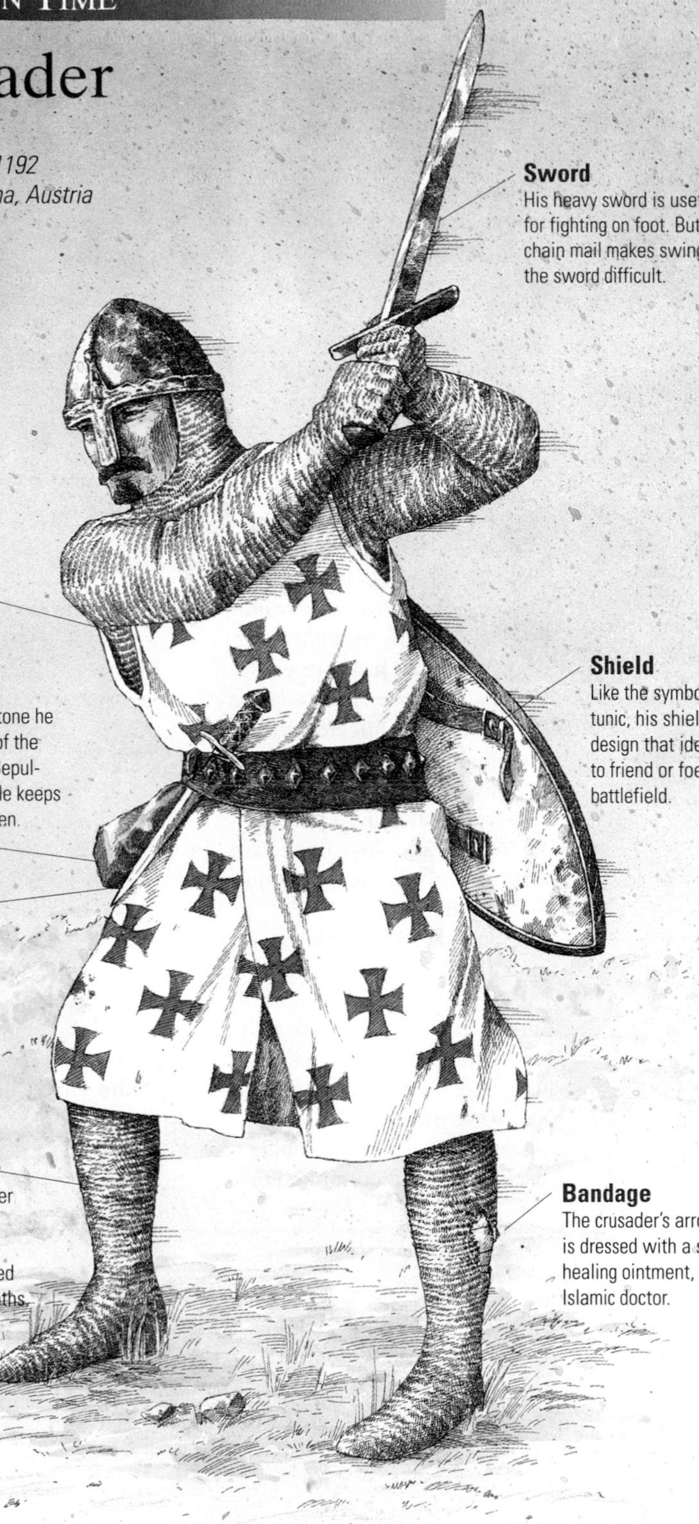

Sword
His heavy sword is useful for fighting on foot. But his chain mail makes swinging the sword difficult.
Chain Mail
His protective chain mail covers him head to toe. Chain mail is made of interlocking metal rings. It is heavy, hot, and hard to keep clean.
Shield
Like the symbols on his tunic, his shield shows a design that identifies him to friend or foe on the battlefield.
Pebble
In his pouch is the stone he picked off the floor of the Church of the Holy Sepulchre in Jerusalem. He keeps it as a good luck token.
Spices
These gifts will delight his friends in England. Black pepper is uncommon in his region, and sugar is a rare treat.
Quilted Body Suit
He wears a cloth suit under his chain mail to keep it from scraping his skin. He has not washed or removed his body suit in many months.
Bandage
The crusader's arrow wound is dressed with a sophisticated healing ointment, applied by an Islamic doctor.

Note: You might wish to use this Moment in Time to preview the text on page 416.

HISTORY

Visual Learning

Use this picture to explain why the crusader only fought on foot in emergencies. *(A knight's chain mail or armor was very heavy, making it hard to move quickly or handle a sword precisely.)*

Knights usually fought on horseback, but they had to be assisted onto their horses because their armor was so heavy! When they fought on horseback, they often used a wooden lance with a metal tip.

Explain to students that the crusades allowed knights from countries typically at war with one another—France and England, for example—to fight a common enemy, the Muslims, who had taken over the holy places of Jerusalem and the Holy Land.

More About the Knight's Chain Mail The springy mesh of interlocking rings that made up the crusader's chain mail could break the force of a sword blow. However, a well-shot arrow could go right through the spaces between the rings.

Writing a Letter

Many knights couldn't read or write, but they could have dictated a letter to someone who did know how to write. Ask students to write a letter that a knight might have dictated to be sent to his family in England. They should be sure to include descriptions of his adventures in Jerusalem and how he feels about being away from home for so long.

Research

The coat of arms emblem developed during the early 1100s was a way to identify crusading knights. The insignia appeared on the knight's shield, on his coat, and on flags carried into battle. Coats of arms also marked possessions and official documents.

Have students research the use of coats of arms. Ask them to construct an emblem that will identify them in the same way the knight's shield told people who he was.

Visual Learning

This picture is bursting with information. Ask students what they can tell or guess about the crusader from looking at the picture and reading the captions. *(He's probably religious, dirty, wounded, superstitious, weighted down with chain-mail armor, and homesick.)*

HISTORY

Visual Learning

Have students study the painting and its caption on this page. Explain that about one third of the people of Europe died from the plague during the 14th century. Discuss what life might have been like during the time of the plague.

ECONOMICS

Critical Thinking

Ask students to consider the positive and negative effects of the increased trade that developed after the crusades. List each effect on the chalkboard.

■ *Trade ships carried infected rats from Asia.*

CLOSE

Have students answer the Thinking Focus. Then draw a timeline on the chalkboard, beginning with the year 476 and ending with 1450. Ask students to locate the years of the Viking raids *(late 700s to mid-900s),* the crusades *(1095–1291),* and the first outbreak of the plague *(1346).* Ask students to recap the developments that led to these events.

Europe at the End of the Middle Ages

➤ *This painting shows Death riding on horseback, striking down people with the plague.*

After the crusades, international trade increased. Peace treaties helped open up new trade routes among Europe, Asia, and Africa. Italian cities such as Venice, Florence, Milan, and Genoa grew rich and powerful. Skilled shipbuilders, merchants, and bankers lived in these Italian cities. They helped supply wealthy Europeans with the foreign goods they demanded —spices, herbs, fine cloth, maps, and jewels.

▲ *Rats helped spread the plague across Europe.*

However, trade ships brought more than just rare goods to Europe. They also carried rats infected with the **plague** *(playg),* a deadly disease. Fleas living on these rats carried the germs that caused plague. When the trade ships docked in the ports of Europe, the infected rats raced to shore.

■ *How did trade ships bring the plague to Europe?*

Around 1347 the plague—known as the Black Death—swept across Europe from Asia. All over Europe, people tried to fight it. Yet nothing cured the plague or stopped it from spreading. In less than 10 years, about 25 million Europeans died from this deadly disease. The plague continued to strike Europe and the rest of the world for centuries. In 1525 Michael V. Behaim, a German teenager, wrote this to his cousin:

> *There has been a terrible plague throughout the land. More than a hundred thousand people have died, men, women, and children. . . . You may well wonder how I survived.*

To learn more about the spread of the plague, read Making a Hypothesis on the opposite page.

For survivors of the Black Death, the future may have looked bleak. People may have felt helpless. Could a new society come about from the ruins of the past? ■

REVIEW

1. **FOCUS** Describe daily life in feudal Europe.
2. **HISTORY** How was feudalism in Europe similar to feudalism in Japan?
3. **ECONOMICS** How did increased trade after the crusades have positive and negative effects on Europe?
4. **CRITICAL THINKING** Did the crusades fail? Explain.
5. **ACTIVITY** Write a short story for young children about life during the Middle Ages. Describe the events of one day in the life of a queen, knight, peasant, or crusader, for example. The setting for your story could be a castle, farming village, or seaport.

Homework Options

Direct students to gather additional information about the Vikings from their school or public library and write a paragraph or two on the topic of their choice. Suggest that they investigate the daily life of the Vikings, their skill as shipbuilders, or their conquests and exploration.

Study Guide: page 72

Answers to Review Questions

1. People of feudal Europe lived in classes—fixed social ranks defined by their occupation. Most people were poor peasants or serfs who belonged to the land.
2. Feudalism in both lands was based on the granting of land in exchange for loyalty and assistance in times of war.
3. Positive effects included new trade routes, a greater supply of foreign goods, and the rise of Italian cities. A negative effect was the plague.
4. From the Christian's point of view, the crusades failed because crusaders did not capture the Holy Land. Also, many people died on the crusades. However, they opened up Europe to increased contact with other parts of the world.
5. Students' stories should show an awareness of the feudal system and may include details about farm life, the plague, the crusades, or increased trade and the spread of ideas.

UNDERSTANDING CRITICAL THINKING

Making a Hypothesis

Here's Why

You have just finished reading about the plague. Perhaps you want to learn why it spread so quickly through Europe from 1347 to 1350. How would you find the answer? You could ask your teacher, or you could do what many scientists do. You could make a hypothesis.

A hypothesis is an educated guess that can be tested. It is based on facts you know from reading, observing nature, or experimenting. Before a hypothesis can be useful, it must be tested.

To test a hypothesis, scientists set up experiments and collect data. However, hypotheses about events in history—such as the plague—cannot be tested by experiment. They can be tested by collecting data from maps, books, and other historical sources. In fact you can use the map on this page and information from Lesson 2 to make and test a hypothesis about the spread of the plague.

Here's How

To make and test a hypothesis of your own, follow these steps:

1. **Define the question.** You could ask: Is there any connection between trade routes and the spread of the plague?
2. **Gather evidence.** Study the map, and review page 418. List the facts that might support your idea. Your list might look like this:
   - From the map it appears that the plague affected Europe in a wavelike pattern.
   - The port cities shown on the trade routes were among the first places affected by the plague.
   - Fleas found on rats carried the disease. These rats lived on many of the ships traveling the trade routes.
3. **Make a hypothesis.** Based on the evidence, your hypothesis might be: Though the development of trade routes helped people to exchange goods and ideas, these routes also helped spread the plague.
4. **Test the hypothesis.** You can test your hypothesis by learning more about the plague in a book, magazine, or another source. If you learn new facts about the plague, change your hypothesis to account for the new information.

Spread of the Plague, c. 1347–1353

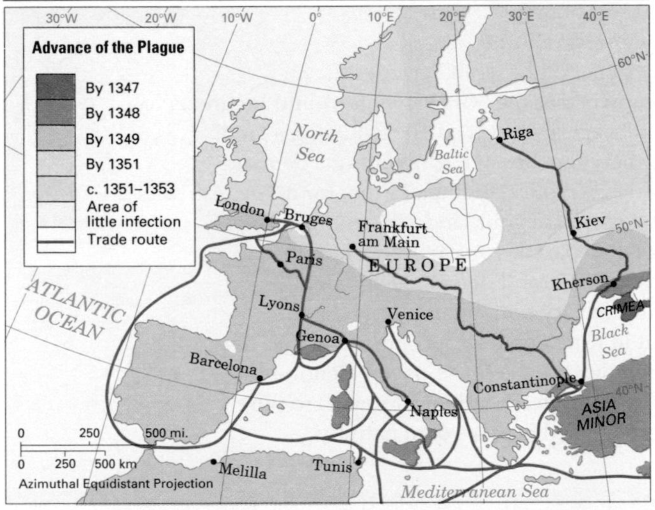

Advance of the Plague
By 1347
By 1348
By 1349
By 1351
c. 1351–1353
Area of little infection
Trade route
30°W
20°W
10°W
0°
10°E
20°E
30°E
40°E
60°N
50°N
40°N
North Sea
Baltic Sea
Riga
London
Bruges
Frankfurt am Main
Kiev
Paris
EUROPE
Kherson
ATLANTIC OCEAN
Lyons
Venice
CRIMEA
Black Sea
Genoa
Barcelona
Constantinople
Naples
ASIA MINOR
Melilla
Tunis
Mediterranean Sea
0 250 500 mi.
0 250 500 km
Azimuthal Equidistant Projection

Try It

Now use the map to form another hypothesis. For example: Why were the northernmost areas on the map the last areas affected by the plague? Use the four-step process to make and test your hypothesis.

Apply It

Make a hypothesis that answers this question: Why do some students make excuses about late homework assignments? Again, use the four-step process.

UNDERSTANDING CRITICAL THINKING

This skills feature uses information students learned about the plague in Lesson 2 to teach students how to make a hypothesis.

SOCIAL SYSTEMS

Critical Thinking

Discuss the hypothesis regarding the spread of the plague. Ask students to recall occasions when they have used a hypothesis to predict the outcome of a science experiment. Have them describe the experiment and their hypothesis to the rest of the class. Did their experiment prove or disprove their hypothesis? How did making a hypothesis help them conduct their experiment? *(Students should recognize that their hypothesis helped them decide what materials to gather for the experiment and what evidence or data to observe and record.)*

Answers to Try It

Be sure that students' hypotheses are supported with evidence. Possible hypothesis: The northernmost areas were the last to be affected by the plague because they had the least amount of trade-route traffic.

Answers to Apply It

Students should base their hypotheses on evidence, including their own experiences and those of their classmates. Possible hypothesis: Some students make excuses about late homework assignments because they have too much to do during the day and can't finish their assignments on time.

Objective

Explain how historical thematic maps can be used to formulate hypotheses. (Critical Thinking 3; Map and Globe Skills 2, 3)

INTRODUCE

Tales of chivalry developed in 12th-century France and spread to the popular literatures of other European countries. They are adventure stories of knightly quests, tournaments fought, and dragons slain. The tales stress the ideals of courage, honor, and mercy to an opponent. They also involve magic, spells, and enchantment. This excerpt, Chapter Six of *Valentine & Orson,* is just such a tale.

READ AND RESPOND

This translation has been written as a dramatic script narrated by an enchanter named Pacolet. Students will find it entertaining to listen to the tale read aloud or to take turns reading it aloud. Point out that the translator has worked hard to create a regular rhythm and rhyme. Based on their listening, have students write brief, imaginative descriptions of the main characters and the setting of the story.

Before students read, point out the vocabulary words and unfamiliar terms defined in the margins. Be sure they understand what the words mean; help with pronunciation if necessary.

LITERATURE

Valentine & Orson

Re-created as a folk play in verse and paintings by Nancy Ekholm Burkert

In Lesson 2 you read about the feudal world of medieval Europe. This story presents the flavor of the period when kings employed knights to protect their kingdoms.

Europe during the Middle Ages was a continent divided into many kingdoms. King Pepin led the Franks between 751 and 768 A.D. The fanciful tale below is chapter six of a long poem that recounts an adventure of King Pepin, his sister Bellicent, and her twin sons, Valentine and Orson. The twins were separated at birth by a strange series of happenings. Bellicent was accused by her husband, Emperor Alexander, of unfaithfulness. He ordered her to leave his realm. During her return to France, she gave birth to twins while traveling through a forest. A bear took one of the babies and raised him in the wild. This earned the child, Orson, the nickname Wild Man because his appearance resembled that of a bear. King Pepin himself found the other child, Valentine, and raised him at the royal court. Valentine and Orson became good friends and learned that they were brothers only after sharing many adventures together. As you read this narrative poem, ask yourself why Valentine agrees to fight the Green Knight.

The good Duke Savary
Ruled in Aquitaine
And was King Pepin's friend.
I shall explain
How he was caught
In a predicament
That for our tale
Is most significant!
A brother of the giant Ferragus,
Renowned as the "Green Knight," and infamous,
Laid siege against the Duke and all his land.
He held him hostage, with but one demand:
"Give me your daughter, Fezon, for my wife,
Or I will burn your land and take your life!
I shall depart, if you can find a knight
To challenge and defeat me in a fight!"
Duke Savary sent letters everywhere.
But in King Pepin's court no one would dare
To undertake the cause, save Valentine,
Who in his heart had never ceased to pine
For knowledge of his own nativity.

Aquitaine a region in southwestern France

predicament difficult situation

infamous having a bad reputation

nativity birth

Thematic Connections

Social Studies: History/A sense of empathy for the past

Houghton Mifflin Literary Readers: Adventure/The Spirit of Survival

Background

The history of this classic tale is a story in itself. The first version, a lost romance in French verse, probably dates to the 12th century. A French prose version, *Valentin et Orson,* was written by Jacques Maillet, c. 1475–1489. Maillet's edition was translated into English by Henry Watson. Watson's first edition survives only in fragments, but his second edition is nearly complete (c. 1548–1558). From Watson's translation, 75 versions and variations in English have followed. Nancy Ekholm Burkert is the first writer to retell the tale since 1919.

Burkert became fascinated by the tale indirectly. A student of art, she was an admirer of the Flemish painter Pieter Bruegel the Elder. At an exhibit in 1982, she was intrigued by one of Bruegel's woodcuts entitled *The Masquerade of Valentine and Orson,* and she began to research the story. Seven years later her translation of the tale was published in both Europe and the United States.

This was a splendid opportunity
To search in realms outside of France, and find
Some tidings of his birth to ease his mind.
He felt obliged, moreover, to defend
The noble man who was King Pepin's friend.

Wild Orson ran beside him, on the route
Toward Aquitaine, and all the world ran out,
Amused to see a man so like a bear,
All rough, and nearly naked. He could hear
Their laughter but the Wild Man paid no heed.
However, Valentine could see his need
And found an armorer nearby who made
A coat of mail, in finest steel. He bade
That Orson pull it on, and ever thence,
The Wild Man had a prouder countenance!

mail flexible armor

countenance appearance

They journeyed on, two fellows glad to be
Companions on the road, and soon could see
The spires of Aquitaine, which rose on high.
By chance, or fate, an aged man passed by
Who had a long white beard and the attire
Of a pilgrim. Actually, he was a squire
On his way from Portugal to France, carrying
A noble lady's message to the King.
He warned them not to enter Aquitaine,
Where forty knights were overcome and slain.
They could be seen, afar, hanging from a tree.
And then, as they were parting company,
Valentine was strangely drawn to this old man,
Who was, as you have guessed, good Blandyman.

Blandyman the queen's loyal squire

They ventured on and soon arrived before
The Duke and his fair daughter. Gathered there
Were fourteen other knights from foreign lands,
To challenge the Green Knight and his demands.
Valentine spoke reverently to Fezon:
"Right dear Lady, I have come from Pepin,
Mighty King of France, and with me, here,
The bravest man on earth. He has no peer."
The maiden gazed upon the simply clad
And rugged Orson. Ah, we hear it said
That when the heart is dealt a blow, no love
Is less than beautiful. And, friends, above
All others, Fezon set her heart on Orson!
"A thousand thanks to both of you," said Fezon.
"Too many noble knights were slain for me.

◄ What qualities seem to attract Fezon to Orson? *(His simplicity and his rugged appearance)*

Access Strategy

Ask students to think about stories or movies that include knights as characters. Have them make a list of all the characteristics they can think of that a knight possesses. *(Courage, loyalty, kindness, and so forth)* Help students understand that in late medieval Europe, the tradition of courtly love required that a knight pledge his spiritual service to a single "fair lady" and that every lady love a knight. It was during this period that the behaviors associated with "courtesy" evolved, and Christians began worshiping the Virgin Mary as "Our Lady." Many modern "romantic" ideals spring from the ideal of courtly love.

➤ How does the Green Knight decide beforehand if a knight is the one who can conquer him? *(If the knight can fetch the green shield, he is the one who can defeat the Green Knight.)*

jeopardy risk

retorted replied sharply

lamented said sadly

balm a soothing oil

quest search

melancholy sad

I beg you not to put your lives in jeopardy!"
But Orson placed his hands across his heart,
And Valentine insisted, for their part.

Thus on the morrow, sixteen men in all
Took counsel with each other in the hall.
The two who asked that they be first to fight
Were soon defeated by the fierce Green Knight,
Who hung them without mercy from the tree.
Now Orson shook his fists ferociously,
But Valentine was next, and when he rode
Onto the field, the evildoer crowed,
"Ha, Knight! On yonder rowan tree, you see
A green shield hanging. Bring it here to me!"
Valentine retorted, "Why? Do I observe
That you have servants? Why not let them serve!"
The villain shouted, "You shall fetch the shield,
Or by my law, we shall not take the field!"
So Valentine complied in fear his foe would try
To use this lame excuse, but could not pry
The shield away. "Now you will understand,"
The villain jeered, "this shield from Fairyland
Will not come loose unless you are the one
Predestined as my conqueror, the son
Of royal rank, but nourished well without
A woman's milk!" "What you have said I doubt
Is true of me," lamented Valentine, "yet
I shall fight!" "Such folly reaps regret,"
The Green Knight said and spurred his horse.
The two fought back and forth along the course
So fiercely all their weapons broke apart.
They stopped as darkness fell, but vowed to start
When it was day. They had sore wounds to tend.
The Green Knight kept a magic balm to mend
His injuries, but this he kept concealed.
Poor Valentine was not so quickly healed.
When he had dressed his wounds, he tried to rest,
But could not sleep as he reviewed his quest
To learn the truth about his origin.
He thought of the enchanted shield, or Orson;
Was he by chance or by a jest of fate
Somehow descended from a high estate?

At dawn, it could be seen that Valentine
Was in a melancholy state of mind.
He gathered all his armor for the fight,
But, friends, imagine Orson's wild delight

422

Collaborative Learning

The prologue to this tale includes these lines, spoken by Pacolet, the narrator:

> Ah, friends, both great and small, come near!
> The right good troupe of players you see here
> Will mime a tale that you shall not forget,
> With verse recited by your Pacolet,
> Of ORSON and his brother, VALENTINE.

Read this introduction to your students and encourage them to organize, rehearse, and perform their own pantomimes of the tale in small groups, with a narrator reading most of the verse. Ask them to imagine that they are a band of itinerant players, roaming the European countryside in the Middle Ages, performing for small villages. Have them use makeshift costumes and simple props made from everyday objects. Encourage groups to perform their plays for the rest of the class or to videotape their efforts.

When Valentine came forth to place it all
Into his hands! Orson, prancing round the hall,
Made signs that he preferred a club of wood
To other weapons, but he understood
The reason he must pose as Valentine.
The shining armor made him look so fine
That all who saw him clapped and cheered, except
His wounded friend, who was forlorn and kept
An anxious watch as Orson rode away,
And prayed for his return, unharmed, that day.

Further Reading

Adam of the Road. Elizabeth J. Gray. Searching for his minstrel father and his dog, Adam wanders through 13th century England. He meets jugglers, minstrels, pilgrims, and nobles on his journeys.

Life in a Fifteenth Century Monastery. Anne Boyd. The author provides a detailed look at the daily life of monks in an English monastery.

A Proud Taste for Scarlet and Minevar. E. L. Konigsberg. This historical fiction brings to life the adventures of Queen Eleanor of Aquitaine.

The Road to Camlann. Rosemary Sutcliff. This book retells the adventures of King Arthur's court and all its colorful figures, including Sir Lancelot and Queen Guenevere.

The Merry Adventures of Robin Hood. Howard Pyle. The book retells the legend of a man who robs from the rich and gives to the poor peasants.

◄ How does the bearlike Orson disguise himself as Valentine? *(He wears a suit of shining armor.)*

EXTEND

Have students write what they think will happen next in this tale, either in prose or in rhyming couplets. Ask them to try to mimic the language and the imagery of what they have read. Encourage them to share, compare, and contrast their stories and, finally, to find out what really happens in the classic tale. *(In the next chapter, Orson pins the evil knight to the ground and mercifully grants him his life. When Orson approaches the green shield, it leaps into his hands, proving that he is the one whom destiny has named to conquer the Green Knight.)*

Further Reading

You may want to have students find the complete tale of *Valentine & Orson* in the local or school library.

INTRODUCE

Have students read the headings in Lesson 3, and scan the illustrations to find out as much as possible about the Renaissance. Define the word Renaissance for students. *(Rebirth or revival)*

Have them read the Thinking Focus and suggest some of the major changes that a rebirth of learning and thinking might bring to feudal Europe. Then have them read the lesson to learn more about some of the major achievements of the Renaissance.

Key Terms

Vocabulary Strategies: T36–T37

Renaissance—the time of renewed interest in the arts and sciences of ancient Greece and Rome that began in northern Italy in the late 1300s

patron—a person who supports the arts and learning

classics—works of ancient Greece and Rome

humanist—a person who studies the classics in order to better understand people and the world

B.C. A.D.
450
625
800
975
1150
1300
1650

LESSON 3

The Renaissance

THINKING FOCUS

What were some of the major achievements of the Renaissance?

Key Terms

- Renaissance
- patron
- classics
- humanist

Take pains and pleasure in constantly copying the best things which you can find done by the hand of great masters [the best painters]. And if you are in a place where many good masters have been, so much the better for you. But I give you this advice: take care to select the best one every time, and the one who has the greatest reputation.

Cennino Cennini, from The Craftsman's Handbook, 1437

Cennini's book gave practical advice for the beginning artist. He wrote about how to mix paint, prepare a canvas, and protect one's hands.

Yet Cennini's book was not just a how-to-paint manual. Cennini also gave advice about life: what to eat, wear, and study, and how to act in public. After the horrors of the Black Death, Europeans were eager to read books such as Cennini's.

A new way of living and thinking took hold in Europe after the Black Death. People of the late 1300s and 1400s wanted to know more about the world. Although religious, they hoped to gain great wealth and lasting fame.

A new era had begun. It was called the **Renaissance** *(rehn ih SAHNS)*, from a Latin word meaning "rebirth" or "revival." The Renaissance was a time of renewed interest in both the arts and sciences of ancient Greece and Rome. It was a rebirth of learning. The Renaissance began in northern Italy during the late 1300s, then spread through Europe.

➤ *Note the rich colors and religious themes in this Raphael painting. Raphael (1483–1520) was called "the prince of painters" for his mastery of the Renaissance style.*

Objectives

1. Describe city life during the Italian Renaissance.
2. Explain how the Renaissance spread throughout Europe.
3. Describe some of the achievements made in the arts and sciences during the Renaissance.

Graphic Overview

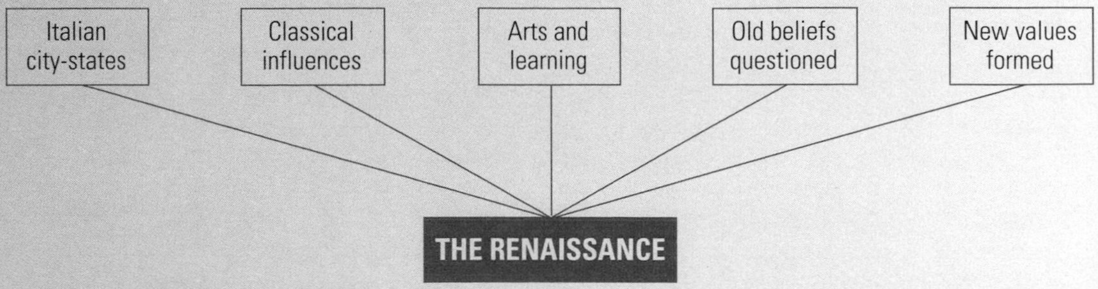
Italian city-states
Classical influences
Arts and learning
Old beliefs questioned
New values formed
THE RENAISSANCE

Italy: Birthplace of the Renaissance

Renaissance Italy was not a unified country. Instead it was made up of individual city-states. Like ancient Athens and Sparta, each Italian city-state ruled itself and the surrounding countryside.

Wealthy families, not kings or queens, ruled the Italian city-states. Often these rulers fought for control of the Mediterranean Sea trade. Their thirst for power led to many murders, riots, and feuds.

In spite of these dangers, Italian cities thrived during the 1400s and 1500s. Italy's location made it a crossroads between Europe, Africa, and Asia. Venice, Florence, Milan, and Genoa were centers of international trade and banking. Their wealth would fuel the rebirth of Europe—the Renaissance.

▲ *Note how this Renaissance painting by Ambrogio Lorenzetti (c. 1290–1348) gives you a sense of depth—some people and buildings appear close, while others appear far away.*

City Life

In these bustling Italian cities, people were divided into social classes, or ranks. The lower classes were made up of unskilled workers, such as boat workers and peddlers. In spite of the wealth in Italian cities, most people of the lower classes were poor. They had no say in running either the government or the powerful guilds, which were like unions.

The middle class was made up of shop owners, carpenters, blacksmiths, and other skilled workers. Each one belonged to a guild. Guilds set prices and quality standards. They decided who could or could not join.

Patrons of the Arts

At the top of the social classes were the wealthy nobles, merchants, and businesspeople. They ran the most powerful guilds. These major guilds included cloth manufacturers, merchants, bankers, and doctors. Wealthy families, such as the Medici *(MEHD uh chee)* family in Florence, ran their cities like personal kingdoms.

The Medicis also used their wealth to enjoy leisure, or free time. Like many other wealthy families of the Renaissance, the Medicis were **patrons,** or supporters of the arts and learning. Patrons hired artists to fill their homes with beautiful paintings and sculptures. They bought rare books and paid scholars to teach their children.

Just as these families competed in business, they competed in the arts and learning. Patrons spent huge sums of money bidding for the services of the best artists and teachers. They also competed with the richest patron of them all—the Catholic church. ■

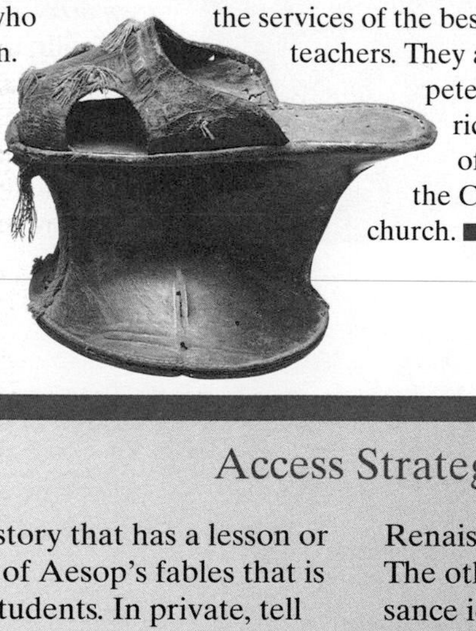

◄ *To keep their dresses from dragging in dust or mud, Italian women often wore platform shoes, like the one shown at left.*

■ *Describe the people who made up the different classes of Renaissance Italy.*

DEVELOP

On the chalkboard draw a timeline with dates so that students can identify some of the contributing factors to the growth and spread of the Renaissance. Ask students to copy the timeline and to write in the appropriate information as they read.

You may want to include these dates: late 1200s *(the end of the crusades and the opening of new trade routes to Italian cities);* 1300s *(the increasing wealth of these cities and their contact with Arab and Byzantine scholars);* 1450s *(the invention of the printing press);* late 1400s and early 1500s *(the fame of Renaissance thinkers and painters).*

■ *The lower classes were made up of unskilled workers; the middle class was made up of small shop owners and skilled workers, including some artists; the upper class was the ruling class and included mostly wealthy merchants and bankers. The middle class formed the minor guilds, such as carpenters, while the ruling class controlled the major guilds, such as bankers.*

Access Strategy

Make up a short story that has a lesson or moral, or select one of Aesop's fables that is unfamiliar to most students. In private, tell one student the story, and then ask that student to tell another and so on, until most of the students have heard the story. Have the last student to hear the story repeat it to the class. Then read your original story to show students how it had changed.

Point out that as information spread from Italy throughout Europe during the Renaissance, that information also changed. The other people of Europe molded Renaissance ideas to fit their own needs, adapting them to fit their way of life, values, and religion. Ask students how people learn about new ideas in our society. *(Schools, books, magazines, newspapers, movies, videos, radio and television, word of mouth)* Tell students they will read in this lesson about how ideas were spread during the Renaissance.

Access Activity

Bring in various books that show examples of Renaissance art. Include examples of architecture, painting, and sculpture from this time. Have students pick out a work of art that appeals to them and describe to the rest of the class what they like about it.

HISTORY

Visual Learning

Have students compare the illustrations from the French book of prayers on page 415 with the visuals in this lesson. Ask them to name two or more characteristics of Renaissance art that is different from that of the Middle Ages. *(Possible answers include: Renaissance art looks more three-dimensional; it has depth or perspective; human figures in it are more lifelike; people in paintings show a broader range of emotions; artists have chosen a variety of subjects.)*

ECONOMICS

Critical Thinking

Ask students why the Renaissance began among the wealthy. *(Wealthy Italians had enough money to allow them the leisure time to study the classics, or to sponsor scholars to study the classics.)* How did increased trade help bring about the Renaissance? *(Increased trade brought Italians into contact with other peoples and ideas. It also provided the money to spend on art and learning.)*

A Flowering of Arts and Learning

Trade did more than just increase the wealth of the Italian cities. It also brought the Italians into contact with people from all over the Mediterranean world. Just as goods were traded, so too were ideas.

Compare Brunelleschi's dome on the Florence cathedral, shown here, with the Byzantine domes on page 412. Brunelleschi's most famous work took 16 years to build. He is buried there.

Looking Forward to the Past

Trade brought the Italians into greater contact with Arab and Byzantine scholars. These scholars were experts in the **classics**—the works of ancient Greece and Rome.

A person who studied the classics was called a **humanist.** By studying the classics, Italian humanists hoped to understand people and the world better. They wanted to re-create classical styles in art, literature, and architecture. All over Italy, artists, writers, and builders turned to the ancient past for inspiration.

Humanists did not want simply to copy ideas from the past. They hoped to use old ideas to create something new—and better.

Age of the Artist

One such humanist was Filippo Brunelleschi (*broo nuh LEHS kee),* an architect and engineer who lived from 1377 to 1446.

Brunelleschi left his home in Florence to study ancient ruins in Rome. Since ancient times no dome had been built in Europe. After years of study, he built a dome for the Florence cathedral. Another architect of the time, Leon Battista Alberti, wrote of Brunelleschi's dome that "it was probably unknown and unthought of to the ancients."

Another famous Renaissance artist designed a dome about 100 years after Brunelleschi had designed his. You may think of Michelangelo *(my kuhl AN juh loh)* only as a painter or sculptor. However, he wrote hundreds of poems. He also designed the dome of St. Peter's cathedral in Rome.

Many of Michelangelo's works, such as his dome, were paid for by one patron—the Catholic church. In 1508 Pope Julius II asked Michelangelo to paint biblical scenes on the ceiling of the Sistine Chapel in Rome. Michelangelo worked while squatting on shaky boards high above the marble floor. Paint splattered into his eyes. His back always ached. Often he grew dizzy and would almost faint.

Finally, in 1512, Michelangelo finished. In all he had painted more than 300 figures from the Bible and classical times. One visitor at the time wrote that "all Rome admired it and crowded to see it."

Study Skills

Explain that Leonardo da Vinci represented the ideals of the Renaissance by his broad range of interests. Da Vinci became an accomplished painter, scientist, inventor, sculptor, musician, writer, and military engineer. Have students use art books and encyclopedias to research da Vinci's interests in one of these areas and prepare a brief oral report for the class.

Historical Context

To help students understand the workings of a guild, explain that metalsmiths, weavers, and other craftsworkers formed guilds to control the quality and quantity of production. Craftspeople who were experts in their trade were called masters. Someone who learned a craft from a master—usually a boy or young man—was called an apprentice. In most cases, an apprentice had to pay the master for this education, as well as for housing and meals.

After serving an apprenticeship ranging from five to nine years, an apprentice could then become a journeyman and be paid wages for his labor. A journeyman who could show proof of his competence by producing a masterpiece could rise to the status of master—and set up his own shop and train his own apprentices.

The Renaissance Man

During the Renaissance, well-educated men were expected to do many things well. They collected art, wrote poetry, played music, and learned Greek. They also took part in politics, were skilled at sports, and could fight if necessary.

Perhaps the most famous Renaissance man was Leonardo da Vinci. Leonardo began his career as a teenage apprentice, working for a master painter in Florence. By 1478, Leonardo had left his master to set up his own workshop.

Leonardo's fame grew—and not just for his painting. Leonardo was in demand for his great knowledge and engineering skills. In Italy and France, patrons such as the Medicis bid for his services. Only after his death were many of his inventions discovered, such as the one shown on page 429.

The Renaissance Woman

Unlike the Renaissance man, the Renaissance woman was not encouraged to develop her abilities. One male writer gave Renaissance women this advice:

> It does not befit [suit] women to handle weapons, to ride, to play tennis, to wrestle, and to do many other things that befit men. . . .
>
> Baldassare Castiglione, *The Book of the Courtier*, 1528

Some Renaissance women ignored this advice. Some became writers or artists. Others became skilled workers or shop owners. A few held political power.

Two exceptional Renaissance women were Isabella d'Este *(DEHS tay)* and Christine de Pizan *(pee ZAHN)*. During the late 1400s, d'Este helped her family rule the Italian city-state of Mantua. She was also a patron to many gifted Renaissance artists.

Christine de Pizan was born in Venice in the late 1300s but spent most of her life in France. She studied the arts and sciences, then married and had children. After her husband died, de Pizan wrote poems and essays to support her family. ■

◄ Leonardo da Vinci made this drawing of Isabella d'Este in 1500.

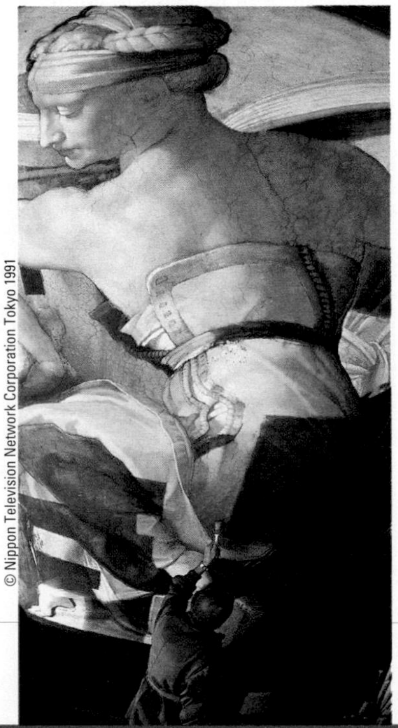

◄ Cleaning and restoring Michelangelo's paintings on the ceiling of the Sistine Chapel took nine years—more than twice as long as it took Michelangelo to paint them.

How Do We Know?

HISTORY *In 1980 art experts began cleaning the dirt from Michelangelo's paintings on the ceiling of the Sistine Chapel. In 1989 the experts finished their work. With the dirt removed, the paintings seemed to come alive with color and light.*

■ Compare the life of a Renaissance woman with that of a Renaissance man.

CULTURE

Social Participation

Have students reread the sections on this page about the Renaissance man and Renaissance woman. Make a list on the chalkboard of some of the characteristics mentioned in the lesson. Then ask students to work in pairs and write a brief biographical sketch describing someone from the past or present who they consider to be an ideal Renaissance person. Have them share their biographies with the class.

■ Women were expected to stay at home and run the household. They were not expected to develop their abilities. An example of an exceptional Renaissance woman is Christine de Pizan, who supported her family by writing professionally after her husband died.

The ideal Renaissance man was expected to do many things well. The best example is probably Leonardo da Vinci, a master painter, engineer, and inventor.

Social Context

Help students understand that most people who lived during this time were not the "ideal" Renaissance man or woman. During the Renaissance the luxury of pursuing one's own individual interests was reserved for the privileged of the middle and upper classes who could afford to do so. However, life for the lower classes—especially for women—did not change significantly from what it had been.

Some Renaissance women did become shop owners or skilled workers. Yet, most were poor peasant women who worked in the fields, milked the cows, and did other farmwork. Most men of this time were merely expected to perform their trade well. Only a few became wealthy or well-known artists.

Social Participation

Have students work in small groups and write a letter to a patron requesting support for a work of art or architecture they would like to create.

GEOGRAPHY

Map and Globe Skills

Have students look at the Atlas map of Europe on page 682 and locate some of the important cities of the Renaissance that exist today, such as Venice and Rome. Then have them trace the spread of the Renaissance from Italy. Ask them to identify Germany, Poland, the Netherlands, England, France, and Spain on the map. Point out Germany as the home of Gutenberg, Poland of Copernicus, the Netherlands of Bruegel, England of Shakespeare, France of Vesalius, and Spain of Miguel de Cervantes (1547–1616), author of *Don Quixote.*

The Spread of the Renaissance

This painting, The Renaissance Classroom, *shows people's thirst for learning during the Renaissance. By 1500 about six million books had been printed in Europe. As more people learned to read and write, demand for books grew.*

The rebirth of the Italian cities attracted visitors from all over Europe. Clergy and pilgrims flocked to Rome. Merchants and bankers hoped to make their fortunes in the Italian city-states. Artists and students sought knowledge, fame, and fortune.

When these travelers returned home, they brought Renaissance ideas—and newly printed books—with them. In the 1450s a German named Johannes Gutenberg *(GOOT n burg)* had developed a new printing press. Gutenberg's press used movable type—individual letters made into small, metal blocks. This movable type was easy to arrange and rearrange into words. Instead of having to be copied by hand, books could be printed quickly, in larger numbers, and for less money than ever before.

By the late 1400s, printers used movable type to print everything from the Bible to cartoons. This explosion of print helped spread the Renaissance north.

Northern Renaissance Ideas

As in Italy, humanists in northern Europe focused on the individual. However, their style of writing and painting was very different from that of the Italians.

England's William Shakespeare may be the best-known northern Renaissance writer. Born in 1564, Shakespeare was a poet, an actor, and a playwright. His plays showed the strengths and weaknesses of all

This painting by Pieter Bruegel is called The Peasant Dance. *Bruegel tried to tell the stories of everyday people in his paintings. Notice the different expression each figure has.*

Visual Learning

Have students carve their names or initials in reverse on a cut potato or sponge. Then coat the initials with paint or ink and print them on paper. Tell them that this is an example of block printing. Next, have each student carve individual letters. Have students get together to form and print words. This is an example of printing with movable type.

Historical Context

Explain the impact of movable type on the printing and paper business. The explosion of print that followed the development of movable type was aided by the mass of discarded clothing left after the Black Death. These garments were shredded to make rag paper, a valuable component of the emerging print revolution. Historians estimate that by 1500 more than six million books were in print, including numerous editions of Greek and Roman classics.

Political Context

Germany was the first country of northern Europe to adopt the ideals of the Italian Renaissance. The German Renaissance flourished from the end of the 1400s to the early 1500s. Historians think that Germany was the first northern country to embrace humanism because, although its central government was unstable at the time, its cities were strong and relatively independent, like the city-states of Italy.

people—past and present. Shakespeare's characters included Roman emperors, British kings and queens, and Italian teenagers. Because his plays mixed slapstick humor with drama, audiences flocked to see them.

The Dutch painter Pieter Bruegel *(BROY guhl)* also wanted to show people as they really were. Many of his paintings showed peasants working, dancing, and eating. Although he had studied Italian painting, Bruegel developed his own style. Compare Bruegel's painting on the previous page with Raphael's on page 424.

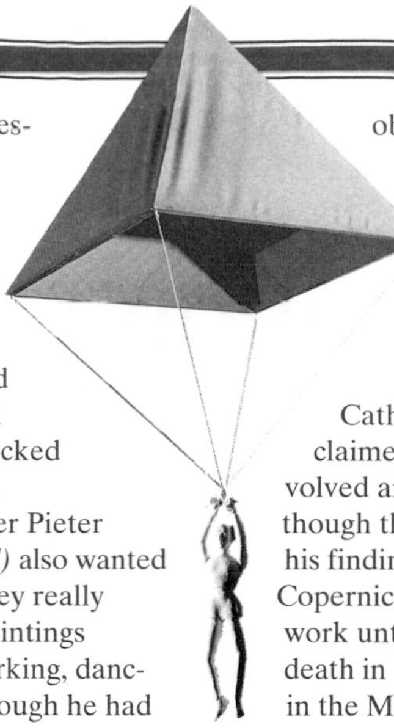

◄ *Leonardo da Vinci drew this design for a parachute in one of his many notebooks around 1485. The first air-to-ground jump wasn't made until 1797—over 300 years later.*

Rebirth of Science in Europe

Interest in the past led to a new age of science in Europe. The first modern European scientists studied science and philosophy from Greece, Egypt, and India. They performed experiments to test their own ideas. The Scientific Revolution had begun in Europe.

The Polish astronomer, Nicolaus Copernicus *(koh PUR nuh kuhs),* was one of its earliest leaders. Copernicus began his studies in 1491—just one year before Columbus's first voyage. Copernicus read ancient scientific works. He also observed the planets, stars, and moon. Finally, he used math to conclude that the sun was the center of the solar system.

For centuries, the Catholic church had claimed that the sun revolved around the earth. Although the Pope approved of his findings, others did not. Copernicus did not publish his work until just before his death in 1543. Turn to page G8 in the Map and Globe Handbook to see how Copernicus's ideas helped to explain the seasons.

While Copernicus explored the night sky, Andreas Vesalius *(vih SAY lee uhs)* roamed French cemeteries. Vesalius was searching for dead bodies. Ancient texts about human anatomy were wrong, Vesalius thought. By studying dead bodies, he hoped to learn how the human body really worked. Vesalius's book, *On the Structure of the Human Body,* helped improve the practice of medicine.

Copernicus and Vesalius questioned long-held beliefs about the world. Other Europeans began to question the teachings of the Catholic church. As you will read next, the Church—and the world—would never be the same. ■

■ *How did the ideas of the Renaissance spread through Europe?*

REVIEW

1. **FOCUS** What were some of the major achievements of the Renaissance?
2. **GEOGRAPHY** How did Italy's location contribute to its role as birthplace of the Renaissance?
3. **CULTURE** What did humanist artists and builders try to teach or show?
4. **CRITICAL THINKING** What role did the printing press play in the spread of the Renaissance through Europe?
5. **ACTIVITY** Study a work of Renaissance art from this chapter or another book. Research the artist's life, and make a report to your class. What ideas from the past influenced this artist? Did he or she influence other artists? How? Illustrate your report with a painting or drawing of your own.

■ *Many people from northern Europe, such as students and merchants, traveled to Italy and brought back Renaissance ideas to their home countries. The invention of the printing press also helped to spread ideas throughout Europe.*

CLOSE

Review the events that students listed on the timelines they started at the beginning of this lesson. Ask students to discuss the Thinking Focus. Then, on the chalkboard, draw three columns. In the first, labeled *Renaissance Achievements,* list the names, terms, and achievements associated with the Renaissance. *(For instance, guilds, Medicis, patrons, Gutenberg press, Copernicus, Sistine Chapel)* Label the other columns *Northern Europe* and *Italy.*

Ask students whether each item in column one applies to the northern European Renaissance or the Italian Renaissance. Have them explain their responses, using information from the text. Then place a check mark in the appropriate column. Elaborate on items as you go, asking students from which countries historical figures originated and what they are famous for, as well as the significance of the terms.

Answers to Review Questions

1. Achievements include Brunelleschi's dome, a sense of depth in painting, and Vesalius's studies, which helped improve the practice of medicine.
2. Italy was at a cultural crossroads between Europe, Asia, and Africa. The Italian city-states had access to ideas by both land and sea.
3. They studied the classics in order to understand people and the world better. Individuals tried to develop their abilities, and interest in science flourished.
4. The printing press helped to spread new ideas. People could read about ideas from other parts of Europe and from ancient times.
5. Suggest that students use encyclopedias or a biographical dictionary to research the lives of Renaissance artists. They may study artists discussed in this chapter, or others such as Giotto, Masaccio, Donatello, Botticelli, or Jan van Eyck.

Homework Options

Tell students that music flourished during the Renaissance. Have students use encyclopedias at school or the public library to research musical instruments that were invented or made popular during the Renaissance. You may also want to bring in recordings of Renaissance music.

Study Guide: page 74

INTRODUCE

Remind students that the Roman Catholic church was the most important religious and political institution in medieval and Renaissance Europe. Tell them that the Reformation was a religious protest movement that struck a great blow to the Catholic church in the mid-1500s.

Have the students read the Thinking Focus. Tell them that they will read about the Reformation and how it changed the course of Christianity in western Europe.

Key Terms

Vocabulary Strategies: T36–T37

indulgence—a pardon issued by the Pope for sins

Protestant—a critic of the Roman Catholic church who protested its practices

Reformation—the protest movement intended to reform the Catholic church

Inquisition—a Catholic court where people suspected of being heretics were brought to trial

B.C. A.D. 450 625 800 975 1150 1325 1500 1600 1675

L E S S O N 4

The Reformation

THINKING FOCUS

What were the causes and the effects of the Reformation?

Key Terms

- indulgence
- Protestant
- Reformation
- Inquisition

On October 31, 1517, Martin Luther marched to All Saints Church in Wittenberg *(VIHT n behrk)*, Germany. Luther was a Catholic priest, and he was angry. He held up the paper he carried. Bang! Bang! Bang! Quickly Luther nailed his challenge to the church doors for all to see. Luther marched back home in silence.

Meanwhile, outside Wittenberg, a noisy crowd had gathered around another man of the Catholic church. People eagerly bought the slips of paper this monk, Johann Tetzel *(TEHT suhl)*, offered. Tetzel was selling indulgences. Issued by the Pope, **indulgences** were pardons, or forgiveness, for sins.

The sale of indulgences had angered Luther. "How could the Catholic church sell forgiveness?" he wondered. Luther felt that only God could forgive sins. In the paper he had nailed to the church doors, Luther protested that the Church had become too worldly. Luther's writings, called the *Ninety-Five Theses,* pointed out the problems he saw:

> *Why doesn't the pope build the basilica of St. Peter [the pope's church] out of his own money?. . . He would do better to sell St. Peter's and give the money to the poor folk who are being fleeced by the hawkers of indulgences.*

Luther's *Ninety-Five Theses* called for a debate. He hoped people would openly discuss his ideas and think about reforming the Church. Luther did not expect anything more than that. Yet in his lifetime, Luther's writings split the Catholic church and rocked the thrones of kings.

➤ *The entrance doors to All Saints Church in Wittenberg, Germany, now show Martin Luther's* Ninety-Five Theses.

Objectives

1. Explain the causes of the Reformation.
2. Explain how the Reformation spread through Europe.
3. Discuss the effects of the Reformation.

Graphic Overview

Chuch Abuses
- Church "too worldly"
- Sale of indulgences

→

Martin Luther
- Luther posts his theses objecting to the sale of indulgences and other Church practices

→

The Reformation
- Luther's ideas spark the Protestant Reformation

→

Europe Splits
- Europe divides into mainly Protestant countries in the north, Catholic in the south

The Reformation Begins

Within a year, printing presses had helped to spread Luther's ideas all over Europe. People debated his ideas. Many agreed with Luther. They began to question the Catholic church: Were its teachings and practices still true to the Bible?

The Church's critics were soon called **Protestants**. Like Luther, they protested what they saw as abuses by the Church. Their protest movement became known as the **Reformation**. These Protestants wanted to reform, or change, the Church from within.

In 1518, Pope Leo X ordered Luther to stop his attacks. Luther refused, so Pope Leo asked the Holy Roman Emperor, Charles V, to bring Luther to trial. Standing before a huge crowd, Luther again refused to take back his words:

I do not accept the authority of popes and councils, for they have contradicted each other—my conscience is captive to the Word of God. I cannot and I will not recant [take back] anything, for to go against conscience is neither right nor safe. God help me. Amen.

Charles then declared Luther an outlaw. Anyone could arrest him. Luckily for Luther, he had a powerful friend. Frederick the Wise, Prince of Saxony, hid Luther.

While in hiding, Luther translated the Bible into German. For the first time, Germans could read the Bible for themselves. Many felt they no longer needed priests to read and interpret it.

Luther's teachings inspired many people to break away from the Catholic church. Some called themselves Lutherans. They based their religious beliefs on Luther's ideas. Soon more people would become Protestants. ■

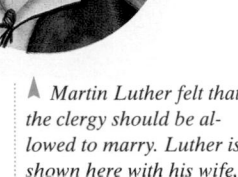

▲ *Martin Luther felt that the clergy should be allowed to marry. Luther is shown here with his wife, Katherina von Bora, a former nun.*

◄ *Johann Tetzel sold so many indulgences that some people made fun of him in a popular rhyme, "As soon as money in the box rings, The soul from Hell's fire springs."*

■ *Why did Luther object to the sale of indulgences?*

DEVELOP

Provide a copy of the Graphic Overview to each student. Have students add supporting sentences to the Graphic Overview as they read the lesson.

Then have students read the selection from Luther's *Ninety-Five Theses* on page 430. Explain that the Roman Catholic church obtained some of the wealth to which Luther alludes through the sale of indulgences. Explain that indulgences were sold by the church as pardons for sin or wrongdoing.

Indulgences did not completely absolve a person from sin. However, they were said to reduce the penalties one had to suffer for committing a sin. Tetzel was so determined to sell indulgences that he gave people the mistaken impression that they could buy God's forgiveness and gain salvation.

■ *Luther thought that it was wrong for the Church to sell forgiveness. He felt that only God could pardon, or forgive, sins.*

Access Strategy

Help students understand the Reformation by asking them if there's some aspect of school life they would like to change. Ask them what they think they could do to bring about this change. Then offer an example. Have them imagine that a student posts on the school's main entrance door a complaint about litter on the playground or schoolyard.

Encourage the class to guess how this student's classmates, teachers, and principal would react. List their ideas on the chalkboard. Would some classmates support the student? What would happen if the principal took action against the student? Would supporters continue to defend him or her then? Explain that, in a similar way, Martin Luther called for reform in church practices and gained support because of many people's determination to bring about change.

Access Activity

Ask students to study the picture at the bottom of this page and read the caption. Then have them answer these questions: What might Johann Tetzel be doing? *(He's selling something.)* What might he be selling? *(Indulgences)* Encourage students to use details from the picture to determine whether the artist supports or objects to this practice.

HISTORY

Social Participation

Explain that the printing press helped spread Luther's ideas throughout Europe. Then read the following statement by the Renaissance thinker Francis Bacon: "Printing, gunpowder, and the compass . . . have changed the appearance and state of the whole world: first in literature, then in warfare, and lastly in navigation." Have students debate which development during this time period (or one not listed by Bacon) changed the world the most, giving reasons for their choice.

HISTORY

Critical Thinking

Ask students to consider the causes and effects of the Reformation. Make a chart on the chalkboard and have the class help you complete it.

The Reformation Spreads in Europe

This illustration comes from one of Luther's printed Bibles.

Across Time & Space

Martin Luther and Martin Luther King, Jr., share more than a name. Both led reform movements that changed the way people live and think. King's policy of civil disobedience promoted racial equality in the United States during the 1950s and 1960s. Under his leadership, the civil rights movement helped reform U.S. society.

The printing press helped to spread Luther's ideas quickly. His teachings were translated from German and printed in English, Dutch, and other languages. As more people read or heard Luther's ideas, the Reformation grew throughout northern Europe.

Other Protestant Movements

In addition to Luther, the Reformation had many other leaders. Because the Catholic church did not change, many reformers decided to leave it and form their own churches.

John Calvin of Switzerland agreed with much of what Luther thought. However, Calvin taught that God had already chosen a special group for heaven. These believers, Calvin thought, could be recognized during their lifetime.

Calvin's followers were called Calvinists. Their church services were plain. No images of saints hung on the walls. No organ played as people sang. Nothing distracted the people from solemn prayer, reading the Bible, or listening to sermons.

Calvinists also followed strict rules outside of church. By the time Calvin died in 1564, his beliefs had taken root in Scotland, the Netherlands, and many other places.

In England during the 1500s, King Henry VIII made himself, rather than the Pope, head of the Church of England, or Anglican *(ANG glih kuhn)* church. King Henry split from the Catholic church because he wanted to divorce his wife, Catherine of Aragon.

Catherine and Henry had only one living child, Mary Tudor. Henry wanted a son to rule after him. He feared a civil war would break out after his death if he did not have a son to take over the throne. Henry thought that a new wife would give him this son. However, the Pope refused to grant him the divorce from Catherine.

In response to the Pope, King Henry took over most of the Church's property in England. He still kept many of the practices of the Catholic church, but he would not obey the Pope.

The Catholic Church Responds

Throughout Europe more and more people joined Protestant churches. Finally, in 1545, Catholic leaders decided to make some important changes.

Social Participation

Divide the class into groups to research Lutheranism, Anglicanism, Calvinism, or another Protestant religion. Ask each group to answer these questions: What is the history of this religious body? How does this church differ from the Roman Catholic church? What are some of its practices today? Have each group make a report to the class.

Historical Context

Help students understand that one of the influences on the Reformation was the translation of the Bible into the vernacular. William Tyndale was the first to translate the Bible into English. Arrested in the Netherlands, he was burned at the stake for his efforts. Yet within several years of Tyndale's death, English Bibles were widely available in England to anyone who could read. This widespread distribution of the Bible helped greatly to increase literacy.

Religious Context

One Protestant group, called the Anabaptists, lived by an even stricter moral code than that of the Calvinists. The Anabaptist movement began in Zurich, Switzerland, around 1525 among a group of dissatisfied followers of Ulrich Zwingli. They believed that the state was made up of sinners. Therefore, the Anabaptists believed, true Christians should withdraw from the state and form a separate community.

The reforms were expressed in different ways. New rules were made to help rid the Catholic church of any abuses. New religious orders were made up of believers who agreed to follow special rules, like the monks of the Middle Ages. One such order was the Jesuits. They took vows of poverty and swore to obey the Pope. Jesuits focused their efforts on education and missionary work.

The Catholic church also tried to stop the spread of Protestantism with the Inquisition *(ihn kwih ZIHSH uhn)*. An **Inquisition** was a Catholic church court. People suspected of being heretics, or nonbelievers, were brought to trial. Many Jewish and Muslim believers were tried as well. Those who were believed to be guilty but refused to admit their wrongdoings were sometimes tortured or sentenced to death. However, no reforms or harsh measures could stop the spread of Protestantism.

Europe Is Divided

During the late 1500s and early 1600s, religious beliefs began to divide the people of Europe. In the north, England, Denmark, Sweden, and parts of Germany and the Netherlands became Protestant. In the south, Spain, France, and Italy remained Catholic. Use the map on this page to see how religion divided Europe. Then compare this map with the Atlas map of religions today on page 688.

Loyalty to the state often meant having the same religion as the ruler. In Spain, England, Russia, and elsewhere, religious differences would lead to violent conflict. You will read about some of these conflicts in the next chapter. ■

The Spread of Protestantism, c. 1560

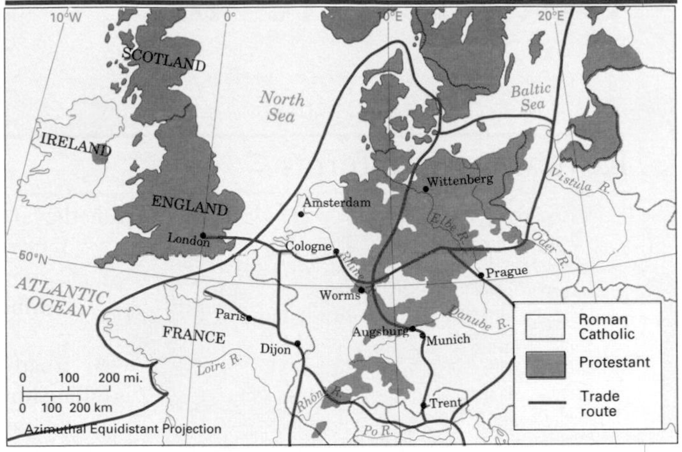
10°W
0°
10°E
20°E
SCOTLAND
North Sea
Baltic Sea
IRELAND
ENGLAND
London
Amsterdam
Wittenberg
Vistula R.
Elbe R.
Oder R.
Cologne
Prague
60°N
ATLANTIC OCEAN
Worms
Paris
FRANCE
Dijon
Augsburg
Munich
Danube R.
Loire R.
Trent
Po R.
0 100 200 mi.
0 100 200 km
Azimuthal Equidistant Projection
Roman Catholic
Protestant
Trade route

▲ *This map shows how religious beliefs divided Europe. Which countries were mostly Protestant in 1560? Which were mostly Catholic?*

◄ *Turn this woodcut portrait upside down to see what Luther's enemies thought about him.*

■ *Why did the Reformation spread?*

REVIEW

1. **FOCUS** What were the causes and the effects of the Reformation?
2. **HISTORY** What role did the printing press play in the Reformation? How does this compare with its role in the Renaissance?
3. **BELIEF SYSTEMS** Why did Martin Luther want to reform the Catholic church? How did the Catholic church respond to the Reformation?
4. **CRITICAL THINKING** Why did the Reformation divide Europe?
5. **ACTIVITY** Think of something you would like to reform or change in your community. For example, should your community recycle more than it does? Write your ideas on the topic and post them on a bulletin board. As in Luther's time, invite other students to debate you and exchange ideas.

◄ *Mostly Protestant countries included England and Scotland, as well as Denmark, Norway, and Sweden. Mostly Catholic countries included France. Germany and the Netherlands were both split into Protestant and Catholic regions.*

■ *Many people agreed with Luther's ideas. In addition, the printing press helped to spread the Reformation.*

CLOSE

Guide students through the Graphic Overviews they completed during the lesson. Then ask for examples of Martin Luther's objections to Church practices. *(The sale of indulgences, the publication of the Bible only in Latin)*

Have students discuss the Thinking Focus. Encourage students to elaborate on the effects of the Reformation. *(The northern part of Europe became mainly Protestant; several different Protestant churches were founded; the Roman Catholic church responded with new orders and with a renewed Inquisition.)*

Answers to Review Questions

1. The Reformation arose out of objections to Roman Catholic church practices such as selling indulgences. The result was the formation of Protestant churches.
2. The printing press helped spread the new ideas of the Reformation and enabled more people to read the Bible. In the Renaissance, too, it helped spread new ideas throughout Europe.
3. Luther believed that many Roman Catholic church practices had strayed from what was taught in the Bible. The Church made new rules to help avoid abuses, formed new religious orders, and renewed the Inquisition.
4. Europe divided between mainly Catholic and Protestant countries.
5. Be sure that students' positions are well-supported. For the recycling issue, some may state that there are already enough laws for recycling. Others may feel that more recycling is needed to reduce waste.

Homework Options

Suggest that students look at the woodcut of Martin Luther on this page. Mention that cartoonists often poke fun at public figures. Have students look in newspapers and magazines for a cartoon that makes fun of a current public figure. Ask them to bring in copies of cartoons to share with the class.

Study Guide: page 75

Anwers to Reviewing Key Terms

A. Sample answers:

1. **Clergy (**Latin word *cléricus,* meaning "clerk, cleric"). The clergy were the priests, archbishops and bishops, and cardinals, in the Church.
2. **Monastery** (Greek word *monazein,* meaning "to live alone"). A monastery is a religious community of monks.
3. **Tithe** (Old English word *téotha,* meaning "tenth"). A tithe was paid to support the Church.
4. **Crusade (**Latin word *crux,* or *cruc,* meaning "cross"). The crusades were campaigns fought against Muslims.
5. **Indulgence** (Latin word *indulgére,* meaning "to be kind to, to yield to"). Indulgences were sold as pardons for sins.
6. **Inquisition** (Latin word *inquírere,* meaning "to inquire"). The Inquisition was a Church court.

B. Sample answers:

1. Both **knights** and **vassals** served as soldiers in feudal society.
2. **Serfs** belonged to the **manor,** which included the land and everything on it.
3. A **humanist** was a person who studied the **classics,** the works of ancient Greece and Rome.
4. The **Protestant** movement to reform the Church became known as the **Reformation.**
5. Increased trade helped spread the **plague** throughout Europe. At the same time, trade helped spark the **Renaissance.**
6. **Patrons** gave financial aid to the artists of the **Renaissance.**

Answers to Exploring Concepts

A. Sample answers:

Cause(s) Germanic tribes divide Europe, and the Church provides people with a common faith. People look to strong rulers to protect them from invaders.

Effect(s): The Church splits into the Roman Catholic church and the Eastern Orthodox church. Peasants, knights, and other European Christians join the Crusades.

B. Sample answers:

1. People depended on the Church for their daily spiritual and practical needs.
2. The two empires differed in the languages used for worship. Byzantine Christians recognized the Byzantine emperor, not the Pope, as head of the Church.
3. Because there were no strong governments, people relied on local leaders.
4. Most people in the Middle Ages were serfs. Without them, feudalism would not have survived.
5. Church leaders promised that anyone killed on a crusade would go to heaven.
6. Trade brought wealth and new ideas to Europe. It also spread the Plague.
7. Many Renaissance scholars and artists wanted to recapture the spirit of the classics.
8. People in the lower classes remained poor. Unskilled workers had no say in running the government or the powerful guilds.
9. Wealthy patrons bid against each other for the services of artists and teachers.
10. In the Middle Ages, most people did not expect life to improve. During the Renaissance, their hopes were raised.
11. For example, Martin Luther questioned the practice of selling indulgences, and John Calvin wanted to simplify worship.
12. The printing press made books more accessible to a wider audience.

Chapter Review

Reviewing Key Terms

classics (p. 426)
clergy (p. 411)
crusades (p. 416)
humanist (p. 426)
indulgence (p. 430)
Inquisition (p. 433)
knight (p. 416)
manor (p. 415)
monastery (p. 411)
patron (p. 425)
plague (p. 418)
Protestant (p. 431)
Reformation (p. 431)
Renaissance (p. 424)
serf (p. 415)
tithe (p. 411)
vassal (p. 415)

A. Use a dictionary to find the origins of the following words. Write down the earliest origin given. Then, write a sentence or two explaining how the meaning of each word applies to the medieval Catholic church.

1. clergy
2. monastery
3. tithe
4. crusades
5. indulgence
6. Inquisition

B. Read each pair of words. Write a sentence telling how the words in each pair are related.

1. knight, vassal
2. serf, manor
3. humanist, classics
4. Protestant, Reformation
5. Renaissance, plague
6. patrons, Renaissance

Exploring Concepts

A. From 476 to 1600, a series of momentous events rocked Europe. Copy the following chart. Then, complete it by writing the cause(s) or effect(s) for the events listed. Use the timeline on pages 408–409 to help you.

Cause(s)	Effect(s)
	The Church becomes very powerful.
Byzantine Christians disagree with the western church on many issues.	
	Feudalism develops in Europe.
The Seljuk Turks capture the Holy Land.	

B. Support each of the following statements with information from the chapter.

1. During the Middle Ages, the Church was the center of the community.
2. The eastern church split from the western church because of several disagreements.
3. Because of people's need for protection, feudalism developed in Europe.
4. Serfs were the backbone of feudalism.
5. Many Christians in Europe were eager to join the crusades.
6. Trade brought many new things to Europe, some good, some bad.
7. Learning about the ancient past helped inspire the Renaissance.
8. The Renaissance had little effect on the lives of people in the lower classes.
9. Wealth, and competition among the leading families in Italy, helped to fuel the Renaissance.
10. The Renaissance changed the way some Europeans looked at their life and their place in the world.
11. Reformers questioned the teachings and practices of the Catholic church.
12. The printing press helped spread the ideas of the Renaissance and the Reformation all over Europe.

Reviewing Skills

1. Write a hypothesis that answers these questions: Why did the Catholic church punish Martin Luther? Why wasn't there an open discussion of his ideas? Use the four-step process on page 419 to test your hypothesis.
2. Reread the passage from Martin Luther's *Ninety-Five Theses* on page 430. What is Luther's main idea, or most important point? Which statements, in the passage or from your reading, support Luther's main idea?
3. Imagine that you are writing a report about various Protestant groups. What information would you include in your report? What topics would you select to compare the different groups?

Using Critical Thinking

1. During the Middle Ages, building a cathedral took a great deal of time and money. Why might people have devoted so much time and energy to the project?
2. The word *renaissance* means "rebirth." In what ways was the Renaissance both a rebirth of classical learning and a rebirth of interest in new ideas? Give examples from your reading.
3. During the Renaissance, a middle class of shop owners and skilled workers emerged. Do you think this was an important development? Explain.
4. Wealthy patrons, many of whom were rulers of Italian city-states, supported artists during the Renaissance. Do you think the government should support the arts today? Give several reasons to support your response.
5. In the 1500s Martin Luther and other reformers hoped to change the Catholic church for the better. Today, many reformers hope to improve governments, businesses, and other institutions around the world. Name two reformers who are active today. What are their goals? Compare these reformers with Luther. How are they alike and how are they different?

Preparing for Citizenship

1. **WRITING ACTIVITY** Michelangelo, Leonardo da Vinci, and Christine de Pizan excelled in the arts. Who do you think is an excellent writer, artist, or builder today? Write a review of the person's work. Be sure to include details that support your opinions about him or her.
2. **COLLECTING INFORMATION** During the Renaissance, Europeans read books by authors such as Cennino Cennini. Europeans wanted to learn all they could about good manners, human achievement, and personal growth. What people do you turn to for advice about life? Make a list of the people and the resources that are available to you. Share the list with your classmates.
3. **ARTS ACTIVITY** In many of his paintings, Pieter Bruegel told stories of everyday life. Create a painting, a sculpture, or a collage that shows a part of everyday life in your community. Write a title for your work. Display your work of art in your classroom.
4. **COLLABORATIVE LEARNING** During the Renaissance, carpenters and other skilled workers belonged to guilds, or unions. Form small groups. Have each group give a presentation on a modern labor union. Divide the following tasks among the members of each group: (a) research the history of the union, (b) find out about the benefits the union offers workers, (c) investigate the problems the union faces today, and (d) interview one or more members of the union (or a similar union in your community). Then, as a group, present your report to the class.

Answers to Reviewing Skills

1. Possible hypothesis: The Church punished Luther to demonstrate how it would deal with critics.
2. Luther's main idea is that the Church is too concerned with worldly affairs. Students may cite Luther's statement that the Pope "would do better to sell St. Peter's . . . ."
3. Students should include information about each group's history, beliefs, and worship service. Topics for comparison might include each group's founders and basic rituals.

Answers to Using Critical Thinking

1. Many of the workers must have found spiritual fulfillment in the work. The work gave many the opportunity to earn money.
2. Humanists wanted to recreate classical styles and use old ideas to create something new. For example, Brunelleschi studied ancient ruins in Rome and then built a dome for the Florence cathedral.
3. Students may note that as the middle class grew, its influence on government and economic affairs increased.
4. Some students may suggest that private individuals alone cannot support the arts. Others may suggest that government support leads to censorship.
5. Students may name political leaders, consumer rights advocates, or local community leaders. Their goals may include achieving political rights for people or improving product safety. Similarities to Luther may include trying to publicize dissatisfaction with an institution in order to change it. Differences may include the methods reformers use to bring about change.

Answers to Preparing for Citizenship

1. **WRITING ACTIVITY** Suggest that students identify local or nationally recognized artists, such as best-selling authors.
2. **COLLECTING INFORMATION** Encourage students to think of specific times when they have needed help and the people who have helped them. Suggest that they also look for books and magazine articles that offer advice to readers.
3. **ARTS ACTIVITY** Refer students to the Bruegel painting, *The Peasant Dance,* on page 428. Encourage students to think of an appropriate title for their work.
4. **COLLABORATIVE LEARNING** Encourage students to divide the four tasks equally among their group members. Have them consult the library resources for information.

CHAPTER ORGANIZER

Chapter 19 The Rise of Spain, Great Britain, and Russia

CHAPTER PLANNING CHART

Pupil's Edition	Teacher's Edition	Ancillaries
Lesson 1: Spain: The First Modern Empire (2–3 days) Objective 1: Explain how Isabella and Ferdinand helped unite Spain. (History 5; Social and Political Systems 1, 2) Objective 2: Explain how Spain built its empire. (History 5; Social and Political Systems 5, 6) Objective 3: Describe Spain's leading role in the Columbian exchange. (Geography 4; Economics 4)	• Graphic Overview (438) • Access Strategy (439) • Access Activity (439) • Visual Learning (440) Historical Context (440) Political Context (441) Collaborative Learning (441) Critical Thinking (441, 442) Language Arts Connection (442)	Study Guide (76) Map Activities (23) Discovery Journal (39)
Lesson 2: Great Britain's Sea Empire (2–3 days) Objective 1: Explain how Great Britain built its empire. (History 5; Social and Political Systems 5, 6) Objective 2: Describe how the industrial revolution changed daily life. (History 3; Culture 2) Objective 3: Explain how Great Britain's empire declined. (History 6)	• Graphic Overview (444) • Access Strategy (445) • Access Activity (445) • Visual Learning (446) Economic Context (446) Collaborative Learning (446) Language Arts Connection (447) Political Context (447) Critical Thinking (447) Map and Globe Skills (448) Writing a Report (448) Reader's Theater (449) Research (449) • Visual Learning (449)	Study Guide (77) Map Activities (23) Discovery Journal (40)
Understanding Graphic Information Objective: Make and read different kinds of graphs and select the appropriate graph for displaying information. (Visual Learning 2)		Study Guide (78)
Lesson 3 : Russia's Land Empire (2–3 days) Objective 1: Explain how Russia's geography influenced its people. (Geography 3, 4) Objective 2: Describe the rise of the Russian state. (Social and Political Systems 5, 6) Objective 3: Describe the changes that Peter and Catherine began in Russia. (Culture 1, 2)	• Graphic Overview (452) • Access Strategy (453) • Access Activity (453) Critical Thinking (454) Cultural Context (454)	Study Guide (79) • Posters (3)
Chapter Review	Answers (456–457)	Tests (73–76)

* Objectives are correlated to the strands and goals in the program Scope and Sequence on pages T41–T49.

• LEP appropriate resources. (For additional strategies, see pages T32–T33.)

CHAPTER RATIONALE

Chapter 19 introduces students to the rise of three empires—Spain, Great Britain, and Russia—in the post-Reformation period. A map and chart strand throughout each lesson allows students to compare the sizes, areas colonized, reasons for empire-building, and items imported from the colonies of each empire. Spain and Great Britain, discussed in the first two lessons, expanded their empires to control large areas outside Europe. Russia's empire is treated in the final lesson, because its development and character are decidedly distinct from those of its western neighbors.

Lesson 1 begins by describing the process by which Spain became united, laying the foundation for a discussion of Spain's exploration and expansion around the globe. This exploration led to Columbus's voyage to the West Indies and the resulting Columbian exchange. A chart illustrating this exchange and a feature on colonialism reveal different perspectives on colonization. Students learn to look at the Columbian exchange through the eyes of both the colonizers and the colonized.

An eyewitness account of the Spanish Armada begins **Lesson 2,** leading to a discussion of the shift in power between Spain and England that this event marked. Students discover that France alone stood as a rival to Great Britain's overseas colonization and that the French were forced to withdraw from the world stage after being defeated by the English in a series of wars in Europe and North America. The lesson then examines the dramatic social and economic changes unleashed by the Industrial Revolution. Students learn that though not everyone benefited from these changes, they were nonetheless felt throughout Britain and the world. A skill feature and A Closer Look reinforce students' understanding of the immense size of Britain's empire.

From Great Britain the students move on to a brief survey of the rise of the Russian Empire in **Lesson 3.** They quickly discover that Russia's rise is quite different from that of the other empires in the chapter. The lesson chronicles Russia's domination by foreign powers and its efforts at modernizing, as the empire expands around its borders rather than overseas. Lesson 3 concludes by observing that the gap between Russia's upper classes and the common people would later bring about a collapse of Russian society.

ACTIVITIES & PROJECTS

Basic: Interviewing

Assign one student to take the role of talk show host, and cast several other students as famous figures from the chapter—Christopher Columbus, Queen Isabella, William Henry Fox Talbot, Rudyard Kipling, Charles Darwin, Marianne North, Ivan III, Peter the Great, and Catherine the Great. Have the host interview each figure about his or her major accomplishments. Why did they do what they did? What were their goals? Direct students to stress the excitement, danger, or uniqueness of their accomplishments when answering the host. (Use after any lesson.)

LEP: Drawing

Have students draw a picture of a Spanish ship or an English ship unloading its cargo after a trip from the Americas. Students should draw some of the plants and animals that were sent to Europe as a result of the Columbian exchange. (Use after Lesson 2.)

Bulletin Board

Have students make an illustrated chart of famous people who lived in Spain, Great Britain, and Russia as each empire grew. Suggest that they collect information from their text as well as from outside sources such as encyclopedias, biographies, or nonfiction books. The chart should include each famous person's name, birthplace, birth and death dates, and achievements. Display the chart on the bulletin board and have students add to it each day. (Use after any lesson.)

Collaborative Learning

Have students work together to create crossword puzzles. Divide the class into four groups, and assign each group the task of designing a puzzle and developing a list of clues and answers. Each puzzle should have a theme drawn from the chapter, such as exploration, colonization, the Columbian exchange, famous figures, or the Industrial Revolution. Have groups exchange their puzzles and compete to see which group can solve its puzzle first. (Use after any lesson.)

Challenge: Debate

Encourage all students to take part in an open debate on the following statement: Colonialism benefited the colonizers and the colonized people equally. Have students use information from the text to back up their arguments. (Use after Lesson 2.)

LEP: Role-Playing

Divide students into groups of five or six people. Select one person from each group to pick an important figure from the chapter and assume the identity of that person. Then have the other members in each group try to determine who that person is by asking the student up to 20 questions that can be answered yes or no. The student who guesses correctly chooses a new identity and becomes the role player. (Use after any lesson.)

CHAPTER PREVIEW

Have students read the chapter title and the paragraph following it. Ask students to examine the visuals on these pages and identify which pertain to each empire. *(Painting—Spain; Bristol, watch, and emu—Great Britain; Church of the Annunciation—Russia)* Discuss how the visuals represent the changes that took place in Europe as these empires developed.

Looking Back

Remind students of how the Protestant Reformation transformed Europe. Have them recall the religions of Great Britain and Spain. *(Great Britain—Protestant; Spain—Catholic)* Ask them which form of Christianity was followed in Russia. *(Eastern Orthodox)*

Looking Forward

Inform students that in the next three lessons—Spain: The First Modern Empire; Great Britain's Sea Empire; and Russia's Land Empire—they will read about how these three nations established extensive empires.

Lesson 1 describes the formation, decline, and lasting influence of the Spanish empire.

Chapter 19
The Rise of Spain, Great Britain, and Russia

The period after the Reformation was a stormy time in Europe. Catholics and Protestants fought for their beliefs. Kings and queens plotted against their enemies. Spain, Great Britain, and Russia each built enormous empires. Meanwhile, European explorers sailed across uncharted waters and claimed new lands. The New World was colonized and a "revolution" began to change the old one.

Christopher Columbus set sail from Spain and landed in the West Indies in 1492. This painting shows Columbus and King Ferdinand of Spain kneeling at the feet of the Virgin Mary as she blesses them and their ships.

800	1040	1280

436

800

988 Kievan Prince Vladimir I becomes an Orthodox Christian. He begins a tradition of deep religious devotion among the Russian people. The Church of the Annunciation (above), built in the 15th century, is a lasting symbol of Russia's religious heritage.

BACKGROUND

The years between 1500 and 1900 witnessed the transformation of Europe from a patchwork of hundreds of separate kingdoms into the beginnings of the countries people recognize today. This ...sformation was not without ...er between compet- ... between

Motives for Expansion

In many respects, the Renaissance set the stage for European exploration. The rediscovery of classical texts, such as Ptolemy's *Geography,* encouraged speculation about the shape and size of the world.

Commercial interests spurred the search for new lands. As the demand for eastern imports grew in Europe, explorers sought alternate routes to Asia, resulting in the European exploration of the Americas. Since the voyages of exploration were designed to find new sources of wealth, countries jealously competed with one another for overseas territories. Early Spanish, Portuguese, and French explorers were also motivated by religious concerns. They sought to convert people to Christianity.

Spain in the New World

Spanish exploration of the Americas began with high hopes—to bring the true God to non-Christians—but ended in disillusion. Spain's rulers through the 16th and 17th centuries saw themselves as the defenders of the Catholic faith. They defended that faith in

At the height of its empire, Great Britain became known as the workshop of the world. Goods and resources flowed between Britain and the rest of the world through busy ports like this one in Bristol, England.

The Industrial Revolution affected all aspects of life, including the way people kept track of time. This 18th-century British watch shows how workers, who once measured their labor in terms of crops and seasons, adapted to the strict schedule of the modern workday.

1588 The Spanish Armada is defeated by the English navy and unfavorable winds in the English Channel.

1770 James Cook of the British navy sights and explores Australia.

1891 Work begins on the Trans-Siberian Railroad in Russia.

1520 | 1760 | 2000

1867 Russia sells Alaska to the United States.

Plants and animals such as the Australian emu were unfamiliar and fascinating to European explorers.

Today

Understanding the Visuals

The picture of the Virgin Mary, on the facing page, is titled *Madonna of the Navigators* and was painted by Alejo Fernández. With Columbus and King Ferdinand at the Madonna's feet are Amerigo Vespucci (for whom America is named) and the Pinzón brothers, who accompanied Columbus on his first voyage.

The Church of the Annunciation was built of stone on the site of an older, wooden church. The cupolas of the cathedral are designed in the tradition of Byzantine architecture.

Direct students' attention to the watch on this page, and then to the smaller circle used for the second hand. During the 18th century, the need to determine longitude at sea stimulated the invention of accurate timepieces.

Understanding Chronology

Ask students to examine the timeline and the images. Note that the Russian Empire grew with little or no interference from other European powers during the period indicated by the timeline.

numerous battles across Europe, paid for with gold from their American colonies. In the end, this zeal to keep Europe Catholic weakened Spain and ultimately helped bring about the demise of its empire.

The Glory That Was the British Empire

In contrast, the British Empire was founded not so much on religious zeal as on economic aspirations. As the British developed technologically, they sought both more markets and more raw materials to fuel their economy. These economic goals brought Great Britain into a number of conflicts with Spain and France.

By the early 1800s, Great Britain emerged as an economic giant due to the enormous changes unleashed by the Industrial Revolution. Starting in the cotton-textile industry, the revolution transformed Britain's economy and culture.

A Vast Empire to the East

Although Russia was geographically vast, it was less economically advanced than the empires to the west. Russia was an agrarian society with little industrial development. However, Russia coveted the role of world power and expanded to gain lands and resources in an effort to modernize its economy.

INTRODUCE

Point out the lesson title and review the concept of empire building. Ask students to recall other empires that they have read about. *(Examples include Alexander's Greek empire and the Aztec, Inca, Roman, Persian, and Mongol empires.)* Have students explain what is common to all empires. *(One political body reaches beyond its borders to control other peoples.)*

Have students read the Thinking Focus. Ask them to determine why a country might build an empire. Then direct them to read the lesson to discover whether their predictions were correct.

Key Terms

Vocabulary Strategies: T36–T37

converso—a Spanish Jew who converted to Christianity

Reconquista—the reconquest of the Iberian Peninsula from the Muslims

colonialism—the policy by which one country occupies another and controls its people, politics, and economy

Columbian exchange—the movement of people, goods, culture, and ideas between the Americas, Europe, Asia, and Africa

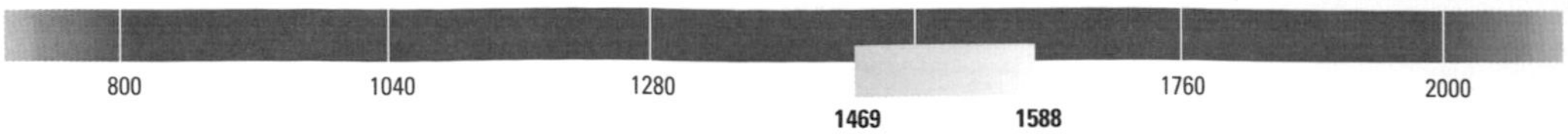

800
1040
1280
1469
1588
1760
2000

L E S S O N 1

Spain: The First Modern Empire

THINKING FOCUS

What did the Spanish people gain and lose by building an empire?

Key Terms

- converso
- Reconquista
- colonialism
- Columbian exchange

It is an October morning in 1469. Eighteen-year-old Princess Isabella of Castile *(kas TEEL)* and seventeen-year-old Prince Ferdinand of Aragon are about to make history. They will soon be married against the wishes of Castile's King Henry IV, Isabella's half brother.

King Henry has ideas of his own about whom Isabella should marry. He wants her to choose between Charles, the brother of the king of France, and Alfonso, the king of Portugal.

However, Isabella has no interest in either of these men. She does not want her kingdom controlled by either France or Portugal. Nor does she want to marry an older man, especially one as old as King Alfonso. He merely wants a queen to bear his children—most important, a male heir. Isabella wants to be a ruler herself. She has made sure of that by drawing up a marriage contract that protects all of her rights as a ruler. Alfonso would never allow it. Ferdinand has already agreed to her terms.

If Isabella marries Ferdinand, they can unite their two kingdoms. One day she hopes to unite all the Spanish peninsula to create one of the strongest crowns in Europe.

➤ *The marriage of Ferdinand and Isabella was the first step toward Spain's becoming an empire.*

Although Isabella is young and inexperienced, she is also intelligent and strong willed. She knows that her choice of a husband is very important; kingdoms are united and allied through royal marriages.

Isabella succeeded in the first step of her plan. She married Ferdinand before her brother could halt the wedding. The question remained, however, as to what kind of a kingdom she and Ferdinand would create and who would be allowed to live in it.

Objectives

1. Explain how Isabella and Ferdinand helped unite Spain.
2. Explain how Spain built its empire.
3. Describe Spain's leading role in the Columbian exchange.

Graphic Overview

Spain Unites Iberian Peninsula → Columbus Claims the Americas for Spain → Columbian Exchange Begins → Spanish Empire Declines

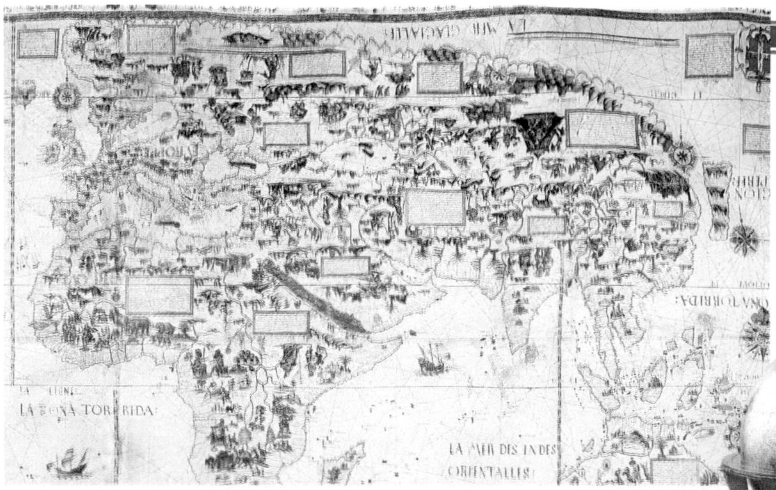

◄ *This map shows the world as it was known in 1546. A united Spain hoped to lead and dominate it.*

▲ *Muslims made many valuable contributions to Spain and Spanish culture. This 12th century celestial globe was made in Persia and aided the Spaniards in their explorations.*

Uniting Spain

Isabella and Ferdinand were determined to make Spain a completely Catholic, united state. To do this, they needed to wrest the kingdom of Granada, to the south, from the control of the Muslims from North Africa. Spain also wanted to drive all Jews, Muslims, and **conversos,** Jews who had converted to Christianity, out of Spain.

The Reconquista

Isabella and Ferdinand needed to capture Granada, the last Muslim stronghold in Spain. They led their armies in the **Reconquista,** or reconquering of the peninsula. Finally, in 1492, the Spanish rulers captured Granada.

The Spanish Inquisition

Some Christians worried that the *conversos* were a threat. They thought some *conversos* had converted only so they could hold offices that were barred to Jews. In reaction to this fear, Isabella and Ferdinand set the Spanish Inquisition in motion. People who were suspected of being non-Catholic were examined. Suspects were sometimes tortured. Several thousand *conversos* and many Muslims who claimed to have converted were persecuted.

In 1492 Ferdinand and Isabella drove out all Jews who refused to be baptized. More than 100,000 Spanish citizens left the country. However, many Jews remained in Spain and became Catholics. Many others returned to Spain later and converted.

By 1492 Isabella's dream of a unified Spain was becoming a reality. For the first time in centuries, efforts to make Spain a unified Catholic state were beginning to show results. ■

◄ *Before the Inquisition, many Spanish Jews were successful merchants, doctors, and scholars. In this picture a wealthy Jew distributes food to the poor.*

■ *What did Ferdinand and Isabella do to unify Spain?*

DEVELOP

Discuss with students Isabella and Ferdinand's goals of uniting the kingdoms of Aragon and Castille and becoming a single Catholic nation. Use the Graphic Overview to focus students' attention on the rise and decline of the Spanish empire. Have students copy the Graphic Overview flow chart on a separate piece of paper. As they read the lesson, have students list supporting details under each part of the flow chart.

HISTORY

Map and Globe Skills

Have students look at the map of Europe in 1546 on this page and compare it with the world map in the Atlas on pages 678–679. How accurate was the 1546 map? *(The 1546 map was fairly accurate as far as Europe was concerned, but Africa and Asia were still largely uncharted; there was no knowledge of North and South America.)*

■ *Ferdinand and Isabella united Castile and Aragon, drove the Muslims out of Granada, and began the Spanish Inquisition to rid the country of all non-Catholics.*

Access Strategy

Ask students to imagine that two large objects in the classroom (possibly a desk and a lectern) are separate continents. Have students use their imaginations to list on the chalkboard the plants and animals that populate each "continent." Ask a volunteer to list the names of the plants and animals of each continent on the chalkboard as other students dictate their ideas. Then stage a visit by a few people from one continent to another. Ask students to suggest the changes that might occur as the visits from continent to continent grew more frequent. *(People learn about other peoples' way of life; some plants and animals are transplanted.)*

Lead into the lesson by telling students that this kind of exchange occurred as a result of Spain's empire building; it was called the Columbian exchange, and it radically changed the world.

Access Activity

Have students examine the visual of the Spanish explorer on page 440. Discuss the dress and other aspects of Spanish culture that the explorer took to the Americas. Speculate with students how Spanish culture differed from the cultures already in the Americas. Ask them to imagine how the native peoples felt upon seeing these Europeans.

ETHICS

Study Skills

Create a chart that describes the advantages and disadvantages of colonialism to both the colonizing country and the colonized peoples. *(Colonizing country, advantages: get raw materials and market for products, place to spread ideas and religion, learn new ideas; disadvantages: become dependent on colonies for health of economy, bear cost of defending and governing colonies. Colonized peoples, advantages: learn new ideas; disadvantages: loss of freedom, culture damaged, dependent on other country for economy, must live under imposed rules)*

ECONOMICS

Critical Thinking

Tell students that the actual total cash expense of Columbus's expedition was 1,167,542 maravedis (the currency of the period). The Spanish monarchs paid one million maravedis, and Columbus paid the rest. Ask students why it took King Ferdinand and Queen Isabella eight years to approve the release of funds for his expedition. *(They were busy with the Reconquista; the costs of fighting the Moors was heavy; they may not have been motivated yet to begin overseas exploration.)*

Building an Empire

With the conquest of Granada, Ferdinand and Isabella concentrated their energies on overseas expansion. They wanted to catch up with rival Portugal, which now led the European world in trade, navigation, and exploration. If Spain could match Portugal's successes, Spain would have to seek its own trade routes and establish its own overseas contacts and colonies. Read Understanding Colonialism below to discover more about colonies.

➤ *Spanish explorers followed Columbus to the Americas to seek their fortunes, to claim land for the Spanish Crown, and to spread Christianity.*

The Voyages of Columbus

Shortly after the defeat of the Muslims, the Italian seaman Christopher Columbus reached an agreement with Queen Isabella. Columbus would sail west and seek a shorter route to Asia. The Spanish monarchs would fund his expedition. As payment for a successful

UNDERSTANDING COLONIALISM

Spain, Portugal, France, England, and the Netherlands were all once great colonial powers. They had colonies in North, South, and Central America as well as Asia, Africa, and the islands in the Pacific.

What Is Colonialism?

Colonialism means that one country occupies another and controls its people, politics, and economy. Colonies were not free to make their own decisions.

Why did the European powers seek colonies? Is colonialism practiced today?

Reasons for Colonialism

Colonies gave the European powers added territory, natural resources, and cheap labor. Since colonies were under a European nation's control, the land, the resources, and the labor of the colonists were used to benefit the ruling country rather than the colony itself.

Most colonial powers believed they were helping the people they had colonized by bringing them Christianity or ideas of Western civilization. However, this view also served to justify their often cruel or unjust treatment of the colonized peoples.

Colonialism Today

Nearly all the colonies of European nations have now won their independence and are recognized as nations themselves. Some made this transition without violence; others had to fight for it. Colonialism is considered wrong today, but many of the economies of less developed countries are still controlled by the industrialized nations. In this way colonialism is still occurring throughout the world.

Visual Learning

Ask students to look through pages 436–443 for illustrations that have to do with Spain. Have students make a list of these illustrations. Then have them select the two illustrations that they think best symbolize the Spanish Empire. Have them share their choices with the class, giving reasons for their selections.

Historical Context

To commemorate the 500th anniversary of Columbus's first transatlantic voyage, Spanish authorities commissioned the construction of replicas of Columbus's ships—the *Niña, Pinta,* and *Santa Maria*—and re-created the voyage from Spain to the Americas. Only Columbus's description of the ships guided the shipbuilders.

After the replicas were completed, one of the shipbuilders said, "We could re-create the tools, the ships, the rigs, but we could not re-create what went on in Columbus's mind. We knew too well where we were going." Not everyone wanted to celebrate Columbus's voyage. Some people pointed out that people were already living in the Americas when Columbus arrived and that the Europeans brought disease and slavery there. On the other hand, many people agree that the Americas could not have remained isolated: if not Columbus, another explorer would have sailed to the Americas.

voyage, Columbus would receive a title, knighthood, and a share of any wealth that he discovered.

In 1492 Columbus reached the West Indies. Upon his return to Spain, rumors spread that the lands he had explored were rich with gold. This news attracted many Spanish fortune seekers to the Americas.

The Empire Grows

Armed adventurers and colonizers poured out of Spain. Most were from poor families. They claimed most of the Caribbean Islands, Panama, Florida, Mexico, Peru, and then much of South America for Spain. In less than 50 years, these explorers had seized for Spain territories that were about the size of the Roman Empire at its height.

The Spanish monarchs did not trust all of these adventurers. These bold fighters were very likely to set up governorships of their own. Colonists and administrators were quickly sent to make sure the new conquests remained under the Crown's control and were well run. Plantations were set up to grow sugar cane and other crops for export to Europe. With native labor, they built cities, towns, and churches in the Spanish style. By 1540 the first printing presses and universities in the Western Hemisphere were quickly established in Santo Domingo and Mexico City.

By the middle of the 1500s, Spain's empire included wide holdings in North, Central, and South America. The map of Spain's empire below shows the full extent of Spanish colonization. Spain also controlled what is now the Netherlands and Belgium as well as parts of France, Italy, Austria, and Germany. ■

▲ *These coins, called pieces of eight, were made in Mexico for use in Asia. They show the vastness of the Spanish Empire in the 16th and 17th centuries.*

◄ *In what regions did most of Spain's overseas trade activity take place?*

Spanish Empire, c. 1600

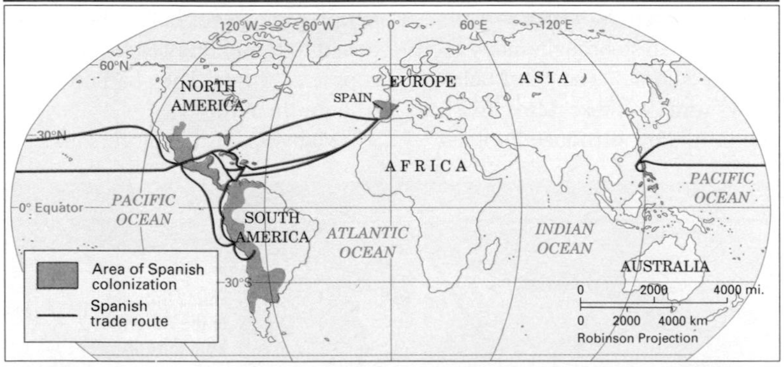
120°W
60°W
0°
60°E
120°E
60°N
30°N
0° Equator
30°S
NORTH AMERICA
SPAIN
EUROPE
ASIA
AFRICA
PACIFIC OCEAN
SOUTH AMERICA
ATLANTIC OCEAN
INDIAN OCEAN
PACIFIC OCEAN
AUSTRALIA
Area of Spanish colonization
Spanish trade route
0 2000 4000 mi.
0 2000 4000 km
Robinson Projection

Spanish Empire, 1492–1898

Reasons for Empire	Imports from Spanish Colonies
Seek private profit, increase national wealth, spread Christianity	Silver, gold, copper, grain, tobacco, cocoa beans, hides, sugar

■ *What was the extent of Spain's empire by the end of the 1500s?*

GEOGRAPHY

Map and Globe Skills

Direct students' attention to the map on this page, and have them locate Spain. Then ask them to categorize Spain's overseas possessions or areas of control by continent. Have them use the scale to determine the distance between Spain and Mexico. *(Roughly 5,000 miles)* Have them tell whether most of Spain's possessions fell in the Eastern or Western Hemisphere. *(Western)*

◄ *Most of Spain's overseas trade activity took place in Central and South America.*

■ *The empire included wide holdings throughout the Americas as well as what are now the Netherlands and Belgium; parts of France, Italy, Austria, and Germany were also part of the empire.*

Political Context

During Spain's pursuit of its empire, it competed with Portugal, which was establishing its own colonial empire. As a result of a series of papal bulls issued by Pope Alexander VI, a Spaniard, Spain and Portugal concluded the Treaty of Tordesillas in 1494. This treaty created an imaginary line in the Atlantic Ocean to divide areas of exploration between Spain and Portugal. Other European nations, such as England and the Netherlands, which were not Catholic, saw no reason to obey the Pope.

Collaborative Learning

Have students work in groups to research legends that spurred explorers or scientists to venture into unknown regions. Suggested legends include Prester John, the Fountain of Youth, El Dorado, and the Holy Grail. Then, have each group write a legend of its own to describe the "wonders" or "mysteries" of another land. Groups can read their legends aloud to the class.

Critical Thinking

Have students review the way Spain built its empire. Then have them brainstorm to suggest problems Spain may have encountered in establishing colonies. *(Possible answers include the unwillingness of Native Americans to be ruled by Spain, the distance from Spain, and the headstrong nature of the explorers.)*

CULTURE

Visual Learning

Have students examine the chart of the Columbian exchange on this page and explain which plants came from Europe and which came from the Americas. Then have them use information from the text to create another visual incorporating other plants and goods that were exchanged. Ask students to include ideas that were involved in the Columbian exchange in their drawing. *(To the Americas: horses, cows, pigs, sheep, many of Spain's brightest citizens, diseases, Christianity; to Europe: chocolate, avocados, tobacco, timber, silver, gold)*

BELIEF SYSTEMS

Critical Thinking

Have students imagine that they are Spanish missionaries sent to convert the Native Americans. When they arrive in the Americas, they find that the native peoples are being badly mistreated. Have students write accounts of what they have seen, to be read by people in Spain. The accounts should express outrage over this treatment of the Native Americans and call for action on the part of the Spanish people and government. Have students read their accounts to the class.

The Columbian Exchange

▲ *This 15th-century cross was found on La Isabella, one of the islands in the West Indies that Columbus visited.*

People, goods, culture, and ideas were exchanged between Spain and its colonies, and with the rest of the world. Soon five continents were involved in the trade: North and South America, Europe, Asia, and Africa. Everything from religion to potatoes traveled back and forth across the Atlantic. This vast movement has become known as the **Columbian exchange.**

The Columbian Exchange

"I believe there are many plants and trees here that would be very much appreciated in Spain," wrote Columbus, as he surveyed the island of Hispaniola *(hihs puhn YOH luh)*. In time, the Americas provided Spain with a number of new foods and other products. Maize, or corn, and chocolate made their way to Europe, along with avocados, beans, tomatoes, tobacco, and timber. Foods such as corn became important crops in Africa as well.

The Spanish brought many foods to their colonies. The chart below shows some of these items. In addition, they introduced horses, cows, pigs, and sheep to the Americas.

Africans brought with them to the Americas their cultures, including African languages and beliefs. The Spaniards brought European beliefs to many parts of the Americas. They also brought their language and Christianity to the colonies.

The Cost of Exchange

Much of Africa's involvement in the Columbian exchange was tragic. Vast numbers of Africans were shipped to the Western Hemisphere as slaves to work on the plantations. In general they were inhumanly treated.

The arrival of the Europeans and slaves from Africa brought death to many Native Americans. Fatal diseases, overwork, and slavery accounted for untold losses.

Measles, smallpox, typhus, and other diseases rapidly spread through the hemisphere. The native peoples had never before been exposed to these illnesses from Europe and Africa. They had no way to fight them off.

Many Spanish explorers and

Foods in the Columbian Exchange

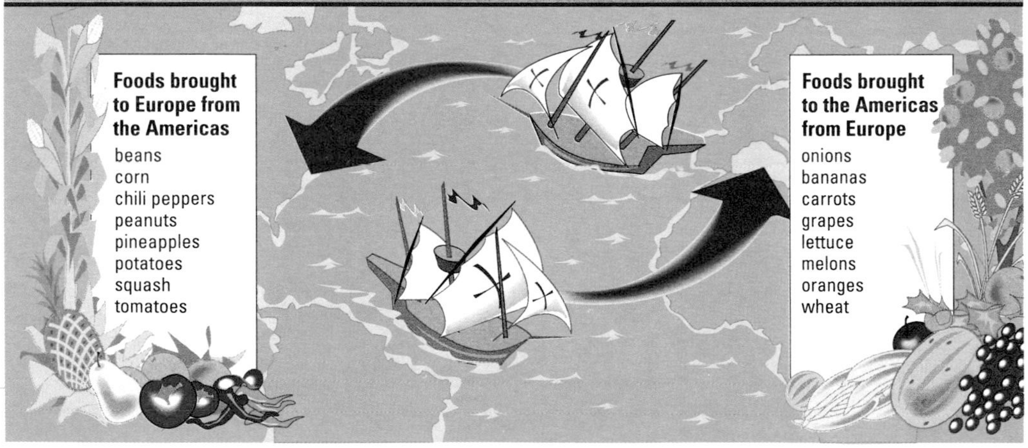
Foods brought to Europe from the Americas
beans
corn
chili peppers
peanuts
pineapples
potatoes
squash
tomatoes
Foods brought to the Americas from Europe
onions
bananas
carrots
grapes
lettuce
melons
oranges
wheat

Critical Thinking

The Smithsonian Institution developed an exhibit that focused on five "seeds" that transformed the history of life on our planet: disease, corn, the potato, the horse, and sugar. Ask students to consider these five items and their relationships to the Columbian exchange.

Language Arts Connection

One of the world's greatest writers lived at the time Spain was building its empire. In 1605 Miguel de Cervantes published *Don Quixote,* often called the first modern novel. In it the moonstruck Don Quixote and his long-suffering servant Sancho try to understand the meaning of life as the novel pokes fun at Spanish politics and culture. Generally, the Spanish Inquisition forbade criticism of Spain's institutions; Cervantes got away with mocking the authorities by speaking through a character—Don Quixote—who presented himself as a lunatic.

Read the following quotations from *Don Quixote.* Have students discuss each quotation's meaning and how the quotations reveal elements of Spanish culture.

"The brave man carves out his fortune."

"Experience, the universal Mother of Sciences."

"My honor is dearer to me than my life."

▲ *Although they outnumbered the English, Spanish ships were big and slow. English ships were faster and easier to handle.*

settlers treated Native Americans cruelly. They forced them to work on plantations or to mine precious metals. Yet a few Spaniards, such as Bartolomé de las Casas *(bahr toh loh MAY day lahs KAH sahs)*, a planter who had become a priest, objected to this mistreatment. In his *History of the Indies,* he describes "the mild and pacific [peaceful] temperament [personality] of the natives" and comments, "but our work was to exasperate, ravage, kill, mangle, and destroy."

Spain's Empire in Decline

Spain's rulers started to rely on shipments of silver and gold from the Americas to solve their financial problems. The flood of precious metals caused prices at home to rise, which created a need for even more wealth. Only a small part of the riches was invested in the country's economy or people. The silver and gold were instead used to pay for the Crown's expenses and for the Spanish armies fighting Protestants in Europe.

Spain experienced a large outflow of population while building its empire. Many of its brightest citizens, most of whom were adventurous young people, went to Spanish America to look for riches.

When Philip II, Isabella and Ferdinand's great-grandson, took the throne in 1556, he wanted to spread Catholicism throughout the world. His desire to convert England back to Catholicism led in 1588 to an unsuccessful attack on England by the so-called Invincible [unbeatable] Armada, a fleet of 130 Spanish galleons. The defeat of the Armada was the beginning of the decline of the Spanish Empire. ■

How Do We Know?

HISTORY *Although the journal Columbus kept during the voyage has been lost, we know much of what he said in it. Bartolomé de las Casas used it to write his* History of the Indies *in the 1500s. It is one of our most important sources of information about the 1492 voyage.*

■ *What was the Columbian exchange?*

REVIEW

1. **FOCUS** What did the Spanish people gain and lose by building an empire?
2. **ECONOMICS** What did Spain receive through the Columbian exchange? What did Spain's colonies receive in return?
3. **HISTORY** Why is 1492 such an important date in Spanish history?
4. **CRITICAL THINKING** Why did Spain and other European nations seek colonies in this period?
5. **ACTIVITY** One of modern Spain's great artists was Pablo Picasso. One of his contributions to art was his development of the collage. Use pictures from magazines or travel brochures to create a collage about Spain.

CULTURE

Critical Thinking

Ask students to think about the ultimate effect of the Columbian exchange on the Spanish Empire. How did exploration eventually cause the empire to suffer? *(Loss of brightest citizens to expeditions, economic disturbances)* Have students consider the impact of space exploration on modern society. How might the effects be the same or different compared to the effects of exploration on the Spanish Empire?

■ *The Columbian exchange was the exchange of people, goods, culture, and ideas between Spain, North and South America, Asia, and Africa.*

CLOSE

Read the Thinking Focus aloud. Ask half the class to list the gains and the other half to list the losses. Then have the groups share their information. Ask them to determine which gains led to losses.

Then refer students to the predictions they made at the beginning of the lesson. Have them see how those predictions matched up with the reasons Spain built an empire.

Answers to Review Questions

1. The Spanish gained many new foods and plants as well as a great deal of gold and other minerals. However, the gold led to inflation and poor economic planning by the Spanish monarchs.
2. Spain received new foods and a steady supply of gold. The colonies received new foods and products as well as the Spanish language and Christianity. Tragically, Europeans also brought fatal diseases and slavery.
3. In 1492 the Moors were driven from the Iberian Peninsula; Muslims and Jews were expelled from Spain; and Columbus made his first voyage to the Western Hemisphere, claiming land for Spain.
4. The desire for riches, power, and the opportunity to spread their religion led monarchs and merchants to seek colonies.
5. Students' collages should show an appreciation for and an understanding of Spanish history and culture.

Homework Options

Ask students to bring in foods that were involved in the Columbian exchange. For example, they might bring popcorn, corn bread, tomato juice, or peanuts. Have a shared feast celebrating the value of the Columbian exchange.

Study Guide: page 76

INTRODUCE

Have students recall the reasons why Spain built an empire. *(To spread Christianity and to gain wealth)* Ask a volunteer to read the introductory paragraph on this page, an eyewitness account of the Spanish Armada. Direct students' attention to the Thinking Focus. Have them suggest reasons why the British might have wanted to build an empire.

Key Terms

Vocabulary Strategies: T36–T37

Industrial Revolution—a change in the way work was done, dramatically increasing the amount and types of goods that could be manufactured

trade union—a society formed by workers to fight for better working conditions and better pay

raw materials—the natural materials needed to produce manufactured goods

800 | 1040 | 1280 | 1520 | 1588 | TODAY

LESSON 2

Great Britain's Sea Empire

THINKING FOCUS

What inspired Great Britain to build an empire?

Key Terms

- Industrial Revolution
- trade union
- raw materials

You could hardly see the sea. The Spanish fleet was stretched out in the form of a half moon. . . . The masts and rigging, the towering sterns and prows which in height and number were so great that they dominated the whole [scene], caused horror mixed with wonder and gave rise to doubt whether that campaign was at sea or on land. . . .

This eyewitness account of the Spanish Armada describes the enormous invasion force Spain sent to attack England. It had been called the Invincible Armada by the Spaniards. Never before had such a military force been put together. The English navy faced an enemy like no other.

Outnumbered, English sailors outwitted the Spanish navy. With the aid of the weather, the English successfully turned the armada away. Spain's navy and spirit were all but destroyed.

Much more was won than just a military victory, however. Spain's power and prestige throughout the world were shaken. As you have read, Spain's empire quickly declined after the defeat of the armada.

Out of the smoke of the battle, a new world power appeared. This power would be known as the British Empire.

➤ *One of the lasting marks of Britain's worldwide empire is the tradition of afternoon tea.*

Objectives

1. Explain how Great Britain built its empire.
2. Describe how the Industrial Revolution changed daily life.
3. Explain how Great Britain's empire declined.

Graphic Overview

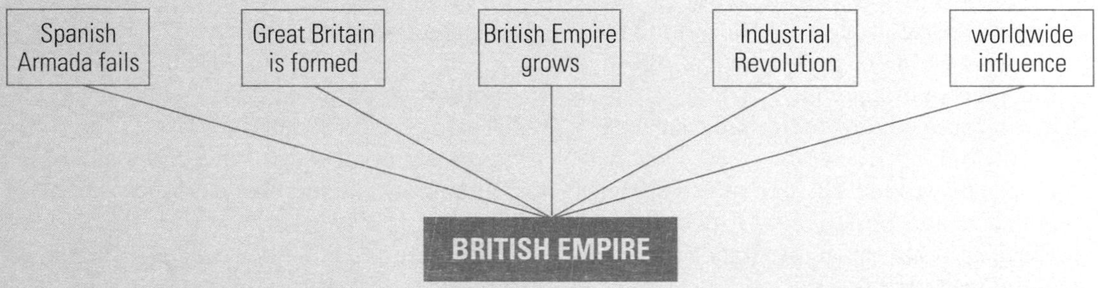
Spanish Armada fails
Great Britain is formed
British Empire grows
Industrial Revolution
worldwide influence
BRITISH EMPIRE

Building the British Empire

At its peak, Britain's empire spanned the globe. The British boasted that "the sun never sets on the British Empire." The map below supports this claim. The process of building this empire, however, was a long one.

The Rise of the British Empire

The early stages of empire building began with the failure of the Spanish Armada. English merchants and sailors became eager to compete with the Spaniards around the world.

Abundant fish and the fur trade first had attracted British ships to the Americas. By 1670, colonies were established in North America. Settlements were also built in Bermuda, Honduras, Antigua, and Barbados.

Spices had attracted ships to India in the early 1600s. As you read in Chapter 14, by the mid-1700s England had become the true ruler of India.

In 1707 the Kingdom of England and the Kingdom of Scotland approved the Act of Union. England had already united with Wales. The entire island was now under a single government. This union was called Great Britain.

Competition with France

With Spain in decline, Britain found itself competing with France for economic control of North America, the West Indies, and India. Several armed conflicts between the British and the French took place. The conflict between them finally boiled over in the French and Indian War.

Begun in 1754, this war was fought in North America. Each side allied itself with Native American peoples and fought throughout the hemisphere. Two years later the

▲ *Among the world's greatest explorers was the British navigator James Cook. This drawing of one of Cook's ships was made by a member of his crew.*

British Empire, c. 1860

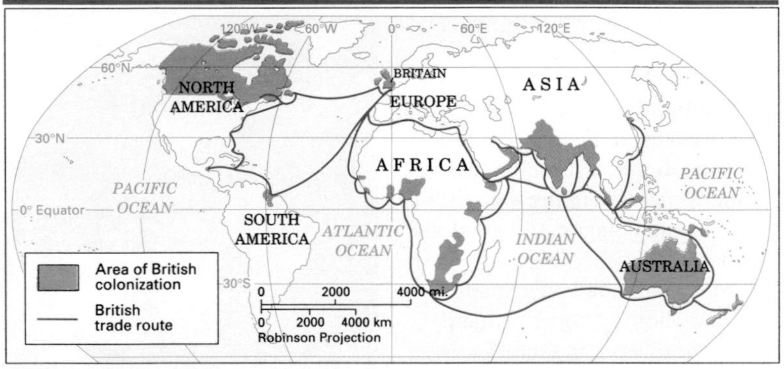
120°W
60°W
0°
60°E
120°E
60°N
30°N
0° Equator
30°S
NORTH AMERICA
BRITAIN
EUROPE
ASIA
AFRICA
PACIFIC OCEAN
PACIFIC OCEAN
SOUTH AMERICA
ATLANTIC OCEAN
INDIAN OCEAN
AUSTRALIA
Area of British colonization
British trade route
0 2000 4000 mi
0 2000 4000 km
Robinson Projection

◄ *On how many continents did Great Britain have colonies?*

Great Britain's Empire, 1600–1931

Reasons for Empire	Imports from British Colonies
Expand trade, improve defense, increase power	Sugar, oil, palm oil, ivory, gold, nuts, cocoa, cotton, copper, tea, spices

DEVELOP

Tell students that they will be reading about reasons that Great Britain built its empire and about how it did so. As they read the lesson, have students list three reasons why the empire expanded and three ways that the empire actually grew.

◄ *The British Empire had colonies on six continents: Europe, North and South America, Africa, Asia, and Australia.*

Access Strategy

Remind students of the meaning of the term *archaeology.* Ask them to think of themselves as archaeologists living thousands of years in the future. They come upon the artifacts of the British Empire that are pictured in this lesson. First, ask students to describe the artifacts they have found. *(Tea set; camera; badminton racquet; items pictured in A Closer Look)* Encourage them to be as descriptive as possible. Next, based on these descriptions, have them hypothesize about the culture of the British Empire at its height. Help them elaborate by suggesting descriptions of dress, leisure activities, preferences, and values. Be sure to encourage students to think of how the people in the various colonies reacted to British rules and ways of living. Let this lead into several general hypotheses about the nature of the British Empire. Explain to students that they will be reading about how England built its empire in the 1700s and 1800s.

Access Activity

Have students list the elements of their daily lives that are influenced by British culture. *(For example, language, laws, music)* Discuss their lists. Explain that because Great Britain played a large role in settling North America, U.S. society kept many English traditions. Point out that part of Canada, settled by France, carries on many French traditions.

■ *Britain became a great colonial power by taking advantage of the decline of Spain and by eliminating France as a rival in North America and India.*

ECONOMICS

Critical Thinking

Point out to students that the Industrial Revolution radically changed the economic structure of the world. Ask them to answer the following questions about aspects of economic structure that were affected by the Industrial Revolution: How did the cost of producing items decrease? *(For example, through mass production workers could make goods at a faster rate and for a lower cost.)* What kinds of resources were in great demand? *(Raw materials that could be turned into goods by machines and fuels to power the machines)* How did the distribution of goods change as the Industrial Revolution developed? *(People now had greater access to all sorts of goods.)* How did the need for labor change? *(Workers were now needed in the cities where the factories were located.)*

conflict spilled over into Europe and was called the Seven Years' War.

Britain emerged victorious and gained French territories throughout North America, including Canada.

The Empire Suffers Setbacks

Britain sought to pay for the expansion and control of its empire by taxing the colonies. The burden of supporting Britain's growth was too much for many colonies.

Taxes such as those on stamps and tea were put into effect in North America. Eventually, the 13 original North American colonies broke away to form the United States. Britain, however, continued to colonize Canada, which it prized for its fur and timber. The chart on page 445 shows more about the empire and the goods it valued.

India's rulers and their peoples struggled with the British taxes. Many Indian rulers revolted. However, India for the time being was unable to break away from Britain. India was too important for Britain to lose.

The cost of fighting France in the Americas and throughout Europe had severely drained the British treasury. In Great Britain itself colonialism was becoming increasingly unpopular. ■

■ *How did Britain become a great colonial power?*

▲ *Isambard Kingdom Brunel was one of Britain's greatest engineers. He is shown standing in front of the launching chains of the ship* Great Western *in 1857.*

The Industrial Revolution

In 1769 James Watt, a poor Scottish instrument maker, built a steam engine that was fast and efficient. A few years later he began manufacturing his engine. Eventually, it powered many different types of machines. Watt's invention helped bring about a revolution—the **Industrial Revolution.**

From Farm to Factory

The Industrial Revolution greatly changed the way workers lived and did their jobs. It caused a dramatic increase in the amount of work human beings could get done in a day.

People who had once made thread or cloth at home by hand now went to work in factories. There they used steam-powered machines to spin thread and weave it into cloth. A 19th-century textile worker using steam-powered machines could make 50 times as much cloth as a worker in the previous century.

As the Industrial Revolution expanded, more and more factories sprang up in Britain's cities. Many people left the countryside for good. They exchanged their old ties to the land for a new and often troubling life.

➤ *Street scenes like this one in 19th-century London were common during the Industrial Revolution.*

Visual Learning

Have students examine the pictures on this page. Explain that the ship in front of which Isambard Kingdom Brunel is standing was the first transatlantic steamer. Then have them make two lists of adjectives, one for each picture. Ask students to contrast the meaning of the two pictures—the two sides of the Industrial Revolution.

Economic Context

Iron production in Britain grew through a number of technological advances. Furnaces for smelting iron were heated by charcoal made from hardwood. When hardwood became scarce around 1700, production declined. During the early to mid-1700s, Abraham Darby and his son developed a way to produce a cheaper substitute from coal, called coke. Coal was plentiful in Britain, and as a result of the new technology, iron production tripled between 1788 and 1806.

Collaborative Learning

Have students work together in small groups to make a mural of inventions and technological advances made during the Industrial Revolution. They can bring in pictures or make drawings after doing research in the school or public library. Have students write a caption below each picture indicating the invention's name, the inventor, and the year it was invented.

APPARATUS

New Machines and Ideas

Many technologies of today can be traced back to this era. For example, in the 1830s William Henry Fox Talbot produced the first photographic negative in Britain. Inventions and discoveries of all sorts changed ordinary life.

A scientific approach to solving problems was behind these inventions. That approach had its roots in the Enlightenment of the 1600s and 1700s. Enlightenment thinkers believed that humans could understand and explain the laws that governed the universe.

In the 1800s some artists, writers, and musicians rebelled against that way of thinking. They valued emotions and nature over science and machines. Their movement was called Romanticism.

Technology Changes Daily Life

Industrialization made life harder for workers. Early factory working conditions were miserable. People who had once made their own decisions about when to work now had to work when the factory boss told them to. Instead of setting their own pace, workers had to match their pace to a machine's.

Yet the growth of industry opened up many new opportunities. People no longer needed large amounts of land to be wealthy. Through hard work, shrewd investing, and luck, they could improve their standard of living and even become rich. More and more people entered the middle class.

Cries for Reform in Great Britain

Britain's House of Lords was still controlled largely by the rich, landowning nobility. The middle class demanded a larger voice as it grew and prospered. In 1832 middle-class males won the right to vote.

Also successful, in the long run, were efforts made by workers themselves. They formed societies and eventually **trade unions** to fight for better working conditions and better pay. Unsafe conditions injured, disabled, and killed many workers, who worked up to 15 hours a day. Gradually, in the face of great opposition, the unions rolled back the worst problems. Eventually, over several decades, pressure from the voters and the unions led to changes such as the 10-hour work day, child labor laws, and required schooling.

No one—rich or poor—could escape the filth caused by the Industrial Revolution. Pollution affected the land, the air, the rivers, and the lakes everywhere. Inadequate sewer systems, polluted water, and dirty streets led to the spread of dangerous diseases. As the 19th century progressed, social reformers pressured the British government to improve sanitation. ■

◄ *The camera was one of the most important inventions of the 19th century.*

Across Time & Space

Augusta Ada Byron, Lady Lovelace (1815–1852), played an important role in the development of the computer. An associate of Charles Babbage, the "Father of the Computer," she was the first to recognize that the machine he had described could be programmed. Her work is recognized as the beginning of computer programming. The U.S. Department of Defense honored her in 1980 by naming its new computer language ADA.

■ *Who benefited most from the Industrial Revolution? Explain your answer.*

SOCIAL SYSTEMS

Study Skills

Ask students to review this page and the previous one. Then have them create a chart summarizing the changes in daily life that took place as a result of the Industrial Revolution. Their charts should include such categories as The Workplace, Living Areas, Wages, Working Hours, Sanitation, and Technological Advances.

ECONOMICS

Critical Thinking

Tell students that Britain's rate of pig-iron production rose about 328 percent between 1831 and 1850. France's production in the same period, on the other hand, rose about 62 percent. Ask students what these statistics tell them about Britain compared with France during this period. *(The rate of industrial growth was far greater in Britain.)*

■ *Many workers were able to enter the middle class and benefited most through an expanded variety of consumer goods and increased political power. The landowning nobility lost some of its power and influence.*

Language Arts Connection

Read to the class the following excerpt from *Hard Times* by Charles Dickens. "It was a town of machinery and tall chimneys, out of which interminable [never-ending] serpents of smoke trailed themselves for ever and ever. . . . It had a black canal in it, and a river that ran purple with ill-smalling [smelling] dye, and vast piles of buildings." Ask students what is being described. *(Polluted Industrial Revolution–era city)* Do they think the author liked what he described?

Political Context

Even more powerful than the House of Lords was the House of Commons, the lower house of Parliament, where legislation and all tax laws affecting the British Empire were enacted. Representation in the House of Commons was based on local units of government, the shires and the boroughs. However, many boroughs were barely villages, while cities such as Manchester and Birmingham had no representation whatsoever. The Reform Acts of 1832 corrected these inequities.

Critical Thinking

Read to the class the following quotation by Oliver Goldsmith, an Anglo-Irish poet and novelist of the 18th century: "Laws grind the poor, and rich men rule the law." Ask students to suggest interpretations of this quotation. Have them predict whether Goldsmith would be sympathetic to labor unions; ask them to support their statements.

HISTORY

Critical Thinking

Ask students to recall the rise and decline of the Spanish Empire, discussed in Lesson 1. Then have them write several paragraphs comparing and contrasting the Spanish and the British empires. Some of the categories they may wish to compare are the time during which each empire was dominant, the reasons for each empire's establishment, the way each handled its wealth, the geographic extent of each empire, the reasons for its decline, and its lasting influences.

CULTURE

Visual Learning

Have students study the visuals on this page. Ask them to speculate on the relationship between the two pictures. *(The English monarchy, which Queen Victoria represents, extended and exerted its influence around the globe by sending troops, such as members of the 93rd Highlanders, to maintain the Crown's rule.)*

Expanding the British Empire

▲ *Great Britain reached the height of its power during the reign of Queen Victoria. The period of her rule is often called the Victorian age.*

The astonishing increase in Britain's wealth brought on by the Industrial Revolution now fueled the growth of the empire. Britain soon dominated world trade.

The Empire Expands

Britain's growing middle class could not buy all the goods that were being produced. By the middle of the 1800s, Britain's workers and machines produced more than 1.75 billion yards of cotton a year. Britain's production of iron made up nearly half the global output.

Because Great Britain had a small population, it had to seek more buyers for its goods all over the world. The British believed that an expanding empire would create markets for their goods.

Britain's own supplies of coal and other important raw materials were too small. **Raw materials** are the basic materials from which industrial goods are produced. Raw materials poured into Britain from its colonies. Manufactured goods were shipped out. All of these exchanges were carried on merchant vessels that were protected around the world by the British navy.

By the close of the 19th century, Britain had established settlements or colonies throughout the world. The map on page 445 shows the extent of Britain's empire.

British Influence Worldwide

As their empire grew to include more distant regions, many Britons grew curious about these lands. Like the Spaniards, some Britons thought they were helping people by bringing them Christianity and Western civilization. Rudyard Kipling captured much of the romance of the British Empire in his poetry. He expressed its best and worst side in his poem "The White Man's Burden."

Take up the White Man's
burden–
Send forth the best ye breed–
Go, bind your sons to exile
To serve your captives' need

Not everyone in Britain thought that foreigners needed to be "civilized." A few naturalists and anthropologists wanted to study the cultures, plants, and wildlife of distant parts of the empire. Marianne North and Charles Darwin are examples of this.

▼ *The costs of maintaining an empire were very high. The British soldiers below are the 93rd Highlanders, on duty in India in the 1890s.*

Map and Globe Skills

Refer students to the map of the British Empire on page 445. Ask whether most of the British Empire lay to the north or south of Great Britain. *(South)* Ask why Britain's empire is called a "sea empire" in the lesson title. *(Because the British developed a navy that reached around the globe)*

Writing a Report

Ask students to select a country that was once a member of the British Empire. Encourage students to choose diverse countries, such as Australia, New Zealand, South Africa, Burma, or Barbados. Point out that as some colonies have won their freedom, they have changed their names, particularly in Africa and Asia. Have students do research and write a report on their country of choice. Some issues they may wish to focus on include the reason the country was colonized by Britain; the dates of possession; the items the colony exported to Britain and how they benefited Britain; the way they won their independence; and their present relationship with Britain. Have students share their reports in class.

A CLOSER LOOK

Britain, Transplanted

Wherever the British went during the days of their empire, they took along their way of life. They packed their trunks with Victorian clothing and games. Tropical heat in foreign lands would force most people indoors at noon—but not the British. Some newcomers even drank hot tea every day at teatime. Most tried to live as if they were still in England.

A pith helmet was lighter and cooler than the top hat, which was worn in England.

Long dresses with tight waists were uncomfortable, especially in hot and humid climates.

This judicial wig and robe might have been worn in a colony courtroom, where British law ruled.

95
R.C.

Rudyard Kipling, a British author, lived in India and wrote several stories about life there.

Croquet was a favorite lawn game. Some carrying cases for the wooden mallets and balls were lined with velvet.

Note: You may wish to use this Closer Look as an extension of the discussion, in Lesson 2, of British culture and influence throughout the world.

More About British Culture Croquet is not the only sport that Great Britain introduced around the globe as the empire grew. Three other sports in particular stand out as vestiges of Britain's colonial past: cricket, rugby, and golf. Cricket, a game played with a bat and a ball by two teams of 11 players each, remains one of Britain's most popular sports. The same is true of rugby, which resembles the game of football played in the United States. The roots of golf have been traced to Scotland, where the game was developed in 1100 from a Roman game called *paganica.* Each of these sports is pursued throughout the world, particularly in countries that were once British colonies.

Reader's Theater

Although Rudyard Kipling is famous for his novels and poetry, he is also well known for his short stories. He won the Nobel Prize for literature in 1907. Obtain several copies of his works from the school or public library. Have students form groups and select a story or poem to interpret orally, such as "The White Man's Burden," mentioned on page 448. Then ask students to present their interpretations to the class.

Research

Ask students to look in the library for more information on British exploration of the world. Suggest that they use the *Readers' Guide* and the card catalog to locate articles and books on one of Britain's famous explorers. Possible subjects include Sir Francis Drake, Sir Martin Frobisher, Henry Hudson, Sir Richard Burton, James Cook, William Dampier, Robert Falcon Scott, and Sir William Parry.

Visual Learning

Have students examine the items pictured as examples of British culture. They can discuss the uses of each item and try to decide what each suggests about British culture in the Victorian age. For example, have them tell why a woman would use a parasol and what that suggests about upper-class British women of that time.

■ *Britain's colonies supplied the markets and the raw materials needed for industrial expansion.*

CLOSE

Ask a volunteer to read the Thinking Focus aloud. Have students list the reasons for British expansion in the order of their occurrence in history. Point out that in addition to economic reasons, many British people believed that they were performing a service to less-developed countries by including them in the empire. Then have students compare the list with their initial predictions.

North traveled throughout the empire and the world, painting the flowers and other plants of various regions. Her paintings are displayed at London's botanical gardens.

Darwin sailed around the world, observing plants and animals. His notes from his journey were the basis for his theory of natural selection, or how he believed life had evolved on the earth. Darwin's theory was considered at the time to be one of the 19th century's most important contributions to science.

At about the same time, a German philosopher named Karl Marx wrote *Das Kapital* in Great Britain. In this work he analyzes the economics of capitalism. His ideas served as the basis for the theories of communism.

The Empire Dwindles

Although it had taken centuries to build, Britain's empire declined in just a few decades. A whole generation of British people were killed or ruined by World War I. The war exhausted the British economy. After the war, independence movements arose in many British colonies. One of the most famous was the nonviolent campaign for India's independence, led by Gandhi. You read in Chapter 14 about his role in India's struggle for independence.

The costs of World War II ended Britain's role as a world power. It was now utterly unable to maintain an empire. Britain withdrew from the Middle East and most of its Asian colonies between 1945 and 1948. In the early 1960s, most of Britain's African colonies won their independence, some after violent struggles.

The Influence of British Culture

Like Spain, Great Britain brought its language and its religion, Protestantism, to its colonies. Today, English is the second most widely spoken language in the world. This language has in turn been enriched by all the peoples who have spoken it. For example, the word *pajamas* comes from India, as does the word *loot*. Read A Closer Look on page 449 to discover more about British culture and Britain's relationship with its territories. ■

Traces of British culture can be found around the world in everything from the use of the English language to the popular sport of badminton.

■ *Why were Britain's colonies important to its industrial expansion?*

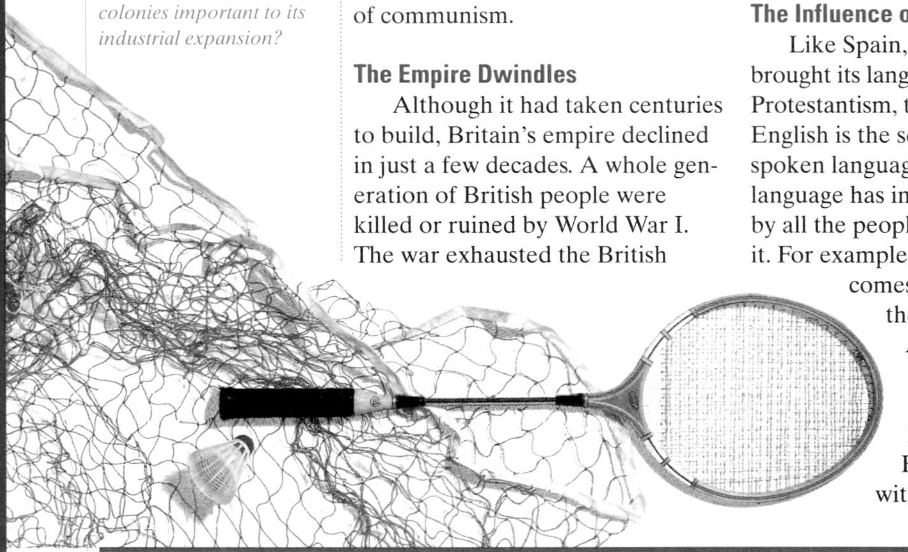

REVIEW

1. **FOCUS** What inspired Great Britain to build an empire?
2. **SOCIAL SYSTEMS** How did the Industrial Revolution change British society?
3. **ECONOMICS** How did the Industrial Revolution contribute to the growth of the British Empire?
4. **POLITICAL SYSTEMS** How did the Industrial Revolution affect the government of Great Britain?
5. **CRITICAL THINKING** Do you think that the Industrial Revolution made life better or worse for people in Britain? Explain your answer.
6. **WRITING ACTIVITY** Imagine you are the editor of a small newspaper in Britain during the Industrial Revolution. Write a positive or negative editorial commenting on an aspect of life that has changed in your town in recent decades.

Homework Options

Have students draw a picture illustrating one way in which British colonization has left a lasting influence on U.S. culture.

Study Guide: page 77

Answers to Review Questions

1. At the beginning the inspiration was trade. With the Industrial Revolution, colonies were needed for their raw materials and as markets for British goods.
2. The middle class grew more wealthy and powerful. The upper class lost some of its power and prestige. Industrialism initially made life harder for the working classes.
3. The need for new markets and sources of raw materials that resulted from the Industrial Revolution led to the continued expansion of the British Empire.
4. The middle class won the right to vote and thus gained a stronger role in government.
5. Students' answers should reflect an awareness that different classes were affected differently by the Industrial Revolution.
6. Students' editorials should comment on a positive (more goods, more broadly based political power) or negative (poor working conditions, urban crowding) aspect of life.

UNDERSTANDING GRAPHIC INFORMATION

Comparing Graphs

Here's Why

Graphs can help you organize information. They can help you see patterns and make comparisons. Some kinds of graphs are best used to present certain kinds of information.

Suppose you want to understand how world trade increased as a result of the Industrial Revolution in Europe. You can use graphs to analyze this information.

The graphs on this page present information on world trade. The graphs show trade information in two very different ways.

By comparing two graphs, you can get more information than you can from one graph. Also, by understanding what each graph does best, you can learn which type of graph to choose to present your own information.

World Trade, 1780–1820

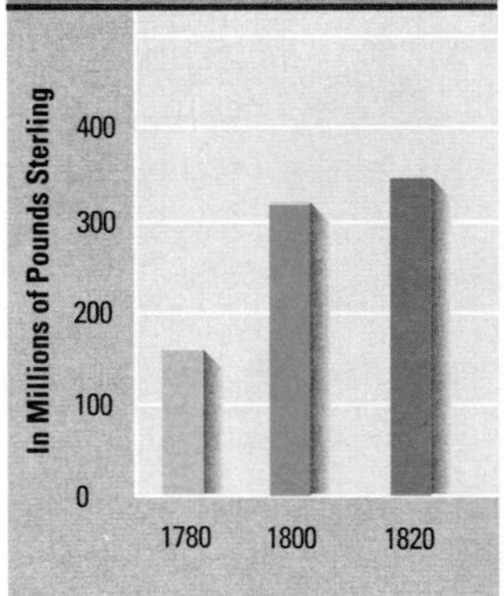
In Millions of Pounds Sterling
400
300
200
100
0
1780
1800
1820

Source: The Dictionary of Statistics, 1892

Here's How

The graph on the left is a bar graph; the other is a pie graph. The bar graph shows change over time. The bar graph at the lower left shows how world trade increased from the year 1780 through the year 1820. The amount of trade is measured in British money, called pounds (£).

You can see that in 1780 world trade was valued at approximately £186 million. By 1820 this figure had risen to about £350 million.

Suppose you want to know what countries were involved in most of the trade at one particular time. You could use a pie graph for this information.

A pie graph shows how something is divided into parts. Each part is a fraction, or a percentage, of the whole. For example, if you made a pie graph of your class, you might show how the class is divided into boys and girls.

The pie graph below shows what countries took part in world trade in the year 1820. Each piece of the pie shows how the amount of trade from one country or region relates to the total world trade. You can see that Great Britain was involved in 22 percent of the total world trade.

World Trade, 1820

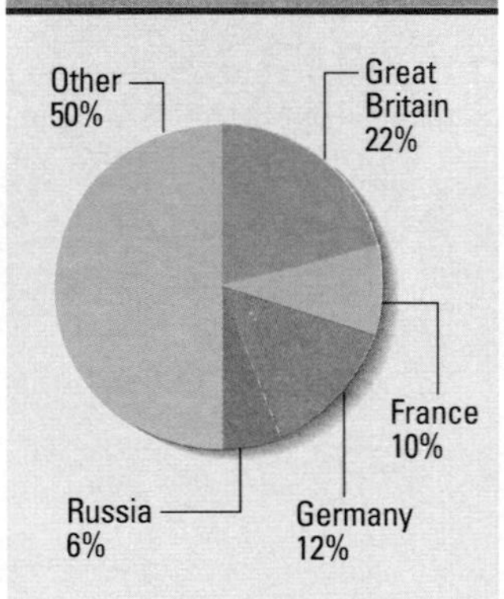
Other 50%
Great Britain 22%
France 10%
Germany 12%
Russia 6%

Source: The Dictionary of Statistics, 1892

Try It

Now try making your own graphs with the following information. Suppose that in 1840 world trade dropped by £100 million. What would your new bar graph look like? Suppose that in 1840 France decreased its trade by 4 percent because of trade barriers. France's loss was split evenly between Germany and Russia. Trade in all the other countries remained the same. What would your new pie graph look like?

Apply It

Keep track of how you spend your free time after school for a week. Your activities might include studying, reading, and playing. What would be the best way to present this information? Draw the graph you have chosen and be prepared to present it to the class.

UNDERSTANDING GRAPHIC INFORMATION

This skills feature uses a bar graph and a pie graph to interpret information about world trade during the Industrial Revolution.

ECONOMICS

Visual Learning

Before beginning the skill lesson, make sure that students understand the meaning of world trade. *(The amount of importing from and exporting to other countries done by all the countries in the world)*

Direct students to read the skill lesson to themselves. Have them explain how the graphs provide information. *(The bar graph shows an increase in trade between 1780 and 1820; the pie graph shows which countries were involved in world trade.)* Ask how we know that the Industrial Revolution was involved in the increase in world trade. *(It took place at this time in Europe and resulted in increased production of goods; when these goods were distributed outside the country of origin, that was part of world trade.)* Ask students what is remarkable about Britain's role in world trade in 1820. *(It's remarkable that a single country was involved in nearly one-fourth of all world trade.)*

Answers to Try It

The bar graph should show an 1840 bar at 250 million pounds. The pie chart for 1840 should show Great Britain with 22 percent; France with 6 percent; Germany with 14 percent; Russia with 8 percent; and Other with 50 percent.

Answers to Apply It

Answers will vary. Some students may choose a bar graph with the various after-school activities on the x-axis and the number of hours spent on each activity on the y-axis. Others may choose a pie chart showing the percentage of time spent on each activity.

Objective

Make and read different kinds of graphs and select the appropriate graph for displaying information. (Visual Learning 2)

INTRODUCE

Introduce Lesson 3 by playing a recording of some Russian music such as Mussorgsky's *Pictures at an Exhibition* or Tchaikovsky's *Russian Easter* or *1812 Overture.* Ask students what emotions this music suggests. *(Possible answers include majesty, tragedy, and great joy or sorrow.)* Tell students that the range of emotions that this music evokes reflects Russia's history: a past of both severe hardships and spirited steps toward progress. Then have students read the lesson title and the Thinking Focus. Ask them to predict how Russia acquired its empire. *(Acquired land around its immediate borders)* Have students read Lesson 3 to find out whether their predictions were correct.

Key Terms

Vocabulary Strategies: T36–T37
steppe—an extensive, rolling grassland
czar—Russian for "emperor," from the Latin *Caesar*

800 — 1917 — 2000

LESSON 3

Russia's Land Empire

THINKING FOCUS

How did the Russian Empire grow?

Key Terms

- steppe
- czar

To the distant east, far from Spain and Great Britain, another empire was growing. For most of this empire's history, wild horses stampeded across the plains and wandering peoples herded cattle. It was a vast land of great beauty.

What did this land look like? Imagine a broad, rolling plain covered with tall, greenish gold grasses higher than your head. Purple, blue, and golden wildflowers dot the grass. The sea of grass goes on for several thousand miles in every direction. This is the **steppe**—a huge grassland like the Great Plains of North America.

North of the steppe is a thick forest. The windy steppe and thick, northern forests dominate the land.

Even today, thick forests cover much of the land. In the north the trees are evergreens. Other forests include oak, birch, and beech trees.

Several large rivers cross this land. They run generally from north to south, many between the Baltic Sea and the Black Sea. Rivers provided the easiest way to travel across the wild land.

People eventually settled in valleys near the rivers. They worshiped statues and figures that they believed controlled the forces of nature and life.

Later, Eastern Slavs *(slahvz)* moved into the area that would become the Russian Empire. The Slavs lacked political unity. There were few natural barriers to protect them from invasions. This lack of natural barriers to invasion was to affect Russia throughout its history.

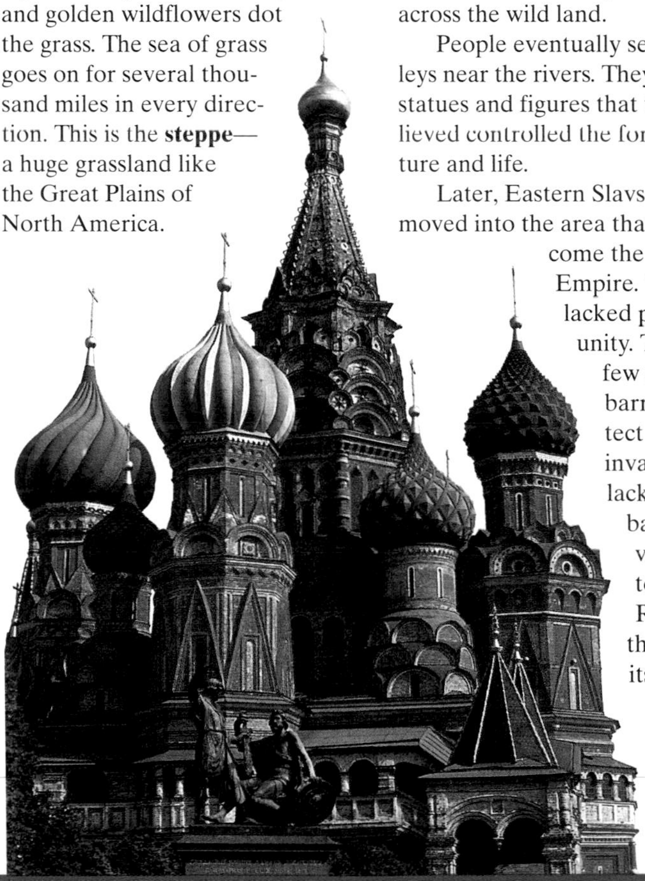

➤ *Saint Basil's Cathedral in Moscow's Red Square was built during the reign of Ivan IV. He celebrated the empire's growth during his reign by having it built.*

Objectives

1. Explain how Russia's geography influenced its people.
2. Describe the rise of the Russian state.
3. Describe the changes Peter and Catherine began in Russia.

Graphic Overview

Slavic Groups Establish Towns ➤ Foreign Invasions ➤ Influence of Byzantines ➤ Ivan III and Ivan IV Strengthen Russia ➤ Romanovs Modernize Russia

The Rise of Russia

By the 800s, Slavic groups had established towns in the western portion of Russia known as the Ukraine. Before long two powerful forces dominated these peoples.

The First Russian State

Probably early in the 800s, the first invading group, the Vikings, discovered that the rivers of Russia were a good trade route. The route ran from the Baltic Sea to Constantinople, one of the main cities of the Byzantine Empire. Vikings took slaves, furs, amber, honey, and beeswax to trade for the Byzantines' gold, silver, and silk.

To protect trade the Vikings fortified their trading posts of Kiev *(KEE ehv)* and Novgorod *(NAWV guh rawd)*.

Vikings soon ruled Kiev and Novgorod. Kiev became a rich trading center due to its position on the Dnieper River, which is between the Baltic Sea and the Black Sea. The ruler of Kiev came to be known as the *grand prince* and ranked above all other Russian princes. Kiev's rulers greatly admired Byzantine culture. In about 988, Prince Vladimir I and all of his subjects became Orthodox Christians.

The Mongol Invasion

Disaster came suddenly to Kievan Russia. Weakened by civil wars and lacking strong leadership, the area fell to the Mongols. This second group of invaders were

A mid-16th-century Russian crown made of engraved gold set with jewels and fur trimming.

Russian Empire, c. 1600

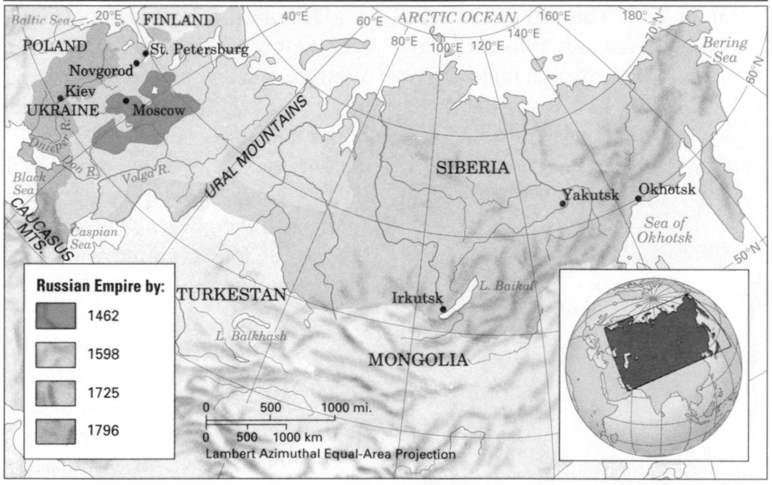

Baltic Sea
FINLAND
POLAND
St. Petersburg
Novgorod
Kiev
UKRAINE
Moscow
Dnieper R.
Don R.
Volga R.
Black Sea
CAUCASUS MTS.
Caspian Sea
URAL MOUNTAINS
ARCTIC OCEAN
SIBERIA
Yakutsk
Okhotsk
Sea of Okhotsk
Bering Sea
L. Baikal
Irkutsk
TURKESTAN
L. Balkhash
MONGOLIA
20°E
40°E
60°E
80°E
100°E
120°E
140°E
160°E
180°
60°N
50°N
Russian Empire by:
1462
1598
1725
1796
0 500 1000 mi.
0 500 1000 km
Lambert Azimuthal Equal-Area Projection

What were the last regions to become part of the Russian Empire?

Russian Empire, 1462–1917

Reasons for Empire	Imports from Russian Colonies
Protect borders, gain seaports, increase trade, add natural resources	Timber, iron ore, gold, fur, grain

Across Time & Space

Only about 55 miles of water separate Siberia, in easternmost Russia, from the State of Alaska. Russian expeditions sent by Peter the Great landed in Alaska in the 1700s, and a rich fur trade grew there. Russians made the first settlement in 1784, and a joint Russian-U.S. company ran the territory. Russia sold Alaska to the United States in 1867, for $7,200,000.

DEVELOP

Duplicate the Graphic Overview on page 452 on the chalkboard. Point out to students that it illustrates the major steps in Russia's growth. Then have students read the subheads in the lesson. Ask them how the subheads show a progression in the development of Russia's empire.

The last regions to become part of the empire were an area to the west running from the Caucasus Mountains to the Baltic Sea and a small region below Finland.

GEOGRAPHY

Map and Globe Skills

Direct students' attention to the map on this page. Have them locate rivers such as the Dnieper, the Volga, and the Don. Ask students to explain how the rivers made the region easily accessible to invasion by foreign cultures. *(Rivers provided easy transportation for foreign invaders.)* Have students use the map scale to estimate the width of the Russian empire in 1796. *(Over 5,000 miles)*

Access Strategy

Discuss some of the differences between Russia and the two other countries covered in this chapter. Ask students what factors contributed to these differences. How did these differences affect the ways these empires grew? Have students examine the map on this page and note the location of Russia's major rivers and its coastline. Ask them how Russia's geography differs from Spain's and Great Britain's. Why might Russia have been less involved in overseas exploration and colonization than Spain or Great Britain? *(Much of the coast is in the North, which freezes during the long winters, effectively shutting these regions down and preventing any sort of boat travel. Russia could never launch a sustained campaign overseas.)*

Access Activity

Point out the Russian crown on this page. What does it represent? *(Power, prestige, authority)* Have students consider the roles of the conqueror and the conquered in building an empire. Help students see that Russia has assumed both roles at various times in history.

■ *The Vikings ruled the Russian people in a more beneficial manner than the Mongols. Interaction with the Vikings led to contact with the Byzantines, resulting in a rich trading economy and the influence of the Eastern Orthodox religion. The Mongols destroyed the region when they invaded. Later, they kept the people poor by making them pay high taxes and by demanding troops to serve in the Mongol army.*

HISTORY

Critical Thinking

Ask students what conditions gave rise to the Russian Empire. *(Powerful leadership in Moscow, strong Romanov family, vision of Peter the Great)* Have the class speculate on the detrimental effects of this expansion. *(Students might mention the limit on peasants' freedoms.)*

fierce warriors from Asia who came galloping in from the plains to the east.

By 1240 Russia had become part of the immense Mongol Empire. The Mongols did not rule the region directly. Instead, they required tribute and troops from the Slavic princes. Paying high taxes to the Mongols kept Russia poor.

■ *Did the Vikings or the Mongols better rule the people of Russia? Why?*

The Rise of Moscow

Deep in the forest, the town of Moscow was becoming strong and rich. Its rulers were clever and ambitious. They took over neighboring lands and fought to escape Mongol control.

In 1480 Ivan III, called "the Great," stopped paying tribute to the Mongols. He declared himself the leader of Russia and defender of its church. He took the title **czar,** from the Latin word for emperor.

Ivan's grandson, Ivan IV, conquered lands along the Volga River. Called "Ivan the Terrible" for his cruelty, he limited peasants' freedoms. Over the centuries Russian peasants became serfs, bound to the land they worked. ■

Russia Becomes a World Power

After Ivan IV died in 1584, wars and revolts swept over Russia during the Time of Troubles. In 1613 a new ruling family, the Romanovs, came to power. The Romanovs would remain in power for the next 300 years until the February Revolution of 1917. You will read about the end of Romanov rule in Chapter 20. The map on page 453 shows the Russia that the Romanovs would rule.

ДЕНГИ
ВЗѦТЫ

➤ *Peter the Great desperately wanted to westernize Russia. He even wanted Russia's nobles to cut off their beards to look more like the upper classes of Europe. A nobleman could keep his beard if he paid a special tax to obtain a beard license like the one above.*

Peter the Great Looks to the West

The reign of Peter the Great was a turning point for Russia. Peter, a Romanov, became czar in 1682. He wanted Russia to catch up with Western Europe's skills, technology, and culture.

Disguised as an ordinary traveler, Peter had explored much of Western Europe before he took power. As czar, Peter began to modernize and westernize Russia. He encouraged the building of modern factories and schools. Peter made changes in the government and improved the quality of the army.

Peter also wanted to enlarge Russia's borders and build an empire. To help him achieve these goals, he began a massive shipbuilding program. He went to war against the Ottoman Empire and against the Persians. His victories allowed Russia to extend south, to the shores of the Caspian Sea.

To gain land and a seaport on the Baltic Sea, Peter went to war against Sweden in 1700. He defeated Sweden and opened up a

Critical Thinking

Russian serfs were required to provide the state with recruits for the army as well as with labor for the construction of state projects such as roads and forts. Ask students to suggest why Peter the Great and Catherine the Great did little to improve their conditions. *(Peasants weren't a group to fear.)*

Cultural Context

Bring to class some pictures of Russian art, such as nesting dolls, painted eggs, or religious icons. Explain to students that Russian art reflects the long-standing influence of Byzantine culture. The use of mosaics, the extraordinary architecture of churches, with their many cupolas, and the depiction of saints—full-faced and haloed—are all examples of this influence.

Of particular interest are the artifacts surrounding the Russian festival of Easter, which in the Eastern Orthodox faith is the most important holiday of the year. The Russians make beautiful decorative paintings on eggshapes; they once used clay and now use lacquered wood. The eggs symbolize springtime and fertility, which, after the severe Russian winters, is particularly welcome.

"window to the West," a needed passageway to the Baltic Sea. Peter then built a brand-new capital city, St. Petersburg, near the Baltic coast.

Imperial Russia

Russia's empire grew most of all during the reigns of Catherine the Great and the two czars who came after her. Catherine, a German princess, became empress in 1762, after her husband was deposed. She ruled until 1796 and made Russia a great power. Land in Poland and Turkey became part of the empire.

Like Peter, Catherine admired the culture of Western Europe. She corresponded with the great thinkers of her time. She encouraged schools and the arts, including ballet. Yet although Europeans were discussing new ideas such as the rights of ordinary people, Catherine did nothing to help the peasants in Russia.

Russia Expands Its Empire

Once Russia was a great power, it had to fight to keep and expand its position. Unlike Spain and Great Britain, Russia continued to look around its own borders for room to expand, as China had done before.

Russia fought the Ottoman Empire, Britain, and France, losing the Crimean War in 1856. Russia then moved eastward toward the Pacific Ocean. It won territories from China and in central Asia.

Russian writer and novelist Leo Tolstoy, pictured here telling a story to his grandchildren in 1909, lived through much of Russia's expansion. A veteran of the Crimean War, he later gave up all his wealth to live and write among peasants.

Life under the Czars

From the time of the first czars, there had been a huge gap between the Russian upper classes and ordinary people. Nobles and wealthy families lived in glittering luxury, often following Western European customs. Russian peasants simply tried to survive.

Some czars after Catherine were truly interested in democratic ideas. They did not want to give up power, however. Writers and young nobles who demanded reforms often faced prison or exile.

In 1861 Czar Alexander II gave the serfs their freedom and some land. Unfortunately, the lives of ordinary Russians did not improve much. As you will read in the next chapter, the growing gap between rich and poor would eventually tear Russian society apart. ■

■ *How did Peter the Great and Catherine the Great modernize Russia?*

REVIEW

1. **FOCUS** How did the Russian Empire grow?
2. **GEOGRAPHY** How did Russia's physical environment play a role in its history?
3. **HISTORY** What changes did Peter and Catherine begin in Russia?
4. **HISTORY** Why was the reign of Peter the Great considered a turning point in Russia's history?
5. **CRITICAL THINKING** What do you think was the greatest difference between Russia's empire and the empires of Spain and Great Britain?
6. **ACTIVITY** Imagine you are living in Russia during the 800s. Give an eyewitness account of the arrival of the Viking raiders. Where did they come from? How do they treat you and your family? What do they want?

CULTURE

Study Skills

Remind students of the admiration both Peter the Great and Catherine the Great felt for the culture of Western Europe. Have students create a chart showing the changes that Peter and Catherine made in Russia. Have them place a check mark beside the changes that originated in Western Europe.

■ *They both tried to bring modern technology to Russia. Peter made changes in the army and the government. Catherine encouraged the development of the arts.*

CLOSE

Ask students to reread the Thinking Focus. Have them create a brief outline, flow chart, or timeline that illustrates how Russia acquired its empire.

Answers to Review Questions

1. The Russian Empire grew as Russia slowly expanded outward, taking land around its borders from its neighbors.
2. Russia's physical environment (especially the lack of mountain barriers) made it susceptible to invasion. The Vikings used Russia's rivers to take over the region. The Mongols came across the easily passable plains in the East.
3. They began to westernize and modernize every aspect of Russian society, including education and the economy.
4. Peter the Great sought to modernize Russia and actually set Russia on the course toward becoming a true world power.
5. The Spanish and the British traveled great distances to build their empires—both overseas. The Russians built their empire by taking lands around its borders.
6. Students' accounts should demonstrate an understanding of the changes that the Vikings initiated.

Homework Options

Have students write an imaginative but historically accurate story of an aspect of Russia's history. Topics might include a firsthand account of the Mongol invasion or of the rise of Moscow, a diary entry by an aide helping Peter the Great, or a description of a day in the life of a Russian peasant.

Study Guide: page 79

Answers to Reviewing Key Terms

A. Sample answers:

1. The **Reconquista,** the reconquering of the Iberian Peninsula from the Muslims, included the persecution of **conversos** (Jews who had converted to Christianity).
2. Because factory working conditions during the **Industrial Revolution** were unhealthy, workers organized **trade unions.**
3. Under **colonialism,** one country occupies and controls another, mainly for land and profit from **raw materials.**

B. Answers:

1. **steppe**
2. **Columbian exchange**
3. **czar**

Answers to Exploring Concepts

A. Sample answers:

To the Americas: Food plants: wheat, carrots, onions, lettuce, bananas, melons, oranges, grapes; Animals and other plants: horses, cows, pigs, oxen; Other: language, Christianity, diseases, slavery

To Europe: Food plants: beans, tomatoes, corn, chocolate, peanuts, potatoes, squash; Animals and other plants: fish, fur, sugar cane, tobacco, timber; Other: silver, gold

B. Answers:

1. Princess Isabella married Prince Ferdinand because he had agreed to rule with her.
2. They wanted to unite Spain, take back land from the Muslims, and make the country completely Catholic.
3. Spain's rival was Portugal.
4. It held lands in North and South America and western Europe.
5. Answers should mention the loss of young, ambitious people to Spanish America; the wars fought for colonies; and the dependence on American gold and silver, which led to higher prices.
6. The English ships were smaller, faster, and easier to handle than the Spanish ships.
7. The kingdoms of England, Wales, and Scotland united to form Great Britain.
8. They competed for colonies and economic control in North America, the West Indies, and India.
9. Answers may include: cloth once made at home by hand was now made in factories by machines; farmers left the land to become factory workers in cities; products were made many times faster.
10. An expanded empire would provide more markets for British goods and more sources of raw materials.
11. The Vikings, the Byzantines, and Mongol invaders influenced early Russia.
12. He wanted to modernize and to introduce Western European customs and technology. He also wanted to expand Russia's borders and build an empire.
13. It seized lands around its borders. Under Peter, Russia gained land from Poland and the Ottoman Empire and from Sweden, access to the Baltic Sea. Under Catherine, Russia gained land from Poland, Turkey, China, and Central Asia.
14. He granted serfs freedom and some land.

Chapter Review

Reviewing Key Terms

colonialism (p. 440)
Columbian exchange (p. 442)
converso (p. 439)
czar (p. 454)
Industrial Revolution (p. 446)
raw materials (p. 448)
Reconquista (p. 439)
steppe (p. 452)
trade union (p. 447)

A. Read each pair of words. Write a sentence telling how the words in each pair are related. Be sure to use the terms themselves in each explanation.

1. Reconquista, converso
2. Industrial Revolution, trade union
3. colonialism, raw materials

B. Write the key term that is described by each sentence below.

1. The Mongols crossed a broad, rolling plain of tall grasses and conquered Kievan Russia.
2. People, goods, culture, and ideas flowed between North and South America, Europe, Asia, and Africa.
3. Ivan the Great created a new title for himself that came from the Latin word for emperor.

Exploring Concepts

A. In this chapter you have read about the Columbian exchange. Copy and complete the table below to show what was brought to the Americas and what was sent to Europe. List at least two items in each box.

Items Exchanged	To the Americas	To Europe
Food plants		
Animals and other plants		
Other		

B. Answer each question with information from the chapter.

1. Why did Princess Isabella want to marry Prince Ferdinand instead of someone like King Alfonso of Portugal?
2. What were Isabella and Ferdinand's main goals for Spain?
3. In the 1400s, what country was Spain's main rival for leadership in trade and exploration throughout the world?
4. On what continents did Spain hold territories by the mid-1500s?
5. In what ways did building an empire weaken Spain?
6. Why was the English navy able to turn the Spanish Armada away from England's shores?
7. What kingdoms were united in 1707 to form Great Britain?
8. In what ways did Britain and France compete during the 1700s?
9. Explain two ways in which the Industrial Revolution changed how goods such as cloth were made.
10. How did the Industrial Revolution increase Great Britain's need to build an empire around the globe?
11. What three outside groups influenced the development of Russia before the 1400s?
12. What were Peter the Great's main goals for Russia?
13. As the Russian Empire expanded, where were the new lands that it acquired?
14. What social reform did Czar Alexander II put into effect in Russia?

Reviewing Skills

1. The table below tells how many millions of tons of coal were used in Great Britain at the height of the British Empire. Would you use a bar graph or a pie graph to show this information?

Year	Coal (in millions of tons)
1890	132
1900	155
1910	168
1913	177
1920	193

2. On your own paper, create a graph using the figures from the table. Make the kind of graph you chose in Question 1.
3. The end of Lesson 3 makes this prediction: "The growing gap between rich and poor would eventually tear Russian society apart." Reread the lesson to find facts and statements on which this prediction is based. From what you have read, would you make the same prediction?
4. The Industrial Revolution greatly increased the variety of goods made in Britain's factories. What graphing method would best show the different types of goods made during this period?

Using Critical Thinking

1. Finding gold and silver was a major goal of Spanish explorers and conquerors in the Americas. How did these new riches prove harmful for Spain? Could Spain's rulers have prevented these problems?
2. When a Spanish official received land and the Indians living on that land, he was expected to provide something in return: to care for them and teach them Catholicism. Based on what you have read in this chapter, did most Spanish officials fulfill their part of this agreement?
3. If the Industrial Revolution had taken place in Russia in the 1800s, how might the country's history have been different?
4. At the close of the 19th century, Great Britain was known as the "workshop of the world." Explain why.

Preparing for Citizenship

1. **COLLECTING INFORMATION** The growth of the empires discussed in this chapter was the result of the efforts of a number of individuals. Choose someone mentioned in a lesson or feature and do research on this person. Prepare a short speech to present to the class about what you have learned about this person's life and work.
2. **ARTS ACTIVITY** The Romantic movement in art and literature began after the Industrial Revolution. English Romantic poets, such as William Wordsworth, Samuel Taylor Coleridge, and William Blake, wrote about nature. Find one or two short poems by one of these writers that you like. Read what you have chosen to the class, or draw a picture that illustrates the poem's meaning.
3. **COLLABORATIVE LEARNING** Working with your classmates, make an illustrated map of the Spanish or the British empire at its height. Some students might work together and draw a large-scale copy of the map of Spain's Empire (page 441) or the map of the British Empire (page 445). Other students could look in magazines for pictures of some of the goods that passed between each empire and its colonies as part of the Columbian exchange. Place each map on the bulletin board and use ribbons and thumbtacks to connect each picture with the right location.

Answers to Reviewing Skills

1. A bar graph is the best way to graphically present this information. Some students may have a knowledge of line graphs and may choose to present the data in this way. A pie graph would not work, however.
2. Students should draw a bar graph (or a line graph) with these figures on coal use.
3. Answers may mention the huge gap between the upper classes and ordinary people; czars who didn't want to give up power; the persecution of those who demanded reforms.
4. A bar graph.

Answers to Using Critical Thinking

1. Students should recall that Spanish rulers came to rely on large amounts of gold and silver from the Americas; rulers got used to spending money on wars. Students may suggest that rulers should have invested in the country's economy and in its people.
2. Students may state that since many officials were cruel, they couldn't have cared for the Native Americans. Others may state that officials did teach Catholicism, as evidenced by the many people in Mexico and South America today who are Catholic.
3. Students may suggest that industry might have brought prosperity to more Russians, created a middle class, and given the serfs a better life. Those who know about the Russian Revolution may suggest that it might have been prevented by an industrial revolution.
4. Great Britain was called the workshop of the world due to its rapid industrial development. It produced a huge quantity of goods and sold them throughout the world.

Answers to Preparing for Citizenship

1. **COLLECTING INFORMATION** This activity can be done by individual students or partners working together. Interesting people include Isabella, Charles V, Elizabeth I, Ivan IV, Charles Darwin, and Robert Owen. If class time does not allow for oral reports, have students write brief biographical sketches.
2. **ARTS ACTIVITY** This activity may be done by one or several students. Students who illustrate a poem can display their work with a copy of the poem on the bulletin board.
3. **COLLABORATIVE LEARNING** Give students whatever help they need in reproducing the map accurately and in finding sources for pictures.

CHAPTER ORGANIZER

Chapter 20 Europe: 1900 to the End of the Cold War

CHAPTER PLANNING CHART

Pupil's Edition	Teacher's Edition	Ancillaries
Lesson 1: World War I (1–2 days) Objective 1: Explain two causes of World War I. (History 5) Objective 2: Describe the outcomes of World War I. (Social and Political Systems 6)	• Graphic Overview (460) • Access Strategy (461) • Access Activity (461) Investigating (462) Cultural Context (462)	Study Guide (80)
Lesson 2: Russia Becomes the Soviet Union (1–2 days) Objective 1: Identify two causes and effects of the Russian Revolution. (History 5) Objective 2: Compare life under the czars with life under Lenin and Stalin. (Social and Political Systems 3, 5)	• Graphic Overview (464) • Access Strategy (465) • Access Activity (465) • Visual Learning (466) Language Arts Connection (466) Reader's Theater (466)	Study Guide (81) Discovery Journal (41)
Lesson 3: World War II and the Cold War (2–3 days) Objective 1: Name two causes of World War II. (History 5; Social and Political Systems 6; Citizenship 7) Objective 2: Describe the outcomes of World War II. (Social and Political Systems 4, 5) Objective 3: Explain the concept of genocide. (Ethics and Belief Systems 2) Objective 4: Describe life behind the iron curtain. (History 6)	• Graphic Overview (468) • Access Strategy (469) • Access Activity (469) • Visual Learning (470) Social Context (470) Historical Context (471) Language Arts Connection (471) Study Skills (471, 472) Collaborative Learning (472) Political Context (472) Science Connection (473) Reader's Theater (473) Critical Thinking (473)	Study Guide (82) Map Activities (24) Discovery Journal (42) • Study Prints (12) Transparency (9)
Understanding Visual Learning Objective: Use a political cartoon to analyze the controversy over economic reforms in Russia. (Visual Learning 1, 3, 4)	Writing Activity (475)	Study Guide (83)
Chapter Review	Answers (476–477)	Tests (77–80)

* Objectives are correlated to the strands and goals in the program Scope and Sequence on pages T41–T49.

• LEP appropriate resources. (For additional strategies, see pages T32–T33.)

CHAPTER RATIONALE

This chapter focuses on five major historic events of the 20th century and examines their effects on the people of Europe. These events are World War I, the Russian Revolution of 1917, World War II, the Cold War, and the collapse of the Soviet Union.

Through the use of maps, photographs, and special features, students better understand these events and thus are able to explain their causes and effects. In addition, students read about how these events have affected Europeans throughout the 20th century.

Lesson 1 examines the role that nationalism, modernization, and the alliance system played in the events leading up to World War I, including the assassination of Archduke Francis Ferdinand of Austria-Hungary. The text describes the war as the first modern war, providing students with a sense of how destructive modern warfare can be. Finally, we explain the outcomes of World War I to help students connect them to the origins of World War II.

In **Lesson 2** we describe the events that led to the Russian Revolution of 1917 and the formation of the world's first Communist state. A Closer Look at the last days of Czar Nicholas II and his family provides students with a portrait of a ruling family that was out of touch with the concerns of ordinary Russians. We examine the role that Lenin played in leading the Russian Revolution and in forming the Soviet Union. We also explain Stalin's dictatorship, his five-year plans, and the costs to the Russian people of building the Soviet Union.

Lesson 3 presents the causes and outcomes of World War II. We describe the rise to power of Hitler and his Nazi party, which was fueled by German nationalism. To provide students with a detailed look at the Second World War, we focus on these events: the Resistance, the Holocaust, turning points in the war, and the costs of the war. The Understanding Genocide feature gives students greater insight into the Holocaust and other examples of genocide. We challenge students to explore what it was like to live during the Cold War, when the fear of a nuclear war was at its height. Finally, we describe the collapse of the Soviet Union and the end of the Cold War. An Understanding Skills feature teaches students how to interpret and appreciate political cartoons.

Throughout this chapter, students gain an understanding of how five major events of the 20th century affected the people of Europe. The illustrations and photographs help students empathize with the lives, thoughts, feelings, and aspirations of Europeans during times of violent conflict and division.

ACTIVITIES & PROJECTS

Role Playing

Have students form six groups, each representing one of these countries: Austria-Hungary, Serbia, Russia, Germany, France, and Great Britain. Ask each student to role play an ambassador or a political leader. Have each group prepare for a summit meeting of all the countries with the goal of trying to prevent World War I from starting. Remind each group of the assassination in Sarajevo and ask them to consider the alliances of the time as they prepare for this meeting. (Use after Lesson 1.)

Basic: Making a Timeline

Prepare a timeline that extends along one wall of the classroom and shows the major events discussed in the chapter: World War I, the Russian Revolution, World War II, and the Cold War. Have students draw pictures to illustrate these and other events as they read. Direct students to post their pictures at the appropriate place on the timeline and explain their significance. (Use after any lesson.)

LEP: Making Maps

Have students use tracing paper to make overlay maps of Europe and Russia. Instruct them to create three maps, depicting Europe and Russia in 1913, 1938, and today, noting carefully the changing borders. The maps should include country and city names and important geographic features mentioned in the chapter. Have students explain the importance of each item they add. (Use after any lesson.)

Challenge: Writing a Report

Have students write a report on any of the events or the people mentioned in the lesson or discussed in class. You might have students focus on how the event affected daily life or the role the person played in culture, politics, economics, or science. (Use after any lesson.)

Collaborative Learning

Divide the class into groups of three or four students each. Have the groups create their own A Moment in Time or A Closer Look feature about one person, place, or event in the chapter. Have the students study the special feature pages in the text before beginning. See the list of features at the beginning of the pupil's text. (Use after Lesson 3.)

CHAPTER PREVIEW

Ask students to read the chapter title and introductory text. Point out that World War I and World War II were global conflicts—and enormously destructive. Tell students that conflicts in Europe and Russia in the first half of this century changed the map of the world and still influence events today.

Looking Back

Remind students that the rise of empires, such as those of Spain, Great Britain, and Russia, led to fierce, international rivalries.

Looking Forward

Inform students that they will be reading about major events in this century that shaped Europe and much of the world in these lessons: World War I, Russia Becomes the Soviet Union, and World War II and the Cold War.

Lesson 1 describes the causes and effects of a war so unlike all previous wars that it was called "the war to end war."

Chapter 20

Europe: 1900 to the End of the Cold War

As the 20th century began, Europeans felt that technology would improve their lives. However, Europeans used gains in technology to build modern weapons. Triggered by nationalism, two world wars exploded in Europe. After World War II, Europe lay in ruins. An "iron curtain" then divided Europe—until the curtain came crashing down, peacefully.

Two world wars destroyed entire cities, such as Warsaw, Poland, shown here. World War I recruiting posters served to raise troops for the war.

'YOU
ARE THE MAN
I WANT'

1860 | 1880 | 1900 | 1920

458

1871

1914–1918 More than eight million people die in World War I, the most destructive war to date.

BACKGROUND

By the late 19th century, most European countries were controlled by central governments. In previous centuries many Europeans had felt loyalty to their village or city, or to their local ruler or religion. Now loyalty to their country—nationalism—began to replace these feelings.

The Great Powers of Europe

In the 19th century, France, Great Britain, Austria, Prussia, and Russia were called the Great Powers because of their ability to influence world affairs. The rise of nationalism threatened the balance of power among the Great Powers—and peace in Europe.

During the first half of the 19th century, Italy was divided into small states, most under the foreign control of Austria and Spain. Germany was a loose collection of 39 states, dominated by Austria and Prussia. However, both Italians and Germans were determined to build their own nation-states. Italian nationalists led by Giuseppe Garibaldi and Camillo di Cavour united Italy in 1861. German nationalists led by Otto von Bismarck, the leader of Prussia, united Germany in 1871.

Competition among the Great Powers

Germans and Italians were now determined to compete with France, Great Britain, Austria, and Russia as Great Powers. Prussia's defeat of France in the Franco-Prussian War (1870–1871) helped pave the way for German

Mother Russia carries the hopes of the Russian people for their revolution of 1917.

Berliners celebrate the fall of the Berlin Wall in 1989. One year later, East and West Germany would reunite. Below, a Lithuanian worker sweeps off the toppled statue of the once-feared Soviet ruler, Josef Stalin.

1940	1960	1980	2000

1939–1945 About 50 million people die in World War II—six times as many as died in World War I. After the war, the United Nations is formed, and the Cold War begins.

1961 The East German government builds the Berlin Wall to prevent its people from fleeing to the West. The wall is a grim symbol of the deep division between Eastern and Western Europe.

1991

Understanding the Visuals

The ruins in Warsaw shown on the previous page illustrate the destructive nature of the weapons that were used in World War II. Point out to students that World War I posters were used to recruit troops and also to sell war bonds to pay for the war.

The Russian poster on this page is typical of Soviet art during the 1920s that depicted the ideals—but not necessarily the realities—of the Soviet Union as a country built by and for the masses. After the Soviet Communist Party was disbanded in 1991, former Communist leaders—such as Josef Stalin on this page—were discredited.

The Berlin Wall was perhaps the most famous symbol of the Cold War. It measured about 29 miles long.

Understanding Chronology

Refer students to the timeline. Ask them to name an event, represented in the visuals, that occurred during each of these periods: 1900–1919, 1920–1945, and 1946–1991. *(1900–1919: World War I; 1920–1945: the destruction of Warsaw and the building of the Soviet Union; 1946–1991: the Cold War and the collapse of communism in East Germany and the Soviet Union)*

unification under the lead of Prussia—and Germany's expansion as a Great Power. After defeating France in this war, Germany took control of the French region of Alsace-Lorraine, a territory rich in coal and iron ore.

Resentment and conflict over this region helped fuel prewar hostilities in Europe. Still, until World War I erupted, no major wars broke out in Europe between 1871 and 1914 even though the six Great Powers competed fiercely to build empires and to modernize. When World War I started on August 4, 1914, most Europeans thought that it would be a short war—over before the year ended—with few casualties.

Mussolini: A Model for Hitler

Billing himself as a "man of the people," Benito Mussolini (1883–1945) rose from humble origins to become dictator of Italy from 1922 until his death. Mussolini became the first fascist dictator in Europe, serving as a model for Adolf Hitler in Germany and Francisco Franco in Spain. Mussolini, like Hitler, was a skilled speaker and promised his people a new empire.

The Role of the United States

U.S. President Woodrow Wilson had won reelection in 1916 by vowing to keep the United States out of World War I. It was only after much debate that the United States joined the fighting. Many U.S. citizens had argued that isolation—remaining neutral—was best for the United States. They reasoned that since these wars were not on "our" soil, "we" should not be fighting them.

INTRODUCE

Explain that World War I, by far the most destructive war up to this time in history, involved the world's great powers. Have students read the Thinking Focus. Ask what generally causes countries to go to war. *(The desire to gain or keep territory and economic, political, or cultural control; the desire of a people to free themselves from control by another group; the failure of compromise or cooperation to gain desired ends)*

Let students predict what might have caused so many countries to enter World War I. Have students read the lesson to learn more about the causes and outcomes of this war.

Key Terms

Vocabulary Strategies: T36–T37

jingoism—extreme and aggressive nationalism

alliance—an agreement among nations to advance a common interest

1860 · 1871 · 1919 · 1940 · 1960 · 1980 · 2000

LESSON 1

World War I

THINKING FOCUS

What were the causes and outcomes of World War I?

Key Terms

- jingoism
- alliance

We don't want to fight,
But, by jingo, if we do,
We've got the ships,
We've got the men,
We've got the money too!

British music-hall song, 1878

During the late 1800s, the people of Europe were extremely proud of their countries. As this song shows, the British were proud of their world empire. The French took great pride in their country as did the Germans in theirs. What these people felt was nationalism—that loyalty to one's country was more important than individual, family, or global interests.

In Europe, nationalism also meant belonging to the same ethnic group. For example, most of the citizens of France considered themselves to be one ethnic group. They shared the same customs and language. Nationalism united the French as it did the Germans and other Europeans.

However, nationalism also divided Europe. Reread the song on this page. It introduced the word *jingo.* In the late 1800s, European nationalism often turned into **jingoism,** or warlike nationalism. "Jingoes" believed their nation could beat anyone at anything.

As a result, France, Germany, Great Britain, and Russia competed for world power. First, they raced to modernize their industries. Second, they competed for control of trade routes, raw materials, and markets around the world. Third, Germany, Great Britain, and France fought to set up colonies in Africa and Asia.

Finally, these nations competed in an arms race. They built up great armies and huge supplies of weapons.

➤ *Before World War I, using new technologies to build a dirigible, or airship, made Europeans proud of what their modern nations could accomplish. This airship's hull, or main body, held hydrogen gas, which made it lighter than air.*

Objectives

1. Explain two causes of World War I.
2. Describe the outcomes of World War I.

Graphic Overview

European Countries Are Nationalistic and Competitive — Alliances Form → **Two-nation Conflict Escalates into Multinational World War I** → **World War I Ends** → **War Costs Lives and Property — Treaty Creates New Boundaries**

▲ *Huge factories owned by the Krupp family of Germany produced tons of steel and weapons in both World War I and World War II.*

Europe in Conflict

Look at the map on page 462 to see where the people of Europe lived in the early 1900s. Notice where Austrians and Hungarians lived. Find the region of southeast Europe surrounded by the Black Sea and the Mediterranean known as the Balkan peninsula, or simply the Balkans. What groups of people did this region include?

Europe's Powder Keg

Nationalism turned the Balkans into Europe's powder keg. Since the late 1400s, the Ottoman Turks had ruled most of the Balkans. Then, in 1867, the Austrians and Hungarians formed the Austro-Hungarian Empire, which was also known as Austria-Hungary.

This empire soon ruled over much of the Balkans. Turn to the map again to see which peoples they ruled. From the map you can see that many Serbs lived in the Austro-Hungarian Empire. Serbs are one of the Slavic peoples you read about in Chapter 19.

By 1878 most of the Serbs had formed an independent country, Serbia. Yet not all Serbs lived in Serbia. Many still lived in areas ruled by Austria-Hungary. Serbia wanted to expand its borders to include all Serbs. Austria-Hungary was determined not to lose any part of its empire.

The Alliance System

In the 1870s, Europeans began forming alliances to try to keep peace in Europe. An **alliance** *(uh LY uhns)* is an agreement among nations to advance a common interest.

Europeans trusted alliances to keep conflicts between nations from leading to war. Germany, Italy, and Austria-Hungary formed one alliance. Great Britain, France, and Russia formed another. Russia also promised its support to Serbia.

This alliance system was thought to be foolproof. For example, attacking Serbia meant probably having to fight Russia, too. Then, if Russia fought, Great Britain and France might back up Russia. After all, they belonged to an alliance. No country would dare attack one that had an alliance—or would it? ■

■ *Explain why the Balkans were known as the powder keg of Europe.*

DEVELOP

Point out that this lesson presents the causes and effects of World War I by exploring the political, economic, and cultural forces involved. To illustrate this, refer students to the music-hall song on the previous page. Notice that the warlike nationalism it so cheerily expresses contributed to the onset of World War I.

Have students keep track of the causes and outcomes of World War I by listing them as they read the lesson.

ECONOMICS

Critical Thinking

Encourage students to study the photograph on this page. Ask them what it reveals or suggests about industrialization during the late 19th and early 20th centuries. *(Sample response: Huge factories could produce enormous quantities of goods; industrialization depended on large numbers of workers.)*

■ *Nationalistic conflicts between Austria-Hungary and Serbia could ignite a war. Because of the alliance system, a local Balkan war could end up involving other European countries.*

Access Strategy

Relate the alliance system to personal loyalties familiar to students. For example, have they been asked "Are you on my side or hers?" or "Why are you speaking to him after what he said to me?" Encourage students to describe situations in which people they know have disagreed with one another and have tried to get supporters, or allies, to side with them. Ask if they found it difficult not to take sides. Encourage a discussion of personal loyalties, or alliances. Try to elicit from students that loyalties could pull them into a conflict.

Tell students that in the late 1800s and early 1900s, European countries formed alliances similar to these personal loyalties. Members of each alliance agreed to support the other members. Explore with students some of the advantages and disadvantages of this system. Point out that while alliances were formed to help promote peace, they also increased the chances of war.

Access Activity

To help students understand how popular culture influences or reflects politics, encourage them to listen carefully to the lyrics of popular songs or advertising jingles. Ask them to describe what these songs and ads say about politics today. Have students bring recordings of songs and ads for the class to listen to. Compare them with the song on the previous page.

➤ *This map shows that ethnic groups in Europe—for example, those in the Balkans—were divided by political borders or were ruled by another ethnic group. These conditions fueled nationalistic conflicts that led to war.*

ETHICS

Social Participation

Divide students into groups of four or five and ask each group to explain how the system of alliances, crafted to prevent war, backfired. *(Because of their commitment to support one another, a two-nation dispute pulled other nations into war.)*

Then have each group discuss these questions: What if an alliance member had refused to honor its commitment to support another? How might this refusal have affected both the war and future relations among the countries? *(The war might not have grown to a global scale, but the broken trust might have made future agreements meaningless.)*

People of Europe, 1914

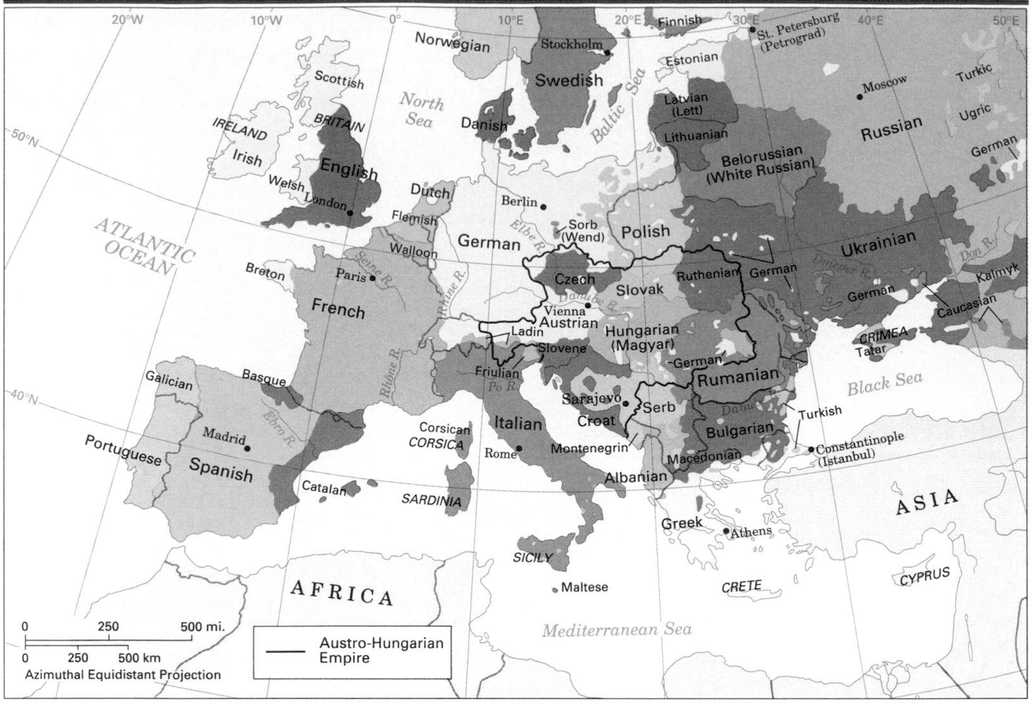

Norwegian
Stockholm
Swedish
Finnish
St. Petersburg (Petrograd)
Estonian
Scottish
North Sea
Danish
Baltic Sea
Latvian (Lett)
Lithuanian
Moscow
Russian
Turkic
Ugric
German
IRELAND
Irish
BRITAIN
English
Welsh
London
Dutch
Berlin
Belorussian (White Russian)
Flemish
Walloon
German
Sorb (Wend)
Polish
Elbe R.
ATLANTIC OCEAN
Breton
Paris
Seine R.
Rhine R.
Czech
Slovak
Ruthenian
Ukrainian
Kalmyk
French
Vienna
Austrian
Ladin
Slovene
Hungarian (Magyar)
German
Caucasian
CRIMEA
Tatar
Galician
Basque
Rhône R.
Friulian
Po R.
Rumanian
Black Sea
Sarajevo
Serb
Croat
Corsican
CORSICA
Italian
Montenegrin
Bulgarian
Turkish
Portuguese
Madrid
Spanish
Ebro R.
Rome
Macedonian
Constantinople (Istanbul)
Albanian
Catalan
SARDINIA
Greek
Athens
ASIA
SICILY
Maltese
CRETE
CYPRUS
AFRICA
Mediterranean Sea
0 250 500 mi.
0 250 500 km
Azimuthal Equidistant Projection
Austro-Hungarian Empire
20°W
10°W
0°
10°E
20°E
30°E
40°E
50°E
50°N
40°N

▲ *This cultural map shows the ethnic groups of Europe before World War I. How does it help explain nationalism as a cause of World War I? For help in using a cultural map, see page G14 of the Map and Globe Handbook.*

"The War to End War"

On the morning of June 28, 1914, Serbs in Sarajevo *(sar uh YAY voh)* watched as a parade of six cars passed. The day was their national holiday. As part of their celebration, Archduke Francis Ferdinand rode through their city. The archduke was the future ruler of Austria-Hungary. This empire still ruled Sarajevo against the Serbs' wishes.

Suddenly, shots rang out, killing the archduke. Austria-Hungary blamed Serbia for his death. It then declared war on Serbia.

Since Russia had promised to support Serbia, it prepared its soldiers to fight Austria-Hungary. As Russian soldiers readied for war, so did the German troops. France and Great Britain also prepared for war. Instead of preventing war, the alliance system was now dragging nations into one.

As armies moved into position, European leaders were not able to back down from the fight. Remember that jingoism was a common feeling in Europe then. Each country believed that its modern armies and navies meant victory.

The First Modern War

On August 4, 1914, World War I began. Germany, Bulgaria, Turkey, and Austria-Hungary fought on one side as the Central Powers. France, Russia, Great Britain, and seven other European countries formed the Allied Powers, or Allies.

Before the war, few Europeans knew the destructive power that modern industry could produce. During the war, railroads quickly

Investigating

Ask students to compare the map on this page with the inset of Europe in the Atlas on page 679. Have them identify the modern nations that once made up the empire of Austria-Hungary. *(Austria, Hungary, Czech Republic, Slovak Republic, Croatia, Slovenia, Bosnia-Herzegovina, and parts of Poland, Romania, Yugoslavia, and Italy)*

Cultural Context

Before World War I, most people felt that women should be restricted to certain roles, for example, mother and homemaker. However, during the war millions of men went to war—and millions of women replaced them in factories, business offices, and shops. Not only did women keep soldiers supplied with weapons and clothing, they also paved streets, ran hospitals, and dug ditches. Working outside the home during the war helped change the role of women in society.

The enormous loss of life in World War I deeply affected the survivors, especially young people. In a war so destructive, they thought, no one was the victor. The young people of this time became known as the Lost Generation. They questioned the values of the older generation. Some became writers and artists who described their grief and bitterness in their works. During the 1920s and 1930s, the arts and literature often reflected a deep sense of loss and pessimism.

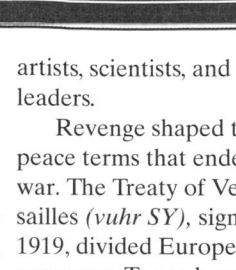

moved huge armies to the war zones. Then machine guns, artillery and poison gas were unleashed, killing millions of soldiers.

For several years neither side could defeat the other. In 1917 Russia began peace talks with Germany, which you'll read about in the next lesson. That same year the United States joined the Allies. After losing several major battles, German leaders asked for peace. On November 11, 1918, in a railroad car in France, they signed a truce. World War I was over.

The Costs of War

World War I was the most destructive war up to that time. In all about 8.5 million soldiers died, and another 21 million were wounded. This enormous loss of life drained Europe of a generation of workers, artists, scientists, and new leaders.

Revenge shaped the peace terms that ended the war. The Treaty of Versailles *(vuhr SY)*, signed in 1919, divided Europe in new ways. To see how, compare the map on the opposite page with the Atlas map on page 682.

The Allies divided Austria-Hungary among seven countries. They took away some of Germany's land and all its colonies. They ordered Germany to admit its "war guilt." Germany was forced to pay huge sums of money for war damages to the Allies.

Many Europeans believed that World War I would be "the war to end war." French army marshal Ferdinand Foch *(fosh)* disagreed: "This is not a peace treaty. It is an armistice [cease-fire] for twenty years." ■

◄ To support the war effort at home, many women on both sides worked in their country's weapons factories.

How Do We Know?

HISTORY *Before television, newsreels helped people see current events. These short films first appeared in movie theaters about 1897. During World War I, efforts were made to produce newsreels that showed battle scenes from Europe, but people didn't get a very good idea of what the war was like. It was not until World War II that newsreels became an effective source of war news.*

◄ For months at a time, soldiers fought from—and lived in—trenches, or deep ditches. Modern weapons made trenches essential for protection.

■ Explain why World War I was so destructive.

REVIEW

1. **FOCUS** What were the causes and outcomes of World War I?
2. **HISTORY** Give two examples of how nationalism divided the people of Europe before 1914.
3. **POLITICAL SYSTEMS** Why did European countries form alliances? Did the alliance system work? Explain why or why not.
4. **CRITICAL THINKING** What does this slogan mean to you: "My country, right or wrong." Explain how this slogan points out the positive and negative aspects of nationalism.
5. **ACTIVITY** Research the changes in communications technology after 1850 and before World War I. Read pages 666–667 in the Minipedia to learn what some of these changes were. Use the library to find more information about a topic that interests you. Then report your findings to your class.

HISTORY

Critical Thinking

Refer students to the lesson titles in this chapter. Then have them reread the words of Ferdinand Foch on this page and discuss their meaning. Based on the title of Lesson 3—World War II and the Cold War—have students make a prediction based on Foch's quotation. Encourage them to support their predictions with information from this lesson.

■ *Powerful new weapons, efficient transportation systems, and modern industries helped make the war so destructive.*

CLOSE

Refer students to the Thinking Focus and the lists of causes and outcomes they recorded as they read the lesson. Suggest that students use their lists to draw illustrations that reflect some aspect of European culture or society before and after World War I.

Answers to Review Questions

1. Causes: Nationalism led countries to compete with one another; alliances obligated them to support member nations at war. Outcomes: Millions were killed, Austria-Hungary was divided into seven countries, and Germany lost territory and was required to pay war damages.
2. Nationalism divided Europe into competing nations. It also created divisions among citizens of the same country.
3. They formed alliances to help prevent war. The system did not work since Serbia and Austria-Hungary dragged their alliance members into war.
4. Possible response: No matter what my country does, I will be loyal to it. Positive aspect: This slogan can help unite people. Negative aspect: It represents a loyalty that is blind and unquestioning.
5. Research projects will vary but could include reports on the radio, phonograph, typewriter, telephone, or movie camera.

Homework Options

Suggest that efforts to resolve conflicts peacefully might help prevent wars. Ask students to imagine themselves as advisors to the head of state of Austria-Hungary in 1914. Have them write possible responses to the assassination in Sarajevo that might have helped prevent World War I.

Study Guide: page 80

INTRODUCE

Remind students of the political system in czarist Russia as described in Chapter 19. Let students discuss how World War I might have affected life in Russia. Then ask students to use the chapter title, the Thinking Focus, and the visuals on this page and the next page to predict how life in Russia might have changed during the period covered by this lesson. Have students read the lesson to see what changed about life in Russia.

Key Terms

Vocabulary Strategies: T36–T37

revolution—the overthrow of a government by those who were previously subject to it

dictator—a ruler who holds absolute power

propaganda—information spread to advance a particular cause or set of ideas

➤ *Russian peasants lived in poverty, with little opportunity to improve the condition of their lives.*

1860
1900
1940
1960
1980
2000

LESSON 2

Russia Becomes the Soviet Union

THINKING FOCUS

How did life under the czars compare with life under Lenin and Stalin?

Key Terms

- revolution
- dictator
- propaganda

Arctic winds blasted the women marching through the streets of Petrograd on March 8, 1917. "Bread! Bread! Bread!" they chanted. Russian soldiers stood by, unsure of what to do. Confused, the soldiers let the women march.

The winter of 1916–1917 was a bitter one for the Russian people. Not only was it extremely cold, but fuel and food supplies were low. Worse, World War I showed no signs of ending. Already hundreds of thousands of Russians had been killed.

At first most Russians had supported the war. Like other people in Europe, they believed it would result in an easy victory for their country. However, Russia was far less modernized than most of Europe. Most Russians were still peasant farmers. Russian soldiers had poor equipment and little training.

As a result, one disaster followed another, both on the battlefield and at home. By March 1917 the Russians had had enough fighting. In Petrograd, formerly St. Petersburg, Russians took to the streets in protest. They demanded peace, land, and bread from their ruler, Czar Nicholas II.

Soon rioting spread throughout Russia. How would the czar respond?

➤ *Examine this photograph of Russian peasants, taken before the revolution. Describe what you think their lives were like.*

Objectives

1. Identify two causes and effects of the Russian Revolution.
2. Compare life under the czars with life under Lenin and Stalin.

Graphic Overview

life under czars
tyranny of czars
food shortages
World War I
landless peasants
life under Lenin and Stalin
tyranny of dictators
collective farms
food shortages
modernized industry
RUSSIAN REVOLUTION

◄ *These Russian children stand next to a toppled statue of Czar Alexander III, Nicholas II's father. After the Russian Revolution, statues of the czars were replaced with those of Lenin and other Communist leaders.*

The Russian Revolution

In the past, soldiers had shot protesters out of loyalty to the czar. Now, Russian soldiers—cold, hungry, and angry—joined the protests. On March 15, 1917, the protesters forced Nicholas to give up his throne. To learn more about Czar Nicholas and his family, read A Closer Look on the next page.

Lenin Takes Control

News of this **revolution,** or overthrow of a government, swept through Russia. Peasants seized land. Workers took over factories. Lacking a strong ruler, Russia soon erupted in chaos, or disorder.

One Russian, known as Lenin, believed communism was Russia's best hope for the future. He called for Russians to own all land and industry in common. Lenin won support by promising "Peace, Land, and Bread."

In November 1917 Lenin and his supporters took control of the weak Russian government by force. Lenin divided farmland among the peasants. Then he signed a peace treaty with Germany to end Russian fighting in World War I.

The Russian Civil War

Many Russians did not support Lenin. In May 1918 his opponents started a civil war in Russia.

Lenin's supporters called themselves the Red Army. Those who opposed Lenin were called the Whites. Some Whites wanted a new czar. Others fought for democracy. Still others were non-Russians, such as Ukrainians, who wanted to form separate countries.

By the end of 1920, the Red Army had defeated the Whites. Lenin set up governments in the separate republics, or states. In 1922 Lenin united these republics, forming the Union of Soviet Socialist Republics, or Soviet Union.

According to Communist ideals, workers were to run the cities, farmers the countryside. Instead, only Lenin and his supporters ruled. ■

СУХИХ, ЧИСТЫХ ПЕЛЕНОК
ГРУДИ МАТЕРИ
АКУШЕРОК А НЕ БАБОК
ЗДОРОВЫХ РОДИТЕЛЕЙ

▼ *Russian Communists used posters such as this one to win support for their revolutionary goals. The dolls, symbols of children, are shown demanding fresh milk, fresh air, and healthy parents.*

■ *What were the causes of the Russian Revolution?*

DEVELOP

Tell students that this lesson will compare and contrast conditions in Russia before and after the Russian Revolution of 1917. You may wish to put the Graphic Overview on the chalkboard, omitting the listed details, and have students complete it as they read.

POLITICAL SYSTEMS

Visual Learning

Have students examine the photograph of the toppled statue of Alexander III and compare it with the photograph of Stalin's statue on page 459. Ask what these two photographs reveal about the attitudes of people who were ruled by the Russian czar in 1917 and by Communist leaders in the Soviet Union in 1991. *(Statues usually symbolize honor and respect. The toppling of these statues indicates that in both the czarist empire of 1917 and the Soviet empire of 1991 people had been forced to honor leaders whom many, in fact, despised.)*

■ *Causes of the Russian Revolution included hunger, poverty, and losses in World War I.*

Access Strategy

Encourage discussion of how students and their families spend their free time. Have students imagine turning on the radio and finding only government-approved music or censored news reports glorifying the government. Discuss the range of foods and products available to students. Tell them to picture in their minds stores with nothing but meager supplies of basic necessities.

Remind students of complaints they can voice about rules and people in authority. Have them imagine being imprisoned, without a trial, for criticizing school rules or government leaders. Explain that in this lesson, they will read about how the people of Russia experienced such conditions under a Communist government headed by Stalin. As they read, have students relate their experiences with law and authority to those of the Soviet people. Ask whether defying the law or overthrowing a government is ever justified.

Access Activity

Invite ideas for a new school policy or program. Have students work in groups or with a partner to create a slogan and propaganda poster for or against the policy or program. Tell students to limit the slogans to five or fewer words that capture the essence of their message. Ask that they use strong images or symbols to illustrate their message.

Note: You may wish to use this Closer Look before students read any of the lesson or after they have read through the first paragraph on the previous page.

More About Rasputin Grigory Rasputin, a Siberian peasant and faith healer, was widely known and despised for mixing religious fervor with earthly pleasures. He won the favor of Empress Alexandra, however, with his apparent healing powers over her son, who suffered from hemophilia.

When Nicholas II took command of the Russian troops in 1915, he left Alexandra and Rasputin in charge of the government. Several noblemen, alarmed by Rasputin's influence on the empress, set out to murder him. Rasputin proved hard to kill. He survived poisoning and shooting by the noblemen. Finally, they drowned him.

A CLOSER LOOK

The Last Czar

Czar Nicholas II lived in lavish palaces with his wife, the empress Alexandra; their daughters Olga, Tatiana, Marie, and Anastasia; and their young son Alexis, heir to the monarchy. In his royal, protected world, the czar was out of touch with the Russian people. Communists killed him and his family in 1917, after his government was overthrown.

Worry tormented Nicholas and Alexandra. Alexis, shown here in 1914 in front of his mother, had hemophilia—a painful and dangerous condition in which blood fails to clot normally.

Rasputin! He posed as a holy man, but his unholy behavior caused many Russians to despise him. Yet Nicholas and Alexandra trusted him because he eased Alexis's suffering.

Fantastic eggs were crafted for the czar by Carl Fabergé and his jewelry firm. This egg is like a cuckoo clock. Inside another egg, a miniature train runs on tiny tracks.

Visual Learning

Refer students to the captions describing the extravagant lifestyle of the Russian royal family and to the photographs of the clock egg. Ask students how peasants might have felt about a czar who lived in such luxury at public expense. *(Possible answers: angry and betrayed; proud and protective)*

Language Arts Connection

Read aloud short selections from *Animal Farm* by George Orwell (Harcourt Brace Jovanovich, 1990). Point out that it is a political fable based on the Russian Revolution. After they have read a few selections, students can identify who some of the book's characters might represent. *(For example, Farmer Jones might stand for the czar. The pigs might stand for Communist dictators such as Stalin.)* For further readings, refer students to the unit bibliography on pages 404–405.

Reader's Theater

Have students select a story or a book about life in Russia under the czars or during the Russian Revolution of 1917. For example, students may enjoy reading about Czar Nicholas II's family in the novel *Nicholas and Alexandra* by Robert K. Massie (Atheneum, 1972). Then have students write a script based on their readings to perform for the class.

Building the Soviet Union

World War I and the civil war left the Soviet Union in ruins. Lenin tried to rebuild the country. In 1921 he allowed peasants to sell some grain for private profit, rather than at set prices to the government. Given a chance to earn a profit, people worked harder. The Soviet Union began to recover.

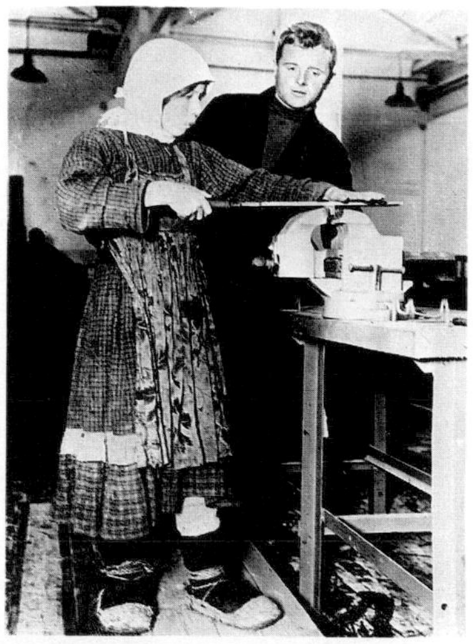

Millions of Soviet peasant farmers, such as the woman shown here, moved to cities to work in heavy industry—steel, cement, and tool factories.

Stalin's Five-Year Plans

After Lenin died in 1924, Josef Stalin took over the Soviet government. Like Lenin, he ruled as a **dictator,** or ruler who holds total power. Stalin wanted to industrialize the Soviet Union. He forced peasants to work on huge collective farms run by his government. He ordered factories to produce only basic goods such as steel.

Stalin set out his goals for the Soviet Union in Five-Year Plans. In some ways his plans were successful. Soviet factories grew quickly in the 1930s. Yet the Soviet people paid a terrible price for Stalin's plans. Collective farms failed to supply enough food for the country. Drought made the famine worse. Millions died from starvation.

A Life of Fear

Stalin held complete power over the Soviet people. He arrested anyone suspected of disloyalty. Many were sent to labor camps in Siberia or were killed by his secret police.

To stay in power, Stalin also used **propaganda** *(prahp uh GAN duh),* or information spread to advance one's cause or ideas. All newspapers, radio stations, and schools were run by the Soviet government. They could print, air, or teach only propaganda that praised Stalin and his plans. Stalin also controlled artists and writers. By the late 1930s, the Soviet Union was a world power again. However, under the dictator Stalin, millions of Soviet people had no say in their government. ■

■ *What were Stalin's economic plans?*

REVIEW

1. **FOCUS** How did life under the czars compare with life under Lenin and Stalin?
2. **HISTORY** Why did the Russian people revolt against Czar Nicholas II?
3. **ECONOMICS** Communism in the Soviet Union had many negative effects. Describe at least one negative effect.
4. **CRITICAL THINKING** Explain why Lenin's slogan, "Peace, Land, and Bread," gained the support of the Russian people. Was Lenin's slogan an example of propaganda? Explain why or why not.
5. **ART ACTIVITY** Design a propaganda poster. You may want to design one that Lenin or Stalin might have used. Or, design a poster that opponents of Lenin or Stalin might have used.

ECONOMICS

Study Skills

Stalin forced millions of people to leave the countryside to supply labor for Soviet industrialization. Have students search the text and visuals for possible reasons why Stalin might want the Soviet Union to industrialize. *(To build up the Soviet Union as a world power, and then to increase his own power)*

■ *Stalin planned to modernize the economy quickly by collectivizing farms and by speeding the growth of factories that produced basic goods such as steel.*

CLOSE

Have students answer the Thinking Focus by reviewing the Graphic Overview they completed as they read the lesson. Point out that comparing life under the czars with life under Lenin and Stalin reveals both similarities and differences. Have students speculate on what might have contributed to the downfall of the Soviet Communist party in 1991.

Answers to Review Questions

1. Similarities: Most people were poor, with few rights or political power. Differences: Under the czars, many peasants were landless, and the economy was based on agriculture. Under Lenin and Stalin, the economy was industrialized, while peasants were forced to work on collective farms run by the government.
2. Hunger and the losses of World War I fueled their revolt.
3. People had no freedom and the country was run like a dictatorship. The failure of the collective farms caused millions to die from starvation.
4. The slogan addressed people's needs and demands, which the czar had ignored. The slogan is a good example of propaganda since it was clearly part of Lenin's effort to win support for communism.
5. Posters will vary but could include an anti-Leninist call for democracy or a pro-Stalinist call for modernization.

Homework Options

To help students understand censorship and propaganda, have them write a paragraph aimed at winning Russian peasants over to collective farms. Tell them that if Stalin thinks their paragraph is not persuasive, they will be arrested by the Russian secret police.

Study Guide: page 81

INTRODUCE

Have students read the lesson title and discuss the meaning of Cold War. Explain that the Cold War began in the years following World War II, the hottest, most destructive war ever. After students have read the Thinking Focus, ask them to recall any terms of the treaty ending World War I that could have sparked a second world war. *(The territorial and financial costs imposed on Germany could have sparked a desire for revenge.)* Have students read the lesson to find out more about World War II.

Key Terms

Vocabulary Strategies: T36–T37

genocide—the planned killing of an entire racial, religious, or ethnic group

Holocaust—large-scale slaughter or destruction, especially of Jews by the Nazis during World War II

superpower—a country that is a military, political, and economic giant

iron curtain—a barrier that prevents free interaction, especially between Eastern and Western Europe after World War II

Cold War—the rivalry that existed between the Soviet bloc and Western nations from the 1940s through the 1980s

1860 1880 1900 **1920** **1991** 2000

LESSON 3

World War II and the Cold War

THINKING FOCUS

What were the causes and outcomes of World War II?

Key Terms

- genocide
- Holocaust
- superpower
- iron curtain
- Cold War

➤ *Hitler is shown here inspecting his Nazi troops. Notice the swastika, or cross with bent arms, on the flags, uniforms, and helmets. Nazi Germany used the swastika for its national symbol.*

Thousands of Germans gathered for a rally in the city of Nuremberg in 1933. "*Sieg heil!* [Hail to victory!]" they shouted. Everyone saluted the *führer (FYUR uhr),* or leader—Adolf Hitler.

Hitler's success grew out of the German people's despair. In the early 1920s, Germany struggled to pay the millions of dollars it owed the Allies for World War I. German money, the *mark,* became almost worthless.

Then, in 1929, a worldwide depression struck. This economic downturn put more than six million Germans out of work. Many Germans were angry and afraid. They wanted a strong leader to restore order and German pride. They turned to Hitler and his political party, the National Socialist German Workers' Party, or Nazis.

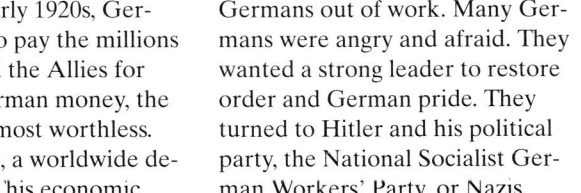

Germany under Nazi Rule

Hitler promised that the Nazis would create new jobs and make Germany a strong military power again. He vowed that Germany would win back all the land it had lost in World War I—and more.

Hitler ruled Germany as a dictator. His goal was "one state, one people, one leader." Like Stalin, Hitler used propaganda and fear to control people. "Storm troopers" and secret police arrested, beat up, or killed anyone viewed as a threat to Hitler.

Hitler preached hatred for the Jews. Germany's troubles, he said, were caused by a "Jewish world conspiracy." Many Germans also wanted someone to blame for their suffering. They shared Hitler's ideas.

Objectives

1. Name two causes of World War II.
2. Describe the outcomes of World War II.
3. Explain the concept of genocide.
4. Describe life behind the iron curtain.

Graphic Overview

Causes
- economic depression in Germany
- Hitler's aggression
- German resentment of Treaty of Versailles

→ **World War II** →

Outcomes
- massive war casualties and destruction
- the Holocaust
- shift in power to U.S.A. and U.S.S.R.
- Cold War

The Night of Broken Glass

On the night of November 9, 1938, Nazis began smashing and burning Jewish stores, homes, and synagogues all over Germany. Afterward, the streets of Germany were littered with broken glass. This night was named *Kristallnacht* —the night of broken glass.

Kristallnacht was Nazi Germany's first official large-scale attack on Jews. Although they had committed no crimes, about 30,000 Jews were arrested that night. The Nazis split up Jewish families and seized their property. However, the worst was yet to come.

Germany's Road to War

Hitler built up Germany's military strength. Then he began to take back what he saw as Germany's rightful territory. In 1938 Hitler forced Austria into his new German Reich, or empire. Then, from 1938 to 1939, he took over Czechoslovakia piece by piece.

Other European leaders tried to ignore Hitler. They did not want to risk another major war by opposing him. They hoped Hitler would stop after Czechoslovakia. Then, on September 1, 1939, Hitler ordered German troops to march again— and invade Poland.

European leaders finally realized that only force could stop Hitler. Two days after the invasion of Poland, France and Great Britain declared war on Germany. World War II had begun.

On one side were the Axis Powers: Germany, Italy, and Japan. On the other side were the Allies, which included France and Great Britain. Later Canada, the Soviet Union, and the United States joined the Allies. ■

Across Time & Space

Between 1936 and 1939, Spain fought a civil war that resulted in General Francisco Franco becoming dictator. Franco ruled Spain until his death in 1975. Germany and Italy used the Spanish Civil War to test modern tanks and warplanes in preparation for a future war.

■ What events led to World War II?

World War II

German tanks rumbled down the muddy roads leading to Poland's capital, Warsaw. Modern German airplanes bombed Poland's cities and countryside. The Polish army fought back, often with soldiers on horseback. However, in just 17 days, Germany conquered Poland.

◄ *Hundreds of thousands of Polish people were forced to flee from their homes after Germany invaded their country in 1939.*

DEVELOP

Explain that this lesson will explore the causes and outcomes of World War II and the subsequent Cold War. Have students complete an outline as they read, using *World War II* and *Cold War* as the major headings, and the subheadings *Causes and Outcomes* under each major heading.

■ *Germany's economic trouble after World War I led to Hitler's rise to power, which in turn led to Germany's military build-up, its takeover of Austria and Czechoslovakia, and its invasion of Poland—the event that led France and Great Britain to declare war on Germany.*

POLITICS

Critical Thinking

Ask students why many Europeans supported dictators such as Hitler and Franco. *(Possible response: During economic hard times of the 1920s and 1930s, many Europeans felt that strong rulers were needed to restore order and prosperity.)*

Access Strategy

Discuss the concept of scapegoat—an innocent person or group blamed for wrongdoings or troubles. Have students consider why some people label an ethnic or religious group that is different from their own as a scapegoat. *(It may seem to be easier to focus hatred or criticize people who appear to be different, rather than take responsibility for problems themselves.)* Tell students that Hitler made the Jewish people scapegoats for his country's problems. Ask students to think about times when they were made the scapegoat or when they made someone else the scapegoat.

Then ask students what a stereotype is. *(An oversimplified idea about a group of people)* You may want students to read the skill feature on identifying stereotypes on page 637 in Chapter 27. Have students read the lesson to see what happened to the Jewish people during Hitler's rise to power and during World War II.

Access Activity

Refer students to the image on this page and ask what it suggests about life in Europe during the war. Have students discuss the effects of war on people when the fighting is done on their own soil. Use the two world wars and the Bosnian War as examples.

GEOGRAPHY

Critical Thinking

Point out that unlike other European Allies, Great Britain was bombed but not conquered or occupied. Refer students to the map of Europe on page 682 of the Atlas. Ask how Great Britain's location helped it resist conquest. *(Great Britain is surrounded by water. Nazi troops could attack it only by sea or by air.)*

ETHICS

Social Participation

Discuss the Resistance, including the individuals who aided Jews at risk to their own lives. Ask students what values these people may have held that inspired their actions. *(Fairness, justice, compassion, loyalty to their defeated country)* Have them discuss the risks that people their age take when they stand up for what they believe is right or fair. *(Risks may involve loss of popularity or privilege.)*

Modern Europe and Russia

1900
1910
1920
1930
1940
1901 Queen Victoria of Great Britain dies.
1905 "Bloody Sunday" in St. Petersburg results in nationwide strikes.
1912 Conflict flares in the Balkans.
1914–1918 World War I
1917 The Russian Revolution begins.
1922 USSR is formed.
1933 Hitler comes to power in Germany.
1939–19 World V

▲ *Londoners shown here used their subways, or "the tube," as air raid shelters when German warplanes bombed Great Britain from 1940 to 1941.*

Hitler's "Lightning War"

In the first year of the war, German armies waged a *blitzkrieg (BLIHTS kreeg),* or "lightning war." After Germany defeated Poland, it conquered Denmark, Norway, the Netherlands, Belgium, and Luxembourg by the spring of 1940. Then Germany forced France to surrender. A proud Hitler made French leaders sign a truce in the same railroad car where the truce ending World War I was signed.

Great Britain was the only western European power left fighting Hitler. Winston Churchill, Britain's new prime minister, proclaimed, "We shall go on to the end; . . . we shall never surrender."

The Resistance

In countries conquered by the Nazis, people tried to fight back in secret. Others helped Jews escape or smuggled secrets to the Allies.

This movement to fight the Nazis was called the Resistance. Resistance groups formed in many of the countries Germany had defeated. One member of a Jewish resistance group wrote, "Our watchword was: Live and die with dignity!"

The Holocaust

In 1942 Hitler began to carry out his "final solution to the Jewish problem." His "final solution" was **genocide,** or the planned killing of an entire race or ethnic group. Nazi soldiers rounded up all the Jews they could find. Some were killed; others were sent to prison camps.

Many Jews tried to hide in cellars, attics, and barns. Anne Frank, a teenager, hid with her family in an attic in Amsterdam, the Netherlands. She wrote:

> The Germans ring at every front door to inquire if there are any Jews living in the house. If there are, then the whole family has to go at once. If they don't find any, they go on to the next house. No one has a chance of evading them unless one goes into hiding.

➤ *Nazis in Poland forced Jewish men, women, and children into a crowded ghetto, or restricted area, of Warsaw. Later, as this photograph shows, they were sent to concentration camps.*

Visual Learning

Refer students to the images on these pages. Ask what they reveal about the human costs of war. *(Possible answer: The danger, fear, and suffering of war affect everyone.)* Have students distinguish between the suffering that affected every European during the war and the abuses inflicted on specific racial and ethnic groups by the Nazis.

Social Context

Ask students if they think that any Germans tried to openly protest or resist Hitler's rule. Then tell them that some Germans did try to resist Hitler. A group of Hitler's own generals plotted to kill him, and several ministers protested his treatment of Jews. A group of women whose Jewish husbands had been seized by the Nazis staged a public protest in Berlin in 1943, which led to the Nazis releasing the men.

Few other Germans opposed Hitler for fear of receiving the same treatment as Jews. You may want to have students discuss whether Hitler could have been stopped if more people had protested or had resisted his rule. Remind students that without popular support—or acquiescence on the part of the majority of the German people—Hitler would not have been able to hold so much power.

1961 Berlin Wall is built.

ited Nations is formed; 'ar begins.

1989 Berlin Wall falls.

950 | 1960 | 1970 | 1980 | 1990

1986 Chernobyl nuclear power plant explodes near Kiev, USSR.

1957 Common Market begins.

1991 USSR breaks up and the Cold War ends.

If caught, Jewish families were sent to prison camps in Poland or Germany—the Nazi concentration camps. Prisoners were often beaten and tortured in the concentration camps. The healthiest were forced to work as slave labor. Most of the rest—the old, the sick, and the young—were killed.

Some camps, such as Treblinka and Auschwitz *(OWSH vihts),* became "death camps." Jews, Gypsies, and other prisoners were brought there and worked to death, or killed. About six million Jews, and several million others—Gypsies, Slavs, Poles, and political prisoners—died in these Nazi camps.

Nazi Germany's murders of Jews and others in Europe is now known as the **Holocaust.** The word *holocaust (HAHL uh kawst)* means "great destruction by fire." To learn more about genocide and the Holocaust, read Understanding Genocide on this page.

Understanding Genocide

Genocide is an attempt to kill all the people or members of a certain group. Why would one group of people want to completely destroy another group of people?

The Roots of Genocide

One reason a group of people commits genocide is hatred. In Nazi Germany, Jewish people were blamed for the country's problems. Hitler accused them of being evil. These false beliefs resulted in the Holocaust.

A second reason one group commits genocide is to gain land. During World War I, Turks forced Armenians to leave Turkey. About 600,000 Armenians died or were killed on this forced march. A group may also commit genocide to stay in power. In Kampuchea (Cambodia), in the 1970s, the Pol Pot regime stayed in power by killing about two million Khmer people.

The UN Resolution of 1948

In 1948 the United Nations declared genocide "a crime under international law." This UN resolution tried to prevent another Holocaust from happening.

HISTORY

Visual Learning

Have students study the timeline on these pages and then copy it onto a large piece of paper. Ask them to write down other important events or details from their reading onto their timelines, such as *Kristallnacht* (1938) and Germany's invasion of Poland (1939). You may also want to have them include pictures or their own drawings on their timelines.

CULTURE

Critical Thinking

Some people survived the Nazi concentration camps through luck, their wits, or some other combination of factors. Discuss how people might have survived the horrible conditions—and have escaped being sent to the gas chambers. *(Possible responses: some prisoners collaborated with the Nazis; others somehow managed to stay healthy and were able to continue working.)*

Historical Context

In the Polish city of Warsaw—which had a thriving Jewish community, numbering in the hundreds of thousands—the Nazis forced Jews to live in a ghetto. Surrounded by a high wall, this ghetto was isolated from the rest of the city. Many Jews died from disease and starvation. Thousands of others were sent to concentration camps. In 1942 alone, more than 300,000 Jews were sent from Warsaw to the gas chambers.

Language Arts Connection

Many prisoners of Nazi concentration camps kept personal journals or wrote letters to friends and family members. Have students use their family histories or library resources to find and read some of these accounts of the Holocaust. You may want to ask students to keep a journal as they read to record their thoughts and feelings about their reading.

Study Skills

Explain that the suffix *-cide* in *genocide* means the "act of killing." Assign students to research examples of genocide in history. For example, they may learn more about the examples presented in the Understanding Genocide feature or the "ethnic cleansing" of Muslims and Croats by Serbs in Bosnia-Herzegovina, which is addressed in Chapter 21.

■ *The Nazis killed millions of people in concentration camps. European countries suffered huge losses of soldiers, civilians, and property.*

GEOGRAPHY

Map and Globe Skills

Remind students that German attacks had devastated Russia, and then the Soviet Union, twice in 30 years. Refer students to the map of Eurasia on pages 682–683 of the Atlas. Point out the East European nations that were formerly part of the Soviet bloc. Have students explain how the location of these countries made them vital to the Soviet Union's security. *(Lined along the Soviets' western border, these countries formed a barrier, separating the Soviet Union from Germany and the West.)*

This picture of Churchill, U.S. President Franklin D. Roosevelt, and Stalin is from the Yalta Conference, held in 1945 to settle differences as World War II neared an end.

■ *How did World War II damage Europe?*

Turning Points of the War

By 1940 Hitler had gained control of much of western Europe. He then tried to defeat Great Britain by bombing its cities. When these air attacks failed, he turned east. In the summer of 1941, Hitler attacked the Soviet Union, which then joined the Allies.

These German attacks—and above all, the Japanese attack on Pearl Harbor—led the United States to join the Allies. On December 8, 1941, the United States declared war on Japan. By the end of the year, the United States was also at war with Germany and Italy.

In 1943 Soviet troops defeated a large German army at Stalingrad (now Volgograd). Soviet troops then pushed the German troops out of the Soviet Union. Next, they moved across eastern Europe and began to attack Germany. Meanwhile, in western Europe, Allied forces defeated Italy in 1943. After the secret invasion known as D-day, on June 6, 1944, the Allies freed France and Belgium in 1944. Finally, the Allies invaded Germany.

The Costs of World War II

On May 8, 1945, Germany surrendered. However, World War II did not end until September 2, 1945, with the surrender of Japan, which you read about on page 371.

About 50 million people, including 35 million civilians, died in World War II. More than 40 million people were left homeless. Bombs had reduced much of Europe to rubble. ■

The Cold War

For centuries western Europe had controlled much of the world. However, after World War II, two new superpowers emerged: the United States and the Soviet Union. A **superpower** is a military, political, and economic giant. For the next 45 years, the United States and the Soviet Union would dominate world affairs.

This East German border guard was never seen again after disobeying orders. He let a boy cross back from West Berlin to East Berlin.

The peace treaties ending World War II divided Europe almost in half. In fact, Germany was split in two, as you can see from the map on page 473. Notice, too, how Germany's capital, Berlin, was also divided. This division was made even more dramatic in 1961. That year, East Germany built a wall separating East and West Berlin.

An iron curtain fell upon Europe. **Iron curtain** was the term used to describe how Eastern Europe was isolated from the West. Many democratic countries of Western Europe aligned with the United States. However, most countries

Study Skills

Explain that the entry of the United States into World War II made the Allies' victory possible. Assign students to use library references to research the involvement of the United States in World War II, including the debate at home over whether to get involved in the war.

Collaborative Learning

Tell students that rebuilding Europe after World War II cost billions of dollars and took years of hard work. Have students form groups of four or five and discuss ways to help a devastated Europe rebuild itself after the war. Encourage students to decide which areas of life would need the most immediate attention—for example, food, shelter, transportation, medical care, and education. Have one person from each group report to the class the decisions their group made.

Political Context

New alliances were created in Europe after World War II. In 1949 the North Atlantic Treaty Organization (NATO) was established by France, Italy, the United Kingdom, the United States, and eight other European nations to defend against possible Soviet aggression. In response the Soviets created the Warsaw Treaty Organization, or Warsaw Pact, an alliance between the Soviet Union and its East European satellites (countries under its control).

Berlin and Germany, 1989

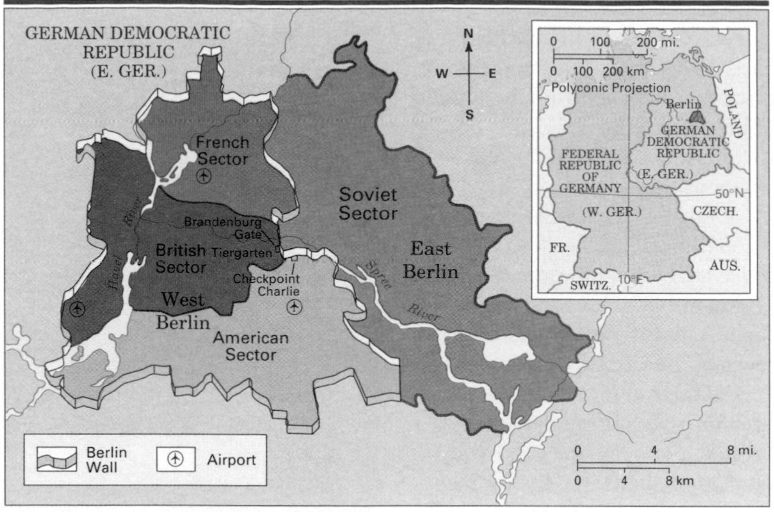

GERMAN DEMOCRATIC REPUBLIC (E. GER.)
N
S
W
E
French Sector
Soviet Sector
Brandenburg Gate
Tiergarten
British Sector
Checkpoint Charlie
East Berlin
West Berlin
American Sector
Havel
Spree River
Berlin Wall
Airport
0 4 8 mi.
0 4 8 km
0 100 200 mi.
0 100 200 km
Polyconic Projection
Berlin
GERMAN DEMOCRATIC REPUBLIC (E. GER.)
POLAND
FEDERAL REPUBLIC OF GERMANY (W. GER.)
50°N
CZECH.
FR.
AUS.
SWITZ.
10°E

◄ *This map shows East and West Germany, and a divided Berlin. Why were West Berliners called "islanders"?*

in Eastern Europe became part of the Soviet bloc. Soviet troops had freed them from the Nazis. After the war, the Soviet government turned them into Communist states and controlled their governments.

Once more Europe was divided by fear and distrust. This tension, called the **Cold War,** lasted from the late 1940s through the 1980s.

Nuclear Standoff

When the United States and the Soviet Union began to build thousands of nuclear bombs, people began to fear a nuclear war.

Soon after World War II, one of the first disputes of the Cold War occurred. As you can see from the map on this page, West Berlin was surrounded by Communist East Germany. At the end of World War II, Allied troops controlled West Berlin, angering Stalin.

In 1948 Stalin ordered Russian troops to prevent supplies from getting to West Berlin by rail or truck. U.S. President Harry S. Truman responded by sending in supplies by airplane. After 277,264 flights, Stalin gave in and let West Berlin exist as a democratic "island" in East Germany.

Life Behind the Iron Curtain

The iron curtain cut off contact between the people of Eastern and Western Europe. Barbed wire lined the borders. Communist governments in Eastern Europe granted their people few freedoms. Workers were told where to work. Newspapers were told what to print, teachers what to teach.

In some ways these Communist governments did take care of their citizens. Food prices were low. Health care was free. Ethnic conflicts, especially in the Balkans and the Soviet Union, were reduced. ■

▼ *News of nuclear weapons tests, such as the one shown here in the Pacific Ocean, frightened people around the world during the Cold War.*

■ *Describe life behind the iron curtain during the Cold War.*

GEOGRAPHY

Map and Globe Skills

For Western Europeans, having to cross Soviet-occupied territory to reach West Berlin was an awkward arrangement at best. Have students draw a map of Germany and Berlin, showing how Germany could have been divided to allow each country access to Berlin through friendly territory. *(Territories will have odd shapes, with a part of each ending in Berlin.)*

◄ *They lived in a Western European city completely surrounded by Communist-controlled territory, as an island is entirely surrounded by water.*

ECONOMICS

Critical Thinking

Explain that in the iron curtain countries, the prices of most goods and services were set by the government. Ask students how citizens benefited from such price controls. *(Food cost little; health care was free.)* Ask students about the possible disadvantages of this system. *(People may not work hard since they can't make a profit; quality may suffer; variety of goods may be lacking.)*

■ *People were cut off from Western Europe, lived highly regulated lives with few freedoms, had low-cost food and free health care, and had reduced ethnic strife.*

Science Connection

To help students understand the gains in science and technology since World War II, have students work in pairs to interview local scientists, engineers, doctors, and so forth. Ask students to write down their questions before going on their interviews. Encourage students to draw diagrams to help explain how their interviewee uses science or technology. Then have each pair share its interview with the class.

Reader's Theater

Have students obtain nonfiction or fiction accounts of World War II or the Cold War and select passages for dramatic readings or skits. *Anne Frank: The Diary of a Young Girl* (Doubleday & Company, 1967), for example, has potential for dramatic readings.

Critical Thinking

Explain that in 1948, only a few countries—the United States, the Soviet Union, and Great Britain—had nuclear weapons. Ask students to consider the impact of nuclear weapons on alliance systems. *(Alliances might be viewed as increasingly vital to the prevention of nuclear war, but they would afford little protection in the event of nuclear war.)*

■ *To retain Communist control, Gorbachev wanted to strengthen the Soviet economy, which was faltering, and provide greater freedom for the Soviet people.*

CLOSE

Have students answer the Thinking Focus by reviewing the outlines they completed as they read the chapter. You may want also to discuss the causes and outcomes of World War II and the Cold War. Ask how World War II led to the onset of the Cold War. *(The United States and the Soviet Union emerged as superpowers whose political systems conflicted. The introduction of nuclear weapons in World War II also increased distrust and fear.)*

The Collapse of Soviet Communism

The Cold War "thawed" in the early 1970s as the two superpowers discussed arms control. The United States and the Soviet Union agreed to limit the number of nuclear weapons they kept.

➤ *Mikhail Gorbachev, shown at right, tried to reform the Soviet government. The people were unhappy with the slow pace of his reforms, however. They preferred the plans of Russian Republic President Boris Yeltsin. These plans called for greater—and quicker—changes.*

Even bigger changes happened when Mikhail Gorbachev *(GAWR buh chawf)* took power in the Soviet Union in 1985. He began to give Soviet citizens more freedom. For instance, he let non-Communist candidates run for office. Gorbachev also hoped to reform the Soviet economic system. The Cold War era had not improved life for most people in the Soviet Union.

Gorbachev also said that Soviet soldiers would no longer crush protests against Communist governments in Eastern Europe. Without Soviet support, Eastern European Communist governments began to collapse in 1989. Some republics within the Soviet Union demanded independence as well.

On August 18, 1991, some Soviet Communist party leaders tried to overthrow Gorbachev. They wanted to stop Gorbachev's reforms. They sent tanks into the streets of Moscow to enforce their takeover. Yet thousands of Russians blocked the tanks in protest. Many soldiers and police joined the protesters, just as they had in the Russian Revolution of 1917.

Gorbachev returned to power in just three days. However, the Russian people no longer trusted Gorbachev or feared the Communist party. They wanted greater changes. Boris Yeltsin, newly elected president of the Russian Republic, won their trust by ending Communist rule. "When I heard they had outlawed communism, I felt like a man freed from jail," one Soviet man said. In the next chapter, you will read about what happened to the Soviet Union—and to all of Europe—after the Cold War. ■

■ *Why did Gorbachev try to reform the Soviet Union?*

REVIEW

1. **FOCUS** What were the causes and outcomes of World War II?
2. **HISTORY** Explain why Hitler's ideas appealed to so many Germans.
3. **HISTORY** What was the Holocaust? Give another example of an attempt at genocide.
4. **CRITICAL THINKING** Why did the United States and the Soviet Union fight the Cold War?
5. **WRITING ACTIVITY** There are many excellent books about World War II. Some, such as *Anne Frank: The Diary of a Young Girl,* are personal accounts of people's wartime experiences. Ask your teacher or librarian for title suggestions. Then write a journal entry based on your reading.

Homework Options

Have students write to imaginary pen pals in today's Russia. Suggest that students include details about life in the United States that may interest their pen pals, and ask questions about life in Russia.

Study Guide: page 82

Answers to Review Questions

1. Causes: Hitler's armed aggression in Europe led France and Great Britain to declare war on Germany. Outcomes: Millions were killed and countries were left in ruins. New political divisions and alliances were created, and the United States and the Soviet Union emerged as superpowers engaged in a Cold War.
2. His ideas tapped their deep desire to restore German pride and power, which they felt had been stripped from them by the Treaty of Versailles and economic difficulties.
3. The Holocaust was Hitler's killing of millions of Jews. Other examples of genocide include Turkey's forced march of Armenians and Pol Pot's killing of the Khmer people.
4. Their opposing political and economic philosophies led to mutual distrust and conflict.
5. Responses will vary, but students could write factual accounts or personal responses to their reading.

Understanding Visual Learning

Interpreting Political Cartoons

Here's Why

Reading political cartoons can be an amusing way to learn how people feel about certain events. By making dramatic, often funny drawings, political cartoonists make strong statements that reflect their feelings or those of their readers.

Suppose you wanted to know more about how people feel about economic reforms in Russia, formerly part of the Soviet Union. Looking for political cartoons in a newspaper or magazine would be a good place to start.

Here's How

Look at the cartoon below, drawn by a Russian artist. Use the following steps to understand it.

1. **Read the captions.** Identify the action and people in the cartoon. The action of this cartoon is easily seen: People in a car are going over a cliff. Who are the people? Boris Yeltsin, the president of Russia, and another Russian leader are the drivers. We can assume the people in the back of the car are the Russian people.
2. **Identify the symbols in the cartoon.** Symbols are objects or people that are used to represent an idea. The cartoonist has used the car as a symbol of the Russian economy. The steep cliff represents the danger that the Russians face as they try to get to the reforms on the other side.
3. **Try to understand the cartoonist's message.** On one hand, the cartoonist may be saying that despite people's fears, the Russian economy will land safely and the reforms will get the economy rolling again. On the other hand, the cartoonist may be saying that the Russian economy will crash, as will Yeltsin and his group of reformers. What do you think the cartoonist is trying to say?

!!?
STOP!
BACK!
ONLY FORWARD!
RUSSIAN ECONOMY
REFORMS

Try It

Examine the cartoon again. What might the cartoonist think life will be like after the reforms? How can you tell?

Apply It

Find a political cartoon in a newspaper or magazine. Write a short paragraph explaining what the cartoonist is trying to say. Be sure to identify the people and symbols in the cartoon.

UNDERSTANDING VISUAL LEARNING

Discuss the use of caricatures in political cartoons. If possible, bring to class a photograph of Boris Yeltsin, and discuss the exaggeration used by the cartoonist. You may also wish to bring in cartoons and photographs of public figures well known to students and have them compare and contrast photographs with caricatures in cartoons.

HISTORY

Visual Learning

Ask students how the cartoonist might have drawn the cartoon differently if the cartoonist had been convinced that the reforms would lead to disaster. *(Sample answers include adding DETOUR to the "reforms" sign, with an arrow pointing to the abyss.)*

Answers to Try It

The cartoonist may think that life in Russia will be more comfortable after the reforms. The soft level grass on the "reforms" side of the gorge supports this idea.

Answers to Apply It

Check to see that students have correctly identified the action, people, and symbols in the cartoon. Check that students' interpretations are supported by these elements.

Writing Activity

Political cartoons often reflect popular feelings of the time. Interpreting them usually requires some understanding of the people and events involved. Select several political cartoons featuring people and events familiar to students. Ask students to imagine that the cartoons will be published in a history textbook in the year 2050. Have students choose one cartoon and write the background information that future readers will need to know in order to understand and interpret it.

Objective

Use a political cartoon to analyze the controversy over economic reforms in Russia.

Answers to Reviewing Key Terms

A. Answers:

1. Incorrect. Countries in an **alliance** would not be likely to fight each other.
2. Correct. Neither **dictator** was voted into office but ruled by force.
3. Incorrect. The Russian **Revolution** of 1917 overthrew the czar's government.
4. Correct. All these groups were **Holocaust** victims.
5. Correct. Both used **propaganda** to strengthen their positions of power.

B. Sample answers:

1. The *Cold War* was a period of tension, but not warfare, between the United States and the Soviet Union. The Cold War went on for more than 40 years between the United States and the USSR and divided Europe into Western and Eastern blocs.
2. The word *genocide* means the destruction of an entire national, cultural, or racial group. Genocide occurred in Stalin's Russia. The Holocaust was the almost total destruction of the Jews in Europe by the Nazis.
3. The phrase *iron curtain* means "a barrier that prevents the free exchange of ideas and information." The iron curtain prevented contact between Eastern and Western Europe during the Cold War.
4. *Jingoism* means "extreme, warlike nationalism." Lesson 1 gives students the song from which this term comes. Jingoistic attitudes made European countries very competitive and led to World War I.
5. *Superpower* describes a country whose military and economic strength make it one of the most powerful in the world. The United States and the Soviet Union emerged as the post–World War II superpowers.

Answers to Exploring Concepts

A. Sample causes:

The future ruler of Austria-Hungary, Archduke Francis Ferdinand, is killed in Sarajevo.

Austria-Hungary's and Serbia's allies prepare to fight.

The German army loses several major battles.

Austria-Hungry and Germany—the Central Powers—lose World War I.

The Austro-Hungarian Empire collapses.

B. Answers should include the following:

1. Competed in modernizing industries, controlling trade, and acquiring colonies.
2. Austrians, Hungarians, Serbs, Romanians, Bulgarians, Albanians, Greeks, and Turks.
3. Took away Germany's colonies and demanded huge payments.
4. Less modern and industrialized.
5. Peasants, workers, and soldiers.
6. To modernize and build power; organized collective farms and improved factories.
7. Conquered most countries of western Europe.
8. The U.S. joined the war in December 1941 after Japan attacked Pearl Harbor.
9. Divided by Allied and Soviet forces, it was surrounded by Communist East Germany.
10. Allowing non-Communists to run for office, changing the economic system, and giving less military support to Eastern Europe.

Chapter Review

Reviewing Key Terms

alliance (p. 461)
Cold War (p. 473)
dictator (p. 467)
genocide (p. 470)
Holocaust (p. 471)
iron curtain (p. 472)
jingoism (p. 460)
propaganda (p. 467)
revolution (p. 465)
superpower (p. 472)

A. Each statement below uses a key term from this chapter. Tell whether each key term is used correctly. Then explain the reason for your answer.

1. Because France and Great Britain were part of an <u>alliance</u> before World War I, they fought each other when war began.
2. Lenin and Stalin, the first two leaders of the Soviet Union, did not establish democracy but ruled as <u>dictators</u>.
3. The 1917 <u>revolution</u> in Russia strengthened the government of the czar.
4. Jews, Slavs, Poles, and gypsies were victims in the <u>Holocaust</u>.
5. Both Stalin and Hitler used <u>propaganda</u> and fear to rule their countries.

B. Use the text or a dictionary to write the meaning of each of these terms in your own words. Then explain how each word was related to the history of Europe after 1900.

1. Cold War
2. genocide
3. iron curtain
4. jingoism
5. superpower

Exploring Concepts

A. Copy this chart of cause-and-effect relationships in World War I. Then supply what you think is the main cause for each effect. One cause has been filled in.

Cause	Effect
Modern industry develops in the late 1800s.	More destructive weapons of war are built.
	Austria-Hungary attacks Serbia.
	World War I begins.
	German leaders ask for peace.
	Austro-Hungarian Empire is divided.

B. Answer each question with information from the chapter.

1. In what ways did Germany, France, and Great Britain compete before World War I?
2. What were some of the ethnic groups living within Austria-Hungary?
3. How did the terms of the Treaty of Versailles affect Germany?
4. In the early 1900s, how was Russia different from its allies France and Britain?
5. What groups of Russians were involved in the 1917 revolution against the czar?
6. What were Stalin's goals for the Soviet Union? How did he try to reach those goals?
7. What were the effects of Germany's "lightning war" in Europe in 1939 and 1940?
8. When and why did the United States become involved in World War II?
9. Why was Berlin a symbol of the Cold War?
10. What were some of the reforms begun in the Soviet Union by Gorbachev?

Reviewing Skills

1. Political cartoons can make a strong statement in a simple, amusing way. Study this cartoon. Identify the people, symbols, and actions it shows. Then write an explanation of what you think the cartoon means. Do you think the cartoonist is sympathetic toward events in the Soviet Union or not?

STAHLER
IT SHRUNK!
SOVIET UNION
DEMOCRACY

2. Events in Europe and Russia in the 20th century were related. To show this, make a timeline for the years 1910 to 1950. Divide your timeline into decades, or 10-year periods, starting with 1910. From the chapter find at least two events that occurred in each decade. Write them in the correct position on the timeline. Place events in Russia (and the Soviet Union) above the timeline. Place events for the rest of Europe below the timeline.
3. Suppose you want to compare the number of civilian and military casualties suffered by different European countries in World War I and World War II. What would be the best way to show this information? Explain your response.

Using Critical Thinking

1. What events after World War I led the German people to support Hitler and his Nazi party's rise to power?
2. Should the leaders of a country encourage people's feelings of nationalism? What are the advantages and dangers of doing so?
3. How do you think dictators such as Hitler and Stalin manage to stay in power for many years? What do people gain and what do they lose when ruled by a dictator?
4. Why did Hitler try to destroy the Jews of Europe? Do you think that genocide could ever become a reality in the United States? Explain your response.

Preparing for Citizenship

1. **COLLECTING INFORMATION** During the first half of the 20th century, many Europeans influenced history, for better or worse. Choose a person mentioned in the chapter or another European from this time period. Use the encyclopedia or other library sources to research his or her life. Then give a biographical report to the class.
2. **WRITING ACTIVITY** Imagine that you are a U.S. newspaper reporter in Germany during the late 1930s. Choose an event such as *Kristallnacht* or a Nazi rally, and write a news story for your paper. Remember that your readers at home may not be aware of what is going on in Germany.
3. **INTERVIEWING** Many people have emigrated from, or left, the former Soviet Union and Eastern Europe. If possible, interview someone from the former Soviet Union or Eastern Europe. Ask why he or she came to the United States. What does he or she miss most? Report your interview to your class.
4. **COLLABORATIVE LEARNING** Imagine you live in a European village about to be taken over by the Nazis during World War II. Divide into groups and discuss the reasons for and against joining the Resistance. After your group discussion, share your ideas with the entire class. As a class, vote on whether your village will join the Resistance.

Answers to Reviewing Skills

1. The man in this cartoon of 1991 represents Soviet officials (not specifically Gorbachev); the "laundry" is the Soviet Union; the "detergent" is democratic reforms. The force that held the Soviet republics together depended greatly on dictatorship, or lack of democratic freedoms.
2. Events appropriate for the timeline include these: (1910–1919) Archduke Francis Ferdinand is killed, 1914; World War I begins, 1914; Russian Revolution, 1917; Treaty of Versailles, 1919. (1920–1929) Soviet Union forms, 1922; Stalin comes to power, 1924. (1930–1939) Famine in USSR, 1930s; *Kristallnacht,* 1938; Hitler invades Poland, 1939. (1940–1949) United States joins war, 1941; USSR joins Allies, 1941; World War II ends, 1945; Berlin blockade and airlift, 1948.
3. The information could be shown in a bar graph or in a table so that people could easily compare the figures.

Answers to Using Critical Thinking

1. Students may mention these causes: loss of land and colonies, hard times paying war damages, job losses.
2. Answers should show that students have considered both the value of patriotic feelings (which can result in cooperation between people) and the dangers of intense nationalism (which can lead to ethnic or national hatred and violent conflict).
3. Guide students in thinking carefully about this question, which is important for people in a democracy to consider. Answers may cite people's fear. A strong dictator may give people pride. People lose many rights and freedoms, such as freedom of speech.
4. Hitler found it useful to make the Jews a scapegoat for Germany's economic troubles. Ask students to think about the causes of genocide to consider whether such situations could develop in the United States.

Answers to Preparing for Citizenship

1. **COLLECTING INFORMATION** This can be either an individual or a small-group activity. Give students whatever help they need in choosing the right resources. Suggest that they research European artists and writers, as well as political leaders.
2. **WRITING ACTIVITY** This activity demands creative imagination as well as skill in research. You may want to have students research events that interest them and read their news stories to the class.
3. **INTERVIEWING** An alternative approach is to invite a recent Russian or Eastern European immigrant to visit the class. A student panel can prepare the interview format.
4. **COLLABORATIVE LEARNING** This discussion can bring up sensitive issues of what people are willing to risk in defense of freedom—such as their own lives. You might want to suggest that students first discuss joining the Resistance as if they had no knowledge of the Holocaust. Would that knowledge change their decision? Why? Suggest that students play roles, perhaps as political leaders, businesspeople, or ordinary citizens.

CHAPTER ORGANIZER

Chapter 21 Europe and Russia Today

CHAPTER PLANNING CHART

Pupil's Edition	Teacher's Edition	Ancillaries
Lesson 1: Europe Today (2–3 days) Objective 1: Describe the climate of Europe. (History 7; Geography 5) Objective 2: Describe some of the major geographic features of Europe. (Geography 2, 5)	• Graphic Overview (480) • Access Strategy (481) • Access Activity (481)	Study Guide (84) Transparency (11)
Understanding Conflict Objective: Find common ground on which to resolve conflicts peacefully. (Social Participation 1, 2)		
Lesson 2: Western Europe Today (3–4 days) Objective 1: Explain the reasons for and against a united Europe. (History 1, 3, 4, 5, 6; Ethics and Belief Systems 5; Social and Political Systems 3) Objective 2: Describe the European Economic Community. (Economics 1, 2, 4; Social and Political Systems 6)	• Graphic Overview (484) • Access Strategy (485) • Access Activity (485) • Visual Learning (486) Research (486) Mathematics Connection (486)	Study Guide (85) Map Activities (25) Discovery Journal (43)
Making Decisions: Voting For or Against a United Europe Objective 1: Understand the developments of Europe's current status. (History 1, 5) Objective 2: Decide whether to vote for or against a united Europe. (History 6; Critical Thinking 3)		Discovery Journal (44) Posters (8)
Lesson 3: Eastern Europe Today (2–3 days) Objective 1: Explain why there has been fighting in the Balkans. (History 5, 6, 7; Culture 3; Ethics and Belief Systems 5; Social and Political Systems 3) Objective 2: Describe the challenges facing Eastern Europe after the fall of communism. (History 7; Economics 3; Culture 3; Ethics and Belief Systems 5)	• Graphic Overview (490) • Access Strategy (491) • Access Activity (491)	Study Guide (86)
Lesson 4: Russia and the Former Soviet Republics (2–3 days) Objective 1: Explain why the USSR collapsed. (History 5, 6, 7; Economics 1) Objective 2: Describe the challenges facing Russia today. (History 5, 7; Economics 1, 2, 3; Ethics and Belief Systems 5) Objective 3: Describe the challenges facing the former Soviet republics today. (History 5, 7; Economics 1, 2, 3; Ethics and Belief Systems 5)	• Graphic Overview (493) • Access Activity (494) • Access Strategy (494) Economic Context (495) Role-Play (495) • Visual Learning (495) Social Participation (496) Historical Context (496)	Study Guide (87) Transparency (10)
Chapter Review	Answers (498–499)	Tests (81–84)

* Objectives are correlated to the strands and goals in the program Scope and Sequence on pages T41–T49.

• LEP appropriate resources.
(For additional strategies, see pages T32–T33.)

CHAPTER RATIONALE

This chapter explores the changes taking place in Europe and Russia today. It analyzes the political, economic, and environmental challenges facing the people of this region in their struggle to build greater unity and overcome division. The chapter discusses how the past, especially ethnic divisions, still affects the people of Europe and Russia.

Lesson 1 examines the role geography and climate play in shaping the lives of Europeans. It explains that Europe's ethnic differences and history of conflicts divide its peoples much more than geography does. Europe's resources and the productivity of Europeans are identified as significant reasons for this continent's wealth.

Lesson 2 focuses on Western Europe's attempts to forge a greater political and economic union. It explains the formation of the Common Market, the effort to create a single economic market, and the debate over the Maastricht Treaty. In the process, the lesson looks at the forces that promote European unity—economic growth and peace—and the nationalism that promotes division.

Lesson 3 covers the challenges facing Eastern Europe today as its peoples adjust to life after communism. It focuses on the struggles that people accustomed to one-party rule face as they build market economies and form democracies. The lesson describes the split of Czechoslovakia, progress toward democratization in Poland, and the challenges of a recently reunited Germany. Finally, students read about the civil war in the former republics of Yugoslavia.

Lesson 4 examines the sweeping political and economic changes taking place in Russia and the other former republics of the Soviet Union. A two-page map of this region provides students with an overview of the diverse people, resources, environmental trouble spots, and major challenges facing these peoples. The lesson also describes the formation of the Commonwealth of Independent States and the struggles of the Baltic states. The chapter concludes by looking at the challenges facing Russia, especially the need to reduce its nuclear weapons.

ACTIVITIES & PROJECTS

Writing a Travelogue

Assign small groups of students a region of Europe such as the Mediterranean or Eastern Europe. Have them plan an imaginary trip through their assigned region. Students should note physical features and major cities as well as whether the region was formerly a republic of the Soviet Union or a separate country. Groups should appoint researchers, scriptwriters, and spokespersons to report their findings to the class. Ask them to present their findings as a travelogue. (Use after Lesson 1.)

Challenge: Writing a Letter

Ask students to imagine that they live in Western Europe. Then have them write a letter to the editor of a local newspaper arguing either in favor of or against the Maastricht Treaty. (Use after Lesson 2.)

LEP: Understanding Key Terms

Assign pairs of students one of the three key terms in Lesson 2. Have each pair make a cartoon or drawing that illustrates the key term.
(Use after Lesson 2.)

Basic: Making a Timeline

To help students understand the chronology of Eastern Europe, have them develop their own timeline for a particular region or country. Ask them to research at least ten highlights for one region within a particular time period. They may want to draw pictures or cut out photos from magazines to illustrate specific events. (Use after Lesson 3.)

Delivering a Speech

Have students work in pairs to write and deliver a short speech that a current leader of Russia might deliver. Students' speeches should take into account issues concerning the environment and the reduction of nuclear weapons. (Use after Lesson 4.)

CHAPTER PREVIEW

Have students read the chapter title and the passage that follows. Explain that in the United States of America, governing power is divided between the central government and the 50 states. The central government, for example, deals with other countries and issues money. The states do such tasks as maintaining roads and determining the curriculum for public schools. Ask students what is meant by the phrase "United States of Europe." *(European nations would keep their own identities but also be members of a larger community.)* Tell students to look for examples of unity and disunity as they read.

Looking Back

Ask students to recall how Russia and Eastern Europe changed under Gorbachev. *(People experienced new freedoms and began to experiment with self-government.)*

Looking Forward

Tell students that in the next four lessons—Europe Today, Western Europe Today, Eastern Europe Today, and Russia and the Former Soviet Republics—they will read about the forces that are shaping Europe.

Lesson 1 describes Europe's geography and climate.

Chapter 21
Europe and Russia Today

As the 20th century neared its end, change swept through Europe. Western Europeans debated whether a "United States of Europe" was a realistic goal. In Eastern Europe, people freed themselves from Communist dictatorships and one-party rule. What would happen as a result? The Soviet Union fell apart. What would take its place? No one knew the answers to these questions.

Russians celebrate independence from the Soviet Union in Moscow's Red Square in 1991.

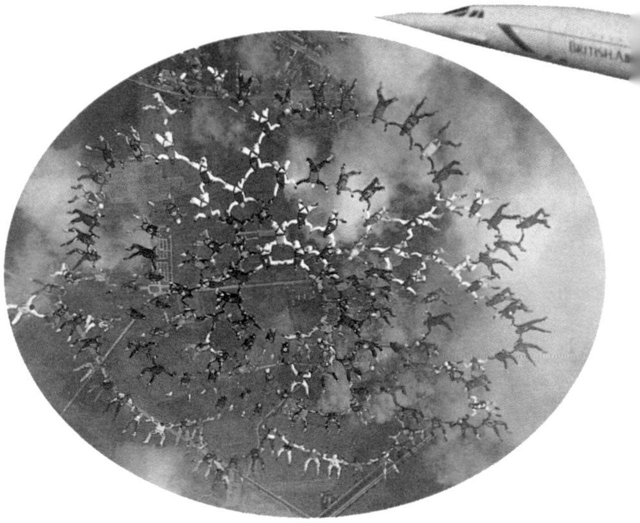

A record-setting group of 150 skydivers joins together over Belgium.

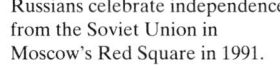

1988 Lech Walesa leads workers on a strike against Poland's Communist government.

1990 Germans celebrate the reunification of their country.

1980 | 1984 | 1988

1984 Sarajevo, Yugoslavia, hosts the Winter Olympics.

1989 Playwright Vaclav Havel leads a peaceful "Velvet Revolution" that topples Czechoslovakia's Communist government.

1984

478

BACKGROUND

Following World War II, European leaders argued that Europe's sufferings resulted from the division of the continent into independent political units, whose separate quarrels dragged everyone into war. The following provides background for the unification movement as well as factors that threaten unification, two main themes of Chapter 21.

Europe Without Frontiers

Progress toward a United States of Europe began when Belgium, the Netherlands, and Luxembourg united in 1948 to form Benelux, the first completely free international labor market. During the 1950s, interest in a united Europe shifted from Benelux to the European Economic Community. The EC originated with the French government's plan for joining the coal and steel industries of France and Germany as a way of fostering peace between the two countries. The founding of the European Coal and Steel Community in 1952 was followed by the establishment of the European Economic Community in 1957. The EC helped to alleviate fears of war and to develop the economies of member states into a single common market.

Ethnic Unrest

Counterbalancing the wish for a united Europe are the continent's centuries-old ethnic rivalries. Problem groups include the Basques and Catalonians in Spain, the Welsh and Scots in Great Britain, and Protestants and Catholics in Northern Ireland. Yet ethnic

Muslim girls study the Qur'an in a mosque in Tajikistan, which was a Soviet republic until 1991. Under Soviet rule, freedom of religion did not exist until 1990.

France and Great Britain cooperated to build the Concorde, a supersonic jetliner.

Civil war erupts in Yugoslavia in 1991. Carrying all she owns, this woman leaves her home near the Croatia-Serbia border, heading to an uncertain future.

1993 Czechoslovakia divides into two countries.

1992 | 1996 | 2000

1992 Violence continues in many of the former Soviet republics. Elsewhere, thousands die in Bosnia, Croatia, and Slovenia—former republics of Yugoslavia.

Today

Understanding the Visuals

The Concorde shown on pages 478–479 is capable of cruising up to twice the speed of sound—about 1,320 miles per hour. The Concorde is a product of the cooperation between Great Britain and France.

The photographs of the Muslim girls and the Yugoslav woman are reminders of the ethnic and religious diversity that exists among the peoples of Europe and Russia.

Understanding Chronology

Refer students to the timeline and ask a volunteer to read aloud the events listed. Point out that there are several entries that indicate political change in Europe and Russia. You may wish to update the timeline by having students work in small groups. They can use newspapers and magazines to add important events.

rivalries are perhaps most apparent in the former Yugoslavia. A patchwork of conflicting cultures, Yugoslavia was formed from parts of the Austro-Hungarian and Ottoman empires after World War I. The boundaries of the new states, however, failed to reflect the ancient settlement patterns of the region's many ethnic groups. Although Yugoslavia enjoyed a period of stability under the dictatorship of Josip Broz Tito, by the time of his death in 1980 old tensions had surfaced, leading to civil war and economic collapse in the 1990s.

Ethnic Tensions in Russia

In the former Soviet Union as well, ethnic diversity has given rise to tensions and conflict. Ethnic tensions, which had long existed, increased during the late 1980s. Violent clashes took place among some ethnic groups, including between Slavs and non-Slavs. Most of the 15 former Soviet republics are facing demands for greater autonomy from smaller national groups within their borders. Borders between republics that were arbitrarily drawn during the Communist era are also a source of conflict.

INTRODUCE

Have students read the lesson title and the Thinking Focus. Then have them look at the map on page 481. Ask volunteers to point out Europe's main geographic features. *(For example, mountains, plains, peninsulas)* Explain that the plains of Europe are very fertile and have many natural resources, making some European countries leading producers of farm products as well as leaders in industry. Then have students read to find out more about Europe's geography, climate, and productivity.

Key Terms

Vocabulary Strategies: T36–T37

marine climate—a climate with constant, mild temperatures

continental climate—a climate with warm, short summers and long, cold winters

Mediterranean climate—a climate with mild winters and hot, dry summers

1980
1984
1988
1992
TODAY

LESSON 1

Europe Today

THINKING FOCUS

Why is Europe such a productive region?

Key Terms

- marine climate
- continental climate
- Mediterranean climate

In a speech he made while he was still leader of the Soviet Union, Mikhail Gorbachev quoted a famous French writer:

> A day will come when you, France; you, Russia; you, Italy; you, Britain; and you, Germany—all of you, all nations of the Continent [Europe] will merge tightly. . . . A day will come when markets, open to trade, and minds, open to ideas, will become the sole battlefields.
>
> Victor Hugo, 1802–1885

When Hugo wrote this passage more than 100 years ago, Europe was a continent of ancient conflicts. Its peoples were divided and often at war.

However, many Europeans such as Hugo hoped for greater unity within Europe. Hugo never saw his dream for a united Europe come true. Yet in your lifetime, a united Europe may become a reality.

Barriers to peace and unity still divide Europe, however. The effects of the iron curtain continue to split Europe into eastern and western halves.

The Land of Europe

The East-West division in Europe is based mainly on political and ethnic differences, not on geography. That is, no natural borders such as mountains or rivers separate Eastern Europe from Western Europe. What continues to divide Europeans today are their ethnic differences and history of conflicts. From the map on the opposite page, you can see how Europe is divided between East and West. Note that no natural borders mark this political division.

The Land Regions of Europe

Take a closer look at this same map. Two mountain systems, one in the north, the other in the south, divide Europe into three land regions: northern, central, and southern Europe.

Northern Europe is marked by a series of mountains that cover northern Great Britain and most of Norway and Sweden. The Alpine

The Alps, stretching across southern Switzerland, give that country a distinct natural border.

Objectives

1. Describe the climate of Europe.
2. Describe some of the major geographic features of Europe.

Graphic Overview

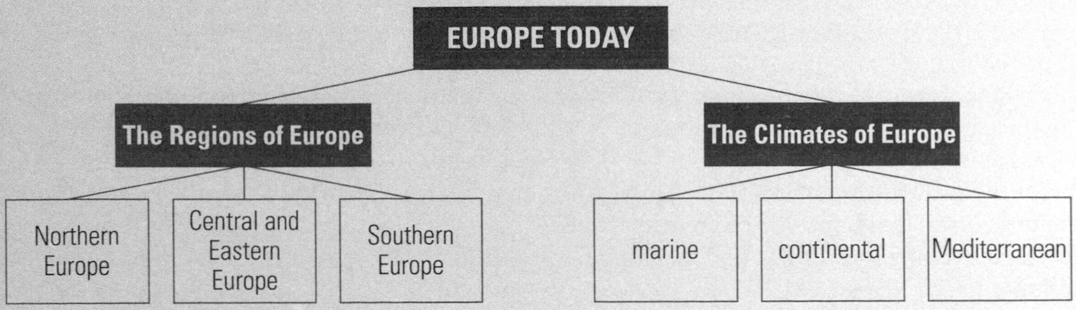
EUROPE TODAY
The Regions of Europe
The Climates of Europe
Northern Europe
Central and Eastern Europe
Southern Europe
marine
continental
Mediterranean

Eastern and Western Europe, 1993

NORWAY
FINLAND
SWEDEN
EST.
LAT.
LITH.
RUS.
RUSSIA
DENMARK
North Sea
Baltic Sea
IRELAND
UNITED KINGDOM
NETH.
GERMANY
POLAND
BELARUS
ATLANTIC OCEAN
BEL.
LUX.
CZECH REP.
SLOVAK REP.
UKRAINE
Don R.
Dnieper R.
Vistula R.
Elbe R.
Rhine R.
Seine R.
Loire R.
FRANCE
LIECH.
SWITZ.
AUSTRIA
HUNGARY
CARPATHIAN MTS.
MOLDOVA
ALPS
Po R.
SLO.
CRO.
ROMANIA
BOS.-H.
YUGO.
BULGARIA
Danube R.
Black Sea
AND.
PYRENEES
MONACO
ITALY
PORTUGAL
SPAIN
Ebro R.
Tagus R.
Rhone R.
MACE.
ALB.
GREECE
TURKEY
Formerly a Communist country or region
Formerly a republic of the Soviet Union
Formerly East Germany
0 250 500 mi.
0 250 500 km
Azimuthal Equidistant Projection
N
W E
S
Mediterranean Sea

mountain system separates central from southern Europe. These mountains run between France and Spain, across northern Italy, and into the Balkans.

The Great Plain of Europe

Between these two mountain systems lies central Europe. At the heart of this region is the Northern European Plain. This plain stretches from the west coast of France to the Ural Mountains in Russia.

In the past, this plain was a battleground. Many of Europe's ethnic groups fought over its land and resources. Today, this region is home to much of Europe's population, agriculture, and industry.

The Northern European Plain has rich farmland. There, European farmers grow wheat, barley, oats, potatoes, and rye. They raise hogs, cattle, and sheep. Using the plain's rich supplies of iron and coal, Europeans also produce steel, cars, airplanes, textiles, and chemical products.

A Productive Land

In spite of being the world's second smallest continent, Europe is an agricultural and industrial giant. Its almost 700 million people are well educated. Much of Europe's wealth results from its people's productivity.

Throughout history, Europeans have made great use of their resources and geographic location. Europe's timber, oil, coal, and other resources are raw materials for its factories. Europe's rivers serve as important shipping routes. European farmers produce most of the food the people of Europe need. They also export their products all over the world. ■

▲ *Notice on the map above how the European plain grows wider west to east. What countries are part of this plain? Below the map, this Greek fisherman sorts a catch of sponges. Many Europeans depend on the sea for their livelihood.*

■ *Where is Europe's great plain located?*

DEVELOP

Have students read the lesson's headings and scan the photos and their captions. Then draw the framework of the Graphic Overview on the chalkboard for students to copy. Tell students that as they read the lesson, they should fill in additional information about the regions and the climate of Europe.

◄ *The European Plain includes France, Belgium, Germany, the Czech Republic, Poland, Belarus, Ukraine, and Russia. It also includes Moldova and the Baltic states of Lithuania, Latvia, and Estonia.*

■ *Europe's great plain, or the Northern European Plain, is located in central Europe. It stretches eastward from the west coast of France, across Central and Eastern Europe, until it ends in the Ural Mountains.*

Access Strategy

To help students understand the climate of Europe, write the words *marine, continental,* and *Mediterranean* on the chalkboard. Explain that these are types of climates found in Europe. Have students turn to the World Climate Map in the Atlas on page 688 and identify Europe. Then ask a volunteer to read the caption in the map legend that explains marine, continental, and Mediterranean climates. Ask students to locate the regions in Europe that have these climates. Have them find and name other regions of the world—especially the United States—that have similar climates. Discuss what students know about the weather in those regions. Then tell them that they will learn more about Europe's climate in this lesson.

Access Activity

From the school or public library, gather an assortment of picture books and encyclopedia articles that include color photos of European countries and regions. Allow students to look through the photos and choose several to describe to the class. They should tell, if possible, where the photo is from and what it suggests about the place where it was taken.

GEOGRAPHY

Map and Globe Skills

Ask students to trace the map on page 481 on a sheet of paper. Have them locate the Alpine mountain system and the Northern European Plain. Then have them compare the climate of your region of the United States with that of western Europe, Mediterranean Europe, and central Europe.

CLOSE

Read the Thinking Focus aloud. Then have students share their Graphic Overviews and the information they added about geography and climate with a partner. Have partners compare the information they added.

■ *Most of Europe has a mild climate because the Gulf Stream warms western Europe and because hot, dry winds from North Africa blowing over the Mediterranean warm southern Europe.*

The Climates of Europe

If you look at the Atlas map on page 680, you can see that most of Europe is farther north than the Great Lakes. Yet most of Europe has a temperate, or mild, climate. Why is this so?

The Winds of Europe

Europe's climate is mainly determined by three prevailing winds, or air masses that blow in a certain pattern. First, moist winds from the Atlantic blow across western Europe. These winds are warmed by the Gulf Stream, a warm ocean current that starts in the Gulf of Mexico and flows to Europe.

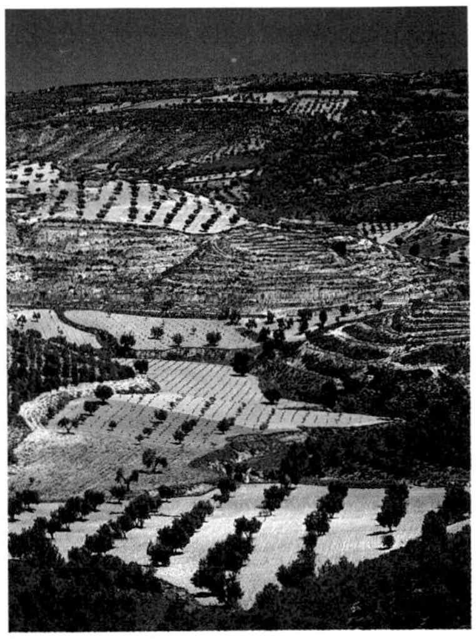

➤ *In spite of Spain's dry climate, Spanish farmers export food all over the world. Modern irrigation and farming methods made this land in Spain a productive olive grove.*

■ Give two reasons why most of Europe has a mild climate.

As a result, most of western Europe enjoys a **marine climate** because its winds form over the ocean. A marine climate has fairly constant, mild temperatures.

Second, the Gulf Stream winds cool as they move across the European plain. Because land cools these winds, most of eastern Europe has what is called a **continental climate.** Summers are warm and short while winters are long and cold.

Third, in southern Europe, hot, dry winds blow across the Mediterranean Sea from North Africa. These winds give much of Spain, Portugal, Italy, and Greece mild winters and hot, dry summers, or a **Mediterranean climate.**

A Longer Growing Season

Since much of Europe has a mild climate, many farmers in southern and western Europe can grow crops for much of the year. In eastern Europe, however, the continental climate greatly reduces the length of the growing season.

In the past, Europeans went to war, seeking control of land and resources. In recent years, ethnic conflicts continue to divide eastern Europe. Western Europe, as you will read in the next lesson, is trying to resolve its past conflicts and unite. ■

REVIEW

1. **FOCUS** Why is Europe such a productive region?
2. **GEOGRAPHY** What mountain system divides southern from central Europe?
3. **GEOGRAPHY** What are the differences between a marine climate, a Mediterranean climate, and a continental climate?
4. **CRITICAL THINKING** In what ways does the mild climate benefit European farmers?
5. **ACTIVITY** Europe's ethnic differences, not its geography, still divide its peoples. One such difference is Europe's many languages. Study the English alphabet chart on page 660 in the Minipedia. Then research one of the other languages of Europe. Make a chart of its alphabet similar to the one in the Minipedia. Compare your chart with those of your classmates. How are they alike and different?

Homework Options

Have students use encyclopedias in the school and public libraries to research the agricultural and industrial products of Europe. If they wish, they may present their findings in the form of a products map.

Study Guide: page 84

Answers to Review Questions

1. Some European countries are world leaders in industry and agriculture because their people are well educated and productive, and they have made efficient use of their resources and geographic location.
2. The Alpine mountain system, extending from Spain to Russia, divides southern Europe from central Europe.
3. A marine climate is marked by fairly constant, mild temperatures year round. A continental climate has short summers and long winters. A Mediterranean climate has mild winters and hot, dry summers.
4. Because of the mild climate in much of Europe, many farmers can produce crops—and earn income—throughout most of the year.
5. You may want to suggest that some students choose from one of the three major Indo-European language groups of Europe: Slavic, Germanic, and Romance.

UNDERSTANDING CONFLICT

Resolving Conflicts Peacefully

Here's Why

Disagreements or conflicts are part of life. After all, not everyone shares the same values, beliefs, or goals. However, people can choose to resolve conflicts positively or negatively. Too often people around the world have gone to war to settle their differences. The results, as you know from reading Chapter 20, have been millions of deaths and widespread destruction.

What if someone calls you names, makes fun of you, or "puts you down"? What if someone hits you? You may be angry and hurt. You may want to strike back with words—or fists. However, striking back in anger often leads to more angry words or more violence.

Resolving conflicts peacefully is difficult. Yet it is an essential skill for getting along with others. Do you know how to resolve your conflicts without violence or name-calling?

Here's How

Suppose the members of your class disagreed about where to go on a class trip. Some students wanted to go to an amusement park. Others wanted to go hiking in a state forest. Here's one way to resolve this conflict:

1. **Define the problem.** Have people from both sides answer this question: What is the problem? The class members disagree about where to go on a trip. Try to understand the reasons for both points of view. Some students may rarely get a chance to go to an amusement park. Others may rarely get a chance to explore nature. You may find areas of common concern. For example, how much money each trip will cost may worry both sides.
2. **Brainstorm for solutions.** Think about solutions—the ways this problem can be resolved. As a class, talk over all the possible solutions. Be sure to give everyone a chance to speak. Don't reject any ideas—the goal is to think up as many solutions as you can together. You do not have to choose one solution at this step.
3. **Choose the best solution.** Aim for the solution that lets both sides feel the resolution is fair. For example, your class may agree to go to the state forest. To be fair to both sides, your class may also decide to raise money and take a trip to the amusement park another time.
4. **Evaluate the solution's success.** If both sides feel good about your solution, it was probably the right one. However, if anyone is still angry or upset, your class may need to talk about it some more. Consider asking your teacher or another adult for advice.

Try It

Reread the solution to this conflict. What are the strengths of the solution? What are the weaknesses?

Apply It

Try using the steps listed above to resolve a conflict at home, in school, or with a friend. What do you think will be the most difficult step in resolving your conflict peacefully?

Define ➡ Brainstorm ➡ Choose ➡ Evaluate

UNDERSTANDING CONFLICT

This skills feature teaches students to resolve conflicts positively by using certain guidelines.

SOCIAL PARTICIPATION

Critical Thinking

Discuss these school situations using the four principles explained under Here's How. Then have students come up with a solution to each problem.

1. Students have been noisy and have misbehaved during assemblies. They say the reason is that the assemblies are boring.
2. Students are getting into fights after eating lunch. They say it's because there's nothing interesting to do.
3. Students are not completing homework assignments. They say the assignments are too hard and too long.

Answers to Try It

Students might answer that strengths include the fact that the resolution avoided conflict and encouraged cooperation. Weaknesses include one side possibly feeling that they had to give up something by delaying the class trip they wanted, while the other side did not have to give up anything.

Answers to Apply It

You may want students to share conflicts and their strategies for solving them. Discuss the obstacles to resolving conflicts peacefully. Encourage students to think of solutions that are fair and that make both sides feel good about the resolution.

Objective

Find common ground on which to resolve conflicts peacefully. (Social Participation 1, 2)

INTRODUCE

Read the lesson title and the Thinking Focus aloud. Then read the first two paragraphs of the lesson. Explain that this ceremony of lights celebrated a new unity among Europeans. Have students read the lesson to find out more about the possibilities for unity in Western Europe.

Key Terms

Vocabulary Strategies: T36–T37
common market—an economic union formed to increase trade and cooperation among nations
tariff—a fee a country charges for imported goods
customs check—a border inspection

1980 1984 **1986** **TODAY**

L E S S O N 2

Western Europe Today

THINKING FOCUS

Is the dream of a united Europe coming true? Explain why or why not.

Key Terms

- common market
- tariff
- customs check

Just before midnight on New Year's Eve, a crowd of people gathers at the Acropolis in Athens. There, where the Parthenon stands, they wait in the cool night air. Other crowds wait near the Eiffel Tower in Paris and at a park in Dublin. Crowds gather at other sites all across Western Europe. Together they will celebrate a historic event in the coming new year of 1993.

At midnight, the first of 1,000 beacons is lit in Athens. This chain of signal lights stretches hundreds of miles across Western Europe. These beacons blaze in Europe's quiet villages and bustling cities.

In the past, Europeans lit beacons out of fear or to spread news. The ancient Greeks used them to signal victories or to warn of attack. In 1588 the English lit beacons to warn of the approach of the Spanish Armada.

CORPORATION OF LONDON

➤ *Lighting this beacon in London, above right, helped mark the beginning of closer unity in Western Europe.*

However, Europeans lit the 1,000 beacons to celebrate a new era. These beacons signaled the beginning of a new economic union in Western Europe. Nearly 350 million Europeans would now be able to work, trade, and move more freely across national borders.

On the morning of January 1, 1993, thousands of Europeans were on the move. For the first time in their lives, most did not have to stop at national borders. These Europeans took steps toward greater unity—and perhaps a lasting peace.

Western Europe Moves to Greater Unity

During the Cold War, Western Europeans formed an economic union, or a **common market.** Europeans created a common market to increase trade and cooperation among countries. If Europeans became economic partners, maybe they would not become enemies again—and all could profit.

Building the Common Market

In 1957 Belgium, France, Italy, Luxembourg, the Netherlands, and West Germany signed the Treaty of

Objectives

1. Explain the reasons for and against a united Europe.
2. Describe the European Economic Community.

Graphic Overview

WESTERN EUROPE TODAY
Unifying Forces
Challenges to Unity
Common Market
Maastricht Treaty
nationalism
ethnic conflict

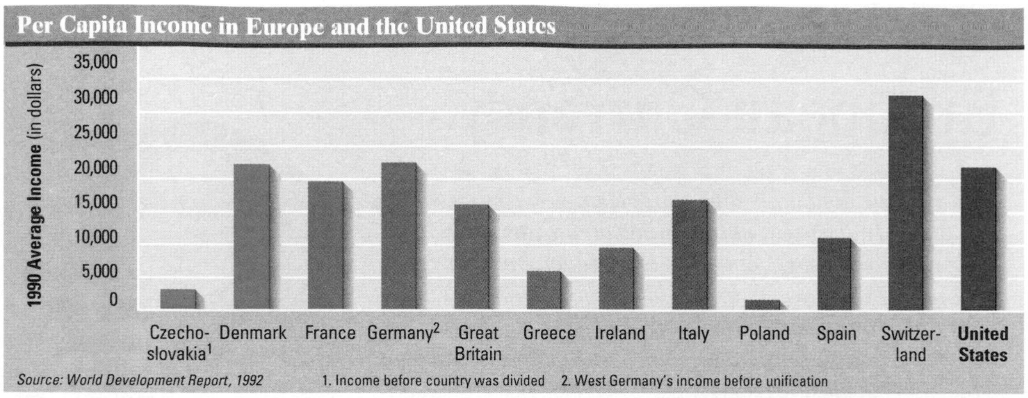
Per Capita Income in Europe and the United States
1990 Average Income (in dollars)
35,000
30,000
25,000
20,000
15,000
10,000
5,000
0
Czecho-slovakia[1]
Denmark
France
Germany[2]
Great Britain
Greece
Ireland
Italy
Poland
Spain
Switzer-land
United States
Source: World Development Report, 1992
1. Income before country was divided
2. West Germany's income before unification

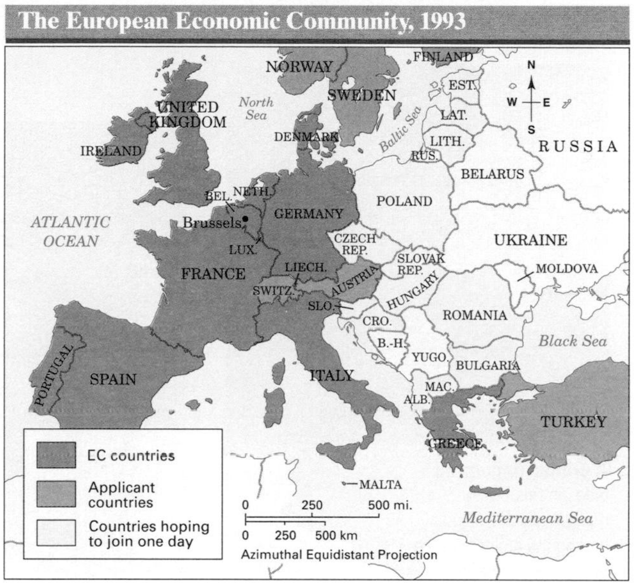
The European Economic Community, 1993
NORWAY
FINLAND
SWEDEN
UNITED KINGDOM
North Sea
IRELAND
DENMARK
Baltic Sea
EST.
LAT.
LITH.
RUS.
RUSSIA
BELARUS
POLAND
NETH.
BEL.
Brussels
GERMANY
ATLANTIC OCEAN
LUX.
CZECH REP.
SLOVAK REP.
UKRAINE
MOLDOVA
FRANCE
LIECH.
AUSTRIA
HUNGARY
SWITZ.
SLO.
ROMANIA
CRO.
B.-H.
YUGO.
Black Sea
BULGARIA
PORTUGAL
SPAIN
ITALY
MAC.
ALB.
TURKEY
GREECE
MALTA
Mediterranean Sea
EC countries
Applicant countries
Countries hoping to join one day
0 250 500 mi.
0 250 500 km
Azimuthal Equidistant Projection

Rome. This treaty created the European Economic Community (EC), or the Common Market.

The Common Market made trade easier among these six countries. For example, it reduced **tariffs,** or fees a country charged for imported goods. Tariffs raised the price of those goods. Higher prices discouraged people from buying imports and slowed the economic growth of all countries.

By 1986 Great Britain, Ireland, Denmark, Greece, Portugal, and Spain had also joined the Common Market. As trade increased among these countries, their economies all grew and their standards of living rose. Study the chart above to learn more about average personal, or per capita, incomes in Europe.

Still, barriers to trade remained. For example, goods and people still had to pass through a **customs check,** or border inspection. A customs check required a person to have certain papers, such as a passport, in order to enter another country. If someone wanted to work in another country, he or she also had to have a work permit. Truck drivers had to stop at each border, fill out forms, and have their goods inspected. Customs checks slowed movement and trade within the Common Market.

Toward Greater Economic Unity

Starting in the late 1980s, Europeans set new goals for the Common Market. Europeans hoped to form a single economic market, like the one in the United States. As in the United States, they would be free to trade, work, and live anywhere within the Common Market.

The lighting of the 1,000 beacons celebrated this new economic union in Western Europe. Customs checks and trade barriers were removed or greatly reduced. Could economic union lead to a "United States of Europe"? ■

▲ *The European Economic Community, or Common Market, includes most of Western Europe. Which Western European countries are not part of this union? Use the chart above to compare the per capita, or per person, income of the United States with that of several European countries.*

■ *What is the Common Market?*

DEVELOP

Have students copy the lesson's main headings—*Western Europe Moves to Greater Unity* and *Western Europe Faces Its Future*—on a sheet of paper, and leave space. Next, have them copy the subheadings under the appropriate headings, again leaving space. Then ask them to fill in two details for each subheading as they read.

ECONOMICS

Critical Thinking

Help students understand a common market by asking them to imagine that they are collecting baseball cards. They hear about a group who swap cards among themselves and arrange swaps with others. Should they join? *(Students might answer yes, because they would have access to more cards through the group.)*

◄ *The Western European countries that were not part of the Common Market according to the map include Switzerland, Iceland, Norway, and Sweden.*

■ *The Common Market is an economic union formed to increase trade and cooperation among the countries of Western Europe.*

Access Strategy

If possible bring a U.S. passport and a passport from a European country to class. Explain that a passport is a government-issued document that permits the holder to cross international borders. Most passports establish the holder's identity with a sealed photograph; they also indicate nationality and request safe passage.

Discuss reasons that a country would require a passport. *(To keep track of who enters the country and for how long the travelers stay)* What are the advantages for travelers if countries do not require passports? *(They experience fewer delays.)*

Have students make their own mock passports. Use a quick-developing camera to take students' passport photos if possible; or have students bring in photos from home; or have them draw self-portraits. Tell students that they are now ready to take an imaginary trip to Europe.

Access Activity

Have students identify the 12 members of the EC on the map on this page. Then have them use an almanac to look up each country's flag. In groups, students can choose one of the flags to draw. Then paste all flags on one sheet to make a single flag. Explain that according to the EC ideal, countries will become part of a larger community while keeping their own identities.

Note: Use this A Closer Look to provide additional information about European currencies and the possibility of a single European currency.

ECONOMICS

Visual Learning

Ask students to study the pictures of the various European currencies on this page. Then have them imagine that each of the 50 states in the United States had its own currency. How might having so many different currencies affect travel and trade among the states? *(Travel and trade would be more complicated and difficult.)*

More About European Currency Although coins survived in the Byzantine Empire after the fall of Rome in A.D. 476, they almost disappeared in the West. Bullion (gold and silver) and barter financed much of the trade and commerce that existed until a money system once again emerged with the rise of the Italian city-states. Paper money did not appear in Europe until after the end of the 13th century, when the art of paper making developed there.

A CLOSER LOOK

European Currency

Most European nations may share a single currency by the year 2000. Today, each nation mints and prints its own money. Special papers and inks and hidden patterns and symbols prevent forgers from making false money. Dutch bank notes, or guilders, include images of a shorebird, astronomer, sunflower, and lighthouse—each with unusual protections against forgery.

Magnifier and design tools

A printed fingerprint hides in this Dutch guilder, which is shown among the guilders at the bottom of this page.

The lighthouse includes part of a poem, which would be difficult to copy. In a one-guilder note, a rabbit is visible only with a filter.

CHANGE
CAMBIO
WECHSEL
CHANGE

At this exchange booth in Paris, people can buy and sell French francs, Spanish pesetas, British pounds, or Italian lire, among other currencies.

vijftig gulden
de nederlandsche bank
tweehonderd gulden

Visual Learning

Have students design a coin for a single European currency. It may be helpful to give each group coins from other countries. Have students present their coins, explaining reasons for the symbols and letters they included.

Research

Have students work in pairs, in the school or public library, to research the currency of a European country of their choice. Ask them to be prepared to answer some of the following questions: What is the country's currency called? What is the approximate exchange rate with the United States? Where is the currency minted and printed? How does the currency prevent forgery? What images appear on coins and bills?

Mathematics Connection

Look in a newspaper or contact a local bank for information on current rates of exchange for U.S. money in various European countries. Then give students a work sheet with problems they might experience if they traveled in Europe. Here are two examples: 1. A meal in Paris costs 25 francs. How much would the meal cost in U.S. dollars? 2. A bus ride in Italy costs 2,000 lire. How much is the fare in U.S. money?

Western Europe Faces Its Future

During the 1980s and early 1990s, Europeans worked on a new treaty. They called it the "Maastricht *(MAHS trihkt)* Treaty" since it was signed in the town of Maastricht, Netherlands. This treaty was a plan for a more united Europe.

The Maastricht Treaty

One of this treaty's most important goals was to create a single currency for Europe. To learn more about currency in Europe, read A Closer Look on the opposite page.

In 1992 Europeans voted country by country on whether to approve the Maastricht Treaty. However, Europeans still held strong feelings of nationalism and ethnic pride. Many feared losing their national identity, or their sense of who they are as a people, if they voted yes.

In Denmark, voters said no. In France, the treaty barely passed. As a result, European leaders decided to revise the Maastricht Treaty and to put it to a new vote.

Challenges to Unity

Feelings of nationalism also led to outbreaks of violence in Germany, France, and other European countries. For instance, a few Germans formed groups inspired by Hitler's Nazis. These "neo-Nazis," or new Nazis, attacked immigrants to Germany.

Anti-immigrant feelings also arose in other Western European countries. Many immigrants to Western Europe were Muslims from Southwest Asia searching for better jobs. When Europe's economy stumbled in the early 1990s, millions of people lost their jobs. Some Europeans blamed immigrants for their economic troubles.

Western Europe also faces the challenge of how best to help Eastern Europe. Should it get involved in Eastern Europe's ethnic conflicts and economic problems? In the next lesson, you will read about the challenges of Eastern Europe. ■

Not everyone in Europe wants free trade. These French farmers protested the removal of trade barriers by dumping their apples in Paris.

■ *What was a goal of the Maastricht Treaty?*

REVIEW

1. **FOCUS** Is the dream of a united Europe coming true? Explain why or why not.
2. **HISTORY** What was the Treaty of Rome?
3. **ECONOMICS** The Common Market formed a single market in 1993. What were three of its goals?
4. **CRITICAL THINKING** Denmark rejected the Maastricht Treaty in 1992. France barely passed it. Suggest some reasons why so many Europeans opposed this treaty.
5. **ROLE-PLAYING ACTIVITY** Form groups of three to five students. Act out what you think it was like to cross national borders in Europe when customs checks were required. Then act out what crossing national borders without customs checks might be like today.

CITIZENSHIP

Critical Thinking

Have students consider what a united Europe would mean to the United States. What benefits might the United States gain from a united Europe? *(A more peaceful world, the ability to negotiate with one trading partner instead of many)* What drawbacks might there be for the United States from a united Europe? *(A united Europe could serve as a powerful military and economic force that could oppose the United States; also it could erect trade barriers that would hurt U.S. exporters.)*

■ *One goal of the Maastricht Treaty is to have one form of European currency.*

CLOSE

Write the lesson's main headings on the chalkboard. Read the Thinking Focus aloud. Have students use the outlines they made as they read the lesson to fill in important details. Be sure that students include the problems that Western Europe faces as it looks to the future: ethnic conflict, anti-immigrant feeling, and the need to help Eastern Europe.

Answers to Review Questions

1. Students answering yes may mention that Western Europeans formed a Common Market and are working toward greater economic unity. Students answering no may say that Europe remains divided, as shown by Denmark's rejecting the Maastricht Treaty and by ethnic violence in Germany.
2. The Treaty of Rome created the Common Market in Western Europe in 1957.
3. The Common Market's goals included allowing people to trade, work, travel, and live anywhere within Western Europe.
4. Some countries may have opposed the treaty because they feared being controlled by more powerful countries or because they were afraid of losing their identities.
5. You may want to suggest that students choose among these roles: truck drivers, tourists, immigrants, and border-patrol guards. Encourage students to have "travelers" fill out forms and have goods inspected.

Homework Options

Have students use newspaper and magazine articles from the school and public libraries to learn more about the Common Market. Have them share their information orally with the class.

Study Guide: page 85

DECISION-MAKING PROCESS

1. Recognize the need for a decision.
2. Define the goals and values involved.
3. Acquire and evaluate necessary information.
4. Identify and analyze possible alternatives.
5. Choose the best alternative.

This Making Decisions feature uses steps 1–5 of the decision-making process.

CULTURE

Critical Thinking

Have volunteers read the opening quotations aloud. Then locate Denmark and Greece on the map on page 485. Ask students why people from two of Europe's smaller countries would have such different views on a united Europe. *(Some people from smaller countries fear that their cultural identity will be swallowed up by the cultures of larger countries; others welcome the economic opportunities that come with being part of a larger community.)*

MAKING DECISIONS

Voting For or Against a United Europe

Oranges from SPAIN
Cars from FRANCE

Free trade between countries

I don't want a United States of Europe. There would be no Denmark. . . . We Danes are less than two percent of the community [the Common Market], and we'll lose everything. Denmark will be just a patch of Europe attached to Germany.

Kim Jensen, glassware artisan, near Copenhagen, Denmark

I am 16 and live in a small village in Greece. My country is not wealthy and I come from a very poor region. Yet I feel like a true European and my dream, like so many others in Europe, is of final union to benefit all Europe's citizens. . . . If Europeans want to unite, then we must start thinking together as one.

Aristides H. Liakopoulos, Kendrico, Greece

Just a few years ago, the London district of Notting Hill, shown here, was the site of riots between ethnic groups. As diversity increases throughout Europe, many wonder how it will affect European unity.

Background

In the early 1990s, Western Europeans debated the idea of a united Europe. As you read in the previous lesson, much of this debate focused on the Maastricht Treaty. This treaty was a plan to form a "United States of Europe" that would be somewhat similar to the way the states of the United States form a union. Although states have their own laws, they are also subject to higher, federal laws.

The Maastricht Treaty had several goals, including:

1. a single currency and a central bank
2. a more powerful European Parliament to make laws
3. a more powerful European Court of Justice

Objectives

1. Understand the developments of Europe's current status. (History 1, 5)
2. Decide whether to vote for or against a united Europe. (History 6, Critical Thinking 3)

Activity

Divide students into small groups to assemble a public-relations package that they can mail to every citizen of Europe. The package will present positive or negative reasons for a united Europe. It should include a letter that briefly summarizes the group's position; a bumper sticker with a short, catchy slogan; and a poster or leaflet that could be placed in a store window or town library. When students finish, have them share their PR plan.

4. European citizenship for residents of the Common Market
5. a common foreign and defense policy.

The terms of the Maastricht Treaty would become law for all the countries of a united Europe. In other words, some laws of a united Europe would override, or overpower, laws of individual countries.

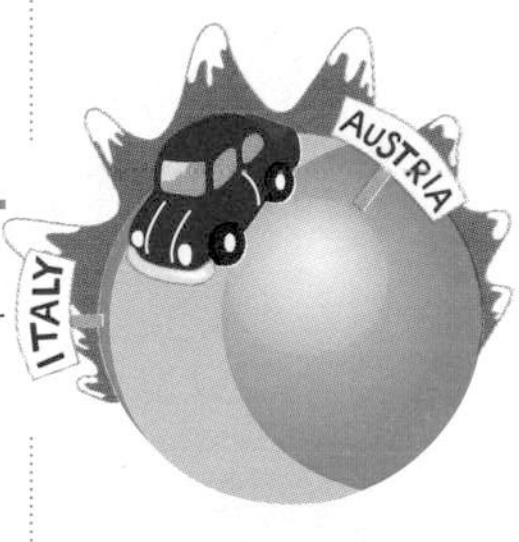
AUSTRIA
ITALY
Free travel between countries

Concerns about a United Europe

Some Europeans—such as the young man from Greece (page 488)—support the idea of a united Europe. They feel it would ensure future peace and economic growth. To compete in a global economy, they say, would require European countries to join together for greater economic strength.

Environmental protection

However, other Europeans—such as Kim Jensen of Denmark (page 488)—do not support the Maastricht Treaty. Many Danes think of themselves as Danish first and European second. Other Europeans feel the same way about their countries. Danes voted to reject the Maastricht Treaty, fearing loss of their national identity.

Some Europeans also fear losing their jobs if Europe is united. They worry that increased competition would force many companies to go out of business.

Partly as a result of the Danish vote and these economic worries, the Maastricht Treaty—and its plan for a united Europe —is being revised.

Can Europeans preserve their national identities in a united Europe? Can the many national groups of Europe get along as one people? Would a united Europe reduce the ethnic tensions within countries? Should creating a united Europe take place before the end of this century? These are just a few of the difficult questions Europeans face as they decide whether to form a united Europe.

Scientific cooperation

Decision Point

1. What are the benefits of a united Europe? What are the costs? (Consider these questions with regard to having one currency, one law-making body, and one supreme court.)
2. What goals and values would cause Europeans to support a united Europe? What goals and values would cause them to reject the idea?
3. Suppose the United States, Mexico, and Canada agreed to form a "United States of North America." Would you support this idea? Explain your response.
4. Collect information from newspapers and magazines about current events in Europe. Discuss how these events could lead to greater unity—or division—in Europe.

▲ *These illustrations reflect some of the benefits of a united Europe. Think about what is not shown—the costs of a united Europe.*

BELIEF SYSTEMS

Social Participation

Have students look at the illustrations on this page that summarize the benefits of the Maastricht Treaty; ask students to rank them according to importance. Then give students two index cards each, and have them write the most compelling reasons for joining the EC on one card and the reasons for not joining it on the other. Collect the cards and read each aloud, having volunteers debate the reasons. Time student responses to keep the activity like a debate.

Answers to Decision Point

1. Benefits include convenience as well as the increased power of a centralized law-making body and supreme court. Costs include loss of autonomy and possible loss of jobs and businesses.
2. Goals and values that support a united Europe include peace and economic growth. Goals and values that reject the idea include preserving national identity and the fear of losing jobs.
3. Yes: The three countries could become more economically competitive and could more easily cooperate to solve problems; travel and trade would be simplified and cultural exchanges would take place more readily. No: The three countries might lose their national identities; the United States might lose jobs to other countries.
4. Students' information should include examples of cooperation among countries as well as ethnic and religious strife.

Collaborative Strategy

For a collaborative learning strategy you can use with this lesson, refer to pages T34–T35.

INTRODUCE

Have students read the lesson title and the Thinking Focus. Point out that only a few years ago Eastern Europe was celebrating freedom from communism. Now many of these same countries are facing a different threat: ethnic and religious conflicts between peoples within one country. Ask students to speculate on how Communist regimes may have prevented these internal conflicts in the past and why they have erupted under more democratic governments. Have students read the lesson to find out more about how freedom and independence from Communist rule have brought new challenges to Eastern Europe.

Key Terms

Vocabulary Strategies: T36–T37

command economy—an economic system in which the government owns all farms and factories, decides what to produce, and sets all prices

market economy—an economic system in which farms and factories are privately owned, and owners decide what to produce and set their own prices according to market forces

1980 | 1984 | 1988 | 1989 | TODAY

LESSON 3

Eastern Europe Today

THINKING FOCUS

What are two challenges facing Eastern Europe?

Key Terms

- command economy
- market economy

For families in Sarajevo, the last night of 1992 passed quietly. No bombs crashed into their city. No gunfire sounded. The war between the Serbs and the Muslims of Bosnia-Herzegovina *(BAHZ nee uh hehrt suh goh VEE nuh)*, once part of Yugoslavia, had not ended. Yet fighting had stopped this cold winter night during a brief cease-fire.

For warmth, families huddled together under piles of blankets. Homes in Sarajevo lacked electricity, heat, and running water. For dinner, most people had only a few pieces of bread to eat.

Meanwhile, in Czechoslovakia people counted down the last minutes of 1992. At midnight, Czechoslovakia would split into two separate countries: the Czech Republic and the Slovak Republic. Unlike people in the former country of Yugoslavia, Czechs and Slovaks did not go to war. Their leaders chose to part peacefully. However, Czechs, Slovaks, and many other East Europeans worried about their futures.

Progress in Eastern Europe

Until recently, Communist dictators ruled Eastern Europe. Today, East Europeans are building democratic governments. They are inexperienced with democracy, however, having lived under one-party rule for so long.

East Europeans are also changing from a command economy to a market economy. In a **command economy,** the government owns all farms and factories. It decides what to produce and sets all prices. Under communism, Eastern Europe had a command economy, as in the Soviet Union. In a **market economy,** as in the United States, farms and factories are privately owned. Owners decide what to produce and set their own prices.

East Europeans hope a free-market economy will help to improve their lives. However, they face ethnic conflict, unemployment, and lack of security. Many are making choices that they have never before had.

➤ *These women register to vote in Warsaw. The first free election to Poland's parliament was held in November 1991.*

Objectives

1. Explain why there has been fighting in the Balkans.
2. Describe the challenges facing Eastern Europe after the fall of communism.

Graphic Overview

	Change	Challenge
Czechoslovakia	Two republics emerge.	Strengthen economies
Poland	Communism ends.	Achieve democracy
Germany	East and West reunite.	Solidify the union
Yugoslavia	Republics divide.	End civil strife

Czechoslovakia Divides

When Czechoslovakia split into two separate nations, the two sides split up their assets, or property and equipment, fairly. They agreed to share the same currency.

The Slovak Republic is poorer and less industrialized than the Czech Republic. Many of its factories were used to build weapons during the Cold War. Converting them to other uses will be costly. However, Slovaks are determined to build their own modern country. One of their first goals is to create their own national currency.

Most Czechs wanted to remain as one country with the Slovaks. However, they too feel they can stand on their own. Many Czechs are well educated. With many modern factories, Czechs hope to build a thriving market economy quickly.

Success in Poland

The 1980s saw Poland in turmoil. Its Communist government was losing control over the country. Hundreds of thousands of workers went on strike. From these strikes, a new leader arose in Poland, Lech Walesa *(wah LEHN sah)*.

Walesa led the unions in toppling Poland's Communist government in 1989. Then he worked to transform Poland into a democracy with a market economy. Poland has suffered from high unemployment and rising prices. However, economists now expect Poland's economy to grow.

A New Germany

East and West Germany reunited in 1990. For the first time since World War II, Germans were one people and one country. Germans celebrated this union. Some other Europeans did not.

Many feared a united Germany. They worried that Germany would once again try to rule over Europe. Their fears were not of military power, but of economic power. ■

▲ *Prague, the capital of the Czech Republic, is noted for its rich cultural life, especially in music and literature.*

How Do We Know?

HISTORY *When events change as quickly as they are changing in Eastern Europe, how do people there make sense of them? In Warsaw, Poland, for example, one way people stay up to date on current affairs is by reading several of the city's 15 newspapers. Just a few years ago, Poland had only one official newspaper.*

■ *Why did East Europeans want to change from a command economy to a market economy?*

DEVELOP

Have students scan the headings and name the Eastern European countries that are discussed in the lesson. *(Czechoslovakia—the Czech and Slovak republics—Poland, Germany, Yugoslavia—Bosnia, Macedonia, Slovenia, and Croatia)* Have them copy the names of these countries on a sheet of paper and write a sentence about each as they read.

HISTORY

Social Participation

Divide students into two groups. Have one group imagine that they are reporters for a newsmagazine investigating the changes taking place in Eastern Europe. Have the other group imagine that they are citizens of one of the Eastern European countries discussed in the lesson. Direct students to use the text and photographs from the lesson to prepare for mock interviews between reporters and citizens. Have students conduct their interviews for the rest of the class.

■ *They thought that the change would improve their standard of living.*

Access Strategy

From the school and public libraries, collect maps from encyclopedias and history books showing the changes that Eastern Europe has undergone since the mid-1700s. If possible, point out that during the period between 1795 and 1981, Poland was part of the Hapsburg Empire, the Prussian Empire of Germany, and the Russian Empire; sometimes, Poland disappeared from the map of Europe entirely. Discuss other changes reflected by the maps.

Draw the Graphic Overview on the chalkboard. Ask which country recently united. *(Germany)* Which countries divided? *(Czechoslovakia, Yugoslavia)* Explain that Czechoslovakia split up peacefully, while civil war broke out in Yugoslavia. Point out that the countries of Eastern Europe recently changed from Communist regimes to democracies. Ask in which country Lech Walesa led the movement to topple the Communist government. *(Poland)*

Access Activity

Have students examine the lesson's photographs and read the captions. Then ask students what they can learn about Eastern Europe from the photos. *(Poland held its first free Parliamentary elections in November 1991; some cities in Eastern Europe, such as Prague, are very beautiful and well known for their rich culture; life in parts of Eastern Europe is difficult and dangerous.)*

GEOGRAPHY

Map and Globe Skills

Ask students to turn back to the cultural map of Europe in Chapter 20 (page 462). Have them locate the Balkan Peninsula in southeastern Europe. Then ask why they think there is ethnic conflict in the Balkans. *(Many different ethnic groups live there and they don't get along with one another.)*

■ *Bosnia declared its independence from Yugoslavia. Serbs, Muslims, and Croats fought over control of Bosnia. The Serbs then tried to kill or drive out all Muslims from Bosnia in order to control this land, and perhaps make it part of Serbia (Yugoslavia).*

CLOSE

Pass out file cards to each student. On the front of each card, have students write the name of a country discussed in the lesson. On the back have them write the sentence that they wrote as part of the Develop activity. Collect the cards and read the sentences. Have students guess which country is on the opposite side of the card. Then have them use the information on the cards to help them answer the Thinking Focus.

Old Conflicts Rise Anew

Across Time & Space

Religious differences have divided Serbs, Croats, and Bosnian Muslims—who speak the same language—for centuries. Charlemagne converted the Croats to western Christianity. Later, Byzantines converted the Serbs to eastern Christianity. After being invaded by the Ottoman Turks in the 1300s, many Bosnians converted to Islam.

After the collapse of one-party rule, violent ethnic conflicts broke out in many regions of Eastern Europe. The worst of these conflicts arose in parts of what was once Yugoslavia.

The Breakup of Yugoslavia

Until 1991, Yugoslavia included the republics of Bosnia-Herzegovina (or Bosnia), Macedonia, Slovenia, and Croatia. Today, Yugoslavia is made up of only two republics: Montenegro and Serbia.

Turn to the map on page 481 to see what Yugoslavia and its former republics look like today.

Several ethnic groups live in Yugoslavia and its former republics. For the most part, each ethnic group calls one republic its home. For example, mostly Eastern Orthodox Serbs live in Serbia. Croatia is home to mainly Roman Catholic Croats. However, Muslims, Serbs, and Croats all live in Bosnia.

▲ *Despite the dangers in Sarajevo, these men must cook their meals outdoors.*

■ *Why are Serbs, Muslims, and Croats at war in Bosnia?*

Civil War in Yugoslavia

In mid-1991 civil war broke out when Croatia and Slovenia declared independence from Yugoslavia. Serbs fought to keep Yugoslavia together. After months of war, Slovenia and Croatia made peace with the Serbs. Then Bosnia declared its independence. As a result, Serbs fought Muslims and Croats for control of Bosnia.The Serbs tried to kill or drive out all the non-Serbs from Bosnia. They hoped to make Bosnia part of Yugoslavia again.

Thousands of people, mostly civilians, died in the fighting. Hundreds of thousands of others fled their homes, becoming war refugees. The city of Sarajevo lay battered.

Serbs were accused of "ethnic cleansing," or genocide, for trying to rid Bosnia of everyone who was not a Serb. Serbs were blamed for horrible war crimes, including attacks on women and children and the use of death camps.

Peace talks between the United Nations and leaders of all sides began in mid-1992. The United Nations also sent a small military force to Bosnia to supply people with food and medicine.

Ethnic tensions are also creating problems in the former Soviet Union. The next lesson describes some of the political, economic, and environmental challenges the former Soviet Union is facing. ■

REVIEW

1. **FOCUS** What are two challenges facing Eastern Europe?
2. **ECONOMICS** What problems do Eastern European countries face in trying to shift from a command economy to a market economy?
3. **GEOGRAPHY** Name the republics that seceded from Yugoslavia in the early 1990s.
4. **HISTORY** What ethnic groups were fighting in Bosnia?
5. **CRITICAL THINKING** Why are some people afraid that war in Bosnia may spread throughout Europe?
6. **ACTIVITY** Compare the Atlas map of modern Europe on page 682 with the cultural map of Europe in 1914 on page 462. Then make a chart showing some of the ways Europe today differs from Europe in 1914.

Homework Options

Have students collect and share newspaper articles on Eastern Europe. Then ask them to imagine they have been sent by the United Nations to try to help solve Eastern Europe's problems. Ask them to write a list of possible solutions.

Study Guide: page 86

Answers to Review Questions

1. One challenge, forming democracies, is difficult for people who are inexperienced with democratic government. Another challenge is making the change to a market economy.
2. Eastern European countries face ethnic conflict, unemployment, and lack of security as they shift to a market economy.
3. The countries that seceded from Yugoslavia were Bosnia-Herzegovina (or Bosnia), Croatia, Slovenia, and Macedonia.
4. Serbs, Muslims, and Croats fought one another for control of Bosnia.
5. They worry that other countries may take sides and become involved in the fighting.
6. Students' charts should show that Austria-Hungary no longer exists. They should also show the many new nations, such as Croatia and Slovenia, that did not exist in 1914.

1980 1984 1988 1991 TODAY

L E S S O N 4

Russia and the Former Soviet Republics

The Kremlin is the heart of Moscow and the center of government. Next to it is Red Square, home to kiosks, such as this one.

THINKING FOCUS

What are two challenges facing the former Soviet republics today?

Key Terms

- entrepreneur
- commonwealth

Vladislav Vasnev owns one of the first private businesses in the former Soviet Union. Vasnev and his partners run a chain of kiosks *(KEE ahsks),* or booths, near Red Square in Moscow. From their kiosks, they sell a variety of goods from video equipment to shoes.

Russian shoppers crowd around Vasnev's many kiosks. Only a few have enough money to buy something there. Still, Vasnev's business continues to grow. Elsewhere in Russia, other **entrepreneurs** *(ahn truh pruh NUHRS),* or people who start businesses, are trying to realize their dreams. However, Russian entrepreneurs risk losing their investments—and businesses.

Although Russians are building a democracy and a market economy, what if they fail? As Vasnev says, "There were never any guarantees, and there still aren't any. We are still at risk, even today."

After the Breakup of the Soviet Union

In Chapter 20 you read how Communist officials tried to overthrow Gorbachev in August 1991. Afterward Gorbachev returned as president of the Soviet Union. His goal was to reform the Soviet Union slowly. However, many people demanded quicker reforms.

INTRODUCE

Have students read the Thinking Focus and the beginning paragraphs about entrepreneurs. Ask them to comment on whether this example of free enterprise could have happened 15 years ago in the former Soviet Union. *(No. Free enterprise was not part of the Communist economic system.)* Explain that it is not easy for a government to change an economic system. When the former Soviet Union collapsed, there was a scramble among its 15 republics to change their economies. This has posed many challenges to the people and government. Tell students to consider, as they read the lesson, the economic challenges that the former Soviet Union faces.

Key Terms

Vocabulary Strategies: T36–T37

entrepreneur—a person who starts and invests in businesses

commonwealth—a group of countries sharing common goals

Graphic Overview

The Soviet Union breaks apart into 15 new countries. → The C.I.S. is formed. The Baltics rule themselves. → Struggles for economic reform continue in Russia and the former Soviet republics.

Objectives

1. Explain why the USSR collapsed.
2. Describe the challenges facing Russia today.
3. Describe the challenges facing the former Soviet republics today.

DEVELOP

Point out that the lesson gives a chronology of Russia and the former Soviet Republics since the breakup of the Soviet Union in 1991. Have students scan the lesson and read the headings to find clues to the region's recent history. Then write the date *1991* on the chalkboard. Tell students that they will be finding out what happened in Russia during this important year and afterwards. Ask them to keep a list of the events of 1991 as they read the lesson.

➤ *From the map, students can see that national borders do not match the colored borders of ethnic groups in the former Soviet Union. As in Eastern Europe, ethnic conflict could result if these groups want the same land and resources or if they want to form their own independent countries.*

The Caspian and Aral Seas—or Deserts?

Rivers supplying fresh water to the Caspian and Aral seas are being diverted to grow cotton. As a result, these two inland seas are drying up—and becoming deserts.

Ethnic Conflict in the Caucasus

Christian Armenia and Muslim Azerbaijan are fighting over Nagorno-Karabakh. This region is located in Azerbaijan, but its people are mostly Armenians.

Russia Today

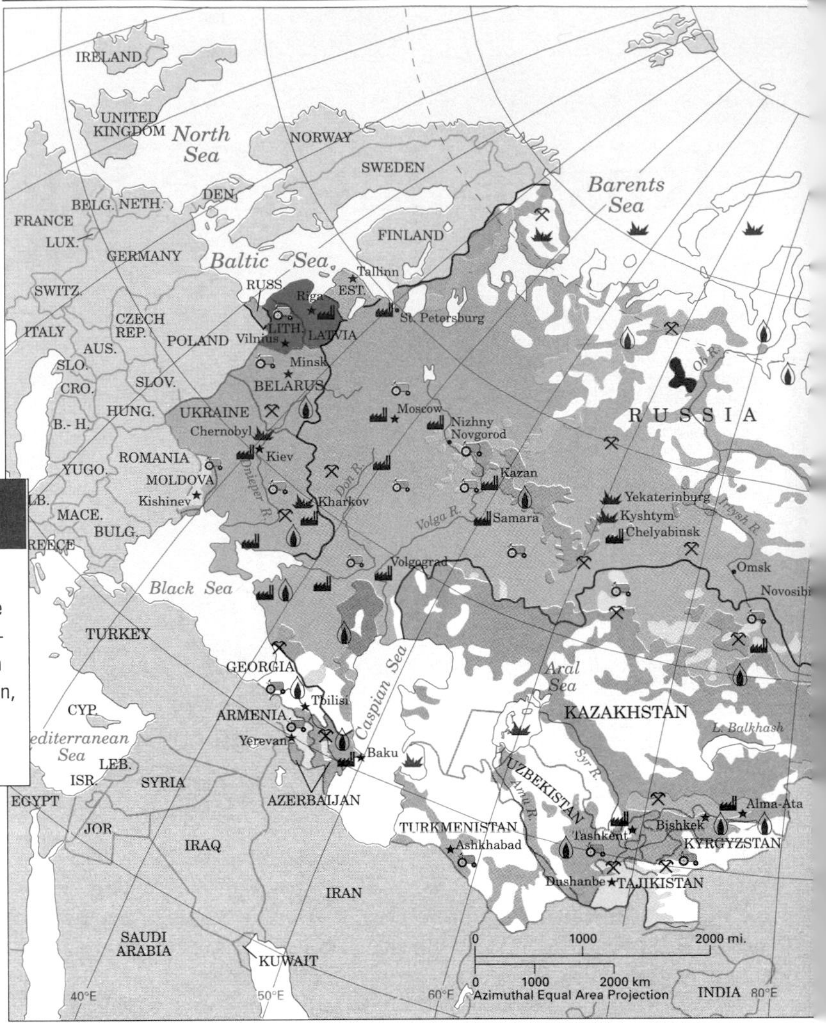
IRELAND
UNITED KINGDOM
North Sea
NORWAY
SWEDEN
Barents Sea
FINLAND
DEN.
BELG.
NETH.
FRANCE
LUX.
GERMANY
Baltic Sea
Tallinn
EST.
RUSS.
Riga
LATVIA
LITH.
Vilnius
St. Petersburg
SWITZ.
CZECH REP.
POLAND
ITALY
AUS.
SLO.
CRO.
SLOV.
Minsk
BELARUS
B.-H.
HUNG.
UKRAINE
Chernobyl
Moscow
Nizhny Novgorod
RUSSIA
ROMANIA
Kiev
YUGO.
MOLDOVA
Kishinev
Dnieper R.
Don R.
Kharkov
Kazan
Volga R.
Samara
Yekaterinburg
Kyshtym
Chelyabinsk
Irtysh R.
Ob R.
MACE.
BULG.
Volgograd
Omsk
Black Sea
TURKEY
GEORGIA
Tbilisi
Caspian Sea
Aral Sea
KAZAKHSTAN
L. Balkhash
ARMENIA
Yerevan
Baku
CYP.
LEB.
ISR.
SYRIA
EGYPT
AZERBAIJAN
UZBEKISTAN
Syr R.
Amu R.
Alma-Ata
Bishkek
KYRGYZSTAN
Tashkent
TURKMENISTAN
Ashkhabad
JOR.
IRAQ
Dushanbe
TAJIKISTAN
IRAN
SAUDI ARABIA
KUWAIT
0 1000 2000 mi.
0 1000 2000 km
Azimuthal Equal Area Projection
INDIA
40°E
50°E
60°E
80°E

➤ *Study this map of Russia and the other former Soviet republics. Why might ethnic conflict become a major problem in these republics?*

The Soviet Union Falls Apart

Fear of Soviet troops had kept the 15 republics from breaking away from the Soviet Union. After the failed takeover, however, people no longer feared Soviet troops.

During the autumn of 1991, the republics took the final steps to become independent countries. Gorbachev was powerless to stop them from leaving the Soviet Union. He could not depend on the loyalty of the Soviet troops. People no longer trusted the slow pace of his reforms.

As a result, the Soviet Union broke apart. Gorbachev resigned as Soviet president. At the end of 1991, the Soviet Union ceased to exist.

Fifteen New Countries Emerge

All of the 15 republics of the Soviet Union were now independent countries. To learn more about these 15 new countries, see the map on this and the opposite page.

Access Activity

Have students use the physical map of the world on page 681 to identify the varied physical regions of the former Soviet Union. Then ask them to think about how the climate might vary across such a vast land area.

Access Strategy

Have students turn to the World Map on pages 678–679 of the Atlas. Point out that the former Soviet Union spanned 11 time zones. Next, ask students to find the Bering Sea in the east and the Baltic Sea in the west. Then give them this puzzler: If you were eating breakfast at your home near the Bering Sea on Wednesday, what might your friend who lives near the Baltic Sea be doing at the same time? *(Eating dinner)* What day would it be for your friend? *(The day before—Tuesday)* If students have questions about time zones, refer them to the Time Zone Map on page G10 of the Map and Globe Handbook. Finally, have students speculate on what some of the problems of uniting such a vast region as the former Soviet Union might be. *(Uniting the many different ethnic groups; distributing food and resources evenly)*

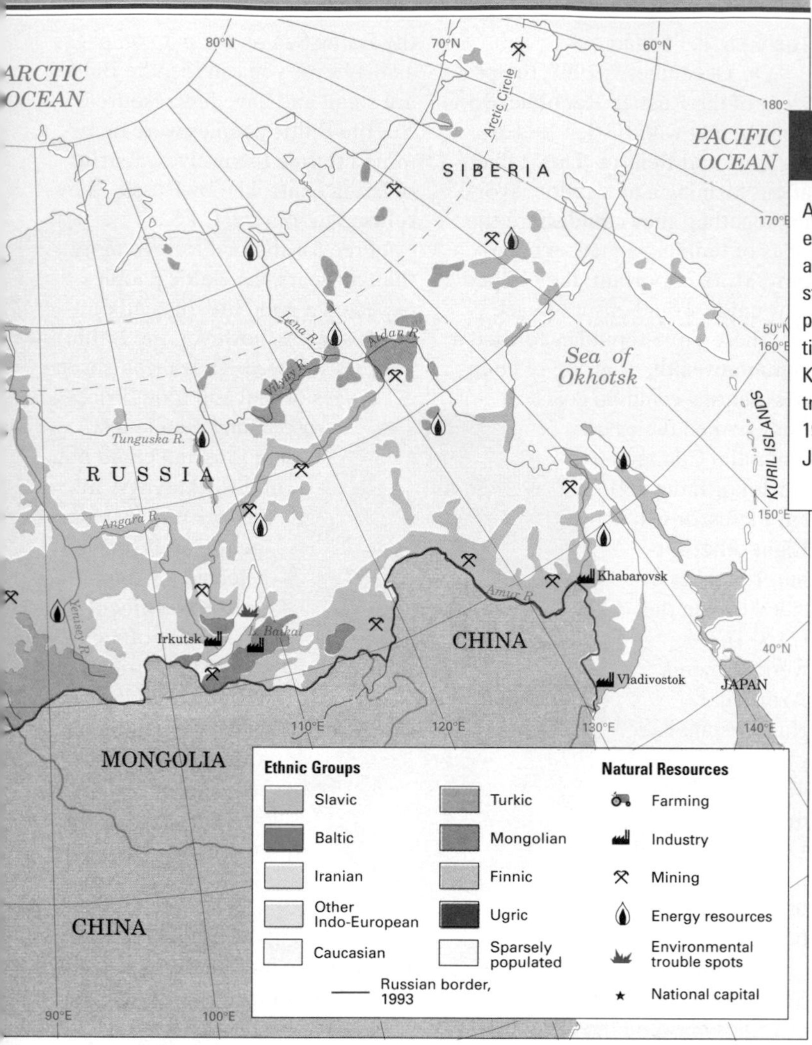
ARCTIC OCEAN
PACIFIC OCEAN
SIBERIA
RUSSIA
CHINA
MONGOLIA
JAPAN
Sea of Okhotsk
KURIL ISLANDS
Arctic Circle
Lena R.
Aldan R.
Vilyuy R.
Tunguska R.
Angara R.
Yenisey R.
Amur R.
L. Baikal
Irkutsk
Khabarovsk
Vladivostok
80°N
70°N
60°N
50°N
40°N
180°
170°E
160°E
150°E
140°E
130°E
120°E
110°E
100°E
90°E
Ethnic Groups
Slavic
Baltic
Iranian
Other Indo-European
Caucasian
Turkic
Mongolian
Finnic
Ugric
Sparsely populated
Russian border, 1993
Natural Resources
Farming
Industry
Mining
Energy resources
Environmental trouble spots
National capital

Friction Between Russia and Japan

Although World War II ended almost 50 years ago, Russia and Japan still have not signed a peace treaty. They continue to argue over the Kuril Islands—controlled by Russia since 1945, but ruled by Japan for centuries.

The Siberian Tiger: Soon to Be Extinct?

The last 300 or so Siberian tigers on earth are in danger of losing their home—and disappearing forever. Their home, the world's largest forest in Siberia, is being cut down for timber.

Like many Eastern European countries, these 15 new countries faced many challenges. Most attempted to form democratic governments. Most struggled to change from a command economy to a market economy.

In the past, the Soviet government controlled the local economies and local governments. Now, the 15 former Soviet republics are in charge of both. Nickolai Karanko, a Ukrainian teenager, said:

> *Five years ago, we had to do what the government wanted. Now, they have to do what we want. That's democracy.*

Still, people in the former Soviet republics worried about the future. People still had to wait in line for food. Worse, unemployment and prices were rising. Could they survive without the Soviet Union?

GEOGRAPHY

Map and Globe Skills

Refer students to the map on these pages. Have volunteers read the information in the boxes next to the map aloud. What does this information explain about the kinds of challenges facing Russia today? *(Environmental problems, ethnic tensions, and quarrels with other nations)* Then have students work in pairs to read more about Russia today in newspapers and newsmagazines in the school and public libraries. Ask them to add a new box to the map, or update an existing one, and share their additions with the class.

Economic Context

To help students understand the concern that many Russians have about their future, explain that new economic policies brought many new economic possibilities, such as private ownership of industries and farms. With these reforms, however, came problems, including higher prices. Inflation rates have been reported at 20 to 40 percent a month, leaving many Russians without the food and comforts they once enjoyed.

Role-Play

Have students discuss the Ukrainian teenager's definition of democracy quoted on this page. Then point out that while the teenager expresses optimism, many Russians are worried about their future. Have students role-play conversations between schoolchildren, parents, or business people. Students might express both feelings of optimism and personal fears, such as unemployment and rising prices for food.

Visual Learning

Have students look at the photographs in the lesson. Ask them these questions: How do the pictures show hope for the future? Are these hopes justified by recent events? To answer the second question, have students clip current newspaper and magazine articles and summarize them.

HISTORY

Critical Thinking

Have students reread the sections about former President Gorbachev on pages 493–494 and review relevant sections of Chapter 20. Then ask them to imagine that they are to meet with Gorbachev. They will be allowed to ask him one question about the events that led to the collapse of the Soviet Union. What will that question be? Have students share their questions with the class. *(Students' questions should show an awareness of Gorbachev's role in the events leading up to the breakup of the Soviet Union.)*

■ *One reason was to share the costs of building market economies. Another reason was to help ensure peace and cooperation among these former republics.*

Across Time & Space

The Soviet Union was home to many ethnic groups, such as Ukrainians and Georgians. For years, Russians had ruled these ethnic groups with czars and later with Communist dictators. Then, in 1991 the Soviet Union broke up, and some of these peoples were free to govern themselves.

The C.I.S. Is Formed

On December 7, 1991, the president of the Russian Republic, Boris Yeltsin, met with the leaders of Ukraine and Belarus. They talked about forming a new union. Working together, they could share the costs of building a market economy. More important, they hoped a new union would ensure peace.

These three republics formed a **commonwealth,** or group of countries sharing common goals. They named their new union the Commonwealth of Independent States, or C.I.S. Eight other former republics decided to join the C.I.S. These were Armenia, Azerbaijan, Kazakhstan, Kyrgyzstan, Moldova, Tajikistan, Turkmenistan, and Uzbekistan. Study the map on pages 494–495 to find the 11 original members of the C.I.S.

➤ *Russian President Boris Yeltsin, shown here, wants to move quickly toward a market economy. However, other government leaders do not.*

Tensions throughout the former Soviet Union have already weakened ties between the republics. Azerbaijan and Armenia, for example, are fighting over territory.

■ *Give two reasons why Russia and several other republics formed the C.I.S.*

The Baltics Struggle Alone

To locate the Baltic countries of Estonia, Latvia, and Lithuania, find the Baltic Sea on the map on pages 494–495. As you can see, the Baltics are small and have few resources. Yet the Baltic peoples were determined to rule themselves. Fearful of being controlled by Russia, they refused to join the C.I.S.

Free for the first time in more than 50 years, the Baltic peoples expected a good life. Instead of quick success, however, the Baltic peoples suffered. They faced shortages of fuel and food. Prices rose. Many people lost their jobs and could not find work. Angry at the lack of progress, people in Lithuania elected a Communist government back into office.

More troubling, Russian soldiers still remained in all three countries. In fact, almost two million Russians call the Baltics their home. However, the Baltic peoples view Russians as their former rulers. Estonia and Latvia passed laws making it difficult for Russians to become citizens there. As a result, ethnic conflict in the Baltics increased.

Just a few years after independence, the high hopes of the Baltic peoples were fading. They wondered if they would survive as independent countries. ■

Challenges for the Future

People in the other former Soviet republics also expected their economies to improve quickly. However, as in the Baltics and Eastern Europe, they did not. Prices and unemployment rose, while many factories closed. In Russia, organized crime greatly increased. People wondered if economic reforms were worth these costs.

Social Participation

Have students imagine that they have a chance to become a Russian entrepreneur. Ask them to work in pairs to answer the following questions: What sort of business would they start? What machinery and workers would they need? What might be some of the obstacles they would face? Have them present their business plan to the rest of the class.

Historical Context

In order to increase students' understanding of the Baltic states, explain that the Soviet Union annexed the Baltic republics in 1940. For the next 50 years, Russians poured into the region, taking control of business and industry. In Latvia, for example, there are almost as many Russians as native-born Latvians. With the weakening of the Soviet Union in the late 1980s, the people of the Baltics saw their chance; in 1990 they voted to secede from the Soviet Union. After the failed coup attempt in 1991, Gorbachev allowed the Baltics to leave the Soviet Union.

The price of independence has been high for this resource-poor region. For example, now people must wait in line for several hours to buy gasoline, which formerly came from the Soviet Union. On the other hand, many people are enjoying their new freedom. One student is quoted as saying, "Before, we only learned the viewpoint of the Communists. Now we hear the views of others, too."

In Russia, President Yeltsin and several former Communist leaders agreed to slow down the change to a market economy. For example, they decided to control the prices of milk, pasta, and bread.

Many of the other former republics also tried to slow their reforms. Some people approved of these slowdowns. Others, however, feared a return to communism.

▲ *These Soviet bombers once carried nuclear weapons. After agreeing to arms control treaties with the United States, Russian officials cut off the tails to prove that these planes no longer posed a nuclear threat.*

Reducing Nuclear Weapons

Almost all Soviet nuclear weapons had been placed in Russia, Ukraine, Belarus, and Kazakhstan. What would happen to these weapons now?

In 1993 Russian President Yeltsin and U.S. President George Bush signed a new treaty, called START II (Strategic Arms Reduction Treaty). Both leaders agreed to destroy many of their country's nuclear weapons. Belarus, Kazakhstan, and Ukraine had signed an earlier treaty to reduce nuclear arms with the United States and Russia. That treaty quickly ran into trouble, however. Some Ukrainians wanted to keep their nuclear weapons to protect the country against Russia. Ukrainian officials asked for more aid from the West. U.S. President George Bush offered millions of dollars to help Ukraine disarm.

Cleaning Up the Environment

Turn back to the map on pages 494–495. Note the locations of some environmental trouble spots facing the former republics today. Cleaning up their air, land, and water will cost billions of dollars. However, these new countries do not have enough money to pay these costs.

Perhaps the greatest challenge facing the former Soviet republics is living with so much uncertainty. Will life improve? Will a Communist dictator again seize power? Only in the future will the answers be known. ■

■ *Why do some Russians and others in the former republics want to slow their economic reforms?*

■ *They do not like the economic problems that have resulted from the free market reforms. For example, prices rose and factories closed. They hope that by slowing the reforms, economic troubles can be reduced.*

REVIEW

1. **FOCUS** What are two challenges facing the former Soviet republics today?
2. **HISTORY** Explain one reason for the breakup of the Soviet Union.
3. **ECONOMICS** Why were the Baltic peoples disappointed in the years following independence?
4. **CRITICAL THINKING** Russia and the former republics need investments to help them succeed. What kind of investments might benefit Russia and the former Soviet republics? Explain how the United States might benefit from making investments there.
5. **ACTIVITY** Imagine you are a Russian entrepreneur, such as Vladislav Vasnev. What would you say to Russian leaders to persuade them to keep your kiosks open and to continue to build a market economy? Write a letter that Vasnev might write on this topic.

CLOSE

Reread the Thinking Focus aloud. Have students share the lists of events of 1991 that they made as they read the lesson; their lists should include the failed coup attempt, President Gorbachev's resignation, and the formation of the Commonwealth of Independent States (C.I.S). Then draw the first two frames of the Graphic Overview on the chalkboard. Provide the heading for the last frame but give no additional information. Have students fill in the last frame.

Answers to Review Questions

1. Sample answer: One challenge is that the republics with nuclear arms must decide what to do with them; another is that the republics face severe environmental problems and cannot afford solutions.
2. Sample answer: The Soviet economy was collapsing, and people wanted reform to move faster than it was under President Gorbachev.
3. They expected to be successful fairly quickly, but economic troubles followed.
4. Students might mention investments to destroy nuclear weapons, clean up the environment, and fund entrepreneurs. Long-term benefits to the United States might include peace and increased trade.
5. Encourage students to think of how Vasnev's business improves the standard of living. For example, he might say that having more shops to choose from will increase jobs and keep prices low because of increased competition.

Homework Options

Have students use magazines and newspapers to learn more about one of the following: nuclear weapons in Russia or Ukraine; environmental trouble spots such as the Caspian and Aral seas; or recent events in the Baltics. Have them write a summary of their findings.

Study Guide: page 87

Chapter Review

Reviewing Key Terms

command economy (p. 490)
common market (p. 484)
commonwealth (p. 496)
continental climate (p. 482)
customs check (p. 485)
entrepreneur (p. 493)
marine climate (p. 482)
market economy (p. 490)
Mediterranean climate (p. 482)
tariff (p. 485)

A. Write a short paragraph explaining how the terms in each of these groups are related. Be sure to use the terms themselves in your explanation.

1. marine climate, Mediterranean climate, continental climate
2. command economy, market economy

B. Answer the following questions, using the key term in parentheses.

1. How did Western European nations hope to increase economic cooperation during the Cold War? (common market)
2. What happens when goods and people cross a country's borders in Europe? (customs check)
3. How might a country whose factories make shoes protect its shoe industry from cheaper imported shoes? (tariff)
4. What was one result of the economic and political changes taking place in Russia? (entrepreneur)
5. What kind of organization brought together some of the former republics of the Soviet Union? (commonwealth)

Exploring Concepts

A. Copy the timeline below. Place these events in their proper positions.

- Czechoslovakia divides in two.
- Germany reunites.
- Civil war erupts in Yugoslavia.
- Poland's Communist government falls.
- Three former Soviet republics form the C.I.S.
- Europeans vote on the Maastricht Treaty.
- Gorbachev resigns as Soviet leader.

B. Answer each question with information from the chapter.

1. Where are the mountain systems of Europe located? What regions do they separate?
2. How has the Northern European Plain contributed to Europe's prosperity?
3. What causes Europe's marine climate?
4. Name at least three of the founding members of the European Economic Community.
5. What were some of the original goals of the European Economic Community?
6. Why did some Europeans oppose the first version of the Maastricht Treaty?
7. Who were the targets of Germany's neo-Nazi groups? Why were they targets?
8. What change occurred in Czechoslovakia at the end of 1992?
9. What were the main causes of the breakup of Yugoslavia?
10. When the Soviet Union fell apart, what became of its former republics?
11. What countries formed the C.I.S.?

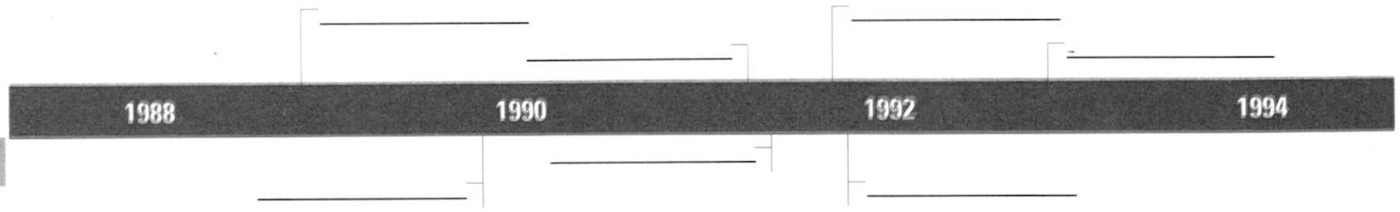

1988
1990
1992
1994

Answers to Reviewing Key Terms

A. Sample answers:

1. The European continent is relatively small but has several different climates. Most of western Europe has a mild, wet **marine climate** because of warm ocean winds. The interior has a more extreme **continental climate,** with short summers and long winters. Warm winds from Africa give much of southern Europe a dry **Mediterranean climate.**
2. The old governments in Eastern Europe owned farms and factories under a **command economy.** As changes came, they worked to switch to a **market economy,** in which private individuals own businesses.

B. Sample answers:

1. Some Western European nations formed an economic union, or **common market.**
2. When people cross into another country in Europe, officials at the border run a **customs check** or border inspection.
3. A country may impose a **tariff** on imported shoes to encourage its people to buy shoes made in their own country.
4. Because of the changes in Russia, an **entrepreneur** was able to start his or her own business.
5. Some former Soviet republics decided to work together as part of a **commonwealth.**

Answers to Exploring Concepts

A. Events should appear on the timeline as follows: Poland's Communist government falls (1989); Germany reunites (1990); Civil war erupts in Yugoslavia (mid-1991); Gorbachev resigns as Soviet leader (August 1991); Three former Soviet republics form the C.I.S. (December 1991); Europeans vote on the Maastricht Treaty (1992); Czechoslovakia divides in two (January 1993).

B. Sample answers:

1. One mountain system crosses northern Europe. The Alpine system separates central Europe from southern Europe.
2. The Northern European Plain has rich farmland and natural resources like iron and coal.
3. The Gulf Stream, which flows northward from the Gulf of Mexico, warms the ocean water and the winds that blow over it.
4. (Any three) Belgium, France, Italy, Luxembourg, the Netherlands, West Germany.
5. The European Economic Community was originally created to increase trade and cooperation among its members.
6. They were afraid of losing their national identity and of possible economic problems.
7. Neo-Nazis attacked mainly immigrants, blaming them for economic problems.
8. After 1992, the country split into two separate republics—the Czech Republic and the Slovak Republic.
9. The main causes were religious and ethnic differences among Serbs, Croats, and Muslims.
10. They became independent countries. Most joined the new Commonwealth of Independent States.
11. Russia, Ukraine, and Belarus formed the C.I.S. in December 1991. Later eight other former republics joined.

Reviewing Skills

1. Suppose that you and a friend or family member want to watch different television shows that are on at the same time. Applying the steps on page 483, describe the first step you would take to resolve this conflict. How might you reach a solution that satisfies both of you?
2. One of the major changes in Europe in the 1990s was the split of Czechoslovakia into two nations. Reread the section of Lesson 3 that discusses this change. From those paragraphs, what predictions would you make about the future of the Slovak Republic and the Czech Republic? Explain the reasons behind your predictions.
3. Study the chart below. If a Russian worker earned 350 rubles a month, how much would he or she have left over after buying one gallon of milk, two loaves of bread, one-half pound of sausage, and one pound of butter?

Basic Food Costs in Russia

Food	Before Price Reforms	After Price Reforms
Milk (1 quart)	.69 Rubles	2.1 Rubles
Bread (1 loaf)	.60 Rubles	2.63 Rubles
Butter (1 pound)	4.5 Rubles	20.35 Rubles
Sausage (1 pound)	35 Rubles	50 Rubles

Note: The average salary is 350–500 rubles ($3.15–$4.50) a month.
Source: Facts on File, 1992

Using Critical Thinking

1. Why would the members of the Common Market want lower tariffs? How do tariffs benefit the people of a country that charges tariffs? How might tariffs hurt those people?
2. Some planners hope for a "United States of Europe." How might this be harder to achieve than a United States of America?
3. In many countries of Eastern Europe, people have never lived under a democratic government. What things about democracy do you think would be surprising or difficult for Eastern Europeans to accept?

Preparing for Citizenship

1. **COLLECTING INFORMATION** Working with one or two classmates, choose one European nation to study. From newspapers, news magazines, and TV or radio reports, gather information about ongoing events in the nation you have chosen. Make a scrapbook of articles, pictures, and notes for that country. Then use this information to prepare a short report that will bring your classmates up to date on events in the country you have studied.
2. **WRITING ACTIVITY** Imagine that you have a pen pal in Russia, Poland, the Baltic states, or the Czech or Slovak republics. Your friend has written you about problems resulting from changes in the government and the economy. Write a letter to your friend in which you describe the good things about democracy and a market economy—the things you feel will make the changes and difficulties worthwhile.
3. **COLLABORATIVE LEARNING** Working with your classmates, make a large-scale illustrated map of modern-day Europe. Use the map on page 481 as a guide. Then look in used magazines or newspapers for pictures you may cut out that show the land and people of Europe. Include pictures of art and handicrafts, as well as your own drawings. Use ribbons and thumbtacks to connect the pictures to the map.

Answers to Reviewing Skills

1. The first step is to define the problem and see each side's position. A possible solution is to watch one program this week, the other next week.
2. Students may suggest that the Czech Republic has advantages, because it is more industrialized, and so may have an easier time establishing itself as an independent country.
3. The solution to the word problem:
   1 gal. milk = 8.40 rubles (2.1 x 4)
   2 lvs. bread = 5.26 (2.63 x 2)
   1/2 lb. saus. = 25.00 (50 ÷ 2)
   1 lb. butter = 20.35 (20.35 x 1)
   total cost = 59.01 rubles
   350 – 59.01 = 290.99 rubles left over

(Total rubles minus costs equals rubles left over.)

Answers to Using Critical Thinking

1. The Common Market members hoped that lowering or reducing tariffs would increase trade. A tariff can protect workers in the industry that makes a certain product, but it can increase prices for consumers.
2. Answers may mention differences in language, ethnic differences, and a long history of conflicts and wars.
3. Encourage students to discuss how freedom can make people feel insecure or unprotected as well as free. For instance, they no longer have guaranteed jobs. They may not be experienced in deciding how to vote when candidates from more than one party are running.

Answers to Preparing for Citizenship

1. **COLLECTING INFORMATION** To encourage student interest in current events, allow class time for each group to give an update on events in countries where situations are changing rapidly.
2. **WRITING ACTIVITY** This activity can be the basis for class discussion about the advantages of a market economy, such as greater choices of goods.
3. **COLLABORATIVE LEARNING** Provide students with the time and materials needed for making and displaying their map.

UNIT
PREVIEW

Explain to students that the photograph on these pages shows folk art from Central America. Ask volunteers to offer definitions of the term *folk art.* How do students think it is different from other kinds of art, for example, *School of Athens* (pages 402–403)?

Then, on a large map of the Western Hemisphere, have students point out Central America, South America, and the Caribbean Sea. In this unit they will read about several countries in this region, from the small nations of Central America to Brazil, the largest country in the region.

Looking Backward

Remind students that in Chapter 6 they studied some of the ancient cultures of this part of the world. Point out that the events discussed in Chapter 19 also shaped the cultures of the present-day nations of this region.

Looking Forward

Unit 7 focuses entirely on the Western Hemisphere. It treats two regions and one major country:

Chapter 22 *The Caribbean*
Chapter 23 *Central and South America*
Chapter 24 *Brazil*

Unit 7
The Caribbean, Central and South America

Wrapped in a hammock, a man is carried off for burial. Hanging above the body are food and prized possessions that will accompany him into the afterlife. This story, told in this brightly colored cloth panel called a mola, reveals part of traditional Kuna culture. Native Americans, such as the Kuna of Panama, are the descendants of Asians who first came to the Americas perhaps 50,000 years ago. Native Americans developed agriculture, complex belief systems, and civilizations that scientists and historians today are still learning about.

1492

A mola (fabric made from stitched pieces of cloth) from the San Blas Islands, Panama, c. 1965

BIBLIOGRAPHY

Books for Students
Anthony, Suzanne. *Haiti.* New York: Chelsea House, 1989. An overview of Haiti's history and geography. Nonfiction.

Bachelis, Faren. *The Central Americans.* New York: Chelsea House, 1990. A history of modern Central America. Nonfiction.

Bender, Evelyn. *Brazil.* New York: Chelsea House, 1990. A short history of Brazil and the economic problems it faces. Nonfiction.

Carter, William E. *South America.* Rev. ed. New York: Watts, 1983. Background information on each country in South America. Nonfiction.

Books to Read Aloud
Lessac, Frané. *Caribbean Canvas.* New York: Lippincott, 1989. A collection of poems, with paintings depicting Caribbean life. Fiction.

Moeri, Louise. *The Forty-Third War.* Boston: Houghton Mifflin, 1989. A war story about a 12-year-old boy in a Central American country and his fight for survival. Fiction.

Today

Understanding Folk Art

The mola is a form of folk art unique to the Caribbean and to South America. Historians believe that this sewing technique originated with the Cuna (or Kuna) people of the San Blas Islands off the eastern coast of Panama. They also think that the designs may have been inspired by the body paintings of ancient cultures and the circular patterns of brain coral.

Have students locate Panama and tell them that the mola in this photograph was made on an island off the coast of Panama. It was created by an unknown Panamanian artist in the 1960s. The design is a little over one foot square. Today molas are used as wall hangings and are prized by collectors.

Understanding Chronology

The events covered in these chapters occurred after Europeans arrived in the Americas in the fifteenth century. The information in this unit should heighten students' awareness that this arrival was truly a significant turning point in world history.

Other Resources

Books for Teachers

Keen, Benjamin. *A History of Latin America.* 2 vols. Boston: Houghton Mifflin, 1992. A comprehensive overview. Nonfiction.

Langley, Lester. *Central America: The Real Stakes: Understanding Central America Before It's Too Late.* Chicago: Dorsey, 1988. An account of Central America, focusing on military and economic problems. Nonfiction.

Visual Media

Americas. Produced by WGBH, Boston and Central Television Enterprises, 1993. Ten one-hour videos from the PBS series on the history and culture of the Americas.

Software

Hidden Agenda. Springboard Software, 1989. A simulation program in which a student becomes president of a Central American country and must solve its problems.

Houghton Mifflin Social Studies

Bookshelf

Joseph, Lynn. *A Wave in Her Pocket: Stories from Trinidad.* New York: Clarion Books, 1991. A wise woman tells children six stories from Trinidad and West Africa.

INTRODUCE

On his quest to find a shorter route to Asia, Christopher Columbus arrived at the islands of the Caribbean instead. Although this part of the world became known as the New World, in contrast to the Old World of Europe, this hemisphere was also an old world, with well-established cultures of its own.

After students have read the unit title and the paragraphs on this page, point out the picture of the Peruvian child, and mention that in rural areas people still wear traditional costumes like this one. Note the picture of the Peruvian landscape. Ask students to name high mountain ranges such as these elsewhere in the world. *(Himalayas, Rockies, Alps)*

Unit 7 Overview

The Caribbean, and Central and South America

The islands of the Caribbean stretch for more than 2,000 miles. Many are part of a vast underwater mountain chain. Some islands are the tops of volcanoes that erupted long ago. Other islands are made of coral that was formed during thousands of years from the skeletons of tiny sea animals.

A funnel-shaped ribbon of land forms Central America. This narrow strip is crisscrossed by steep mountains and volcanoes. The region is often shaken by earthquakes. At its southern end, Central America meets South America, the world's fourth largest continent.

Native American cultures had prospered in this region long before Columbus sailed into the hemisphere. Spanish and Portuguese sailors began to arrive in the late 1400s and found highly developed civilizations. The explorers overpowered the Indians, took their lands, and forced them to work on farms and in mines. Later, Africans and Asians were brought to the region to work for European plantation owners.

The people of the Caribbean and Central and South America are descendants of Indians, Europeans, Africans, and Asians. Their music, dance, literature, art, and religion all show the influence of many different cultures.

This young girl's Incan ancestry is revealed in her style of dress.

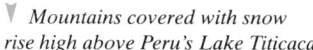

Mountains covered with snow rise high above Peru's Lake Titicaca.

Objectives

1. Explain how four different cultures—Native American, European, African, and Asian—blended to form the cultures of Central and South America and the Caribbean.
2. Identify the influence of the main colonizers of this region, the Spaniards and the Portuguese.
3. Describe the varied geography of this region.

Historical Context

Christopher Columbus first landed on one of the islands of the Bahamas on October 12, 1492. Everything he saw persuaded Columbus that he was among what he called "the islands which are set down in the maps at the end of the Orient." He left quickly to see "whether I can come across the Island of Cipango [Japan]." When Columbus landed on the island now occupied by the Dominican Republic and Haiti, he named it Hispaniola, or "the Spanish Island."

Gulf of Mexico
Nassau
BAHAMAS
Havana
CUBA
Tropic of Cancer
Santiago de Cuba
Port-au-Prince
HAITI
DOMINICAN REPUBLIC
Santo Domingo
PUERTO RICO (U.S.)
VIRGIN ISLANDS (U.S., U.K.)
ANGUILLA (U.K.)
ANTIGUA AND BARBUDA
GUADELOUPE (Fr.)
DOMINICA
MARTINIQUE (Fr.)
ST. LUCIA
BARBADOS
ST. KITTS AND NEVIS
ST. VINCENT AND THE GRENADINES
GRENADA
CAYMAN ISLANDS (U.K.)
JAMAICA
Kingston
BELIZE
Belmopan
Caribbean Sea
HONDURAS
Tegucigalpa
NICARAGUA
Managua
MOSQUITO COAST
SAN JOSÉ
COSTA RICA
PANAMA
Panama City
ISTHMUS OF PANAMA
Gulf of Panama
NETHERLANDS ANTILLES (Neth.)
ARUBA (Neth.)
TRINIDAD AND TOBAGO
Barranquilla
Cartagena
Maracaibo
Caracas
ATLANTIC OCEAN
VENEZUELA
LLANOS
Orinoco River
Angel Falls
Georgetown
Paramaribo
Cayenne
GUYANA
SURINAME
FRENCH GUIANA (Fr.)
GUIANA HIGHLANDS
Medellín
Bogotá
COLOMBIA
OCCIDENTAL MTS.
Magdalena River
Cauca R.
MALPELO (Colombia)
Rio Negro
Equator
Quito
ECUADOR
GALAPAGOS ISLANDS (Ecuador)
Guayaquil
Gulf of Guayaquil
Iquitos
AMAZON
BASIN
Manaus
Amazon River
Solimões River
Belém
Fortaleza
Tapajós River
Xingu River
Madeira River
BRAZIL
Tocantins River
Recife
São Francisco River
Trujillo
PERU
ANDES
Lima
Cuzco
PLATEAU OF MATO GROSSO
BRAZILIAN HIGHLANDS
Salvador
Brasília
PACIFIC OCEAN
Lake Titicaca
La Paz
Arequipa
BOLIVIA
ALTIPLANO
Sucre
Belo Horizonte
GRAN CHACO
PARAGUAY
Paraguay River
Paraná River
Rio de Janeiro
São Paulo
Santos
Antofagasta
ATACAMA DESERT
Asunción
Tropic of Capricorn
SAN FÉLIX ISLAND (Chile)
SAN AMBROSIO ISLAND (Chile)
Salado River
Pôrto Alegre
CHILE
Córdoba
Rosario
URUGUAY
Valparaíso
Santiago
Buenos Aires
Montevideo
Río de la Plata
JUAN FERNÁNDEZ ISLANDS (Chile)
ARGENTINA
PAMPAS
Concepción
Colorado R.
Bahía Blanca
Valdivia
Gulf of San Matías
PATAGONIA
Comodoro Rivadavia
Gulf of San Jorge
National capital
Major city
National boundary
0 400 800 mi.
0 400 800 km
Azimuthal Equal-Area Projection
Strait of Magellan
TIERRA DEL FUEGO
FALKLAND ISLANDS (U.K.)
Cape Horn
Drake Passage
SOUTH GEORGIA (U.K.)
90°W
80°W
70°W
60°W
50°W
40°W
30°W
20°W
100°W
20°N
10°N
0°
10°S
20°S
30°S
40°S
50°S
503

The Caribbean, and Central and South America

Learning from Maps

Make sure that students understand the locator map at the upper right corner of the large map on this page. Ask students to identify on the large map some of the islands of the Caribbean that they know. Then have them identify the Andes, the backbone of South America; the Amazon River, which carries more water than any other river in the world; the two landlocked countries *(Bolivia and Paraguay);* Peru and its capital *(Lima);* a country named for Columbus *(Colombia);* and one named for its location at the equator *(Ecuador).*

Geographic Context

Like South America, Central America is dominated by a mountainous backbone. Many of these mountains are volcanoes. In Central America there are more than 100 large and 150 minor volcanoes. Guatemala City was almost completely destroyed by volcanoes in 1917 and 1918 and again in 1976. Managua, Nicaragua, was ravaged in 1931 and again in 1972.

Not only volcanoes but earthquakes as well wreak damage on Central America. El Salvador experiences such frequent seismic disturbances that the surroundings are called the Valley of the Hammocks *(Valle de las Hamacas).* Residents say that during an earthquake the ground moves more than a swinging hammock does.

Map and Globe Skills

Have students turn to the world religions map in the Atlas on page 688. Ask them which religion prevails in Central and South America and the Caribbean. *(Christianity, specifically Roman Catholicism)* Explain that this religious influence stems from the Spanish and Portuguese colonizers, who sent religious missionaries to help spread Christian beliefs.

LOOK AND RESPOND

Have students scan the captions and images on these two pages. Make a list on the chalkboard of their impressions and observations.

Learning from the Map

Ask students to look at the map on this page. Have them identify the desert and rain forest areas. Tell them that the Amazon rain forest is the largest in the world. Ask what they know about this rain forest. *(Some students may know that the rain forest is shrinking as more and more people cut its trees in an attempt to farm on the land.)* Tell students that, as they will read in this unit, the destruction of the rain forest could have devastating effects on the region and even on the rest of the world.

The Land and People

Much of the Caribbean and Central America have a tropical climate and rain forest vegetation. As you might expect in so large an area, South America is a land of great variety. South America is home to soaring mountains and wide, grass-covered plains. The vast Amazon rain forest is the largest forest in the world. Thousands of kinds of plants and animals live in this rain forest. These include one of the world's longest snakes, the anaconda—and the largest rodent, the capybara.

South America's climate ranges from the tropics in the north to the polar regions of the south.

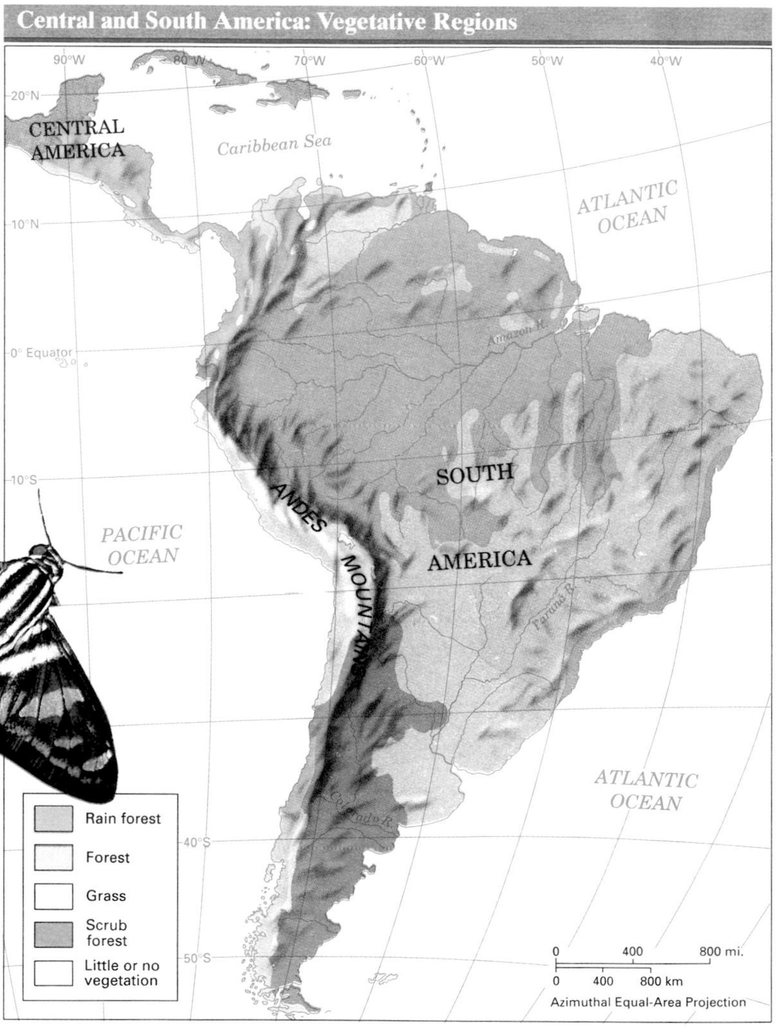
Central and South America: Vegetative Regions
90°W
80°W
70°W
60°W
50°W
40°W
20°N
10°N
0° Equator
10°S
40°S
50°S
CENTRAL AMERICA
Caribbean Sea
ATLANTIC OCEAN
PACIFIC OCEAN
SOUTH AMERICA
ANDES MOUNTAINS
Amazon R.
Paraná R.
ATLANTIC OCEAN
Rain forest
Forest
Grass
Scrub forest
Little or no vegetation
0 400 800 mi.
0 400 800 km
Azimuthal Equal-Area Projection

This skipper butterfly is one of the many animals and plants that live in the Amazon rain forest.

504

Writing to Learn

Have students write poems about what they know already about the Caribbean or Central or South America—perhaps the Native Americans' first view of Europeans; the Amazon rain forest; or navigating the Amazon. After reading the unit, have students revise their poems, or write new poems, based on what they have learned.

Scientific Context

The Galapagos Islands that lie about 600 miles west of Ecuador and belong to that country are actually volcanic peaks. These islands are host to a variety of unusual birds and other animals, including a cormorant that cannot fly, the penguin, unique mockingbirds, four-foot-long iguanas, and turtles that weigh more than 500 pounds. In fact, the Spanish word for these turtles gave the islands their name. In 1835 Charles Darwin studied the unusual animals found on these islands. He was inspired to write his book *The Origin of Species,* in which he theorized about the evolution of animals.

Central and South America separate the Caribbean Sea and Atlantic Ocean from the Pacific Ocean. At one time, people had to sail around South America to get from the Atlantic to the Pacific by ship. In 1904, however, the United States began to build a canal in Panama that would link the oceans. To dig a passage through the rain forest took thousands of workers. Many lives were lost from disease and landslides. Most African Americans who live in Central America today descend from those who came to the region to build the Panama Canal.

When Portuguese and Spanish explorers arrived, many were looking for gold. They had heard tall tales of El Dorado, a ruler so rich that he covered himself in gold. Some did return home with riches. More important, they brought their languages and religion. Today Spanish and Portuguese are the region's major languages. Roman Catholicism is the main religion.

Much of the region's culture is a blend of traditions, however. The festival of Carnival, for example, began with the Catholic custom of feasting before Lent. Today, the people of the region bring their own cultural traditions to Carnival's music, dance, costumes, and parades.

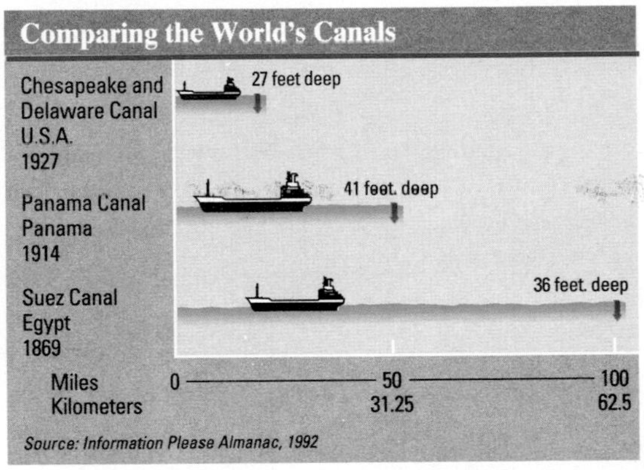

Comparing the World's Canals
Chesapeake and Delaware Canal U.S.A. 1927
27 feet deep
Panama Canal Panama 1914
41 feet. deep
Suez Canal Egypt 1869
36 feet. deep
Miles
Kilometers
0
50
31.25
100
62.5
Source: Information Please Almanac, 1992

Shippers depend on the world's canals to transport their goods. The canals on the chart above are three of the world's longest and most important ones.

Spanish and Portuguese sailors returned to Europe with gold and jewels. They transported their treasure in heavy wooden ships called galleons.

The festival of Carnival in Trinidad and Tobago reflects its European, African, Indian, and Asian heritage.

Learning from the Photographs

The world the Spanish and Portuguese colonizers found was full of riches. Some riches, such as gold and jewels, were plundered. Others, such as peoples' rich cultural heritage, were ignored or forcibly repressed. Ask students why they think that people from this region continue to use traditional objects and participate in traditional activities. *(To maintain continuity with the past, to strengthen family and community ties, or to mark religious rites)*

Learning from the Chart

Have students study the chart of ship canals on this page. Ask which of the three canals is the longest *(Suez)*, which is the deepest *(Panama)*, and which is the oldest *(Suez)*.

ENRICH

Students can use the library to research the Amazon rain forest and the efforts that have been made to save it. Have them answer these questions: What importance does this rain forest hold for the entire world? What can we do as U.S. citizens to save the rain forest and promote economic growth in the region?

Making a Model

Interested students might like to build a model of the Panama Canal. Encourage them to research how a canal works. Then help them build a model to scale and use it to demonstrate how ships pass through the complex series of locks. Explain that the tropical climate of Central America, with its heavy rainfall, unstable soils, and the risk of landslides, makes maintaining the Panama Canal a challenge.

Making a Carnival Float

Have groups of students work on planning and designing a float for Carnival. Direct each group to reach a consensus on theme, costumes, decorations, and props. Group members should work on specific tasks. Have each group submit illustrations and make an oral presentation to the class.

Collaborative Learning

During the 1500s Spanish galleons carried hundreds of tons of gold and silver across the Atlantic Ocean from the Americas to Spain. Divide the class into small groups and have them work together to research, write, and present a television documentary about the treasure and the galleons. Each member of the group should have a task to help with the presentation.

CHAPTER ORGANIZER

Chapter 22 The Caribbean

CHAPTER PLANNING CHART

Pupil's Edition	Teacher's Edition	Ancillaries
Lesson 1: Geography of the Caribbean (2–3 days) Objective 1: Describe the overall geography and climate of the Caribbean islands. (History 7; Geography 2, 3, 5) Objective 2: Name at least two distinctive geographic features of a typical Caribbean island. (Geography 2, 5)	• Graphic Overview (508) • Access Strategy (509) • Access Activity (509) Critical Thinking (510) Geographic Context (510)	Study Guide (88) Map Activities (26) Transparency (12)
Lesson 2: The Caribbean: Cradle of the Americas (3–4 days) Objective 1: Describe the colonial past of the Caribbean. (History 1, 2, 7; Economics 2, 4; Social and Political Systems 1, 4) Objective 2: Show how colonialism led to a mixing of people. (Culture 1, 2) Objective 3: Show how Caribbean people gained emancipation and resisted colonial rule. (History 5, 8; Economics 2, 3; Social and Political Systems 3, 4)	• Graphic Overview (512) • Access Strategy (513) • Access Activity (513) Study Skills (514) Historical Context (514) • Collaborative Learning (515) Map and Globe Skills (515)	Study Guide (89)
Understanding Others Objective: Develop strategies for giving and receiving constructive criticism. (Social Participation 1, 2)	Understanding Criticism (517)	Study Guide (90)
Lesson 3: The Caribbean Today (2–3 days) Objective 1: Describe at least two cultural characteristics shared by the Caribbean islands. (Geography 5; Culture 1, 2, 3) Objective 2: Name at least one challenge facing Caribbean nations today. (History 7; Economics 4, 5)	• Graphic Overview (518) • Access Strategy (519) • Access Activity (519) Critical Thinking (520) Cooperative Learning (520) Music Connection (521) • Visual Learning (521) Critical Thinking (522) Mathematics Connection (522)	Study Guide (91) Discovery Journal (45) • Posters (5)
Chapter Review	Answers (524–525)	Tests (85–88)

* Objectives are correlated to the strands and goals in the program Scope and Sequence on pages T41–T49.

• LEP appropriate resources. (For additional strategies, see pages T32–T33.)

CHAPTER RATIONALE

Chapter 22, which covers the diverse region of the Caribbean, opens the unit on the Caribbean, and Central and South America. To Europeans, the Caribbean was the gateway to the Western Hemisphere. Native peoples living on these islands 500 years ago were the first to have contact with explorers from Western Europe. Today, as a result of a shared history of colonialism, many diverse cultures have met and interacted in the Caribbean. For this reason, the island nations of this region provide students with excellent examples of complex multicultural societies. In addition, the history of the islands illustrates a pattern that has repeated itself throughout the Americas.

Lesson 1 explains the geography of the Caribbean. It discusses what and where the islands are and gives an overview of their climate, flora and fauna, and natural resources. The lesson ends by introducing the idea of the region's multicultural past, which is examined in depth in the next lesson.

Lesson 2 highlights certain aspects of Caribbean history that would repeat themselves throughout the Western Hemisphere: colonialism, slavery, emancipation, independence. It examines how peoples indigenous to the islands were wiped out after the arrival of the Europeans. The lesson spans the Caribbean islands' history of colonialism, discussing the importation and enslavement of African peoples, the successful battle for emancipation, and the importation of Asians as indentured servants. Last, students read how emancipation led to the end of colonialism on most islands.

Lesson 3 looks at how the culture of sports reflects Caribbean unity on certain islands. Students read about aspects of contemporary life in the Caribbean and about how the Caribbean today reflects the colonial history of the region. The lesson highlights Puerto Rico and Cuba as examples of two islands that, despite their close proximity to each other and historical affiliation with Spain, contrasted greatly in their political and social development. The lesson concludes with a look at economic challenges that face Caribbean nations today, as well as the phenomenon of emigration from the Caribbean to other parts of the world.

ACTIVITIES & PROJECTS

Bulletin Board

Illustrate the importance of tourism to the economies of many Caribbean nations. Have students design a display intended to persuade people to travel to the Caribbean. Suggest that they use their own drawings or make a collage from travel posters and brochures. (Use after Lesson 3.)

LEP: Labeling a Map

Provide students with an outline map of the Caribbean or have them trace the text map on page 509. Have them label the following: Gulf of Mexico, Caribbean Sea, Atlantic Ocean, Trinidad, Jamaica, Haiti, Virgin Islands, Cuba, Puerto Rico, Dominica, and the Bahamas. Then ask students to show on their maps the following cities: San Juan; Santo Domingo; Port-au-Prince; Havana; Nassau; and Kingston. (Use after Lesson 1.)

Basic: Reader's Theater

Ask students to read the literature selection and explanatory text on page 512 and adapt it for a reader's theater presentation. Ask them to think of ways to heighten the drama of their reading. Give them time to practice before they present their reading to the class. (Use after Lesson 2.)

Challenge: Research

Have students use encyclopedias or other library resources to find out more about the game of cricket. They should discover that cricket teams, including those from the Caribbean islands, enjoy a wide following in many parts of the world. Suggest that students investigate the history, membership, and activities of the International Cricket Conference, the organization that regulates international cricket competitions, called "test matches." (Use after Lesson 3.)

Basic: Writing a Letter

Check travel guides for the Caribbean islands to find addresses of national tourist bureaus. Help students draft a sample letter identifying themselves as students and requesting information on points of interest in selected islands. Send letters to several travel bureaus and post the brochures received on the bulletin board. (Use after Lesson 3.)

CHAPTER
PREVIEW

Ask students to read the chapter title and the paragraph that follows. Tell students that when Columbus first encountered the Americas, he landed in the Caribbean. Point out that Columbus found a thriving Native American culture in the Caribbean. Explain that this culture soon came to be dominated by Europeans and that many social and political changes would take place on the islands.

Looking Forward

Tell students that they will read about both Caribbean history and about the Caribbean region today in three lessons, Geography of the Caribbean; The Caribbean: Cradle of the Americas; and The Caribbean Today.

Lesson 1 describes the geography of the Caribbean and tells how the region was shaped by the influence of many cultures.

Chapter 22
The Caribbean

From Cuba to Guadeloupe to Trinidad and Tobago, the tropical world of the Caribbean is a region of diversity. Different cultures have met and influenced one another, and they all have been shaped by the history of colonialism. Although different ethnic traditions have been kept, a unique Caribbean culture has been produced.

The tropical beauty of t islands, admired long a by European explorers continues to draw peop to the Caribbean today

This woodcut shows Arawak women baking cassava bread. Cassava, a starchy root, is still used today in Caribbean cooking.

1492 The images of Ferdinand and Isabella adorn the Spanish coin shown above. Columbus gives coins like these to the Native Americans of the Caribbean.

1375 | **1500** | **1625**

1502 Santo Domingo, the first permanent European settlement in the Americas, is established by Spaniards.

1492

BACKGROUND

The Caribbean islands stretch 2,200 miles from the southern tip of Florida to the coast of Venezuela. To some people, the image of the Caribbean is of a tropical paradise of white sand, palm trees, and blue seas. Selling this "paradise" has become the basis of many island economies.

The islands host 2 million tourists annually, and the tourist industry employs two-thirds of the Caribbean workforce. Yet the beauty of the islands is shadowed by problems rooted in a colonial past, a past that began with Columbus's voyages of exploration.

European Exploration

Christopher Columbus made four voyages from Spain. He intended to find gold and a new route to Asia. When he first sailed into the islands of the Caribbean, he thought he had reached Asian islands. When he explored the Caribbean, he met three peoples indigenous to the islands. The Arawaks, the largest group, were primarily farmers; the Ciboney, who lived on Hispaniola and Cuba, were quickly enslaved and soon disappeared; and the Caribs, the third group, were warlike hunters and fishers. Originally from the South American mainland, the Caribs had driven most Arawaks from the Lesser Antilles and were expanding by the time the Spanish arrived on the islands. The skillful and cruel Carib warriors fiercely resisted European attempts to enslave and control them.

These children enjoy their leisure time after school under the warm sun of the Bahamas.

This colorful Carnival mask from Puerto Rico shows how people of the Caribbean celebrate Spanish cultural traditions.

1804 Haiti is the first country in the Caribbean to gain independence from colonial rule.

1750 | 1875 | 2000

1952 After years under U.S. control, Puerto Rico is established as a commonwealth. Though its residents are U.S. citizens, Puerto Rico is a self-governing island.

Today

Understanding the Visuals

Direct students' attention to the illustration of the Arawak women. The Arawak had been living in the Caribbean for many generations before the arrival of Columbus in 1492. Based on radio-carbon dating of artifacts, scientists believe that the Arawak may have inhabited the islands between A.D. 1300 and A.D. 1500.

The Arawak lived in communities of a few hundred to a thousand people. They had a well-developed political system. They farmed cassava (a root crop) and corn, and they fished in the seas.

Understanding Chronology

Refer students to the timeline. Point out that the timeline entries illustrate the historical involvement of Europe and the United States in the Caribbean.

A Colonial Heritage

Due to European colonization, four separate empires developed in the Caribbean—Spanish, Dutch, English, and French. In their fashion, the colonial governments fostered ties to the colonizer and not to neighboring islands. Caribbean students were taught in the language of the colonizer, thus setting up language barriers among the islands that remain to this day. This helps to account for the fact that attempts to form political unity after independence were not successful among the Caribbean islands. Only competitive sports—cricket among the English-speaking islands, and baseball among the Spanish-speaking islands—have helped to build bridges in the region.

Facing the Future

Slavery and indentured labor at the hands of the European colonizers are things of the past, but daily life in the Caribbean reflects its history. In Trinidad, for example, Hinduism is practised as widely as Christianity, and Trinidad also has the highest Muslim population in the region. Today, the people of the Caribbean islands face major challenges. Some islands must import food; most islands have limited natural resources. A lot of hope has been invested in CARICOM, the Caribbean Community and Common Market. This group is working to promote trade and to stimulate industrial growth in all the Caribbean islands.

INTRODUCE

Have students locate the Caribbean islands on the world political inset map in the Atlas, on pages 678–679. Then ask students to find the equator on the map. Ask the students what they know about places located near the equator. *(They usually have warm climates.)* Tell the class that the Caribbean islands are in the tropical zone (between the Tropic of Cancer and the equator), where the climate is warm all year round. Have students read the Thinking Focus and make predictions about what the land and people of the Caribbean are like. Tell them to read the lesson to find out if their predictions are correct.

Key Term

Vocabulary Strategies: T36–T37

tropical—having a hot, humid climate, characteristic of most areas between the tropics of Cancer and Capricorn

1375
1492
TODAY

L E S S O N 1

Geography of the Caribbean

THINKING FOCUS

Describe the land and the people of the Caribbean islands.

Key Term

- tropical

We started driving down into a beautiful valley. The sea sprang up all around. It was sparkling like a blue Carnival costume. The waves were smacking the rocks with big kisses and then ducking back into the sea. The trees were green and spread out wide like fans. Even the rocks looked different here. They jutted out from the land like big, brown fishermen waiting to catch fish.

Writer Lynn Joseph knows all about the beauty of the Caribbean *(kar uh BEE uhn)*. Joseph grew up on the island of Trinidad, one of the thousands of islands in the Caribbean Sea. In the passage above from her book *A Wave in Her Pocket,* she describes a special trip to Toco, a beach on the north-eastern tip of Trinidad. This passage reveals some characteristics common to Caribbean geography.

➤ *This painting reveals Caribbean artist Frané Lessac's view of an island fishing scene.*

508

Objectives

1. Describe the overall geography and climate of the Caribbean islands.
2. Name at least two distinctive geographic features of a typical Caribbean island.

Graphic Overview

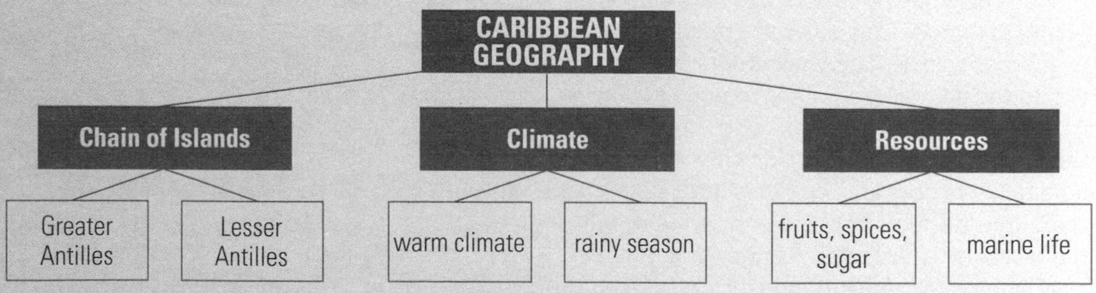

CARIBBEAN GEOGRAPHY
Chain of Islands
Climate
Resources
Greater Antilles
Lesser Antilles
warm climate
rainy season
fruits, spices, sugar
marine life

Caribbean: Natural Resources

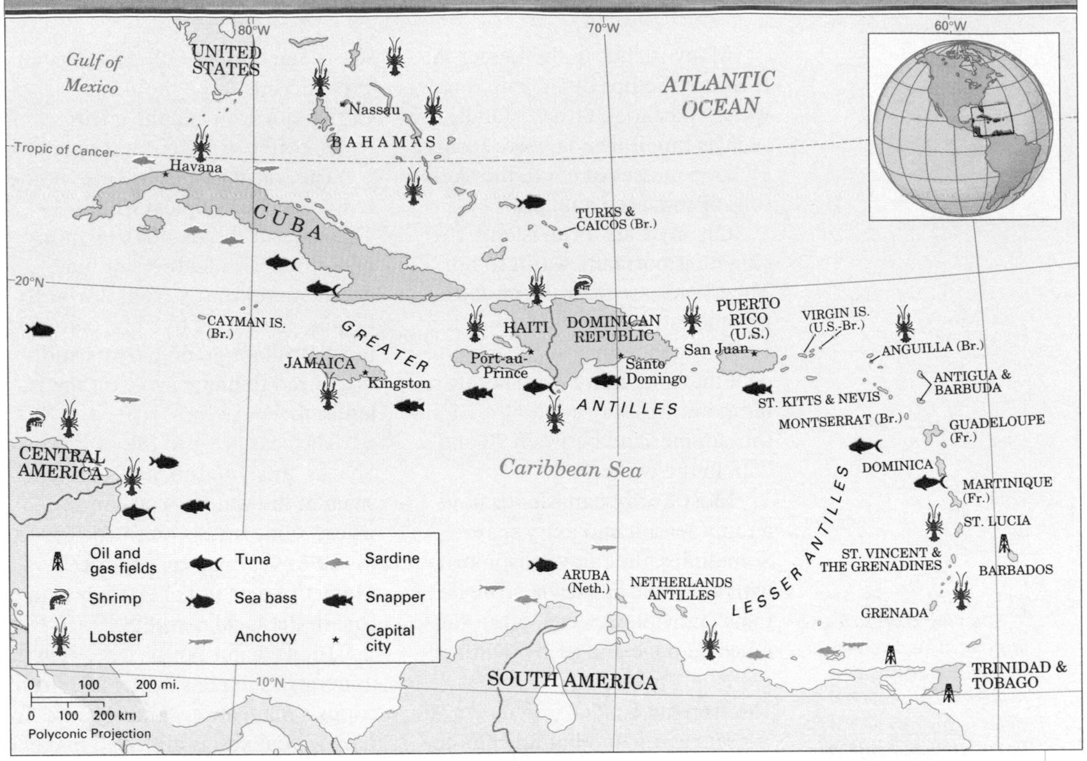

Gulf of Mexico
UNITED STATES
80°W
70°W
60°W
ATLANTIC OCEAN
Nassau
BAHAMAS
Tropic of Cancer
Havana
CUBA
TURKS & CAICOS (Br.)
20°N
CAYMAN IS. (Br.)
GREATER ANTILLES
JAMAICA
Kingston
HAITI
Port-au-Prince
DOMINICAN REPUBLIC
Santo Domingo
PUERTO RICO (U.S.)
San Juan
VIRGIN IS. (U.S.-Br.)
ANGUILLA (Br.)
ANTIGUA & BARBUDA
ST. KITTS & NEVIS
MONTSERRAT (Br.)
GUADELOUPE (Fr.)
DOMINICA
MARTINIQUE (Fr.)
ST. LUCIA
ST. VINCENT & THE GRENADINES
BARBADOS
GRENADA
LESSER ANTILLES
TRINIDAD & TOBAGO
CENTRAL AMERICA
Caribbean Sea
ARUBA (Neth.)
NETHERLANDS ANTILLES
SOUTH AMERICA
10°N
Oil and gas fields
Shrimp
Lobster
Tuna
Sea bass
Anchovy
Sardine
Snapper
Capital city
0 100 200 mi.
0 100 200 km
Polyconic Projection

A Chain of Islands

Find Trinidad on the map above. It is one of the southernmost islands in the Caribbean Sea. The Caribbean refers to a chain of islands in the Caribbean Sea that stretches from Florida to South America.

People often call the Caribbean region the West Indies. When Christopher Columbus bumped into a Caribbean island in 1492, he thought he had reached islands in Asia called the Indies. Later, people began calling the Caribbean islands the West Indies, to tell them apart from the East Indies.

Look again at the map. Find the islands of the Bahamas off the tip of Florida. South of the Bahamas are the largest islands of the Caribbean. This group, called the Greater Antilles *(an TIHL eez)*, includes Cuba, Jamaica, Puerto Rico, and Hispaniola. The island of Hispaniola is split into two countries: Haiti and the Dominican Republic.

To the south and east of Puerto Rico is a group of islands called the Lesser Antilles. At the end of the chain are Barbados, Trinidad and Tobago, the Netherlands Antilles, and Aruba, off the coast of South America.

A Tropical World

Many islands in the Greater Antilles are the tips of huge, underwater mountains in the Caribbean Sea. Large islands such as Jamaica or Cuba have rugged mountains and lush, green rain forests.

(above) Colorful fish thrive in the warm Caribbean Sea. (top) Study the map. Some kinds of marine life are considered natural resources. Name the kinds that are caught in the waters around the Greater Antilles.

DEVELOP

Create a web on the chalkboard. In the center of the web write *The Caribbean.* Tell students to use their prior knowledge as well as the headings and visuals in the lesson to fill in the web with descriptions of the Caribbean. Their descriptions should include the climate, the land, and the plants and animals they read about in the lesson. *(Students may describe hundreds of islands; clear blue waters filled with fish; sunshine; hurricanes; and so forth.)*

◄ *Sardine, snapper, tuna, anchovy, shrimp, and lobster are caught in the waters around the Greater Antilles.*

GEOGRAPHY

Critical Thinking

So that students will understand the proximity of the Caribbean islands to Florida, have them use the map on this page to calculate the distance between the southernmost tip of mainland Florida and Havana, Cuba. *(The distance is roughly 150 miles.)* Point out that the islands stretch for about 2,200 miles from Florida in North America to Venezuela in South America.

Access Strategy

Read aloud the descriptions of Caribbean geography found on this page and the next page. Tell students to imagine that they have been asked to find a site for an action-adventure movie that will be filmed in the Caribbean. First, students should examine the map and visuals in this lesson; then they can collect photographs of different Caribbean islands from magazines and travel brochures. Encourage students to try to find photographs that show as much variety as possible. After students have collected the photographs, the group can decide on the most suitable sites to propose for the movie's setting.

Access Activity

Suggest that students use clay, paper, markers, and pipe cleaners to create a model of a tropical landscape in the Caribbean. Have them use the visuals in this lesson, as well as information in outside sources, as a guide. Tell students to label the geographic features they have included in their models.

GEOGRAPHY

Critical Thinking

Direct students' attention to the photograph of the hurricane on this page. Point out that hurricanes bring very heavy rains (as much as 18 inches in one day) and violent winds with velocities of more than 75 miles an hour. Ask students to speculate about why a hurricane would be especially damaging to the economy of an island that relies on tourism. *(The economy is hurt when weather conditions keep tourists from the island; hurricanes destroy hotels, take down power lines, destroy beaches, and so forth.)*

■ *Valuable natural resources include minerals, such as the iron and bauxite used for industry in the Greater Antilles; a good climate for growing many crops; and the beautiful sea and landscape that attract tourists.*

Many islands in the Lesser Antilles are the tips of ancient, underwater volcanoes. Other islands, such as tiny Barbuda, were formed by large masses of coral, the skeletons of small sea animals.

On any Caribbean island, the climate is normally warm to hot. The islands are near the equator, the hottest, or **tropical** part of the earth. Surrounding waters help to cool the land, however. Therefore, temperatures stay at about 81°F in the summer and between 70 and 75°F in the winter.

Most Caribbean islands have a rainy season and a dry season. Sometimes, the rainy season brings with it terrible hurricanes. The heavy rains and violent winds often cause much damage and many deaths.

The Tropical Land

The warm and humid climate of most islands is ideal for certain crops. Caribbean markets are filled with stands stacked with fruits—juicy pineapples, tart limes, and sweet mangoes, to name just a few.

Some islands have special crops. Spices such as nutmeg gave Grenada the nickname Spice Island. In Antigua people grow fine sea-island cotton. Other important export crops throughout the Caribbean are bananas, citrus fruits, coffee, tobacco, and sugar.

The warm islands are also home to a variety of tropical wildlife. Throughout the islands tiny hummingbirds with feathers of blue, green, or yellow fly from flower to flower. They look like big, colorful bugs. Brilliant green parrots and bright red flamingos live on the islands, too.

The seas are also full of life. Sharks, tuna, marlin, and sailfish swim in the waters. You can see where some of this marine life is found on the map on page 509. Many types of fish are caught and sold in the local markets.

The Greater Antilles are rich in minerals. Cuba has deposits of iron, copper, manganese, and chrome. In Jamaica bauxite is mined to make aluminum. Trinidad, in the Lesser Antilles, has oil and oil refineries.

On many Caribbean islands, however, the greatest natural resources are the climate, sea, and landscape. Like birds flying south each winter, more than eight million tourists flock to the Caribbean to enjoy the beauty around them. ■

Shipping ports such as this one in the Dominican Republic hold goods ready for export. Hurricanes frequently lash West Indian islands, badly damaging their economies.

■ *What are some of the most valuable natural resources in the Caribbean?*

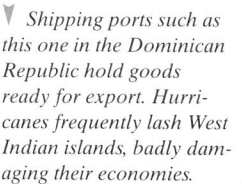

Critical Thinking

Point out that the islands of Trinidad and Tobago were once part of the continent of South America. Point out Venezuela on the Atlas map on pages 678–679. Ask students to predict what geographic features Trinidad and Tobago might share with Venezuela. *(Trinidad and Tobago have the same soil, rocks, and plant and animal life as Venezuela.)*

Geographic Context

Where do some of the names and terms used to describe the geography of the Caribbean come from? The name *Caribbean* comes from one of the Native American peoples who first inhabited the islands—the Caribs.

The Lesser Antilles are divided into a northern cluster, called the Leeward Islands, and a southern cluster, called the Windward Islands. *Windward* is a sailing term that means "the direction or side from which the wind blows." *Leeward* means "the direction or side toward which the wind blows." While sailboats have a hard sail going against the prevailing tradewinds to get to the Windward group, they have an easy sail when they are going with the wind, toward the Leeward group.

A Multicultural Past

Callaloo is the name of a special soup served in the Caribbean. It is made from a tasty mixture of soft-shell crab, coconut, curry, taro leaf, and hot peppers. As one writer remarked, "The more diverse the ingredients, the sweeter the soup."

Like callaloo, the people of the Caribbean are a diverse group. Among their ancestors are Native Americans, Africans, Europeans, and Asians. Although their family backgrounds are different, the people share a common history.

▲ *This Carnival band called China the Forbidden City shows how Trinidadians celebrate their Asian origins.*

A Shared Colonial Past

The story of the Caribbean is one of colonialism. European nations fought for land and control in the Caribbean. Today many islands are independent nations. Yet a few are still associated with France, Great Britain, the Netherlands, or the United States.

On all the islands, you can see the remains of this colonial past. People speak a wide variety of languages in the Caribbean—from English in Jamaica and French in Martinique to Spanish in the Dominican Republic. Governments vary too. Jamaica, for example, has a British-style, elected government. Guadeloupe and Martinique are overseas departments of France. Their people are French citizens.

A Special Caribbean Culture

The people of the West Indies have combined their backgrounds into a shared Caribbean culture. You can see the influence of different traditions in many ways.

In Haiti the people speak French Creole, a language influenced by African languages and French. In Trinidad thousands of people gather for a huge Carnival celebration each year. Carnival was introduced by European settlers. Trinidadians, however, have made Carnival a celebration of their own culture. Through this blend of traditions, people of the Caribbean seem to embody the national slogan of Jamaica, "Out of Many, One People." ■

■ *In what ways can you find evidence of a colonial past in the Caribbean?*

■ *Different languages and different types of government reveal the islands' colonial past.*

REVIEW

1. **FOCUS** Describe the land and the people of the Caribbean islands.
2. **HISTORY** Why are the Caribbean islands also called the West Indies?
3. **GEOGRAPHY** Why are the Caribbean islands warm to hot all year round?
4. **CRITICAL THINKING** Why is it important for people of the Caribbean to preserve the beauty of the natural landscape?
5. **ACTIVITY** Use the map on page 509 to make a chart of the Caribbean islands and their major natural resources. You may want to illustrate your chart with drawings or photographs.

CLOSE

Have students answer the Thinking Focus by examining the webs students created as they read the lesson. Ask students to compare their present understanding of the land and people of the Caribbean with the predictions they made at the beginning of the lesson.

Answers to Review Questions

1. The land is warm and tropical; the people have ancestors from many different cultural backgrounds, such as Native Americans, Africans, Europeans, and Asians.
2. When Columbus sailed into the Caribbean in 1492, he thought he had reached islands in Asia called the Indies. Later, people called the islands the West Indies, to tell them apart from the East Indies.
3. The islands are near the equator, where the sun shines from directly overhead. The climate of the islands is relatively mild, however, because of the cooling effect of the surrounding waters.
4. On many islands, the landscape is the most valuable natural resource. If that beauty is destroyed, the islands will lose the money that tourism brings in.
5. Check to see that students' charts correspond to the information found on the map on page 509. You may want to display the charts on a class bulletin board.

Homework Options

Have students write promotional copy for a travel brochure that encourages people in northern climates to visit the Caribbean in the wintertime. Tell students to use information from the lesson and from library resources to describe the Caribbean landscape and its people.

Study Guide: page 88

INTRODUCE

Point out that when Columbus explored the Caribbean islands he met Native Americans who had been living there for many generations. Write the words *New World* and *Old World* on the chalkboard. Ask students to think about ways in which this world was new to the Spanish explorers of the 1400s and 1500s. *(Europeans had never before seen this world. From their point of view it was new.)* Then ask students in what ways this world was "old" for Native Americans. *(Native Americans had been living there long before the Europeans arrived.)* Have students read the Thinking Focus. Tell them to read the lesson to learn about what happened to the peoples of the Caribbean after the arrival of the Europeans.

Key Terms

Vocabulary Strategies: T36–T37

indentured servant—a person who signed a contract to work without pay for three to seven years

triangle trade—a system by which Europeans exchanged European goods for enslaved Africans, who were in turn exchanged for island products that Europeans wanted

emancipation—the act of freeing people from slavery

1375
1492
1900
2000

L E S S O N 2

The Caribbean: Cradle of the Americas

THINKING FOCUS

What was the impact of European arrival on Caribbean history?

Key Terms

- indentured servant
- triangle trade
- emancipation

I swam closer to get a better look and had to stop myself from laughing. The strangers had wrapped every part of their bodies with colorful leaves and cotton. Some had decorated their faces with fur and wore shiny rocks on their heads. Compared to us, they were very round. Their canoe was short and square, and, in spite of all their dipping and pulling, it moved so slowly. What a backward, distant island they must have come from. But really, to laugh at guests, no matter how odd, would be impolite, especially since I was the first to meet them. If I was foolish, they would think they had arrived at a foolish place.

You have just read a passage from *Morning Girl*, a book of fiction by Michael Dorris. The book tells about the arrival of Christopher Columbus in the Caribbean. As the passage above shows, Dorris's story is unusual. It is told from the point of view of a young Native American girl.

The visitors whom Morning Girl saw were Columbus and other explorers from Spain. When these Europeans stepped onto the islands, they changed the lives of the people who lived there—the Arawaks, Caribs, and Ciboneys. The Spaniards brought back accounts of the islands and the Caribbean peoples. Soon other Europeans also sailed to this so-called New World.

➤ *Doña Carmen is a Cuban descendant of the Arawaks, one of many groups who once lived in the beautiful Dominican Republic, shown below.*

Objectives

1. Describe the colonial past of the Caribbean.
2. Show how colonialism led to a mixing of people.
3. Show how Caribbean people gained emancipation and resisted colonial rule.

Graphic Overview

Thriving Native American Cultures Europeans not yet arrived. ➤ **European Arrival** European settlers attack Native Americans. ➤ **Development of Plantations** A need for cheap plantation labor encourages slavery. ➤ **Emancipation of Enslaved Africans** Asian indentured servants are introduced. ➤ **Independence for Many Islands** Most Caribbean islands become nations.

The Arrival of the Europeans

Wading ashore on an island in the Bahamas, Columbus thought he had found a new route to the gold and spices of Asia. After a few days on the island, Columbus and his men explored Cuba and Hispaniola.

Returning to Spain, Columbus got a royal welcome. He also received orders to colonize Hispaniola. On this second voyage, he took 17 ships and more than 1,000 men. They founded Santo Domingo, the first permanent European colony in America.

Columbus made two more voyages to the Caribbean. His travels touched off enormous changes on three continents. Europeans would soon be scrambling for land and riches in the Americas. Africans would soon be captured and forced to work on plantations there. Also, Native Americans were already dying as a result of contact with Columbus's men.

Many of these Native Americans were killed in battle. Others died of measles, smallpox, and other diseases brought from Europe by the explorers. Many others died of overwork in the mines or on plantations that the Spaniards set up. Millions of Native Americans died within 50 years of Columbus's arrival.

Competing for Gold

Spanish explorers did not intend to remain only on the islands. They used them as stepping stones to the treasures of Aztec and Inca societies in Mexico and Peru.

At first the English and the French were too busy with problems at home to try to get riches from the Americas. However, individual Frenchmen like François *(frahn SWAH)* le Clerq *(luh KLAIRK)* and English sailors like Francis Drake became pirates in the Caribbean. Their ships attacked Spanish trading vessels carrying gold from Mexico and Peru.

Some pirates worked for themselves. Others, like Francis Drake, worked for their monarchs. Drake stole so much gold from Spain that he was knighted by Queen Elizabeth I in 1581 despite Spanish protests.

European Settlement

Like the Spaniards before them, English and French colonists began building settlements on some Caribbean islands in the 1620s. The Dutch did the same in the 1630s.

The settlers grew tobacco, indigo, and spices. At first they depended on indentured servants from Europe to do the work. **Indentured servants** were people who signed contracts to work without pay for three to seven years. Their life on the Caribbean plantations was one of hard, physical labor and abusive conditions. The few who survived the hard work and terrible treatment usually became farmers. ■

▼ *This engraving depicts the* Santa María, *Columbus's flagship on his first voyage to the Americas. The ship lasted the voyage but ran aground off Haiti on December 25, 1492, and was lost.*

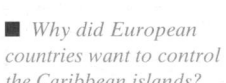

■ *Why did European countries want to control the Caribbean islands?*

DEVELOP

Draw students' attention to the title of the lesson. Ask students what words and images come to mind when they hear the word *cradle. (Babies; birth)*

Explain that the arrival of Europeans in the Caribbean can be considered the "birth" of European exploration and settlement in the Americas.

CULTURE

Study Skills

Tell students that scholars are unsure about the exact number of Native Americans who died on Hispaniola from 1492 to 1542. Scholars' estimates range from 100,000 to millions of people. To help students get a sense of what one million means, direct them to page 664 of the Minipedia. Tell students to find a U.S. city with a population close to one million people. *(Detroit—1,203,399)*

■ *European countries used the Caribbean islands as a gateway to riches in Mexico and Peru. They also began to establish plantations on the islands to grow certain crops.*

Access Strategy

Tell students to imagine that a spaceship full of aliens lands in their backyard. The aliens decide that they have "discovered" the neighborhood.

Explain that the aliens have far more sophisticated weapons and technology than the people on Earth. When the aliens decide to take over the land, the Earth people cannot fight back to reclaim their land. In addition, many Earth people begin to die from strange diseases brought from outer space.

Ask students how they would feel in this situation. *(Terrorized, frightened, angry)* Ask them to compare the plight of the Earth people with the plight of the Native American people in the Caribbean.

Access Activity

Have students improvise a scene in which aliens from space and people from Earth first meet. Then have them perform a scene in which the Earth people find out that the aliens think they have "discovered" their land and decide to take control of it.

ECONOMICS

Critical Thinking

Use the map on this page or a larger map in the Atlas on pages 678–679 to review the course of the triangle trade in the Caribbean colonies. Ask students why slaves were used on sugar cane plantations. *(Planters wanted cheap labor in order to increase their profits.)* Ask students to speculate about why slaves were not imported in large numbers to Europe. *(Europe did not have a labor shortage. European farming did not need large numbers of workers. Families could manage the work of a small farm.)*

■ *The triangle trade was a system through which European goods were exchanged for enslaved Africans. Those slaves were then exchanged for island products that Europeans wanted. One of the major consequences of this system was the brutal treatment and often death of tens of millions of Africans and their descendants.*

European Presence in the Caribbean

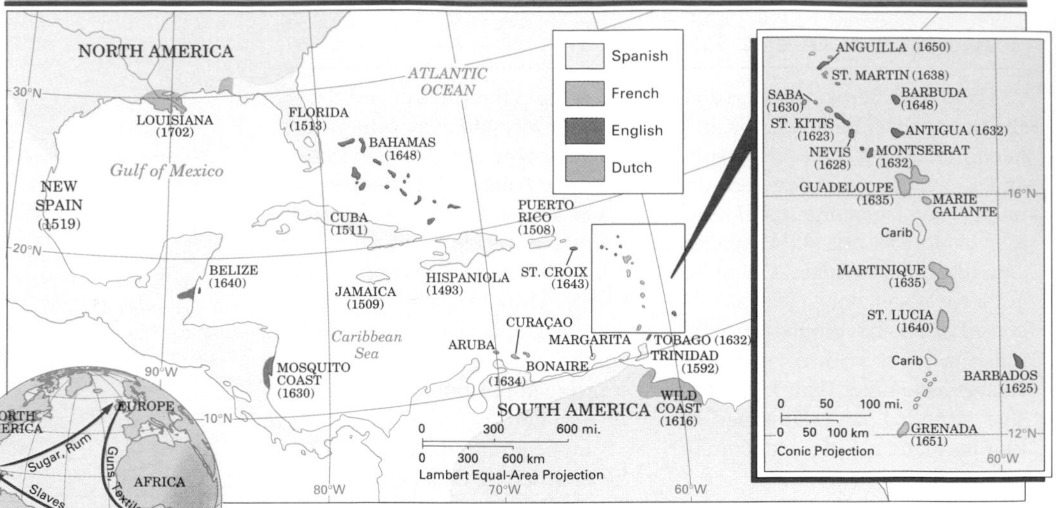

NORTH AMERICA
ATLANTIC OCEAN
Spanish
French
English
Dutch
30°N
LOUISIANA (1702)
FLORIDA (1513)
BAHAMAS (1648)
Gulf of Mexico
NEW SPAIN (1519)
CUBA (1511)
PUERTO RICO (1508)
20°N
BELIZE (1640)
JAMAICA (1509)
HISPANIOLA (1493)
ST. CROIX (1643)
Caribbean Sea
CURAÇAO
ARUBA
MARGARITA
TOBAGO (1632)
TRINIDAD (1592)
BONAIRE
(1634)
MOSQUITO COAST (1630)
90°W
10°N
WILD COAST (1616)
SOUTH AMERICA
0 300 600 mi.
0 300 600 km
Lambert Equal-Area Projection
80°W
70°W
60°W
ANGUILLA (1650)
ST. MARTIN (1638)
SABA (1630)
BARBUDA (1648)
ST. KITTS (1623)
ANTIGUA (1632)
NEVIS (1628)
MONTSERRAT (1632)
GUADELOUPE (1635)
MARIE GALANTE
16°N
Carib
MARTINIQUE (1635)
ST. LUCIA (1640)
Carib
BARBADOS (1625)
0 50 100 mi.
0 50 100 km
GRENADA (1651)
12°N
Conic Projection
60°W

NORTH AMERICA
EUROPE
Sugar, Rum
Guns, Textiles
AFRICA
Slaves
SOUTH AMERICA
ATLANTIC OCEAN

European countries claimed the Caribbean islands as their territories. The circular map shows the triangle trade.

The business of growing, harvesting, and processing sugar cane shaped the history of the islands.

The Development of Plantations

Sugar was becoming popular in Europe. The English and the French quickly took advantage of this popularity. By the 1650s, Caribbean sugar plantations and mills brought their owners large profits. This profit was mainly due to the low cost of labor. To lower their costs even further, the planters replaced the indentured servants with persons in bondage for life, or slaves. African people were brought in for this purpose.

The Slave Trade

This was not the first appearance of slavery in the Caribbean. Spanish explorers had brought in Africans as slaves when the local Native American population died.

It was the Dutch, however, who developed the **triangle trade** system. Through this system, they exchanged European goods for enslaved Africans. African men, women, and even children were taken to prisons on the coast of Africa where they spent months waiting for the ships. As the map on this page shows, the enslaved people were then exchanged for the sugar, salt, and other island products that Europeans wanted.

The Middle Passage

The number of Africans who died on the Middle Passage, the second leg of the triangle, is unknown. Thousands suffocated, packed in the holds of ships. Many died of disease.

Those who survived faced more abuses on the plantations. The planters split up families. They prevented the enslaved Africans from being educated. African men, women, and children were forced to work in the fields for 12 or more hours a day. They often had to work under the hot sun with little to eat or drink. ■

■ *What was the triangle trade system developed by the Dutch, and what were its consequences?*

Study Skills

To keep Africans alive during the Middle Passage, slave traders fed them traditional African foods. As a result, foods such as the yam were introduced to the Western Hemisphere. Have students use library resources to research other foods that came to the Western Hemisphere from Africa. *(Other foods from Africa include okra, millet, cow pea, and watermelon.)*

Historical Context

The British-controlled island of Montserrat (in the Leeward Islands) provides a good example of how labor in the Caribbean colonies shifted from indentured servants to enslaved Africans. In the early years of settlement on the island, plantation owners brought Irish and a few Scottish indentured servants to do the work on the expanding plantations. These were political refugees, prisoners from English jails, or impoverished people in search of a better life. Relations were not good between the Irish workers and their British masters. The Irish openly scorned the plantation owners and often tried to leave Montserrat for other islands or for North America. Africans were cheaper than European workers, and they were more easily identified. As a result, British planters began to replace these indentured workers with enslaved Africans. By the 1730s Africans outnumbered Europeans on the island by five to one, and by the late 1700s by nearly ten to one.

Resistance and Revolution

In spite of the planters' efforts, the enslaved Africans began to organize. Many rose up against the plantation owners and escaped.

In August 1791 the largest and most successful slave rebellion in human history took place. It happened in the French colony of Saint Domingue, now known as Haiti. Boukman, a slave from a northern plantation, had held secret meetings all summer. At these meetings, the slave leaders sang political songs with words such as "We swear to destroy the whites and all that they possess; let us die rather than fail to keep this vow."

After attracting more than 10,000 slaves to his cause, Boukman planned a revolt for the night of August 22. Carrying pruning hooks, sugar cane knives, and torches, the slaves surrounded the homes of planters, killed most of them, and set fire to the plantations. As one survivor wrote:

The most striking feature of this terrible spectacle was a rain of fire composed of burning cane-straw which whirled thick before the blast like snow and which the wind whipped, now toward the harbor and ships, now over the houses of the town.

The rebellion spread like wildfire throughout the colony. The revolution was taking hold. A new leader emerged named Toussaint L'Ouverture *(too SAN loo vehr TUR).* With Toussaint's leadership and military knowledge, the former slaves took over the countryside within a few weeks. This rebellion marked the beginning of the end of slavery throughout the Caribbean. ■

This portrait of Toussaint L'Ouverture was painted by Gerard, a Haitian artist.

■ *How did blacks forge a path to freedom and leadership in the Caribbean?*

The End of Colonialism

Emancipation, the act of freeing people from slavery, came at different times to each of the Caribbean islands. Slavery ended in 1794 in Saint Domingue, in 1833 in the British colonies, and as late as 1886 in Cuba.

The Cost of Slavery

Emancipation was the result of many forces. First was the great resistance of the enslaved Africans. As slave rebellions became more frequent, European investors lost property, and sugar production fell.

The costs of maintaining slavery grew even more when European governments sent armed forces to the islands to stop the revolts. In addition, many Europeans were beginning to think that slavery was wrong. These different pressures ended slavery in the Caribbean.

Many former slaves left the plantations and became farmers and fishers. Others went to the Latin American mainland. The Africans who stayed on the plantations demanded more money and better working conditions.

How Do We Know?

HISTORY *Toussaint L'Ouverture was born François Dominique Toussaint à Bréda. Because the French word* ouverture *means "opening," scholars think the name may have come from his military victories: a man who "makes an opening everywhere."*

HISTORY

Visual Learning

Ask students to look carefully at the painting of Toussaint L'Ouverture on this page. Point out that the painting was done by Gerard, a Haitian artist. Ask students how they think the artist viewed Toussaint L'Ouverture. What evidence can they find in the painting to support their opinion? *(The artist admired Toussaint L'Ouverture. This is shown in the painting by the figure's formal uniform and dignified posture.)*

CITIZENSHIP

Critical Thinking

Have students read the section The End of Colonialism. Encourage them to consider the actions of plantation owners who hired people from India and other parts of Asia to work on the plantations. Ask students how colonialism led to a mixing of people. *(Students should infer that Native Americans, Africans, Asians, and Europeans all contributed to the culture of the islands.)*

■ *The enslaved blacks on the Caribbean nation of Haiti fought their way to freedom by gathering together and organizing mass rebellions against the planters.*

Collaborative Learning

Many students may know about Haiti because of the large number of desperate Haitians who have tried to immigrate to the United States in recent years. Have students divide into groups to create a television news program about the plight of the Haitian people. Groups can use news magazines, newspapers, and library books to help them find out more about this immigration issue. The groups should address questions such as these: Why are the people in Haiti so desperate to leave their country to come to the United States? Historically, what has been the relationship between the United States and Haiti? How have current U.S. leaders reacted to the efforts of the Haitian people to come to the United States? In the groups each member should take a different role, such as researcher, writer and editor, director, anchorperson, and so forth.

Map and Globe Skills

Point out for most of the islands in the Caribbean, independence did not immediately follow the emancipation of the slaves. Have students use an almanac to find out when various islands in the Caribbean were officially declared independent from the ruling country. Students should create a map and label it with dates of independence.

CLOSE

Have students answer the Thinking Focus by creating a flow chart of the history of the Caribbean after the arrival of the Europeans. *(Students' charts should show how Europeans enslaved Native Americans and Africans, turned the land into plantations, and set up governments on many Caribbean islands.)*

➤ *Most of them came from Asia.*

■ *Many forces combined to put an end to slavery in the Caribbean: First, the resistance of the enslaved blacks; second, the great expense to European countries of sending armed forces to the islands to stop the revolts; third, the fact that many Europeans at this time were beginning to think that slavery was wrong. The recruitment of thousands of people from Asia as indentured servants, as well as the end of colonialism on many islands, were two events that followed emancipation.*

Indentured Servants to the Caribbean

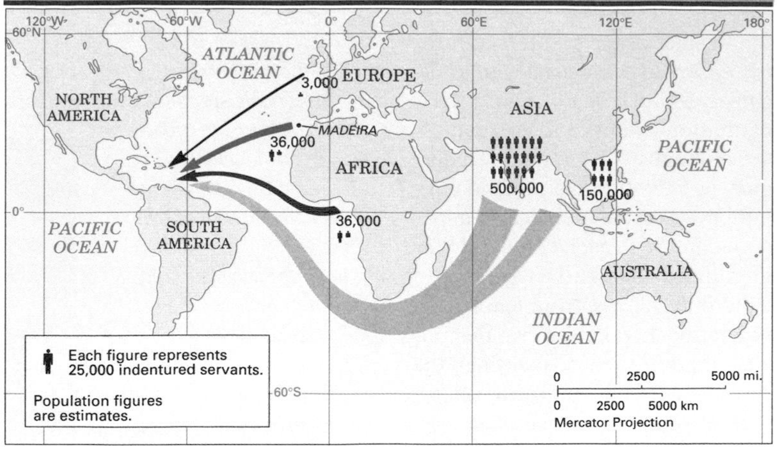
120°W
60°W
0°
60°E
120°E
180°
60°N
0°
60°S
ATLANTIC OCEAN
NORTH AMERICA
EUROPE
3,000
MADEIRA
36,000
AFRICA
ASIA
500,000
150,000
PACIFIC OCEAN
PACIFIC OCEAN
SOUTH AMERICA
36,000
AUSTRALIA
INDIAN OCEAN
Each figure represents 25,000 indentured servants.
Population figures are estimates.
0 2500 5000 mi.
0 2500 5000 km
Mercator Projection

➤ *After the end of slavery, hundreds of thousands of people were brought to the Caribbean as indentured servants. Where did most of these people come from?*

The plantation owners, however, still wanted a cheap work force. As a result, they brought in hundreds of thousands of people from India and other places in Asia as indentured servants.

Struggle for Independence

After emancipation, people living on some islands demanded self-government. As a result, colonialism in parts of the West Indies began to come apart.

The French colony of Saint Domingue, under the leadership of Toussaint L'Ouverture until his death in 1803, was the first to gain independence. Following years of warfare, the colony declared its independence in 1804. It was renamed Haiti, its original Arawak name. Other colonies would not gain independence until much later.

Although most Caribbean islands are independent nations today, some remain politically tied to other countries. For example, the Cayman Islands is a British dependency, and Puerto Rico is a U.S. commonwealth.

As you can see, much of Caribbean history has been brutal, marked by terrible conflict. Throughout this history, however, Caribbean peoples have built a culture that is complex, creative, and proud. This culture has shown its ability to stand up against abusive situations. It has flourished in the face of great hardships. ■

■ *Why did slavery end in the Caribbean, and what events followed emancipation?*

REVIEW

1. **FOCUS** What was the impact of European arrival on Caribbean history?
2. **ECONOMICS** In what ways did the plantation system support colonialism, the triangle trade system, and slavery?
3. **HISTORY** What conditions made it difficult for the Africans to organize and rebel when they were first brought to the Caribbean?
4. **CRITICAL THINKING** What are some advantages and disadvantages of a small Caribbean island nation remaining tied to a large political power?
5. **WRITING ACTIVITY** Suppose you are someone living in the early 1800s who is against slavery. Write a speech or an editorial in which you describe the Middle Passage or life on a plantation. Persuade your audience to take action against slavery.

Homework Options

Have students write five headlines for news stories that could have been written about the Caribbean during the period covered in this lesson. *(Possible headlines: Christopher Columbus Explores the Americas; Native Americans Forced to Work for Europeans)*

Study Guide: page 89

Answers to Review Questions

1. The arrival of the Europeans in the Caribbean caused the deaths of most of the peoples living there. European nations influenced economic, social, and political life in the Caribbean.
2. The plantation system reinforced colonialism because plantations were profitable for colonial powers; it reinforced the triangle trade because cheap labor increased profits, and it provided West Indian products for trade; and it reinforced slavery because of the need for cheap labor.
3. The planters fed and housed the Africans poorly, overworked them, and split up their families.
4. Two advantages are military protection and economic support; a disadvantage is the possibility that the larger power will use the smaller nation solely for its own gain.
5. Students should use material from the lesson to write an argument against slavery.

UNDERSTANDING OTHERS

Using Constructive Criticism

Here's Why

We have all had our feelings hurt because of something critical someone said to us. Perhaps the criticism was well-intended, but it hurt because of the way it was said.

In school you and your classmates are often asked to present your work to the rest of the class. How can you comment on other people's work without hurting their feelings? Learning to give constructive criticism will help you.

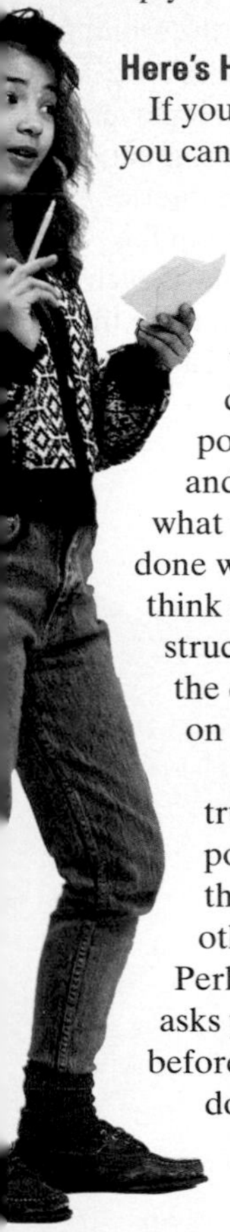

Here's How

If you try hard enough, you can usually find something good to say about anyone's presentation. Suppose you are listening while another student presents a report. Listen carefully, and try to comment on what the student has done well. If you can't think of anything constructive to say, consider the questions in the box on this page.

Sometimes, to be truthful, you need to point out something that is wrong with another person's work. Perhaps a good friend asks you to read a report before turning it in. How do you handle this?

Always remember to criticize the work, not the person. Also, give your good comments first. If you start with something positive, then your criticism won't be so difficult to hear. Your friend will probably thank you for your help.

Try It

Take your turn at presenting to the class the speech you wrote against slavery. (See Lesson 2 Review, Question 5.) Review the presentations of your classmates. Listen carefully to each student, and pay attention to how each speech is presented. Use the suggestions in the box, or use your own words to say something positive about each speech.

Apply It

Keep a diary during a 24-hour period at home and at school. Make a note every time you say something constructive about a person. What reactions did you get? Were your family and friends pleased? Did your constructive criticism help others?

Evaluating a Presentation

1. Were the facts accurate?
2. Did the presenter speak clearly, without hesitation?
3. Did the presenter look directly at the audience while speaking?
4. Were the ideas creative and original?
5. Did the presentation really work for you?

UNDERSTANDING OTHERS

This skills feature teaches students how to use constructive criticism in a classroom setting.

ETHICS

Critical Thinking

Ask students to name some basic differences between criticism and constructive criticism. *(Criticism usually involves simply pointing out what is wrong. Constructive criticism involves pointing out flaws and making suggestions about how to make things better.)* Ask students to relate situations in which they have been criticized. Then ask students to relate situations in which they have had to give criticism. Challenge them to decide which is more difficult—giving or receiving criticism.

Understanding Criticism

Have students gather clippings of critical reviews in newspapers and magazines. Students may choose reviews of movies, restaurants, artwork, music, and so forth. Tell students to read the review and to write a short paragraph that addresses this question: Does the review offer constructive criticism? They should then explain their answer. Students can share their reviews and their opinions of them with the class.

Answers to Try It

Possible answer: Your speech expressed great feeling, but I think you need to support your arguments with more facts.

Answers to Apply It

Possible answer: Family members respond favorably when they hear something constructive instead of constant negative comments.

Objective

Develop strategies for giving and receiving constructive criticism. (Social Participation 2)

INTRODUCE

Have a student read the opening paragraphs on this page to the class. Then read the Thinking Focus. Tell students that life in the Caribbean today reflects parts of its colonial past—for instance, the cricket game described in the text. Based on their knowledge of other countries with a colonial past (for example, India, many countries in Africa, the United States), ask students to predict what challenges the people of the Caribbean islands faced as they forged new nations after colonialism. *(Establishing new governments; arranging for self-defense; uniting politically; diversifying economies)*

Key Terms

Vocabulary Strategies: T36–T37
monocrop—the only major crop in a region
labor-intensive—requiring large numbers of workers

1375 | 1500 | 1625 | 1750 | 1875 | **1900** | **TODAY**

LESSON 3

The Caribbean Today

THINKING FOCUS

What is life like in the Caribbean today?

Key Terms

- monocrop
- labor-intensive

Dressed all in white, the player slams the hard, maroon ball with a paddle-shaped bat. Crack! The ball sails over the far wall, and the crowd roars. It's a 6—cricket's version of a home run.

Under the hot sun, people crowd together in the Jamaican stadium to watch the best cricket players in the West Indies take on Great Britain's team. Since the 1960s the West Indians, with their expert, hard-hitting play, have ruled the sport.

A British game, cricket is a favorite sport on the islands once ruled by Great Britain. The West Indians take great pride in their teams. "Whatever we are, we are cricketers," wrote one West Indian.

What cricket is to the former British islands, baseball is to the Spanish-speaking Caribbean. There are thousands of baseball fans in Cuba, Puerto Rico, and the Dominican Republic. These places have produced some of the best players in the world, including the great Roberto Clemente from Puerto Rico, and Manuel Lee from the Dominican Republic. Sports such as baseball and cricket help unite the different peoples of the Caribbean.

DUNCAN FEARNLEY
SUPREME
The MAGNUM

Cricketers play in Queen's Park, known as the Savannah, in Trinidad. All ages and social groups enjoy cricket.

Objectives

1. Describe at least two cultural characteristics shared by the Caribbean islands.
2. Name at least one challenge facing Caribbean nations today.

Graphic Overview

Economies based on monocrops, labor-intensive industries, tourism, low wages → **Emigrants** establish Caribbean communities in North America and Europe → **Immigrants** maintain close ties to home and support the economies of the Caribbean islands

Life in the Caribbean

On many Caribbean islands, most people live in small rural villages. Villages might include small homes, a police station, a church, a post office, and a school.

Life in the Countryside

In the villages, school children play cricket, baseball, or soccer. Their families live in small houses. Many of the houses are built of brightly painted wood with tin roofs.

When colonial rule ended, many West Indians left the huge plantations to farm small plots of land. The people grow vegetables and raise chickens, cows, and goats. Today, fewer than half the people in the Caribbean still make their living this way. Many people fish in small boats. What their families don't eat, the fishers sell in the local markets.

To earn extra money, some family members may look for seasonal or part-time work on the large, mostly foreign-owned sugar and coffee plantations. Others find jobs related to tourism as waiters, drivers, hotel staff, and guides.

Life in the Cities

Throughout the islands, you'll also find cities bustling with activity. San Juan, the capital of Puerto Rico, is a lively mix of modern life and Spanish heritage.

When Spain first ruled the island, the city's name was *Puerto Rico,* or "rich port." Here ships loaded with treasure set sail for the trip back to Spain. Although the name has changed to San Juan, the city is still a rich port, one of the busiest in the Caribbean.

In "Old San Juan," you'll find Spanish-style houses and shops with tiled roofs and floors. El Morro, a fortress built in 1539 to guard the port from pirates, still stands. Another old Spanish fort serves as the governor's palace.

Outside Old San Juan lies the modern-looking part of the city, complete with tall apartment buildings and offices, factories, large stores, and a luxurious shopping mall. Traffic fills the streets. San Juan and its suburbs are home to about one-third of Puerto Rico's population.

In Caribbean cities the rich and the very poor live near each other. Many cities are overcrowded. Rural people who move to the cities often cannot find work. Thousands live just outside the city in crude shacks in shantytowns, without any running water or electricity.

No matter where you are, in the country or in the city, in the poorest or the richest areas, you'll hear the distinctive sounds of Caribbean music. Through their music West Indians are able to express many political and social views.

(top) These women are sewing lace in front of their home in Saba, one of the islands of the Netherlands Antilles. (bottom) These children are eating conch salad, a favorite dish on many of the islands.

DEVELOP

Point out that this lesson will discuss the Caribbean today. Draw the Graphic Overview on the chalkboard or overhead projector. Ask students to think about what aspects of life pose the greatest challenges for the Caribbean people today as they read the lesson.

CULTURE

Visual Learning

Have students study the photos and read the captions that show some aspects of life in the Caribbean. Ask the students to identify cultural elements that reflect European culture. *(The architecture of the house; the women sewing lace)*

Access Strategy

Help students to understand the economic difficulties that the Caribbean nations have experienced as a result of the colonial sugar economy. Tell students to imagine that they have taken over a business. For years and years that business has produced only one product—pencils. Now, however, people don't want to buy nearly as many pencils. As the owners of the new business, students should try to imagine that they want to modernize, for example, by producing computers and other types of supplies, such as disks and printers. Ask students what kinds of challenges they might face as they try to change the business. Tell students to think about issues such as educating workers to build computers, getting the money needed to build the computers, and so forth. This discussion should lead to a discussion about the economic challenges that people in the Caribbean face.

Access Activity

Write the word *monocrop* on the chalkboard. Help students to find the prefix *mono-* in a dictionary. Write the definition on the chalkboard. *(One, alone, single)* Ask students if they can guess the meaning of the word *monocrop.* *(One crop)*

POLITICAL SYSTEMS

Critical Thinking

Draw students' attention to the chart on this page. Ask students to speculate about which governments have the most strained relations with the United States. *(The governments are those of Cuba and Haiti: The United States has traditionally had strained relationships with Communist countries and does not support the military dictatorship in Haiti.)*

This chart shows the diversity of some of the largest islands of the Caribbean.

The Largest Caribbean Islands

	Country	Area/Population	Language	Government
	Cuba	42,804 square miles 110,862 square kilometers 10,700,000 people	Spanish	One-party Communist republic
	Dominican Republic*	18,704 square miles 48,443 square kilometers 7,320,000 people	Spanish	Republic
	Haiti*	10,714 square miles 27,749 square kilometers 6,617,000 people	French, Creole	Temporary military-dominated government
	Jamaica	4,244 square miles 10,992 square kilometers 2,500,000 people	English	Parliamentary republic
	Puerto Rico	3,515 square miles 9,104 square kilometers 3,500,000 people	Spanish, English	Self-governing commonwealth of U.S.A.

*shares island of Hispaniola

Source: Britannica Book of the Year, 1992

Flowers decorate many of the Caribbean islands.

Two Islands in Contrast

Puerto Rico and Cuba have some things in common. Both Caribbean islands were once Spanish colonies, and both were occupied by the United States. These two neighbors, however, have developed differently.

After a war with Spain in 1898, the United States gained Puerto Rico. Today it is a self-governing commonwealth in free association with the United States. Puerto Ricans are U.S. citizens, but island residents can't vote for President.

After Cuba gained independence from Spain in 1899, the island went through periods of U.S. occupation, rule by presidents, and rule by dictators. In 1959 Fidel Castro and a small band of rebels took over the government. Soon Castro turned Cuba into a Communist state. It remains so today.

The two islands today differ economically as well. Once sugar cane was the heart of Puerto Rico's economy. Now it is industry. Since the 1950s, thousands of factories have opened all over Puerto Rico. Puerto Ricans manufacture textiles, clothing, medicines, metal products, processed foods, and chemicals.

Cuba, on the other hand, still depends largely on agriculture and especially on growing and refining sugar cane. In the past the Cuban economy was heavily supported by the Soviet Union. Since the Soviet breakup, the Cuban economy has suffered greatly.

For both islands, the future is uncertain. Puerto Ricans heatedly debate whether their island should remain a commonwealth, become the 51st state, or seek independence from the United States. (See the Making Decisions feature in Chapter 27.) Cubans wonder whether their nation will withstand its economic problems. They also wonder whether their country will continue

Critical Thinking

Ask students to think about the strength of cultural ties between people. Discuss how cultural ties resulting from music, sports, and celebrations can sometimes be stronger than political ties. *(Students should recognize that cultural ties are very strong because they affect an individual's daily life. Because they are personal, cultural ties are stronger than political ones.)*

Cooperative Learning

Divide the class into groups. Tell the students that each group will contribute to a class project called The Caribbean Today. Group members should collect articles from news magazines and newspapers, and they should summarize television news reports about events in the Caribbean. Strong visual learners in the group may be responsible for adding photographs and other illustrations.

Once the groups have gathered their information, they should come together as a class to decide how to present their materials. They may decide to create a Caribbean Today magazine or bulletin-board display; or they might stage a Caribbean Today news broadcast. Whatever the project, each group should be responsible for completing a certain task. For example, one group could choose the stories, another could decide how to present the information, and so forth.

to be Communist after Fidel Castro passes from the scene.

Caribbean Connections

The West Indies have never been politically unified. However, between 1957 and 1962, most British colonies briefly joined together in the West Indies Federation. The federation collapsed when the islands of Jamaica and Trinidad decided to withdraw from the group. The leaders of these larger, more industrialized islands did not want to support the smaller, poorer islands in the region.

Look at the chart on page 520 and you can see just how varied the islands are. Still, a common West Indian spirit is found on some of the islands. This spirit is expressed in different forms—including music and the popular Carnival celebrations that are held throughout the islands. A Closer Look (below) examines one kind of music.

Moving Around the Islands

West Indians form ties when they migrate or move from island to island in search of jobs. People usually travel from small, mostly agricultural islands such as Grenada to islands such as Trinidad with more industry. There they might find jobs in construction or factories.

Farm workers move from island to island to harvest crops. In this way the people of different islands build connections. ■

■ *What unites the people of the West Indies, and how are these bonds expressed?*

A CLOSER LOOK

Steel Drums

Music of the Caribbean islands often relies on drums for strong dance rhythms. You may have heard calypso and reggae music. Steel drums got their start at Carnival in Trinidad in the 1930s and 1940s, when drummers beat large oil barrels. Before long, they refined the barrels into steel drums, which are called pans.

Steel bands, which play and compete at festivals, may include more than 100 drummers.

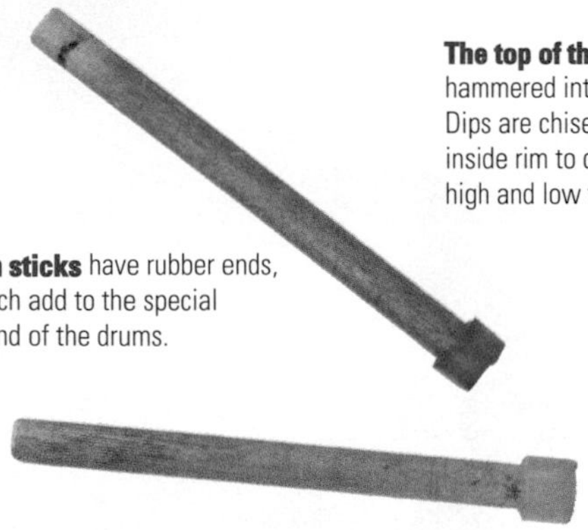

Pan sticks have rubber ends, which add to the special sound of the drums.

The top of the drum is hammered into a dish shape. Dips are chiseled around the inside rim to create a range of high and low tones.

Note: You may want to introduce this page after students read the section Life in the Caribbean.

HISTORY

Critical Thinking

In 1937 the Trinidadian government passed a law that outlawed skin drums and bamboo rhythm sticks on the island; the authorities feared they would be used for secret communications and would encourage rebellion. To replace their drums, people used their voices and created new instruments, including the steel drum. Ask students to speculate about how banning music can help one group dominate or control another. *(Suppress ideas of rebellion and protest)*

More About Caribbean Music

Steel drums are an integral part of the West Indian music called calypso. The rumba and cha-cha began in Cuba; the merengue is popular in the Dominican Republic, reggae in Jamaica, and salsa in Puerto Rico. Each type of music is heavily influenced by African rhythms.

■ *The people are united through migration among the islands and through sports such as cricket and baseball. Caribbean bonds are expressed through music and celebrations such as Carnival.*

Music Connection

Calypso is one of the earliest authentic Caribbean art forms. It is rooted in the African oral tradition, in which songs were sung as a form of pointed social comment. Today, much of the Caribbean calypso music is infused with expressions of political and social commentary about the islands. Have students bring in tapes of calypso music from home or from the public library. Write out the lyrics and discuss what the artist is trying to say.

Visual Learning

The steel drum and pan sticks pictured on this page have particular physical characteristics that help to create a unique sound. Ask students to compare these instruments with other types of drums and sticks.

VISUAL LEARNING

Critical Thinking

Have students look carefully at the photograph of shantytowns of San Juan on this page. In what ways does this photograph reflect the economic situation in many countries they have studied thus far? *(The photograph shows very poor people and wealthy people living side by side. Uneven distribution of wealth is a common problem in most nations.)*

■ *Growing sugar created a monocrop economy, one that was not diversified. It also led to large numbers of unskilled workers and contributed to overpopulation.*

Economic Challenges

The shantytowns of San Juan contrast greatly with the rest of the city. This sight is common in many cities throughout the islands.

Today people throughout the Caribbean must respond to many economic challenges. Most of these problems can be traced back to one crop: sugar cane.

Relying on Sugar

European landowners in the Caribbean had one interest—making money by exporting sugar cane. Sugar cane became a **monocrop,** or the only major crop in the region. This reliance on sugar led to a number of problems on the islands.

The sugar industry created a surplus of unskilled workers on the islands. Growing and processing sugar cane is **labor-intensive.** That is, it requires huge numbers of people. In some places machines can do much of the harvesting, but hilly fields of cane still must be cut by hand.

In the past the sugar industry kept the number of sugar workers high by importing slaves and indentured servants. With the introduction of modern medicine and the decline in infant deaths, the result was overpopulation. Today the islands have more people than they can support with their present economies. Unemployment is very high, and wages are very low.

Creating New Businesses

Many Caribbean islands are creating jobs for their people in assembly plants. These factories offer the people jobs, but the wages are usually low. The workers perform simple tasks and do not develop skills for better-paying jobs.

Haiti, for example, is the world's largest producer of baseballs. The companies pay women low wages to stitch baseballs all day. Yet since most of these factories are owned by people in other countries, they add little wealth to the local economy.

In recent years tourism has boosted the economies of the islands. Tourism, however, has become a "monocrop" on some islands. When tourism slumps, for reasons such as a hurricane, the economy is hurt badly.

Tourism presents other problems. It, too, is labor-intensive. It calls for many unskilled workers who are often poorly paid. Foreign owners often reap most of the profits from the large hotels and resorts. In some areas the building of hotels and resorts threatens the beauty that brings people to the Caribbean. ■

CENTRAL BANK OF BARBADOS
THESE NOTES ARE LEGAL TENDER FOR THE PAYMENT OF ANY AMOUNT
TWO DOLLARS
CO CENTRAL DE LA REPUBLICA DOMINICA
CIEN PESOS ORO
100

The currency of the Dominican Republic and Barbados reflects European influence in the Caribbean.

■ What economic problems did growing sugar bring to the Caribbean islands?

Critical Thinking

Point out that although tourism brings large sums of money and low-skilled jobs into many Caribbean islands, many islanders resent the influx of visitors each year. Ask students to think about reasons for this resentment. *(Possible answers: Most of the profits reaped from tourism are made by foreign investors; Caribbean people resent having limited employment options.)*

Mathematics Connection

Have students refer to a current world almanac to research the number of Caribbean people who have immigrated to the United States since 1980. Have them present their findings in clear graphs on posters. Encourage students to present the information in various forms, such as a simple chart of the statistics, or a circle graph showing how this region contributes to the total number of immigrants for a given year or for a five- or ten-year period.

Spread of Caribbean Culture

Every summer in Toronto, Canada; Brooklyn, New York; and London, England, people from the Caribbean organize huge Carnival celebrations. These are people who have left the islands in search of better-paying jobs and a higher standard of living for their families.

Moving Throughout the World

Many islanders have moved to Europe and Canada, but the highest number have come to the United States. By the mid-1980s, about one million West Indians were living in the New York City area alone. More than one million Cubans live in the United States, the majority in Florida.

These islanders bring their culture with them. Caribbean culture can be seen not only at Carnival, but in radio shows, restaurants, and food shops in cities everywhere. There are many Caribbean writers and artists at work throughout the world as well. In 1992 Caribbean poet Derek Walcott was awarded the Nobel Prize in Literature. Walcott, born in St. Lucia, lives in both Trinidad and Massachusetts.

Maintaining Close Ties

Caribbean immigrants keep close ties to their island homes. West Indian doctors, taxi drivers, nurses, and postal workers living in North America and Europe send money back to their relatives. The money helps island families buy houses or land. It also benefits the whole economy as tens of millions of dollars are sent back to the larger islands each year.

West Indians often return to the islands to visit. They bring consumer goods such as clothes, radios, and furniture for babies, which help improve the standard of living of their families.

One group of West Indian doctors returns regularly to give free medical care to the island people. As one Jamaican woman now living in the United States said, "You never really leave the islands; they're always with you in your heart." ■

Across Time & Space

In 1989 four-star General Colin Powell was named the chairman of the U.S. Joint Chiefs of Staff, the highest military post in the United States. Powell, born and raised in New York City, is the son of Jamaican immigrants.

A Caribbean-style Carnival is held every year in Brooklyn, New York.

■ *In what ways is Caribbean culture spread throughout the world?*

■ *Caribbean culture is spread by emigrating peoples, who take Caribbean food, music, arts, and other aspects of their culture to other parts of the world.*

REVIEW

1. **FOCUS** What is life like in the Caribbean today?
2. **ECONOMICS** How did most people in the Caribbean earn a living after the end of colonialism?
3. **CULTURE** How do West Indians keep their culture alive in other countries of the world?
4. **CRITICAL THINKING** Why is it difficult to build a strong economy based on unskilled workers?
5. **ACTIVITY** Review the chart on page 520. With a partner, record the population density, or the number of people per square mile, for each island listed. Which of the islands has the highest population density? Form groups to make a class graph.

CLOSE

Read the Thinking Focus aloud. Have students review the visuals in this lesson. On the chalkboard create one column that briefly describes each visual and another column that tells the significance of the visual for life in the Caribbean today. For example, write *cricket players* in the first column. In the second column write *Cricket is an important cultural tie in the Caribbean.*

Answers to Review Questions

1. On many Caribbean islands, most people live in villages. People celebrate their culture through Carnival and express political and social views through music. Caribbean leaders are trying to find ways to solve their countries' economic problems. These problems force many islanders to move to other countries or among the islands.
2. Most people began to farm small plots of their own land or they became fishers.
3. People in the Caribbean keep their culture alive through language, music, food, celebrations, politics, literature, and art.
4. Unskilled workers are paid low wages. Islands with a surplus of unskilled workers do not attract companies that need more skilled workers.
5. Students should use the population and area figures listed on the chart to determine the population density of each island. Puerto Rico has the highest population density—995.73 people per square mile.

Homework Options

Have students draw a scene that illustrates some aspect of modern life in the Caribbean. Tell students to use the visuals in the lesson as a guide.

Study Guide: page 91

Chapter Review

Reviewing Key Terms

emancipation (p. 515)
indentured servant (p. 513)
labor-intensive (p. 522)
monocrop (p. 522)
triangle trade (p. 514)
tropical (p. 510)

A. Use each word below in a sentence that shows what the word means. Write your sentence as if it were the beginning of a story.

1. tropical
2. indentured servant
3. triangle trade
4. emancipation
5. monocrop
6. labor-intensive

B. Write whether each of the following statements is *true* or *false.* Then rewrite the false statements to make them true.

1. Tropical areas have dry seasons and rainy seasons.
2. Indentured servants had to work for a plantation owner for a certain period of time before they were free to work where they wanted.
3. The triangle trade refers to trade between three European countries.
4. The act of emancipation freed people from slavery.
5. Sugar cane was called a monocrop because one person owned all the sugar plantations.
6. Labor-intensive industries are those that require small numbers of people for a long time.

Exploring Concepts

A. The cause-and-effect chart below lists facts about the Caribbean. Copy the chart. Then fill in a sentence to the right of each cause that tells an effect. The first one has been done for you.

Cause	Effect in Caribbean
Christopher Columbus thought he had reached the East Indies in Asia.	He called the Caribbean the "Indies."
The Caribbean islands were colonies of different European countries.	
Sugar growers in the Caribbean wanted to increase their profits by lowering the cost of labor.	
Enslaved blacks organized themselves and rebelled against their slave masters.	
After emancipation, the sugar growers wanted to find another source of cheap labor.	
Today, tourism is a monocrop on many Caribbean islands.	

B. Support each of the following statements with information from the chapter.

1. Geography and climate have been important influences on Caribbean culture.
2. The people of the Caribbean must be careful to safeguard their environment.
3. There are many diverse cultural influences in the Caribbean.
4. The desire for freedom and independence has been very important to the development of the Caribbean nations.
5. The sugar cane plant shaped the history of people in the Caribbean.
6. The people of the Caribbean are unified in a number of ways.
7. Cities in the Caribbean are very much like cities in the rest of the world.
8. Caribbean culture has spread to countries all over the world.
9. Tourism is important to the economies of many Caribbean nations.

Answers to Reviewing Key Terms

A. Sample answers:

1. The Caribbean islands are popular with tourists, because of their hot, or **tropical,** climates.
2. The **indentured servant** was required to work without pay for three to seven years.
3. The **triangle trade** brought enslaved Africans to the Caribbean Islands, in exchange for European goods.
4. Resistance and revolution led to **emancipation,** or freedom from slavery, for Caribbean Islanders of African descent.
5. Under European landowners, sugar cane became a **monocrop,** or the only major crop, on many Caribbean islands.
6. The work on the sugar cane plantation was **labor-intensive,** requiring huge numbers of workers to cut the cane.

B. Answers:

1. True.
2. True.
3. False. The **triangle trade** was a trade system developed by the Dutch in which Europeans exchanged European goods for enslaved Africans. These Africans were then exchanged for the island products that Europeans wanted.
4. True.
5. False. Sugar was called a **monocrop** because it was the only major crop in the Caribbean region.
6. False. **Labor-intensive** industries require huge numbers of workers.

Answers to Exploring Concepts

A. Sample answers:

1. He called the Caribbean the "Indies."
2. The people of the Caribbean speak different languages, and the islands have different political systems.
3. Sugar growers brought enslaved Africans to the Caribbean to work on their plantations.
4. Africans gained emancipation, and colonialism began to decline.
5. Sugar growers recruited workers as indentured servants from other countries.
6. Caribbean economies that rely on tourism are hurt when bad weather strikes.

B. Sample answers:

1. Many island economies depend on the money generated by tourists who are attracted by the beautiful Caribbean environment.
2. If the people of the Caribbean spoil the environment, they stand to lose this tourism money.
3. The Caribbean culture is a complex blend of cultures from areas such as Africa, Europe, and India.
4. Slave rebellions and other protests helped to end colonialism.
5. Because of the sugar business, enslaved Africans and their African cultures were brought to the Caribbean.
6. The people of the Caribbean are held together by common cultural interests, such as sports and music.
7. San Juan, Puerto Rico has similarities to other cities. For example, there are modern buildings, factories, and rich and poor areas.
8. There are West Indian celebrations of Carnival in Toronto, Brooklyn, and London.
9. To many islands in the Caribbean, tourism is a monocrop. Bad weather or economic slumps in other nations can cause the economy of these islands to decline.

Reviewing Skills

1. Imagine that you and your classmates are going to evaluate the oral reports that students give in social studies class. You have been asked to create a form that your classmates will fill in with constructive criticism after they listen to each oral report. Review the suggestions about constructive criticism on page 517. Use these suggestions to create the one-page form.
2. Look at the map on page 509. What kind of prediction could you make about the future success or failure of the economies of the Caribbean nations if the seas around these islands were to become severely polluted?
3. Reread the description of the slave revolt in Haiti on page 515. Is this a primary source or a secondary source? Explain your reasoning.
4. Reread the literature excerpt on page 508. What kind of organization pattern did author Lynn Joseph use to write her description—chronological, cause-and-effect, or spatial order? How can you tell?

Using Critical Thinking

1. Why can the Caribbean region be called a true "melting pot" of cultures? Support your answer with at least two cultural examples.
2. In 1973 a Native American named Adam Nordwall flew to Italy on an airplane. When he stepped off the plane onto the ground, Nordwall "claimed" Italy for the Indian people "by right of discovery." What point was Adam Nordwall trying to make with this action?
3. What factors have kept the nations of the Caribbean from unifying into one political nation? Support your answer with both historical and cultural information.
4. In what ways does the sugar economy continue to hurt the Caribbean economy today?

Preparing for Citizenship

1. **WRITING ACTIVITY** Today many people disagree about whether or not Christopher Columbus should be honored as a hero, considering the fate of Native Americans after his arrival in the Caribbean. Columbus once wrote about the Native Americans, "They are completely defenseless . . . and so they are fit to be ordered about and made to work. . . ." Imagine that you have been asked to write a guest column in a local newspaper about the following issue: Is Christopher Columbus a U.S. hero? Write a rough outline for your column. Be sure to support your opinions with concrete facts.
2. **COLLABORATIVE LEARNING** Many different types of governments exist in the West Indies, from the Communist government of Cuba and the temporary military-dominated government of Haiti, to the parliamentary government of Barbados and the commonwealth status of Puerto Rico. As a class, find out more about different governmental systems. Divide into small groups, with each group choosing a different Caribbean island country to research. Use the chart on page 520 as a starting point for your research. Each member of a group should research different aspects of the island government. Questions to investigate include: Who is allowed to take part in the government? How are the people of the country represented? Who are their leaders? How are government decisions made? How did this type of government develop in this island country? Together your group should prepare and present a government fact sheet that answers these questions.

Answers to Reviewing Skills

1. Check that student forms follow the guidelines on page 517.
2. Prediction: If the Caribbean seas were to become severely polluted, the Caribbean economy would be seriously hurt.
3. This excerpt is a primary source because it describes the slave revolts from the point of view of an eyewitness.
4. The description uses spatial order because it gives the reader a visual "snapshot" of the area.

Answers to Using Critical Thinking

1. In the Caribbean, people from many different cultures have merged to create something totally new. Two examples include French Creole, a language spoken in Haiti; and Carnival, a celebration that was introduced by Europeans but became a celebration of Trinidad's culture.
2. Just as he has no right to "claim" Italy, Nordwall was trying to point out that Europeans had no right to claim Native American land that had been occupied for thousands of years.
3. The islands are separated by social, political, and economic structures as a result of their colonial past. Also, many of the larger islands are reluctant to unite with smaller, poorer islands.
4. The sugar industry created a surplus of unskilled workers and led to overpopulation and unemployment on many Caribbean islands.

Answers to Preparing for Citizenship

1. **WRITING ACTIVITY** Answers will vary. Check that students have supported their opinions with facts. Possible answer: Yes, Christopher Columbus should be honored as a hero because he did accomplish a spectacular feat at the time—crossing the Atlantic Ocean and uncovering a part of the earth that Europeans did not know existed.
2. **COLLABORATIVE ACTIVITY** Direct students to the library to do their research. They may find the information in encyclopedias, almanacs, and books about the Caribbean.

CHAPTER ORGANIZER

Chapter 23 Central and South America

CHAPTER PLANNING CHART

Pupil's Edition	Teacher's Edition	Ancillaries
Lesson 1: The Land and Its History (2–3 days) Objective 1: Describe the climate and geography of Central and South America. (History 7; Geography 2, 5) Objective 2: Identify the mixture of people who live in Central and South America. (History 7, 8; Geography 5; Culture 1, 2, 3, 4) Objective 3: Describe how South Americans live. (Geography 3, 5; Economics 3; Culture 5, 6; Ethics and Belief Systems 1, 3; Social and Political Systems 1, 2)	• Graphic Overview (528) • Access Strategy (529) • Access Activity (529) • Visual Learning (530) Cultural Context (530) Geographic Context (531) Historical Context (531) Critical Thinking (531, 532) Political Context (532)	Study Guide (92) • Posters (5) • Study Prints (13)
Literature: From *The Captive*	Access Strategy (535) Reader's Theater (535)	Discovery Journal (46)
Lesson 2: South America (2–3 days) Objective 1: Compare the populations of Venezuela and Argentina. (History 7; Geography 5; Economics 4; Social and Political Systems 6) Objective 2: Describe the move from dictatorship to democracy in Venezuela and Argentina. (History 5; Social and Political Systems 3, 5) Objective 3: Contrast the economies of Venezuela and Argentina. (Economics 1, 2, 4, 5)	• Graphic Overview (536) • Access Strategy (537) • Access Activity (537) • Visual Learning (538) Bulletin Board (538) Cultural Context (538) Historical Context (539) Conducting a Survey (539) Critical Thinking (539)	Study Guide (93) Discovery Journal (47)
Understanding Oral Reports Objective: Plan, write, and deliver an oral report. (Study Skills 3)	Preparing an Oral Report (541)	Study Guide (94)
Lesson 3: Central America (2–3 days) Objective 1: Explain the problems facing the people of El Salvador, Nicaragua, and Panama. (History 1, 7, 8; Geography 5; Economics 1, 3, 4, 5; Ethics and Belief Systems 5; Social and Political Systems 2, 4) Objective 2: Describe the importance of Central America to the United States. (History 7; Geography 4; Economics 4; Culture 1; Ethics and Belief Systems 5; Social and Political Systems 6) Objective 3: Explain why democracy has prospered in Costa Rica. (Economics 3, 4; Social and Political Systems 1, 2, 5, 6)	• Graphic Overview (542) • Access Strategy (543) • Access Activity (543) • Visual Learning (544) Reader's Theater (544) Mathematics Connection (544)	Study Guide (95) Map Activities (27)
Chapter Review	Answers (546–547)	Tests (89–92)

* Objectives are correlated to the strands and goals in the program Scope and Sequence on pages T41–T49.

• LEP appropriate resources. (For additional strategies, see pages T32–T33.)

CHAPTER RATIONALE

Chapter 23 presents students with the history, geography, and culture of Central and South America. Material on Native American cultures introduced in Chapter 6 is now discussed in more detail. The text also highlights the political and economic struggles of modern nations in this region.

Lesson 1 begins with an overview of important geographic features and climates of Central and South America. Charts on pages 530 and 531 detail the ethnic mix, the main languages, and the literacy rates of countries in the region. Students learn how Native American populations were affected by Spanish and Portuguese colonization starting around 1500. To help students appreciate the global spread of influential ideas, the independence movement in North America is shown as a catalyst to the independence movement led by Simon Bolívar and José de San Martín. Finally, students are made aware of some of the problems that still need to be solved, such as urban expansion and wide disparities in the distribution of wealth and land.

Lesson 2 focuses on two South American countries that are representative of the region in different ways: Venezuela and Argentina. The countries are compared and contrasted in terms of ethnic composition, geography, and economy. Discussion of problems related to a dependence on oil in Venezuela and the political turmoil in Argentina helps students understand the complexities of modern South American societies. A Moment in Time features the gaucho, an Argentinian cowhand who works on the open range.

In **Lesson 3** the focus is on Central America. A special map featuring major products from this region helps students appreciate the trade relationship that the United States has had with Central American nations. The lesson introduces two recent Nobel Peace Prize winners, Rigoberta Menchú of Guatemala and Oscar Arias Sánchez of Costa Rica. A section on Costa Rica—a traditional, stable democracy—concludes the chapter.

ACTIVITIES & PROJECTS

LEP: Making a Relief Map

Have students refer to the physical map on page 687 of the Atlas to make a model of Central and South America. Students can copy the map and then create a textured surface with clay to show land features. Tell them to include the Amazon and its basin, as well as the Andes. Students should use different colors of Plasticine, if possible, and should create an appropriate key. (Use after Lesson 1.)

Investigating

Have students investigate what effect each of these had on South American history: the Andes, the Amazon Basin, and the pampas. (For example, because of its vastness, much of the Amazon Basin remained unexplored by outsiders until the 20th century.) Students may also want to research the role of river systems during the development of the South American interior. (Use after Lesson 1.)

Basic: Role-Playing

Divide the class into pairs and have students take roles as Venezuelans and Argentinians. List some key topics on the chalkboard, such as *economic resources, ethnic composition, and political system.* Ask students to role-play a conversation between modern citizens of the two countries. Invite them to be specific with their concerns and to refer to facts that fall under the topics you listed. (Use after Lesson 2.)

Challenge: Writing a Diary Entry

Costa Rica enjoys a relatively stable economy, and its citizens participate in a democratic government. As Lesson 3 points out, refugees from neighboring Central American countries often flee to Costa Rica. Invite students to imagine themselves as Costa Ricans and to write a brief diary entry about the refugees. Encourage them to refer to details about the other nations as well as about Costa Rica. (Use after Lesson 3.)

CHAPTER PREVIEW

Have students read the chapter title and the paragraph that follows. Point out that often when people think of Central and South America, they think first of Spain and Portugal's influence on the region. Have students speculate on why this might be true. Then have them examine the illustrations for evidence of cultures other than Spanish and Portuguese. *(Native American influence in the fish tapestry; terraces built by Incas in the Andes; and Native American, African, and European faces depicted in the storefront sign)*

Looking Back

Help students recall that Chapter 22 showed how the Caribbean was shaped by geography and European settlement. Tell students that Central and South America are influenced by these same factors, but in different ways.

Looking Forward

Explain to students that this chapter includes three lessons: The Land and Its History, South America, and Central America.

Lesson 1 describes the geography and climate of the region, as well as the history of its people.

Chapter 23
Central and South America

An Andean woman weaves a rich tapestry with the secret symbols of her ancient culture. Dancers swing to the rhythms of the rumba, a dance of African origin. A visitor thinks of Spain as he walks on cobblestone streets, past courtyards and red-tiled roofs. These scenes of Central and South America have their roots in the past—in the cultures of Native Americans, Africans, and Europeans. Together these people will shape the future of the region.

A sign on a storefront symbolizes the ethnic origins of the people of Venezuela—Africans, Europeans, and Native Americans.

Many explorers wore armor such as this Spanish helmet.

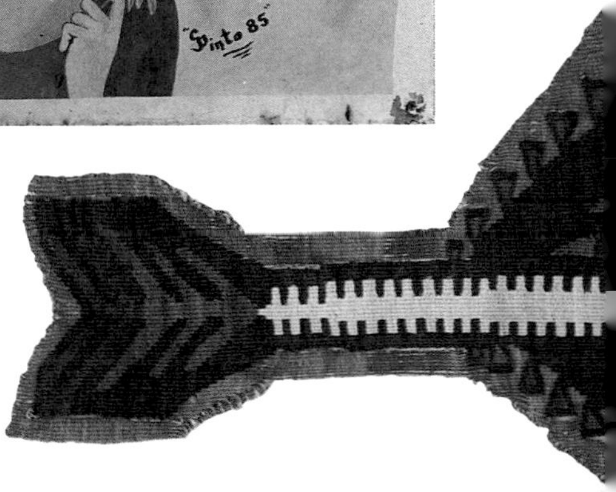

1498 Columbus lands in South America, the first European explorer to arrive there.

1475	1550	1625	1700

1600s Most of Central and South America is under Spanish or Portuguese control.

1498

BACKGROUND

In addition to constructing the Panama Canal and establishing plantations in the region, the United States has played an active role in the political life of Central America, especially in the late 1900s. This interest is due in large part to the strategic location of the region, the only land bridge between North and South America.

The United States Stays Involved

Both El Salvador and Nicaragua have experienced serious political upheaval in recent decades. Since 1979 the United States has backed ambitious programs to distribute land among the peasants of war-torn El Salvador. Conflicts between government troops and guerrilla forces persist in that country. The United States continues to give economic aid to El Salvador in the hope that the nation can settle its internal disputes over land reform and the direction of its government.

In 1981 the United States resisted the Nicaraguan Communist coalition, called the Sandinistas, with U.S.-backed opposition groups called *contras.* After much bloodshed, the Sandinistas prevailed, eventually electing Daniel Ortega as president. Since that time, a new president—Violeta Chamorro—has emerged, and the nation is working toward policies of national reconciliation. The United States now offers political and economic support to democratic leadership in Nicaragua.

Music, dance, and playing musical instruments is central to the life of many people, as it is with this Guatemalan boys' chorus.

This ancient fish-shaped tapestry was woven in the same style used by Native Americans long before Europeans arrived.

This village is set in the fertile foothills of the Andes, near Cuzco. Peru still has many of the features of the Inca Empire—terraces built into the steep mountainsides and water brought through canals to grow crops.

1775 | 1850 | 1925 | 2000

c. 1812 Bolívar and San Martín begin to lead the struggle for independence for South America.

1992 Rigoberta Menchú is awarded the Nobel Peace Prize.

Today

Understanding the Visuals

Direct the students' attention to the picture of the Guatemalan schoolboys on this page. About 20 different languages, mostly of Mayan origin, are spoken in Guatemala. Remind students of the Mayan civilization they learned about in Chapter 6.

Invite students to examine the fish-shaped tapestry on these pages. Dating from A.D. 1000, this textile originated in the central coast region of Peru. Ask students what the design might tell them about the early Peruvians. *(Fish, and probably fishing, were important to them.)*

Understanding Chronology

Ask students to calculate how long the Spaniards and Portuguese ruled in South America. Columbus landed in South America in 1498, six years after his first voyage to the Caribbean in 1492. Independence forces led by generals Simon Bolívar and José de San Martín defeated the Spaniards by 1826. *(1826 – 1498 = 328 years of Spanish rule in South America)* Ask whether the South American countries are older or younger nations than the United States. (*They are younger—the United States declared its independence in 1776.)*

An Organization for the Americas

Internal political struggles continue to dominate the lives of Central and South Americans. The region is also undergoing other changes, as increased industrialization has exposed serious problems with health care, education, and drugs. In 1948 almost all the independent states in the Western Hemisphere came together to form the Organization of American States (OAS); its main purpose is to foster peace and cooperation among nations in the Western Hemisphere. Today the OAS makes policy on collective security and helps improve social conditions throughout the region. For example, OAS members have established a special commission on youth drug addiction to address problems in the new urban areas of South America. The nations of Central and South America now face an important challenge to strengthen their independence as they look toward the next century.

INTRODUCE

Read the Thinking Focus aloud. Review the concepts of physical features (landforms, climate) and cultural features (languages, ethnic composition) by asking students to offer examples of such features in the United States. *(Physical: mountains and plains spanning almost an entire continent; cultural: large numbers of immigrants, democracy, many different religions)* Tell students that they will use maps and photos to help them determine the physical and cultural features of Central and South America.

Key Terms

Vocabulary Strategies: T36–T37

pampas—grassy plains of Argentina

basin—an area drained by a river and its tributaries

vertical zone—the climate and vegetation conditions that exist at a certain altitude level

1475
1498
TODAY

LESSON 1

The Land and Its History

THINKING FOCUS

What are the physical and cultural features of Central and South America?

Key Terms

- pampas
- basin
- vertical zone

All grass and sky, and sky and grass, and still more sky and grass, the pampa stretched . . . a thousand miles away. . . .

Well did the ancient Quichuas name the plains, with the word signifying "space," for all was spacious—earth, sky, the waving continent of grass, the enormous herds of cattle and of horses, the strange effects of light, the fierce and blinding storms and, above all, the feeling in men's minds of freedom, and of being face to face with nature. . . .

These words by R. B. Cunninghame Graham in the 1800s describe the Argentine **pampas,** the grassy plains. You will learn about other features of Central and South America and the region's history.

Land of Variety

Central and South America is a land of extremes. The region has the world's longest mountain range—the Andes *(AN deez)*. It has the highest waterfall—Angel Falls—and the world's largest river—the Amazon.

The map on page 529 shows that Central America is the region stretching south from the border of Mexico through the narrow strip of Panama. Pear-shaped South America extends nearly to Antarctica.

Mountains and Rivers

A long chain of majestic mountains runs along the western region of South America. This range, called the Andes, curves northward for about 5,500 miles. Many peaks are more than 20,000 feet high. Only a narrow coastal plain lies between the Andes and the Pacific Ocean.

The land under the Andes is restless and unstable. Active volcanoes and earthquakes shape these mountains.

The Andes affect all of South America. They cut through the region,

Vertical Zones

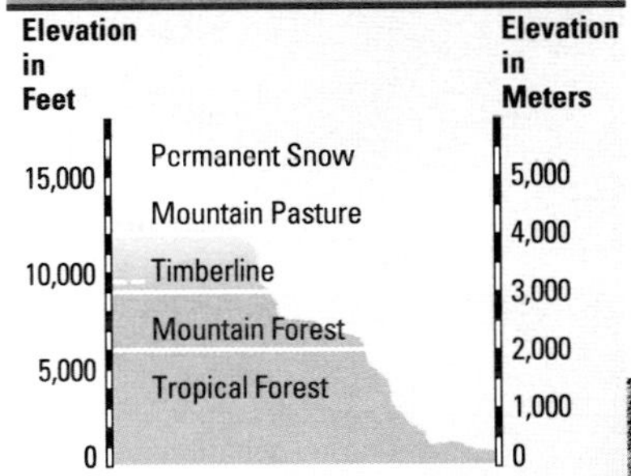
Elevation in Feet
Elevation in Meters
15,000
10,000
5,000
0
Permanent Snow
Mountain Pasture
Timberline
Mountain Forest
Tropical Forest
5,000
4,000
3,000
2,000
1,000
0

Source: *Elements of Physical Geography, 1989*

These vertical zones are found on the eastern side of the Andes in Peru, where llamas (right) are used for transportation, food, wool, and hides.

Objectives

1. Describe the climate and geography of Central and South America.
2. Identify the mixture of people who live in Central and South America.
3. Describe how South Americans live.

Graphic Overview

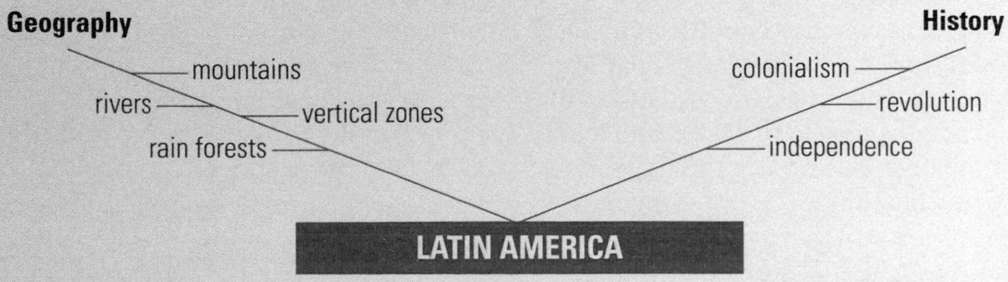
Geography
mountains
rivers
vertical zones
rain forests
History
colonialism
revolution
independence
LATIN AMERICA

creating borders and making communication difficult. The Andes also form a divide, from which the rivers flow east or west.

East of the Andes and south of the Guiana Highlands is the Amazon River. The river forms a huge basin covering about 2.7 million square miles. A **basin** is an area drained by a river and its tributaries. The Amazon basin is the largest in the world.

Central and South America: Climate Regions

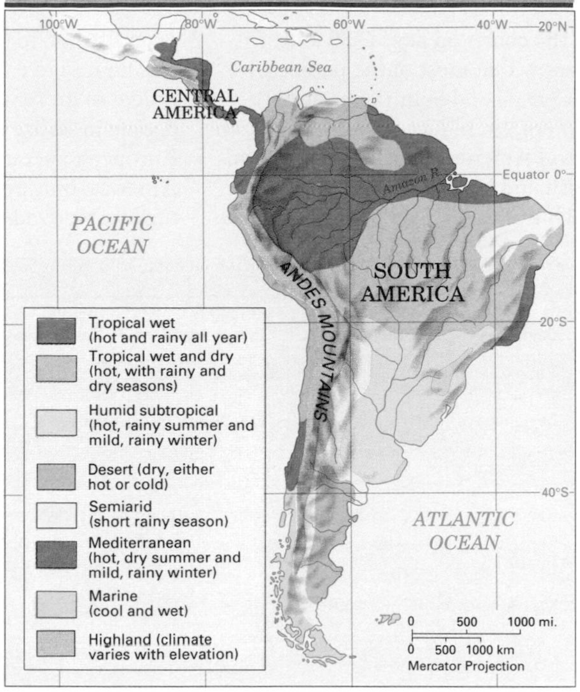
100°W
80°W
60°W
40°W
20°N
Caribbean Sea
CENTRAL AMERICA
Amazon R.
Equator 0°
PACIFIC OCEAN
SOUTH AMERICA
ANDES MOUNTAINS
20°S
40°S
ATLANTIC OCEAN
Tropical wet (hot and rainy all year)
Tropical wet and dry (hot, with rainy and dry seasons)
Humid subtropical (hot, rainy summer and mild, rainy winter)
Desert (dry, either hot or cold)
Semiarid (short rainy season)
Mediterranean (hot, dry summer and mild, rainy winter)
Marine (cool and wet)
Highland (climate varies with elevation)
0 500 1000 mi.
0 500 1000 km
Mercator Projection

Four-fifths of Central America is hilly or mountainous. Most people live in these cool highlands rather than in the tropical coastal lowlands. Destructive earthquakes and volcanoes are common.

Climates

Because Central and South America extend over a vast region, the climate varies greatly. Yet many areas are tropical in climate.

The equator crosses South America near the continent's widest point. South of the equator in the Southern Hemisphere the seasons are opposite from those in the Northern Hemisphere.

If you have ever climbed a mountain, you know that the air gets colder as you go higher. The climate and vegetation at different altitude levels make up **vertical zones.** As the chart on page 528 shows, you can begin your climb in tropical forests and end in snow!

Farming in the Andes depends on the climate in these vertical zones. It is difficult to grow bananas at high altitudes or to grow wheat in the tropical forest zone.

Rain Forests

Heavy rains—150 inches or more a year—fall in parts of tropical South America. Dense tropical rain forests cover much of the Amazon Basin, coastal Brazil, the Pacific coast of Colombia, and much of the eastern lowland area of Central America.

The trees provide timber and protect the soil. Even more important, the rain forest contains types of plants and animals that exist nowhere else on earth. ■

◄ *What regions of Central and South America do not have a tropical climate?*

▲ *Central and South America have climate extremes. A tropical climate is found in Panama (top). Appliqué mola art is on display in this picture. A cold climate is typical at the southern tip of Argentina (bottom). In the distance is Upsala Glacier.*

■ *How do the land forms affect the climate in Central and South America?*

DEVELOP

Invite students to make two headings in their notebooks: *Land* and *History.* As they read the lesson, have them list features under each heading. Ask them to speculate about what effect the land might have had on the history of this area of the world. *(The Andes cut through the region, making communication difficult; farming is possible only in certain regions.)*

◄ *Regions in the southern portion of the South American continent do not have a tropical climate.*

GEOGRAPHY

Map and Globe Skills

Have students locate Quito, Ecuador, on the map of South America in the Atlas on page 687. Compare it with the map on this page. Note that although the equator crosses Quito, its climate is cold and dry. Have students study its location and physical features and offer an explanation. *(Quito is located in the Andes, where an upper vertical zone contributes to a colder climate.)*

■ *The Andes create distinctive vertical zones, even at the equator. At the upper vertical zones, temperatures decrease, leading to a colder climate.*

Access Strategy

Ask students to look at the picture of Peruvian women on page 533 and to read the caption. Then invite them to name ways that differences in social status are represented in U.S. culture. *(Clothes, cars, houses, ownership of property or goods such as televisions or watches)* Point out that in some societies, family background and ethnic group tend to be more important determinants of status. In other societies education and ability count as well. Draw a ladder on the chalkboard and explain that a social system is often described as a ladder—not only because it has places at the top and the bottom but also because people can climb, or move from one rung of social standing to another. Tell students that while economic mobility is improving in modern Central and South America, there are still more people of European ancestry on the top rungs of the ladder and more native peoples on the bottom rungs.

Access Activity

Remind students that volcanoes, as well as earthquakes, are common in Central America. Students should discuss the consequences of natural disasters in their own region. Write their responses on the chalkboard. *(Floods, earthquakes, and hurricanes destroy property and cause deaths; often they necessitate rebuilding and can use up economic resources.)*

POLITICAL SYSTEMS

Critical Thinking

Introduce the term *adult literacy* and explain that it means the ability of adults to read and write. Then ask the students to consider why increased literacy would benefit a nation as well as an individual. *(Citizens would be better informed about political and social issues and would be able to vote more intelligently. It would benefit the economy, too, since educated people can hold better-paying jobs.)*

SOCIAL SYSTEMS

Critical Thinking

The mix of peoples described on this page was the result of large-scale immigration, among other factors. Have students consider the expectations and hopes that many arriving immigrants to Central and South America had for their new lives. Ask them to list them with you on the chalkboard. As the chapter progresses, consult this list. *(Expectations and hopes might include making money, starting an adventure, and escaping hardships in their native land.)*

Looking at the People

The charts on pages 530 and 531, show that most of the people of Central and South America are *mestizos*. In fact, two-thirds of Central Americans are of mixed Spanish and Native American ancestry. Until the early 1800s, immigration from Europe to Central America was limited to citizens of Spain, except in present-day Belize. Many people in Belize are of African and European ancestry. In South America, only Spaniards and Portuguese were admitted to their

Central America

Country	Percent Urban	Largest Ethnic Group	Official Languages	Percent Adult Literacy
Belize	52	Creole	English	93
Costa Rica	54	European	Spanish	93
El Salvador	44	Mestizo	Spanish	73
Guatemala	35	American-Ladino	Spanish	60
Honduras	40	Mestizo	Spanish	73
Nicaragua	60	Mestizo	Spanish	74
Panama	53	Mestizo	Spanish	88

Source: Britannica Book of the Year, 1992

A wooden folk mask from Guatemala is worn by this boy during a dance festival.

Hand-carved painted toys like this one from El Salvador capture children's imaginations.

Visual Learning

Encourage students to analyze the charts on this page and the next by asking them whether this statement is true: The most rural country always has the lowest literacy rate. *(False)* Then have students write their own true or false statements about the data and take turns testing the class with them.

Cultural Context

South America has a long history of literary excellence. The works of many of its leading writers are available in English translation. Their novels provide excellent windows into South American culture and history. *Don Segundo Sombra* (1926), by Ricardo Güiraldes, tells the story of a young Argentine gaucho. *One Hundred Years of Solitude* (1967), by the Colombian writer Gabriel García Márquez, helped earn him the Nobel Prize in Literature. In 1929 the Venezuelan novelist Rómulo Gallegos wrote a powerful novel called *Doña Bárbara.* The novel presents the history and culture of Venezuela in terms of a struggle between the European civilization of the cities and the rustic life of the countryside. Owing in part to the popularity of his novel, Gallegos was elected president of his country in 1948. A military coup, however, quickly overthrew his government.

colonies until the end of the colonial period.

The native peoples of Central and South America influenced the populations that settled there later. Today Peru, Bolivia, Ecuador, and Guatemala—which once had dense native populations—now have many descendants of these native peoples. As the charts show, large European populations are found in Argentina and Costa Rica, which are areas that had fewer native peoples. Along the coast of Brazil, and in Belize, Honduras, and Nicaragua, people of African ancestry are a significant part of the population. ■

South America

Country	Percent Urban	Largest Ethnic Group	Official Languages	Percent Adult Literacy
Argentina	86	European	Spanish	95
Bolivia	51	Mestizo/Quechua	Spanish, Aymara, Quechua	78
Brazil	75	European	Portuguese	81
Chile	81	Mestizo	Spanish	93
Colombia	67	Mestizo	Spanish	87
Ecuador	55	Mestizo/Quechua	Spanish	69
Guyana	28	East Indian	English	96
Paraguay	46	Mestizo	Spanish	90
Peru	69	Mestizo/Quechua	Spanish, Quechua	87
Suriname	65	Indo-Pakistani	Dutch	95
Uruguay	86	Mixed Spanish-Italian	Spanish	95
Venezuela	84	Mestizo	Spanish	91

Source: Britannica Book of the Year, 1992

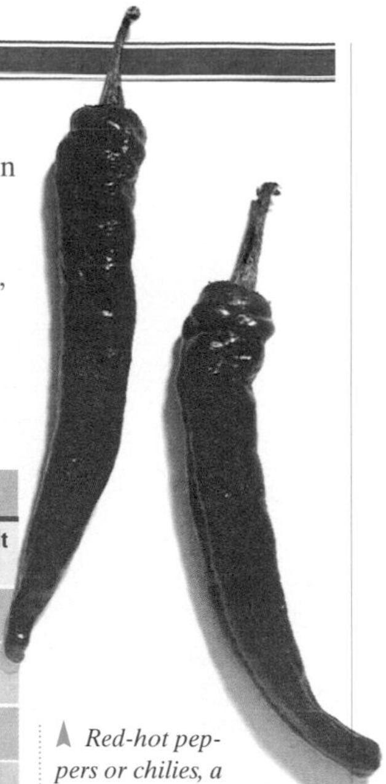

▲ *Red-hot peppers or chilies, a very hot seasoning, come from a tropical plant. Chilies may first have been grown by native peoples in South America.*

■ *What countries in Central and South America have the highest literacy rates?*

➤ *Weddings like this one in Peru, family gatherings, and other local traditions are an important part of the culture of Central and South America.*

SOCIAL SYSTEMS

Critical Thinking

Invite students to consider the wide variety of peoples in Central and South America, as described on this page and the previous page. What problems do these differences pose? *(Language and cultural differences make communication between peoples difficult. People in different regions cannot easily share information and resources.)*

■ *In Central America, Belize and Costa Rica have the highest literacy rate; in South America, Guyana has the highest literacy rate.*

GEOGRAPHY

Visual Learning

Have students locate photographs in the Chapter Opener and Lesson 1 that show different landscapes of Central and South America. Ask them to point out important features of the region, using these visuals. *(For example, students might notice the high mountains in the wedding photo on this page.)*

Geographic Context

Students might review the Closer Look in Chapter 17, on page 388, which highlighted the natural forces and cultural impact of volcanoes. Central America experiences frequent volcanic eruptions and severe earthquakes. More than 40 volcanoes extend along the Pacific coast of Central America for 900 miles, from the Guatemalan-Mexican border to Costa Rica. In recent times earthquakes in Central America have caused more destruction than have active volcanoes.

Historical Context

After the South American countries gained their independence in the early 1800s, large-scale European immigration began. From 1870 to 1930, between 11 and 12 million immigrants came to South America—most of them from Europe. Over half of these new arrivals went to Argentina, and another third went to Brazil. During the 1930s and early 1940s, Europeans fleeing Hitler came. After World War II, a smaller wave of Europeans moved to Venezuela and Argentina.

Critical Thinking

Have students compare the data on the charts on these two pages and make generalizations about differences between Central and South America. Possible topics for comparison include most common language *(Spanish)*, largest ethnic group overall *(mestizo)*, and differences in population patterns *(South American countries are more urban)*.

HISTORY

Critical Thinking

In 1776 North American colonists declared their independence from Great Britain. Ask students why they think the American Revolution had an impact on the independence movements in South America in the early 1800s. In what way were the struggles in North and South America similar? *(Both were rebellions against colonial rulers and had as their goal freedom from overseas control.)*

HISTORY

Social Participation

Have students work in groups to list the events that led to independence for many South American countries. *(Frustration with colonial government, inspiration from North American revolution, strong leadership by Simon Bolívar)* Ask each group to present its answer to the class, adding details from the lesson to support all assertions.

Colonialism to Independence

In Chapter 6 you read that many Native American cultures flourished in Central and South America before Europeans first arrived in the late 1400s. Here you will learn how the colonial era changed this region.

Native Peoples and Europeans

The years following the arrival of the conquistadors brought disease and disaster to Native Americans. Many were killed in warfare. Millions more died of diseases, such as measles and smallpox, brought by the Europeans and enslaved Africans. The Native Americans were forced to farm the land and work in the mines for the Spaniards. Many died because of the harsh working conditions.

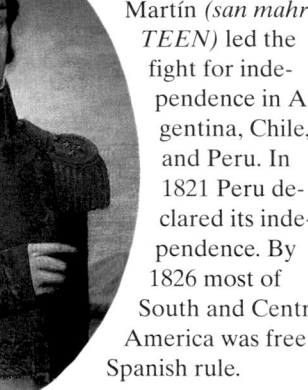

➤ *In the 1800s Simon Bolívar led the movement for liberation from colonialism. He hoped to unite all of South America but failed in his attempt.*

Yet some Native Americans in Central and South America continue to live in groups that have great cultural influence. In Paraguay, for example, the original language, Guarani *(gwah ruh NEE)*, is spoken as widely as Spanish. In Peru one of the official languages is Quechua *(KEHCH wuh)*, the language of the ancient Inca.

Revolution and Independence

By the 1600s Spain and Portugal controlled nearly all of Central and South America. Then, in the late 1700s, the spirit of freedom swept through the Western Hemisphere. British colonists in North America declared their independence in 1776. Haitians rebelled against the French monarchy in 1804.

The idea of independence led the peoples of South America to demand their freedom. The leader of the fight for independence from Spain was the wealthy Venezuelan general Simon Bolívar *(boh LEE vahr)*. By 1822 his armies had won major victories. José de San Martín *(san mahr TEEN)* led the fight for independence in Argentina, Chile, and Peru. In 1821 Peru declared its independence. By 1826 most of South and Central America was free of Spanish rule.

A Mix of Peoples

In the colonial period and later, Native American peoples mingled with people from Europe and Africa. Most of the early European settlers spoke Spanish and Portuguese, which are Latin-based languages (see charts on pages 530 and 531). Therefore, Central and South America, along with Mexico and the Spanish- and French-speaking islands of the Caribbean, are often called Latin America.

Spanish colonial society in Central and South America was divided into distinct classes. These social groups were ranked according to race and wealth. At the top, holding much of the wealth and power, were

How Do We Know?

HISTORY *Quechua Indians hold on to their past by weaving and wearing traditional clothes. Women have brightly colored shawls; men wear ponchos. Nearly everyone wears patterned hats. Archaeologists have found looms and textiles of early Andean peoples. By studying these artifacts, we learn the origin of some of the patterns, symbols, and weaves that are used today.*

Critical Thinking

Have students speculate on how life in South America might be different today if Simon Bolívar's dream of a United States of South America had succeeded. *(Students might give answers that suggest a unified nation more like the United States—having one official language and improved transportation within the country, for example.)*

Political Context

Ideas of freedom, equality, and democracy from the Enlightenment inspired Latin America's independence leaders. As explained in this lesson, Bolívar and San Martín also drew inspiration from the examples of the French and American revolutions. In the mid-1800s, some newly independent Latin American nations used the American Constitution as a model in writing their own constitutions.

a few officials and merchants born in Spain.

Creoles made up the next class. They were born in the Americas to Spanish or Portuguese families. Although many *creoles* were wealthy and owned large pieces of land, they had little political power. Many leaders—such as Bolívar and San Martín—were *creoles.*

Much of the population was of mixed ancestry. These people were a blend of Spaniards, Portuguese, Africans, and Native Americans.

At the bottom of the social ladder were Native Americans and enslaved Africans. In the 1500s, Africans were brought in as slaves to replace the dying Native American population. By the 1850s, most African slaves, except those in Brazil, had been freed.

Independence changed Central and South American society. Being Native American, African, or of mixed ancestry affected a person's class and culture. It did not necessarily keep the person from rising to a higher class, however.

Ability and education as well as race and family background continue to be important today. Yet there are still more Europeans at the top and more Native Americans and mixed peoples at the bottom of the social ladder.

▲ Peruvian women display their produce at the marketplace. The styles of their colorful clothes and straw or felt hats represent different social status.

Urban and Rural Life

Today less than one-half of the people of Central America live in rural areas. The percentage of people who live in rural areas in South America is even less.

Most of the people live in cities, where rapid growth has led to pollution, crime, job and housing shortages, and poverty. On the edge of the cities, the poorest people often live in shacks. The cities are working to solve these problems.

Throughout Central and South America modern architecture blends with ancient native structures and old Spanish buildings. Many people enjoy a rich cultural life. Many of the oldest universities in the Western Hemisphere are located here. The oldest, founded in 1551, is in Lima, Peru. ■

■ *What were the main ethnic groups in colonial Central and South America?*

R E V I E W

1. **FOCUS** What are the physical and cultural features of Central and South America?
2. **GEOGRAPHY** What effect do the vertical zones in the Andes have on vegetation in the region?
3. **POLITICAL SYSTEMS** How did the colonists in North America affect the movement for independence led by Bolívar and San Martín in South America?
4. **SOCIAL SYSTEMS** How did the ethnic background of the people and their place of birth affect social classes in colonial South America?
5. **CULTURE** In what ways are the countries of Central and South America centers of culture today?
6. **ACTIVITY** The Andes have affected many areas of life in South America. Choose one aspect of the Andes to research in the library: for instance, animal life, plant life, products grown, people who live in the area. Then either write a short description or draw a detailed picture of this feature.

SOCIAL SYSTEMS

Visual Learning

Invite students to leaf through this lesson and the rest of the chapter. Ask them to point to photos that give evidence of the economic mix in the region: rich and poor, ancient and modern, rural and urban. Ask students to help you list adjectives on the chalkboard that apply to Central and South American society.

■ *Native Americans, Europeans from Spain and Portugal, Africans, and people of mixed ancestry were the main ethnic groups in colonial Central and South America.*

C L O S E

Read the Thinking Focus aloud and have students consult their *Land* and *History* lists from the beginning of the lesson. You may want to copy the Graphic Overview onto the chalkboard for students to consider. Choose a few students to answer the Thinking Focus for the class.

Answers to Review Questions

1. Most of Central America is hilly, with tropical lowlands along the coasts. South America has a mountain range, rain forests, and long rivers. The culture is a blend of Native American, European, and African influences.
2. The lower vertical zones support tropical rain forests. At higher altitudes there are mountain forests and pastures.
3. The idea of freedom spread to Central and South America after Britain's 13 colonies declared their independence in 1776.
4. Those born in Spain had the highest status. At the bottom were Native Americans and people of African descent.
5. Historic Spanish-style buildings and some of the oldest universities in the Western Hemisphere are located in Central and South America.
6. You might want to have several students combine their reports into a class presentation.

Homework Options

Challenge students to list three ways the histories of the United States and Latin America are alike. *(Latin America had a large native population before European discovery, had a colonial past under European power, endured a period of slavery, and won a struggle for independence.)*

Study Guide: page 92

INTRODUCE

Students have read in Lesson 1 about the arrival of the Spanish in Latin America. Scott O'Dell's historical novel *The Captive* is the story of a 16-year-old Spanish theology student caught up in this adventure. In this excerpt, Julián Escobar, the narrator, takes a stand against the leaders of the expedition, who have enslaved the local Carib Indians.

READ AND RESPOND

Students may need some background about the novel before they read. Tell them that the narrator, Julian, is a young Spaniard studying for the priesthood who has come with an expedition to the Caribbean. Discovering gold, the leaders of the expedition (Guzmán and Don Luis) have used the island Indians as slaves and have killed their leader. As students read, ask them to consider these questions: What is most important to Guzmán and Don Luis? What is most important to Julian? What do you think will happen in the story?

Before students read, point out the vocabulary words and unfamiliar terms defined in the margins. Be sure they understand what the words mean; help with pronunciation if necessary.

In Lesson 1 you learned that the people of Central and South America today are descended from a blend of many cultures. This story tells of the early contact between Native Americans and the Spanish explorers and missionaries.

LITERATURE

The Captive

Scott O'Dell

As the Spaniards began to explore and settle the Caribbean islands and Central and South America, they brought with them Christian missionaries. These representatives of the Church were intent on bringing Christian beliefs to the peoples living in the Western Hemisphere in the 16th century. Scott O'Dell tells a gripping tale of a young seminary student, Julian Escobar, who stands up to the leaders of an expedition when they enslave the island people and force them to mine gold. As you read the excerpt from The Captive, *try to answer this question: Why was Julian angry about the happenings on the island?*

By noon Señor Guzmán had collected his band, six in all, as well as the lone Indian who knew where his tribe had hidden in the past and where they were apt to hide now, and Esteban, our translator. At the last minute, though he thoroughly mistrusted me, Guzmán decided that I should also go along.

Don Luis and I were standing at the head of the lagoon, watching members of the crew empty the storehouse. He had decided to move the gold onto the *Santa Margarita* in case the camp was overrun by the Caribs. There was danger in this, because the ruffian crew could take it into their heads to sail off with the treasure while we were ashore. But it seemed to be less than the danger from marauding Caribs. There was another and more important reason as well. The *encomendero* who now owned the island might appear and, finding the shed overflowing with gold, rightfully claim it.

ruffian tough and rowdy

marauding raiding

encomendero Spanish agent

Señor Guzmán came up with his band. "We need you," he said, laying a hand on my shoulder. "The savages will believe what you tell them."

"And what will that be?"

"Say that the Caribs have been vanquished, so it's safe to return to their village."

"The Caribs haven't been vanquished," I replied.

Guzmán went on as if I hadn't spoken.

"Say we regret that it was necessary to do away with the cacique."

"It was not necessary."

***cacique* (kah SEEK)** Indian chief

Thematic Connections

Social Studies: History/Relationships between ideas and events

Houghton Mifflin Literary Readers: Realistic Fiction/Becoming

Background

The author of more than two dozen books, Scott O'Dell said that he wrote novels to "acquaint young readers with their past and then persuade them that history, especially their own, has relevance to the lives they will lead and the choices they will make." His first book, *Island of the Blue Dolphins* (1960), won the 1961 Newbery Medal and has become a classic. *The Captive* (1979) is the first book in a trilogy about Spanish exploration in Latin America. It continues with *The Feathered Serpent* (1981) and *The Amethyst Ring* (1983). Julian Escobar is the central figure in all three.

From the start, Julian is confused by the conflict of cultures he witnesses in the Americas, and his sympathy for the native peoples increases throughout the trilogy. By the last book, he has made his way to the Inca Empire in Peru; his love for an Incan princess ends sadly in the mountaintop city of Machu Picchu, and he returns to Spain and a different future.

"I gave him fair warning."

"Why should you warn him? It's his island and his people. Why should you order him to do anything? You are not a king."

Guzmán's mottled face grew pale.

Don Luis said, "We need the men and the women also. We can't mine without them."

Guzmán swallowed hard but went on, "Say that we forgive them for running away. That we'll share the gold they mine; share and share alike."

"You're a friend. They'll listen to you," Don Luis said.

"I have nothing to tell them."

"Say what Guzmán has told you to tell them."

"I would have trouble speaking the words."

"Then say that we need them." He was growing impatient. "Go. Every moment counts."

I did not move.

"You want the Indians back as much as I do."

I spoke slowly so that there would be no doubt about what I was saying. "The truth is, sir, I don't wish them back. I wish them to stay where they are. Wherever it is, they are far better off than here."

Guzmán held in his hand the musket he had used upon the Caribs. He glanced at Don Luis, as if asking his permission to use it at that moment upon me. He had large white teeth, and his drawn-back lips showed that they were clamped tight together.

musket gun

The young Indian who had given him information about the tribe's whereabouts was watching. He sat huddled on the ground. Around his neck from ear to ear I saw that he wore a thin red welt.

I listened in silence as Don Luis repeated his request.

"You are a member of this expedition," he said. "I, Don Luis de Arroyo, Duke of Cantavara y Llorente, am its leader. I have asked you to accompany us on a mission of great importance. You give me evasive answers."

evasive indirect

"What makes you think that our Indians will return to their village if only I speak to them? They have been worked close to death. Some, close to a dozen, have died. Many more have sickened from hard work. And now their chieftain has been cruelly slain. They trust neither you nor Guzmán. They shouldn't trust *me*."

"But they do trust you."

"That, sir, is the point. They trust me, and I will not betray them."

Further Reading

The Forty-Third War. Louise Moeri. A war story about a fictional Central American country where a 12-year-old boy fights for his survival.

◄ To whom might the book title *The Captive* refer? *(It most likely refers to Julian. At this point he is literally held captive by the leaders of the expedition. He is also held captive in other ways—by his beliefs and sympathies. The title might also refer to the Indian who can lead the Spaniards to the rest of the Caribs or to the entire group whom the Spaniards have enslaved.)*

EXTEND

Have students read the entire novel *The Captive* to see how Julian has gotten into this situation and what becomes of him. Some students may want to read the other two books in the trilogy. Have them give oral book reports about the novels to the class.

Access Strategy

Ask students to think about books, stories, films, examples from history, or real life events they know about in which people have disagreed with an authority figure because they believed strongly in their own ideas. What happens when the rebels are successful? What happens when they are not? Finally, tell students that in this story they will read about a young man who takes a stand against a powerful authority: the Spanish explorers.

Reader's Theater

Because the dialogue in this excerpt is strong yet simple, groups of six students can perform the excerpt as Reader's Theater. Three students can read the parts of Señor Guzmán, Don Luis, and Julian; another can read Julian's expository narration; a fifth can serve as director; and a sixth can be production manager, in charge of simple props, sound effects, and lighting. Encourage them to tape-record or videotape their productions for other classes to hear or see.

Further Reading

You may want to have students look for other historical novels by Scott O'Dell in the school or local library.

INTRODUCE

Locate Venezuela and Argentina in the Atlas on page 687. Explain that they are both among South America's wealthiest nations but that there are also many differences between them. Read the Thinking Focus aloud. Have students locate both countries on the chart on page 531 and compare their data with those of other South American nations. Students should also preview the chapter and speculate on answers to the Thinking Focus. Then have students read to find out if their answers are correct.

Key Terms

Vocabulary Strategies: T36–T37

caudillo—a military dictator

nationalize—government taking ownership of an industry or resource

coup—a takeover of government

guerrilla—a member of a small, organized group fighting a government

1475 1498 TODAY

LESSON 2

South America

THINKING FOCUS

How do the ethnic groups and the source of economic wealth of Venezuela and Argentina differ?

Key Terms

- caudillo
- nationalize
- coup
- guerrilla

We discovered a very large population, who dwelt in houses having foundations that had been built in the water, like Venice, with much ingenuity.

From the writings of Amerigo Vespucci

Amerigo Vespucci *(vehs POO chee)*, an Italian explorer, may have named the place in South America where he landed in 1499. Because it reminded him of Venice, Italy, it became known as Venezuela, or "little Venice."

Several years later, a mapmaker suggested that all the newly discovered lands in South America be called America after Amerigo Vespucci. Later, the name was extended to include North America.

This lesson examines two South American countries—Venezuela and Argentina. Both are wealthy nations, yet their people, history, and resources are quite different.

Venezuela: Land of Liquid Gold

In 1498, on his third trip to the Caribbean, Christopher Columbus landed in Venezuela in South America. It seemed to him like an earthly paradise.

A Blend of Cultures

Venezuela was one of the first South American lands to be colonized by Europeans. Yet it was ignored for many years because it lacked the natural resources of other colonies. The Spaniards who settled there raised cattle and grew cacao and tobacco. These products, however, did not interest Spain nearly as much as gold and silver.

The colonists forced the Native Americans to work the land for them. When many died from the harsh working conditions, Africans were brought in as slaves to work on the plantations. Today most Venezuelans are a blend of European, Native American, and African descent.

▼ *Venezuelan houses on stilts reminded Amerigo Vespucci of the houses along the canals in Venice, Italy.*

Striking Oil

In the early 1500s, Spanish explorers saw Native Americans using a gooey black substance in their

Objectives

1. Compare the populations of Venezuela and Argentina.
2. Describe the move from dictatorship to democracy in Venezuela and Argentina.
3. Contrast the economies of Venezuela and Argentina.

Graphic Overview

	Venezuela	Argentina
Sources of Wealth	oil	cattle, grain, industry
People	mixed	mostly European
Political System	stable democracy	democracy
Challenges	oil dependence	political instability

canoe-making. Yet no one realized until about 400 years later that this substance, oil, was valuable.

By the early 1900s, industries in the United States and Europe needed oil for fuel in factories. In 1913 European companies began to drill for oil in Lake Maracaibo. U.S. companies joined in and by the 1920s, the oil business in Venezuela was booming.

Suddenly Venezuela changed from a quiet farming country into a major world oil producer and exporter. Good wages drew thousands of farmers and other workers from rural areas to the oil fields and the cities. Venezuela now had to import food it once had grown.

When the drilling began, Venezuela was ruled by a military dictator, or **caudillo** *(kaw DEE yoh)*. The *caudillo* encouraged foreign oil companies to set up drilling rigs. Under the *caudillo,* most of the profits went to government officials. Few oil profits went to improving health or schools.

Although the country's leaders were rich, most Venezuelans remained poor. Discontent grew until a group overthrew the dictator and changed the government. In 1958 Venezuela held democratic elections. Rómulo Betancourt, a political reformer, became president.

Betancourt launched programs to help Venezuelans. In 1960 the government passed a law that gave land to small farmers. Betancourt also used oil profits to fund education and health programs.

Effect of Oil on Venezuelan Life

Foreigners from Europe and from other South American countries poured into Venezuela to work in the oil industry. These jobs provided a way for many people to become part of the middle class. Today the country has a prosperous, educated middle class.

To distribute the wealth, Venezuela sought to gain ownership of, or **nationalize,** its most valuable resource—oil. In 1976 the government nationalized the oil industry.

Oil is a risky business, however. Prices go up and down. When oil prices dropped in the 1980s, many people lost their jobs. As a result, Venezuelans recognized the need for other industries. The discovery of iron ore deposits and the growth of the steel and aluminum industries have helped the economy. ■

Across Time & Space

In 1960 it was Venezuela that took the lead in forming OPEC, the Organization of Petroleum Exporting Countries (see Chapter 8, page 196). OPEC meets to set world oil prices. Although most OPEC members are Arab states, other members include nations in Asia, Africa, and Latin America.

▼ *Oil pumps operate near Lake Maracaibo (left) in Venezuela. The oil wealth of the country is evident in downtown Caracas (below).*

■ *How did the oil industry change Venezuela?*

DEVELOP

Point out that the lesson compares life in Venezuela and Argentina, with particular attention to differences in ethnic groups, history, natural resources, and sources of wealth. Draw a Venn diagram on the chalkboard. Label the left section *Venezuela* and the right section *Argentina.* Have students copy the diagram into their notebooks. Shade in the area where the circles overlap. Have students read to find similarities for the shaded area and to identify differences for the remainder of each circle.

■ *Immigrants came to Venezuela to work, exports shifted from farm products to oil, and the nation became economically dependent on oil.*

ECONOMICS

Study Skills

Have students list one or more effects of each of these developments in Venezuela's recent history: Foreign countries find oil in Lake Maracaibo; Betancourt comes to power; the oil industry is nationalized. Write responses on the chalkboard. Then have students name one way the events will affect Venezuela's future. *(The country now recognizes the need for industries other than oil.)*

Access Strategy

To help students appreciate the uniqueness of successful democracies worldwide, tell them that countries in South America have been struggling to establish stable democracies. Have students imagine that they are setting up a new club. You may wish to divide the class into small groups for this activity. Ask the students to agree on a purpose for this club. How will decisions be made? How will they raise funds for club events?

After 10 minutes gather the students together and tell them that South Americans faced similar decisions when they gained their independence. Ask students why democracy is the preferred form of government in the United States. Suggest to them that many democracies protect rights of all citizens, such as freedom of speech, press, and religion. Democracies often encourage people to participate in free elections in order to work through the political process.

Access Activity

The name *Venezuela* ("Little Venice") reflects the way towns in that area adapted to water. Tell the class that the country of Bolivia got its name from the leader Simon Bolívar. Ask students to speculate on the origins of the names of the countries Ecuador *(location on the equator)* and Colombia *(Christopher Columbus).*

Note: Expand on the changing role of the Argentinean pampas by directing the students' attention to the figure of the gaucho on this page.

CULTURE

Visual Learning

The gaucho lived his life on the pampas and depended on the grazing cattle for his livelihood. Have the class study the picture of the gaucho and imagine his daily life. Ask students what food they imagine a gaucho would most likely eat. *(Beef was his everyday fare.)* Tell the class that the gaucho sometimes enjoyed cornmeal mush or squash. He might also have sipped tea from a hollowed gourd.

More About the *Bombachas*
Early gauchos wore a *chiripa,* or a loincloth over leggings. The favored pants then changed to the *bombachas* like those pictured here; they narrowed at the bottom to fit inside the gaucho's handmade boots. A variation of these pants is still worn by modern Argentinean cowhands.

A MOMENT IN TIME

A Gaucho

7:20 A.M., December 21, 1893
Pampas near the Rio Colorado, Argentina

Poncho
Last night he slept on his wool poncho on the ground, his usual bed under summer stars. Proud and rugged, he scorns the comforts of town life.
Leather Belt
Wearing his best belt, he leaves his grazing cattle and heads for today's fiesta. Since the last fiesta, he has sewn more coins on his belt. He enjoys praise for the large silver buckle.
Pants *(Bombachas)*
Miles of high pampas grass brush against these tough baggy pants as he herds his cattle. He knows the land well. From the taste of grass shoots, he can tell whether water is nearby.
Saddle
Thick cloth padding under the leather protects his horse. The gaucho rides all day, working in the saddle. He shows off his expert riding skills in fiesta contests.

538

Visual Learning

Remind the class that gauchos worked to oversee the herds of cattle. The figure depicted here roamed the huge expanse of a frontier region. Have students describe the gaucho's environment, based on this lesson. Ask them what modern devices might have displaced the gaucho at the end of the 19th century. *(Fencing and more settlement on the pampas)*

Bulletin Board

The gaucho has been a symbol of Argentinean identity since the 19th century. Introduce the idea of national identity to the class, comparing the U.S. cowboy with the Argentinean gaucho. Invite the class to find multiple images of the gaucho for a bulletin-board display on Argentinean cultural life. Suggest that they research other cultural elements of Argentina, such as the tango and troubadours, and add appropriate images to the display.

Cultural Context

In Venezuela, as in Argentina and the United States, cowhands played an important role in the nation's history. Venezuela's cowhands, called *llaneros (yah NARE os),* herded cattle and rode the plains, or *llanos (YAH nos),* in the interior of Venezuela, near the Orinoco River. During the independence wars, these cowhands fought as cavalry against the Spaniards. They helped win the war for independence from Spain.

Argentina: European Influences

Like Venezuela, Argentina was a disappointment to Spanish colonists because it lacked silver and gold. Even so, in 1860 *Argentina,* a Latin word for "silver," became the official name of the country. Today Argentina is one of South America's wealthiest nations, with resources such as iron ore, oil, and natural gas.

Buenos Aires *(BWAY nuhs AIR eez),* the capital of Argentina, is an important cultural center in South America. The city has a distinct European flavor, with spacious parks and tree-lined avenues. About 80 percent of Argentina's people live in or near a city.

Immigrants from Europe

The racial and ethnic character of Argentineans is different from that of other South American peoples. In the colonial period, there were a few Spaniards, many *mestizos,* and a small population of Africans and Native Americans. Then in the late 1800s and early 1900s, about six million Europeans moved to the farms, ranches, and factories of Argentina.

The government lured Europeans to Argentina to work as farmers and ranchers. The largest number of immigrants came from Italy and Spain. Swiss, German, and British settlers also arrived.

After the 1930s many people immigrated to Argentina from Eastern Europe. European Jews came to escape the Nazis. After World War II, more Europeans arrived. Today nearly 85 percent of the people are of European descent. Only a small number are *mestizo,* Native American, or of African descent.

Cattle, Grain, and Industry

The wealth of Argentina comes mainly from the pampas, the fertile grasslands. This flat plain is much like the prairies of North America. Gauchos, or Argentinean cowhands, work the open range (see A Moment in Time, page 538). Grains are also grown here. During the late 1800s, Argentina exported meat and grain to Europe. Beef, corn, and wheat are still important exports. Look at your shoes or billfold. The leather may come from cattle raised on the pampas.

Industry also has thrived in Argentina. Refrigeration, invented in the 1870s, made meat processing and the shipment of meat safer. Mills were built to make flour. Factories turn out cars and machinery.

From Dictatorship to Democracy

By the mid-1800s, Argentina set up a constitutional government modeled after that of the United States. One of its first presidents,

Comercial
El diario de negocios mejor informado.

▲ *The capital and main port in Argentina is Buenos Aires. Notice the ornate European-style buildings with balconies.*

▼ *A gaucho rides the range, herding beef cattle on the Argentine pampas. Most of the country's cattle and wheat come from this region.*

ECONOMICS

Critical Thinking

Remind students that the pampas, or grassy plains, are the source of Argentina's wealth. Ask them to consider how technology has made that fertile area even more profitable. (*Modern refrigeration is used to preserve beef, and improved mills process flour more efficiently.*) Have students contrast this economic base to that of Venezuela. (*Venezuela's dependence on oil is less stable, since oil is a depletable resource and crops and livestock are not. However, oil is generally worth more than crops and livestock.)*

Historical Context

The Falkland Islands are located about 300 miles off the east coast of Argentina in the Atlantic Ocean. After gaining its independence from Spain, Argentina claimed the islands in 1820. In 1833, however, the British occupied the islands and evicted the Argentineans, claiming that Great Britain had land rights. In April of 1982, the military rulers of Argentina ordered an invasion. An abrupt defeat of Argentina brought down the military government there.

Conducting a Survey

After taking office in 1983, President Alfonsín of Argentina tried to correct a formerly corrupt government. Some supporters of these reforms demanded trials of the military officials who were responsible for human-rights violations, such as torture and disappearances. This process might destabilize the government. What is more important, punishing the violators or maintaining a stable government? Have students conduct a survey and present the results to the class.

Critical Thinking

Ask students to identify factors that have made democracy difficult to establish in Venezuela and Argentina. *(Monopoly of political power by* caudillos *in Venezuela, elite rule by the few, military coups that overthrew constitutional governments in Argentina, absence of free elections for long periods)*

POLITICAL SYSTEMS

Visual Learning

Have students study the picture of the mothers of the "disappeared ones" on this page. Ask them to describe how the mothers might feel about the disappearance of their children. Students might think about why the families chose this form of protest. Discuss other ways the mothers might express their concern now that democracy has returned to Argentina. *(This form of protest appeals to basic human rights; the mothers have lost their children and are hoping for international support.)*

■ *Nearly 85 percent of Argentineans are of European descent, as opposed to* mestizo *or Native American descent.*

CLOSE

Have students complete their Venn diagrams from the beginning of the lesson and share them with the class. Ask a student to reread the Thinking Focus aloud, and encourage the class to answer it together, comparing their earlier predictions with their answers.

Domingo Sarmiento, created the public education system. For the first time, Argentina opened its schools to women. As the country thrived, foreign investors poured money into trade and business.

A period of conflict followed, however. Argentina faced economic and political crises. In 1930 a group of army officers staged a **coup** *(koo)*, or takeover of the government. After this coup, a series of undemocratic governments held power.

One military officer became a leader who would change Argentina's history. In 1946 Juan Domingo Perón *(puh ROHN)*, an army officer, was elected president. Perón's policy, called *peronismo*, helped poor city workers. He gave the workers higher pay and provided other benefits.

The workers backed Perón and adored his gifted wife, Eva Duarte de Perón, a former actress, better known as Evita *(ay VEE tuh)*. She helped women gain the right to vote in 1947. She also set up a foundation to aid the poor.

Perón was less popular after Evita died in 1952. As opposition grew, he became ruthless. He banned political parties and shut down newspapers that disagreed with him. Then in 1955 he was driven from power. Although Perón returned to power in 1973, he died soon after.

A time of violence and terror followed. In 1976 new military leaders took over. **Guerrillas** *(guh RIHL uhz)*, or small groups of fighters, organized against the government. However, the government forces crushed the guerrillas and arrested, tortured, or killed thousands. Some people have never been found; they have simply "disappeared."

In 1982 Argentina suffered a humiliating defeat by Britain in the Falklands War. The military government resigned, and in 1983 a new president was elected. The democratic leaders who followed have faced problems of debt and high prices. Argentina's recovery depends on the wise use of its natural resources and its well-educated population. ■

Mothers and grandmothers of the "disappeared ones" protest. Carrying photographs, they demand to know what has happened to their children.

■ *How does the population of Argentina differ from that of most other South American countries?*

REVIEW

1. **FOCUS** How do the ethnic groups and the sources of economic wealth of Venezuela and Argentina differ?
2. **ECONOMICS** Why did Venezuela face economic problems in the 1980s?
3. **GEOGRAPHY** Describe the geographic feature in Argentina that is similar to one in the United States. In what other ways are the two countries similar?
4. **POLITICAL SYSTEMS** What kind of rulers did Argentina have between the 1930s and the early 1980s?
5. **CRITICAL THINKING** Why do you think Argentina has a large European population but Venezuela does not?
6. **ACTIVITY** Imagine you are a European farmer who migrated to Argentina around 1900. Write a letter home telling your family about your new country and your way of life. Persuade them to join you in South America.

Homework Options

Introduce the word *diversify*, and explain that Argentina has had a more diversified economy than Venezuela. Have students write a paragraph explaining the advantages of economic diversity and the risks of depending on a single industry, using Venezuela and Argentina as examples.

Study Guide: page 93

Answers to Review Questions

1. Venezuela has a mixed ethnic population; Argentina has a high percentage of Europeans. Venezuela's primary source of wealth is oil; Argentina depends on cattle and grain.
2. When world prices for oil dropped in the 1980s, many Venezuelans lost their jobs. They responded by developing steel and aluminum industries.
3. Argentina's pampas are like our Great Plains. Wheat and cattle are important to both countries.
4. During that period Argentina's rulers were dictators or groups of military dictators.
5. In the 1800s Argentina encouraged Europeans to immigrate to work on farms and in factories. In colonial times Venezuela brought in Africans to work on plantations.
6. Students might describe the beauty of the pampas, its gauchos, or the growing city of Buenos Aires.

UNDERSTANDING ORAL REPORTS

Presenting Information

Here's Why

Oral reports are one way to share information with others. Suppose you were assigned to give an oral report about the role of Eva Duarte de Perón in gaining women's rights and aiding the poor. How would you do it?

Here's How

In Chapter 15, you read about preparing a written report. Use those steps and the steps below to prepare an oral presentation on the social programs of Eva Perón.

1. **Identify your audience.** How much does your audience already know about Eva Perón and Argentina? How much background information do they need?
2. **Identify the time limit for your presentation.** Five or ten minutes may seem like a short period of time, but if you're not prepared, five minutes in front of the class can seem like forever.

   Try reading your information aloud. How long does it take to get a sense of how much information you have? Cut back or add information so that you're close to your time limit.
3. **Create note cards to help you as you speak.** You won't be reading directly from the note cards. They will serve as guides. Try not to write long sentences on your note cards. Instead, write key words and phrases. Below are some student note cards about Eva Perón.
4. **Sharpen your memory.** The best speakers look directly at their audiences. Try to memorize as much of your information as possible, so you won't have to look at your notes as often. Eye contact holds the listeners' attention.
5. **Practice your report.** Speaking in front of people may make you nervous. Practice is the best way to help you get past your fear. At first practice your report alone. Remember these public speaking hints:
   - Keep eye contact with your audience.
   - Stand up straight.
   - Speak loudly and clearly.
   - Avoid saying "um" and "you know."

   Later, practice in front of a friend. Ask your friend to evaluate your presentation. The more you practice your report, the easier it will be to give it in class.

Try It

Imagine you have been assigned to give an oral report on the political situation in a country in Central America, such as Honduras. Your audience will be your classmates. Think about your audience. What do they already know about politics in Central America? What do they know about Honduras?

Apply It

Use the steps above to prepare an oral report about a special hobby or interest you may have. You might want to give a report about a political leader whom you admire.

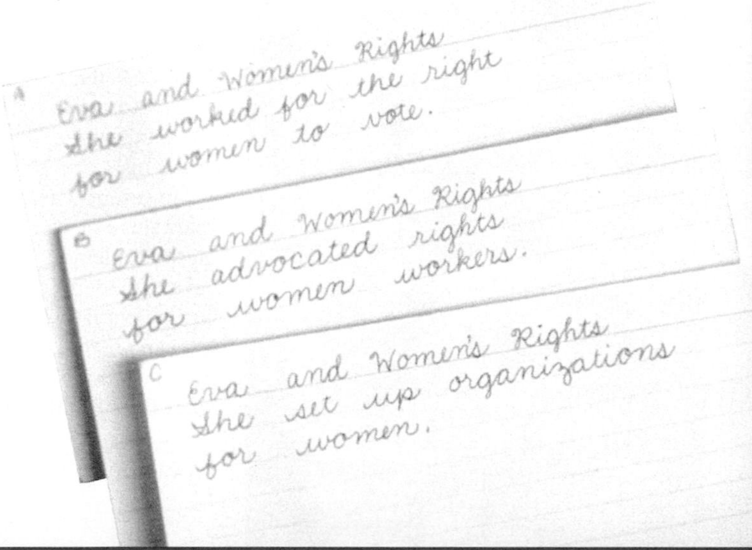
A
Eva and Women's Rights
She worked for the right
for women to vote.
B
Eva and Women's Rights
She advocated rights
for women workers.
C
Eva and Women's Rights
She set up organizations
for women.

UNDERSTANDING ORAL REPORTS

This skills feature teaches students how to prepare and deliver an oral report.

HISTORY

Study Skills

Have students read the information on Eva Perón in Lesson 2 and examine the note cards on this page. Tell students to imagine that their audience is made up of classmates who have not yet studied South America. Ask students how much background information will be needed to introduce the topic. *(Possible answers: Perón's country of origin, her birth and death dates, her role in politics, reasons for her popularity and influence with Argentinean people)*

Preparing an Oral Report

Divide students into groups. Have each group prepare a three-minute oral report entitled "The Latin American Country I Would Most Like to Visit." Have groups brainstorm possible topics for an outline and decide if the topics they have chosen will be interesting. Groups can prepare notes and select a representative to report to the class. Before the presentation, speakers can practice their reports; they should use the guidelines in this lesson to give constructive criticism.

Answers to Try It

A possible answer is that while they know about the political strife in neighboring Central American countries, they may not know anything about the situation in Honduras.

Answers to Apply It

Check to be sure that students have sufficiently narrowed their topics. Have students practice their presentations with partners.

Objective

Plan, write, and deliver an oral report. (Study Skills 3)

INTRODUCE

Read the Thinking Focus aloud. Based on what students have learned about Argentina, Venezuela, and other South American countries, have them make predictions about the types of economic and political challenges Central American nations face. Have students write down their predictions. After completing the lesson, students can revise their predictions to reflect what they have learned.

Key Terms

Vocabulary Strategies: T36–T37

migrant worker—a worker who moves from place to place to tend crops

negotiate—to discuss issues in order to reach an agreement

1475
1550
1625
1700
1775
1800
TODAY

LESSON 3

Central America

THINKING FOCUS

What common challenges do many countries of Central America face?

Key Terms

- migrant worker
- negotiate

The only thing I wish for is freedom for Indians wherever they are.

Rigoberta Menchú, 1992 Nobel Peace Prize winner

Rigoberta Menchú of Guatemala expressed this hope for her people after she was awarded the Nobel Peace Prize in 1992. It was given in honor of her work for the rights of Native Americans.

Menchú is a Mayan Indian of the Quiché *(kee CHAY)* group. Her father organized groups to protest the unfair treatment of Indian farm laborers. As a result, her parents and brother were tortured and killed by government forces in Guatemala.

Death squads killed thousands of others who rebelled against the government. Fearing for her safety, in 1981 Menchú fled to Mexico.

Countries in Turmoil

The seven countries of Central America—Guatemala, Belize, Honduras, El Salvador, Nicaragua, Costa Rica, and Panama—lie in the narrow land bridge connecting North and South America (see Atlas, page 686). Although they have much in common, each nation has its own history and faces its own problems.

In recent years some of these problems have exploded into violence. Civil wars and revolutions have torn apart El Salvador and Nicaragua. Dictators in Guatemala and Panama have ruled by terror. Many young people have lived with war all their lives. Why is this region so troubled?

This 11-year-old girl is part of a guerrilla unit in El Salvador.

Influence of History

Most of Central America—like South America—was part of Spain's empire. By the early 1800s, most countries had gained independence. Yet centuries of colonial rule had set the stage for conflict.

As in South America, a small group of people in Central America controlled most of the land and wealth. The rest of the people lived in poverty. The class system remained rigidly in place. Today a deep division between rich and poor still exists in most of these Central American nations.

Objectives

1. Explain the problems facing the people of El Salvador, Nicaragua, and Panama.
2. Describe the importance of Central America to the United States.
3. Explain why democracy has prospered in Costa Rica.

Graphic Overview

CHALLENGES
Costa Rica
Other Nations
coffee price dependency
flood of refugees
no democratic traditions
single crop economies

Central America: Major Products

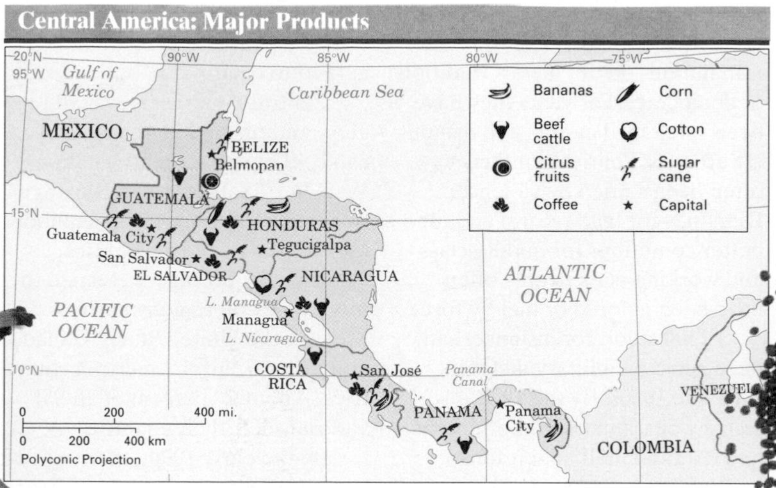

Gulf of Mexico
Caribbean Sea
MEXICO
BELIZE
Belmopan
GUATEMALA
HONDURAS
Guatemala City
Tegucigalpa
San Salvador
EL SALVADOR
NICARAGUA
L. Managua
Managua
L. Nicaragua
PACIFIC OCEAN
ATLANTIC OCEAN
COSTA RICA
San José
Panama Canal
PANAMA
Panama City
VENEZUELA
COLOMBIA
Bananas
Corn
Beef cattle
Cotton
Citrus fruits
Sugar cane
Coffee
Capital
20°N
15°N
10°N
95°W
90°W
85°W
80°W
75°W
0 200 400 mi.
0 200 400 km
Polyconic Projection

▲ *Exporting agricultural products is essential to the economies of Central American countries. Bananas and coffee beans are some of the most valuable exports in Central America. Which countries produce coffee and bananas?*

In addition, these countries have often depended on one crop. If prices for that one crop went down, the country's economy was in trouble.

The United States has long had a close connection with Central America. By the 1930s U.S. companies owned huge tracts of land there, mostly banana plantations. Two large U.S. fruit companies had the power to influence local laws.

To protect U.S. business interests, the government has sent troops to Central America many times. As recently as 1989, U.S. troops landed in Panama. They removed Manuel Noriega, the corrupt military ruler, from power. However, sending in the army has often caused bad feelings toward the United States.

The Panama Canal is another reason for U.S. involvement in this region. Built by the United States, the canal is a vital link for ships between the Atlantic and Pacific oceans. Since 1903 the Canal Zone, the land on either side of the canal, has been controlled by the United States. Then in 1977 the United States and Panama signed treaties agreeing to turn over control of the canal to Panama on December 31, 1999.

A Land-Based Economy

Crops like coffee, cocoa, and bananas, along with sugar and cotton, grow well in Central America. Coffee became a valuable export as early as the 1830s. Many workers are needed to pick plantation crops. Often they are **migrant workers,** workers who move from place to place as crops ripen.

Tropical crops have become important exports for Central America because these crops cannot be grown in cool climates. The profits from these crop sales are used to buy manufactured goods.

Many Central Americans have moved to the cities. However, about half the people of the region make their living in some way from the land. Some work in factories making wood products or processing food.

Conflicts and Civil Wars

In the past 20 years, much of Central America has been caught

DEVELOP

Copy the Graphic Overview on the chalkboard and share it with the class. Point out that both Costa Rica and neighboring countries face challenges. Tell students that the lesson will compare and contrast the struggles of most Central American countries with the relative peace and prosperity enjoyed by Costa Rica. Have students read to find reasons for these differences.

◄ *Costa Rica and Honduras produce coffee and bananas. Guatemala, El Salvador, and Nicaragua produce coffee; Panama produces bananas.*

GEOGRAPHY

Map and Globe Skills

Have students study the map on this page. Have them locate Panama. Then ask students why they think the United States chose this particular location for a major canal. *(The narrowness of the landmass at that point made it a shorter distance to have to cut through the land.)* You might also want to review here the term *isthmus,* from Chapter 10.

Access Strategy

Divide the class into two groups. One group works as a democracy, while the other is run by a military dictator. The democracy group discusses and votes on a series of choices, such as favorite musical groups, places to travel, books, or cafeteria menus. Each student has one vote (political equality), and the will of the majority rules. In the dictator group, the dictator gives his or her opinion first. Other group members may try to voice opinions, but the dictator should acknowledge them only if their opinion agrees with his or her own. The dictator can remove all group members who express opposing opinions. After 10 minutes, groups can exchange roles. Then, as a class, have democratic leaders, dictators, and other group members discuss their experiences of political participation in each group. By reminding students that democracy and dictatorship play important roles in Central America, link this exercise to the lesson.

Access Activity

Read the quote from Rigoberta Menchú on page 542. Discuss Menchú's life. Have students create a drawing depicting what they wish for themselves or for others. *(For example, students might draw symbols of peace, prosperity, or natural beauty.)* Then have students explain their drawings to the class.

SOCIAL SYSTEMS

Critical Thinking

The war-torn areas of El Salvador and Nicaragua have resulted in a flood of refugees to Costa Rica, as well as to North America. Ask students why some countries might not welcome refugees. *(Students might answer that refugees would strain the nations' economies or that some people in the host nations would be prejudiced against foreigners.)*

■ *A tropical climate allows Central American countries to grow crops that other nations want to import—coffee, fruits, bananas. The profits from these crop sales are used to buy manufactured goods.*

POLITICAL SYSTEMS

Study Skills

Make a two-column chart on the chalkboard, labeling one column *Cause* and the other column *Effect.* In the second column, list these effects of the cycle of political instability in many Central American countries: political conflicts settled by violence, a powerless middle class, and uneven distribution of land. Have students supply the causes. *(Causes for all three can be linked to military dictatorships and dependence on single crops.)*

up in violence. Most Central American nations do not have a tradition of democracy. For years they have been ruled by dictators and dishonest officials. Political conflicts have often been settled by violence. Demands for land reform and for better conditions for middle-class and working-class people often have been ignored or met by force.

El Salvador, for instance, had been ruled by military dictators since the 1930s. By the 1970s protests by peasants and labor unions had led to limited land reforms. Landowners and army officers violently opposed these reforms.

Civil war followed in El Salvador. At least 70,000 Salvadorans died in the war. Finally, in 1992, after 12 years of civil war, the government and the opposition groups signed a peace agreement and agreed to disarm.

Central America is a small region, and turmoil in one country can spill over into nearby nations. Wars in El Salvador and Nicaragua were a threat to peace in neighboring Honduras and Costa Rica. Thousands of refugees escaped to more peaceful regions, such as Mexico, the United States, Canada, and other Central American countries. About 20 percent of all Salvadorans left their country.

By the early 1990s, there was an uneasy calm in Central America. In Guatemala, government and guerrilla groups reached a truce and began to **negotiate,** or discuss the issues. Civil war was over in El Salvador. In Nicaragua, voters democratically elected a new leader. ■

■ *How has geography affected the economies of Central American countries?*

Costa Rica

Unlike governments in other Central American nations, Costa Rica's government is politically stable and democratically elected. Wealth and land have been more evenly divided than elsewhere in the region. As a result, the country has a large middle class. Costa Rica has stayed out of its neighbors' wars. In fact, it has not had an army since 1949. A civil guard keeps order.

In Central America, Costa Rica is the most Spanish in character. The people of Spanish descent have kept much of their culture.

Democratic Tradition

The roots of democracy in Costa Rica were formed during the colonial period. The land held no gold or silver. No large Native American population existed. As a result, the colonists owned small family farms. Early in the 1800s, Costa Ricans began to grow coffee beans. It was by exporting coffee that the country first became prosperous.

Costa Rica held its first free democratic elections more than 100 years ago. Except for two short periods, the nation has maintained democracy since then.

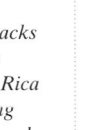

▼ *Many army barracks were converted into schools after Costa Rica replaced the standing army with a civil guard.*

Visual Learning

Ask students to study the section called Countries in Turmoil in this lesson. Then have them create a timeline of U.S. involvement in Central America in this century. *(Should include the following: 1930s—the United States manages plantations; c. 1903—the United States builds Panama Canal; 1989—the United States ousts Noriega from Panama.)*

Reader's Theater

In 1992, at age 33, Rigoberta Menchú won the Nobel Peace Prize. The story of her difficult life can be found in her autobiography, *I, Rigoberta Menchú,* published in 1983. The book is about the hardships suffered by her family and the Mayan people under brutal military dictatorship in Guatemala. The book has been translated into nearly a dozen languages, including English. Select some of the most colorful passages from her book and have students read them aloud.

Mathematics Connection

Population density can lead to conflict over land. Have students look up areas and populations for El Salvador, Costa Rica, and Nicaragua on pages 674–676 in Countries of the World and compute population densities. Tell them to divide the population by the area in square miles to determine the number of people per square mile. Round off numbers. *(Example: El Salvador's population of about 5,600,000 divided by 8,260 sq. mi. = 678 persons per square mile)*

◄ *Oscar Arias Sánchez of Costa Rica is greeted warmly by his enthusiastic supporters.*

Oscar Arias Sánchez

Oscar Arias Sánchez *(AH ryahs SAHN chez)* became president in 1986. He not only kept his country out of war, but he also negotiated a peace in the region.

In 1987 Arias persuaded the leaders of Guatemala, El Salvador, Honduras, and Nicaragua to sign a peace plan. Soon after, he was awarded the Nobel Peace Prize.

Looking Forward

The people of Costa Rica enjoy a fairly high standard of living. With a stable economy, the government has established far-reaching educational and social programs.

However, the country still depends on imports, such as wheat, corn, beans, and oil. It has had to borrow money to pay for these goods. In addition, Costa Rica's wealth depends largely on world coffee prices.

Costa Rica's population is growing rapidly. Retired people from North America have moved there because of the climate and the political stability. The civil wars of the 1980s have led many refugees from other Central American countries—especially from El Salvador and Nicaragua—to settle there. These newcomers strain the country's economy and resources.

When Arias received the peace prize, he said, "It has been given to a magnificent country and to the values we share: freedom, peace, and democracy." ■

▼ *The Pan American Games—like this one between Costa Rica and Brazil—build good relations among the nations of Central, South, and North America.*

■ *What features make Costa Rica different from other Central American countries?*

REVIEW

1. **FOCUS** What common challenges do many countries of Central America face?
2. **ECONOMICS** Why has depending on one crop for export caused problems for Central American countries?
3. **HISTORY** Why has the United States been involved in the politics and economies of many Central American countries?
4. **SOCIAL SYSTEMS** How is the social structure in most Central American countries different from that in Costa Rica?
5. **CRITICAL THINKING** Why do you think Costa Rica developed a tradition of democracy while other Central American countries did not?
6. **ACTIVITY** You have read about two people who won the Nobel Peace Prize. Imagine you are a member of the committee that awards this prize. Write two or three paragraphs describing the things you would look for in choosing a person for the Nobel Peace Prize. If you think of any specific people, name them.

ETHICS

Critical Thinking

Have students reread the statement from Oscar Arias's Nobel Peace Prize acceptance speech, which appears at the end of this lesson. Note that the first free democratic elections in all of Central America took place in Costa Rica in 1890. Ask students to find evidence in the lesson that Costa Ricans are committed to "freedom, peace, and democracy." *(Freedom: absence of military dictatorships; peace: stayed out of neighbors' wars; democracy: long tradition of free elections)*

■ *A fairly high standard of living, a long democratic tradition, political and economic stability, no large Native American population, and a large middle class make Costa Rica different from its neighbors.*

CLOSE

Examine the Thinking Focus by writing students' responses from the beginning of the lesson on the chalkboard. Invite students to revise their predictions, based on what they've learned from the lesson. Then encourage them to organize the challenges into categories such as *economic challenges, ethnic challenges,* and *political challenges.*

Answers to Review Questions

1. Most have unstable governments, often run by military dictators. Civil wars and political battles are frequent and violent. The countries depend on exports. Wealth is in the hands of a few people.
2. When a country depends on one crop, the country's economy declines if the price of that crop goes down or if the crop fails.
3. The United States wants to protect the Panama Canal and the large investments U.S. companies have made in land and in tropical-food products.
4. In Costa Rica the wealth and land are more evenly divided. As a result, there is a large middle class which is not true of its neighbors.
5. Small family farms there provided a stable economic base and were well suited to democratic government.
6. Students might use a world almanac to find names of other Nobel Prize winners.

Homework Options

Have students look up one of these products and write a paragraph describing where it was originally grown: bananas, coffee, cocoa, tobacco, cotton, corn, and sugar. Students may be surprised to learn that only cocoa and corn are native to Central and South America.

Study Guide: page 95

Chapter Review

Reviewing Key Terms

basin (p. 529)
caudillo (p. 537)
coup (p. 540)
guerrilla (p. 540)
migrant worker (p. 543)
nationalize (p. 537)
negotiate (p. 544)
pampas (p. 528)
vertical zone (p. 529)

A. Use each of the following key terms in a sentence that shows clearly what the word means.

1. caudillo
2. coup
3. nationalize
4. negotiate

B. Answer the following questions regarding selected key terms.

1. Which three key terms are related to the geography of Central and South America? Write a sentence that uses each term correctly and shows that you understand its meaning.
2. Which two terms refer to people? For each term, write a sentence that describes the role of those people in events that have occurred in present-day Central and South America.
3. Compound terms are discussed on page 264. Which key terms here are compound terms?

Exploring Concepts

A. On a separate sheet of paper, copy and complete the chart below to compare three countries of Latin America.

Country	Population Makeup	Important Products	Government
Argentina		beef, corn	
Costa Rica			
Venezuela		oil	

B. Answer each question with information from the chapter.

1. What are the major geographic features of Central and South America?
2. What river forms a huge basin in South America?
3. Why is the climate in Central and South America generally tropical? What factors influence the continent's climate?
4. Why are the rain forests so important?
5. What European colonial powers controlled Central and South America in the 1800s?
6. What three ethnic groups are blended in almost all Latin American populations?
7. What kind of changes did the oil industry bring to Venezuela?
8. What different reasons brought immigrants to Venezuela and to Argentina in the 20th century?
9. How has Argentina's geography influenced its history and economy?
10. What makes Costa Rica unusual among Central American countries? Explain differences fully.

Answers to Reviewing Key Terms

A. Sample answers:

1. The ruler of the country was a **caudillo** chosen by a group of military officers.
2. After a **coup** ended the old government, the country had new leaders.
3. A country with valuable resources like oil may **nationalize** them so that the national government, not private business, will get the profits.
4. The two sides in the civil war agreed to **negotiate** about what they each wanted.

B. Sample answers:

1. The three terms are **basin, pampas,** and **vertical zone.** The Amazon River and its tributaries form a huge **basin.** Cattle graze on the grassy **pampas.** The explorers in the Andes encountered a warm climate and tropical vegetation at the lowest **vertical zone.**
2. The two terms are **guerrilla** and **migrant worker.** Groups of **guerrillas** have fought against the governments of several Latin American countries. Some of the poorest people in Latin America are **migrant workers,** who move from place to place to tend crops.
3. **migrant worker, vertical zone**

Answers to Exploring Concepts

A. Sample answers:

Argentina: many Europeans; democracy since 1983, dictators earlier

Costa Rica: European, mostly Spanish descent; coffee; tradition of democracy

Venezuela: mixed European, Native American, African; democracy since 1958

B. Sample answers:

1. A chain of high mountains, the Andes, runs along the west side of South America. The continent also has vast grasslands, tropical rain forests, and long rivers.
2. The Amazon River and its tributaries form a huge basin in South America.
3. Central and South America are near the equator and experience a tropical climate. At higher altitudes, the climate is cooler. It is also cooler toward the southern tip of South America, which is near the Antarctic.
4. The rain forest contains types of plants and animals found nowhere else on earth.
5. Spain controlled almost all of South and Central America. Portugal held Brazil.
6. Most populations include people of European, African, and Native American descent.
7. Oil changed Venezuela from a farming country to an oil exporter. Many people gave up farming; many foreigners came to work in the oil industry.
8. People came to Venezuela mainly to work in the oil industry. People came to Argentina to work on farms and ranches and to escape war in Europe.
9. Argentina became prosperous mainly because it had huge, fertile grasslands for growing grain and raising cattle.
10. Costa Rica has a democratic tradition, a history of peace and stability, and a fairly large middle class. The country was never a destination for settlers in search of quick economic gain.

Reviewing Skills

1. Imagine that you are planning an oral report on someone who has been important in the history of Latin America, such as Simon Bolívar, Domingo Sarmiento, or Eva Perón. First, list five questions you want to answer in your report. Then list the places where you might look for this information.
2. Put the following steps for preparing an oral report in the right order:
   - Create note cards as guides.
   - Identify your audience.
   - Practice giving your report.
   - Memorize as much as you can.
   - Test your time limit by reading your information aloud.
3. Look at the Atlas map on pages 680–681. Different colors show elevation, or height above sea level. The map key shows the elevation range represented by each color on the map. Looking at South America, answer these questions: (a) At about what elevation are the highest parts of the two "highlands" regions? (b) Where are the highest parts of the Andes? (See also the political map on pages 678–679.) (c) What is the elevation of the pampas region?
4. Suppose you want to show the amount of oil exported by Venezuela between 1920 and 1990. What would be the best way to show this information?

Using Critical Thinking

1. From your reading, which country in Central or South America do you think is most like the United States? What qualities do you think make the two countries alike? How are they different?
2. How has the history of Central and South America led to deep divisions between the rich and the poor in this region? Do you think it is better for a society when most people are in the middle class rather than being very rich or very poor? Or do you think that very wealthy people would be able to look after the rest of the population? Explain your answer.
3. Depending on one crop or product—such as coffee or oil—has caused economic problems for some Central and South American countries. What would you predict these countries will do? Give evidence from the text to back up your prediction.

Preparing for Citizenship

1. **ARTS ACTIVITY** Choose any country in Central or South America and make a poster for it. Either draw your own pictures or use pictures cut from magazines to create a collage. The poster can show people, landscapes, works of art, or anything else you believe represents the country you have chosen.
2. **INTERVIEWING** If possible, talk to someone who has come to the United States from a country in Central or South America. What does this person see as the country's future?
3. **COLLECTING INFORMATION** Find and bring to class a tape cassette of music from the Andes or another part of Central or South America. Look in an encyclopedia or in library books for information about the flutes, pipes, drums, and other musical instruments that are used on the tape or played elsewhere in the region. Give a report to the class about your findings.
4. **COLLABORATIVE LEARNING** Working with your classmates, plan a meal for your class that includes foods typical of Central and South America. Your local supermarket, for example, is likely to have bananas, mangoes, papayas, and other tropical fruits and fruit juices. If anyone in your class has friends or relatives from the region, ask them for suggestions about typical and easy-to-make dishes.

Answers to Reviewing Skills

1. Questions might include: When did this person live? What did he or she do? What effect did this person have on Latin American history? What was this person like? Sources for contemporary subjects are magazines and newspapers; for historical figures, encyclopedias, biographies, and history books.
2. Identify your audience. Test your time limit by reading your information aloud. Create note cards as guides. Memorize as much as you can. Practice giving your report.
3. (a) 1,000–2,000 meters or 3,280–6,580 feet. (b) In parts of Peru, Chile, and Bolivia. (c) From 0 to 1,000 meters or 0 to 3,280 feet.
4. Students should suggest a line graph or bar graph.

Answers to Using Critical Thinking

1. In Central America, Costa Rica is most like the United States because of its long tradition of democracy. In South America, Argentina is similar to the United States because of its plains region, wheat growing, cattle ranching, and its large European population. Students should be aware of the great differences between these nations and the United States.
2. Students should mention the long-lasting effects of the colonial pattern, with a small ruling class and the mass of poor farmers or laborers. Students should recognize that the wealthy have often not looked after the rest of the population in these countries.
3. The logical prediction is that countries will continue to try to vary what they produce and import or export. Venezuela is already developing its iron ore resources.

Answers to Preparing for Citizenship

1. **ARTS ACTIVITY** Encourage students to research the country they have chosen before starting to work on the poster. Travel guides and travel magazines can provide good ideas.
2. **INTERVIEWING** Although this is a sensitive area, it can provide the class with important insights into the conditions and problems in many countries of Central and South America. Students can work in small groups to prepare a list of appropriate questions.
3. **COLLECTING INFORMATION** Give students whatever help they need in finding examples of Andean or other South American music, which is quite widely available.
4. **COLLABORATIVE LEARNING** If possible, provide class time or a lunch-time meeting when students can sample and share the meal they have assembled.

CHAPTER ORGANIZER

Chapter 24 Brazil

CHAPTER PLANNING CHART

Pupil's Edition	Teacher's Edition	Ancillaries
Lesson 1: The History of Brazil (2–3 days) Objective 1: Explain how Brazil came to be settled by the Portuguese. (History 5, 6, 7; Geography 4; Economics 3, 4) Objective 2: Describe the role of slavery in the development of Brazil. (History 8; Economics 1; Social and Political Systems 4) Objective 3: Explain how Brazil gained its independence. (History 7)	• Graphic Overview (550) • Access Strategy (551) • Access Activity (551) Critical Thinking (552) Cultural Context (552)	Study Guide (96) Map Activities (28) • Posters (5)
Understanding Critical Thinking Objective: Recognize and evaluate assumptions in decision making. (Critical Thinking 2)		Study Guide (97)
Lesson 2: The Geography and Economy of Brazil (1–2 days) Objective 1: Describe the geography and regions of Brazil. (Geography 4, 5) Objective 2: Describe the pattern of boom-and-bust in Brazil's economy. (Economics 3, 4) Objective 3: Describe the steps taken to industrialize Brazil. (Geography 5; Economics 5)	• Graphic Overview (555) • Access Activity (556) • Access Strategy (556) Geographic Context (557) Map and Globe Skills (557) • Visual Learning (558) Research (558) Writing a Journal (558) Economic Context (559) Study Skills (559) • Visual Learning (560) Political Context (560)	Study Guide (98) Discovery Journal (48, 49) Transparency (13)
Lesson 3: Brazil Today (3–4 days) Objective 1: Describe the role of the rain forest as it relates to Brazil's economic development. (History 7; Geography 5; Economics 1, 3, 4) Objective 2: Describe the three major groups that make up the population of Brazil. (History 8; Culture 2) Objective 3: Give examples of the contributions of different groups to Brazilian culture. (Culture 1, 2, 3, 6) Objective 4: Describe some new developments in Brazilian culture. (Culture 1, 5)	• Graphic Overview (562) • Access Strategy (563) • Access Activity (563) • Visual Learning (564) Music Connection (564)	Study Guide (99)
Making Decisions: Rain Forests: Preserve Them? Use Them? Objective 1: Name the issues involved in making a decision about the destruction of the rain forest. (Citizenship 5) Objective 2: Find and analyze information on the issues involved in making a decision about rain forests. (Citizenship 5)		Discovery Journal (50) Posters (8)
Chapter Review	Answers (568–569)	Tests (93–96)

* Objectives are correlated to the strands and goals in the program Scope and Sequence on pages T41–T49.

• LEP appropriate resources. (For additional strategies, see pages T32–T33.)

CHAPTER RATIONALE

Chapter 24 introduces students to the vast country of Brazil beginning with a look at the role of the Portuguese Empire during the period of European exploration. Brazil is studied within a unit that examines South American culture. The chapter begins with a discussion of Brazil's history and gradually expands into a detailed exploration of the development of the multicultural nation called modern Brazil.

Lesson 1 begins on board a caravel, a type of 15th-century ship used by the Portuguese to explore the Mediterranean and the coast of Africa. The lesson helps students understand the roots of Brazil's current culture. Discussions of Portuguese influences on the economy, religious and political life, and the blending of Indian, African, and Portuguese colonial culture help students understand modern events in Brazil.

Lesson 2 gives students a view of the diverse geography of Brazil and provides a solid foundation for further study of Brazil's economic crisis and future as a democratic country. Students are introduced to Brazil's five geographic regions—the northeast, the south, the southeast, the north, and the central west. The text discusses the cultural diversity of the people who inhabit each region. A Closer Look at the Amazon River on page 558 explores this natural wonder and gives it a human dimension. A discussion of Brazil's economy and a feature on Understanding Inflation on page 560 help students understand this difficult issue within a context to which they can easily relate.

Students are introduced to the nation's capital city, Brasília, in **Lesson 3.** Built in the 1960s, the city lies in the center of the Brazilian Highlands. Students read about the conflict between development of the rain forest and preservation of natural resources. The contributions of Indians, African Brazilians, and peoples of European ancestry are offered as a possible solution to the problems Brazil faces today.

ACTIVITIES & PROJECTS

Basic: Writing an Advertisement

Have students write an advertisement for Prince Henry's school for sailors. Have students try to persuade young people to attend the school. Some students might prefer to create a poster to advertise for a school for young explorers. (Use after Lesson 1.)

Making a Chronological List

Write the following phrases on the chalkboard (without the numbers) and ask students to number them from one through six to indicate the order in which the events took place. (Use after Lesson 1.)

3. *Napoleon Bonaparte attacks Portugal.*
5. *Princess Isabel signs the Golden Law that frees all slaves in Brazil.*
2. *Pope Alexander VI draws a Line of Demarcation that splits the non-Christian world in two.*
6. *President Collor de Mello is removed from office.*
1. *Prince Henry the Navigator starts a school for sailors.*
4. *Dom Pedro I declares Brazil independent.*

Writing a Letter

Have students study A Closer Look on page 558 before they begin this activity. Ask them to imagine that they are Brazilian Indians who have left their Amazonia homesteads to work in the city. It is harvest time and all family members have been called back to help with the crops. They've worked for a week. Ask students to write a letter to a friend in the city, telling about a typical day in the life of the Indian people. (Use after Lessons 2 or 3.)

Challenge: Research

Inform students that Brazilian *favelas* have grown to immense proportions in some sections of the cities. For example, the Rocin'Ha *favela* in Rio de Janeiro has 350,000 inhabitants. Ask students to gather more information about the daily lives of the inhabitants of these poor Brazilian communities, known as *favelas.* Direct students to encyclopedias and other reference books. They should take notes and give an oral report on the results of their research. (Use after Lesson 3.)

LEP: Making a Display

Have students do picture research on the endangered species of the Amazon rain forests. Instruct students to make copies in any form they wish—drawings, paintings, colored photocopy enlargements, clay models—and then arrange their own display of the living treasures of the rain forests. (Use after Lessons 2 and 3.)

CHAPTER PREVIEW

Ask students to look at the photographs on these facing pages and to read the captions that accompany them. Invite them to identify the different types of people mentioned or depicted in the photographs. *(Students may suggest Portuguese, Indian, African, and migrant workers.)* Ask the students what these photographs convey about Brazilian culture. *(Students may say that it is based on Portuguese, Indian, and African cultures, that people live in urban and rural settings.)*

Looking Back

Ask students to recall other countries that, as in the case of Brazil, achieved independence after a period of European colonial rule. *(Suggestions may include Egypt, Ghana, India, countries in the Caribbean, and Argentina.)*

Looking Forward

The chapter covers the physical and cultural diversity of Brazil in three lessons—The History of Brazil, The Geography and Economy of Brazil, and Brazil Today. Lesson 1 relates the history of Brazil from Portuguese colonization to the present.

Chapter 24
Brazil

Brazil is a vast and modern industrial nation with busy cities, high technology, and many natural resources. Like other South American countries, however, Brazil has had to face the challenges of poverty, crime, and political corruption. As the 20th century draws to a close, the Brazilian people are striving to fulfill their country's motto: "Order and Progress."

When the Portuguese sailors landed in Brazil in 1500, they may have met the ancestors of this Indian boy. Many Indian groups, such as the Tupí, retreated to the Amazon rain forest to escape slavery.

When the Indians could not provide enough labor, Africans were brought in to work on the big sugar cane and coffee plantations, like the one shown above.

1375 | 1500 | 1625

1500 Pedro Alvares Cabral lands on the Brazilian coast and claims the region for Portugal.

548

1492

BACKGROUND

Modern Brazil has been described as a fusion of three continents—the Americas, Africa, and Europe. Peoples from all three areas have made lasting contributions to the Brazilian way of life. The people of Brazil are proud of this legacy of cultural blending.

The Peoples of the Forest

The Brazilian Indian groups that escaped death in slavery or from European diseases, continued their close connection to the land. Many escaped to the rain forests. Until recently, however, the Indians of Brazil stood almost alone in their respect for the precious rain forests. Today, their way of life has earned widespread acclaim from people concerned about the future of the environment. In 1989, for example, a committee of rubber tappers and Indians came together as the Alliance of the People of the Forest. In part, their first declaration read as follows: "This alliance embraces all efforts to protect and preserve this immense but fragile life-system, the source of our wealth and the basis of our cultures."

The African Legacy

The enslaved Africans transported to Brazil by the Portuguese soon outnumbered the Indian peoples. This helps explain, in part, why African traditions and beliefs have had a considerable impact on modern Brazil. Today, Brazil has the largest population

Famous for its beautiful beaches and large harbor, Rio de Janeiro, settled in 1555, is the cultural capital of Brazil.

This folk art sculpture shows migrant workers from the northeast region of Brazil.

1750 | 1875 | 2000

1822 Brazil becomes independent.

1888 Slavery is abolished in Brazil.

1992 Earth Summit on world environmental problems held in Rio de Janeiro.

Today

Understanding the Visuals

Rio de Janeiro was Brazil's capital from 1763 until 1960, when the capital was moved to newly built Brasília (see page 562). Spectacular beaches and imposing mountains press against Rio from both sides. Tropical parks and gardens are found within and around the city. Ask students what features make a city a cultural capital. *(Students may suggest annual carnivals, sports, music, museums, libraries, and historical buildings.)* Tell them that all of these features are associated with Rio de Janeiro. Add that Brazilian culture is noted for its acceptance of folk art, or the art of ordinary people. Popular painting and sculpture have been little influenced by international fads and fashions.

Understanding Chronology

Ask students to look at the timeline to find the date when Brazil became independent from Portuguese rule. *(1822)* How many years elapsed between Cabral's landing and Brazilian independence? *(322 years)* How many years elapsed between Brazil's independence and the abolition of slavery? *(66 years)*

of African descendants in the Western Hemisphere.

African Brazilians are now part of a huge multicultural society. At the same time, Benedita da Silva, the first African Brazilian woman elected to Brazil's congress, speaks for many who say Brazilian society has a long way to go: "Now I'm a federal congresswoman but I am still an Afro-Brazilian woman from the favelas." Fighting for the rights of people of the *favelas,* Brazil's poorest urban communities, is the focus of much of da Silva's work.

The Legacy of Colonialism

During colonial times, in the style of the British and other colonial systems, manufacturing industries were discouraged in Brazil. This ensured that Brazilians bought Portuguese goods. In the 1950s, many years after independence, however, the Brazilian government poured foreign investment into manufacturing. Then a worldwide recession slowed Brazil's growth and left it with the largest debt of any developing country. In addition, while Brazil's industrialization program was under way, its cities expanded at a rate that could not meet the needs of millions of new migrants. Today, the federal government of Brazil is struggling to maintain democracy in the face of huge debts and internal corruption. The unique blend of people who call themselves Brazilians face a challenging future.

INTRODUCE

Tell students that Brazil was the only country in South America that was colonized by Portugal. Point out that there were more than two million Indians, or native people, living in Brazil when the first European explorers landed there. Add that more than three million enslaved peoples were brought to Brazil from Africa by the Portuguese colonists. Invite students to predict what this may mean for Brazil today. *(Students may suggest Portuguese, Indian, and African influences on language, religion, food, and culture.)* Have students read the Thinking Focus, and then tell them they will find out how the people of Brazil finally gained independence from Portugal.

Key Terms

Vocabulary Strategies: T36–T37

Line of Demarcation—an imaginary line drawing a border, or boundary, intended to divide the non-Christian world between Spain and Portugal

convert—to adopt a new religion or set of beliefs

1400
1492
TODAY

LESSON 1

The History of Brazil

THINKING FOCUS

How did Brazil gain its independence?

Key Terms

- Line of Demarcation
- convert

Prince Henry the Navigator was the driving force behind Portuguese explorations. This portrait of the prince appears in a book titled The Chronicle of the Discovery and Conquest of Guinea, *written in the mid-1400s.*

In the 1400s Portuguese explorers sailed the Atlantic Ocean on small ships called *caravels.* Their sails were marked with a red-bordered cross, a symbol of the Catholic church. They were searching for new lands and new trade routes.

When they visited a land unknown to them, the Portuguese claimed it for their king. Stone markers, called *padrões (pa DROENS),* were placed on the ground for everyone to see. The Portuguese believed that this land now belonged to them.

Prince Henry the Navigator (1394–1460), the son of the king of Portugal, supported the search for new lands. He started a school for sailors in 1419. Prince Henry's school trained sailors to find a sea route to Asia. He also wanted Portugal to profit from the gold found in West Africa. Sailors at his school learned to read maps and use the compass. They made voyages farther and farther south along the African coast.

Spain was also interested in trade. Over the years competition between Portugal and Spain grew fiercer. Soon the Pope had to step in to keep peace between these two Catholic powers.

In 1492 and 1493, Pope Alexander VI drew a **Line of Demarcation** that split the non-Christian world in two. Spain could have the lands on the west side of the line. Portugal could have the lands on the east side of the line. As a result, most of Brazil was placed in Portugal's half of the world.

Objectives

1. Explain how Brazil came to be settled by the Portuguese.
2. Describe the role of slavery in the development of Brazil.
3. Explain how Brazil gained its independence.

Graphic Overview

Cabral Claims Brazil for Portugal → Portuguese Settlers Enslave Indians and Africans → Dom Pedro I Rules Independent Brazil → Brazil Becomes a Democracy

Portuguese Exploration and Settlement

Vasco da Gama made the long ocean trip from Portugal around Africa to India and back, from 1497 to 1499. Thus, nearly 40 years after Prince Henry's death, Portugal had a sea route to Asia. The Portuguese explorer Admiral Pedro Álvares Cabral began another trip to India in the spring of 1500. On the way south, he sailed off course to the west. He reached a land the Portuguese had not visited before and named it *Terra da Vera Cruz*—the Land of the True Cross.

Later explorers found trees there that could be used to make a red dye. The Portuguese called the trees brazilwood. Soon people began to call the land *Terra do Brasil (TEHR rah du brah ZEEL)*, the Land of the Brazilwood. This was later shortened to Brazil.

Brazil: Geographic Regions

80°W
70°W
60°W
50°W
40°W
Equator 0°
10°S
20°S
30°S
VENEZUELA
COLOMBIA
GUYANA
SURINAME
FRENCH GUIANA
ECUADOR
Belém
Manaus
Amazon R.
AMAZON BASIN
Olinda
Recife
BRAZIL
PERU
PARECIS RANGE
São Francisco R.
BRAZILIAN HIGHLANDS
Salvador
Brasília
PLATEAU OF MATO GROSSO
BOLIVIA
Belo Horizonte
Rio de Janeiro
CHILE
PARAGUAY
São Paulo
Santos
ARGENTINA
URUGUAY
North
Northeast
South
Southeast
Central West
Capital city
0 300 600 mi.
0 300 600 km
Azimuthal Equal-Area Projection

This map shows Brazil's five different regions. Which regions might the Brazilians have settled first? Why?

Making Contact

The Tupí Indians had lived and worked in Brazil for thousands of years before Cabral. The Indians' first meeting with the Portuguese was described in a letter to King Manuel in Portugal.

> *They carried in their hands bows with their arrows. All came boldly towards the boat, and Nicolau Coelho made a sign to them that they should lay down their bows, and they laid them down. . . . He gave them only a red cap and a cap of linen, which he was wearing on his head, and a black hat. And one of them gave him a hat of long bird feathers with a little tuft of red and grey feathers like those of a parrot.*
>
> From the letter of Pero Vaz de Caminha to King Manuel, written at Porto Seguro, Brazil, May 1, 1500

This detail from an early Portuguese map shows the brazilwood trees that gave the country its name. What product came from the brazilwood trees?

These good feelings didn't last long. The Portuguese soon began to enslave the Indians as a source of cheap labor for their plantations.

DEVELOP

Tell students that the Portuguese were not really looking for land in the Americas when they landed in Brazil. Even after they arrived, they did not consider it very important for many decades. Brazil did eventually become colonized by Portugal. Ask if students can recall other parts of the world that were colonized by Europeans. *(Students may suggest the Caribbean, Africa, North America, or India.)* Instruct students as they read this lesson to follow the stages that led Brazil from colonization to independence.

Students may suggest that the Portuguese settlers would have first settled along the coastal areas. The map shows that many cities were founded on the Brazilian coast.

Red dye was extracted from brazilwood trees.

Access Strategy

Begin a discussion about the advantages and disadvantages of political independence. Invite students to give reasons why some American colonists wanted independence from Britain. *(Students may suggest the desire to rule themselves, dislike of the British monarchy, new ideas of the social contract between people and government, and the requirement to pay high taxes on British goods.)*

Explain that the road to independence for the people of Brazil was similar in some respects and different in other respects from the North American experience. Ask students to keep notes about these similarities and differences as they work through this lesson.

Access Activity

Copy the Graphic Overview on the chalkboard or display it on an overhead projector. Invite students to use the information in the Overview to help them identify the major stages of Brazilian history from European settlement to independence. *(Students may suggest Portuguese exploration, colonization, slavery, monarchy, abolishment of slavery, and democracy.)*

CULTURE

Visual Learning

Ask students to study the pie chart on this page. Ask these questions: What information does the pie chart provide? *(The percentage of slaves compared to the rest of the population of Brazil in 1818)* Which group was the largest segment of the population? *(Slaves)* Suggest that students convert the information in the pie chart to a bar graph.

■ *Admiral Pedro Álvares Cabral; he was bound for India.*

BELIEF SYSTEMS

Visual Learning

Have students study the sculpture by Aleijadinho *(ah lay zha DEEN yu)* shown on this page, and ask a volunteer to read the caption. Since they know that this is a biblical figure and that it is located in a church, ask students what these facts imply about Brazilian culture. *(Religion is an important part of the culture.)*

➤ *The owners of early plantations, like this coffee plantation outside São Paulo, depended on slave labor. Use the chart to compare the percentage of slaves to the rest of the population of Brazil in 1818.*

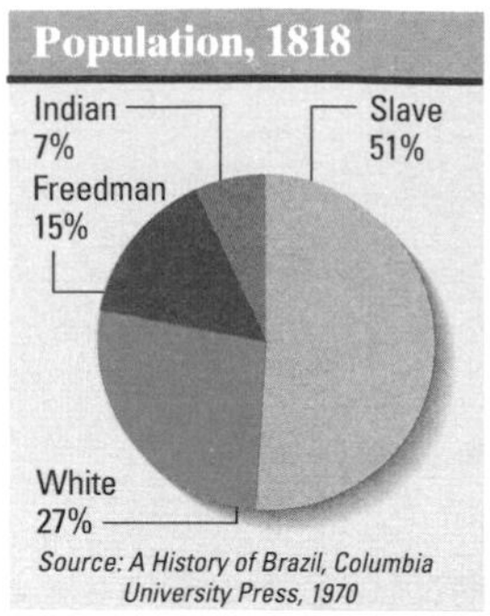
Population, 1818
Indian 7%
Slave 51%
Freedman 15%
White 27%
Source: A History of Brazil, Columbia University Press, 1970

How Do We Know?

HISTORY *One way we know that slaves were treated badly is from advertisements for runaway slaves in 19th-century Brazilian newspapers. Descriptions of runaway slaves nearly always included injuries resulting from hard work or punishment.*

■ *Who was the first Portuguese explorer to land in Brazil? What was his original destination?*

Slavery and Settlement

About two to five million Indians lived in Brazil in 1500. In less than a century, two-thirds of the Indians were dead. Hundreds of thousands died working for the Portuguese as slaves.

The first permanent Portuguese colony was founded in 1532 at São Vicente, near the present-day city of Santos. Other Portuguese colonists settled what are now the cities of Salvador, São Paulo *(sown POW lu),* and Rio de Janeiro *(REE u dee zhuh NAI ru).*

Along with the first Portuguese settlers came Jesuits. They tried to make the Indians **convert,** or change, from their own religions to Catholicism.

While the number of Indians in Brazil grew smaller and smaller, Portuguese landowners there still wanted people to work on their large plantations. The Portuguese began to use slaves from Africa. They brought about three and one-half million Africans to Brazil during more than three centuries of slave trading. ■

Brazilian Independence

The American Revolution gave Brazilians the idea of rebelling against their Portuguese rulers. In 1789 the rebels were led by a cavalry officer and part time dentist called Tiradentes *(tee ruh DEHN tees),* the Tooth Puller. The rebels failed, and Tiradentes was put to death.

From Colony to Country

In the early 1800s, the French ruler Napoleon Bonaparte had conquered much of Europe. In 1807 he turned his armies toward Portugal. To escape Napoleon, the Portuguese royal family fled to Brazil. There Prince Dom João *(dahm zhwown)* took over the government. He made changes that made Brazil more independent. Brazil became the center of the Portuguese Empire.

In 1821 things changed. To stop unrest in Portugal, Dom João, now king, had to return there to rule. João's son, Dom Pedro, stayed to govern Brazil. In Portugal, parliament tried to undo most of

➤ *This sculpture of the biblical prophet Daniel was created by 18th-century master sculptor Aleijadinho. It stands in a church near the historic city of Ouro Prêto.*

Critical Thinking

Have students prepare a presentation that Dom Pedro I might have used to justify his declaration of Brazil's independence. The presentation could take the form of a speech, a letter to the king of Portugal, or a letter to the people of Brazil. Suggest that they compare the U.S. Declaration of Independence with their own creations.

Cultural Context

You may wish to provide students with some background information about the creator of the sculpture pictured on this page. Born of a Portuguese carpenter and an African slave in 1738, António Francisco Lisbôa was one of Brazil's greatest artists. He is always called O Aleijadinho, or "The Little Cripple," because of a disease, probably leprosy, that twisted his legs, disfigured his face, and crippled his hands.

In spite of his physical challenges, Aleijadinho created larger-than-life sculptures of Old Testament prophets, as well as many other biblical images. The faces and bodies of Aleijadinho's statues are notable for the ornate way they convey emotion.

Though he never left Brazil or received a formal education, Aleijadinho learned about art from books and missionaries. Today his works are considered among the finest examples of baroque art in the world.

João's reforms. The Brazilians became angry with Portugal.

Dom Pedro took the side of the Brazilians. When an order came for him to return to Portugal, he refused to go. On September 7, 1822, with the words "Independence or death!" Dom Pedro declared Brazilian independence. Unlike many other South American countries, Brazil had become free with little bloodshed.

Pedro I ruled Brazil for only a short time, but his son, Pedro II, ruled for 49 years. Pedro II's long reign improved farming, trade, and business. He also worked to keep political unity. However, slavery was still legal.

The government had been slowly working to end slavery. In 1850 the slave trade became illegal. In 1871 a law was passed that freed all children born to slaves. However, Pedro II needed the help of the big plantation owners to stay in power. The plantation owners used slaves to keep their plantations running.

In 1888, while Pedro II was on vacation in Europe, his daughter Princess Isabel was left in charge. She signed the Golden Law. This law freed all the slaves in Brazil. The landowners were angry because they were not paid for the loss of their slaves. They stopped supporting Pedro II, and the next year he was overthrown.

Movement Toward Democracy

When Pedro II's rule ended, Brazil became a republic. It has had several constitutions, some modeled on the Constitution of the United States. However, dictators have ruled Brazil until recently.

This pattern seemed to change with the election of Fernando Collor de Mello *(COH lawr dee MEHL lu)* as president in 1990. He was popular with the people of his country when first elected. Improving trade with other countries and helping Brazilian businesses to grow were just two of his important achievements. He also stopped Brazil's nuclear bomb program, helped the Indians, and started to save the rain forest.

In the fall of 1992, however, the government discovered that the president had broken the law. He was legally removed from office. This peaceful change in government gave Brazilians hope that they finally had a real democracy. ■

Some farmers, like this woman, are very wealthy and live in fine homes on their plantations.

■ *Why do many Brazilians have hope for a democratic government?*

REVIEW

1. **FOCUS** How did Brazil gain its independence?
2. **CULTURE** Why did Prince Henry the Navigator start his school for sailors?
3. **HISTORY** What effect did the arrival of the Portuguese have on the Native American population of Brazil?
4. **CRITICAL THINKING** Pedro II was afraid to abolish slavery because he needed the support of big landowners to stay in power. After his daughter Princess Isabel abolished slavery in 1888, the empire was overthrown. Do you think that Isabel was right or wrong to abolish slavery? Explain your answer.
5. **WRITING ACTIVITY** Imagine you are Princess Isabel and you have just signed the Golden Law. Write a letter to your father, Pedro II, explaining why you signed the law in spite of the anger of the landowners.

■ *Because the people were able to remove President Collor legally, without causing the government to fall, many Brazilians feel that democracy has finally come to Brazil.*

CLOSE

Have students reread the Thinking Focus. Instruct them to respond to the question by creating a class timeline of events leading to the independence of Brazil. Provide mural paper and markers, or have students work on the chalkboard. Then display the Graphic Overview on an overhead projector—or copy it on a chalkboard—and suggest that students compare their timelines to the entries on the Overview chart.

Answers to Review Questions

1. Brazil achieved independence in 1822, when Dom Pedro, son of the king of Portugal, declared it independent.
2. Prince Henry wanted access to trade with Asia. He wanted to find gold in West Africa, and he wanted to claim new lands for Portugal.
3. The Portuguese enslaved the Native Americans. In less than a century, two-thirds of the Indian population was dead from cruel treatment.
4. Students' answers should show an awareness of the importance of human rights and political stability.
5. Students' letters should show an understanding of why the government would want to end slavery despite the anger of the powerful landowners.

Homework Options

Tell students to imagine that they are Portuguese sailors who have just landed in 16th-century Brazil. Ask them to write a brief essay describing how they would explain their presence to the Brazilian Indians they have met.

Study Guide: page 96

UNDERSTANDING CRITICAL THINKING

This skills feature asks students to identify some of the assumptions made by the Portuguese when they first came to Brazil. It also asks students to identify assumptions they themselves make.

HISTORY

Critical Thinking

Ask students to state their assumption about the Portuguese view of the Brazilian Indians. *(Possible answer: The Portuguese thought the Indians were less than human.)* Then ask students to identify the basis of this assumption. *(Possible answer: The Portuguese took the Indians' land and enslaved them.)*

Have volunteers test the assumption by rereading Lesson 1 to find facts that support or refute it. Then ask them to revise the assumption, if necessary, to fit the facts. *(For example, students might note that the Jesuits tried to convert the Indians, which is evidence that the Jesuits considered the Indians human. A revised statement of the assumption could be as follows: The Portuguese knew the Indians were human, but they were so desperate for cheap labor that they enslaved them anyway.)*

UNDERSTANDING CRITICAL THINKING

Recognizing Assumptions

Here's Why

Suppose you are in charge of ordering food for a special after-school event. You choose to serve pizza. Your decision has been made based on an assumption: most students like to eat pizza.

An assumption is an idea that is accepted as fact without proof or demonstration. Most assumptions can be proved either true or false, depending on the facts.

Correct assumptions can help you make sound decisions quickly when you aren't able to gather all the facts. Incorrect assumptions, on the other hand, can cause you to make poor and even harmful decisions.

Here's How

Suppose you want to identify some of the assumptions made by the Portuguese when they first came to Brazil. You can use the following steps to help you identify and evaluate their assumptions.

1. **Put the assumption into words.** In Lesson 1 you read about the Portuguese treatment of the Brazilian Indians. What assumptions do you think the Portuguese settlers made about the Indians? You might say the Portuguese assumed that the Indians had no rights to the land.
2. **Identify the basis of the assumption.** Think about why people hold certain assumptions. Many assumptions are based on experience. Others are an unquestioned part of a culture or set of beliefs. Portuguese assumptions were based on their cultural beliefs.
3. **Check assumptions for accuracy.** Always try to test assumptions against accurate information. In Lesson 3 you will read many facts about the Brazilian Indians. You will read about the many ways in which they helped the Portuguese adapt to life in a tropical climate. These facts show that the Indians had a dynamic culture and held strong beliefs about the land.

Try It

Many people are concerned about resources. What assumption might you have made about the people who are trying to protect the rain forests of Brazil? Follow the three steps listed in Here's How to identify and test your assumption.

Apply It

Write a sentence or two identifying the assumptions that might have led to each situation listed below. Explain the basis of each assumption.

1. The radio announcer says it is going to rain tonight. You decide to leave your windows open anyway.
2. You are going camping at a campground you've never been to before. It's the middle of summer. You decide to bring insect repellent.

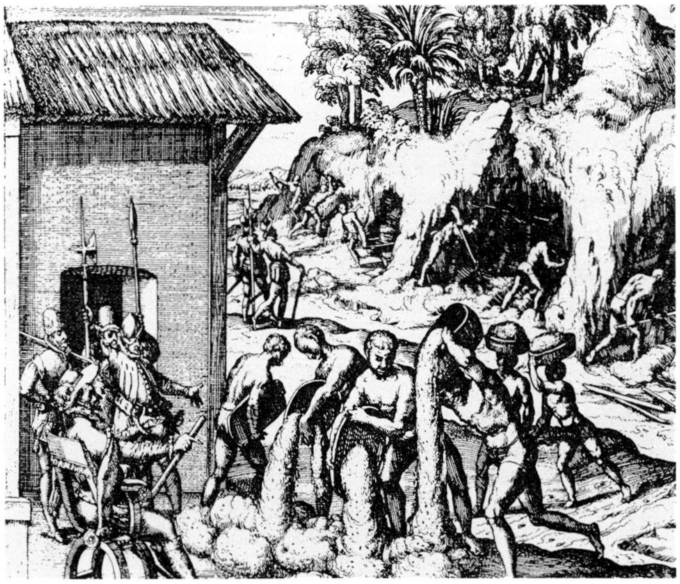

Objective

Recognize and evaluate assumptions in decision making. (Critical Thinking 2)

Answers to Try It

Be sure that students correctly identify and evaluate their assumptions. Possible answer: Students may have made the assumption that only naturalists were involved in the effort to save the rain forest. From their reading, they will find that workers, such as rubber tappers, and the local Indian populations also want to preserve the forests.

Answers to Apply It

Assumption 1: The radio announcer is wrong. This assumption may be based on earlier forecasts that weren't right. Assumption 2: There will be insects at the campground. This assumption may be based on previous camping trips made during the summer.

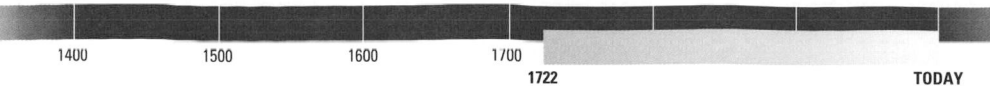

1400 1500 1600 1700 1722 TODAY

L E S S O N 2

The Geography and Economy of Brazil

A group of men struggle through a dense forest. Parrots cry in the branches overhead. An Indian slave stops to listen. African slaves carry heavy loads of supplies.

The men leading this group are called *bandeirantes (bahn dee RAHN tehs). Bandeirantes* means "flag bearers" in Portuguese. They are named after soldiers who carried banners, or flags, into battle.

Many of these men were once soldiers in São Paulo. They have tired of barracks life and poor pay. They hope to get rich quickly in the areas of Brazil that Europeans have not yet explored. They are often cruel, but their raw courage is undeniable. They are making trails that other, more respectable settlers will follow later:

> Sometimes they fell upon the land and sometimes upon man. Sometimes they went in search of gold and sometimes in search of slaves. But one thing they did do was to discover huge tracts of land—land which they did not cultivate and which, it might be, they left more of a desert than it was before. . . .
>
> Euclides da Cunha, *Rebellion in the Backlands*

THINKING FOCUS

Why does Brazil have serious economic problems in spite of its many exports and natural resources?

Key Terms

- boom-and-bust
- capital
- inflation

Brazil is a huge country with a variety of terrains. What are some physical features of Brazil visible in this picture?

INTRODUCE

Tell students that Brazil is larger than the continental United States. Ask them to list some of the physical features and climate found in the United States. *(Students may suggest the seasonal changes; warm, humid swamp regions; midwestern farmland; flat, dry plains; dense forests; deserts; and mountains.)* Point out that Brazil is equally diverse in its climate and terrain. Then ask students to read the Thinking Focus aloud, and tell them to look for answers as they read the lesson.

Key Terms

Vocabulary Strategies: T36–T37

boom-and-bust—a rapid expansion in economic activity, followed by a rapid decline

capital—money used to start, or invest, in businesses

inflation—a continuing rise in prices due to an increase in available money or to rising costs of the materials needed to make goods

Physical features include highlands or plateaus, forests, and brush vegetation.

Graphic Overview

Pre-industrialization
brazilwood
coffee
rubber
gold
sugar
Post-industrialization
military weapons
soybeans
gold and metal ores
cocoa
orange juice
coffee
BRAZIL'S MAJOR EXPORTS

Objectives

1. Describe the geography and regions of Brazil.
2. Describe the pattern of boom-and-bust in Brazil's economy.
3. Describe the steps taken to industrialize Brazil.

DEVELOP

Tell students that many factors, such as geography, culture, and technology, affect the economy of a country. Ask them how a country's geography affects its economy. *(Students may suggest the kinds of crops grown; that a shortage of natural resources will mean a country must buy some products from other countries; an abundance of natural resources could mean that the country could export these resources or products made from these resources.)* Point out that different cultures may use similar environments in very different ways. Then, as they read this lesson, suggest students list ways that Brazil's geography affects its economy.

➤ *Students' responses may include that having a good education helps one obtain a good job.*

➤ *Students' responses may point out that São Paulo is the center of Brazil's coffee industry and that the city has the capital to invest in new businesses.*

The Geography of Brazil

Brazil is the largest country in South America. It is the world's fifth largest country, stretching across nearly half of South America. Brazil can be divided into five regions: the northeast, the south, the southeast, the north, and the central west. (See the map on page 551.)

The Northeast

The population of the northeast is largely African Brazilian. The 1,800-mile São Francisco River is the major source of water for the region. Today areas of dry land called *sertão (SEHR town)* cover the region. Most of the *sertão* is flat and dry, with few trees, and it is hard to make a living here. Some people do raise cattle. Others work on the cocoa and sugar cane plantations along the Atlantic coast. These large farms created Brazil's first big cash crop—sugar.

Times of drought and flooding have made this region one of the poorest in the country. For example, in 1984 a drought that had lasted for more than five years ended with heavy floods. These natural disasters forced thousands of people in the northeast to move to Brazil's crowded cities.

Although poor, northeastern Brazil is known for its history and culture. Cities like Recife *(reh SEE fe)* and Olinda *(oh LEEN dah)* reflect Brazil's rich past. These cities are filled with art treasures and historic churches.

➤ *There is a large and thriving community of Japanese in Brazil. They came to Brazil in search of a better life. How does education help people advance economically?*

The South and Southeast

The south is the smallest of Brazil's five regions. It is also the only region that has four seasons. Many people from Europe moved to this region because of its mild climate. Today southern Brazil

▼ *São Paulo is one of Brazil's fastest growing cities. It is also the largest. What makes São Paulo a good industrial city? See the Minipedia, pages 660–673, for the worldwide ranking of Brazil's cities.*

Access Activity

Have students examine the map of Brazil on page 551, in Lesson 1. Then write on the chalkboard the five geographic regions: north, south, central west, northeast, and southeast. You may want to use a wall map of South America. Invite a volunteer to point out each of these five regions for the rest of the class.

Access Strategy

Extend the Access Activity by asking students to form groups, representing each of Brazil's five regions, to play "Ask the Question" on the subject of Brazil's geography and resources. Instruct students to begin by comparing the map of Brazil's resources and states on page 557 to the map of Brazil's geographic regions on page 551. Tell the groups to form answers to questions to ask another group or "region." Start them off with sample questions, such as these: "Which region contains rubber and gold?" *(The Amazon Basin)* "The capital city of Brasília is in which region?" *(Central west)*

Brazil: Resources and States

80°W
70°W
60°W
50°W
40°W
30°W
0° Equator
10°S
20°S
30°S
VENEZUELA
COLOMBIA
GUYANA
SURINAME
FRENCH GUIANA
ECUADOR
PERU
BOLIVIA
CHILE
PARAGUAY
ARGENTINA
URUGUAY
BRAZIL
PACIFIC OCEAN
ATLANTIC OCEAN
Roraima
Amapá
Amazonas
Pará
Maranhão
Ceará
Rio Grande do Norte
Paraíba
Pernambuco
Alagoas
Sergipe
Piauí
Bahia
Acre
Rondônia
Tocantins
Mato Grosso
Goiás
Distrito Federal
Minas Gerais
Espírito Santo
Mato Grosso do Sul
São Paulo
Rio de Janeiro
Paraná
Santa Catarina
Rio Grande do Sul
Belém
São Luís
Manaus
Pôrto Velho
Recife
Salvador
Brasília
Goiânia
Belo Horizonte
Rio de Janeiro
São Paulo
Pôrto Alegre
Amazon R.
Negro R.
Solimões R.
Marañón R.
Juruá R.
Purus R.
Madeira R.
Tapajós R.
Xingu R.
Branco R.
Tocantins R.
Araguaia R.
São Francisco R.
Paranaíba R.
Rio Grande
Paraná R.
Paraguay R.
Uruguay R.
Cattle
Coffee
Sugar cane
Soya beans
Rubber
Gold
Hydroelectric power
0 300 600 mi.
0 300 600 km
Azimuthal Equal-Area Projection

▲ *As this map shows, Brazil is a nation rich in resources. What are the three most common resources in Brazil? Where are they found?*

shows traces of Germany, France, Poland, Italy, and Switzerland in its buildings, food, and music.

The major landforms in the south are a low mountain range covered with evergreen forests and a flat grassland called the pampas. Most of Brazil's cattle are raised on the pampas. The south is also the site of the world's largest hydroelectric plant.

The southern regions are the engines that drive Brazil's economy. São Paulo, Rio de Janeiro, and Belo Horizonte *(BAY loh hawr ah ZAHT ee)* are here. They are the country's three largest cities. Most of Brazil's businesses are based here. Much of the world's coffee grows in the rich, red soil of São Paulo state. The southeast is rich in minerals and gems. Forty-four percent of Brazil's population now lives in this region. The state of São Paulo has the largest Japanese population outside Japan.

The North and Central West

Brazilians view their northern and western regions as the land of the future. The north includes Amazonia, a land of rain forests and rivers. The Amazon is the largest river in Brazil and, indeed, the largest on the earth. Along with the rain forest the river is a very important natural resource. It holds about one-fifth of the earth's fresh water. (See A Closer Look at the Amazon River on page 558.)

The central west region on the Central Plateau is covered with

GEOGRAPHY

Visual Learning

Have students recall each of Brazil's geographic regions. *(Northeast, south, southeast, north, central west)* List the names on the chalkboard. Then ask students to make a chart that lists the geographic features of each of these regions. *(Northeast: São Francisco River, sertão; south: evergreen forests, pampas; southeast: rich soil, mineral resources; north: Amazon River, rain forests; central west: plateau, brush, fertile soil, swampland)*

◄ *Cattle in the south, central west, and southeast are Brazil's most common resource, followed by sugar cane in the south. Rubber in the north and coffee in the northeast, south, and southeast are the third most common resources.*

Geographic Context

Help students understand the ways the Brazilian government is trying to meet the challenges of industrialization. Brazil is one of the richest countries in the world in terms of mineral wealth. However, much of its mineral resources are buried beneath dense rain forests, and extreme tropical-weather conditions have leached the land, obscuring evidence of trace minerals.

Many of Brazil's mineral resources are great distances from markets and ports. The Brazilian government has had to borrow massive amounts of money from foreign investors to build the necessary transportation routes and energy sources to make mining economical. In 1984 the government opened the gigantic Tucurui Dam in Amazonia, where one of the world's largest deposits of iron ore is mined. The Itaipu Dam, the world's largest, was opened that same year to service the industrial needs of both São Paulo and Rio de Janeiro.

Map and Globe Skills

Have students examine the map on this page. Ask how land use differs from west to east in Brazil. *(Students may suggest that the west, or Amazon region, is much less developed, has less hydroelectric power, and has less access to the coast.)*

Note: You may wish to refer to this feature when you discuss the illustration of the rain forest on page 561.

GEOGRAPHY

Visual Learning

Explain the importance of preserving the Amazon region by planning an "ecosystem" class project. Tell students that soil and plant life are delicately balanced and that every living thing depends on another for its existence. Bring in, or invite students to help collect, pictures of plants and animals found in the rain forests. Ask them what the wildlife of the rain forests, such as the bird and the frog in the photographs on this page, depends on for its existence. *(Students may suggest plants, insects, grubs, trees.)* Create a mural with the pictures collected in class. For additional ideas for the project, suggest that students study the illustration of the rain forest on page 561.

More About the Amazon River
The Amazon is the greatest river in South America; it is the largest in the world in volume and in the area of its drainage basin. Its almost 4,000-mile length is a distance nearly equivalent to that between New York City and Rome. Its source is high in the Andes, about 100 miles from the Pacific Ocean, and it empties into the Atlantic.

A CLOSER LOOK

The Amazon River

The Amazon begins as a stream high in the Andes. It flows across Brazil, transporting more water than any other river on the earth. Every hour it empties more than 170 billion gallons of water into the Atlantic Ocean. The river winds through rain forests, where the Indians grow many crops, including yams, corn, manioc, and medicinal herbs. Their ancient farming methods renew, rather than destroy, the forests.

Wildlife by the millions thrives in the river and forests—insects, birds, monkeys, frogs, eels, water snakes, fish, and more.

On dugout canoes, hollowed out of tree trunks, the Indians travel the river and its tributaries.

Visual Learning

Have students look closely at the frog in the photograph on this page. Ask them what purpose might the stripes and spots of color on its body have. *(Probably protective coloration)* Invite students to suggest two uses of the Amazon portrayed by the photograph of the girl in the dugout. *(Students may suggest transportation or fishing.)*

Research

Suggest that students research the early European exploration of the Amazon. One of the first European explorers of the mighty river was Spanish adventurer Francisco de Orellana, who named the river. Suggest that some students might compile a list of Amazing Amazon Facts. The list can begin with the facts that, besides ranking first in volume and area of drainage basin, the Amazon has 1,000 known tributaries, and carries one-fifth of all the flowing water in the world.

Writing a Journal

Ask students to write an entry about a typical day in the life of an Amazon family for a group journal. Point out that although the family may lack many of the labor-saving conveniences of an urban family, their life is likely to have advantages unavailable to urban and suburban people in the United States. Have students brainstorm what these advantages might be. *(Students may suggest freedom from urban traffic jams and crime; closeness to wildlife and exotic animals.)*

brush and small trees. It has rich, red soil that is good for farming. To encourage Brazilians to move to this region, the government began building a new city, called Brasília *(Brah ZIL yah),* there in the 1950s. In 1960 it became the capital of Brazil.

In the 1950s the government also built the Belém *(beh LEHM)* Brasília Highway to connect the northeast to Brasília. The Trans-Amazonian Highway was built in the 1970s to cross the Amazon rain forest at Brazil's widest point.

The Panatal is a low swampland off the Central Plateau. Between October and April, heavy rains flood this area. More than 350 kinds of fish and exotic plants can be found in this isolated region. ■

■ *Which of Brazil's five regions drives the economy? What features give it this power?*

■ *The south and southeast can be considered the economic engines of Brazil because Brazil's largest cities are located there, along with most of its businesses. These regions are also the center of Brazil's important coffee industry and are rich in mineral resources.*

The Economy of Brazil

Thousands of settlers poured into Brazil's interior in search of riches, after gold was discovered there in 1722. A century later the gold was gone. The gold boom had gone bust.

A Boom-and-Bust Economy

The gold rush is only one example of the **boom-and-bust** pattern of the Brazilian economy. In a boom-and-bust cycle, a new product first brings high profits. People and businesses rush to invest in the new product. Often, they borrow money to do so. When the product stops bringing in big profits, many people lose all their money and the economy is weakened.

In the 1500s and 1600s, there was a sugar boom in Brazil. Brazil was the number one exporter of sugar in the world. Then Caribbean plantations began to produce sugar more cheaply than Brazilian plantations. The Brazilian sugar market failed, or crashed.

In the late 1800s, there was a sudden boom in Brazilian rubber. Then rubber trees were planted in British colonies in Asia. Rubber from countries such as Malaysia quickly won the largest share of the world market. By 1913 the price of rubber was less than one-fourth of what it had been in 1910. Many Brazilian rubber merchants went bankrupt. Wealthy communities in the Amazon became ghost towns.

Coffee was also an important crop and major export in the 19th century. The families who controlled Brazil's coffee crop also controlled its land and politics. Thus, changes in world coffee prices affected not only Brazil's economy but also its politics.

Industrial Development

From the 1930s on, Brazil's leaders worked to end the ups and downs of a boom-and-bust economy. Although sugar, rubber, coffee, and gold mining had promised a better future, the dreams had not come true.

◄ *Rubber tappers like this worker took part in the great rubber boom of the late 19th century.*

Across Time & Space

Like the Brazilian government, the U.S. government once encouraged its people to settle the West by offering cheap land and supporting the building of railroads. Many American Indians were driven from their homelands, and the buffalo that once covered the Great Plains nearly became extinct.

HISTORY

Critical Thinking

Brazil is not the only economy to suffer from boom-and-bust economic cycles. Regions of the western United States experienced boom-and-bust during the gold, silver, and oil rushes, and during searches for other resources in the late 19th century. In the long term, few people make money from these booms. Still, thousands of people rush to get involved. Ask students why so many people are willing to risk their money, time, and sometimes even their lives in such ventures. *(Students may suggest that people convince themselves that the boom will never end and that if it does, they will be among the few to make money.)*

Economic Context

To help students understand the importance of rubber to the economy of Brazil, tell them that Indians used rubber for bottles and boots before the Portuguese arrived. Rubber did not, however, become a major export for Brazil until it was needed for automobile tires in the late 19th century.

Manaus, a remote city situated about 960 miles (or 1,600 kilometers) into the Amazonian interior, was the center of the rubber boom. It had the first electric public transport system in South America and the first telephone system in the Amazon. Every modern convenience— banks, luxury hotels, and an opera house—was available to the rubber "barons."

By the early 1900s, Manaus had a population of more than one million. Five thousand people arrived each week to take advantage of the boom. But when British rubber came on the market, many Brazilian rubber families lost everything, and Manaus could not even afford to light its streets.

Study Skills

Gold is believed to be one of the first metals used by human beings. Ask students to prepare fact sheets with drawings or photographs showing some aspect of gold. Some topics might include the history of gold, industrial and medical uses of gold, famous gold rushes, the role of gold in currencies, and myths and legends about gold.

ECONOMIC SYSTEMS

Critical Thinking

Ask students to read the feature Understanding Inflation on this page. Allow them a few minutes to review the two types of inflation discussed in the feature. Ask students to explain what happens when the prices of new materials or labor rise. *(Higher materials and labor costs push up the prices of goods.)* Then ask what happens when people have a lot of money to spend and there is a shortage of available goods or services. *(The price of goods and services gets "pulled" up.)* Ask students how rising prices—or inflation—might affect the following people: senior citizens on a fixed income, poor people, middle-income people, and rich people. *(Students may suggest that, in all cases, higher prices force people to make choices, to substitute, and to find better ways to economize. In all cases the standard of living decreases because people get less for the same amount of money.)*

Because Brazil has little oil and no coal, the government has built dams, which use the power of water.

The economy needed to be made stronger. Brazil's leaders decided to industrialize. If the people of Brazil built their own businesses and factories, they could create their own products and services. They could also export finished goods instead of raw materials.

São Paulo seemed like the perfect place to start building. It was the center of the coffee industry and had the capital needed for

Understanding Inflation

Inflation occurs when the prices of many goods and services in a country or a region rise. Why should we worry about rising prices? Let's look at a personal example.

What Is Inflation?

Suppose you have just earned $2 for selling a birdhouse you made to your neighbor. What can you do with your money? You can save it in the bank and earn interest (a payment the bank makes to you), or you can spend your money for goods and services. For example, with $2 you can buy an ice cream cone and one of your favorite magazines.

What would happen if the prices of ice cream, magazines, haircuts, gasoline, bicycle tires, and lots of other prices in your region increased? Your $2 just wouldn't go as far as before. With rising prices, or inflation, your money might buy only an ice cream cone. To continue buying an ice-cream cone and a magazine, you might be tempted to raise the price of your birdhouses.

Pushing the Price Up

If you raise the price of your birdhouse, you have just contributed to inflation. The price of the birdhouse also depended on the cost of making it. You had to buy lumber, glue, and plastic. If there is a shortage of lumber, the price of wood will increase, and so will the cost of producing your birdhouse. Think about the raw materials, human skills, and machinery needed to make the products you see around you. What would happen to your birdhouse business if the costs of all these materials increased?

Pulling the Price Up

Sometimes, people have so much money to spend on goods and services that producers cannot supply all the goods people want to buy. Then people are willing to pay more for these goods and services. When this happens, producers can raise prices. Thus, prices rise as a result of the actions of both producers and consumers. This causes inflation.

Inflation can cause problems for individuals and for a country. People with low or limited incomes suffer because their money doesn't go as far as it went before. The prices of exports increase along with other prices. People from other countries buy fewer of the exported products. Thus, the economy of the exporting country is hurt because fewer of its goods are sold on the global market.

Visual Learning

Have students examine the illustration of the rain forest on page 561; ask a volunteer to read the captions aloud. Then create a class flow chart showing how the destruction of the rain forests is threatening the ecological cycle. *(Students may include extinction of plant and animal species, the warming of the atmosphere, and the destruction of Indian groups.)*

Political Context

The following information may help students understand some of the complex reasons behind Brazil's high national debt. Although Brazil's leaders bear some responsibility for its high rate of debt, some of the blame must go to the lenders.

The booming Brazilian economy of the 1970s made Brazil the favorite investment of international bankers. Although rising oil prices pushed up the cost of Brazil's imports, it also created a glut of money for the rich oil-producing regions in Southwest Asia. Bankers seeking investment opportunities looked to Brazil, whose massive expansion and development projects made it one of the fastest growing economies in the world. It was not until the end of the decade that bankers suddenly decided that Brazil's deficit made the country a poor credit risk.

Rare plant and animal species that rely on the unique habitats found in rain forests become extinct.
The slash and burn method pollutes the air and may contribute to the "greenhouse effect," the gradual warming of the earth's atmosphere.
The livelihoods of native people, such as those who extract material from rubber trees for making rubber, are destroyed.
When logging operations clear vast areas, topsoil is washed away, so nothing will grow.
When the roots of trees and plants that soak up water are removed, flooding can result.

business growth. **Capital** is money that is used to start businesses. The city was also well located. It was near mines that could provide raw materials. It was also near farms that could produce food for a growing population. It had a network of roads and railroads for bringing goods into the factories.

Industry grew in São Paulo and other cities. By the early 1990s, Brazil had the world's eighth largest economy. It exported the most coffee and orange juice concentrate in the world. Soybeans, cocoa, metal ore, gold, and military weapons are other important products of Brazil.

Yet Brazil paid a high price for this development. The government had borrowed money—too much money. Money that should have gone to improve the country had to go to other countries to pay off loans. This debt caused **inflation,** or a general increase in prices. ■

▲ *Cutting down trees for lumber and other wood products and clearing the land for farming helps Brazil's economy. Still, what are the long-term effects of destroying the country's rain forests?*

■ *Why did the Brazilian government decide to industrialize the country?*

REVIEW

1. **FOCUS** Why does Brazil have serious economic problems in spite of its many exports and natural resources?
2. **GEOGRAPHY** How did the geography and climate of the northeast region force thousands of people into the cities?
3. **ECONOMICS** Why has the government of Brazil encouraged people to settle in the western regions?
4. **CRITICAL THINKING** Can you think of examples of boom-and-bust economies in other countries?
5. **ACTIVITY** Locate the regions, features, and cities you read about in this lesson on a map of Brazil. Mark rivers in blue, cities in red, and regions in green.

▲ *The long-term effects of destroying the rain forests include extinction of plant and animal life, soil erosion, flooding, the warming of the earth's atmosphere, and the destruction of Indian groups.*

■ *To break the cycle of boom-and-bust economics, the government decided to industrialize so that Brazilians could produce goods and services for themselves instead of relying on a single export.*

CLOSE

Have students review the lists they made of how geography affected Brazil's economy. Then copy the Graphic Overview on the chalkboard, or display it on an overhead projector. Ask a volunteer to read the Thinking Focus aloud. Suggest that students use the diagram to help them answer the question. *(Students may suggest the impact of drought and floods, boom-and-bust economics, overcrowded cities, inflation, and a huge national debt.)*

Answers to Review Questions

1. Brazilwood, sugar, coffee, and rubber provided the country with great wealth until other countries entered the same markets. Also, high unemployment, the high cost of borrowing money, and rapid inflation continue to challenge Brazil today.
2. The northeast is mostly flat and dry, with large areas of *sertão.* Drought and flooding caused widespread unemployment and forced thousands of people to move.
3. As Brazil industrialized, its cities became overcrowded. The government hoped to create jobs and living space for Brazilians by opening the western region to settlement.
4. Some students may mention the gold, silver, and oil rushes in the western United States. Others may note Ghana's reliance on cocoa.
5. Students' maps should show the five regions; the major cities; the São Francisco River; the Amazon River, the *sertão;* and the pampas.

Homework Options

Orange juice, soybeans, and cocoa are important export products of Brazil. Instruct students to read the labels on food products they find at home and that they purchase in the course of a week. Ask them to list how many times they eat a food containing one of these Brazilian products.

Study Guide: page 98

INTRODUCE

The rapid urbanization of parts of Brazil has brought some problems, as in other countries throughout the world. Have students read the Thinking Focus aloud. Invite them to predict answers based on what they have already learned about Brazil. *(Students may suggest saving the rain forests, improving the cities, slowing the inflation rate, and lowering the foreign debt.)*

Key Term

Vocabulary Strategies: T36–T37

favela—a poor community made up of shacks and built on the outskirts of a Brazilian city

1400
1500
1600
1700
1800
1891
TODAY

LESSON 3

Brazil Today

THINKING FOCUS

What are some of the problems facing the people of Brazil today?

Key Term

- favela

The capital city of Brasília was built in the 1960s. Yet the idea for this city is much older. More than 100 years ago, in 1891, a large area of land was set aside for the new capital. This area, called the Federal District, was modeled after the District of Columbia, the capital of the United States.

However, not all the citizens of Brazil were included in the plans for this city of the future. Indians living in the area lost land to the new development. The poor people who came looking for work had no homes built for them. That is why there are **favelas** *(fuh VEH luhz)*, poor communities made up of shacks, all around the city.

➤ *Although Brasília was built to symbolize the unity of the people, it also highlights their differences.*

Problems and Solutions

Some people think that developing the rain forests will solve Brazil's economic problems. Others believe that developing the rain forests may harm Brazil and the world (see page 561). Many scientists think that the rain forests help control the earth's temperature and protect its atmosphere.

Chico Mendes *(SHEE ku MEHN dehz)* was one of the most famous protectors of the Amazon rain forest. He worked as a rubber tapper. When developers began to destroy millions of acres of trees, Mendes organized nonviolent protests called *empates (ehm PAH tees)*. The *empates* saved up to three million acres of forest. Chico Mendes was murdered in 1988 by ranchers who wanted to stop him.

Objectives

1. Describe the role of the rain forest as it relates to Brazil's economic development.
2. Describe the three major groups that make up the population of Brazil.
3. Give examples of the contributions of different groups to Brazilian culture.
4. Describe some new developments in Brazilian culture.

Graphic Overview

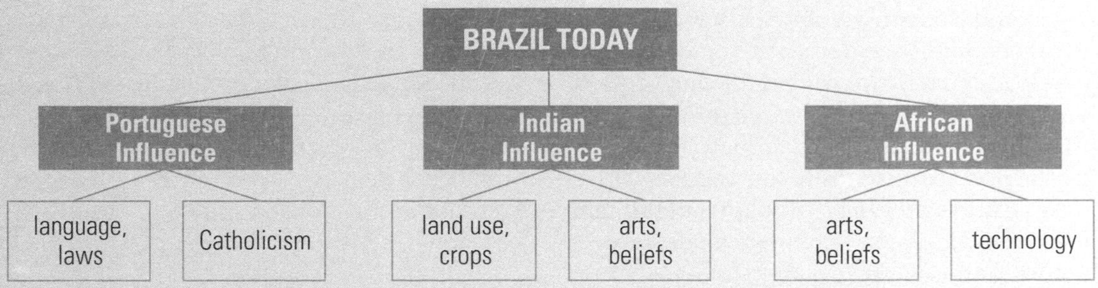
BRAZIL TODAY
Portuguese Influence
Indian Influence
African Influence
language, laws
Catholicism
land use, crops
arts, beliefs
arts, beliefs
technology

Mendes believed that the forest could be saved by sustainable development, or using natural resources in a way that doesn't harm them or use them up. Harvesting forest products that will grow back, such as rubber and nuts, are examples of sustainable development.

Scientists have learned a great deal by studying Indian farming methods. The Kaiapó *(kay ah POH)* live in the Amazonia region of northern Brazil. They clear circular fields and mix crops so that the fragile rain forest soil is not harmed.

In 1992 Brazil hosted an Earth Summit. People from all over the world met to talk about different ways to protect the world's environment.

◄ *Conservationist Chico Mendes, shown in the painting, made his living tapping rubber trees, like the man in the photo on page 559.*

Brazilians, like people everywhere, do not want other nations telling them how to use their natural resources. However, with help from other countries, Brazil might find a way to meet the needs of its citizens without destroying its natural treasures. ■

■ *Why have scientists and concerned citizens of other countries criticized Brazil's efforts to develop its rain forests?*

Brazilian Life

Brazil's cities are lively and modern. However, many city-dwellers are very poor, living in shacks without running water or electricity. About 40 percent of the people of Rio de Janeiro live in *favelas*.

More than half the workers in Brazil earned less than $170 a month in 1990. Perhaps as many as eight of every ten children living in the northeast suffer from hunger. In the southeast, nearly one-fifth of São Paulo's children are homeless. Many of them were forced out of their homes because their parents couldn't feed them. In spite of their problems, Brazilians struggle to survive and hope for better days.

There are few African Brazilians or Indians in the government. This is starting to change. Benedita da Silva became the first African Brazilian woman in Brazil's congress in 1987. In 1992 she almost won the race for mayor of Rio de Janeiro.

City-dwellers enjoy simple pleasures. Many Brazilians live a short bus ride from a beach. Soccer matches are also popular events in Brazil. Soccer players are big stars, like football players in the United States. African Brazilian Edson Arantes do Nascimento, known as Pelé *(pay LAY)*, is said to have been the greatest soccer player of all time. He may even run for president sometime in the future. ■

▼ *Thousands of poor people live in* favelas *on the edges of the modern capital city. In this respect, Brasília is just like Brazil's older cities.*

■ *Describe some of the problems facing people living in Brazil today.*

DEVELOP

Ask students to think back to Lesson 1 and the different groups of people that contributed to Brazil's history. Have volunteers name those groups and list them on the chalkboard. *(Students may suggest Indians, Portuguese traders and settlers, Christian missionaries, and Africans.)* Then have students read the major heads of this lesson. Ask them to write each head on a separate sheet of paper. Suggest they take notes that give the details for each section of text as they read.

■ *Scientists and others have been worried about the impact of developing the rain forests on the world's temperature and atmosphere.*

■ *Some of the problems facing Brazil today are poverty, hunger, homelessness, and the need for greater representation for Indian and African Brazilians in government.*

Access Strategy

Ask students to think of people they regard as heroes. *(Students may suggest personal heroes, such as family members; others may suggest public figures in sports, politics, history, or the arts.)* Direct their attention to the photograph of the Brazilian rubber tapper, Chico Mendes, on this page. Tell students that Chico Mendes lost his life in the struggle for the protection of the Brazilian rain forests. To many people in his own country and in the international community, Mendes was a hero. At the same time, however, to many developers and farmers of the rain forest, Mendes was a villain. Explain that in this lesson students will be learning more about the struggle to save the Brazilian rain forests without slowing down the growth of the country's economy.

Access Activity

Ask students to look through the lesson pages for visual clues to modern Brazil. Invite them to answer this question: What do these photographs depict about life in Brazil today? *(Students may suggest modern buildings; wealthy cities; poor, crowded communities; religious festivals; Carnivals; and multicultural heritage.)*

CULTURE

Critical Thinking

Ask students to imagine that they are working on a committee that is preparing the 175th anniversary celebration of Brazil's independence in 1997. Each student must prepare a 15- to 30-second "spot" to appear on Brazilian television. Suggest that the televised announcements salute the contributions diverse groups have made to Brazil. *(Students may suggest Indian farming methods, foods, and canoe and raft building; African mining, farming, and cooking; and Portuguese religion, laws, and language. Also, the Brazilian way of blending cultures in music and the arts should be noted.)*

Students may complete their televised announcements in writing by creating a series of cartoons to portray the ad, role-playing the spot with other students, or making an actual video.

Religion is an important part of life to many Brazilians, as attendance at this festival of Corpus Christi shows.

The Culture of Brazil

It is almost 500 years since Cabral reached the shores of Brazil. In the years following his arrival, Portuguese and African people came to the country. They joined the Indians already living there, and as these people mixed, so did their cultures.

The Historic Blend

The Portuguese brought their language, religion, legal system, and noble families to Brazil. They set up the government, plantations, and other institutions that have shaped Brazil's economy and society.

The Indians taught Portuguese settlers traditional skills and showed them local foods and materials. They taught the Portuguese to eat manioc *(MAN ee ohk),* made from the cassava plant, instead of bread. The Indians also taught them how to build dugout canoes and rafts.

The methods used by African slaves improved Brazilian mining, farming, cattle ranching, and iron working. African cooks added red peppers, okra, and ginger to European and South American foods. African music, stories, and games are part of the lives of all Brazilians.

Most Indians and Africans in Brazil became Catholics. For other Brazilians, however, many old and new beliefs have been brought together. For example, *candomblé (kuhn dawm BLEH)* is an important Brazilian

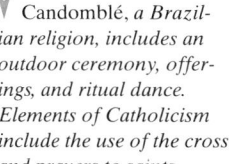

Candomblé, *a Brazilian religion, includes an outdoor ceremony, offerings, and ritual dance. Elements of Catholicism include the use of the cross and prayers to saints.*

Visual Learning

Have students study the three images on these facing pages. Each portrays a religious festival or ceremony. Ask students to infer what these images depict about Brazilian culture. *(Brazilians keep religious traditions alive through regular festivals and activities.)*

Music Connection

This activity should extend your teaching of the part diverse groups play in Brazilian music. Brazil's music, like every other aspect of its culture, combines European, Indian, and African traditions. Indians contributed the chant, the one-word chorus, pipes, and percussion instruments such as rattles to Brazil's folk music. Indian music has little melody but is rhythmically complex. The Portuguese contributed folk dances, the accordion, and stringed instruments such as the guitar. Africans provided the backbone of Brazil's music, however. Africa's infectious rhythms became the samba, and a variety of string and percussion instruments contribute to the distinctive sound of Brazil's music. Bring in records of Brazilian music. Have students listen and try to identify the instruments they hear.

religion. It honors African Gods, called *orixás (aw ri SHAS)*. However, the *orixás* are sometimes given the names of Catholic saints, such as Saint Anthony or the Virgin Mary.

Modern Brazilian Culture

Music is an important part of Brazilian culture. The music of Brazil is based on a blend of Indian, Portuguese, and African influences. Perhaps Brazil's most famous musical export is the samba rhythm.

The samba comes from what is now the African country Angola. The samba is a major part of the Carnival of Brazil. Carnival is a four-day festival that marks the beginning of the Christian Lent.

Thousands of Brazilians belong to neighborhood groups called samba schools. During Carnival the samba schools perform in the parades for big cash prizes. Today Brazilian musicians like Milton Nascimento and Gilberto Gil use Indian, Portuguese, and African-based music to create popular music that has a special Brazilian sound.

Brazil's artists and writers have learned much from the different traditions found there. For example, landscape architect Roberto Burle Marx uses native Brazilian plants to create gardens and parks around the world. Brazilian writers, such as Euclides da Cunha and Abdias do Nascimento, have based their works on the real lives and culture of their fellow Brazilians. ■

◄ *A wild mix of color and music, Carnival is the last celebration before the Christian season of Lent. Samba schools, whose members have been rehearsing, planning, sewing, and building since last year's Carnival, compete against one another in Carnival parades for big cash prizes.*

■ *How has Brazil's popular music been affected by Brazil's cultural mix?*

REVIEW

1. **FOCUS** What are some of the problems facing the people of Brazil today?
2. **SOCIAL AND POLITICAL SYSTEMS** What is the importance of the election of Benedita da Silva to Brazil's Congress in 1987?
3. **CULTURE** What were the cultural contributions of different ethnic groups in Brazil?
4. **CRITICAL THINKING** At one time most African and Indian Brazilians were slaves. Yet Brazil's religion, food, and music have been strongly influenced by African and Indian culture. How do you explain this?
5. **WRITING ACTIVITY** Arbor Day, a holiday for planting trees, is celebrated in some U.S. communities. For an Arbor Day celebration in your city or town, write a brief speech about the importance of preserving rain forests using what you have read about Brazil.

■ *Brazilian music includes many Indian, Portuguese, and African rhythms. This legacy enlivens traditional Brazilian festivals, such as Carnival, with street dancing, folk plays, extravagant costumes, and friendly competition.*

CLOSE

Have students answer the Thinking Focus. List their suggestions about problems on the chalkboard. Then tell students that *Ordem e Progresso* ("Order and Progress") is the motto on Brazil's flag. Ask them to think about the meaning of this motto. Then direct students to review this lesson by listing examples of things Brazil has done to achieve order and progress. *(Students may suggest democratic government; the blending of African, Indian, and Portuguese cultures; industrialization; and the beginning of sustainable development of the Amazon region.)*

Answers to Review Questions

1. Poverty, sustainable development of the rain forests, and a huge national debt are some problems facing Brazil today.
2. Benedita da Silva was the first African Brazilian woman in Brazil's congress. Her election may give African Brazilians more hope for the future.
3. The Portuguese brought their language, Catholicism, and laws to Brazil. Indians taught survival techniques. Africans brought mining, ranching, and ironworking skills. Brazil's religions and music are a blend of all three cultures.
4. Students' answers should reflect knowledge of the fact that the Portuguese settlers had to survive in Brazil with unfamiliar food, climate, and resources. Indians taught them to do this. The sheer number of Africans has influenced Brazilian culture in many ways.
5. Students should demonstrate an understanding of the effects of deforestation.

Homework Options

Have students find out more about the samba by interviewing family or neighbors, or by reading about the dance in an encyclopedia or geographic magazine.

Study Guide: page 99

DECISION-MAKING PROCESS

1. Recognize the need for a decision.
2. Define the goals and values involved.
3. Acquire and evaluate necessary information.
4. Identify and analyze possible alternatives.
5. Choose the best alternative.

This Making Decisions lesson is entitled Rain Forests: Preserve Them? Use Them? It uses steps 1, 2, 3, and 4 of the decision-making process.

CITIZENSHIP

Critical Thinking

Have students read the quotations on this page. Ask them to state the goals each represents. *(Rep. Porter states the environmental goal of conserving global resources; the Brazilian president states the economic goal of decreasing Brazil's national debt.)* Ask why it is important that all sides are considered when deciding what to do about the rain forests. *(Students may suggest that focusing only on economic goals could destroy Amazon rain forests, causing plant and animal extinction and atmospheric decay. Ignoring Brazilian needs could increase its debt and rate of unemployment.)*

MAKING DECISIONS

Rain Forests: Preserve Them? Use Them?

We simply cannot replace this invaluable resource once it is gone. The rain forests . . . once lost, can never be regained. Every second of every day, we are losing a tropical forest the size of a football field.

Hon. John E. Porter
U.S. Representative, Illinois

How can Brazil be expected to control its economic development, [Brazil's President José Sarney] asks, when it is staggering under a $111 billion foreign-debt load? By what right does the U.S. . . . lecture poor countries like Brazil on their responsibilities to mankind?

Time, September 18, 1989

Background

From the air Brazil's great forests look like a giant, green cushion. Once the earth nourished many such rain forests. Now only a few remain. The loss of these rain forests affects the entire world.

How? Like all plants, the huge trees of the forest take in carbon dioxide from the air. They use this gas to make their food. In the process, they release oxygen into the atmosphere. The enormous forests, therefore, help balance the carbon dioxide and the oxygen in the earth's atmosphere. When the trees are cut down, we reduce the amount of carbon dioxide taken from the air. At the same time, we are burning more gasoline and other fossil fuels, releasing more carbon dioxide into the air. Some scientists predict that this buildup of carbon dioxide in the atmosphere will cause the world's climates to grow warmer and warmer. We cannot foresee all the results of this global warming. One possibility, though, is that fertile farmland could someday become barren desert.

A close look at the rain forests reveals bare patches, some as big as Connecticut. Other effects of deforestation are more difficult to see. When trees go, so do mammals, plants, insects, and birds. Species as unique as the frogs shown here may also become extinct if this trend continues. Such extinctions could have far-reaching effects. For example, many of our

Objectives

1. Name the issues involved in making a decision about the destruction of the rain forest. (Citizenship 5)
2. Find and analyze information on the issues involved in making a decision about rain forests. (Citizenship 5)

Activity

Divide students into five groups. Group members are to assume these identities: Group 1—the poor and landless who have cleared land to farm it; Group 2—miners who extract gold or other metals; Group 3—rubber tappers; Group 4—loggers; Group 5—wildlife (a jaguar, a woolly monkey, a giant anteater, and a tarantula). Have each group do a joint written report on its own successes, problems, and failures in the rain forest. For example, do the farmers have fertile soil for raising plentiful crops? Are they happy there? Do miners have good wages and working conditions? The report should also include how each group affects the environment of the rain forest. Collect written reports. Each group will then prepare a skit to present its information to the class. Source material might include "Unquiet on the Brazilian Front," *Audubon,* January/February 1992; "Brazil's Two Faces," *Time,* June 8, 1992.

medicines come from plants. What if a plant growing in a rain forest today contains a cure for a form of cancer? What if the plant becomes extinct as the forest shrinks?

Roots of the Problem

If you look only at the effects of this loss of the rain forests, the solution may seem clear: Put a stop to it. To see how complicated the problem really is, you have to study the causes—the reasons for clearing the rain forests.

As you have read, Brazil has a large and rapidly growing population. Providing jobs and housing requires space. Some forests are cleared to build homes, factories, roads, and bridges.

Like most other countries, Brazil wants to keep a balance of trade. This means that Brazil tries to sell to other nations as much as it buys from them. Brazil imports steel and other products. It exports beef, rubber, and lumber. Forests are cleared to provide grazing land for cattle. Lumber, of course, comes from the forests.

In addition, Brazilian miners bring 70 tons of gold a year out of the rain forests. Some areas of the forests are cleared to give the miners room to work.

Brazilians want to raise their standard of living. If the rain forests can be useful, why shouldn't they benefit the nation in which they grow?

Decision Point

1. After reading about the problem of the rain forests, what questions do you have?
2. Where would you look for more information about global warming? About Brazil's economy?
3. Are there ways to both preserve and use the rain forests? How can you find out?
4. Choose one topic related to the rain forest problem. What more do you need to know about it? Find the information in newspapers and magazines.
5. Discuss the new information you and your classmates found. Based on this limited information, what ideas and alternatives can you suggest?

SOCIAL SYSTEMS

Critical Thinking

Remind students that many groups of Brazilian Indians still live in the rain forest. If the rain forests are destroyed, their way of life is also destroyed. Ask this question: Should the Indians of Brazil have a greater, lesser, or equal say in how the rain forest is used? *(Students may point out that the Brazilian Indians are the oldest human inhabitants of the rain forests and therefore should have a greater say. Their way of life has shown environmentalists how to protect the rain forests.)*

Answers to Decision Point

1. Helpful references for students' research include Rainforest Action Network, 450 Sansome, Suite 700, San Francisco, CA 94111 and *The State of the Ark: An Atlas of Conservation in Action* by Lee Durrell.
2. For information on global warming, see the *Readers' Guide* for articles in news, geographic, and environmental magazines. For information on Brazil's economy, consult the *Readers' Guide* for magazine articles; *New York Times Index* and *Wall Street Journal Index* for newspaper articles.
3. Yes, landless Brazilians can earn their living from rain forests without destroying them, but it's difficult for companies to make profits without destruction. See answer 2 for resources.
4. Students' suggestions may include the future of the Brazilian Indian residents of the rain forest.
5. Students' suggestions should reflect information gained in questions 1 through 4.

Collaborative Learning

For a recommended collaborative learning strategy you can use with this lesson, refer to pages T34–T35.

Answers to Reviewing Key Terms

A. Answers:

1. False. The **Line of Demarcation** was a line drawn by Pope Alexander in 1492 and 1493 that split the non-Christian parts of the world between Spain and Portugal.
2. True.
3. True.
4. False. São Paulo was a thriving economic center and did have the **capital,** or the money, needed to start businesses.
5. False. **Inflation** causes a general increase in prices.
6. False. Most of Brasília's poor people live in **favelas.**

B. Sample answers:

1. People hope to improve life for all Brazilian city residents by building better housing. This will mean replacing the **favelas** with well-serviced communities.
2. For many years, Brazil's economy followed a **boom-and-bust** pattern. Products such as gold and rubber first brought high profits, then they stopped bringing much profit at all.
3. Jesuits were among the first Portuguese settlers in Brazil. They tried to **convert** Indians from their religions to Catholicism.

Answers to Exploring Concepts

A. Sample answers:

1. Brazil was a colony of Portugal; it won its independence from Portugal in 1822.
2. Brazil has been a republic since the late 1880s, but military and civilian dictators ran the government until 1990.
3. The people of Brazil are primarily a mix of African, Indian, and European peoples. There is also a large Japanese population in Brazil.
4. Economic challenges include industrializing, keeping inflation under control, and fighting widespread poverty in Brazil.

B. Sample answers:

1. He wanted Portugal to profit from the trade with Asia, and from the gold in West Africa.
2. The Pope created the Line of Demarcation that split the non-Christian areas of the world in half. Spain could have the lands on the west side of the line. Portugal could have the lands on the east side of the line.
3. The Portuguese enslaved the Indians. Hundreds of thousands died.
4. As the number of Indians in Brazil decreased, the Portuguese brought enslaved Africans to work on their plantations.
5. Brazil became independent in 1822.
6. The Amazon River is located in the north.
7. Gold, sugar, rubber, and coffee fueled Brazil's boom-and-bust economy.
8. Brazil's leaders hope to stabilize the economy through industrialization.
9. *Empates* were nonviolent protests to save the rain forests.
10. Indians introduced local foods such as manioc and taught people farming methods and how to build dugout canoes and rafts; Africans added new foods to Brazilian cuisine, contributed music, stories, and games, and introduced mining and cattle ranching techniques.

Chapter Review

Reviewing Key Terms

boom-and-bust (p. 559)
capital (p. 561)
convert (p. 552)
favela (p. 562)
inflation (p. 561)
Line of Demarcation (p. 550)

A. Write whether each of the following statements is *true* or *false.* Then rewrite the false statements to make them true.

1. The Line of Demarcation is the boundary between the countries of Portugal and Spain.
2. Jesuits tried to make Indians convert, or change from their own religions, to Catholicism.
3. In a boom-and-bust cycle, a product first brings high profits, then it stops bringing much profit at all.
4. São Paulo lacked the capital to create businesses in Brazil.
5. Inflation causes a general decrease in prices.
6. Most of Brasília's wealthy population lives in *favelas.*

B. Write sentences according to the directions below. Your sentences should show your understanding of each term.

1. Write two sentences about the future of Brazil's cities using the term favela.
2. Write two sentences about Brazil's economy using the term boom-and-bust.
3. Write two sentences about Brazil's history using the term convert.

Exploring Concepts

A. Copy and complete the chart below. Fill it in with three to four major ideas from the chapter.

Brazil Fact Sheet	
Brazil's Colonial History	
Government of Brazil	
People of Brazil	
Modern Economic Challenges	development causes inflation and environmental problems

B. Answer each question with information from the chapter.

1. Why was Prince Henry interested in sea travel?
2. How did Pope Alexander VI settle a dispute between Spain and Portugal in 1493?
3. Why did conflict arise between the Indians of Brazil and the Portuguese?
4. Why were Africans brought to Brazil?
5. When did Brazil gain its independence from Portugal?
6. In which of Brazil's five regions is the Amazon River located?
7. What products fueled Brazil's boom-and-bust economy?
8. How did Brazil's leaders hope to stabilize their economy?
9. What were the *empates*?
10. Name at least two contributions made by the native Indians and the Africans to the culture of Brazil.

Reviewing Skills

1. What is an assumption? Why is it important to always test an assumption against facts? What types of assumptions do adults make about young people today? Do you think that their assumptions are true? Why or why not?
2. Look at the graph on page 552. What kind of graph is this? What kind of graph would you use if you want to show the shrinking Indian population in Brazil from the 1500s to today? Explain your answer.
3. Imagine that you have been asked to write an essay about the importance of preserving the rain forest in Brazil. What types of supporting evidence found in this chapter could you use in your essay?
4. As you write your essay, you realize that you would like more information about efforts to preserve the rain forest. Where would you find a list of magazine articles about the rain forest that were written during the past year?

Using Critical Thinking

1. Compare the histories of the Caribbean and Brazil. In what ways are they similar? Think about each region's colonial experiences, including their economies, the Europeans' treatment of Native Americans, the types of people who were brought into or came to each area, and the blend of cultures in each region.
2. Why did the development of Caribbean sugar plantations in the 1500s and 1600s result in problems for Brazil's economy?
3. Why do Brazilians view their northern and western regions as the land of the future? Why are some people opposed to this way of thinking?
4. You have read about many nations that are trying to combat poverty. Based on your readings, how can nations such as Brazil hope to bring their people a better standard of living?

Preparing for Citizenship

1. WRITING ACTIVITY When Princess Isabel signed the Golden Law freeing Brazil's slaves in 1888, she angered the landowners of Brazil. In this case, Isabel went against their wishes in order to do what she thought was right. Think about leaders in the United States. Is it ever right for an elected U.S. representative to act against the wishes of the people to do what he or she thinks is right? Why or why not? Give reasons to support your answer.
2. ART ACTIVITY Make a map of the landforms, climate, and major geographic features of the community in which you live. You may want to use the map of North America: Political and Physical in the Atlas on page 686. Do geography and climate affect the ways that people in your community make a living? Do the people in your community share environmental concerns similar to those of the Brazilian people?
3. INTERVIEWING Every community has people working to improve the environment. Some people are active in cleaning up polluted streams or lakes. Others are concerned about the future of endangered animals. Find a person to interview in your community who is active in environmental issues. They may be employed by an environmental organization. Or, they may volunteer in their spare time to help protect our environment. You may find a suitable person who is willing to come and discuss their work with your class.
4. COLLABORATIVE LEARNING As a class, create a Community Environmental Report. Your report may include maps of your area showing places of concern to environmentalists, and clippings from local newspapers about environmental issues.

Answers to Reviewing Skills

1. An assumption is an idea that is accepted as fact without proof or demonstration. It is important to test an assumption because it may be based on incomplete or misleading information. Answers will vary about adult assumptions about young people. Possible answer: Some adults assume that all young people are not willing to work hard. This assumption is wrong because many young people do work hard. Adults may base their views on news stories about young people who get into trouble.
2. It is a pie graph. You would use a line graph or a bar graph to show the decline, because these graphs show change over time.
3. Examples of supporting evidence: Many scientists think that the dense rain forests help control the earth's temperature and protect its atmosphere. Important foods and medicines come from the rain forest.
4. The *Readers' Guide to Periodical Literature* is the source for this information.

Answers to Using Critical Thinking

1. Both regions were European colonies; native peoples in both regions were enslaved and killed in huge numbers; both regions were used for European sugar plantations that were worked by Indians and enslaved Africans; both regions are a complex blend of African, Native American, and European cultures.
2. When sugar was produced more cheaply in the Caribbean, the Brazilian sugar market crashed.
3. The people of Brazil hope that the vast lands of rain forests and rivers in the northern and western regions will be the land of the future. Some people may oppose developing these areas because new economic ventures could threaten the fragile ecosystem of the Brazilian rain forests.
4. Answers will vary. Possible answer: The best way to bring people a better standard of living is to educate them so they can find jobs that are more profitable.

Answers to Preparing for Citizenship

1. WRITING ACTIVITY Answers will vary. Possible answer: Yes, it can be right for a representative to act against the wishes of the people because the people often do not have all the information they need to make an informed decision.
2. ART ACTIVITY Maps should illustrate the impact of geographic conditions and environmental issues on the students' communities.
3. INTERVIEWING Interviews should show genuine interest in the person's activities in the area of environmental issues.
4. COLLABORATIVE LEARNING This activity should heighten students' awareness of environmental issues in their community. As in Brazil, people all over the world are struggling with issues related to protecting the environment while maintaining and expanding economic growth. You might suggest that students research area landfills, recycling efforts, and zoning codes or disputes in your community (for example, use of wetland areas). You may want students to share their final reports with community leaders.

UNIT PREVIEW

Show students a map of North America and make sure that they can name and locate the three largest countries that share the continent. Explain that Canada, the United States, and Mexico share similar political and economic systems.

Geography also links the three nations. The Rocky Mountains—shown in the photograph—are part of a mountain range that runs the length of North America.

Looking Back

Remind students that in Chapter 6 they studied the earliest civilizations in the Americas. This unit looks at the changes that occurred as other peoples arrived there.

Looking Forward

Three of the four upcoming chapters explore the history, geography, and cultures of the three countries of North America. The last chapter examines the work of the United Nations, particularly its role in the development of the modern nations of Israel and South Korea.

Chapter 25 *Mexico*
Chapter 26 *Canada*
Chapter 27 *From Many, One Nation*
Chapter 28 *The United Nations, Israel, and South Korea*

Unit 8

North America

Over millions of years, great upheavals of earth and vast movements of ice and water formed the huge mountain chains of North America. The first humans reached these mountains from Asia perhaps 50,000 years ago. Around 500 years ago, explorers and conquerors came from Europe. They were followed by waves of settlers from many parts of the world.

1400

The San Juan Mountains in Colorado

BIBLIOGRAPHY

Books for Students

Canada in Pictures. Minneapolis: The Company, 1990. An Overview of Canada.

Farley, Carol. *Korea: Land of the Morning Calm.* Minneapolis: Dillon, 1991. A depiction of the two Koreas. Nonfiction.

Freedman, Russell. *Immigrant Kids.* New York: Dutton, 1980. An account of the immigrants who came to the United States from 1890 to the early 1900s. Nonfiction.

Stefoff, Rebecca. *West Bank/Gaza Strip.* New York: Chelsea House, 1988. A history of the occupied territories. Nonfiction.

Woods, Harold and Geraldine Woods. *The United Nations.* New York: Watts, 1985. A description of UN activities.

Books to Read Aloud

Hudson, Jan. *Sweetgrass.* New York: Philomel, 1989. The story of the life of a Blackfoot girl in nineteenth-century Canada. Fiction.

Books for Teachers

Franck, Thomas. *Nation Against Nation: What Happened to the UN Dream and What the U.S. Can Do About It.* New York: Oxford, 1985. A study of the UN Nonfiction.

Today
571

Understanding the Photograph

The Rocky Mountains are part of the North American Cordillera system, a chain of mountains linking Canada, the United States, and Mexico (where it becomes the Sierra Madre Oriental). This range forms the Continental Divide. Rivers on one side flow south and east to the Gulf of Mexico and the Atlantic Ocean; on the other, they flow west to the Pacific Ocean. Rich in mineral wealth, wildlife, and wilderness areas, the Rockies provide some of the continent's most spectacular scenery.

Understanding Chronology

The focus of these chapters is on relatively recent history and 20th-century concerns, from European settlement of North America to the present. The United States played an important role in founding the United Nations after World War II; the last chapter looks at current UN activities.

Khouri, Fred. *The Arab-Israeli Dilemma.* 3rd ed. Syracuse: Syracuse University Press, 1985. A history of the Arab-Israeli conflict. Nonfiction.

Meyer, Michael, and William Sherman. *The Course of Mexican History.* 4th ed. New York: Oxford University Press, 1991. A history of Mexico. Nonfiction.

Yi, Ki-baek. *A New History of Korea.* Cambridge: Harvard University Press, 1984. A comprehensive history of Korea. Nonfiction.

Other Resources

Visual Media

In the Holy Land. Optical Data, 1989. An interactive videodisk that provides background on the Israeli-Palestinian conflict through interviews with Palestinian and Israeli children, biographies, political history, and narration in English and Spanish.

HOUGHTON MIFFLIN SOCIAL STUDIES

Bookshelf

Silverthorne, Elizabeth. *Fiesta! Mexico's Great Celebrations.* Brookfield, Conn.: Millbrook Press, 1992. This entertaining look at Mexican holidays and customs includes instructions on making crafts and foods.

INTRODUCE

Read aloud the unit title and the paragraphs on this page. Then refer to the photograph of the cloverleaf highway and read its caption with the students. Ask students to guess in which country people drive more miles than any other country in the world. *(The United States)* Then ask them to guess the average number of miles people in the United States drive each year. *(Between 7,000 and 8,000 miles, three times more than the Japanese, twice the British average)* Ask students to suggest possible reasons why the Europeans and Japanese drive so much less than people in the United States. *(They have smaller areas to cover; they may have better transit and rail systems; higher gasoline taxes in Europe and Japan.)*

Learning from the Photograph

Refer to the photograph of the boy. Discuss how there is no one "typical" North American and that North America is a land having varied cultural heritages—like every other region students have studied.

Unit 8 Overview
North America

North America stretches "from sea to shining sea." The continent measures 3,300 miles at its widest point—from St. John's, Newfoundland, to the Pacific coast. From Alaska to Mexico, the continent extends 4,900 miles. Unlike Europe, which is made up of many small nations, North America is composed of only three large nations: Canada, the United States, and Mexico.

The earliest North Americans crossed the Bering Strait from Asia thousands of years ago. Over time, groups of people settled in every part of the continent. Each group created its own culture and way of life. The Zuni hunted and herded in the southwestern desert. The Inuit adapted to the frozen, snowy climate of what is now Canada and Alaska.

In time North America came under the control of the English, French, and Spaniards. The arrival of Europeans greatly changed Native American culture. Many place names, including New York City, San Francisco, and Montreal, show their European origins. Today people from almost every country in the world make their home in North America.

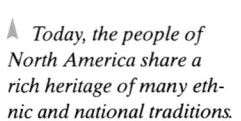

▲ *Today, the people of North America share a rich heritage of many ethnic and national traditions.*

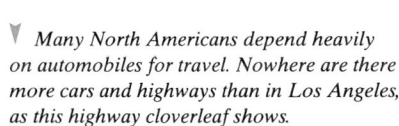

▼ *Many North Americans depend heavily on automobiles for travel. Nowhere are there more cars and highways than in Los Angeles, as this highway cloverleaf shows.*

Objectives

1. Identify North America as a multicultural continent.
2. Recognize the major geographic features of North America.
3. Preview important political, economic, and social issues facing North Americans.

Historical Context

A gasoline-powered automobile was first developed in Germany in 1876. By 1898 there were about 50 car manufacturers in the United States. However, early cars were very expensive and most people could not afford them.

Then in 1908 Henry Ford introduced the Model T automobile in the United States. Ford created one of the first modern factories that used the mechanized assembly line. That made the price of cars affordable for many people. Today there are more than 140 million cars in the United States, more than 11 million in Canada, and more than 5 million in Mexico.

ASIA
ARCTIC OCEAN
Bering Sea
Bering Strait
Beaufort Sea
Prime Meridian
BROOKS RANGE
QUEEN ELIZABETH ISLANDS
ELLESMERE ISLAND
GREENLAND (Denmark)
Baffin Bay
BANKS ISLAND
VICTORIA ISLAND
BAFFIN ISLAND
ALASKA RANGE
Fairbanks
Anchorage
KODIAK ISLAND
Gulf of Alaska
ALEXANDER ARCHIPELAGO
QUEEN CHARLOTTE ISLANDS
COAST MOUNTAINS
LAURENTIAN SHIELD
UNGAVA PENINSULA
Hudson Bay
Labrador Sea
LABRADOR
NEWFOUNDLAND
VANCOUVER ISLAND
Edmonton
CANADA
ROCKY MOUNTAINS
Vancouver
Seattle
Calgary
Winnipeg
PRINCE EDWARD ISLAND
CAPE BRETON ISLAND
Portland
Quebec
Montreal
Ottawa
Bay of Fundy
BLACK HILLS
Minneapolis
Toronto
Boston
Cape Cod
Milwaukee
Chicago
Detroit
Cleveland
New York
Philadelphia
Baltimore
Washington
ATLANTIC OCEAN
San Francisco
COAST RANGES
SIERRA NEVADA
Salt Lake City
Omaha
Denver
Kansas City
Indianapolis
St. Louis
Louisville
APPALACHIAN MTS.
Wichita
UNITED STATES
Nashville
Charlotte
Cape Hatteras
BERMUDA (U.K.)
Los Angeles
San Diego
MOJAVE DESERT
GRAND CANYON
Phoenix
Atlanta
Birmingham
PACIFIC OCEAN
Fort Worth
Ciudad Juárez
Austin
Houston
New Orleans
Jacksonville
Cape Canaveral
Tropic of Cancer
Chihuahua
San Antonio
BAJA CALIFORNIA
Monterrey
Miami
Gulf of Mexico
Cabo San Lucas
MEXICO
PLATEAU OF MEXICO
SIERRA MADRE OCCIDENTAL
SIERRA MADRE ORIENTAL
Guadalajara
Mexico City
Puebla
Veracruz
YUCATÁN PENINSULA
ISTHMUS OF TEHUANTEPEC
Acapulco
Caribbean Sea
CENTRAL AMERICA
KAUAI
OAHU
MOLOKAI
Honolulu
LANAI
MAUI
HAWAII
100 mi.
100 km
National capital
Major city
National boundary
SOUTH AMERICA
0 400 800 mi.
0 400 800 km
Azimuthal Equal-Area Projection
Equator

North America

Learning from the Map

Make sure that students understand the locator map at the upper right corner of the page. Then refer them to the political map of North America. Which country is the largest? *(Canada)* How many countries share a land border with Canada? *(One, the United States)* Explain that about 80 percent of Canadians live within 100 miles of the United States border. How might this affect Canadian-U.S. relations? *(Extensive trade and travel, similar cultures)*

Have students use the Atlas map on page 686 and the map of the United States on page 43 to answer the following questions. Which countries share a land border with Mexico? *(The United States, Guatemala and Belize)* Which states in the United States share a land border with Mexico? *(California, Arizona, New Mexico, and Texas)*

573

Debate

Should United States citizens be allowed to live and work in Canada or Mexico without restrictions? Should citizens of Mexico be allowed to live and work in the United States or Canada without restrictions? Should Canadians be allowed to live and work in the United States or Mexico without restrictions?

Organize a debate in which one side argues for unrestricted immigration and the other side argues for immigration restrictions. Explain that each team will plan and then present an opening statement presenting three or four reasons for its position. Students will want to use newspaper and magazine articles to help them gather background information for their arguments.

After each team has presented its opening arguments, have teams debate the opposite team's position. Take the role of moderator. Invite another class to watch the debate and vote on which team is the winner.

Map and Globe Skills

Using the world climate map in the Atlas on page 688, have students locate North America. Ask them to list the types of climates that exist throughout the continent. *(Polar, subpolar, continental, semi arid, desert, humid subtropical, Mediterranean, marine tropical wet, and tropical wet and dry)*

LOOK AND RESPOND

Ask students to scan the images and captions on these two pages. Make a web of their observations and impressions on the chalkboard.

Learning from the Maps and Diagram

Have students study the maps and read the captions. What do they tell us about the physical geography of North America? *(The landscape of North America was shaped over a long period of time by many natural events such as melting glaciers, volcanoes, and earthquakes.)*

Using the map of the last ice age on this page, the U.S. region map on page 43, and the map of Canada on page 599, ask students which provinces in Canada and which states in the United States were either all or partially covered by glaciers. *(All Canadian provinces; Alaska, Washington, Idaho, Montana, North and South Dakota, Nebraska, Kansas, Minnesota, Iowa, Missouri, Michigan, Wisconsin, Illinois, Indiana, Ohio, New York, Pennsylvania, New Jersey, Connecticut, Rhode Island, Massachusetts, Vermont, New Hampshire, Maine)* Then have students study the diagram of how a glacier changes a landscape.

The Land and People

North America might be called a land of fire and ice. Huge glaciers—great rivers of ice—covered much of North America thousands of years ago. Glaciers act like giant bulldozers, scooping up rocks and soil as they move over the land. Sometimes, glaciers pile up rocks in narrow ridges. They also carve out U-shaped valleys between mountains.

The western coast of North America is part of the Ring of Fire—the region of earthquakes and volcanoes that circles the Pacific Ocean. In 1985 one of the largest earthquakes of the 1900s destroyed part of Mexico City. Major earthquakes have badly shaken California and Alaska.

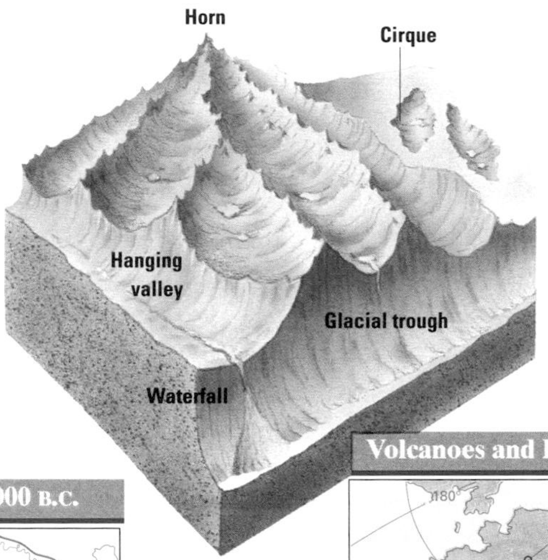
Horn
Cirque
Hanging valley
Glacial trough
Waterfall

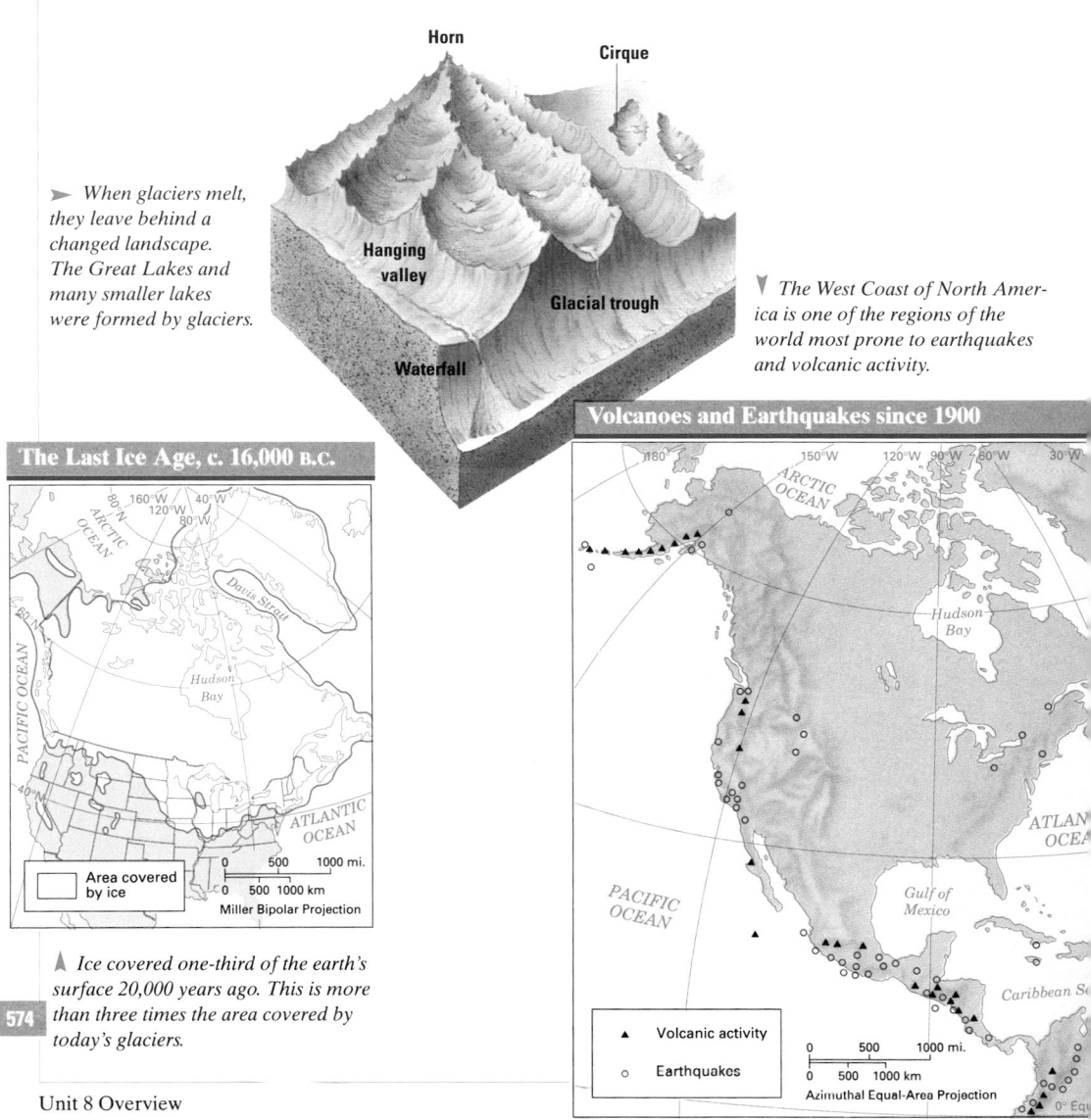

➤ *When glaciers melt, they leave behind a changed landscape. The Great Lakes and many smaller lakes were formed by glaciers.*

▼ *The West Coast of North America is one of the regions of the world most prone to earthquakes and volcanic activity.*

The Last Ice Age, c. 16,000 B.C.

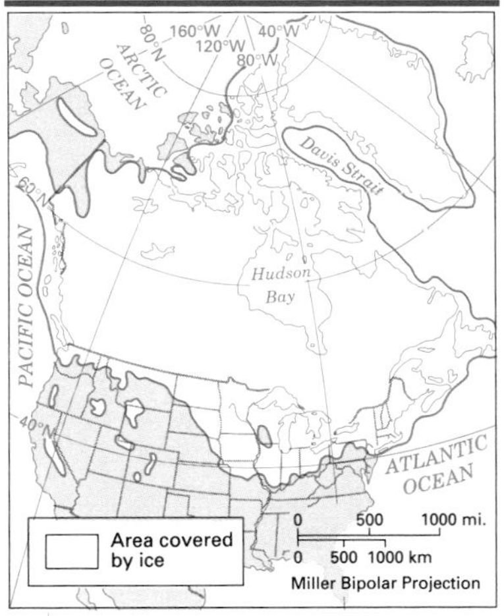
ARCTIC OCEAN
Davis Strait
Hudson Bay
PACIFIC OCEAN
ATLANTIC OCEAN
Area covered by ice
0 500 1000 mi.
0 500 1000 km
Miller Bipolar Projection

▲ *Ice covered one-third of the earth's surface 20,000 years ago. This is more than three times the area covered by today's glaciers.*

Volcanoes and Earthquakes since 1900

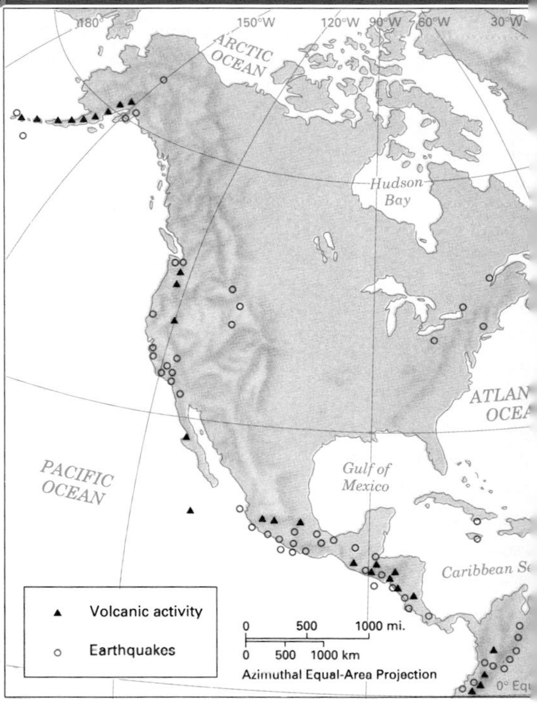
ARCTIC OCEAN
Hudson Bay
PACIFIC OCEAN
ATLANTIC OCEAN
Gulf of Mexico
Caribbean Sea
Volcanic activity
Earthquakes
0 500 1000 mi.
0 500 1000 km
Azimuthal Equal-Area Projection

Writing to Learn

Divide the class into writing teams. Based on what they know so far, half the teams should write about Canada, the other half about Mexico. Encourage students to include information about major cities, industry, climate, language, recreation, and traditions. Explain that students will revise their writing after completing the unit.

Language Arts Connection

Have students write a poem or a short story about a melting glacier from the point of view of a glacier. Explain that they will write in the first person, pretending that they are the glacier. They should imagine where the glacier began, in what direction it is moving, and where it stops.

Students should include the provinces in Canada and the states in the United States that the glacier covers and how it changes the landscape (lakes, valleys, plains, waterfalls, mountains, and so forth). Ask them to name their glaciers, give their poems or stories titles, and display them with their own drawings on a bulletin board.

North America is rich with minerals. Its other natural resources include vast forests and a large supply of fresh water and fertile soil. North America uses its many natural resources to produce about one-third of the world's manufactured goods. The United States and Canada also are major exporters of agricultural products.

Most North Americans live in cities. Each of these cities has been enriched by the traditions of the peoples from all over the world who settled there.

The jaguar symbol has been used in ceremonies and festivals throughout Mexico for hundreds of years. Masks such as this one are still worn in parades and ceremonies today.

Holidays reflect each nation's geography, history, and traditions. During long, cold winters, Canadians create amazing shapes from ice and snow.

On the first Thanksgiving, the English Pilgrims who settled in Plymouth cooked Native American foods. These included squash, wild turkey, and corn.

Learning from the Photographs

Have students study the photographs and read their captions. What information do they give about traditions in Canada, Mexico, and the United States? *(Since winters in some parts of Canada are cold and long, winter sports and activities are very important; the Mexican mask looks very old and shows the importance of ancient festivals; Thanksgiving is a major holiday in the United States. Tell students that Canadians celebrate their Thanksgiving in October.)*

Explain that the jaguar has been an important symbol in Mexico and other areas of Central and South America for more than 3,000 years: For the Aztecs the jaguar was a symbol of courage, daring, and pride. Today in southern Mexico the jaguar is associated with rain.

ENRICH

Arrange a penpal exchange for the class with students from Canada and/or Mexico. For sources of penpals, check with your school or local librarian, or the nearest Canadian and Mexican consulate general offices.

Science Connection

Study the map on page 574 showing North American earthquakes. Explain that earthquakes are disturbances within the earth that cause a series of seismic waves. The most severe earthquakes are caused by shifts in very deep parts of the earth, more than 190 miles, or 300 kilometers, below the earth's surface. Seismographs can find the location of earthquakes and measure their size, expressed on the Richter scale. The 1906 earthquake in San Francisco measured 8.3 on this scale.

Assign students to find magazine and newspaper accounts of recent major North American earthquakes, such as the 1985 earthquake in Mexico City that killed over 7,000 people and the 1989 earthquake in northern California that killed 67 people. Ask students to report their findings to the class, using maps, models, and other visuals.

Collaborative Learning

Divide the class into groups. Ask each group to write the names of some traditions they share. Then ask them to research one tradition and share their findings with the class. Have groups make and display models, masks, or illustrations to represent the traditions.

CHAPTER ORGANIZER

Chapter 25 Mexico

CHAPTER PLANNING CHART

Pupil's Edition	Teacher's Edition	Ancillaries
Lesson 1: The Forming of Mexico (2–3 days) Objective 1: Describe the effects of Spanish colonialism in Mexico. (Ethics and Belief Systems 3; Social and Political Systems 4) Objective 2: Describe Mexico's struggle for independence. (History 7; Geography 3) Objective 3: Describe Mexico's social and economic revolution. (Social and Political Systems 3; Economics 1)	• Graphic Overview (578) • Access Strategy (579) • Access Activity (579) Map and Globe Skills (580) Collaborative Learning (580) Political Context (581) Historical Context (581) Study Skills (581)	Study Guide (100) Transparency (14)
Understanding Historical Evidence Objective: Interpret information presented in an artifact. (Visual Learning 1)		Study Guide (101) • Study Prints (14)
Lesson 2: Regions and Resources (2–3 days) Objective 1: Describe the main geographic features of Mexico. (Geography 2; Economics 1) Objective 2: Identify the main natural resources of Mexico. (Geography 2; Economics 1) Objective 3: Identify some of the major industries of Mexico today. (Economics 2; Geography 3)	• Graphic Overview (584) • Access Strategy (585) • Access Activity (585) Critical Thinking (586) Economic Context (586)	Study Guide (102) Discovery Journal (51)
Lesson 3: A Blending of Cultures (1–2 days) Objective 1: Compare life in rural and urban Mexico. (Culture 2; Ethics and Belief Systems 1) Objective 2: Give some examples of different traditions expressed in Mexican fiestas and folk art. (Culture 1, 5; Ethics and Belief Systems 2) Objective 3: Describe recent trends in Mexico's political life. (Social and Political Systems 5; Economics 1)	• Graphic Overview (588) • Access Strategy (589) • Access Activity (589) • Visual Learning (590) Geographic Context (590) Art Connection (591) Study Skills (591) • Visual Learning (592) Research (592)	Study Guide (103) Map Activities (29) Discovery Journal (52) • Posters (7)
Chapter Review	Answers (594–595)	Tests (97–100)

* Objectives are correlated to the strands and goals in the program Scope and Sequence on pages T41–T49.

• LEP appropriate resources. (For additional strategies, see pages T32–T33.)

CHAPTER RATIONALE

For several reasons, the study of Mexico opens this unit on North America. Mexico was the first country on this continent to be settled by Europeans. In the past 150 years, Mexican history has been closely connected with that of its northern neighbors. Mexico is also the northernmost Latin American country and therefore provides a good transition from the previous unit.

As they read, students will observe that Mexican society is truly *mestizo.* From the encounter of the Spanish and Aztec civilizations institutions emerged that shared characteristics of both. Since its break from Spain, Mexico has been gaining a sense of its own identity. At the same time, it has been taking its place in the industrialized world and as a partner with other North American countries.

Lesson 1 shows how the political, social, economic, and religious institutions of colonial Mexico reflect the blend of the Spanish and Indian cultures. The lesson then briefly describes Mexico's struggle for independence, its development of its own identity, and the beginnings of industrialization. The lesson concludes with Mexico's ongoing social and economic revolutions, as the country seeks to modernize and develop its industries.

Lesson 2 gives an overview of the geographic resources and the economic development of Mexico. As a result of a paucity of agricultural land and a wealth of mineral resources, Mexico has shifted from an agricultural subsistence economy to one of producing raw materials for export, and finally to developing its own manufacturing base. Underlying this shift is Mexico's dilemma over whether to opt for a subsistence economy that is self-sufficient or for an export economy that depends on international markets. The lesson describes Mexico's oil reserves as a major factor in its decision to favor international trade. As Mexico's economy has grown, Mexico and the United States have become increasingly interdependent.

Lesson 3 describes Mexican culture today as a blend of two traditions. Indian and Spanish customs survive in the language, fiestas, religion, art, and many aspects of daily living, particularly in rural areas. In the cities, where 70 percent of Mexicans live today, modern ways have changed traditional roles. Mexico's growing cities face problems shared by large cities everywhere. The lesson concludes by observing that Mexico is moving in the direction of greater democracy and free trade.

ACTIVITIES & PROJECTS

Bulletin Board

Have students draw a large outline map of Mexico and place it on the bulletin board. As the class works through the chapter, they can add facts about Mexico to the map in the form of drawings, pictures, or index cards with the fact or facts written on them. Facts will include geographic features, historic sites, and historical events. Where possible, the fact should be linked to a specific area of Mexico. Have students explain the significance of the features that they add each day. (Use after any lesson.)

LEP: Making a Mural

Divide the class into groups of three or four people. Ask each group to draw or paint a place or an event from the chapter, such as the arrival of the Spaniards, the peasant revolt led by Emiliano Zapata, the central plateau, a local village, or Mexico City. Arrange the completed scenes in a logical order on a mural. Ask each group to explain what their scene represents. (Use after any lesson.)

Collaborative Learning

Have students put on a lively fiesta. Let them first decide what foods they would like to have and who will bring them in. Then volunteers can research some of the dances and music that are typical of fiestas and prepare or bring in samples of each. Students should also plan on dressing up in lively clothing, possibly sporting a mask or a headdress. Other classes could be invited to the fiesta. After the fiesta, have students write a paragraph describing what it is like to attend a fiesta. (Use after Lesson 3.)

Challenge: Writing a News Account

Have students write a one-page news account about any event discussed in the previous lessons. Students might report on the arrival of the Europeans, the friction between the *creoles* and the *peninsulares,* the rule of Porfirio Díaz, the "Mexican Miracle," Mexico's recent economic recovery, pollution and overpopulation problems, or the signing of the North American Free Trade Agreement. Students should explain the *who, what, when,* and *where* of the event they have chosen, and make predictions regarding its consequences. (Use after any lesson.)

LEP: Speaking and Listening

Have one group of students represent Mexicans living in a small village and a second group represent Mexicans living in a large city like Mexico City. Ask each group to discuss their lives. Topics might include what they do all day, what their homes are like, and what is important to them. After each group has spoken, have them explain how their lives differ from those of the other group. (Use after Lesson 3.)

Basic: Making a Timeline

Have students help you make a timeline on the chalkboard that includes events from all three lessons. After each lesson, ask for volunteers to update the timeline. Events should include the following: the arrival of Hernán Cortés, Mexico's fight for independence from Spain, the rule of Porfirio Díaz, the peasant revolt, and the signing of the North American Free Trade Agreement. (Use after Lesson 3.)

CHAPTER PREVIEW

Have students read the chapter title and the paragraph that follows it. Use a large map of the Western Hemisphere to help students locate Mexico. Tell students that although located in North America, Mexico has strong ties with its neighbors to the south because of similar history and heritage. Have students preview the chapter by briefly looking at section headings and illustrations, and then speculate on the peoples and events that have shaped Mexico's history.

Looking Forward

Tell students that they will learn about Mexico's history, its geography and climate, and its rich cultural traditions and changing population profile in the next three lessons: The Forming of Mexico, Regions and Resources, and A Blending of Cultures.

Lesson 1 traces Mexico's history from the first encounter between the Aztec Empire and the Spaniards to the social and economic revolutions of the early 1900s.

Chapter 25
Mexico

Mexico's culture, formed through the meeting of Spanish and ancient Indian civilizations, has kept traditions from both. In recent history, Mexico and the United States have had a close relationship. Mexicans are a proud people who honor their past as they look toward the promising future of North American unity.

The patterned fabric sold in a Mexico City market reveals the influence of both Spanish and Indian designs.

Before the arrival of the Spaniards, Indians had never seen people wearing armor or riding horses. This figure of Santiago (Saint James) was made by a Mexican artist during the colonial period.

1500 | 1600 | 1700

1521 Spaniards conquer Tenochtitlan, the capital of the Aztec Empire.

1519

BACKGROUND

Mexico, which covers about 756,000 square miles, has the third largest land area (after Brazil and Argentina) of Latin America. Mexico's large size, varied climate, and ethnic mix have created a cultural mosaic. Indian influences remain strong. As many as five million Mexicans speak one of more than fifty Indian languages. Because of the long border it shares with Mexico, the United States is an important neighbor.

Mineral Wealth

During the colonial period, the Indian laborers and enslaved Africans dug huge quantities of silver from mines at Guanajuato, San Luis Potosí, and Zacatecas. Mexico remains one of the world's leading silver producers.

Important copper deposits exist in the northern state of Sonora. Discontented copper miners at the Cananea mines in Sonora helped fuel the discontent against Porfirio Díaz that erupted in the Mexican Revolution of 1910.

By the 1920s Mexico ranked second only to the United States in oil production. In 1938 Mexican President Lázaro Cárdenas nationalized the foreign-owned oil companies in Mexico. In the 1970s Mexico discovered huge oil and natural gas deposits along its Gulf coast.

Boom to Bust

Mexicans hoped that with new mineral wealth, the government would fulfill the

Mexico City spreads over a high plateau surrounded by mountains. In the foreground is the Palace of Fine Arts, which contains many murals by Mexico's most famous painters.

Thick tortillas and meat and sausage flavored with chilies are being served at this market stand.

1800 1900 2000

1810 Struggle for independence begins.

1910 Mexican Revolution begins.

1988 President Salinas is elected.

Today

Understanding the Visuals

Situated in the Valley of Mexico, Mexico City (pictured on this page) is the nation's capital. Reminders of the city's past are everywhere, from still-standing Aztec ruins to ornate palaces built during the Spanish colonial period.

Understanding Chronology

Refer students to the time-line. Point out the lengths of three major periods in Mexican history: the colonial period of Spanish rule (289 years), the period of *creole* rule (lasted for 100 years, from the beginning of independence in 1810 until the outbreak of the Mexican Revolution in 1910), and the period of *mestizo* rule with dramatic social and economic changes and reforms (1910 to the present).

promise of the Mexican Revolution. Mexican presidents began many ambitious projects—schools, hospitals, and apartment buildings. Mexico borrowed billions of dollars from the United States and other foreign countries, using its oil reserves as collateral. When oil prices and the demand for oil dropped sharply in the late 1970s, Mexico had to abandon many projects and could not pay the interest on its huge foreign debt. Although Mexico still struggles with its debt problem, Mexicans hope that increased tourism and expanding industry and trade will continue to improve their economy.

New North American Trade Agreement

The North American Free Trade Agreement (NAFTA) was planned to produce greater economic exchanges among the United States, Mexico, and Canada. Opinion is divided on the benefits of this treaty. Many believe that NAFTA may increase competition between U.S. and Mexican workers. Mexican workers are paid so much less than U.S. workers that this competition could lower wages in the United States and encourage factory owners to relocate south of the border. Some in the United States also worry about the effects of the treaty on the environment. Pollution standards and enforcement of laws against polluters are not yet as rigorous in Mexico as they are in the United States.

INTRODUCE

Tell students that Mexico experienced a long period of colonial rule by a European power. While it was a colony of Spain, Mexico was known as "New Spain." Have students read the Thinking Focus. Ask what kind of complaints colonial subjects might have against the colonial power that controls them. *(Taxation without representation, lack of political or economic power, favoritism for those from the home country and for wealthy and powerful colonists, discrimination against colonial subjects, lack of respect for and little understanding of the culture of local peoples)* Have students read the lesson to see if any of these complaints were causes of Mexico's fight for independence.

Key Terms

Vocabulary Strategies: T36–T37

conquistador—one of the Spanish people who conquered New Spain

hacienda—a large estate in a Spanish-speaking region

peon—an Indian who became a peasant after losing land to the Spaniards

1500 | 1519 | TODAY

LESSON 1

The Forming of Mexico

THINKING FOCUS

What were the major causes of Mexico's fight for independence?

Key Terms

- conquistador
- hacienda
- peon

Montezuma, the Aztec emperor, was worried. For some time messengers had told him of floating mountains in the water offshore and of bearded men who rode deerlike animals (horses) and had weapons such as the Aztecs had never seen.

Montezuma feared that the leader of these men might be a God who had come to reclaim his kingdom. On November 8, 1519, he let Hernán Cortés and his followers into the city of Tenochtitlan.

At their first meeting with Cortés and his men, the Aztecs were amazed at the horses and the iron armor of the Spaniards.

Colonization of Mexico

Two years later the Spaniards and their Native American allies conquered the city. Tenochtitlan had been the political, religious, and marketing center of the Aztec Empire. Under Spanish rule, the city was rebuilt and became Mexico City, the capital of New Spain.

Setting Up a Spanish Colony

After the conquest two urban civilizations blended. The Spaniards took over the Aztecs' centralized system of government. Through this system, tribute from all over the empire had poured into Tenochtitlan. The **conquistadors**—the new Spanish overlords—allowed the local lords and chiefs to keep their titles, gather tribute payments, and recruit free labor.

After the conquest the Spaniards recruited Indian craftworkers to rebuild the city destroyed by warfare. New cities blended Spanish and traditional Indian styles.

Most Spanish settlers stayed in the cities. Here they mixed with the Indians and had children with Indian women. These children were the first Mexican *mestizos.*

Objectives

1. Describe the effects of Spanish colonialism in Mexico.
2. Describe Mexico's struggle for independence.
3. Describe Mexico's social and economic revolution.

Graphic Overview

Spaniards Conquer the Aztec Empire ➤ Spanish, Indian, and African Cultures Blend ➤ Mexico Gains Independence ➤ Peasants Revolt Against Díaz ➤ Mexico Modernizes

◄ *The Spaniards and the peoples of the Americas loved gold. Examples of this love are the detailed golden ceiling of this Spanish church and the ceremonial cup (below) created by people of northwest Peru.*

Across Time & Space

English colonists arrived in New England with their families and tended to establish colonies separate from the Indians. Most early Spanish settlers, on the other hand, came without wives or families. They tended to marry Indian women.

Following the conquistadors, missionaries from Spain arrived to convert the Indians to Catholicism. The friars learned Indian languages and set up schools and missions.

Some Indians believed the God of the Christians had defeated their Gods. As Indians came to accept Christianity, they often blended the new religion with their old beliefs.

Sometimes, Indian workers hid images of their Gods in the new churches they built. Thus Indians could secretly continue to honor their Gods while worshiping in Christian churches. You can read more about this in Understanding Historical Evidence on page 583.

Extracting Wealth from Mexico

The conquistadors brought many other changes to Mexico. They imported sheep, pigs, horses, and cattle and let them roam freely over Indian land. They brought in wheat, barley, and a variety of vegetables.

As new settlers came from Spain, more food was needed for the cities. Spanish settlers formed large estates called **haciendas** *(hah see EHN duhz)*. Many took over part of the communal lands owned by Indian villages.

Many Indians who had lost their lands became **peons,** or peasants. Often they received pay in advance from their employers, whom they could not repay. The peons would then lose the freedom to leave their masters' *haciendas.*

Spanish settlers had been dazzled by the Aztecs' gold and silver and were eager to find more for themselves. The Native Americans had practiced surface mining, but now the Spaniards opened underground silver mines. Some Indians were forced to work in these mines. Soon the Spaniards needed more workers. They brought enslaved Africans to do this work.

When the conquistadors arrived, about 21 million Indians lived in central Mexico. By 1700 just over one million remained. Most died from diseases brought by the Spaniards or enslaved Africans. Many others died from bad treatment and overwork. ■

■ How did life change for the Indians after the Spanish conquest?

DEVELOP

Refer students to the timeline, and draw the Graphic Overview on the chalkboard. Explain that the lesson is presented chronologically. Students may want to keep a list of important events, dates, and Mexican leaders as they read. Have students decide to which box in the Graphic Overview each listed item belongs.

■ *Millions of Indians died from diseases and poor treatment at the hands of the Spaniards. Many Indians who survived lost their lands, intermixed with the Spaniards, converted to Christianity, and worked for the Spaniards as peons.*

Access Strategy

Explain to students that in most societies cultural exchange goes on constantly. Have students name some foods from other countries that are now an accepted part of the U.S. diet—for example, tacos, sushi, and pasta. Ask them to think of musical styles that have originated in other cultures—such as reggae and samba from Central and South America. Then consider fashion styles or words from other languages that have become a part of U.S. society. Students might identify some of the products and ideas brought to the Americas by the Spaniards. *(Animals, foods, religious beliefs, weapons, political institutions)* List responses on the chalkboard. Have students put a plus or a minus sign next to each and tell why the borrowed item either enriched or harmed Native American cultures.

Access Activity

Ask students to examine the visuals on this page and consider the following questions. What cultures are represented? *(Spanish and Peruvian cultures)* What might the gold in these visuals indicate about Spain's presence in Mexico? *(The Spanish love of gold fueled much of the exploration and exploitation in early Mexico.)*

ECONOMICS

Critical Thinking

Have students examine the impact of *haciendas* on the Indians. Ask them to compare the communal land-owning practices of the Indians with their roles and rights as workers on *haciendas.* Point out that under the Spaniards, the life of peasants was similar to that of serfs or indentured servants in other parts of the world. What tied the Indians to *haciendas*? *(Debt, fear of force, lack of other alternatives)* What impact did this system have on their ability to earn a living? *(It kept the peasants poor.)* Point out that the Mexican peasants who were descendants of the Indians made landless by the Spaniards were firm supporters of Emiliano Zapata in the 1910 Revolution.

➤ *Texas won its independence from Mexico after the two had gone to war in 1836. The United States took over the territories of northern Mexico after the war with Mexico, 1846–1848.*

Mexican Independence

The rulers of Mexico were often sent from Spain. They were called *peninsulares,* after the peninsula where Spain is located. The children of Spaniards who settled in Mexico were called *creoles.* In the 1800s the *creoles* came to resent the new *peninsulares* who ruled Mexico.

Fighting for Independence

In 1810 the parish priest of the town of Dolores was a *creole* called Miguel Hidalgo y Costilla. He felt that the Indians had been treated unjustly by the Spaniards. With *creole* friends he planned a revolt against the government.

On September 16, 1810, Hidalgo heard that their plot had been discovered. Quickly he had the church bells rung, calling his people to church. With the now-famous *Grito de Dolores*, "the cry of Dolores," he told them to rise up against their Spanish rulers:

> *My children: . . . Will you free yourselves? Will you recover the lands stolen three hundred years ago from your forefathers by the hated Spaniards? We must act at once. . . . Long live our Lady of Guadalupe! Death to the Spaniards! . . .*

Heading an army of poor Indians and *mestizos,* Hidalgo marched to Mexico City. There his army was defeated. Later, he was executed.

Ten years later, a group of *creoles* succeeded in making the break from Spanish rule. For *mestizos* and Indians, little was gained. The *creoles* were now their masters.

Defending Independence

Soon Mexico faced new dangers. In 1836 Texas fought against Mexico and won its independence. Ten years later the United States went to war with Mexico and, in 1848, seized over half of its territory. The map on this page shows how much land Mexico eventually lost to the United States. Even today some descendants of families from

How did Mexico lose Texas? When did the United States take over the territories of northern Mexico?

Mexico: Changing Borders, 1835–1853

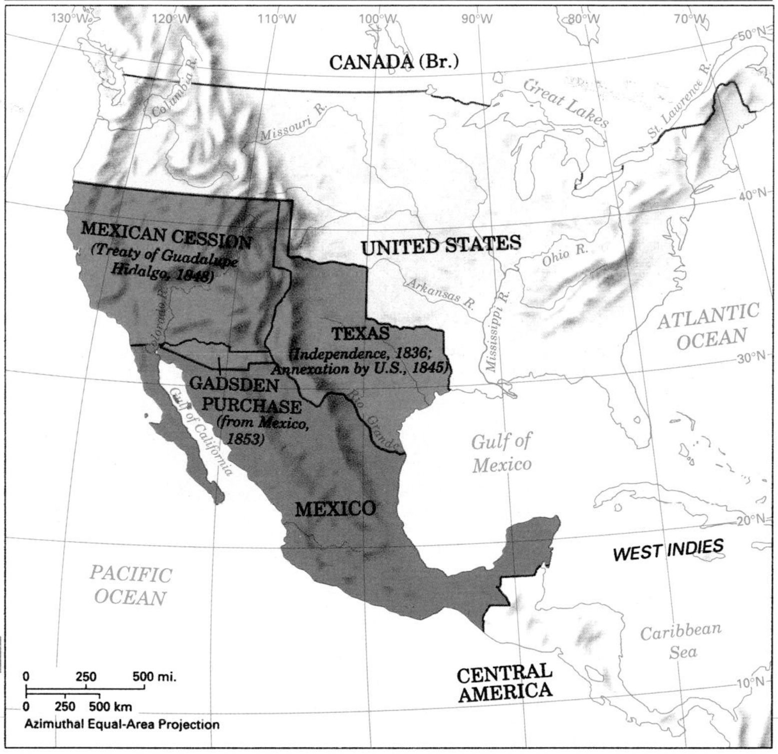
130°W
120°W
110°W
100°W
90°W
80°W
70°W
50°N
40°N
30°N
20°N
10°N
CANADA (Br.)
Great Lakes
St. Lawrence R.
Columbia R.
Missouri R.
MEXICAN CESSION
(Treaty of Guadalupe Hidalgo, 1848)
UNITED STATES
Ohio R.
Arkansas R.
Mississippi R.
Colorado R.
TEXAS
(Independence, 1836; Annexation by U.S., 1845)
GADSDEN PURCHASE
(from Mexico, 1853)
Gulf of California
Rio Grande
ATLANTIC OCEAN
Gulf of Mexico
MEXICO
WEST INDIES
PACIFIC OCEAN
Caribbean Sea
CENTRAL AMERICA
0 250 500 mi.
0 250 500 km
Azimuthal Equal-Area Projection

Map and Globe Skills

Ask students to study the map on this page carefully. Have them name some different kinds of information that can be learned from studying this map. What can they learn about the Mexican Cession, Texas, and the Gadsden Purchase? Have them trace with their fingers the current U.S.-Mexican border.

Collaborative Learning

Have students role-play the struggle for Mexican independence. Assign students the roles of Spaniards, *creoles,* and Indians. Have the members of each group draw up a speech representing their point of view on Mexico's drive for independence. Students representing the Spaniards should urge the people to remain loyal to the king (the Spaniards would profit the most by keeping in place the existing economic and political system). Students role-playing *creoles* should demand access to higher political and religious offices and greater economic freedom. Finally, students representing Indians should demand the return of their land and an end to the abuses. After hearing the speeches of role-players calling for acceptance of their positions, the class can decide whether the differing goals of these groups could have been resolved without conflict.

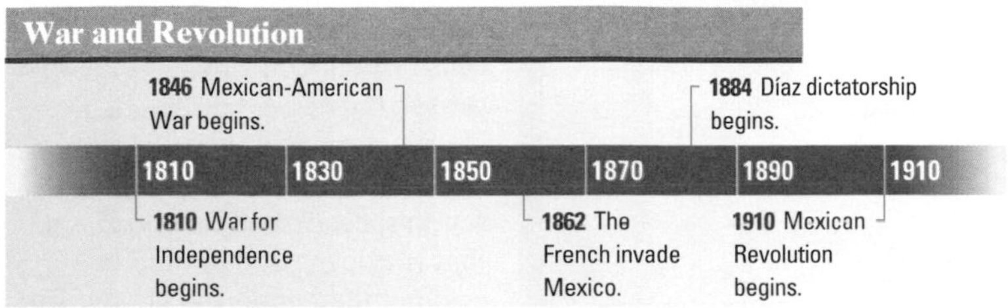
War and Revolution
1846 Mexican-American War begins.
1884 Díaz dictatorship begins.
1810
1830
1850
1870
1890
1910
1810 War for Independence begins.
1862 The French invade Mexico.
1910 Mexican Revolution begins.

Mexico's lost territories still think of these as Mexican lands.

In 1862, France tried to expand its empire by attacking Mexico. Mexicans defeated the French at the Battle of Puebla on May 5, 1862. Mexicans continue to celebrate this victory every Cinco de Mayo (fifth of May).

Their victory did not last. The French again invaded. This time they chose an emperor. Three years later the French were forced to withdraw, and Mexico was free. ■

◄ How many wars did Mexicans fight in the 1800s?

■ How did the fight for Mexican independence begin?

Social and Economic Revolution

As an independent nation, Mexico wrestled with problems dating back to the Spanish conquest. New leaders, some Indian and some *mestizo,* came to power.

New Leaders

Benito Juárez, a Zapotec Indian, had been president before the French invasion. He became president again. During his rule he encouraged the building of railroads. He also supported free education for young children.

In 1876 Porfirio Díaz, a *mestizo* general, took control and ruled first as president and later as dictator. He encouraged foreign investment and built thousands of miles of railroads. Now trains whisked cotton, iron ore, and other raw materials to factories throughout Mexico.

In spite of these improvements, many Mexicans resented Díaz. The profits from industry went to foreigners and enriched few Mexicans. Díaz also let big landowners take over *ejidos (ay HEE dohs)*, the communal native lands. Many Indians were now forced to work for others on what had been their own property.

Revolution and Land Reform

By 1910 simmering anger exploded into revolution against Díaz. Fighting began in the north and spread throughout Mexico. Leaders formed bands of armed peons.

One of these leaders was Emiliano Zapata, a *mestizo* from southern Mexico. A few months after the revolution had begun, Zapata called on local villagers to join the fight. He commanded fierce loyalty from the peasants because of his demand for *Tierra y Libertad!*—"Land and Liberty!"

Zapata turned the landless peasants of his region into a tough army that swooped down on the haciendas. When a hacienda surrendered, he divided the land among the peons who had worked on it.

▲ Porfirio Díaz, in the center of the photo above, resigned the presidency of Mexico in May 1911. He then went into exile.

◄ Mexicans fought four wars (including the fight against the French invasion in 1862).

■ Creoles, mestizos, *and Indian peasants led by Miguel Hidalgo began the uprising against Spain. Ten years later Spanish rule ended.*

POLITICAL SYSTEMS

Critical Thinking

Ask students to compare the attitudes of Porfirio Díaz and Emiliano Zapata regarding land distribution and the rights of peasants. *(Díaz gave the communal native lands to big landowners and failed to improve the lives of the peasants; Zapata wanted to give the land back to the peasants and win them greater freedom and power.)* Based on this information, students should comment on why the overthrow of Díaz was successful.

Political Context

In 1965 Mexican scholar Pablo González published *Democracy in Mexico.* He reminded Mexicans that the lives of Indians had improved little since Spanish colonialism: "The Indian problem is essentially one of internal colonialism. The Indian communities are Mexico's internal colonies. . . . [I]n those regions in which both Indians and [*mestizos*] live, we find prejudice, discrimination, colonial types of exploitation, dictatorial forms, and . . . dominant and dominated populations."

Historical Context

A Mexican writer, Mariano Azuela, wrote a short novel that captured the agony of the Mexican Revolution. He published *The Underdogs* during the revolution in 1915, and it remains a powerful description of the time. Azuela wrote from the point of view of an illiterate peasant, Demetrio. Azuela's novel ends on a pessimistic note. Despite all the violence, life does not seem much better. Most Mexicans believe that the suffering of the time was necessary to bring about needed reforms.

Study Skills

Have students research one of the following figures in Mexico's history: Miguel Hidalgo, Santa Anna, Benito Juárez, Maximilian, Porfirio Díaz, Francisco "Pancho" Villa, Emiliano Zapata. Tell them to organize their notes and then present their findings in an outline in which all items are complete sentences.

CULTURE

Visual Learning

The Mexican Revolution that began in 1910 inspired many artists, including Diego Rivera and José Clemente Orozco. These artists created murals and paintings that glorified the revolution and the Mexican nation. How did such murals, like this one by Orozco, painted on a public building, create support for the revolution among the peasants?

■ *The goals of the revolution were to end Díaz's dictatorship and bring about land reform.*

CLOSE

Read the Thinking Focus aloud. Have students respond. Point out that Mexicans of all social classes became discontented with Spanish colonial rule. Ask students to specify the major source of discontent for each social class. *(Upper-class* creoles *wanted economic control, self-government, and an end to discrimination against them; middle-class* mestizos *wanted economic opportunity; Indians wanted land; enslaved Africans wanted freedom; people disliked Spain's taxes, monopolies, and favoritism toward* peninsulares.)

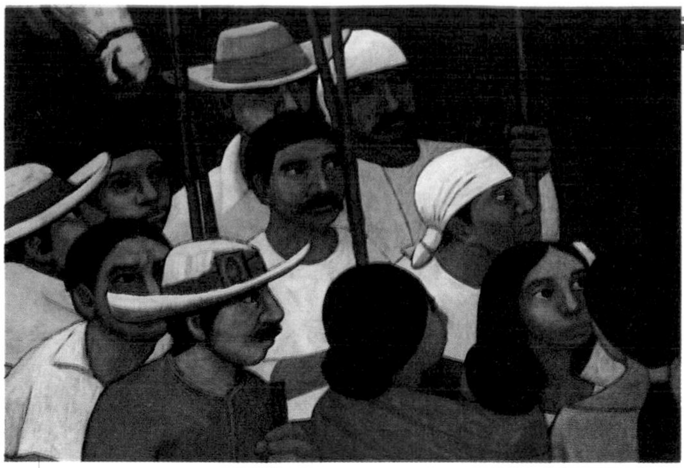

▲ *José Clemente Orozco, a famous painter from the time of the revolution, painted this mural of Mexican peasants in revolt.*

■ *What were the goals of the Mexican Revolution?*

When the revolution finally ended in the 1920s, its ideals were written into a new constitution. However, land reform didn't begin until Lázaro Cárdenas, a *mestizo,* became president in 1934.

Cárdenas turned 50 million acres of hacienda land into *ejidos*. He also encouraged workers in the cities to organize. In 1938, when the foreign-owned oil companies had refused to increase workers' pay, Cárdenas decided that the government should take over the oil companies. In a rush of national pride, thousands of Mexicans gave whatever they had to pay off the foreign owners.

Modernizing Mexico

World War II brought about many changes in the Mexican economy. For years Mexico had exported raw materials and imported consumer goods. Now the United States, Mexico's main supplier, was busy producing arms for war. Mexicans responded by developing their own industries.

After the war the government encouraged growing industries. It set up special taxes on imports so that Mexican goods would be cheaper than imported goods. The government also built roads, railroads, and dams to provide electricity. Large foreign corporations, mostly from the United States, opened branches in Mexico where wages were low. The Mexican government also encouraged tourism.

At this time the government ended its program of land reform. It began large irrigation projects that increased the amount of farmland. Its policies favored large farms that could grow huge amounts of cotton and winter vegetables for export. Many small farmers could not keep up and went to the cities to find jobs.

Profits from the booming economy still went mostly to foreigners. However, the increased number of jobs did help many Mexicans rise into the middle class. At the same time, government spending on health care reduced infant deaths and helped adults live longer. Mexico's population increased rapidly.

Mexico called the "Mexican Miracle" by many—became Latin America's greatest success. During this time Mexico's economy became more closely tied to U.S. markets and capital. ■

REVIEW

1. **FOCUS** What were the major causes of Mexico's fight for independence?
2. **POLITICAL SYSTEMS** Did Indians and *mestizos* gain much from independence before the French invaded?
3. **ECONOMICS** How did events in World War II affect Mexico's economy?
4. **CRITICAL THINKING** Why might Spain have kept important government positions for the *peninsulares*?
5. **ACTIVITY** Write and deliver a one-minute speech supporting or opposing Díaz's modernization plans.

Homework Options

After students have read the lesson, ask them to choose an event or a development in Mexico's history that they think was important in shaping life in Mexico today. Have them write a paragraph explaining the importance of the event or development they choose.

Study Guide: page 100

Answers to Review Questions

1. The *creoles* wanted more say in the government and to control the economy, and the *mestizos* a greater share of the economy.
2. The Indians and *mestizos* gained little from independence. The *creoles* took over power from the Spaniards.
3. Since fewer manufactured goods were available from the United States, Mexico began industries to manufacture some goods for itself.
4. Answers may vary, but students might indicate that the *peninsulares* secured positions of power because they were newly arrived from Spain and would be more loyal to the Spanish king and his policies.
5. Supporting speeches might stress how Díaz's work laid the basis for Mexico's industry. Opposing speeches might argue that the few profited at the expense of the many and that the Indian peasants in particular suffered from the loss of land.

UNDERSTANDING HISTORICAL EVIDENCE

Interpreting Artifacts

Here's Why

In Chapter 4, you read about examining art to get a better understanding of how people live. You also can learn from artifacts, or the things that people made and used in their daily lives, to understand people of the past.

Artifacts you might examine include weapons, clothes, pots and pans, tools, furniture, and even toys. The list is endless. How these things were made and used can shed light on what was important in people's lives.

In this chapter you read about the meeting of the Aztec and Spanish civilizations. Artifacts of the time can reveal the way people's beliefs changed or adapted.

Here's How

Here are some steps you might take to learn from the artifact on this page.

1. **Study the artifact carefully.** What does it look like? What is it made of? Does it have any decorations? What do they represent? You see that the artifact is a block of stone, wider and flatter on one side. It looks like the base of a column lying on its side. It has a carving on the flat side. An archaeologist might tell you that this carving represents the Aztec God Tlaltecuhtli, lord of the earth. The carving was made to face the earth; it is the underside of the artifact.
2. **What is already known about the artifact?** Where was it found? How was it used? This stone came from an ancient Aztec temple. It was reused by Indian workers to build a church. They shaped the stone into a column base, with the carving facing down.
3. **What does this information tell us?** Why was it used this way? Did it have a special meaning for those who used it? By using this ancient carving as a column base for a Christian church, Indian builders secretly placed their God within the church building. As they prayed to the God of the Spaniards, they could also continue to worship their own God.

Try It

This artifact is an excellent example of the cultural *mestizaje (mehs tee ZUH hay)*, or the blending of Indian and Spanish cultures. Explain why.

Apply It

Your entire bedroom is filled with artifacts that tell about the daily life of a student living in the United States! Imagine you are a historian examining an artifact from your room, such as a tape player or a pair of jeans. Write a paragraph describing your "artifact" and what it could tell about its user.

Mexico

583

UNDERSTANDING HISTORICAL EVIDENCE

This skill feature uses an illustration of a stone from an Aztec temple to teach students how artifacts can provide valuable information about the culture and way of life of people in the distant past.

CULTURE

Visual Learning

Have students examine the figure of Saint James on horseback on page 576. Ask them to imagine that they are the first archaeologists to uncover this figure. Have them try to answer these questions about the artifact: What does it show? *(A man riding a horse)* What might it be made of? *(Stone)* When was it made? *(The colonial period)* Does it have any decorations? *(Armor, cross on man's chest)* If so, what do they represent? *(Santiago was a knight and a Christian.)* Where was it found? *(Not known)* How was it used? *(Possibly in a church or in processions during a fiesta honoring this saint)* Next, have students speculate on how they might find information on any of the questions they could not answer from looking at the figure.

Answers to Try It

The stone represents the combination of the Spanish and Native American cultures on two levels. Physically, the stone from an Aztec temple was used to build a Spanish church. Religiously, the stone's presence in the church allowed Native Americans to worship their own God while they prayed to the God of the Spaniards.

Answer to Apply It

Students' paragraphs should give a full description of their artifacts: shape, size, color, and so on. Then students should speculate on how a visitor from the future might interpret the artifacts' uses and what they reveal about the users' beliefs and values.

Objective

Interpret information presented in an artifact. (Visual Learning 1)

INTRODUCE

Direct students to the lesson title. Have them distinguish between human and natural resources. Ask them to identify some of Mexico's natural resources they learned about in Lesson 1. Ask students why climate can be considered a resource. *(Possible answer: Climate determines whether conditions are right for farming.)* In what kinds of industry might a warm climate be important? *(Farming, fishing)* Note that Mexico is a country of many different climates and diverse resources. Tell students to read the Thinking Focus, and then have them preview the lesson to predict how the question might be answered.

Key Term

Vocabulary Strategies: T36–T37

border—an area or line that separates two regions or nations

1500 1519 TODAY

L E S S O N 2

Regions and Resources

THINKING FOCUS

What natural resources have helped Mexico's economy grow?

Key Term

- border

Emperor Charles V, Spain's ruler during the conquest of Mexico, never saw his new colony. When a messenger arrived to report on Mexico, Charles V asked, "What is the land like?"

The messenger took a sheet of paper and crushed it in his hand. Then opening his palm, he showed the crumpled paper to the emperor. "It is like this, sire," he said.

Like the messenger's crumpled paper, two-thirds of Mexico's land is folded into huge, ragged mountains. The rest is made up of high plateaus and coastal plains.

The forces that shaped the land of Mexico are still at work. In 1943 and again in 1982, volcanoes erupted, and seas of lava swallowed up land and crops. In 1985 a terrible earthquake shook and damaged Mexico City.

The Land and Its Resources

Look back at the map on page 580. You can see that Mexico lies between the United States and Central America. In the past, agriculture supported a limited population. The minerals and oil discovered in later times are Mexico's greatest natural resources. These and the labor of its growing population are the main assets of Mexico today.

Diversity of Land and Climate

Mexico's mountains divide the land into six very diverse regions. The largest is the high, dry plateau of Mexico. It is ringed by high mountains often crested with snow. Most of Mexico's cities and half of its population are on the plateau. Mexico's five other regions surround this area.

It is harvest time in the high Valley of Toluca, central Mexico. Maguey plants grow in the foreground. Their tough fiber is used to make mats.

Objectives

1. Describe the main geographic resources of Mexico.
2. Identify the main natural resources of Mexico.
3. Identify some of the major industries of Mexico today.

Graphic Overview

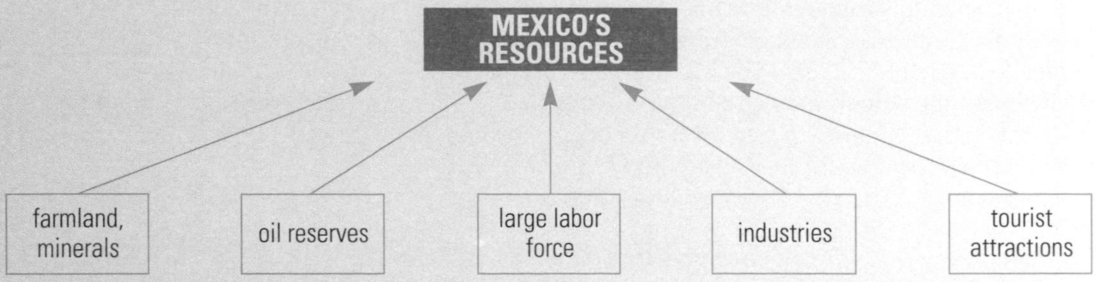
MEXICO'S RESOURCES
farmland, minerals
oil reserves
large labor force
industries
tourist attractions

Mexico: Physical Regions and Resources

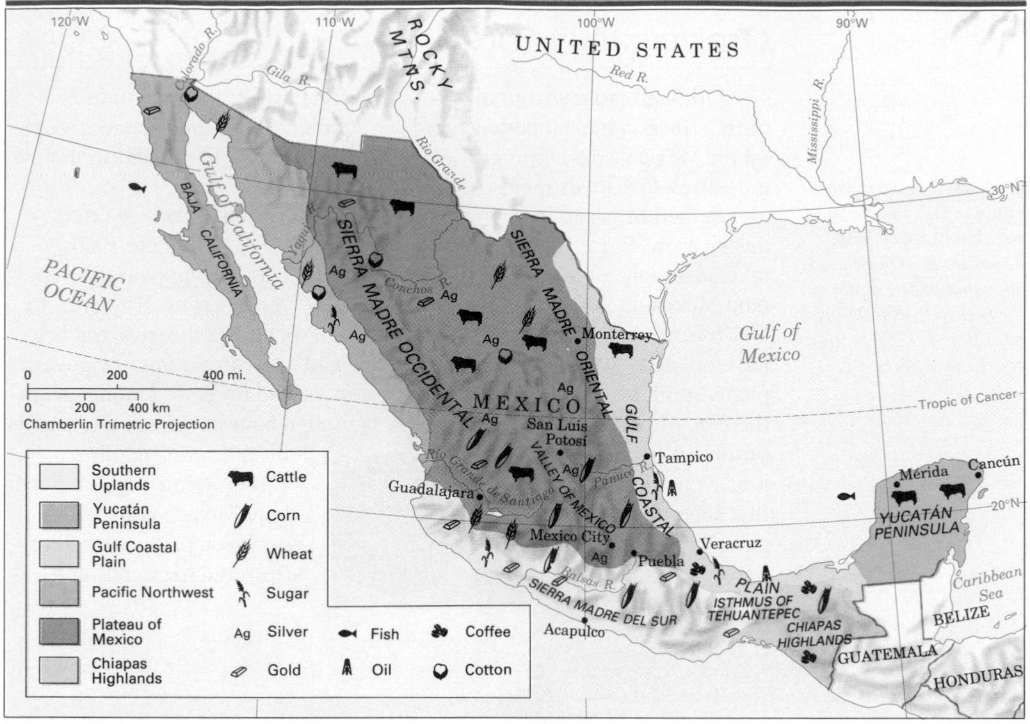
120°W
110°W
100°W
90°W
UNITED STATES
ROCKY MTNS.
Colorado R.
Gila R.
Red R.
Mississippi R.
Rio Grande
30°N
PACIFIC OCEAN
Gulf of California
BAJA CALIFORNIA
Yaqui R.
Conchos R.
SIERRA MADRE OCCIDENTAL
SIERRA MADRE ORIENTAL
Monterrey
Gulf of Mexico
MEXICO
San Luis Potosí
GULF COASTAL PLAIN
Tampico
Pánuco R.
Tropic of Cancer
Mérida
Cancún
YUCATÁN PENINSULA
20°N
Guadalajara
Rio Grande de Santiago
VALLEY OF MEXICO
Mexico City
Puebla
Veracruz
Balsas R.
SIERRA MADRE DEL SUR
Acapulco
ISTHMUS OF TEHUANTEPEC
CHIAPAS HIGHLANDS
Caribbean Sea
BELIZE
GUATEMALA
HONDURAS
0 200 400 mi.
0 200 400 km
Chamberlin Trimetric Projection
Southern Uplands
Yucatán Peninsula
Gulf Coastal Plain
Pacific Northwest
Plateau of Mexico
Chiapas Highlands
Cattle
Corn
Wheat
Sugar
Ag Silver
Gold
Fish
Oil
Coffee
Cotton

Within each region the mountains create areas with very different climates and vegetation. The mountains also isolated the valleys, so people in each valley often had their own culture.

Agriculture

By some estimates only one-third of Mexico's land can be farmed. Today much of Mexico's best land is divided into large, irrigated farms and ranches. Their products are mostly for export: winter vegetables and fruits, cotton, coffee, and cattle. Most of these are sold to the United States.

By contrast, most of the *ejidos* that were given to the Indians were small, dry pieces of land. Since these small farmlands cannot produce enough food to feed the growing population, Mexico imports corn and wheat.

Mexico's coastal waters are an important source of food and export. Each year Mexico's fisheries catch large amounts of shrimp, tuna, sardines, and oysters.

Mining and Oil

Mexico's rugged land may be poor for farming, but it holds a treasure of minerals. Mexico is the world's largest producer of silver. It is also a major producer of 14 other minerals including lead, zinc, copper, gold, and iron. Exports of these minerals earn millions of dollars for Mexico's economy.

In the 1970s, drillers found huge oil reserves in Mexico, giving the country the fourth largest oil supply in the world. Soon Mexico gained billions of dollars from oil exports. It used this income to develop and improve its roads and industries. ■

▲ *Which is the largest of Mexico's regions? Which crops are grown only on low-lying plains?*

■ *How do Mexico's mountains affect the lives of Mexicans?*

DEVELOP

In this lesson students will learn about Mexico's land and resources and how the Mexican people have used the resources to develop their industries. As students read, have them make a list of the industries that have developed from each of the following natural resources: land, climate, coastal waters, and mineral resources.

◄ *The plateau of Mexico is the country's largest region. Sugar and coffee are grown only on low-lying plains.*

■ *Because of the mountains, Mexicans have different climates and vegetation in each valley. The mountains have served as barriers between the valleys. As a result, people in different valleys often developed unique cultures.*

Access Strategy

Discuss with students the concept of borders. Point out that states, cities, and even neighborhoods can have borders. Have students give examples of physical borders or landmarks that separate different parts of their neighborhood or city from one another. *(Streets, bridges, railroad tracks, buildings, highways, rivers)* Then have students identify cultural borders within their community. For example, many cities have ethnic neighborhoods where restaurants serve ethnic foods and grocery stores offer specialty foods for neighborhood residents. Note differences in the kinds of jobs and services offered in areas that border one another. End by considering how the borders within a community both separate people and bring them together.

Access Activity

Have students locate landforms and water bodies in Mexico on a map of North America. Then have them name similar physical features in the United States. *(Both have active volcanoes, such as Mount Saint Helens. The countries share the Rocky Mountain range, the Rio Grande, and coasts on the Pacific Ocean and the Gulf of Mexico.)*

ECONOMICS

Critical Thinking

Ask students to pretend they are Mexican business executives deciding where to build a factory. What are the advantages of locating their factory near the U.S. border? *(Access and lower transportation costs to U.S. markets, access to needed technology and machinery in the United States, potential for growing markets in the United States and Canada because of NAFTA)*

GEOGRAPHY

Map and Globe Skills

Explain that the location of a valley and the mountains around it can determine the amount of sun and rain it receives. Altitude is also a critical factor in climate. Differences in altitude create three temperature zones in Mexico: below 3,000 feet is the *tierra caliente* (hot land); between 3,000 and 6,000 feet is the *tierra templada* (temperate land); and above 6,000 feet, is the *tierra fria* (cold land). Have students use an elevation map of Mexico to identify each of these zones. This activity will help students understand why so little of Mexico's land is well suited to farming.

Growing Industries

Although money from oil exports provided much needed capital for Mexico's developing industries, U.S. investment also helped Mexican industry grow. Eager to take advantage of low-paid Mexican labor, U.S. businesses have opened plants south of the U.S.-Mexican border. A **border** is an area or line that separates two regions or nations. The importance of borders, particularly in the case of the United States and Mexico, is explained in the feature below.

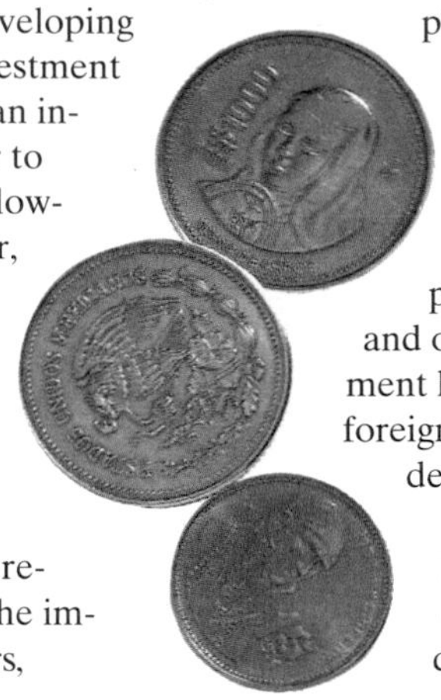

➤ *In 1993 the Mexican Finance Ministry began circulating a new peso. Today three of these pesos are equal to one dollar in the United States. Before 1993 it took 3,000 pesos to equal one dollar.*

From Miracle to Crisis

In the late 1960s, Mexico appeared to be prosperous. However, to pay for industries, roads, and other programs, the government had borrowed money from foreign banks. It planned to pay its debt by exporting oil.

For a time high oil prices kept Mexico going. Suddenly, oil prices started to drop, and Mexico found

Understanding Borders

Mexico and the United States share a 2,000-mile border. It stretches from the Pacific Ocean to the Gulf of Mexico.

Kinds of Borders

A border can be formed by a physical barrier such as a river or a mountain range. As you can see by the map on page 585, the Rio Grande (a river called the Rio Bravo del Norte in Mexico) forms part of the border between Mexico and the United States.

A border can also be cultural. For instance, the Mexican-U.S. border separates two societies with very different histories and cultural roots. Mexico's culture is the result of a unique mix of Spanish-Catholic influence and Indian traditions. The United States is mostly Protestant in religion and English in language.

Borders are also economic. The U.S.-Mexican border is one of the few places in the world where two countries with very different economic systems and resources meet.

The Role of Borders

Borders are lines that both separate and join. People divided by a border are almost sure to have contact.

In spite of their differences, Mexico and the United States depend upon and influence each other. Of the world's countries, Mexico is third in the value of goods it buys from the United States. It is about fourth in the value of goods it sells to the United States. U.S. investments were crucial in Mexico's industrial development. On the other hand, U.S. businesses have drawn heavily on Mexican labor and raw materials.

As you cross the border, differences between the two countries strike you immediately. However, the mixing of people and exchange of goods that take place create a region where U.S. and Mexican cultures blend.

Critical Thinking

Have students explain the differences in the three kinds of borders between Mexico and the United States: physical, cultural, and economic. Ask students which kind of border is easiest to bridge today. *(Physical)* Which is most difficult? *(Students may respond that either the cultural or economic border is the most difficult to bridge.)*

Economic Context

In 1988 Carlos Salinas de Gortari, an economist trained at Harvard University in the United States, became president of Mexico. His philosophy was to use free enterprise to improve Mexico's economy. He decreased the government's role in the economy by "privatizing" industries such as banks, the telephone company, and the steel industry.

Salinas also favored free trade. Mexico and the United States have long-standing economic and trade links. As a part of its plan to repay its debt, Mexico committed itself to opening up its economy. This has meant less government protection for Mexican industries, because the government has lowered taxes, or duties, on foreign imports. Beginning in the mid-1980s, imports from the United States increased as they became cheaper for the Mexican consumer.

itself in trouble in the early 1980s. It was $80 billion in debt with no money to repay its loans.

The Mexican Miracle quickly fell apart. The government cut its support to industry and stopped some major construction projects. Tens of thousands of people lost their jobs. The value of the peso, the Mexican unit of currency, dropped. As a result, inflation soared. The price of a hamburger that once cost 10 pesos zoomed to 100 pesos.

Today Mexico is recovering from these problems. The government has cut spending. It has cut back on protecting Mexican industry and has sold many state-owned businesses to private owners. Forced to compete, these businesses have become more profitable.

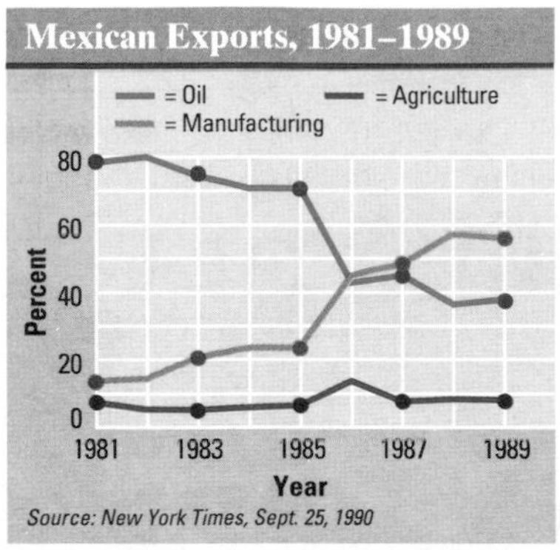

Mexican Exports, 1981–1989
= Oil
= Agriculture
= Manufacturing
80
60
40
20
0
Percent
1981
1983
1985
1987
1989
Year
Source: New York Times, Sept. 25, 1990

▲ *(left) As oil prices fell, Mexican oil exports became less important than manufacturing exports. (right) Many women find work in the* maquiladora *assembly plants.*

Mexican Industry Today

Today Mexico's industries produce about one-fourth of the national income. Many products such as cars, chemicals, electrical products, and processed foods are made for export, mostly to the United States. As you can see on the graph above, exports of manufactured goods have become very important.

Most of Mexico's factories are located in the central plateau region. Mexico City alone has half of the nation's industries. Monterrey is a major steel manufacturing center. Puebla and Guadalajara are two of Mexico's major industrial centers.

Many U.S. manufacturing plants have been opened in Mexico. These plants, called *maquiladoras (mah kee lah DAW rahs)* in Spanish, import parts to be assembled at low cost by Mexican workers. Today the number of *maquiladoras* is growing, and their workers are often highly skilled technicians.

Tourism is also a growing source of jobs and income for Mexicans. More than six million tourists visit Mexico each year.

Although expanding, Mexico's industry cannot provide work for the 800,000 workers who join the labor force each year. As a result, thousands slip across the U.S. border to look for work. ■

■ *What are Mexico's major industries, and what is their importance to the economy?*

REVIEW

1. **FOCUS** What natural resources have helped Mexico's economy grow?
2. **GEOGRAPHY** What geographic features dominate Mexico's landscape?
3. **ECONOMICS** How has oil affected Mexico's economic growth?
4. **CRITICAL THINKING** How do you think Mexicans feel about the *maquiladoras*? Explain the reasons for your opinion.
5. **ACTIVITY** Imagine that you have been traveling around the Mexican countryside. Write a letter to a friend describing the scenery, farming, and industry you have seen. What route did you travel? What places did you visit?

ECONOMY

Social Participation

Hecho en Mexico means "made in Mexico." Have students search their homes or look in stores for items made in Mexico. Among the items they may find are clothing, computers, radios, TVs, small appliances, bicycles, and other items. Many products sold in the United States are assembled in the *maquiladoras.* In class have students compile a list of the items they found.

■ *Mexico's major industries produce cars, chemicals, electrical products, processed food, and steel, and earn one-fourth of the nation's income.*

CLOSE

Have students review the list of resources that they began earlier and tell how each has contributed to the development of Mexican industries. Then have students answer the Thinking Focus. Also ask why it might be said that the country's oil resources have been both a blessing and a curse. *(Oil has brought the country both wealth and debt and has made it dependent on world oil prices over which it has little control.)*

Answers to Review Questions

1. Mexico's minerals, including silver, gold, lead, zinc, copper, and iron, as well as its oil deposits, have helped the economy grow.
2. Mountains and plateaus dominate Mexico's landscape.
3. Sales of oil brought in billions of dollars and helped to finance Mexico's growing industry. Growing oil revenues encouraged government spending and borrowing from other countries. When oil prices dropped, Mexico could no longer pay its foreign debt. Government programs were reduced, people lost jobs, and inflation soared.
4. Answers will vary. Students may say that Mexicans are glad to have jobs; yet the *maquiladoras* do not provide enough jobs.
5. Letters will vary based on itineraries. They should include description of the land and climate and, if possible, they should mention the type of farming or mining that might exist in the area.

Homework Options

Have students list ways that tourism contributes to Mexico's economy. Encourage students to think of both manufacturing and service jobs. *(Jobs open up for, among other people, construction workers, tour guides, hotel and restaurant workers, and crafts workers who sell goods to tourists.)*

Study Guide: page 102

INTRODUCE

Have students name the groups that created Mexico's unique cultural blend. *(Native Americans, Africans, Spanish colonists)* Remind students of the historical origins of Mexico's ethnic diversity by referring to Lesson 1. Then note that, although Mexico has held on to its rich cultural traditions, it is also changing and modernizing. Students might speculate on what kinds of changes rapid population growth, movement from rural areas to cities, and increased trade with the United States might bring. Then ask students to read aloud the Thinking Focus and to find answers to this question in their reading.

Key Terms

Vocabulary Strategies: T36–T37
fiesta—a religious or patriotic holiday
trade agreement—an agreement among countries on rules about the exchange of goods or services

1500
1600
1700
1800
1900
1929
TODAY

LESSON 3

A Blending of Cultures

THINKING FOCUS

How does Mexico blend traditional and modern ways?

Key Terms

- fiesta
- trade agreement

Hardly a week passes in Mexico without a fiesta. A **fiesta** is a religious or patriotic festival. It may be a village celebration for the local saint. Or it may be a feast day observed all over Mexico such as Independence Day or Día de los Muertos (Day of the Dead), described on page 592.

Sometimes, pilgrimages are part of a fiesta. Then thousands travel from all over Mexico to honor saints at shrines like that of the Virgin of Guadalupe. Tourists also flock to these festivals.

Mexican fiestas are outpourings of emotion and color. As Mexican writer Octavio Paz explains, fiestas release deep feelings:

> Thanks to the fiesta the Mexican opens out, participates, communes [shares thoughts] with his fellows and with the values that give meaning to his religious or political existence. And it is significant that a country [like] ours should have so many and such joyous fiestas. Their frequency, their brilliance and excitement, the enthusiasm with which we take part, all suggest that without them we would explode.

Daily Life

This Parachico dancer is from Chiapas. He wears a mask and uses a rattle. This dance recalls events of the Spanish conquest.

Age-old traditions come alive in fiestas in the countryside. Isolated Indian villages in particular have preserved their way of life. Although Spanish is spoken throughout Mexico, many native groups in the rural areas still speak their own language. In the fast-moving cities, however, signs of the past are changing.

Rural Family Life

Many villages and small towns reflect Mexico's past. The plaza at the center, with its church and town hall, is typically Spanish. The open market is an Indian tradition as you read in Chapter 6.

For villagers, life centers around the extended family. Such a family includes the immediate family, as well as aunts, uncles, cousins, and godparents. Children get a set of godparents for every ceremony that marks a new stage in their lives. Godparents are trusted friends and advisers of the entire family.

The father is the head of the family and its main provider. The

588

Objectives

1. Compare life in rural and urban Mexico.
2. Give some examples of different traditions expressed in Mexican fiestas and folk art.
3. Describe recent trends in Mexico's political life.

Graphic Overview

MEXICAN CULTURE
Daily Life
Folk Traditions
Public Life
rural
urban; Mexico City
food, music, dance
folk art
changes in government
changes in trade

◄ *Tortilla making for a large family is a lot of work. It can become a social occasion when several women work together.*

mother takes care of the home and children and controls the money. She may also earn money by growing vegetables or raising chickens. Some women weave cloth or make pottery. Their products bring in good money at the local market.

Traditionally, parents expect their sons to be tough and independent. Daughters learn to be reserved and dependent. They share in household chores and prepare for their future duties as wives and mothers.

Village houses, often made of adobe, or sun-baked clay, are centered around a courtyard. The courtyard usually is full of color from flowering and green plants. Here the family gathers for meals and social occasions.

Religion is the most important influence in the lives of villagers. Religious rituals mark every important event of their lives. In addition to a village church, each neighborhood has a roadside chapel for its favorite saint. These are often built in places the Indians considered holy. Homes also have shrines for the family's favorite saint. People pray to the saints for good health or a plentiful harvest.

Urban Living

For 70 percent of all Mexicans, daily life involves skyscrapers, traffic, crowds, and industries in the cities. Each year more families leave the countryside to seek jobs in the growing urban areas.

Most Mexican cities can't keep up with these newcomers' needs for housing and jobs. Those who are lucky enough to find jobs often receive low pay. To make ends meet, newcomers tend to move in

▼ *Middle-class households in the city usually have modern kitchens with the latest appliances.*

DEVELOP

Explain to students that in this lesson they will have a chance to compare many aspects of Mexican life: rural and urban, traditional and modern, middle-income and poor. They will also learn about national politics and Mexico's relations with other nations. Display the Graphic Overview and ask students to consider some of the ways folk traditions link daily life with public life. *(Most traditions have both private and public aspects. They help unite families and build a sense of community among villagers or city residents.)*

SOCIAL SYSTEMS

Critical Thinking

In the United States, family life revolves around a nuclear family typically made up of one or two parents and one or more children. In Mexico the extended family is much more in evidence. Have students describe the social and economic advantages of living in a large extended family. *(It offers more sources of affection and emotional support, and more help with household tasks; child care can be provided by grandparents; and resources can be pooled.)* Students might speculate about what effect migration to the cities might have on the extended family.

Access Strategy

Ask students if they have ever moved from one part of a city to another or from one state or country to another. What were the biggest differences between the old place and the new? Which changes were the easiest to adjust to? The most difficult to get used to? Write responses on the chalkboard, and group them under such headings as Cultural, Economic, and Social Differences. Explore reasons why people's lives change when they move from a rural to an urban area. Point out that the mass media, such as television, movies, radio, and newspapers, spread knowledge of new ideas, places, and products among urban people. Rural life often follows the daily and seasonal rhythms of nature and agriculture, so people in rural areas are usually on the same schedule. In cities individual schedules may vary more widely. Access to private and public transportation enables each family member to go his or her own way.

Access Activity

Have students examine the pictures in the chapter and list items that reflect Mexico's ancient traditions and items that reflect modern society. *(Sample answers: Traditional statue of Santiago, textile designs, Parachico dancer, making tortillas. Modern—skyscrapers and modern buildings in Mexico City, a home with modern appliances, a factory worker)*

➤ *Mexico City, Puebla, Guadalajara, and Monterrey. The cluster of dots is thickest for these cities.*

GEOGRAPHY

Map and Globe Skills

Explain to students that Mexicans leave rural villages because of inadequate farmland and jobs. Mexico City has acted as a magnet for rural villagers because of its job opportunities and many educational and cultural activities. Today Ciudad Juárez, Mexicali, and Tijuana are among the nation's fastest-growing cities. Ask students to locate these cities on a map of North America. What do these cities have in common? *(Near the U.S. border)* How might their location help them grow? *(More U.S. businesses may open plants in these cities.)*

■ *In rural areas, traditional ways are strongest. Families play a central role. The father is usually the authority; the mother cares for the children and household. In urban areas, families are important centers of social life, but middle-class families tend to be less traditional and adopt modern ways. Women tend to be more independent, working outside the home and having careers.*

Mexico: Population, 1990

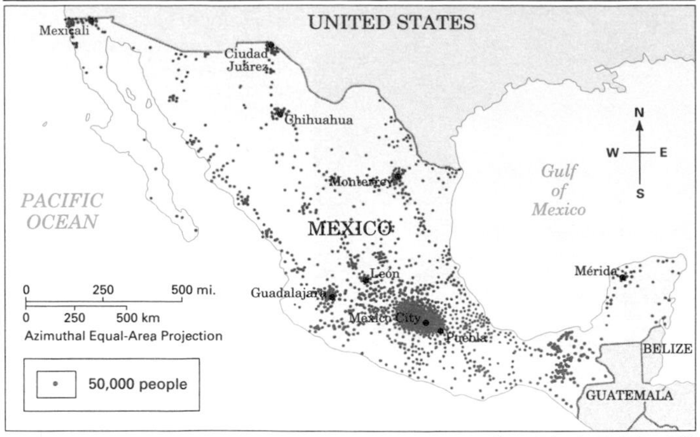

UNITED STATES
Mexicali
Ciudad Juárez
Chihuahua
Monterrey
PACIFIC OCEAN
MEXICO
Gulf of Mexico
N
W
E
S
Mérida
León
Guadalajara
Mexico City
Puebla
BELIZE
GUATEMALA
0 250 500 mi.
0 250 500 km
Azimuthal Equal-Area Projection
50,000 people

Source: Britannica World Data, 1992

▲ *What are the four largest population centers shown on this map? How do you know?*

How Do We Know?

SOCIAL SCIENCE *Population figures are gathered by the government through a process called census taking. Mexico's households answer questionnaires about who lives there, their gender, age, occupation, and other information. A census is usually taken every 10 years.*

➤ *Suburban neighborhoods in Mexico are often modern and colorful.*

■ *How does rural life differ from middle-class urban living?*

with family members. Others live in shacks outside the city close to people from the same town or village.

People do whatever they can to earn a living. They may work as household servants, shoe shiners, or vendors on busy downtown streets. No matter how hard life is for these Mexicans, the family continues to be a source of strength.

Middle-class families in the city lead very different lives. Many live in modern houses in the suburbs. Both men and women may hold jobs outside the home. They may work in offices in government and business, or they may be professional people such as doctors, lawyers, and teachers. Some even own their own small businesses. Many women in this class are well educated. They tend to be more outgoing and independent than women in the villages. In some middle-class households, children go to private schools, and there are servants who live with the family.

In the cities Mexicans use many U.S. products. They enjoy fast food, rock music, U.S. films, and even baseball. Those that can afford it dress in styles that are popular in the United States.

The Largest City in the World

The rapid growth of cities has caused big problems in Mexico, especially in the capital. Mexico City has a population of around 20 million, and it is growing very fast. You can compare it with other large cities in the Minipedia on page 664.

Because Mexico City is surrounded by mountains, pollution from about 30,000 factories and three million motor vehicles hovers overhead. When the pollution level is too high, the government closes schools, limits driving, and closes some factories until the air clears.

In spite of its problems, Mexico City is an exciting place. Glass skyscrapers and fancy hotels, fashion shops and restaurants line its wide streets. Mexico City's university, founded in 1551, is the second oldest in North America. Historic churches, splendid museums, and theaters provide a rich cultural life. Find some of these places in the Map and Globe Handbook on page G3. You will also see that the city is dotted with plazas and parks. ■

Visual Learning

What details in the picture of Mexico City on page 577 indicate that it is a major city? *(Many buildings, busy streets, traffic)* What details would students expect to see in a photograph of a rural village that do not appear in this picture of Mexico City? *(Farmland, farm animals, large areas of open space, fewer buildings, and a different kind of housing)*

Geographic Context

In Mexico City rapid development and population growth have created serious environmental problems. Health and sanitation services cannot keep pace with population growth. Mexico City faces a special problem because it is surrounded by mountains. At certain times of the year, the ring of mountains traps polluted air close to the ground. A brown cloud made up of gases such as carbon monoxide, sulfur dioxide, and ozone often hangs over the city. The fumes cause respiratory infections, nosebleeds, and lung problems such as emphysema. To reduce air pollution will require making hard economic choices. Key causes of pollution are aging buses, taxis, and cars and smokestack industries. To curb pollution, the city has had to reduce the work hours for hundreds of factories employing large numbers of workers.

Folk Traditions

Even as Mexico modernizes, its heart and soul stay linked to its cultural traditions. Religious and historic celebrations and traditional arts express the deepest feelings of Mexican people.

Food, Music, and Dance

As you read earlier, Mexicans love fiestas. At these lively gatherings, there is usually plenty of good food, music, and dance that have their own ancient traditions.
One traditional fiesta food is *mole (MOH lay)* sauce. It is made from hot chilies and chocolate and is often served with turkey.

Dances are an important part of most festivals. Some, like the *quetzal* dance—also called the Bird Dance—are reminders of Aztec rituals. Huge, feathered headdresses make the dancers appear to be twice their height. Other dances tell stories from the time of the Spanish conquest. Dancers wear masks to play the roles of saints, heroes, or animals.

Musicians accompany the dances. Sometimes they play the *concha*, a stringed instrument made from the shell of an armadillo. Trumpets, drums, rattles, and flutes are also used. Then there are the famous *mariachi* bands. These musicians wear big *sombreros* (hats) and dark suits with silver trim. A young man might hire a *mariachi* band to play for his favorite woman friend.

Folk Art

Mexico's folk art remains deeply rooted in its Spanish and Indian traditions. Each region, and often each village, has its own specialty.

Some folk artists make practical items such as clay bowls, colorful woven rugs and shawls, and cotton embroidered clothing. Patterns used to decorate these are often old Indian designs.

Other craftworkers make religious objects such as carved masks and figures of saints. Still others make toys, games, or perhaps figures of playful skeletons or devils. Each feast day has its own traditional candies or baked goods. You can see some of these in A Closer Look, Día de los Muertos, on page 592. Papier-mâché figures and puppets also change with the seasons. Huge puppets are sold around Easter. They are made to be destroyed by fireworks or burnt on the streets the day before Easter. ■

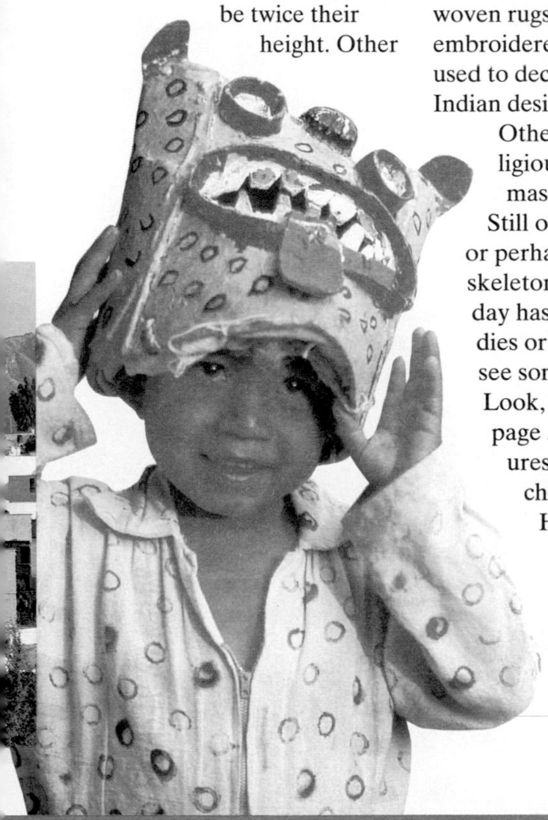

◄ *The jaguar mask worn by this boy goes back to an Aztec jaguar-warrior tradition.*

■ *How do fiestas and folk art link Mexicans to their culture?*

BELIEF SYSTEMS

Critical Thinking

In all cultures holiday celebrations express values. Make a list of holidays celebrated in the United States. Have students describe the various ways these holidays are celebrated. Then compare these ways with the way the Mexican fiesta is celebrated. Students should note similarities and differences. *(Similarities: Celebrations in both places mark significant historic and religious events and are likely to include family, food, and music. Differences: Music, dance, and religion may be more important to the fiesta. Fiestas often involve the entire community and blend and keep alive Indian and Spanish religious traditions.)*

■ *They serve as steady reminders of Mexico's past as the nation modernizes.*

Art Connection

Every part of Mexico produces fascinating folk art. Morelos produces wooden bowls, colonial-style furniture, and palm-leaf baskets. Puebla produces blue tiles for countertops or walls. One village in Oaxaca makes distinctive black pottery. In the colder climate of Chiapas, Indians weave woolen clothing. In the Yucatán, people weave hammocks out of cotton or cactus fiber. Campeche produces fine mahogany furniture. Obtain tourist brochures from different parts of Mexico. Divide students into groups to make a Folk Art Tourist Map promoting Mexico's folk arts and crafts. Have each group pick a different Mexican state and create a colorful map showing folk arts of that state. Combine the maps for a bulletin-board display.

Study Skills

Have students go through this chapter and compile one list with examples of traditional Mexico and another with examples of modern Mexico. *(Traditional—fiestas, shrines, Day of the Dead, open market, extended family, small villages, adobe houses; modern—skyscrapers, industries, heavy traffic, fast food, rock music, U.S. films, baseball)*

Note: You may wish to use this Closer Look as an extension of the discussion of Mexican fiestas on page 591.

More About the Day of the Dead
The celebrating that takes place on the Day of the Dead is joyous. Relatives offer special foods and flowers—usually yellow and orange marigolds—at the graves of their ancestors. Tombs are swept and cleaned and decorative black paper flags and colored ribbons are hung about. Candles are generally lit and a picture of the ancestor is displayed.

Some families hold these feasts at home and hang marigold wreaths over their doors. Trails of flower petals from the street to the house are laid out to guide the ancestor home.

A CLOSER LOOK

Día de los Muertos

Many Mexicans honor their ancestors on November 1, All Saints' Day, and November 2, All Souls' Day or the Day of the Dead. This is a happy event. In many places All Saints' Day is spent at home honoring children who have died and are believed to have become saints. Families prepare the favorite foods and drinks of their ancestors. They decorate tables with flowers and candles. In the evening they bring the food and decorations to the graves of their ancestors. The souls of the dead are believed to enjoy the pleasures of life again. The celebration usually continues into the following day, the Day of the Dead.

This ancient tradition is celebrated differently from region to region. In some communities, the people decorate their churches.

The Aztecs considered marigolds the favorite flowers of the dead. Here the flowers are displayed to guide souls to their feasts.

Sugar treats, fruits, tamales, special breads, and other foods are offered for souls to savor.

Visual Learning

Ask students to examine the visuals on this page. Is this a joyous or a sad event? Why? *(Joyous, because people are smiling, bright colorful flowers are displayed, and the church is decorated.)* What does this celebration indicate about the beliefs of these people? *(They probably believe in life after death; they may not see death as a horrible end to life.)*

Research

Ask students to look in the library for more information on Mexican fiestas and celebrations. Have them write a paragraph or two explaining some aspect of the Mexican celebration they have chosen.

Public Life

As Mexico faces the 21st century, changes are being made in government and trade. These offer great promise.

Mexican Government

For the past 10 years, Mexicans have struggled through hard economic times. Many citizens have asked for reforms.

Since 1929 every Mexican president and state governor has been a member of the Institutional Revolutionary Party, or PRI. A change came in 1988. For the first time, candidates other than those of the PRI had a chance of winning. Carlos Salinas de Gortari, the PRI candidate, had a difficult fight to win the presidency. Two other political parties won many seats in the congress.

Mexico and the World

During this century Mexico has developed strong economic ties with the United States. It has become Mexico's biggest trading partner and a major source of loans. Some Mexicans feel that their country has become too dependent on the United States.

In Latin America, however, Mexico has acted on its own. In the mid-1980s, it presented a peace plan for war-torn Central America. Mexico suggested ways to settle conflicts between Central American countries and the United States.

Balancing independence and economic needs remains a challenge for the people of Mexico. This is especially true of the North American Free Trade Agreement that President Salinas strongly supports. In a **trade agreement,** different countries agree on rules about exchanging goods. According to the new trade agreement, goods and money will move freely among Mexico, the United States, and Canada. Those who favor the agreement hope that many Mexican workers will find work at home instead of having to emigrate to the United States. ■

In October 1992 the North American Free Trade Agreement was signed. The representatives of each signing nation (from left to right, standing at lecterns) were President Carlos Salinas of Mexico, President George Bush of the United States, and Prime Minister Brian Mulroney of Canada.

■ *How is Mexico both dependent on and independent of the United States?*

REVIEW

1. **FOCUS** How does Mexico blend traditional and modern ways?
2. **CULTURE** How does modern tourism help keep Indian and Spanish traditions alive?
3. **CULTURE** Why are fiestas and folk art very important to Mexican culture?
4. **CRITICAL THINKING** How do you think the North American Free Trade Agreement will affect Mexico's relations with the United States and Canada? Give reasons for your opinion.
5. **ACTIVITY** Imagine you are preparing a fiesta for a holiday such as Thanksgiving, the Fourth of July, or some other holiday of your choice. What food, costumes, masks, music, or rituals might you use? How would these remind you and your friends of the traditions of this special day?

POLITICAL SYSTEMS

Critical Thinking

Discuss the reasons the PRI has controlled Mexican politics for more than 60 years. Tell students that Mexicans support the party out of loyalty to and pride in the Mexican Revolution and that the PRI uses the spoils system to reward supporters with jobs and contracts. It also controls the counting of votes and much of the press coverage of elections. Have students describe the strengths and weaknesses of one-party rule. *(Strengths: Continuity, stability, less money expended on elections. Weaknesses: Potential for corruption, voter apathy due to a lack of real choices, lack of innovation in policies, strong candidates discouraged from running for office, restricted political freedom)*

■ *Mexico depends on the United States for a large part of its trade and also for loans. Yet Mexico's government has made changes in its economy so the nation is better able to be self-sufficient.*

CLOSE

Have students respond to the Thinking Focus. Ask students if they agree with the text statement that new changes in government and trade "offer great promise."

Answers to Review Questions

1. Traditions thrive in Mexico's rural way of life, its festivals, and its folk art. Modern ways also thrive, as shown by its cities, its modern architecture, its industry, and the influences from the United States.
2. Tourists in Mexico enjoy fiestas and folk art; thus these Indian and Spanish traditions are kept alive.
3. Fiestas bring people together to honor religious and historic events and give them release from the struggles of daily life. Folk art provides traditional items that meet practical, religious, and entertainment needs.
4. Students may respond that free trade may bring yet more industries and foreign investment and thus more jobs to Mexico. It may also make Mexico more dependent on its northern neighbors.
5. Answers should reflect the celebratory nature of the day chosen.

Homework Options

Have students make lists of arguments in favor of Mexico's signing a free trade agreement and lists of reasons for opposing it. Have students use their lists to write a short position paper, supporting or opposing such a treaty and explaining why the benefits outweigh the negatives or vice versa.

Study Guide: page 103

Answers to Reviewing Key Terms

A. Sample answers:

1. **Conquistadors** took over the Aztecs' centralized system of government.
2. **Peons** often found themselves bound to their employers.
3. The Mexico–United States **border** is 2,000 miles long.
4. Many feel that a **trade agreement** will help goods and money move freely among Mexico, the United States, and Canada.

B. Answers:

1. False. A **hacienda** is a large estate, not a house.
2. False. A **trade agreement** contains rules about exchanging goods, not about military groups.
3. True
4. True
5. False. **Peons** were peasants.

Answers to Exploring Concepts

A. Sample answers:

Cultural—Mexico has a Spanish-Catholic influence and Indian traditions. The United States is largely Protestant, and most people speak English; Economic—Each country has its own currency. The U.S. economy is fully developed, while Mexico's is developing; Physical—Mexico and the United States share a 2,000-mile border. The Rio Grande forms part of the border between the two countries.

B. Sample answers:

1. Tenochtitlan was destroyed by the Spaniards and rebuilt as Mexico City.
2. Haciendas provided food for the Spanish settlers who lived in the cities.
3. Missionaries set up schools and missions and learned Indian languages. Some Indians believed that the God of the Christians had defeated their Gods.
4. Mexico fought with Texas, the United States, and France in the 1800s.
5. Mexico lost the area that now constitutes much of the southwestern United States.
6. Díaz encouraged foreign investment, improved the economy, and modernized the nation. However, he allowed profits from industry to go to foreigners and did little to improve things for most Mexicans.
7. Cárdenas formed *ejidos,* encouraged workers in cities to organize, and nationalized the foreign oil companies.
8. Mexico's greatest assets are minerals, oil, and the labor of its growing population.
9. U.S. businesses open plants in Mexico to take advantage of cheap Mexican labor.
10. Mexico had borrowed money from foreign banks to pay for programs and had planned to pay these loans by exporting oil. Trouble began when oil prices dropped.
11. For Mexicans the family is a source of strength and the center of social life.
12. Religion is the most important influence on the lives of Mexico's villagers.
13. Mexico has had to import food, pollution has increased, industries have not been able to provide enough jobs, and, many people have emigrated to the United States.
14. Mexico City is surrounded by mountains that prevent the city's air pollution from being dispersed by wind.

Chapter Review

Reviewing Key Terms

border (p. 586)
conquistador (p. 578)
fiesta (p. 588)
hacienda (p. 579)
peon (p. 579)
trade agreement (p. 593)

A. Be sure you understand the meanings of the key terms. Use each of the words below in a sentence that gives a specific fact about Mexico.

1. conquistador
2. peon
3. border
4. trade agreement

B. Write whether each of the following statements is *true* or *false*. Then rewrite the false statements to make them true.

1. Baskets and clay pottery were used to decorate large rooms in the hacienda.
2. The United States, Mexico, and Canada agreed to limit the size of their armed forces in a recent trade agreement.
3. A border between two nations can be a cultural, economic, or physical barrier that separates them.
4. Fiestas are held throughout Mexico on Independence Day.
5. The peons owned enormous farms where they grew cotton, tobacco, and a variety of vegetables.

Exploring Concepts

A. Mexico and the United States are separated by different kinds of borders. Three types of borders are listed on the following chart. Copy and complete the chart. List at least two examples of each kind of border that separates Mexico and the United States.

Types of Borders	Characteristics
Cultural	
Economic	
Physical	

B. Answer each question with information from the chapter.

1. What happened to Tenochtitlan after the arrival of the Spaniards?
2. Why did the Spaniards form haciendas?
3. Why did some Indians come to accept Christianity?
4. Who did Mexico fight in the 1800s?
5. What territories did Mexico lose to the United States in 1848?
6. In what ways did Porfirio Díaz improve Mexico as a nation? How did he hurt Mexico?
7. What changes did Lázaro Cárdenas make in Mexico after he became the nation's president?
8. What are the greatest assets of Mexico today?
9. Why do U.S. businesses open manufacturing plants in Mexico?
10. Why did Mexico find itself in economic trouble in the early 1980s?
11. What role does the institution of the family play in Mexico?
12. What is the most important influence on the lives of Mexico's villagers?
13. What effect has Mexico's growing population had on the nation?
14. Why is air pollution a major problem in Mexico City?

Reviewing Skills

1. Find a photograph of an artifact from Mexico's colonial period. For sources look in an encyclopedia or in books on Mexico's history at your local library. Study the artifact carefully. Then write a paragraph describing the artifact. Tell what it looks like, what it is made of, where it was found, how it was used, and why it was used in this way.
2. Find Mexico on the political map of the world on page 372 of your text. Then find Mexico on the cartogram of world petroleum resources on page 373. How do the United States, Canada, and Brazil compare with Mexico in terms of actual size? How do they compare with Mexico in terms of petroleum resources?
3. Imagine you are a naturalist studying the armadillo. What information about this animal would you need in order to pinpoint areas in Mexico where the animal could be found? What type of map would be most useful to you?

Using Critical Thinking

1. After the conquest of Tenochtitlan, how were the Spaniards able to extend their control over the peoples living in the rest of Mexico?
2. Throughout Mexico's history, governmental policies concerning foreign investment have frequently changed. Describe some of these changes.
3. Today government policies favor large farms that contain Mexico's best land. By contrast, the *ejidos* given to the Indians are often small, dry pieces of land. What has been the effect of these policies? Do you think the government should continue to favor large farms? Why or why not?
4. In his office, President Carlos Salinas de Gortari displays only two figures from Mexico's past. One is a painting of Benito Juárez and the other is a bronze statue of Emiliano Zapata. What do you think these choices reveal about Salinas?
5. Each year more and more families leave the countryside to seek jobs in urban areas. Today, about 70 percent of all Mexicans live in the cities. What effect has this shift in population had on Mexico? How do you think this trend will affect the future of Mexico?

Preparing for Citizenship

1. WRITING ACTIVITY Imagine you are a Mexican whose business failed when the Mexican Miracle fell apart. Write a letter to a friend describing what has happened to your country. Who do you blame for the decline of the economy? How can Mexico recover?
2. INTERVIEWING The North American Free Trade Agreement has stirred debate in the United States between those who favor the treaty and those who oppose it. Interview one or two adults in your community to discover how they feel about the agreement. Report your findings to the class.
3. ARTS ACTIVITY Tourism is an important part of Mexico's economy. Create a travel poster that encourages people to vacation in Mexico. What is there to do? What places should people visit? Be prepared to present your poster to the class.
4. GROUP ACTIVITY Benito Juárez has often been compared to Abraham Lincoln. With a classmate, find out more about Juárez. Compare the lives of these two leaders.
5. COLLABORATIVE LEARNING Mexicans have many fiestas. In small groups, plan a Mexican-style fiesta. Have one group prepare some traditional Mexican dishes. Have another group research Mexican music and dances to play and perform. Have another group design and make costumes and masks.

Answers to Reviewing Skills

1. Students should give a complete description of the artifact, including its shape, size, color, and so on. They should also describe its use and what it reveals about the user's beliefs and values.
2. Although Mexico is smaller in size than the United States, Canada, and Brazil, it has greater petroleum resources.
3. Students should recognize that they would need information on the armadillo's habitat. Then, political, vegetation, and topographic maps of Mexico would help them locate this habitat.

Answers to Using Critical Thinking

1. The Spaniards made use of the Aztecs' centralized system of government to gather tribute from all over the empire. Missionaries converted Indians to Catholicism. Spaniards formed haciendas and took over Indian land. Many Spanish settlers had children with the native peoples.
2. Díaz encouraged foreign investment. Cárdenas took over foreign-owned oil companies. In recent years the government has encouraged foreign corporations to open branches in Mexico.
3. The produce from the large farms is mainly for export. Because the *ejidos* cannot produce enough food for the growing population, Mexico imports corn and wheat. Some students will suggest that while large farms are probably necessary, the government should give some of the better land to the *ejidos*.
4. Both Juárez and Zapata identified with the peasants and worked diligently to improve their plight. Most students will probably suggest that Salinas, too, wants to improve conditions for Mexico's poor.
5. Overcrowding in the cities has caused unemployment, low pay, and inadequate housing. These conditions will likely worsen if the trend continues. Moreover, ties to the extended family may weaken under the pressures of modern urban living.

Answers to Preparing for Citizenship

1. WRITING ACTIVITY Students should describe the drop in oil prices that brought about the collapse of the Mexican Miracle. They might say they blame the government. Ideas for improving the economy will vary.
2. INTERVIEWING Discuss arguments for and against the agreement. Pro: More Mexicans will find jobs at home, so fewer will come to compete for U.S. jobs. Con: The United States may lose jobs, as companies move more of their operations to Mexico.
3. ARTS ACTIVITY Posters should reflect aspects of Mexico presented in the chapter.
4. GROUP ACTIVITY Have students make a chart listing facts about the two leaders' lives.
5. COLLABORATIVE LEARNING The following sources may be helpful: Alfonso Cruz Jiménez, *Mexican Folk Songs* (Folkways, 1958); Frances Toor, *Treasury of Mexican Folkways* (Bonanza Books, 1985); Patricia Quintana, *Mexico's Feasts of Life* (Council Oak Books, 1989); Henrietta Yurchenco, *Children's Songs and Games from Ecuador, Mexico, and Puerto Rico* (Folkways Records, 1977).

CHAPTER ORGANIZER

Chapter 26 Canada

CHAPTER PLANNING CHART

Pupil's Edition	Teacher's Edition	Ancillaries
Lesson 1: Geography and Native Peoples (2–3 days) Objective 1: Describe the geography of Canada. (Geography 1, 2, 3) Objective 2: Describe selected native North American cultures. (Culture 1, 2, 5) Objective 3: Describe and locate the resources of Canada. (Geography 1, 3; Economics 1) Objective 4: Explain and describe the provinces and territories of Canada including Nunavut. (Geography 1)	• Graphic Overview (598) • Access Strategy (599) • Access Activity (599)	Study Guide (104) Transparency (15) • Posters (7)
Lesson 2: History of Canada (2–3 days) Objective 1: Understand the British and French heritage of Canada. (History 1, 7; Culture 1, 2, 3) Objective 2: Explain the history of westward expansion. (History 1, 5; Culture 3) Objective 3: Explain the key steps in independence from British rule. (Social and Political Systems 3) Objective 4: Understand the influence of Britain on Canada. (Culture 1, 2, 4)	• Graphic Overview (601) • Access Activity (602) • Access Strategy (602) Historical Context (603) Critical Thinking (603) • Visual Learning (604) Economic Context (604)	Study Guide (105) • Posters (4) • Study Prints (16)
Understanding Diagrams Objective: Read and make a process diagram. (Visual Learning 2)	Map and Globe Skills (606)	Study Guide (106)
Lesson 3: Canada Today (2–3 days) Objective 1: Understand the bilingual, multicultural, and urban nature of Canada today. (History 5, 7; Culture 3, 4) Objective 2: Describe industry, education, and the arts in Canada. (Economics 3; Culture 2, 5) Objective 3: Understand Canada's view of its role in the world today. (Social and Political Systems 6)	• Graphic Overview (607) • Access Activity (608) • Access Strategy (608) Mathematics Connection (609) Study Skills (609) Social Participation (610) Geographic Context (610) Research (611) Creating Animation (611) • Visual Learning (611) Critical Thinking (612) Political Context (612)	Study Guide (107) Map Activities (30) Discovery Journal (53)
Chapter Review	Answers (614–615)	Tests (101–104)

* Objectives are correlated to the strands and goals in the program Scope and Sequence on pages T41–T49.

• LEP appropriate resources. (For additional strategies, see pages T32–T33.)

CHAPTER RATIONALE

Chapter 26 traces Canada's geography and history and shows how its original peoples lived and adapted to the land. A review of Canada's history sets the stage for understanding the continuing tensions between Canadians of French and of English heritage. The aim is to help the student to understand Canada as a thriving, multicultural nation.

Lesson 1 explains Canada's location in North America and gives students a sense of its relative size. The lesson continues with a description of the geographic regions of Canada and an introduction to the political divisions of provinces and territories. The natural resources and climate of each region are discussed. Students are introduced to several of the many Native American peoples of Canada—where they lived and continue to live—with an emphasis on how they have adapted to their environment.

Lesson 2 opens with a brief glimpse of how Native Americans probably viewed the arrival of the French and English explorers. The lesson then summarizes the rivalry between France and Great Britain, concluding with the Seven Years' War (known in North America as the French and Indian War) and the resulting British dominance. Students read about westward expansion and growing immigration to Canada. The lesson concludes by summarizing the major steps in Canada's road to independence from Great Britain and by describing lasting British influences.

Lesson 3 focuses on contemporary Canada, highlighting Toronto as an example of urban Canada. The multicultural, bilingual nature of this vast nation is examined. Students read about Canadian achievements in industry, education and health, and the arts. The chapter concludes with a discussion of relations with the United States, emphasizing that although Canadians share many cultural experiences with the United States, they are proud of their own nation's characteristics and distinctions.

ACTIVITIES & PROJECTS

LEP: Making a Mural

Ask students to reread the text section on The Native Peoples of Canada, page 600. Then place a long piece of butcher paper along a wall. Have students use markers or paint to depict the different cultures of the native peoples of Canada. (Use after Lesson 1.)

Social Participation

Have students review the section in Lesson 2 entitled The Immigration Boom, page 604. Then ask them to try to persuade people from other parts of the world to move to Canada. List their suggestions on the chalkboard. Have volunteers copy the list onto a large poster to serve as an advertisement for new immigrants. (Use after Lesson 2.)

Writing News Reports

Have students write news accounts of an imaginary sea traveler who travels with Alexander Mackenzie on his explorations of Canada's inland waterways. Students should pretend their stories will be aired on a TV evening news show, so their reports should be brief and include pictures. Suggest the use of headlines to attract viewers' attention, and have students include references to Canada's diverse geographic features. (Use after Lesson 2.)

Basic: Writing a Song

Allow students several minutes to read the lines from Canada's national anthem at the beginning of Lesson 3, page 607, and the explanatory text to the right of the verse. Ask them to write their own verse to the anthem. Suggest that their verses reflect the rich diversity of Canada's people. (Use after Lesson 3.)

Challenge: Writing Commentary

Have students write a paragraph commenting on former Canadian prime minister Trudeau's comparison of Canada's position in relation to the United States to that of "a mouse next to an elephant." (Use after Lesson 3.)

CHAPTER PREVIEW

Direct students' attention to the text on this page. Point out that the writer has called Canada a "chilly giant." Discuss reasons why this is—or is not—a good description of our northern neighbor. *(Although much of Canada has a cold climate, it has a diverse climate and geography, covering a vast area.)*

Looking Back

Point out that as the students read more about Canada, they will discover some similarities to its southern neighbors, the United States and Mexico, such as colonization, then independence, and a blending of European, Native American, and many other cultures.

Looking Forward

Explain that in Lessons 1–3, students will read about the geography, history, and distinctive culture of Canada.

Lesson 1 focuses on Canada's diversity of native peoples and geography.

Chapter 26

Canada

Like a chilly giant, Canada sprawls across the top of North America. Canada's massive land area stretches from the Pacific coast to the Atlantic coast, and extends to the Arctic. Its landforms include lofty mountain ranges, fertile plains, and frozen tundra. Only about one-fifth of this huge nation has been settled. Immigrants from many nations have joined the Native Americans living there to create Canada's cultural pattern.

The bright red maple leaf, part of Canada's flag and its national symbol, is painted on barn doors in Saskatchewan.

A portion of a map drawn in 1655 shows part of the east coast of North America. From what is now Massachusetts, the coast stretches northward into Canada.

1497 Giovanni Caboto (John Cabot) claims Newfoundland for England.

1300	1400	1500	1600

1608 Samuel de Champlain establishes the first permanent French settlement.

1400

BACKGROUND

One of Canada's prime ministers, William Lyon Mackenzie King, remarked that while some countries have too much history, Canada has "too much geography." The country has thousands of lakes and islands, and prairie lands that are larger than India, Pakistan, and Nepal combined.

Geography As Art

Canada's vast area and striking geography have been the subjects of the work of many of the country's artists and writers. Much of the art of the Native Americans focuses on the vast northern landscape or on animals that are indigenous to their regions.

During the late 1800s, a unique Canadian style evolved through the work of seven landscape painters known as the Group of Seven.

Emily Carr was an artist who devoted much of her work to capturing the landscape of the West. She, like many other artists descended from European settlers, found the life and the culture of Native Americans to be compelling subjects for her work.

European Influences

The artwork of Maurice Cullen and James Wilson Morrice united the Canadian style with the impressionist and fauvist influences of Europe. However, sharing ideas—and history—with Europe is not unusual in Canada.

Historically, Canada served as a backdrop to conflicts that were taking place in Europe. The French and Indian War (1755–1763), for

These colorful fabrics represent a few of the many cultures present in Canada. From left to right are typical patterns of Scotland, India, the West Indies, and Asia.

The beautiful coastline of Cape Breton in Nova Scotia remains much as it appeared to the first European explorers.

The Inuit people of Canada, including this mother and child, will have their own official territory in 1999.

1992 The Canadian government and Canadian citizens agree to the plan for the Nunavut Territory.

1700 | 1800 | 1900 | 2000

1756–1763 The Seven Years' War is fought between Great Britain and France. Great Britain is the victor.

597

Today

Understanding the Visuals

The maple leaf has long been a Canadian emblem. It became the symbol on the national flag on February 15, 1965.

The historical map section on the previous page illustrates one of the links between Canada and the United States—their common British heritage. Parts of both countries were once colonies of Great Britain.

The background bolts of fabrics from other nations give some idea of the many cultural groups who add to the Canadian mosaic. In addition, native peoples of Canada, including the Inuit, make up about 1.5 percent of Canada's population.

Understanding Chronology

Ask students to examine the timeline. Tell them how the first two events, the claiming of land first by English and then by French settlers, might have led to the third event, the Seven Years' War. *(Students may speculate that both groups wanted to expand their land claims and fought over the right to do so. Native Americans, who wanted to protect their ancient homelands, were drawn into these conflicts over their lands.)*

example, was the North American version of what was known in Europe as the Seven Years' War—a struggle between France and Britain for power. At the conclusion of that war, Canada became part of the powerful British Empire that would one day stretch around the globe.

Canada's independence from Great Britain has come gradually. In 1867, Canada became a dominion of Great Britain, with some measure of self-rule. In 1931 the Statute of Westminster established Canada as an independent nation. In 1982 through the efforts of Prime Minister Pierre Trudeau, the Constitution Act went into effect, granting Canada alone the right to vote on amendment issues that would affect its citizens.

However, the nation is still a constitutional monarchy with ties to Great Britain. The British queen remains the nominal head of government. She has delegated her powers to the governor-general. In essence, she reigns, but she does not govern.

Current Conflicts

The effects of the early French-British conflict are still felt in Canada. The province of Quebec, with its primarily French population, continues its struggle for more recognition. In 1992, Canadians voted on what is called the Charlottetown Agreement. It called Quebec a "distinct society" with special privileges such as a guarantee of a quarter of the seats in the House of Commons. The agreement also offered special rights to other groups of peoples. However, the agreement failed to pass.

INTRODUCE

After students read the Thinking Focus, ask them to predict what geographic features might be found in Canada. *(Mountains, coasts, rivers, lakes, plains, forests, tundra)* Remind students that some Native Americans in Canada also inhabited parts of what is today the United States.

Key Term

Vocabulary Strategies: T36–T37

permafrost—ground that is permanently frozen

GEOGRAPHY

Map and Globe Skills

Ask students to study the map on the next page and identify Canada's provinces and and resources, using the text and the map on page 689. *(Fishing, wood, iron, and coal in the Maritimes. Gold, silver, and copper in Ontario and Quebec. Oil, natural gas, and farming in Prairie Provinces. Fishing and farming in British Columbia. Gold in the Northwest Territories and Yukon Territory.)*

1300 1400 TODAY

L E S S O N 1

Geography and Native Peoples

THINKING FOCUS

What are the geographic regions of Canada, and how did its early native peoples adapt to each region?

Key Term

- permafrost

> The air was fresh and crisp, and little smoke-blue mists curled through the valleys and floated off from the hills. Sometimes the road went through woods where maples were beginning to hang out scarlet banners; . . . sometimes it wound along a harbor shore and passed by a little cluster of weather-gray fishing huts . . .
>
> L. M. Montgomery, *Anne of Green Gables*

These words of a Canadian author describe autumn on Prince Edward Island, a province of Canada. Canada is the world's second largest nation—covering about seven percent of the earth's surface. Each region has its own features and natural beauty.

Canada's Regions, Climate, and Resources

Canada's political regions are made up of two northern territories and ten provinces to the south.

On the Atlantic coast are the four Atlantic Provinces, or the Maritimes: Nova Scotia, New Brunswick, Prince Edward Island, and Newfoundland. Long ago, moving glaciers there ground out rocky islands and peninsulas. Resources of these provinces include rich Atlantic Ocean fishing grounds,

The majestic Canadian Rockies in Alberta (below) and the golden wheat fields of the Saskatchewan prairies (right) display some of the varied beauty of Canada.

Objectives

1. Describe the geography of Canada.
2. Describe selected native North American cultures.
3. Describe and locate the resources of Canada.
4. Explain and describe the provinces and territories of Canada, including Nunavut.

Graphic Overview

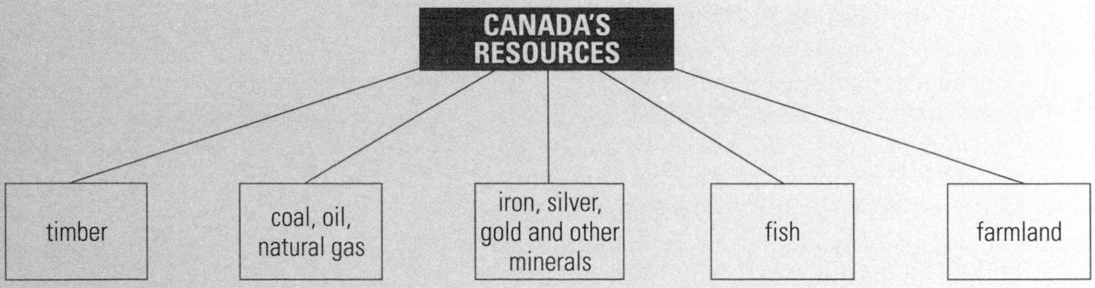
CANADA'S RESOURCES
timber
coal, oil, natural gas
iron, silver, gold and other minerals
fish
farmland

Canada: Vegetation Regions

Yukon R.
UNITED STATES
Alaska
60°N
140°W
110°W
90°W
50°W
Baffin Bay
0 300 600 mi.
0 300 600 km
Lambert Conic Projection
Arctic Circle
Great Bear Lake
Mackenzie R.
MACKENZIE MTS
Yukon Territory
Whitehorse
NUNAVUT
GREENLAND (Den.)
Northwest Territories
Yellowknife
Great Slave Lake
Labrador Sea
Peace R.
50°N
British Columbia
ROCKY MOUNTAINS
Alberta
Hudson Bay
Newfoundland
St. John's
PACIFIC OCEAN
Edmonton
Manitoba
Victoria
Vancouver
Calgary
Lake Winnipeg
Québec
Prince Edward Island
Saskatchewan
Regina
Winnipeg
Ontario
New Brunswick
Halifax
WASH.
MONT.
Québec
Nova Scotia
ATLANTIC OCEAN
Tundra
Farmland
Forest
Proposed Nunavut territory
Grassland
National capital
N. DAK.
MINN.
L. Superior
Montréal
Ottawa
VT.
MAINE
N.H.
MASS.
Toronto
L. Ont.
N.Y.
R.I.
CONN.
S. DAK.
WIS.
MICH.
L. Michigan
L. Huron
L. Erie
PA.
N.J.
NEBR.
IOWA

dense forests that are an important source of pulpwood for paper, and abundant iron and coal.

West of the Maritimes are the St. Lawrence River and Great Lakes lowlands, the southern parts of the provinces of Ontario and Quebec. The St. Lawrence River flows from Lake Ontario to the Atlantic Ocean. This southern, warmer region of Canada is the most populated.

Ontario and Quebec stretch north to the remote shores of chilly Hudson Bay. Here ancient glaciers shaped the Canadian Shield, a vast wilderness plateau filled with thick forests, fast-flowing rivers, glacial lakes, and rich deposits of gold, silver, and copper. The shield curves around Hudson Bay and into Newfoundland and the Northwest Territories.

The flat grasslands of the Great Plains are west of the shield. Here lie the Prairie Provinces of Manitoba, Saskatchewan, and Alberta. Spring rains and dry autumns have helped make this region a major producer of wheat and other grains. Resources include large amounts of oil and natural gas.

West of the plains rise the Rocky Mountains, part of the eastern border of the province of British Columbia. The Coast Mountains lie along Canada's western border near the Pacific Ocean. Here warm, moist air makes the climate mild. Between the mountain ranges are wide valleys with forests, orchards, and vineyards.

The Northwest Territories and the Yukon Territory lie farthest north. They cover 40 percent of Canada's total area. Chilled by the arctic winds, most of the area has **permafrost**; all the soil, except the top few feet, is permanently frozen. Summers are cool and brief; winter is long, dark, and icy. ■

▲ *This map of Canada shows the provinces and territories, including a proposed territory called Nunavut. Which provinces have most of Canada's farmland?*

How Do We Know?

HISTORY *We know that ancient moving glaciers formed much of the geography of Canada through the study of glacial geology. By analyzing the age, types, and layers of rock and land formations, scientists can recreate the movement of glaciers that melted years ago.*

■ *How do the landforms and climate of Canada's regions differ?*

DEVELOP

Draw students' attention to the map on this page. Have them locate the different kinds of terrain defined in the map key. Review the meaning of each term. You may want to have students look up some of these terms in the Glossary of Geographic Terms on page 690. Then, as students read about each region of Canada, have them locate the region on the map and identify the kinds of terrain they find.

◄ *The provinces of Alberta, Manitoba, and Saskatchewan have most of the farmland.*

■ *The Northwest Territories and the Yukon Territory are cold and icy, mostly covered by permafrost. The Atlantic Provinces are hilly and coastal. The St. Lawrence valley has fertile farmland and has become a major population center. The Canadian Shield, which curves around Hudson Bay, is a rocky, wooded wilderness. The Great Plains, to the west of the Canadian Shield, are vast, flat grasslands. British Columbia has two large mountain ranges and a wide valley with forests, fertile plains for farms, and orchards.*

Access Strategy

Help students compare the place where they live with a region directly north of them in Canada. Talk about the land, water bodies, and climate in their community. Discuss whether or not their local geography is similar to the northern region in Canada or to any other Canadian region. Also, discuss any differences in climate the students might expect.

Next, look at the map of North America on page 686 of the Atlas. Have students locate the national capitals of both Canada and Mexico. Then ask them to decide whether their homes are closer to Canada's capital (Ottawa) or to Mexico's capital (Mexico City).

Access Activity

Locate a relief map that includes all of North America. (The map should have raised areas to identify heights above sea level.) Help students get a sense of Canadian geography by asking them to close their eyes as they run their fingers over the map. As they touch the map, tell them what part of the country they are in—north, south, east, or west.

ECONOMICS

Study Skills

Have students determine what resources are richest in the areas where the Inuit live. Judging from the geography and the resources available, students should identify what industries they think might be the most prevalent among the Inuit. *(Students may suggest that because the Inuit live near water, fishing could be one of the biggest industries.)*

■ *The Algonquin were nomads and hunters; the Iroquois farmed and had a representative government; the Assiniboine hunted buffalo for food, clothing, shelter, and weapons; and the Inuit lived in igloos or sod houses, and hunted whales and seals for food and clothing.*

CLOSE

Read the Thinking Focus aloud. Encourage students to think about the advantages and the disadvantages of living in each region. Ask students why it might be beneficial for a nation to have such variety and why such a large and diverse area might present challenges. *(A large country may offer a variety of natural resources and space. Challenges might include difficulties in governing a population whose political concerns are diverse.)*

The Native Peoples of Canada

▲ *Inuit children expect to have their own territory, Nunavut, in 1999.*

Native peoples already living in Canada when Europeans arrived include the Haida *(HY duh)* and the Tsimshian *(CHIM shee uhn)* of Canada's Pacific coast. When the English explorer, James Cook, arrived there in the late 1780s he noted that these people were "ingenious sculptors." From cedar trees they built longhouses. They also made 70-foot dugout canoes for hunting whales and seals and carved tall, beautiful, wooden totem poles.

The Algonquin were hunters, so they did not build permanent settlements. Instead, they moved through the northern forests, following moose, herds of caribou, and other animals.

In contrast, the Iroquois *(IHR uh kwoy)* were farmers. They built permanent farming villages along the St. Lawrence River and lower Great Lakes. Many of their villages united with other Native Americans to form the League of the Five Nations. Each member nation sent a representative to a council that decided issues by voting.

The Assiniboine *(uh SIHN uh boyn)*, Blood, Cree, and Ojibwa *(oh JIHB way)* hunted the buffalo that roamed the Great Plains of Canada. From the buffalo they obtained food and clothing, as well as materials for shelters and weapons.

The ancestors of the Inuit *(IHN yoo iht)* probably first arrived in Canada about 1,000 years ago. Some lived in ice houses, or igloos, but most lived in homes of matted soil called sod. They hunted whales and seals for food and clothes and made tools from the animals' bones.

Native peoples thrived for thousands of years in Canada. Yet, their lives changed drastically when Europeans sailed to their shores. ■

➤ *Restored totem poles carved by native peoples of Canada's northwest stand in Stanley Park in Vancouver.*

■ *Describe the way of life of three Native American groups in Canada before Europeans arrived.*

REVIEW

1. **FOCUS** What are the geographic regions of Canada, and how did its early native peoples adapt to each region?
2. **GEOGRAPHY** Refer to the map of Canada on page 599. Why do you think most Canadians live in the St. Lawrence and Great Lakes lowlands?
3. **GEOGRAPHY** Look at the map of North America in the Atlas on page 686. Compare the overall physical geography of Canada with that of the United States.
4. **CRITICAL THINKING** The European explorers took the name Canada from the Native American word *kanata*, which means "settlement." Why might they have chosen that name?
5. **WRITING ACTIVITY** The sacred tales of Native Americans explained their world. Choose a natural event such as a rainstorm. Write a myth using animal characters that explains the natural event.

Homework Options

Have students pretend that they are among the first explorers to come to one of Canada's regions from Europe. Ask them to design a flag for that region. Their flag design should suggest something of the area's geography and resources and, if possible, of the population as well.

Study Guide: page 104

Answers to Review Questions

1. The major geographic regions of Canada are the Arctic territories, the coastal Atlantic Provinces, the St. Lawrence and Great Lakes lowlands, the Canadian Shield plateau around Hudson Bay, the grasslands of the Prairie Provinces, and the mountainous Pacific coast. Students should look for ways in which each Native American society adapted to the physical features and natural resources of its region.
2. The climate is milder, the land is good for farming, and water is plentiful.
3. Canada is larger. Physical features, such as the Rocky Mountains, the plains, and the Appalachians, extend across the border.
4. Native Americans may have used the word to describe their communities. Early European settlers may have used the word as a synonym for their settlements.
5. Myths should express individual interests and values.

1300 1400 1500 1534 TODAY

L E S S O N 2

History of Canada

Imagine that the year is 1536 and you are a Native American living along the St. Lawrence River. Your people have met a man called Jacques Cartier (ZHAHK kahr tee AY) who has come with ships and men from France. All of these strangers want to reach a place called China.

You have shown Cartier and his crew your homes and villages. You have filled their longboats with loaves of bread made from corn. You have welcomed them to your hearths and treated them to feasts of beans, soup, fish, and broiled meat. You have shown them where to fish and hunt. Still, they ask if your rivers lead west to another land of riches.

THINKING FOCUS

How have France and Britain influenced the history of Canada?

Britain and France Vie for Power

Before Cartier, Giovanni Caboto—called John Cabot by the English—had sailed across the Atlantic. He reached Canada in 1497. Yet neither man ever found an ocean route west to Asia and its riches of silks and spices.

However, they did find other riches—a wealth of fish and furs to sell to Europeans and a beautiful land. Cabot claimed Newfoundland for England; Cartier claimed lands around what is now called the St. Lawrence River for France. On this river in 1608 Samuel de Champlain established the first permanent French settlement in Canada. The French named the settlement Quebec, from an Algonquin word meaning "narrowing of waters."

By the mid-1700s, France had claimed about half of Canada and the Mississippi River valley. Britain had established colonies along the Atlantic coast. In 1756 fierce competition for lands and profitable trade finally led to the Seven Years' War. In North America that war is called the French and Indian War.

Both England and France received help from Native Americans during the war. They taught the French new fighting strategies.

Key Terms

- confederation
- dominion

The Death of General Wolfe *by Benjamin West shows the British commander dying during the successful British battle for Quebec in 1759.*

INTRODUCE

Remind students that in Mexico Spanish explorers found gold. Then have students use what they read about the land and the peoples of Canada in Lesson 1 to help them predict what valuable resources French and English explorers might have found in Canada. *(Students may suggest animals for fur, timber for building, fish, and tillable farmland.)* Have the students discuss the possible reactions of Native Americans to the newcomers. *(They may have resented the newcomers; they may have feared that the newcomers would threaten their land and beliefs; or they may have been eager to trade and make friends.)*

Key Terms

Vocabulary Strategies: T36–T37

confederation—a group of unified states or provinces in which power is divided between national and local governments

dominion—a territory of another country with some self-rule

Graphic Overview

Native Americans Inhabit Canada ➤ French and English Settlers Arrive ➤ Canada Becomes Dominion ➤ Country Expands from Sea to Sea ➤ Canada Becomes Independent

Objectives

1. Understand the British and French heritage of Canada.
2. Explain the history of westward expansion.
3. Explain the key steps in independence from British rule.
4. Understand the influence of Britain on Canada.

DEVELOP

This lesson traces Canada's development from the time of the first European exploration through Canada's evolution as a modern nation. Introduce students to the Graphic Overview to help them keep track of the development of Canada as a nation. Then have them read aloud the Thinking Focus. Advise students to pay special attention to the story of British-French relations in Canada as they read this lesson.

■ *Britain became the dominant power by defeating France in the French and Indian War. In the peace treaty, France ceded not only Canada, but all of North America east of the Mississippi River.*

➤ *He called it the River of Disappointment because he had hoped that it would lead to the Pacific Ocean and a route to Asia. When he arrived at the Arctic Ocean instead, he gave it a name that reflected his feelings.*

■ *How did Britain become the dominant power in Canada?*

However, many Native Americans fought at the side of the British.

In 1758 the British won a key battle when they defeated the French with the siege of Louisburg. From then on, British victories increased. In 1763 the British won the war. In defeat, the French gave up control of Canada and nearly all of North America east of the Mississippi River.

In 1774, to avoid possible revolt, the British agreed to let the French people of Quebec keep their civil laws, religion, and customs. Then, after the American Revolution broke out in 1775, thousands of Loyalists—colonists loyal to Britain—fled from the American colonies to Quebec. Although they wanted British rule, they did not want to live according to French laws and customs. Thus, in 1791, the British split Quebec into Upper Canada and Lower Canada. Most British Loyalists lived in Upper Canada—today, the province of Ontario. Most French Canadians lived in Lower Canada—today, the province of Quebec. ■

Westward Expansion and Immigration

Much of Britain's huge new territory remained uncharted. The task of exploring and mapping it fell to the "Nor'Westers," explorers and fur traders from the North West Company. They were greatly helped by Native American guides.

"From Sea to Sea"

"Thus I have fully completed the survey of this part of North America from sea to sea," wrote David Thompson in 1811, "and . . . have determined the positions of the Mountains, Lakes and Rivers, and other remarkable places. . . ."

More than any other early surveyor and mapmaker, Thompson deserves credit for the first accurate map of western Canada. He took two years to complete it after many years of exploration.

Thompson was not the first Nor'Wester to venture into Canada's vast western lands. One of the most successful was Alexander Mackenzie. In 1789, almost 300 years after John Cabot had tried to find a route to Asia, Mackenzie set off to do the same. He was looking for an inland waterway to the Pacific Ocean.

For many weeks, he and his guides paddled canoes down an icy, unknown river. The land they passed through was frozen. Finally, they reached the ocean. However, it was filled with floating ice; obviously, it was not the Pacific.

Below is a portrait of the famed Canadian explorer Alexander Mackenzie. Trace his routes in 1789 and 1793 on the map to the right. Locate the Mackenzie River. Why did he first name it the River of Disappointment?

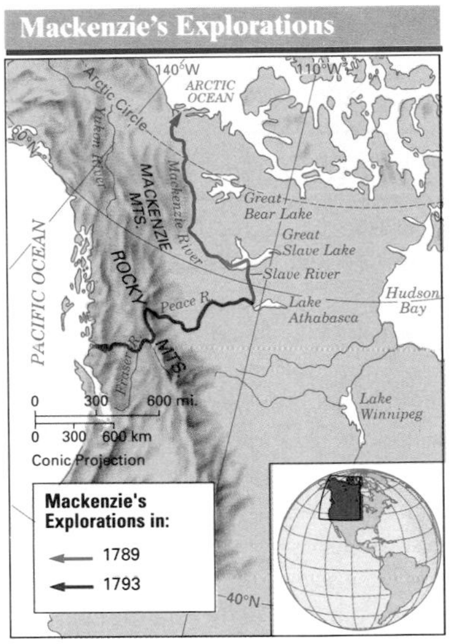

Mackenzie's Explorations
140°W
110°W
ARCTIC OCEAN
Arctic Circle
60°N
Yukon River
MACKENZIE MTS.
Mackenzie River
Great Bear Lake
Great Slave Lake
Slave River
ROCKY MTS.
Peace R.
Fraser R.
Lake Athabasca
Hudson Bay
PACIFIC OCEAN
Lake Winnipeg
0 300 600 mi.
0 300 600 km
Conic Projection
Mackenzie's Explorations in:
1789
1793
40°N

Access Activity

Have students examine the painting and the caption on the previous page. Tell them that the British defeated the French in this battle for Quebec. Then invite the students to make predictions about the future of Quebec. *(Students may suggest that the French people of Quebec will resent the British or that Quebec will remain a troubled region.)*

Access Strategy

Several of the pictures in this lesson show groups of people. Students can use these visuals to help them understand a specific historical period or event. Ask students to study one of the pictures. Then suggest that they choose to be one of the people in the picture. Ask them, if they were that person, what they would see, hear, and feel. Then have them create a short dialogue between themselves and another person in the picture. Ask volunteers to perform their dialogues for the class.

Mackenzie had found a route to the Arctic Ocean. Still, Mackenzie was determined to find an inland waterway to the Pacific Ocean. The feat would gain him fame and a large reward offered by the British Parliament.

So, in 1793, he set off on a different route west. This time he traveled in a 25-foot canoe with French explorers, Native American guides, and a dog. The river took them to the Rocky Mountains. They scaled the steep river banks on foot, carrying the canoe and all their supplies. Then Native Americans they met told them which river would lead to the Pacific.

After weeks of dangerous passage through raging waters, they finally reached the Pacific Ocean. Mackenzie had become the first European in the far north to reach the Pacific Ocean by inland waterway.

Others followed Mackenzie's route, and Thompson would eventually map the western wilderness. These explorers opened the way for Canada's westward expansion and settlement.

Expansion and Unity

By 1821, there were six colonies in Canada—Newfoundland, Prince Edward Island, New Brunswick, Nova Scotia, Upper Canada (now Ontario), and Lower Canada (now Quebec). In the 1830s the British government considered uniting the colonies. Later, Canadians drew up plans for a **confederation**—a unified state in which power is shared between the national and local governments. Fears of U.S. expansion convinced many that confederation was necessary.

On July 1, 1867, many Canadians celebrated when the confederation became a reality. The provinces of New Brunswick and present-day Ontario and Quebec had voted to unite to form the dominion of Canada. Nova Scotia also became part of the dominion. Becoming a **dominion** of Great Britain meant having self-rule. Canada was ruled by a governor general appointed by the British crown and a Parliament made up of the House of Commons and the Senate. In 1873 the dominion had grown to include Prince Edward Island, British Columbia, and Manitoba.

To keep law and order during westward

▲ An Inuit husband and wife add information to a chart for the British explorer Captain John Ross aboard his ship in 1830.

▼ The quadrant was an instrument used by the early European explorers to measure altitudes.

ECONOMICS

Critical Thinking

Explain that people who explored and settled the West had many motives: they were seeking land, food, adventure, a wilderness experience, personal glory, or a fresh start. Underlying these reasons, however, were economic ones. Ask students to hypothesize some economic reasons for frontier exploration. *(Students may suggest: They wanted a trade route to Asia, furs to sell in Europe, farmland for raising crops, a railroad to transport goods to market, or simply a job.)* Ask students to look for these economic motives as they read the lesson.

Historical Context

Tell students that one of the most famous battles of the Seven Years' War (the French and Indian War) was the fight for Quebec. The French city of Quebec was completely fortified by tall, stone walls and stood atop high cliffs beside the St. Lawrence River. British General Wolfe's daring attack came under cover of darkness, when he sailed his troops up the river to a point just above the city. Silently, soldiers climbed the steep cliffs. At daybreak French General Montcalm awoke to find British troops arrayed across the Plains of Abraham, just outside the city walls. In panic, he made a fatal error. He led his French troops out of the walled city to fight. Had he stayed inside and forced the British to scale the walls, he might have won the battle. Both generals suffered mortal wounds in the fighting. You may want to use Study Print 16 here.

Critical Thinking

In the late 19th century, railroads and telegraph lines tied the vast spaces of Canada together. Ask students to identify new communication methods that link Canada today. *(Today, snowmobiles and airplanes have made the Northwest Territory more accessible; television, computers, and fax machines have linked people across Canada.)*

▲ *Immigrants in Canada in the late 1800s included a railroad crew of Chinese workers in British Columbia (left) and Russian women sorting grain on the prairies (right).*

expansion, Canada created the North-West Mounted Police in 1873. Known today as the Royal Canadian Mounted Police, or "Mounties," this force of men and women continues its work.

The Immigration Boom

Before British Columbia would join the dominion in 1871, it insisted that a railroad be built to connect the nation from east to west. The government agreed. It encouraged people from other countries to help build the railroad and to settle along its route.

Thousands of immigrants came. Canada's western plains promised rich farmland and natural resources. Meanwhile, the Canadian Pacific Railway promised work. People came from as far away as China to build the railroad. When it was completed in 1885, many of those workers stayed. Between 1900 and 1911, Canada's population increased by nearly two million. Many immigrants came from Britain, Russia, Germany, and India. Some settled in the Prairie Provinces to grow wheat and other crops. Others settled farther east in Ontario and the Maritime Provinces. They brought many new languages and religious traditions and added to Canada's cultural diversity. ■

■ *How did exploration, expansion, and immigration cause Canada to spread "From Sea to Sea"?*

■ *Canadian explorers and fur traders pushed the boundaries westward from the Atlantic coast in the 1800s. After the Dominion of Canada was formed in 1867, the government sought to expand to the Pacific coast to include the province of British Columbia. That province agreed to become part of the dominion if a railroad was built linking it to the East. Immigrants who came to build the railroad increased the population.*

From Dominion to Independence

Canadians had considerable power over the workings of their government. However, as a dominion of Britain, they could not enjoy total independence.

Many English-speaking Canadians felt closely connected to Great Britain. For example, when Britain went to war in South Africa in 1899, some English speakers demanded involvement in the fight. French speakers, on the other hand, were against participation. In a compromise, Canadian volunteers served under British command in that war. Yet French Canadians continued to resent many aspects of British control of their lives.

Steps to Independence

World War I erupted in 1914. Hundreds of thousands of Canadians volunteered to fight. At first they fought under British command. Then, in 1917, a Canadian officer took command of Canadian forces. These units became the first truly independent Canadian groups in the eyes of the world. Following the war, Canada signed the peace treaty and joined the newly formed League of Nations, another move toward independence.

In 1931 Great Britain agreed to cut another major tie. With the Statute of Westminster, Britain declared Canada an independent

Visual Learning

Make a timeline on the chalkboard from 1867 to the present. Help students plot the steps to independence on it. Determine how many years from this point Canadian independence took. (From the time Canada became a dominion to the Constitution Act was 115 years.)

Economic Context

Extend students' understanding of immigration booms by providing details of the upsurge in population that began in 1896 when gold was discovered on Klondike Creek, a tributary of the Yukon River. More than 100,000 prospectors poured in, primarily from the United States. Most were disappointed. While some gold could be picked up on the surface or panned from rivers, most of it was buried beneath more than a yard of permafrost. The only way to reach the gold was to thaw the ground with fires. Within three years, most of the gold had been found. It yielded around $50 million, about what it cost all of those prospectors to get to the fields.

The gold rush was the first of many mineral discoveries. Shortly after gold had been found, someone discovered silver near James Bay. Subsequent finds of cobalt and radium continued the influx of speculators and settlers. This excitement led to Canada's emergence as a major supplier of mineral resources.

nation, but kept control over the amendment process of the Canadian constitution.

Canada fought with the Allies in World War II. In 1949, Canada joined the North Atlantic Treaty Organization (NATO). In 1982, Britain completed the final step of Canada's peaceful transition to total independence. It gave up its power to change or influence the Canadian constitution in any way.

British Influence Today

Today Canada is a politically independent nation. However, many effects of British rule remain.

In many ways Britain's influence has served Canada as the wise advice of a favorite teacher might serve a student. The Canadian government is based on the British parliamentary system. The laws of Canada, like those of the United States, are based firmly on the principles of British law. The province of Quebec is the exception, with a legal system based on its French origins.

On its dollar bills, Canada continues to print the picture of the ruling king or queen of Britain and Canada. Yet the legacy and influence of Britain does not rest well with all Canadians. As you will read in the next lesson, sharp tensions continue to separate many English-speaking citizens from French-speaking citizens. Groups of native peoples are also seeking new rights. ■

▼ *The image of Britain's Queen Elizabeth II appears on many Canadian coins and bills. Although she is Canada's queen, she does not govern Canada.*

BANK OF CANADA – BANQUE DU CA
20
TWENTY
VINGT
DOLLARS
CANADA
20
TWO DOLLARS DEUX

◄ *On July 1, 1967, Canadians celebrated the hundredth anniversary of the creation of the dominion of Canada.*

■ *What were the major steps that led to Canadian independence from Britain?*

REVIEW

1. **FOCUS** How have France and Britain influenced the history of Canada?
2. **GEOGRAPHY** Why was it important to the people of British Columbia that Canada build a transcontinental railroad?
3. **HISTORY** How did the building of the railway contribute to the diversity of Canada's population?
4. **CRITICAL THINKING** How might the history of Canada have been different if the French had won the Seven Years' War instead of the British?
5. **WRITING ACTIVITY** Imagine that you are Alexander Mackenzie on his first trek, which would lead to the Arctic Ocean. Write three diary entries describing his experiences and feelings. The first entry is for June 3, 1789, just before Mackenzie sets off. The second is on July 12, 1789, when ice is spotted. The final entry is on September 13, 1789, a day after Mackenzie has returned to his camp.

CITIZENSHIP

Visual Learning

Allow students a few minutes to study the photographs of Canadian money on this page. Remind them that many Canadians are uncomfortable with the legacy and the influence of Great Britain. Ask students to design new coins or bank notes for Canada that they think would represent its multicultural heritage. For ideas, suggest that students examine all the photographs in this chapter.

■ *Canada achieved self-rule when it became a dominion in 1867; after World War I, it joined the League of Nations as an independent nation; in 1931, in the Statute of Westminster, Great Britain accepted Canadian independence but kept control of the constitutional amendment process; in 1982 Great Britain gave up its power to change Canada's constitution in any way.*

CLOSE

Ask a volunteer to reread the Thinking Focus. Have students work in pairs. One will write a list of French influences; the other will list British influences. Then have the two compare their lists to see what they have in common.

Answers to Review Questions

1. Both nations sent explorers who started settlements that still have British or French names and ethnic populations. Both used Canada as a source of raw materials. The French and Indian War led to British dominance. Canada's government and laws are based on those of Britain. However, French is still spoken by a large population in Canada, and Quebec has a French legal system.
2. It would speed transportation of goods and people across vast stretches of land; it would connect them to the rest of Canada.
3. People came from many parts of the world to build the railway; many stayed.
4. Possible answer: French language, culture, government, and legal systems would have been dominant.
5. Answers should show an understanding of feelings that range from excitement to disappointment.

Homework Options

Have students hold a debate for and against Canadian independence from Great Britain. Encourage them to prepare their arguments as a group activity.

Study Guide: page 105

UNDERSTANDING DIAGRAMS

This skills feature uses a diagram of how the St. Lawrence Seaway works to teach students to interpret and use process diagrams.

VISUAL LEARNING

Creating a Process Diagram

Ask the students to create their own process diagram illustrating an everyday task, such as making a peanut butter sandwich, sweeping a floor, or playing a game. Tell them to show at least four steps in the process. Then have students exchange their diagrams with classmates. The one who receives the diagram pantomimes the steps it shows. Others in the class guess what process is being acted out.

UNDERSTANDING DIAGRAMS

Reading a Process Diagram

Here's Why

The St. Lawrence Seaway is a very important transportation route for both Canada and the United States. It is a 2,350-mile inland route that makes it possible for ocean-going vessels to travel from the Atlantic Ocean to the Great Lakes and into the heart of Canada.

Look at the diagram on this page. It is a process diagram. A process diagram usually uses pictures to explain the steps of an entire process more clearly. For example, instructions for assembling a bike are likely to include a process diagram.

A process diagram can help you understand how the St. Lawrence Seaway works. Much of the waterway depends on locks that raise and lower ocean-going vessels so they can travel from one body of water to another.

Here's How

Now look at the process diagram more carefully. The numbers tell you how to follow each part of the diagram. For example, the first part of the diagram shows the ship entering the lock from the higher level.

The second part of the diagram shows that after the gates have been shut, water is let out of the lock through openings. What are these openings called?

In the third part of the diagram, you see that as the water passes to the lower level, the water level and the ship are lowered. Now look at the fourth part of the diagram. When are the gates to the lock finally opened?

Try It

See if you can use the diagram to write a paragraph that explains why the gates to the lower channel aren't opened after the vessel first enters the lock.

Apply It

Find a process diagram in your science textbook or another source. Explain each step of the diagram.

How a Lock Works

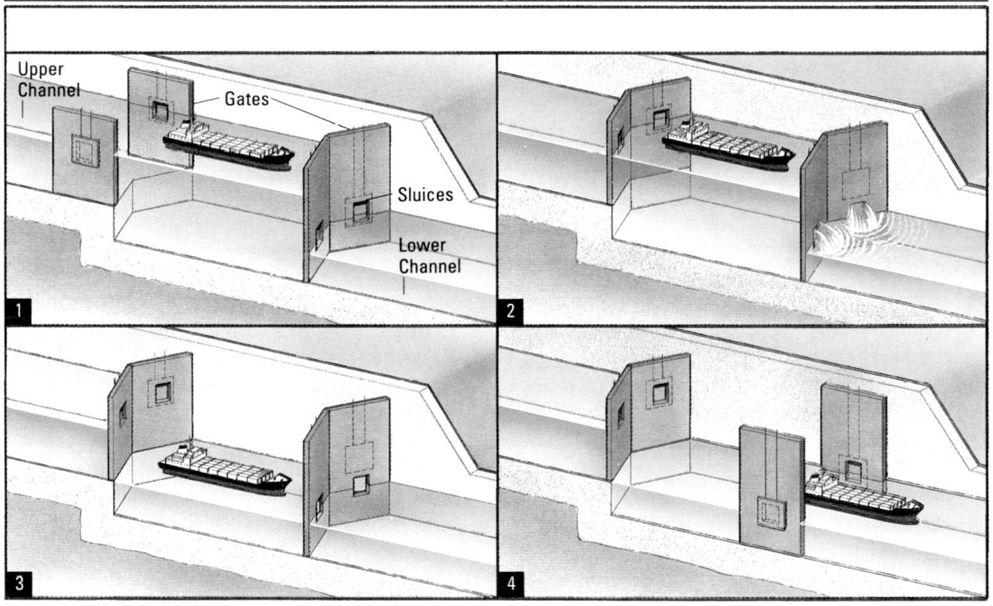
Upper Channel
Gates
Sluices
Lower Channel
1
2
3
4

Objective

Read and make a process diagram. (Visual Learning 2)

Map and Globe Skills

Have students use the Atlas to locate the Panama Canal and the Suez Canal. Ask what bodies of water each canal links. *(Panama Canal—Caribbean Sea with the Pacific Ocean; Suez Canal—Mediterranean Sea with the Red Sea)* Tell students that the St. Lawrence Seaway is the world's longest canal system. Ask what bodies of water are linked by the St. Lawrence Seaway. *(The Atlantic Ocean with the Great Lakes)*

Answer to Try It

Students should be able to use the diagram to explain that if the gates are immediately opened, a massive rush of water could capsize the ship.

Answers to Apply It

Check students' diagrams to see that they have correctly identified a process diagram. You may want to check their understanding of the diagram by asking them to write a brief paragraph explaining the process.

1300 1400 1500 1600 1700 1800 1900 1960 TODAY

L E S S O N 3

Canada Today

O Canada! Our home and native land!
True patriot love in all thy sons command.
With glowing hearts we see thee rise,
The True North strong and free!
From far and wide, O Canada,
We stand on guard for thee.

These lines from Canada's national anthem express the pride and commitment its peoples of many different cultures feel for their "home and native land." Modern Canada is indeed a multicultural nation. In fact, Canadians were among the earliest users of the term **multicultural**, which means "of many cultures."

THINKING FOCUS

What factors make modern Canada a prosperous, multicultural nation?

Key Terms

- multicultural
- bilingual
- separatism

A Multicultural, Bilingual, Urban Nation

In 1991 there were more than 27 million people living in Canada. Of these, about 60 percent are English-speaking and about 24 percent are French-speaking. About 20 percent have other international roots. Native peoples including the Inuit make up about 1.5 percent of Canada's total population.

A Cultural Quilt

Canada's many ethnic groups are like the pieces of a patchwork quilt. Instead of blending, separate pieces combine to make one nation.

For example, most people in Newfoundland are of British heritage, while most people in the province of Quebec are of French heritage. Saskatchewan has Ukrainian, French, German, and many other ethnic communities. A large community of Asian people lives in British Columbia.

Cultural identity and pride are, of course, important to each group.

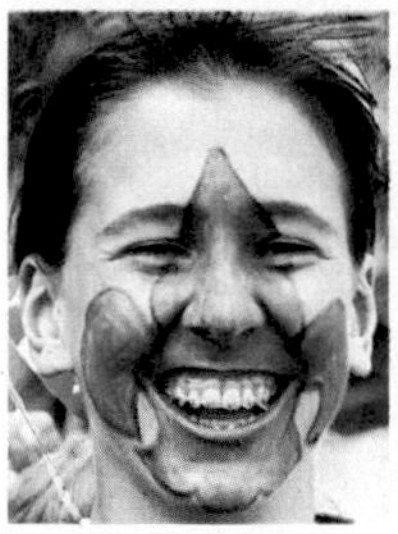

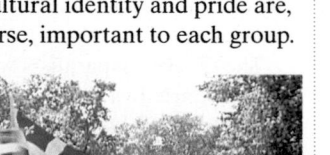

Members of the Parti Québecois rally to gain support for a separate Quebec. The fleur-de-lis *painted on the woman's face (far left) is a symbol of French culture.*

INTRODUCE

Remind students that they have read about a variety of cultures from all parts of the world. Tell them that peoples from most of these cultures have found a home in Canada today. Ask students to read the words of Canada's national anthem for clues about what holds such a multicultural nation together. *(Students may suggest that all the peoples call Canada home. Canadians share a love of the country, of the land, and of freedom.)*

Key Terms

Vocabulary Strategies: T36–T37
multicultural—of many cultures
bilingual—using, or capable of using, two languages
separatism—a policy or a belief in breaking away and being separate

Graphic Overview

Divisions
Unity
geography
separatism
Native American independence
federal government
communications
bilingualism
CANADA TODAY

Objectives

1. Understand the bilingual, multicultural, and urban nature of Canada today.
2. Describe industry, education, and the arts in Canada.
3. Understand Canada's view of its role in the world today.

DEVELOP

Explain to students that as they read this lesson, they will learn about many elements—such as language, cultural differences, politics, and vast landforms that divide Canadians. At the same time, students will also find out what aspects of the nation's government, economy, education system, and cultural life hold the disparate elements together. Students can use the Graphic Overview to help them keep track of these components.

GEOGRAPHY

Map and Globe Skills

Have students list the names of the teams in the National Hockey League. They can find this information in a newspaper during the hockey season or in an almanac. Ask students to locate the cities that are home to these teams on a map of Canada and the United States. Have students use the map scale to measure distances between Canadian cities. Suggest they write a paragraph on how a sport can link people in two different countries.

■ *Some of Canada's provinces are dominated by one ethnic group. Combining to make one nation lends itself to the comparison with a patchwork quilt.*

▼ Caribana *is a joyous two-week Caribbean festival enjoyed by the people of Toronto. It boasts a parade with elaborate, colorful costumes.*

Canada's government has tried to help by supporting all cultures. The Multiculturalism Act of 1988 states that every citizen, regardless of origin, has equal rights.

People speak several languages in Canada. Canada's constitution states that it is a **bilingual** nation. That is, it has two official languages, English and French. Many Canadians are bilingual, speaking two languages with ease.

The discontent of Quebec's French Canadians with English-speaking influence led to the growth of separatism in the 1960s. Supporters of **separatism** believe that if French Canadian culture is to survive, Quebec must become an independent nation. A separatist party called Parti Québecois *(pahr TEE keh beh KWAH)* came to power in Quebec in 1976. Then a new law made French the only official language of the province.

The Quebec separatists want independence. In 1992 the federal government, led by Prime Minister Brian Mulroney, proposed a constitutional reform to persuade Quebec to remain part of Canada. The reform, called the Charlottetown Agreement, proposed special rights to Quebec as a "distinct society" within the nation. For many complex reasons, the voters defeated it. In general, the separatists voted no because they want nothing less than total independence for Quebec. Other Canadians felt that one province should not have special rights that others do not have. Thus the struggle over Quebec's status continues.

The Inuit are native people who have long struggled to preserve their cultural heritage. Today thousands of Inuit live in northern Canada. They have been working to regain land that they believe was always theirs. In 1992 the citizens of the Northwest Territories voted to split that region into two parts. The new part shown on the map on page 599 will become official in 1999. It will be called Nunavut Territory. In Inuit the word *nunavut* means "our land."

Urban Life: Toronto

About 75 percent of all Canadians live in cities and towns, and about 80 percent live within 200 miles of the U.S. border. This southern region is one of the warmer parts of the nation. Toronto, the capital of Ontario, is Canada's largest city. Its location on the St. Lawrence Seaway makes it one of the nation's busiest ports.

In the 1880s the completion of Canada's transcontinental railway system linked the port of Toronto with Canada's timber and mining regions. This link added to the city's industrial growth. Later, its closeness to Detroit, the U.S. car manufacturing center, created an even greater boom in industrial growth.

Toronto is one of the most ethnically diverse cities in the world. More than 80 ethnic groups live there, and approximately 100 languages are spoken. ■

■ *Why can Canada be described as a "cultural quilt"?*

Access Activity

Ask students to identify Canada's two official languages. *(English and French)* Explain that this lesson will describe the rifts between French- and English-speaking Canadians, and how Canada's government is trying to decrease tensions among its ethnic groups.

Access Strategy

Have students recite or sing the first verse of "The Star-Spangled Banner" and then recite or listen to the words of "O Canada!" Then ask students to compare the two songs and note the themes that are similar, such as freedom and patriotism. Ask them to note any differences they find between the two songs, such as the focal point. *(The flag for "The Star-Spangled Banner" and the land in "O Canada!")*

Canada's Achievements

The United Nations has singled out Canada as the world's best place to live based on the education, life expectancy, and income of Canadians. Canadian women live an average of 80 years; men live an average of 73 years.

What other factors make Canada such a great place to live? Some of these include thriving industries, high-quality education, a national health care system, and a wealth of artistic attractions.

Industry

Canada's economy today reflects its urban character. Service industries, including health care, education, and tourism, employ about 72 percent of Canada's workers. Manufacturing, mining, and agriculture follow, with only about 5 percent of the work force employed in agricultural jobs. Canada's major industrial region includes the St. Lawrence River and Great Lakes lowlands.

Canada's economy is strong. It ranks among the top 10 nations in terms of its gross national product (GNP). As you read in Chapter 16, gross national product is the total market value of all goods and services produced yearly by a nation. One reason that Canada's GNP is so high is that the nation has a wealth of natural resources. For example, Canada's natural gas, uranium, crude oil, timber, and coal are purchased by many nations. In fact, the United States buys about 90 percent of Canada's heavy crude oil.

Along with oil and natural gas, Canada has an abundant supply of other energy sources, such as uranium and hydroelectric power. Energy is Canada's second most important export, following cars.

Education and Health

Canada's system of free public schools is similar to that of the United States. Children go to kindergarten and proceed through the system until they graduate from high school.

Across Time & Space

Something that unifies Canadians is their most popular sport—ice hockey. It probably began as a blend of field hockey, a British game, and kolf, a Dutch game played on ice. In 1893 the Canadian governor general, Lord Stanley, donated a silver bowl—the Stanley Cup—for the winners of an annual hockey tournament.

The bustling port city of Toronto takes its name from a Huron word meaning "meeting place." Today it is a center of culture, trade, and industry.

ECONOMICS

Critical Thinking

Explain that when business managers look for places to locate their industries, they consider a number of factors. They need access to raw materials, a reliable and capable work force, good transportation, and a healthy business climate. In addition, companies are interested in so-called quality-of-life factors, such as good schools, safe neighborhoods, a healthy environment, and cultural attractions. Have students discuss why each of these factors is important and then read the lesson to find out which factors are offered in various cities in Canada.

Mathematics Connection

In some Canadian provinces, a special provision allows teachers to take off a year after teaching for four. However, their pay is prorated over the five years, so that a teacher who opts for this plan receives only 80 percent of her or his pay for each of the five years, including the year off. Present this information to students. Then pose the following problem: A teacher works at a job for which he or she could earn $30,000 a year. However, the teacher wants to take advantage of the year-off program. How much money would he or she receive for each of the five years under this plan? *(80 percent of $30,000, or $24,000)*

Study Skills

Show students how to outline the information in Canada's Achievements. Have them list the three subheadings: Industry, Education and Health, and The Arts. Under each heading, have them list important facts from the text. These facts may be written as single words or short phrases. They need not be complete sentences.

POLITICAL SYSTEMS

Critical Thinking

Control of public education policy is an issue that students may want to debate. Ask them to consider the advantages of keeping education under local or provincial control. *(Each region can respond to the specific needs of its population.)* Then ask students to consider what might be the disadvantages of local or provincial control. *(Areas with lesser populations or resources might not have the same advantages as those with facilities such as well-stocked libraries or access to cultural events.)* Then talk about the advantages and disadvantages of having the national government set education policy.

■ *Industry: Canada ranks among the top 10 nations in terms of its GNP. Education: Each province administers its own public education system. As in the bilingual programs in the United States, the Heritage Language Program enables students to learn other languages. The federal and provincial governments subsidize college education. Health Care: All Canadians are guaranteed free medical care, supported by federal and provincial taxes. The Arts: Canada has a long, artistic heritage, beginning with its indigenous peoples.*

▲ *Founded in 1938, the Royal Winnipeg Ballet is the oldest ballet company in Canada. Other famed cultural attractions include the Canadian Opera Company and the Montreal Symphony Orchestra.*

A federal law guarantees all Canadians free health care, funded by federal and provincial taxes. Each province has established its own specific laws regarding the medical services that are available. For example, the province of Quebec extends coverage to include children's dental care.

Each province in Canada has the authority to run its public schools. This system allows each region to shape its schools to the specific needs of its multicultural population. Many schools have students from 20 or more different ethnic or cultural groups.

To aid students from different cultures, some Canadian schools have had the Heritage Language Program in use for more than 20 years. Students who wish to learn a language other than English or French can choose from about 60 other languages.

➤ *Unique Inuit sculptures are prized by many art collectors. This sculpture is of an Inuit woman holding a cutting tool called an* ulu.

In some provinces teachers in the public schools are allowed to take a year off from teaching every four years. This enables teachers to pursue further training.

Canada also has many excellent public and private trade schools, colleges, and universities. McGill University and the University of Toronto are two examples. The government supports these schools so that the fees students must pay are greatly reduced.

■ *What are some of Canada's major achievements in industry, education, health care, and the arts?*

The Arts

Let there be room for magic, room for hope, and room for the imagination.

Paul-Émile Borduas,
French-Canadian painter

Canada has a rich tradition of artistic expression that began thousands of years ago. This unique art includes the towering totem poles of the native peoples of the northwest and the smooth, soapstone sculptures of the Inuit.

Many Canadians have achieved excellence as musicians, writers, and filmmakers. Some Canadian popular musicians who have gained worldwide fame include Anne Murray, Gordon Lightfoot, Neil Young, k. d. lang, and the bands Rush and Triumph. L. M. Montgomery, the author of *Anne of Green Gables* and its sequels, based these famous books on her own childhood on Prince Edward Island. Films produced by the National Film Board of Canada have won many awards. You can read about the art of animation in Canada's films in A Closer Look on page 611. ■

Social Participation

Have students work in groups of from three to five. Have the group plan a trip in Canada by preparing a written travel itinerary. Remind group members that they should try to accommodate the interests of all members.

Geographic Context

To expand students' understanding of the Inuit peoples, explain that Canada is home to 25 percent of the world's Inuit population. The Inuit had no vote in Canadian elections until 1962 but are now politically active. In 1999, in part of what is now the Northwest Territories, the Canadian Inuit will officially claim their own territory—Nunavut. The Inuit territory will have the same degree of political and economic sovereignty as the other northern territories of Canada.

The Inuit are working with the government to establish a stable economic base for Nunavut. At the same time, Canada's Inuit, along with other indigenous peoples of the polar regions of Greenland, Alaska, and the former Soviet Union, are charter members of the Inuit Circumpolar Conference. This body addresses the key issues of the entire Arctic world. Will Canada's Inuit be content to remain part of Canada, or will they look outward to the other peoples of the Arctic?

Canadian Animation

Many of Canada's animated films are world famous. Artists paint pictures on film cels, but they also use clay and other unusual materials. For many years, they have broken the rules of animation to invent new effects. To make an animated film, pictures, called cels, are repeated with slight changes, one after another. Run at the high speed of 24 frames per second, the changes blend into movement that looks real.

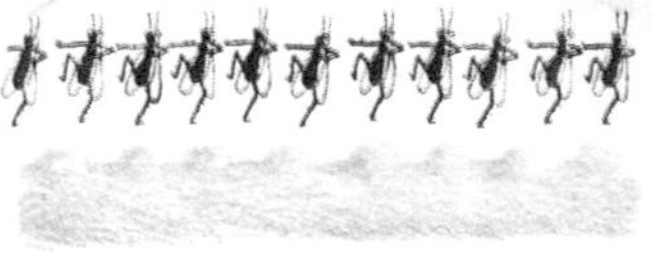

"A-crawlin' in your whiskers, a-crawlin' in your hair . . ." *Blackfly* pits a swarm of pesky flies against Canadian surveyors, and the flies win.

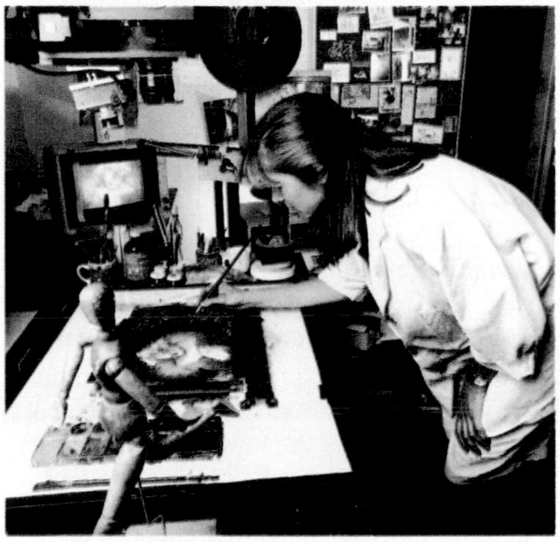

Animator Wendy Tilby creates different textures by painting and scratching film cels.

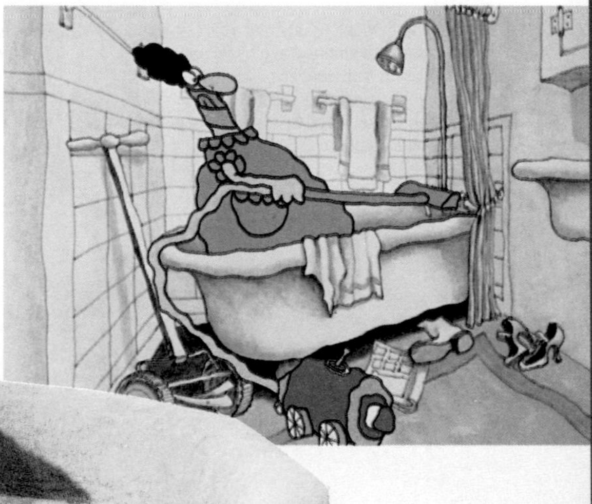

A comical moment from the award winning film *The Big Snit.*

From the Oscar winning film *The Sand Castle*

Note: This feature can be used to extend the discussion (see the previous page) of the arts in Canada.

More About Canadian Animation Most animation is created on cels, single pieces of film or paper that are repeated to create the effect of movement. However, some animators, like Wendy Tilby, work on one large surface, such as glass and, using watercolors, move the paint around while taking repetitive pictures to create a spontaneous effect. In some cases animators like Tilby do not even know the exact effect they are creating until they look at the film. Many animation artists are sponsored by the National Film Board of Canada, which offers no restrictions about the kind of work animators do. In this way, animators are given complete creative license.

611

Research

Assign small groups of students to research United States' innovations in animation. Did the Canadian animation industry have an effect on the United States industry? If so, how? Have a spokesperson from each group present a brief oral report to the class.

Creating Animation

Ask students to create a "flip book" to create the effect of animation. First, they should cut at least 10 small pieces of paper. Next, they should think of a subject to draw and then change the subject very slightly each time they draw it. They may want to choose an active subject, such as a person walking or diving into a pool. Finally, have them staple their drawings together to form a small book and then quickly flip the pages to see the effects of their animation.

Visual Learning

Have students look at each of the pictures on this page. Have them imagine that they are an animation artist about to create movement for each of the photos. Ask students to predict what kind of movement might happen with each of the photos.

BELIEF SYSTEMS

Critical Thinking

Ask students what qualities make a good neighbor. *(Students may suggest: willingness to work together; friendliness; willingness to avoid doing harm to the other.)* List their responses on the chalkboard. Then have them give examples of neighborliness in their personal lives and translate those qualities to neighborliness among nations. *(Example: A good neighbor might bring food to a sick person; a nation might send food to help starving people in a foreign country.)*

Canada's World Vision

Strong domestic antipollution policy has reduced acid rain caused by Canadian industries. However, much of Canada's acid rain starts as air pollution blown across the border from U.S. industries.

Canada's foreign policy has always been one of cooperation and peace. Canada is a member of both the North Atlantic Treaty Organization (NATO) and the United Nations.

Domestic and Foreign Policy

Canada is the only nation in the world to have been involved in every international peacekeeping mission that the United Nations has undertaken. In 1992 Canada joined other nations in sending troops and food supplies to war-torn Somalia.

The Canadian government has sponsored many assistance programs for poor nations. Such programs bring money, food, medicine, agricultural supplies, and knowledge to nations all over the world.

Canada also has a history as a refuge—a place of safety—for people of other nations. Before the U.S. Civil War, Canadians welcomed many African American slaves who reached Canada, where they lived as free men and women. Canada has also welcomed many European and Caribbean immigrants fleeing war or political unrest. During the Vietnam War, Canada's door was open to many young people from the United States. These people came to Canada because they did not support U.S. policies in Vietnam.

Canada and the United States

Canada and the United States share the longest undefended border in the world. This 5,525-mile border stretches from the Atlantic

Acid Rain

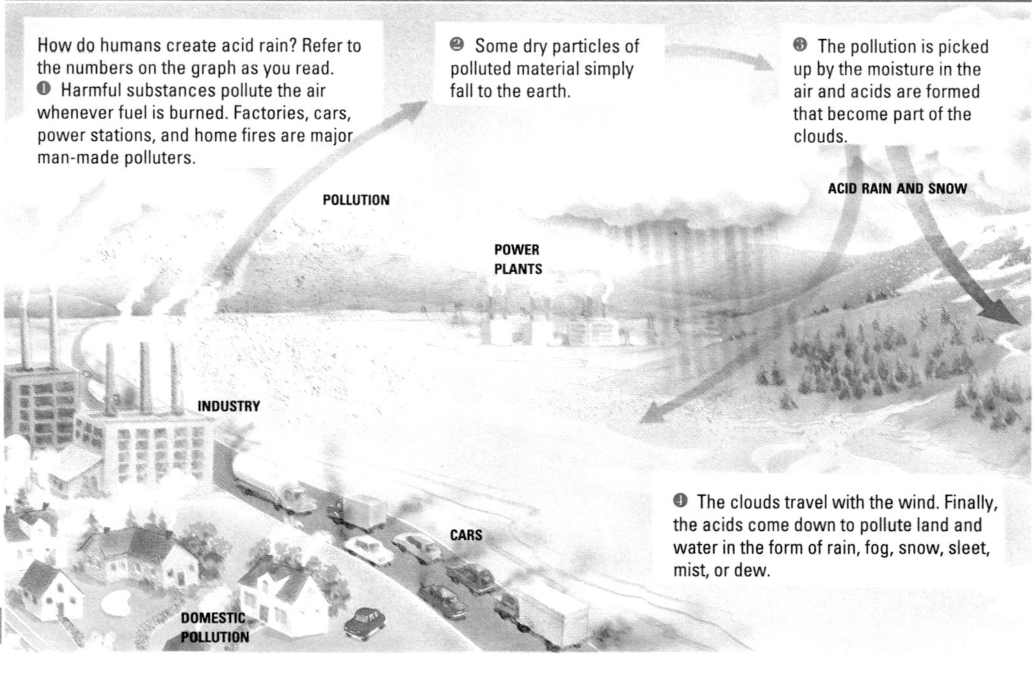
How do humans create acid rain? Refer to the numbers on the graph as you read.
❶ Harmful substances pollute the air whenever fuel is burned. Factories, cars, power stations, and home fires are major man-made polluters.
❷ Some dry particles of polluted material simply fall to the earth.
❸ The pollution is picked up by the moisture in the air and acids are formed that become part of the clouds.
ACID RAIN AND SNOW
POLLUTION
POWER PLANTS
INDUSTRY
❹ The clouds travel with the wind. Finally, the acids come down to pollute land and water in the form of rain, fog, snow, sleet, mist, or dew.
CARS
DOMESTIC POLLUTION

Critical Thinking

Remind students that the boundary between the United States and Canada is a political line that is unmarked except on maps. Have students think about how the existence of this border affects people's lives. *(People on each side of the border salute different flags, use their country's money and stamps, and have separate governments.)*

Political Context

Help students understand why Canada is held in respect around the world as a peacekeeping nation. This reputation probably began with the policies of former Canadian prime minister Lester Pearson. In 1952 he was elected president of the UN General Assembly. In 1956 trouble erupted in the Middle East. Egypt seized control of the Suez Canal and forbade its use by other nations, particularly Israel. France and Britain sent in troops. Despite its close ties to those nations, Canada remained neutral. Then Pearson formed the United Nations Emergency Force. He brought in Canadian troops and supplies to try to foster peace. The troops were stationed on the border of Egypt and Israel and succeeded in ending the conflict. For his leadership role as a peacemaker, Pearson was awarded the Nobel Peace Prize in 1957. In 1963 he became prime minister of Canada. For more information about the UN's involvement in Israel, read Chapter 28.

Ocean and runs through the Great Lakes, which Canada shares with the United States. It then extends west to the Pacific Ocean and along the border of Alaska.

In the 1970s former Canadian prime minister Pierre Trudeau compared Canada's position in relation to the United States as that of "a mouse next to an elephant." Although Canada's world influence has grown, history has taught Canadians to view the United States with some caution. For example, during both the American Revolution and the War of 1812, the United States invaded Canadian soil to attempt to defeat British forces there.

Today, as neighbors and major trading partners, the United States and Canada work together. A Free Trade Agreement in effect since 1989 has enabled Canadian and U.S. exports to cross the border with reduced tariffs, or fees.

The two nations have also cooperated in trying to solve environmental concerns. Pollution of Canada's air and water has come from its own industrial plants and from the U.S. industrial plants across the border. One of the greatest problems is acid rain. The diagram on page 612 explains how acid rain is created. Canada and the United States are working to solve the problem through environmental agreements and a commitment to find clean sources of energy.

In spite of neighborly agreements, Canada has no desire to be thought of as an extension of the United States. Although the nation shares many aspects of U.S. culture, Canada wants to keep its own separate identity. Canadians take pride in their independent nation. They have worked hard throughout their history to maintain a peaceful, prosperous "home and native land." ■

▲ *A 20-foot-wide path, called a vista, shows a portion of the boundary between Quebec, on the left, and Maine. This wintry scene is typical of the many miles of undefended border between Canada and the United States.*

■ What factors of Canada's foreign and domestic policy make it a "good neighbor" to people of other nations?

REVIEW

1. **FOCUS** What factors make modern Canada a prosperous, multicultural nation?
2. **POLITICAL SYSTEMS** Explain the change the French-speaking separatists of Quebec want in Canada's political system.
3. **CULTURE** How does life in Toronto provide an example of a multicultural society?
4. **CRITICAL THINKING** The relationship between Canada and the United States has sometimes been described as a "guarded friendship across an unguarded border." Explain what you think that phrase means.
5. **WRITING ACTIVITY** Canada has several programs designed to help its citizens learn and prosper. Two examples are the Heritage Language Program and the national health care policy. Write a letter to an imaginary Canadian penpal. Include questions you would like to have answered about each program.

■ *Canada's foreign policy is based on cooperation and peace. It has supported many assistance programs to poor nations.*

CLOSE

Read the Thinking Focus aloud. Have students work in pairs, with one person writing a list of factors that make Canada prosperous and the other listing factors that make it multicultural. Then have students exchange lists and brainstorm additions to their partner's list.

Answers to Review Questions

1. Canada's GNP is among the top 10 in the world. The nation has abundant natural resources and sources of energy. Its 26.5 million people include Native Americans and those who have roots in Europe, the Caribbean, and Asia.
2. The separatists want complete independence for Quebec.
3. In Toronto about 100 languages are spoken. The city has newspapers in many languages and many ethnic festivals. People of many cultural backgrounds share in and contribute to life in the city.
4. Despite many years of peace, issues come between the United States and Canada, such as the loss of cultural independence; previous interference in politics; free trade; and acid rain problems.
5. Answers will vary but should indicate comprehension of the features and the benefits of each program and a reasoned point of view on the question.

Homework Options

Have students fold a sheet of paper into thirds and use it to create a pictorial brochure of Canada. Their brochures should advertise cultural attractions that are uniquely Canadian.

Study Guide: page 107

Answers to Reviewing Key Terms

A. Sample answers:

1. In a **confederation,** power is divided between the national and the local governments.
2. As a **dominion,** Canada had self-rule. Canada was governed by a governor general, appointed by the British monarch, and a Parliament consisting of a House of Commons and a Senate.
3. Canadian supporters of **separatism** want Quebec to become an independent nation. The root word *separate* provides a clue.
4. All but the top few feet of soil that has **permafrost** is permanently frozen. Permafrost exists in the northernmost regions of Canada, specifically the Northwest Territory and the Yukon Territory.

B.

1. **Bilingual** means "able to speak two languages." The prefix *bi-* provides the clue "two."
2. **Multicultural** means "of many cultures." The prefix *multi-* provides the clue "many."
3. Examples: *Bicultural* means "of, or having, two cultures." *Multilingual* means "able to speak many languages."

Answers to Exploring Concepts

A. Sample answers:

The Atlantic Provinces: John Cabot claimed Newfoundland for England in 1497.

Ontario: Ontario was named "Upper Canada" in 1791, when the British split Quebec into two parts.

The Prairie Provinces: Immigrants from many countries settled here in the 1900s.

British Columbia: British Columbia joined the Dominion of Canada in 1871, on the condition that a real road be built that connected the nation from east to west.

The Territories: In 1992 the citizens of the Northwest Territory voted to split into two parts, creating the new Nunavut Territory.

Chapter Review

Reviewing Key Terms

bilingual (p. 608)
confederation (p. 603)
dominion (p. 603)
multicultural (p. 607)
permafrost (p. 599)
separatism (p. 608)

A. Answer the following questions regarding selected key terms.

1. What two types of government share the power in a confederation?
2. As a dominion, what was Canada's relationship with Great Britain?
3. What is the goal of the Canadian supporters of separatism? What root word in *separatism* provides a clue to the term's meaning?
4. What are the characteristics of land that has permafrost?

B. The prefix *bi-* means "two." The prefix *multi-* means "many." On your own paper, answer these questions.

1. What does the key term bilingual mean? What clue does the meaning of the prefix give you?
2. What does the key term multicultural mean? What clue does the meaning of the prefix give you?
3. What other words begin with the prefixes *bi-* and *multi-*? List as many words as you can that begin with these prefixes. What do the words mean?

Exploring Concepts

A. Copy the following chart, which lists the political regions of Canada. In the second column, write at least one historical or cultural fact about the region. One entry has been filled in for you.

Region	Historical or Cultural Fact
The Atlantic Provinces	
Ontario	
Québec	Many French-speaking people of Québec want to separate from the rest of Canada.
The Prairie Provinces	
British Columbia	
The Territories	

B. Support each of the following statements with information from the chapter.

1. Canada's Native Americans were helpful to early explorers and settlers.
2. The names of several locations in Canada come from languages spoken by its Native Americans.
3. Canada's motto, "From Sea to Sea," could accurately be changed to "From Sea to Sea to Sea."
4. Unlike many nations who struggled to become independent from their colonial governments, Canada's major steps toward independence were peaceful.
5. Many French-speaking Canadian citizens continue to struggle for independence from the rest of the nation.
6. Canada has worked hard to create laws and programs to benefit all Canadians.
7. Canada is one of the best places to live.
8. Other nations of the world might call Canada "a friendly giant."

B. Sample answers:

1. Canada's Native Americans gave food and supplies to the early explorers and settlers. They showed them how to fish and hunt.
2. For example, the name *Canada* comes from the Native American word *kanata,* which means "settlement." The new territory, to become official in 1999, is named *Nunavut,* which is an Inuit word meaning "our land."
3. Canada stretches from the Atlantic Ocean in the east, to the Pacific Ocean in the west, and northward to the Arctic Ocean.
4. Canada gradually gained its independence through peaceful evolution of its government.
5. Many Québécois voted against the Charlottetown Agreement because they wanted total independence.
6. Canada provides free public education and free health care to all Canadians.
7. Canada has an excellent education system and high life expectancy and personal income.
8. Canada earns the adjective "friendly" through its historic approach to foreign policy—promoting cooperation and peace.

Reviewing Skills

1. Study the process diagram on page 606. Then create a process diagram of your own. Use it to explain a simple process to a younger student. Choose something like how to tie a shoe, play a board or video game, make directional signals while riding a bike, or load a camera with film.
2. European explorers searched the rivers and ocean inlets of Canada, hoping to find a route leading west to Asia. Study the map of the world in the Atlas on pages 680–681. Where does that route exist? What types of modern ships might be able to use it? Why might the early explorers have found the route impossible to navigate?
3. Turn to page 602, and reread the account of Alexander Mackenzie's first attempt to find a route to the Pacific Ocean, in 1789. Imagine that you are with him, paddling along the river. Based on your knowledge of the features of the Arctic region, what assumptions would you make about where the river might lead? Support your assumptions with facts. Then summarize the advice you might give Mackenzie.
4. Using the map on page 599, draw an outline map of Canada that includes the provinces and territories. Fill in the major mountain ranges. Do research to find out where most of the people live in Canada today, and complete a population map. Use clusters of dots to show where people are living.

Using Critical Thinking

1. Look at the picture of the maple leaf on page 596. Why do you think the Canadians selected a maple leaf for their national symbol? Based on facts from your reading, what other symbols do you think they might have selected? Explain your answers.
2. Imagine that the Canadian Prime Minister has asked your advice on how to persuade Quebec to remain part of Canada. What ideas would you offer? Explain how your ideas might help solve the conflict.
3. Think about the fact that Canada, the world's second-largest nation, covers over 3.8 million square miles. In what ways does Canada's size, as well as other facts about Canada that you have read in the chapter, make unifying Canada so difficult?

Preparing for Citizenship

1. **COLLECTING INFORMATION** Use the *Readers' Guide to Periodical Literature* to locate current magazine articles about both sides of the separatist issue in Canada. Use this background information to make a list of supporting arguments for each position. Then predict what would result if Quebec separated from Canada.
2. **ARTS ACTIVITY** Make a travel poster to encourage tourists to visit Canada. Combine pictures and written material to emphasize what you consider Canada's most interesting attractions.
3. **COLLABORATIVE LEARNING** In a small group, create an exhibit that might appear at a Canadian multicultural fair. First, work together to select a specific ethnic group of Canadians, from early or current times. For example, you might pick the Inuit, the Iroquois, the Haida, the Algonquin, the British, the French, or the Chinese. Do research to find out about a specific feature of their ethnic culture, such as their foods, religious beliefs, and community values. Then plan and create your group's exhibit, combining pictures with written facts. Share your exhibit with your classmates. After viewing the exhibits, discuss this statement together: "A multicultural society is greater than the sum of its individual parts."

Answers to Reviewing Skills

1. Process diagrams will vary. Using the process diagram that shows how a lock works on page 606 as a model, students should effectively use labeled pictures or diagrams to explain the steps in the selected process.
2. Students will probably note that the route exists through the small islands north of Hudson Bay, or under the polar cap. Submarines or surface ships equipped with ice cutters could use such a passage. The early explorers, in small wooden ships, would probably have found the route impassable.
3. Students should use the following facts to support the assumption that the river leads to the Arctic Ocean rather than to the Pacific Ocean: The river was icy; the land was frozen and eventually became treeless; the ocean was filled with floating ice. Based on this information, students might advise Mackenzie to turn back.
4. Maps should be as accurate as possible and based on recent population figures.

Answers to Using Critical Thinking

1. Answers will vary. Students may respond that the maple tree is common in Canada, and that it is an important resource because it provides physical beauty as well as products such as lumber and maple syrup. Other symbols that students might suggest include logos symbolizing multiculturalism, abundant natural resources, and so on. Each suggestion should be supported by facts and details taken from the chapter.
2. Answers will vary, but they should indicate students' comprehension of the facts behind the conflict as well as logical ideas for negotiating a settlement that is acceptable to the separatists as well as to other Canadians.
3. Answers will vary, but they should include some of these factors: the physical expanse of the nation makes it difficult to establish communication and transportation links for people in all regions; also, rather than blending, separate groups have usually remained distinct.

Answers to Preparing for Citizenship

1. **COLLECTING INFORMATION** Answers will vary. Students' predictions should be logical and based on what they have read.
2. **ARTS ACTIVITY** Posters should effectively combine pictures and written text to illustrate students' choices.
3. **COLLABORATIVE LEARNING** Students' exhibits should indicate collaborative research and creativity. Provide ample time for each group to present and explain its exhibit. During the ensuing discussion, encourage students to support the statement about a multicultural society, using facts and details from the exhibits, from their texts, and from their own experiences.

CHAPTER ORGANIZER

Chapter 27 *From Many, One Nation*

CHAPTER PLANNING CHART

Pupil's Edition	Teacher's Edition	Ancillaries
Lesson 1: Land of Diversity (2–3 days) Objective 1: Identify the different regions of the United States. (Geography 1, 2; Culture 2, 3) Objective 2: Identify ways in which the use of the land has changed since the days before European settlers arrived. (Geography 3; Economics 3)	• Graphic Overview (618) • Access Strategy (619) Writing a Letter (619) • Access Activity (619) Social Participation (620) Historical Context (620)	Study Guide (108) Map Activities (31) • Posters (7)
Lesson 2: People from Many Lands (3–4 days) Objective 1: Describe how U.S. immigration has changed over the years. (History 5, 6; Culture 1) Objective 2: Describe how different groups of immigrants have contributed to U.S. culture. (Culture 1, 2, 3; National Identity 1) Objective 3: Identify some values and beliefs that have helped unite the many different peoples of the United States. (Ethics and Belief Systems 1, 2, 3, 4, 5; Social and Belief Systems 3, 6)	• Graphic Overview (622) • Access Strategy (623) • Access Activity (623) Study Skills (624) Language Arts Connection (624) Geographic Context (624) Social Context (625) Social Participation (625) Study Skills (626) Cultural Context (626)	Study Guide (109) Discovery Journal (54)
Literature: Ginger for the Heart	Access Strategy (629) Research (630) Writing a Journal Entry (631)	Discovery Journal (55)
Lesson 3: For the Good of All (2–3 days) Objective 1: Define *discrimination* and give examples of ways in which it affects people's lives. (Social and Political Systems 3; National Identity 4; Citizenship 4, 6) Objective 2: Explain why education is important to all people. (History 8; Economics 1; Culture 5, 6; Ethics and Belief Systems 1, 2; National Identity 2; Citizenship 6) Objective 3: Explain how and why U.S. citizens volunteer to help one another. (Ethics and Belief Systems 2; Citizenship 2)	• Graphic Overview (632) • Access Strategy (633) • Access Activity (633) • Visual Learning (634) Bulletin Board (634) Interviewing (634) Social Context (635) • Visual Learning (635)	Study Guide (110) Discovery Journal (56) • Study Prints (16)
Understanding Relationships Objective: Identify and respond to stereotypes presented in photographs and pictures. (Visual Learning 1, 3; Social Participation 2)		Study Guide (111)
Making Decisions: Should Puerto Rico Be the 51st State? Objective 1: Understand the background of Puerto Rico's current status. (History 1, 5) Objective 2: Describe the pros and cons of statehood for Puerto Rico. (History 1, 5; Social and Political Systems 3, 6; Critical Thinking 1, 2) Objective 3: Decide on a point of view on the issue and support the position. (Critical Thinking 3)		Discovery Journal (57)
Chapter Review	Answers (640–641)	Tests (105–108)

* Objectives are correlated to the strands and goals in the program Scope and Sequence on pages T41–T49.

• LEP appropriate resources. (For additional strategies, see pages T32–T33.)

CHAPTER RATIONALE

Chapter 27 provides a portrait of the United States—geography, resources, and, above all, people. Within the historical context of immigration, it examines the "patchwork quilt" of contemporary U.S. society. Students study examples of real problems, such as intolerance and pollution, that have confronted—and continue to confront—U.S. citizens. They also learn about ways in which citizens work together and help one another to overcome these problems.

In **Lesson 1** students take a tour of the U.S. landscape, from the varied coastal regions to the interior plains and mountains, from the Alaskan Arctic to tropical Hawaii. The lesson also offers a bird's-eye view of the nation's rich resources and encourages students to think about using and conserving these resources carefully.

In **Lesson 2** students find themselves in the middle of a Cinco de Mayo festival in the Southwest, where people from many backgrounds mingle. This festival becomes the starting point for an exploration of the historical patterns of immigration to the United States. Within this context, students learn about both diversity and intolerance in U.S. culture. A special feature on naturalization explains citizenship and how people from other countries can become citizens of the United States.

Lesson 3 expands on the concept of discrimination and briefly traces the history of the civil rights movement. As an example of the progress made by groups that have faced discrimination, A Moment in Time focuses on an African American woman serving in the U.S. armed forces. The lesson then presents education as a tool both for eliminating prejudice and for creating a body of educated, skilled citizens. Finally, it looks at a typical U.S. approach to community problems: volunteering.

ACTIVITIES & PROJECTS

Challenge: Investigating

Nearly every community in the United States has some Native American heritage, although this is more evident in some places than in others. Have students do research in local libraries or historical societies to find out what Indian peoples originally lived in the area. Suggest that they look for information about houses, crafts, clothing, beliefs, ways of living (farming, hunting, trading). Also have them look for evidence of Native American influence today. Do Native Americans still live in the community or nearby? Students can report on their findings to the class. (Use after Lesson 1.)

Writing a Letter

Tell students to write a letter in which they introduce themselves to a pen pal in another country. Their letters should describe the region of the United States in which they live: climate, geographical features, and resources. Students may want to read their letters to the class. (Use after Lesson 1.)

LEP: Illustrating Citizenship

Review with students some of the requirements of citizenship described in Lesson 2. Then ask them to illustrate an ending to the following sentence: Good citizenship is . . . (Use after Lesson 2 or 3.)

Basic: Interviewing

Have students make a list of community organizations in which volunteers are important (such as the library, zoo, hospital, or sports team). Assign small groups (two or three students) to interview someone connected with each organization about the volunteer work they do and why they do it. Each group should report briefly to the class on what they learned. (Use after Lesson 3.)

CHAPTER PREVIEW

Read the chapter title and the first paragraph on this page aloud. On the chalkboard write the word *diversity.* Remind students of its definition *(varied, having differences).* Then have them review some of the diverse cultures and lands they have learned about in this book. Ask students how the pictures on these two pages illustrate diversity in the United States. *(Possible answers: The photo and tray show racial diversity. Pictures of St. Louis and the buffalo illustrate diversity of human and natural environments.)*

Looking Forward

Explain to students that in the next three lessons—Land of Diversity, People from Many Lands, and For the Good of All—they will be reading about the diversity of the land and people of the United States and some common political beliefs and experiences that encourage U.S. citizens to work together for the good of all.

Lesson 1 describes the diversity of landforms and resources found in the United States.

Chapter 27

From Many, One Nation

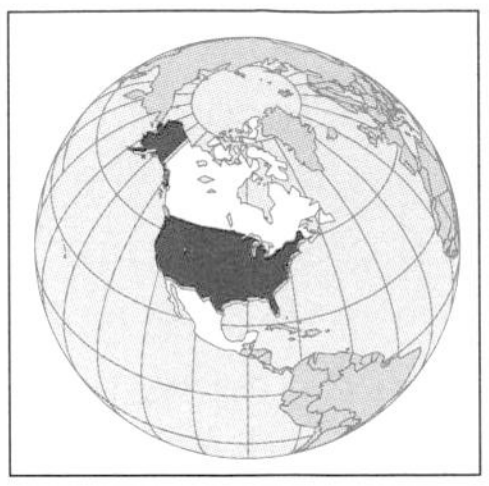

The United States is a land of great diversity—in its geography, its climate, its resources, and above all, its people. Wave after wave of immigrants from the world over have contributed to the growth and the culture of the nation. Today U.S. citizens confront a variety of problems: from discrimination to poverty to pollution. Many people believe that the United States can tackle these problems if citizens work together and help one another.

Starting in colonial times, women held quilting parties where they worked together to sew beautiful quilts like this one. In many families, quilts were passed down from generation to generation.

Millions of buffalo once roamed the Great Plains. Many Native Americans counted on buffalo as a source of food, clothing, and shelter.

1375 | 1500 | 1625

1400

1565 Spain establishes St. Augustine, Florida, the first permanent European settlement in what is now the United States.

BACKGROUND

The United States is a "land of diversity" in both landscape and peoples. While later immigrants from Europe, Africa, and Asia brought a diversity of cultures, the Native Americans who first settled North America were also diverse in languages, customs, and cultures. Several regions had highly developed cultures as early as 1000 B.C.

The Northwest Pacific Coast

By about 1000 B.C., peoples such as the Nootka, Chinook, and Tlingit were living along the Pacific coast, from present-day California to Alaska. Their prosperous cultures were based mainly on fishing and hunting.

Many crafts of the Northwest Coast peoples used wood from the thick forests of the region. They built wooden canoes, made ceremonial masks and objects, and carved wooden totem poles bearing symbols of their family or clan.

The Southwest

In the dry lands of the Southwest, the Anasazi created a farming culture by about the first century A.D. With farming techniques perhaps learned from Mesoamericans, they grew maize, beans, and squash and raised turkeys. The Anasazi built huge "apartment house" complexes of stone or adobe, often in canyons or on cliffs. Networks of roads linked settlements throughout what are now Arizona, New Mexico, southern Colorado, and Utah.

When Spanish explorers arrived several centuries later, they called the buildings

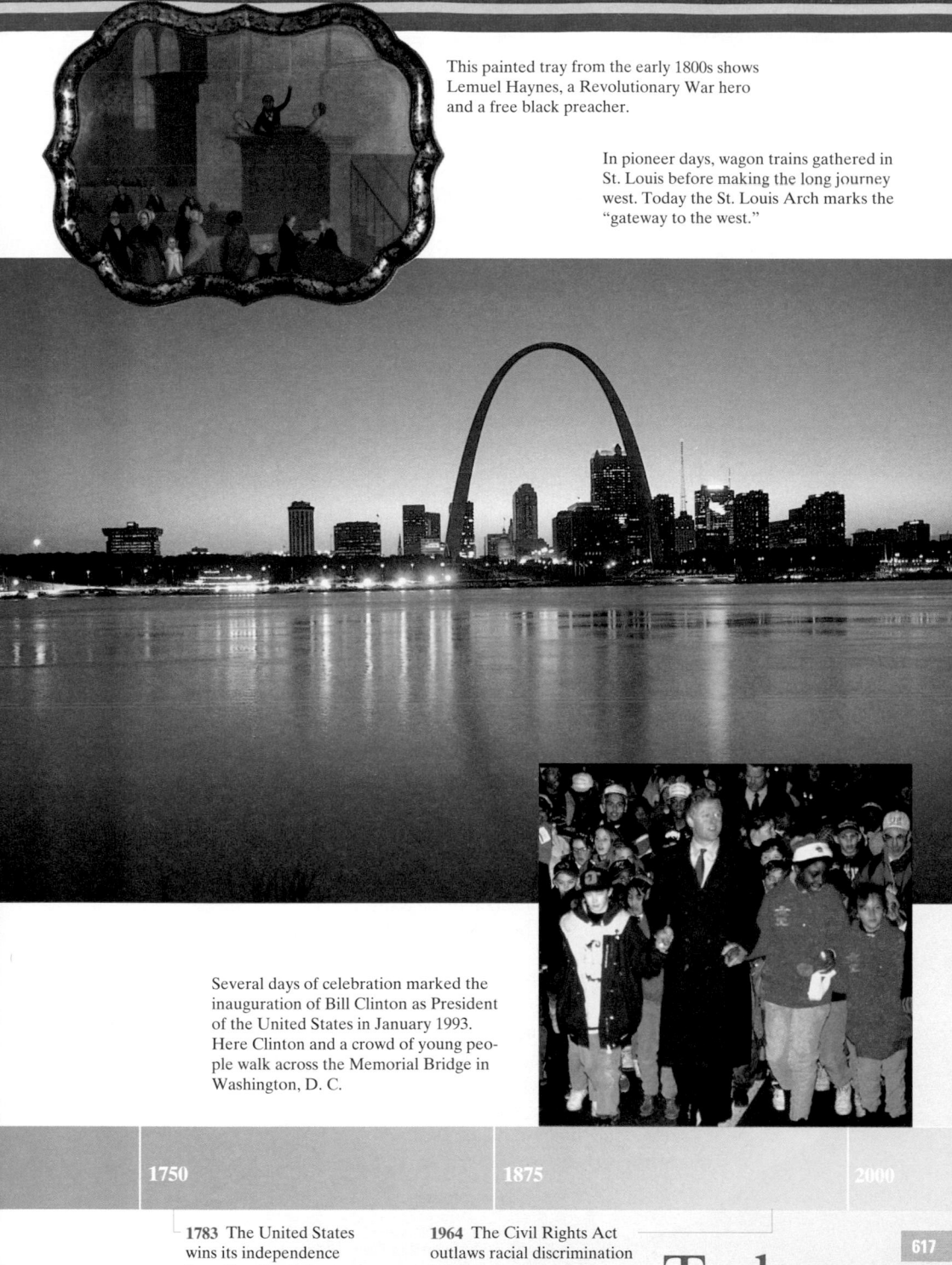

This painted tray from the early 1800s shows Lemuel Haynes, a Revolutionary War hero and a free black preacher.

In pioneer days, wagon trains gathered in St. Louis before making the long journey west. Today the St. Louis Arch marks the "gateway to the west."

Several days of celebration marked the inauguration of Bill Clinton as President of the United States in January 1993. Here Clinton and a crowd of young people walk across the Memorial Bridge in Washington, D. C.

1750 — 1875 — 2000

1783 The United States wins its independence from Great Britain.

1964 The Civil Rights Act outlaws racial discrimination in jobs and public places.

Today

Understanding the Visuals

The American bison (buffalo) symbolizes how the people of the United States have shaped their environment. Native Americans once hunted bison from the Appalachians west to the Rockies. By 1850 about 20 million bison were left, only in the western part of the Great Plains. The rest had been killed off by settlers for farms and by the U.S. government to make way for the transcontinental railroad. By 1899 only 551 bison were left.

The Gateway Arch in St. Louis is the tallest monument constructed in the United States. Made of stainless steel, it stands 630 feet (192 meters) high and honors Thomas Jefferson, the Louisiana Purchase, and the pioneers who settled the West.

Understanding Chronology

Refer students to the timeline. Ask them to compare the length of time between the first European settlement of present-day United States and independence from Great Britain with the time span from independence to the present. *(1783 minus 1565 [St. Augustine] = 218 years; present date minus 1783 = approx. 210 years)*

pueblos, the Spanish word for "town." The name Pueblo was later applied to Native American peoples of the Southwest.

Hopewell Culture

In the central part of what is now the United States, people of the Hopewell culture farmed and traded over a wide area. The culture may have developed as early as 400 B.C. and may have lasted about a thousand years. The Hopewell people are sometimes called Mound Builders because of the large earthworks they built for burials or ceremonies, sometimes in the shape of birds, snakes, and other animals. The culture evidently was centered near the Ohio River but spread over much of the Midwest.

Mississippi River Valley

In the southeast and along the Mississippi River, another culture took shape about A.D. 700. The Mississippians were also traders and farmers. Like people in Mesoamerica, they lived in a strictly hierarchical society and built flat-topped pyramids with temples at the top. They built some of the earliest cities in North America. The largest, Cahokia in Illinois, had at one time a population of about 40,000 people. Monk's Mound at Cahokia covers more than 16 acres and rises 100 feet into the air. This culture was still in existence when French explorers arrived in the 1600s.

INTRODUCE

Ask students to recall the regions of the United States they studied in Chapter 2 (page 43). *(Northeast, Southeast, Midwest, Rocky Mountains, Pacific Coast, Southwest)* Point out that the nation can be divided into regions in other ways. Have students look at the Political/Physical map of North America in the Atlas (page 686). Point out the three coastal regions. *(Pacific, Atlantic, and Gulf coasts)* Point out other major land and water forms. *(Rocky Mountains, Appalachian Mountains, Great Plains, Mojave Desert, Great Lakes)*

Read the Thinking Focus aloud. Ask students how differences in landforms and climate in different regions might affect the way people make use of the land. Why might land use change over time? *(Human interaction with the environment, such as the building of cities, highways, railroads; changing farming patterns; population increase)* Tell students that the lesson tells more about the land and resources of the United States.

Key Term

Vocabulary Strategies: T36–T37
conservation—preserving or protecting resources

1500 TODAY

LESSON 1

Land of Diversity

THINKING FOCUS

How have people used the land and the resources of the United States?

Key Term

- conservation

I am a feather in the bright sky.
I am the blue horse that runs in the plain.
I am the fish that rolls, shining, in the water.
I am the shadow that follows a child.
I am the evening light, the lustre of meadows.
I am an eagle playing with the wind.
I am a cluster of bright beads.
I am the farthest star.
I am the cold of the dawn.
I am the roaring of the rain.
I am the glitter on the crust of the snow.
I am the long track of the moon in a lake.
I am a flame of four colors.
I am a deer standing away in the dusk.
I am a field of sumac and the pomme blanche.
I am an angle of geese upon the winter sky.
I am the hunger of a young wolf.
I am the whole dream of these things.

You see, I am alive, I am alive.
I stand in good relation to the earth.
I stand in good relation to the gods.
I stand in good relation to all that is beautiful.
I stand in good relation to the daughter of Tsen-tainte.
You see, I am alive, I am alive.

Native Americans of the Pacific Northwest held many ceremonies to celebrate the resources of their region. The mask shown here was worn by a singer during ceremonies.

Many Native Americans who lived in what is now the United States believed that every part of the earth is alive with meaning. Soil, rivers, trees—all things in the natural world—were parts of a whole.

The poem above, "The Delight Song of Tsoai-talee," is by N. Scott Momaday, a Native American. It captures the idea that all things in nature are connected and holy.

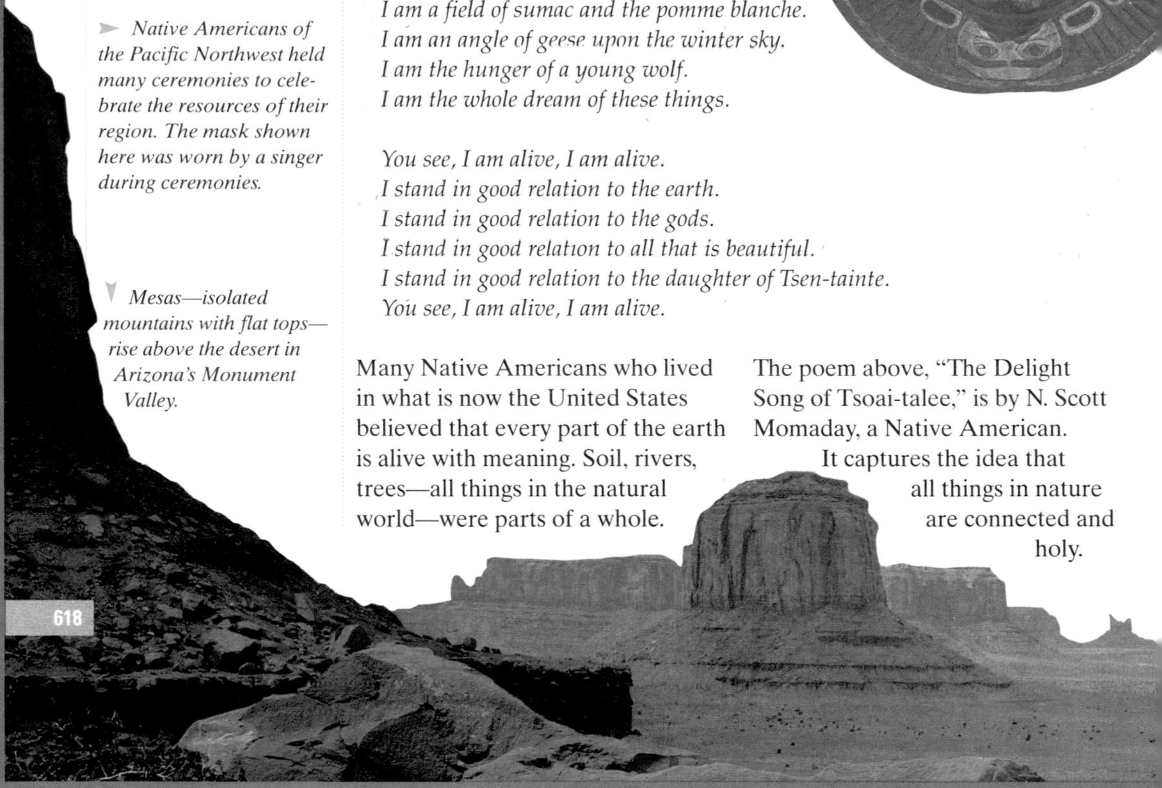

Mesas—isolated mountains with flat tops—rise above the desert in Arizona's Monument Valley.

Objectives

1. Identify the different regions of the United States.
2. Identify ways in which the use of the land has changed since the days before European settlers arrived.

Graphic Overview

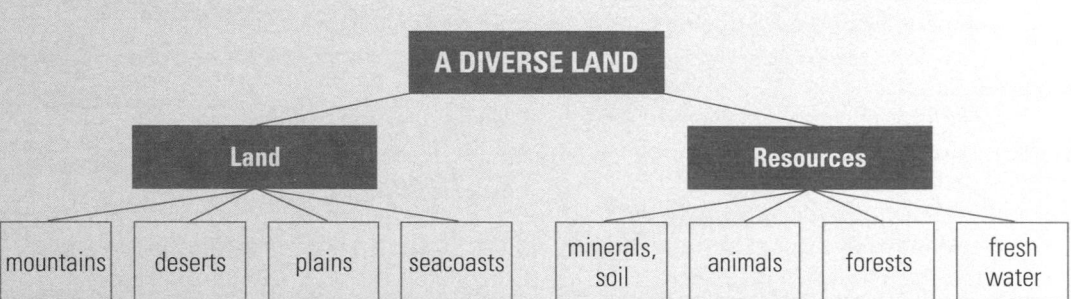

- **A DIVERSE LAND**
  - **Land**
    - mountains
    - deserts
    - plains
    - seacoasts
  - **Resources**
    - minerals, soil
    - animals
    - forests
    - fresh water

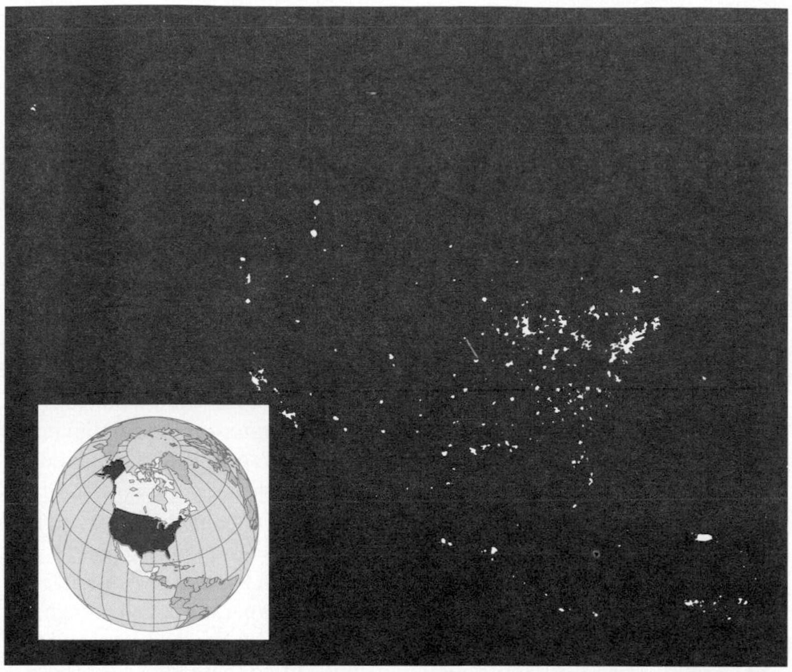

White areas on this satellite map of the United States show population concentration by light use at night. Which side of the country shows the most light, east or west?

A Varied Land

Since the early days of U.S. history, the land has changed forever. Yet it is still a vast and beautiful country.

As you read in Chapter 2, the United States is divided into six regions. Sometimes, however, it is divided in other ways. For example, the northern states are known as the Snowbelt. This name refers to their cold, snowy winters. The band of southern states stretching from the Carolinas to California is often called the Sunbelt.

The map above shows that many people in the United States live along the Gulf coast. Many also live in cities in the Northeast, along the Pacific coast, and along the Great Lakes. In fact, the United States is a nation of cities. Outside the cities, the country is thinly populated. As writer Gertrude Stein put it, "In the United States there is more space where nobody is than where anybody is."

The Coasts of the Country

Use the map on page 573 in the Unit Overview to locate the three coastal regions. They border the Pacific and Atlantic oceans and the Gulf of Mexico.

The Pacific coast is dramatic. Mountains descend to the ocean along a 434-mile road that winds between Los Angeles and San Francisco.

How Do We Know?

SOCIAL SCIENCE *In Native American burial grounds along the Mississippi River, archaeologists have found artifacts of copper. The copper is from the Lake Superior region. Finding this copper so far from Lake Superior suggests that Native Americans along the Mississippi carried on long-distance river trade.*

DEVELOP

Draw the Graphic Overview on the chalkboard and have students give examples of ways in which people use and depend on each of the natural resources shown. Ask them to brainstorm how their lives might change if resources such as forests, fresh water, or coal and oil (minerals) were destroyed or completely used up. *(Possible answers: Without wood pulp, there would be no newspapers and books. People, plants, and animals need fresh water. Without oil, coal, and natural gas, homes and schools could not be heated, and automobiles would not run.)*

The most light appears to be on the eastern seaboard.

GEOGRAPHY

Critical Thinking

Have students compare the satellite map with the physical map of the United States in the Unit Overview. Ask students to point out regions of the satellite map where there are few lights. Why do so few people live in these areas? *(On the Great Plains are large farms with a few scattered settlements. In the desert regions and the Rocky Mountains, climate and landscape discourage settlement.)*

Access Strategy

Have students locate their own state and hometown on a large-scale physical U.S. map or map transparency. Then ask them to name the states, major cities, and significant land and water forms that are at approximately the same latitude across the country. Ask students what resources *not* found in their own region might be found in any of these other locations. Why? Encourage students to explain what differences might exist in climate, vegetation, and wildlife.

Writing a Letter

Have each student use what has been discovered in the Access Strategy to write a letter to a student in some other part of the United States at the same latitude. In their letters students should describe the region where they live and ask questions about life in the other student's region based on what they have interpreted from the map.

Access Activity

N. Scott Momaday is a Kiowa who grew up among the Jemez peoples. For a choral reading of his poem on page 618, have students take turns reading aloud one line each. What phrase is repeated four times? *("I stand in good relation to")* What words might describe "good relations" with a person or nature? *(Respect, love, joy, harmony)*

GEOGRAPHY

Map and Globe Skills

Have students imagine that they are photographers assigned to illustrate a U.S. geography book. Using information from their text and maps in the Atlas, ask them where they would go to photograph wheat fields *(Great Plains),* a mountainous coastline *(Pacific Coast, Hawaii),* snow-capped mountains *(Rocky Mountains, Alaska),* a frozen Arctic land *(Alaska),* and tropical beaches *(Hawaii, southern Florida).*

ECONOMICS

Critical Thinking

Discuss with students the differences between using resources to meet *needs* and to fulfill *wants.* Draw a three-column chart on the chalkboard and label the column heading *Resources, Needs,* and *Wants.* Ask students to identify specific resources. Then have the class suggest entries for the other columns. *(Example: Land—needed for crops; wanted for an amusement park)*

■ *The United States stretches from the Atlantic Ocean to the Pacific Ocean and also includes Alaska in the north and the tropical Pacific islands of Hawaii. It contains forests, mountains, broad plains, large lakes, great rivers, and deserts.*

This painting from the 1580s shows a Native American village in the Southeast woodlands. Villagers planted crops such as corn and arranged their houses in orderly rows.

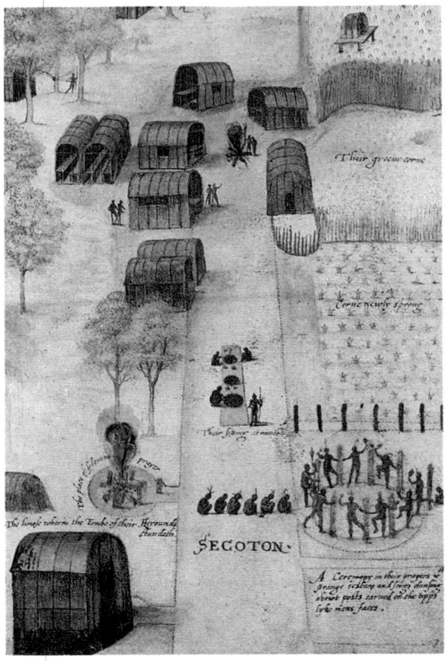
SECOTON.

In contrast, the Atlantic coast is mostly flat and dotted with harbors. It also has stretches of beach, rolling hills, and smaller mountains.

The Gulf coast hooks around the Gulf of Mexico. It has much rich soil and many grassy swamps. Many rivers flow into the gulf. The greatest of these is the Mississippi. It has many tributaries, smaller rivers that stretch east and west.

Interior Plains

The Mississippi River links the Gulf coast with the interior of the country. Native Americans once grew corn in the rich soil of the Mississippi valley. Today barges travel from Minneapolis to New Orleans. They carry raw materials and industrial goods.

West of the Mississippi, forests and mountains give way to the flat, treeless Great Plains. Millions of buffalo once grazed on these plains. Native Americans counted on these herds as a source of food, clothing, and shelter. During the 1800s settlers drove the original inhabitants from the plains. These settlers and newcomers also hunted the buffalo nearly to extinction. Today farms and fields of wheat stretch for miles across the Great Plains.

To the west of the plains are the Rocky Mountains—the "backbone" of North America. They rise to more than 14,000 feet above sea level. The Rocky Mountains are far higher than their eastern cousins, the Appalachians.

From the Arctic to the Tropics

Much of the United States is in the temperate—or mild—climate zone. Some people in the United States, however, must work hard to adapt to their climate. Nowhere in the United States is the climate colder than in parts of Alaska. Winter temperatures can plunge to –30°F. The Yupik, Aleut, and Inuit settled there long ago. These Native Americans had to adapt to a region with no trees or farmland. In south-central Alaska, however, the climate is milder. In the summer, people travel there to fish, sail, and swim.

At the opposite extreme are the tropical islands of Hawaii. Volcanic mountains make up most of the state. It has a warm, wet climate and dense rain forests. One part of Hawaii, in fact, is often called the wettest spot in the world. Its yearly rainfall is 444 inches. ■

■ *Find evidence to support the following statement: The United States is a vast and diverse land.*

Rich Natural Resources

The United States is rich in resources. People have often acted as though these resources were unlimited. In recent years, however, the people of the United States have started to understand that they must use their resources more wisely than they have in the past.

Resources of Land and Sea

Resources of the United States include dense forests, rich soil, fresh water, and varied animal life. The five Great Lakes make up the largest freshwater system in the world. Valuable mineral deposits lie beneath the soil. Alaska's Arctic

Social Participation

Have students work in small groups, each to research and report on a community's attempt to conserve and protect resources, such as recycling, air or water quality, protection of green spaces, waste disposal, or wildlife protection. Students might get information from city and county governments, disposal companies, or local environmental groups.

Historical Context

Chief Seattle, a leader of the Suquamish and other groups of the Puget Sound (Washington), is supposed to have made the speech below at the signing of a treaty with the U.S. government in 1855. Ask students how Chief Seattle's attitude about the land compares with theirs.

"Every part of this soil is sacred. . . . Every hillside, every valley, every plain and grove, has been hallowed [made holy] by some sad or happy event in days long vanished. Even the rocks . . . thrill with the memories of stirring events connected with the lives of my people. . . . When your children's children think themselves alone in the field, the shore, the shop, upon the highway, or in the silence of the pathless woods, they will not be alone. In all the earth there is no place dedicated to solitude. . . . At night when the streets of your cities and villages are silent and you think them deserted, they will throng with the returning hosts that once filled them and still love this beautiful land."

coast holds the largest oil reserves in North America. Oil and natural gas are also found in Texas, Oklahoma, California, and other states.

The early inhabitants of the Pacific Northwest once used trees for building and carving. Today these forests provide much of the nation's lumber. Forests in the Southeast supply wood pulp to make paper. Some southeastern forests are planted and harvested much like any other crop.

Conserving Resources

Native Americans regarded the land as the giver of life, as holy. They were generally careful not to destroy the resources that fed and clothed them. Europeans, however, saw the land as something to be owned and used. To them the resources of the great new land seemed limitless. Today we know that the resources of this land are limited. We understand the need to use them with care. Yet **conservation**—saving resources—is not always easy. Sometimes, conservation seems to conflict with economic growth. In other cases people must learn new habits of saving rather than consuming or wasting.

For example, 90 percent of the U.S. population own at least one car or truck. Many depend on cars for work and recreation. Yet there is a great price to pay in terms of pollution of the environment.

In addition, people in the United States use huge amounts of coal, oil, and natural gas. After people have used these resources, they are gone for good. Much more can be done to save these fuels for the future. More can also be done to clean up the pollution they produce. ■

▲ *The Mississippi River is one of the nation's most important transportation and trade routes. Ships and barges on the Mississippi and its tributaries can travel far into the country's interior.*

◄ *The Tlingit, Native Americans of the Pacific Northwest, carved this wooden ceremonial rattle. Wood continues to be an important resource in the Northwest today.*

■ *Identify three resources of the United States and one place where each is found.*

REVIEW

1. **FOCUS** How have people used the land and the resources of the United States?
2. **GEOGRAPHY** Look back at the map showing the regions of the United States in Chapter 2 (page 43). Which regions border the Atlantic coast? The Gulf coast? The Pacific coast?
3. **CULTURE** Contrast the climates of Alaska and Hawaii with the temperate climate of many of the other 48 states. How might the climate of Alaska and Hawaii affect the way people live there?
4. **CRITICAL THINKING** Should people living in the United States change the way they use the resources? Tell why or why not.
5. **WRITING ACTIVITY** Make a list of all the resources you use in a single day. Include the reason you use each one. List ways in which you could conserve these resources.

NATIONAL IDENTITY

Visual Learning

Artists have portrayed the North American landscape in many different ways. Have students look in art history books, magazines, or wildlife calendars to find a landscape painting or photograph by artists such as these: George C. Bingham, Thomas Cole, Frederic Church, Albert Bierstadt, Winslow Homer, Georgia O'Keeffe, Eliot Porter, or Ansel Adams. Have students write one or two paragraphs describing the picture they have chosen and what features of the landscape the artist emphasized.

■ *Resources include forests (Northwest, Southeast, and elsewhere), fresh water (Great Lakes, rivers, and streams), and oil (Texas, Alaska, Oklahoma, California).*

CLOSE

Divide the class into groups. Using a classroom map, point to a region of the United States and ask one group to tell how people have used the land and resources in that region. Point to various regions and ask groups to take turns giving answers. Finally, have students use the different responses to create a general statement that answers the Thinking Focus.

Answers to Review Questions

1. People in the United States have used soil to grow food, built houses from lumber cut from forests, and used fuels that originate in the earth. They have used water for crops, drinking, and transportation.
2. The Northeast and Southeast border the Atlantic coast. The Southeast and part of Texas (in the Southwest) also border the Gulf coast. The Pacific coast states and Alaska are on the Pacific coast of North America; Hawaii is in the Pacific.
3. Alaska is generally colder than most of the lower 48 states; Hawaii is the most tropical of the states. Students may mention clothing, houses, jobs, and recreation.
4. Students may point out that resources have helped make the country prosperous but that people often use them wastefully.
5. Students may mention water, paper, and fuel. Conservation measures include walking, using less heat or air conditioning, and recycling papers or aluminum cans.

Homework Options

Have students draw pictures or collect illustrations from magazines and newspapers they have at home to illustrate the variety of uses to which people have put a single resource mentioned in this chapter.

Study Guide: page 108

INTRODUCE

Ask a student to read aloud the Thinking Focus, and have the class speculate about why the United States came to be a nation of people with so many different ethnic, racial, and religious backgrounds. *(People thought that they would find freedom or land or better opportunities; they wanted to escape persecution or poverty.)* List responses on the chalkboard or chart paper. Encourage students to suggest additions or corrections for the list as they study the lesson.

Key Terms

Vocabulary Strategies: T36–T37

quota—a specific number of people or things allowed to enter a nation or institution

naturalized citizen—immigrant who has met certain requirements to become a citizen of a new country

1500 — TODAY

LESSON 2

People from Many Lands

THINKING FOCUS

Why is the United States called a nation of many peoples?

Key Terms

- quota
- naturalized citizen

It is May 5 in a city in the Southwest. For days people have been looking forward to a holiday. It is Cinco de Mayo, the Fifth of May. From all over the city, people hurry to the fiesta.

At school, children have learned about Cinco de Mayo. They know that on May 5, 1862, Mexicans turned back French invaders in the Battle of Puebla. This victory lives on in Cinco de Mayo festivals. They are held in Los Angeles, San Antonio, and other southwestern cities with Mexican American communities.

Today people are coming together to celebrate this victory. As they near the park, they see Mexican flags. They hear the Mexican music. It is played by *mariachis,* Mexican musicians, dressed in black. These musicians wander through the crowd. Near a stage at one end of the park, people gather to watch costumed dancers.

Good smells drift over the crowd. At one food stand, a woman makes tacos. She fills thin pancakes, called tortillas, with beans, lettuce, and tomatoes. Italian pizza and ices as well as hot dogs and ice cream are for sale.

All day people enjoy picnics, parades, street dancing, and games. Not everyone at the fiesta is Mexican, however. African Americans, Asian Americans, and people of many other different ethnic groups join the celebration.

▼ *At this Cinco de Mayo celebration in San Antonio, Texas, dancers wear traditional Mexican costumes.*

622

Objectives

1. Describe how U.S. immigration has changed over the years.
2. Describe how different groups of immigrants have contributed to U.S. culture.
3. Identify some values and beliefs that have helped unite the many different peoples of the United States.

Graphic Overview

First Arrivals in the Americas → **Early Settlers and Slaves** → **Nation Builders** → **Today's Diverse Population**

Patterns of Immigration

Any time citizens of the United States get together, the crowd probably will be made up of people whose ancestors came from all over the world. Every ethnic group now living in the United States once came from another land.

Native Americans came first. As you read in Chapter 6, their ancestors crossed a land bridge that linked Asia and Alaska many thousands of years ago.

Settlement by others of what is now the United States began in the early 1500s. This was soon after European explorers arrived and laid claims in the Americas. Spanish missionaries were the first European settlers. They hoped to convert the Native Americans to Catholicism. Spanish missions became centers for settlement in what is now the Southwest, the West, and Florida. In 1565, the Spanish founded St. Augustine in present-day Florida. It became the first permanent European settlement in what is now the United States.

In the early 1600s, French traders and trappers set up forts in the far Northeast and along the Mississippi. At about the same time, the Dutch founded a colony in what became the state of New York. English settlers established their first colonies on the Atlantic coast in the early 1600s. During this period Europeans brought another group to the Americas—Africans. Most Africans came as slaves, taken by force.

Welcoming the World

In time, the English colonies on the Atlantic coast became a new nation. At first, the United States welcomed immigrants. In the 1800s the nation needed people to farm the land and build cities. Immigrants were eager to come to the United States.

Many immigrants had been driven from their countries by war, persecution, disease, and poverty. For them the United States was a "golden land." People came with dreams of freedom and fortune. As one Russian immigrant said, to come to the United States "was the wish, the dream, and the hope of every person."

Between 1820 and 1930, more than 37 million immigrants came to

Across Time & Space

Australia, like the United States, is a land of immigrants. Native Australians, like Native Americans, had crossed an ancient land bridge to enter the country long before European settlers arrived. In the late 1700s, the British arrived. The first British settlers were convicts and their jailors. Australia soon began attracting free British settlers, too. Like U.S. immigrants, they were seeking a better life.

◄ *Europeans brought their knowledge of farming to the United States. These farmers settled in North Dakota.*

▼ *These Jewish children were one of the many groups to immigrate to the United States in the early 20th century. They had been made orphans by war in Europe.*

DEVELOP

Copy the Graphic Overview onto the chalkboard. Have each student copy the Overview across the top of a sheet of paper, leaving plenty of space below. As students read the lesson and study immigrants from a particular nation or region, have them write the names below the appropriate box or boxes on the Overview, along with the time period(s) during which those people arrived in large numbers.

HISTORY

Map and Globe Skills

Display a globe or wall-sized world map, or hand out individual copies of a U.S. map. As students read the lesson, call for volunteers to locate on the world map the nations and regions mentioned as places from where immigrants came. Then ask students to locate U.S. regions mentioned as places where immigrants settled. Why might certain groups of immigrants have chosen certain places to settle? *(Available jobs or land; familiar-seeming landscape; family ties; existing settlements by members of same ethnic or religious group; U.S. sponsors or friends)*

Access Strategy

Have students study the photo of Cinco de Mayo on page 622 and ask them if they have ever gone to this celebration or one similar to it. Point out that today many communities in the United States have ethnic festivals, parades, or celebrations that all people can enjoy. Even though the celebration is in honor of a particular people or event, such as St. Patrick's Day, all members of a community can attend and participate. Point out that this is not necessarily the case in some other countries, where minority religious, ethnic, or political groups might be afraid to publicize their differences from the rest of the community.

Access Activity

Ask students to use the world map on page 624 to identify countries and regions from which U.S. immigrants came. Have them trace the arrows, identifying both the country of origin and the U.S. region or city. Ask them to think about why the immigrants left their country. Let student volunteers who know their family's immigrant background share their experiences.

NATIONAL IDENTITY

Social Participation

Divide the class into groups and assign each group a nation or region of the world from which a major wave of immigrants came to the United States. Have each group research, write, and then act out a short (5–10 minute) play, illustrating one of the hardships they imagine those people faced upon arriving in this country. Suggest that students think about such topics as language, prejudice, money, living conditions, and new social or religious customs.

➤ *In the early 1900s, the greatest number of immigrants came from eastern and southern Europe. By the late 1900s (1980 onward), they came mostly from Southeast Asia and Latin America.*

CULTURE

Critical Thinking

Have students suggest reasons why, despite great difficulties, people chose to emigrate to the United States. *(For instance, freedom to worship, economic opportunities, political freedom, racial or ethnic tolerance)* What might have caused them to leave their homelands? *(Lack of land and economic opportunity, religious or political persecution, war, famine)*

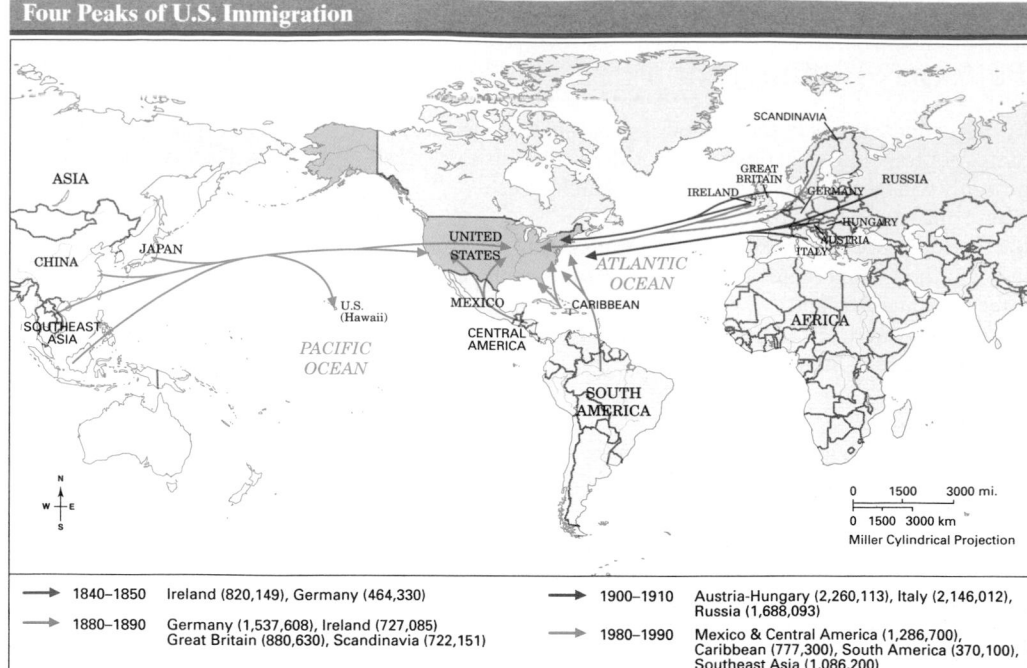

Four Peaks of U.S. Immigration

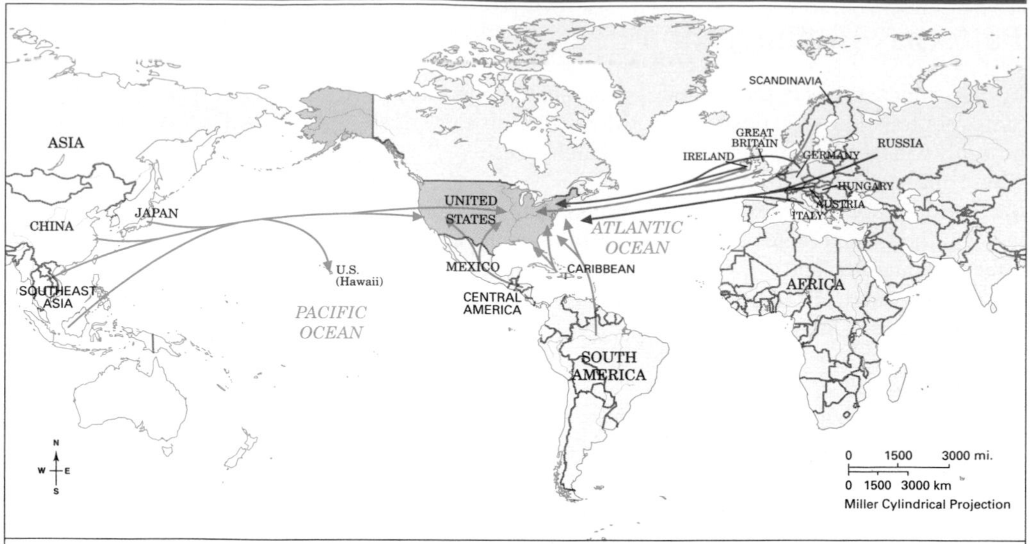
ASIA
CHINA
JAPAN
SOUTHEAST ASIA
U.S. (Hawaii)
PACIFIC OCEAN
UNITED STATES
MEXICO
CENTRAL AMERICA
CARIBBEAN
ATLANTIC OCEAN
SOUTH AMERICA
SCANDINAVIA
GREAT BRITAIN
IRELAND
GERMANY
RUSSIA
HUNGARY
AUSTRIA
ITALY
AFRICA
N
W
E
S
0 1500 3000 mi.
0 1500 3000 km
Miller Cylindrical Projection

Period	Source (number)
1840–1850	Ireland (820,149), Germany (464,330)
1880–1890	Germany (1,537,608), Ireland (727,085) Great Britain (880,630), Scandinavia (722,151)
1900–1910	Austria-Hungary (2,260,113), Italy (2,146,012), Russia (1,688,093)
1980–1990	Mexico & Central America (1,286,700), Caribbean (777,300), South America (370,100), Southeast Asia (1,086,200)

▲ *This map shows some of the peak periods of U.S. immigration. It also shows when immigrants came, where they came from, and where they settled. How did the immigrants' places of origin change from the first part of the 1900s to the last part?*

the United States. Some arrived from Asia and South America. Most, however, came from Europe. In the 1840s and 1850s, for instance, over one and a half million people fled Ireland and came to the United States. The map above and the chart on page 625 show where many other immigrant groups came from and when they arrived.

Closing the Door

Most immigrants faced hardship in their new land. They had to learn a new way of life. Many had to learn a new language. Often the foods were not familiar. Many immigrants arrived with little money. Those who lived in the cities often shared dark, crowded rooms.

To make matters worse, many immigrants had to deal with prejudice. The settled population sometimes feared or hated the newest arrivals. They worried that the newcomers would take their jobs. They feared the immigrants would change their way of life. Immigrants looking for jobs found signs saying NO IRISH NEED APPLY—or a variation of this idea.

The huge number of immigrants and the fears of settled citizens led many people to call for immigration limits. Chinese applicants were excluded beginning in 1882.

In the 1920s the U.S. Congress passed immigration laws that set quotas. These **quotas** put limits on the number of people allowed into the country.

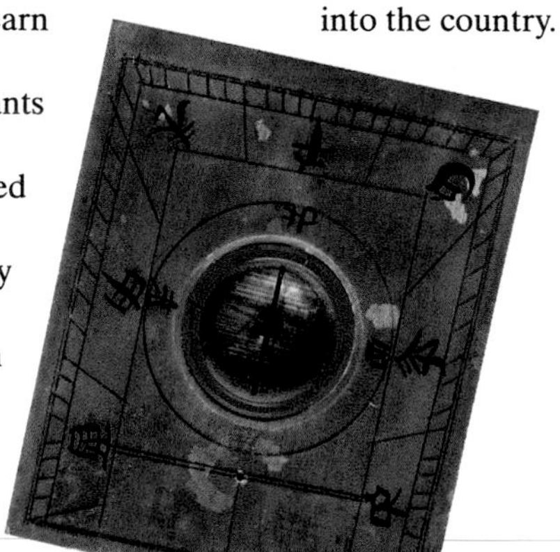

➤ *A Chinese immigrant brought this compass from China to help him find his way in his new country.*

Study Skills

Ask students to identify and research the immigrant groups that have settled in their local communities. Who were the earliest settlers? How has the population changed over time? Have students make a chart, giving names of immigrant groups and dates when they arrived in the students' communities.

Language Arts Connection

To help students understand the challenge of learning a new language, invite someone who has recently moved from another country to talk to the class about the challenges of learning English. Students can also listen to a foreign language radio or TV broadcast or look at a foreign language newspaper. Ask students to write a short paragraph describing what they think was said or written, compare their interpretations, and discuss what clues or cues they were able to use.

Geographic Context

Have students use maps of their own region to look for names of cities, towns, rivers, and so forth, that may reflect the backgrounds of immigrants who settled there. *(Examples: Paris, ME; New London, CT; Detroit, MI [French]; Los Angeles, CA[Spanish]; El Paso, TX [Spanish]; Baton Rouge, LA [French])* Students can also look for names of Native American origin. *(Examples: Tallahassee, FL; Mississippi (state and river); Manhattan (New York); Milwaukee, WI)*

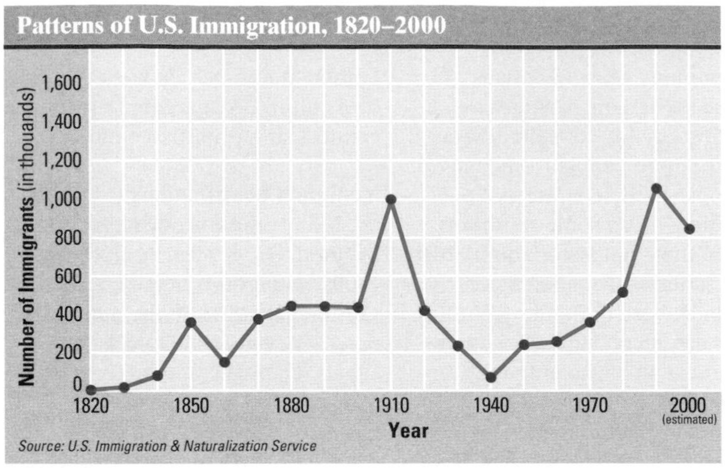
Patterns of U.S. Immigration, 1820–2000
Number of Immigrants (in thousands)
1,600
1,400
1,200
1,000
800
600
400
200
0
1820
1850
1880
1910
1940
1970
2000 (estimated)
Year
Source: U.S. Immigration & Naturalization Service

◄ *No one knows exactly how many immigrants will come to the United States by the year 2000. However, scientists make educated guesses, as this chart shows.*

The laws favored northern Europeans. Congress set low quotas for southern and eastern Europeans. The new laws made it difficult for people fleeing war to enter the United States.

Present Immigration Laws

In the 1950s and 1960s, the United States economy began to boom again. There seemed to be enough jobs for everyone. In 1952 Congress removed the ban on Asian immigration. In 1965 Congress changed U.S. immigration policy even more dramatically. New laws greatly expanded quotas in an attempt to treat every country equally. Quotas also favored uniting families who had relatives already living in the United States.

From 1950 to 1980, immigration increased. Many newcomers were fleeing from their governments. These refugees came from Cuba, Central America, South Vietnam, Haiti, Hungary, and the Soviet Union. Immigrants also arrived from Ethiopia, Mozambique, Angola, and the Middle East. Large numbers of Asians arrived from the Philippines, South Korea, China, and India. Other new immigrants came from Mexico and the Caribbean islands.

During these years more people entered the United States than the quotas allowed. In 1986 the government set up new rules to stop illegal immigration. These rules also helped some illegal immigrants in the country become citizens. Understanding Naturalization on page 626 explains how an immigrant becomes a **naturalized citizen.** ■

▼ *This family had fled Armenia at the turn of the century to come to the United States.*

■ *How have immigration laws changed over the years?*

NATIONAL IDENTITY

Critical Thinking

Explain to students that the 1920s immigration quotas mentioned on page 624 not only set a total number of immigrants allowed into the country each year, but also limited the number from any particular country to three percent of the number of that nationality already in the United States in 1910. Ask students why they think that lawmakers chose this particular formula. *(They were trying to keep the ethnic balance of the U.S. population the same as it had been, favoring people from northern and western Europe.)*

■ *Laws in the late 1800s and early 1900s limited the numbers of immigrants from Asia and southern and eastern Europe. These limits were relaxed in the 1950s and even more in 1965 and later. In 1986, laws were enacted to discourage illegal immigration.*

Social Context

One common idea in industrialized Western nations in the late 19th and early 20th centuries was that racial or ethnic background affected a person's abilities. This erroneous idea was the basis for many pseudo-scientific theories and for restrictions on immigration, particularly those on immigrants from China and Japan.

Some scholars contributed to the problem by claiming that "desirable" and "undesirable" traits were clustered in particular racial and ethnic groups. Because many people in groups considered "undesirable" also were illiterate (through lack of education or opportunity), a literacy test became a means of preventing some people from immigrating to the United States.

Social Participation

Divide the class into small groups and ask each group to design a program in which students could help new students from foreign countries adjust and feel comfortable in their school. Have each group give a brief oral report to the class explaining its plan.

SOCIAL SYSTEMS

Critical Thinking

Write the phrases *melting pot* and *patchwork quilt* on the chalkboard. Remind students that both images have been used to describe how people from various national cultures combine to form a new U.S. culture. (The term *salad bowl* is also used.) Have students identify characteristics of a society described by each image. *(In a melting pot, people lose their differences. In a patchwork quilt, people share basic national beliefs but may keep some distinct cultural traditions and identities.)* Have students discuss which kind of society they believe is preferable. Which image do students think more accurately describes the United States today? Why?

CITIZENSHIP

Visual Learning

Have students look at the photo on this page. Point out the man taking the naturalization oath. Explain that he is Albert Einstein, the Nobel Prize winner in physics in 1921, who was born in Germany and became a U.S. citizen in 1940. Have students research Einstein's career or that of another famous immigrant and give a short report to the class on what that person contributed to the United States.

Becoming One Nation

Physicist Albert Einstein, one of the most famous immigrants to the United States, became a U.S. citizen on October 1, 1940. In the photo below he is shown taking the oath of citizenship with his daughter.

For many years historians described the United States as a "melting pot." By this they meant a place where people from many lands lose their separate, national identities. Today some historians believe that "patchwork quilt" better describes the United States. In a patchwork quilt, the separate pieces are each unique. Together they make up a whole. In the "patchwork quilt" that is the United States, people keep their own culture. At the same time, they create a single, unified nation.

Immigrant Contributions

Many ethnic groups have contributed to U.S. growth. In the late 1800s, immigrants helped build the railroads that linked the nation's cities. They also built roads and canals. They dug mines. They set up farms and ranches. In cities

Understanding Naturalization

What is a citizen? A citizen is any person who was born or naturalized in a country. Many immigrants to the United States go through a process called naturalization to become citizens. A naturalized citizen has all the rights and responsibilities of a citizen born in this country.

U.S. citizens have the right to vote. Citizens also have many freedoms that are guaranteed by the Constitution of the United States. For example, citizens have the freedom to worship in the religion of their choice, to speak their minds, and to own property.

All citizens have legal responsibilities as well. They must obey the law, pay taxes, and serve on a jury when called. They also have civic responsibilities not required by law. They are supposed to vote and to respect and protect the rights of others.

How Does a Person Become a Citizen?

Any person born in this country is a citizen. Any person whose parent is a citizen is also a citizen. In order for an immigrant to become a naturalized citizen, that person must: (1) be at least 18 years old, (2) be in the country legally, (3) have lived here five years in a row, (4) be able to use English, (5) know about U.S. history and government.

There are several steps in the naturalization process. Immigrants must have their fingerprints taken. They must prove that they meet the naturalization requirements; for example, that they have lived here at least five years. They must take a test to show that they can read, write, and speak English. They must also take a test to show their knowledge of U.S. history and government.

Becoming a naturalized citizen is not simple. Yet thousands of people go through the naturalization process each year. They believe that the rights and benefits of U.S. citizenship are worth the effort.

Study Skills

Direct students to research and write a brief (1–2 page) report on the history of Ellis Island (New York Harbor, closed in 1954), Angel Island (the immigration station in San Francisco Bay, where many Asians entered), or the Statue of Liberty and how this place relates to the experience of immigrants who came to the United States in the early 1900s.

Cultural Context

The contributions of immigrants to U.S. culture are so widespread that they have become familiar and easy to overlook. One influence of a diverse population is very evident in the U.S. diet. Some popular foods in the United States that reflect this diversity include frankfurters and hamburgers (both German), chile, nachos, and tacos (Mexican), pizza and pasta (Italian), noodles (Chinese), yogurt (Southwest Asian), doughnuts (Dutch), and gumbo (African). Suggest to students that they make a list of foods they eat during the week that have an ethnic background.

Many holidays, songs, and sports also were brought into this country by people from other cultural traditions. The use of Christmas trees, for example, was brought to North America in the 1600s by German immigrants.

immigrants ran the machines that made everything from textiles to steel.

Immigrants have enriched life in the United States. They have given much more than muscle power alone. They also have brought their ideas, their traditions, and their dreams.

Music, art, food, writing, and dance in the United States show the influences of many lands. For example, jazz, blues, gospel, and rap are African American contributions to music. Reggae developed in the Caribbean. In any big U.S. city, you can eat foods from all over the world.

A Brighter Future

Many immigrants come to the United States looking for freedom. They want to make their own choices and elect their own leaders. Many find their own dreams through their children. The hope of a brighter future continues to unite many U.S. citizens. Farm worker José Urbina expresses a dream that many can understand.■

Our dream is to be able to give the children the best of everything. We know that, for them to have a better future and purpose in life, they need a good education. . . . We are going to sacrifice for them, so that they can have the profession that they desire.

▲ *Visitors in Washington, D.C., in 1993 view the Emancipation Proclamation, the Civil War document that freed slaves in the United States. On display for the first time since being signed by President Lincoln, it held out hope for a brighter future for African Americans.*

Ros-Lehtinen

◄ *Ileana Ros-Lehtinen, a Republican from Florida, was born in Havana, Cuba. She is the first Hispanic woman elected to Congress and the first Cuban American to serve. She is shown at a political rally in this photograph.*

■ *What gives many U.S. citizens a common purpose?*

REVIEW

1. **FOCUS** Why is the United States called a nation of many peoples?
2. **HISTORY** What situations in their birthplaces have led immigrants to come to the United States? Why did the United States seem attractive to them?
3. **GEOGRAPHY** Where did the first European settlers in the Americas come from? Why did they come? Where did they settle?
4. **CRITICAL THINKING** Give two reasons to explain why the United States first began to limit immigration. Do you think that these are good reasons for limiting immigration today? Explain your answer.
5. **ACTIVITY** Imagine that you are a 20-year-old, unmarried man or woman deciding whether to immigrate to the United States. Choose a country of origin. Then fold a sheet of notebook paper in half lengthwise. On one half list the reasons for immigrating, and on the other half list the reasons against.

NATIONAL IDENTITY

Critical Thinking

Ask students what they think people mean when they refer to the American Dream. *(Economic opportunity, social equality, religious and political freedom)* Ask students to what extent, based on their own experience and knowledge, they think the American Dream is a reality. Do they think that it is a reality for today's immigrants? Why?

■ *The desire for freedom and the hope of a better future for themselves and their children give many U.S. citizens of different ethnic groups a common purpose.*

CLOSE

Again draw the Graphic Overview on the chalkboard. Under it, write these headings: *Who Came?, When?, Why?* Have students fill out the chart by giving you the information from the lists they created as they read the text. When the chart has been completed, ask students to give examples of contributions immigrants have made to the United States.

Answers to Review Questions

1. The U.S. population is made up of mostly immigrants and their descendants.
2. Many immigrants were fleeing war, religious or political persecution, disease, and poverty. For them the United States offered peace, freedom, land, health, and prosperity.
3. The first European settlers in the Americas were Spanish missionaries who came to convert Native Americans to Roman Catholicism. In North America they built missions in the Southwest, the West, and Florida.
4. Laws restricting immigration were passed in the 1880s because of economic competition and ethnic and racial prejudice. Students may think that these reasons might still contribute to laws or attitudes today.
5. Answers depend on the country chosen, on the year (if not the present), and on current events there. Students should take into account U.S. immigration policy and past biases against Asians, Irish, southern and eastern Europeans, or other groups.

Homework Options

Encourage students to imagine what it would be like to emigrate from the United States to another country. Ask them to write a short paragraph telling what parts of their own U.S. culture they would want to take with them.

Study Guide: page 109

INTRODUCE

This selection is from *Tales from Gold Mountain: Stories of the Chinese in the New World* by Paul Yee. The Gold Mountain of the title comes from tales told about the United States after the gold rush began in California in 1848. According to stories told in China, gold nuggets lay on the hillsides and in stream beds. (In fact, the Chinese characters for San Francisco meant "nine gold mountains," referring to the city's hills.) News of the gold discoveries drew many Chinese to the United States. The selection supports Lesson 2 of Chapter 27, in which students learned about immigration to California.

READ AND RESPOND

Many students will enjoy reading this story on their own, because it has qualities that are similar to a folktale or a fairy tale. Before they read, ask students to think about why a story like this might be comforting to immigrants in a new land.

Before students read, point out the vocabulary words and unfamiliar terms defined in the margins. Be sure they understand what the words mean; help with pronunciation if necessary.

In Lesson 2 you learned about Chinese immigration to California. The author of this tale has used realistic details about immigrant life as he tells his story of two young lovers living in a California Chinatown.

LITERATURE

Ginger for the Heart

Paul Yee

In 1848 gold was discovered in northern California. This discovery started a world gold rush. People from the East Coast of the United States as well as people from other countries traveled thousands of miles to reach California and try their luck at gold mining. Chinese immigrants poured into California at this time. Many were hired as laborers to help construct the new transcontinental railroad, but others headed for the mountain streams of the Sierra Nevadas, where they panned for gold dust and nuggets that were mixed with the sand in the bottom of the streams. The story below comes from a collection of fictional stories about Chinese immigrants living in the United States. Can you find examples of Chinese traditions in this story?

The buildings of Chinatown are stoutly constructed of brick, and while some are broad and others thin, they rise no higher than four solid storeys. Many contain stained-glass windows decorated with flower and diamond patterns, and others boast balconies with fancy wrought-iron railings.

Only one building stands above the rest. Its turret-like tower is visible even from the harbor, because the cone-shaped roof is made of copper.

In the early days, Chang the merchant tailor owned this building. He used the main floor for his store and rented out the others. But he kept the tower room for his own use, for the sun filled it with light. This was the room where his wife and daughter worked.

His daughter's name was Yenna, and her beauty was beyond compare. She had ivory skin, sparkling eyes, and her hair hung long and silken, shining like polished ebony. All day long she and her mother sat by the tower window and sewed with silver needles and silken threads. They sang songs while they worked, and their voices rose in wondrous harmonies.

ebony a tropical, dark-colored wood often finished to look shiny black

In all Chinatown, the craftsmanship of Yenna and her mother was considered the finest. Search as they might, customers could not discern where holes had once pierced their shirts. Buttonholes never stretched out of shape, and seams were all but invisible.

discern to perceive or detect

One day, a young man came into the store laden with garments for mending. His shoulders were broad and strong, yet his eyes

628

Thematic Connections

Social Studies: Culture/Groups within a multicultural society

Houghton Mifflin Literary Readers: Realistic Fiction/Becoming

Background

Despite the prospect of becoming rich in the United States, many Chinese found it difficult to leave their homeland. The Mountain of Gold was 7,000 miles away across the Pacific Ocean; ship passage was expensive, and family ties were strong. Moreover, the emperor forbade his subjects to leave China. The first Chinese immigrants were men who left secretly and arrived at the height of the gold rush. Soon the emperor relaxed the emigration ban. Within a few years, some 25,000 Chinese had moved to California.

Although most of the immigrants had been farmers in China, laws in many states kept Chinese from owning land. After the gold rush, large numbers of Chinese immigrants found work building the transcontinental railroad or as workers on farms or in garment factories. Others, like the merchant tailor Chang in this story, opened small businesses in the Chinese neighborhoods of large cities.

were soft and caring. Many times he came, and many times he saw Yenna. For hours he would sit and watch her work. They fell deeply in love, though few words were spoken between them.

Spring came and boats bound for the northern gold fields began to sail again. It was time for the young man to go. He had borrowed money to pay his way over to the New World, and now he had to repay his debts. Onto his back he threw his blankets and tools, food and warm jackets. Then he set off with miners from around the world, clutching gold pans and shovels.

Yenna had little to give him in farewell. All she found in the kitchen was a ginger root as large as her hand. As she stroked its brown knobs and bumpy eyes, she whispered to him, "This will warm you in the cold weather. I will wait for you, but, like this piece of ginger, I, too, will age and grow dry." Then she pressed her lips to the ginger, and turned away.

"I will come back," the young man said. "The fire burning for you in my heart can never be extinguished."

extinguished put out

Thereafter, Yenna lit a lamp at every nightfall and set it in the tower window. Rains lashed against the glass, snow piled low along the ledge, and ocean winds rattled the frame. But the flame did not waver, even though the young man never sent letters. Yenna did not weep uselessly, but continued to sew and sing with her mother.

There were few unmarried women in Chinatown, and many men came to seek Yenna's hand in marriage. Rich gold miners and sons of successful merchants bowed before her, but she always looked away. They gave her grand gifts, but still she shook her head, until finally the men grew weary and called her crazy. In

◄ In what ways did Yenna show her steady love for the young man while he was away? *(She did not weep when he did not write but kept working. She kept a lamp burning in the tower window at night as a symbol of her love. She rejected offers of marriage from other men.)*

Access Strategy

Bring a piece of ginger to class and have students touch it, smell it, and taste a small bit. Tell them that in this story a gift of ginger takes on a new meaning—as a symbol of love that lasts through separation. Ask students if they have ever been separated from a close family member or good friend for a long time. Did they have a way to stay in touch? How would they feel if they had no way to communicate with someone far away? What might they give to the person as a reminder of who they are or of good times they shared? *(A picture, a treasured object, a souvenir of a shared experience)*

Remind students that immigrants often came alone to the United States. Even after their families joined them, the search for work frequently led to further separations from loved ones, as occurs in "Ginger for the Heart." Tell students that the story could be about any young couple whose love is tested by a long separation.

China, parents arranged all marriages, and daughters became the property of their husbands. But Chang the merchant tailor treasured his daughter's happiness and let her be.

One winter, an epidemic ravaged the city. When it was over, Chang had lost his wife and his eyesight. Yenna led him up to the tower where he could feel the sun and drifting clouds move across his face. She began to sew again, and while she sewed, she sang for her father. The lamp continued to burn steadily at the tower window as she worked. With twice the amount of work to do, she labored long after dusk. She fed the flame more oil and sent her needle skimming through the heavy fabrics. Nimbly her fingers braided shiny cords and coiled them into butterfly buttons. And when the wick sputtered into light each evening, Yenna's heart soared momentarily into her love's memories. Nights passed into weeks, months turned into years, and four years quickly flew by.

One day a dusty traveler came into the store and flung a bundle of ragged clothes onto the counter. Yenna shook out the first shirt, and out rolled a ginger root. Taking it into her hand, she saw that pieces had been nibbled off, but the core of the root was still firm and fragrant.

She looked up. There stood the man she had promised to wait for. His eyes appeared older and wiser.

"Your gift saved my life several times," he said. "The fire of the ginger is powerful indeed."

"Why is the ginger root still firm and heavy?" she wondered. "Should it not have dried and withered?"

"I kept it close to my heart and my sweat coated it. In lonely moments, my tears soaked it." His calloused hands reached out for her. "Your face has not changed."

"Nor has my heart," she replied. "I have kept a lamp burning all these years."

"So I have heard," he smiled. "Will you come away with me now? It has taken many years to gather enough gold to buy a farm. I have built you a house on my land."

For the first time since his departure, tears cascaded down Yenna's face. She shook her head. "I cannot leave. My father needs me."

"Please come with me," the young man pleaded. "You will be very happy, I promise."

Yenna swept the wetness from her cheeks. "Stay with me and work this store instead," she implored.

implored pleaded

The young man stiffened and stated proudly, "A man does not live in his wife's house." And the eyes that she remembered so well gleamed with determination.

"But this is a new land," she cried. "Must we forever follow the old ways?"

➤ How were Yenna and her family unusual among the people of Chinatown? In what ways did Yenna face a conflict between old and new ways when her lover returned? *(Yenna's father did not force her to accept a marriage she did not want, while most daughters in Chinese families had to follow their parents' choices. When her lover returned, she followed Chinese tradition in wanting to help her father, but she broke with that tradition in asking the young man to live in her house.)*

Research

Have students find out more about the Chinatown districts of large cities such as San Francisco, New York, Boston, or Toronto. Remind them that most Chinese immigrants in cities congregated in their own communities, which grew into large, distinct neighborhoods. There Chinese immigrants could speak their own language, eat their own food, wear traditional clothes, and follow their traditional customs in comfort. They could also turn to other Chinese for support. Community associations helped people find employment, write letters home, and ship deceased relatives back to China for burial.

Suggest that students use travel guides, other library resources, and possibly personal knowledge to find out more about a specific Chinatown or about another ethnic immigrant neighborhood in your own town. Ask them to make notes on population, location, history, architecture, and types of businesses. Then have students share their findings in class.

She reached out for him, but he brushed her away. With a curse, he hurled the ginger root into the fireplace. As the flames leapt up, Yenna's eyes blurred. The young man clenched and unclenched his fists in anger. They stood like stone.

At last the man turned to leave, but suddenly he knelt at the fireplace. Yenna saw him reach in with the tongs and pull something out of the flames.

tongs a grasping tool made of two hinged arms

"Look!" he whispered in amazement. "The ginger refuses to be burnt! The flames cannot touch it!"

Yenna looked and saw black burn marks charring the root, but when she took it in her hand, she found it still firm and moist. She held it to her nose, and found the fragrant sharpness still there.

The couple embraced and swore to stay together. They were married at a lavish banquet attended by all of Chinatown. There, the father passed his fingers over his son-in-law's face and nodded in satisfaction.

Shortly after, the merchant Chang died, and the young couple moved away. Yenna sold the business and locked up the tower room. But on nights when boats pull in from far away, they say a flicker of light can still be seen in that high window. And Chinese women are reminded that ginger is one of their best friends.

Further Reading

Dragonwings. Laurence Yep. Moon Shadow is a Chinese immigrant boy who helps his father test their homemade airplane.

Immigrant Girl: Becky of Eldridge Street. Brett Harvey. This book tells of a young Russian girl who grows up in a busy immigrant neighborhood of New York City in 1910.

My Name is San Ho. Jayne Pettit. San Ho is a 12-year-old Vietnamese boy. He travels to the United States to live with his mother and his stepfather, a U.S. Marine, during the Vietnam War.

Summer Endings. Sollace Hotz. This story tells of a young Polish girl who has to come to the United States during the summer of 1945. The family awaits news of the father, who was detained in Poland because he was a political activist.

◄ How does the ginger root illustrate that true love can overcome obstacles? *(The ginger root remains fresh and solid instead of drying out as years go by. Similarly, the couple's love remains strong even though they are separated for a long time. Also, just as the fire does not destroy the ginger root, disagreements and anger cannot destroy the couple's love.)*

EXTEND

The story mentions that ginger root has a biting, fiery taste. Have students find out how it is used in Chinese and other Asian dishes. *(It is sliced or minced and added as a seasoning to hot and cold dishes. In Western cooking ground ginger flavors gingerbread and often is used in fruit dishes.)*

Writing a Journal Entry

Ask students to write a response in their journals to Yenna's question (page 630): "But this is a new land. Must we forever follow the old ways?" Before they write, point out that family unity is a traditional value in Chinese families and in many other cultures. Yenna has strong loyalty to her father. However, she also wants her future husband to abandon the idea that "a man does not live in his wife's house."

Do students agree with Yenna? Can immigrants benefit by adopting the ways of their new country? Do they think second-generation immigrants are more likely to adopt new ways of acting and thinking? Ask students to give examples in their responses and to write from their own experience if appropriate. Students may want to focus on language, jobs, marriage customs, or holiday celebrations.

Further Reading

You may wish to have students look in the school or local library for more stories about immigrants' experiences in the United States.

INTRODUCE

Have a student read the Thinking Focus aloud. Ask students to speculate about what common goals are shared by most people in the United States. Point out that common goals are based on shared values, such as respect for all peoples, equality of opportunity, and help for the poor and the sick. Tell students that the lesson will describe some of the ways people in this country work together for the common good.

Key Terms

Vocabulary Strategies: T36–T37
discrimination—unfair treatment of a person because of race, religion, nationality, gender, or some other differences
volunteer—a person who gives his or her labor without being paid

1500 1600 1700 1800 TODAY

i don't
put up w
put dow

LESSON 3

For the Good of All

THINKING FOCUS

In what ways have people in the United States worked for the good of all citizens?

Key Terms

- discrimination
- volunteer

Most of the students looked at me because the way I was dressing was strange. It was so cold, I wore everything I'd bought. I didn't know where anything was. I came late to every class. I was confused and I could not ask people. They told me in sign language, "Go to eat." I went into the cafeteria. There were hundreds of people. . . . A supervisor knew I was a new student. He took me to the head of the line to get a hamburger and the other students got angry. "Why does that boy get to go first?" I told the supervisor, "I want to wait in the line. Please." He said, "Don't worry about it. Take the food."

This is how Von, an immigrant from Vietnam, remembers how difficult his first day in a Detroit school was. Part of what made it hard was the reaction of other students.

Fighting Discrimination

Sometimes, people react to differences in the same way the students did to Von. Discrimination often occurs when people fear differences between themselves and others. **Discrimination** means treating a person unfairly because of race, religion, nationality, gender, or other differences. If a person is kept from a job, from housing, or from education for one of these reasons, this is called discrimination.

In the United States, discrimination is an old problem. As you have already read in this chapter, new immigrants often faced hatred and fear. Other groups, such as women and nonwhites, also have had trouble getting fair treatment in the United States.

African Americans have

PRACTICE
BROTHERHOOD

no justice,
NO PEACE

In this photograph, people of many ages, backgrounds, and professions are marching to protest discrimination. The buttons above express their hopes.

Objectives

1. Define *discrimination* and give examples of ways in which it affects people's lives.
2. Explain why education is important to all people.
3. Explain how and why U.S. citizens volunteer to help one another.

Graphic Overview

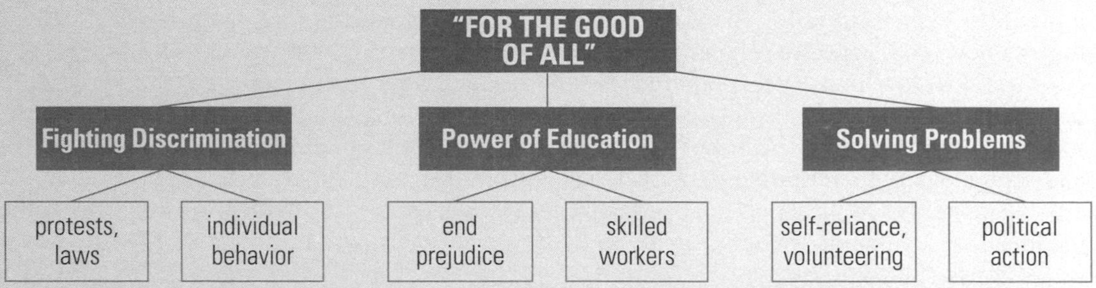

"FOR THE GOOD OF ALL"
Fighting Discrimination
Power of Education
Solving Problems
protests, laws
individual behavior
end prejudice
skilled workers
self-reliance, volunteering
political action

fought a long battle against discrimination. The Civil War (1861–1865) ended slavery and gave African Americans citizenship. However, they did not get equal opportunities for jobs, housing, or education along with their freedom.

In 1955 Rosa Parks, an African American from Montgomery, Alabama, refused to give up her bus seat to a white woman. In those days, bus companies in the South often made African Americans sit behind whites. Parks was jailed for defying this rule. To fight this discrimination, the black community boycotted the city buses for more than a year.

Martin Luther King, Jr., joined the struggle. He became a leader of the civil rights movement—or "freedom struggles." The civil rights protests spread. Volunteers from all over the country joined boycotts, marches, and court actions.

The result of the "freedom struggles" was the Civil Rights Act of 1964 and the Voting Rights Act of 1965. The Civil Rights Act made it illegal to keep people from a public place—such as a store or a bathroom—because of their race. It also outlawed racial discrimination in jobs or schools. The Voting Rights Act allowed more African Americans to register to vote.

The African American "freedom struggles" changed our society. Many schools and colleges that once were closed to African Americans are now desegregated. More African Americans now hold political office. The "freedom struggles" also helped open doors for all minorities and women in the United States.

A Moment in Time on page 634 explains how a young black woman was able to find opportunity in the United States armed services. ■

Projected U.S. Population, 1990–2090

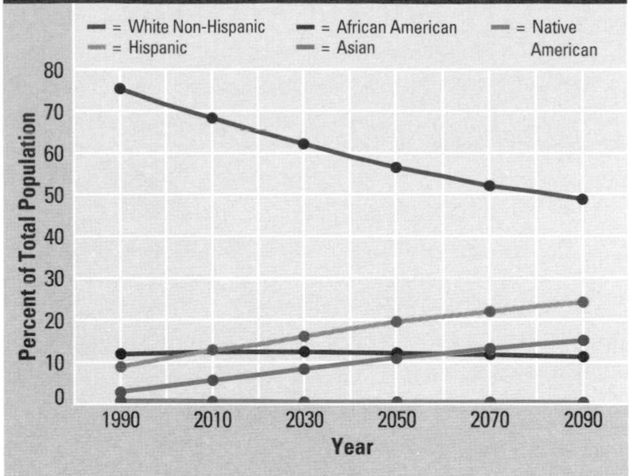

= White Non-Hispanic
= African American
= Native American
= Hispanic
= Asian
Percent of Total Population
80
70
60
50
40
30
20
10
0
1990
2010
2030
2050
2070
2090
Year

Source: Population Studies Center at the Urban Institute, 1991

▲ *The percentages of Asian and Hispanic populations of the United States are growing rapidly while the percentage of the white population is declining. These changes will, in proportion to the whole, affect the nation's ethnic mix in the next century.*

■ *What effect does discrimination have on people's lives?*

The Power of Education

The first step in stopping discrimination is beginning to overcome prejudice. Prejudice is hatred, distrust, or fear of people because of their race, religion, gender, national background, or other differences. Often education helps people to overcome prejudice. They learn to respect and appreciate the differences of others.

The chart on this page shows that the ethnic mix of the United States is changing. Experts predict that by the middle of the 21st century, U.S. citizens of European ancestry will no longer be the majority. Learning to respect others will continue to be important.

The Tradition of Education

The tradition of education goes back to the early days of U.S.

DEVELOP

Have students look at U.S. coins and locate the motto "E pluribus unum." Explain that this motto is Latin and means "from many, one," or "one out of many." Ask students how this motto applies to what they have already read about the United States. *(Immigrants from many nations have come to this land and have become part of a new nation.)* Display the Graphic Overview. Tell students that in this lesson they will learn some ways in which people in the United States join in activities that bring us together as a nation.

■ *Discrimination can deprive people of a fair chance at jobs, housing, education, or political rights. It can also lead to harmful or even violent actions.*

POLITICAL SYSTEMS

Critical Thinking

Write *jobs, housing, education,* and *government* on the chalkboard. Ask students what two important laws were the result of the "freedom struggles." *(Civil Rights Act of 1964 and Voting Rights Act of 1965)* Then ask them to suggest how these landmark laws might have improved life in the United States—not just for African Americans but also for other groups.

Access Strategy

Have a volunteer read aloud the anecdote (primary source) that begins the lesson on page 632. Ask students why they think that people who look and act differently from others sometimes meet unfriendliness or unfair treatment. Tell students that in this lesson they will read about some things that people have done to eliminate this kind of treatment. Point out that they will also read about ways in which people have worked to make sure that all people of the United States have the same opportunities.

Invite students to talk about their experiences in school. How has school encouraged them to treat everyone with fairness? How is it preparing them to live with diversity? Conclude by asking why fairness and cooperation are such important values for this nation.

Access Activity

Ask students to identify some volunteer activities that they, their family members, or friends take part in to help others. *(For example, hospital volunteering, tutoring, neighborhood clean-ups, helping at a playground or day-care center, church activities)* Ask why these activities are important to the whole nation, not just to those involved in the local community.

Note: You may want to use this Moment in Time after students have read the section "Fighting Discrimination," in this lesson. The feature applies to two significant changes in the kinds of discrimination discussed there—against African Americans and against women in the armed forces.

HISTORY

Visual Learning

Until 1978, women in the U.S. Army served in a separate unit called the Women's Army Corps (WAC), established during World War II. Today they serve in all army units that do not engage in combat.

Ask students to study this feature and answer these questions: What range of temperatures can this soldier expect to encounter? *(Deserts may be hot during the day, cold at night.)* How can you tell this soldier's rank? *(Insignia on uniform)* Why do you suppose that this soldier is not wearing her helmet? Besides heat and cold—and bullets—what else do you think that this uniform might protect its wearer against?

More About Her Orders Supplies are moved to combat areas by air and sea. Food is dehydrated so that it is lighter and does not take up as much space or require cooking. Soldiers add hot water to the food.

A MOMENT IN TIME

A Gulf War Soldier

2:16 P.M., February 20, 1991
Close to the front line in Saudi Arabia

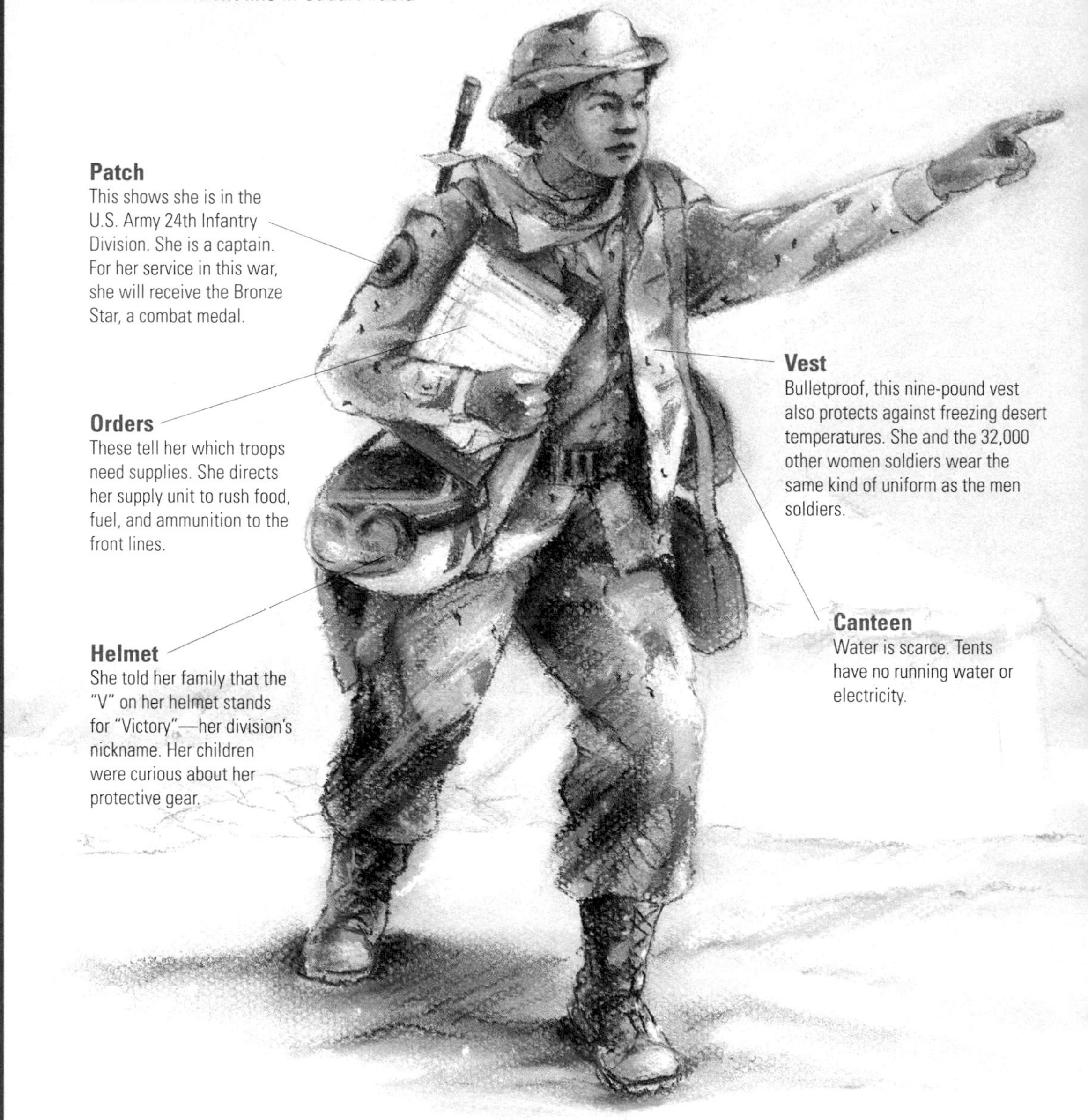
Patch
This shows she is in the U.S. Army 24th Infantry Division. She is a captain. For her service in this war, she will receive the Bronze Star, a combat medal.
Orders
These tell her which troops need supplies. She directs her supply unit to rush food, fuel, and ammunition to the front lines.
Helmet
She told her family that the "V" on her helmet stands for "Victory"—her division's nickname. Her children were curious about her protective gear.
Vest
Bulletproof, this nine-pound vest also protects against freezing desert temperatures. She and the 32,000 other women soldiers wear the same kind of uniform as the men soldiers.
Canteen
Water is scarce. Tents have no running water or electricity.

634

Visual Learning

Ask students to imagine that they are a soldier like the one shown in the picture. Have them write a letter home telling how their clothing and equipment helps keep them safe as they do their job.

Bulletin Board

Have students look in encyclopedias and other references to find illustrations of uniforms worn by the various U.S. armed forces: army, navy, air force, marines. To create a bulletin board display, ask them to copy or draw different uniforms and write captions explaining their features. Some students may research historical uniforms, such as those worn during the American Revolution, the Civil War, World War I, and World War II.

Interviewing

Direct students to interview a family member, friend, or neighbor who has served in the armed forces. Ask students to write down questions about time, location, combat experience, clothing, personal equipment, and food before conducting the interview. Encourage students to ask questions mainly about clothing and personal equipment and their purposes. Have students take notes or use tape recorders and then share the completed interviews with the class.

history. New England Puritans wanted their children to know how to read so that they could study the Bible. Other early settlers also worked to educate their children.

After the American Revolution, a major concern in education was to create good citizens. The new nation needed people who would support the government and choose capable leaders. Some people born in the United States believed that education was a way for immigrants to learn about their new culture. Many immigrants also saw education as a way for their children to get ahead.

Yet many children received little education. Often they had to work to help their families survive.

In the mid-1800s, Horace Mann, a Massachusetts educator, led a movement to improve public schools. Mann worked with the state government to ensure that all children would go to school for at least six months of the year.

The Need for Educated Citizens

By the mid-1900s, the United States needed fewer unskilled workers. More and more jobs required special training. Many jobs called for at least a high school education. College became a dream of more and more people. School attendance increased steadily.

Today the need for skilled workers remains a priority. Yet many people are worried that the nation is falling behind other countries in educating and training its citizens. On tests taken by students of many nations, U.S. students no longer score among the highest.

In order for the United States to be competitive in the modern world, it will need to strengthen its schools. Some experts believe that our present educational system will have to change in the future. ■

BE LOYAL

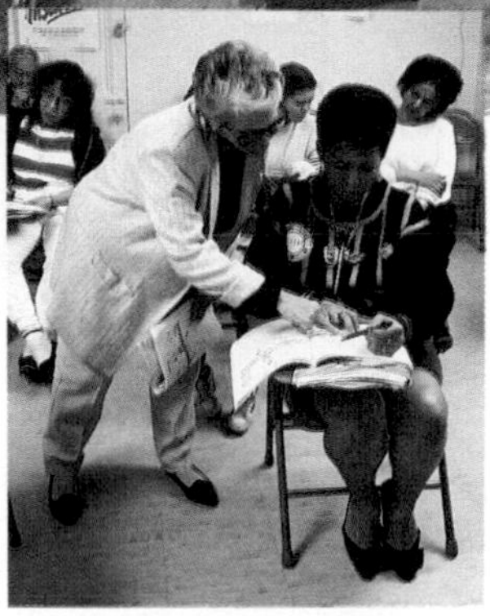

▲ *A turn-of-the-century class in New York City (above) and an English-language class today (inset).*

■ *List three reasons why education is important.*

Solving Problems

Education is an old tradition in the United States. So is self-reliance. The early settlers had to depend on themselves, their family, and their neighbors for survival. Native Americans have also counted on themselves and their communities for support. Today many people still believe that this nation can tackle its problems if citizens help themselves and one another.

A History of Volunteering

A **volunteer** gives his or her free labor. Volunteer labor means that organizations such as Goodwill, the United Fund, and the Red Cross can give more to the people they serve. Volunteers also help the federal government with certain problems.

When John F. Kennedy became President in 1961, he inspired many

SOCIAL SYSTEMS

Critical Thinking

Have students describe ways they or their families and friends may have supported organizations like Goodwill, UNICEF, Oxfam, or the Red Cross. Ask them to name any similar organizations they know about. Ask students to recall specific situations they have read about or have seen on television in which these organizations have been involved. *(Possible responses: Goodwill responding to homelessness; UNICEF and Oxfam responding to hunger in Somalia or other nations; the Red Cross helping victims of earthquakes, hurricanes, and other disasters in the United States and abroad)* Have students identify the beliefs and values that lead people to create or join such organizations.

■ *(Any three) To preserve knowledge and information, improve people's opportunities for jobs and careers, create good citizens and national leaders, build a united nation*

Social Context

Attempts to reform U.S. education often have coincided with attempts to reform society as a whole. Horace Mann's campaign to improve and extend public education began in the late 1830s, a period when reformers were working for temperance, abolition, help for the mentally ill, and women's suffrage. Convinced that democracy depended on educated citizens, Mann toured the nation, campaigning for publicly supported education for all children.

A later educator, John Dewey, worked to improve education in another period of reform, the Progressive era (1893–1917). By the late 1800s, most people in the United States supported the tax-supported schools for which Mann had worked so hard. However, education was still based mainly on memorization and recitation. Dewey wanted children to learn by doing; he wanted schools to relate education to children's real-life experiences.

Visual Learning

Direct students to look at the details of the two photographs of classrooms on this page. Have them discuss the similarities and differences they see in both the students and their surroundings. How are these classrooms like and unlike their own school?

CITIZENSHIP

Social Participation

Ask students to discuss how they would decide whether a problem or emergency should be dealt with by the government or should be left to citizen volunteers. After a brief discussion, divide the class into small groups. Assign each group a problem or emergency (homelessness, an earthquake, racial discrimination, a flood, illiteracy, drug abuse, AIDS, a tornado, air or water pollution, and so forth). Ask groups to discuss whether this particular issue is best handled by government agencies, by volunteers, or by both. Ask them to list their reasons. Have each group report their conclusions and their reasons to the class. Allow time for class discussion and debate.

■ *Volunteers have helped with problems of health care, homelessness, hunger, and education, and have also given help in emergencies, both in the United States and in other countries.*

CLOSE

Read the Thinking Focus aloud. Copy the Graphic Overview again from the beginning of the lesson onto the chalkboard. Point to different boxes in the Graphic Overview, asking students to identify specific examples for each case.

▲ *Former President Jimmy Carter helps build houses for the homeless. His volunteer organization is called Habitat for Humanity.*

U.S. citizens to become volunteers. "Ask not what your country can do for you," he urged. "Ask what you can do for your country."

Many Americans responded to Kennedy's challenge. For example, college graduates from across the United States signed up as Peace Corps volunteers. They helped people in poor countries learn new farming methods. They taught them ways to stay healthy. Other volunteers for VISTA worked in low-income communities in the United States.

■ *Identify two problems that volunteers have worked to solve.*

Volunteers Today

Today volunteers from all walks of life, including former President Jimmy Carter and his wife, Rosalynn Carter, are active in the struggle for civil rights. They work on behalf of women, Native Americans, Hispanic Americans, the homeless, people with AIDS, and other minorities.

Why do so many United States citizens volunteer? Some people have a personal interest in the groups they serve. Other people do volunteer work to prepare for a job. Volunteering in a hospital, for instance, might lead the way to a job in the medical profession.

Many others just feel good about helping others. As one volunteer speaker on AIDS prevention told a teenage audience, "If I can prevent one of you from getting infected, it's worth my time."

Still others see volunteering as a responsibility. For these people, volunteer work is part of being a good citizen.

Whatever their reasons, the volunteers of the United States are following an old and honored tradition. ■

REVIEW

1. **FOCUS** In what ways have people in the United States worked for the good of all of its citizens?
2. **HISTORY** What were the Civil Rights Act of 1964 and the Voting Rights Act of 1965?
3. **HISTORY** In addition to African Americans, what groups were helped by the "freedom struggles" of the 1960s?
4. **CRITICAL THINKING** Why is it important for U.S. schoolchildren to be able to keep up with schoolchildren from other countries?
5. **WRITING ACTIVITY** Identify a problem in your community. Make a list of suggestions explaining how volunteers could help solve the problem.

Homework Options

Tell students to choose a local, national, or international volunteer organization and write a letter asking for information about the group's work and goals.

Study Guide: page 110

Answers to Review Questions

1. To benefit all citizens, people in the United States have worked to end discrimination, tried to provide a good education for everyone, and worked together in the tradition of volunteering.
2. They were laws intended to end social and political discrimination against African Americans and others.
3. The civil rights movement also helped women and other minorities, such as Hispanics and Asian Americans.
4. Some people worry that without a good education to prepare our citizens for work, the U.S. economy will fall behind other nations.
5. Answers will depend on the community in which students live. Some students may identify problems such as environmental pollution, drug abuse, or racial discrimination. Possible solutions may include getting volunteers to educate others about the problem or petition the government to help solve it.

UNDERSTANDING RELATIONSHIPS

Identifying Stereotypes

Here's Why

A stereotype is an overgeneralized idea about a group of people. For example, "Scandinavians are blond" is a stereotype. So is the statement "All Italians are dark haired." These stereotypes are too simple. Not all Scandinavians are blond. Nor are all Italians dark haired.

Stereotypes are often based on partial truths, like the examples above. As a result, stereotypes can be hard to recognize. You may have some general, partly true ideas about people from a certain country or people of a certain race, religion, age, or gender.

Stereotyping can be harmful. During the 1500s, Europeans made slaves of the peoples of Africa and the Americas. Because those Europeans accepted the stereotype of Africans and Indians as less than human, they did not treat them as fellow humans.

Relating to people as individuals rather than as members of groups will help you overcome stereotypes.

Here's How

This picture shows a family in the United States in the 1950s packing their car for a vacation. Look carefully at the picture to see what it tells you about the stereotypes people had about boys and girls in the 1950s. Notice that the girl holds a doll, and the boy holds a baseball bat. Like her mother, the girl wears a skirt and dressy shoes. The boy wears clothing more suitable for play. Some stereotypes that this picture suggests are that only boys play active games and that girls always wear pretty dresses and play quietly with dolls.

Try It

What stereotypes about males and females do people have today? Look through a magazine for pictures of men and women. Think about what the men and the women are doing in the pictures. Could they change roles?

What stereotypes about men and women do the pictures suggest? Do any of the pictures avoid stereotypes? Write a paragraph about one or two of the most interesting examples. Compare your observations with those of your classmates.

Apply It

The humor in television comedies is sometimes based on stereotypes. Make a list of stereotypes that you notice in a show you watch. Discuss your list with others in your class.

637

From Many, One Nation

UNDERSTANDING RELATIONSHIPS

This skills feature uses the concept of overgeneralization and a photograph from the 1950s to teach students how to recognize stereotypes.

NATIONAL IDENTITY

Visual Learning

Tell students to use the photograph on this page to identify and describe what made up the "perfect (stereotypical) U.S. family" of the 1950s. *(Two parents, two children [boy and girl], a dog, nice neighborhood, sports equipment, family vacation; family is well dressed)* Ask students how many families they know that fit this stereotype. Point out that it is not an accurate portrayal of most families.

SOCIAL SYSTEMS

Visual Learning

Explain to students that stereotypes often change over time or even disappear completely. Focusing on stereotypes presented in the photo of the 1950s family, ask students what things have changed. *(Women and girls dress for active sports; boys and girls play the same games and sports. There are many single-parent families.)*

Answers to Try It

Students will encounter a wide range of pictures, particularly in advertisements, that support longtime stereotypes about men and women. They are also likely to find some pictures that are intended to counter particular stereotypes. You may want to have students share their pictures and observations with the class.

Answers to Apply It

You may want to view a television program in class as the starting point for a group discussion on stereotypes. As students discuss their lists of stereotypes in class, categorize their examples on the chalkboard. Possible general headings include these: *men, women, fathers, mothers, brothers, sisters, people with certain jobs, elderly people, teenagers, race or nationality groups.* Students should suggest additional appropriate headings.

Objective

Identify and respond to stereotypes presented in photographs and pictures. (Visual Learning 1, 3; Social Participation 2)

DECISION-MAKING PROCESS

1. Recognize the need for a decision.
2. Define the goals and values involved.
3. Acquire and evaluate necessary information.
4. Identify and analyze possible alternatives.
5. Choose the best alternative.

This Making Decisions lesson uses all five steps of the decision-making process.

HISTORY

Study Skills

Have students use both a dictionary and an encyclopedia to define *commonwealth,* particularly as it applies to Puerto Rico. Ask them to find out how being a commonwealth is different from being a state. *(Puerto Rico has its own governor and a relatively independent government at the local level but is otherwise governed by the United States. Puerto Ricans are represented in the U.S. Congress by an elected resident commissioner, who can only vote in House committees. Residents of the island do not pay federal income taxes.*

MAKING DECISIONS

Should Puerto Rico Be the 51st State?

Puerto Rico is a Latin American nation . . . except for political expression of the fact.

Puerto Rican Senator
Fernando Martin

One half of the electorate in Puerto Rico would stand to gain economically and personally from a vote for statehood.

Former Governor
Rafael Hernández Colón

Background

Consider these facts:

- Puerto Rico is an island about half the size of New Jersey.
- Puerto Rico's population is about 3.5 million people.
- Spanish is the island's official language.
- About 40 percent of the population speak some English.
- The island's per capita [per person] income is about $6,000.
- Its per capita income is higher than that of most other Caribbean islands.
- Its per capita income is about half that of Mississippi, the poorest state.
- Its unemployment rate is about 14 percent, higher than any state's.

U.S. involvement in Puerto Rico dates back to 1898. Up to that time, Puerto Rico had been a Spanish territory.

In April 1898 the United States went to war with Spain. The war lasted only four months. In that time the United States smashed Spanish fleets near the Philippines and Cuba. In July U.S. troops occupied Puerto Rico with little opposition. After the war Puerto Rico became a U.S. territory.

The following are other important dates in U.S.–Puerto Rican relations:

- **1917** Puerto Ricans were granted U.S. citizenship.
- **1948** Puerto Ricans elected their first governor.
- **1952** The island received U.S. commonwealth status. Thus, Puerto Rico would have its own government and constitution.
- **1967** Puerto Ricans voted to continue commonwealth status.

Luis Muñoz Marín
USA
05
Governor, Puerto Rico

Luis Muñoz Marín was elected the first governor of Puerto Rico in 1948.

Objectives

1. Understand the background of Puerto Rico's current status. (History 1, 5)
2. Describe the pros and cons of statehood for Puerto Rico. (History 5; Social & Political Systems 3, 6; Critical Thinking 1, 2)
3. Decide on a point of view on the issue and support that position. (Critical Thinking 3)

Activity

Have students divide into three groups: advocates of Puerto Rican statehood, supporters of independence, and those who want to continue commonwealth status. Tell the members of each group that they are to plan a political campaign to persuade people to support their viewpoint. Their campaign might include speeches that students have written and practiced; slogans, political banners and cartoons; graphs and charts, letters to local newspapers and to members of Congress. After students have discussed their campaign strategy, have assigned tasks within groups, and have completed their work, ask the groups to present their campaign strategy in class.

Considering the Alternatives

WE WANT
STATEHOOD
NOW
THE-SOLUTION

Puerto Ricans demonstrate in favor of statehood. What are some of the reasons they favor this change?

Puerto Ricans have long been divided over the question of whether Puerto Rico should become the 51st state.

About 41 percent of the Puerto Ricans favor statehood, according to a 1990 poll. They argue that becoming a state would give them representation in the world's most powerful nation. The United States, they say, protects the island from extreme poverty and from dictators. Both have weakened other Caribbean islands. They believe that statehood would also bring Puerto Rico greater benefits and social service programs.

About 36 percent of the islanders, according to this poll, want to continue commonwealth status. They say that Puerto Rico should not give up the benefits of its special association with the United States. However, like those who favor independence, they claim that statehood would weaken Puerto Ricans' culture. What's more, they do not want to pay U.S. taxes. They also fear that statehood would cost them jobs. That's because U.S. companies on the island get special tax benefits that would be lost if the island became a state.

About five percent of the population now want their island to become an independent nation, according to the poll. They say that Puerto Rico is different from the 50 states that make up the United States. They are proud of Puerto Rico's unique Spanish-Caribbean tradition and history. They fear that becoming a state might change their culture.

Puerto Ricans may vote again soon on the question of statehood. How do you think they should vote?

Decision Point

1. If you were a Puerto Rican, which point of view would you support? Why?
2. If you were a member of the U.S. Congress, would you favor Puerto Rican statehood? Why or why not?
3. If you owned a factory in Puerto Rico, would you argue for independence, statehood, or commonwealth status? Give your reasons.
4. What changes might result from adding a new state to the Union? For example, consider the U.S. flag.

?

POLITICAL SYSTEMS

Critical Thinking

Write three headings on the chalkboard: *Statehood, Independence,* and *Commonwealth Status.* Then ask students to identify the positions of advocates of each, as you write their answers in chart form. *(Statehood advocates want political representation in the United States and believe that it would bring greater economic benefits. Commonwealth supporters favor present benefits and federal tax exemptions and think that statehood would weaken their own culture. Those who favor independence resent U.S. intervention and want to preserve Puerto Rico's distinct culture.)* Conclude by having students identify the underlying values of each position, then decide which position they would take if they were Puerto Rican.

CULTURE

Social Participation

Divide the class into small groups to work together in researching various aspects of Puerto Rican life and culture such as education, agriculture, the arts, ethnic influences, daily life, colonial history, cities, and holidays. Tell each group to prepare a short oral report to give to the class.

Answers to Decision Point

1. Like Puerto Ricans, students are likely to be divided on the question. Answers should be consistent with the viewpoints given in the text.
2. Answers should include consideration of Puerto Rico's military base and strategic location in the Caribbean Sea.
3. Answers should mention tax exemptions and lower labor costs, which encourage businesses to locate in Puerto Rico. Loss of tax benefits might cause businesses to choose other locations.
4. Answers might include having additional members in the U.S. House and Senate; increased amount of federal dollars expended on benefits in Puerto Rico; an increase in the amount of money collected from federal taxes; changes on maps; one more star—and a new arrangement—on the U.S. flag.

Collaborative Strategy

A recommended strategy for this lesson is Pair Debate. For further information turn to pages T34–T35.

Answers to Reviewing Key Terms

1. Incorrect. A **volunteer** is one who gives his or her labor without being paid.
2. Incorrect. **Conservation** involves saving resources; consequently, they are used at a slower, not a faster, rate.
3. Incorrect. An immigrant must live in the United States for at least five years in a row before becoming a **naturalized citizen.**
4. Correct. **Discrimination** means treating a person unfairly because of race, religion, nationality, gender, or other differences.
5. Correct. **Quotas** in the 1920s set limits on the number of people allowed into the United States.

Answers to Exploring Concepts

A. Sample answers:
Requirements: [at least 18 years old]; in the country legally; resident for five years in a row; able to use English; knowledge of U.S. history and government
Responsibilities: [obey the law]; pay taxes; serve on a jury when called; should vote; respect and protect rights of others

B. Sample answers:

1. Answers may include the Mississippi River, the Great Plains, the Rocky Mountains, the Appalachians, and the Great Lakes.
2. Most of the United States is in the temperate zone.
3. The Mississippi River links the interior of the United States with the Gulf coast; Native Americans farmed in its valley; river barges carry freight today.
4. Native Americans regarded the land as the giver of life and used its resources carefully. Europeans saw the land as something to be owned and used; resources seemed limitless and were used wastefully.
5. Immigrants leave their countries because of war, persecution, disease, and poverty. Patterns of immigration reflect changes in conditions. Today, for example, unrest in Central America, Southwest Asia, Africa, and Southeast Asia have prompted many people to emigrate from their homelands.
6. Immigrants had to face a new way of life; many arrived with little money, had to learn a new language, encountered prejudice and discrimination.
7. Immigrants worked in industry and agriculture, building the U.S. economy; they brought their ideas, traditions, and culture.
8. The "freedom struggles" led to the passage of the Civil Rights Act of 1964 and the Voting Rights Act of 1965. Schools were desegregated; minorities and women have more opportunities.
9. People in the United States have valued education: to become good citizens and skilled workers; to get ahead. Early settlers helped one another survive. Today, many people still believe problems can be solved if citizens help themselves and volunteer to help one another.

Chapter Review

Reviewing Key Terms

conservation (p. 621)
discrimination (p. 632)
naturalized citizen (p. 625)
quota (p. 624)
volunteer (p. 635)

Each statement below uses a key term from this chapter. Tell whether each key term is used correctly. Then explain the reason for your answer.

1. Each volunteer at the Red Cross receives an annual salary from that organization.
2. As a result of applying new conservation methods, natural resources in the United States are being used up at a faster rate than ever before.
3. As soon as an immigrant arrives in the United States, he or she becomes a naturalized citizen.
4. A woman who fails to get a job because of her gender is a victim of discrimination.
5. Because of quotas set in the 1920s, fewer people from southern Europe and eastern Europe were able to immigrate to the United States.

Exploring Concepts

A. Many immigrants to the United States eventually become citizens. Copy and complete the following chart. List the requirements and responsibilities of naturalized citizens. One is done for you.

Becoming a Naturalized Citizen

Requirements	Responsibilities of Citizenship
You must be at least 18 years old.	You must obey the law.

B. Answer each question with information from the chapter.

1. What geographic features dominate the U.S. landscape?
2. To what climate zone does most of the United States belong?
3. What has been the role of the Mississippi River in the United States?
4. How did the Europeans' view of the land differ from that of the Native Americans? What were the consequences of the Europeans' view?
5. Why have the places of origin of immigrants changed over the years? Give an example to support your answer.
6. What hardships did immigrants face in the United States?
7. What contributions have immigrants made to the United States?
8. How did the "freedom struggles" change U.S. society?
9. Tell how the traditions of education and of volunteering in the United States have influenced this nation and its citizens.

Reviewing Skills

1. How can stereotypes be harmful? What can people do to overcome them?
2. What are some stereotypes that relate to age? How do you think these stereotypes came to be?
3. Look through a newspaper or magazine for advertisements. Think about the messages in the ads and what the person or persons are doing. Do they suggest any stereotypes about people from a certain country or of a certain race, age, or sex? Make a list of stereotypes that you notice. Share your list with your classmates. Rewrite an ad to remove stereotypes.

Using Critical Thinking

1. In Lesson 1 you read that "sometimes conservation seems to conflict with economic growth." Do you think conservation limits growth? Tell why or why not. What new jobs might be created by protecting the environment?
2. Prejudice may lead to discrimination. Why do you think this is so? What can be done to stop prejudice?
3. Every ethnic group in the United States once came from another land. Despite this fact, the settled population sometimes reacts to new immigrants with fear and hatred and treats them unfairly. Do you think the condition of the economy in the United States may affect the attitudes of the settled population toward immigrants? Tell why or why not.
4. In Lesson 2 you read that historians often described the United States as a "melting pot." Today, however, some historians believe that "patchwork quilt" better describes the United States. How is it possible for people to keep their own culture and traditions and, at the same time, be part of a single, unified nation?
5. One of the responsibilities of all citizens is to work to improve life in their community. What can you do to improve life in your community?

Preparing for Citizenship

1. **COLLECTING INFORMATION** Imagine you are planning a trip to one of the six regions in the United States. Research the geographic features, the food, customs, climate, resources, recreation areas, and historic places of the region. You may wish to write to the Chamber of Commerce of one or more states in that region for information. Then compile a scrapbook with facts, maps, and photographs. Share the scrapbook with your classmates.
2. **INTERVIEWING** Investigate the national origins of your family or of the family of someone you know. From what country did they come? Why did they come to the United States? How were they received by the settled population? Interview an older family member to find the answers to these questions. Share your findings with the class.
3. **GROUP ACTIVITY** In Lesson 3 you read about Von's first day in school. Interview students in your school who have come from another region or country to learn about their experiences. In small groups, discuss ways you can help newcomers adjust to the school and the community.
4. **COLLABORATIVE LEARNING** Celebrate the contributions of the various ethnic groups in the United States. Plan a Multicultural Festival. Prepare ethnic foods. Research and share stories about immigration to the United States. Tell about customs from another country. Play tapes or records of songs from other countries. Decorate your classroom with flags of different countries. You may wish to invite relatives or another class to the festival.

Answers to Reviewing Skills

1. Possible answers: stereotypes can lead to prejudice and mistreatment of others; awareness of stereotypes can help people to overcome them.
2. Possible answers: some stereotypes about youth include: young people are impulsive and irresponsible, idealistic rather than realistic, energetic. Some stereotypes about old age include: older people lack energy but are wise. These stereotypes come from people making generalizations about a group, based on knowing a few members of the group.
3. Encourage students to examine the advertisements carefully for stereotypes. Discuss why stereotypes can be hard to recognize, that is, they are sometimes based on partial truths.

Answers to Using Critical Thinking

1. Most students will recognize that conservation may limit growth in the short term but should help it in the long term. New environmental technology might create new jobs.
2. If people distrust or fear others because of prejudice, they may treat them unfairly just because they are different. Often education helps people overcome prejudice.
3. In economic hard times, people may fear that newcomers will compete with them for the limited number of jobs. In the 1950s and 1960s, on the other hand, when there seemed to be enough jobs for everyone, the U.S. Congress removed the ban on Asian immigration.
4. Most students should recognize that keeping one's own culture and being part of a unified nation are not mutually exclusive goals. Today, most U.S. citizens are united by their desire for freedom and their hope of a better future for their children.
5. Answers may include supporting recycling efforts, encouraging family members to practice energy conservation, respecting the differences of classmates, throwing trash into the proper receptacles, obeying laws, respecting others' property, and so forth.

Answers to Preparing for Citizenship

1. **COLLECTING INFORMATION** Encourage students to draw a map of the region and trace the route of their proposed trip. Students can find information and photographs in travel or regional magazines. Suggest that students explain why they chose a particular region.
2. **INTERVIEWING** Have students brainstorm a list of questions to ask in the interview. You may wish to have students write the interview as a dialogue or as a feature article. Encourage them to find photographs of family members who emigrated to the United States and share them with classmates.
3. **GROUP ACTIVITY** Discuss prejudice and the ways to combat it in the context of the experiences of new students in the school. Have students discuss ways to carry out their ideas, such as forming a "welcoming committee" or pairing the newcomer with a student in the class to ease the transition.
4. **COLLABORATIVE LEARNING** Encourage students of the same ethnic background to work together in this activity.

CHAPTER ORGANIZER

Chapter 28 The United Nations, Israel, and South Korea

CHAPTER PLANNING CHART

Pupil's Edition	Teacher's Edition	Ancillaries
Lesson 1: The United Nations (2–3 days) Objective 1: State the two main purposes of the United Nations. (Ethics and Belief Systems 1; History 5) Objective 2: Examine the organization of the United Nations and discuss how its role has changed over time. (Social and Political Systems 6; History 5) Objective 3: Identify some achievements of the United Nations. (Social and Political Systems 6)	• Graphic Overview (644) • Access Strategy (645) • Access Activity (645) • Visual Learning (646) Political Context (646) Reader's Theater (646)	Study Guide (112, 115)
Lesson 2: Israel and the United Nations (2–3 days) Objective 1: Explain how Israel became a nation. (Ethics and Belief Systems 3; Social and Political Systems 3) Objective 2: Describe everyday life in Israel. (Ethics and Belief Systems 3; Culture 3)	• Graphic Overview (648) • Access Strategy (649) • Access Activity (649) • Visual Learning (650) Mathematics Connection (650) Political Context (650) Religious Context (651) Social Participation (651)	Study Guide (113, 115) Map Activities (32) Transparency (16)
Lesson 3: South Korea and the United Nations (2–3 days) Objective 1: Recognize Korea's ancient culture. (Culture 2; History 1) Objective 2: Explain the role of the United Nations in the creation of South Korea. (History 6; Social and Political Systems 1) Objective 3: Describe life in South Korea today. (Culture 2, 4; Economics 3)	• Graphic Overview (653) • Access Activity (654) • Access Strategy (654) Historical Context (655) • Visual Learning (655) Map and Globe Skills (656) Collaborative Learning (656) Social Context (656)	Study Guide (114, 115)
Chapter Review	Answers (658)	Tests (109–112)

* Objectives are correlated to the strands and goals in the program Scope and Sequence on pages T41–T49.

• LEP appropriate resources. (For additional strategies, see pages T32–T33.)

CHAPTER RATIONALE

In the foregoing chapters, we explored the wonderful diversity of cultures around the world. Yet there were often conflicts and problems. Growing interdependence among nations has led people to realize the need for an organization to deal with these problems on a worldwide basis. The same awareness makes it imperative at the end of this book to address the United Nations and its role in the world today.

In this chapter, after giving an overview of the United Nations and its activities, we discuss two countries where the United Nations has played a key role—Israel and South Korea. Either one could have become a powder keg that might have ignited world conflicts. Although there has been violence in both places, UN action has kept it contained.

In **Lesson 1**, students read about the goals and organization of the United Nations as well as study examples of the work of the United Nations and its agencies. The lesson mentions some UN achievements and describes new challenges that the organization faces today.

Lesson 2 describes the establishment of the modern State of Israel and the role played by the United Nations. After giving a brief history of the conflict between Jews and Arabs in Palestine, the lesson explains the UN decision in favor of partitioning the territory between Jews and Arabs. As Israel became a nation, conflicts continued between the new state and its Arab neighbors. UN observers and agencies remain involved in this situation. Students can sharpen visual learning skills as they study the photo essay and text section on life in Israel today.

Although both countries have been significantly affected by UN actions, **Lesson 3** shows that the situation in Korea was very different from that in Israel. The lesson opens with a primarily visual overview of Korea's long history as a united country. It describes how Cold War rivalries led to the division of the country and how the United Nations eventually took military action to defend South Korea. Another photo essay looks at South Korean culture and daily life.

ACTIVITIES & PROJECTS

Oral Reports

Supply students with a list of some UN specialized agencies or committees, such as UNESCO, UNICEF, the World Health Organization (WHO), the UN Environment Program, the World Bank, the Food and Agriculture Organization, or the World Meteorological Organization (WMO). Have students choose one agency to research, making sure that a wide range has been covered. Ask each student to prepare a short (two- to three-minute) report to give to the class. If class size demands, have small groups prepare reports, and choose one student as speaker. (Use after Lesson 1.)

Challenge: Interviewing

Ask students to imagine that they are hosting a radio talk show whose next guests will be an Israeli official and a representative of Palestinian Arabs. Tell students to prepare a list of questions that they will ask each of these people on the show. Remind students to create questions that cannot be answered with a simple yes or no. (Use after Lesson 2.)

LEP: Making a Map

To help students understand a relationship between geography and history, have them draw a large relief map of the Korean peninsula, using shading and colors to show highlands and rivers. For reference, have them find a large-scale map in an atlas or an encyclopedia. Tell students to label the rivers and the major cities in both North and South Korea. (Use after Lesson 3.)

Basic: Illustrating

The flag of a nation or an organization usually carries significant symbols. Have students look in an almanac or an encyclopedia under Flag to find the flags of the United Nations, Israel, and South Korea. *(The UN flag, showing a polar projection, appears on the opening page of the chapter. The Israeli flag features the Star of David; the flag of South Korea has a red and blue yin/yang symbol.)* Tell students to choose one flag and make a drawing of it. To accompany the drawing, they should write one or two paragraphs explaining the symbols on the flag. Flag drawings can be shown on the bulletin board. (Use after Lesson 3.)

CHAPTER PREVIEW

Have students read the page and study the pictures. Then ask these questions: What is the United Nations? *(An organization that helps countries settle their conflicts and discuss world problems together)* Why does this chapter discuss Israel and South Korea? *(The modern histories of both countries have been greatly affected by UN actions.)*

Looking Back

Point out that this chapter, the last in the book, tells about an organization that brings countries together. Ask students to name some earlier world conflicts and to suggest how an organization like the United Nations might have been helpful. *(For example, the two world wars might have been shortened or prevented.)*

Looking Forward

Tell students that in the lessons of this chapter—The United Nations, Israel and the United Nations, and South Korea and the United Nations—they will look at events that are influencing both today's events and the future.

Lesson 1 describes the United Nations and its roles as a world forum for peace and a humanitarian organization.

Chapter 28

The United Nations, Israel, and South Korea

In the world today, conflicts threaten many nations. The people of the world need to work together to solve political and environmental problems. After the chaos of World War II, many nations joined together to form the United Nations. This international organization has intervened in many places around the world. The histories of two nations, Israel and South Korea, have been shaped by actions of the United Nations.

DES OCEANS PROPRES
NATIONS UNIES
FS0.80

Korea University students demonstrate in Seoul in 1987.

This carved *menorah,* a candelabrum or candlestick with many branches, is a symbol of Judaism. It stands in front of the Knesset—Israel's parliament—and depicts scenes from Jewish history.

1948 The State of Israel is created.

1930 | 1940 | 1950 | 1960

1945 The United Nations is founded.

1950 UN troops fight in the Korean War.

1945

BACKGROUND

Although the need for a world peacekeeping organization was evident for many years, it was not easy to establish such an organization. The horror of the two world wars finally made the need seem urgent enough.

The immediate precursor of the United Nations was the League of Nations, an international organization established by key European countries after World War I. The League, however, was weakened because it had no way to enforce its decisions. In addition, although U.S. President Woodrow Wilson was the leading planner of the League, he could not persuade the U.S. Congress to allow the United States to join it.

The League of Nations was dissolved in 1946, after the establishment of the United Nations. Some of the League's responsibilities and structure were passed along to the new organization.

Agreements During World War II

The United Nations grew out of an alliance among European governments-in-exile in London during World War II. These nations declared that lasting peace could be secured only if nations worked together. In 1941 the U.S. President, Franklin D. Roosevelt, and the British Prime Minister, Winston Churchill, signed the Atlantic Charter, which voiced their hope for a better system of security and for economic opportunities for all nations.

The term *United Nations* became widely known in 1942, when nations allied against

UNITED NATIONS
22c

The United Nations has its home in this building in New York City. Here the General Assembly and Security Council meet. These UN stamps illustrate some UN efforts: (far left) promotion of clean oceans, (top) World Bank funding for hydroelectric dams, (right) UN cooperation.

1987 The *intifada* begins.

1970 | 1980 | 1990 | 2000

1967 Israel conquers land in neighboring countries—the Gaza Strip, the West Bank, and the Golan Heights.

1991 North Korea and South Korea are admitted to the United Nations.

Today

Understanding the Visuals

The UN symbol (far left on facing page) uses a polar projection as part of its design. For more information about map projections, refer students to Understanding Projections in the Map and Globe Handbook (page G6).

The "Clean Oceans" *(Des oceans propres)* stamps (facing page), issued by the United Nations, emphasize the beauty and diversity of sea life. Growing populations worldwide strain the earth's natural resources, and the United Nations works to raise awareness of problems such as pollution.

Understanding Chronology

Refer the students to the timeline. The United Nations was founded in 1945, just after World War II. The new organization soon became involved in both the establishment of Israel and the conflict in Korea. Ask students to identify the earliest key events on the timeline and to relate them to the work of the United Nations.

the three Axis powers (Germany, Italy, and Japan) signed a short document stating their goals. It was called the *Declaration of the United Nations.* Eventually, 46 nations signed it. In 1944, diplomats from the Big Four—the United States, the United Kingdom, the Soviet Union, and China—met at Dumbarton Oaks (an estate in Washington, D.C.) to discuss a permanent organization.

The United Nations Is Born

After several meetings among world leaders, the United Nations was born in April 1945 at a meeting in San Francisco. There, China, the Soviet Union, Great Britain, the United States, and other nations met to prepare the UN Charter. (Note the excerpt from the Preamble to the UN Charter that begins Lesson 1.) The United Nations officially came into being on October 24, 1945, after a majority of the signing nations had ratified the charter. The first session of the General Assembly met in London in 1946. It voted to build the headquarters of the United Nations in New York City; this project was completed in 1952. (Refer students to the photo of the building above.)

Eleanor Roosevelt, the widow of President Roosevelt, was a member of the UN General Assembly from its beginnings until 1953. Her important work led to the Universal Declaration of Human Rights.

INTRODUCE

Ask students to discuss how countries could work together to avoid war and solve world problems. *(Possible answers: discuss or vote on disagreements instead of going to war; serve as objective observers and peacemakers when countries disagree)* Remind students that the United Nations was founded right after World War II, and have them speculate about why it was formed at that time. Have a volunteer read the Thinking Focus aloud. Tell students that they will learn the answer as they read the lesson.

Key Terms

Vocabulary Strategies: T36–T37

forum—a place for talking and exchanging views

veto—to block or overrule

humanitarian—concerned with basic human needs

1930
1940
1945
TODAY

LESSON 1

The United Nations

THINKING FOCUS

What two main goals have guided the United Nations since its founding?

Key Terms

- forum
- veto
- humanitarian

We, the peoples of the United Nations, determined to save succeeding generations from the scourge of war, which twice in our lifetime has brought untold sorrow to mankind, and to reaffirm faith in fundamental human rights, in the dignity and worth of the human person, in the equal rights of men and women and of nations large and small, and . . . to promote social progress and better standards of life in larger freedom. . . .

From the Preamble to the UN Charter

In 1945 the representatives of 51 nations created a new world organization, the United Nations (UN). World War II was the most devastating war in the world's history. Weary of its horrors, people wanted, in the words of U.S. President Harry S. Truman, to win "a victory against war itself."

This chapter will explain how the United Nations works to meet its goals and will give some examples of its achievements. You will then learn how the United Nations helped two countries, Israel and South Korea, to be born.

Zagreb

This UN observer in Bosnia is from France. He carries a sign that was knocked down by bullets.

The United Nations at Work

Membership in the United Nations has more than tripled since its founding in 1945. However, the two main purposes of the organization have remained the same. The first is to keep the peace. The second is to encourage respect for all people and to ease suffering from abuse, ignorance, and disease.

Organization

The two main parts of the United Nations are the General Assembly and the Security Council.

The General Assembly is the world's **forum,** or place for talking and exchanging views. Here, all member nations can safely bring up their concerns and discuss them with friend or foe. All nations are equal in that each has one vote.

The Security Council has real power. Unlike the General Assembly, it can use force to keep the peace. It has 15 members. Of these, five are permanent. They are the major powers that won World War II: the United States, the Soviet Union (now Russia), Britain, France, and China. Any one of these nations can **veto,** or block, decisions of the Security Council.

Objectives

1. State the two main purposes of the United Nations.
2. Examine the organization of the United Nations and discuss how its role has changed over time.
3. Identify some achievements of the United Nations.

Graphic Overview

UN ACTIVITIES
Peacekeeping
Humanitarian
political action
sanctions
military action
food, shelter
education, culture
health care

The United Nations has one person who can speak for the whole organization, the secretary-general. A strong secretary-general can have great influence on world public opinion.

Special agencies carry out the **humanitarian** efforts of the United Nations. Humanitarian means having concern for and encouraging human welfare.

Many agencies work together to bring food, shelter, and health care to people in need. In addition, the UN Educational, Scientific, and Cultural Organization (UNESCO) organizes schools, trains and sends out teachers, and provides technical advice in countries that request it. The UN Children's Fund (UNICEF) works to relieve the suffering of children and provide for their future.

Achievements

Some important activities of UN agencies include:

Sarajevo, Bosnia: Security Council

—In 1992 the Security Council approved the use of force to stop all trade with Serbia during its conflict with Bosnia. UN troops from several countries were authorized to board and search vessels entering the Adriatic Sea, to stop all but humanitarian supplies from reaching Serbian forces.

Mogadishu, Somalia: World Food Program

—In 1993 supply jets brought food supplied by the United Nations, after U.S. troops reopened Mogadishu's airport. Civil war had closed supply routes, and thousands had died of starvation. The Security Council voted to send a force to protect food deliveries, leading to the arrival of U.S. and French troops.

Geneva, Switzerland: World Health Organization (WHO)

—The number of children dying every day is in decline. This is in part due to the WHO vaccination programs that are now reaching 80 percent of the world's children.

Paris, France: UNESCO

—UNESCO's program to save places of unique importance in the world includes 358 sites in 83 countries. Among these is the ancient city of Venice in Italy. ■

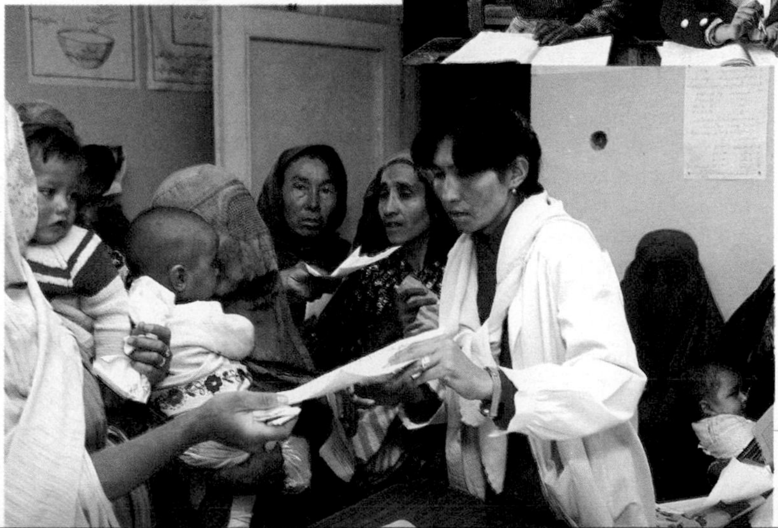

(top) Palestinian refugees attend a school run by UNESCO. (bottom) UNICEF doctors and nurses help mothers to care for their children in Afghanistan.

■ *How is the United Nations organized?*

DEVELOP

On the chalkboard, draw the Graphic Overview for this lesson, leaving some of the boxes blank. Ask students to fill in the blank boxes and then to give examples of the two UN purposes as they read the lesson. *(1. Peacekeeping: using military force to stop an aggressive country from abusing a weaker country; controlling trade between conflicting nations 2. Humanitarian: airdrops of food, vaccination programs)* Point out that the United Nations also has a World Court (the International Court of Justice), which makes judgments in arguments between countries.

ETHICS

Critical Thinking

Ask students if they think richer nations have special international responsibilities to help maintain world peace. *(Possible answer: While richer nations have more power and economic resources, world peace benefits all nations, and all should take part in peacekeeping efforts.)*

■ *The General Assembly is a forum in which all member nations take part; the 15-member Security Council makes peacekeeping decisions; and special agencies carry out the UN humanitarian mission. The secretary-general is the UN spokesperson.*

Access Strategy

In ancient Rome, the term *forum* referred to an open area where citizens went to discuss public issues. Today, forums are held in community centers and even on call-in radio shows. Tell students that this lesson is about another kind of forum, the United Nations, which provides a setting for free discussion of world problems. Choose a local problem that students can understand (such as the school's hot-lunch program, recycling, lack of playgrounds, or streets in need of repair) and have them hold a forum. Write the problem on the chalkboard; then ask for possible solutions. If necessary, suggest some approaches. Encourage students to state different opinions and suggestions for solutions. The forum might end with the class voting on and adopting key action steps.

Access Activity

With the whole class, list on the chalkboard some of the efforts UNICEF might make to help suffering children in the world. *(For example, provide food, health care, housing, clothing, books; build schools and hospitals; supply teachers and medical personnel)* If possible, bring in UNICEF greeting cards or calendars that illustrate various cultures and peoples.

POLITICAL SYSTEMS

Critical Thinking

Tell your students that by 1993 there were more than 170 members of the United Nations, and that many of the new member countries were small. Ask students to consider why a small nation might be interested in joining the United Nations. *(To take part in the world community, to protect itself against aggressors, to benefit from aid programs)* Then ask if they think it is fair for smaller nations, with relatively few people, to have an equal vote in the General Assembly with larger nations that have many millions of people. Point out that the two houses of the U.S. Congress were set up to solve such a conflict. *(The House of Representatives is elected on the basis of population, the Senate state by state.)* Ask students to discuss whether the United Nations should adopt the U.S. solution.

GEOGRAPHY

Map and Globe Skills

Have students look at the map on page 647, and point out the area where the most UN missions have been directed. *(Middle East)* Why might that be the case? *(It is one of the world's most volatile areas, because of its central location, religious conflicts, and valuable oil supplies.)*

New Roles and Challenges

World events are changing how the United Nations functions today. New kinds of conflicts are spreading, bringing untold suffering. At the same time, the world is more than ever challenged by problems of poverty, hunger, and pollution.

Changing Roles

The end of the Cold War has enabled democratic and former Communist nations to work together on some major issues. Security Council members do not use their veto power as often as in the past, which makes it easier for the United Nations to take a stand.

However, divisions between the rich and poor nations of the world are increasing. Many poorer nations are heavily in debt to the richer nations. This inequality between nations has also caused distrust to grow among members of the United Nations.

New leaders are also beginning to emerge. Germany and Japan are challenging the status of the United States and Russia as the world's most powerful and successful nations. They are claiming a greater role in the United Nations.

The United Nations is also taking on new roles. In Cambodia, for example, it is helping to rebuild a country destroyed by civil war. It is organizing elections, rebuilding roads, constructing bridges, and helping more than 360,000 refugees resettle in their homelands there.

New Challenges

The end of the Cold War has increased—not reduced—the UN peacekeeping mission. Look at the map on the next page. In what parts of the world have new UN missions recently started?

The problems of war today are often harder to solve than they were in the past. Ancient ethnic and religious strife—some of it much older than communism—is causing bitter conflicts.

The fight against poverty, hunger, and lack of education is more challenging than ever. Although some diseases like smallpox have been wiped out, new diseases like AIDS are spreading fast.

The growing world population has stretched food supplies to the

➤ *This statue, called* We Shall Beat Our Swords into Ploughshares, *stands in front of the UN building in New York City.*

Visual Learning

Read aloud the title of the statue shown on this page: *We Shall Beat Our Swords into Ploughshares* (from Isaiah 2:4). Explain that a ploughshare is the cutting blade of a plow, and discuss what the title means. Then ask students to write two paragraphs explaining why this statue is appropriate for the UN building. *(Encourages people to turn from war to peace)*

Political Context

The UN General Assembly can have an unlimited number of members. While it is a forum in which nations can express their opinions, as a body it cannot take direct action, as the Security Council can. The nonpermanent members of the Security Council are chosen to represent different groups and the regions of the world; rotated every two years, these members do not have veto power. The secretary-general is chosen by the Security Council and approved by members of the General Assembly.

Reader's Theater

Students can better understand the need for an organization like the United Nations if they appreciate that people everywhere need peace, health care, and a clean environment. Remind them, for example, of the growing AIDS threat or the damage being done to the valuable Amazon rain forest. Using the school or local library, select short poems or articles about the environment from various countries around the world. Divide the class into groups, and help students select passages to read aloud.

Peace Missions of the United Nations

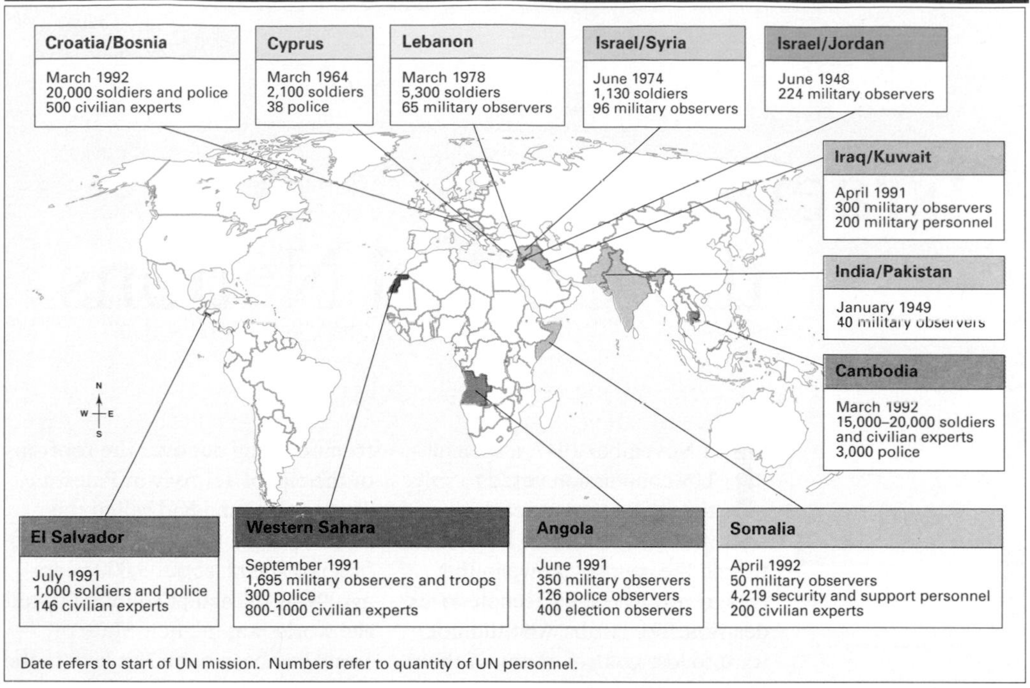

Croatia/Bosnia
March 1992
20,000 soldiers and police
500 civilian experts
Cyprus
March 1964
2,100 soldiers
38 police
Lebanon
March 1978
5,300 soldiers
65 military observers
Israel/Syria
June 1974
1,130 soldiers
96 military observers
Israel/Jordan
June 1948
224 military observers
Iraq/Kuwait
April 1991
300 military observers
200 military personnel
India/Pakistan
January 1949
40 military observers
Cambodia
March 1992
15,000–20,000 soldiers
and civilian experts
3,000 police
N
W
E
S
El Salvador
July 1991
1,000 soldiers and police
146 civilian experts
Western Sahara
September 1991
1,695 military observers and troops
300 police
800-1000 civilian experts
Angola
June 1991
350 military observers
126 police observers
400 election observers
Somalia
April 1992
50 military observers
4,219 security and support personnel
200 civilian experts
Date refers to start of UN mission. Numbers refer to quantity of UN personnel.

Source: UN Peace-keeping Operations Information Notes, September 1992

breaking point. More than 500 million people are undernourished.

As poorer nations struggle to improve their economies, richer nations warn of global dangers to the environment. People in poorer countries are cutting down forests to grow more crops. Cattle and sheep, grazing on land that is already poor, are causing erosion. Whole regions are becoming more desertlike every year. The United Nations is trying to offer new solutions for improving food supplies and protecting the environment. It also has to find a way of paying for the rising costs of its many projects.

Although it faces many new challenges, the United Nations remains a forum where nations can talk instead of fight. Through it, worldwide problems and threats of war may be resolved.

Early in its history, the United Nations took a role in shaping the future of Israel and South Korea. As you will learn in the next lessons, the United Nations took action in both countries and may still have a role to play there. ■

▲ *Which is the oldest UN mission still active in 1992?*

■ *What are some new challenges faced by the United Nations?*

R E V I E W

1. **FOCUS** What two main goals have guided the United Nations since its founding?
2. **HISTORY** Why are the United States, Great Britain, France, Russia, and China permanent members of the General Assembly?
3. **POLITICAL SYSTEMS** What effect did the end of the Cold War have on the United Nations?
4. **CRITICAL THINKING** Usually the United Nations does not get involved in a country without the country's permission. How might civil war bring about a change in UN policy?
5. **ACTIVITY** Find a recent newspaper story about UN activities and explain to the class how its action fits in with the UN mission.

◄ *The oldest UN mission that is still active was started in Israel and Jordan in 1948.*

■ *Some new challenges are posed by bitter ethnic and religious strife, new diseases (such as AIDS), the world's growing population, food shortages, and the rising cost of UN programs.*

C L O S E

Read the Thinking Focus aloud. As students suggest the main goals of the United Nations, write them on the chalkboard. Then ask which two answers best summarize the UN goals. *(Peacekeeping and humanitarian aid)* You might then discuss whether one of these goals is more important, and whether it would be possible to have one without the other. *(Students will probably say that it is difficult to have peace when people's basic human needs are not being met and that wars and conflicts make it hard to deliver humanitarian aid.)*

Answers to Review Questions

1. The two main goals are peacekeeping and humanitarian aid.
2. They were the major powers that won World War II, and they wanted to maintain world peace. (Russia holds the seat of the former Soviet Union.)
3. The UN Security Council was blocked in decision-making by vetoes of one or another of its permanent members. After the Cold War ended, members of the Security Council were better able to act on peacekeeping issues without the threat of a veto.
4. A country's internal conflicts might prevent it from requesting aid; the United Nations might begin to intervene in order to end long-term civil wars.
5. Students' findings will vary, depending on current events. Students should be able to link the actions of the United Nations to its peacekeeping or humanitarian goals.

Homework Options

Ask students to bring in newspaper and magazine photos that show the activities of the special agencies of the United Nations; have them write a caption to go with each photo. Display the photos and captions on a bulletin board under the title "UN Humanitarian Aid at Work."

Study Guide: page 112

INTRODUCE

Read the Thinking Focus aloud. Give students an opportunity to discuss what they already know about both modern Israel and the ancient Israelites (see Chapter 3). Help them make the distinction between ancient and modern Israel. Have students speculate about how Israel became established as a nation.

Key Terms

Vocabulary Strategies: T36–T37

partition—a division or separation

kibbutz—a collective farm in modern Israel

intifada—the uprising of Palestinian Arabs that began in 1987. (The Arabic word means, literally, "the shaking.")

1930 1940 1947 TODAY

LESSON 2

Israel and the United Nations

THINKING FOCUS

How did Israel become a nation?

Key Terms

- partition
- kibbutz
- intifada

In November 1947, a special UN commission voted to solve the conflicts between Jews and Arabs in Palestine. It decided to split the country between the two groups. The Jews accepted this decision. The Arabs, who did not want to lose control of any of their land, did not.

On May 14, 1948, the sound of an ancient shofar, or ram's horn trumpet, rang out over the rooftops of the city of Tel Aviv in Palestine. This same sound had called the Jewish people to prayer in the time of King David, about 3,000 years ago. Now the shofar sounded to tell the world that the new State of Israel had been born. For Jews in the new nation, this was a deeply moving moment—their dream of many years had come true.

Israel and Its Borders

The new State of Israel was to be carved out of Palestine, the land west of the Jordan River, as shown on the map on page 649. A UN decision established its original borders.

The Problem of Palestine

As you read in Chapter 3, many Jews left ancient Palestine in the Diaspora. Through the centuries, they were often unwelcome guests in their new countries.

The six-pointed Star of David, a bas-relief, stands for Judaism. During World War II, the Nazis forced Jews to wear a yellow Star of David, so that everyone would know they were Jews.

By the late 1800s, some Jews—called Zionists—felt that their people could be safe only in a separate Jewish state. They got together in 1897 and set as their goal "to create for the Jewish people a home in Palestine secured by public law."

In 1917, in the Balfour Declaration, the British government agreed with the Zionists. However, Palestine was already home to an ancient Arab people. The British also promised that the rights of Palestinian Arabs would not be harmed. Soon, it became clear that these two promises were in conflict.

At the end of World War I, Britain was put in charge of Palestine. As more Jewish settlers arrived in Palestine, local Arabs felt threatened. Violence broke out between Jews and Arabs. The British tried to limit the

Objectives

1. Explain how Israel became a nation.
2. Describe everyday life in Israel.

Graphic Overview

Jewish Diaspora → Rise of Zionism → • Balfour Declaration • Holocaust • End of World War II → UN partition of Palestine and founding of Israel / Arab-Israeli Conflict

The Founding of Israel

1897	First Zionist Congress meets.
1917	Balfour Declaration promises Jewish homeland in Palestine.
1922	British Mandate of Palestine begins.
1933	Nazis come to power in Germany.
1945	World learns of the Holocaust.
1947	United Nations votes in favor of partition of Palestine.
1948	British Mandate ends. Israel declares its independence.

flow of Jewish settlers. After World War II, however, Jewish immigration to Palestine gained support.

The UN Plan

The British turned the Palestine problem over to the United Nations. The United Nations came up with two plans. One called for the **partition,** or division, of Palestine between Jews and Arabs as shown in the first map below. Jerusalem—a holy city for Jews, Christians, and Muslims—was to be international. The other plan called for a united Palestine in which Jews and Arabs would rule themselves.

In 1947, the United Nations voted for the first plan. On May 14, 1948, the Jews proclaimed the State of Israel. The next day, five Arab states invaded Israel. The Jews fought back and extended their borders beyond the UN partition lines to those shown on the second map.

Many Palestinians refused to accept the existence of Israel. They fled and settled in UN refugee camps along Israel's borders.

In 1967, Israel won another war. It gained the lands shown on the third map. Some of these were later returned to Egypt. The others remain Israeli-occupied territories. ■

▲ *(left) Israeli soldiers stay on the lookout along the country's borders. (right) The founding of Israel was the fulfillment of the Zionist dream. (below) How did the 1967 war change the borders of Israel? How have they changed since then?*

■ *How did the United Nations try to solve the Arab-Jewish conflict in Palestine?*

Changing Boundaries of Palestine and Israel

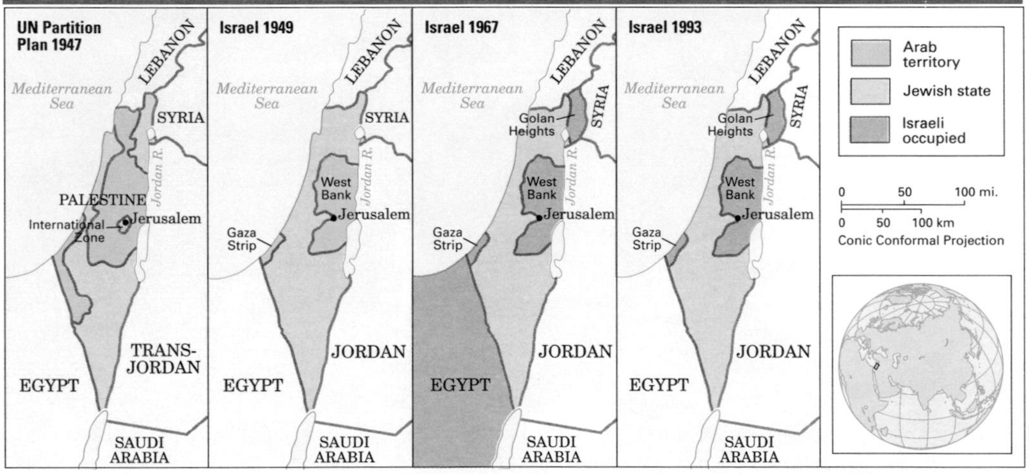
UN Partition Plan 1947
Mediterranean Sea
LEBANON
SYRIA
PALESTINE
Jordan R.
International Zone
Jerusalem
TRANS-JORDAN
EGYPT
SAUDI ARABIA
Israel 1949
West Bank
Gaza Strip
JORDAN
Israel 1967
Golan Heights
Israel 1993
Arab territory
Jewish state
Israeli occupied
0 50 100 mi.
0 50 100 km
Conic Conformal Projection

DEVELOP

Direct students to study the maps on this page, paying special attention to the dates. Then ask students to explain how the area has changed since 1947. Ask them to offer at least one reason for the changes. *(For example, Israel has gained more territory through war and occupation.)* Point out that the situation in the area is very changeable.

■ *The United Nations divided Palestine into separate Jewish and Arab areas.*

◄ *In 1967 Israel captured all territories west of the Jordan River, including the West Bank, the Gaza Strip, and some Egyptian territory. It also took the Golan Heights from Syria. Later, it returned the Egyptian territory.*

Access Strategy

Explain to students that tradition—especially religious tradition—was central to the formation of the State of Israel. One important factor in the founding of Israel was the Jews' desire to return to their homeland, the lands where they believed God first led them. For almost 2,000 years, Jews all over the world prayed for the rebirth of their nation. The Zionist movement changed religious hope into a national liberation movement. The persecution of Jews in many countries—notably the Holocaust during World War II—speeded the flow of refugees to Israel and led the United Nations to act on their behalf.

Have students share their experiences of moving to a new place. With the class, make a list on the chalkboard of the reasons people move. *(For example, better job, nicer place to live)* Explain that many of the Jews who helped found Israel, or who moved there later, had a common religious goal that was an even stronger motivation.

Access Activity

Have students work in small groups to discuss the Arab-Israeli conflict. Encourage them to study the map on this page and to list some problems that arise when two or more distinct national groups attempt to share the same geographic area. *(Natural resources may be strained; cultures clash; governing becomes difficult.)*

SOCIAL SYSTEMS

Critical Thinking

Tell students that the population of Palestine in 1945 was roughly 30 percent Jewish and 70 percent Arab. By 1948 the population of the same area had shifted to about 80 percent Jewish and 20 percent Arab. Ask students to account for these changing percentages. *(Arabs moved away once Israel became a nation; Jews immigrated to Israel.)* How did the increase in Jewish population support the existence of Israel as a new nation? *(It made it easier for the nation to grow and to resist invasion.)*

Everyday Life in Israel

Jewish immigrants have come to Israel from many countries. Since the breakup of the Soviet Union, hundreds of thousands more hope to immigrate.

Israel has created a modern economy along socialist lines. In the **kibbutz,** a type of collective farm, people share the work, daily living, and products of their efforts. Israel has also built factories and modern cities.

At the same time, Israel has to support expensive military forces. This effort uses up the resources needed to solve problems of housing, employment, and water shortages.

Today, UN observers still patrol some of Israel's borders. Palestinian refugees and their children continue to live in UN camps, now in Israeli-occupied territories. ■

Most Christians and Muslims in Israel are Palestinian Arabs.

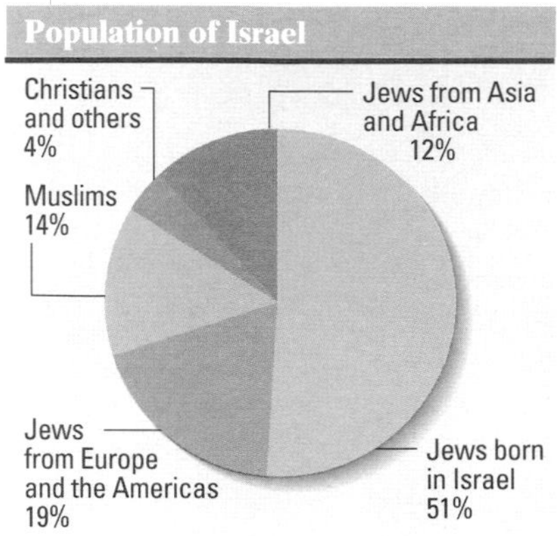
Population of Israel
Christians and others 4%
Jews from Asia and Africa 12%
Muslims 14%
Jews from Europe and the Americas 19%
Jews born in Israel 51%
Source: Israel Central Bureau of Statistics, 1991

This kibbutz in the Negev in southern Israel grows tomatoes in the desert. Water is piped in from the Sea of Galilee, far to the north.

Women serve in the Israeli army.

Visual Learning

Have students work in pairs to study the pictures on these pages. Then ask them to write down what they can learn about Israel from the pictures. *(Parts of the country are dry; some cities are busy and modern, with shops and stores, but they also have old, historic buildings; there are people of different races and religions.)*

Mathematics Connection

Have your students practice reading and interpreting a pie chart by using the population graph on this page to answer the following questions: What percentage of Israel's population is made up of Jews who migrated from other areas? *(12 + 19 = 31 percent)* What percentage of the population is not Jewish? *(4 + 14 = 18 percent)* What is the total percentage of the population that is Jewish? *(19 + 51 + 12 = 82 percent)*

Political Context

The British occupied Palestine in 1918, after the Balfour Declaration. But the increase in Jewish population during the Holocaust (especially after 1941) stirred Palestinian resentment. The Palestinian Liberation Organization was founded in 1964. Point out to students that the *intifada* (page 652) was one result of the Palestinians' feelings of anger and displacement. When the Israelis built new settlements in the occupied territories, Palestinians were deeply resentful.

This refugee camp in Gaza has been home to Palestinians for over 40 years.

In Jerusalem, people shop in a street mall.

Orthodox Jews, who strictly follow ancient traditions, wear prayer shawls on their way to pray at the Wailing Wall.

The Wailing Wall in Jerusalem is a remnant of a wall surrounding the Second Temple. Behind it is the Dome of the Rock, a holy site for Islam. In the distance, a church marks a Christian holy site on the Mount of Olives.

These Jewish children are newly arrived from Ethiopia. It is their third day of school. They are learning to speak Hebrew.

■ *How do the pictures on these pages show the diversity of people and ways of life in Israel?*

BELIEF SYSTEMS

Study Skills

Point out that the central photograph shows sites in Jerusalem that are important in three major religions: Judaism, Christianity, and Islam. Assign small groups of students to prepare short research reports about these sites, explaining why they are important to believers in each faith. Tell students to look for other sites in Jerusalem, or elsewhere in Israel, that are important to religions other than Judaism and to include them in their reports. They can share their findings with the whole class.

■ *Possible answers: The pictures show that people are of different origins and that they work and live in different ways. Some people are Jews and some are Palestinians; some are farmers, others live in modern cities, and still others live in refugee camps; women serve in the army; many people are very religious.)*

Religious Context

The Jewish Sabbath begins at sundown Friday and continues until complete darkness Saturday. Worship services are held at a synagogue, or temple. These services are often led by a teacher called a rabbi. When a boy reaches the age of 13, he has a special ceremony called a *bar mitzvah,* in which he becomes a full member of the Jewish community. Some synagogues have a similar ceremony, called the *bas* (or *bat*) *mitzvah,* for girls. (Refer students to the photo of the young boy reading from the Torah on page 151 of the Unit 3 Overview.) Some of your students may be participating in or preparing for these celebrations; others may have attended them.

Jews remember many major events in their history with feasts and fasts throughout the year, including Hanukkah, Yom Kippur, Purim, and Passover. In addition, Jewish celebrations of births, weddings, and funerals are filled with time-honored ritual.

Social Participation

Have students role-play Israeli citizens and prepare skits that show the kind of assistance they would provide for new immigrants to Israel. *(For example, greeting them at the airport, providing food and shelter, finding them jobs, teaching them to speak Hebrew, taking them to school, and so forth)*

POLITICAL SYSTEMS

Critical Thinking

Have students suggest where a future Palestinian state might be located. *(It would probably be made up mainly of land in the West Bank. If it were, the Gaza Strip and the Golan Heights would not be physically connected. Students may suggest that Syria and Jordan might give some territory. Continuing efforts to make peace could change this picture.)*

■ *Some favor giving up some of the occupied territories in exchange for peace. Others think that the West Bank and the Golan Heights are necessary to ensure Israel's safety.*

CLOSE

Ask volunteers to answer the Thinking Focus. To guide them, ask questions such as these: Who first made plans to establish a Jewish state in Palestine and when did they do so? *(Zionists, 1897)* What effect did the Holocaust have on this cause? *(Increased Jewish emigration to Palestine)* What problems did Jews face in Palestine? *(Conflict with the Arabs who already lived there)* What was the role of the United Nations? *(Voted to partition Palestine between Jews and Arabs)* When was the State of Israel established? *(1948)*

The Future of Israel

Since December 1987, Palestinian anger in the occupied lands has taken the form of an uprising called **intifada** *(ihn tih FAHD ah).* Palestinians—including women and young boys—have protested against Israel's rule by stone throwing, violent demonstrations, and strikes.

In 1992, Israel, its neighbors, and Palestinians began to discuss terms for peace. Some Israelis favor giving up occupied lands in exchange for peace. Others argue that these lands must not be returned because they are important to Israel's safety. However, the Palestinian population is growing quickly in these territories. If these areas become part of Israel, Arabs might soon outnumber Jews. Palestinians want their own country. What areas would this country include? Perhaps the United Nations will again take a role in solving some of these problems. ■

▼ *Israeli settlements in the occupied territories (shown on the map) concern Palestinians, who greatly outnumber Jewish settlers there, as the chart below shows. During the* intifada, *Palestinian women from the West Bank argue with Israeli soldiers (below).*

■ *What are some Israeli opinions about Israel's borders today?*

Israel and the Occupied Territories, 1993

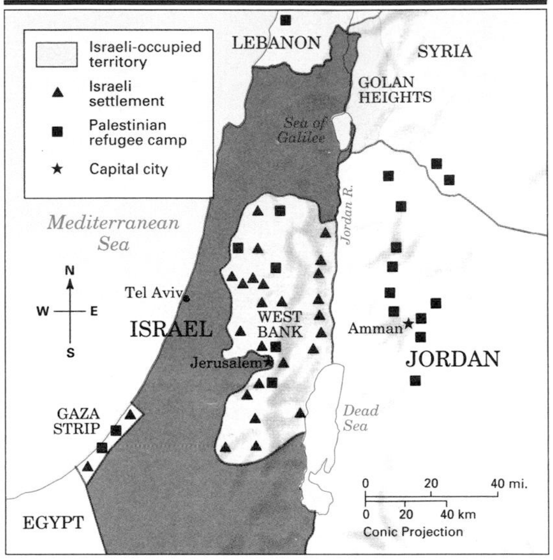
Israeli-occupied territory
Israeli settlement
Palestinian refugee camp
Capital city
LEBANON
SYRIA
GOLAN HEIGHTS
Sea of Galilee
Jordan R.
Mediterranean Sea
N
W
E
S
Tel Aviv
ISRAEL
WEST BANK
Amman
JORDAN
Jerusalem
GAZA STRIP
Dead Sea
EGYPT
0 20 40 mi.
0 20 40 km
Conic Projection

Population

	Jews	Palestinians
Israel	3,946,700	750,000
Occupied Territory	110,000	1,900,000
Total	4,056,700	2,650,000

Source: Israeli Embassy, Information Department

REVIEW

1. **FOCUS** How did Israel become a nation?
2. **HISTORY** What was the aim of the Zionists?
3. **GEOGRAPHY** Why might Israel want to extend its border to the Jordan River?
4. **CRITICAL THINKING** How might the rapid growth of the Palestinian population living in the occupied territories influence Israel's decision to add these territories to the country?
5. **ACTIVITY** Imagine that you are interviewing an Israeli who lived through the founding of Israel in 1948. Write some questions that you have about this person's life since Israel was founded.

Homework Options

Have students write a short paragraph on each of the Key Terms of this lesson, telling how each term is related to the history of the nation of Israel. Then ask students to share their paragraphs with the class.

Study Guide: page 113

Answers to Review Questions

1. To end tensions in Palestine after World War II, the United Nations voted to partition Palestine between Jews and Arabs. The Jews proclaimed the State of Israel in the part allotted to them.
2. The Zionists wanted to establish a separate Jewish homeland, which they thought was the only way to ensure Jewish safety.
3. Natural borders like rivers are easier to defend and often provide valuable transportation and trade routes.
4. Palestinians outnumber Jewish settlers in the occupied territories. If Israel annexed the occupied territories, Palestinians would be a large, hostile majority in that part of Israel.
5. Students' interview questions might ask about the Israeli's pride in Israel's growth and achievements; they might also ask the person how he or she feels about the continued unrest in the area.

1930 1940 **1945** **TODAY**

L E S S O N 3

South Korea and the United Nations

I t is a tense but quiet place. A strip of land two and a half miles wide divides the Korean peninsula between north and south. Soldiers stand by on either side with machine guns and peer at each other through field glasses.

This no man's land forms the border between North Korea and South Korea. It stretches generally along the 38th parallel, or 38° latitude north. In 1950, UN forces, including troops from many countries, defended this border.

THINKING FOCUS

What role did the United Nations play in South Korea's history?

History of Korea

The partition of Korea into North Korea and South Korea first took place in 1945. The years of partition are a tiny slice of time in the history of this ancient land.

Land of the Morning Calm

For more than 1,300 years, Korea was united. Its ancient name, Choson, means "Land of the Morning Calm." The chart on the next page shows different

Key Term

- sanction

North and South Korea, 1993

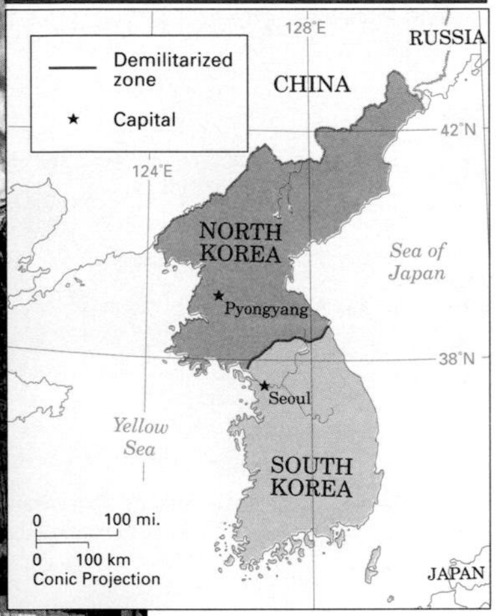
Demilitarized zone
Capital
128°E
RUSSIA
CHINA
42°N
124°E
NORTH KOREA
Sea of Japan
Pyongyang
38°N
Seoul
Yellow Sea
SOUTH KOREA
0 100 mi.
0 100 km
Conic Projection
JAPAN

(left) These cold hillsides behind the barbed wire form the border between North Korea and South Korea. (right) Where is the border between North Korea and South Korea located?

INTRODUCE

Tell your students that, as in the case of Israel, the United Nations played an important role in the creation of South Korea. Point out that the nation of Korea, however, had existed in the same territory for centuries—united by customs, language, and religion. Have your students read the Thinking Focus and prepare to look for the answers in this lesson.

Key Term

Vocabulary Strategies: T36–T37

sanction—a penalty used against a nation that is breaking international law

The border is located at about the 38th parallel of latitude.

Graphic Overview

Causes
- Japanese occupation
- World War II
- U.S.–Soviet Cold War rivalry

→ **Partition of Korea** →

Effects
- North Korean invasion
- UN military action
- South Korean economic success

Objectives

1. Recognize Korea's ancient culture.
2. Explain the role of the United Nations in the creation of South Korea.
3. Describe life in South Korea today.

DEVELOP

Direct students to the map on page 653 and explain that the separate nations of North Korea and South Korea were for many centuries the single country of Korea. Ask what countries are nearby. *(China, Russia, and Japan)* To get a better idea of the size and location of Korea, refer your students to the map of Eurasia on pages 682–683 of the Atlas. Help students identify Korea as a peninsula; tell them that Korea's geographic isolation was yet another reason it was called the Hermit Kingdom. Explain that this lesson will tell about ancient Korea and about what life is like in South Korea today.

HISTORY
Visual Learning

Suggest to students that they can learn a lot about ancient Korea by looking at the examples of Korean artwork on this page. Mention that shamanism—the belief in spirits—was a practice common to many cultures. Have students read the captions, and then ask what each object might show about Korean history. *(Turtle ships: ancient Koreans were experts at sea and at war. Celadon pot: people were skilled in crafts, valued beauty and art. Dragon and rattle: spiritual powers were respected.)*

Modern Korea is built on centuries of tradition. Just as an archaeologist uncovers new layers in a dig, you can see the many layers of Korea's history in this chart.

civilizations that have formed Korea. If you look at the Atlas on page 684, you will see that Korea served as a natural bridge between China and Japan. Korea borrowed from both of these cultures, but it also developed its own language, alphabet, and traditions.

Koreans adopted Buddhism and Confucianism from China. Confucianism still influences daily life and social relationships. Today many Koreans also practice Christianity, which was brought by missionaries in the 1800s. Shamanism, or belief in spirits, still plays a role in the lives of many Koreans.

From the 1600s to 1910, Korea was called the Hermit Kingdom because it closed its borders to outsiders, hoping to prevent new invasions. However, in 1910, Korea was invaded by Japan. It remained a colony of Japan until 1945.

Partition and War

As World War II drew to a close, Koreans hoped to regain their independence. Instead, the Allies divided the country, placing Soviet troops in the north and U.S. troops in the south. (The map on page 653 shows how Korea is divided today.) The superpowers were supposed to cooperate and join the two parts into a single, independent Korea. Instead, the Cold War began, and Korea became a center of conflict.

In 1947 the United Nations decided that free elections should be

The History of Korea

1945–Present	**Divided North and South Korea**	
1910–1945	**Japanese Occupation**	
1392–1910	**Choson Dynasty**	Hermit Kingdom Manchu and Japanese invasions Korean alphabet Confucianism: state religion
936–1392	**Koryo Dynasty**	Buddhism: state religion Fighting against Mongols First movable type
c. A.D. 668–936	**Unified Silla Dynasty**	Golden age Buddhism Strong Chinese influence
c. A.D. 100–c. A.D. 668	**Three Kingdoms: Koguryo, Paekche, and Silla**	Korean influence on Japan Buddhism
c. 2333 B.C.–c. A.D. 100	**Old Choson**	Shamanism Founding of Korea

Turtle ships, covered with armor, were invented by Admiral Yi Sun-sin. They helped the Choson dynasty defeat the Japanese navy in 1592.

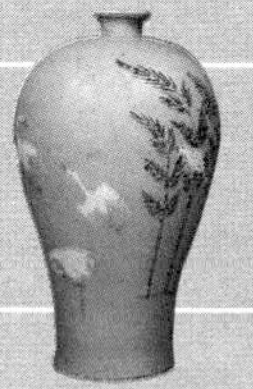

Celadon pottery was a specialty of the Koryo dynasty.

Dragons, believed to be powerful creatures, were often used in the Unified Silla kingdom to decorate ancient Korean temples.

This observatory, built in 647 in the kingdom of Silla, was used to study the stars. It is the oldest observatory in East Asia.

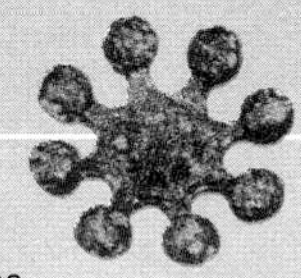

This Old Choson rattle was used during shaman rituals in second to third century B.C.

Access Activity

To help students understand the chart, compare it to a ladder and explain that it can be read either from the top (the present) down or from the bottom up. Move up the "ladder" with your students, explaining how cultures build on earlier achievements. As the caption suggests, you can also compare the chart to the layers of a dig at an archaeologist's field site (refer to Chapter 1).

Access Strategy

Tell students that one of the most celebrated achievements of the Choson kingdom was the creation of the Korean alphabet, called *han-gul,* in about 1446. Before that time, reading and writing for Koreans involved learning thousands of Chinese characters, although the two languages are not related. The revised form of writing had a short alphabet and was phonetic (that is, spelling followed pronunciation); it was much simpler and easier for Koreans to learn. With the new system, all Koreans—not just scholars—could learn to read and write. To highlight the importance of literacy, ask students how such a decision might have affected Korea's culture and history. *(More people could learn to read; more books would be written and printed. People would be better educated and could get better jobs.)*

held in all of Korea. In South Korea, elections were held under UN supervision, and the Republic of Korea was created in 1948. In the north, the Soviets set up a Communist government and closed the border to UN observers.

In 1950, North Korean forces, supplied with Soviet arms, poured into South Korea, occupying most of the country. Because of a Soviet boycott, the United Nations was able to use **sanctions** and military force against North Korea. Sanctions are penalties used against a nation breaking international law. After three years of war, the border between North Korea and South Korea was back about where it had been—near the 38th parallel.

Land of Miracles

The war devastated South Korea. Many families were separated. The United Nations formed the Korean Reconstruction Agency in 1950. From 1951 to 1958 the agency helped South Korea as it recovered from the war.

South Koreans worked very hard to start up new industries. The country has done so well in the last 40 years that it has been called the Land of Miracles. Today, South Korea is one of the "four tigers" of Asia, a major producer of heavy machinery, textiles, and electronics. It is also an important trading partner with other countries of the Pacific Rim (see the Atlas, page 684).

Many Koreans have moved from the countryside into the cities. The population of Seoul *(sohl),* the capital, has grown from 500,000 after the Korean War to over 10 million. As you can see in the Minipedia, page 664, it is now the fourth largest city in the world.

Korea's Political Future

In 1948, after UN-supervised elections, South Korea became a republic. Since then it has actually known little political freedom. In the 1980s huge student demonstrations led to some reforms.

In the 1950s and 1960s, many South Koreans emigrated to the United States, seeking greater freedom. Today they are one of the fastest-growing U.S. minorities.

In North Korea, a dictator named Kim Il Sung has ruled since 1948. Under his rule, North Korea has cut itself off from most of the non-Communist world.

The end of the Cold War has eased relations between North Korea and South Korea. In 1991, both were admitted to the United Nations. Representatives from the two countries have started talks to reunite their countries. ■

Countries Receiving Korean Exports

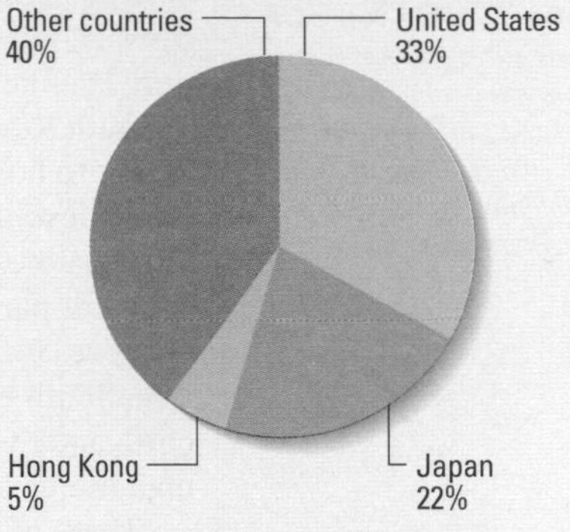
Other countries 40%
United States 33%
Hong Kong 5%
Japan 22%

Source: Britannica Book of the Year, 1992

▲ *The United States is South Korea's most important trading partner.*

▼ *Namdae-mun (Great South Gate) is one of the largest gates in Seoul's ancient city wall.*

■ *Why were Koreans hoping for independence at the end of World War II?*

POLITICAL SYSTEMS
Critical Thinking

Explain to students that in recent decades leaders in South Korea took so much power that they acted like dictators. They changed the method of electing a president from the popular vote to a more limited vote by members of a select body. Refer students to the photo on page 642 of Korea University students demonstrating. What goals might the students have had? *(Weaken president's power; reinstate popular vote; obtain rights such as freedom of press or speech)*

ECONOMICS
Critical Thinking

Ask students to suggest some factors that led to South Korea's rapid economic growth. *(Possible answers: UN recovery aid; determination and ambition; strong trade activity; a purposeful economic plan for the country)* Have them speculate on the effect Korean unification might have on the economy. *(Two very different economic systems would need to blend; tensions might arise from having to share resources and property.)*

■ *Korea was an ancient country with a long history of unity. Ever since the Japanese invaded their country in 1910, the Koreans had wanted to regain their independence.*

Historical Context

Before World War II, Japan held Korea as a colony. At the Yalta conference, the United States and the Soviet Union agreed that in return for entering the war against Japan, the USSR could disarm Japanese troops in northern Korea, while U.S. troops would receive their surrender south of the 38th parallel. When the war ended, Soviet troops moved into the north. The USSR agreed to UN-supervised elections but then refused to let UN officials enter the north.

When North Korean troops invaded South Korea, the United Nations acted to help South Korea. Normally, the Soviet Union would have vetoed such a decision. However, the Soviets were boycotting the Security Council, and the Soviet ambassador was not there to veto the decision. This was the first major military action taken by the United Nations. The UN forces, representing 16 nations, fought under U.S. command.

Visual Learning

Ask students to explain the information given in the pie chart on this page. Be sure they understand the term *trading partner.* Then ask them to name South Korea's major trading partners. *(The United States, Japan, Hong Kong)* What percentage of South Korea's exports go to other places? *(40 percent)*

ECONOMICS

Study Skills

This page and page 655 give students information on South Korea's social and economic patterns. Ask students to review these pages and tell them that South Korea's economic system is a free-market system like the economy of the United States—that is, private companies are free to set up and run their own businesses. Ask students to identify items manufactured and exported by South Korea *(heavy machinery, textiles, electronics)*. Then have them use an almanac or other reference book to learn more about the country's economy. For instance, what products does it import? From where?

■ *Koreans value family, tradition, education, social order, economic success, sports, art, and music.*

Life in South Korea

Across Time & Space

Korea, like Germany, was divided in two parts after World War II. One part has a free-market economy; the other is Communist. As in Germany, if Korea reunites, its people will have to blend two very different ways of life.

South Korea has blended modernization with respect for tradition. Confucianism teaches respect for ancestors, the need for order in society, and the importance of education. Families are very important in South Korea, and children are taught to honor their elders. Koreans believe that education is the key to success in life. It is not unusual for parents to make great sacrifices for their children's education. South Korean students study hard, and the country has a very high literacy rate.

Koreans enjoy sports. Apart from traditional self-defense, wrestling, and archery, they have taken up several western sports. Soccer has become a great favorite. In 1988, South Korea hosted the summer Olympic Games. Its athletes won gold medals in archery, boxing, judo, table tennis, and wrestling. Korea also has a long artistic tradition. This tradition continues to be reflected in its dance, music, and festivals. For example, the National Classic Music Institute serves as a training center for Korean folk music. Folk dances are performed at many ceremonies throughout South Korea. ■

■ *What is important in the life of South Koreans today?*

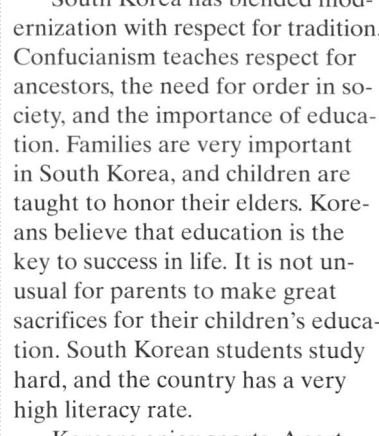

Education is very important to Korean children and their parents. (below) The Korean martial art of tae kwon do, *which means "hand and foot fighting," is very popular in many countries.*

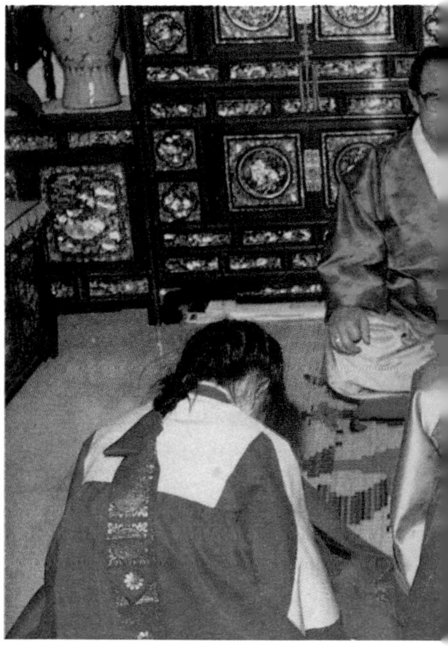

On New Year's Day, families gather to honor the souls of their ancestors. Children bow deeply to their elders and are given advice and presents.

Map and Globe Skills

Have students look at the map of the Pacific Rim on page 684 in the Atlas and locate South Korea's main trading partners. How does geography relate to the country's trade patterns? What influences might it also have on contemporary Korean culture?

Collaborative Learning

To increase your students' knowledge of contemporary life in South Korea, ask each student to sign up to be part of a research team on one of these topics: education, sports, foods, religion, and city life. Then have each group prepare a short oral report on its topic to present to the class; encourage students to include pictures or drawings. (If possible, provide library books and encyclopedias that the groups can consult in the classroom.)

Social Context

South Korea's remarkable urban expansion during recent decades has altered the look of the nation. Old and new buildings often stand next to each other, and in many areas services such as water and sewage systems cannot keep up with the rapid growth. This sometimes creates difficult living conditions for city dwellers.

Seoul has become a huge city with skyscrapers, fast traffic, and parks. To the left is an ancient palace begun in 1392.

This street market in Seoul offers a choice of spicy Korean foods.

Families work together threshing the harvest.

Musicians play the *komun-go*, a six-stringed zither invented in the seventh century during the Koguryo kingdom.

REVIEW

1. **FOCUS** What role did the United Nations play in South Korea's history?
2. **HISTORY** Following World War II, the Cold War began. How did the Cold War affect Korea?
3. **BELIEF SYSTEMS** What religions and philosophies can be found in Korea?
4. **ECONOMICS** Why has South Korea been called the Land of Miracles?
5. **CRITICAL THINKING** If North Korea and South Korea agree to reunite, how is life likely to change for North Koreans? For South Koreans?
6. **ACTIVITY** Imagine that you are South Korean. Write a letter to the secretary-general of the United Nations explaining how you feel about the partition of your country and what you would like the United Nations to do about it.

CLOSE

Have a volunteer reread the Thinking Focus, and then ask students to explain what role the United Nations played in the history of South Korea. *(Called for and supervised elections; sent troops; provided recovery assistance after war)* What role does the United Nations currently play in Korea? *(Both North and South Korea were admitted to the United Nations in 1991. The United Nations still oversees the armistice and the border between the two.)* How might the United Nations be asked to help Korea in the future? *(The United Nations might be asked to help North Korea and South Korea agree on a way to reunite.)*

Answers to Review Questions

1. The United Nations called for and supervised elections in South Korea, sent troops to defend against North Korea's aggression, and helped South Korea's postwar recovery.
2. The Cold War prevented the reunification of Korea and led to the Soviet Union's support of North Korea's invasion.
3. Buddhism and Confucianism were brought from China; many Koreans are Christians; others still follow shamanism.
4. Although its economy was damaged by both World War II and the war with North Korea, South Korea quickly rebuilt and prospered.
5. North Koreans would gain more freedom, but they might lose their jobs and have to learn new skills. South Koreans might have to help North Koreans. Families on both sides could be reunited.
6. Students may focus on the suffering of divided families or on Korea's long history of unity. They may call on the United Nations to sponsor unification talks.

Homework Options

Invite students to plan a visit to South Korea as tourists. Ask them to prepare an itinerary listing things they would want to see and do there.

Study Guide: pages 114–115

Chapter Review

Reviewing Key Terms

forum (p. 644)
humanitarian (p. 645)
intifada (p. 652)
kibbutz (p. 650)
partition (p. 649)
sanction (p. 655)
veto (p. 644)

Answer the following questions using the key term or terms in parentheses.

1. What are the goals and powers of the United Nations? (forum, humanitarian, veto, sanction)
2. How do Israelis earn a living? (kibbutz)
3. What was the result of Allied decisions about Korea after World War II? (partition)
4. How did Palestinians react to Israeli occupation? (intifada)

Exploring Concepts

Answer each question with information from the chapter.

1. What role did the United Nations play in the creation of Israel?
2. What was unusual about the UN role in Korea in 1950?
3. Why have conflicts between Arabs and Jews continued in Israel?
4. Why did Zionist leaders of the early 1900s believe that the Jewish people needed a nation of their own?
5. What was unusual about South Korea's recovery after the war?
6. What is the relationship between the United Nations and the two Korean governments today?

Using Critical Thinking

1. What qualities do you think the UN secretary-general should have? Make up a list of questions you would ask someone who is being considered for this position. Then write the answers you think he or she should give.
2. Having veto power gives the five permanent members of the Security Council a great deal of influence over UN decisions. Do you think that it is a good idea for these five nations to have this power? Explain why or why not.

Preparing for Citizenship

1. **COLLECTING INFORMATION** Make a scrapbook of news articles about the ongoing activities of the United Nations and its agencies.
2. **COLLABORATIVE LEARNING** With your classmates, organize a "model United Nations." Choose five people to represent the permanent members of the Security Council. Choose one person (perhaps your teacher) to act as both secretary-general and moderator. Other class members should choose the nations they want to represent from a list of current UN members. In an almanac or encyclopedia, each delegate should look up basic information about the country he or she represents. Then choose a committee to research and present three to five issues that your model United Nations will address.

Answers to Reviewing Key Terms

Sample answers:

1. The UN General Assembly is a **forum** where nations can talk things over and avoid open war. UN agencies help children as part of their **humanitarian** work. The Security Council can impose **sanctions** on member nations that break international law, but permanent members of the Security Council can **veto** its decisions.
2. Many Israelis are farmers who live and work together on a **kibbutz.**
3. An agreement between the USSR and the United States led to a long-lasting **partition** of Korea.
4. Palestinians' anger took the form of the **intifada,** a violent uprising.

Answers to Exploring Concepts

Sample answers:

1. The United Nations was called on to find a peaceful solution to conflicts in Palestine. Its solution was to divide the country between Jews and Arabs, making it possible for the Jewish state of Israel to be formed.
2. The United Nations took military action.
3. Causes of conflict include: Palestinians' belief that their land was stolen; lack of a place for refugees to go; increasing Jewish occupation of territories taken in war.
4. Jews were persecuted and discriminated against in many nations. Zionists believed Jews would not be safe unless they had their own homeland.
5. Although Korea was occupied in World War II and devastated by the war with North Korea, it quickly became a modern industrial nation.
6. Both nations are UN members. Talks on reunification are going on.

Answers to Using Critical Thinking

1. Students are likely to suggest qualities such as patience, even temper, ability to compromise, persuasiveness. Their questions and answers should show that they understand the need for these qualities.
2. Answers will vary, but students may suggest that the five permanent members are no longer representative of the world as a whole.

Answers to Preparing for Citizenship

1. **COLLECTING INFORMATION** This can be either an individual or a group activity. Encourage students to use library sources (such as *Readers' Guide*) in looking for material other than everyday news stories.
2. **COLLABORATIVE LEARNING** Give students whatever help they need in organizing their delegations and choosing a topic for discussion. Either the teacher or a mature student can act as secretary-general/moderator. (The role also can be divided between two people.) Earlier classroom experience in discussing and debating issues will be useful here.

Time/Space Databank

Minipedia 660
- Alphabet 660
- Architecture 662
- City 664
- Highlights in the History of Communication 665
- History of the World 669

Countries of the World 674

Atlas 678
- World: Political 678
- World: Physical 680
- Eurasia: Political/Physical 682
- Pacific Rim: Political/Physical 684
- Africa: Political/Physical 685
- North America: Political/Physical 686
- South America: Political/Physical 687
- World: Religions 688
- World: Climate 688
- World: Population (Cartogram) 689
- World: Land Use, Land and Ocean Resources 689

Glossary of Geographic Terms 690

Gazetteer 692

Biographical Dictionary 696

Glossary 701

Index 708

Alphabet

Alphabet is the series of letters used in writing a language. The name means exactly what the term ABC's means as a name for the 26 letters of our alphabet. The word comes from *alpha* and *beta,* the first two letters of the Greek alphabet.

Most books, magazines, and newspapers are printed in the 26-letter alphabet called *Roman.* But the Romans did not invent it. They put finishing touches on a system that had been growing for thousands of years.

The earliest writing

In early times, people could communicate with one another only by speaking or by making gestures. They had no way to keep records of important events, unless they memorized the story of a great battle or important happening. They had no way to send messages over long distances unless they passed them from one person to the next by word of mouth, or had one person memorize the message and then deliver it.

The first stage in writing came when people learned to draw pictures to express their ideas. In *ideography,* each picture conveyed an idea. Ideography enabled even people who did not speak the same language to communicate with each other. Then people learned *logography,* expressing ideas indirectly by using signs to stand for the words of the idea. Instead of drawing pictures of five sheep to show a herd of five animals, a person could draw one sign for the numeral "five" and one for "sheep." Gradually people learned to use a *syllabic* system, in which a sign that stood for one word could be used not only for that word but also for any phonetic combination that sounded like that word. This is what we call *rebus writing.* If we used rebus writing in English, we could draw a sign for the word "bee" followed by a sign for the word "leaf" to stand for the word "belief." Finally, people developed alphabets in which indi-

Development of the English alphabet The English alphabet developed from a number of early writing systems, beginning with the sign writing of Ancient Egypt. The Romans had given most capital letters their modern form by A.D. 114. But the letters *J, U,* and *W* were not added to the alphabet until the Middle Ages.

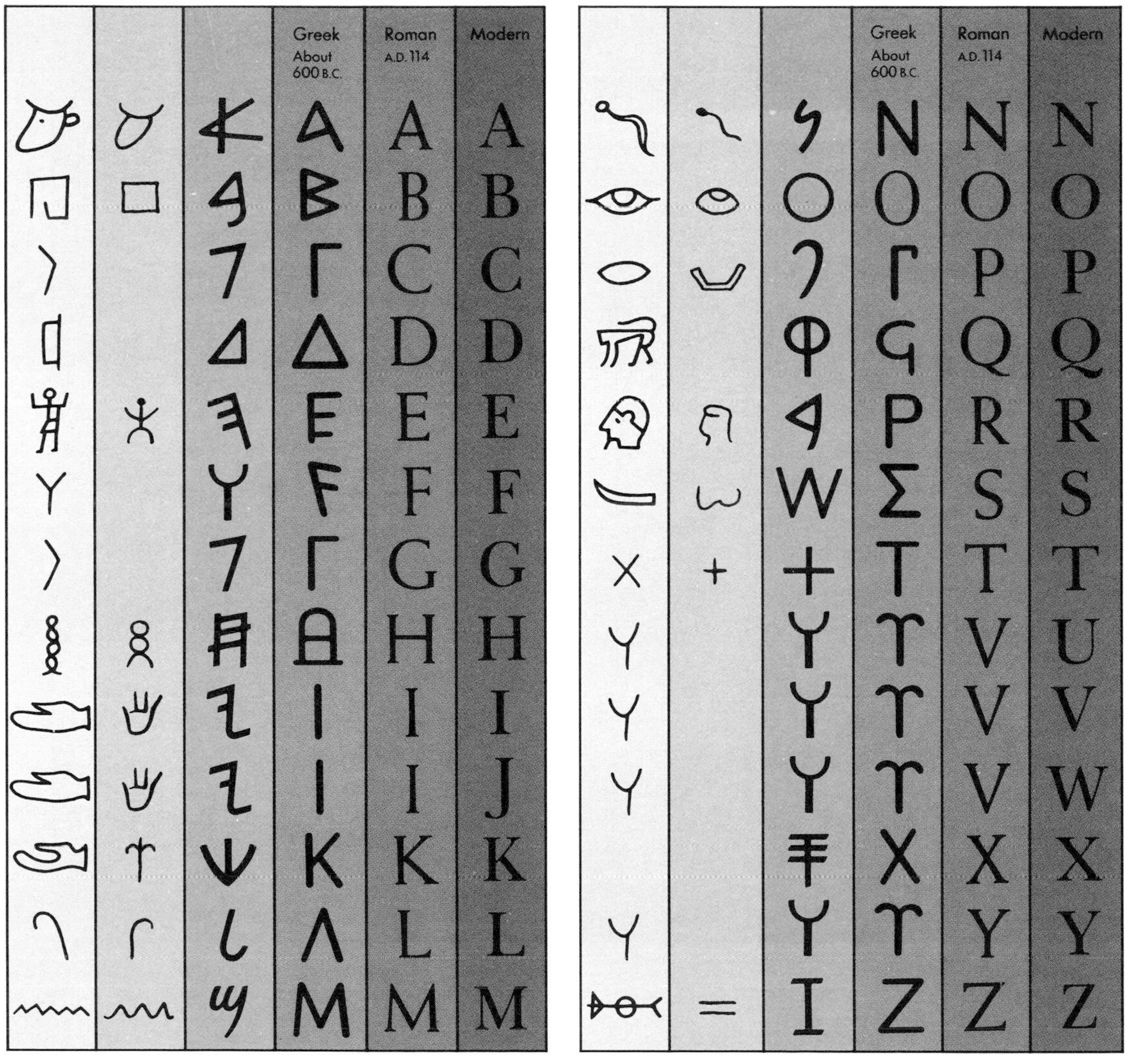
Greek About 600 B.C.
Roman A.D. 114
Modern
Greek About 600 B.C.
Roman A.D. 114
Modern

Some important alphabets The alphabets of five important languages are shown below. Hindi is India's most widely spoken language. People throughout the Middle East and northern Africa use Arabic, which is read from right to left. Gaelic, along with English, is the official language of Ireland.

Greek	Α Β Γ Δ Ε Ζ Η Θ Ι Κ Λ Μ Ν Ξ Ο Π Ρ Σ Τ Υ Φ Χ Ψ Ω
Russian	АБВГДЕЁЖЗИЙКЛМНОПРСТУФХЦЧШЩЪЫЬЭЮЯ
Hindi	अ आ इ ई उ ऊ ऋ ए ऐ ओ औ क ख ग घ ङ च छ ज झ ञ ट ठ ड ढ ण त थ द ध न प फ ब भ म य र ल व श ष स ह
Arabic	ا ب ت ث ج ح خ د ذ ر ز س ش ص ض ط ظ ع غ ف ق ك ل م ن ه و ي
Gaelic	a b c d e f g h i l m n o p r s t u

vidual signs stood for particular sounds. Today, most written languages in the world use alphabetic writing systems.

The earliest alphabets

The Egyptians used a system of several hundred signs that stood for full words or for syllables. They could write the word *nefer,* or *good,* with a single sign for the whole word, or with three signs, for the sounds *n, f,* and *r.* These signs specified the consonants in syllables, but not the vowels. Egyptian writing, which developed around 3000 B.C., was formally a picture writing, and structurally a word and syllabic writing.

The Semites, who lived in Syria and Palestine, knew something of the Egyptian writing system. They worked out an alphabetic writing about 1500 B.C. They used signs to show the consonants of syllables, just as the Egyptians did. The Semites seem to have adapted some of the pictures from Egyptian hieroglyphics, but they used these symbols for sounds in their own language. The oldest Semitic alphabet comes from the Sinai Peninsula.

The Phoenicians, who lived along the coast of the Mediterranean Sea, developed a system of 22 signs about 1000 B.C. Their alphabet was structurally related to Semitic and Egyptian, with signs for consonant sounds, not vowel sounds. Early Phoenician writing consists partly of pictographic forms, which they may have borrowed from older pictographic systems, and partly of geometric or diagrammatic signs that they invented. Historians find it difficult to trace the formal relations between Semitic and Phoenician signs, because Phoenician has both pictographic and diagrammatic signs, and because so little is known of the ancient systems used in Syria and Palestine.

The Cypriots, the people of the island of Cyprus, developed an alphabet of their own. Starting with an unknown word-syllable system, they worked out an alphabet of 56 signs, each standing for an initial consonant and a different vowel. The next step was to create separate signs for vowels and consonants.

The Greeks came in contact with Phoenician traders, and learned from them the idea of writing individual sounds of the language. Sometime during the period before 800 B.C., they borrowed Phoenician symbols and modified them to form the Greek alphabet. The Phoenician alphabet included more consonants than the Greeks needed for their language, so they used the extra signs for vowel sounds. In this way, the Greeks improved on both Phoenician and Cypriot ideas, because they could combine individual letters for both consonants and vowels to spell any word they wanted.

The Greeks took over the Phoenician names for their signs, and in most cases the signs themselves. The first letter of the Phoenician alphabet, , and its name, *aleph,* meaning *ox,* became , or *alpha* in Greek. The second letter, , or *beth,* meaning *house,* became , or *beta* in Greek. The Greeks later modified the shapes of these letters, adding and dropping some letters, to form the 24-letter Greek alphabet of today.

The Roman alphabet

The Etruscans moved to central Italy from somewhere in the eastern Mediterranean region sometime after 1000 B.C. They carried the Greek alphabet with them. The Romans learned the alphabet from the Etruscans, and gave it much the same form we use today. The early Roman alphabet had about 20 letters, and gradually gained 3 more.

Capital letters were the only forms used for hundreds of years. Many people consider the Roman alphabet to have been perfected by A.D. 114. That year, sculptors carved the inscriptions on a memorial column built to honor the emperor Trajan. The style of lettering they used is considered one of the most beautiful in the world.

Carving letters in stone is not an easy job, and Roman stonecutters rounded or squared, simplified, and polished their letters. They developed the beautiful thick-and-thin strokes we use today. They also added *serifs* (little finishing strokes) at the tops and bottoms of many letters. The practical reason for serifs was that the carvers found it difficult to end wide strokes without ugly blunt lines. And if a chisel slipped while squaring off an end, they could not erase the mistake. But serifs also added a touch of strength and grace to Roman lettering, and are still used today.

Small letters gradually developed from capitals. Scribes who copied books often used *uncials* (rounded letters) that were easier to form than some capitals. True lower-case letters developed later, when scribes saved space in books by using the smaller letters.

Architecture

Architectural terms

Ambulatory is a continuous aisle in a circular building. In a church, the ambulatory serves as a semicircular aisle that encloses the apse.

Apse is a semicircular area. In most churches, the apse is at one end of the building and contains the main altar.

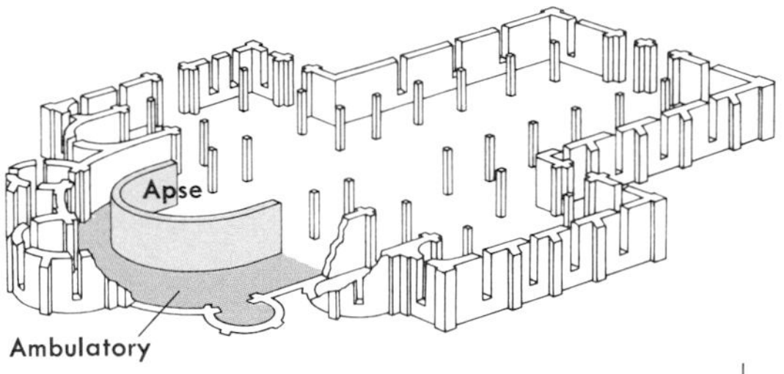
Apse
Ambulatory

Arcade refers to a series of arches supported by columns or piers. A passageway formed by the arches is also called an arcade.

Arch is a curved structure used to support the weight of the material above it. A stone at the top of an arch, called the *keystone,* holds the other parts in place.

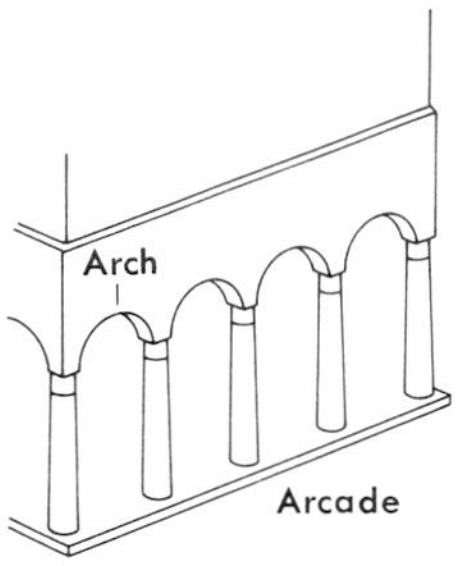
Arch
Arcade

Architrave makes up the lowest part of an entablature. It rests on the capital of a column. For a drawing of an architrave, see Entablature on the opposite page.

Buttress is a support built against an outside wall of a building. A *flying buttress* is an arched support that extends from a column or pier to the wall.

Buttress

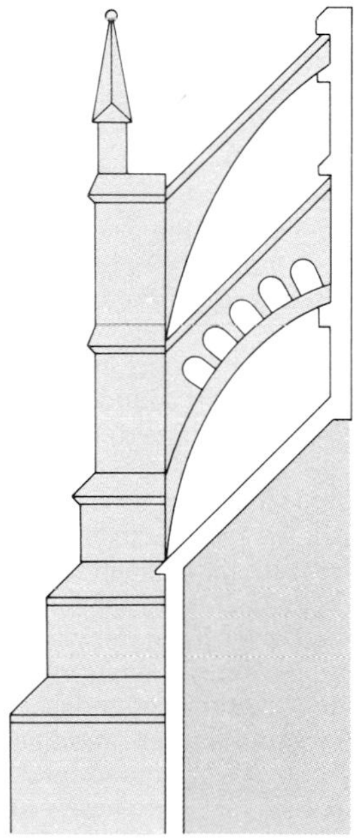

Flying Buttress

Cantilever is a horizontal projection, such as a balcony or a beam, which is supported only at one end.

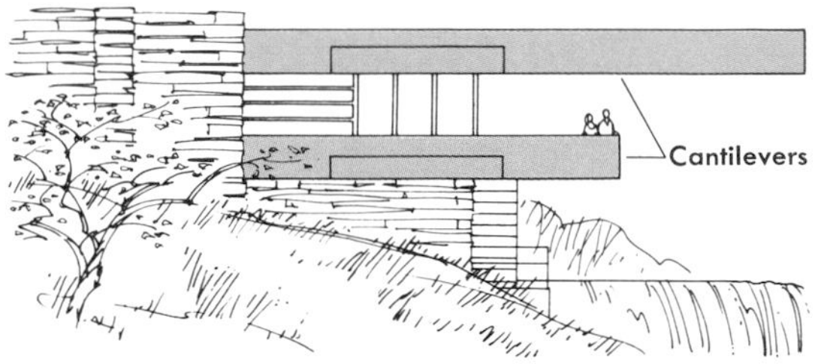
Cantilevers

Capital, in an order, forms the upper part of a column. It separates the shaft from the entablature.

Doric Ionic Corinthian

Colonnade means a row of columns, each set an equal distance apart.

Column is a vertical support. In an order, it consists of a shaft and a capital and often rests on a base.

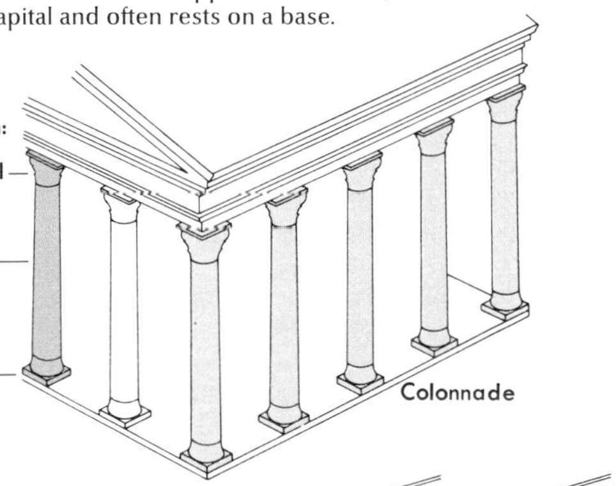
Column:
Capital
Shaft
Base
Colonnade

Composite order is a Roman order. It resembles the Corinthian order but has a capital that combines the Corinthian acanthus leaf decoration with volutes from the Ionic order.

Corinthian order became the last of the three Greek orders. It resembles the Ionic order but has an elaborate capital that is decorated with carvings of leaves of the acanthus plant.

Composite Order Corinthian Order

Cornice forms the upper part of an entablature and extends beyond the frieze.

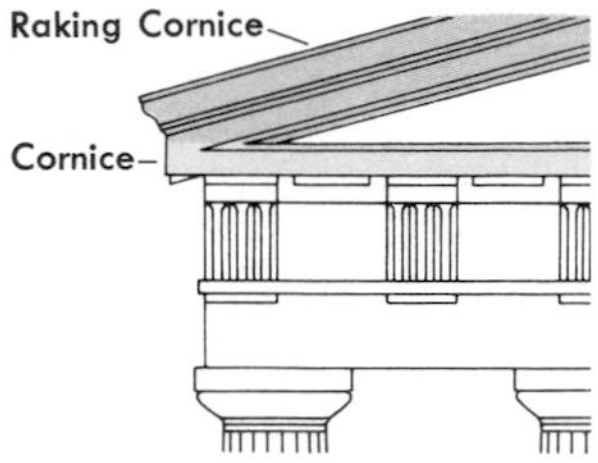
Raking Cornice
Cornice

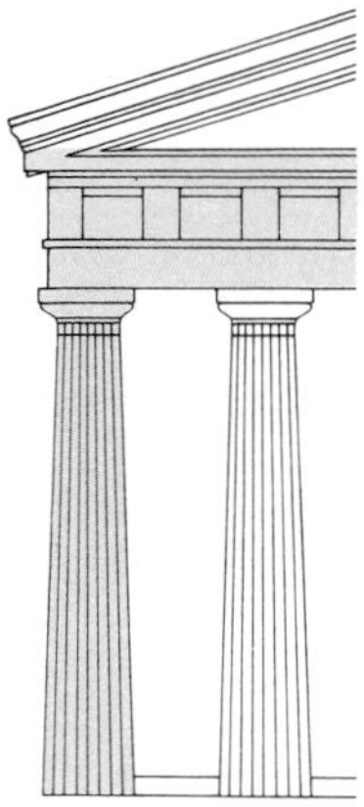

Doric Order

Doric order was the first and simplest of the three Greek orders. The Doric is the only order that normally has no base.

Entablature refers to the upper horizontal part of an order between a capital and the roof. It consists of three major parts—the architrave, frieze, and cornice.

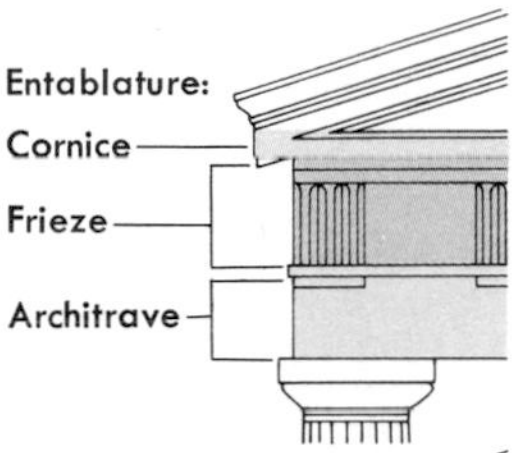
Entablature:
Cornice
Frieze
Architrave

Facade is the front of a building. Most facades contain an entrance.

Frieze forms the middle part of an entablature and is often decorated with a horizontal band of relief sculpture.

Ionic order was the second of the three Greek orders. It has a capital decorated with carved spiral scrolls called *volutes.*

Ionic Order

Module is a measurement, such as the diameter of a column, which architects use to establish the proportions of an entire structure.

Nave is the chief area within a church. It extends from the main entrance to the transept.

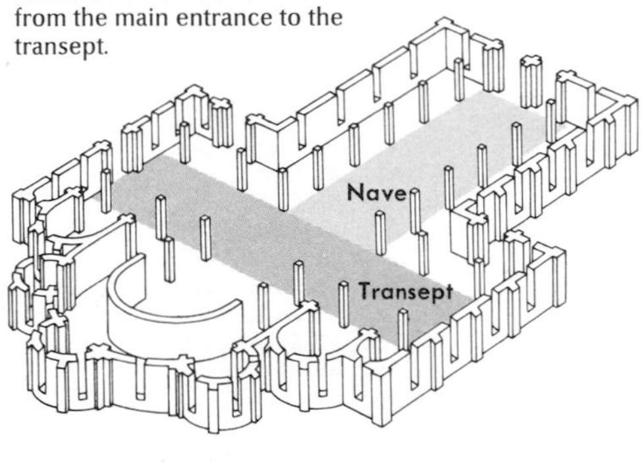
Nave
Transept

Order, in classical architecture, consisted of a column and an entablature. Orders served as the basic elements of Greek and Roman architecture and influenced many later styles.

Pediment is a triangular segment between the horizontal entablature and the sloping roof at the front of a classical-style building.

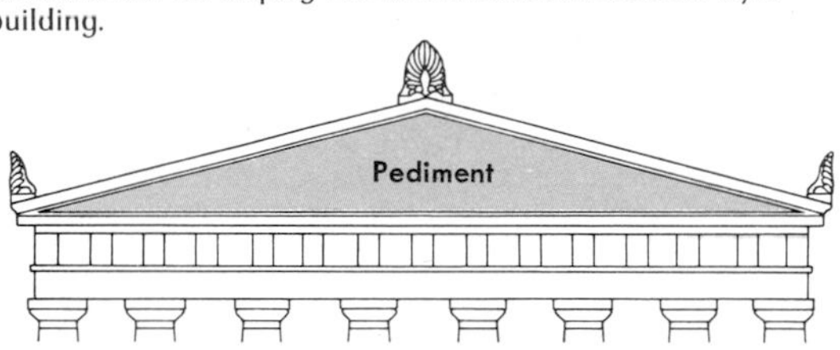
Pediment

Pendentive is a curved support shaped like an inverted triangle. Pendentives hold up a dome.

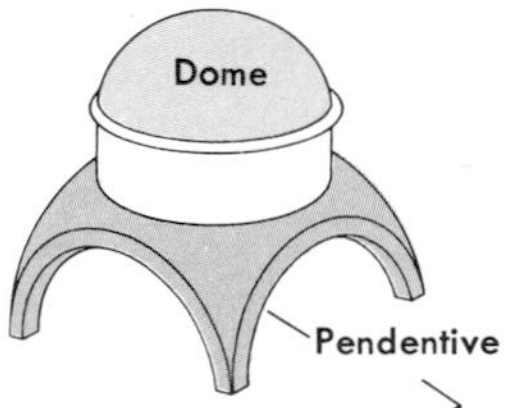
Dome
Pendentive

Pier refers to a large pillar used to support a roof.

Post and lintel is a method of construction in which vertical beams (posts) support a horizontal beam (lintel).

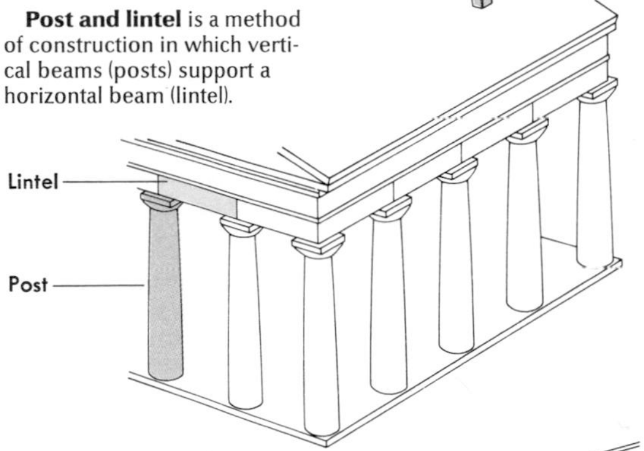
Lintel
Post

Shaft is the main part of a column below the capital. Many shafts have shallow vertical grooves called *fluting.*

Transept forms the arms in a T- or cross-shaped church.

Tuscan order, a Roman order, resembles the Doric order, but the shaft has no fluting.

Tuscan Order

Vault is an arched brick or stone ceiling or roof. A *barrel vault,* the simplest form of vault, is a single continuous arch. A *groined vault* is formed by joining two barrel vaults at right angles. A *ribbed vault* has diagonal arches that project from the surface.

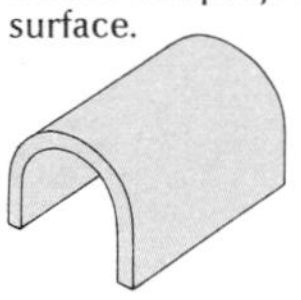

Barrel Vault

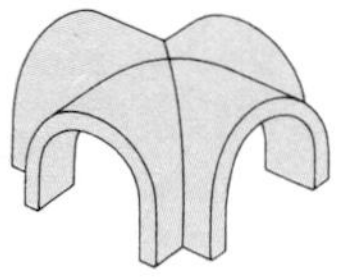

Groined Vault

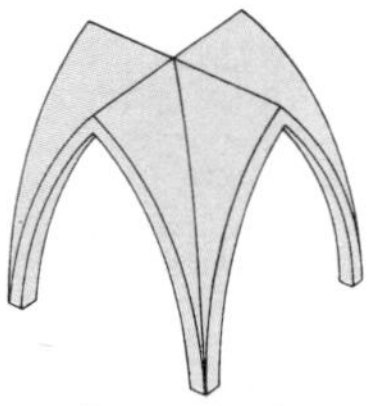

Ribbed Vault

WORLD BOOK illustrations by Robert Keys

Comparing the sizes of cities

A city determines its population by counting the people who live within its political boundaries. But cities of the world define their city limits differently, making population comparisons difficult. United States cities fix their limits so that they do not overlap or include other cities and towns. Some foreign cities include other urban and rural areas.

Countries also determine metropolitan areas in various ways. In the United States, metropolitan area boundaries follow county lines. Each metropolitan area includes a county with a large city and perhaps nearby counties. But in most countries, a metropolitan area does not have definite political boundaries. In these countries, metropolitan areas include the major city and urban and rural areas that are socially or economically identified with the city.

Mexico City has the largest population of any city in the world. Mexico City also has the largest metropolitan area population in the world.

Some governments do not report separate city and metropolitan area populations in their censuses and population estimates. In such cases, the same city proper figure appears in both the cities and the metropolitan areas tables, *below,* to show the existence of a metropolitan area.

50 largest cities in the world

1.	**Mexico City**	10,061,000	27.	**Ho Chi Minh City**	3,419,978
2.	**Seoul**	9,645,932	28.	**Wuhan**	3,340,000
3.	**Tokyo**	8,353,674	29.	**Calcutta**	3,305,006
4.	**Moscow**	8,275,000	30.	**Madras**	3,276,622
5.	**Bombay**	8,227,332	31.	**Guangzhou**	3,220,000
6.	**New York City**	7,071,639	32.	**Madrid**	3,123,713
7.	**São Paulo**	7,033,529	33.	**Berlin (East and West)**	3,062,979
8.	**Shanghai**	6,880,000	34.	**Chicago**	3,005,072
9.	**London**	6,767,500	35.	**Yokohama**	2,992,644
10.	**Jakarta**	6,503,449	36.	**Sydney**	2,989,070
11.	**Cairo**	6,052,836	37.	**Baghdad**	2,969,000
12.	**Beijing**	5,760,000	38.	**Los Angeles**	2,968,579
13.	**Teheran**	5,734,199	39.	**Lahore**	2,952,689
14.	**Hong Kong**	5,705,000	40.	**Alexandria**	2,917,327
15.	**Istanbul**	5,475,982	41.	**Buenos Aires**	2,908,001
16.	**Tianjin**	5,300,000	42.	**Rome**	2,830,569
17.	**Karachi**	5,208,170	43.	**Chongqing**	2,730,000
18.	**Bangkok**	5,153,902	44.	**Melbourne**	2,645,484
19.	**Rio de Janeiro**	5,093,232	45.	**Pyongyang**	2,639,448
20.	**Delhi**	4,884,234	46.	**Osaka**	2,636,260
21.	**Leningrad**	4,295,000	47.	**Harbin**	2,590,000
22.	**Santiago**	4,225,299	48.	**Hanoi**	2,570,905
23.	**Lima**	4,164,597	49.	**Chengdu**	2,540,000
24.	**Shenyang**	4,130,000	50.	**Bangalore**	2,476,355
25.	**Bogotá**	3,982,941			
26.	**Pusan**	3,516,807			

50 largest metropolitan areas in the world

1.	**Mexico City**	15,505,000	26.	**Bangkok**	5,153,902
2.	**São Paulo**	12,588,439	27.	**Leningrad**	4,827,000
3.	**Shanghai**	12,050,000	28.	**Philadelphia**	4,716,818
4.	**Tokyo**	11,618,281	29.	**Lima**	4,608,010
5.	**Cairo**	10,000,000	30.	**Detroit**	4,488,072
6.	**Buenos Aires**	9,927,404	31.	**Madras**	4,289,347
7.	**Seoul**	9,645,932	32.	**Santiago**	4,225,299
8.	**Beijing**	9,470,000	33.	**Shenyang**	4,130,000
9.	**Calcutta**	9,194,018	34.	**Bogotá**	3,982,941
10.	**Rio de Janeiro**	9,018,637	35.	**Pusan**	3,516,807
11.	**Paris**	8,706,963	36.	**Toronto**	3,427,168
12.	**Moscow**	8,537,000	37.	**Ho Chi Minh City**	3,419,978
13.	**New York City**	8,274,961	38.	**Wuhan**	3,340,000
14.	**Bombay**	8,227,332	39.	**Caracas**	3,310,236
15.	**Tianjin**	7,990,000	40.	**Washington, D.C.**	3,250,822
16.	**Los Angeles-Long Beach**	7,447,503	41.	**Guangzhou**	3,220,000
17.	**London**	6,767,500	42.	**Madrid**	3,123,713
18.	**Jakarta**	6,503,449	43.	**Berlin (East and West)**	3,062,979
19.	**Chicago**	6,060,387	44.	**Athens**	3,027,331
20.	**Manila**	5,926,000	45.	**Yokohama**	2,992,644
21.	**Teheran**	5,734,199	46.	**Sydney**	2,989,070
22.	**Delhi**	5,729,283	47.	**Baghdad**	2,969,000
23.	**Hong Kong**	5,705,000	48.	**Lahore**	2,952,689
24.	**Istanbul**	5,475,982	49.	**Bangalore**	2,921,751
25.	**Karachi**	5,208,170	50.	**Montreal**	2,921,357

50 largest cities in the United States

1.	**New York City**	7,071,639	26.	**St. Louis**	452,801
2.	**Chicago**	3,005,072	27.	**Kansas City, Mo.**	448,033
3.	**Los Angeles**	2,968,579	28.	**El Paso**	425,259
4.	**Philadelphia**	1,688,210	29.	**Atlanta**	425,022
5.	**Houston**	1,595,138	30.	**Pittsburgh**	423,959
6.	**Detroit**	1,203,399	31.	**Oklahoma City**	403,484
7.	**Dallas**	904,078	32.	**Cincinnati**	385,457
8.	**San Diego**	875,538	33.	**Fort Worth**	385,164
9.	**Phoenix**	789,704	34.	**Minneapolis**	370,951
10.	**Baltimore**	786,741	35.	**Portland, Ore.**	366,383
11.	**San Antonio**	786,023	36.	**Honolulu**	365,048
12.	**Indianapolis**	700,807	37.	**Long Beach**	361,355
13.	**San Francisco**	678,974	38.	**Tulsa**	360,919
14.	**Memphis**	646,174	39.	**Buffalo**	357,870
15.	**Washington, D.C.**	638,432	40.	**Toledo**	354,635
16.	**Milwaukee**	636,297	41.	**Miami**	346,865
17.	**San Jose**	629,531	42.	**Austin**	345,890
18.	**Cleveland**	573,822	43.	**Oakland**	339,337
19.	**Columbus, O.**	565,032	44.	**Albuquerque**	332,239
20.	**Boston**	562,994	45.	**Tucson**	330,537
21.	**New Orleans**	557,927	46.	**Newark**	329,248
22.	**Jacksonville, Fla.**	540,920	47.	**Omaha**	327,558
23.	**Seattle**	493,846	48.	**Charlotte**	314,447
24.	**Denver**	492,365	49.	**Louisville**	298,694
25.	**Nashville**	455,651	50.	**Birmingham**	284,413

50 largest cities and towns in Canada

1.	**Montreal**	1,015,420	28.	**Markham**	114,597
2.	**Calgary**	636,104	29.	**Halifax**	113,577
3.	**Toronto**	612,289	30.	**Thunder Bay**	112,272
4.	**Winnipeg**	594,551	31.	**Richmond**	108,492
5.	**Edmonton**	573,982	32.	**St. John's**	96,216
6.	**North York**	556,297	33.	**Nepean**	95,490
7.	**Scarborough**	484,676	34.	**Montréal-Nord**	90,303
8.	**Vancouver**	431,147	35.	**Glouster**	89,810
9.	**Mississauga**	374,005	36.	**Sudbury**	88,717
10.	**Hamilton**	306,728	37.	**Saanich**	82,940
11.	**Etobicoke**	302,973	38.	**Gatineau**	81,244
12.	**Ottawa**	300,763	39.	**Sault Ste. Marie**	80,905
13.	**Laval**	284,164	40.	**Cambridge**	79,920
14.	**London**	269,140	41.	**Delta**	79,610
15.	**Windsor**	193,111	42.	**Guelph**	78,235
16.	**Brampton**	188,498	43.	**Saint John**	76,381
17.	**Surrey**	181,447	44.	**Brantford**	76,146
18.	**Saskatoon**	177,641	45.	**St.-Léonard**	75,947
19.	**Regina**	175,062	46.	**La Salle**	75,621
20.	**Quebec**	164,580	47.	**Sherbrooke**	74,438
21.	**Kitchener**	150,604	48.	**Niagara Falls**	72,107
22.	**Burnaby**	145,161	49.	**Ste.-Foy**	69,615
23.	**York**	135,401	50.	**Coquitlam**	69,291
24.	**Longueuil**	125,441			
25.	**Oshawa**	123,651			
26.	**St. Catherines**	123,455			
27.	**Burlington**	116,675			

Sources: 1980 census for the United States cities; 1986 census for Canadian cities; 1976-1990 censuses and estimates for other cities.

Highlights in the history of communication

- **About 20,000 B.C.** — Prehistoric people used paintings and drawings to tell stories.
- **About 3500 B.C.** — The Sumerians developed the first known system of writing.
- **About 1500-1000 B.C.** — The Semites developed the first real alphabet.
- **59 B.C.** — The Romans began a handwritten newssheet that was a forerunner of today's newspapers.

WORLD BOOK illustration by Richard Hook

Smoke signals were one of the earliest forms of long-distance communication. Such signals could send only limited information—a warning, for example.

Deutsches Museum, Munich, West Germany

Cuneiform writing consists of wedge-shaped characters stamped on clay. The clay cylinder above was inscribed during the 500's B.C. in Babylon.

Deutsches Museum, Munich, West Germany

Wax tablets were once a common writing surface. The early Greeks wrote on such tablets with a pointed tool called a *stylus* and laced the tablets together.

- **About A.D. 105** — T'sai Lun, a Chinese government official, invented paper.
- **About 1045** — Pi Sheng, a Chinese printer, invented movable type.
- **Mid-1400's** — The German metalsmith Johannes Gutenberg reinvented movable type.
- **Mid-1500's** — The English made the first pencils of *graphite,* the substance used today.
- **1600's** — Printed newssheets called *corantos* appeared.

Detail of an Italian manuscript (about 1331) by Giovanni de' Nuxiglia; Bibliothèque Nationale, Paris (SCALA/EPA)

During the Middle Ages, artists copied books by hand, letter by letter. They covered their work with gold, silver, and colored decorations called *illumination.*

Bettmann Archive

Printing from movable type was invented in Asia during the 1000's and in Europe during the 1400's. A shop of the 1600's is shown above. At the left, typesetters assemble type to form pages. In the background, an assistant inks a page. At the right, a printer turns a huge screw on the printing press to push paper against the type.

Communication

- Late 1700's — The French engineer Claude Chappe developed a visual telegraph.
- 1811 — Friedrich Koenig, a German printer, invented a steam-powered printing press.
- 1826 — Joseph Nicéphore Niépce, a French physicist, made the first permanent photograph.
- 1830's — The French painter Louis J. M. Daguerre developed an improved photograph.

American Antiquarian Society, Worcester, Mass.

Postal service was established in many nations during the 1700's. This postrider carried mail between Boston and other cities in the American Colonies.

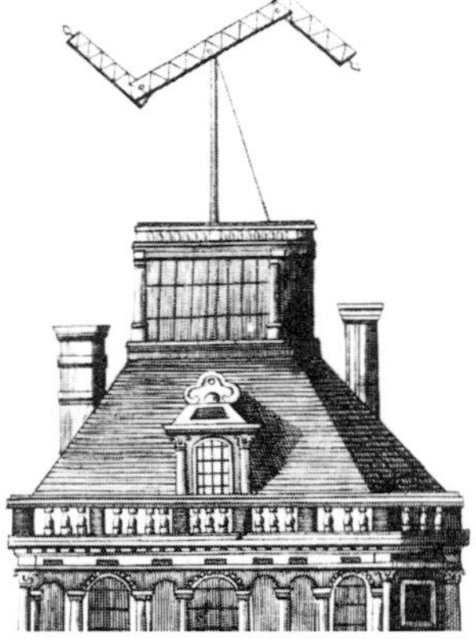

Deutsches Museum, Munich, West Germany

The Chappe telegraph consisted of a series of towers. An operator in each tower moved a crossbar and two large, jointed arms to send coded messages.

Detail of *Intérieur d'un Cabinet de Curiosités;* Société Française de Photographie, Paris

A daguerreotype was an early type of photograph printed on a metal plate. Louis J. M. Daguerre took this picture of a collection of rare objects in 1837.

- 1877 — Thomas A. Edison developed the first practical phonograph.
- 1880's — The German physicist Heinrich Hertz discovered electromagnetic waves.
- 1884 — Ottmar Mergenthaler, a German-born mechanic, patented the Linotype machine.
- 1895 — The Italian inventor Guglielmo Marconi developed the *wireless telegraph* (radio).

Bettmann Archive

Thomas A. Edison's phonograph recorded sound on a cylinder covered with foil. This picture shows the inventor with an early version of his phonograph.

Historical Pictures Service

Linotype machines used a keyboard to set type mechanically. Their introduction sped the production of newspapers and other publications.

The Marconi Company

Guglielmo Marconi combined the ideas of several scientists to send signals through the air. His invention, the *wireless telegraph,* led to present-day radio.

1840 — The American painter Samuel F. B. Morse patented his electric telegraph.

1864 — The British physicist James Clerk Maxwell reported his theory of electromagnetism, which led to radio.

1866 — The first successful transatlantic telegraph cable linked Europe and North America.

1868 — Three American inventors patented the first practical typewriter.

1876 — Alexander Graham Bell patented a type of telephone.

Bettmann Archive

Samuel F. B. Morse developed one of the first successful electric telegraphs. He also developed Morse code, a system of sending messages by dots and dashes.

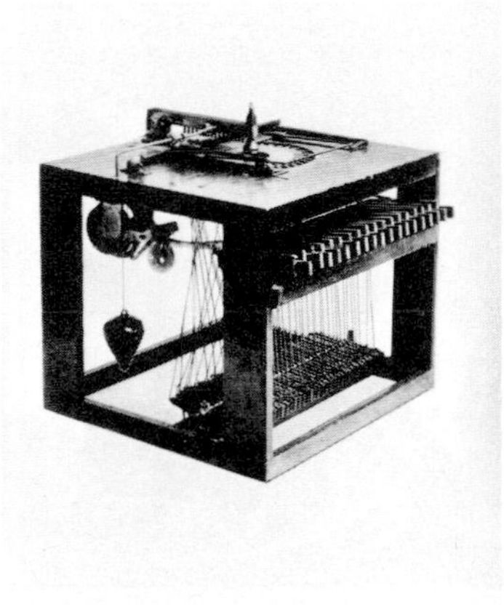

Bettmann Archive

An early typewriter was patented in the 1860's by three American inventors—Carlos Glidden, Christopher Latham Sholes, and Samuel W. Soulé.

Bettmann Archive

Alexander Graham Bell designed one of the first successful telephones and demonstrated it at the 1876 Centennial Exposition in Philadelphia.

1906 — Reginald A. Fessenden, a Canadian-born physicist, transmitted voice by radio.

1907 — The American inventor Lee De Forest patented the *triode,* an improved vacuum tube.

1929 — Vladimir K. Zworykin, a Russian-born physicist, demonstrated the first all-electronic TV system.

1936 — The British Broadcasting Corporation made the world's first TV broadcasts.

Bettmann Archive

A motion picture camera of about 1915 was used to film silent movies. Several inventors developed movie cameras in the late 1800's and early 1900's.

Bettmann Archive

Radio became a major source of family entertainment during the 1920's. This photograph shows a singer making a broadcast during the early days of radio.

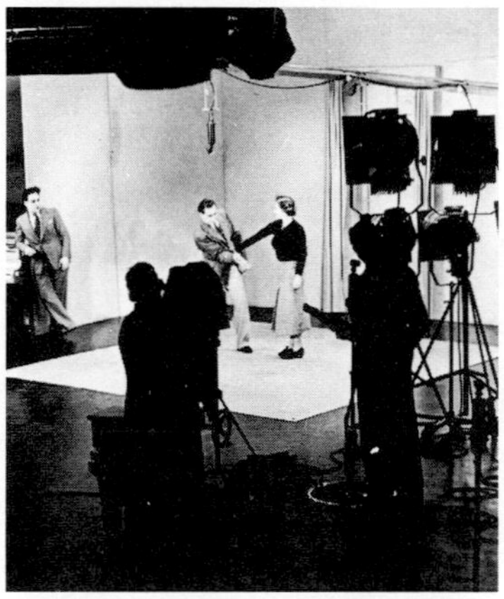

British Broadcasting Corporation

One of the first TV broadcasts was a demonstration of self-defense techniques. It appeared in 1936 on the British Broadcasting Corporation (BBC).

Communication

1947 — Bell Telephone Laboratories developed the transistor.

1947 — Dennis Gabor, a British engineer, invented *holography* (3-D photography).

Mid-1950's — Television networks began to record programs on videotape.

1960 — Xerox Corporation perfected *xerography,* a copying process.

1960 — *Echo 1* became the first satellite to receive radio signals from a ground station and reflect them back to earth.

Ampex Corporation

Tape recorders that recorded sounds on magnetic tape were developed in the 1930's. This 1948 recorder was the first one manufactured in the United States.

American Telephone & Telegraph Co.

Telstar I, a communications satellite launched in 1962, relayed telephone calls, TV shows, and other communications between the United States and Europe.

WORLD BOOK photo

Computers revolutionized communication in the 1960's and 1970's. A computer terminal at an airport, *above,* relays information about flights and reservations.

1970 — Corning Glass Works produced the first optical fiber suitable for long-range communication.

1970's — Several manufacturers developed cassette videotape recorders.

1974 — The first mailgram was transmitted by satellite.

Early 1980's — Several companies began marketing cellular mobile telephones.

WORLD BOOK photo

Fiber-optic communication uses a laser to send signals through glass strands called *optical fibers,* shown above.

WORLD BOOK photo

A home computer, *above,* helps a girl practice arithmetic problems. Small computers that perform a variety of jobs gained popularity in the late 1970's.

© Paul Robert Perry

A cellular mobile telephone enables a motorist to make and receive calls. These devices, introduced in the 1980's, greatly improved mobile phone communication.

Major developments in early centers of civilization

WORLD BOOK illustrations by Tak Murakami

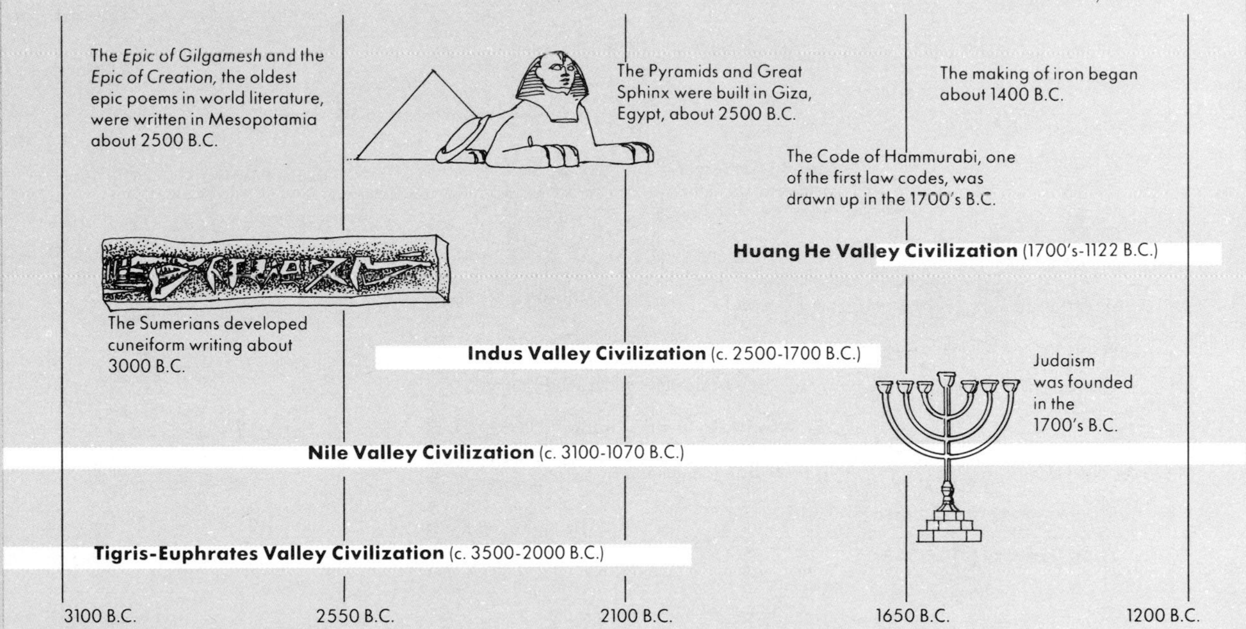

The *Epic of Gilgamesh* and the *Epic of Creation*, the oldest epic poems in world literature, were written in Mesopotamia about 2500 B.C.
The Pyramids and Great Sphinx were built in Giza, Egypt, about 2500 B.C.
The making of iron began about 1400 B.C.
The Code of Hammurabi, one of the first law codes, was drawn up in the 1700's B.C.
Huang He Valley Civilization (1700's-1122 B.C.)
The Sumerians developed cuneiform writing about 3000 B.C.
Indus Valley Civilization (c. 2500-1700 B.C.)
Judaism was founded in the 1700's B.C.
Nile Valley Civilization (c. 3100-1070 B.C.)
Tigris-Euphrates Valley Civilization (c. 3500-2000 B.C.)
3100 B.C.
2550 B.C.
2100 B.C.
1650 B.C.
1200 B.C.

The earliest civilizations arose in four river valleys in Asia and Africa between about 3500 B.C. and the 1700's B.C. The fertile soil of the valleys supported flourishing farming villages. Civilization began when such villages developed into cities.

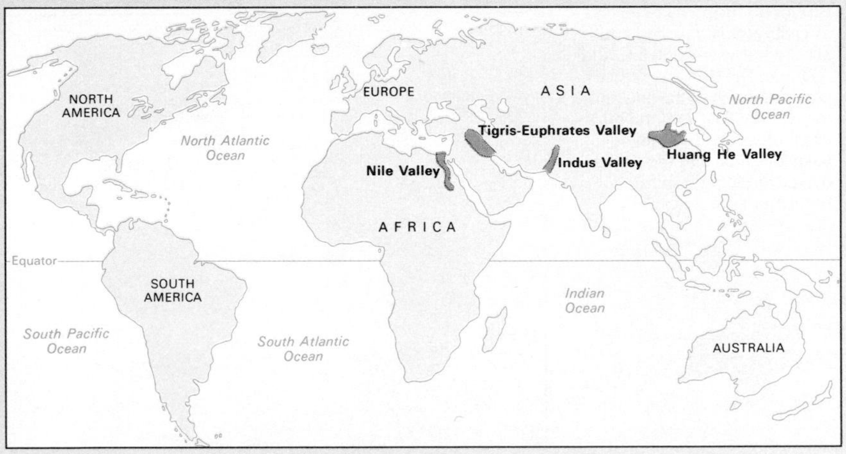

NORTH AMERICA
EUROPE
ASIA
North Pacific Ocean
North Atlantic Ocean
Tigris-Euphrates Valley
Indus Valley
Huang He Valley
Nile Valley
AFRICA
Equator
SOUTH AMERICA
Indian Ocean
South Pacific Ocean
South Atlantic Ocean
AUSTRALIA

WORLD BOOK map

Important dates

c. 9000 B.C. The development of agriculture began with the growing of crops and the domestication of animals in the Middle East.

c. 3500 B.C. A number of small cities, centers of the world's first civilization, appeared in Sumer, the lower part of the Tigris-Euphrates Valley.

c. 3500 B.C. The Sumerians invented the first form of writing. It was later simplified to produce wedge-shaped *cuneiform* writing, which spread throughout the Middle East.

c. 3100 B.C. King Menes of Upper Egypt united Lower and Upper Egypt.

c. 2500 B.C. The Indus Valley civilization began to flourish in the cities of Moen-jo-Daro and Harappa in what is now Pakistan.

c. 2500-1100 B.C. The Minoan civilization on the island of Crete rose and fell.

2300's B.C. Sargon of Akkad conquered the Sumerians and united all Mesopotamia under his rule, creating the world's first empire.

1700's B.C. The Shang dynasty began its rule in the Huang He Valley of China.

c. 1792-1750 B.C. Babylonia flourished under King Hammurabi.

1500's-c. 1100 B.C. The city of Mycenae was the leading political and cultural center on the Greek mainland.

c. 1595 B.C. The Hittites, a warlike people from what is now central Turkey, conquered the Babylonians.

c. 1500 B.C. The Aryans of central Asia began migrating to India.

Major developments from about 1200 B.C. to A.D. 500

WORLD BOOK illustrations by Tak Murakami

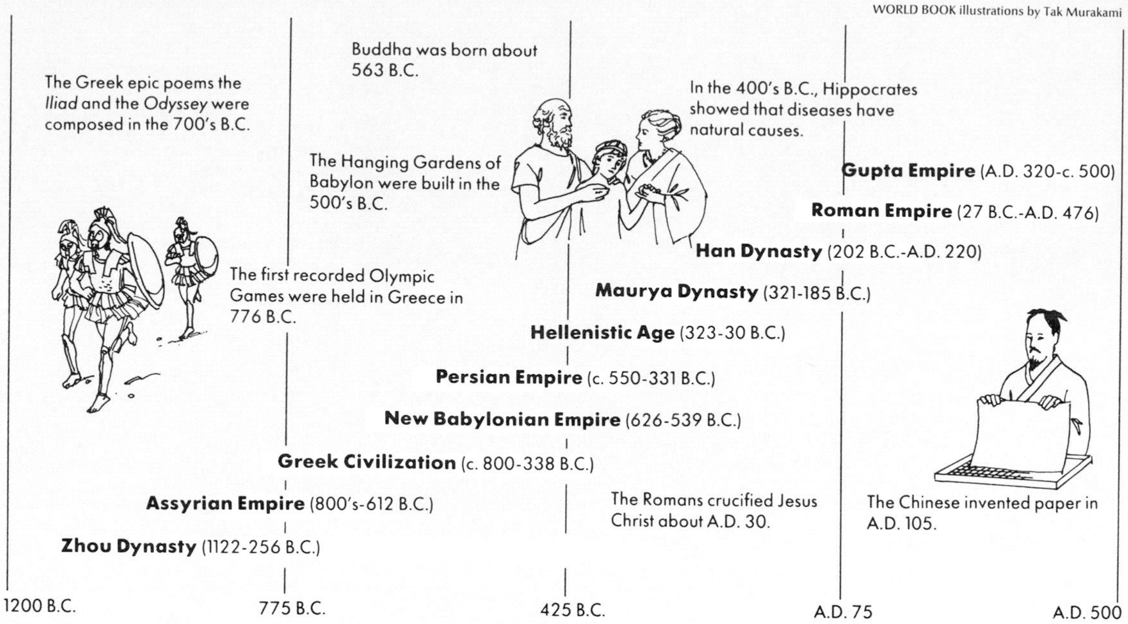
The Greek epic poems the *Iliad* and the *Odyssey* were composed in the 700's B.C.
Buddha was born about 563 B.C.
In the 400's B.C., Hippocrates showed that diseases have natural causes.
The Hanging Gardens of Babylon were built in the 500's B.C.
Gupta Empire (A.D. 320-c. 500)
Roman Empire (27 B.C.-A.D. 476)
Han Dynasty (202 B.C.-A.D. 220)
The first recorded Olympic Games were held in Greece in 776 B.C.
Maurya Dynasty (321-185 B.C.)
Hellenistic Age (323-30 B.C.)
Persian Empire (c. 550-331 B.C.)
New Babylonian Empire (626-539 B.C.)
Greek Civilization (c. 800-338 B.C.)
Assyrian Empire (800's-612 B.C.)
The Romans crucified Jesus Christ about A.D. 30.
The Chinese invented paper in A.D. 105.
Zhou Dynasty (1122-256 B.C.)
1200 B.C.
775 B.C.
425 B.C.
A.D. 75
A.D. 500

Powerful empires emerged as civilization advanced and spread between 1200 B.C. and A.D. 500. The Roman Empire covered much of Europe and the Middle East, and the north coast of Africa. The Han dynasty of China and the Gupta dynasty of India also ruled huge empires.

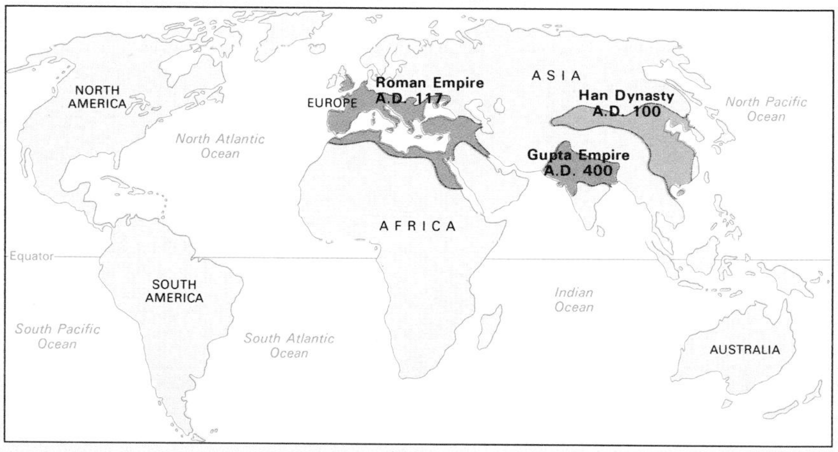
NORTH AMERICA
EUROPE
Roman Empire A.D. 117
ASIA
Han Dynasty A.D. 100
North Pacific Ocean
North Atlantic Ocean
Gupta Empire A.D. 400
AFRICA
Equator
SOUTH AMERICA
Indian Ocean
South Pacific Ocean
South Atlantic Ocean
AUSTRALIA

WORLD BOOK map

Important dates

1020 B.C. The Hebrews founded a kingdom in what is now Palestine.

800's B.C. The Etruscans settled in west-central Italy.

750-338 B.C. Athens, Corinth, Sparta, and Thebes were the chief city-states of Greece.

c. 550 B.C. Cyrus the Great established the Persian Empire.

509 B.C. The people of Rome revolted against their Etruscan rulers and established a republic.

338 B.C. Philip II of Macedonia conquered the Greeks.

331 B.C. Alexander the Great defeated the Persians at Arbela, opening the way to his conquest of northern India.

221-206 B.C. The Qin dynasty established China's first strong central government.

202 B.C. The Han dynasty began its 400-year rule of China.

146 B.C. The Romans conquered Greece.

55-54 B.C. Julius Caesar led the Roman invasion of Britain.

27 B.C. Augustus became the first Roman emperor.

c. A.D. 250 The Maya Indians developed an advanced civilization in Central America and Mexico.

313 Constantine issued the Edict of Milan, which granted freedom of worship to Christians of the Roman Empire.

320 India began its golden age under the Gupta dynasty.

395 The Roman Empire split into the East Roman, or Byzantine, Empire and the West Roman Empire.

476 The Germanic chieftain Odoacer overthrew Romulus Augustulus, the last emperor of the West Roman Empire.

World, History of the

Major developments from A.D. 500 to about 1500

WORLD BOOK illustrations by Tak Murakami

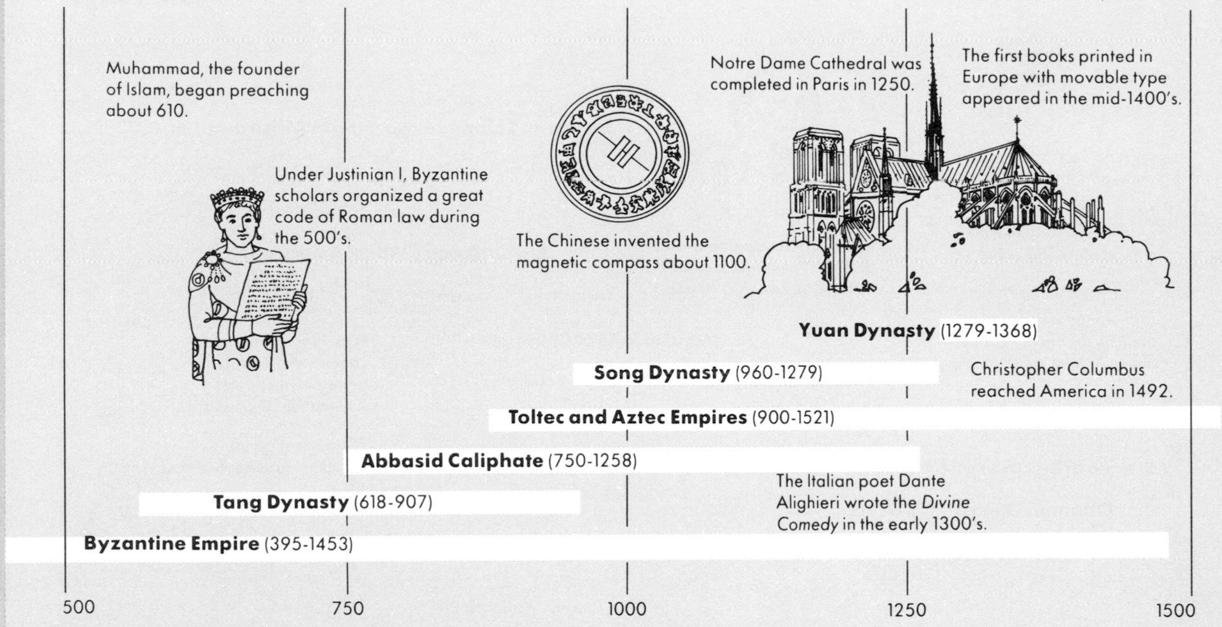
Muhammad, the founder of Islam, began preaching about 610.
Under Justinian I, Byzantine scholars organized a great code of Roman law during the 500's.
The Chinese invented the magnetic compass about 1100.
Notre Dame Cathedral was completed in Paris in 1250.
The first books printed in Europe with movable type appeared in the mid-1400's.
Yuan Dynasty (1279-1368)
Song Dynasty (960-1279)
Christopher Columbus reached America in 1492.
Toltec and Aztec Empires (900-1521)
Abbasid Caliphate (750-1258)
The Italian poet Dante Alighieri wrote the Divine Comedy in the early 1300's.
Tang Dynasty (618-907)
Byzantine Empire (395-1453)
500
750
1000
1250
1500

Between 500 and 1500, new civilizations appeared in Africa and the Americas. In the Middle East, the Muslim Arabs rose to power and conquered a huge empire by the mid-700's. In the 1200's, Mongol warriors swept through Asia, creating one of the largest empires in history.

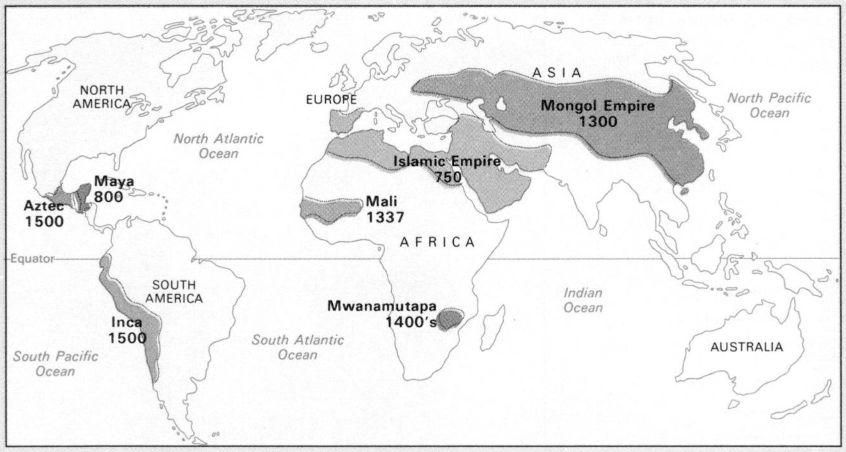
NORTH AMERICA
EUROPE
ASIA
Mongol Empire 1300
North Pacific Ocean
North Atlantic Ocean
Islamic Empire 750
Maya 800
Aztec 1500
Mali 1337
AFRICA
Equator
SOUTH AMERICA
Inca 1500
Mwanamutapa 1400's
Indian Ocean
South Atlantic Ocean
South Pacific Ocean
AUSTRALIA

WORLD BOOK map

Important dates

527-565 The Byzantine Empire reached its greatest extent under Emperor Justinian I.

622 Muhammad, founder of Islam, fled from Mecca to Medina. His flight, called the Hegira, marks the beginning of the Islamic calendar.

700's-mid-1000's The Ghana Empire, the first great black empire in western Africa, flourished as a trading state.

732 Charles Martel and the Franks defeated invading Muslims in fighting in west-central France. The victory prevented the Muslims from overrunning Europe.

750 The Abbasids became the caliphs of the Islamic world.

800 Pope Leo III crowned Charlemagne, ruler of the Franks, emperor of the Romans.

c. 988 Vladimir I converted the Russians to Christianity.

1054 Rivalries between the church in Rome and the church in Constantinople resulted in their separation as the Roman Catholic Church and Eastern Orthodox Churches, respectively.

1192 Yoritomo became the first shogun to rule Japan.

1215 English barons forced King John to grant a charter of liberties called Magna Carta.

1279 The Mongols gained control of all China.

1300's The Renaissance began in Italy.

1368 The Ming dynasty began its nearly 300-year rule of China.

1453 The Ottoman Turks captured Constantinople (Istanbul) and overthrew the Byzantine Empire.

Major developments from A.D. 1500 to about 1900

WORLD BOOK illustrations by Tak Murakami

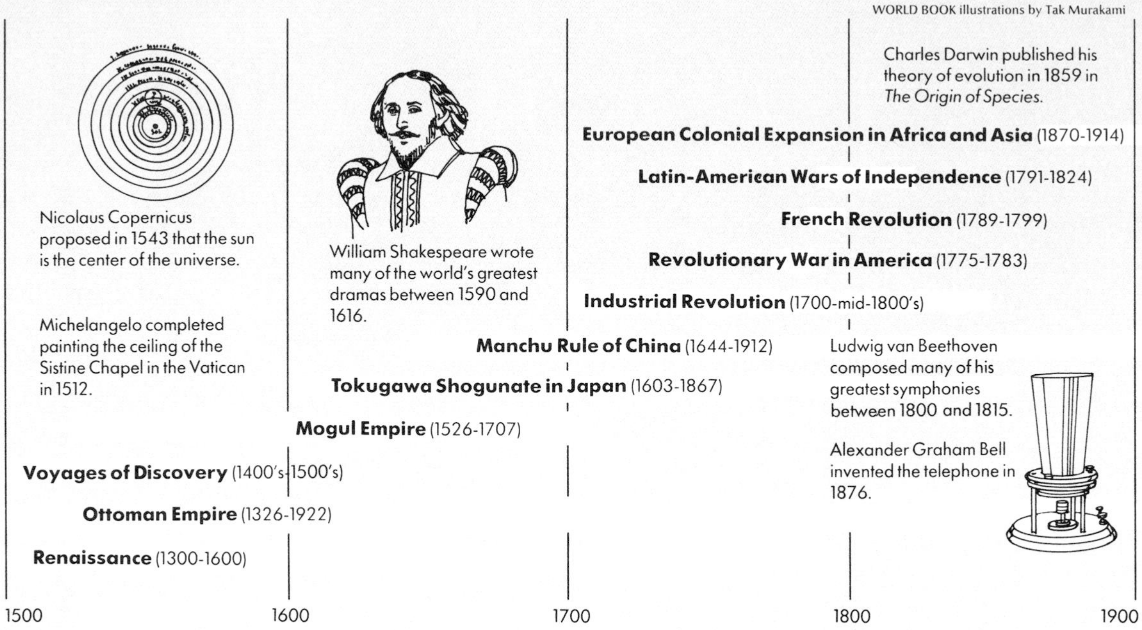
Charles Darwin published his theory of evolution in 1859 in *The Origin of Species*.
European Colonial Expansion in Africa and Asia (1870-1914)
Latin-American Wars of Independence (1791-1824)
French Revolution (1789-1799)
Revolutionary War in America (1775-1783)
Industrial Revolution (1700-mid-1800's)
Manchu Rule of China (1644-1912)
Tokugawa Shogunate in Japan (1603-1867)
Mogul Empire (1526-1707)
Voyages of Discovery (1400's-1500's)
Ottoman Empire (1326-1922)
Renaissance (1300-1600)
Nicolaus Copernicus proposed in 1543 that the sun is the center of the universe.
Michelangelo completed painting the ceiling of the Sistine Chapel in the Vatican in 1512.
William Shakespeare wrote many of the world's greatest dramas between 1590 and 1616.
Ludwig van Beethoven composed many of his greatest symphonies between 1800 and 1815.
Alexander Graham Bell invented the telephone in 1876.
1500
1600
1700
1800
1900

European colonial empires had spread over much of the world by the late 1800's. The largest empires of the period belonged to Great Britain, France, and Germany.

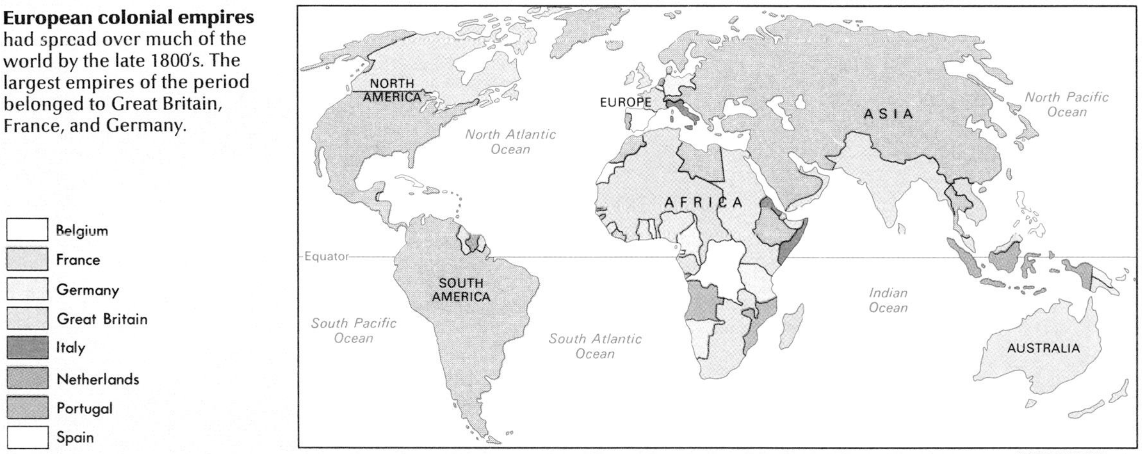
Belgium
France
Germany
Great Britain
Italy
Netherlands
Portugal
Spain
NORTH AMERICA
EUROPE
ASIA
AFRICA
SOUTH AMERICA
AUSTRALIA
North Atlantic Ocean
North Pacific Ocean
South Pacific Ocean
South Atlantic Ocean
Indian Ocean
Equator

WORLD BOOK map

Important dates

1500's The Reformation led to the birth of Protestantism.

1519-1521 Ferdinand Magellan commanded the first globe-circling voyage, completed in 1522 after his death.

1521 The Spanish conquistador Hernando Cortés defeated the Aztec Indians of Mexico.

1526 Babar, a Muslim prince, invaded India and founded the Mogul Empire.

1588 The Royal Navy of England defeated the Spanish Armada, establishing England as a great naval power.

1644-1912 The Manchus ruled China as the Qing dynasty.

1776 The 13 American Colonies adopted the Declaration of Independence, establishing the United States of America.

1789 The French Revolution began.

1815 Napoleon Bonaparte was defeated in the Battle of Waterloo, ending his attempt to rule Europe.

1853-1854 Commodore Matthew Perry visited Japan and opened two ports to U.S. trade, ending Japan's isolation.

1858 Great Britain took over the rule of India from the East India Company after the Sepoy Rebellion.

1865 Union forces defeated the Confederates in the American Civil War after four years of fighting.

1869 The Suez Canal opened.

1871 Germany became united under the Prussian king, who ruled the new empire as Kaiser Wilhelm I.

1898 The United States took control of Guam, Puerto Rico, and the Philippines following the Spanish-American War.

Major developments from 1900 to 1990

WORLD BOOK illustrations by Tak Murakami

1900

Sigmund Freud developed psychoanalysis about 1900.

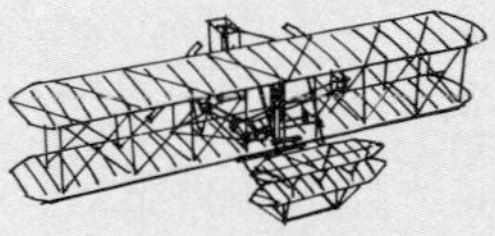

The Wright brothers made the first successful airplane flights in 1903.

Albert Einstein published his special theory of relativity in 1905.

World War I (1914-1918)

1925

Alexander Fleming discovered penicillin in 1928.

The first computers were developed in the 1930's and 1940's.

The British Broadcasting Corporation made the world's first TV broadcasts in 1936.

World War II (1939-1945)

1950

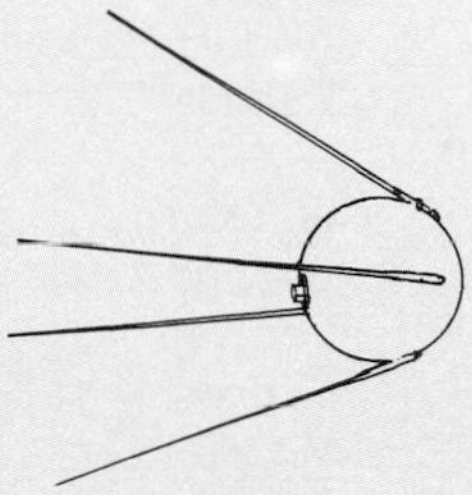

The Soviet Union launched the first artificial satellite in 1957.

Space Age (1957-)

Vietnam War (1957-1975)

Korean War (1950-1953)

1975

Researchers developed the first successful recombinant DNA procedure in 1974.

2000

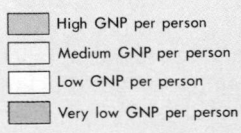

The wealth of nations can be compared on the basis of each country's *gross national product* (GNP). The GNP is the value of all goods and services produced by a country in a year. The developing countries of Africa and Asia have the lowest GNP per person.

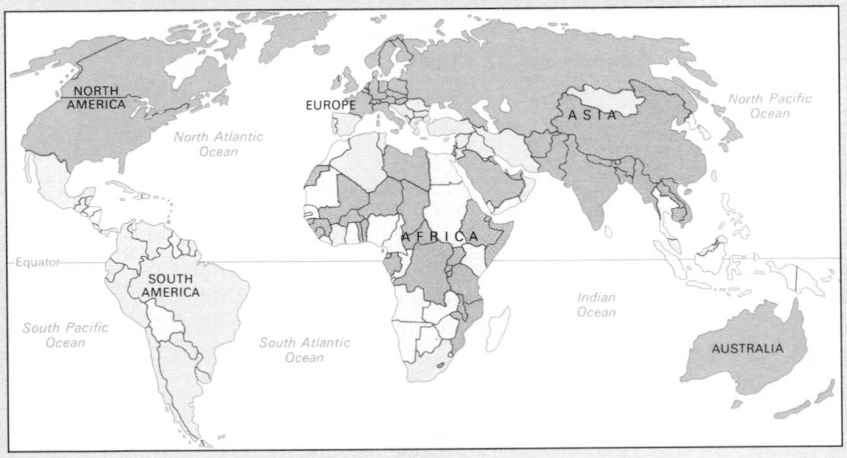
NORTH AMERICA
EUROPE
ASIA
North Pacific Ocean
North Atlantic Ocean
AFRICA
Equator
SOUTH AMERICA
Indian Ocean
South Pacific Ocean
South Atlantic Ocean
AUSTRALIA

- High GNP per person
- Medium GNP per person
- Low GNP per person
- Very low GNP per person

WORLD BOOK map
Map is based on U.S. government GNP estimates for 1982.

Important dates

1914 The assassination of Archduke Francis Ferdinand of Austria-Hungary started World War I.

1917 The Bolsheviks (Communists) seized power in Russia.

1933 Adolf Hitler became dictator of Germany.

1939 Germany invaded Poland, starting World War II.

1941 The Japanese attacked Pearl Harbor, and the United States entered World War II.

1945 The United Nations was established.

1945 The first atomic bombs used in warfare were dropped by U.S. planes on Hiroshima and Nagasaki.

1945 World War II ended in Europe on May 7 and in the Pacific on September 2.

1949 The Chinese Communists conquered China.

1950 North Korean Communist troops invaded South Korea, starting the Korean War.

1957 The Vietnam War started when South Vietnamese rebels known as the Viet Cong attacked the U.S.-backed South Vietnamese government.

1962 The Soviet Union agreed to U.S. demands that its missiles be removed from Cuba, ending a serious Cold War crisis.

1969 U.S. astronauts made the first manned moon landing.

1975 The Vietnam War ended when South Vietnam surrendered to the Viet Cong and North Vietnam.

1979 Soviet troops invaded Afghanistan to support the leftist Afghan government against rebel tribes.

1989 The Soviet Union completed withdrawal of its troops from Afghanistan.

Country	Location	Capital	Population*	Area	Area (Metric)
Afghanistan	SW-central Asia	Kabul	16,900,000	250,000 sq mi.	647,500 sq km.
Albania	SE Europe	Tirana	3,300,000	11,100 sq mi.	28,748 sq km.
Algeria	NW Africa	Algiers	26,000,000	919,595 sq mi.	2,381,751 sq km.
Andorra	SW Europe	Andorra la Vella	55,400	175 sq mi.	453 sq km.
Angola	SW Africa	Luanda	8,900,000	481,350 sq mi.	1,246,700 sq km.
Antigua and Barbuda	Caribbean	St. John's	100,000	171 sq mi.	442 sq km.
Argentina	S South America	Buenos Aires	33,100,000	1,072,067 sq mi.	2,776,654 sq km.
Armenia	SW Asia	Yerevan	3,376,000	11,500 sq mi.	29,800 sq km.
Australia	SE of Asia	Canberra	17,800,000	2,966,150 sq mi.	7,682,300 sq km.
Austria	central Europe	Vienna	7,900,000	32,375 sq mi.	83,851 sq km.
Azerbaijan	SW Asia	Baku	7,100,000	33,400 sq mi.	86,600 sq km.
Bahamas	Caribbean	Nassau	254,685	5,380 sq mi.	13,939 sq km.
Bahrain	SW Asia	Manama	500,000	240 sq mi.	620 sq km.
Bangladesh	S Asia	Dhaka	111,400,000	55,598 sq mi.	143,998 sq km.
Barbados	Caribbean	Bridgetown	300,000	166 sq mi.	431 sq km.
Belarus	E Europe	Minsk	10,300,000	80,200 sq mi.	207,600 sq km.
Belgium	W Europe	Brussels	10,000,000	11,781 sq mi.	30,513 sq km.
Belize	Central America	Belmopan	200,000	8,867 sq mi.	22,965 sq km.
Benin	W Africa	Porto-Novo	5,000,000	43,483 sq mi.	112,622 sq km.
Bhutan	central Asia	Thimphu	700,000	18,000 sq mi.	46,620 sq km.
Bolivia	South America	Sucre; La Paz	7,800,000	424,162 sq mi.	1,098,581 sq km.
Bosnia and Herzegovina	SE Europe	Sarajevo	4,200,000	19,741 sq mi.	51,129 sq km.
Botswana	central S Africa	Gaborone	1,400,000	231,800 sq mi.	600,360 sq km.
Brazil	E South America	Brasília	156,275,000	3,286,470 sq mi.	8,511,957 sq km.
Brunei	island of Borneo	Bandar Seri Begawan	300,000	2,226 sq mi.	5,765 sq km.
Bulgaria	SE Europe	Sofia	8,900,000	42,823 sq mi.	110,912 sq km.
Burkina Faso	W Africa	Ouagadougou	9,600,000	105,870 sq mi.	274,200 sq km.
Burma	(see Myanmar)				
Burundi	E Africa	Bujumbura	5,800,000	10,747 sq mi.	27,834 sq km.
Cambodia	SE Asia	Phnom Penh	9,100,000	69,884 sq mi.	181,000 sq km.
Cameroon	W Africa	Yaoundé	12,700,000	183,569 sq mi.	475,442 sq km.
Canada	N North America	Ottawa	27,400,000	3,851,809 sq mi.	9,976,186 sq km.
Cape Verde	W of Africa	Praia	400,000	1,557 sq mi.	4,033 sq km.
Central African Republic	central Africa	Bangui	3,200,000	241,313 sq mi.	625,000 sq km.
Chad	central Africa	N'Djamena	5,200,000	495,752 sq mi.	1,284,000 sq km.
Chile	W South America	Santiago	13,600,000	292,132 sq mi.	756,622 sq km.
China	E Asia	Beijing	1,165,800,000	3,691,521 sq mi.	9,561,000 sq km.
Colombia	NW South America	Bogotá	34,300,000	440,829 sq mi.	1,141,748 sq km.
Comoros	E. of Africa	Moroni	500,000	690 sq mi.	1,787 sq km.
Congo	central Africa	Brazzaville	2,400,000	132,046 sq mi.	342,000 sq km.
Costa Rica	Central America	San José	3,200,000	19,652 sq mi.	50,898 sq km.
Côte D'Ivoire	W Africa	Abidjan; Yamoussoukro	13,000,000	124,502 sq mi.	322,462 sq km.
Croatia	E Europe	Zagreb	4,600,000	21,829 sq mi.	56,537 sq km.
Cuba	Caribbean	Havana	10,800,000	44,218 sq mi.	114,524 sq km.
Cyprus	S. of Europe	Nicosia	710,000	3,572 sq mi.	9,251 sq km.
Czech Republic	central Europe	Prague	10,362,000	30,441 sq mi.	78,864 sq km.
Denmark	N Europe	Copenhagen	5,200,000	16,631 sq mi.	43,075 sq km.
Djibouti	E Africa	Djibouti	400,000	8,490 sq mi.	22,000 sq km.

*Populations are mid-1992 estimates.

Country	*Location*	*Capital*	*Population**	*Area*	*Area (Metric)*
Dominica	Caribbean	Roseau	100,000	290 sq mi.	751 sq km.
Dominican Republic	Caribbean	Santo Domingo	7,500,000	18,704 sq mi.	48,442 sq km.
Ecuador	NW South America	Quito	10,300,000	106,927 sq mi.	276,840 sq km.
Egypt	NE Africa	Cairo	57,758,000	386,900 sq mi.	1,002,000 sq km.
El Salvador	Central America	San Salvador	5,600,000	8,260 sq mi.	21,393 sq km.
Equatorial Guinea	W Africa	Malabo	400,000	10,830 sq mi.	28,051 sq km.
Estonia	NE Europe	Tallinn	1,600,000	18,370 sq mi.	47,549 sq km.
Ethiopia	E Africa	Addis Ababa	54,300,000	472,432 sq mi.	1,223,600 sq km.
Fiji	SW Pacific Ocean	Suva	800,000	7,078 sq mi.	18,333 sq km.
Finland	N Europe	Helsinki	5,000,000	130,119 sq mi.	337,009 sq km.
France	W Europe	Paris	56,900,000	212,918 sq mi.	547,026 sq km.
Gabon	W Africa	Libreville	1,100,000	103,346 sq mi.	267,667 sq km.
Gambia	W Africa	Banjul	900,000	4,093 sq mi.	10,600 sq km.
Georgia	SW Asia	Tbilisi	5,550,000	26,900 sq mi.	69,940 sq km.
Germany	W Europe	Berlin	80,600,000	137,838 sq mi.	357,000 sq km.
Ghana	W Africa	Accra	16,000,000	92,100 sq mi.	238,537 sq km.
Greece	SE Europe	Athens	10,300,000	50,961 sq mi.	131,990 sq km.
Grenada	Caribbean	St. George's	100,000	133 sq mi.	344 sq km.
Guatemala	Central America	Guatemala City	9,700,000	42,042 sq mi.	108,889 sq km.
Guinea	W Africa	Conakry	7,800,000	94,925 sq mi.	245,857 sq km.
Guinea-Bissau	W Africa	Bissau	1,000,000	13,948 sq mi.	36,125 sq km.
Guyana	N South America	Georgetown	800,000	83,000 sq mi.	214,969 sq km.
Haiti	Caribbean	Port-au-Prince	6,400,000	10,714 sq mi.	27,750 sq km.
Honduras	Central America	Tegucigalpa	5,500,000	43,277 sq mi.	112,088 sq km.
Hungary	central Europe	Budapest	10,300,000	35,919 sq mi.	93,030 sq km.
Iceland	N Atlantic Ocean	Reykjavík	300,000	39,709 sq mi.	102,846 sq km.
India	S Asia	New Delhi	882,600,000	1,229,737 sq mi.	3,185,019 sq km.
Indonesia	SE Asia	Jakarta	184,500,000	735,268 sq mi.	1,904,344 sq km.
Iran	SW Asia	Tehran	59,700,000	636,293 sq mi.	1,648,000 sq km.
Iraq	SW Asia	Baghdad	18,200,000	167,920 sq mi.	434,913 sq km.
Ireland	N Atlantic Ocean	Dublin	3,500,000	27,136 sq mi.	70,282 sq km.
Israel	SW Asia	Jerusalem	5,200,000	8,020 sq mi.	20,772 sq km.
Italy	S Europe	Rome	58,000,000	116,500 sq mi.	301,278 sq km.
Jamaica	Caribbean	Kingston	2,500,000	4,411 sq mi.	11,424 sq km.
Japan	E Asia	Tokyo	124,400,000	145,874 sq mi.	377,815 sq km.
Jordan	SW Asia	Amman	3,600,000	34,573 sq mi.	89,544 sq km.
Kazakhstan	W-central Asia	Alma-Ata	16,900,000	1,049,000 sq mi.	2,717,300 sq km.
Kenya	E Africa	Nairobi	26,200,000	224,960 sq mi.	582,646 sq km.
Kiribati	Pacific Ocean	Tarawa	72,298	280 sq mi.	726 sq km.
Kuwait	SW Asia	Kuwait	1,400,000	6,880 sq mi.	17,820 sq km.
Kyrgyzstan	W-central Asia	Bishkek	4,500,000	76,000 sq mi.	198,500 sq km.
Laos	SE Asia	Vientiane	4,400,000	91,429 sq mi.	236,800 sq km.
Latvia	NE Europe	Riga	2,700,000	25,400 sq mi.	65,786 sq km.
Lebanon	SW Asia	Beirut	3,400,000	4,015 sq mi.	10,400 sq km.
Lesotho	S Africa	Maseru	1,900,000	11,720 sq mi.	30,355 sq km.
Liberia	W Africa	Monrovia	2,800,000	43,000 sq mi.	111,370 sq km.
Libya	N Africa	Tripoli	4,500,000	679,536 sq mi.	1,759,998 sq km.
Liechtenstein	W-central Europe	Vaduz	30,000	61 sq mi.	157 sq km.
Lithuania	NE Europe	Vilnius	3,700,000	25,174 sq mi.	64,445 sq km.
Luxembourg	NW Europe	Luxembourg	400,000	999 sq mi.	2,586 sq km.
Macedonia	SE Europe	Skopje	1,900,000	9,928 sq mi.	25,713 sq km.

*Populations are mid-1992 estimates.

Country	Location	Capital	Population*	Area	Area (Metric)
Madagascar	off SE Africa	Antananarivo	11,900,000	226,660 sq mi.	587,050 sq km.
Malawi	E-central Africa	Lilongwe	8,700,000	45,747 sq mi.	118,484 sq km.
Malaysia	SE Asia	Kuala Lumpur	18,700,000	128,328 sq mi.	332,370 sq km.
Maldives	Indian Ocean	Malé	200,000	115 sq mi.	298 sq km.
Mali	W Africa	Bamako	8,500,000	478,819 sq mi.	1,240,142 sq km.
Malta	Mediterranean Sea	Valletta	400,000	122 sq mi.	316 sq km.
Marshall Islands	W-central Pacific Ocean	Majuro	48,000	70 sq mi.	181 sq km.
Mauritania	W Africa	Nouakchott	2,100,000	397,953 sq mi.	1,030,700 sq km.
Mauritius	Indian Ocean	Port Louis	1,100,000	787 sq mi.	2,040 sq km.
Mexico	S North America	Mexico City	87,700,000	761,600 sq mi.	1,972,547 sq km.
Micronesia	W Pacific Ocean	Kolonia	100,000	271 sq mi.	703 sq km.
Moldova	E Europe	Kishinev	4,400,000	13,000 sq mi.	33,700 sq km.
Monaco	S Europe	Monaco	29,700	.73 sq mi.	1.9 sq km.
Mongolia	central Asia	Ulan Bator	2,300,000	604,250 sq mi.	1,565,000 sq km.
Morocco	NW Africa	Rabat	26,200,000	172,413 sq mi.	446,550 sq km.
Mozambique	SE Africa	Maputo	16,600,000	303,073 sq mi.	799,380 sq km.
Myanmar	SE Asia	Yangon	42,500,000	261,220 sq mi.	676,560 sq km.
Namibia	SW Africa	Windhoek	1,500,000	318,261 sq mi.	824,296 sq km.
Nauru	W-central Pacific Ocean	Yaren	9,500	8.2 sq mi.	21 sq km.
Nepal	central Asia	Kathmandu	19,900,000	54,463 sq mi.	141,059 sq km.
Netherlands	NW Europe	Amsterdam; The Hague	15,300,000	16,041 sq mi.	41,548 sq km.
New Zealand	Pacific Ocean	Wellington	3,400,000	103,884 sq mi.	269,062 sq km.
Nicaragua	Central America	Managua	4,100,000	50,180 sq mi.	130,000 sq km.
Niger	W Africa	Niamey	8,300,000	489,206 sq mi.	1,267,044 sq km.
Nigeria	W Africa	Abuja	88,500,000	356,700 sq mi.	923,853 sq km.
North Korea	E Asia	Pyongyang	22,200,000	46,768 sq mi.	121,129 sq km.
Norway	N Europe	Oslo	4,300,000	125,049 sq mi.	323,877 sq km.
Oman	SW Asia	Muscat	2,070,000	82,030 sq mi.	212,458 sq km.
Pakistan	S Asia	Islamabad	121,700,000	310,400 sq mi.	803,936 sq km.
Panama	Central America	Panama City	2,400,000	29,761 sq mi.	77,082 sq km.
Papua New Guinea	SW Pacific Ocean	Port Moresby	3,900,000	178,704 sq mi.	462,840 sq km.
Paraguay	South America	Asunción	4,500,000	157,047 sq mi.	406,752 sq km.
Peru	W South America	Lima	22,500,000	496,222 sq mi.	1,285,216 sq km.
Philippines	E Asia	Manila	63,700,000	115,830 sq mi.	300,000 sq km.
Poland	E Europe	Warsaw	38,400,000	120,727 sq mi.	312,683 sq km.
Portugal	S Europe	Lisbon	10,500,000	35,550 sq mi.	92,075 sq. km.
Qatar	SW Asia	Doha	500,000	4,000 sq mi.	11,437 sq km.
Romania	E-central Europe	Bucharest	22,760,000	91,700 sq mi.	237,500 sq km.
Russia	E Europe; N Asia	Moscow	148,542,700	6,592,800 sq mi.	17,075,400 sq km.
Rwanda	E Africa	Kigali	7,700,000	10,169 sq mi.	26,338 sq km.
St. Kitts and Nevis	Caribbean	Basseterre	40,000	100 sq mi.	260 sq km.
St. Lucia	Caribbean	Castries	200,000	238 sq mi.	616 sq km.
St. Vincent and the Grenadines	Caribbean	Kingstown	100,000	150 sq mi.	389 sq km.
San Marino	N Italy	San Marino	20,000	23.6 sq mi.	62 sq km.
São Tomé and Príncipe	off W Africa	São Tomé	100,000	370 sq mi.	958 sq km.

*Populations are mid-1992 estimates.

Country	*Location*	*Capital*	*Population**	*Area*	*Area (Metric)*
Saudi Arabia	SW Asia	Riyadh	16,100,000	865,000 sq mi.	2,250,070 sq km.
Senegal	W Africa	Dakar	7,900,000	75,954 sq mi.	196,722 sq km.
Seychelles	off E Africa	Victoria	100,000	175 sq mi.	453 sq km.
Sierra Leone	W Africa	Freetown	4,400,000	27,700 sq mi.	71,740 sq km.
Singapore	SE Asia	Singapore	2,800,000	246.7 sq mi.	639 sq km.
Slovakia	E Europe	Bratislava	5,278,700	18,928 sq mi.	49,035 sq km.
Slovenia	E Europe	Ljubljana	1,962,600	7,819 sq mi.	20,251 sq km.
Solomon Islands	SW Pacific Ocean	Honiara	400,000	11,500 sq mi.	29,785 sq km.
Somalia	E Africa	Mogadishu	8,300,000	246,199 sq mi.	637,655 sq km.
South Africa	S Africa	Pretoria	41,700,000	471,440 sq mi.	1,221,030 sq km.
South Korea	E Asia	Seoul	44,300,000	38,031 sq mi.	98,500 sq km.
Spain	W Europe	Madrid	39,301,000	194,884 sq mi.	504,750 sq km.
Sri Lanka	off SE India	Colombo	17,600,000	25,332 sq mi.	65,610 sq km.
Sudan	E Africa	Khartoum	26,500,000	967,491 sq mi.	2,505,802 sq km.
Suriname	N South America	Paramaribo	400,000	63,251 sq mi.	163,820 sq km.
Swaziland	SE Africa	Mbabane	800,000	6,704 sq mi.	17,363 sq km.
Sweden	N Europe	Stockholm	8,700,000	173,800 sq mi.	449,964 sq km.
Switzerland	W Europe	Bern	6,900,000	15,941 sq mi.	41,288 sq km.
Syria	W Asia	Damascus	13,700,000	71,498 sq mi.	185,180 sq km.
Taiwan	off SE China	Taipei	20,800,000	13,895 sq mi.	35,988 sq km.
Tajikistan	W Asia	Dushanbe	5,500,000	55,300 sq mi.	143,100 sq km.
Tanzania	E Africa	Dar es Salaam	27,400,000	364,879 sq mi.	945,037 sq km.
Thailand	SE Asia	Bangkok	56,300,000	198,455 sq mi.	514,000 sq km.
Togo	W Africa	Lomé	3,800,000	21,925 sq mi.	56,785 sq km.
Tonga	SW Pacific Ocean	Nuku'alofa	96,800	290 sq mi.	751 sq km.
Trinidad and Tobago	Caribbean	Port-of-Spain	1,300,000	1,980 sq mi.	5,128 sq km.
Tunisia	N Africa	Tunis	8,400,000	63,379 sq mi.	164,152 sq km.
Turkey	S Europe/SW Asia	Ankara	59,200,000	300,947 sq mi.	779,452 sq km.
Turkmenistan	W Asia	Ashkhabad	3,900,000	188,500 sq mi.	488,100 sq km.
Tuvalu	W Pacific Ocean	Funafuti	9,300	10 sq mi.	26 sq km.
Uganda	E Africa	Kampala	17,500,000	91,459 sq mi.	236,880 sq km.
Ukraine	E Europe	Kiev	52,100,000	233,000 sq mi.	603,700 sq km.
United Arab Emirates	SW Asia	Abu Dhabi	2,500,000	32,000 sq mi.	82,880 sq km.
United Kingdom	off W Europe	London	57,533,000	94,247 sq mi.	244,100 sq km.
United States	North America	Washington, D.C.	255,600,000	3,536,341 sq mi.	9,159,123 sq km.
Uruguay	E South America	Montevideo	3,100,000	68,040 sq mi.	176,224 sq km.
Uzbekistan	W Asia	Tashkent	21,300,000	172,700 sq mi.	447,400 sq km.
Vanuatu	SW Pacific Ocean	Port Vila	200,000	5,700 sq mi.	14,763 sq km.
Vatican City	central Italy	—	778	.17 sq mi.	.44 sq km.
Venezuela	N South America	Caracas	18,900,000	352,143 sq mi.	912,050 sq km.
Vietnam	SE Asia	Hanoi	69,200,000	127,246 sq mi.	329,566 sq km.
Western Samoa	S Pacific	Apia	200,000	1,093 sq mi.	2,831 sq km.
Yemen	SW Asia	Sanaa	10,400,000	203,850 sq mi.	527,970 sq km.
Yugoslavia**	SE Europe	Belgrade	10,000,000	26,940 sq mi.	69,775 sq km.
Zaire	central Africa	Kinshasa	37,900,000	905,365 sq mi.	2,344,885 sq km.
Zambia	S Africa	Lusaka	8,400,000	290,586 sq mi.	752,618 sq km.
Zimbabwe	S Africa	Harare	10,300,000	150,698 sq mi.	390,308 sq km.

*Populations are mid-1992 estimates.
**Present-day Yugoslavia comprises the republics of Serbia and Montenegro.

WORLD: *Political*

ABBREVIATIONS

BOS. AND HERZ. Bosnia and Herzegovina
CEN. AFR. REP. Central African Republic
DEN. Denmark
FR. France
GR. Greece
IT. Italy
N. North, Northern
NETH. Netherlands
N.Z. New Zealand
PORT. Portugal
S. South
SP. Spain
U.A.E. United Arab Emirates
U.K. United Kingdom
U.S. United States
W. Western

— National boundary

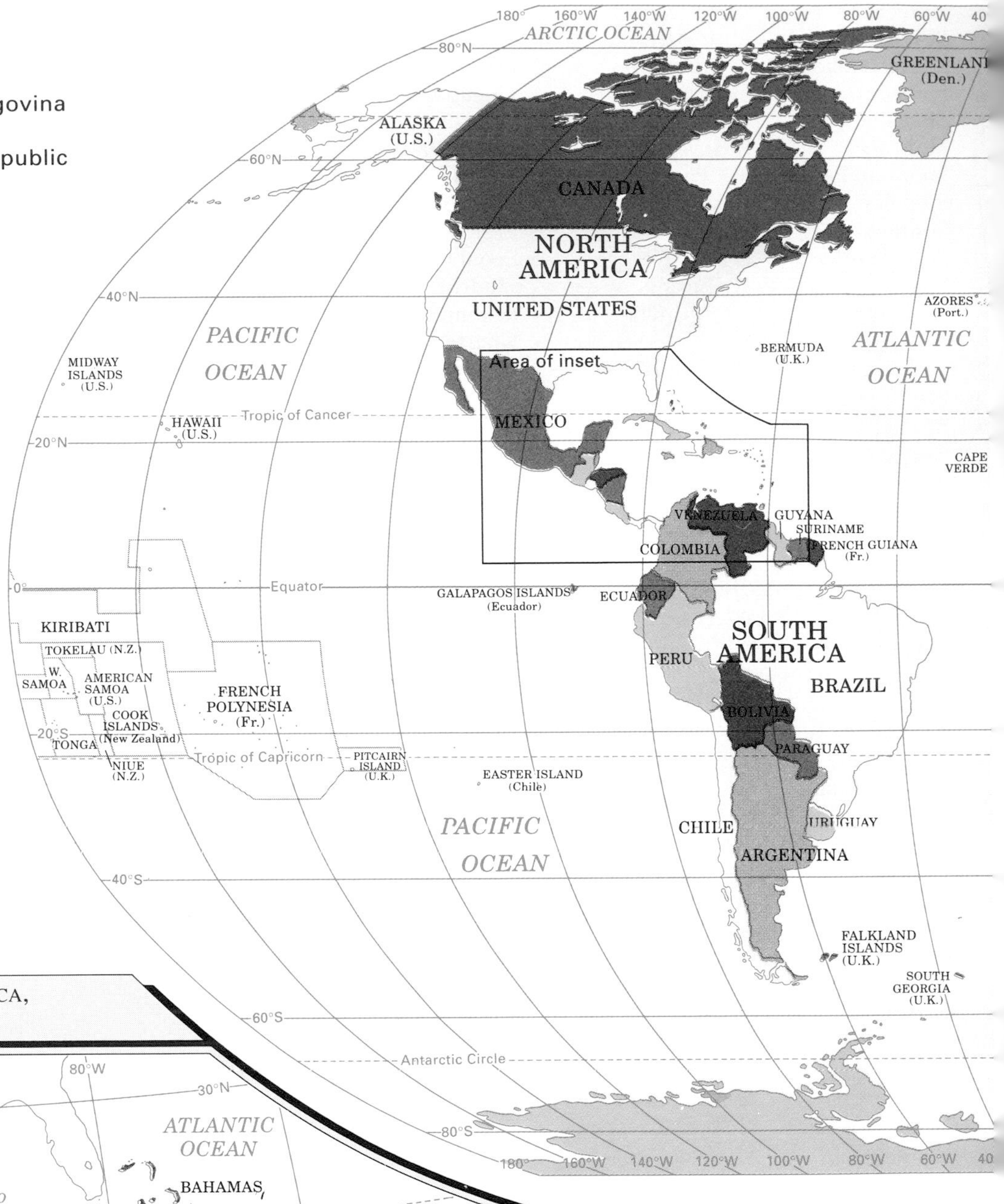

180°
160°W
140°W
120°W
100°W
80°W
60°W
ARCTIC OCEAN
80°N
GREENLAND (Den.)
ALASKA (U.S.)
60°N
CANADA
NORTH AMERICA
40°N
AZORES (Port.)
UNITED STATES
PACIFIC OCEAN
MIDWAY ISLANDS (U.S.)
Area of inset
BERMUDA (U.K.)
ATLANTIC OCEAN
HAWAII (U.S.)
Tropic of Cancer
MEXICO
20°N
CAPE VERDE
GUYANA
VENEZUELA
SURINAME
FRENCH GUIANA (Fr.)
COLOMBIA
0°
Equator
GALAPAGOS ISLANDS (Ecuador)
ECUADOR
KIRIBATI
TOKELAU (N.Z.)
SOUTH AMERICA
PERU
W. SAMOA
AMERICAN SAMOA (U.S.)
FRENCH POLYNESIA (Fr.)
BRAZIL
COOK ISLANDS (New Zealand)
BOLIVIA
20°S
TONGA
PARAGUAY
Tropic of Capricorn
PITCAIRN ISLAND (U.K.)
NIUE (N.Z.)
EASTER ISLAND (Chile)
PACIFIC OCEAN
CHILE
URUGUAY
ARGENTINA
40°S
FALKLAND ISLANDS (U.K.)
SOUTH GEORGIA (U.K.)
60°S
Antarctic Circle
80°S

MEXICO, CENTRAL AMERICA, AND THE CARIBBEAN

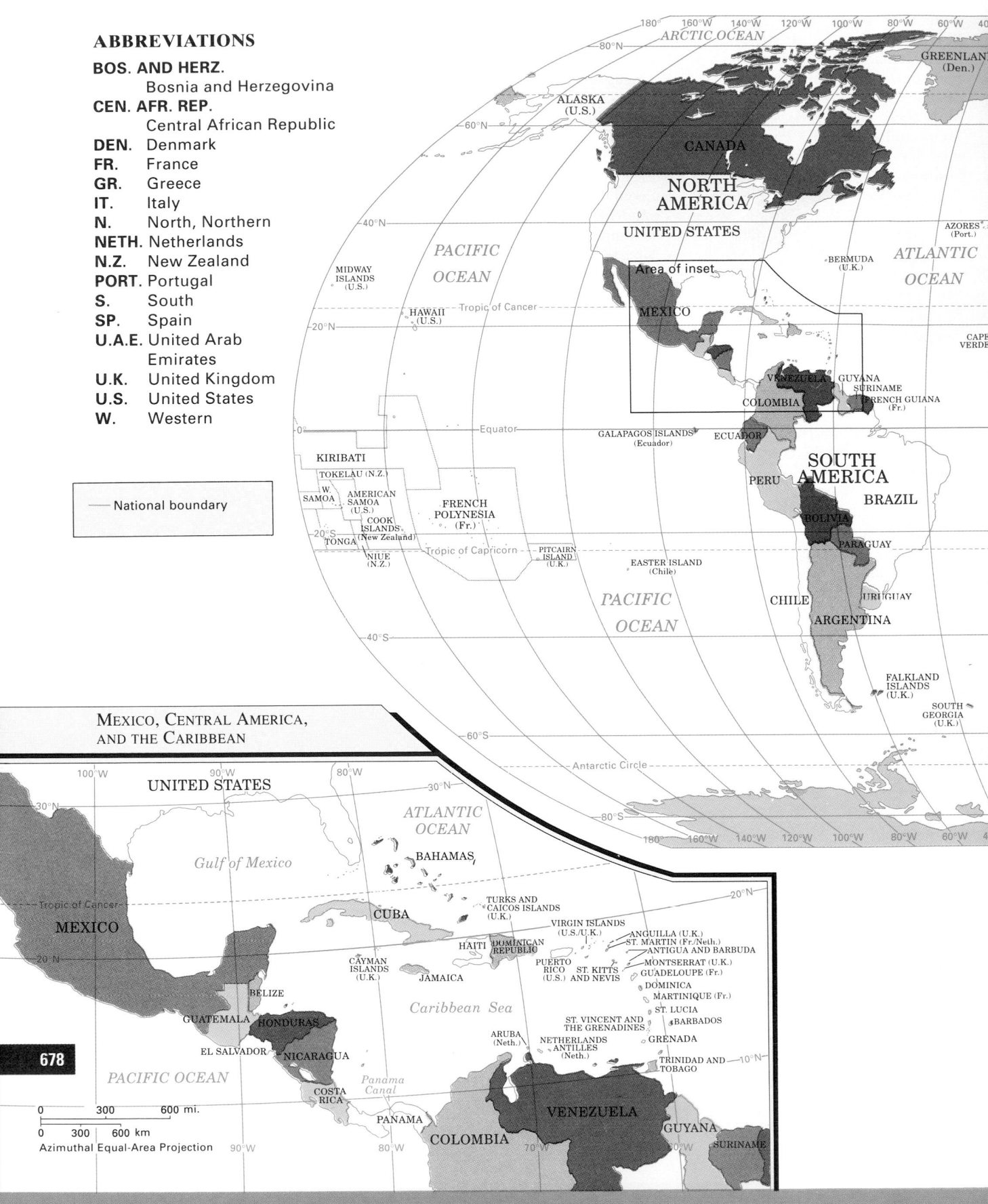

100°W
90°W
80°W
UNITED STATES
30°N
ATLANTIC OCEAN
Gulf of Mexico
BAHAMAS
Tropic of Cancer
20°N
TURKS AND CAICOS ISLANDS (U.K.)
MEXICO
CUBA
VIRGIN ISLANDS (U.S./U.K.)
ANGUILLA (U.K.)
ST. MARTIN (Fr./Neth.)
ANTIGUA AND BARBUDA
HAITI
DOMINICAN REPUBLIC
CAYMAN ISLANDS (U.K.)
PUERTO RICO (U.S.)
ST. KITTS AND NEVIS
MONTSERRAT (U.K.)
GUADELOUPE (Fr.)
JAMAICA
DOMINICA
MARTINIQUE (Fr.)
BELIZE
Caribbean Sea
ST. LUCIA
GUATEMALA
HONDURAS
ST. VINCENT AND THE GRENADINES
BARBADOS
ARUBA (Neth.)
NETHERLANDS ANTILLES (Neth.)
GRENADA
EL SALVADOR
NICARAGUA
TRINIDAD AND TOBAGO
10°N
PACIFIC OCEAN
Panama Canal
COSTA RICA
VENEZUELA
PANAMA
GUYANA
COLOMBIA
SURINAME
70°W
60°W
0 300 600 mi.
0 300 600 km
Azimuthal Equal-Area Projection

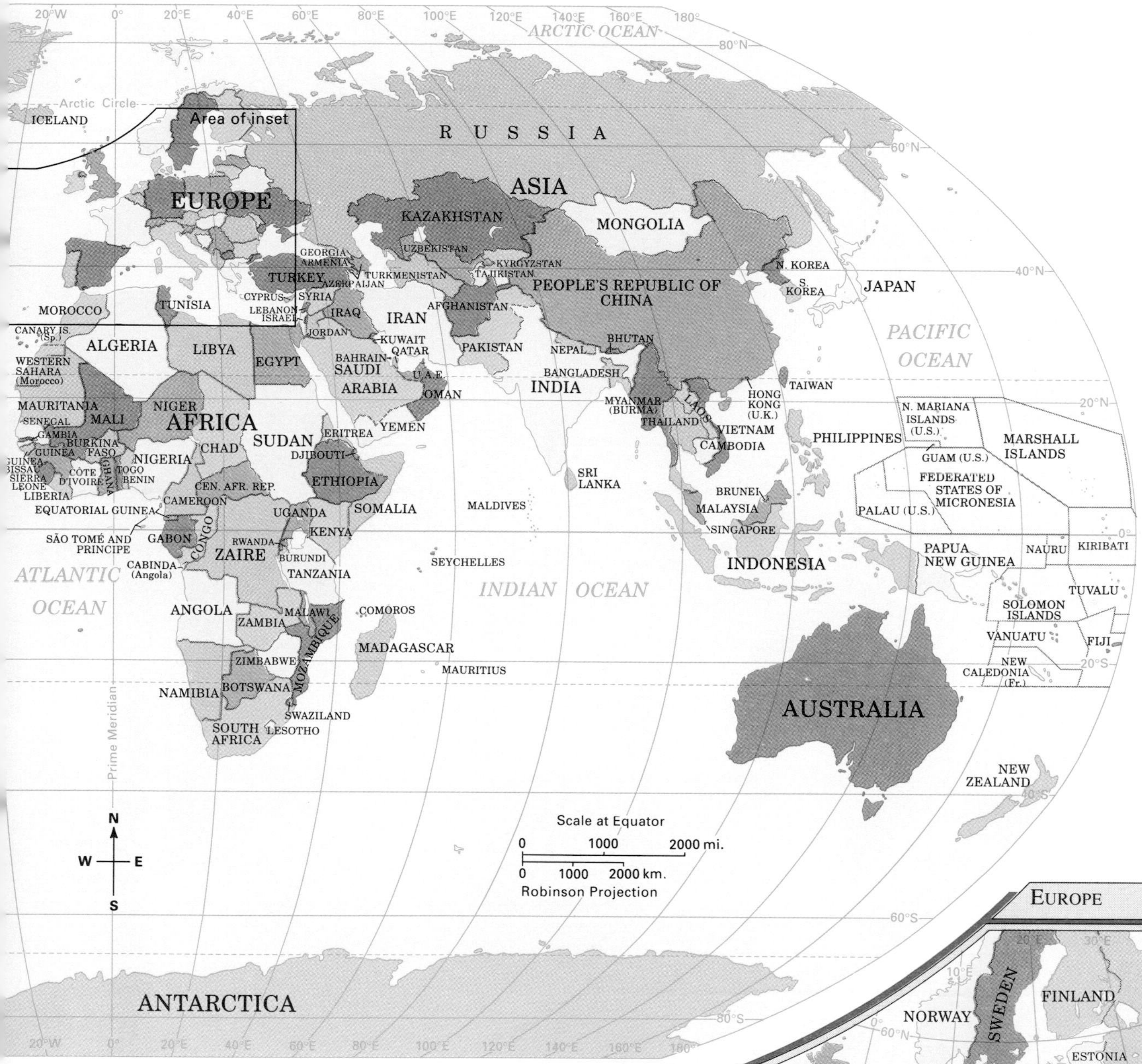
ARCTIC OCEAN
Arctic Circle
Area of inset
ICELAND
RUSSIA
EUROPE
ASIA
KAZAKHSTAN
MONGOLIA
UZBEKISTAN
GEORGIA
ARMENIA
AZERBAIJAN
TURKMENISTAN
KYRGYZSTAN
TAJIKISTAN
TURKEY
N. KOREA
S. KOREA
JAPAN
PEOPLE'S REPUBLIC OF CHINA
CYPRUS
SYRIA
LEBANON
ISRAEL
IRAQ
IRAN
AFGHANISTAN
MOROCCO
TUNISIA
JORDAN
KUWAIT
QATAR
BAHRAIN
CANARY IS. (Sp.)
ALGERIA
LIBYA
EGYPT
SAUDI ARABIA
U.A.E.
OMAN
PAKISTAN
NEPAL
BHUTAN
BANGLADESH
INDIA
PACIFIC OCEAN
WESTERN SAHARA (Morocco)
MAURITANIA
MALI
NIGER
AFRICA
SENEGAL
GAMBIA
GUINEA
BURKINA FASO
GUINEA-BISSAU
SIERRA LEONE
LIBERIA
CÔTE D'IVOIRE
GHANA
TOGO
BENIN
NIGERIA
CHAD
SUDAN
ERITREA
DJIBOUTI
YEMEN
ETHIOPIA
SOMALIA
CEN. AFR. REP.
CAMEROON
EQUATORIAL GUINEA
SÃO TOMÉ AND PRINCIPE
GABON
CONGO
ZAIRE
UGANDA
KENYA
RWANDA
BURUNDI
TANZANIA
CABINDA (Angola)
ATLANTIC OCEAN
ANGOLA
ZAMBIA
MALAWI
MOZAMBIQUE
COMOROS
ZIMBABWE
MADAGASCAR
MAURITIUS
NAMIBIA
BOTSWANA
SWAZILAND
SOUTH AFRICA
LESOTHO
MYANMAR (BURMA)
LAOS
THAILAND
CAMBODIA
VIETNAM
HONG KONG (U.K.)
TAIWAN
PHILIPPINES
SRI LANKA
MALDIVES
SEYCHELLES
INDIAN OCEAN
BRUNEI
MALAYSIA
SINGAPORE
INDONESIA
N. MARIANA ISLANDS (U.S.)
GUAM (U.S.)
MARSHALL ISLANDS
FEDERATED STATES OF MICRONESIA
PALAU (U.S.)
PAPUA NEW GUINEA
NAURU
KIRIBATI
SOLOMON ISLANDS
TUVALU
VANUATU
FIJI
NEW CALEDONIA (Fr.)
AUSTRALIA
NEW ZEALAND
Prime Meridian
N
W
E
S
Scale at Equator
0 1000 2000 mi.
0 1000 2000 km.
Robinson Projection
ANTARCTICA

EUROPE
NORWAY
SWEDEN
FINLAND
RUSSIA
ESTONIA
LATVIA
LITHUANIA
(Russia)
North Sea
Baltic Sea
DENMARK
IRELAND
UNITED KINGDOM
BELARUS
POLAND
0 300 600 mi.
0 300 600 km
Azimuthal Equal-Area Projection
NETHERLANDS
BELGIUM
GERMANY
UKRAINE
LUXEMBOURG
CZECH REPUBLIC
SLOVAK REPUBLIC
FRANCE
LIECHTENSTEIN
AUSTRIA
SWITZERLAND
HUNGARY
MOLDOVA
ATLANTIC OCEAN
SLOVENIA
CROATIA
ROMANIA
BOS. AND HERZ.
YUGOSLAVIA
Black Sea
MONACO
ANDORRA
SAN MARINO
Adriatic Sea
BULGARIA
PORTUGAL
SPAIN
CORSICA (Fr.)
ITALY
MACEDONIA
VATICAN CITY
ALBANIA
BALEARIC IS. (Sp.)
SARDINIA (It.)
TURKEY
GREECE
Mediterranean Sea
GIBRALTAR (U.K.)
SICILY (It.)
MOROCCO
ALGERIA
MALTA
CRETE (Gr.)
Prime Meridian

WORLD: *Physical*

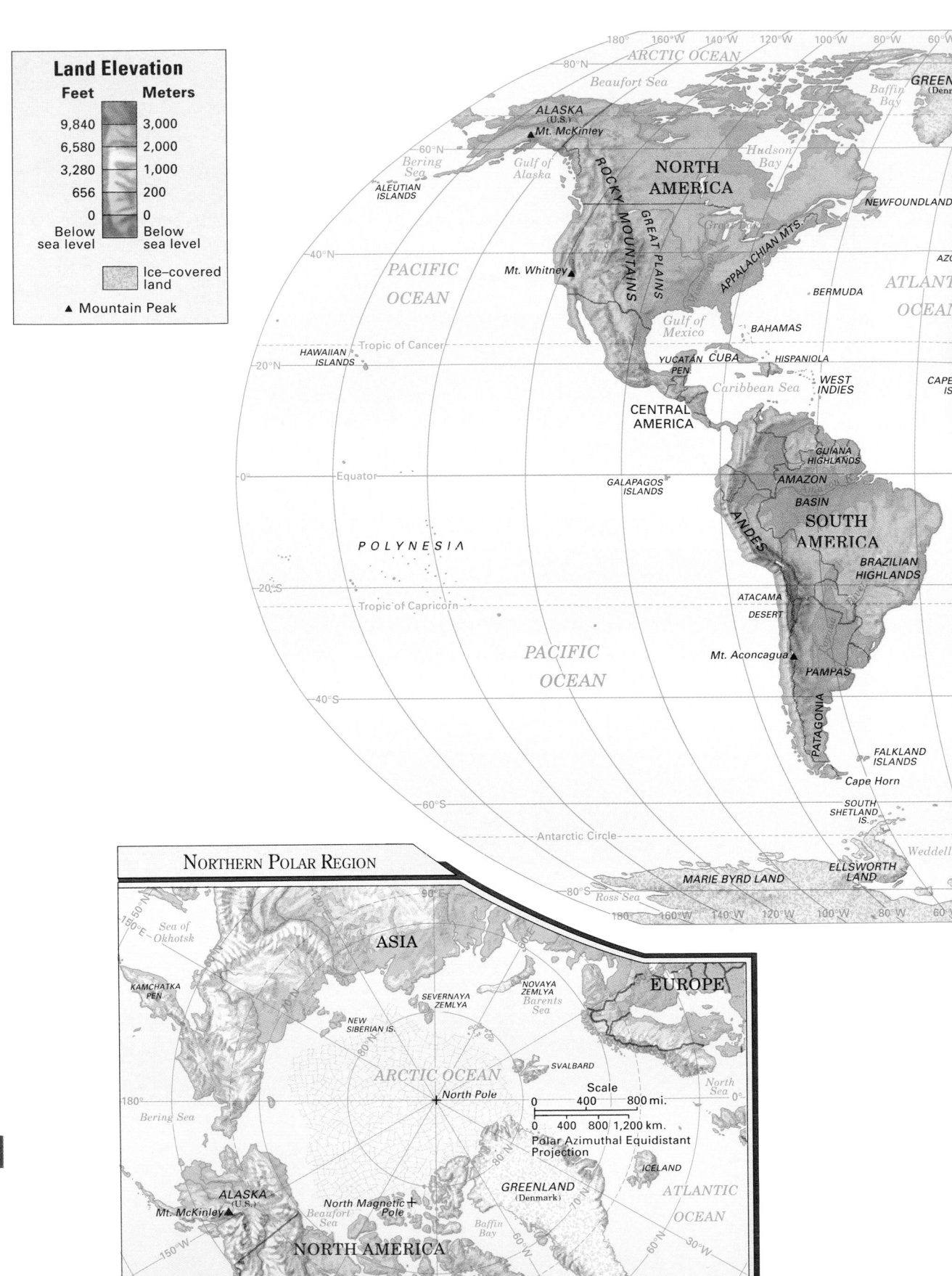

Land Elevation

Feet	Meters
9,840	3,000
6,580	2,000
3,280	1,000
656	200
0	0
Below sea level	Below sea level

Ice–covered land

▲ Mountain Peak

ARCTIC OCEAN
Beaufort Sea
ALASKA (U.S.)
Mt. McKinley
Baffin Bay
GREEN
Bering Sea
ALEUTIAN ISLANDS
Gulf of Alaska
ROCKY MOUNTAINS
NORTH AMERICA
Hudson Bay
GREAT PLAINS
NEWFOUNDLAND
APPALACHIAN MTS.
PACIFIC OCEAN
Mt. Whitney
BERMUDA
ATLANT
OCEAN
Gulf of Mexico
BAHAMAS
Tropic of Cancer
HAWAIIAN ISLANDS
YUCATÁN PEN.
CUBA
HISPANIOLA
Caribbean Sea
WEST INDIES
CENTRAL AMERICA
GUIANA HIGHLANDS
Equator
GALAPAGOS ISLANDS
AMAZON
BASIN
ANDES
SOUTH AMERICA
POLYNESIA
BRAZILIAN HIGHLANDS
ATACAMA DESERT
Tropic of Capricorn
PACIFIC OCEAN
Mt. Aconcagua
PAMPAS
PATAGONIA
FALKLAND ISLANDS
Cape Horn
SOUTH SHETLAND IS.
Antarctic Circle
Weddell S
MARIE BYRD LAND
ELLSWORTH LAND
Ross Sea

NORTHERN POLAR REGION

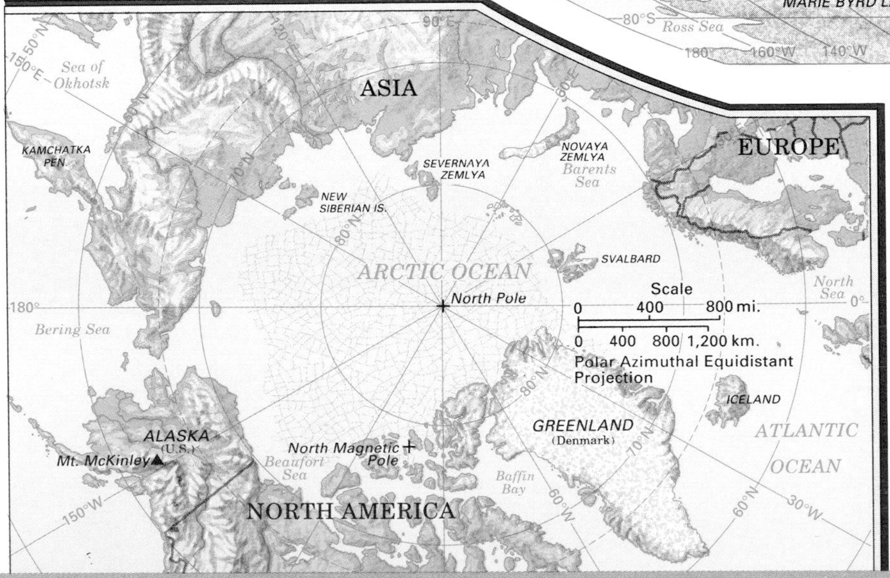

Sea of Okhotsk
ASIA
KAMCHATKA PEN.
SEVERNAYA ZEMLYA
NOVAYA ZEMLYA
Barents Sea
EUROPE
NEW SIBERIAN IS.
SVALBARD
ARCTIC OCEAN
North Pole
Scale
0 400 800 mi.
0 400 800 1,200 km.
Polar Azimuthal Equidistant Projection
North Sea
Bering Sea
ICELAND
GREENLAND (Denmark)
ALASKA (U.S.)
Mt. McKinley
North Magnetic Pole
Beaufort Sea
Baffin Bay
ATLANTIC OCEAN
NORTH AMERICA

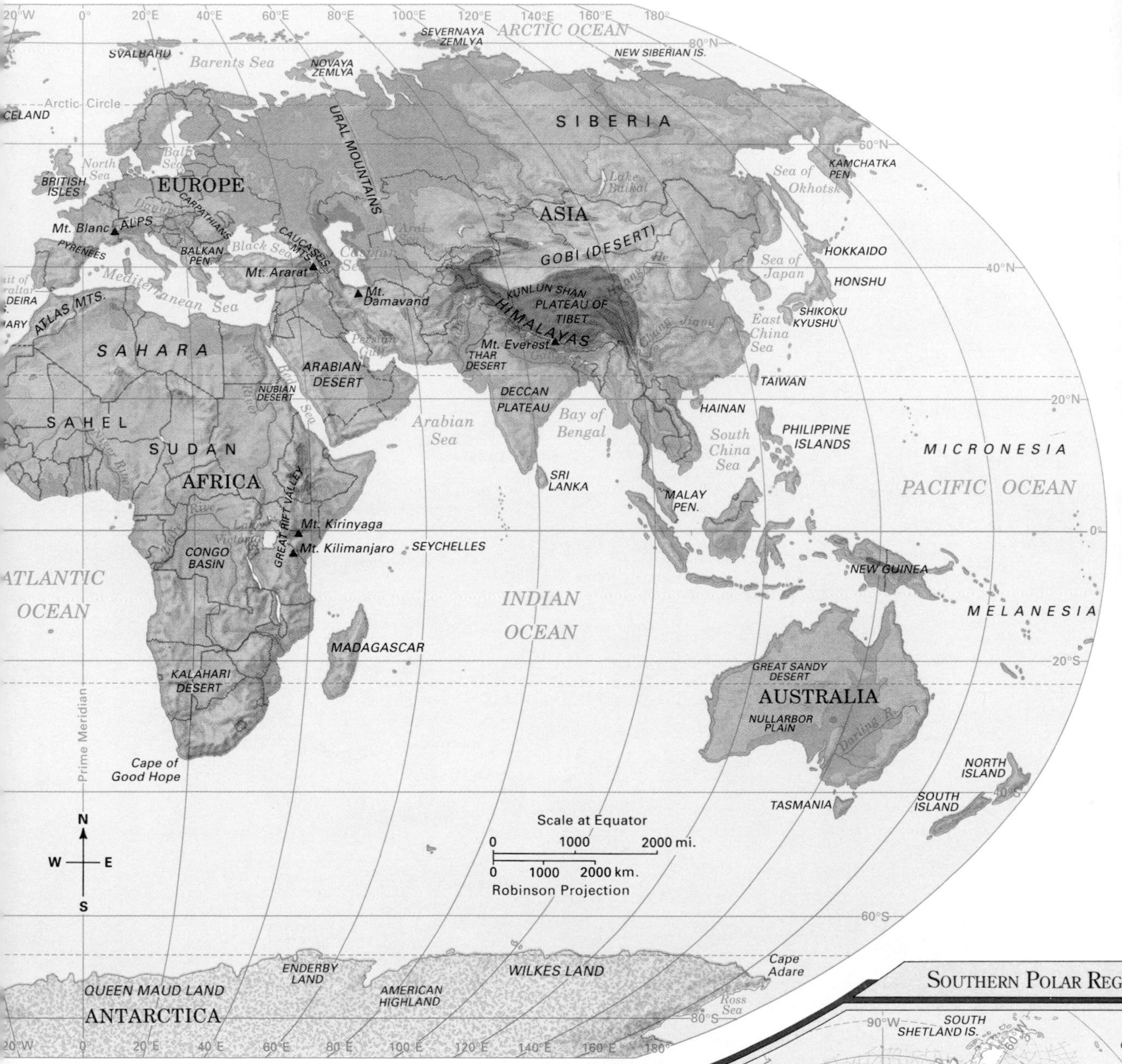
ARCTIC OCEAN
SEVERNAYA ZEMLYA
SVALBARD
Barents Sea
NOVAYA ZEMLYA
NEW SIBERIAN IS.
Arctic Circle
ICELAND
SIBERIA
URAL MOUNTAINS
North Sea
Baltic Sea
BRITISH ISLES
EUROPE
CARPATHIANS
Mt. Blanc
ALPS
PYRENEES
BALKAN PEN.
Black Sea
CAUCASUS MTS.
Caspian Sea
Aral Sea
Mt. Ararat
Mt. Damavand
Lake Baikal
Sea of Okhotsk
KAMCHATKA PEN.
ASIA
GOBI (DESERT)
Sea of Japan
HOKKAIDO
HONSHU
KUNLUN SHAN
PLATEAU OF TIBET
HIMALAYAS
Mt. Everest
THAR DESERT
SHIKOKU
KYUSHU
East China Sea
TAIWAN
Mediterranean Sea
ATLAS MTS.
MADEIRA
SAHARA
ARABIAN DESERT
Persian Gulf
NUBIAN DESERT
Red Sea
DECCAN PLATEAU
Arabian Sea
Bay of Bengal
HAINAN
South China Sea
PHILIPPINE ISLANDS
MICRONESIA
PACIFIC OCEAN
SAHEL
SUDAN
AFRICA
GREAT RIFT VALLEY
SRI LANKA
MALAY PEN.
Mt. Kirinyaga
Mt. Kilimanjaro
SEYCHELLES
CONGO BASIN
ATLANTIC OCEAN
NEW GUINEA
MELANESIA
INDIAN OCEAN
MADAGASCAR
GREAT SANDY DESERT
AUSTRALIA
NULLARBOR PLAIN
Darling R.
KALAHARI DESERT
Prime Meridian
Cape of Good Hope
NORTH ISLAND
SOUTH ISLAND
TASMANIA
Scale at Equator
0 1000 2000 mi.
0 1000 2000 km.
Robinson Projection
N
W
E
S
60°S
ENDERBY LAND
WILKES LAND
Cape Adare
QUEEN MAUD LAND
AMERICAN HIGHLAND
Ross Sea
ANTARCTICA
80°S
20°W 0° 20°E 40°E 60°E 80°E 100°E 120°E 140°E 160°E 180°
80°N
60°N
40°N
20°N
0°
20°S

Southern Polar Region

SOUTH SHETLAND IS.
SOUTH GEORGIA
ANTARCTIC PENINSULA
ELLSWORTH LAND
Weddell Sea
PACIFIC OCEAN
ATLANTIC OCEAN
MARIE BYRD LAND
Ross Sea
TRANSANTARCTIC MOUNTAINS
POLAR PLATEAU
South Pole
ANTARCTICA
QUEEN MAUD LAND
Cape Adare
Scale
0 400 800 mi.
0 400 800 1,200 km.
Polar Azimuthal Equidistant Projection
South Magnetic Pole
WILKES LAND
AMERICAN HIGHLAND
ENDERBY LAND
90°W
120°W
150°W
180°
150°E
120°E
90°E
60°E
30°E
0°
30°W
60°W
60°S
70°S
80°S

EURASIA: Political/Physical
90°W
75°W
60°W
45°W
30°W
15°W
0°
15°E
30°E
45°E
60°E
75°N
60°N
45°N
30°N
15°N
0°
15°S
Arctic Circle
Tropic of Cancer
Equator
Prime Meridian
SVALBARD (Norway)
FRANZ JOSEF LAND
NOVAYA ZEMLYA
Barents Sea
NORTH AMERICA
Norwegian Sea
Murmansk
White Sea
ICELAND
Reykjavik
Trondheim
NORWAY
SWEDEN
Gulf of Bothnia
FINLAND
RUSSIA
Ob River
URAL MOUNTAINS
Oslo
Helsinki
Tallinn
Stockholm
ESTONIA
Lake Ladoga
St. Petersburg
Volga River
North Sea
ATLANTIC OCEAN
Edinburgh
UNITED KINGDOM
Copenhagen
DENMARK
Baltic Sea
Riga
LATVIA
LITHUANIA
Moscow
Gdansk
(Russia)
Vilnius
Dublin
IRELAND
Amsterdam
The Hague
NETH.
Berlin
Minsk
BELARUS
Samara
London
BELG.
GERMANY
Warsaw
POLAND
Bonn
Brussels
LUX.
Prague
CZECH REP.
Vistula R.
SLOVAK REP.
Kiev
UKRAINE
Kharkov
Don River
Dnieper River
Volgograd
KIRGHIZ STEPPE
KAZAKHSTAN
Lake Balkhash
Paris
Rhine River
Loire R.
LIECH.
Vienna
AUST.
Bratislava
HUNG.
Budapest
CARPATHIANS
Dniester R.
MOLDOVA
Kishinev
Sea of Azov
Bern
SWITZ.
ALPS
SLO.
Sea of Biscay
FRANCE
Venice
Zagreb
CRO.
BOS.
Danube R.
ROMANIA
Bucharest
Aral Sea
MONACO
SAN MARINO
Belgrade
YUGO.
Sarajevo
BULGARIA
Sofia
Black Sea
GEORGIA
CAUCASUS MTS.
Caspian Sea
UZBEKISTAN
Tashkent
KYR.
Bishkek
ANDORRA
PYRENEES
CORSICA (Fr.)
APENNINES
Adriatic Sea
MACE.
Tbilisi
Barcelona
Rome
ITALY
ALB.
Tirana
Istanbul
ARMENIA
Yerevan
Baku
AZERBAIJAN
TURKMENISTAN
Dushanbe
PAMIRS
TAJIKISTAN
PORTUGAL
Lisbon
Madrid
SPAIN
SARDINIA (Italy)
Tyrrhenian Sea
GREECE
Athens
Ankara
ASIA MINOR
TURKEY
KURDISTAN
Ashkhabad
BALEARIC ISLANDS (Sp.)
SICILY (Italy)
Ionian Sea
Aegean Sea
ELBURZ MTS.
Tehran
HINDU KUSH
MALTA
Nicosia
CYPRUS
SYRIA
Euphrates R.
Tigris R.
Kabul
Islamabad
Mediterranean Sea
LEBANON
Beirut
Damascus
Baghdad
ZAGROS MOUNTAINS
IRAN
PLATEAU OF IRAN
AFGHANISTAN
Indus River
Jerusalem
Amman
ISRAEL
JORDAN
IRAQ
Kuwait
KUWAIT
New Delhi
PAKISTAN
THAR DESERT
Persian Gulf
BAHRAIN
QATAR
OMAN
Abu Dhabi
Karachi
INDIA
Riyadh
U.A.E.
Muscat
SAUDI ARABIA
Red Sea
Mecca
RUB AL KHALI (DESERT)
DECCAN PLATEAU
Bombay
Arabian Sea
WESTERN GHATS
Sanaa
YEMEN
AFRICA
Aden
Gulf of Aden
SOCOTRA (Yemen)
LACCADIVE ISLANDS (India)
Colombo
Male
MALDIVES
INDIAN OCEAN
N
W
E
S
National capital
Major city
National boundary
0
400
800 mi.
0
400
800 km.
Robinson Projection
15°E
30°E
45°E
60°E
75°E

105°E
120°E
135°E
150°E
165°E
180°
165°W
150°W
135°W
120°W
ARCTIC OCEAN
75°N
NORTH AMERICA
SIBERIA
Lena River
60°N
Bering Sea
STANOVOI RANGE
Sea of Okhotsk
Lake Baikal
Irkutsk
DA HINGGAN LING
Amur River
SAKHALIN
180°
KURIL ISLANDS
Ulan Bator
MONGOLIA
Harbin
45°N
GOBI (DESERT)
Vladivostok
Sapporo
Sea of Japan
N. KOREA
Beijing
Pyongyang
Seoul
JAPAN
S. KOREA
Tokyo
Huang He
Yellow Sea
Osaka
PEOPLE'S REPUBLIC OF CHINA
Jiang
Shanghai
30°N
East China Sea
Taipei
TAIWAN
PACIFIC OCEAN
Xi Jiang
Guangzhou
MACAO (Port.)
HONG KONG (U.K.)
MYANMAR (BURMA)
Hanoi
LAOS
Gulf of Tonkin
HAINAN
Philippine Sea
Vientiane
Yangon (Rangoon)
Mekong
Da Nang
THAILAND
15°N
Bangkok
CAMBODIA
VIETNAM
Manila
PHILIPPINES
Phnom Penh
Ho Chi Minh City (Saigon)
South China Sea
Bandar Seri Begawan
BRUNEI
MALAYSIA
Kuala Lumpur
MALAYSIA
Singapore
SINGAPORE
SUMATRA
BORNEO
0°
CELEBES
INDONESIA
Java Sea
NEW GUINEA
Jakarta
JAVA
Arafura Sea
Timor Sea
15°S
AUSTRALIA
105°E
120°E
135°E
150°E
165°E

ATLAS

PACIFIC RIM: *Political/Physical*

120°E
150°E
180°
150°W
120°W
90°W
ARCTIC OCEAN
Arctic Circle
RUSSIA
60°N
ALASKA (U.S.)
Anchorage
Bering Sea
KAMCHATKA
ASIA
SAKHALIN
MONGOLIA
CANADA
Vancouver
NORTH AMERICA
Seattle
Ottawa
Vladivostok
KURIL IS. (Russia)
NORTH KOREA
Beijing
Pyongyang
Seoul
JAPAN
PEOPLE'S REPUBLIC OF CHINA
SOUTH KOREA
Tokyo
PACIFIC OCEAN
San Francisco
UNITED STATES
Washington
Los Angeles
30°N
Shanghai
East China Sea
RYUKYU IS. (Japan)
VOLCANO IS. (Japan)
International Date Line
MIDWAY ISLANDS (U.S.)
Taipei
Hanoi
HONG KONG (U.K.)
TAIWAN
Tropic of Cancer
Honolulu
HAWAII (U.S.)
MEXICO
Mexico City
WAKE ISLAND (U.S.)
LAOS
VIETNAM
THAILAND
CAMBODIA
Philippine Sea
NORTHERN MARIANA ISLANDS (U.S.)
MARSHALL ISLANDS
BELIZE
HONDURAS
GUATEMALA
EL SALVADOR
NICARAGUA
COSTA RICA
PANAMA
Manila
PHILIPPINES
GUAM (U.S.)
MICRONESIA
Kolonia
Majuro
South China Sea
Kuala Lumpur
BRUNEI
MALAYSIA
SINGAPORE
PALAU (U.S.)
FEDERATED STATES OF MICRONESIA
Tarawa
Equator
GALAPAGOS IS. (Ecuador)
ECUADOR
Yaren
NAURU
INDONESIA
PAPUA NEW GUINEA
NEW GUINEA
SOLOMON ISLANDS
TUVALU
Funafuti
KIRIBATI
Jakarta
Port Moresby
Honiara
TOKELAU (N.Z.)
POLYNESIA
INDIAN OCEAN
Arafura Sea
Timor Sea
Gulf of Carpentaria
Great Barrier Reef
VANUATU
WALLIS AND FUTUNA IS. (Fr.)
WESTERN SAMOA
Apia
AMERICAN SAMOA (U.S.)
FRENCH POLYNESIA (Fr.)
Lima
GREAT SANDY DESERT
GREAT DIVIDING RANGE
Port-Vila
Suva
TONGA
NIUE (N.Z.)
COOK ISLANDS (N.Z.)
SOUTH AMERICA
Coral Sea
FIJI
Nuku'alofa
Tropic of Capricorn
MACDONNELL RANGE
NEW CALEDONIA (Fr.)
PITCAIRN I. (U.K.)
EASTER I. (Chile)
DARLING RANGE
AUSTRALIA
30°S
NORFOLK I. (Aust.)
KERMADEC ISLANDS (N.Z.)
Valparaíso
Santiago
Sydney
Canberra
Great Australian Bight
Auckland
PACIFIC OCEAN
NEW ZEALAND
TASMANIA
Wellington
Tasman Sea
CHATHAM IS. (N.Z.)
Scale at Equator
0 1000 2000 mi.
0 1000 2000 km
Miller Cylindrical Projection
60°S
Antarctic Circle
National capital
Major city
National boundary
ANTARCTICA

AFRICA: *Political/Physical*

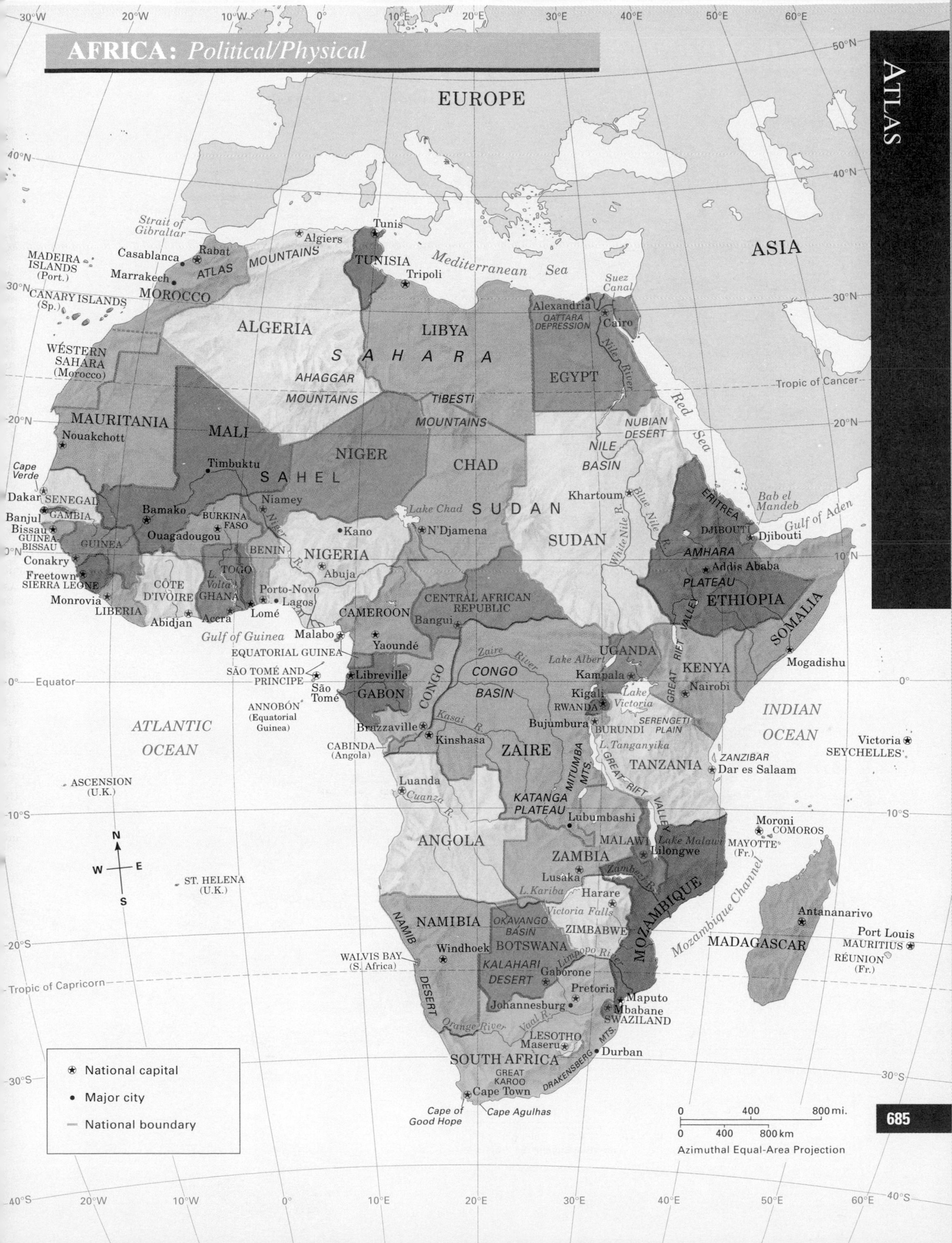
EUROPE
ASIA
Strait of Gibraltar
MADEIRA ISLANDS (Port.)
CANARY ISLANDS (Sp.)
WESTERN SAHARA (Morocco)
Casablanca
Rabat
Marrakech
ATLAS MOUNTAINS
MOROCCO
Algiers
Tunis
TUNISIA
Mediterranean Sea
Tripoli
ALGERIA
LIBYA
S A H A R A
AHAGGAR MOUNTAINS
TIBESTI MOUNTAINS
Suez Canal
Alexandria
QATTARA DEPRESSION
Cairo
Nile River
EGYPT
Red Sea
Tropic of Cancer
NUBIAN DESERT
NILE BASIN
MAURITANIA
Nouakchott
MALI
NIGER
CHAD
Timbuktu
S A H E L
Cape Verde
Dakar
SENEGAL
Banjul
GAMBIA
Bissau
GUINEA-BISSAU
Bamako
BURKINA FASO
Niamey
Niger R.
Ouagadougou
GUINEA
Conakry
Freetown
SIERRA LEONE
Monrovia
LIBERIA
CÔTE D'IVOIRE
Abidjan
GHANA
L. Volta
Accra
TOGO
Lomé
BENIN
Porto-Novo
Lagos
NIGERIA
Kano
Abuja
Lake Chad
N'Djamena
S U D A N
SUDAN
Khartoum
White Nile R.
Blue Nile R.
ERITREA
Bab el Mandeb
Gulf of Aden
DJIBOUTI
Djibouti
AMHARA PLATEAU
Addis Ababa
ETHIOPIA
SOMALIA
Mogadishu
CAMEROON
Yaoundé
CENTRAL AFRICAN REPUBLIC
Bangui
Gulf of Guinea
Malabo
EQUATORIAL GUINEA
SÃO TOMÉ AND PRINCIPE
São Tomé
Libreville
GABON
CONGO
ANNOBÓN (Equatorial Guinea)
Zaire River
CONGO BASIN
Lake Albert
UGANDA
Kampala
KENYA
Nairobi
GREAT RIFT VALLEY
Lake Victoria
Kigali
RWANDA
Bujumbura
BURUNDI
SERENGETI PLAIN
Brazzaville
Kinshasa
Kasai R.
ZAIRE
CABINDA (Angola)
MITUMBA MTS.
L. Tanganyika
TANZANIA
ZANZIBAR
Dar es Salaam
ATLANTIC OCEAN
INDIAN OCEAN
Equator
ASCENSION (U.K.)
Luanda
Cuanza R.
KATANGA PLATEAU
Lubumbashi
ANGOLA
MALAWI
Lake Malawi
Lilongwe
ZAMBIA
Lusaka
Zambezi R.
L. Kariba
Harare
Victoria Falls
ZIMBABWE
MOZAMBIQUE
Mozambique Channel
Victoria
SEYCHELLES
Moroni
COMOROS
MAYOTTE (Fr.)
MADAGASCAR
Antananarivo
Port Louis
MAURITIUS
RÉUNION (Fr.)
ST. HELENA (U.K.)
N
S
E
W
NAMIBIA
NAMIB DESERT
Windhoek
WALVIS BAY (S. Africa)
OKAVANGO BASIN
BOTSWANA
KALAHARI DESERT
Gaborone
Limpopo River
Pretoria
Johannesburg
Maputo
Mbabane
SWAZILAND
Orange River
Vaal R.
LESOTHO
Maseru
Durban
DRAKENSBERG MTS.
SOUTH AFRICA
GREAT KAROO
Cape Town
Cape of Good Hope
Cape Agulhas
Tropic of Capricorn
National capital
Major city
National boundary
0 400 800 mi.
0 400 800 km
Azimuthal Equal-Area Projection

NORTH AMERICA: *Political/Physical*

ARCTIC OCEAN
ASIA
EUROPE
Bering Sea
Bering Strait
Beaufort Sea
BROOKS RANGE
Yukon River
ALASKA RANGE
Fairbanks
Anchorage
Gulf of Alaska
KODIAK ISLAND
ALEXANDER ARCHIPELAGO
QUEEN CHARLOTTE ISLANDS
VANCOUVER ISLAND
COAST MOUNTAINS
QUEEN ELIZABETH ISLANDS
ELLESMERE ISLAND
BANKS ISLAND
VICTORIA ISLAND
BAFFIN ISLAND
Baffin Bay
GREENLAND (Denmark)
Arctic Circle
Great Bear Lake
Mackenzie River
Great Slave Lake
LAURENTIAN SHIELD
Hudson Bay
UNGAVA PENINSULA
LABRADOR
Labrador Sea
NEWFOUNDLAND
PRINCE EDWARD ISLAND
CAPE BRETON ISLAND
CANADA
Edmonton
Calgary
Lake Winnipeg
Winnipeg
ROCKY MOUNTAINS
Vancouver
Puget Sound
Seattle
Portland
Quebec
Montreal
Ottawa
St. Lawrence River
Bay of Fundy
L. Superior
Lake Michigan
Lake Huron
L. Ontario
Lake Erie
Toronto
Detroit
Cleveland
Boston
Cape Cod
New York
Philadelphia
Baltimore
Washington
APPALACHIAN MTS.
ATLANTIC OCEAN
BLACK HILLS
Minneapolis
Milwaukee
Chicago
Missouri River
Omaha
Snake R.
Great Salt Lake
Salt Lake City
San Francisco
SIERRA NEVADA
COAST RANGES
Denver
Indianapolis
Ohio River
Kansas City
St. Louis
Louisville
Colorado River
Wichita
Los Angeles
MOJAVE DESERT
GRAND CANYON
UNITED STATES
San Diego
Phoenix
Nashville
Charlotte
Cape Hatteras
BERMUDA (U.K.)
Red River
Atlanta
Birmingham
Mississippi River
Fort Worth
Ciudad Juárez
Rio Grande
PACIFIC OCEAN
Gulf of California
Chihuahua
Austin
Houston
San Antonio
New Orleans
Jacksonville
Cape Canaveral
Tropic of Cancer
BAJA CALIFORNIA
SIERRA MADRE OCCIDENTAL
SIERRA MADRE ORIENTAL
Monterrey
Miami
Nassau
BAHAMAS
Gulf of Mexico
Cabo San Lucas
MEXICO
PLATEAU OF MEXICO
Havana
CUBA
Guadalajara
Mexico City
Veracruz
Puebla
YUCATÁN PENINSULA
Santiago de Cuba
DOMINICAN REPUBLIC
San Juan
VIRGIN ISLANDS (U.S., U.K.)
ANGUILLA (U.K.)
ANTIGUA AND BARBUDA
PUERTO RICO (U.S.)
ST. KITTS AND NEVIS
GUADELOUPE (Fr.)
MARTINIQUE (Fr.)
Port-au-Prince
HAITI
Santo Domingo
CAYMAN ISLANDS (U.K.)
JAMAICA
Kingston
DOMINICA
Roseau
Castries
ST. LUCIA
Bridgetown
BARBADOS
Kingstown
ST. VINCENT AND THE GRENADINES
St. George's
GRENADA
Port-of-Spain
TRINIDAD AND TOBAGO
ISTHMUS OF TEHUANTEPEC
Acapulco
Belmopan
BELIZE
GUATEMALA
Caribbean Sea
NETHERLANDS ANTILLES (Neth.)
ARUBA (Neth.)
Guatemala City
HONDURAS
Tegucigalpa
San Salvador
EL SALVADOR
NICARAGUA
Managua
MOSQUITO COAST
Lago de Nicaragua
San José
COSTA RICA
ISTHMUS OF PANAMA
Panama City
PANAMA
SOUTH AMERICA
Equator
N
S
E
W
National capital
Major city
National boundary
0
400
800 mi.
0
400
800 km
Azimuthal Equal-Area Projection
70°N
80°N
60°N
50°N
40°N
30°N
20°N
10°N
170°E
180°
160°W
150°W
140°W
130°W
120°W
110°W
100°W
90°W
80°W
70°W
60°W
30°W
20°W

SOUTH AMERICA: *Political/Physical*

CENTRAL AMERICA
Caribbean Sea
ATLANTIC OCEAN
Barranquilla
Cartagena
Maracaibo
Caracas
Orinoco River
LLANOS
VENEZUELA
Angel Falls
Gulf of Panama
Cauca R.
Magdalena River
OCCIDENTAL MTS.
Medellín
Bogotá
COLOMBIA
GUIANA HIGHLANDS
Georgetown
GUYANA
Paramaribo
SURINAME
Cayenne
FRENCH GUIANA (Fr.)
MALPELO (Colombia)
Rio Negro
AMAZON
Manaus
Amazon River
Quito
ECUADOR
Equator
GALAPAGOS ISLANDS (Ecuador)
Guayaquil
Gulf of Guayaquil
Iquitos
Solimões River
BASIN
Madeira River
Tapajós River
Xingu River
Belém
Fortaleza
BRAZIL
Tocantins River
São Francisco River
Recife
Trujillo
PERU
ANDES
Lima
Cuzco
PLATEAU OF MATO GROSSO
BRAZILIAN HIGHLANDS
Salvador
Brasília
PACIFIC OCEAN
Lake Titicaca
La Paz
Arequipa
BOLIVIA
ALTIPLANO
Sucre
Paraguay River
Paraná River
Belo Horizonte
ATACAMA DESERT
GRAN CHACO
PARAGUAY
São Paulo
Rio de Janeiro
Santos
Antofagasta
Asunción
Tropic of Capricorn
SAN FÉLIX ISLAND (Chile)
SAN AMBROSIO ISLAND (Chile)
Salado River
Pôrto Alegre
CHILE
Córdoba
Rosario
URUGUAY
Valparaíso
Santiago
Buenos Aires
Montevideo
Río de la Plata
JUAN FERNÁNDEZ ISLANDS (Chile)
ARGENTINA
PAMPAS
ATLANTIC OCEAN
Concepción
Colorado R.
Bahía Blanca
Valdivia
Gulf of San Matías
N
W
E
S
PATAGONIA
Comodoro Rivadavia
Gulf of San Jorge
National capital
Major city
National boundary
Strait of Magellan
FALKLAND ISLANDS (U.K.)
TIERRA DEL FUEGO
0 400 800 mi.
0 400 800 km
Azimuthal Equal-Area Projection
Cape Horn
Drake Passage
SOUTH GEORGIA (U.K.)
90°W 80°W 70°W 60°W 50°W 40°W
20°N 10°N 0° 10°S 20°S 30°S 40°S 50°S
100°W 90°W 80°W 70°W 60°W 50°W 40°W 30°W 20°W

WORLD: *Religions*

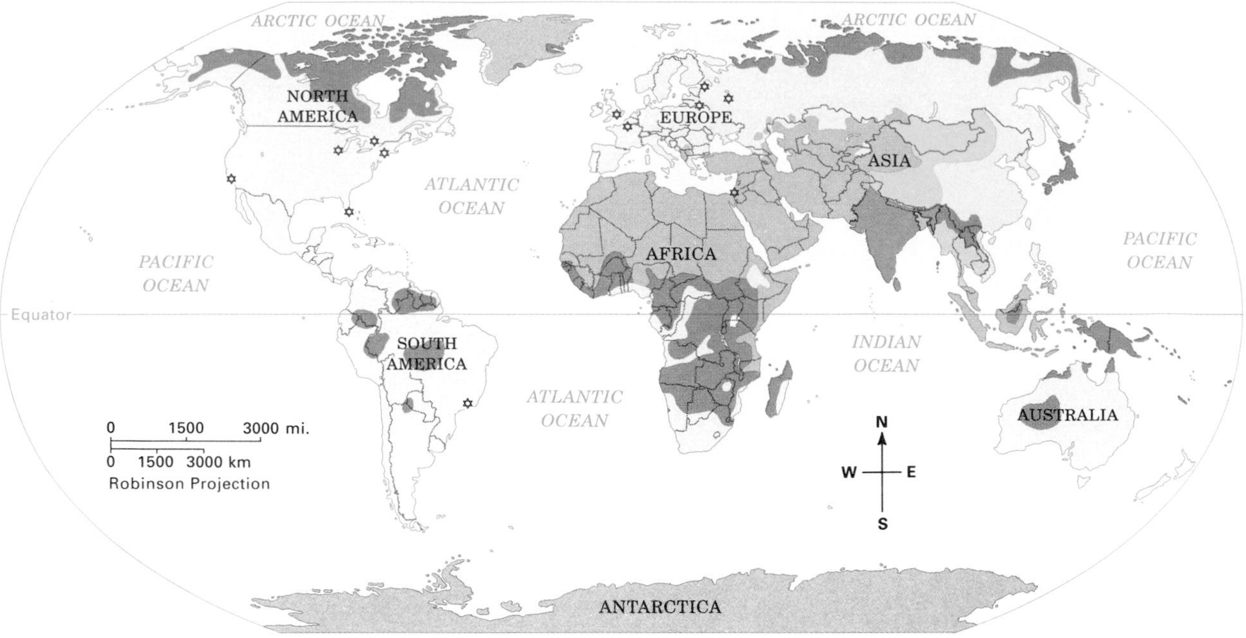
ARCTIC OCEAN
ARCTIC OCEAN
NORTH AMERICA
EUROPE
ASIA
ATLANTIC OCEAN
AFRICA
PACIFIC OCEAN
PACIFIC OCEAN
Equator
SOUTH AMERICA
INDIAN OCEAN
ATLANTIC OCEAN
AUSTRALIA
0 1500 3000 mi.
0 1500 3000 km
Robinson Projection
N
W E
S
ANTARCTICA

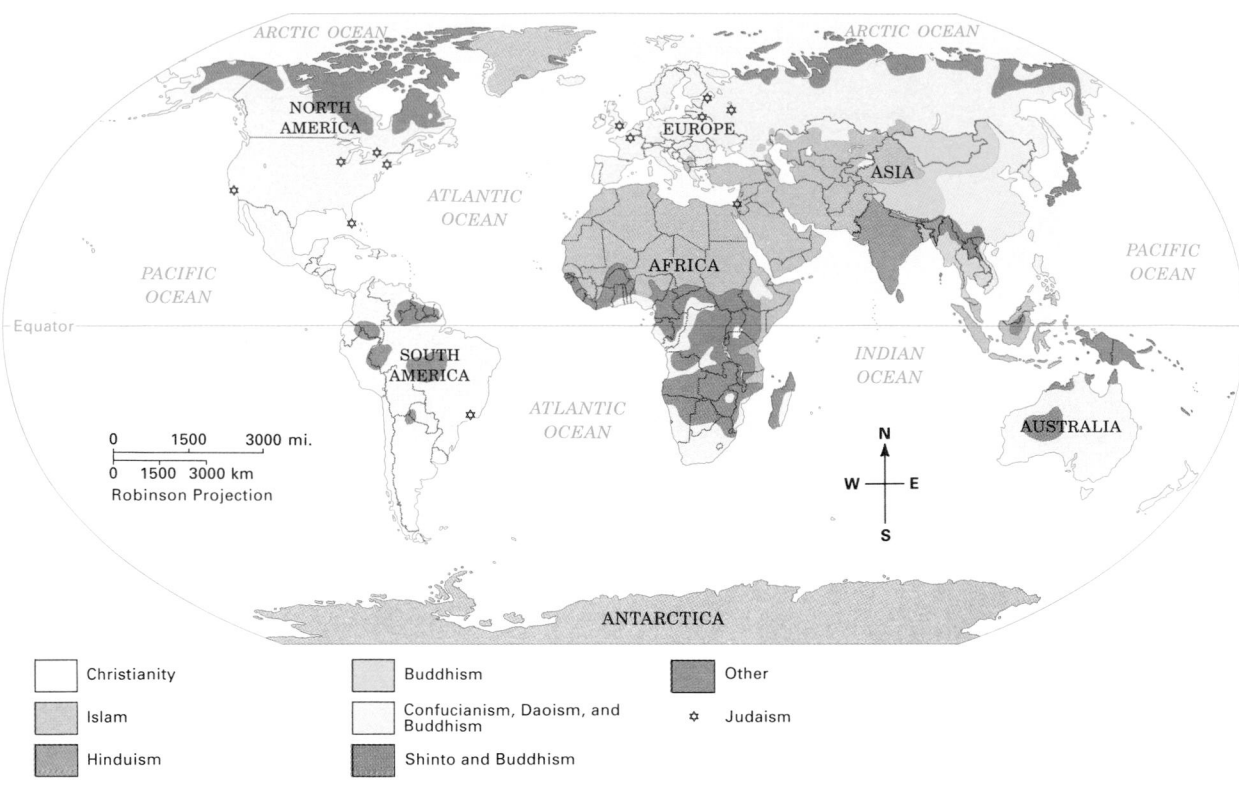

- Christianity
- Islam
- Hinduism
- Buddhism
- Confucianism, Daoism, and Buddhism
- Shinto and Buddhism
- Other
- ✡ Judaism

WORLD: *Climate*

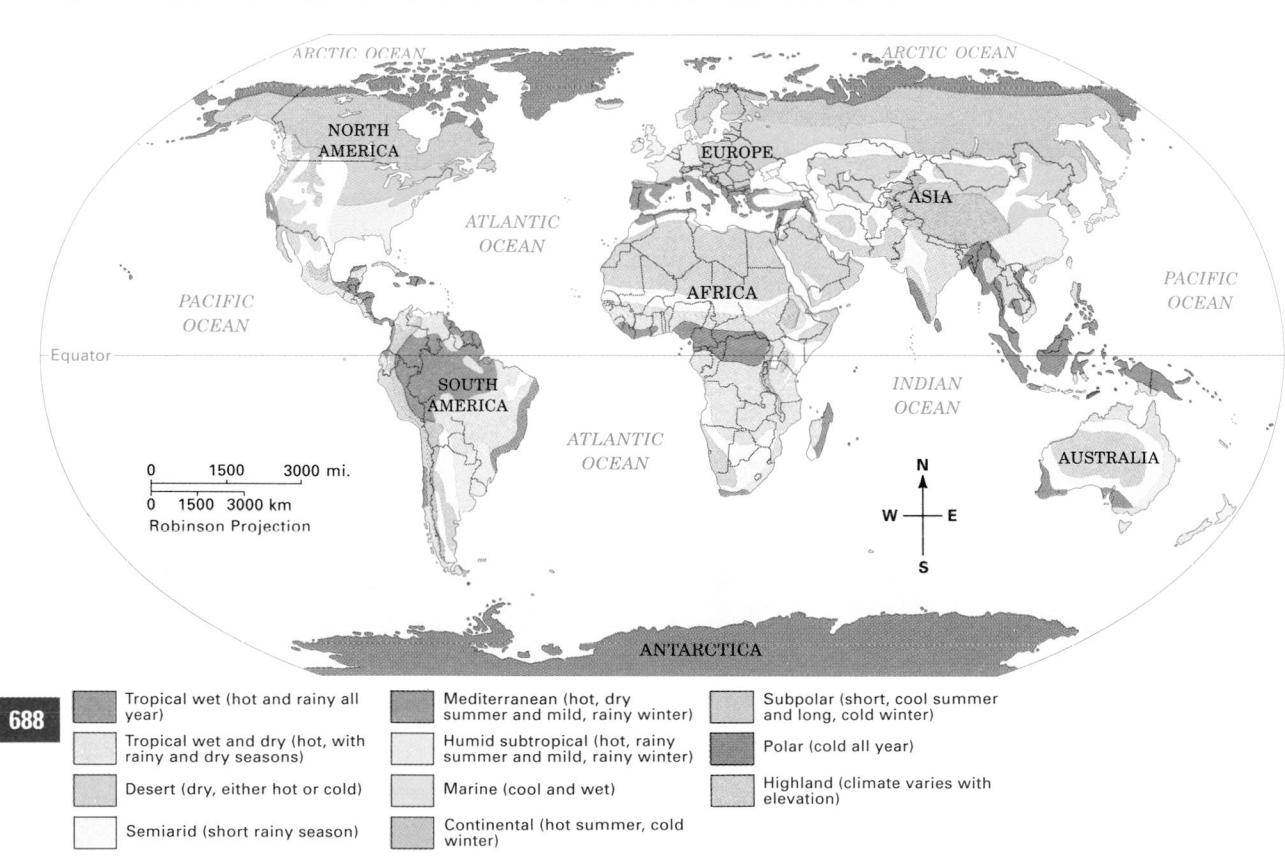

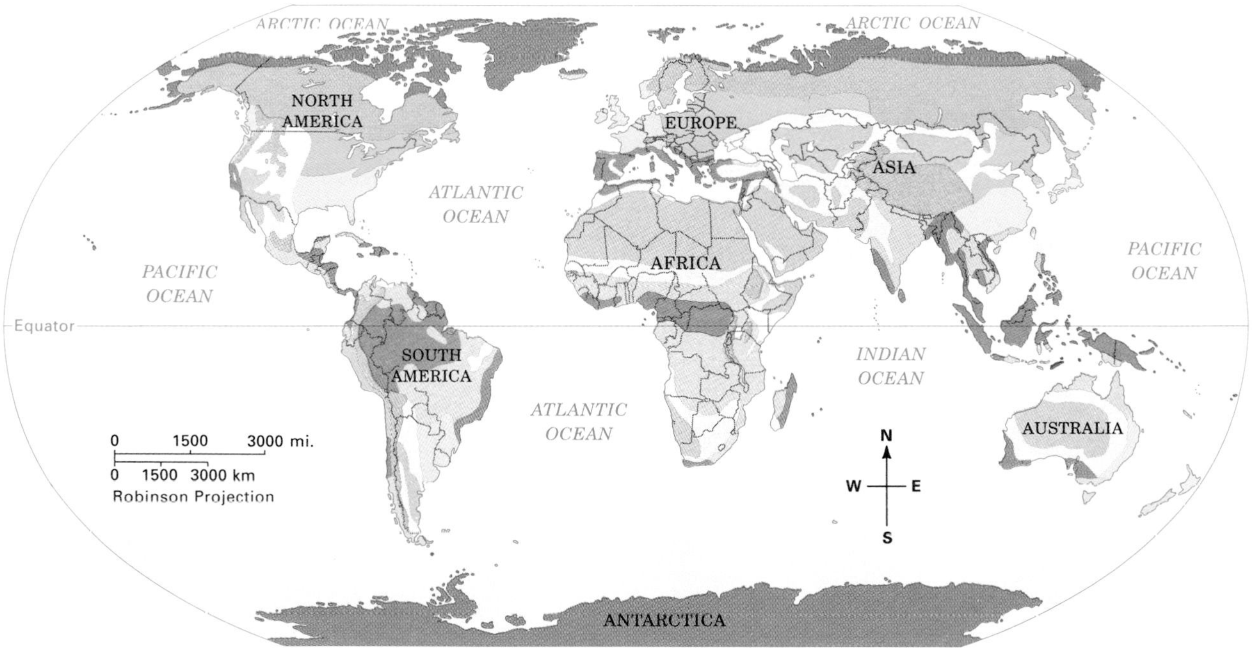
ARCTIC OCEAN
ARCTIC OCEAN
NORTH AMERICA
EUROPE
ASIA
ATLANTIC OCEAN
AFRICA
PACIFIC OCEAN
PACIFIC OCEAN
Equator
SOUTH AMERICA
INDIAN OCEAN
ATLANTIC OCEAN
AUSTRALIA
0 1500 3000 mi.
0 1500 3000 km
Robinson Projection
N
W E
S
ANTARCTICA

- Tropical wet (hot and rainy all year)
- Tropical wet and dry (hot, with rainy and dry seasons)
- Desert (dry, either hot or cold)
- Semiarid (short rainy season)
- Mediterranean (hot, dry summer and mild, rainy winter)
- Humid subtropical (hot, rainy summer and mild, rainy winter)
- Marine (cool and wet)
- Continental (hot summer, cold winter)
- Subpolar (short, cool summer and long, cold winter)
- Polar (cold all year)
- Highland (climate varies with elevation)

WORLD: *Population*

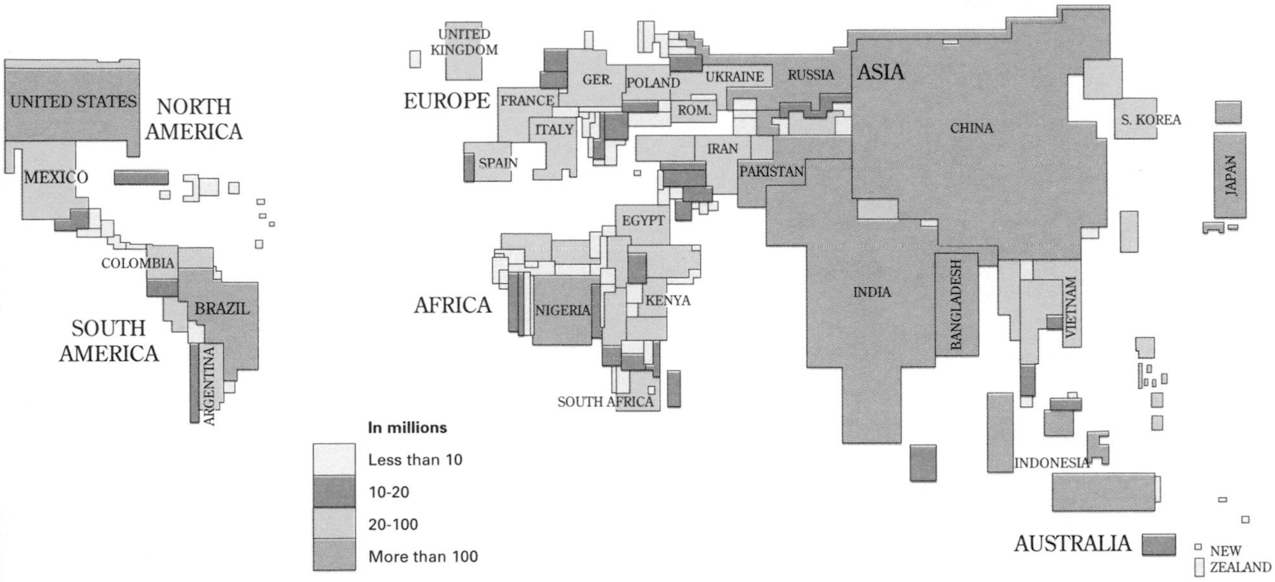
UNITED STATES
NORTH AMERICA
MEXICO
COLOMBIA
BRAZIL
SOUTH AMERICA
ARGENTINA
UNITED KINGDOM
EUROPE
FRANCE
GER.
POLAND
UKRAINE
RUSSIA
ROM.
ITALY
SPAIN
IRAN
PAKISTAN
EGYPT
AFRICA
NIGERIA
KENYA
SOUTH AFRICA
ASIA
CHINA
S. KOREA
JAPAN
INDIA
BANGLADESH
VIETNAM
INDONESIA
AUSTRALIA
NEW ZEALAND
In millions
Less than 10
10-20
20-100
More than 100

Each country's size in the cartogram represents the size of its population compared with those of other countries in the world. Based on information in *Statistical Abstract of the United States 1995.*

WORLD: *Land Use, Land and Ocean Resources*

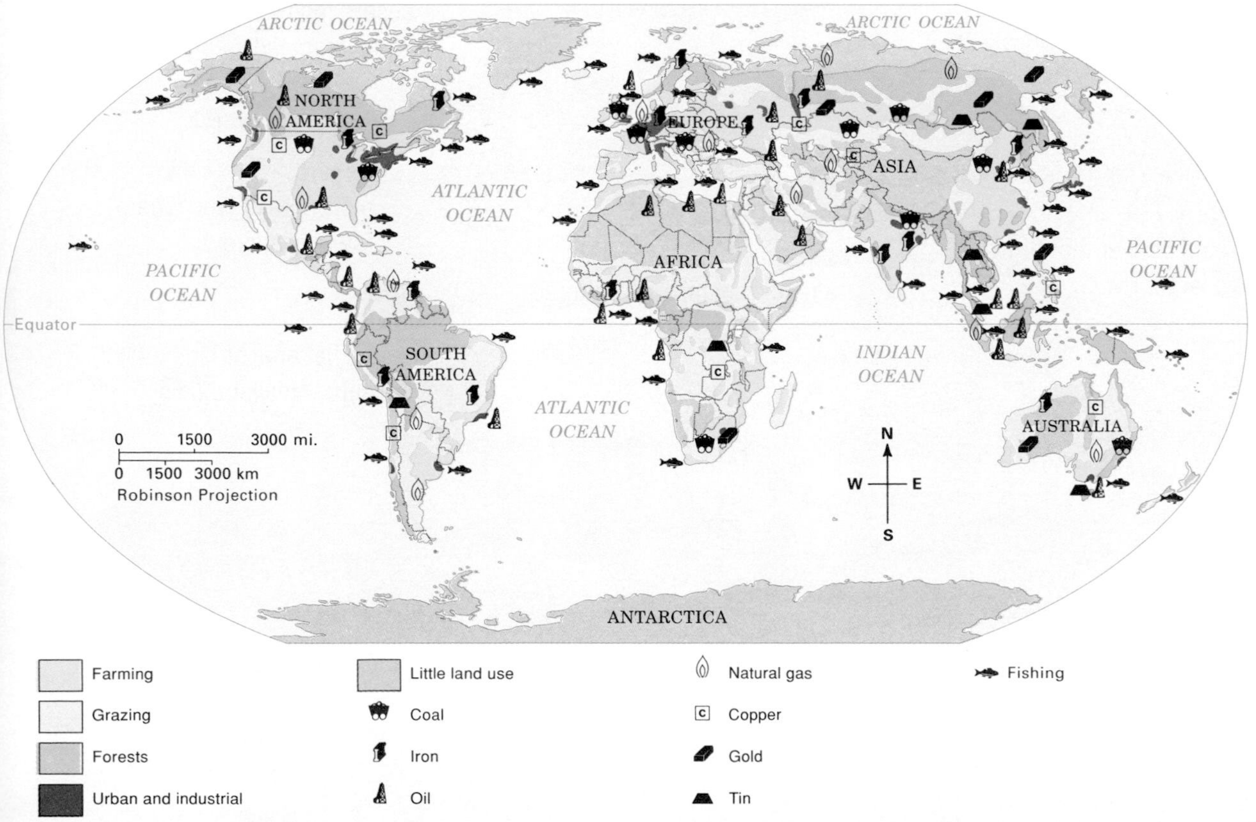
ARCTIC OCEAN
ARCTIC OCEAN
NORTH AMERICA
EUROPE
ASIA
ATLANTIC OCEAN
PACIFIC OCEAN
AFRICA
PACIFIC OCEAN
Equator
SOUTH AMERICA
INDIAN OCEAN
ATLANTIC OCEAN
AUSTRALIA
0 1500 3000 mi.
0 1500 3000 km
Robinson Projection
N
W
E
S
ANTARCTICA
Farming
Grazing
Forests
Urban and industrial
Little land use
Coal
Iron
Oil
Natural gas
Copper
Gold
Tin
Fishing

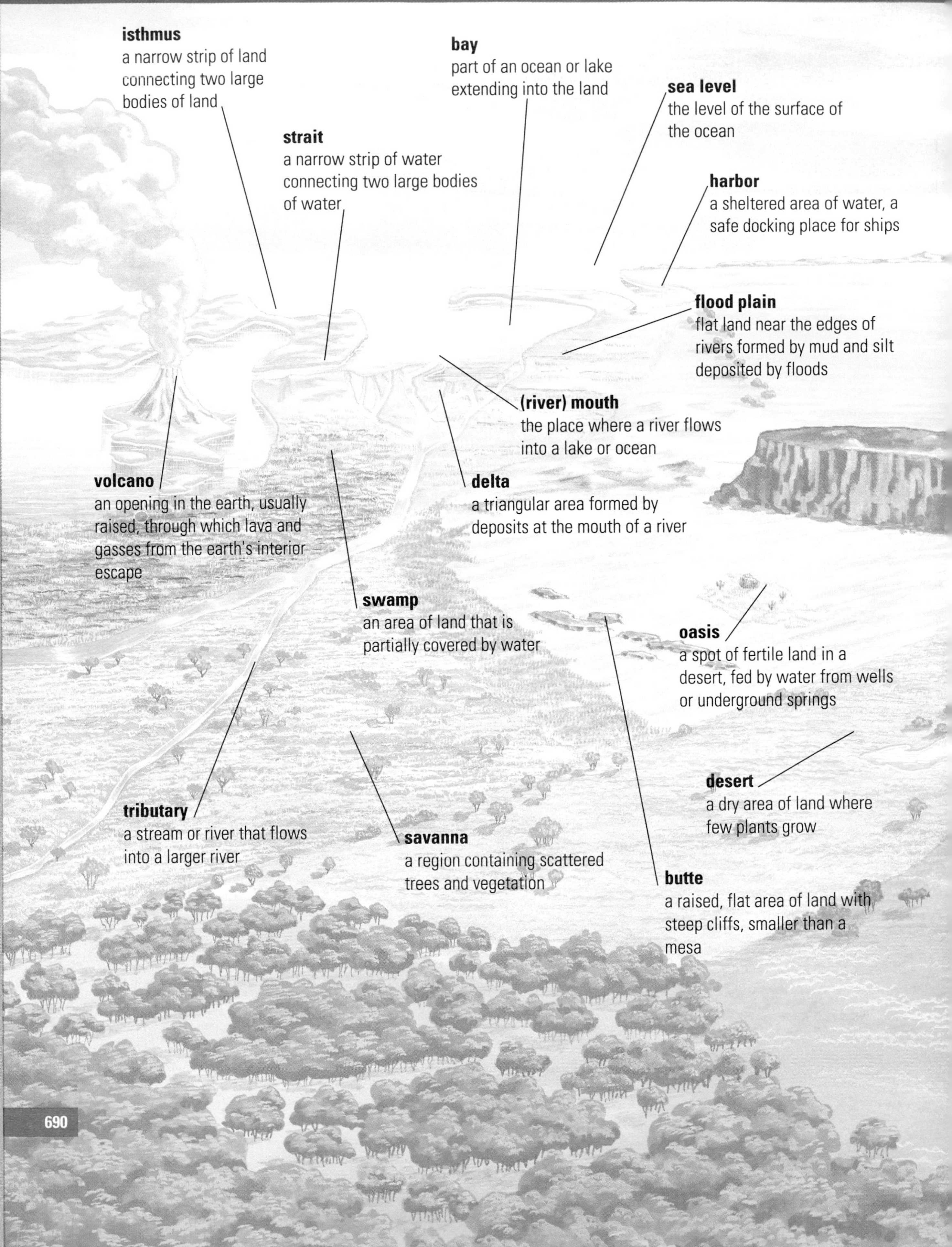
isthmus
a narrow strip of land connecting two large bodies of land
bay
part of an ocean or lake extending into the land
sea level
the level of the surface of the ocean
strait
a narrow strip of water connecting two large bodies of water
harbor
a sheltered area of water, a safe docking place for ships
flood plain
flat land near the edges of rivers formed by mud and silt deposited by floods
(river) mouth
the place where a river flows into a lake or ocean
volcano
an opening in the earth, usually raised, through which lava and gasses from the earth's interior escape
delta
a triangular area formed by deposits at the mouth of a river
swamp
an area of land that is partially covered by water
oasis
a spot of fertile land in a desert, fed by water from wells or underground springs
desert
a dry area of land where few plants grow
tributary
a stream or river that flows into a larger river
savanna
a region containing scattered trees and vegetation
butte
a raised, flat area of land with steep cliffs, smaller than a mesa

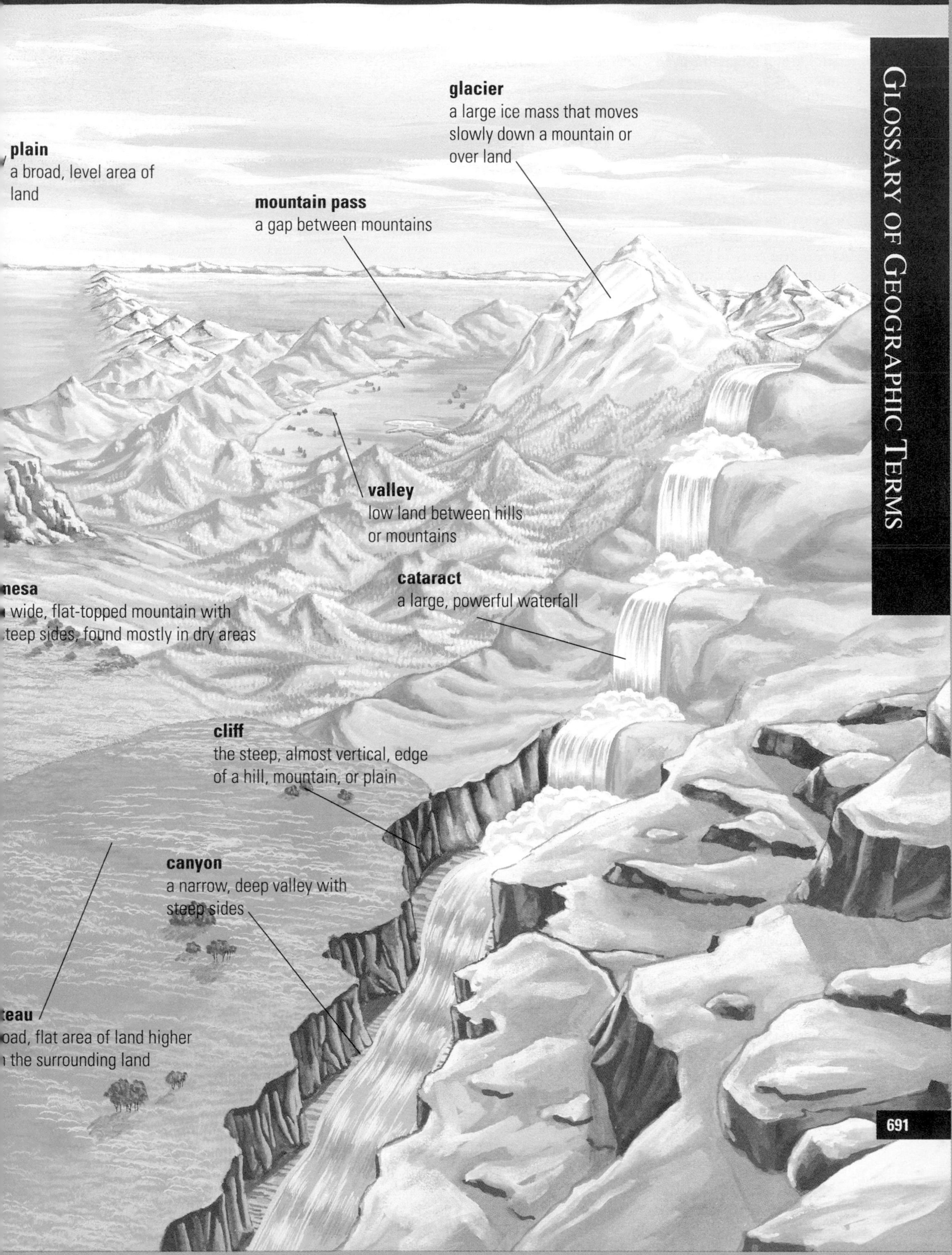
glacier
a large ice mass that moves slowly down a mountain or over land
plain
a broad, level area of land
mountain pass
a gap between mountains
valley
low land between hills or mountains
cataract
a large, powerful waterfall
nesa
wide, flat-topped mountain with teep sides, found mostly in dry areas
cliff
the steep, almost vertical, edge of a hill, mountain, or plain
canyon
a narrow, deep valley with steep sides
teau
oad, flat area of land higher
the surrounding land

Gazetteer

This Gazetteer will help you locate many of the places discussed in this book. Latitude and longitude given for large areas of land and water refer to the centermost point of the area; latitude and longitude of rivers refer to the river mouth. The page number tells you where to find each place on a map.

A

PLACE	LAT.	LONG.	PAGE
Accra (capital of Ghana)	6°N	0°	**282**
Aegean Sea (part of the Mediterranean Sea)	39°N	25°E	**155**
Alexandria (city in Egypt founded by Alexander the Great)	31°N	30°E	**178**
altiplano (high plateau, as in the Andes region)	19°S	68°W	**687**
Amazon R. (in South America; largest in the world)	1°S	52°W	**557**
Andes (mountain system in South America)	13°S	75°W	**687**
Angel Falls (in S.E. Venezuela; world's highest waterfall)	5°N	62°W	**687**
Arabian Sea (in Asia; meets the Indian Ocean)	16°N	65°E	**190**
Aral Sea (inland sea between Kazakhstan and Uzbekistan)	45°N	60°E	**494**
Argos (ancient Greek city-state)	38°N	23°E	**155**
Ashanti (region in central Ghana)	7°N	2°W	**282**
Assur (ancient city of Assyria; in modern Iraq)	35°N	43°E	**71**
Athens (ancient city-state; capital of modern Greece)	38°N	24°E	**155**
Attica (ancient region in central Greece)	38°N	24°E	**155**

B

PLACE	LAT.	LONG.	PAGE
Babylon (ancient city-kingdom and capital of Babylonia)	33°N	44°E	**67**
Baghdad (capital of modern Iraq)	33°N	44°E	**215**
Baikal, Lake (in S. Siberia)	53°N	109°E	**494**
Baja California (peninsula in N.W. Mexico; between the Pacific Ocean and the Gulf of California)	27°N	114°W	**585**
Baltic Sea (in N. Europe)	55°N	17°E	**494**
Beijing (capital of China)	40°N	116°E	**348**
Benares (city in north-central India; now known as Varanasi)	25°N	83°E	**324**
Bengal, Bay of (part of the Indian Ocean)	18°N	87°E	**324**
Bering Strait (waterway separating Asia and North America)	65°N	169°W	**686**
Berlin (capital of Germany)	53°N	13°E	**473**
Black Sea (between Europe and Asia)	43°N	35°E	**178**
Bombay (city in W. India where the British first traded)	19°N	73°E	**324**
Brasília (capital of Brazil)	16°S	48°W	**551**
Buenos Aires (capital of Argentina)	34°S	59°W	**687**

C

PLACE	LAT.	LONG.	PAGE
Cairo (capital of Egypt)	30°N	31°E	**240**
Calcutta (chief commercial port in India)	23°N	88°E	**324**
Cape Town (capital of South Africa)	34°S	18°E	**294**
Caribbean Sea (area of the western Atlantic Ocean bounded by Central and S. America and West Indies)	15°N	73°W	**509**
Caspian Sea (largest salt lake and inland sea in the world; between Europe and Asia)	42°N	51°E	**169**
Chang Jiang (river in China; also known as the Yangtze R.)	32°N	121°E	**115**
Constantinople (modern Istanbul; capital of the Byzantine and Ottoman empires)	41°N	29°E	**413**
Corinth (ancient Greek commercial city)	38°N	23°E	**155**
Crete (island of Greece; in the Mediterranean Sea)	35°N	25°E	**155**
Crimea (in Ukraine; peninsula extending into the Black Sea)	45°N	34°E	**419**
Cuzco (in Peru; capital of the Inca Empire)	14°S	72°W	**139**

D

PLACE	LAT.	LONG.	PAGE
Danube R. (second longest river in Europe)	45°N	30°E	**169**
Dasht-e-Kavir (salt desert in north-central Iran)	35°N	54°E	**205**
Dasht-e-Lut (desert in east-central Iran)	32°N	59°E	**205**
Delhi (in India; capital of the Mughal Empire)	29°N	77°E	**324**

E

PLACE	LAT.	LONG.	PAGE
Elburz Mts. (mountain range in N. Iran)	37°N	51°E	**205**
Elmina (seaport in Ghana)	2°W	5°N	**269**

PLACE	LAT.	LONG.	PAGE
Ephesus (ancient city in modern Turkey)	38°N	27°E	**155**
Euphrates R. (in S.W. Asia; along with the Tigris R., the site of several ancient civilizations)	31°N	47°E	**67**
Everest, Mt. (part of the Himalaya range; highest mountain in the world)	28°N	87°E	**115**
F			
Fuji, Mt. (volcano in Japan, inactive since 1707)	35°N	139°E	**361**
G			
Ganges R. (in India; Hindu holy river)	23°N	91°E	**331**
Gao (in Mali; capital of the Songhai Empire)	16°N	0°	**256**
Good Hope, Cape of (on the S.W. coast of Africa)	34°S	19°E	**298**
Great Rift Valley (land depression stretching from Jordan to S.E. Africa)	0°	36°E	**224**
Guadalajara (city in S.W. Mexico)	21°N	103°W	**585**
Guangzhou (city in China)	23°N	113°E	**348**
Guiana Highlands (plateau and mountain region in northern South America)	3°N	60°W	**687**
Guinea, Gulf of (part of the Atlantic Ocean off the coast of western Africa)	2°N	1°E	**269**
H			
Hanoi (capital of Vietnam)	21°N	106°E	**387**
Himalayas (mountain system in Asia)	28°N	84°E	**115**
Hindu Kush (mountain range in central Asia)	36°N	70°E	**324**
Hiroshima (city in S.W. Japan)	34°N	132°E	**361**
Hormuz, Strait of (connects the Persian Gulf to the Gulf of Oman)	27°N	57°E	**205**
Horn, Cape (southernmost tip of South America)	56°S	67°W	**503**
Huang He (river in China; also known as the Yellow R.)	38°N	117°E	**115**
Hudson Bay (inland sea in Canada)	60°N	86°W	**599**

PLACE	LAT.	LONG.	PAGE
I			
Indus R. (in Pakistan; longest of the Himalayan rivers)	24°N	68°E	**331**
Isfahan (city in Iran)	33°N	52°E	**209**
Ithaca (Greek island)	38°N	21°E	**155**
J			
Jakarta (capital of Indonesia)	6°S	107°E	**387**
Jericho (ancient city in present-day Occupied Territory)	32°N	35°E	**67**
Johannesburg (city in South Africa)	26°S	28°E	**294**
Jordan R. (forms the boundary between Israel and Jordan, and Israel and Syria)	32°N	36°E	**652**
K			
Khyber Pass (narrow mountain pass on the border between W. Afghanistan and N. Pakistan)	34°N	71°E	**324**
Kiev (capital of Ukraine)	50°N	31°E	**494**
Kumasi (capital of the Ashanti Region in Ghana)	7°N	2°W	**269**
Kunlun Shan (mountain range in China)	36°N	88°E	**115**
Kyoto (city in Japan)	35°N	136°E	**361**
L			
Lima (capital of Peru)	12°S	77°W	**687**
London (capital of the United Kingdom)	52°N	0°	**682**
M			
Machu Picchu (in Peru; ruined Inca citadel)	13°S	73°W	**139**
Mackenzie Mts. (mountain range in N.W. Canada)	64°N	129°W	**599**
Mackenzie R. (in N.W. Canada)	69°N	134°W	**599**
Manila (capital of the Philippines)	15°N	121°E	**387**
Mecca (in Saudi Arabia; holiest city of Islam)	21°N	40°E	**190**
Medina (in Saudi Arabia; holy city of Islam)	24°N	40°E	**190**
Mediterranean Sea (between Europe and Africa)	35°N	20°E	**178**

PLACE	LAT.	LONG.	PAGE
Memphis (ancient city in Lower Egypt; capital of most rulers of the Old Kingdom)	30°N	31°E	**86**
Meroë (ancient city on east bank of the Nile; capital of Nubia)	17°N	34°E	**86**
Mesopotamia (region in S.W. Asia; site of Babylonia and Assyria)	34°N	44°E	**67**
Mexico City (capital of Mexico)	19°N	99°W	**585**
Montréal (in Canada; French settlement)	46°N	74°W	**599**
Moscow (capital of Russia)	56°N	38°E	**494**

N

PLACE	LAT.	LONG.	PAGE
Napata (ancient capital of Nubia in Egypt)	19°N	32°E	**86**
Nile R. (in Africa; longest river in the world)	30°N	31°E	**83**
North Sea (part of the Atlantic Ocean, between Great Britain and the European continent)	56°N	3°E	**494**
Nubia (ancient empire in N.E. Africa)	21°N	33°E	**83**

O

PLACE	LAT.	LONG.	PAGE
Olympus, Mt. (highest mountain in Greece; on the Macedonia-Thessaly border)	40°N	22°E	**155**
Orinoco R. (river in Venezuela)	9°N	61°W	**687**

P

PLACE	LAT.	LONG.	PAGE
Pampas (plains in S. South America)	37°S	65°W	**687**
Panama Canal (in Panama; opened in 1914)	9°N	81°W	**543**
Paraná R. (in S.E. South America)	34°S	59°W	**557**
Paris (capital of France)	49°N	2°E	**682**
Peloponnesus (peninsula of Greece)	38°N	22°E	**155**
Persepolis (in Iran; ancient capital of Persia)	30°N	53°E	**205**
Persian Gulf (part of the Arabian Sea; between Iran and the Arabian Peninsula)	27°N	51°E	**215**
Pinatubo, Mt. (volcano in the Philippines; erupted in June 1991)	15°N	120°E	**401**
Pretoria (administrative capital of South Africa)	26°S	28°E	**294**
Pyongyang (capital of North Korea)	39°N	126°E	**653**

Q

PLACE	LAT.	LONG.	PAGE
Québec (in Canada; French settlement)	47°N	71°W	**599**
Quito (capital of Ecuador)	0°	79°W	**687**

R

PLACE	LAT.	LONG.	PAGE
Red Sea (between the Arabian Peninsula and N.E. Africa)	20°N	38°E	**234**
Rhone R. (in Switzerland and France)	43°N	5°E	**169**
Rio de Janeiro (seaport in Brazil)	23°S	43°W	**557**
Rio Grande (river that forms the boundary between Texas and Mexico)	26°N	97°W	**585**
Rome (capital of Italy; center of ancient Roman Empire)	42°N	13°E	**169**

S

PLACE	LAT.	LONG.	PAGE
Sahara (largest desert on the earth; stretches across northern Africa)	24°N	2°W	**224**
San José (capital of Costa Rica)	10°N	84°W	**543**
São Paulo (city in Brazil)	24°S	47°W	**557**
Seoul (capital of South Korea)	38°N	127°E	**653**
Siberia (vast region in Russia; covers the northern third of Asia)	57°N	97°E	**683**
Sicily (island of Italy in the Mediterranean Sea)	38°N	14°E	**178**
Sierra Madre del Sur (part of the Sierra Madre range on the coast of southern Mexico)	17°N	100°W	**585**
Sierra Madre Occidental (part of the Sierra Madre range in Mexico; runs almost parallel to the Gulf of California and the Pacific Ocean)	21°N	105°W	**585**
Sierra Madre Oriental (part of the Sierra Madre range in Mexico; runs almost parallel to the Gulf of Mexico)	21°N	99°W	**585**
Sinai Peninsula (easternmost part of Egypt; between the Gulf of Suez and the Gulf of Aqaba)	30°N	34°E	**240**
Sparta (ancient city-state of Greece)	37°N	22°E	**155**

PLACE	LAT.	LONG.	PAGE
St. Petersburg (in Russia; Peter the Great's capital)	60°N	30°E	**494**
Susa (ancient city in Persia)	32°N	49°E	**209**

T

PLACE	LAT.	LONG.	PAGE
Tehran (capital of Iran)	36°N	52°E	**205**
Tema (city in Ghana)	6°N	0°	**282**
Tenochtitlan (modern Mexico City; capital of the Aztec Empire)	19°N	99°W	**130**
Tian Shan (mountain range in Asia)	42°N	80°E	**115**
Tibet, Plateau of (region of China; highest plateau in the world)	33°N	92°E	**115**
Tigris R. (in S.W. Asia; along with the Euphrates R., site of several ancient civilizations)	31°N	47°E	**67**
Timbuktu (in modern Mali; city in Songhai Empire)	17°N	3°W	**256**
Titicaca, Lake (in Bolivia and Peru; center of early South American civilizations)	16°S	69°W	**139**
Tokyo (Edo; center of the Tokugawa shogunate; capital of Japan)	36°N	140°E	**361**
Toronto (city in Ontario, Canada)	44°N	79°W	**599**

U

PLACE	LAT.	LONG.	PAGE
Ur (city in ancient Sumer)	31°N	46°E	**67**
Ural Mts. (mountain range in Russia; form the border between Europe and Asia)	56°N	58°E	**453**
Uxmal (in Mexico; capital of the later Mayan Empire)	20°N	90°W	**130**

V

PLACE	LAT.	LONG.	PAGE
Vancouver (city in British Columbia, Canada)	49°N	123°W	**599**
Veracruz (city in Mexico)	19°N	96°W	**585**
Vladivostok (seaport in Russia)	43°N	132°E	**494**
Volga R. (in Russia; longest river in Europe)	46°N	49°E	**494**
Volta R. (in Ghana)	5°N	1°E	**269**
Volta, Lake (reservoir in Ghana)	7°N	1°W	**282**

X

PLACE	LAT.	LONG.	PAGE
Xi'an (early capital of China; on Wei He)	34°N	109°E	**341**

Y

PLACE	LAT.	LONG.	PAGE
Yucatán Peninsula (mainly in S.E. Mexico)	20°N	89°W	**130**
Yukon R. (in North America; flows from Canada across Alaska)	62°N	165°W	**599**

Z

PLACE	LAT.	LONG.	PAGE
Zagros Mts. (mountain range in western Iran)	34°N	47°E	**205**

This dictionary lists many of the important people introduced in this book. The page number refers to the main discussion of that person in the book. For more complete references see the Index.

Pronunciation Key
This chart presents the system of phonetic respellings used to indicate pronunciation in the Biographical Dictionary and in the chapters of this book.

Spellings	Symbol	Spellings	Symbol	Spellings	Symbol
pat	a	**k**ick, **c**at, pi**que**	k	**th**in, **th**is	th
p**ay**	ay	**l**id, need**le**	l	c**u**t	uh
c**are**	air	**m**u**m**	m	**ur**ge, t**er**m, f**ir**m, w**or**d, h**ear**d	ur
f**a**ther	ah	**n**o, sudde**n**	n	**v**al**v**e	v
bi**b**	b	thi**ng**	ng	**w**ith	w
chur**ch**	ch	p**o**t, h**o**rrid	ah	**y**es	y
dee**d**, mille**d**	d	t**oe**	oh	**z**ebra, **x**ylem	z
p**e**t	eh	c**au**ght, p**aw**, f**o**r	aw	vi**s**ion, plea**s**ure, gara**ge**	zh
b**ee**	ee	n**oi**se	oy	**a**bout, it**e**m, ed**i**ble, gall**o**p, circ**u**s	uh
li**f**e, **ph**ase, rou**gh**	f	t**oo**k	u	butt**er**	ur
ga**g**	g	b**oo**t	oo		
hat	h	**ou**t	ow		
which	hw	**p**o**p**	p		
p**i**t	ih	**r**oa**r**	r		
p**ie**, b**y**	eye, y	**s**au**ce**	s		
p**ier**	ihr	**sh**ip, di**sh**	sh		
ju**dge**	j	**t**igh**t**, stopp**ed**	t		

Capital letters indicate stressed syllables.

A

Abbas I 1571–1629, shah of Persia (1587–1629) who strengthened the Safavid dynasty and encouraged great artistic and cultural achievements (p. 210).
Abdul Aziz *(AHB dul, ah ZEEZ)* c. 1880–1953, also known as ibn-Saud, founder of the Kingdom of Saudi Arabia and its first king, (1932–1953) (p. 194).
Abraham c. 2000 B.C., according to the Bible, the ancestor of the Israelites (p. 73).
Akbar *(AK bahr)* 1542–1605, Mughal emperor of India (1556–1605) who transformed the region into a major cultural center (p. 323).
Alexander II 1818–1881, czar of Russia (1855–1881) who emancipated the serfs (1861) (p. 455).
Alexander the Great 356–323 B.C., king of Macedonia, (336–323 B.C.) who conquered the Persians and established an empire stretching from Egypt to India. His conquests spread Greek culture (p. 159).
Aquino, Benigno 1932–1983, opposition leader in the Philippines during a period of martial law under President Marcos; assassinated by the military upon his return to the Philippines from the United States (p. 393).
Aquino, Corazón (Cory) 1933–, president of the Philippines (1986–1992) after succeeding her husband, Benigno, as the leader of the opposition to Marcos (p. 393).
Arias Sánchez, Oscar *(AH ryahs SAHN chez)* 1941–, president of Costa Rica (1986–1990) and Nobel Peace Prize winner (1987) (p. 545).
Aristotle *(AIR ihs taht uhl)* 384–332 B.C., Greek philosopher and scientist, student of Plato, and teacher of Alexander the Great (p. 160).
Aryabhata *(ah ree ah BAHT uh)* 476–c. 550, Indian mathematician who worked mainly in the fields of astronomy and trigonometry (p. 318).
Ashoka *(ah SHOH kah)* died c. 238 B.C., last major emperor of the Mauryan dynasty in India; responsible for spreading Buddhism in India and beyond (p. 113).
Ashurbanipal *(ah shur BAH nuh pahl)* seventh century B.C., last great Assyrian king; known for assembling a major library in the ancient Middle East (p. 72).
Augustus 63 B.C.–A.D. 14, first Roman emperor (27 B.C.–A.D. 14) who defeated Antony and Cleopatra and ruled the Greco-Roman world (p. 169).
Aurangzeb *(AWR ehng zehb)* 1618–1707, last great ruler of the Mughal Empire in India (p. 323).

B

Begin, Menachem 1913–1992, prime minister of Israel (1977–1983) who negotiated with President Sadat of Egypt in an attempt to settle the Arab-Israeli conflict (p. 237).
Bolívar, Simon *(boh LEE vahr)* 1783–1830, Venezuelan leader who led the independence movement in South America (p. 532).
Bonaparte, Napoleon 1769–1821, French general, emperor of France (1804–1814) who controlled Continental Europe (p. 552).
Botha, Louis *(BOH tuh)* 1862–1919, first prime minister of the Union of South Africa (p. 301).
Botha, Pieter Willem 1916–, prime minister of South Africa (1978–1989) who refused to abolish the policy of apartheid (p. 305).
Bowdich, Thomas Edward 1791–1824, British traveler who negotiated peace with the Ashanti kingdom, leading to an increase in British influence in Africa (p. 274).
Bruegel, Pieter (the Elder) *(BROY guhl)* c. 1525–1569, Flemish Renaissance painter known for landscapes and scenes of peasant life (p. 428).

Brunelleschi, Filippo *(broo nuh LEHS kee)* 1377–1446, Italian Renaissance architect; best known for the dome of the Florence cathedral (p. 426).

Buthelezi, Mangosuthu *(boo tuh LEH zee)* 1928–, Zulu chief and head of the Inkatha Freedom Party in South Africa (p. 305).

C

Caboto, Giovanni (John Cabot) c. 1450–c. 1498, Italian-born navigator who led the first English expedition to North America (p. 601).

Cabral, Pedro Álvares 1467/1468–1520, Portuguese explorer who claimed Brazil for Portugal in 1500 (p. 551).

Caesar, Julius 100–44 B.C., Roman general who ruled Rome as a dictator from 49 B.C. until his assassination (p. 169).

Calvin, John 1509–1564, French-born Swiss Protestant reformer, whose ideas heavily influenced the development of Protestantism in Europe (p. 432).

Cárdenas, Lázaro 1895–1970, president of Mexico (1934–1940) who worked to carry out the goals of the Mexican Revolution (p. 582).

Cartier, Jacques *(ZHAHK kahr tee AY)* 1491–1557, French navigator who explored the St. Lawrence River and claimed the region for France (p. 601).

Castro, Fidel 1926/1927–, Communist leader of Cuba since 1959, after leading a revolution to overthrow the Batista regime (p. 520).

Catherine the Great 1729–1796, empress of Russia (1762–1796); greatly increased the size of the empire and brought Russia closer to Europe politically and culturally (p. 455).

Champlain, Samuel de c. 1567–1635, French explorer who founded the Canadian city of Québec in 1608 (p. 601).

Charlemagne *(SHAR luh mayn)* c. 742–814, king of the Franks who conquered and united most of western Europe (p. 412).

Chiang Kai-shek *(chang ky shehk)* 1887–1975, Chinese general; head of the Nationalist government in China (1928–1949); later headed the Chinese Nationalist government in exile in Taiwan (p. 344).

Churchill, Winston 1874–1965, British prime minister (1940–1945 and 1951–1955) who led Great Britain through World War II (p. 470).

Cleopatra VII 69–30 B.C., queen of Egypt; Cleopatra's and Mark Antony's forces were defeated by Octavian's Roman forces (p. 229).

Collor de Mello, Fernando *(COH lawr dee MEHL lu)* 1949–, president of Brazil (1990–December 1992) (p. 553).

Columbus, Christopher 1451–1506, Italian explorer who reached the Americas in 1492 and claimed the area for Spain while attempting to find a westward sea route to Asia (pp. 440, 513).

Confucius (K'ung Ch'iu) *(kung chee oo)* c. 551–479 B.C., Chinese teacher and philosopher whose ideas influenced all the Asian civilizations (p. 118).

Constantine I c. 280–337, first Roman emperor to support Christianity; protected Christians in the empire and made Constantinople its new capital (pp. 178, 412).

Copernicus, Nicolaus *(koh PUR nuh kuhs)* 1473–1543, Polish astronomer who developed the theory that Earth and the other planets revolve around the sun (p. 429).

Cortés, Hernán 1485–1547, Spaniard who conquered the Aztec Empire and claimed Mexico for Spain (p. 578).

D

da Silva, Benedita 1942–, first African Brazilian woman elected to the Brazilian congress (1987) (p. 563).

Darius I *(duh RY uhs)* 550–486 B.C., king of Persia (522–486 B.C.) who enlarged the empire, standardized gold and silver coins, and built Persepolis (p. 209).

Darwin, Charles 1809–1882, British naturalist famous for his theory of evolution, as set forth in his work, *Origin of Species* (p. 448).

David second king of Israel who ruled from c. 1000 B.C. until his death (c. 962 B.C.); made Jerusalem the capital of Israel and founded a lasting dynasty (p. 75).

de Klerk, Frederik Willem 1936–, president of South Africa since 1989 who released Nelson Mandela from prison and began repealing apartheid laws (p. 305).

Deng Xiaoping *(duhng shyow pihng)* 1904–, strongest leader of the Chinese Communist party late 1970s–1990 (p. 348).

d'Este, Isabella *(DEHS tay)* 1474–1539, Renaissance patron of the arts who helped her husband's family rule the Italian city-state of Mantua (p. 427).

Dias, Bartolomeu *(DEE uhs)* c. 1450–1500, Portuguese explorer who led the first European expedition to sail around the Cape of Good Hope (1488) (p. 297).

Díaz, Porfirio 1830–1915, president of Mexico (1877–1880 and 1884–1911) who created a strong central government (p. 581).

Djoser *(DZOH suhr)* second king of the Third Dynasty of Egypt (c. 2650–c. 2575 B.C.) who ordered the construction of the Step Pyramid (p. 93).

Drake, Sir Francis c.1540–1596, first English navigator to circumnavigate the globe; vice admiral of the fleet that defeated the Spanish Armada (p. 513).

E

Einstein, Albert 1879–1955, German-born U.S. physicist who developed the theory of relativity (p. 626).

F

Farouk 1920–1965, king of Egypt from 1936 until his overthrow by Nasser in 1952 (p. 236).

Ferdinand 1452–1516, king of Aragon who, with his wife, Isabella of Castile, united and ruled Spain (p. 438).

Foch, Ferdinand *(fosh)* 1851–1929, French marshal and commander-in-chief on the western front during World War I; helped lead the Allied forces to victory (p. 463).

Francis Ferdinand 1863–1914, archduke of Austria whose assassination triggered World War I (p. 462).

G

Gama, Vasco da c. 1460–1524, Portuguese navigator who led the first European expedition to India, helping make Portugal a world power (p. 551).

Gandhi, Mohandas K. 1869–1948, Indian leader of the independence movement against the British; known for his use of nonviolent civil disobedience (pp. 299, 326, 450).

Gorbachev, Mikhail *(GAWR buh chawf)* 1931–, general secretary of the Communist party of the USSR (1985–1991) and president of the USSR (1990–1991) who began reforms that helped bring about the end of the Cold War and the breakup of the USSR (p. 474).

Gutenberg, Johannes *(GOOT n burg)* c. 1400–c. 1468, German printer who invented a printing press that used moveable type (p. 428).

H

Hammurabi ruler of Babylonia 1792–1750 B.C., recorded a system of laws known as the Code of Hammurabi (p. 69).
Hatshepsut *(haht SHEHP soot)* ruler of ancient Egypt (c. 1472–1458 B.C.) who took the title of pharaoh for herself (p. 85).
Havel, Václav 1936–, Czech playwright, poet, and protest leader; became Czechoslovakia's president in 1989 after the collapse of communism; president of the newly formed Czech Republic (1993) (p. 478).
Haynes, Lemuel 1753–1833, African American minister and Revolutionary War soldier (p. 617).
Henry (the Navigator) 1394–1460, Portuguese prince who sponsored voyages to Africa and advanced shipbuilding, cartography, and commerce (p. 550).
Henry VIII 1491–1547, king of England (1509–1547). His refusal to obey the Pope led to the establishment of the Church of England (p. 432).
Hidalgo y Costilla, Miguel 1753–1811, Mexican priest who led an uprising against Spanish domination; known as the father of Mexican independence (p. 580).
Hippocrates *(hih PAHK ruh teez)* c. 460–c. 377 B.C., ancient Greek physician who is considered the founder of medicine (p. 160).
Hitler, Adolf 1889–1945, leader of the Nazi party in Germany from 1921; dictator of Germany's Third Reich (1933–1945); ordered the killing of millions of Jews and others during World War II (p. 468).
Ho Chi Minh *(hoh chee minh)* 1890–1969, founder of the Indochina Communist party; president of North Vietnam (1945–1969) (p. 397).
Homer ninth or eighth century B.C., Greek poet considered the creator of the two great epic poems, the *Iliad* and the *Odyssey* (p. 154).
Hugo, Victor 1802–1885, French author of *The Hunchback of Notre Dame, Les Misérables,* and many other works (p. 480).

I

Ibn Battuta 1304–1368/1369, Arab traveler and author who journeyed throughout the Muslim countries and to the Far East (p. 250).
Ibn Khaldun *(IHB uhn kal DOON)* 1332–1406, Arab historian who wrote the first significant history of Muslim North Africa (p. 232).
Imhotep *(ihm HOH tehp)* 27th century B.C., architect, physician, and chancellor under Djoser, later worshiped in Egypt and Greece as the God of medicine (p. 93).
Isabella 1451–1504, queen of Castile who, with her husband, Ferdinand of Aragon, united and ruled Spain; sponsored the voyages of Christopher Columbus (p. 438).
Ivan III (the Great) 1440–1505, prince of Moscow (1462–1505) who fought off the dominance of the Tatars and laid the foundation for a unified Russian state (p. 454).
Ivan IV (the Terrible) 1530–1584, first czar of Russia (1547–1584); fought unsuccessful wars with Sweden; carried out a reign of terror against the aristocracy (p. 454).

J

Jacob (or Israel) according to the Bible, grandson of Abraham. His 12 sons became the ancestors of the 12 tribes of Israel (p. 74).
Jesuit a member of the Society of Jesus (S.J.), the Roman Catholic order founded in 1530 by Ignatius of Loyola for teaching and missionary work (p. 433).
Jesus c. 6 B.C.–A.D. 30, great religious leader called the Christ by his followers; believed by most Christians to be the son of God (p. 175).
João VI 1767–1826, king of Portugal (1816–1826). During the time of his rule Brazil was declared independent (1822) (pp. 552–553).
Juárez, Benito 1806–1872, president of Mexico (1861–1872); fought against foreign domination by Napoleon III of France and Maximilian of Austria (p. 581).

K

Khomeini, (Ayatollah) Ruholla *(AY uh tohl lah koh MAY nee)* 1900–1989, Shiite religious leader, although in exile, directed the Iranian revolution that overthrew the shah in 1979; head of state of Iran (1979–1989) (p. 214).
Khufu *(KOO foo)* second king of Egypt's Fourth Dynasty (2500s B.C.), who built the Great Pyramid at Giza (p. 88).
King, Martin Luther, Jr. 1929–1968, U.S. minister, leader of the U.S. civil rights movement from the mid-1950s until his assassination (pp. 432, 633).
Krishna eighth incarnation of the Hindu God Vishnu (p. 109).

L

Las Casas, Bartolomé de 1474–1566, Spanish missionary in the Americas who called for the abolition of Indian slavery (p. 443).
Lenin 1870–1924, founder of the Bolsheviks (Russian Communist party); a leader of the Russian Revolution (1917); first head of the Soviet Union (p. 465).
Leo Africanus 1485–c. 1554, Arabian traveler who wrote about Africa and Islam (p. 251).
Leonardo da Vinci 1452–1519, Italian Renaissance artist, inventor, and scientist whose paintings include *Mona Lisa* and *The Last Supper* (p. 427).
Luther, Martin 1483–1546, German priest whose ideas inspired the Protestant Reformation; translated the Bible from Latin to German (p. 430).

M

MacArthur, Douglas 1880–1964, U.S. general who commanded the Allied troops in Asia in World War II; headed the U.S. occupation forces in Japan (p. 392).
Mackenzie, Alexander c. 1755–1820, Scottish-born explorer of Canada for whom the Mackenzie River in Canada is named (p. 602).
Magellan, Ferdinand c. 1480–1521, Portuguese navigator and explorer whose European expedition was the first to complete the trip around the globe (p. 390).
Mahmud *(mah MOOD)* 971–1030, sultan (ruler) of the kingdom of Ghazna; one of the early Muslim leaders who invaded India (p. 322).
Mandela, Nelson 1918–, South African activist and head of the African National Congress (p. 292).
Mann, Horace 1796–1859, U.S. educator whose work led to reforms in public education, including a longer school year and teacher training programs (p. 635).
Mansa Musa died c. 1332/1337, emperor of Mali (1307–1332) who made an extravagant pilgrimage to Mecca (p. 248).

Mao Zedong *(mow dzuh dahng)* 1893–1976, Chinese leader who helped found the Chinese Communist party; established the People's Republic of China (1949) (p. 345).
Marconi, Guglielmo 1874 –1937, Italian physicist who invented the wireless (p. 12).
Marcos, Ferdinand 1917–1989, Philippine head of state (1966–1986) who was overthrown by a popular rebellion (p. 392).
Margaret I of Denmark 1353–1412, queen who united the Scandinavian countries of Denmark, Norway, and Sweden (p. 415).
Marie de France flourished late 12th century; earliest known French woman poet whose famous work was *Ysopet,* a collection of fables (p. 415).
Marx, Karl 1818–1883, German philosopher whose political theories started the movement called Marxism and whose famous book with Friedrich Engels is the *Communist Manifesto* (p. 450).
Medici (family) *(MEHD uh chee)* wealthy Italian family that ruled Florence during the Renaissance, making important contributions to the arts, politics, and religion (p. 425).
Menchú, Rigoberta 1959–, Guatemalan Nobel Peace Prize winner (1992) (p. 542).
Mendes, Chico *(SHEE ku MEHN dehz)* 1944?–1988, Brazilian environmental activist who promoted sustainable development (p. 562).
Mengzi c. 371–289 B.C., Chinese philosopher and follower of Confucius (p. 340).
Michelangelo *(my kuhl AN juh loh)* 1475–1564, Italian Renaissance sculptor, painter, and architect whose works include paintings in the Sistine Chapel and the sculpture *David* (p. 426).
Montezuma c. 1466–1520, Aztec emperor defeated by Cortés in 1520 (p. 578).
Moses c. 14th–13th century B.C., according to the Bible, Hebrew prophet and law giver who led the Israelites out of slavery in Egypt (p. 74).
Mubarak, Hosni 1928–, president of Egypt since 1981 (p. 237).
Muhammad c. 570–632, religious prophet and founder of Islam (p. 186).
Muhammad Ali *(ah LEE)* 1769–1849, founder of the Egyptian dynasty that ruled from the early 1800s to the mid-1900s (p. 234).

N

Nasser, Gamal Abdel (*NAS uhr*) 1918–1970, Egyptian revolutionary and president (1956–1970) who instituted broad reforms and ordered the building of the Aswan Dam (p. 236).
Nebuchadnezzar II c. 630–562 B.C., king of Babylonia who captured Jerusalem and had the Israelites brought to Babylon (p. 76).
Nehru, Jawaharlal *(juh wah hur LAHL NAY roo)* 1889–1964, activist for independence in India; first prime minister of independent India (1947–1964) (p. 327).
Nicholas II 1868–1918, last Russian czar who was killed by the Bolsheviks (Communists) during the Russian Revolution (p. 464).
Nkrumah, Kwame *(KWAH may uhng KROO muh)* 1909–1972, leader of the Ghanaian independence movement against British rule, president of Ghana (1960–1966) (p. 280).
Noriega, Manuel 1940–, military dictator of Panama (1983–1989) (p. 543).

O

Odysseus *(oh DIHS ee uhs)* Perhaps mythical Greek hero and central character in Homer's epic poem the *Odyssey.* (p. 154).

P

Pachacuti *(pah chah KOO tee)* Inca emperor 1438–1471, who greatly expanded the Inca Empire in South America (p. 142).
Pahlavi, Mohammed Reza Shah 1919–1980, shah of Iran (1941–1979) overthrown by Islamic fundamentalists (p. 214).
Pahlavi, Reza Shah 1878–1944, Iranian general who became the shah of Iran and started reform of the country (p. 213).
Parks, Rosa 1913–, African American civil rights activist whose refusal in 1955 to give up her seat to a white bus rider stirred the U.S. civil rights movement (p. 633).
Paul c. A.D. 5–c. A.D. 67, Jewish convert to Christianity who became one of its most important apostles (p. 175).
Pedro I 1798–1834, Portuguese prince who declared Brazil's independence from Portugal (1822); served as its first emperor (1822–1831) (p. 553).
Pedro II 1825–1891, second and last emperor of Brazil (1831–1889); during his reign slavery was abolished (p. 553).
Pericles *(PEHR ih kleez)* c. 495–429 B.C., political and cultural leader of Athens during its Golden Age (p. 158).
Perón, Eva Duarte de *(puh ROHN)* 1919–1952, Argentinean social reformer and supporter of women's rights (p. 540).
Perón, Juan Domingo *(puh ROHN)* 1895–1974, president of Argentina (1946–1955 and 1973–1974) (p. 540).
Perry, Matthew C. 1794–1858, U.S. naval officer who led the expedition to force Japan to open its doors to foreign trade (1853–1854) (p. 370).
Peter the Great 1672–1725, czar of Russia (1682–1725) who extended Russian territory, introduced Western technology, greatly reformed the government and military forces, and built St. Petersburg (p. 454).
Philip II 1527–1598, king of Spain (1556–1598) who sent the Spanish Armada on an unsuccessful invasion of England (1588) (p. 443).
Philip II 382–336 B.C., king of Macedonia who conquered Greek city-states; father of Alexander the Great (p. 159).
Pizan, Christine de *(pee ZAHN) c.* 1365–1430, French poet known for her love poems and writings about women (p. 427).
Plaatje, Solomon *(PLAHT juh)* 1877–1932, black South African interpreter and journalist whose diary provides an important account of the South African War (p. 301).
Plato c. 427–c. 348 B.C., ancient Greek philosopher; a student of Socrates who recorded his teacher's ideas (p. 160).

R

Raffles, Sir (Thomas) Stamford 1781–1826, administrator of British holdings in East India and founder of Singapore (1819) (p. 395).
Ramesses II *(RAM ih seez)* king of Egypt (1279–1213 B.C.), known for his major building projects and the many statues of himself in Egypt and Nubia (p. 85).

Ramos, Fidel 1928–, army chief of staff in the Philippines who led the protest against Marcos; elected president in 1992 (p. 393).
Roosevelt, Franklin D. 1882–1945, U.S. president (1933–1945) who brought the country through the Great Depression (1929–1941) with the economic reform program called the New Deal; led the country during World War II (p. 472).

S

Sadat, Anwar *(suh DAHT)* 1918–1981, Egyptian military leader and president of Egypt (1970–1981) who worked for peace with Israel (p. 236).
Saladin 1138–1193, Muslim sultan of Egypt who captured Jerusalem and defended it during the Third Crusade (p. 233).
San Martín, José de *(san mahr TEEN)* 1778–1850, Argentinian general and leader of the independence movement against Spanish rule in Argentina, Chile, and Peru (p. 532).
Shaka c. 1787–1828, Zulu chief and founder of the Zulu kingdom in southern Africa (p. 299).
Shakespeare, William 1564–1616, English playwright and poet, often considered the greatest dramatist in history whose plays include *Romeo and Juliet* and *Hamlet* (p. 428).
Shakti Hindu deity who is worshiped as the mother Goddess of Hinduism (p. 109).
Shi huangdi *(see hwahng dee)* c. 259–210 B.C., first emperor of the Qin dynasty who built the Great Wall and unified most of China (p. 121).
Shōtoku 574–622, Japanese ruler (593–622) who made major changes in culture and education (p. 363).
Siddhartha Gautama *(sihd DAHR tah GAW tah mah)* c. 563–c. 483 B.C., the Buddha or "Enlightened One" whose teachings formed the basis of Buddhism (p. 110).
Socrates *(SOK ruh teez)* c. 470–399 B.C., ancient Greek philosopher; teacher of Plato (p. 160).
Solomon flourished mid-10th century B.C., generally considered the greatest king of Israel; built the famous temple in Jerusalem (p. 75).
Sonni 'Ali *(SOH nee AHL ee)* died 1492, leader of the Songhai Empire that conquered the ancient Mali Empire (p. 251).
Stalin, Josef 1879–1953, Soviet head of state (1922–1953) who ruled as a dictator and made the USSR a world power (p. 467).
Sun Yat-sen 1866–1925, leader of the revolution against the Manchu dynasty; first leader of the new Republic of China (p. 344).
Sundiata *(sun dee AHT ah)* died 1255, West African monarch who founded the empire of Mali (p. 249).

T

Thompson, David 1770–1857, English explorer who mapped much of western Canada (p. 602).
Tokugawa Ieyasu *(ih yeh YAH soo)* 1543–1616, founder of the last shogunate (military government) in Japan, which lasted from 1603 until 1867 (p. 368).
Tolstoy, Leo 1828–1910, Russian writer whose novels include *War and Peace* and *Anna Karenina* (p. 455).
Toussaint L'Ouverture *(too SAN loo vehr TUR)* 1743–1803, leader of the Haitian independence movement who helped emancipate enslaved Africans (p. 515).
Trudeau, Pierre 1919–, prime minister of Canada (1969–1979 and 1980–1984), during whose administration Canada was granted full independence from Great Britain (p. 613).
Truman, Harry S. 1884–1972, U.S. president (1945–1953) who ordered the dropping of two atomic bombs on Japan, which ended World War II; led the United States during the Korean War (p. 473).
Tutankhamon *(toot ahng KAH muhn)* Egyptian king (1333–1323 B.C.) whose tomb was discovered intact in 1922 (p. 85).
Tutu, Osei late 17th century, launched the Ashanti Empire by uniting the Akan tribes in what is now Ghana (p. 273).

V

Vesalius, Andreas *(vih SAY lee uhs)* 1514–1564, Flemish Renaissance biologist who wrote one of the first textbooks on anatomy (p. 429).
Vespucci, Amerigo *(vehs POO chee)* 1454–1512, Italian explorer of South America; gave his name to the American continents (p. 536).
Vladimir I c. 956–1015, Russian prince who is credited with bringing Orthodox Christianity to Russia; later made a saint (p. 453).

W

Walesa, Lech *(wah LEHN sah)* 1943–, Polish labor leader, chairman of the trade union Solidarity and president of Poland since 1990 (p. 491).

Y

Yaa Asantewa c. 1840/1860–1921, leader of the Asante in West Africa who stirred her people to resist British attempts to take power (p. 276).
Yeltsin, Boris 1931–, first secretary of Moscow City Party Committee who became Russia's first freely elected president (p. 474).

Z

Zapata, Emiliano 1879–1919, Mexican revolutionary who fought for land reform (p. 581).

Pronunciation Key
This chart presents the pronunciation key used in this Glossary. For a key to the phonetic respellings used to indicate pronunciation in the text of the chapters, see page 696.

Spellings	Symbol	Spellings	Symbol	Spellings	Symbol
p**a**t	ă	**k**i**ck**, **c**at, pi**que**	k	**th**in	th
p**ay**	ā	**l**id, need**le**	l	**th**is	*th*
c**are**	âr	**m**u**m**	m	c**u**t	ŭ
f**a**ther	ä	**n**o, sudd**en**	n	**ur**ge, t**er**m, f**ir**m, w**or**d, h**ear**d	ûr
bi**b**	b	thi**ng**	ng	**v**al**ve**	v
chur**ch**	ch	p**o**t, h**o**rrid	ŏ	**w**ith	w
dee**d**, mill**ed**	d	t**oe**	ō	**y**es	y
p**e**t	ĕ	c**au**ght, p**aw**, f**or**	ô	**z**ebra, **x**ylem	z
b**ee**	ē	n**oi**se	oi	vi**s**ion, plea**s**ure, gara**ge**	zh
li**f**e, **ph**ase, rou**gh**	f	t**oo**k	o͝o	**a**bout, it**e**m, ed**i**ble, gall**o**p, circ**u**s	ə
ga**g**	g	b**oo**t	o͞o	butt**er**	ər
hat	h	**ou**t	ou		
which	hw	**p**o**p**	p		
p**i**t	ĭ	**r**oa**r**	r		
p**ie**, b**y**	ī	**s**au**c**e	s		
p**ier**	îr	**sh**ip, di**sh**	sh	Primary stress ˊ	
ju**dge**	j	**t**igh**t**, stopp**ed**	t	Secondary stress ˊ	

A

acid rain (ăsˊĭd rān) rain that has very high amounts of acids; caused by pollution.

adapt (ə-dăptˊ) to adjust to meet new situations (p. 33).

Afrikaner (ăfˊ rĭ-käˊnər) an Afrikaans-speaking South African descended from the early Dutch, German, and French settlers (p. 297).

afterlife (ăfˊtər-līf) according to some beliefs, the life that follows death (p. 89).

agriculture (ăgˊrĭ-kŭlˊ chər) the practice of cultivating the soil to produce crops and to raise livestock; farming (p. 59).

alliance (ə-līˊəns) agreement made between nations for a common cause (p. 461).

anthropologist (ănˊ thrə-pŏlˊə-jĭst) a scientist who studies the origins, behavior, and development of human beings (anthropology) (p. 23).

apartheid (ə-pärtˊhītˊ) an official policy of racial separation and white supremacy practiced in the Republic of South Africa, now being reversed (p. 293).

apostle (ə-pŏsˊəl) one of Jesus' twelve original followers and other missionaries of the early Christian Church (p. 175).

aqueduct (ăkˊwĭ-dŭktˊ) a large pipe built to carry water from a distant source; also, the structure that carries the pipe (p. 173).

archaeologist (ärˊkē-ŏlˊə-jĭst) a scientist who recovers and studies the tools, graves, buildings, pottery, and other remains of past human life and culture (p. 58).

archipelago (ärˊkə-pĕlˊə-gō) a large number of islands in a group (p. 387).

arid (ărˊĭd) having little rainfall, or none at all (p. 205).

B

ban (băn) to forbid by law or policy.

bankrupt (băngkˊrŭptˊ) declared by law as being without the means to pay off debts.

barter (bärˊtər) a system of trading in which people exchange goods or services directly, without using money (p. 134).

basin (bāˊsĭn) an area drained by a river and its tributaries (p. 529).

belief (bĭ-lēfˊ) an idea that a person holds to be true (p. 8).

bilingual (bī-lĭngˊgwəl) able to speak two languages fluently; written in two languages (p. 608).

boom-and-bust (bo͞om ənd bŭst) a rapid expansion in economic activity, followed by a rapid decline (p. 559).

border (bôrˊdər) an area or line that separates two regions or nations (p. 586).

boycott (boiˊkŏtˊ) an organized form of protest by a group that refuses to use, deal in, or buy certain products or services from specific businesses or nations (p. 295).

Buddhism (bo͞oˊdĭzˊəm) a religion founded in India by Siddhartha Guatama; Buddhism stresses freedom from worldly desires and nonviolence (p. 110).

C

caliph (kăˊlĭf) religious head of a Muslim state (p. 189).

capital (kăp´ĭ-təl) money used to start, or invest in, businesses; also, a city where the head of a state or federal government is located (p. 561).
caravan (kăr´ə-văn) a group of merchants or pilgrims journeying together, usually through desert regions (p. 277).
cash crop (kăsh krŏp) a crop that is grown primarily to sell rather than to keep (p. 277).
caste (kăst) one of the four social classes in Hindu society in India (p. 106).
cataract (kăt´ə-răkt´) a steep rapid in a river (p. 83).
caudillo (kô-dēl´yō) a military dictator (p. 537).
censor (sĕn´sər) to control what people read, write, hear, or see; to prohibit free expression of ideas (p. 197).
circumnavigate (sûr´kəm-năv´ĭ-gāt´) to travel completely around; for example, to sail around the earth (p. 390).
citizen (sĭt´ĭ-zən) a person who owes loyalty to a town, city, state, or nation and in return is protected by its government (p. 156).
citizenship (sĭt´ĭ-zən-shĭp´) the possession of rights, duties, and privileges of every citizen of a city, state, or country.
city-state (sĭt´ē-stāt´) an independent state including a city and the surrounding area (p. 155).
civil disobedience (sĭv´əl dĭs´ə-bē´dē-əns) the refusal to obey certain laws because they are thought to be unjust and in order to effect change in government policy or laws (p. 326).
civilization (sĭv´ə-lĭ-zā´shən) a complex society with, among other features, a highly developed government and culture (p. 67).
civil war (sĭv´əl wôr) a war fought between groups or regions within a country.
class (klăs) a group of people who share similar economic and social conditions (p. 67).
classics (klăs´ĭks) the collection of literature of the ancient Greek and Roman cultures (p. 426).
clergy (klûr´jē) the group of people ordained to serve as religious leaders; for example, priests, ministers, and rabbis (p. 411).
climate (klī´mĭt) the average weather conditions of a particular region, including temperature, wind, and precipitation.
cold war or **Cold War** (kōld wôr) an intense rivalry between countries, stopping short of military engagement, especially as existed between Soviet-bloc and Western-bloc countries after World War II (p. 473).
collective (kə-lĕk´tĭv) a large farm or business where people work together to produce a product, usually under government supervision.
colonialism (kə-lō´nē-ə-lĭz´əm) a policy by which a nation obtains and controls foreign lands as colonies, usually for economic gain (p. 440).
Columbian exchange (kə-lŭm´bē-ən ĭks-chānj´) the exchange of people, goods, culture, and ideas that occurred among Europe, Asia, Africa, and the Americas after the arrival of Columbus in America (p. 442).
command economy (kə-mănd´ ĭ-kŏn´ə-mē) a system of government ownership and control of farms and factories in which the government decides what to produce and sets all prices (p. 490).
common market (kŏm´ən mär´kĭt) an economic union formed to increase trade and cooperation among its member countries (p. 484).
commonwealth (kŏm´ən-wĕlth´) union of countries that share common goals (p. 496).
communism (kôm´yə nĭz´əm) a social system without social classes or private ownership in which the state controls the production and distribution of goods (p. 344).
community (kə-myōō´nĭ-tē) a group of people living in the same area and usually having common ties of language or culture.
confederation (kən-fĕd´ə-rā´shən) a unified political state in which power is shared between national and local governments (p. 603).
Confucianism (kən-fyōō´shən-ĭz-əm) the ethical teachings of Confucius, emphasizing social harmony, devotion to family, and personal virtue (p. 118).
conquistador (kŏn-kwĭs´tə-dôr´) a leader in the Spanish conquest of Mexico, Central America, and Peru during the 16th century (p. 578).
conservation (kŏn´sûr-vā´shən) the careful use and protection of natural resources, such as forests and rivers (p. 621).
continental climate (kôn´tə-nĕn´təl klī´mĭt) a climate marked by warm, short summers and long, cold winters (p. 482).
contribution (kŏn´trĭ-byōō´shən) the act of giving something for a special purpose.
converso (kŏn-vĕr´sō) a person of the Jewish faith who converted to Christianity during the reign of Ferdinand and Isabella (p. 439).
convert (kən-vûrt´) to change from one religion to another (p. 552).
Coptic Church (kôp´tĭk chûrch) a Christian church of Egyptian origin.
coup (kōō) a sudden takeover of the government (p. 540).
Creole (krē´ōl´) in Latin America, people whose ancestors came from Europe; a person of European descent born in Spanish America; in the United States, people descended from French settlers.
crusade (krōō-sād´) one of the military expeditions carried out by European Christians during the Middle Ages in an attempt to recapture the Holy Land from the Muslims (p. 416).

cultural diffusion (kŭl′chər-əl dĭ-fyo͞o′zhən) the spreading of elements of one culture (arts, customs, beliefs, ideas, institutions) to another culture (p. 15).
culture (kŭl′chər) the institutions, beliefs, values, art, technology, and other achievements of a group of people, passed on from one generation to the next (p. 5).
currency (kûr′ən-sē) any items used as a medium of exchange during a given time (p. 134).
custom (kŭs′təm) a way of doing things that has become accepted by a people (p. 6).
customs check (kŭs′təmz chĕk) a border inspection (p. 485).
czar (zär) any of the male emperors who ruled Russia before the revolution of 1917 (p. 454).

D

deforestation (dē-fôr′ĭ-stā′shən) the removal, usually by fire or clear-cutting, of forest trees and other plants (p. 35).
delta (dĕl′tə) a triangular area of fertile land at the mouth of a river (p. 83).
demilitarized zone (dē-mĭl′ĭ-tə-rīzd′ zōn) an area where no military personnel or equipment are allowed.
democracy (dĭ-mŏk′rə-sē) a form of government in which the citizens are entitled to influence the making of laws and policies, either directly or through elected representatives (p. 158).
depression (dĭ-prĕsh′ən) a period marked by severe economic decline. It is usually a time of enormous unemployment and hardship.
desalination (dē-săl′ə-nā′shən) the process of taking away salts and other chemicals, especially from ocean water or soil (p. 198).
diagnosis (dī′əg-nō′sĭs) an identification of an illness and its cause (p. 189).
dictator (dĭk′tā′tər) a ruler who holds absolute power, usually by force (p. 467).
discrimination (dĭ-skrĭm′ə-nā′shən) the unfair treatment of a person because of the person's race, nationality, gender, age, disabilities, or other factors (p. 632).
dissident (dĭs′ĭ-dənt) a person who does not agree with an accepted opinion or belief; a protester (p. 350).
distribution (dĭs′trə-byo͞o′shən) the act of allotting or apportioning specific goods or resources; the geographic occurrence of a given feature (p. 142).
diversity (dĭ-vûr′sĭ-tē) the variety or differences characterizing a group of people, things, or places (p. 129).
divine right (dĭ-vīn′ rīt) the belief that monarchs receive their right to rule directly from God.
dominion (də-mĭn′yən) a self-governing nation within the British Commonwealth (p. 603).
drought (drout) a long period in which there is little or no rainfall (p. 256).
dynasty (dī′nə-stē) a series of rulers from the same family (p. 84).

E

ejido (ĕ-hē′dō) Mexican rural lands recognized by the government as belonging to Native Americans and commonly used for agricultural purposes.
elevation (ĕl′ə-vā′shən) the height of a given point above sea level, usually expressed in feet or meters (p. 138).
emancipation (ĭ-măn′sə-pā′shən) the act of freeing people from bondage or slavery (p. 515).
embargo (ĕm-bär′gō) a ban by a government on trade with a foreign nation (p. 398).
emigrant (ĕm′ĭ-grənt) a person who leaves a native land to make a new home in another place (p. 41).
endangered (ĕn-dān′jərd) threatened with extinction (p. 35).
entrepreneur (ŏn′trə-prə-nûr) one who organizes and operates a business (p. 493).
environment (ĕn-vī′rən-mənt) all the living and nonliving things surrounding a person or organism (p. 12).
epic (ĕp′ĭk) a long poem or literary work that tells the story of a heroic character (p. 319).
ethnic group (ĕth′nĭk gro͞op) a group of people who can be characterized by their similar culture, religion, race, ancestry, or language (p. 21).
exile (ĕg′zīl) to banish; also, the state of being banished from one's native land (p. 215).
export (ĭk-spôrt′) to send the goods of a country abroad for sale or trade; a good sent out of the country (p. 277).
extinct (ĭk-stĭngkt′) no longer living or existing (p. 35).

F

famine (făm′ĭn) an extreme shortage of food, leading to hunger and starvation (p. 341).
favela (fə-vĕl′ə) a poor community in Brazilian cities (p. 562).
fellahin (fĕl′ə-hēn′) farmers or peasants in an Arab country, such as Egypt (p. 228).
felucca (fə-lo͞o′kə) a narrow sailing vessel used on the Nile or in the Mediterranean (p. 240).
feudalism (fyo͞od′əl-ĭz′əm) a political and economic system in which lords granted land to vassals in exchange for protection and other services (p. 367).
fiesta (fē-ĕs′tə) a religious or patriotic festival, generally held in Spanish-speaking countries to celebrate an important person or event (p. 588).
foreign policy (fôr′ĭn pŏl′ĭ-sē) set of guidelines that a government adopts in order to define its interactions with other nations.
forum (fôr′əm) a public meeting place for discussion (p. 644).

free enterprise (frē ĕn´tər-prīz´) the freedom of private businesses to operate for profit, with little government control (p. 347).
fundamentalism (fŭn´də-mĕn´təl-ĭz´əm) a movement based on the strict following of certain beliefs, such as those put forth in the Bible or Qur'an.

G

galleon (găl´ē-ən) a large, three-masted wooden trading ship or warship, with a square rig and two or more decks; used by Spain from the 15th to the 17th century (p. 391).
genocide (jĕn´ə-sīd´) the planned killing of an entire racial, national, political, or ethnic group (p. 470).
geography (jē-ŏg´rə-fē) the study of the earth and the relationship between human beings and the earth, including the study of natural features, population, and resources (p. 29).
glacier (glā´shər) a huge mass of ice that flows slowly over land (p. 128).
global (glō´bəl) worldwide in scope or influence.
Gospel (gŏs´pəl) one of the first four books of the New Testament, in which the life and teachings of Jesus are recorded (p. 176).
gross national product (grōs năsh´ə-nəl prŏd´əkt) the total value of all goods and services that a nation produces in a given time period (p. 374).
guerrilla (gə-rĭl´ə) a member of a small group of fighters who organize against the government (p. 540).
guild (gĭld) an association of artisans who do the same type of work, or of merchants who engage in the same type of business.

H

hacienda (hä´sē-ĕn´də) a large ranch or estate in Spanish-speaking countries (p. 579).
hierarchy (hī´ə-rär´kē) a body of authority figures, such as the clergy, organized by rank.
hieroglyphics (hī´ər-ə-glĭf´ĭks) a type of writing in which pictorial symbols stand for meanings or sounds (p. 87).
Hinduism (hĭn´do͞o-ĭz´əm) the major religion in India, based on a belief in a supreme being of many forms (p. 108).
Holocaust (hŏl´ə-kôst´) the genocide of Jews and others by the Nazis during World War II (p. 471).
homogeneous (hō´mə-jē´nē-əs) having the same ethnic or racial composition (p. 378).
hostage (hŏs´tĭj) a person who is held by one party so that certain terms will be met by an opposing party (p. 216).
humanist (hyo͞o´mə-nĭst) someone who studies the classics; someone concerned with the welfare of humankind (p. 426).
humanitarian (hyo͞o-măn´ĭ-târ´ē-ən) concerned with the welfare and needs of people (p. 645).
hunter-gatherer (hŭn´tər-ga*th*´ər-ər) a person who gets food by hunting wild animals and gathering wild plants (p. 59).

I

ideology (ī´dē-ŏl´ə-jē) a system of ideas and beliefs (p. 348).
immigration (ĭm´ĭ-grā´shən) the act of entering and permanently resettling in a country to which one is not native (p. 39).
imperialism (ĭm-pîr´ē-ə-lĭz´əm) the policy of increasing a nation's authority by acquiring or controlling other nations (p. 325).
import (ĭm-pôrt´) to bring goods into one country from another through trade; a good brought into a country (p. 277).
indentured servant (ĭn-dĕn´chərd sûr´vənt) a person under contract to serve another for a specified amount of time (p. 513).
independence (ĭn´dĭ-pĕn´dəns) the state of being free or self-governing.
indulgence (ĭn-dŭl´jəns) in the Roman Catholic church, the medieval practice of pardoning sin in exchange for a gift of money (p. 430).
Industrial Revolution (ĭn-dŭs´trē-əl rĕv´ə-lo͞o´shən) the far-reaching changes brought about by technological advances in the way goods were produced; it began in England around 1760 and spread to other countries (p. 446).
inflation (ĭn-flā´shən) a continuing rise in prices due to an increase in available money (p. 561).
infrastructure (ĭn´frə-strŭk´chər) the basic public services and facilities, such as roads, canals, and bridges, needed by a community or society (p. 230).
Inquisition (ĭn´kwĭ-zĭsh´ən) during the Middle Ages, the tribunal, or church court, set up by the Roman Catholic church to find and punish people considered heretics (p. 433).
institution (ĭn´stĭ-to͞o´shən) an organization, especially one that is dedicated to public service (p. 7).
interaction (ĭn´tər-ăk´shən) the act of two or more parties affecting each other.
intervene (ĭn´tər-vēn´) to enter into in order to change a course of events.
intifada (ĭn-tĭ-fă´də) the Arab uprising started in 1987 against the Israeli occupation of the Gaza Strip, the West Bank, and parts of Jerusalem (p. 652).
iron curtain (ī´ərn kûr´tən) the military, political, and ideological barrier that separated the Soviet bloc from Western Europe and the United States after World War II (p. 472).
irrigation (ĭr´ĭ-gā´shən) the practice of supplying dry lands with water by means of canals, ditches, pipes, and streams (p. 67).
isolation (ī´sə-lā´shən) the state of being separated from others (p. 362).
isthmus (ĭs´məs) a thin strip of land connecting two larger pieces of land (p. 235).

J

jingoism (jĭng′gō-ĭz′əm) a warlike feeling of extreme nationalism (p. 460).

K

kabuki (kə-bo͞o′kē) the traditional Japanese drama that evolved from No theater, with songs and dances performed in costume (p. 650).

kibbutz (kĭ-bo͞ots′) a collective farm in Israel (p. 650).

kinship (kĭn′shĭp′) relationship by blood, marriage, or adoption (p. 271).

knight (nīt) a mounted, armed soldier in medieval Europe who served a monarch or feudal lord (p. 416).

L

labor-intensive (lā′bər-ĭn-tĕn′sĭv) requiring a greater amount of human power than resources (p. 522).

landform (lănd′fôrm′) a feature on the surface of the earth, such as a hill, plain, or valley (p. 29).

landlocked (lănd′lŏkt′) enclosed by land (p. 256).

latitude (lăt′ĭ-to͞od′) how far north or south of the equator a place is (p. 29).

legion (lē′jən) a unit of the ancient Roman army, consisting of 3,000 to 6,000 foot soldiers, along with some cavalry; a large number (p. 170).

liberation (lĭb′ə-rā′shən) the act of being set free from confinement or control.

life expectancy (līf ĭk-spĕk′tən-sē) the number of years a person is expected to live (p. 261).

Line of Demarcation (līn əv dē′mär-kā′shən) an imaginary line that split the non-Christian world (p. 550).

lineage (lĭn′ē-ĭj) the descendants of a common ancestor (p. 271).

literacy rate (lĭt′ər-ə-sē rāt) the percentage of a given population that can read and write (p. 283).

longitude (lŏnj′jĭ-to͞od′) how far east or west of the prime meridian a place is (p. 29).

M

Mandate of Heaven (măn′dāt′ əv hĕv′ən) the doctrine that an emperor has received the right to rule from heaven (p. 116).

manor (măn′ər) the estate of a feudal lord in medieval Europe (p. 415).

marine climate (mə-rēn′ klī′mĭt) a fairly mild climate; its main air mass forms over oceans (p. 482).

market economy (mär′kĭt ĭ-kŏn′ə-mē) the private ownership of land, farms, and factories; free enterprise (p. 490).

martial law (mär′shəl lô) temporary military rule during an emergency (p. 392).

matrilineal (măt′rə-lĭn′ē-əl) relating to tracing ancestry through the maternal line (p. 270).

media (mē′dē-ə) the means used to communicate in society, such as newspapers, magazines, radio, and television (p. 21).

Mediterranean climate (mĕd′ĭ-tə-rā′nē-ən klī′mĭt) the climate of the Mediterranean region, characterized by mild winters and sunny, hot summers (p. 482).

mestizo (mĕs-tē′zō) a person of mixed racial ancestry (p. 391).

middleman (mĭd′l-măn′) a trader who buys goods from one party and sells to another; a go-between (p. 250).

migrant worker (mī′grənt wûr′kər) a worker who moves from place to place, as crops ripen (p. 543).

migration (mī-grā′shən) the movement of people from one country, place, or region to another (p. 39).

modernize (mŏd′ər-nīz′) to update, or make modern, in order to meet current needs (p. 214).

monarchy (mŏn′ər-kē) government by a monarch (a ruler such as a king, queen, or emperor).

monastery (mŏn′ə-stĕr′ē) a community of persons living under religious vows, especially monks (p. 411).

monocrop (mŏn′ō-krŏp) the only major crop in a region (p. 522).

monotheism (mŏn′ə-thē-ĭz′əm) the belief that there is only one God (p. 73).

mosque (mŏsk) a house of worship for Muslims (p. 186).

Mughal (mo͞o′gəl) the Muslim dynasty that ruled India from 1526 to 1857 (p. 323).

multicultural (mŭl′tē-kŭl′chər-əl) including many cultures (p. 607).

mummy (mŭm′ē) a body embalmed after death in the manner practiced by the ancient Egyptians (p. 89).

N

nationalism (năsh′ə-nə-lĭz′əm) devotion to a nation and its interests and culture; desire for national independence (p. 280).

nationalize (năsh′ə-nə-līz′) to transfer control of an industry from private ownership to government ownership (p. 537).

naturalization (năch′ər-ə-lĭ-zā′shən) the act of giving full citizenship to a person of foreign birth.

naturalized citizen (năch′ər-ə-līzd sĭt′ĭ-zən) an immigrant who has met naturalization requirements to become a citizen of the new country (p. 625).

navigable (năv′ĭ-gə-bəl) being wide and deep enough to allow passage of a vessel.

Nazi (nät′sē) a member of the National Socialist German Workers' Party, which ruled Germany under Adolf Hitler from 1933 to 1945.

negotiate (nĭ-gō′shē-āt′) to discuss with another party in order to come to an agreement (p. 544).

nuclear (no͞o′klē-ər) using energy that is derived from the nuclei of atoms.

O

oasis (ō-ā′sĭs) a fertile area around a spring or water hole in the desert (p. 185).

P

pampas (păm´pəz) the grassy, treeless plains of Argentina and some other parts of South America (p. 528).

papyrus (pə-pī´rəs) a long, thin reed; a type of paper made from this plant by ancient people, especially Egyptians (p. 94).

parliament (pär´lə-mənt) a body of representatives that makes laws for a country.

partition (pär-tĭsh´ən) division or separation of something into parts (p. 649).

patriarch (pā´trē-ärk´) the male leader of a family.

patrilineal (păt´rə-lĭn´ē-əl) relating to tracing ancestry through the paternal line (p. 270).

patron (pā´trən) one who supports the arts, an institution, or a cause (p. 425).

peninsula (pə-nĭn´syə-lə) a piece of land mostly surrounded by water and attached to a larger land mass (p. 155).

peon (pē´ŏn´) a landless peasant laboring in Spanish America (p. 579).

permafrost (pûr´mə-frôst´) the permanently frozen subsoil of the Arctic (p. 599).

pharaoh (fâr´ō) a ruler of ancient Egypt (p. 85).

philosophy (fĭ-lŏs´ə-fē) the study and love of wisdom; the search for knowledge (p. 160).

pilgrimage (pĭl´grə-mĭj) a journey to a place that is sacred, like Mecca or Jerusalem (p. 184).

plague (plāg) a highly contagious, widespread disease, which is often fatal (p. 418).

plateau (plă-tō´) an elevated area of relatively flat land (p. 205).

pluralism (plŏŏr´ə-lĭz´əm) the state of having many different ethnic and cultural groups existing together in a society.

pollute (pə-lōōt´) to make dirty; to contaminate (p. 35).

prehistoric (prē´hĭ-stôr´ĭk) of the time before the development of writing (p. 59).

prejudice (prĕj´ə-dĭs) hatred or suspicion of persons of a particular race, ethnic group, or religion (p. 23).

propaganda (prŏp´ə-găn´də) information designed to win people over to a certain doctrine (p. 467).

prophet (prŏf´ĭt) a religious leader who is believed to proclaim the wishes of a God (p. 76).

Protestant (prŏt´ĭ-stənt) a member of one of the Christian churches that broke away from the Roman Catholic church starting in the 16th century (p. 431).

province (prŏv´ĭns) a territory governed as a unit within a country or empire (p. 170).

pyramid (pĭr´ə-mĭd) a large monument such as those found in ancient Egypt and Mexico, with a rectangular base and four triangular sides, built as a tomb or temple.

Q

quota (kwō´tə) an allotment; the maximum number of people allowed to enter a country, group, or institution (p. 625).

R

rabbi (răb´ī) a teacher and spiritual leader of Jews (p. 77).

racism (rā´sĭz´əm) discrimination based on race (p. 23).

rain forest (rān fôr´ĭst) a dense forest, usually tropical, that is green throughout the year and has an annual rainfall of at least 100 inches (p. 130).

raw materials (rô mə-tîr´ē-əls) the natural products used for industry and manufacturing (p. 448).

Reconquista (rē´kŏng-kē´stə) the Spanish re-conquest of the Iberian peninsula from the Muslims in a series of wars in the 1400s (p. 439).

Reformation (rĕf´ər-mā´shən) a political and religious movement in 16th-century Europe to reform the Roman Catholic church; the result was the establishment of Protestant churches (p. 431).

region (rē´jən) an area with shared features that set it apart from surrounding areas (p. 42).

reincarnation (rē´ĭn-kär-nā´shən) the rebirth of a soul into another body after death, according to some religious traditions (p. 109).

Renaissance (rĕn´ĭ-säns´) the period of intellectual and artistic rebirth in Europe that began in Italy in the late 1300s (p. 424).

republic (rĭ-pŭb´lĭk) a nation without a monarch, in which political power may lie with the citizens (p. 169).

resistance (rĭ-zĭs´təns) the act of opposing, especially an enemy or an attack.

reunification (rē-yōō´nə-fĭ-kā´shən) the process of making whole again something that has been separated.

revolution (rĕv´ə-lōō´shən) political rebellion that results in overthrow of a government and formation of a new government (p. 465).

rhythm (rĭ*th*´əm) a movement that occurs repeatedly and in a regular sequence.

rural (rŏŏr´əl) pertaining to the country (p. 41).

S

Sahel (sə-hāl´) the hot, dry region in Africa that lies between the Sahara and the savanna vegetation zone (p. 256).

samurai (săm´ə-rī´) the Japanese warriors who owed their allegiance to the nobility in feudal times (p. 367).

sanction (săngk´shən) a penalty against nations for breaking international law (p. 655).

satrap (sā´trăp) a provincial governor in ancient Persia (p. 208).

savanna (sə-văn´ə) the flat, largely treeless grasslands found in warm or tropical regions (p. 257).

scribe (skrīb) a writer, secretary, or copyist, especially

in ancient times (p. 88).
segregation (sĕg´rĭ-gā´shən) the act of separating or isolating one group of people from another group, based on race or social class (p. 293).
separatism (sĕp´ər-ə-tĭz-əm) being in favor of separating from a group, a nation, or an established church (p. 608).
serf (sûrf) a peasant; a member of the lowest feudal class, bound to the land and controlled by a lord (p. 415).
shah (shä) the title of a hereditary monarch of Iran, used before the 1979 revolution (p. 208).
Shinto (shĭn´tō) the earliest Japanese religion, which emphasizes worship of nature and spirits (p. 362).
shogun (shō´gən) a military ruler of Japan from 1192 to 1867 (p. 366).
silt (sĭlt) a material of very fine particles (p. 243).
social interaction (sō´shəl ĭn´tər-ăk´shən) the way that people relate to each other at all levels in a community (p. 14).
social justice (sō´shəl jŭs´tĭs) fairness for all people in a society (p. 305).
specialization of labor (spĕsh´ə-lĭ-zā´shən ŭv lā´bər) having specific people performing specific jobs; a feature of civilization (p. 67).
standard of living (stăn´dərd əv lĭv´ĭng) the economic level at which an individual, family, or nation lives (p. 376).
steppe (stĕp) a vast, grassy plain (p. 452).
subcontinent (sŭb´kŏn´tə-nənt) a large landmass, such as India, that is to some extent separate but still part of a continent (p. 329).
sultan (sŭl´tən) a ruler of the former Ottoman Empire or of a Muslim country (p. 234).
superpower (so͞o´pər-pou´ər) a country that is a military, political, and economic giant (p. 472).
surplus (sûr´pləs) an excess amount or quantity (p. 67).
synagogue (sĭn´ə-gŏg´) a house of worship for people of the Jewish faith.

T

taiga (tī´gə) the northern region of Europe and Asia that is covered with forest. The ground is frozen during winter and swampy in summer.
Talmud (tăl´mo͝od) the collection of ancient books containing the laws and customs that developed in the Jewish tradition (p. 77).
tariff (tăr´ĭf) a government tax on imports or exports (p. 485).
technology (tĕk-nŏl´ə-jē) the application of scientific knowledge, particularly in industry (p. 16).
tithe (tī*th*) one-tenth of a person's income, which is paid to a church each year (p. 411).
Torah (tôr´ə) the first five books of the Hebrew scriptures (p. 74).
toxic (tŏk´sĭk) poisonous.
trade agreement (trād ə-grē´mənt) an agreement on the rules about exchanging goods and services between different countries (p. 593).
trade imbalance (trād ĭm-băl´əns) when a country exports more than it imports from another country (p. 379).
trade union (trād yo͞on´yən) an organization of workers formed to look after their interests (p. 447).
tradition (trə-dĭsh´ən) elements of a culture that are handed down from generation to generation.
trek (trĕk) a long and difficult journey (p. 298).
triangle trade (trī´ăng´gəl trād) a three-way trade system, originated by the Dutch. The original triangle included the exchange of European goods for slaves, and the exchange of slaves for sugar and other Caribbean goods (p. 514).
tributary (trĭb´yə-tĕr´ē) a river or stream that flows into a larger river or stream (p. 103).
tribute (trĭb´yo͞ot) a gift or payment made for protection, or to show respect, submission, or admiration (p. 137).
tropical (trŏp´ĭ-kəl) hot and humid; characteristic of the tropics (p. 510).
tundra (tŭn´drə) the treeless area of the Arctic region, with only low-growing plants.
typhoon (tī-fo͞on´) a severe tropical cyclone that develops in the western Pacific and Indian oceans (p. 387).

U

unemployment (ŭn´ĕm-ploi´mənt) being without a job.
untouchable (ŭn-tŭch´ə-bəl) a member of the class that is excluded from Hindu rituals and is considered unclean (p. 106).
urban (ûr´bən) pertaining to cities (p. 43).

V

value (văl´yo͞o) an amount considered fair in an exchange; a principle, standard, or quality considered worthwhile or desirable (p. 9).
vassal (văs´əl) a person who was granted land by a feudal monarch, in exchange for military service or tribute (p. 415).
vertical zone (vûr´tĭ-kəl zōn) a climate and vegetation at different altitude levels (p. 529).
veto (vē´tō) refusal to approve a bill or a decision that otherwise would be enforced (p. 644).
volunteer (vŏl´ən-tîr´) a person who provides labor or services without expectation of financial reward (p. 635).

W

westernize (wĕs´tər-nīz´) to adapt to the culture and technology of the West (p. 370).
work unit (wûrk yo͞o´nĭt) in Communist China, a team of state workers who are provided with housing, education, health care (p. 353).

INDEX

Italic numbers refer to pages on which illustrations appear.

A

Abbas I, shah of Persia, 210, 212
Abbasid family, 210
Abdul Aziz, king of Saudi Arabia, 183, 194–195, 196, 199
Abraham, 56–57, 73–74, 151
Abu Simbel, 241
Abu-Bakr, caliph, 189
Acacia trees, 253
Accra, Ghana, 267, *270,* 282, 283
Acid rain, 406, *612*
Acropolis, *152,* 484
Adaptation, 32–33
Aegean Sea, 155
Afghanistan, United Nations presence in, *645*
Africa
  in Columbian exchange, 442
  crafts in, 278–279
  festivals in, *21*
  geography of, 222, *223*
  history of, 225
  maps of, G6–G7, G9, *685*
  population of, *225*
  rainfall in, 49
  storytelling in, 284–286
  topography of, 224, *224*
African Americans
  in Brazil, *548,* 556, 563, *564*
  in Canada, 612
  in the Caribbean, *507,* 511, *515,* 515, *519*
  in Central America, 505, 530, 531
  discrimination against, 633
  forebears of, 514
  migration of, 40, 41
  in South America, *526,* 536, 539
  in the U.S., *20, 21,* 40, *40,* 523, *523,* 622, 627, 632–633, *634*
African National Congress (ANC), 292
Afrikaans language, 302
Afrikaners, 297–302
Afterlife, 89
Agriculture, 59
  origins of, 129
Agyeman-Rawlings, Nana Konadu, 267
Akbar, Mughal emperor, 323
Akhenaton, pharaoh of Egypt, 85
Akosombo Dam, 267
Al-Azhar University, 234, 242
Al-Fustat, 233
Al-Idrisi, 182
Alaska, *151,* 437, *453,* 572
  climate of, 620
  earthquakes in, 574
  oil in, 621
Albania, 461
Alberta, *598,* 599
Alberti, Leon, 426
Aleijadinho, *552*
Aleut people, 620
Alexander II, czar of Russia, 455
Alexander III, czar of Russia, 465
Alexander the Great, 152, 159, 160, 209–210, 226, 229
  conquests of, *G12*
Alexander VI, pope, 550
Alexandra, empress of Russia, 466
Alexandria, Egypt, G15, 226, 229
Alexis, prince of Russia, 466
Alfonso, king of Portugal, 438
Algeria, immigration into, 261
Algonquin people, 600
Ali, caliph, 190
Alliance, defined, 461
Alpenhorn, 406
Alphabets, 660–661
  Hebrew, *73*
Alps, *45,* 480, *480*
Altiplano, 139
Amazon Basin, 529, 557
Amazon rain forest, 504
  as resource, 566–567
  wildlife in, 504, *504*
Amazon River, 528, 529, 557, 558
Amber, *279*
American Indians. *See* Native Americans.
American Revolution, 532, 613, 617, 635
Amish, 45
Amsterdam, the Netherlands, 470
Anastasia, princess of Russia, 466
ANC (African National Congress), 292
Anchorage, Alaska, 47
Andes (mountains), G13, 32, *32,* 54, *502, 527,* 528–529
  civilizations in, 138–142
  zones of, *528*
Angel Falls, 528
Angola, emigration to U.S. from, 625
Antarctica, 528
Anthropologist, *22*
  defined, 23
Antigua, British rule over, 445
Antilles, Greater and Lesser, 509–510
Antoninus Pius, emperor of Rome, *146–147*
Apache people, 14, *14*
Apartheid, 293–295, 302
  combating of, 295, 305
  defined, 293
  world view of, 295, 307
Apostles, 175
Appalachian Mountains, 620
Aqueducts, *171,* 173
Aquino, Benigno, 393
Aquino, Corazón, *385,* 393
Ar-Razi, 189
Arabia
  rule over Egypt, 228, 232–234
  trade with China, 384
  trade with India, 319, 384
  trade with Southeast Asia, 384, 389
  See also Saudi Arabia.
Arabian peninsula, 185
Arabian Sea, 185
Arabic language, 187
Arafat, Plain of, 184, 194
Aral Sea, *494*
Arawak people, *506,* 512
Archaeology, 58
Archipelago, 387
Architectural terms, 662–663
Argentina
  agriculture in, 539
  climate of, *529*
  demography of, 531, *531,* 539
  education in, 540
  gauchos in, *538, 539*
  government of, 539–540
  independence of, 532
  industry in, 539
  land regions of, *G13*
  population density of, *G13*
  women in, 540
Arias Sánchez, Oscar, 545, *545*
Arid, defined, 205
Aristotle, 152, 160
Arizona, *618–619*
  Apache ceremony in, 14, *14*
Armenia, *494*
  emigration to U.S. from, *625*
  membership in CIS, 496
  Turkish persecution of, 471
Armistice, 463
Arthur, king of England, 415
Artifacts, interpreting, 583
Aryabhata, 318
Aryans, 105–106
Asante people, 266, 268–270
  kinship system of, 270–271
  modern, 282–283
Ashanti Empire, 266, 267, 273–274, 276
Ashoka, king of India, 113
Ashura, 207, 213
Ashurbanipal, 72
Asia
  economy of, 314
  geography of, 312–314, *313*
  physical map of, *683*
  Southeast. *See* Southeast Asia.
  transportation in, *312*
Assiniboine people, 600
Assumptions, recognizing, 554
Assyria, 57, 70, 71–72, *71,* 92
Astronomy
  Arabic, 191
  Egyptian, 229
  Korean, *654*
Aswan, Egypt, *86,* 239, 240
Aswan High Dam, *227,* 239, *239,* 241, 243
Athens, Greece, *152,* 156, 158, 484
Atlantic City, New Jersey, *26*
Atlas, 679–689
Atlas mountains, *224*
Attica, Greece, 156
Augustus Caesar, 169, 175
Aurangzeb, Mughal emperor, 323
Auschwitz concentration camp, 471
Australia, *58,* 315
  aboriginal customs, 6
  geography of, G2
  settlement of, 623
  Sydney, 33, *33*
  wildlife of, *437*
Austria, 461
  German invasion of, 469

Austro-Hungarian Empire, 461
end of, 463
World War I alliances of, 461, 462
Axis powers, 371, 469
Azerbaijan, *494*
membership in CIS, 496
people of, 206
Azeri language, 206
Aztecs, 136–137, 145, 576
culture of, *127*, 135–137, 583
economy of, 134
fall of, 578, 579
modern borrowings from, 591
origin of, 132
religion of, 135–136
riches of, 513
society of, 137

B

Babbage, Charles, 447
Babylonia, G12, 69, 71
Baghdad, *66*
Bahamas, *507*, 509, 513
Bahasa Indonesia language, 396
Balfour Declaration, 648, 649
Bali, agriculture in, *310–311*, *388*
Balkans, 461
modern conflict in, 492
Baltic states, 496
Bamako, Mali, 254, 259, 261, *262*
Bambara people, 258, 259
Bananas, 543
Banda Aceh, Indonesia, *396*
Banerji, R. D., 102
Bangladesh
formation of, 327, 331
Muslims in, 190
Bani River, 256
Bantu languages, G14, 296
Bantu people, migration of, G14
Barbados, 509
British rule over, 445
currency of, *522*
Barbuda, 510
Barter, 134
Baseball, 518
Bashō, 364
Basin, defined, 529
Bataan, 392
Bay, defined, 690
Bedouins, 185
Begin, Menachem, 237
Beijing, China, *338*, 346, 349–350
Belarus
membership in CIS, 496
nuclear weapons in, 497
Belém, Brazil, 559
Belgium, *478*
Common Market and, 484
Spanish rule over, 441
in World War II, 470, 472
Beliefs, 8–9
Belize, 542
demography of, 530, *530*, 531
Belo Horizonte, Brazil, 557
Beringia, 128, 129, *129*
Berlin, Germany, division of, 472, 473
Berlin blockade, 473
Berlin Wall, *459*, 471, *472*
Bermuda, British rule over, 445
Betancourt, Romulo, 537
Bible, 175–176, 412
art based on, 426, 432
book of Psalms in, 75–76
Gospels in, 175–176
and Gutenberg's press, 428
preservation of, 411
and prophets, 75–76
translated into German, 431
Bilingual, defined, 608
Biographical dictionary, 696–700
Bishops, 179
Black Death, 418
Blacks. *See* African Americans.
Blake, William, 457
Boer War, 301
Boers. *See* Afrikaners.
Bolívar, Simon, 527, 532, *532*
Bolivia, 32, *32*
demography of, 531, *531*
Bombay, India, 324
population density of, *315*
Bonaparte, Napoleon, 552
Bonsai, 363
Boom-and-bust, defined, 559
Bora, Katherine von, *431*
Border
defined, 586
types and functions of, 586
Borduas, Paul-Émile, 610
Borobudur, *384*
Bosnia-Herzegovina, conflict in, 479, 490, 492, *644*, 645
Botha, Louis, 301
Botha, P. W., 305
Botswana, 293
Boukman, 515
Bowdich, Edward, 274
Boycott, defined, 295
Bozo people, 258
Brasília, Brazil, 559, 562
Brazil, *34*
abolition of slavery in, 553, 569
culture of, 564–565
democracy movement in, 553
demography of, 531, *531*
economy of, 559–561
ethnic population in, 556
festivals in, 565, *565*
geography of, 555–557, *557*, 559
history of, 548–549
independence of, 549, 552
industry in, 559–560
life in, 563–564
modern, 562–563
plantations in, *548*
Portuguese settlement of, 550–552
rain forests of, 529, 566–567
religion in, 564–565, *564*
Bristol, England, *437*
Britain
Norse settlements in, 414
Roman rule of, 153, 170
See also British Empire; Great Britain.
British Columbia, 599
ethnic communities in, 607
British East India Company, 317, 324–325, 395
British Empire, *26*, *445*, *449*
decline and fall of, 450
expansion of, 448
rise of, 443
setbacks to, 446
Brooklyn, New York, Caribbean influence on, 523, *523*
Bruegel, Pieter, *428*, 429, 435
Brunei, population of, 387
Brunel, Isambard K., *446*
Brunelleschi, Filippo, 426, *426*
Buddhism, 110–112
in China, 101
in Korea, 654
Buenos Aires, Argentina, G13, 539, *539*
Buildings, purposes of, *9*
Bulgaria, 461
Burma
religion in, 112
See also Myanmar.
Bush, George, 497
Buthelezi, Mangosuthu, 305
Butte, defined, 690
Byron, Augusta Ada, Lady Lovelace, 447
Byzantine Empire, 178, 231, 412
architecture of, *408*
influence on Egypt, 228

C

Caboto, Giovanni (Cabot, John), 596, 601
Cabral, Pedro Álvares, 548, 551, 564
Caesar Julius, 153, 169
Cai Lung, 120
Cairo, Egypt, 191, *227*, 232, 233, 236, *236*, 242–243, 249
Calcutta, India, 324
California, *16*, 619
migrant workers in, 39
Chinese immigrants in, 628–631
earthquakes in, 574
gold rush in, 628
migrant workers in, 39
oil in, 621
Caliph, defined, 189
Calvin, John, 432
Calvinists, 432
Cambodia, 386, 471, 647
Communist rule over, 398
population of, 387
United Nations presence in, 646
Caminha, Pero Vaz de, 551
Canaan, 56, 57, 75
Canada, 12, *13*, 31 , 572
achievements of, 609
African Americans in, 612
arts in, 610, 611
border with U.S., 612–613, *613*
British rule over, 446
climates and topography of, 599
cultures of, 596–597, 607–608, 615
economy of, 609
education in, 609–610
festivals in, *575*
French and British settlement of, 601–602

geography of, *599*
government of, 604–605
health care in, 610
immigration to, 604
industry in, 609
international relations of, 612–613
legal system of, 605
Native Americans in, *597,* 600
natural resources of, 599
North American trade of, 593
provinces of, 598–599
quality of life in, 609
separatism in, 615
trade with U.S., 613
transportation in, 606
westward expansion of, 602–604
in World War I, 604
in World War II, 605
World War II alliances of, 469
Canadian Rockies, *598*
Canadian Shield, 599
Canal Zone, 543
Canals, *505*
Candomblé, 564–565
Canyon, defined, 691
Cape Breton, *597*
Cape Colony, 301
Cape of Good Hope, 297
Cape Town, South Africa, *291*
Capital, defined, 561
Caracas, Venezuela, *537*
Caravan, defined, 185
Cárdenas, Lázaro, 582
Carib people, 512
Caribana, 608
Caribbean islands
agriculture in, 510 , 519
city life in, 519
climate of, 504, 510, 523
cultures of, 502, 511
economy of, 522
emigration to U.S. from, 625
geography of, 502, 509–510
history of, 511
languages of, 511
music of, 521, 627
Native Americans in, 512
plantations on, 513, 514
Spanish rule over, 441
sports in, 518
wildlife in, 510
Caribbean Sea, 508, 509
marine life in, *509*
Carnival, 504, *504,* 511, *511,* 521, *523,* 565, *565*
Carter, Jimmy, 237, 238, 636, *636*
Carter, Rosalynn, 636
Carthage, 169
Cartier, Jacques, 601
Cartograms, 372–373
Cartoons, 475
Cash crop, defined, 277
Caspian Sea, *494*
Caste system, 106, 320, 335
Castiglione, Baldassare, 427
Castro, Fidel, 520
Catacombs, *177*
Cataract, defined, 83, 691
Cathedral, defined, 411
Catherine the Great, empress of Russia, 455
Catholic Church
medieval, 410–412
Orthodox split from, 408, 412–413, *413*
post-Reformation, 433
in Reformation, 432–433
Caudillo, defined, 537
Cause and effect, 107
Cayman Islands, 516
Cebu, Philippines, 390
Celadon pottery, *654*
Cennini, Cennino, 424, 435
Censor, defined, 197
Census, described, 590
Central America
African Americans in, 505
agriculture of, 543
cities of, 533
climate of, 504, 529
cultures of, 502
economy of, 543
exports of, 543, *543*
geography of, 502, 528
independence movements in, 532
migrant workers in, 543
peace plan for, 545
peoples of, 530–531, *530,* 531–532
social injustice in, 542
unrest in, 542, 543–544
Champlain, Samuel de, 596, 601
Chang Jiang (river), *53,* 54, 115
Chapultepec Park, G2
Charlemagne, king of France, 408, 412–413, 492
Charles I, king of Spain, 390
Charles V, Holy Roman Emperor, 431
Charles V, king of Spain, 584
Charlottetown Agreement, 608
Chavín civilization, 126, 139
Chernobyl nuclear disaster, 471
Cherrapunji, India, 312
Chesapeake and Delaware Canal, *505*
Chiang Kai-shek, 344
Chiapas, Mexico, *588*
Chicago, Illinois, 40, 46–47
Chichén Itzá, *126,* 131
Chile, 139
demography of, *531*
independence of, 532
Chili peppers, *531*
China, 38, *52,* 101, 192, 356
achievements of, 120–121
agriculture in, 352
ancient, 114
ancient, history of, 100–101, 116
civil service in, 101, 120
cultural heritage of, 117–120
daily life in, 351–353
democracy movement in, 349–350
economic and social reform in, 348
emigration to U.S. from, 624, 625
festivals in, 7, *7*
future of, 354
geography of, 115, *115, 348*
history of, 338–339
international trade of, 342–343
Manchu rule over, 342–343
modern, 347–349
Mongol rule over, 341
Nationalist, 344
population of, 312, *348*
relations with West, 343–344
religion in, 101, 112
trade with Arabs, 384
trade with India, 319
trade with Philippines, 391
trade with Southeast Asia, 389
transportation in, *339*
urban life in, 353
war with Japan, *344,* 345, 371
Chinese Americans, 21
Chinese language, 117
dialects of, 355
Chinese New Year, 7
Choson kingdom, 653, *654*
Christianity, 73
Coptic, 231
crusades of, 416
east-west division of, 408, 412–413, *413*
growth of, 177–179, *178*
Islam on, 188
Jerusalem and, 649, *651*
Jesus in, 175–177
medieval, 410–412
origins of, 148, 151, 153
Chronological order, 107
Chu Yüan-chang, 342
Churchill, Winston, *472*
Ciboney people, 512
Cinco de Mayo, 581, 622, *622*
Circumnavigate, defined, 390
Circus Maximus, 170
CIS (Commonwealth of Independent States)
economic situation in, *475*
environmental problems in, 497
ethnic conflict in, *494*
formation of, 496
future of, 496–497
nuclear weapons in, 497
Citizen, defined, 156
Citizenship, 156–158
rights and responsibilities of, 626
Roman, 170, 171
U.S., by naturalization, 625, 626
City-state, defined, 155
Civil disobedience, 326
Civil Rights Act of 1964, 617, 633
Civil War (U.S.), 633
Civilization, 67
ancient, *53,* 54–55
See also names of individual civilizations.
Class structure
Aryan, 106
defined, 67
Mesopotamian, 68
Classics, defined, 426
Clemente, Roberto, 518
Cleopatra VII, queen of Egypt, 226, 229
Clergy, defined, 411
Cliff, defined, 691
Clinton, Bill, 617
Clovis, New Mexico, 128
Clovis point, *128*
Cocoa, 281, *281*
Code of Hammurabi, 69, 71, 209

Codex Mendoza, *136,* 137
Coffee, 543, *543,* 544, 559
Cold War, 471, 472–473
  end of, 646
  Korea in, 655
Coleridge, Samuel Taylor, 457
Colombia, 139
  demography of, *531*
  rain forests of, 529
Colonialism, 440
Color de Mello, Fernando, 553
Colorado, *570–571*
Colosseum, 153, 170
Columbian exchange, 442–443
Columbus, Christopher
  discovery of Venezuela by, 536
  racial attitudes of, 525
  voyages of, 440–441, 502, 506, 509, 512, 513, 526
Command economy, 490
Commerce. *See* Trade.
Common Market, *485,* 497
  building, 484–485
  defined, 484
Commonwealth, defined, 496
Commonwealth of Independent States. *See* CIS; Russia; Soviet Union.
Communication
  advances in, 17
  history of, 665–668
Communism
  defined, 344
  functioning of, 345
  in Russia, 465
Comparison and contrast, 107
Compass rose, defined, G2
Concentration camps, 471
Concorde (airplane), *479*
Confederation, defined, 603
Conflicts, resolving, 483
Confucianism, 118, 120
  in Korea, 654, 656
Confucius, 118, 120
Congo Basin, G9
Conquistadors, 578
Conservation, 621
Constantine, emperor of Rome, 153, 178, 179
Constantinople, 178, 412, 413
  international trade of, 409, 453
  See also Istanbul, Turkey.
Constitution, Roman antecedents of, 171
Constructive criticism, 517
Continental climate, defined, 482
Conversion, religious, 552
Converso, defined, 439
Cook, James, 437, *445,* 600
Copán, 131
Copernicus, Nicolaus, 429
Coptic Christianity, 231
Coptic language, 231
Córdoba, Spain, 192
Cortés, Hernán, 578
Costa Rica, 542
  democracy in, 544–545
  demography of, *530*
  future of, 545
  tranquility of, 544, *545*
Cotton, 235
Countries of the world, 43, 675–677
Coup, defined, 540
Courlander, Harold, 262
Cree people, 600
Creole language, 511
Creoles, 533
Cricket, 518
Criticism, constructive, 517
Croatia
  modern, 492
  unrest in, 479
Crusade
  defined, 416
  knights of, *417*
Cuba, 391, 506, 509, 638
  abolition of slavery in, 515
  demographics of, 520
  economy of, 520
  emigration to U.S. from, 625
  future of, 520–521
  sports in, 518
Cultural diffusion, 15
Cultural Revolution, 346, 347
Culture
  in civilization, 67
  defined, 5
  diversity of, 4, 21, 23
  elements of, 6–9
  factors affecting, 12–17, 138–139
  regional, 45
  spread of, 15
  in U.S., 20–21
Cuneiform, 70
Cunha, Euclides da, 555, 565
Cunninghame Graham, R. B., 528
Currency, 134
Customs, 6
Customs check, defined, 485
Cuzco, Peru, 140, *527*
Cyrus, shah of Persia, 202, 209
Czar, defined, 454
Czech Republic, 490, 491
Czechoslovakia
  breakup of, 479, 490, 491
  German invasion of, 469
  per capita income in, *485*
  Velvet Revolution of, 478

D

Dagomba people, 274
Dai Jin, 342
Damascus, Syria, 192
Damavand, Mount, 205
Darius I, king of Persia, 209
Dark Ages. *See* Middle Ages.
Darwin, Charles, 448, 450
David, king of Israel, 75
Deforestation, *34,* 35, *561*
Degrees, 29
De Klerk, F. W., 305
Delhi, India, *334*
Delphi, Greece, 148
Delta, defined, 83, 690
Democracy
  birth of, 156–157
  defined, 157
  forms of, 157
Deng Xiaoping, 348, 349, 350
Denmark, 414, 415
  Common Market and, 485
  German invasion of, 470
  per capita income in, *485*
  Reformation in, 433
  rejection of Maastricht Treaty, 487
Desalination, *198*
  defined, 198
Desert, 224
  defined, 690
Desert Storm, Operation, 197
Detroit, Michigan, 40, 608
Dhaka, Bangladesh, population density of, *315*
Di-xin, Chinese emperor, 340
Día de los Muertos, 588, 592
Diagnosis, 189
Dialects, 355
Dias, Bartolomeu, 297
Diaspora, 648
Díaz, Porfirio, 581, *581*
Dictator, defined, 467
Dionysus Exiguus, 75
Diossé, Koumi, 254
Diré, Mali, 247
Direct democracy, 157
Discrimination
  defined, 632
  in South Africa, 301–302
  in U.S., 632–633
Disease, introduction to the Americas, 442, 513, 532
Dissident, defined, 350
Distribution, defined, 142
Diversity, defined, 129
Djenné, Mali, 249, *251*
Djoser, pharaoh of Egypt, 93
Dolores, Mexico, 580
Dominican Republic, 509, *510*
  currency of, *522*
  language of, 511
  sports in, 518
Dominion, defined, 603
Dorris, Michael, 512
Drake, Francis, 513
Drought
  defined, 256
  effects of, 260–261
Dublin, Ireland, 484
Dubois, Eugene, 396
Dutch East India Company, 297
Dutch language, 406
Dynasty
  defined, 84
  in China, 116

E

Earth Summit, 549, 563
Earthquakes, 204, 361
Easter Island, 18–19, *18*
Eastern Europe
  conflicts in, 492
  democracy in, 490
  progress in, 491
EC. *See* Common Market.
Economic systems, 8
Economics, defined, 23
Economy
  boom-and-bust, 559
  command, 490
  market, 490
Ecuador, 139
  demography of, 531, *531*
Edelweiss, 406
Edo (Tokyo), Japan, 370
Education
  Argentine, 540
  Canadian, 609–610
  importance of, 635
  Japanese, 375–376, 380–381
  Japanese vs. U.S., 380–381

Peruvian, 533
South Korean, *656*
U.S., 633, 635
UN and, 645
Egypt, *54,* 55, 245, 249
agriculture in, 235
ancient, 82–85
ancient, achievements of, 93–94
ancient, death rituals in, 99
ancient, history of, 80–81
ancient, religion in, 89
ancient, society in, 87–88
Arab rule over, 232–234
art of, 96–97
British rule over, 235–236
Byzantine rule over, 226–227
foreign influences in, 228–229
history of, 226–227
international trade of, 234, 235–236
modern, 236–237, *240*
Muslims in, 190, 226
Ottoman rule over, 234–235
religion in, 231, 233, 237
Roman rule over, 229, 230
Suez Canal, *505*
wars with Israel, 236–237, 649
Eiffel, A. G., 29
Einstein, Albert, *626*
El Dorado, 505
El Salvador, G15, 542
crafts in, *530*
demography of, 530
government of, 544
peace plan for, 545
unrest in, 542, 544, 545
Elevation, G9
defined, 138
maps of, 399
Elizabeth I, queen of England, 513
Elizabeth II, queen of England, *407, 605*
Elmina, Ghana, 266, 274
Emancipation, 515, 553, 569
Embargo, defined, 398
Emigrant, defined, 41
Empire, defined, 136
Empty Quarter (Arabia), 185, 194
Endangered species, 35, *35*
England, 414
defeat of Spanish Armada, 437, 443, 444
Reformation in, 432, 433
religious conflict in, 433
See also British Empire; Great Britain.
English Channel, tunnel under, *407*
Enlightenment, 447
Enrile, Juan Ponce, 393
Entrepreneur, defined, 493
Environment, 12–13
changing, 33–34
culture and, 138–139
Epic, defined, 319
Epidaurus, *161*
Equator, G4
Eratosthenes, 160
Este, Isabella d', 427
Estonia, independence of, 496
Ethiopia, 225
emigration to Israel from, *651*
emigration to U.S. from, 625
famine in, 243
marriage customs of, 6
Muslims in, 190
Ethnic group, defined, 21
Euphrates River, 54, *54,* 66, 67
Europe, *481*
eastern. *See* Eastern Europe.
economic unity of, 496–497
ethnic diversity of, *462*
geography of, *404,* 406–407
great plain of, 481
physical map of, *682*
regions of, 480–481
western. *See* Western Europe.
European Economic Community. *See* Common Market.
Evidence, identifying, 263
Ewe people, 272
Exchange, currency, 486
Exile, 215
Export, defined, 277
Extinct, defined, 35

F

Fabergé, Carl, 466
Facts, 18–19
Fahd, king of Saudi Arabia, 195
Faisal, king of Saudi Arabia, 195, 199
Falkland Islands, *26*
Family, as institution, 8
Famine, defined, 341
Fante people, 274
Farming. *See* Agriculture.
Farouk, king of Egypt, 236
Farsi language, 206, 210
Fatima, 190
Favela, defined, 562
Faxian, 321
Fellahin, defined, 228
Felucca, defined, 242
Ferdinand, king of Spain, 436, 438, 439, 440, 506
Fertile Crescent, *56–57,* 67, *67*
Festa Del Gallo, 7
Festivals, 6–7
Feudalism, 367, 414–418
structure of, 415
Fez, Morocco, 192
Fiesta, defined, 588
Flood plain, defined, 690
Florence, Italy, 427
as trade center, 418, 425
Florida, 509, 616, 623
Cuban emigration to, 523
Spanish rule over, 441
Flow charts, 61
Foch, Ferdinand, 463
Folsom, New Mexico, 128
Forbidden City, *338*
Forum, defined, 644
Fossils, *26*
France, *29,* 29–31, *30,* 155
Caribbean possessions of, 511, 513, 514
Catholicism in, 433
colonial expansion of, 460
competition with Britain, 445–446
currency of, 486
economic isolationism in, *487*
influence over Canada, 602, 608
medieval empire of, 412–413
nationalism of, 460
Norse settlements in, 414
per capita income in, *485*
resistance to Nazis in, 470
rule over Egypt, 228
rule over Mali, 247, *251,* 253–254
rule over Mexico, 581
rule over Vietnam, 397
Seven Years' War with Britain, 597
trade with China, 342
trade with Southeast Asia, 389
World War I alliances of, 461, 462
in World War II, 470, 472
World War II alliances of, 469
Francis Ferdinand, archduke of Austria, 462
Franco, Francisco, 469
Frank, Anne, 470
Frankincense, 185
Frederick the Wise, prince of Saxony, 431
Free enterprise, defined, 347
French and Indian War, 445–446, 601–602
French language, 406
Fuji, Mount, 314
Fulani people, 258

G

Galilee, Sea of, *650*
Galleons, 391
Gama, Vasco da, 225, 324
Gandhi, Indira, 327, *327*
Gandhi, Mohandas, 299, 326–327, *326,* 337
Ganges River, *329*
Gao, Mali, 249, 250
Gauchos, *538, 539*
Gaza, *651*
Gazetteer, 692–695
Geneva, Switzerland, 645
Genghis Khan, 341
Genoa, Italy, as trade center, 418, 425
Genocide, 470, 471, 492
Geographic terms, 690–691
Geography, G15
Arabic, 191
defined, 21, 29
five themes of, 28
See also Maps.
George V, king of England, 299
Georgics (Virgil), 168
Germany
aggression of, 469
alliance with Japan, 371
colonial expansion of, 460
Common Market and, 484
division of, 472, *473*
economy of, 373
emigration to U.S. from, 625
Gulf War and, 197
industrialization of, *461*
inflation in, 468
manners in, 6
Nazi, 468–470
neo-Nazism in, 487
oil resources of, 373
per capita income in, *485*

Reformation in, 430–431, 433
reunification of, 459, 491, 655
World War I alliances of, 461, 462
World War I peace talks, 463, 465
in World War II, 470–472
World War II alliances of, 469
Ghana, 225, 289
colonization of, 267, 276–277
crafts in, *266,* 271, 275
demographics of, 283
festivals in, 268, 273
geography of, 269
history of, 266
independence of, 280–281
international trade of, 274–275
modern, 282–283
natural resources of, 277, 281, 282
proverbs of, 272
religion in, 271, 276
Gil, Gilberto, 565
Gilgamesh, 62–65
Giza, Egypt, 242
pyramids at, 88–89, *88, 227*
Glacier, defined, 128, 574, 691
Globe, using, G4
Glossary, 701–708
of geographic terms, 690–691
GNP (gross national product), 374
Gokason, 365
Gold Coast, 276, 277, 280
Golden Stool, 273, 276
Good, Paul, G7
Goodwill, 635
Gorbachev, Mikhail, 474, *474,* 480, 493, 494
Gospels, 175–176
Government
as institution, 8
Roman influences on, 171
types of, 525
Granada, Spanish conquest of, 440
Grand Canal (China), *338*
Graphs, comparing, 451
Great Britain, 12
Caribbean possessions of, 511, 513, 514, 515, 516
colonial expansion of, 460
colonization of Ghana, 267, 276–277
Common Market and, 485
competition with France, 445–446
culture of, 450
currency of, 486
economy of, 373
empire of. *See* British Empire.
festivals in, 7
fuel consumption of, 457
government of, 407
international influence of, 448, 450
mountains of, 480
oil resources of, 373
per capita income in, *485*
reform efforts in, 447
rule over Canada, 601, 602, 603–605
rule over Egypt, 228, 236
rule over India, 317, 324–325
rule over Palestine, 648, 649
rule over South Africa, 298, 301
Seven Years' War with France, 597
sports in, 518
trade with China, 342
trade with Southeast Asia, 389
transportation in, 16
World War I alliances of, 461, 462
in World War II, 450, 470, 472
World War II alliances of, 469
Great Lakes, *574,* 599, 600, 609, 620
Great Leap Forward, 346
Great Migration, 40
Great Plains, 33, *616,* 620
Canadian, 600
Great Rift Valley, G9, 224, *224*
Great Trek, 290, 298–299, *298*
Great Wall, 121, 342
benefits and costs of, 122–123
Greater Antilles, 509, 510
natural resources of, 510
Greece, 461, *481*
climate of, 482
Common Market and, 485
culture of, 148
geography of, 155
per capita income in, *485*
resources of, 155
Greek Empire, *149*
achievements of, 159–161
conquest of Persia, 209–210
culture of, 161
engineering in, 174
Golden Age of, 156–158
influence on Egypt, 228
mythology of, 164–166
philosophy in, 160
religion in, 159–160
science in, 160
size of, 155
Greek language, 406, 412
Greenland, G6
Grenada, 521
Grid, map, G2, G3
Gross national product (GNP), 374
Guadeloupe, 506
government of, 511
Guangzhou, China, *344*
Guarani language, 532
Guatemala, G15, *44,* 134, 542
arts in, *527*
demography of, *530,* 531
dictatorship in, 542
festivals of, *530*
peace plan for, 545
unrest in, 544
Guerrillas, defined, 540
Guiana Highlands, 529
Guild, defined, 425
Gulf of Mexico, 620
Gulf Stream, 482
Gulf War, 197, 199, *634*
Gum arabic, 253
Gupta dynasty, 316, 320
achievements of, 318–319
decline of, 321
Gutenberg, Johannes, 428
Guyana, demography of, *531*

H

Habitat for Humanity, *636*
Hacienda, defined, 579
Haida people, 600
Haiti, 509, 515
economy of, 522
emigration to U.S. from, 625
independence of, 507, 516, 532
language of, 511
Halloween, 21
Hammurabi, 69, 71
Hanoi, Vietnam, 398
Harappa, 104
Harbor, defined, 690
Hatshepsut, queen of Egypt, 85
Havel, Václav, 478
Hawaii, climate of, 620
volcanoes in, *26*
Haynes, Lemuel, *617*
Hebrew language, *73*
Heian period, 363
Hemisphere, 529
of globe, G4
Henry IV, king of Castile, 438
Henry the Navigator, prince of Spain, 550
Heritage Language Program, 610
Hermit, defined, 654
Herodotus, 94
Hidalgo y Castillo, Miguel, 580
Hieroglyphics, 87, 95
Hijra, 186
Himalayas, 115, 312, 314, 331
Hindi language, 332, 333
Hindu Kush (mountains), 105, 331
Hindu New Year, *108*
Hinduism, 108–110
culture of, 100
customs of, 316, 320–321
funeral customs of, 6
suppression by Muslims, 322
Hippocrates, 160
Hiroshima, Japan, 371
Hispaniola, 442, 509, 513
History, defined, 21, 23
History of the Indies (de las Casas), 443
Hitler, Adolf, 468, *468,* 469, 470, 472
Ho Chi Minh, 397
Ho Chi Minh City, Vietnam, 398, *398*
population density of, *315*
Ho-ti, emperor of China, 120
Hockey, 609
Hodgson, Frederick, 276
Hokkaido, 360
Holland. *See* Netherlands.
Holocaust, 470–471, 649
Holy Land, 416
Homer, 93, 154
Homo sapiens, 59–60
Homogeneous, defined, 378
Honduras, G15, 542, 544
British rule over, 445
demography of, *530*
peace plan for, 545

Hong Kong
economy of, *315*
future of, 354
population density of, 315
Honolulu, Hawaii, G10
Honshu, 360
Hostage, defined, 216
House of Commons, 407
House of Lords, 447
Housing, 31
Houston, Texas, 31
Huang He (river), 54, *54*, 115
Hudson Bay, 599
Hugo, Victor, 480
Humanism, defined, 426
Humanitarian, defined, 645
Hung-wu, Chinese emperor, 342
Hungary, 461
emigration to U.S. from, 625
Huns, white, 321
Hunter-gatherers, 58, 129
Husayn, 207, 214
Hypotheses, making, 419

I

Ibn Battuta, 191, 250, 251
Ibn Juzayy, 251
Ibn Khaldun, 232
Ideology, defined, 348
Idioms, 25
Iffat, queen of Saudi Arabia, 195
Imhotep, 93
Immigration, 39, 623–624
current laws on, 625
patterns of, *625*
quotas on, 624–625
value of, 626–627
Imperialism, defined, 325
Import, defined, 277
Inca Empire, 142, 145
accomplishments of, 143
culture of, 140
heritage of, *502*
people of, 140, 143
riches of, 513
roads of, 141
ruins of, *527*
Indentured servants, 513, 516, *516*
India, 38, 192
ancient, 100
ancient, arts in, 319
ancient, civilization of, 102–103
ancient, crafts in, 319
ancient, governments in, 321
ancient, religion in, 105, 316
ancient, science and medicine in, 318–319
ancient, social system in, 106
ancient, trade in, 103–104, 319
British rule over, 317, 324–325, 445
conflict with Pakistan, 332
cultures of, 332
democracy in, 335
emigration to U.S. from, 625
festivals in, *108*
funeral customs of, 6
geography of, 329, 331–332
history of, 316–317
independence movement in, 325–327
international trade of, 319, 324
languages and peoples of, 332–333
Mughal rule over, 323–324, *324*
Muslims in, 190, *191*
overthrow of British rule, 337
population of, 312, 335
providing labor to Saudi Arabia, 198
rainfall in, 312
religion in, 112, 333
revolts against Britain, 446
self-government for, 327
social progress in, 333–335
trade with Arabs, 384
trade with Southeast Asia, 389
See also Hinduism.
Indo-European languages, 206
Indo-Europeans, 105
Indonesia, 396–397, *399*
agriculture in, *310–311, 388*
arts in, *384*
economy of, *315*
climate of, *G8*
Muslims in, 190
population of, 387
trade with India, 319
Indulgences, defined, 430
Indus River, G12, 54, *54*, 103, 389
civilizations along, 100
Industrial Revolution, 437, 446–447
Inflation, 560, 587
defined, 561
Information, recording, 303
Infrastructure, defined, 230
Inquisition
defined, 433
Spanish, 439
Inset, defined, G2
Institutions, 7–8
International Date Line, 610
Inti Raymi, *142*
Intifada, 652
Inuit people, 597, 600, *600*, 607, 608, 620
art of, *610*
Ipuky, 96
Iran, 219
agriculture in, 205
commerce in, *203*
earthquakes in, 204
festivals in, 207, 213
geography of, 205
government of, 214, 215, 216
history of, 202–203
languages of, 206
modernization of, 213–214
Muslims in, 190
natural resources of, 196
oil in, *215*
peoples of, 206
plateau of, 205
relations with U.S., 214–216
religions of, 206
war with Iraq, 197, 216
See also Persian Empire.
Iraq
Gulf War and, 197
natural resources of, 196
war with Iran, 197, 216
Ireland, 38
Common Market and, 485
emigration to U.S. from, 624
Norse settlements in, 414
per capita income in, *485*
potato famine in, 624
Irish Americans, 41, 624
Iron curtain, 472
Iroquois people, 600
Irrigation, 34, 67, 206
Isabel, princess of Brazil, 553, 569
Isabella, queen of Spain, 438, 439, 440, 506
Isfahan, 210, 212
Islam, *479*
growth of, 189–191, *190*
origins of, 148, 151, 186–187
sects of, 190, 207, 210
Shi'a, 190, 203, 206, 207, 210, 232
in Southeast Asia, 384
Sunni, 190
teachings of, 187–188
See also Muslims.
Ismail, 235, 237
Isolation, defined, 362
Israel, 416
ancient, 56–57, 75
borders of, 648
demography of, *650*
everyday life in, 650, *651*
founding of, 642
future of, 652
immigration to, 650, *651*
independence of, 649
population of, *652*
religion in, *650, 651*
territories occupied by, 643, *652*
UN and, 648–649, 650
wars with Egypt, 236–237, 649
women in, *650*
Istanbul, Turkey, 178, 412
See also Constantinople.
Isthmus, defined, 235, 690
Italy, 155
Catholicism in, 433
climate of, 482
culture of, 148
currency of, 486
festivals in, 7
per capita income in, *485*
Renaissance, 425
World War I alliances of, 461
in World War II, 472
World War II alliances of, 469
See also Roman Empire.
Ivan the Great, czar of Russia, 454
Ivan the Terrible, czar of Russia, 454

J

Jacob, 74
Jakarta, Indonesia, 396
population density of, *315*
Jamaica, 509
government of, 511
language of, 511
natural resources of, 510
sports in, 518
Japan
arts in, *358–359*
Chinese influence in, 363
colonization of Korea, 363, *654*
conflict with Russia, 495

economy of, *315,* 373, 374–376
education in, 375–376, 380–381
environment of, 378
family life in, 376–377
future of, 378–379
geography of, G1, 360–362, *361*
Gulf War and, 197
history of, 358–359, 366–371
international relations of, 379
language in, 363
leisure in, 377–378
literacy rate of, 375
minorities in, 378
natural resources of, 361–362
occupation of Philippines, 392
oil resources of, 373
poetry of, 364–365
religion in, 112, 362, 363
shogunates of, 366–368, 370
standard of living in, 376
tea ceremony in, *369*
war with China, *344,* 345, 371
war with Russia, 371
in World War II, 371, 472
World War II alliances of, 469
Java, 396, *384*
Java man, 396
Jerusalem, 75, *75,* 649
Turkish rule over, 416
Jesuits, 433, 552
Jesus
life of, 175–177
See also Christianity.
Jingoism, 460
João, prince of Portugal, 552, 553
Johannesburg, South Africa, 299, *305*
John, apostle, 175
Jomon people, 362–363
Jordan, Gulf War and, 197
Joseph, Lynn, 508
Juárez, Benito, 581
Judah, 75
Judaism
Christianity and, 175
in Egypt, 229, 230
holy days of, 7, 74, *77*
inquisitions against, 433
Islam on, 188
Israel and, 648
Jerusalem and, 416, 649, *651*
marriage customs of, 6
Nazi persecution of, 468, 469, 470, 648
origins of, 73–77, 148, 151
Spanish persecution of, 439
symbols of, *642*
in U.S., *77, 623*
Judgments, making, 18–19
Julius II, pope, 426
Justice, social, 306

K

Kabuki theater, 315
Kaiapó people, 563
Kalahari Desert, *224*
Kampuchea, genocide in, 471
Kapital, Das (Marx), 450
Kayes, Mali, 254
Kazakhstan
membership in CIS, 496
nuclear weapons in, 497
Ka'bah, *183,* 184, 185, *186,* 187
Keita, Modibo, 254
Kennedy, John F., 635–636
Kente cloth, 271, 274, 275
Kenya, *222*
Kenya, Mount, *224*
Kerinci, Mount, 399
Kerma kingdom, 81, *86,* 90
Khadijah, 186
Khafre, pharaoh of Egypt, 88
Khartoum, Sudan, 83
Khmer people, persecution of, 471
Khoikhoi people, 296
Khoisan people, 290, 296, 297
Khomeini, ayatollah of Iran, 214–216
Khufu, pharaoh of Egypt, 88, 89–90
Khyber Pass, 322
Kibbutz, defined, 650
Kiev, Ukraine, 471
Kievan Russia, Viking rule over, 453
Kilimanjaro, Mount, G9, *224*
Kim Il Sung, 655
King, Martin Luther, Jr., 350, 633
Kinship, 270–271
defined, 271
Kipling, Rudyard, 448, 449
Knesset, *642*
Knight, *417*
defined, 416
Koguryo kingdom, *654*
Konaré, Alpha Oumar, 247, 262
Koran. *See* Qu'ran.
Korea
arts in, *3, 654*
in Cold War, 655
geography of, G1, 654
history of, 653–654, *654*
Japanese control over, 363, *654*
partition of, 653, 654–655
religion in, 112, 654
science in, *654*
UN and, 653, 655
See also North Korea; South Korea.
Korean Reconstruction Agency, 655
Korean War, 642
Koryo kingdom, *654*
Kraft, Adam, *409*
Kremlin, *493*
Kristallnacht, 469
Krupp family, *461*
Kublai Khan, 338, 341
Kumasi, Ghana, 273, 274, 276, 277, 283
Kuna people, 500
Kurile Islands, 495
Kush, 86, 90, 92, 94
Kuwait
Gulf War and, 197
natural resources of, 196
Kwanzaa, *21*
Kyoto, Japan, 363, 366
Kyrgyzstan, membership in CIS, 496
Kyushu, 360

L

La Paz, Bolivia, 32, *32*
Labor
indentured, 513, 516, *516*
migrant, 39, 543
specialization of, 67
trade unions, 447
Labor-intensive, defined, 522
Lancaster, Pennsylvania, 45
Landform, defined, 29
Landlocked, defined, 256
Lang, k. d., 610
Language
alphabets, 660–661
development of, 39
Indo-European, 206
Laos, 386
Communist rule over, 398
population of, 387
Las Casas, Bartolomé de, 442–443
Last Supper, 176–177, *179*
Latin America, 45, *52*
See also Central America; South America.
Latin language, 173, 413
Latitude
defined, G2, 29
lines of, G4
using, G5
Latvia, independence of, 496
Lawrence, Jacob, 40
Le Clerq, François, 513
League of Nations, 604
League of the Five Nations, 600
Leakey, Louis, 222
Leakey, Mary, 222
Lebanon, unrest in, 197
Lee, Manuel, 518
Legend, map, G2, G3, G9
Legion, defined, 170
Lenin, Vladimir, 465, 467
Leo Africanus, 251, 253
Leo III, pope, 408, 412
Leo X, pope, 431
Leonardo da Vinci, 427, *429*
Lessac, Frané, *508*
Lesser Antilles, 509, 510
Liberia, 225
Libya, Gulf War and, 197
Life expectancy, defined, 261
Lightfoot, Gordon, 610
Lima, Peru, 533
Line of demarcation, 550
Lineage, defined, 271
Lintong, China, 119
Literacy rate, defined, 283
Literature, 10–11, 62–65, 164–166, 284–286, 364–365, 420–423, 534–537, 628–631
Lithuania, independence of, 496
Location, 30
Locator inset, G2, G3
Lock, functioning of, *606*
London, England, Caribbean influence on, 523
Longitude
defined, G2, 29
lines of, G4
using, G5
Lord, feudal, 415
Lorenzetti, Ambrogio, *425*
Los Angeles, California, G10, *16, 572,* 622
Lothal, 104
Louisburg, Canada, 602
Louisiana, 43
Louvre museum, 407, *407*

Luke, apostle, 175, 176
Luther, Martin, 409, 430–431, 432
Lutherans, 431
Luxembourg
Common Market and, 484
German invasion of, 470
Luxor, Egypt, 242
Luzon, Philippines, 390

M
Maastricht Treaty, 487, 496–497
MacArthur, Douglas, 371, 392
Macedonia, 461
Machu Picchu, *126,* 140
Mackenzie, Alexander, 602–603, *602*
MacNeish, Richard, 128
Madras, India, 324
Magellan, Ferdinand, 385, 389, 390
Mahabharata, 319
Mahmud of Ghazna, 316, 322
Main idea, identifying, 143
Maine, border with Quebec, *613*
Malaya, natural resources of, 550
Malaysia, 386
Malaysia, population of, 387
Mali, 21, 225
agriculture in, 255, 257
crafts in, 252, 265
culture of, 262
demographics of, 261
empire of, 246–250
French rule over, 247, *251,* 253–254
future of, 262
history of, 246–247
international trade of, 250
Islam in, 248–249, 250, 251, 258
life expectancy in, 265
natural resources of, 260
peoples of, 258
Malinke people, 249, 258
Manchus, rule over China, 339, 342–343
Mandate of Heaven, 116, 340
Mandela, Nelson, 291, 292, 294, 295, 305, 309
Manetho, 84
Manila, Philippines, 391, 394
Manitoba, 599
Mann, Horace, 635
Manners, 6
Manor, defined, 415
Mansa Musa, king of Mali, 246, 248–249, 250
Mantua, Italy, 427
Manuel, king of Portugal, 551
Mao Zedong, 339, 345–346, 348
Map and Globe Handbook, G1–G15
Maps
comparing, G13
cultural, G14
defined, G1
elevation, 399
geographic references on, G15
historical, G11
physical, G9
reading, G2–G3
symbols on, 372–373
thematic, 46–47
types of, G9–G12
using, 29–30
world, 679–689
Maquiladoras, 587, *587*
Maracaibo, Lake, 537, *537*
Marathon, Battle of, 158
Marconi, Guglielmo, 12, 25
Marcos, Ferdinand, 385, 392–393
Marcos, Imelda, 393
Margaret I, queen of Denmark, 415
Marie de France, 415
Marine climate, defined, 482
Maritime provinces, 598, 599, 604
Maritz, Gert, *290*
Mark, apostle, 175
Market, defined, 415
Market economy, 490
Marseilles, France, 155
Martial law, defined, 392–393
Martinique
government of, 511
language of, 511
Marx, Karl, 450
Marx, Roberto Burle, 565
Massachusetts, 523, 596
Matrilineal, defined, 270
Matthew, apostle, 175, 176
Mauritania, *279*
Mauryas, 113
May Day, *7*
Mayans, *52, 55, 126,* 130–131
achievements of, 131
McGill University, 610
Mecca, 151, *183,* 184, 185, 186, 187, 233, 248
Media
defined, 21
effect on democracy, 157
Medici family, 425, 427
Medicine
Arabic, 189, 191
Indian, 319
Medina, 186, 188
Mediterranean Sea, *149*
climate of, 150, 482
trade around, 150
Meiji Restoration, 370–371
Mekong River, 398
Memphis, Egypt, *86*
Menchú, Rigoberta, 527, 542
Mendes, Chico, 562–563, *563*
Mengzi, 340
Mercator, Gerardus, G6
Meroë, *86,* 94, 95
Mesa, defined, 618, 691
Mesoamerica, *130*
early cultures in, 129–131
Mesopotamia, *55,* 66–72
Mestizos, 391, 530
Mexica. *See* Aztecs.
Mexico, 572
agriculture in, 585
border with U.S., 586
climates of, 585
colonization of, 578–579
crafts in, 3
cultures of, 591
emigration to U.S. from, 625
family life in, 589
festivals in, *575,* 588, *588,* 591, 592
folk traditions in, 591
French rule of, 581
geography of, 584–585
government of, 593
history of, 576–577
independence of, 580–581
industry in, 582, 586–587
international relations of, 593
land reform in, 582
modernization of, 582
native cultures in, 513
natural resources of, 585
relations with U.S., 582, 586, 593
religion in, 579, 589
revolutions in, 577, 581–582
rural life in, 588–589
Spanish rule over, 441
unrest in, *581*
urban life in, 589–590
war with U.S., 580
women's role in, 589
Mexico City, G2, *576, 577,* 590
earthquakes in, 574
Meyer, Elana, 304
Mfecane, 299
Miami, Florida, G10
Michelangelo, 426, 427
Middle Ages, 410
Christianity in, 410–413
crusades in, 416, 417
daily life in, *408,* 415
end of, 418
feudalism in, 415
Middle East, emigration to U.S. from, 625
Middleman, defined, 250
Midwest, of U.S., 43
Migrant workers, 543
Migration, 39, 41
Milan, Italy, as trade center, 418, 425
Minamoto family, 366
Mindanao, Philippines, 394
Minerals, *26*
Ming dynasty, 338, 342
Minneapolis, Minnesota, 620
Missionaries, 177, 276
Mississippi, 638
Mississippi River, 620, *621,* 623
Moche civilization, 139
Montezuma, Aztec emperor, 578
Modernization, defined, 214
Mogadishu, Somalia, 645
Mohammed Reza Pahlavi, shah of Iran, 214, 215, 216
Mohenjo-Daro, *12,* 102–103, *103,* 125
Moldova, membership in CIS, 496
Moluccas, 387
Momaday, N. Scott, 618
Monastery, defined, 411
Mongols
invasion of Russia, 453–454
rule over China, 338, 341
Monocrop, defined, 522
Monotheism, 73
Monsoons, 314, 329, 330, 387
Mont Blanc, France, *1*
Montenegro, modern, 492
Montgomery, Alabama, boycotts in, 633
Montgomery, L. M., 598, 610
Montreal, Quebec, 572, 610

Morocco, Muslims in, 190
Moscow, Russia, *405,* 474, *478*
rise of, 454
Moses, 74
Mosques, 186
Mosul, Iraq, 192
Mount of Mercy, 184
Mountain pass, defined, 691
Mouth (river), defined, 690
Mozambique, 293
emigration to U.S. from, 625
Mubarak, Hosni, 237
Mughal Empire, 323–324, *324*
Muhammad, 151, 182, 184, 188, 190
life of, 186–187
Muhammad Ali, 226, 234, 235
Mulroney, Brian, 608
Multicultural, defined, 607
Multiculturalism Act (Canada), 608
Mummy, defined, 89–90
Murray, Anne, 610
Muslims, 73
achievements of, 191–192
in Balkans, 492
crusades against, 416
inquisitions against, 433
Jerusalem and, 416, 649, *651*
and Spanish culture, 439
See also Islam.
Myanmar, 386
population of, 387

N

Nagasaki, Japan, 371
Nagorno-Karabakh, *494*
Nairobi, Kenya, *222*
Nalanda, India, 318
Namibia, 293
Napata, *86,* 92
Nascimento, Abdias do, 565
Nascimento, Milton, 565
Nasser, Gamal Abdel, 227, 236, 239
Natal, 301, 302
National Film Board of Canada, 610
Nationalism, 460
defined, 280
in modern Europe, 487
Nationalization, defined, 537
Native Americans
in Alaska, 620, 620
arrival in North America, 623
art of, 527
Canadian, *597,* 600, *600,* 607, 608
Caribbean, *506,* 512
in Central and South America, 532
Columbus on, 525
in French and Indian War, 601–602
North American, 14, *14*
in Pacific Northwest, *621*
philosophy of, 618
pre-Columbian cultures of, 502
trade by, 619
villages of, *620*
NATO (North Atlantic Treaty Organization), 612
Natural resources, 34
Naturalized citizen
becoming, 626
defined, 625
Nazi party, 468–470, 649
Nebamun, 96
Negev Desert, *650*
Negotiate, defined, 544
Nehru, Jawaharlal, 317, 327
Netherlands, 34
colonization of Africa by, *277,* 290, 297–298
Caribbean possessions of, 511, 513
Common Market and, 484
currency of, 486
German invasion of, 470
Reformation in, 432, 433
resistance to Nazis in, 470
rule over Indonesia, 396
settlement of New York, 623
Spanish rule over, 441
and triangle trade, 514, *514*
trade with Southeast Asia, 389
Netherlands Antilles, 509, *519*
New Brunswick, 598
confederation of, 603
in dominion of Canada, 603
New Jersey, *27*
New Mexico, archaeological excavations in, 128
New Orleans, Louisiana, 620
New Testament, 175–176
New York, 572
New York, New York, *38*
Caribbean influence on, 523, *523*
population density of, *315*
settlement of, 623
United Nations in, *643*
Newfoundland, 12, 598, 599, 601
confederation of, 603
ethnic communities in, 607
Nicaragua, 542, 544
demography of, *530,* 531
elections in, 544
peace plan for, 545
unrest in, 542, 544, 545
Nicholas, bishop of Myra, 416
Nicholas II, czar of Russia, 464, 465, 466
Niger, immigration into, 261
Niger River, 255, 256, 263
Nigeria, Muslims in, 190
Nile River, 54, *54,* 80, *227,* 245
civilizations on, 82–93
geography of, 83
lower, 240, 242
upper, 242–243
Nîmes, France, G11
Ninety-Five Theses (Luther), 430
Nineveh, 71
Nkrumah, Kwame, 280, *280,* 281
Nobunaga, Oda, 367–368
Noh theater, 315
Noriega, Manuel, 543
Norsemen, 414
North America
ethnic communities in, *572*
European rule of, 572
exploration of, 596
geography of, *573,* 574–575
map of, *686*
natural resources of, 575
North American Free Trade Agreement, 593
North Atlantic Treaty Organization (NATO), 612
North Dakota, *624*
North Korea, 643
government of, 655
military aggression of, 655
relations with South Korea, 655
North, Marianne, 448, 450
Northeast, of U.S., 43
Northern Hemisphere, G4
tilt of, G8
Northwest Territory, 599, 608
Norway, 414, 415
German invasion of, 470
mountains of, 480
Note taking, 303
Nova Scotia, *597,* 598
confederation of, 603
in dominion of Canada, 603
Novgorod, Viking rule over, 453
Now Rouz, 207, 208
Nubia, 85–86, *85,* 90, 92
achievements of, 94–95
modern, 95, 240
nobility of, *91*
relations with Egypt, 81
Nuclear weapons, 371, 473
control of, 497
Nunavut Territory, 597, 608
Nuremberg, Germany, 468
Nzima people, 280

O

Oasis, defined, 185, 690
Octavian. *See* Augustus Caesar.
Odwira festival, 268, 273, 282
Odysseus, 154
Odyssey (Homer), 154
Oil
importance of, 196–198, 199
Saudi Arabian, 196–198
U.S. reserves of, 621
Venezuelan, 536–537
world resources of, 373
Ojibwa people, 600
Oklahoma, oil in, 621
Old Testament, 175, *176*
Olinda, Brazil, 556
Olmec, *126,* 130
Olympia, Greece, 148
Olympic Games, 148
Ontario, 599, 602, 608
confederation of, 603
in dominion of Canada, 603
Ontario, Lake, 599
OPEC (Organization of Petroleum Exporting Countries), 196, 199, 537
Operation Desert Storm, 197
Opinions, 18–19
Opium War, 344
Oral report, presenting, 541

Orange Free State, 298, 299
Organization of Petroleum Exporting Countries (OPEC), 196, 199, 537
Organization, patterns of, 107
Orientus, 410
Orinoco River, 529
Orthodox Church, 408, 412–413, *413, 436*
Ottoman Empire, *234,* 461
  rule over Egypt, 234–235
  war with Russia, 454
Ouro Prêto, Brazil, 552

P

Pacific Northwest, 621
Pacific Rim, 315, 655
  map of, *684*
Paekche kingdom, *654*
Pahlavi family, 213–214
Pakistan, *12,* 13
  conflict with India, 332
  formation of, 327, 331–332
  Muslims in, 190
  providing labor to Saudi Arabia, 198
Palestine
  British rule over, 648, 649
  partition of, 649, *649*
  refugees from, *645,* 650, *651,* 652
Pamir mountains, *50–51*
Pampas, G13, 528
Pan American games, *545*
Panama, 528, 542
  climate of, *529*
  crafts in, *500–501*
  demography of, *530*
  dictatorship in, 542
  Spanish rule over, 441
Panama Canal, 505, *505,* 543
Panatal, Brazil, 559
Panchatantra, 319
Papyrus, 94, *94*
Parachico people, *588*
Paraguay
  ancient languages of, 532
  demography of, *531*
Parallel timelines, 199
Paris, France, *29,* 29–31, *30,* 484, 645
Parks, Rosa, 633
Parthenon, *152,* 158, 484
Partition, defined, 649
Pass, mountain, 691
Passover, 74, *77*
Patagonia, G13
Patrilineal, 270
Patrilocal, defined, 270
Patron, defined, 425
Patterns, identifying, 107
Paul, apostle, 175, 176, 177
Pax Romana, 169
Paz, Octavio, 588
Peace Corps, 636
Pearl Harbor, Hawaii, 371, 392, 472
Pearl Mosque, 192
Pedro I, king of Brazil, 552–553
Pedro II, king of Brazil, 553
Peksowa, Ewelina, *3*
Pelé (Edson Arantes do Nascimento), 563
Peloponnesian War (Thucydides), 158
Peloponnesus, *155,* 156
Peninsula, defined, 155
Pennsylvania, 45
Peon, defined, 579
Pepin, king of France, 420
Pericles, 158
Permafrost, defined, 599
Perón, Eva Duarte de, 540, 541
Perón, Juan, 540
Perry, Matthew C., 370
Persepolis, 208, *208*
Persian Empire, *149,* 158, *209*
  achievements of, 210–212
  crafts in, *202,* 219
  history of, 209–210, 212
  religion in, 202, 203
  trade in, *208,* 209
  war with Russia, 454
  See also Iran.
Persian Gulf War, 197, 199, *634*
Peru, 54, 55, *502,* 528
  ancient languages of, 532
  commerce in, *533*
  cultures of, 138–142
  demography of, 531, *531*
  education in, 533
  festivals in, *142*
  independence of, 532
  native cultures in, 513
  Spanish rule over, 441
  wedding customs of, *531*
Peter the Great, czar of Russia, *453,* 454–455
Peters, Arno, G6
Petrograd, 464, 470
Pharaoh, defined, 85
Philip II, king of Spain, 390, 443
Philip, king of Macedon, 159
Philippines, 638
  colonial rule over, 390–392
  economy of, *315*
  emigration to U.S. from, 625
  festivals in, *385*
  independence of, 392–393
  Japanese occupation of, 392
  literacy rate of, 394
  modern, 394
  population of, 387
  providing labor to Saudi Arabia, 198
  religion in, 390–391, 393
  Spanish Rule over, 385, 390–391
  volcanoes in, 388
Philosophy, 160
Physical environment, 12–13
Physical features, 31
Pilgrimage, defined, 184
Pilipino language, 394
Pinatubo, Mount, 388
Pizan, Christine de, 427
Plague, 409, *419*
  defined, 418
Plain, defined, 691
Plantations, 514, 553, 559
  labor force for, 513, 514, 516, 552
Plateau, defined, 205, 691
Plato, 160
Pol Pot, 471
Poland
  arts in, *3*
  democracy in, 491
  German invasion of, 469
  per capita income in, *485*
  resistance to Nazis in, 470
  science in, 429
  trade unions in, 478
  in World War I, *458*
Political cartoons, 475
Pollution, 35
  industrial, 447
Population, of large cities, 664
Porter, John, 566
Portugal
  climate of, 482
  colonization of Ghana, 266, 274
  colonization of South America, 526, 532, 548, 550–552
  Common Market and, 485
  rivalry with Spain, 550
Portuguese language, 45
Porus, Indian prince, G12
Potato famine, 38, 41
Powell, Colin, 523
Prague, Czechoslovakia, *491*
Predictions, making, 217
Prehistoric, defined, 50
Prejudice, 624
  combating, 633
  defined, 23
Prime meridian, G4
Prince Edward Island, 598
  confederation of, 603
  in dominion of Canada, 603
Printing, movable-type, 428, 432
Process diagram, reading, 606
Profile, G9
Projection
  defined, G2
  examples of, G6–G7
Pronunciation key, 701
Propaganda, defined, 467
Prophets, 76–77
Protestant
  and Anglican church, 432
  and biblical art, *432*
  Calvinists as, 432
  defined, 431
  and Inquisition, 433
  and John Calvin, 432
  Lutherans as, 431
  and Martin Luther, 409, 430–431
  and spread of Reformation, 432, *433*
Proverbs, 272
Province, defined, 170
Psalms, 75
Ptolemy dynasty, 229, 233
Pu Yi, Chinese emperor, 344
Puebla, Battle of, 581, 622
Puerto Rico, 509
  demographics of, 520
  economy of, 520
  festivals in, *507*
  government of, 507, 638
  Spanish rule over, 638
  sports in, 518
  statehood and independence movements in, 520, 639
  U.S. rule over, 638
  urban life in, 519, *522*
Punic Wars, 169
Pyramids, 88–89, *88, 92,* 242

Q

Qing dynasty, 342–343
Qu'ran, 73, *182,* 187, 188, 192, 195, 201
Quadrant, *603*

Quebec, 599, 601, 602
border with Maine, *613*
confederation of, 603
in dominion of Canada, 603
ethnic communities in, 607
health care in, 610
legal system of, 605
separatist movement in, *607,* 608
Quechua language, 532
Quechua people, 528
crafts of, 532
Quotas, immigration, 624–625
Qustul, *86*

R

Rabbi, defined, 77
Racism, defined, 23
Raffles, Stamford, 395
Rain forests, 130, 529, 566–567
Rajputs, 324
Ramayana, 319
Ramesses II, pharaoh, 85, 241
Ramos, Fidel, 393, 394
Raphael, *402–403, 424*
Rashid family, 194
Rasputin, *466*
Rattray, R. S., 268
Raw materials, defined, 448
Rawlings, Jerry, 267, 282
Readers' Guide, 328
Recife, Brazil, 556
Reconquista, 439
Red Cross, 635
Red Guard, 346
Red River (Vietnam), 398
Red Sea, 185
Red Square, *478,* 493
Reformation, 409
beginning of, 430–431
spread of, 432–433, *433*
Regions
defined, 42
of U.S., 42–43
of world, 44–45
Reincarnation, 109, 111
Religion
ancient Egyptian, 89
ancient Indian, 105, 316
Aryan, 105–106
Aztec, 135–136
Brazilian, 564–565, *564*
Burmese, 112
Chinese, 101, 112
conversion, 552
Egyptian, 231, 233, 237
Ghanaian, 271, 276
Greek, 159–160
as institution, 8
Indian, 112, 333
Iranian, 206
Israeli, *650, 651*
Japanese, 112, 362, 363
Korean, 112, 654
Mexican, 579, 589
Persian, 202, 203
Philippine, 390–391, 393
Russian, 436
South American, 505
world distribution of, *688*
See also names of individual religions.
Remus, 168
Renaissance
arts in, *409,* 426–427
city life in, 425
defined, 424
Italian, 425
northern, 428–429
science in, 429
Reports, oral, 541
Representative democracy, 157
Republic, defined, 169
Resistance, 470
Revolution, 465
Reza Shah Pahlavi, 203, 213–214
Rig-Veda, 105
Ring of Fire, 574
Rio Bravo del Norte (Rio Grande), 586
Rio de Janeiro, Brazil, 549, *549,* 552, 557
Riyadh, Saudi Arabia, *183,* 194
Robinson, Arthur, G7
Rocky Mountains, 43, 47
Canadian, 620
Roman Empire, *149, 153*
achievements of, 171, 173
agriculture in, *230*
culture of, 148
decline of, 171
engineering in, *172,* 174
expansion of, G11
extent of, *153, 169*
fall of, 410
influence on Egypt, 228
laws of, 171, 173
origins of, 168
military organization of, 174
rise of, 168–169
rule over Egypt, 229, 230
trade with India, 319
Romance languages, 173
Romanian language, 406
Romanov family, 454
Romantic movement, 447, 457
Rome, 413, 426
Treaty of, 484–485
See also Roman Empire.
Romulus, 168
Roosevelt, Franklin D., *472*
Rosen, Barry, 216
Rosetta stone, 87
Rosh Hashanah, 7, 74
Ross, John, *603*
Royal Canadian Mounted Police, 604
Rubber, *315*
as natural resource, 559, *559*
Rudbar, 204
Rumania, 461
Rural, defined, 41
Russia, 155, 192
colonial expansion of, 460
conflict with Japan, 495
early history of, 453–454
economic conditions in, 499
emigration to U.S. from, 623, 625
empire of, *453,* 454–455
expansionism of, 454–455
geography of, 452
modernization of, 454–455
Mongol invasion of, 453–454
Norse settlements in, 414
rail travel in, 436
religion in, 436
religious conflict in, 433
rise of, 454–455
war with Japan, 371
World War I alliances of, 461, 462
World War I peace talks, 463, 465
See also CIS; Soviet Union.
Russian language, 406
Russian Republic, 474
Russian Revolution of 1905, 470
Russian Revolution of 1917, *459,* 464–465

S

Saba, Netherlands Antilles, 519
Sadat, Anwar, 236–237, 238
Sadat, Jehan, 237, 238
Safavid Empire, 210, 212
Sahara (desert), 82, *224,* 274
Sahel, 13, 31, 39, 41, *224,* 256–257, 260, 261, 263
St. Augustine, Florida, 616, 623
Saint Domingue, 515, 516
St. John, Newfoundland, 572
St. Lawrence River, 599, 600, 601, 609
St. Lawrence Seaway, 606, 608
St. Louis, Missouri, *617*
St. Lucia, 523
St. Peter's cathedral, 426, 430
St. Petersburg. *See* Petrograd.
Sako, Ousmane, 262
Salamis, Battle of, 158
Salinas de Gortari, Carlos, 593
Salvador, Brazil, 552
Samba, 565
Samurai, 359, 367
San Antonio, Texas, 622
San Francisco, California, 572
San Juan Mountains (Colorado), *570–571*
San Juan, Puerto Rico, 519, *522*
San Martín, José de, 527, 532
San people, 296
Sanctions, defined, 655
Sankoré Mosque, *246*
Sanpū, 364
Sanskrit language, 105, 319
Santayana, George, 402
Santiago (St. James), *576*
Santo Domingo, Dominican Republic, 506, 513
Santos, Brazil, 552
São Francisco River, 556
São Paulo, Brazil, 552, 555, *556,* 557, 560
São Vicente, Brazil, 552
Saqqara, 93
Sarajevo, Bosnia, 462, 645
destruction of, 490
Olympics in, 478
Sardis, Persia, 209
Sarmiento, Domingo, 540
Saskatchewan, *598,* 599
ethnic communities in, 607
Sassanian Empire, 209–210
Satrap, defined, 209
Saud family, 194
Saudi Arabia, *13,* 151, *183,* 184
agriculture in, *198*
customs of, 193
history of, 194–196
resources of, 196–198

rainfall of, *150*
Savafids, 203
SAVAK, 214, 215
Savanna, *257*
defined, 257, 690
Scale, defined, G2
Scandinavia
unification of, 415
Vikings in, 414
Science
Arabic, 191
Egyptian, 229
Indian, 318–319
Renaissance, 429
Scotland, Reformation in, 432
Scribe, defined, 88
Sea level, defined, 690
Seasons, G8
Segregation, defined, 293
Seljuk Turks, rule over Jerusalem, 416
Senegal River, 253, 256
Seoul, South Korea, *642, 655,* 656
Separatism, defined, 608
Serbia, 461
modern, 492
unrest in, 479
World War I alliances of, 461, 462
Serf, defined, 415
Seven Years' War, 446, 597
Shah, defined, 208
Shaka, Zulu king, 299
Shakespeare, William, 428–429
Shamanism, 654, *654*
Shang dynasty, 100, 340
Sharpeville, South Africa, 295
Shi huang-di, emperor of China, 119, 121, 122–123
Shiite Muslims, 190
in Egypt, 232
in Iran, 203, 206, 207, 210
Shikoku, 360
Shinto, 362
Shogun, defined, 366
Shogun government, 359, 366–370
Shōtoku, prince of Japan, 363
Siberia, *453*
environmental crisis in, 495
Siddhartha Gautama, 110–111
Sierra Madre, 39
Sikhs, 324, *332*
Silk Road, *50*, 121, 341
Silla kingdom, *654*
Silt, defined, 243
Silva, Benedita da, 563
Sima Xiangru, 114
Singapore, G5, 395–396
economy of, *315*
population of, 387
Sisal fiber, *225*
Sistine Chapel, 426, *427*
Slavery, 623
abolition of, 515, 553, 569
in Brazil, 552, 553
in Ghana, 274–275
in Latin America, 533
triangle trade, 514, *514*
Slavs, 452
Slovak Republic, 490, 491
Slovakia, *8*
Slovenia, 492
unrest in, 479
Social interaction, 14–15
Social justice, 306
Social sciences, defined, 21, 23
Socrates, 160
Solomon, king of Israel, 75
Somalia, *220–221*
relief efforts in, 612, 645
Songhai Empire, 246, 250–251, 253
Songhai people, 258
Sonni 'Ali, 246, 250, 251
Sources, evaluating, 238
South Africa, 225, 292, 326
apartheid in, 293–295
demography of, *294*
government of, 293
history of, 290–291, 296–299, 301–302
mining in, 299, 300
modern, 304–306
world relations of, 307
South African War, 301
South America, 528
cities of, 533
climates of, 504, *504,* 529
cultures of, 502, 505
emigration to U.S. from, 625
geography of, 502, *503*
independence movements in, 532
languages of, 505
map of, *687*
peoples of, 530–531, *531,* 531–532
religion in, 505
Spanish rule over, 441
topography of, 528–529
South Korea, 643
border with North Korea, 653, *653*
daily life in, 656, *656, 657*
economy of, *315*
education in, *656*
emigration to U.S. from, 625, 655
family life in, 656, *656*
holidays in, *656*
industrialization of, 655
international trade of, *656*
protests in, *642,* 655
sports in, 656, *656*
Southeast Asia
climate and resources of, 387
cultures of, 389
international trade in, 384, 389
physical geography of, 386–387
Southeast, of U.S., 43
Southern Hemisphere, G4
tilt of, G8
Soviet Union
breakup of, *478,* 493–495
collapse of, 474
emigration to Israel from, 650
emigration to U.S. from, 625
ethnic problems in, 492
foreign aid to Cuba, 520
formation of, 465
modernization of, 467
transformation into CIS, 496
World War II alliances of, 469
See also CIS; Russia.
Soweto, South Africa, *291,* 292, 295
Space exploration, *41*
Spain, 155, 190
agriculture in, *482*
Catholicism in, 433
civil war in, 469
climate of, 482
colonization of South America, 442–443, 513, 532
Common Market and, 485
currency of, 486
empire of, 440–443, *441*
Inquisition in, 439
per capita income in, *485*
religious conflict in, 433
rivalry with Portugal, 550
rule over Central America, 542
rule over Mexico, 578–579
rule over Philippines, 385, 390–391
rule over South America, 420–423, 526
settlement of North America, 442–443, 506, 519
unification of, 438, 439
Spanish Armada, 437, 443, 444, 484
Spanish language, 45, 406
Spanish-American War, 385, 391
Sparta, Greece, 156, 158
Spatial order, 107
Specialization of labor, defined, 67
Sphinx, *80–81*
Spice Islands, 387
Sri Lanka, providing labor to Saudi Arabia, 198
Stalin, Josef, *459,* 467, 468, *472,* 473
Stalingrad, 472
Standard of living, defined, 376
Stanley Cup, 609
States, 43
Statute of Westminster, 604–605
Steel drums, 521
Stein, Gertrude, 619
Stephens, John Lloyd, 131
Steppe, defined, 452
Stereotypes, identifying, 637
Stockholm, *3*
Strait, defined, 690
Strategic Arms Reduction Treaty (START II), 497
Subcontinent, defined, 329
Sudan, 83, 95
famine in, 243
Suez Canal, 235–236, *505*
Sugar, as natural resource, 522, 556, 559
Sultan, defined, 234
Sumatra, 399, *399*
Sumer, 68
birth of writing in, 56
culture of, 69
Sun Yat-sen, 344
Sunbelt, 619
Sundiata, king of Mali, 249, 250
Sung dynasty, 101
Sunni Muslims, 190
Superpower, defined, 472
Suriname, demography of, *531*
Surplus, defined, 67
Susa, Persia, 209
Sustainable development, defined, 563
Swamp, defined, 690
Swaziland, 293

Sweden, 414, 415
  mountains of, 480
  Reformation in, 433
  war with Russia, 454–455
Swedish Americans, 21
Switzerland, *480*
  per capita income in, *485*
  Reformation in, 432
Sydney, Australia, 33, *33*
Syria, agriculture in, *56*

T

Tagalog language, 394
Taharka, emperor of Nubia, *81*
Taira family, 366
Taj Mahal, 323
Tajikistan, membership in CIS, 496
  religion in, *479*
Takoma, Washington, *9*
Talbot, William Henry Fox, 447
Talmud, 77
Tangier, Morocco, 191
Tanzania, *224*
  human origins in, 222
Tarahumara Indians, 39, 41
Tariffs, defined, 485
Technology
  and culture, 16–17
  space exploration, *41*
Tehran, Iran, *205,* 215, 216
Tel Aviv, Israel, 648
Television, 17, 21
  effect on democracy, 157
Tema, Ghana, *282*
Ten Commandments, 74
Tenochtitlan, *127,* 132, 133, *133, 135,* 576
  destruction of, 578
Teotihuacán, 127, 132, 134
Tetzel, Johannes, 430, 431
Texas, 31
  independence of, 580, *580*
  oil in, 621
Texcoco, Lake, 132, 133
Thailand, 386
  population of, 387
Thanksgiving, 21, *575*
Thebes, *86*
Thompson, David, 602
Thucydides, 158
Tiananmen Square, 346, 349–350, *350*
Tibet, religion in, 112
Tigris River, 54, *54, 66,* 67
Tilby, Wendy, *611*
Timbuktu, 246, *246,* 250–251, 253
Time zones, G10
Timelines, parallel, 199
Tiradentes, 552
Tithe, defined, 411
Titicaca, Lake, *138,* 502
Tlatelolco, 132, 134
Tlingit people, *621*
Tokugawa Ieyasu, 368
Tokugawa shogunate, 359, 368–370
Tokyo, Japan, 370, 374, 376
Tolstoy, Leo, *455*
Toluca, Mexico, *584*
Torah, *57,* 74, *74*
Toronto, Ontario, 608, *608, 609*
Toronto, University of, 610
Tourism, 522, 587
Toussaint L'Ouverture, 515, *515,* 516
Toxic waste, 35
Trade agreement, defined, 593
Trade imbalance, defined, 379
Trade
  Arab, 319, 384, 389
  Byzantine, 171
  British, 342, 389
  Canadian, 613
  Chinese, 319, 342–343, 384, 389, 391
  Dutch, 389
  Egyptian, 93, 234, 235–236
  French, 342, 389
  Ghanaian, 274–275
  in India, 103–104, *104,* 319, 324, 384, 389
  Indonesian, 319
  in Italy, 418, 425
  Japanese, 374–376
  in Mali, 250
  Mediterranean, 150
  Native American, 619
  in Persian Empire, 208, 209
  Roman, 319
  South Korean, *656*
  Southeast Asian, 384, 389
  triangle, 514, *514*
  U.S., 342, 593, 613
  world, 451
Trade unions, 447
Tradition, defined, 268
Trans-Siberian Railway, 436
Transportation, 16–17, 31, 38–39
Transvaal, 299
Treblinka concentration camp, 471
Trek, defined, 298
Triangle trade, 514, *514*
Tributary, defined, 103, 690
Tribute, defined, 137–138
Trinidad and Tobago, 506, 508, 509, 521, 523
  festivals in, *504, 511*
  natural resources of, 510
  sports in, *518*
Trinity, 179
Trojan War, 154
Tropical, defined, 509
Trudeau, Pierre, 613
Truman, Harry S., 473, 644
Tsumshian people, 600
Tuareg people, 261
Tulu, Derartu, 304
Tundra, 387
Tupi people, *548,* 551
Turkey, 155, 178, 461
  Muslims in, 190
  persecution of Armenians, 471
  rule over Egypt, 228
  See also Ottoman Empire.
Turkmenistan, membership in CIS, 496
Tusaik Palace, 195
Tutankhamon, pharaoh of Egypt, 85
Tutu, Osei, 225, 267, 273
Typhoons, 387

U

Ukraine
  membership in CIS, 496
  nuclear weapons in, 497
Umar, caliph, 232
Umayyad family, 190
Ummayyads, 210
UNESCO (UN Educational, Scientific, and Cultural Organization), 645
UNICEF (United Nations Children's Fund), 645
United Fund, 635
United Nations, *643*
  achievements of, 645
  formation of, 459, 471, 642
  Gulf War and, 197
  importance of, 646–647
  Israel and, 649, 650
  Korea and, 655–656
  peacekeeping role of, 492, 642, 646, *647*
  structure of, 644–645
United Silla kingdom, *654*
United States, 572
  border with Canada, 612–613, *613*
  border with Mexico, 586
  Caribbean possessions of, 511, 516
  Civil War of, 633
  climates of, 620
  crafts in, 616
  cultures of, 626–627
  demographic changes in, *633*
  diversity of, 616
  economy of, 373
  education in, 380–381, 633, 635
  energy consumption of, 621
  festivals in, 7, *7, 21,* 622, *622*
  formation of, 446
  geography of, 46–47, *46, 47*
  Gulf War and, 197
  immigration to, 623–627
  independence of, 532, 617
  literacy rate of, 375
  manners in, 6
  marriage customs of, 6
  natural resources of, 620–621
  North American trade of, 593
  occupation of Japan, 359
  oil dependency of, 196, 199
  oil resources of, 373
  overthrow of British rule, 337
  per capita income in, 485
  purchase of Alaska, 437, 453
  regions of, 42–43, 43, 619–620
  relations with Central America, 543
  relations with Iran, 214–216
  relations with Japan, 379
  relations with Mexico, 582, 586, 593
  relations with Saudi Arabia, 196
  relations with South Korea, *656*
  relations with Vietnam, 385, 397, 398
  religion in, 623
  rule over Philippines, 391–392
  satellite map of, *619*
  trade with Canada, 613
  trade with China, 342
  transportation in, 16–17, 31, 38–39, 621
  war with Mexico, 580
  World War I alliances of, 46
  in World War II, 472

World War II alliances of, 469
Untouchable, defined, 106
Ur, 68, 103
Urban, defined, 43
Uruguay, demography of, *531*
USSR. *See* Soviet Union.
Uzbekistan, membership in CIS, 496

V
Valley, defined, 691
Values, defined, 8
Vancouver, British Columbia, 600
Vassal, defined, 415
Vedas, 105
Velvet Revolution, 478
Venezuela
agriculture in, 536
cultures of, 526, 536
natural resources of, 536–537
demography of, *531*
native peoples of, *536*
natural resources of, 196
Venice, Italy, 536
restoration of, 645
as trade center, 418, 425
Versailles, Treaty of, 463
Vertical zones, 529
Vesalius, Andreas, 429
Vespucci, Amerigo, 536
Veto, defined, 644
Victoria, queen of England, 325, 448, 470
Vietnam, 386, 397–398
Communist rule over, 397–398
emigration to U.S. from, 625
population of, 387
Vietnam War, 385, 397, 612
Vikings, 414
rule over Russia, 453
Virgil, 168
Virgin Islands, 516
VISTA, 636
Vladimir I, Kievan prince, 436, 453
Volcanoes, G15, *26,* 361, 387, 388
defined, 690
Volga River, 454
Volta River, 267, 269
Volunteer, defined, 635
Voting Rights Act of 1965, 633

W
Wailing Wall, *651*
Walcott, Derek, 523
Walesa, Lech, 478, 491
Warfare
Greek, 158, 159
modern, 462–463, 472–473
Roman, 174
nuclear, 371, 473
War of 1812, 613
Warsaw, Poland, 469, *470, 458, 490,* 491
Washington, D.C., 617
West, Benjamin, *601*
West Indies Federation, 521
West Indies. *See* Caribbean Islands.
Western Europe
climates of, 482
economic union in, 484–485
future of, 487
productivity of, 481, 482
Westernization, defined, 371
Winnipeg, Manitoba, *610*
Wittenberg, Germany, 430
Wolfe, James, *601*
Women
in Argentina, 540
in Babylonia, 69
in China, 351
in Ghana, 267, 270
in Inca culture, 140
in India, 335
in Iran, 214, 215, 216
in Israel, *650*
in Japan, 363, 376
in Mexico, 589
in Muslim culture, 187, 193
in Renaissance, 427
in Rome, 170
in Saudi Arabia, 196
in U.S., 632
stereotypes of, 637
Wordsworth, William, 457
Work unit, 353
World Bank, *643*
World
climates of, *688*
countries of, 675–677
hemispheres of, 44
history timetables of, 669–673
largest cities of, 664
physical map of, *680–681*
population distribution of, *689*
regions of, 44–45, *44*
religions of, *688*
resource distribution of, *689*
World Food Program, 645
World Health Organization (WHO), 645
World War I, 462–463
alliances of, 462
antecedents of, 460
costs of, 458
World War II
aftermath of, 472–473
costs of, 459, 472
Writing
alphabetic, *73,* 660–661
birth of, 56
cuneiform, 70
hieroglyphics, 87, 95
Wu, Chinese emperor, 340

X
Xhosa language, 292
Xhosa people, 298
Xochimilco, 134

Y
Yaa Asantewa, queen mother of Ghana, 276, *277*
Yalta peace conference, *472*
Yamato people, 358, 363
Yamin, Mohammad, 386
Yangdi, emperor of China, 123
Yangtse. *See* Chang Jiang.
Yathrib, 186
Yeltsin, Boris, 474, *475,* 496, *496,* 497
Yemen, 194, 234
Gulf War and, 197
Yi Sun-sin, *654*
Yom Kippur, 74
Yoritomo, shogun, 366
Young, Neil, 610
Yoyoi people, 363
Yuan dynasty, 341
Yugoslavia, breakup of, 479, 490, 492
Yukon Territory, 599
Yupik people, 620

Z
Zagros mountains, 205
Zapata, Emiliano, 581
Zapotec people, 582
Zheng He, 343
Zhou dynasty, 340
Zimbabwe, 293
Zionists, 648
Zoroaster, 206–207
Zoroastrianism, 206–207, 210
Zulu kingdom, 299
Zuni people, 572

ACKNOWLEDGMENTS

Text (continued from page iv)

ii From "Auguries of Innocence" by William Blake from the Pickering Manuscript, about 1803. **10** "I Love the World," "The Pier," "A Wish," "Winter" from *Miracles: Poems by Children of the English-speaking World,* collected by Richard Lewis. Copyright © 1966 by Richard Lewis. Reprinted by permission of Richard Lewis. **11** "Sailing Homeward" by Chang Fang-Sheng from *Translations from the Chinese,* by Arthur Waley, New York: Alfred E. Knopf, Inc., 1941. **38** Quote by Elihu Burritt as it appears in *Eyewitness to History,* edited by John Carey, Cambridge, Massachusetts: Harvard University Press, 1987. **64** "The Luring of Enkidu" from *Gilgamesh* by Bernarda Bryson. Copyright © 1966 by Bernarda Bryson. Reprinted by permission of Bernarda Bryson Shahn. **73** Genesis 12: 1–2 from *The Holy Bible,* New Revised Standard Version, Oxford University Press, © 1989. **89** From Spell 125 from *The Book of the Dead* translated by Raymond O. Faulkner, edited by Carol Andrews, New York: Macmillan Publishing Company, 1985. **113** From *The Edicts of Asoka* translated by N. A. Nikam and Richard McKeon, Chicago: University of Chicago Press, 1959. **114** From "The Shang-lin Park" translated by Burton Watson, in *Anthology of Chinese Literature,* compiled and edited by Cyril Birch. Copyright © 1965 by Grove Press. Reprinted by permission of the publisher. **132** From a Náhuatl lyric poem in *Pre-Columbian Literatures of Mexico* by Miguel León-Portilla, translated from the Spanish by Grace Lobanov and the author. Copyright © 1969 by the University of Oklahoma Press. Reprinted by permission of University of Oklahoma Press. **154** Quote from *The Odyssey of Homer* translated by Richmond Lattimore, New York: Harper and Row, 1965. **158** Quote by Pericles from "Pericles' Funeral Speech" as it appears in "Athens at War," from *The History of the Peloponnesian War of Thucydides* retold by Rex Warner, New York: E. P. Dutton & Company, 1970. **164** "Demeter and Persephone" from *D'Aulaires' Book of Greek Myths* by Ingri and Edgar Parin D'Aulaire. Copyright © 1962 by Ingri and Edgar Parin D'Aulaire. Used by permission of Doubleday, a division of Bantam Doubleday Dell Publishing Group, Inc. **175** Acts 16:30–1 from *The Holy Bible,* New Revised Standard Version, Oxford University Press, © 1989. **176** Matthew 22:37–40 from *The Holy Bible,* New Revised Standard Version, Oxford University Press, © 1989. **188** From *The Holy Koran: An Introduction with Selections* by A. J. Arberry, New York: Macmillan, 1953. **189** Quote by ar-Razi from *A History of Medicine* by Arturo Castiglioni, translated from the Italian and edited by E.B. Krumbhaar, New York: Jason Aronson, 1975. **212** Poem by an unknown Sufi poet as it appears in *Fall of the Peacock Throne* by William H. Forbis, New York: Harper & Row Publishers, 1980. **216** Quote by Barry Rosen as it appears in *444 Days: The Hostages Remember* by Tim Wells, Orlando: Harcourt Brace Jovanovich, 1985. **232** Quote by ibn Khaldun as it appears in *Egypt* by Mary Cross, Orlando: Harcourt Brace Jovanovich, 1991. **235** Quote by Nasser as it appears in "Letter from Alexandria" by Amos Elon, *The New Yorker,* July 18, 1988. **236** From a 1935 letter by Gamal Abdel Nasser to a friend in *Nasser* by Anthony Nutting, London: Constable and Company, 1972. **236** Quote by King Farouk as it appears in "Letter from Alexandria" by Amos Elon in *The New Yorker,* July 18, 1988. **237** From a letter by Jihan Sadat as it appears in *Sadat and His Statecraft* by Felipe Fernández-Armesto, London: The Kensal Press, 1982. **245** From *Those I Have Known* by Anwar el-Sadat, New York: Continuum, 1984. **249** Quote by al-Omari from *History of African Civilization* by E. J. Murphy, New York: Delta, 1972. **250** Quote by Ibn Battuta as it appears in *Ancient Ghana and Mali* by Nehemia Levtzion, New York: Africana Publishing Company, 1980. **253** Quote by Leo Africanus as it appears in "Bound and Free in 1508" by Mahmud Kati in *The African Past* by Basil Davidson, Boston: Atlantic Monthly Press, 1964. **262** From *The Heart of the Ngoni* by Harold Courlander with Ousamane Sakeo. Copyright © 1982 by Harold Courlander. Reprinted by permission of Harold Courlander. **268** From *Religion and Art in Ashanti* by R. S. Rattray, Oxford, England: Clarendon Press, 1927. **280** From *I Speak of Freedom* by Kwame Nkrumah, London: Panaf Books, 1973. **280** Quote by Kwame Nkrumah from *The Africans* by David Lamb, New York: Random House, 1982. **284** "The Cow-Tail Switch" from *The Cow-Tail Switch and Other West African Stories* retold by Harold Courlander and George Herzog. Copyright © 1947 by Harold Courlander, renewed 1975 by Harold Courlander. Reprinted by permission of Henry Holt, Inc. **294** From an excerpt of an April 20, 1964, speech by Nelson Mandela as it appears in *The Land and People of South Africa* by Jonathan Paton, New York: J. B. Lippincott, 1990. **307** Quote by Jane Mogase as it appears in The Open School Children's Art Calendar, 1992. Reprinted by permission of the publisher. **322** From *The Book of Kings* by Firdawsi, quoted in *A History of the World* by Stanley Chodorow, New York: Harcourt Brace Jovanovich, 1986. **327** From an excerpt of an August 14, 1947, speech by Nehru in *Nehru: A Political Biography* by Michael Brecher, Abridged Edition, Boston: Beacon Press, 1962. **347** From "Joining Forces" in *Chinese Lives: An Oral History of Contemporary China* by Zhang Xinxin and Sang Ye, translated by W. J. F. Jenner and Delia Davin, London: Macmillan London, 1987. Previously published in China as *Beijingren,* Shanghai: Shanghai Cultural Publishing House, 1986. **350** From a 36-line poem displayed in a shop window in Tiananmen Square as it appears in *The Iron House* by Michael S. Duke, Layton, Utah: Gibbs-Smith Publisher, 1990. **351** Quotes from Meng Maying and Xiao Wenxin as they appear in *Portraits of Ordinary Chinese* edited by Liu Bing-Wen and Xiong Lei, Peking: Foreign Language Press, 1990. **352** Adapted from "Population, Plenty and Poverty" by Paul R. Ehrlich and Anne H. Ehrlich from *National Geographic,* December 1988. **364** From *An Introduction to Haiku* by Harold G. Henderson. Copyright © 1958 by Harold G. Henderson. Reprinted by permission of Doubleday, a division of Bantam Doubleday Dell, Inc. **364** "The kite with a full stomach . . ." "When I think it's mine . . ." and "Wondering . . ." text and accompanying art from *Senryu Poems of the People,* calligraphy and illustrations by J. C. Brown. Copyright © 1991 by Charles E. Tuttle, Co., Inc. Reprinted by permission of Charles E. Tuttle, Co., Inc. **366** From *The Tale of the Heike,* anonymous, translated by Helen Craig McCullough, Stanford: Stanford University Press, 1988. **368** Quote from Ieyasu Tokugawa as it appears in *The Japanese* by Peter Tasker, New York: E. P. Dutton, 1987. Originally published in Great Britain as *Inside Japan,* London: Sidgwick & Jackson, Ltd. **386** Excerpt from poem by Mohammed Yamin and translated by Burton Raffel as it appears in *The Development of Modern Indonesian Poetry* edited by Burton Raffel. Translation copyright © 1967. Reprinted by permission of Burton Raffel. **394** Quote by Pope Pius XII as it appears in *Corazon Aquino: The Story of a Revolution* by Lucy Komisar, New York: George Braziller, 1987. **402** From *The Life of Reason* by George Santayana, New York: Scribners, 1905. **414** Translation of a Latin prayer which appears in *The Vikings in History* by F. Donald Logan, Second Edition, London: HarperCollins Academic, 1991. **415** From a song of the Second Crusade as it appears in *English in the Making of the Middle Ages* by R. W. Southern, New Haven: Yale University Press, 1953, and cited to *Les Chansons de Croisade* Paris: J. Bédier and P. Aubrey, 1909. **418** From a March 14, 1525, letter by Michael Behaim to his cousin in *Three Behaim Boys* by Steven Ozment, New Haven: Yale University Press, 1990. **420** Chapter 6 from *Valentine and Orson* by Nancy Ekholm Burkert. Copyright © 1989 by Nancy Ekholm Burkert. Reprinted by permission of Farrar, Straus, and Giroux, Inc. **424** From *The Craftsman's Handbook* by Cennino d'Andrea Cennini, translated by Daniel V. Thompson, Jr., New Haven: Yale University Press, 1933. **426** Quote by Leon Battista Alberti as it appears in *The Day the Universe Changed* by James Burke, Boston: Little, Brown and Company, 1985. **426** Quote by a contemporary of Michaelangelo as it appears in "The Sistine Restoration" by David Jeffrey in *National Geographic,* Vol. 176, No. 6, December 1989. **427** Quote by The Magnifico from *The Book of the Courtier* by Count Baldesar Castiglione, translated by Leonard Eckstein Opdycke, New York: Horace Liveright, 1901. **430** Quote by Martin Luther from "The Ninety-Five Theses" in *Here I Stand: A Life of Martin Luther* by Roland H. Bainton, Nashville: Abingdon Press, 1950. **431** Quote by Martin Luther as it appears in *Here I Stand: A Life of Martin Luther* by Roland H. Bainton, Nashville: Abingdon Press, 1950. **442** Quote by Christopher Columbus as it appears in "Edible Treasures" by Shari Lyn Zuber in *Cobblestone,* January 1992. **443** Quote by Bartolomé de las Casas as it appears in *A People's History of the United States* by Howard Zinn, New York: Harper Colophon, 1980. **444** Quote by Bentivollo as it appears in *The Spanish Armadas* by Winston Graham, Garden City: Doubleday and Company, 1972. **447** Quote by William Wordsworth from *Evening Voluntaries* by William Wordworth. **448** From *The White Man's Burden* (The United States and the Philippines Islands) by Rudyard Kipling, 1899. **460** From a song by Gilbert Hastings McDermott as it appears in *Age of Progress* by S. C. Burchell, Amsterdam, Holland: Time-Life Books, 1966. **463** Quote by Ferdinand Foch as it appears in *World War II: A 50th Anniversary History* by the writers and photographers of The Associated Press, New York: Henry Holt, 1989. **470** Quote from the "Report of the Jewish Resistance Movement" as it appears in *The Holocaust: The Nazi Destruction of Europe's Jews* by Gerhard Schoenberner, translated from the German by Susan Sweet, Edmunton: Hurtig Publishers, 1985. **470** From *Anne Frank: The Diary of a Young Girl,* New York: Doubleday & Company, 1967. **474** Quote from "Good-bye Soviet Union" by Bill Walter in *Junior Scholastic,* October 19, 1991. **480** Quote by Victor Hugo as it appears in *Euroquake* by Daniel Burstein, New York: Simon & Schuster, 1991. **488** Quote by Kim Jensen as it appears in "Making the Pieces Fit" by David Lawday in *U.S. News and World Report,* June 1, 1992. **488** From a letter by Aristides H. Liakopoulos as it appears in in *The European,* July 16–19, 1992. **493** From "It's a Kiosk! It's a Mall! No, It's Slavyansky Ryad!" by Celestine Bohlen in *The New York Times,* December 23, 1992. **495** Quote by Nikolai Karanko from "Glasnost's Children" by Lauren Tarshis and Judith Goldberg in *Scholastic Update,* Vol. 124, No. 7, December 6, 1991. **508** From *A Wave in Her Pocket: Stories from Trinidad* by Lynn Joseph, New York: Clarion Books, 1991. **512** From *Morning Girl* by Michael Dorris, New York: Hyperion Books for Children, 1992. **515** Quote from a letter which appeared in *Written in Blood: The Story of the Haitian People, 1492–1971,* by Robert Debs Heinl, Jr., and Nancy Gordon Heinl, Boston: Houghton Mifflin, 1978. **528** From "La Pampa" in *The South American Sketches of R. B. Cunninghame Graham,* selected and edited by John Walker, Norman: University of Oklahoma Press, 1978. **534** From *The Captive* by Scott O'Dell. Copyright © 1979 by Scott O'Dell. Reprinted by permission of Houghton Mifflin Company. **536** Quote by Amerigo Vespucci as it appeared in "Letter from Seville" from *Amerigo Vespucci: Pilot Major* by Frederick J. Pohl, New York: Octagon Books, 1944. **551** From a May 1, 1500, letter of Pero Vaz de Caminha to King Manuel, written at Porto Seguro (Brazil) as it appeared in *Portugal Brazil: The Age of Atlantic Discoveries* by Bertrand Editora, Franco Maria Ricci, and the Brazilian Cultural Foundation, New York: Brazilian Cultural Foundation, 1990. **555** From *Rebellion in the Backlands* by Euclides da Cunha, translated by Samuel Putnam, Chicago: University of Chicago Press, 1944. **588** From *The Labyrinth of Solitude* by Octavio Paz, translated by Lysander Kemp, New York: Grove Press, 1961. **598** From *Anne of Green Gables* by L. M. Montgomery, Boston: L. C. Page & Company, 1908. **600** Quote by James Cook as it appears in *Canada* by the Editors of Time-Life Books, Amsterdam, Holland: Time-Life Books, 1987. **602** Quote by David Thompson as it appeared in *The Canadians* by George Woodcock, Cambridge: Harvard University Press, 1979. **618** "The Delight Song of Tsai-talee" in *The Gourd Dancer* by N. Scott Momaday. Copyright © 1976 by N. Scott Momaday. Reprinted by permission of N. Scott Momaday. **627** Quote by José Luis as it appears in "Mojados" from *New Americans: An Oral History* by Al Santoli, New York: Viking Penguin, 1988. **628** "Ginger for the Heart" from *Tales from Gold Mountain* by Paul Yee. Copyright © 1989 by Paul Yee. Reprinted by permission of Macmillan and Douglas & McIntyre, Ltd. **632** From *New Kids on the Block: Oral Histories of Immigrant Teens* by Janet Bode, New York: Franklin Watts, 1989. **636** Quote from a volunteer speaker as it appears in the *AIDS Action Committee of Massachusetts Update,* Vol. 7, No. 3, Summer 1992.

Illustrations

Ligature 9, 17, 36, 41, 60, 61, 76, 78, 85, 95, 98, 107, 111, 112, 117, 120–121, 187, 190, 199, 298–299, 308, 336, 356, 357, 387, 400, 441, 445, 451, 451, 453, 456, 457, 470, 471, 476, 483, 499, 521, 524, 530, 531, 594, 639, 640, 649, 652, 654, 674–675, 676, 677. **Precision Graphics** 6, 54, 134, 150, 198, 214, 215, 227, 237, 261, 281, 294, 314, 315, 316, 333, 334, 348, 374, 413, 415, 485, 505, 528, 552, 581, 587, 625, 633, 650, 656. **Brian Battles** 112. **John T. Burgoyne** 298. **Young Sook Cho** 22, 634. **Ebet Dudley** 55, 226, 241, 574, 612. **Amy Fagin** 73. **Simon Galkin** 561. **Tyrone Geter** 252. **Andrea Golden** 489, 602, 603. **Hank Iken** 135, 171, 606. **Charley Liu** 118. **Al Lorenz** 102, 184, 260, 271. **Chuck MacKey** 88 (adapted from an illustration by Mark Lehner), 407, 442. **Judy Reed** 84. **Mike Rodericks** 369, 538. **Kirsten Tarnowski** 30. **Richard Waldrep** 91, 172.

Maps

R. R. Donnelley & Sons Company Cartographic Services 149(t), 223, 313, 372, 373, 375, 404, 503, 573, 678–689. **Mapping Specialists** G1–G14, 43, 44, 46, 47, 49, 53, 59, 67, 71, 83, 86, 104, 115, 129, 130, 139, 149(b), 150, 155, 169, 178, 184, 190, 205, 209, 215, 224, 230, 234, 240, 250, 251, 256, 269, 282, 294, 297, 298, 314, 318, 324, 331, 333, 341, 348, 355, 361, 387, 391, 399, 401, 406, 413, 416, 419, 433, 441, 445, 453, 462, 473, 481, 485, 494, 504, 509, 514, 516, 529, 543, 551, 557, 574, 580, 585, 590, 599, 602, 624, 647, 649, 652, 653.

Photographs

AR—Art Resource, New York; **BM**—British Museum, London; **P.A.I.**—Polish Information Agency; **PR**—Photo Researchers; **RHPL**—Robert Harding Picture Library; **SP**—Schlowsky Photography; **TM, SAP**—Tony Morrison, South American Pictures

Front Cover Globe courtesy of Replogle Globes, Inc.; photo by Peter Bosy. **Back Cover** The British Library, London, Bridgeman. **G8** Tony Stone Images (l). **G12** Scala, AR (bl). **G1** T. Van Sant, Geosphere Project, SPL, PR (l,r). **G11** © Michael Holford. **ii** Sovfoto (b); BM, Bridgeman (t). **iii** Museum Expedition courtesy of Museum of Fine Arts, Boston (r); © Jerry Howard, Positive Images (l). **vi** © Lee Boltin (c); By courtesy of the Board of Trustees of the Victoria & Albert Museum (b). **vii** Nelson Gallery-Atkins Museum (Nelson Fund), Kansas City (t); © Popperfoto (c); © Wolfgang Kaehler (b). **viii** © D. Donne Bryant (c); © Craig Duncan, D. Donne Bryant (b). **ix** SP. **x** © Loren McIntyre, Woodfin Camp & Assoc. **0–1** Hubert Le Campion, ANA, Viesti Assoc. **2** © O'Connor School Portraits & Assoc. (b). **3** J. Langevin, Sygma (tr); Stanislaw Momot, P.A.I. (bl); TM, SAP (tl); © Martha Copper, Viesti Assoc. (br). **4** © 1993 Steven Greenberg (l); © Linc Cornell, Light Sources Stock (r). **5** © 1993 Steven Greenberg. **6** SP (cr); © Laura Dwight, Peter Arnold Inc. (tl). **7** SP (both).**8** © Dean Conger, © National Geographic Society (l); © Eastcott, Momatiuk, The Image Works (r). **9** Eric Simmons, Stock Boston. **12** © Dilip Mehta, Woodfin Camp & Assoc. **13** James Balog, Black Star (t); © Robert Azzi, Woodfin Camp & Assoc.(b). **14** © Stephen Trimble (b). **14–15** Addison Geary, Stock Boston. **16** © Al Zwiazek, Tony Stone Images (t); © Chad Ehlers, Tony Stone Images (br); Culver Pictures (bl). **18** Werner Forman Archive. **20** Jerry Howard, Positive Images. **21** Maddy Miller (t); Julie Bidwell, Stock Boston (b). **23** SP (r); © Gerd Ludwig, Woodfin Camp & Assoc. (t). **26** SP (b); Steven Raymer, © National Geographic Society (l); © Lee Allen Thomas (c). **26–27** © Joe Viesti, Viesti Assoc. **27** SP (b); NASA (r). **28–29** SP. **29** © Mark Antman, The Image Works. **30** © Arthus-Bertrand, Explorer. **31** SP. **32** © TM, SAP. **33** Hiroyuki Matsumoto, Black Star. **34** © Michael Nichols, Magnum. **35** Courtesy of David Clendenen, Hooper Mountain National Wildlife Refuge California Condor Recovery Program. **36** SP. **37** SP. **38** Museum of The City of New York, 33.169, Gift of Mrs. Robert M. Littlejohn. **38–39** UPI/Bettmann. **40** The Phillips Collection, Washington, D.C. (c); © The Library of Congress (tr); SP (br, l). **41** NASA. **42** Rhoda Sidney, Stock Boston. **44** © Robert Frerck, Odyssey Productions. **45** © Hubert Le Campion, Viesti Assoc. **50–51** © R. & S. Michaud, Woodfin Camp & Assoc. **52** © Henri Cartier-Bresson, Magnum (b); Werner Forman Archive, National Museum of Anthropology, Mexico City (t). **54** Georg Gerster, Comstock (l); © U.S. Geological Survey (r). **55** John Ross, RHPL (l); TM, SAP (c); Georg Gerster, Comstock (r). **56** Ralph J. Brunke. **56–57** Michael Jennes, RHPL. **57** Jewish Museum, AR (b); © Michael Holford, BM (t). **58** BM (br); Ralph J. Brunke (bl). **59** Scala, AR. **60** © Michael Holford, BM. **66** Georg Gerster, Comstock. **68** BM, Bridgeman (t); Georg Gerster, Comstock (b). **69** Erich Lessing, AR (b); Scala, AR (t). **70** SP (b); BM (r); Kelsey Museum of Ancient and Medieval Archaeology, University of Michigan, Ann Arbor (t). **72** BM. **74** By permission of the British Library, ADDMS 10456-Folio. **75** © Photographic Archive of the the Jewish Theological Seminary of America, New York. **77** SP (t); Richard T. Nowitz (b). **80** AR. **80–81** John Ross, RHPL (c); Harvard University-MFA Expedition, courtesy of Museum of Fine Arts, Boston (t). **81** Museum Expedition, courtesy of Museum of Fine Arts, Boston (r,b). **82** Photothèque du Musée de l'Homme, Paris (t); © Susan Lapides, Woodfin Camp & Assoc. (c). **84** © Michael Holford, BM. **85** Erich Lessing, Scala, AR. **86** Museum Expedition, courtesy of Museum of Fine Arts, Boston. **87** © Michael Holford, BM. **89** © Michael Holford, BM (tr); The Metropolitan Museum of Art (bl); The Metropolitan Museum of Art, Rogers Fund, 1915 (bc). **90** Peter Clayton (b); Museum Expedition, courtesy of Museum of Fine Arts, Boston (t). **92** © Francis Geus (r); BM (l). **93** Ashmolean Museum, Oxford. **94** BM. **95** © Timothy Kendall, Museum of Fine Arts, Boston. **96** The Metropolitan Museum of Art. **97** The Metropolitan Museum of Art. **100** Ralph J. Brunke (b); J.H.C. Wilson, RHPL (l). **100–101** Laurie Platt Winfrey, Inc. (t). **101** Laurie Platt Winfrey, Inc. (r); © Ralph J. Brunke (b). **102** P. Koch, PR (b). **103** SP (bl); © Christine Pemberton, Hutchison Library (r). **104** AR (r); © Josephine Powell (l). **105** © R. & S. Michaud, Woodfin Camp & Assoc. **106** K. Rodgers, Hutchison Library. **108** SUPERSTOCK. **109** © Michael Holford, Musée Guimet. **110** © Michael Holford, BM. **111** AR. **113** Asoka School of Oriental and African Studies. **114** © George Bosio, Gamma-Liaison (c); © Manfred Gotschalk, Tom Stack & Associates (b). **116** © Michael Holford, BM. **117** In the Collection of the C. V. Starr East Asian Library, Columbia University. **118** BM. **119** SP (bl); Tony Waltham,

RHPL (full); Eastfoto (br); © Audrey Topping (tr); Sovfoto (cl). **120** Keren Su, Stock Boston. **120–121** SP. **121** © Wan-go Weng (tr). **122** The Image Bank, Harold Sund (t); National Numismatic Society, Smithsonian Institution (b). **123** © Photo R.M.N., Paris (r); Xi'an Visual Art Company, China (l). **126** © Justin Kerr (l); TM, SAP (r). **126–127** TM, SAP. **127** © Lee Boltin (b); Stuart Cohen, Comstock (t). **128** © Lee Boltin. **129** SP. **130** Laurie Platt Winfrey, Inc. **131** I. Graham, PR (t); TM, SAP (cr). **132** Dumbarton Oaks Research Library & Collections, Washington, D.C. **133** The Granger Collection, NY. **134** The Saint Louis Art Museum, Gift of Morton D. May (t); SP (b). **136** *Codex Mendoza,* Courtesy of Frances Berdan. **137** © Lee Boltin. **138** TM, SAP. **139** © H. Brooks Walker (both). **140** © Gift of Edward W. Hooper, Courtesy Museum of Fine Arts, Boston. **141** SP (t); © Museum fur Volkerkunde SMPK, Berlin (l); © Craig Duncan, D. Donne Bryant (r). **142** M. Fantin, PR. **146–147** Scala, AR. **148** Erich Lessing, AR (l); © Explorer (b). **150** SP (bl); © Lynn Abercrombie (cl). **151** © Wolfgang Kaehler (bl); © Abbas, Magnum (tl); © Cary Wolinsky, Tony Stone Images (br). **152** AR (l); © C. O'Rear, Woodfin Camp & Assoc. (r). **153** © The Image Bank, Clark Weinberg (r); The Granger Collection, NY (b); © Michael Holford, BM (l). **154** © Michael Kuh, PR (b). **155** SP. **156** © Michael Holford, BM. **157** Ancient Art & Architecture Collection (b); Scala, AR(t). **158** © Michael Holford, BM. **159** Scala, AR (t); Scala, AR (r). **160** Scala, AR. **161** Scala, AR (both). **163** © The LEGO Group (t). **165** Scala, AR. **168** AR. **170** © Capitoline Museum, Rome, Newsweek Books (t); © BM, Michael Holford (b). **171** © Paolo Koch. **173** Erich Lessing, AR. **174** Ralph J. Brunke. **175** © Ara Juler, Newsweek Books. **176** © The University Museum, University of Pennsylvania. **177** Scala, AR. **179** Scala, AR. **182–183** M. Biber, PR. **182** © Bodleian Library, Oxford, UK (b); Camerapix (l). **183** © Robert Azzi, Woodfin Camp & Assoc. (t). **185** SP(b); Robert Azzi, Woodfin Camp & Assoc. (t). **186** © Nabeel Turner, Tony Stone Images. **187** Aral, SIPA. **188** Musée Condé, Chantilly, Giraudon, Bridgeman. **189** The Metropolitan Museum of Art, Rogers Fund, 1913. **191** The Granger Collection, NY. **192** B. Norman, Ancient Art & Architecture Collection (l); © Bruno Barbey, Magnum (r). **193** SP(b); Gentile, SIPA (t). **194** M. Biber, PR. **195** R. Ellis, PR. **196** © Bill Strode, Woodfin Camp & Assoc. **197** J. Langevin, Sygma (r); © Abbas, Magnum (l). **198** The Image Bank, Ronald R. Johnson. **202** Courtesy of the Freer Gallery of Art, Smithsonian Institution. **202–203** SUPERSTOCK. **203** Courtesy of The Arthur M. Sackler Museum, Harvard University Art Museums (t). **204** Witt, SIPA. **205** © Bruno Barbey, Magnum. **206** © Abbas, Magnum (t); © Christina Dodwell, Hutchison Library (b). **207** SP. **208** Georg Gerster, Comstock (l); SEF, AR (r). **210** Ancient Art & Architecture Collection. **211** SP (background); by Permission of the British Library (l); by Courtesy of the Board of Trustees of the Victoria & Albert Museum (b). **212** By Courtesy of the Board of Trustees of the Victoria & Albert Museum, Bridgeman. **213** © M.M.J. Fischer, Department of Anthropology, Rice University. **214** © Marilyn Silverstone, Magnum. **215** Alain Keler, Sygma. **216** © Jean Guamy, Magnum. **220–221** Peter Menzel. **222** © Wolfgang Kaehler (both). **224–225** © Wolfgang Kaehler. **225** SP (br); Adam Tanner, Comstock (c). **226** © Michael Holford, BM (bl). **226–227** © Luc Girard. **227** © Schiller, The Image Works (b); © Brun J, Explorer (t). **228** The Brooklyn Museum 16.105, Gift of the Estate of Charles Edwin Wilbour. **229** Donald McLeish Collection, RHPL (tr); BM (bl). **230** AR. **231** © Schiller, The Image Works. **232–233** © Robert Azzi, Woodfin Camp & Assoc. **235** SP (tr); The Image Bank, Guido Alberto Rossi (b). **236** Culver Pictures. **237** SP (tl); J. Giannini, Sygma (tr). **239** F. Keating, PR. **240** © James Nachtwey, Magnum. **241** SP (c); Georg Gerster, © National Geographic Society (t,l,b). **243** Peter Turnley, Black Star. **246** © David Simpson, Magnum (r); photo P.- A. Ferrazzini, Musée Barbier-Mueller, Genève (b); Ralph J. Brunke (l). **246–247** © Larry C. Price. **247** photo P.- A. Ferrazzini, Musée Barbier-Mueller, Genève (t). **248** © Bibliothèque Nationale, Paris. **249** © Michael Holford, BM (t); © The Israel Museum, Jerusalem (b). **250** Georg Gerster, Comstock. **251** Georg Gerster, Comstock. **253** Betty Press, Picture Group. **254** Courtesy of Weldon D. Burson. **255** SP (r); David Poole, RHPL (b). **257** © Crispin Hughes, Hutchison Library (b); © Timothy Beddow, Hutchison Library (tl); V. Engelbert, PR (tr). **258** © M. Renaudeau, Hoa-Qui. **259** © Wolfgang Kaehler (b); © Werner Forman, Schindler Collection, NY (r). **260** Georg Gerster, Comstock. **261** Betty Press, Picture Group (c). **262** Betty Press, Picture Group. **266** Photograph by Eliot Elisofon, National Museum of African Art, Eliot Elisofon Archives, Smithsonian Institution (b). **266–267** Betty Press, Picture Group. **267** Photograph by Eliot Elisofon, National Museum of African Art, Eliot Elisofon Archives, Smithsonian Institution (b); © Richard Allen (cl, br). **268** © Fred Mayer, Magnum **269** © Ian Berry, Magnum. **270** © Richard Allen. **271** Nelson Gallery–Atkins Museum (Nelson Fund), Kansas City. **272** Mike Dye, *The White Men*, Julia Blackburn, Orbis Publishing, London (t); © Richard Allen (b). **273** Photo P.- A. Ferrazzini, Musée Barbier-Mueller, Genève **274** Photo P.- A. Ferrazzini, Musée Barbier-Mueller, Genève (tr); © Dennis Stock, Magnum (b). **275** © SP (c); © Herbert M. Cole (tr); © Fred Mayer, Magnum (bl). **276** © Marc & Evelyne Bernheim, Woodfin Camp & Assoc. (bl). **277** The National Archives of Zimbabwe (br); © Richard Allen (t). **278** SP (all). **278–279** SP. **279** © Angela Fisher, Robert Estall Photographs (l); SP (br). **280** UPI/Bettmann. **281** © Ian Berry, Magnum (br). **282** SUPERSTOCK (b). **283** SUPERSTOCK (tr). **290** © Roger de La Harpe, Anthony Bannister Photo Library (r); © Anthony Bannister, Anthony Bannister Photo Library (l). **291** © M. Kahn, Hutchison Library (t); Seowyn Tait, Black Star (c); SP (b). **292** David Turnley, Black Star (bl); © University Microfilms Inc. (bl). **293** SP (tr); © Peter Jordan, Gamma-Liaison. **294** Africana Museum, Johannesburg (b). **295** P. Duran, Sygma (tr). **296–297** SP. **296** © South African Tourism Board (t). **298** © Phillip Richardson, Anthony Bannister Photo Library (tr); © Africana Museum, Johannesburg (tl). **299** Postage Stamp reproduced under Government Printer's Copyright Authority 8893 of 5.7.1988; Source unknown. (tr); Popperfoto (tc). **300** SP (background); © Abbas, Magnum (l); © World Gold Council (br); Comstock (t). **301** © Africana Museum, Johannesburg (both). **302** © A. Venzago, Magnum. **303** SP. **304** © Mike Powell, Allsport. **305** Peters, SIPA (b); © G. Mendel, Magnum (t). **307** Benny Gool, Impact Visuals (tr). **310–311** © Abbas, Magnum. **312–313** Lisa Quinones, Black Star. **312** Carl Purcell, Words & Pictures (bl). **315** SP (bl); Orion Press (tr). **316** By Courtesy of the Board of Trustees of the Victoria & Albert Museum (t); © New Delhi Museum, India, AR (b); © Alain Felix, Explorer (c). **316–317** © Steve McCurry, Magnum. **317** M. Oppersdorff, PR (r). **318–319** © Anil A. Dave, Dinodia. **319** SP (cr). **320** © Ranjit Sen, Dinodia (t); © Thierry Borredon, Explorer (b). **321** S. Nagendra, PR. **322** © Pramod Mistry, Dinodia. **323** © Saraj N. Sharma, Dinodia (t); © Tony Stone Images (b). **324** © R. A. Acharya, Dinodia. **325** Culver Pictures. **326** UPI/Bettmann (cl); Popperfoto (b). **327** © Henri Cartier-Bresson, Magnum. **329** Henry Georgi, Comstock. **330** SP (tr); © Steve McCurry, Magnum (cl, both r); © DPA, MP, The Image Works (b). **332** © Suraj N. Sharma, Dinodia (bl); © Mike Yamashita, Woodfin Camp & Assoc. (bc); © Saraj N. Sharma, Dinodia (cl); © H. Mahidhar, Dinodia (br). **334** © Jagdish Agarwal, Dinodia (cl); Henry Georgi, Comstock (tr). **335** © Robert Frerck, Odyssey Productions. **338** SEF, AR (l); © George Holton, PR (r). **339** J. P. Laffont, Sygma (r); Superstock (tl); Peabody Museum of Salem, photo by Mark Sexton (bl). **340** Minneapolis Institute of Arts. **341** Private Collection. **343** From the Western Sea Cruises of Eunuch San Pao, by L. O. Mouteng, 1597 (r); The Image Bank, Edward Bower (l); AR (cr); The Image Bank, K. Wothe (bl); Ralph J. Brunke (tc); Chait Galleries, New York (br). **344** UPI/Bettmann (b); Peabody Museum of Salem, photo by Mark Sexton (t). **345** © William Sewell, E.T. Archive. **346** SP. **347** Bruce Dale, © National Geographic Society (r); Diego Goldberg, Sygma (l); **349** © David Wells, The Image Works. **350** © Stuart Franklin, Magnum. **351** Carl Purcell, Words & Pictures. **352** Bruce Dale, © National Geographic Society (bl); The Image Bank, P. & G. Bowater (br). **353** © Alon Reininger, Woodfin Camp & Assoc. (t); © Michael MacIntyre, Hutchison Library (b). **354** © Bellavia, REA, SABA. **358** The Tokyo National Museum, photo courtesy of The International Society for Educational Information, Inc. (c). **358–359** Orion Press (c); Asian Art Museum of San Francisco (b). **359** Werner Forman, Victoria & Albert Museum, London (cl); Michael Holford (cr); Diego Goldberg, Sygma (tr). **360** William Sturgis Bigelow Collection, courtesy, Museum of Fine Arts, Boston. **361** Gift of Frederick Weisman Company, Los Angeles County Museum of Art. **362** Orion Press. **362–363** Sybil Sassoon, RHPL (t). **365** Courtesy of the Charles E. Tuttle Company, Inc. (both). **366** Orion Press. **367** The Granger Collection, NY. **368** © Tokugawa Reimeikai Foundation. **369** National Institute of Japanese Literature, photo courtesy of the International Society for Educational Information, Inc. **371** © Yuichiro Sasaki, Wide World (t); UPI/Bettmann (r). **374** Courtesy of Consulate General of Japan, Boston. **375** © Mark S. Wexler, Woodfin Camp & Assoc. **376** © Dallas & John Heaton, Westlight. **377** SP (b); Karen Kamauski, © National Geographic Society (t); Orion Press (l). **378** Orion Press (b); Consulate General of Japan in Boston (l). **379** © Burbank, The Image Works. **380** Joel Sackett, Michael O'Mara Books, Ltd.(t); Ralph J. Brunke (b). **381** Ralph J. Brunke (both). **384** © Kal Muller, Woodfin Camp & Assoc. **384–385** Andy Hernandez, Picture Group(t); © Kal Muller, Woodfin Camp & Assoc. (b). **385** A. Evrard, PR (r). **386** © Kal Muller, Woodfin Camp & Assoc. **388** SP (b); AP/Wide World (r); The Image Bank, Don King (bl); AP/Wide World (full). **389** S. Summerhays, PR. **390** AR. **391** SP. **392** © John Hatt, Hutchison Library. **393** © REZA (tr); SP (cr); © Michael MacIntyre, Hutchison Library (bl). **394** A. Evrard, PR. **395** © Robin Smith, Tony Stone Images (bl); © Cameramann International (br). **396** © Kal Muller, Woodfin Camp & Assoc. **397** © Kal Muller, Woodfin Camp & Assoc. (both tr); © Catherine Karnow, Woodfin Camp & Assoc. (b). **398** Earl Young, RHPL. **402–403** Scala, AR. **404** © Cotton Coulson, Woodfin Camp & Assoc. **405** Charles O. Hyman, © National Geographic Society. **406** Swiss National Tourist Office (br); © Meininger, Explorer (b). **407** © Topham-PA, The Image Works (tr); © Pesle B., Explorer (l). **408** Scala, AR (l); Giraudon, AR (r). **409** Isabella Stewart Gardner Museum, Boston, AR (t); © Ingeborg Limmer (c); © Ralph J. Brunke (b). **410** © Erich Hartmann, Magnum. **411** The Image Bank, Francisco Hidalgo. **412** The British Library. **414** © Michael Holford, BM. **415** Museum of London, Archeology Service (tr); Giraudon, AR (tl,c,br). **416** Laurie Platt Winfrey, Inc. (tr). **418** Scala, AR (tr); © Jane Burton, Bruce Coleman, Inc. (cl). **424** Scala, AR. **425** Scala, AR (t); Musée de Cluny, Paris (b). **426** Allen Birnbach, Westlight. **427** AR (t); Nippon Television Network Corporation Tokyo 1991 (b). **428** Scala, AR (t); AR (b). **429** IBM. **430** AR. **431** Scala, AR (tr); Lutherhalle, Wittenberg (b). **432** Cambridge University Library, Cambridge, Bridgeman. **433** Worms, Museum der Stadt Andreasstift. **436** Laurie Platt Winfrey, Inc. (l); © Douglas Armand, Tony Stone Images (r). **437** BM, Bridgeman (r); City of Bristol Museum & Art Gallery, Bridgeman (t); © Jean-Paul Nacivet, Explorer (b). **438** Giraudon, AR. **439** Edimedia (t); © BM (r); © The British Library (b). **440** Laurie Platt Winfrey, Inc. **441** © Sisse Brimberg, Matrix. **442** James A. Sugar, Black Star (t). **443** © ET Archive. **444** SP. **445** The Granger Collection, NY (t). **446** Mary Evans Picture Library (l); The Granger Collection, NY (r). **447** © Michael Holford, Science Museum. **448** Mary Evans Picture Library (t); Culver Pictures (b). **449** SP. **450** SP. **452** © Wolfgang Kaehler. **453** Kremlin Museums, Moscow, Bridgeman (tr). **454** Culver Pictures (b); NOVOSTI from Sovfoto (l). **455** NOVOSTI from Sovfoto (tr). **458** P.A.I. (b); Mary Evans Picture Library (l). **459** © Larry Price (r); © Fotomas (l); A. Nogues, Sygma (t). **460** Culver Pictures. **461** UPI, Bettman. **463** Mary Evans Picture Library (both). **464** Sovfoto. **465** David King Collection (both). **466** SP (tl); NOVOSTI from Sovfoto (tl,bl); © Larry Stein, Forbes Magazine (r). **467** TASS from Sovfoto. **468** Culver Pictures. **469** P.A.I. **470** P.A.I. (br); Culver Pictures (l). **471** P.A.I. **472** Sygma (b); Franklin D. Roosevelt Library (t). **473** UPI/Bettmann (b). **474** © Francis Apesteguy, Gamma-Liaison (tr). **475** by Vladimir Mochalov, Izvestia. **477** Jeff Stahler, Cincinnati Post 1991. **478** © Willy Boeykens, Allsport (r); Laski, SIPA (l). **478–479** British Airways. **479** © Zelijko, Gamma-Liaison (b); © Abbas, Magnum (t). **480** © Liba Taylor, Hutchison Library (bl). **481** © Paul Solomon, Woodfin Camp & Assoc. **482** © Mike Yamashita, Woodfin Camp & Assoc. **484** Syndication International. **486** SP (cl,cr,b,t); Richemond, The Image Works (l). **487** © Raymond Roig, Gamma-Liaison (br). **488** © Crispin Hughes, Hutchison Library. **490** P.A.I. **491** © Israel Talby, Woodfin Camp & Assoc. **492** Patrick Robert, Sygma. **493** Georges de Keerle, Sygma. **496** © Roberto Koch, Contrasto, SABA. **497** © Samuel Hutchinson, GLMR. **500–501** Curing Scene Molas, San Blas Islands, Panama, c. 1965, Cloth, 14 1/2" x 20 1/4", Collection of the Museum of American Folk Art, New York. **502** The Image Bank, Anne Rippy (l); TM, SAP (br). **504** © Michael Fogden, DRK Photo. **505** © Noel Norton (b); © Jonathan Blair, Woodfin Camp & Assoc. (t). **506** By Permission of the Houghton Library, Harvard University (t); BM, Michael Holford (b). **507** Suzanne L. Murphy, D. Donne Bryant (b); Kit Kittle, Viesti Assoc. (t). **508** Frané Lessac, Art to Beat. **509** © Mickey Gibson, Animals, Animals. **510** © Bernard Regent, Hutchison Library (br); K. B. Sandved, PR (bl). **511** © Noel Norton. **512** © Zui Dorner, WGBH, Boston (bl). **512–513** © Noel Norton. **514–515** SP. **515** Courtesy of Daniel Segal. **517** Ralph J. Brunke (both). **518** SP (l); © Noel Norton (br). **519** Porterfield-Chickering, PR (tr); Milt & Joan Mann, Cameramann International (cr). **520** The Image Bank, Kaz Mori (br). **521** © Ian Berry, Magnum (tr); SP (l,tr,br). **522** SP (br); © Stephanie Maze, Woodfin Camp & Assoc. (cl). **523** © Martha Cooper, Viesti Assoc. (br). **526** The Granger Collection, NY (b); The Three Potencies Shop Sign, "El Negro," Merida, Venezuela, c. 1985, oil on tin, 24" x 39 1/4" x 1", Collection of the Museum of American Folk Art, New York (c). **526–527** Harriet Otis Cruft Fund, courtesy of Museum of Fine Arts, Boston (b). **527** TM, SAP (r); © D. Donne Bryant (tl). **528** TM, SAP. **529** Hillary Bradt, TM, SAP (b); TM, SAP (t). **530** Photo by Marion Oettinger, Jr. (l); Girard Foundation Collection in the Museum of International Folk Art, a unit of the Museum of New Mexico (r). **531** SP (t); The Image Bank, Paul E. Loven (b). **532** Giraudon, AR. **533** © Elizabeth Harris, Tony Stone Images. **536** TM, SAP. **537** The Image Bank, Max Hilaire (r); TM, SAP (l). **539** TM, SAP (both). **540** TM, SAP. **541** Marek Jurkowski. **542** Timothy Ross, Picture Group. **543** SP (both). **544** © Ed Gallo, Gamma-Liaison. **545** Cindy Karp, Black Star (t); © Pool Mondiale, Gamma-Liaison (b). **548** © Jesco Von Puttkamer, Hutchison Library (l); Courtesy of the Edward E. Ayer Collection, The Newberry Library, Chicago (r). **549** © George Anacona (r); © Stephanie Maze, Woodfin Camp & Assoc. (l). **550** The Granger Collection, NY (t). **551** Bibliothèque Nationale, Paris. **552** TM, SAP (both). **553** Claus Meyer, TYBA, Black Star. **554** The Folger Shakespeare Library. **555** Mauricio Simonetti, D. Donne Bryant. **556** D. McIntyre, PR (b); © Stephanie Maze, Woodfin Camp & Assoc. (t). **558** Robert Perron (background); © Loren McIntyre, Woodfin Camp & Assoc. (bl, br); © Luiz C. Marigo, Peter Arnold Inc. (tl); SP (tr). **559** © Paula Lerner, Woodfin Camp & Assoc. **560** Claus Meyer, Black Star. **561** Simon Galkin (b). **562** TM, SAP. **563** Gustavo Gilbert, JB Pictures (t); Claus Meyer, Black Star (b). **564** © Carlos Freire, Hutchison Library (b); Claus Meyer, Black Star (t). **565** Photri. **566** Ralph J. Brunke (t); © D. G. Barker, Tom Stack and Associates (b). **567** The Image Bank, Peter Frey (b); Ralph J. Brunke (t); © D. G. Barker, Tom Stack and Associates (c). **570–571** © David Muench. **572** © Mark Downey, Viesti Assoc. (b); © Carol Palmer (l). **575** SP, Mask courtesy of Eden Thibeault (r); SP (b); Peter Menzel (l). **576** Museo Franz Mayer, Mexico City. 18-057 00486. BEA-004. Photograph courtesy of The Metropolitan Museum of Art (l); TM, SAP (r). **576–577** TM, SAP. **577** TM, SAP. **578** Bibliothèque Nationale, Paris. **579** TM, SAP (t); © Michael Holford, BM (b). **581** INDH, Casasola Archive, Hidalgo, Mexico. **582** © Robert Frerck, Odyssey Productions (tl). **583** CNCA-INAH, Museo Nacional de Antropologia, Mexico City, 11-3369, 10-46639. Photograph courtesy of The Metropolitan Museum of Art. **584** Charles Lenars, Explorer. **586** SP. **587** © Peter Chautrand, D. Donne Bryant. **588** © D. Donne Bryant. **589** TM, SAP (b); © Kal Muller, Woodfin Camp & Assoc. (t). **590–91** TM, SAP. **591** David Hiser, Photographers, Aspen (br). **592** SP (br,c); © Patricia Cué (cl,tr). **593** © Dirck Halstead, Gamma-Liaison. **596** © Mante, ZEFA-Germany (l); © Michael Holford, National Maritime Museum (r). **596–597** SP. **597** F. Lewis, PR (c); © The Boston Globe (b). **598** © Craig Aurness, Woodfin Camp and Assoc. (r); © Jim Brandenburg, Minden Pictures (l). **600** © Fred Bruemmer (t); SUPERSTOCK (b). **601** © Royal Ontario Museum. **602** © British Columbia Archives (l). **603** © Rare Book Collection, National Library of Canada (t); © Fred Maroon (b). **604** © National Archives of Canada (r); © Glenbow Museum (l). **605** SP (r); © Malak Photography (l). **607** Sygma (l); Julienne, SIPA (r). **608** SP (background); Hiroyuki Matsumoto, Black Star (tl). **609** © George Hunter, Tony Stone Images. **610** Gift of Mr. George J. Rosengarten, Canadian Museum of Civilization, Hull, Quebec (b); David Cooper, photo courtesy of Royal Winnipeg Ballet (l). **611** SP (tr); National Film Board of Canada (br,tl,bl,b). **613** © Sarah Leen, Matrix (r); Ralph J. Brunke (c). **616** Photo courtesy of M. Finkel & Daughter, Private Collection (c); © Grant Heilman Photography (b). **617** Museum of Art, Rhode Island School of Design, Gift of Miss Lucy T. Aldrich (t); © Donovan Reese, Tony Stone Images (c); Sygma (b). **618** American Museum of Natural History, photo by A. Singer (r). **618–619** © David Muench 1992. **619** © Woodruff Sullivan (tl). **620** © Michael Holford, BM. **621** © The Burke Museum (l); © Tom Tracy, FPG (r). **622** © Reed Kaestner, Zephyr. **623** © Minnesota Historical Society (t); photo courtesy of The American Jewish Joint Distribution Committee, Inc. (b). **624** © Chermayeff & Geismar, Karen Yamouchi (b). **625** National Park Service: Statue of Liberty Monument (b). **626** UPI/Bettmann. **627** AP/Wide World (both). **629** Brown Brothers. **632** SP (bl); © Kashi, Gamma-Liaison (br). **635** Brown Brothers (tr); © Mark Sherman, Bruce Coleman (br). **636** SP (tl); © Ben van Hook, Gamma-Liaison (tc). **637** Willinger, FPG International. **638** Courtesy Stamps Magazine. **639** © Gary Williams, Gamma-Liaison. **642** © Kim Newton, Woodfin Camp and Assoc. (l); Richard T. Nowitz (r). **642–643** SP. **643** Comstock. **644** © Karian Daher, Gamma-Liaison. **645** © James Nachtwey, Magnum (r); © Nickelsberg, Gamma-Liaison (b). **646** The Image Bank, Bill Carter. **648** Richard T. Nowitz. **649** © Micha Bar Am, Magnum. **650** Richard T. Nowitz (tr,bl). **650–651** David Harris. **651** © James Nachtwey, Magnum (tl); © Harry Uvegi, Gamma-Liaison (c); ZEFA-London (tr); © Alon Reininger, Woodfin Camp & Assoc. (br). **652** © Alon Reininger, Woodfin Camp & Assoc. (bl). **653** © Nathan Benn, Woodfin Camp & Assoc. **654** SP (bl, br); Milt & Joan Mann, Cameramann International (t); © Charles B. Hoyt Collection, courtesy of Museum of Fine Arts, Boston (cr); © Michael MacIntyre, Hutchison Library (c). **655** © Wolfgang Kaehler. **656** Milt & Joan Mann, Cameramann International (t); Robert, SIPA (b). **656–657** SP. **657** © Michael MacIntyre, Hutchison Library (tl); The Image Bank, P. & G. Bowater (tr); Milt & Joan Mann, Cameramann International (b); © Maurice Harvey, Hutchison Library (c).